Safety Symbols

These symbols appear in laboratory activities.
They alert you to possible dangers and remind
you to work carefully.

General Safety Awareness Read all directions for an experiment several times. Follow the directions exactly as they are written. If you are in doubt, ask your teacher for assistance.

Physical Safety If the lab includes physical activity, use caution to avoid injuring yourself or others. Tell your teacher if there is a reason that you should not participate.

Safety Goggles Always wear safety goggles to protect your eyes in any activity involving chemicals, heating, or the possibility of broken glassware.

Lab Apron Wear a laboratory apron to protect your skin and clothing from harmful chemicals or hot materials.

Plastic Gloves Wear disposable plastic gloves to protect yourself from contact with chemicals that can be harmful. Keep your hands away from your face. Dispose of gloves according to your teacher's instructions.

Heating Use a clamp or tongs to hold hot objects. Test an object by first holding the back of your hand near it. If you feel heat, the object may be too hot to handle.

Heat-Resistant Gloves Hot plates, hot water, and hot glassware can cause burns. Never touch hot objects with your bare hands. Use an oven mitt or other hand protection.

Flames Tie back long hair and loose clothing, and put on safety goggles before using a burner. Follow instructions from your teacher for lighting and extinguishing burners.

No Flames If flammable materials are present, make sure there are no flames, sparks, or exposed sources of heat.

Electric Shock To avoid an electric shock, never use electrical equipment near water, or when the equipment or your hands are wet. Use only sockets that accept a three-prong plug. Be sure cords are untangled and cannot trip anyone. Disconnect equipment that is not in use.

Fragile Glassware Handle fragile glassware, such as thermometers, test tubes, and beakers, with care. Do not touch broken glass. Notify your teacher if glassware breaks. Never use chipped or cracked glassware.

Corrosive Chemical Avoid getting corrosive chemicals on your skin or clothing, or in your eyes. Do not inhale the vapors. Wash your hands after completing the activity.

Poison Do not let any poisonous chemical get on your skin, and do not inhale its vapor. Wash your hands after completing the activity.

Fumes When working with poisonous or irritating vapors, work in a well-ventilated area. Never test for an odor unless instructed to do so by your teacher. Avoid inhaling a vapor directly. Use a wafting motion to direct vapor toward your nose.

Sharp Object Use sharp instruments only as directed. Scissors, scalpels, pins, and knives are sharp and can cut or puncture your skin. Always direct sharp edges and points away from yourself and others.

Disposal All chemicals and other materials used in the laboratory must be disposed of safely. Follow your teacher's instructions.

Hand Washing Before leaving the lab, wash your hands thoroughly with soap or detergent, and warm water. Lather both sides of your hands and between your fingers. Rinse well.

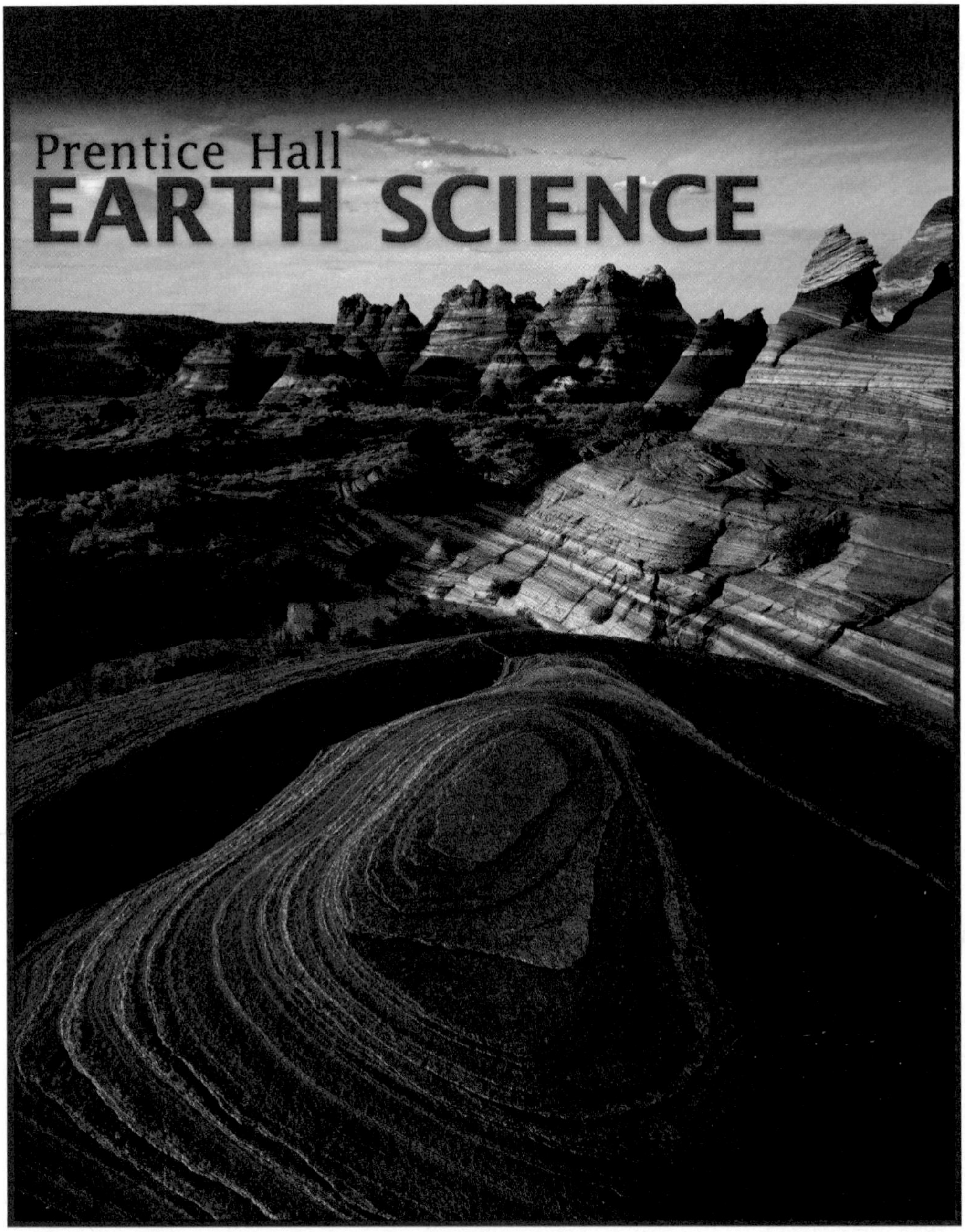

Prentice Hall
EARTH SCIENCE

Edward J. Tarbuck   Frederick K. Lutgens
Both Illinois Central College, Emeritus

Illustrated by **Dennis Tasa**

Needham, Massachusetts
Upper Saddle River, New Jersey

Prentice Hall
EARTH SCIENCE

Cover Sandstone formations in the Paria Canyon-Vermillion Cliffs Wilderness, Arizona

Print Components
Student Edition
Teacher's Edition
Lesson Plans
Laboratory Manual
Laboratory Manual, Annotated Teacher's Edition
Teaching Resources
Guided Reading and Study Workbook
Guided Reading and Study Workbook, Annotated
  Teacher's Edition
Chapter Tests

Technology
Earth Science Interactive Textbook
Earth Science Computer Test Bank CD-ROM
Earth Science Transparencies
Discovery Channel Earth Science Video Field Trips
Prentice Hall Earth Science Web Site
Prentice Hall Earth Science Teacher Express CD-ROM
GEODe: Earth Science CD-ROM

Credits begin on page 802, which constitutes an extension of this copyright page.

ISBN 0-13-125852-4

4 5 6 7 8 9 10   10 09 08 07 06 05

Edward J. Tarbuck

Edward J. Tarbuck served twenty-nine years as Professor of geosciences at Illinois Central College. During twenty of those years he was also Chair of the Math, Science and Engineering Department. Ed now holds a place as Professor Emeritus at Illinois Central College.

Frederick K. Lutgens

For thirty years, Frederick K. Lutgens served as Professor of geosciences at Illinois Central College. During his career he was awarded "The Faculty Who Make a Difference" honor in recognition of his outstanding academic performance and dedication to students. He is also Professor Emeritus at Illinois Central College.

Tarbuck and Lutgens

The term *synergistic* applies to the combined efforts of Tarbuck and Lutgens, two names widely recognized and respected in the field of geosciences. Early in their careers, they shared frustrations with the limited availability of textbooks designed for non-majors. Out of their dilemma sprang a series of textbooks that are utilized nationwide and have been published in English, Spanish, Italian and Korean. They have co-authored over forty editions of college textbooks including *Earth Science,* now in its 10th edition, *Earth: Introduction to Physical Geology,* and *The Atmosphere.* Tarbuck and Lutgens have received several publishing honors including the *Texty Award* for *Earth,* and the *McGuffy Award* for *Earth Science,* both from the Text and Academic Authors Association.

With unfailing interest in exposing students to the broad world of geosciences, Tarbuck and Lutgens collaborated on the development and implementation of a field studies program that continues today at Illinois Central College.

Illustration by Dennis Tasa

Dennis Tasa has been illustrating college textbooks since 1978, specializing in the area of geology and geography. In 1993, he expanded his illustration work to develop and produce Earth Science educational CD-ROMs. Dennis has won numerous awards for his illustration and software products including EDDIE Awards by ComputEd Education Software Review for both Middle School and High School Science; Silver Awards, Summit Creative Awards; and the Children's Software and New Media Review School All Star Award.

It is with great pride that Prentice Hall brings the talents of this superb author team to the high school classroom.

High School Earth Science Consultant, Writer, and Reviewer
Michael Wysession

Michael Wysession received his Ph.D. in geophysics from Northwestern University in 1991. He is an Associate Professor in Earth and Planetary Sciences at Washington University in St. Louis, Missouri. His area of specialization is using seismic waves to explore Earth's interior. Dr. Wysession is an author on more than 50 scientific publications. For his research, he was awarded a Presidential Faculty Fellowship at the White House. He also has created educational simulations to accurately show how seismic waves propagate.

Teacher Reviewers

Helen A. Bastin
Bloomington High
   School North
Bloomington, Indiana

David R. Blakely
Arlington High School
Arlington, Massachusetts

Joseph M. Bosco Jr.
New Britain High School
New Britain, Connecticut

Jo A. Combs
Broward County Schools
Ft. Lauderdale, Florida

Scott Cordell
Earth Science Teacher
Armarillo, TX

**Elizabeth Elixman
Campbell**
Warren Central High School
Indianapolis, Indiana

Glen Dolphin
Union-Endicott High School
Endicott, New York

Richard P. Filson
Edison High School
Stockton, California

Greg J. Geisen
New Albany High School
New Albany, Indiana

Georgina Koch Hidalgo
Miami-Dade County
   Public Schools
Miami, Florida

Kristine J. Kelley
Wilkes Central High School
Wilkesboro, North Carolina

Kevin Leineweber
Tippecanoe School
   Corporation
Lafayette, Indiana

Marian J. Marley
Wilkes Central High School
Wilkesboro, North Carolina

Bruce A. Mellin
Brooks School
North Andover, Massachusetts

George Mumford
Dover, Massachusetts

Michael Passow
White Plains MS
White Plains, NY

Gregory S. Small
William Henry Harrison
   High School
Evansville, Indiana

Thomas J. Vaughn
Arlington High School
Arlington, Massachusetts

Donald G. Wafer
Muncie Central High School
Muncie, Indiana

Jeffrey A. Williams
New Albany High School
New Albany, Indiana

Content Reviewers

Glen C. Kroeger, Ph.D.
Associate Professor and Chair
   Geosciences Department
Trinity University
San Antonio, Texas

**George S. Mumford,
Ph.D.**
Professor of Astronomy,
   Emeritus
Tufts University
Medford, Massachusetts

Scott M. Rochette, Ph.D.
Department of the
   Earth Sciences
State University of New York
   at Brockport
Brockport, New York

Ronald Sass
Ecology and Evolutionary
   Biology
Rice University
Houston, Texas

Paul R. Stoddard, Ph.D.
Department of Geology and
   Environmental Geosciences
Northern Illinois University
DeKalb, Illinois

Contents in Brief

Contents

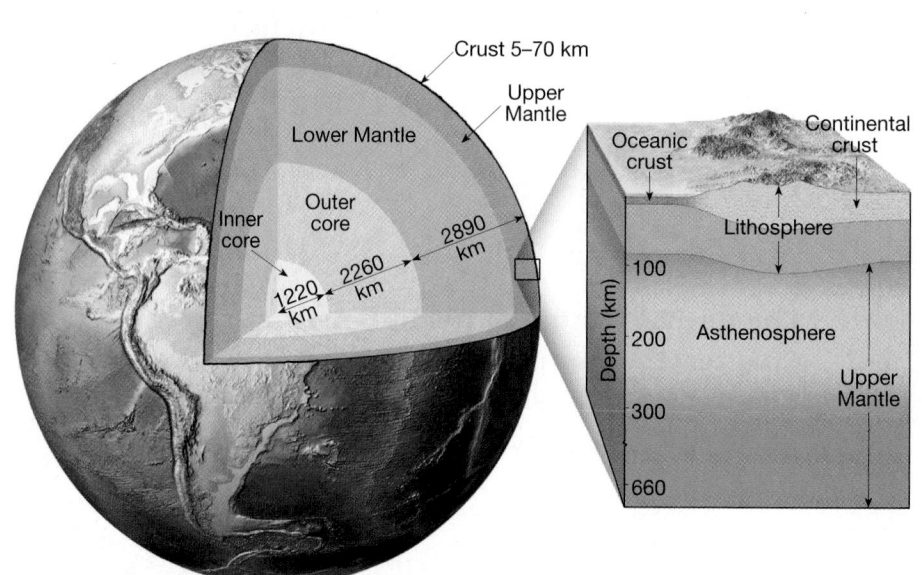

Unit 2 Sculpturing Earth's Surface

Unit 3 Forces Within

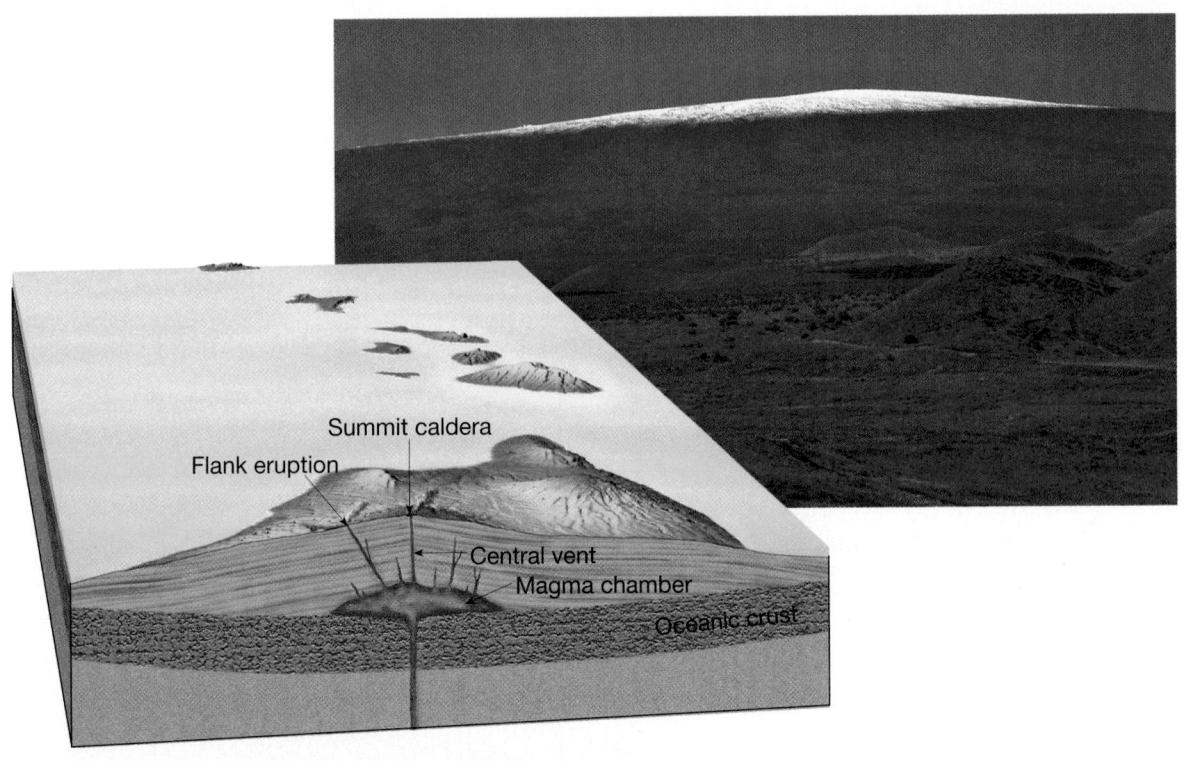

Summit caldera

Flank eruption

Central vent

Magma chamber

Oceanic crust

Unit 4 Historical Geology

Unit 5 Oceanography

Unit 6 Meteorology

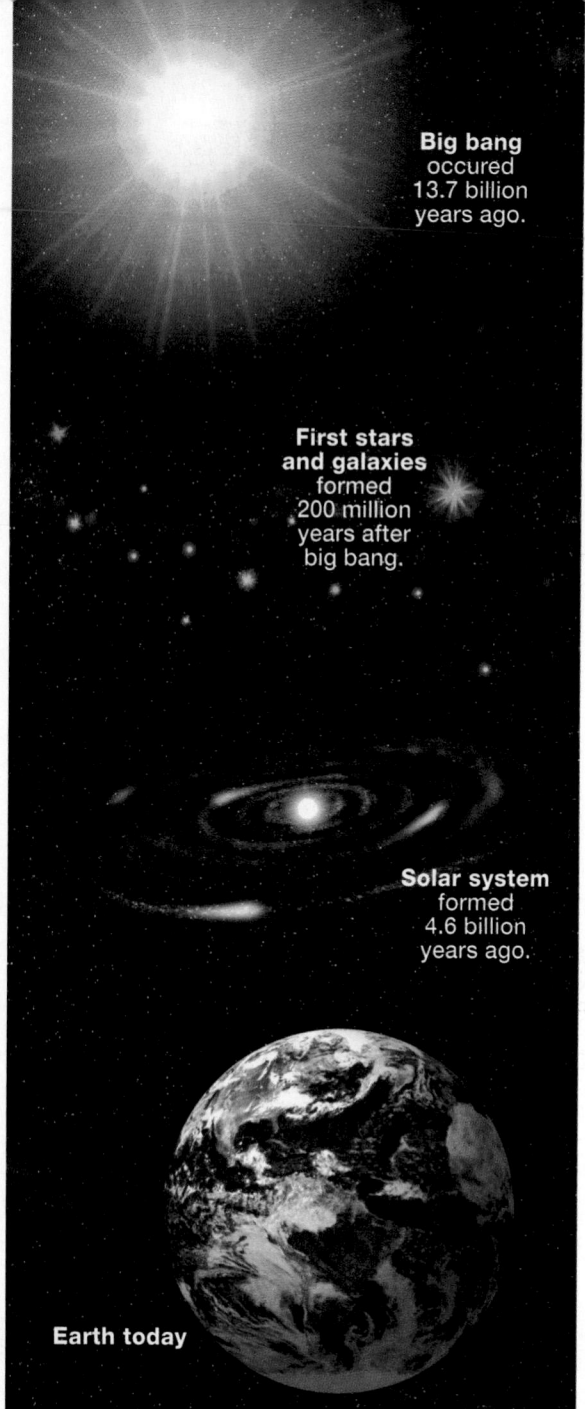

Big bang occured 13.7 billion years ago.

First stars and galaxies formed 200 million years after big bang.

Solar system formed 4.6 billion years ago.

Earth today

Unit 7 Astronomy

Skills and Reference Handbook

Labs and Activities

Inquiry › Activity

**Begin each chapter with an activity
that sets a purpose for reading.**

Features

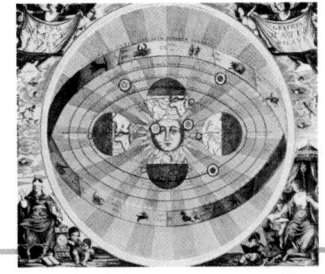

earth as a SYSTEM

Recognize some of the important interrelationships among Earth's spheres.

people and the ENVIRONMENT

Develop a better understanding of the effects of human activity on the natural environment.

understanding EARTH

Examine some of the difficulties encountered by scientists as they collect reliable data about our planet.

How the Earth Works

MAP✦MASTER™
Skills Activity

Discovery CHANNEL SCHOOL™ **Video Field Trip**

These videos will take you to places all over the world to explore some Earth Science topics that make our planet so unique in the universe.

GEODe EARTH SCIENCE

This engaging CD-ROM takes you on an audiovisual tour of the key concepts in the text. Through the wonder of animation, you can actually see in just a few seconds the dynamic processes that occur on Earth over millions of years. To be sure that you understand what you've learned, you'll work with a number of interesting interactive exercises to test your knowledge of each topic.

Careers in Earth and Space Science

The career opportunities available in Earth and space science are far reaching—from exploring distant galaxies to investigating deep inside Earth. Here are a few of these exciting careers.

Meteorologist

Meteorologists study how the physical characteristics, processes, and movements of the atmosphere affect the environment. They use this information to forecast the weather and study the patterns of weather change, such as droughts and global warming.

Educational requirements Four-year college degree, majoring in meteorology or atmospheric science

Seismologist

Seismologists are Earth scientists who investigate earthquakes. They determine the location and size of earthquakes, and use seismic waves to study Earth's interior. Some seismologists help the building industry design earthquake-proof structures.

Educational requirements Four-year college degree, majoring in geology, geophysics, or mathematics

Surveying Technician

Helping to measure and map Earth's surface are the responsibilities of surveying technicians. They assist land surveyors who measure distances, directions, and contours on, above, or below Earth's surface. Surveying technicians use surveying instruments to collect data and then enter the data into computers.

Educational requirements Two-year junior or community college program, one to three years of technical school

For: Career links
Visit: PHSchool.com
Web Code: ccb-3000

Commercial Diver

Just about anywhere there is water, there is a need for commercial divers. Their work ranges from operating submersibles to helping map the ocean floor. They may perform underwater surveys or carry out underwater rescue and salvage operations.

Educational requirements High-school diploma, diving-school certification or naval training

Archaeologist

Archaeologists excavate, preserve, study, and classify objects and structures from past cultures. In order to interpret what they see at a particular site, archaeologists must be able to identify different types of soil and notice the smallest of changes in soil characteristics.

Educational requirements Master's degree in anthropology or archaeology

Astronomer

Astronomers use the laws of physics and mathematics to study the universe. They may specialize to investigate the moon, sun, planets, stars, or galaxies, such as the Andromeda Galaxy shown in the photo at the left. They also may use what they know about astronomy to help develop satellites and spacecraft.

Educational requirements Doctoral degree in physics, astrophysics, or space physics

xix

CHAPTER 1 Introduction to Earth Science

CONCEPTS in Action

Exploration Lab
Determining Latitude and Longitude

Earth as a System
Earth's Place in the Universe

Understanding Earth
Studying Earth From Space

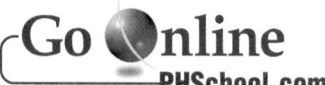

Discovery Channel School — Video Field Trip
Mapping the World

Take a field trip with Discovery Channel to learn more about maps. Answer the following questions after watching the video.

1. Name and describe two types of maps.
2. What is the significance of the prime meridian, and what European city does it run through?

Go Online PHSchool.com

For: Chapter 1 Resources
Visit: PHSchool.com
Web Code: cjk-9999

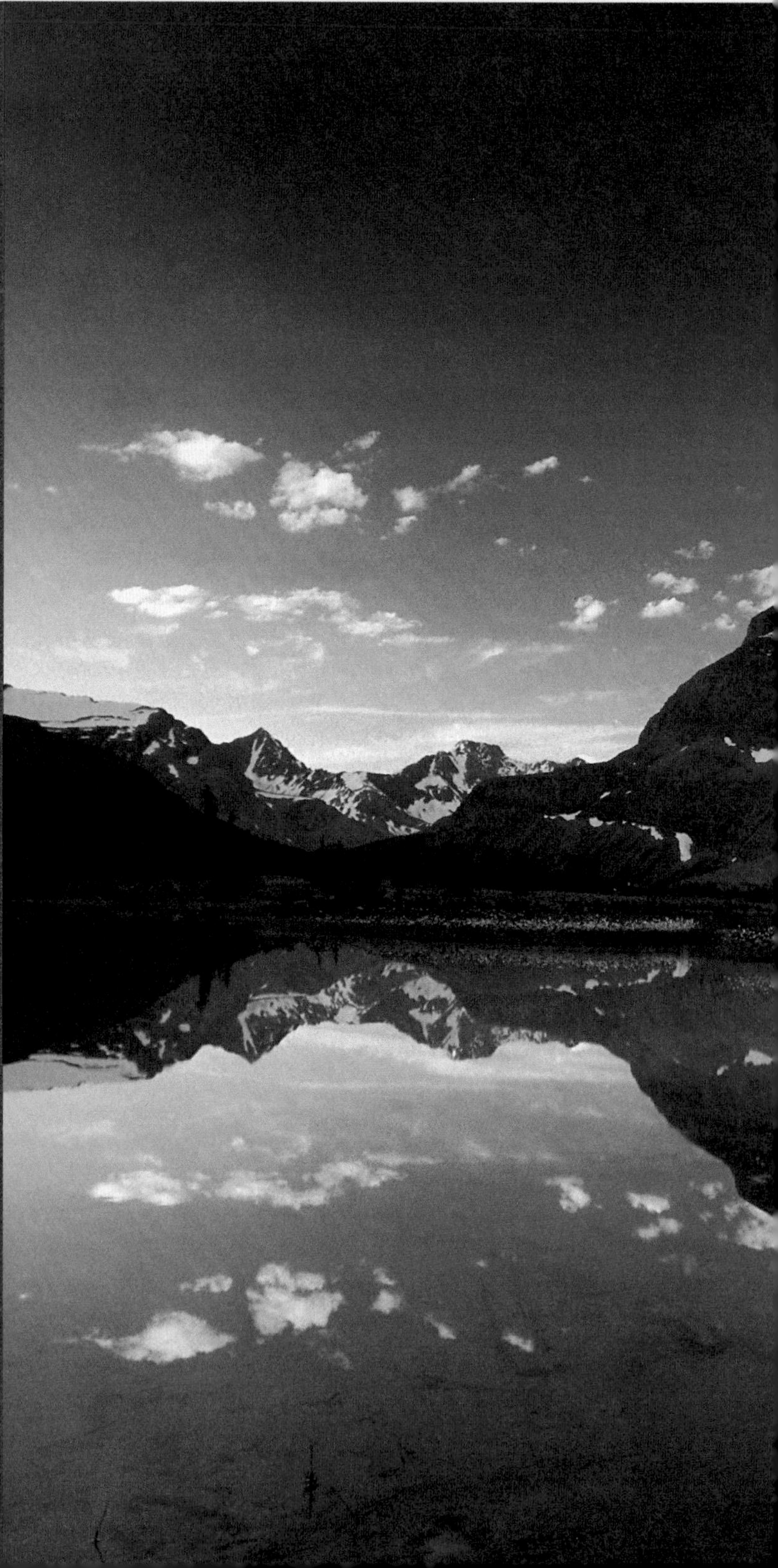

This photograph shows British Columbia's ▶ Mount Robson, the highest point in the Canadian Rockies.

Chapter Preview

Inquiry ⟩ Activity

Developing Your Observation Skills

Procedure
Look at the photograph on this page. Have you ever seen anything like it?

Think About It

1. **Observing** What features can you identify in the photograph?

2. **Inferring** Where do you think this photograph came from?

3. **Designing Experiments** If you were an Earth scientist, how could you use this photograph in your work?

1.1 What Is Earth Science?

Reading Focus

Key Concepts

- What is the study of Earth science?
- How did Earth and the solar system form?

Vocabulary

- ◆ Earth science
- ◆ geology
- ◆ oceanography
- ◆ meteorology
- ◆ astronomy

Reading Strategy

Categorizing As you read about the different branches of Earth science, fill in the column with the name of each branch and list some of the things that are studied.

geology	a. _____?_____
b. ____?____	c. _____?_____
d. ____?____	e. ____?____
f. ____?____	g. ____?____

The spectacular eruption of a volcano, the magnificent scenery of a rocky coast, and the destruction created by a hurricane are all subjects for Earth science. The study of Earth science deals with many fascinating and practical questions about our environment. What forces produced the mountains shown on page 1? Why does our daily weather change? Is our climate changing? How old is Earth? How is Earth related to the other planets in the solar system? What causes ocean tides? What was the Ice Age like? Will there be another?

Understanding Earth is not an easy task because our planet is always changing. Earth is a dynamic planet with a long and complex history.

Overview of Earth Science

Earth science is the name for the group of sciences that deals with Earth and its neighbors in space. Earth science includes many subdivisions of geology such as geochemistry, geophysics, geobiology and paleontology, as well as oceanography, meteorology, and astronomy.

Units 1 through 4 focus on the science of **geology,** a word that means "study of Earth." Geology is divided into two broad areas—physical geology and historical geology.

Physical geology includes the examination of the materials that make up Earth and the possible explanations for the many processes that shape our planet. Processes below the surface create earthquakes, build mountains, and produce volcanoes. Processes at the surface break rock apart and create

Figure 1 Scientists called paleontologists study fossils, which are signs of life in the distant past, to find out how life-forms have changed through time.
Posing Questions *What questions do you have about this fossil?*

different landforms. Erosion by water, wind, and ice results in different landscapes. You will learn that rocks and minerals form in response to Earth's internal and external processes. Understanding the origin of rocks and minerals is an important part of understanding Earth.

In contrast to physical geology, the aim of historical geology is to understand Earth's long history. Historical geology tries to establish a timeline of the vast number of physical and biological changes that have occurred in the past. See Figure 1. We study physical geology before historical geology because we must first understand how Earth works before we try to unravel its past.

 **Reading Checkpoint** *What are the two main areas of geology?*

Unit 5 is devoted to **oceanography.** Oceanography integrates the sciences of chemistry, physics, geology, and biology. Oceanographers study the composition and movements of seawater, as well as coastal processes, seafloor topography, and marine life. See Figure 2.

Unit 6 examines the composition of Earth's atmosphere. The combined effects of Earth's motions and energy from the sun cause the atmosphere to produce different weather conditions. This, in turn, creates the basic pattern of global climates. **Meteorology** is the study of the atmosphere and the processes that produce weather and climate. Like oceanography, meteorology also involves other branches of science.

Unit 7 demonstrates that understanding Earth requires an understanding of Earth's position in the universe. The science of **astronomy,** the study of the universe, is useful in probing the origins of our own environment. All objects in space, including Earth, are subject to the same physical laws. Learning about the other members of our solar system and the universe beyond helps us to understand Earth.

Throughout its long existence, Earth has been changing. In fact, it is changing as you read this page and will continue to do so. Sometimes the changes are rapid and violent, such as when tornados, landslides, or volcanic eruptions occur. Many changes, however, take place so gradually that they go unnoticed during a lifetime.

Figure 2 Oceanographers study all aspects of the ocean—the chemistry of its waters, the geology of its seafloor, the physics of its interactions with the atmosphere, and the biology of its organisms.

Formation of Earth

Earth is one of nine planets that revolve around the sun. Our solar system has an orderly nature. Scientists understand that Earth and the other planets formed during the same time span and from the same material as the sun. ⬤**The nebular hypothesis suggests that the bodies of our solar system evolved from an enormous rotating cloud called the solar nebula. It was made up mostly of hydrogen and helium, with a small percentage of heavier elements.** Figure 3 on page 4 summarizes some key points of this hypothesis.

Figure 3 Formation of the Solar System According to the Nebular Hypothesis A Our solar system began as an enormous cloud of dust and gases made up mostly of hydrogen and helium with a small percentage of heavier elements. **B** This cloud, called a nebula, started to rotate and collapse toward the center of the cloud. Heat was generated at the center, which eventually formed the sun. **C** Cooling of the nebula caused rocky and metallic materials to form tiny solid particles. **D** Repeated collisions of these particles resulted in the formation of asteroid-sized bodies. **E** These asteroids eventually combined to form the four inner planets—Mercury, Venus, Earth, and Mars. The lighter materials and gases combined farther away from the center to form the four outer planets—Jupiter, Saturn, Uranus, and Neptune.

High temperatures and weak fields of gravity characterized the inner planets. As a result, the inner planets were not able to hold onto the lighter gases of the nebular cloud. The lightest gases, hydrogen and helium, were whisked away toward the heavier planets by the solar wind. Earth, Mars, and Venus were able to retain some heavier gases including water vapor and carbon dioxide. The materials that formed by outer planets contained high percentages of water, carbon dioxide, ammonia, and methane. The size and frigid temperatures of the outer planets provided the surface gravity to hold these heavier gases.

Layers Form on Earth Shortly after Earth formed, the decay of radioactive elements, combined with heat released by colliding particles, produced some melting of the interior. This allowed the denser elements, mostly iron and nickel, to sink to Earth's center. The lighter, rocky components floated outward, toward the surface. This sinking and floating is believed to still be occurring, but on a much smaller scale. As a result of this process, Earth's interior is not made of uniform materials. It consists of layers of materials that have different properties.

 **Reading Checkpoint** *Why does Earth have layers?*

An important result of this process is that gaseous materials were allowed to escape from Earth's interior, just as gases escape today during volcanic eruptions. In this way, an atmosphere gradually formed along with the ocean. It was composed mainly of gases that were released from within the planet.

Section 1.1 Assessment

Reviewing Concepts
1. What are the sciences that are included in Earth science?
2. What topics are included in the study of physical geology?
3. Explain how physical geology differs from historical geology.
4. Describe the nebular hypothesis.

Critical Thinking
5. **Forming Conclusions** Explain why Earth is called a dynamic planet.

6. **Inferring** Would meteorology be a useful science to apply to the study of planets such as Mercury and Mars? Explain.
7. **Hypothesizing** Suppose that as Earth formed, all lighter elements were released to surrounding space. How might this affect the structure of Earth today?

Connecting Concepts

Summarizing Earth science is composed of many different areas of study. Why is it important to include all of these areas in the study of Earth and the solar system?

Earth's Place in the Universe

For centuries, people who have gazed at the night sky have wondered about the nature of the universe, Earth's place within it, and whether or not we are alone. Today many exciting discoveries in astronomy are beginning to provide answers about the origin of the universe, the formation and evolution of stars, and how Earth came into existence.

The realization that the universe is immense and orderly began in the early 1900s. Edwin Hubble and other scientists demonstrated that the Milky Way galaxy is one of hundreds of billions of galaxies, each of which contains billions of stars. Evidence supports that Earth, its materials, and all living things are the result of the Big Bang theory. The universe began between 13 and 14 billion years ago as a dense, hot, massive amount of material exploded with violent force. See Figure 4. Within about one second, the temperature of the expanding universe cooled to approximately 10 billion degrees. Basic atomic particles called protons and neutrons began to appear. After a few minutes, atoms of the simplest elements—hydrogen and helium—had formed. The initial conversion of energy to matter in the young universe was completed.

During the first billion years or so, matter (essentially hydrogen and helium) in the expanding universe clumped together to form enormous clouds that eventually collapsed to become galaxies and clusters of galaxies. Inside these collapsing clouds, smaller concentrations of matter formed into stars. One of the billions of galaxies to form was the Milky Way.

During the life of most stars, energy produced as hydrogen nuclei (protons) fuses with other hydrogen nuclei to form helium. During this process, called nuclear fusion, matter is converted to energy. Stars begin to die when their nuclear fuel is used up. Massive stars often have explosive deaths. During these events, called supernovas, nuclear fusion produces atoms such as oxygen, carbon, and iron. These atoms may become the materials that make up future generations of stars. From the debris scattered during the death of a preexisting star, our sun, and the solar system formed

Our star, the sun, is at the very least a second-generation star. Along with the planets in our solar system, the sun began forming nearly 5 billion years ago from a large interstellar cloud called a nebula. This nebula consisted of dust particles and gases enriched in heavy elements from supernova explosions. Gravitational energy caused the nebula to contract, rotate, and flatten. Inside, smaller concentrations of matter began condensing to form the planets. At the center of the nebula there was sufficient pressure and heat to initiate hydrogen nuclear fusion, and our sun was born.

It has been said that all life on Earth is related to the stars. This is true because the atoms in our bodies and the atoms that make up everything on Earth, owe their origin to a supernova event that occurred billions of years ago, trillions of kilometers away.

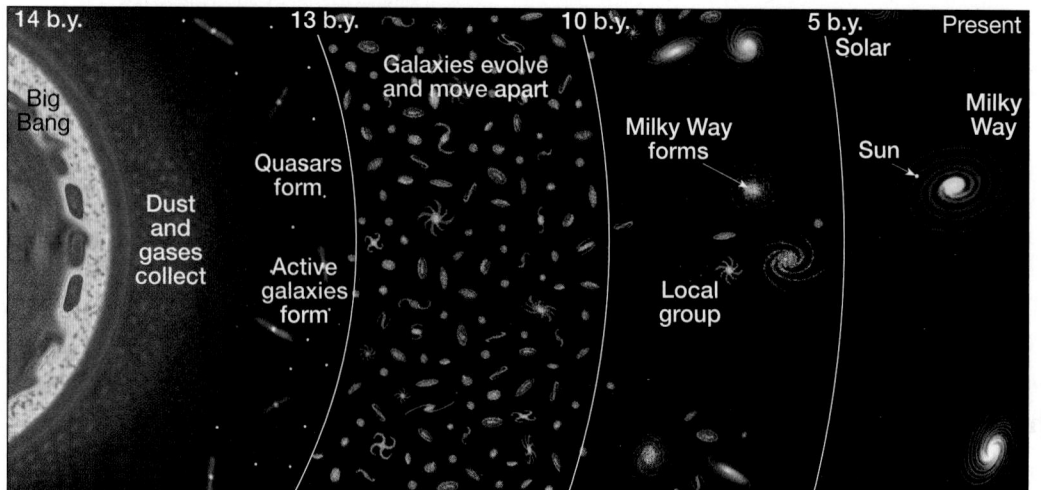

Figure 4 Big Bang Theory Between 13 and 14 billion years ago, a huge explosion sent all of the universe's matter flying outward at great speed. After a few billion years, the material cooled and condensed into the first stars and galaxies. About 5 billion years ago, our solar system began forming in a galaxy that is now called the Milky Way galaxy.

1.2 A View of Earth

Reading Focus

Key Concepts

- What are the four major spheres into which Earth is divided?
- What defines the three main parts of the solid Earth?
- Which model explains the position of continents and the occurrence of volcanoes and earthquakes?

Vocabulary

- hydrosphere
- atmosphere
- geosphere
- biosphere
- core
- mantle
- crust

Reading Strategy

Predicting Before you read, predict the meaning of the vocabulary words. After you read, revise your definition if your prediction was incorrect.

Vocabulary Term	Before You Read	After You Read
hydrosphere	a. _____?_____	b. _____?_____
atmosphere	c. _____?_____	d. _____?_____
geosphere	e. _____?_____	f. _____?_____
biosphere	g. _____?_____	h. _____?_____
core	i. _____?_____	j. _____?_____
mantle	k. _____?_____	l. _____?_____
crust	m. _____?_____	n. _____?_____

A view such as the one in Figure 5A provided the *Apollo 8* astronauts with a unique view of our home. Seen from space, Earth is breathtaking in its beauty. Such an image reminds us that our home is, after all, a planet—small, self-contained, and in some ways even fragile.

If you look closely at Earth from space, you may see that it is much more than rock and soil. The swirling clouds and the vast global ocean emphasize the importance of water on our planet.

Figure 5 A View that greeted the *Apollo 8* astronauts as their spacecraft emerged from behind th Moon. **B** Africa and Arabia are prominent in this image of Earth taken from *Apollo 17*. The tan areas are desert regions. The bands of clouds over central Africa are associated with rainforests. Antarctica, which is covered by glacial ice, is visible at the south pole. The dark blue oceans and white swirling clouds remind us of the importance of oceans and the atmosphere.

Earth's Major Spheres

The view of Earth shown in Figure 5B should help you see why the physical environment is traditionally divided into three major spheres: the water portion of our planet, the **hydrosphere;** Earth's gaseous envelope, the **atmosphere;** and the **geosphere.**

Our environment is characterized by the continuous interactions of air and rock, rock and water, and water and air. The **biosphere,** which is made up of all the life-forms on Earth, interacts with all three of these physical spheres. **Earth can be thought of as consisting of four major spheres: the hydrosphere, atmosphere, geosphere, and biosphere.**

Hydrosphere Water is what makes Earth unique. All of the water on Earth makes up the hydrosphere. Continually on the move, water evaporates from the oceans to the atmosphere, falls back to Earth as rain, and runs back to the ocean. The oceans account for approximately 97 percent of the water on Earth. The remaining 3 percent is fresh water and is present in groundwater, streams, lakes, and glaciers.

Although these freshwater sources make up a small fraction of the total amount of water on Earth, they are quite important. Streams, glaciers, and groundwater are responsible for sustaining life and creating many of Earth's varied landforms.

Atmosphere A life-sustaining, thin, gaseous envelope called the atmosphere surrounds Earth. It reaches beyond 100 kilometers above Earth, yet 90 percent occurs within just 16 kilometers of Earth's surface. This thin blanket of air is an important part of Earth. It provides the air that we breathe. It protects us from the sun's intense heat and dangerous radiation. The energy exchanges that continually occur between space, the atmosphere, and Earth's surface produce weather and climate.

If Earth had no atmosphere, life on our planet as we know it could not exist. Many of the processes and interactions that make the surface such a dynamic place would not occur. For example, without weathering and erosion, the face of our planet might more closely resemble the moon.

Geosphere Lying beneath both the atmosphere and the ocean is the geosphere. **Because the geosphere is not uniform, it is divided into three main parts based on differences in composition—the core, the mantle, and the crust.** Figure 6A shows the dense or heavy inner sphere that is the core; the less dense mantle; and the lighter, thin crust. The crust is not uniform in thickness. It is thinnest beneath the oceans and thickest beneath the continents. Figure 6B shows that the crust and uppermost mantle make up a rigid outer layer called the lithosphere. Beneath the lithosphere, the rocks become partially molten, or melted. They are able to slowly flow because of the uneven distribution of heat deep within Earth. This region is called the asthenosphere. Beneath the asthenosphere, the rock becomes more dense. This region of Earth is called the lower mantle.

Figure 6 A On this diagram, the inner core, outer core, and mantle are drawn to scale but the thickness of the crust is exaggerated by about 5 times. **B** There are two types of crust—oceanic and continental. The lithosphere is made up of the crust and upper mantle. Below the lithosphere are the asthenosphere and the lower mantle.

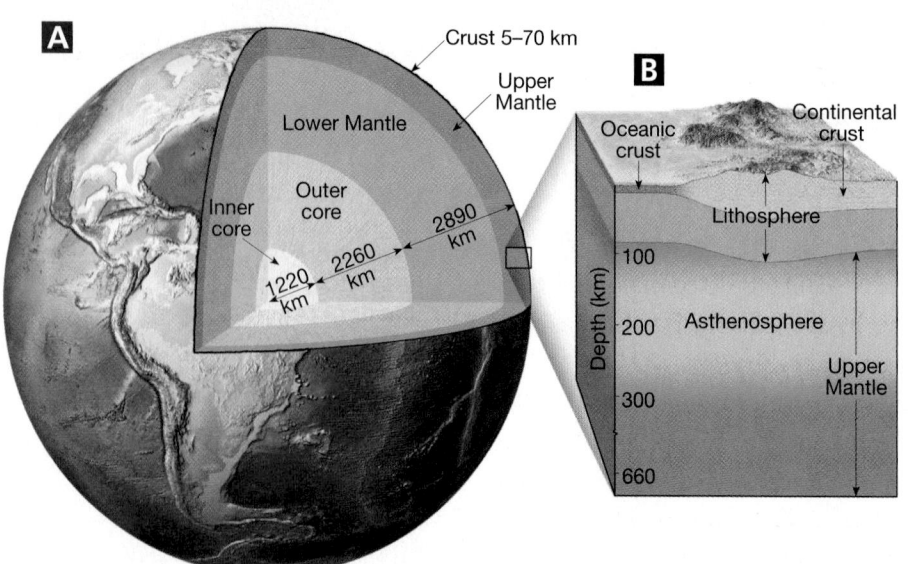

Biosphere The biosphere includes all life on Earth. It is concentrated in a zone that extends from the ocean floor upward for several kilometers into the atmosphere. Plants and animals depend on the physical environment for life. However, organisms do more than just respond to their physical environment. Through countless interactions, organisms help maintain and alter their physical environment. Without life, the makeup and nature of the solid Earth, hydrosphere, and atmosphere would be very different.

 **Reading Checkpoint** *What are Earth's four major spheres?*

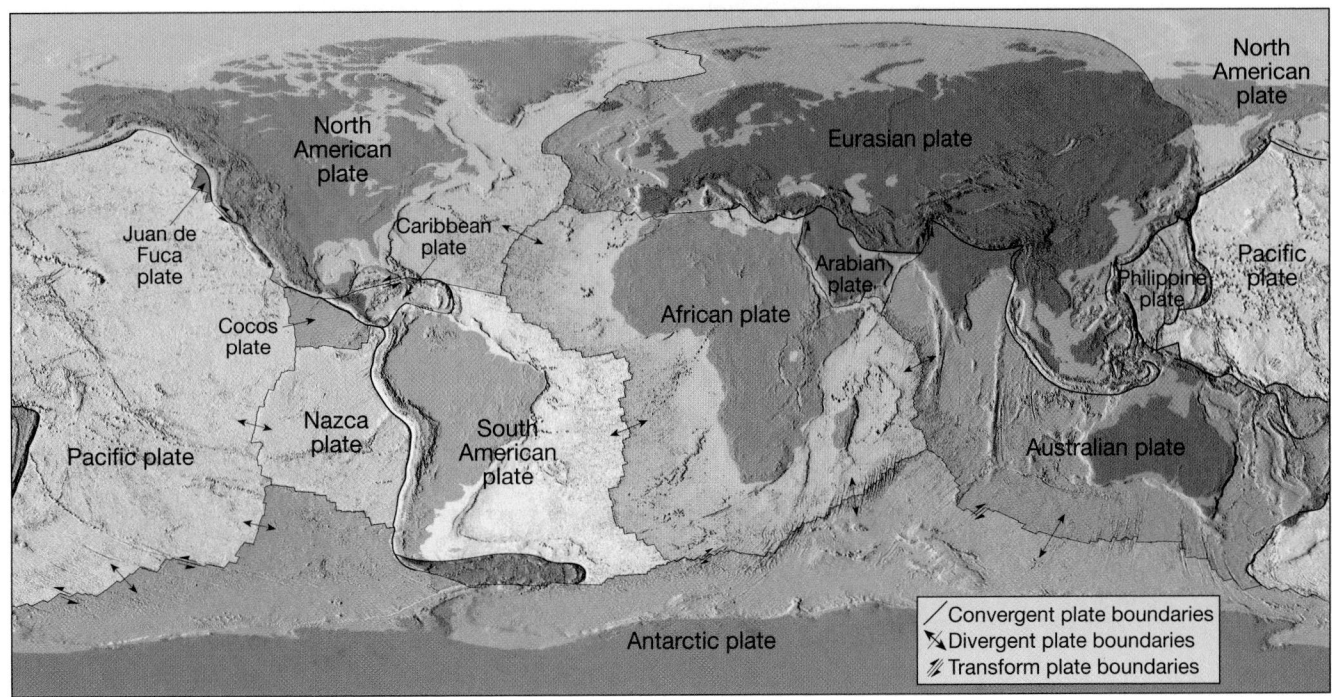

Antarctic plate

/ Convergent plate boundaries
⬟ Divergent plate boundaries
⫽ Transform plate boundaries

Plate Tectonics

You have read that Earth is a dynamic planet. If we could go back in time a billion years or more, we would find a planet with a surface that was dramatically different from what it is today. Such prominent features as the Grand Canyon, the Rocky Mountains, and the Appalachian Mountains did not exist. We would find that the continents had different shapes and were located in different positions from those of today.

There are two types of forces affecting Earth's surface. *Destructive forces* such as weathering and erosion work to wear away high points and flatten out the surface. *Constructive forces* such as mountain building and volcanism build up the surface by raising the land and depositing new material in the form of lava. These constructive forces depend on Earth's internal heat for their source of energy.

Figure 7 Plate Tectonics There are currently 7 major plates recognized and numerous smaller plates.
Relating Cause and Effect
What is the relationship between mountain chains and plate boundaries?

Within the last several decades, a great deal has been learned about the workings of Earth. In fact, this period is called a revolution in our knowledge about Earth. This revolution began in the early part of the twentieth century with the idea that the continents had moved about the face of the Earth. This idea contradicted the accepted view that the continents and ocean basins are stationary features on the face of Earth. Few scientists believed this new idea. More than 50 years passed before enough data were gathered to transform this hypothesis into a widely accepted theory. **The theory that finally emerged, called plate tectonics, provided geologists with a model to explain how earthquakes and volcanic eruptions occur and how continents move.**

Reading Checkpoint *What is the difference between destructive forces and constructive forces?*

According to the plate tectonics model, Earth's lithosphere is broken into several individual sections called plates. Figure 7 on page 9 shows their current position. These plates move slowly and continuously across the surface. This motion is driven by the result of an unequal distribution of heat within Earth. Ultimately, this movement of Earth's lithospheric plates generates earthquakes, volcanic activity, and the deformation of large masses of rock into mountains. You will learn more about the powerful effects of plate tectonics in Chapter 9.

Section 1.2 Assessment

Reviewing Concepts

1. Which of Earth's spheres do each of these features belong: lake, meadow, canyon, cloud?
2. What are the three main parts of the geosphere?
3. Why is the solid Earth layered?
4. The plate tectonics theory explains the existence and occurrence of what features?
5. What sort of energy allows the tectonic plates to move?
6. Describe an example of how water moves through the hydrosphere.

Critical Thinking

7. **Inferring** Using the definitions of spheres as they occur on Earth, what spheres do you think are present on Venus?
8. **Applying Concepts** Describe a situation in which two or more of Earth's spheres are interacting.
9. **Classifying** Choose an Earth science branch. List how some of its studies relate to Earth's spheres.

Connecting Concepts

Earth's Spheres You learned in Section 1.1 that Earth is a dynamic planet. Explain how features in each of Earth's spheres are changing over time.

1.3 Representing Earth's Surface

Key Concepts

- What lines on a globe are used to indicate location?
- What problems do mapmakers face when making maps?
- How do topographic maps differ from other maps?

Vocabulary

- ◆ latitude
- ◆ longitude
- ◆ topographic map
- ◆ contour line
- ◆ contour interval

Reading Strategy

Monitoring Your Understanding Preview the Key Concepts, topic headings, vocabulary, and figures in this section. List two things you expect to learn. After reading, state what you learned about each item you listed.

What I Expect to Learn	What I Learned
a. _____?_____	b. _____?_____
c. _____?_____	d. _____?_____

Determining Location

Today we use maps and computer programs to help us plan our routes. Long ago, people had to rely on maps that were made using data and information that were collected by travelers and explorers. Today computer technology is available to anyone who wants to use it. Mapmaking has changed a lot throughout recorded history.

After Christopher Columbus and others proved that Earth was not flat, mapmakers began to use a global grid to help determine location.

Global Grid Scientists use two special Earth measurements to describe location. The distance around Earth is measured in degrees. **Latitude is the distance north or south of the equator, measured in degrees. Longitude is the distance east or west of the prime meridian, measured in degrees.** Earth is 360 degrees in circumference. Lines of latitude are east-west circles around the globe. All points on the circle have the same latitude. The line of latitude around the middle of the globe, at 0 degrees (°), is the equator. Lines of longitude run north and south. The prime meridian is the line of longitude that marks ° of longitude as shown in Figure 8.

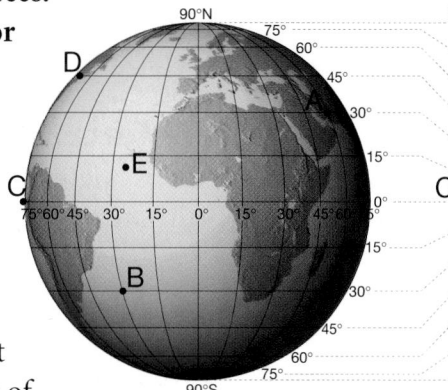
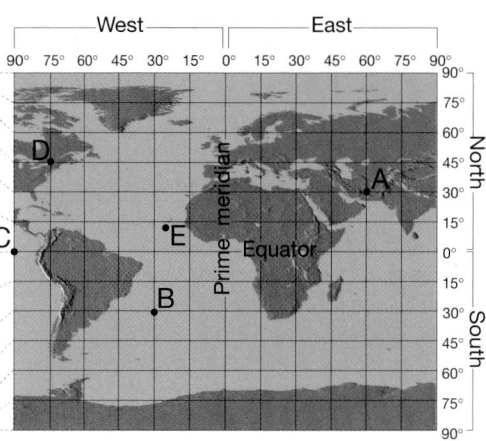

Figure 8 Global Grid

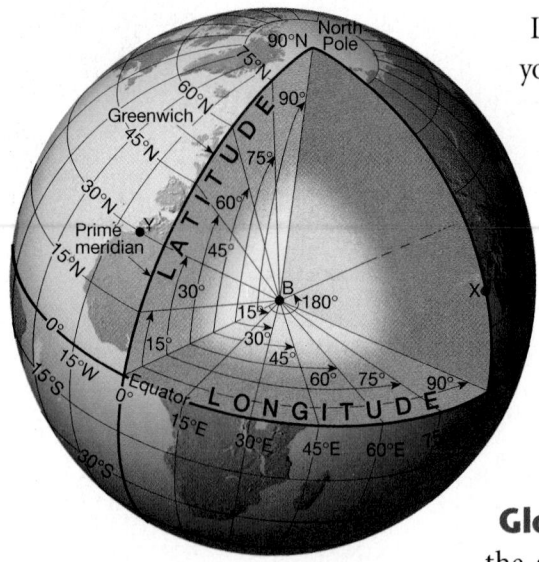

Figure 9 Measuring Latitude and Longitude

Lines of latitude and longitude form a global grid. This grid allows you to state the absolute location of any place on Earth. For example, Savannah, Georgia, is located at 32° north latitude and 81° west longitude.

The equator divides Earth in two. Each half is called a hemisphere. The equator divides Earth into northern and southern hemispheres. The prime meridian and the 180° meridian divide Earth into eastern and western hemispheres.

✓ **Reading Checkpoint** *How does the global grid divide Earth?*

Globes As people explored Earth, they collected information about the shapes and sizes of islands, continents, and bodies of water. Mapmakers wanted to present this information accurately. The best way was to put the information on a model, or globe, with the same round shape as Earth itself. By using an accurate shape for Earth, mapmakers could show the continents and oceans of Earth much as they really are. The only difference would be the scale, or relative size.

But there is a problem with globes. Try making a globe large enough to show the streets in your community. The globe might have to be larger than your school building! A globe can't be complete enough to be useful for finding directions and at the same time small enough to be convenient for everyday use.

Maps and Mapping

A map is a flat representation of Earth's surface. But Earth is round. Can all of Earth's features be accurately represented on a flat surface without distorting them? The answer is no. **No matter what kind of map is made, some portion of the surface will always look either too small, too big, or out of place. Mapmakers have, however, found ways to limit the distortion of shape, size, distance, and direction.**

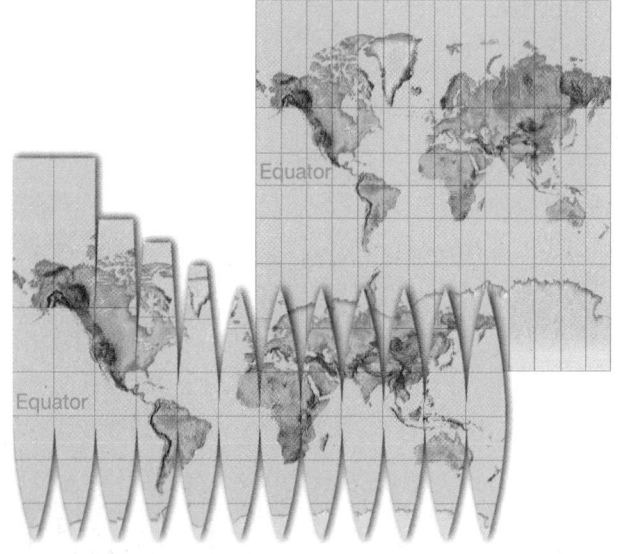

Figure 10 Mercator Map To make a Mercator map, mapmakers have to carve an image of Earth's surface into slices and then stretch the slices into rectangles. Stretching the slices enlarges parts of the map. The enlargement becomes greater toward the north and south poles. **Observing** *What areas on the map appear larger than they should?*

The Mercator Projection In 1569, a mapmaker named Gerardus Mercator created a map to help sailors navigate around Earth. On this map, the lines of longitude are parallel, making this grid rectangular, as shown on the map in Figure 10. The map was useful because, although the sizes and distances were distorted, it showed directions accurately. Today, more than 400 years later, many seagoing navigators still use the Mercator projection map.

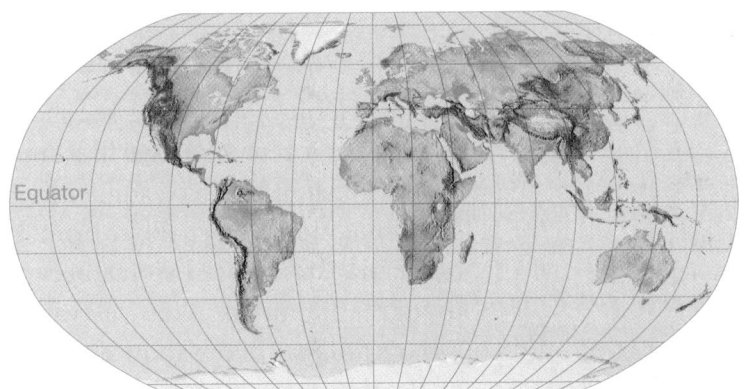

Figure 11 Robinson Projection Map Compare this map to the Mercator projection.
Comparing and Contrasting *How do the shapes in the continents differ between these maps? Are there any other differences?*

Different Projection Maps for Different Purposes

The best projection is always determined by its intended use. The Robinson projection map is one of the most widely used. Maps that use this projection show most distances, sizes, and shapes accurately. However, even a Robinson projection has distortions, especially in areas around the edges of the map. You can see this in Figure 11. Conic projection maps are made by wrapping a cone of paper around a globe at a particular line of latitude, as shown in Figure 12. Various points and lines are projected onto the paper. There is almost no distortion along the line of latitude that's in contact with the cone, but there can be much distortion in areas away from this latitude. Because accuracy is great over a small area, these maps are used to make road maps and weather maps. Gnomonic projections, as shown in Figure 13, are made by placing a piece of paper on a globe so that it touches a single point on the globe's surface. Various points and lines are then projected onto the paper. Although distances and directions are distorted on these maps, they are useful to sailors and navigators because they show with great accuracy the shortest distance between two points.

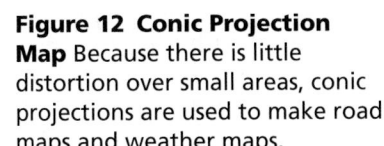

Figure 12 Conic Projection Map Because there is little distortion over small areas, conic projections are used to make road maps and weather maps.

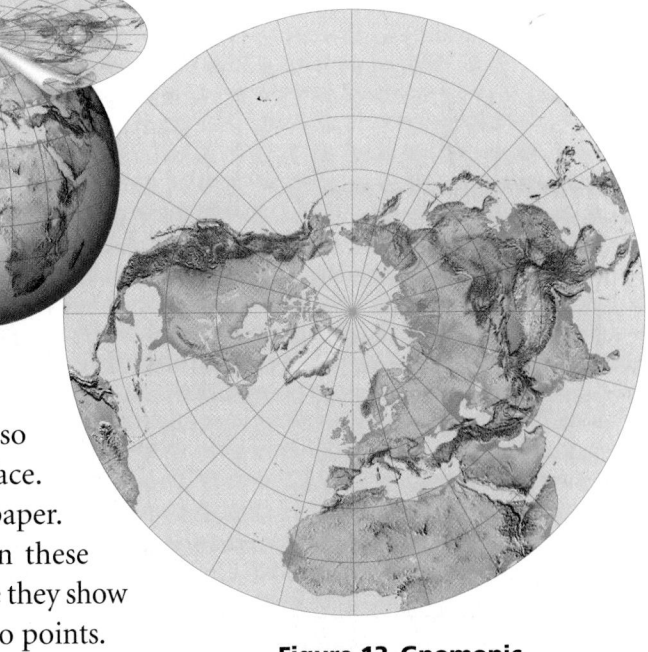

Figure 13 Gnomonic Projection Map Gnomonic projections allow sailors to accurately determine distance and direction across the oceans.

Reading Checkpoint *What major problem must mapmakers overcome?*

Introduction to Earth Science **13**

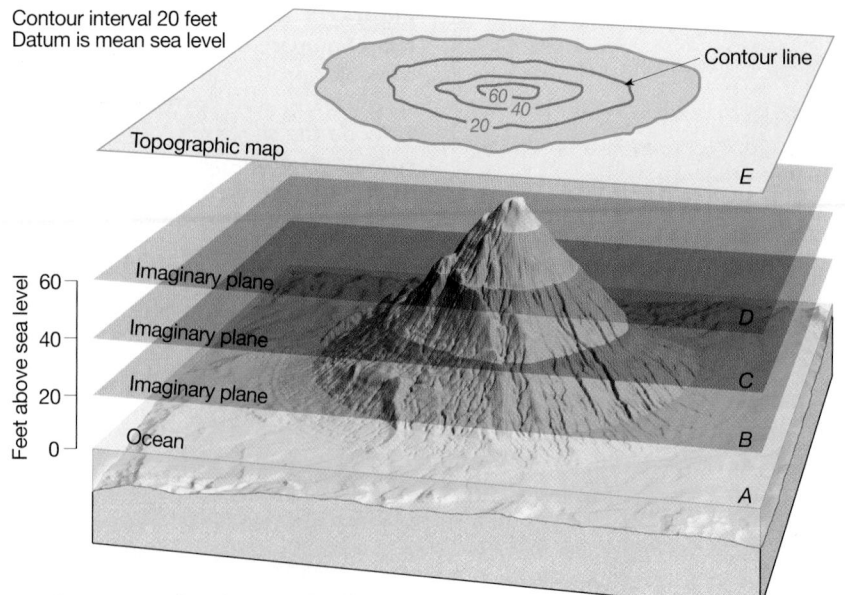

Contour interval 20 feet
Datum is mean sea level

Contour line

Topographic map

Feet above sea level

60 — Imaginary plane
40 — Imaginary plane
20 — Imaginary plane
0 — Ocean

E
D
C
B
A

Figure 14 This illustration shows how contour lines are determined when topographic maps are constructed.

Topographic Maps

A **topographic map,** like the one shown in Figure 15, represents Earth's three-dimensional surface in two dimensions. 🔑 **Topographic maps differ from the other maps discussed so far because topographic maps show elevation. Topographical maps show elevation of Earth's surface by means of contour lines.** Most also show the presence of bodies of water, roads, government and public buildings, political boundaries, and place names. These maps are important for geologists, hikers, campers and anyone else interested in the three-dimensional lay of the land.

Contour Lines The elevation of the land is indicated by using contour lines. Every position along a single contour line is the same elevation. Adjacent contour lines represent a change in elevation. Every fifth line is bold and labeled with the elevation. It is called an index contour. The **contour interval** tells you the difference in elevation between adjacent lines. The steepness of an area can be determined by examining a map. Lines that are closer together indicate a steeper slope, while lines farther apart indicate a gentler slope. You can see this relationship on the illustration in Figure 14. Contour lines that form a circle represent a hill. A depression is represented by circular contours that have hachure marks, which are small lines on the circle that point to the center. Contour lines never touch or intersect.

Figure 15 Topographic Map
This is a portion of the Holy Cross, Colorado, topographic map. Contour lines are shown in brown.

Reading Checkpoint

How do topographic maps indicate changes in elevation?

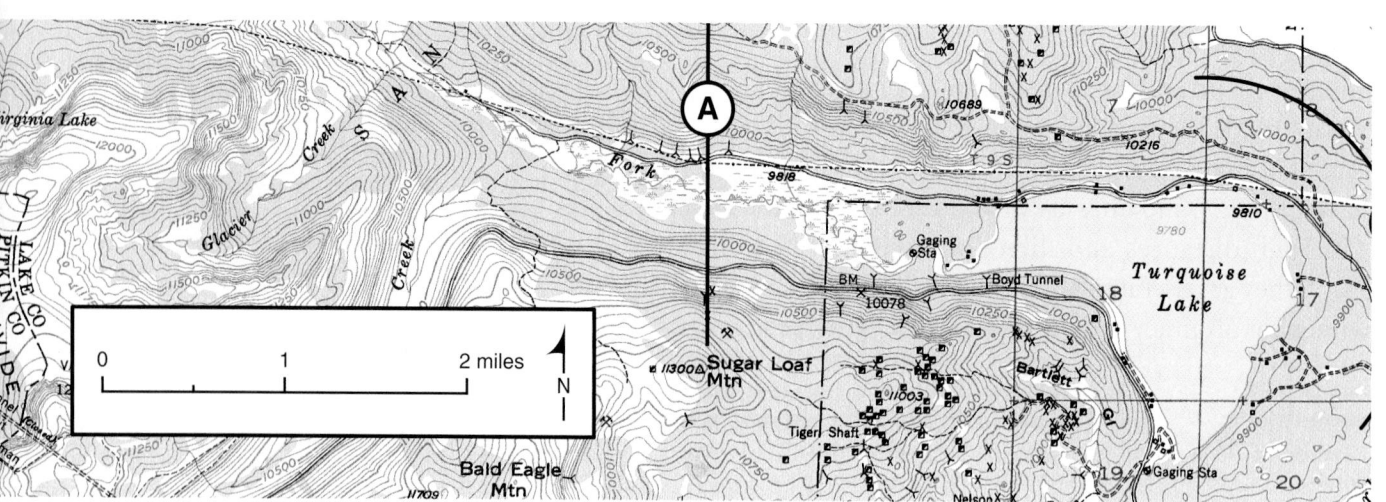

Scale A map represents a certain amount of area on Earth's surface. So it is necessary to be able to determine distances on the map and relate them to the real world. Suppose you want to build a scale model of a boat that is 20 feet long. If your model is a 1/5-scale model, then it is 4 feet long.

In a similar way, a map is drawn to scale where a certain distance on the map is equal to a certain distance at the surface. Because maps model Earth's surface, the scale must be larger than that of the model boat. Look at the scale on the map in Figure 16. The ratio reads 1:24,000. This means that 1 unit on the map is equal to 24,000 units on the ground. Because the ratio has no units, it may stand for anything. We usually use inches or centimeters for our units. If the 1 stands for 1 centimeter on the map, how many kilometers does the 24,000 stand for on the ground?

Another scale provided on a map is a bar scale. See Figure 15. This allows you to use a ruler to measure the distance on the map and then line the ruler up to the bar to determine the distance represented.

Geologic Maps It is often desirable to know the type and age of the rocks that are exposed, or crop out, at the surface. This kind of map is shown in Figure 16. ⟵ **A map that shows this information is called a geologic map.** Once individual rock formations are identified, and mapped out, their distribution and extent are drawn onto the map. Each rock formation is assigned a color and sometimes a pattern. A key provides the information needed to learn what formations are present on the map. Contour lines are often included to provide a more detailed and useful map.

Go Online
SciLINKS NSTA

For: Links on mapping
Visit: www.SciLinks.org
Web Code: cjn-1013

Figure 16 Geologic Map The color coding on the map represents some rock formations in Montana. Each color and pattern represents a different type of rock.

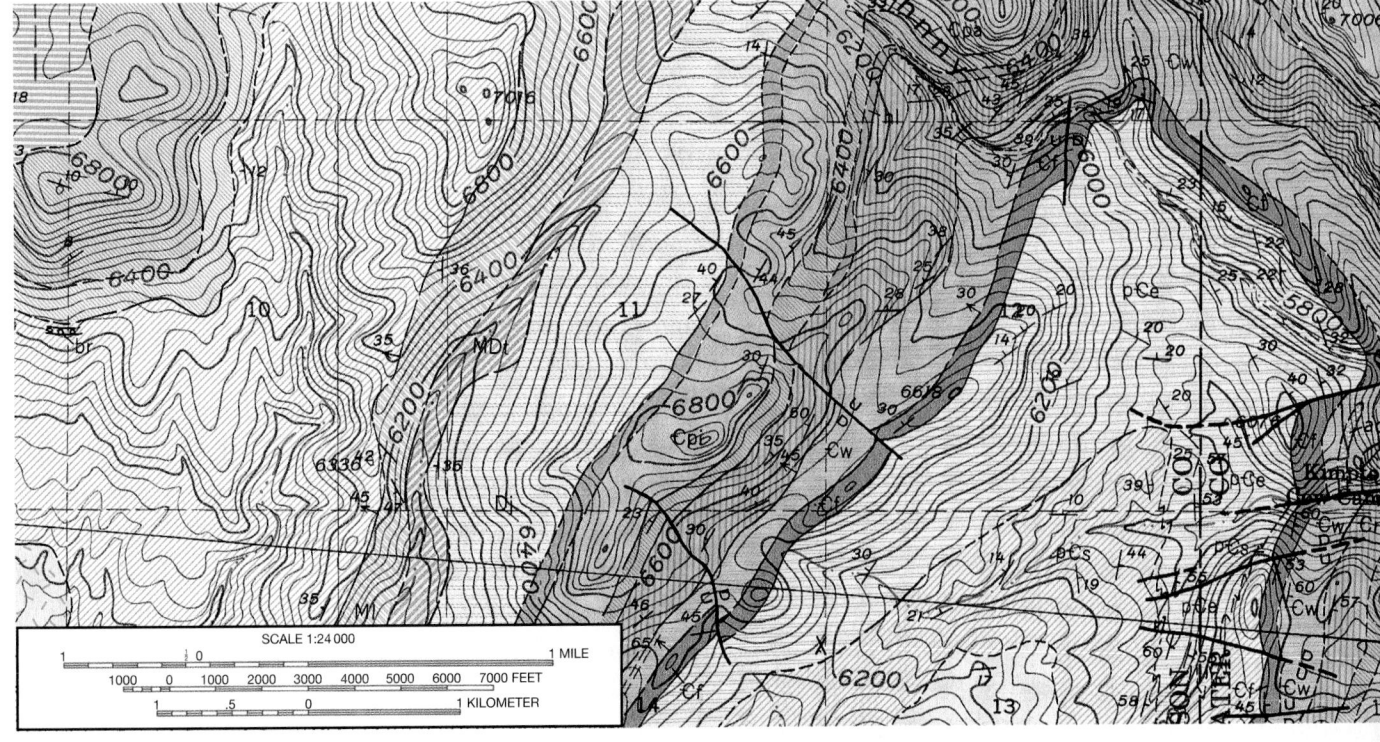

SCALE 1:24 000

1   0   1 MILE

1000   0   1000   2000   3000   4000   5000   6000   7000 FEET

1   .5   0   1 KILOMETER

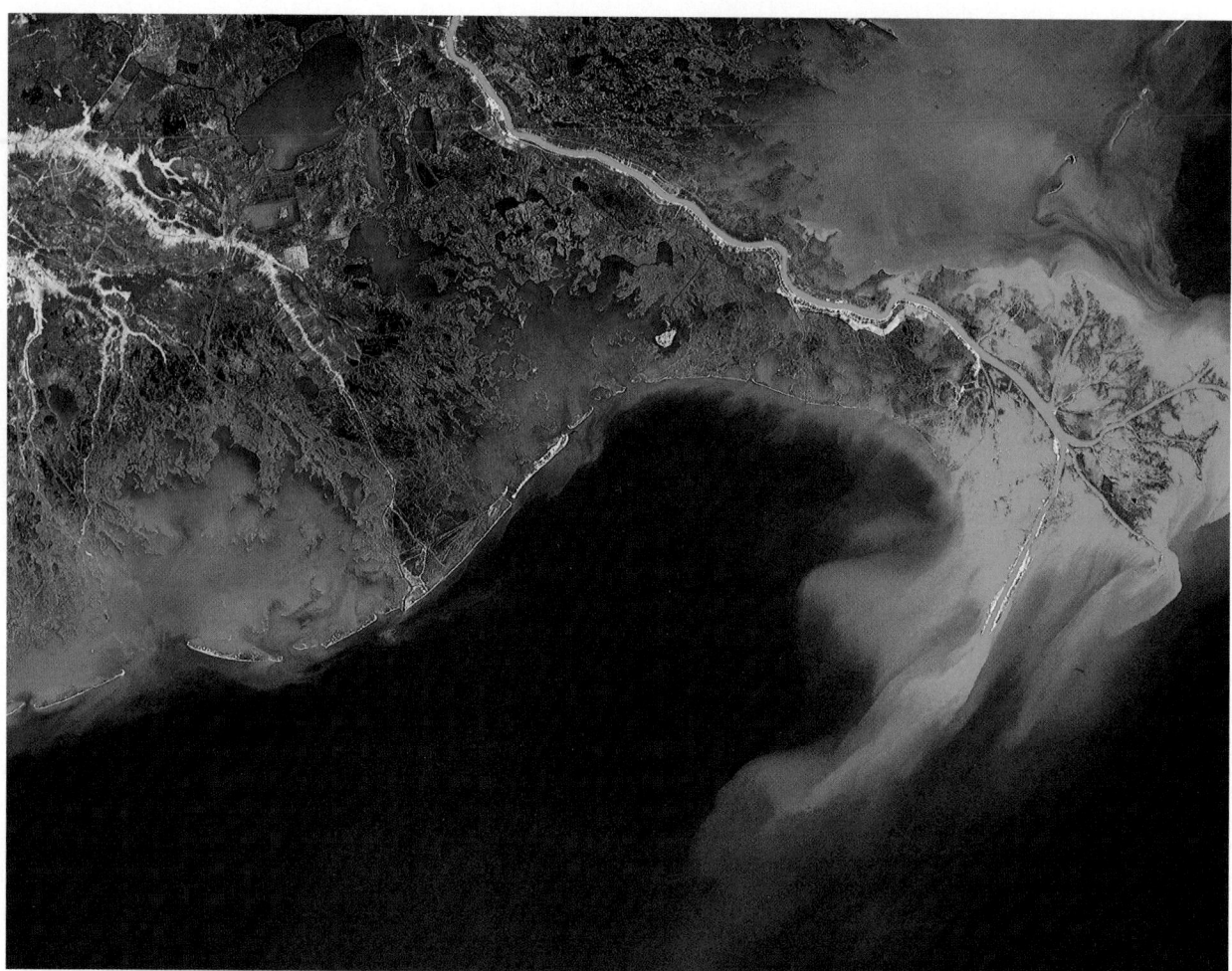

Figure 17 Satellite Image of the Mississippi River Delta
Moving sediment (light blue) indicates current patterns. Red shows vegetation.

Advanced Technology

Advanced technology is used to make maps that are more accurate than ever before. **Today's technology provides us with the ability to more precisely analyze Earth's physical properties.** Scientists now use satellites and computers to send and receive data. These data are converted into usable forms such as pictures and numerical summaries.

The process of collecting data about Earth from a distance, such as from orbiting satellites, is called remote sensing. Satellites use remote sensing to produce views of Earth that scientists use to study rivers, oceans, fires, pollution, natural resources, and many other topics. How might a scientist use the image shown in Figure 17?

We can use this technology in our daily lives too. For example, Global Positioning Systems (GPS) can provide maps in our cars to help us reach our destinations. GPS consists of an instrument that receives signals to compute the user's latitude and longitude as well as speed, direction, and elevation. GPS is an important tool for navigation by ships and airplanes. Scientists use GPS to track wildlife, study earthquakes, measure erosion, and many other purposes. Table 1 describes some of the technology that is particularly useful in the study of Earth science.

Table 1 Technology and Earth Science

Type of Equipment	Capabilities
Weather Satellites	• These monitor atmospheric temperature and humidity, ground and surface seawater temperature, cloud cover, and water-ice boundaries. • They can help locate sources of distress signals. • They are able to scan Earth's surface in one 24-hour period.
Navigation Satellites	• These assist ships and submarines to determine their exact location at any time.
Landsat Satellites	• The first Landsat satellite was launched in 1972. Landsat 7 was launched in 1999. • They provide data on Earth's landmasses, coastal boundaries, and coral reefs. • Pictures taken are transmitted to ground stations around the world. • They orbit Earth every 99 minutes and complete 14 orbits per day. • Total coverage of Earth is achieved in 16 days.
Global Positioning System (GPS)	• This system combines satellite information with computer technology to provide location information in three dimensions: latitude, longitude, and altitude. • Three satellite signals are detected by a receiver. The distance from the satellites to the receiver is calculated, and the location is determined using the triangulation method. A fourth signal is then used to mathematically determine exact position.
Very Long Baseline Interferometry (VLBI)	• VLBI utilizes a large network of antennas around the world to receive radio waves from space objects such as quasars. • In Earth science, VLBI is used in geodesy, or the measurement of the geosphere. • Using the arrival times of radio waves from quasars, the position of radio telescopes on Earth are determined to within millimeters of their position. • Small changes in the telescope positions allow scientists to study tectonic plate motions and other movements of Earth's crust with great precision and accuracy.

Section 1.3 Assessment

Reviewing Concepts

1. Describe the two sets of lines that are used on globes and some maps.

2. What happens to the images on the globe when they are transferred to a flat surface?

3. What is the purpose of contour lines on topographic maps?

4. What two lines mark zero degrees on the globe? In which directions do these lines run?

5. Why is the Mercator projection map still in use today?

6. What types of advanced technology are used in mapmaking today?

Critical Thinking

7. **Applying Concepts** Why are there so many different types of maps?

8. **Drawing Conclusions** How can data from VLBI be used in mapmaking today?

9. **Conceptualizing** An area on a topographic map has the following contour line configuration: First, the lines are fairly widely spaced. Then they are closely spaced. Finally, they are circular. Describe the topography represented by these lines.

Math Practice

Use the bar scale on Figure 15 to answer the following question.

10. Determine the distance along the shoreline of Turquoise Lake from the gaging station on the west shore to the gaging station on the south shore. Record your answer in kilometers.

1.4 Earth System Science

Reading Focus

Key Concepts

- How is Earth a system?
- What is a system?
- Where does the energy come from that powers Earth's systems?
- How do humans affect Earth's systems?
- What makes a resource renewable or nonrenewable?

Vocabulary

- system

Reading Strategy

Outlining As you read, make an outline of the most important ideas in this section. Begin with the section title, then list the green headings as the next step of the outline. Outline further as needed.

```
I. Earth System Science
   A. What is a System?
      1. _____?_____
      2. _____?_____
   B. _____?_____
```

As we study Earth, we see that it is a dynamic planet with many separate but interactive parts or spheres. Earth scientists are studying how these spheres are interconnected. **This way of looking at Earth is called Earth system science. Its aim is to understand Earth as a system made up of numerous interacting parts, or subsystems.** Instead of studying only one branch of science, such as geology, chemistry, or biology, Earth system science tries to put together what we know from our study of all of these branches. Using this type of approach, we hope to eventually understand and solve many of our global environmental problems.

 **Reading Checkpoint**   *What Is Earth system science?*

What Is a System?

Most of us hear and use the term system frequently. You might use your city's transportation system to get to school. A news report might inform us of an approaching weather system. We know that Earth is just a small part of the much larger solar system.

A system can be any size group of interacting parts that form a complex whole. Most natural systems are driven by sources of energy that move matter and/or energy from one place to another. A simple analogy is a car's cooling system. It contains a liquid (usually water and antifreeze) that is driven from the engine to the radiator and back again. The role of this system is to transfer the heat generated by combustion in the engine to the radiator, where moving air removes the heat from the system.

This kind of system is called a closed system. Here energy moves freely in and out of the system, but no matter enters or leaves the system. In the case of the car's cooling system, the matter is the liquid. By contrast, most natural systems are open systems. Here both energy and matter flow into and out of the system. In a river system, for example, the amount of water flowing in the channel can vary a great deal. At one time or place, the river may be fuller than it is at another time or place.

Earth as a System

The Earth system is powered by energy from two sources. **One source is the sun, which drives external processes that occur in the atmosphere, hydrosphere, and at Earth's surface.** Weather and climate, ocean circulation, and erosional processes are driven by energy from the sun. **Earth's interior is the second source of energy.** There is heat that remains from the time Earth formed. There is also heat continuously generated by the decay of radioactive elements. These sources power the internal processes that produce volcanoes, earthquakes, and mountains.

The parts of the Earth system are linked so that a change in one part can produce changes in any or all of the other parts. For example, when a volcano erupts, lava may flow out at the surface and block a nearby valley. This new obstruction influences the region's drainage system by creating a lake or causing streams to change course. Volcanic ash and gases that can be discharged during an eruption might be blown high into the atmosphere and influence the amount of solar energy that can reach Earth's surface. The result could be a drop in air temperatures over the entire hemisphere.

Figure 18 When Mount St. Helens erupted in May 1980, the area shown here was buried by a volcanic mudflow. Now, plants are reestablished and new soil is forming.

How do we know that Earth's systems are connected?

Over time, soil will develop on the lava or ash-covered surface and, as shown in Figure 18, plants and animals will reestablish themselves. This soil will reflect the interactions among many parts of the Earth system—the original volcanic material, the type and rate of weathering, and the impact of biological activity. Of course, there would also be significant changes in the biosphere. Some organisms and their habitats would be eliminated by the lava and ash, while new settings for life, such as the lake, would be created. The potential climate change could also have an effect on some life-forms.

The Earth system is characterized by processes that occur over areas that range in size from millimeters to thousands of kilometers. Time scales for Earth's processes range from milliseconds to billions of years. Despite this great range in distance and time, many processes are connected. A change in one component can influence the entire system.

Humans are also part of the Earth system. **Our actions produce changes in all of the other parts of the Earth system.** When we burn gasoline and coal, build breakwaters along a shoreline, dispose of our wastes, and clear the land, we cause other parts of the Earth system to respond, often in unforeseen ways. Throughout this book, you will learn about many of Earth's subsystems, such as the hydrologic (water) system, the tectonic (mountain-building) system, and the climate system. Remember that these components and we humans are all part of the complex interacting whole we call the Earth system.

People and the Environment

Environment refers to everything that surrounds and influences an organism. Some of these things are biological and social. Others are nonliving such as water, air, soil and rock as well as conditions such as temperature, humidity, and sunlight. These nonliving factors make up our physical environment. Because studying the Earth sciences leads to an understanding of the physical environment, most of Earth science can be characterized as environmental science.

 *What are examples of nonliving factors?*

Today the term *environmental science* is usually used for things that focus on the relationships between people and the natural environment. For example, we can dramatically influence natural processes. A river flooding is natural, but the size and frequency of flooding can be changed by human activities such as clearing forests, building cities, and constructing dams. Unfortunately, natural systems do not always adjust to artificial changes in ways we can anticipate. An alteration to the environment that was intended to benefit society may have the opposite effect, as shown in Figure 19.

Resources Resources are an important focus of the Earth sciences. They include water and soil, metallic and nonmetallic minerals, and energy. Together they form the foundation of modern civilization. The Earth sciences deal not only with the formation and occurrence of

Figure 19 The benefit that was intended by the construction of the Aswan Dam in Egypt was not achieved.
Drawing Conclusions *How might the flooding here have been avoided?*

these vital resources but also with maintaining supplies and the environmental impact of their mining and use.

Resources are commonly divided into two broad categories—renewable resources and nonrenewable resources. **Renewable resources can be replenished over relatively short time spans.** Common examples are plants and animals for food, natural fibers for clothing, and forest products for lumber and paper. Energy from flowing water, wind, and the sun are also considered renewable resources.

Important metals such as iron, aluminum, and copper plus our most important fuels of oil, natural gas, and coal are classified as nonrenewable resources. **Although these and other resources continue to form, the processes that create them are so slow that it takes millions of years for significant deposits to accumulate.** Earth contains limited quantities of these materials. Although some nonrenewable resources, such as aluminum, can be used over and over again, others, such as oil, cannot. When the present supplies are exhausted, there will be no more.

Reading Checkpoint *How do renewable and nonrenewable resources differ?*

Go Online
SciLINKS NSTA

For: Links on environmental decision-making
Visit: www.SciLinks.org
Web Code: cjn-1014

Population Figure 20 shows that the population of Earth is growing rapidly. Although it took until the beginning of the nineteenth century for the population to reach 1 billion, just 130 years were needed for the population to double to 2 billion. Between 1930 and 1975, the figure doubled again to 4 billion, and by about 2010, as many as 7 billion people may inhabit Earth. Clearly, as population grows, so does the demand for resources. However, the rate of mineral and energy resource usage has increased more rapidly than the overall growth of the population.

How long will the remaining supplies of basic resources last? How long can we sustain the rising standard of living in today's industrialized countries and still provide for the growing needs of developing regions? How much environmental deterioration are we willing to accept to obtain basic resources? Can alternatives be found? If we are to cope with the increasing demand on resources and a growing world population, it is important that we have some understanding of our present and potential resources.

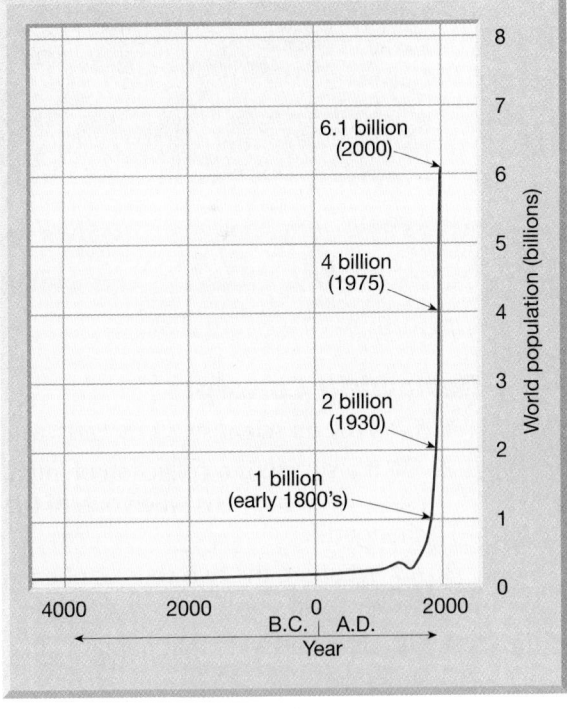

Figure 20 Growth of World Population

Environmental Problems

In addition to the search for mineral and energy resources, the Earth sciences must also deal with environmental problems. Some of these problems are local, some are regional, and still others are global. Humans can cause problems, such as the one shown in Figure 21. **Significant**

Figure 21 Air pollution in the Chinese city of Guangzhou. Air quality problems affect many cities. **Interpreting Photographs** *What may have contributed to this air pollution problem?*

threats to the environment include air pollution, acid rain, ozone depletion, and global warming. The loss of fertile soils to erosion, the disposal of toxic wastes, and the contamination and depletion of water resources are also of considerable concern. The list continues to grow.

People must cope with the many natural hazards that exist such as the one shown in Figure 22. Earthquakes, landslides, floods, hurricanes, and drought are some of the many risks. Of course, environmental hazards are simply natural processes. They become hazards only when people try to live where these processes occur.

It is clear that as world population continues to grow, pressures on the environment will increase as well. Therefore, an understanding of Earth is essential for the location and recovery of basic resources. It is also essential for dealing with the human impact on the environment and minimizing the effects of natural hazards. Knowledge about Earth and how it works is necessary to our survival and well being. Earth is the only suitable habitat we have, and its resources are limited.

Figure 22 The damage here was caused by a landslide that was triggered by an earthquake.

Section 1.4 Assessment

Reviewing Concepts

1. Why do scientists study Earth as a system?
2. If a system is a collection of interacting parts, what happens when one of the parts is changed?
3. What are the two sources of energy that power Earth's systems?
4. List three ways that humans affect Earth's systems.
5. Large numbers of tiny ocean organisms die every day, fall to the ocean floor, are buried, and are eventually converted to oil and natural gas. Why are these two fuels considered nonrenewable?

Critical Thinking

6. **Applying Concepts** Describe the parts of a tree in terms of it being a system.
7. **Evaluating** Is it possible for humans to have no effect on any of Earth's systems? Explain.
8. **Applying Concepts** How can scientists help to prevent a natural process from becoming an environmental hazard?

Connecting Concepts

City Planning In Section 1.3, you learned about Landsat satellite imaging. How can data from Landsat help city planners determine where and where not to build?

1.5 What Is Scientific Inquiry?

Reading Focus

Key Concepts
- What is a hypothesis?
- What is a theory?

Vocabulary
- hypothesis
- theory

Reading Strategy
Comparing and Contrasting Complete the Venn diagram by listing the ways hypothesis and theory are alike and how they differ.

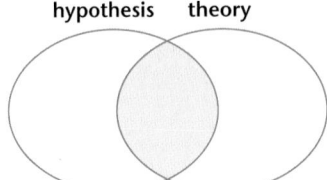

hypothesis   theory

All science is based on two assumptions. First, the natural world behaves in a consistent and predictable manner. Second, through careful, systematic study, we can understand and explain the natural world's behavior. We can use this knowledge to make predictions about what should or should not be expected. For example, by knowing how oil deposits form, geologists are able to predict the most likely sites for exploration.

The development of new scientific knowledge involves some basic steps. First, scientists collect data through observation and measurement. These data are essential to science and serve as the starting point for the development of scientific theories.

Hypothesis

Once data have been gathered, scientists try to explain how or why things happen in the manner observed. Scientists do this by stating a possible explanation called a scientific hypothesis. Sometimes more than one hypothesis is developed to explain a given set of observations. Just because a hypothesis is stated doesn't mean that it is correct or that the scientific community will automatically accept it.

Before a hypothesis can become an accepted part of scientific knowledge, it must be tested and analyzed. If a hypothesis can't be tested, it is not scientifically useful, no matter how interesting it might seem. Hypotheses that fail rigorous testing are discarded. The history of science is filled with discarded hypotheses. One of the best known is the Earth-centered model of the universe. This hypothesis was based on the apparent movement of the sun, moon, and stars around Earth.

For: Links on scientific methods
Visit: www.SciLinks.org
Web Code: cjn-1015

As the mathematician Jacob Bronowski stated, "Science is a great many things, but in the end they all return to this: Science is the acceptance of what works and the rejection of what does not."

Theory

When a hypothesis has survived extensive testing and when competing hypotheses have been eliminated, a hypothesis may become a scientific **theory**. 🔵**A scientific theory is well tested and widely accepted by the scientific community and best explains certain observable facts.** For example, the theory of plate tectonics provides the framework for understanding the origin of continents and ocean basins, plus the occurrence of mountains, earthquakes, and volcanoes.

Scientific Methods

The process of gathering facts through observations and formulating scientific hypotheses and theories is called the scientific method. There is no set path that scientists must follow in order to gain scientific knowledge. However, many scientific investigations involve the following steps: (1) the collection of scientific facts through observation and measurement, (2) the development of one or more working hypotheses or models to explain these facts, (3) development of observations and experiments to test the hypotheses, and (4) the acceptance, modification, or rejection of the hypothesis based on extensive testing.

Section 1.5 Assessment

Reviewing Concepts

1. 🔵 You have just come up with an explanation to a question that has bothered you for some time. What must you do to have your explanation become a hypothesis?

2. 🔵 Explain how a hypothesis can become a theory.

3. According to the scientific community, how does the natural world behave?

4. What happens if more than one hypothesis is put forward to explain the same observations?

5. When is a model useful in scientific investigations?

Thinking Critically

6. **Applying Concepts** Why do most scientists follow a set order of steps when carrying out a scientific investigation?

7. **Designing Experiments** While carrying out an investigation, a scientist observes some unexpected results. What are the scientist's next steps?

8. **Understanding Concepts** Why is it necessary to use careful and systematic methods when carrying out scientific investigations?

Writing in Science

Explanatory Paragraph It took a long time for the scientific community to accept the theory of plate tectonics. Write a paragraph suggesting how the use of proper scientific methods helped the theory gain acceptance.

Studying Earth From Space

Scientific facts are gathered in many ways, such as laboratory studies, field observations, and field measurements. Satellite images like the one in Figure 23 are another useful source of data. Such images provide perspectives that are difficult to get from more traditional sources. The high-tech instruments aboard many satellites enable scientists to gather information from remote regions where data are otherwise scarce.

The image in Figure 23 makes use of the Advanced Spaceborne Thermal Emission and Reflection Radiometer (ASTER). Because different materials reflect and give off energy in different ways, ASTER can provide detailed information about the composition of Earth's surface. Figure 23 is a three-dimensional view looking north over Death Valley, California. The data have been computer enhanced to exaggerate the color variations that highlight differences in types of surface materials.

Figure 23 This satellite shows detailed information about the composition of surface materials in Death Valley, California. It was produced by superimposing nighttime thermal infrared data, acquired on April 7, 2000, over topographic data from the U.S. Geological survey. (Image courtesy of NASA)

Salt deposits on the floor of Death Valley appear in shades of yellow, green, purple, and pink. These indicate the presence of carbonate, sulfate, and chloride minerals. The Panamint Mountains to the west and the Black Mountains to the east are made up of sedimentary limestones, sandstones, shales, and metamorphic rocks. The bright red areas are dominated by the mineral quartz, found in sandstone; the green areas are limestone. In the lower center of the image is Badwater, the lowest point in North America.

Determining Latitude and Longitude

*Using maps and globes to find places and features on Earth's surface is an essential skill required of all Earth scientists. The grid that is formed by lines of latitude and longitude form the basis for locating points on Earth. Latitude lines indicate north-south distance and longitude lines indicate east-west distance. Degrees are used to mark latitude and longitude distances on Earth's surface. Degrees can be divided into sixty equal parts called minutes (') and a minute of angle can be divided into sixty parts, called seconds (").
Thus, 31°10'20" means 31 degrees, 10 minutes, and 20 seconds. This exercise will introduce you to the systems used for determining location on Earth.*

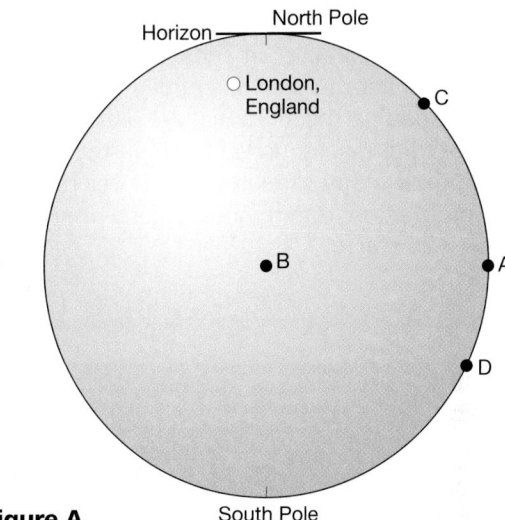

Figure A

Problem
How are latitude and longitude calculated and how do they indicate a particular location's position on the globe?

Materials
- globe
- protractor
- ruler
- compass or round object for tracing
- pencil
- world map

Skills
Interpreting, Measuring, Inferring

Procedure

Part A: Determining Latitude

1. Figure A represents Earth, with point B its center. Draw this figure on a separate piece of paper. Locate the equator on the globe. Sketch and label the equator on your diagram. Label the Northern Hemisphere and Southern Hemisphere on your diagram.

2. On your diagram, make an angle by drawing a line from point A on the equator to point B (the center of Earth). Then extend the line from point B to point C in the Northern Hemisphere. The angle you have drawn (∠ABC) is 45°. By definition of latitude, point C is located at 45° N latitude.

3. Draw a line on your figure through point C that is also parallel to the equator. What is the latitude at all points on this line? Record this number on the line.

4. Using a protractor, measure ∠ABD on your paper. Then draw a line parallel to the equator that also goes through point D. Label the line with its proper latitude.

5. How many degrees of latitude separate the latitude lines (or parallels) on the globe that you are using? Record this on your paper.

6. Refer to Figure B. Determine the latitude for each point A–F. Be sure to indicate whether it is north or south of the equator and include the word "latitude." Record these numbers on your paper.

7. Use a globe or map to locate the cities listed below. On your paper, record their latitude to the nearest degree.
   A. Moscow, Russia
   B. Durban, South Africa
   C. Your home city

8. Use the globe or map to give the name of a city or feature that is equally as far south of the equator as your home city is north.

Part B: Determining Longitude

9. Locate the prime meridian on Figure C. Sketch and label it on your diagram. Label the Eastern and Western Hemispheres.

10. How many degrees of longitude separate each meridian on your globe? Record this on your paper.

11. Refer to Figure C. Determine the longitude for each point A–F. Be sure to indicate whether it is east or west of the Prime Meridian. Record these numbers on your paper.

12. Use the globe or map to give the name of a city or feature that is equally as far east of the prime meridian as your home city is west.

Analyze and Conclude

1. **Applying Concepts** What is the maximum number of 1 degree longitude or latitude lines that can be drawn on a globe?

2. **Comparing and Contrasting** How are longitude and latitude lines the same and how are they different?

3. **Thinking Critically** Amelia Earhart, her flight engineer, and her plane are believed to have been lost somewhere over the Pacific Ocean. It is now thought that the coordinates that she was given for her fuel stop at Howley Island in the Pacific Ocean were wrong. Knowing what you do about how latitude and longitude coordinates are written, why would a wrong number have been so catastrophic for her?

Go Further Use reference books or the Internet to research the number of time zones on Earth. Find out how many there are and draw their boundaries on the figure you created for this lab. What time zone do you live in? What time zone is the location that you chose in question 12? What is the time difference between these two locations?

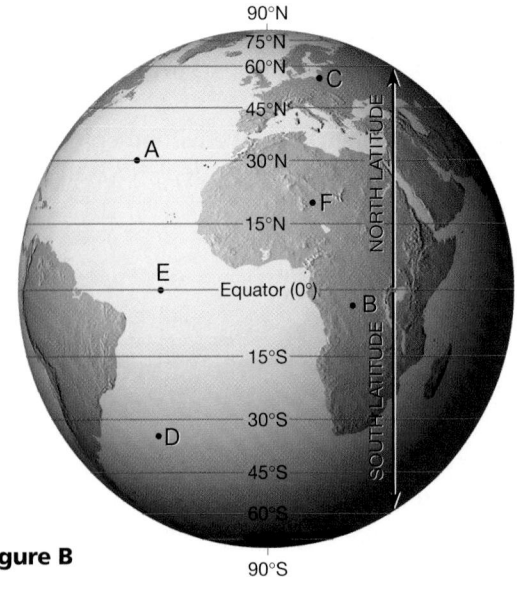

Figure B

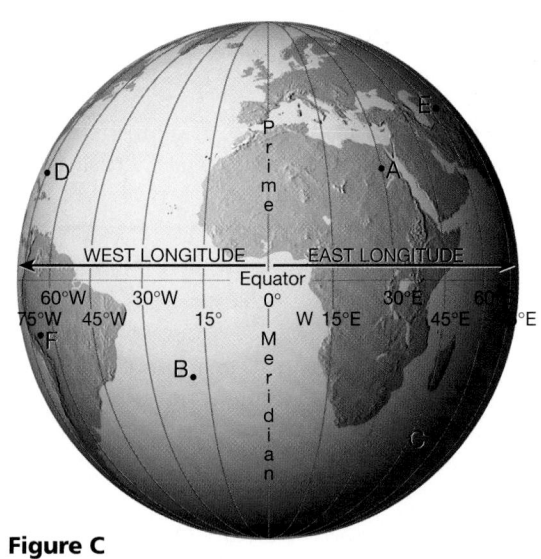

Figure C

Study Guide

1.1 What Is Earth Science?

🖰 Key Concepts

- Earth science is the name for the group of sciences that deals with Earth and its neighbors in space.
- The nebular hypothesis suggests that the bodies of our solar system eevolved from an enormous rotating cloud called the solar nebula. It was made up mostly of hydrogen and helium, with a small percentage of heavier elements.

Vocabulary

Earth science, *p. 2;* geology, *p. 2;* oceanography, *p. 3;* meteorology, *p. 3;* astronomy, *p. 3*

1.2 A View of Earth

🖰 Key Concepts

- Earth can be thought of as consisting of four major spheres: the hydrosphere, atmosphere, geosphere, and biosphere.
- Because the geosphere is not uniform, it is divided into three main parts based on differences in composition—the core, the mantle, and the crust.
- The model that explains the position of continents and the occurrence of volcanoes and earthquakes is called plate tectonics.

Vocabulary

hydrosphere, *p. 7* atmosphere, *p. 7;* geosphere, *p. 7;* biosphere, *p. 7;* core, *p. 8;* mantle, *p. 8;* crust, *p. 8*

1.3 Representing Earth's Surface

🖰 Key Concepts

- Latitude is the distance north or south of the equator, measured in degrees. Longitude is the distance east or west of the prime meridian, measured in degrees.
- No matter what kind of map is made, some portion of the surface will always look either too small, too big, or out of place. Mapmakers have, however, found ways to limit the distortaion of shape, size, distance, and direction.
- Topographic maps differ from other maps because topographic maps show elevation.

- The elevation of the land is indicated by using contour lines.
- A map that shows the type and age of exposed rock is called a geologic map.
- Today's technology provides us with the ability to more precisely analyze Earth's physical properties.

Vocabulary

latitude, *p. 11;* longitude, *p. 11;* topographic map, *p. 14;* contour line, *p. 14;* contour interval, *p. 14*

1.4 Earth System Science

🖰 Key Concepts

- Earth system science aims to study Earth as a system made up of numerous interacting parts, or subsystems.
- A system can be any size group of interacting parts that form a complex whole.
- The sun drives external processes that occur in the atmosphere, hydrosphere, and at Earth's surface. Earth's interior is also a source of energy.
- Our actions produce changes in all other parts of the Earth system.
- Renewable resources can be replenished over relatively short time spans. Nonrenewable resources form over such a long period of time that it takes millions of years for significant deposits to accumulate.
- Significant threats to the environment include air pollution, acid rain, ozone depletion, and global warming.

Vocabulary

system, *p. 18*

1.5 What Is Scientific Inquiry?

🖰 Key Concepts

- A hypothesis is a statement made by scientists to explain how or why things happen in the manner observed.
- A scientific theory is well tested and widely accepted by the scientific community and best explains certain observable facts.

Vocabulary

hypothesis, *p. 23;* theory, *p. 24*

Reviewing Content

Choose the letter that best answers the question or completes the statement.

1. The science that deals with the study of the atmosphere is
   a. oceanography.   b. meteorology.
   c. geology.   d. astronomy.

2. What caused Earth to develop layers as it cooled?
   a. differences in composition
   b. the magnetic field
   c. the speed of rotation
   d. escaping gases

3. What drives the process of plate tectonics, the currently accepted explanation for the movement of drifting continents?
   a. gravity
   b. ocean currents
   c. unequal heat distribution
   d. earthquakes

4. Lines of latitude describe position
   a. north or south of the equator.
   b. east or west of the equator.
   c. north or south of the prime meridian.
   d. east or west of the prime meridian.

5. The Robinson map projection is considered very useful because
   a. all of the continents are the same size.
   b. most distances, sizes, and shapes are accurate.
   c. it shows landmasses in three dimensions.
   d. features along latitude lines are accurate.

6. Which of the following maps shows the three dimensions of Earth's surface?
   a. Mercator projection
   b. topographic
   c. gnomonic
   d. conic

7. Which type of technology can scientists use to monitor coral reef development?
   a. Landsat satellites   b. VLBI
   c. computer imaging d. weather satellites

8. What makes a hypothesis scientifically useful?
   a. Many people think it is a good idea.
   b. It can be tested.
   c. It contains numerical data.
   d. It applies directly to Earth science.

9. The theory that Earth's lithosphere is broken into large sections that move is called
   a. biosphere.   b. global positioning.
   c. nebular.   d. plate tectonics.

10. On a topographic map, contour lines that are closer together indicate
    a. forest.   b. a steeper slope.
    c. a mountain top.   d. roads.

Understanding Concepts

11. Briefly list the events that led to the formation of the solar system.

12. Which of Earth's spheres do mountains, lakes, trees, clouds, ice, and snow represent?

13. List the three parts of the geosphere indicated at the letters in the figure below.

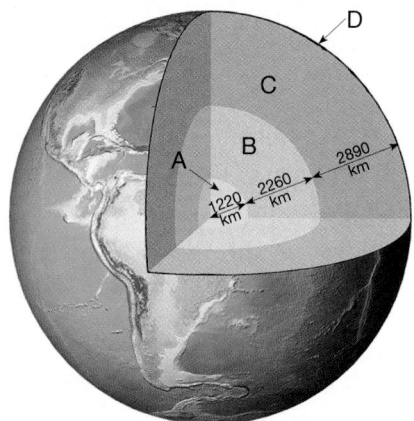

14. The Mercator projection map shows Earth's features on a grid. Why is this map useful to sailors?

15. Why is the contour interval included on a topographic map?

16. What type of satellite is used to monitor cloud cover and air temperature?

17. What happens to matter and energy in a closed system?

18. What types of factors make up our nonliving environment?

19. What are the two sources of energy for the Earth system?

20. What requirements must be satisfied in order for a resource to be considered renewable?

21. List at least four processes that could be regarded as natural hazards.

22. Briefly describe the four steps that most scientific investigations follow.

Critical Thinking

23. **Comparing and Contrasting** How is a scientific hypothesis different from a scientific theory?

24. **Applying Concepts** If oceans cover nearly 71 percent of Earth's surface, why is it important to conserve water?

25. **Inferring** Explain the following statement: If Earth had no atmosphere, our planet would be lifeless.

26. **Hypothesizing** Predict what the effect will be on some of Earth's systems if a forest is cut down for lumber.

27. **Comparing and Contrasting** As part of the Great Plains of the United States, the topography of the state of Kansas is relatively flat. On the other hand, portions of the state of Colorado are mountainous. Describe how the contour interval and the contour lines might vary on topographic maps of these two states.

Math Skills

Use the bar graph to answer Questions 28 and 29.

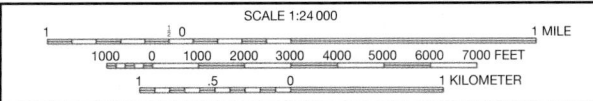

SCALE 1:24 000

1   0   1 MILE
1000   0   1000 2000 3000 4000 5000 6000 7000 FEET
1   .5   0   1 KILOMETER

28. **Using Graphs** Approximately how many miles is 1 kilometer equal to?

29. **Calculating** If 1 kilometer is equal to 1 centimeter on the map, what is the distance in km between two cities that are 7.5 cm apart?

30. **Calculating** Recall that Earth is divided into 360 degrees. If you travel to a location that is 90 degrees starting from the prime meridian, how far around the globe have you gone? What about a location that is 120 degrees from the prime meridian?

Map Skills

Use the topographic map in Figure 15 on page 14 to answer Questions 31–33.

31. **Reading Maps** About how wide is Turquoise Lake at its widest point from east to west?

32. **Reading Maps** What is the elevation of Sugar Loaf Mountain?

33. **Reading Maps** How does the land on the east side of Turquoise Lake differ from the land on the southwest side of the lake? How do you know?

Concepts in Action

34. **Applying Concepts** List at least three examples of how you can influence one or more of Earth's major spheres.

35. **Applying Concepts** A local company wants to open a new limestone quarry. Explain what type of map they should use to determine if limestone is present in your area.

36. **Classifying** The planet Mars has been in the news recently. Based on the information that has been reported, list and explain the spheres that are present or might have been present on Mars.

37. **Writing in Science** You are given the opportunity to address the city council about the proposed construction of a dam on the river in your community. Prepare a list of questions about the project that you would like to ask the city council and the dam engineers before deciding whether or not you would support the project.

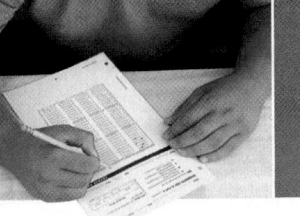

Standardized Test Prep

Choose the letter that best answers the question or completes the statement.

1. The _____ strongly influences the other three "spheres" because without life their makeup and nature would be much different.
  (A) atmosphere
  (B) hydrosphere
  (C) geosphere
  (D) biosphere

2. The science that includes the study of the composition and movements of water, as well as coastal processes, the seafloor, and marine life is _____.
  (A) geology
  (B) oceanography
  (C) meteorology
  (D) astronomy

3. Which of these situations is(are) an example of an open system?
  I.   a car's cooling system
  II. a boiling teakettle
  III. a loaf of bread in a sealed plastic bag.
  IV. your digestive system
   (A) I only
   (B) II & IV
   (C) I & III
   (D) I, II, III & IV

Use the figure below to answer Questions 4, 5, and 6.

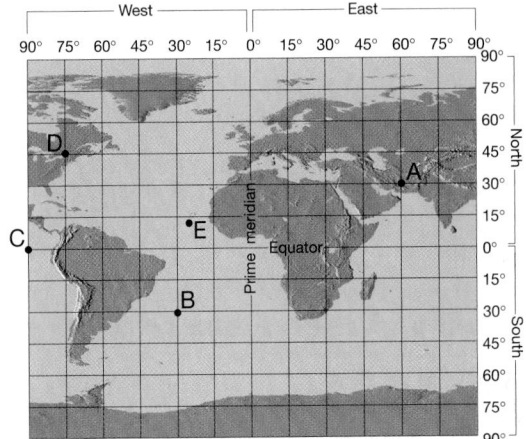

4. What is the latitude and longitude for point A on the map?

5. Locate the state of Florida on the map. What is the approximate location of its southernmost point?

6. Why does the continent of Antarctica appear to be stretched out?

7. The three principal layers of Earth are differentiated by their density. List these three layers by increasing density.

2 Minerals

CONCEPTS
in Action

Exploration Lab
Mineral Identification

Understanding Earth
Gemstones

 Earth Materials
↳ Rock Cycle

 **Video Field Trip**
Gold

Take a trip to Brazil with the Discovery Channel and see how gold on the Rio Medeira River is mined. Answer the following questions after watching the video.

1. In what two parts of Earth is gold found?

2. Describe what happens to gold during the "smelting" process.

For: Chapter 2 Resources
Visit: PHSchool.com
Web Code: cjk-9999

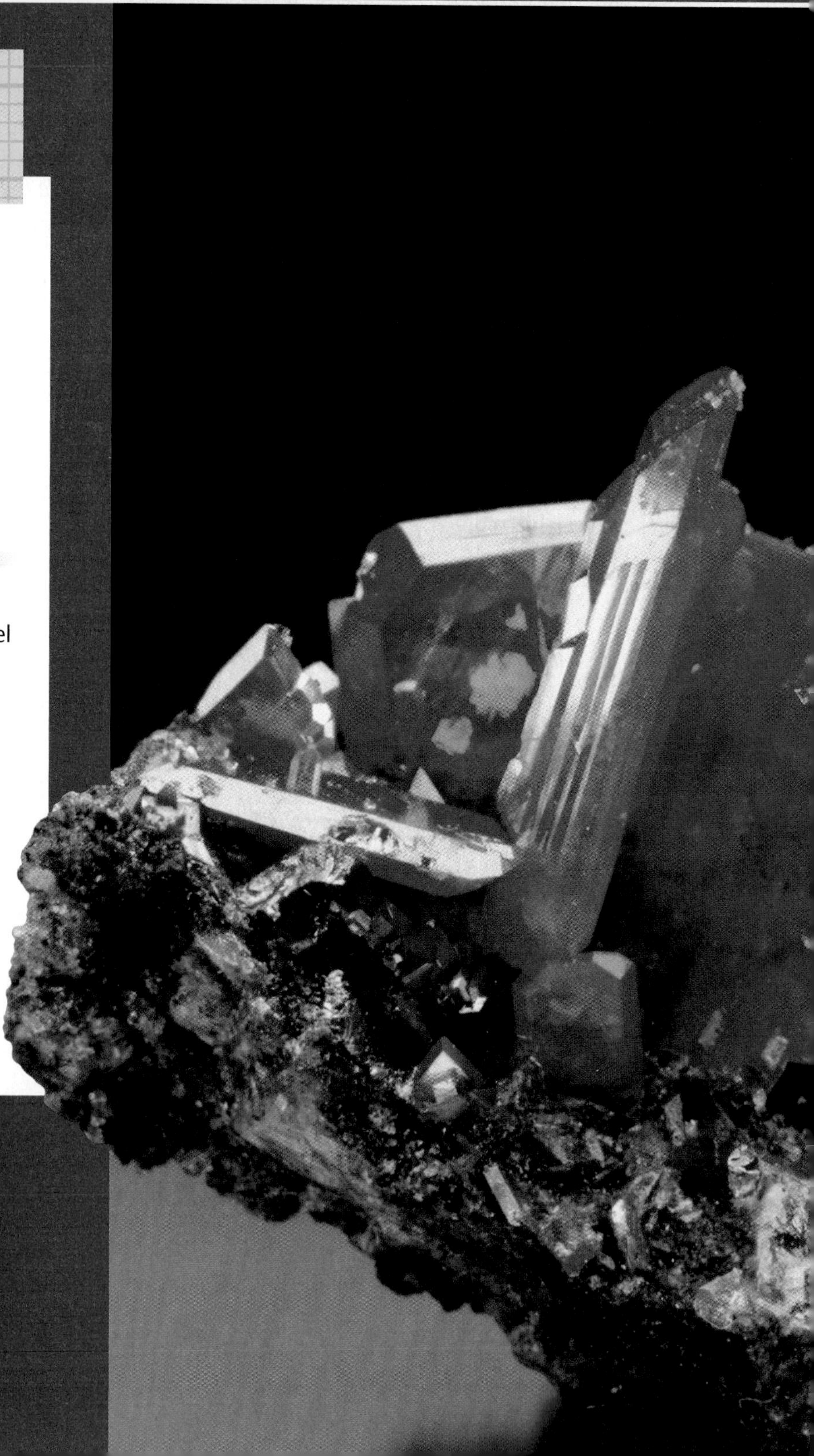

The large reddish-orange crystals are ▶ crystals of wulfenite. Wulfenite is one of more than 3800 minerals found on Earth.

Chapter Preview

Inquiry Activity

How Are a Group of Minerals Alike and Different?

Procedure

1. Obtain the mineral samples from your teacher. Examine them closely.

2. Make a data table to record at least three ways that the samples are alike.

3. Now record at least three ways that the samples differ.

4. Classify the minerals into two groups based on your observations. Give reasons for your classification scheme.

5. Put on safety goggles. Gently strike each sample with a hammer and observe the pieces of each sample. If necessary, use these results to reclassify the minerals into two groups.

Think About It

1. **Observing** What kinds of characteristics did you observe in all of the samples?

2. **Contrasting** How did the samples differ?

3. **Formulating Hypotheses** Each of the minerals you just observed belongs to a different group. Design a scheme for how these minerals might be classified into four different groups.

2.1 Matter

Reading Focus

Key Concepts
- What is an element?
- What particles make up atoms?
- What are isotopes?
- What are compounds and why do they form?
- How do chemical bonds differ?

Vocabulary
- element
- atomic number
- energy level
- isotope
- mass number
- compound
- chemical bond
- ion
- ionic bond
- covalent bond
- metallic bond

Reading Strategy
Comparing and Contrasting Copy the graphic organizer. As you read, complete the organizer to compare and contrast protons, neutrons, and electrons.

Protons	Electrons	Neutrons
Differences		
Similarities		

You and everything else in the universe are made of matter. Matter is anything that has volume and mass. On Earth, matter usually exists in one of three states—solid, liquid, or gas. A solid is a type of matter that has a definite shape and a definite volume. Rocks and minerals are solids. A liquid is matter that has a definite volume, but not a definite shape. Earth's oceans, rivers, and lakes are liquids. A gas is matter that has neither a definite shape nor a definite volume. Most of Earth's atmosphere is composed of the gases nitrogen and oxygen. Though matter can be classified by its physical state: solid, liquid, or gas, it is more useful to look at its chemical composition and structure. Each of Earth's nearly 4000 minerals is a unique substance. The building blocks of minerals are **elements.**

Elements and the Periodic Table

The names of many elements are probably very familiar to you. Many common metals are elements, such as copper, iron, silver, and gold. **An element is a substance that cannot be broken down into simpler substances by chemical or physical means.** There are more than 112 known elements, and new elements continue to be discovered. Of these, 92 occur naturally, the others are produced in laboratories.

The elements have been organized by their properties in a document called the periodic table, which is shown in Figure 1 on pages 36 and 37. You see from the table that the name of each element is represented by a symbol consisting of one, two, or three letters. Symbols provide a shorthand way of representing an element. Each element is

Go Online

For: Links on the periodic table
Visit: www.SciLinks.org
Web Code: cjn-1021

also known by its atomic number, which is shown above each symbol on the table. Look at the block for sulfur, element 16, and gold, element 79. Sulfur and gold are minerals made of one element. Most elements are not stable enough to exist in pure form in nature. Thus, most minerals are combinations of elements.

The rows in the periodic table are called periods. The number of elements in a period varies. Period 1, for example, contains only two elements. These elements are hydrogen (H) and helium (He). Period 2 contains the elements lithium (Li) through neon (Ne). Periods 4 and 5 each contain 18 elements while Period 6 includes 32 elements.

The columns in the periodic table are called groups. Note that there are 18 groups in the periodic table shown on pages 36 and 37. Elements within a group have similar properties.

Of the known elements, only eight make up most of Earth's continental crust. These eight elements are listed in Table 1. Notice that six of the eight elements in Table 1 are classified as metals. Metals have specific properties such as the ability to be shaped and drawn into wire. Metals are also good conductors of heat and electricity. They combine in thousands of ways to form compounds, the building blocks of most Earth materials. To understand how elements form compounds we need to review their building blocks which are atoms.

Table 1 Relative Abundance of the Most Common Elements in Earth's Continental Crust	
Element	Approximate Percentage by Weight
Oxygen (O)	46.6
Silicon (Si)	27.7
Aluminum (Al)	8.1
Iron (Fe)	5.0
Calcium (Ca)	3.6
Sodium (Na)	2.8
Potassium (K)	2.6
Magnesium (Mg)	2.1
All others	1.7

Source: Data from Brian Mason.

Atoms

As you might already know, all elements are made of atoms. **An atom is the smallest particle of matter that contains the characteristics of an element.**

The central region of an atom is called the nucleus. The nucleus contains protons and neutrons. Protons are dense particles with positive electrical charges. Neutrons are equally dense particles that have no electrical charge. Electrons, which are small particles with little mass and negative electrical charges, surround an atom's nucleus.

Protons and Neutrons A proton has about the same mass as a neutron. Hydrogen atoms have only a single proton in their nuclei. Other atoms contain more than 100 protons. The number of protons in the nucleus of an atom is called the **atomic number.** All atoms with six protons, for example, are carbon atoms. The atomic number of carbon is 6. Likewise, every atom with eight protons is an oxygen atom. The atomic number of oxygen is 8.

Atoms have the same number of protons and electrons. Carbon atoms have six protons and therefore six electrons. Oxygen atoms have eight protons in their nuclei and have eight electrons surrounding the nucleus.

Figure 1

	Nonmetals	Metals	Metalloids	
	C	Li	B	Solid
	Br	Hg		Liquid
	H			Gas
		Tc		Not found in nature

1A (1)

| 1 H Hydrogen 1.0079 |

2A (2)

| 3 Li Lithium 6.941 | 4 Be Beryllium 9.0122 |
| 11 Na Sodium 22.990 | 12 Mg Magnesium 24.305 |

	3B (3)	4B (4)	5B (5)	6B (6)	7B (7)	8B (8)	8B (9)
19 K Potassium 39.098 / 20 Ca Calcium 40.08	21 Sc Scandium 44.956	22 Ti Titanium 47.90	23 V Vanadium 50.941	24 Cr Chromium 51.996	25 Mn Manganese 54.938	26 Fe Iron 55.847	27 Co Cobalt 58.933
37 Rb Rubidium 85.468 / 38 Sr Strontium 87.62	39 Y Yttrium 88.906	40 Zr Zirconium 91.22	41 Nb Niobium 92.906	42 Mo Molybdenum 95.94	43 Tc Technetium (98)	44 Ru Ruthenium 101.07	45 Rh Rhodium 102.91
55 Cs Cesium 132.91 / 56 Ba Barium 137.33	71 Lu Lutetium 174.97	72 Hf Hafnium 178.49	73 Ta Tantalum 180.95	74 W Tungsten 183.85	75 Re Rhenium 186.21	76 Os Osmium 190.2	77 Ir Iridium 192.22
87 Fr Francium (223) / 88 Ra Radium (226)	103 Lr Lawrencium (262)	104 Rf Rutherfordium (261)	105 Db Dubnium (262)	106 Sg Seaborgium (263)	107 Bh Bohrium (264)	108 Hs Hassium (265)	109 Mt Meitnerium (268)

Lanthanide Series

| 57 La Lanthanum 138.91 | 58 Ce Cerium 140.12 | 59 Pr Praseodymium 140.91 | 60 Nd Neodymium 144.24 | 61 Pm Promethium (145) | 62 Sm Samarium 150.4 |

Actinide Series

| 89 Ac Actinium (227) | 90 Th Thorium 232.04 | 91 Pa Protactinium 231.04 | 92 U Uranium 238.03 | 93 Np Neptunium (237) | 94 Pu Plutonium (244) |

Metals—elements that are good conductors of heat and electric current

Nonmetals—elements that are poor conductors of heat and electric current

Metalloids—elements with properties that are somewhat similar to metals and nonmetals

	Atomic number —	6								18 **8A**

Atomic number — 6

Element symbol — C

Element name — Carbon

Atomic mass — 12.011

			13 **3A**	14 **4A**	15 **5A**	16 **6A**	17 **7A**	18 **8A** 2 **He** Helium 4.0026

5 **B** Boron 10.81	6 **C** Carbon 12.011	7 **N** Nitrogen 14.007	8 **O** Oxygen 15.999	9 **F** Fluorine 18.998	10 **Ne** Neon 20.179
13 **Al** Aluminum 26.982	14 **Si** Silicon 28.086	15 **P** Phosphorus 30.974	16 **S** Sulfur 32.06	17 **Cl** Chlorine 35.453	18 **Ar** Argon 39.948

10	11 **1B**	12 **2B**						

28 **Ni** Nickel 58.71	29 **Cu** Copper 63.546	30 **Zn** Zinc 65.38	31 **Ga** Gallium 69.72	32 **Ge** Germanium 72.59	33 **As** Arsenic 74.922	34 **Se** Selenium 78.96	35 **Br** Bromine 79.904	36 **Kr** Krypton 83.80
46 **Pd** Palladium 106.4	47 **Ag** Silver 107.87	48 **Cd** Cadmium 112.41	49 **In** Indium 114.82	50 **Sn** Tin 118.69	51 **Sb** Antimony 121.75	52 **Te** Tellurium 127.60	53 **I** Iodine 126.90	54 **Xe** Xenon 131.30
78 **Pt** Platinum 195.09	79 **Au** Gold 196.97	80 **Hg** Mercury 200.59	81 **Tl** Thallium 204.37	82 **Pb** Lead 207.2	83 **Bi** Bismuth 208.98	84 **Po** Polonium (209)	85 **At** Astatine (210)	86 **Rn** Radon (222)
110 *****Uun** Ununnilium (269)	111 *****Uuu** Unununium (272)	112 *****Uub** Ununbium (277)		114 *****Uuq** Ununquadium				

*Name not officially assigned.

63 **Eu** Europium 151.96	64 **Gd** Gadolinium 157.25	65 **Tb** Terbium 158.93	66 **Dy** Dysprosium 162.50	67 **Ho** Holmium 164.93	68 **Er** Erbium 167.26	69 **Tm** Thulium 168.93	70 **Yb** Ytterbium 173.04

95 **Am** Americium (243)	96 **Cm** Curium (247)	97 **Bk** Berkelium (247)	98 **Cf** Californium (251)	99 **Es** Einsteinium (252)	100 **Fm** Fermium (257)	101 **Md** Mendelevium (258)	102 **No** Nobelium (259)

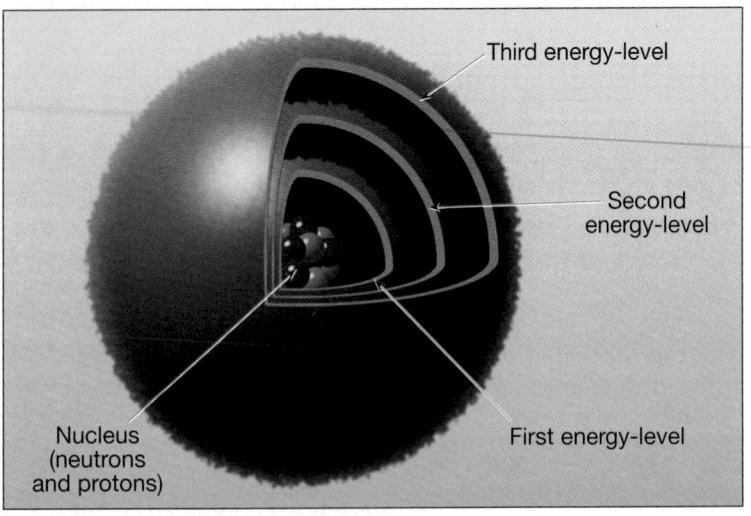

Third energy-level

Second energy-level

First energy-level

Nucleus (neutrons and protons)

Figure 2 Model of an Atom
The electrons that move about an atom's nucleus occupy distinct regions called energy levels.

Q *Are the minerals in this chapter the same as those in dietary supplements?*

A Not ordinarily. Most minerals found in dietary supplements are compounds made in the laboratory. These dietary minerals often contain elements that are metals, such as calcium, potassium, magnesium, and iron. From the geologist's point of view, a mineral must be a naturally occurring crystalline solid.

Electrons An electron is the smallest of the three fundamental particles in an atom. An electron has a mass of about 1/1836 the mass of a proton or a neutron. Electrons move about the nucleus so rapidly that they create a sphere-shaped negative zone. You can picture moving electrons by imagining a cloud of negative charges surrounding the nucleus, as shown in Figure 2.

Electrons are located in regions called **energy levels.** Each energy level contains a certain number of electrons. Interactions among electrons in the outermost energy levels explains how atoms form compounds, as you will find out later in the chapter.

 **Reading Checkpoint** *How are electrons, protons, and neutrons alike and how are they different?*

Isotopes

Atoms of the same element always have the same number of protons. For example, every carbon atom has 6 protons. Carbon is element number 6 on the periodic table. But the number of neutrons for atoms of the same element can vary. **Atoms with the same number of protons but different numbers of neutrons are isotopes of an element.** Isotopes of the same element are labeled using a convention called the mass number and with the element's name or symbol. The **mass number** of an atom is the total mass of the atom (protons plus neutrons) expressed in atomic mass units. The proton and the neutron each have a mass that is slightly larger than the atomic mass unit. Recall that the mass of an electron is so small that the number of electrons has no effect on the mass number of an atom.

Carbon has 15 different isotopes. Models for three of these are shown in Figure 3. Carbon-12 makes up almost 99 percent of all carbon on Earth. Carbon-12 has 6 protons and 6 neutrons. Carbon-13 makes up much of the remaining naturally occurring carbon atoms on Earth. Carbon-13 has 6 protons and 7 neutrons. Though only traces of carbon-14 are found in nature, the presence of this isotope is often used to determine the age of once-living things. Carbon-14 has 6 protons and 8 neutrons

The nuclei of most atoms are stable. However, many elements have atoms whose nuclei are unstable. Such atoms disintegrate through a process called radioactive decay. Radioactive decay occurs because the forces that hold the nucleus together are not strong enough.

During radioactive decay, unstable atoms radiate energy and particles. Some of this energy powers the movements of Earth's crust and upper mantle. The rates at which unstable atoms decay are measurable. Therefore certain radioactive atoms can be used to determine the ages of fossils, rocks, and minerals.

 **Reading Checkpoint** *What are isotopes?*

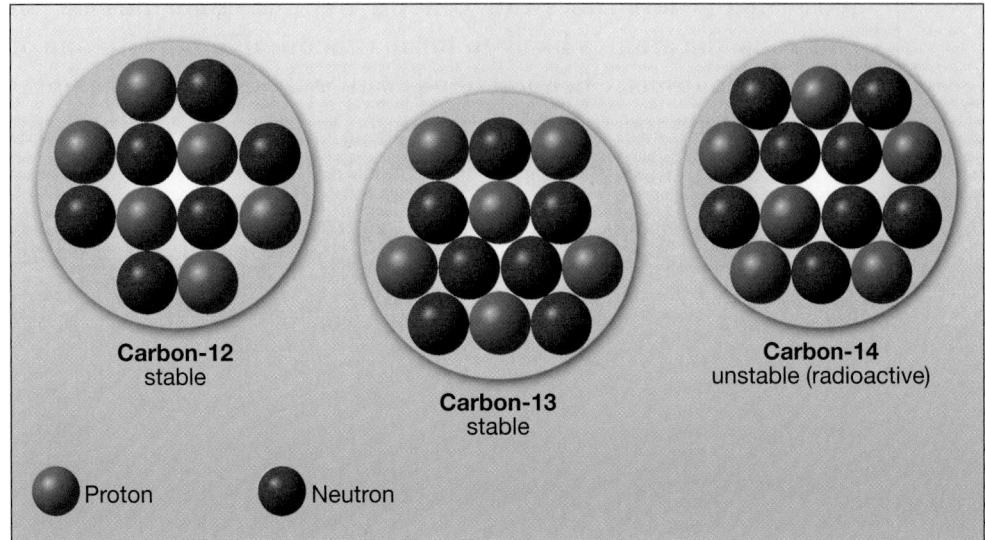

Carbon-12
stable

Carbon-13
stable

Carbon-14
unstable (radioactive)

● Proton   ● Neutron

Figure 3 Nuclei of Isotopes of Carbon
Carbon has many isotopes. Of these, three occur in nature.
Comparing and Contrasting *How are the nuclei of these isotopes the same, and how do they differ?*

Why Atoms Bond

Most elements exist combined with other elements to form substances with properties that are different from the elements themselves. Sodium is often found combined with the element chlorine as the mineral halite. Lead ore is really the mineral galena, which is the element, lead, combined with the element, sulfur. Chemical combinations of the atoms of elements are called **compounds.** **A compound is a substance that consists of two or more elements that are chemically combined in specific proportions.** Compounds form when atoms are more stable (exist at a lower energy state) in a combined form. The chemical process, called bonding, centers around the electron arrangements of atoms. Thus, when atoms combine with others to form compounds, they gain, lose, or share electrons.

Scientists have discovered that the most stable elements are found on the right side of the periodic table in Group 8A (18). These elements have a very low reactivity and exist in nature as single atoms. Scientists explain why atoms form compounds by considering how an atom undergoes changes to its electron structure to be more like atoms in Group 8A.

Look at Figure 4. It shows the shorthand way of representing the number of electrons in the outer energy level. Recall that electrons move about the nucleus of an atom in a region called an electron cloud. Within this cloud, only a certain number of electrons can occupy each energy level. For example, a maximum of two electrons can occupy the first energy level. From Figure 4, you see that helium (He) is shown with two electrons. A maximum of eight electrons can be found in the second energy level. You also see from the figure that neon (Ne) is shown with eight electrons. ⬤ **When an atom's outermost energy level does not contain the maximum number of electrons, the atom is likely to form a chemical bond with one or more other atoms. Chemical bonds** can be thought of as the forces that hold atoms together in a compound. The principal types of chemical bonds are ionic bonds, covalent bonds, or metallic bonds.

Figure 4 In an electron dot diagram, each dot represents an electron in the atom's outer energy level. These electrons are sometimes called valence electrons.
Observing *How many electrons do sodium and chlorine have in their outer energy levels?*

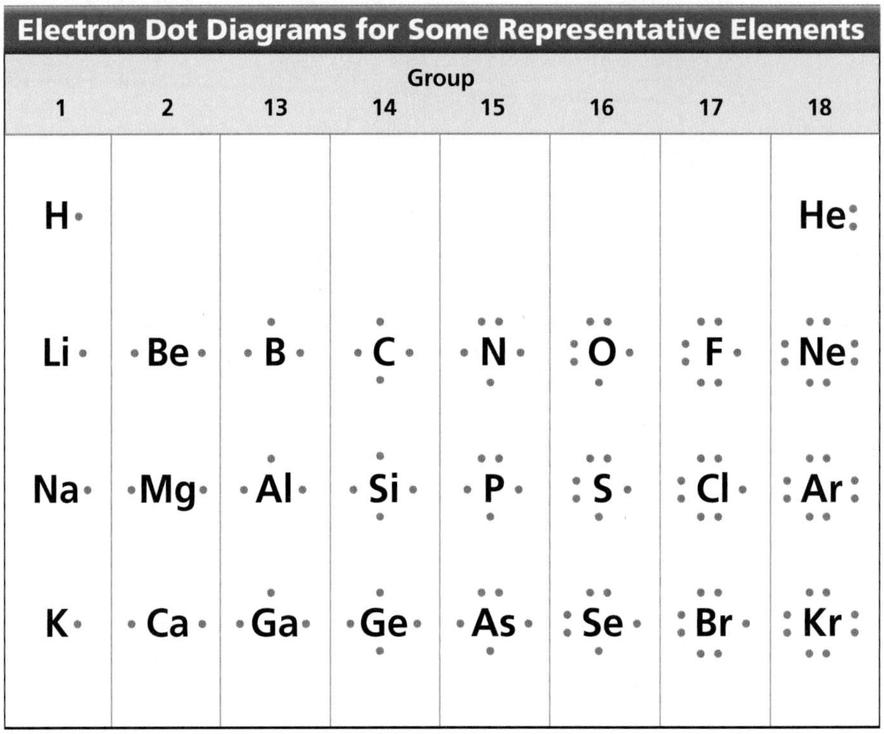

Electron Dot Diagrams for Some Representative Elements

			Group				
1	2	13	14	15	16	17	18
H·							He:
Li·	·Be·	·B·	·C·	·N·	:O·	:F·	:Ne:
Na·	·Mg·	·Al·	·Si·	·P·	:S·	:Cl·	:Ar:
K·	·Ca·	·Ga·	·Ge·	·As·	:Se·	:Br·	:Kr:

Types of Chemical Bonds

Ionic Bonds An atom that gains electrons becomes negatively charged. This happens because the atom now has more electrons than protons. An atom that loses electrons becomes positively charged. This happens because the atom now has more protons than electrons. An atom that has an electrical charge because of a gain or loss of one or more electrons is called an **ion.** Oppositely charged ions attract each other to form crystalline compounds. ⬤ **Ionic bonds form between positive and negative ions.**

Some common compounds on Earth have both a chemical name and a mineral name. For example, table salt has a chemical name, sodium chloride, and a mineral name, halite. Salt forms when sodium (Na) reacts with chlorine (Cl) as shown in Figure 5A. Sodium is very unstable and reactive. Sodium atoms lose one electron and become positive ions. Chlorine atoms gain one electron and become negative ions. These oppositely charged ions are attracted to each other and form the compound called sodium chloride.

The properties of a compound are different from the properties of the elements in the compound. Sodium is a soft, silvery metal that reacts vigorously with water. If you held it in your hand, sodium could burn your skin. Chlorine is a green poisonous gas. Chemically combined these atoms produce table salt, the familiar crystalline solid that is essential to health.

 **Reading Checkpoint** *What happens when two or more atoms react?*

Formation of Sodium Chloride

Figure 5 A When sodium metal comes in contact with chlorine gas, a violent reaction occurs. **B** Sodium atoms transfer one electron to the outer energy levels of chlorine atoms. Both ions now have filled outer energy levels **C** The positive and negative ions formed attract each other to form a crystalline solid with a rigid structure.

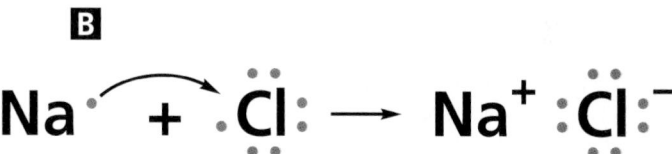

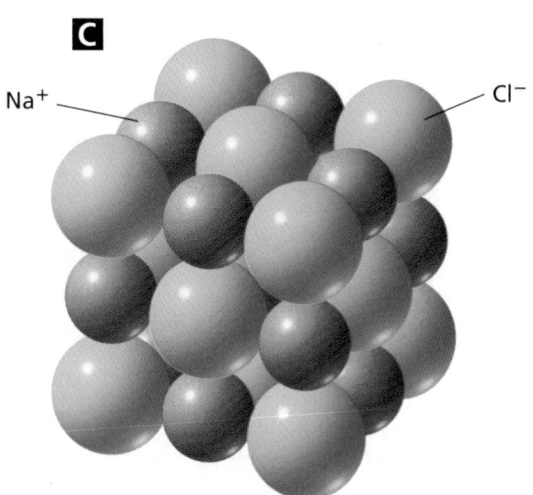

A

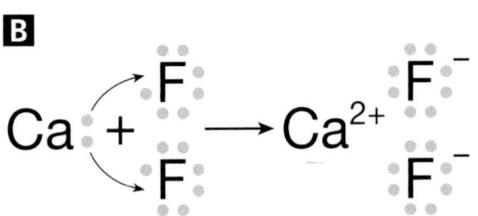

B

Figure 6 Ionic Compound A Fluorite is an ionic compound that forms when calcium reacts with fluorine. **B** The dots shown with the element's symbol represent the electrons in the outermost levels of the ions.
Explaining *Explain what happens to the electrons in calcium atoms and fluorine atoms when fluorite forms.*

A

B

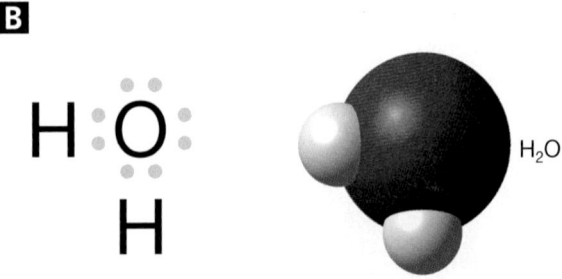

Figure 7 Covalent Compounds A Quartz is a covalent compound that forms when silicon and oxygen atoms bond. **B** Water consists of molecules formed when hydrogen and oxygen share electrons.

Compounds that contain ionic bonds are called ionic compounds. Figure 6 shows calcium fluoride, a common ionic compound. Our model for ionic bonding suggests that one calcium atom transfers two electrons from its outermost energy level to two atoms of fluorine. This transfer gives all atoms the right numbers of electrons in their outer energy levels. The compound that forms is known as the mineral fluorite.

Ionic compounds are rigid solids with high melting and boiling points. These compounds are poor conductors of electricity in their solid states. When melted, however, many ionic compounds are good conductors of electricity. Most ionic compounds consist of elements from groups 1 and 2 on the periodic table reacting with elements from groups 16 and 17 of the table.

 **Reading Checkpoint** *How do ionic bonds form, and what are some properties of ionic compounds?*

Covalent Bonds Covalent bonds form when atoms share electrons. Compounds with covalent bonds are called covalent compounds. Figure 7 shows silicon dioxide, one of the most common covalent compounds on Earth. Silicon dioxide forms when one silicon atom and two oxygen atoms share electrons in their outermost energy levels. Silicon dioxide is also known as the mineral quartz.

The bonding in covalent compounds results in properties that differ from those of ionic compounds. Unlike ionic compounds, many covalent compounds have low melting and boiling points. For example, water, a covalent compound, boils at 100°C at standard pressure. Sodium chloride, an ionic compound, boils at 1413°C at standard pressure. Covalent compounds also are poor conductors of electricity, even when melted.

The smallest particle of a covalent compound that shows the properties of that compound is a molecule. A molecule is a neutral group of atoms joined by one or more covalent bonds. Water, for example, consists of molecules. These molecules are made of two hydrogen atoms covalently-bonded to one oxygen atom. The many gases that make up Earth's atmosphere, including hydrogen, oxygen, nitrogen, and carbon dioxide, also consist of molecules.

Metallic Bonds Metals are malleable, which means that they can be easily shaped. You've observed this property when you wrapped aluminum foil around food or crushed an aluminum can. Metals are also ductile, meaning that they can be drawn into thin wires without breaking. The wiring in your school or home is probably made of the metal copper. Metals are excellent conductors of electricity.

Metallic bonds form when electrons are shared by metal ions. Figure 8 shows a model for this kind of bond. The sharing of an electron pool gives metals their characteristic properties. Using the model you can see how an electrical current is easily carried through the pool of electrons. Later in this chapter, you will learn about some metals that are classified as minerals.

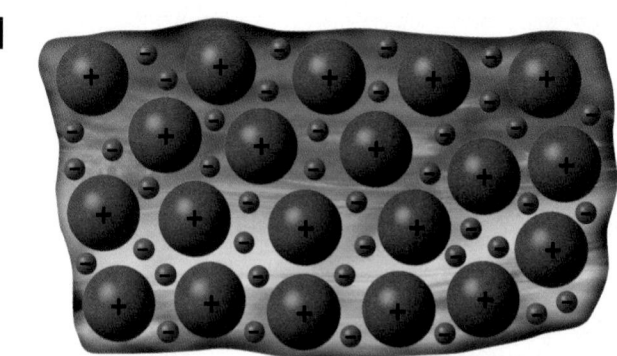

Figure 8 Metallic Bonds A Metals form bonds with one another by sharing electrons. **B** Such bonds give metals, such as this copper, their characteristic properties. Metals can be easily formed and shaped.

Section 2.1 Assessment

Reviewing Concepts

1. What is an element?
2. What kinds of particles make up atoms?
3. What are isotopes?
4. What are compounds and why do they form?
5. Contrast ionic, covalent, and metallic bonds.

Critical Thinking

6. **Comparing and Contrasting** Compare and contrast solids, liquids, and gases.
7. **Applying Concepts** What elements in Table 1 are metals?
8. **Applying Concepts** A magnesium atom needs two electrons to fill its outermost energy level. A chlorine atom needs one electron to fill its outermost shell. If magnesium reacts with chlorine, what type of bond will most likely form? Explain.
9. **Applying Concepts** Which elements in the periodic table might combine with oxygen to form compounds similar to magnesium dioxide (MgO_2)?

Math ▶ Practice

10. The isotopes of carbon have from 2 to 16 neutrons. Use this information to make a table that shows the 15 isotopes of carbon and the atomic number and mass number of each.

2.2 Minerals

Reading Focus

Key Concepts

- What are five characteristics of a mineral?
- What processes result in the formation of minerals?
- How can minerals be classified?
- What are some of the major groups of minerals?

Vocabulary

- mineral
- silicate
- silicon-oxygen tetrahedron

Reading Strategy

Previewing Copy the organizer below. Skim the material on mineral groups on pages 47 to 49. Place each group name into one of the ovals in the organizer. As you read this section, complete the organizer with characteristics and examples of each major mineral group.

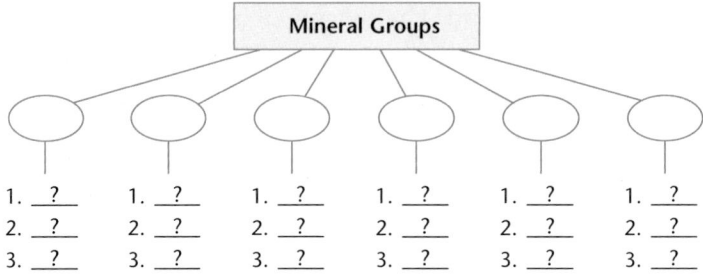

Mineral Groups

1. ?	1. ?	1. ?	1. ?	1. ?	1. ?
2. ?	2. ?	2. ?	2. ?	2. ?	2. ?
3. ?	3. ?	3. ?	3. ?	3. ?	3. ?

A

B

Look at the salt shaker in Figure 9B. This system is made up of the metal cap, glass container, and salt grains. Each component is made of elements or compounds that either are minerals or that are obtained from minerals. In fact, practically every manufactured product that you might use in a typical day contains materials obtained from minerals. What other minerals do you probably use regularly? The lead in your pencils actually contains a soft black mineral called graphite. Most body powders and many kinds of make-up contain finely ground bits of the mineral talc. Your dentist's drill bits contain tiny pieces of the mineral diamond. It is hard enough to drill through your tooth enamel. The mineral quartz is the main ingredient in the windows in your school and the drinking glasses in your family's kitchen. What do all of these minerals have in common? How do they differ?

Figure 9 A Table salt is the mineral halite. **B** The glass container is made from the mineral quartz. Bauxite is one of the minerals that provides aluminum for the cap.

Minerals

A mineral in Earth science is different from the minerals in foods. ⬭**A mineral is a naturally occurring, inorganic solid with an orderly crystalline structure and a definite chemical composition.** For an Earth material to be considered a mineral, it must have the following characteristics:

1. **Naturally occurring** A mineral forms by natural geologic processes. Therefore, synthetic gems, such as synthetic diamonds and rubies, are not considered minerals.

2. **Solid substance** Minerals are solids within the temperature ranges that are normal for Earth's surface.

3. **Orderly crystalline structure** Minerals are crystalline substances which means that their atoms or ions are arranged in an orderly and repetitive manner. You saw this orderly type of packing in Figure 5 for halite (NaCl). The gemstone opal is not a mineral even though it contains the same elements as quartz. Opal does not have an orderly internal structure.

4. **Definite chemical composition** Most minerals are chemical compounds made of two or more elements. A few, such as gold and silver, consist of only a single element (native form). The common mineral quartz consists of two oxygen atoms for every silicon atom. Thus the chemical formula for quartz would be SiO_2.

5. **Generally considered inorganic** Most minerals are inorganic crystalline solids found in nature. Table salt (halite) is one such mineral. However, sugar, another crystalline solid is not considered a mineral because it is classified as an organic compound. Sugar comes from sugar beets or sugar cane. We say "generally inorganic" because many marine animals secrete inorganic compounds, such as calcium carbonate (calcite). This compound is found in their shells and in coral reefs. Most geologists consider this form of calcium carbonate a mineral.

How Minerals Form

Minerals form nearly everywhere on Earth under different conditions. For example, minerals called silicates often form deep in the crust or mantle where temperatures and pressures are very high. Most of the minerals known as carbonates form in warm, shallow ocean waters. Most clay minerals form at or near Earth's surface when existing minerals are exposed to weathering. Still other minerals form when rocks are subjected to changes in pressure or temperature. ⬭**There are four major processes by which minerals form: crystallization from magma, precipitation, changes in pressure and temperature, and formation from hydrothermal solutions.**

Feldspar

Quartz

Muscovite

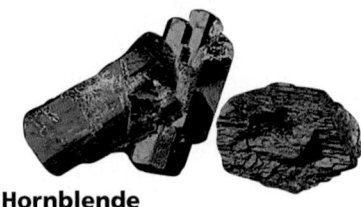

Hornblende

Figure 10 These minerals often form as the result of crystallization from magma.

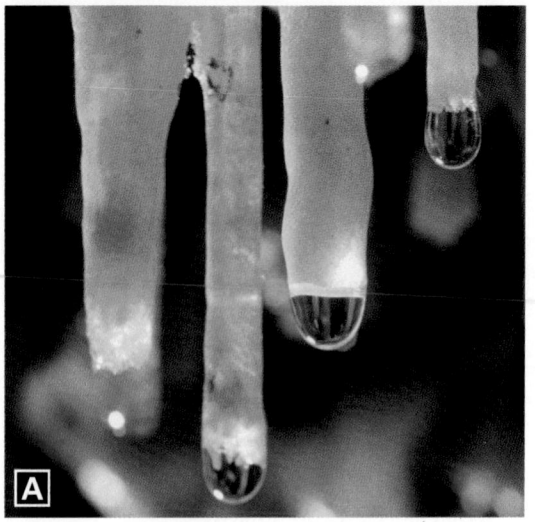

A

B

←— 5 cm —→

Figure 11 **A** This limestone cave formation is an obvious example of precipitation. **B** Halite and calcite are also formed by precipitation.

Figure 12 Bornite (blue and purple) and chalcopyrite (gold) are sulfur minerals that form from thermal solutions.

Crystallization from Magma Magma is molten rock. It forms deep within Earth. As magma cools, elements combine to form minerals such as those shown in Figure 10 on page 45. The first minerals to crystallize from magma are usually those rich in iron, calcium, and magnesium. As minerals continue to form, the composition of the magma changes. Minerals rich in sodium, potassium, and aluminum then form.

Precipitation The water in Earth's lakes, rivers, ponds, oceans, and beneath its surface contains many dissolved substances. If this water evaporates, some of the dissolved substances can react to form minerals. Changes in water temperature may also cause dissolved material to precipitate out of a body of water. The minerals are left behind, or precipitated, out of the water. Two common minerals that form in this way are shown in Figure 11.

Pressure and Temperature Some minerals, including talc and muscovite, form when existing minerals are subjected to changes in pressure and temperature. An increase in pressure can cause a mineral to recrystallize while still solid. The atoms are simply rearranged to form more compact minerals. Changes in temperature can also cause certain minerals to become unstable. Under these conditions, new minerals form, which are stable at the new temperature.

Hydrothermal Solutions A hydrothermal solution is a very hot mixture of water and dissolved substances. Hydrothermal solutions have temperatures between about 100°C and 300°C. When these solutions come into contact with existing minerals, chemical reactions take place to form new minerals. Also, when such solutions cool, some of the elements in them combine to form minerals such as quartz and pyrite. The sulfur minerals in the sample shown in Figure 12 formed from thermal solutions.

 Reading Checkpoint

Describe what happens when a mineral is subjected to changes in pressure or temperature.

Mineral Groups

Over 3800 minerals have been named, and several new ones are identified each year. You will be studying only the most abundant minerals.  **Common minerals, together with the thousands of others that form on Earth, can be classified into groups based on their composition.** Some of the more common mineral groups include the silicates, the carbonates, the oxides, the sulfates and sulfides, the halides, and the native elements. First, you will learn about the most common groups of minerals on Earth—the **silicates.**

Silicates If you look again at Table 1, you can see that the two most abundant elements in Earth's crust are silicon and oxygen. **Silicon and oxygen combine to form a structure called the silicon-oxygen tetrahedron.** This structure is shown in Figure 13. The tetrahedron, which consists of one silicon atom and four oxygen atoms, provides the framework of every silicate mineral. Except for a few silicate minerals, such as pure quartz (SiO_2), most silicates also contain one or more other elements.

Silicon-oxygen tetrahedra can join in a variety of ways, as you can see in Figure 14 on the next page. The silicon-oxygen bonds are very strong. Some minerals, such as olivine, are made of millions of single tetrahedra. In minerals such as augite, the tetrahedra join to form single chains. Double chains are formed in minerals such as hornblende. Micas are silicates in which the tetrahedra join to form sheets. Three-dimensional network structures are found in silicates such as quartz and feldspar. As you will see, the internal structure of a mineral affects its properties.

Reading Checkpoint *What is the silicon-oxygen tetrahedron, and in how many ways can it combine?*

Figure 13 A The silicon-oxygen tetrahedron is made of one silicon atom and four oxygen atoms. The rods represent chemical bonds between silicon and the oxygen atoms. **B** Quartz is the most common silicate mineral. A typical piece of quartz like this contains millions of silicon-oxygen tetrahedra.

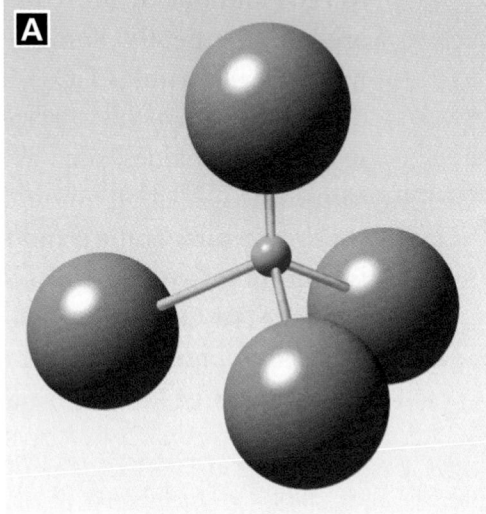

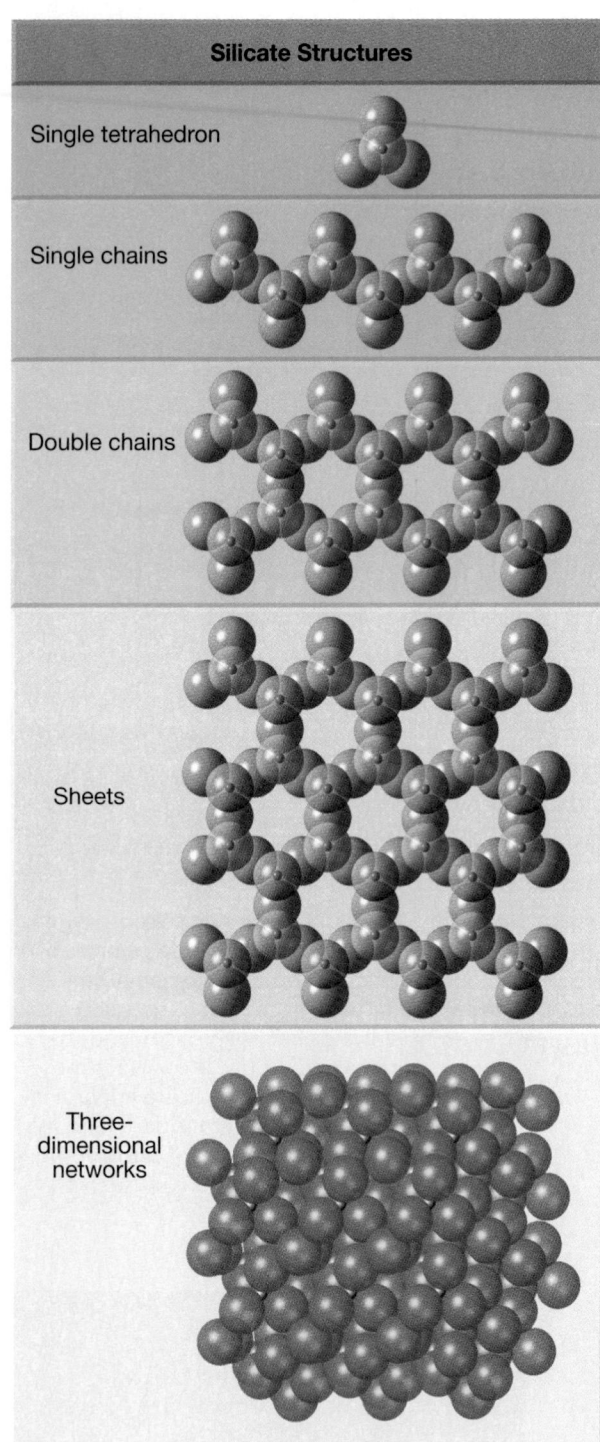

Silicate Structures

Single tetrahedron

Single chains

Double chains

Sheets

Three-dimensional networks

Figure 14 Silicon-oxygen tetrahedra can form chains, sheets, and three-dimensional networks.
Formulating Hypotheses *What type of chemical bond is formed by silicon atoms in an SiO₄ tetrahedron?*

Recall that most silicate minerals crystallize from magma as it cools. This cooling can occur at or near Earth's surface, where temperatures and pressures are relatively low. The formation of silicates can also occur at great depths, where temperatures and pressures are high. The place of formation and the chemical composition of the magma determine which silicate minerals will form. For example, the silicate olivine crystallizes at temperatures of about 1200°C. Quartz crystallizes at about 700°C.

Some silicate minerals form at Earth's surface when existing minerals are exposed to weathering. Clay minerals, which are silicates, form this way. Other silicate minerals form under the extreme pressures that occur with mountain building. Therefore, silicate minerals can often provide scientists with clues about the conditions in which the minerals formed.

Carbonates Carbonates are the second most common mineral group. **Carbonates are minerals that contain the elements carbon, oxygen, and one or more other metallic elements.** Calcite ($CaCO_3$) is the most common carbonate mineral. Dolomite is another carbonate mineral that contains magnesium and calcium. Both limestone and marble are rocks composed of carbonate minerals. Both types of rock are used in building and construction.

Oxides **Oxides are minerals that contain oxygen and one or more other elements, which are usually metals.** Some oxides, including the mineral called rutile (TiO_2), form as magma cools deep beneath Earth's surface. Rutile is titanium oxide. Other oxides, such as corundum (Al_2O_3), form when existing minerals are subjected to changes in temperature and pressure. Corundum is aluminum oxide. Still other oxides, such as hematite (Fe_2O_3), form when existing minerals are exposed to liquid water or to moisture in the air. Hematite is one form of iron oxide.

Sulfates and Sulfides

Sulfates and sulfides are minerals that contain the element sulfur. Sulfates, including anhydrite ($CaSO_4$) and gypsum ($CaSO_4 \cdot 2H_2O$), form when mineral-rich waters evaporate. Sulfides, which include the minerals galena (PbS), sphalerite (ZnS), and pyrite (FeS_2), often form from thermal, or hot-water, solutions. Figure 15 shows two of these sulfides.

Halides

Halides are minerals that contain a halogen ion plus one or more other elements. Halogens are elements from Group 7A of the periodic table. This group includes the elements fluorine (F) and chlorine (Cl). The mineral halite (NaCl), table salt, is a common halide. Fluorite (CaF_2) is also a common halide and is used in making steel. It forms when salt water evaporates.

Native Elements

Native elements are a group of minerals that exist in relatively pure form. You are probably familiar with many native elements, such as gold (Au), silver (Ag), copper (Cu), sulfur (S), and carbon (C). Native forms of carbon are diamond and graphite. Some native elements form from hydrothermal solutions.

Figure 15 Sulfides A Galena is a sulfide mineral that can be mined for its lead. **B** Pyrite is another sulfide that is often called fool's gold.
Inferring *What element do you think pyrite is generally mined for?*

Section 2.2 Assessment

Reviewing Concepts

1. What are five characteristics of a mineral?
2. Describe four processes that result in the formation of minerals.
3. How can minerals be classified?
4. Name the major groups of minerals, and give at least two examples of minerals in each group.

Critical Thinking

5. **Comparing and Contrasting** Compare and contrast sulfates and sulfides.
6. **Formulating Conclusions** When hit with a hammer, quartz shows an uneven breakage pattern. Using Figure 14, what can you suggest about its structure?
7. **Applying Concepts** To which mineral group do each of the following minerals belong: bornite (Cu_5FeS_4), cuprite (Cu_2O), magnesite ($MgCO_3$), and barite ($BaSO_4$)?

Writing in Science

Explanatory Paragraph Coal forms from ancient plant matter that has been compressed over time. Do you think coal is a mineral? Write a paragraph that explains your reasoning.

2.3 Properties of Minerals

Reading Focus

Key Concepts

- What properties can be used to identify minerals?
- What is the Mohs scale?
- What are some distinctive properties of minerals?

Vocabulary

- ◆ streak
- ◆ luster
- ◆ crystal form
- ◆ hardness
- ◆ Mohs scale
- ◆ cleavage
- ◆ fracture
- ◆ density

Reading Strategy

Outlining Before you read, make an outline of this section, following the format below. Use the green headings as the main topics. As you read, add supporting details.

I. Properties of Minerals
   A. Color
      1. _____
      2. _____
   B. Luster
      1. _____
      2. _____

As you can see from the photographs in this chapter, minerals occur in different colors and shapes. Now you will learn that minerals vary in the way they reflect light and in the way in which they break. You will also find out that some minerals are harder than others and that some minerals smell like rotten eggs. All of these characteristics, or properties, of minerals can be used to identify them.

Color

One of the first things you might notice about a mineral is its color. While color is unique to some minerals, this property is often not useful in identifying many minerals. **Small amounts of different elements can give the same mineral different colors.** You can see examples of this in Figure 16.

Figure 16 Small amounts of different elements give these sapphires their distinct colors. **Observing** *Why is color often not a useful property in mineral identification?*

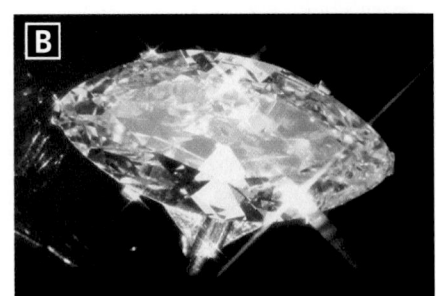

Figure 17 A The mineral copper has a metallic luster. **B** The brilliant luster of diamond is also known as an adamantine luster.

Streak

Streak is the color of a mineral in its powdered form. Streak is obtained by rubbing a mineral across a streak plate, a piece of unglazed porcelain. While the color of a mineral may vary from sample to sample, the streak usually doesn't. Therefore, streak can be a good indicator. Streak can also help to see the difference between minerals with metallic lusters and minerals with nonmetallic lusters. Metallic minerals generally have a dense, dark streak. Minerals with nonmetallic lusters do not have such streaks.

Luster

Luster is used to describe how light is reflected from the surface of a mineral. Minerals that have the appearance of metals, regardless of their color, are said to have a metallic luster. The piece of copper shown in Figure 17A has a metallic luster. Minerals with a nonmetallic luster are described by many adjectives. These include vitreous or glassy, like the quartz crystals in Figure 5. Other lusters include pearly, silky, and earthy. Diamond has an adamantine, or brilliant luster. Some minerals appear *somewhat* metallic and are said to have a sub-metallic luster.

Crystal Form

Crystal form is the visible expression of a mineral's internal arrangement of atoms. Every mineral has a distinct crystal form.

Usually, when a mineral forms slowly and without space restrictions, it will develop into a crystal with well-formed faces—sides, top, and bottom—as shown in Figure 18. Most of the time, however, minerals compete for space. This crowding results in an intergrown mass of small crystals. None of these crystals shows its crystal form.

 **Reading Checkpoint** *What two conditions produce crystals with well-defined faces?*

Figure 18 Crystal Form A This quartz sample shows hexagonal (six-sided) crystals. The ends of the crystals have a pyramid shape. **B** Fluorite often forms cubic crystals.

Hardness

One of the most useful properties to identify a mineral is hardness. **Hardness** is a measure of the resistance of a mineral to being scratched. You can find this property by rubbing the mineral against another mineral of known hardness. One will scratch the other, unless they have the same hardness.

Geologists use a standard hardness scale called the Mohs scale. The Mohs scale consists of 10 minerals arranged from 10 (hardest) to 1 (softest). See Figure 19. Any mineral of unknown hardness can be rubbed against these to determine its hardness. Other objects can also be used to determine hardness. Your fingernail, for example, has a hardness of 2.5. A copper penny has a hardness of 3.5. A piece of glass has a hardness of about 5.5. Look again at Figure 19. The mineral gypsum, which has a Mohs hardness of 2, can be easily scratched by your fingernail. The mineral calcite, which resembles gypsum, has a hardness of 3. Calcite cannot be scratched by your fingernail. Calcite, which can resemble the mineral quartz, cannot scratch glass, because its hardness is less than 5.5. Quartz, the hardest of the common minerals with a Mohs hardness of 7, will scratch a glass plate. Diamond, the hardest mineral on Earth, can scratch anything.

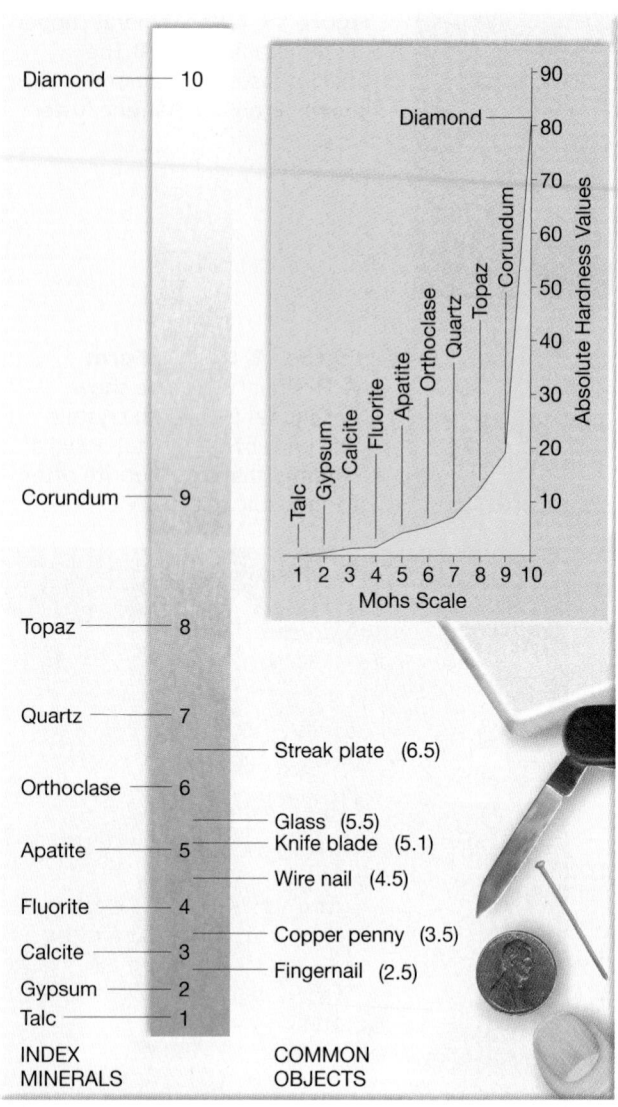

Figure 19 Mohs Scale of Hardness Common objects can be used with the Mohs scale to determine mineral hardness. **Using Tables and Graphs** *A mineral has a hardness of 4.2. Which common items on the chart will that mineral scratch?*

 **Reading Checkpoint**

Describe three or four of the most useful properties for identifying unknown minerals.

Cleavage

In the atomic structure of a mineral, some bonds are weaker than others. These weak bonds are places where a mineral will break when it is stressed. **Cleavage is the tendency of a mineral to cleave, or break, along flat, even surfaces.**

Minerals called micas show the simplest type of cleavage. Because the micas have weak bonds in one direction, they cleave to form thin, flat sheets, as shown in Figure 20A. Look again at Figure 14. Can you see the relationship between mica's internal structure and the cleavage it shows? Mica, and all other silicates, tend to cleave between the silicon-oxygen structures rather than across them. This is because the silicon-oxygen bonds are strong. The micas' sheet structure causes them to cleave into flat plates. Quartz has equally strong silicon-oxygen bonds in all directions. Therefore, quartz has no cleavage but fractures instead.

Some minerals have cleavage in more than one direction. Look again at Figure 11. Halite (11A) has three directions of cleavage. The cleavage planes of halite meet at 90-degree angles. Calcite (11B) also has three directions of cleavage. The cleavage planes of calcite, however, meet at 75-degree angles.

Fracture

 **Minerals that do not show cleavage when broken are said to fracture. Fracture** is the uneven breakage of a mineral. For example, quartz shows a curvy and glassy fracture. Like cleavage, there are different kinds of fracture. Minerals that break into smooth, curved surfaces like the quartz in Figure 20B have a conchoidal fracture. Other minerals, such as asbestos, break into splinters or fibers. Many minerals have an irregular fracture.

Reading Checkpoint *How are cleavage and fracture different?*

Figure 20 A Mica has cleavage in one direction and therefore cleaves into thin sheets. **B** The bonds in quartz are very strong in all directions, causing quartz to display conchoidal fracture.

Density

 **Density is a property of all matter that is the ratio of an object's mass to its volume.** Density is a ratio and can be expressed using the following equation.

$$Density \ (D) = \frac{mass \ (m)}{Volume \ (V)}$$

Density is expressed using derived units with a unit of mass over a unit of volume. For example, the density of copper is 8.96 g/cm^3 (grams per cubic centimeter). Therefore, any sample of pure copper with a volume of one cubic centimeter will have a mass of 8.96 grams.

Many common minerals have densities between 2 and 5 g/cm^3. Some metallic minerals have densities that are often greater than rock-forming minerals. Galena, the ore of lead, has a density around 7.5 g/cm^3. The density of gold is 19.3 g/cm^3. The density of a pure mineral is a constant value. Thus, density can be used to determine the purity or identity of some minerals.

For: Links on mineral identification
Visit: www.SciLinks.org
Web Code: cjn-1023

Table 2 Some Common Minerals and Their Properties

Name	Chemical Formula and Mineral Group	Common Color(s)	Density (g/cm³)	Hardness	Comments
Quartz	SiO_2 silicates	colorless, milky white, pink, brown	2.65	7	glassy luster; conchoidal fractures
Orthoclase feldspar	$KAlSi_3O_8$ silicates	white to pink	2.57	6	cleaves in two directions at 90°
Plagioclase feldspar	$(Na,Ca)AlSi_3O_8$ silicates	white to gray	2.69*	6	cleaves in two directions at 90°; striations common
Galena	PbS sulfides	metallic silver	7.5*	2.5	cleaves in three directions at 90°; lead gray streak
Pyrite	FeS_2 sulfides	brassy yellow	5.02	6–6.5	fractures; forms cubic crystals; greenish-black streak
Sulfur	S native elements	yellow	2.07*	1.5–2.5	fractures; yellow streak smells like rotten eggs
Fluorite	CaF_2 halides	colorless, purple	3.18	4	perfect cleavage in three directions; glassy luster
Olivine	$(Mg,Fe)_2SiO_4$ silicates	green, yellowish-green	3.82*	6.5–7	fractures; glassy luster; often has granular texture
Calcite	$CaCO_3$ carbonates	colorless, gray	2.71	3	bubbles with HCl; cleaves in three directions
Talc	$Mg_3Si_4O_{10}(OH)_2$ silicates	pale green, gray, white	2.75*	1	pearly luster; feels greasy; cleaves in one direction
Gypsum	$CaSO_4 \cdot 2H_2O$ sulfates	colorless, white, gray	2.32	2	glassy or pearly luster; cleaves in three directions
Muscovite mica	$KAl_3Si_3O_{10}(OH)_2$ silicates	colorless in thin sheets to brown	2.82*	2–2.5	silky to pearly luster; cleaves in one direction to form flexible sheets

* Average density of the mineral

Figure 21 Calcite shows the property of double refraction.

Distinctive Properties of Minerals

Some minerals can be recognized by other distinctive properties. Talc and graphite, for example, both have distinctive feels. Talc feels soapy. Graphite feels greasy. Metallic minerals, such as gold, silver, and copper, are easily shaped. Some types of magnetite are magnetic and can be used to pick up paper clips and small nails. When a piece of transparent calcite is placed over printed material, the letters appear doubled as Figure 21 shows. This property is called double refraction. Streaks of a few minerals that contain sulfur smell like rotten eggs. Carbonate minerals, such as calcite, will fizz when they come into contact with hydrochloric acid.

A mineral's properties depend on the elements that compose the mineral (its composition) and its structure (how its atoms are arranged). Table 2 lists some of the more common minerals and their properties. You will use this table to identify minerals in the lab on pages 58 and 59.

Table 2 Some Common Minerals and Their Properties, *continued*

Name	Chemical Formula and Mineral Group	Common Color(s)	Density (g/cm³)	Hardness	Comments
Biotite mica	$K(Mg,Fe)_3(AlSi_3O_{10})$ $(OH)_2$ silicates	dark green to brown to black	3.0*	2.5–3	perfect cleavage in one direction to form flexible sheets
Halite	$NaCl$ halides	colorless, white	2.16	2.5	has a salty taste; dissolves in water; cleaves in three directions
Augite	$(Ca, Na)(Mg, Fe, Al)$ $(Si, Al)_2O_6$ silicates	dark green to black	3.3*	5–6	glassy luster; cleaves in two directions; crystals have 8-sided cross section
Hornblende	$(Ca, Na)_{2-3}(Mg, Fe, Al)_5$ $Si_6(Si, Al)_2O_{22}(OH)_2$ silicates	dark green to black	3.2*	5–6	glassy luster; cleaves in two directions; crystals have 6-sided cross section
Hematite	Fe_2O_3 oxides	reddish brown to black	5.26	5.5–6.5	metallic luster in crystals; dull luster in earthy variety; dark red streak
Dolomite	$CaMg(CO_3)_2$ carbonates	pink, colorless, white, gray	2.85	3.5–4	does not react to HCl as quickly as calcite; cleaves in three directions
Magnetite	Fe_3O_4 oxides	black	5.18	6	metallic luster; black streak; strongly magnetic
Copper	Cu native elements	copper-red on fresh surface	8.9	2.5–3	metallic luster; fractures; can be easily shaped
Graphite	C native elements	black to gray	2.3	1–2	black to gray streak; marks paper; feels slippery

Section 2.3 Assessment

Reviewing Concepts

1. 🔵 Describe five common properties of minerals that can be used to identify them.

2. 🔵 How is the Mohs scale used?

3. 🔵 What are some unique properties that can be used to identify minerals?

Critical Thinking

4. **Applying Concepts** What kind of luster do the minerals shown in Figure 15 have? Explain your choice.

5. **Applying Concepts** Hornblende is a double-chain silicate. How many planes of cleavage do you think hornblende has when it breaks? Explain your answer.

6. **Applying Concepts** A mineral scratches a piece of fluorite but cannot be scratched by a piece of glass. What is this mineral's hardness?

Connecting C Concepts

Mineral Properties Choose one of the minerals pictured in this chapter. Find out to which mineral system it belongs as well as its luster, streak, hardness, specific gravity, and whether it cleaves or fractures. Also note any unique properties of the mineral.

Gemstones

Precious stones have been prized by people since ancient times. Unfortunately, much misinformation exists about the nature of gems and the minerals of which they are composed. Part of the misinformation stems from the ancient practice of grouping precious stones by color rather than mineral makeup.

For example, the more common red spinels were often passed off to royalty as rubies, which are more valuable gems. Even today, when modern techniques of mineral identification are commonplace, yellow quartz is frequently sold as topaz.

What's In a Name?

Compounding the confusion is the fact that many gems have names that are different from their mineral names. For example, diamond is composed of the mineral of the same name, whereas sapphire is a form of corundum, an aluminum oxide-rich mineral. Although pure aluminum oxide is colorless, a tiny amount of a foreign element can produce a vividly colored gemstone. Therefore, depending on the impurity, sapphires of nearly every color exist. Pure aluminum oxide with trace amounts of titanium and iron produce the most prized blue sapphires. If the mineral corundum contains enough chromium, it exhibits a brilliant red color, and the gem is called ruby. Large gem-quality rubies are much rarer than diamonds and thus command a very high price.

If the specimen is not suitable as a gem, it simply goes by the mineral name corundum. Although common corundum is not a gemstone, it does have value as an abrasive material. Whereas two gems—rubies and sapphires—are composed of the mineral corundum, quartz is the parent mineral of more than a dozen gems. Table 3 lists some well-known gemstones and their mineral names.

Figure 22 Emerald is the dark green variety of the mineral beryl. More common blue-green beryl is aquamarine.

Precious or Semiprecious?

What makes a gem a gem instead of just another mineral? Basically, certain mineral specimens, when cut and polished, possess beauty of such quality that they can command a price that makes the process of producing the gem profitable. Gemstones can be divided into two categories: precious and semiprecious. A *precious* gem has beauty, durability, size, and rarity, whereas a *semiprecious* gem usually has only one or two of these qualities. The gems that have traditionally enjoyed the highest esteem are diamonds, rubies, sapphires, emeralds, and some varieties of opal. All other gemstones are classified as semiprecious. It should be noted, however, that large, high-quality specimens of semiprecious stones can often command a very high price.

Obviously, beauty is the most important quality that a gem can possess. Today we prefer translucent stones with evenly tinted colors. The most favored hues appear to be red, blue, green, purple, rose,

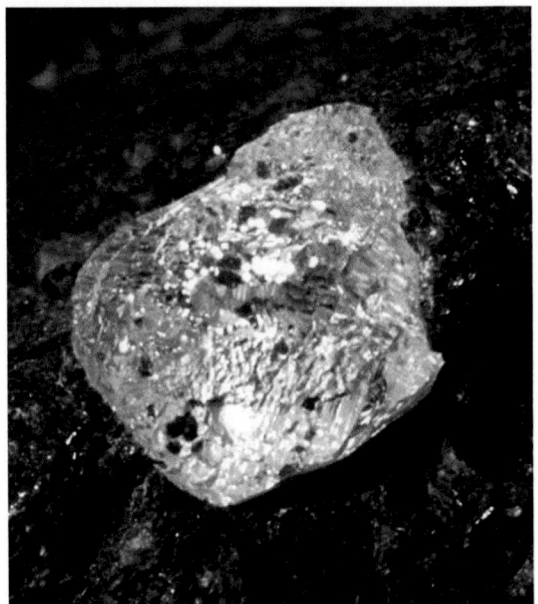 

Figure 23 A diamond in the rough looks very different from the brilliant, multi-faceted gem it can become.

and yellow. The most prized stones are deep red rubies, blue sapphires, grass-green emeralds, and canary-yellow diamonds. Colorless gems are generally less than desirable except in the case of diamonds that display "flashes of color" known as brilliance.

Notice in figure 23 that gemstones in the "rough" are dull and would be passed over by most people as "just another mineral." Gemstones must be cut and polished by experienced artisans before their true beauty can be displayed.

The durability of a gem depends on its hardness—that is, its resistance to abrasion by objects normally encountered in everyday living. For good durability, gems should be as hard or harder than quartz, as defined by the Mohs scale of hardness. One notable exception is opal, which is comparatively soft (hardness 5 to 6.5) and brittle. Opal's esteem comes from its fire, which is a display of a variety of brilliant colors including greens, blues, and reds.

It seems to be human nature to treasure that which is rare. In the case of gemstones, large, high-quality specimens are much rarer than smaller stones. Thus, large rubies, diamonds, and emeralds, which are rare in addition to being beautiful and durable, command the very highest prices.

Table 3 Some Important Gemstones		
Gem	**Mineral Name**	**Prized Hues**
Precious		
Diamond	Diamond	Colorless, yellows
Emerald	Beryl	Greens
Opal	Opal	Brilliant hues
Ruby	Corundum	Reds
Sapphire	Corundum	Blues
Semiprecious		
Alexandrite	Chrysoberyl	Variable
Amethyst	Quartz	Purples
Aquamarine	Beryl	Blue-greens
Cat's-eye	Chrysoberyl	Yellows
Chalcedony	Quartz (agate)	Banded
Citrine	Quartz	Yellows
Garnet	Garnet	Reds, greens
Jade	Jadeite or nephrite	Greens
Moonstone	Feldspar	Transparent blues
Peridot	Olivine	Olive greens
Smoky quartz	Quartz	Browns
Spinel	Spinel	Reds
Topaz	Topaz	Purples, reds
Tourmaline	Tourmaline	Reds, blue-greens
Turquoise	Turquoise	Blues
Zircon	Zircon	Reds

Mineral Identification

Most minerals can be easily identified by using the properties discussed in this chapter. In this lab, you will use what you have learned about mineral properties and the table on pages 54 and 55 to identify some common rock-forming minerals. In the next chapter, you will learn about rocks, which are mixtures of one or more minerals. Being able to identify minerals will enable you to understand more about the processes that form and change the rocks at and beneath Earth's surface.

Problem How can you use simple tests and tools to identify common minerals?

Materials
- mineral samples
- hand lens
- streak plate
- copper penny
- steel knife blade
- glass plate
- piece of quartz
- dilute hydrochloric acid
- magnet
- hammer
- 50 mL graduated cylinder
- tap water
- balance
- thin thread
- scissors
- paper or cloth towels
- Table 2 on pages 54–55

Skills Observing, Comparing and Contrasting, Measuring

Procedure

Part A: Color and Luster

1. Examine each mineral sample with and without the hand lens. Examine both the central part of each mineral as well as the edges of the samples.

2. Record the color and luster of each sample in a data table like the one shown on the next page.

Part B: Streak and Hardness

3. To determine the streak of a mineral, gently drag it across the streak plate and observe the color of the powdered mineral. If a mineral is harder than the streak plate (H = 7), it will not produce a streak.

4. Record the streak color for each mineral in your data table.

5. Use your fingernail, the penny, the glass plate, the knife blade, and the piece of quartz to test the hardness of each mineral. Remember that if a mineral scratches an object, the mineral is harder than the object. If an object scratches a mineral, the mineral is softer than the object.

6. Record the hardness values for each sample in your data table.

Part C: Cleavage and Fracture

7. With your goggles on and everyone out of your way, gently strike one of the mineral samples with a hammer.

8. Observe the broken mineral pieces. Does the mineral cleave or fracture? Remember that cleavage is breakage along flat, even surfaces and fracture is uneven breakage. Record your observations in your data table.

9. Repeat Steps 7 and 8 for the other minerals.

Data Table

Mineral Number	Color	Luster	Streak	Relative Hardness	Cleavage/ Fracture	m	V₁	V₂	d	Other Properties
						\multicolumn{4}{c}{Density}				
1										
2										
3										
4										
5										
6										
7										
8										

Part D: Density

10. Using a balance, determine the mass of your mineral sample. Record the mass in the first column under Density.

11. Cut a piece of thread about 20 cm long. Tie a small piece of your mineral sample to one end of the thread.

12. Securely tie the other end of the thread to a pencil or pen.

13. Fill the graduated cylinder about half full with water. Record the volume of the water in the second column under Density.

14. Lower the mineral into the graduated cylinder. Read the volume of the water now. Record the volume in the third column under Density.

15. Calculate the density of the mineral using the following equation:

$$\frac{mass_1}{volume_2 - volume_1}$$

Record this value in the fourth column.

Part E: Other Properties

16. Use the magnet to determine if any of the minerals are magnetic. Record your observations in the data table.

17. Place the transparent minerals over a word on this page to see if any have the property of double refraction. If a mineral has this property, you will see two sets of the word. Record your observations.

18. Compare the feel of the minerals. In the data table, note any differences.

19. Carefully place one or two drops of dilute hydrochloric acid on each mineral. Record your observations. When you are finished with this test, wash the minerals well with tap water to rinse away the acid.

Analyze and Conclude

1. **Identifying** Use your data and Table 2 to identify each of the minerals tested.

2. **Evaluating** Which of the properties did you find most useful? Least useful? Give reasons for your answers.

3. **Comparing and Contrasting** In general, how did the minerals with metallic luster differ from those with non-metallic luster?

4. **Classifying** Classify your minerals into at least three groups based on your observations. How does your classification scheme differ from those of at least two other students?

Go Further Obtain some rock samples from your teacher or collect some of your own. Use the hand lens to try to identify the minerals in each rock. Make a table in which to record your observations. Compare your table to the information presented in Chapter 3.

2.1 Matter

Key Concepts

- An element contains only one type of atom. Therefore, an element cannot be broken down, chemically or physically, into a simpler substance.

- An atom is a submicroscopic particle made of even smaller components called protons, neutrons, and electrons.

- Atoms with the same number of protons but different numbers of neutrons are isotopes of an element.

- A compound is a substance that consists of two or more elements. Compounds form when electrons are transferred or shared to form bonds.

- When an atom's outermost energy level does not contain the maximum number of electrons, the atom is likely to form a chemical bond with one or more other atoms.

- Ionic bonds form between positive and negative ions. Covalent bonds form when atoms share electrons. Metallic bonds form when electrons are shared by metal ions.

Vocabulary

element, *p. 34*; atomic number, *p. 35*; energy level, *p. 38*; isotope, *p. 38*; mass number, *p. 38*; compound, *p. 39*; chemical bond, *p. 40*; ion, *p. 40*; ionic bond, *p. 40*; covalent bond, *p. 42*; metallic bond, *p. 43*

2.2 Minerals

Key Concepts

- A mineral is a naturally occurring, inorganic solid with an orderly internal structure and a definite chemical composition.

- There are four major processes by which minerals form: crystallization from magma, precipitation, changes in pressure and temperature, and formation from hydrothermal solutions.

- Common minerals, together with the thousands of others that form on Earth, can be classified into groups based on their composition.

- Silicates are the most common minerals on Earth and are made of millions of silicon-oxygen tetrahedra. Carbonates contain carbon, oxygen, and one or more other elements. Oxides contain oxygen and one or more other elements, usually metals. Sulfates and sulfides are minerals that contain sulfur. Halides contain a halogen ion plus one or more other elements. Native elements are minerals that exist in relatively pure form.

Vocabulary

mineral, *p. 45*; silicate, *p. 47*; silicon-oxygen tetrahedron, *p. 47*

2.3 Properties of Minerals

Key Concepts

- Small amounts of different elements can give the same mineral many different colors.

- Streak is the color of a mineral in its powdered form.

- Luster describes how light is reflected from the surface of a mineral.

- Crystal form is the visual expression of a mineral's internal arrangement of atoms.

- The Mohs scale is a scale that can be used to determine a mineral's hardness.

- Cleavage is the tendency of a mineral to cleave, or break along flat, even surfaces; fracture is uneven breakage.

- Density is a property of all matter that is the ratio of an object's mass to its volume.

- Some minerals can be recognized by other distinctive properties.

Vocabulary

streak, *p. 51*; luster, *p. 51*; crystal form, *p. 51*; hardness, *p. 52*; Mohs scale, *p. 52*; cleavage, *p. 52*; fracture, *p. 53*; density, *p. 53*

Thinking Visually

Observing Use what you have learned about minerals and Table 2 to list as many properties as possible of the mineral below.

Reviewing Content

Choose the letter that best answers the question or completes the statement.

1. Which of the following is neutrally charged?
   - **a.** an ion
   - **b.** a compound
   - **c.** an electron
   - **d.** a proton

2. Atoms combine when
   - **a.** their outer electron shells are filled.
   - **b.** their electrons are shared or transferred.
   - **c.** the number of protons and neutrons is the same.
   - **d.** the number of electrons and protons is the same.

3. Compounds with low boiling points have
   - **a.** metallic bonds.
   - **b.** ionic bonds.
   - **c.** covalent bonds.
   - **d.** no chemical bonds.

4. Minerals that form from magma form as the result of
   - **a.** crystallization.
   - **b.** evaporation.
   - **c.** precipitation.
   - **d.** condensation.

5. The mineral barite ($BaSO_4$) is a(n)
   - **a.** oxide.
   - **b.** silicate.
   - **c.** carbonate.
   - **d.** sulfate.

6. Color is often not a useful identification property because
   - **a.** some minerals are colorless.
   - **b.** the same mineral can be different colors.
   - **c.** different minerals can be different colors.
   - **d.** some minerals are single elements.

7. What is a mineral's streak?
   - **a.** the resistance to being scratched
   - **b.** the color of the mineral in powder form
   - **c.** the way in which the mineral reflects light
   - **d.** the way the mineral reacts to hydrochloric acid

8. A particular mineral breaks like a piece of glass does. Which of these describes the breakage?
   - **a.** cleavage
   - **b.** hardness
   - **c.** metallic luster
   - **d.** fracture

9. Mineral properties depend on composition and
   - **a.** structure.
   - **b.** luster.
   - **c.** cleavage.
   - **d.** streak.

Understanding Concepts

10. Name the three types of particles found in an atom and explain how they differ.

11. Compare and contrast ionic and covalent bonds.

12. What are five characteristics of a mineral?

13. Explain three ways in which new minerals can form from existing minerals.

14. Contrast the composition of minerals in each of the mineral groups discussed in the chapter.

15. How is cleavage related to a mineral's atomic structure?

16. Give examples of four minerals that can be identified by unique properties. Describe each property.

Use this diagram to answer Questions 17–21.

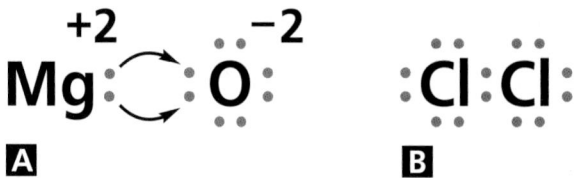

17. Briefly describe the kind of bond that is formed when two atoms shown in **A** bond.

18. Describe the kind of bond that forms when the atoms shown in **B** bond.

19. Is the atom on the left in **A** an ion? Explain your answer.

20. Use the periodic table to determine the atomic number of the atom on the left side of **A**. What group is this element in?

21. The atoms in **B** contain 17 protons. Are these atoms ions when they bond with each other? Can these atoms form ions when they react with other elements? Explain your answers.

Critical Thinking

22. **Comparing and Contrasting** Three atoms have the same atomic number but different mass numbers. What can you say about the atoms?

23. **Predicting** Potassium metal in group 1 of the periodic table is very reactive. When placed in chlorine gas, potassium reacts to form a halide compound. Using Figure 4 and the periodic table propose the formula and name for the compound.

24. **Formulating Hypotheses** Why do you think metals can easily be rolled into thin sheets and drawn into wires? (*Hint:* Think about the arrangement of electrons in metals.)

25. **Explaining** Explain the processes that result in the formation of silicate minerals.

26. **Formulating Hypotheses** A mineral forms deep beneath the surface. It reaches Earth's surface during mountain building. Describe two things that might happen to this mineral at the surface.

27. **Applying Concepts** Classify the following minerals based on their chemical formulas.

   a. $NaCO_3$ b. PbS
   c. $FeCr_2O_4$ c. CaF_2

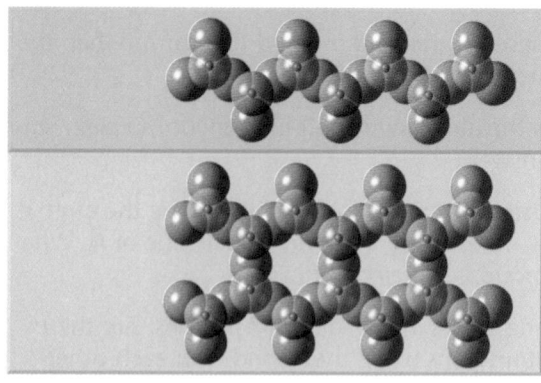

Use the diagrams to answer Questions 28–31.

28. **Identifying** What is the basic structural unit in these two diagrams?

29. **Classifying** What are the names given to these two silicate structures?

30. **Applying Concepts** How do these two structures affect mineral breakage?

31. **Formulating Hypotheses** Which of the two structures is more complex? Explain your choice.

Concepts in Action

32. **Applying Concepts** Your friend shows you a crystal that he thinks is a diamond. Without asking an expert, how could you tell if the crystal is really a diamond?

33. **Hypothesizing** Which two minerals discussed in this chapter would be useful as abrasives? Which could be used as a lubricant? Which might be used in sparkly eye shadows?

34. **Calculating** Gold has a density of 19.3 g/cm^3. What would be the mass of a gold brick that is 30 cm long, 8 cm wide, and 4 cm tall?

Performance-Based Assessment

Applying Concepts Go on a scavenger hunt around your school or home to find at least 20 items that are minerals, that contain minerals, or that were obtained from minerals. Make a poster that shows what you found and display it for the class.

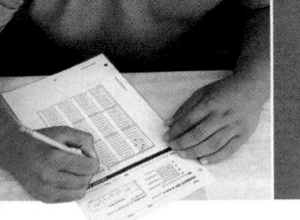

Standardized Test Prep

Use the graph to answer Questions 4–6.

Evaluating

Sometimes an answer to a test question contains accurate information, but does not actually answer the question being asked. When this happens, follow the suggestions given below. Use this test-taking tip to answer Questions 1–3 on this page.

- Reread the question several times if necessary.
- Check to see that the information in each answer choice is accurate.
- Eliminate answers you know are incorrect.
- Check to see that your answer choice answers the question being asked.

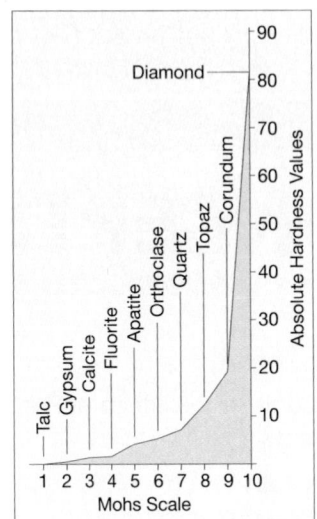

Choose the letter that best answers the question or completes the statement.

1. The central region of an atom includes
   - (A) only neutrons.
   - (B) only electrons.
   - (C) electrons and protons.
   - (D) neutrons and protons.

2. Protons in an atom
   - (A) make up the atom's electron cloud.
   - (B) are equal in number to the atom's neutrons.
   - (C) determine the kind of element.
   - (D) are NOT used to determine atomic mass.

3. If the atomic number of an element is 6 and its mass number is 14, how many neutrons are in the atom's nucleus?
   - (A) 0   (B) 6
   - (C) 8   (D) 20

4. What does this graph show?

5. How does talc's hardness on the Mohs scale compare with its absolute hardness?

6. Describe the relationship between Mohs hardness and absolute hardness.

Answer the following questions in complete sentences.

7. How do the isotopes of an element differ?

8. Define a mineral.

CHAPTER

3 Rocks

CONCEPTS in Action

Quick Lab
Observing Some of the Effects of Pressure on Mineral Grains

Exploration Lab
Rock Identification

Earth as a System
The Carbon Cycle

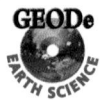

GEODe EARTH SCIENCE
Earth Materials
↳ Rock Cycle
Igneous Rocks
Sedimentary Rocks
Metamorphic Rocks

Discovery Channel School **Video Field Trip**

The Rock Cycle

Take a field trip through the rock cycle with Discovery Channel and learn about how rocks are constantly forming, changing, and eroding.

1. Name two natural forces that lead to rock erosion.
2. What can happen to rock that is buried beneath Earth's surface?

Go Online PHSchool.com

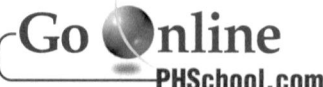

For: Chapter 3 Resources
Visit: PHSchool.com
Web Code: cjk-9999

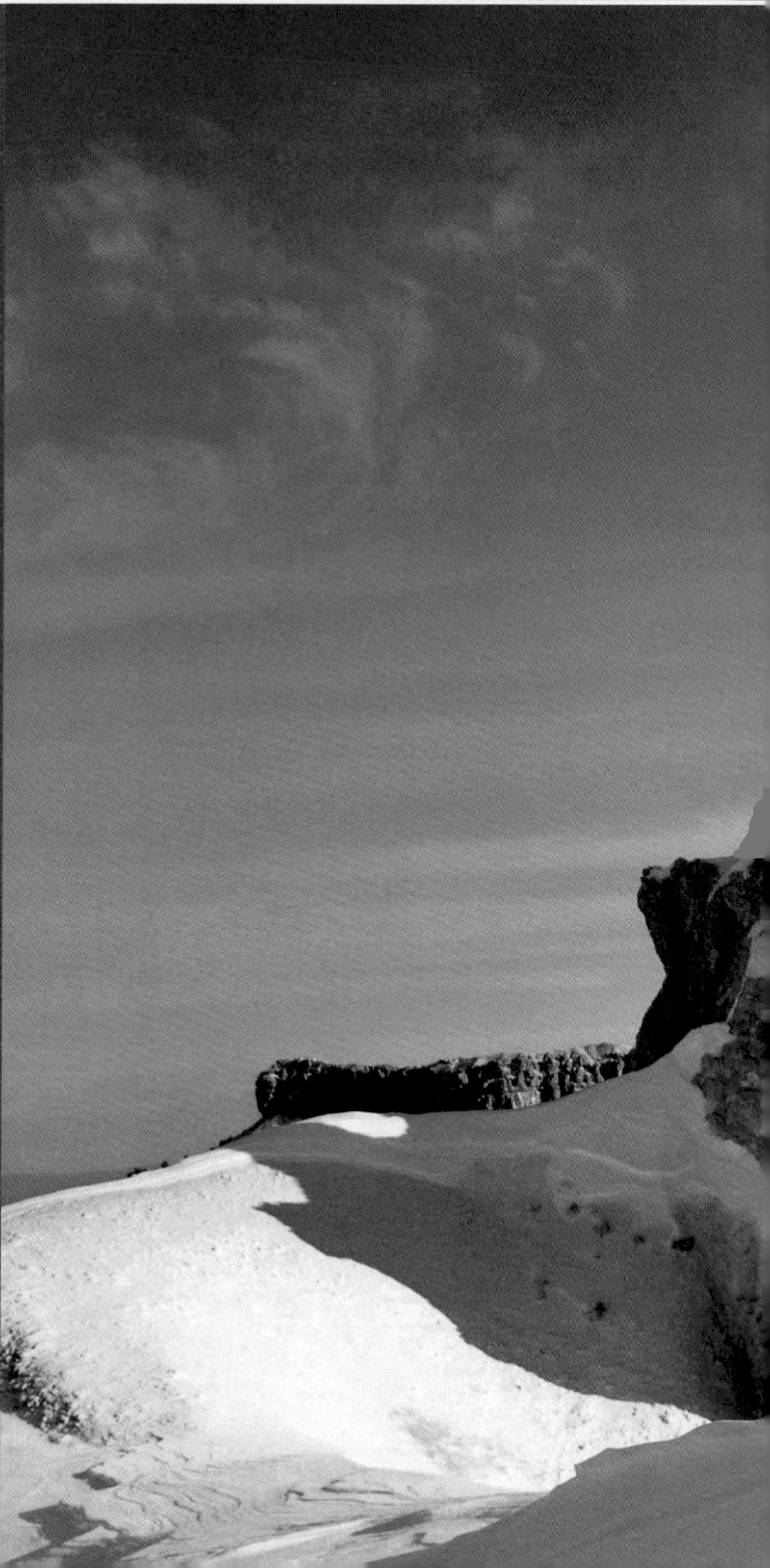

Columns of rock called hoodoos dot ▶ Bryce Canyon National Park.

Chapter Preview

Inquiry **Activity**

What Are Some Similarities and Differences Among Rocks?

Procedure

1. Your teacher will provide you with six rock samples. Examine them closely.

2. Record at least three ways in which the rocks are alike.

3. Now determine and record at least three ways in which the rocks differ.

4. Classify the rock samples into three groups based on your observations. Give reasons for your groupings.

Think About It

1. **Comparing and Contrasting** How are the rock samples similar? How do they differ?

2. **Comparing and Contrasting** How does your classification scheme compare with the classification schemes of at least two other students? How do they differ?

3. **Formulating Hypotheses** Each of the rocks used in this activity belongs to one of the three major groups of rocks. Hypothesize what makes one group of rocks different from the others.

3.1 The Rock Cycle

Reading Focus

Key Concepts
- What is a rock?
- What are the three major types of rocks?
- How do igneous, sedimentary, and metamorphic rocks differ?
- What is the rock cycle?
- What powers Earth's rock cycle?

Vocabulary
- rock
- igneous rock
- sedimentary rock
- metamorphic rock
- rock cycle
- magma
- lava
- weathering
- sediments

Reading Strategy
Building Vocabulary Copy and expand the table to include each vocabulary term. As you read, write down the definition for each term.

Term	Definition
rock	a. _____?_____
igneous rock	b. _____?_____
sedimentary rock	c. _____?_____
sediments	d. _____?_____

Why do we study rocks? All Earth processes such as volcanic eruptions, mountain building, weathering, erosion, and even earthquakes involve rocks and minerals. Rocks contain clues about the environments in which they were formed. For example, if a rock contains shell fragments, it was probably formed in a shallow ocean environment. The locations of volcanic rocks tell a story of volcanic activity on Earth through time. Thus, you can see that a basic knowledge of rocks is essential to understanding the Earth.

Rocks

A rock is any solid mass of mineral or mineral-like matter that occurs naturally as part of our planet. A few rocks are composed of just one mineral. However, most rocks, like granite, occur as solid mixtures of minerals. A characteristic of rock is that each of the component minerals retains their properties in the mixture. A few rocks are composed of nonmineral matter. Coal is considered a rock even though it consists of organic material. Obsidian and pumice, shown in Figure 1, are volcanic rocks that do not have a crystalline structure.

Rocks are classified into three groups based on how they were formed. The three major types of rocks are igneous rocks, sedimentary rocks, and metamorphic rocks. Before examining each group, you will look at a model for the rock cycle, which is the process that shows the relationships between the rock groups.

Figure 1 A Obsidian and **B** pumice are two examples of rocks that do not have a crystalline structure.

← 5 cm →
A

← 5 cm →
B

 Reading Checkpoint *What are the three types of rocks?*

The Rock Cycle

Earth is a system. It consists of many interacting parts that form a complex whole. ☞**Interactions among Earth's water, air, and land can cause rocks to change from one type to another. The continuous processes that cause rocks to change make up the rock cycle.** Most changes in the rock cycle take place over long periods of time.

Figure 2 shows some key events in the rock cycle. Refer to the figure throughout this section as you examine how rock might change over time. Look at Figures 2A and 2B. **Magma** is molten material that forms deep beneath Earth's surface. ☞**When magma cools and hardens beneath the surface or as the result of a volcanic eruption, igneous rock forms.** Magma that reaches the surface is called **lava.**

Rock Cycle

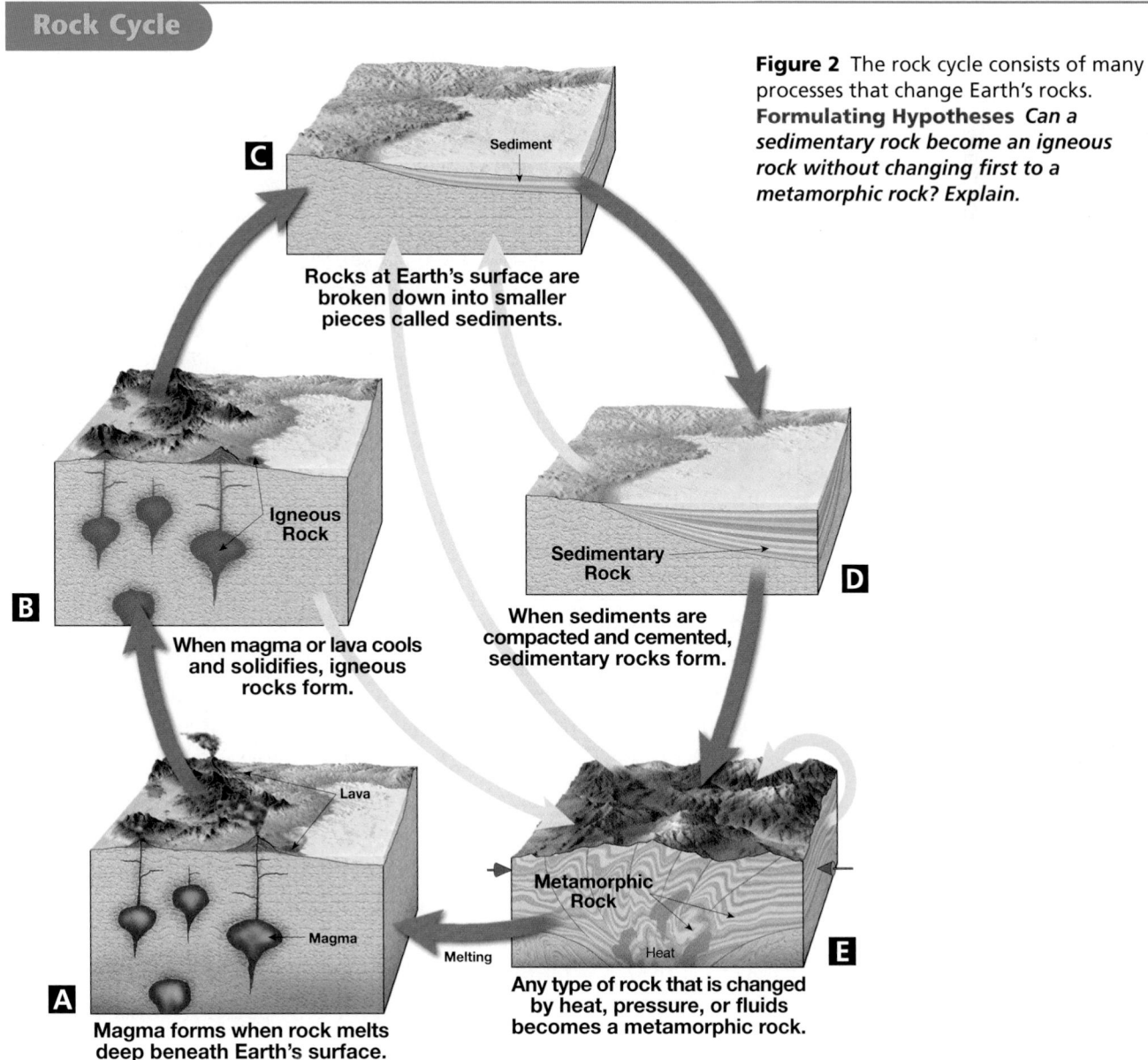

Sediment

C

Rocks at Earth's surface are broken down into smaller pieces called sediments.

Figure 2 The rock cycle consists of many processes that change Earth's rocks. **Formulating Hypotheses** *Can a sedimentary rock become an igneous rock without changing first to a metamorphic rock? Explain.*

Igneous Rock

B

When magma or lava cools and solidifies, igneous rocks form.

Sedimentary Rock

D

When sediments are compacted and cemented, sedimentary rocks form.

Lava

Magma

A

Magma forms when rock melts deep beneath Earth's surface.

Metamorphic Rock

Melting

Heat

E

Any type of rock that is changed by heat, pressure, or fluids becomes a metamorphic rock.

Figure 3 El Capitan in Yosemite National Park This granite was once buried deep beneath Earth's surface. Now that it is exposed, it will eventually weather and form sediments.

What will happen if an igneous rock that formed deep within Earth is exposed at the surface? Any rock at Earth's surface, including the granite shown in Figure 3, will undergo weathering. **Weathering** is a process in which rocks are physically and chemically broken down by water, air, and living things. These weathered pieces of earth materials are **sediments**. Sediments are often moved by water, gravity, glaciers, or wind. **Eventually, sediments are compacted and cemented to form sedimentary rock, as shown in Figure 2C and 2D.**

If the sedimentary rocks become buried deep within Earth, they will be subjected to increases in pressure and/or temperature. **Under extreme pressure and temperature conditions, sedimentary rock will change into metamorphic rock, as shown in Figure 2E.** If the metamorphic rocks are subjected to additional pressure changes or to still higher temperatures, they may melt to form magma. The magma will eventually crystallize to form igneous rock once again.

Alternate Paths

The purple arrows in Figure 2 show only one way in which an igneous rock might form and change. Other paths are just as likely to be taken as an igneous rock goes through the rock cycle. The blue arrows show a few of these alternate paths.

Suppose, for example, that an igneous rock remained deeply buried. Eventually, the rock could be subjected to strong forces and high temperatures such as those associated with mountain building. Then, the igneous rock could change into one or more kinds of metamorphic rock. If the temperatures and pressures were high enough, the igneous rock could melt and recrystallize to form new igneous rock.

Metamorphic and sedimentary rocks, as well as sediment, do not always remain buried. Often, overlying rocks are stripped away, exposing the rock that was once buried. When this happens, the rocks weather to form sediments that eventually become sedimentary rocks. However, if the sedimentary rocks become buried again, metamorphic rocks, like those used for the roof tiles in Figure 4, will form.

Where does the energy that drives Earth's rock cycle come from? **Processes driven by heat from Earth's interior are responsible for forming both igneous and metamorphic rocks. Weathering and the movement of weathered materials are external processes powered by energy from the sun. External processes produce sedimentary rocks.**

Figure 4 The roof on this house is made of slate. Slate is a metamorphic rock that forms from the sedimentary rock shale. **Explaining** *How can shale become slate?*

Section 3.1 Assessment

Reviewing Concepts

1. What is a rock?
2. What are the three major types of rocks?
3. How do igneous, sedimentary, and metamorphic rocks differ?
4. What is the rock cycle?
5. What powers Earth's rock cycle?

Critical Thinking

6. **Comparing and Contrasting** Compare and contrast igneous and metamorphic rocks.

7. **Applying Concepts** How might a sedimentary rock become an igneous rock?

8. **Applying Concepts** List in order the processes that could change one sedimentary rock into another sedimentary rock.

Writing in Science

Writing to Persuade Coral reefs are made of calcite that is secreted by the corals and algae that make up the reefs. Over time, this calcite accumulates to form limestone. Use what you know about minerals and rocks to write a paragraph explaining whether or not you think that this limestone is a rock.

3.2 Igneous Rocks

Key Concepts

- How are intrusive and extrusive igneous rocks alike and different?
- How does the rate of cooling affect an igneous rock's texture?
- How are igneous rocks classified according to composition?

Vocabulary

- intrusive igneous rock
- extrusive igneous rock
- porphyritic texture
- granitic composition
- basaltic composition
- andesitic composition
- ultramafic

Reading Strategy

Outlining Copy the outline and complete it as you read. Include points about how each of these rocks form, some of the characteristics of each rock type, and some examples of each.

```
I.  Igneous Rocks
    A. Intrusive Rocks
       1. ____?____
       2. ____?____
    B. Extrusive Rocks
       1. ____?____
       2. ____?____
```

Recall from the discussion of the rock cycle that igneous rocks form when magma or lava cools and hardens. When the red hot lava shown in Figure 5 cools, a dark-colored igneous rock called basalt will form. If this melted material had stayed deep beneath Earth's surface, a very different kind of igneous rock would have been produced as the material cooled. Different kinds of igneous rocks form when magma and lava cool and harden.

Figure 5 Basaltic Lava
Lava from this Hawaiian volcano flows easily over Earth's surface. When this lava cools and hardens, the igneous rock called basalt will form.

Formation of Igneous Rocks

The word *igneous* comes from the Latin word *ignis,* which means "fire." Perhaps that is why people often associate igneous rock with fiery volcanic eruptions like the one shown in Figure 5. Igneous rock also forms deep beneath Earth's surface.

Intrusive Igneous Rocks 🔑 **Rocks that form when magma hardens beneath Earth's surface are called intrusive igneous rocks.** That is because they *intrude* into the existing rocks. We would never see these deep rocks were it not for erosion stripping away the overlying rock.

Magma consists mainly of the elements silicon and oxygen, plus aluminum, iron, calcium, sodium, potassium, and magnesium. Magma also contains some gases, including water vapor. These gases are kept within the magma by the pressure of the surrounding rocks. Because magma is less dense than the surrounding rocks, it slowly works its way toward the surface. As magma rises, it cools, allowing elements to combine and form minerals. Gradually, the minerals grow in size, forming a solid mass of interlocking crystals. Granite, shown in Figure 6A, is a common intrusive igneous rock.

Extrusive Igneous Rocks You know that when magma reaches Earth's surface, it is called lava. Lava is similar to magma, except that in lava, most of the gases have escaped. 🔑 **When lava hardens, the rocks that form are called extrusive igneous rocks.** That is because they are *extruded* onto the surface. The rhyolite shown in Figure 6B is an extrusive igneous rock.

Figure 6 A Granite is an intrusive igneous rock that forms when magma cools slowly beneath Earth's surface. **B** Rhyolite is an extrusive igneous rock that forms when lava cools quickly at Earth's surface.

Q *How are magma and lava the same, and how are they different?*

A Magma and lava are both terms used to describe melted rock. The composition of magma and lava can be the same. However, magma is melted material beneath Earth's surface. Lava is melted material at Earth's surface.

Q *Native Americans used obsidian for making arrowheads and cutting tools. Is this the only material they used?*

A No. Native Americans used whatever materials were locally available to make tools, including any hard dense rock material that could be shaped. This includes materials such as the metamorphic rocks slate and quartzite, sedimentary deposits made of silica called jasper, chert, opal, flint, and even jade. Some of these deposits occur in only a few areas. That helps anthropologists reconstruct trade routes between different Native Americans groups.

Figure 7 This sample of andesite displays igneous rock with a porphyritic texture.
Describing *Describe how this rock probably formed.*

Classification of Igneous Rocks

A quick glance at the two rocks in Figure 6 tells you that they are different. The granite contains large mineral grains. Only a few of the mineral grains in the sample of rhyolite can be seen with the unaided eye. **Texture and composition are two characteristics used to classify igneous rocks.** Texture describes the appearance of an igneous rock based on its size, shape, and the arrangement of its interlocking crystals. The composition classes of igneous rocks are based on the proportions of light and dark minerals in the rock.

Coarse-Grained Texture The rate of cooling strongly affects the textures of igneous rocks. If magma cools very slowly, few centers of crystal growth develop. Slow cooling also allows charged atoms, or ions, to move large distances within the magma. **Slow cooling results in the formation of large crystals.** Igneous rocks with large crystals exhibit a coarse-grained texture.

Fine-Grained Texture If cooling of magma or lava occurs rapidly, the ions in the melted material lose their motion and quickly combine. This results in a large number of tiny crystals that all compete for the available ions. **Rapid cooling of magma or lava results in rocks with small, interconnected mineral grains.** Igneous rocks with small grains are said to have a fine-grained texture.

Glassy Texture When lava spews onto Earth's surface, there may not be enough time for the ions in the lava to arrange themselves into a network of crystals. So the solids produced this way are made of randomly distributed ions. Such rocks have a glassy texture. The obsidian and pumice shown in Figure 1 on page 66 are igneous rocks with glassy textures.

Porphyritic Texture A large body of magma located deep within Earth may take tens of thousands of years to harden. Minerals that crystallize from the magma do not form at the same rate or at the same time. It is possible for some crystals to become quite large before others even start to form. The resulting rock can have large crystals, called phenocrysts, surrounded by fine-grained minerals. Rocks with very different-size minerals experience different rates of cooling. These rocks have a **porphyritic texture.** The igneous rock shown in Figure 7 has a porphyritic texture.

Reading Checkpoint *How does the rate of cooling of magma or lava affect the texture of igneous rocks?*

Granitic Composition One group of igneous rocks includes those that are made almost entirely of the light-colored silicate minerals quartz and feldspar. Igneous rocks in which these are the main minerals are said to have a **granitic composition.** In addition to quartz and feldspar, most granitic rocks contain about 10 percent dark silicate minerals. These dark minerals are often biotite mica and amphibole. Granitic rocks contain about 70 percent silica and are the major rocks of the continental crust. Rhyolite is an extrusive granitic rock. Compare granite and rhyolite again in Figure 6 on page 71.

For: Links on igneous rocks
Visit: www.SciLinks.org
Web Code: cjn-1032

Basaltic Composition Rocks that contain many dark silicate minerals and plagioclase feldspar have a **basaltic composition.** Basaltic rocks are rich in the elements magnesium and iron. Because of their iron content, basaltic rocks are typically darker and denser than granitic rocks. The most common basaltic rock is basalt, shown in Figure 8. Gabbro is an intrusive igneous rock with a basaltic composition.

Other Compositional Groups
Rocks with a composition between granitic and basaltic rocks have an **andesitic composition.** This group of igneous rocks is named after the common volcanic rock andesite. Andesitic rocks contain at least 25 percent dark silicate minerals—mainly amphibole, pyroxene, and biotite mica. The other dominant mineral in andesitic rocks is plagioclase feldspar.

Another important igneous rock is peridotite. This rock contains mostly the minerals olivine and pyroxene. Because peridotite is composed almost entirely of dark silicate minerals, its chemical composition is referred to as **ultramafic.** Although ultramafic rocks are rare at Earth's surface, much of the upper mantle is thought to be made of peridotite.

Figure 8 Basalt is an igneous rock made mostly of dark-colored silicate minerals.
Describing *Describe the texture of this igneous rock.*

Reading Checkpoint *Describe the main differences between granitic and basaltic rocks.*

To summarize, igneous rocks form when magma or lava cools and hardens. Intrusive rocks form when magma cools and hardens deep within Earth. Extrusive rocks form when lava cools and hardens on Earth's surface. Igneous rocks can be classified according to texture and composition. A general classification scheme based on texture and mineral composition is shown in Table 1.

Table 1 Classification of Major Igneous Rocks

Chemical Composition		Granitic	Andesitic	Basaltic	Ultramafic
Dominant Minerals		Quartz Potassium feldspar Sodium-rich plagioclase feldspar	Amphibole Sodium- and calcium-rich plagioclase feldspar	Pyroxene Calcium-rich plagioclase feldspar	Olivine Pyroxene
T E X T U R E	Coarse-grained	Granite	Diorite	Gabbro	Peridotite
	Fine-grained	Rhyolite	Andesite	Basalt	Komatiite (rare)
	Porphyritic	"Porphyritic" precedes any of the above names whenever there are appreciable phenocrysts.			Uncommon
	Glassy	Obsidian (compact glass) Pumice (frothy glass)			
Rock Color (based on % of dark minerals)		0% to 25%	25% to 45%	45% to 85%	85% to 100%

Section 3.2 Assessment

Reviewing Concepts

1. Compare and contrast the formation of intrusive and extrusive igneous rocks.

2. How do coarse-grained igneous rocks form?

3. How are igneous rocks classified according to composition?

4. How do fine-grained igneous rocks form?

5. How do igneous rocks with glassy textures form?

Critical Thinking

6. **Contrasting** Contrast basalt and granite in terms of how each forms, the texture of each rock, the color of each rock, and each rock's composition.

7. **Formulating Hypotheses** The extrusive igneous rock pumice contains many small holes. Hypothesize how these holes might form.

Writing in Science

Explanatory Paragraph Write a paragraph to explain how one of the igneous rocks pictured in this chapter may have formed.

3.3 Sedimentary Rocks

Reading Focus

Key Concepts

- Describe the major processes involved in the formation of sedimentary rocks.
- What are clastic sedimentary rocks?
- What are chemical sedimentary rocks?
- What features are unique to some sedimentary rocks?

Vocabulary

- ◆ erosion
- ◆ deposition
- ◆ compaction
- ◆ cementation
- ◆ clastic sedimentary rock
- ◆ chemical sedimentary rock

Reading Strategy

Outlining Copy this outline beneath the outline you made for Section 3.2. Complete this outline as you read. Include points about how each of these rocks form, some of the characteristics of each rock type, and some examples of each.

> II. Sedimentary Rocks
>   A. Clastic Rocks
>   1. _____?_____
>   2. _____?_____
>   B. Chemical Rocks
>   1. _____?_____
>   2. _____?_____

All sedimentary rocks begin to form when existing rocks are broken down into sediments. Sediments, which consist mainly of weathered rock debris, are often transported to other places. When sediments are dropped, they eventually become compacted and cemented to form sedimentary rocks. The structures shown in Figure 9 are made of the sedimentary rock called sandstone. It is only one of many types of sedimentary rocks.

Figure 9 Sedimentary Rocks in Canyonlands National Park, Utah The rocks shown here formed when sand and other sediments were deposited and cemented. Weathering processes created this arch.

Formation of Sedimentary Rocks

The word *sedimentary* comes from the Latin word *sedimentum,* which means "settling." Sedimentary rocks form when solids settle out of a fluid such as water or air. The rocks shown in Figure 10 formed when sediments were dropped by moving water. The sediments eventually became cemented to form rocks. Several major processes contribute to the formation of sedimentary rocks.

Weathering, Erosion, and Deposition Recall that weathering is any process that breaks rocks into sediments. Weathering is often the first step in the formation of sedimentary rocks. Chemical weathering takes place when the minerals in rocks change into new substances. Weathering also takes place when physical forces break rocks into smaller pieces. Living things, too, can cause chemical and physical weathering.

Weathered sediments don't usually remain in place. Instead, water, wind, ice, or gravity carries them away. **Erosion involves weathering and the removal of rock. When an agent of erosion—water, wind, ice, or gravity—loses energy, it drops the sediments. This process is called deposition.** Sediments are deposited according to size. The largest sediments, such as the rounded pebbles in the conglomerate in Figure 10A, are deposited first. Smaller sediments, like the pieces of sand that make up the sandstone in Figure 10B, are dropped later. Some sediments are so small that they are carried great distances before being deposited.

Compaction and Cementation After sediments are deposited, they often become lithified, or turned to rock. **Compaction** and **cementation** change sediments into sedimentary rock. **Compaction is a process that squeezes, or compacts, sediments.** Compaction is caused by the weight of sediments. During compaction, much of the water in the sediments is driven out.

Cementation takes place when dissolved minerals are deposited in the tiny spaces among the sediments. Much of the cement in the conglomerate shown in Figure 10A can be seen with the unaided eye. The cement holding the sand grains together in the sandstone in Figure 10B, however, is microscopic.

Figure 10 Although these two rocks appear quite different, both formed when sediments were dropped by moving water. **A** Conglomerate is made of rounded pebbles cemented together. **B** Sandstone is made of sand grains cemented together.

 *Briefly describe the five major processes involved in the formation of sedimentary rocks.*

Classification of Sedimentary Rocks

Just like igneous rocks, sedimentary rocks can be classified into two main groups according to the way they form. The first group includes rocks that are made of weathered bits of rocks and minerals. These rocks are called **clastic sedimentary rocks.** The second group forms when dissolved minerals precipitate from water solutions. These rocks are called **chemical sedimentary rocks.**

Clastic Sedimentary Rocks Many different minerals are found in clastic rocks. The most common are the clay minerals and quartz. This is because clay minerals, like those that make up much of the shale in Figure 11A, are the most abundant products of chemical weathering. Quartz, which is a major mineral in the breccia shown in Figure 11B, is a common sedimentary mineral for a different reason. It is very durable and resistant to chemical weathering.

Clastic sedimentary rocks can be grouped according to the size of the sediments in the rocks. When rounded, gravel-size or larger particles make up most of the rock, the rock is called conglomerate. If the particles are angular, the rock is called breccia. Sandstone is the name given to rocks when most of the sediments are sand-size grains. Shale, the most common sedimentary rock, is made of very fine-grained sediment. Siltstone is another fine-grained rock.

 **Reading Checkpoint** *Describe the major types of clastic sedimentary rocks.*

Figure 11 A Shale and **B** breccia are common clastic sedimentary rocks. This sample of shale contains plant fossils.
Formulating Hypotheses *How do you think this breccia might have formed?*

Chemical and Biochemical Sedimentary Rocks

Chemical sedimentary rocks form when dissolved substances precipitate, or separate, from water solution. This precipitation generally occurs when the water evaporates or boils off leaving a solid product. Examples of this type of chemical rock are some limestones, rock salt, chert, flint, and rock gypsum.

For: Links on sedimentary rocks
Visit: www.SciLinks.org
Web Code: cjn-1034

Figure 12 This biochemical rock, called coquina, is a type of limestone that is made of hundreds of shell fragments.

About 90 percent of limestones are formed from biochemical sediments. Such sediments are the shells and skeletal remains of organisms that settle to the ocean floor. The coquina in Figure 12 is one obvious example. You can actually see the shells cemented together. Another biochemical rock is chalk, the material used to write on a chalkboard.

Features of Some Sedimentary Rocks

Sedimentary rocks, like other types of rocks, are used to unravel what may have happened in Earth's long history. **The many unique features of sedimentary rocks are clues to how, when, and where the rocks formed.** Each layer of a sedimentary rock, for example, records a period of sediment deposition. In undisturbed rocks, the oldest layers are found at the bottom. The youngest layers are found at the top of the rocks. Ripple marks like the ones shown in Figure 13A may indicate that the rock formed along a beach or stream bed. The mud cracks in Figure 13B formed when wet mud or clay dried and shrank, leaving a rock record of a dry environment.

Fossils, which are the traces or remains of ancient life, are unique to some sedimentary rocks. Fossils can be used to help answer many questions about the rocks that contain them. For example, did the rock form on land or in the ocean? Was the climate hot or cold, rainy or dry? Did the rock form hundreds, thousands, millions, or billions of years ago? Fossils also play a key role in matching up rocks from different places that are the same age.

To summarize, sedimentary rocks are rocks that form as the result of four major processes. *Weathering* produces particles called sediments. Wind, water, ice, and gravity *erode* and *deposit* these sediments. Over time, the sediments are *compacted and cemented* to form rocks. Sedimentary rocks can be classified according to how they form. A general classification scheme based on a rock's formation, texture, and composition is shown in Table 2.

Figure 13 A Ripple marks and **B** mud cracks are features of sedimentary rocks that can be used to learn about the environments in which the rocks formed.

A

B

Table 2 Classification of Major Sedimentary Rocks

Clastic Sedimentary Rocks

Texture (grain size)		Sediment Name	Rock Name
Coarse (over 2 mm)		Gravel (rounded fragments)	Conglomerate
		Gravel (angular fragments)	Breccia
Medium (1/16 to 2 mm)		Sand	Sandstone
Fine (1/16 to 1/256 mm)		Mud	Siltstone
Very fine (less than 1/256 mm)		Mud	Shale

Chemical Sedimentary Rocks

Composition	Texture (grain size)	Rock Name	
Calcite, $CaCO_3$	Fine to coarse crystalline	Crystalline Limestone	
		Travertine	
	Visible shells and shell fragments loosely cemented	Coquina	Biochemical Limestone
	Various size shells and shell fragments cemented with calcite cement	Fossiliferous Limestone	
	Microscopic shells and clay	Chalk	
Quartz, SiO_2	Very fine crystalline	Chert (light colored) Flint (dark colored)	
Gypsum $CaSO_4 \cdot 2H_2O$	Fine to coarse crystalline	Rock Gypsum	
Halite, NaCl	Fine to coarse crystalline	Rock Salt	
Altered plant fragments	Fine-grained organic matter	Bituminous Coal	

Section 3.3 Assessment

Reviewing Concepts

1. ⬤ Contrast weathering, erosion, and deposition.

2. ⬤ Name four clastic sedimentary rocks and explain how these rocks form.

3. ⬤ Name four chemical sedimentary rocks and explain how these rocks form.

4. ⬤ Explain how three different features of sedimentary rocks can be used to determine how, where, or when the rocks formed.

5. What is compaction?

6. Where do the cements that hold sediments together come from?

Critical Thinking

7. **Applying Concepts** Briefly describe how the rock shown in Figure 12 may have formed.

8. **Predicting** Which type of sediments do you think would undergo more compaction—grains of sand or grains of clay? Explain your choice.

9. **Formulating Conclusions** Suppose you found a sedimentary rock in which ripple marks were pointing toward the ground. What could you conclude about the rock?

Connecting Concepts

Sedimentary Rocks Choose one of the sedimentary rocks pictured in this section. Find out how the rock is useful to people.

3.4 Metamorphic Rocks

Reading Focus

Key Concepts

- Where does most metamorphism take place?
- How is contact metamorphism different from regional metamorphism?
- What are three agents of metamorphism, and what kinds of changes does each cause?
- What are foliated metamorphic rocks, and how do they form?
- How are metamorphic rocks classified?

Vocabulary

- ◆ metamorphism
- ◆ contact metamorphism
- ◆ regional metamorphism
- ◆ hydrothermal solution
- ◆ foliated metamorphic rock
- ◆ nonfoliated metamorphic rock

Reading Strategy

Outlining Copy this outline beneath the outline you made for Section 3.3. Complete it as you read. Include points about how each of these rocks form, some of the characteristics of each rock type, and some examples of each.

III. Metamorphic Rocks
   A. Foliated Rocks
      1. ____?____
      2. ____?____
   B. Nonfoliated Rocks
      1. ____?____
      2. ____?____

Figure 14 Deformed Rock
Intense pressures metamorphosed these rocks by causing them to fold as well as change composition.

Recall that metamorphic rocks form when existing rocks are changed by heat and pressure. **Metamorphism** is a very appropriate name for this process because it means *to change form*. Rocks produced during metamorphism often look much different from the original rocks, or parent rocks. The folds in the rocks shown in Figure 14 formed when the parent rocks were subjected to intense forces. These highly folded metamorphic rocks may also develop a different composition than the parent rocks had.

Formation of Metamorphic Rocks

Most metamorphic changes occur at elevated temperatures and pressures. These conditions are found a few kilometers below Earth's surface and extend into the upper mantle. Most metamorphism occurs in one of two settings—contact metamorphism or regional metamorphism.

Contact Metamorphism When magma intrudes—forces its way into—rock, contact metamorphism may take place. **During contact metamorphism, hot magma moves into rock.** Contact metamorphism often produces what is described as low-grade metamorphism. Such changes in rocks are minor. Marble, like that used to make the statue in Figure 15, is a common contact metamorphic rock. Marble often forms when magma intrudes a limestone body.

Regional Metamorphism During mountain building, large areas of rocks are subjected to extreme pressures and temperatures. The intense changes produced during this process are described as high-grade metamorphism. **Regional metamorphism results in large-scale deformation and high-grade metamorphism.** The rocks shown in Figure 14 on page 80 were changed as the result of regional metamorphism.

Agents of Metamorphism

The agents of metamorphism are heat, pressure, and hydrothermal solutions. During metamorphism, rocks are usually subjected to all three of these agents at the same time. However, the effect of each agent varies greatly from one situation to another.

Heat The most important agent of metamorphism is heat. Heat provides the energy needed to drive chemical reactions. Some of these reactions cause existing minerals to recrystallize. Other reactions cause new minerals to form. The heat for metamorphism comes mainly from two sources—magma and the change in temperature with depth. Magma essentially "bakes" any rocks that are in contact with it. Heat also comes from the gradual increase in temperature with depth. In the upper crust, this increase averages between 20°C and 30°C per kilometer.

When buried to a depth of about 8 kilometers, clay minerals are exposed to temperatures of 150°C to 200°C. These minerals become unstable and recrystallize to form new minerals that are stable at these temperatures, such as chlorite and muscovite. In contrast, silicate minerals are stable at these temperatures. Therefore, it takes higher temperatures to change silicate minerals.

 **Reading Checkpoint** *Compare and contrast contact and regional metamorphism.*

Figure 15 Statue Carved from Marble Marble is a common metamorphic rock that forms as the result of contact metamorphism of limestone.

Q *How hot is it deep in the crust?*

A The deeper a person goes beneath Earth's surface, the hotter it gets. The deepest mine in the world is the Western Deep Levels mine in South Africa, which is about 4 kilometers deep. Here, the temperature of the surrounding rock is so hot that it can scorch human skin. In fact, miners in this mine often work in groups of two. One miner mines the rock, and the other operates a large fan that keeps the worker cool.

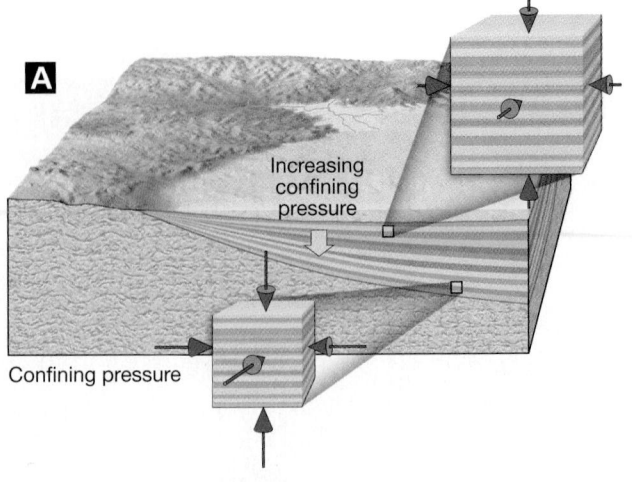

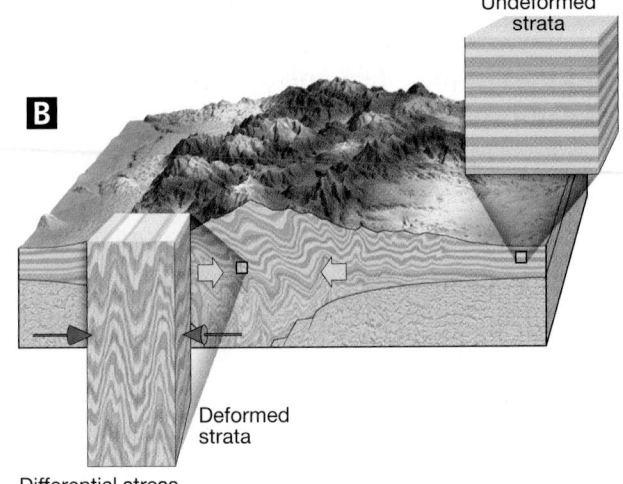

Figure 16 Pressure (Stress) As a Metamorphic Agent
A Forces in all directions are applied equally to buried rocks.
B During mountain building, rocks subjected to differential stress are shortened in the direction that pressure is applied.

Figure 17 Imagine the tremendous amounts of pressure that caused these rocks to fold.

Pressure (Stress) Pressure, like temperature, also increases with depth. Like the water pressure you might have experienced at the bottom of a swimming pool, pressure on rocks within Earth is applied in all directions. See Figure 16. Pressure on rocks causes the spaces between mineral grains to close. The result is a more compact rock with a greater density. This pressure also may cause minerals to recrystallize into new minerals.

Increases in temperature and pressure cause rocks to flow rather than fracture. Under these conditions, mineral grains tend to flatten and elongate.

≡Quick Lab

Observing Some of the Effects of Pressure on Mineral Grains

Materials

soft modeling clay; 2 pieces of waxed paper (each 20 cm × 20 cm); 20–30 small, round, elongated plastic beads; small plastic knife

Procedure

1. Use the clay to form a ball about the size of a golf ball. Randomly place all of the beads into this model rock.

2. Make a sketch of the rock. Label the sketch *Before.*

3. Sandwich the model rock between the two pieces of waxed paper. Use your weight to apply pressure to the model rock.

4. Remove the waxed paper and observe your "metamorphosed" rock.

5. Draw a top view of your rock and label it *After.* Include arrows to show the directions from which you applied pressure.

6. Make a cut through your model rock. Sketch this view of the rock.

Analyze and Conclude

1. **Comparing and Contrasting** How did the *Before* sketch compare with the *After* sketch of your model rock?

2. **Drawing Conclusions** How does pressure affect the mineral grains in a rock?

3. **Inferring** Was pressure the only agent of change that affected your rock? Explain.

During mountain building, horizontal forces metamorphose large segments of Earth's crust. This often produces intricately folded rocks like those shown in Figure 17.

Reactions in Solution Water solutions containing other substances that readily change to gases at the surface play an important role in some types of metamorphism. Solutions that surround mineral grains aid in recrystallization by making it easier for ions to move. When solutions increase in temperature reactions among substances can occur at a faster rate. When these hot, water-based solutions escape from a mass of magma, they are called **hydrothermal solutions.** These hot fluids also promote recrystallization by dissolving original minerals and then depositing new ones. As a result of contact with hydrothermal solutions, a change in a rock's overall composition may occur.

Classification of Metamorphic Rocks

Like igneous rocks, metamorphic rocks can be classified by texture and composition. ☞ **The texture of metamorphic rocks can be foliated or nonfoliated.**

Foliated Metamorphic Rocks When rocks undergo contact metamorphism, they become more compact and thus more dense. A common example is the metamorphic rock slate. Slate forms when shale is subjected to temperatures and pressures only slightly greater than those at which the shale formed. The pressure on the shale causes the microscopic clay minerals to become more compact. The increase in pressure also causes the clay minerals to align in a similar direction.

Under more extreme conditions, certain minerals will recrystallize. Some minerals recrystallize with a preferred orientation, which is at right angles to the direction of the force. The resulting alignment usually gives the rock a layered or banded appearance. This rock is called a **foliated metamorphic rock.** Gneiss, the metamorphic rock shown in Figure 18, is a foliated rock. Another foliated metamorphic rock is schist.

Nonfoliated Metamorphic Rocks A metamorphic rock that does not have a banded texture is called a **nonfoliated metamorphic rock.** Most nonfoliated rocks contain only one mineral. Marble, for example, is a nonfoliated rock made of calcite. When its parent rock, limestone, is metamorphosed, the calcite crystals combine to form the larger interlocking crystals seen in marble. A sample of marble is shown in Figure 19. Quartzite and anthracite are other nonfoliated metamorphic rocks.

 **Reading Checkpoint** *Contrast foliated and nonfoliated metamorphic rocks.*

Figure 18 Gneiss is a foliated metamorphic rock.
Inferring *In which directions was pressure exerted on this rock?*

For: Links on metamorphic rocks
Visit: www.SciLinks.org
Web Code: cjn-1033

Figure 19 Marble is a nonfoliated metamorphic rock.

To summarize, metamorphic rocks form when existing rocks are changed by heat, pressure, or hydrothermal solution. Contact metamorphism is often caused when hot magma intrudes a body of rock. Changes during this type of metamorphism are minor. Regional metamorphism is associated with mountain building. Such metamorphic changes can be extreme. Metamorphic rocks can be classified by texture as foliated or nonfoliated, as shown in Table 3.

Table 3 Classification of Major Metamorphic Rocks

Rock Name			Texture		Grain Size	Comments	Parent Rock
Slate	Increasing	Metamorphism	Foliated		Very fine	Smooth dull surfaces	Shale, mudstone, or siltstone
Phyllite					Fine	Breaks along wavy surfaces, glossy sheen	Slate
Schist					Medium to Coarse	Micaceous minerals dominate	Phyllite
Gneiss					Medium to Coarse	Banding of minerals	Schist, granite, or volcanic rocks
Marble			Nonfoliated		Medium to coarse	Interlocking calcite or dolomite grains	Limestone, dolostone
Quartzite					Medium to coarse	Fused quartz grains, massive, very hard	Quartz sandstone
Anthracite					Fine	Shiny black organic rock that fractures	Bituminous coal

Section 3.4 Assessment

Reviewing Concepts

1. ☒ Where does most metamorphism take place?

2. ☒ Compare and contrast contact metamorphism and regional metamorphism.

3. ☒ Name the agents of metamorphism and explain how each changes a rock.

4. ☒ What are foliated rocks, and how do they form?

5. ☒ How are metamorphic rocks classified?

Critical Thinking

6. **Applying Concepts** What is the major difference between igneous and metamorphic rocks?

7. **Predicting** What type of metamorphism—contact or regional—would result in a schist? Explain your choice.

8. **Formulating Conclusions** Why can the composition of gneiss vary but overall texture cannot?

Writing in Science

Explanatory Paragraph Write a short paragraph that explains the major differences and similarities among the three major rock groups.

The Carbon Cycle

To illustrate the movement of material and energy in the Earth system, we can take a brief look at the carbon cycle, shown in Figure 20. Pure carbon is rare in nature. It is found mainly as two minerals—diamond and graphite. Most carbon is bonded to other elements to form compounds. Carbon dioxide (CO_2), for example, is an important gas in Earth's atmosphere. Calcite ($CaCO_3$) is a mineral found in many sedimentary and metamorphic rocks. Hydrocarbons, such as coal, oil, and natural gas, are compounds made of carbon and hydrogen. Carbon also combines with hydrogen and oxygen to form the basic compounds that make up living things. This important element moves continually among Earth's major spheres by way of the carbon cycle.

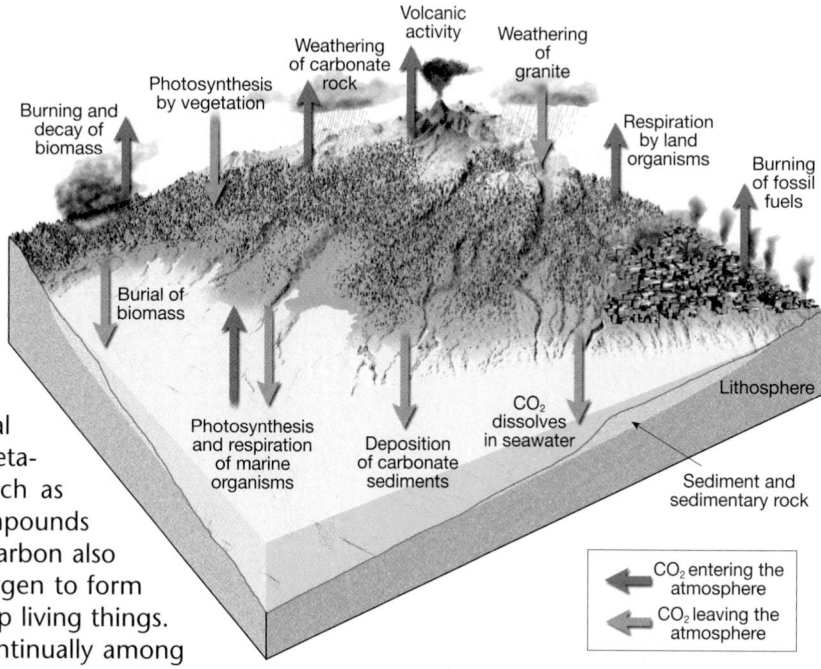

Figure 20 The Carbon Cycle

Carbon Dioxide on the Move

In the atmosphere, carbon is found mainly as carbon dioxide. This gas absorbs much of the energy given off by Earth. Therefore, carbon dioxide influences the heating of the atmosphere. Carbon dioxide constantly moves into and out of the atmosphere by way of four major processes: photosynthesis, respiration, organic decay, and combustion of organic material.

Carbon and Fossil Fuels

Some carbon from decayed organic matter is deposited as sediment. Over long periods of time, this carbon becomes buried. Under the right conditions, some of these carbon-rich deposits are changed to fossil fuels, such as coal. When fossil fuels are burned, huge quantities of carbon dioxide enter into the air.

The Role of Marine Animals

Chemical weathering of certain rocks produce bicarbonate ions that dissolve water. Groundwater, rivers, and streams carry these ions to the ocean. Here, some organisms extract this substance to produce body parts—shells, skeletons, and spines—made of calcite. When the organisms die, these hard parts settle to the ocean floor and become the sedimentary rock called limestone.

The Complete Cycle

The source of most CO_2 in the atmosphere is thought to be from volcanic activity early in Earth's history. When CO_2 combines with water, it forms carbonic acid. This substance reacts with rock through chemical weathering to form bicarbonate ions that are carried by groundwater and streams to the ocean. Here, marine organisms take over and sedimentary rock is eventually produced. If this rock is then exposed at the surface and subjected to chemical weathering, CO_2 is also produced. Use Figure 20 to trace the path of carbon from the atmosphere to the hydrosphere, the geosphere, the biosphere, and back to the atmosphere.

Rock Identification

Most rocks can be easily identified by texture and composition. In this lab, you will use what you have learned about rocks as well as the information on minerals from Chapter 2 to identify some common rocks.

Problem
How can you use composition and texture to identify common rocks?

Materials
- rock samples
- hand lens
- pocket knife
- dilute hydrochloric acid
- colored pencils
- Chapter 2, Table 4 and Chapter 3, Tables 1, 2, 3

Skills
Observing, Comparing and Contrasting, Measuring

Procedure

1. On a separate sheet of paper, make a copy of the data table shown below. Add any other columns that you think might be useful.

2. Examine each rock specimen with and without the hand lens. Determine and record the overall color of each rock.

3. Try to identify all of the minerals in each rock, using the information in Chapter 2 Table 4. Record your observations.

Data Table

Rock	Overall Color	Composition	Texture	Sketch	Rock Type	Rock Name
1.						
2.						
3.						
4.						
5.						

4. Determine and record the presence of any organic matter in any of the samples.

5. Observe the relationships among the minerals in each rock to determine texture. Refer to Chapter 3 Tables 1, 2, and 3 if necessary. Record your observations.

6. Note and record any other unique observations of the samples.

7. In your data table, make and color a detailed sketch of each sample.

8. Identify each sample as being an igneous rock, a sedimentary rock, or a metamorphic rock.

9. Name each sample. Use the photographs in this chapter and Tables 1, 2, and 3 if necessary.

3. **Applying Concepts** Match the metamorphic rocks with their probable parent rocks.

4. **Applying Concepts** Choose two pairs of rocks used in this investigation. Write a brief description for each pair that explains how one rock can be changed into the other. Refer to the diagram of the rock cycle on page 67.

Go Further Obtain permission to collect some local rock samples from a park or nearby road. Use what you have learned about rocks and minerals to identify the rocks. Then write a brief history of each sample to explain how it formed and how it has changed since being formed.

Analyze and Conclude

1. **Evaluating** Which of the rock identification characteristics did you find most useful? Which of the characteristics did you find least useful? Give reasons for your answers.

2. **Comparing and Contrasting** How did identifying rocks compare with the mineral identification lab you did in Chapter 2? How is identifying rocks different from identifying the minerals that compose the rocks?

3.1 The Rock Cycle

Key Concepts

- A rock is any solid mass of mineral or mineral-like matter that occurs naturally.
- The three major types of rocks are igneous, sedimentary, and metamorphic.
- Interactions among Earth's water, air, and land can cause rocks to change from one type to another. The continuous processes that cause rocks to change make up the rock cycle.
- When magma cools and hardens beneath the surface or as the result of a volcanic eruption, igneous rock forms.
- Eventually sediments are compacted and cemented to form sedimentary rocks.
- Under extreme pressure and temperature conditions, sedimentary rock will change into metamorphic rock.
- Heat from Earth's interior and energy from the sun power the rock cycle.

Vocabulary

rock, *p. 66;* igneous rock, *p. 66;* sedimentary rock, *p. 66;* metamorphic rock, *p. 66;* rock cycle, *p. 67;* magma, *p. 67;* lava, *p. 67;* weathering, *p. 68;* sediments, *p. 68*

3.2 Igneous Rocks

Key Concepts

- Rocks that form when magma hardens beneath Earth's surface are called intrusive igneous rocks.
- When lava hardens, the rocks that form are called extrusive igneous rocks.
- Texture and composition are two characteristics used to classify igneous rocks.
- Slow cooling results in the formation of large crystals.
- Rapid cooling of magma or lava results in rocks with small, interconnected mineral grains.

Vocabulary

intrusive igneous rock, *p. 71;* extrusive igneous rock, *p. 71;* porphyritic texture, *p. 72;* granitic composition, *p. 73;* basaltic composition, *p. 73;* andesitic composition, *p. 73;* ultramafic, *p. 73*

3.3 Sedimentary Rocks

Key Concepts

- Erosion involves weathering and the removal of rock. When an agent of erosion—water, wind, ice, or gravity—loses energy, it drops the sediments. This process is called deposition.
- Compaction is a process that squeezes, or compacts, sediments.
- Cementation takes place when dissolved minerals are deposited in the tiny spaces among the sediments.
- Just like igneous rocks, sedimentary rocks can be classified into two main groups according to the way they form.
- The many unique features of sedimentary rocks are clues to how, when, and where the rocks formed.

Vocabulary

erosion, *p. 76;* deposition, *p. 76;* compaction, *p. 76;* cementation, *p. 76;* clastic sedimentary rock, *p. 77;* chemical sedimentary rock, *p. 77*

3.4 Metamorphic Rocks

Key Concepts

- Most metamorphic changes occur at elevated temperatures and pressures. These conditions are found a few kilometers below Earth's surface and extend into the upper mantle.
- During contact metamorphism, hot magma moves into rock.
- Regional metamorphism results in large-scale deformation and high-grade metamorphism.
- The agents of metamorphism are heat, pressure, and hydrothermal solutions.
- Metamorphic rocks can be classified by texture as foliated or nonfoliated.

Vocabulary

metamorphism, *p. 80;* contact metamorphism, *p. 81;* regional metamorphism, *p. 81;* hydrothermal solution, *p. 83;* foliated metamorphic rock, *p. 83;* nonfoliated metamorphic rock, *p. 83*

Reviewing Content

Choose the letter that best answers the question or completes the statement.

1. Which of the following is NOT one of the three major types of rocks?
   a. anthracite   b. igneous
   c. metamorphic   d. sedimentary

2. Which of the following forms partly as the result of surface processes?
   a. metamorphic slate
   b. igneous basalt
   c. magma
   d. intrusive granite

3. Which of the following would NOT be a major process in the formation of sedimentary rocks?
   a. erosion   b. melting
   c. deposition   d. compaction

4. The formation of igneous rocks is powered by
   a. internal heat.   b. the rock cycle.
   c. erosion.   d. the sun.

5. A fine-grained igneous rock forms
   a. deep within Earth.
   b. from magma.
   c. as the result of slow cooling.
   d. as the result of quick cooling.

6. Cementation often occurs after Earth materials are
   a. eroded.   b. weathered.
   c. intruded.   d. deposited.

7. Ripple marks indicate that the rock formed
   a. underground.   b. under a glacier.
   c. in water.   d. from lava.

8. A major process in the formation of clastic sedimentary rocks is
   a. contact with magma.
   b. cementation.
   c. hardening.
   d. foliation.

9. Metamorphic rocks that have a banded appearance due to the alignment of minerals are called
   a. foliated.   b. nonfoliated.
   c. clastic.   d. glassy.

10. Which rock is made of the smallest sediments?
    a. shale   b. conglomerate
    c. breccia   d. sandstone

Understanding Concepts

11. Use what you have learned about the rock cycle to explain the following statement: One rock is the raw material for another rock.

12. Which igneous rock forms when basaltic lava hardens? When basaltic magma hardens?

13. A rock has a porphyritic texture. What can you conclude about the rock?

14. How are granite and rhyolite the same, and how do they differ?

15. Explain three types of weathering.

16. What are the most common minerals in clastic rocks? Why?

17. Distinguish between regional and contact metamorphism.

18. How could you easily distinguish a black and white gneiss from a similar-colored granite?

Use the following diagram to answer Questions 19–22.

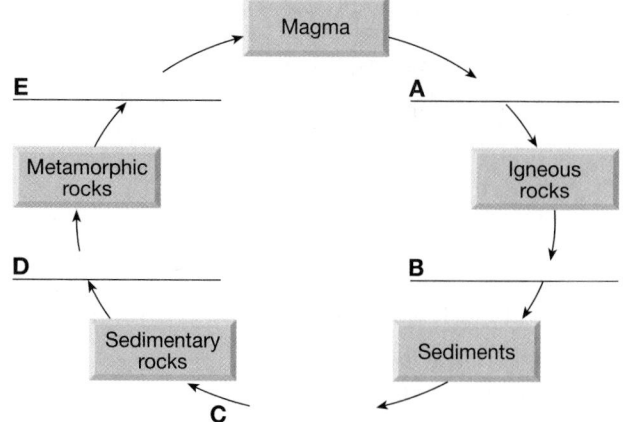

19. What process occurs at point A?

20. What three processes can occur at point B?

21. Name two processes that occur at point C.

22. What two processes occur at points D and E?

Critical Thinking

23. Synthesizing Is it possible for two different types of igneous rocks to have the same composition and the same texture? Explain.

24. Comparing and Contrasting Compare and contrast the two types of sedimentary rocks and give at least two examples of each type.

25. Formulating Hypotheses Think about the sediments that compose both conglomerate and breccia. What one sedimentary process makes these two rocks different? Explain.

26. Comparing and Contrasting Compare and contrast the effects of heat and pressure in the formation of metamorphic rocks.

27. Explaining Explain all of the processes that might change a sandstone into a quartzite.

28. Synthesizing In what ways do metamorphic rocks differ from the sedimentary and igneous rocks from which they form?

Use the photograph to answer Questions 29–33.

29. Observing Describe the texture of the rock.

30. Identifying To which of the three major groups of rocks does the rock belong?

31. Classifying Classify the rock as specifically as possible.

32. Formulating Hypotheses Briefly describe how this rock formed.

33. Applying Concepts Explain how this rock might become an igneous rock.

Concepts in Action

34. Applying Concepts Your friend shows you a rock with distinct layers. How can you and your friend determine if the rock is a sedimentary rock or a metamorphic rock?

35. Applying Concepts Name two rocks discussed in this chapter that might be used as flooring, countertops, or facades on museums and government buildings. Name two rocks that might be used for monuments and statues.

36. Calculating Each year, roughly 9100 kilograms of rock, sand, and gravel are mined for each person in the United States. Calculate how many kilograms of rock, sand, and gravel have been mined for you thus far in your life. Then calculate how much will be mined when you are 75 years old.

37. Writing in Science Suppose you're a writer for the school newspaper. You have been asked to do a story on one of the rocks described in this chapter. Pick a rock and write a short, newspaper-type story. Include facts about the rock—its texture, mineral composition, and how it formed. Also describe how the rock might change into a rock in each of the other two categories of rocks. Be creative, but scientifically accurate.

Performance-Based Assessment

Applying Concepts Go on field trip around your house, neighborhood, and community to find at least 10 items that are made from rocks or show ways in which rocks are used. Make a poster that shows what you found and display it for the class.

Standardized Test Prep

Use the photographs to answer Questions 1–9.

Choose the letter that best answers the question or completes the statement.

1. Which of the rocks has a fine-grained texture?
   (A) A
   (B) B
   (C) C
   (D) D

2. Which rock cooled the fastest?
   (A) A
   (B) B
   (C) C
   (D) D

3. Which of the rocks formed deep beneath the surface?
   (A) only A
   (B) only B
   (C) both A and D
   (D) both B and C

4. Which of the following best describes the texture of the rock labeled D?
   (A) porphyritic
   (B) glassy
   (C) fine-grained
   (D) coarse-grained

Write one or two complete sentences to answer each of the following questions.

5. What kinds of conditions produced the rock labeled A?

6. How and where did the rock labeled B form?

7. Compare and contrast the rocks labeled A and D.

8. How is the rock labeled C different from the other rocks shown?

9. Describe the conditions that led to the formation of the rock labeled D.

10. Use what you have learned about rocks to describe the color and texture of the rock below. What type of rock is this? How did it form?

CHAPTER

4 Earth's Resources

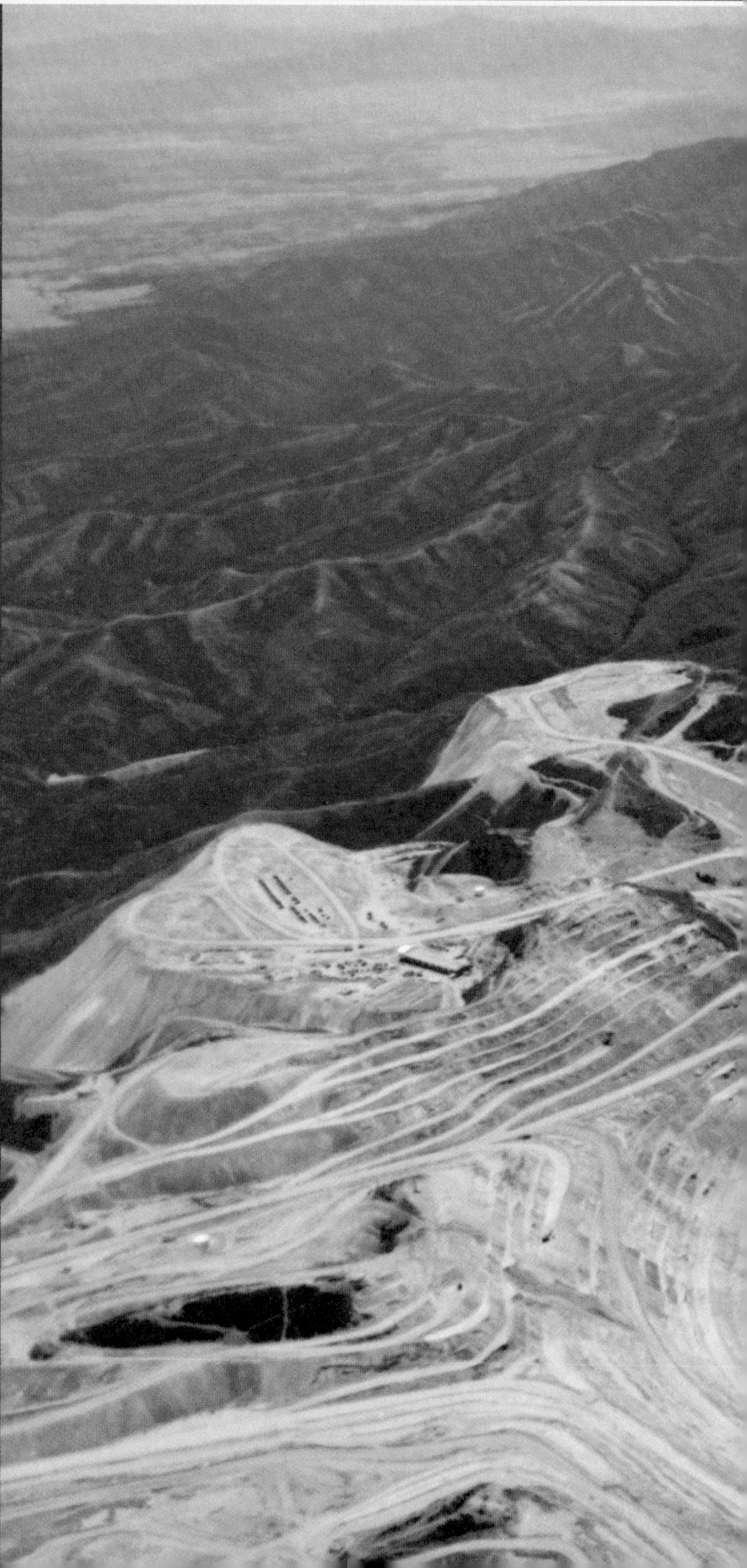

CONCEPTS in Action

Application Lab
Finding the Product that Best Conserves Resources

Understanding Earth
Bingham Canyon, Utah: The Largest Open-Pit Copper Mine

Discovery Channel School **Video Field Trip**
PET Clothes

Take a field trip to a recycling facility with Discovery Channel and find out how plastic bottles can be turned into clothes you can actually wear. Answer the following questions after watching the video.

1. Approximately how many plastic bottles end up in landfills every year?
2. Name two ways that using PET bottles in manufacturing clothes can help preserve the environment.

Go Online PHSchool.com

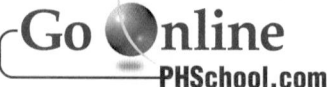

For: Chapter 4 Resources
Visit: PHSchool.com
Web Code: cjk-9999

Once a mountain, this hole is now the ▶ world's largest open-pit mine.

Inquiry Activity

How Can You Determine the Resources You Use?

Procedure

1. List three objects that you are using now or objects that are around you.

2. Observe the objects. Try to determine which resources they might contain. List possible resources for each object.

3. Your teacher will list several objects chosen by students on the board, along with the resources students believe they contain. Use these objects to answer the following questions.

Think About It

1. **Observing and Analyzing** How did you determine the resources that might be in each object?

2. **Designing Experiments** How could you actually test each object to determine what resources it contains?

Reading Focus

Key Concepts

- What is the difference between renewable and nonrenewable resources?
- Which energy resources are fossil fuels?
- Which energy resources might replace dwindling petroleum supplies in the future?
- What processes concentrate minerals into deposits sufficiently large enough to mine?
- How are nonmetallic mineral resources used?

Vocabulary

- ◆ renewable resource
- ◆ nonrenewable resource
- ◆ fossil fuel
- ◆ ore

Reading Strategy

Monitoring Your Understanding Copy this table onto a separate piece of paper before you read this section. List what you know about energy and mineral resources in the first column and what you'd like to know in the second column. After you read, list what you have learned in the last column.

Energy and Mineral Resources		
What I Know	What I Would Like to Know	What I Learned
a. _____?_____	c. _____?_____	e. _____?_____
b. _____?_____	d. _____?_____	f. _____?_____

Figure 1 Mineral resources went into the construction of every building in this New York skyline. Energy resources keep the lights on, too.

Mineral and energy resources are the raw materials for most of the things we use. Mineral resources are used to produce everything from cars to computers to basketballs. Energy resources warm your home, fuel the family car, and light the skyline in Figure 1.

Renewable and Nonrenewable Resources

There are two categories of resources—renewable and nonrenewable. **A renewable resource can be replenished over fairly short time spans such as months, years, or decades.** Common examples are plants and animals for food, natural fibers for clothing, and trees for lumber and paper. Energy from flowing water, wind, and the sun are also renewable resources.

By contrast, a nonrenewable resource takes millions of years to form and accumulate. When the present supply of nonrenewable resources run out, there won't be any more. Fuels such as coal, oil, and natural gas are nonrenewable. So are important metals such as iron, copper, uranium, and gold.

Earth's population is growing fast which increases the demand for resources. Because of a rising standard of living, the rate of mineral and energy resource use has climbed faster than population growth. For example, 6 percent of the world's population lives in the United States, yet we use 30 percent of the world's annual production

Average
Heat Value

Anthracite
12,700 Btu/lb

Bituminous coal
13,100 Btu/lb

Subbituminous coal
9500 Btu/lb

Lignite
6700 Btu/lb

0   500
kilometers

0   500
kilometers

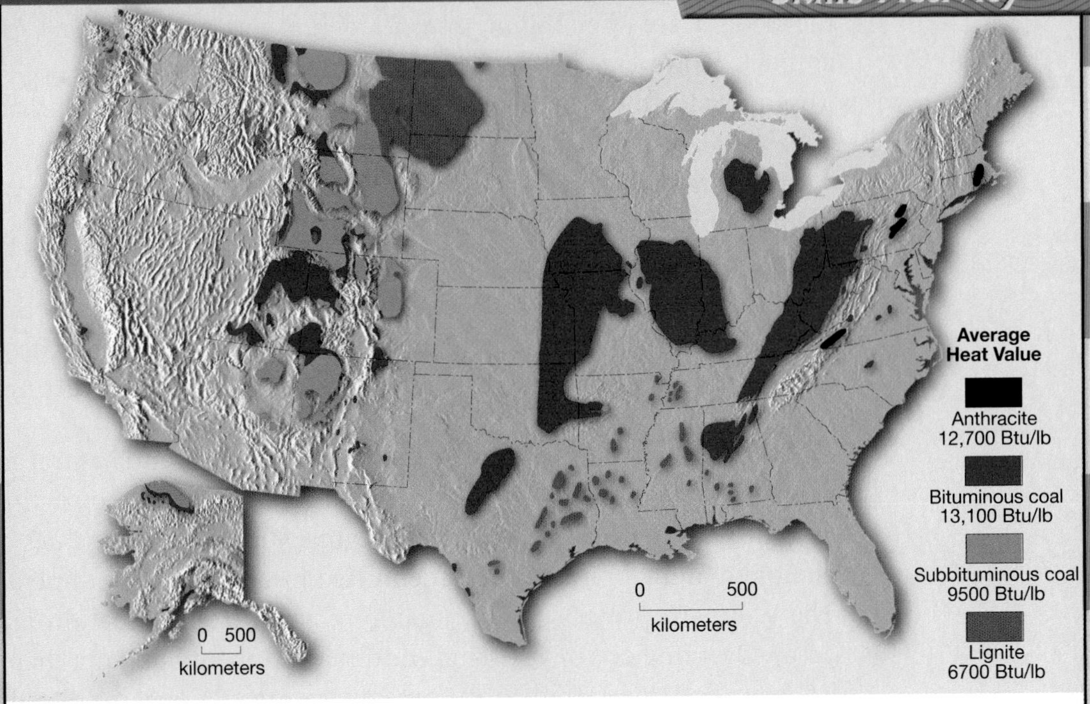

Figure 2

Location This map shows the location of major coal deposits in the United States.
Identify Which type of coal is most plentiful? **Locate** Where are the anthracite
deposits in the U.S. located?

of mineral and energy resources. How long can existing resources
provide for the needs of a growing population?

Fossil Fuels

Nearly 90 percent of the energy used in the United States comes from
fossil fuels. A **fossil fuel** is any hydrocarbon that may be used as a
source of energy. ◑ **Fossil fuels include coal, oil, and natural gas.**

Coal Coal forms when heat and pressure transform plant material
over millions of years. Coal passes through four stages of development.
The first stage, peat, is partially decayed plant material that sometimes
look like soil. Peat then becomes lignite, which is a sedimentary rock
that is often called brown coal. Continued heat and pressure transforms
lignite into bituminous coal, or soft coal. Bituminous coal is another
sedimentary rock. Coal's last stage of development is a metamorphic
rock called anthracite or hard coal. As coal develops from peat to bituminous, it becomes harder and releases more heat when burned.

Power plants primarily use coal to generate electricity. In fact, electric power plants use more than 70 percent of the coal mined today.
The world has enormous coal reserves. Figure 2 shows coal fields in
the United States.

Go Online
SCi LINKS™ NSTA

For: Links on fossil fuels
Visit: www.SciLinks.org
Web Code: cjn-1041

Although coal is plentiful, its recovery and use present problems. Surface mining scars the land. Today, all U.S. surface mines must restore the land surface when mining ends. Underground mining doesn't scar as much. However, it has been costly in terms of human life and health. Mining is safer today because of federal safety regulations. Yet, the hazards of collapsing roofs and gas explosions remain.

Burning coal—much of which is high in sulfur—also creates air pollution problems. When coal burns, the sulfur becomes sulfur oxides in the air. A series of chemical reactions turns the sulfur oxides into sulfuric acid, which falls to Earth as acid precipitation—rain or snow that is more acidic than normal. Acid precipitation can have harmful effects on forests and aquatic ecosystems, as well as metal and stone structures.

Petroleum and Natural Gas Petroleum (oil) and natural gas form from the remains of plants and animals that were buried in ancient seas. Petroleum formation begins when large quantities of plant and animal remains become buried in ocean-floor sediments. The sediment protects these organic remains from oxidation and decay. Over millions of years and continual sediment build up, chemical reactions slowly transform some of the organic remains into the liquid and gaseous hydrocarbons we call petroleum and natural gas.

These materials are gradually squeezed from the compacting, mud-rich sediment layers. The oil and gas then move into nearby permeable beds such as sandstone. The oil and gas are squeezed out of the sedimentary rock layers along with water. However, oil and natural gas are less dense than water, so they migrate upward through the water-filled spaces of the enclosing rocks. If nothing stops this migration, the fluids will eventually reach the surface.

Sometimes an oil trap—a geologic structure that allows large amounts of fluids to accumulate—stops upward movement of oil and gas. Several geologic structures may act as oil traps, but all have two things in common. First, an oil trap has a permeable reservoir rock that allows oil and gas to collect in large quantities. Second, an oil trap has a cap rock that is nearly impenetrable and so keeps the oil and gas from escaping to the surface. One structure that acts as an oil trap is an anticline. An anticline is an uparched series of sedimentary rock layers, as shown in Figure 3.

When a drill punctures the cap rock, pressure is released, and the oil and gas move toward the drill hole. Then a pump lifts the petroleum out.

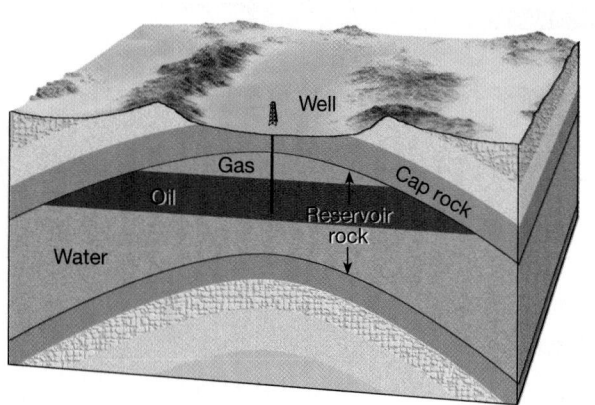

Figure 3 Anticlines are common oil traps. The reservoir rock contains water, oil, and gas. The fluids collect at the top of the arch with less dense oil and gas on top.
Interpreting Diagrams Why is the water located beneath the oil and gas?

 **Reading Checkpoint** *What two features must an oil trap have?*

Tar Sands and Oil Shale

In the years to come, world petroleum supplies will dwindle. ⬤ **Some energy experts believe that fuels derived from tar sands and oil shales could become good substitutes for dwindling petroleum supplies.**

Tar Sands Tar sands are usually mixtures of clay and sand combined with water and varying amounts of a black, thick tar called bitumen. Deposits occur in sands and sandstones, as the name suggests, but also in shales and limestones. The oil in these deposits is similar to heavy crude oils pumped from wells. The oil in tar sands, however, is much more resistant to flow and cannot be pumped out easily. The Canadian province of Alberta (Figure 4) has the largest tar sand deposits, which accounts for about 15 percent of Canada's oil production.

Currently, tar sands are mined at the surface, much like the strip mining of coal. The excavated material is then heated with pressurized steam until the bitumen softens and rises. The material is processed to remove impurities, add hydrogen, and refine into oil. However, extracting and refining tar sand requires a lot of energy—nearly half as much as the end product yields.

Obtaining oil from tar sand has significant environmental drawbacks. Mining tar sand causes substantial land disturbance. Processing also requires large amounts of water. When processing is completed, contaminated water and sediment accumulate in toxic disposal ponds.

Only about 10 percent of Alberta's tar sands can be economically recovered by surface mining. In the future, other methods may be used to obtain the more deeply buried material, reduce the environmental impacts, and make mining tar sands more economical.

 **Reading Checkpoint** *What are some environmental drawbacks to mining tar sands?*

Oil Shale Oil shale is a rock that contains a waxy mixture of hydrocarbons called kerogen. Oil shale can be mined and heated to vaporize the kerogen. The kerogen vapor is processed to remove impurities, and then refined.

Roughly half of the world's oil shale supply is in the Green River Formation of Colorado, Utah, and Wyoming. See Figure 5 on page 98. The oil shales are part of sedimentary layers that accumulated at the bottom of two extremely large, shallow lakes 57 to 36 million years ago.

Figure 4 Tar Sand Deposits In North America, the largest tar sand deposits occur in the Canadian province of Alberta. They contain an estimated reserve of 35 billion barrels of oil.

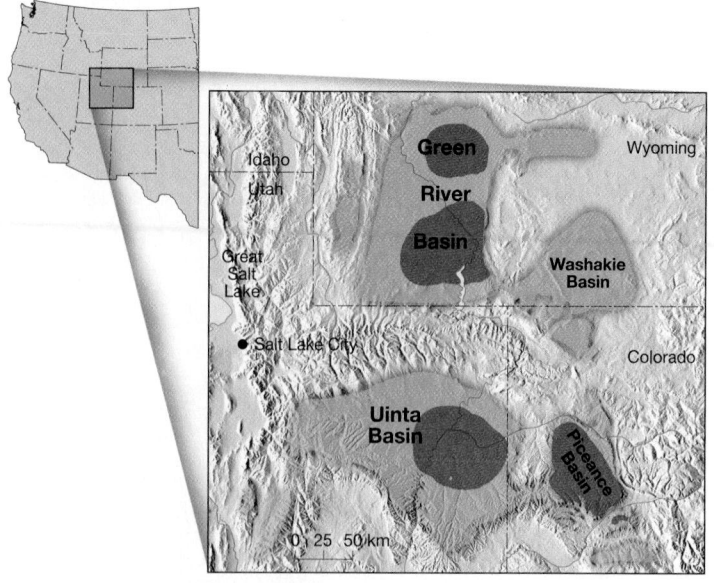

Some people see oil shale as a partial solution to dwindling fuel supplies. However, the heat energy in oil shale is only about one-eighth that in crude oil because oil shale contains large amounts of minerals. This mineral material adds costs to the mining, processing, and waste disposal of oil shale. The processing of it requires large amounts of water, which is scarce in the semi-arid region where the shales are found. Current technology makes mining oil shale an unprofitable solution.

Figure 5 Distribution of Oil Shale in the Green River Formation The areas in red are the richest deposits.
Posing Questions *How might the mining and processing of oil shale become more economically attractive?*

Formation of Mineral Deposits

Practically every manufactured product contains substances that come from minerals. Mineral resources are deposits of useful minerals that can be extracted. Mineral reserves are deposits from which minerals can be extracted profitably. **Ore** is a useful metallic mineral that can be mined at a profit.

There are also known deposits that are not yet economically or technologically recoverable. These deposits, as well as deposits that are believed to exist, are also considered mineral resources.

The natural concentration of many minerals is rather small. A deposit containing a valuable mineral is worthless if the cost of extracting it exceeds the value of the material that is recovered. For example, copper makes up about 0.0135 percent of Earth's crust. However, for a material to be considered a copper ore, it must contain a concentration of about 50 times this amount.

Geologists have established that the occurrences of valuable mineral resources are closely related to Earth's rock cycle. The rock cycle includes the formation of igneous, sedimentary, and metamorphic rock as well as the processes of weathering and erosion. **Some of the most important mineral deposits form through igneous processes and from hydrothermal solutions.**

Mineral Resources and Igneous Processes Igneous processes produce important deposits of metallic minerals, such as gold, silver, copper, mercury, lead, platinum, and nickel. For example, as a large body of magma cools, heavy minerals crystallize early and settle to the bottom of the magma chamber. Chromite (chromium ore), magnetite, and platinum sometimes form this way. Such deposits produced layers of chromite at Montana's Stillwater Complex. Another deposit is found in the Bushveld Complex in South Africa. This deposit contains over 70 percent of the world's known platinum reserves.

Hydrothermal Solutions

Hydrothermal (hot-water) solutions generate some of the best-known and most important ore deposits. Examples of hydrothermal deposits include the gold deposits of the Homestake Mine in South Dakota; the lead, zinc, and silver ores near Coeur D'Alene, Idaho; the silver deposits of the Comstock Lode in Nevada; and the copper ores of Michigan's Keweenaw Peninsula.

Most hydrothermal deposits form from hot, metal-rich fluids that are left during the late stages of the movement and cooling of magma. Figure 6 shows how these deposits form. As the magma cools and becomes solid, liquids and various metal ions collect near the top of the magma chamber. These ion-rich solutions can move great distances through the surrounding rock. Some of this fluid moves along openings such as fractures or bedding planes. The fluid cools in these openings and the metallic ions separate out of the solution to produce vein deposits, like those shown in Figure 7. Many of the most productive gold, silver, and mercury deposits occur as hydrothermal vein deposits.

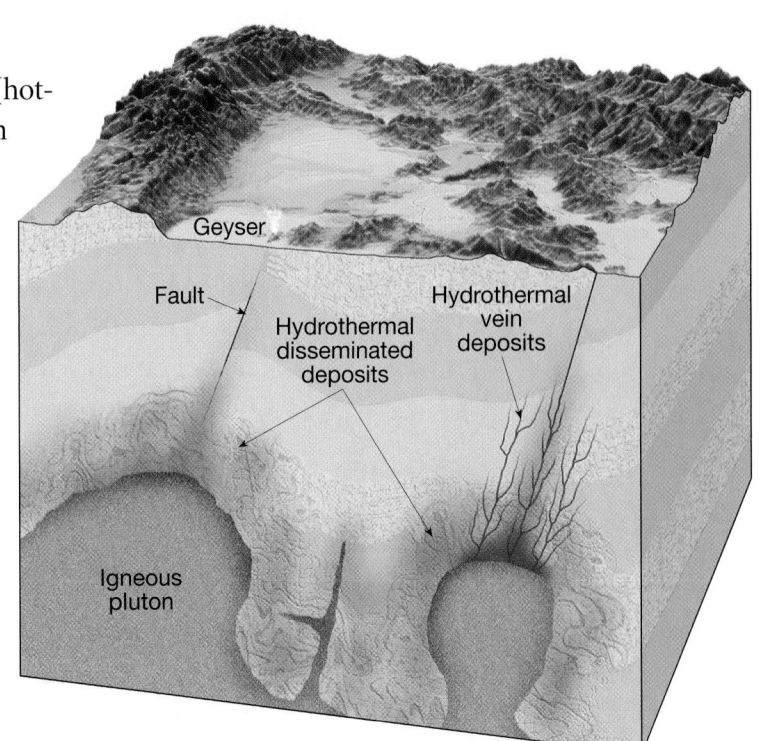

Figure 6 Mineral-rich hot water seeps into rock fractures, cools, and leaves behind vein deposits.

Placer Deposits

Placer deposits are formed when eroded heavy minerals settle quickly from moving water while less dense particles remain suspended and continue to move. This settling is a means of sorting in which like-size grains are deposited together due to the density of the particles. Placer deposits usually involve minerals that are not only heavy but also durable and chemically resistant. Common sites of accumulation include point bars on the inside of bends in streams, as well as cracks, depressions, and other streambed irregularities.

Figure 7 Light veins of quartz lace a body of darker gneiss in Washington's North Cascades National Park.

Figure 8 Placer deposits led to the California gold rush. Here, a prospector in 1850 swirls his gold pan, separating sand and mud from flecks of gold.

Q *How big was the largest gold nugget ever discovered?*

A The largest gold nugget ever discovered was the Welcome Stranger Nugget found in 1869 as a placer deposit in the gold-mining region of Victoria, Australia. It weighed a massive 2520 troy ounces (210 pounds, or 95 kilograms) and, at today's gold prices, was worth over $700,000. The largest gold nugget known to remain in existence today is the Hand of Faith Nugget, which was found in 1975 near Wedderburn, Victoria, Australia. It was found with a metal detector and weighs 875 troy ounces (73 pounds, or 33 kilograms). Sold in 1982, it is now on display in the Golden Nugget Casino in Las Vegas, Nevada.

Gold is the best-known placer deposit. In 1848, placer deposits of gold were discovered in California, sparking the famous California gold rush. Early prospectors searched rivers by using a flat pan to wash away the sand and gravel and concentrate the gold "dust" at the bottom. Figure 8 shows this common method. Years later, similar deposits created a gold rush to Alaska. Sometimes prospectors follow the placer deposits upstream. This method may lead prospectors to the original mineral deposit. Miners found the gold-bearing veins of the Mother Lode in California's Sierra Nevadas by following placer deposits.

Reading Checkpoint *What are mineral resources?*

Nonmetallic Mineral Resources

Nonmetallic mineral resources are extracted and processed either for the nonmetallic elements they contain or for their physical and chemical properties. People often do not realize the importance of nonmetallic minerals because they see only the products that resulted from their use and not the minerals used to make the products.

Examples of nonmetallic minerals include the fluorite and limestone that are part of the steelmaking process and the fertilizers needed to grow food, as shown in Table 1.

Nonmetallic mineral resources are divided into two broad groups—building materials and industrial minerals. For example, natural aggregate (crushed stone, sand, and gravel), is an important material used in nearly all building construction.

Some substances, however, have many uses in both construction and industry. Limestone is a good example. As a building material, it is used as crushed rock and building stone. It is also an ingredient in cement. As an industrial mineral, limestone is an ingredient in the manufacture of steel. Farmers also use it to neutralize acidic soils.

Many nonmetallic resources are used for their specific chemical elements or compounds. These resources are important in the manufacture of chemicals and fertilizers. In other cases, their importance is related to their physical properties. Examples include abrasive minerals such as corundum and garnet.

Although industrial minerals are useful, they have drawbacks. Most industrial minerals are not nearly as abundant as building materials. Manufacturers must also transport nonmetallic minerals long distances, adding to their cost. Unlike most building materials, which need a minimum of processing before use, many industrial minerals require considerable processing to extract the desired substance at the proper degree of purity.

Table 1 Occurrences and Uses of Nonmetallic Minerals

Mineral	Uses	Geological Occurrences
Apatite	Phosphorus fertilizers	Sedimentary deposits
Asbestos (chrysotile)	Incombustible fibers	Metamorphic alteration
Calcite	Aggregate; steelmaking; soil conditioning; chemicals; cement; building stone	Sedimentary deposits
Clay minerals (kaolinite)	Ceramics; china	Residual product of weathering
Corundum	Gemstones; abrasives	Metamorphic deposits
Diamond	Gemstones; abrasives	Kimberlite pipes; placers
Fluorite	Steelmaking; aluminum refining; glass; chemicals	Hydrothermal deposits
Garnet	Abrasives; gemstones	Metamorphic deposits
Graphite	Pencil lead; lubricant; refractories	Metamorphic deposits
Gypsum	Plaster of Paris	Evaporite deposits
Halite	Table salt; chemicals; ice control	Evaporite deposits, salt domes
Muscovite	Insulator in electrical applications	Pegmatites
Quartz	Primary ingredient in glass	Igneous intrusions, sedimentary deposits
Sulfur	Chemicals; fertilizer manufacture	Sedimentary deposits, hydrothermal deposits
Sylvite	Potassium fertilizers	Evaporite deposits
Talc	Powder used in paints, cosmetics, etc.	Metamorphic deposits

Section 4.1 Assessment

Reviewing Concepts

1. ⬭ What is the difference between a renewable and a nonrenewable resource?

2. ⬭ What are the three major fossil fuels?

3. ⬭ What are tar sands and oil shale?

4. ⬭ How do hydrothermal deposits form?

5. ⬭ What are the two broad categories of nonmetallic mineral resources?

6. Compare and contrast the formation of coal with that of petroleum and natural gas.

Critical Thinking

7. **Drawing Conclusions** Why isn't the use of tar sands more widespread in the United States?

8. **Applying Concepts** Explain how following placer deposits upstream would help prospectors find the original deposit.

Writing in Science

Compare-Contrast Paragraph Write a paragraph describing the difference in the use of nonmetallic building minerals and nonmetallic industrial minerals.

4.2 Alternate Energy Sources

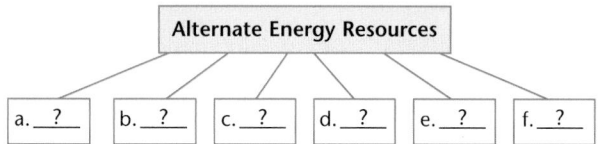

Reading Focus

Key Concepts
- What are the advantages of using solar energy?
- How do nuclear power plants use nuclear fission to produce energy?
- What is wind power's potential for providing energy in the future?
- How do hydroelectric power, geothermal energy, and tidal power contribute to our energy resources?

Vocabulary
- hydroelectric power
- geothermal energy

Reading Strategy
Previewing Skim the section and start a concept map for the various alternate energy resources.

```
                Alternate Energy Resources
    ┌──────┬──────┬──────┬──────┬──────┬──────┐
  a. ?   b. ?   c. ?   d. ?   e. ?   f. ?
```

Figure 9 Solar One is a solar installation used to generate electricity in the Mojave Desert near Barstow, California.

There's no doubt that we live in the age of fossils fuels. These non-renewable resources supply nearly 90 percent of the world's energy. But that can't last forever. At the present rates of consumption, the amount of recoverable fossil fuels may last only another 170 years. As the world population soars, the rate of consumption will climb as well. This will leave fossil fuel reserves in even shorter supply. In the meantime, the burning of huge quantities of fossil fuels will continue to damage the environment. Our growing demand for energy along with our need for a healthy environment will likely lead to a greater reliance on alternate energy sources.

Solar Energy

Solar energy is the direct use of the sun's rays to supply heat or electricity. **Solar energy has two advantages: the "fuel" is free, and it's non-polluting.** The simplest and perhaps most widely used solar energy systems are passive solar collectors such as south-facing windows. As sunlight passes through the glass, objects in the room absorb its heat. These objects radiate the heat, which warms the air.

More elaborate systems for home heating use an active solar collector. These roof-mounted devices are usually large, blackened boxes covered with glass or plastic. The heat they collect can be transferred to areas where it is needed by circulating air or liquids through piping. Solar collectors are also used to heat water for domestic and commercial needs. For example, solar collectors provide hot water for more than 80 percent of Israel's homes.

There are a few drawbacks to solar energy. While the energy collected is free, the necessary equipment and installation is not. A supplemental heating unit is also needed when there is less solar energy—on cloudy days or in the winter—or at night when solar energy is unavailable. However, over the long term, solar energy is economical in many parts of the United States. It will become even more cost effective as the prices of other fuels increase.

Research is currently underway to improve the technologies for concentrating sunlight. Scientists are examining a way to use mirrors to track the sun and keep its rays focused on a receiving tower. Figure 9 shows a solar collection facility with 2000 mirrors that was built near Barstow, California. This facility heats water in pressurized panels to over 500°C by focusing solar energy on a central tower. The superheated water is then transferred to turbines, which turn electrical generators.

Another type of collector, shown in Figure 10, uses photovoltaic (solar) cells. They convert the sun's energy directly into electricity.

Figure 10 Solar cells convert sunlight directly into electricity. This array of solar panels is near Sacramento, California.
Applying Concepts *What characteristics would you look for if you were searching for a location for a new solar plant?*

 **Reading Checkpoint** *What are the two main advantages of using solar energy?*

Nuclear Energy

Nuclear power meets about 7 percent of the energy demand of the United States. The fuel for nuclear plants, like the one in Figure 11, comes from radioactive materials that release energy through nuclear fission. **In nuclear fission, the nuclei of heavy atoms such as uranium-235 are bombarded with neutrons. The uranium nuclei then split into smaller nuclei and emit neutrons and heat energy.** The neutrons that are emitted then bombard the nuclei of adjacent uranium atoms, producing a chain reaction. If there is enough fissionable material and if the reaction continues in an uncontrolled manner, fission releases an enormous amount of energy as an atomic explosion.

Figure 11 Diablo Canyon Nuclear Plant Near San Luis Obispo, California Reactors are in the dome-shaped buildings. You can see cooling water being released to the ocean.
Analyzing *The siting of this plant was controversial because it is close to faults. Why would that be a cause for concern?*

In a nuclear power plant, however, the fission reaction is controlled by moving neutron-absorbing rods into or out of the nuclear reactor. The result is a controlled nuclear chain reaction that releases great amounts of heat. The energy drives steam turbines that turn electrical generators. This is similar to what occurs in most conventional power plants.

At one time, energy experts thought nuclear power would be the cheap, clean energy source that would replace fossil fuels. But several obstacles have slowed its development. First, the cost of building safe nuclear facilities has increased. Second, there are hazards associated with the disposal of nuclear wastes. Third, there is concern over the possibility of a serious accident that could allow radioactive materials to escape. The 1979 accident at Three Mile Island in Pennsylvania made this concern a reality. A malfunction in the equipment led the plant operators to think there was too much water in the primary system. Instead there was not enough water. This confusion allowed the reactor core to lie uncovered for hours. Although there was little danger to the public, the malfunction resulted in substantial damage to the reactor.

Unfortunately, the 1986 accident at Chernobyl in Ukraine was far more serious. In this case, the reactor went out of control. Two small explosions lifted the roof of the structure, and pieces of uranium spread over the surrounding area. A fire followed the explosion. During the 10 days that it took to put out the fire, the atmosphere carried high levels of radioactive material as far away as Norway. Eighteen people died within six weeks of the accident. Thousands more faced an increased risk of death from cancers associated with the fallout.

 **Reading Checkpoint** *What is nuclear fission?*

Wind Energy

According to one estimate, if just the winds of North and South Dakota could be harnessed, they would provide 80 percent of the electrical energy used in the United States. Wind is not a new energy source. People have used it for centuries to power sailing ships and windmills for grinding grains.

Following the "energy crisis" brought about by the oil embargo of the 1970s, interest in wind power and other alternative forms of energy grew. In 1980, the federal government started a program to develop wind-power systems, such as the one shown in Figure 12. The U.S. Department of Energy set up experimental wind farms in mountain passes with strong, steady winds. One of these facilities, at Altamont Pass near San Francisco, now operates more than 7000 wind turbines. In the year 2000, wind supplied a little less than one percent of California's electricity.

 Some experts estimate that in the next 50 to 60 years, wind power could meet between 5 to 10 percent of the country's demand for electricity. Islands and other isolated regions that must import fuel for generating power are major candidates for wind energy expansion.

The future for wind power looks promising, but there are difficulties. The need for technical advances, noise pollution, and the cost of large tracts of land in populated areas are obstacles to development.

Go Online
SCLINKS NSTA

For: Links on wind
Visit: www.SciLinks.org
Web Code: cjn-1042

Figure 12 These wind turbines are operating near Palm Springs, California.

Figure 13 Glen Canyon Dam and Lake Powell on the Colorado River As dam operators release water in the reservoir, it passes through machinery that drives turbines and produces electricity.

Hydroelectric Power

Like wind, moving water has been an energy source for centuries. The mechanical energy that waterwheels produce has powered mills and other machinery. Today, the power that falling water generates, known as **hydroelectric power,** drives turbines that produce electricity. In the United States, hydroelectric power plants produce about 5 percent of the country's electricity. Large dams, like the one in Figure 13, are responsible for most of it. The dams allow for a controlled flow of water. **The water held in a reservoir behind a dam is a form of stored energy that can be released through the dam to produce electric power.**

Although water power is a renewable resource, hydroelectric dams have finite lifetimes. Rivers deposit sediment behind the dam. Eventually, the sediment fills the reservoir. When this happens, the dam can no longer produce power. This process takes 50 to 300 years, depending on the amount of material the river carries. An example is Egypt's Aswan High Dam on the Nile River, which was completed in the 1960s. It is estimated that half the reservoir will be filled with sediment by 2025.

The availability of suitable sites is an important limiting factor in the development of hydroelectric power plants. A good site must provide a significant height for the water to fall. It also must have a high rate of flow. There are hydroelectric dams in many parts of the United States, with the greatest concentration in the Southeast and the Pacific Northwest. Most of the best U.S. sites have already been developed. This limits future expansion of hydroelectric power.

Geothermal Energy

Geothermal energy is harnessed by tapping natural underground reservoirs of steam and hot water. **Hot water is used directly for heating and to turn turbines to generate electric power.** The reservoirs of steam and hot water occur where subsurface temperatures are high due to relatively recent volcanic activity.

Figure 14 The Geysers is the world's largest electricity-generating geothermal facility. Most of the steam wells are about 3,000 meters deep.

Q *Is power from ocean waves a practical alternative energy source?*

A It's being seriously explored now. In November 2000, the world's first commercial wave power station opened on the Scottish island of Islay. It provides power for the United Kingdom. The 500-kilowatt power station uses an oscillating water column, in which incoming waves push air up and down inside a concrete tube that is partly under the ocean's surface. Air rushing in and out of the top of the tube drives a turbine to produce electricity. If the facility succeeds, it could open the door for wave power to become a significant contributor of renewable energy in some coastal areas.

In the United States, areas in several western states use hot water from geothermal sources for heat. The first commercial geothermal power plant in the United States was built in 1960 at The Geysers, shown in Figure 14. The Geysers is an important source of electrical power for nearby San Francisco and Oakland. Although production in the plant has declined, it remains the world's premier geothermal field. It continues to provide electrical power with little environmental impact. Geothermal development is now also occurring in Nevada, Utah, and the Imperial Valley of California.

Geothermal power is clean but not inexhaustible. When hot fluids are pumped from volcanically heated reservoirs, the reservoir often cannot be recharged. The steam and hot water from individual wells usually lasts no more than 10 to 15 years. Engineers must drill more wells to maintain power production. Eventually, the field is depleted.

As with other alternative methods of power production, geothermal sources are not expected to provide a high percentage of the world's growing energy needs. Nevertheless, in regions where people can develop its potential, its use will no doubt grow.

 *In what two ways is geothermal energy used?*

Tidal Power

Several methods of generating electrical energy from the oceans have been proposed, yet the ocean's energy potential still remains largely untapped. The development of tidal power is one example of energy production from the ocean.

Tides have been a power source for hundreds of years. Beginning in the 12th century, tides drove water wheels that powered gristmills and sawmills. During the seventeenth and eighteenth centuries, a tidal mill produced much of Boston's flour. But today's energy demands require more sophisticated ways of using the force created by the continual rise and fall of the ocean.

Tidal power is harnessed by constructing a dam across the mouth of a bay or an estuary in coastal areas with a large tidal range. The strong in-and-out flow that results drives turbines and electric generators. An example of this type of dam is shown in Figure 15.

The largest tidal power plant ever constructed is at the mouth of France's Rance River. This tidal plant went into operation in 1966. It produces enough power to satisfy the needs of Brittany—a region of 27,000 square kilometers—and parts of other regions. Much smaller experimental facilities have been built near Murmansk in Russia, near Taliang in China, and on an arm of the Bay of Fundy in Canada.

Tidal power development isn't economical if the tidal range is less than eight meters or if a narrow, enclosed bay isn't available. Although the tides will never provide a high portion of the world's ever-increasing energy needs, it is an important source at certain sites.

Tidal Dam

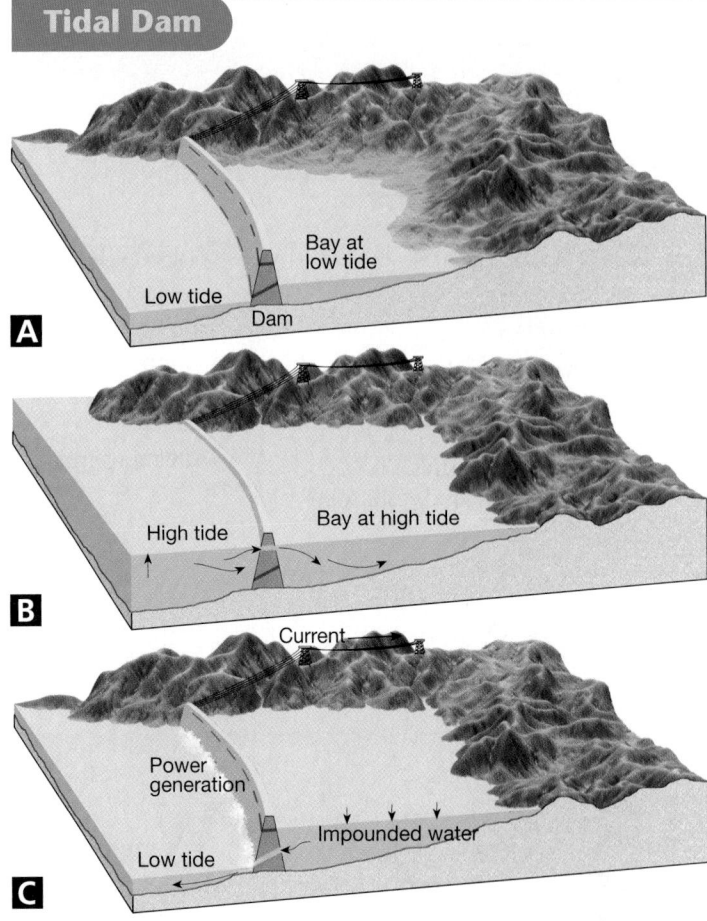

Figure 15 A At low tide, water is at its lowest level on either side of the dam. **B** At high tide, water flows through a high tunnel. **C** At low tide, water drives turbines as it flows back to sea through a low tunnel.
Analyzing Concepts *Why is a large tidal range (difference in water level between high and low tide) needed to produce power?*

Section 4.2 Assessment

Reviewing Concepts

1. What are the advantages and drawbacks of using solar energy?
2. How do nuclear power plants produce energy?
3. What percentage of our energy might be met by wind power over the next 60 years?
4. What are the advantages and drawbacks of hydroelectric power, geothermal energy, and tidal power?

Critical Thinking

5. **Predicting** Why will the interest in alternate energy sources probably grow in the future?
6. **Classifying** Identify solar, nuclear, and wind power as renewable or nonrenewable energy sources. Explain your answers.

Explain a Concept Write a letter to a family member explaining how tidal power works.

4.3 Water, Air, and Land Resources

Reading Focus

Key Concepts

- Why is fresh water a vital resource?
- Why is the chemical composition of the atmosphere important?
- What are Earth's important land resources?

Vocabulary

- point source pollution
- nonpoint source pollution
- runoff
- global warming

Reading Strategy

Building Vocabulary Copy the table below. As you read, add definitions and examples to complete the table.

Definitions		Examples
point source pollution: Pollution that can be traced to a location		factory pipes, sewer pipes
nonpoint source pollution: a. __?__		b. __?__
runoff:	c. __?__	d. __?__
greenhouse gas:	e. __?__	f. __?__

Water, air, and land resources are essential for life. You need clean air and water every day. What's more, soil provides nutrients that allow plants—the basis of our own food supply—to grow. How do people use—and sometimes misuse—these vital resources?

The Water Planet

Figure 16 shows Earth's most prominent feature—water. Water covers nearly 71 percent of Earth's surface. However, most of this water is saltwater, not fresh water. Oceans have important functions. Their currents help regulate and moderate Earth's climate. They are also a vital part of the water cycle, and a habitat for marine organisms. Fresh water, however, is what people need in order to live. **Each day, people use fresh water for drinking, cooking, bathing, and growing food.** While fresh water is extremely important, Earth's reserves are relatively small. Less than one percent of the water on the planet is usable fresh water.

Freshwater Pollution Pollution has contaminated many freshwater supplies. In general, there are two types of water pollution sources—point sources and nonpoint sources. **Point source pollution** is pollution that comes from a known and specific location, such as the factory pipes in Figure 17. Other examples include a leaking landfill or storage tank.

Figure 16 Oceans cover almost three fourths of Earth surface, making Earth a unique planet.

Nonpoint source pollution is pollution that does not have a specific point of origin. Runoff, the water that flows over the land rather than seeping into the ground, often carries nonpoint source pollution. Runoff can carry waste oil from streets. It can wash sediment from construction sites or pesticides off farm fields and lawns. Water filtering through piles of waste rock from coal mines can carry sulfuric acid into rivers or lakes. This contaminated water can kill fish and other aquatic life.

As you can see in Table 2, water pollution has adverse health effects. Pollutants can damage the body's major organs and systems, cause birth defects, lead to infectious diseases, and cause certain types of cancers. Contaminated fresh water can sicken or kill aquatic organisms and disrupt ecosystems. What's more, fish and other aquatic life that live in contaminated waters often concentrate poisons in their flesh. As a result, it is dangerous to eat fish taken from some polluted waters.

Figure 17 Pollution from point sources, such as these factory pipes, is easy to locate and control.

 **Reading Checkpoint** *What is the difference between a point and non-point water pollution source?*

Table 2 Major Types of Water Pollution			
Type	**Examples**	**Sources**	**Effects**
Disease organisms	Bacteria, viruses	Wastes from people and animals	Typhoid, cholera, dysentery, infectious hepatitis
Wastes that remove oxygen from water	Animal manure and plant debris that bacteria decompose	Sewage, animal feedlots	Great amounts of bacteria can remove oxygen from water, killing fish
Inorganic chemicals	Acids, toxic metals	Industrial effluent, urban runoff, household cleaners	Poisons fresh water and can sicken those who drink it
Organic chemicals	Oil, gasoline, plastic, pesticides, detergent	Farm and yard runoff, industrial waste, household cleaners	Some cancers, disorders of nervous and reproductive systems
Plant fertilizer	Water soluble compounds with nitrate, phosphorus ions	Sewage, manure, farm and garden runoff	Spurs rapid growth of algae that decay and deplete water's oxygen; fish die
Sediment	Soil	Erosion	Disrupts aquatic food webs, clogs lakes and reservoirs, reduces photosynthesis of aquatic plants
Radioactive substances	Radon, uranium, radioactive iodine	Nuclear power plants, uranium ore mining and processing	Some cancers, birth defects, genetic mutations

Figure 18 Cars, trucks, and buses are the biggest source of air pollution. Laws that control motor vehicle emissions have helped make the air cleaner in many areas.

Primary Pollutants

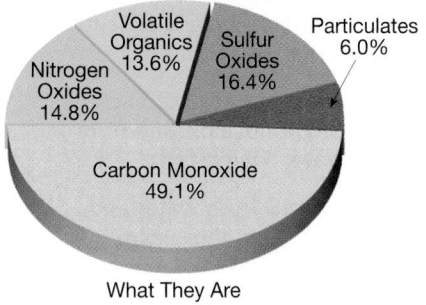

What They Are

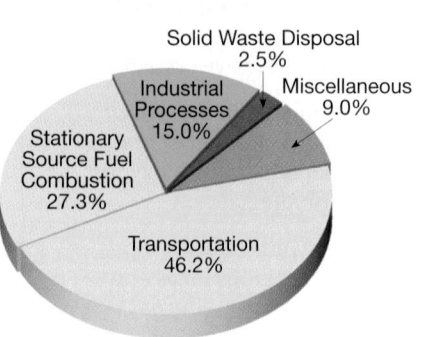

Where They Come From

Figure 19 Major Primary Pollutants and Their Sources Percentages are calculated on the basis of weight.
Using Graphs *What are the three major primary pollutants? What is the major source of air pollution?*

Earth's Blanket of Air

Earth's atmosphere is a blanket of nitrogen, oxygen, water vapor and other gases. **The chemical composition of the atmosphere helps maintain life on Earth.** First and foremost, people and other animals could not live without the oxygen in Earth's atmosphere. But the atmosphere is also part of several other cycles, such as the carbon cycle, that make vital nutrients available to living things.

The atmosphere also makes life on land possible by shielding Earth from harmful solar radiation. There is a layer of protective ozone high in the air. Ozone is a three-atom form of oxygen that protects Earth from 95 percent of the sun's harmful ultraviolet (UV) radiation.

Certain greenhouse gases in the atmosphere—such as carbon dioxide, methane, and water vapor—help maintain a warm temperature near Earth's surface. When solar energy hits Earth, the Earth gives off some of this energy as heat. The gases absorb the heat Earth emits, keeping the atmosphere warm enough for life as we know it.

 **Reading Checkpoint** *What is the role of ozone in the atmosphere?*

Pollution in the Air Pollution can change the chemical composition of the atmosphere and disrupt its natural cycles and functions. Fossil-fuel combustion is the major source of air pollution. Most of this pollution comes from motor vehicles and coal or oil-burning power plants. Motor vehicles, like those in Figure 18, release carbon monoxide, nitrogen oxide, soot, and other pollutants. Some of the pollutants react to form smog. Power plants release sulfur dioxide and nitrogen oxides. These pollutants combine with water vapor in the air to create acid precipitation. Figure 19 shows the primary air pollutants and the sources of those pollutants.

The burning of fossil fuels also produces carbon dioxide, an important greenhouse gas. The amount of carbon dioxide in the atmosphere has increased since industrialization began in the nineteenth century. This increase has altered the carbon cycle and contributed to the unnatural warming of the lower atmosphere, known as **global warming.** Global warming could lead to enormous changes in Earth's environment. These changes could include the melting of glaciers, which would contribute to a rise in sea level and in the flooding of coastal areas.

Chlorofluorocarbons (CFCs) once used in air conditioners and plastic foam production destroy ozone in the stratosphere layer of the atmosphere. Researchers say that a significant loss of ozone could result in an increased incidence of health problems like cataracts and skin cancers because more of the sun's UV radiation would reach Earth's surface.

Air pollution is a major public health problem. It can cause coughing, wheezing, headaches, as well as lung, eye, and throat irritation. Long-term health effects include asthma, bronchitis, emphysema, and lung cancer. The U.S. Environmental Protection Agency estimates that as many as 200,000 deaths each year are associated with outdoor air pollution.

Land Resources

Earth's land provides soil and forests, as well as mineral and energy resources. How do land resources impact your daily life? Soil is needed to grow the food you eat. Forests provide lumber for your home, wood for furniture, and pulp for paper. Petroleum provides energy and is in the plastic of your computer and CD boxes. Minerals such as zinc, copper, and nickel make up the coins in your pocket. Removing and using resources from Earth's crust can take a heavy environmental toll.

Damage to Land Resources There are an estimated 500,000 mines in the United States. Mines are essential because they produce many of the mineral resources we need. But mining tears up Earth's surface and destroys vegetation, as you can see in Figure 20. It can also cause soil erosion and create pollution that contaminates surrounding soil and water and destroys ecosystems.

Agriculture has many impacts on the land as well. Today, farmers can produce more food per hectare from their land. Extensive irrigation also has allowed many dry areas to be farmed for the first time. But heavy pumping for irrigation of dry areas is depleting the groundwater. And over time, irrigation causes salinization, or the build-up of salts in soil. When irrigation water on the soil evaporates, it leaves behind a salty crust. Eventually, the soil becomes useless for plant growth.

Go Online

SciLINKS™ NSTA

For: Links on environmental toxins
Visit: www.SciLinks.org
Web Code: cjn-1043

Figure 20 Surface mining destroys vegetation, soil, and the contours of Earth's surface. However, laws now require mine owners to restore the surface after mining operations cease.

MAP MASTER™
Skills Activity

Virgin Forests 1620–1998

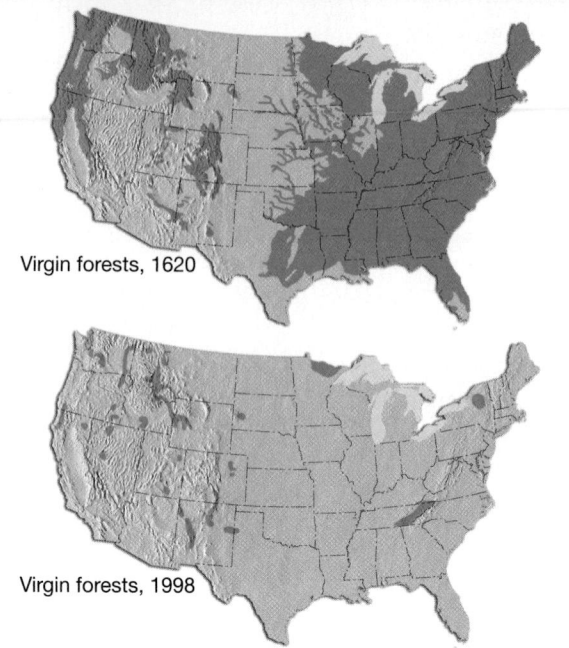

Virgin forests, 1620

Virgin forests, 1998

Figure 21

Location These maps compare the location of virgin forests in the contiguous 48 states of the U.S. in 1620 and in 1998. **Identifying Effects** How has the amount of virgin forest changed? How has the location of virgin forest changed?

Trees must be cut to supply our need for paper and lumber. But the removal of forests, especially through clear-cutting, can damage land. Clear-cutting is the removal of all trees in an area of forest. Cleared areas are susceptible to soil erosion. Forest removal also destroys ecosystems and wildlife habitat. The United States actually has more hectares of forest today than it did a century ago. That's because much of the virgin forest (forest that had never been cut down) that was cut long ago has regrown as second-growth forest. The forest is not as diverse as the virgin forest—it does not contain as much variety of plant species. Some forestland has also become tree plantations, with even fewer species. As you see in Figure 21, the United States has lost most of its virgin forest during the last few centuries.

Finally, land serves as a disposal site. You may have seen landfills and other waste facilities. When disposal is done correctly, there is minimal impact on land. But many old landfills leak harmful wastes that get into soil and underground water. The same is true of buried drums of chemicals, which were often disposed of illegally. Waste is inevitable. But there is a need for ways to reduce it and make the disposal safer.

Section 4.3 Assessment

Reviewing Concepts

1. 🌐 Why is fresh water a vital resource?
2. 🌐 Why is the chemical composition of Earth's atmosphere important?
3. What is the difference between point source pollution and nonpoint source pollution?
4. 🌐 What do Earth's land resources provide?

Critical Thinking

5. **Applying Concepts** How would Earth be different if there were no greenhouse gases?
6. **Classifying** Which of the following is a nonpoint source pollution of water: rainwater pouring from an eroded bank into a river, a boat emptying a waste tank into a lake, or a sewage plant sending sewage into a river through a pipe?
7. **Relating Cause and Effect** How would the removal of sulfur from coal affect the type of air pollution in a local area? Explain your answer.

Connecting Ⲥ Concepts

Write a brief paragraph that connects the following: waste of paper, loss of species diversity of forests, and the increase in second-growth forest area.

4.4 Protecting Resources

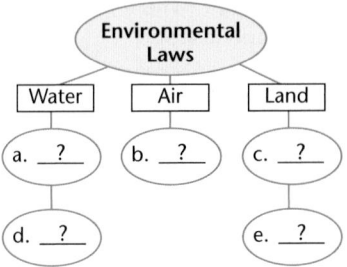

Reading Focus

Key Concepts

- When were the first laws passed to deal with water pollution?
- What was the most important law passed to deal with air pollution?
- What is involved in protecting land resources?

Vocabulary

- conservation
- compost
- recycling

Reading Strategy

Summarizing After reading this section, complete the concept map below to organize what you know about the major laws that help keep water, air, and land resources clean.

Environmental Laws
- Water
  - a. ?
    - d. ?
- Air
  - b. ?
- Land
  - c. ?
    - e. ?

Each year, Americans throw out about 30 million cell phones, 18 million computers, 8 million TV sets, and enough tires to circle the Earth about three times. With just 6 percent of the world's population, Americans use about one third of the world's resources—and produce about one third of the world's garbage.

This high rate of consumption squanders resources, many of which are nonrenewable. The manufacture and disposal of these products uses enormous amounts of energy and creates pollution, as shown in Figure 22. Is there a way to have the products and services we want and still protect resources and create less pollution?

Many people think conservation and pollution prevention are the answer. **Conservation** is the careful use of resources. Pollution prevention means stopping pollution from entering the environment.

Between the late 1940s and 1970, a number of serious pollution problems got the public's attention. Severe air pollution events killed hundreds and sickened thousands in the United States and elsewhere. In the late 1960s, many beaches closed due to pollution. An oil spill off the California coast killed wildlife. Then in 1969, Americans watched news reports of Ohio's polluted Cuyahoga River catching fire and burning for days.

Figure 22 Strict laws have helped curb air pollution, though it remains a problem.

Table 3 How You Can Prevent Water Pollution
• Never pour household chemicals (paints, thinners, cleaners, pesticides, waste oil) down the drain or into the toilet.
• Never dump toxic chemicals in the gutter or onto the ground.
• Don't put items that contain hazardous substances, such as batteries or old computer monitors, into the trash.
• Find out about hazardous waste collection sites and times from your local sanitation or public works department.
• Avoid using hazardous substances in the first place.

Keeping Water Clean and Safe

Both the public and government officials became increasingly concerned about pollution. **Starting in the 1970s, the federal government passed several laws to prevent or decrease pollution and protect resources.**

America's polluted rivers and lakes got early attention. In 1972, the U.S. Congress passed the Clean Water Act (CWA). Among other provisions, the law requires industries to reduce or eliminate point source pollution into surface waters. It also led to a huge increase in the number of sewage treatment plants, which eliminated the discharge of raw sewage into many lakes, rivers, and bays. There are still water pollution problems. But because of the CWA, the percentage of U.S. surface waters safe for fishing and swimming increased from 36 percent to 62 percent between 1972 and the end of the 1990s.

The Safe Drinking Water Act of 1974 helped protect drinking resources. It set maximum contaminant levels for a number of pollutants that could harm the health of people. Public water resources are cleaner today because of this law. See Table 3 for ways that individuals can help conserve water and keep it clean.

Reading Checkpoint   *What did the Clean Water Act do?*

Protecting the Air

As lawmakers were tackling water pollution in the 1970s, air pollution was also on the agenda. **In 1970, Congress passed the Clean Air Act, the nation's most important air pollution law.** It established National Ambient Air Quality Standards (NAAQS) for six "criteria" pollutants known to cause health problems—carbon monoxide, ozone, lead, sulfur dioxide, nitrogen oxides, and particulates (fine particles). Air monitors, such as the one in Figure 23, sample the air. If the maximum permissible level of pollutants in the air is exceeded, local authorities must come up with plans to bring these levels down. Between 1970 and 2001, the emissions of the six criteria pollutants regulated under the Clean Air Act decreased 24 percent. Over the same time span, energy consumption increased 42 percent and the U.S. population grew by 39 percent.

Today, power plants and motor vehicles use pollution control devices to reduce or eliminate certain byproducts of fossil fuel combustion. Power plants are also more likely to use low-sulfur coal. These controls cut down on emissions of sulfur and nitrogen oxides that often produce acid rain.

Figure 23 Air Sampler

Increased use of clean, alternate energy sources such as solar, wind, and hydroelectric power, can also help clear the air. These energy sources don't create air or water pollution, and they're based on renewable resources.

Cars with electric and hybrid (combination of electric and either natural gas, gasoline, or diesel) motors produce fewer or no tailpipe emissions. Several of these lower-emissions models are now available. Some of the hybrid models are also very efficient and get high gas mileage. When a car can go farther on a tank of gas, it uses less fuel and creates less pollution.

Energy conservation is an important air pollution control strategy. Fossil-fuel combustion produces most of the electricity in the United States. If we can use less electricity we would have to burn less fossil fuel. Less fossil-fuel combustion means less air pollution. You can see several energy conservation tips in Table 4.

 **Reading Checkpoint** *What did the Clean Air Act do?*

Table 4 How You Can Save Energy
• Recycle when possible.
• Let the sun in on bright winter days using solar energy to warm rooms.
• Use energy-saving fluorescent bulbs instead of incandescent bulbs where you can.
• Turn off lights when you leave a room. Turn off the radio, TV, or computer when you're not using them.
• Walk or ride a bike when you can.
• When buying electric products, look for the Energy Star sticker which denotes energy-saving products.

Caring for Land Resources

Protecting land resources involves preventing pollution and managing land resources wisely. Farmers, loggers, manufacturers, and individuals can all take steps to care for land resources.

Farmers now use many soil conservation practices to prevent the loss of topsoil and preserve soil fertility. In contour plowing, farmers plow across the contour of hillsides. This method of farming decreases water runoff that washes away topsoil. Another conservation method is strip cropping—crops with different nutrient requirements are planted in adjacent rows. Strip cropping helps preserve the fertility of soil.

Selective cutting conserves forest resources. In this method of logging, some trees in an area of a forest are cut, while other trees remain. This practice preserves topsoil as well as the forest habitat. Clear-cutting, on the other hand, removes whole areas of forest and destroys habitats and contributes to the erosion of topsoil.

Some farmers and gardeners now use less pesticides and inorganic fertilizers to decrease chemicals in soil and on crops. Natural fertilizers such as compost or animal manure have replaced inorganic commercial fertilizers on some fields. **Compost** is partly decomposed organic material that is used as fertilizer. Integrated Pest Management (IPM) uses natural predators or mechanical processes (such as vacuuming pests off leaves) to decrease the number of pests. Pesticide use is a last resort.

For: Links on emerging technologies
Visit: www.SciLinks.org
Web Code: cjn-1044

Some laws reduce the possibility of toxic substances getting into the soil. Since 1977, sanitary landfills have largely replaced open dumps and old-style landfills. Sanitary landfills have plastic or clay liners that prevent wastes from leaking into the surrounding soil or groundwater. The Resource Conservation and Recovery Act (RCRA) of 1976 has decreased the illegal and unsafe dumping of hazardous waste. The law requires companies to store, transport, and dispose of hazardous waste according to strict guidelines. The 1980 Comprehensive Environmental Response, Compensation, and Liability Act (Superfund) mandates the cleaning up of abandoned hazardous waste sites that are a danger to the public or the environment.

 Reading Checkpoint *What is the RCRA and what does it do?*

Creating less waste by using fewer products and recycling products also helps preserve land resources. **Recycling** is the collecting and processing of used items so they can be made into new products, as Figure 24 shows. By conserving resources and producing less waste, everyone can contribute to a cleaner, healthier future.

Figure 24 Recycling saves resources, reduces energy consumption, and prevents pollution.

Section 4.4 Assessment

Reviewing Concepts

1. When were the first laws passed to deal with water pollution?

2. Identify the most important air pollution control law.

3. What are National Ambient Air Quality Standards?

4. How does selective cutting of forests conserve topsoil?

5. How can gardeners care for land resources?

Critical Thinking

6. **Applying Concepts** How can turning off lights when you're not using them help decrease air pollution?

7. **Relating Cause and Effect** Explain how the Superfund law helps prevent pollution from entering underground water sources.

 **Writing in Science**

Explanatory Paragraph Write a brief paragraph explaining how recycling your aluminum soda cans helps conserve resources and energy.

Bingham Canyon, Utah: The Largest Open-Pit Mine

This huge pit was once where a mountain stood. It's Bingham Canyon copper mine, the largest open-pit mine in the world. The mine, southwest of Salt Lake City, Utah, is 4 kilometers across and covers almost 8 square kilometers. It's so deep—900 meters—that if a steel tower were built at the bottom, it would have to be five times taller than France's Eiffel Tower to reach the pit's rim.

Figure 25 Aerial view of Utah's Bingham Canyon copper mine, the largest open-pit copper mine on Earth.

The pit began in the late 1800s as an underground silver and lead mine. Miners later discovered copper. There are similar deposits at several sites in the American Southwest and in a belt from southern Alaska to northern Chile.

The ore at Bingham Canyon formed after magma was intruded to shallow depths. After this, shattering created extensive fractures in the rock. Hydrothermal solutions penetrated these cracks, and ore minerals formed from the solutions.

Although the percentage of copper in the rock is small, the total volume of copper is huge. Ever since open-pit operations started in 1906, some 5 billion tons of material have been removed, yielding more than 1.2 million tons of copper. Miners have also recovered significant amounts of gold, silver, and molybdenum.

The ore body is far from exhausted. Over the next 25 years, the mine's owners plan to remove and process an additional 3 billion tons of material. This mining operation has generated most of Utah's mineral production for more than 80 years. People have called it the "richest hole on Earth."

Like many older mines, the Bingham pit was unregulated during most of its history. Development occurred before today's awareness of the environmental impacts of mining and prior to effective environmental laws. Today, problems of groundwater and surface water contamination, air pollution, and land reclamation are receiving long overdue attention at Bingham Canyon.

Finding the Product that Best Conserves Resources

When you buy a product, you usually consider factors such as price, brand name, quality, and how much is in the package. But do you consider the amount of resources the package uses? Many products come in packages of different types and materials. You might buy a larger pack if you use a lot, or a tiny pack if you like the convenience of individual servings. But how much cardboard, plastic, or glass are you using—or wasting—depending on your choice? How about the trees, petroleum, and other resources needed to make those packages? In this lab, you will compare three sets of packages that hold the same amount of juice to determine how your decisions about packaging affect the use of resources.

Problem Which packaging conserves resources the best?

Materials
- 1 1.89-L (64 fl. oz) cardboard juice carton
- 1 946-mL (32 fl. oz) cardboard juice carton
- 1 240-mL (8 fl. oz) cardboard juice carton
- scissors
- metric ruler

CAUTION *Be careful when using scissors.*

Skills Observing, Measuring, Calculating, Comparing and Contrasting, Relating Cause and Effect, Drawing Conclusions

Procedure

Part A: Determine the Amount of Material in Each Package

1. Work in groups of three or four. Use scissors to cut apart the three cartons your teacher gives your group. Then spread each one out as you see here.

2. Measure the dimensions of the cartons with the ruler.

3. Calculate the area of each carton on a separate sheet of paper. Use these equations:
   - Area of a rectangle:
     $A = l \times w$
     (l = length; w = width)
   - Area of a square:
     $A = s^2$
     (s = length of a side of the square)

Data Table			
	Area of Cardboard in One Carton	Number of Cartons Needed to Hold 1.89 L	Area of Cardboard to Hold 1.89 L
1.89 L		1	
946 mL		2	
240 mL		8	

4. Copy the data table above on a separate sheet of paper. Then record the data you calculated.

Part B: Compare the Amount of Material in the Packages

5. On a separate sheet of paper, calculate how much more cardboard is used when you buy 1.89 L of juice in the two 946-mL cartons instead of one 1.89-L carton.

Use this procedure:

a) Subtract the area of material in the 1.89-L carton from the area of material in the two 946-mL cartons.

b) Divide the answer you get in part a by the area of material in the 1.89-L carton.

c) Multiply the answer you get in part b by 100. This is how much more material is in the two containers, expressed as a percentage.

6. Repeat this procedure for the material in eight small containers.

Analyze and Conclude

1. **Comparing and Contrasting** Based on your data, does buying the juice in one large carton or in an 8-pack of small individual cartons use more cardboard? How does buying the juice in two medium-size cartons compare.

2. **Relating Cause and Effect** How does buying the juice in several cartons instead of one large carton impact the use of resources?

3. **Drawing Conclusions** Suppose you have determined which set of cardboard cartons uses the least resources. Then you find out that the same size carton of juice comes in plastic and glass as well as cardboard. How would you decide which of these containers would be the best choice, in terms of saving resources?

4.1 Energy and Mineral Resources

Key Concepts

- A renewable resource can be replenished over fairly short time spans, whereas a nonrenewable resource takes millions of years to form and accumulate.
- Fossil fuels include coal, oil, and natural gas.
- Some energy experts believe that fuels derived from tar sands and oil shales could become good substitutes for dwindling petroleum supplies.
- Some of the most important mineral deposits form through igneous processes and from hydrothermal solutions.
- Nonmetallic mineral resources are extracted and processed either for the nonmetallic elements they contain or for their physical and chemical properties.

Vocabulary

renewable resources, *p. 94;* nonrenewable resource, *p. 94;* fossil fuel, *p. 95;* ore, *p. 98*

4.2 Alternate Energy Sources

Key Concepts

- Solar energy has two advantages: the "fuel" is free, and it's non-polluting.
- In nuclear fission, the nuclei of heavy atoms such as uranium-235 are bombarded with neutrons. The uranium nuclei then split into smaller nuclei and emit neutrons and heat energy.
- Some experts estimate that in the next 50 to 60 years, wind power could provide between 5 to 10 percent of the country's demand for electricity.
- The water held in a reservoir behind a dam is a form of stored energy that can be released through the dam to produce electric power.
- Hot water is used directly for heating and to turn turbines to generate electric power.

- Tidal power is harnessed by constructing a dam across the mouth of a bay or an estuary in coastal areas with a large tidal range. The strong in-and-out flow that results drives turbines and electric generators.

Vocabulary

hydroelectric power, *p. 105;* geothermal energy, *p. 105*

4.3 Water, Air, and Land Resources

Key Concepts

- Each day, people use fresh water for drinking, cooking, bathing, and growing food.
- The chemical composition of the atmosphere helps maintain life on Earth.
- Earth's land provides soil and forests, as well as mineral and energy resources.

Vocabulary

point source pollution, *p. 108;* nonpoint source pollution, *p. 109;* runoff, *p. 109;* global warming, *p. 110*

4.4 Protecting Resources

Key Concepts

- Starting in the 1970s, the federal government passed several laws to prevent or decrease pollution and protect resources.
- In 1970, Congress passed the Clean Air Act, the nation's most important air pollution law.
- Protecting land resources involves preventing pollution and managing land resources wisely.

Vocabulary

conservation, *p. 113;* compost, *p. 115;* recycling, *p. 116*

Reviewing Content

Choose the letter that best answers the question or completes the statement.

1. Nonrenewable resources are those that
   a. will never run out.
   b. take one or two decades to replace.
   c. have finite supplies.
   d. are contaminated by pollution.

2. Which of the following is a fossil fuel?
   a. uranium
   b. coal
   c. wood
   d. ozone

3. Petroleum and natural gas form from
   a. the remains of plants and animals buried in seas long ago.
   b. the decay of radioactive sediments underground.
   c. plant material that collected millions of years ago in swamps.
   d. heating and cooling of magma in underground chambers.

4. Hydroelectric power produces electricity using
   a. the sun's rays.
   b. wind.
   c. moving water.
   d. storms.

5. Which of the following substances is a fuel used in nuclear power plants?
   a. sulfur dioxide
   b. uranium
   c. petroleum
   d. carbon dioxide

6. Point source pollution comes from sources that are
   a. basically unknown.
   b. directly identifiable.
   c. very small.
   d. dumped illegally.

7. An unnatural warming of the atmosphere near Earth's surface is called
   a. solar wind.
   b. ozone accumulation.
   c. acid precipitation.
   d. global warming.

8. The careful use of resources is
   a. conservation.
   b. recycling.
   c. composting.
   d. deposition.

9. The Clean Air Act
   a. makes all air pollution illegal.
   b. limits greenhouse gases in outdoor air.
   c. limits nonpoint source pollution.
   d. set limits on certain pollutants in outdoor air.

10. What type of pollution did the Clean Water Act succeed in limiting?
    a. carbon dioxide
    b. sewage
    c. solid waste
    d. acid precipitation

Understanding Concepts

11. What are the three major types of fossil fuels?

12. What is a major negative impact of the use of fossil fuels?

13. What is the difference between a mineral resource and an ore?

14. Briefly explain how active solar collectors work.

15. Why do hydroelectric dams have limited lifetimes?

16. Explain why fresh water is a vital resource.

17. How can farmers help protect land resources?

18. When were some of the earliest laws passed to deal with water pollution? Why were they passed at that time?

19. Explain why an anticline might be a good place to search for petroleum and natural gas.

20. What are three things that you can do to prevent water pollution?

21. What are three things that you can do to save energy?

Critical Thinking

22. Applying Concepts Some people predict that tar sands and oil shale will one day supply much of our energy needs. Are tar sands and oil shale a good long-term energy solution? Explain.

23. Relating Cause and Effect What effect can recycling paper have on the use of resources and the creation of pollution?

24. Inferring How might an increased use of alternate energy sources such as wind and solar radiation affect the lifetime of fossil fuel resources?

25. Summarizing Describe how a hydrothermal solution can produce a vein deposit of ore.

26. Comparing and Contrasting What is the difference between how electricity is produced with tides and how it's produced in a nuclear power plant?

Analyzing Data

Use the diagram below to answer Questions 27–29.

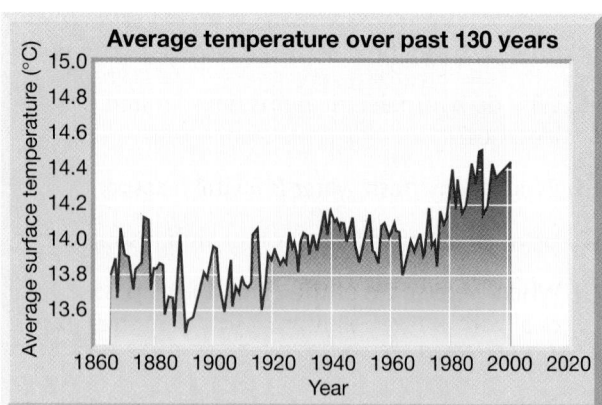

Average temperature over past 130 years

27. Interpreting Graphs What does this graph show?

28. Using Graphs What is the general temperature trend during the time period shown on the graph? What was the average temperature in 2000?

29. Drawing Conclusions How would you expect the graph to be different between 1700 and 1800, before the start of widespread industrialization? Explain.

Concepts in Action

30. Classifying Limestone is a nonmetallic mineral that has several uses: as a stone used for structures; as a substance used to neutralize acidic soils; as an ingredient in the manufacture of steel. Should limestone be classified as an industrial mineral or a building mineral? Explain.

31. Analyzing Concepts The factors in favor of the use of solar power include the fact that the fuel it uses is free, it's renewable, and it doesn't create pollution. Identify drawbacks of the use of solar power.

32. Summarizing What is the effect of the destruction of ozone on human life?

33. Connecting Concepts What is the relationship between petroleum production, the increased use of hybrid cars, and the level of air pollutants regulated by the Clean Air Act that are in the air?

Performance-Based Assessment

Drawing Conclusions Locate an electric power plant that is in or close to your community. Find out which method it uses to produce electricity. Take into consideration the way the plant produces power, its location, the pollution it produces, and the number of people it serves. Write a short essay on the plant's impact on the environment and on your community in general.

Standardized Test Prep

Test-Taking Tip

Make Logical Connections

A cause-and-effect statement may seem to be true when it is actually false. The statement may seem true because the stated cause and effect are both accurate. However, there may be no logical connection between the cause and the effect. In the question below, the opening phrase contains an accurate statement about fossil fuels. But only one answer provides a logical effect of the statement in the opening phrase.

Because fossil fuels are nonrenewable resources,

(A) solar energy is renewable.
(B) petroleum and natural gas often form together.
(C) supplies of coal, oil, and natural gas are finite.
(D) most power plants in the United States use fossil fuels to produce electricity.

(Answer: C)

Choose the letter that best answers the question or completes the statement, or write a brief answer to the question.

1. Which one of the substances listed below is a fossil fuel?
   (A) uranium
   (B) petroleum
   (C) carbon dioxide
   (D) granite

2. Recycling is an important way to reduce resource consumption because
   (A) reducing waste is better than recycling it.
   (B) it decreases the use of new resources to make products.
   (C) recycling is not a new way to save resources.
   (D) curbside pick-up makes recycling more convenient in many communities.

Answer Questions 3–5 using the line graph below, which shows U.S. energy consumption between 1970 and 2000, and projected consumption between 2000 and 2020.

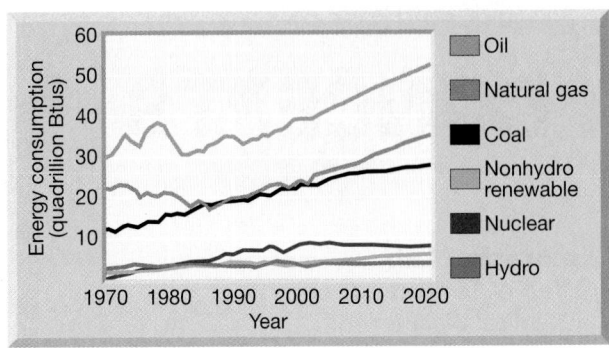

3. Which fuel source had the highest rate of consumption during this period?
   (A) coal
   (B) nuclear
   (C) oil
   (D) hydroelectric

4. Which renewable energy source is most widely used?
   (A) solar
   (B) hydroelectric
   (C) natural gas
   (D) nuclear

5. Look at the part of the graph that shows projections for U.S. energy consumption between 2000 and 2020. Explain why this pattern of consumption is, or is not, a good long-term energy strategy.

6. Explain how air pollutants can change the chemical composition of the atmosphere and how that affects Earth.

CHAPTER 5 Weathering, Soil, and Mass Movements

CONCEPTS in Action

Exploration Lab
Effect of Temperature on Chemical Weathering

How Earth Works
Soil

 **GEODe EARTH SCIENCE** Sculpturing Earth's Surface
↳ External vs Internal Process

Earth Materials
↳ Sedimentary Rocks

 **Video Field Trip**

Weathering and Erosion

Take a rugged field trip through the great outdoors with Discovery Channel and find out the roles weathering and erosion play in the creation of Earth's most beautiful features. Answer the following questions after watching the video.

1. Describe the creative forces of erosion.

2. How is soil created?

Go Online
PHSchool.com

For: Chapter 5 Resources
Visit: PHSchool.com
Web Code: cjk-9999

Weathering caused these spectacular rock ▶ formations in Arizona's Monument Valley.

Chapter Preview

Inquiry Activity

What Causes Weathering?

Procedure

1. Fill a 1-L plastic container about half full of rocks. Add enough water to barely cover the rocks.

2. Place a tight-fitting lid on the container, and shake the container vigorously 100 times.

3. Hold a strainer over a clear glass jar. Pour the water and rocks into the strainer.

4. Use a hand lens to observe the bottom and sides of the empty container. Then use the hand lens to observe the water in the glass jar.

Think About It

1. **Observing** What did you see on the bottom or sides of the empty container during Step 4? How did shaking the rock-and-water mixture change the appearance of the water?

2. **Predicting** How do you think your observations would change if you put the rocks and water back in the container and repeated Steps 2 through 4 several more times?

3. **Predicting** Suppose you found a stream where water ran over a rock ledge into a pool. What would you expect to find at the bottom of the pool?

5.1 Weathering

Figure 1 Weathering Ice, rain, and wind are slowly breaking down the rock in this mountain. The rock fragments accumulate in sloped deposits at the base of the mountain.

Earth's surface is constantly changing. Internal forces gradually raise some parts of the surface through mountain building and volcanic activity. At the same time, external processes continually break rock apart and move the debris to lower elevations, as shown in Figure 1. The breaking down and changing of rocks at or near Earth's surface is called weathering. Weathering is a basic part of the rock cycle and a key process in the Earth system. There are two types of weathering—mechanical and chemical. Though these processes are different, they are at work at the same time.

Mechanical Weathering

Mechanical weathering occurs when physical forces break rock into smaller and smaller pieces without changing the rock's mineral composition. Each piece has the same characteristics as the original rock. Breaking a rock into smaller pieces increases the total surface area of the rock. Look at Figure 2. When rock is broken apart, more surface area is exposed to chemical weathering. In nature, three physical processes are especially important causes of mechanical weathering: frost wedging, unloading, and biological activity.

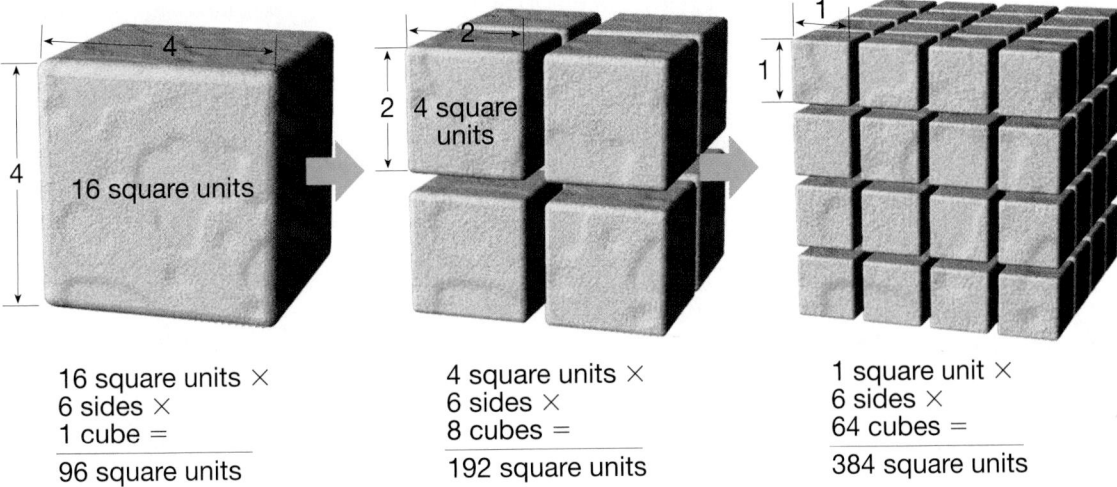

16 square units ×
6 sides ×
1 cube =
_____
96 square units

4 square units ×
6 sides ×
8 cubes =
_____
192 square units

1 square unit ×
6 sides ×
64 cubes =
_____
384 square units

Frost Wedging When liquid water freezes, it expands by about 9 percent, exerting a tremendous outward force. This force is great enough to burst water pipes during the winter. In nature, water works its way into every crack in rock. When water freezes and expands, it enlarges the cracks. After many freeze-thaw cycles, the rock breaks into pieces. This process, which is shown in Figure 3, is called **frost wedging.** Frost wedging is most common in mountainous regions in the middle latitudes. Here daily freezing and thawing often occur. Sections of rock that are wedged loose may tumble into large piles called **talus,** which typically form at the base of steep, rocky cliffs.

 **Reading Checkpoint** *Explain how water can cause mechanical weathering.*

Figure 2 By breaking a rock into smaller pieces, mechanical weathering increases the rock's surface area that can be exposed to chemical weathering.
Calculating *Calculate the total surface area if each of the 64 cubes shown in the right diagram were broken into 8 equal-sized cubes.*

Figure 3 Frost Wedging Rainwater entered cracks in this boulder. Each time the water froze, it expanded. Eventually, the boulder split.

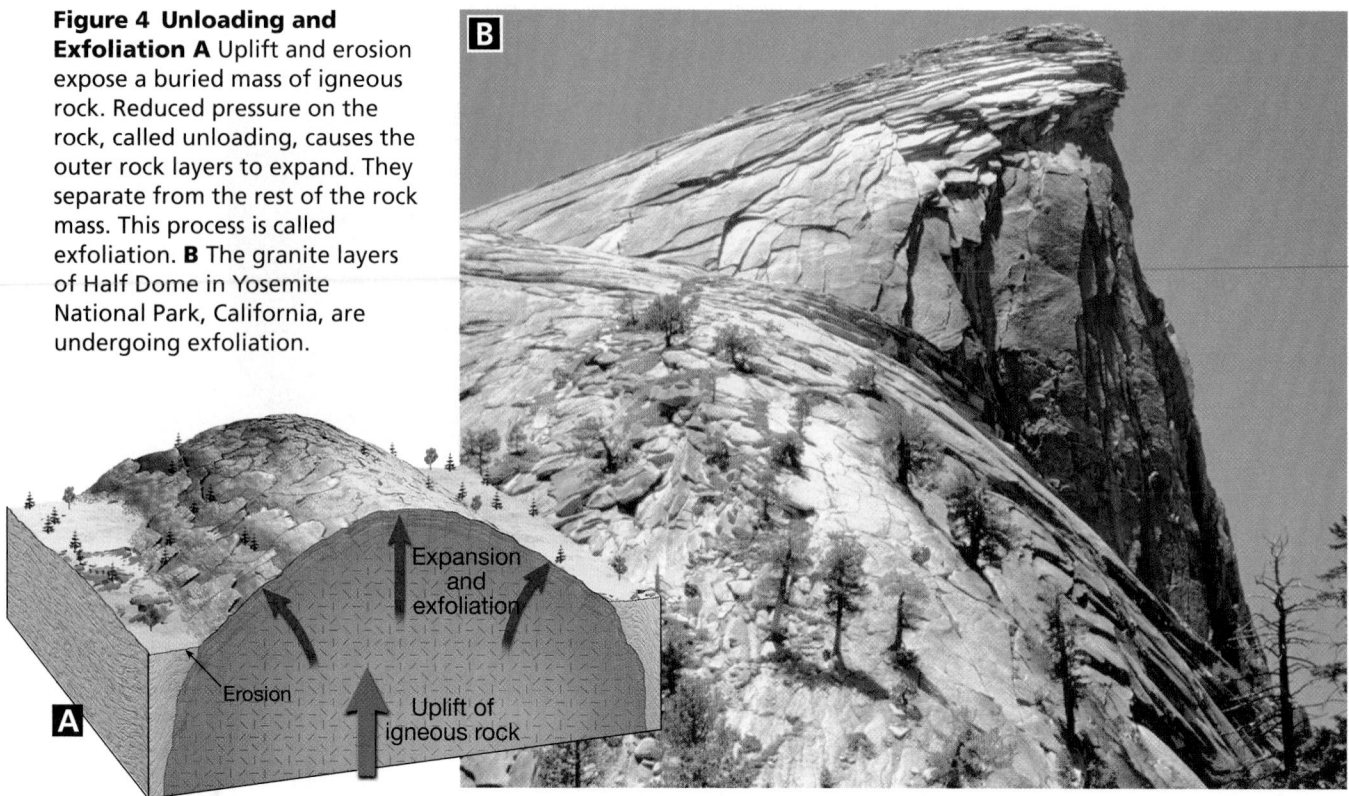

Figure 4 Unloading and Exfoliation A Uplift and erosion expose a buried mass of igneous rock. Reduced pressure on the rock, called unloading, causes the outer rock layers to expand. They separate from the rest of the rock mass. This process is called exfoliation. **B** The granite layers of Half Dome in Yosemite National Park, California, are undergoing exfoliation.

Expansion and exfoliation

Erosion

Uplift of igneous rock

Figure 5 The roots of this tree are causing mechanical weathering by widening the cracks in the rock.

Unloading Large masses of igneous rock may be exposed through uplift and erosion of overlying rocks. When that happens, the pressure exerted on the igneous rock is reduced. This is known as unloading. As illustrated in Figure 4A, unloading causes the outer layers of the rock to expand more than the rock below. Slabs of outer rock separate like the layers of an onion and break loose in a process called **exfoliation.** Exfoliation is especially common in rock masses made of granite. It often produces large, dome-shaped rock formations. Figure 4B shows one of these formations. Other important exfoliation domes are Stone Mountain, Georgia, and Liberty Cap also in Yosemite National Park.

A striking example of the weathering effects of unloading is shown in deep underground mining. Newly cut mine tunnels suddenly reduce the pressure on the surrounding rock. As a result, large rock slabs sometimes explode off the walls of the tunnels.

Biological Activity The activities of organisms, including plants, burrowing animals, and humans, can also cause mechanical weathering. As Figure 5 shows, plant roots grow into cracks in rock, wedging the rock apart as they grow. Burrowing animals move rocks to the surface, where weathering is more rapid. Decaying organisms produce compounds called acids that cause chemical weathering.

Humans accelerate mechanical weathering through deforestation and blasting in search of minerals or in the creation of new roads.

Chemical Weathering

⬭Chemical weathering is the transformation of rock into one or more new compounds. The new compounds remain mostly unchanged as long as the environment in which they formed does not change. You can contrast chemical weathering and mechanical weathering with a sheet of paper. Tearing the paper into small pieces is like mechanical weathering of rock. Burning the paper, which changes it into carbon dioxide and water, is like chemical weathering.

Water Water is the most important agent of chemical weathering. Water promotes chemical weathering by absorbing gases from the atmosphere and the ground. These dissolved substances then chemically react with various minerals. Oxygen dissolved in water reacts easily with certain minerals, forming oxides. For example, iron-rich minerals get a yellow to reddish-brown coating of iron oxide when they react with oxygen. Iron oxide is the rust that forms when iron-containing objects are exposed to water. Figure 6A shows this rust on barrels.

Water absorbs carbon dioxide when rain falls through the atmosphere. Water that seeps through the ground also picks up carbon dioxide from decaying organic matter. The carbon dioxide dissolved in water forms carbonic acid. This is the weak acid in carbonated soft drinks. Carbonic acid reacts with many common minerals.

 *How are water, oxygen, and carbon dioxide involved in chemical weathering?*

Figure 6 A Oxygen reacted with the iron in these barrels, forming iron oxide, or rust. **B** This granite gravestone, placed in 1868, shows little evidence of chemical weathering. **C** The inscription date (1872) on this marble gravestone is nearly illegible due to chemical weathering.

Water in the atmosphere also absorbs sulfur oxides and nitrogen oxides. These oxides are produced by the burning of coal and petroleum. Through a series of chemical reactions, these pollutants are converted into acids that are the major cause of acid precipitation. Acid precipitation accelerates the chemical weathering of stone monuments and structures, such as the one shown in Figure 7.

Figure 7 One Effect of Acid Precipitation Acid precipitation contributed to the chemical weathering of this stone building facade in Leipzig, Germany.

Chemical Weathering of Granite

To illustrate how chemical weathering can change the properties of rock, let's consider granite. Recall that granite consists mainly of the minerals feldspar and quartz. When granite is exposed to water containing carbonic acid, the feldspar is converted mostly to clay minerals. Quartz, in contrast, is much more resistant to carbonic acid and remains unchanged. As the feldspar slowly changes to clay, the quartz grains are released from the granite. Rivers transport some of this weathered debris to the sea. The tiny clay particles may be carried far from shore. The quartz grains are deposited near the shore where they become the main component of beaches and sand dunes.

Chemical Weathering of Silicate Minerals

Recall that silicate minerals make up most of Earth's crust and are composed largely of just eight elements. When silicate minerals undergo chemical weathering, the sodium, calcium, potassium, and magnesium they contain dissolve and are carried away by groundwater. Iron reacts with oxygen, producing iron oxide. The three remaining elements are aluminum, silicon, and oxygen. These elements usually combine with water and produce clay minerals. See Table 1 for a list of products of weathering.

Spheroidal Weathering

Chemical weathering can change the physical shape of rock as well as its chemical composition. For example, when water enters along the joints in a rock, it weathers the corners and edges most rapidly. These parts of the rock have a greater surface area than the faces have. As a result, the corners and edges become more rounded. The rock takes on a spherical shape, as shown in Figure 8A. This process is called spheroidal weathering.

Table 1 Products of Weathering		
Mineral	**Residual Products**	**Materials in Solution**
Quartz	Quartz grains	Silica
Feldspars	Clay minerals	Silica K^+, Na^+, Ca^{2+}
Amphibole (hornblende)	Clay minerals Limonite Hematite	Silica Ca^{2+}, Mg^{2+}
Olivine	Limonite Hematite	Silica Mg^{2+}

As Figure 8B shows, spheroidal weathering sometimes causes the outer layers of a rock to separate from the rock's main body. This can happen when the minerals in the rock turn to clay, which swells by adding water. The swelling exerts a force that causes the layers to break loose and fall off. This allows chemical weathering to penetrate deeper into the boulder. Although the effects of this type of spheroidal weathering resemble exfoliation, the two processes are different. Spheroidal weathering is a form of chemical weathering. Exfoliation is caused by unloading. The layers that separate from the rock are not chemically changed.

Rate of Weathering

Mechanical weathering affects the rate of chemical weathering. By breaking rock into smaller pieces, mechanical weathering accelerates chemical weathering by increasing the surface area of exposed rock. **Two other factors that affect the rate of weathering are rock characteristics and climate.**

Rock Characteristics Physical characteristics of rock, such as cracks, are important in weathering because they influence the ability of water to penetrate rock. However, a rock's mineral composition also dramatically affects its rate of weathering. You can see this by visiting a cemetery and comparing old gravestones made from different rock types. Gravestones made of granite, like the one in Figure 6B on page 129, are relatively resistant to chemical weathering. You can easily read the inscriptions on a granite gravestone that is over 100 years old. In contrast, marble gravestones undergo much more rapid chemical weathering, as shown in Figure 6C on page 129. Marble is composed of calcite (calcium carbonate), which easily dissolves even in weak acids.

Figure 8 Spheroidal Weathering A The edges of these granite rocks in California's Joshua Tree National Monument were rounded through spheroidal weathering. **B** Spheroidal weathering has caused the outer layers of this rock to loosen and separate.

Figure 9 These boldly sculpted pinnacles in Bryce Canyon National Park show differential weathering. **Drawing Conclusions** *In which parts of these formations is weathering happening most rapidly?*

Silicates are the most abundant mineral group. Silicates weather in the same sequence as their order of crystallization. Olivine crystallizes first and weathers most rapidly. Quartz, which crystallizes last, is the most resistant to weathering.

Climate Climatic factors, especially temperature and moisture, have a strong effect on the rate of weathering. For example, these factors control the frequency of freeze-thaw cycles, which affect the amount of frost wedging. Temperature and moisture also affect the rate of chemical weathering. They influence the kind of vegetation and how much is present. Regions with lush vegetation generally have a thick layer of soil rich in decaying organic matter that releases acids into the water.

The climate most favorable for chemical weathering has high temperatures and abundant moisture. So, chemical weathering is very slow in arid regions. It is also slow in polar regions because the low temperatures there keep moisture locked up as ice.

Differential Weathering Different parts of a rock mass often weather at different rates. This process, called differential weathering, has several causes. Differences in mineral composition are one cause. More resistant rock protrudes as pinnacles, or high peaks, such as those shown in Figure 9. Another cause is the variations in the number and spacing of cracks in different parts of a rock mass.

Section 5.1 Assessment

Reviewing Concepts

1. What happens to a rock's mineral composition during mechanical weathering?
2. What is unloading? How does it contribute to weathering?
3. How does chemical weathering affect the compounds in rock?
4. Name two rock characteristics and two climatic factors that affect the rate of weathering.

Critical Thinking

5. **Using Analogies** Think about the following processes: dissolving a piece of rock salt in a pan of water and grinding a peach pit in a garbage disposal. Which process is more like mechanical weathering, and which is more like chemical weathering?

6. **Applying Concepts** The level of carbon dioxide in the atmosphere is increasing. How might this affect the rate of chemical weathering of Earth's surface rocks? Explain your reasoning.

Math ▶ Practice

7. Suppose frost wedging splits a spherical rock 2 m in diameter into two equal-sized hemispheres. Calculate the total surface area of the original rock and of the two hemispheres. (The area of a circle $= \pi r^2$, and the surface area of a sphere $= 4\pi r^2$, where r is the radius.)

5.2 Soil

Reading Focus

Key Concepts

- What are the major components of soil?
- What are the most important factors in soil formation?
- How does soil vary with depth?
- What are three common types of soil?
- How do human activities affect the rate of soil erosion?

Vocabulary

- regolith
- soil
- soil horizon
- soil profile
- pedalfer
- pedocal
- laterite

Reading Strategy

Comparing and Contrasting Copy the table. After you read, compare the three types of soils by completing the table.

Soil Type	Where It's Found
Pedalfer	a. _____?_____
Pedocal	b. _____?_____
Laterite	c. _____?_____

Soil, an important product of weathering, covers most land surfaces. Along with air and water, it is one of our most important resources. All life depends on a dozen or so elements that come from Earth's crust. Once weathering and other processes create soil, plants absorb the elements and make them available to animals, including humans.

Characteristics of Soil

Weathering produces a layer of rock and mineral fragments called **regolith,** which covers nearly all of Earth's land surface. **Soil is the part of the regolith that supports the growth of plants.** Three important characteristics of soil are its composition, texture, and structure.

Soil Composition **Soil has four major components: mineral matter, or broken-down rock; organic matter, or humus, which is the decayed remains of organisms; water; and air.** The proportions of these components vary in different soils. Figure 10 shows that in a good-quality surface soil, mineral matter and organic matter make up half the total volume. The organic matter in soil, or humus, consists of the decayed remains of animal and plant life. The other half consists of pore spaces where air and water circulate.

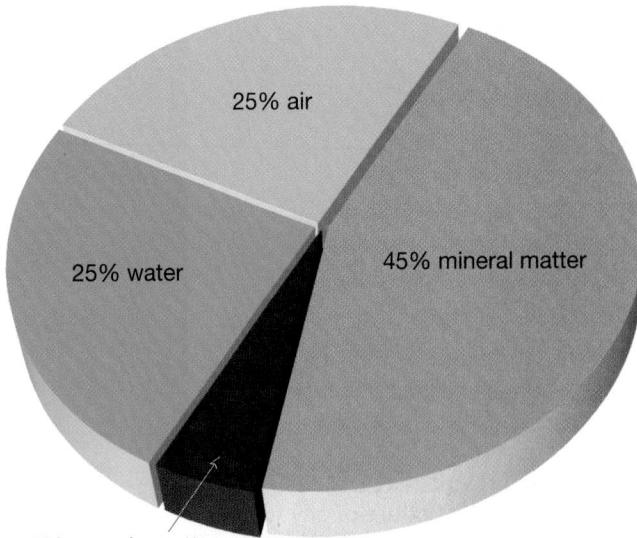

Figure 10 Composition by Volume of Good-Quality Soil Using Graphs *What percentage of this soil consists of water and mineral matter?*

The percentage of organic matter in soil varies greatly. Certain bog soils are composed almost entirely of organic matter. Desert soils may contain only a tiny amount. In most soils, organic matter or humus is an essential component. It is an important source of plant nutrients and increases the soil's ability to retain water. Poor soils can be enriched with the addition of humus.

The water and air components of soil are also vital for plant growth. Soil water provides the moisture needed for chemical reactions that sustain life. Soil water provides nutrients in a form that plants can use. Air is the source of the carbon dioxide plants use to produce sugar during photosynthesis.

Soil Texture Most soils contain particles of different sizes. Soil texture refers to the proportions of different particle sizes. To classify soil texture, the U.S. Department of Agriculture has established categories based on the percentages of clay, silt, and sand in soil. The diagram in Figure 11 shows how the percentages differ for each category. For example, point A, near the left-center part of the diagram, represents a soil composed of 40 percent clay, 10 percent silt, and 50 percent sand. Such a soil is called a sandy clay. In soils called loam, which occupy the central part of the diagram, neither clay, silt, nor sand is dominant.

Texture strongly influences a soil's ability to support plant life. Sandy soils may drain and dry out too quickly, while clay-rich soils drain very slowly. Plant roots often have difficulty penetrating soils that contain a high percentage of clay and silt. Loam soils are usually best for plant growth. They retain water better and store more nutrients than do soils composed mainly of clay or sand.

Figure 11 Soil-Texture Diagram The texture of any soil can be represented by a point on this diagram.
Interpreting Diagrams *What type of soil consists of 10 percent clay, 60 percent silt, and 30 percent sand?*

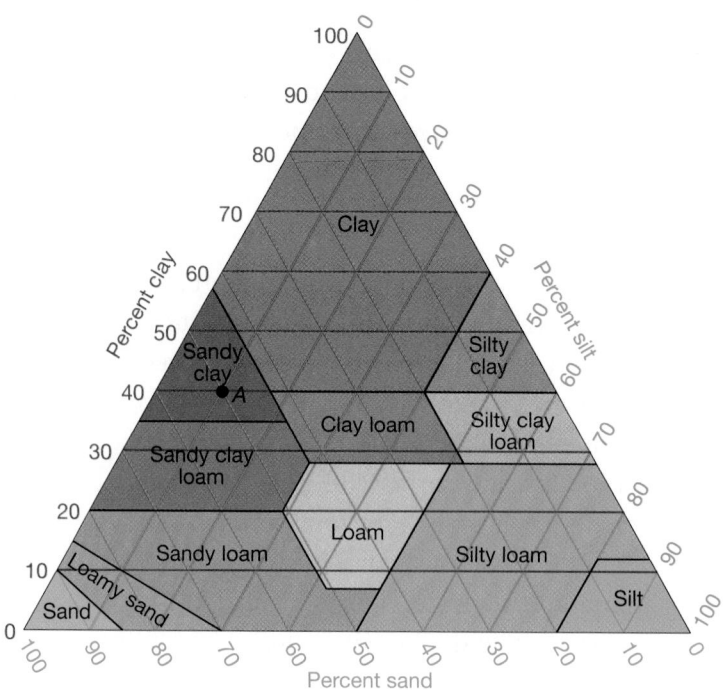

Soil Structure Soil particles usually form clumps that give soils a particular structure. Soil structure determines how easily a soil can be cultivated and how susceptible it is to erosion. Soil structure also affects the ease with which water can penetrate the soil. This, in turn, influences the movement of nutrients to plant roots.

Soil Formation

Soil forms through the complex interaction of several factors. **The most important factors in soil formation are parent material, time, climate, organisms, and slope.** Although these factors all interact, we'll examine them separately.

For: Links on soil
Visit: www.SciLinks.org
Web Code: cjn-2052

Figure 12 Parent Materials and Soils

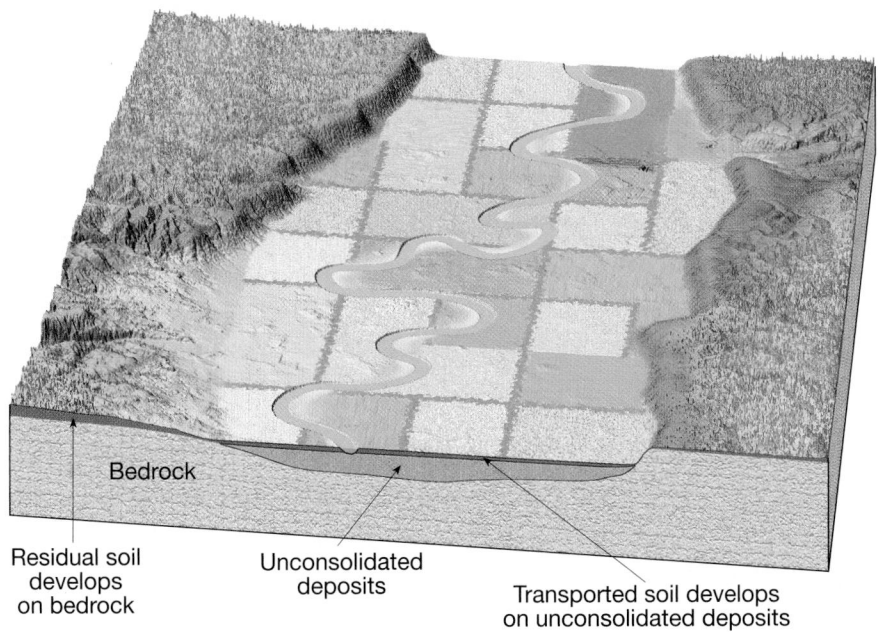

Bedrock

Residual soil develops on bedrock

Unconsolidated deposits

Transported soil develops on unconsolidated deposits

Parent Material The source of the mineral matter in soil is known as the parent material. Notice in Figure 12 that parent material may be either bedrock or unconsolidated deposits, such as those in a river valley. The soil that forms on bedrock is called residual soil. The soil that forms on unconsolidated deposits is called transported soil. Its parent material was moved from another location by gravity, water, wind, or ice.

Reading Checkpoint *What is the difference between residual soil and transported soil?*

The nature of the parent material influences soils in two ways. First, it affects the rate of weathering and the rate of soil formation. Because unconsolidated deposits are already partly weathered, they provide more surface area for chemical weathering. Therefore, transported soil usually develops more rapidly than residual soil develops. Second, the chemical makeup of the parent material affects the soil's fertility. Fertility influences the types of plants the soil can support.

Time The longer a soil has been forming, the thicker it becomes. The parent material largely determines the characteristics of young soils. As weathering continues, however, the influence of the parent material can be overshadowed by the other factors, especially climate.

Climate Climate has the greatest effect on soil formation. Variations in temperature and precipitation influence the rate, depth, and type of weathering. For example, a hot, wet climate may produce a thick layer of chemically weathered soil. In the same amount of time, a cold, dry climate might produce only a thin layer of mechanically weathered debris. The amount of precipitation also influences soil fertility by affecting the rate at which nutrients are removed from the soil. Finally, climate has a big effect on the types of organisms that live on and in the soil.

The influence of climate is so great that soil scientists have found that similar soils can be produced from different parent materials in the same climate. Dissimilar soils can be produced from the same parent material in different climates.

Organisms The types of organisms and how many there are in a soil have a major impact on its physical and chemical properties. In fact, scientists name some soils—such as prairie soil, forest soil, and tundra soil—based on the soils' natural vegetation.

Plants are the main source of organic matter in soil. Animals and microorganisms may also contribute. Because organic matter releases nutrients when it decays, it contributes to soil fertility. As you read in Section 5.1, the decay of organic matter also produces acids that speed up weathering.

Microorganisms, including fungi, bacteria, and single-celled protozoans, play an active role in decomposing dead plants and animals. Some bacteria also aid soil fertility by converting nitrogen gas into nitrogen compounds that plants can use.

Burrowing animals mix the mineral and organic matter in soil. Earthworms, for example, feed on organic matter as they burrow through soil. The earthworms in a single hectare (10,000 square meters) can mix thousands of kilograms of soil each year. The holes made by burrowing animals also help water and air to penetrate into soil.

Slope

The slope of the land can vary greatly over short distances. Such variations can result in very different soil types. Many of the differences are related to the amount of erosion and the water content of the soil.

On steep slopes, erosion is accelerated. Little water can soak in, so the soil generally holds too little moisture for vigorous plant growth. As a result, soils are usually thin or nonexistent on steep slopes, as shown in Figure 13A. In contrast, flat areas have little erosion and poor drainage. As Figure 13B shows, the waterlogged soils that form here are typically thick and dark. The dark color results from large amounts of organic matter.

The direction a slope faces also affects soil formation. In the temperate zone of the Northern Hemisphere, south-facing slopes receive much more sunlight than do north-facing slopes. Consequently, soils on south-facing slopes are usually warmer and drier. These differences may influence the types of plants that grow in the soil.

Although you have read about five separate factors that affect soil formation, remember that they all work together to form soil. No single factor is responsible for a soil's composition.

 **Reading Checkpoint** *Explain how the slope of the land affects soil thickness.*

Figure 13 Slope and Soil Thickness A Little or no soil develops on steep slopes. **B** Flat areas often have very thick soil.

The Soil Profile

The processes that form soil operate from the surface downward. 🔘 **Soil varies in composition, texture, structure, and color at different depths.** These variations divide the soil into zones known as **soil horizons.** A vertical section through all of the soil horizons is called a **soil profile.** In some soil profiles, the soil horizons blend gradually from one to another. In others, like the one shown in Figure 14A, the soil horizons are quite distinct. Mature soils usually have three distinct soil horizons, which are identified in Figure 14B. From the surface downward, these horizons are called the A, B, and C horizons.

A Horizon The A horizon is commonly known as topsoil. Its upper part consists mostly of organic matter, including loose leaves and partly decomposed plant structures. It is teeming with insects, fungi, and microorganisms. The lower part of the A horizon is a mixture of mineral matter and organic matter.

B Horizon The B horizon, or subsoil, contains fine clay particles washed out of the A horizon by water that filters through pore spaces. In some soils, the clay that accumulates in the B horizon forms a compact, impenetrable layer called hardpan. The B horizon is the lower limit of most plant roots and burrowing animals.

C Horizon Between the B horizon and the unaltered parent material is the C horizon, which contains partially weathered parent material. While the A and B horizons barely resemble the parent material, the C horizon does.

Figure 14 Soil Profiles A The A, B, and C horizons have different characteristics. **B** Three soil horizons are visible in this soil. **Interpreting Photographs** *Using the diagram in B as a guide, identify the soil horizons in A.*

Loose and partly decayed organic matter

A horizon (Topsoil)

Mineral matter mixed with some organic matter

B horizon (Subsoil)

Clay transported from above

C horizon Partially weathered parent material

Unweathered parent material

A

B

Soil Types

Recall that climate is the most important factor in soil formation. Climate also has a major effect on the type of soil that forms. ⊙ **Three common types of soil are pedalfer, pedocal, and laterite.**

Pedalfer Pedalfers usually forms in temperate areas that receive more than 63 cm of rain each year. This soil type is present in much of the eastern half of the United States, most often in forested areas. The B horizon in pedalfers contains large amounts of iron oxide and aluminum-rich clays, giving it a brown to red-brown color.

Pedocal Pedocals are found in the drier western United States in areas that have grasses and brush vegetation. Because chemical weathering is slower in dry climates, pedocals generally contains less clay than pedalfers. Pedocals contain abundant calcite, or calcium carbonate, and are typically a light gray-brown.

Figure 15 The Temple at Angkor Wat, Cambodia This temple was constructed of laterite bricks between 1113 and 1150.

Laterite Laterites form in hot, wet tropical areas. Chemical weathering is intense under such conditions. So laterites are usually deeper than soils that develop over a similar period in temperate areas. The large quantity of water that filters through these soils removes most of the calcite and silica. Iron oxide and aluminum oxide are left behind. The iron oxide gives laterite a distinctive orange or red color.

When dried, laterite becomes very hard and practically waterproof. For centuries, people in portions of South and Southeast Asia have made bricks by digging up laterite, shaping it, and allowing it to harden in the sun. Ancient structures built of laterite bricks, such as the one shown in Figure 15, are well preserved even today.

Plants that die in a tropical rain forest decompose rapidly because bacterial activity is high in hot and wet climates. As a result, laterite contains almost no organic matter. The roots of living rain forest plants quickly absorb the nutrients released during decomposition. So, even though the vegetation may be dense, the soil itself contains few available nutrients. Most of the nutrients in a tropical rain forest are present in the plants themselves.

Today, large areas of tropical rain forest are being cleared for timber and to provide land for agriculture, as shown in Figure 16.

Figure 16 Clearing a Tropical Rain Forest in Borneo The laterite soil cannot support agriculture for more than a few years.

However, laterite is one of the poorest soils for agriculture. Because laterite contains little organic matter and few nutrients, it cannot nourish crops. The nutrients it does have are soon washed out by the plentiful rainwater that filters through the soil. In only a few years, the soil in a freshly cleared area may be completely useless for growing crops. Without trees or crop plants to anchor the soil and shield the ground from the full force of heavy rains, the soil erodes quickly.

 *Why is the soil in a tropical rain forest poorly suited for agriculture?*

Soil Erosion

Soils are just a tiny fraction of all Earth materials, yet they are a vital resource. Because soils are necessary for the growth of rooted plants, they are the foundation of the human life-support system. However, soils are among our most abused resources. The loss of fertile topsoil is a growing problem as human activities disturb more of Earth's surface.

How Water Erodes Soil Soil erosion is a natural part of the constant recycling of Earth materials known as the rock cycle. Water, wind, and other agents move soil from one place to another. Every time it rains, raindrops strike the soil surface with surprising force. As Figure 17 shows, each drop acts like a tiny bomb, blasting soil particles off the surface. Water flowing across the surface then carries away the dislodged particles. Because thin sheets of water move the soil particles, this process is called sheet erosion.

Figure 17 Soil Erosion by Raindrops A raindrop can splash soil particles more than a meter away from where it strikes the soil.

After flowing as a thin sheet for a short distance, the water forms tiny streams called rills. As more water enters the rills, they erode the soil further, creating trenches known as gullies, like those shown in Figure 18. Although most dislodged soil particles do not move far during each rainfall, large quantities eventually make their way downslope to a stream. The stream transports these soil particles, which are now called sediment, and eventually deposits them.

Rates of Erosion In the past, soil eroded more slowly than it does today because more land was covered by trees, grasses, and other plants. However, human activities that remove natural vegetation, such as farming, logging, and construction, have greatly accelerated erosion. Without plants, soil is more easily carried away by wind and water.

Scientists can estimate the rate of erosion due to water by measuring the amount of sediment in rivers. These estimates indicate that before humans appeared, rivers carried about 9 trillion kg of sediment to the oceans each year. In contrast, the amount of sediment currently transported to the sea by rivers is about 24 trillion kg per year.

Wind generally erodes soil much more slowly than water does. During a prolonged drought, however, strong winds can remove large quantities of soil from unprotected fields. That's exactly what happened during the 1930s in the part of the Great Plains that came to be known as the Dust Bowl.

The rate of soil erosion depends on soil characteristics and on factors such as climate, slope, and type of vegetation. In many regions, including about one-third of the world's croplands, soil is eroding faster than it is being formed. This results in lower productivity, poorer crop quality, and a threatened world food supply.

Figure 18 Gullies The unprotected soil in this field in southern Colombia is deeply eroded.

 *How do human activities affect rates of erosion?*

Sediment Deposition Another problem caused by excessive soil erosion is the deposition of sediment. Rivers that accumulate sediment must be dredged to remain open for shipping. As sediment settles in reservoirs, they become less useful for storing water, controlling floods, and generating electricity.

Some sediments are contaminated with agricultural pesticides. When these chemicals enter a river or lake, they endanger organisms that live in or use the water, including humans. Sediments also contain soil nutrients, which may come from natural processes and from added fertilizers. Excessive nutrient levels in lakes stimulate the growth of algae and plants. This can accelerate a process that eventually leads to the early death of the lake.

Controlling Erosion Although we cannot completely eliminate soil erosion, we can significantly slow it by using soil conservation measures. You have seen how a misunderstanding of the composition of rain forest soil has led to the destruction of millions of acres leaving only severely leached, unproductive land. Conservation measures include steps taken to preserve environments and protect the land. These measures include planting rows of trees called windbreaks, terracing hillsides, plowing along the contours of hills, and rotating crops. Preserving fertile soil is essential to feeding the world's rapidly growing population.

Section 5.2 Assessment

Reviewing Concepts

1. List the four major components of soil.
2. How does climate affect soil formation?
3. Describe the contents of the three soil horizons found in most mature soils.
4. What climates are usually associated with pedalfer, pedocal, and laterite?
5. How can an activity such as road construction affect the rate of soil erosion?

Critical Thinking

6. **Relating Cause and Effect** A gardener notices that rain showers usually produce long-lasting puddles on the soil in her garden. Is it more likely that the soil contains too much sand or too much clay? Explain.

7. **Predicting** Which activity would cause more sediment to be deposited in a river that flows through a gently sloping valley—cultivating the valley or cultivating the hills that surround the valley? Explain.

Connecting Concepts

Weathering and Soil Using what you learned about chemical weathering in Section 5.1, explain why the soils formed in a hot, wet climate and a cold, dry climate are different.

5.3 Mass Movements

Reading Focus

Key Concepts

- What is mass movement?
- What factors trigger mass movements?
- How do geologists classify mass movements?

Vocabulary

- mass movement
- rockfall
- rockslide
- slump
- mudflow
- earthflow
- creep

Reading Strategy

Previewing Copy the table. Before you read the section, rewrite the green topic headings as *what* questions. As you read, write an answer to each question.

Question	Answer
a. _____?_____	b. _____?_____
c. _____?_____	d. _____?_____

Earth's land surface consists of slopes, some steep and others very gradual. While most slopes appear stable, they are always changing. The force of gravity causes material to move downslope. **The transfer of rock and soil downslope due to gravity is called mass movement.** Some types of mass movement are so slow that you cannot see them. Others, such as landslides like the one illustrated in Figure 19, are very sudden.

The combined actions of weathering and mass movement produce most landforms. Once weathering weakens and breaks rock apart, mass movement moves the debris downslope. There a stream usually carries it away. Stream valleys are the most common of Earth's landforms.

Q *Are snow avalanches a type of mass movement?*

A Yes. These thundering downslope movements of snow and ice can also transport large quantities of rock, soil, and trees. About 10,000 snow avalanches occur each year in the mountainous western United States. Besides damaging buildings and roads at the bottom of slopes, they are especially dangerous to skiers. In an average year, snow avalanches claim between 15 and 25 lives in the United States and Canada. Snow avalanches are a growing problem as more people participate in winter sports and recreation.

Figure 19 Landslide This home in Pacific Palisades, California, was destroyed by a landslide triggered by the January 1994 Northridge earthquake.

Figure 20 Mudflow In October 1998, heavy rains from Hurricane Mitch led to massive mudflows in Central America.
Formulating Hypotheses *What human activities before the rains might have contributed to the mudflows?*

Triggers of Mass Movements

Gravity is the force behind mass movements. Several factors make slopes more susceptible to the pull of gravity. **Among the factors that commonly trigger mass movements are saturation of surface materials with water, oversteepening of slopes, removal of vegetation, and earthquakes.**

Water Heavy rains and rapid melting of snow can trigger mass movement by saturating surface materials with water. This was the case when torrential downpours associated with Hurricane Mitch caused devastating mudflows, as shown in Figure 20. When the pores in sediment become filled with water, the particles slide past one another more easily. You can demonstrate this effect with sand. If you add water until the sand becomes slightly moist, the sand grains will stick together. However, if you add enough water to fill all the pores between the sand grains, the sand-water mixture will ooze downhill. Clay also becomes very slick when it is wet.

Oversteepened Slopes Loose soil particles can maintain a relatively stable slope up to a certain angle. That angle ranges from about 25 to 40 degrees, depending on the size and shape of the particles. If the steepness of a slope exceeds the stable angle, mass movements become more likely. Such slopes are said to be oversteepened. An oversteepened slope can result when a stream undercuts a valley wall or waves pound against the base of a cliff. People may also create oversteepened slopes by excavating during the construction of roads and buildings.

 *How do oversteepened slopes trigger mass movements?*

Removal of Vegetation Plants make slopes more stable because their root systems bind soil and regolith together. When plants are removed by forest fires or by human activities such as logging or farming, the likelihood of mass movement increases. An example that illustrates the stabilizing effect of plants occurred several decades ago on steep slopes near Menton, France. Farmers replaced olive trees, which have deep roots, with carnations, a more profitable but shallow-rooted crop. Planting carnations made the slopes less stable. A landslide on one of the slopes killed 11 people.

Earthquakes Earthquakes are one of the most dramatic triggers of mass movements. An earthquake and its aftershocks can dislodge enormous amounts of rock and unconsolidated material. In many areas, these mass movements cause more damage than the ground vibrations themselves. The landslide shown in Figure 19 was triggered by an earthquake.

Types of Mass Movements

Geologists classify mass movements based on the kind of material that moves, how it moves, and the speed of movement. We'll consider five basic types of mass movement: rockfalls, slides, slumps, flows, and creep.

Rockfalls A **rockfall** occurs when rocks or rock fragments fall freely through the air. This type of mass movement is common on slopes that are too steep for loose material to remain on the surface. Many rockfalls result from the mechanical weathering of rock caused by freeze-thaw cycles or plant roots. Rockfalls sometimes trigger other mass movements.

Slides In a slide, a block of material moves suddenly along a flat, inclined surface. Slides that include segments of bedrock are called **rockslides.** They often occur in high mountain areas such as the Andes, Alps, and Canadian Rockies. Rockslides are among the fastest mass movements, reaching speeds of over 200 km per hour. Some rockslides, such as the one shown in Figure 21, are triggered by rain or melting snow.

Figure 21 Rockslide The scar on the side of this mountain in northwestern Wyoming was made by an enormous rockslide that happened more than 75 years ago. The debris in the slide formed a dam 70 m high across the Gros Ventre River.

Figure 22 Slump Heavy rains triggered this slump in Santa Barbara, California. Notice the crescent-shaped cliff just above the slump.

Slumps

A **slump** is the downward movement of a block of material along a curved surface. The material in a slump usually does not travel very fast or very far. As the block moves, its upper surface sometimes tilts backward. Slumps leave a crescent-shaped cliff just above the slump, which you can see in Figure 22. They are common on oversteepened slopes where the soil contains thick accumulations of clay.

Flows

Flows are mass movements of material containing a large amount of water, which move downslope as a thick fluid. Flows that move quickly, called **mudflows,** are common in semiarid mountainous regions, such as parts of southern California. In these regions, protective vegetation is sparse. A heavy downpour or rapid snowmelt can flood canyons with a mixture of soil, rock, and water. The mixture may have the consistency of wet concrete. It follows the contours of the canyon, taking large boulders and trees along with it. As you saw in Figure 20, mudflows in populated areas are very dangerous and destructive. In 1988, a massive mudflow triggered by the eruption of Nevado del Ruiz, a volcano in Colombia, killed 25,000 people.

Earthflows are flows that move relatively slowly—from about a millimeter per day to several meters per day. Their movement may continue for years. Earthflows occur most often on hillsides in wet regions. When water saturates the soil and regolith on a hillside, the material breaks away, forming a tongue-shaped mass like the one shown in Figure 23. Earthflows range in size from a few meters long and less than 1 m deep to over 1 km long and more than 10 m deep.

 *How do mudflows differ from earthflows?*

Figure 23 Earthflow This small, tongue-shaped mass movement occurred on a newly formed slope along a recently built highway. **Comparing and Contrasting** *Which other type of mass movement looks most similar to an earthflow?*

Creep The slowest type of mass movement is **creep**, which usually travels only a few millimeters or centimeters per year. One factor that contributes to creep is alternating between freezing and thawing, as Figure 24A shows. Freezing expands the water in soil, lifting soil particles at right angles to the slope. Thawing causes contraction, which allows the particles to fall back to a slightly lower level. Each freeze-thaw cycle moves the particles a short distance downhill.

Because creep is so slow, you cannot observe it directly as it happens. However, the effects of creep are easy to recognize. As Figure 24B shows, creep causes structures that were once vertical to tilt downhill. Creep can also displace fences and crack walls and underground pipes.

Figure 24 Creep A Repeated expansion and contraction of the soil on a slope results in a gradual downhill movement of the soil. **B** Years of creep have caused these gravestones to tilt. **Inferring** *In which direction is creep occurring in this photograph?*

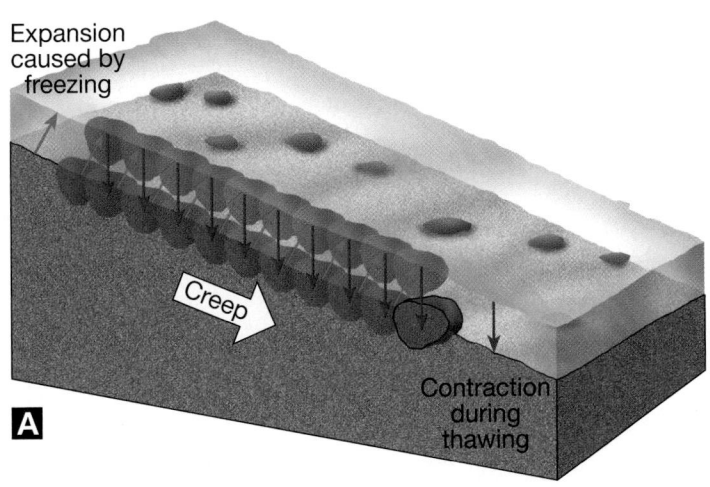

Expansion caused by freezing

Creep

Contraction during thawing

A

B

Section 5.3 Assessment

Reviewing Concepts

1. What is mass movement?
2. How does water trigger mass movements?
3. How does a rockfall differ from a rockslide?
4. What is the slowest type of mass movement?

Critical Thinking

5. **Applying Concepts** When highway engineers build a road in a mountainous area, they insert drainage pipes into the slopes alongside the road. Explain why.

6. **Making Judgments** Which mass movement—a slump, a mudflow, or an earthflow—poses the greatest risk to human life? Explain your reasoning.

Writing in Science

Explanatory Paragraph Explain how people can make mass movements more likely. Include two examples in your explanatory paragraph.

Soil

On the surface of the Earth, **soil** is the thin layer of loose material in which plants grow. Soil consists partly of mineral particles, and partly of **organic matter** derived from living plants and animals and their remains. Other key components of soil are water and air. Complex natural processes build soil over many thousands of years. The process begins when rock is broken down by weathering. Next, plants take root in the weathered rock. Then, organic material in the soil, called **humus,** is formed from decaying vegetation and animals. Different types of soil occur because of variations in climate, types of vegetation, and types of rock. In large countries like Russia, there is a wide variety of soil types.

SOIL FORMATION
Typically, the first step in soil building is the development of **regolith,** or weathered rock. Next, immature soil is formed as organic material begins to decay. Finally, mature soil supports abundant life both above and below the surface.

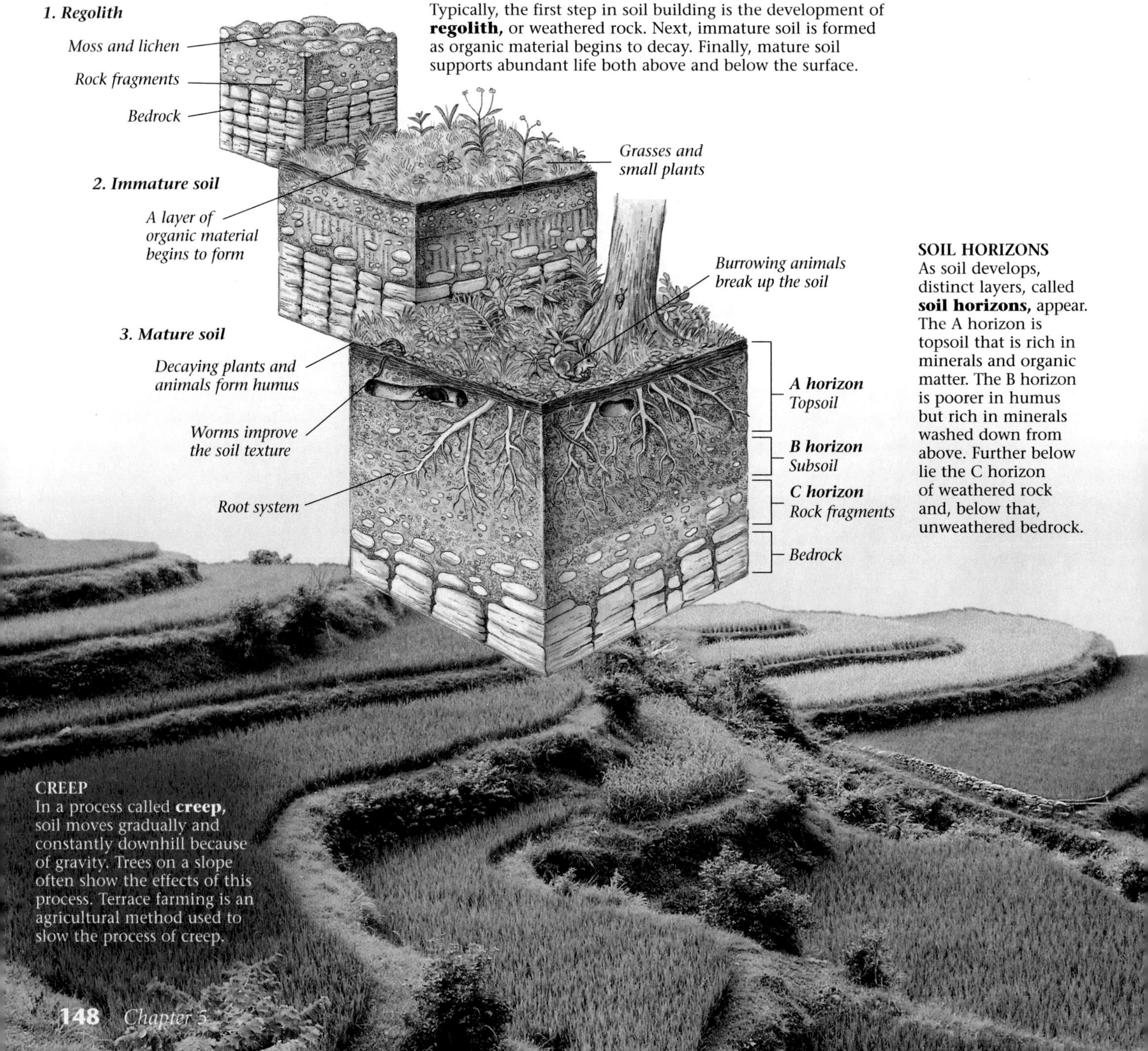

1. Regolith

Moss and lichen

Rock fragments

Bedrock

2. Immature soil

A layer of organic material begins to form

3. Mature soil

Decaying plants and animals form humus

Worms improve the soil texture

Root system

Grasses and small plants

Burrowing animals break up the soil

A horizon
Topsoil

B horizon
Subsoil

C horizon
Rock fragments

Bedrock

SOIL HORIZONS
As soil develops, distinct layers, called **soil horizons,** appear. The A horizon is topsoil that is rich in minerals and organic matter. The B horizon is poorer in humus but rich in minerals washed down from above. Further below lie the C horizon of weathered rock and, below that, unweathered bedrock.

CREEP
In a process called **creep,** soil moves gradually and constantly downhill because of gravity. Trees on a slope often show the effects of this process. Terrace farming is an agricultural method used to slow the process of creep.

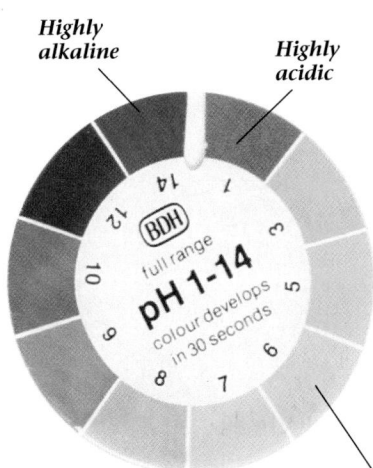

Highly alkaline · **Highly acidic** · **Neutral**

SOIL pH
The pH scale measures acidity or alkalinity on a scale of 0 to 14. When a chemical solution called an indicator is added to a soil sample, the indicator changes color, showing the soil's pH. Most plants thrive only in soils with a pH between 5 and 9.

Clay soil

Silty soil

SOIL TEXTURE
Soil texture depends on the size and nature of soil particles. Clay soils have the smallest grains, silty soils have medium-sized grains, and sandy soils have the largest grains. **Loam,** a mixture of clay, silt, and sand, is the best soil for agriculture.

Sandy soil

Wildflowers · **Grass** · **Snail** · **Decomposing leaf** · **Slug** · **Roots**

LIFE IN THE SOIL
Soil is home to a vast array of life, including microorganisms, ants, termites, worms, and rodents. Fungi and bacteria convert dead plant and animal matter into chemicals that enrich the soil. Burrowing creatures improve the soil by mixing it.

Spodosol is a sandy soil found in northern coniferous forests.

Aridisols, found in deserts, have high concentrations of salts

SOIL CLASSIFICATION
Some experts recognize thousands of different soil types. The U.S. Department of Agriculture has devised a comprehensive soil classification system for categorizing soils. Each type of soil can be identified by the characteristics of its horizons.

ASSESSMENT

1. **Key Terms** Define **(a)** soil, **(b)** organic matter, **(c)** humus, **(d)** regolith, **(e)** soil horizon, **(f)** creep, **(g)** loam.

2. **Physical Processes** Describe the three stages of soil formation.

3. **Physical Characteristics** How do various types of soil differ from one another?

4. **Natural Resources** What soil characteristics are most beneficial for agriculture?

5. **Critical Thinking Making Comparisons** Study the cross-sections of spodosol and aridisol. **(a)** How are they alike? **(b)** How do they differ? **(c)** Do research to learn more about their different characteristics.

Effect of Temperature on Chemical Weathering

Water is the most important agent of chemical weathering. One way water promotes chemical weathering is by reacting with the minerals in rocks. In this lab, you will examine the effect of temperature on chemical weathering by measuring the rate at which antacid tablets dissolve in water at different temperatures. These tablets contain calcium carbonate, the mineral found in rocks such as limestone and marble.

Problem
How does temperature affect the rate of chemical weathering?

Materials
- 250-mL beaker
- thermometer
- hot water (40–50°C)
- ice
- 5 antacid tablets
- stopwatch
- graph paper

Skills
Measuring, Using Tables and Graphs, Drawing Conclusions, Inferring

Procedure

1. On a sheet of paper, copy the data table.

2. Add a mixture of hot water and ice to the beaker. Use the thermometer to measure the temperature of the mixture. Add either more hot water or more ice until the temperature is between 0°C and 10°C. The total volume of the mixture should be about 200 mL.

3. When the temperature is within the correct range, remove any remaining ice from the beaker. Record the starting temperature of the water in your data table. Remove the thermometer from the beaker.

4. Drop an antacid tablet into the beaker. Start the stopwatch as soon as the tablet enters the water. Stop the stopwatch when the tablet has completely dissolved and no traces of the tablet are visible. (Don't wait for the bubbling to stop.) Record the time in your data table.

5. Place the thermometer in the beaker and wait for the temperature of the water to stabilize. Record the final temperature of the water in your data table.

Data Table			
Starting Temperature (°C)	Dissolving Time(s)	Final Temperature (°C)	Average Temperature (°C)

6. Calculate the average temperature by adding the starting and final temperatures and dividing by 2. Record the result in your data table.

7. Repeat Steps 2 through 6 four more times, once at each of the following temperature ranges: 10–20°C, 20–30°C, 30–40°C, and 40–50°C. Adjust the relative amounts of hot water and ice to produce the correct water temperatures. The total volume of water and ice should always be about 200 mL.

8. On graph paper, make a graph with average temperature on the x-axis and dissolving time on the y-axis. Plot your data on the graph. Draw a smooth curve through the data points.

Analyze and Conclude

1. **Analyzing Data** At which temperature did the antacid tablet dissolve most rapidly?

2. **Analyzing Data** At which temperature did the antacid tablet dissolve most slowly?

3. **Drawing Conclusions** What is the relationship between temperature and the rate at which antacid tablets react with water?

4. **Formulating Hypotheses** Based on your observations, form a hypothesis about the relationship between temperature and the rate of chemical weathering.

5. **Designing Experiments** How could you test your hypothesis?

6. **Predicting** What would your results have been if you had ground each tablet into a fine powder before dropping it into the water? Would your conclusion be the same or different? Explain.

7. **Inferring** Would a limestone building weather more rapidly in Homer, Alaska, or in Honolulu, Hawaii? (Both cities receive about the same amount of precipitation in an average year.) Explain your reasoning.

Go Further Look for signs of chemical weathering on old stone buildings in your community. Consult your local library or historical society to find out when the buildings were constructed and what type of stone they are made of.

5.1 Weathering

Key Concepts

- Mechanical weathering occurs when physical forces break rock into smaller and smaller pieces without changing the rock's mineral composition.
- In nature, three physical processes are especially important causes of mechanical weathering: frost wedging, unloading, and biological activity.
- Chemical weathering is the transformation of rock into one or more new compounds.
- Two factors that affect the rate of weathering are rock characteristics and climate.

Vocabulary

mechanical weathering, *p. 126;* frost wedging, *p. 127;* talus, *p. 127;* exfoliation, *p. 128;* chemical weathering, *p. 129*

5.2 Soil

Key Concepts

- Soil is the part of the regolith that supports the growth of plants.
- Soil has four major components: mineral matter, or broken down rock; organic matter, or humus, which is the decayed remains of organisms; water; and air.
- The most important factors in soil formation are parent material, time, climate, organisms, and slope.
- Soil varies in composition, texture, structure, and color at different depths.
- Three common types of soil are pedalfer, pedocal, and laterite.
- Human activities that remove natural vegetation, such as farming, logging, and construction, have greatly accelerated erosion.

Vocabulary

regolith, *p. 133;* soil, *p. 133;* soil horizon, *p. 138;* soil profile, *p. 138;* pedalfer, *p. 139;* pedocal, *p. 139;* laterite, *p. 139*

5.3 Mass Movements

Key Concepts

- The transfer of rock and soil downslope due to gravity is called mass movement.
- Among the factors that commonly trigger mass movements are saturation of surface materials with water, oversteepening of slopes, removal of vegetation, and earthquakes.
- Geologists classify mass movements based on the kind of material that moves, how it moves, and the speed of movement.

Vocabulary

mass movement, *p. 143;* rockfall, *p. 145;* rockslide, *p. 145;* slump, *p. 146;* mudflow, *p. 146;* earthflow, *p. 146;* creep, *p. 147*

Reviewing Content

Choose the letter that best answers the question or completes the statement.

1. The breaking down and changing of rocks at or near Earth's surface is called
   a. mass movement.   b. sheet erosion.
   c. weathering.   d. uplift.

2. Which of the following is NOT a cause of mechanical weathering?
   a. dissolving   b. frost wedging
   c. unloading   d. burrowing

3. In which type of climate does chemical weathering occur most rapidly?
   a. cold, dry   b. cold, wet
   c. warm, dry   d. warm, wet

4. Organic matter in soil is also called
   a. regolith.   b. humus.
   c. talus.   d. loam.

5. A soil's texture is determined by its
   a. water content.
   b. mineral composition.
   c. thickness.
   d. particle sizes.

6. In soils with distinct soil horizons, the topmost zone is the
   a. parent material. b. A horizon.
   c. B horizon.   d. C horizon.

7. Compared to past rates of soil erosion, the current rate is
   a. lower.
   b. about the same.
   c. higher.
   d. impossible to determine.

8. Which of the following does NOT usually trigger mass movements?
   a. growth of native vegetation on slopes
   b. formation of oversteepened slopes
   c. saturation of surface materials with water
   d. vibration of the ground during an earthquake

9. When a block of material moves downward along a curved surface, the process is called
   a. a rockslide.   b. a rockfall.
   c. a slump.   d. an earthflow.

10. Which of the following best describes a mudflow?
    a. movement too slow to be observed directly
    b. material moving downslope as a thick fluid
    c. material falling freely through the air
    d. sudden movement along a flat, inclined surface

Understanding Concepts

11. What happens to the total surface area of the cubes in the process shown below? What type of weathering does this process represent?

12. What is exfoliation? Give an example of a feature produced by exfoliation.

13. How does mechanical weathering promote chemical weathering?

14. How is carbonic acid formed in nature? What happens when this acid reacts with feldspar?

15. Which factor has the greatest effect on soil formation? Explain.

16. How does slope affect the formation of soil?

17. Describe the major characteristics of A, B, and C horizons.

18. Distinguish between pedalfer and pedocal.

19. List three negative effects of soil erosion.

20. Explain how weathering and mass movement together produce most landforms.

21. What is the force behind mass movements? What other factors can trigger mass movements?

22. Distinguish between rockfalls and rockslides.

23. Distinguish between mudflows and earthflows.

24. How do freezing and thawing contribute to creep?

Assessment *continued*

Critical Thinking

25. Inferring Roads in northern states such as Maine and Michigan need to be repaired more often than roads in southern states such as Florida and Louisiana. What form of mechanical weathering could account for this?

26. Comparing and Contrasting How do the effects of mechanical weathering on rock differ from the effects of chemical weathering?

27. Predicting Granite and marble are exposed at the surface in a hot, wet region. Which of the rocks will weather more rapidly? Why?

28. Applying Concepts Heat speeds up most chemical reactions. Why then does chemical weathering happen slowly in a hot desert?

29. Making Judgments Do you think that soil erosion is an artificial byproduct of careless land use by humans? Explain.

Analyzing Data

Use the diagram below to answer Questions 30–32.

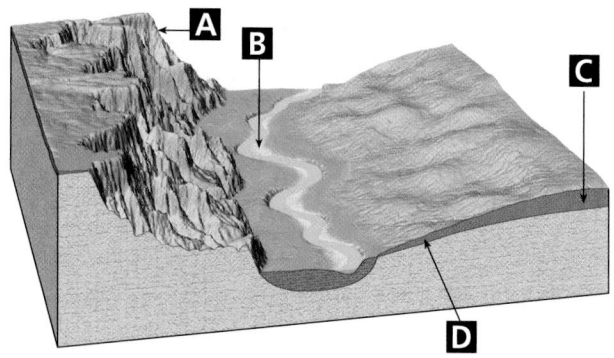

30. Comparing and Contrasting Compare the thickness of the soil in the areas labeled A and B.

31. Interpreting Diagrams What name is given to the soil that develops in the area labeled B? In the area labeled C?

32. Inferring Why is the soil in the area labeled D thinner than the soil in the area labeled C?

Concepts in Action

33. Using Analogies Explain how the following scenario is analogous to weathering: One evening you place a sealed jar full of water in a freezer. The next morning, the water has turned to ice and the jar is cracked.

34. Applying Concepts A committee has been established to design a stone memorial commemorating 100 soldiers who died in battle. The committee decides to use a large block of marble for the memorial. Considering only the memorial's durability, would it be better to use the whole block as a single memorial for all 100 soldiers or to divide it into 100 blocks of equal size, one for each soldier?

35. Classifying How would you determine the texture of the soil in your area?

36. Making Judgments Should a homeowner in a dry, mountainous area remove all vegetation from surrounding slopes to reduce fire danger? Explain why or why not.

37. Writing in Science Write a paragraph describing one type of mass movement. Include a specific example of a time when such a mass movement made the news.

Performance-Based Assessment

Observing Look for places in your community where people have taken specific actions to reduce erosion. Such places may include sites where buildings are being constructed or roads are being built or repaired. Make a list of each action and explain how it is intended to reduce erosion.

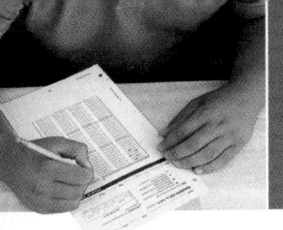

Standardized Test Prep

Use the diagram below to answer Questions 3 and 4.

Test-Taking Tip

Watch for Qualifiers
The words *best* and *least* are examples of qualifiers. If a question contains a qualifier, more than one answer will contain correct information. However, only one answer will be complete and correct for the question asked. Look at the question below. Eliminate any answers that are clearly incorrect. Then choose the remaining answer that offers the best explanation for the question asked.

Which mass movement is LEAST dangerous to people walking below a slope?
(A) rockslide
(B) rockfall
(C) creep
(D) mudflow

(Answer: C)

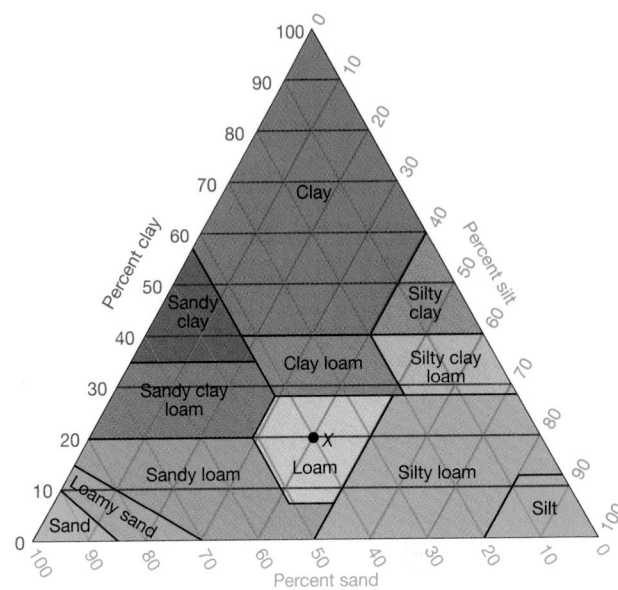

Choose the letter that best answers the question or completes the statement.

1. Which of the following best describes regolith?
   (A) a soil that contains large amounts of iron oxide and aluminum-rich clays
   (B) a mixture of mineral matter, organic matter, water, and air
   (C) a large pile of rock fragments at the base of a steep cliff
   (D) the layer of rock and mineral fragments that covers nearly all of Earth's land surface

2. In which mass movement do rock fragments fall freely through the air?
   (A) rockslide
   (B) rockfall
   (C) slump
   (D) earthflow

3. What are the percentages of clay, silt, and sand in the soil at the point labeled X?
   (A) 60 percent clay, 80 percent silt, and 60 percent sand
   (B) 0 percent clay, 40 percent silt, and 60 percent sand
   (C) 20 percent clay, 40 percent silt, and 40 percent sand
   (D) 50 percent clay, 40 percent silt, and 10 percent sand

4. The name given to soil that contains 60 percent clay, 20 percent silt, and 20 percent sand is
   (A) clay.   (B) loam.
   (C) silty clay loam.   (D) sandy loam.

Answer the following questions in complete sentences.

5. How does the surface area of an exposed rock affect its rate of weathering?

6. What role does acid precipitation play in weathering?

7. When a tropical rain forest is cleared, why does the soil usually become useless for growing crops after only a few years?

8. Explain how water can trigger an earthflow.

Running Water and Groundwater

CONCEPTS in Action

Exploration Lab
Investigating the Permeability of Soils

People and the Environment
The Ogallala Aquifer—How Long Will the Water Last?

GEODe Sculpturing Earth's Surface
EARTH SCIENCE
↳ Hydrologic Cycle
Running Water
Groundwater

DISCOVERY CHANNEL SCHOOL **Video Field Trip**

Dams

Take a field trip to China with the Discovery Channel and learn about the construction of the Three Gorges dam on the Yangtze River. Answer the following questions after watching the video.

1. What led to the decision to build a dam on the Yangtze River?

2. Name two disadvantages of the Three Gorges Dam.

Go Online PHSchool.com

For: Chapter 6 Resources
Visit: PHSchool.com
Web Code: cjk-9999

This photograph shows Lost Yak Rapids ▶ on Chile's Rio Bio Bio.

Chapter Preview

Inquiry ➤ Activity

How Do Local Bodies of Water Affect Your Community?

Procedure

1. Identify an important body of water in or near your community. It could be a river, lake, dam reservoir, stream, ocean, or estuary.

2. List the ways the people of your community use this body of water.

3. Observe and record the ways this body of water has affected (or still affects) the local landscape.

Think About it

1. **Classifying** Is the body of water used for recreation (boating, swimming, fishing), for industry and business (transportation or waste disposal for factories and power plants), for drinking water, or a combination of these purposes?

2. **Inferring** If your community uses this body of water as a source of drinking water, how might that affect other possible uses of the water?

3. **Drawing Conclusions** Has this body of water shaped the landscape in the area? How?

Reading Focus

Key Concepts

- What is the water cycle?
- What does it mean to say Earth's water cycle is balanced?
- What is the most important factor in determining the power of a stream to erode and transport material?
- How do gradient and discharge change between a stream's source and its mouth?
- What is a stream's base level?

Vocabulary

- water cycle
- infiltration
- transpiration
- gradient
- stream channel
- discharge
- tributary
- base level
- meander

Reading Strategy

Building Vocabulary Copy the table. As you read the section, define in your own words each vocabulary term listed in the table.

Vocabulary Term	Definition
Water cycle	?
Infiltration	?
Transpiration	?

W ater is everywhere on Earth—oceans, glaciers, rivers, lakes, air, soil, and living tissue. All of these reservoirs make up Earth's hydrosphere. Most of it—about 97.2 percent—is stored in oceans, as Figure 1 shows. Ice sheets and glaciers account for another 2.15 percent, leaving only 0.65 percent to be divided among lakes, streams, groundwater, and the atmosphere. The water found in glaciers, ice sheets, lakes, streams, groundwater, and the atmosphere may seem like a tiny percent of Earth's water, but the actual quantities are great.

The Water Cycle

Water constantly moves among the oceans, the atmosphere, the solid Earth, and the biosphere. This unending circulation of Earth's water supply is the water cycle. This cycle is possible because water readily changes from one state of matter—solid, liquid, or gas—to another at temperatures and pressure common on Earth's surface.

The water cycle, shown in Figure 2, is a gigantic worldwide system powered by energy from the sun. The atmosphere provides the most important link between the oceans and land. Water evaporates into the atmosphere from the ocean, and to a lesser extent from the continents. Winds transport this moisture-rich air until conditions cause the moisture to condense into clouds. Precipitation—rain and snow—then falls to Earth. Precipitation that falls into oceans has completed

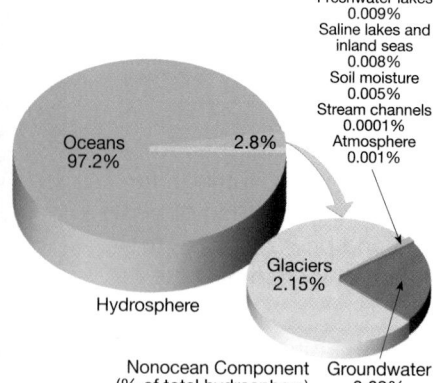

Freshwater lakes
0.009%
Saline lakes and
inland seas
0.008%
Soil moisture
0.005%
Stream channels
0.0001%
Atmosphere
0.001%

Oceans
97.2%   2.8%

Glaciers
2.15%

Hydrosphere

Nonocean Component   Groundwater
(% of total hydrosphere)   0.62%

Figure 1 Distribution of Earth's Water
Using Graphs *What percentage of Earth's water is not held in its oceans?*

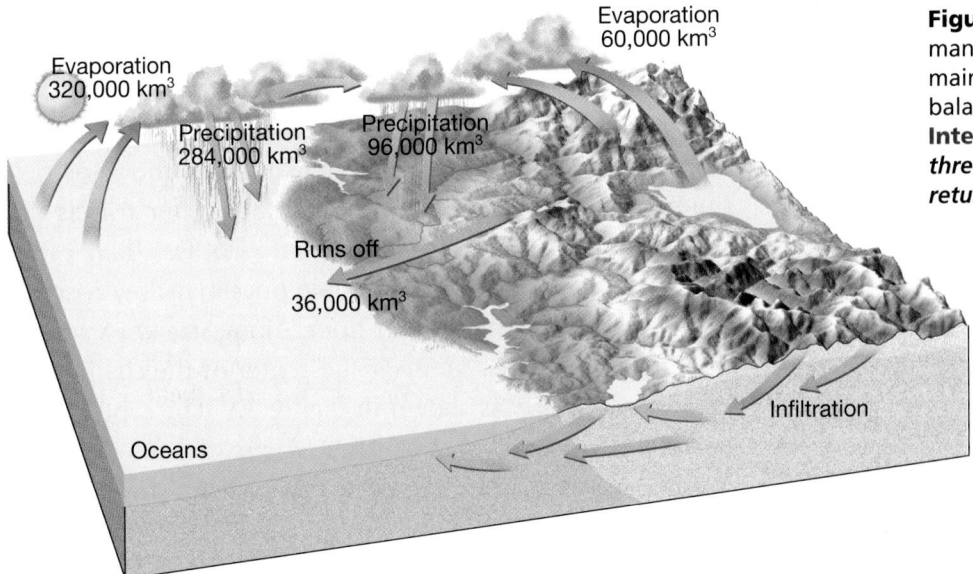

Evaporation
320,000 km³

Evaporation
60,000 km³

Precipitation
284,000 km³

Precipitation
96,000 km³

Runs off

36,000 km³

Infiltration

Oceans

Figure 2 The Water Cycle The many processes of the water cycle maintain Earth's overall water balance.
Interpreting Diagrams *In which three ways does precipitation return to oceans?*

one full cycle and is ready to begin another. However, water that falls on land must make its way back to the ocean to complete the full cycle.

 Reading Checkpoint) *What is Earth's hydrosphere?*

What happens to precipitation that falls on land? Some of it slowly soaks into the ground through infiltration. **Infiltration** is the movement of surface water into rock or soil through cracks and pore spaces. The water gradually moves through the land and actually seeps into lakes, streams, or the ocean. When the rate of rainfall exceeds Earth's ability to absorb it, the excess water flows over the surface into lakes and streams in a process called runoff. Much of that runoff returns to the atmosphere because of evaporation from the soil, lakes, and streams. Plants also absorb water and release it into the atmosphere through **transpiration.**

When precipitation falls in very cold areas—at high elevations or high latitudes—the water may not immediately soak in, run off, or evaporate. Instead, it may become part of a glacier. Glaciers store large amounts of water on land. If present-day glaciers were to melt and release all their water, ocean levels would rise by several dozen meters.

Earth's Water Balance

Even with all these processes occurring, Earth's water cycle is balanced. **Balance in the water cycle means the average annual precipitation over Earth equals the amount of water that evaporates.** There are local imbalances. For example, precipitation exceeds evaporation over continents. Over oceans, evaporation exceeds precipitation. However, the fact that the level of world oceans is not changing very much indicates the system is balanced.

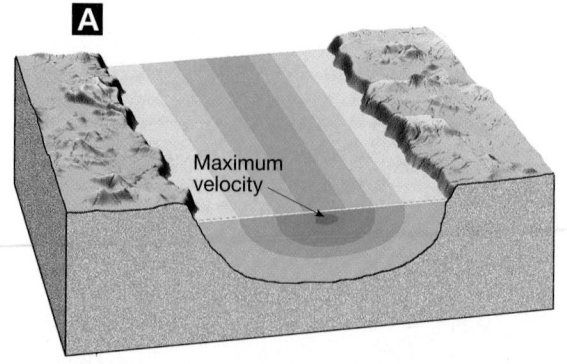

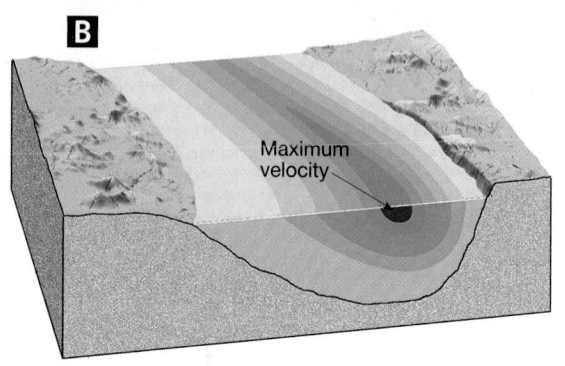

Figure 3 A Along straight stretches, stream velocity is highest at the center of the channel. **B** When a stream curves, its zone of maximum speed shifts toward the outer bank.
Interpreting Diagrams *How does velocity change with depth in the middle of the stream?*

Streamflow

Gravity influences the way water makes its way to the oceans. Streams and rivers carry water downhill from the land to the sea. The time this journey takes depends on the velocity of the stream. Velocity is the distance that water travels in a period of time. Some slow streams flow at less than 1 kilometer per hour, whereas a few rapid ones may flow at speeds that exceed 30 kilometers per hour. Along straight stretches, the highest velocities are near the center of the channel just below the surface, as shown in Figure 3A. The center of the channel is where friction is lowest. A stream's zone of maximum speed shifts toward its outer bank when a stream curves, as Figure 3B shows.

⬤ **The ability of a stream to erode and transport materials depends largely on its velocity.** Even slight changes in velocity greatly change the amount of sediment that water can transport. Several factors determine the velocity of a stream. They include its gradient; the shape, size, and roughness of its channel; and its discharge.

Gradient Gradient is the slope or steepness of a stream channel. Gradient is usually expressed as the vertical drop of a stream over a certain distance. Portions of the Mississippi River have very low gradients of 10 centimeters per kilometer or less. By contrast, some mountain streams tumble downhill at a rate of more than 40 meters per kilometer. This mountain stream's gradient is 400 times steeper than that of the lower Mississippi. Gradient varies over a stream's length and between streams. The steeper the gradient, the more energy the stream has as it flows downhill. Compare the steep and gentle gradients in Figure 4.

Figure 4 This cross section along the length of a stream shows a steeper gradient upstream, and a gentler gradient downstream.

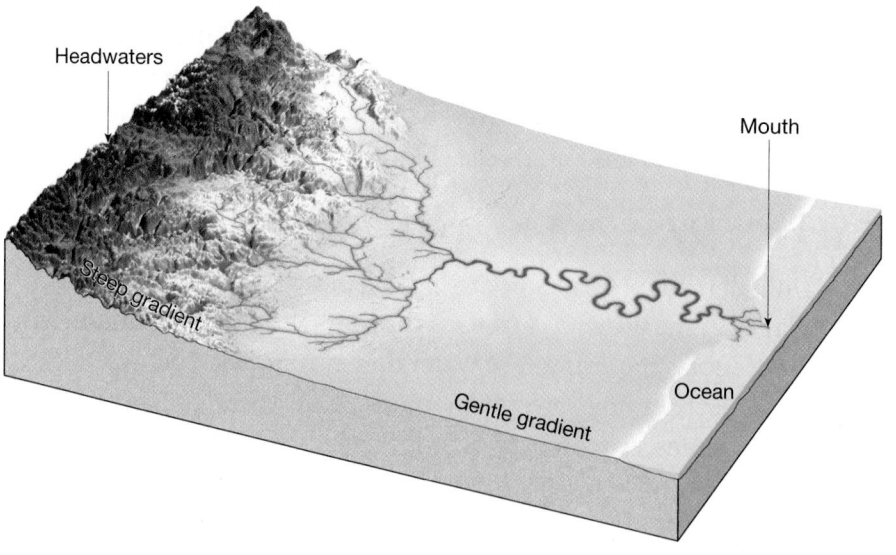

Channel Characteristics A **stream channel** is the course the water in a stream follows. As the water flows, it encounters friction from the sides and the bottom of its channel. This friction slows its forward movement. The shape, size, and roughness of the channel affect the amount of friction. For example, an irregular channel filled with boulders creates enough turbulence to slow the stream significantly. Water in a smooth channel flows more easily. Larger channels also have more efficient water flow because a smaller proportion of water is in contact with the channel surfaces.

Discharge The **discharge** of a stream is the volume of water flowing past a certain point in a given unit of time. Discharge is usually measured in cubic meters per second. Table 1 lists the world's largest rivers in terms of discharge. The discharges of most rivers change with rainfall and snowmelt. The size and velocity of the stream also changes when discharge changes. The stream channel widens and deepens to handle additional water. As the size of the channel increases, there is less friction and the water flows more swiftly .

Building urban centers around a stream channel can also affect discharge. For example, the magnitude and frequency of floods can increase. The construction of streets, parking lots, and buildings covers soil that once soaked up water. Less water soaks into the ground and runoff increases, especially at times of heavy rainfall. Also, because less water soaks into the ground, the dry season flow of streams is reduced greatly. Urbanization is just one example of how humans can interfere with the normal flow of streams.

 **Reading Checkpoint** *What factors determine the velocity of a stream?*

Table 1 World's Largest Rivers Ranked by Discharge			
Rank	River	Country	Average Discharge m³/s
1	Amazon	Brazil	212,400
2	Congo	Zaire	39,650
3	Yangtze	China	21,800
4	Brahmaputra	Bangladesh	19,800
5	Ganges	India	18,700
6	Yenisei	Russia	17,400
7	Mississippi	United States	17,300
8	Orinoco	Venezuela	17,000
9	Lena	Russia	15,500
10	Parana	Argentina	14,900

Changes from Upstream to Downstream

One useful way to study a stream is to look at its profile. A profile is a cross-sectional view of a stream from its source, or headwaters, to its mouth—the point downstream where the river empties into another body of water. In Figures 4 and 5, you can see that the most obvious feature of a typical stream profile is a decreasing gradient or slope from its headwaters to its mouth.

 **While gradient decreases between a stream's headwaters and mouth, discharge increases.** The amount of discharge increases because more and more tributaries enter the main channel as it moves downstream. A **tributary** is a stream that empties into another stream. In most humid regions, the groundwater supply adds even more water. As the river moves downstream, its width, depth, and velocity change with the increased volume of water it carries.

The observed increase in the average velocity of the water downstream contradicts what people may think about mountain streams. Most people believe that mountain streams are swift and lowland rivers are slow. Although a mountain stream may look like a violent, gushing flow of water, its average velocity is often less than the average velocity of a river near its mouth.

The difference in velocity is mostly due to the great efficiency of the larger downstream channel. In the headwaters area where the gradient may be steep, water often flows in a small channel over many boulders. The small channel and rough bed increase fiction. This increase in friction scatters the water in all directions and slows its movement. However, downstream the channel is usually smoother so that it offers less resistance to flow. The width and depth of the channel also increase toward the mouth to handle the greater discharge. These factors permit the water to flow more rapidly.

✓ **Reading Checkpoint** *What is a stream profile?*

Figure 5 Sea level is the ultimate base level of any stream.

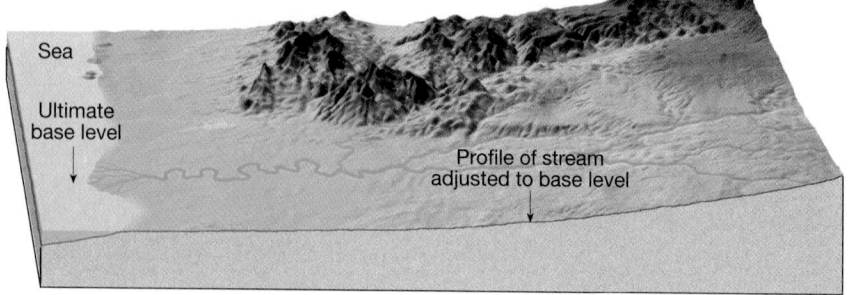

Sea

Ultimate base level

Profile of stream adjusted to base level

Base Level

Streams can't erode their channels endlessly. There is a lower limit to how deep a stream can erode. **Base level is the lowest point to which a stream can erode its channel.** The base level is the level at which the mouth of a stream enters the ocean, a lake, or another stream.

Figure 6 A river in a broad, flat-floored valley near base level often has a channel with many meanders. **Inferring** *Is the river in this picture close to or high above its base level?*

There are two types of base level—ultimate base level and temporary base level. As Figure 5 shows, sea level is the ultimate base level because it's the lowest level that stream erosion can lower the land. Temporary base levels include lakes, resistant layers of rock, and main streams that act as base level for their tributaries. For example, when a stream enters a lake, its velocity quickly approaches zero. Its ability to erode ceases. The lake prevents the stream from eroding below its level at any point upstream from the lake. However, because the outlet of the lake can cut downward and drain the lake, the lake is only a temporary obstacle to the stream's ability to erode its channel.

A stream in a broad, flat-bottomed valley that is near its base level often develops a course with many bends called **meanders,** as shown in Figure 6. If base level dropped or the land was uplifted the river, which is now considerably above base level, would have excess energy and would downcut its channel. The result could be incised meanders—a winding river in a steep, narrow valley, as shown in Figure 7.

Figure 7 When land is gradually uplifted, a meandering river adjusts to being higher above base level by downcutting. The result can be a landscape with incised meanders, such as these in Utah's Canyonlands National Park.

For: Links on river systems
Visit: www.SciLinks.org
Web Code: cjn-2062

Section 6.1 Assessment

Reviewing Concepts

1. What is the water cycle?
2. How is Earth's water cycle balanced?
3. Where is most of Earth's water located?
4. What part does infiltration play in the water cycle?
5. What factor most influences the power of a stream to erode and transport material?
6. How do gradient and discharge change between a stream's headwaters and its mouth?
7. How might lowering base level affect stream erosion?

Critical Thinking

8. **Relating Cause and Effect** What would happen if evaporation exceeded precipitation over the continents and oceans?
9. **Comparing and Contrasting** How does the development of urban areas along streams and rivers affect discharge during periods of heavy rainfall?

Math **Practice**

10. A stream that is 27 kilometers long drops 90 meters in elevation from its headwaters to its mouth. What is the stream's gradient?

6.2 The Work of Streams

Reading Focus

Key Concepts

 How do streams erode their channels and transport sediment?

How does stream deposition occur?

What are the two types of stream valleys?

What causes floods, and what are the major flood control measures?

What is the relationship between a stream and a drainage basin?

Vocabulary

- bed load
- capacity
- alluvium
- delta
- natural levee
- floodplain
- flood
- drainage basin
- divide

Reading Strategy

Monitoring Your Understanding Preview the Key Concepts, topic headings, vocabulary, and figures in this section. List two things you expect to learn about each. After reading, state what you learned about each item you listed.

What I Expect to Learn	What I Learned

Streams are Earth's most important agents of erosion. They can downcut or erode their channels. They can also transport enormous amounts of sediment. Most of the sediment a stream carries comes from weathering. Weathering produces huge amounts of material that are delivered to the stream by sheet flow, mass movements, and groundwater. Eventually, streams drop much of this material to create many different depositional features.

Erosion

Streams generally erode their channels lifting loose particles by abrasion, grinding, and by dissolving soluble material. When the flow of water is turbulent enough, it can dislodge loose particles from the channel and lift them into the moving water. In this manner, the force of running water rapidly erodes some streambeds and banks. The stronger the current is, the more erosional power it has and the more effectively the water will pick up particles.

Sand and gravel carried in a stream can erode solid rock channels like sandpaper grinds down wood. Moreover, pebbles caught in swirling stream currents can act like cutting tools and bore circular "potholes" into the channel floor.

 **Reading Checkpoint** *What are three ways that streams erode their channels?*

Sediment Transport

Streams transport sediment in three ways.
1. in solution (dissolved load)
2. in suspension (suspended load)
3. scooting or rolling along the bottom (bed load)

Dissolved Load Most of the dissolved load enters streams through groundwater. Some of this load also enters by dissolving rock along the stream's course. The amount of material the stream carries in solution changes depending on climate and the geologic setting. Usually the dissolved load is expressed as parts of dissolved material per million parts of water (parts per million, or ppm). Some rivers may have a dissolved load of 1000 ppm or more. However, the average figure for the world's rivers is estimated at 115 to 120 ppm. Streams supply almost 4 billion metric tons of dissolved substances to the oceans each year.

Suspended Load Most streams carry the largest part of their load in suspension. The visible cloud of sediment suspended in the water is the most obvious portion of a stream's load. Streams usually carry only sand, silt, and clay this way. However, streams also transport larger particles during a flood because water velocity increases. The total amount of material a stream carries in suspension increases dramatically during floods, as shown in Figure 8.

Bed Load Bed load is that part of a stream's load of solid material that is made up of sediment too large to be carried in suspension. These larger, coarser particles move along the bottom, or bed, of the stream channel. The suspended and dissolved loads are always moving. But the bed load moves only when the force of the water is great enough to move the larger particles. The grinding action of the bed load is very important in eroding the stream channel.

Figure 8 During this 1997 flood, the suspended load in the muddy Ohio River is clearly visible. The greatest erosion and sediment transport occur during floods. **Applying Concepts** *What other types of load might account for the muddiness of the river?*

Competence and Capacity The ability of streams to carry a load is determined by two factors: the stream's competence and its capacity. Competence of a stream measures the largest particles it can transport. A stream's competence increases with its velocity. In fact, the competence of a stream increases four times when the velocity doubles.

The **capacity** of a stream is the maximum load it can carry. Capacity is directly related to a stream's discharge. The greater the volume of water in a stream is, the greater its capacity is for carrying sediment.

Mississippi Delta Region

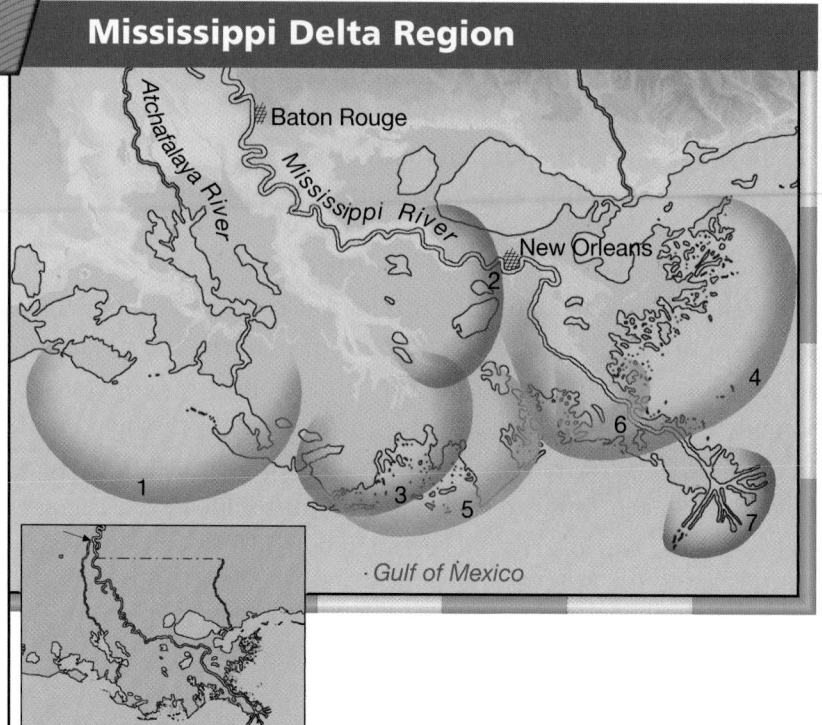

Figure 9

Movement This map shows the growth of the Mississippi River delta over the past 5,000 to 6,000 years. As you can see, the river has built a series of sub-deltas, one after the other. The numbers indicate the order in which they were deposited.
Locating In which overall direction has the Mississippi River built its delta over the past few thousand years?
Locating How has the growth of the delta changed the location of the mouth of the Mississippi River in relation to New Orleans?

Deposition

Whenever a stream slows down, the situation reverses. As a stream's velocity decreases, its competence decreases and sediment begins to drop out, largest particles first. Each particle size has a critical settling velocity. 🔊 **Deposition occurs as streamflow drops below the critical settling velocity of a certain particle size. The sediment in that category begins to settle out.** Stream transport separates solid particles of various sizes, large to small. This process is called sorting. It explains why particles of similar size are deposited together.

The sorted material deposited by as stream is called **alluvium.** Many different depositional features are made of alluvium. Some occur within stream channels. Some occur on the valley floor next to the channel. And others occur at the mouth of a stream.

Deltas When a stream enters the relatively still waters of an ocean or lake, its velocity drops. As a result, the stream deposits sediment and forms a delta. A **delta** is an accumulation of sediment formed where a stream enters a lake or ocean. As a delta grows outward, the stream's gradient lessens and the water slows down. The channel becomes choked with sediment settling out of the slow-moving water. As a result, the river changes direction as it seeks a shorter route to base level. The main channel often divides into several smaller channels called distributaries as shown in sub-delta 7 in Figure 9. These shifting channels act in the opposite way of tributaries.

Rather than carrying water into the main channel like tributaries, distributaries carry water away. After many shifts of the channel, a delta may grow into a triangular shape, like the Greek letter delta (Δ). However, not all deltas have this idealized shape. Differences in the shapes of shorelines and variations in the strength of waves and currents result in different shapes of deltas.

Natural Levees Some rivers occupy valleys with broad, flat floors. Successive floods over many years can build natural levees along them. A **natural levee** is a landform that parallels some streams. They form when a stream overflows its banks. When it overflows, its velocity rapidly decreases and leaves coarse sediment deposits in strips that border the channel. As the water spreads out over the valley, less sediment is deposited. This uneven distribution of material produces the gentle slope of the natural levee.

Stream Valleys

Narrow Valleys The Yellowstone River, shown in Figure 10, is an excellent example of a narrow valley. **A narrow V-shaped valley shows that the stream's primary work has been downcutting toward base level.** Rapids and waterfalls are the most prominent features of a narrow valley. Both rapids and waterfalls occur where the stream profile drops rapidly. The variations in the erosion of the underlying bedrock cause these rapid drops.

Wide Valleys Once a stream has cut its channel closer to base level, downward erosion becomes less dominant. More of the stream's energy is directed from side to side. The result is a widening of the valley as the river cuts away first at one bank and then at the other.

The side-to-side cutting of a stream eventually produces a flat valley floor, or **floodplain.** A floodplain is appropriately named because during a flood the river overflows its banks and floods the plain.

Streams that flow on floodplains move in meanders. Once a bend in a channel begins to form, it grows larger. Most of the erosion occurs on the outside of the meander—often called the cut bank—where velocity and turbulence are greatest. Much of the debris the stream removes at the cut bank moves downstream where it is deposited as point bars. Point bars form in zones of decreased velocity on the insides of meanders. In this way, meanders move side to side by eroding the outside of bends and depositing on the inside.

Figure 10 The Yellowstone River is an example of a V-shaped valley. The rapids and waterfall show that the river is vigorously downcutting the channel.

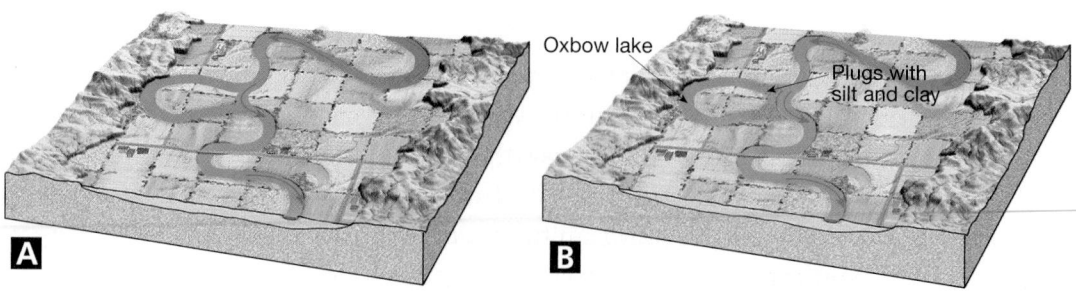

Figure 11 A One meander has overtaken the next, forming a ring of water on the floodplain. **B** After deposits of sediment cut off the ring, an oxbow lake forms.

Oxbow lake

Plugs with silt and clay

A

B

Erosion is more effective on the downstream side of a meander because of the slope of the channel. The bends gradually travel down the valley. Sometimes the downstream movement of a meander slows when it reaches a more resistant portion of the floodplain. This resistance allows the next meander upstream to overtake it, as shown in Figure 11. Gradually the neck of land between the meanders is narrowed. Eventually the river may erode through the narrow neck of land to the next loop. The new, shorter channel segment is called a cutoff and, because of its shape, the abandoned bend is called an oxbow lake. Such a situation is shown in the bottom portion of Figure 6 on page 163.

Floods and Flood Control

A **flood** occurs when the discharge of a stream becomes so great that it exceeds the capacity of its channel and overflows its banks. Floods are the most common and most destructive of all natural geologic hazards.

Most floods are caused by rapid spring snow melt or storms that bring heavy rains over a large region. Heavy rains caused the devastating floods in the upper Mississippi River Valley during the summer of 1993, as shown in Figure 12.

Unlike far-reaching regional floods, flash floods are more limited in extent. However, flash floods occur with little warning, and they can be deadly as walls of water sweep through river valleys. Several factors

MAP✦MASTER™ Skills Activity

Mississippi River Flooding

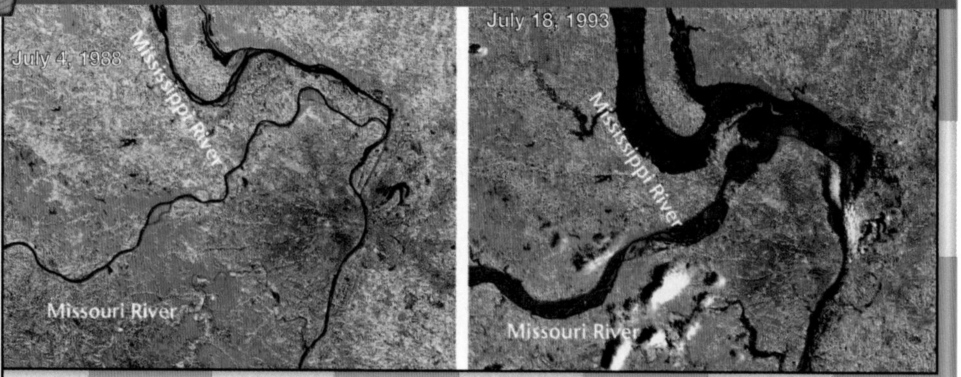

Figure 12

Region These satellite images show the confluence of the Missouri and Mississippi rivers. The first photo shows the rivers during normal flow.
Interpreting Photographs What does the second satellite image show? How do you know?

July 4, 1988

July 18, 1993

Mississippi River

Mississippi River

Missouri River

Missouri River

influence flash floods: rainfall intensity and duration, surface conditions, and topography. As you have learned, many urban areas are susceptible to flash floods. Mountainous areas are also susceptible because steep slopes can send runoff into narrow canyons.

Human interference with the stream system can worsen or even cause floods. A prime example is the failure of a dam or an artificial levee. These structures are designed to contain floods of a certain size. If that size is exceeded, water can then spill over or break through a dam or levee and rush downstream causing a disastrous flood.

There are several flood control strategies.  **Measures to control flooding include artificial levees, flood control dams, and placing limits on floodplain development.**

Artificial Levees Artificial levees are earthen mounds built on the banks of a river. These levees increase the volume of water a channel can hold. When levees confine a river during periods of high water, the river often deposits material in its channel as the discharge diminishes. This discharge is sediment that would have been dropped on the floodplain. Because the stream cannot deposit material outside of its channel the bottom of the channel is gradually built up. When the channel is built up, it takes less water to overflow the levee. As a result, people may have to raise the height of the levee periodically to protect the floodplain behind it. Moreover, many artificial levees are not built to withstand periods of extreme flooding. For example, there were many levee failures in the Midwest during the summer of 1993 when the upper Mississippi experienced record flooding.

Flood-Control Dam Flood-control dams store floodwater and then let it out slowly. Since the 1920s, thousands of dams have been built on nearly every major river in the United States. Many dams have other non-flood related functions, such as providing water for irrigation and for hydroelectric power generation.

Although dams may reduce flooding and provide other benefits, building dams has consequences. For example, dams trap sediment. Deltas and floodplains downstream can erode because silt no longer replenishes them during floods. Built up sediment behind a dam means the volume of the stored water will gradually diminish. This build-up reduces the effectiveness of the dam for flood control. Large dams also cause ecological damage to river environments.

Limiting Development Today many scientists and engineers advocate sound floodplain management instead of building structures. That often means preserving floodplains in their natural state. Minimizing development on floodplains allows them to absorb floodwaters with little harm to homes and businesses.

Q Sometimes a major flood is described as a 100-year flood. What does that mean?

A The phrase "100-year flood" is misleading because it makes people believe that such an event happens only once every 100 years. In truth, a huge flood can happen any year. The phrase "100-year flood" is really a statistical designation. It indicates that there is a 1-in-100 chance that a flood this size will happen during any year. Perhaps a better term would be the "1-in-100 chance flood."

Drainage Basins

Every stream has a drainage basin. ⬬ **A drainage basin is the land area that contributes water to a stream.** An imaginary line called a **divide** separates the drainage basins of one stream from another. Divides range in scale from a ridge separating two small gullies on a hillside to a continental divide, which splits continents into enormous drainage basins. The Mississippi River has the largest drainage basin in North America. See Figure 13. The river and its tributaries collect water from more than 3.2 million square kilometers of the continent.

Figure 13 Mississippi River Drainage Basin Divides are the boundaries that separate drainage basins from each other.

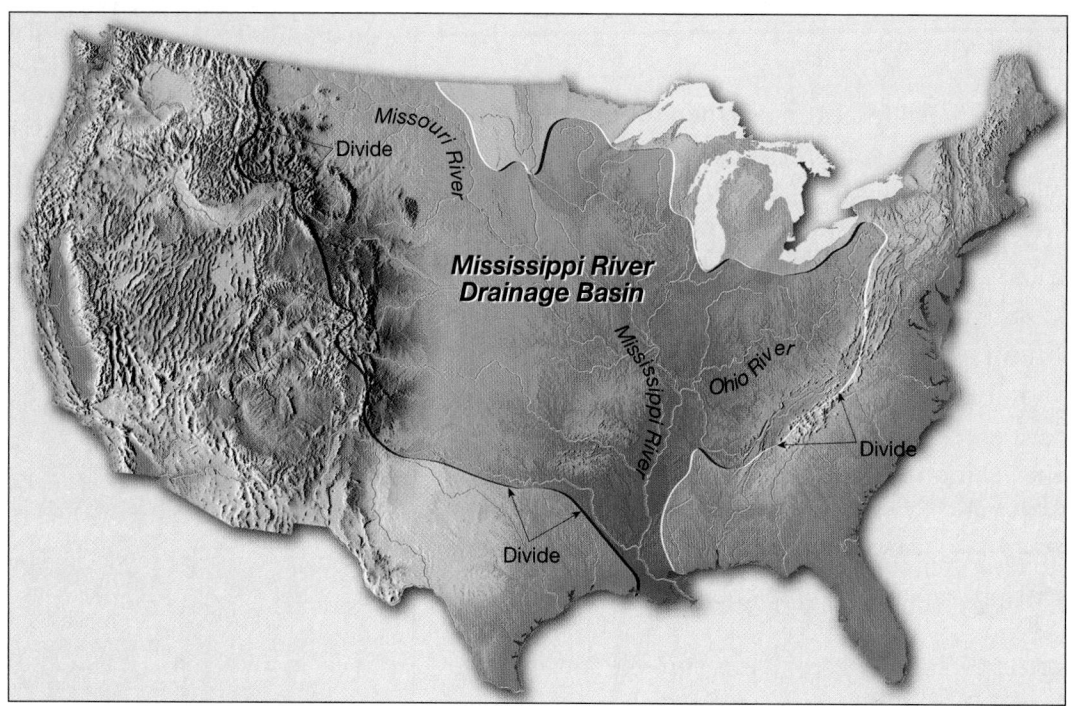

Missouri River

Divide

Mississippi River Drainage Basin

Mississippi River

Ohio River

Divide

Divide

Section 6.2 Assessment

Reviewing Concepts

1. ⬬ How do streams erode their channels?
2. ⬬ What causes floods?
3. ⬬ What is the relationship between a stream and a drainage basin?
4. ⬬ How do streams transport sediments?

Critical Thinking

5. **Analyzing Concepts** How does urban development interfere with the natural function of floodplains?

6. **Summarizing** Explain the formation of one of the landforms that streams create by deposition.

Writing in Science

Descriptive Paragraph Use library sources or the Internet to research the causes of a recent major flood. Write a paragraph that tells the name of the flood, when it happened, where it happened, and the conditions that led to the flood itself.

6.3 Water Beneath the Surface

Reading Focus

Key Concepts

- Where is groundwater and how does it move?
- How do springs form?
- What are some environmental threats to groundwater supplies?
- How and where do most caverns form?
- What landforms are common in an area of karst topography?

Vocabulary

- zone of saturation
- groundwater
- water table
- porosity
- permeability
- aquifer
- spring
- geyser
- well
- artesian well
- cavern
- travertine
- karst topography
- sinkhole

Reading Strategy

Previewing Copy the table below. Before you read the section, rewrite the green topic headings as how, why, and what questions. As you read, write an answer to each question.

Question	Answer
How does water move underground?	

The ground beneath your feet isn't as solid as you might think. It includes countless tiny pore spaces between grains of soil and sediment. It also contains narrow joints and fractures in bedrock. Together these spaces add up to an immense volume of tiny openings where water collects underground and moves.

Underground water in wells and springs provides water for cities, crops, livestock, and industry. In the United States, it is the drinking water for more than 50 percent of the population. It also provides 40 percent of the irrigation water and more than 25 percent of industry's needs.

Distribution and Movement of Water Underground

When rain falls, some of the water runs off, some evaporates, and the rest soaks into the ground to become subsurface water. The amount of water that ends up underground in an area depends on the steepness of slopes, the nature of surface materials, the intensity of rainfall, and the type and amount of vegetation.

Distribution Some of the water soaks into the ground, but it does not travel far. Molecular attraction holds it in place as a surface film on soil particles. This near-surface zone is called the belt of soil moisture. Roots, voids left by decayed roots, and animal and worm burrows crisscross this zone. These features help rainwater seep into soil.

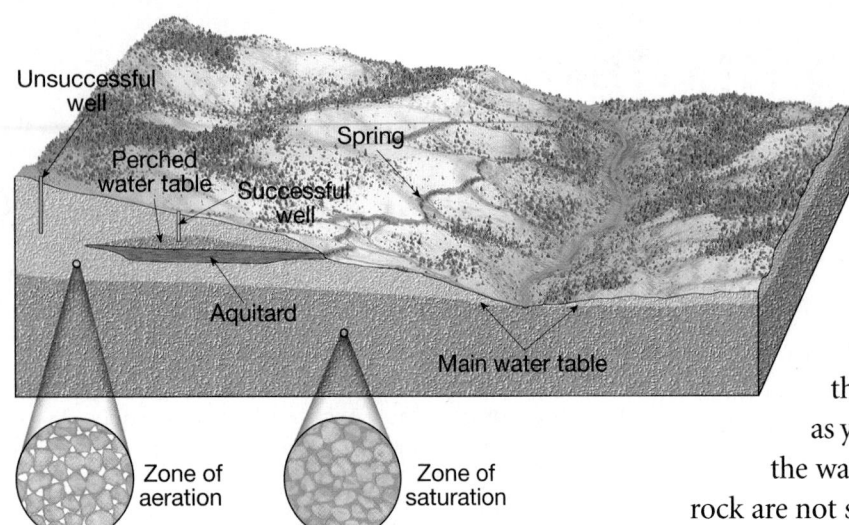

Unsuccessful well

Perched water table

Spring

Successful well

Aquitard

Main water table

Zone of aeration

Zone of saturation

Figure 14 This diagram shows the relative positions of many features associated with subsurface water.
Applying Concepts *What is the source of the spring in the center of the illustration?*

Figure 15 A spring flows from a valley wall into a stream.

🔵 Much of the water in soil seeps downward until it reaches the zone of saturation. The zone of saturation is the area where water fills all of the open spaces in sediment and rock. Groundwater is the water within this zone. The upper limit of the zone of saturation is the **water table,** as you can see in Figure 14. The area above the water table where the soil, sediment, and rock are not saturated is the zone of aeration. Wells cannot pump water from this zone. The water clings too tightly to the rocks and soil. Only below the water table—where water pressure is great enough to allow water to enter wells—can water be pumped.

Movement The flow and storage of groundwater vary depending on the subsurface material. The amount of groundwater that can be stored depends on porosity. **Porosity** is the percentage of the total volume of rock or sediment that consists of pore spaces. Spaces between sedimentary particles form pore spaces. Joints, faults, and cavities also are formed by the dissolving of soluble rocks such as limestone.

Rock or sediment may be very porous and still block water's movement. The **permeability** of a material is its ability to release a fluid. 🔵 **Groundwater moves by twisting and turning through interconnected small openings. The groundwater moves more slowly when the pore spaces are smaller.** If the spaces between particles are too small, water cannot move at all. For example, clay has high porosity. But clay is impermeable because its pore spaces are so small that water can't move through them.

Impermeable layers that get in the way or prevent water movement are aquitards. Larger particles, such as sand, have larger pore spaces. Water moves through them easily. Permeable rock layers or sediments that transmit groundwater freely are **aquifers.** Aquifers are important because they are the source of well water.

Springs

🔵 **A spring forms whenever the water table intersects the ground surface.** A **spring** is a flow of groundwater that emerges naturally at the ground surface, as shown in Figure 15. Springs form when an aquitard blocks downward movement of groundwater and forces it to move laterally.

Hot Springs A hot spring is 6°C to 9°C warmer than the mean annual air temperature where the spring occurs. There are more than 1000 hot springs in the United States

Temperatures in deep mines and oil wells usually rise with an increase in depth at an average of 2°C per 100 meters. So when groundwater circulates at great depths, it becomes heated. If it rises to the surface, the water may emerge as a hot spring. This process heats many hot springs in the eastern United States. However, more than 95 percent of the hot springs in the United States are in the West. The source of heat for most of these hot springs is cooling igneous rock. In some places, hot acidic groundwater mixes with minerals from adjacent rock to form thick, bubbling mineral springs called mudpots.

Geysers A **geyser** is an intermittent hot spring or fountain in which a column of water shoots up with great force at various intervals. Geysers often shoot up columns of water 30 to 60 meters. After the jet of water stops, a column of steam rushes out—usually with a thundering roar. Perhaps the most famous geyser in the world is Old Faithful in Yellowstone National Park. It erupts about once each hour.

Geysers occur where extensive underground chambers exist within hot igneous rocks. Follow the formation of a geyser in Figure 16. As relatively cool groundwater enters the chambers, the surrounding rock heats it. The weight of the overlying water creates great pressure at the bottom of the chamber. This pressure prevents the water from boiling at the normal surface temperature of 100°C. However, the heat makes the water expand, and it forces some of the water out at the surface. This loss of water reduces the pressure in the chamber. The boiling point drops. Some of the water deep within the chamber then turns to steam and makes the geyser erupt. Following the eruption, cool groundwater again seeps into the chamber. Then the cycle begins again.

 *What is a geyser?*

Geyser Eruption Cycle

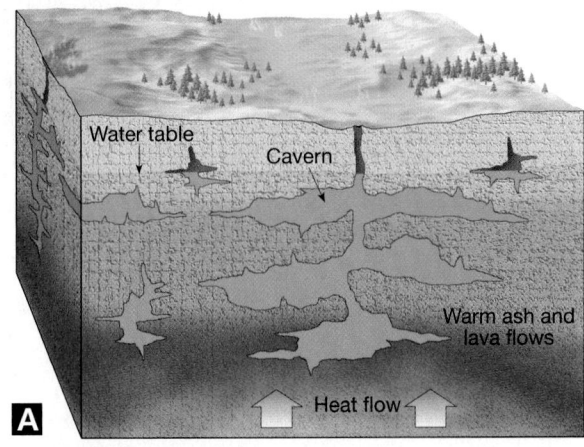

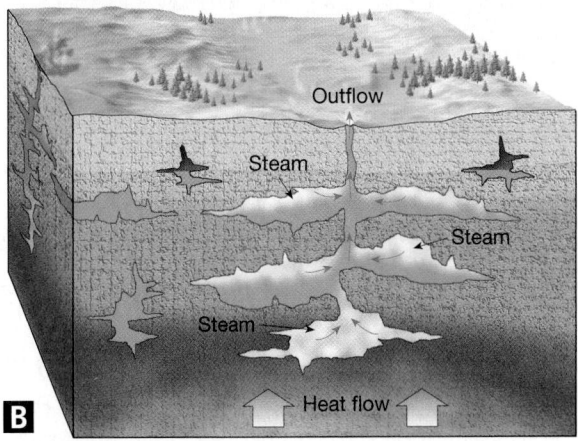

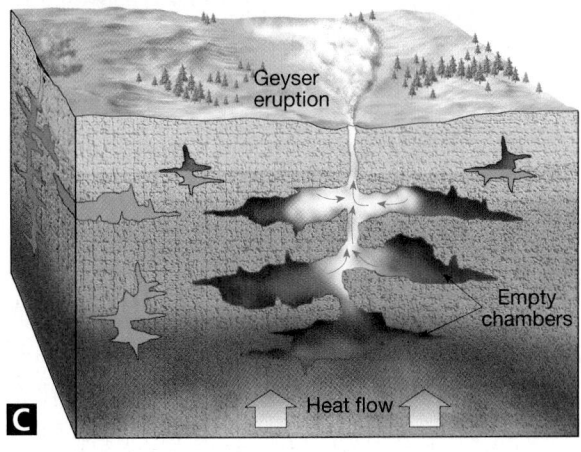

Figure 16 A Groundwater enters underground caverns and fractures in hot igneous rock where it is heated to near its boiling point. **B** Heating causes the water to expand, with some being forced out at the surface. The loss of water reduces the pressure on the remaining water, thus reducing its boiling temperature. Some of the water flashes to steam. **C** The rapidly expanding steam forces the hot water out of the chambers to produce a geyser. The empty chambers fill again, and the cycle starts anew.

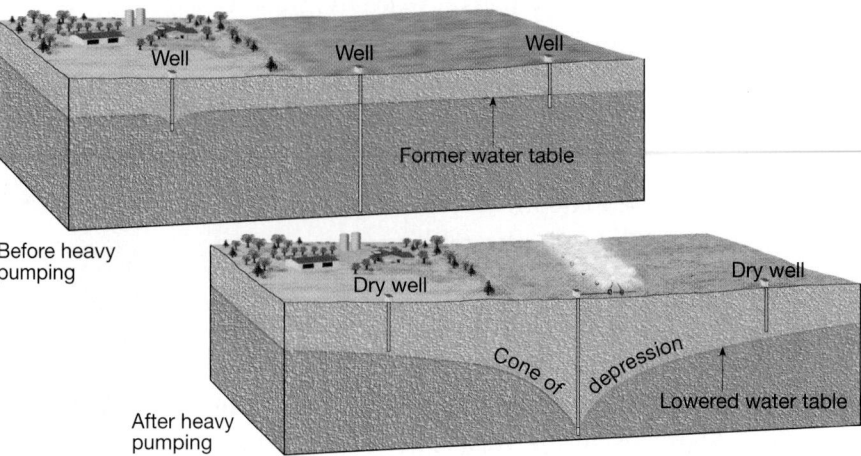

Figure 17 A cone of depression in the water table often forms around a pumping well. If heavy pumping lowers the water table, some wells may be left dry.

Before heavy pumping

After heavy pumping

Q *I have heard people say that supplies of groundwater can be located using a forked stick. Can this actually be done?*

A What you describe is a practice called "water dowsing." In the classic method, a person holding a forked stick walks back and forth over an area. When water is detected, the bottom of the "Y" is supposed to be attracted downward.

Geologists and engineers are extremely doubtful, to say the least. Case histories and demonstrations may seem convincing, but when dowsing is exposed to scientific scrutiny, it fails. Most "successful" examples of water dowsing occur in places where water would be hard to miss. In a region of adequate rainfall and favorable geology, it is difficult to drill and *not* find water!

For: Links on aquifers
Visit: www.SciLinks.org
Web Code: 2064

Wells

A **well** is a hole bored into the zone of saturation. Irrigation for agriculture is by far the single greatest use of well water in the United States—more than 65 percent of groundwater used annually. Industrial uses of groundwater rank a distant second, followed by the amount used by homes.

The level of the water table may change considerably during a year. The level can drop during the dry season and rise following periods of rain. To ensure a continuous water supply, a well must penetrate far below the water table. The water table around the well drops whenever a substantial amount of water is withdrawn from a well. This effect is called drawdown, and it decreases with an increase in distance from the well. The result of a drawdown is a cone of depression in the water table. This cone of depression is shown in Figure 17. For most small domestic wells, the cone of depression is tiny. However, when wells are used for irrigation or industry, a very wide and steep cone of depression can result.

Water must be pumped out of most wells. However, water rises on its own in some wells, sometimes overflowing the surface. An **artesian well** is any formation in which groundwater rises on its own under pressure. For such a situation to occur, two conditions must exist. First, water must be in an aquifer that is tilted so that one end is exposed at the surface, where it can receive water. Second, there must be aquitards both above and below the aquifer to stop the water from escaping. The pressure created by the weight of the water above forces the water to rise when a well taps the aquifer.

 *How does an artesian well differ from most wells?*

Environmental Problems Associated with Groundwater

As with many valuable natural resources, groundwater is being threatened at an increasing rate. **Overuse and contamination threatens groundwater supplies in some areas.**

Treating Groundwater as a Nonrenewable Resource

Groundwater seems like an endlessly renewable resource. However, supplies are finite. In some regions, the amount of water available to recharge an aquifer is much less than the amount being withdrawn.

The High Plains provides one example of severe groundwater depletion. In some parts of the region, intense irrigation has gone on for a long time. Even if pumping were to stop now, it could take thousands of years for the groundwater to be fully replenished.

The ground may sink when water is pumped from wells faster than natural processes can replace it. As water is withdrawn, the ground subsides because the weight of the overburden packs relatively loose sediment grains more tightly together.

This type of subsidence is extreme in the San Joaquin Valley of California, as shown in Figure 18. Land subsidence due to groundwater withdrawal for irrigation began there in the mid-1920s. It exceeded eight meters by 1970. During a drought in 1976 and 1977, heavy groundwater pumping led the ground to sink even more. Land subsidence affected more than 13,400 square kilometers of irrigable land—one half the entire valley.

Groundwater Contamination

The pollution of groundwater is a serious matter, particularly in areas where aquifers provide much of the water supply. Common sources of groundwater pollution are sewage from septic tanks, farm wastes, and inadequate or broken sewers.

If sewage water that is contaminated with bacteria enters the groundwater system, it may become purified through natural processes. The harmful bacteria can be mechanically filtered by the sediment through which the water passes, destroyed by chemical oxidation, and/or assimilated by other organisms. For purification to occur, however, the aquifer must be of the correct composition.

For example, extremely permeable aquifers have such large openings that contaminated groundwater may travel long distances without being cleansed. In this case, the water flows too quickly and is not in contact with the surrounding material long enough for purification to occur. This is the problem at Well 1 in Figure 19A.

 **Reading Checkpoint** *What are some common sources of groundwater pollution?*

Figure 18 The marks on the utility pole indicate the level of the surrounding land in years past. Between 1925 and 1975 this part of the San Joaquin Valley sank almost 9 meters because of the withdrawal of groundwater and the resulting compaction of sediments.

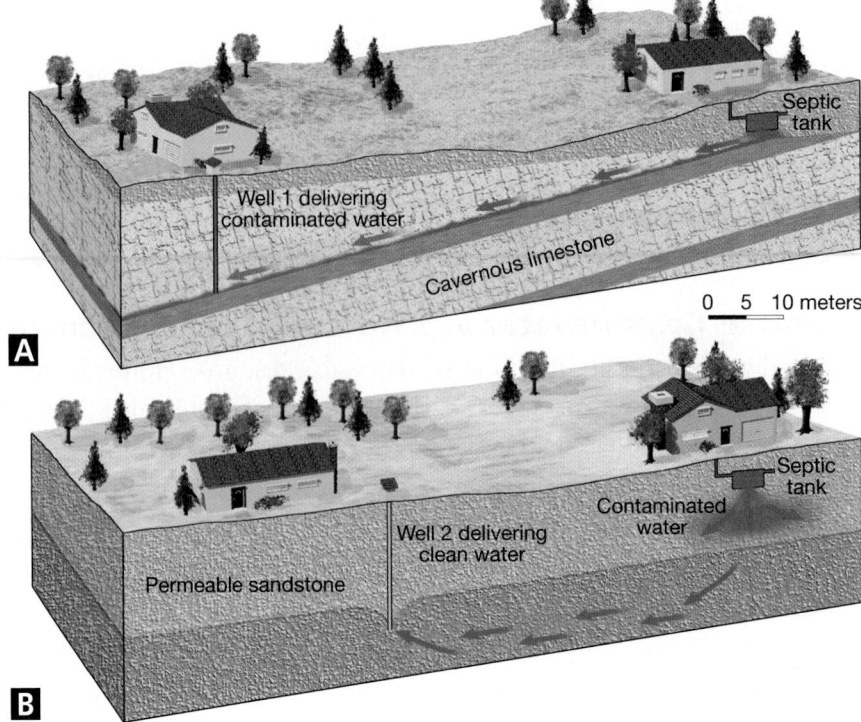

Figure 19 A Although the contaminated water has traveled more than 100 meters before reaching Well 1, the water moves too quickly through the cavernous limestone to be purified. **B** As the discharge from the septic tank percolates through the permeable sandstone, it is purified in a short distance.

Figure 20 Agricultural chemicals sprayed on farm fields can seep into soil and contaminate underground water supplies.

Figure 21 If landfills leak, harmful waste buried in them can escape into groundwater.

However, when the aquifer is composed of sand or permeable sandstone, the water can sometimes be purified after traveling only a few dozen meters through it. The openings between sand grains are large enough to permit water movement, yet the movement of the water is slow enough to allow enough time for its purification. This is the case at Well 2 in Figure 19B.

Other sources and types of contamination also threaten supplies, as you can see in Figures 20 and 21. These include fertilizers that are spread across the land, pesticides, and highway salt. In addition, chemicals and industrial materials—some hazardous—may leak from pipelines, storage tanks, landfills, and holding ponds. As rainwater oozes through the refuse, it may dissolve contaminants. If this material reaches the water table, it will mix with and contaminate groundwater. In coastal areas, heavy use can deplete aquifers, causing underground saltwater to enter wells.

Once the source of the problem has been identified and eliminated, the most common practice is to abandon the water supply. Abandoning the water supply allows the pollutants to flush out gradually. It's the least costly and easiest solution, but the aquifer must stay unused for years. To speed up this process, engineers sometimes pump out and treat polluted water. The aquifer then recharges naturally, or the treated water is pumped back in. This process can be risky, because there is no way to be sure that treatment has removed all the pollution. Prevention remains the most effective solution to groundwater contamination.

Some substances in groundwater are natural. Ions of substances (from adjacent rock) such as calcium and iron make some water "hard." Hard water forms scum with soap instead of suds. It can also deposit residue that clogs pipes. But hard water is generally not a health risk.

Caverns

The most spectacular results of ground-water's ability to erode rock are limestone caverns. Soluble rocks, especially limestone, underlie millions of square kilometers of Earth's surface. Limestone is nearly insoluble in pure water. But water containing small quantities of carbonic acid dissolves it easily. Most natural water contains the weak acid because rainwater dissolves carbon dioxide from the air and decaying plants. Therefore, when groundwater comes in contact with limestone, the carbonic acid reacts with calcite in the rocks. Calcium bicarbonate forms. As groundwater carries away calcium carbonate in solution, it slowly erodes rock. A **cavern** is a naturally formed underground chamber, such as the one you see in Figure 22. There are thousands of caverns in the United States. Most are fairly small, but some have spectacular dimensions. Carlsbad Caverns in southeastern New Mexico is a famous example. One chamber has an area equivalent to 14 football fields, and it is high enough to fit the U.S. Capitol building inside it.

Figure 22 The dissolving action of groundwater creates caverns. These dripstone features are in Three Fingers Cave in New Mexico.

Erosion forms most caverns at or below the water table in the zone of saturation. Here, acidic groundwater follows lines of weakness in the rock, such as joints and bedding planes. As time passes, the dissolving process slowly creates cavities and enlarges them into caverns. Material the groundwater dissolves eventually flows into streams and then the ocean.

The features that produce the greatest curiosity for most cavern visitors are depositional stone formations. These formations give some caverns a wonderland appearance. They form from seemingly endless dripping of water over great spans of time. The calcium carbonate that is left behind produces the limestone we call **travertine.** These cave deposits are commonly called dripstone.

Although the formation of caverns takes place in the zone of saturation, the deposition of dripstone features is not possible until the caverns are above the water table in the zone of aeration. The formation of caverns in the zone of aeration commonly occurs as nearby streams cut their valleys deeper. As the elevation of the stream drops, the water table also lowers, leaving the caverns high and largely dry.

Figure 23 Soda straw stalactites in Great Basin National Park's Lehman Caves.
Relating Cause and Effect
What part do these drops of water play in the formation of the stalactites?

Dripstone Features Perhaps the most familiar dripstone features are stalactites. Stalactites are icicle-like stone pendants that hang from the ceiling of a cavern. They form when water seeps through cracks in the cavern ceiling. When water reaches air in the cave, some of the dissolved carbon dioxide escapes from the drop and calcite begins to separate out. Deposition occurs as a ring around the edge of the water drops. As drops fall, each one leaves a tiny trace of calcite behind. This calcite creates a hollow limestone tube called a soda straw, as shown in Figure 23. Often the hollow tube becomes plugged or its supply of water increases. When a stalactite becomes plugged or the water supply increases, the water flows and deposits along the outside of the tube. As deposition continues, the stalactite takes on the more common conical shape.

Stalagmites are formations that develop on the floor of a cavern and reach up toward the ceiling. The water supplying the calcite for stalagmite growth falls from the ceiling and splatters over the surface of the cavern floor. As a result, stalagmites do not have a central tube. They are usually more massive and more rounded on their upper ends than stalactites. Given enough time, a downward-growing stalactite and an upward-growing stalagmite may join to form a column.

 **Reading Checkpoint** *What is a dripstone deposit?*

Karst Topography

Many areas of the world have landscapes that have been shaped largely by the dissolving power of groundwater. These areas are said to have **karst topography.** This term comes from the *Krs* region of Slovenia, where such topography is strikingly developed. In the United States, karst landscapes occur in many areas that are underlain by limestone. These areas include parts of Kentucky, Tennessee, Alabama, southern Indiana, and central northern Florida.

Karst areas typically have irregular terrain, with many depressions called sinkholes. A **sinkhole** is a depression produced in a region where groundwater has removed soluble rock. In the limestone areas of Florida, Kentucky, and southern Indiana, there are tens of thousands of these depressions. They vary in depth from just a meter or two to more than 50 meters.

Sinkholes commonly form in one of two ways. Some develop gradually over many years without any physical disturbance to the rock. In these situations, downward-seeping rainwater containing carbon dioxide dissolves limestone below the soil. These depressions are fairly shallow and have gentle slopes. Sinkholes can also form suddenly when the roof of a cavern collapses. The depressions created in this way are steep-sided and deep. When they form in populated areas, they may be a serious geologic hazard, as shown in Figure 24.

In addition to a surface pockmarked by sinkholes, karst regions usually show a striking lack of surface drainage (streams). Following a rainfall, runoff is quickly funneled below ground through sinkholes. It then flows through caverns until it finally reaches the water table. Where streams do exist at the surface, their paths are usually short. The names of such streams often give a clue to their fate. In the Mammoth Cave area of Kentucky, for example, there is Sinking Creek, Little Sinking Creek, and Sinking Branch. Some sinkholes become plugged with clay and debris, creating small lakes or ponds.

Figure 24 This small sinkhole formed suddenly in 1991 when the roof of a cavern collapsed. It destroyed this home in Frostproof, Florida.

Section 6.3 Assessment

Reviewing Concepts

1. Where is groundwater located under the surface?
2. How does water move underground?
3. What are some environmental threats to groundwater supplies?
4. How and where do most caverns form?
5. What landforms are common in an area of karst topography?

Critical Thinking

6. **Comparing and Contrasting** What is the difference between stalactites and stalagmites?

7. **Analyzing Concepts** How is groundwater a nonrenewable resource?
8. **Analyzing Concepts** Explain why caverns form in the zone of saturation, while dripstone features form in the zone of aeration?

Writing in Science

Relating Cause and Effect Write a paragraph that connects these three concepts: land subsidence, extensive farming in dry regions, and water conservation.

The Ogallala Aquifer—How Long Will the Water Last?

The High Plains extend from the western Dakotas south to Texas. Despite being a land of little rain, this is one of the most important agricultural regions in the United States. The reason is a vast supply of groundwater that makes irrigation possible throughout most of the region. The source of most of this water is the Ogallala Formation, the largest aquifer in the United States.

Geologically, the Ogallala Formation consists of a number of sandy and gravelly rock layers. The sediments came from the erosion of the Rocky Mountains and were carried eastward by sluggish streams. Erosion has removed much of the formation from eastern Colorado, severing the Ogallala's connection to the Rockies.

The Ogallala Formation, the largest aquifer in the United States, averages 60 meters thick. However, in some places it is as thick as 180 meters thick. Groundwater in the aquifer originally traveled downslope from the Rocky Mountains and from surface precipitation that soaked into the ground over thousands of years. Because of its high porosity and great size, the Ogallala Formation accumulated a large amount of groundwater—enough to fill Lake Huron! Today, with the connection between the aquifer and the Rockies gone (erosion has removed much of the formation in eastern Colorado), all of the Ogallala's recharge must come from the meager rainfall of the Plains.

In the late 1800s, people first started to use the Ogallala for irrigation. However, the capacity of pumps available at the time limited water withdrawal. Then in the 1920s, large-capacity irrigation pumps were invented. High Plains' farmers began tapping the Ogallala for irrigation. Today, there are nearly 170,000 wells irrigating more than 65,000 square kilometers of land.

The increase in irrigation has caused a drastic drop in the Ogallala's water table, especially in the High Plains. Declines in the water table of 3 to 15 meters are common. In places, however, the water table is now 60 meters below its original level.

Although the decline in the water table has slowed in parts of the southern High Plains, substantial pumping continues—often in excess of recharge. The future of irrigated farming here is clearly in jeopardy.

The southern High Plains will return sooner or later to dry-land farming. The transition will come sooner and with fewer ecological and economic crises if the agricultural industry is weaned gradually from its dependence on groundwater irrigation. If nothing is done until all the accessible water in the Ogallala aquifer has been removed, the transition will be ecologically dangerous and economically dreadful.*

*National Research Council. *Solid-Earth Sciences and Society.* Washington, DC: National Academy Press, 1993, p. 148.

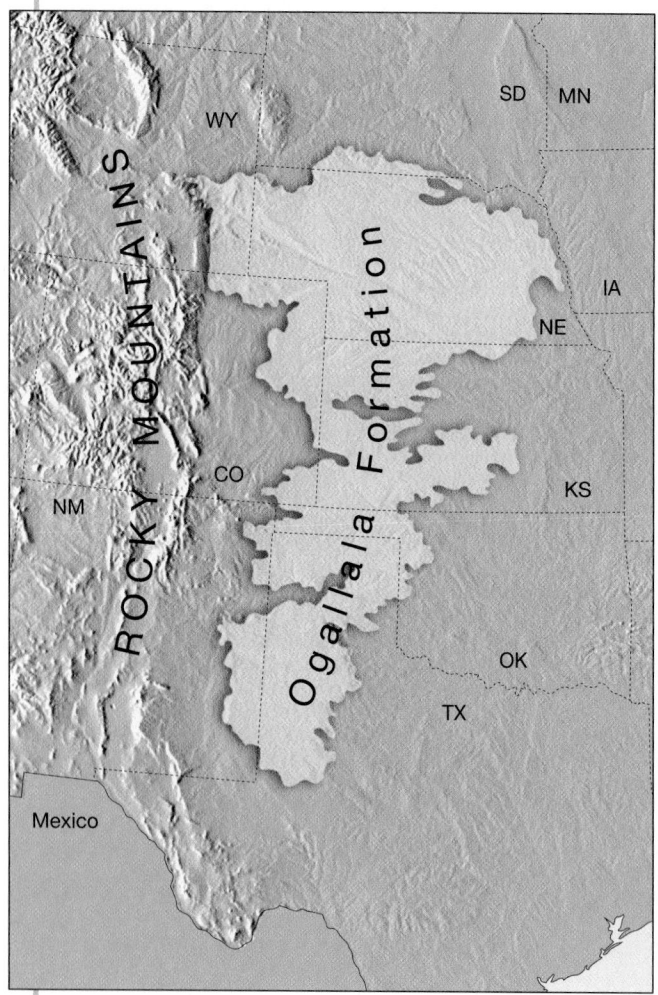

Figure 25 The Ogallala Formation underlies about 450,000 square kilometers of the High Plains, making it the largest aquifer in the United States.

Investigating the Permeability of Soils

The permeability of soils affects the way groundwater moves—or if it moves at all. Some soils are highly permeable, while others are not. In this lab, you will determine the permeability of various soils, and draw conclusions about their effect on the movement of water underground.

Problem
How does the permeability of soil affect its ability to move water?

Materials
- 100 mL graduated cylinder
- beaker
- small funnel
- 3 pieces of cotton
- samples of coarse sand, fine sand, and soil
- clock or watch with a second hand

Skills
Observing, Measuring, Comparing and Contrasting, Analyzing Data, Interpreting Data

Procedure

1. Place a small, clean piece of cotton in the neck of the funnel. Fill the funnel above the cotton with coarse sand. Fill the funnel about two-thirds of the way.

2. **Measure** Pour water into the graduated cylinder until it reaches the 50 mL mark.

3. With the bottom of the funnel over the beaker, pour the water from the graduated cylinder slowly into the sand in the funnel.

4. **Measure** In a data table like the one shown, keep track of the time from the second you start to pour the water into the funnel. Measure the amount of time that it takes the water to drain through the funnel filled with coarse sand.

5. Record the time it takes for the water to drain through the sand in the data table.

6. Empty and clean the measuring cylinder, funnel, and beaker.

7. Repeat Steps 1 through 7, first using fine sand, and then using soil.

Analyze and Conclude

1. **Comparing and Contrasting** Of the three materials you tested, which has the greatest permeability? Which had the least permeability?

2. **Analyzing Data** Why were different amounts of water recovered in the beaker for each material tested?

3. **Interpreting Data** What effect would the differences you observed in this lab have on the movement of groundwater through different soils?

Data Table		
	Time Needed for Water to Drain Through Funnel	Water Collected in Beaker (mL)
Coarse Sand		
Fine Sand		
Soil		

6 | Study Guide

6.1 Running Water

Key Concepts

- Water constantly moves among the oceans, the atmosphere, the solid Earth, and the biosphere. This unending circulation of Earth's water supply is the water cycle

- Balance in the water cycle means the average annual precipitation over Earth equals the amount of water that evaporates.

- The ability of a stream to erode and transport materials depends largely on its velocity.

- While gradient decreases between a stream's headwaters and mouth, discharge increases.

- Base level is the lowest point to which a stream can erode its channel.

Vocabulary

water cycle, *p. 158;* infiltration, *p. 159;* transpiration, *p. 159;* gradient, *p. 160;* stream channel, *p. 161;* discharge, *p. 161;* tributary, *p. 162;* meander, *p. 163*

6.2 The Work of Streams

Key Concepts

- Streams generally erode their channels by dissolving soluble material, by lifting loose particles, and by abrasion, or grinding.

- Streams transport their load of sediment in three ways: (1) in solution (dissolved load), (2) in suspension (suspended load), and (3) scooting or rolling along the bottom (bed load).

- Deposition occurs as streamflow drops below the critical settling velocity of a certain particle size.

- There are two general types of stream valleys: narrow V-shaped valleys and wide valleys with flat floors.

- Most floods are caused by rapid spring snow melt and storms that bring heavy rains over a large region.

- Measures to control flooding include the construction of artificial levees, building flood control dams, and placing limits on floodplain development.

- A drainage basin is the land area that contributes water to a stream.

Vocabulary

bed load, *p. 165;* capacity, *p. 165;* delta, *p. 166;* natural levee, *p. 167;* floodplain, *p. 167;* flood, *p. 168;* drainage basin, *p. 170;* divide, *p. 170*

6.3 Water Beneath the Surface

Key Concepts

- Much of the water in soil seeps downward until it reaches the zone of saturation. The zone of saturation is the area where water fills all of the open spaces in sediment and rock. Groundwater is the water within this zone.

- Groundwater moves by twisting and turning through interconnected small openings. The groundwater moves more slowly when the pore spaces are smaller.

- A spring forms whenever the water table intersects the ground surface.

- Overuse and contamination threatens groundwater supplies in some areas.

- Erosion forms most caverns at or below the water table in the zone of saturation.

- Karst areas typically have irregular terrain, with many depressions called sinkholes.

Vocabulary

zone of saturation, *p. 172;* groundwater, *p. 172;* water table, *p. 172;* porosity, *p. 172;* permeability, *p. 172;* aquifer, *p. 172;* spring, *p. 172;* geyser; *p. 173;* well, *p. 174;* artesian well; *p. 174;* cavern, *p. 177;* travertine, *p. 177;* karst topography, *p. 178;* sinkhole, *p. 178*

Reviewing Content

Choose the letter that best answers the question or completes the statement.

1. The energy for the water cycle comes from the
   a. ocean.
   b. sun.
   c. atmosphere.
   d. soil.

2. How does water move from plants to the atmosphere ?
   a. infiltration
   b. precipitation
   c. transpiration
   d. condensation

3. By what process do streams and rivers move material?
   a. weathering
   b. infiltration
   c. mass wasting
   d. erosion

4. A river's discharge is generally greatest
   a. at its source.
   b. on its floodplain.
   c. at its mouth.
   d. at the sides of its channel.

5. When do streams and rivers deposit sediment?
   a. when their velocity decreases
   b. when they are in the midst of flooding
   c. when their velocity increases
   d. when they plunge over waterfalls

6. A stream's drainage basin is all the water that
   a. flows into it.
   b. infiltrates from it into the ground.
   c. is removed from it for drinking water.
   d. is within 100 kilometers of its channel.

7. What is a stream's bed load?
   a. material that moves along its bottom
   b. material that is carried in solution
   c. material that floats on its surface
   d. material that is carried in suspension

8. Where is groundwater located?
   a. zone of aeration
   b. zone of reduction
   c. zone of saturation
   d. zone of distribution

9. Water in an artesian well
   a. dries up after a short amount of time.
   b. rises on its own under pressure.
   c. has been contaminated by saltwater.
   d. is heated by cooling igneous rocks.

10. Caverns form when rocks such as limestone are dissolved by a mixture of water and
    a. carbonic acid.
    b. sulfur dioxide.
    c. nitrogen.
    d. ammonia.

11. Which of these landforms is characteristic of an area with karst topography?
    a. mountains
    b. canyons
    c. sinkholes
    d. drumlins

Understanding Concepts

12. Write a list of numbered statements that summarize the major steps in the water cycle.

13. How does a stream's gradient affect is velocity?

14. Why does a stream's base level affect how it downcuts its channel?

15. Which type of stream valley is formed primarily by downcutting?

16. What are the main causes of floods?

17. What is the relationship between a spring and the water table?

18. Why are leaking landfills and septic tanks of concern to people who use groundwater?

19. How do stalactites form?

20. What type of rock is often associated with the formation of caverns and karst topography?

21. How do dripstone columns form?

Critical Thinking

22. Analyzing Concepts Why must Earth's water cycle be balanced in order for the system to work?

23. Relating Cause and Effect How would a reduction in friction in a stream channel affect the stream's velocity?

24. Applying Concepts A stream's discharge decreases. Explain how this affects the stream's capacity?

25. Summarizing Briefly explain how a material can be porous but also impermeable.

26. Drawing Conclusions The bedrock under a region is primarily a very hard rock that doesn't easily erode. The area is also very arid. Is it likely that this area has a karst landscape? Explain your answer.

Analyzing Data

Use the graph below to answer Questions 27–30.

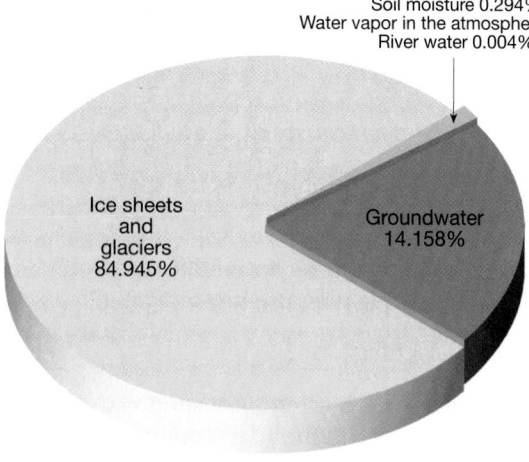

Lakes and reservoirs 0.549%
Soil moisture 0.294%
Water vapor in the atmosphere 0.049%
River water 0.004%

Ice sheets and glaciers 84.945%

Groundwater 14.158%

27. Using Graphs Where is the greatest percentage of Earth's fresh water located?

28. Calculating What percentage of Earth's fresh water is held in rivers, lakes, and reservoirs?

29. Calculating Oceans hold about 97 percent of Earth's water. The rest of the water is fresh. What percentage of Earth's water is freshwater that people can use for drinking, cooking, and growing crops?

30. Drawing Conclusions Taking into account your answer to Question #29 above, explain why many people think of Earth's supply of fresh water as a resource that must be protected.

Concepts in Action

31. Applying Concepts A person drills a well into an area where there is a known aquifer underground. But the well doesn't produce water. What might be the cause of the problem? What does this person need to know about the water table in this area to solve the problem?

32. Predicting Erosion reduces the size of pebbles on the bottom of a stream channel. Which of the following would be most affected: the stream's competence, velocity, or discharge? Explain your answer.

33. Connecting Concepts Explain what deltas and natural levees have in common.

34. Writing in Science Imagine you live in a town that floods often. The people in your community want to take measures to decrease the amount of flooding and property damage. The community has identified three choices: a set of natural levees, a flood control dam, or clearing development from the river floodplain. Write a letter to the editor supporting one of these choices.

Performance-Based Assessment

Drawing Diagrams Draw a graphic organizer that shows the major steps of the water cycle. Label each step.

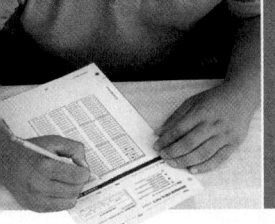

Standardized Test Prep

Test-Taking Tip

Evaluating and Revising
Frequently, a scientifically accurate answer choice may not answer the question that is being asked. Keep these tips in mind.

- Verify what the question is asking.
- Determine if an answer choice is a true statement or not.
- Determine if a true answer choice actually answers the question.
- Be cautious with inserted or deleted words that make a false statement seem accurate.

Practice using these tips in Question 3.

Choose the letter that best answers the question or completes the statement, or write a brief answer to the question.

1. Which of these processes of the water cycle is a direct effect of the sun's energy?
   (A) formation of precipitation
   (B) runoff of water over soil
   (C) evaporation
   (D) seeping of water into soil

2. Which factor is most important in determining the erosive power of a stream?
   (A) stream discharge
   (B) dissolved load
   (C) stream velocity
   (D) channel width

3. Rejuvenation causes streams to resume downcutting their channels because
   (A) the stream's greatest velocity is at its bottom.
   (B) the stream's bed load helps erode the stream's bottom.
   (C) natural levees restrict the lateral movement of stream waters.
   (D) uplift creates a new base level for the stream.

4. When a soil is impermeable, it
   (A) allows water to flow freely through it.
   (B) has no water in it at all.
   (C) does not allow water to pass through it.
   (D) has large pore spaces.

5. Which of these features is a landform associated with karst topography?
   (A) sinkholes
   (B) streams
   (C) natural levees
   (D) deltas

6. What are the major environmental problems associated with the use of groundwater?

7. What is a cone of depression and how does it form?

8. Which of the following drawings shows a feature of stream deposition?

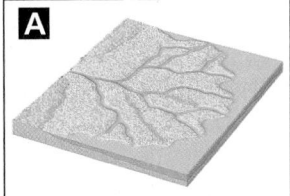
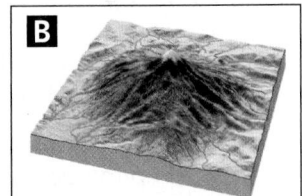
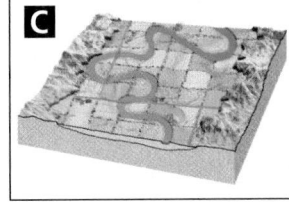
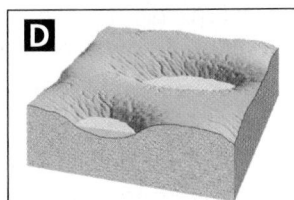

CHAPTER 7

Glaciers, Deserts, and Wind

CONCEPTS in Action

Exploration Lab
Interpreting a Glacial Landscape

How the Earth Works
Erosion

 **GEODe** EARTH SCIENCE
Sculpturing Earth's Surface
↳ Glaciers
Deserts

Discovery CHANNEL SCHOOL **Video Field Trip**

Glaciers

Take a field trip through cold waters with Discovery Channel and find out how glaciers helped shape Earth. Answer the following questions after watching the video.

1. What happened to the glaciers at the end of the last ice age? How did the end of the ice age affect Earth?

2. How are icebergs formed?

Go Online PHSchool.com

For: Chapter 7 Resources
Visit: PHSchool.com
Web Code: cjk-9999

 This fjord at Tracy Arm, Alaska, formed as ▶
a glacier carved the valley that became

SCULPTURING EARTH'S SURFACE

Inquiry Activity

How Does Pressure Affect Ice Crystals?

Procedure

1. Obtain a beaker full of ice crystals, either by collecting snow outside or by scraping ice crystals from the inside surfaces of a freezer. Use a magnifying glass to observe the loose crystals. Sketch their appearance in your science notebook.

2. Use your hands to mold a snowball from the crystals. Then squeeze the snowball as hard as you can, making the snowball compact.

3. Use a table knife to cut the snowball in half. Observe the compressed crystals with your magnifying glass and sketch them.

Think About It

1. **Drawing Conclusions** How did the ice crystals change after you squeezed them? Describe how pressure seems to affect ice crystals.

2. **Predicting** The raw material for glaciers is snow. Predict how snowflakes will change under the increasing pressure of overlying snow.

7.1 Glaciers

Reading Focus

Key Concepts

- What types of glaciers exist, and where is each type found?
- How do glaciers move?
- What distinguishes the various types of glacial drift?
- What landscape features do glaciers form?

Vocabulary

- ice age
- glacier
- snowline
- valley glacier
- ice sheet
- glacial trough
- till
- stratified drift
- moraine

Reading Strategy

Building Vocabulary Draw a table similar to the one below that includes all the vocabulary terms listed for the section. As you read the section, define each vocabulary term in your own words.

Vocabulary Term	Definition
Glacier	a. _____?_____
Ice Sheet	b. _____?_____
Moraine	c. _____?_____
Till	d. _____?_____

Figure 1 Valley Glacier Barry Glacier, in Alaska's Chugach Mountains, slowly advances down this valley.

Earth's climate strongly influences the processes that shape its surface. In this section, you will see the strong link between climate and geology in studying how glaciers shape the land.

Types of Glaciers

As recently as 15,000 years ago—the blink of an eye in geologic history—up to 30 percent of Earth was covered by glacial ice. At that time, Earth was coming out of an **ice age**—a period of time when much of Earth's land is covered in glaciers. Sheets of ice that were thousands of meters thick shaped places like the Alps, Cape Cod, and Yosemite Valley. Long Island, the Great Lakes, and the fjords of Norway were all formed by glaciers. A **glacier** is a thick ice mass that forms over hundreds or thousands of years. Today glaciers still cover nearly 10 percent of Earth's land area. In these regions they continue to sculpt the landscape.

Glaciers originate on land in places where more snow falls each winter than melts each summer. The **snowline** is the lowest elevation in a particular area that remains covered in snow all year. At the poles, the snowline occurs at sea level. Closer to the equator, the snowline is near the top of tall mountains. Instead of completely melting away, snow above the snowline accumulates and compacts. The compressed snow first recrystallizes into coarse grains of ice. Further pressure from added snow above changes the coarse grains into interlocking crystals of glacial ice.

A glacier appears to be motionless, but it's not. Sit beside a glacier for an hour and you may hear a sporadic chorus of creaks, cracks, and groans as the mass of ice slowly moves downhill. Just like running water, groundwater, wind, and waves, glaciers are dynamic agents of erosion. They accumulate, transport, and deposit sediment. Thus, glaciers are an important part of the rock cycle.

Valley Glaciers Thousands of small glaciers exist in high mountains worldwide. Unlike fast-flowing mountain streams, glaciers advance only a few centimeters to meters each day. **Valley glaciers** are ice masses that slowly advance down valleys that were originally occupied by streams. **A valley glacier is a stream of ice that flows between steep rock walls from a place near the top of the mountain valley.** Like rivers, valley glaciers can be long or short, wide or narrow, single or with branching tributaries. Figure 1 shows a valley glacier in Alaska.

Ice Sheets Ice sheets are enormous ice masses that flow in all directions from one or more centers and cover everything but the highest land. **Ice sheets are sometimes called continental ice sheets because they cover large regions where the climate is extremely cold. They are huge compared to valley glaciers.** Ice sheets covered much of North America during the recent ice age. Figure 2 shows the two remaining ice sheets, which combined cover almost 10 percent of Earth's land area. One ice sheet covers about 80 percent of Greenland. It averages nearly 1500 meters thick, and in places it rises to 3000 meters above the island's surface.

The huge Antarctic Ice Sheet in the Southern Hemisphere is nearly 4300 meters thick in places. This glacier accounts for 80 percent of the world's ice, and it holds nearly two-thirds of Earth's fresh water. If it melted, sea level could rise 60 to 70 meters and many coastal cities would flood.

 **Reading Checkpoint** *Where do ice sheets exist on Earth today?*

Go Online
SciLINKS NSTA

For: Links on glaciers
Visit: www.SciLinks.org
Web Code: cjn-2071

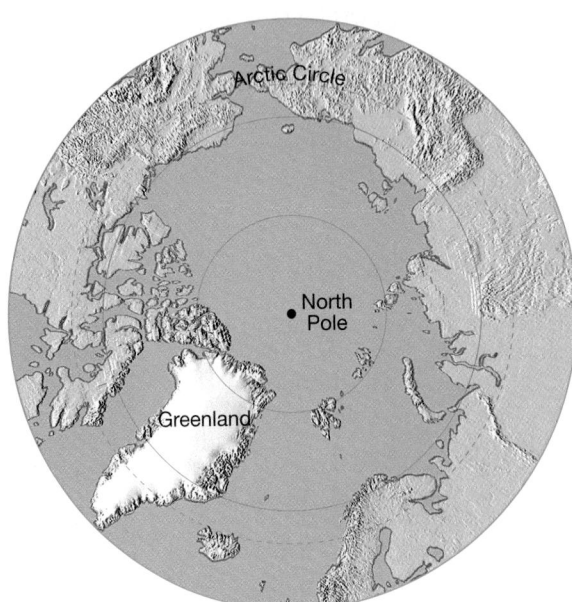

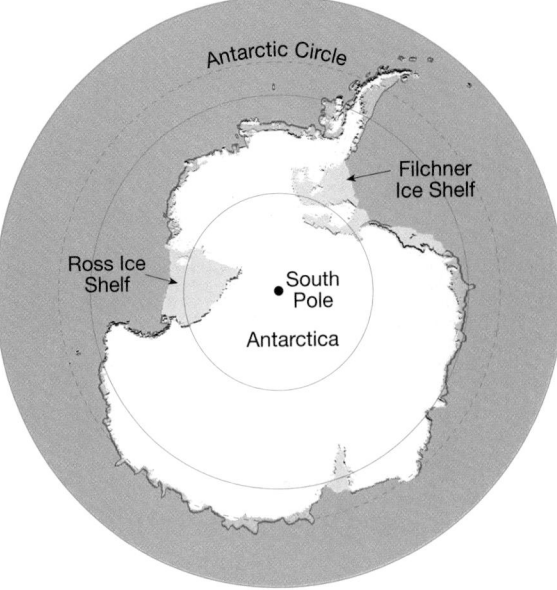

Figure 2 The only present-day ice sheets are those covering Greenland and Antarctica.

Glaciers, Deserts, and Wind **189**

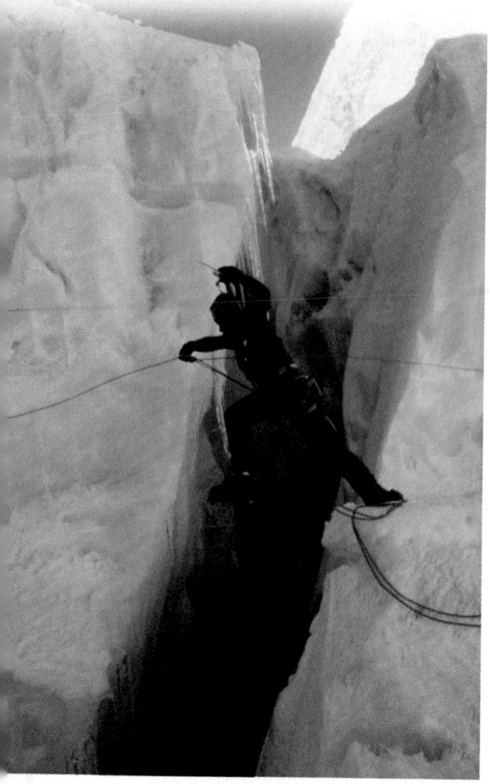

How Glaciers Move

You might wonder how a glacier, which is solid, can move. 🔑 **The movement of glaciers is referred to as flow. Glacial flow happens two ways: plastic flow and basal slip.** Plastic flow involves movement within the ice. Under high enough pressure, the normally brittle ice begins to distort and change shape—a property known as plasticity. The weight of overlying ice exerts this pressure on the ice below, causing it to flow. Plastic flow begins at about 50 meters below the glacier surface.

Basal slip is the second cause of glacial movement. Due to gravity, the entire ice mass actually slips and slides downhill along the ground. The upper 50 meters of a glacier is not under enough pressure to have plastic flow. The surface of the glacier behaves differently than the ice below. This uppermost zone of a glacier is brittle, and it is referred to as the zone of fracture. This brittle topmost ice piggybacks a ride on the flowing ice below. The zone of fracture experiences tension when the glacier moves over irregular terrain. This tension results in gaping cracks called crevasses. Crevasses can be 50 meters deep. They are often hidden by snow and make travel across glaciers dangerous, as shown in Figure 3.

Figure 3 Crevasses like this one in Pakistan can extend 50 meters into a glacier's brittle surface ice.

Rates of Glacial Movement Different glaciers move at different speeds. Some flow so slowly that trees and other vegetation grow in the debris on their surface. Other glaciers can advance several meters per day. Some glaciers alternate between periods of rapid movement and periods of no movement whatsoever.

Budget of a Glacier Glaciers form where more snow falls in winter than can melt during the summer. They constantly gain and lose ice. Snow accumulates, and ice forms at the head of the glacier in the zone of accumulation, shown in Figure 4. Here new snowfall thickens the glacier and promotes movement. The area of the glacier beyond the snowline is called the zone of wastage. Here the glacier loses ice—and any new snow—to melting.

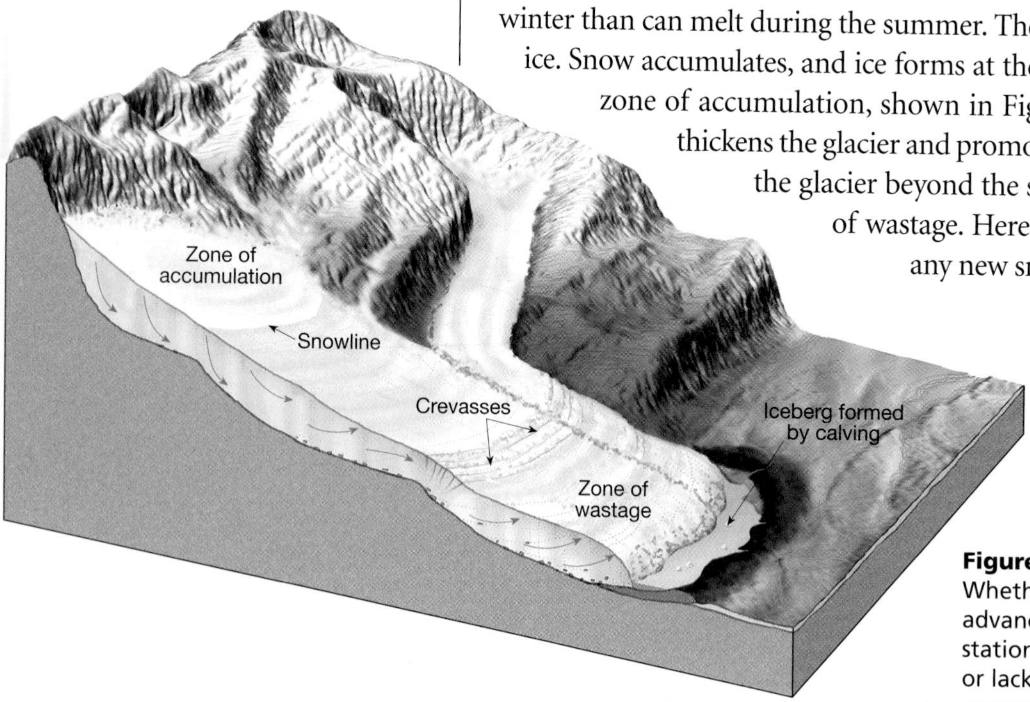

Zone of accumulation

Snowline

Crevasses

Zone of wastage

Iceberg formed by calving

Figure 4 How a Glacier Moves Whether the margin of a glacier advances, retreats, or remains stationary depends on the balance or lack of balance between accumulation and wastage.

Glaciers also lose ice when large pieces break off their fronts in a process called calving. Calving creates icebergs where glaciers meet the ocean. Because icebergs are just slightly less dense than seawater, they float low in the water. Only about 10 percent of their mass is visible above the surface, as shown in Figure 5. The Greenland Ice Sheet calves thousands of icebergs each year. Many drift southward into the North Atlantic where they are navigational hazards.

The foot of a glacier can advance, retreat, or remain in place. Which course it follows depends on the glacier's budget. ⬭ **The glacial budget is the balance or lack of balance between accumulation at the upper end of a glacier and loss, or wastage, at the lower end.** If more ice accumulates at the glacier head than melts or calves at the glacier foot, then the glacier advances. The glacier retreats when it loses ice faster than it gains ice. If a glacier gains ice at the same rate as ice melts or calves off, the front or terminus of the glacier remains stationary. Whether the front of a glacier advances, retreats, or remains stationary, the ice within the glacier continues to flow forward. In the case of a receding glacier, the ice still flows forward, but not rapidly enough to offset wastage.

Figure 5 Calving A Ice calves from the front of the Hubbard glacier in Alaska's Wrangell-St. Elias National Park. Once it lands in the water the ice is called an iceberg. Icebergs float on their sides. **B** Just 10 percent of their mass is visible above the surface.

Reading Checkpoint *What causes a glacier to retreat?*

Figure 6 Glacial Abrasion A glacier smoothed and polished this rock surface in Alaska's Glacier Bay. Rock fragments embedded in the glacier carved the scratches and grooves.

Glacial Erosion

Glaciers are nature's bulldozers. Their ice scrapes, scours, and tears rock from valley floors and walls. Glaciers then carry the rocks down the valley. The rock fragments that are eroded by the glacier drop at the glacier's foot where the ice melts. Unlike streams, which drop sediments while they flow, glaciers hold everything until they melt. They can carry rocks as big as buses over long distances. **Many landscapes were changed by the widespread glaciers of the recent ice age.**

How Glaciers Erode Glaciers mainly erode the land in two ways: plucking and abrasion. Rock surfaces beneath glaciers break up as melted water from the glacier penetrates the cracks. When the water refreezes it expands and pries the rock apart. As a glacier flows over the fractured bedrock surface, it loosens and lifts blocks of rock and incorporates them into the ice. This type of glacial erosion is called plucking.

A second form of glacial erosion is called abrasion. As the glacial ice and its load of rock fragments slide over bedrock, they work like sandpaper to smooth and polish the surface below. The pulverized rock produced by this glacial gristmill is appropriately called rock flour. So much rock flour may be produced that streams of meltwater leaving the glacier often have the grayish appearance of skim milk—visible evidence of the grinding power of the ice. When the ice at the bottom of a glacier contains large rock fragments, long scratches and grooves may be gouged in the bedrock, shown in Figure 6. These glacial striations provide valuable clues to the direction of past glacial movement. By mapping the striations over large areas, geologists often can reconstruct the direction the ice flowed.

As with other agents of erosion, the rate of glacial erosion is highly variable. These differences are mainly controlled by four factors: 1) rate of glacial movement; 2) thickness of the ice; 3) shape, abundance, and hardness of the rock fragments in the ice at the base of the glacier; and 4) the type of surface below the glacier.

Reading Checkpoint

How do glaciers cause erosion?

Landforms Created by Glacial Erosion

Erosion by valley glaciers produces many spectacular features in mountainous areas. ◉ **Glaciers are responsible for a variety of erosional landscape features, such as glacial troughs, hanging valleys, cirques, arêtes, and horns.** Compare and contrast the mountain setting before, during, and after glaciation as shown is Figure 7.

Glaciated Valleys Before glaciation, alpine valleys are usually V-shaped because streams are well above base level and are downcutting. However, in mountain regions that have been glaciated, the valleys are no longer narrow. As a glacier moves down a valley once occupied by a stream, the glacier widens, deepens, and straightens the valley. The once narrow V-shaped valley is changed into a U-shaped **glacial trough.**

The amount of glacial erosion depends in part on the thickness of the ice. Main glaciers cut U-shaped valleys that are deeper than those carved by smaller side glaciers. When the ice recedes, the valleys of the smaller side glaciers are left standing higher than the main glacial trough. These higher valleys are called hanging valleys. Rivers flowing from hanging valleys sometimes produce spectacular waterfalls, such as those in Yosemite National Park, California.

Reading Checkpoint *What is a glacial trough?*

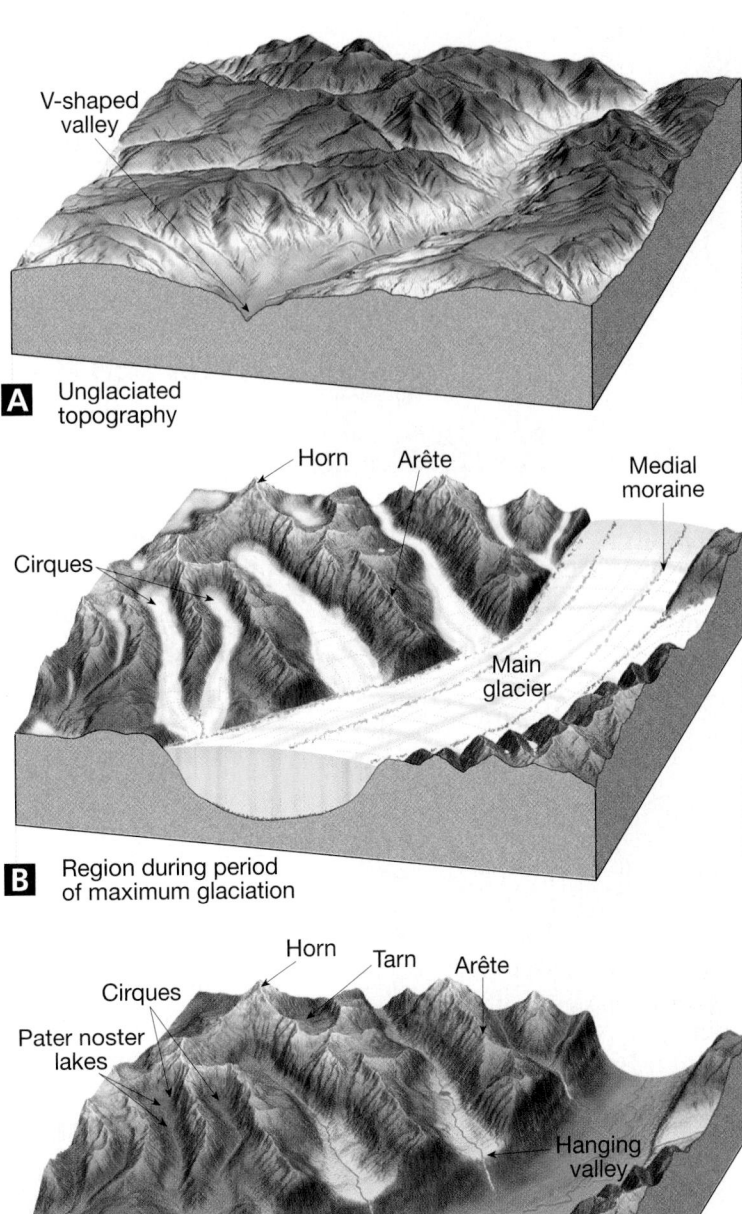

A Unglaciated topography

B Region during period of maximum glaciation

C Glaciated topography

Figure 7 Erosional Landforms Caused by Valley Glaciers
A shows what the valley glaciers looked like in this mountainous region. **B** reveals the modified landscape and its features.
Inferring *What direction did the main valley glacier flow? How do you know?*

Figure 8 Cirque Natural amphitheaters like this one in Canada's Yukon Territory result from the plucking action of ice in a glacier's zone of accumulation.

Figure 9 Glacial till is an unsorted mixture of many different sediment sizes. A close look often reveals cobbles that have been scratched as they were dragged along by the glacier.

Cirques A cirque is a bowl-shaped depression at the head of a glacial valley that is surrounded on three sides by steep rock walls, as shown in Figure 8. These impressive features are the focal point of the glacier's growth because they form where snow and ice accumulate at the head of a valley glacier. Cirques begin as irregularities in the mountainside. Glaciers carve cirques by plucking rock from along the sides and the bottom. The glaciers then act as conveyor belts that carry away the debris. Sometimes the melting glacier leaves a small lake in the cirque basin.

Arêtes and Horns Other mountain landscapes carved by valley glaciers reveal more than glacial troughs and cirques. Snaking, sharp-edged ridges called arêtes and sharp pyramid-like peaks called horns project above the surroundings. You can see these features in the Alps and the northern Rockies. Horns like the Matterhorn in Switzerland form where several cirques surround a single high mountain. The converging cirques create one distinctive horn. Arêtes form where cirques occur on opposite sides of a divide. As these cirques grow, the divide separating them is reduced to a narrow, sharp ridge.

Glacial Deposits

Glaciers transport huge loads of debris as they slowly advance across the land. When a glacier melts it deposits its sediment. For example, in many areas once covered by the ice sheets of the recent ice age, the bedrock is rarely exposed because glacial deposits that are dozens—or even hundreds—of meters thick completely cover the terrain. Rocky pastures in New England, wheat fields in the Dakota plains, and rolling Midwest farmland are all landscapes resulting from glacial deposition.

Types of Glacial Drift ⬩ **Glacial drift applies to all sediments of glacial origin, no matter how, where, or in what form they were deposited. There are two types of glacial drift: till and stratified drift.** Till is material deposited directly by the glacier. It is deposited as the glacier melts and drops its load of rock debris. Unlike moving water and wind, ice cannot sort the sediment it carries. Therefore, till deposits are usually unsorted mixtures made up of many particle sizes. Notice the unsorted till in Figure 9.

Stratified drift is sediment laid down by glacial meltwater. Stratified drift contains particles that are sorted according to size and weight of the debris. Some deposits of drift are made by streams coming directly from the glacier. Stratified drift often consists of sand and gravel, because the meltwater cannot move large boulders and finer sediments remain suspended and are carried far from the glacier.

Boulders found in till or lying free on the ground are glacial erratics. Their mineral content is different from the underlying bedrock, which shows they were carried there by some means. In parts of New England and other glaciated areas, glacial erratics are scattered throughout pastures and farm fields. Early settlers cleared the smaller ones from their fields and piled them into stone fences that remain today. Geologists can sometimes determine the path of a long-gone glacier by studying the minerals in glacial erratics.

 **Reading Checkpoint**   *What is glacial drift?*

Moraines, Outwash Plains, and Kettles

Glaciers are responsible for a variety of depositional features, including moraines, outwash plains, kettles, drumlins, and eskers.

When glaciers melt, they leave layers or ridges of till called **moraines.** These widespread glacial features come in several varieties.

Lateral Moraines The sides of a valley glacier gather large amounts of debris from the valley walls. Lateral moraines are ridges that form along the sides of glacial valleys when the glacier melts and leaves the material it has gathered. Medial moraines are formed when two valley glaciers join to form a single ice stream. Observe the medial and lateral moraines in Figure 10. The till that was once carried along the edges of each glacier joins to form a dark stripe of debris within the newly enlarged glacier.

Figure 10 The dark stripe running down the middle of this glacier is a medial moraine. It formed from the lateral moraines of these two merging valley glaciers.

End Moraines and Ground Moraines Glaciers can remain stationary for long periods of time. When a glacier is stationary it means snow and ice accumulate at the head of the glacier at the same rate snow and ice melt at the foot of the glacier. Within the glacier, the ice still flows. It acts as a conveyor belt to carry rock debris to the end of the glacier. When the ice there melts, it deposits the debris and forms a ridge called an end moraine. The longer the glacier remains stationary, the larger the end moraine grows.

Ground moraines form when glaciers begin to recede. The glacier front continues to deliver debris. The glacier deposits sediment as the ice melts away. However, instead of forming a ridge, the retreating glacier creates a rock-strewn, gently rolling plain. This ground moraine fills in low spots and clogs old stream channels. Ground moraine can thus result in poorly drained swamp lands.

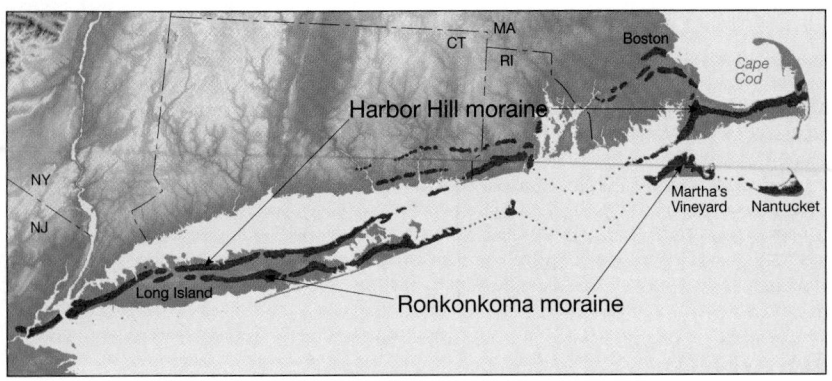

Figure 11 Long Island, Cape Cod, Martha's Vineyard, and Nantucket are remnants of an end moraine.

Terminal and Recessional Moraines

Glaciers can periodically retreat, then find equilibrium again and remain stationary for some time. A glacier forms a new end moraine during the stationary period, then another ground moraine once it starts retreating again. This pattern can repeat many times before the glacier completely melts. The farthest end moraine is the terminal end moraine. The end moraines that form when the ice front occasionally becomes stationary during its retreat are recessional end moraines.

End moraines that formed in the recent ice age are prominent in the landscapes of the Midwest and Northeast. The Kettle Moraine is a scenic one that occurs in Wisconsin near Milwaukee. New York's Long Island is part of a series of end moraines stretching from eastern Pennsylvania to Cape Cod, Massachusetts. Figure 11 shows the locations of these end moraines that form part of the Northeast coast.

Outwash Plains

At the same time that an end moraine is forming, streams of fast-moving meltwater emerge from the bases of glaciers. As mentioned before, this water is often so choked with fine sediment that it looks like milk. Once it leaves the glacier, the water slows and drops the sediment in a broad, ramp-like accumulation downstream from the end moraine. This type of sediment ramp resulting from an ice sheet is called an outwash plain.

Kettles

You can often find depressions and small lakes called kettles within end moraines and outwash plains, as shown in Figure 12. Kettles form when blocks of stagnant ice become buried in drift and eventually melt. This melting leaves pits in the glacial sediment. A well-known example of a kettle is Walden Pond near Concord, Massachusetts. Thousands of kettles dot the landscape of the Upper Midwest in Wisconsin and Minnesota.

Drumlins and Eskers

Moraines are not the only landforms deposited by glaciers. Some landscapes have many elongated parallel hills made of till. Other areas have conical hills and narrow winding ridges made mainly of stratified drift. If you know what to look for, the signs of a once-glaciated landscape are unmistakable—especially from an airplane.

Drumlins are streamlined hills composed of till. Drumlins are taller and steeper on one end, and they range in height from 15 to 60 meters and average 0.4 to 0.8 kilometer long. The steep side of the hill faces the direction the ice came from, and the gentler slope points in the direction the ice moved. Drumlins occur in clusters called drumlin fields. Near Rochester, New York, one cluster contains nearly 10,000 drumlins. Their streamlining shows they were molded by active glaciers.

Eskers are snake-like ridges composed of sand and gravel that were deposited by streams once flowing in tunnels beneath glaciers. They can be several meters high and many kilometers long. Many eskers are mined for the sand and gravel they contain.

 **Reading Checkpoint** *What depositional features do glaciers form?*

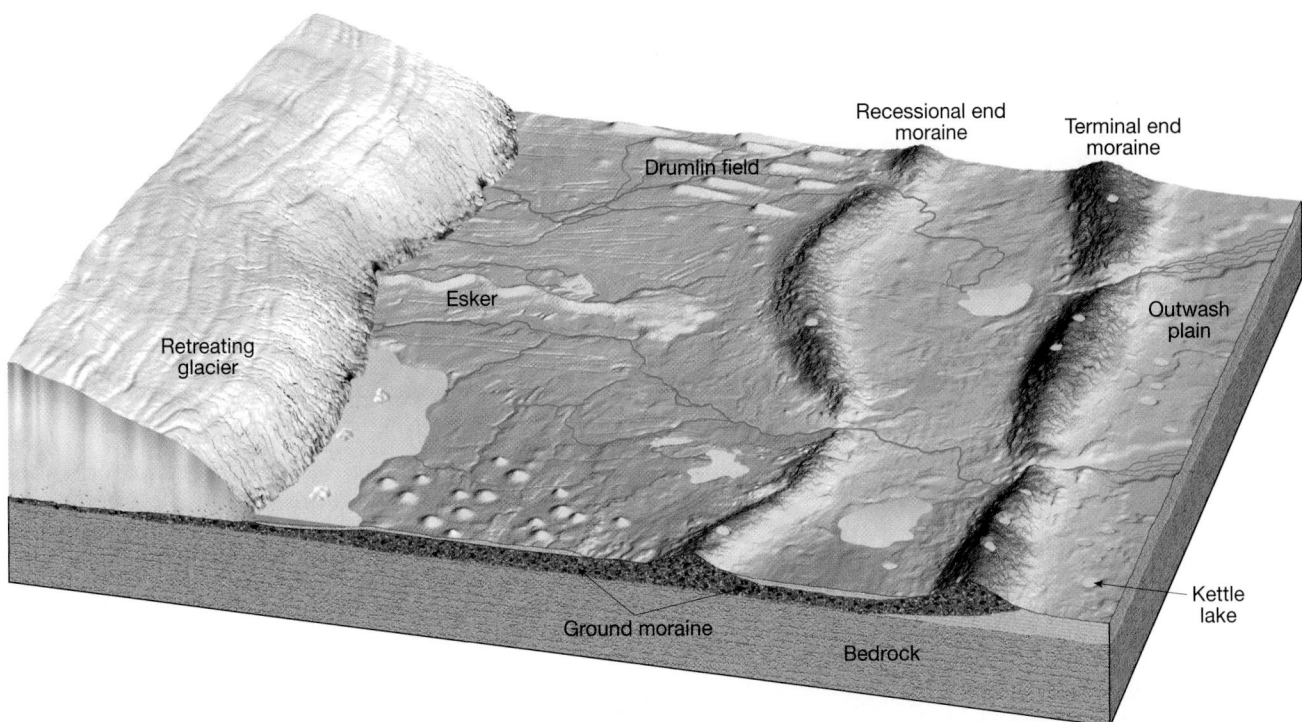

Figure 12 The landscape left by a retreating glacier includes a number of distinctive features. The terminal end moraine marks the farthest extent of the glacier. Recessional moraines occur where a retreating glacier temporarily becomes stationary.
Using Analogies *How is a glacier like a conveyor belt?*

Glaciers of the Ice Age

During the recent ice age continental ice sheets and alpine glaciers covered a lot more land than they do today. People once thought that glacial deposits had drifted in on icebergs or that they swept across the landscape in a catastrophic flood. However, scientific field investigations during the nineteenth century provided convincing evidence that an extensive ice age explained these deposits and many other features.

During the recent ice age, glaciers covered almost 30 percent of Earth's land, including large portions of North America, Europe, and Siberia, as shown in Figure 13. The Northern Hemisphere had twice the ice of the Southern Hemisphere. The Southern Hemisphere has far less land, so glaciation was mostly confined to Antarctica. By contrast, North America and Eurasia have plenty of land where the ice sheets could spread.

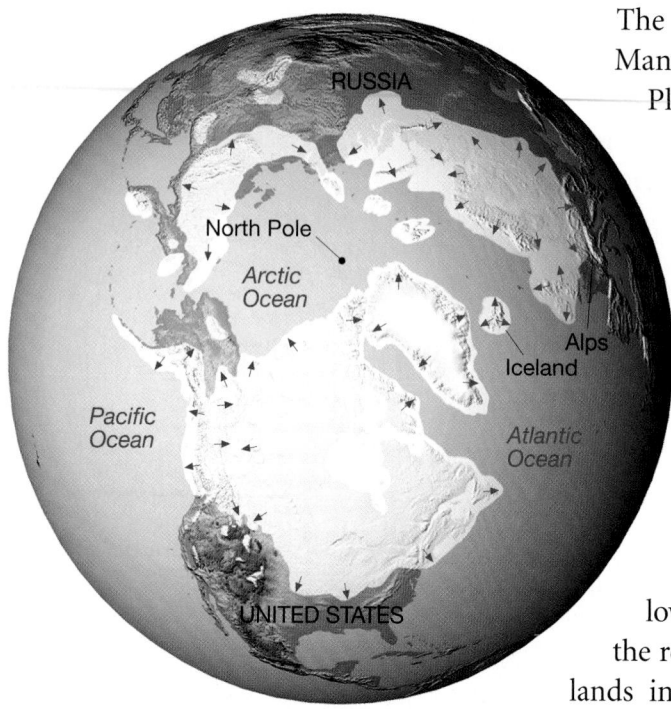

Figure 13 This map shows the extent of Northern Hemisphere ice sheets during the recent ice age.

The recent ice age began two to three million years ago. Many of the major glacial episodes occurred during the Pleistocene epoch when wooly mammoths and saber-toothed cats roamed the landscape. To some people the Pleistocene is synonymous with the recent ice age, but it actually began before this epoch on the geologic time scale.

Ice Age Effects on Drainage The ice sheets greatly affected the drainage patterns over large regions. For example, before glaciation, the Missouri River flowed northward toward Hudson Bay in Canada. The Mississippi River flowed through central Illinois. Furthermore, the Great Lakes did not exist. Their locations were marked by lowlands with rivers that flowed toward the east. During the recent ice age, glacial erosion transformed these lowlands into wide, deep basins that filled with water and eventually became the Great Lakes.

The formation and growth of ice sheets triggered changes in climates beyond the glacial margins. Regions that are arid today became cooler and wetter. This change in climate resulted in the formation of lakes in such areas as the Basin and Range region of Nevada and Utah. One of these lakes was ancient Lake Bonneville, which covered much of western Utah. The Great Salt Lake is all that remains of this glacial lake.

Section 7.1 Assessment

Reviewing Concepts

1. What are the two basic types of glaciers? Where is each type found?
2. Describe how glaciers move. Which property or properties of ice allow this movement?
3. How does glacial till differ from stratified drift? Describe one glacial feature made of each type of sediment.
4. Name three glacial features formed by erosion and three that are formed by deposition. What does each feature look like?

Critical Thinking

5. **Comparing and Contrasting** Compare and contrast advancing and retreating glaciers.
6. **Inferring** The snowline at the poles is sea level. Close to the equator, the snowline occurs high up on the tallest mountains. What is the relationship between the distance from the equator and snowline?

Math Practice

7. A glacier advances 20 meters over a period of about two months. What is its approximate rate of advance per day?

7.2 Deserts

Reading Focus

Key Concepts

- How does running water affect deserts?
- What roles do mechanical and chemical weathering play in forming deserts?

Reading Strategy

Summarizing Write each blue heading in the section on a sheet of paper. Write a brief summary of the text for each heading.

Vocabulary

- alluvial fan
- playa lake

Weathering
?
?

The Role of Water
?
?

Desert landscapes reveal the effects of both running water and wind. As you will see, these combine in different ways in different places to result in a variety of desert landscapes.

Geologic Processes in Arid Climates

If you live in a humid region, visiting a desert might at first seem like encountering an alien planet. Rounded hills and curving slopes are typical of humid regions. By contrast, deserts have angular rocks, sheer canyon walls, and surfaces covered in pebbles or sand, shown in Figure 14. Despite their differences, the same geologic processes operate in both humid regions and deserts.

Weathering In humid regions, well-developed soils support an almost continuous cover of vegetation. In these regions, the slopes and rock edges are rounded and the landscape reflects the strong influence of chemical weathering . **By contrast, much of the weathered debris in deserts has resulted from mechanical weathering.** That debris consists of rock whose minerals remain unchanged. In dry lands, rock weathering of any type is greatly reduced because of the lack of moisture and scarcity of organic acids from decaying plants. **Chemical weathering, however, is not completely absent in deserts. Over long time spans, clays and thin soils do form.** Many iron-bearing silicate minerals oxidize, producing the rust-colored stain found tinting some desert landscapes.

Figure 14 Desert landscapes vary a great deal. This landscape is in California's Death Valley.

Figure 15 A Most of the time stream channels in deserts remain dry. **B** This is the same stream shortly after a heavy shower. Ephemeral streams can cause a large amount of erosion in a short time.
Predicting *How long will the water flow in this stream?*

A

B

 Reading Checkpoint   *Why do deserts experience less chemical weathering than humid regions?*

The Role of Water Permanent streams are normally found in humid regions. However, in the desert, you'll find bridges with no water beneath them and dips in the road where empty stream channels cross. ⬤ **In the desert, most streams are ephemeral—they only carry water after it rains.** A typical ephemeral stream might flow for only a few days or just a few hours during a year. In some years, the channels may not carry any water. In the western states people call these dry creeks *washes* or *arroyos.*

Figure 16 Alluvial Fans Over the years, alluvial fans enlarge and merge with fans from adjacent canyons to produce an apron of sediment along the mountain front.

Ephemeral streams are known for dangerous flash flooding after heavy rains. During heavy showers, so much rain falls that the soil cannot absorb it. The lack of vegetation allows water to quickly run off the land, as shown in Figure 15. The floods end as quickly as they start. Because there are fewer plants in deserts to anchor the soil, the amount of erosion caused during a single-short lived rain event is impressive. Floods in humid regions are different. A flood on a river like the Mississippi can take days to reach its crest and days to subside.

Basin and Range: A Desert Landscape

Because arid regions typically lack permanent streams, they have interior drainage. This means that they have intermittent streams that do not flow out of the desert to the ocean. In the United States, the dry Basin and Range provides an excellent example. The region includes southern Oregon, all of Nevada, western Utah, southeastern California, southern Arizona, and southern New Mexico. The name Basin and Range is an apt description for this region, because it contains more than 200 relatively small mountain ranges that rise 900 to 1500 meters above the basins that separate them.

When the occasional torrents of water produced by sporadic rains move down the mountain canyons, they are heavily loaded with sediment. Emerging from the confines of the canyon, the runoff spreads over the gentler slopes at the base of the mountains and quickly loses velocity. Consequently, most of its load is dumped within a short distance. The result is a cone of debris known as an **alluvial fan** at the mouth of a canyon, as shown in Figure 16.

Q *I heard that deserts are expanding. Is that true?*

A Yes. The problem is called desertification, and it refers to the alteration of land to desert-like conditions as the result of human activities. It commonly takes place on the margins of deserts and results mostly from inappropriate land use. It is triggered when the modest natural vegetation in marginal areas is removed by plowing or grazing. When drought occurs, as it often does in these regions, and the vegetative cover has been destroyed beyond the minimum to hold the soil against erosion, the destruction becomes irreversible. Desertification is occurring in many places but is particularly serious in the region south of the Sahara Desert known as the Sahel.

On the rare occasions of abundant rainfall, or snowmelt in the mountains, streams may flow across the alluvial fans to the center of the basin, converting the basin floor into a shallow **playa lake.** Playa lakes last only a few days or weeks, before evaporation and infiltration remove the water. The dry, flat lake bed that remains is called a *playa.*

Humid regions have complex systems of rivers and streams that drain the land. Streams in dry regions lack this extensive drainage system. **Most desert streams dry up long before they ever reach the ocean. The streams are quickly depleted by evaporation and soil infiltration.**

Some permanent streams do manage to cross arid regions. The Colorado and Nile Rivers begin in well-watered mountains with huge water supplies. The rivers are full enough at the beginning to survive their desert crossings. The Nile River, for example, leaves the lakes and mountains of central Africa and covers almost 3000 kilometers of the Sahara without a single tributary adding to its flow. In humid regions, however, rivers generally gain water from both incoming tributaries and groundwater.

The point to remember about running water in the desert is this: although it is infrequent, it is an important geological force. **Most desert erosion results from running water. Although wind erosion is more significant in deserts than elsewhere, water does most of the erosional work in deserts.** Wind plays a different primary role in the desert. It transports and deposits the sediments to create dunes.

Section 7.2 Assessment

Reviewing Concepts

1. How are ephemeral streams different form streams in humid locations?

2. How do weathering processes affect deserts?

3. Why is erosion by running water important in deserts?

4. How does a river survive crossing an arid region?

Critical Thinking

5. **Comparing and Contrasting** Compare and contrast the Nile River with the Mississippi River. Which factor is most responsible for their differences?

6. **Applying Concepts** Explain how evaporation affects drainage systems in desert areas.

Writing in Science

Suppose you are standing on a bridge over an ephemeral stream in the desert. Write a paragraph describing what you might see following a sudden downpour.

7.3 Landscapes Shaped by Wind

Reading Focus

Key Concepts

- How does deflation cause erosion in the desert?
- How does abrasion shape desert landscapes?
- What types of landforms are deposited by wind?
- How do sand dunes differ?

Vocabulary

- deflation
- desert pavement
- loess
- dune

Reading Strategy

Outlining Before you read, make an outline of this section. Use the green headings as the main topics and the blue headings as subtopics. As you read, add supporting details.

Landscapes Shaped by Wind
I. Wind Erosion
A. Deflation
B. Abrasion
II. _____?
A. _____?

Wind Erosion

Compared with running water, wind does not do nearly as much erosional work on the land, even in deserts. But wind is still an important force. Humid areas can resist wind erosion because moisture binds soil particles together and plants anchor the soil. But desert soils are dry and have less vegetation to hold soil in place. Therefore, wind does its most effective erosional work in deserts.

Strong desert winds pick up, transport, and deposit great quantities of fine sediment. Farmers of the Great Plains experienced the power of wind erosion during the 1930s. After they plowed the natural vegetation from this semi-arid region, a severe drought set in. The land was left exposed to wind erosion. Vast dust storms swept away the fertile topsoil. The area became known as the Dust Bowl.

Wind erodes in the desert in two ways: deflation and abrasion. Deflation is the lifting and removal of loose particles such as clay and silt. Coarser sand particles roll or skip along the surface in a process called saltation. These large sand particles make up the bed load. In portions of the Dust Bowl, deflation lowered the land by a meter or more in only a few years, as shown in Figure 17.

Deflation also results in shallow depressions called blowouts. You can see thousands of blowouts in the Great Plains. They range from small dimples less than 1 meter deep and 3 meters wide to depressions more than 45 meters deep and several kilometers across.

Figure 17 The mounds in this photo show the level of the land before deflation removed the topsoil. The mounds are 1.2 meters tall and are anchored by vegetation. The photo was taken in July 1936 in Granville, North Dakota and reveals the extent of the damage in the Dust Bowl. **Applying Concepts** *How did farmers contribute to ruining the land during the Dust Bowl?*

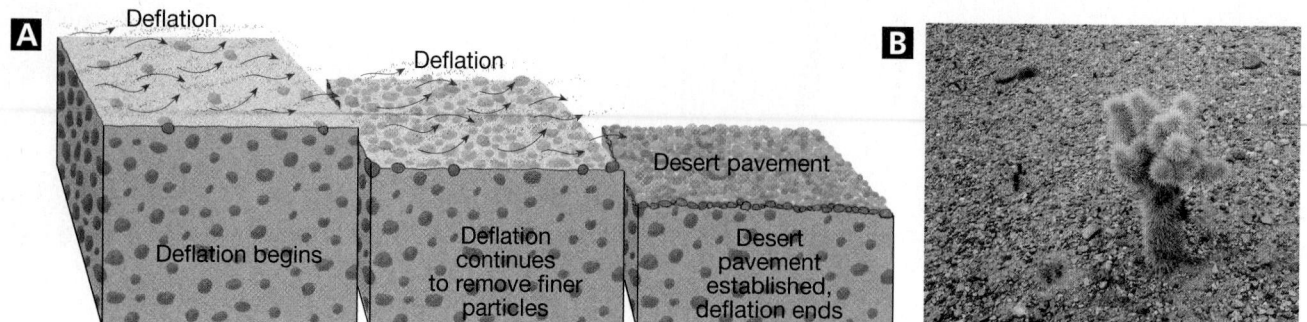

A Deflation

Deflation

Desert pavement

Deflation begins

Deflation continues to remove finer particles

Desert pavement established, deflation ends

B

Figure 18 A These cross sections show how deflation removes the sand and silt of the desert surface until only coarser particles remain. These coarser particles concentrate into a tightly packed layer called desert pavement. **B** Desert pavement like this in Arizona's Sonoran Desert protects the surface from further deflation. **Predicting** *What will happen if a vehicle disturbs this desert pavement?*

In portions of many deserts, the surface is characterized by a layer of course pebbles and cobbles that are too large to be moved by the wind. Deflation creates a stony surface layer called **desert pavement** when it removes all the sand and silt and leaves only coarser particles. See Figure 18. The remaining surface of coarse pebbles and cobbles is protected from further deflation—unless vehicles or animals break it up. If something does disturb the surface, the wind begins eroding once again.

Wind can erode by abrasion, too. Abrasion happens when wind-blown sand cuts and polishes exposed rock surfaces. Blowing sand can grind away at boulders and smaller rocks, sometimes sandblasting them into odd shapes. Abrasion is often credited for features such as balanced rocks that stand high atop narrow pedestals or the detailing on tall pinnacles. However, these features are not the results of abrasion. Sand rarely travels more than a meter above the surface, so the wind's sandblasting effect is limited in a vertical extent. However, in some areas, telephone poles have been cut through near the base.

 **Reading Checkpoint** *What is deflation?*

Wind Deposits

The wind can create landforms when it deposits its sediments, especially in deserts and along coasts. Both layers of loess and sand dunes are landscape features deposited by wind. These blankets of silt and mounds of sand are striking features in some parts of the world.

Loess Loess is windblown silt that blankets the landscape. Dust storms over thousands of years picked up this material, transported it, and then deposited it. The thickest and most extensive deposits of loess on Earth occur in western and northern China. The silt was derived from nearby deserts. This fine, buff-colored sediment gives the Yellow River its name. You also can find loess in the United States. See Figure 19. Strong winds sweeping across glacial sediments created significant loess deposits in portions of South Dakota, Nebraska, Iowa, Missouri, Illinois, and the Columbia Plateau in the Pacific Northwest.

Figure 19 This loess bluff near the Mississippi River in southern Illinois is about 3 meters high.

Figure 20 Sand slides down the steeper face of a dune in New Mexico's White Sands National Monument. Wind blows sand up the opposite, windward, face of the dune, then it drops down this sheltered side. Slippage along the steep side results in migration of the dune in the direction the wind blows.

Figure 21 These cross beds are part of the Navajo Sandstone in Zion National Park, Utah.

Sand Dunes Like running water, wind releases its load of sediment when its velocity falls and the energy available for transport diminishes. Sand begins to accumulate wherever an obstruction crosses its path and slows its movement. ⊙ **Unlike deposits of loess, which form blanket-like layers over broad areas, winds commonly deposit sand in mounds or ridges called dunes.** Dunes can occur in places where the wind encounters an obstruction. The wind's velocity falls and the sand particles drop to the ground. Dunes can begin near obstructions as small as a clump of vegetation or a rock. Once the sand starts to mound up it serves as its own obstruction, and it traps more and more sand. With enough sand and long periods of steady wind, the mound of sand becomes a dune.

Dunes often are steeper on the sheltered side and more gently sloping inclined on the side facing the wind. Wind blows sand grains up the gentler windward side. Once the sand blows over the crest of the dune, the wind slows and the sand drops out. The sheltered side of the dune becomes steeper, and the sand eventually slides down the slope, as shown in Figure 20. In this way, the dune tends to migrate in the direction the wind blows.

As sand is deposited on the sheltered side of the dune, it forms layers inclined in the direction the wind is blowing. These sloping layers are called cross beds. When the dunes are eventually buried under other layers of sediment and become sedimentary rock, the cross beds remain as a record of their origin, as shown in Figure 21.

 **Reading Checkpoint** *How do obstructions help to form dunes?*

For: Links on wind erosion
Visit: www.SciLinks.org
Web Code: cjn-2073

Types of Sand Dunes

Dunes are not just random heaps of sand. They occur in a variety of consistent forms worldwide. ◯ **What form sand dunes assume depends on the wind direction and speed, how much sand is available, and the amount of vegetation.** Figure 22 shows six different types of dunes.

Barchan Dunes Solitary sand dunes shaped like crescents are called barchan dunes. These form on flat, hard ground where supplies of sand and vegetation are limited. Barchan dunes move slowly and only reach heights of about 30 meters. If the wind direction is constant, barchan dunes remain symmetrical. One tip of the dune can grow larger than the other if the wind direction varies somewhat.

Transverse Dunes If prevailing winds are steady, sand is plentiful, and vegetation is sparse, dunes form in a series of long ridges. They are called transverse dunes because these ridges are perpendicular to the direction of the wind. Transverse dunes are typical in many coastal areas.

Types of Sand Dunes

Figure 22

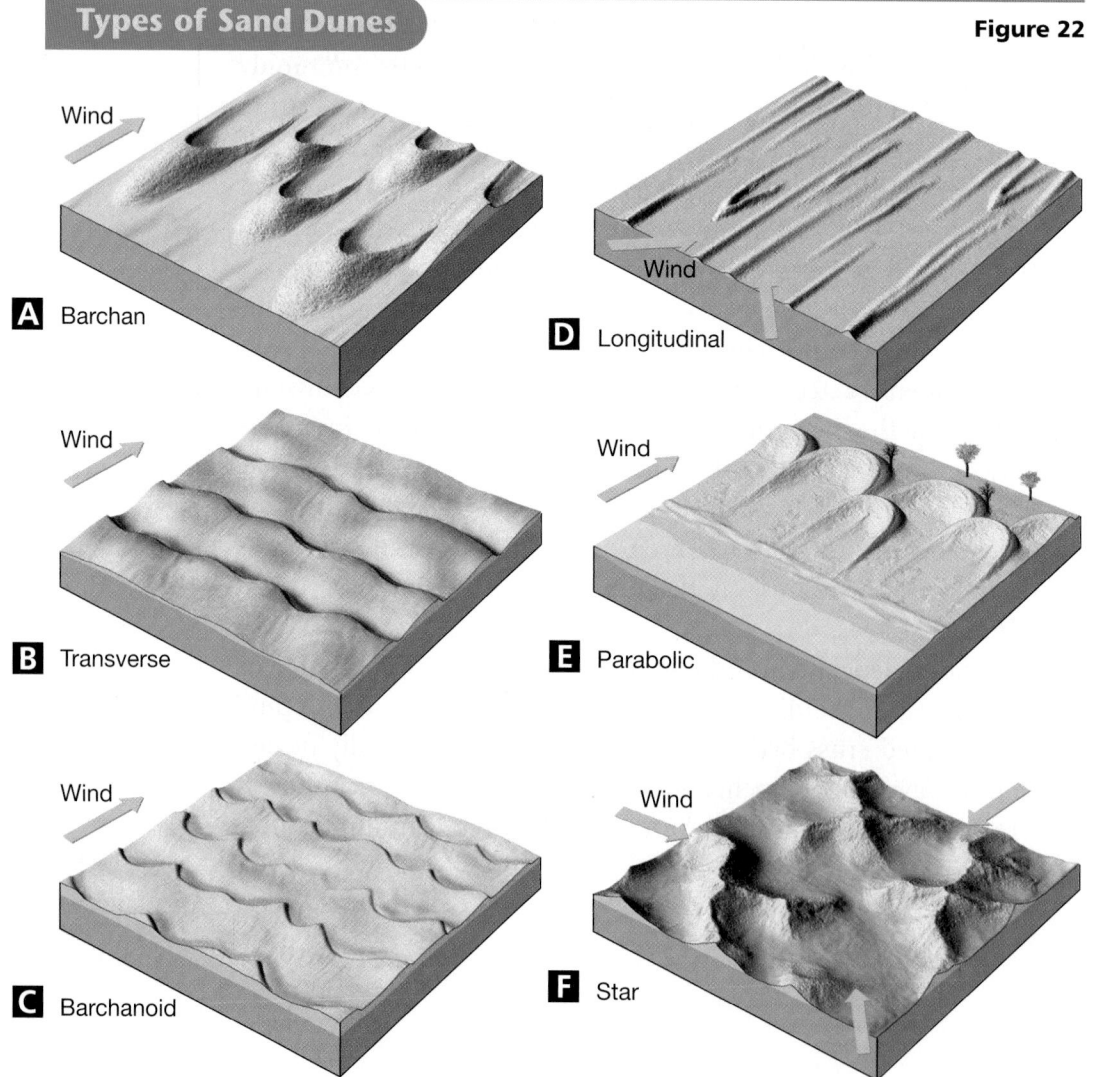

A Barchan

B Transverse

C Barchanoid

D Longitudinal

E Parabolic

F Star

They also comprise the "sand seas" found in parts of the Sahara and Arabian deserts. Transverse dunes in both of these deserts reach heights of 200 meters, measure 1 to 3 kilometers across, and extend for distances of 100 kilometers or more.

Barchanoid Dunes A common dune form that is intermediate between a barchan and transverse dune is the barchanoid dune. These scalloped rows of sand form at right angles to the wind. The rows resemble a series of barchans that have been positioned side by side. You can see them at White Sands National Monument in New Mexico.

Longitudinal Dunes Longitudinal dunes are long ridges of sand that form parallel to the prevailing wind. These dunes occur where sand supplies are moderate and the prevailing wind direction varies slightly. In portions of North Africa, Arabia, and central Australia, longitudinal dunes can reach nearly 100 meters high and extend for more than 100 kilometers.

Parabolic Dunes Parabolic dunes look like backward barchans. Their tips point into the wind instead of away from it. They form where some vegetation covers the sand. Parabolic dunes often form along the coast where strong onshore winds and abundant sand are available.

Star Dunes Star dunes are isolated hills of sand mostly found in parts of the Sahara and Arabian deserts. Their bases resemble stars and they usually have three or four sharp ridges that meet in the middle. Star dunes develop in areas of variable wind direction, and they sometimes reach heights of 90 meters.

Q *Aren't deserts mostly covered with sand dunes?*

A Many people think a desert is covered in drifting sand dunes. Some deserts do have striking sand dunes. But sand dunes worldwide represent only a small percentage of the total desert area. Dunes cover only one-tenth of the world's largest desert, the Sahara, and only one-third of the world's sandiest desert, the Arabian, is covered in dunes.

Section 7.3 Assessment

Reviewing Concepts

1. How does deflation lower the surface of the desert?
2. What would you expect to see in areas subject to abrasion?
3. What was the Dust Bowl, and why did it occur?
4. How does a dune help itself to grow?
5. What factors determine the shape of sand dunes?

Critical Thinking

5. **Comparing and Contrasting** Compare and contrast loess and sand dunes.
6. **Designing Experiments** Describe how you would conduct an experiment to determine the wind speed necessary to suspend sand, silt, and clay particles.

Connecting Concepts

Which dune type would you expect to travel the least? Explain your answer.

# How the Earth Works

Erosion

Erosion is the process by which rocks are broken down by weathering and the loose material is carried away. Rock material can be moved by streams and rivers, by waves, by glacial ice, or by wind. The number of fragments that are moved and the distance that they travel are affected by factors such as the size and weight of the particles and the speed at which the eroding agent is moving. The eroded material is carried to another site where it is deposited as **sediment.** Erosion affects the landscapes of Central Asia, the Caucasus, and all regions of the world.

WATER FLOWING
As water flows from highlands to the sea, sharp descents result in rapids and waterfalls. Flowing water is an important agent of erosion.

SAND DUNES
A dune begins to form where a plant or other obstacle slows the wind, which drops its load of sand. As the sand piles up, it creates an ever-growing barrier to the wind, causing more sand to be dropped. Eventually the dune crest may collapse like an ocean wave.

Sand dunes

Rock arch

Wadi

Rock fragments collect in wadi

EROSION IN ARID LANDS
When rare torrential rain comes to arid areas in Central Asia and elsewhere, entire mountainsides may be swept clean of boulders, rock fragments, sand, and clay. Flash floods wash eroded material down **wadis**—the valleys of streams that are usually dry.

SEAS OF SAND
The huge amounts of sand that comprise some deserts started out as rock that was weathered to form fine particles. The finer the particle, the farther it can be transported by agents of erosion.

EROSION BY GLACIAL ICE

Huge masses of moving ice are called **glaciers.** Over thousands or millions of years, they can scour mountainsides and dramatically change the shapes of valleys.

1. Before glaciation
A narrow, V-shaped river valley is surrounded by rounded mountains.

2. During glaciation
Moving ice erodes mountaintops and carves wider valleys.

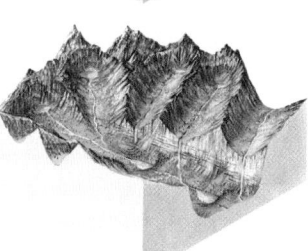

3. After glaciation
The result is a U-shaped valley with rugged, sharp peaks above.

STREAM EROSION

Streams erode their banks and beds, continually widening and deepening them. In some cases, a canyon may result. A **canyon,** such as this one in Utah, is a deep valley with vertical sides that have been eroded by river water.

WAVE ACTION

Coastlines are constantly eroded by waves that are formed by winds blowing over water. Cracked and soft rocks are eroded away first, leading to the creation of arches. If the arch roof collapses, a **sea stack** results.

1. Waves curve around headland.

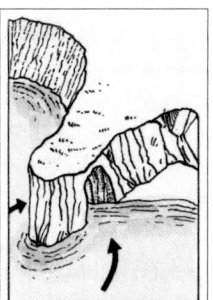

2. An arch forms.

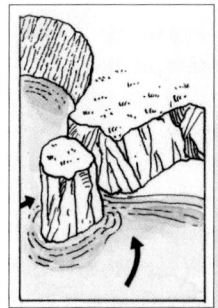

3. A sea stack results.

Sea stack off the British Isles

ASSESSMENT

1. **Key Terms** Define **(a)** erosion, **(b)** sediment, **(c)** wadi, **(d)** glacier, **(e)** canyon, **(f)** sea stack.

2. **Environmental Change** How does water gradually reshape the land?

3. **Physical Characteristics** What are some major physical characteristics of an arid landscape eroded by wind and rain?

4. **Physical Processes** Analyze the three diagrams of glacial erosion. How can glaciers change the shapes of mountain valleys?

5. **Critical Thinking Analyzing Causes and Effects** How can erosion on farmlands cause a reduction in agricultural production?

Interpreting a Glacial Landscape

Topographic maps are valuable tools geologists use to interpret landscapes. Especially in the field—when your view can be limited—these maps not only help you determine your location, they can offer a bigger landscape picture than what is actually visible. See how well you can do at identifying glacial features on the map and interpreting them to reconstruct geologic history.

Problem How can a topographic map allow you to interpret a glacially formed landscape?

Materials
- topographic map
- piece of blank paper
- pencil

SOUTH / NORTH

Sugar Loaf Mountain / Bear Lake

Skills Graphing, Inferring, Drawing Conclusions

Procedure

1. Following line A on the map, sketch a topographic profile of the Lake Fork Valley onto the grid above. Place the straight edge of your blank paper along the line and mark in pencil where it meets every fifth contour line (the darker guide contours). Be sure to write the elevation of every fifth contour line along the *y*-axis of the profile grid.

2. How can you tell from your profile that the valley was formed by a glacier?

3. Was the valley shaped by a continental ice sheet or by a valley glacier? Explain how you know.

4. Use the map to help you describe the direction the glacier flowed through this valley. How can you tell?

5. Which letter arrow points to cirques? You can refer to Figure 7 in your textbook for help.

6. The lakes inside cirques are called tarns. Identify the tarns inside the cirques you just found.

7. Which letter arrows point to hanging valleys?

8. Which letter arrows point to arêtes?

9. Name a peak on the map that is a horn.

10. Feature E on the map is composed of glacial till. What type of glacial feature is E, and how did it form?

11. Explain how Turquoise Lake formed.

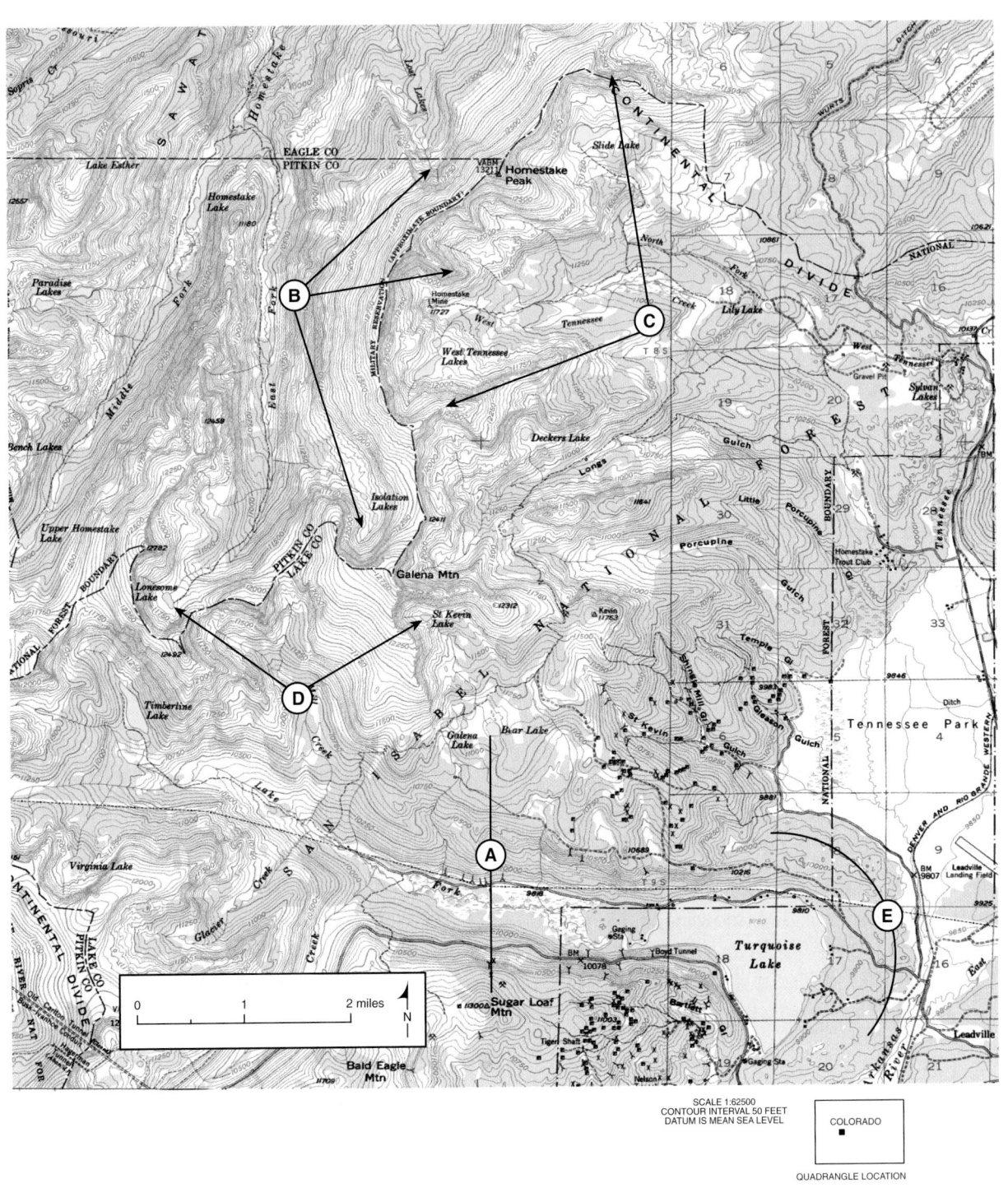

SCALE 1:62500
CONTOUR INTERVAL 50 FEET
DATUM IS MEAN SEA LEVEL

COLORADO

QUADRANGLE LOCATION

Study Guide

7.1 Glaciers

Key Concepts

- Valley glaciers are found in mountains. They are streams of ice that flow between steep rock walls from a place near the top where snow accumulates.

- Ice sheets cover large regions where the climate is extremely cold. They are huge compared to valley glaciers.

- The movement of glaciers is referred to as flow. Glacial flow happens two ways: plastic flow and basal slip.

- The glacial budget is the balance or lack of balance between accumulation at the upper end of a glacier and its loss at the lower end.

- Many landscapes were changed by the widespread glaciers of the recent ice age.

- Glaciers are responsible for a variety of erosional landscape features, such as hanging valleys, cirques, arêtes, and horns.

- Glacial drift applies to all sediments of glacial origin, no matter how, where, or in what form they were deposited. There are two types of glacial drift: till and stratified drift.

- Glaciers are responsible for a variety of depositional landscape features, including moraines, outwash plains, kettles, drumlins, and eskers.

Vocabulary

ice age, *p. 188;* glacier, *p. 188;* snowline, *p. 189;* valley glacier, *p. 189;* ice sheet, *p. 189;* glacial trough, *p. 193;* till, *p. 194;* stratified drift, *p. 194;* moraine, *p. 195*

7.2 Deserts

Key Concepts

- Mechanical weathering produces most of the debris in most deserts. Chemical weathering does exist in the desert; however, the process is slow. Chemical weathering results in thin soils and the familiar rust-tinted desert landscapes.

- In the desert, most streams are ephemeral—they only carry water after it rains.

- Because there are fewer plants in deserts to anchor the soil, the amount of erosion caused during a single short-lived rain event is impressive.

- Most desert streams dry up long before they ever reach the ocean. The streams are quickly depleted by evaporation and soil infiltration.

- Most desert erosion results from running water. Although deserts experience more wind erosion than other places, water is still the foremost agent that carves arid landscapes.

Vocabulary

alluvial fan, *p. 201;* playa lake, *p. 202*

7.3 Landscapes Shaped by Wind

Key Concepts

- Wind erosion is more effective in deserts than in humid regions.

- There are two types of wind erosion: deflation and abrasion.

- The wind can create landforms when it deposits its sediments. Layers of loess and sand dunes are landscape features deposited by wind.

- A sand dune's form depends on the wind direction and speed, the amount of sand available, and the amount of vegetation.

Vocabulary

deflation, *p. 203;* desert pavement, *p. 204;* loess, *p. 204;* dune, *p. 205*

Reviewing Content

Choose the letter that best answers the question or completes the statement.

1. Icebergs are produced when large pieces of ice break from the front of glacier during a process called
   a. plucking.
   b. deflation.
   c. calving.
   d. abrasion.

2. What type of dune forms at right angles to the wind when there is abundant sand, a lack of vegetation, and a constant wind direction?
   a. barchan
   b. transverse
   c. longitudinal
   d. parabolic

3. During which division of geologic time did the most recent ice age occur?
   a. Pliocene
   b. Paleocene
   c. Pleistocene
   d. Miocene

4. All sediments of glacial origin are
   a. till.
   b. glacial drift.
   c. stratified drift.
   d. outwash.

5. What term is used to describe desert streams that carry water only during periods of rainfall called?
   a. playas
   b. ephemeral
   c. episodic
   d. occasional

6. The two major ways that glaciers erode land are abrasion and
   a. plucking.
   b. tension.
   c. deflation.
   d. slipping.

7. The most noticeable result of deflation in some places are shallow depressions called
   a. sinkholes.
   b. blowouts.
   c. ventifacts.
   d. kettles.

8. In which of these places do extensive yellow loess deposits occur?
   a. Canada
   b. Cambodia
   c. China
   d. Australia

9. Which of the following is NOT a feature associated with valley glaciers?
   a. horn
   b. cirque
   c. arête
   d. arroyo

10. The broad, ramp-like surface of stratified drift built adjacent to the downstream edge of most end moraines is a (an)
    a. kettle.
    b. drumlin.
    c. outwash plain.
    d. terminal moraine.

Understanding Concepts

11. Why is the uppermost 50 m of a glacier called the zone of fracture?

12. How do the erosional processes of plucking and abrasion work?

Use the diagram below to answer Question 13.

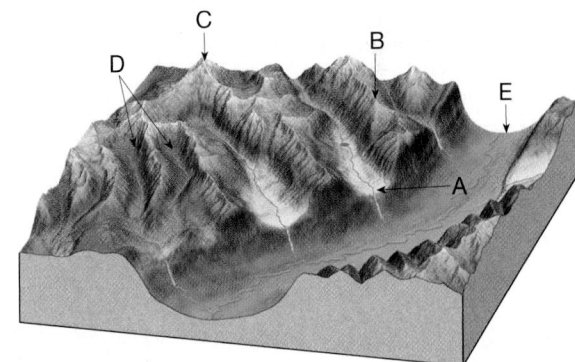

13. The area in the diagram was eroded by valley glaciers. For each feature listed below, write the letter of that feature in the diagram.
    a) cirque
    b) glacial trough
    c) hanging valley
    d) horn
    e) arête

14. Describe each type of moraine:
   a) end moraine
   b) lateral moraine
   c) ground moraine

15. Identify the glacier features in the diagram.

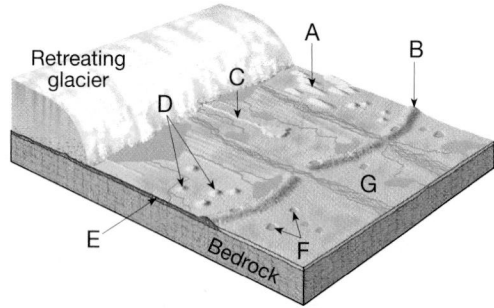

   a) drumlin
   b) outwash plain
   c) esker
   d) end moraine

16. Describe how sand dunes migrate.

17. How does the transport of sediment by glaciers differ from transport by water?

18. How do desert streams differ from those in humid regions?

19. What results when desert pavement is disturbed?

20. Describe the relative importance of wind and running water in eroding the desert landscape.

21. How is if possible for ice to flow?

22. Why do crevasses only extend 50 meters or so beneath the surface of a glacier?

Critical Thinking

23. Relating Cause and Effect Explain how a glacier's budget determines whether it advances, retreats, or remains stationary.

24. Comparing and Contrasting In what ways are the erosional actions of wind, water, and glaciers similar? How are they different?

25. Inferring Explain why glacial erratics will usually contain different minerals than the rock outcropping where they are found.

Analyzing Data

Use the graph below to answer Questions 26–28.

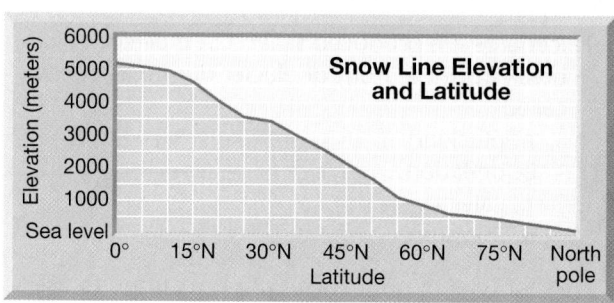

26. Inferring What is the minimum elevation required for year-round snow on a mountain located on the equator?

27. Inferring Suppose a 2000-meter mountain was located at 75 degrees north of the equator. What percentage of its height would have year-round snow?

28. Drawing Conclusions Write a statement that summarizes the information in the graph.

Concepts in Action

29. Using Models Explain how you would model each type of sand dune using a fan, a pan full of sand, and some playing cards.

30. Classifying Which types of landscape features described in this chapter resulted from erosion? Which types resulted from deposition?

31. Writing in Science Write a paragraph that summarizes the role of climate in the development of the landscapes discussed in this chapter.

Performance-Based Assessment

Researching Eskers are one glacial feature that people have transformed into a resource. Find out why glacial sediments are useful, who mines them, how they mine them, and the extent of their commercial value. Explain whether glacial deposits are considered renewable or non-renewable resources.

Standardized Test Prep

Avoiding Careless Mistakes

Students often make mistakes when they fail to read a test question and the possible answers carefully. Read the question carefully and underline key words that may change the meaning of the question, such as *not, except,* or *excluding.* After choosing an answer, reread the question to check your selection.

Choose the letter that best answers the question or completes the statement.

1. Which of the following is NOT associated with water?
   (A) ephemeral stream
   (B) kettle
   (C) hanging valley
   (D) blowout

   (Answer: D)

2. Which of the following statements about ice sheets is NOT true?
   (A) They cover 30 percent of Earth's land surface.
   (B) They form where more snow accumulates than melts.
   (C) They are more effective agents of erosion than running water.
   (D) They can flow.

3. Which is NOT true of loess?
   (A) Loess is a blanket of silt covering the landscape.
   (B) The Yellow River in China is named for the loess that it transports.
   (C) Wind carries and deposits the sediments that comprise loess.
   (D) There are no loess deposits in the United States.

4. What is the main factor that causes barchan dunes to form in the opposite direction of parabolic dunes?
   (A) Parabolic dunes are partially anchored by vegetation.
   (B) Barchan dunes have a greater supply of available sand than parabolic dunes.
   (C) The wind that creates barchan dunes is more variable in direction than the wind forming parabolic dunes.
   (D) Barchan dunes can migrate; parabolic dunes cannot.

5. When a stream emerges from a mountain canyon, the stream slope is greatly reduced. As a result the sediment is deposited within a short distance and forms a (an)
   (A) playa lake.
   (B) alluvial fan.
   (C) sinkhole.
   (D) arête.

Answer the following questions in complete sentences.

6. Name the four basic types of moraines. How are they similar? How are they different?

7. Glaciers are solid, but they are a basic part of Earth's water cycle. Are glaciers a part of solid Earth or part of Earth's hydrosphere? Explain your answer.

8. What role do glaciers play in Earth's rock cycle?

Earthquakes and Earth's Interior

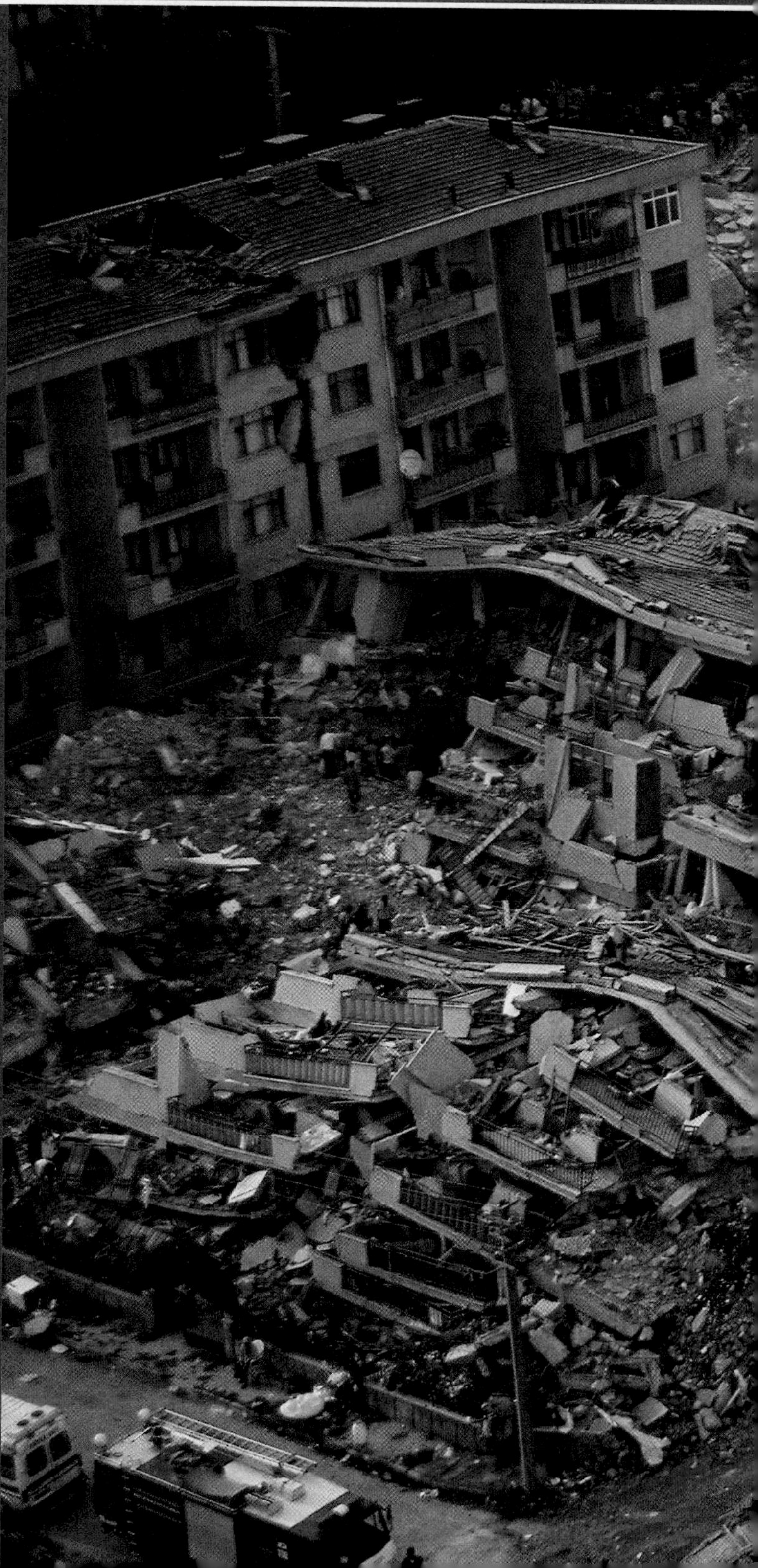

CONCEPTS
— in Action —

Quick Lab
Measuring the Distance to Epicenters

Exploration Lab
Locating an Earthquake

How the Earth Works
Effects of Earthquakes

 **GEODe** Forces Within
EARTH SCIENCE ↳ Earthquakes

 **Video Field Trip**

Earth in Motion

Take a field trip to the center of the Earth with the Discovery Channel and find out how earthquakes occur. Answer the following questions after watching the video.

1. Describe how the meeting of two tectonic plates can lead to an earthquake.

2. Where does the greatest damage occur during an earthquake?

Go Online
PHSchool.com

For: Chapter 8 Resources
Visit: PHSchool.com
Web Code: cjk-9999

Destruction caused by a major earthquake ▶ that struck northwestern Turkey on August 17, 1999. More than 17,000 people died.

Chapter Preview

Inquiry Activity

How Can Buildings Be Made Earthquake-Safe?

Procedure

1. Construct a model of a one-story brick building using two thin pieces of cardboard as the floor and roof. Use sugar cubes as bricks and peanut butter, frosting, or double-sided tape to hold the bricks together.

2. Construct a second building. Make this building a two-story structure.

3. To test how well your buildings stand up to a simulated earthquake, place the one-story building on a table or desk. Then either drop a large book on the table, or gently shake the edge of the table. Record your observations.

4. Repeat Step 3 with the two-story model building. Record your observations.

5. Construct a third building using small pieces of window screen as reinforcement. This building should be a one-story structure. Spread a thin layer of peanut butter or frosting on the inside of the walls and carefully attach pieces of screen to each of the inside walls. Use extra peanut butter or frosting to reinforce the inside corners.

6. Repeat Step 3 with the reinforced building. Record your observations.

Think About It

1. **Observing** What happened to each building during the simulated earthquakes?

2. **Comparing and Contrasting** Compare the amount of earthquake damage in the three model buildings.

8.1 What Is an Earthquake?

Reading Focus

Key Concepts

- What is a fault?
- What is the cause of earthquakes?

Vocabulary

- earthquake
- focus
- epicenter
- fault
- elastic rebound hypothesis
- aftershock
- foreshock

Reading Strategy

Building Vocabulary Copy the table below. Then as you read the section, write a definition for each vocabulary term in your own words.

Vocabulary	Definition
earthquake	a. _____?_____
b. _____?_____	c. _____?_____
d. _____?_____	e. _____?_____
f. _____?_____	g. _____?_____

Each year, more than 30,000 earthquakes occur worldwide that are strong enough to be felt. Fortunately, most of these earthquakes are minor tremors and do very little damage. Generally, only about 75 major earthquakes take place each year. Most of these occur in remote regions. However, occasionally a large earthquake occurs near a city. Under these conditions, an earthquake is one of the most destructive natural forces on Earth, as shown in Figure 1.

Earthquakes

An **earthquake** is the vibration of Earth produced by the rapid release of energy. Earthquakes are often caused by slippage along a break in Earth's crust.

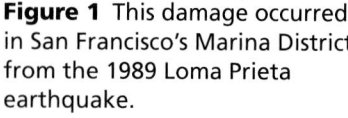

Figure 1 This damage occurred in San Francisco's Marina District from the 1989 Loma Prieta earthquake.

Focus and Epicenter The point within Earth where the earthquake starts is called the **focus.** The released energy radiates in all directions from the focus in the form of waves. These waves are similar to the waves produced when a stone is dropped into a calm pond. The impact of the stone sets water waves in motion. An earthquake is similar because it produces seismic waves that radiate throughout Earth.

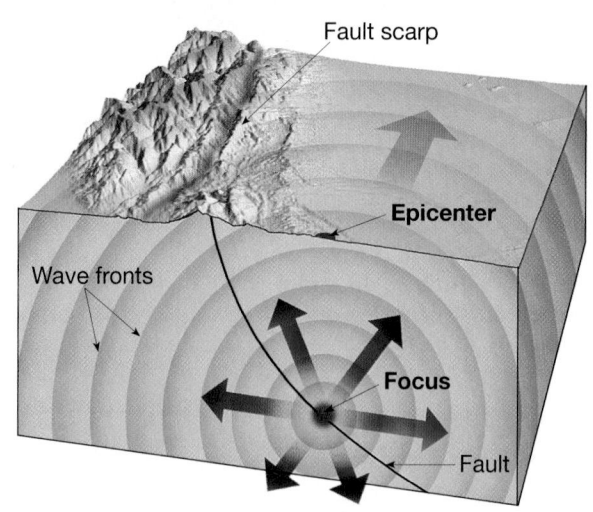

Fault scarp

Epicenter

Wave fronts

Focus

Fault

The focus of an earthquake is the place within Earth where the earthquake originates. When you see a news report about an earthquake, the reporter always mentions the place on Earth's surface where the earthquake has been located. The **epicenter** is the location on the surface directly above the focus, as shown in Figure 2.

Faults A lot of evidence shows that Earth is constantly changing. We know that Earth's crust has been uplifted at times. We have found many ancient wave-cut features meters above the level of the highest tides. Offsets in fence lines, roads, and other structures indicate that horizontal movements of Earth's crust are also common, as seen in Figure 3. Earthquakes are usually associated with large fractures in Earth's crust and mantle called **faults**. 🔑 Faults are fractures in Earth where movement has occurred.

 **Reading Checkpoint** *What is a fault?*

Figure 2 The focus of each earthquake is the place within Earth where the earthquake originated. The foci (plural of focus) are located along faults. The surface location directly above the focus is called the epicenter.
Predicting *Where do you think the damage from an earthquake is usually greatest?*

Cause of Earthquakes

Before the great 1906 San Francisco earthquake, the actual causes and effects of earthquakes were not understood. The San Fransisco earthquake caused horizontal shifts in Earth's surface of several meters along the northern portion of the San Andreas Fault. The 1300-kilometer San Andreas fracture extends north and south through southern California. Studies following the 1906 quake found that during this single event, the land on the western side of the San Andreas Fault moved as much as 4.7 meters to the north compared to the land on the eastern side of the fault.

Based on these measurements and related studies, a hypothesis was developed to explain what had been observed. Figure 4 on page 220 illustrates this hypothesis. Part A shows an existing fault. In part B, forces within Earth slowly deform the crustal rocks on both sides of the fault, shown by the bent features of the rocks. These forces cause the rocks to bend and store elastic energy, just like a wooden stick does if it is bent. Elastic energy is the same kind of energy that is stored when you stretch a rubber band. Eventually, the resistance caused by internal friction that holds the rocks together is overcome. The rocks slip at the weakest point (the focus). The movement will exert forces farther along the fault, where additional slippage will occur until most of the built-up energy is released. This slippage allows the deformed rock to snap back in place. The vibrations we call an earthquake occur as the rock elastically returns to its original shape.

Figure 3 Slippage along a fault caused an offset in this orange grove east of Calexico, California. The white arrows show the direction of movement on either side of the fault.

Figure 4 As rock is stressed it bends, storing elastic energy. Once the rock is strained beyond its breaking point, it ruptures and releases the stored energy in the form of seismic waves.
Inferring *How do you think the temperature of rock would affect its ability to bend or break?*

Elastic Rebound Hypothesis

The springing back of the rock into its original place is called elastic rebound. The rock behaves much like a stretched rubber band does when it is released. The explanation says that when rocks are deformed, they first bend and then break, releasing stored energy. This explanation for the release of energy stored in deformed rocks is called the **elastic rebound hypothesis.**

Elastic Rebound

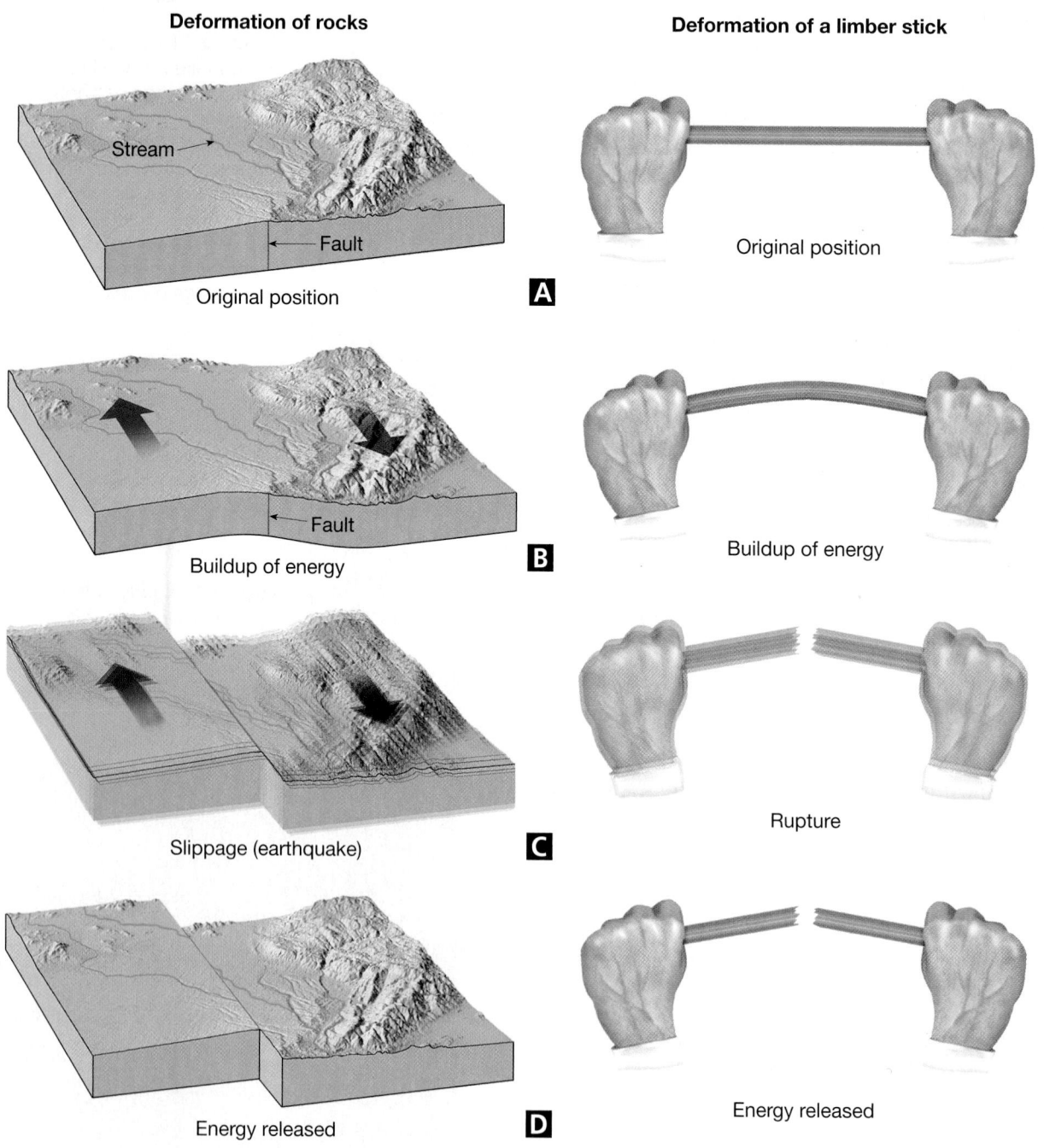

Deformation of rocks

Stream

Fault

Original position **A**

Fault

Buildup of energy **B**

Slippage (earthquake) **C**

Energy released **D**

Deformation of a limber stick

Original position

Buildup of energy

Rupture

Energy released

Most earthquakes are produced by the rapid release of elastic energy stored in rock that has been subjected to great forces. When the strength of the rock is exceeded, it suddenly breaks, causing the vibrations of an earthquake. Earthquakes most often happen along existing faults. They occur when the frictional forces on the fault surfaces are overcome.

For: Links on earthquakes
Visit: www.SciLinks.org
Web Code: cjn-3081

Aftershocks and Foreshocks The intense shaking of the 1906 San Francisco earthquake lasted about 40 seconds. Most of the movement along the fault occurred in this short time period. However, additional movements along this and nearby faults continued for several days. The movements that follow a major earthquake often produce smaller earthquakes called **aftershocks.** These aftershocks are usually much weaker than the main earthquake, but they can sometimes destroy structures weakened by the main quake. Small earthquakes called **foreshocks** often come before a major earthquake. These foreshocks can happen days or even years before the major quake.

The San Andreas Fault is the most studied fault system in the world. Studies have shown that displacement has occurred along segments that are 100 to 200 kilometers long. Each fault segment behaves a bit differently than the other segments. Some parts of the San Andreas show a slow, gradual movement known as fault creep. This movement happens fairly smoothly. Other segments regularly slip and produce small earthquakes. However, some segments stay locked and store elastic energy for hundreds of years before they break and cause great earthquakes.

Section 8.1 Assessment

Reviewing Concepts

1. What is a fault?
2. Describe the cause of earthquakes.
3. What is an earthquake?
4. What is the source of an earthquake called?
5. What are foreshocks and aftershocks?

Critical Thinking

6. **Connecting Concepts** How are faults, foci, and epicenters related?

7. **Inferring** What is meant by elastic rebound?
8. **Making Judgments** Why do most earthquakes cause little damage and loss of life?

Math Practice

9. In 25 years, how much movement will result from a fault that slowly slips 1.5 centimeters per year?

8.2 Measuring Earthquakes

Key Concepts

- What are the types of seismic waves?
- How is an earthquake epicenter located?
- How is the size of an earthquake measured?

Vocabulary

- seismograph
- seismogram
- surface wave
- P wave
- S wave
- moment magnitude

Reading Strategy

Outlining As you read, make an outline of the important ideas in this section. Use the green headings as the main topics and the blue headings as subtopics.

Measuring Earthquakes
I. Earthquake Waves
A. Surface Waves
B. _____?_____
II. _____?_____
A. _____?_____

Figure 5 The seismograph (*seismos* = shake, *graph* = write) amplifies and records ground motion.

Weight hinged to allow movement

Support moves with Earth

Weight does not move with ground motion due to inertia

Pen

Rotating drum records motion

Bedrock

Earth moves

Bedrock

The study of earthquake waves, or seismology, dates back almost 2000 years. The first attempts to discover the direction of earthquakes were made by the Chinese. **Seismographs** are instruments that record earthquake waves. The idea behind seismographs can be demonstrated with a weight suspended from a support attached to bedrock as shown in Figure 5. When waves from an earthquake reach the instrument, the inertia of the weight keeps it stationary, while Earth and the support vibrate. Because the weight stays almost motionless, it provides a reference point to measure the amount of movement that occurs as waves pass through the ground below. The movement of Earth compared to the stationary weight can be recorded on a rotating drum, shown in Figure 5.

Modern seismographs amplify and electronically record ground motion, producing a trace, called a **seismogram.** A typical seismogram (*seismos* = shake, *gramma* = what is written) is shown in Figure 6.

Earthquake Waves

The energy from an earthquake spreads outward as waves in all directions from the focus. Seismograms show that two main types of seismic waves are produced by an earthquake—surface waves and body waves.

Surface Waves **Surface waves** are seismic waves that travel along Earth's outer layer. The motion of surface waves is complex. Surface waves travel along the ground and cause the ground and anything resting upon it to move. This movement is like ocean waves that toss a ship. Surface waves move in an up-and-down motion as well as a side-to-side motion, as shown in Figures 7E and 7F. The side-to-side motion is especially damaging to the foundations of buildings. These movements make surface waves the most destructive earthquake waves.

Body Waves The other waves that travel through Earth's interior are called body waves. Body waves are identified as either P waves or S waves, depending on how they travel through the materials within Earth. Figures 7B and 7D shows differences between the two kinds of waves. **P waves** are push-pull waves—they push (compress) and pull (expand) rocks in the direction the waves travel. P waves are also known as compression waves. In contrast, **S waves** shake the particles at right angles to their direction of travel. This can be shown by fastening one end of a rope and shaking the other end, as in Figure 7C. S waves are transverse waves. P waves temporarily change the volume of the material they pass through by alternately compressing and expanding it, as in Figure 7A. S waves temporarily change the shape of the material they pass through. Gases and liquids will not transmit S waves because they do not rebound elastically to their original shape.

 A seismogram shows all three types of seismic waves—surface waves, P waves, and S waves. By observing a typical seismic record, as shown in Figure 8 on page 225, you can see that the first P wave arrives at the recording station, then the first S wave, and then surface waves. The waves arrive at different times because they travel at different speeds. Generally, in any solid material, P waves travel about 1.7 times faster than S waves. Surface waves travel the slowest at about 90 percent of the speed of the S waves.

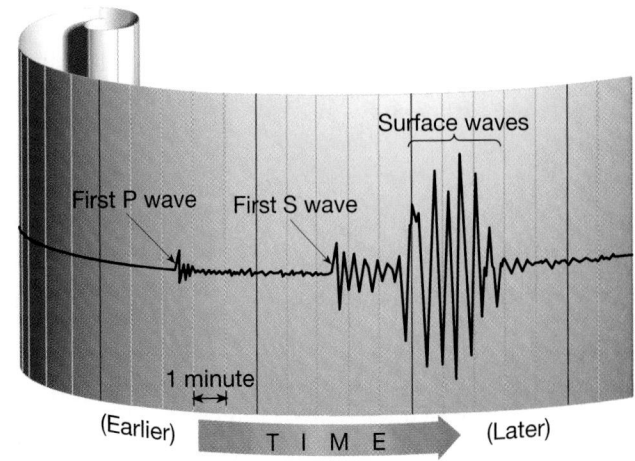

Figure 6 Typical Seismogram
The first wave to arrive is the P wave, followed later by S waves. The last waves recorded are the surface waves.
Measuring *What is the time interval in minutes between the start of the first P wave and the start of the first S wave?*

 **Reading Checkpoint** *Which seismic wave travels fastest?*

Locating an Earthquake

The difference in velocities of P and S waves provides a way to locate the epicenter. You can compare this difference to a race between two cars. The winning car is faster than the losing car. The P wave always wins the race, arriving ahead of the S wave. The longer the race, the greater will be the difference in arrival times of the P and S waves at the finish line (the seismic station). The greater the interval measured on a seismogram between the arrival of the first P wave and the first S wave, the greater the distance to the earthquake source.

Figure 7 Each type of seismic wave has characteristic motions.

Seismic Waves

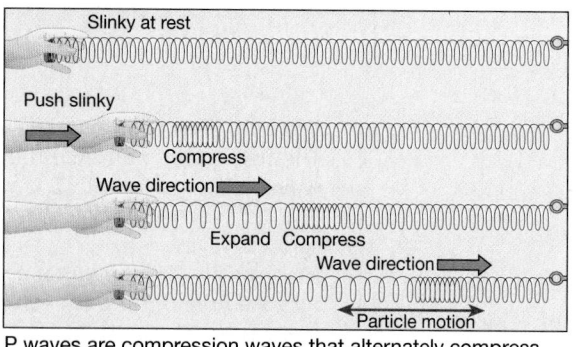

A P waves are compression waves that alternately compress and expand the material through which they pass.

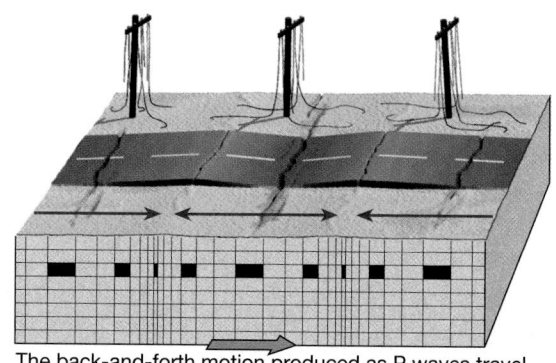

B The back-and-forth motion produced as P waves travel along the surface can cause the ground to buckle and fracture.

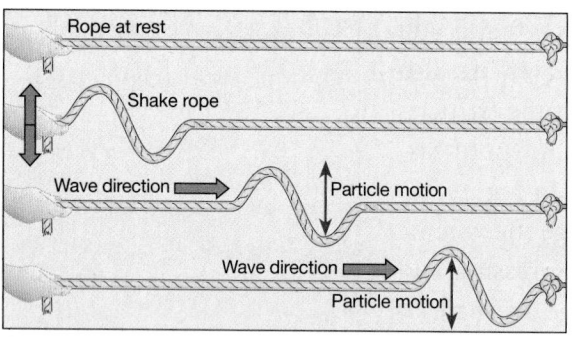

C S waves are transverse waves which cause material to shake at right angles to the direction of wave motion. The length of the red arrow is the displacement, or amplitude, of the S wave.

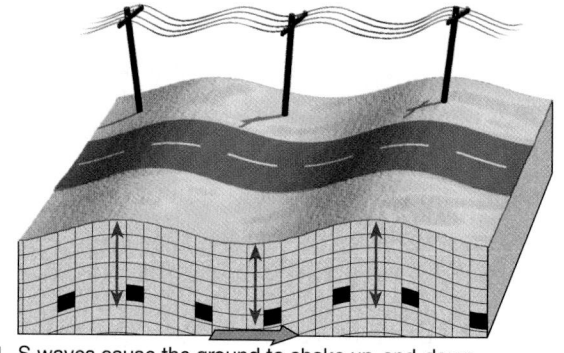

D S waves cause the ground to shake up-and-down and sideways.

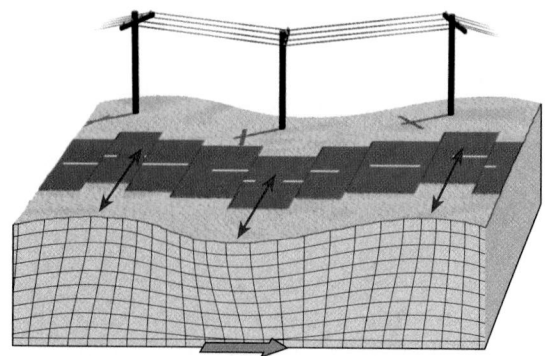

E One type of surface wave moves the ground from side to side and can damage the foundations of buildings.

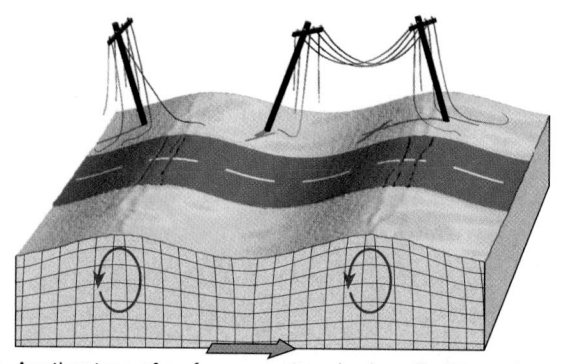

F Another type of surface wave travels along Earth's surface much like rolling ocean waves. The arrows show the movement of rock as the wave passes. The motion follows the shape of an ellipse.

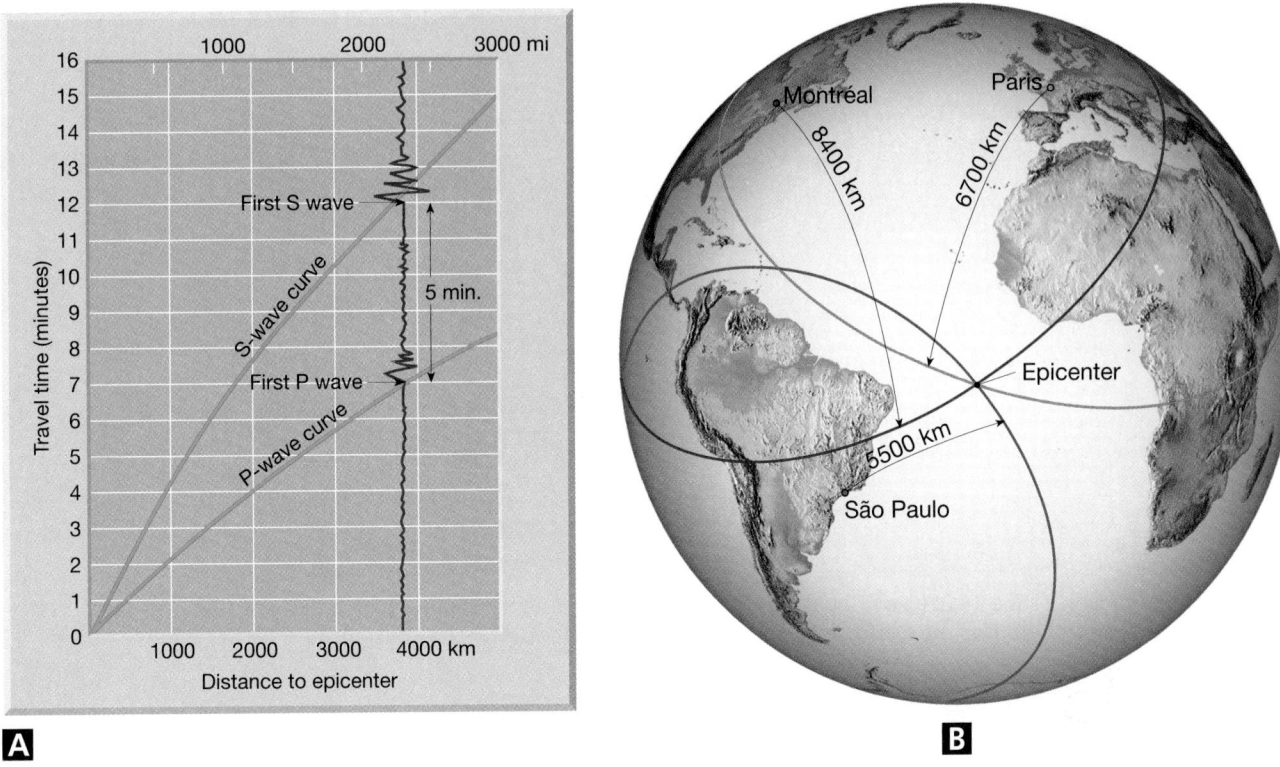

A

B

Figure 8 Locating an Earthquake A A travel-time graph is used to determine the distance to the epicenter. The difference in arrival times of the first P wave and the first S wave in the graph is 5 minutes. So the epicenter is roughly 3800 kilometers away. **B** The epicenter is located using the distance obtained from three seismic stations. The place the circles intersect is the epicenter.

Earthquake Distance A system for locating earthquake epicenters was developed by using seismograms from earthquakes whose epicenters could be easily pinpointed from physical evidence. Travel-time graphs are constructed from these seismograms, as shown in Figure 8A. Using the sample seismogram in Figure 6 and the travel-time curves in Figure 8A, we can determine the distance from the recording station to the earthquake in two steps. First, find the time interval between the arrival of the first P wave and the first S wave on the seismogram. Second, find on the travel-time graph the equivalent time spread between the P and S wave curves. From this information, you can see that this earthquake occurred 3800 kilometers from the seismograph.

Earthquake Direction Now we know the distance, but what about the direction? The epicenter could be in any direction from the seismic station. As shown in Figure 8B, the precise location can be found when the distance is known from three or more different seismic stations. On a globe, we draw a circle around each seismic station. Each circle represents the distance of the epicenter from each station. The point where the three circles intersect is the epicenter of the quake. **Travel-time graphs from three or more seismographs can be used to find the exact location of an earthquake epicenter.**

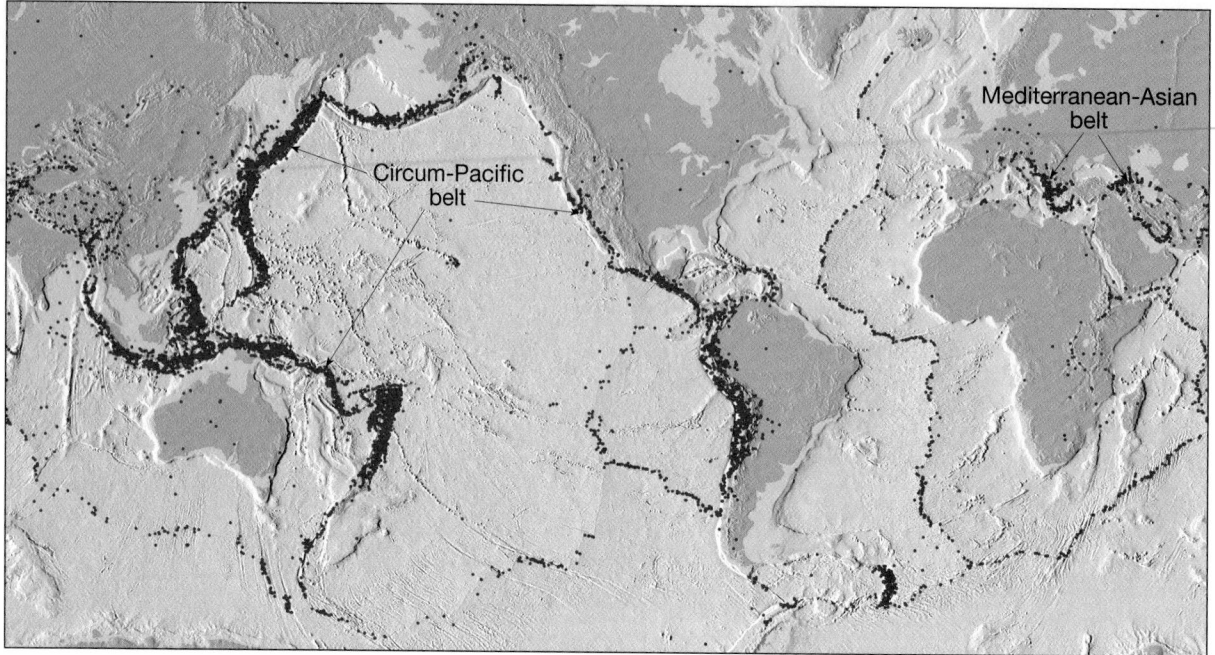

Figure 9 Distribution of the 14,229 earthquakes with magnitudes equal to or greater than 5 from 1980 to 1990. **Observing** *Where do you find most of the earthquakes—in the interiors of the continents or at the edges?*

Measuring the Distance to Epicenters

Procedure

1. Look at Figures 6 and 8A. Figure 6 is a seismogram and Figure 8A is a travel-time graph. Use the graph to answer the Analyze and Conclude questions.

2. Make sure to use only the bottom scale on the x-axis, measured in kilometers, to answer the questions.

Analyze and Conclude

1. **Reading Graphs** What is the difference in arrival times in minutes between the first P wave and first S wave for stations that are the following distances from an epicenter: 1000 km, 2000 km, 2400 km, and 3000 km?

2. **Inferring** How does the difference in arrival times of the first P wave and first S wave on a seismogram change? How does it change if the station is farther from the epicenter?

3. **Predicting** How do you think the vibrations recorded on a seismogram would change as the distance to the epicenter increases?

Earthquake Zones About 95 percent of the major earthquakes occur in a few narrow zones, as shown in Figure 9. Most of these earthquakes occur around the outer edge of the Pacific Ocean. This zone is known as the circum-Pacific belt. Active earthquake areas in this zone include Japan, the Philippines, Chile, and Alaska's Aleutian Islands. A second zone of earthquake activity occurs along the Mediterranean Sea. This is the Mediterranean-Asian belt. Another continuous belt extends for thousands of kilometers through the world's oceans. This zone coincides with the oceanic ridge system.

 *Where do most earthquakes occur?*

Measuring Earthquakes

Historically, scientists have used two different types of measurements to describe the size of an earthquake—intensity and magnitude. Intensity is a measure of the amount of earthquake shaking at a given location based on the amount of damage. Intensity is not a quantitative measurement because it is based on uncertain personal damage estimates. Quantitative measurements, called magnitudes, were developed that rely on calculations using seismograms. Magnitudes are a measure of the size of seismic waves or the amount of energy released at the source of the earthquake.

Richter Scale A familiar but outdated scale for measuring the magnitude of earthquakes is the Richter scale. The Richter scale is based on the amplitude of the largest seismic wave (P, S, or surface wave) recorded on a seismogram. Earthquakes vary greatly in strength, so Richter used a logarithmic scale. A tenfold increase in wave amplitude equals an increase of 1 on the magnitude scale. For example, the amount of ground shaking for a 5.0 earthquake is 10 times greater than the shaking produced by an earthquake of 4.0 on the Richter scale.

Seismic waves weaken as the distance between the earthquake focus and the seismograph increases. The Richter scale is only useful for small, shallow earthquakes within about 500 kilometers of the epicenter. Most of the earthquake measurements you hear on news reports use the Richter scale. Scientists, however, no longer use it.

Moment Magnitude In recent years, scientists have been using a more precise means of measuring earthquakes. It is called the moment magnitude scale. The **moment magnitude** is derived from the amount of displacement that occurs along a fault zone. It doesn't measure the ground motion at some distant point. The moment magnitude is calculated using several factors. These factors include the average amount of movement along the fault, the area of the surface break, and the strength of the broken rock: (surface area of fault) × (average displacement along fault) × (rigidity of rock). Together these factors provide a measure of how much energy rock can store before it suddenly slips and releases this energy during an earthquake. **Moment magnitude is the most widely used measurement for earthquakes because it is the only magnitude scale that estimates the energy released by earthquakes.**

Table 1 describes the damage and incidence of earthquakes of different magnitudes. Compare this information to the earthquakes listed in Table 2 on page 228.

Table 1 Earthquake Magnitudes and Expected World Incidence		
Moment Magnitudes	Effects Near Epicenter	Estimated Number per Year
< 2.0	Generally not felt, but can be recorded	> 600,000
2.0–2.9	Potentially perceptible	> 300,000
3.0–3.9	Rarely felt	> 100,000
4.0–4.9	Can be strongly felt	13,500
5.0–5.9	Can be damaging shocks	1,400
6.0–6.9	Destructive in populous regions	110
7.0–7.9	Major earthquakes; inflict serious damage	12
8.0 and above	Great earthquakes; destroy communities near epicenter	0–1

Table 2 Some Notable Earthquakes

Year	Location	Deaths (est.)	Magnitude†	Comments
*1886	Charleston, South Carolina	60		Greatest historical earthquake in the eastern United States
*1906	San Francisco, California	1500	7.8	Fires caused extensive damage.
1923	Tokyo, Japan	143,000	7.9	Fire caused extensive destruction.
1960	Southern Chile	5700	9.6	Possibly the largest-magnitude earthquake ever recorded
*1964	Alaska	131	9.2	Greatest North American earthquake
1970	Peru	66,000	7.8	Large rockslide
*1971	San Fernando, California	65	6.5	Damages exceeded $1 billion.
1985	Mexico City	9500	8.1	Major damage occurred 400 km from epicenter.
1988	Armenia	25,000	6.9	Poor construction practices caused great damage.
*1989	Loma Prieta, California	62	6.9	Damages exceeded $6 billion.
1990	Iran	50,000	7.3	Landslides and poor construction practices caused great damage.
1993	Latur, India	10,000	6.4	Located in stable continental interior
*1994	Northridge, California	57	6.7	Damages exceeded $40 billion.
1995	Kobe, Japan	5472	6.9	Damages estimated to exceed $100 billion.
1999	Izmit, Turkey	17,127	7.4	Nearly 44,000 injured and more than 250,000 displaced.
1999	Chi Chi, Taiwan	2300	7.6	Severe destruction; 8700 injuries
2001	El Salvador	1000	7.6	Triggered many landslides
2001	Bhuj, India	20,000†	7.9	1 million or more homeless

*U.S. earthquakes
†Widely differing magnitudes have been estimated for some earthquakes. When available, moment magnitudes are used.
SOURCE: U.S. Geological Survey

Section 8.2 Assessment

Reviewing Concepts

1. List the two categories of seismic waves.
2. Briefly describe how the epicenter of an earthquake is located.
3. Describe the two different ways to measure the size of an earthquake.
4. In what order do the basic types of seismic waves reach a seismograph?

Critical Thinking

5. **Comparing and Contrasting** Describe the differences in speed and mode of travel between primary waves and secondary waves.

6. **Applying Concepts** How does a seismograph measure an earthquake?

Writing in Science

Descriptive Paragraph Write a paragraph describing in your own words what would occur in an earthquake that has been measured as a moment magnitude of 6.0.

8.3 Destruction from Earthquakes

Reading Focus

Key Concepts

- What destructive events can be triggered by earthquakes?

- Can earthquakes be predicted?

Vocabulary

- liquefaction
- tsunami
- seismic gap

Reading Strategy

Monitoring Your Understanding Preview the Key Concepts, topic headings, vocabulary, and figures in this section. List two things you expect to learn. After reading, state what you learned about each item you listed.

What I Expect To Learn	What I Learned
a. _____ ? _____	b. _____ ? _____
c. _____ ? _____	d. _____ ? _____

The Good Friday Alaskan Earthquake in 1964 was the most violent earthquake to jar North America in the 20th century. The earthquake was felt throughout Alaska. It had a moment magnitude of 9.2 and lasted 3 to 4 minutes. The quake left 131 people dead and thousands homeless. The state's economy was also badly damaged because the quake affected major ports and towns. Had the schools and businesses been open on this holiday, the death toll would surely have been much higher.

Seismic Vibrations

The 1964 Alaskan earthquake gave geologists new insights into the role of ground shaking as a destructive force. **The damage to buildings and other structures from earthquake waves depends on several factors. These factors include the intensity and duration of the vibrations, the nature of the material on which the structure is built, and the design of the structure.**

Building Design All multistory buildings in Anchorage, Alaska, were damaged by the vibrations. However, the more flexible wood-frame buildings, such as homes, were less damaged. Figure 10 offers an example of how differences in construction can affect earthquake damage. You can see that the steel-frame building on the left withstood the vibrations. However, the poorly designed building on the right was badly damaged. Engineers have learned that unreinforced stone or brick buildings are the most serious safety threats during earthquakes.

Figure 10 Earthquake Damage This five-story building in Anchorage, Alaska, collapsed from the great earthquake of 1964. Very little structural damage was incurred by the steel-framed building to the left.
Inferring *Why do some buildings undergo little damage, while nearby buildings are nearly destroyed?*

A The largest wave ever recorded occurred in Lituya Bay, about 200 kilometers west of Juneau, Alaska. On July 9, 1958, an earthquake triggered an enormous rockslide that dumped 90 million tons of rock into the upper part of the bay. The rockslide created a huge splash wave that swept over the ridge facing the rockslide. The splash uprooted or snapped off trees 522 meters above the bay. Even larger splash waves may have occurred 65 million years ago when an estimated 900-meter wave is thought to have resulted from a meteorite impact in the Gulf of Mexico.

Liquefaction Where loosely consolidated sediments are saturated with water, earthquakes can cause a process known as **liquefaction.** Under these conditions, what had been stable soil turns into a liquid that is not able to support buildings or other structures. Buildings and bridges may settle and collapse. Underground storage tanks and sewer lines may float toward the surface.

 **Reading Checkpoint** *When does liquefaction occur?*

Tsunamis

Most deaths associated with the 1964 Alaskan quake were caused by seismic sea waves, or **tsunamis.** These destructive waves often are called tidal waves by news reporters. However, this name is incorrect because these waves are not produced by the tidal effect of the moon or sun.

Causes of Tsunamis A tsunami triggered by an earthquake occurs where a slab of the ocean floor is displaced vertically along a fault. A tsunami also can occur when the vibration of a quake sets an underwater landslide into motion. Once formed, a tsunami resembles the ripples created when a pebble is dropped into a pond. A tsunami travels across the ocean at speeds of 500 to 950 kilometers per hour. Despite this speed, a tsunami in the open ocean can pass without notice because its height is usually less than 1 meter, and the distance between wave crests can range from 100 to 700 kilometers. However, when the wave enters shallower coastal water, the waves are slowed and the water begins to pile up to heights that sometimes are greater than 30 meters, as shown in Figure 11.

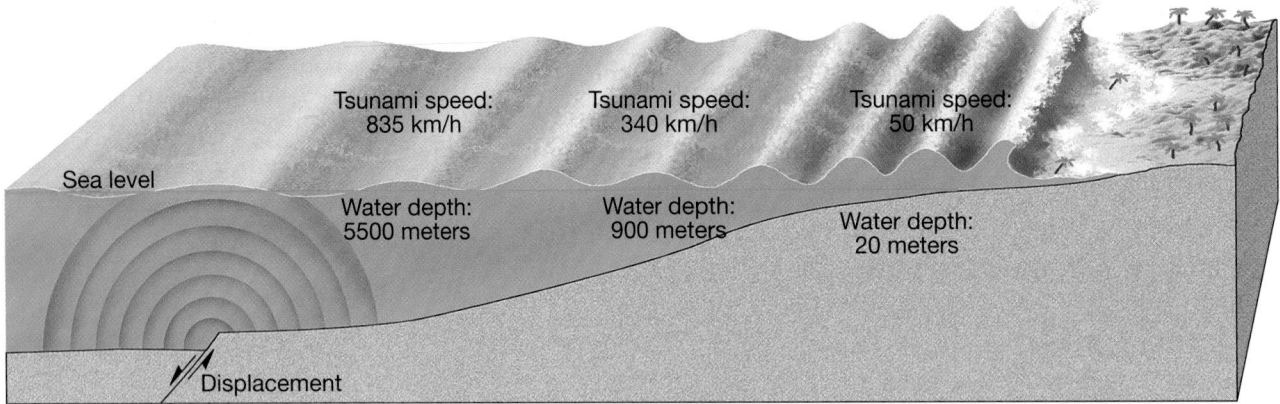

Figure 11 Movement of a Tsunami A tsunami is generated by movement of the ocean floor. The speed of a wave moving across the ocean is related to the ocean depth. Waves moving in deep water travel more than 800 kilometers per hour. Speed gradually slows to 50 kilometers per hour at depths of 20 meters. As waves slow down in shallow water, they grow in height until they topple and hit shore with tremendous force.

Tsunami Warning System The destruction from a large tsunami in the Hawaiian Islands led to the creation of a tsunami warning system for coastal areas of the Pacific. Large earthquakes are reported to the Tsunami Warning Center in Honolulu from seismic stations around the Pacific. Scientists use water levels in tidal gauges to determine whether a tsunami has formed. Within an hour of the reports, a warning is issued. Although tsunamis travel very rapidly, there is sufficient time to evacuate all but the area closest to the epicenter. Fortunately, most earthquakes do not generate tsunamis. On the average, only one or two destructive tsunamis are generated worldwide every year. Only about one tsunami in every 10 years causes major damage and loss of life.

 **Reading Checkpoint** *What areas are protected by the tsunami warning system?*

Other Dangers

The vibrations from earthquakes cause other dangers, including landslides, ground subsidence, and fires.

Landslides **With many earthquakes, the greatest damage to structures is from landslides and ground subsidence, or the sinking of the ground triggered by the vibrations.** The violent shaking of an earthquake can cause the soil and rock on slopes to fail, resulting in landslides. Figure 12 shows some of the damage landslides can cause. Earthquake vibration can also cause large sections of the ground to collapse, liquefy, or subside. Ground subsidence can cause foundations to collapse, as shown in Figure 12. It can also rupture gas and water pipelines.

Figure 12 This landslide caused by the 1964 Alaskan earthquake destroyed many homes. More than 200 acres of land slid toward the ocean.
Interpreting Photos *Assuming the land was originally horizontal, to what angle have the trees on the left side of the photo been tilted?*

Fire The 1906 San Francisco earthquake reminds us of the major threat of fire. The city contained mostly large wooden structures and brick buildings. The greatest destruction was caused by fires that started when gas and electrical lines were cut. Many of the city's water lines had also been broken by the quake, which meant that the fires couldn't be stopped. A 1923 earthquake in Japan caused an estimated 250 fires. They devastated the city of Yokohama and destroyed more than half the homes in Tokyo. The fires spread quickly due to unusually high winds. More than 100,000 people died in the fires.

Predicting Earthquakes

The earthquake in Northridge, California, in 1994 caused 57 deaths and about $40 billion in damage. Scientists warn that quakes of similar or greater strength will occur. But can earthquakes be predicted?

Short-Range Predictions The goal of short-range prediction is to provide an early warning of the location and magnitude of a large earthquake. Researchers monitor possible precursors—things that precede and may warn of a future earthquake. They measure uplift, subsidence, and strain in the rocks near active faults. They measure water levels and pressures in wells. Radon gas emissions from fractures and small changes in the electromagnetic properties of rocks are also monitored. So far, methods for short-range predictions of earthquakes have not been successful.

Long-Range Forecasts Long-range forecasts give the probability of a certain magnitude earthquake occurring within 30 to 100-plus years. These data are important for updating building codes, which have standards for designing earthquake-resistant structures. Long-range forecasts are based on the idea that earthquakes are repetitive or cyclical. In other words, as soon as one earthquake is over, the forces in Earth will begin to build strain in the rocks again. Eventually the rocks will slip again, causing another earthquake. Scientists study historical records of earthquakes to see if there are any patterns of recurrence. They also study seismic gaps. A **seismic gap** is an area along a fault where there has not been any earthquake activity for a long period of time. There has been only limited success in long-term forecasting. Scientists don't yet understand enough about how and where earthquakes will occur to make accurate long-term predictions.

Figure 13 Effects of Subsidence Due to Liquefaction This tilted building rests on unconsolidated sediment that imitated quicksand during the 1985 earthquake in Mexico.

Go Online
SCi LINKS ™ NSTA

For: Links on predicting earthquakes
Visit: www.SciLinks.org
Web Code: cjn-3082

Section 8.3 Assessment

Reviewing Concepts

1. What destructive events can be triggered by an earthquake?

2. What physical changes have been used in the attempts to predict earthquakes?

3. What is a tsunami?

4. What is a seismic gap?

Critical Thinking

5. **Making Judgments** Do you think scientists are close to being able to accurately predict earthquakes? Explain your answer.

6. **Drawing Conclusions** Why is it incorrect to refer to tsunamis as tidal waves?

Connecting Concepts

Earthquakes In Section 8.1, you learned about the elastic energy stored in rocks before an earthquake and the elastic rebound hypothesis. How could this information be used to try to predict earthquakes?

8.4 Earth's Layered Structure

Reading Focus

Key Concepts
- What is Earth's internal structure?
- What is the composition of Earth's interior?

Vocabulary
- crust
- mantle
- lithosphere
- asthenosphere
- outer core
- inner core
- Moho

Reading Strategy
Sequencing Copy the flowchart. After you read, complete the sequence of layers in Earth's interior.

Earth's Internal Structure

Lithosphere → a. ___?___ → b. ___?___ → Outer core → c. ___?___

Earth's interior lies not very far beneath our feet, but we can't reach it. The deepest well has drilled only 12 kilometers into Earth's crust. With such limited access, how do we know what Earth's interior is like? Most knowledge of the interior comes from the study of earthquake waves that travel through Earth.

Layers Defined by Composition

If Earth were made of the same materials throughout, seismic waves would spread through it in straight lines at constant speed. However, this is not the case. Seismic waves reaching seismographs located farther from an earthquake travel at faster average speeds than those recorded at locations closer to the event. This general increase in speed with depth is due to increased pressure, which changes the elastic properties of deeply buried rock. As a result, the paths of seismic waves through Earth are refracted, or bent, as they travel. Figure 14 shows this bending. **Earth's interior consists of three major zones defined by its chemical composition—the crust, mantle, and core.**

Crust The **crust,** the thin, rocky outer layer of Earth, is divided into oceanic and continental crust. The oceanic crust is roughly 7 kilometers thick and composed of the igneous rocks basalt and gabbro. The continental crust is 8–75 kilometers thick, but averages a thickness of 40 kilometers. It consists of many rock types. The average composition of the continental crust is granitic rock called granodiorite. Continental rocks have an average density of about 2.7 g/cm^3 and some are over 4 billion years old. The rocks of the oceanic crust are younger (180 million years or less) and have an average density of about 3.0 g/cm^3.

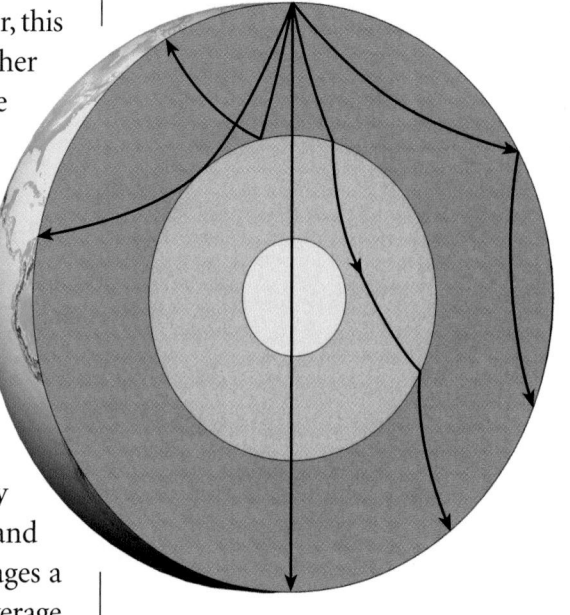

Figure 14 The arrows show only a few of the many possible paths that seismic waves take through Earth.
Inferring *What causes the wave paths to change?*

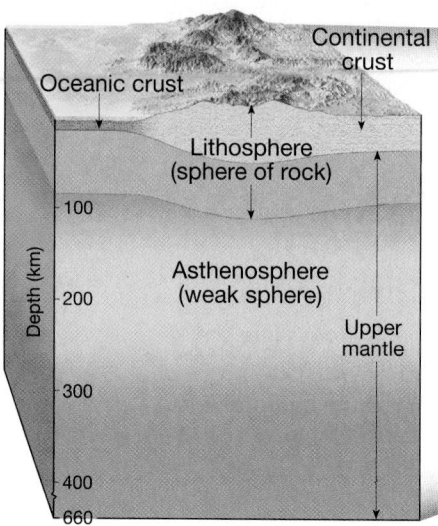

Figure 15 Earth's Layered Structure The left side of the globe shows that Earth's interior is divided into three different layers based on compositional differences—the crust, mantle, and core. The right side of the globe shows the five main layers of Earth's interior based on physical properties and mechanical strength— the lithosphere, asthenosphere, mesosphere, outer core, and inner core. The block diagram shows an enlarged view of the upper portion of Earth's interior.

Mantle Over 82 percent of Earth's volume is contained in the **mantle**—a solid, rocky shell that extends to a depth of 2890 kilometers. The boundary between the crust and mantle represents a change in chemical composition. The dominant rock type in the uppermost mantle is peridotite, which has a density of 3.4 g/cm³.

Core The core is a sphere composed of an iron-nickel alloy. At the extreme pressures found in the center of the core, the iron-rich material has an average density of almost 13 g/cm³ (13 times heavier than water).

 **Reading Checkpoint** *What is the composition of the core?*

Layers Defined by Physical Properties

Earth's interior has a gradual increase in temperature, pressure, and density with depth. When a substance is heated, the transfer of energy increases the vibrations of particles. If the temperature exceeds the melting point, the forces between particles are overcome and melting begins.

If temperature were the only factor that determined whether a substance melted, our planet would be a molten ball covered with a thin, solid outer shell. Fortunately, pressure also increases with depth and increases rock strength. Depending on the physical environment (temperature and pressure), a material may behave like a brittle solid, a putty, or a liquid. **Earth can be divided into layers based on physical properties—the lithosphere, asthenosphere, outer core, and inner core.**

Lithosphere and Asthenosphere Earth's outermost layer consists of the crust and uppermost mantle and forms a relatively cool, rigid shell called the **lithosphere**. This layer averages about 100 kilometers in thickness.

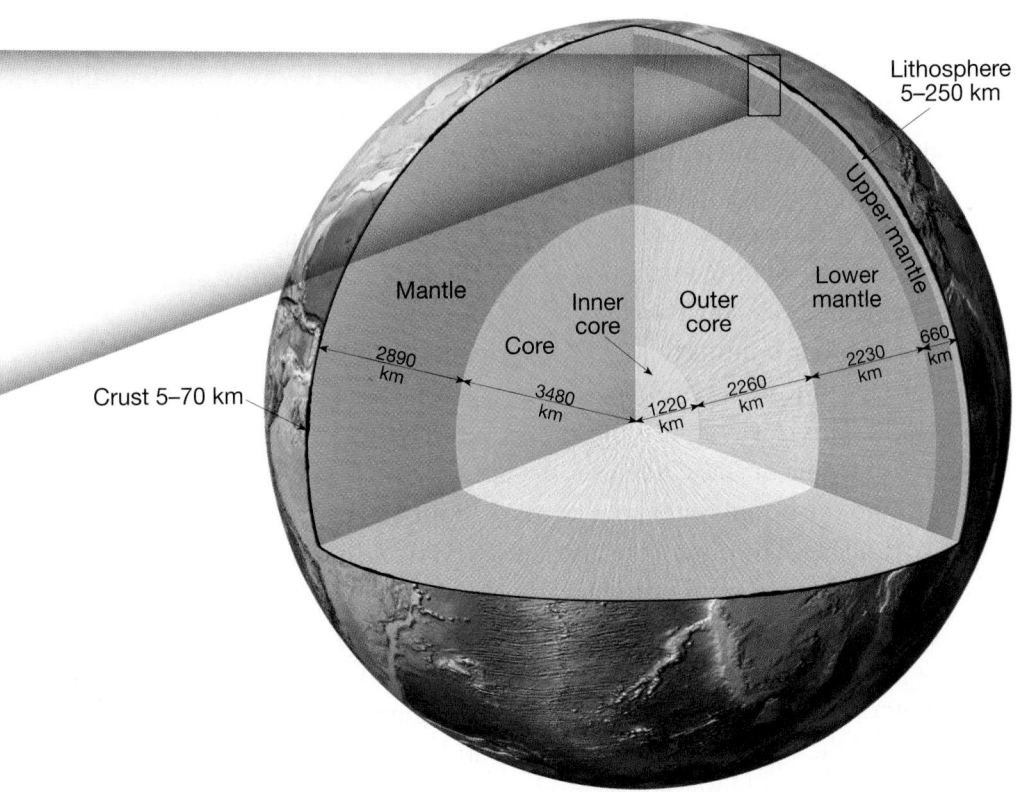

Lithosphere 5–250 km

Upper mantle

Mantle

Inner core

Outer core

Core

Lower mantle

2890 km

3480 km

1220 km

2260 km

2230 km

660 km

Crust 5–70 km

Beneath the lithosphere lies a soft, comparatively weak layer known as the **asthenosphere.** The asthenosphere has temperature/pressure conditions that may result in a small amount of melting. Within the asthenosphere, the rocks are close enough to their melting temperatures that they are easily deformed. Thus, the asthenosphere is weak because it is near its melting point, just as hot wax is weaker than cold wax. The lower lithosphere and asthenosphere are both part of the upper mantle.

Lower Mantle From a depth of about 660 kilometers down to near the base of the mantle lies a more rigid layer called the lower mantle. Despite their strength, the rocks of the lower mantle are still very hot and capable of gradual flow. The bottom few hundred kilometers of the mantle, laying on top of the hot core, contains softer, more flowing rock like that of the asthenosphere.

Inner and Outer Core The core, which is composed mostly of an iron-nickel alloy, is divided into two regions with different physical properties. The **outer core** is a liquid layer 2260 kilometers thick. The flow of metallic iron within this zone generates Earth's magnetic field. The **inner core** is a sphere having a radius of 1220 kilometers. Despite its higher temperature, the material in the inner core is compressed into a solid state by the immense pressure.

 Reading Checkpoint   *Why is the inner core solid?*

Discovering Earth's Layers

In 1909, a Croatian seismologist, Andrija Mohorovičić, presented evidence for layering within Earth. By studying seismic records, he found that the velocity of seismic waves increases abruptly below about 50 kilometers of depth. This boundary separates the crust from the underlying mantle and is known as the Mohorovičić discontinuity. The name is usually shortened to **Moho.**

Another boundary was discovered between the mantle and outer core. Seismic waves from even small earthquakes can travel around the world. This is why a seismograph in Antarctica can record earthquakes in California or Italy. However, it was observed that P waves were bent around the liquid outer core beyond about 100 degrees away from an earthquake. The outer core also causes P waves that travel through the core to arrive several minutes later than expected. This region, where bent P waves arrive, is sometimes called the shadow zone.

The bent wave paths can be explained if the core is composed of material that is different from the overlying mantle. The P waves bend around the core in a way similar to sound waves being bent around the corner of a building. For example, you can hear people talking from around the side of a building even if you cannot see them. In this way, rather than actually stopping the P waves in the shadow zone, the outer core bends them, as you can see modeled in Figure 16. It was further shown that S waves could not travel through the outer core. Therefore, geologists concluded that this region is liquid.

> ✓ **Reading Checkpoint** *What is the Moho?*

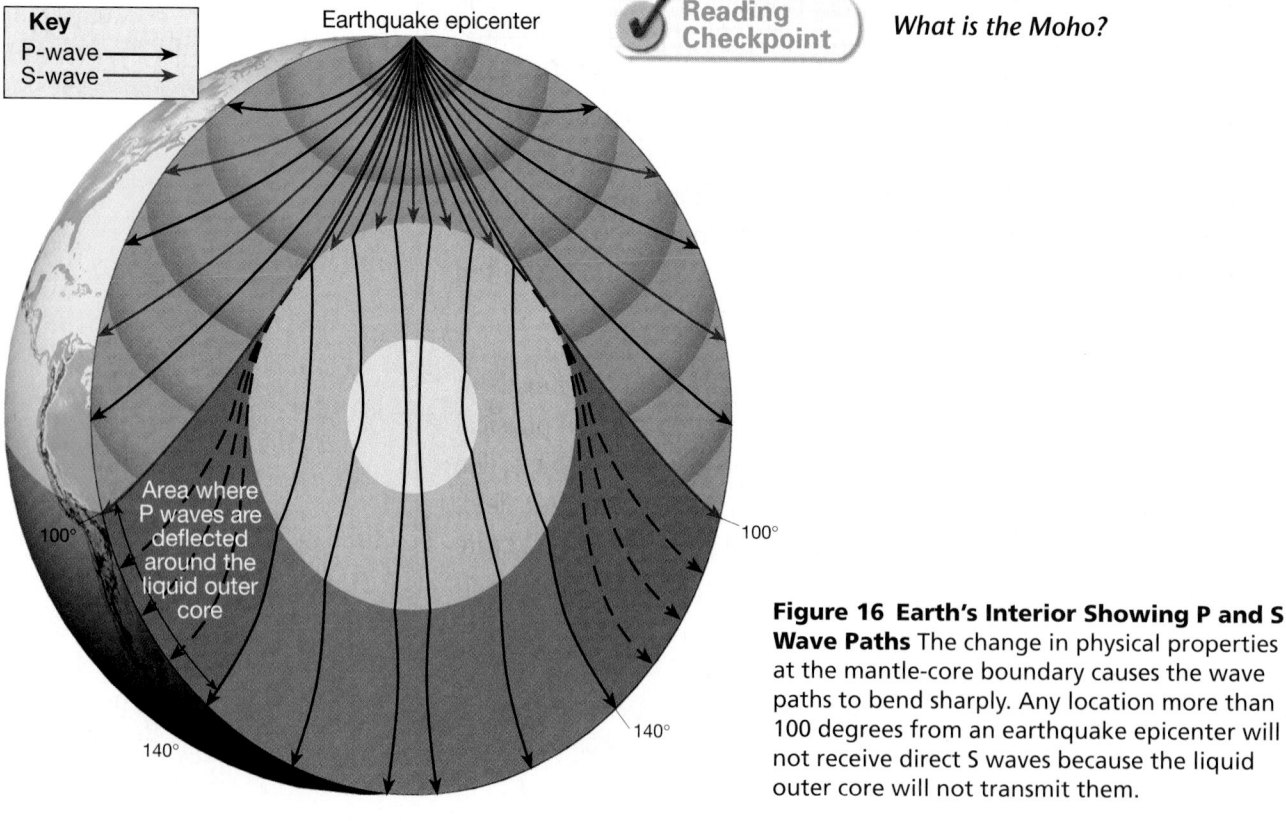

Key
P-wave →
S-wave →

Earthquake epicenter

Area where P waves are deflected around the liquid outer core

100°

100°

140°

140°

Figure 16 Earth's Interior Showing P and S Wave Paths The change in physical properties at the mantle-core boundary causes the wave paths to bend sharply. Any location more than 100 degrees from an earthquake epicenter will not receive direct S waves because the liquid outer core will not transmit them.

Discovering Earth's Composition

We have examined Earth's structure, so now let's look at the composition of each layer. ⬡ **Early seismic data and drilling technology indicate that the continental crust is mostly made of lighter, granitic rocks.** Until the late 1960s, scientists had only seismic evidence they could use to determine the composition of oceanic crust. The recovery of ocean-floor samples was made possible with the development of deep-sea drilling technology. ⬡ **The crust of the ocean floor has a basaltic composition.**

The composition of the rocks of the mantle and core is known from more indirect data. Some of the lava that reaches Earth's surface comes from the partially melted asthenosphere within the mantle. In the laboratory, experiments show that partially melting the rock called peridotite produces a substance that is similar to the lava that erupts during volcanic activity of islands such as Hawaii.

Surprisingly, meteorites that collide with Earth provide evidence of Earth's inner composition. Meteorites are assumed to be composed of the original material from which Earth was formed. Their composition ranges from metallic meteorites made of iron and nickel to stony meteorites composed of dense rock similar to peridotite. Because Earth's crust contains a smaller percentage of iron than do meteorites, geologists believe that the dense iron, and other dense metals, sank toward Earth's center during the planet's formation. Lighter substances may have floated to the surface, creating the less-dense crust. ⬡ **Earth's core is thought to be mainly dense iron and nickel, similar to metallic meteorites. The surrounding mantle is believed to be composed of rocks similar to stony meteorites.**

Section 8.4 Assessment

Reviewing Concepts

1. ⬡ List the major layers of Earth's internal structure based on physical properties. List the layers in order from Earth's center to the surface.

2. ⬡ What is the composition of Earth's core?

3. What evidence indicates that Earth's outer core is liquid?

4. What is the composition of the mantle?

Critical Thinking

5. **Comparing and Contrasting** Compare the physical properties of the asthenosphere and the lithosphere.

6. **Inferring** Why are meteorites considered important clues to the composition of Earth's interior?

Writing in Science

Creative Writing Write a short fictional story about a trip to Earth's core. Make sure the details about the layers of Earth's interior are scientifically accurate.

How the Earth Works

Effects of Earthquakes

An **earthquake** is a shaking of the ground caused by sudden movements in the Earth's crust. The biggest quakes are set off by the movement of tectonic plates. Some plates slide past one another gently. However, others get stuck, and the forces pushing the plates build up. The stress mounts until the plates suddenly shift their positions and cause the Earth to shake. Most earthquakes last less than one minute. Even so, the effects of an earthquake can be devastating and long-lasting.

TSUNAMI
In 1755, an earthquake in Lisbon, Portugal, caused a tsunami, as illustrated in this painting. A **tsunami** is a huge sea wave that is set off by an undersea earthquake or volcanic eruption. When tsunamis break on shore, they often devastate coastal areas. Tsunamis can race at speeds of about 450 miles per hour and may reach heights of about 100 feet (30.5 m).

LANDSLIDE
In January 2001, an earthquake struck El Salvador. It caused the landslide that left these Salvadoran women homeless. A **landslide** is a sudden drop of a mass of land down a mountainside or hillside. Emergency relief workers from around the world often rush to the site of an earthquake disaster like the one that occurred in El Salvador.

INFRASTRUCTURE DAMAGE

When an earthquake occurred in Los Angeles in 1994, underground gas and water lines burst, causing fires and floods. Earthquakes often cause tremendous damage to the **infrastructure**—the network of services that supports a community. Infrastructure includes power utilities, water supplies, and transportation and communication facilities.

AVALANCHE

Earthquakes may trigger an **avalanche**—a sudden fall of a mass of ice and snow. In 1970, a severe earthquake off the coast of Peru caused a disastrous slide of snow and rock that killed some 18,000 people in the valley below.

WHEN THE EARTH CRACKS

Most people killed or injured by an earthquake are hit by debris from buildings. Additional damage can be caused by **aftershocks**—tremors that can occur hours, days, or even months after an earthquake. The scene above shows the city of Anchorage, Alaska, after a major earthquake. Extensive ground tremors caused the street to break up as the soil below it collapsed. Buildings and cars were dropped more than 10 feet (3 m) below street level.

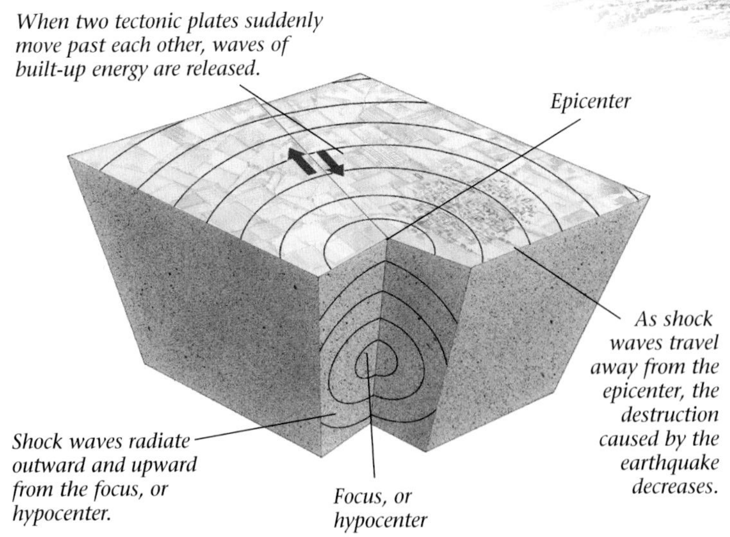

When two tectonic plates suddenly move past each other, waves of built-up energy are released.

Epicenter

As shock waves travel away from the epicenter, the destruction caused by the earthquake decreases.

Shock waves radiate outward and upward from the focus, or hypocenter.

Focus, or hypocenter

SEISMIC WAVES

As tectonic forces build, rock beneath the surface bends until it finally breaks. The tectonic plates suddenly move, causing **seismic waves,** or vibrations, to travel through the ground. The waves radiate outward from an underground area called the focus, or hypocenter. Damage is usually greatest near the **epicenter,** the point on the surface directly above the focus.

ASSESSMENT

1. **Key Terms** Define **(a)** earthquake, **(b)** tsunami, **(c)** landslide, **(d)** infrastructure, **(e)** avalanche, **(f)** aftershock, **(g)** seismic wave, **(h)** epicenter.

2. **Physical Processes** What physical processes cause an earthquake to occur?

3. **Environmental Change** How can an earthquake cause changes to the physical characteristics of a place?

4. **Natural Hazards** **(a)** How can an earthquake change the human characteristics of a place? **(b)** How does the international community respond to a devastating earthquake?

5. **Critical Thinking** **Solving Problems** What can a community do to reduce the amount of earthquake damage that might occur in the future?

239

Exploration Lab

Locating an Earthquake

The focus of an earthquake is the actual place within Earth where the earthquake originates. When locating an earthquake on a map, scientists plot the epicenter, the point on Earth's surface directly above the focus. To locate an epicenter, records from three different seismographs are needed.

Problem How can you determine the location of an earthquake's epicenter?

Materials

- pencil
- drawing compass
- world map or atlas
- photocopy of map on page 241

Skills Measuring, Interpreting Maps, Interpreting Graphs

Procedure

1. These three seismograms recorded the same earthquake, in New York City, Seattle, and Mexico City. Use the travel-time graph to determine the distance that each station is from the epicenter. Record your answers in a data table like the one shown.

2. Refer to a world map or atlas for the locations of the three seismic stations. Place a small dot showing the location of each of the three stations on the photocopy of the map on the next page. Neatly label each city on the map.

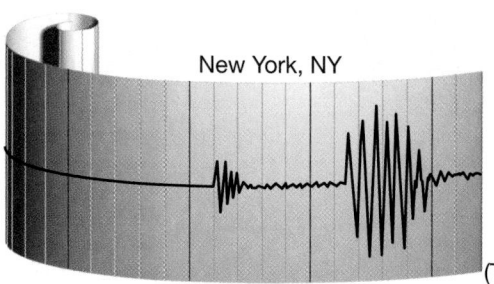

New York, NY

(Time marks in minutes)

9:00 UTC

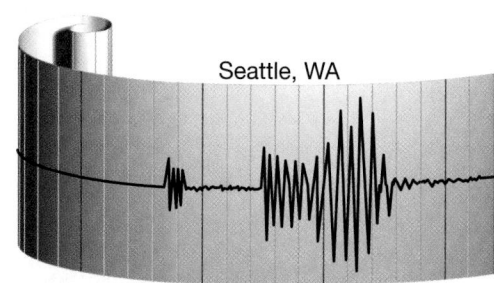

Seattle, WA

9:00 UTC

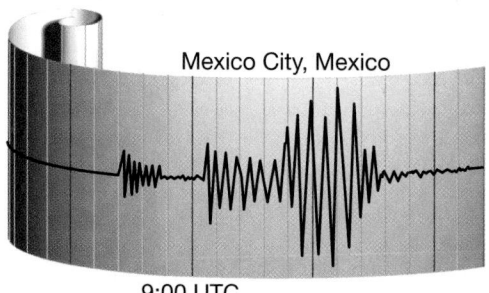

Mexico City, Mexico

9:00 UTC

Data Table			
	New York	Seattle	Mexico City
Elapsed time between first P and first S waves			
Distance from epicenter in miles			

3. On the map, use a drawing compass to draw a circle around each of the three stations. The radius of the circle, in miles, should be equal to each station's distance from the epicenter. Use the scale on the map to set the distance on the drawing compass for each station. **CAUTION** *Use care when handling the drawing compass.*

Analyze and Conclude

1. **Using Graphs** How far from the epicenter are the three cities located?

2. **Calculating** What would the distances from the epicenter to the cities be in kilometers?

3. **Interpreting Maps** What is the approximate latitude and longitude of the epicenter of the earthquake that was recorded by the three stations?

4. **Drawing Conclusions** On the New York seismogram the first P wave was recorded at 9:01 UTC. UTC is the international standard on which most countries base their time. At what time (UTC) did the earthquake actually occur? Explain.

Go Further Use the Internet or the library to find the locations of recent earthquake epicenters. Make a data table displaying the location, date, and magnitude of ten recent earthquakes. Report your findings to the class.

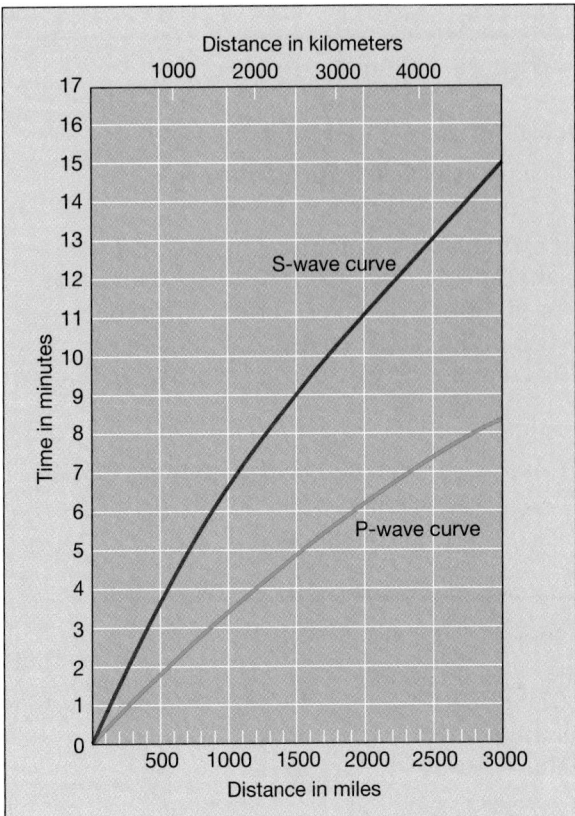

Study Guide

8.1 What Is an Earthquake?

Key Concepts

- Faults are fractures in Earth along which movement has occurred.
- Most earthquakes are produced by the rapid release of elastic energy. This energy is stored in rock that has been subjected to great forces. When the strength of the rock is exceeded, it suddenly breaks, causing the vibrations of an earthquake.

Vocabulary

earthquake, *p. 218;* focus, *p. 218;* epicenter, *p. 219;* fault, *p. 219;* elastic rebound hypothesis, *p. 220;* aftershock, *p. 221;* foreshock, *p. 221*

8.2 Measuring Earthquakes

Key Concepts

- A seismogram shows the three main types of seismic waves—surface waves, P waves, and S waves.
- Travel-time graphs from three or more seismographs can be used to find the exact location of an earthquake epicenter.
- Historically, scientists have used two different measurement types to describe the size of an earthquake—intensity and magnitude.
- Moment magnitude is the most widely used measurement for earthquakes because it is the only magnitude scale that estimates the energy released by earthquakes.

Vocabulary

seismograph, *p. 222;* seismogram, *p. 222;* surface wave, *p. 223;* P wave, *p. 223;* S wave, *p. 223;* moment magnitude, *p. 227*

8.3 Destruction from Earthquakes

Key Concepts

- The damage to buildings and other structures from earthquake waves depends on several factors. These factors include the intensity and the duration of the vibrations, the nature of the material on which the structure is built, and the design of the structure.
- A tsunami triggered by an earthquake occurs where a slab of the ocean floor is displaced vertically along a fault. A tsunami also can occur when the vibration of a quake sets an underwater landslide into motion.
- With many earthquakes, the greatest damage to structures is from landslides and ground subsidence, or the sinking of the ground triggered by the vibrations.
- So far, methods for short-range predictions of earthquakes have not been successful.
- Scientists don't yet understand enough about how and where earthquakes will occur to make accurate long-term predictions.

Vocabulary

liquefaction, *p. 230;* tsunami, *p. 230;* seismic gap, *p. 232*

8.4 Earth's Layered Structure

Key Concepts

- Earth's interior consists of three major zones defined by its chemical composition—the crust, mantle, and core.
- Earth can be divided into layers based on physical properties—the lithosphere, asthenosphere, outer core, and inner core.
- Early seismic data and drilling technology indicate that the continental crust is mostly made of lighter, granitic rocks.
- The crust of the ocean floor has a basaltic composition.
- Earth's core is thought to be mainly dense iron and nickel, similar to metallic meteorites. The surrounding mantle is believed to be composed of rocks similar to stony meteorites.

Vocabulary

crust, *p. 233;* mantle, *p. 234;* lithosphere, *p. 234;* asthenosphere, *p. 235;* outer core, *p. 235;* inner core, *p. 235;* Moho, *p. 236*

Reviewing Content

Choose the letter that best answers the question or completes the statement.

1. Approximately how many earthquakes are strong enough to be felt each year worldwide?
   a. 500 **b.** 1000
   c. 10,000 **d.** 30,000

2. What is the location on the surface directly above the earthquake focus called?
   a. epicenter **b.** fault
   c. magnitude **d.** Moho

3. The rigid layer of Earth that includes the entire crust and the uppermost part of the mantle is called the
   a. asthenosphere. **b.** mesosphere.
   c. lithosphere. **d.** Moho.

4. The instrument that records earthquakes is called
   a. a seismogram. **b.** a seismologist.
   c. seismology. **d.** a seismograph.

5. Which of the following regions has the greatest amount of earthquake activity?
   a. central Europe
   b. the circum-Pacific belt
   c. the eastern United States
   d. central Africa

6. What material do scientists believe makes up a large part of the upper mantle?
   a. basalt **b.** granite
   c. iron **d.** peridotite

7. The point at which an earthquake begins is called
   a. a foreshock. **b.** the epicenter.
   c. the focus. **d.** the Moho.

8. In areas where loosely consolidated materials are saturated with water, earthquakes can turn stable soil into a liquid during a process called
   a. faulting. **b.** liquefaction.
   c. tsunamis. **d.** subsidence.

9. To find the epicenter of an earthquake, what is the minimum number of seismic stations that are needed?
   a. three **b.** nine
   c. five **d.** two

10. What scale is currently used to express the magnitude of an earthquake?
    a. Richter scale
    b. moment magnitude
    c. tsunami scale
    d. Moho scale

Understanding Concepts

Use the diagram below to answer Questions 11 and 12.

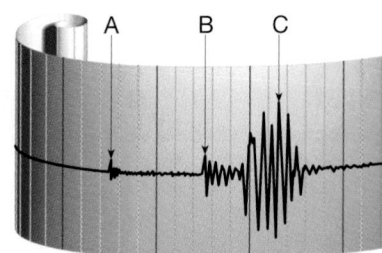

11. The diagram shows a typical recording of an earthquake. What is the record called?

12. Identify the waves recorded at A, B, and C on the diagram.

13. Does all motion along large faults occur in the form of destructive earthquakes?

14. What type of seismic wave causes the greatest destruction to buildings?

15. In addition to the damage caused directly by seismic vibrations, list three other types of destructive events that can be triggered by earthquakes.

16. Describe the composition and physical properties of the crust.

17. What is liquefaction and how can earthquakes cause liquefaction to occur?

18. List the major differences between P waves and S waves.

19. How much does the amplitude of the waves increase between an earthquake that measures 4.2 on the Richter scale and an earthquake that measures 6.2 on the Richter scale?

20. What are two factors that can determine the amount of destruction that results from an earthquake?

Critical Thinking

21. Applying Concepts Give two reasons why an earthquake with a moderate magnitude might cause more extensive damage than an earthquake with a high magnitude.

22. Comparing and Contrasting How are the moment magnitude scale and the Richter scale different?

23. Inferring How did scientists determine the structure and composition of Earth's interior?

Analyzing Data

Use the diagram below to answer Questions 24–26.

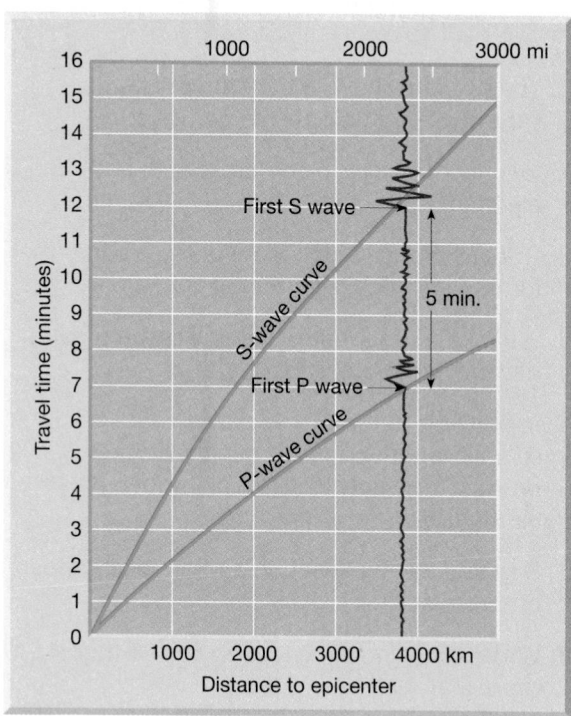

24. Using Graphs Determine the distance between an earthquake and seismic station if the first S wave arrives three minutes after the first P wave.

25. Using Graphs If a seismic station is 2500 kilometers from the earthquake's epicenter, approximately when will the first P wave be received? When will the first S wave be received?

26. Calculating What is the difference in the travel-times of the first P wave and the first S wave if the seismic station is 1000 kilometers from the earthquake epicenter?

Concepts in Action

27. Applying Concepts Why is the moment magnitude the most commonly used scale by scientists for measuring earthquakes?

28. Classifying In what major earthquake zone would an earthquake in Indonesia be located?

29. Hypothesizing You are on a large ocean research ship. You have generated seismic waves by causing an explosion on a platform towed behind the ship. What seismic waves will be recorded by a seismograph located on the ocean floor beneath the ship? Explain your answer.

30. Writing in Science Research a recent earthquake and write about the earthquake damage in the style of a newspaper article.

Performance-Based Assessment

Designing an Experiment Design a model seismograph to record simulated earthquakes. When your model is completed, test it for the class. Then determine how your seismograph design could be improved or changed if it doesn't work well.

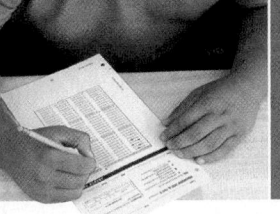

Standardized Test Prep

Use the diagram below to answer Questions 4–6.

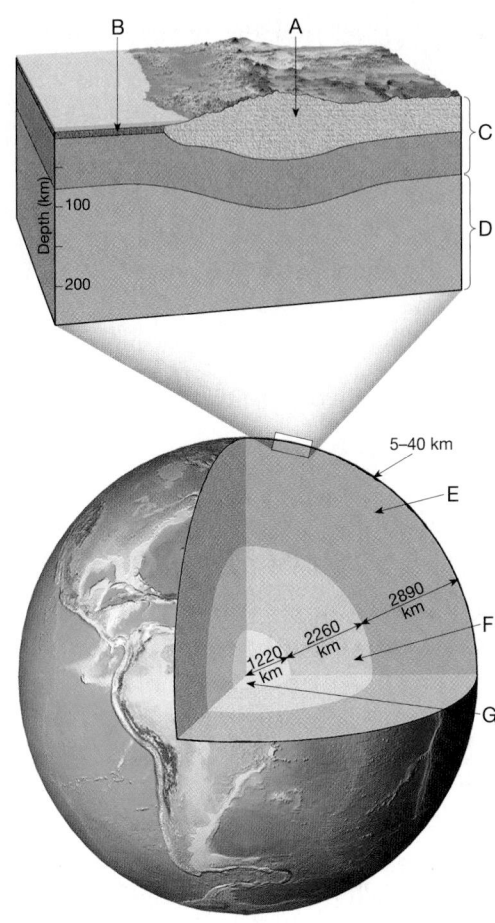

Test-Taking Tip

Narrowing the Choices

If, after reading all the answer choices, you are not sure which one is correct, eliminate those answers that you know are wrong. In the question below, first eliminate the choices you know are wrong. For example, answer choice A can be eliminated since the fact that earthquakes are destructive does not affect long-range forecasting. Then focus on the remaining choices.

Long-range earthquake forecasts are based on the assumption that earthquakes are

(A) destructive.
(B) random.
(C) fully understood.
(D) repetitive.

(Answer: D)

Choose the letter that best answers the question or completes the statement.

1. What property that is different for P and S waves provides a method for locating the epicenter of an earthquake?
   (A) magnitude
   (B) foci
   (C) modes of travel
   (D) speed

2. Movements that follow a major earthquake often generate smaller earthquakes called
   (A) aftershocks.
   (B) foreshocks.
   (C) surface waves.
   (D) landslides.

3. An earthquake in the ocean floor can cause a destructive sea wave called a
   (A) P wave.
   (B) S wave.
   (C) Moho.
   (D) tsunami.

4. What layer of Earth's interior is labeled F in the diagram? Explain this layer.

5. What layer is labeled A in the diagram? What type of rock makes up this layer?

6. In the diagram which letters would indicate layers that form the lithosphere? Explain the layers.

7. Describe the composition (mineral/rock makeup) of Earth's crust, mantle, and core. How did scientists determine the composition of each layer?

8. Discuss the conditions that cause earthquakes to occur.

CHAPTER

9 Plate Tectonics

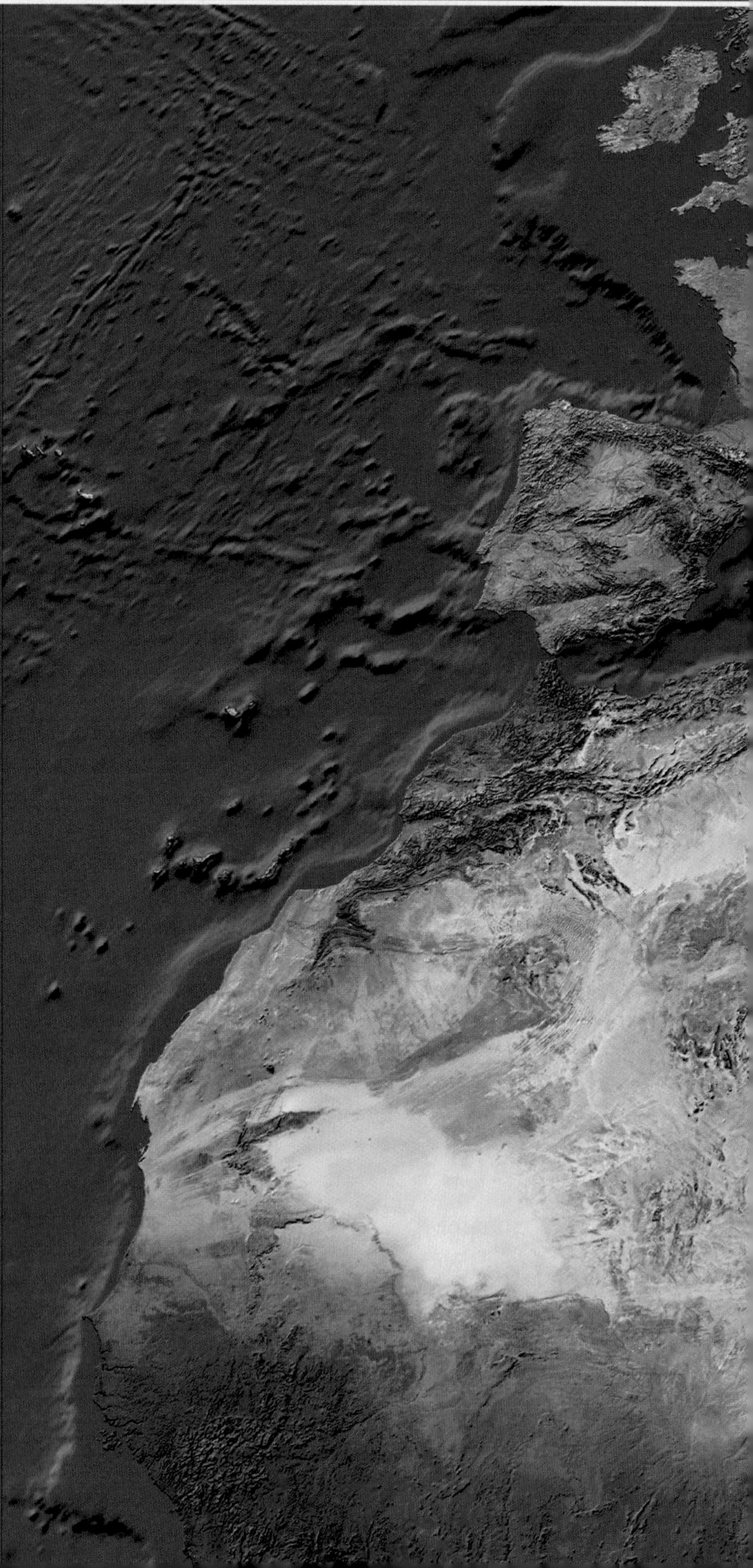

CONCEPTS
— in Action —

Quick Lab
Charting the Age of the Atlantic Ocean

Exploration Lab
Paleomagnetism and the Ocean Floor

Understanding Earth
Plate Tectonics into the Future

GEODe   Forces Within
          ↳ Plate Tectonics

Discovery CHANNEL **Video Field Trip**
SCHOOL™
Plate Tectonics

Take a plate tectonics field trip with Discovery
Channel and see how the crust of Earth is in
constant motion. Answer the following
questions after watching the video.

1. What does the discovery of identical basalt
   rock in South America and Africa help to
   prove?

2. How was the Atlantic Ocean formed?

For: Chapter 9 Resources
Visit: PHSchool.com
Web Code: cjk-9999

► This photograph is a composite satellite
image of Europe, North Africa, and the
Arabian Peninsula.

Chapter Preview

Inquiry Activity

How Do the Continents Fit Together?

Procedure

1. Get a copy of a world map from your teacher. Cut out the major continents along their coastlines. **CAUTION** *Be careful when using scissors.*

2. Try to fit together the pieces into one large landmass. Look for a "best-fit" configuration.

3. Compare your large landmass with those of other students. Did anyone come up with a landmass that was very different from the others?

Think About It

1. **Observing** From your continental reconstruction, where did the continents fit together well? Where did problems occur?

2. **Developing Hypotheses** Use your observations to develop a hypothesis on how to get a better fit of the continents. How could the overlaps and large gaps be explained? (*Hint:* What if the outline of the coasts was not the same as the boundaries of the continents themselves?)

9.1 Continental Drift

Reading Focus

Key Concepts

- What is the hypothesis of continental drift?
- What evidence supported continental drift?

Vocabulary

- continental drift
- Pangaea

Reading Strategy

Summarizing Copy the table. Fill it in as you read to summarize the evidence of continental drift.

Hypothesis	Evidence
Continental Drift	a. continental puzzle
	b. _____?_____
	c. _____?_____
	d. _____?_____

Figure 1 A Curious Fit This map shows the best fit of South America and Africa at a depth of about 900 meters. The areas where continents overlap appear in brown.
Inferring *Why are there areas of overlap?*

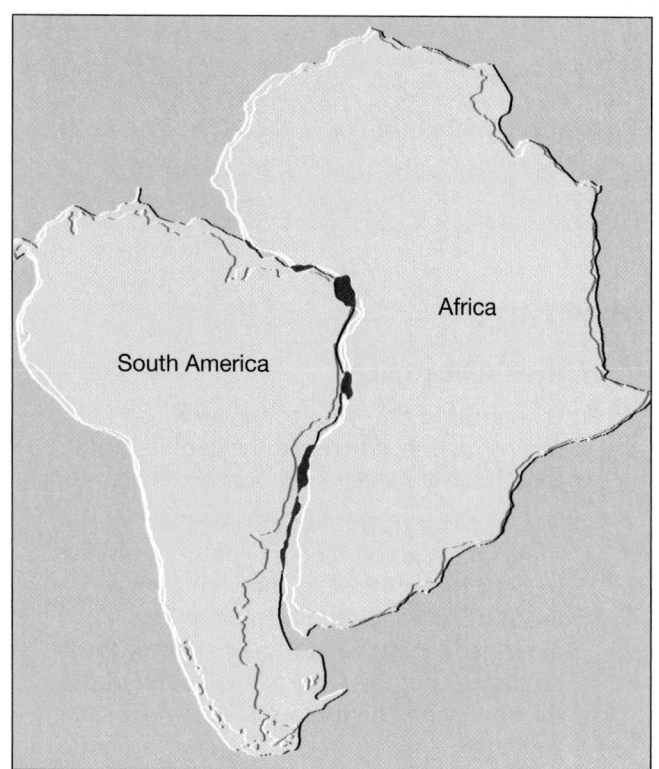

Will California eventually slide into the ocean? Have continents really drifted apart over the centuries? Early in the twentieth century, most geologists thought that the positions of the ocean basins and continents were fixed. During the last few decades, however, new data have dramatically changed our understanding of how Earth works.

An Idea Before Its Time

The idea that continents fit together like pieces of a jigsaw puzzle came about when better world maps became available. Figure 1 shows the two most obvious pieces of this jigsaw puzzle. However, little significance was given this idea until 1915, when Alfred Wegener, a German scientist, proposed his radical hypothesis of **continental drift.** **Wegener's continental drift hypothesis stated that the continents had once been joined to form a single supercontinent.** He called this supercontinent **Pangaea,** meaning *all land.*

Wegener also hypothesized that about 200 million years ago Pangaea began breaking into smaller continents. These continents then drifted to their present positions, as shown on page 250. Wegener and others collected much evidence to support these claims. Let's examine their evidence.

Evidence: The Continental Puzzle

Wegener first thought that the continents might have been joined when he noticed the similarity between the coastlines on opposite sides of the South Atlantic Ocean. He used present-day shorelines to show how the continents fit together. However, his opponents correctly argued that erosion continually changes shorelines over time.

Evidence: Matching Fossils  Fossil evidence for continental drift includes several fossil organisms found on different landmasses. Wegener reasoned that these organisms could not have crossed the vast oceans presently separating the continents. An example is *Mesosaurus*, an aquatic reptile whose fossil remains are limited to eastern South America and southern Africa, as shown in Figure 2. If *Mesosaurus* had been able to swim well enough to cross the vast South Atlantic Ocean, its fossils should be more widely distributed. This is not the case. Therefore, Wegener argued, South America and Africa must have been joined somehow.

The idea of land bridges was once the most widely accepted explanation for similar fossils being found on different landmasses. Most scientists believed that during a recent glacial period, the lowering of sea level allowed animals to cross the narrow Bering Strait between Asia and North America. However, if land bridges did exist between South America and Africa, their remnants should still lie below sea level. But no signs of such land bridges have ever been found in the Atlantic Ocean.

Reading Checkpoint *How does the distribution of* Mesosaurus *fossils provide evidence for continental drift?*

Q *If all the continents were once joined as Pangaea, what did the rest of Earth look like?*

A When all the continents were together, there must also have been one huge ocean surrounding them. This ocean is called *Panthalassa* (*pan* = all, *thalassa* = sea). Today all that remains of Panthalassa is the Pacific Ocean, which has been decreasing in size since the breakup of Pangaea.

Figure 2 Location of Mesosaurus Fossils of *Mesosaurus* have been found on both sides of the South Atlantic and nowhere else in the world. Fossil remains of this and other organisms on the continents of Africa and South America appear to link these landmasses at some time in Earth's history.

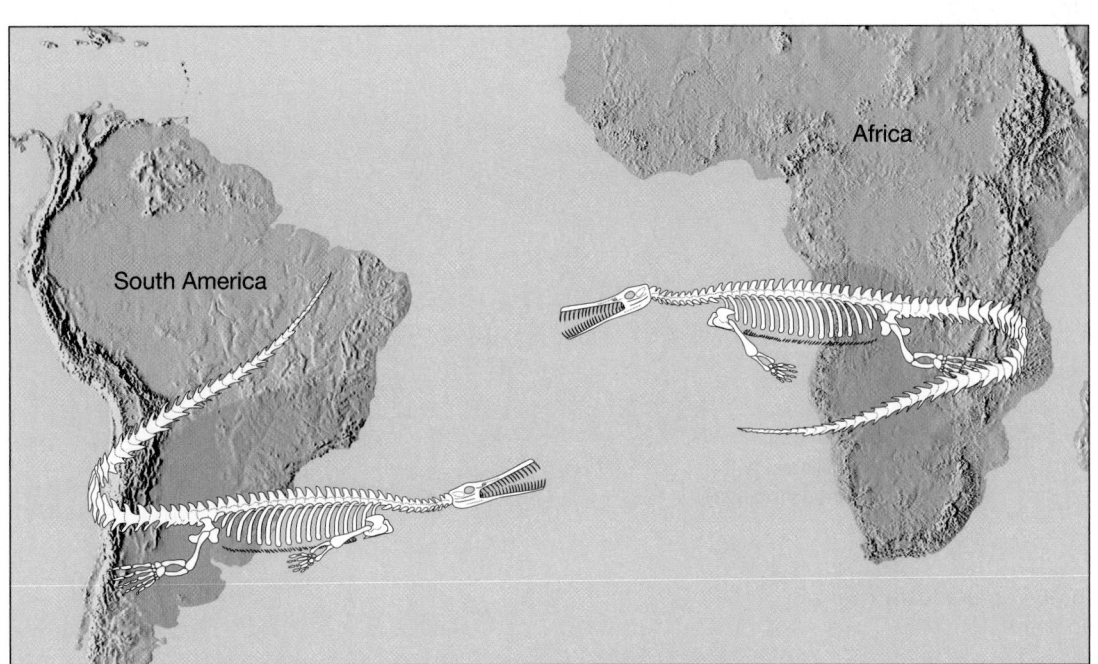

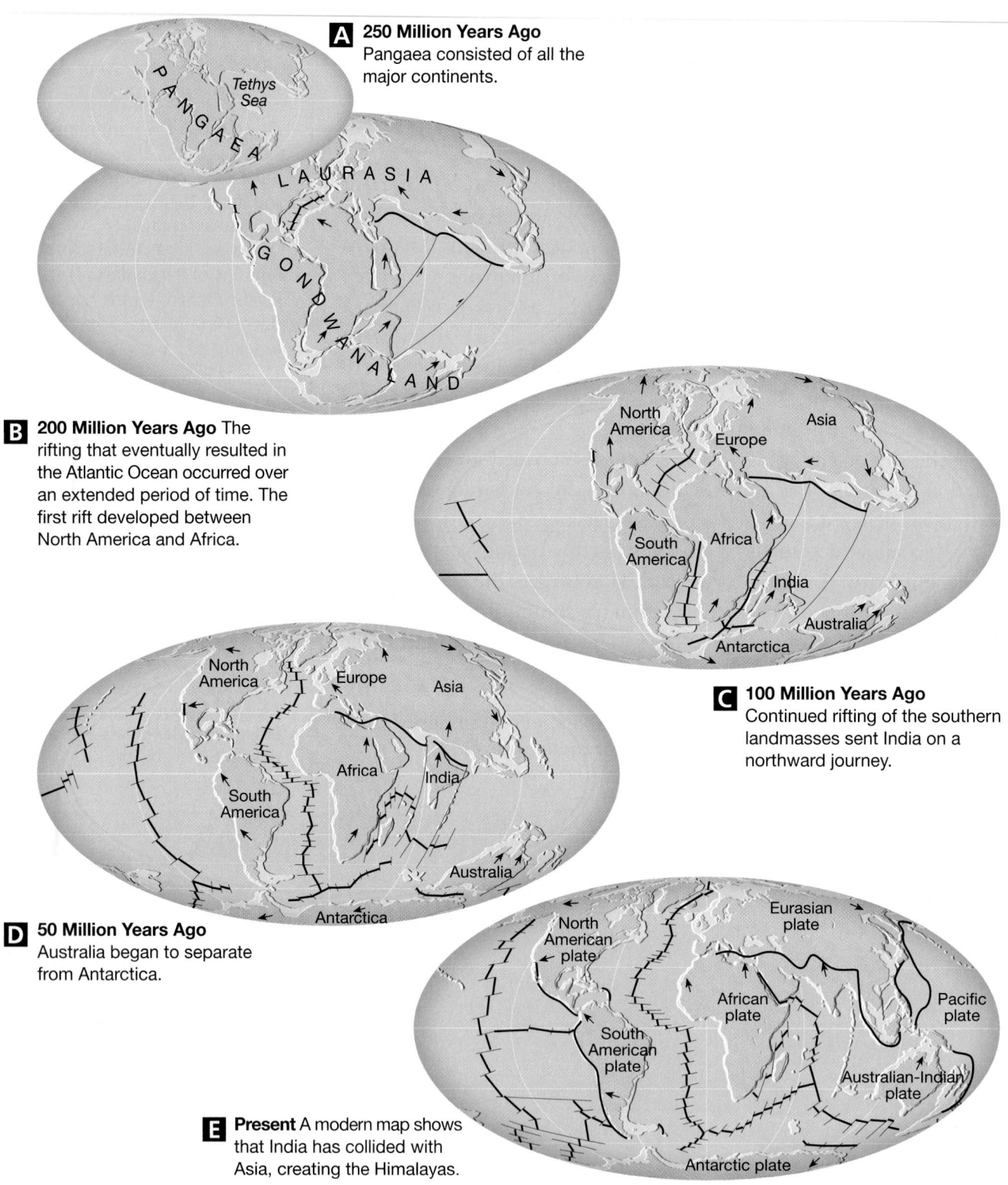

A **250 Million Years Ago**
Pangaea consisted of all the major continents.

B **200 Million Years Ago** The rifting that eventually resulted in the Atlantic Ocean occurred over an extended period of time. The first rift developed between North America and Africa.

C **100 Million Years Ago**
Continued rifting of the southern landmasses sent India on a northward journey.

D **50 Million Years Ago**
Australia began to separate from Antarctica.

E **Present** A modern map shows that India has collided with Asia, creating the Himalayas.

Figure 3 Pangaea broke up gradually over a period of 200 million years.

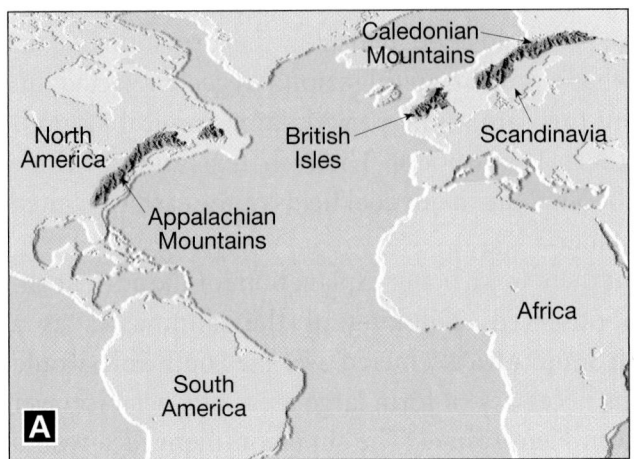

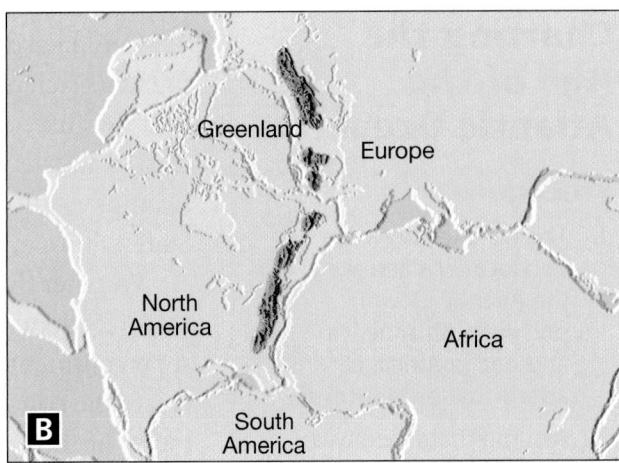

Evidence: Rock Types and Structures

Anyone who has worked a jigsaw puzzle knows that the pieces must fit together to form a clear picture. The clear picture in the continental drift puzzle is one of matching rock types and mountain belts. If the continents existed as Pangaea, the rocks found in a particular region on one continent should closely match in age and type those in adjacent positions on the adjoining continent.

Rock evidence for continental drift exists in the form of several mountain belts that end at one coastline, only to reappear on a landmass across the ocean. For example, the Appalachian mountain belt runs northeastward through the eastern United States, ending off the coast of Newfoundland, as shown in Figure 4A. Mountains of the same age with similar rocks and structures are found in the British Isles and Scandinavia. When these landmasses are fit together as in Figure 4B, the mountain chains form a nearly continuous belt.

 *How does the location of mountain chains provide evidence of continental drift?*

Evidence: Ancient Climates

Wegener was a meteorologist, so he was interested in obtaining data about ancient climates to support continental drift. And he did find evidence for dramatic global climate changes. Wegener found glacial deposits showing that between 220 million and 300 million years ago, ice sheets covered large areas of the Southern Hemisphere. Layers of glacial till were found in southern Africa and South America, as well as in India and Australia. Below these beds of glacial debris lay scratched and grooved bedrock carved by the ice. In some locations, the scratches and grooves showed that the ice had moved from what is now the sea onto land. It is unusual for large continental glaciers to move from the sea

Figure 4 A The Appalachian Mountains run along the eastern side of North America and disappear off the coast of Newfoundland. Mountains that are similar in age and structure are found in the British Isles and Scandinavia. **B** When these landmasses are united as Pangaea, these ancient mountain chains form a nearly continuous belt.

For: Links on continental drift
Visit: www.SciLinks.org
Web Code: cjn-3091

Charting the Age of the Atlantic Ocean

Procedure

1. The distance between two locations across the Atlantic Ocean, one in South America and one in Africa, is approximately 4300 km.

2. Assume that these two locations were once joined as part of Pangaea.

Analyze and Conclude

1. **Calculating** If the two landmasses moved away from each other at a rate of 3.3 cm/y, how long did it take these two locations to move to their current positions?

2. **Inferring** Do you think the Atlantic Ocean would have formed at a constant rate or would that rate have varied over time? Why?

onto land. It is also interesting that much of the land area that shows evidence of this glaciation now lies near the equator in a subtropical or tropical climate.

Could Earth have been cold enough to allow the formation of continental glaciers in what is now a tropical region? Wegener rejected this idea because, during this same time period, large tropical swamps existed in the Northern Hemisphere. The lush vegetation of these swamps eventually became the major coal fields of the eastern United States, Europe, and Siberia.

Wegener thought there was a better explanation for the ancient climate evidence he observed. Thinking of the landmasses as a supercontinent, with South Africa centered over the South Pole, would create the conditions necessary to form large areas of glacial ice over much of the Southern Hemisphere. The supercontinent idea would also place the northern landmasses nearer the tropics and account for their vast coal deposits, as shown in Figure 5.

 *Summarize the climate evidence for continental drift.*

Glacier Evidence

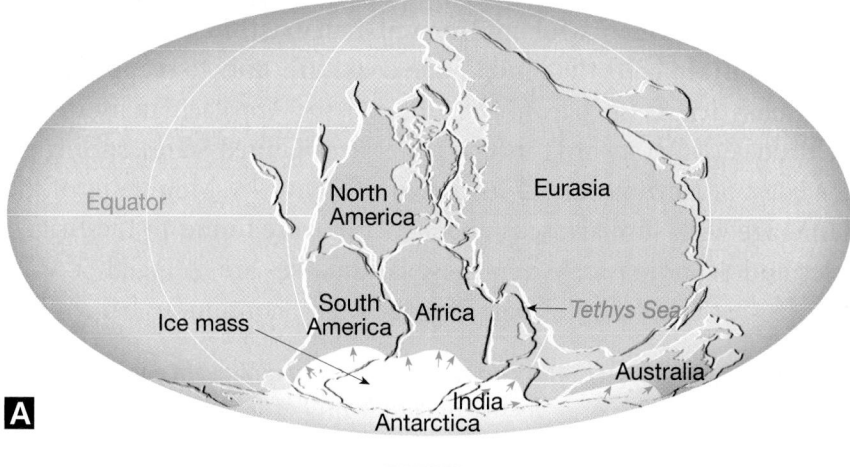

A

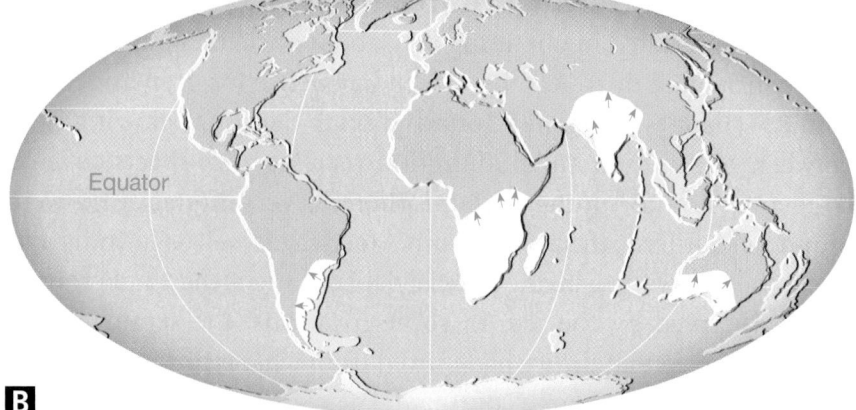

B

Figure 5 A The area of Pangaea covered by glacial ice 300 million years ago. **B** The continents as they are today. The white areas indicate where evidence of the old ice sheets exists.
Interpreting Diagrams *Where were the continents located when the glaciers formed?*

Rejecting a Hypothesis

Wegener's drift hypothesis faced a great deal of criticism from other scientists. One objection was that Wegener could not describe a mechanism that was capable of moving the continents across the globe. Wegener proposed that the tidal influence of the Moon was strong enough to give the continents a westward motion. However, physicists quickly responded that tidal friction of the size needed to move the continents would stop Earth's rotation.

Wegener also proposed that the larger and sturdier continents broke through the oceanic crust, much like ice breakers cut through ice. However, no evidence existed to suggest that the ocean floor was weak enough to permit passage of the continents without the ocean floors being broken and deformed in the process.

Most scientists in Wegener's day rejected his hypothesis. However, a few geologists continued to search for additional evidence of continents in motion.

 **Reading Checkpoint** *Why was Wegener's hypothesis rejected?*

A New Theory Emerges During the years that followed Wegener's hypothesis, major strides in technology enabled scientists to map the ocean floor. Extensive data on earthquake activity and Earth's magnetic field also became available. By 1968, these findings led to a new theory, known as plate tectonics. This theory provides the framework for understanding most geologic processes, such as the formation of the mountains shown in Figure 6.

Q *Some day will the continents come back together and form a single landmass?*

A Yes, but not anytime soon. Based on current plate motions, it appears that the continents may meet up again in the Pacific Ocean—in about 300 million years.

Figure 6 Mountain ranges are commonly formed at plate boundaries. This photograph shows part of the Canadian Rockies in Banff National Park, Alberta, Canada.

Section 9.1 Assessment

Reviewing Concepts

1. 🔵 What is the hypothesis of continental drift?
2. 🔵 List the evidence that supported the hypothesis of continental drift.
3. What was one of the main objections to Wegener's continental drift hypothesis?
4. What is Pangaea?

Critical Thinking

5. **Applying Concepts** Would the occurrence of the same plant fossils in South America and Africa support continental drift? Explain.

6. **Drawing Conclusions** How did Wegener explain the existence of glaciers in the southern landmasses, and the lush tropical swamps in North America, Europe, and Siberia?

Writing in Science

Descriptive Paragraph Write a paragraph describing Pangaea. Include the location and climate of Pangaea. Use the equator as your reference for position.

9.2 Plate Tectonics

Earth's Major Plates

According to the plate tectonics theory, the uppermost mantle, along with the overlying crust, behaves as a strong, rigid layer. This layer is known as the lithosphere. The outer shell lies over a weaker region in the mantle known as the asthenosphere. The lithosphere is divided into segments called **plates,** which move and continually change shape and size. Figure 8 on pages 256-257 shows the seven major plates. The largest is the Pacific plate, covering most of the Pacific Ocean. Notice that several of the large plates include an entire continent plus a large area of the seafloor. This is a major departure from Wegener's continental drift hypothesis, which proposed that the continents moved through the ocean floor, not with it. Note also that none of the plates is defined entirely by the margins of a continent.

The lithospheric plates move relative to each other at a very slow but continuous rate that averages about 5 centimeters per year—about as fast as your fingernails grow. This movement is driven by the unequal distribution of heat within Earth. Hot material found deep in the mantle moves slowly upward as part of Earth's internal convection system. At the same time, cooler, denser slabs of oceanic lithosphere descend into the mantle, setting Earth's rigid outer shell into motion. The grinding movements of Earth's lithospheric plates generate earthquakes, create volcanoes, and deform large masses of rock into mountains.

 *What is plate tectonics?*

Types of Plate Boundaries

All major interactions among individual plates occur along their boundaries. ⬭ **The three main types of boundaries are convergent, divergent, and transform fault boundaries.**

Divergent boundaries Divergent boundaries (also called spreading centers) occur when two plates move apart. This process results in upwelling of material from the mantle to create new seafloor, as shown in Figure 7A. A relatively new divergent boundary is located in Africa, in a region known as the East African Rift valley.

Convergent boundaries Convergent boundaries form where two plates move together. This process results in oceanic lithosphere plunging beneath an overriding plate, and descending into the mantle, as shown in Figure 7B. At other locations, plates carrying continental crust are presently moving toward each other. Eventually, these continents may collide and merge. Thus, the boundary that once separated two plates disappears as the plates become one.

Transform fault boundaries Transform fault boundaries are margins where two plates grind past each other without the production or destruction of lithosphere, as shown in Figure 7C. The San Andreas Fault zone in California is an example of a transform fault boundary.

Each plate contains a combination of these three types of boundaries. Although the total surface area of Earth does not change, plates may shrink or grow in area. This shrinking or growing depends on the locations of convergent and divergent boundaries. The Antarctic plate is growing larger. The Philippine plate is descending into the mantle along its margins and is becoming smaller. New plate boundaries can be created because of changes in the forces acting on these rigid slabs.

Figure 7 Three Types of Plate Boundaries

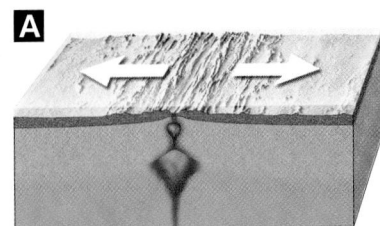

Divergent boundary

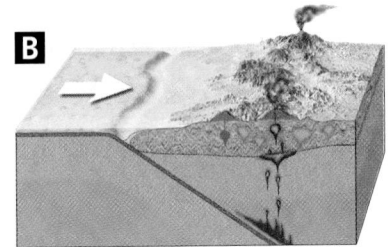

Convergent boundary

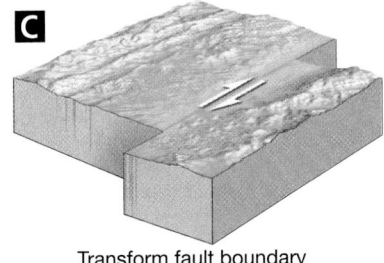

Transform fault boundary

Section 9.2 Assessment

Reviewing Concepts

1. ⬭ Define the term *lithospheric plate*.
2. ⬭ List the three types of plate boundaries.
3. ⬭ What theory proposes that Earth's outer shell consist of a number of rigid slabs?

Critical Thinking

4. **Comparing and Contrasting** Compare the plate motions in the three types of boundaries.

5. **Drawing Conclusions** What is the major difference in the role of the ocean floor between the continental drift hypothesis and the theory of plate tectonics?

Connecting Concepts

Plate Boundaries Use what you have learned about plate tectonics to compare Wegener's continental drift hypothesis to the theory of plate tectonics.

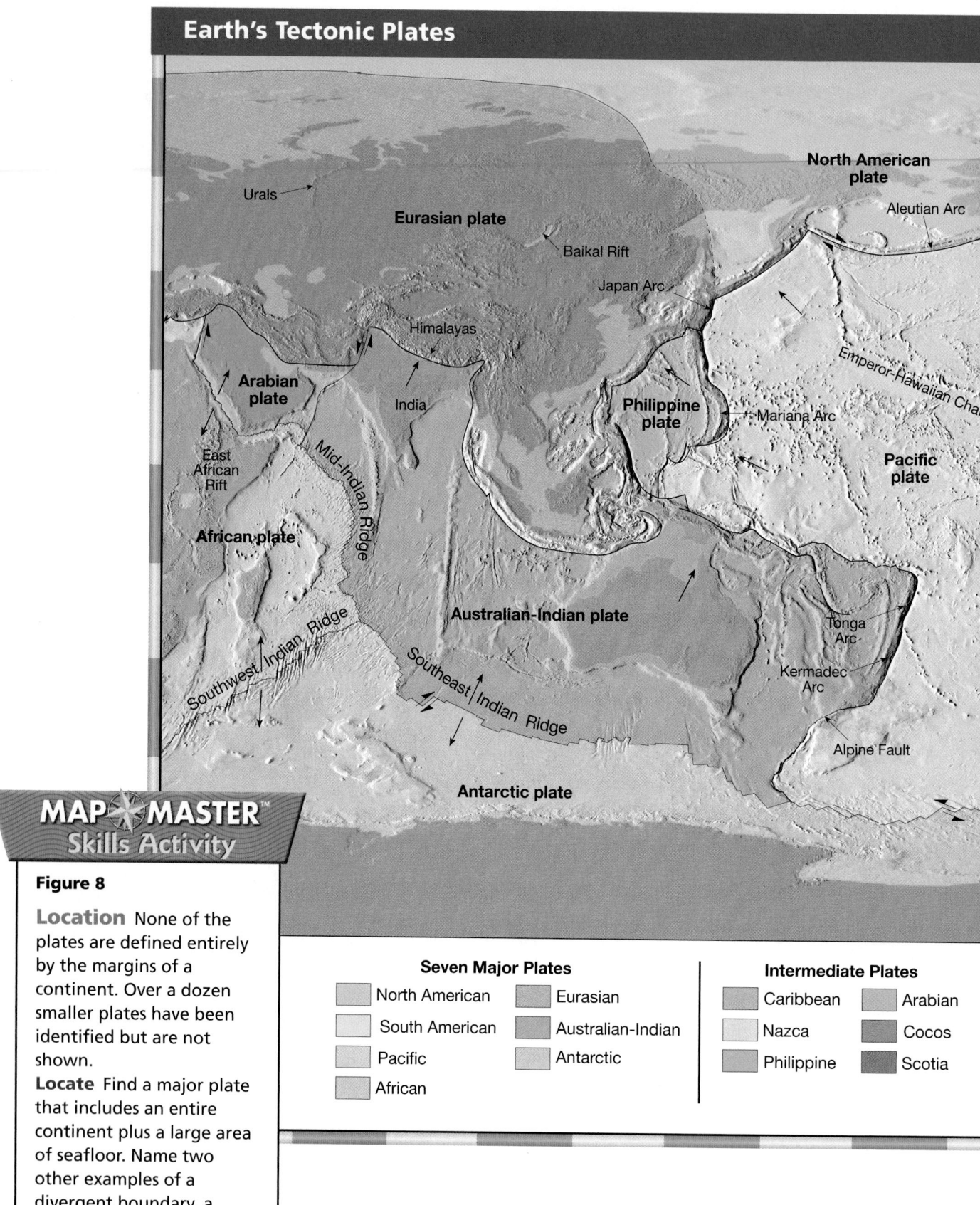

Earth's Tectonic Plates

Urals

Eurasian plate

Baikal Rift

North American plate

Aleutian Arc

Japan Arc

Himalayas

Emperor-Hawaiian Chain

Arabian plate

India

Philippine plate

Mariana Arc

East African Rift

Mid-Indian Ridge

Pacific plate

African plate

Southwest Indian Ridge

Australian-Indian plate

Tonga Arc

Southeast Indian Ridge

Kermadec Arc

Alpine Fault

Antarctic plate

MAP★MASTER™
Skills Activity

Figure 8

Location None of the plates are defined entirely by the margins of a continent. Over a dozen smaller plates have been identified but are not shown.

Locate Find a major plate that includes an entire continent plus a large area of seafloor. Name two other examples of a divergent boundary, a convergent boundary, and a transform fault boundary.

Seven Major Plates

- North American
- South American
- Pacific
- African
- Eurasian
- Australian-Indian
- Antarctic

Intermediate Plates

- Caribbean
- Nazca
- Philippine
- Arabian
- Cocos
- Scotia

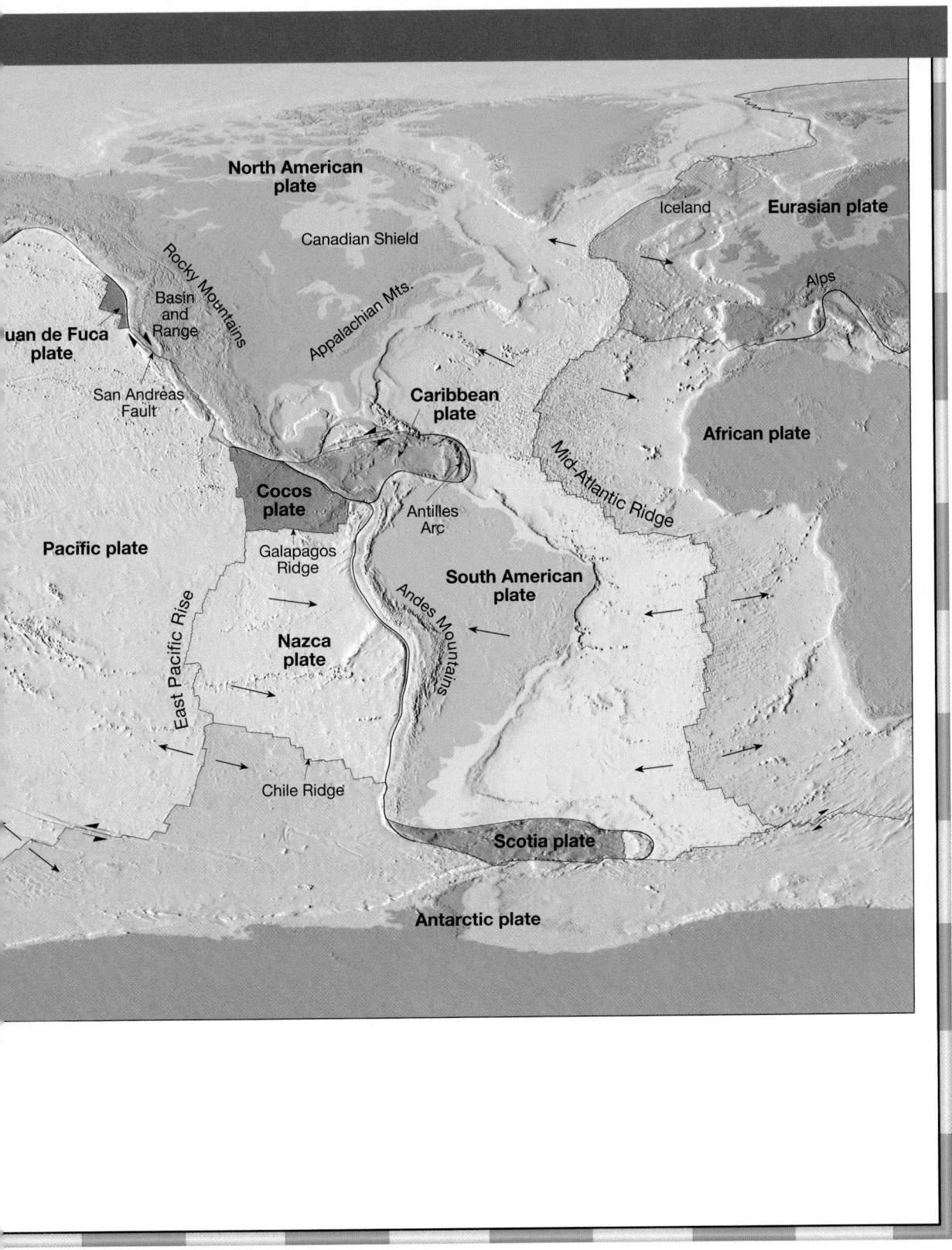

North American
plate

Canadian Shield

Iceland

Eurasian plate

Alps

Rocky Mountains

Basin
and
Range

uan de Fuca
plate

San Andreas
Fault

Appalachian Mts.

Caribbean
plate

African plate

Mid-Atlantic Ridge

Cocos
plate

Antilles
Arc

Pacific plate

Galapagos
Ridge

South American
plate

Andes Mountains

East Pacific Rise

Nazca
plate

Chile Ridge

Scotia plate

Antarctic plate

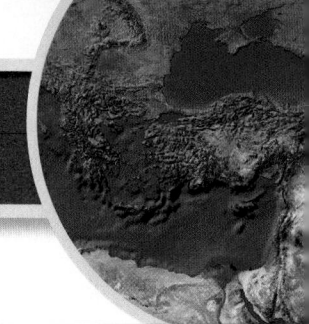

9.3 Actions at Plate Boundaries

Reading Focus

Key Concepts

- What is seafloor spreading?
- What is a subduction zone?

Vocabulary

- ◆ oceanic ridge
- ◆ rift valley
- ◆ seafloor spreading
- ◆ subduction zone
- ◆ trench
- ◆ continental volcanic arc
- ◆ volcanic island arc

Reading Strategy

Outlining Before you read, make an outline of this section. Use the green headings as the main topics and the blue headings as subtopics. As you read, add supporting details.

Actions at Boundaries
I. Divergent Boundaries
A. _____?
B. _____?
II. _____?

Tremendous forces are at work where tectonic plates meet. Let's take a closer look at what happens at the three types of plate boundaries.

Divergent Boundaries

Most divergent plate boundaries are located along the crests of oceanic ridges. These plate boundaries can be thought of as *constructive plate margins* because this is where new oceanic lithosphere is generated. Look again at the divergent boundary in Figure 7A on page 255. As the plates move away from the ridge axis, fractures are created. These fractures are filled with molten rock that wells up from the hot mantle below. Gradually, this magma cools to produce new slivers of seafloor. Spreading and upwelling of magma continuously adds oceanic lithosphere between the diverging plates.

Oceanic Ridges and Seafloor Spreading Along well-developed divergent plate boundaries, the seafloor is elevated, forming the **oceanic ridge**. The system of ocean ridges is the longest physical feature on Earth's surface, stretching more than 70,000 kilometers in length. This system winds through all major ocean basins like the seam on a baseball. The term *ridge* may be misleading. These features are not narrow like a typical ridge. They are 1000 to 4000 kilometers wide. Deep faulted structures called **rift valleys** are found along the axes of some segments. As you can see in Figure 9, rift valleys and spreading centers can develop on land, too.

For: Links on plate boundaries
Visit: www.SciLinks.org
Web Code: cjn-3093

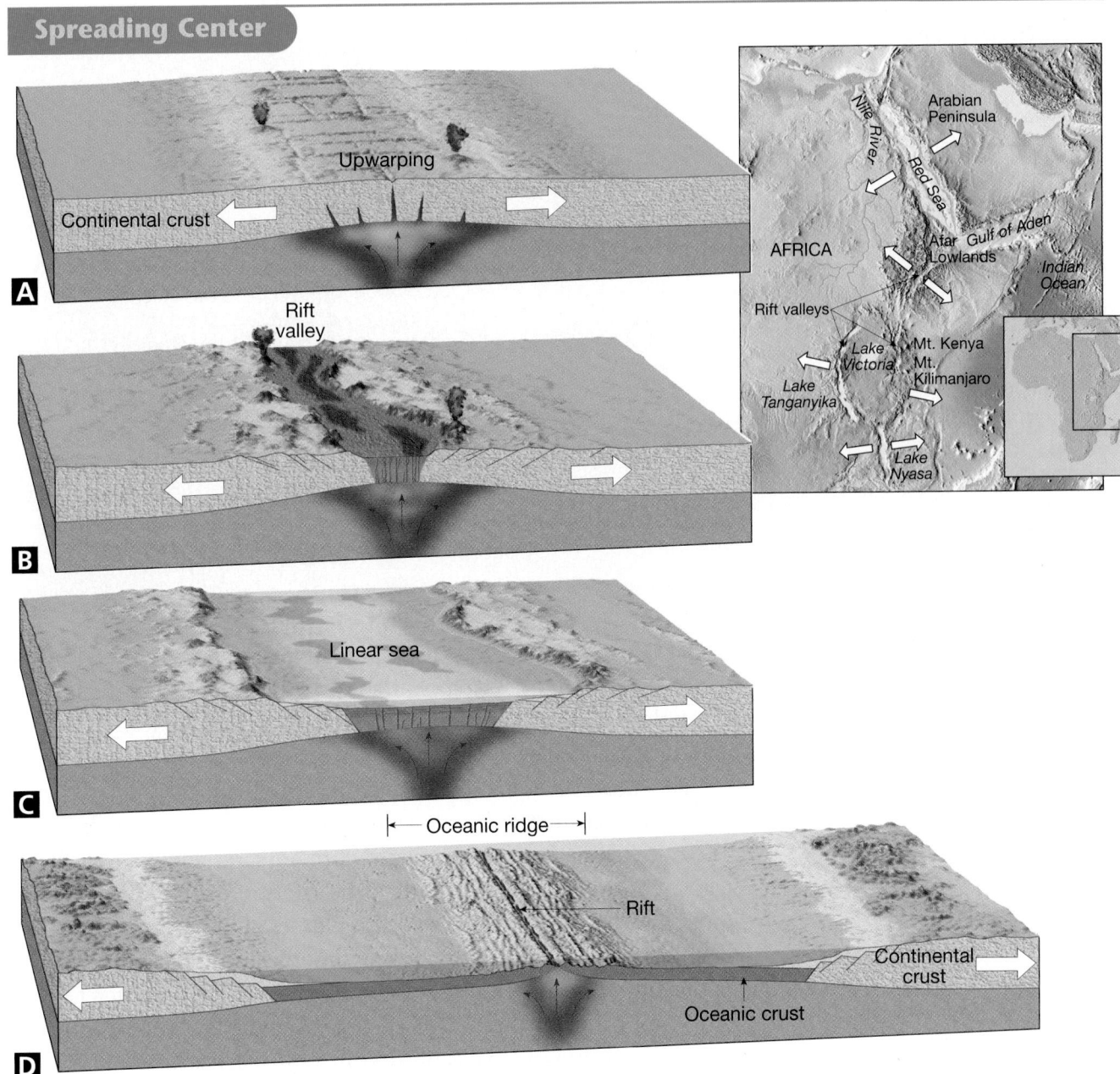

A

Continental crust ← Upwarping →

B

Rift valley

C

Linear sea

|← Oceanic ridge →|

D

Rift

Oceanic crust

Continental crust →

Arabian Peninsula
Nile River
Red Sea
Afar Gulf of Aden
Lowlands
AFRICA
Indian Ocean
Rift valleys
Lake Victoria
Mt. Kenya
Lake Tanganyika
Mt. Kilimanjaro
Lake Nyasa

🖱 **Seafloor spreading is the process by which plate tectonics produces new oceanic lithosphere.** Typical rates of spreading average around 5 centimeters per year. These rates are slow on a human time scale. However, they are rapid enough so that all of Earth's ocean basins could have been generated within the last 200 million years. In fact, none of the ocean floor that has been dated is older than 180 million years.

Figure 9 The East African rift valleys may represent the initial stages of the breakup of a continent along a spreading center. **A** Rising magma forces the crust upward, causing numerous cracks in the rigid lithosphere. **B** As the crust is pulled apart, large slabs of rock sink, causing a rift zone. **C** Further spreading causes a narrow sea. **D** Eventually, an ocean basin and ridge system is created.
Relating Cause and Effect
What causes the continental crust to stretch and break?

Figure 10 East African Rift Valley This valley may be where the African continent is splitting apart.
Interpreting Diagrams *What stage in the drawings on page 259 does this photograph show?*

Continental Rifts When spreading centers develop within a continent, the landmass may split into two or more smaller segments. Examples of active continental rifts include the East African rift valley and the Rhine Valley in Northwest Europe.

The most widely accepted model for continental breakup suggests that forces that are stretching the lithosphere must be acting on the plate. These stretching forces by themselves are not large enough to actually tear the lithosphere apart. Rather, the rupture of the lithosphere is thought to begin in those areas where plumes of hot rock rise from the mantle. This hot-spot activity weakens the lithosphere and creates domes in the crust directly above the hot rising plume. Uplifting stretches the crust and makes it thinner, as shown in Figure 9A. Along with the stretching, faulting and volcanism form a rift valley, as in Figure 9B

The East African rift valley, shown in Figure 10, may represent the beginning stage in the breakup of a continent. Large mountains, such as Kilimanjaro and Mount Kenya, show the kind of volcanic activity that accompanies continental rifting. If the stretching forces continue, the rift valley will lengthen and deepen, until the continent splits in two. At this point, the rift becomes a narrow sea with an outlet to the ocean, similar to the Red Sea. The Red Sea formed when the Arabian Peninsula rifted from Africa about 20 million years ago. In this way, the Red Sea provides scientists with a view of how the Atlantic Ocean may have looked in its infancy.

 **Reading Checkpoint** *How do rifts begin to form?*

Convergent Boundaries

Although new lithosphere is constantly being added at the oceanic ridges, our planet is not growing larger. Earth's total surface area remains the same. How can that be? To accommodate the newly created lithosphere, older portions of oceanic plates return to the mantle along convergent plate boundaries. Because lithosphere is "destroyed" at convergent boundaries, they are also called *destructive plate margins*. As two plates slowly converge, the leading edge of one is bent downward, allowing it to slide beneath the other. Destructive plate margins where oceanic crust is being pushed down into the mantle are called **subduction zones.** The surface feature produced by the descending plate is an ocean **trench,** as shown in Figure 11. ⬤ **A subduction zone occurs when one oceanic plate is forced down into the mantle beneath a second plate.**

Convergent boundaries are controlled by the type of crust involved and the forces acting on the plate. Convergent boundaries can form between two oceanic plates, between one oceanic plate and one continental plate, or between two continental plates.

Oceanic-Continental When the leading edge of a continental plate converges with an oceanic plate, the less dense continental plate remains floating. The denser oceanic slab sinks into the asthenosphere. When a descending plate reaches a depth of about 100 to 150 kilometers, some of the asthenosphere above the descending plate melts. The newly formed magma, being less dense than the rocks of the mantle, rises. Eventually, some of this magma may reach the surface and cause volcanic eruptions.

The volcanoes of the Andes, located along western South America, are the product of magma generated as the Nazca plate descends beneath the continent. Figure 11 shows this process. The Andes are an example of a **continental volcanic arc.** Such mountains are produced in part by the volcanic activity that is caused by the subduction of oceanic lithosphere.

Figure 11 Oceanic-Continental Convergent Boundary Oceanic lithosphere is subducted beneath a continental plate.
Inferring *Why doesn't volcanic activity occur closer to the trench?*

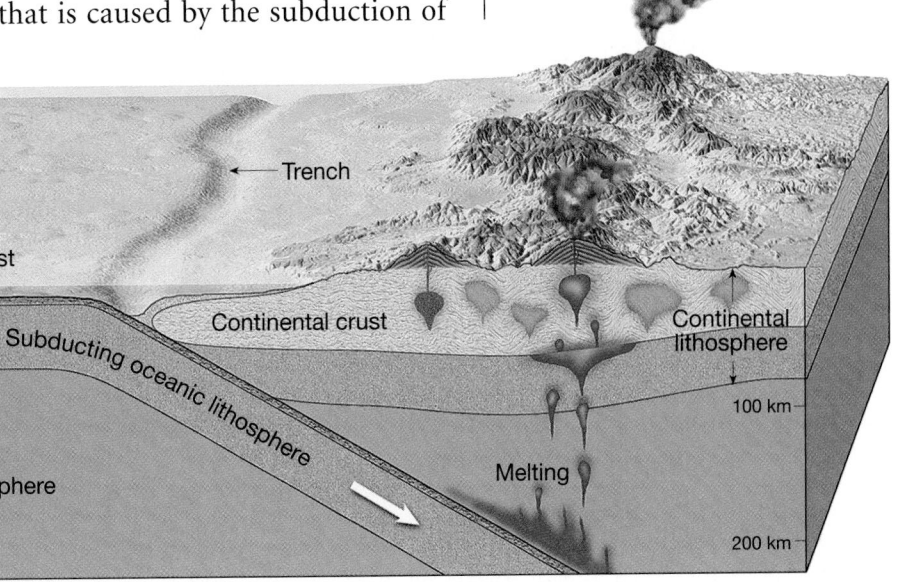

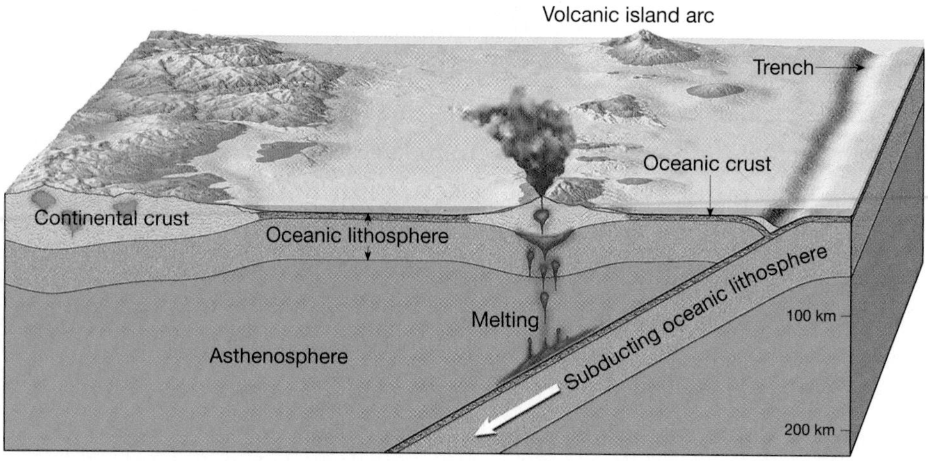

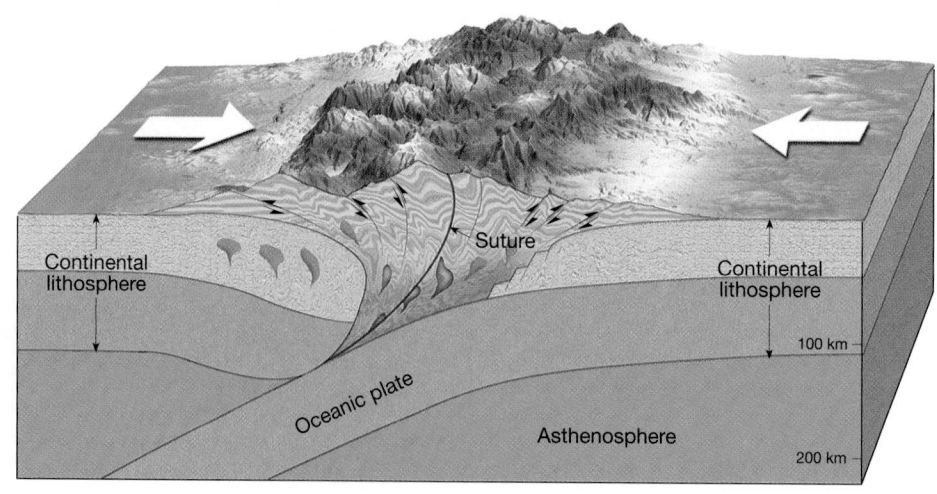

Volcanic island arc

Trench

Oceanic crust

Continental crust

Oceanic lithosphere

Melting

Asthenosphere

Subducting oceanic lithosphere

100 km

200 km

Figure 12 Oceanic-Oceanic Convergent Boundary One oceanic plate is subducted beneath another oceanic plate, forming a volcanic island arc. **Predicting** *What would happen to the volcanic activity if the subduction stopped?*

Oceanic-Oceanic When two oceanic slabs converge, one descends beneath the other. This causes volcanic activity similar to what occurs at an oceanic-continental boundary. However, the volcanoes form on the ocean floor instead of on a continent, as shown in Figure 12. If this activity continues, it will eventually build a chain of volcanic structures that become islands. This newly formed land consisting of an arc-shaped chain of small volcanic islands is called a **volcanic island arc.** The Aleutian Islands off the shore of Alaska are an example of a volcanic island arc. Next to the Aleutians is the Aleutian trench.

Continental-Continental When an oceanic plate is subducted beneath continental lithosphere, a continental volcanic arc develops along the margin of the continent. However, if the subducting plate also contains continental lithosphere, the subduction eventually brings the two continents together, as shown in Figure 13. Continental lithosphere is buoyant, which prevents it from being subducted to any great depth. The result is a collision between the two continents, which causes the formation of complex mountains such as the Himalayas in South Asia.

Figure 13 Continental-Continental Convergent Boundary Continental lithosphere cannot be subducted because it floats. The collision of two continental plates forms mountain ranges.

Continental lithosphere

Suture

Continental lithosphere

100 km

Oceanic plate

Asthenosphere

200 km

Before continents collide, the landmasses involved are separated by an ocean basin. As the continents move toward each other, the seafloor between them is subducted beneath one of the plates. When the continents collide, the collision folds and deforms the sediments along the margin as if they were placed in a giant vise. A new mountain range forms that is composed of deformed and metamorphosed sedimentary rocks, fragments of the volcanic arc, and possibly slivers of oceanic crust.

This kind of collision occurred when the subcontinent of India rammed into Asia and produced the Himalayas, as shown in Figure 14. During this collision, the continental crust buckled and fractured. Several other major mountain systems, including the Alps, Appalachians, and Urals, were also formed as a result of continental collisions.

Figure 14 A The leading edge of the plate carrying India is subducted beneath the Eurasian plate. **B** The landmasses collide and push up the crust. **C** India's collision with Asia continues today.

Collision of India and Asia

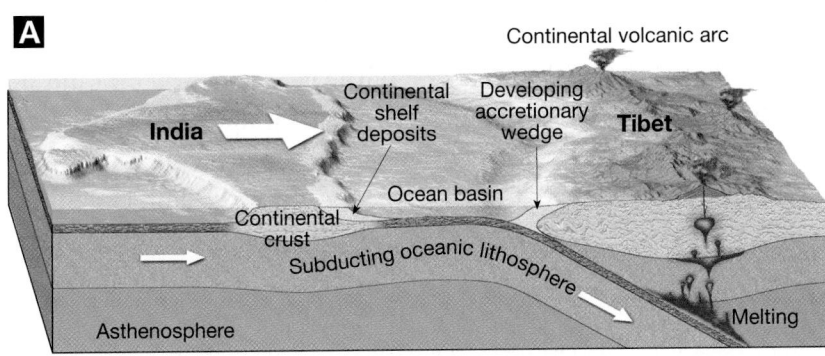

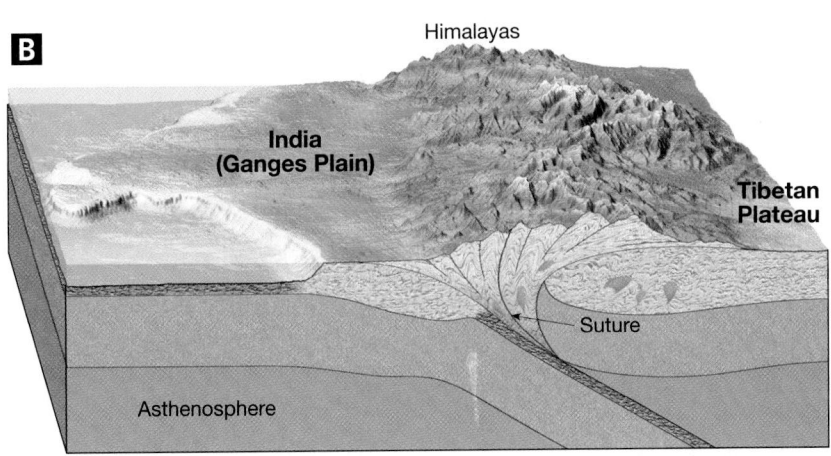

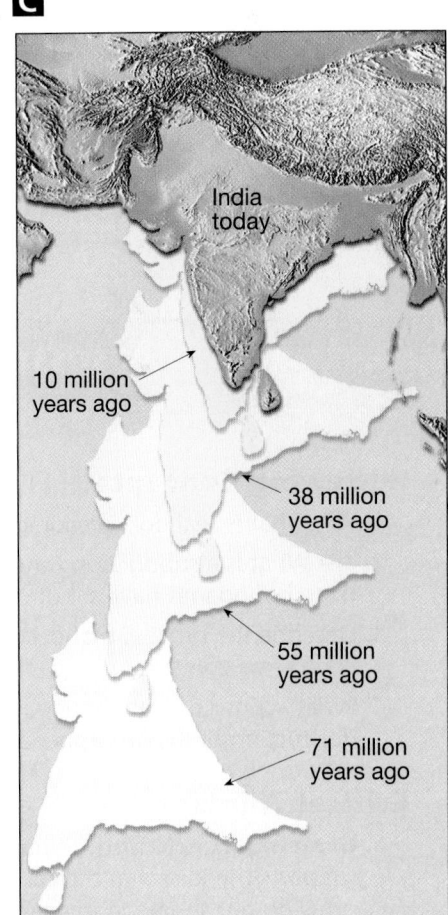

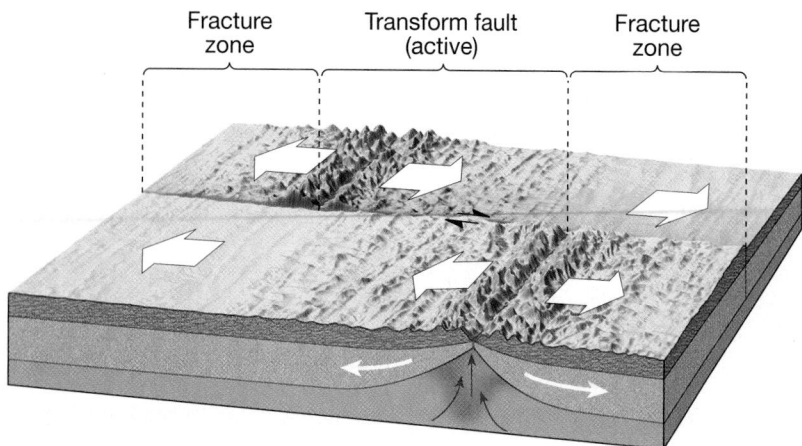

Fracture zone | Transform fault (active) | Fracture zone

Figure 15 A transform fault boundary offsets segments of a divergent boundary at an oceanic ridge.

Transform Fault Boundaries

The third type of plate boundary is the transform fault boundary. ◗ **At a transform fault boundary, plates grind past each other without destroying the lithosphere.** Most transform faults join two segments of a mid-ocean ridge, as shown in Figure 15. These faults are present about every 100 kilometers along the ridge axis. Active transform faults lie between the two offset ridge segments. The seafloor produced at one ridge axis moves in the opposite direction as seafloor is produced at an opposing ridge segment. So between the ridge segments these slabs of oceanic crust are grinding past each other along a transform fault.

Although most transform faults are located within the ocean basins, a few cut through the continental crust. One example is the San Andreas Fault of California. Along the San Andreas, the Pacific plate is moving toward the northwest, past the North American plate. If this movement continues, that part of California west of the fault zone will become an island off the west coast of the United States and Canada. It could eventually reach Alaska. However, a more immediate concern is the earthquake activity triggered by movements along this fault system.

Section 9.3 Assessment

Reviewing Concepts

1. ◗ What is seafloor spreading?
2. ◗ What is a subduction zone? What types of plate boundaries have subduction zones?
3. Describe the process that occurs when continents converge.
4. What actions of plate boundaries cause the destruction of the lithosphere?

Critical Thinking

5. **Drawing Conclusions** What evidence supports the idea that the Earth is neither growing nor shrinking in size?

6. **Relating Cause and Effect** During the collision between two continents, why doesn't a subduction zone form?
7. **Predicting** How will the angle at which an oceanic plate is subducted affect the distance from the volcanic arc to the trench?

Writing in Science

Creative Writing Write a paragraph that describes the rifting apart of a continent to form a new ocean. The paragraph should be written from the point of view of a person witnessing the events.

9.4 Testing Plate Tectonics

Key Concepts

- What evidence supports the theory of plate tectonics?
- How does paleomagnetism support the theory of plate tectonics?

Vocabulary

- ◆ paleomagnetism
- ◆ normal polarity
- ◆ reverse polarity
- ◆ hot spot

Reading Strategy

Predicting Copy the table. Write a prediction of where earthquakes will occur. After you read, if your prediction was incorrect or incomplete, write where earthquakes actually occur.

Probable Locations	Actual Locations
a. _____?_____	b. _____?_____

Evidence for Plate Tectonics

With the birth of the plate tectonics model, researchers from all of the Earth sciences began testing it. You have already seen some of the evidence supporting continental drift and seafloor spreading. Additional evidence for plate tectonics came as new technologies developed.

Paleomagnetism If you have ever used a compass to find direction, you know that the magnetic field has a north pole and a south pole. These magnetic poles align closely, but not exactly, with the geographic poles.

In many ways, Earth's magnetic field is much like that produced by a simple bar magnet. Invisible lines of force pass through Earth and extend from one pole to the other. A compass needle is a small magnet that is free to move about. The needle aligns with these invisible lines of force and points toward the magnetic poles.

Certain rocks contain iron-rich minerals, such as magnetite. When heated above a certain temperature, these magnetic minerals lose their magnetism. However, when these iron-rich mineral grains cool down, they become magnetized in the direction parallel to the existing magnetic field. Once the minerals solidify, the magnetism they possess stays frozen in this position. So magnetized rocks behave much like a compass needle because they point toward the existing magnetic poles. If the rock is moved or if the magnetic pole changes position, the rock's magnetism retains its original alignment. Rocks formed millions of years ago thus show the location of the magnetic poles at the time of their formation, as shown in Figure 16. These rocks possess **paleomagnetism.**

Figure 16 Paleomagnetism Preserved in Lava Flows As the lava cools, it becomes magnetized parallel to the magnetic field present at that time. When the polarity randomly reverses, a record of the paleomagnetism is preserved in the sequence of lava flows.

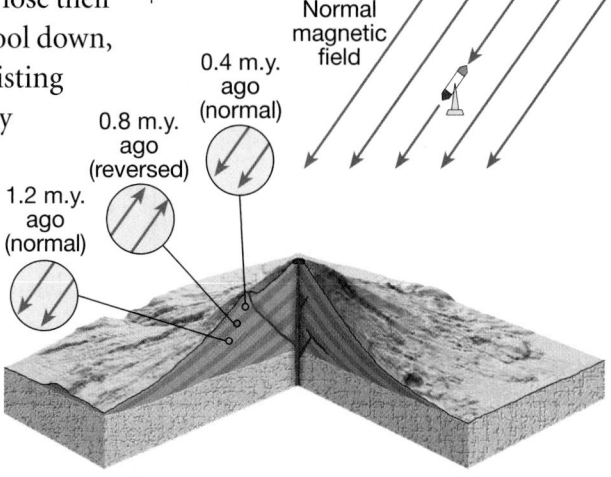

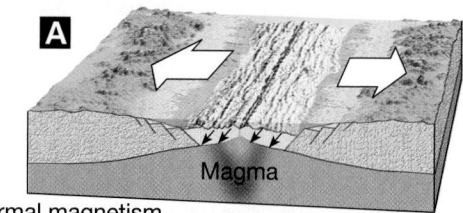

Period of normal magnetism

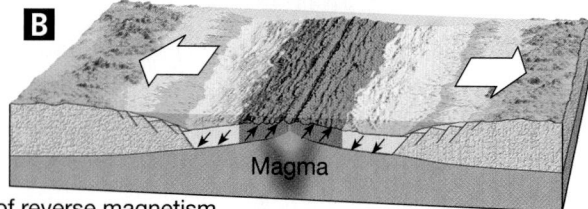

Period of reverse magnetism

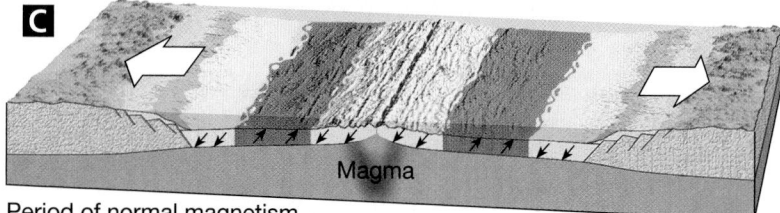

Period of normal magnetism

Figure 17 A As new material is added to the ocean floor at the oceanic ridges, it is magnetized according to Earth's existing magnetic field. **B** This process records each reversal of Earth's magnetic field. **C** Because new rock is added in approximately equal amounts to the trailing edges of both plates, strips of equal size and polarity parallel both sides of the ocean ridges. **Applying Concepts** *Why are the magnetized strips about equal width on either side of the ridge?*

Geophysicists learned that Earth's magnetic field periodically reverses polarity. The north magnetic pole becomes the south magnetic pole, and vice versa. A rock solidifying during one of the periods of reverse polarity will be magnetized with the polarity opposite that of rocks being formed today.

When rocks show the same magnetism as the present magnetic field, they are described as having **normal polarity.** Rocks that show the opposite magnetism are said to have **reverse polarity.** A relationship was discovered between the magnetic reversals and the seafloor-spreading hypothesis. Ships towed instruments called magnetometers across segments of the ocean floor. This research revealed alternating strips of high- and low-intensity magnetism that ran parallel to the ridges. The strips of high-intensity magnetism are regions where the paleomagnetism of the ocean crust is of the normal type. These positively magnetized rocks enhance the existing magnetic field. The low-intensity strips represent regions where the ocean crust is polarized in the reverse direction and, therefore, weaken the existing magnetic field. As new basalt is added to the ocean floor at the oceanic ridges, it becomes magnetized according to the existing magnetic field, as shown in Figure 17. **The discovery of strips of alternating polarity, which lie as mirror images across the ocean ridges, is among the strongest evidence of seafloor spreading.**

Earthquake Patterns **Scientists found a close link between deep-focus earthquakes and ocean trenches. Also, the absence of deep-focus earthquakes along the oceanic ridge system was shown to be consistent with the new theory.**

Compare the distribution of earthquakes shown in Chapter 8 on page 226 with the map of plate boundaries on pages 256–257. The close link between plate boundaries and earthquakes is obvious. When the depths of earthquake foci and their locations within the trench systems are plotted, a pattern emerges.

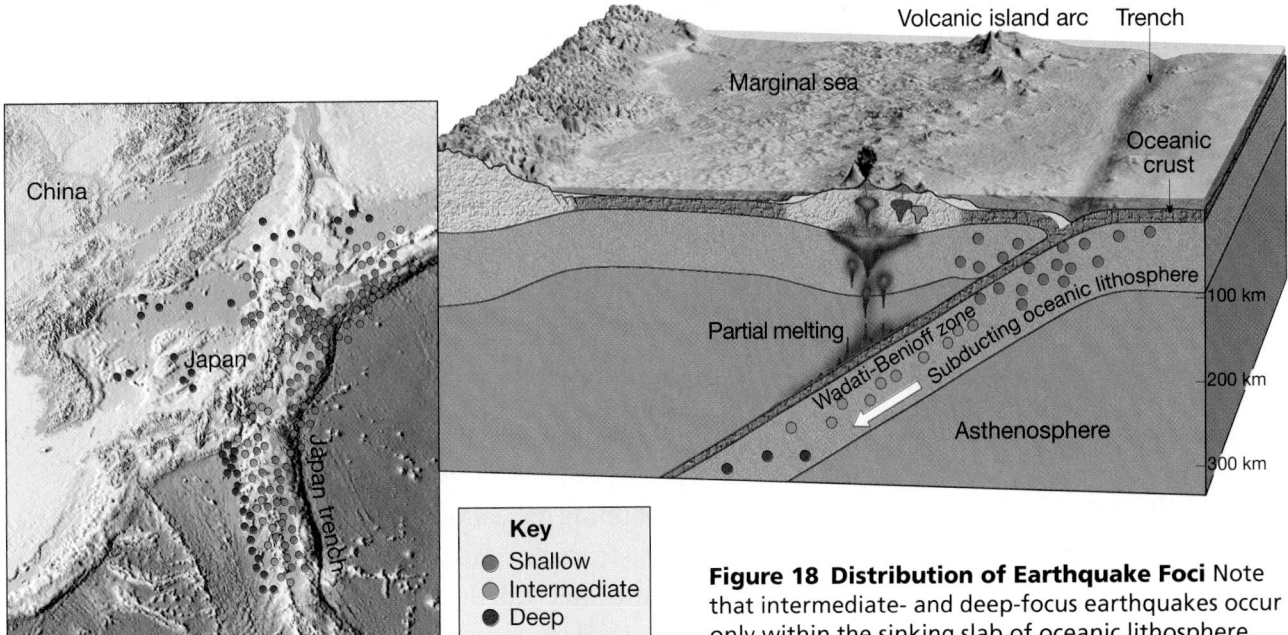

Figure 18 Distribution of Earthquake Foci Note that intermediate- and deep-focus earthquakes occur only within the sinking slab of oceanic lithosphere.

Look at Figure 18. It shows the distribution of earthquakes near the Japan trench. Here, most shallow-focus earthquakes occur within or adjacent to the trench. Intermediate- and deep-focus earthquakes occur toward the mainland.

In the plate tectonics model, deep-ocean trenches are produced where cool, dense slabs of oceanic lithosphere plunge into the mantle. Shallow-focus earthquakes are produced as the descending plate interacts with the lithosphere above it. As the slab descends farther into the mantle, deeper-focus earthquakes are produced. No earthquakes have been recorded below 700 kilometers. At this depth, the slab has been heated enough to soften.

Ocean Drilling Some of the most convincing evidence confirming the plate tectonics theory has come from drilling directly into ocean-floor sediment. The Deep Sea Drilling Project from 1968 to 1983 used the drilling ship *Glomar Challenger* to drill hundreds of meters into the sediments and underlying crust.

When the oldest sediment from each drill site was plotted against its distance from the ridge crest, it was revealed that the age of the sediment increased with increasing distance from the ridge. **The data on the ages of seafloor sediment confirmed what the seafloor-spreading hypothesis predicted. The youngest oceanic crust is at the ridge crest and the oldest oceanic crust is at the continental margins.**

The data also reinforced the idea that the ocean basins are geologically young. No sediment older than 180 million years was found. By comparison, some continental crust has been dated at 4.0 billion years.

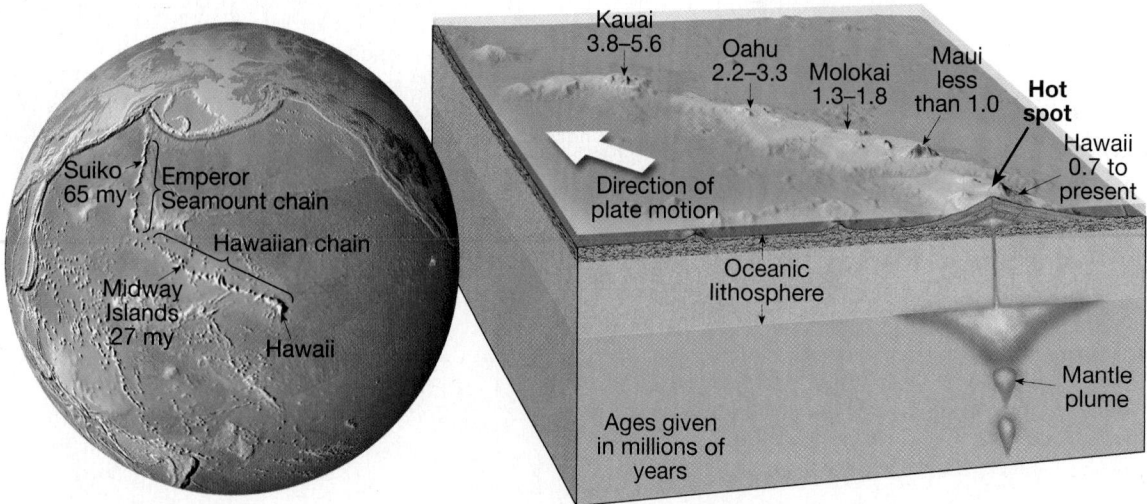

Kauai
3.8–5.6

Oahu
2.2–3.3 Molokai
1.3–1.8

Maui
less
than 1.0

Hot
spot

Hawaii
0.7 to
present

Direction of
plate motion

Oceanic
lithosphere

Mantle
plume

Ages given
in millions of
years

Suiko
65 my

Emperor
Seamount chain

Hawaiian chain

Midway
Islands
27 my

Hawaii

Figure 19 Hot Spot The chain of islands and seamounts that extends from Hawaii to the Aleutian trench results from the movement of the Pacific plate over a stationary hot spot. **Predicting** *Where will a new Hawaiian island be located?*

Hot Spots

Mapping of seafloor volcanoes in the Pacific revealed a chain of volcanic structures extending from the Hawaiian Islands to Midway Island and then north to the Aleutian trench, as shown in Figure 19. Dates of volcanoes in this chain showed that the volcanoes increase in age with increasing distance from Hawaii. Suiko Seamount is 65 million years old. Midway Island is 27 million years old. The island of Hawaii formed less than a million years ago and is still forming today.

A rising plume of mantle material is located below the island of Hawaii. Melting of this hot rock as it nears the surface creates a volcanic area, or **hot spot**. As the Pacific plate moves over the hot spot, successive volcanic mountains have been created. The age of each volcano indicates the time when it was situated over the hot spot. Kauai is the oldest of the large islands in the Hawaiian chain. Its volcanoes are extinct. The youthful island of Hawaii has two active volcanoes— Mauna Loa and Kilauea. 🌐 **Hot spot evidence supports the idea that the plates move over Earth's surface.**

Section 9.4 Assessment

Reviewing Concepts

1. 🌐 List and describe the evidence for the plate tectonics theory.

2. 🌐 Define the term *paleomagnetism.*

3. What is the age of the oldest ocean crust? How do the ages of the ocean crust compare to the age of continental rocks?

4. What is a hot spot?

Critical Thinking

5. **Applying Concepts** How do hot spots and the plate tectonics theory account for the different ages of the Hawaiian Islands?

6. **Predicting** Would earthquakes occur at depths of over 700 kilometers? Why or why not?

Explanatory Paragraph Write a paragraph explaining why the age pattern of the ocean floor supports seafloor spreading.

9.5 Mechanisms of Plate Motion

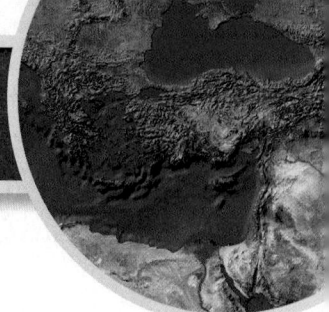

Reading Focus

Key Concepts

- What are the mechanisms of plate motion?
- What causes plate motion?

Vocabulary

- convective flow
- slab-pull
- ridge-push
- mantle plume

Reading Strategy

Identifying Main Ideas Copy the table. As you read, write the main ideas for each topic.

Topic	Main Idea
Slab-pull	a. _____?_____
Ridge-push	b. _____?_____
Mantle convection	c. _____?_____

Causes of Plate Motion

Scientists generally agree that convection occurring in the mantle is the basic driving force for plate movement. During convection, warm, less dense material rises and cooler, denser material sinks. The motion of matter resulting from convection is called **convective flow.** The slow movements of the plates and mantle are driven by the unequal distribution of Earth's heat. The heat is generated by the radioactive decay of elements, such as uranium, found within Earth's mantle and crust.

Slab-Pull and Ridge-Push Several mechanisms produce forces that cause plate motion. One mechanism, called **slab-pull,** occurs because old oceanic crust, which is relatively cool and dense, sinks into the asthenosphere and "pulls" the trailing lithosphere along. Slab-pull is thought to be the primary downward arm of convective flow in the mantle. By contrast, **ridge-push** results from the elevated position of the oceanic ridge system. Ridge-push causes oceanic lithosphere to slide down the sides of the oceanic ridge. The downward slide is the result of gravity acting on the oceanic lithosphere. Ridge-push, although active in some spreading centers, is probably less important than slab-pull.

Mantle Convection Most models suggest that hot plumes of rock are the upward flowing arms in mantle convection. These rising **mantle plumes** sometimes show themselves on Earth's surface as hot spots and volcanoes.

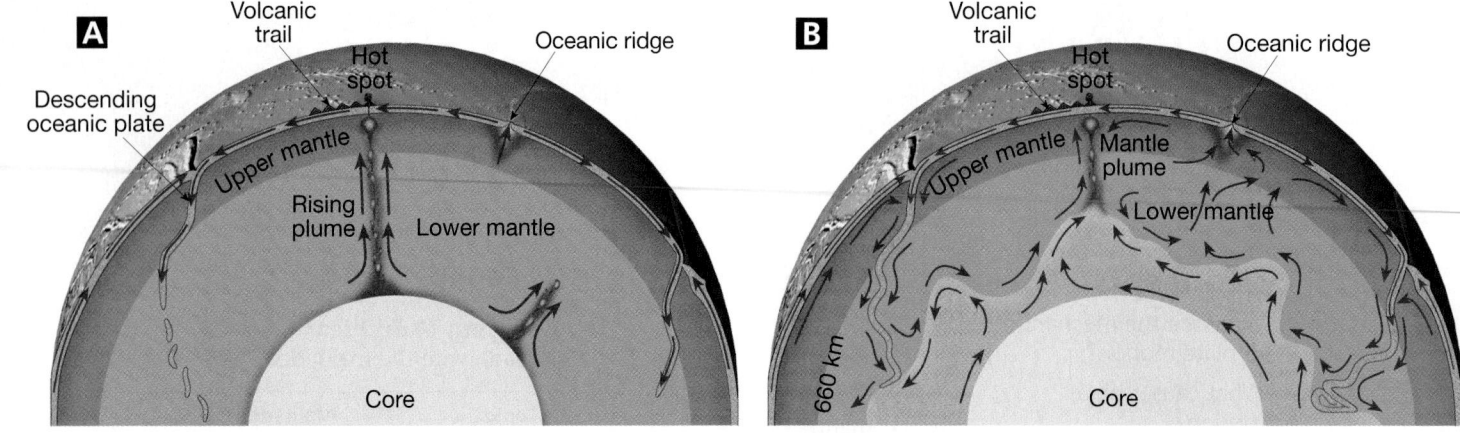

Figure 20 Mantle Convection Models A In the whole-mantle convection model, cold oceanic lithosphere descends into the mantle. Hot mantle plumes transport heat toward the surface. **B** The deep-layer model suggests that Earth's heat causes these layers of convection to slowly swell and shrink in complex patterns. Some material from the lower layer flows upward as mantle plumes.

One recent model is called whole-mantle convection. In this model, slabs of cold oceanic lithosphere descend into the lower mantle. This process provides the downward arm of convective flow, as shown in Figure 20A. At the same time, hot mantle plumes originating near the mantle-core boundary move heat toward the surface. Another model is the deep-layer model. You might compare this model to a lava lamp on a low setting. As shown in Figure 20B, the lower mantle is like the colored fluid in the bottom layer of a lava lamp. Like a lava lamp, heat from Earth's interior causes the two layers to slowly swell and shrink in complex patterns without much mixing. A small amount of material from the lower layer flows upward as mantle plumes, creating hot-spot volcanism at the surface.

There is still much to be learned about the mechanisms that cause plates to move. But one thing is clear. **The unequal distribution of heat within Earth causes the thermal convection in the mantle that ultimately drives plate motion.** Exactly how this convection operates is still being debated.

Section 9.5 Assessment

Reviewing Concepts

1. Describe the mechanisms of plate motion.
2. What drives the slow movement of the plates and the convection in the mantle?
3. What is the main source of heat in Earth's interior?

Critical Thinking

4. **Relating Cause and Effect** How is the theory of plate tectonics related to the radioactive decay of elements within Earth's interior?

5. **Calculating** If Africa and Australia are moving apart at a rate of 4.4 centimeters per year, approximately how long will it take for the ocean between the two continents to increase by 1000 kilometers?

Connecting Concepts

Heat Flow Review Section 9.1. How would the flow of heat generated by radioactive decay benefit the theory of continental drift?

understanding EARTH

Plate Tectonics into the Future

Two geologists, Robert Dietz and John Holden, used present-day plate movements to predict the locations of landmasses in the future. The map below shows where they predict Earth's landmasses will be 50 million years from now if plate movements remain at their present rates.

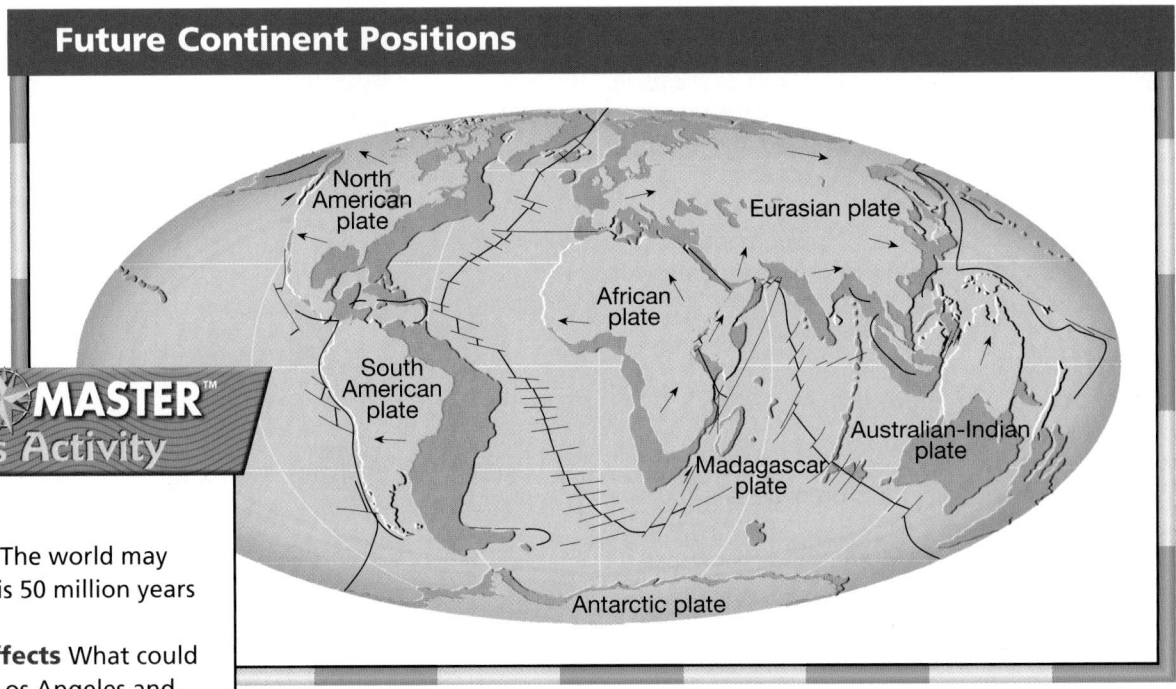

Future Continent Positions

North American plate

Eurasian plate

African plate

South American plate

Australian-Indian plate

Madagascar plate

Antarctic plate

MAP★MASTER™ Skills Activity

Figure 21

Location The world may look like this 50 million years from now.
Identify Effects What could happen to Los Angeles and San Francisco if this proposed movement occurs?

L.A. on the Move

In North America, the Baja Peninsula and the portion of southern California that lies west of the San Andreas Fault will have slid past the North American plate. If this northward motion takes place, Los Angeles and San Francisco will pass each other in about 10 million years. In about 60 million years Los Angeles will begin to descend into the Aleutian trench.

New Sea in Africa

Major changes are seen in Africa, where a new sea emerges as East Africa is ripped away from the mainland. In addition, Africa will have moved slowly into Europe, perhaps creating the next major mountain-building stage on Earth. Meanwhile, the Arabian Peninsula continues to move away from Africa, allowing the Red Sea to widen and close the Persian Gulf.

Atlantic Ocean Grows

In other parts of the world, Australia will be located across the equator and, along with New Guinea, will be on a collision course with Asia. Meanwhile, North and South America will begin to separate, while the Atlantic and Indian oceans will continue to grow as the Pacific Ocean shrinks.

These projections into the future, although interesting, must be viewed with caution because many assumptions must be correct for these events to occur. We can be sure that large changes in the shapes and positions of continents will occur for millions of years to come.

Paleomagnetism and the Ocean Floor

In the continental drift hypothesis, the ocean floors were not really involved. The continents were proposed to move through the oceans like icebreaking ships plowing through ice. Later studies of the oceans provided one of the keys to the plate tectonic theory. You will observe how the magnetic rocks on the ocean floor can be used to understand plate tectonics.

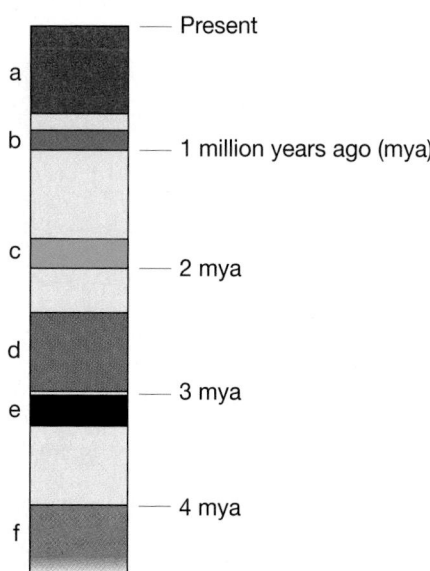

Present
a
b — 1 million years ago (mya)
c — 2 mya
d — 3 mya
e
f — 4 mya

Problem
How are the paleomagnetic patterns on the ocean floor used to determine the rate of seafloor spreading?

Materials
- pencil
- metric ruler
- calculator
- photocopy of diagrams on page 273

Skills
Measuring, Interpreting Diagrams, Calculating

Procedure

1. Scientists have reconstructed Earth's magnetic polarity reversals over the past several million years. A record of these reversals is shown above. Periods of normal polarity, when a compass would have pointed north as it does today, are shown in color. Periods of reverse polarity are shown in white. Record the number of times Earth's magnetic field has had reversed polarity in the last 4 million years.

2. The three diagrams on the next page illustrate the magnetic polarity reversals across sections of the mid-ocean ridges in the Pacific, South Atlantic, and North Atlantic oceans. Periods of normal polarity are shown in color and match the colors in the illustration above. Observe that the patterns of polarity in the rock match on either side of the ridge for each ocean basin.

3. On the photocopy of the three ocean-floor diagrams, identify and mark the periods of normal polarity with the letters *a–f*. Begin at the ridge crest and label along both sides of each ridge. (*Hint:* The left side of the South Atlantic has already been done and can act as a guide.)

4. Using the South Atlantic as an example, label the beginning of the normal polarity period c, "2 million years ago," on the left sides of the Pacific and North Atlantic diagrams.

5. Using the distance scale shown with the ocean floor diagrams, determine which ocean basin has spread the greatest distance during the last 2 million years.

6. Refer to the distance scale. Notice that the left side of the South Atlantic basin has spread approximately 39 kilometers from the center of the ridge crest in 2 million years.

Analyze and Conclude

1. **Analyzing Data** How many kilometers has the left side of the Pacific basin spread in 2 million years?

2. **Analyzing Data** How many kilometers has the left side of the North Atlantic basin spread in 2 million years?

3. **Inferring** How many kilometers has each ocean basin opened in the past 2 million years?

4. **Calculating** If both the distance that each ocean basin has opened and the time it took to open that distance are known, the rate of seafloor spreading can be calculated. Determine the rate of seafloor spreading for the South Atlantic Ocean basin in centimeters per year. (*Hint:* To determine the rate of spreading in centimeters per year for each ocean basin, first convert the distance from kilometers to centimeters and then divide this distance by the time, 2 million years.)

5. **Calculating** Determine the rate of seafloor spreading for the North Atlantic and Pacific Ocean basins.

6. **Drawing Conclusions** Which ocean basin is spreading the fastest? The slowest?

7. **Inferring** Do ocean basins spread uniformly over the entire basin? Explain.

Go Further Use the library or the Internet to research the spreading rates for other divergent plate boundaries on Earth. Where is the fastest spreading rate? The slowest spreading rate?

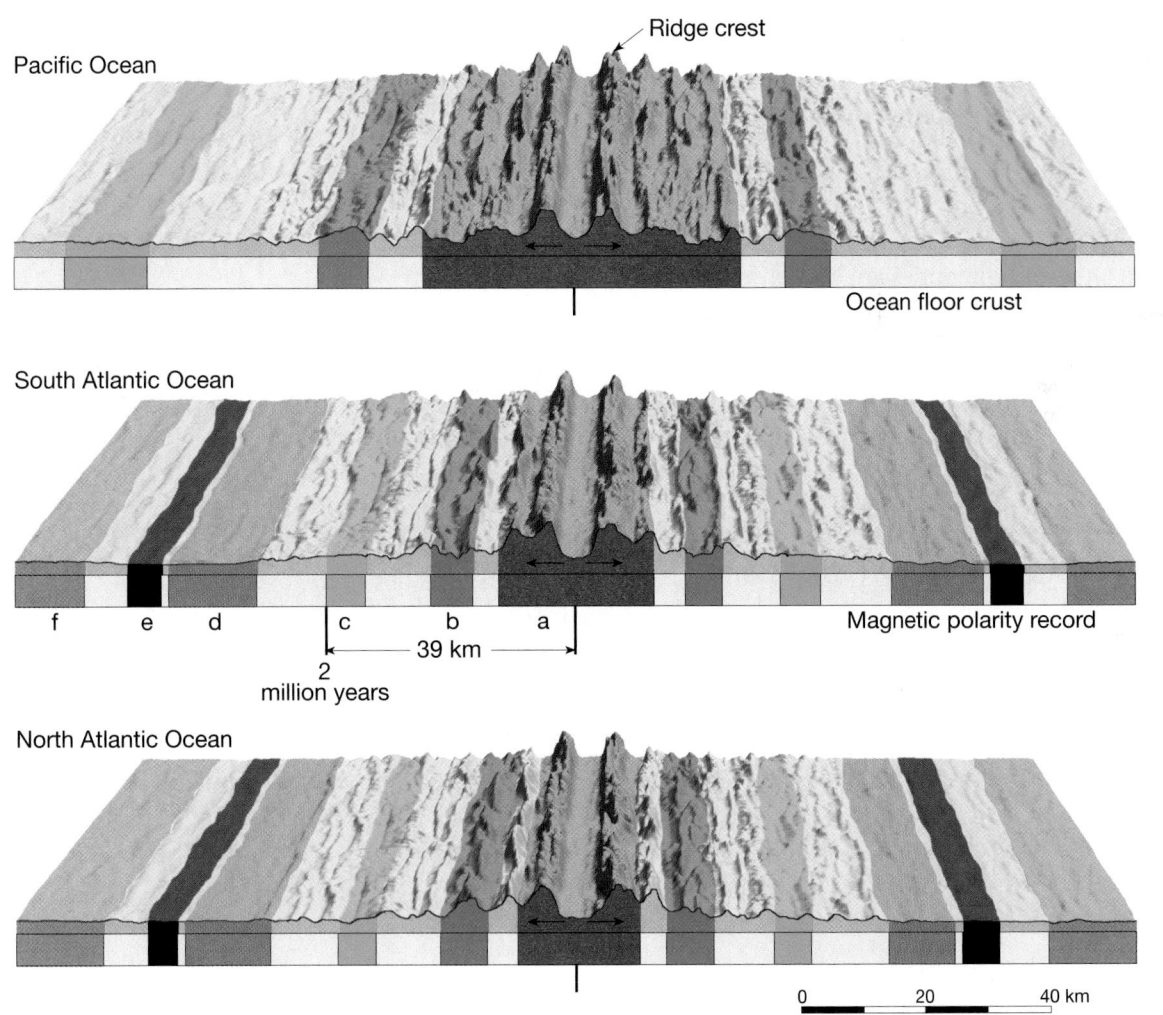

Pacific Ocean

Ridge crest

Ocean floor crust

South Atlantic Ocean

f   e   d   c   b   a

Magnetic polarity record

|← 39 km →|

2 million years

North Atlantic Ocean

0   20   40 km

Scale

9.1 Continental Drift

Key Concepts

- Wegener's continental drift hypothesis stated that the continents had once been joined to form a single supercontinent.
- Fossil evidence for continental drift includes several fossil organisms found on different landmasses.
- Rock evidence for continental drift exists in the form of several mountain belts that end at one coastline, only to reappear on a landmass across the ocean.

Vocabulary

continental drift, *p. 248;* Pangaea, *p. 248*

9.2 Plate Tectonics

Key Concepts

- According to the plate tectonics theory, the uppermost mantle, along with the overlying crust, behaves as a strong, rigid layer. This layer is known as the lithosphere.
- The three types of boundaries are convergent, divergent, and transform fault boundaries.

Vocabulary

plate tectonics, *p. 254;* plate, *p. 254;* divergent boundary, *p. 255;* convergent boundary, *p. 255;* transform fault boundary, *p. 255*

9.3 Actions at Plate Boundaries

Key Concepts

- Seafloor spreading is the process by which plate tectonics produces new oceanic lithosphere.
- A subduction zone occurs when one oceanic plate is forced down into the mantle beneath a second plate.
- At a transform fault boundary, plates grind past each other without destroying the lithosphere.

Vocabulary

oceanic ridge, *p. 258;* rift valley, *p. 258;* seafloor spreading, *p. 259;* subduction zone, *p. 261;* trench, *p. 261;* continental volcanic arc, *p. 261;* volcanic island arc, *p. 262*

9.4 Testing Plate Tectonics

Key Concepts

- The discovery of strips of alternating polarity, which lie as mirror images across the ocean ridges, is among the strongest evidence of seafloor spreading.
- Scientists found a close link between deep-focus earthquakes and ocean trenches. Also, the absence of deep-focus earthquakes along the oceanic ridge system was shown to be consistent with the new theory.
- The data on the ages of seafloor sediment confirmed what the seafloor-spreading hypothesis predicted. The youngest oceanic crust is at the ridge crest and the oldest oceanic crust is at the continental margins.
- Hot spot evidence supports that the plates move over Earth's surface.

Vocabulary

paleomagnetism, *p. 265;* normal polarity, *p. 266;* reverse polarity, *p. 266;* hot spot, *p. 268*

9.5 Mechanisms of Plate Motion

Key Concepts

- Scientists generally agree that convection occurring in the mantle is the basic driving force for plate movement.
- Slab-pull is thought to be the primary downward arm of convective flow in the mantle.
- Ridge-push causes oceanic lithosphere to slide down the sides of the oceanic ridge.
- The unequal distribution of heat within Earth causes the thermal convection in the mantle that ultimately drives plate motion.

Vocabulary

convective flow, *p. 269;* slab-pull, *p. 269;* ridge-push, *p. 269;* mantle plume, *p. 269*

Reviewing Content

Choose the letter that best answers the question or completes the statement.

1. What is the weaker, hotter zone beneath the lithosphere that allows for motion of Earth's rigid outer shell?
   a. crust   **b.** asthenosphere
   c. outer core   **d.** inner core

2. Most of Earth's earthquakes, volcanoes, and mountain building occur
   a. in the center of continents.
   b. in the Himalayas.
   c. at plate boundaries.
   d. at volcanic island arcs.

3. Alfred Wegener is best known for what hypothesis?
   a. plate tectonics   **b.** seafloor spreading
   c. continental drift   **d.** subduction

4. Complex mountain systems such as the Himalayas are the result of
   a. oceanic-oceanic convergence.
   b. hot spots.
   c. continental volcanic arcs.
   d. continental-continental convergence.

5. The best approximation of the true outer boundary of the continents is the seaward edge of
   a. continental shelf.
   b. mid-ocean ridge.
   c. present-day shorelines.
   d. ocean trenches.

6. What is the name given by Wegener to the supercontinent he proposed existed before the current continents?
   a. Euroamerica   **b.** Atlantis
   c. Pangaea   **d.** Panamerica

7. Which of the following mountain ranges was NOT the result of continental-continental convergence?
   a. Himalayas   **b.** Alps
   c. Appalachians **d.** Andes

8. What is the type of plate boundary where two plates move together, causing one of the slabs of lithosphere to descend into the mantle beneath an overriding plate?
   a. oceanic-continental convergent
   b. divergent
   c. transform fault
   d. continental-continental convergent

9. Most deep-focus earthquakes are linked to
   a. hot spots.
   b. ocean trenches.
   c. ocean ridges.
   d. transform fault boundaries.

10. One of the main objections to Wegener's hypothesis of continental drift was that he was unable to provide an acceptable
    a. rate of continental drift.
    b. date of continental drift.
    c. mechanism of continental drift.
    d. direction of continental drift.

Understanding Concepts

11. What are the three types of convergent plate boundaries?

12. Briefly explain the theory of plate tectonics.

13. How have earthquake patterns been used to support the theory of plate tectonics?

14. What type of plate boundary is shown? What types of lithosphere are involved?

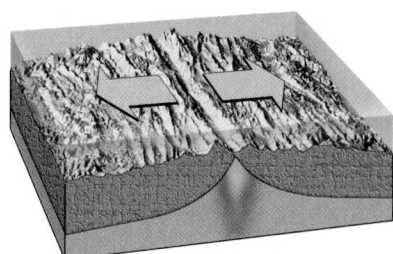

15. At what location is most lithosphere created? At what location is most lithosphere destroyed?

16. What feature produces volcanoes that do not occur at plate boundaries?

17. At what types of boundaries do subduction zones form?

Critical Thinking

18. Drawing Conclusions In the Atlantic Ocean basin, where would the oldest oceanic lithosphere be found?

19. Summarizing Describe the evidence that supported the hypothesis of continental drift.

20. Applying Concepts Some people predict that California will sink into the ocean. Does this idea fit with the theory of plate tectonics? Explain.

21. Inferring Why did the discovery of *Mesosaurus*, in both South America and Africa but nowhere else, support the hypothesis of continental drift?

22. Comparing and Contrasting What is the difference between the collision of an oceanic plate with a continental plate and the collision of two continental plates?

Analyzing Data

Use the diagram below to answer Questions 23–25.

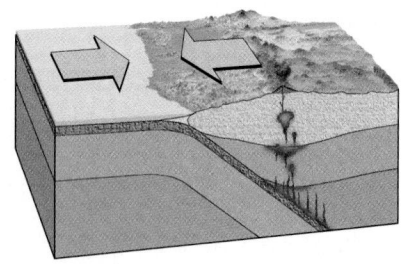

23. Interpreting Diagrams What type of boundary is shown? What types of lithosphere are involved?

24. Inferring What process is triggered as the slab descends beneath the other plate?

25. Drawing Conclusions How would the foci of earthquakes change if they were plotted in the diagram?

Concepts in Action

26. Inferring If the spreading rate at an ocean ridge increased, how would that affect the width of the paleomagnetic strips found on the ocean floor?

27. Classifying What type of plate boundary is formed when two plates grind past each other? Give an example of this type of boundary.

28. Formulating Hypotheses Form a hypothesis to explain what you think would happen if the direction of motion between India and Asia would change and India began to move in a southward direction.

29. Calculating How much wider would the Atlantic Ocean become in 10 million years if the spreading rate at the Mid-Atlantic Ridge was 2.5 cm/yr? Give your answer in kilometers.

30. Connecting Concepts What relationship exists between the ages of the Hawaiian Islands, hot spots, and plate tectonics?

31. Writing in Science Write a paragraph explaining why it is less likely that there will be a large earthquake in a location in the middle of North America, such as in Chicago, Illinois.

Performance-Based Assessment

Classifying Use a world map to choose ten different locations around the world. Then use Figure 8 on pages 256–257 to find the plate boundary nearest each location. Classify each boundary.

Standardized Test Prep

Use the diagram below to answer Questions 3 and 4.

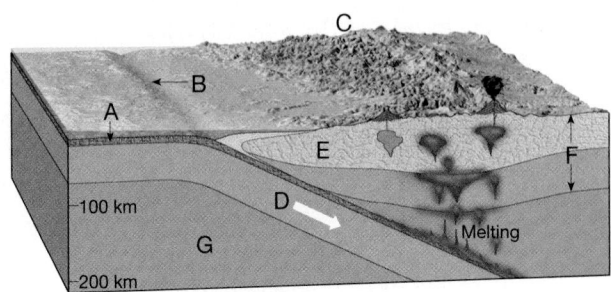

Test-Taking Tip

Eliminating Unreasonable Answers
When you answer a multiple-choice question, you can often eliminate at least one answer choice because it is clearly incorrect. If you eliminate one or more choices, you increase your odds of choosing the correct answer.

In the question below, you can immediately eliminate choice B because the outer core is located deep in Earth's interior. The mantle, answer choice A, is another layer that is found in Earth's interior. So you can eliminate A. You have narrowed your choices down to either C, the lithosphere, or D, the asthenosphere. The asthenosphere is not rigid. It is a weak layer over which the plates move. The remaining choice, C, must be the correct answer.

What is Earth's strong, rigid outer layer called?

(A) the mantle
(B) the outer core
(C) the lithosphere
(D) the asthenosphere

Choose the letter that best answers the question or completes the statement.

1. Which one of the following was NOT used as support of Wegener's continental drift hypothesis?
   (A) fossil evidence
   (B) paleomagnetism
   (C) the fit of South America and Africa
   (D) ancient climates

2. At what type of plate boundary do plates move apart, resulting in the upwelling of material from the mantle to create new seafloor?
   (A) divergent
   (B) convergent
   (C) transform fault
   (D) subduction

3. What feature is labeled F?
   (A) a continental volcanic arc
   (B) a subduction zone
   (C) continental lithosphere
   (D) an ocean ridge

4. The process occurring at the location labeled D is
   (A) oceanic lithosphere being created.
   (B) continental lithosphere being created.
   (C) a continental-continental collision occurring.
   (D) oceanic lithosphere being subducted.

Answer the following questions in complete sentences.

5. How does the age of the ocean lithosphere and deepest sediment in an ocean basin change with increasing distance from the oceanic ridge?

6. Why is Earth not getting larger even though new lithosphere is constantly being added at the oceanic ridges?

7. Describe two events that occur on Earth that you would not expect to find on Mars because of the lack of plate movements.

8. At some time in the distant future, Earth's interior will cool to the point that plate movement will stop. Describe how Earth would be different form that point onward.

Volcanoes and Other Igneous Activity

CONCEPTS
— in Action —

Quick Lab
Why are some volcanoes explosive?

Exploration Lab
Melting Temperatures of Rocks

How the Earth Works
Effects of Volcanoes

GEODe Forces Within
↳ Igneous Activity

DISCOVERY CHANNEL SCHOOL **Video Field Trip**

Death and Destruction

Take a field trip to the ancient city of Pompeii with Discovery Channel and find out how the eruption of Mount Vesuvius destroyed a civilization. Answer the following questions after watching the video.

1. Judging from its eruption, what type of volcano is Vesuvius?

2. Are the cities near Vesuvius any safer today than they were in 79 A.D.? Why or why not?

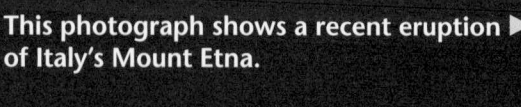
Go Online
PHSchool.com

For: Chapter 10 Resources
Visit: PHSchool.com
Web Code: cjk-9999

This photograph shows a recent eruption ▶ of Italy's Mount Etna.

Chapter Preview

Inquiry Activity

Where Are Volcanoes Located?

Procedure

1. Use the Internet and library resources to locate at least 15 active volcanoes and 10 historical volcanic eruptions.

2. Plot the locations of these volcanoes on a copy of a world map or on an overlay for a world atlas.

3. Neatly label the volcanoes on the map or overlay.

4. Compare your volcano map with the map of earthquake epicenters in Figure 9 on page 226 and the map of plate boundaries in Figure 8 on pages 256 and 257.

Think About It

1. **Observing** What is the relationship between the locations of the volcanoes you plotted and the earthquake epicenters and plate boundaries on the maps?

2. **Inferring** If there have been numerous volcanic eruptions in an area, would the area be a likely place for earthquakes to occur? Explain your answer.

3. **Predicting** Use your volcano map to predict if a volcanic eruption would be likely or not likely in each of the following areas: eastern coast of North America, Spain, eastern coast of South America, Italy, and Japan.

10.1 The Nature of Volcanic Eruptions

Reading Focus

Key Concepts

- What determines the type of volcanic eruption?
- What materials are ejected from volcanoes?
- What are the three main types of volcanoes?
- What other landforms are associated with volcanic eruptions?

Vocabulary

- viscosity
- vent
- pyroclastic material
- volcano
- crater
- shield volcano
- cinder cone
- composite cone
- caldera

Reading Strategy

Previewing Copy the table. Before you read the section, rewrite the green topic headings as questions. As you read, write the answers to the questions.

The Nature of Volcanic Eruptions	
What factors affect an eruption?	a. _____?_____

Volcanic eruptions are more than spectacular sights. They are windows to Earth's interior. Because volcanoes eject molten rock that formed at great depth, they provide opportunities to observe the processes that occur deep beneath Earth's surface.

On May 18, 1980, one of the largest volcanic eruptions to occur in North America changed a scenic volcano into the smoldering wreck shown in Figure 1. On this date, Mount St. Helens erupted with tremendous force. The blast blew out the entire north flank of the volcano, leaving a gaping hole. The eruption ejected nearly a cubic kilometer of ash and rock debris. The air over Yakima, Washington, 130 kilometers to the east, was so filled with ash that noon became almost as dark as midnight. Why do volcanoes like Mount St. Helens erupt explosively, while others like Kilauea in Hawaii are relatively quiet?

Figure 1 A Mount St. Helens before the May 18, 1980, eruption. **B** After the eruption, Spirit Lake filled with debris.

Spirit Lake

Table 1 Magma Composition					
Composition	Silica Content	Viscosity	Gas Content	Tendency to Form Pyroclastics (ejected rock fragments)	Volcanic Landform
Basaltic	Least (~50%)	Least	Least (1–2%)	Least	Shield Volcanoes Basalt Plateaus Cinder Cones
Andesitic	Intermediate (~60%)	Intermediate	Intermediate (3–4%)	Intermediate	Composite Cones
Rhyolitic	Most (~70%)	Greatest	Most (4–6%)	Greatest	Pyroclastic Flows Volcanic Domes

Factors Affecting Eruptions

The primary factors that determine whether a volcano erupts violently or quietly include magma composition, magma temperature, and the amount of dissolved gases in the magma.

Viscosity Viscosity is a substance's resistance to flow. For example, maple syrup is more viscous than water and flows more slowly. Magma from an explosive eruption may be thousands of times more viscous than magma that is extruded quietly.

The effect of temperature on viscosity is easy to see. If you heat maple syrup, it becomes more fluid and less viscous. In the same way, the mobility of lava is strongly affected by temperature. As a lava flow cools and begins to harden, its viscosity increases, its mobility decreases, and eventually the flow halts.

The chemical composition of magmas has a more important effect on the type of eruption. The viscosity of magma is directly related to its silica content. In general, the more silica in magma, the greater is its viscosity. Because of their high silica content, rhyolitic lavas are very viscous and don't flow easily. Basaltic lavas, which contain less silica, tend to be more fluid.

Dissolved Gases During explosive eruptions, the gases trapped in magma provide the force to eject molten rock from the **vent,** an opening to the surface. These gases are mostly water vapor and carbon dioxide. As magma moves nearer the surface, the pressure in the upper part of the magma is greatly reduced. The reduced pressure allows dissolved gases to be released suddenly.

Very fluid basaltic magmas allow the expanding gases to bubble upward and escape relatively easily. Therefore, eruptions of fluid basaltic lavas, such as those that occur in Hawaii, are relatively quiet. At the other extreme, highly viscous magmas slow the upward movement of expanding gases. The gases collect in bubbles and pockets that increase in size until they explosively eject the molten rock from the volcano. The result is a Mount St. Helens.

Why are some volcanoes explosive?

Procedure

1. Obtain two bottles of noncarbonated water and two bottles of club soda.

2. Open one bottle of the noncarbonated water and one bottle of the club soda. Record your observations.

3. Gently shake each of the remaining unopened bottles. **CAUTION:** *Wear safety goggles and point the bottles away from everyone.*

4. Carefully open each bottle over a sink or outside. Record your observations.

Analyze and Conclude

1. **Observing** What happened when the bottles were opened?

2. **Inferring** Which bottle represents lava with the most dissolved gas?

Figure 2 Lava Flows A Typical pahoehoe (ropy) lava flow, Kilauea Hawaii. **B** Example of a slow-moving aa flow.
Drawing Conclusions *Which of the flows has more viscous lava?*

Volcanic Material

Lava may appear to be the main material extruded from a volcano, but this is not always the case. Just as often, explosive eruptions eject huge quantities of broken rock, lava bombs, fine ash, and dust. All volcanic eruptions also emit large amounts of gas.

Lava Flows Hot basaltic lavas are usually very fluid because of their low silica content. Flow rates of 10 to 300 meters per hour are common. In contrast, the movement of silica-rich (rhyolitic) lava is often too slow to be visible. When fluid basaltic lavas harden, they commonly form a relatively smooth skin that wrinkles as the still-molten subsurface lava continues to move. These are known as pahoehoe (pah HOH ee hoh ee) flows and resemble the twisted braids in ropes, as shown in Figure 2. Another common type of basaltic lava called aa (AH ah) has a surface of rough, jagged blocks with dangerously sharp edges and spiny projections.

Gases Magmas contain varied amounts of dissolved gases held in the molten rock by confining pressure, just as carbon dioxide is held in soft drinks. As with soft drinks, as soon as the pressure is reduced, the gases begin to escape. The gaseous portion of most magmas is only about 1 to 6 percent of the total weight. The percentage may be small, but the actual quantity of emitted gas can exceed thousands of tons each day. Samples taken during a Hawaiian eruption consisted of about 70 percent water vapor, 15 percent carbon dioxide, 5 percent nitrogen, 5 percent sulfur, and lesser amounts of chlorine, hydrogen, and argon. Sulfur compounds are easily recognized because they smell like rotten eggs and readily form sulfuric acid, a natural source of air pollution. The composition of volcanic gases is important because they have contributed greatly to the gases that make up the atmosphere.

Pyroclastic Materials When basaltic lava is extruded, dissolved gases propel blobs of lava to great heights. Some of this ejected material may land near the vent and build a cone-shaped structure. The wind will carry smaller particles great distances. Viscous rhyolitic magmas are highly charged with gases. As the gases expand, pulverized rock and lava fragments are blown from the vent. **Pyroclastic material** is the name give to particles produced in volcanic eruptions. **The fragments ejected during eruptions range in size from very fine dust and volcanic ash (less than 2 millimeters) to pieces that weigh several tons.**

Particles that range in size from small beads to walnuts (2–64 millimeters) are called lapilli or more commonly cinders. Particles larger than 64 millimeters in diameter are called blocks when they are made of hardened lava and bombs when they are ejected as glowing lava. Because bombs are semimolten upon ejection, they often take on a streamlined shape as they hurtle through the air.

 **Reading Checkpoint** *What is a volcanic bomb?*

For: Links on volcanic eruptions
Visit: www.SciLinks.org
Web Code: cjn-3101

Types of Volcanoes

Volcanic landforms come in a wide variety of shapes and sizes. Each structure has a unique eruptive history. **The three main volcanic types are shield volcanoes, cinder cones, and composite cones.**

Anatomy of a Volcano Volcanic activity often begins when a fissure, or crack, develops in the crust as magma is forced toward the surface. The gas-rich magma moves up this fissure, through a circular pipe, ending at a vent, as shown in Figure 3. Repeated eruptions of lava or pyroclastic material often separated by long inactive periods eventually build the mountain called a **volcano.** Located at the summit of many volcanoes is a steep-walled depression called a **crater.**

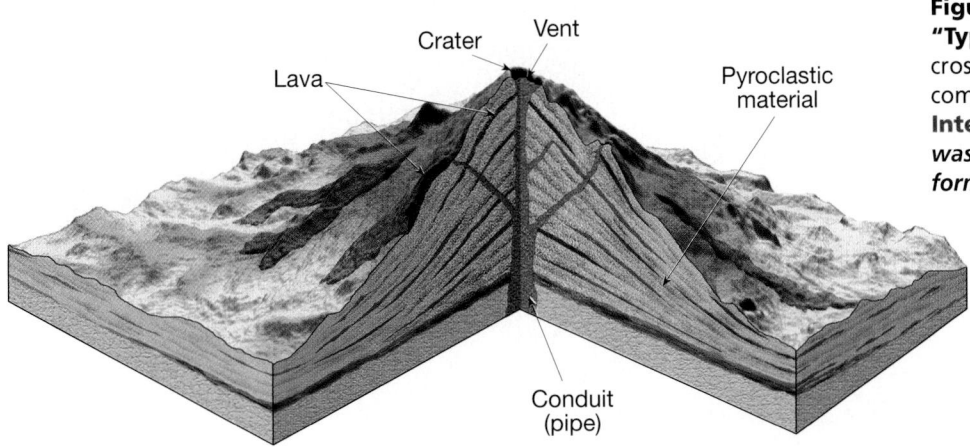

Lava

Crater

Vent

Pyroclastic material

Conduit (pipe)

Figure 3 Anatomy of a "Typical" Volcano This cross section shows a typical composite cone.
Interpreting Diagrams *How was the volcano in the diagram formed?*

The form of a volcano is largely determined by the composition of the magma. As you will see, fluid lavas tend to produce broad structures with gentle slopes. More viscous silica-rich lavas generate cones with moderate to steep slopes.

Shield Volcanoes **Shield volcanoes** are produced by the accumulation of fluid basaltic lavas. Shield volcanoes have the shape of a broad, slightly domed structure that resembles a warrior's shield, as shown in Figure 4. Most shield volcanoes have grown up from the deep-ocean floor to form islands. Examples of shield volcanoes include the Hawaiian Islands and Iceland.

Cinder Cones Ejected lava fragments the size of cinders, which harden in the air, build a **cinder cone.** These fragments range in size from fine ash to bombs but consist mostly of lapilli, or cinders. Cinder cones are usually a product of relatively gas-rich basaltic magma. Although cinder cones are composed mostly of loose pyroclastic material, they sometimes extrude lava.

Cinder cones have a very simple shape as shown in Figure 5A. The shape is determined by the steep-sided slope that loose pyroclastic material maintains as it comes to rest. Cinder cones are usually the product of a single eruption that sometimes lasts only a few weeks and rarely more than a few years. Once the eruption ends, the magma in the pipe connecting the vent to the magma chamber solidifies, and the volcano never erupts again. Because of this short life span, cinder cones are small, usually between 30 meters and 300 meters and rarely exceed 700 meters in height.

Figure 4 Shield Volcanoes
Shield volcanoes are built mainly of fluid basaltic lava flows. They contain only a small amount of pyroclastic materials. These broad, slightly domed structures are the largest volcanoes on Earth. An example is Kilauea in Hawaii.

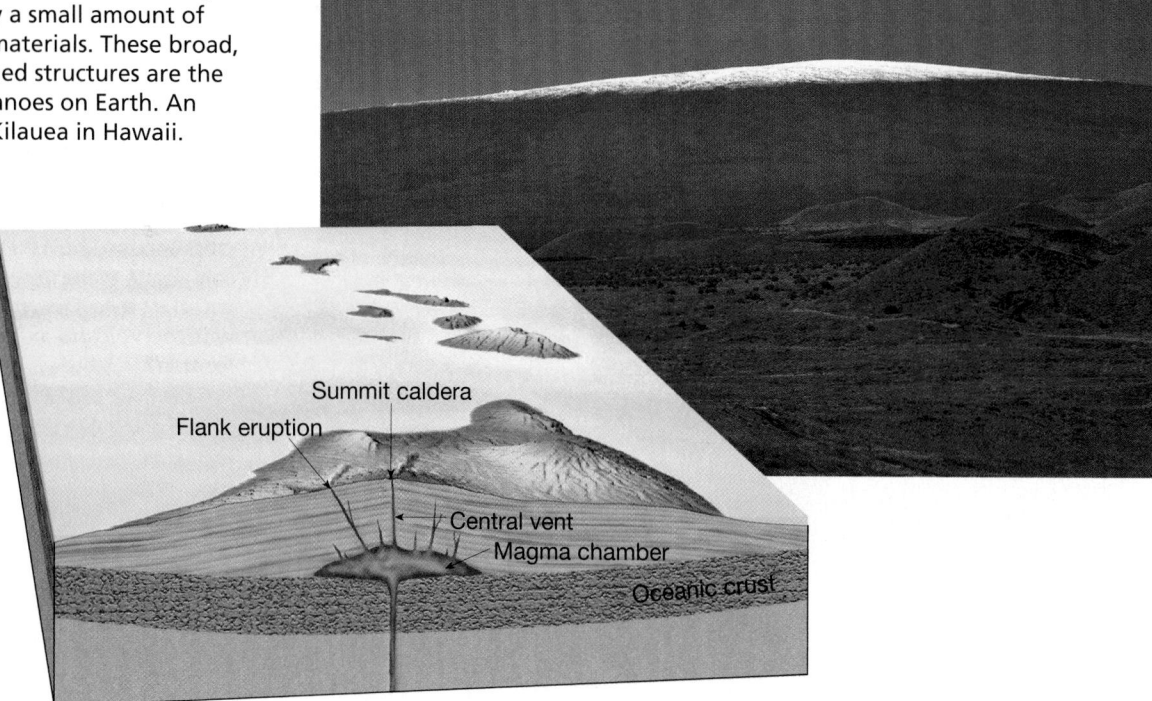

Summit caldera

Flank eruption

Central vent

Magma chamber

Oceanic crust

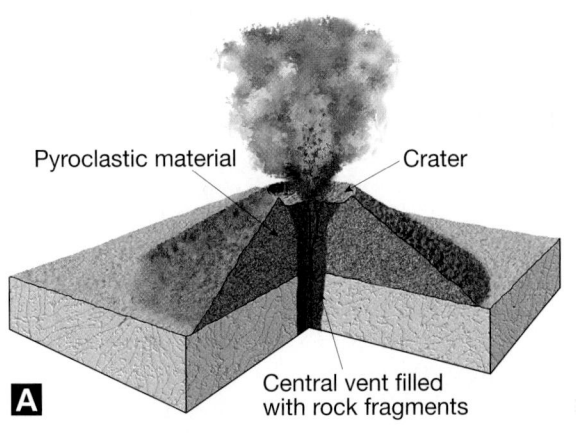

Cinder cones are found by the thousands all around Earth. Some, like the one shown in Figure 5B, near Flagstaff, Arizona, are located in volcanic fields. This field consists of about 600 cones. Others form on the sides of larger volcanoes. Mount Etna, for example, has dozens of cinder cones dotting its flanks.

Composite Cones Earth's most beautiful and potentially dangerous volcanoes are composite cones, or stratovolcanoes. Most are located in a relatively narrow zone that rims the Pacific Ocean, appropriately called the Ring of Fire. The Ring of Fire includes the large cones of the Andes in South America and the Cascade Range of the western United States and Canada. The Cascade Range includes Mount St. Helens, Mount Rainier, and Mount Garibaldi. The most active regions in the Ring of Fire are located along curved belts of volcanic islands next to the deep ocean trenches of the northern and western Pacific. This nearly continuous chain of volcanoes stretches from the Aleutian Islands to Japan, the Philippines, and New Zealand.

A **composite cone** is a large, nearly symmetrical structure composed of layers of both lava and pyroclastic deposits. For the most part, composite cones are the product of gas-rich magma having an andesitic composition. The silica-rich magmas typical of composite cones generate viscous lavas that can only travel short distances. Composite cones may generate the most explosive eruptions that eject huge quantities of pyroclastic material. Compare the shape and height of composite cones with other types of volcanoes in Figure 6.

Figure 5 Cinder Cones
A A typical cinder cone has steep slopes of 30–40 degrees. **B** This photograph shows SP Crater, a cinder cone north of Flagstaff, Arizona.
Inferring *What feature is shown in the lower part of the photograph?*

Figure 6 Profiles of Volcanic Landforms A Profile of Mauna Loa, Hawaii, the largest shield volcano in the Hawaiian chain. **B** Profile of Mount Rainier, Washington, a large composite cone. **C** Profile of Sunset Crater, Arizona, a typical steep-sided cinder cone.

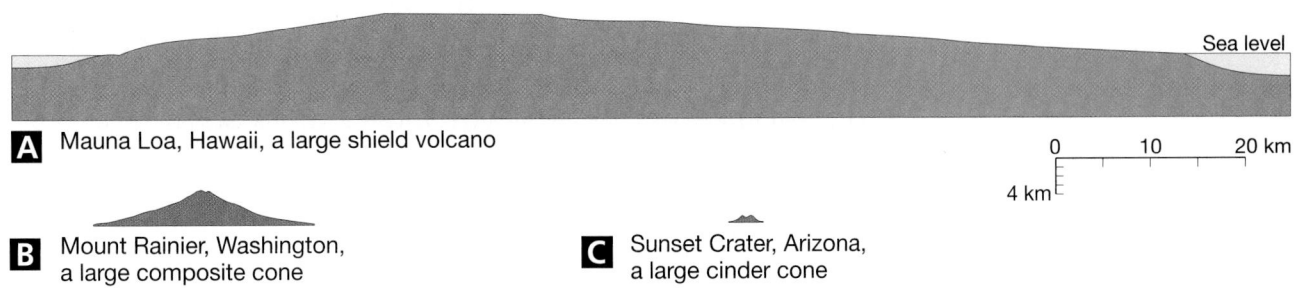

A Mauna Loa, Hawaii, a large shield volcano

0   10   20 km

4 km

B Mount Rainier, Washington, a large composite cone

C Sunset Crater, Arizona, a large cinder cone

Volcanoes and Other Igneous Activity **285**

Figure 7 Composite Cone
Mount Shasta, California, is one of the largest composite cones in the Cascade Range. Shastina is the smaller cone that formed on the left flank of Mt. Shasta.

Fujiyama in Japan and Mount Shasta in California show the classic shape you would expect of a composite cone, with its steep summit and gently sloping flanks, as shown in Figure 7. About 50 such volcanoes have erupted in the United States in the past 200 years. On a global scale, numerous destructive eruptions of composite cones have occurred during the past few thousand years. A few of these have had a major influence on human civilization.

Dangers from Composite Cones One of the most devastating features associated with composite cones are pyroclastic flows. They consist of hot gases, glowing ash, and larger rock fragments. The most destructive of these fiery flows are capable of racing down steep volcanic slopes at speeds of nearly 200 kilometers per hour. Some pyroclastic flows result when a powerful eruption blasts material out the side of a volcano. Usually they form from the collapse of tall eruption columns that form over a volcano during an explosive event. Once gravity overcomes the upward thrust provided by the escaping gases, the material begins to fall. Massive amounts of hot fragments, ash, and gases begin to race downhill under the influence of gravity.

Large composite cones may also generate mudflows called lahars. These destructive mudflows occur when volcanic debris becomes saturated with water and rapidly moves down steep volcanic slopes, often following stream valleys. Some lahars are triggered when large volumes of ice and snow melt during an eruption. Others are generated when heavy rainfall saturates weathered volcanic deposits. Lahars can occur even when a volcano is not erupting.

 **Reading Checkpoint** *What is a lahar?*

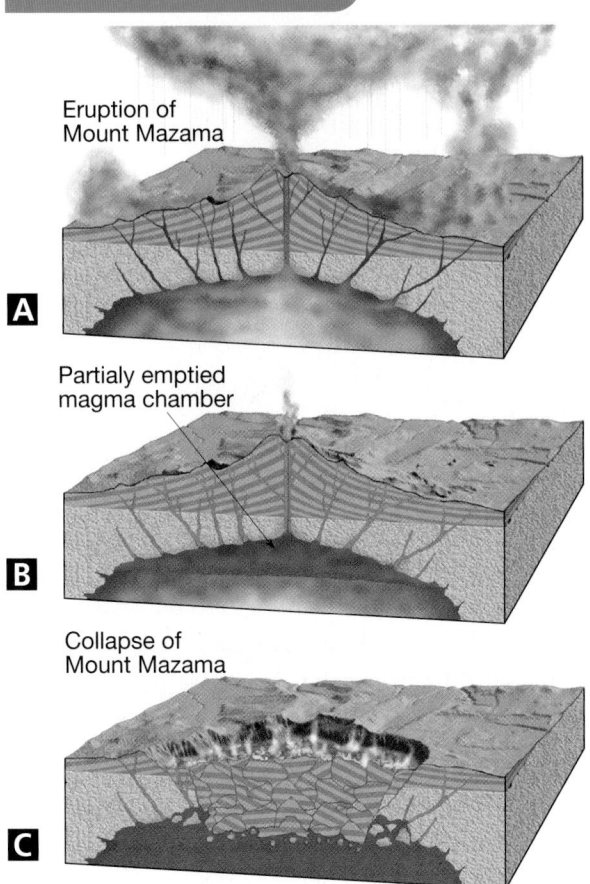

Eruption of
Mount Mazama

A

Partialy emptied
magma chamber

B

Collapse of
Mount Mazama

C

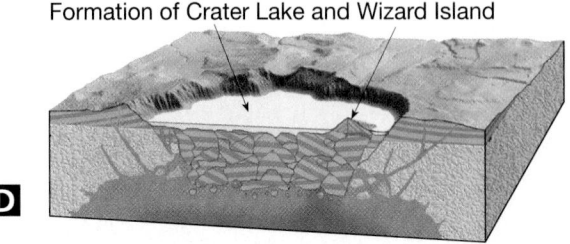

Formation of Crater Lake and Wizard Island

D

E

Other Volcanic Landforms

Calderas A caldera is a large depression in a volcano. Most calderas form in one of two ways: by the collapse of the top of a composite volcano after an explosive eruption, or from the collapse of the top of a shield volcano after the magma chamber is drained. Crater Lake, Oregon, is located in a caldera. This caldera formed about 7000 years ago when a composite cone, Mount Mazama, violently erupted and collapsed, as shown in Figure 8.

Necks and Pipes Most volcanoes are fed magma through conduits, called pipes, connecting a magma chamber to the surface. Volcanoes are always being weathered and eroded. Cinder cones are easily eroded because they are made up of loose materials. When the rock in the pipe is more resistant and remains standing above the surrounding terrain after most of the cone has been eroded, the structure is called a volcanic neck, as shown in Figure 9A on page 288.

The best-known volcanic pipes are the diamond-bearing pipes of South Africa. The rocks filling these pipes formed at depths of at least 150 kilometers, where pressure is high enough to form diamonds. The process of moving unaltered magma through 150 kilometers of solid rock is unusual, resulting in the rarity of diamonds.

Figure 8 Crater Lake in Oregon occupies a caldera about 10 kilometers in diameter. About 7000 years ago, the summit of former Mount Mazama collapsed following a violent eruption that partly emptied the magma chamber. Rainwater then filled the caldera. Later eruptions produced the cinder cone called Wizard Island.

Figure 9 Other Volcanic Landforms A Ship Rock, New Mexico, is a volcanic neck. Ship Rock consists of igneous rock that crystallized in the pipe of a volcano that then was eroded away. **B** Lava erupting from a fissure forms fluid lava flows called flood basalts. **C** These dark-colored basalt flows are near Idaho Falls, Idaho.

Lava Plateaus You probably think of volcanic eruptions as building a mountain from a central vent. But the greatest volume of volcanic material is extruded from fissures. Rather than building a cone, low-viscosity basaltic lava flows from these fissures, covering a wide area, as shown in Figure 9B. The extensive Columbia Plateau in the northwestern United States was formed this way. Here, numerous fissure eruptions extruded very fluid basaltic lava, shown in Figure 9C. Successive flows, some 50 meters thick, buried the landscape, building a lava plateau nearly 1.6 kilometers thick.

Section 10.1 Assessment

Reviewing Concepts

1. ● What factors determine the type of volcanic eruption?
2. ● List the materials ejected from volcanoes.
3. ● Describe the three types of volcanoes.
4. ● What is a caldera?

Critical Thinking

5. **Comparing and Contrasting** Compare the formation of a lava plateau with the formation of a cinder cone.

6. **Applying Concepts** What type of eruption produces a viscous magma containing 53 percent silica and a gas content of 2 percent?

7. **Calculating** If a pyroclastic flow was traveling 145 kilometers per hour, how long would it take to reach a town 2.5 kilometers from the volcano's crater?

Writing in Science

Summary Research a volcanic eruption. Write a paragraph describing the eruption. Make sure to classify what type of volcano erupted.

10.2 Intrusive Igneous Activity

Reading Focus

Key Concepts

- How are intrusive igneous features classified?
- What are the major intrusive igneous features?
- What is the origin of magma?

Vocabulary

- pluton
- sill
- laccolith
- dike
- batholith
- geothermal gradient
- decompression melting

Reading Strategy

Comparing and Contrasting After you read the section, compare the types of plutons by completing the table.

Types of Plutons	Description
Sill	a. _____?_____
Laccolith	b. _____?_____
Dike	c. _____?_____
Batholith	d. _____?_____

Although volcanic eruptions are among the most violent and spectacular events in nature, most magma cools deep within Earth. The structures that result form the roots of mountain ranges and some of the most familiar features in the landscape.

Plutons

The structures that result from the cooling and hardening of magma at depth are called **plutons.** Because all plutons form beneath Earth's surface, they can be studied only after uplift and erosion have exposed them. Plutons occur in a great variety of sizes and shapes. **Intrusive igneous bodies, or plutons, are generally classified according to their shape, size, and relationship to the surrounding rock layers.**

Sills and Laccoliths

Sills and laccoliths are plutons that form when magma is intruded close to the surface. Sills and laccoliths differ in shape and often differ in composition. A **sill** forms when magma is injected along sedimentary bedding surfaces, parallel to the bedding planes. Horizontal sills, like the one shown in Figure 10, are the most common.

For a sill to form, the overlying sedimentary rock must be lifted to a height equal to the thickness of the sill. Although this is a not an easy task, at shallow levels it often requires less energy than forcing the magma up to the surface. Because of this, sills form only at shallow depths, where the pressure exerted by the weight of overlying rock layers is low. As shown in Figure 11A on page 290, sills look like buried lava flows.

Figure 10 Sills This dark, horizontal band is a sill of basalt that intruded into horizontal layers of sedimentary rock in Salt River Canyon, Arizona.
Inferring *How could you determine if a horizontal igneous rock layer was a lava flow or a sill?*

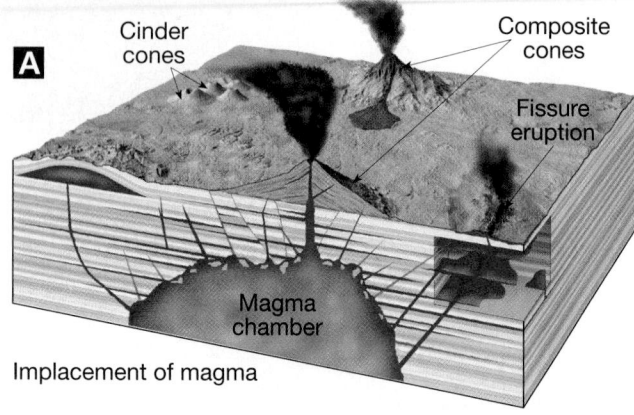

A

Cinder cones Composite cones

Fissure eruption

Magma chamber

Implacement of magma

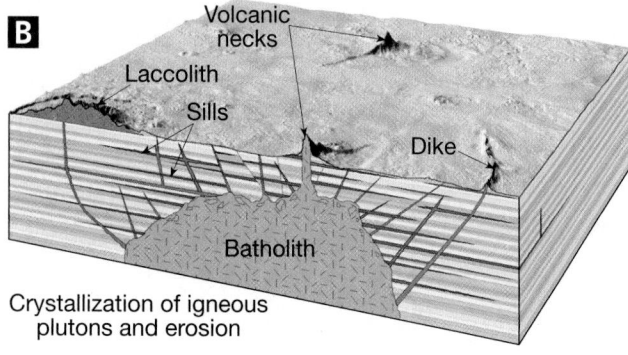

B

Volcanic necks

Laccolith

Sills

Dike

Batholith

Crystallization of igneous plutons and erosion

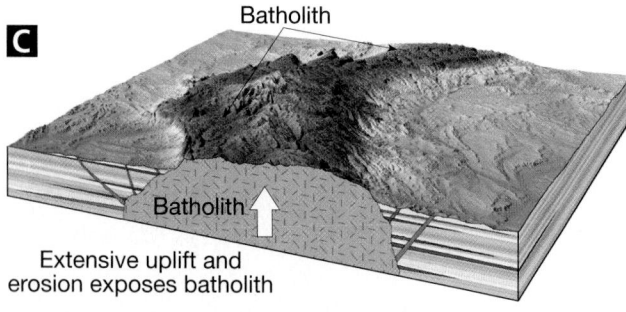

C

Batholith

Batholith

Extensive uplift and erosion exposes batholith

Figure 11 A This diagram shows the relationship between volcanism and intrusive igneous activity. **B** This view shows the basic intrusive igneous structures, some of which have been exposed by erosion long after their formation. **C** After millions of years of uplift and erosion, a batholith is exposed at the surface.

Laccoliths are similar to sills because they form when magma is intruded between sedimentary layers close to the surface. However, the magma that generates laccoliths is more viscous. This less-fluid magma collects as a lens-shaped mass that pushes the overlying strata upward. Most laccoliths are not much wider than a few kilometers.

 **Reading Checkpoint** *Compare and contrast sills and laccoliths.*

Dikes Some plutons form when magma is injected into fractures, cutting across preexisting rock layers. Such plutons are called **dikes,** as in Figure 11B. These sheetlike structures have thicknesses ranging from less than a centimeter to more than a kilometer. Most dikes, however, are a few meters thick and extend laterally for no more than a few kilometers.

Some dikes radiate, like spokes on a wheel, from an eroded volcanic neck. The movement of magma probably formed fissures in the volcanic cone from which the magma flowed to form the dikes. **Many dikes form when magma from a large magma chamber invades fractures in the surrounding rocks.**

Batholiths The largest intrusive igneous bodies are **batholiths.** The Idaho batholith, for example, covers an area of more than 40,000 square kilometers and consists of many individual plutons. Indirect evidence from gravity and seismic studies indicates that batholiths are also very thick, possibly extending dozens of kilometers into the crust.

An intrusive igneous body must have a surface exposure greater than 100 square kilometers to be considered a batholith. Smaller plutons are called stocks. Many stocks appear to be portions of batholiths that are not yet fully exposed. Batholiths may form the core of mountain ranges, as shown in Figure 12. In this case, uplift and erosion have removed the surrounding rock, exposing the batholith.

Origin of Magma

The origin of magma has been controversial in geology for a long time. Based on available scientific evidence, Earth's crust and mantle are composed primarily of solid, not molten, rock. Although the outer core is a fluid, its iron-rich material is very dense and stays deep within Earth. What is the source of magma that produces igneous activity? **Geologists conclude that magma originates when essentially solid rock, located in the crust and upper mantle, partially melts. The most obvious way to generate magma from solid rock is to raise the temperature above the level at which the rock begins to melt.**

Role of Heat What source of heat is sufficient to melt rock? Workers in underground mines know that temperatures get higher as they go deeper. The rate of temperature change averages between 20°C and 30°C per kilometer in the upper crust. This change in temperature with depth is known as the **geothermal gradient.** Estimates indicate that the temperature at a depth of 100 kilometers ranges between 1400°C and 1600°C. At these high temperatures, rocks in the lower crust and upper mantle are near, but not quite at their melting point temperatures. So they are very hot but still essentially solid.

There are several ways that enough additional heat can be generated within the crust or upper mantle to produce some magma. First, at subduction zones, friction generates heat as huge slabs of crust slide past each other. Second, crustal rocks are heated as they descend into the mantle during subduction. Third, hotter mantle rocks can rise and intrude crustal rocks. All of these processes only form relatively small amounts of magma. As you'll see, the vast bulk of magma forms without an additional heat source.

Figure 12 Batholiths Mount Whitney in California makes up just a tiny portion of the Sierra Nevada batholith, a huge structure that extends for approximately 400 kilometers.

Reading Checkpoint *What is a geothermal gradient?*

Figure 13 Basaltic Magma at the Surface Lava extruded along the East Rift Zone, Kilauea, Hawaii.
Observing *Does this lava appear to have a high viscosity or a low viscosity? Explain.*

Role of Pressure If temperature were the only factor that determined whether or not rock melts, Earth would be a molten ball covered with a thin, solid outer shell. This is not the case because pressure also increases with depth. Melting, which causes an increase in volume, occurs at higher temperatures at depth because of greater confining pressure. In this way, an increase in confining pressure causes an increase in the rock's melting temperature. The opposite is also true. Reducing confining pressure lowers a rock's melting temperature. When confining pressure drops enough, **decompression melting** is triggered. This process generates magma beneath Hawaii where plumes of hot rock melt as they rise toward the surface.

Role of Water Another important factor affecting the melting temperature of rock is its water content. Water causes rock to melt at lower temperatures. Because of this, "wet" rock buried at depth has a much lower melting temperature than does "dry" rock of the same composition and under the same pressure. Laboratory studies have shown that the melting point of basalt can be lowered by up to 100°C by adding only 0.1 percent water. In addition to a rock's composition, its temperature, depth (confining pressure), and water content determine if it is a solid or liquid.

In summary, magma can be formed in three ways. First, heat may be added when a magma body from a deeper source intrudes and melts crustal rock. Second, a decrease in pressure (without the addition of heat) can result in decompression melting. Third, water can lower the melting temperature of mantle rock enough to form magma.

Section 10.2 Assessment

Reviewing Concepts

1. How are intrusive features classified?
2. List the major intrusive igneous bodies.
3. What are the three major ways that magma forms?
4. What is a pluton?

Critical Thinking

5. **Comparing and Contrasting** Describe the difference between a sill and a dike.

6. **Relating Cause and Effect** What effect does a decrease in confining pressure have on the melting temperature of rocks in the upper mantle?

Connecting Concepts

Convection Currents Recall what you learned about convection currents in Chapter 9. Explain how convection currents could affect the depth at which molten rocks are found.

10.3 Plate Tectonics and Igneous Activity

Reading Focus

Key Concepts

- What is the relationship between plate boundaries and igneous activity?
- Where does intraplate volcanism occur?

Vocabulary

- intraplate volcanism

Reading Strategy

Outlining After you read, make an outline of the most important ideas in the section.

> I. Plate Tectonics and Igneous Activity
>   A. Convergent Plate Boundaries
>   1. _____?_____
>   2. _____?_____

More than 800 active volcanoes have been identified worldwide. Most of them are located along the margins of the ocean basins, mainly within the circum-Pacific belt known as the Ring of Fire. A second group of volcanoes is found in the deep-ocean basins, including on Hawaii and Iceland. A third group includes volcanic structures that are irregularly distributed in the interiors of the continents. Until the late 1960s, geologists had no explanation for the distribution of volcanoes. With the development of the theory of plate tectonics, the picture became clearer.

Convergent Plate Boundaries

The basic connection between plate tectonics and volcanism is that plate motions provide the mechanisms by which mantle rocks melt to generate magma. At convergent plate boundaries, slabs of oceanic crust are pushed down into the mantle. As a slab sinks deeper into the mantle, the increase in temperature and pressure drives water from the oceanic crust. Once the sinking slab reaches a depth of about 100 to 150 kilometers, the fluids reduce the melting point of hot mantle rock enough for melting to begin. The magma formed slowly migrates upward forming volcanoes such as Mount St. Helens shown here. As you read about the relationships between plate tectonics and igneous activity, refer to Figure 17 on pages 296–297, which summarizes the relationships.

Figure 14 Convergent Boundary Volcano Mount St. Helens emitting volcanic ash on July 22, 1980, two months after the huge May eruption. Mount St. Helens is located at a convergent boundary between the Juan de Fuca plate and the North American plate.

Major Volcanoes

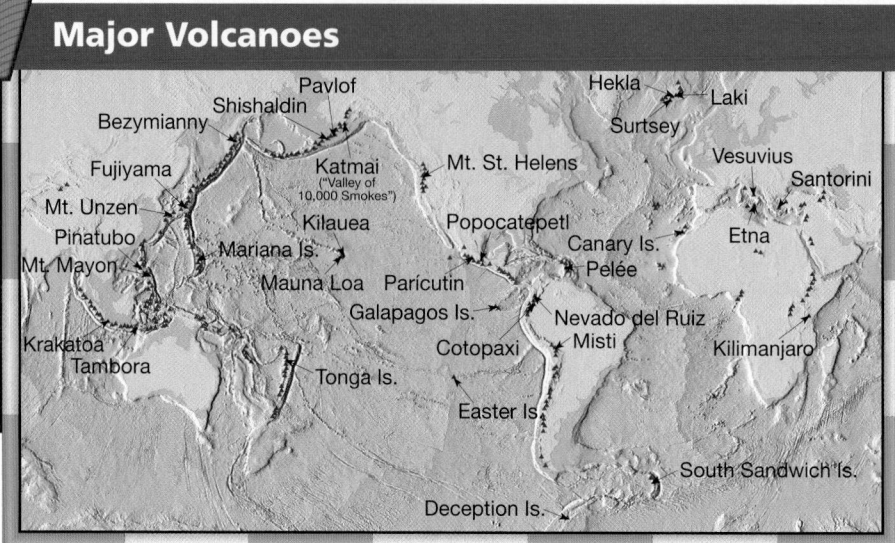

Figure 15

Location Note the concentration of volcanoes encircling the Pacific basin, known as the Ring of Fire.
Inferring How are the volcanoes in the middle of the Atlantic Ocean related to a plate boundary?

Ocean-Ocean Volcanism at a convergent plate where one oceanic slab descends beneath another results in the formation of a chain of volcanoes on the ocean floor. Eventually, these volcanic structures grow large enough to rise above the surface and are called volcanic island arcs. Several volcanic island arcs border the Pacific basin, including the Aleutians.

Ocean-Continent Volcanism associated with convergent plate boundaries may also develop where slabs of oceanic lithosphere are subducted under continental lithosphere to produce a continental volcanic arc. The mechanisms are basically the same as those at island arcs. The major difference is that continental crust is much thicker and is composed of rocks with a higher silica content than oceanic crust. As the silica-rich crustal rocks melt, the magma may change composition as it rises through continental crust. The volcanoes of the Andes Mountains along the western edge of South America are an example of a continental volcanic arc, as shown in Figure 15.

Divergent Plate Boundaries

Most magma is produced along the oceanic ridges during seafloor spreading. Below the ridge axis where the plates are being pulled apart, the solid yet mobile mantle rises upward to fill in the rift where the plates have separated. As rock rises, confining pressure decreases. The rock undergoes decompression melting, producing large amounts of magma. This newly formed basaltic magma is less dense than the mantle rock from which it was formed, so it buoyantly rises.

Partial melting of mantle rock at spreading centers produces basaltic magma. Although most spreading centers are located along the axis of an oceanic ridge, some are not. The East African Rift in Africa is a site where continental crust is being rifted apart.

Intraplate Igneous Activity

Kilauea is Earth's most active volcano, but it is in the middle of the Pacific plate, thousands of kilometers from a plate boundary. **Intraplate volcanism** occurs within a plate, not at a plate boundary. Another site of intraplate volcanism is Yellowstone National Park.

Most intraplate volcanism occurs where a mass of hotter than normal mantle material called a mantle plume rises toward the surface. Most mantle plumes appear to form deep within Earth at the core-mantle boundary. These plumes of hot mantle rock rise toward the surface in a way similar to the blobs that form within a lava lamp. Once the plume nears the top of the mantle, decompression melting forms basaltic magma. The result may be a small volcanic region a few hundred kilometers across called a hot spot. More than 40 hot spots have been identified, and most have lasted for millions of years. By measuring the heat flow at hot spots, geologists found that the mantle beneath some hot spots may be 100–150°C hotter than normal.

The volcanic activity on the island of Hawaii, shown in Figure 16, is the result of a hot spot. Where a mantle plume has persisted for long periods of time, a chain of volcanoes may form as the overlying plate moves over it. Mantle plumes are also thought to cause the vast outpourings of lava that create large lava plateaus such as the Columbia Plateau in the northwestern United States.

Figure 16 Intraplate Volcano An eruption of Hawaii's Kilauea volcano. The Hawaiian hot spot activity is currently centered beneath Kilauea and is an example of intraplate volcanic activity.

Section 10.3 Assessment

Reviewing Concepts

1. How are the locations of volcanoes related to plate boundaries?
2. What causes intraplate volcanism?
3. Where is most of the magma produced on Earth on a yearly basis?
4. What is the Ring of Fire?

Critical Thinking

5. **Comparing and Contrasting** What are the differences between volcanic island arcs and continental volcanic arcs?

6. **Predicting** Would it be more likely for a major explosive eruption to occur at an ocean ridge or at a convergent ocean-continental boundary? Explain your answer.

Writing in Science

Explanatory Paragraph Write a paragraph to explain how magma is formed in the crust without adding heat.

Three Zones of Volcanism

Convergent plate volcanism

Volcanic island arc

Trench

Oceanic crust

Marginal sea

Continental crust

Mantle rock melts

Water driven from plate

Subducting oceanic lithosphere

Asthenosphere

Oceanic crust

Hot spot

Hawaii

Decompression melting

Rising mantle plume

Intraplate volcanism

Continental volcanic arc

Trench

Oceanic crust

Subducting oceanic lithosphere

Continental crust

Mantle rock melts

Water driven from plate

Convergent plate volcanism

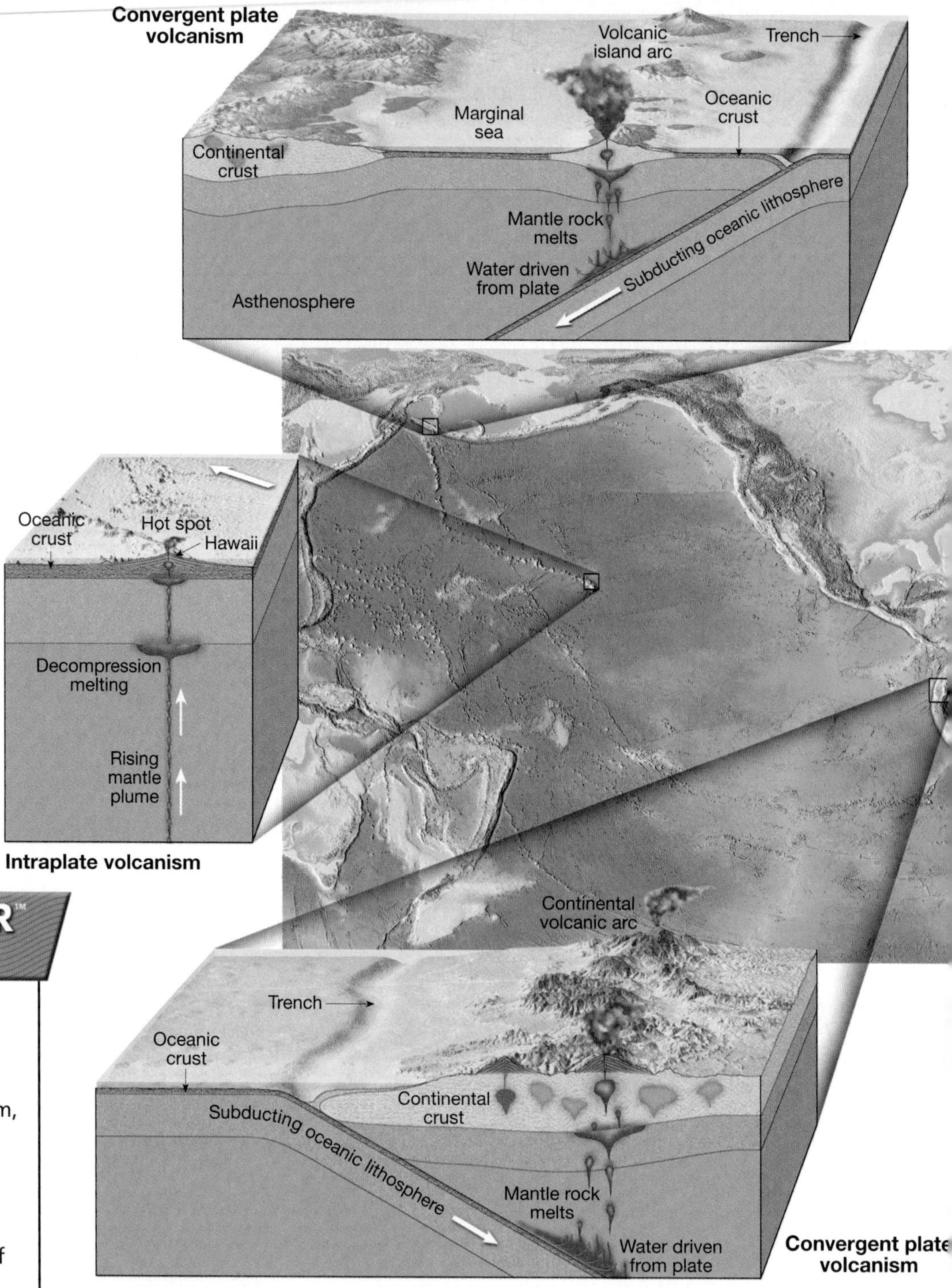

MAP MASTER™
Skills Activity

Figure 17

Regions The three zones of volcanism are convergent plate volcanism, divergent plate volcanism, and intraplate volcanism. Two of these zones are plate boundaries, and the third is the interior area of the plates.

Drawing Conclusions In which zones do volcanoes occur on both continental plates and oceanic plates?

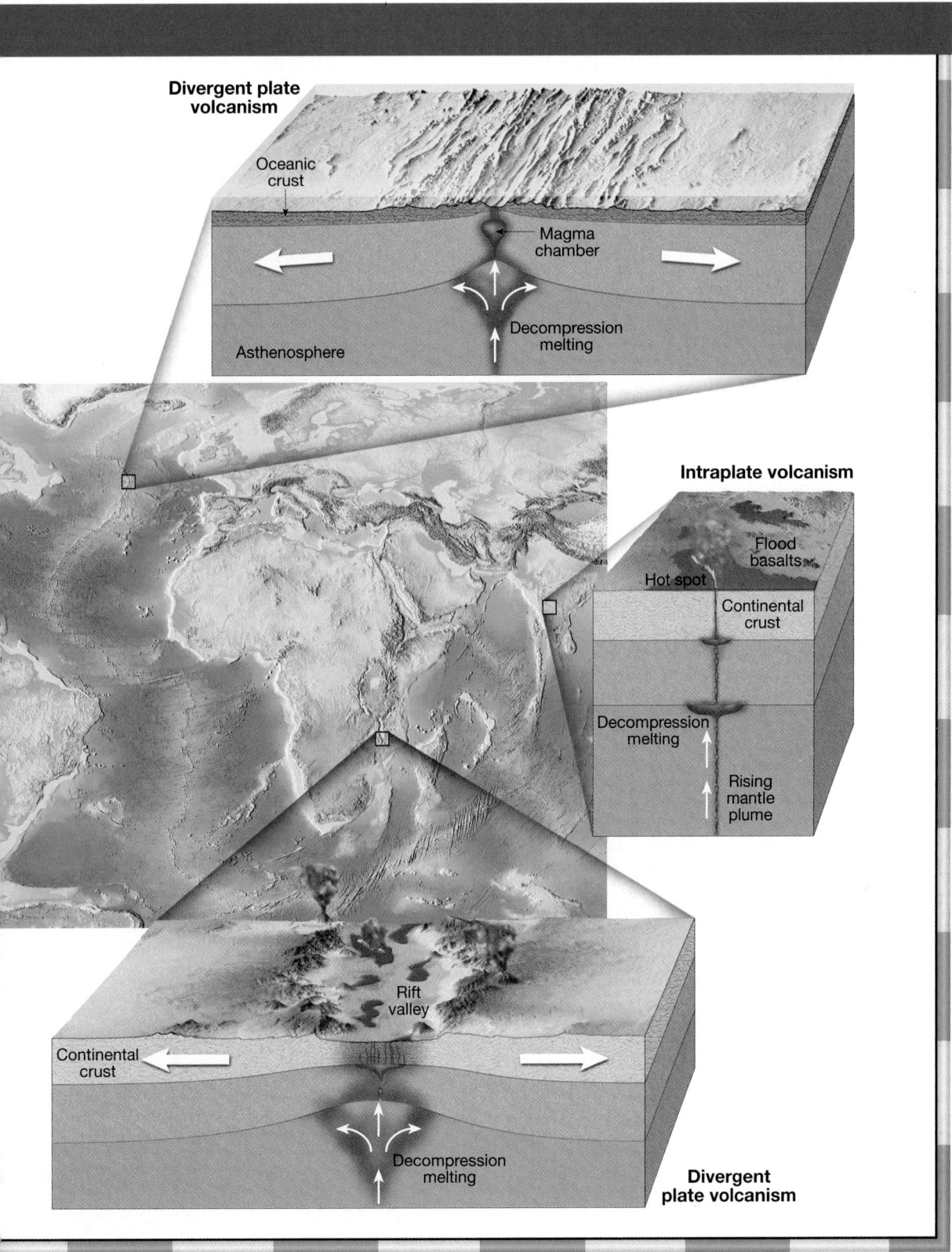

Divergent plate volcanism

Oceanic crust

Magma chamber

Asthenosphere

Decompression melting

Intraplate volcanism

Flood basalts

Hot spot

Continental crust

Decompression melting

Rising mantle plume

Rift valley

Continental crust

Decompression melting

Divergent plate volcanism

How the Earth Works

Effects of Volcanoes

A **volcano** is an opening in the Earth's crust from which **lava,** or molten rock, escapes to the surface. The impact of powerful volcanic eruptions is both immediate and long-lasting. Burning rocks are flung out in all directions. Huge clouds of scorching ash and fiery gases billow high into the sky. As a result, the landscape and even the weather can be changed. Soil may become more fertile when enriched with nutrients from volcanic ash. Islands, mountains, and other landforms may be created from the material emitted by volcanoes.

The Giant's Causeway in Northern Ireland

DRAMATIC ROCK FORMATIONS
Lava flows can form amazing rock formations. **Columnar rocks** are volcanic rocks that split into columns as the lava cools. The Devil's Tower in Wyoming (below) is one example of a columnar rock. Another example is the Giant's Causeway (left). This rock formation in Northern Ireland is the result of a lava flow that erupted millions of years ago.

The Devil's Tower in Wyoming

DUST AND GAS
Explosive volcanoes, like Mount St. Helens in Washington (right), spit clouds of ash and fumes into the sky. The debris can completely cover human communities. Another hazard is that volcanic gases may be deadly poisons.

ERUPTING LAVA
Red-hot lava is hurled into the air during an eruption of a volcano on Stromboli, an island off the coast of southern Italy. The Stromboli volcano is one of only a few volcanoes to display continuous eruptive activity over a period of more than a few years.

AFFECTING THE WORLD'S WEATHER

Powerful eruptions emit gas and dust that can rise high into the atmosphere and travel around the world. Volcanic material can reduce average temperatures in parts of the world by filtering out some of the sunlight that warms the Earth.

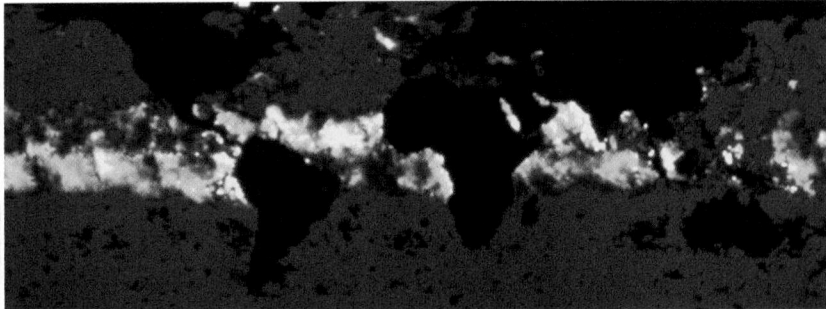

A satellite image shows the global spread of emissions from the 1991 eruptions of Mount Pinatubo in the Philippines.

A STRING OF ISLANDS

The Hawaiian Islands are the tops of volcanic mountains. They have developed over millions of years as a **plume,** or a very hot spot in the Earth's mantle, erupted great amounts of lava. As the Pacific Plate moves over the stationary plume, it carries older islands in the chain to the northwest. Today, active volcanoes are found on the island of Hawaii and the newly forming island of Loihi.

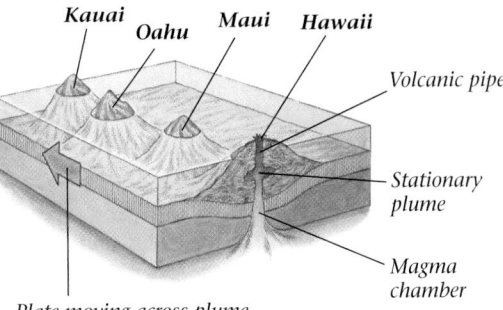

Plate moving across plume

A CRATER LAKE

A **crater lake** is a body of water that occupies a bowl-shaped depression around the opening of an extinct or dormant volcano. An eruption can hurl the water out of the crater. The water can then mix with hot rock and debris and race downhill in a deadly mudslide.

A crater lake in Iceland

LIFE RETURNS TO THE LAVA

In time, plant life grows on lava. Lichen and moss often appear first. Grass and larger plants slowly follow. The upper surface of the rock is gradually weathered, and the roots of plants help break down the rock to form soil. After many generations, the land may become lush and fertile again.

A few lichens find a home on the lava.

Plants take root in the beginnings of topsoil.

ASSESSMENT

1. **Key Terms** Define **(a)** volcano, **(b)** lava, **(c)** columnar rock, **(d)** plume, **(e)** crater lake.

2. **Natural Resources** How can soil become more fertile as a result of volcanic eruptions?

3. **Environmental Change (a)** How can volcanic activity create new landforms? **(b)** How can explosive volcanic eruptions affect the atmosphere and weather around the world?

4. **Natural Hazards** What are some of the ways in which a volcanic eruption can devastate nearby human settlements?

5. **Critical Thinking** **Sequencing** Study the diagram of the Hawaiian Islands and the caption that accompanies it. **(a)** Which island on the diagram is probably the oldest? Why do you think so? **(b)** What will happen to the volcanoes on the island of Hawaii as a result of plate movement?

299

Melting Temperatures of Rocks

Measurements of temperatures in wells and mines have shown that Earth's internal temperatures increase with depth. Recall that this rate of temperature increase is called the geothermal gradient. Although the geothermal gradient varies from place to place, it is possible to calculate an average. In this lab, you will investigate Earth's internal temperatures and the temperatures at which rocks melt. You will also investigate the effect of water on the melting temperatures of rock.

Problem How can rocks melt to form magma in the crust and uppermost mantle?

Materials
- photocopy of Temperature Curves graph
- colored pencils (three different colors)
- ruler

Skills Analyzing Data, Graphing, Calculating

Procedure

1. Obtain a photocopy of the Temperature Curves graph on page 301. You will use it to plot the average temperature gradient for Earth's interior. Plot the temperature gradient on graph paper labeled like the graph shown.

2. Plot the temperature values from Table 1 on your graph. Then draw a single best-fit line through the points with a colored pencil. Extend your line from the surface to 200 kilometers. Label the line "Temperature Gradient."

3. The melting temperature of a rock changes as pressure increases deeper within Earth. The approximate melting points of the igneous rocks, granite and basalt, under various pressures (depths) have been determined in the laboratory and are shown in Table 2. Granite and basalt were used because they are common materials in the upper layer of Earth. Plot the melting temperatures from Table 2 on the same graph you made above. Use a different colored pencil to plot each set of points and draw the best-fit lines.

4. Label the two lines "Melting Curve for Wet Granite" and "Melting Curve for Basalt."

Table 1 Idealized Internal Temperatures of Earth	
Depth (kilometers)	Temperature (°C)
0	20
25	600
50	1000
75	1250
100	1400
150	1700
200	1800

Table 2 Melting Temperatures of Granite (with water) and Basalt at Various Depths Within Earth			
Granite (with water)		Basalt	
Depth (km)	Melting Temperature (°C)	Depth (km)	Melting Temperature (°C)
0	950	0	1100
5	700	25	1160
10	660	50	1250
20	625	100	1400
40	600	150	1600

Analyze and Conclude

1. **Using Graphs** Does the rate of increase of Earth's internal temperature stay the same or change with increasing depth?

2. **Using Graphs** Is the rate of temperature increase greater from the surface to 100 kilometers or below 100 kilometers?

3. **Interpreting Data** What is the temperature at 100 kilometers below the surface?

4. **Calculating** Use the data and your graph to calculate the average temperature gradient for the upper 100 kilometers of Earth in °C/100 kilometers and in °C/kilometer.

5. **Drawing Conclusions** Based on your data, at approximately what depth within Earth would wet granite reach its melting temperature and begin to form magma? Explain.

6. **Drawing Conclusions** Based on your data, at what depth will basalt have reached its melting temperature and begin to form magma?

Go Further What is the name of the layer within Earth's upper mantle that is below about 100 kilometers? Why do scientists theorize that this zone is capable of "flowing" more easily than other mantle rock, allowing the lithosphere to move across it?

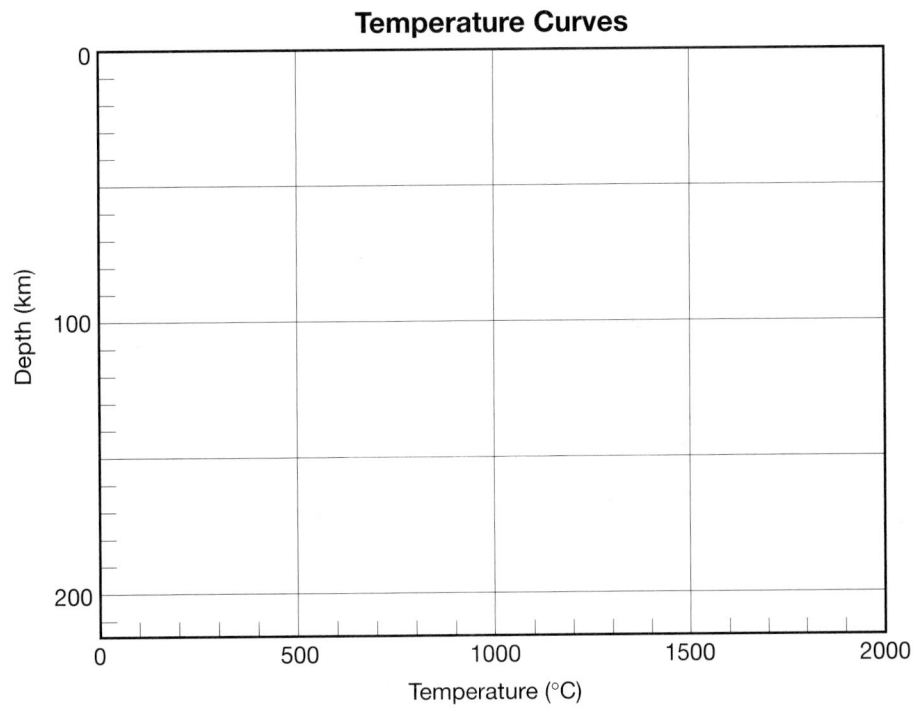

Temperature Curves

10 | Study Guide

10.1 The Nature of Volcanic Eruptions

Key Concepts

- The primary factors that determine whether a volcano erupts violently or quietly include magma composition, magma temperature, and the amount of dissolved gases in the magma.

- The fragments ejected during eruptions range in size from very fine dust and volcanic ash (less than 2 millimeters) to pieces that weigh several tons.

- The three main volcanic types are shield volcanoes, cinder cones, and composite cones.

- A caldera is a large depression in a volcano.

- Most volcanoes are fed magma through conduits, called pipes, connecting a magma chamber to the surface.

Vocabulary

viscosity, *p. 281*; vent, *p. 281*; pyroclastic material, *p. 283*; volcano, *p. 283*; crater, *p. 283*; shield volcano, *p. 284*; cinder cone, *p. 284*; composite cone, *p. 285*; caldera, *p. 287*

10.2 Intrusive Igneous Activity

Key Concepts

- Intrusive igneous bodies, or plutons, are generally classified according to their shape, size and relationship to the surrounding rock layers.

- Sills and laccoliths are plutons that form when magma is intruded close to the surface.

- Many dikes form when magma from a large magma chamber invades fractures in the surrounding rocks.

- An intrusive igneous body must have a surface exposure greater than 100 square kilometers to be considered a batholith.

- Geologists conclude that magma originates when essentially solid rock, located in the crust and upper mantle, partially melts. The most obvious way to generate magma from solid rock is to raise the temperature above the level at which the rock begins to melt.

Vocabulary

pluton, *p. 289*; sill, *p. 289*; laccolith, *p. 290*; dike, *p. 290*; batholith, *p. 290*; geothermal gradient, *p. 291*; decompression melting, *p. 292*

10.3 Plate Tectonics and Igneous Activity

Key Concepts

- The basic connection between plate tectonics and volcanism is that plate motions provide the mechanisms by which mantle rocks melt to generate magma.

- Most intraplate volcanism occurs where a mass of hotter than normal mantle material called a mantle plume rises toward the surface.

Vocabulary

intraplate volcanism, *p. 295*

Thinking Visually

Web Diagram Copy the web diagram below and use information from the chapter to complete it.

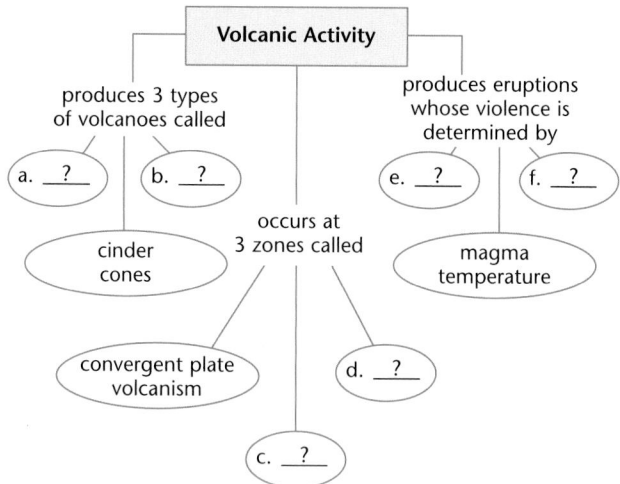

Reviewing Content

Choose the letter that best answers the question or completes the statement.

1. Underground igneous rock bodies are called
   a. lava flows.
   b. plutons.
   c. volcanoes.
   d. calderas.

2. The greatest volume of volcanic material is produced by
   a. eruptions of cinder cones.
   b. eruptions of composite cones.
   c. eruptions along ocean ridges.
   d. eruptions of shield volcanoes.

3. The most violent type of volcanic activity is associated with
   a. cinder cones.
   b. sills.
   c. composite cones.
   d. shield volcanoes.

4. A magma's viscosity is directly related to its
   a. depth.
   b. age.
   c. color.
   d. silica content.

5. What are the pulverized rock, lava, ash, and other fragments ejected from the vent of a volcano called?
   a. sills
   b. craters
   c. pahoehoes
   d. pyroclastic material

6. Which type of volcano consists of layers of lava flows and pyroclastic material?
   a. composite cone
   b. cinder cone
   c. shield volcano
   d. laccolith

7. Fluid basaltic lavas, like those in Hawaii, commonly form
   a. aa flows.
   b. pahoehoe flows.
   c. pyroclastic flows.
   d. lapilli flows.

8. What is the very large depression at the top of some volcanoes called?
   a. a vent
   b. a lava plateau
   c. a volcanic neck
   d. a caldera

9. When silica-rich magma is extruded, ash, hot gases, and larger fragments may be propelled from the vent at high speeds and produce which of the following?
   a. a lava plateau
   b. a lahar
   c. a pahoehoe flow
   d. a pyroclastic flow

10. What feature may form in an intraplate area over a rising plume of hot mantle material?
    a. a hot spot
    b. a dike
    c. a subduction zone
    d. an ocean ridge

Understanding Concepts

11. What is a volcanic neck and how does it form?

12. Describe the Ring of Fire.

13. The Hawaiian Islands and Yellowstone National Park are associated with which of the three zones of volcanism?

14. What is the chain of volcanoes called that forms at a convergent boundary between a subducting oceanic plate and a continental plate? What type of volcano commonly forms?

15. Explain how most magma is theorized to originate.

Use the diagram below to answer Questions 16 and 17.

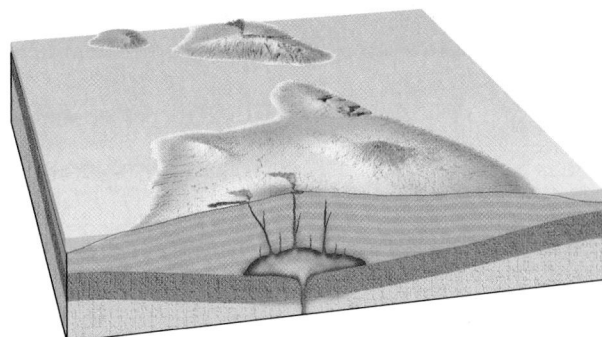

16. Identify the type of volcano shown in the diagram.

17. What types of eruptions are commonly associated with this type of volcano?

18. How do hot spots form?

19. How are pyroclastic materials classified?

20. What is viscosity and how does it affect volcanic eruptions?

21. Give an example of each of the three types of volcanoes.

22. How do dikes form?

Critical Thinking

23. Applying Concepts Why might a laccolith be detected at Earth's surface before being exposed by erosion?

24. Inferring Why is a volcano fed by a highly viscous magma likely to be a greater threat to people than a volcano fed by very fluid magma?

25. Comparing and Contrasting Compare pahoehoe lava flows and aa lava flows.

26. Relating Cause and Effect What is a lahar? Explain why a lahar can occur on a volcano without an eruption.

27. Drawing Conclusions Why are cinder cones usually small?

Analyzing Data

Use the data table below to answer Questions 28–31.

Notable Volcanic Eruptions

Volcano	Date	Volume Ejected	Height of Plume
Toba	74,000 years ago	2800 km³	50–80 km
Vesuvius	A.D. 79	4 km³	32 km
Tambora	1815	150 km³	44 km
Krakatau	1883	21 km³	36 km
Mount St. Helens	1980	1 km³	19 km
Mount Pinatubo	1991	5 km³	35 km

28. Interpreting Data What volcanic eruption listed in the data table produced the most pyroclastic material?

29. Calculating The volume of material ejected by the eruption of Tambora in 1815 was how many times larger than the volume of material ejected in 1883 by the eruption of Krakatau?

30. Forming Hypotheses Develop a hypothesis to explain why the eruption of Mount Vesuvius in A.D. 79 was more deadly than the eruption of Mount Pinatubo in 1991, even though the eruptions were approximately the same size.

31. Calculating Calculate how much higher the plume of volcanic debris was during the eruption of Tambora in 1815 compared to the plume from the 1980 eruption of Mount St. Helens. Calculate the increase in kilometers and in percentage of increase.

Concepts in Action

32. Hypothesizing Large volcanic eruptions eject large amounts of gas, dust, and ash into the atmosphere. This volcanic material can affect the world's climate by blocking incoming solar radiation. An eruption from what type of volcano is most likely to cause global climate changes? Explain your answer.

33. Classifying On the side of a composite cone you see a large area where there are no trees and the ground surface looks disturbed. What possible volcanic feature or event could have caused this?

34. Applying Concepts Would you be safer from a violent, explosive eruption while vacationing in Arizona near a cinder cone or while skiing in the Andes Mountains of South America? Explain.

35. Writing in Science Write a paragraph describing what an eruption of a nearby composite cone might be like.

Performance-Based Assessment

Making a Poster Make a poster illustrating the internal and external features that are typical of a composite cone. Include on your poster copies of photographs of some classic composite cones. Also explain some of the possible dangers associated with living near a composite cone.

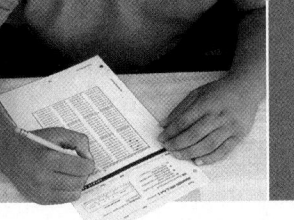

Standardized Test Prep

Choose the letter that best answers the question or completes the statement.

1. Which of the following is NOT a factor that determines if a volcano erupts violently or quietly?
   (A) temperature of the magma
   (B) size of the volcanic cone
   (C) the magma's composition
   (D) amount of dissolved gases in the magma

2. How does an increase in confining pressure affect a rock's melting temperature?
   (A) The melting temperature increases.
   (B) The melting temperature decreases.
   (C) The melting temperature is stabilized.
   (D) It has no effect on the melting temperature.

Use the diagram below to answer Questions 3 and 4.

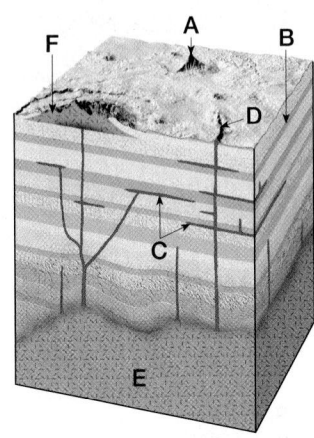

3. What intrusive igneous feature in the diagram is labeled C?
   (A) a dike
   (B) a sill
   (C) a batholith
   (D) a laccolith

4. If the feature labeled E when exposed to erosion extended for over 100 square kilometers, what would it be classified as?
   (A) a dike
   (B) a stock
   (C) a laccolith
   (D) a batholith

Answer the following questions in complete sentences.

5. Briefly describe the relative sizes and shapes of the three types of volcanoes.

6. Explain how a volcanic eruption is affected by magma composition, magma temperature, and the amount of dissolved gases in the magma.

7. Most volcanic eruptions occur at tectonic plate boundaries, but some occur within a tectonic plate, far from plate boundaries.

   Part A Explain the tectonic setting of volcanoes that occur at plate boundaries.

   Part B Explain how volcanoes form in areas that are not associated with a plate boundary. Give an example.

11 Mountain Building

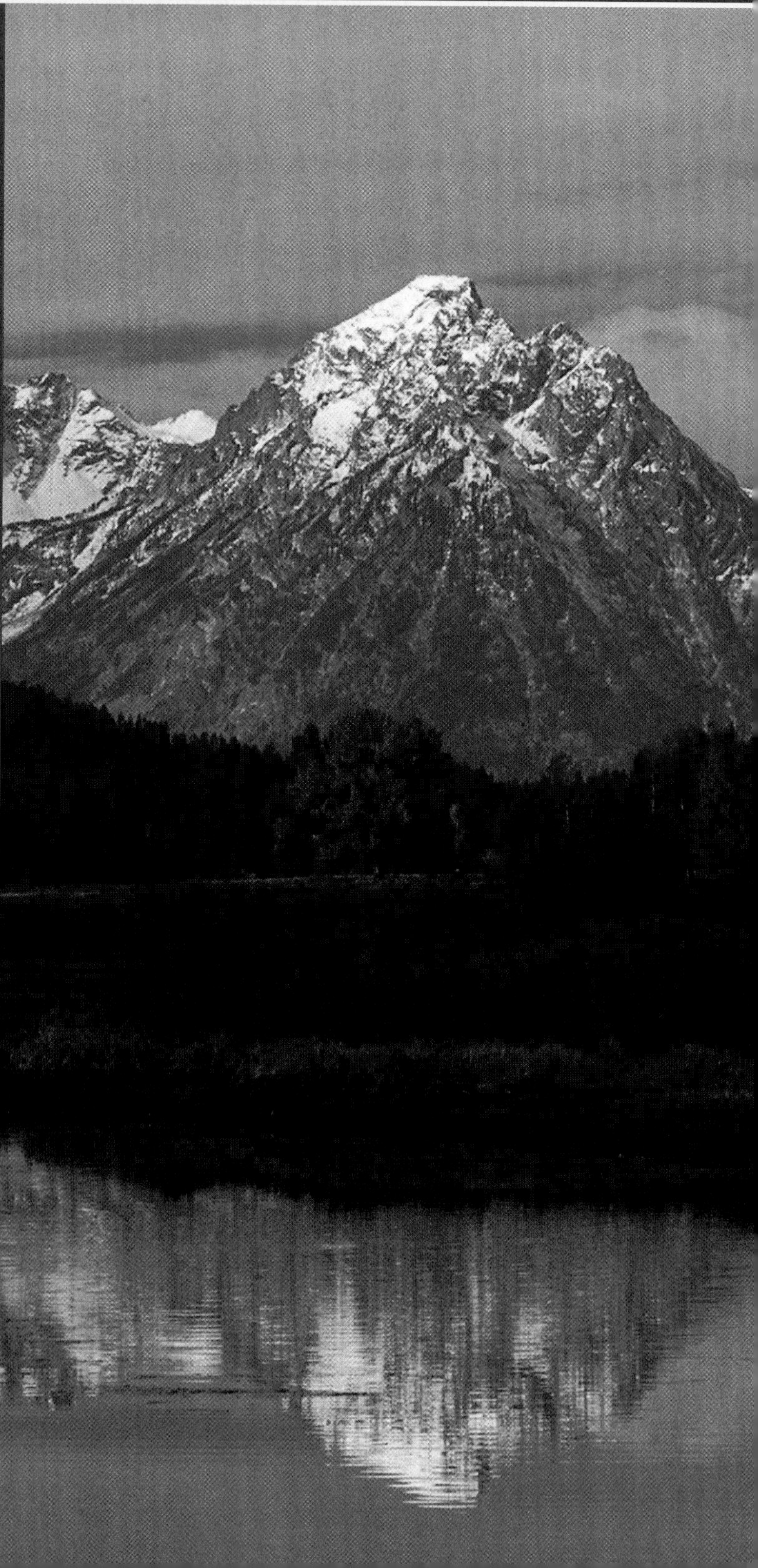

CONCEPTS
— in Action —

Exploration Lab
Investigating Anticlines and Synclines

Understanding Earth
Mountain Building away from Plate Margins

People and the Environment
The San Andreas Fault System

Problem Solving
Rates of Mountain Building

 GEODe Forces Within
⤷ Igneous Activity

 **Video Field Trip**

Earthquake Zone

Take a field trip to the Himalayas with Discovery Channel and learn about the excitement and danger that surround the world's most dramatic mountain range. Answer the following questions after watching the video.

1. How were the Himalayas formed?

2. Why is the convergence of tectonic plates surrounding the Himalayas so dangerous?

For: Chapter 11 Resources
Visit: PHSchool.com
Web Code: cjk-9999

▶ Mount Moran (on right) in Wyoming's
Grand Teton National Park

Chapter Preview

Inquiry Activity

Can You Model How Rocks Deform?

Procedure

1. Take a large, thick rubber band and stretch it out a few centimeters. Then let it relax. **CAUTION:** *Be sure to hold on to both ends of the rubber band so it does not snap your fingers. Record your observations.*

2. Take a chunk of plastic putty. Pull on the ends of the piece of putty rapidly. Record your observations.

3. Now take the chunk of plastic putty, and work it gently until it is warm and flexible. Slowly stretch it. Record your observations.

4. Take a straight, thin wooden stick about 25 centimeters long, and gently bend the ends of the stick until it breaks. **CAUTION:** *Be sure to wear safety goggles when bending the stick.* Record your observations.

Think About It

1. **Observing** Describe how the rubber band, plastic putty, and wooden stick behaved when you deformed them.

2. **Observing** Which item or items returned to the original shape and size after the force was removed?

3. **Drawing Conclusions** Which item was the easiest to deform? The hardest to deform?

4. **Inferring** Under what conditions do you think rocks are easier to bend? Under what conditions to you think rocks will break?

11.1 Rock Deformation

Reading Focus

Key Concepts

- What determines the strength of a rock?
- What are the types of stresses that affect rocks?
- What are the three main types of folds?
- What are the main types of faults?

Vocabulary

- deformation
- stress
- strain
- anticline
- syncline
- monocline
- normal fault
- reverse fault
- thrust fault
- strike-slip fault

Reading Strategy

Comparing and Contrasting After you read the section, compare types of faults by completing the table below.

Types of Fault	Description
Normal fault	a. _____?_____
b. _____?_____	c. _____?_____
d. _____?_____	e. _____?_____
f. _____?_____	g. _____?_____

Mountains, like those shown in Figure 1, provide some of the most spectacular scenery on our planet. It is theorized that all continents were once mountainous masses and grow by the addition of mountains to their edges. As geologists unravel the secrets of mountain formation, they also gain a deeper understanding of the evolution of Earth's continents. However, if continents do grow by adding mountains to their edges, then how do mountains exist in the interior of continents?

Factors Affecting Deformation

Every body of rock, no matter how strong, has a point at which it will bend or break. **Deformation** is a general term that refers to all changes in the original shape and/or size of a rock body. Most crustal deformation occurs along plate margins. Plate motions and interactions at plate boundaries create forces that cause rock to deform.

Stress is the force per unit area acting on a solid. When rocks are under stresses greater than their own strength, they begin to deform, usually by folding, flowing, or fracturing. The change in shape or volume of a body of rock as a result of stress is called **strain.** How can rock masses be bent into folds without being broken? When stress is gradually applied, rocks first respond by deforming elastically. Changes that result from elastic deformation are recoverable. Like a rubber band, the rock will return to almost its original size and shape once the force is removed. Once the elastic limit or strength of a rock is surpassed, it either flows or fractures. The factors that influence the strength of a rock and how it will deform include temperature, confining pressure, rock type, and time.

Figure 1 Mountain Ranges This peak is part of the Karakoram Range in Pakistan.

Temperature and Pressure ⬭ Rocks deform permanently in two ways: brittle deformation and ductile deformation. Rocks near the surface, where temperatures and confining pressures are low, usually behave like brittle solids and fracture once their strength is exceeded. This type of deformation is called brittle failure or brittle deformation. You know that glass objects, wooden pencils, china plates, and even our bones show brittle failure once their strength is exceeded.

At depth, where temperatures and confining pressures are high, rocks show ductile behavior. Ductile deformation is a type of solid-state flow that produces a change in the size and shape of an object without fracturing the object. Objects that display ductile behavior include modeling clay, bee's wax, caramel candy, and most metals. For example, a copper penny placed on a railroad track will be flattened and deformed without breaking by the force applied by a passing train. Ductile deformation of a rock that is strongly aided by high temperature and high confining pressure is somewhat similar to the deformation of a penny flattened by a train.

Rock Type The mineral composition and texture of a rock also greatly affect how it will deform. Rocks like granite and basalt that are composed of minerals with strong internal molecular bonds usually fail by brittle fracture. Sedimentary rocks that are weakly cemented or metamorphic rocks that contain zones of weakness—such as foliation—are more likely to deform by ductile flow. Rocks that are weak and most likely behave in a ductile manner when under force include rock salt, gypsum, and shale. Limestone, schist, and marble are of intermediate strength and may also behave in a ductile manner.

Time In nature small stresses applied over long time spans play an important role in the deformation of rock. You can see the effects of time on deformation in everyday settings. For example, marble benches have been known to sag under their own weight over a span of a hundred years or so. ⬭ Forces that are unable to deform rock when first applied may cause rock to flow if the force is maintained over a long period of time.

Reading Checkpoint *What is brittle deformation?*

Types of Stress

Rocks are exposed to many different forces due to plate motions. ⬭ The three types of stresses that rocks commonly undergo are tensional stress, compressional stress, and shear stress. Look at Figure 2. When rocks are squeezed or shortened the stress is compressional. Tensional stress is caused by rocks being pulled in opposite directions. Shear stress causes a body of rock to be distorted.

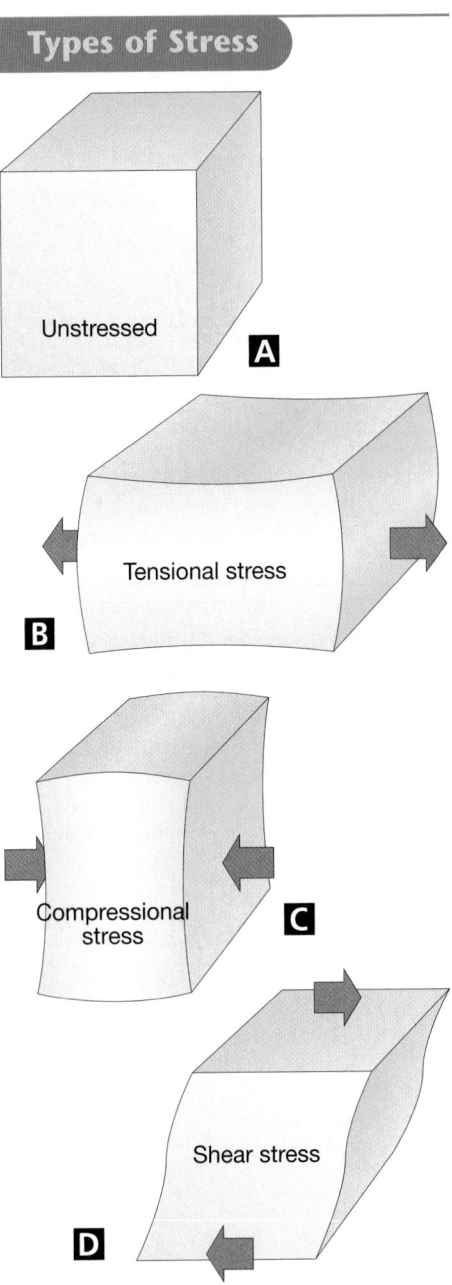
Figure 2 Undeformed material is changed as it undergoes different types of stress. The arrows show the direction of maximum stress. **A** Compressional stress causes a material to shorten. **B** Tensional stress causes a material to be stretched or to undergo extension. **C** Shear stress causes a material to be distorted with no change in volume.

Types of Stress

Unstressed **A**

Tensional stress **B**

Compressional stress **C**

Shear stress **D**

Folds

During mountain building, flat-lying sedimentary and volcanic rocks are often bent into a series of wavelike ripples called folds. Folds in sedimentary strata are much like those that would form if you were to hold the ends of a sheet of paper and then push them together. In nature, folds come in a wide variety of sizes and shapes. ⬭ **The three main types of folds are anticlines, synclines, and monoclines.**

Anticlines The two most common types of folds are anticlines and synclines. An **anticline** is most commonly formed by the upfolding, or arching, of rock layers, as shown in Figure 3.

Synclines Often found in association with anticlines are downfolds, or troughs, called **synclines**. Notice in Figure 3 that the limb of an anticline is also a limb of the adjacent syncline. Folds do not continue forever. Instead their ends die out much like the wrinkles in cloth.

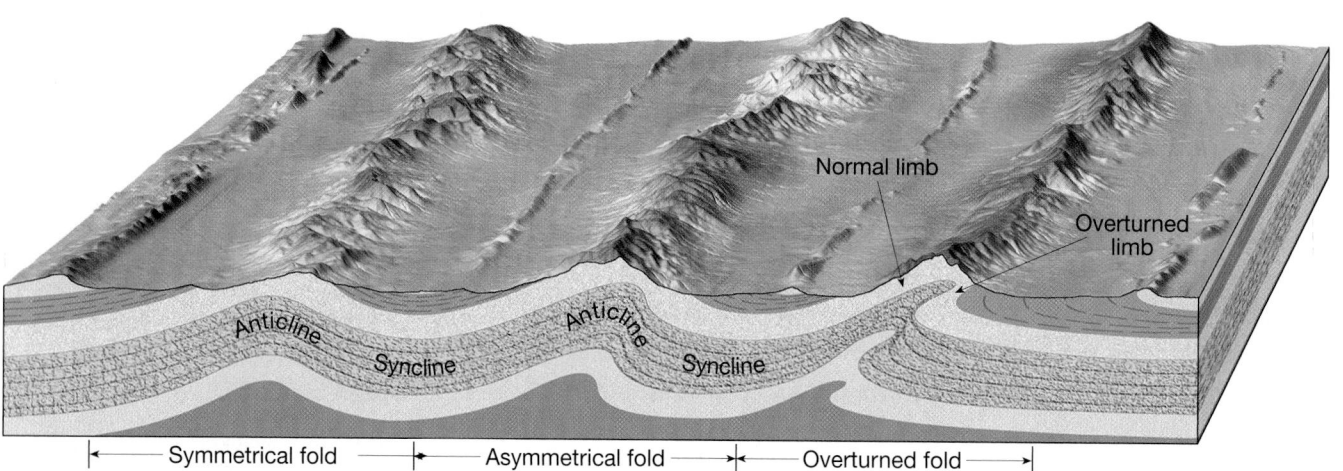

Figure 3 Anticlines and Synclines The upfolded or arched structures are anticlines. The downfolds or troughs are synclines. Notice that the limb of an anticline is also the limb of the adjacent syncline.

Monoclines Although we will discuss folds and faults separately, in the real world folds are generally closely associated with faults. Examples of this close association are broad, regional features called monoclines. **Monoclines** are large, step-like folds in otherwise horizontal sedimentary strata. Monoclines seem to occur as sedimentary layers have been folded over a large faulted block of underlying rock. Monoclines are prominent features of the Colorado Plateau area in Colorado, New Mexico, Utah, and Arizona, as shown in Figure 4 on the next page.

What is a syncline?

Figure 4 Monocline
A Monocline located near Mexican Hat, Utah. **B** This monocline consists of bent sedimentary beds that were deformed by faulting in the bedrock below.

Faults

Recall that faults are fractures in the crust along which movement has taken place. Small faults can be recognized in road cuts where sedimentary beds have been offset a few meters, as shown in Figure 5. Faults of this size usually occur as single breaks. By contrast, large faults, like the San Andreas fault in California, have displacements of hundreds of kilometers and consist of many interconnecting fault surfaces. These fault zones can be many kilometers wide and are often easier to identify from high-altitude photographs than at ground level.

The rock surface that is immediately above the fault is commonly called the hanging wall, and the rock surface below the fault is called the footwall. ⬤ **The major types of faults are normal faults, reverse faults, thrust faults, and strike-slip faults.**

Figure 5 Normal Fault Faulting caused the vertical displacement of these beds located near Kanab, Utah. Arrows show the relative motion of rock units.
Observing *Which side of the fault is the hanging wall?*

Normal Faults A **normal fault** occurs when the hanging wall block moves down relative to the footwall block. Most normal faults have steep dips of about 60°, as shown in Figure 6A on the next page. These dips often flatten out with depth. The movement in normal faults is mainly in a vertical direction, with some horizontal movement. Because of the downward motion of the hanging wall block, normal faults result in the lengthening, or extension, of the crust.

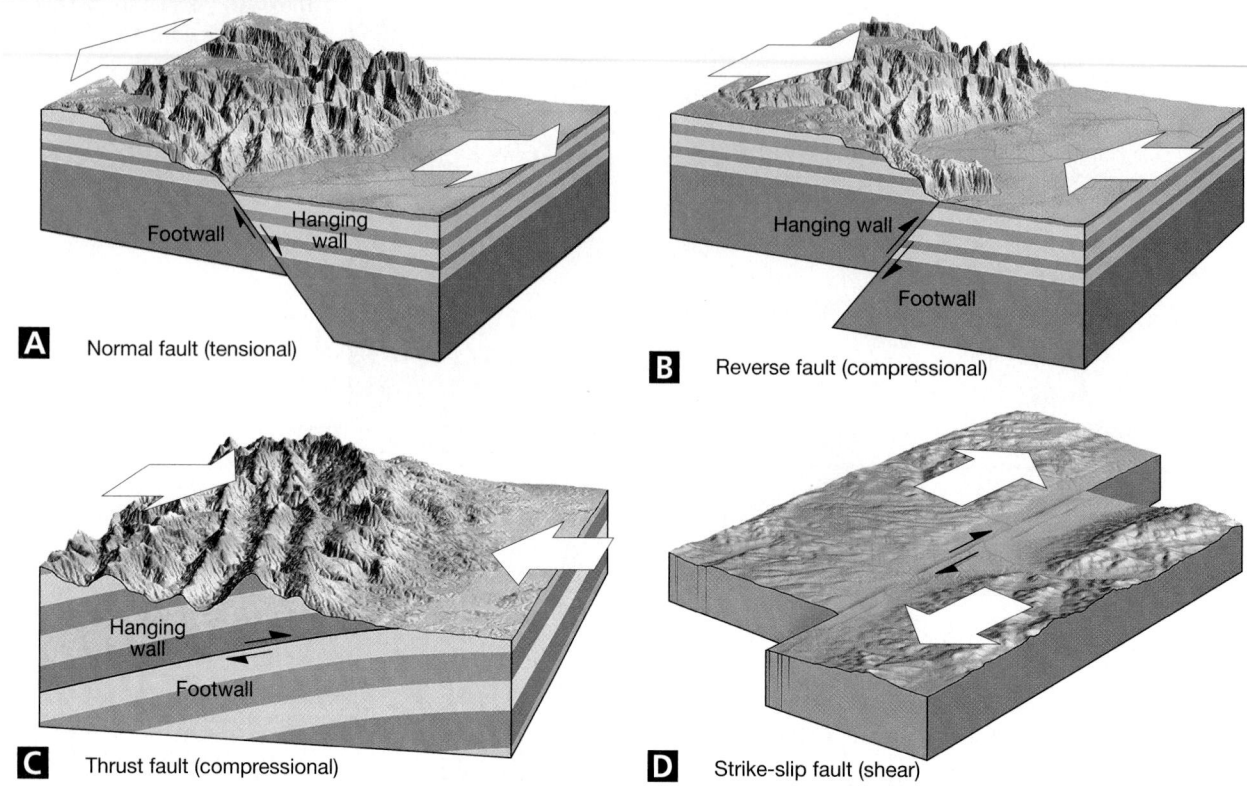

A Normal fault (tensional)

B Reverse fault (compressional)

C Thrust fault (compressional)

D Strike-slip fault (shear)

Figure 6 A Normal fault
B Reverse fault **C** Thrust fault
D Strike-slip fault
Interpreting Diagrams *Which*
type of fault would cause
extension in an area?

Q *How do you determine which*
side of a fault has moved?

A For the fault shown in
Figure 5, did the left side move
down, or did the right side
move up? Since the surface at
the top of the photo has been
eroded flat, either side could
have moved, or both sides
could have moved, with one
side moving more than the
other. That's why geologists
talk about *relative* motion across
faults. In this case, the left side
moved down *relative* to the right
side, and the right side moved
up *relative* to the left side.

Reverse Faults and Thrust Faults A **reverse fault** is a fault
in which the hanging wall block moves up relative to the footwall block.
Reverse faults are high-angle faults with dips greater than 45°. **Thrust
faults** are reverse faults with dips of less than 45°. Because the hanging
wall block moves up and over the footwall block, reverse and thrust
faults result in a shortening of the crust, as shown in Figure 6B and 6C.

Most high-angle reverse faults are small. They cause only local displacements in regions dominated by other types of faulting. Thrust
faults, on the other hand, exist at all scales. In mountainous regions
such as the Alps, northern Rockies, Himalayas, and Appalachians,
thrust faults have displaced rock layers as far as 50 kilometers over adjacent rocks. The result of this large-scale movement is that older rocks
end up on top of younger rocks.

Normal faults occur due to tensional stresses, and reverse and
thrust faults result from compressional stresses. Compressional forces
generally produce folds as well as faults. These compressional forces
result in a thickening and shortening of the rocks.

**Reading
Checkpoint** *What are the major types of faults?*

Strike-Slip Faults Faults in which the movement is horizontal and parallel to the trend, or strike, of the fault surface are called **strike-slip faults,** as shown in Figure 6D. Because of their large size and linear nature, many strike-slip faults produce a trace that is visible over a great distance. Rather than a single fracture, large strike-slip faults usually consist of a zone of roughly parallel fractures. The zone may be up to several kilometers wide. The most recent movement, however, is often along a section only a few meters wide, which may offset features such as stream channels. Crushed and broken rocks produced during faulting are more easily eroded, often producing linear valleys or troughs that mark the locations of strike-slip faults. Scientific records of strike-slip faulting were made following surface ruptures that produced large earthquakes. Strike-slip faults are commonly caused by shear stress. The San Andreas fault in California and the Great Glen fault in Scotland are well-known examples of strike-slip faults.

Joints Among the most common rock structures are fractures called joints. Unlike faults, joints are fractures along which no appreciable movement has occurred. Although some joints have a random orientation, most occur in roughly parallel groups, as shown in Figure 7. Joints usually form as the result of large-scale regional stresses.

Figure 7 Joints These joints are found in Arches National Park, near Moab, Utah. The joints in the sandstone stand out because chemical weathering is enhanced along them.

Section 11.1 Assessment

Reviewing Concepts

1. What factors determine the strength of a rock?

2. In what ways do rocks deform? Explain the differences in these deformations.

3. Describe the different types of stress.

4. List the three types of folds.

5. Explain the direction of movement in the four types of faults.

Critical Thinking

6. **Inferring** What type of deformation would a rock in the lower part of the mantle be more likely to undergo? Explain.

7. **Comparing and Contrasting** How is an anticline different from a syncline?

8. **Applying Concepts** What type of faults should be most common at a spreading ocean ridge? Explain.

Connecting Concepts

Compressional Stress Review the types of plate boundaries in Chapter 9. At which type of boundary would compressional stresses be the dominant force?

11.2 Types of Mountains

Reading Focus

Key Concepts

- How are mountains classified?
- What are the major types of mountains?

Vocabulary

- orogenesis
- folded mountain
- fault-block mountain
- graben
- horst

Reading Strategy

Previewing Make a table like the one below. Before you read the section, rewrite the green topic headings as questions. As you read, write answers to the questions.

Types of Mountains
What are folded mountains?
a. _____?_____
b. _____?_____
c. _____?_____

Mountains are one of the most inspiring features on Earth. The collection of processes that produce a mountain belt is called **orogenesis.** The rocks in mountains provide striking evidence of the enormous compressional forces that have deformed and lifted Earth's crust. Folding is often the most obvious sign of these forces, but thrust faulting, metamorphism, and igneous activity are also important processes in mountain building. **Mountains are classified by the dominant processes that have formed them.**

Figure 8 Folded Mountains
Folded sedimentary layers are exposed in the northern Rocky Mountains on the face of Mount Kidd, Alberta, Canada.

Folded Mountains

Many mountains contain huge spectacular folds of rocks, as shown in Figure 8. **Mountains that are formed primarily by folding are called folded mountains.** Compressional stresses are the major force that forms folded mountains.

Thrust faulting is also important in the formation of folded mountains, which are often called fold-and-thrust belts. Folded mountains often contain numerous stacked thrust faults that have displaced the folded rock layers many kilometers horizontally. The Appalachian Mountains, the northern Rocky Mountains, and the Alps in Europe are examples of folded mountain ranges.

Fault-Block Mountains

Most normal faults are small and have displacements of only a meter or so. Others extend for tens of kilometers where they may outline the boundary of a mountain front. ◯ **Large-scale normal faults are associated with structures called fault-block mountains.** These mountains form as large blocks of crust are uplifted and tilted along normal faults.

In the western United States, examples of fault-block mountains include the Teton Range of Wyoming and the Sierra Nevada of California. Both are faulted along their eastern flanks, which were uplifted as the blocks tilted downward to the west. These steep mountain fronts were produced over a period of 5 million to 10 million years by many episodes of faulting. Each event produced just a few meters of displacement.

Normal faulting occurs where tensional stresses cause the crust to be stretched or extended. As the crust is stretched, a block called a **graben,** which is bounded by normal faults, drops down. *Graben* is the German word for ditch or trench. Grabens produce an elongated valley bordered by relatively uplifted structures called **horsts.** The Basin and Range Province of Nevada, Utah, and California, shown in Figure 9, is made of elongated grabens. Above the grabens, tilted fault-bound blocks or horsts produce linear fault-block mountains.

Reading Checkpoint *What is a horst?*

B

Figure 9 Fault-Block Mountains A Part of the Basin and Range Province of Nevada, California, and Utah **B** Here, tensional stresses have elongated and fractured the crust into numerous blocks. Movement along these fractures has tilted the blocks producing parallel mountain ranges called fault-block mountains.

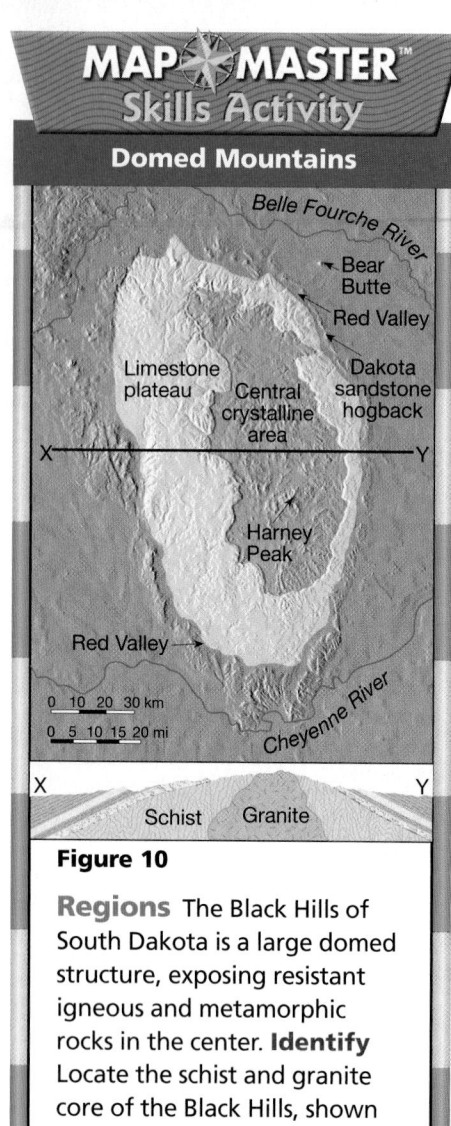

Domed Mountains

X ——— Y

X ——— Y

Schist   Granite

Figure 10

Regions The Black Hills of South Dakota is a large domed structure, exposing resistant igneous and metamorphic rocks in the center. **Identify** Locate the schist and granite core of the Black Hills, shown on the cross section.

Domes and Basins

The Black Hills of western South Dakota form a large domed structure thought to be formed by upwarping. Broad upwarping in basement rock may deform the overlying cover of sedimentary strata. This upwarping can generate large folds. ◯**When upwarping produces a circular or elongated structure, the feature is called a dome.** Erosion has stripped away the highest portion of the sedimentary beds in the Black Hills, exposing older igneous and metamorphic rocks in the center. Look at the map in Figure 10. The remnants of the sedimentary layers surround the crystalline core of the mountains. The oldest rocks form the core.

✓ **Reading Checkpoint** *Where are the oldest rocks found in a dome?*

Downwarped structures having a circular shape are called basins. Several large basins exist in the United States. The basins of Michigan and Illinois have very gently sloping beds similar to saucers. These basins are thought to be the result of large accumulations of sediment, whose weight caused the crust to subside.

Because large basins usually contain sedimentary beds sloping at very low angles, the basins are usually identified by the age of the rocks composing them. The youngest rocks are found near the center. The oldest rocks are at the flanks. A geologic map of lower Michigan, for example, looks somewhat like a bull's-eye. The oldest rocks are near the center of the state. Progressively younger rocks ring the center. This is just the opposite order of a domed structure, such as the Black Hills, where the oldest rocks form the core.

Section 11.2 Assessment

Reviewing Concepts

1. ◯ Describe how mountains are classified.
2. ◯ List the major types of mountains.
3. What is a graben? In what type of mountains are grabens most commonly found?
4. What is the dominant type of stress associated with folded mountains?

Critical Thinking

5. **Applying Concepts** In a mountain range, you observe a series of anticlines and synclines and numerous thrust faults. How would you classify the type of mountains in this mountain range?

6. **Comparing and Contrasting** Compare uplifted mountains and fault-block mountains.

Writing in Science

Descriptive Paragraph Write a paragraph describing a trip across an uplifted mountain. Describe the types of rocks and structures you might observe.

11.3 Mountain Formation

Reading Focus

Key Concepts

- What mountains are associated with convergent plate boundaries?

- What mountains are associated with divergent plate boundaries?

- How is isostatic adjustment involved in mountain formation?

Vocabulary

- accretionary wedge
- accretion
- terrane
- isostasy
- isostatic adjustment

Reading Strategy

Outlining As you read, make an outline of the important ideas in this section. Use the green topic headings as the main topics and the blue headings as subtopics.

> **I. Mountain Formation**
>   A. Mountain Building at Convergent Boundaries
>   1. Ocean-Ocean Convergence
>   2. a. _____?_____
>   3. b. _____?_____
>   B. Mountain Building at Divergent Boundaries

Mountain building still occurs in several places worldwide. For example, the Himalayas began to form 45 million years ago and are still rising. Older mountain ranges, such as the Appalachians in the eastern United States, are deeply eroded, but they have many features found in younger mountains.

Many hypotheses have been proposed to explain mountain formation. One early proposal suggested that mountains are wrinkles in Earth's crust, produced as the planet cooled from its early semi-molten state. People believed that as Earth cooled, it contracted and shrank. In this way, the crust was deformed the way an apple peel wrinkles as it dries out. However, this early hypothesis and many others were not able to withstand careful analysis and had to be discarded.

Figure 11 Young Mountains The Grand Tetons of Wyoming are an example of relatively young mountains.

Mountain Building at Convergent Boundaries

With the development of the theory of plate tectonics, a widely accepted model for orogenesis became available. **Most mountain building occurs at convergent plate boundaries. Colliding plates provide the compressional forces that fold, fault, and metamorphose the thick layers of sediments deposited at the edges of landmasses.** The partial melting of mantle rock also provides a source of magma that intrudes and further deforms these deposits.

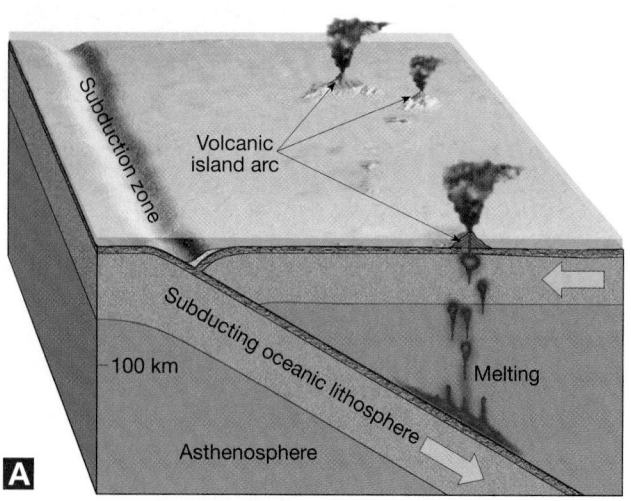

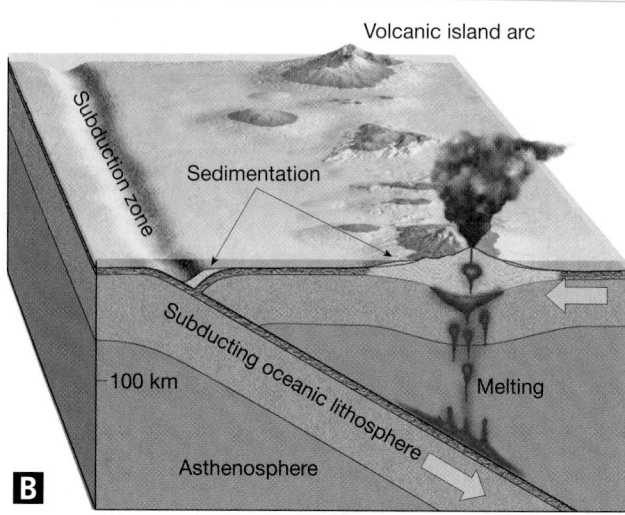

Figure 12 A A volcanic island arc develops due to the convergence of two oceanic plates. **B** Continued subduction along this type of convergent boundary results in the development of volcanic mountains.

Ocean-Ocean Convergence

Ocean-ocean convergence occurs where two oceanic plates converge and one is subducted beneath the other, as shown in Figure 12. The converging plates result in partial melting of the mantle above the subducting plate and can lead to the growth of a volcanic island arc on the ocean floor. Because they are associated with subducting oceanic lithosphere, island arcs are typically found on the margins of a shrinking ocean basin, such as the Pacific. These features tend to be relatively long-lived. Here, somewhat sporadic volcanic activity, the depth of magma, as well as the accumulation of sediment that is scraped off the subducting plates, increases the volume of the crust. An example of an active island arc is the Aleutian arc, which forms the Aleutian Islands in Alaska. Some volcanic island arcs, such as Japan, appear to have been built up by two or three different periods of subduction. As shown by Japan, the continued development of a volcanic island arc can result in the formation of mountains made up of belts of igneous and metamorphic rocks. **Ocean-ocean convergence mainly produces volcanic mountains.**

Ocean-Continental Convergence

Mountain building along continental margins involves the convergence of an oceanic plate and a plate whose leading edge contains continental crust. A good example is the west coast of South America. In this area, the Nazca plate is being subducted beneath the South American plate along the Peru-Chile trench. As shown by the Andes Mountains, ocean-continental convergence results in the formation of a continental volcanic arc inland of the continental margin.

The convergence of the continental block and the subduction of the oceanic plate leads to deformation and metamorphism of the continental margin. Partial melting of mantle rock above the subducting slab generates magma that migrates upward. This melting and fluid migration occurs once the oceanic plate moves down to about 100 kilometers. During the development of this continental volcanic arc, sediment derived from the land and scraped from the subducting plate is stuck against the landward side of the trench. This accumulation of different sedimentary and metamorphic rocks with some scraps of ocean crust is called an **accretionary wedge.** A long period of subduction can build an accretionary wedge of rock that is large enough to stand above sea level, as shown in Figure 13.

Ocean-continental convergence produces mountain ranges composed of two roughly parallel belts. The continental volcanic arc develops on the continental block. The arc consists of volcanoes and large intrusive bodies mixed with high-temperature metamorphic rocks. The seaward belt is the accretionary wedge. It consists of folded, faulted sedimentary and metamorphic rocks. ⬤ **The types of mountains formed by ocean-continental convergence are volcanic mountains and folded mountains.**

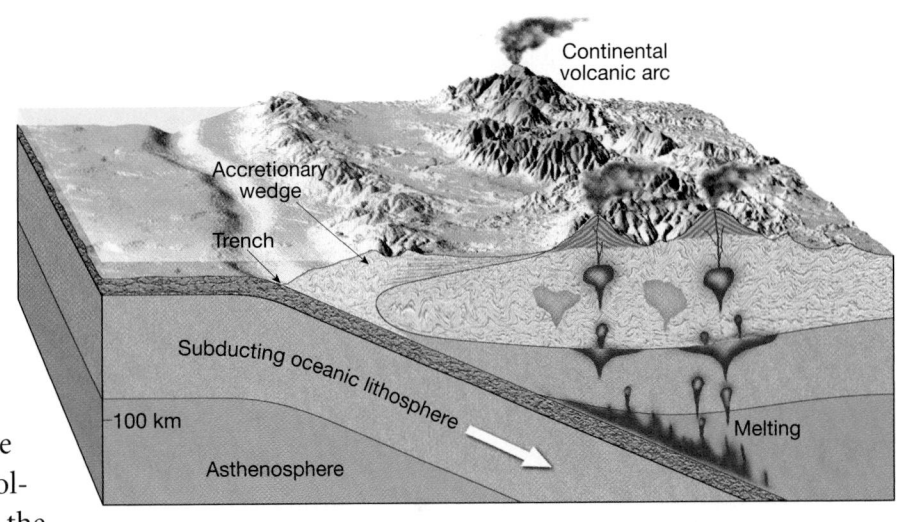

Figure 13 Ocean-Continental Convergence Plate convergence generates a subduction zone, and partial melting produces a continental volcanic arc. Continued convergence and igneous activity further deforms the crust and forms a roughly parallel folded mountain belt. **Observing** *What type of mountains result from the partial melting?*

Problem-Solving ⟩ Activity

Rates of Mountain Building

The mighty Himalayas between India and Tibet are the tallest mountains on Earth, rising to more than 8 kilometers. These mountains are still rising at about 1 centimeter per year. Mount Everest is the tallest peak with an elevation of 8848 meters above sea level. The Himalayas formed as a result of India colliding with the Eurasian plate.

1. **Calculating** If you assume that the Himalayas will continue to be uplifted at the current rate of 1 centimeter per year, how long will it take the mountains to rise another 500 meters?

2. **Calculating** Assuming a rate of uplift of 1 centimeter per year, how much higher could the Himalayas be in one million years?

3. **Applying Concepts** If the convergence of tectonic plates is causing the Himalayas to rise in elevation, what common surface processes are working to decrease their elevations?

4. **Inferring** Do you think it is reasonable for the Himalayas to continue to rise in elevation indefinitely? Explain your answer.

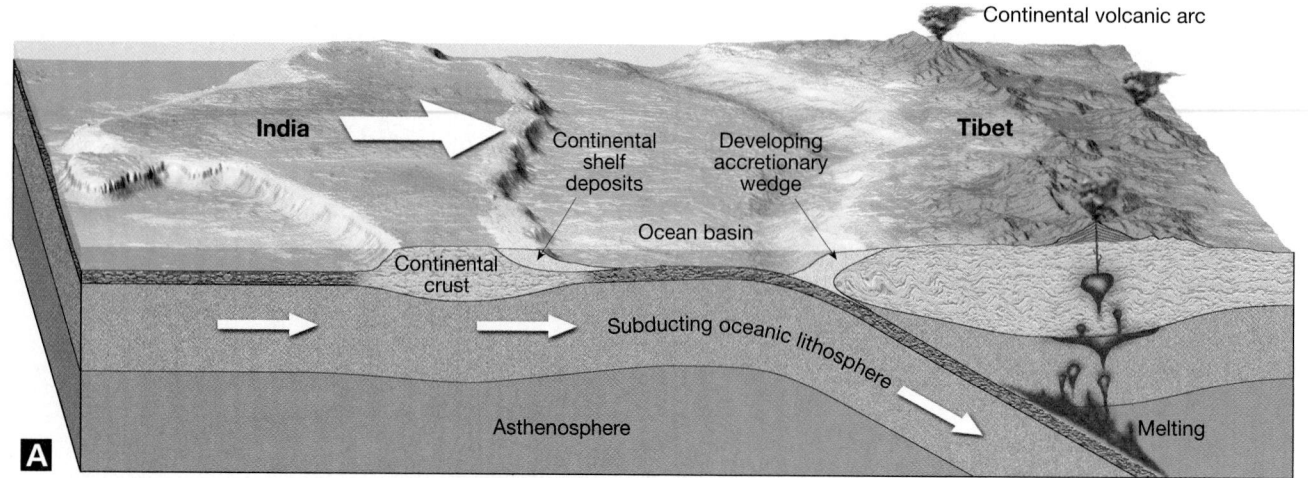

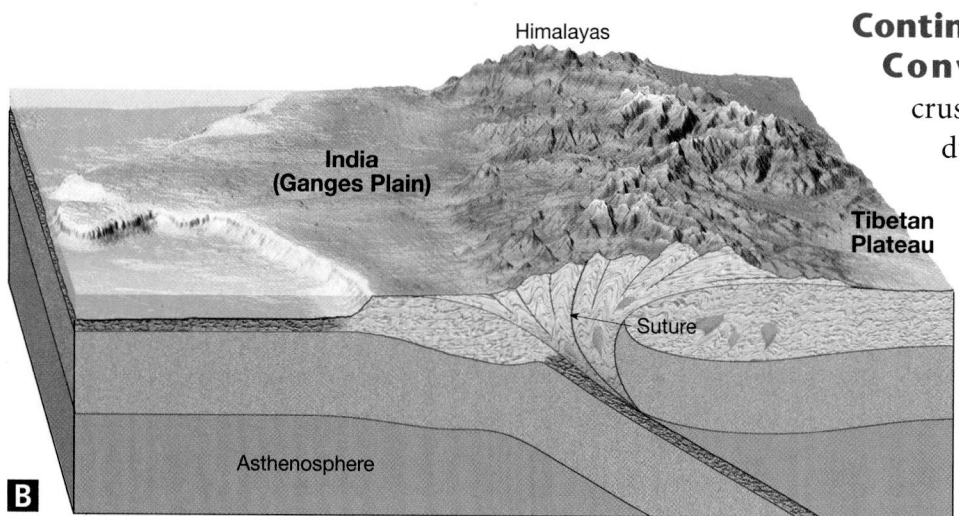

Figure 14 Continental-Continental Convergence The ongoing collision of India and Asia started about 45 million years ago and produced the majestic Himalayas. **A** Converging plates generated a subduction zone, producing a continental volcanic arc. **B** Eventually the two landmasses collided, which deformed and elevated the mountain range.

Continent-Continent Convergence

Continental crust floats too much to be subducted. At a convergent boundary between two plates carrying continental crust, a collision between the continental fragments will result and form folded mountains.

An example of such a collision began about 45 million years ago when India collided with the Eurasian plate, as shown in Figure 14. Before this event, India was once part of Antarctica, and it had split from that continent over the course of millions of years. It slowly moved a few thousand kilometers due north. The result of the collision was the formation of the spectacular Himalaya Mountains and the Tibetan Plateau. Most of the oceanic crust that separated these landmasses before the collision was subducted, but some was caught up in the collision zone, along with the sediment along the shoreline. Today these sedimentary rocks and slivers of oceanic crust are elevated high above sea level.

A similar but much older collision is believed to have taken place when the European continent collided with the Asian continent to produce the Ural Mountains in Russia. Before the theory of plate tectonics, geologists had difficulty explaining mountain ranges such as the Urals, which are located far within continents.

 *Why can't continental crust be subducted?*

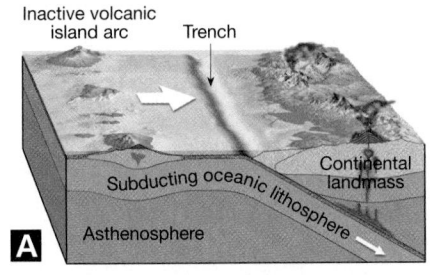

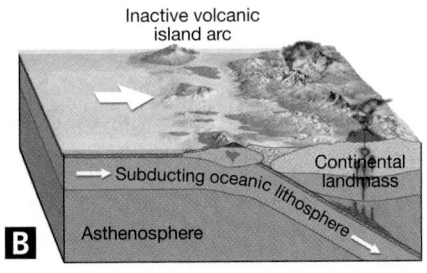

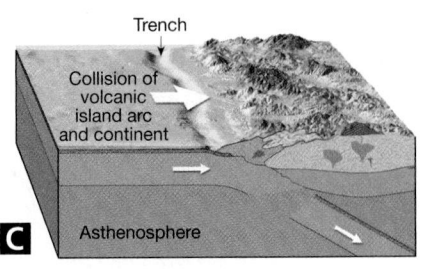

Mountain Building at Divergent Boundaries

Most mountains are formed at convergent boundaries, but some are formed at divergent boundaries, usually on the ocean floor. These mountains form a chain that curves along the ocean floor at the ocean ridges. This mountain chain is over 65,000 kilometers long and rises to 2000 to 3000 meters above the ocean floor. 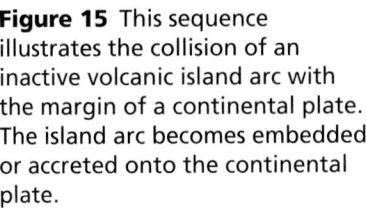 **The mountains that form along ocean ridges at divergent plate boundaries are fault-block type mountains.** The mountain chain that makes up the Mid-Atlantic Ridge is an example.

Non-Boundary Mountains

Even though most mountains are formed at plate boundaries, some are found far from any boundaries. Some upwarped mountains, fault-block mountains, and volcanic mountains are not formed at plate boundaries. Volcanic mountains such as the Hawaiian Islands are formed at a hot spot, far from any plate boundary. Many fault-block mountains occur in areas that are undergoing regional extension or stretching. These areas may possibly become a plate boundary if the plate rifts apart.

 *Where is the longest mountain range?*

Continental Accretion

Plate tectonics theory originally suggested two major mechanisms for orogenesis at convergent boundaries: continental collisions and subduction of oceanic lithosphere to form volcanic arcs. Further studies have lead to another mechanism in which smaller crustal fragments collide and merge with continental margins. When the fragments collide with a continental plate they become stuck to or embedded into the continent in a process called **accretion**. Many of the mountainous regions rimming the Pacific have been produced through the process of collision and accretion.

Figure 15 This sequence illustrates the collision of an inactive volcanic island arc with the margin of a continental plate. The island arc becomes embedded or accreted onto the continental plate.

For: Links on mountain building
Visit: www.SciLinks.org
Web Code: cjn-3113

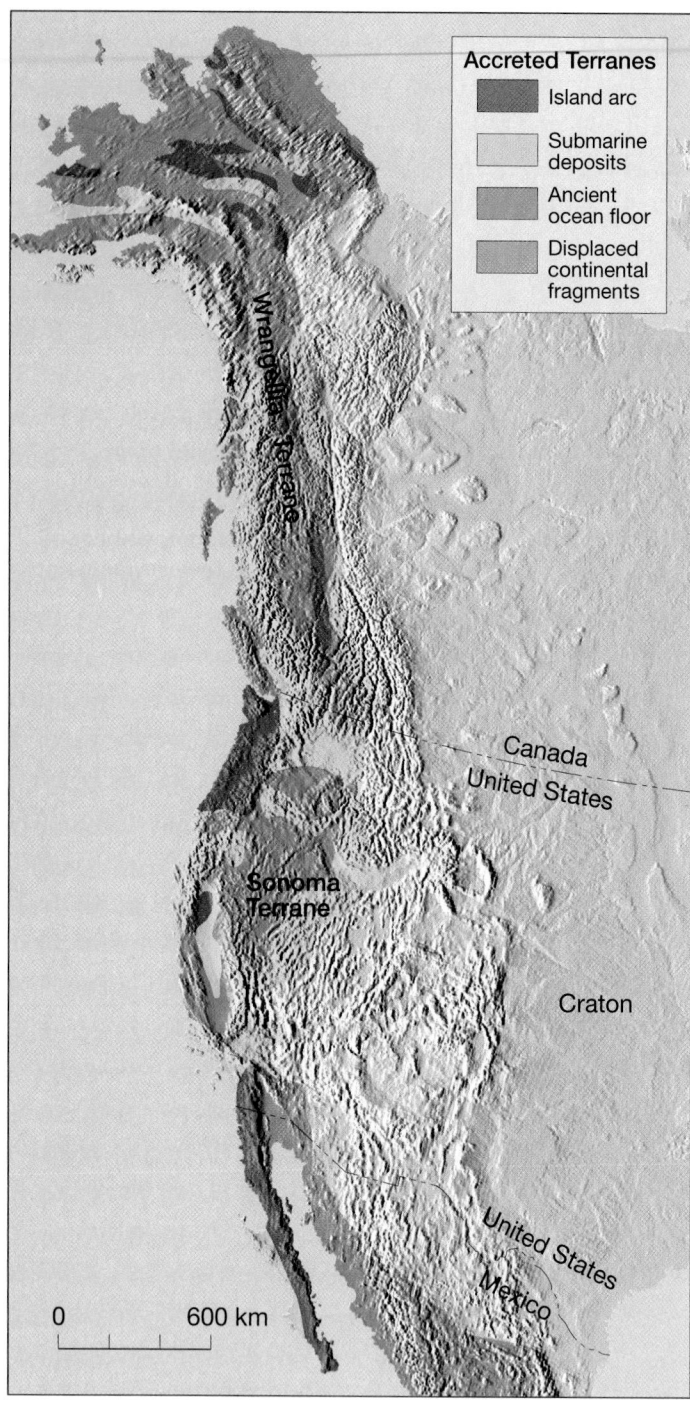

Accreted Terranes

- Island arc
- Submarine deposits
- Ancient ocean floor
- Displaced continental fragments

Wrangellia Terrane

Canada
United States

Sonoma Terrane

Craton

United States
Mexico

0   600 km

Figure 16 Accretion in Western North America These terranes are thought to have been added to western North America during the past 200 million years.
Interpreting Maps *What do the areas in blue represent?*

Terranes Geologists refer to accreted crustal blocks as terranes. A **terrane** is any crustal fragment that has a geologic history distinct from that of the adjoining terranes. Terranes come in many shapes and sizes. Some are no larger than volcanic islands, while others are immense, such as the one making up the entire Indian subcontinent. Before their accretion to a continental block, some of the fragments may have been microcontinents similar to the present-day island of Madagascar, located in the Indian Ocean east of Africa. Many others were island arcs like Japan and the Philippines.

As oceanic plates move, they carry the embedded volcanic island arcs and microcontinents along with them. Eventually a collision between the crustal fragment and the continent occurs. Relatively small crustal pieces are peeled from the oceanic plate at a subduction zone, and thin sheets of the crustal fragment are thrust onto the continental block. This newly added material increases the width and thickness of the continental crust. The material may later be displaced farther inland by the addition of other fragments.

Mountains from Accretion The accretion of larger crustal fragments, such as a mature island arc, may result in a mountain range. These mountain ranges are much smaller than the ones that result from a continent–continent collision. Because of its buoyancy, or ability to float, an island arc will not subduct beneath the continental plate. Instead, it will plow into the continent and deform both blocks.

The idea that mountain building occurs in connection with the accretion of crustal fragments to a continental mass came mainly from studies in western North America. See Figure 16. Areas in the mountains of Alaska and western Canada were found to contain rocks, fossils, and structures that were different from those in surrounding areas. These areas have been accreted to the western margin of North America.

 **Reading Checkpoint** *What is a terrane?*

Principle of Isostasy

In addition to the horizontal movements of lithospheric plates, gradual up-and-down motions of the crust are seen at many locations around the globe. Although much of this vertical movement occurs along plate margins and is linked to mountain building, some of it is not. The up-and-down motions also occur in the interiors of continents far from plate boundaries.

Earth's crust floats on top of the denser and more flexible rocks of the mantle. The concept of a floating crust in gravitational balance is called **isostasy** (*iso* = equal and *stasis* = standing). One way to understand the concept of isostasy is to think about a series of wooden blocks of different heights floating in water, as shown in Figure 17. Note that the thicker wooden blocks float higher than the thinner blocks. In a similar way, many mountain belts stand high above the surface because they have buoyant (less dense) crustal "roots" that extend deep into the denser mantle. The denser mantle supports the mountains from below.

What would happen if another small block of wood were placed on top of one of the blocks in Figure 17? The combined block would sink until a new isostatic balance was reached. However, the top of the combined block would actually be higher than before, and the bottom would be lower. This process of establishing a new level of gravitational equilibrium is called **isostatic adjustment.**

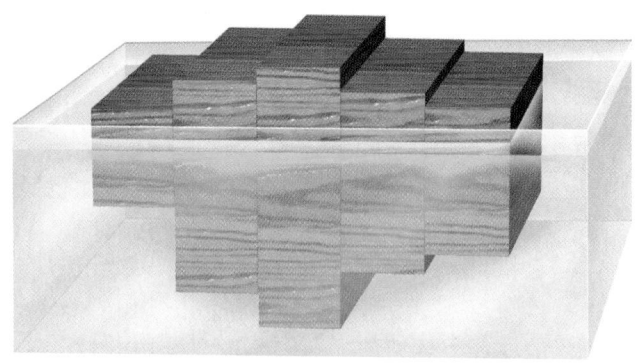

Figure 17 Isostatic Adjustment This drawing illustrates how wooden blocks of different thicknesses float in water. In a similar manner, thick sections of crustal material float higher than thinner crustal slabs. **Inferring** *Would a denser wooden block float at a higher or lower level?*

Isostatic Adjustment in Mountains

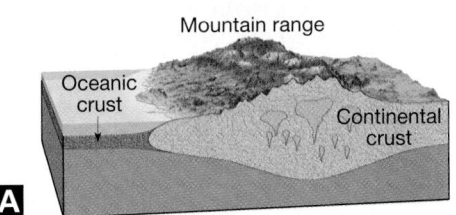

A When mountains are young, the continental crust is thickest.

Figure 18 This sequence illustrates how the combined effect of erosion and isostatic adjustment results in a thinning of the crust in mountainous regions.

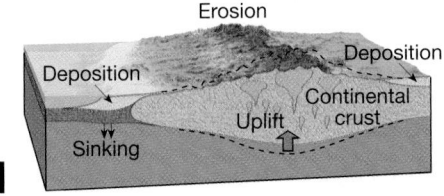

B As erosion lowers the mountains, the crust rises in response to the reduced load.

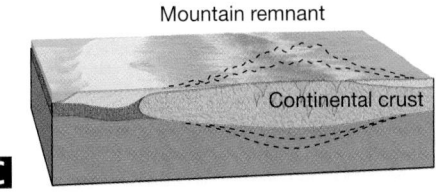

C Erosion and uplift continue until the mountains reach "normal" crustal thickness.

Isostatic Adjustment for Mountains Applying the concept of isostasy, we should expect that when weight is added to the crust, the crust responds by subsiding. Also when weight is removed, the crust will rebound. Evidence of crustal subsidence followed by crustal rebound is provided by the continental ice sheets that covered parts of North America during the Pleistocene epoch. The added weight of a 3-kilometer-thick mass of ice depressed Earth's crust by hundreds of meters. In the 8000 years since the last ice sheet melted, uplift of as much as 330 meters has occurred in Canada's Hudson Bay region, where the ice was thickest.

 **Reading Checkpoint** *How are ice sheets related to isostatic adjustment?*

Crustal buoyancy can account for considerable vertical movement. Most mountain building causes the crust to shorten and thicken. **Because of isostasy, deformed and thickened crust will undergo regional uplift both during mountain building and for a long period afterward.** As the crust rises, the processes of erosion increase, and the deformed rock layers are carved into a mountainous landscape.

As erosion lowers the summits of mountains, the crust will rise in response to the reduced load, as shown in Figure 18 on page 323. The processes of uplifting and erosion will continue until the mountain block reaches "normal" crustal thickness. When this occurs, the mountains will be eroded to near sea level, and the once deeply buried interior of the mountain will be exposed at the surface.

Section 11.3 Assessment

Reviewing Concepts

1. ⬤ What types of mountains are associated with convergent plate boundaries?

2. ⬤ What mountains are associated with divergent plate boundaries?

3. ⬤ How is isostatic adjustment involved in mountain building?

4. How is accretion involved in mountain formation?

Critical Thinking

5. **Comparing and Contrasting** Compare mountain building along an ocean-continent convergent boundary and a continent-continent convergent boundary.

6. **Drawing Conclusions** How does the theory of plate tectonics help explain the existence of marine fossils in sedimentary rocks on top of the Himalayas?

7. **Applying Concepts** How would the accretion of a large microcontinent affect the isostatic adjustment of the region around a mountain range?

Writing in Science

Creative Writing Describe a trip through a mountain range like the Andes that has formed at an ocean-continent convergent boundary.

The San Andreas Fault System

The San Andreas, the largest fault system in North America, first attracted attention after the 1906 San Francisco earthquake. But this dramatic event is just one of many thousands of earthquakes that have resulted from movements along the San Andreas over the last 29 million years.

The San Andreas fault system, as shown in the map, trends in a north-westerly direction for nearly 1300 kilometers through much of western California. In many places, a linear trough marks the trace of the San Andreas fault. From the air, linear scars, offset stream channels, and elongated ponds mark the location of the fault. On the ground, however, evidence of the fault is harder to find. Some of the most distinctive landforms include long, straight cliffs, narrow ridges, and sag ponds formed by the settling of blocks within the fault zone.

Transform Boundary Mountains

The San Andreas fault is a transform fault boundary separating two crustal plates that move very slowly. The Pacific plate, located to the west, moves northwestward in relation to the North American plate.

Some large blocks of crust within the fault zone are pushed up forming hills or mountains of various sizes. Other blocks are forced down

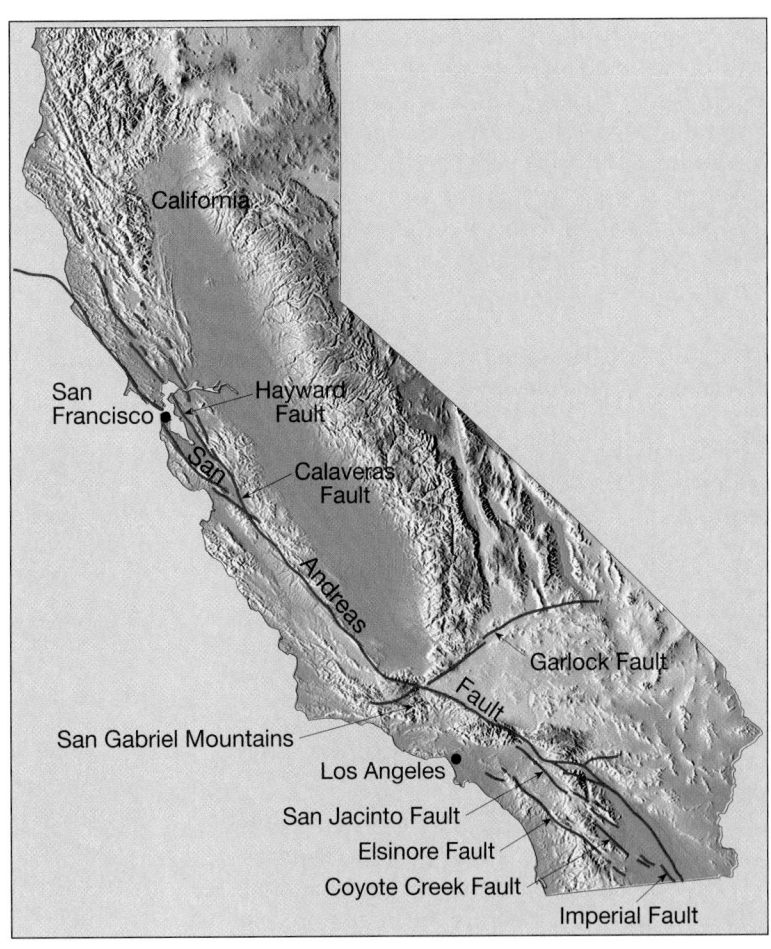

and form depressions called sag ponds. The fault trace is not straight. It has many bends along its length. In one of these major bends, the force of the two sides of the fault moving past one another has caused the uplift of the San Gabriel Mountains north of Los Angeles.

Fault System

Different segments of the San Andreas behave differently. Some portions creep slowly with little noticeable seismic activity. Other segments regularly slip, producing small earthquakes. Still other segments seem to store elastic energy for hundreds of years and rupture in great earthquakes.

Because of the great length and complexity of the San Andreas fault, it is more appropriately referred to as a "fault system." This major fault system consists primarily of the San Andreas fault and several major branches, including the Hayward and Calaveras faults of central California and the San Jacinto and Elsinore faults. By matching rock units across the fault, geologists have determined that the total displacement from earthquakes and creep along the San Andreas is greater than 560 kilometers.

Investigating Anticlines and Synclines

The axial plane of a fold is an imaginary plane drawn through the long axis of a fold. The axial plane divides the fold into two halves called limbs as shown in Figure 1. In a symmetrical fold, the limbs are mirror images of each other and move away at the same angle. In an asymmetrical fold, the limbs dip or tilt at different angles. Folds do not continue forever. Where the fold axis dips and is no longer horizontal, the fold is said to be plunging, as shown in Figure 2. A geologic principle known as the principle of superposition states that in most situations with layered rocks, the oldest rocks are at the bottom of the sequence.

Problem
How are rocks oriented in anticlines and synclines?

Materials
- pencil
- protractor
- tracing paper

Skills
Observing, Measuring, Classifying, Interpreting Diagrams

Procedure

1. Study the two diagrams, labeled Fold A and Fold B in Figures 3 and 4.

2. Use a protractor to measure the angles of the rock layers in both limbs of Fold A. Repeat your measurements for both limbs of Fold B. For consistency, measure the angles on both folds at the surface between layers 3 and 4.

3. Use Figures 3 and 4 and Figure 3 on page 310 to determine what types of folds are shown by Fold A and Fold B.

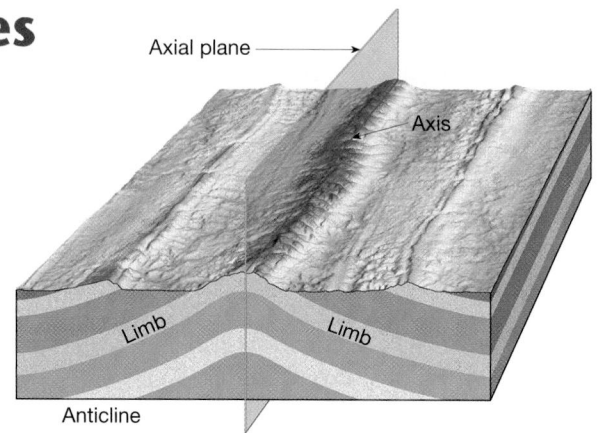

Figure 1 Horizontal Axis

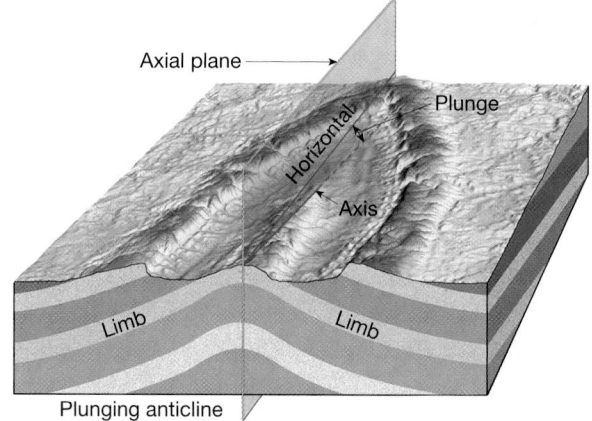

Figure 2 Plunging Axis

4. Anticlines and synclines are linear features caused by compressional stresses. Two other types of folds—domes and basins—are often nearly circular and result from vertical displacement. Uplift produces domes like those shown in Figure 3. A basin is a downwarped structure, as shown in Figure 4.

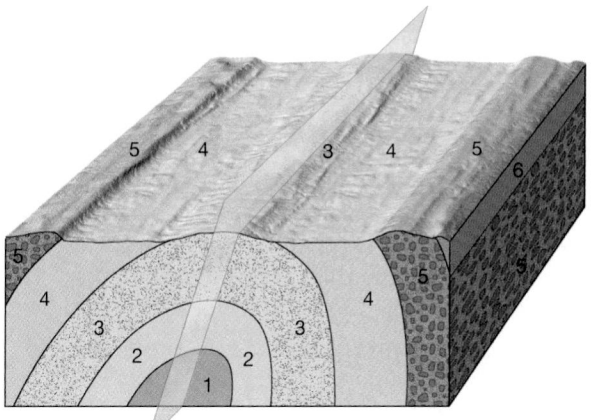

Figure 3 Fold A

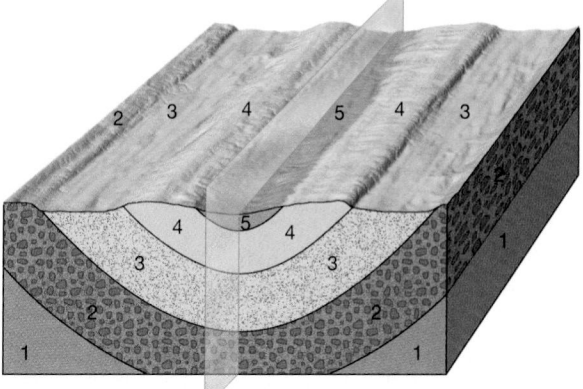

Figure 4 Fold B

5. Use tracing paper to make a copy of the blank block diagram shown below. Complete all three sides of the diagram to show an eroded fold consistent with the rock layer shown on the right side of the block.

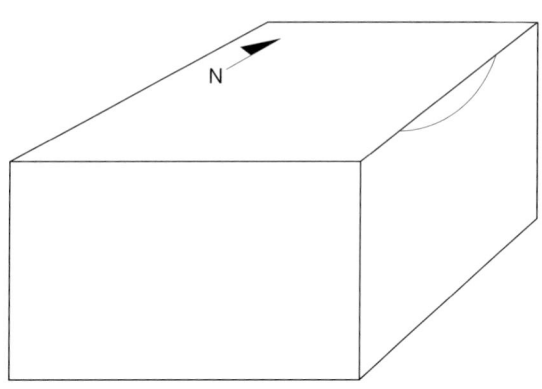

Analyze and Conclude

1. **Interpreting Diagrams** What type of fold is shown by Fold A? In what direction do the limbs dip or tilt from the axial plane?

2. **Interpreting Diagrams** What type of fold is shown by Fold B? In what direction do the limbs dip or tilt from the axial plane?

3. **Drawing Conclusions** In Fold A, which rock layer is the oldest shown? Which rock layer is the youngest shown?

4. **Measuring** In Fold A, at what angle are the rock layers in both limbs dipping or tilted?

5. **Drawing Conclusions** In Fold B, which rock layer is the oldest shown? Which rock layer is the youngest shown?

6. **Measuring** In Fold B, at what angle are the rock layers in both limbs dipping or tilted?

7. **Classifying** What type of fold did you draw in the blank block diagram on your tracing paper?

8. **Observing** Is Fold A symmetrical or asymmetrical? Is Fold B symmetrical or asymmetrical?

9. **Observing** Is Fold A plunging or nonplunging? Is Fold B plunging or nonplunging?

10. **Applying Concepts** If you walk away from the axis on an eroded anticline, do the rocks get older or younger? How do the ages of the rocks change as you walk away from the axis in a syncline?

Go Further Use library or Internet sources to research the geologic terms "strike" and "dip." Draw a block diagram showing rocks layers that illustrate these terms. Give a presentation to the class, and explain the terms using your diagram as a visual aid.

11.1 Rock Deformation

Key Concepts

- The factors that influence the strength of a rock and how it will deform include temperature, confining pressure, rock type, and time.
- Rocks deform permanently in two ways: brittle deformation and ductile deformation.
- Forces that are unable to deform rock when first applied may cause rock to flow if the force is maintained over a long period of time.
- The three types of stresses that deform rocks are tensional stress, compressional stress, and shear stress.
- The three main types of folds are anticlines, synclines, and monoclines.
- The major types of faults are normal faults, reverse faults, thrust faults, and strike-slip faults.

Vocabulary

deformation, *p. 308;* stress, *p. 308;* strain, *p. 308;* anticline, *p. 310;* syncline, *p. 310;* monocline, *p. 310;* normal fault, *p. 311;* reverse fault, *p. 312;* thrust fault, *p. 312;* strike-slip fault, *p. 313*

11.2 Types of Mountains

Key Concepts

- Mountains are classified by the dominant processes that have formed them.
- Mountains that are formed primarily by folding are called folded mountains.
- Large-scale normal faults are associated with structures called fault-block mountains.
- Mountains formed by the upwarping of a large block of basement rock are called domed mountains. Downwarped structures having a circular shape are called basins.

Vocabulary

orogenesis, *p. 314;* folded mountain, *p. 314;* fault-block mountain, *p. 315;* graben, *p. 315;* horst, *p. 315*

11.3 Mountain Formation

Key Concepts

- Most mountain building occurs at convergent plate boundaries. Colliding plates provide the compressional forces that fold, fault, and metamorphose the thick layers of sediments deposited at the edges of landmasses.
- Ocean-ocean convergence mainly produces volcanic mountains.
- The types of mountains formed by ocean-continental convergence are volcanic mountains and folded mountains.
- At a convergent boundary between two continental plates, a collision between the continental fragments will result and form folded mountains.
- The mountains that form along ocean ridges at divergent plate boundaries are fault-block mountains.
- Because of isostasy, deformed and thickened crust will undergo regional uplift both during mountain building and for a long period afterward.

Vocabulary

accretionary wedge, *p. 319;* accretion, *p. 321;* terrane, *p. 322;* isostasy, *p. 323;* isostatic adjustment, *p. 323*

Thinking Visually

Concept Map Copy the concept map onto a sheet of paper. Use information from the chapter to complete it.

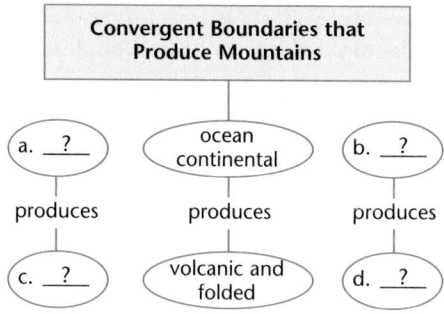

Reviewing Content

Choose the letter that best answers the question or completes the statement.

1. Which one of the following is NOT a form of rock deformation?
   a. elastic deformation
   b. ductile deformation
   c. brittle deformation
   d. oblique deformation

2. The two most common types of linear folds are
   a. anticlines and synclines.
   b. basins and monoclines.
   c. domes and synclines.
   d. thrusts and anticlines.

3. Orogenesis refers to those processes that produce
   a. spreading centers.
   b. earthquakes.
   c. mountains.
   d. subduction zones.

4. Which one of the following is NOT a factor that affects the strength of a rock?
   a. time
   b. age of the rock
   c. rock type
   d. temperature

5. The rock surface immediately above a fault surface is commonly called the
   a. anticline.
   b. foot wall.
   c. hanging wall.
   d. syncline.

6. Folding is usually the result of what type of stress?
   a. tensional stress
   b. compressional stress
   c. shear stress
   d. faulting

7. The collision and joining of crustal fragments to a continent is called
   a. subduction.
   b. isostasy.
   c. accretion.
   d. extension.

8. The San Andreas Fault is an example of what type of fault?
   a. normal fault
   b. strike-slip fault
   c. reverse fault
   d. thrust fault

9. What type of mountains form at convergent boundaries where two oceanic plates meet?
   a. volcanic mountains
   b. upwarped mountains
   c. folded mountains
   d. fault-block mountains

10. What is the most important difference between faults and joints?
    a. Joints occur along folds.
    b. Joints are often parallel.
    c. Joints have no displacement.
    d. Joints are always vertical.

Understanding Concepts

11. How does tensional stress deform a body of rock?

12. What is ductile deformation?

13. How is a syncline different from an anticline?

14. What types of faults are most commonly associated with fault-block mountains?

15. Define graben.

16. What types of faults are most commonly formed by compressional stresses?

Use the diagram below to answer Questions 17–18.

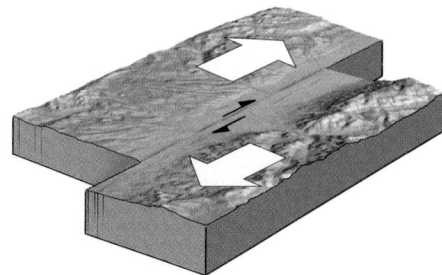

17. What type of fault is shown in the diagram?

18. What type of stress formed the fault shown in the diagram?

19. In the plate tectonics theory, what type of plate boundary is associated with the formation of the Himalayas and Appalachians?

20. What is an accretionary wedge? Briefly describe its formation.

21. Define terrane.

22. Describe folded mountains. Give an example of folded mountains.

23. How do volcanic mountains form at locations that are not near plate boundaries? Give an example.

24. How do the ages of rock layers change as you go from the axial plane of an anticline outwards towards the limbs?

25. What type of stress is most common at divergent boundaries? What type of mountains are most often found at this type of boundary? Give an example.

Critical Thinking

26. Applying Concepts How would a period of major erosion affect the isostatic adjustment of a mountain range?

27. Comparing and Contrasting Compare normal faults and reverse faults.

28. Predicting What would most likely happen if a continental fragment the size of Greenland was carried by an oceanic plate into a subduction zone along the margin of a continental plate?

29. Inferring Why don't anticlines always appear as hills, even though the rocks beneath the surface are folded upward?

30. Comparing and Contrasting How are a dome and a basin similar? How are they different?

Analyzing Data

Use the diagram below to answer Questions 31–34.

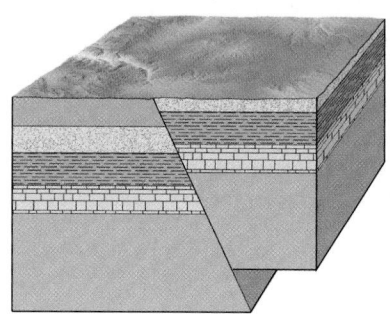

31. Inferring What is the block on the right side of the fault called?

32. Observing Describe the movement along the fault.

33. Interpreting Diagrams What type of fault is shown in the diagram?

34. Drawing Conclusions What type of stress was responsible for forming this fault?

Concepts in Action

35. Designing an Experiment Put together an experiment that models the isostatic adjustment that results from a continent-continent collision and the erosion that takes place on the resulting mountain range.

36. Hypothesizing Explain how a slice of ocean crust could be found on top of a peak in the Himalayas.

37. Writing in Science Write a paragraph briefly describing the development of volcanic mountains at an oceanic-oceanic convergent boundary.

Performance-Based Assessment

Classifying Use a world physiographic map or a world atlas and Figure 8 in Chapter 9 to classify the following mountains or mountain ranges: Mount Baker in Washington State, the Zagros Mountains in Iran, Mount Fuji in Japan, and the mountains in western Egypt.

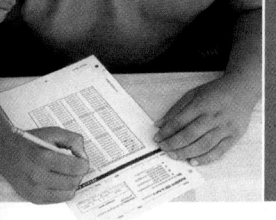

Standardized Test Prep

Choose the letter that best answers the question or completes the statement.

1. A fracture with horizontal displacement parallel to its surface trend is called a
   (A) joint.
   (B) normal fault.
   (C) strike-slip fault.
   (D) reverse fault.

2. Compared to the elevation of a thin piece of continental crust, the highest elevation of a thick piece in isostatic balance will be
   (A) the same.
   (B) higher.
   (C) lower.
   (D) older.

3. The removal of material by erosion will cause the crust to
   (A) subduct.
   (B) fold.
   (C) rise.
   (D) subside.

4. Which of the following are NOT generally associated with convergent margins?
   (A) volcanic mountains
   (B) folded mountains
   (C) thrust faulted mountains
   (D) fault-block mountains

Use the diagram below to answer Questions 5–6.

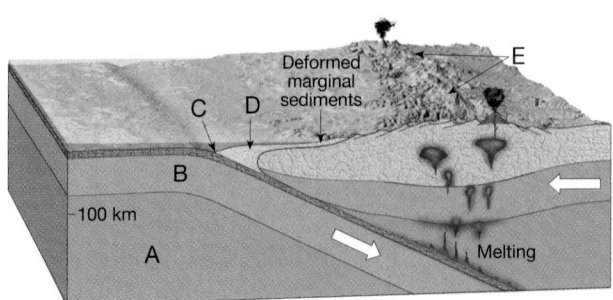

5. What feature is illustrated at the area labeled D in the diagram?
   (A) accretionary wedge
   (B) subducting continental lithosphere
   (C) ocean trench
   (D) continental volcanic arc

6. What types of mountains can form at the type of plate boundary illustrated in the diagram?
   (A) upwarped mountains and volcanic mountains
   (B) volcanic mountains and fault-block mountains
   (C) volcanic mountains and folded mountains
   (D) folded mountains and upwarped mountains

7. Describe the concept of isostasy.

8. Briefly describe what grabens and horsts are and how they form.

9. What type of tectonic settings are grabens and horsts commonly associated with? Give an example of an area where these structures are found.

Mountain Building away from Plate Margins

In the American West, extending from the Front Range of the southern Rocky Mountains across the Colorado Plateau and through the Basin and Range Province, the topography consists of lofty peaks and elevated plateaus. According to the plate tectonics model, you would expect mountain belts to be produced along continental margins and convergent plate boundaries. But this mountainous region extends inland almost 1600 kilometers, far from the nearest plate boundary.

The Laramide Orogeny

The portion of the Rocky Mountains that extends from southern Montana to New Mexico was produced by a period of uplift known as the Laramide Orogeny. This event, which created some of the most picturesque scenery in the United States, peaked about 60 million years ago.

The event that may have triggered the Laramide Orogeny started with the nearly horizontal subduction of the Farallon plate eastward beneath North America. As the diagrams show, this plate extended inland as far as the Black Hills of South Dakota. As the subducted slab scraped beneath the continent, compressional forces started a period of tectonic activity. About 65 million years ago the Farallon plate began to sink into the mantle. As this relatively cool plate gradually separated from the lithosphere above, it was replaced by hot rock that upwelled from the mantle. Thus, according to this scenario, the hot mantle provided the buoyancy to raise the southern Rockies, as well as the Colorado Plateau and the Basin and Range Province.

Basin and Range

In the southern Rockies this event uplifted large blocks of ancient basement rocks along high-angle faults. This produced mountains separated by large basins that became filled with sediment as the mountains eroded. The upwelling that is associated with the Basin and Range Province started about 50 million years ago and remains active today. Here the buoyancy of the warm material caused upwarping and rifting that elongated the overlying crust by 200 to 300 kilometers. The lower crust is ductile and easily stretched. The upper crust, on the other hand, is brittle and deforms by faulting. The extension and faulting broke the uplifted crust, causing individual blocks to shift. The high portions of these tilted blocks make up the mountain ranges, whereas their low areas form the basins, now partially filled with sediment.

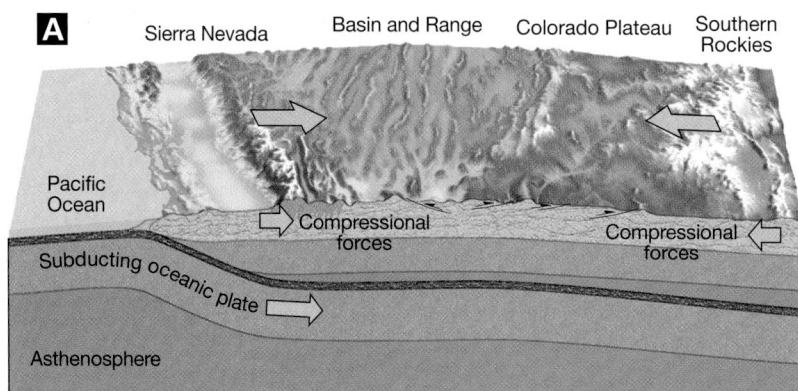

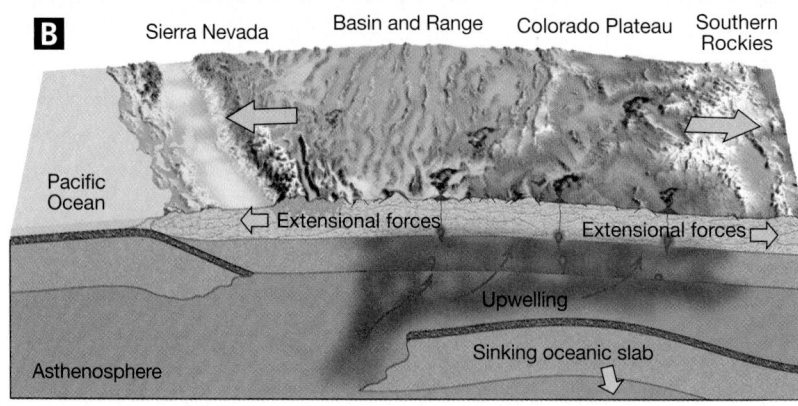

A Nearly horizontal subduction of an oceanic plate initiated a period of tectonic activity. **B** Sinking of this oceanic slab allowed for upwelling of hot mantle material that buoyantly raised the crust.

people and the ENVIRONMENT

Damaging Earthquakes East of the Rockies

When you think of earthquakes, you probably think of California and Japan. However, six major earthquakes have occurred in the central and eastern United States since colonial times. Three of these had estimated moment magnitudes of 7.3, 7.0, and 7.5, and they were centered near the Mississippi River Valley in southeastern Missouri. Occurring on December 16, 1811, January 23, 1812, and February 7, 1812, these earthquakes, plus numerous smaller tremors, destroyed the town of New Madrid, Missouri, triggered massive landslides, and caused damage over a six-state area. The course of the Mississippi River was altered, and Tennessee's Reelfoot Lake was enlarged. Chimneys toppled in Cincinnati, Ohio, and Richmond, Virginia, while Boston residents, located 1770 kilometers away, felt the tremor.

Damage to Charleston, South Carolina, caused by the August 31, 1886 earthquake.

Memphis, Tennessee, the largest population center in the New Madrid area today, is located on unconsolidated floodplain deposits. Therefore, buildings are more susceptible to damage than similar structures built on bedrock. It has been estimated that if earthquakes the size of New Madrid events were to strike in the next decade, they would result in casualties in the thousands and damages in tens of billions of dollars.

Damaging earthquakes that occurred in Aurora, Illinois (1909), and Valentine, Texas (1931), remind us that other areas in the central United States are vulnerable.

The greatest historical earthquake in the eastern states occurred August 31, 1886, in Charleston, South Carolina. The event, which spanned 1 minute, caused 60 deaths, numerous injuries, and great economic loss within 200 kilometers of Charleston. Within 8 minutes, effects were felt as far away as Chicago and St. Louis, where strong vibrations shook the upper floors of buildings, causing people to rush outdoors. In Charleston alone, over 100 buildings were destroyed, and 90 percent of the remaining structures were damaged. It was difficult to find a chimney still standing as the photograph shows.

Numerous other strong earthquakes have been recorded in the eastern United States. New England and adjacent areas have experienced sizable shocks since colonial times. The first reported earthquake in the Northeast took place in Plymouth, Massachusetts, in 1683, and was followed in 1755 by the destructive Cambridge, Massachusetts, earthquake. Moreover, ever since records have been kept, New York State alone has experienced over 300 earthquakes large enough to be felt.

Earthquakes in the central and eastern United States occur far less frequently than in California. Yet history indicates that the East is vulnerable. Further, these shocks east of the Rockies have generally produced structural damage over a larger area than counterparts of similar magnitude in California. The reason is that the underlying bedrock in the central and eastern United States is older and more rigid. As a result, seismic waves are able to travel greater distances with less weakening than in the western United States. It is estimated that for earthquakes of similar magnitude, the region of maximum ground motion in the East may be up to 10 times larger than in the West. Therefore, the higher rate of earthquake occurrence in the western United States is balanced somewhat by the fact that central and eastern U.S. quakes can damage larger areas.

12 Geologic Time

CONCEPTS
— in Action —

Exploration Lab
Fossil Occurrence and the Age of Rocks

Understanding Earth
Using Tree Rings to Date and Study the Recent Past

 **GEODe** Geologic Time
EARTH SCIENCE ↳ Relative Dating
Radiometric Dating
Geologic Time Scale

 **Video Field Trip**

Grand Canyon

Take a field trip to the Grand Canyon with Discovery Channel and get a scenic glimpse of Earth's history. Answer the following questions after watching the video.

1. How was the Grand Canyon formed?

2. What kinds of historic records are contained within the Canyon's walls?

Go Online
PHSchool.com

For: Chapter 12 Resources
Visit: PHSchool.com
Web Code: cjk-9999

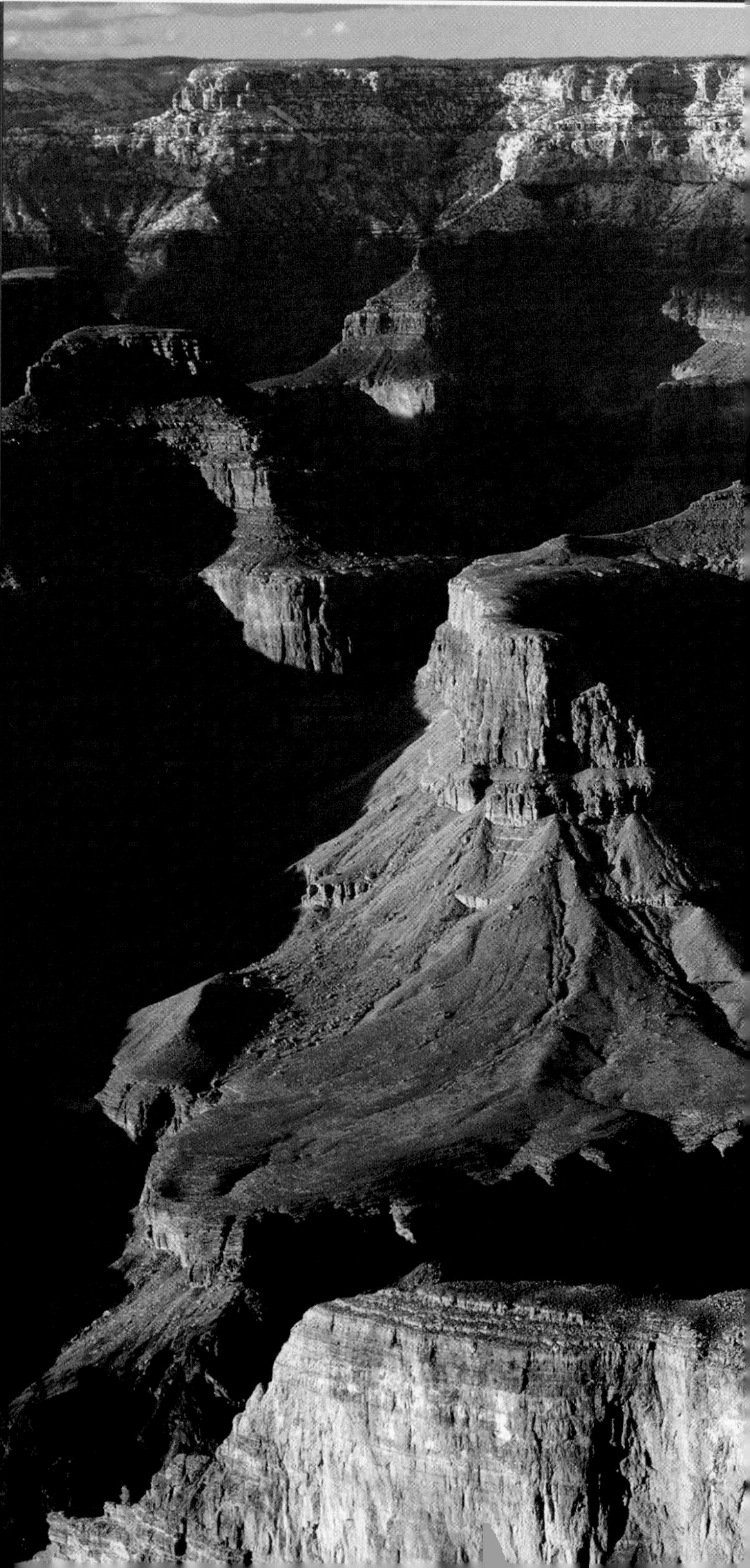

The rock layers exposed in Arizona's Grand ▶ Canyon contain clues to hundreds of millions of years of Earth history.

HISTORICAL GEOLOGY

Chapter Preview

Inquiry Activity

What Can Become a Fossil?

Procedure

1. Obtain a set of samples from your teacher.

2. Using a magnifying glass and microscope, examine each sample carefully.

3. Separate those items that you think have a good chance of becoming a fossil.

Think About It

1. **Observing and Inferring** What characteristics do the samples have that led you to select them as possible candidates for fossilization?

2. **Hypothesizing** What do you think needs to happen to these objects in order for them to become fossilized?

3. **Designing Experiments** Outline an experiment to test your answers to Questions 1 and 2.

Reading Focus

Key Concepts

- How do rocks allow geologists to interpret Earth's history?
- How does uniformitarianism help explain Earth's features?
- How do geologists use relative dating in their work?
- What are the key principles of relative dating?
- What do unconformities represent?

Vocabulary

- uniformitarianism
- relative dating
- law of superposition
- principle of original horizontality
- principle of cross-cutting relationships
- unconformity
- correlation

Reading Strategy

Identifying Main Ideas Copy and expand the table below. As you read, fill in the first column with a main idea and add details that support it in the second column.

Main Idea	Details
1. _____a. ?_____	_____b. ?_____
2. _____c. ?_____	_____d. ?_____
3. _____e. ?_____	_____f. ?_____

Figure 1 Exploring the Grand Canyon A John Wesley Powell, pioneering geologist and the second director of the U.S. Geological Survey. **B** Start of the expedition from Green River station.

In the 18th and 19th centuries, scientists recognized that Earth had a very long history and that Earth's physical features must have taken a long time to form. But they had no way of knowing Earth's true age. A geologic time scale was developed that showed the sequence, or order, of events based on several principles of relative dating. What are these principles? What part do fossils play? In this chapter you will learn the answers to these questions.

Rocks Record Earth History

In 1869, Major John Wesley Powell, shown in Figure 1A, led an expedition down the Colorado River and through the Grand Canyon, shown in Figure 1B. Powell realized that the evidence for an ancient Earth was concealed in its rocks. Powell was impressed with the record of Earth's history contained in the rocks exposed along the walls of the Grand Canyon. **Rocks record geological events and changing life forms of the past.** Erosion has removed a lot of Earth's rock record but enough of it remains to allow much of the story to be studied and interpreted.

Geological events by themselves, however, have little meaning until they are put into a time perspective. The geologic time scale revolutionized the way people think about time and how they perceive our planet. **We have learned that Earth is much older than anyone had previously imagined and that its surface and interior have been changed by the same geological processes that continue today.**

A Brief History of Geology

The primary goal of geologists is to interpret Earth's history. By studying rocks, especially sedimentary rocks, geologists can begin to understand and explain the past.

In the mid-1600s, Archbishop James Ussher constructed a chronology or time line of both human and Earth history in which he determined that Earth was more than five thousand years old. He believed Earth had been created in 4004 B.C. Ussher published his chronology, and his book earned widespread acceptance among Europe's scientific and religious leaders.

In the late 1700s, James Hutton, a Scottish physician and gentleman farmer, published his *Theory of the Earth*. In this work, Hutton put forth the fundamental principle of **uniformitarianism,** which simply states that the physical, chemical, and biological laws that operate today have also operated in the geologic past. **Uniformitarianism means that the forces and processes that we observe today have been at work for a very long time.** To understand the geologic past, we must first understand present-day processes and their results.

Today, scientists understand that these same processes may not always have had the same relative importance or operated at precisely the same rate. Moreover, some important geologic processes are not currently observable, but evidence that they occur is well established. For example, we know that Earth has been hit by large meteorites even though we have no human witnesses. Such events altered Earth's crust, modified its climate, and strongly influenced life on the planet.

The acceptance of uniformitarianism meant the acceptance of a very long history for Earth. It is important to remember that although many features of our physical landscape may seem to be unchanging over our lifetimes, they are still changing, but on time scales of hundreds, thousands, or even millions of years.

 **Reading Checkpoint** *How do the laws that govern geological processes change through time?*

Relative Dating—Key Principles

During the late 1800s and early 1900s, several attempts were made to determine the age of Earth. To establish a relative time scale, a few basic principles or rules had to be discovered and applied. These principles were major breakthroughs in thinking at the time, and their discovery and acceptance was an important scientific achievement.

Relative dating means identifying which rock units formed first, second, third, and so on. **Relative dating tells us the sequence in which events occurred, not how long ago they occurred.**

Figure 2 Ordering the Grand Canyon's History The law of superposition can be applied to the layers exposed in the Grand Canyon. **Interpreting Illustrations** *Which layer is the oldest? youngest?*

Kaibab Limestone

Younger

Toroweap Formation

Coconino Sandstone

Hermit Shale

Supai Group

Law of Superposition Nicolaus Steno, a Danish anatomist, geologist, and priest (1636–1686), is credited with describing a set of geologic observations that are the basis of relative dating. The first observation is the **law of superposition.** 🔑 **The law of superposition states that in an undeformed sequence of sedimentary rocks, each bed is older than the one above it and younger than the one below it.** Although it may seem obvious that a rock layer could not be deposited unless it had something older beneath it for support, it was not until 1669 that Steno stated the principle. This rule also applies to other surface-deposited materials, such as lava flows and beds of ash from volcanic eruptions. Applying the law of superposition to the beds exposed in the upper portion of the Grand Canyon, shown in Figure 2, you can easily place the layers in their proper order.

Figure 3 Disturbed Rock Layers Rock layers that are folded or tilted must have been moved into that position by crustal disturbances after their deposition. These folded layers are exposed in the Namib Desert (southwestern Africa).

Principle of Original Horizontality

Another of Steno's observations is called the **principle of original horizontality.** 🔑 **The principle of original horizontality means that layers of sediment are generally deposited in a horizontal position.** If you see rock layers that are flat, it means they haven't been disturbed and they still are in their original horizontal position. The layers in the Grand Canyon shown on pages 334–335 and in Figure 2 clearly demonstrate this. However, the rock layers shown in Figure 3 have been tilted and bent. This tilting means they must have been moved into this position sometime after their deposition.

Reading Checkpoint

To what rock type can the law of superposition and the principle of original horizontality be best applied?

Principle of Cross-Cutting Relationships

The principle of cross-cutting relationships is Steno's third observation. The **principle of cross-cutting relationships** states that when a fault cuts through rock layers, or when magma intrudes other rocks and crystallizes, we can assume that the fault or intrusion is younger than the rocks affected. For example, in Figure 4 you can see that fault A occurred after the sandstone layer was deposited because it "broke" the layer. However, fault A occurred before the conglomerate was laid down, because that layer is unbroken. Because they cut through the layers of sedimentary rock, the faults and dikes clearly must have occurred after the sedimentary layers were deposited.

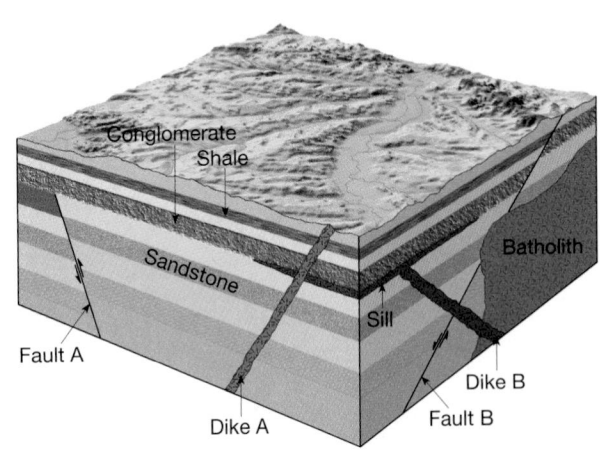

Inclusions Sometimes inclusions can help the relative dating process. Inclusions are pieces of one rock unit that are contained within another. The rock unit next to the one containing the inclusions must have been there first in order to provide the rock fragments. Therefore, the rock unit containing inclusions is the younger of the two. Figure 5 provides an example. The photograph in Figure 5C shows inclusions of igneous rock within a layer of sedimentary rock. How did they get there? The inclusions indicate that the sedimentary layer was deposited on top of the weathered igneous mass. The sedimentary layer must be younger than the igneous rock because the sedimentary layer contains pieces of the igneous rock. We know the layer was not intruded upon by magma from below that later crystallized because the sedimentary rock is still horizontal.

Figure 4 Applying Steno's Principles Cross-cutting relationships are an important principle used in relative dating. An intrusive rock body is younger than the rocks it intrudes. A fault is younger than the rock layers it cuts.
Interpreting Diagrams *What is the age relationship between the batholith, dike B, dike A, and the sill?*

Formation of Inclusions

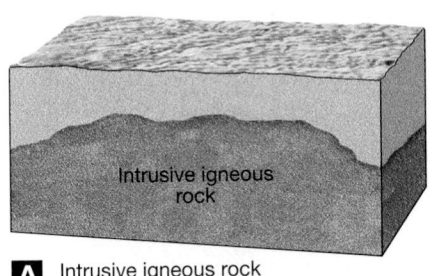

A Intrusive igneous rock

B Exposure and weathering of intrusive igneous rock

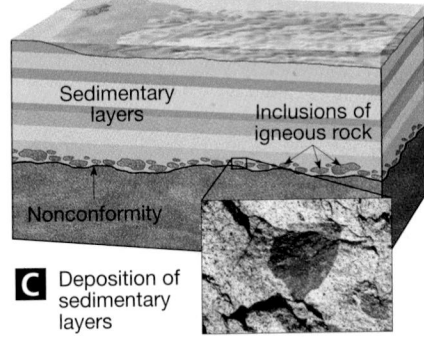

C Deposition of sedimentary layers

Figure 5 A A mass of igneous rock formed from magma that intruded an older rock body. **B** The older rock erodes and exposes the igneous rock to weathering. **C** Sedimentary rock layers form on top of the weathered igneous rock.

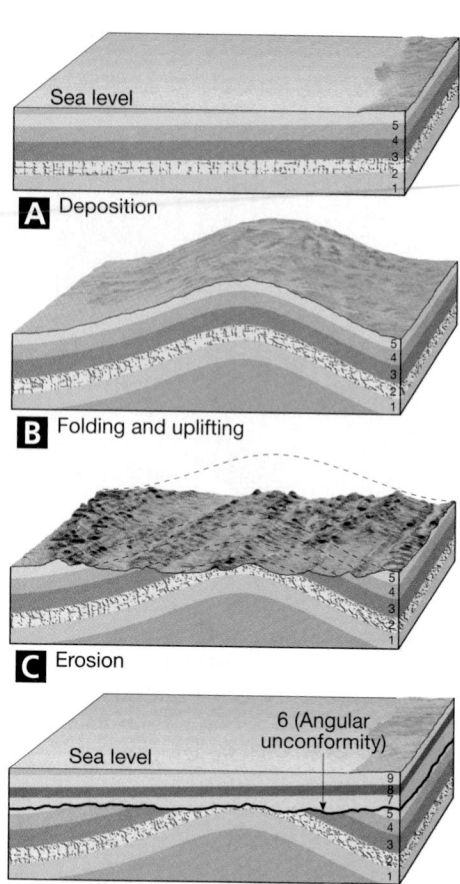

A Deposition

B Folding and uplifting

C Erosion

6 (Angular unconformity)

Sea level

D Subsidence and renewed deposition

Figure 6 Formation of an Angular Conformity
An angular unconformity represents an extended period during which deformation and erosion occurred.

Figure 7 A Record of Uplift, Erosion, and Deposition This cross section through the Grand Canyon illustrates the three basic types of unconformities.

Unconformities Casual observation of layers of rock may look like they represent a complete geologic history of an area. However, no place on Earth is geologically complete. Throughout Earth's history, the deposition of sediment has been interrupted again and again. All such breaks in the rock record are termed **unconformities.** 🔑 **An unconformity represents a long period during which deposition stopped, erosion removed previously formed rocks, and then deposition resumed.** In each case uplift and erosion are followed by subsidence and renewed sedimentation, as shown in Figure 6. Unconformities are important features because they represent significant geologic events in Earth history. Moreover, their recognition helps us identify what intervals of time are not represented in the rock record.

A geologic cross section of the Grand Canyon is shown in Figure 7. It shows the three basic types of unconformities: angular unconformities, disconformities, and nonconformities. Perhaps the most easily recognized unconformity is an angular unconformity. It appears as tilted or folded sedimentary rocks that are overlain by younger, more flat-lying strata. 🔑 **An angular unconformity indicates that during the pause in deposition, a period of deformation (folding or tilting) and erosion occurred.**

Two sedimentary rock layers that are separated by an erosional surface are called a disconformity. Disconformities are more common than angular unconformities, but they are more difficult to recognize. The third basic type of unconformity is a nonconformity. Nonconformities mean the erosional surface separates older metamorphic or intrusive igneous rocks from younger sedimentary rocks.

 **Reading Checkpoint** *What are the three basic types of unconformities?*

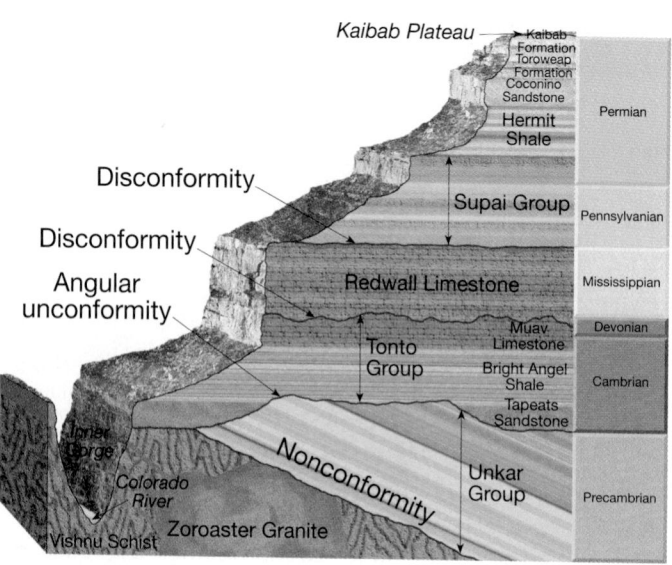

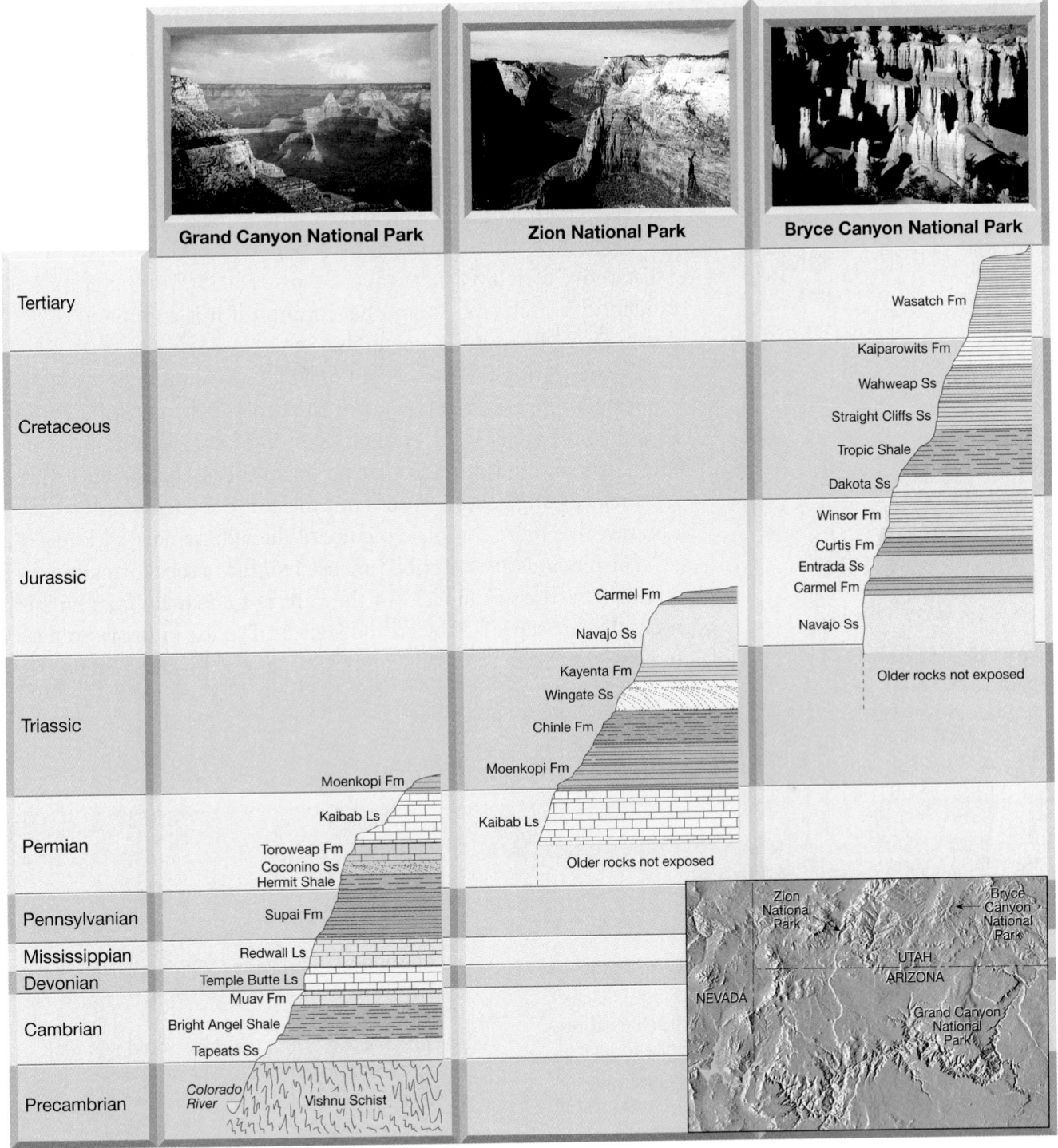

Grand Canyon National Park

Zion National Park

Bryce Canyon National Park

Tertiary

Cretaceous

Jurassic

Triassic

Permian

Pennsylvanian

Mississippian

Devonian

Cambrian

Precambrian

Wasatch Fm

Kaiparowits Fm

Wahweap Ss

Straight Cliffs Ss

Tropic Shale

Dakota Ss

Winsor Fm

Curtis Fm

Entrada Ss

Carmel Fm

Navajo Ss

Older rocks not exposed

Carmel Fm

Navajo Ss

Kayenta Fm

Wingate Ss

Chinle Fm

Moenkopi Fm

Kaibab Ls

Older rocks not exposed

Moenkopi Fm

Kaibab Ls

Toroweap Fm

Coconino Ss

Hermit Shale

Supai Fm

Redwall Ls

Temple Butte Ls

Muav Fm

Bright Angel Shale

Tapeats Ss

Colorado River

Vishnu Schist

Zion National Park

Bryce Canyon National Park

UTAH

ARIZONA

NEVADA

Grand Canyon National Park

Figure 8 Correlation of strata at three locations on the Colorado Plateau reveals a more complete view of the extent of sedimentary rocks in the region.

Correlation of Rock Layers

To develop a geologic time scale that can be applied to the entire Earth, rocks of similar age in different regions must be matched up. This task is called **correlation.**

Within a small area, you can correlate the rocks of one locality with those of another by simply walking along the outcropping edges. However, this might not be possible when the rocks are covered by soil and vegetation. You can correct this problem by noting the position of a distinctive rock layer in a sequence of strata. Or, you might be able to identify a rock layer in another location if it is composed of very distinctive or uncommon minerals.

By correlating the rocks from one place to another, it is possible to create a more complete view of the geologic history of a region. Figure 8 on page 341, for example, shows the correlation of strata at three sites on the Colorado Plateau in southern Utah and northern Arizona. No single location contains the entire sequence. But correlation reveals a more complete picture of the sedimentary rock record.

The methods just described are used to trace a rock formation over a relatively short distance. But they are not adequate for matching rocks that are separated by great distances. The use of fossils comes in to play when trying to correlate rocks separated by great distances.

Go Online

SciLINKS NSTA

For: Links on relative dating
Visit: www.SciLinks.org
Web Code: cjn-4122

Section 12.1 Assessment

Reviewing Concepts

1. 🔵 What information do rocks provide to geologists?

2. 🔵 What does uniformitarianism tell us about processes at work on Earth's surface today?

3. 🔵 How can relative dating be used in geology?

4. 🔵 List and briefly describe Steno's principles.

5. 🔵 What is an unconformity?

6. What is the name of the process in which rock layers in different regions are matched?

Critical Thinking

7. **Applying Concepts** How did the acceptance of uniformitarianism change the way scientists viewed Earth?

8. **Comparing and Contrasting** How does Archbishop Ussher's work compare to that of James Hutton? What did each do to back up their ideas?

9. **Summarizing** What features would you look for to correlate rocks from one area to another?

Writing in Science

Descriptive Paragraph Imagine that you are hiking down into the Grand Canyon. Use some of Steno's principles to write a paragraph describing what you see, how old it all is, and how it was deposited.

12.2 Fossils: Evidence of Past Life

Key Concepts

- What are fossils?
- What determines if an organism will become a fossil?
- What is the principle of fossil succession?

Vocabulary

- fossil
- index fossil

Reading Strategy

Monitoring Your Understanding Draw and complete a chart like the one below. After you finish this section, correct or add details as needed.

Fossils	How Fossils Form	How Fossils are Used
a. ___?___	b. ___?___	c. ___?___

Fossils are important tools for interpreting the geologic past. **Fossils are the remains or traces of prehistoric life. They are important components of sediment and sedimentary rocks.** Knowing the nature of the life forms that existed at a particular time helps researchers understand past environmental conditions. Further, fossils are important time indicators. They play a key role in correlating rocks of similar ages that are from different places.

Fossil Formation

There are many types of fossils. **The type of fossil that is formed is determined by the conditions under which an organism died and how it was buried.**

Unaltered Remains Some remains of organisms—such as teeth, bones, and shells—may not have been altered, or changed, hardly at all over time. It is far less common to find the remains of an entire animal, including flesh. In Siberia, archaeologists recently found a fully preserved, frozen mammoth, shown in Figure 9. This is an excellent example of unaltered remains.

Altered Remains The remains of an organism are likely to be changed over time. Fossils often become petrified, or "turned into stone." When a fossil is petrified, mineral-rich water soaks into the small cavities and pores of the original organism. The minerals precipitate from the water and fill the spaces. The log of petrified wood in Figure 10E shows the result. In other instances, the cell walls or other solid material of an organism are replaced with mineral matter. Sometimes the microscopic details of the replaced structure are preserved.

Figure 9 Unaltered Remains
Frozen animals are an extreme and unusual type of fossilization.

Figure 10 Types of Fossilization
Six examples are shown here.
A A fossil bee was preserved as a thin carbon film. **B** Impressions are common fossils and often show considerable detail. **C** An insect in amber **D** This dinosaur footprint was found in fine-grained limestone near Tuba City, Arizona. **E** Petrified wood in Petrified Forest National Park, Arizona **F** Natural casts of shelled organisms called ammonites

Molds and casts are another common type of fossil. A fossil mold is created when a shell or other structure is buried in sediment and then dissolved by underground water. The mold accurately reflects only the shape and surface markings of the organism. It doesn't reveal any information about its internal structure. Cast fossils (Figure 10F) are created if the hollow spaces of a mold are later filled with mineral matter.

A type of fossilization called carbonization is particularly effective in preserving leaves and delicate animal forms. Carbonization occurs when an organism is buried under fine sediment. As time passes, pressure squeezes out the liquid and gaseous components of an organism and leaves behind a thin residue of carbon, like that shown in Figure 10A. Black shale often contains abundant carbonized remains. If the carbon film is lost from a fossil preserved in fine-grain sediment, a replica of the surface, or an impression, may remain. The impression may still show considerable detail. An impression is shown in Figure 10B.

Delicate organisms, such as insects, are difficult to preserve, so they are relatively rare in the fossil record. For a fossil of an insect to form, the insect must be protected from any pressure that would crush it. Some insects have been preserved in amber—the hardened resin of ancient trees. The fly in Figure 10C was preserved after being trapped in a drop of the sticky resin.

Indirect Evidence Trace fossils are indirect evidence of prehistoric life. Tracks, like those in Figure 10D, are animal footprints made in soft sediment that was later compacted and cemented. Burrows are holes made by an animal in sediment, wood, or rock that were later filled with mineral matter and preserved. Some of the oldest known fossils are believed to be worm burrows. Coprolites are fossils of dung and stomach contents. These can often provide useful information regarding the food habits of organisms. Gastroliths are highly polished stomach stones that were used in the grinding of food by some extinct reptiles.

Reading Checkpoint

What are three types of fossils?

Conditions Favoring Preservation  **Two conditions are important for preservation: rapid burial and the possession of hard parts.** The soft parts of a dead animal are usually eaten by scavengers or decomposed by bacteria. However, if the remains are buried quickly by sediment, they are protected from the environment. Then there is a chance that the organism will become a fossil. In addition, organisms have a better chance of being preserved if they have hard parts such as shells, bones, and teeth. Fossils of hard parts dominate the fossil record even though fossils of soft-bodied animals such as jellyfish and worms do exist.

Reading Checkpoint *Why are soft parts of dead animals rarely preserved?*

Fossils and Correlation

In the late 18th century, William Smith, an English engineer and canal builder, demonstrated the usefulness of fossils to geology. He found that fossils weren't randomly distributed throughout the rock layers he cut through. Instead, each layer contained a distinct assortment of fossils that did not occur in the layers above or below it. Smith also noted that sedimentary rock layers in distant areas could be identified and correlated by the distinct fossils they contained.

Based on Smith's observations and the findings of many geologists who followed, one of the most important principles in historical geology was formulated. **The principle of fossil succession states that fossil organisms succeed one another in a definite and determinable order. Therefore, any time period can be recognized by its fossil content.**

Based on the rock record from around the world, geologists have identified an order of fossils: an Age of Trilobites, an Age of Fishes, an Age of Coal Swamps, an Age of Reptiles, and an Age of Mammals. These "ages" correspond to particular time periods and are characterized by distinct and abundant fossils. This same order of dominant organisms is found on every continent.

Once fossils were recognized as time indicators, they became the most useful means of correlating rocks of similar age in different regions. Geologists pay particular attention to **index fossils.** **Index fossils are widespread geographically, are limited to a short span of geologic time, and occur in large numbers.** Their presence provides an important method of matching rocks of the same age. Rock formations, however, do not always contain a specific index fossil. Then groups of fossils are used to establish the age of a rock layer. Figure 11 shows how an assemblage of fossils can be used to date rocks more precisely than using only one kind of fossil.

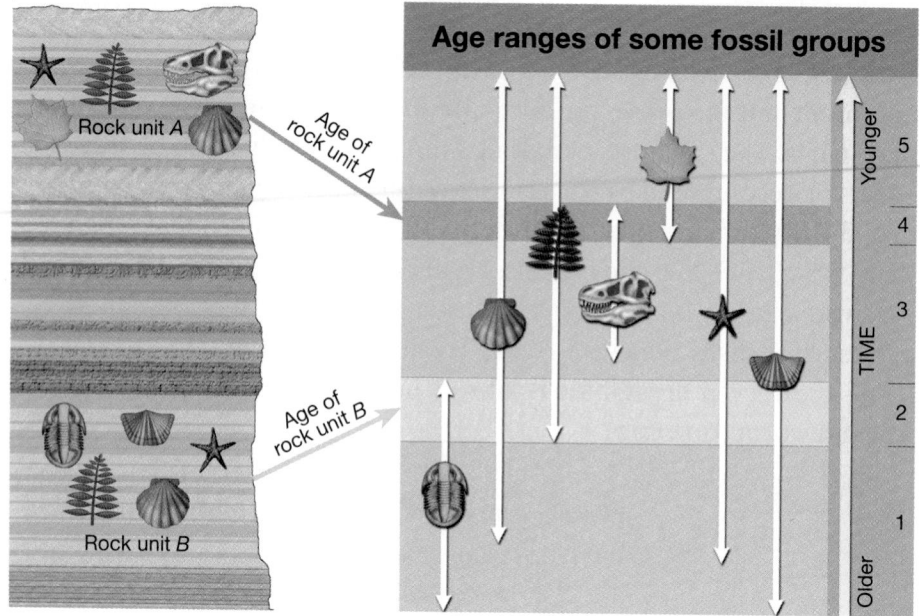

Figure 11 Overlapping ranges of fossils help date rocks more exactly than using a single fossil. The fossils contained in rock unit A all have overlapping age ranges in time 4. The fossils in rock unit B have overlapping age ranges in time 2.

Age ranges of some fossil groups

Age of rock unit A

Age of rock unit B

Rock unit A

Rock unit B

Younger

Older

TIME

5
4
3
2
1

Interpreting Environments Fossils can also be used to interpret and describe ancient environments. For example, geologists can conclude that a region was once covered by a shallow sea when the remains of certain clam shells are found in the limestone of that region. The geologists might also be able to conclude the approximate position of the ancient shoreline by observing the types and locations of fossils. For instance, fossil animals with thick shells capable of withstanding pounding waves must have lived near shorelines.

Fossils can also indicate the former temperature of the water. Certain present-day corals require warm and shallow tropical seas—like those around Florida and the Bahamas. When similar corals are found in ancient limestones, they indicate that a Florida-like marine environment must have existed when the corals were alive. These examples illustrate how fossils can help unravel the complex story of Earth history.

Section 12.2 Assessment

Reviewing Concepts

1. What are fossils?
2. What conditions are necessary to insure fossilization?
3. What is the principle of fossil succession?

Critical Thinking

4. **Sequencing** Describe how a clam might become a fossil.

5. **Inferring** The remains of a large animal are found in a cave along with a large pile of fossilized dung. How can you incorporate this dung into your studies of this unknown animal?

Connecting Concepts

Relating Ideas How are the law of superposition and the principle of fossil succession related?

12.3 Dating with Radioactivity

Reading Focus

Key Concepts

- What is radioactivity?
- What is half-life?
- What is radiometric dating?
- How is carbon-14 used in radiometric dating?

Vocabulary

- ◆ radioactivity
- ◆ half-life
- ◆ radiometric dating
- ◆ radiocarbon dating

Reading Strategy

Monitoring Your Understanding Preview the key concepts, topics, headings, vocabulary, and figures in this section. Copy the chart below. List two things you expect to learn about each. After reading, state what you learned about each item you listed.

What I expect to learn	What I learned
1. a. ?	b. ?
2. c. ?	d. ?

Today, it is possible to obtain reliable numerical dates for events in the geologic past. For example, we know that Earth is about 4.56 billion years old and that the last dinosaurs became extinct about 65 million years ago. Although these great spans of time are hard to imagine, the vast expanse of geologic time is a reality. In this section you will learn how scientists measure time using radioactivity and radiometric dating.

Basic Atomic Structure

Recall from Chapter 2 that each atom has a nucleus containing protons and neutrons and that the nucleus is orbited by electrons. Electrons have a negative electrical charge and protons have a positive charge. A neutron has no charge. The atomic number of an element is the number of protons in its nucleus. Different elements have different atomic numbers, but atoms of the same element always have the same atomic number. An atom's mass number is the number of protons and neutrons in an atom's nucleus. The number of neutrons can vary, and these variants, or isotopes, have different mass numbers.

Radioactivity

The forces that bind protons and neutrons together in the nucleus are usually strong. However, in some isotopes, the forces binding the protons and neutrons together are not sufficiently strong and the nuclei are unstable. **When nuclei are unstable, they spontaneously break apart, or decay, in a process called radioactivity.** An unstable or radioactive isotope of an element is called the parent. The isotopes that result from the decay of the parent are called the daughter products.

Figure 12 Common Types of Radioactive Decay in each case, the number of protons (atomic number) in the nucleus changes, thus producing a different element.

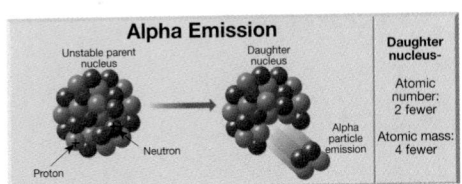

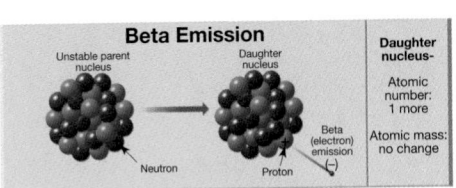

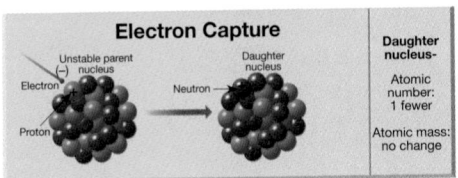

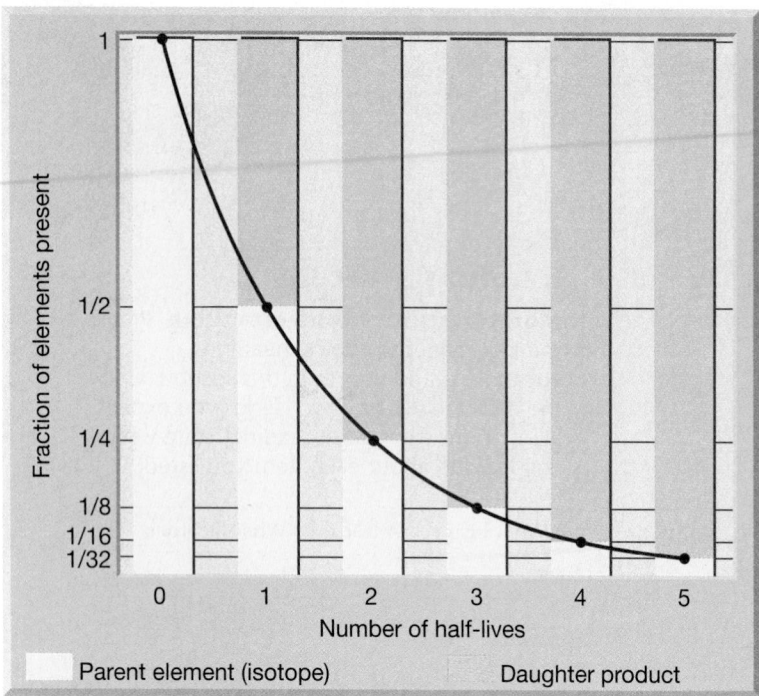

Parent element (isotope)   Daughter product

Figure 13 The Half-Life Decay Curve The radioactive decay curve shows change that is exponential. Half of the radioactive parent remains after one half-life. After a second half-life, one quarter of the parent remains, and so forth. **Interpreting Graphs** *If $\frac{1}{32}$ of the parent material remains, how many half-lives have passed?*

What happens when unstable nuclei break apart? Radioactive decay continues until a stable or non-radioactive isotope is formed. A well-documented decay series is uranium-238, which decays over time to form the stable isotope lead-206. Three common types of radioactive decay are shown in Figure 12 on page 347.

Half-Life

A **half-life** is a common way of expressing the rate of radioactive decay. ●**A half-life is the amount of time necessary for one half of the nuclei in a sample to decay to its stable isotope.** Figure 13 illustrates what occurs when a radioactive parent decays directly into its stable daughter product. If the half-life of a radioactive isotope is known and the parent/daughter ratio can be measured, the age of the sample can be calculated. For example, if the half-life of an unstable isotope is 1 million years, and the parent/daughter ratio is 1:16, the ratio indicates that four half-lives have passed. The sample must be 4 million years old.

What is a half-life?

Radiometric Dating

One of the most important results of the discovery of radioactivity is that it provides a way to calculate the ages of rocks and minerals that contain certain radioactive isotopes. The procedure is called **radiometric dating.** The rates of decay for many isotopes have been precisely measured and do not vary under the physical conditions that exist in Earth's outer layers. ●**Each radioactive isotope has been decaying at a constant rate since the formation of the rocks in which it occurs.** The products of decay have also been accumulating at a constant rate. For example, when uranium is incorporated into a mineral that crystallizes from magma, lead isn't present from previous decay. The radiometric "clock" starts at this point. ●**As the uranium decays, atoms of the daughter product are formed, and measurable amounts of lead eventually accumulate.**

What is a radiometric dating?

Of the many radioactive isotopes that exist in nature, five have proved particularly useful in providing radiometric ages for ancient rocks. The five radioactive isotopes are listed in Table 1.

Table 1 Radioactive Isotopes Frequently Used in Radiometric Dating		
Radioactive Parent	**Stable Daughter Product**	**Currently Accepted Half-Life Values**
Uranium-238	Lead-206	4.5 billion years
Uranium-235	Lead-207	713 million years
Thorium-232	Lead-208	14.1 billion years
Rubidium-87	Strontium-87	47.0 billion years
Potassium-40	Argon-40	1.3 billion years

An accurate radiometric date can be obtained only if the mineral remained in a closed system during the entire period since its formation. If the addition or loss of either parent or daughter isotopes occurs, then it is not possible to calculate a correct date. For example, an important limitation of the potassium-argon method stems from the fact that argon is a gas. Argon may leak from minerals and throw off measurements. Cross-checking of samples, using two different radiometric methods, is done where possible to ensure accuracy. Although the basic principle of radiometric dating is simple, the actual procedure is quite complex. The analysis that determines the quantities of parent and daughter must be painstakingly precise. In addition, some radioactive materials do not decay directly into the stable daughter product. Uranium-238, for example, produces thirteen intermediate unstable daughter products before the fourteenth and final daughter product, the stable isotope lead-206, is produced.

 **Reading Checkpoint** *Why is a closed system necessary in radiometric dating?*

Dating with Carbon-14

To date recent events, carbon-14 is used in a method called **radiocarbon dating.** Carbon-14 is the radioactive isotope of carbon. Carbon-14 is continuously produced in the upper atmosphere. It quickly becomes incorporated into carbon dioxide, which circulates in the atmosphere and is absorbed by living matter. As a result, all organisms—including you—contain a small amount of carbon-14.

Q *In radioactive decay, is there ever a time when all of the parent material is converted into the daughter product?*

A Theoretically, no. During a half-life, half of the parent material is converted into the daughter product. Then half of the remaining parent material is converted to the daughter product in another half life, and so on. By converting only half of the parent material with each half-life, there is never a time when all the parent material would be converted. However, after many half-lives, the parent material can exist in such small amounts that it is essentially undetectable.

For: Links on radioactive dating
Visit: www.SciLinks.org
Web Code: cjn-4124

Figure 14 Carbon-14 is used to date recent events and objects.

While an organism is alive, the decaying radiocarbon is continually replaced. Thus, the ratio of carbon-14 to carbon-12—the stable isotope of carbon—remains constant. **When an organism dies, the amount of carbon-14 gradually decreases as it decays. By comparing the ratio of carbon-14 to carbon-12 in a sample, radiocarbon dates can be determined.**

Because the half-life of carbon-14 is only 5730 years, it can be used to date recent geologic events up to about 75,000 years ago. The age of the object shown in Figure 14 was determined using radiocarbon dating. Carbon-14 has become a valuable tool for anthropologists, archaeologists, and historians, as well as for geologists who study recent Earth history.

Reading Checkpoint *What is compared when dating with carbon-14?*

Importance of Radiometric Dating

Radiometric dating methods have produced thousands of dates for events in Earth's history. Rocks formed on Earth have been dated to be as much as 4 billion years old. Meteorites have been dated at 4.6 billion years old.

Radiometric dating has supported the ideas of James Hutton, Charles Darwin, and others who inferred that geologic time must be immense. Modern dating methods have proved that there has been enough time for the processes we observe to have accomplished tremendous tasks.

Section 12.3 Assessment

Reviewing Concepts

1. What happens to atoms that are radioactive?
2. Explain the concept of half-life.
3. What is needed to do radiometric dating?
4. Describe radiocarbon dating.

Critical Thinking

5. **Explaining Data** A grain of zircon in a sandstone is dated at 3 billion years. But the sandstone is from a unit of rock dated at 250 million years old. Explain how this can be.

6. **Understanding Concepts** How do scientists use half-lives in radiometric dating?

Connecting Concepts

Comparing and Contrasting Discuss the use of radiocarbon dating in determining the age of an ancient civilization.

Using Tree Rings to Date and Study the Recent Past

If you look at the top of a tree stump or at the end of a log, you will see that it is made of a series of concentric rings, like those shown in Figure 15. Every year in temperate regions trees add a layer of new wood under the bark. Each of these tree rings becomes larger in diameter outward from the center. During favorable environmental conditions, a wide ring is produced. During unfavorable environmental conditions, a narrow ring is produced. Trees growing at the same time in the same region show similar tree-ring patterns.

Because a single growth ring is usually added each year, you can determine the age of the tree by counting the rings. Cutting down a tree to count the rings is not necessary anymore. Scientists can use small, non-destructive core samples from living trees. The dating and study of annual rings in trees is called dendrochronology.

To make the most effective use of tree rings, extended patterns known as ring chronologies are established. They are produced by comparing the patterns of rings among trees in an area. If the same pattern can be identified in two samples, one of which has been dated, the second sample can be dated from the first by matching the ring pattern common to both. This technique, called cross dating, is illustrated in Figure 16. Tree-ring chronologies extending back for thousands of years have been established for some regions. To date a timber sample of unknown age, its ring pattern is matched against the reference chronology.

Tree-ring chronologies have important applications in such disciplines as climate, geology, ecology, and archaeology. For example, tree rings are used to reconstruct long-term climate variations within a certain region. Knowledge of such variations is of great value in studying and understanding the recent record of climate change.

Dendrochronology provides useful numerical dates for events in the historic and recent prehistoric past. Because tree rings are a storehouse of data, they are a valuable tool in the reconstruction of past environments.

Figure 15 Each year's growth for a tree can be seen as a ring. Because the amount of growth (thickness of a ring) depends upon precipitation and temperature, tree rings are useful records of past climates.

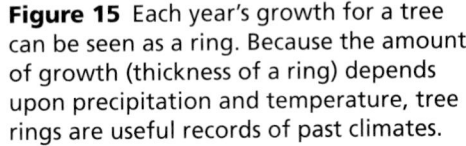

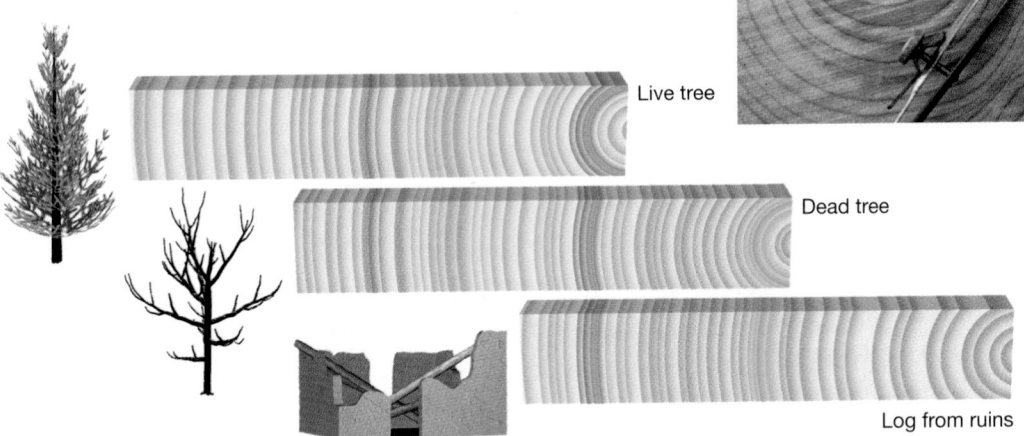

Live tree

Dead tree

Log from ruins

Figure 16 Using Tree Rings to Date Ancient Civilizations Cross dating is used to date an archaeological site by correlating tree-ring patterns using wood from trees of three different ages. First, a tree-ring chronology for the area is established using cores extracted from living trees. This chronology is extended further back in time by matching overlapping patterns from older, dead trees. Finally, cores taken from beams inside the ruin are dated using the chronology established from the other two sites.

12.4 The Geologic Time Scale

Reading Focus

Key Concepts

- What is the geologic time scale?
- How is the geologic time scale constructed?
- What are some complications in dating rocks?

Vocabulary

- geologic time scale
- eon
- era
- period
- epoch

Reading Strategy

Outlining As you read, make an outline of the important ideas in this section. Use the green headings as the main topics and fill in details from the remainder of the text.

The Geologic Time Scale
I. Structure of the Time Scale
A. _____?_____
B. _____?_____

Historians divide human history into certain periods, such as the Renaissance and the Industrial Revolution, based on human events. Thus you can produce a timeline of human history. Geologists have done something similar. **Based on their interpretations of the rock record, geologists have divided Earth's 4.56-billion-year history into units that represent specific amounts of time. Taken together, these time spans make up the geologic time scale.** The geologic time scale is shown in Figure 17. The major units of the time scale were described during the nineteenth century, principally by scientists working in Western Europe and Great Britain. Because radiometric dating was unavailable at that time, the entire time scale was created using methods of relative dating. It was only in the twentieth century that radiometric dating permitted numerical dates to be added.

Structure of the Time Scale

As shown in Figure 17, the geologic time scale is divided into eons, eras, periods, and epochs. **Eons represent the greatest expanses of time. Eons are divided into eras. Each era is subdivided into periods. Finally, periods are divided into still smaller units called epochs.** The eon that began about 540 million years ago is the **Phanerozoic,** a term derived from Greek words meaning "visible life." It is an appropriate description because the rocks and deposits of the Phanerozoic Eon contain abundant fossils that document major changes in life-forms over time.

 *What is the geologic time scale divided into?*

 There are three eras within the Phanerozoic. The Paleozoic, which means "ancient life," the Mesozoic, which means "middle life," and the Cenozoic, which means "recent life." As the names imply, the eras are bounded by profound worldwide changes in life forms.  Each era is subdivided into periods, each of which is characterized by a somewhat less profound change in life forms as compared with the eras.

Reading Checkpoint *What do each of the eras within the Phanerozoic Eon mean?*

The periods of the Cenozoic are divided into still smaller units called epochs. The epochs of other periods, however, are not usually referred to by specific names. Instead, the terms early, middle, and late are generally applied to the epochs of these earlier periods.

Precambrian Time

Notice that the detail of the geologic time scale doesn't begin until the start of the Cambrian Period, about 540 million years ago. The more than 4 billion years prior to the Cambrian is divided into eons, as shown in Figure 17. The common name for this huge expanse of time is the Precambrian. The view of the time scale on page 357 gives you a better idea of the expanse of time represented by the Precambrian.

Although it represents about 88 percent of Earth history, the Precambrian is not divided into nearly as many smaller time units as is the Phanerozoic eon. The reason is simple. Precambrian history is not known in great enough detail. The amount of information that geologists have acquired about Earth's past decreases substantially the farther back in time you go. During Precambrian time, there were fewer life forms. These life forms are more difficult to identify and the rocks have been disturbed often.

Reading Checkpoint *Why does detail in the geologic time scale begin at the Cambrian Period?*

Eon	Era	Period	Epoch	Millions of years ago
Phanerozoic	Cenozoic	Quaternary	Holocene	0.01
			Pleistocene	1.8
		Tertiary	Pliocene	5.3
			Miocene	23.8
			Oligocene	33.7
			Eocene	54.8
			Paleocene	65.0
	Mesozoic	Cretaceous		144
		Jurassic		206
		Triassic		248
	Paleozoic	Permian		290
		Carboniferous — Pennsylvanian		323
		Carboniferous — Mississippian		354
		Devonian		417
		Silurian		443
		Ordovician		490
		Cambrian		540
Proterozoic		Precambrian		
Archean				
Hadean				

Figure 17 The Geologic Time Scale The numerical dates were added long after the time scale had been established using relative dating techniques.

For: Links on the geologic time scale
Visit: www.SciLinks.org
Web Code: cjn-4125

Difficulties With the Geologic Time Scale

Although reasonably accurate numerical dates have been determined for the periods of the geologic time scale, the task is not easy. The basic problem comes from the fact that not all rocks can be dated by radiometric methods. For a radiometric date to be useful, all minerals in the rock must have formed at about the same time. For this reason, radioactive isotopes can be used to determine when minerals in an igneous rock crystallized and when pressure and heat made new minerals in a metamorphic rock.

However, samples of sedimentary rock can rarely be dated directly by radiometric means. **A sedimentary rock may contain particles that contain radioactive isotopes, but these particles are not the same age as the rock in which they occur.** The sediments that are eventually cemented together into a sedimentary rock have been weathered from older rocks. Radiometric dating would not be accurate since sedimentary rock forms from so many older rock particles.

Radiometric dating of metamorphic rocks may also be difficult. **The age of a particular mineral in a metamorphic rock does not necessarily represent the time when the rock first formed. Instead, the date may indicate when the rock was metamorphosed.**

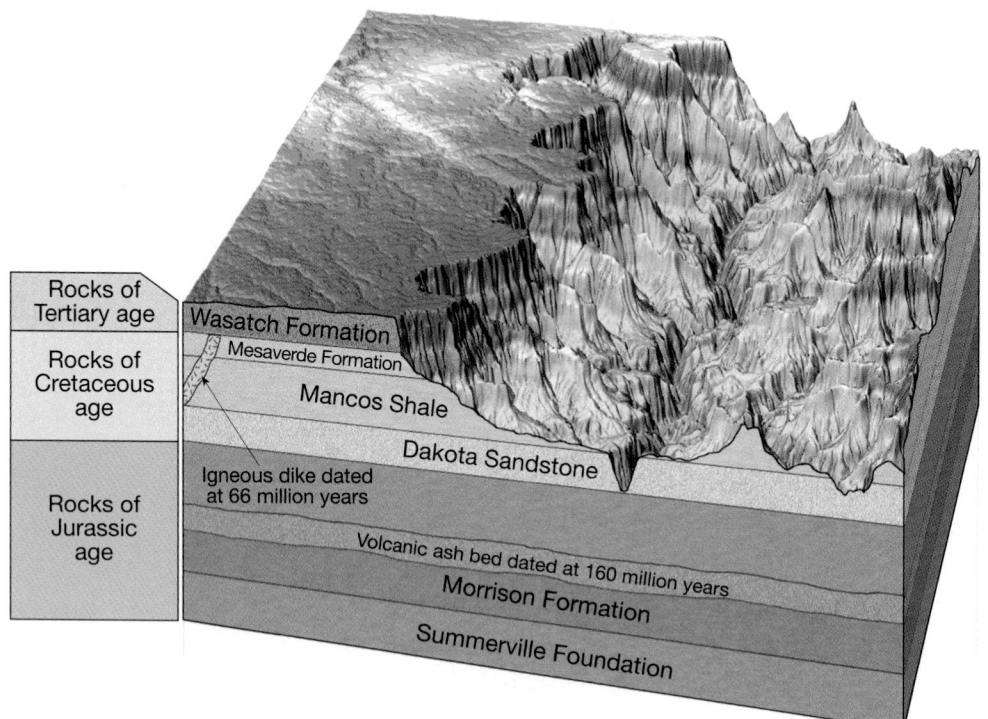

Figure 18 Using Radiometric Methods to Help Date Sedimentary Rocks
Numerical dates for sedimentary layers are usually determined by examining their relationship to igneous rocks.
Interpreting Illustrations *Which of Steno's principles (pages 338–339) can you use to interpret the relative ages of these rock layers?*

If samples of sedimentary rocks rarely produce reliable radiometric ages, how can numerical dates be assigned to sedimentary layers? Usually geologists must relate sedimentary rocks to datable igneous masses, as shown in Figure 18. In this example, radiometric dating has determined the ages of the volcanic ash bed within the Morrison Formation and the dike cutting the Mancos Shale and Mesaverde Formation. Both formations are igneous rock. The area covered by the Morrison Formation includes the following states: Montana, North and South Dakota, Nebraska, Kansas, Oklahoma, Texas, New Mexico, Arizona, Colorado, Utah, Wyoming, and Idaho. Using the principle of superposition, you can tell that the sedimentary beds below the ash are older than the ash, and all the layers above the ash are younger. Using the principle of cross-cutting relationships, you can see that the dike is younger than the Mancos Shale and the Mesaverde Formation. But the dike is older than the Wasatch Formation because the dike does not intrude the Tertiary rocks.

 **Reading Checkpoint** *How can geologists overcome the problem of sedimentary rocks and dating the time units of the geologic time scale?*

The Morrison Formation is one example of literally thousands that illustrates how datable materials are used to bracket the various episodes in Earth history within specific time periods. It shows the necessity of combining laboratory methods with field observations of rocks.

Section 12.4 Assessment

Reviewing Concepts

1. What is the geologic time scale?
2. What subdivisions make up the geologic time scale?
3. What is the basis on which the subdivisions are made?
4. What is the geologic time scale used for?
5. Why can it be difficult to assign dates to the divisions of the geologic time scale?

Thinking Critically

6. **Connecting Ideas** Explain how igneous intrusions and Steno's laws help geologists get around the problem of dating sedimentary rock layers.

7. **Inferring** What might have happened at the end of the Precambrian Eon and the beginning of the Phanerozoic Eon to allow geologists to mark this boundary on the time scale?

Connecting Concepts

Hypothesizing The boundaries of the geologic time scale are based on significant geologic events, while the epochs of the Cenozoic are based on the percentage occurrence of different fossil animals. Explain why you think it is possible to do this.

Fossil Occurrence and the Age of Rocks

Groups of fossil organisms occur throughout the geologic record for specific intervals of time. This time interval is called the fossil's range. Knowing the range of the fossils of specific organisms or groups of organisms can be used to relatively date rocks and sequences of rocks. In this laboratory exercise, you will use such information to assign a date to a hypothetical unit of rock.

Problem How can the occurrence of fossils and their known age ranges be used to date rocks?

Materials
- geologic time scale
- graph paper
- pencil

Skills Interpreting Diagrams, Graphing, Hypothesizing, Inferring

Procedure

1. A section of rock made up of layers of limestone and shale has been studied and samples have been taken. A large variety of fossils were collected from the rock samples. Use a sheet of graph paper to make a bar graph using the information shown in the Fossil Data Table. Begin by listing the individual fossils on the horizontal axis. Use Figure A to list the units of the geologic time scale on the vertical axis.

2. Transfer the range data of each fossil onto your graph. Draw an X in each box, beginning at the oldest occurrence of the organism up to the youngest occurrence. Shade in the marked boxes. You will end up with bars depicting the geologic ranges of each of the fossils listed.

3. Examine your graph. Are there any time units that contain all of the fossils listed? Write this time period at the bottom of the graph.

		Fossil Data Table	
	Type of Fossil	Oldest occurrence	Youngest occurrence
1	Foraminifera	Silurian	Quaternary
2	Bryozoan	Silurian	Permian
3	Gastropod	Devonian	Pennsylvanian
4	Brachiopod	Silurian	Mississippian
5	Bivalve	Silurian	Permian
6	Gastropod	Ordovician	Devonian
7	Trilobite	Silurian	Devonian
8	Ostracod	Devonian	Tertiary
9	Brachiopod	Cambrian	Devonian

Analyze and Conclude

1. **Reading Graphs** What is the age of the hypothetical rock layer that these fossils were collected from?

2. **Inferring** Based on the age determined, do you think that this group of fossils could be considered index fossils? Why or why not?

3. **Inferring** A species of the trilobite listed in line 7 of the data table (phacops logani) is limited to rocks of lower Devonian age. Trilobite fossils are widespread throughout North America. Can this fossil be considered an index fossil? Why or why not?

4. **Connecting Concepts** These fossils were collected from limestone and shale rocks. Based on what you have learned about the formation of these rock types, what type of environment did these organisms live in?

5. **Understanding Concepts** Shale often contains fossils of leaves. If the gastropods listed in line 3 and line 6 were collected from shale containing leaf fossils, could you use radiocarbon dating to assign a numerical date to this rock unit? Explain.

Go Further Use the library or Internet to research these fossils. Find out how some of them are used in the oil industry or the cosmetics industry.

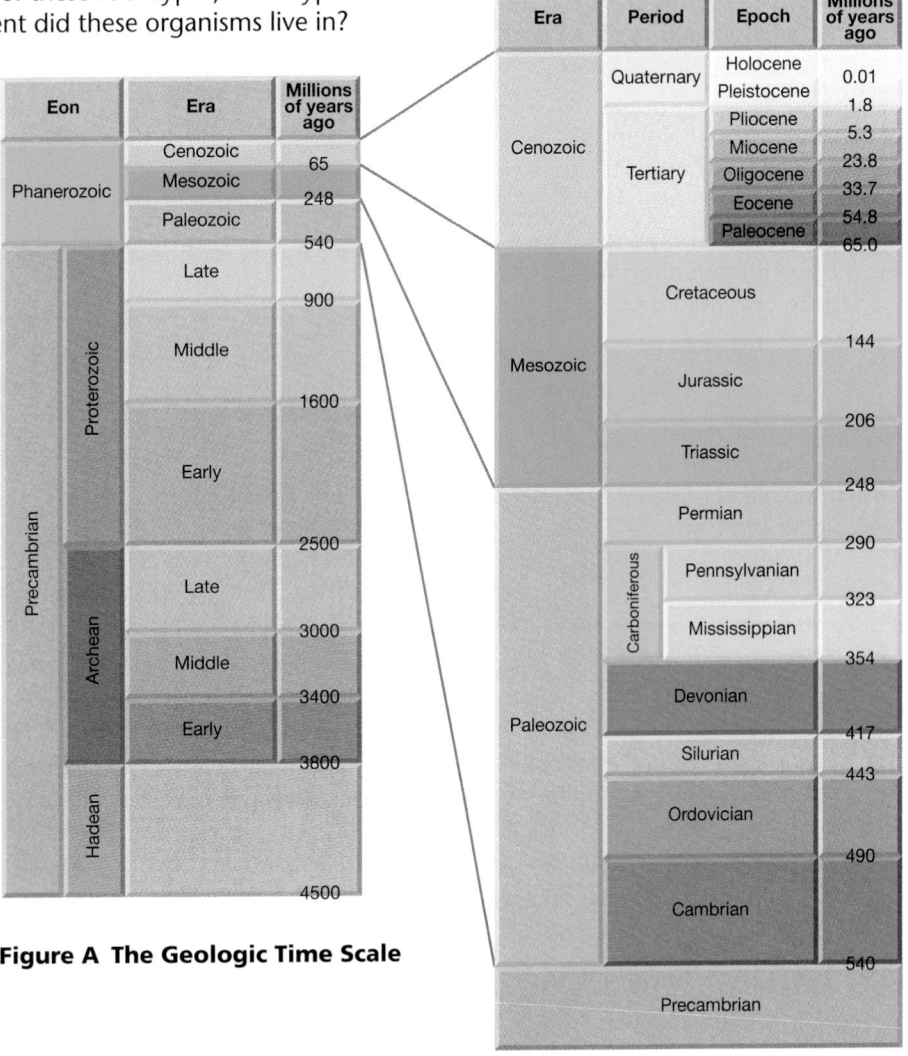

Figure A The Geologic Time Scale

12 | Study Guide

12.1 Discovering Earth's History

Key Concepts

- Rocks record geological events and changing life of the past.

- We have learned that Earth is much older than anyone had previously imagined and that its surface and interior have been changed by the same geologic processes that continue today.

- Uniformitarianism means that the forces and processes that we observe today have been at work for a very long time.

- Relative dating can't tell us how long ago something took place. It can only tell us the sequence in which events occurred.

- The law of superposition states that in an undeformed sequence of sedimentary rocks, each bed is older than the one above it and younger than the one below it.

- The principle of original horizontality means that layers of sediment are generally deposited in a horizontal position.

- An unconformity represents a long period during which deposition stopped, erosion removed previously formed rocks, and then deposition resumed.

Vocabulary

uniformitarianism, *p. 337;* relative dating, *p. 339;* law of superposition, *p. 340;* principle of original horizontality, *p. 340;* principle of cross-cutting relationships, *p. 341;* unconformity, *p. 341;* correlation, *p. 342*

12.2 Fossils: Evidence of Past Life

Key Concepts

- Fossils are the remains or traces of prehistoric life, and they are important components of sediment and sedimentary rocks.

- The type of fossil that is formed is determined by the conditions under which an organism died and how it was buried.

- The principle of fossil succession combines the law of superposition and the study of the fossils the rock layers contain.

Vocabulary

fossil, *p. 343;* index fossil, *p. 346*

12.3 Dating with Radioactivity

Key Concepts

- A half-life is the amount of time necessary for one half of the nuclei in a sample to decay to its stable isotope.

- An accurate radiometric date can be obtained only if the mineral remained a closed system during the entire period since its formation.

- When an organism dies, the amount of carbon-14 gradually decreases at is decays. By comparing the ratio of carbon-14 to carbon-12 in a sample, radiocarbon dates can be determined.

Vocabulary

radioactivity, *p. 347;* half-life, *p. 348;* radiometric dating, *p. 348;* radiocarbon dating, *p. 349*

12.4 The Geologic Time Scale

Key Concepts

- Geologists have divided Earth's 4.56 billion year history into specific time units.

- Eons represent the greatest expanses of time. Eons are divided into eras. Each era is subdivided into periods. Finally periods are divided into still smaller units called epochs.

- A sedimentary rock may contain particles that contain radioactive isotopes, but these particles are not the same age as the rock in which they occur.

- The age of a particular mineral in a metamorphic rock does not necessarily represent the time when the rock first formed. Instead, the date may indicate when the rock was metamorphosed.

Vocabulary

geologic time scale, *p. 353;* eon, *p. 353;* era, *p. 353;* period, *p. 353;* epoch, *p. 353*

12 | Assessment

Reviewing Content

1. What is the name of the doctrine that states the physical, chemical and biological laws that operate today have also operated in the geologic past?
   - a. uniformitarianism
   - b. unity
   - c. Earth science
   - d. law of superposition

2. What is the name of the process that matches up rocks of similar ages in different regions?
   - a. indexing
   - b. correlation
   - c. succession
   - d. superposition

3. What name is given to fossils that are widespread geographically, are abundant in number, and are limited to a short span of time?
   - a. key
   - b. succeeding
   - c. relative
   - d. index

4. What is the name of the process during which atomic nuclei decay?
   - a. fusion
   - b. fission
   - c. nucleation
   - d. radioactivity

5. Which unit of geologic time is the greatest span of time?
   - a. era
   - b. eon
   - c. period
   - d. epoch

6. What are remains or traces of prehistoric life called?
   - a. indicators
   - b. replicas
   - c. fossils
   - d. fissures

7. What name is given to layers of tilted rocks that are overlain by younger, more flat-lying rock layers?
   - a. disconformity
   - b. angular unconformity
   - c. nonconformity
   - d. fault

8. What are atoms with the same atomic number but different mass numbers called?
   - a. protons
   - b. isotopes
   - c. ions
   - d. nucleotides

9. Which of Steno's principles states that most layers of sediments are deposited in a horizontal position?
   - a. original horizontality
   - b. cross-cutting relationships
   - c. fossil succession
   - d. superposition

10. What name is given to pieces of rock that are contained within another, younger rock?
   - a. intrusions
   - b. interbeds
   - c. hosts
   - d. inclusions

11. About how old is Earth?
    - a. 4,000 years
    - b. 4.0 million years
    - c. 5.8 million years
    - d. 4.56 billion years

Understanding Concepts

12. How have the processes that affect Earth's surface changed through time?

13. Why does the law of superposition apply primarily to sedimentary rocks?

14. How are cross-cutting relationships used in relative dating?

15. How do unconformities form?

16. List and briefly describe three different types of fossils.

17. What two conditions increase an organism's chance of becoming a fossil?

18. Why can certain fossils, such as corals, be used to indicate former water temperature?

19. What is a half-life?

20. Explain how radioactivity and radiometric dating are related.

21. Why can't radiometric dating be used with accuracy on metamorphic rocks?

Critical Thinking

22. Comparing and Contrasting Compare the techniques of relative dating to those of numerical dating.

23. Drawing Conclusions Why can't carbon-14 be used to date material that is older than 75,000 years?

24. Making Connections Why is it important to have a closed system when using radiometric dating?

25. Predicting An analysis of some sedimentary rocks suggests the environment was close to the shoreline where high energy waves hit the shore. Corals and shelled organisms lived here. Describe what their fossils would be like.

26. Applying Concepts Why is radiometric dating the most reliable method of dating the geologic past?

Analyzing Data

Refer to the diagram to answer Questions 27 and 28.

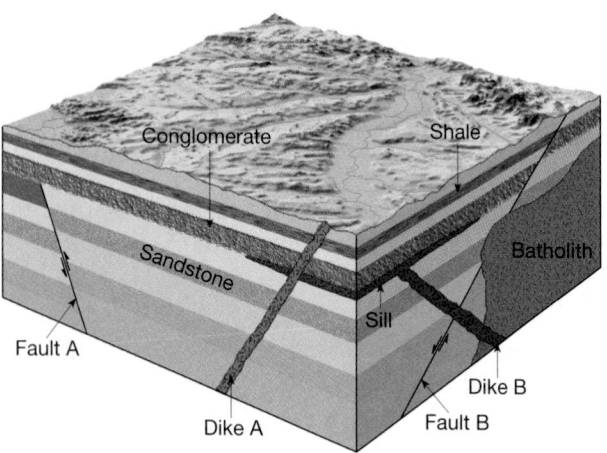

27. Which fault is older, A or B? Explain how you know.

28. Which dike is older, A or B? Explain how you know.

29. Calculating A sample of potassium-40 has a mass of 12.5 grams. If the sample originally had 50 grams of potassium-40 at the start of radioactive decay, how many half-lives have passed? The decay rate of potassium-40 is 1.3 billion years. How old is the sample?

Concepts in Action

30. Applying Concepts Fossilized human remains called bog bodies are often found in bogs, which are wet, low-oxygen areas that contain decaying plant material. How would you go about dating such a fossil?

31. Comparing and Contrasting Apply the concept of uniformitarianism to explain how a particular sequence of rock layers could be interpreted as a former ocean coastline. (*Hint:* compare what you might see at a modern shoreline to what you would see in the rocks).

32. Analyzing Data A sunken Spanish ship containing a treasure in gold coins has recently been found at the bottom of the Atlantic Ocean. What types of dating techniques can be used to date the ship?

33. Calculating Nuclear power plants produce radioactive waste that must be stored properly until it is no longer harmful to life on Earth. Uranium-238 has a half-life of 4.5 billion years. If, in order to be safe, a uranium sample must decay to 1/64 of its original amount, how many years must we wait?

Performance-Based Assessment

Describing and Classifying Create a poster illustrating the different ways that fossils can form. Be sure to include altered and unaltered remains with examples of both. Include samples of fossils that are found in your area.

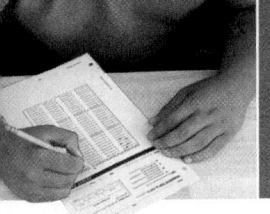

Standardized Test Prep

Simplify the Diagram

When examining a diagram, it is important not to be confused by unnecessary information. It helps to identify only the features that relate to the question being asked. Reread the question with these features in mind and then answer the question. In the diagram below, you do not need to know what rock types are present.

How can you tell that dike C is older than fault H?

(A) The top of dike C is eroded.
(B) Dike C is broken by fault H.
(C) Fault H ends at the eroded layer E.
(D) Both dike C and fault H end at layer E.

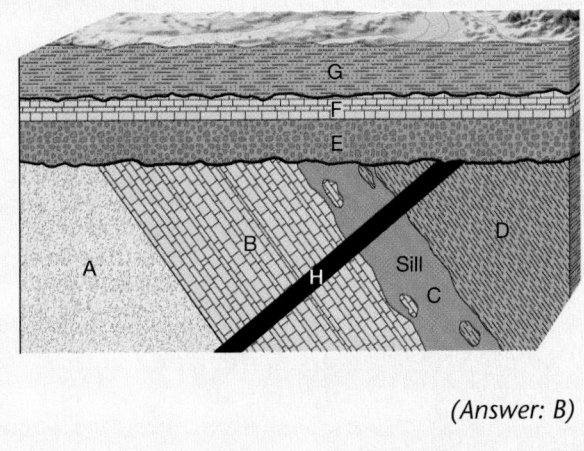

(Answer: B)

Choose the letter that best answers the question or completes the statement.

1. Who was the scientist that formulated the theory of uniformitarianism?
   (A) Archbishop Ussher
   (B) James Hutton
   (C) William Smith
   (D) Louis Agassiz

2. Using relative dating methods, which of the following are scientists able to do?
   (A) Identify the order in which rock units formed.
   (B) Assign a numerical date to each rock layer studied.
   (C) Determine the age of the fossils within each layer.
   (D) Identify what rock types are present.

Use the diagram below to answer Questions 3–5.

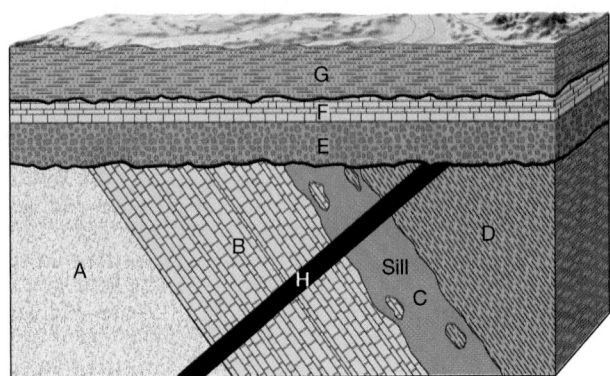

3. Which choice correctly lists the order of deposition of rock layers A through D?
   (A) A, B, C, D
   (B) D, C, B, A
   (C) B, C, D, A
   (D) A, B, D, C

4. When were rock layers A though D uplifted and tilted?
   (A) after deposition of layer G
   (B) after deposition of layer F and before deposition of layer G
   (C) after deposition of layer D and before deposition of layer E
   (D) after deposition of layer A and before deposition of layer G

5. When was sill C intruded? Explain.

Answer the following in complete sentences.

6. Explain why decay rates can be used with confidence in radiometric dating.

7. Describe the relationship between uniformitarianism and time.

8. Explain the difference in fossilization between a mammoth frozen in ice and a seashell embedded in rock.

9. Explain why the time periods of the Paleozoic and Mesozoic are subdivided into early, middle, and late instead of named epochs, as they are in the Cenozoic.

CHAPTER

13 Earth's History

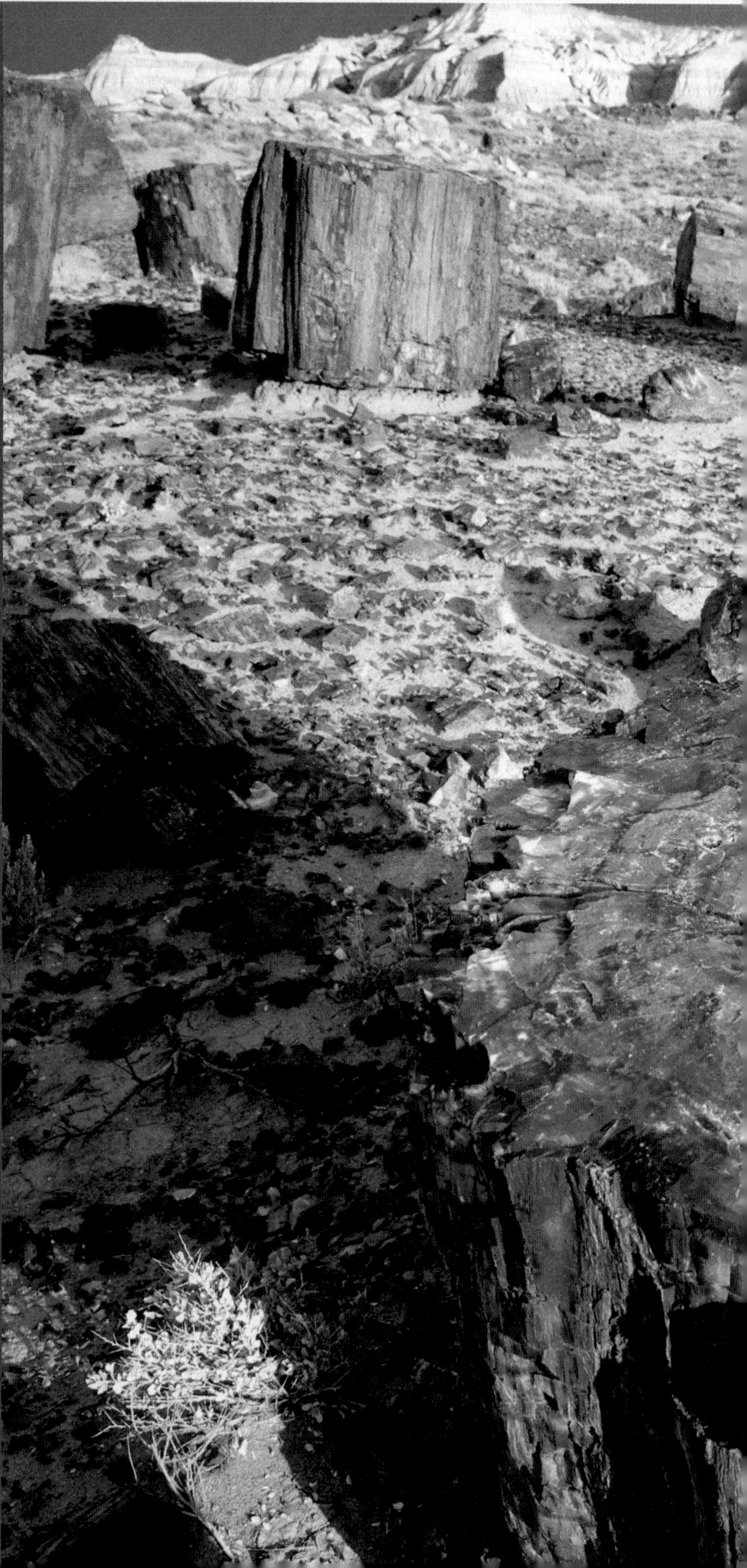

CONCEPTS in Action

Quick Lab
Relative Dating

Exploration Lab
Modeling the Geologic Time Scale

Understanding Earth
Demise of the Dinosaurs

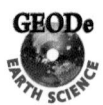

GEODe EARTH SCIENCE Geologic Time
↳ Geologic Time Scale

Discovery Channel School **Video Field Trip**

Extinction

Take a prehistoric field trip with Discovery Channel and learn some theories about why the dinosaurs disappeared. Answer the following questions after watching the video.

1. Why could the collision of a giant meteor and Earth have led to dinosaur extinction?
2. What types of species flourished after the extinction of the dinosaurs? Why?

Go Online PHSchool.com

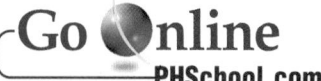

For: Chapter 13 Resources
Visit: PHSchool.com
Web Code: cjk-9999

This photograph shows petrified logs in the Triassic Chinle Formation of Petrified Forest National Park in Arizona. ▶

Chapter Preview

Inquiry Activity

What Are Fossils?

Procedure

1. Obtain and observe some examples of fossils. You may either find and collect examples of real fossils, get them from your teacher, or use pictures of fossils.

2. Share the fossils with your classmates so that you can observe several examples.

Think About It

1. **Observing** What kinds of organisms do the fossils show? What can you tell about the ancient organisms from these fossils?

2. **Inferring** How do you think these fossils were formed? What conditions were necessary for their formation?

13.1 Precambrian Time: Vast and Puzzling

Reading Focus

Key Concepts

- How much of Earth's history is included in Precambrian time?
- What was the atmosphere and surface like after Earth's formation?
- What evidence exists about conditions during Precambrian time?

Vocabulary

- ◆ shields
- ◆ stromatolites

Reading Strategy

Building Vocabulary Use the information about the vocabulary terms in this section to complete these phrases.

1. Shields are composed of a. ? ; are evidence of b. ? ; and are significant to Precambrian time because c. ? .

2. Stromatolites are composed of d. ? ; are evidence of e. ? ; and are significant to Precambrian time because f. ? .

As you read in Chapter 12, geologists have many tools at their disposal for interpreting the clues about Earth's past. Using these tools and clues that are contained in the rock record, geologists have been able to unravel many of the complex events of the geological past. Figure 1 shows a scientist examining fossil evidence of ancient life. The goal of this chapter is to provide a brief overview of the history of our planet and its life forms.

Precambrian History

The Precambrian encompasses immense geological time, from Earth's distant beginnings 4.56 billion years ago until the start of the Cambrian period, over 4 billion years later. To get a visual sense of this proportion, look at the right side of Figure 2, which shows the relative time span of eras. The Precambrian comprises about 88 percent of the geologic time scale.

Most Precambrian rocks do not contain fossils, which makes correlating rock layers difficult. Many rocks of this great age are metamorphosed and deformed, extremely eroded, and hidden by overlaying strata. As a result, Precambrian history is written in scattered, speculative episodes, like a long book with many missing pages.

Figure 1 Paleontologists study fossils to learn about ancient life. This researcher is examining the skull of a *Tyrannosaurus rex*.

Reading Checkpoint *Why are specific events in Precambrian history difficult to determine?*

Geologic Time Scale

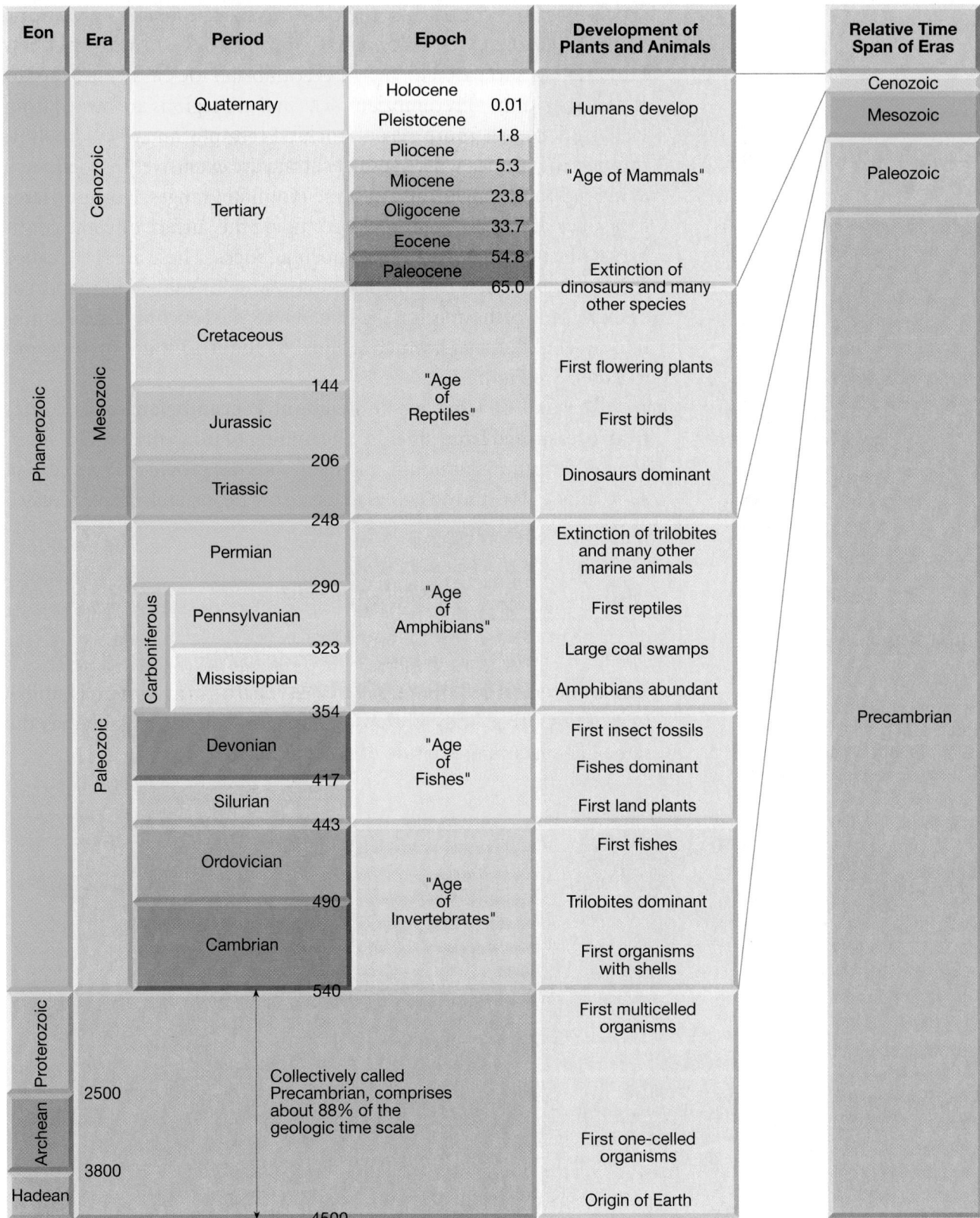

Eon	Era	Period	Epoch		Development of Plants and Animals	Relative Time Span of Eras
Phanerozoic	Cenozoic	Quaternary	Holocene	0.01	Humans develop	Cenozoic
			Pleistocene	1.8		Mesozoic
		Tertiary	Pliocene	5.3	"Age of Mammals"	Paleozoic
			Miocene	23.8		
			Oligocene	33.7		
			Eocene	54.8	Extinction of dinosaurs and many other species	
			Paleocene	65.0		
	Mesozoic	Cretaceous	"Age of Reptiles"	144	First flowering plants	
		Jurassic		206	First birds	
		Triassic		248	Dinosaurs dominant	
	Paleozoic	Permian	"Age of Amphibians"	290	Extinction of trilobites and many other marine animals	Precambrian
		Carboniferous — Pennsylvanian		323	First reptiles	
		Carboniferous — Mississippian		354	Large coal swamps / Amphibians abundant	
		Devonian	"Age of Fishes"	417	First insect fossils / Fishes dominant / First land plants	
		Silurian		443		
		Ordovician	"Age of Invertebrates"	490	First fishes / Trilobites dominant	
		Cambrian		540	First organisms with shells	
Proterozoic				2500	First multicelled organisms	
Archean			Collectively called Precambrian, comprises about 88% of the geologic time scale	3800	First one-celled organisms	
Hadean				4500	Origin of Earth	

Figure 2 Numbers on the time scale represent time millions of years before the present.

Analyzing *The Precambrian accounts for approximately what percentage of geologic time?*

Precambrian Rocks Looking at Earth from the space shuttle, astronauts see mostly ocean and much less land area. Over large expanses of the continents, the orbiting space scientists gaze upon many Paleozoic, Mesozoic, and Cenozoic rock surfaces, but few Precambrian surfaces. The lack of Precambrian rock illustrates the law of superposition—Precambrian rocks in these regions are buried from view underneath more recent rocks. Precambrian rocks do show through the surface where younger strata are extensively eroded, such as in the Grand Canyon and in some mountain ranges. However, large core areas of Precambrian rocks dominate the surface of some continents, mostly as deformed metamorphic rocks. These areas are called **shields** because they roughly resemble a warrior's shield in shape. For example, in North America, the Canadian Shield encompasses 7.2 million square kilometers, which is equal to about 10 states of Texas put together. See Figure 3.

Much of what we know about Precambrian rocks comes from ores mined from shields. The mining of iron, nickel, gold, silver, copper, chromium, uranium, and diamonds has provided Precambrian rock samples for study. Surveys to locate ore deposits also have revealed much about the rocks.

Reading Checkpoint *What are shields?*

Figure 3 Remnants of Precambrian rocks are the continental shields. They are largely made up of metamorphosed igneous and sedimentary rocks.

Earth's Atmosphere Evolves Earth's atmosphere is unlike that of any other body in the solar system. No other planet has the same life-sustaining mixture of gases as Earth.

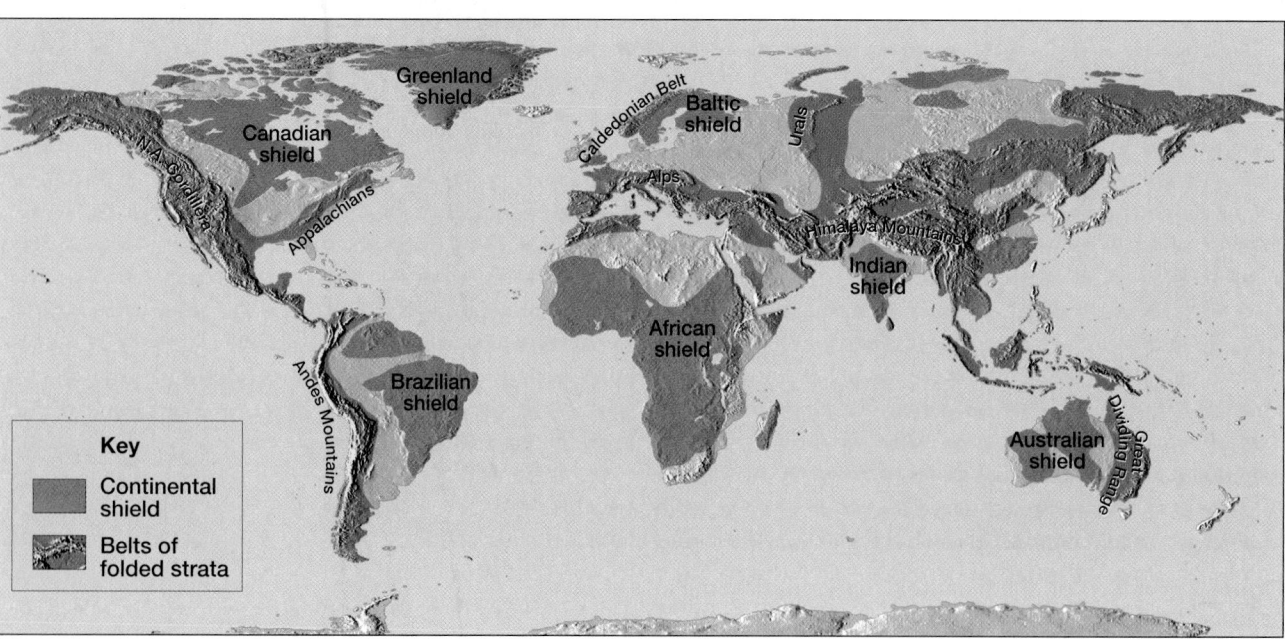

Key

Continental shield

Belts of folded strata

Today, the air you breathe is a stable mixture of nitrogen, oxygen, a small amount of argon, and trace gases like carbon dioxide and water vapor. But our planet's original atmosphere, several billion years ago, was far different.

Early in Earth's history, the high-velocity impact of nebular debris caused at least the outer shell of our planet to melt. After this period of bombardment subsided, Earth slowly cooled and the molten surface solidified into a crust. The gases that had been dissolved in the molten rock were gradually released. **Earth's original atmosphere was made up of gases similar to those released in volcanic eruptions today—water vapor, carbon dioxide, nitrogen, and several trace gases, but no oxygen.**

As the planet continued to cool, the water vapor condensed to form clouds, and great rains began. At first the rain water evaporated in the hot air before reaching the ground or quickly boiled or evaporated when it did reach the ground. This evaporation sped up the cooling of Earth's surface. Torrential rains continued and slowly filled low areas, forming the oceans. This rain and the forming of the oceans reduced not only the water vapor in the air but also the amount of carbon dioxide, which became dissolved in the water. A nitrogen-rich atmosphere remained.

The first life forms on Earth did not need oxygen. **Later, primitive organisms evolved that used photosynthesis and released oxygen.** These organisms, primarily cyanobacteria, did not adapt to Earth's atmosphere. They actually influenced it, dramatically changing the make up of Earth's atmosphere by using carbon dioxide and releasing oxygen. Slowly, the oxygen content of Earth's atmosphere increased. The influence the ancestors of plants had on the atmosphere is a good example of how Earth operates as a giant system in which living things interact. The Precambrian rock record suggests that much of the first free oxygen did not remain free because it combined with iron. Iron combines with oxygen to form iron oxides, or rust, at any opportunity.

Once the available iron finished reacting, oxygen began to accumulate in the atmosphere. By the beginning of the Paleozoic era—about 4 billion years into Earth's existence—the fossil record reveals abundant ocean-dwelling organisms that require oxygen to live. These fossils show that the composition of Earth's atmosphere has evolved together with its life forms, from an oxygen-free envelope to today's oxygen-rich environment. **Oxygen began to accumulate in the atmosphere about 2.5 billion years ago.**

 **Reading Checkpoint** *How did Earth's oceans form?*

Q *The era names refer to "ancient," "middle," and "recent" life. What is the origin of period names?*

A There is no overall scheme for naming the periods; rather, these names have diverse origins. Several names refer to places that have prominent strata of that age. For example, the Cambrian period is taken from the Roman name for Wales (Cambria). The Permian is named for the province of Perm in Russia, while the Jurassic period gets its name from the Jura Mountains located between France and Switzerland.

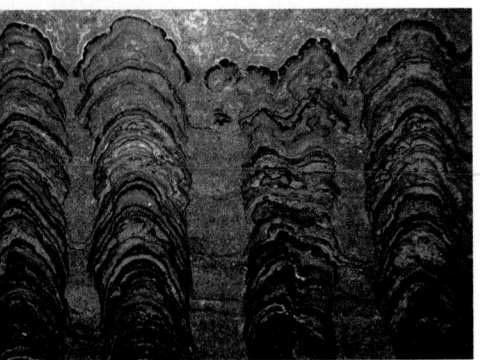

Figure 4 Stromatolites are among the most common Precambrian fossils. **Interpreting** *What are stromatolites made of?*

Precambrian Fossils Precambrian fossils are disappointing if you are expecting to see fascinating plants and large animals, for these organisms had not yet evolved. ☁**The most common Precambrian fossils are stromatolites.** Stromatolites are distinctively layered mounds or columns of calcium carbonate, as shown in Figure 4. They are not the remains of actual organisms but are material deposited by algae. Stromatolites are indirect evidence of algae because they closely resemble similar deposits made by modern algae.

Stromatolites did not become common until the middle Precambrian, around 2 billion years ago. Although stromatolites are large, most actual organisms preserved in Precambrian rocks are microscopic. Remains of cyanobacteria have been discovered, which extend the record of life back beyond 3.5 billion years.

Many of these ancient fossils are preserved in chert—a hard, dense chemical sedimentary rock. Chert must be sliced very thin and studied under a powerful microscope to see the bacteria and algae fossils within it. These fossils are the most primitive organisms, called prokaryotes. More advanced organisms called eukaryotes evolved later, and are among billion-year-old fossils discovered.

The development of eukaryotes may have dramatically increased the rate of evolutionary change. Plant fossils date from the middle Precambrian, but animal fossils date to the late Precambrian. Many are trace fossils. Trace fossils are not fossils of the animals themselves but rather impressions of their activities, such as trails and worm holes.

Section 13.1 Assessment

Reviewing Concepts

1. ☁ What time span is encompassed by Precambrian time?

2. ☁ Describe the components that made up Earth's first atmosphere.

3. Why did the amount of oxygen in Earth's atmosphere increase dramatically?

4. ☁ What kinds of fossils of Precambrian life have been found?

5. Describe how shields play an important role in providing information about Earth's formation.

Critical Thinking

6. **Comparing and Contrasting** Compare and contrast Earth's early atmosphere with today's atmosphere.

7. **Inferring** Why did life not develop on the other planets in our solar system?

Math Practice

8. Using Figure 2, create a circle graph that shows the percentages of relative time encompassed by the Cenozoic, Mesozoic, Paleozoic, and Precambrian eras. Then estimate the percentage of time in Earth's history that humans have existed.

13.2 Paleozoic Era: Life Explodes

Reading Focus

Key Concepts

- When was the Paleozoic era?

- How did tectonic movements affect the locations and formations of the continents during the Paleozoic era?

- What kind of life existed in the early Paleozoic?

- How did life evolve during the Paleozoic era?

Vocabulary

- Gondwana
- Laurasia

Reading Strategy

Identifying Details Copy the table below. As you read the section, fill out the table with notes.

	Continental positions	Plant life	Animal life
Early Paleozoic			
Middle Paleozoic			
Late Paleozoic			

As the Precambrian came to a close, the fossil record disclosed diverse and complete multicelled organisms. This set the stage for more complex plants and animals to evolve at the dawn of the Paleozoic era. **Following the long Precambrian, the most recent 540 million years of Earth's history are divided into three eras: Paleozoic, Mesozoic, and Cenozoic.** The Paleozoic era encompasses about 292 million years and is by far the longest of the three.

Before the Paleozoic, life forms possessed no hard parts, such as shells, scales, bones, or teeth. Hard parts greatly enhanced a life form's chance of being preserved as part of the fossil record. The Paleozoic era contains many more diverse fossils due to the emergence of life forms with hard parts.

Abundant Paleozoic fossils have allowed geologists to construct a far more detailed time scale for the last one-eighth of geologic time than for the preceding seven-eighths, the Precambrian. Moreover, because every organism is associated with a particular environment, the greatly improved fossil record provided invaluable information for learning about ancient environments. For our brief tour of the Paleozoic, we divide it into Early Paleozoic (Cambrian, Ordovician, Silurian periods) and Late Paleozoic (Devonian, Mississippian, Pennsylvanian, Permian periods).

Early Paleozoic

The early Paleozoic consists of a 123-million-year span that includes the Cambrian, Ordovician, and Silurian periods. Looking at Earth from space at this time, you would have seen the familiar blue planet with many clouds, but the arrangement of the continents would be very different from today.

Early Paleozoic History  During the Cambrian, Ordovician, and Silurian periods, the vast southern continent of Gondwana encompassed five continents (South America, Africa, Australia, Antarctica, and parts of Asia).

North America and several other landmasses were not part of Gondwana. Although the exact position of these northern continents is uncertain, they are thought to have been near the equator and separated by a narrow sea, as shown on the map in Figure 5.

At the beginning of the Paleozoic, North America was a land with no living things, plant or animal. Soon, a mountain-building event affected eastern North America. The final chapter in this story was the formation of the Appalachian Mountains, over 200 million years later.

During the Silurian period, much of North America was once again covered by shallow seas. This time, large barrier reefs restricted circulation between shallow marine basins and the open ocean. Water in these basins evaporated, depositing large quantities of rock salt and gypsum.

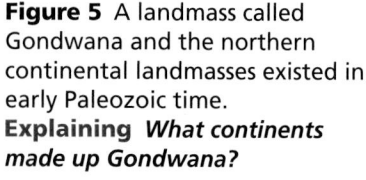 **Reading Checkpoint** *Why are more fossils found from the Paleozoic era than Precambrian time?*

Figure 5 A landmass called Gondwana and the northern continental landmasses existed in early Paleozoic time.
Explaining *What continents made up Gondwana?*

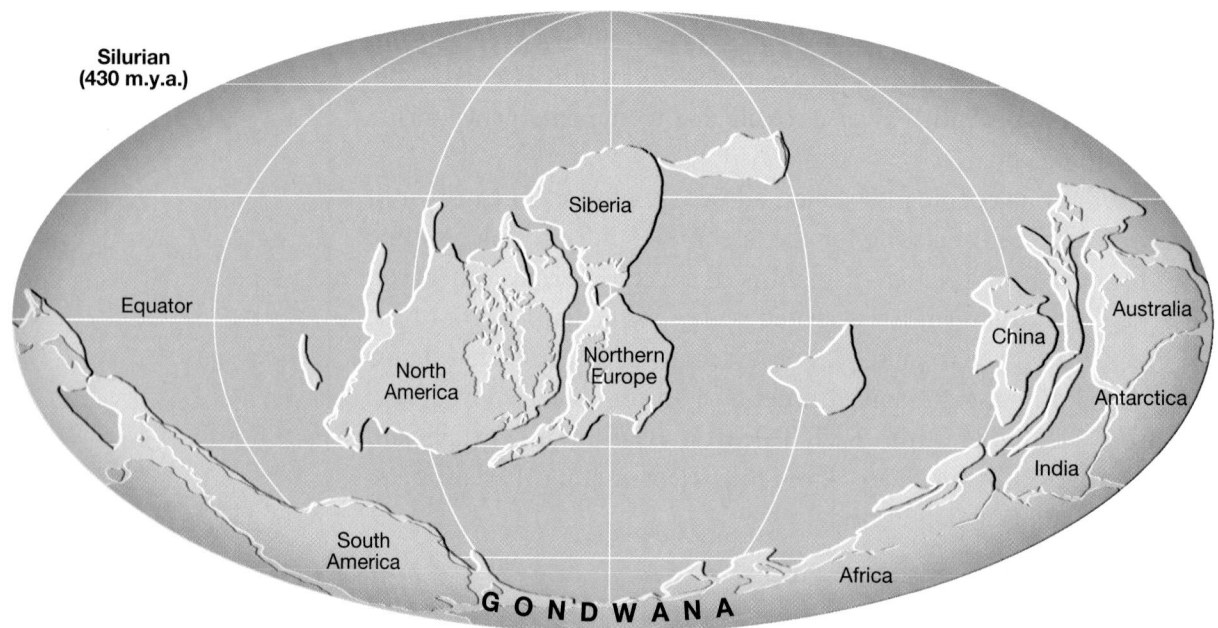

Figure 6 Cephalopods, trilobites, brachiopods, snails, and corals inhabited the waters of the Ordovician period.

Early Paleozoic Life ⬭ **Life in early Paleozoic time was restricted to the seas.** Vertebrates had not yet evolved, so life consisted of several invertebrate groups. The Cambrian period was the golden age of trilobites. More than 600 types of these mud-burrowing scavengers flourished worldwide. By Ordovician times, brachiopods outnumbered the trilobites. Brachiopods are among the most widespread Paleozoic fossils and, except for one modern group, are now extinct. The adult brachiopods lived attached to the seafloor, but the young larvae were free swimming. This mobility accounts for the group's wide geographic distribution.

The Ordovician also marked the appearance of cephalopods—mobile and highly developed mollusks that became the major predators of the time. Squid and octopus are descendents of these early cephalopods. Cephalopods were the first truly large organisms on Earth. Figure 6 shows some cephalopods and other organisms of the Ordovician.

The beginning of the Cambrian period marks an important event in animal evolution. For the first time, organisms appeared that secreted material that formed hard parts, such as shells. Hard parts clearly served many useful purposes and aided adaptations to new ways of life. Mollusks, such as clams and snails, secreted external shells that protected them and allowed body organs to function in a more controlled environment. The successful trilobites developed an exoskeleton of a protein called chitin, which permitted them to burrow through soft sediment in search of food. The fossil in Figure 7 shows the exoskeleton of a trilobite.

**Figure 7 Trilobite Fossil
Inferring** *When did trilobites live?*

 **Reading Checkpoint** *How did the formation of hard parts benefit animals?*

Relative Dating

Geologists can relatively date the fossils they uncover with respect to their positions in the ground. Assume the playing cards shown are layers of rocks viewed from above. Using the cards, answer the questions below.

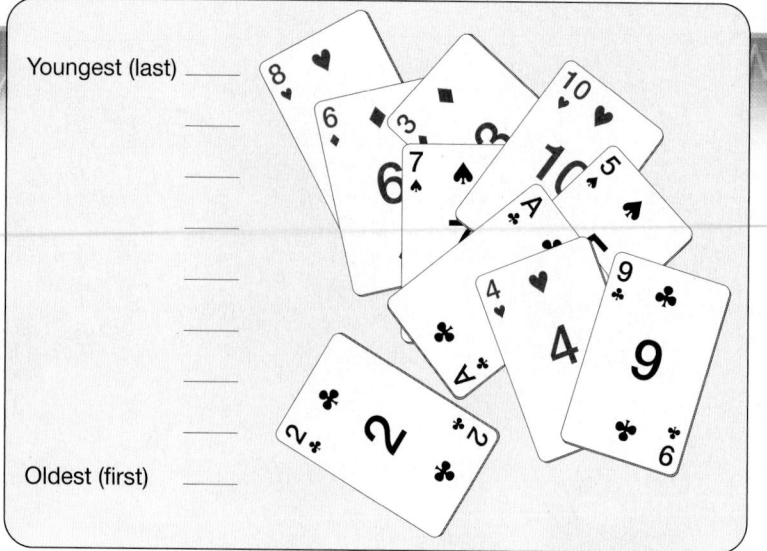

Youngest (last) ____

Oldest (first) ____

Analyze and Conclude

1. **Observing** List the order, first (oldest) to last (youngest), that the cards were laid down.

2. **Inferring** Were you able to place all of the cards in sequence? If not, which one(s) could not be "relatively" dated and why not?

3. **Applying** What geologic process would be represented by slipping a card in from the side?

Late Paleozoic

The late Paleozoic consists of four periods—the Devonian, Mississippian, Pennsylvanian, and Permian—that span about 160 million years. Tectonic forces reorganized Earth's landmasses during this time, creating the supercontinent Pangaea.

Late Paleozoic History As ancestral North America collided with Africa, the narrow sea that separated these landmasses began to close slowly, as compared in Figure 8B and 8C. Strong forces of compression from this collision deformed the rocks to produce the Appalachian Mountains of eastern North America.

During the union of North America and Africa, the other northern continents began to join, as shown in Figure 8. By the Permian period, this newly formed landmass had collided with western Asia and the Siberian landmass along the line of the Ural Mountains. Through this union, the northern continent of **Laurasia** was born, made up of present-day North America, Europe, western Asia.

As Laurasia was forming, Gondwana moved northward. By the Pennsylvanian period, Gondwana collided with Laurasia, forming a mountainous belt through central Europe. **By the end of the Paleozoic, all the continents had fused into the supercontinent of Pangaea.** With only a single vast continent, the world's climate changed dramatically. The interior of this large continent, located far from a source of moisture became quite arid. In addition, these regions became very seasonal, having extremes far greater than those we experience today.

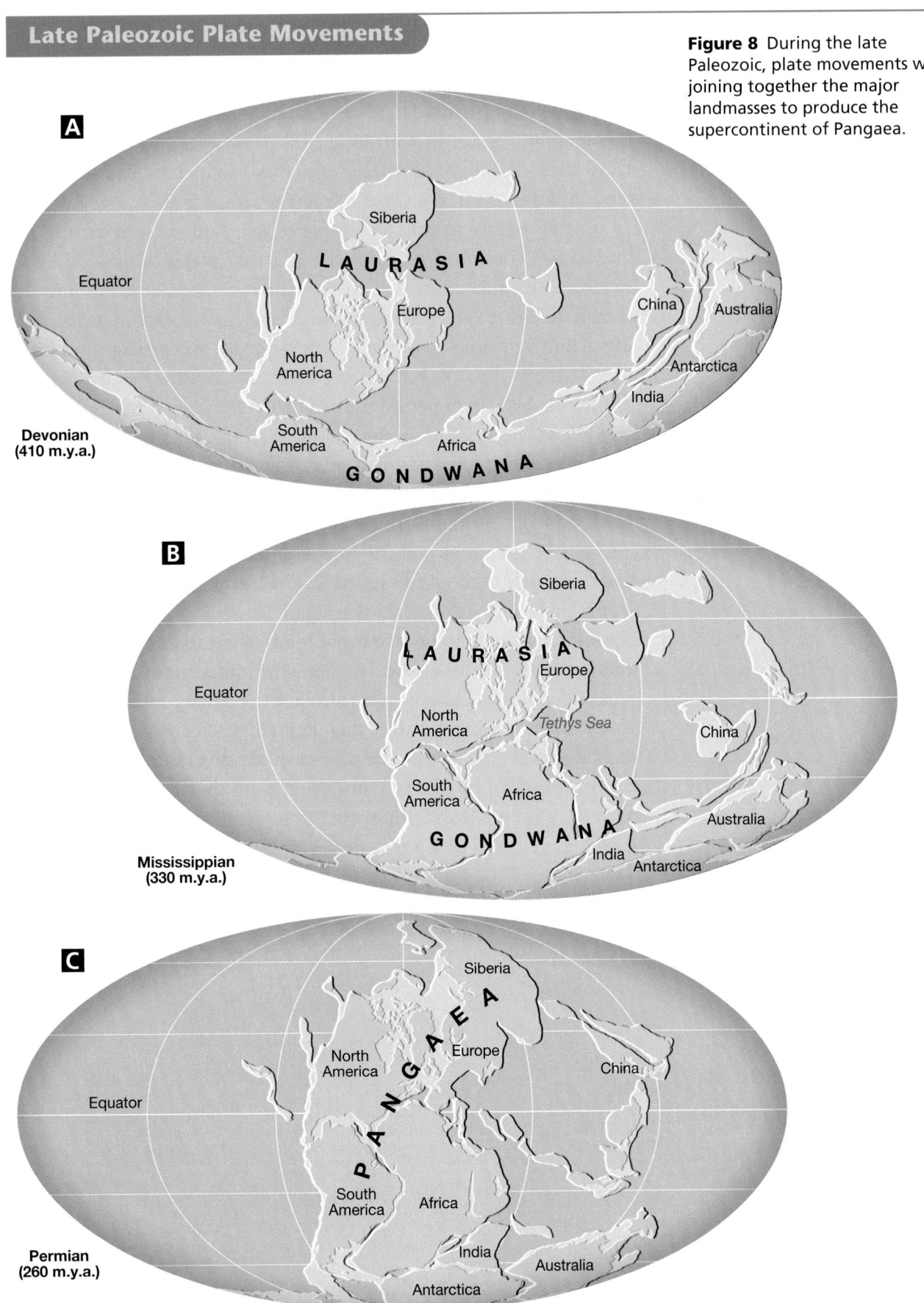

Figure 8 During the late Paleozoic, plate movements were joining together the major landmasses to produce the supercontinent of Pangaea.

A

Siberia

L A U R A S I A

Equator

Europe

China

Australia

North America

Antarctica

India

South America

Africa

G O N D W A N A

Devonian (410 m.y.a.)

B

Siberia

L A U R A S I A

Europe

Equator

Tethys Sea

North America

China

South America

Africa

Australia

G O N D W A N A

India

Antarctica

Mississippian (330 m.y.a.)

C

Siberia

P A N G A E A

North America

Europe

China

Equator

South America

Africa

India

Australia

Antarctica

Permian (260 m.y.a.)

Late Paleozoic Life During most of the late Paleozoic, organisms diversified dramatically. ⬭**Some 400 million years ago, plants that had adapted to survive at the water's edge began to move inland, becoming land plants.** These earliest land plants were leafless vertical spikes about the size of your index finger. However, by the end of the Devonian, 40 million years later, the fossil record indicates the existence of forests with trees tens of meters high.

In the oceans, armor-plated fishes that had evolved during the Ordovician continued to adapt. Their armor plates thinned to lightweight scales that increased the organisms' speed and mobility, as shown in Figure 9. Other fishes evolved during the Devonian, including primitive sharks that had a skeleton made of cartilage and bony fishes—the groups to which virtually all modern fishes belong. Because of this, the Devonian period is often called the "age of fishes."

By late Devonian time, several fish became adapted to land environments. The fishes had primitive lungs that supplemented their breathing through gills. Lobe-finned fish likely occupied tidal flats and small ponds. Through time, the lobe-finned fish began to use their lungs more than their gills. By the end of the Devonian period, they had developed lungs and eventually evolved into true air-breathing amphibians with fishlike heads and tails.

Modern amphibians, like frogs, toads, and salamanders, are small and occupy limited biological niches. However, conditions during the remainder of the Paleozoic were ideal for these newcomers to the land. Plants and insects, which were their main diet, already were very abundant and large. ⬭**The amphibians rapidly diversified because they had minimal competition from other land dwellers.** Some groups took on roles and forms that were more similar to modern reptiles, such as crocodiles, than to modern amphibians.

Figure 9 Armor-plated fish were common during the Devonian period.
Inferring *What steps were involved in the evolution of armor-plated fish into modern day fish?*

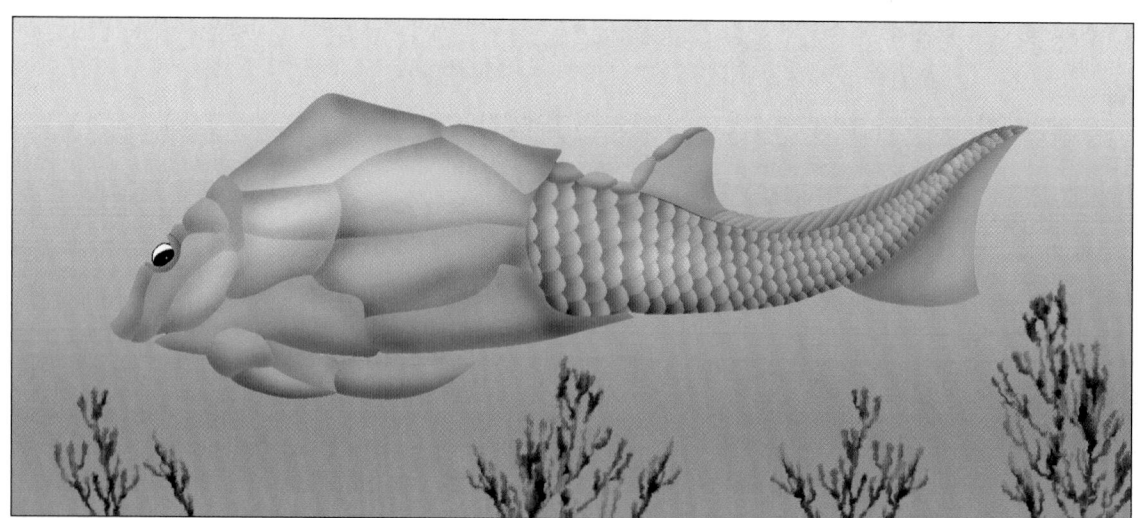

By the Pennsylvanian period, large tropical swamps extended across North America, Europe, and Siberia. Trees approached 30 meters, with trunks over a meter across. The coal deposits that we use today for fuel originated in these swamps. See Figure 10. These lush swamps allowed the amphibians to evolve quickly into a variety of species.

Figure 10 Model of a Pennsylvanian Coal Swamp Shown are scale trees (left), seed ferns (lower left), and scouring rushes (right). Note the large dragonfly.

The Great Paleozoic Extinction

The Paleozoic ended with the Permian period, a time when Earth's major landmasses joined to form the supercontinent Pangaea. This redistribution of land and water and changes in the elevations of landmasses brought pronounced changes in world climates. Broad areas of the northern continents became elevated above sea level, and the climate became drier. These climate changes are believed to have triggered extinctions of many species on land and sea.

By the close of the Permian, 75 percent of the amphibian families had disappeared, and plants had declined in number and variety. Although many amphibian groups became extinct, their descendants, the reptiles, would become the most successful and advanced animals on Earth. Much of the marine life did not adapt and survive. At least 80 percent, and perhaps as much as 95 percent, of marine life disappeared. Many marine invertebrates that had been dominant during the Paleozoic, including all the remaining trilobites as well as some types of corals and brachiopods, could not adapt to the widespread environmental changes.

The late Paleozoic extinction was the greatest of at least five mass extinctions to occur over the past 500 million years. Each of the mass extinctions drastically changed the existing biosphere and wiped out large numbers of species. In each case, however, the survivors formed new biological communities that were more diverse than their predecessors. Thus, mass extinctions actually allowed life on Earth to flourish, as the few hardy survivors eventually filled more niches than the ones left by the victims.

The cause of the great Paleozoic extinction is uncertain. The climate changes from the formation of Pangaea and the associated drop in sea level undoubtedly stressed many species. In addition, at least 2 million cubic kilometers of lava flowed across Siberia to produce what is called the Siberian Traps. Perhaps debris from these volcanic eruptions blocked incoming sunlight, or perhaps enough sulfuric acid was emitted to make the seas virtually unfit to live in. Some recent research suggests that an impact with an extraterrestrial body may have contributed to the mass extinction. Whatever caused the late Paleozoic extinction, it is clear that without it a very different population of organisms would exist today.

Section 13.2 Assessment

Reviewing Concepts

1. What are the seven periods that make up the Paleozoic era?

2. Which present-day continents made up Gondwana, Laurasia, and Pangaea?

3. Which life forms dominated the early, middle, and late parts of the Paleozoic era?

4. What allowed amphibians to flourish on land?

Critical Thinking

5. **Comparing and Contrasting** Compare and contrast the life that existed at the beginning of the Paleozoic era with the life that existed at the end of the era.

6. **Applying Concepts** Explain how life made the transition from water to land.

Writing in Science

Descriptive Paragraph Imagine you are uncovering rocks and fossils from a site that was formed during the Paleozoic era. Write a paragraph describing what kinds of fossils you would expect to find as you dug from the surface and moved downward.

13.3 Mesozoic Era: Age of Reptiles

Reading Focus

Key Concepts

- What continental movements occurred during the Mesozoic era?
- What plant and animal life dominated the Mesozoic?
- What caused the extinction that marks the end of the Mesozoic?

Vocabulary

- dinosaur
- gymnosperm

Reading Strategy

Summarizing List the blue headings from the section, leaving space to write after each heading. Use a bulleted list to write a brief summary of the text for each heading.

I. Mesozoic History

- Begins with most areas above sea level.
- Shallow seas invade most continents.
- _____ ? _____

Mesozoic Era

The Mesozoic era spanned about 183 million years, and it is divided into three periods: the Triassic, Jurassic, and Cretaceous. The Mesozoic era marked the beginning of the breakup of the supercontinent Pangaea. During this era, organisms that survived the great Permian extinction began to diversify in amazing ways. On land, **dinosaurs** became dominant and remained unchallenged for over 100 million years.

Mesozoic History The Mesozoic era began with much of the world's land above sea level. In fact, very few marine fossils are found in North America from the Triassic period.

As the Jurassic period gave way to the Cretaceous, shallow seas invaded much of western North America, the Atlantic, and Gulf coastal regions. These shallow seas created great swamps like those of the Paleozoic era, forming Cretaceous coal deposits that are very important economically to the western United States and Canada.

A major event of the Mesozoic era was the breakup of Pangaea. Follow this breakup in Figure 11. A rift developed between what is now the eastern United States and western Africa, marking the birth of the Atlantic Ocean and the beginning of the breakup of Pangaea, a process that continued for 200 million years, through the Mesozoic and into the Cenozoic.

For: Links on CAT scanning fossils
Visit: www.SciLinks.org
Web Code: cjn-4133

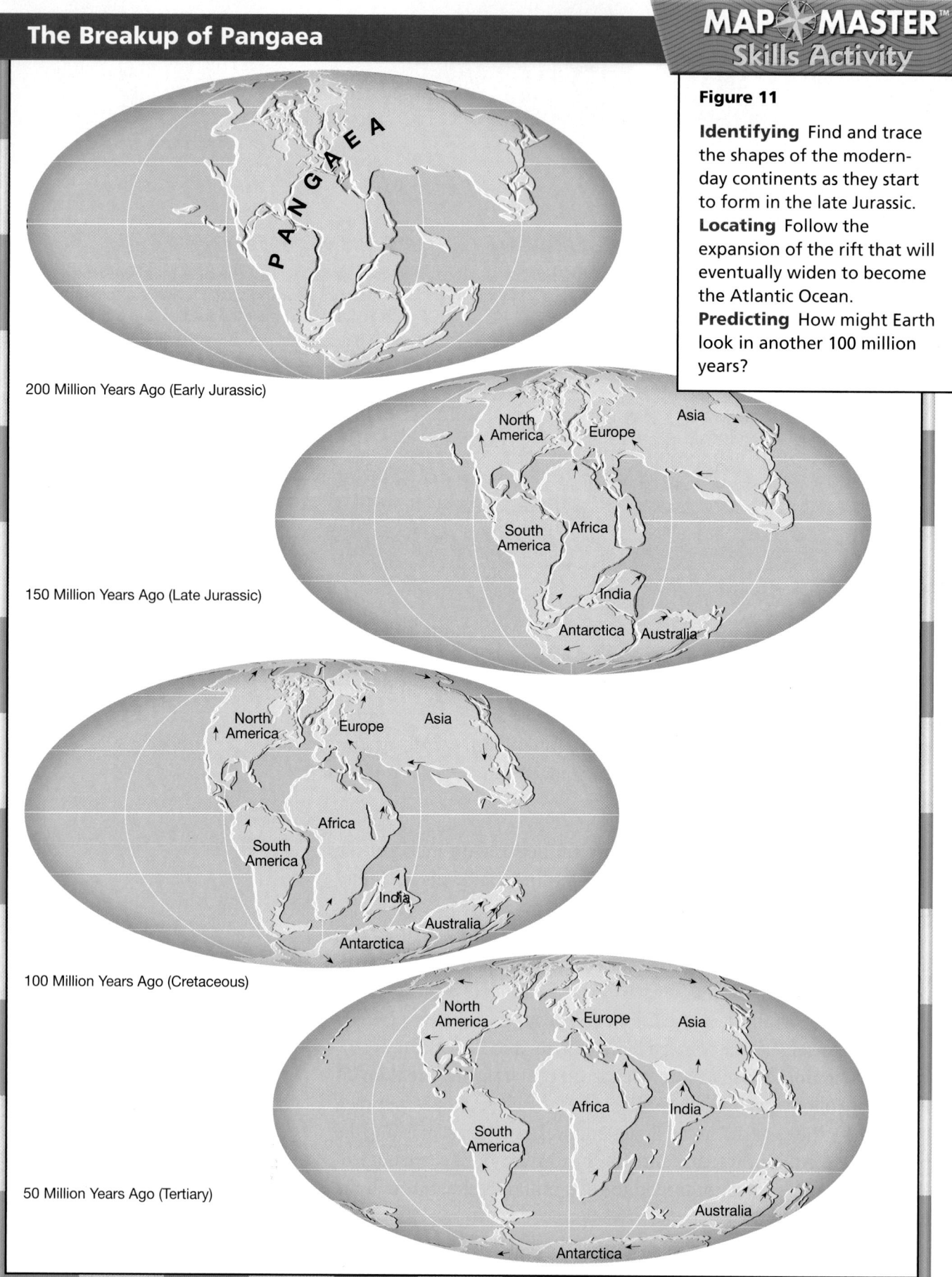

200 Million Years Ago (Early Jurassic)

150 Million Years Ago (Late Jurassic)

100 Million Years Ago (Cretaceous)

50 Million Years Ago (Tertiary)

MAP★MASTER™ Skills Activity

Figure 11

Identifying Find and trace the shapes of the modern-day continents as they start to form in the late Jurassic.
Locating Follow the expansion of the rift that will eventually widen to become the Atlantic Ocean.
Predicting How might Earth look in another 100 million years?

As Pangaea broke apart, the westward-moving North American plate began to override the Pacific plate. Tectonic activity began a continual wave of deformation that moved inland along the entire western part of the continent. The tectonic activity that began in the Jurassic continued throughout the Cretaceous. This activity formed the vast mountains of western North America, like those in Figure 12. Toward the end of the Mesozoic, the ranges of the Rocky Mountains located in Colorado and surrounding states began to form.

 **Reading Checkpoint** *Explain how the Atlantic Ocean was formed.*

Mesozoic Life When the Mesozoic era began, its life forms were the survivors of the great Paleozoic extinction. These survivors were diversified in many ways and filled the biological emptiness created at the end of the Paleozoic. On land, conditions favored life that could adapt to drier climates. Among plants, the **gymnosperms** were a group of seed-bearing plants that did not depend on free-standing water for fertilization. Unlike the first plants to invade the land, gymnosperms were not restricted to living near the water's edge, and they could take advantage of nutrients and space available in dry areas.

 The gymnosperms quickly became the dominant plants of the Mesozoic. Gymnosperm trees included the cycads, the conifers, and the ginkgoes. The cycads resembled a large pineapple plant. The ginkgoes had fan-shaped leaves, much like their modern relatives. The largest plants were the conifers, whose modern descendants include the pines, firs, and junipers.

Figure 12 Mountain ranges such as the Canadian Rockies were formed throughout the Cretaceous.
Relating Cause and Effect *What forces created the mountains?*

The Shelled Egg Among the animals, reptiles readily adapted to the drier Mesozoic environment. They were the first true land animals. Unlike amphibians, reptiles have shell-covered eggs that can be laid on land. The elimination of a water-dwelling stage (like the tadpole stage in frogs) was an important evolutionary step.

Reptiles Dominate  **With the perfection of the shelled egg, reptiles quickly became the dominant land animals.** They continued this dominance for more than 160 million years. The dinosaurs were the most awesome of the Mesozoic reptiles. Some of the huge dinosaurs were carnivorous—meat eaters—while others were herbivorous—plant eaters. For example, *Tyrannosaurus* was a carnivorous dinosaur. *Apatosaurus* (formerly *Brontosaurus*) was an herbivore. However, not all dinosaurs were large. Some small dinosaurs resembled the fleet-footed lizards that exist today.

The reptiles made a spectacular adaptation that had already occurred for insects. One group, the pterosaurs, began to fly. These "dragons of the sky" possessed huge membranous wings that allowed them basic flight, as shown in Figure 13. Another group of reptiles, demonstrated by the fossil *Archaeopteryx*, led to more successful flyers—the birds. Whereas some reptiles took to the skies, others returned to the sea, including the fish-eating plesiosaurs and ichthyosaurs. These reptiles became proficient swimmers but retained their reptilian teeth and breathed by means of lungs.

Reading Checkpoint *How did reptiles become the dominant land animals?*

Figure 13 The flying reptile Pteranodon had a wingspan of 7 meters.

At the end of the Mesozoic, many reptile groups became extinct. Only a few types of reptiles survived to recent times, including the turtles, snakes, crocodiles, and lizards. The huge land-dwelling dinosaurs, the marine plesiosaurs, and the flying pterosaurs are known only through the fossil record. Most scientists believe that the extinction of these reptiles was caused by a large meteorite that collided with Earth. They believe this collision created huge quantities of dust that blocked out the sun, causing plants to die because they could not turn sunlight into food. Without plants, the huge herbivores could not find enough to eat and eventually could not survive. Then, the carnivores who ate the herbivores could no longer find food. The smaller animals probably survived because they needed less food than the huge dinosaurs.

Q *Many dinosaurs were very large. Were they the only large reptiles?*

A No. One well-publicized example is a crocodile known as *Sarcosuchus imperator*, shown in Figure 14. This huge river dweller lived in Africa about 110 million years ago during the Cretaceous period. By age 50 or 60, the animal weighed 8 metric tons and was about 12 meters long—as long as *Tyrannosaurus rex* and much heavier. Its jaws were roughly as long as an adult human. This animal has appropriately been dubbed "supercroc." Paleontologists indicate that the teeth and jaw suggest a diet of large vertebrates, including fish and dinosaurs.

Figure 14 A fossil skull of a large crocodile—*Sarcosuchus imperator*

Section 13.3 Assessment

Reviewing Concepts

1. How did plate tectonics create dramatic changes in the continental land mass during the Mesozoic?
2. What advantage allowed both reptiles and gymnosperms to dominate as life forms in the Mesozoic?
3. What caused the extinction of so many of the reptile groups that had flourished?

Critical Thinking

4. **Comparing and Contrasting** Compare and contrast the physical environment of the Mesozoic era with the Paleozoic.

5. **Predicting** Why do scientists find so many more fossils from the Mesozoic era than from the Paleozoic?

Connecting Concepts

Hypothesizing The fluid in many eggs is similar to seawater, causing some scientists to refer to shelled eggs as "private aquariums." Propose a hypothesis on how environmental conditions might cause shelled eggs to develop and allow animals to move onto land.

13.4 Cenozoic Era: Age of Mammals

Reading Focus

Key Concepts

- What time period is defined by the Cenozoic era?
- Which land formations were created during the Cenozoic era?
- What types of life forms became prominent in the Cenozoic?
- What adaptations enabled mammals to diversify?

Vocabulary

- mammal
- angiosperm

Reading Strategy

Identifying Details Copy the table below. As you read, list the adaptations of each life form.

Angiosperms	Mammals

The Cenozoic era, or "era of recent life," encompasses the past 65 million years of Earth history. It is the "post-dinosaur" era, the time of mammals, including humans. It is during this span that the physical landscapes and life forms of our modern world came into being. The Cenozoic era represents a much smaller fraction of geologic time than either the Paleozoic or the Mesozoic. The Cenozoic era is shorter than the other eras, but it possesses a rich history because the completeness of the geologic record improves as time approaches the present. The rock formations of this time span are more widespread and less disturbed than those of any preceding time.

The Cenozoic era is divided into two periods of very unequal duration, the Tertiary period and the Quaternary period. The Tertiary period embraces about 63 million years, practically all of the Cenozoic era. The Quaternary period represents only the last 2 million years of geologic time.

Cenozoic North America

Most of North America was above sea level throughout the Cenozoic era. However, the eastern and western margins of the continent experienced contrasting events because of their different relationships with plate boundaries. The Atlantic and Gulf coastal regions were far removed from an active plate boundary, so they were tectonically stable. In contrast, western North America was the leading edge of the North American plate. **Plate interactions during the Cenozoic caused many events of mountain building, volcanism, and earthquakes in the West.**

Cenozoic Life

⊙ **Mammals replaced reptiles as the dominant land animals in the Cenozoic.** The Cenozoic is often called the "age of mammals" because land animals came to dominate land life. It could also be called the "age of flowering plants" because the angiosperms enjoyed a similar status in the plant world. ⊙ **Angiosperms—flowering plants with covered seeds—replaced gymnosperms as the dominant land plants.** Marine invertebrates took on a modern look.

The advances in seed fertilization and dispersal allowed angiosperms to experience a rapid development and expansion as the Mesozoic drew to a close. As the Cenozoic era began, angiosperms were already the dominant land plants.

Development of the flowering plants strongly influenced the evolution of both birds and mammals. Birds that feed on seeds and fruits, for example, evolved rapidly during the Cenozoic in close association with the flowering plants. During the middle Tertiary, grasses developed rapidly and spread over the plains. This fostered the emergence of herbivorous mammals that were mainly grazers. In turn, the development and spread of grazing animals established the setting for the evolution of the carnivorous mammals that preyed upon them.

Mammals Replace Reptiles Back in the Mesozoic, an important evolutionary event was the appearance of primitive mammals in the late Triassic, about the same time the dinosaurs emerged. Yet throughout the period of dinosaur dominance, mammals remained as small and primitive. By the close of the Mesozoic era, dinosaurs and other reptiles no longer dominated the land. It was only after these large reptiles became extinct that mammals became the dominant land animals. The transition is a major example in the fossil record of the replacement of one large group by another.

Mammals are distinct from reptiles in important ways. Mammalian young are born alive rather than in eggs, and mammals maintain a steady body temperature—they are "warm-blooded." Because mammals are warm-blooded, they could survive in cold regions and search for food during any season or time of day. Other adaptations included the development of insulating body hair and more efficient heart and lungs. ⊙ **These adaptations allow mammals to lead more active lives than reptiles.**

Figure 15 Fossils being excavated from the La Brea tar pits in 1914. **Inferring** *What kinds of fossils were found in the La Brea tar pits?*

Go Online
SciLINKS
NSTA

For: Links on environmental disruptions
Visit: www.SciLinks.org
Web Code: cjn-4134

With the demise of most Mesozoic reptiles, Cenozoic mammals diversified rapidly. The many forms that exist today evolved from small primitive mammals that were characterized by short legs, flat five-toed feet, and small brains. Their development and specialization took four principal directions: (1) increase in size, (2) increase in brain capacity, (3) specialization of teeth to better accommodate a particular diet, and (4) specialization of limbs to better equip the animal for life in a particular environment.

 **Reading Checkpoint** *What adaptations caused mammals to be successful?*

Large Mammals and Extinction Some groups of mammals became very large. For example, by the Oligocene epoch a hornless rhinoceros that stood nearly 5 meters high had evolved. It is the largest land mammal known to have existed. Many large forms of mammals were common as recently as 11,000 years ago. However, a wave of late Pleistocene extinctions rapidly eliminated these animals from the landscape.

In North America, the mastodon and mammoth, both huge relatives of the elephant, became extinct. In addition, saber-toothed cats, giant beavers, large ground sloths, horses, camels, giant bison, and others died out. The reason for this recent wave of extinctions puzzles scientists. These animals had survived several major glacial advances and interglacial periods, so it is difficult to say that climatic change caused the extinctions. Some scientists believe that early humans hurried the decline of these mammals by selectively hunting large forms. Although this hypothesis is preferred by many, it is not yet accepted by all.

Section 13.4 Assessment

Reviewing Concepts

1. What proportion of the Cenozoic era do each of the two periods make up?
2. How were the mountains of western North America created?
3. What adaptations caused angiosperms to surpass the success of gymnosperms?
4. How did the extinctions at the end of the Mesozoic era allow mammals to be successful?

Critical Thinking

5. **Making Generalizations** How did mobility play a role in the evolutionary success of plants and animals?

6. **Inferring** Although the Quaternary period encompasses much less time than any of the other periods you've studied, a vast majority of fossils and remains found are from this period. Why?

Connecting **Concepts**

Evolutionary Development In what ways were the evolutionary development of plants and animals tied to each other?

Demise of the Dinosaurs

The boundary between the Mesozoic era—"middle life"—and Cenozoic era—"recent life"—about 65 million years ago is of special interest. Around this time, more than half of all plant and animal species died out in a mass extinction. This boundary marks the end of the era in which dinosaurs and other reptiles dominated the landscape and the beginning of the era when mammals become very important.

The extinction of the dinosaurs is generally attributed to the group's inability to adapt to some radical change in the environment's conditions. What event could have caused the rapid extinction of the dinosaurs—one of the most successful groups of land animals ever to have lived?

The most strongly supported hypothesis about the extinction of the dinosaurs states that about 65 million years ago a large meteorite about 10 kilometers in diameter collided with Earth, see Figure 16. The speed of the meteorite impact was believed to be 70,000 kilometers per hour. The force of the impact vaporized the meteorite and trillions of tons of Earth's crust. Huge quantities of dust and other metamorphosed debris were blasted high into the atmosphere.

For months the encircling dust cloud would have greatly restricted the sunlight reaching Earth's surface. Without sunlight for photosynthesis, delicate food chains would have collapsed. By the time the sunlight returned, more than half of the species on Earth, including numerous marine organisms, had become extinct.

What evidence points to such a catastrophic collision 65 million years ago? First, a thin layer of sediment nearly 1 centimeter thick has been discovered worldwide. This sediment contains a high level of the element iridium, which is rare in Earth's crust but is found in high proportions in stony meteorites. Could this layer be the scattered remains of the meteorite that was responsible for the environmental changes that led to the demise of many reptile groups?

Despite its growing support, some scientists disagree with the impact hypothesis. These scientists suggest that huge volcanic eruptions led to the breakdown in the food chain. They cite enormous outpourings of lavas in the Deccan Plateau of northern India about 65 million years ago as support for their thesis. It could be that both volcanism and a catastrophic impact played a role.

Whatever caused the extinction, we now have a greater appreciation of the role of catastrophic events in shaping the history of our planet and the life that occupies it. Could a catastrophic event having similar results occur today? This possibility may explain why an event that occurred 65 million years ago has captured the interest of so many.

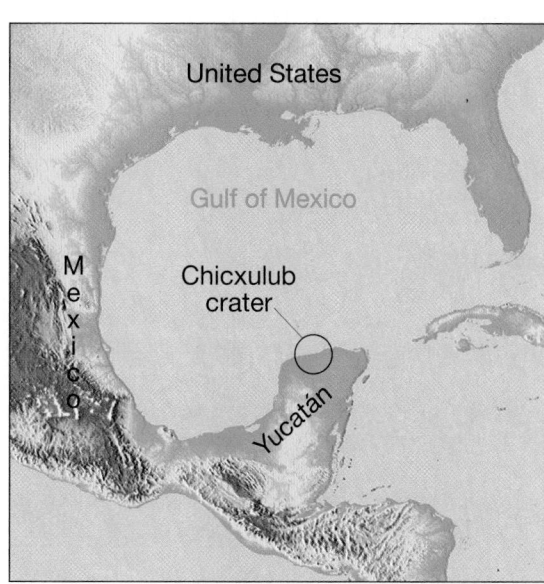

Figure 16 Some researchers believe that the Chicxulub crater is the impact site that resulted in the demise of the dinosaurs.

Modeling the Geologic Time Scale

Applying the techniques of geologic dating, the history of Earth has been subdivided into several different units that provide a meaningful time frame. The events that make up Earth's history can be arranged within this time frame to provide a clearer picture of the past. The span of a human life is like the blink of an eye compared to the age of Earth. Because of this, it can be difficult comprehending the magnitude of geologic time.

Problem
How can the geologic time scale be represented in a way that allows a clearer visual understanding?

Materials
- strip of adding machine paper measuring 5 meters or longer
- meterstick or metric measuring tape
- pencil

Skills
Measuring, Calculating, Interpreting Diagrams

Procedure
1. Obtain a piece of adding machine paper slightly longer than 5 meters in length. Draw a line at one end of the paper and label it "Present."

2. Using the following scale, construct a timeline by completing Steps 3 and 4.

Scale
1 meter = 1 billion years

10 centimeters = 100 million years

1 centimeter = 10 million years

1 millimeter = 1 million years

3. Using the geologic time scale on page 387 as a reference, divide your timeline into the eons and eras of geologic time. Label each division with its name and indicate its absolute age.

4. Using the scale, plot and label the plant and animal events on your timeline that are listed on the geologic time scale.

Analyze and Conclude

1. **Calculating** What fraction or percent of geologic time is represented by the Precambrian eon?

2. **Explaining** Using your text and class notes as references, explain why the approximate time of 540 million years ago was selected to mark the end of the Precambrian eon and the beginning of Phanerozoic eon.

3. **Inferring** Suggest one reason why the periods of the Cenozoic era have been further subdivided into several epochs with reasonably reliable accuracy.

4. **Analyzing Data** How many times longer is the whole of geologic time than the time represented by the 5000 years of recorded history?

5. **Calculating** For what fraction or percent of geologic time have land plants been present on Earth?

Geologic Time Scale

Eon	Era	Millions of years ago
Phanerozoic	Cenozoic	65
	Mesozoic	248
	Paleozoic	540
Precambrian	Proterozoic — Late	900
	Proterozoic — Middle	1600
	Proterozoic — Early	2500
	Archean — Late	3000
	Archean — Middle	3400
	Archean — Early	3800
	Hadean	
	Origin of Earth	4500

Era	Period	Epoch	Development of Plants and Animals
Cenozoic	Quaternary	Holocene 0.01	Humans develop
		Pleistocene 1.8	
	Tertiary	Pliocene 5.3	"Age of Mammals"
		Miocene 23.8	
		Oligocene 33.7	
		Eocene 54.8	
		Paleocene 65.0	Extinction of dinosaurs and many other species
Mesozoic	Cretaceous 144	"Age of Reptiles"	First flowering plants
	Jurassic 206		First birds
	Triassic 248		Dinosaurs dominant
Paleozoic	Permian 290	"Age of Amphibians"	Extinction of trilobites and many other marine animals
	Carboniferous — Pennsylvanian 323		First reptiles
	Carboniferous — Mississippian 354		Large coal swamps
			Amphibians abundant
	Devonian 417	"Age of Fishes"	First insect fossils
			Fishes dominant
	Silurian 443		First land plants
	Ordovician 490	"Age of Invertebrates"	First fishes
			Trilobites dominant
	Cambrian 540		First organisms with shells
	Precambrian		First multicelled organisms

13.1 Precambrian Time: Vast and Puzzling

🌐 Key Concepts

- The Precambrian encompasses immense geological time, from Earth's distant beginning 4.56 billion years ago until the start of the Cambrian period, over 4 billion years later.

- Much of what we know about Precambrian rocks comes from data gathered in exploring the mineral resources in shields.

- Earth's original atmosphere was made up of gases similar to those released in volcanic emissions today—water vapor, carbon dioxide, nitrogen, and several trace gases.

- Primitive organisms evolved that used photosynthesis and released oxygen.

- Oxygen began to accumulate in the atmosphere about 2.5 billion years ago.

- The most common Precambrian fossils are stromatolites.

Vocabulary

shields, *p. 366*; stromatolites, *p. 368*

13.2 Paleozoic Era: Life Explodes

🌐 Key Concepts

- Following the long Precambrian, the most recent 540 million years of Earth history are divided into three eras: Paleozoic, Mesozoic, and Cenozoic.

- During the Cambrian, Ordovician, and Silurian periods, the vast southern continent of Gondwana encompassed five continents (South America, Africa, Australia, Antarctica, and parts of Asia).

- Life in early Paleozoic time was restricted to the seas.

- By the end of the Paleozoic, all the continents had fused into the supercontinent of Pangaea.

- Some 400 million years ago, plants that had adapted to survive at the water's edge began to move inland, becoming land plants.

- The amphibians rapidly diversified because they had minimal competition from other land dwellers.

Vocabulary

Gondwana, *p. 370*; Pangaea, *p. 372*; Laurasia, *p. 372*

13.3 Mesozoic Era: Age of Reptiles

🌐 Key Concepts

- A major event of the Mesozoic era was the breakup of Pangaea.

- Gymnosperms quickly became the dominant plants of the Mesozoic.

- With the perfection of the shelled egg, reptiles quickly became the dominant land animals of the Mesozoic era.

- At the end of the Mesozoic, many reptile groups became extinct.

Vocabulary

dinosaur, *p. 377*; gymnosperm, *p. 379*

13.4 Cenozoic Era: Age of Mammals

🌐 Key Concepts

- The Cenozoic era is divided into two periods of very unequal duration, the Tertiary period and the Quaternary period.

- Plate interaction during the Cenozoic caused many events of mountain building, volcanism, and earthquakes in the West.

- Mammals replaced reptiles as the dominant land animals in the Cenozoic.

- Angiosperms—flowering plants with covered seeds—replaced gymnosperms as the dominant land plants.

- Several adaptations, including hair and live birth of offspring, allowed mammals to lead more active lives than reptiles.

Vocabulary

mammal, *p. 383*; angiosperm, *p. 383*

Reviewing Content

Choose the letter that best answers the question or completes the statement.

1. Which era spans the least amount of time on the geologic scale?
   a. Cenozoic **b.** Mesozoic
   c. Paleozoic **d.** Precambrian

2. The most common Precambrian fossils are
   a. fish.
   b. stromatolites.
   c. trilobites.
   d. ferns.

3. Which era is known as the "age of reptiles"?
   a. Cenozoic **b.** Mesozoic
   c. Paleozoic **d.** Proterozoic

4. Modern squids descended from what type of early Paleozoic organisms?
   a. cephalopods **b.** trilobites
   c. brachiopods **d.** amphibians

5. The Devonian period is known as the
   a. "age of reptiles."
   b. "age of amphibians."
   c. "age of fishes."
   d. "age of invertebrates."

6. Which adaptation allowed gymnosperm plants to colonize and dominate land?
   a. stems **b.** seeds
   c. leaves **d.** flowers

7. Reptiles that were adapted to fly included the
   a. plesiosaurs. **b.** pterosaurs.
   c. ichthyosaurs. **d.** tyrannosaurs.

8. Humans first appeared during the
   a. Cretaceous period.
   b. Jurassic period.
   c. Quaternary period.
   d. Tertiary period.

9. Insulating body hair is a characteristic of
   a. mammals.
   b. amphibians.
   c. reptiles.
   d. invertebrates.

10. What development caused the emergence of animals that were grazing herbivores?
    a. seed plants
    b. grasses
    c. fruits
    d. carnivorous mammals

Understanding Concepts

11. How did plants help change Earth's early atmosphere?

12. What are shields? What kind of information is gained from shields?

Use the photograph below to answer Question 13.

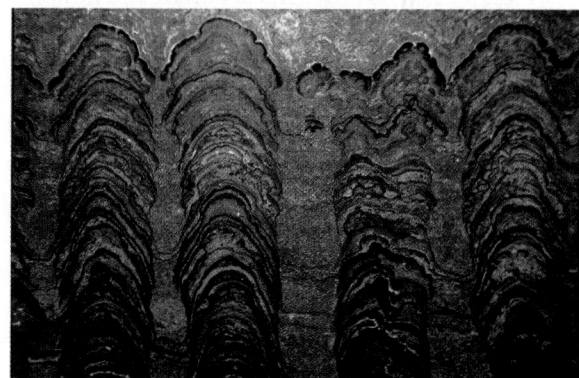

13. This photograph shows evidence of what kind of organism?

14. What significant tectonic activity occurred during the Mesozoic?

15. What present-day continents made up Gondwana?

16. Which kind of animals are trilobites and cephalopods?

17. Modern fishes and sharks both evolved from what type of ancient animals?

18. What development allowed mammals to adapt to different environments successfully?

Critical Thinking

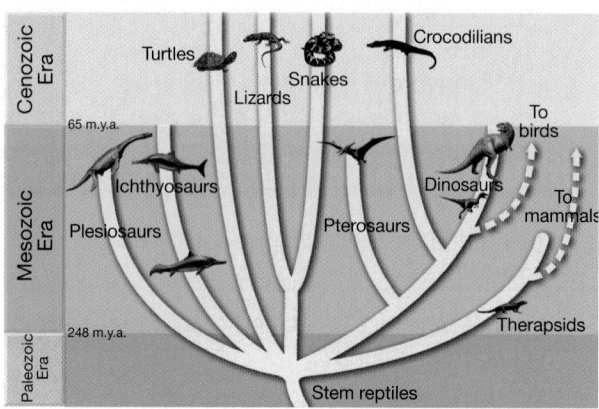

19. Interpreting Diagrams Examine the figure above, which shows the origin and development of reptile groups. Arrange these groups in relative chronological order from first appearance: crocodilians, lizards, plesiosaurs, and pterosaurs.

20. Interpreting Photographs Most of the vast North American coal resources located from Pennsylvania to Illinois began forming during the Pennsylvanian and Mississippian periods. Using Figure 10 on page 375, describe the climatic and biological conditions associated with this environment.

21. Interpreting Diagrams Examine Figure 8B and C. Where, relative to the equator, was North America located during the time of coal formation? What role did plate tectonics play in determining the conditions that produced North America's coal reserves?

22. Making Generalizations Why is so little known about the Precambrian time?

23. Relating Cause and Effect Describe the role of the biosphere, hydrosphere, and solid Earth in forming the current level of atmospheric oxygen.

24. Inferring What is the major source of free oxygen in Earth's atmosphere?

25. Comparing and Contrasting Make a list of differences between amphibians and reptiles.

Concepts in Action

26. Classifying Match the following words and phrases to the most appropriate time span. Select among the following: Precambrian, early Paleozoic, late Paleozoic, Mesozoic, and Cenozoic.
  (a) Pangaea came into existence
  (b) Encompasses the least amount of time
  (c) Shields
  (d) Age of dinosaurs
  (e) Triassic, Jurassic, and Cretaceous
  (f) Formation of most of the world's major iron-ore deposits
  (g) Age of fishes
  (h) Cambrian, Ordovician, and Silurian
  (i) Golden age of trilobites
  (j) Gymnosperms were dominant

27. Writing in Science Write a paragraph explaining the relationship between the development and movement of plants, herbivore animals, and carnivore animals.

Performance-Based Assessment

Researching Research and select several different types of gymnosperm and angiosperm plants that are mentioned in the chapter. Also, research more primitive plants that existed before gymnosperms. Write a paragraph describing each plant, including information on its physical structure, reproduction, and characteristics that might cause it to be more successful in some eras than others.

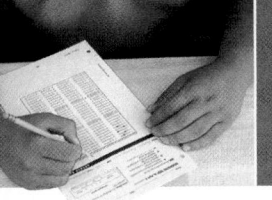

Standardized Test Prep

Test-Taking Tip

Anticipate the Answer

When answering multiple-choice questions, a useful strategy is to cover up the given answers and supply your own answer. Then compare your answer with those listed and select the one that most closely matches.

Practice anticipating the answer in this question.

Early in Earth's history, which gas was largely removed from the atmosphere and became more concentrated in seawater?

(A) oxygen
(B) carbon dioxide
(C) argon
(D) hydrogen

(Answer: B)

Choose the letter that best answers the question or completes the statement.

1. Which of the following modern-day continents was NOT a part of Gondwana?
   (A) Africa
   (B) North America
   (C) South America
   (D) Antarctica

2. Where did the water that makes up Earth's oceans originally come from?
   (A) Water vapor as part of the original atmosphere.
   (B) Water vapor dissolved in molten rock.
   (C) Liquid water came from beneath Earth's surface and from comets.
   (D) Liquid water settled into low areas of the surface.

Use the diagram below to answer Questions 3 and 4.

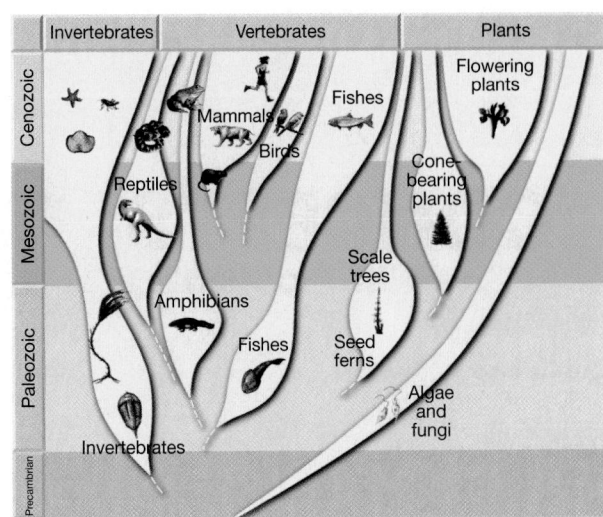

3. According to the diagram, which group of organisms appeared first?
   (A) invertebrates
   (B) flowering plants
   (C) algae and fungi
   (D) fishes

4. According to the diagram, when did the first mammals appear?
   (A) Precambrian
   (B) Paleozoic
   (C) Mesozoic
   (D) Cenozoic

Answer the following questions in complete sentences.

5. What are two hypotheses for the extinction of the dinosaurs and many other plant and animal groups at the end of the Mesozoic era?

6. Why is so little known about the Precambrian era?

7. List and describe four traits that separate mammals from reptiles.

14 The Ocean Floor

CONCEPTS
— in Action —

Quick Lab
Evaporative Salts

Exploration Lab
Modeling Seafloor Depth Transects

Understanding Earth
Explaining Coral Atolls—Darwin's Hypothesis

 **GEODe** Oceans
↳ Floor of the Ocean

DISCOVERY **Video Field Trip**
CHANNEL
SCHOOL *Seafloor Maps*

Take a field trip to the bottom of the sea with Discovery Channel and learn how the ocean floor can be measured. Answer the following questions after watching the video.

1. Describe how sonar technology can help scientists map an area of sea floor.

2. Does sonar technology provide realistic measurements for the entire ocean floor? Why or why not?

For: Chapter 14 Resources
Visit: PHSchool.com
Web Code: cjk-9999

This photograph shows a view of the ▶ Atlantic Ocean near Cape Canaveral, Florida.

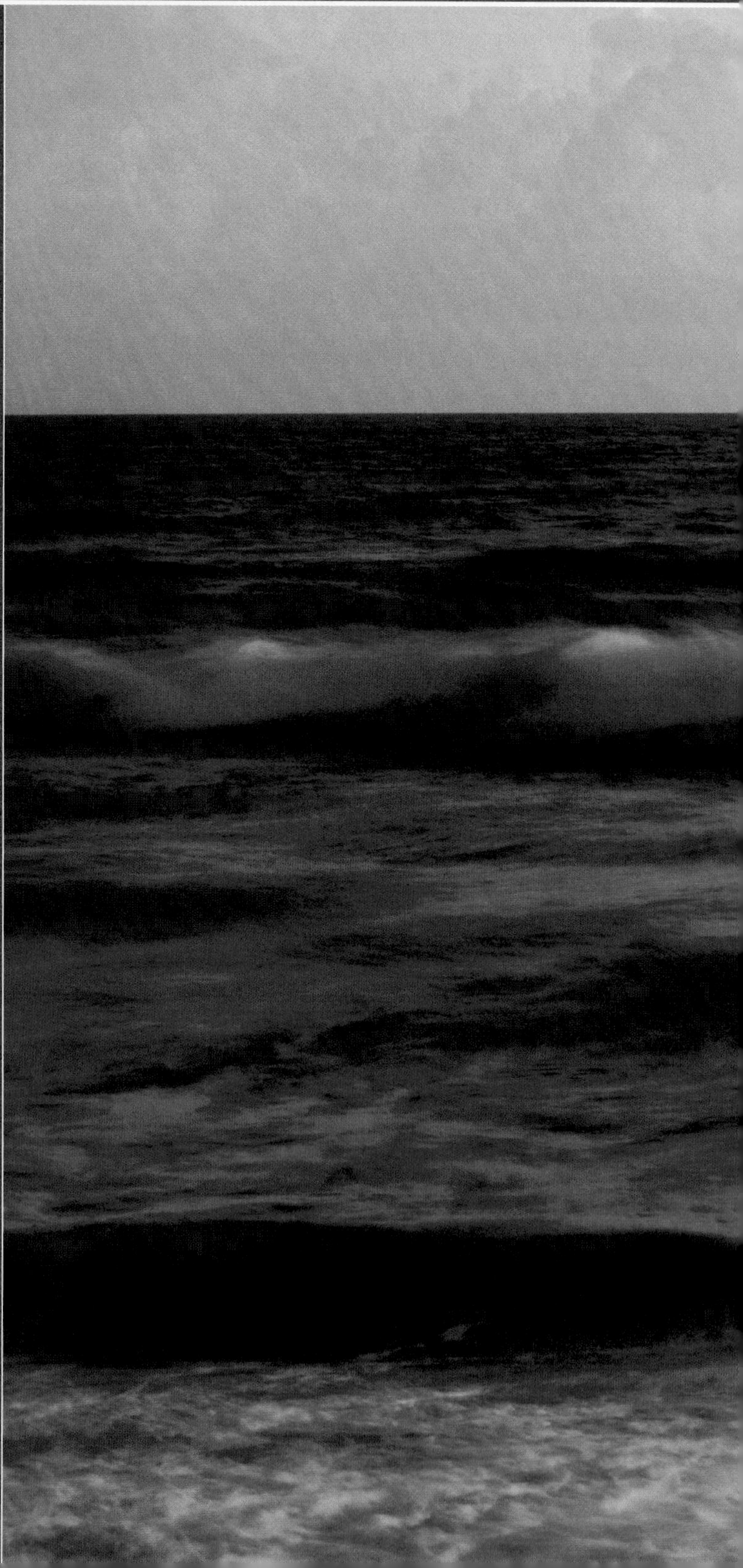

Chapter Preview

Inquiry Activity

How Does Particle Size Affect Settling Rates?

Procedure

1. Fill two large transparent containers with water. Place two samples of sediment, one clay and one sand, on separate sheets of white paper. Examine the sediments with a hand lens. Determine which sediment sample has larger-sized particles. Record your observations.

2. Carefully measure 1 tbsp of the clay sample. Hold the spoon directly above the first container and pour the clay into the water. Using a stopwatch, time how long it takes for the entire clay sample to reach the bottom of the container and settle. Record the time.

3. Repeat Step 2 using the second container and the sand sample. Be sure to hold the spoon the same distance from the container as you did in the clay sample.

Think About It

1. **Drawing Conclusions** Which sample had smaller particles? Which sample took longer to settle in the water? Explain the general relationship between sediment size and settling rates.

2. **Predicting** Both of these sediments enter ocean water from rivers. Predict which type of sediment would be found closest to the coast. Which will be found father away? Explain.

14.1 The Vast World Ocean

Reading Focus

Key Concepts

- How much of Earth's surface is covered by water?
- How can the world ocean be divided?
- How does the topography of the ocean floor compare to that on land?
- What types of technology are used to study the ocean floor?

Vocabulary

- oceanography
- bathymetry
- sonar
- submersible

Reading Strategy

Building Vocabulary Draw a table similar to the one below that includes all the vocabulary terms listed for the section. As you read the section, define each term in your own words.

Vocabulary Term	Definition
oceanography	a. _____?_____
bathymetry	b. _____?_____
sonar	c. _____?_____
submersible	d. _____?_____

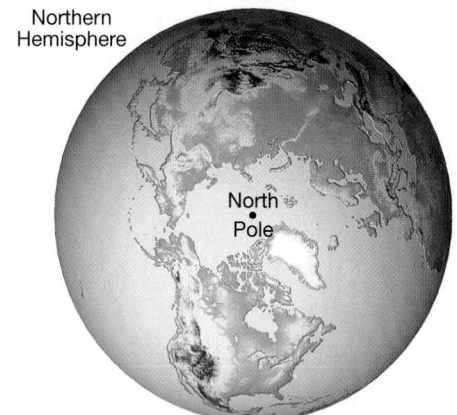

North Pole

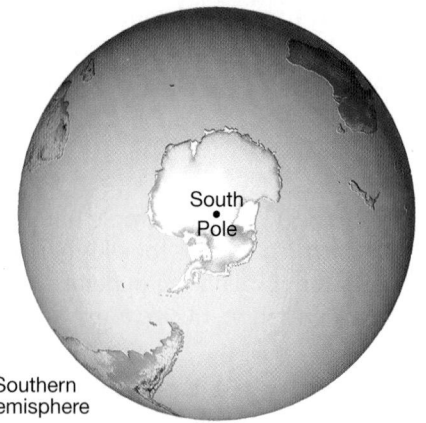

South Pole

Figure 1 The World Ocean These views of Earth show the planet is dominated by a single interconnected world ocean.

How deep is the ocean? How much of Earth is covered by the global ocean? What does the ocean floor look like? Humans have long been interested in finding answers to these questions. However, it was not until relatively recently that these simple questions could be answered. Suppose, for example, that all of the water were drained from the ocean. What would we see? Plains? Mountains? Canyons? Plateaus? You may be surprised to find that the ocean conceals all of these features, and more.

The Blue Planet

Look at Figure 1. You can see why the "blue planet" or the "water planet" are appropriate nicknames for Earth. **Nearly 71 percent of Earth's surface is covered by the global ocean.** Although the ocean makes up a much greater percentage of Earth's surface than the continents, it has only been since the late 1800s that the ocean became an important focus of study. New technologies have allowed scientists to collect large amounts of data about the oceans. As technology has advanced, the field of oceanography has grown. **Oceanography** is a science that draws on the methods and knowledge of geology, chemistry, physics, and biology to study all aspects of the world ocean.

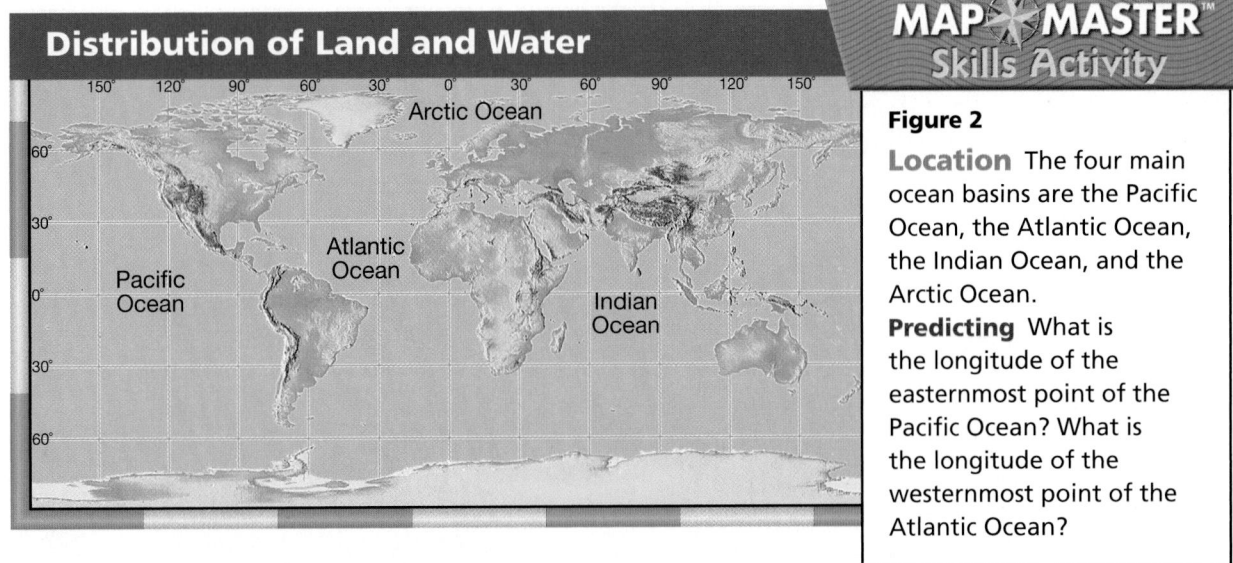

Distribution of Land and Water

Arctic Ocean

Atlantic Ocean

Pacific Ocean

Indian Ocean

Figure 2

Location The four main ocean basins are the Pacific Ocean, the Atlantic Ocean, the Indian Ocean, and the Arctic Ocean.
Predicting What is the longitude of the easternmost point of the Pacific Ocean? What is the longitude of the westernmost point of the Atlantic Ocean?

Geography of the Oceans

The area of Earth is about 510 million square kilometers. Of this total, approximately 360 million square kilometers, or 71 percent, is represented by oceans and smaller seas such as the Mediterranean Sea and the Caribbean Sea. Continents and islands comprise the remaining 29 percent, or 150 million square kilometers. **The world ocean can be divided into four main ocean basins—the Pacific Ocean, the Atlantic Ocean, the Indian Ocean, and the Arctic Ocean.** These ocean basins are shown in Figure 2.

The Pacific Ocean is the largest ocean. In fact, it is the largest single geographic feature on Earth. It covers more than half of the ocean surface area on Earth. It is also the world's deepest ocean, with an average depth of 3940 meters.

The Atlantic Ocean is about half the size of the Pacific Ocean, and is not quite as deep. It is a relatively narrow ocean compared to the Pacific. The Atlantic and Pacific Oceans are bounded to the east and west by continents.

The Indian Ocean is slightly smaller than the Atlantic Ocean, but it has about the same average depth. Unlike the Pacific and Atlantic oceans, the Indian Ocean is located almost entirely in the southern hemisphere.

The Arctic Ocean is about 7 percent of the size of the Pacific Ocean. It is only a little more than one-quarter as deep as the rest of the oceans.

Reading Checkpoint *What are the four main ocean basins?*

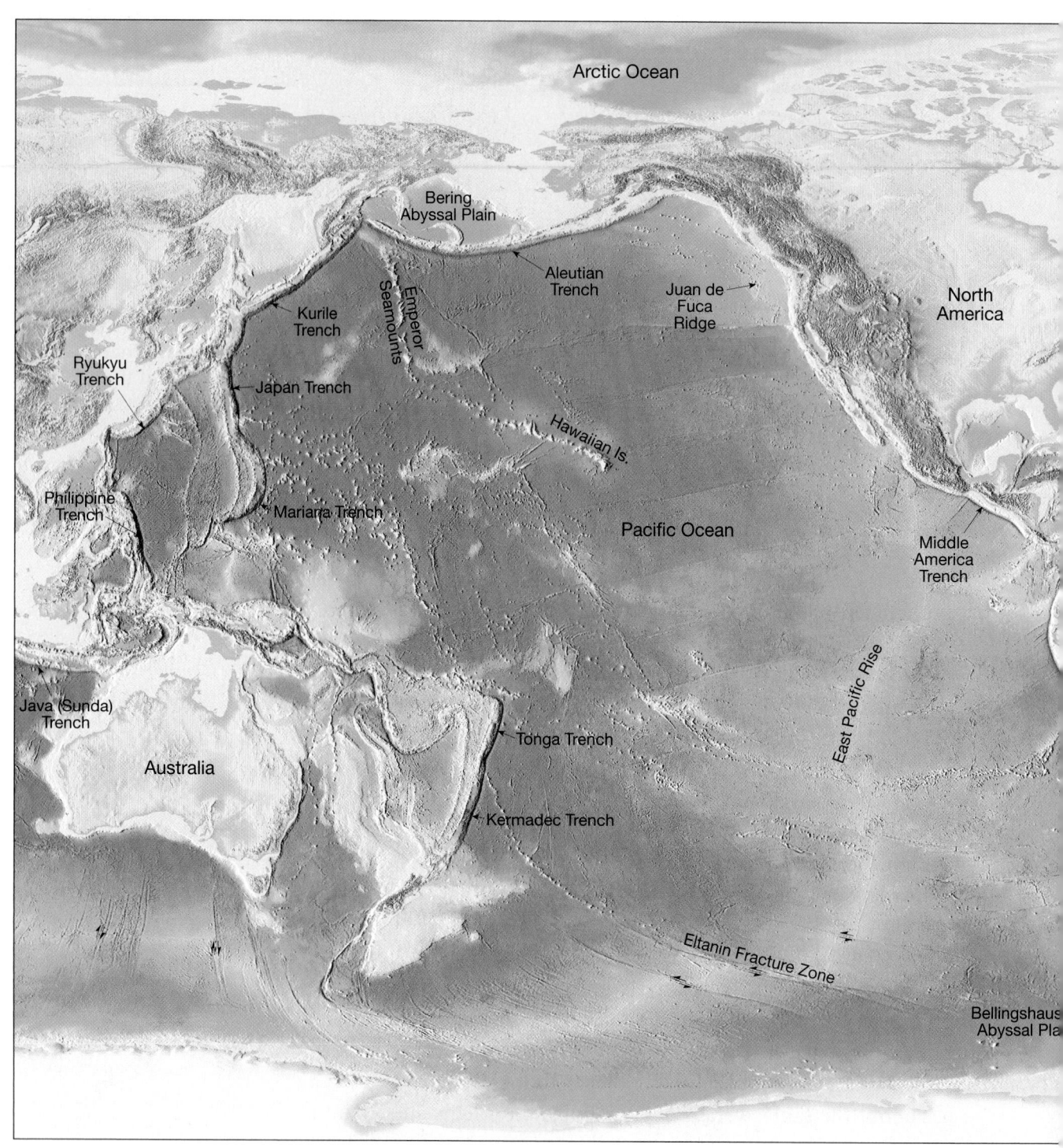

Arctic Ocean

Bering
Abyssal Plain

Aleutian
Trench

Juan de
Fuca
Ridge

North
America

Kurile
Trench

Emperor
Seamounts

Ryukyu
Trench

Japan Trench

Hawaiian Is.

Philippine
Trench

Mariana Trench

Pacific Ocean

Middle
America
Trench

Java (Sunda)
Trench

East Pacific Rise

Australia

Tonga Trench

Kermadec Trench

Eltanin Fracture Zone

Bellingshaus
Abyssal Pla

Figure 3 The topography
of the ocean floor is as
varied as the topography of
the continents. The ocean
floor contains mountain
ranges, trenches, and flat
regions called abyssal
plains.
Interpreting Diagrams
*List all of the features you
can identify in the figure.*

Mapping the Ocean Floor

If all the water were drained from the ocean basins, a variety of features
would be seen. These features include chains of volcanoes, tall
mountain ranges, trenches, and large submarine plateaus. 🔵 **The
topography of the ocean floor is as diverse as that of continents.** The
topographic features of the ocean floor are shown in Figure 3.

An understanding of ocean-floor features came with the development of techniques to measure the depth of the oceans. **Bathymetry**

Greenland

Arctic
Mid-Ocean Ridge

Asia

Gibbs
Fracture
Zone

uerto-Rico
Trench

Atlantic
Ocean

Red Sea
Rift

Mid-Atlantic Ridge

Demerara
Abyssal
Plain

Africa

Mid-Indian Ridge

South
America

St. Paul
Fracture
Zone

Indian
Ocean

Peru-Chile
trench

Southwest Indian Ridge

Southeast Indian Ridge

South Sandwich
Trench

Weddell Abyssal Plain

Key: ⟳ transform fault

(*bathos* = depth, *metry* = measurement) is the measurement of ocean depths and the charting of the shape or topography of the ocean floor.

The first understanding of the ocean floor's varied topography did not unfold until the historic three-and-a-half-year voyage of the HMS *Challenger*. From December 1872 to May 1876, the *Challenger* expedition made the first—and perhaps still the most comprehensive—study of the global ocean ever attempted by one agency. The 127,500 kilometer trip took the ship and its crew of scientists to every ocean

Go Online

SciLINKS
NSTA

For: Links on oceans
Visit: www.SciLinks.org
Web Code: cjn-5141

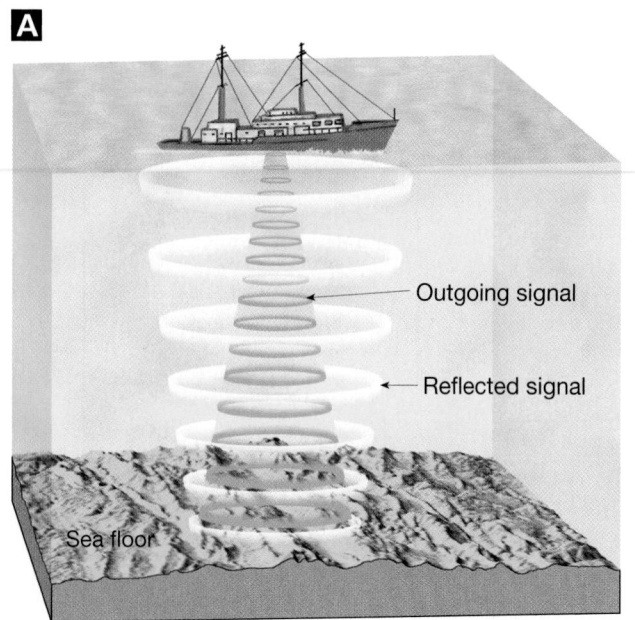

A

Outgoing signal

Reflected signal

Sea floor

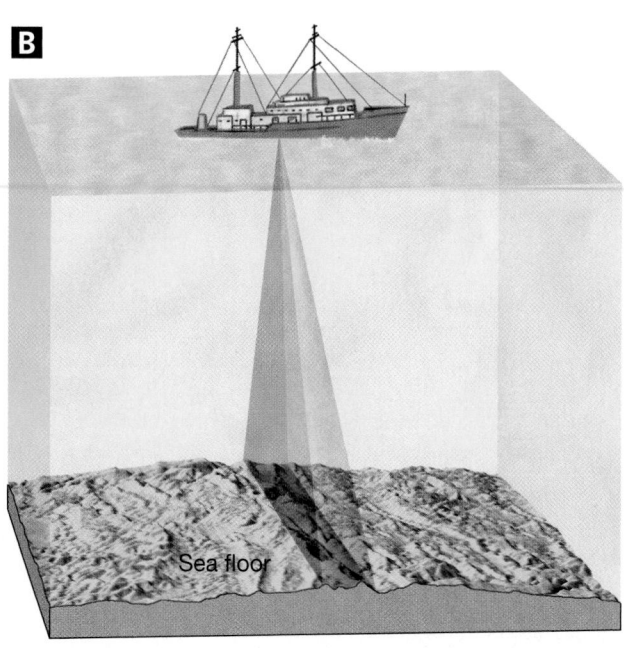

B

Sea floor

Figure 4 Sonar Methods
A By using sonar, oceanographers can determine the depth of the ocean floor in a particular area. **B** Modern multibeam sonar obtains a profile of a narrow swath of seafloor every few seconds.

except the Arctic. Throughout the voyage, they sampled various ocean properties. They measured water depth by lowering a long, weighted line overboard. 🌐 **Today's technology—particularly sonar, satellites, and submersibles—allows scientists to study the ocean floor in a more efficient and precise manner than ever before.**

Sonar In the 1920s, a technological breakthrough occurred with the invention of sonar, a type of electronic depth-sounding equipment. Sonar is an acronym for **so**und **na**vigation **a**nd **r**anging. It is also referred to as echo sounding. Sonar works by transmitting sound waves toward the ocean bottom, as shown in Figure 4A. With simple sonar, a sensitive receiver intercepts the echo reflected from the bottom. Then a clock precisely measures the time interval to fractions of a second. Depth can be calculated from the speed of sound waves in water— about 1500 meters per second—and the time required for the energy pulse to reach the ocean floor and return. The depths determined from continuous monitoring of these echoes are plotted. In this way a profile of the ocean floor is obtained. A chart of the seafloor can be produced by combining these profiles.

In the last few decades, researchers have designed even more sophisticated sonar to map the ocean floor. In contrast to simple sonar, multibeam sonar uses more than one sound source and listening device. As you can see from Figure 4B, this technique obtains a profile of a narrow strip of ocean floor rather than obtaining the depth of a single point every few seconds. These profiles are recorded every few seconds as the research vessel advances. When a ship uses multibeam sonar to make a map of a section of ocean floor, the ship travels through the area in a regularly spaced back-and-forth pattern. Not surprisingly, this method is known as "mowing the lawn."

Satellites Measuring the shape of the ocean surface from space is another technological breakthrough that has led to a better understanding of the ocean floor. After compensating for waves, tides, currents, and atmospheric effects, scientists discovered that the ocean surface is not perfectly flat. This is because gravity attracts water toward regions where massive ocean floor features occur. Therefore, mountains and ridges produce elevated areas on the ocean surface. Features such as canyons and trenches cause slight depressions.

The differences in ocean-surface height caused by ocean floor features are not visible to the human eye. However, satellites are able to measure these small differences by bouncing microwaves off the ocean surface. Figure 5 shows how the outgoing radar pulses are reflected back to a satellite. The height of the ocean surface can be calculated by knowing the satellite's exact position. Devices on satellites can measure variations in sea-surface height as small as 3 to 6 centimeters. This type of data has added greatly to the knowledge of ocean-floor topography. Cross-checked with traditional sonar depth measurements, the data are used to produce detailed ocean-floor maps, such as the one previously shown in Figure 3.

 **Reading Checkpoint** *How do satellites help us learn about the shape of the seafloor?*

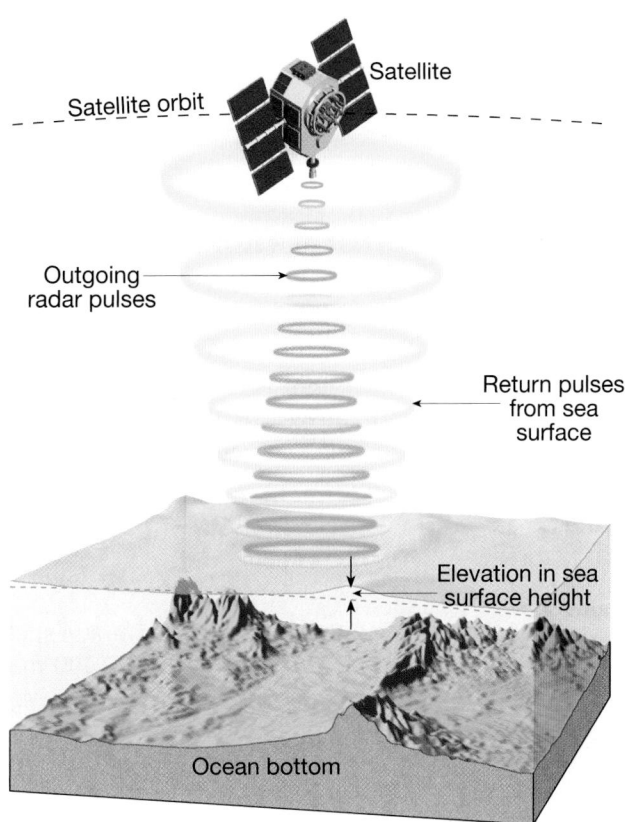

Satellite

Satellite orbit

Outgoing radar pulses

Return pulses from sea surface

Elevation in sea surface height

Ocean bottom

Figure 5 Satellite Method
Satellites can be used to measure sea-surface height. The data collected by satellites can be used to predict the location of large features on the seafloor. This method of data collection is much faster than using sonar.

Submersibles A **submersible** is a small underwater craft used for deep-sea research. Submersibles are used to collect data about areas of the ocean that were previously unreachable by humans. Submersibles are equipped with a number of instruments ranging from thermometers to cameras to pressure gauges. The operators of submersibles can record video and photos of previously unknown creatures that live in the abyss. They can collect water samples and sediment samples for analysis.

The first submersible was used in 1934 by William Beebe. He descended to a depth of 923 meters off of Bermuda in a steel sphere that was tethered to a ship. Since that time, submersibles have become more sophisticated. In 1960, Jacques Piccard descended in the untethered submersible *Trieste* to 10,912 meters below the ocean surface into the Mariana Trench. *Alvin* and *Sea Cliff II* are two other manned submersibles used for deep-sea research. *Alvin* can reach depths of 4000 meters, and *Sea Cliff II* can reach 6000 meters.

Today, many submersibles are unmanned and operated remotely by computers. These remotely operated vehicles (ROVs) can remain under water for long periods. They collect data, record video, use sonar, and collect sample organisms with remotely operated arms. Another type of submersible, the autonomous underwater vehicle (AUV), is under development. Its goal is to collect long-term data without interruption.

Section 14.1 Assessment

Reviewing Concepts

1. How does the area of Earth's surface covered by the oceans compare with the area covered by land?

2. Name the four ocean basins. Which of the four ocean basins is the largest? Which is located almost entirely in the southern hemisphere?

3. How does the topography of the ocean floor compare to that on land? Name three topographic features found on the ocean floor.

4. What types of technology are used to study the ocean floor?

5. Describe how sonar is used to determine seafloor depth.

Critical Thinking

6. **Comparing and Contrasting** Compare and contrast the use of satellites and submersibles to collect data about the topography of the seafloor.

7. **Inferring** Why is deep-sea exploration and data collection difficult?

Math Practice

8. Assuming the average speed of sound waves in water is 1500 meters per second, determine the water depth in meters if a sonar signal requires 4.5 seconds to hit the bottom and return to the recorder.

Reading Focus

Key Concepts

- What are the three main regions of the ocean floor?
- How do continental margins in the Atlantic Ocean differ from those in the Pacific Ocean?
- How are deep-ocean trenches formed?
- How are abyssal plains formed?
- What is formed at mid-ocean ridges?

Vocabulary

- ◆ continental margin
- ◆ continental shelf
- ◆ continental slope
- ◆ submarine canyon
- ◆ turbidity current
- ◆ continental rise
- ◆ ocean basin floor
- ◆ abyssal plains
- ◆ seamounts
- ◆ mid-ocean ridge
- ◆ seafloor spreading

Reading Strategy

Outlining Before you read, make an outline of this section. Use the green headings as the main topics and the blue headings as subtopics. As you read, add supporting details.

> **I.** Continental Margins
>   **A.** Continental Shelf
>   **B.** Continental Slope
>   **C.** _____ ?
> **II.** _____ ?
>   **A.** _____ ?

Oceanographers studying the topography of the ocean floor have divided it into three major regions. ⬤ **The ocean floor regions are the continental margins, the ocean basin floor, and the mid-ocean ridge.** The map in Figure 6 outlines these regions for the North Atlantic Ocean. The profile at the bottom of the illustration shows the varied topography. Scientists have discovered that each of these regions has its own unique characteristics and features.

Figure 6 Topography of the North Atlantic Ocean Basin
Beneath the map is a profile of the area between points A and B. The profile has been exaggerated 40 times to make the topographic features more distinct.

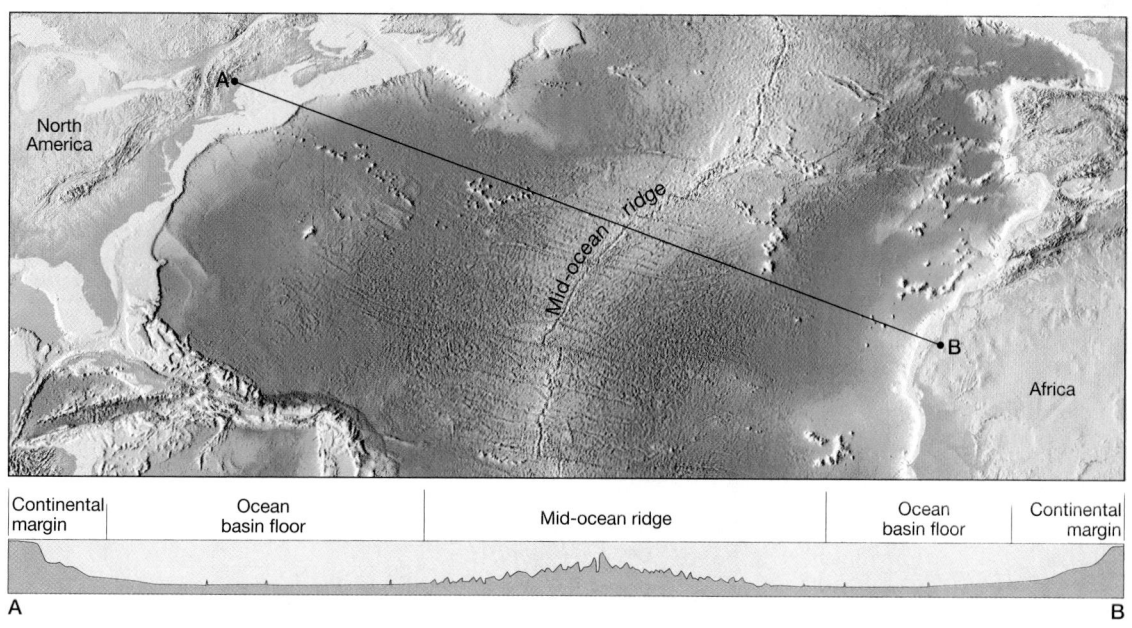

Continental Margins

The zone of transition between a continent and the adjacent ocean basin floor is known as the **continental margin.** 🔑 **In the Atlantic Ocean, thick layers of undisturbed sediment cover the continental margin. This region has very little volcanic or earthquake activity.** This is because the continental margins in the Atlantic Ocean are not associated with plate boundaries, unlike the continental margins of the Pacific Ocean. 🔑 **In the Pacific Ocean, oceanic crust is plunging beneath continental crust. This force results in a narrow continental margin that experiences both volcanic activity and earthquakes.** Figure 7 shows the features of a continental margin found along the Atlantic coast.

Continental Shelf What if you were to begin an underwater journey eastward across the Atlantic Ocean? The first area of ocean floor you would encounter is the continental shelf. The **continental shelf** is the gently sloping submerged surface extending from the shoreline. The shelf is almost nonexistent along some coastlines. However, the shelf may extend seaward as far as 1500 kilometers along other coastlines. On average, the continental shelf is about 80 kilometers wide and 130 meters deep at its seaward edge. The average steepness of the shelf is equal to a drop of only about 2 meters per kilometer. The slope is so slight that to the human eye it appears to be a horizontal surface.

Continental shelves have economic and political significance. 🔑 **Continental shelves contain important mineral deposits, large reservoirs of oil and natural gas, and huge sand and gravel deposits.** The waters of the continental shelf also contain important fishing grounds, which are significant sources of food.

Figure 7 Atlantic Continental Margin The continental margins in the Atlantic Ocean are wider than in the Pacific Ocean and are covered in a thick layer of sediment.
Explaining *Why are continental margins in the Pacific Ocean narrower and associated with earthquakes and volcanic activity?*

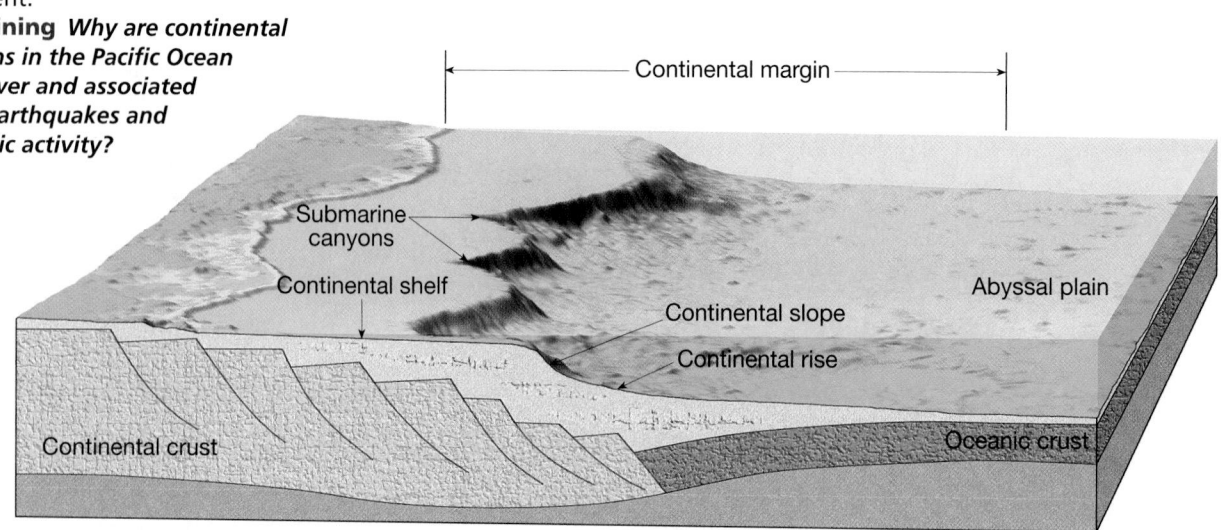

Continental Slope Marking the seaward edge of the continental shelf is the **continental slope.** This slope is steeper than the shelf, and it marks the boundary between continental crust and oceanic crust. The continental slope can be seen in Figure 7 on page 402. Although the steepness of the continental slope varies greatly from place to place, it averages about 5 degrees. In some places the slope may exceed 25 degrees. The continental slope is a relatively narrow feature, averaging only about 20 kilometers in width.

Deep, steep-sided valleys known as **submarine canyons** are cut into the continental slope. These canyons may extend to the ocean basin floor. Figure 8 shows how submarine canyons are formed. Most information suggests that submarine canyons have been eroded, at least in part, by turbidity currents. **Turbidity currents** are occasional movements of dense, sediment-rich water down the continental slope. They are created when sand and mud on the continental shelf and slope are disturbed—perhaps by an earthquake—and become suspended in the water. Because such muddy water is denser than normal seawater, it flows down the slope. As it flows down, it erodes and accumulates more sediment. Erosion from these muddy torrents is believed to be the major force in the formation of most submarine canyons. Narrow continental margins, such as the one located along the California coast, are marked with numerous submarine canyons.

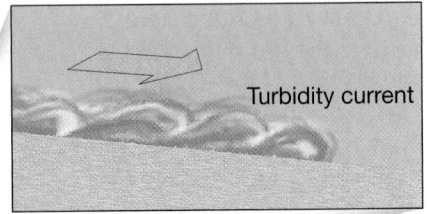

Submarine canyons

Turbidity current

Figure 8 Submarine Canyons Most evidence suggests that submarine canyons probably formed as river valleys during periods of low sea level during recent ice ages. Turbidity currents continue to change the canyons.

Turbidity currents are known to be an important mechanism of sediment transport in the ocean. Turbidity currents erode submarine canyons and deposit sediments on the deep-ocean floor.

Continental Rise In regions where trenches do not exist, the steep continental slope merges into a more gradual incline known as the **continental rise.** Here the steepness of the slope drops to about 6 meters per kilometer. Whereas the width of the continental slope averages about 20 kilometers, the continental rise may be hundreds of kilometers wide.

Reading Checkpoint *Compare and contrast the continental slope and continental rise.*

For: Links on ocean floor features
Visit: www.SciLinks.org
Web Code: cjn-5142

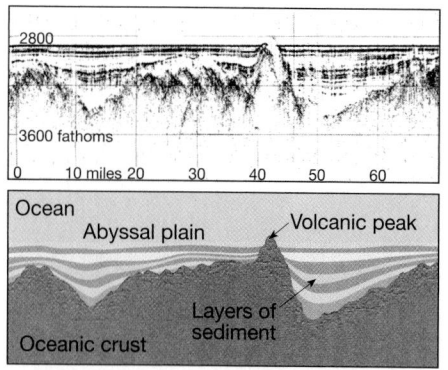

Figure 9 Abyssal Plain Cross Section This seismic cross section and matching sketch of a portion of the Madeira abyssal plain in the eastern Atlantic Ocean shows how the irregular oceanic crust is buried by sediments.

Ocean Basin Floor

Between the continental margin and mid-ocean ridge lies the **ocean basin floor.** The size of this region—almost 30 percent of Earth's surface—is comparable to the percentage of land above sea level. This region includes deep-ocean trenches, very flat areas known as abyssal plains, and tall volcanic peaks called seamounts and guyots.

Deep-Ocean Trenches Deep-ocean trenches are long, narrow creases in the ocean floor that form the deepest parts of the ocean. Most trenches are located along the margins of the Pacific Ocean, and many exceed 10,000 meters in depth. A portion of one trench—the Challenger Deep in the Mariana Trench—has been measured at a record 11,022 meters below sea level. It is the deepest known place on Earth.

Trenches form at sites of plate convergence where one moving plate descends beneath another and plunges back into the mantle. Earthquakes and volcanic activity are associated with these regions. The large number of trenches and the volcanic activity along the margins of the Pacific Ocean give the region its nickname as the *Ring of Fire.*

Abyssal Plains **Abyssal plains** are deep, extremely flat features. In fact, these regions are possibly the most level places on Earth. Abyssal plains have thick accumulations of fine sediment that have buried an otherwise rugged ocean floor, as shown in Figure 9. **The sediments that make up abyssal plains are carried there by turbidity currents or deposited as a result of suspended sediments settling.** Abyssal plains are found in all oceans of the world. However, the Atlantic Ocean has the most extensive abyssal plains because it has few trenches to catch sediment carried down the continental slope.

Seamounts and Guyots The submerged volcanic peaks that dot the ocean floor are called **seamounts.** They are volcanoes that have not reached the ocean surface. These steep-sided cone-shaped peaks are found on the floors of all the oceans. However, the greatest number have been identified in the Pacific. Some seamounts form at volcanic hot spots. An example is the Hawaiian-Emperor Seamount chain, shown in Figure 3 on page 396. This chain stretches from the Hawaiian Islands to the Aleutian trench.

Once underwater volcanoes reach the surface, they form islands. Over time, running water and wave action erode these volcanic islands to near sea level. Over millions of years, the islands gradually sink and may disappear below the water surface. This process occurs as the moving plate slowly carries the islands away from the elevated oceanic ridge or hot spot where they originated. These once-active, now-submerged, flat-topped structures are called guyots.

Reading Checkpoint *What are abyssal plains?*

Mid-Ocean Ridges

The **mid-ocean ridge** is found near the center of most ocean basins. It is an interconnected system of underwater mountains that have developed on newly formed ocean crust. This system is the longest topographic feature on Earth's surface. It exceeds 70,000 kilometers in length. The mid-ocean ridge winds through all major oceans similar to the way a seam winds over the surface of a baseball.

The term *ridge* may be misleading because the mid-ocean ridge is not narrow. It has widths from 1000 to 4000 kilometers and may occupy as much as one half of the total area of the ocean floor. Another look at Figure 3 shows that the mid-ocean ridge is broken into segments. These are offset by large transform faults where plates slide past each other horizontally, resulting in shallow earthquakes.

Seafloor Spreading A high amount of volcanic activity takes place along the crest of the mid-ocean ridge. This activity is associated with seafloor spreading. **Seafloor spreading** occurs at divergent plate boundaries where two lithospheric plates are moving apart. **New ocean floor is formed at mid-ocean ridges as magma rises between the diverging plates and cools.**

Hydrothermal Vents Hydrothermal vents form along mid-ocean ridges. These are zones where mineral-rich water, heated by the hot, newly-formed oceanic crust, escapes through cracks in oceanic crust into surrounding water. As the super-heated, mineral-rich water comes in contact with the surrounding cold water, minerals and metals such as sulfur, iron, copper, and zinc precipitate out and are deposited.

Section 14.2 Assessment

Reviewing Concepts

1. What are the three main regions of the ocean floor?

2. How do continental margins in the Atlantic Ocean differ from those in the Pacific Ocean?

3. What are trenches? How are deep-ocean trenches formed?

4. What are abyssal plains? How are abyssal plains formed?

5. What is formed at mid-ocean ridges?

Critical Thinking

6. **Comparing and Contrasting** Compare and contrast seamounts and guyots.

7. **Applying Concepts** Explain how turbidity currents are related to submarine canyons.

Writing in Science

Descriptive Paragraph Imagine you are about to take an underwater journey in a submersible across the Atlantic Ocean. Your journey begins at the coast, and you travel out toward the mid-ocean ridge. Write a paragraph describing the ocean floor features you will likely see on your journey.

understanding EARTH

Explaining Coral Atolls— Darwin's Hypothesis

Coral atolls are ring-shaped structures that often extend several thousand meters below sea level. Corals are colonial animals about the size of an ant. They are related to jellyfish and feed with stinging tentacles. Most corals protect themselves by precipitating a hard external skeleton made of calcium carbonate. Coral reefs occur where corals reproduce and grow over many centuries. Their skeletons fuse into large structures called coral reefs.

The Problem with Corals

Corals require specific environmental conditions to grow. For example, reef-building corals grow best in waters with an average annual temperature of about 24°C. They cannot survive prolonged exposure to temperatures below 18°C or above 30°C. Reef-building corals also need clear sunlit water. As a result, the limiting depth of most active reef growth is only about 45 meters.

Gathering Data

How can corals—which require warm, shallow, sunlit water no deeper than a few dozen meters to live—create thick structures like coral atolls that extend into deep water? The naturalist Charles Darwin was one of the first to formulate a hypothesis on the origin of atolls. From 1831 to 1836, he sailed aboard the British ship HMS *Beagle* during its famous voyage around the world. In various places Darwin noticed a series of stages in coral-reef development. Development begins with a fringing reef, like the one shown in Figure 10A. The fringing reef forms along the sides of a volcanic island. As the volcanic island slowly sinks, the fringing reef becomes a barrier reef, as shown in Figure 10B. Figure 10C shows the final stage of development of the atoll. The volcano sinks completely underwater but the coral reef remains near the surface.

Darwin's Hypothesis

Figure 10 is a drawing that summarizes Darwin's hypothesis about atoll formation. As a volcanic island slowly sinks, the corals continue to build the reef upward. This explained how living coral reefs, which are restricted to shallow water, can build structures that now exist in much deeper water. The theory of plate tectonics supports Darwin's hypothesis. Plate tectonics explains how a volcanic island can become extinct and experience a change in elevation over long periods of time. As the hot ocean seafloor moves away from the mid-ocean ridge, it becomes denser and sinks. This is why islands also sink. Darwin's hypothesis is also supported by evidence from drilling that shows volcanic rock is beneath the oldest and deepest coral reef structures. Atolls owe their existence to the gradual sinking of volcanic islands containing coral reefs that build upward through time.

Figure 10 Formation of a Coral Atoll **A** A fringing coral reef forms around a volcanic island. **B** As the volcanic island sinks, the fringing reef slowly becomes a barrier reef. **C** Eventually, the volcano is completely underwater and a coral atoll remains.

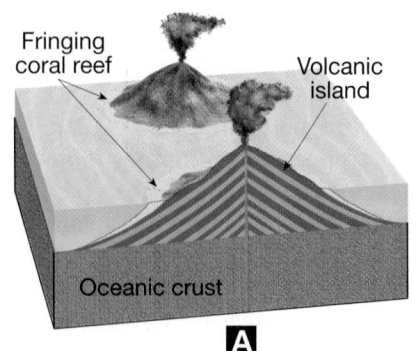

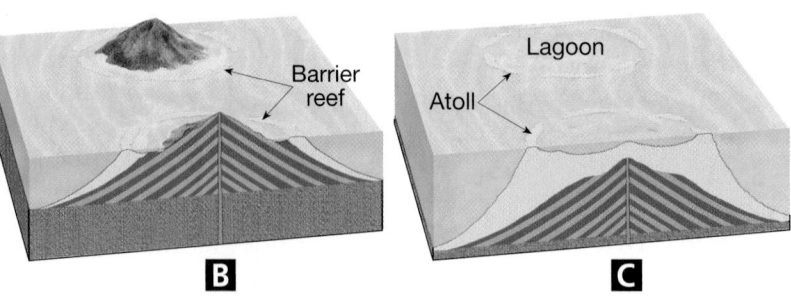

14.3 Seafloor Sediments

Reading Focus

Key Concepts

- What are the three types of ocean-floor sediments?
- What does terrigenous sediment consist of?
- What is the composition of biogenous sediment?
- How is hydrogenous sediment formed?

Vocabulary

- terrigenous sediment
- biogenous sediment
- calcareous ooze
- siliceous ooze
- hydrogenous sediment

Reading Strategy

Summarizing Make a table like the one below that includes all the headings for the section. Write a brief summary of the text for each heading.

Actions at Boundaries
I. Types of Seafloor Sediments • Terrigenous sediments originated on land. • Biogenous sediments are biological in origin. • _____ ? _____

Except for steep areas of the continental slope and the crest of the mid-ocean ridge, most of the ocean floor is covered with sediment. Some of this sediment has been deposited by turbidity currents. The rest has slowly settled onto the seafloor from above. The thickness of ocean-floor sediments varies. Some trenches act as traps for sediment originating on the continental margin. The accumulation may approach 10 kilometers in thickness. In general, however, accumulations of sediment are much less—about 500 to 1000 meters.

Generally, coarser sediments, such as sand, cover the continental shelf and slope while finer sediments, such as clay, cover the deep-ocean floor. Figure 11 shows the distribution of the different types of ocean-floor sediments. Various types of sediment accumulate on nearly all areas of the ocean floor in the same way dust accumulates in all parts of your home. Even the deep-ocean floor, far from land, receives small amounts of windblown material and microscopic parts of organisms.

Figure 11 Distribution of Ocean-Floor Sediments Coarse-grained terrigenous deposits dominate continental margin areas. Fine-grained clay, or mud, is more common in the deepest areas of the ocean basins.
Infer *Why is it more common to find fine-grained sediments in the deepest areas of the ocean basins?*

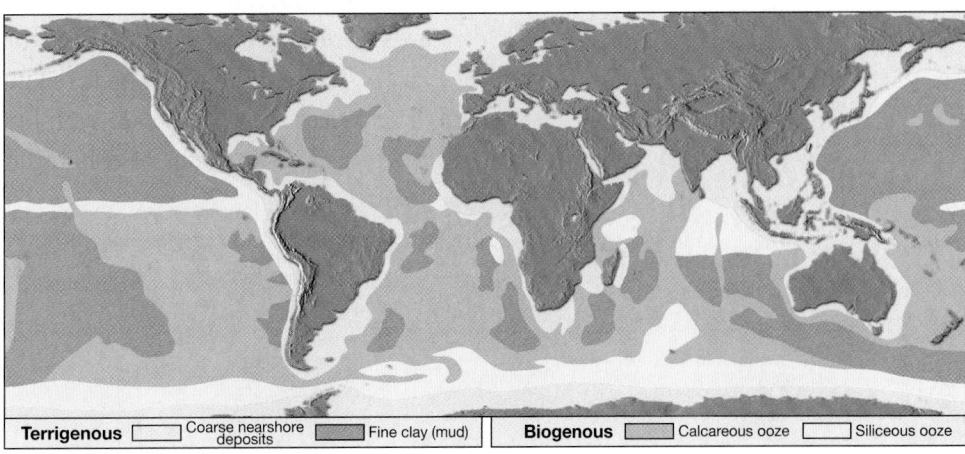

| Terrigenous | ☐ Coarse nearshore deposits | ☐ Fine clay (mud) | **Biogenous** | ☐ Calcareous ooze | ☐ Siliceous ooze |

Types of Seafloor Sediments

Ocean-floor sediments can be classified according to their origin into three broad categories: terrigenous sediments, biogenous sediments, and hydrogenous sediments. Ocean-floor sediments are usually mixtures of the various sediment types.

Terrigenous Sediment

Terrigenous sediment is sediment that originates on land. **Terrigenous sediments consist primarily of mineral grains that were eroded from continental rocks and transported to the ocean.** Larger particles such as gravel and sand usually settle rapidly near shore. Finer particles such as clay can take years to settle to the ocean floor and may be carried thousands of kilometers by ocean currents. Clay accumulates very slowly on the deep-ocean floor. To form a 1-centimeter abyssal clay layer, for example, requires as much as 50,000 years. In contrast, on the continental margins near the mouths of large rivers, terrigenous sediment accumulates rapidly and forms thick deposits. In the Gulf of Mexico, for instance, the sediment is many kilometers thick.

Biogenous Sediment

Biogenous sediment is sediment that is biological in origin. **Biogenous sediments consist of shells and skeletons of marine animals and algae.** This debris is produced mostly by microscopic organisms living in surface waters. Once these organisms die, their hard shells sink, accumulating on the seafloor.

The most common biogenous sediment is calcareous ooze. **Calcareous ooze** is produced from the calcium carbonate shells of organisms. Calcareous ooze has the consistency of thick mud. When calcium carbonate shells slowly sink into deeper parts of the ocean, they begin to dissolve. In ocean water deeper than about 4500 meters, these shells completely dissolve before they reach the bottom. As a result, calcareous ooze does not accumulate in the deeper areas of ocean basins.

Other biogenous sediments include siliceous ooze and phosphate-rich material. **Siliceous ooze** is composed primarily of the shells of diatoms—single-celled algae—and radiolarians—single-celled animals that have shells made out of silica. The shells of these organisms are shown in Figure 12. Phosphate-rich biogenous sediments come from the bones, teeth, and scales of fish and other marine organisms.

 *Name two types of biogenous sediments.*

Hydrogenous Sediment 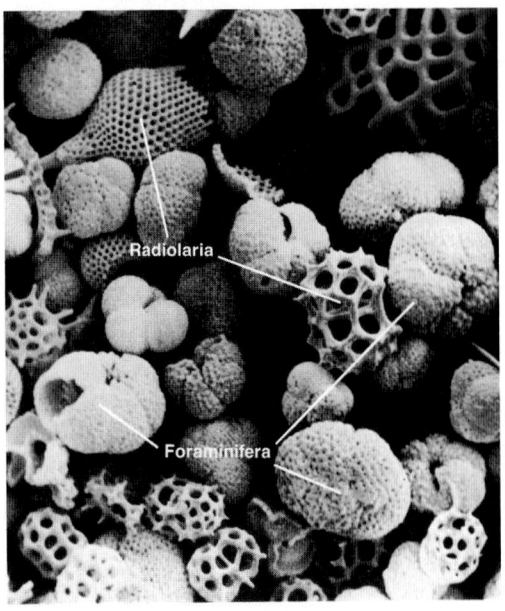 **Hydrogenous sediment consists of minerals that crystallize directly from ocean water through various chemical reactions.** Hydrogenous sediments make up only a small portion of the overall sediment in the ocean. They do, however, have many different compositions and are distributed in many different environments. Some of the most common types of hydrogenous sediment are listed below.

- Manganese nodules are rounded, hard lumps of manganese, iron, and other metals. These metals precipitate around an object such as a grain of sand. The nodules can be up to 20 centimeters in diameter and are often scattered across large areas of the deep ocean floor.

- Calcium carbonates form by precipitation directly from ocean water in warm climates. If this material is buried and hardens, a type of limestone forms. Most limestone, however, is composed of biogenous sediment.

- Evaporites form where evaporation rates are high and there is restricted open-ocean circulation. As water evaporates from such areas, the remaining ocean water becomes saturated with dissolved minerals that then begin to precipitate. Collectively termed "salts," some evaporite minerals do taste salty, such as halite, or common table salt. Other salts do not taste salty, such as the calcium sulfate minerals anhydrite ($CaSO_4$) and gypsum.

Figure 12 Biogenous Sediments The microscopic shells of radiolarians and foraminifers are examples of biogenous sediments. This photomicrograph has been enlarged hundreds of times.

Section 14.3 Assessment

Reviewing Concepts

1. What are the three types of ocean floor sediments?
2. What does terrigenous sediment consist of?
3. What is the composition of biogenous sediment?
4. How is hydrogenous sediment formed?

Critical Thinking

5. **Comparing and Contrasting** Compare and contrast calcareous ooze and siliceous ooze.
6. **Predicting** Would you expect to find more evaporites in an area of warm water that receives large amounts of sunlight such as the Red Sea or in an area of cold water that receives less sunlight such as the Greenland Sea?

Connecting Concepts

Origin of Sediments An oceanographer is studying sediment samples from the Bahama Banks. The sediments have a high amount of calcium carbonate. They are labeled biogenous but are later found to contain no shells from organisms that typically make up calcareous ooze. What other explanation is there for the origin of these sediments?

14.4 Resources from the Seafloor

Key Concepts
- Which ocean resources are used for energy production?
- How are gas hydrates formed?
- What other resources are derived from the ocean?

Vocabulary
- gas hydrates
- manganese nodule

Reading Strategy
Identifying Details Copy the concept map below. As you read, complete it to identify details about resources from the ocean.

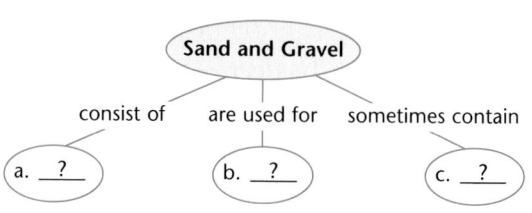

Sand and Gravel

consist of — a. ___?___

are used for — b. ___?___

sometimes contain — c. ___?___

The ocean floor is rich in mineral and organic resources. Recovering them, however, involves technological challenges and high costs. As technology improves we are able to access some of these resources more efficiently. However, other resources, such as manganese nodules, remain untouched.

Energy Resources

Most of the value of nonliving resources in the ocean comes from their use as energy products. **Oil and natural gas are the main energy products currently being obtained from the ocean floor.** Other resources have the potential to be used as a source of energy in the future.

Oil and Natural Gas The ancient remains of microscopic organisms are the source of today's deposits of oil and natural gas. These organisms were buried within marine sediments before they could decompose. After millions of years of exposure to heat from Earth's interior and pressure from overlying rock, the remains were transformed into oil and natural gas. The percentage of world oil produced from offshore regions has increased from trace amounts in the 1930s to more than 30 percent today. Most of this increase is due to the continual update of the technology used by offshore drilling platforms such as the one shown in Figure 13.

Major offshore reserves exist in the Persian Gulf, in the Gulf of Mexico, off the coast of southern California, in the North Sea, and in the East Indies. Additional reserves are probably located off the north coast of Alaska and in the Canadian Arctic, Asian seas, Africa, and Brazil. One

Figure 13 Offshore drilling rigs tap the oil and natural gas reserves of the continental shelf. These platforms are near Santa Barbara, California.
Inferring *What changes to the marine environment may occur as a result of drilling for oil?*

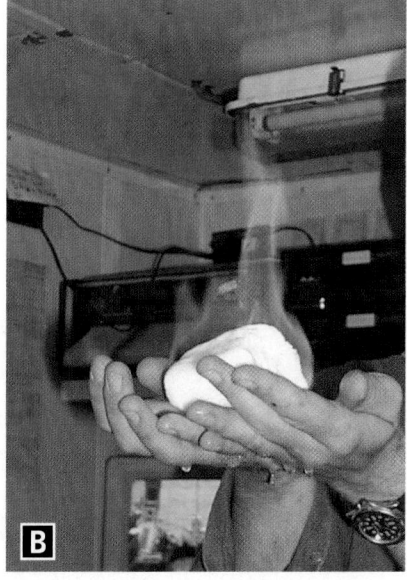

environmental concern about offshore petroleum exploration is the possibility of oil spills caused by accidental leaks during the drilling process.

Gas Hydrates Gas hydrates are compact chemical structures made of water and natural gas. The most common type of natural gas is methane, which produces methane hydrate. Gas hydrates occur beneath permafrost areas on land and under the ocean floor at depths below 525 meters.

Most oceanic gas hydrates are created when bacteria break down organic matter trapped in ocean-floor sediments. The bacteria produce methane gas along with small amounts of ethane and propane. These gases combine with water in deep-ocean sediments in such a way that the gas is trapped inside a lattice-like cage of water molecules.

Vessels that have drilled into gas hydrates have brought up samples of mud mixed with chunks of gas hydrates like the one shown in Figure 14A. These chunks evaporate quickly when they are exposed to the relatively warm, low-pressure conditions at the ocean surface. Gas hydrates resemble chunks of ice but ignite when lit by a flame, as shown in Figure 14B. The hydrates burn because methane and other flammable gases are released as gas hydrates evaporate.

An estimated 20 quadrillion cubic meters of methane are locked up in sediments containing gas hydrates. This amount is double the amount of Earth's known coal, oil, and natural gas reserves combined. One drawback to using gas hydrates as an energy source is that they rapidly break down at surface temperatures and pressures. In the future, however, these ocean-floor reserves of energy may help provide our energy needs.

 **Reading Checkpoint** *What happens when gas hydrates are brought to the surface?*

Figure 14 Gas Hydrates
A A sample from the ocean floor has layers of white, ice-like gas hydrate mixed with mud.
B Gas hydrates evaporate when exposed to surface conditions, releasing natural gas that can be burned.

For: Links on ocean resources
Visit: www.SciLinks.org
Web Code: cjn-5144

Other Resources

⬤ Other major resources from the ocean floor include sand and gravel, evaporative salts, and manganese nodules.

Sand and Gravel The offshore sand-and-gravel industry is second in economic value only to the petroleum industry. Sand and gravel, which include rock fragments that are washed out to sea and shells of marine organisms, are mined by offshore barges using suction devices. Sand and gravel are used for landfill, to fill in recreational beaches, and to make concrete.

In some cases, materials of high economic value are associated with offshore sand and gravel deposits. Gem-quality diamonds, for example, are recovered from gravels on the continental shelf offshore of South Africa and Australia. Sediments rich in tin have been mined from some offshore areas of Southeast Asia. Platinum and gold have been found in deposits in gold-mining areas throughout the world. Some Florida beach sands are rich in titanium.

Manganese Nodules As described earlier, **manganese nodules** are hard lumps of manganese and other metals that precipitate around a smaller object. Figure 15 shows manganese nodules on the deep-ocean floor. They contain high concentrations of manganese, iron, and smaller concentrations of copper,

Figure 15 These manganese nodules lie 5323 meters on the Pacific Ocean floor south of the island of Tahiti.
Applying Concepts *How do manganese nodules form?*

☰Quick Lab

Evaporative Salts

Materials

400 mL beaker, table salt, tablespoon, balance, glass stirrer

Procedure

1. Place the empty beaker on the balance and add between 3 and 5 tablespoons of the salt. Measure the combined mass of the balance and the salt. Record the measurement and remove the beaker from the balance.

2. Add 100 mL of water to the beaker and stir until the salt is dissolved.

3. Place the beaker in a warm, sunny area and allow the water to evaporate.

4. When all of the water has evaporated, place the beaker and its remaining contents on the balance and record the measurement.

Analyze and Conclude

1. **Comparing** How did the mass of the beaker and salt before the water was added compare to the mass of the beaker and salt after the water evaporated?

2. **Drawing Conclusions** What happened to the salt when the water evaporated?

3. **Predicting** How could the oceans be used as a source of salt?

nickel, and cobalt, all of which have a variety of economic uses. Cobalt, for example, is important because it is required to produce strong alloys with other metals. These alloys are used in high-speed cutting tools, powerful permanent magnets, and jet engine parts. With current technology, mining the deep-ocean floor for manganese nodules is possible but not economically profitable.

Manganese nodules are widely distributed along the ocean floor, but not all regions have the same potential for mining. Good locations for mining must have a large amount of nodules that contain an optimal mix of copper, nickel, and cobalt. Sites like this are limited. In addition, it is difficult to establish mining rights far from land. Also, there are environmental concerns about disturbing large portions of the deep-ocean floor.

Figure 16 Common table salt, or halite, is harvested from the salt left behind when ocean water evaporates. About 30 percent of the world's salt is produced by evaporating seawater.

Evaporative Salts When seawater evaporates, the salts increase in concentration until they can no longer remain dissolved. When the concentration becomes high enough, the salts precipitate out of solution and form salt deposits. These deposits can then be harvested, as shown in Figure 16. The most economically important salt is halite—common table salt. Halite is widely used for seasoning, curing, and preserving foods. It is also used in agriculture, in the clothing industry for dying fabric, and to de-ice roads.

Section 14.4 Assessment

Reviewing Concepts

1. 🌐 What are the main energy resources from the ocean?

2. 🌐 How are gas hydrates formed?

3. What drawbacks are associated with harvesting ocean resources for energy use?

4. 🌐 What other resources are derived from the ocean?

5. What are the uses of evaporative salts?

6. What are manganese nodules? Why is it difficult to recover them from the ocean?

Critical Thinking

7. **Making Generalizations** How does technology influence the availability of resources from the ocean?

8. **Inferring** Near-shore mining of sand and gravel can result in large amounts of sediments being suspended in water. How might this affect marine organisms living in the area?

Connecting Concepts

Sand and Gravel Why are most sand and gravel deposits found on the continental shelf? What type of sediment is sand and gravel?

Modeling Seafloor Depth Transects

Oceanographers use a number of methods to determine the depth and topography of the ocean floor. Technology, such as sonar, satellites, and submersibles, have allowed scientists to produce detailed maps of the ocean floor in each ocean basin. In this lab, you will model a seafloor depth transect to determine the topography of an ocean basin created by your classmates.

Problem How can the topography of an ocean basin be determined?

Materials
- shoe box
- modeling clay
- aluminum foil
- pencil
- scalpel
- graph paper
- ruler

Skills Measuring, Graphing, Inferring, Drawing Conclusions

Procedure

Part A: Making a Model of the Seafloor

1. Reexamine Figure 3, Figure 7, and the figure below to determine which area of the ocean floor you will model. Be sure to identify the specific features that would be found in the area you choose to model. For example, if you were to model the continental margin you would want to include the continental shelf, continental slope, continental rise, and maybe some submarine canyons in your model. If you were to model the ocean basin floor you would want to include abyssal plains, trenches, seamounts, and guyots. Do not discuss the plan for your model with students outside your group.

2. Once you have determined which area of the ocean floor you will model, use the clay to make a contoured model of the seafloor inside the shoebox.

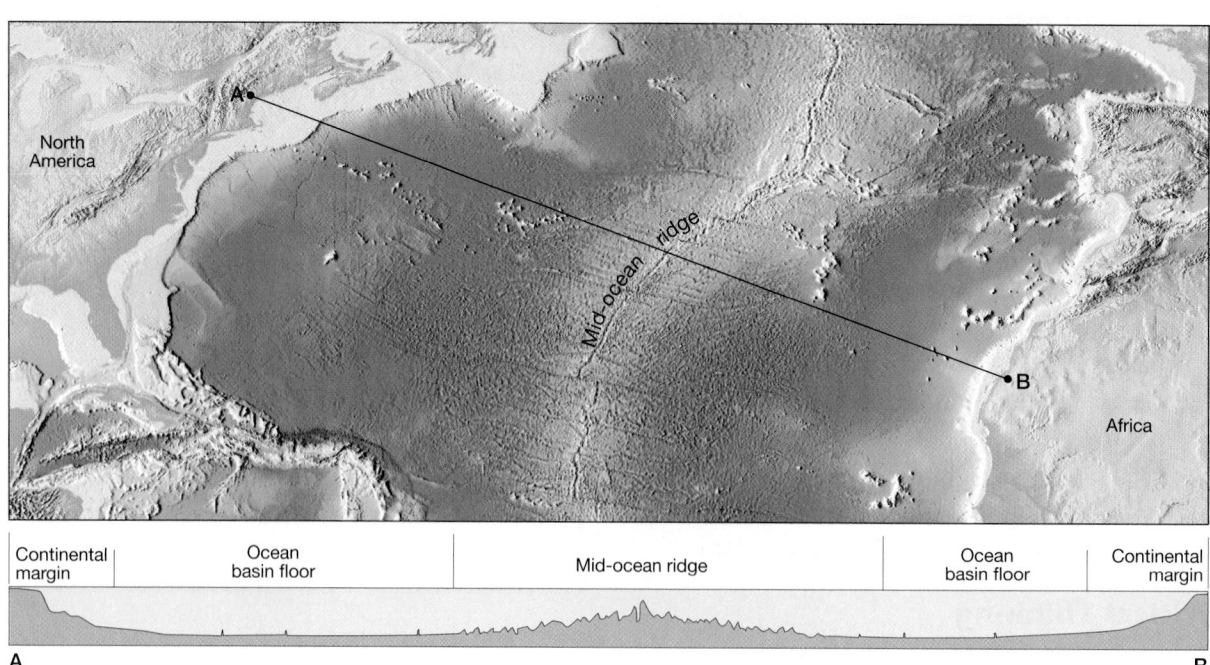

3. Cover the box with its top and exchange boxes with another group from your class. Do not remove the top of the box that you receive from another group.

Part B: Completing a Depth Transect

4. Obtain a piece of aluminum foil that is large enough to cover the top of the shoebox and fold over the sides of the box about an inch all the way around.

5. Spread the foil flat on your lab table. Place the ruler lengthwise on the foil, parallel to the edge of the foil. The ruler can be in the middle of the foil or off to the side. The line formed by the edge of the ruler will be your transect line.

6. Use a pencil to make tick marks on the foil piece every centimeter along the entire length of the foil.

7. Hold the foil in place over the top of the box. Quickly and carefully remove the top of the box and set the foil piece down in place of the top. Do not look in the box. Secure the foil in place on top of the box by turning down the foil over the sides of the box. Be sure the foil is taut across the top.

8. Label your graph paper. The *x*-axis will be "Distance along Transect Line" in centimeters, and the *y*-axis will be "Depth" in centimeters. Make tick marks along the *x*-axis once every centimeter. Make tick marks along the *y*-axis every half of a centimeter.

9. Use the scalpel to carefully make a slit in the foil along the first centimeter mark.
   CAUTION *The scalpel is extremely sharp. Handle it carefully.* After cutting the foil, gently place the ruler through the slit until it makes contact with the clay in the box. Be sure to hold the ruler straight and take the depth measurement. Record your data on the graph.

10. Repeat Step 9 for each point along the foil. When you are done, you should have a depth profile for the entire length of the box along your transect line.

11. Remove the foil from the box and examine the contour of the model.

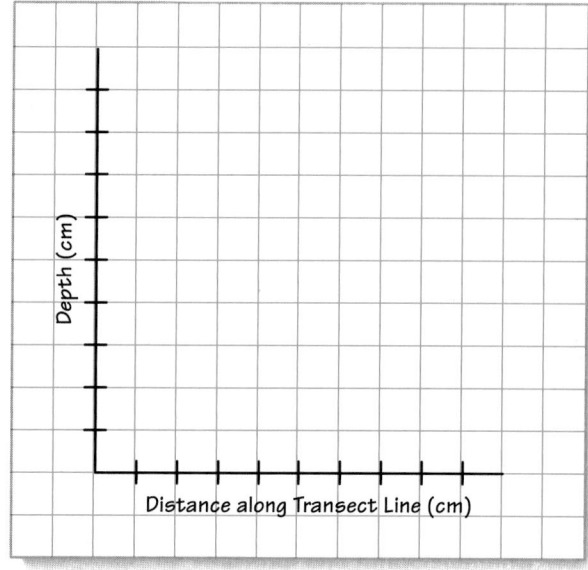

Analyze and Conclude

1. **Inferring** Based on your contour profile, what part of the ocean floor was being modeled? Check your answer with the group that created the model. Were you correct? Why or why not?

2. **Comparing** How does the profile on your graph compare with the contour of the model? Are there any major features in the model that did not appear on your graph? Why or why not?

3. **Analyzing Data** What could you have done to make your profile match the contour more accurately?

4. **Explaining** Before sonar was used to measure ocean depth, a less sophisticated method was used. A long line of rope with a lead weight on the end was tossed over the side of a ship and lowered until the weight hit the bottom. How is this method similar to what you did in the lab? How can the rope method lead to inaccuracies when trying to build an ocean floor profile?

14 | Study Guide

14.1 The Vast World Ocean

Key Concepts

- Nearly 71 percent of Earth's surface is covered by the global ocean.
- The world ocean can be divided into four main ocean basins—the Pacific Ocean, the Atlantic Ocean, the Indian Ocean, and the Arctic Ocean.
- The topography of the ocean floor is as diverse as that of continents.
- Today, technology—particularly sonar, satellites, and submersibles—allows scientists to study the ocean floor in a more efficient and precise manner.

Vocabulary

oceanography, *p. 394*; bathymetry, *p. 396*; sonar, *p. 398*; submersible, *p. 400*

14.2 Ocean Floor Features

Key Concepts

- The ocean floor regions are the continental margins, the ocean basin floor, and the mid-ocean ridge.
- In the Atlantic Ocean thick layers of undisturbed sediment cover the continental margin. This region has very little volcanic or earthquake activity.
- In the Pacific Ocean oceanic crust is plunging beneath continental crust. This force results in a narrow continental margin that experiences both volcanic activity and earthquakes.
- Continental shelves contain important mineral deposits, large reservoirs of oil and natural gas, and huge sand and gravel deposits.
- Trenches form at sites of plate convergence where one moving plate descends beneath another and plunges back into the mantle.
- The sediments that make up abyssal plains are carried there by turbidity currents or are deposited as a result of suspended sediments settling.
- New ocean floor is formed at mid-ocean ridges as magma rises between the diverging plates and cools.

Vocabulary

continental margin, *p. 402*; continental shelf, *p. 402*; continental slope, *p. 403* submarine canyon, *p. 403*; turbidity current, *p. 403*; continental rise, *p. 403*; ocean basin floor, *p. 404*; abyssal plains, *p. 404*; seamounts, *p. 404*; mid-ocean ridge, *p. 405*; seafloor spreading, *p. 405*

14.3 Seafloor Sediments

Key Concepts

- Ocean-floor sediments can be classified according to their origin into three broad categories: terrigenous sediments, biogenous sediments, and hydrogenous sediments.
- Terrigenous sediments consist primarily of mineral grains that were eroded from continental rocks and transported to the ocean.
- Biogenous sediments consist of shells and skeletons of marine animals and algae.
- Hydrogenous sediments consist of minerals that crystallize directly from ocean water through various chemical reactions.

Vocabulary

terrigenous sediment, *p. 408*; biogenous sediment, *p. 408*; calcareous ooze, *p. 408*; siliceous ooze, *p. 408*; hydrogenous sediment, *p. 409*

14.4 Resources from the Seafloor

Key Concepts

- Oil and natural gas are the main energy products currently being obtained from the ocean floor.
- Most oceanic gas hydrates are created when bacteria break down organic matter trapped in ocean-floor sediments.
- Other major resources from the seafloor include sand and gravel, evaporative salts, and manganese nodules.

Vocabulary

gas hydrates, *p. 411*; manganese nodule, *p. 412*

Reviewing Content

Choose the letter that best answers the question or completes the statement.

1. Approximately what percentage of Earth's surface is covered by oceans?
   a. 40   **b.** 50
   c. 60   **d.** 70

2. Which ocean basin is the largest?
   a. the Atlantic   **b.** the Indian
   c. the Pacific   **d.** the Arctic

3. The use of sound waves to determine the depth of the ocean is called
   a. submarine sounding.
   b. sonar.
   c. satellite altimetry.
   d. submersible sounding.

4. The gently sloping submerged surface that extends from the shoreline toward the ocean basin floor is the continental
   a. shelf.   **b.** slope.
   c. rise.   **d.** margin.

5. Submarine canyons are believed to have been created by
   a. rivers during the ice age.
   b. earthquakes.
   c. lost ships.
   d. subduction.

6. Important mineral deposits, including large reservoirs of oil and natural gas, are associated with
   a. the ocean basin floor.
   b. the continental shelf.
   c. abyssal plains.
   d. the continental rise.

7. Calcareous ooze is an example of
   a. terrigenous sediment.
   b. biogenous sediment.
   c. hydrogenous sediment.
   d. a combination of hydrogenous and terrigenous sediment.

8. Sediments that consist of mineral grains that were eroded from continental rocks are called
   a. terrigenous.   **b.** biogenous.
   c. hydrogenous.   **d.** hydrates.

9. What could gas hydrates be used for?
   a. as landfill
   b. to make concrete
   c. as a source of energy
   d. as a source of cobalt and copper

10. Economically valuable materials such as diamonds, tin, and platinum are associated with which ocean floor resource?
    a. oil and natural gas
    b. sand and gravel
    c. evaporative salts
    d. manganese nodules

Understanding Concepts

11. Why is Earth called the "blue planet"?

12. What is bathymetry? What techniques do scientists use to discover more about the bathymetry of ocean basins?

13. Why is multibeam sonar more efficient than simple sonar at collecting data from the ocean floor?

14. Compare and contrast the size and topography of the Atlantic Ocean basin to that of the Pacific Ocean basin.

15. What is a continental shelf? What economic significance do continental shelves have?

16. Compare and contrast deep-ocean trenches and mid-oceanic ridges.

17. In which ocean basin are most trenches found? Why?

18. What is the difference between terrigenous sediments and biogenous sediments?

19. Explain the process by which hydrogenous sediments are formed.

20. Why is it uncommon to find calcareous ooze in deep-ocean basins?

21. From which area of the ocean basin are the resources of oil and natural gas harvested?

22. What current disadvantages exist to using gas hydrates as a form of energy?

23. What are the uses for sand and gravel harvested from the continental shelf?

Critical Thinking

24. **Interpreting Diagrams** Reexamine Figure 1. Why do you think that the Northern Hemisphere is called the "land hemisphere" and the Southern Hemisphere is called the "water hemisphere"?

25. **Making Generalizations** A friend says that because of gravity we can learn about the topography of the ocean floor. Explain why this is true.

26. **Inferring** The continental margin of the Atlantic Ocean is often referred to as a "passive" continental margin whereas Pacific Ocean continental margins are referred to as "active." Infer what the characteristics of passive and active continental margins would be.

27. **Inferring** There is usually very little sediment accumulation found at mid-ocean ridges. Why do you think this is true?

28. **Applying Concepts** Imagine you have been asked to invent a device that would be used to retrieve manganese nodules. What characteristics would the device have in order to successfully achieve this goal?

Math Skills

29. **Calculating** Assuming the average speed of sound waves in water is 1500 meters per second, determine, in seconds, how long it would take a sonar signal to hit the bottom and return to the recorder if the water depth is 7500 meters.

30. **Calculating** The rate of seafloor spreading in the Atlantic Ocean has been estimated to be about 2.5 centimeters per year. By how many centimeters will the Atlantic Ocean basin increase over a period of 7 years?

31. **Calculating** If the settling rate of very fine sand in the open ocean is 360 meters per day, how many days will it take for the sediment to reach the ocean floor at a depth of 4 kilometers?

Concepts in Action

Use the table below to answer Questions 32 and 33.

The table shows the kind of data that a simple sonar echo sounder would provide. The sonar is taken along a transect line in the Pacific Ocean. The stations are approximately 500 meters apart from each other.

Sonar Data			
Station Number	Depth (in meters)	Station Number	Depth (in meters)
1	5500	7	3110
2	5550	8	3285
3	4540	9	3490
4	4000	10	4000
5	3675	11	4675
6	3355	12	5000

32. **Making Graphs** Plot these points on a sheet of graph paper.

33. **Interpreting Data** The data recorded in the table was taken over a portion of the ocean basin floor in the Pacific Ocean. What ocean basin feature could be between stations 2 and 12?

Performance-Based Assessment

Researching Choose a resource that is harvested from the ocean. Research information about how the resource is formed, where in the ocean it is harvested, what methods and equipment are used in the harvesting of the resource, what it is used for, and if there are any negative impacts on the marine environment as a result of harvesting the resource. Present the results of your research to your class in the form of an oral presentation.

Standardized Test Prep

Test-Taking Tip

Avoiding Careless Mistakes

Students often make mistakes when they fail to examine a test question and possible answers thoroughly. Read the question carefully and underline key words that may change the meaning of the question, such as *not, except, excluding,* and so on. After choosing an answer, reread the question to check your selection.

Which of the following is NOT one of the four major topographic features of the ocean basin floor?

(A) deep-ocean trench
(B) abyssal plain
(C) submarine canyon
(D) seamount

(Answer: C)

Choose the letter that best answers the question or completes the statement.

1. Which of the following is NOT true of deep ocean trenches?
   (A) They are long and narrow depressions in the ocean floor.
   (B) They are sites where plates plunge back into the mantle.
   (C) They are geologically very stable.
   (D) They may act as sediment traps.

2. Movements of sediment-rich water down the continental slope are known as
   (A) streaming currents.
   (B) longshore currents.
   (C) turbidity currents.
   (D) avalanches.

Use the diagram below to answer Questions 3 and 4.

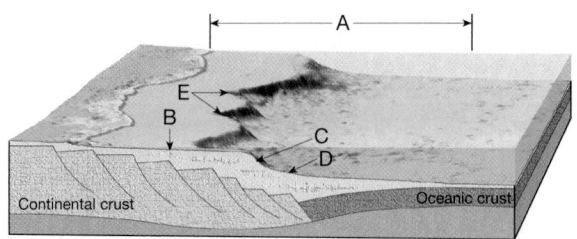

3. Which portion of the ocean floor is represented by the letter A? Describe its physical features.

4. Which ocean floor area is represented by the letter D? What are its characteristics?

5. What is the most economically important salt? Why is it important?

6. What are abyssal plains? What is underneath the plains, and how do they form?

Use the diagram below to answer Question 7.

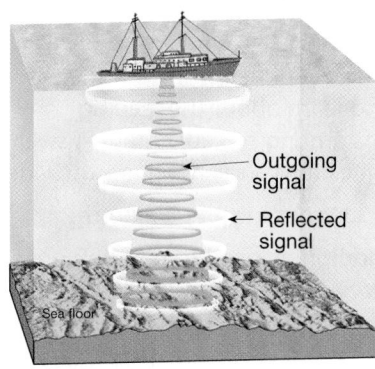

7. How is sonar used to determine the topography of ocean basins?

8. Sediment on the seafloor often leaves clues about various conditions that existed during deposition. What do the following layers in a seafloor sample tell about the environment in which each layer was deposited?
   Layer 5 (top): Fine clay
   Layer 4: Siliceous ooze
   Layer 3: Calcareous ooze
   Layer 2: Fragments of coral reef
   Layer 1 (bottom): Volcanic rock

CHAPTER 15

Ocean Water and Ocean Life

CONCEPTS in Action

Exploration Lab
How Does Temperature Affect Water Density?

How the Earth Works
Ocean Life

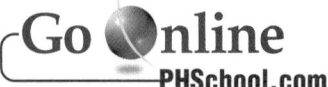

Discovery Channel School **Video Field Trip**
Ocean Water and Ocean Life

Take an underwater field trip with the Discovery Channel and learn about the feeding relationships among sea creatures. Answer the following questions after watching the video.

1. How do sardines ingest plankton?
2. Why do dolphins need to pin their prey close to the ocean surface?

Go Online PHSchool.com

For: Chapter 15 Resources
Visit: PHSchool.com
Web Code: cjk-9999

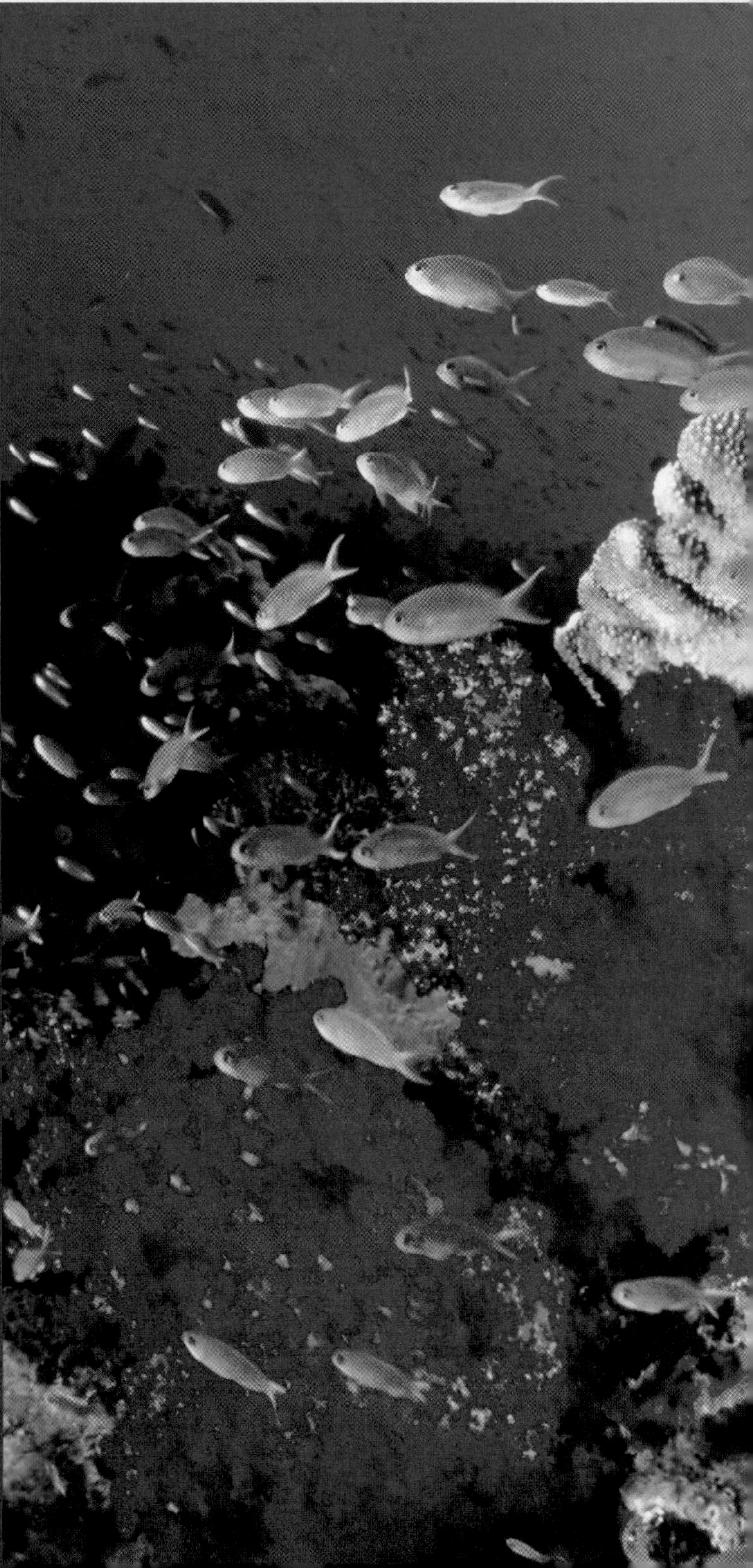

The marine environment is a habitat for ▶ thousands of species of organisms, including the damselfish and corals shown here in the south Pacific near Fiji.

Chapter Preview

Inquiry Activity

How Does Salinity Affect the Density of Water?

Procedure

1. Fill a 500-mL graduated cylinder with 400 mL of fresh water. Fill a second 500-mL graduated cylinder with 400 mL of salt water. Precise measurement is important.

2. Gently place a small rubber ball or stopper in the fresh water. Record the new water level. Remove the object from the water, and dry it off thoroughly.

3. Repeat Step 2 using the salt water. The object should float.

Think About It

1. **Calculating** What volume of fresh water was displaced by the object? What volume of salt water was displaced by the floating object?

2. **Drawing Conclusions** As the density of water increases, the volume of liquid displaced by an object decreases. Which water is more dense—fresh water or salt water?

3. **Drawing Conclusions** How does salinity affect the density of water?

15.1 The Composition of Seawater

Reading Focus

Key Concepts

- What units are used to express the salinity of ocean water?

- What are the sources of salt in ocean water?

- What factors affect the density of ocean water?

- What are the three main zones of the open ocean?

Vocabulary

- salinity
- thermocline
- density
- pycnocline
- mixed zone

Reading Strategy

Previewing Copy the table below. Before you read, preview the figures in this section and add three more questions to the table. As you read, write answers to your questions.

Questions About Seawater		Answers
What processes affect seawater salinity?		a. ___?___
b. _____?_____	?	c. ___?___
d. _____?_____	?	e. ___?___
f. _____?_____	?	g. ___?___

Figure 1 Salts in Seawater This circle graph shows that 1000 grams of seawater with a salinity of 35‰ consists of 965 grams of water and 35 grams of various salts and other solids dissolved in the water.

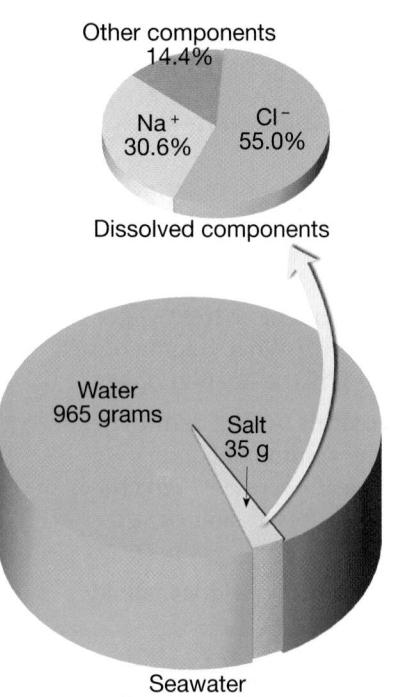

Other components 14.4%

Na⁺ 30.6%

Cl⁻ 55.0%

Dissolved components

Water 965 grams

Salt 35 g

Seawater Salinity = 35‰

What is the difference between pure water and seawater? One of the most obvious differences is that seawater contains dissolved substances that give it a salty taste. These dissolved substances include sodium chloride, other salts, metals, and even dissolved gases. In fact, every known naturally occurring element is found dissolved in at least trace amounts in seawater. The salt content of seawater makes it unsuitable for drinking or for irrigating most crops and causes it to be highly corrosive to many materials. However, many parts of the ocean are full of life adapted to this environment.

Water is the major component of nearly every life form on Earth. Our own body fluid chemistry is similar to the chemistry of seawater. Seawater consists of about 3.5 percent dissolved mineral substances that are collectively termed "salts." Although the percentage of dissolved components may seem small, the actual quantity is huge because the ocean is so vast.

Salinity

Salinity (*salinus* = salt) is the total amount of solid material dissolved in water. It is the ratio of the mass of dissolved substances to the mass of the water sample. Many common quantities are expressed in percent (%), which is parts per hundred. **Because the proportion of dissolved substances in seawater is such a small number, oceanographers typically express salinity in parts per thousand (‰).** The average salinity of seawater is 3.5% or 35‰. Figure 1 shows the principal elements that contribute to the ocean's salinity. **Most of the salt in seawater is sodium chloride, common table salt.**

Sources of Sea Salts What are the primary sources of dissolved substances in the ocean? 🔵**Chemical weathering of rocks on the continents is one source of elements found in seawater.** These dissolved materials reach oceans through runoff from rivers and streams at an estimated rate of more than 2.3 billion metric tons per year. 🔵**The second major source of elements found in seawater is from Earth's interior.** Through volcanic eruptions, large quantities of water vapor and other gases have been emitted into the atmosphere during much of geologic time. Scientists believe that this is the principal source of water in the oceans. About 4 billion years ago, as Earth's temperature cooled, the water vapor condensed and torrential rains filled the ocean basins with water. Certain elements—particularly chlorine, bromine, sulfur, and boron—were emitted along with the water. These elements exist in the ocean in much greater quantities than could be explained by weathering of rocks alone.

Processes Affecting Salinity Because the ocean is well mixed, the relative concentrations of the major components in seawater are essentially constant, no matter where the ocean is sampled. Surface salinity variation in the open ocean normally ranges from 33‰ to 38‰. Variations in salinity result from changes in the water content of the solution.

Figure 2 shows some of the different processes that affect the amount of water in seawater, thereby affecting salinity. Some processes add large amounts of fresh water to seawater, decreasing salinity. These processes include precipitation, runoff from land, icebergs melting, and sea ice melting.

Q *Is the ocean getting saltier?*

A Evidence suggests that the composition of seawater has been relatively stable for millions of years. Material is being removed just as rapidly as it is added by rivers and volcanic activity. Some dissolved components are removed from sea water by organisms as they build hard structures. Other components are lost when they chemically precipitate out of the water as sediment. Still others are exchanged at the oceanic ridge at hydrothermal vents. The net effect is that the overall makeup of seawater has remained relatively constant for a long time.

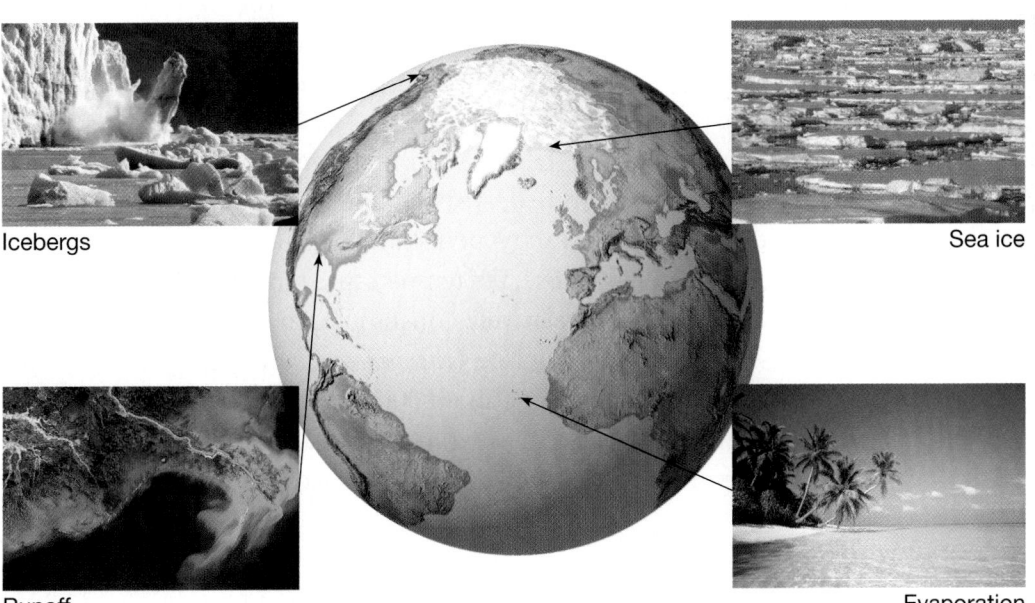

Icebergs

Sea ice

Runoff

Evaporation

Figure 2 Natural processes affect the salinity of seawater. **Applying Concepts** *Which processes decrease the salinity of seawater? Which processes increase it?*

Other processes remove large amounts of fresh water from seawater, increasing salinity. These processes include evaporation and the formation of sea ice. High salinities, for example, are found where evaporation rates are high, as is the case in the dry subtropical regions. In areas where large amounts of precipitation dilute ocean waters, as in the mid-latitudes and near the equator, salinity is lower. Both of these examples are shown on the graph in Figure 3.

Surface salinity in polar regions varies seasonally due to the formation and melting of sea ice. When seawater freezes in winter, salts do not become part of the ice. Therefore, the salinity of the remaining seawater increases. In summer when sea ice melts, the addition of relatively fresh water dilutes the solution and salinity decreases.

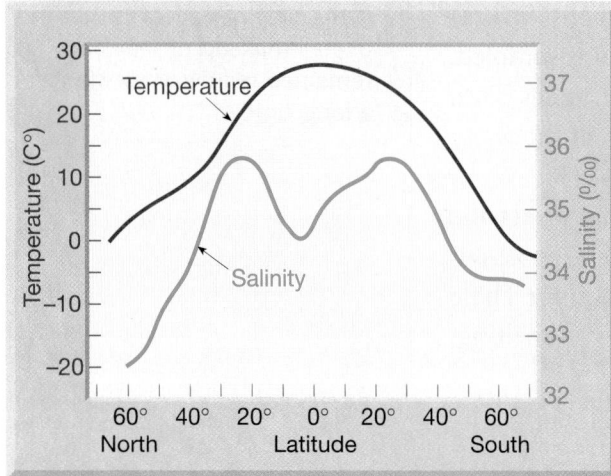

Figure 3 This graph shows the variations in ocean surface temperature (top curve) and surface salinity (lower curve). **Interpreting Diagrams** *At which latitudes is sea surface temperature highest? Why?*

Ocean Temperature Variation

The ocean's surface water temperature varies with the amount of solar radiation received, which is primarily a function of latitude.

The graph in Figure 3 shows this relationship. The intensity of solar radiation in high latitudes is much less than the intensity of solar radiation received in tropical latitudes. Therefore, lower sea surface temperatures are found in high-latitude regions. Higher sea surface temperatures are found in low-latitude regions.

Temperature Variation with Depth If you lowered a thermometer from the surface of the ocean into deeper water, what temperature pattern do you think you would find? Surface waters are warmed by the sun, so they generally have higher temperatures than deeper waters. However, the observed temperature pattern depends on the latitude.

Figure 4 on page 425 shows two graphs of temperature versus depth: one for low-latitude regions and one for high-latitude regions. The low-latitude curve begins with high temperature at the surface. However, the temperature decreases rapidly with depth because of the inability of the sun's rays to penetrate very far into the ocean. At a depth of about 1000 meters, the temperature remains just a few degrees above freezing and is relatively constant from this level down to the ocean floor. The **thermocline** (*thermo* = heat, *cline* = slope) is the layer of ocean water between about 300 meters and 1000 meters, where there is a rapid change of temperature with depth. The thermocline is a very important structure in the ocean because it creates a vertical barrier to many types of marine life.

The high-latitude curve in Figure 4 shows a very different pattern from the low-latitude curve. Surface water temperatures in high latitudes are much cooler than in low latitudes, so the curve begins at the surface with a low temperature. Deeper in the ocean, the temperature of the water is similar to that at the surface, so the curve remains vertical. There is no rapid change of temperature with depth. A thermocline is not present in high latitudes. Instead, the water column is isothermal (*iso* = same, *thermo* = heat).

 **Reading Checkpoint** *What is the thermocline?*

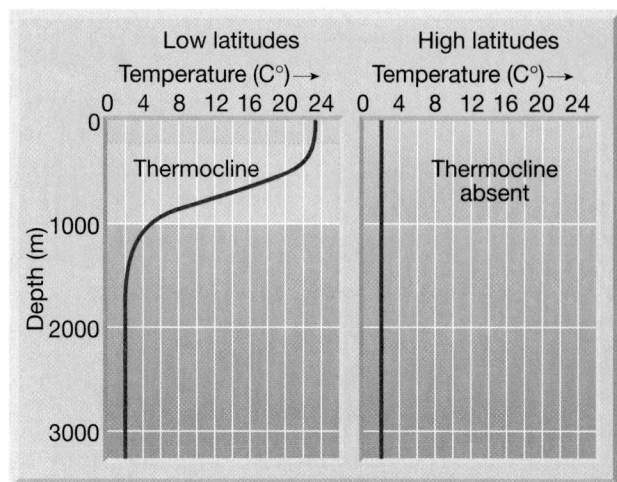

Figure 4 These graphs show the variations in ocean water temperature with depth for low-latitude and high-latitude regions. **Applying Concepts** *Why is the thermocline absent in the high latitudes?*

Ocean Density Variation

Density is defined as mass per unit volume. It can be thought of as a measure of how heavy something is for its size. For example, an object that has low density is lightweight for its size, such as a dry sponge, foam packing, or a surfboard. An object that has high density is heavy for its size, such as cement, most metals, or a large container full of water.

Density is an important property of ocean water because it determines the water's vertical position in the ocean. Density differences cause large areas of ocean water to sink or float. When high-density seawater is added to low-density fresh water, the denser seawater sinks below the fresh water.

Factors Affecting Seawater Density ⬤ Seawater density is influenced by two main factors: salinity and temperature. An increase in salinity adds dissolved substances and results in an increase in seawater density. An increase in temperature results in a decrease in seawater density. Temperature has the greatest influence on surface seawater density because variations in surface seawater temperature are greater than salinity variations. In fact, only in the extreme polar areas of the ocean—where temperatures are low and remain relatively constant—does salinity significantly affect density. Cold water that also has high salinity is some of the highest-density water in the world.

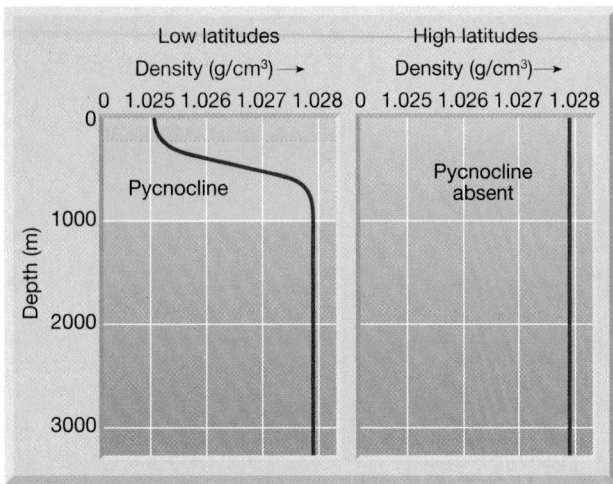

Low latitudes
Density (g/cm³) →
0 1.025 1.026 1.027 1.028

High latitudes
Density (g/cm³) →
0 1.025 1.026 1.027 1.028

Pycnocline

Pycnocline absent

Figure 5 The graphs show variations in ocean water density with depth for low-latitude and high-latitude regions.
Interpreting Diagrams
What is the difference between the low-latitude graph and the high-latitude graph? Why does this difference occur?

Density Variation with Depth By sampling ocean waters, oceanographers have learned that temperature and salinity—and the water's resulting density—vary with depth. Figure 5 shows two graphs of density versus depth. One graph shows the density for low-latitude regions and the other for high-latitude regions. Compare the density curves in Figure 5 to the temperature curves in Figure 4. They are similar. This similarity demonstrates that temperature is the most important factor affecting seawater density. It also shows that temperature is inversely proportional to density. When two quantities are inversely proportional, they can be multiplied together to equal a constant. Therefore, if the value of one quantity increases, the value of the other quantity decreases proportionately. When water temperature increases, its density decreases.

Reading Checkpoint

How does temperature affect the density of seawater?

The **pycnocline** (*pycno* = density, *cline* = slope) is the layer of ocean water between about 300 meters and 1000 meters where there is a rapid change of density with depth. A pycnocline presents a significant barrier to mixing between low-density water above and high-density water below. A pycnocline is not present in high latitudes; instead, the water column is about the same density throughout.

Ocean Layering

The ocean, like Earth's interior, is layered according to density. Low-density water exists near the surface, and higher-density water occurs below. Except for some shallow inland seas with a high rate of evaporation, the highest-density water is found at the greatest ocean depths. **Oceanographers generally recognize a three-layered structure in most parts of the open ocean: a shallow surface mixed zone, a transition zone, and a deep zone.** These zones are shown in Figure 6.

Surface Zone Because solar energy is received at the ocean surface, it is here that water temperatures are warmest. The **mixed zone** is the area of the surface created by the mixing of water by waves, currents, and tides. The mixed zone has nearly uniform temperatures. The depth and temperature of this layer vary, depending on latitude and season. The zone usually extends to about 300 meters, but it may extend to a depth of 450 meters. The surface mixed zone accounts for only about 2 percent of ocean water.

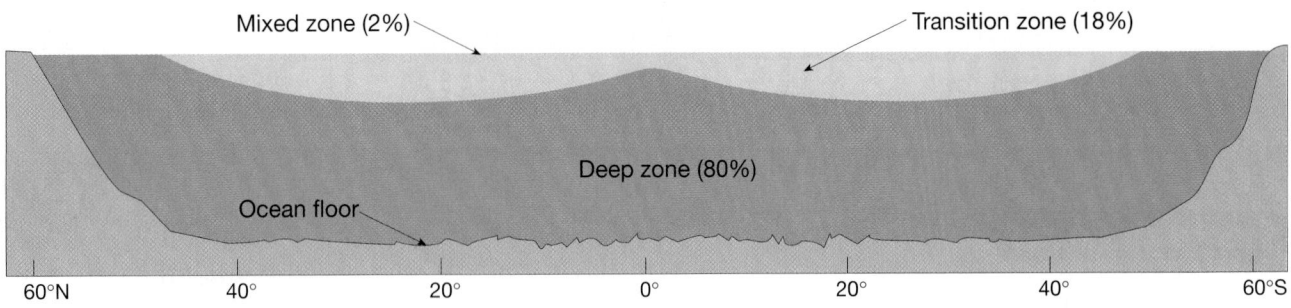

Mixed zone (2%)   Transition zone (18%)

Deep zone (80%)

Ocean floor

60°N   40°   20°   0°   20°   40°   60°S

Transition Zone Below the sun-warmed zone of mixing, the temperature falls abruptly with depth as was seen in Figure 4. Here, a distinct layer called the transition zone exists between the warm surface layer above and the deep zone of cold water below. The transition zone includes a thermocline and associated pycnocline. This zone accounts for about 18 percent of ocean water.

Deep Zone Below the transition zone is the deep zone. Sunlight never reaches this zone, and water temperatures are just a few degrees above freezing. As a result, water density remains constant and high. The deep zone includes about 80 percent of ocean water.

In high latitudes, this three-layered structure of the open ocean does not exist as seen in Figure 6. The three layers do not exist because there is no rapid change in temperature or density with depth. Therefore, good vertical mixing between surface and deep waters can occur in high-latitude regions. Here, cold high-density water forms at the surface, sinks, and initiates deep-ocean currents, which are discussed in Chapter 16.

Figure 6 Ocean Zones
Oceanographers recognize three main zones of the ocean based on water density, which varies with temperature and salinity.

Section 15.1 Assessment

Reviewing Concepts

1. What is salinity? What units are used to express the salinity of ocean water?

2. What are the six most abundant elements in seawater?

3. What are the sources of salt in ocean water?

4. Explain the relationship between latitude and sea surface temperature.

5. What factors affect the density of ocean water?

6. What are the three main zones of the open ocean?

Critical Thinking

7. **Inferring** Why does the salinity of seawater remain relatively constant over time?

8. **Summarizing** Explain the general pattern of temperature variation with depth in low-latitude oceans.

Writing in Science

Descriptive Paragraph Write a paragraph that describes the different characteristics of the three zones of the open ocean. Include an explanation of why polar regions do not exhibit the same pattern of water stratification.

Key Concepts

- How can marine organisms be classified?
- What is the difference between plankton and nekton?
- In which area of the ocean can most benthos organisms be found living?
- What factors are used to divide the ocean into marine life zones?

Vocabulary

- plankton
- phytoplankton
- zooplankton
- nekton
- benthos
- photic zone
- intertidal zone
- neritic zone
- oceanic zone
- pelagic zone
- benthic zone
- abyssal zone

Reading Strategy

Building Vocabulary Copy the table below. As you read, add definitions and examples to complete the table.

Definitions	Examples
Plankton: organisms that drift with ocean currents	bacteria
Phytoplankton: a. _____?_____	b. ___?___
Zooplankton: c. _____?_____	d. ___?___
Nekton: e. _____?_____	f. ___?___
Benthos: g. _____?_____	h. ___?___

A wide variety of organisms inhabit the marine environment. These organisms range in size from microscopic bacteria and algae to the largest organisms alive today—blue whales, which are as long as three buses lined up end to end. Marine biologists have identified over 250,000 marine species. This number is constantly increasing as new organisms are discovered.

Most marine organisms live within the sunlit surface waters. Strong sunlight supports photosynthesis by marine algae. Algae either directly or indirectly provide food for the majority of organisms. All marine algae live near the surface because they need sunlight to survive. Most marine animals also live near the surface because this is where they can find food.

Classification of Marine Organisms

Marine organisms can be classified according to where they live and how they move. They can be classified as either plankton (floaters) or nekton (swimmers). All other organisms are benthos, or bottom dwellers.

Plankton **Plankton** (*planktos* = wandering) **include all organisms—algae, animals, and bacteria—that drift with ocean currents.** Just because plankton drift does not mean they are unable to swim. Many plankton can swim but either move very weakly or move only vertically.

Figure 7 Plankton are organisms that drift with ocean currents. **A** This photo shows a variety of phytoplankton from the Atlantic Ocean. **B** The zooplankton shown here include copepods and the larval stages of other common marine organisms.

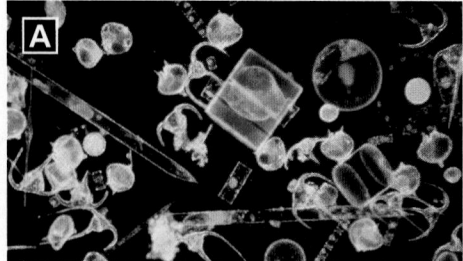

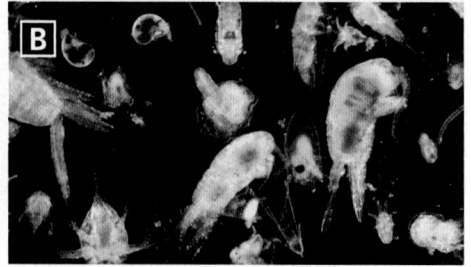

Among plankton, the algae that undergo photosynthesis are called **phytoplankton.** Most phytoplankton, such as diatoms, are microscopic. Animal plankton, are called **zooplankton.** Zooplankton include the larval stages of many marine organisms such as fish, sea stars, lobsters, and crabs. Figure 7 shows members of each group.

Nekton

Nekton (*nektos* = swimming) **include all animals capable of moving independently of the ocean currents, by swimming or other means of propulsion.** Nekton are able to determine their position within the ocean and in many cases complete long migrations. Nekton include most adult fish and squid, marine mammals, and marine reptiles. Figure 8 shows examples of nekton.

Fish may appear to exist everywhere in the oceans, but they are more abundant near continents and islands and in colder waters. Some fish, such as salmon, swim upstream in fresh water rivers to spawn. Many eels do just the reverse, growing to maturity in fresh water and then swimming out of the streams to breed in the depths of the ocean.

Benthos

The term *benthos* (*benthos* = bottom) **describes organisms living on or in the ocean bottom.** Figure 9 shows some examples of benthos organisms. The shallow coastal ocean floor contains a wide variety of physical conditions and nutrient levels. Most benthos organisms can be found living in this area. Shallow coastal areas are the only locations where large marine algae, often called seaweeds, are found attached to the bottom. These are the only areas of the seafloor that receive enough sunlight for the algae to survive.

Throughout most of the deeper parts of the seafloor, animals live in perpetual darkness, where photosynthesis cannot occur. They must feed on each other or on whatever nutrients fall from the productive surface waters. The deep-sea bottom is an environment of coldness, stillness, and darkness. Under these conditions, life progresses slowly. Organisms that live in the deep sea usually are widely distributed because physical conditions vary little on the deep-ocean floor.

Figure 8 Nekton includes all animals capable of moving independently of ocean currents. **A** This squid can use propulsion to move through the water. **B** This school of grunts swims through the water with ease.
Inferring *Why do you think some organisms, such as fish, are classified as plankton during some stages of their lives and nekton during other stages?*

Figure 9 Benthos describes organisms living on or in the ocean bottom. **A** Sea star **B** Coral crab

Marine Life Zones

The distribution of marine organisms is affected by the chemistry, physics, and geology of the oceans. Marine organisms are influenced by a variety of physical factors. **Three factors are used to divide the ocean into distinct marine life zones: the availability of sunlight, the distance from shore, and the water depth.** Figure 10 shows the different zones in which marine life can be found.

Availability of Sunlight The upper part of the ocean into which sunlight penetrates is called the **photic zone** (*photos* = light). The clarity of seawater is affected by many factors, such as the amount of plankton, suspended sediment, and decaying organic particles in the water. In addition, the amount of sunlight varies with atmospheric conditions, time of day, season of the year, and latitude.

The euphotic zone is the portion of the photic zone near the surface where light is strong enough for photosynthesis to occur. In the open ocean, this zone can reach a depth of 100 meters, but the zone will be much shallower close to shore where water clarity is typically reduced. In the euphotic zone, phytoplankton use sunlight to produce food and become the basis of most oceanic food webs.

Although photosynthesis cannot occur much below 100 meters, there is enough light in the lower photic zone for marine animals to avoid predators, find food, recognize their species, and locate mates. Below this zone is the aphotic zone, where there is no sunlight.

Reading Checkpoint *What is the difference between the photic zone and the aphotic zone?*

Figure 10 Marine Life Zones
The ocean is divided into marine life zones, based on availability of light, distance from shore, and water depth.
Interpreting Diagrams *Why are phytoplankton and larger algae found only in surface waters?*

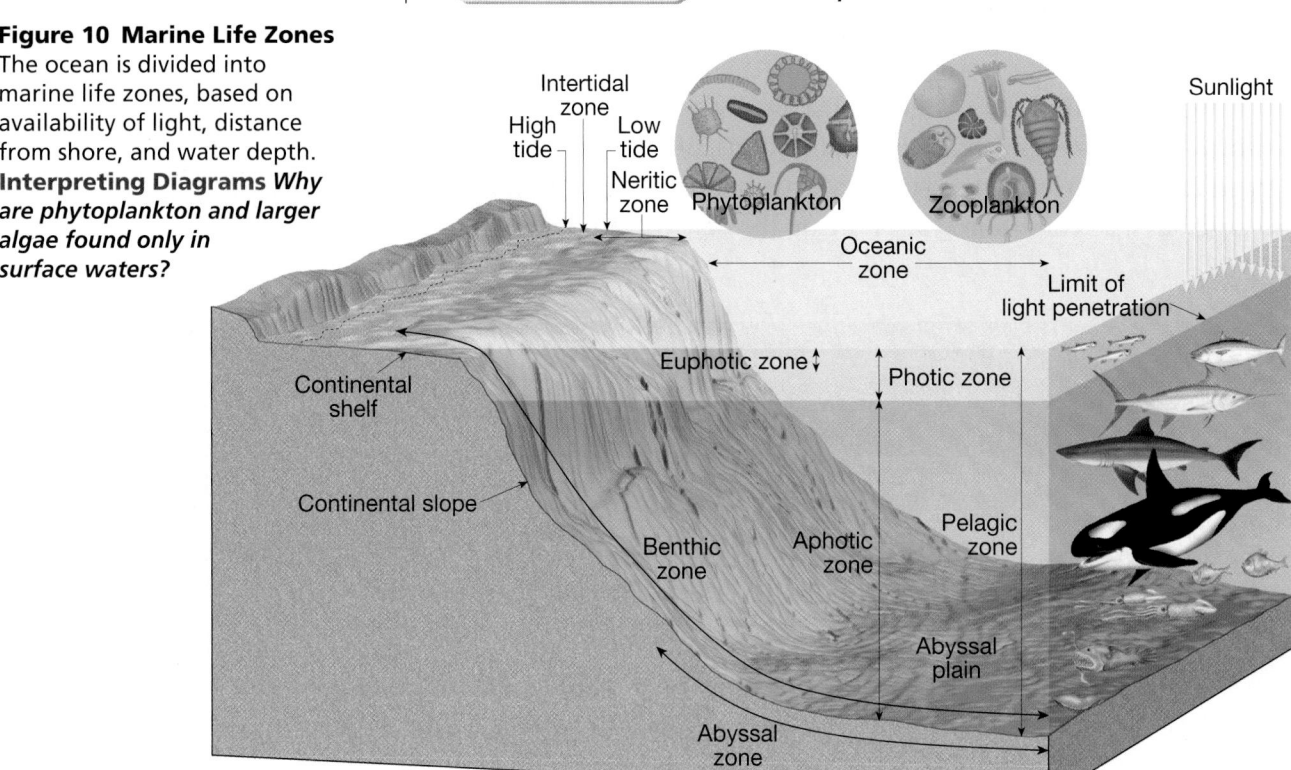

Distance from Shore Marine life zones can also be subdivided based on distance from shore. The area where the land and ocean meet and overlap is the **intertidal zone.** This narrow strip of land between high and low tides is alternately covered and uncovered by seawater with each tidal change. It appears to be a harsh place to live with crashing waves, periodic drying out, and rapid changes in temperature, salinity, and oxygen concentrations. However, the species that live here are well adapted to the constant environmental changes.

Seaward from the low-tide line is the **neritic zone.** This zone covers the gently sloping continental shelf. The neritic zone can be very narrow or may extend hundreds of kilometers from shore. It is often shallow enough for sunlight to reach all the way to the ocean floor, putting it entirely within the photic zone.

Although the neritic zone covers only about 5 percent of the world ocean, it is rich in both biomass and number of species. Many organisms find the conditions here ideal because photosynthesis occurs readily, nutrients wash in from the land, and the bottom provides shelter and habitat. This zone is so rich that it supports 90 percent of the world's commercial fisheries.

Beyond the continental shelf is the **oceanic zone.** The open ocean reaches great depths. As a result, surface waters typically have lower nutrient concentrations because nutrients tend to sink out of the photic zone to the deep-ocean floor. This low nutrient concentration usually results in smaller populations than the more productive neritic zone.

Water Depth A third method of classifying marine habitats is based on water depth. Open ocean of any depth is called the **pelagic zone.** Animals in this zone swim or float freely. The photic part of the pelagic zone is home to phytoplankton, zooplankton, and nekton, such as tuna, sea turtles, and dolphins. The aphotic part of this zone has giant squid and other species that are adapted to life in deep water.

Benthos organisms such as giant kelp, sponges, crabs, sea anemones, sea stars, and marine worms that attach to, crawl upon, or burrow into the seafloor occupy parts of the benthic zone. The **benthic zone** includes any sea-bottom surface regardless of its distance from shore and is mostly inhabited by benthos organisms.

The **abyssal zone** is a subdivision of the benthic zone. The abyssal zone includes the deep-ocean floor, such as abyssal plains. This zone is characterized by extremely high water pressure, consistently low temperature, no sunlight, and sparse life. Food sources at abyssal depths typically come from the surface. Some food is in the form of tiny decaying particles that steadily "rain" down from the surface. These particles provide food for filter-feeders, brittle stars, and burrowing worms. Other food arrives as large fragments or entire carcasses of organisms that sink from the surface. These pieces supply meals for actively searching fish, such as the grenadier, tripodfish, and hagfish.

Q *Do any deep-sea organisms produce light themselves?*

A Over half of deep-sea organisms—including fish, jellies, crustaceans, and deep-sea squid—can bioluminesce, which means they can produce light organically. These organisms produce light through a chemical reaction in specially designed structures or cells called photophores. Some of these cells contain luminescent bacteria that live symbiotically within the organism. In a world of darkness, the ability to produce light can be used to attract prey, define territory, communicate with others, or avoid predators.

Hydrothermal Vents

Among the most unusual seafloor discoveries of the past 30 years have been the hydrothermal vents along the oceanic ridge. Here seawater seeps into the ocean floor through cracks in the crust.

The water becomes super-heated and saturated with minerals. Eventually the heated water escapes back into the ocean. When the hot water comes in contact with the surrounding cold water, the minerals precipitate out, giving the water the appearance of black smoke. These geysers of hot water are referred to as black smokers, like the one shown in Figure 11.

At some vents water temperatures of 100°C or higher support communities of organisms found nowhere else in the world. In fact, hundreds of new species have been discovered surrounding these deep-sea habitats since scientists found some vents along the Galápagos Rift in 1977. Chemicals from the vents become food for bacteria. The bacteria produce sugars and other foods that enable them and many other organisms to live in this very unusual and extreme environment. Look at Figure 12 for another example of organisms found along hydrothermal vents.

Figure 11 When super-heated water meets cold seawater, minerals and metals precipitate out of the water to form this black smoker.

Figure 12 Tube worms up to 3 meters in length are among the organisms found along hydrothermal vents.

Section 15.2 Assessment

Reviewing Concepts

1. How can marine organisms be classified?
2. What is the difference between plankton and nekton?
3. In which area of the ocean do most benthos organisms live?
4. What factors are used to divide the ocean into marine life zones?
5. Why is the neritic zone rich in life?

Critical Thinking

6. **Inferring** Why do many fish in the abyssal zone locate food through chemical sensing?

7. **Inferring** Organisms that live in the intertidal zone must deal with harsh and changing conditions. What types of adaptations would benefit organisms living in this zone?

Writing in Science

Making Tables Make a table to organize the information about marine life zones presented in this section. Include the basis by which the zone is classified, any subdivisions of the zone, and the characteristics of each zone within the table.

15.3 Oceanic Productivity

Reading Focus

Key Concepts

- What factors influence a region's photosynthetic productivity?
- Describe the transfer efficiency between trophic levels.
- What advantage do organisms in a food web have over those in a food chain?

Vocabulary

- primary productivity
- photosynthesis
- chemosynthesis
- trophic level
- food chain
- food web

Reading Strategy

Identifying Main Ideas Copy the table below. As you read, write the main idea of each topic.

Topic	Main Idea
Productivity in polar oceans	a. ___?___
Productivity in tropical oceans	b. ___?___
Productivity in temperate oceans	c. ___?___

Like other ecosystems on Earth, organisms in the marine environment are interconnected through the web of food production and consumption. Marine producers include phytoplankton, larger algae such as seaweeds, and bacteria. Consumers include crabs, clams, sea stars, fish, dolphins, and whales. Why are some regions of the ocean teeming with life, while other areas seem barren? The answer is related to the amount of primary productivity in various parts of the ocean.

Primary Productivity

Primary productivity is the production of organic compounds from inorganic substances through photosynthesis or chemosynthesis. **Photosynthesis** is the use of light energy to convert water and carbon dioxide into energy-rich glucose molecules. **Chemosynthesis** is the process by which certain microorganisms create organic molecules from inorganic nutrients using chemical energy. Bacteria in hydrothermal vents use hydrogen sulfide as an energy source. Acting as producers, these bacteria support the hydrothermal vent communities.

Two factors influence a region's photosynthetic productivity: the availability of nutrients and the amount of solar radiation, or sunlight. Primary producers need nutrients such as nitrogen, phosphorus, and iron. Lack of nutrients can be a limiting factor in productivity. Thus, the most abundant marine life exists where there are ample nutrients and good sunlight. Oceanic productivity, however, varies dramatically because of the uneven distribution of nutrients throughout the photosynthetic zone and the availability of solar energy due to seasonal changes.

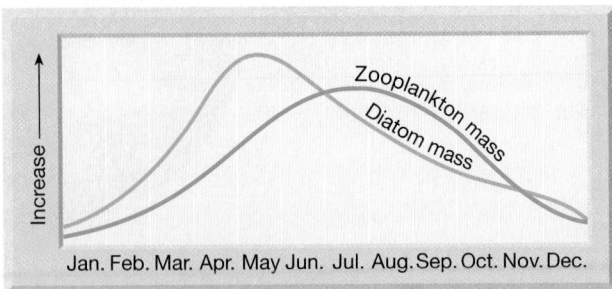

Figure 13 One example of productivity in polar oceans is illustrated by the Barents Sea. **Interpreting Diagrams** *Describe the relationship between the zooplankton and phytoplankton populations.*

Productivity in Polar Oceans

Polar regions such as the Arctic Ocean's Barents Sea, off the northern coast of Europe, experience continuous darkness for about three months of winter and continuous illumination for about three months during summer. Productivity of phytoplankton, mostly single-celled algae called diatoms, peaks there during May. This trend is shown in the graph in Figure 13. During May the sun rises high enough in the sky so that sunlight penetrates deep into the water. As soon as the diatoms develop, zooplankton begin feeding on them. As Figure 13 shows, the zooplankton biomass peaks in June and continues at a relatively high level until winter darkness begins in October.

Recall that density and temperature change very little with depth in polar regions and mixing occurs between surface waters and deeper, nutrient-rich waters. In the summer, however, melting ice creates a thin, low-salinity layer that does not readily mix with the deeper waters. This lack of mixing between water masses is crucial to summer production, because it helps prevent phytoplankton from being carried into deeper, darker waters. Instead, they are concentrated in the sunlit surface waters where they reproduce continuously.

Because of the constant supply of nutrients rising from deeper waters below, high-latitude surface waters typically have high nutrient concentrations. **The availability of solar energy, however, is what limits photosynthetic productivity in polar areas.**

Productivity in Tropical Oceans

You may be surprised to learn that productivity is low in tropical regions of the open ocean. Because the sun is more directly overhead, light penetrates much deeper into tropical oceans than in temperate and polar waters. Solar energy also is available year-round. However, productivity is low because a permanent thermocline prevents mixing between surface waters and nutrient-rich deeper waters. Figure 14 shows how water masses are separated in the tropics. The thermocline is a barrier that cuts off the supply of nutrients from deeper waters below. **Productivity in tropical regions is limited by the lack of nutrients.** These areas have so few organisms that they are considered biological deserts.

Figure 14 Water Layers in the Tropics The permanent thermocline in tropical oceans prevents the mixing of surface and deep water masses. Productivity is limited by the amount of nutrients in surface waters.

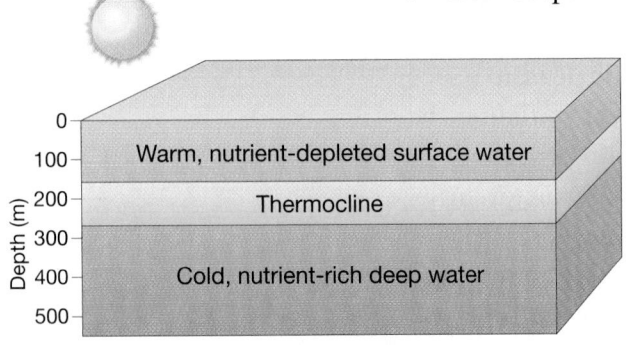

Productivity in Temperate Oceans Productivity is limited by available sunlight in polar regions and by nutrient supply in the tropics. **In temperate regions, which are found at mid-latitudes, a combination of these two limiting factors, sunlight and nutrient supply, controls productivity.** These relationships are shown in Figure 15.

- **Winter** Productivity in temperate oceans is very low during winter, even though nutrient concentration is highest at this time. The reason is that solar energy is limited because days are short, and the sun angle is low. As a result, the depth at which photosynthesis can occur is so shallow that phytoplankton do not grow much.

- **Spring** The sun rises higher in the sky during spring, creating a greater depth at which photosynthesis can occur. A spring bloom of phytoplankton occurs because solar energy and nutrients are available, and a seasonal thermocline develops. The thermocline traps algae in the euphotic zone. This creates a tremendous demand for nutrients in the euphotic zone, so the supply is quickly depleted, causing productivity to decrease sharply. Even though the days are lengthening and sunlight is increasing, productivity during the spring bloom is limited by the lack of nutrients.

- **Summer** The sun rises even higher in the summer, so surface waters in temperate parts of the ocean continue to warm. A strong seasonal thermocline is created that prevents the mixing of surface and deeper waters. So nutrients depleted from surface waters cannot be replaced by those from deeper waters. Throughout summer, the phytoplankton population remains relatively low.

- **Fall** Solar radiation decreases in the fall as the sun moves lower in the sky. Surface temperatures drop and the summer thermocline breaks down. Nutrients return to the surface layer as increased wind strength mixes surface waters with deeper waters. These conditions create a fall bloom of phytoplankton, which is much less dramatic than the spring bloom. The fall bloom is very short-lived because sunlight becomes the limiting factor as winter approaches to repeat the seasonal cycle.

Figure 15 Productivity in Northern Hemisphere, Temperate Oceans The graph shows the relationship among phytoplankton, zooplankton, amount of sunshine, and nutrient levels for surface waters. **Analyzing** *What happens to phytoplankton in the spring and in the fall?*

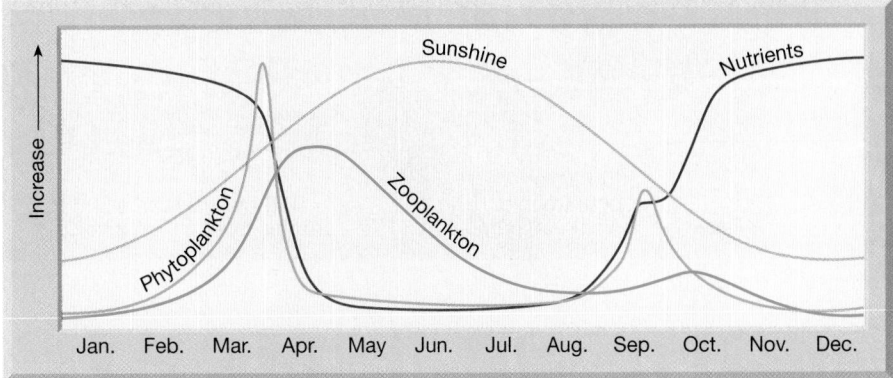

Oceanic Feeding Relationships

Marine algae, plants, bacteria, and bacteria-like organisms are the main oceanic producers. As producers make food available to the consuming animals of the ocean, energy passes from one feeding population to the next. Only a small percentage of the energy taken in at any level is passed on to the next because energy is consumed and lost at each level. As a result, the producers' biomass in the ocean is many times greater than the mass of top consumers, such as sharks or whales.

Trophic Levels Chemical energy stored in the mass of the ocean's algae is transferred to the animal community mostly through feeding. Zooplankton are herbivores (*herba* = grass, *vora* = eat), so they eat algae. Larger herbivores feed on the larger algae and marine plants that grow attached to the ocean bottom near shore. The herbivores are then eaten by carnivores (*carni* = meat, *vora* = eat). Smaller carnivores are eaten by another population of larger carnivores, and so on. Each of these feeding stages is called a **trophic level.**

Transfer Efficiency The transfer of energy between trophic levels is very inefficient. The efficiencies of different algal species vary, but the average is only about 2 percent. This means that 2 percent of the light energy absorbed by algae is ultimately changed into food and made available to herbivores. Figure 16 shows the passage of energy between trophic levels through an entire ecosystem—from the solar energy used by phytoplankton to a top-level carnivore, humans.

Figure 16 Energy Flow and Transfer Efficiency in an Ecosystem For every 500,000 units of radiant energy input available to the producers, only one unit of mass is added to the fifth trophic level.
Analyzing *What is the average transfer efficiency for phytoplankton? What is it for all of the other trophic levels?*

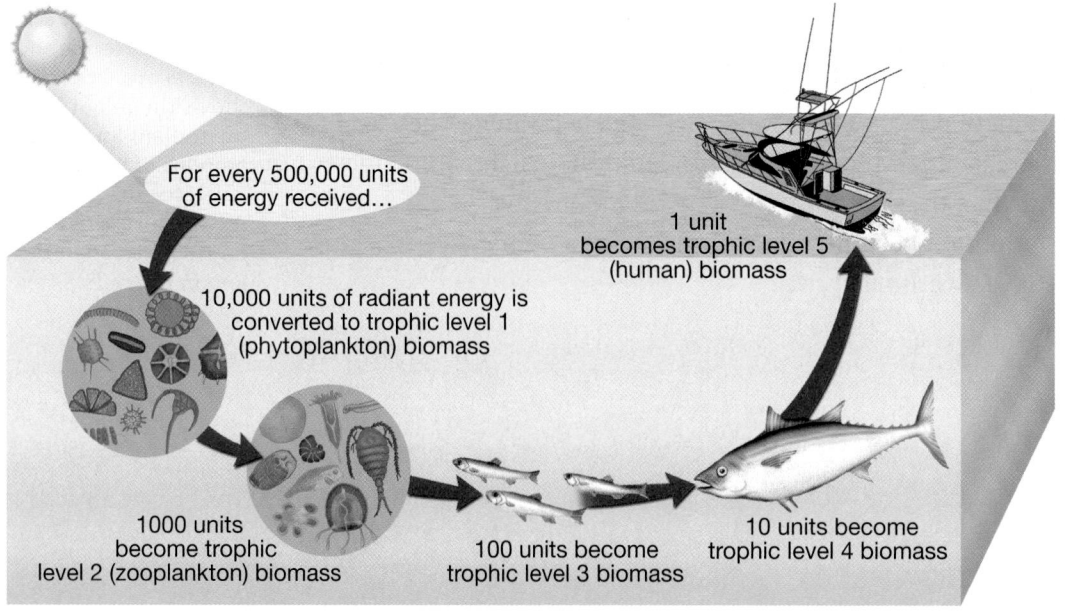

For every 500,000 units of energy received…

10,000 units of radiant energy is converted to trophic level 1 (phytoplankton) biomass

1 unit becomes trophic level 5 (human) biomass

1000 units become trophic level 2 (zooplankton) biomass

100 units become trophic level 3 biomass

10 units become trophic level 4 biomass

Food Chains and Food Webs

A **food chain** is a sequence of organisms through which energy is transferred, starting with the primary producer. A herbivore eats the producer, then one or more carnivores eats the herbivore. The chain finally culminates with the "top carnivore," which is not usually preyed upon by any other organism.

Figure 17A shows a simple food chain. Feeding relationships are rarely as simple as this food chain suggests. More often, top carnivores in a food chain feed on a number of different animals, each of which feeds on a variety of organisms. These feeding relationships form a **food web,** as shown in Figure 17B for North Sea herring.

◉Animals that feed through a food web rather than a food chain are more likely to survive because they have alternative foods to eat should one of their food sources diminish or disappear. Newfoundland herring, on the other hand, eat only copepods, so the disappearance of copepods would greatly affect their population.

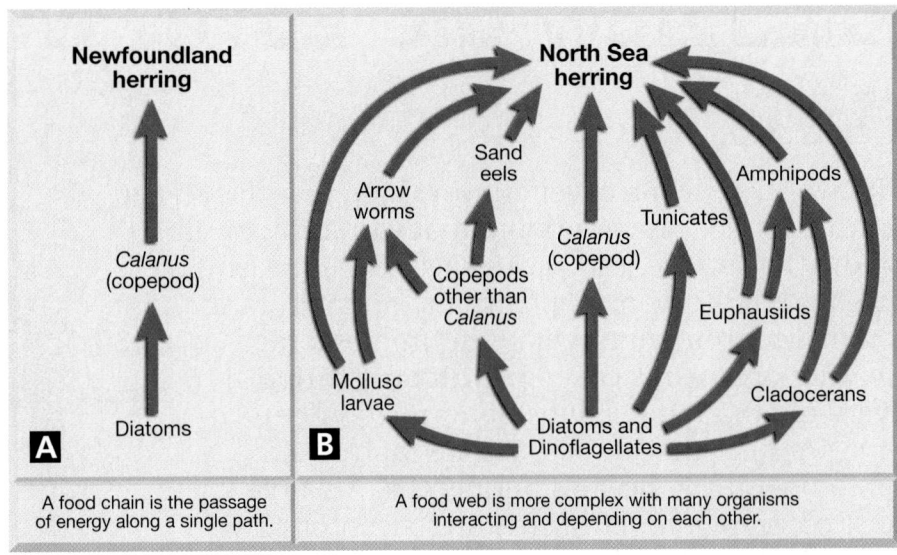

A A food chain is the passage of energy along a single path.

B A food web is more complex with many organisms interacting and depending on each other.

Figure 17 A A food chain is the passage of energy along a single path. **B** A food web is a complex series of feeding relationships with many organisms interacting and depending on each other.

Section 15.3 Assessment

Reviewing Concepts

1. ◉ What factors influence a region's photosynthetic productivity?

2. ◉ Describe the transfer efficiency between trophic levels.

3. ◉ What advantage do organisms in a food web have over those in a food chain?

4. ◉ What limits primary productivity in tropical oceans? Why?

Critical Thinking

5. **Comparing and Contrasting** Compare and contrast photosynthesis and chemosynthesis. Give examples of organisms that undergo each process.

6. **Drawing Conclusions** Explain why producers are always the first tropic level in a food chain or food web.

7. If 700,000 energy units are received by phytoplankton in the ocean surface, how many energy units will reach a consumer that is on the fourth trophic level of a food chain?

How the Earth Works

Ocean Life

The world's oceans cover almost three quarters of the Earth's surface and are home to a vast array of life. Below the surface, the oceans become increasingly cold and dark. Even so, plants and animals, ranging in size from giant whales to microscopic floating organisms called **plankton,** thrive at every depth. Some jellyfish and turtles float or swim near the surface. Whales and squid often live in the ocean's middepths. A whole host of strange-looking creatures swim or crawl around the darkest ocean depths.

Distribution of world's major oceans

ARCTIC OCEAN
NORTH AMERICA
EUROPE
ASIA
TROPIC OF CANCER
PACIFIC OCEAN
AFRICA
EQUATOR
SOUTH AMERICA
ATLANTIC OCEAN
INDIAN OCEAN
AUSTRALIA
TROPIC OF CAPRICORN
SOUTHERN OCEAN
ANTARCTICA

BIOLUMINESCENCE
Some fish have special organs called photophores that give off a glow. In this process, called **bioluminescence,** fish use the light to recognize members of their own species or as lures for attracting prey.

Black snaggletooth fish

VERTICAL ZONES
Oceanographers divide the oceans into zones based on depth. Each zone is home to living things that are adapted to survive at that depth. For example, deep-water animals cope with darkness, very cold temperatures, and pressures that would crush a human. Some creatures can survive in more than one zone.

A school of chromis swims among the coral in Australia's Great Barrier Reef.

Life in the ocean zones

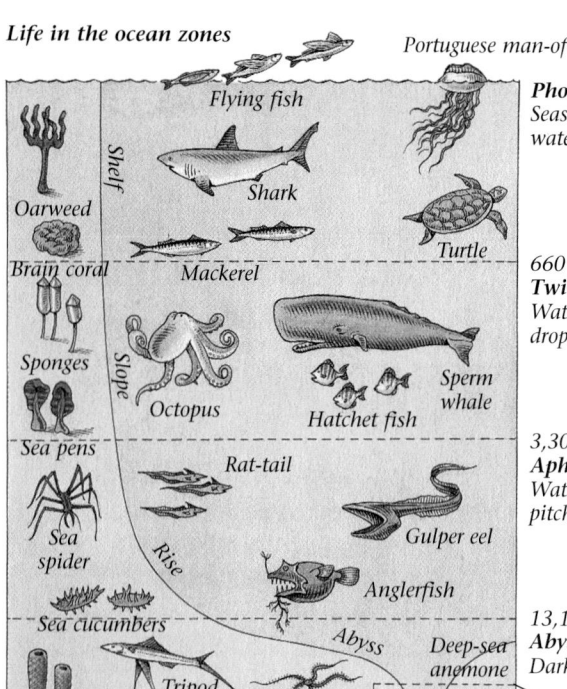

Portuguese man-of-war
Flying fish
Shark
Shelf
Oarweed
Turtle
Brain coral
Mackerel
Sponges
Slope
Octopus
Hatchet fish
Sperm whale
Sea pens
Rat-tail
Sea spider
Rise
Gulper eel
Anglerfish
Sea cucumbers
Abyss
Deep-sea anemone
Sponges
Tripod fish
Brittle star

Photic zone
Seasonal changes in water temperature

660 ft (200 m)
Twilight zone
Water temperature drops

3,300 ft (1,000 m)
Aphotic zone
Water very cold and pitch black

13,120 ft (4,000 m)
Abyss
Dark and cold

19,700 ft (6,000 m)

Deep-sea trench
Life exists below this depth.

CORAL REEFS

A coral is a tubular animal with tentacles. Most corals attach to a surface and build reefs that can rise above sea level around islands and continents. Other reefs are ring-shaped **atolls** around a lagoon of shallow water. Atolls grow over millions of years.

Growth of a coral atoll

1. Coral starts to grow around a volcanic island.

2. The island sinks. Sand collects on the growing coral reef and forms land.

3. The island disappears. Vegetation grows on the atoll that remains.

Australian sea lions are marine mammals that breathe air, feed at sea, and breed on land.

PHOTIC ZONE

Sunlight supports the growth of algae, sea grasses, and other plants on which some sea creatures feed. Marine mammals, squid, fish, and other animals have to be strong swimmers to move in the surface currents. Sea grasses and coral reefs provide food, shelter, and breeding sites for a variety of creatures.

HYDROTHERMAL VENTS

On the deep ocean floor, hot, mineral-rich water gushes from cracks, called **hydrothermal vents.** Bacteria feed on chemicals in this water, forming the basis of a food chain that does not rely on sunlight and plants. Giant tube worms, clams, and blind white crabs live around these vents.

Worms and crabs live near a hydrothermal vent.

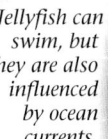

Jellyfish can swim, but they are also influenced by ocean currents.

Forcepsfish

False eyespot

ASSESSMENT

1. **Key Terms** Define **(a)** plankton, **(b)** bioluminescence, **(c)** atoll, **(d)** hydrothermal vent.

2. **Ecosystems** Why does plant life grow near the ocean surface but not on the deep ocean floor?

3. **Physical Processes** How can the emergence of a volcano lead to the growth of coral and the formation of an atoll?

4. **Ecosystems** How are some fish specially adapted to attract prey or to escape predators?

5. **Critical Thinking Analyzing Processes** Suppose that changes in the environment cause a decline in the population of ocean plants and corals. How might that environmental change also cause damage to populations of fish, marine mammals, and other sea creatures?

BRIGHT COLORS

Many fish have bright colors that attract mates and confuse predators. Complex coloration makes it hard to detect the outline of a fish. Some fish have eyespots, or false eyes. As a predator attacks the false head, the fish darts off in the opposite direction.

How Does Temperature Affect Water Density?

Ocean water temperatures vary from equator to pole and change with depth. Temperature, like salinity, affects the density of seawater. However, the density of seawater is more sensitive to temperature fluctuations than salinity. Cool surface water, which has a greater density than warm surface water, forms in the polar regions, sinks, and moves toward the tropics.

Problem
How can you determine the effects of temperature on water density?

Materials
- 100 mL graduated cylinders (2)
- test tubes (2)
- beakers (2)
- food coloring or dye
- stirrer
- ice
- tap water
- graph paper
- colored pencils

Skills
Observing, Graphing, Inferring, Drawing Conclusions

Procedure

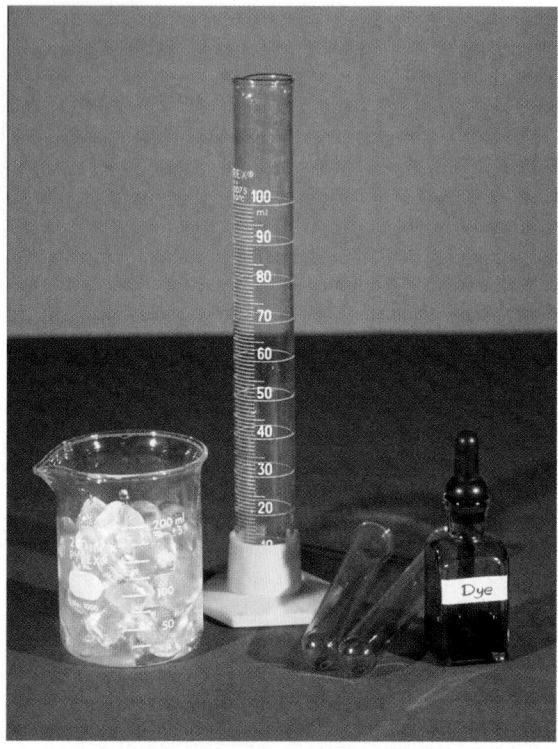

Part A

1. In a beaker, mix cold tap water with several ice cubes. Stir until the water and ice are well mixed.

2. Fill the graduated cylinder with 100 mL of the cold water from the beaker. The graduated cylinder should not contain any pieces of ice.

3. Put 2 to 3 drops of dye in a test tube and fill it 1/2 full with hot tap water.

4. Pour the contents of the test tube slowly into the graduated cylinder and record your observations.

5. Add a test tube full of cold tap water to a beaker. Mix in 2 to 3 drops of dye and a handful of ice to the beaker. Stir the solution thoroughly.

6. Fill the test tube 1/2 full of the solution from Step 5. Do not allow any ice into the test tube.

7. Fill the second graduated cylinder with 100 mL of hot tap water.

8. Pour the test tube of cold liquid slowly into the cylinder of hot water. Record your observations.

9. Clean the glassware and return it along with other materials to your teacher.

Part B

1. Photocopy the graph on the next page or copy it onto a separate sheet of graph paper.

2. Using the data in Table 1, plot a line on your graph for temperature. Using a different colored pencil, plot a line for density on the same graph.

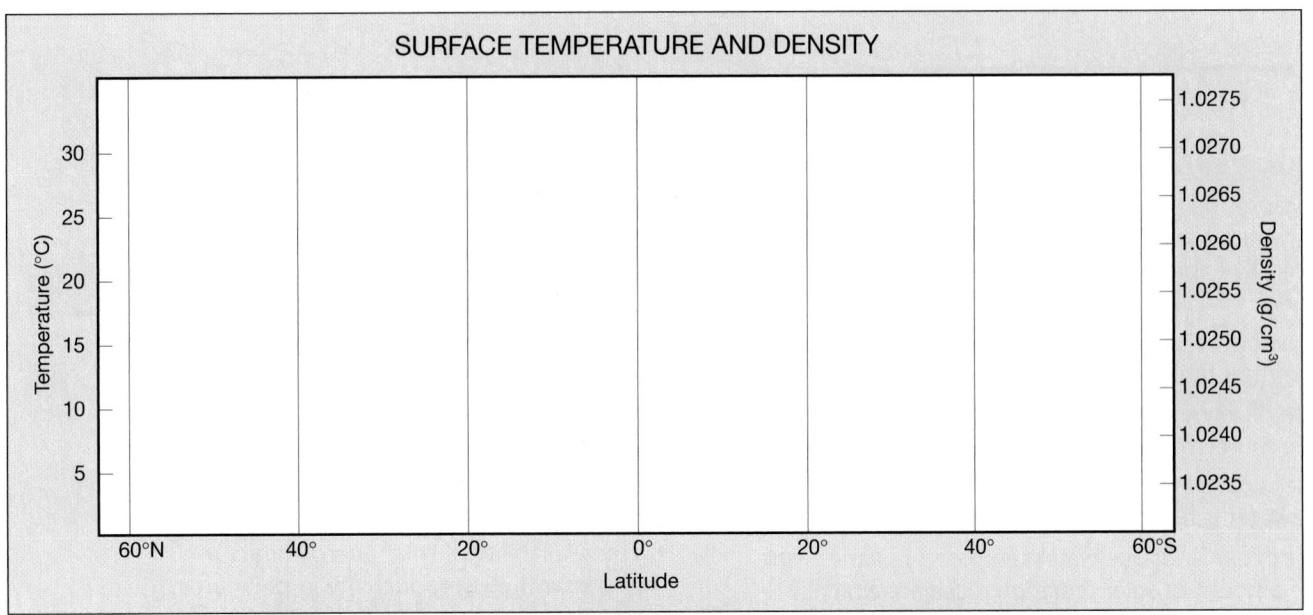

SURFACE TEMPERATURE AND DENSITY

Table 1 Idealized Ocean Surface Water Temperatures and Densities at Various Latitudes		
Latitude	**Surface Temperature (C°)**	**Surface Density (g/cm³)**
60°N	5	1.0258
40°N	13	1.0259
20°N	24	1.0237
0°	27	1.0238
20°S	24	1.0241
40°S	15	1.0261
60°S	2	1.0272

Analyze and Conclude

1. **Observing** What differences did you observe in the behavior of the water samples from Part A and Part B? Which water sample was the most dense in each experiment?

2. **Inferring** How does temperature affect the density of water?

3. **Drawing Conclusions** If two water samples of equal mass had equal salinities, which sample would be more dense: Water Sample A, which has a temperature of 25°C or water Sample B, which has a temperature of 14°C?

4. **Interpreting Diagrams** Describe the density and temperature characteristics of water in equatorial regions. Compare these characteristics to water found in polar regions.

5. **Inferring** What is the reason that higher average surface densities are found in the Southern Hemisphere?

15.1 The Composition of Seawater

🌐 Key Concepts

- Because the proportion of dissolved substances in seawater is such a small number, oceanographers typically express salinity in parts per thousand (‰).

- Most of the salt in seawater is sodium chloride—common table salt.

- Chemical weathering of rocks on the continents is one source of elements found in seawater.

- The second major source of elements found in seawater is from Earth's interior.

- The ocean's surface water temperature varies with the amount of solar radiation received, which is primarily a function of latitude.

- Seawater density is influenced by two main factors: salinity and temperature.

- Oceanographers generally recognize a three-layered structure in most parts of the open ocean: a shallow surface mixed zone, a transition zone, and a deep zone.

Vocabulary

salinity, *p. 422*; thermocline, *p. 424*; density, *p. 425*; pycnocline, *p. 426*; mixed zone, *p. 426*

15.2 The Diversity of Ocean Life

🌐 Key Concepts

- Marine organisms can be classified according to where they live and how they move.

- Plankton include all organisms—algae, animals, and bacteria—that drift with ocean currents.

- Nekton include all animals capable of moving independently of the ocean currents, by swimming or other means of propulsion.

- The term *benthos* describes organisms living on or in the ocean bottom.

- Three factors are used to divide the ocean into distinct marine life zones: the availability of sunlight, the distance from shore, and the water depth.

Vocabulary

plankton, *p. 428*; phytoplankton, *p. 429*; zooplankton, *p. 429*; nekton, *p. 429*; benthos, *p. 429*; photic zone, *p. 430*; intertidal zone, *p. 431*; neritic zone, *p. 431*; oceanic zone, *p. 431*; pelagic zone, *p. 431*; benthic zone, *p. 431*; abyssal zone, *p. 431*

15.3 Oceanic Productivity

🌐 Key Concepts

- Two factors influence a region's photosynthetic productivity: the availability of nutrients and the amount of solar radiation, or sunlight.

- The availability of solar energy limits photosynthetic productivity in polar areas.

- Productivity in tropical regions is limited by the lack of nutrients.

- In temperate regions, which are found at mid-latitudes, a combination of these two limiting factors, sunlight and nutrient supply, controls productivity.

- The transfer of energy between trophic levels is very inefficient.

- Animals that feed through a food web rather than a food chain are more likely to survive because they have alternative foods to eat should one of their food sources diminish in quantity or even disappear.

Vocabulary

primary productivity, *p. 433*, photosynthesis, *p. 433*, chemosynthesis, *p. 433*, trophic level, *p. 436*, food chain, *p. 437*, food web, *p. 437*

Thinking Visually

Web Diagram Use the information in the chapter to complete the web diagram on marine life zones.

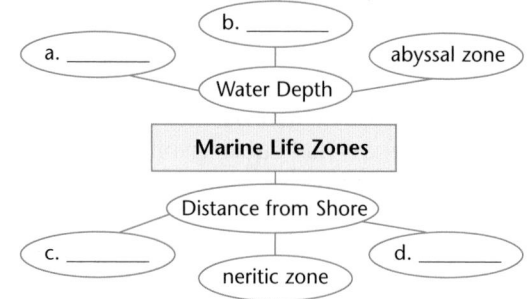

Reviewing Content

Choose the letter that best answers the question or completes the statement.

1. The most abundant salt in seawater is
   a. calcium chloride.
   b. magnesium chloride.
   c. sodium chloride.
   d. sodium fluoride.

2. Which process does NOT lead to a decrease in the salinity of seawater?
   a. runoff from land
   b. precipitation
   c. evaporation
   d. sea ice melting

3. Which term refers to the layer of water in which there is a rapid change of temperature with depth in the ocean?
   a. pycnocline
   b. abyssal zone
   c. thermocline
   d. isothermal line

4. Which is NOT a zone in the three-layered structure of the ocean according to density?
   a. mixed zone
   b. deep zone
   c. transition zone
   d. intertidal zone

5. Organisms that drift with ocean currents are
   a. nekton.
   b. plankton.
   c. neritic.
   d. pelagic.

6. Which term describes the upper part of the ocean into which sunlight penetrates?
   a. neritic zone
   b. intertidal zone
   c. oceanic zone
   d. photic zone

7. Phytoplankton are usually found in the
   a. benthic zone.
   b. photic zone.
   c. abyssal zone.
   d. aphotic zone.

8. The use of light energy by organisms to convert water and carbon dioxide into organic molecules is
   a. chemosynthesis.
   b. decomposition.
   c. photosynthesis.
   d. consumption.

9. During which season does primary productivity reach its peak in polar oceans?
   a. spring
   b. summer
   c. fall
   d. winter

10. In temperate oceans, primary productivity is limited by
    a. nutrients and oxygen concentration.
    b. nutrients and water temperature.
    c. sunlight and oxygen concentration.
    d. sunlight and nutrients.

Understanding Concepts

11. Why is salinity expressed in parts per thousand instead of percent?

12. What is the principal source of water in oceans? Why do scientists reach this conclusion?

13. Explain how the salinity of water in polar regions varies seasonally.

14. What is the range of salinity for surface waters in the open ocean?

15. Is there a thermocline present in high-latitude ocean waters? Why or why not?

16. Compare and contrast phytoplankton and zooplankton.

17. What factors may affect the depth of the photic zone in any given area of the ocean?

18. What is the oceanic zone? What limits the amount of production in the oceanic zone?

19. What is the difference between the pelagic zone and the benthic zone?

20. How does the permanent thermocline in tropical oceans affect primary productivity in those areas?

Copy the diagram onto a separate sheet of paper and use it to answer Questions 21 and 22.

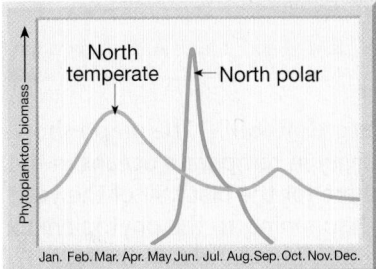

21. Draw a line on the graph that correctly represents the productivity of tropical oceans year-round.

22. Draw a line on the graph that represents the changes in zooplankton population in north temperate oceans throughout the course of a year.

23. What is the difference between a food chain and a food web?

Assessment continued

Critical Thinking

24. Analyzing In the Red Sea, evaporation values are higher than the values of precipitation and river runoff, particularly in summer months. Do you think that the salinity of the water here is higher or lower than average ocean water salinity? Why?

25. Drawing Conclusions Water Mass A is 2°C with a salinity of 34.50‰. Water Mass B is 2°C with a salinity of 34.00‰. Water Mass C is 2°C with a salinity of 34.78‰. Order the water masses from lowest density to highest density. Which water mass will be nearest the surface? Which will be closest to the bottom?

26. Relating Cause and Effect Explain how the phytoplankton productivity in polar waters is related to the fact that density and temperature change very little with depth in polar waters.

Use the figure below to answer Questions 27–29.

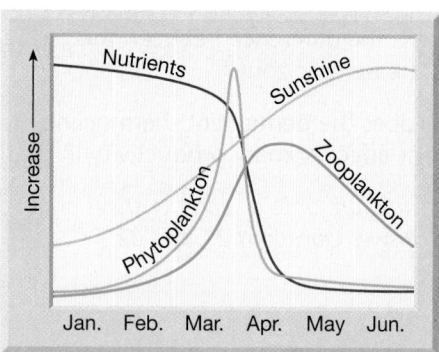

27. Applying Concepts The graph shows the productivity in temperate oceans in the northern hemisphere for the first half of the year. Describe what is happening to the phytoplankton and zooplankton populations in the graph. Explain what factors are affecting productivity.

28. Inferring Describe what the graph would look like if it were extended through December. How is it different than the January through June portion?

29. Drawing Conclusions How would this graph be different if it were for a temperate ocean in the southern hemisphere?

Concepts in Action

Use the table below to answer Questions 30 and 31.

Depth (m)	Temperature (°C)
0	23
200	22.5
400	20
600	14
800	8
1000	5
1200	4.5
1400	4.5
1600	4

30. Interpreting Data An oceanographer records the following temperature data for an area of ocean water. Graph the data on a sheet of graph paper. What feature exists between 400 and 1200 meters?

31. Applying Concepts For which area of the world oceans would this temperature variation with depth be present? What processes cause this to occur?

32. Formulating Hypotheses It has been observed that some species of zooplankton migrate vertically in ocean water. They spend the daylight hours at deeper depths of about 200 meters and at night move to the surface. Formulate a hypothesis that might explain this behavior.

Performance-Based Assessment

Designing Equipment Imagine you have been asked to collect marine plankton samples from surface waters near the coast. Recall that many plankton are microscopic or nearly so and that by definition, plankton drift with currents. Design a piece of equipment that will allow you to collect the plankton so that they can be brought to the lab and examined under a microscope. Include the materials you will use to construct the equipment, a drawing of it, and an explanation of how it should be used in the field.

Standardized Test Prep

Choose the letter that best answers the question or completes the statement.

1. The total amount of solid material dissolved in water is known as
   (A) sediment load.
   (B) salinity.
   (C) total dissolved solids.
   (D) density.

2. Thermoclines in oceans are *best* developed at
   (A) lower latitudes.
   (B) higher latitudes.
   (C) both high and low latitudes.
   (D) regions close to continents.

3. Which term describes a rapid change in density with depth?
   (A) thermocline
   (B) halocline
   (C) isocline
   (D) pycnocline

4. Animals capable of moving independently of ocean currents, by swimming or other means of propulsion are called
   (A) benthos.
   (B) plankton.
   (C) nekton.
   (D) pelagic.

5. During which season is productivity the *greatest* in temperate waters?
   (A) spring
   (B) summer
   (C) fall
   (D) winter

Use the diagram below to answer Questions 6 and 7.

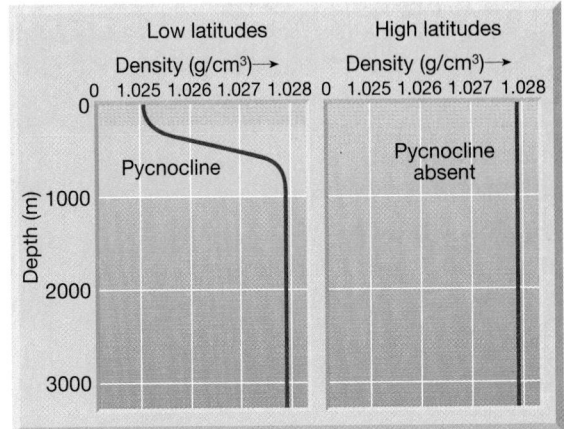

6. Explain what influences the formation of the pycnocline at low latitudes.

7. Why is the pycnocline absent at high latitudes?

8. What changes would occur to the food web below if the population of copepods was killed by a bacterial disease?

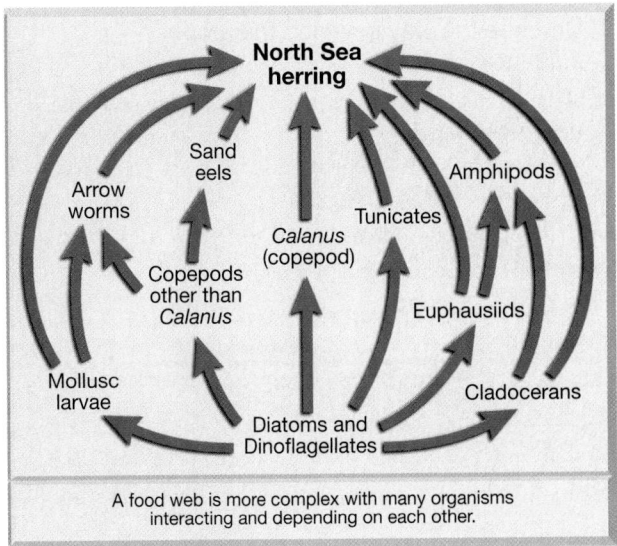

A food web is more complex with many organisms interacting and depending on each other.

CONCEPTS
— in Action —

Exploration Lab
Graphing Tidal Cycles

Understanding Earth
Shoes and Toys as Drift Meters

 Oceans
↳ Coastal Processes

 **Video Field Trip**

Waves and Tides

Take a surfing field trip with Discovery Channel and learn about waves, swells, and tides. Answer the following questions after watching the video.

1. How are waves created?

2. Describe the way in which the moon influences the tides.

For: Chapter 16 Resources
Visit: PHSchool.com
Web Code: cjk-9999

Waves break along California's rocky ▶
Big Sur coast.

Chapter Preview

Inquiry > Activity

How Do Ocean Waves Form?

Procedure

1. Fill a rectangular, clear, plastic container with water to within about 3 cm of the top of the container.

2. Place a fan next to the container, aiming the flow of air toward the water. **CAUTION:** *Make sure the cord and the fan do not come in contact with the water in the container.*

3. Turn the fan on low power for 2–3 minutes. Observe what effect this has on the water in the container. Using a ruler, measure the size of the waves produced. Record your observations and data.

4. Turn the fan off and allow the water in the container to settle. Repeat Step 3 with the fan on high power.

Think About It

1. **Inferring** Where does the energy to produce most ocean waves come from?

2. **Drawing Conclusions** What is the relationship between the speed of the wind and the size of a wave?

16.1 Ocean Circulation

Reading Focus

Key Concepts

- How do surface currents develop?
- How do ocean currents affect climate?
- Why is upwelling important?
- How are density currents formed?

Vocabulary

- ◆ ocean current
- ◆ surface current
- ◆ gyre
- ◆ Coriolis effect
- ◆ upwelling
- ◆ density current

Reading Strategy

Identifying Main Ideas Copy and expand the table below. As you read, write the main idea of each topic.

Topic	Main Idea
Surface currents	a. _____?_____
Gyres	b. _____?_____
Ocean currents and climate	c. _____?_____
Upwelling	d. _____?_____

Figure 1 Wind not only creates waves, but it also provides the force that drives the ocean's surface circulation.

Ocean water is constantly in motion, powered by many different forces. Winds, for example, generate surface currents, which influence coastal climate. Winds also produce waves like the ones shown in Figure 1. Some waves carry energy from powerful storms to distant shores, where their impact erodes the land. In some areas, density differences create deep-ocean circulation. This circulation is important for ocean mixing and recycling nutrients.

Surface Circulation

Ocean currents are masses of ocean water that flow from one place to another. The amount of water can be large or small. Ocean currents can be at the surface or deep below. The creation of these currents can be simple or complex. In all cases, however, the currents that are generated involve water masses in motion.

Surface Currents Surface currents are movements of water that flow horizontally in the upper part of the ocean's surface. **Surface currents develop from friction between the ocean and the wind that blows across its surface.** Some of these currents do not last long, and they affect only small areas. Such water movements are responses to local or seasonal influences. Other surface currents are more permanent and extend over large portions of the oceans. These major horizontal movements of surface waters are closely related to the general circulation pattern of the atmosphere.

Ocean Surface Currents

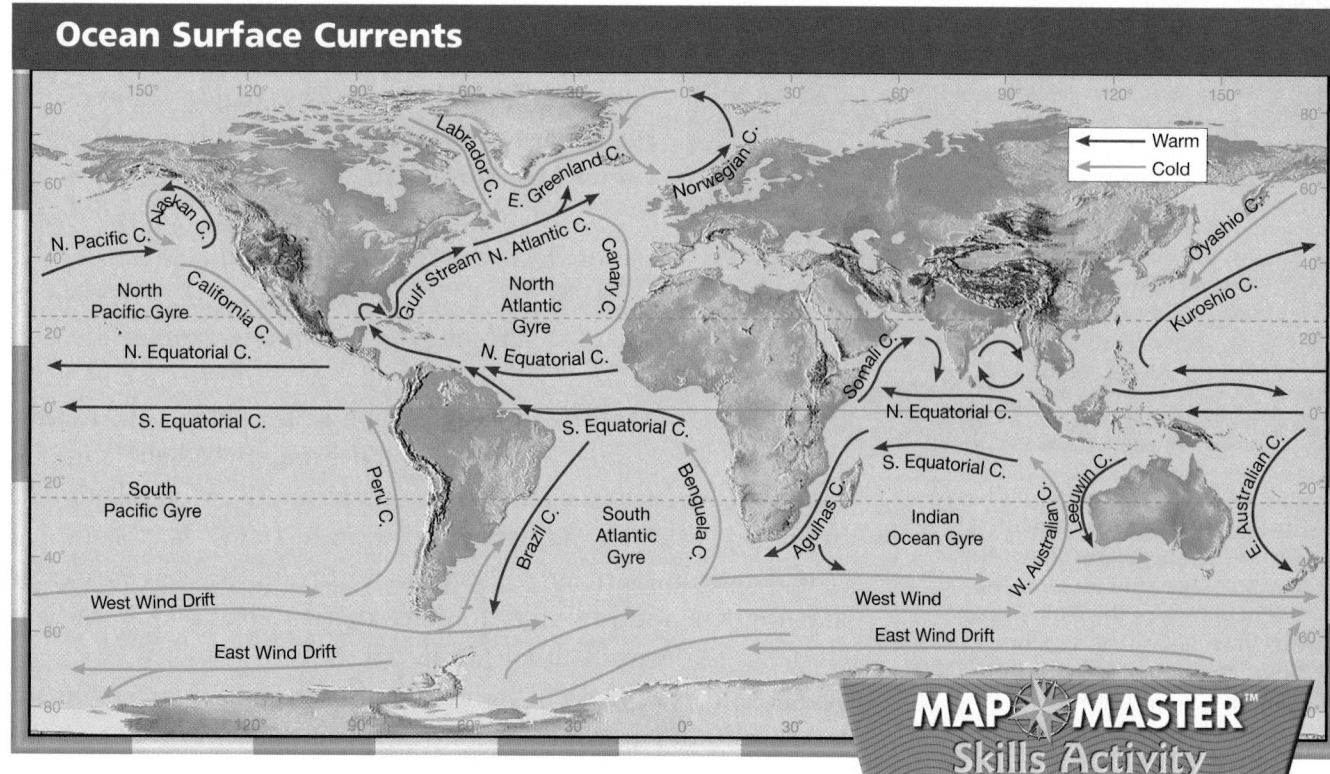

MAP MASTER™
Skills Activity

Figure 2
The ocean's circulation is organized into five major gyres, or circular current systems. The West Wind Drift flows around the continent of Antarctica.

Movement
Locate Which currents make up the North Atlantic Gyre?
Locate Find the West Wind Drift on the map. Explain why the West Wind Drift is the only current that completely encircles Earth.
Drawing Conclusions Why is there not another comparable current that encircles Earth at the same latitude in the Northern Hemisphere?

Gyres Huge circular-moving current systems dominate the surfaces of the oceans. These large whirls of water within an ocean basin are called **gyres** (*gyros* = a circle). There are five main ocean gyres: the North Pacific Gyre, the South Pacific Gyre, the North Atlantic Gyre, the South Atlantic Gyre, and the Indian Ocean Gyre. Find these gyres in Figure 2.

Although wind is the force that generates surface currents, other factors also influence the movement of ocean waters. The most significant of these is the Coriolis effect. The **Coriolis effect** is the deflection of currents away from their original course as a result of Earth's rotation. ⬤**Because of Earth's rotation, currents are deflected to the right in the Northern Hemisphere and to the left in the Southern Hemisphere.** As a consequence, gyres flow in opposite directions in the two different hemispheres.

Four main currents generally exist within each gyre. For example, the North Pacific Gyre consists of the North Equatorial Current, the Kuroshio Current, the North Pacific Current, and the California Current. The tracking of floating objects that are released into the ocean reveals that it takes about six years for the objects to go all the way around the loop.

Reading Checkpoint *Why do gyres in the Northern Hemisphere flow in the opposite direction of gyres in the Southern Hemisphere?*

The Dynamic Ocean **449**

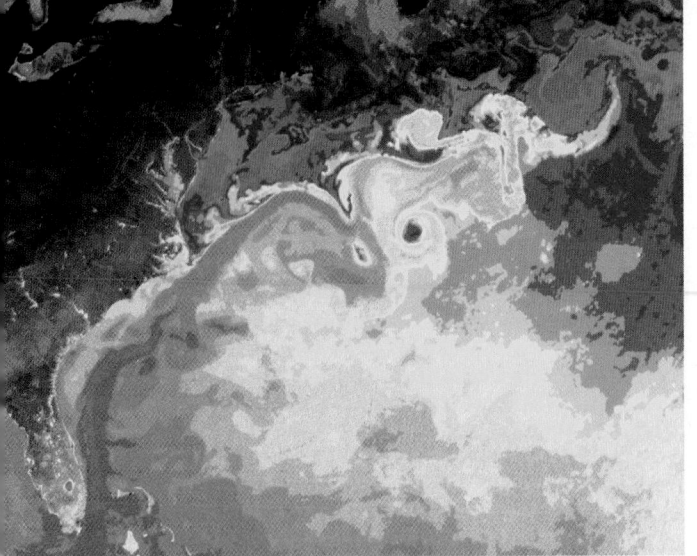

Figure 3 Gulf Stream This false-color satellite image of sea surface temperatures shows the course of the Gulf Stream. The warm waters of the Gulf Stream are shown in red and orange along the east coast of Florida and the Carolinas. The surrounding colder waters are shown in green, blue, and purple. Compare this image to the map of the Gulf Stream in Figure 2.

Ocean Currents and Climate Ocean currents have an important effect on climates. **When currents from low-latitude regions move into higher latitudes, they transfer heat from warmer to cooler areas on Earth.** The Gulf Stream, a warm water current shown in Figure 3, is an excellent example of this phenomenon. The Gulf Stream brings warm water from the equator up to the North Atlantic Current, which is an extension of the Gulf Stream. This current allows Great Britain and much of northwestern Europe to be warmer during the winter than one would expect for their latitudes, which are similar to the latitudes of Alaska and Newfoundland. The prevailing westerly winds carry this warming effect far inland. For example, Berlin, Germany (52 degrees north latitude), has an average January temperature similar to that experienced at New York City, which lies 12 degrees latitude farther south.

The effects of these warm ocean currents are felt mostly in the middle latitudes in winter. In contrast, the influence of cold currents is most felt in the tropics or during summer months in the middle latitudes. Cold currents begin in cold high-latitude regions. **As cold water currents travel toward the equator, they help moderate the warm temperatures of adjacent land areas.** Such is the case for the Benguela Current along western Africa, the Peru Current along the west coast of South America, and the California Current. These currents are shown in Figure 2.

Ocean currents also play a major role in maintaining Earth's heat balance. They do this by transferring heat from the tropics, where there is an excess of heat, to the polar regions, where less heat exists. Ocean water movement accounts for about a quarter of this heat transport. Winds transport the remaining three-quarters.

Upwelling In addition to producing surface currents, winds can also cause vertical water movements. **Upwelling** is the rising of cold water from deeper layers to replace warmer surface water. Upwelling is a common wind-induced vertical movement. One type of upwelling, called coastal upwelling, is most characteristic along the west coasts of continents, most notably along California, western South America, and West Africa.

Coastal upwelling occurs in these areas when winds blow toward the equator and parallel to the coast. Coastal winds combined with the Coriolis effect cause surface water to move away from shore. As the surface layer moves away from the coast, it is replaced by water that "upwells" from below the surface. This slow upward movement of water from depths of 50 to 300 meters brings water that is cooler than

Go Online

For: Links on ocean currents
Visit: www.SciLinks.org
Web Code: cjn-5161

the original surface water and results in lower surface water temperatures near the shore.

 **Upwelling brings greater concentrations of dissolved nutrients, such as nitrates and phosphates, to the ocean surface.** These nutrient-enriched waters from below promote the growth of microscopic plankton, which in turn support extensive populations of fish and other marine organisms. Figure 4 is a satellite image that shows high productivity due to coastal upwelling off the southwest coast of Africa.

Reading Checkpoint *What is upwelling?*

Deep-Ocean Circulation

In contrast to the largely horizontal movements of surface currents, deep-ocean circulation has a significant vertical component. It accounts for the thorough mixing of deep-water masses.

Density Currents Density currents are vertical currents of ocean water that result from density differences among water masses. Denser water sinks and slowly spreads out beneath the surface. **An increase in seawater density can be caused by a decrease in temperature or an increase in salinity.** Processes that increase the salinity of water include evaporation and the formation of sea ice. Processes that decrease the salinity of water include precipitation, runoff from land, icebergs melting, and sea ice melting. Density changes due to salinity variations are important in very high latitudes, where water temperature remains low and relatively constant.

High Latitudes Most water involved in deep-ocean density currents begins in high latitudes at the surface. In these regions, surface water becomes cold, and its salinity increases as sea ice forms. When this water becomes dense enough, it sinks, initiating deep-ocean density currents. Once this water sinks, it is removed from the physical processes that increased its density in the first place. Its temperature and salinity remain largely unchanged during the time it is in the deep ocean. Because of this, oceanographers can track the movements of density currents in the deep ocean. By knowing the temperature, salinity, and density of a water mass, scientists are able to map the slow circulation of the water mass through the ocean.

Figure 4 Effects of Upwelling
This image from the SeaStar satellite shows chlorophyll concentration along the southwest coast of Africa. High chlorophyll concentrations, in red, indicate high amounts of photosynthesis, which is linked to upwelling nutrients.

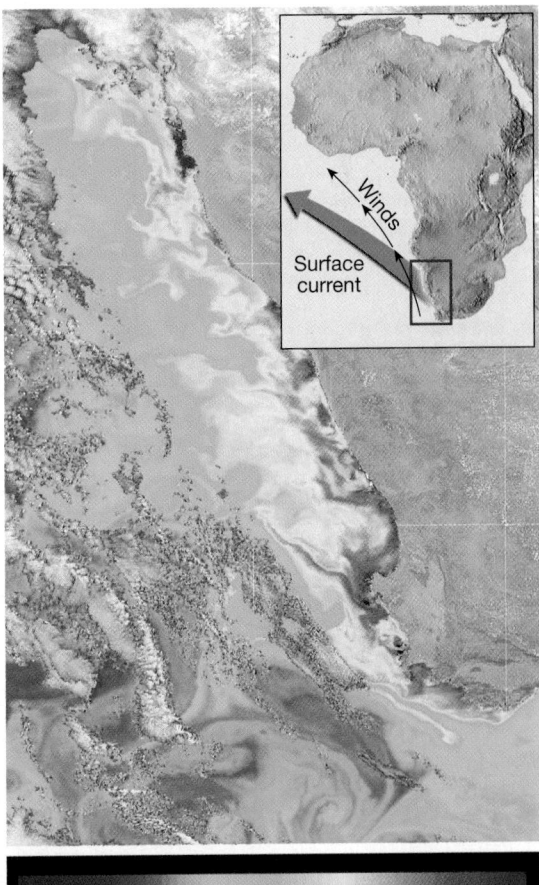

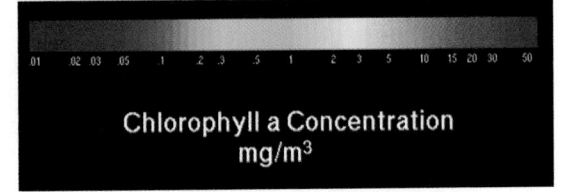

Chlorophyll a Concentration
mg/m^3

Figure 5 Sea Ice in the Arctic Ocean When seawater freezes, sea salts do not become part of the ice, leading to an increase in the salinity of the surrounding water.
Drawing Conclusions *How does this process lead to the formation of a density current?*

Near Antarctica, surface conditions create the highest density water in the world. This cold, salty water slowly sinks to the sea floor, where it moves throughout the ocean basins in slow currents. After sinking from the surface of the ocean, deep waters will not reappear at the surface for an average of 500 to 2000 years.

Evaporation Density currents can also result from increased salinity of ocean water due to evaporation. In the Mediterranean Sea conditions exist that lead to the formation of a dense water mass at the surface that sinks and eventually flows into the Atlantic Ocean. Climate conditions in the eastern Mediterranean include a dry northwest wind and sunny days. These conditions lead to an annual excess of evaporation compared to the amount of precipitation. When seawater evaporates, salt is left behind, and the salinity of the remaining water increases. The surface waters of the eastern Mediterranean Sea have a salinity of about 38‰ (parts per thousand). In the winter months, this water flows out of the Mediterranean Sea into the Atlantic

Figure 6 This cross section of the Atlantic Ocean shows the deep-water circulation of water masses formed by density currents.

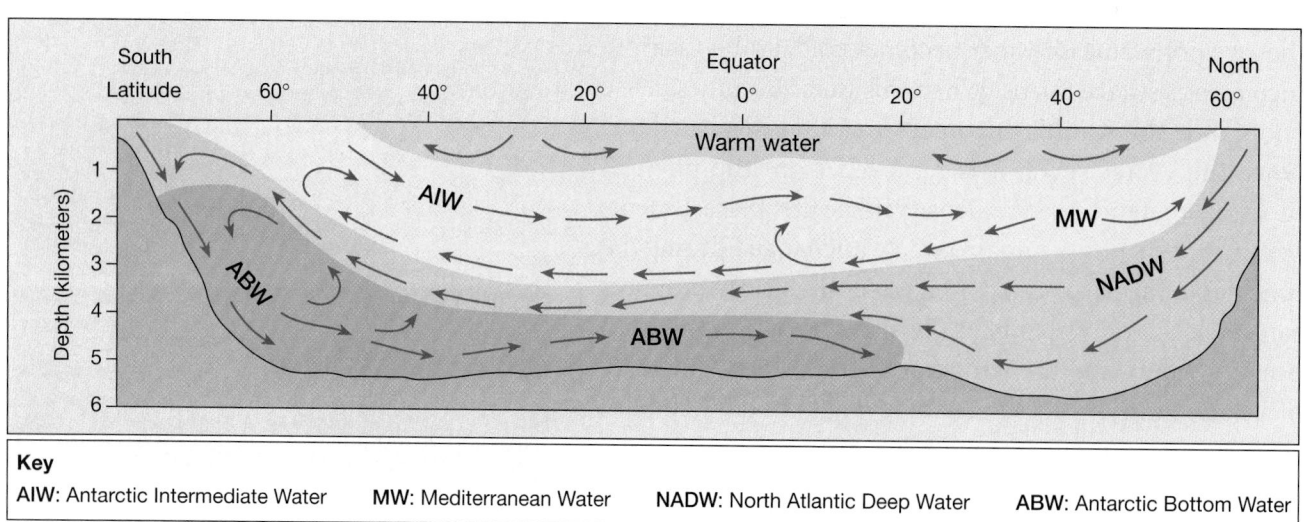

Key

AIW: Antarctic Intermediate Water   **MW:** Mediterranean Water   **NADW:** North Atlantic Deep Water   **ABW:** Antarctic Bottom Water

Ocean. At 38‰, this water is more dense than the Atlantic Ocean surface water at 35‰, so it sinks. This Mediterranean water mass can be tracked as far south as Antarctica. Figure 6 shows some of the different water masses created by density currents in the Atlantic Ocean.

A Conveyor Belt A simplified model of ocean circulation is similar to a conveyor belt that travels from the Atlantic Ocean through the Indian and Pacific oceans and back again. Figure 7 shows this conveyor belt model. In this model, warm water in the ocean's upper layers flows toward the poles. When the water reaches the poles, its temperature drops and salinity increases, making it more dense. Because the water is dense, it sinks and moves toward the equator. It returns to the equator as cold, deep water that eventually upwells to complete the circuit. As this "conveyor belt" moves around the globe, it influences global climate by converting warm water to cold water and releasing heat to the atmosphere.

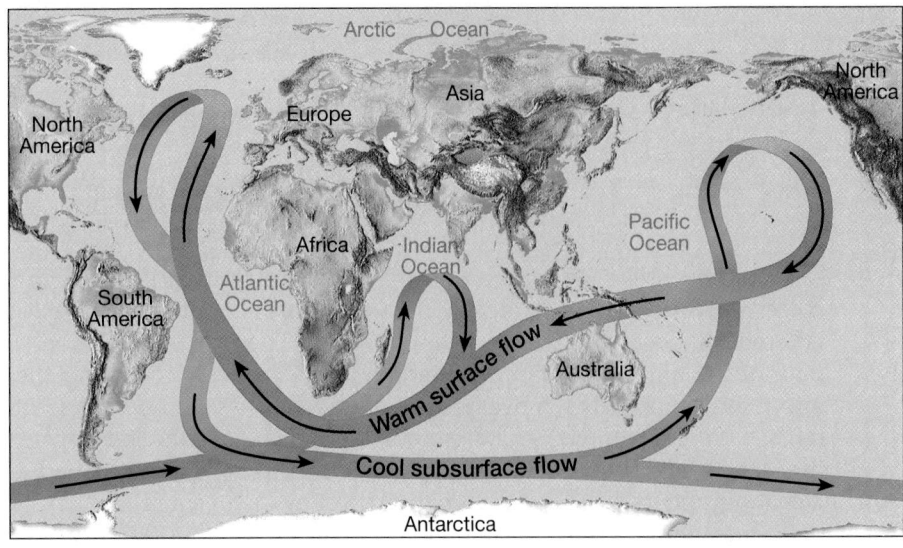

Figure 7 This "conveyor belt" model of ocean circulation shows a warm surface current with an underlying cool current.

Section 16.1 Assessment

Reviewing Concepts

1. 🕮 How do surface currents develop?
2. What is the Coriolis effect? How does it influence the direction of surface currents flowing in the ocean?
3. 🕮 How do ocean currents affect climate?
4. 🕮 Why is upwelling important?
5. 🕮 How are density currents formed?

Thinking Critically

6. **Applying Concepts** The average surface water temperature off of the coast of Ecuador is 21°C. The average surface water temperature off of the coast of Brazil at the same latitude is about 27°C. Explain why there is such a difference in water temperature between these areas at the same latitude.

7. **Inferring** During an El Niño event, the upwelling of cold, nutrient-rich water stops in areas off the coast of Peru. How might this affect the food web in this area?

Writing in Science

Explanatory Paragraph During the 1700s, mail ships sailed back and forth between England and America. It was noted that it took the ships two weeks longer to go from England to America than to travel the same route from America to England. It was determined that the Gulf Stream was delaying the ships. Write a paragraph explaining why this is true. Use Figure 2 to explain how sailors could avoid the Gulf Stream when sailing to America.

Shoes and Toys as Drift Meters

Any floating object can serve as a makeshift drift meter, as long as it is known where the object entered the ocean and where it was retrieved. The path of the object can then be inferred, providing information about the movement of surface currents. If the times of release and retrieval are known, the speed of currents can also be determined. Oceanographers have long used drift bottles—a radio-transmitting device set adrift in the ocean—to track the movement of currents and, more recently, to refine computer models of ocean circulation.

Many objects have accidentally become drift meters when ships have lost some (or all) of their cargo at sea. In this way, athletic shoes have helped oceanographers advance the understanding of surface circulation in the North Pacific Ocean. In May 1990, the container vessel *Hansa Carrier* was traveling from Korea to Seattle, Washington, when it encountered a severe North Pacific storm. During the storm the ship lost 21 deck containers overboard, including five that held athletic shoes. The shoes that were released from their containers floated and were carried east by the North Pacific Current. Within six months, thousands of the shoes began to wash up along the beaches of Alaska, Canada, Washington, and Oregon—over 2400 kilometers from the site of the spill. The inferred course of the shoes is shown in Figure 8. A few shoes were found on beaches in northern California, and over two years later shoes from the spill were even recovered from the north end of the main island of Hawaii.

With help from the beachcombing public and remotely based lighthouse operators, information on the location and number of shoes collected was compiled during the months following the spill. Serial numbers inside the shoes were traced to individual containers, which indicated that only four of the five containers had released their shoes. Most likely, one entire container sank without opening. A maximum of 30,910 pairs of shoes (61,820 individual shoes) were released. Before the shoe spill, the largest number of drift bottles purposefully released at one time by oceanographers was about 30,000. Although only 2.6 percent of the shoes were recovered, this compares favorably with the 2.4 percent recovery rate of drift bottles released by oceanographers conducting research.

In January 1992, another cargo ship lost 12 containers overboard during a storm to the north of where the shoes had previously spilled. One of these containers held 29,000 packages of small, floatable, colorful plastic bathtub toys in the shapes of blue turtles, yellow ducks, red beavers, and green frogs. Even though the toys were housed in plastic packaging glued to a cardboard backing, studies showed that after 24 hours in seawater, the glue deteriorated, thereby releasing over 100,000 individual floating toys.

The floating bathtub toys began to come ashore in southeast Alaska 10 months later, which verified computer models of North Pacific circulation. The models indicate that many of the bathtub toys will continue to be carried by the Alaska Current and will eventually disperse throughout the North Pacific Ocean.

Since 1992, oceanographers have continued to study ocean currents by tracking other floating items spilled from cargo ships, including 34,000 hockey gloves, 5 million plastic Lego pieces, and an unidentified number of small plastic doll parts.

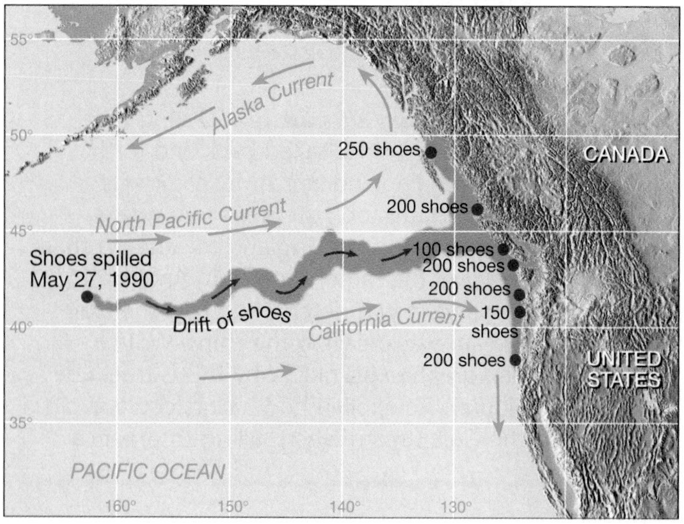

Figure 8 The map shows the path of drifting shoes and recovery locations from a spill in 1990.

16.2 Waves and Tides

Reading Focus

Key Concepts

- From where do ocean waves obtain their energy?
- What three factors affect the characteristics of a wave?
- How does energy move through a wave?
- What force produces tides?

Vocabulary

- ◆ wave height
- ◆ wavelength
- ◆ wave period
- ◆ fetch
- ◆ tide
- ◆ tidal range
- ◆ spring tide
- ◆ neap tide

Reading Strategy

Building Vocabulary Copy the table below. As you read the section, define in your own words each vocabulary word listed in the table.

Vocabulary Term	Definition
Wave height	a. _____?_____
Wavelength	b. _____?_____
Wave period	c. _____?_____
Fetch	d. _____?_____

The movement of ocean water is a powerful thing. Waves created by storms release energy when they crash along the shoreline. Sometimes the energy of water movement can be harnessed and used to generate electricity.

Waves

Ocean waves are energy traveling along the boundary between ocean and atmosphere. Waves often transfer energy from a storm far out at sea over distances of several thousand kilometers. That's why even on calm days the ocean still has waves that travel across its surface. The power of waves is most noticeable along the shore, the area between land and sea where waves are constantly rolling in and breaking. Sometimes the waves are low and gentle. Other times waves, like the ones shown in Figure 9, are powerful as they pound the shore. If you make waves by tossing a pebble into a pond, or by splashing in a pool, or by blowing across the surface of a cup of coffee, you are giving energy to the water. The waves you see are just the visible evidence of the energy passing through the water. When observing ocean waves, remember that you are watching energy travel through a medium, in this case, water. In Chapter 24, you will study waves of the electromagnetic spectrum (which includes light). These waves transfer energy without matter as a medium.

Figure 9 The Force of Breaking Waves These waves are slamming into a seawall that has been built at Sea Bright, New Jersey, to protect the nearby electrical lines and houses from the force of the waves.

A Not in all cases. Most surface waves travel in the same direction as the wind blows, but waves radiate outward in all directions from the disturbance that creates them. In addition, as waves move away from the sea area where they were generated, they enter areas where other currents exist. As a result, the direction of wave movement is often unrelated to that of currents. In fact, waves can even travel in a direction completely opposite to that of a current. A rip current, for example, moves away from the shoreline, opposite to the direction of incoming waves.

Wave Characteristics Most ocean waves obtain their energy and motion from the wind. When a breeze is less than 3 kilometers per hour, only small waves appear. At greater wind speeds, more stable waves gradually form and advance with the wind.

Characteristics of ocean waves are illustrated in Figure 10. The tops of the waves are the crests, which are separated by troughs. Halfway between the crests and troughs is the still water level, which is the level that the water would occupy if there were no waves. The vertical distance between trough and crest is called the **wave height.** The horizontal distance between two successive crests or two successive troughs is the **wavelength.** The time it takes one full wave—one wavelength—to pass a fixed position is the **wave period.**

The height, length, and period that are eventually achieved by a wave depend on three factors: (1) wind speed; (2) length of time the wind has blown; and (3) fetch. Fetch is the distance that the wind has traveled across open water. As the quantity of energy transferred from the wind to the water increases, both the height and steepness of the waves also increase. Eventually, a critical point is reached where waves grow so tall that they topple over, forming ocean breakers called whitecaps.

Wave Motion Waves can travel great distances across ocean basins. In one study, waves generated near Antarctica were tracked as they traveled through the Pacific Ocean basin. After more than 10,000 kilometers, the waves finally expended their energy a week later along the shoreline of the Aleutian Islands of Alaska. The water itself does not travel the entire distance, but the wave does. As a wave travels, the water particles pass the energy along by moving in a circle. This movement, shown in Figure 10, is called circular orbital motion.

Observations of a floating object reveals that it moves not only up and down but also slightly forward and backward with each successive wave.

Figure 10 Anatomy of a Wave
The diagram of a non-breaking wave shows the parts of a wave as well as the movement of particles at depth.

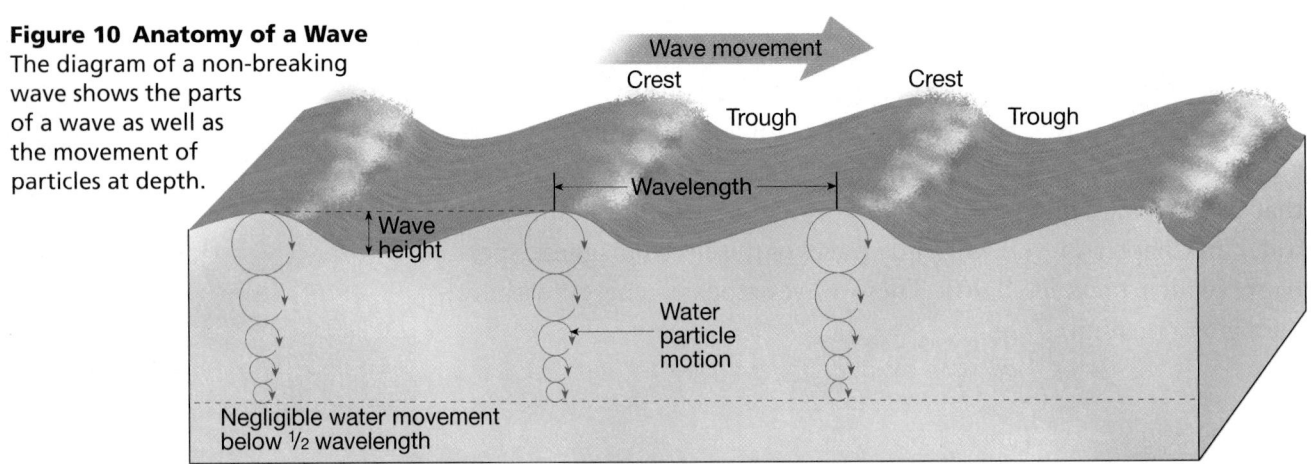

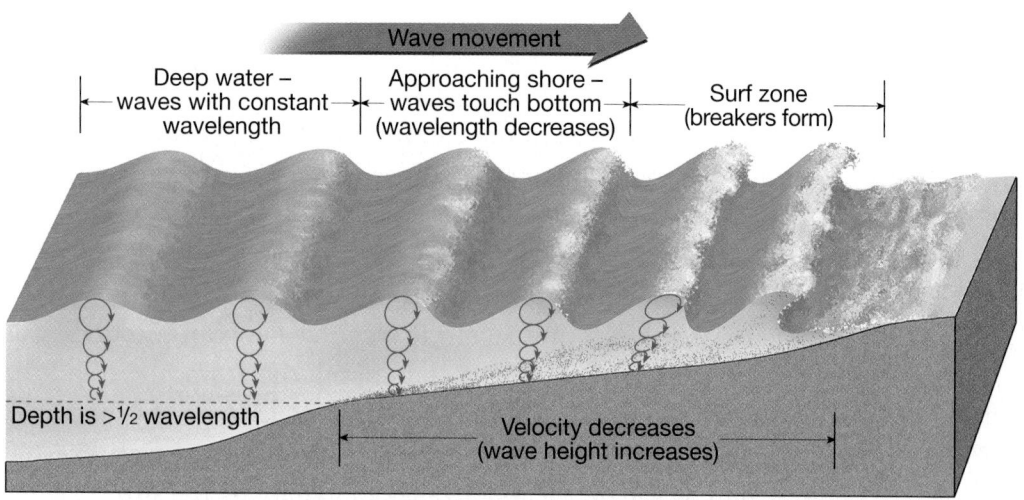

Deep water – waves with constant wavelength

Approaching shore – waves touch bottom (wavelength decreases)

Surf zone (breakers form)

Wave movement

Depth is >½ wavelength

Velocity decreases (wave height increases)

Figure 11 Breaking Waves Changes occur as a wave moves onto shore. As the waves touch bottom, wave speed decreases. The decrease in wave speed results in a decrease in wavelength and an increase in wave height.

This movement results in a circle that returns the object to essentially the same place in the water. **Circular orbital motion allows energy to move forward through the water while the individual water particles that transmit the wave move around in a circle.**

The energy contributed by the wind to the water is transmitted not only along the surface of the sea but also downward. However, beneath the surface, the circular motion rapidly diminishes until—at a depth equal to one-half the wavelength measured from still water level—the movement of water particles becomes negligible. The dramatic decrease of wave energy with depth is shown by the rapidly decreasing diameters of water-particle orbits in Figure 10.

Breaking Waves As long as a wave is in deep water, it is unaffected by water depth. However, when a wave approaches the shore, the water becomes shallower and influences wave behavior. The wave begins to "feel bottom" at a water depth equal to half of its wavelength. Such depths interfere with water movement at the base of the wave and slow its advance. Figure 11 shows the changes that occur as a wave moves onto shore.

As a wave advances toward the shore, the slightly faster waves farther out to sea catch up and decrease the wavelength. As the speed and length of the wave decrease, the wave steadily grows higher. Finally, a critical point is reached when the wave is too steep to support itself, and the wave front collapses, or breaks, causing water to advance up the shore.

The turbulent water created by breaking waves is called surf. On the landward margin of the surf zone, the turbulent sheet of water from collapsing breakers, called swash, moves up the slope of the beach. When the energy of the swash has been expended, the water flows back down the beach toward the surf zone as backwash.

At what depth do the characteristics of a wave begin to change as it approaches the shore?

For: Links on ocean waves
Visit: www.SciLinks.org
Web Code: cjn-5162

Q *Where is the world's largest tidal range?*

A The world's largest tidal range is found in the northern end of Nova Scotia's 258-kilometer-long Bay of Fundy. During maximum spring tide conditions, the tidal range at the mouth of the bay is only about 2 meters. However, the tidal range progressively increases from the mouth of the bay inward because the natural geometry of the bay concentrates tidal energy. In the northern end of Minas Basin, the maximum spring tidal range is about 17 meters. This extreme tidal range leaves boats high and dry during low tide.

Figure 12 Tidal Bulges on Earth Caused by the Moon *Analyzing What force is involved in causing the tidal bulges?*

Tides

Tides are daily changes in the elevation of the ocean surface. Their rhythmic rise and fall along coastlines have been noted throughout history. Other than waves, they are the easiest ocean movements to observe. Although known for centuries, tides were not well explained until Sir Isaac Newton applied the law of gravitation to them. Newton showed that there is a mutual attractive force between two bodies, as between Earth and the moon. Because both the atmosphere and the ocean are fluids and are free to move, both are changed by this force. **Ocean tides result from the gravitational attraction exerted upon Earth by the moon and, to a lesser extent, by the sun.**

Tide-Causing Force The primary body that influences the tides is the moon, which makes one complete revolution around Earth every 29 and a half days. The sun, however, also influences the tides. It is far larger than the moon, but because it is much farther away, its effect is considerably less. In fact, the sun's tide-generating effect is only about 46 percent that of the moon's.

To illustrate how tides are produced, consider the Earth as a rotating sphere covered to a uniform depth with water. Think about the tide-generating forces that result from the Earth-moon system, ignoring the influence of the sun for now. **The force that produces tides is gravity.** Gravity is the force that attracts Earth and the moon to each other. On the side of Earth closest to the moon, the force of the moon's gravity is greater. At this time, water is pulled in the direction of the moon and produces a tidal bulge. On the side of Earth furthest from the moon, water is pulled away from the direction of the moon and produces an equally large tidal bulge on the side of Earth directly opposite the moon. These idealized tidal bulges are shown in Figure 12.

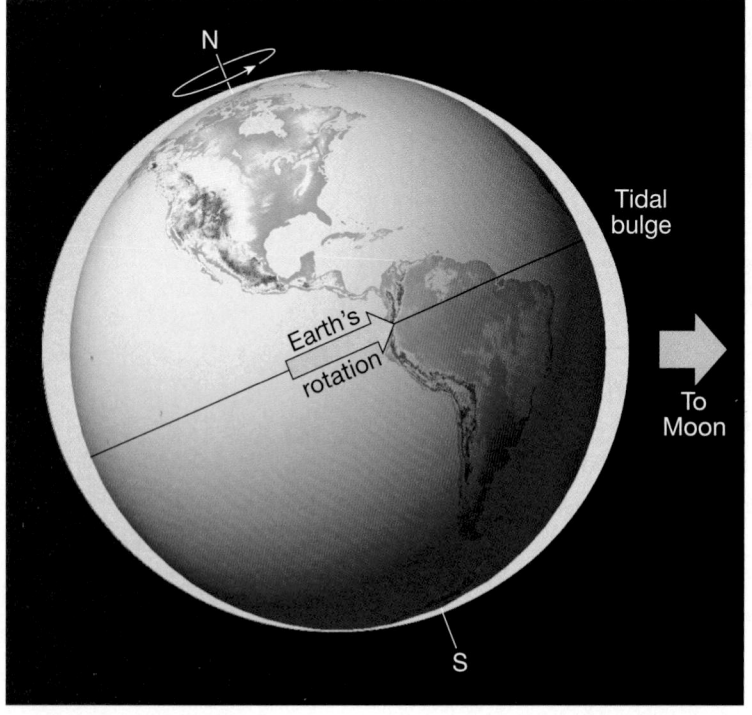

Because the position of the moon changes only moderately in a single day, the tidal bulges remain in place while Earth rotates "through" them. For this reason, if you stand on the seashore for 24 hours, Earth will rotate you through alternating areas of higher and lower water. As you are carried into each tidal bulge, the tide rises. As you are carried into the intervening troughs between the tidal bulges, the tide falls. Therefore, most places on Earth experience two high tides and two low tides each day.

Tidal Cycle Although the sun is farther away from Earth than the moon, the gravitational attraction between the sun and Earth does play a role in producing tides. The sun's influence produces smaller tidal bulges on Earth. These tidal bulges are the result of the same forces involved in the bulges created by the moon. The influence of the sun on tides is most noticeable near the times of new and full moons. During these times, the sun and moon are aligned, and their forces are added together, as shown in Figure 13A. The combined gravity of these two tide-producing bodies causes larger tidal bulges (higher high tides) and larger tidal troughs (lower low tides). This combined gravity produces a large tidal range. The **tidal range** is the difference in height between successive high and low tides. **Spring tides** are tides that have the greatest tidal range due to the alignment of the Earth–moon–sun system. They are experienced during new and full moons. Conversely, at about the time of the first and third quarters of the moon, the gravitational forces of the moon and sun act on Earth at right angles. The sun and moon partially offset the influence of the other, as shown in Figure 13B. As a result, the daily tidal range is less. These tides are called **neap tides.** Each month there are two spring tides and two neap tides, each about one week apart.

 **Reading Checkpoint** *What is the tidal range?*

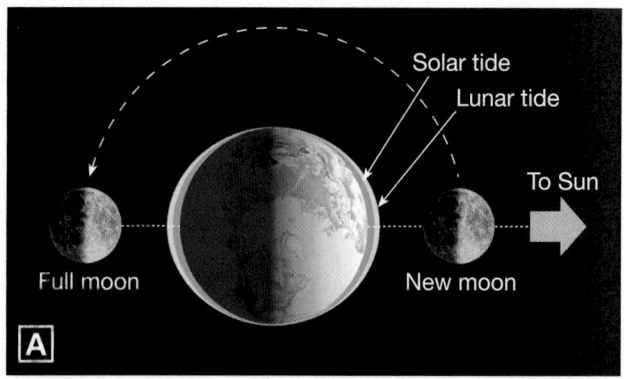

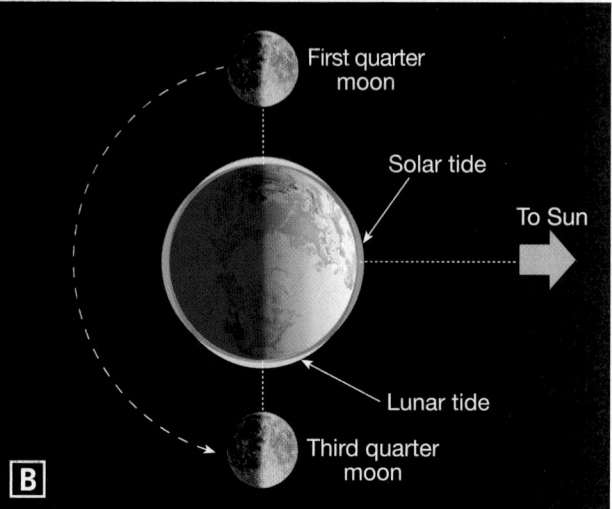

Figure 13 Earth-Moon-Sun Positions and the Tides
A When Earth, moon, and sun are aligned, spring tides are experienced. **B** When Earth, moon, and sun are at right angles to each other, neap tides are experienced.
Describing *How does the sun influence the formation of spring and neap tides?*

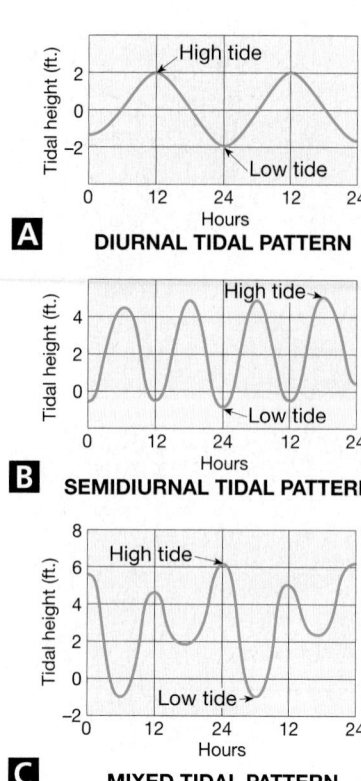

A DIURNAL TIDAL PATTERN

B SEMIDIURNAL TIDAL PATTERN

C MIXED TIDAL PATTERN

Figure 14 Tidal patterns

Tidal Patterns You now know the basic causes and types of tides. However, many factors—including the shape of the coastline, the configuration of ocean basins, and water depth—greatly influence the tides. Consequently, tides at various locations respond differently to the tide-producing forces. This being the case, the nature of the tide at any coastal location can be determined most accurately by actual observation. The predictions in tidal tables and tidal data on nautical charts are based on such observations.

⬤ **Three main tidal patterns exist worldwide: diurnal tides, semidiurnal tides, and mixed tides.** A diurnal tidal pattern is characterized by a single high tide and a single low tide each tidal day, as shown in the graph in Figure 14A. Tides of this type occur along the northern shore of the Gulf of Mexico.

A semidiurnal tidal pattern exhibits two high tides and two low tides each tidal day. The two highs are about the same height, and the two lows are about the same height. Figure 14B shows a semidiurnal tide pattern. This type of tidal pattern is common along the Atlantic Coast of the United States.

A mixed tidal pattern, shown in Figure 14C, is similar to a semidiurnal pattern except that it is characterized by a large inequality in high water heights, low water heights, or both. In this case, there are usually two high and two low tides each day. However, the high tides are of different heights, and the low tides are of different heights. Such tides are found along the Pacific Coast of the United States and in many other parts of the world.

Section 16.2 Assessment

Reviewing Concepts

1. ⬤ From where do ocean waves obtain their energy?

2. ⬤ What three quantities are used to describe a wave?

3. ⬤ How does energy move by means of a wave?

4. What changes occur in a wave as it approaches shore?

5. Which celestial bodies influence Earth tides?

6. ⬤ What force produces tides?

7. What are the three types of tidal patterns?

Thinking Critically

8. **Inferring** Two waves have the same fetch and were created by winds of equal speed. Why might one wave be higher than the other?

9. **Relating Cause and Effect** Explain how the forces of gravity and inertia lead to tides in Earth's oceans.

10. **Comparing and Contrasting** Compare and contrast spring tides and neap tides.

Math ▶ Practice

11. **Calculating** Wavelength, wave period, and wave speed can be related to each other in the equation:

$$\frac{\text{wavelength}}{\text{wave period}} = \text{wave speed}.$$

If wavelength = 187 meters, and wave speed = 16.8 meters per second, what is the period of this wave?

16.3 Shoreline Processes and Features

Reading Focus

Key Concepts

- How are sediments along the shoreline moved?
- How does refraction affect wave action along the shore?
- What do longshore currents do?
- By which processes do shoreline features form?
- What structures can be built to protect a shoreline?
- What is beach nourishment?

Vocabulary

- beach
- wave refraction
- longshore current
- barrier islands

Reading Strategy

Summarizing Read the section on wave refraction. Then copy and complete the concept map below to organize what you know about refraction.

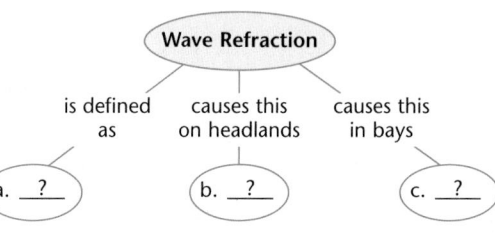

Beaches and shorelines are constantly undergoing changes as the force of waves and currents act on them. A **beach** is the accumulation of sediment found along the shore of a lake or ocean. Beaches are composed of whatever sediment is locally available. They may be made of mineral particles from the erosion of beach cliffs or nearby coastal mountains. This sediment may be relatively coarse in texture. Some beaches have a significant biological component. For example, most beaches in southern Florida are composed of shell fragments and the remains of organisms that live in coastal waters. Regardless of the composition, the sediment that makes up the beach does not stay in one place. The waves that crash along the shoreline are constantly moving it. Beaches can be thought of as material in transit along the shoreline.

Forces Acting on the Shoreline

Waves along the shoreline are constantly eroding, transporting, and depositing sediment. Many types of shoreline features can result from this activity.

Wave Impact During calm weather, wave action is minimal. During storms, however, waves are capable of causing much erosion. The impact of large, high-energy waves against the shore can be awesome in its violence. Each breaking wave may hurl thousands of tons of water against the land, sometimes causing the ground to tremble.

Figure 15 Erosion has undercut this sandstone cliff at Gabriola Island, British Columbia, Canada.

It is no wonder that cracks and crevices are quickly opened in cliffs, coastal structures, and anything else that is subjected to these enormous impacts. Water is forced into every opening, causing air in the cracks to become highly compressed by the thrust of crashing waves. When the wave subsides, the air expands rapidly. This expanding air dislodges rock fragments and enlarges and extends preexisting fractures.

Abrasion In addition to the erosion caused by wave impact and pressure, erosion caused by abrasion is also important. In fact, abrasion is probably more intense in the surf zone than in any other environment. Abrasion is the sawing and grinding action of rock fragments in the water. Smooth, rounded stones and pebbles along the shore are evidence of the continual grinding action of rock against rock in the surf zone. Such fragments are also used as "tools" by the waves as they cut horizontally into the land, like the sandstone shown in Figure 15. Waves are also very effective at breaking down rock material and supplying sand to beaches.

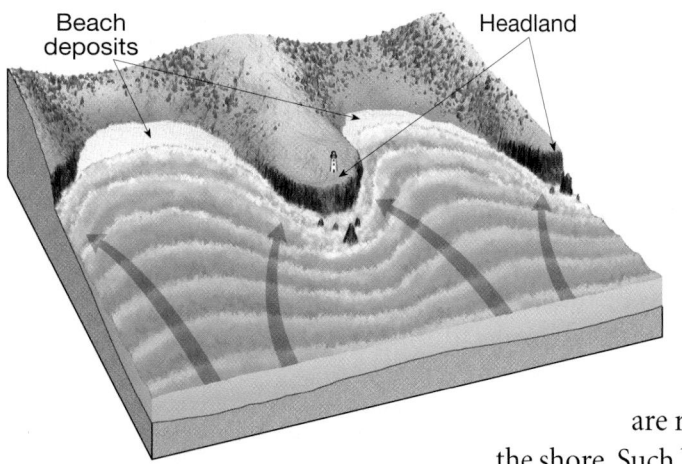

Figure 16 Wave Refraction
Waves are refracted as they come into shore. Wave energy is concentrated at the headlands and dispersed in the bays.
Inferring *What processes occur as a result of wave refraction on this shoreline?*

Wave Refraction **Wave refraction** is the bending of waves, and it plays an important part in shoreline processes. Wave refraction affects the distribution of energy along the shore. It strongly influences where and to what degree erosion, sediment transport, and deposition will take place.

Waves seldom approach the shore straight on. Rather, most waves move toward the shore at a slight angle. However, when they reach the shallow water of a smoothly sloping bottom, the wave crests are refracted, or bent, and tend to line up nearly parallel to the shore. Such bending occurs because the part of the wave nearest the shore touches bottom and slows first, whereas the part of the wave that is still in deep water continues forward at its full speed. The change in speed causes wave crests to become nearly parallel to the shore regardless of their original orientation.

🔑 **Because of refraction, wave energy is concentrated against the sides and ends of headlands that project into the water, whereas wave action is weakened in bays.** This type of wave action along irregular coastlines is illustrated in Figure 16. Waves reach the shallow water in front of the headland sooner than they do in adjacent bays. Therefore, wave energy is concentrated in this area, leading to erosion. By contrast, refraction in the bays causes waves to spread out and expend less energy. This refraction leads to deposition of sediments and the formation of sandy beaches.

Reading Checkpoint *What is wave refraction?*

Longshore Transport Although waves are refracted, most still reach the shore at a slight angle. As a result, the uprush of water, or swash, from each breaking wave is at an oblique angle to the shoreline. These angled waves produce currents within the surf zone. The currents flow parallel to the shore and move large amounts of sediment along the shore. This type of current is called a **longshore current,** shown in Figure 17.

The water in the surf zone is turbulent. **Turbulence allows longshore currents to easily move the fine suspended sand and to roll larger sand and gravel particles along the bottom.** At Sandy Hook, New Jersey, for example, the quantity of sand transported along the shore over a 48-year period averaged almost 680,000 metric tons annually. For a 10-year period at Oxnard, California, more than 1.4 million metric tons of sediment moved along the shore each year. Longshore currents can change direction because the direction that waves approach the beach changes with the seasons. Nevertheless, longshore currents generally flow southward along both the Atlantic and Pacific shores of the United States.

Longshore current

Reading Checkpoint *What causes longshore currents?*

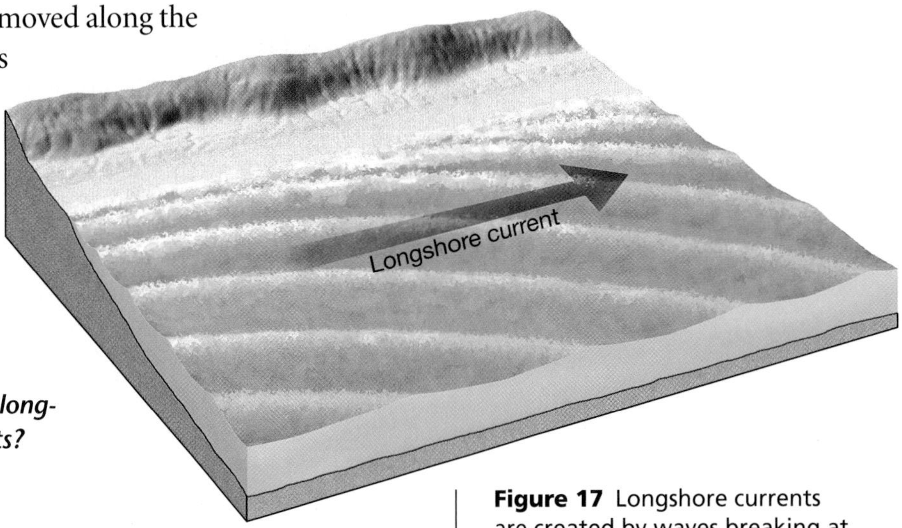

Figure 17 Longshore currents are created by waves breaking at an angle.
Applying Concepts *Explain how longshore currents can change direction.*

Erosional Features

A fascinating assortment of shoreline features can be observed along the world's coastal regions. These shoreline features vary depending on the type of rocks exposed along the shore, the intensity of waves, the nature of coastal currents, and whether the coast is stable, sinking, or rising. **Shoreline features that originate primarily from the work of erosion are called erosional features. Sediment that is transported along the shore and deposited in areas where energy is low produce depositional features.**

Many coastal landforms owe their origin to erosional processes. Such erosional features are common along the rugged and irregular New England coast and along the steep shorelines of the West Coast of the United States.

Figure 18 In time, the sea arch will collapse and form a sea stack like the one on the left.

Wave-Cut Cliffs and Platforms Wave-cut cliffs, like the one shown in Figure 20C, result from the cutting action of the surf against the base of coastal land. As erosion progresses, rocks that overhang the notch at the base of the cliff crumble into the surf, and the cliff retreats. A relatively flat, benchlike surface, called a wave-cut platform, is left behind by the receding cliff. The platform broadens as the wave attack continues. Some debris produced by the breaking waves remains along the water's edge as sediment on the beach. The rest of the sediment is transported farther seaward.

Sea Arches and Sea Stacks Headlands that extend into the sea are vigorously attacked by waves because of refraction. The surf erodes the rock selectively and wears away the softer or more highly fractured rock at the fastest rate. At first, sea caves may form. When two caves on opposite sides of a headland unite, a sea arch like the one in Figure 18 results. Eventually, the arch falls in, leaving an isolated remnant, or sea stack, on the wave-cut platform.

Reading Checkpoint *How does a sea arch form?*

Depositional Features

Recall that a beach is the shore of a body of water that is covered in sand, gravel, or other larger sediments. Sediment eroded from the beach is transported along the shore and deposited in areas where wave energy is low. Such processes produce a variety of depositional features.

Figure 19 This high-altitude image shows a baymouth bar along the coast of Martha's Vineyard, Massachusetts.

baymouth bar

Spits, Bars, and Tombolos Where longshore currents and other surf zone currents are active, several features related to the movement of sediment along the shore may develop. As shown in Figure 20B and C, a spit is an elongated ridge of sand that projects from the land into the mouth of an adjacent bay. Often the end in the water hooks landward in response to the dominant direction of the longshore current. The term baymouth bar is applied to a sandbar that completely crosses a bay, sealing it off from the open ocean. Find the baymouth bar in Figure 19. Such a feature tends to form across bays where currents are weak. The weak currents allow a spit to extend to the other side and form a baymouth bar. A tombolo is a ridge of sand that connects an island to the mainland or to another island. A tombolo forms in much the same way as a spit. Follow the formation of tombolos and other shoreline features in Figure 20.

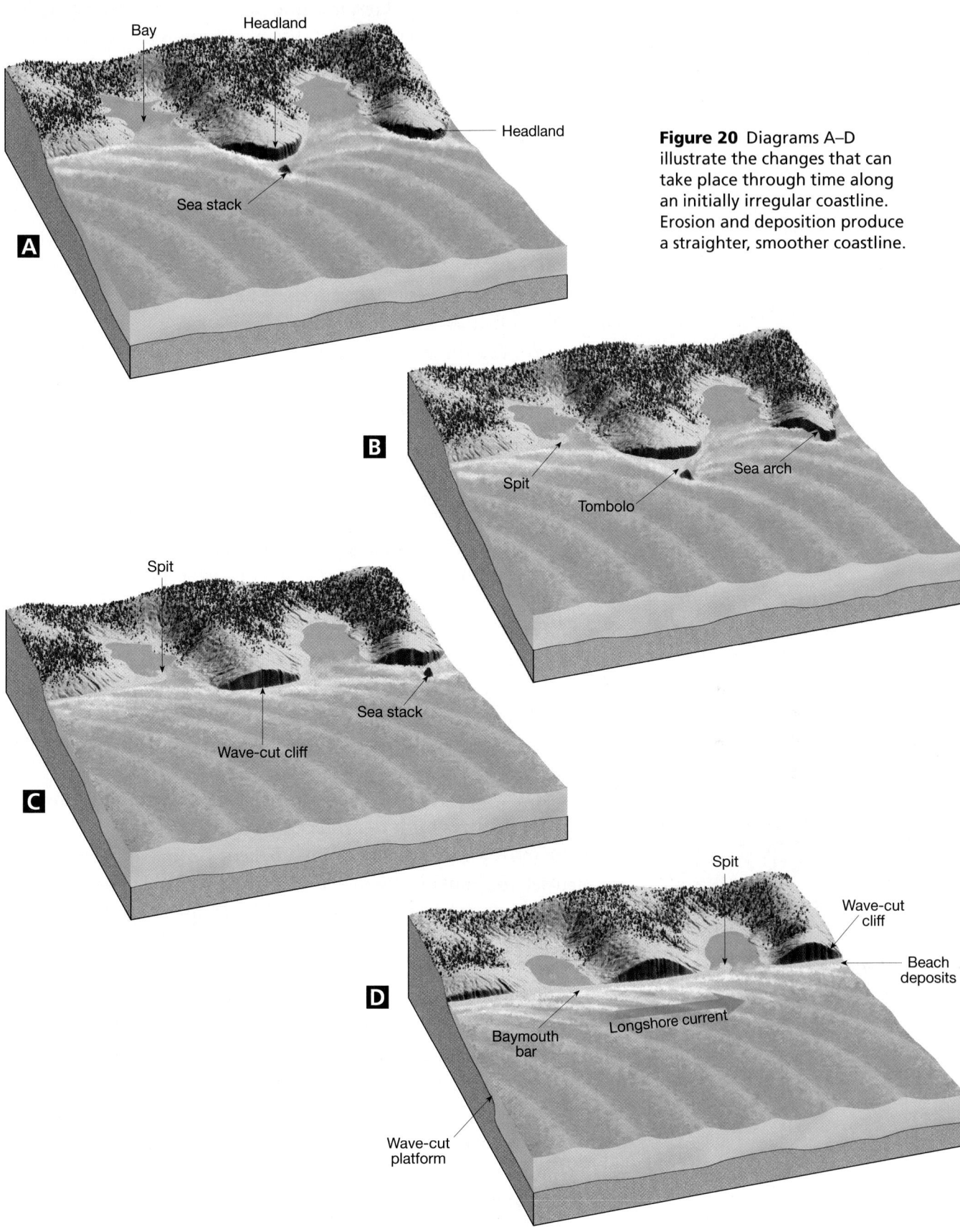

Figure 20 Diagrams A–D illustrate the changes that can take place through time along an initially irregular coastline. Erosion and deposition produce a straighter, smoother coastline.

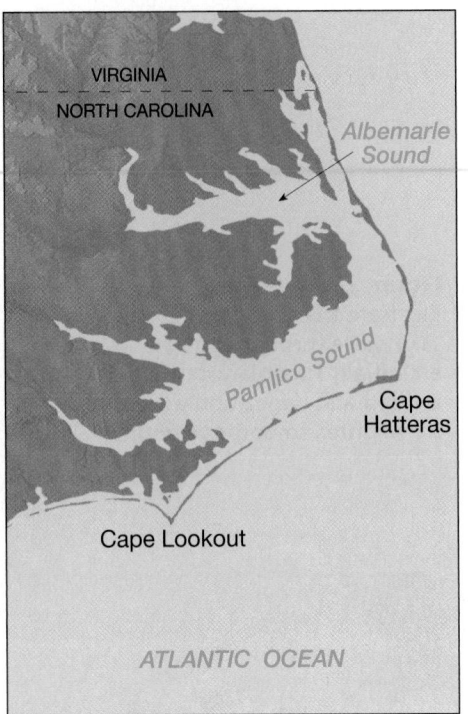

Figure 22 A series of groins traps sand along the shore in Sussex, England.
Inferring *In which direction does the sand move along the coast in this photo? How do you know?*

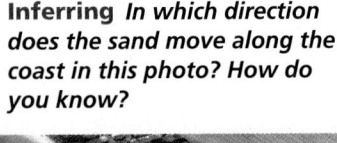

For: Links on coastal changes
Visit: www.SciLinks.org
Web Code: cjn-5163

Barrier Islands The Atlantic and Gulf Coastal Plains are relatively flat and slope gently seaward. The shore zone in these areas is characterized by barrier islands. **Barrier islands** are narrow sandbars parallel to, but separated from, the coast at distances from 3 to 30 kilometers offshore. From Cape Cod, Massachusetts, to Padre Island, Texas, nearly 300 barrier islands rim the coast. The barrier islands along the coast of North Carolina are shown in Figure 21.

Barrier islands probably formed in several ways. Some began as spits that were later cut off from the mainland by wave erosion or by the general rise in sea level following the last glacial period. Others were created when turbulent waters in the line of breakers heaped up sand that had been scoured from the bottom. Finally, some barrier islands may be former sand-dune ridges that began along the shore during the last glacial period, when sea level was lower. As the ice sheets melted, sea level rose and flooded the area behind the beach-dune complex.

 **Reading Checkpoint** *What is a barrier island?*

Stabilizing the Shore

Shorelines are among Earth's most dynamic places. They change rapidly in response to natural forces. Storms are capable of eroding beaches and cliffs at rates that far exceed the long-term average erosion. Such bursts of accelerated erosion not only affect the natural evolution of a coast but can also have a profound impact on people who reside in the coastal zone. Erosion along the coast causes significant property damage. Huge sums of money are spent annually not only to repair damage but also to prevent or control erosion.

Protective Structures 🔵 **Groins, breakwaters, and seawalls are some structures built to protect a coast from erosion or to prevent the movement of sand along a beach.** Groins are sometimes constructed to maintain or widen beaches that are losing sand. A groin is a barrier built at a right angle to the beach to trap sand that is moving parallel to the shore. Notice how a series of groins has trapped sand along the shore in Figure 22.

Protective structures can also be built parallel to the shoreline. A breakwater is one such structure. Its purpose is to protect boats from the force of large breaking waves by creating a quiet water zone near the shore. A seawall is another protective structure built parallel to the shore. A seawall is designed to shield the coast and defend property from the force of breaking waves. Waves expend much of their energy as they move across an open beach. Seawalls reduce this process by reflecting the force of unspent waves seaward.

Protective structures often only offer temporary solutions to shoreline problems. The structures themselves interfere with the natural processes of erosion and deposition. Then more structures often need to be built in order to counteract the new problems that arise. Many scientists feel that using protective structures to divert the ocean's energy causes more harm than good.

Beach Nourishment

Beach nourishment is the addition of large quantities of sand to the beach system. It is an attempt to stabilize shoreline sands without building protective structures. Examine the before and after photos shown in Figure 23. By building the beaches seaward, both beach quality and storm protection are improved. However, the same processes that removed the sand in the first place will eventually wash away the replacement sand as well.

Beach nourishment can be very expensive because huge volumes of sand must be transported to the beach from offshore areas, nearby rivers, or other source areas for sand. Beach nourishment can also have detrimental effects on local marine life. For example, beach nourishment at Waikiki Beach, Hawaii, involved replacing the natural coarse beach sand with softer, muddier sand. Destruction of the softer sand by breaking waves increased the water's turbidity, or "cloudiness," and killed offshore coral reefs.

Figure 23 Miami Beach
A Before beach nourishment
B After beach nourishment
Analyzing *What are the advantages and disadvantages of beach nourishment?*

Section 16.3 Assessment

Reviewing Concepts

1. How are sediments along the shoreline moved?
2. What effect does wave impact have on shorelines?
3. How does refraction affect wave action along the shore?
4. What do longshore currents do?
5. By which processes do shoreline features form?
6. Name three examples of shoreline features formed by erosion.
7. How do barrier islands form?
8. What structures can be built to protect a shoreline?
9. What is beach nourishment?

Thinking Critically

10. **Analyzing** How can beach nourishment be helpful? How can it be harmful?
11. **Comparing and Contrasting** Compare and contrast a tombolo and a barrier island.
12. **Relating Cause and Effect** A breakwater is built to reduce wave action in near-shore areas. How might the reduced wave action along the shore behind the breakwater affect sediment deposition? What problems might this cause?

Connecting Concepts

Wave Refraction Relate the concept of wave refraction to the changes that occur as a wave enters shallow water and goes into shore.

Graphing Tidal Cycles

Tides are the cyclical rise and fall of sea level caused by the gravitational attraction of Earth to the moon and, to a lesser extent, to the sun. Gravitational pull creates a bulge in the ocean on the side of Earth nearest the moon. This inertia creates a similar bulge on the opposite side of Earth from the moon. Tides develop as the rotating Earth moves through these bulges causing periods of high and low water. In this lab, you will make a graph of tidal data to determine whether an area has diurnal, semidiurnal, or mixed tides.

High tide in Nova Scotia's Bay of Fundy

Problem How can you determine the tidal pattern an area experiences?

Materials
- graph paper
- pencil

Skills
Graphing, Interpreting Data, Inferring, Drawing Conclusions

Procedure
1. Label the graph paper as below to make a graph of the tidal cycle. The *x*-axis should be in days, and the *y*-axis should be in feet. It is often easier to place the *x*-axis at the top of the graph, rather than at the bottom, when graphing a tidal cycle.
2. Use the data in Table 1 to make a graph of the tidal cycle.

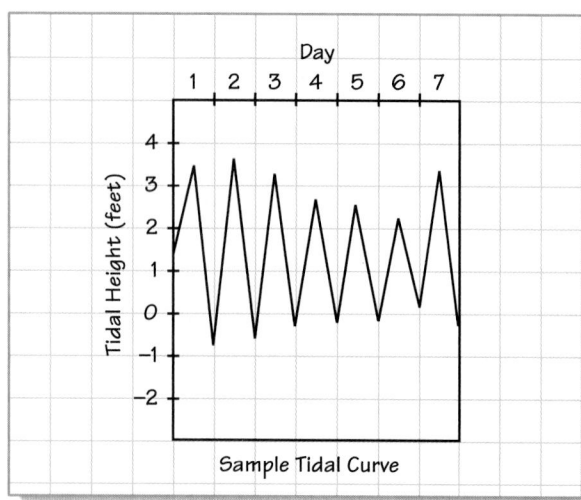

Sample Tidal Curve

Low tide in the same area

Analyze and Conclude

1. **Applying Concepts** What tidal pattern does this area experience? Explain how you determined this.

2. **Calculating** What is the greatest tidal range for the data you graphed? What is the least tidal range? What types of tides correspond to each of these tidal ranges?

3. **Draw Conclusions** Based on your graph, identify the days when each moon phase could have occurred: new moon, first quarter moon, full moon, last quarter moon. How do you know this?

4. **Applying Concepts** On January 5th (Day 5 on the table) at 9:00 A.M., Jarred anchored his boat in about 4 feet of water at the beach. When he returned to his boat at 3:30 that afternoon, the boat was completely in the sand. What had happened? How long did Jarred have to wait to leave the area in his boat?

Table 1 Tidal Data for Long Beach, New York, January 2003

All times are listed in Local Standard Time (LST). All heights are in feet.

Day	Time	Height	Time	Height	Time	Height	Time	Height
1	05:45 A.M.	5.5	12:16 P.M.	−0.7	06:12 P.M.	4.4	———	—
2	12:18 A.M.	−0.5	06:35 A.M.	5.6	01:07 P.M.	−0.8	07:03 P.M.	4.4
3	01:10 A.M.	−0.5	07:23 A.M.	5.5	01:56 P.M.	−0.8	07:53 P.M.	4.4
4	01:59 A.M.	−0.4	08:11 A.M.	5.4	02:42 P.M.	−0.7	08:42 P.M.	4.3
5	02:45 A.M.	−0.2	08:59 A.M.	5.1	03:25 P.M.	−0.5	09:32 P.M.	4.2
6	03:30 A.M.	0.0	09:47 A.M.	4.8	04:07 P.M.	−0.3	10:23 P.M.	4.0
7	04:14 A.M.	0.3	10:35 A.M.	4.6	04:49 P.M.	−0.1	11:12 P.M.	3.9
8	05:01 A.M.	0.6	11:22 A.M.	4.3	05:32 P.M.	0.2	11:59 P.M.	3.9
9	05:54 A.M.	0.8	12:09 P.M.	4.0	06:18 P.M.	0.4	———	—
10	12:45 A.M.	3.9	06:56 A.M.	0.9	12:57 P.M.	3.7	07:10 P.M.	0.5
11	01:31 A.M.	3.9	07:59 A.M.	0.9	01:47 P.M.	3.5	08:02 P.M.	0.5
12	02:19 A.M.	4.0	08:57 A.M.	0.8	02:41 P.M.	3.4	08:53 P.M.	0.5
13	03:10 A.M.	4.1	09:50 A.M.	0.6	03:39 P.M.	3.5	09:41 P.M.	0.4
14	04:02 A.M.	4.3	10:38 A.M.	0.3	04:34 P.M.	3.6	10:28 P.M.	0.2
15	04:51 A.M.	4.6	11:26 A.M.	0.1	05:23 P.M.	3.7	11:15 P.M.	0.1
16	05:36 A.M.	4.8	12:12 P.M.	−0.1	06:08 P.M.	3.9	———	—
17	12:02 A.M.	−0.1	06:17 A.M.	5.0	12:57 P.M.	−0.3	06:51 P.M.	4.1
18	12:49 A.M.	−0.2	06:58 A.M.	5.1	01:40 P.M.	−0.5	07:32 P.M.	4.2
19	01:35 A.M.	−0.4	07:38 A.M.	5.2	02:22 P.M.	−0.6	08:15 P.M.	4.3
20	02:20 A.M.	−0.4	08:21 A.M.	5.2	03:30 P.M.	−0.7	09:01 P.M.	4.4
21	03:05 A.M.	−0.4	09:07 A.M.	5.1	03:44 P.M.	−0.7	09:51 P.M.	4.5
22	03:52 A.M.	−0.3	09:58 A.M.	4.9	04:27 P.M.	−0.6	10:44 P.M.	4.6
23	04:43 A.M.	−0.1	10:52 A.M.	4.7	05:13 P.M.	−0.4	11:37 P.M.	4.7
24	05:43 A.M.	0.1	11:48 A.M.	4.4	06:08 P.M.	−0.2	———	—
25	12:32 A.M.	4.7	06:53 A.M.	0.2	12:47 P.M.	4.2	07:11 P.M.	−0.1
26	01:30 A.M.	4.8	08:06 A.M.	0.2	01:50 P.M.	3.9	08:17 P.M.	0.0
27	02:31 A.M.	4.8	09:12 A.M.	0.1	02:57 P.M.	3.8	09:19 P.M.	0.0
28	03:35 A.M.	4.8	10:13 A.M.	−0.1	04:05 P.M.	3.9	10:17 P.M.	−0.1
29	04:37 A.M.	5.0	11:09 A.M.	−0.3	05:07 P.M.	4.0	11:13 P.M.	−0.2
30	05:33 A.M.	5.1	12:01 P.M.	−0.5	06:01 P.M.	4.2	———	—
31	12:06 A.M.	−0.3	06:22 A.M.	5.2	12:51 P.M.	−0.6	06:50 P.M.	4.3

Source: Center for Operational Oceanographic Products and Services, National Oceanographic and Atmospheric Association, National Ocean Service.

16 | Study Guide

16.1 Ocean Circulation

🔵 Key Concepts

- Surface currents develop from friction between the ocean and the wind that blows across its surface.
- Because of Earth's rotation, currents are deflected to the right in the Northern Hemisphere and to the left in the Southern Hemisphere.
- When currents from low-latitude regions move into higher latitudes, they transfer heat from warmer to cooler areas on Earth.
- As cold water currents travel toward the equator, they help moderate the warm temperatures of adjacent land areas.
- Upwelling brings greater concentrations of dissolved nutrients, such as nitrates and phosphates, to the ocean surface.
- An increase in seawater density can be caused by a decrease in temperature or an increase in salinity.

Vocabulary

ocean current, *p. 448*; surface current, *p. 448*; gyre, *p. 449*; Coriolis effect, *p. 449*; upwelling, *p. 450*; density current, *451*

16.2 Waves and Tides

🔵 Key Concepts

- Most ocean waves obtain their energy and motion from the wind.
- The height, length, and period that are eventually achieved by a wave depend on three factors: (1) wind speed; (2) length of time the wind has blown; and (3) fetch.
- Circular orbital motion allows energy to move forward through the water while the individual water particles that transmit the wave move around in a circle.
- Ocean tides result from the gravitational attraction exerted upon Earth by the moon and, to a lesser extent, by the sun.
- The force that produces tides is gravity.
- Three main tidal patterns exist worldwide: diurnal tides, semidiurnal tides, and mixed tides.

Vocabulary

wave height, *p. 456*; wavelength, *p. 456*; wave period, *p. 456*; fetch, *p. 456*; tide, *p. 458*; tidal range, *p. 459*; spring tide, *p. 459*; neap tide, *p. 459*

16.3 Shoreline Processes and Features

🔵 Key Concepts

- Waves are responsible for the movement of sediment along the shoreline.
- Because of refraction, wave energy is concentrated against the sides and ends of headlands that project into the water, whereas wave action is weakened in bays.
- Turbulence allows longshore currents to easily move the fine suspended sand and to roll larger sand and gravel particles along the bottom.
- Shoreline features that originate primarily from the work of erosion are called erosional features. Sediment is transported along the shore and deposited in areas where energy is low produce depositional features.
- Groins, breakwaters, and seawalls are some structures built to protect a coast from erosion or to prevent the movement of sand along a beach.
- Beach nourishment is the addition of large quantities of sand to the beach system.

Vocabulary

beach, *p. 461*; wave refraction, *p. 462*; longshore current, *p. 463*; barrier island, *p. 466*

Reviewing Content

Choose the letter that best answers the questions or completes the statement.

1. An ocean current moving from the equator toward a pole is
   a. cold.
   b. warm.
   c. cold in the Northern Hemisphere and warm in the Southern Hemisphere.
   d. warm in the Northern Hemisphere and cold in the Northern Hemisphere.

2. Because of the Coriolos effect, surface currents in the Southern Hemisphere are deflected
   a. to the left.   b. to the right.
   c. north.   d. south.

3. Which term describes the rising of cold water from deeper layers to replace warmer surface water?
   a. density current   b. downwelling
   c. surface current   d. upwelling

4. The energy and motion of most waves is derived from
   a. currents.   b. tides.
   c. wind.   d. gravity.

5. The five huge circular-moving systems of ocean surface currents are called
   a. density currents.   b. fetches.
   c. drifts.   d. gyres.

6. Daily changes in the elevation of the ocean surface are called
   a. surface currents.   b. tides.
   c. waves.   d. density currents.

7. Which of the following results from wave refraction?
   a. Wave energy is concentrated on headlands projecting into the water.
   b. Wave energy is concentrated in the recessed areas between headlands.
   c. Wave energy is largely dissipated before waves reach the shore.
   d. Headlands are enlarged because sediment is deposited on their seaward side.

8. The movement of water within the surf zone that parallels the shore is called
   a. tidal current.   b. density current.
   c. longshore current. d. surface current.

9. Which describes a ridge of sand that connects an island to the mainland or another island?
   a. baymouth bar   b. sea arch
   c. sea stack   d. tombolo

10. Which is created through the process of erosion?
    a. baymouth bar   b. sea arch
    c. spit   d. tombolo

Understanding Concepts

11. Describe the influence that the Coriolis effect has on the movement of ocean waters.

12. Describe the effect that cold ocean currents have on the climates of adjacent land areas.

13. What role do ocean currents play in maintaining Earth's heat balance?

14. Describe coastal upwelling and the effect it has on fish populations.

15. Where and how is the densest water in all the oceans formed?

Use the figure below to answer Questions 16–18.

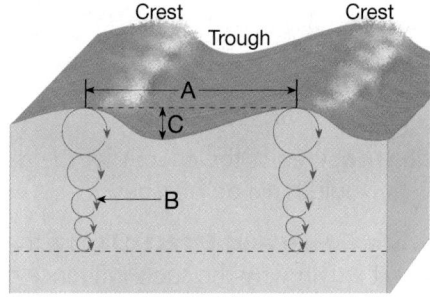

16. Identify which wave characteristics are represented by A and C.

17. Explain what B represents. What happens to a floating object as a wave passes through the water?

18. What factors can lead to an increase in the height of this wave?

19. Compare and contrast a diurnal tidal pattern with a semidiurnal tidal pattern.

20. How does wave refraction result in sediment deposition in some shoreline areas?

21. How are a wave-cut cliff and wave-cut platforms related?

22. What are two types of protective structures used to stop erosion on beaches?

Critical Thinking

23. **Creating Models** Create a diagram that models the steps involved in the process of upwelling.

24. **Applying Concepts** The figure below shows the Earth–moon–sun system. What type of tide is experienced when Earth, the moon, and the sun are in these positions? What is the phase of the moon in the diagram?

25. **Predicting** Predict the effect that the damming of rivers would have on beaches.

26. **Relating Cause and Effect** Discuss the origin of tides. Explain why the sun's influence on Earth's tides is only about half that of the moon's, even though the sun is much more massive than the moon.

Math Skills

27. **Calculating** As waves enter shallow water and decrease in speed, wave height increases and eventually a wave will break. The point at which a wave will break can be calculated using the formula for wave steepness: steepness = wave height/wavelength. When the steepness of a wave reaches 1/7, the wave will break. If the wavelength of a wave is 50 m, at what height will the wave break?

Concepts in Action

28. **Applying Concepts** Re-examine Figure 6. Describe the probable temperature and salinity characteristics for each water mass: Antarctic Bottom Water, North Atlantic Deep Water, and Mediterranean Water.

29. **Inferring** How do you think an increase in Earth's surface temperature would affect the "conveyor belt" model of currents in the ocean?

30. **Interpreting Diagrams** The graph below shows a tidal curve for Seattle, Washington. What type of tidal pattern does Honolulu experience?

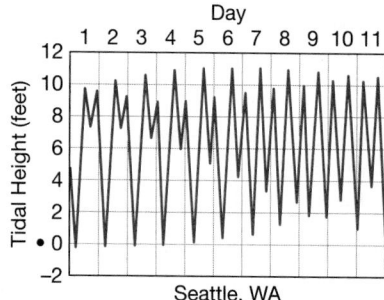

Performance-Based Assessment

Synthesizing Investigate the problems associated with shoreline development. Choose a coastal area that is experiencing problems with shoreline erosion. What actions have been taken to try to resolve the problems? Have the actions been effective? Why or why not? What are the advantages and disadvantages to different methods of preventing shoreline erosion? Offer a solution for the area you investigated.

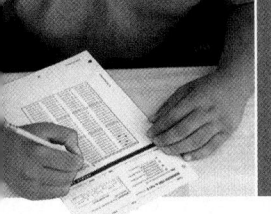

Standardized Test Prep

Choose the letter that best answers the question or completes the statement.

1. Which of the following statements correctly explains a wave in the open ocean?
  (A) Water particles move in a circular path.
  (B) Waves continue to move without change, regardless of depth.
  (C) The waveform moves forward, and the water particles also advance.
  (D) A floating object does not move at all as a wave passes through the water.

2. A barrier built at a right angle to the beach to trap sand that is moving parallel to the shore is known as a
  (A) seawall.   (B) groin.
  (C) headland.   (D) sea stack.

3. In the open sea, the movement of water particles in a wave becomes negligible at a depth equal to
  (A) one-fourth the wavelength.
  (B) one-third the wavelength.
  (C) one-half the wavelength.
  (D) three-fourths the wavelength.

4. Which term refers to the time interval between the passage of successive wave crests?
  (A) wave height
  (B) wavelength
  (C) wave period
  (D) wave speed

5. What happens as a wave approaches the shore?
  (A) wavelength decreases and wave height increases
  (B) wavelength increases and wave height increases
  (C) wave speed decreases and wave height decreases
  (D) wave period decreases and wave height decreases

Answer the following questions in complete sentences.

Use the figure below to answer Question 6.

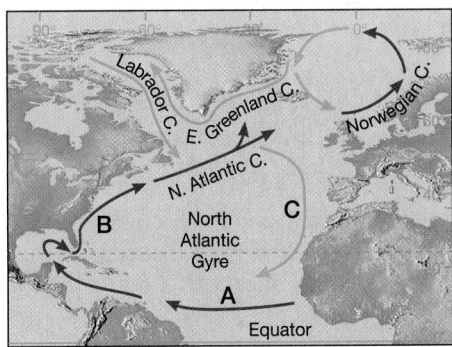

6. Identify the currents in the North Atlantic Gyre represented by A, B, and C. Specify whether each current is a warm water current or a cold water current. How does the North Atlantic Current affect weather in northwestern Europe?

7. What is the primary driving force of surface currents in the ocean? How do the distribution of continents on Earth and the Coriolis effect influence these currents?

CHAPTER

17 The Atmosphere: Structure and Temperature

CONCEPTS
in Action

Exploration Lab
Heating Land and Water

How the Earth Works
Earth's Atmosphere

 The Atmosphere
↳ Heating the Atmosphere

 **Video Field Trip**

About Weather

Take a weather field trip with Discovery Channel and learn about Earth's atmosphere. Answer the following questions after watching the video.

1. What protects Earth from the hot and cold extremes of space?

2. How do clouds form?

Go Online
PHSchool.com

For: Chapter 17 Resources
Visit: PHSchool.com
Web Code: cjk-9999

A bald eagle, found only in North America, ▶
soars over Mount Rainier National Park in

Chapter Preview

17.1 Atmosphere Characteristics

17.2 Heating the Atmosphere

17.3 Temperature Controls

Inquiry Activity

Modeling the Angle of the Sun

Procedure

1. Place a sheet of dark construction paper on a desk or table top. Hold a flashlight approximately 10 cm above the paper. The flashlight should be held at a 90° angle and pointed toward the paper.

2. Darken the room, and turn on the flashlight. Have a partner trace the perimeter of the light on the paper.

3. Repeat step 2, but this time, tilt the flashlight so that it is at 45 degrees to the paper. The end of the light should be 10 cm above the paper. Have a partner trace the perimeter of the light on the paper.

Think About It

1. **Observing** Describe the sizes and shapes of the light on the paper for steps 2 and 3.

2. **Modeling** Suppose the flashlight represents the sun, and the paper represents Earth's surface. Which angle gives more energy, per unit area, on the surface of Earth?

17.1 Atmosphere Characteristics

Reading Focus

Key Concepts

- How does weather differ from climate?
- Why do seasonal changes occur?

Vocabulary

- ◆ ozone
- ◆ troposphere
- ◆ stratosphere
- ◆ mesosphere
- ◆ thermosphere
- ◆ summer solstice
- ◆ winter solstice
- ◆ autumnal equinox
- ◆ spring equinox

Reading Strategy

Comparing and Contrasting Copy the Venn diagram below. As you read, complete the diagram by comparing and contrasting summer and winter solstices.

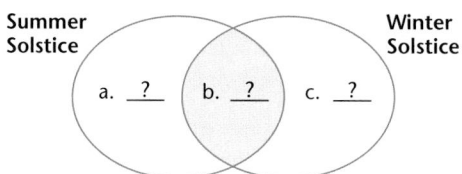

Summer Solstice   Winter Solstice

a. ? b. ? c. ?

Figure 1 Buffalo, New York, was under a state of emergency in late December 2001 after receiving almost 2 meters of snow.

Earth's atmosphere is unique. No other planet in our solar system has an atmosphere with the exact mixture of gases or the moisture conditions and heat needed to sustain life as we know it. The gases that make up Earth's atmosphere and the controls to which they are subject are vital to our existence. In this chapter, you will begin to examine the ocean of air in which we live.

The state of the atmosphere at a given time and place is known as weather. The combination of Earth's motions and energy from the sun produce a variety of weather. As shown in Figure 1, weather strongly influences our everyday activities. **Weather is constantly changing, and it refers to the state of the atmosphere at any given time and place. Climate, however, is based on observations of weather that have been collected over many years. Climate helps describe a place or region.** Climate often is defined simply as "average weather," but this is not a complete description. For example, farmers need to know not only the average rainfall during a growing season, but they also need to know the frequency of extremely wet and extremely dry years. The most important measurable properties of weather and climate are air temperature, humidity, type and amount of precipitation, air pressure, and the speed and direction of the wind.

Reading Checkpoint   *How does weather differ from climate?*

Composition of the Atmosphere

The composition of the atmosphere has changed dramatically over Earth's nearly 4.6 billion year history. The atmosphere is thought to have started as gases that were emitted during volcanic eruptions. Evidence indicates that oxygen did not start to accumulate in the atmosphere until about 2.5 billion years ago. The atmosphere continues to exchange material with the oceans and life on Earth's surface.

Major Components Sometimes the term *air* is used as if it were a specific gas, which it is not. Air is a mixture of different gases and particles, each with its own physical properties. The composition of air varies from time to time and from place to place. However, if the water vapor, dust, and other variable components were removed from the atmosphere, its makeup would be very stable worldwide up to an altitude of about 80 kilometers.

Look at Figure 2. Two gases—nitrogen and oxygen—make up 99 percent of the volume of clean, dry air. Although these gases are the most common components of air, they don't affect the weather much. The remaining 1 percent of dry air is mostly the inert gas argon (0.93 percent) plus tiny quantities of a number of other gases. Carbon dioxide is present in only small amounts (approximately 0.039 percent), but it is an important component of air. Carbon dioxide is an active absorber of energy given off by Earth. Therefore, it plays a significant role in heating the atmosphere.

Variable Components Important materials that vary in the air from time to time and place to place include water vapor, dust particles, and ozone. These components also can have significant effects on weather and climate.

The amount of water vapor varies from almost none to about 4 percent by volume. Why is such a small quantity so significant? **Water vapor is the source of all clouds and precipitation. Like carbon dioxide, water vapor absorbs heat given off by Earth. It also absorbs some solar energy.**

Movements of the atmosphere allow a large quantity of solid and liquid particles to be suspended within it. Although visible dust sometimes clouds the sky, these relatively large particles are too heavy to stay in the air for very long. Still, many particles are microscopic and remain suspended for longer periods of time. These particles include sea salts from breaking waves, fine soil blown into the air, smoke and soot from fires, pollen and microorganisms lifted by the wind, and ash and dust from volcanic eruptions.

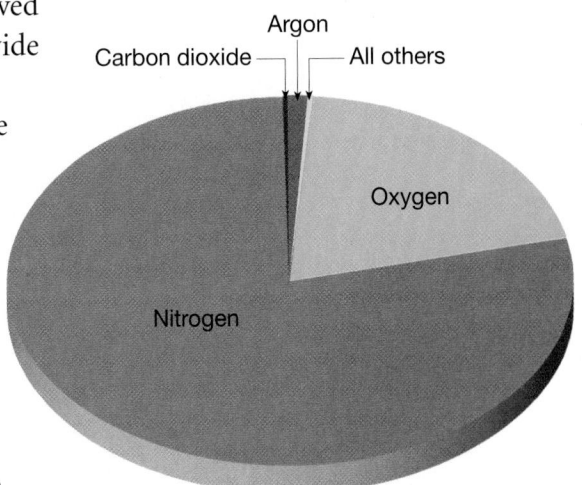

Figure 2 Volume of Clean, Dry Air Nitrogen and oxygen dominate the volume of gases composing dry air.

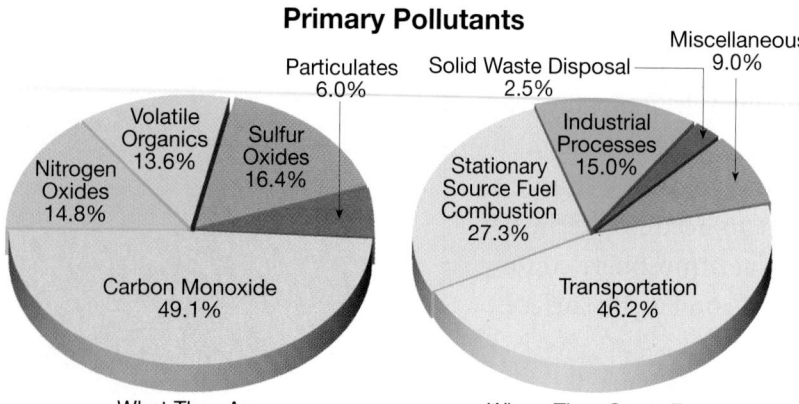

Primary Pollutants

What They Are

- Volatile Organics 13.6%
- Nitrogen Oxides 14.8%
- Sulfur Oxides 16.4%
- Particulates 6.0%
- Carbon Monoxide 49.1%

Where They Come From

- Solid Waste Disposal 2.5%
- Miscellaneous 9.0%
- Industrial Processes 15.0%
- Stationary Source Fuel Combustion 27.3%
- Transportation 46.2%

Figure 3 Primary Pollutants
These circle graphs show major primary pollutants and their sources. Percentages are calculated by weight.
Source: U.S. Environmental Protection Agency.

Another important variable component of the atmosphere is ozone. **Ozone** is a form of oxygen that combines three oxygen atoms into each molecule (O_3). Ozone is not the same as the oxygen we breathe, which has two atoms per molecule (O_2). There is very little ozone in the atmosphere, and it is not distributed evenly. It is concentrated in a layer located between 10 and 50 kilometers above Earth's surface.

In this altitude range, oxygen molecules (O_2) are split into single atoms of oxygen (O) when they absorb ultraviolet (UV) radiation emitted by the sun. Ozone is then produced when a single atom of oxygen (O) and a molecule of oxygen (O_2) collide. This collision must happen in the presence of a third, neutral molecule that acts as a catalyst. A catalyst allows a reaction to take place without being consumed in the process. Ozone is concentrated 10 to 50 kilometers above Earth because the UV radiation from the sun is sufficient to produce single atoms of oxygen. In addition, there are enough gas molecules to bring about the required collisions.

The ozone layer is crucial to life on Earth. Ozone absorbs potentially harmful UV radiation from the Sun. **If ozone did not filter most UV radiation and all of the sun's UV rays reached the surface of Earth, our planet would be uninhabitable for many living organisms.**

Human Influence Air pollutants are airborne particles and gases that occur in concentrations large enough to endanger the health of organisms. Primary pollutants, shown in Figure 3, are emitted directly from identifiable sources. Emissions from transportation vehicles account for nearly half the primary pollutants by weight.

Secondary pollutants are not emitted directly into air. They form in the atmosphere when reactions take place among primary pollutants and other substances. For example, after the primary pollutant sulfur dioxide enters the atmosphere, it combines with oxygen to produce sulfur trioxide. Then the sulfur trioxide combines with water to create sulfuric acid, an irritating and corrosive substance.

Reactions triggered by strong sunlight are called photochemical reactions. For instance, when nitrogen oxides absorb solar radiation, a chain of complex reactions begins. If certain volatile organic compounds are present, secondary products form that are reactive, irritating, and toxic. This noxious mixture of gases and particles is called photochemical smog.

 **Reading Checkpoint** *What are secondary pollutants?*

Height and Structure of the Atmosphere

Where does the atmosphere end and outer space begin? There is no sharp boundary. **The atmosphere thins as you travel away from Earth until there are too few gas molecules to detect.**

Pressure Changes To understand the vertical extent of the atmosphere, examine Figure 4, which shows changes in atmospheric pressure with height. Atmospheric pressure is simply the weight of the air above. At sea level, the average pressure is slightly more than 1000 millibars, or slightly more than 1 kilogram per square centimeter. One half of the atmosphere lies below an altitude of 5.6 kilometers. Above 100 kilometers, only 0.00003 percent of all the gases making up the atmosphere exist.

Temperature Changes The pictures of snow-capped mountains rising above snow-free valleys shown in Figure 5 might remind you that Earth's atmosphere becomes colder as you climb higher. But not all layers of the atmosphere show this temperature pattern.

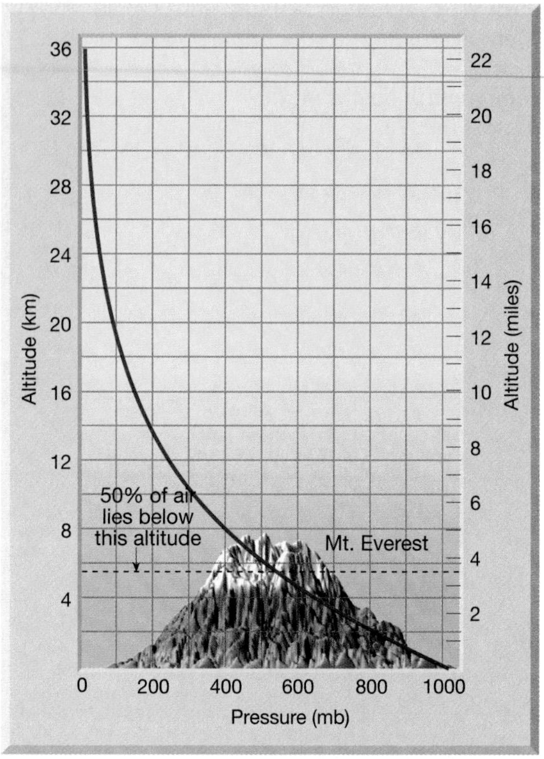

Figure 4 Atmospheric Pressure vs. Altitude This graph shows how atmospheric pressure varies with altitude.
Comparing *How do changes in air pressure at low altitudes compare with air pressure changes at high altitudes?*

Figure 5 In Jasper National Park in Alberta, Canada, snowy mountaintops contrast with warmer, snow-free lowlands below.

Figure 6 This diagram illustrates the thermal structure of the atmosphere. **Interpret** *How do air temperatures change with height in the mesosphere?*

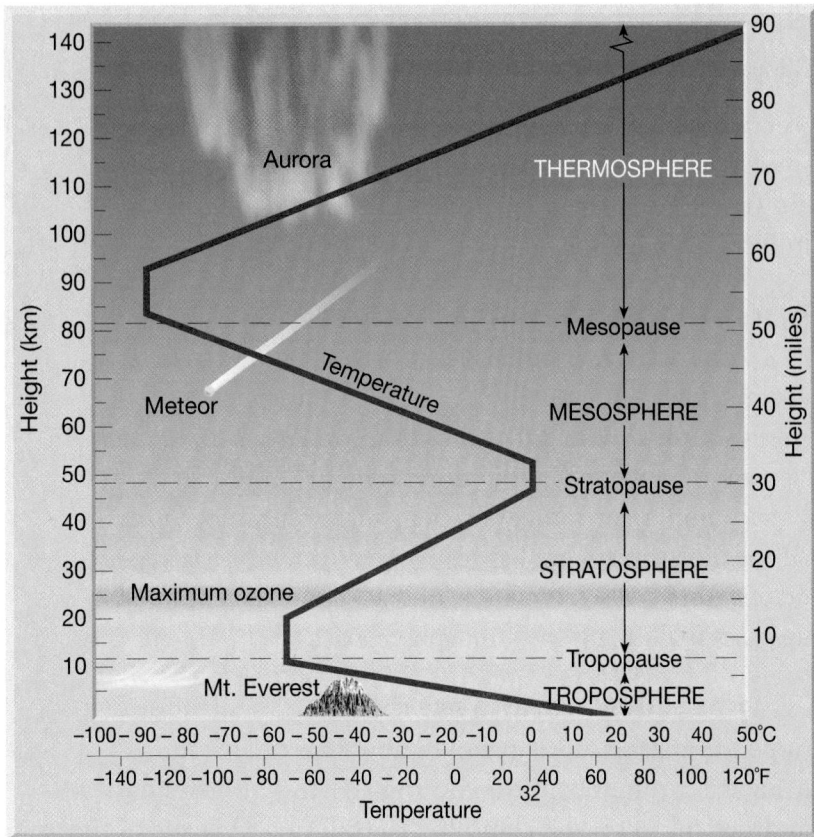

The atmosphere can be divided vertically into four layers based on temperature. Figure 6 illustrates these layers. The bottom layer, where temperature decreases with an increase in altitude, is the **troposphere.** It is in this layer that essentially all important weather phenomena occur. The thickness of the troposphere is not the same everywhere. It varies with latitude and the season. On average, the temperature drop continues to a height of about 12 kilometers, where the outer boundary of the troposphere, called the tropopause, is located.

Beyond the tropopause is the **stratosphere.** In the stratosphere, the temperature remains constant to a height of about 20 kilometers. It then begins a gradual increase in temperature that continues until the stratopause, at a height of nearly 50 kilometers above Earth's surface. Temperatures increase in the stratosphere because the atmosphere's ozone is concentrated here. Recall that ozone absorbs ultraviolet radiation from the sun. As a result, the stratosphere is heated.

In the third layer, the **mesosphere,** temperatures again decrease with height until the mesopause. The mesopause is more than 80 kilometers above the surface and the temperatures approach −90°C. The fourth layer extends outward from the mesopause and has no well-defined upper limit. It is the **thermosphere,** a layer that contains only a tiny fraction of the atmosphere's mass. Temperatures increase in the thermosphere because oxygen and nitrogen absorb short-wave, high-energy solar radiation.

Earth-Sun Relationships

Nearly all of the energy that drives Earth's variable weather and climate comes from the sun. Earth absorbs only a tiny percentage of the energy given off by the sun—less than one two-billionth. This may seem insignificant, but the amount is several hundred thousand times the electrical-generating capacity of the United States.

Solar energy is not distributed evenly over Earth's surface. The amount of energy received varies with latitude, time of day, and season of the year. As you will see, the variations in solar heating are caused by the motions of Earth relative to the sun and by variations in Earth's land and ocean surface. It is the unequal heating of Earth that creates winds and drives the ocean's currents. These movements transport heat from the tropics toward the poles in an attempt to balance energy differences. The results of these processes are the phenomena we call weather.

Earth's Motions Earth has two principal motions—rotation and revolution. Rotation is the spinning of Earth about its axis. The axis is an imaginary line running through the north and south poles. Our planet rotates once every 24 hours, producing the daily cycle of daylight and darkness. Revolution is the movement of Earth in its orbit around the sun. Earth travels at nearly 113,000 kilometers per hour in an elliptical orbit about the sun.

Earth's Orientation We know that it is colder in the winter than in the summer. But why? Length of day and a gradual change in the angle of the noon sun above the horizon affect the amount of energy Earth receives. ⬛ **Seasonal changes occur because Earth's position relative to the sun continually changes as it travels along its orbit.** Earth's axis is not perpendicular to the plane of its orbit around the sun. Instead it is tilted 23.5 degrees from the perpendicular, as shown in Figure 7. Because the axis remains pointed toward the North Star as Earth moves around the sun, the position of Earth's axis to the sun's rays is constantly changing. If the axis were not tilted, we would not have seasonal changes.

The orientation of Earth relative to the sun and the constant movement of Earth cause the angle of the noon sun to vary by up to 47 degrees (−23.5 degrees to +23.5 degrees) for many locations during the year. For example, a mid-latitude city like New York, located about 40 degrees north latitude, has a maximum noon sun angle of 73.5 degrees when the sun's vertical rays reach their farthest northward location in June. Six months later, New York has a minimum noon sun angle of 26.5 degrees.

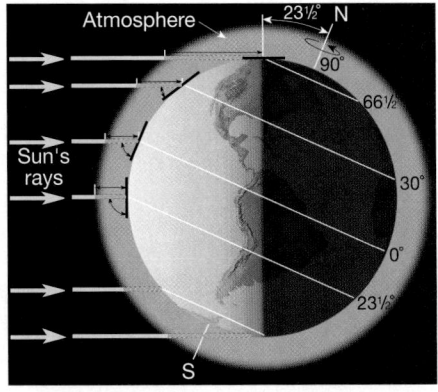

Figure 7 Tilt of Earth's Axis
Earth's axis always points toward the North Star as it revolves around the sun.

 **Reading Checkpoint** *In which direction does Earth's axis point?*

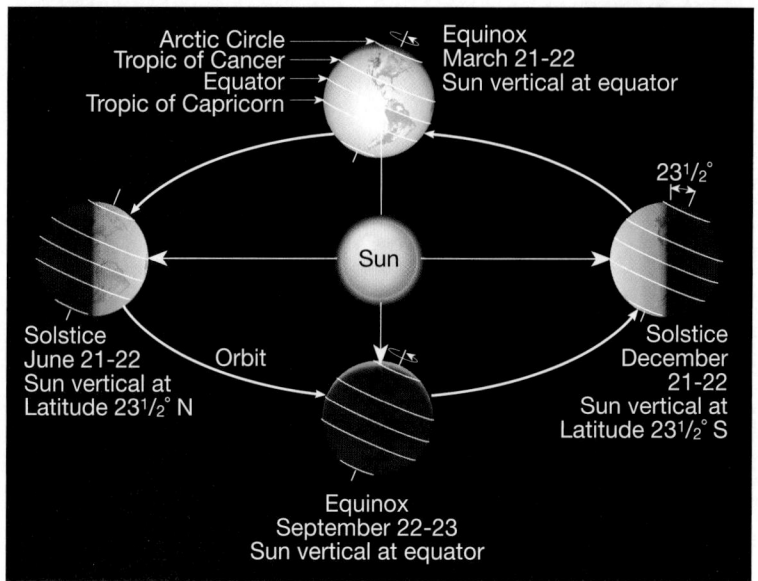

Figure 8 Solstices and equinoxes are important events in Earth's yearly weather cycle.

Solstices and Equinoxes On June 21 or 22 each year the axis is such that the Northern Hemisphere is "leaning" 23.5 degrees toward the sun. This date, shown on the left side of Figure 8, is known as the **summer solstice,** or the first "official" day of summer. Six months later, in December, when Earth has moved to the opposite side of its orbit, the Northern Hemisphere "leans" 23.5 degrees away from the sun. December 21 or 22 is the **winter solstice,** the first day of winter. On days between these extremes, Earth's axis is leaning at amounts less than 23.5 degrees to the rays of the sun.

The equinoxes occur midway between the solstices. September 22 or 23 is the date of the **autumnal equinox** in the Northern Hemisphere. March 21 or 22 is the date of the **spring equinox** for the Northern Hemisphere. On these dates, the vertical rays of the sun strike the equator (0 degrees latitude) because Earth is in a position in its orbit so that the axis is tilted neither toward nor away from the sun.

Length of Daylight The length of daylight compared to darkness also is determined by Earth's position in orbit. All latitudes receive 12 hours of daylight during the vernal and autumnal equinoxes (equal night). The length of daylight on the summer solstice in the Northern Hemisphere is greater than the length of darkness. The farther you are north of the equator on the summer solstice, the longer the period of daylight. When you reach the Arctic Circle, at 66.5 degrees N latitude, the length of daylight is 24 hours.

Section 17.1 Assessment

Reviewing Concepts

1. Compare and contrast weather and climate.

2. Why do seasonal changes occur?

3. How much of Earth's atmosphere is located below about 5.6 kilometers?

4. How do ozone molecules form in the stratosphere?

5. In which layers of the atmosphere does temperature increase with increasing height?

Critical Thinking

6. **Applying Concepts** Explain what would happen to air temperatures in the troposphere if carbon dioxide were removed from air.

Connecting Concepts

Connecting Concepts Using Figure 8, explain why solstices and equinoxes are opposite for the Northern and Southern hemispheres.

17.2 Heating the Atmosphere

Reading Focus

Key Concepts

- How are heat and temperature related?
- What are the three major mechanisms of heat transfer?
- How is the atmosphere affected by each of the heat transfer mechanisms?

Vocabulary

- heat
- temperature
- conduction
- convection
- radiation
- reflection
- scattering
- greenhouse effect

Reading Strategy

Using Prior Knowledge Before you read, copy the table below and write your definition for each vocabulary term. After you read, write the scientific definition of each term and compare it with your original definition.

Term	Your Definition	Scientific Definition
Heat	a. ___?___	b. ___?___
Temperature	c. ___?___	d. ___?___

The concepts of heat and temperature often are confused. The phrase "in the heat of the day" is one common expression in which the word "heat" is misused to describe the concept of temperature. **Heat is the energy transferred from one object to another because of a difference in their temperatures.** Recall that all matter is composed of atoms or molecules that possess kinetic energy, or the energy of motion. **Temperature** is a measure of the average kinetic energy of the individual atoms or molecules in a substance. When energy is transferred to the gas atoms and molecules in air, those particles move faster and air temperature rises. When air transfers energy to a cooler object, its particles move slower, and air temperature drops.

Energy Transfer as Heat

Three mechanisms of energy transfer as heat are conduction, convection, and radiation. All three processes, illustrated in Figure 9, happen simultaneously in the atmosphere. These mechanisms operate to transfer energy between Earth's surface (both land and water) and the atmosphere.

Conduction Anyone who has touched a metal spoon that was left in a hot pan has experienced the result of heat conducted through the spoon. **Conduction** is the transfer of heat through matter by molecular activity. The energy of molecules is transferred by collisions from one molecule to another. Heat flows from the higher temperature matter to the lower temperature matter.

Figure 9 Energy Transfer as Heat A pot of water on the campfire illustrates the three mechanisms of heat transfer.

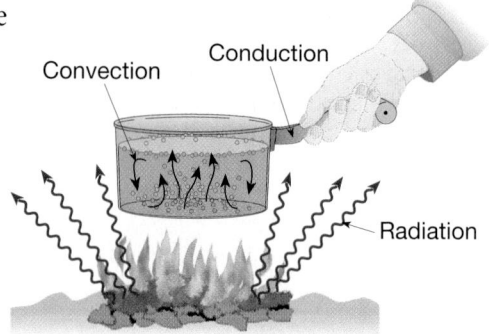

The Atmosphere: Structure and Temperature **483**

The ability of substances to conduct heat varies greatly. Metals are good conductors, as those of us who have touched hot metal have quickly learned. Air, however, is a very poor conductor of heat. Because air is a poor conductor, conduction is important only between Earth's surface and the air directly in contact with the surface. For the atmosphere as a whole, conduction is the least important mechanism of heat transfer.

Convection Much of the heat transfer that occurs in the atmosphere is carried on by convection. **Convection** is the transfer of heat by mass movement or circulation within a substance. It takes place in fluids, like the ocean and air, where the atoms and molecules are free to move about. Convection also takes place in solids, such as Earth's mantle, that behave like fluids over long periods of time.

The pan of water in Figure 9 shows circulation by convection. Radiation from the fire warms the bottom of the pan, which conducts heat to the water near the bottom of the container. As the water is heated, it expands and becomes less dense than the water above. The warmer water rises because of its buoyancy. At the same time, cooler, denser water near the top of the pan sinks to the bottom, where it becomes heated. As long as the water is heated unequally, it will continue to circulate. In much the same way, most of the heat acquired by radiation and conduction in the lowest layer of the atmosphere is transferred by convective flow.

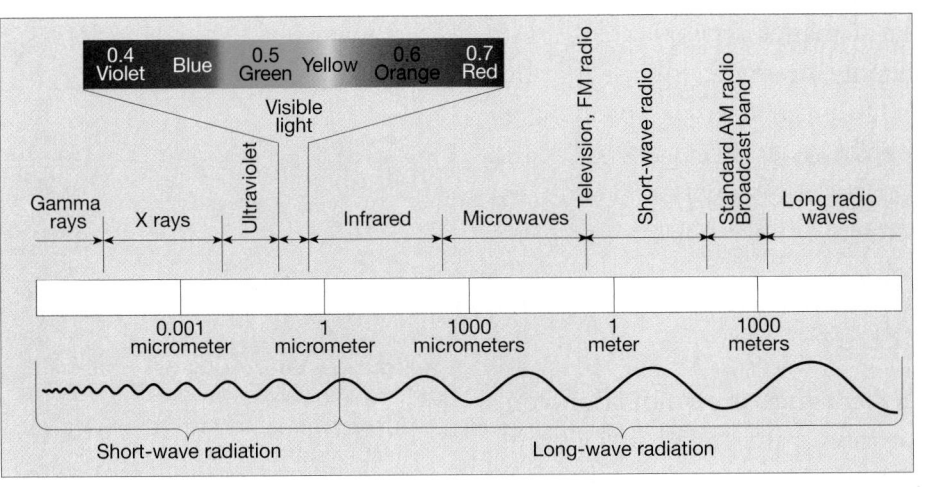

Figure 10 Electromagnetic Spectrum Electromagnetic energy is classified according to wavelength in the electromagnetic spectrum.

Electromagnetic Waves

The sun is the ultimate source of energy that creates our weather. You know that the sun emits light and heat as well as the ultraviolet rays that cause a suntan. These forms of energy are only part of a large array of energy called the electromagnetic spectrum. This spectrum of electromagnetic energy is shown in Figure 10. All radiation, whether X-rays, radio waves, or heat waves, travel through the vacuum of space at 300,000 kilometers per second. They travel only slightly slower through our atmosphere.

 **Reading Checkpoint** *What is convection?*

Imagine what happens when you toss a pebble into a pond. Ripples are made and move away from the location where the pebble hit the water's surface. Much like these ripples, electromagnetic waves move out from their source and come in various sizes. The most important difference among electromagnetic waves is their wavelength, or the distance from one crest to the next. Radio waves have the longest wavelengths, ranging to tens of kilometers. Gamma waves are the shortest, and are less than a billionth of a centimeter long.

Visible light is the only portion of the spectrum you can see. White light is really a mixture of colors. Each color corresponds to a specific wavelength, as shown in Figure 11. By using a prism, white light can be divided into the colors of the rainbow, from violet with the shortest wavelength—0.4 micrometer (1 micrometer is 0.0001 centimeter)—to red with the longest wavelength—0.7 micrometer.

Figure 11 Visible light consists of an array of colors commonly called the colors of the rainbow.

Radiation The third mechanism of heat transfer is radiation. As shown in Figure 9, **radiation** travels out in all directions from its source. **Unlike conduction and convection, which need material to travel through, radiant energy can travel through the vacuum of space.** Solar energy reaches Earth by radiation.

To understand how the atmosphere is heated, it is useful to think about four laws governing radiation.

1. **All objects, at any temperature, emit radiant energy.** Not only hot objects like the sun but also Earth—including its polar ice caps—continually emit energy.

2. **Hotter objects radiate more total energy per unit area than colder objects do.**

3. **The hottest radiating bodies produce the shortest wavelengths of maximum radiation.** For example, the sun, with a surface temperature of nearly 6000°C radiates maximum energy at 0.5 micrometers, which is in the visible range. The maximum radiation for Earth occurs at a wavelength of 10 micrometers, well within the infrared range.

4. **Objects that are good absorbers of radiation are good emitters as well.** Gases are selective absorbers and radiators. The atmosphere does not absorb certain wavelengths of radiation, but it is a good absorber of other wavelengths.

For: Links on conduction and convection
Visit: www.SciLinks.org
Web Code: cjn-6172

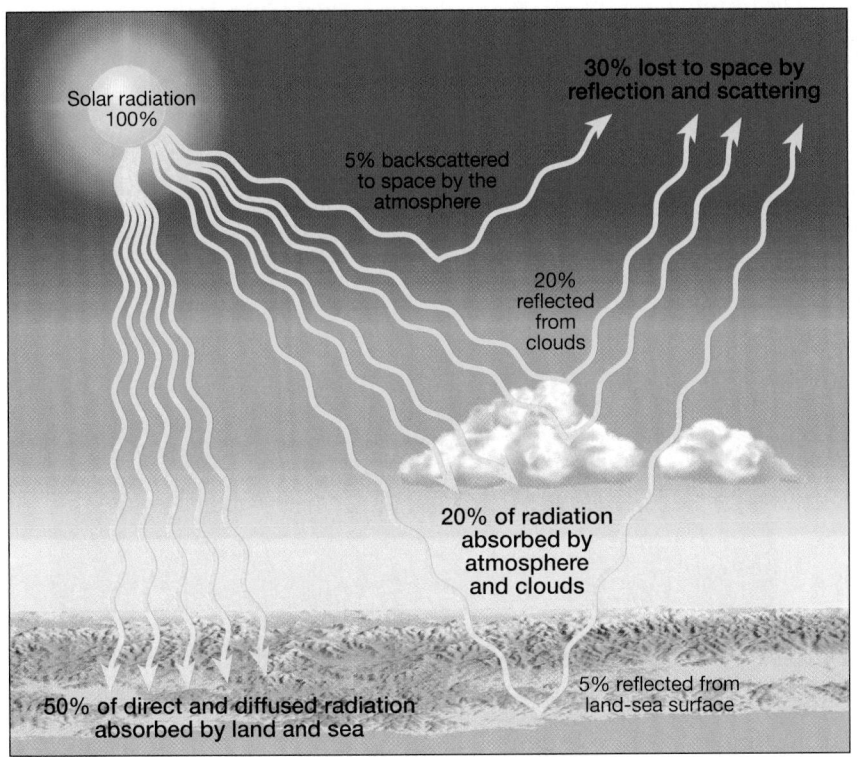

Solar radiation 100%

30% lost to space by reflection and scattering

5% backscattered to space by the atmosphere

20% reflected from clouds

20% of radiation absorbed by atmosphere and clouds

50% of direct and diffused radiation absorbed by land and sea

5% reflected from land-sea surface

What Happens to Solar Radiation?

When radiation strikes an object, there usually are three different results.

1. **Some energy is absorbed by the object.** When radiant energy is absorbed, it is converted to heat and causes a temperature increase.

2. **Substances such as water and air are transparent to certain wavelengths of radiation.** These substances transmit the radiant energy. Radiation that is transmitted does not contribute energy to the object.

3. **Some radiation may bounce off the object without being absorbed or transmitted.** Figure 12 shows what happens to incoming solar radiation, averaged for the entire globe.

Figure 12 Solar Radiation This diagram shows what happens, on average, to incoming solar radiation by percentage.

Reflection and Scattering Reflection occurs when light bounces off an object. The reflected radiation has the same intensity as the incident radiation. In contrast, **scattering** produces a larger number of weaker rays that travel in different directions. See Figure 13. Scattering disperses light both forward and backward. However, more energy is dispersed in the forward direction. About 30 percent of the solar energy reaching the outer atmosphere is reflected back to space. This 30 percent also includes the amount of energy sent skyward by scattering. This energy is lost and does not play a role in heating Earth's atmosphere.

Small dust particles and gas molecules in the atmosphere scatter some incoming radiation in all directions. This explains how light reaches into the area beneath a shade tree, and how a room is lit in the absence of direct sunlight. Scattering also accounts for the brightness and even the blue color of the daytime sky. In contrast, bodies like the moon and Mercury—which are without atmospheres—have dark skies and "pitch-black" shadows even during daylight hours. About half of the solar radiation that is absorbed at Earth's surface arrives as scattered light.

Figure 13 Reflection vs. Scattering
A Reflected light bounces back with the same intensity.
B Scattering produces more light rays with a weaker intensity.

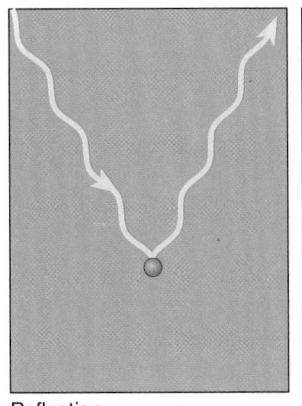

Reflection

A

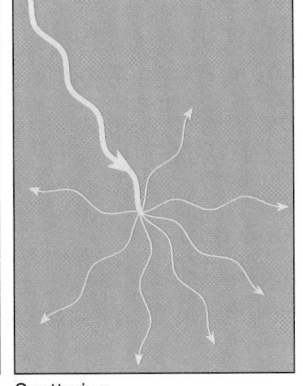

Scattering

B

Reading Checkpoint

What causes the blue color of the daytime sky?

Absorption About 50 percent of the solar energy that strikes the top of the atmosphere reaches Earth's surface and is absorbed, as shown in Figure 12. Most of this energy is then reradiated skyward. Because Earth has a much lower surface temperature than the sun, the radiation that it emits has longer wavelengths than solar radiation does.

The atmosphere efficiently absorbs the longer wavelengths emitted by Earth. Water vapor and carbon dioxide are the major absorbing gases. When a gas molecule absorbs light waves, this energy is transformed into molecular motion that can be detected as a rise in temperature. Gases in the atmosphere eventually radiate some of this energy away. Some energy travels skyward, where it may be reabsorbed by other gas molecules. The remainder travels Earthward and is again absorbed by Earth. In this way, Earth's surface is continually being supplied with heat from the atmosphere as well as from the sun.

Without these absorbing gases in our atmosphere, Earth would not be a suitable habitat for humans and other life forms. This important phenomenon has been termed the **greenhouse effect** because it was once thought that greenhouses were heated in a similar manner. A more important factor in keeping a greenhouse warm is the fact that the greenhouse itself prevents the mixing of air inside with cooler air outside. Nevertheless, the term greenhouse effect is still used.

Q *Isn't the greenhouse effect responsible for global warming?*

A It is important to note that the greenhouse effect and global warming *are not* the same thing. Without the greenhouse effect, Earth would be uninhabitable. We do have mounting evidence that human activity (particularly the release of carbon dioxide into the atmosphere) is responsible for a rise in global temperatures. Thus, human activities seem to be enhancing an otherwise natural process (the greenhouse effect) to increase Earth's temperature. Nevertheless, to equate the greenhouse effect, which makes life possible, with undesirable changes to our atmosphere caused by human activity is incorrect.

Section 17.2 Assessment

Reviewing Concepts

1. 🔵 How are heat and temperature related?
2. 🔵 List and describe the three major mechanisms of heat transfer in the atmosphere.
3. 🔵 How is the atmosphere affected by
   a. convection?
   b. conduction?
   c. radiation?
4. 🔵 Describe what happens to solar radiation when it strikes an object.
5. Contrast reflection and scattering.

Critical Thinking

6. **Applying Concepts** Dark objects tend to absorb more radiation than light-colored objects. Explain whether dark objects or light objects on Earth's surface would be better radiators of heat.

Writing in Science

Descriptive Paragraph Write a paragraph that describes the four laws governing radiation discussed in this chapter. Make sure to use your own words. Use examples to reinforce concepts wherever possible.

17.3 Temperature Controls

Reading Focus

Key Concepts
- What is a temperature control?
- How do the heating of land and water differ?
- Why do some clouds reflect a portion of sunlight back to space?

Vocabulary
- albedo
- isotherm

Reading Strategy
Previewing Copy the table below. Before you read, use Figure 15 to describe the temperature variations for Vancouver and Winnipeg.

Temperature Variations	
Vancouver	a. _____?_____
Winnipeg	b. _____?_____

Figure 14 This modern instrument shelter contains an electrical thermometer called a thermistor.

Temperature is one of the basic elements of weather and climate. When someone asks what it is like outside, air temperature is often the first element we mention. At a weather station, the temperature is read on a regular basis from instruments mounted in an instrument shelter like the one in Figure 14. The shelter protects the instruments from direct sunlight and allows a free flow of air.

Why Temperatures Vary

A temperature control is any factor that causes temperature to vary from place to place and from time to time. Earlier in this chapter you examined the most important cause for temperature variations—differences in the receipt of solar radiation. Because variations in the angle of the sun's rays and length of daylight depend on latitude, they are responsible for warmer temperatures in the tropics and colder temperatures toward the poles. Seasonal temperature changes happen as the sun's vertical rays move toward and away from a particular latitude during the year. **Factors other than latitude that exert a strong influence on temperature include heating of land and water, altitude, geographic position, cloud cover, and ocean currents.**

Reading Checkpoint *List three factors that influence temperature.*

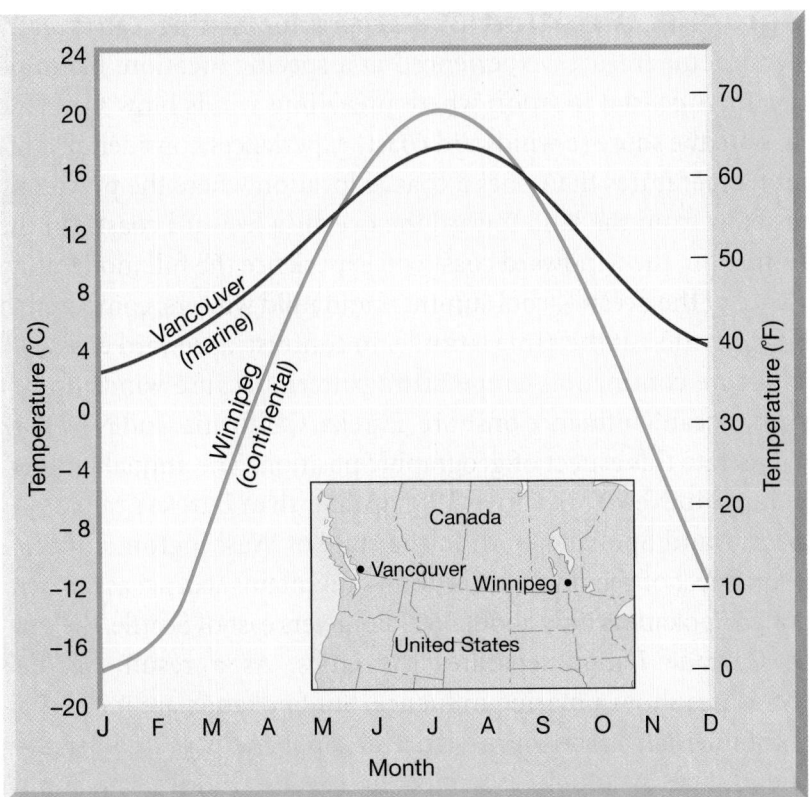

Figure 15 Mean Monthly Temperatures for Vancouver and Winnipeg Winnipeg illustrates the greater extremes associated with an interior location.
Calculating *How much lower is Winnipeg's January mean temperature than Vancouver's? Calculate the temperature to the nearest degree.*

Land and Water The heating of Earth's surface controls the temperature of the air above it. To understand variations in air temperature, we consider the characteristics of the surface. Different land surfaces absorb varying amounts of incoming solar energy. The largest contrast, however, is between land and water. 🔑 **Land heats more rapidly and to higher temperatures than water. Land also cools more rapidly and to lower temperatures than water.** Temperature variations, therefore, are considerably greater over land than over water.

Monthly temperature data for two cities, shown in Figure 15, show the influence of a large body of water. Vancouver, British Columbia, is located along the windward Pacific coast. Winnipeg, Manitoba, is far from the influence of water. Both cities are at about the same latitude, so they experience similar lengths of daylight and angles of the sun's rays. Winnipeg, however, has much greater temperature extremes than Vancouver does. Vancouver's moderate year-round climate is due to its location by the Pacific Ocean.

Temperature variations in the Northern and Southern hemispheres are compared in Table 1. Water accounts for 61 percent of the Northern Hemisphere, and land accounts for the remaining 39 percent. In the Southern Hemisphere, 81 percent of the surface is water and only 19 percent of the surface is land. The Southern Hemisphere shows smaller annual temperature variations.

Table 1 Variation in Annual Mean Temperature Range (°C) with Latitude		
Latitude	Northern Hemisphere	Southern Hemisphere
0	0	0
15	3	4
30	13	7
45	23	6
60	30	11
75	32	26
90	40	31

Geographic Position The geographic setting can greatly influence temperatures experienced at a specific location. Examine Figure 16. A coastal location where prevailing winds blow from the ocean onto the shore (a windward coast) experiences considerably different temperatures than does a coastal location where the prevailing winds blow from the land toward the ocean (a leeward coast). In the first situation, the windward coast will experience the full moderating influence of the ocean—cool summers and mild winters, compared to an inland station at the same latitude. In contrast, a leeward coast will have a more continental temperature pattern because winds do not carry the ocean's influence onshore. Eureka, California, and New York City illustrate this aspect of geographic position. The annual temperature range in New York City is 19°C greater than Eureka's range.

Seattle and Spokane, both in the state of Washington, illustrate another aspect of geographic position—mountains that act as barriers. Although Spokane is only about 360 kilometers east of Seattle, the towering Cascade Range separates the cities. As a result, Seattle's temperatures show a marine influence, but Spokane's are more typically continental, as shown in Figure 17. Spokane is 7°C cooler than Seattle in January and 4°C warmer than Seattle in July. The annual range in Spokane is 11°C greater than in Seattle. The Cascade Range cuts Spokane off from the moderating influence of the Pacific Ocean.

Figure 16 Mean Monthly Temperatures for Eureka and New York City Eureka is strongly influenced by prevailing ocean winds, and New York City is not.

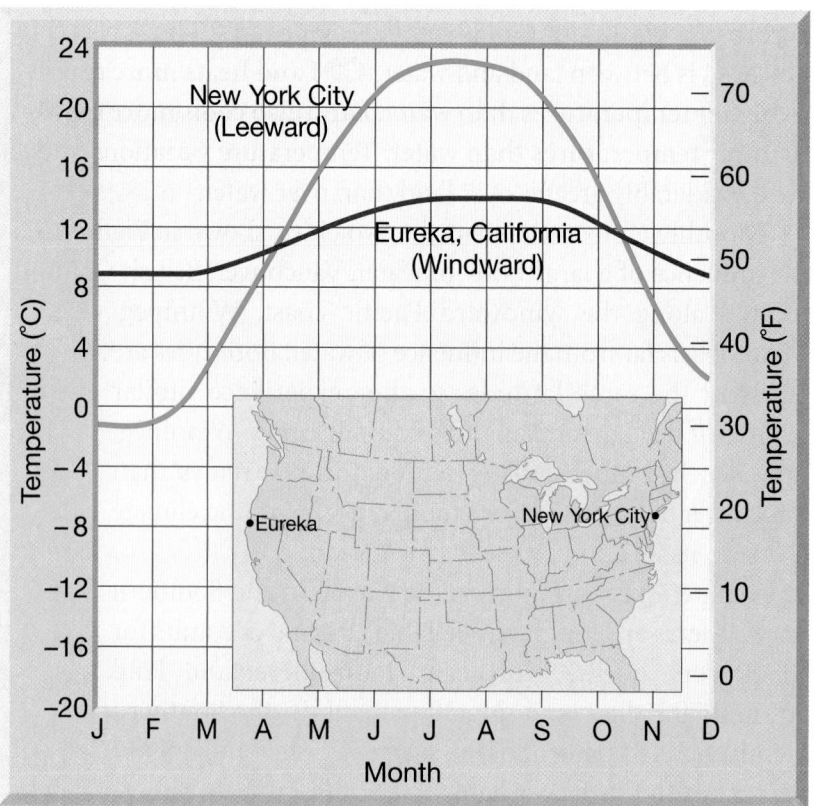

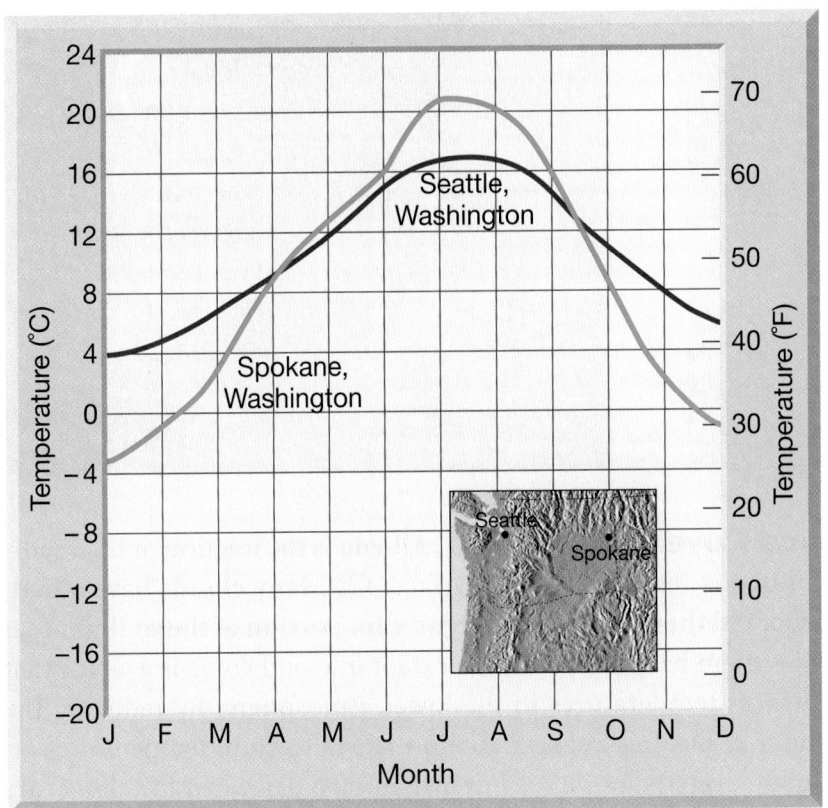

Figure 17 Mean Monthly Temperatures for Seattle and Spokane The Cascade Mountains cut off Spokane from the moderating influence of the Pacific Ocean. **Relating Cause and Effect** *How does this affect Spokane's annual temperature range?*

Figure 18 Mean Monthly Temperatures for Quito and Guayaquil Quito's altitude is much higher than Guayaquil's, causing Quito to experience cooler temperatures than Guayaquil.

Altitude Two cities in Ecuador, Quito and Guayaquil, demonstrate the influence of altitude on mean temperature. Both cities are near the equator and relatively close to one another, as shown in Figure 18. The annual mean temperature at Guayaquil is 25°C, compared to Quito's mean of 13°C. If you note these cities' elevations, you can understand the temperature difference. Guayaquil is only 12 meters above sea level, whereas Quito is high in the Andes Mountains at 2800 meters.

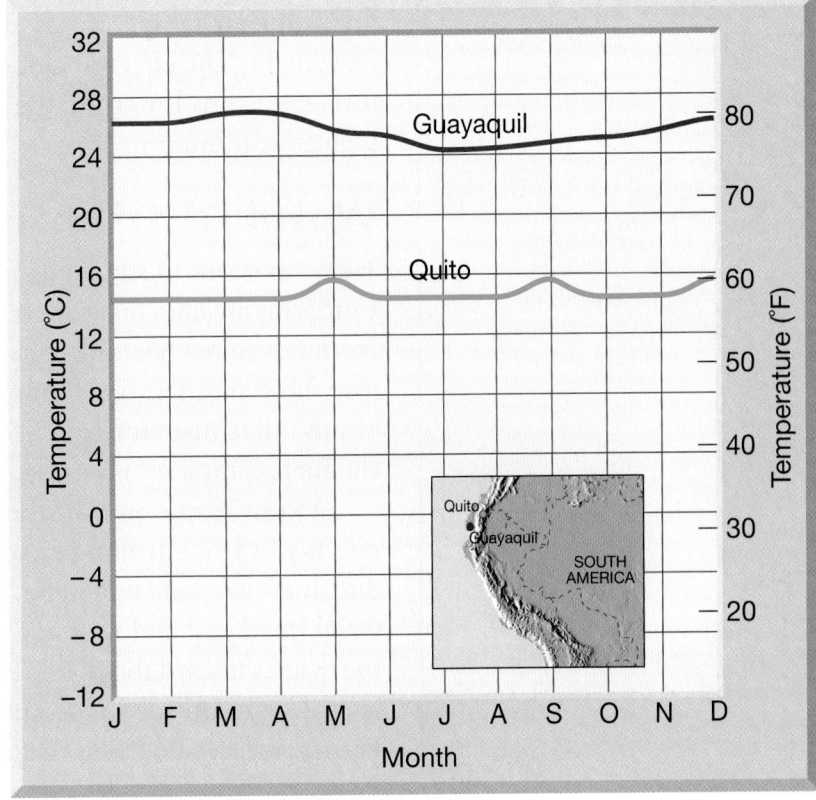

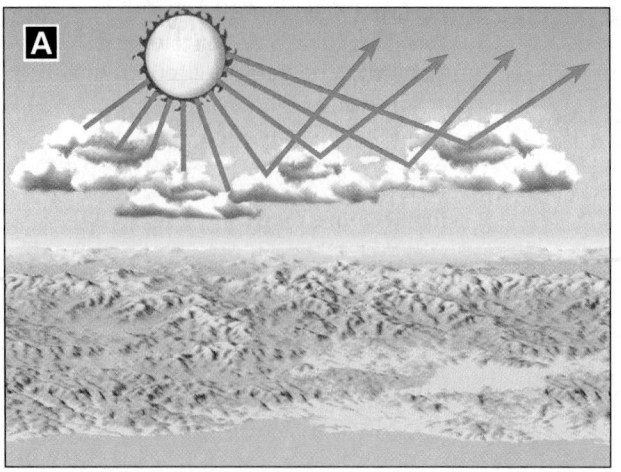

Figure 19 A During daylight hours, clouds reflect solar radiation back to space. **B** At night, clouds absorb radiation from the land and reradiate some of it back to Earth, increasing nighttime temperatures.

Cloud Cover and Albedo Albedo is the fraction of total radiation that is reflected by any surface. **Many clouds have a high albedo, and therefore reflect a significant portion of the sunlight that strikes them back to space.** The extent of cloud cover is a factor that influences temperatures in the lower atmosphere. By reducing the amount of incoming solar radiation, the maximum temperatures on a cloud-covered day will be lower than on a day when the clouds are absent and the sky is clear, as shown in Figure 19A.

At night, clouds have the opposite effect, as shown in Figure 19B. Clouds act as a blanket by absorbing outgoing radiation emitted by Earth and reradiating a portion of it back to the surface. Thus, cloudy nighttime air temperatures do not drop as low as they would on a clear night. The effect of cloud cover is to reduce the daily temperature range by lowering the daytime maximum and raising the nighttime minimum.

World Distribution of Temperature

Take a moment to study Figure 20, which is a world isothermal map. **Isotherms** are lines that connect points that have the same temperature. From hot colors near the equator to cool colors toward the poles, this map shows mean sea-level temperatures in the seasonally extreme month of July. All temperatures on this map have been reduced to sea level to eliminate complications caused by differences in altitude.

On this map, you can study global temperature patterns and the effects of the controlling factors of temperature, especially latitude, distribution of land and water, and ocean currents. The isotherms generally trend east and west and show a decrease in temperatures from the tropics toward the poles. This map emphasizes the importance of latitude as a control on incoming solar radiation, which in turn heats Earth's surface and the atmosphere above it.

World Isothermal Map

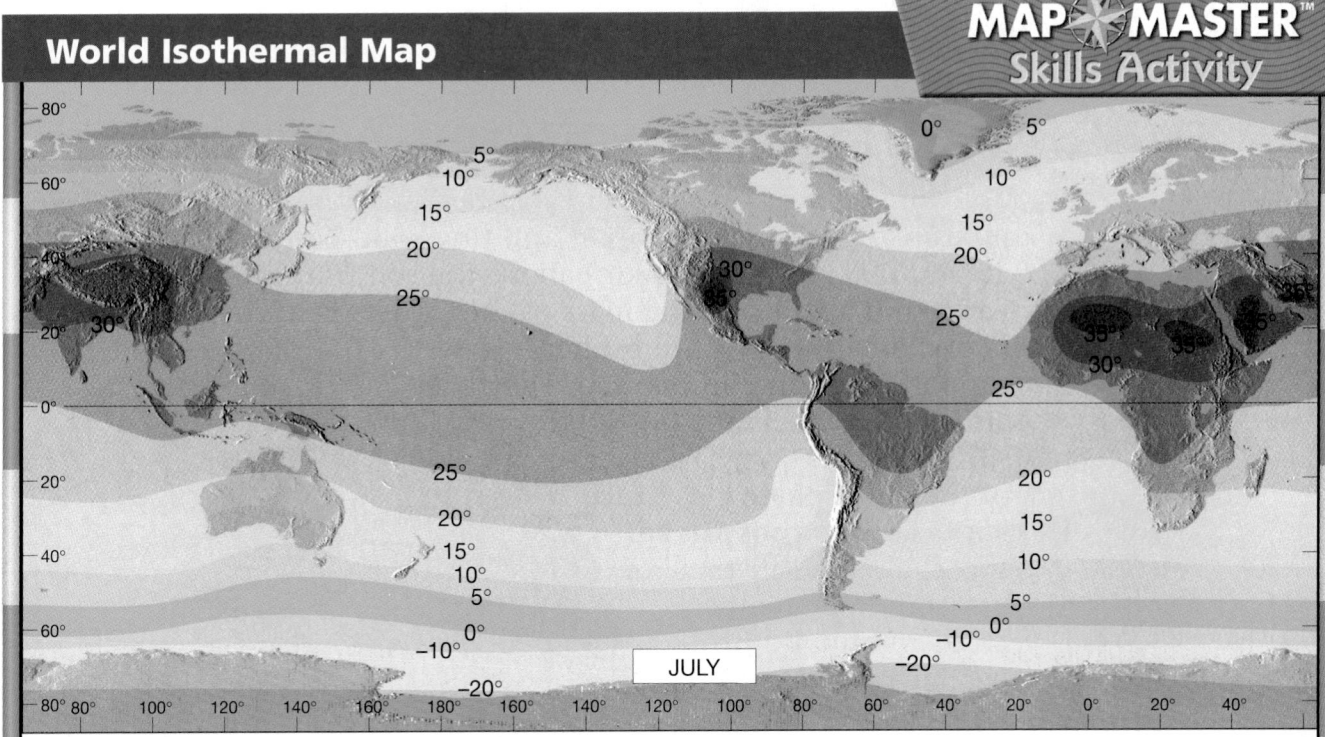

Figure 20

Regions The map shows the distribution of world mean sea-level temperatures averaged for the month of July.
Locating Estimate the latitude range for temperatures between 20 and 25 degrees Celsius in the Northern Hemisphere. Approximate to the nearest 5 degrees latitude for each extreme.
Predicting Do you expect the color of the temperature band to change near the equator for the month of January? Explain your prediction.

Section 17.3 Assessment

Reviewing Concepts

1. 💬 What is a temperature control?
2. 💬 How do the heating of land and water differ?
3. 💬 Why do many clouds reflect a significant amount of sunlight back to space?
4. Why do some coastal cities experience a moderation of temperature from water, while others do not?
5. List four specific controls of atmospheric temperature.

Critical Thinking

6. **Inferring** Look back at the graph in Figure 18. Why do the temperatures of these two cities stay within a limited range throughout the year?

Math ▶ Practice

7. Using the data in Table 1, determine the latitude that shows the greatest variation in average mean temperature between the Northern and Southern Hemispheres.

The Atmosphere: Structure and Temperature **493**

How the Earth Works

Earth's Atmosphere

The outermost part of the Earth is the atmosphere, a multilayered mixture of gases, water vapor, and tiny solid particles. It extends at least 600 miles (1,000 km) above the solid surface of the Earth, but about half the mass of these gases is in the lowest (5.6 kilometers). The atmosphere's gases support plant and animal life. They also protect the Earth from the sun's harmful rays. The layer of the atmosphere closest to land is the **troposphere.** It contains the air that we breathe. Here, temperature and humidity change rapidly, and the air is turbulent, creating weather patterns.

OXYGEN FROM PHOTOSYNTHESIS
Oxygen is a relative newcomer in the Earth's atmosphere. It has come from plants that, during **photosynthesis,** use carbon dioxide to make their food, while giving out oxygen. The earliest photosynthesizing plants, which probably looked like these algae, evolved about 3,500 million years ago.

THE ATMOSPHERE FROM SPACE
Viewed from space, the Earth looks totally unlike other planets of our solar system. It is partly shrouded in white clouds, which swirl in patterns, making weather. **Clouds** are masses of tiny particles of water and dust floating in the atmosphere. A very low cloud is called fog.

OXYGEN CYCLE
A vast store of oxygen exists in oceans, rocks, and the atmosphere. Oxygen created by plant photosynthesis balances oxygen used by people and animals.

A large amount of oxygen is stored in the atmosphere

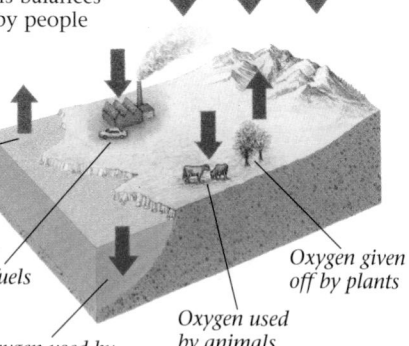

Oxygen given off by marine plants

Oxygen used in burning fossil fuels

Oxygen used by marine animals

Oxygen used by animals and humans

Oxygen given off by plants

FERTILE LAND
The atmosphere helps life to flourish on the Earth. It offers protection from harmful radiations and provides nourishment for both plants and animals. Winds in the troposphere moderate daily and seasonal temperatures by distributing heat around the world.

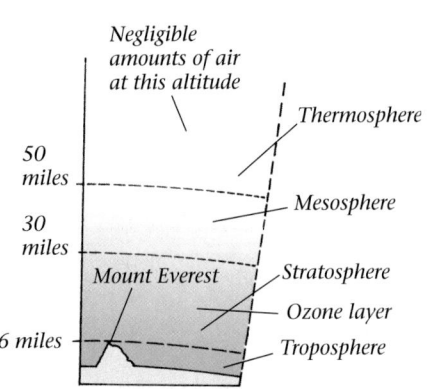

Negligible amounts of air at this altitude

Thermosphere

50 miles

Mesosphere

30 miles

Stratosphere

Ozone layer

Mount Everest

6 miles

Troposphere

LAYERS OF ATMOSPHERE
The Earth's atmosphere has several layers. The heights of these layers vary with season and latitude. Weather is confined to the troposphere, and almost all clouds are below this level. In the stratosphere lies the important ozone layer that filters the sun's rays.

OZONE HOLE
Within the stratosphere is the **ozone layer,** a band of ozone gas that absorbs the sun's harmful ultraviolet rays. In recent years, the ozone layer has been getting thinner. Certain pollutant gases, such as chlorofluorocarbons, cause ozone molecules to break down. Some scientists suggest that ozone depletion also may be caused by natural phenomena. Holes in the ozone layer were first detected over Antarctica and the Arctic. At times, the southern hole has expanded over populated areas of South America, as shown by the dark blue color in this NASA satellite photograph.

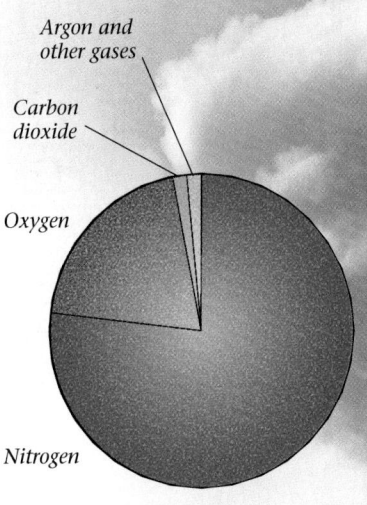

Argon and other gases

Carbon dioxide

Oxygen

Nitrogen

GASES IN THE ATMOSPHERE
The most abundant gas in the lower atmosphere is nitrogen, which makes up about 78 percent of air. Oxygen, about 21 percent of air, is essential for supporting animal life. Carbon dioxide is just a tiny fraction of the atmosphere, but it is vital in sustaining plant life.

VOLCANIC GASES
About 4 billion years ago, the Earth had no atmosphere and its surface was covered with erupting volcanoes. The Earth's atmosphere was formed mostly from gases spewed out by volcanoes since the Earth began, although some gases, like oxygen, are a later contribution.

ASSESSMENT

1. **Key Terms** Define **(a)** troposphere, **(b)** photosynthesis, **(c)** cloud, **(d)** ozone layer.

2. **Physical Processes** How was the earth's atmosphere formed?

3. **Natural Resources** How does carbon dioxide support life?

4. **Geographic Tools** How does the NASA satellite photograph display the growing problem of ozone holes?

5. **Critical Thinking Analyzing Processes** Study the diagram showing the oxygen cycle. **(a)** How would extensive deforestation affect the oxygen cycle? **(b)** Which part of the cycle can damage the ozone layer?

Heating Land and Water

In this lab you will model the difference in the heating of land and water when it is subjected to a source of radiation. You first will assemble simple tools. Then you will observe and record temperature data. Finally, you will explain the results of the experiment and how they relate to the moderating influence of water on air temperatures near Earth's surface.

Problem How do the heating of land and water compare?

Materials

- 2 250-mL beakers
- dry sand
- tap water
- ring stand
- light source
- 2 flat wooden sticks
- 2 thermometers
- graph paper
- 3 colored pencils

Skills Modeling, Observing, Measuring, Analyzing Data

Procedure

Part A: Preparing for the Experiment

1. On a separate sheet of paper, copy the data table shown.

2. Pour 200 mL of dry sand into one of the beakers. Pour 200 mL of water into the other beaker.

	Land and Water Heating Data Table										
	Starting Temperature	1 min	2 min	3 min	4 min	5 min	6 min	7 min	8 min	9 min	10 min
Water											
Dry sand											
Damp sand											

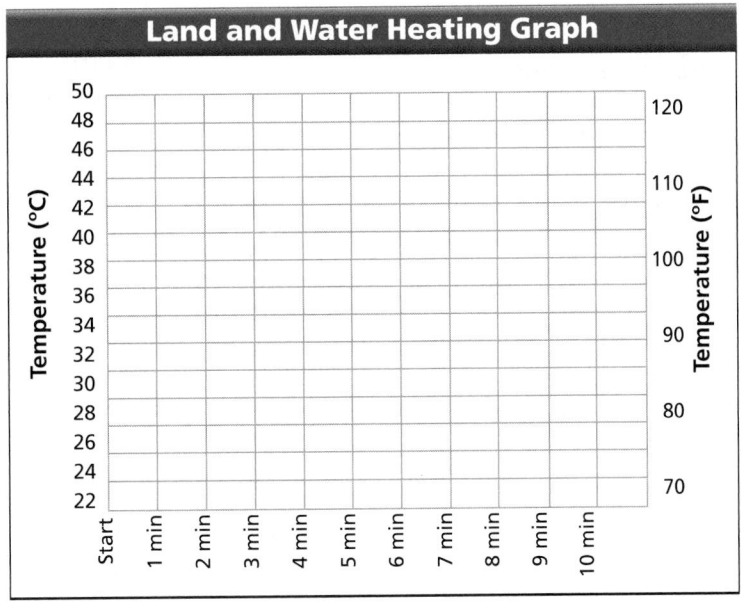

Land and Water Heating Graph

3. Hang a light source from a ring stand so that it is about 5 inches above the beaker of sand and the beaker of water. The light should be situated so that it is at the same height above both beakers.

4. Using the wooden sticks, suspend a thermometer in each beaker. The thermometer bulbs should be just barely below the surfaces of the sand and the water.

5. Record the starting temperatures for both the dry sand and the water in the data table.

Part B: Heating the Beakers

CAUTION *Do not touch the light source or the beakers without using thermal mitts.*

6. Turn on the light. Observe and record the temperatures in the data table at one-minute intervals for 10 minutes.

7. Turn off the light for several minutes. Dampen the sand with water and record the starting temperature for damp sand. Repeat step 6 for the damp sand.

Analyze and Conclude

1. **Using Tables and Graphs** Copy the sample land and water heating graph sheet onto a separate piece of graph paper. Use the data you collected to plot the temperatures for the water, dry sand, and damp sand. Use a different color line to connect the points for each material.

2. **Comparing and Contrasting** How does the changing temperature differ for dry sand and water when they are exposed to equal amounts of radiation?

3. **Comparing and Contrasting** How does the changing temperature differ for dry sand and damp sand when they are exposed to equal amounts of radiation?

4. **Applying** Locate Eureka, California, and Lafayette, Indiana, on a map. Infer which city would show the greatest annual temperature range. Explain your answer.

17.1 Atmosphere Characteristics

🔑 Key Concepts

- Weather is constantly changing, and it refers to the state of the atmosphere at any given time or place. Climate is the sum of all statistical weather information that helps describe a place or region.

- Water vapor is the source of all clouds and precipitation. Like carbon dioxide, it absorbs heat given off by Earth as well as some solar energy.

- If ozone did not filter most UV radiation, Earth would be uninhabitable for many living organisms.

- The atmosphere thins as you travel away from Earth, until there are too few gas molecules to detect.

- The atmosphere can be divided vertically into four layers based on temperature.

- Seasonal changes occur because Earth's position relative to the sun continually changes as it travels along its orbit.

Vocabulary

ozone, *p. 478;* troposphere, *p. 480;* stratosphere, *p. 480;* mesosphere, *p. 480;* thermosphere, *p. 480;* summer solstice, *p. 482;* winter solstice, *p. 482;* autumnal equinox, *p. 482;* spring equinox, *p. 482*

17.2 Heating the Atmosphere

🔑 Key Concepts

- Heat is the transfer of energy between two objects resulting from differences in their temperatures. Temperature is a measure of the average kinetic energy of individual particles.

- Three mechanisms of heat transfer are conduction, convection, and radiation. Unlike conduction and convection, radiant energy can travel through the vacuum of space.

- All objects, at any temperature, emit radiant energy. Hotter objects radiate more total energy per unit area than colder objects do. The hottest radiating bodies produce the shortest wavelengths of maximum radiation. Objects that are good absorbers of radiation are good emitters as well.

- Objects can absorb, transmit, scatter, or reflect radiation that strikes them.

Vocabulary

heat, *p. 483;* temperature, *p. 483;* conduction, *p. 483;* convection, *p. 484;* radiation, *p. 485;* reflection, *p. 486;* scattering, *p. 486;* greenhouse effect, *p. 487*

17.3 Temperature Controls

🔑 Key Concepts

- Factors other than latitude that exert a strong influence on temperature include heating of land and water, altitude, geographic position, cloud cover, and ocean currents.

- Land heats more rapidly and to higher temperatures than water. Land also cools more rapidly and to lower temperatures than water.

Vocabulary

albedo, *p. 492;* isotherm, *p. 492*

Thinking Visually

Concept Map Copy the concept map below onto a sheet of paper. Use information from the chapter to complete the concept map.

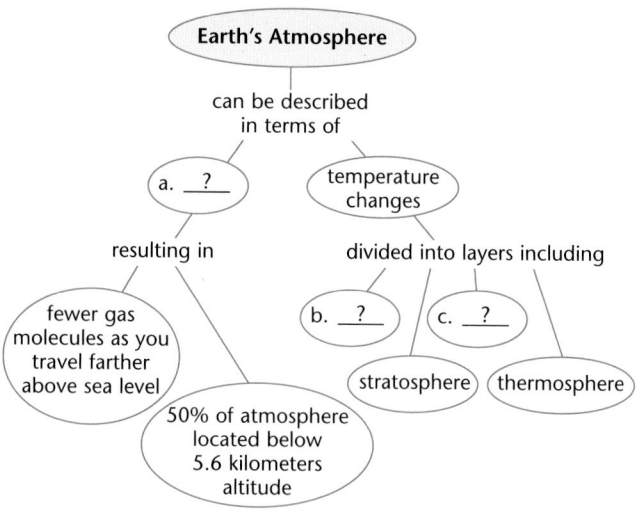

Reviewing Content

Choose the letter that best answers the question or completes the statement.

1. What is a description of atmospheric conditions over a long period of time?
   - **a.** climate
   - **b.** meteorology
   - **c.** precipitation
   - **d.** weather

2. The bottom layer of the atmosphere in which we live is called the
   - **a.** mesosphere.
   - **b.** stratosphere.
   - **c.** thermosphere.
   - **d.** troposphere.

3. Which form of radiation has the longest wavelength?
   - **a.** blue light
   - **b.** infrared
   - **c.** radio waves
   - **d.** ultraviolet

4. This layer of atmosphere contains ozone that filters UV radiation.
   - **a.** mesosphere
   - **b.** stratosphere
   - **c.** thermosphere
   - **d.** troposphere

5. The average kinetic energy of all the atoms and molecules that make up a substance is referred to as
   - **a.** radiation.
   - **b.** greenhouse effect.
   - **c.** temperature.
   - **d.** heat.

6. The two principle absorbers of radiation emitted by Earth's surface are carbon dioxide and
   - **a.** nitrogen.
   - **b.** oxygen.
   - **c.** ozone.
   - **d.** water vapor.

7. On a map showing temperature distributions, what are the lines connecting points of equal temperature?
   - **a.** isobars
   - **b.** isotemps
   - **c.** isotherms
   - **d.** equigrads

8. Which gas is most abundant in clean, dry air?
   - **a.** argon
   - **b.** carbon dioxide
   - **c.** nitrogen
   - **d.** oxygen

9. Select the best description of air.
   - **a.** It is a compound.
   - **b.** It is an element.
   - **c.** It is a mixture.
   - **d.** It is mainly oxygen and carbon dioxide.

10. Earth's atmosphere is thought to have become enriched in which gas about 2.5 billion years ago?
    - **a.** argon
    - **b.** carbon dioxide
    - **c.** nitrogen
    - **d.** oxygen

Understanding Concepts

11. Why are temperature variations greater over dry land than they are over water?

12. Describe how the ozone in the stratosphere forms.

13. Describe the three types of heat transfer in the atmosphere.

14. In what ways can geographic position be considered a temperature control?

15. Describe the two principle motions of Earth.

16. Explain why Earth's atmosphere is mainly heated from the ground up.

17. Describe the effects of cloud cover on air temperature.

18. Why do temperatures increase in the stratosphere?

19. What causes the position of the noon sun to vary by up to 47 degrees over a year's time?

Use the figure below to answer Question 20.

20. The illustration below shows two ways that radiation bounces off objects. Identify the process shown in each diagram. What clues in the illustration helped you identify these processes?

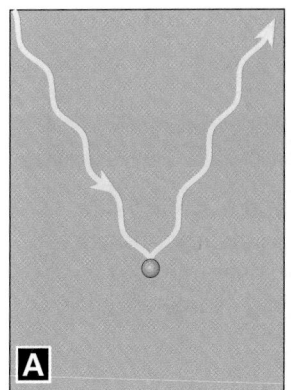
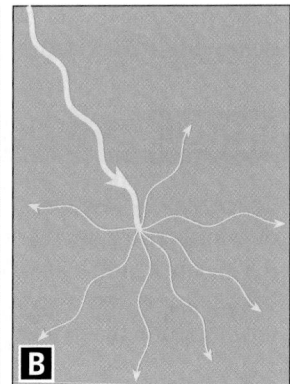

The Atmosphere: Structure and Temperature **499**

Critical Thinking

Use the table below to answer Questions 21 and 22.

Albedo of Various Surfaces	
Surface	**Percent Reflected**
Clouds, stratus	
<meters thick	25–63
150–300 meters thick	45–75
300–600 meters thick	59–84
Average of all types and thicknesses	50–55
Concrete	17–27
Crops, green	5–25
Forest, green	5–10
Meadows, green	5–25
Ploughed field, moist	14–17
Road, blacktop	5–10
Sand, white	30–60
Snow, fresh-fallen	80–90
Snow, old	45–70
Soil, dark	5–15
Soil, light (or desert)	25–30
Water	8*

*Typical albedo value for a water surface. The albedo of a water surface varies greatly depending upon the sun angle.

21. Analyzing Data Using the data in the table, determine which types of surfaces have the highest average albedos.

22. Applying Concepts Determine the date after which the length of daylight gets progressively longer going south from the equator. Use Figure 8 to explain your answer.

23. Inferring Give an example of how the Earth system might be affected if Earth's axis were perpendicular to the plane of its orbit instead of being tilted 23.5 degrees.

Math Skills

24. Calculating Assume that the average rate of temperature decrease in the troposphere is 6.5°C/km. Using this rate, determine the air temperature at a height of 2 kilometers if the temperature at sea level were 23°C.

Concepts in Action

25. Inferring Yakutsk is located in Siberia at about 60 degrees north latitude. This Russian city has one of the highest average annual temperature ranges in the world: 62.2°C. Explain the reasons for the very high annual temperature range.

26. Making Generalizations Speculate on the changes in global temperatures that might occur if Earth had substantially more land area and less ocean area than it does at present. How might such changes influence the biosphere?

27. Applying Concepts Why are carbon dioxide and water vapor such important components in Earth's atmosphere? What would happen to life forms on Earth if these gases were no longer present in the atmosphere?

28. Generalizing State the relationship between the temperature of a radiating body and the wavelengths of radiation that it emits.

29. Interpreting Illustrations Refer to Figure 20. What can you determine about temperatures in regions where isotherms are closely spaced, compared with regions where isotherms are farther apart?

30. Writing in Science Write a paragraph that describes two environmental settings where you would expect the albedo of surfaces to be high. Your scenarios can describe any reasonable area on Earth's surface. Be sure to include as much detail as possible in your paragraph.

Performance-Based Assessment

Designing an Experiment Design and conduct an experiment that models how variations in color of an object can affect the amount of radiation it absorbs. As a first step, write a clear hypothesis statement. Then plan the materials you will need to design the experiment. Have your teacher approve your plan before you begin.

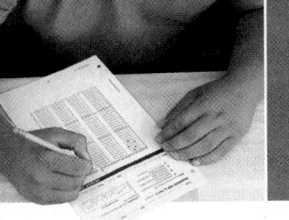

Standardized Test Prep

Choose the letter that best answers the question or completes the statement.

1. Which of these gases plays a more important role in weather processes than the others?
   (A) argon
   (B) carbon dioxide
   (C) nitrogen
   (D) oxygen

2. Practically all clouds and storms occur in this layer of the atmosphere.
   (A) mesosphere
   (B) stratosphere
   (C) thermosphere
   (D) troposphere

3. The primary wavelengths of radiation emitted by Earth's surface are
   (A) longer than those emitted by the sun.
   (B) shorter than those emitted by the sun.
   (C) about the same as those emitted by the sun.
   (D) about the same as UV radiation.

4. Which of the following is true about equinoxes?
   (A) They occur in June and December.
   (B) The sun's vertical rays are striking either the Tropic of Cancer or the Tropic of Capricorn.
   (C) Lengths of daylight and darkness are equal everywhere.
   (D) The length of daylight in the Arctic and Antarctic Circles is 24 hours.

Use the graph below to answer Questions 5 and 6.

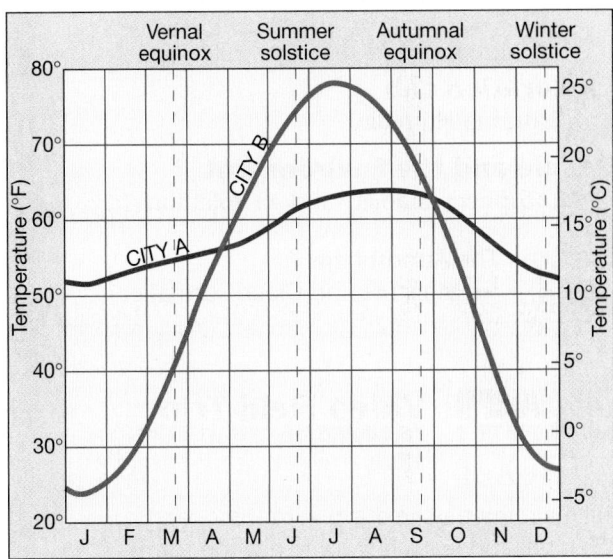

5. Determine the difference in December mean temperatures for cities A and B. Express your answer to the nearest degree C.

6. In which hemisphere are the cities located? Use information given in the graph to explain your answer.

CHAPTER 18 Moisture, Clouds, and Precipitation

CONCEPTS
— in Action —

Exploration Lab
Measuring Humidity

People and the Environment
Atmospheric Stability and Air Pollution

 **GEODe** The Atmosphere
↳ Moisture and Cloud Formation

DISCOVERY **Video Field Trip**
SCHOOL *Rain*

Take a rainy-day field trip with Discovery Channel and learn how precipitation forms. Answer the following questions after watching the video.

1. Why do cold fronts cause the heaviest rains?

2. The top of the Grand Canyon gets twenty times as much rain as the bottom. Why?

PHSchool.com

For: Chapter 18 Resources
Visit: PHSchool.com
Web Code: cjk-9999

Towering cumulonimbus cloud develops ▶ over San Carlos, Mexico.

Inquiry > Activity

What Causes Condensation?

Procedure

1. Fill a 250-mL beaker about one-third full of tap water. Gradually add ice to the beaker. Gently stir the water-ice mixture with a thermometer.

2. Be sure to keep the thermometer in the water-ice mixture. Record the temperature at the moment water begins to form on the outside surface of the beaker.

Think About It

1. **Observing** At what temperature did water first appear on the outside of the beaker?

2. **Inferring** Where did the water that formed on the beaker's outer surface come from?

3. **Applying Concepts** Describe a process in nature that results from condensation with a change in temperature.

18.1 Water in the Atmosphere

Reading Focus

Key Concepts

- Which gas is most important for understanding atmospheric processes?
- What happens during a change of state?
- How do warm and cold air compare in their ability to hold water vapor?
- What is relative humidity?
- What can change the relative humidity of air?

Vocabulary

- precipitation
- latent heat
- evaporation
- condensation
- sublimation
- deposition
- humidity
- saturated
- relative humidity
- dew point
- hygrometer

Reading Strategy

Monitoring Your Understanding Before you read, copy the table. List what you know about water in the atmosphere and what you would like to learn. After you read, list what you have learned.

What I Know	What I Would Like to Learn	What I Have Learned
a. ___?___	b. ___?___	c. ___?___
d. ___?___	e. ___?___	f. ___?___

As you observe day-to-day weather changes, you can see the powerful role of water in the air. Water vapor is the source of all condensation and **precipitation,** which is any form of water that falls from a cloud. Look at Figure 1. Clouds and fog, as well as rain, snow, sleet, and hail, are examples of some of the more noticeable weather conditions. When it comes to understanding atmospheric processes, water vapor is the most important gas in the atmosphere.

Water vapor makes up only a small fraction of the gases in the atmosphere, varying from nearly 0 to about 4 percent by volume. But the importance of water in the air greatly exceeds what these small percentages would indicate.

Water's Changes of State

The three states of matter are solid, liquid, and gas. Water can change from one state of matter to another—at temperatures and pressures experienced on Earth. This unique property allows water to freely leave the oceans as a gas and return again as a liquid, producing the water cycle. All water in the cycle must pass through the atmosphere as water vapor, even though the atmosphere only holds enough to make a global layer about 2 mm deep.

 Reading Checkpoint

What is the range in volume percent of water in the atmosphere?

Figure 1 This downpour shows how precipitation can affect daily activities.

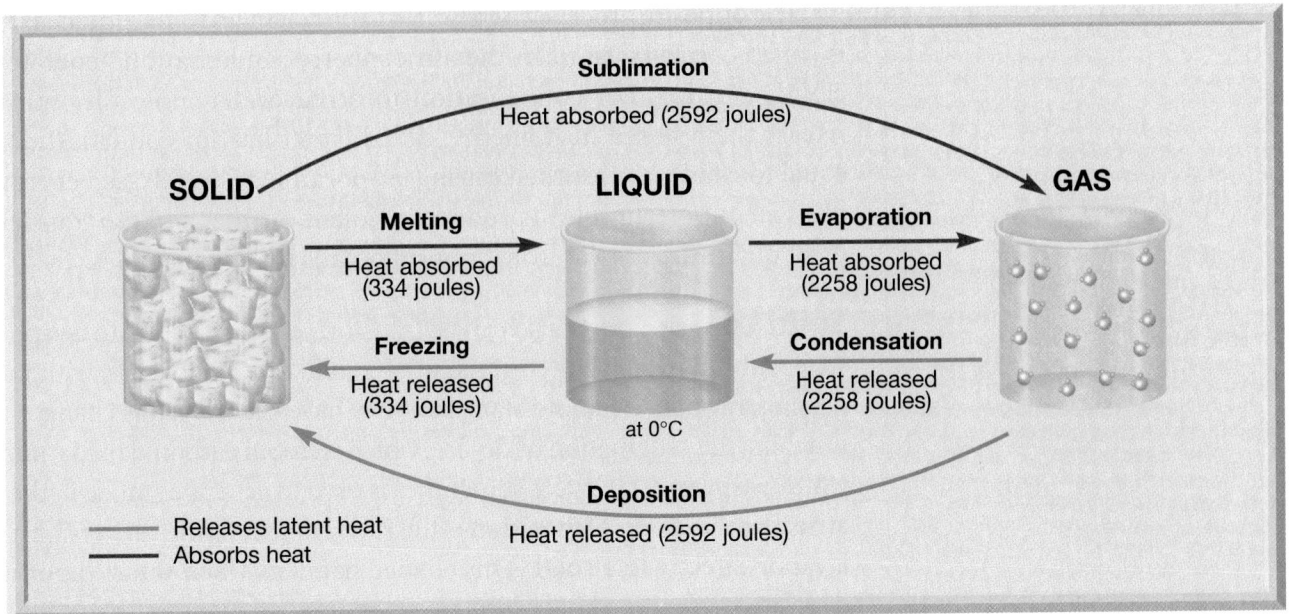

Figure 2 Changes of State The heat energy, in joules, is indicated for 1 gram of water.

Solid to Liquid 🔹 **The process of changing state requires that energy is transferred in the form of heat.** When heat is transferred to a glass of ice water, the temperature of the ice water remains a constant 0°C until all the ice has melted. If adding heat does not raise the temperature, then where does this energy go? In this case, the added heat breaks apart the crystal structure of the ice cubes. The bonds between water molecules in the ice crystals are broken forming the noncrystalline substance liquid water. You know this process as melting.

The heat used to melt ice does not produce a temperature change, so it is referred to as **latent heat.** *Latent* means "hidden," like the latent fingerprints hidden at a crime scene. This energy, measured in joules or calories, becomes stored in the liquid water and is not released as heat until the liquid returns to the solid state.

Latent heat plays a crucial role in many atmospheric processes. For example, the release of latent heat aids in forming the towering clouds often seen on warm summer days. It is the major source of energy for thunderstorms, tornadoes, and hurricanes.

Liquid to Gas The process of changing a liquid to a gas is called **evaporation.** You see in Figure 2 that it takes approximately 2258 joules of energy to convert 1 gram of liquid water to water vapor. The energy absorbed by the water molecules during evaporation gives them the motion needed to escape the surface of the liquid and become a gas. This energy is referred to as latent heat of vaporization.

You might have experienced a cooling effect when stepping dripping wet from a swimming pool or bathtub. This cooling results because it takes considerable energy to evaporate water. In this situation, the energy comes from your skin—hence the expression that "evaporation is a cooling process."

The opposite process where water vapor changes to the liquid state is called **condensation.** In the atmosphere, condensation generates clouds and fog. For condensation to occur, water molecules must release their stored heat energy, called latent heat of condensation, equal to what was absorbed during evaporation. This released energy plays an important role in producing violent weather and can transfer great quantities of heat from tropical oceans toward the poles.

Solid to Gas Water also can be transformed from a solid to a vapor state. **Sublimation** is the conversion of a solid directly to a gas, without passing through the liquid state. You may have observed this change in watching the sublimation of dry ice, which is frozen carbon dioxide, into white, wispy vapor. Dry ice sometimes is used to generate smoke in theatrical productions. **Deposition** is the reverse process, the conversion of a vapor directly to a solid. This change happens when water vapor is deposited as frost on cold objects such as grass or windows.

Humidity

The general term for the amount of water vapor in air is **humidity.** Meteorologists use several methods to express the water-vapor content of the air. These include relative humidity and dew-point temperature.

Table 1 Water Vapor Needed for Saturation		
Temperature		**Water Vapor Content at Saturation (g/kg)**
°C	**(°F)**	
−40	(−40)	0.1
−30	(−22)	0.3
−20	(−4)	0.75
−10	(14)	2
0	(32)	3.5
5	(41)	5
10	(50)	7
15	(59)	10
20	(68)	14
25	(77)	20
30	(86)	26.5
35	(95)	35
40	(104)	47

Saturation Imagine a closed jar half full of water and half full of dry air. As the water begins to evaporate from the water surface, a small increase in pressure can be detected in the air above. This increase is the result of the motion of the water-vapor molecules that were added to the air through evaporation. As more and more molecules escape from the water surface, the pressure in the air above increases steadily. This forces more and more water molecules to return to the liquid. Eventually, the number of vapor molecules returning to the surface will balance the number leaving. At that point, the air is said to be **saturated.** The amount of water vapor required for saturation depends on temperature as shown in Table 1. **When saturated, warm air contains more water vapor than saturated cold air.**

Relative Humidity The most familiar and most misunderstood term used to describe the moisture content of air is relative humidity. **Relative humidity is a ratio of the air's actual water-vapor content compared with the amount of water vapor air can hold at that temperature and pressure.** Relative humidity indicates how near the air is to saturation, rather than the actual quantity of water vapor in the air.

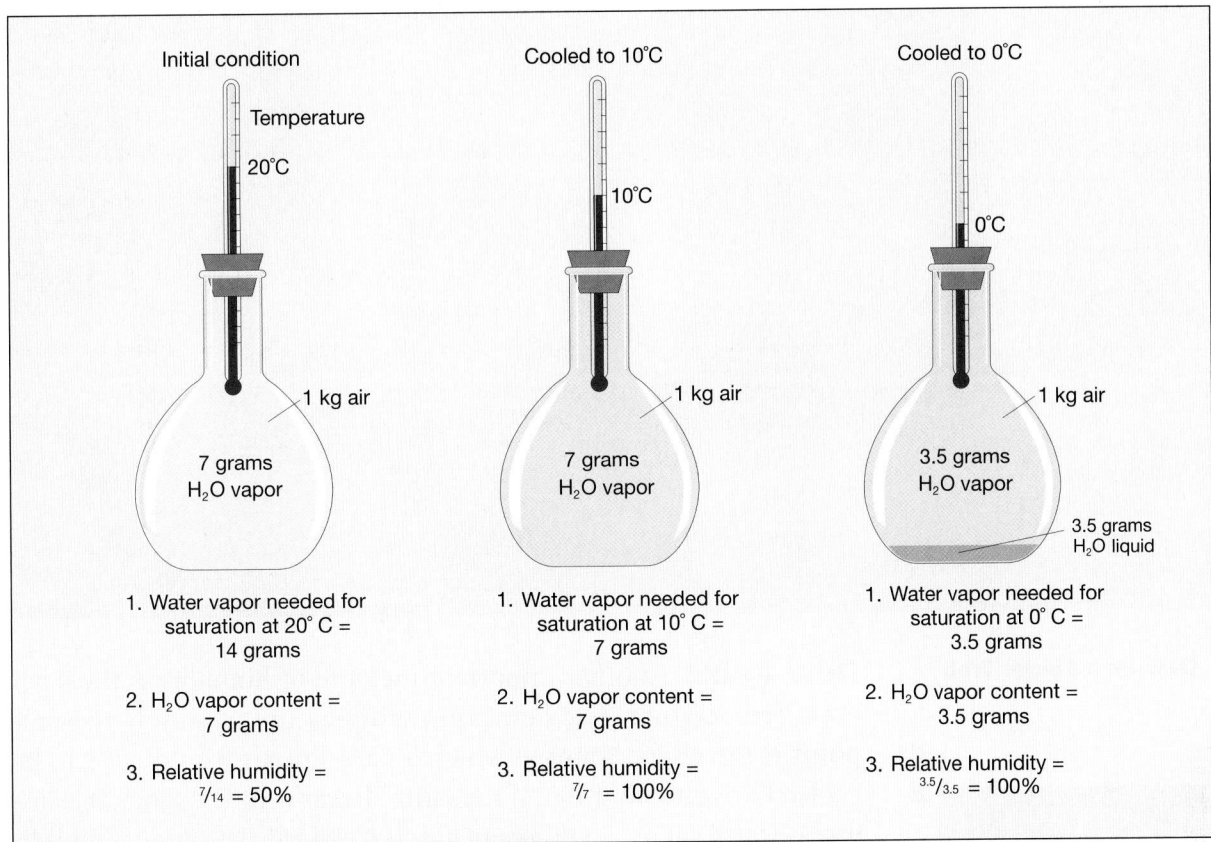

Initial condition

Temperature

20°C

1 kg air

7 grams
H₂O vapor

1. Water vapor needed for
   saturation at 20° C =
   14 grams

2. H₂O vapor content =
   7 grams

3. Relative humidity =
   $^7/_{14}$ = 50%

Cooled to 10°C

10°C

1 kg air

7 grams
H₂O vapor

1. Water vapor needed for
   saturation at 10° C =
   7 grams

2. H₂O vapor content =
   7 grams

3. Relative humidity =
   $^7/_7$ = 100%

Cooled to 0°C

0°C

1 kg air

3.5 grams
H₂O vapor

3.5 grams
H₂O liquid

1. Water vapor needed for
   saturation at 0° C =
   3.5 grams

2. H₂O vapor content =
   3.5 grams

3. Relative humidity =
   $^{3.5}/_{3.5}$ = 100%

Relative humidity can be changed in two ways. First, it can be changed by adding or removing water vapor. In nature, moisture is added to air mainly by evaporation from the oceans and smaller bodies of water.

Second, because the amount of moisture needed for saturation depends on temperature, relative humidity varies with temperature. Notice in Figure 3 that when the flask is cooled from 20°C to 10°C, the relative humidity increases from 50 to 100 percent. However, once the air is saturated, further cooling does not change the relative humidity. Further cooling causes condensation, which keeps the air at its saturation level for the temperature. When air far above Earth's surface is cooled below its saturation level, some of the water vapor condenses to form clouds. Because clouds are made of liquid droplets, this moisture is no longer part of the water-vapor content of the air. 🔑 **To summarize, when the water-vapor content of air remains constant, lowering air temperature causes an increase in relative humidity, and raising air temperature causes a decrease in relative humidity.**

Figure 3 Relative humidity varies with temperature.

Go Online

For: Links on atmospheric moisture
Visit: www.SciLinks.org
Web Code: cjn-6181

Figure 4 Dew on a Spider Web

Figure 5 Sling Psychrometer
This psychrometer is used to measure both relative humidity and dew point.
Interpreting Photographs
Identify the wet bulb and the dry bulb in this photograph.

Dew Point Another important measure of humidity is the dew-point temperature. The dew-point temperature or simply the **dew point** is the temperature to which a parcel of air would need to be cooled to reach saturation. If the same air was cooled further, the air's excess water vapor would condense, typically as dew, fog, or clouds. During evening hours, objects near the ground often cool below the dew-point temperature and become coated with water. This is known as dew, shown on the spider web in Figure 4.

For every 10°C increase in temperature, the amount of water vapor needed for saturation doubles. Therefore, relatively cold saturated air at 0°C contains about half the water vapor of saturated air at a temperature of 10°C, and roughly one-fourth that of hot saturated air with a temperature of 20°C as shown in Table 1 on page 506. Because the dew point is the temperature at which saturation occurs, high dew-point temperatures indicate moist air, and low dew-point temperatures indicate dry air.

Measuring Humidity Relative humidity is commonly measured by using a **hygrometer.** One type of hygrometer, called a psychrometer, consists of two identical thermometers mounted side by side. See Figure 5. One thermometer, the dry-bulb thermometer, gives the present air temperature. The other, called the wet-bulb thermometer, has a thin cloth wick tied around the end.

To use the psychrometer, the cloth wick is saturated with water and air is continuously passed over the wick. This is done either by swinging the instrument freely in the air or by fanning air past it. Water evaporates from the wick, and the heat absorbed by the evaporating water makes the temperature of the wet bulb drop. The loss of heat that was required to evaporate water from the wet bulb lowers the thermometer reading. This temperature is referred to as the wet-bulb temperature.

The amount of cooling that takes place is directly proportional to the dryness of the air. The drier the air, the more moisture evaporates, and the lower is the temperature of the wet bulb. The larger the difference is between temperatures observed on the thermometers, the lower the relative humidity. If the air is saturated, no evaporation will occur, and the two thermometers will have identical readings. To determine the precise relative humidity and to calculate the dew point, standard tables are used.

A sling psychrometer would not be all that useful in a weather balloon used to monitor conditions in the upper atmosphere. A different type of hygrometer is used in instrument packages that transmit data back to a station on the ground. The electric hygrometer contains an electrical conductor coated with a chemical that absorbs moisture. The passage of current varies with the amount of moisture absorbed.

Q *Why is the air in buildings so dry in the winter?*

A If the water-vapor content of air stays constant, an increase in temperature lowers the relative humidity, and a drop in temperature raises the relative humidity. During winter months, outside air is comparatively cold. When this air is drawn into a building, it is heated to room temperature. This causes the relative humidity to drop, often to uncomfortably low levels of 10 percent or lower. Living with dry air can mean static electrical shocks, dry skin, sinus headaches, or even nosebleeds.

Section 18.1 Assessment

Reviewing Concepts

1. What is the most important gas for understanding atmospheric processes?

2. What happens to heat during a change of state?

3. How does the temperature of air influence its ability to hold water?

4. What does relative humidity describe about air?

5. List two ways that relative humidity can be changed.

6. What does a low dew point indicate about the moisture content of air?

Critical Thinking

7. **Interpreting Illustrations** Study Figure 2. For 1 gram of water, how do the energy requirements for melting and evaporation compare?

Math Practice

8. The air over Fort Myers, Florida, has a dew point of 25°C. Fort Myers has twice the water vapor content of the air over St. Louis, Missouri, and four times the water vapor content as air over Tucson, Arizona. Determine the dew points for St. Louis and Tucson.

18.2 Cloud Formation

Reading Focus

Key Concepts

- What happens to air when it is compressed or allowed to expand?
- List four mechanisms that can cause air to rise.
- Contrast movements of stable and unstable air.
- What conditions in air favor condensation of water?

Vocabulary

- dry adiabatic rate
- wet adiabatic rate
- orographic lifting
- front
- temperature inversion
- condensation nuclei

Reading Strategy

Identifying Main Ideas Copy the table. As you read, write the main idea for each topic.

Topic	Main Idea
Adiabatic temperature changes	a. _____?_____
Stability measurements	b. _____?_____
Degrees of stability	c. _____?_____

Figure 6 Clouds form when air is cooled to its dew point.

Recall that condensation occurs when water vapor changes to a liquid. Condensation may form dew, fog, or clouds. Although these three forms are different, all require saturated air to develop. Saturation occurs either when enough water vapor is added to air or, more commonly, when air is cooled to its dew point.

Near Earth's surface, heat is quickly exchanged between the ground and the air above. During evening hours, the surface radiates heat away, causing the surface and adjacent air to cool rapidly. This radiational cooling causes the formation of dew and some types of fog. In contrast, clouds, like those shown in Figure 6, often form during the warmest part of the day. Clearly, some other process must cool air enough to generate clouds.

Air Compression and Expansion

If you have pumped up a bicycle tire, you might have noticed that the pump barrel became warm. The increase in temperature you felt resulted from the work you did on the air to compress it. When air is compressed, the motion of gas molecules increases and the air temperature rises. The opposite happens when air is allowed to escape from a bicycle tire. The air expands and cools. The expanding air pushes on the surrounding air and cools by an amount equal to the energy used up.

Adiabatic Temperature Changes Temperature changes that happen even though heat isn't added or subtracted are called *adiabatic temperature changes*. They result when air is compressed or allowed to expand. **When air is allowed to expand, it cools, and when it is compressed, it warms.**

Expansion and Cooling As you travel from Earth's surface upward through the atmosphere, the atmospheric pressure decreases. This happens because there are fewer and fewer gas molecules. Any time a volume of air moves upward, it passes through regions of successively lower pressure. As a result, the ascending air expands and cools. Unsaturated air cools at the constant rate of 10°C for every 1000 meters of ascent. In contrast, descending air encounters higher pressures, compresses, and is heated 10°C for every 1000 meters it moves downward. This rate of cooling or heating applies only to unsaturated air and is called the **dry adiabatic rate.**

If a parcel of air rises high enough, it will eventually cool to its dew point. Here the process of condensation begins. From this point on as the air rises, latent heat of condensation stored in the water vapor will be released. Although the air will continue to cool after condensation begins, the released latent heat works against the adiabatic cooling process. This slower rate of cooling caused by the addition of latent heat is called the **wet adiabatic rate.** Because the amount of latent heat released depends on the quantity of moisture present in the air, the wet adiabatic rate varies from 5–9°C per 1000 meters.

Figure 7 shows the role of adiabatic cooling in the formation of clouds. Note that from the surface up to the condensation level the air cools at the dry adiabatic rate. The wet adiabatic rate begins at the condensation level.

 **Reading Checkpoint** *What happens to heat stored in water vapor when it is cooled to its dew point?*

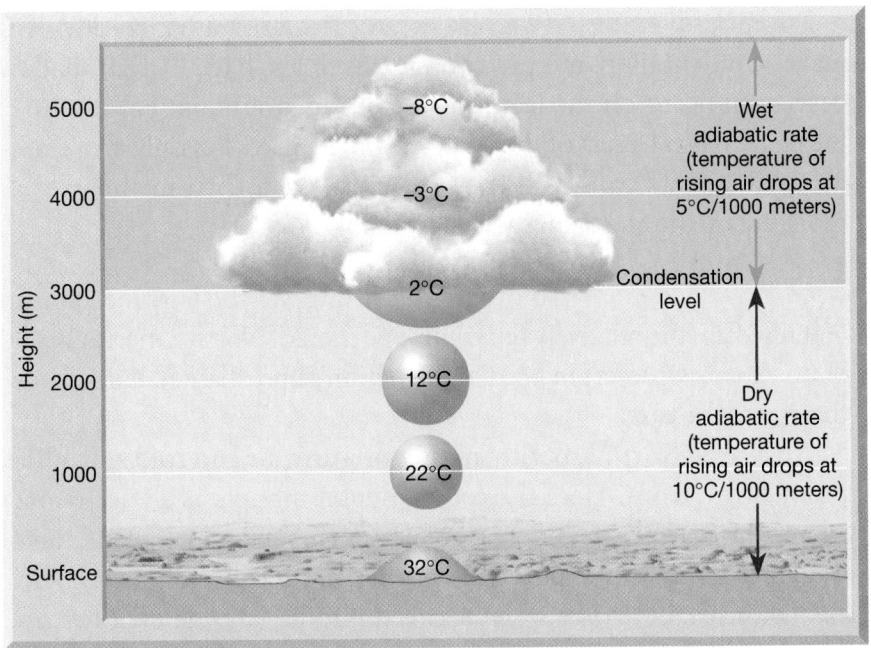

Figure 7 Cloud Formation by Adiabatic Cooling Rising air cools at the dry adiabatic rate of 10°C per 1000 meters, until the air reaches the dew point and condensation (cloud formation) begins. As air continues to rise, the latent heat released by condensation reduces the rate of cooling.
Interpreting Diagrams *Use this diagram to determine the approximate air temperature at 3500 m.*

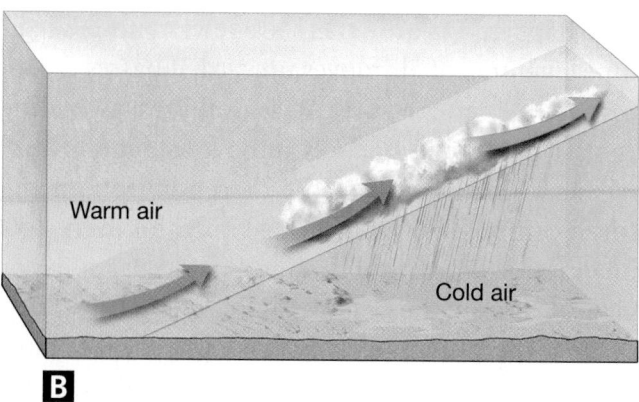

**Figure 8 A Orographic Lifting
B Frontal Wedging
Relating Cause and Effect** *Why
does the warm air mass move
upward over the cold air mass?*

Processes That Lift Air

In general, air resists vertical movement. Air located near the surface tends to stay near the surface. Air far above the surface tends to remain far above the surface. Some exceptions to this happen when conditions in the atmosphere make air buoyant enough to rise without the aid of outside forces. In other situations, clouds form because there is some mechanical process that forces air to rise. ⊙ **Four mechanisms that can cause air to rise are orographic lifting, frontal wedging, convergence, and localized convective lifting.**

Orographic Lifting When elevated terrains, such as mountains, act as barriers to air flow, **orographic lifting** of air occurs. Look at Figure 8A. As air goes up a mountain slope, adiabatic cooling often generates clouds and precipitation. Many of the rainiest places on Earth are located on these windward mountain slopes.

By the time air reaches the leeward side of a mountain, much of its moisture has been lost. If the air descends, it warms adiabatically. This makes condensation and precipitation even less likely. A rain shadow desert can occur on the leeward side of the mountain. For example, the Great Basin Desert of the western United States lies only a few hundred kilometers from the Pacific Ocean, cut off from the ocean's moisture by the Sierra Nevada Mountains.

Frontal Wedging If orographic lifting was the only mechanism that lifted air, the relatively flat central portion of North America would be an expansive desert instead of the nation's breadbasket. Fortunately, this is not the case.

In central North America, masses of warm air and cold air collide, producing a **front.** Here the cooler, denser air acts as a barrier over which the warmer, less dense air rises. This process, called frontal wedging, is shown in Figure 8B. Weather-producing fronts are associated with specific storm systems called middle-latitude cyclones. You will study these in Chapter 20.

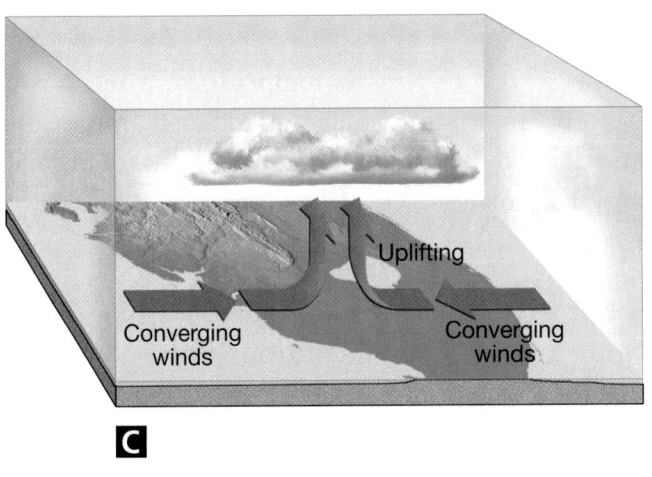

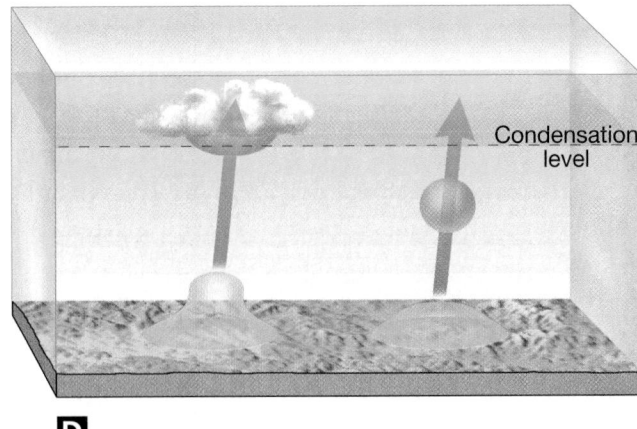

C

D

**Figure 8 C Convergence
D Localized Convective Lifting**

Convergence Recall that the collision of contrasting air masses forces air to rise. In a more general sense, whenever air in the lower atmosphere flows together, lifting results. This is called convergence. When air flows in from more than one direction, it must go somewhere. Because it cannot go down, it goes up, as shown in Figure 8C. This leads to adiabatic cooling and possibly cloud formation.

The Florida peninsula provides an example of how convergence can cause cloud development and precipitation. On warm days, the airflow is from the ocean to the land along both coasts of Florida. This leads to a pileup of air along the coasts and general convergence over the peninsula. This pattern of air movement and the uplift that results is helped along by intense solar heating of the land. The result is that the peninsula of Florida experiences the greatest number of mid-afternoon thunderstorms in the United States.

Localized Convective Lifting On warm summer days, unequal heating of Earth's surface may cause pockets of air to be warmed more than the surrounding air. For example, air above a paved parking lot will be warmed more than the air above an adjacent wooded park. Consequently, the parcel of air above the parking lot, which is warmer and less dense than the surrounding air, will move upward, as shown in Figure 8D. These rising parcels of warmer air are called thermals. The process that produces rising thermals is localized convective lifting. Birds such as hawks and eagles use these thermals to carry them to great heights where they can gaze down on unsuspecting prey. People have learned to use these warm parcels effectively for hang gliding. When warm parcels of air rise above the condensation level, clouds form. These clouds may produce mid-afternoon rain showers.

 *What are thermals?*

Stability

If a volume of air was forced to rise, its temperature would drop because of expansion. If this volume of air was cooler than the surrounding environment, it would be denser, and if allowed to do so, it would sink to its original position. Air of this type, called stable air, resists vertical movement.

Density Differences If this imaginary volume of rising air was warmer and therefore less dense than the surrounding air, it would continue to rise until it reached an altitude where its temperature equaled that of its surroundings. This is exactly how a hot-air balloon works. The balloon rises as long as it is warmer and less dense than the surrounding air, as shown in Figure 9. This type of air is classified as unstable air. **Stable air tends to remain in its original position, while unstable air tends to rise.**

Stability Measurements Air stability is determined by measuring the temperature of the atmosphere at various heights. The rate of change of air temperature with height is called the environmental lapse rate. This rate is determined from observations made by aircraft and by radiosondes. A radiosonde is an instrument designed to collect weather data high in the atmosphere. Radiosondes are often carried into the air by balloons. It is important not to confuse the environmental lapse rate with adiabatic temperature changes.

Figure 9 Hot-air balloons will rise as long as the air inside them is warmer than the air in the atmosphere surrounding them.

Degrees of Stability Air is stable when the temperature decreases gradually with increasing altitude. The most stable conditions happen when air temperature actually increases with height, called a **temperature inversion.** Temperature inversions frequently happen on clear nights as a result of radiation cooling off Earth's surface. The inversion is created because the ground and the air immediately above the ground will cool more rapidly than air higher above the ground. Under these conditions, there is very little vertical air movement. In contrast, air is considered unstable when the air close to the surface of Earth is significantly warmer than the air higher above the surface, indicating a large environmental lapse rate. Under these conditions, the air actually turns over, as the warm air below rises and is displaced by the colder air higher above the ground.

Stability and Daily Weather Recall that stable air resists vertical movement and that unstable air rises freely. But how do these facts apply to the daily weather?

Because stable air resists upward movement, you might conclude that clouds won't form when stable conditions are present in the atmosphere. Although this seems reasonable, remember that there are processes that force air above Earth's surface. These include orographic lifting, frontal wedging, and convergence. When stable air is forced above Earth's surface, the clouds that form are widespread and have little vertical thickness when compared to their horizontal dimension. Precipitation, if any, is light to moderate.

In contrast, clouds associated with the lifting of unstable air are towering and often generate thunderstorms and occasionally even a tornado. For this reason, on a dreary, overcast day with light drizzle, stable air has been forced above Earth's surface. During a day when cauliflower-shaped clouds appear to be growing as if bubbles of hot air are surging upward, the air moving up is unstable. Figure 10 shows cauliflower-shaped clouds caused by the rising of unstable air.

Figure 10 These clouds provide evidence of unstable conditions in the atmosphere.

 *What types of weather can result when stable air rises?*

Condensation

Recall that condensation happens when water vapor in the air changes to a liquid. This may be in the form of dew, fog, or clouds. ◖➤ **For any of these forms of condensation to occur, the air must be saturated.** Saturation occurs most commonly when air is cooled to its dew point, or less often when water vapor is added to the air.

Types of Surfaces Generally, there must be a surface for water vapor to condense on. When dew forms, objects at or near the ground, such as grass and car windows, serve this purpose. But when condensation occurs in the air above the ground, tiny bits of particulate matter, called **condensation nuclei,** serve as surfaces for water-vapor condensation. These nuclei are important because if they are absent, a relative humidity much above 100 percent is needed to produce clouds.

Condensation nuclei such as microscopic dust, smoke, and salt particles from the ocean are abundant in the lower atmosphere. Because of these plentiful particles, relative humidity rarely exceeds 100 percent. Some particles, such as ocean salt, are especially good nuclei because they absorb water. When condensation takes place, the initial growth rate of cloud droplets is rapid. It diminishes quickly because the excess water vapor is quickly absorbed by the numerous competing particles. This results in the formation of a cloud consisting of millions upon millions of tiny water droplets. These droplets are all so fine that they remain suspended in air. In the next section, you will examine types of clouds and the precipitation that forms from them.

Section 18.2 Assessment

Reviewing Concepts

1. ◖➤ Describe what happens to air temperature when work is done on the air to compress it.

2. ◖➤ What does stability mean in terms of air movement?

3. ◖➤ List four mechanisms that cause air to rise.

4. ◖➤ Describe conditions that cause condensation of liquid water in air.

5. What is a temperature inversion?

6. Which types of condensation nuclei are especially good for condensation to form?

Critical Thinking

7. **Hypothesizing** Study a world map. Hypothesize about other regions on Earth, other than the Florida peninsula, where convergence might cause cloud development and precipitation.

Connecting C Concepts

Air Temperature Review the description of atmospheric temperature changes in Section 17.1. Then write a paragraph explaining how these differ from adiabatic temperature changes in parcels of air.

18.3 Cloud Types and Precipitation

Reading Focus

Key Concepts

- How are clouds classified?
- How are clouds and fogs similar and different?
- What must happen in order for precipitation to form?
- What controls the type of precipitation that reaches Earth's surface?

Vocabulary

- cirrus
- cumulus
- stratus
- Bergeron process
- supercooled water
- supersaturated air
- collision-coalescence process

Reading Strategy

Building Vocabulary Copy the table. As you read, add definitions.

Vocabulary Term	Definition
Cirrus	a. _____?_____
Cumulus	b. _____?_____
Stratus	c. _____?_____
Coalescence	d. _____?_____

Clouds are among the most striking and noticeable effects of the atmosphere and its weather. Clouds are a form of condensation best described as visible mixtures of tiny droplets of water or tiny crystals of ice. Clouds are of interest to meteorologists because clouds show what is going on in the atmosphere. If you try to recognize different types of clouds, you might find it hard to do. But, if you learn the basic classification scheme for clouds, recognizing cloud types will be easy.

Figure 11 Cirrus Clouds

Types of Clouds

Clouds are classified on the basis of their form and height. The three basic forms are: cirrus, cumulus, and stratus. All other clouds reflect one of these three basic forms or are combinations or modifications of them.

Cirrus (*cirrus* = a curl of hair) clouds are high, white, and thin. They can occur as patches or as delicate veil-like sheets or extended wispy fibers that often have a feathery appearance. An example of cirrus clouds is shown in Figure 11.

Cumulus (*cumulus* = a pile) clouds consist of rounded individual cloud masses. Refer to Figure 10 on page 515. Normally, they have a flat base and the appearance of rising domes or towers. These clouds are frequently described as having a cauliflower structure.

Stratus (*stratum* = a layer) clouds are best described as sheets or layers that cover much or all of the sky. While there may be minor breaks, there are no distinct individual cloud units.

There are three levels of cloud heights: high, middle, and low, as shown in Figure 12. High clouds normally have bases above 6000 meters. Middle clouds generally occupy heights from 2000 to 6000 meters. Low clouds form below 2000 meters. The altitudes listed for each height category are not hard and fast. There is some seasonal and latitudinal variation. For example, at high latitudes or during cold winter months in the mid-latitudes, high clouds often are found at lower altitudes.

High Clouds Three cloud types make up the family of high clouds: cirrus, cirrostratus, and cirrocumulus. Look at Figure 12. Cirrocumulus clouds consist of fluffy masses, while cirrostratus clouds are flat layers. All high clouds are thin and white and are often made up of ice crystals. This is because of the low temperatures and small quantities of water vapor present at high altitudes. These clouds are not considered precipitation makers. However, when cirrus clouds are followed by cirrocumulus or cirrostratus clouds and increased sky coverage, they may warn of approaching stormy weather.

Middle Clouds Clouds that appear in the middle range, from about 2000 to 6000 meters, have the prefix *alto-* as part of their name. Altocumulus clouds are composed of rounded masses that differ from

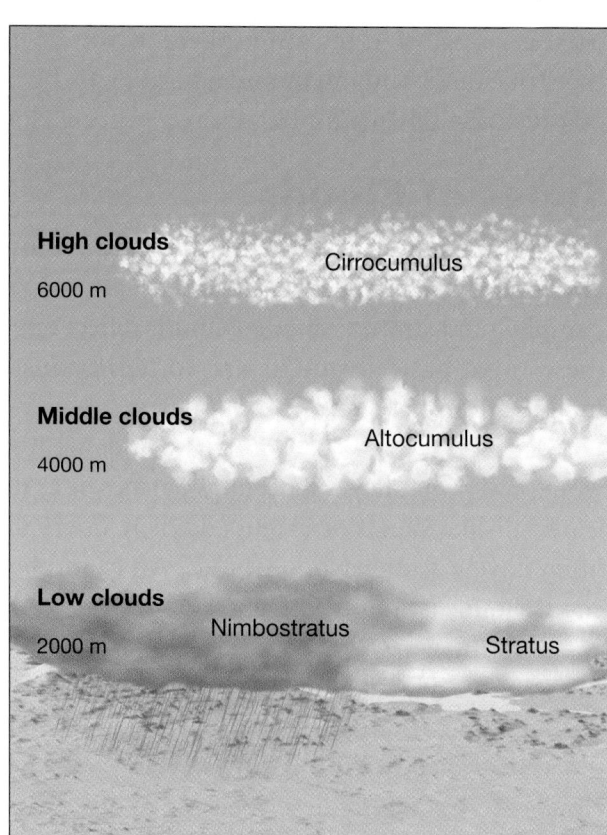

Figure 12 Cloud Classification
Clouds are classified according to form and height.
Interpreting Diagrams *Which cloud types are the chief precipitation makers?*

High clouds
6000 m
Cirrocumulus

Middle clouds
4000 m
Altocumulus

Low clouds
2000 m   Nimbostratus
Stratus

cirrocumulus clouds in that altocumulus clouds are larger and denser, as shown in Figure 12. Altostratus clouds create a uniform white to grayish sheet covering the sky with the sun or moon visible as a bright spot. Infrequent light snow or drizzle may accompany these clouds.

Low Clouds There are three members in the family of low clouds: stratus, stratocumulus, and nimbostratus. As illustrated in Figure 12, stratus clouds are a uniform, fog-like layer of clouds that frequently covers much of the sky. Occasionally, these clouds may produce light precipitation. When stratus clouds develop a scalloped bottom that appears as long parallel rolls or broken rounded patches, they are called stratocumulus clouds.

Nimbostratus clouds derive their name from the Latin word *nimbus,* which means "rainy cloud," and *stratus,* which means "to cover with a layer." As the name suggests, nimbostratus clouds are one of the main precipitation makers. Nimbostratus clouds form during stable conditions. You might not expect clouds to develop in stable air. But cloud growth of this type is common when air is forced upward, as occurs along a mountain range, a front, or where converging winds cause air to rise. Such a forced upward movement of stable air can result in a cloud layer that is largely horizontal compared to its depth.

 Reading Checkpoint **What does the Latin word stratus mean?**

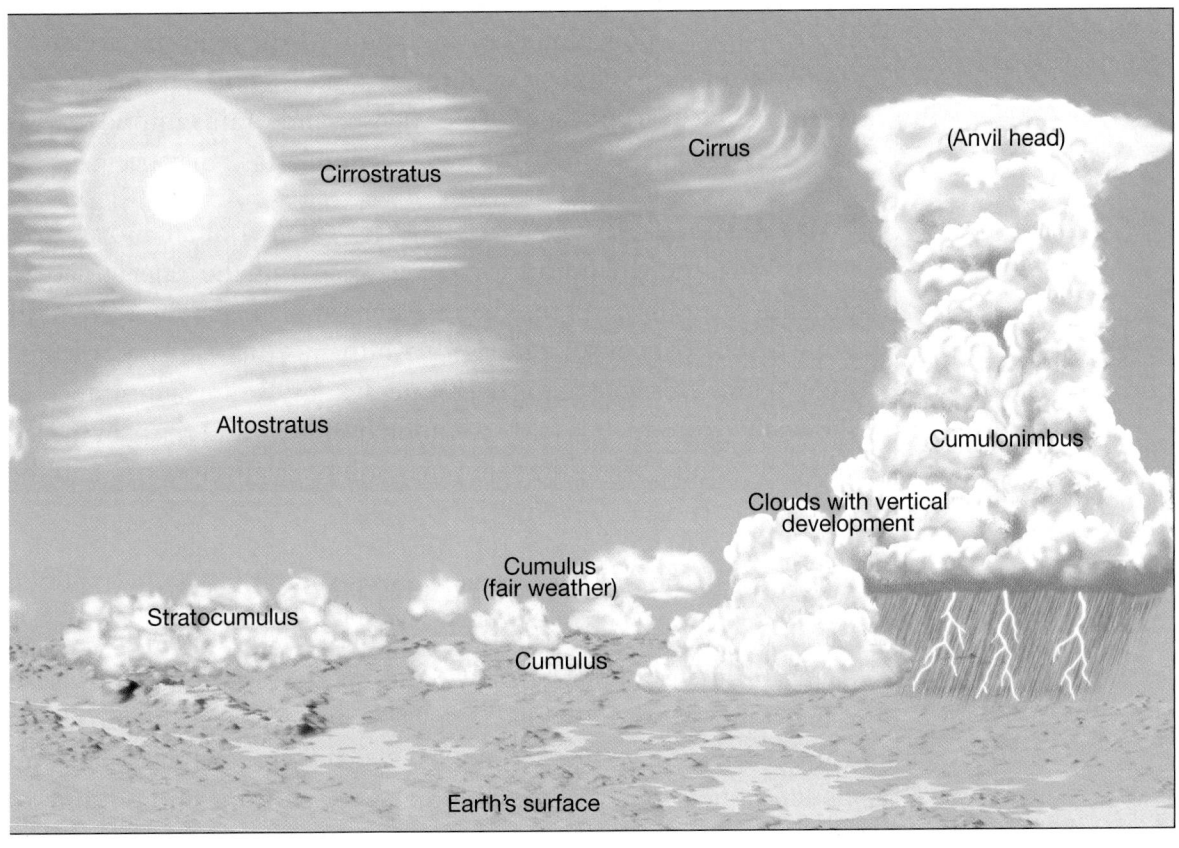

Figure 13 This steam fog rose from upper St. Regis Lake, Adirondack Mountains, New York.

Clouds of Vertical Development Some clouds do not fit into any one of the three height categories mentioned. Such clouds have their bases in the low height range but often extend upward into the middle or high altitudes. They all are related to one another and are associated with unstable air. Although cumulus clouds are often connected with fair weather, they may grow dramatically under the proper circumstances. Once upward movement is triggered, acceleration is powerful, and clouds with great vertical range form. The end result often is a cumulonimbus cloud that may produce rain showers or a thunderstorm.

Fog

Physically, there is no difference between a fog and a cloud. Their appearance and structure are the same. The difference is the method and place of formation. Clouds result when air rises and cools adiabatically. Most fogs are the result of radiation cooling or the movement of air over a cold surface. Fogs also can form when enough water vapor is added to the air to bring about saturation. **Fog is defined as a cloud with its base at or very near the ground.** When fog is dense, visibility may be only a few dozen meters or less, making travel not only difficult but often dangerous.

Fogs Caused by Cooling A blanket of fog is produced in some West Coast locations when warm, moist air from the Pacific Ocean moves over the cold California Current and then is carried onshore by prevailing winds. Fogs also can form on cool, clear, calm nights when Earth's surface cools rapidly by radiation. As the night progresses, a thin layer of air in contact with the ground is cooled below its dew point. As the air cools, it becomes denser and drains into low areas such as river valleys, where thick fog accumulations may occur.

Fogs Caused by Evaporation When cool air moves over warm water, enough moisture may evaporate from the water surface to produce saturation. As the rising water vapor meets the cold air, it immediately condenses and rises with the air that is being warmed from below. This type of fog over water has a steaming appearance, as shown in Figure 13. It is fairly common over lakes and rivers in the fall and early winter, when the water may still be relatively warm and the air is rather crisp.

How Precipitation Forms

Cloud droplets are very tiny, averaging less than 20 micrometers in diameter. Because of their small size, the rate at which cloud droplets fall is incredibly slow. Most cloud droplets would evaporate before falling a few meters into unsaturated air below. **For precipitation to form, cloud droplets must grow in volume by roughly one million times.**

Cold Cloud Precipitation

The **Bergeron process,** shown in Figure 14, relies on two physical processes: supercooling and supersaturation. Cloud droplets do not freeze at 0°C as expected. In fact, pure water suspended in air does not freeze until it reaches a temperature of nearly −40°C. Water in the liquid state below 0°C is said to be **supercooled.** Supercooled water will readily freeze if it impacts a solid object. Freezing nuclei are materials that have a crystal form that closely matches that of ice. Freezing nuclei can cause supercooled water to freeze.

When air is saturated (100% relative humidity) with respect to water, it is **supersaturated** with respect to ice (greater than 100% humidity). Ice crystals cannot coexist with water droplets in the air because the air "appears" supersaturated to the ice crystals. Any excess water vapor becomes ice that lowers the relative humidity near the surrounding droplets. Water droplets then evaporate to provide a continual source of water vapor for the growth of ice crystals.

Because the level of supersaturation with respect to ice can be quite high, the growth of ice crystals is rapid enough to produce crystals that are large enough to fall. As they fall the ice crystals contact cloud drops causing them to freeze. A chain reaction can occur and large crystals, called snowflakes form. When the surface temperature is above 4°C, snowflakes usually melt before they reach the ground. Even on a hot summer day, a heavy downpour may have started as a snowstorm high in the clouds.

Warm Cloud Precipitation

Much rainfall can be associated with clouds located well below the freezing level, especially in the tropics. In warm clouds, the mechanism that forms raindrops is the **collision-coalescence process.** Some water-absorbing particles, such as salt, can remove water vapor from the air at relative humidities less than 100 percent, forming drops that are quite large. As these large droplets move through the cloud, they collide and coalesce (join together) with smaller, slower droplets.

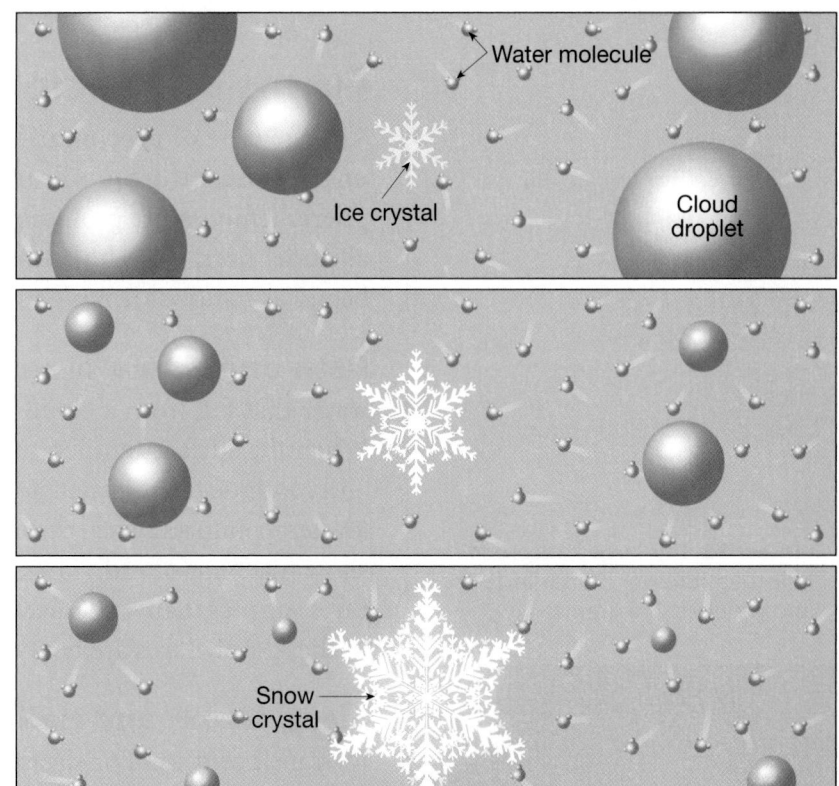

Figure 14 The Bergeron Process Ice crystals grow at the expense of cloud droplets until they are large enough to fall. The size of these particles has been greatly exaggerated.

For: Links on precipitation
Visit: www.SciLinks.org
Web Code: cjn-6184

Forms of Precipitation

The type of precipitation that reaches Earth's surface depends on the temperature profile in the lowest few kilometers of the atmosphere. Temperature profile is the way the air temperature changes with altitude. Even on a hot summer day, a heavy downpour may have begun as a snowstorm high in the clouds overhead.

Rain and Snow In meteorology, the term *rain* means drops of water that fall from a cloud and have a diameter of at least 0.5 mm. When the surface temperature is above 4°C, snowflakes usually melt and continue their descent as rain before they reach the ground. At very low temperatures (when the moisture content of air is small) light, fluffy snow made up of individual six-sided ice crystals forms. At temperatures warmer than −5°C, ice crystals join into larger clumps. Snowfalls of these snowflakes are heavy and have high moisture contents.

Sleet, Glaze, and Hail Sleet is the fall of small particles of clear-to-translucent ice. For sleet to form, a layer of air with temperatures above freezing must overlie a subfreezing layer near the ground. Glaze, also known as freezing rain, results when raindrops become supercooled (below 0°C) as they fall through subfreezing air near the ground and turn to ice when they impact objects.

Hail is produced in cumulonimbus clouds. Hailstones begin as small ice pellets that grow by collecting supercooled water droplets as they fall through a cloud. If the ice pellets encounter a strong updraft, they may be carried upward and begin the downward journey once more. Each trip through the supercooled portion of the cloud may be represented by another layer of ice, as shown in Figure 15.

Figure 15 This largest recorded hailstone fell over Kansas in 1970 and weighed 766 grams.

Section 18.3 Assessment

Reviewing Concepts

1. How are clouds classified?

2. Compare and contrast clouds and fogs.

3. What must happen in order for precipitation to form?

4. Describe how the temperature profile of air near Earth's surface controls the type of precipitation that falls to the ground.

Critical Thinking

5. **Predicting** What type of precipitation would fall to Earth's surface if a thick layer of air near the ground was −8°C?

6. **Classifying** Identify the following cloud types as producers of heavy, light, or generally no precipitation.

   a. cirrocumulus   b. cumulonimbus

   c. stratus   d. nimbostratus

Writing in Science

Compare-Contrast Paragraph Write a paragraph comparing the Bergeron and collision-coalescence processes. Relate each to the type(s) of precipitation that can result.

and the **ENVIRONMENT**

Atmospheric Stability and Air Pollution

Air quality is closely linked to the atmosphere's ability to scatter pollutants. Perhaps you've heard "Dilution is the solution to pollution." To a large degree, this is true. If the air into which pollution is released is not dispersed, the air will become more toxic. Two of the most important atmospheric conditions affecting the distribution of pollutants are wind strength and air stability.

When winds are weak or calm, the concentration of pollutants is higher than when winds are strong. High wind speeds mix polluted air into a larger volume of surrounding air, causing the pollution to be more diluted. When winds are light, there is less turbulence and mixing, so the concentration of pollutants is higher.

Atmospheric stability affects vertical movements of air. In general, the larger the extent of vertical mixing, the better the air quality is. During a temperature inversion, the atmosphere is very stable and it does not move much vertically. Warm air overlying cooler air acts as a lid and prevents upward movement, which leaves pollutants trapped near the ground, as shown in Figure 16.

Some inversions form near the ground, while others form higher above the ground. A surface inversion develops close to the ground on clear and relatively calm nights because the ground is a better radiator of heat than the air above it. Radiation from the ground to the clear night sky causes more rapid cooling at the surface than higher in the atmosphere. The result is that the air close to the ground is cooled more than the air above, yielding a temperature profile similar to the one shown in Figure 17. After sunrise, the ground is heated and the inversion disappears.

Although surface inversions usually are shallow, they may be thick in regions where the land surface is uneven. Because cold air is denser than warm air, the chilled air near the surface gradually drains from slopes into adjacent lowlands and valleys. As might be expected, these thicker surface inversions will not spread out as quickly after sunrise.

Figure 16 Air Pollution in Downtown Los Angeles Temperatures inversions act as lids to trap pollutants below.

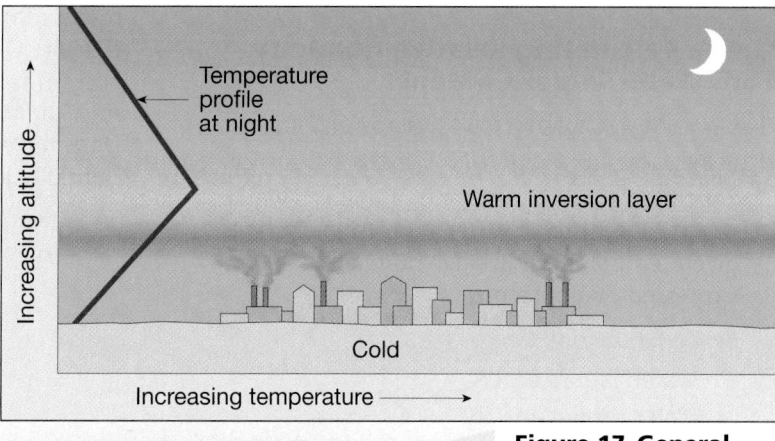

Figure 17 General Temperature Profile for a Surface Inversion

Measuring Humidity

Relative humidity is a measurement used to describe water vapor in the air. In general, it expresses how close the air is to saturation. In this lab, you will use a psychrometer and a data table to determine the relative humidity of air.

Problem How can relative humidity be determined?

Materials
- calculator
- water at room temperature
- psychrometer

Alternative materials for psychrometer:
- 2 thermometers
- cotton gauze
- paper fan
- string

Skills Observing, Measuring, Analyzing Data, Calculating

Procedure

Part A: Calculating Relative Humidity From Water Vapor Content

1. On a sheet of paper, make a copy of Data Table 1.

2. Relative humidity is the ratio of the air's water vapor content to its water vapor capacity at a given temperature. Relative humidity is expressed as a percent.

Relative humidity (%) =

$$\frac{\text{Water vapor content}}{\text{Water vapor capacity}} \times 100$$

3. At 25°C, the water vapor capacity is 20 g/kg. Use this information to complete Data Table 1.

Part B: Determining Relative Humidity Using a Psychrometer

4. A psychrometer consists of two thermometers. The wet-bulb thermometer has a cloth wick that is wet with water and spun for about 1 minute. Relative humidity is determined by the difference in temperature reading between the dry-bulb temperature and the wet-bulb temperature, and using Data Table 2. For example, suppose a dry-bulb temperature is measured as 20°C, and a wet-bulb temperature is 14°C. Read the relative humidity from Data Table 2.

5. If a psychrometer is not available, construct a wet-bulb thermometer by tying a piece of cotton gauze around the end of a thermometer. Wet it with room-temperature water and fan it until the temperature stops changing.

6. Make wet-bulb and dry-bulb temperature measurements for air in your classroom and air outside. On a separate sheet of paper, make a copy of Data Table 3. Record your measurements. Use your measurements and Data Table 2 to determine the relative humidity inside and outside.

Data Table 1 Relative Humidity Determination Based on Water Vapor Content			
Air Temperature (°C)	Water Vapor Content (g/kg)	Water Vapor Capacity (g/kg)	Relative Humidity (%)
25	5	20	25
25	12		
25	18		

Data Table 2 Relative Humidity (percent)																						
Dry-bulb Temperature (°C)	Depression of Wet-bulb Temperature (Dry-bulb Temperature − Wet-bulb Temperature = Depression of the Wet Bulb)																					
	1	2	3	4	5	6	7	8	9	10	11	12	13	14	15	16	17	18	19	20	21	22
−20	28																					
−18	40																					
−16	48	0																				
−14	55	11																				
−12	61	23																				
−10	66	33	0																			
−8	71	41	13																			
−6	73	48	20	0																		
−4	77	54	43	11																		
−2	79	58	37	20	1																	
0	81	63	45	28	11																	
2	83	67	51	36	20	6																
4	85	70	56	42	27	14																
6	86	72	59	46	35	22	10	0														
8	87	74	62	51	39	28	17	6														
10	88	76	65	54	43	33	24	13	4													
12	88	78	67	57	48	38	28	19	10	2												
14	89	79	69	60	50	41	33	25	16	8	1											
16	90	80	71	62	54	45	37	29	21	14	7	1										
18	91	81	72	64	56	48	40	33	26	19	12	6	0									
20	91	82	74	66	58	51	44	36	30	23	17	11	5	0								
22	92	83	75	68	60	53	46	40	33	27	21	15	10	4	0							
24	92	84	76	69	62	55	49	42	36	30	25	20	14	9	4	0						
26	92	85	77	70	64	57	51	45	39	34	28	23	18	13	9	5						
28	93	86	78	71	65	59	53	47	42	36	31	26	21	17	12	8	2					
30	93	86	79	72	66	61	55	49	44	39	34	29	25	20	16	12	8	4				
32	93	86	80	73	68	62	56	51	46	41	36	32	27	22	19	14	11	8	4			
34	93	86	81	74	69	63	58	52	48	43	38	34	30	26	22	18	14	11	8	5		
36	94	87	81	75	69	64	59	54	50	44	40	36	32	28	24	21	17	13	10	7	4	
38	94	87	82	76	70	66	60	55	51	46	42	38	34	30	26	23	20	16	13	10	7	5
40	94	89	82	76	71	67	61	57	52	48	44	40	36	33	29	25	22	19	16	13	10	7

Relative Humidity Values

Data Table 3 Relative Humidity Determinations Using Dry- and Wet-Bulb Thermometers		
	Inside	Outside
Dry-bulb temperature (°C)		
Wet-bulb temperature (°C)		
Difference between dry-bulb and wet-bulb temperatures (°C)		
Relative humidity (%)		

Analyze and Conclude

1. **Comparing and Contrasting** How do the relative humidity measurements for inside and outside compare? Why are your determinations similar or different?

2. **Applying Concepts** Explain the principle behind using a psychrometer to determine relative humidity.

3. **Applying Concepts** Suppose you hear on the radio that the relative humidity is 90 percent on a winter day. Can you conclude that this air contains more moisture than air on a summer day with a 40 percent relative humidity? Explain why or why not.

4. **Applying Concepts** Why is a cool basement often damp in the summer?

18.1 Water in the Atmosphere

Key Concepts

- Water vapor is the most important gas in the atmosphere for understanding atmospheric processes.
- The process of changing state requires that energy is transferred in the form of heat.
- When saturated, warm air contains more water vapor than cold air.
- Relative humidity is a ratio of the air's actual water-vapor content compared with the amount of water vapor needed for saturation at that temperature and pressure.
- When the water-vapor content of air remains constant, lowering air temperature causes an increase in relative humidity, and raising air temperature causes a decrease in relative humidity.

Vocabulary

precipitation, *p. 504;* latent heat, *p. 505;* evaporation, *p. 505;* condensation, *p. 506;* sublimation, *p. 506;* deposition, *p. 506;* humidity, *p. 506;* saturated, *p. 506;* relative humidity, *p. 506;* dew point, *p. 508;* hygrometer, *p. 508*

18.2 Cloud Formation

Key Concepts

- When air is allowed to expand, it cools, and when it is compressed, it warms.
- Four mechanisms that can cause air to rise are orographic lifting, frontal wedging, convergence, and localized convective lifting.
- Stable air tends to remain in its original position, while unstable air tends to rise.
- For condensation of water to occur, the air must be saturated.

Vocabulary

dry adiabatic rate, *p. 511;* wet adiabatic rate, *p. 511;* orographic lifting, *p. 512;* front, *p. 512;* temperature inversion, *p. 514;* condensation nuclei, *p. 516*

18.3 Cloud Types and Precipitation

Key Concepts

- Clouds are classified on the basis of their form and height.
- Fog is a cloud with its base at or very near the ground.
- In order for precipitation to form, cloud droplets must grow in volume by roughly one million times.
- The type of precipitation that reaches Earth's surface depends on the temperature profile in the lowest few kilometers of the atmosphere.

Vocabulary

cirrus, *p. 517;* cumulus, *p. 517;* stratus, *p. 518;* Bergeron process, *p. 521;* supercooled water, *p. 521;* supersaturated air, *p. 521;* collision-coalescence process, *p. 521*

Thinking Visually

Concept Map Copy the concept map below onto a sheet of paper. Use information from the chapter to complete the concept map.

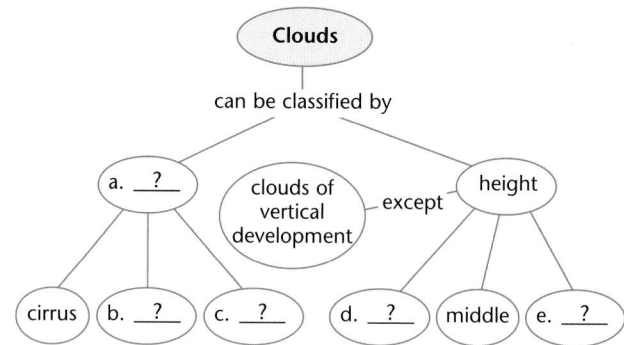

Reviewing Content

Choose the letter that best answers the question or completes the statement.

1. What is the general term for water vapor in air?
   a. capacity
   b. condensation
   c. humidity
   d. saturation

2. During which process does water vapor change to the liquid state?
   a. condensation
   b. deposition
   c. melting
   d. sublimation

3. The ratio of air's actual water-vapor content to the amount of water needed for saturation is the
   a. adiabatic rate.
   b. dew point.
   c. relative humidity.
   d. water capacity.

4. What are visible mixtures of tiny water droplets or ice crystals suspended in air?
   a. clouds
   b. dew
   c. hail
   d. sleet

5. Air that has a 100 percent relative humidity is said to be
   a. dry.
   b. saturated.
   c. stable.
   d. unstable.

6. Compared to clouds, fogs are
   a. a different composition.
   b. at lower altitudes.
   c. colder.
   d. thicker.

7. Which of the following clouds are high, white, and thin?
   a. cirrus
   b. cumulus
   c. nimbostratus
   d. stratus

8. Which of the following words means "rainy cloud"?
   a. cirrus
   b. cumulus
   c. nimbus
   d. stratus

9. Which of the following substances changes from one state of matter to another at temperatures and pressures experienced at Earth's surface?
   a. carbon dioxide
   b. nitrogen
   c. oxygen
   d. water

10. Which of the following forms when supercooled raindrops freeze on contact with solid objects near Earth's surface?
    a. glaze
    b. hail
    c. sleet
    d. snow

Understanding Concepts

11. What happens when unstable air is forced to rise?

12. Describe the conditions that might cause convergence.

13. As you drink an ice-cold beverage on a hot day, the outside of the glass becomes wet. Explain why this happens.

14. What is the difference between condensation and precipitation?

15. Why does air cool when it rises through the atmosphere? What is this type of cooling known as?

16. Write a general statement relating air temperature and the amount of water vapor needed to saturate the air.

17. Describe the difference between clouds and water vapor.

18. List two changes of state for water that cause latent heat to be released.

Use the figure below to answer Questions 19 and 20.

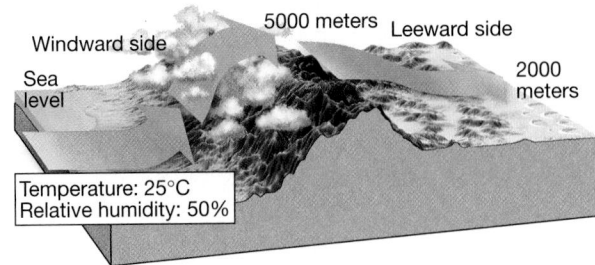

Windward side   5000 meters   Leeward side
Sea level   2000 meters

Temperature: 25°C
Relative humidity: 50%

19. Which air-lifting mechanism is shown?

20. Use the dry adiabatic rate of 10°C per kilometer to determine the air temperature on the windward side of the mountains at an altitude of 500 meters.

Critical Thinking

21. **Applying Concepts** What is the physical property of thermals that helps birds of prey? Describe how this physical property helps these birds.

22. **Applying Concepts** Explain how urban areas contribute to localized convective lifting.

23. **Identifying Cause and Effect** Describe how atmospheric stability affects daily weather. Include specific examples.

24. **Applying Concepts** In general, when traveling in foggy conditions, what types of topography should you be most cautious of?

Math Skills

Use the table below to answer Questions 25–27.

Water Vapor Needed for Saturation		
Temperature		Mass of water vapor per kg of air (g/kg)
°C	(°F)	
−40	(−40)	0.1
−30	(−22)	0.3
−20	(−4)	0.75
−10	(14)	2
0	(32)	3.5
5	(41)	5
10	(50)	7
15	(59)	10
20	(68)	14
25	(77)	20
30	(86)	26.5
35	(95)	35
40	(104)	47

25. **Analyzing Data** According to the table, how much water vapor is required to saturate a kilogram of air at each of the following temperatures?
    a. 40°C
    b. 0°C
    c. −10°C

26. **Calculating** How does the amount of water vapor required to saturate 1 kilogram of air change when it is cooled from 10°C to 0°C?

27. **Calculating** Use the table to determine the relative humidity of air at 15°C when its water vapor content is 7 g/kg.

Concepts in Action

28. **Inferring** Mount Waialeale, Hawaii, is located on a windward mountain slope. A weather station there records the highest average annual rainfall at 1234 cm. Explain what processes could contribute to this extreme rainfall.

29. **Interpreting Illustrations** After studying Figure 2, summarize the processes by which water changes from one state of matter to another. For each case, point out whether heat energy is absorbed or released.

30. **Writing in Science** The amount of precipitation that falls at any particular place and time is controlled by the quantity of moisture in the air and many other factors, which may include (1) an increase in the elevation of the land, (2) a decrease in the area covered by forests and other types of vegetation, and (3) an increase in the percentage of time that the winds blow from an adjacent body of water. Write a paragraph explaining how each of these factors might change the precipitation at a particular location.

Performance-Based Assessment

Designing an Experiment Design and conduct an experiment that explores daily variations in temperature and relative humidity. As a first step, write a clear hypothesis statement. Then plan and design the experiment. Include sample data tables in your plan. Have your teacher approve your plan before you begin.

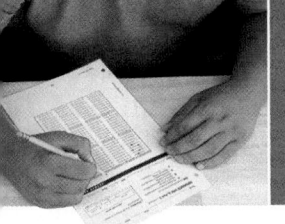

Standardized Test Prep

When answering a question with a graph, keep these tips in mind:

- Read the question thoroughly to identify what the question is asking.
- Study the title of the graph. This may help you identify what information is available from the graph.
- Examine the graph and note the axes labels.
- Identify the scale of the axes.
- Recall information, equations, definitions, relationship, and so forth that may be required to interpret the graph.
- Once you have chosen your answer, check it against the graph.

Graph 1 Temperature and Relative Humidity

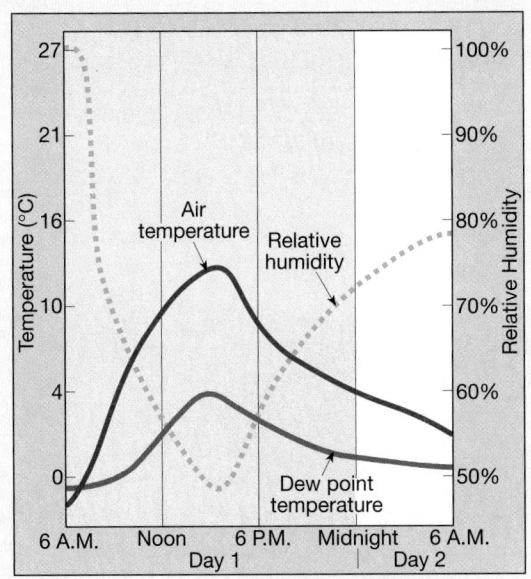

The graph above depicts variations in temperature and relative humidity on a spring day. Which of the following statements is true?

(A) When temperature increases, relative humidity increases.

(B) When temperature decreases, relative humidity decreases.

(C) When temperature increases, relative humidity decreases.

(D) Temperature and relative humidity are not related.

(Answer: C)

Choose the letter that best answers the question or completes the statement.

1. The dew point is the temperature at which
   (A) cumulus clouds change to cirrus clouds.
   (B) hailstones are formed.
   (C) liquid water changes to vapor.
   (D) water vapor condenses to liquid.

2. Which process is most important for cloud formation?
   (A) cooling by compression of air
   (B) cooling by contact with a cold surface
   (C) cooling by expansion of air
   (D) cooling by radiation from Earth's surface

3. The process by which water vapor changes directly to a solid is
   (A) condensation.
   (B) deposition
   (C) evaporation.
   (D) sublimation.

Use the graph below to answer Questions 4–5.

Graph 2 Temperature and Relative Humidity

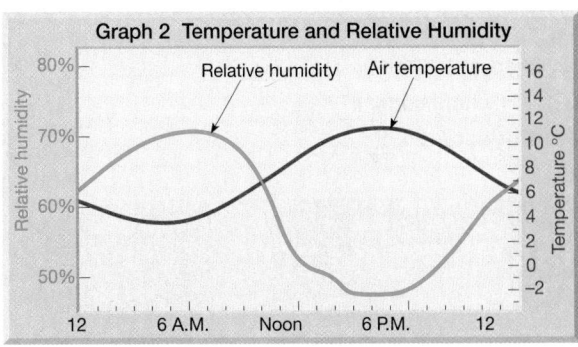

4. According to this graph, when is relative humidity at its maximum?

5. When does the lowest relative humidity occur?

CONCEPTS
— in Action —

Go Online
PHSchool.com

For: Chapter 19 Resources
Visit: PHSchool.com
Web Code: cjk-9999

Sailboats in this Norwegian fjord get their ▶
power from the wind.

Chapter Preview

Inquiry Activity

How Do Gradients Influence Speed?

Procedure

1. Build a steep ramp using textbooks, wood blocks, or other items in your classroom. Roll a tennis ball down the ramp.

2. Now build another ramp. This ramp should have a slope, or gradient, that is much less steep. Keep the length of the ramp the same as in step 1.

3. Roll the tennis ball down the second ramp. Compare the speeds of the ball for both ramps.

Think About It

1. **Observing** Which ramp setup caused the ball to roll the fastest?

2. **Applying Concepts** Like the ramps you built, air pressure also forms gradients. Wind is air that flows down the "slopes" of air pressure gradients. What air pressure conditions do you think would favor faster wind speeds?

Reading Focus

Key Concepts

- Describe how air pressure is exerted on objects.
- What happens to the mercury column of a barometer when air pressure changes?
- What is the ultimate energy source for wind?
- How does the Coriolis effect influence free-moving objects?

Vocabulary

- air pressure
- barometer
- pressure gradient
- Coriolis effect
- jet stream

Reading Strategy

Identifying Main Ideas Copy the table below. As you read, write the main ideas for each topic.

Topic	Main Ideas
Air Pressure Defined	Air pressure is the weight of air above. It is exerted in all directions.
Measuring Air Pressure	a. _____?_____
Factors Affecting Wind	b. _____?_____

Figure 1 These palm trees in Corpus Christi, Texas, are buffeted by hurricane-force winds.

Of the various elements of weather and climate, changes in air pressure are the least noticeable. When you listen to a weather report, you probably focus on precipitation, temperature, and humidity. Most people don't wonder about air pressure. Although you might not perceive hour-to-hour and day-to-day variations in air pressure, they are very important in producing changes in our weather. For example, variations in air pressure from place to place can generate winds like those shown in Figure 1. The winds, in turn, bring change in temperature and humidity. Air pressure is one of the basic weather elements and is an important factor in weather forecasting. Air pressure is closely tied to the other elements of weather in a cause-and-effect relationship.

Air Pressure Defined

Air pressure is simply the pressure exerted by the weight of air above. Average air pressure at sea level is about 1 kilogram per square centimeter. This pressure is roughly the same pressure that is produced by a column of water 10 meters in height. You can calculate that the air pressure exerted on the top of a 50-centimeter-by-100-centimeter school desk exceeds 5000 kilograms, which is about the mass of a 50-passenger school bus. Why doesn't the desk collapse under the weight of the air above it? Air pressure is exerted in all directions—down, up, and sideways. The air pressure pushing down on an object exactly balances the air pressure pushing up on the object.

Reading Checkpoint *What is average air pressure at sea level?*

Imagine a tall aquarium that has the same dimensions as the desktop in the previous example. When this aquarium is filled to a height of 10 meters, the water pressure at the bottom equals 1 atmosphere, or 1 kilogram per square centimeter. Now imagine what will happen if this aquarium is placed on top of a student desk so that all the force is directed downward. The desk collapses because the pressure downward is greater than the pressure exerted in the other directions. When the desk is placed inside the aquarium and allowed to sink to the bottom, however, the desk does not collapse in the water because the water pressure is exerted in all directions, not just downward. The desk, like your body, is built to withstand the pressure of 1 atmosphere.

Measuring Air Pressure

When meteorologists measure atmospheric pressure, they use a unit called the millibar. Standard sea-level pressure is 1013.2 millibars. You might have heard the phrase "inches of mercury," which is used by the media to describe atmospheric pressure. This expression dates from 1643, when Torricelli, a student of the famous Italian scientist Galileo, invented the mercury barometer. A **barometer** is a device used for measuring air pressure (*bar* = pressure, *metron* = measuring instrument).

Torricelli correctly described the atmosphere as a vast ocean of air that exerts pressure on us and all objects around us. To measure this force, he filled a glass tube, closed at one end, with mercury. He then put the tube upside down into a dish of mercury, as shown in Figure 2A. The mercury flowed out of the tube until the weight of the column was balanced by the pressure that the atmosphere exerted on the surface of the mercury in the dish. In other words, the weight of mercury in the column (tube) equaled the weight of the same size column of air that extended from the ground to the top of the atmosphere.

When air pressure increases, the mercury in the tube rises. When air pressure decreases, so does the height of the mercury column. With some improvements, the mercury barometer is still the standard instrument used today for measuring air pressure.

The need for a smaller and more portable instrument for measuring air pressure led to the development of the aneroid barometer. The aneroid barometer uses a metal chamber with some air removed. This partially emptied chamber is extremely sensitive to variations in air pressure. It changes shape and compresses as the air pressure increases, and it expands as the pressure decreases. One advantage of the aneroid barometer is that it can be easily connected to a recording device, shown in Figure 2B. The device provides a continuous record of pressure changes with the passage of time.

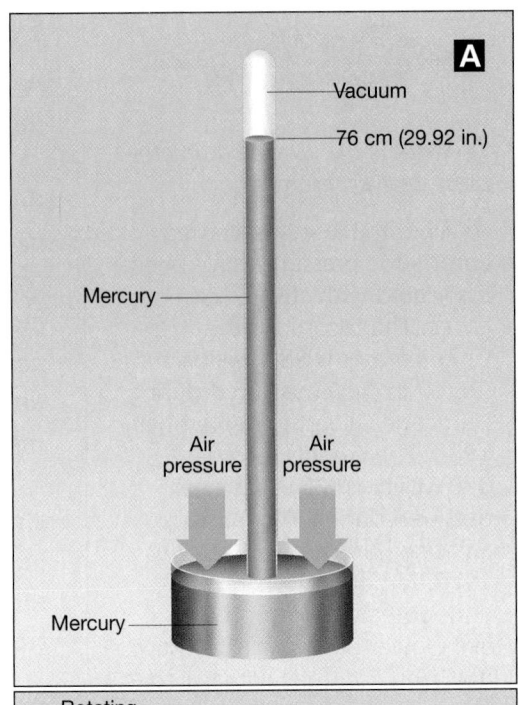

Vacuum

76 cm (29.92 in.)

Mercury

Air pressure   Air pressure

Mercury

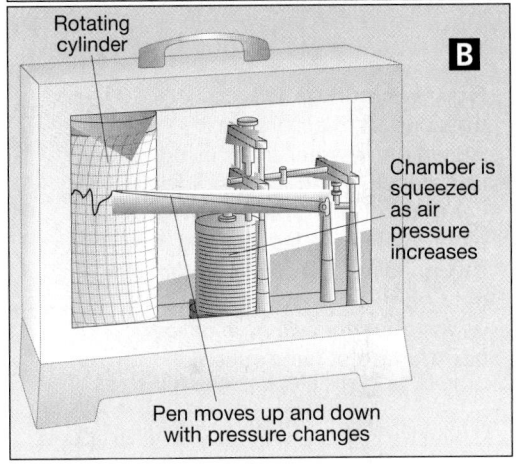

Rotating cylinder

Chamber is squeezed as air pressure increases

Pen moves up and down with pressure changes

Figure 2 A Mercury Barometer Standard atmospheric pressure at sea level is 29.92 inches of mercury. **B Aneroid Barometer** The recording mechanism provides a continuous record of pressure changes over time. **Applying Concepts** *Why would a continuous record help weather forecasters?*

Q *What is the lowest barometric pressure ever recorded?*

A All of the lowest recorded barometric pressures have been associated with strong hurricanes. The record for the United States is 888 millibars (26.20 inches) measured during Hurricane Gilbert in September 1988. The world's record, 870 millibars (25.70 inches), occurred during Typhoon Tip, a Pacific hurricane, in October 1979. Although tornadoes undoubtedly have produced even lower pressures, they have not been accurately measured.

Figure 3 Isobars The distribution of air pressure is shown on weather maps using isobar lines. Wind flags indicate wind speed and direction. Winds blow toward the station circles. **Interpreting Visuals** *Use the data on this map to explain which pressure cell, high or low, has the fastest wind speeds.*

Factors Affecting Wind

As important as vertical motion is, far more air moves horizontally, the phenomenon we call wind. What causes wind?

Wind is the result of horizontal differences in air pressure. Air flows from areas of higher pressure to areas of lower pressure. You may have experienced this flow of air when opening a vacuum-packed can of coffee or tennis balls. The noise you hear is caused by air rushing from the higher pressure outside the can to the lower pressure inside. Wind is nature's way of balancing such inequalities in air pressure. **The unequal heating of Earth's surface generates pressure differences. Solar radiation is the ultimate energy source for most wind.**

If Earth did not rotate, and if there were no friction between moving air and Earth's surface, air would flow in a straight line from areas of higher pressure to areas of lower pressure. But both factors do exist so the flow of air is not that simple. **Three factors combine to control wind: pressure differences, the Coriolis effect, and friction.**

Pressure Differences Wind is created from differences in pressure—the greater these differences are, the greater the wind speed is. Over Earth's surface, variations in air pressure are determined from barometric readings taken at hundreds of weather stations. These pressure data are shown on a weather map, like the one in Figure 3, using isobars. Isobars are lines on a map that connect places of equal air pressure. The spacing of isobars indicates the amount of pressure change occurring over a given distance. These pressure changes are expressed as the **pressure gradient.**

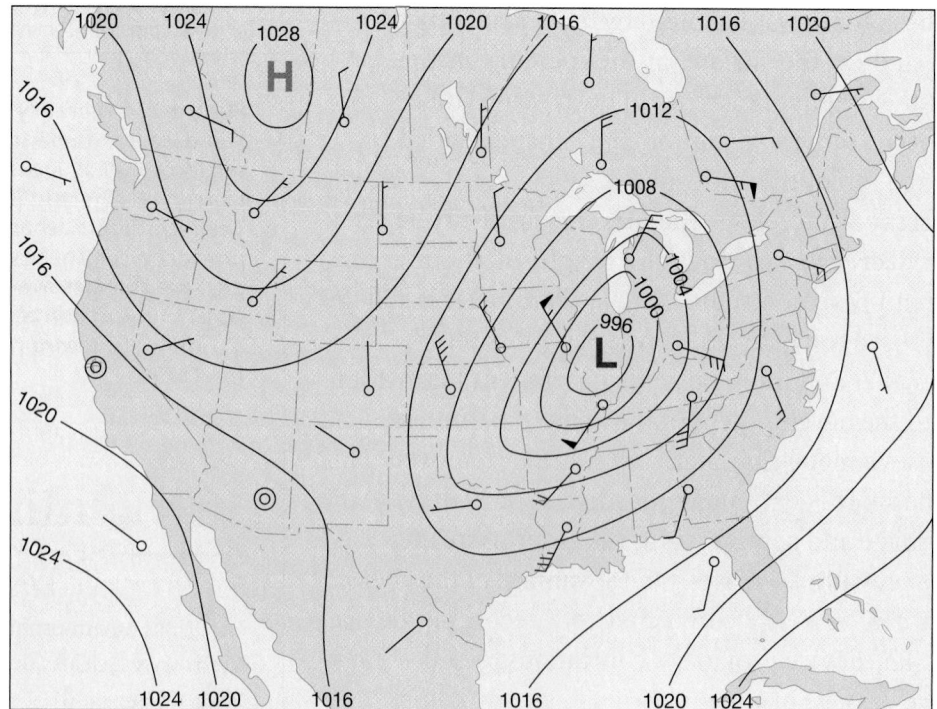

A steep pressure gradient, like a steep hill, causes greater acceleration of a parcel of air. A less steep pressure gradient causes a slower acceleration. **Closely spaced isobars indicate a steep pressure gradient and high winds. Widely spaced isobars indicate a weak pressure gradient and light winds.** The pressure gradient is the driving force of wind. The pressure gradient has both magnitude and direction. Its magnitude is reflected in the spacing of isobars. The direction of force is always from areas of higher pressure to areas of lower pressure and at right angles to the isobars. Friction affects wind speed and direction. The Coriolis effect affects wind direction only.

Coriolis Effect The weather map in Figure 3 shows typical air movements associated with high- and low-pressure systems. Air moves out of the regions of higher pressure and into the regions of lower pressure. However, the wind does not cross the isobars at right angles as you would expect based solely on the pressure gradient. This change in movement results from Earth's rotation and has been named the **Coriolis effect.**

The Coriolis effect describes how Earth's rotation affects moving objects. All free-moving objects or fluids, including the wind, are deflected to the right of their path of motion in the Northern Hemisphere. In the Southern Hemisphere, they are deflected to the left. The reason for this deflection is illustrated in Figure 4. Imagine the path of a rocket launched from the North Pole toward a target located on the equator. The true path of this rocket is straight, and the path would appear to be straight to someone out in space looking down at Earth. However, to someone standing on Earth, it would look as if the rocket swerved off its path and landed 15 degrees to the west of its target.

This slight change in direction happens because Earth would have rotated 15 degrees to the east under the rocket during a one-hour flight. The counterclockwise rotation of the Northern Hemisphere causes path deflection to the right. In the Southern Hemisphere, the clockwise rotation produces a similar deflection, but to the left of the path of motion.

The apparent shift in wind direction is attributed to the Coriolis effect. This deflection: 1) is always directed at right angles to the direction of airflow; 2) affects only wind direction and not wind speed; 3) is affected by wind speed—the stronger the wind, the greater the deflection; and 4) is strongest at the poles and weakens toward the equator, becoming nonexistent at the equator.

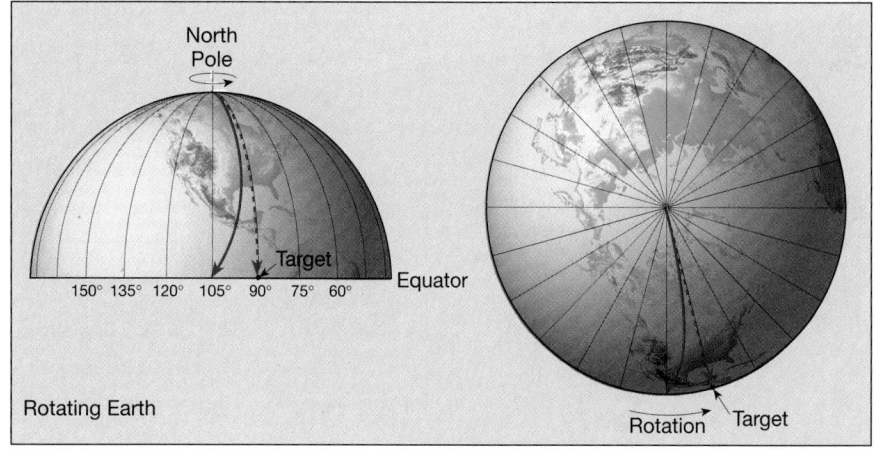

Figure 4 The Coriolis Effect
Because Earth rotates 15° each hour, the rocket's path is curved and veers to the right from the North Pole to the equator.
Calculating *How many degrees does Earth rotate in one day?*

A

B

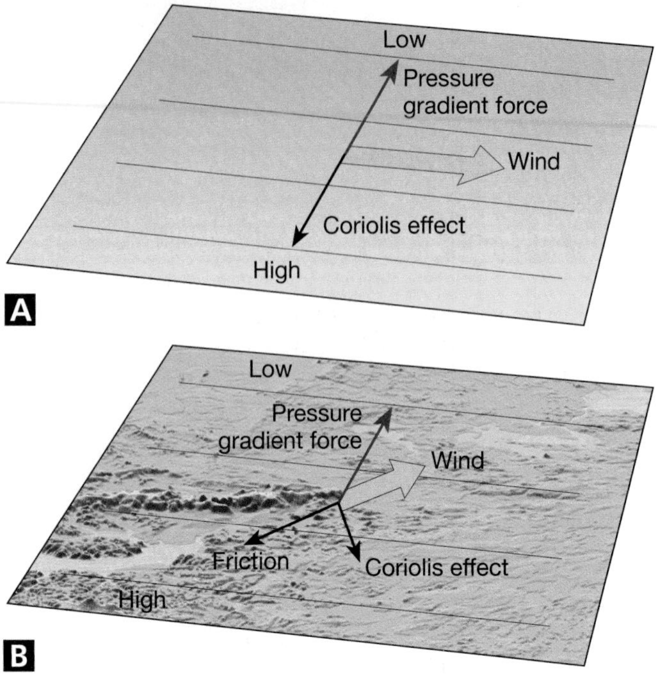

Figure 5 A Upper-level wind flow is balanced by the Coriolis effect and pressure gradient forces. **B** Friction causes surface winds to cross isobars and move toward lower pressure areas.

Friction The effect of friction on wind is important only within a few kilometers of Earth's surface. Friction acts to slow air movement, which changes wind direction. To illustrate friction's effect on wind direction, first think about a situation in which friction does not play a role in wind's direction.

When air is above the friction layer, the pressure gradient causes air to move across the isobars. As soon as air starts to move, the Coriolis effect acts at right angles to this motion. The faster the wind speed, the greater the deflection is. The pressure gradient and Coriolis effect balance in high-altitude air, and wind generally flows parallel to isobars, as shown in Figure 5A. The most prominent features of airflow high above the friction layer are the jet streams. **Jet streams** are fast-moving rivers of air that travel between 120 and 240 kilometers per hour in a west-to-east direction. One such jet stream is situated over the polar front, which is the zone separating the cool polar air from warm subtropical air. Jet streams originally were encountered by high-flying bombers during World War II.

For air close to Earth's surface, the roughness of the terrain determines the angle of airflow across the isobars. Over the smooth ocean surface, friction is low, and the angle of airflow is small. Over rugged terrain, where the friction is higher, winds move more slowly and cross the isobars at greater angles. As shown in Figure 5B, friction causes wind to flow across the isobars at angles as great as 45 degrees. Slower wind speeds caused by friction decrease the Coriolis effect.

Section 19.1 Assessment

Reviewing Concepts

1. Why don't objects such as a table collapse under the weight of air above them?

2. Suppose the height of a column in a mercury barometer is decreasing. What is happening?

3. What is the ultimate energy source for most wind?

4. How does the Coriolis effect influence motion of free-moving objects?

5. Why do jet streams flow parallel to isobars?

Critical Thinking

6. **Interpreting illustrations** Study Figures 5A and 5B. Why are the wind arrows drawn to different lengths in these figures?

Connecting Concepts

Solar Radiation Review section 17.3. Describe examples of unequal heating of Earth's atmosphere that could lead to air pressure differences that ultimately influence wind.

19.2 Pressure Centers and Winds

Reading Focus

Key Concepts

- Describe how winds blow around pressure centers in the Northern and Southern Hemispheres.

- What are the air pressure patterns within cyclones and anticyclones?

- How does friction control net flow of air around a cyclone and an anticylone?

- How does the atmosphere attempt to balance the unequal heating of Earth's surface?

Vocabulary

- cyclone
- anticyclone
- trade winds
- westerlies
- polar easterlies
- polar front
- monsoon

Reading Strategy

Comparing and Contrasting Copy the table below. As you read about pressure centers and winds, fill in the table indicating to which hemisphere the concept applies. Use N for Northern Hemisphere, S for Southern Hemisphere, and B for both.

Cyclones rotate counterclockwise.	a. _____?_____
Net flow of air is inward around a cyclone.	b. _____?_____
Anticyclones rotate counterclockwise.	c. _____?_____
Coriolis effect deflects winds to the right.	d. _____?_____

Pressure centers are among the most common features on any weather map. By knowing just a few basic facts about centers of high and low pressure, you can increase your understanding of present and forthcoming weather. You can make some weather generalizations based on pressure centers. For example, centers of low pressure are frequently associated with cloudy conditions and precipitation. By contrast, clear skies and fair weather may be expected when an area is under the influence of high pressure, as shown in Figure 6.

Figure 6 These sunbathers at Cape Henlopen, Delaware, are enjoying weather associated with a high-pressure center.

Highs and Lows

Lows, or **cyclones** (*kyklon* = moving in a circle) are centers of low pressure. Highs, or **anticyclones,** are centers of high pressure. **In cyclones, the pressure decreases from the outer isobars toward the center. In anticyclones, just the opposite is the case—the values of the isobars increase from the outside toward the center.**

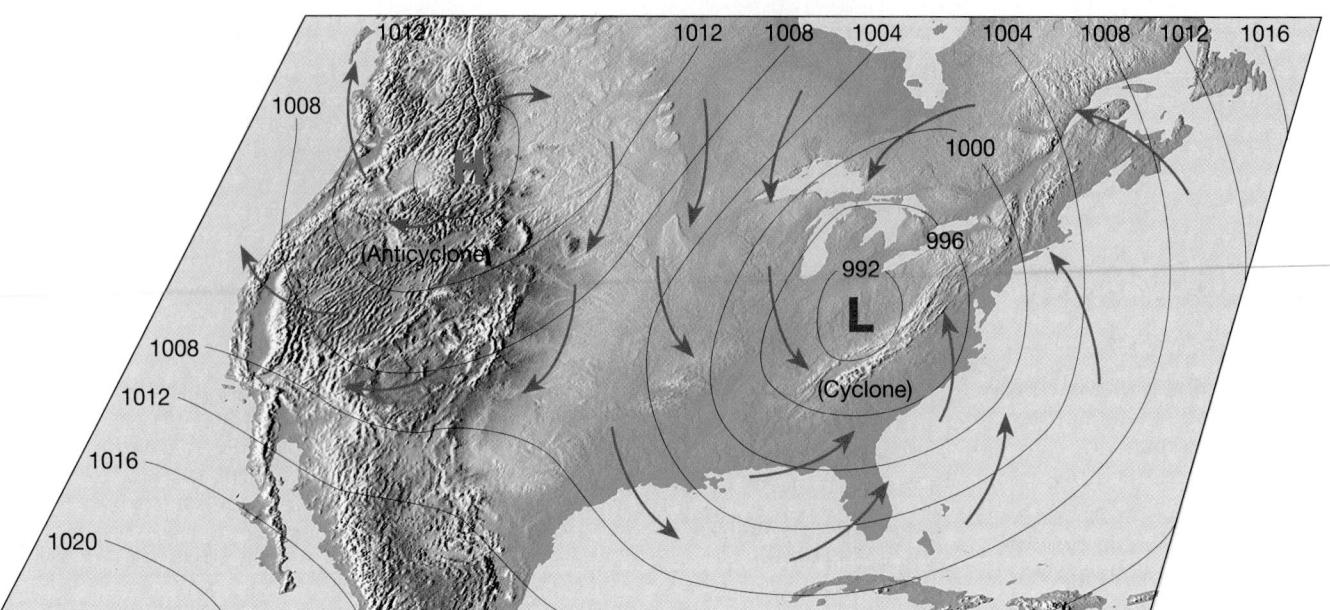

Figure 7 This map shows cyclonic and anticyclonic winds in the Northern Hemisphere.

Cyclonic and Anticyclonic Winds

You learned that the two most significant factors that affect wind are the pressure gradient and the Coriolis effect. Winds move from higher pressure to lower pressure and are deflected to the right or left by Earth's rotation.  **When the pressure gradient and the Coriolis effect are applied to pressure centers in the Northern Hemisphere, winds blow counterclockwise around a low. Around a high, they blow clockwise.** Notice the wind directions in Figure 7.

In the Southern Hemisphere, the Coriolis effect deflects the winds to the left. Therefore, winds around a low move clockwise. Winds around a high move counterclockwise.  **In either hemisphere, friction causes a net flow of air inward around a cyclone and a net flow of air outward around an anticyclone.**

Weather and Air Pressure

Rising air is associated with cloud formation and precipitation, whereas sinking air produces clear skies.

Imagine a surface low-pressure system where the air is spiraling inward. Here the net inward movement of air causes the area occupied by the air mass to shrink—a process called horizontal convergence. Whenever air converges (or comes together) horizontally, it must increase in height to allow for the decreased area it now occupies. This increase in height produces a taller and heavier air column. A surface low can exist only as long as the column of air above it exerts less pressure than does the air in surrounding regions. This seems to be a paradox—a low-pressure center causes a net accumulation of air, which increases its pressure.

Reading Checkpoint *With what type of weather is rising air associated?*

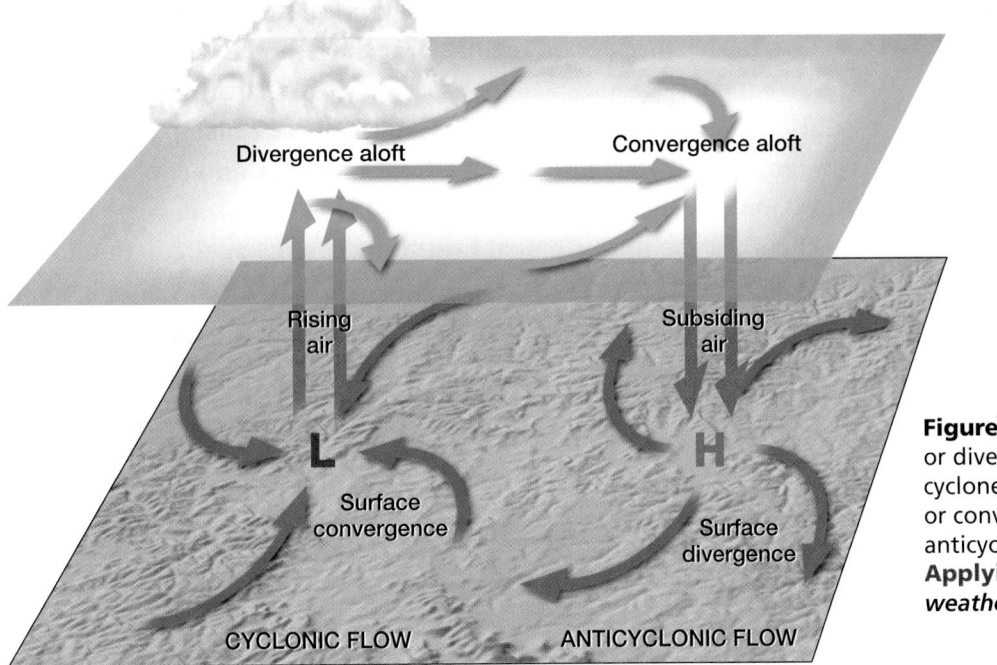

Figure 8 Air spreads out, or diverges, above surface cyclones, and comes together, or converges, above surface anticyclones.
Applying Concepts *Why is fair weather associated with a high?*

In order for a surface low to exist for very long, converging air at the surface must be balanced by outflows aloft. For example, surface convergence could be maintained if divergence, or the spreading out of air, occurred above the low at a rate equal to the inflow below. Figure 8 shows the relationship between surface convergence (inflow) and divergence (outflow) needed to maintain a low-pressure center. Surface convergence around a cyclone causes a net upward movement. Because rising air often results in cloud formation and precipitation, a low-pressure center is generally related to unstable conditions and stormy weather.

Like cyclones, anticyclones also must be maintained from above. Outflow near the surface is accompanied by convergence in the air above and a general sinking of the air column, as shown in Figure 8.

Weather Forecasting Now you can see why weather reports emphasize the locations and possible paths of cyclones and anticyclones. The villain in these reports is always the low-pressure center, which can produce bad weather in any season. Lows move in roughly a west-to-east direction across the United States, and they require a few days, and sometimes more than a week, for the journey. Their paths can be somewhat unpredictable, making accurate estimation of their movement difficult. Because surface conditions are linked to the conditions of the air above, it is important to understand total atmospheric circulation.

Global Winds

The underlying cause of wind is the unequal heating of Earth's surface. In tropical regions, more solar radiation is received than is radiated back to space. In regions near the poles the opposite is true—less solar energy is received than is lost. ⬤ **The atmosphere balances these differences by acting as a giant heat-transfer system. This system moves warm air toward high latitudes and cool air toward the equator.** On a smaller scale, but for the same reason, ocean currents also contribute to this global heat transfer. Global circulation is very complex, but you can begin to understand it by first thinking about circulation that would occur on a non-rotating Earth.

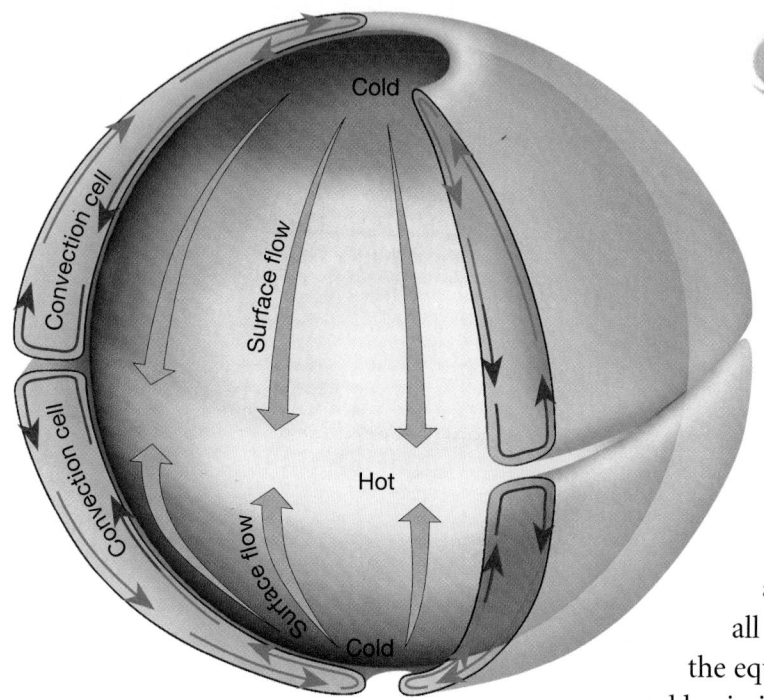

Figure 9 Circulation on a Non-Rotating Earth A simple convection system is produced by unequal heating of the atmosphere.
Relating Cause and Effect *Why would air sink after reaching the poles?*

> ✓ **Reading Checkpoint** *How does the atmosphere balance the unequal heating of Earth's surface?*

Non-Rotating Earth Model On a hypothetical non-rotating planet with a smooth surface of either all land or all water, two large thermally produced cells would form, as shown in Figure 9. The heated air at the equator would rise until it reached the tropopause—the boundary between the troposphere and the stratosphere. The tropopause, acting like a lid, would deflect this air toward the poles. Eventually, the upper-level airflow would reach the poles, sink, spread out in all directions at the surface, and move back toward the equator. Once at the equator, it would be reheated and begin its journey over again. This hypothetical circulation system has upper-level air flowing toward the pole and surface air flowing toward the equator.

Rotating Earth Model If the effect of rotation were added to the global circulation model, the two-cell convection system would break down into smaller cells. Figure 10 illustrates the three pairs of cells that would carry on the task of redistributing heat on Earth. The polar and tropical cells retain the characteristics of the thermally generated convection described earlier. The nature of circulation at the middle latitudes, however, is more complex.

Near the equator, rising air produces a pressure zone known as the equatorial low—a region characterized by abundant precipitation. As shown in Figure 10, the upper-level flow from the equatorial low reaches 20 to 30 degrees, north or south latitude, and then sinks back toward the surface. This sinking of air and its associated heating due to compression produce hot, arid conditions. The center of this zone of sinking dry air is the subtropical high, which encircles the globe near 30 degrees north and south latitude. The great deserts of Australia, Arabia, and the Sahara in North Africa exist because of the stable dry conditions associated with the subtropical highs.

At the surface, airflow moves outward from the center of the subtropical high. Some of the air travels toward the equator and is deflected by the Coriolis effect, producing the trade winds. **Trade winds** are two belts of winds that blow almost constantly from easterly directions. The trade winds are located between the subtropical highs and the equator. The remainder of the air travels toward the poles and is deflected, generating the prevailing **westerlies** of the middle latitudes. The westerlies make up the dominant west-to-east motion of the atmosphere that characterizes the regions on the poleward side of the subtropical highs. As the westerlies move toward the poles, they encounter the cool polar easterlies in the region of the subpolar low. The **polar easterlies** are winds that blow from the polar high toward the subpolar low. These winds are not constant winds like the trade winds. In the polar region, cold polar air sinks and spreads toward the equator. The interaction of these warm and cool air masses produces the stormy belt known as the **polar front.**

This simplified global circulation is dominated by four pressure zones. The subtropical and polar highs are areas of dry subsiding (sinking) air that flows outward at the surface, producing the prevailing winds. The low-pressure zones of the equatorial and subpolar regions are associated with inward and upward airflow accompanied by clouds and precipitation.

 Reading Checkpoint   *What is the polar front?*

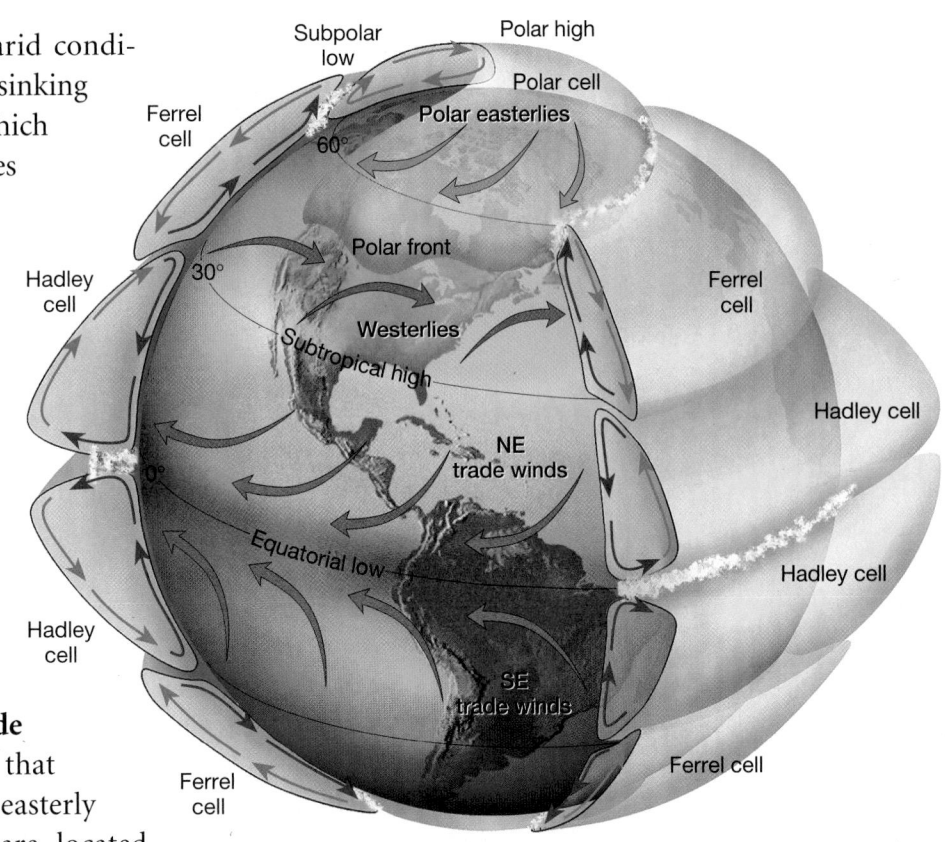

Figure 10 Circulation on a Rotating Earth This model of global air circulation proposes three pairs of cells.
Interpreting Diagrams *Describe the patterns of air circulation at the equatorial and subpolar lows.*

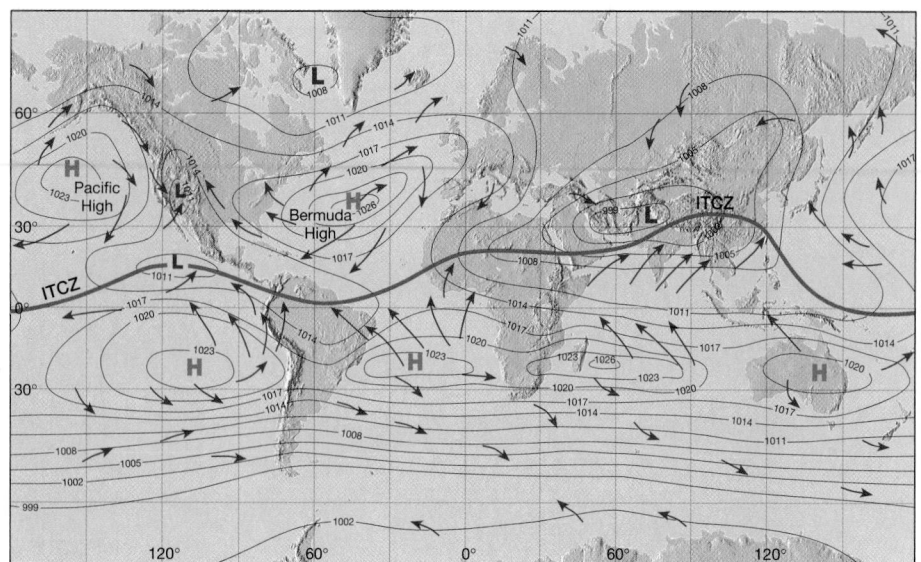

Figure 11 Average Surface Pressure and Associated Global Circulation for July. The ITCZ line stands for the Intertropical Convergence Zone.

Influence of Continents

The only truly continuous pressure belt is the subpolar low in the Southern Hemisphere. Here the ocean is uninterrupted by landmasses. At other latitudes, particularly in the Northern Hemisphere where landmasses break up the ocean surface, large seasonal temperature differences disrupt the pressure pattern. Large landmasses, particularly Asia, become cold in the winter when a seasonal high-pressure system develops. From this high-pressure system, surface airflow is directed off the land. In the summer, landmasses are heated and develop low-pressure cells, which permit air to flow onto the land as shown in Figure 11. These seasonal changes in wind direction are known as the **monsoons.** During warm months, areas such as India experience a flow of warm, water-laden air from the Indian Ocean, which produces the rainy summer monsoon. The winter monsoon is dominated by dry continental air. A similar situation exists to a lesser extent over North America.

Section 19.2 Assessment

Reviewing Concepts

1. Describe how winds blow around pressure centers in the Northern Hemisphere.

2. Compare the air pressure for a cyclone with an anticyclone.

3. How does friction control the net flow of air around a cyclone and an anticyclone?

4. Describe how the atmosphere balances the unequal heating of Earth's surface.

5. What is the only truly continuous pressure belt? Why is it continuous?

6. In general, what type of weather can you expect if a low-pressure system is moving into your area?

Critical Thinking

7. **Identifying Cause and Effect** What must happen in the air above for divergence at the surface to be maintained? What type of pressure center accompanies surface divergence?

Math Practice

8. Examine Figure 7. What is the approximate range of barometric pressure indicated by the isobars on the map? What is the pressure interval between adjacent isobars?

19.3 Regional Wind Systems

Reading Focus

Key Concepts

- What causes local winds?
- Describe the general movement of weather in the United States.
- What happens when unusually strong, warm ocean currents flow along the coasts of Ecuador and Peru?
- How is a La Niña event triggered?

Vocabulary

- prevailing wind
- anemometer
- El Niño

Reading Strategy

Previewing Copy the table below. Before you read, use Figure 17 to locate examples of the driest and wettest regions on Earth. After you read, identify the dominant wind system for each location.

Precipitation	Location	Dominant Wind System
Extremely low	a. ____?____	b. ____?____
Extremely high	c. ____?____	d. ____?____

Circulation in the middle latitudes is complex and does not fit the convection system described for the tropics. Between about 30 and 60 degrees latitude, the general west-to-east flow, known as the westerlies, is interrupted by migrating cyclones and anticyclones. In the Northern Hemisphere, these pressure cells move from west to east around the globe.

Local Winds

Small-scale winds produced by a locally generated pressure gradient are known as local winds. **The local winds are caused either by topographic effects or by variations in surface composition—land and water—in the immediate area.**

Land and Sea Breezes In coastal areas during the warm summer months, the land surface is heated more intensely during the daylight hours than an adjacent body of water is heated. As a result, the air above the land surface heats, expands, and rises, creating an area of lower pressure. As shown in Figure 12, a sea breeze then develops because cooler air over the water at higher pressure moves toward the warmer land and low pressure air. The breeze starts developing shortly before noon and generally reaches its greatest intensity during the mid- to late afternoon. These relatively cool winds can be a moderating influence on afternoon temperatures in coastal areas.

Figure 12 Sea Breeze During daylight hours, the air above land heats and rises, creating a local zone of lower air pressure.

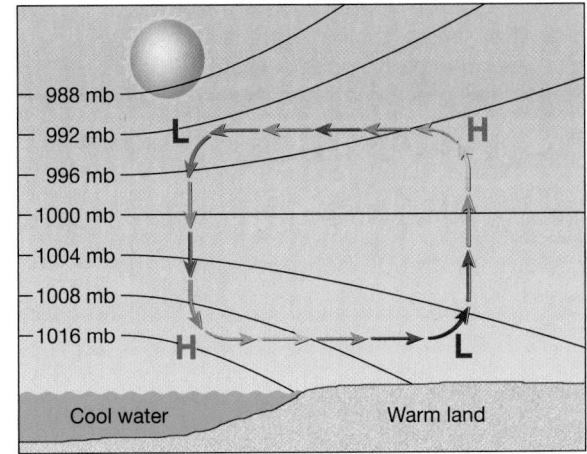

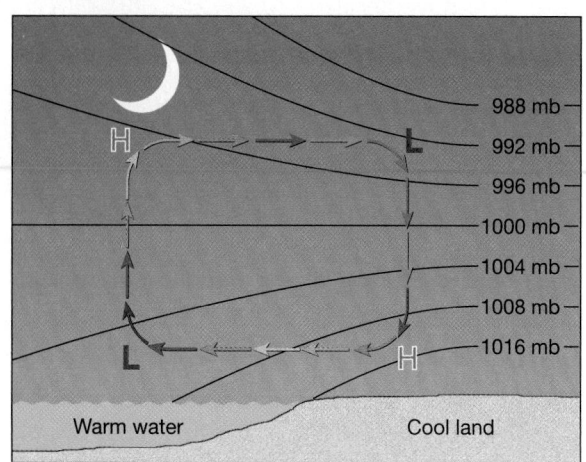

Figure 13 Land Breeze At night, the land cools more rapidly than the sea, generating an offshore flow called a land breeze.
Inferring *How would the isobar lines be oriented if there was no air pressure change across the land–water boundary?*

At night, the reverse may take place. The land cools more rapidly than the sea, and a land breeze develops, as shown in Figure 13. The cooler air at higher pressures over the land moves to the sea, where the air is warmer and at lower pressures. Small-scale sea breezes also can develop along the shores of large lakes. People who live in a city near the Great Lakes, such as Chicago, recognize this lake effect, especially in the summer. They are reminded daily by weather reports of the cool temperatures near the lake as compared to warmer outlying areas.

Valley and Mountain Breezes A daily wind similar to land and sea breezes occurs in many mountainous regions. During daylight hours, the air along the slopes of the mountains is heated more intensely than the air at the same elevation over the valley floor. Because this warmer air on the mountain slopes is less dense, it glides up along the slope and generates a valley breeze, as shown in Figure 14A. The occurrence of these daytime upslope breezes can often be identified by the cumulus clouds that develop on adjacent mountain peaks.

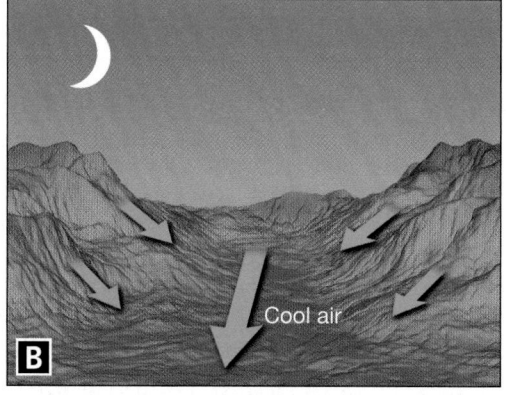

Figure 14 A Valley Breeze Heating during the day generates warm air that rises from the valley floor. **B Mountain Breeze** After sunset, cooling of the air near mountain slopes can result in cool air moving into the valley.

After sunset, the pattern may reverse. The rapid cooling of the air along the mountain slopes produces a layer of cooler air next to the ground. Because cool air is denser than warm air, it moves downslope into the valley. Such a movement of air, illustrated in Figure 14B, is called a mountain breeze. In the Grand Canyon at night, the sound of cold air rushing down the sides of the canyon can be louder than the sound of the Colorado River below.

The same type of cool air drainage can occur in places that have very modest slopes. The result is that the coldest pockets of air are usually found in the lowest spots. Like many other winds, mountain and valley breezes have seasonal preferences. Although valley breezes are most common during the warm season when solar heating is most intense, mountain breezes tend to be more dominant in the cold season.

Reading Checkpoint *What type of local wind can form in the Grand Canyon at night?*

How Wind Is Measured

Two basic wind measurements—direction and speed—are particularly important to the weather observer. Winds are always labeled by the direction from which they blow. A north wind blows from the north toward the south. An east wind blows from the east toward the west. The instrument most commonly used to determine wind direction is the wind vane, shown in the upper right of Figure 15. Wind vanes commonly are located on buildings, and they always point into the wind. The wind direction is often shown on a dial connected to the wind vane. The dial indicates wind direction, either by points of the compass—N, NE, E, SE, etc.—or by a scale of 0° to 360°. On the degree scale, 0° or 360° are north, 90° is east, 180° is south, and 270° is west.

Figure 15 Wind Vane and Cup Anemometer
Interpreting Photographs *How does the position of a wind vane tell you which direction the wind is blowing?*

 **Reading Checkpoint** *Toward which direction does a SE wind blow?*

Wind Direction When the wind consistently blows more often from one direction than from any other, it is called a **prevailing wind.** Recall the prevailing westerlies that dominate circulation in the middle latitudes. **In the United States, the westerlies consistently move weather from west to east across the continent.** Along within this general eastward flow are cells of high and low pressure with the characteristic clockwise and counterclockwise flows. As a result, the winds associated with the westerlies, as measured at the surface, often vary considerably from day to day and from place to place. In contrast, the direction of airflow associated with the trade winds is much more consistent.

Wind Speed Shown in the upper left of Figure 15, a cup **anemometer** (*anemo* = wind, *metron* = measuring instrument) is commonly used to measure wind speed. The wind speed is read from a dial much like the speedometer of an automobile. Places where winds are steady and speeds are relatively high are potential sites for tapping wind energy.

Go Online
SciLINKS
For: Links on winds
Visit: www.SciLinks.org
Web Code: cjn-6193

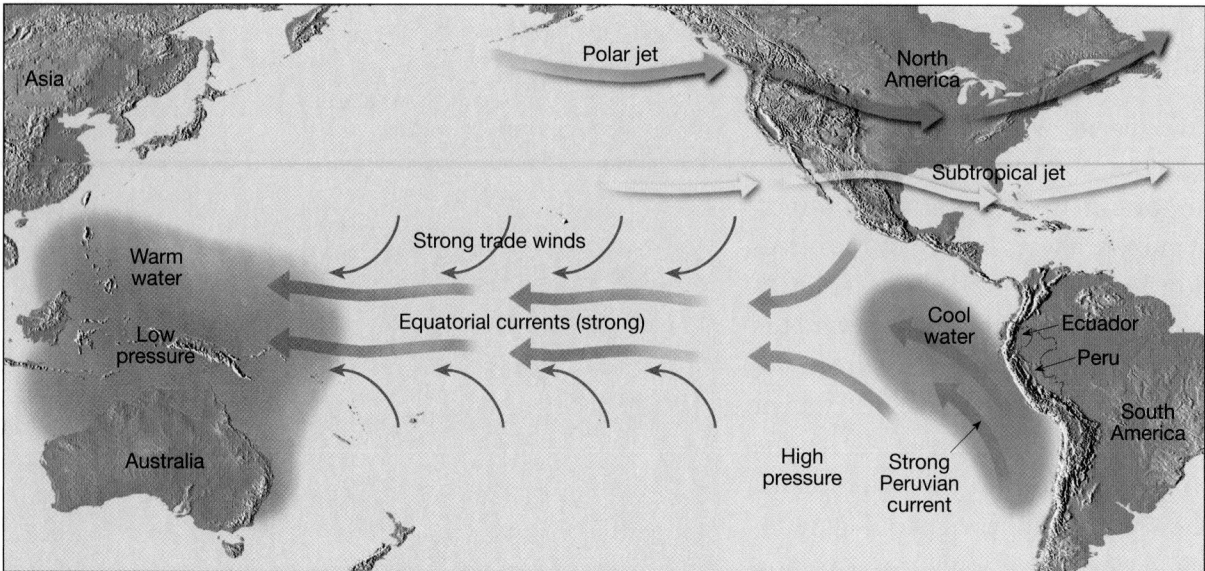

Figure 16 Normal Conditions
Trade winds and strong equatorial ocean currents flow toward the west.

El Niño and La Niña

Look at Figure 16. The cold Peruvian current flows toward the equator along the coasts of Ecuador and Peru. This flow encourages upwelling of cold nutrient-filled waters that are the primary food source for millions of fish, particularly anchovies. Near the end of the year, however, a warm current that flows southward along the coasts of Ecuador and Peru replaces the cold Peruvian current. During the nineteenth century, the local residents named this warm current El Niño ("the child") after the Christ child because it usually appeared during the Christmas season. Normally, these warm countercurrents last for a few weeks and then give way to the cold Peruvian flow again.

El Niño At irregular intervals of three to seven years, these warm countercurrents become unusually strong and replace normally cold offshore waters with warm equatorial waters. Scientists use the term **El Niño** for these episodes of ocean warming that affect the eastern tropical Pacific.

The onset of El Niño is marked by abnormal weather patterns that drastically affect the economies of Ecuador and Peru. As shown in Figure 17, these unusually strong undercurrents accumulate large quantities of warm water that block the upwelling of colder, nutrient-filled water. As a result, the anchovies starve, devastating the local fishing industry. At the same time, some inland areas that are normally arid receive an abnormal amount of rain. Here, pastures and cotton fields have yields far above the average. These climatic fluctuations have been known for years, but they were originally considered local phenomena. It now is understood that El Niño is part of the global circulation and that it affects the weather at great distances from Peru and Ecuador.

When an El Niño began in the summer of 1997, forecasters predicted that the pool of warm water over the Pacific would displace the

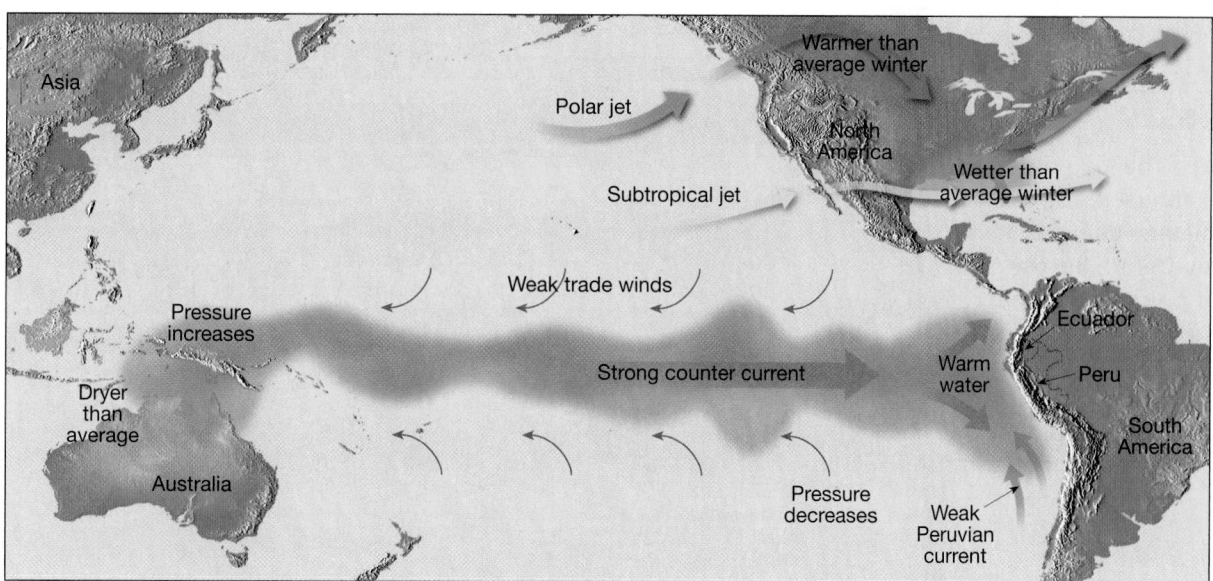

paths of both the subtropical and midlatitude jet streams, as shown in Figure 17. The jet streams steer weather systems across North America. As predicted, the subtropical jet brought rain to the Gulf Coast. Tampa, Florida, received more than three times its normal winter precipitation. The mid-latitude jet pumped warm air far north into the continent. As a result, winter temperatures west of the Rocky Mountains were significantly above normal.

 **Reading Checkpoint** *What is an El Niño and what effect does it have on weather?*

Figure 17 El Niño Warm countercurrents cause reversal of pressure patterns in the western and eastern Pacific.

La Niña The opposite of El Niño is an atmospheric phenomenon known as La Niña. Once thought to be the normal conditions that occur between two El Niño events, meteorologists now consider La Niña an important atmospheric phenomenon in its own right. **Researchers have come to recognize that when surface temperatures in the eastern Pacific are colder than average, a La Niña event is triggered that has a distinctive set of weather patterns.** A typical La Niña winter blows colder than normal air over the Pacific Northwest and the northern Great Plains. At the same time, it warms much of the rest of the United States. The Northwest also experiences greater precipitation during this time. During the La Niña winter of 1998–99, a world-record snowfall for one season occurred in Washington State. La Niña impact can also increase hurricane activity. A recent study concluded that the cost of hurricane damages in the United States is 20 times greater in La Niña years as compared to El Niño years.

The effects of both El Niño and La Niña on world climate are widespread and vary greatly. These phenomena remind us that the air and ocean conditions of the tropical Pacific influence the state of weather almost everywhere.

For: Links on La Niña and El Niño
Visit: www.SciLinks.org
Web Code: cjn-6211

Global Precipitation

Figure 18

Regions The map shows average annual precipitation in millimeters. **Using the Map Key** Determine the range of precipitation that dominates Northern Africa. **Identify Causes** Which weather pattern influences precipitation in this area?

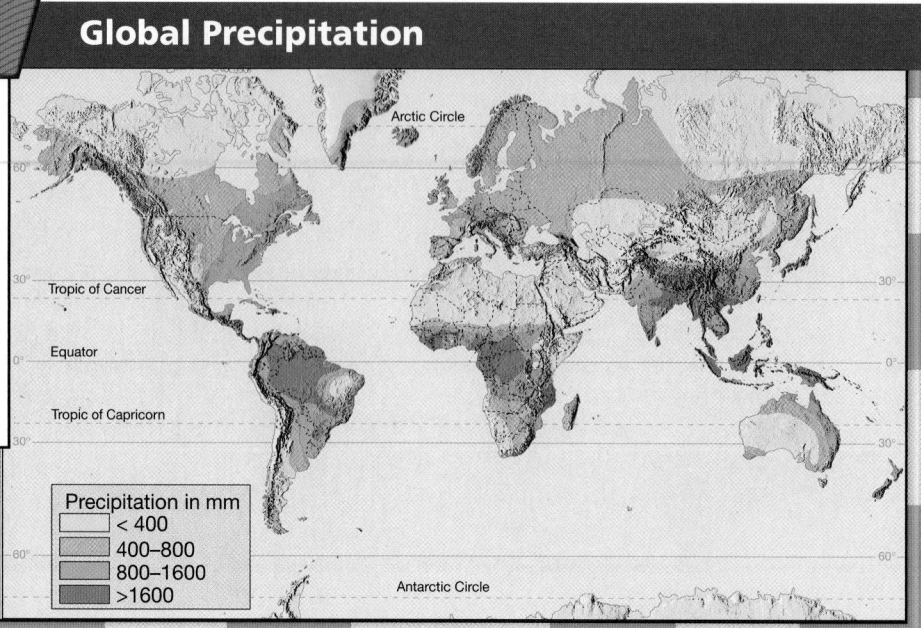

Arctic Circle
Tropic of Cancer
Equator
Tropic of Capricorn
Antarctic Circle

Precipitation in mm
< 400
400–800
800–1600
>1600

Global Distribution of Precipitation

Figure 18 shows that the tropical region dominated by the equatorial low is the rainiest region on Earth. It includes the rain forests of the Amazon basin in South America and the Congo basin in Africa. In these areas, the warm, humid trade winds converge to yield abundant rainfall throughout the year. In contrast, areas dominated by the subtropical high-pressure cells are regions of extensive deserts. Variables other than pressure and wind complicate the pattern. For example, the interiors of large land masses commonly experience decreased precipitation. However, you can explain a lot about global precipitation if you apply your knowledge of global winds and pressure systems.

Section 19.3 Assessment

Reviewing Concepts

1. ⬤ What are local winds, and how are they caused?
2. ⬤ Describe the general movement of weather in the United States.
3. ⬤ What happens when strong, warm countercurrents flow along the coasts of Ecuador and Peru?
4. ⬤ How is a La Niña event recognized?
5. What two factors mainly influence global precipitation?

Critical Thinking

6. **Interpreting illustrations** Study Figure 17. How could air pressure changes influence weather patterns in this region?

Writing in Science

Compare-Contrast Paragraph Write a paragraph comparing the features and effects of El Niño and La Niña. Include specific weather patterns associated with each phenomenon.

Tracking El Niño from Space

The images in Figure 19 show the progression of the 1997–98 El Niño. They were derived from data collected by the satellite TOPEX/Poseidon.* This satellite bounces radar signals off the ocean surface to precisely measure the distance between the satellite and the sea surface. When combined with high-precision data from the Global Positioning System (GPS) of satellites, maps of sea-surface topography like these can be produced. These maps show the topography of the sea surface. The presence of hills indicates warmer-than-average water, and the areas of low topography, or valleys, indicate cooler-than-normal water. Using water topography, scientists can determine the speed and direction of surface ocean currents.

The colors in these images show sea-level height relative to the average. When you focus on the images, remember that hills are warm colors and valleys are cool colors. The white and red areas indicate places of higher-than-normal sea-surface heights. In the white areas, the sea surface is between 14 and 32 centimeters above normal. In the red areas, sea level is elevated by about 10 centimeters. Green areas indicate average conditions, whereas purple shows zones that are at least 18 centimeters below average sea level.

The images show the progression of the large warm-water mass from west to east across the equatorial Pacific Ocean. At its peak in November 1997, the surface area covered by the warm water mass was about one and one half times the size of the 48 contiguous United States. The amount of warm water added to the eastern Pacific with a temperature between 21°C and 30°C was about 30 times the combined volume of the water in all of the United States Great Lakes.

*Source: NASA's Goddard Space Flight Center

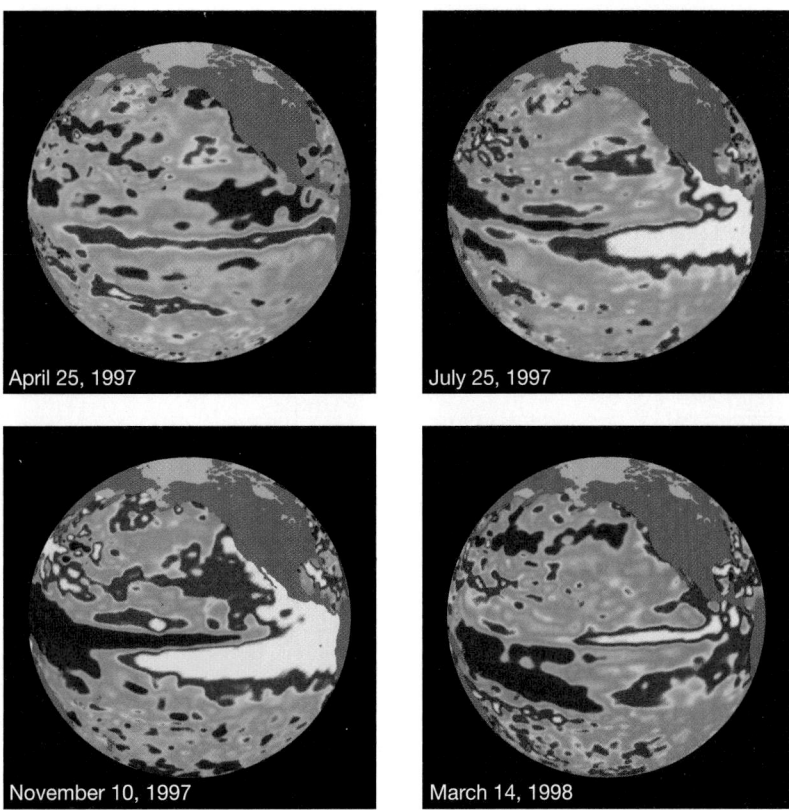

April 25, 1997

July 25, 1997

November 10, 1997

March 14, 1998

Figure 19 Progression of the 1997–98 El Niño

Observing Wind Patterns

Atmospheric pressure and wind are two elements of weather that are closely interrelated. Most people don't usually pay close attention to the pressure given in a weather report. However, pressure differences in the atmosphere drive the winds that often bring changes in temperature and moisture.

Problem
How can surface barometric pressure maps be interpreted?

Materials
- 1 copy each of Figure 1 and Figure 2
- paper
- pencil

Skills
Observing, Analyzing Data, Calculating

Procedure

1. Look at Figure 2. This map shows global wind patterns and average global barometric pressure for the month of January.

2. Examine the individual pressure cells in Figure 2. Then complete the diagrams in your copy of Figure 1. Label the isobars with appropriate pressures, and use arrows to indicate the surface air movement in each pressure cell.

3. Copy the data table below. Indicate the movements of air in high and low pressure cells by completing the table.

Northern Hemisphere

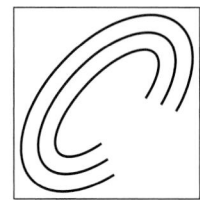 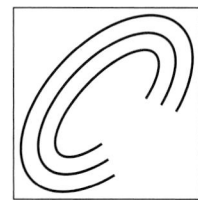

Southern Hemisphere

 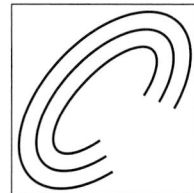

Figure 1

Air Movement in Pressure Cells Data Table				
Air Movement	N. Hem. High	N. Hem. Low	S. Hem High	S. Hem. Low
into/out of				
rises/sinks				
rotates CW/CCW*				

* CW = clockwise; CCW = counterclockwise

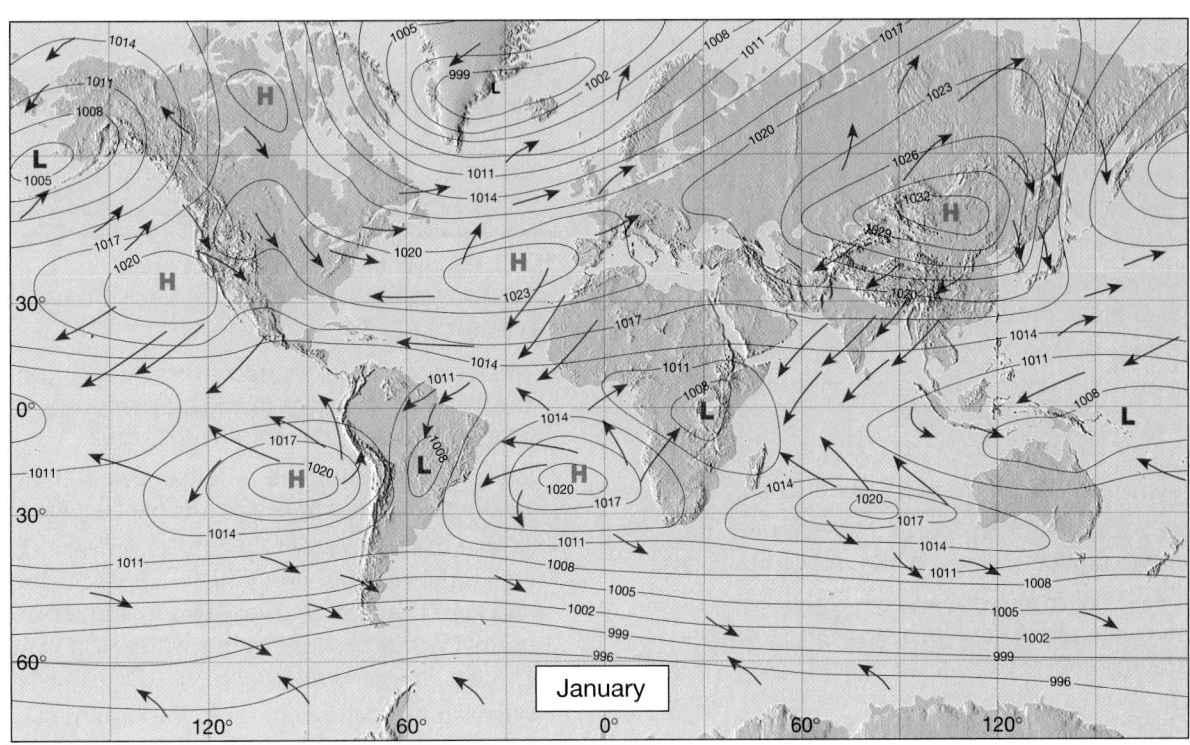

January

Figure 2

Analyze and Conclude

1. **Comparing and Contrasting** Summarize the differences and similarities in surface air movement between a Northern Hemisphere cyclone and a Southern Hemisphere cyclone.

2. **Interpreting Illustrations** Use your textbook as a reference to locate and write the name of each global wind belt at the appropriate location on your copy of the map in Figure 2. Also indicate the region of the polar front.

3. **Applying** Label areas on your copy of Figure 2 where you would expect high wind speeds to occur.

4. **Applying** Label areas on your copy of Figure 2 where circulation is most like the idealized global wind model for a rotating Earth. Explain why this region on Earth is so much like the model.

19.1 Understanding Air Pressure

🌀 Key Concepts

- Air pressure is exerted in all directions—down, up, and sideways. The air pressure pushing down on an object exactly balances the air pressure pushing up on the object.

- When air pressure increases, the mercury in the tube rises. When air pressure decreases, so does the height of the mercury column.

- Wind is the result of horizontal differences in air pressure. Air flows from areas of higher pressure to areas of lower pressure.

- The unequal heating of Earth's surface generates pressure differences. Solar radiation is the ultimate energy source for most wind.

- Three factors combine to control wind: pressure differences, the Coriolis effect, and friction.

- Closely spaced isobars indicate a steep pressure gradient and high winds. Widely spaced isobars indicate a weak pressure gradient and light winds.

- The Coriolis effect describes how Earth's rotation affects moving objects. All free-moving objects or fluids, including the wind, are deflected to the right of their path of motion in the Northern Hemisphere. In the Southern Hemisphere, they are deflected to the left.

Vocabulary

air pressure, *p. 532;* barometer *p. 533;* pressure gradient, *p. 534;* Coriolis effect, *p. 535;* jet stream, *p. 536*

19.2 Pressure Centers and Winds

🌀 Key Concepts

- In the Northern Hemisphere, winds blow inward and counterclockwise around a low. Around a high, they blow outward and clockwise.

- In cyclones, the pressure decreases from the outer isobars toward the center. In anticyclones, just the opposite is the case—the values of the isobars increase from the outside toward the center.

- In either hemisphere, pressure difference, the Coriolis effect, and friction causes a net flow of air inward around a cyclone and a net flow of air outward around an anticyclone.

- The atmosphere balances differences in solar radiation in the tropics and the poles by acting as a giant heat-transfer system. This system moves warm air toward high latitudes and cool air toward the equator.

Vocabulary

cyclone, *p. 538;* anticyclone, *p. 538;* trade winds, *p. 541;* westerlies, *p. 541;* polar easterlies, *p. 541;* polar front, *p. 541;* monsoon, *p. 542*

19.3 Regional Wind Systems

🌀 Key Concepts

- The local winds are caused either by topographic effects or by variations in surface composition—land and water—in the immediate area.

- In the United States, the westerlies consistently move weather from west to east across the continent.

- At irregular intervals of three to seven years, warm equatorial currents along the coasts of Ecuador and Peru become unusually strong and replace normally cold offshore waters with warm waters. This occurrence is referred to as an El Niño event.

- When surface temperatures in the eastern Pacific are colder than average, a La Niña event is triggered that has a distinctive set of weather patterns.

Vocabulary

prevailing wind, *p. 545;* anemometer, *p. 545;* El Niño, *p. 546;* La Niña, *p. 547*

Thinking Visually

Concept Map Copy the concept map below onto a sheet of paper. Use information from the chapter to complete the concept map.

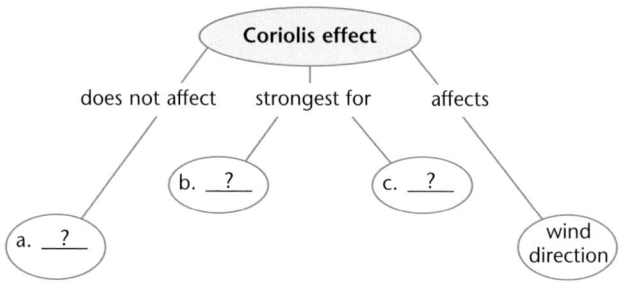

Reviewing Content

Choose the letter that best answers the question or completes the statement.

1. The mercurial barometer was invented by
   - **a.** Galileo.
   - **b.** Newton.
   - **c.** Torricelli.
   - **d.** Watt.

2. The force exerted by the air above is called
   - **a.** air pressure.
   - **b.** convergence.
   - **c.** divergence.
   - **d.** the Coriolis effect.

3. What are centers of low pressure called?
   - **a.** air masses
   - **b.** anticyclones
   - **c.** cyclones
   - **d.** jet streams

4. Variations in air pressure from place to place are the principal cause of
   - **a.** clouds.
   - **b.** lows.
   - **c.** hail.
   - **d.** wind.

5. In the winter, large landmasses often develop a seasonal
   - **a.** high-pressure system.
   - **b.** low-pressure system.
   - **c.** typhoon.
   - **d.** trade wind.

6. A sea breeze is most intense
   - **a.** during mid- to late afternoon.
   - **b.** in the late morning.
   - **c.** late in the evening.
   - **d.** at sunrise.

7. What is the pressure zone that is associated with rising air near the equator?
   - **a.** equatorial low
   - **b.** equatorial high
   - **c.** subtropical low
   - **d.** subtropical high

8. What are high-altitude, high-velocity winds?
   - **a.** cyclonic currents
   - **b.** isobars
   - **c.** jet streams
   - **d.** pressure gradients

9. Where is deflection of wind due to the Coriolis effect the strongest?
   - **a.** near the equator
   - **b.** in the midlatitudes
   - **c.** near the poles
   - **d.** near the westerlies

10. In what stormy region do the westerlies and polar easterlies converge?
    - **a.** equatorial low
    - **b.** subpolar high
    - **c.** polar front
    - **d.** subtropical front

Understanding Concepts

11. Describe how an aneroid barometer works.

12. Write a general statement relating the spacing of isobars to wind speed.

13. Describe the weather that usually accompanies a
    a. drop in barometric pressure.
    b. rise in barometric pressure.

14. How does the Coriolis effect modify air movement in the Southern Hemisphere?

15. The trade winds originate from which pressure zone?

16. List and briefly describe three examples of local winds.

17. On a wind vane with a degree scale, which type of wind is indicated by 90 degrees?

Use the figure below to answer Questions 18–20.

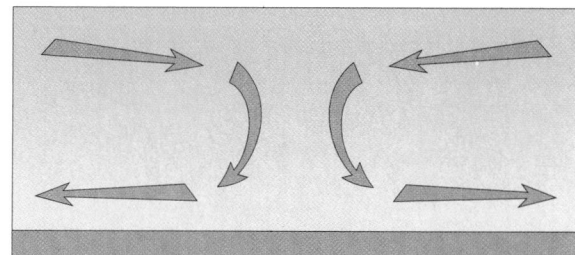

A

B

18. In diagram A, what type of surface air flow is shown?

19. What type of surface pressure system is illustrated in diagram B?

20. Select the diagram in which air at the surface first begins to pile up.

Critical Thinking

21. **Predicting** If you are in the Northern Hemisphere and are directly west of the center of a cyclone, what most likely will be the wind direction? What will the wind direction be if you are west of an anticyclone in the Northern Hemisphere?

22. **Applying Concepts** If you were looking for a location to place a wind turbine to generate electricity, how would you use the spacing of isobars in making your decision?

23. **Hypothesizing** What differences in the biosphere would you predict for areas dominated by low-pressure systems compared to those dominated by high-pressure systems?

Math Skills

Use the illustration below to answer Questions 24–26.

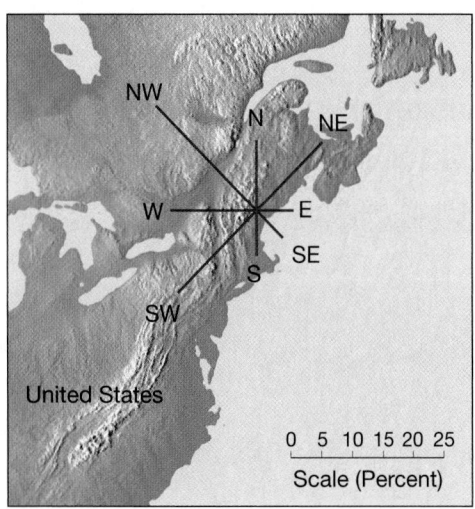

NW
N
NE
W — E
SE
S
SW

United States

0 5 10 15 20 25
Scale (Percent)

24. **Analyzing Data** According to the map, which winds dominate this region?

25. **Measuring** About what percent of the time do winds blow from the east?

26. **Calculating** Determine the approximate percent of time that winds blow from either the west or the northwest in this area.

Concepts in Action

27. **Predicting** How might a La Niña event impact the weather in your area?

28. **Applying Concepts** Mercury is 13 times heavier than water. If you built a barometer using water rather than mercury, how tall would it have to be to record standard sea-level pressure? Express your answer in centimeters. (Hint: How many centimeters of mercury represent standard sea-level pressure?)

29. **Interpreting Illustrations** After studying Figure 16, explain the relationship between water temperature and the type of air pressure system that develops.

Performance-Based Assessment

Observing For two weeks, keep a daily air pressure, wind, and precipitation log in your science notebook. Be sure to note any changes, and note if any of the changes occur over the course of a single day. At the end of two weeks, organize your information into a data table. Prepare a short summary that includes any patterns you determine among these variables. Report the results orally to your class.

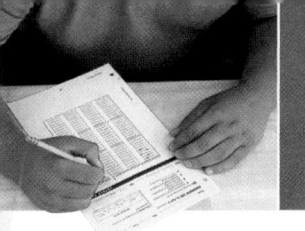

Standardized Test Prep

Test-Taking Tip

Anticipate the Answer
When answering multiple choice questions, a useful strategy is to cover up the given answers and supply your own answer. Then compare your answer with those listed and select the one that most closely matches.

Practice anticipating the answer in Questions 1–4.

Choose the letter that best answers the question or completes the statement.

1. The Sahara in North Africa and the Australian desert, as well as others, are associated with which pressure zone?
   (A) equatorial low
   (B) polar high
   (C) subpolar low
   (D) subtropical high

2. What does a steep air pressure gradient cause?
   (A) high winds
   (B) light winds
   (C) variable winds
   (D) north winds

3. Low-pressure systems are usually associated with
   (A) descending air.
   (B) diverging surface winds.
   (C) clear weather.
   (D) precipitation.

4. A sea breeze usually originates during the
   (A) evening and flows toward the land.
   (B) day and flows toward the land.
   (C) evening and flows toward the water.
   (D) day and flows toward the water.

Use the illustration below to answer Questions 5 and 6.

5. Using this scale, determine the standard sea level pressure in millibars and inches of mercury. Express your answers to the nearest millibar and to the nearest hundredth of an inch.

6. What is the corresponding pressure, in millibars, for a pressure measurement of 30.30 inches of mercury?

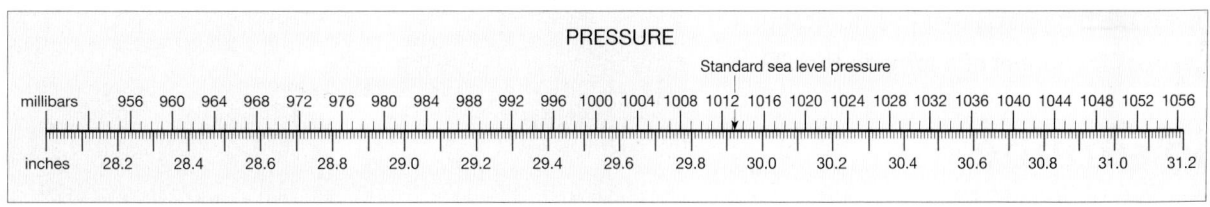

PRESSURE

Standard sea level pressure

millibars 956 960 964 968 972 976 980 984 988 992 996 1000 1004 1008 1012 1016 1020 1024 1028 1032 1036 1040 1044 1048 1052 1056

inches 28.2 28.4 28.6 28.8 29.0 29.2 29.4 29.6 29.8 30.0 30.2 30.4 30.6 30.8 31.0 31.2

CHAPTER 20

Weather Patterns and Severe Storms

CONCEPTS in Action

Application Lab
Middle-Latitude Cyclones

How the Earth Works
Winds and Storms

GEODe EARTH SCIENCE
The Atmosphere
↳ Basic Weather Patterns

Discovery Channel School

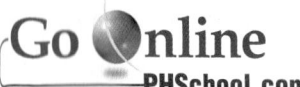

Video Field Trip

Violent Weather

Take a stormy field trip with Discovery Channel and find out how hurricanes and tornadoes occur. Answer the following questions after watching the video.

1. What is the biggest danger in a hurricane?
2. How does the funnel of a tornado form?

Go Online
PHSchool.com

For: Chapter 20 Resources
Visit: PHSchool.com
Web Code: cjk-9999

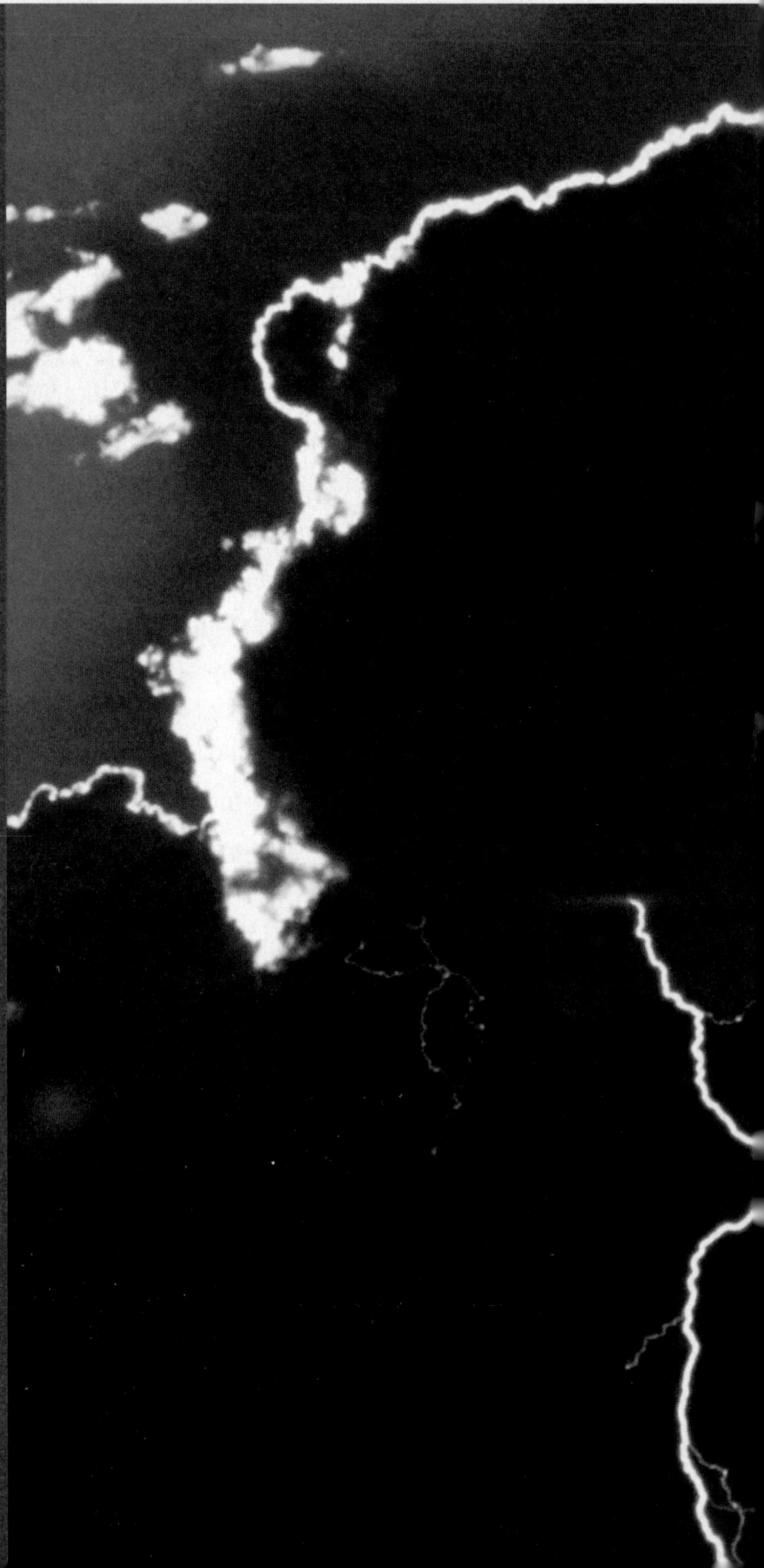

Lightning forms suddenly when negative charges near the bottom of a cloud flow toward the positively charged ground. ▶

Chapter Preview

Inquiry Activity

How Can You Model the Movement of Air in a Tornado?

Procedure

1. Pour tap water into a 1-L plastic bottle until it is about two-thirds full. Wipe off any water from the outside of the bottle as well as from the opening.

2. Without getting any of either substance on the outside of the bottle, add about 30 mL of liquid dishwashing soap and a spoonful of glitter to the water in the bottle.

3. Center a washer on the mouth of the bottle.

4. Invert another 1-L empty bottle and place its mouth over the washer.

5. Wrap about 10 cm of duct tape around the mouths of the bottles to seal them. Be careful not to move the washer as you do this.

6. Quickly invert the bottles so that the bottle holding the water is on top. Then, while holding the top bottle, swirl the bottles in a counterclockwise direction.

7. Observe your mini-tornado.

Think About It

1. **Observing** How did the water move in the bottle?

2. **Modeling** What might the glitter represent?

3. **Formulating Hypotheses** What kinds of forces do you think acted on the water to make it move as it did?

20.1 Air Masses

Reading Focus

Key Concepts

- What is an air mass?
- What happens as an air mass moves over an area?
- How are air masses classified?
- Which air masses influence much of the weather in North America?
- Why do continental tropical air masses have little effect on weather in North America?

Vocabulary

- air mass

Reading Strategy

Building Vocabulary Copy the table. As you read this section, write a definition for each of the terms in the table. Refer to the table as you read the rest of the chapter.

Term	Definition
Air mass	a. _____?_____
Source region	b. _____?_____
Polar air mass	c. _____?_____
Tropical air mass	d. _____?_____
Continental air mass	e. _____?_____
Maritime air mass	f. _____?_____

Figure 1 Tornado Damage in Kansas The force of the wind during a tornado was strong enough to drive a piece of metal into the utility pole.

Severe storms are among nature's most destructive forces. Every spring, for example, newspapers and newscasts report the damage caused by tornadoes, which are short but violent windstorms that move quickly over land. The forces associated with these storms can be incredibly strong, as you can see from the damage shown in Figure 1. During late summer and early fall, you have probably heard reports about severe storms known as hurricanes. Unlike tornadoes, hurricanes form over Earth's tropical oceans. As they move toward land, the strong winds and heavy rains produced by these storms can destroy anything in their paths. You are probably most familiar with a type of severe storm known as a thunderstorm. Thunderstorms are a type of severe weather that produces heavy rains, loud noises you know as thunder, and flashes of light called lightning. Before learning more about these different types of violent weather, you will learn about the atmospheric conditions that most often affect the day-to-day weather.

Air Masses and Weather

For the many people who live in the middle latitudes, which include much of the United States, summer heat waves and winter cold spells are familiar experiences. During summer heat waves, several days of high temperatures and high humidity often end when a series of storms pass through the area. This stormy weather is followed by a few days of relatively cool weather. By contrast, winter cold spells are often characterized by periods of frigid temperatures under clear skies. These bitter cold periods are usually followed by cloudy, snowy, relatively warm days that seem mild when compared to those just a day earlier. In both of these situations, periods of fairly constant weather conditions are followed by a short period of changes in the weather. What do you think causes these changes?

Air Masses The weather patterns just described result from movements of large bodies of air called air masses. **An air mass is an immense body of air that is characterized by similar temperatures and amounts of moisture at any given altitude.** An air mass can be 1600 kilometers or more across and several kilometers thick. Because of its size, it may take several days for an air mass to move over an area. This causes the area to experience fairly constant weather, a situation often called air-mass weather. Some day-to-day variations may occur, but the events will be very unlike those in an adjacent air mass.

Movement of Air Masses When an air mass moves out of the region over which it formed, it carries its temperature and moisture conditions with it. An example of the influence of a moving air mass is shown in Figure 2. A cold, dry air mass from northern Canada is shown moving southward. The initial temperature of the air mass is −46°C. It warms 13 degrees by the time it reaches Winnipeg. The air mass continues to warm as it moves southward through the Great Plains and into Mexico. Throughout its southward journey, the air mass becomes warmer. But it also brings some of the coldest weather of the winter to the places in its path. **As it moves, the characteristics of an air mass change and so does the weather in the area over which the air mass moves.**

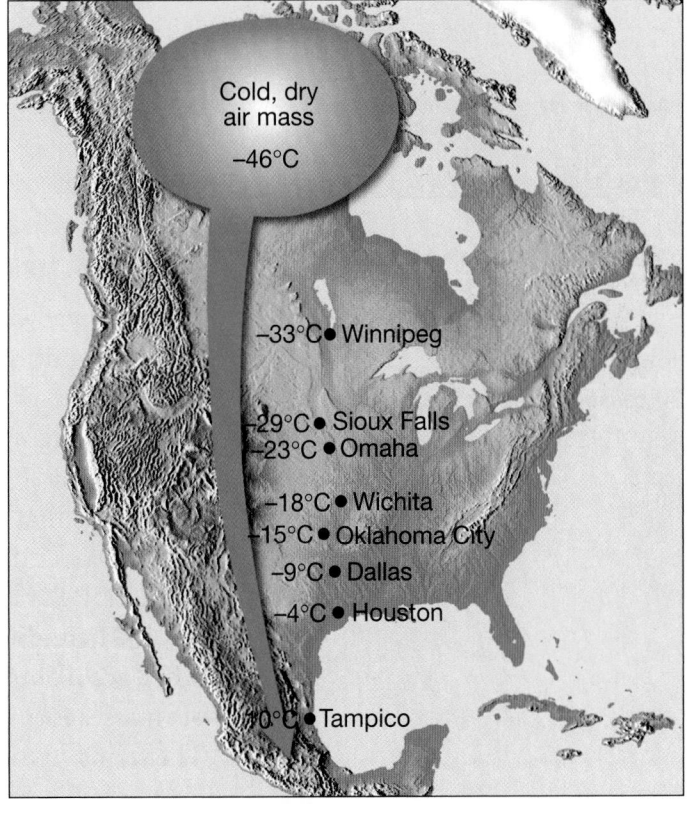

Figure 2 As a frigid Canadian air mass moves southward, it brings colder weather to the area over which it moves.
Computing *How much warmer was the air mass when it reached Tampico, Mexico, than when it formed?*

Reading Checkpoint *What is an air mass, and what happens as it moves over an area?*

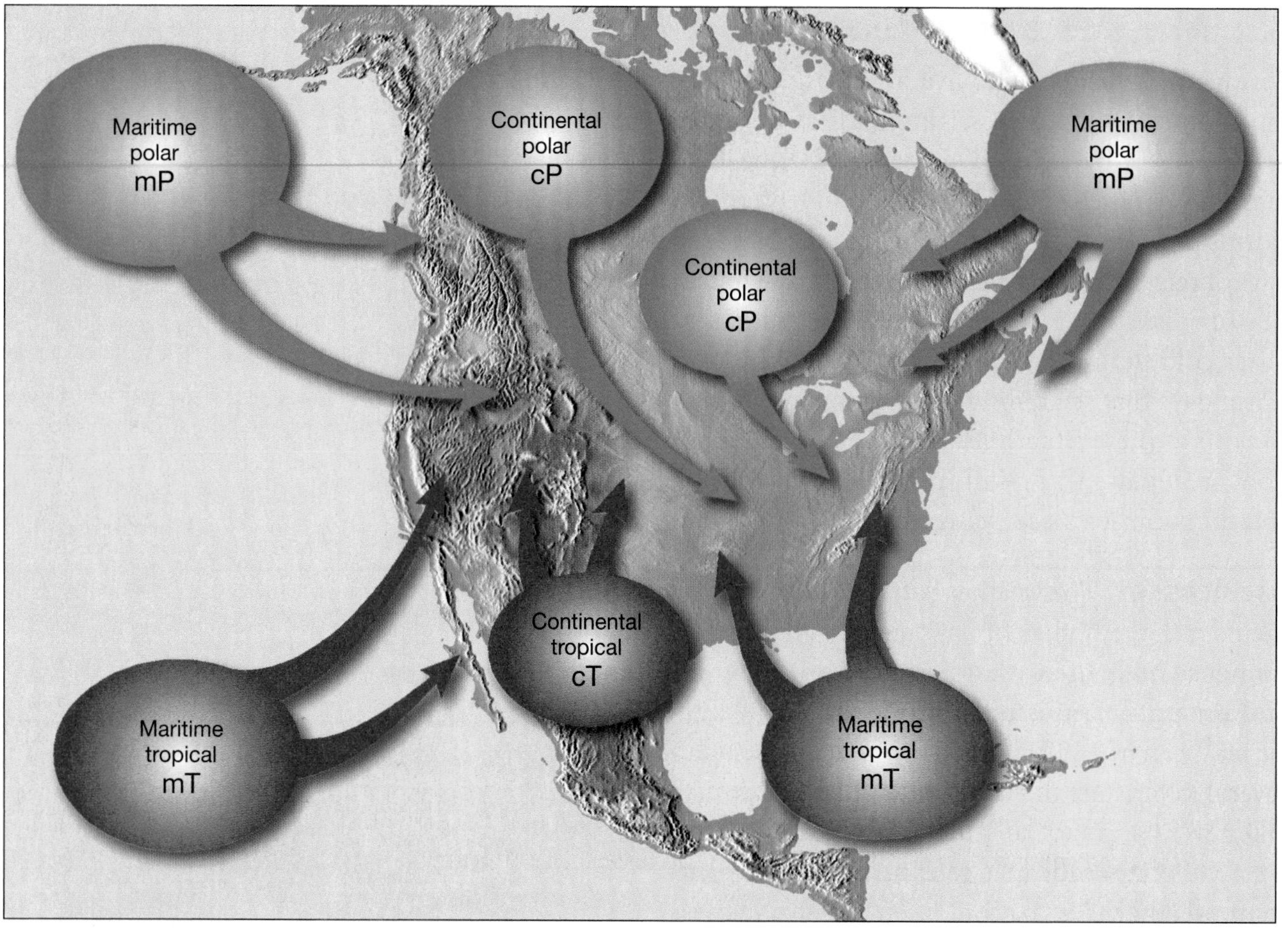

Figure 3 Air masses are classified by the region over which they form. **Interpreting Maps** *What kinds of air masses influence the weather patterns along the west coast of the United States?*

Classifying Air Masses

The area over which an air mass gets its characteristic properties of temperature and moisture is called its source region. The source regions that produce air masses that influence the weather in North America are shown in Figure 3. Air masses are named according to their source region. Polar (P) air masses form at high latitudes toward Earth's poles. Air masses that form at low latitudes are tropical (T) air masses. The terms *polar* and *tropical* describe the temperature characteristics of an air mass. Polar air masses are cold, while tropical air masses are warm.

🔑 **In addition to their overall temperature, air masses are classified according to the surface over which they form.** Continental (c) air masses form over land. Maritime (m) air masses form over water. The terms *continental* and *maritime* describe the moisture characteristics of the air mass. Continental air masses are likely to be dry. Maritime air masses are humid.

Using this classification scheme, there are four basic types of air masses. A continental polar (cP) air mass is dry and cool. A continental tropical (cT) air mass is dry and warm or hot. Maritime polar (mP) and maritime tropical (mT) air masses both form over water. But a maritime polar air mass is much colder than a maritime tropical air mass.

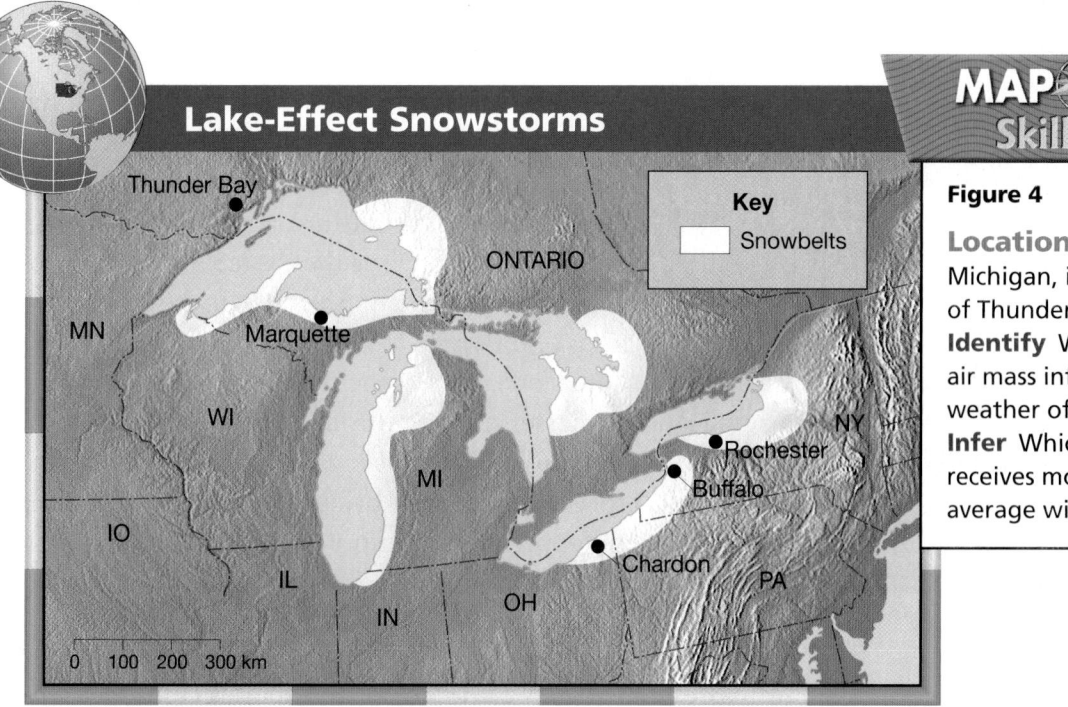

Lake-Effect Snowstorms

Key
Snowbelts

Thunder Bay
ONTARIO
MN
Marquette
WI
MI
NY
Rochester
Buffalo
IO
IL
Chardon
IN
OH
PA

0 100 200 300 km

Figure 4

Location Marquette, Michigan, is southeast of Thunder Bay, Ontario. **Identify** What type of air mass influences the weather of these two cities? **Infer** Which of these cities receives more snow in an average winter? Why?

Weather in North America

🔑 **Much of the weather in North America, especially weather east of the Rocky Mountains, is influenced by continental polar (cP) and maritime tropical (mT) air masses.** The cP air masses begin in northern Canada, the interior of Alaska, and the Arctic areas. The mT air masses most often begin over the warm waters of the Gulf of Mexico, the Caribbean Sea, or the adjacent Atlantic Ocean.

Continental Polar Air Masses Continental polar air masses are uniformly cold and dry in winter and cool and dry in summer. In summer, cP air masses may bring a few days of relatively cooler weather. In winter, this continental polar air brings the clear skies and cold temperatures you associate with a cold wave.

Continental polar air masses are not, as a rule, associated with heavy precipitation. However, those that cross the Great Lakes during late autumn and winter sometimes bring snow to the leeward shores, as shown in Figure 4. These localized storms, which are known as lake-effect snows, make Buffalo and Rochester, New York, among the snowiest cities in the United States. What causes lake-effect snow? During late autumn and early winter, the difference in temperature between the lakes and adjacent land areas can be large. The temperature contrast can be especially great when a very cold cP air mass pushes southward across the lakes. When this occurs, the air gets large quantities of heat and moisture from the relatively warm lake surface. By the time it reaches the opposite shore, the air mass is humid and unstable. Heavy snow, like that shown in Figure 5, is possible.

Figure 5 A six-day lake-effect snowstorm in November 1996 dropped a record 175 cm (69 in.) of snow on Chardon, Ohio.

Reading Checkpoint *What causes large amounts of snow to fall on the southern and eastern shores of the Great Lakes?*

Maritime Tropical Air Masses

Maritime tropical air masses also play a dominant role in the weather of North America. These air masses are warm, loaded with moisture, and usually unstable. Maritime tropical air is the source of much, if not most, of the precipitation received in the eastern two thirds of the United States. The heavy precipitation shown in Figure 6 is the result of maritime tropical air masses moving through the area. In summer, when an mT air mass invades the central and eastern United States, it brings the high temperatures and oppressive humidity typically associated with its source region.

Figure 6 Rain Storm over Florida Bay in the Florida Keys

Maritime Polar Air Masses

During the winter, maritime polar air masses that affect weather in North America come from the North Pacific. Such air masses often begin as cP air masses in Siberia. The cold, dry continental polar air changes into relatively mild, humid, unstable maritime polar air during its long journey across the North Pacific, as shown in Figure 7. As this maritime polar air arrives at the western shore of North America, it is often accompanied by low clouds and showers. When this maritime polar air advances inland against the western mountains, uplift of the air produces heavy rain or snow on the windward slopes of the mountains.

Maritime polar air masses also originate in the North Atlantic off the coast of eastern Canada. These air masses influence the weather of the northeastern United States. In winter, when New England is on the northern or northwestern side of a passing low-pressure center, the counterclockwise winds draw in maritime polar air. The result is a storm characterized by snow and cold temperatures, known locally as a nor'easter.

Figure 7 During winter, maritime polar (mP) air masses in the northern Pacific Ocean usually begin as continental polar (cP) air masses in Siberia.
Inferring *What happens to the mP air masses as they cross the Pacific?*

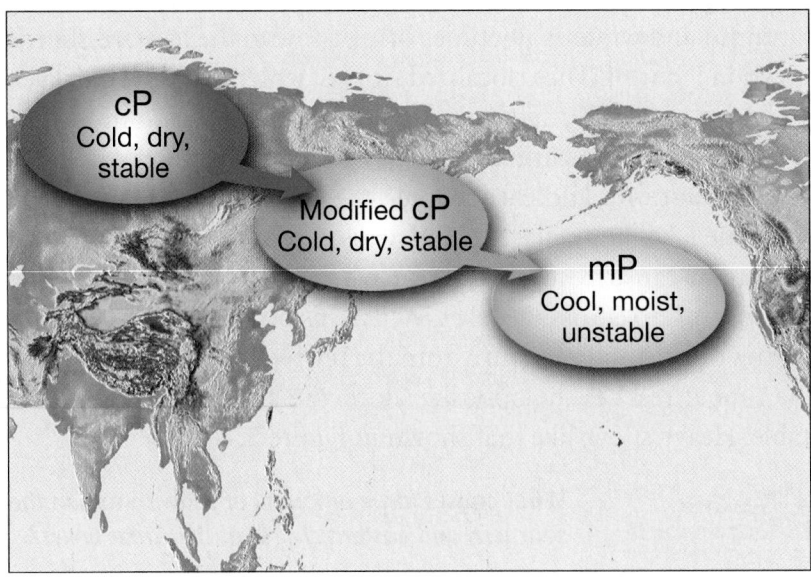

Continental Tropical Air Masses Continental tropical air masses have the least influence on the weather of North America. These hot, dry air masses begin in the southwestern United States and Mexico during the summer. ⬡ **Only occasionally do cT air masses affect the weather outside their source regions.** However, when a cT air mass does move from its source region, it can cause extremely hot, droughtlike conditions in the Great Plains in the summer. Movement of such air masses in the fall results in mild weather in the Great Lakes region, often called Indian summer. Conditions during Indian summer are unseasonably warm and mild, as shown in Figure 8.

Figure 8 A cT air mass produces a few days of warm weather amid the cool days of fall in the Great Lakes region.

Section 20.1 Assessment

Reviewing Concepts

1. ⬡ What is an air mass?
2. ⬡ What happens as an air mass moves over an area?
3. ⬡ How are air masses classified?
4. ⬡ Which types of air masses have the greatest effect on weather in North America?
5. ⬡ Why do continental tropical air masses have little effect on weather in North America?

Critical Thinking

6. **Comparing and Contrasting** Compare and contrast the four types of air masses.
7. **Explaining** Explain which type of air mass could offer relief from a scorching summer to the Midwestern United States. Justify your choice.

8. **Applying Concepts** How can continental polar air be responsible for lake-effect snowstorms in the Great Lakes region?
9. **Identifying** Look again at Figure 3. What kinds of air masses influence the weather patterns over Florida?
10. **Synthesizing** What kind of weather could be expected in southern Canada if an mT air mass was to invade the region in mid-July?

Writing in Science

Explanatory Paragraph Pick one of the air masses shown in Figure 3 that affects the weather in your area. Write a paragraph that explains the weather typically associated with the air mass in both the summer and the winter.

20.2 Fronts

Reading Focus

Key Concepts

- What happens when two air masses meet?
- How is a warm front produced?
- What is a cold front?
- What is a stationary front?
- What are the stages in the formation of an occluded front?
- What is a middle-latitude cyclone?
- What fuels a middle-latitude cyclone?

Vocabulary

- front
- warm front
- cold front
- stationary front
- occluded front

Reading Strategy

Outlining As you read, make an outline like the one below. Include information about how each of the weather fronts discussed in this section forms and the weather associated with each.

Fronts
I. Warm front
A. _____?_____
B. _____?_____
II. Cold front
A. _____?_____
B. _____?_____

Formation of Fronts

Recall that air masses have different temperatures and amounts of moisture, depending on their source regions. Recall also that these properties can change as an air mass moves over a region. What do you think happens when two air masses meet? **When two air masses meet, they form a front, which is a boundary that separates two air masses.** Fronts can form between any two contrasting air masses. Fronts are often associated with some form of precipitation, such as that shown in Figure 9.

In contrast to the vast sizes of air masses, fronts are narrow. Most weather fronts are between about 15 and 200 km wide. Above Earth's surface, the frontal surface slopes at a low angle so that warmer, less dense air overlies cooler, denser air. In the ideal case, the air masses on both sides of a front move in the same direction and at the same speed. When this happens, the front acts simply as a barrier that travels with the air masses. In most cases, however, the distribution of pressure across a front causes one air mass to move faster than the other. When this happens, one air mass advances into another, and some mixing of air occurs.

Figure 9 Precipitation from a Storm in South Africa

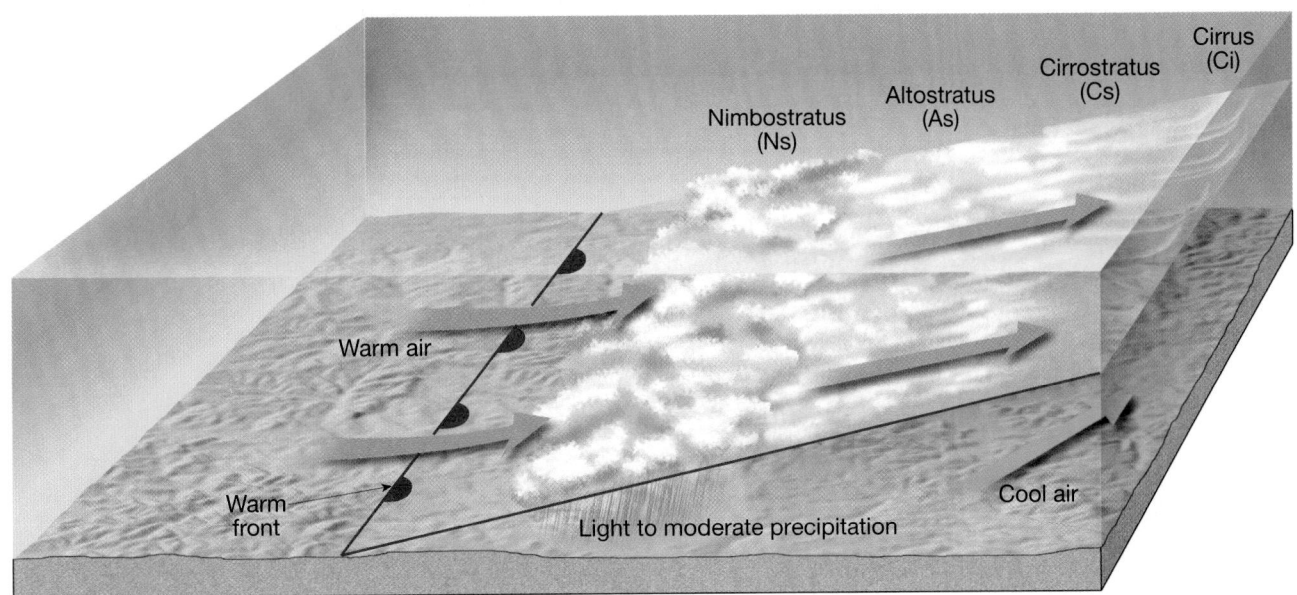

Nimbostratus
(Ns)

Altostratus
(As)

Cirrostratus
(Cs)

Cirrus
(Ci)

Warm air

Warm
front

Cool air

Light to moderate precipitation

Types of Fronts

Fronts are often classified according to the temperature of the advancing front. There are four types of fronts: warm fronts, cold fronts, stationary fronts, and occluded fronts.

Warm Fronts  **A warm front forms when warm air moves into an area formerly covered by cooler air.** On a weather map, the surface position of a warm front is shown by a red line with red semicircles that point toward the cooler air.

The slope of the warm front is very gradual, as shown in Figure 10. As warm air rises, it cools to produce clouds, and frequently precipitation. The sequence of clouds shown in Figure 10 typically comes before a warm front. The first sign of the approaching warm front is the appearance of cirrus clouds. As the front nears, cirrus clouds change into cirrostratus clouds, which blend into denser sheets of altostratus clouds. About 300 kilometers ahead of the front, thicker stratus and nimbostratus clouds appear, and rain or snow begins.

Because of their slow rate of movement and very low slope, warm fronts usually produce light-to-moderate precipitation over a large area for an extended period. A gradual increase in temperature occurs with the passage of a warm front. The increase is most apparent when a large temperature difference exists between adjacent air masses. Also, a wind shift from the east to the southwest is associated with a warm front.

Reading Checkpoint *What causes a warm front to form?*

Figure 10 Formation of a Warm Front A warm front forms when warm air glides up over a cold, dense air mass. The affected area has warmer temperatures, and light to moderate precipitation.

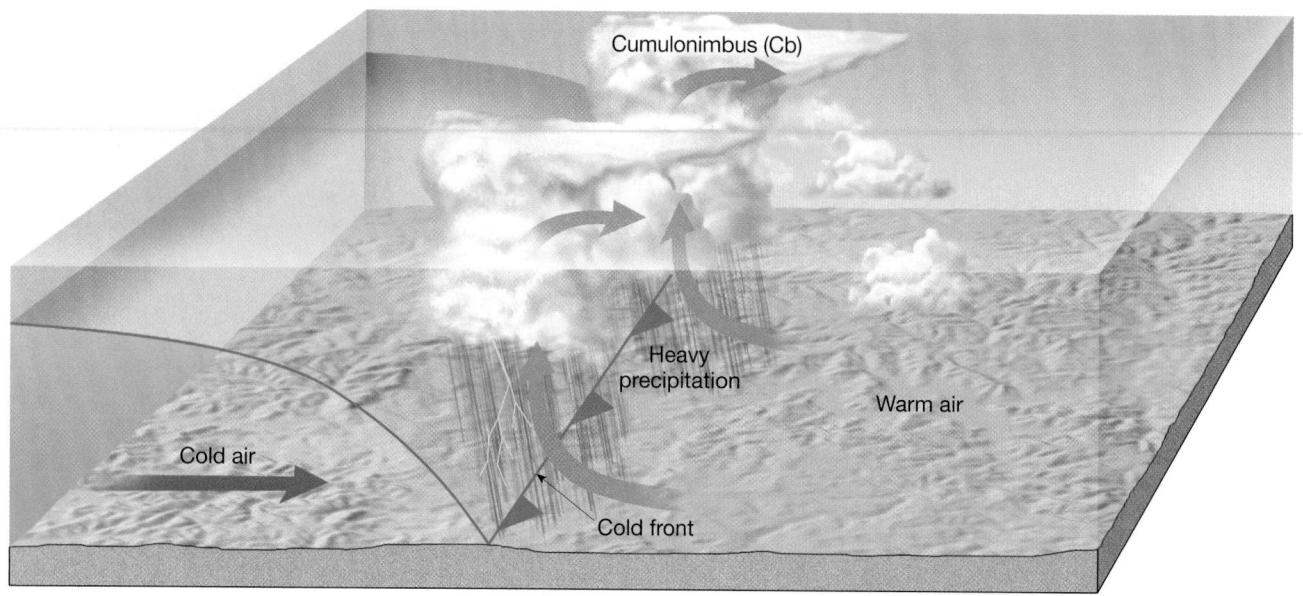

Cumulonimbus (Cb)

Heavy
precipitation

Warm air

Cold air

Cold front

Figure 11 Formation of a Cold Front A cold front forms when cold air moves into an area occupied by warmer air. The affected area experiences thunderstorms if the warm air is unstable.

Cold Fronts  A cold front forms when cold, dense air moves into a region occupied by warmer air. On a weather map, the surface position of a cold front is shown by a blue line edged with blue triangles that point toward the warmer air mass.

Figure 11 shows how a cold front develops. As this cold front moves, it becomes steeper. On average, cold fronts are about twice as steep as warm fronts and advance more rapidly than warm fronts do. These two differences—rate of movement and steepness of slope—account for the more violent weather associated with a cold front.

The forceful lifting of air along a cold front can lead to heavy downpours and gusty winds. As a cold front approaches, towering clouds often can be seen in the distance. Once the cold front has passed, temperatures drop and wind shifts. The weather behind a cold front is dominated by a cold air mass. So, weather clears soon after a cold front passes. When a cold front moves over a warm area, low cumulus or stratocumulus clouds may form behind the front.

Stationary Fronts Occasionally, the flow of air on either side of a front is neither toward the cold air mass nor toward the warm air mass, but almost parallel to the line of the front. In such cases, the surface position of the front does not move, and a stationary front forms. On a weather map, stationary fronts are shown by blue triangles on one side of the front and red semicircles on the other. Sometimes, gentle to moderate precipitation occurs along a stationary front.

✓ **Reading Checkpoint** *How are cold fronts different from warm fronts?*

Occluded Fronts 🌀**When an active cold front overtakes a warm front, an occluded front forms.** As you can see in Figure 12, an occluded front develops as the advancing cold air wedges the warm front upward. The weather associated with an occluded front is generally complex. Most precipitation is associated with the warm air's being forced upward. When conditions are suitable, however, the newly formed front is capable of making light precipitation of its own.

It is important to note that the descriptions of weather associated with fronts are general descriptions. The weather along any individual front may or may not conform to the idealized descriptions you've read about. Fronts, like all aspects of nature, do not always behave as we would expect.

Middle-Latitude Cyclones

Now that you know about air masses and what happens when they meet, you're ready to apply this information to understanding weather patterns in the United States. The main weather producers in the country are middle-latitude cyclones. On weather maps, these low-pressure areas are shown by the letter L.

🌀**Middle-latitude cyclones are large centers of low pressure that generally travel from west to east and cause stormy weather.** The air in these weather systems moves in a counterclockwise direction and in toward the center of the low. Most middle-latitude cyclones have a cold front, and frequently a warm front, extending from the central area. Forceful lifting causes the formation of clouds that drop abundant precipitation.

How do cyclones develop and form? The first stage is the development of a front, which is shown in Figure 14A on page 569. The front forms as two air masses with different temperatures move in opposite directions. Over time, the front takes on a wave shape, as shown in Figure 14B. The wave is usually hundreds of kilometers long.

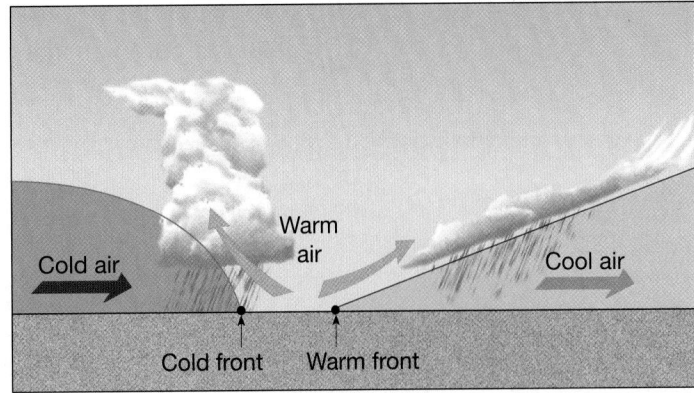

A A cold front moves toward a warm front, forcing warm air aloft.

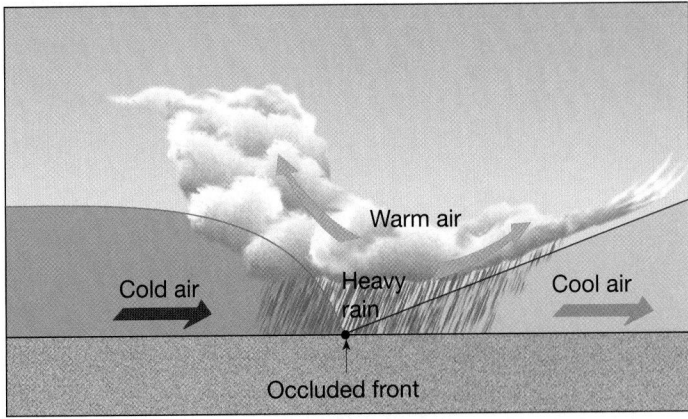

B A cold front merges with the warm front to form an occluded front that drops heavy rains.

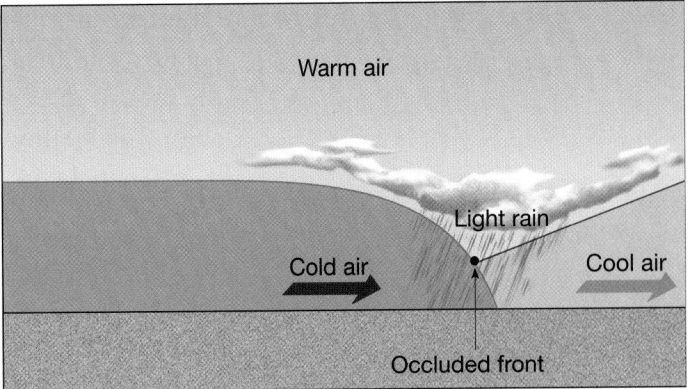

C Because occluded fronts often move slowly, light precipitation can fall for several days.

Figure 12 An occluded front forms when a cold front overtakes a warm front, producing a complex weather pattern.

As the wave develops, warm air moves towards Earth's poles. There it invades the area formerly occupied by colder air. Meanwhile, cold air moves toward the equator. This change in airflow near the surface is accompanied by a change in pressure. The result is airflow in a counterclockwise direction, as Figure 14C shows.

Recall that a cold front advances faster than a warm front. When this occurs in the development of a middle-latitude cyclone, the cold front closes in and eventually lifts the warm front, as Figure 14D shows. This process, which is known as occlusion, forms the occluded front shown in Figure 14E. As occlusion begins, the storm often gets stronger. Pressure at the storm's center falls, and wind speeds increase. In the winter, heavy snowfalls and blizzard-like conditions are possible during this phase of the storm's evolution. A satellite view of this phase of a mature cyclone is shown in Figure 13.

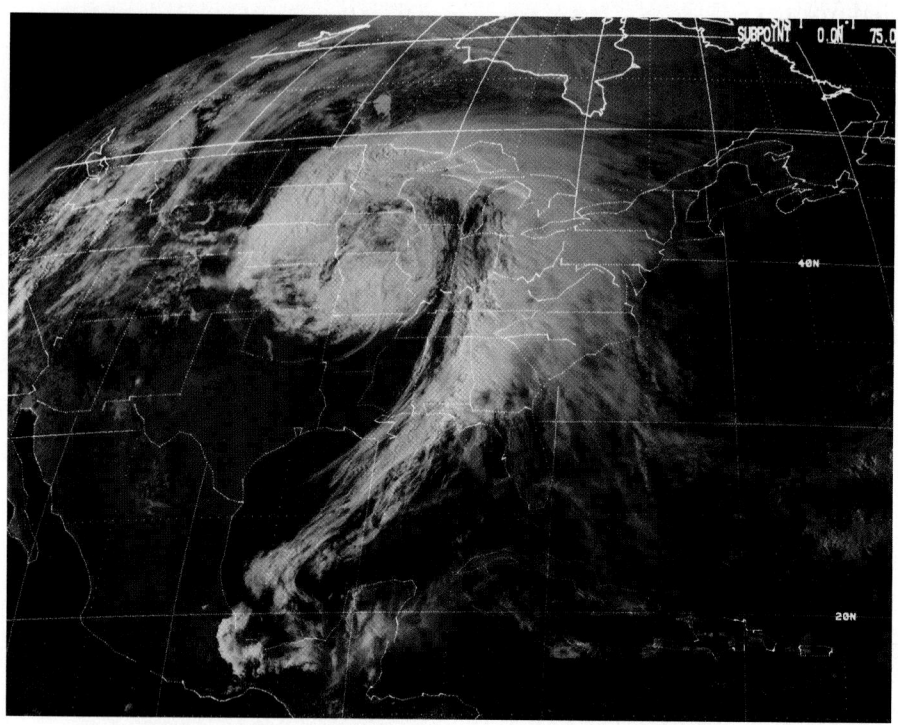

Figure 13 This is a satellite view of a mature cyclone over the eastern United States.

As more of the warm air is forced to rise, the amount of pressure change weakens. In a day or two, the entire warm area is displaced. Only cold air surrounds the cyclone at low levels. The horizontal temperature difference that existed between the two air masses is gone. At this point, the cyclone has exhausted its source of energy. Friction slows the airflow near the surface, and the once highly organized counterclockwise flow ceases to exist (Figure 14F).

The Role of Airflow Aloft

Airflow aloft plays an important role in maintaining cyclonic and anticyclonic circulation. In fact, these rotating surface wind systems are actually generated by upper-level flow.

Cyclones often exist for a week or longer. For this to happen, surface convergence must be offset by outflow somewhere higher in the atmosphere. As long as the spreading out of air high up is equal to or greater than the surface inflow, the low-pressure system can be sustained. ⬤ **More often than not, air high up in the atmosphere fuels a middle-latitude cyclone.**

Reading Checkpoint   *How do middle-latitude cyclones form and develop?*

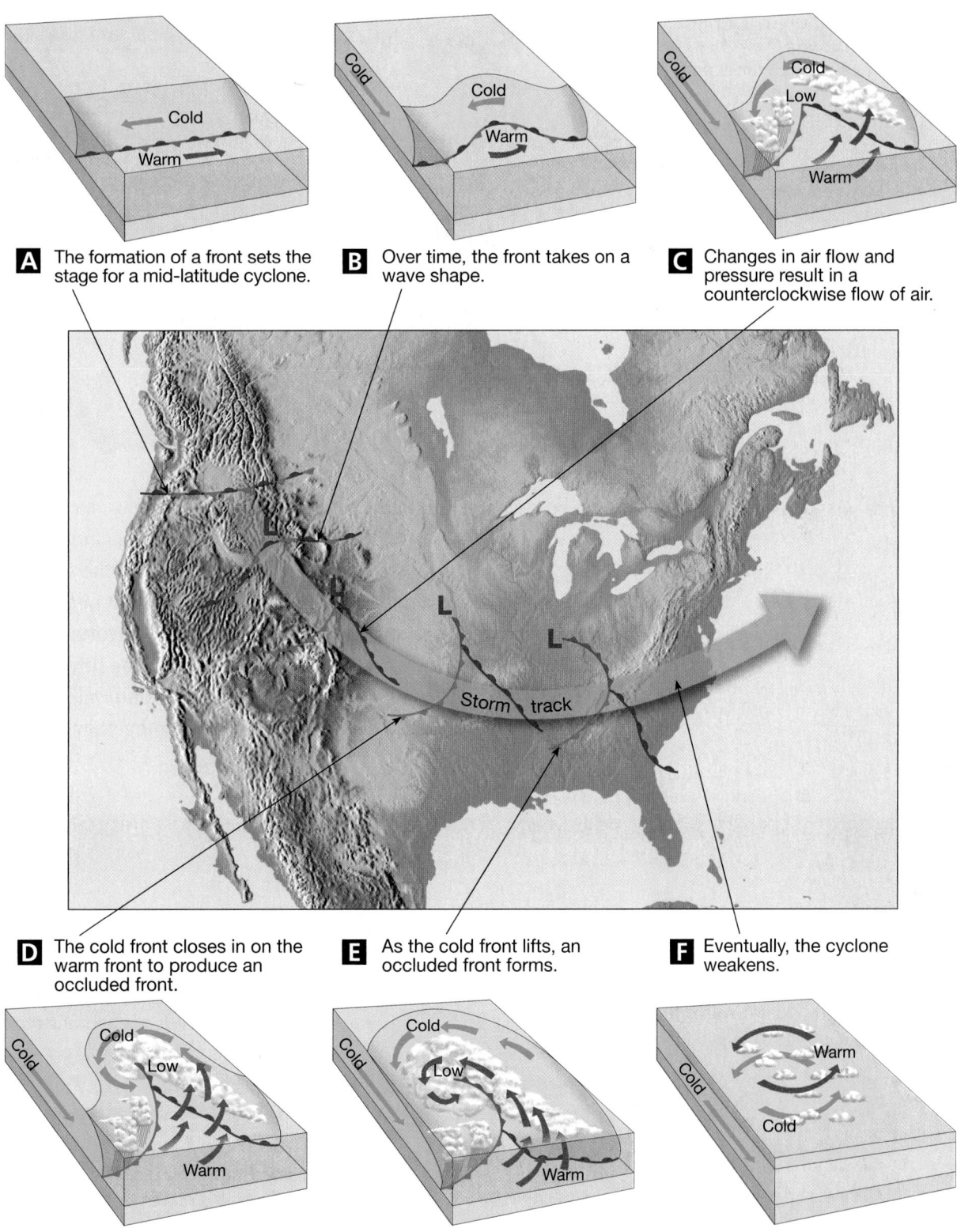

A The formation of a front sets the stage for a mid-latitude cyclone.

B Over time, the front takes on a wave shape.

C Changes in air flow and pressure result in a counterclockwise flow of air.

D The cold front closes in on the warm front to produce an occluded front.

E As the cold front lifts, an occluded front forms.

F Eventually, the cyclone weakens.

Figure 14 Cyclones have a fairly predictable life cycle.

Figure 15 Movements of air high in the atmosphere fuel the cyclones and anticyclones near Earth's surface.
Comparing and Contrasting *Compare and contrast the movement of air in cyclones and anticyclones.*

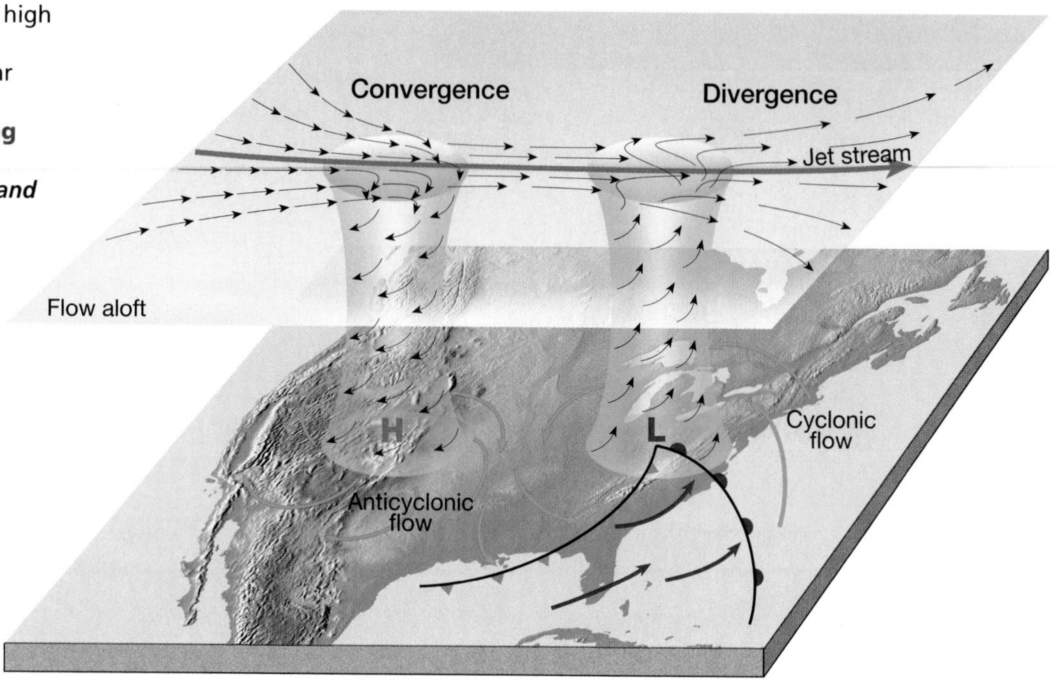

Because cyclones bring stormy weather, they have received far more attention than anticyclones. However, a close relationship exists between these two pressure systems. As shown in Figure 15, the surface air that feeds a cyclone generally originates as air flowing out of an anticyclone. As a result, cyclones and anticyclones typically are found next to each other. Like a cyclone, an anticyclone depends on the flow of air high in the atmosphere to maintain its circulation. In an anticyclone, air spreading out at the surface is balanced by air coming together from high up.

Section 20.2 Assessment

Reviewing Concepts

1. What happens when two air masses meet?
2. How does a warm front form?
3. What is a cold front?
4. What is a stationary front?
5. What are the stages in the formation of an occluded front?
6. What is a middle-latitude cyclone?
7. What causes a middle-latitude cyclone to sustain itself?

Critical Thinking

8. **Comparing and Contrasting** Compare and contrast warm fronts and cold fronts.

9. **Synthesizing** Use Figure 15 and what you know about Earth's atmosphere to describe the air movement and pressure conditions associated with both cyclones and anticyclones.

Writing in Science

Explanatory Paragraph Write a paragraph to explain this statement: The formation of an occluded front marks the beginning of the end of a middle-latitude cyclone.

20.3 Severe Storms

Reading Focus

Key Concepts

- What is a thunderstorm?
- What causes a thunderstorm to form?
- What is a tornado?
- How does a tornado form?
- What is a hurricane?
- How does a hurricane form?

Vocabulary

- thunderstorm
- tornado
- hurricane
- eye wall
- eye
- storm surge

Reading Strategy

Identifying Cause and Effect Copy the table and complete it as you read this section.

Severe Storms		
	Causes	Effects
Thunderstorms	a. ___?___	b. ___?___
Tornadoes	c. ___?___	d. ___?___
Hurricanes	e. ___?___	f. ___?___

Severe weather has a fascination that everyday weather does not provide. For example, a thunderstorm with its jagged lightning and booming thunder can be an awesome sight. The damage and destruction caused by these storms, as well as other severe weather, can also be frightening. A single severe storm can cause billions of dollars in property damage as well as many deaths. This section discusses three types of severe storms and their causes.

Thunderstorms

Have you ever seen a small whirlwind carry dust or leaves upward on a hot day? Have you observed a bird glide effortlessly skyward on an invisible updraft of hot air? If so, you have observed the effects of the vertical movements of relatively warm, unstable air. These examples are caused by a similar thermal instability that occurs during the development of a thunderstorm. **A thunderstorm is a storm that generates lightning and thunder. Thunderstorms frequently produce gusty winds, heavy rain, and hail.** A thunderstorm may be produced by a single cumulonimbus cloud and influence only a small area. Or it may be associated with clusters of cumulonimbus clouds that stretch for kilometers along a cold front.

Figure 16 Lightning is a spectacular and potentially dangerous feature of a thunderstorm.

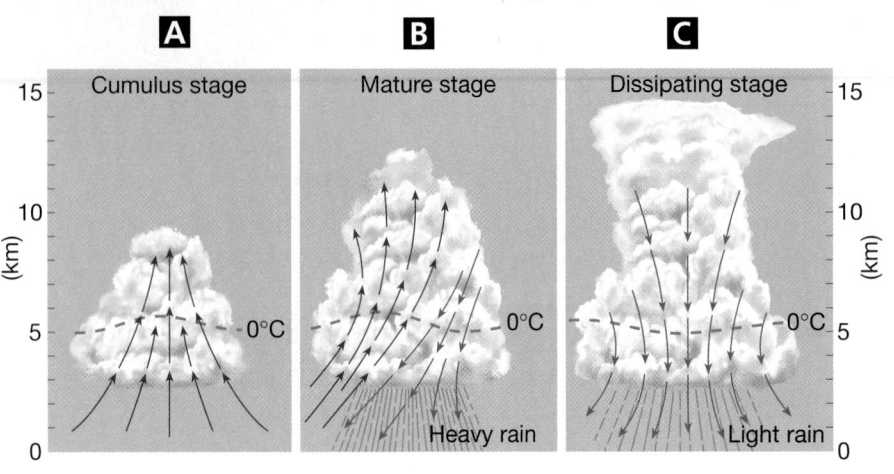

Stages in the Development of a Thunderstorm

A Cumulus stage

B Mature stage

C Dissipating stage

Heavy rain

Light rain

Figure 17 A During the cumulus stage, warm, moist air is supplied to the cloud. **B** Heavy precipitation falls during the mature stage. **C** The cloud begins to evaporate during the dissipating stage. **Observing** *How do the clouds involved in the development of a thunderstorm vary?*

Occurrence of Thunderstorms How common are thunderstorms? Consider these numbers. At any given time, there are an estimated 2000 thunderstorms in progress on Earth. As you might expect, the greatest number occurs in the tropics where warmth, plentiful moisture, and instability are common atmospheric conditions. About 45,000 thunderstorms take place each day. More than 16 million occur annually around the world. The United States experiences about 100,000 thunderstorms each year, most frequently in Florida and the eastern Gulf Coast region. Most parts of the country have from 30 to 100 storms each year. The western margin of the United States has little thunderstorm activity because warm, moist, unstable maritime tropical air seldom penetrates this region.

Development of Thunderstorms 🔑 **Thunderstorms form when warm, humid air rises in an unstable environment.** The development of a thunderstorm generally involves three stages. During the cumulus stage, shown in Figure 17A, strong updrafts, or upward movements of air, supply moist air. Each new surge of warm air rises higher than the last and causes the cloud to grow vertically.

Usually within an hour of the initial updraft, the mature stage begins, as shown in Figure 17B. At this point in the development of the thunderstorm, the amount and size of the precipitation is too great for the updrafts to support. So, heavy precipitation is released from the cloud. The mature stage is the most active stage of a thunderstorm. Gusty winds, lightning, heavy precipitation, and sometimes hail are produced during this stage.

Eventually, downdrafts, or downward movements of air, dominate throughout the cloud, as shown in Figure 17C. This final stage is called the dissipating stage. During this stage, the cooling effect of the falling precipitation and the flowing in of colder air from high above cause the storm to die down.

The life span of a single cumulonimbus cell within a thunderstorm is only about an hour or two. As the storm moves, however, fresh supplies of warm, humid air generate new cells to replace those that are scattering.

 **Reading Checkpoint** *Describe the stages in the development of a thunderstorm.*

Tornadoes

Tornadoes are violent windstorms that take the form of a rotating column of air called a vortex. The vortex extends downward from a cumulonimbus cloud. Some tornadoes consist of a single vortex. But within many stronger tornadoes, smaller vortexes rotate within the main funnel. These smaller vortexes have diameters of only about 10 meters and rotate very rapidly. Smaller vortexes explain occasional observations of tornado damage in which one building is totally destroyed, while another one, just 10 or 20 meters away, suffers little damage.

Occurrence and Development of Tornadoes In the United States, about 770 tornadoes are reported each year. These severe storms can occur at any time during the year. However, the frequency of tornadoes is greatest from April through June. In December and January, tornadoes are far less frequent.

Most tornadoes form in association with severe thunderstorms. An important process in the formation of many tornadoes is the development of a mesocyclone. A mesocyclone is a vertical cylinder of rotating air that develops in the updraft of a thunderstorm. The formation of this large vortex begins as strong winds high up in the atmosphere cause winds lower in the atmosphere to roll, as shown in Figure 18A. In Figure 18B, you can see that strong thunderstorm updrafts cause this rolling air to tilt. Once the air is completely vertical (Figure 18C), the mesocyclone is well established. The formation of a mesocyclone does not necessarily mean that a tornado will follow. Few mesocyclones produce tornadoes like the one shown in Figure 19 on page 574.

Go Online

SC*LINKS* NSTA

For: Links on fronts and severe weather
Visit: www.SciLinks.org
Web Code: cjn-6203

Q *What is the most destructive tornado on record?*

A The Tri-State Tornado, which occurred on March 18, 1925, started in southeastern Missouri and remained on the ground over a distance of 352 kilometers, until it reached Indiana. Casualties included 695 people dead and 2027 injured. Property losses were also great, with several small towns almost totally destroyed.

Formation of a Mesocyclone

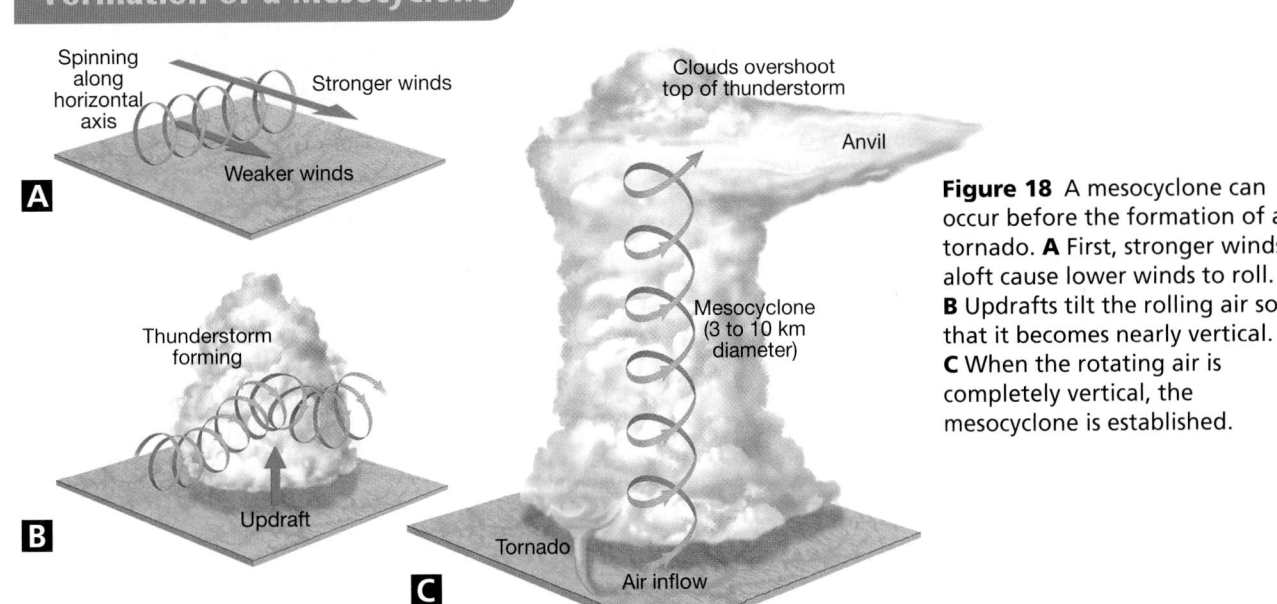

Spinning along horizontal axis

Stronger winds

Weaker winds

A

Thunderstorm forming

Updraft

B

Clouds overshoot top of thunderstorm

Anvil

Mesocyclone (3 to 10 km diameter)

Tornado

Air inflow

C

Figure 18 A mesocyclone can occur before the formation of a tornado. **A** First, stronger winds aloft cause lower winds to roll. **B** Updrafts tilt the rolling air so that it becomes nearly vertical. **C** When the rotating air is completely vertical, the mesocyclone is established.

Figure 19 The tornado shown here descended from the lower portion of a mesocyclone in the Texas Panhandle in May, 1996.

Tornado Intensity Pressures within some tornadoes have been estimated to be as much as 10 percent lower than pressures immediately outside the storm. The low pressure within a tornado causes air near the ground to rush into a tornado from all directions. As the air streams inward, it spirals upward around the core. Eventually, the air merges with the airflow of the cumulonimbus cloud that formed the storm. Because of the tremendous amount of pressure change associated with a strong tornado, maximum winds can sometimes approach 480 kilometers per hour. One scale used to estimate tornado intensity is the Fujita tornado intensity scale, shown in Table 1. Because tornado winds cannot be measured directly, a rating on this scale is determined by assessing the worst damage produced by a storm.

Tornado Safety The Storm Prediction Center (SPC) located in Norman, Oklahoma, monitors different kinds of severe weather. The SPC's mission is to provide timely and accurate forecasts and watches for severe thunderstorms and tornadoes. Tornado watches alert people to the possibility of tornadoes in a specified area for a particular time period. A tornado warning is issued when a tornado has actually been sighted in an area or is indicated by weather radar.

	Table 1 Fujita Tornado Intensity Scale	
Intensity	**Wind Speed Estimates (kph)**	**Typical Damage**
F0	< 116	Light damage. Some damage to chimneys; branches broken off trees; shallow-rooted trees pushed over; sign boards damaged.
F1	116–180	Moderate damage. Peels surface off roofs; mobile homes pushed off foundations or overturned; moving cars blown off roads.
F2	181–253	Considerable damage. Roofs torn off frame houses; mobile homes demolished; large trees snapped or uprooted; light-object missiles generated; cars lifted off ground.
F3	254–332	Severe damage. Roofs and some walls torn off well-constructed houses; trains overturned; most trees in forest uprooted; heavy cars lifted off the ground and thrown.
F4	333–419	Devastating damage. Well-constructed houses leveled; structures with weak foundations blown some distance; cars thrown; large missiles generated.
F5	> 419	Incredible damage. Strong frame houses lifted off foundations and carried away; automobile-sized missiles fly through the air in excess of 100 m; bark torn off trees.

Hurricanes

If you've ever been to the tropics or seen photographs of these regions, you know that warm breezes, steady temperatures, and heavy but brief tropical showers are the norm. It is ironic that these tranquil regions sometimes produce the most violent storms on Earth. **Whirling tropical cyclones that produce winds of at least 119 kilometers per hour are known in the United States as hurricanes.** In other parts of the world, these severe tropical storms are called typhoons, cyclones, and tropical cyclones.

Regardless of the name used to describe them, hurricanes are the most powerful storms on Earth. At sea, they can generate 15-meter waves capable of destruction hundreds of kilometers away. Should a hurricane hit land, strong winds and extensive flooding can cause billions of dollars in damage and great loss of life. Hurricane Floyd, which is shown in a satellite image in Figure 20, was one such storm. In September 1999, Floyd brought flooding rains, high winds, and rough seas to a large portion of the Atlantic coast. More than 2.5 million people evacuated their homes. Torrential rains caused devastating inland flooding. Floyd was the deadliest hurricane to strike the U.S. mainland since Hurricane Agnes in 1972. Most of the deaths caused by Hurricane Floyd were the result of drowning from floods.

Hurricanes are becoming a growing threat because more and more people are living and working near coasts. At the close of the twentieth century, more than 50 percent of the U.S. population lived within 75 kilometers of a coast. This number is expected to increase even more in the early decades of this century. High population density near shorelines means that hurricanes and other large storms place millions of people at risk.

Q *Why are hurricanes given names, and who picks the names?*

A Actually, the names are given once the storms reach tropical-storm status (winds between 61–119 kilometers per hour). Tropical storms are named to provide ease of communication between forecasters and the general public regarding forecasts, watches, and warnings. Tropical storms and hurricanes can last a week or longer, and two or more storms can be occurring in the same region at the same time. Thus, names can reduce the confusion about what storm is being described.

The World Meteorological Organization creates the lists of names. The names for Atlantic storms are used again at the end of a six-year cycle unless a hurricane was particularly destructive or otherwise noteworthy. Such names are retired to prevent confusion when the storms are discussed in future years.

Figure 20 This satellite image of Hurricane Floyd shows its position off the coast of Florida a few days before the hurricane moved onto land. Floyd eventually made landfall near Cape Fear, North Carolina.

Occurrence of Hurricanes Most hurricanes form between about 5 and 20 degrees north and south latitude. The North Pacific has the greatest number of storms, averaging 20 per year. The coastal regions of the southern and eastern United States experience fewer than five hurricanes, on average, per year. Although many tropical disturbances develop each year, only a few reach hurricane status. A storm is a hurricane if the spiraling air has winds blowing at speeds of at least 119 kilometers per hour.

Development of Hurricanes A hurricane is a heat engine that is fueled by the energy given off when huge quantities of water vapor condense. ◖**Hurricanes develop most often in the late summer when water temperatures are warm enough to provide the necessary heat and moisture to the air.** A hurricane begins as a tropical disturbance that consists of disorganized clouds and thunderstorms. Low pressures and little or no rotation are characteristic of these storms.

Occasionally, tropical disturbances become hurricanes. Figure 21 shows a cross section of a well-developed hurricane. An inward rush of warm, moist surface air moves toward the core of the storm. The air then turns upward and rises in a ring of cumulonimbus clouds. This doughnut-shaped wall that surrounds the center of the storm is the **eye wall.** Here the greatest wind speeds and heaviest rainfall occur. Surrounding the eye wall are curved bands of clouds that trail away from the center of the storm. Notice that near the top of the hurricane, the rising air is carried away from the storm center. This outflow provides room for more inward flow at the surface.

At the very center of the storm is the **eye** of the hurricane. This well-known feature is a zone where precipitation ceases and winds subside. The air within the eye gradually descends and heats by compression, making it the warmest part of the storm.

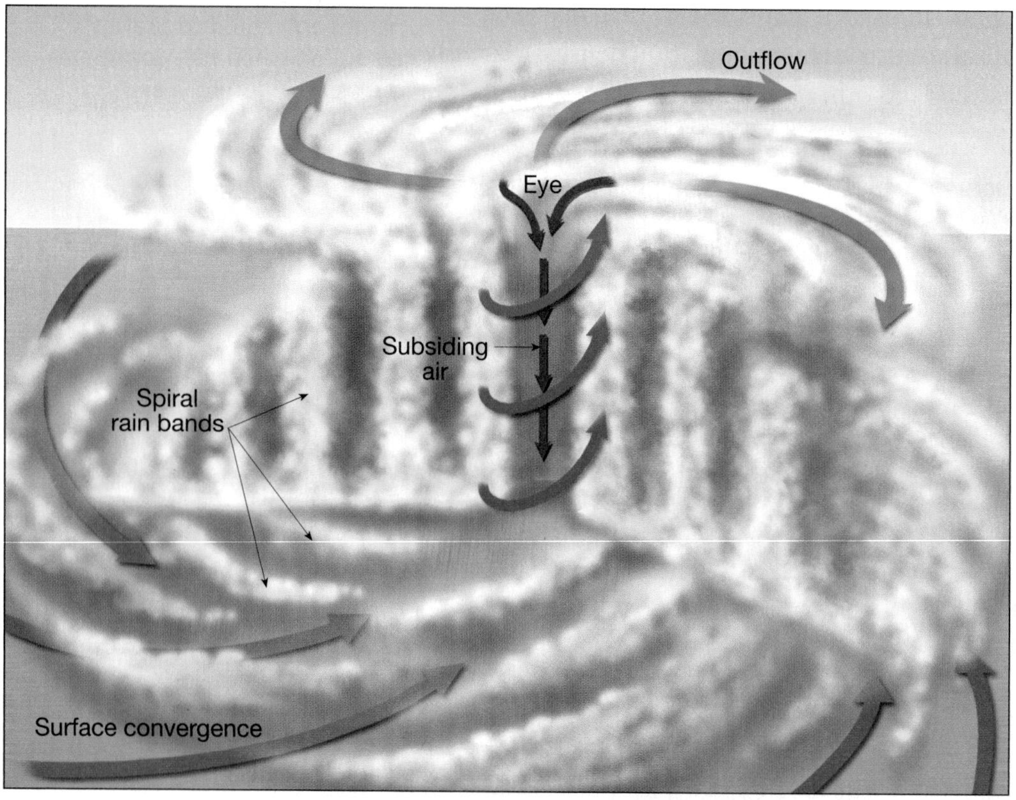

Figure 21 Cross Section of a Hurricane The eye of the hurricane is a zone of relative calm, unlike the eye wall region where winds and rain are most intense.
Describing *Describe the airflow in different parts of a hurricane.*

Outflow

Eye

Subsiding air

Spiral rain bands

Surface convergence

Hurricane Intensity The intensity of a hurricane is described using the Saffir-Simpson scale shown in Table 2. The most devastating damage from a hurricane is caused by storm surges. A **storm surge** is a dome of water about 65 to 80 kilometers wide that sweeps across the coast where a hurricane's eye moves onto land.

A hurricane weakens when it moves over cool ocean waters that cannot supply adequate heat and moisture. Intensity also drops when storms move over land because there is not sufficient moisture. In addition, friction with the rough land surface causes winds to subside. Finally, if a hurricane reaches a location where the airflow aloft is unfavorable, it will die out.

Table 2 Saffir-Simpson Hurricane Scale		
Category	**Sustained Wind Speeds (kph)**	**Typical Damage**
1	119–153	Storm surge 1.2–1.5 meters; some damage to unanchored mobile homes, shrubbery, and trees; some coastal flooding; minor pier damage.
2	154–177	Storm surge 1.6–2.4 meters; some damage to buildings' roofs, doors, and windows; considerable damage to mobile homes and piers; moderate coastal flooding.
3	178–209	Storm surge 2.5–3.6 meters; some structural damage to small buildings; some large trees blown over; mobile homes destroyed; some coastal and inland flooding.
4	210–249	Storm surge 3.7–5.4 meters; severe damage to trees and signs; complete destruction of mobile homes; extensive damage to doors and windows; severe flooding inland.
5	> 249	Storm surge >5.4 meters; complete roof failure on many buildings; some complete building failure; all treees and signs blown away; major inland flooding.

Section 20.3 Assessment

Reviewing Concepts

1. ⬤ What is a thunderstorm?
2. ⬤ What causes a thunderstorm?
3. ⬤ What is a tornado?
4. ⬤ How does a tornado form?
5. ⬤ What is a hurricane?
6. ⬤ How does a hurricane form?

Critical Thinking

7. **Formulating Hypotheses** What kind of front is associated with the formation of tornadoes? Explain.

8. **Synthesizing** Explain why a hurricane quickly loses its strength as the storm moves onto land.

Writing in Science

Explanatory Paragraph Examine Tables 1 and 2 to contrast the damage caused by tornadoes and hurricanes. Use the data to explain why even though hurricanes have lower wind speeds, they often cause more damage than tornadoes do.

How the Earth Works

Winds and Storms

The world's atmosphere is forever on the move. **Wind,** or air in motion, occurs because solar radiation heats up some parts of the sea and land more than others. Air above these hot spots becomes warmer and lighter than the surrounding air and therefore rises. Elsewhere, cool air sinks because it is heavier. Winds blow because air squeezed out by sinking, cold air is sucked in under rising, warm air. Wind may move slowly as in a gentle breeze. In extreme weather, wind moves rapidly, creating terrifyingly destructive storms.

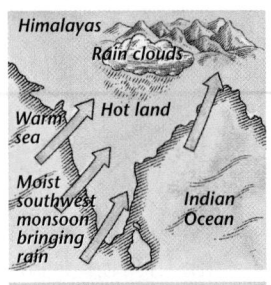

Southwest Monsoon
During the early summer, the hot, dry lands of Asia draw in cooler, moist air from the Indian Ocean.

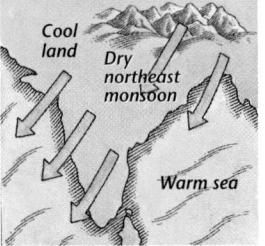

Northeast Monsoon
The cold, dry winter air from Central Asia brings chilly, dusty conditions to South Asia.

MONSOONS
Seasonal winds called monsoons affect large areas of the tropics and subtropics. They occur in South Asia, southern North America, eastern Australia, and other regions of the world. In South Asia, southwest monsoons generally bring desperately needed rain from May until October.

THUNDERSTORMS
Thunderclouds are formed by powerful updrafts of air that occur along cold fronts or over ground heated very strongly by the sun. Ice crystals and water droplets high in the cloud are torn apart and smashed together with such ferocity that they become charged with electricity. Thunderstorms can unleash thunder, lightning, wind, rain, and hail.

LIGHTNING AND THUNDER
Electricity is discharged from a thundercloud in the form of lightning. A bolt of lightning can heat the air around it to a temperature four times as hot as the sun. The heated air expands violently and sends out a rumbling shock wave that we hear as thunder.

TORNADOES

Tornadoes may strike wherever thunderstorms occur. A **tornado** begins when a column of strongly rising warm air is set spinning by high winds at a cloud's top. A funnel is formed and may touch the ground. With winds that can rise above 419 kph, tornadoes can lift people, cars, and buildings high into the air and then smash them back to the ground.

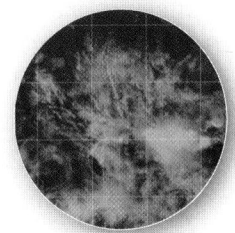

BLIZZARDS

In a **blizzard,** heavy snowfall and strong winds often make it impossible to see. Winds pile up huge drifts of snow. Travel and communication can grind to a halt.

HOW TROPICAL STORMS DEVELOP

Tropical storms begin when water evaporates over an ocean in a hot tropical region to produce huge clouds and thunderstorms. When the storms cluster together and whirl around a low-pressure center, they form a **tropical cyclone.** Tropical cyclones with winds of at least 119 kph are called hurricanes in some regions and **typhoons** in other regions. The sequence below shows satellite images of an Atlantic hurricane.

Stage 1: Thunderstorms develop over the ocean.

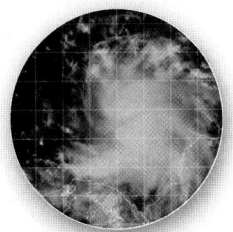

Stage 2: Storms group to form a swirl of cloud.

IMPACT OF TROPICAL STORMS

Tropical storms are often devastating. The strongest winds, with gusts sometimes more than 249 kph, occur at the storm's center, or eye. When a tropical storm strikes land, raging winds can uproot trees and destroy buildings. Vast areas may be swamped by torrential rain, and coastal regions may be overwhelmed by a **storm surge,** a wall of water some 8 m high sucked up by the storm's eye.

These women wade through the streets of Dhaka, Bangladesh, flooded by a tropical cyclone. In 1991, a cyclone killed more than 130,000 Bangladeshis.

A Pacific typhoon struck this ship off the coast of Taiwan in November 2000. Many of the crew members fell victim to the raging sea.

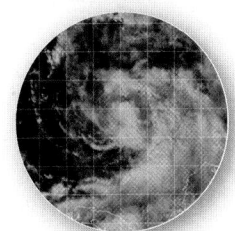

Stage 3: Winds grow and a distinct center forms in the cloud swirl.

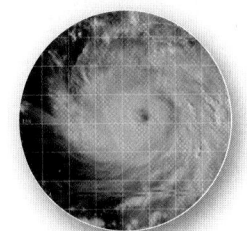

Stage 4: Eye forms. The hurricane is now at its most dangerous.

Stage 5: Eye passes over land. The hurricane starts to weaken.

ASSESSMENT

1. **Key Terms** Define **(a)** wind, **(b)** tornado, **(c)** blizzard, **(d)** tropical cyclone, **(e)** typhoon, **(f)** storm surge.

2. **Physical Processes** How do thunderstorms come into being?

3. **Economic Activities** **(a)** How can storms have a negative impact on economic activities? **(b)** How can monsoons benefit economic activities?

4. **Natural Hazards** How can a tropical cyclone result in the loss of thousands of lives?

5. **Critical Thinking** **Developing a Hypothesis** Since 1991, the Bangladeshi government has constructed hundreds of concrete storm shelters in coastal regions of the country. **(a)** Why do you think the government decided on this policy? **(b)** How do you think the policy has benefited the country?

Middle-Latitude Cyclones

You've learned that much of the day-to-day weather in the United States is caused by middle-latitude cyclones. In this lab, you will identify some of the atmospheric conditions associated with a middle-latitude cyclone. Then you will use what you know about Earth's atmosphere and weather to predict how the movement of the low-pressure system affects weather in the area.

Problem
How do middle-latitude cyclones affect weather patterns?

Materials
- tracing paper
- sharp pencil
- paper clips or removable tape
- metric ruler
- colored pencils

Skills
Observing, Comparing and Contrasting, Predicting

Procedure

1. Use the paper clips or removable tape to secure the tracing paper over the map on the facing page.

2. Carefully trace all of the features and boundaries on the map. Be sure to include the isobars—the lines that show atmospheric pressure. Use the ruler to trace lines EA and GF.

3. Remove the tracing paper. Place it next to the map.

4. Transfer all of the letters and numbers on the map to your tracing.

5. Use the colored pencils to color the land and water areas on the tracing. Also color the symbols used to designate the fronts.

6. Identify and label the cold front, warm front, and occluded front on your tracing.

7. Draw arrows that show the direction of surface winds at points A, C, E, F, and G.

Analyze and Conclude

1. **Describing** In which direction are the surface winds moving?

2. **Identifying** At which stage of formation is the cyclone? Explain your answer. Refer to Figure 14 if necessary.

3. **Explaining** Is the air in the center of the cyclone rising or falling? What effect does this have on the potential for condensation and precipitation?

4. **Inferring** Find the center of the low, which is marked with the letter L. What type of front has formed here? What happens to the maritime tropical air in this type of front?

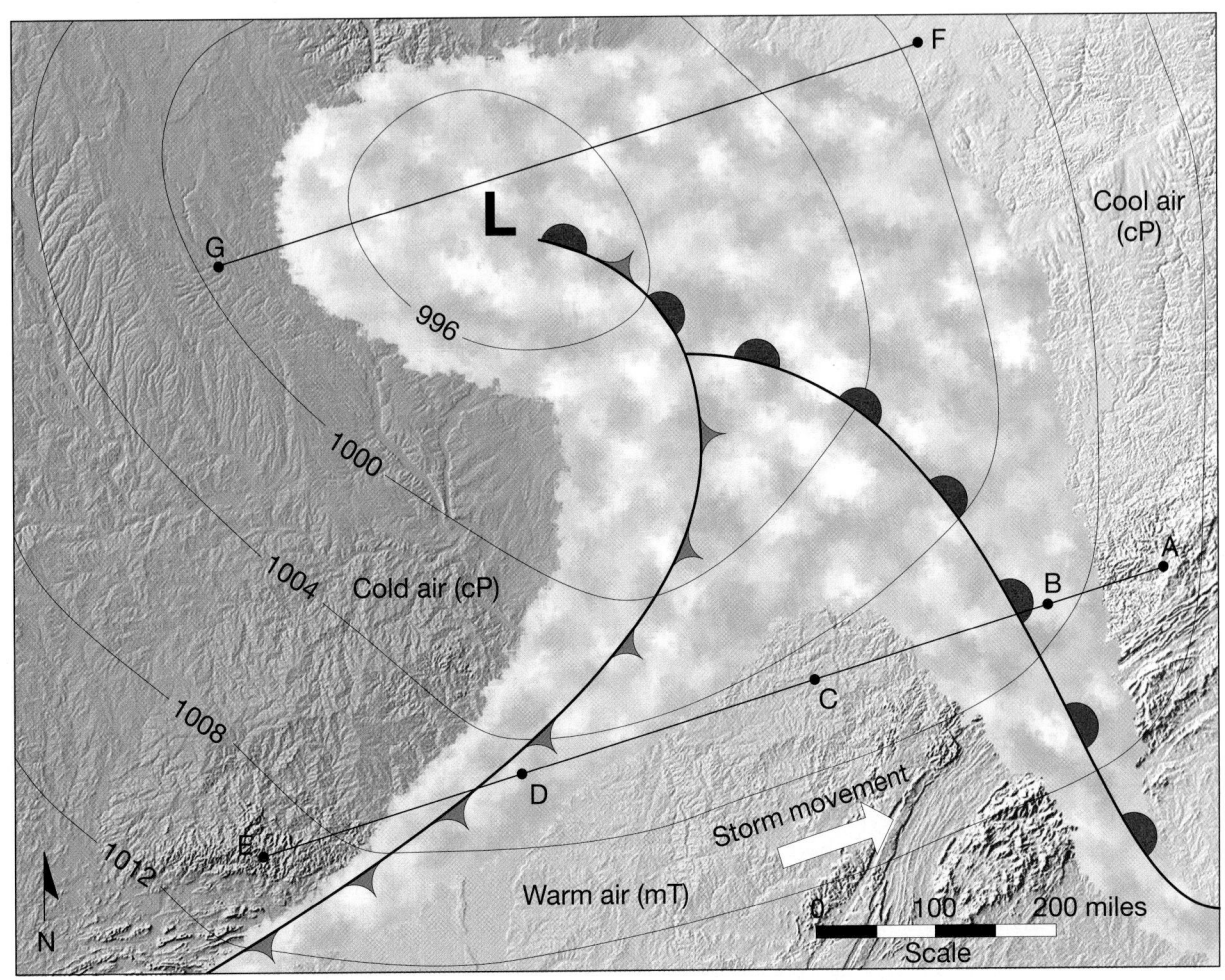

5. **Predicting** Once the warm front passes, in which direction will the wind at point B blow?

6. **Synthesizing** Describe the changes in wind direction and moisture in the air that will likely occur at point D after the cold front passes.

7. **Synthesizing** Describe the wind directions, humidity, and precipitation expected for a city as the cyclone moves and the city's relative position changes from point A to B, point C, point D, and finally from point D to E.

Go Further Find out and explain how subpolar lows affect middle-latitude cyclones over the United States in winter.

20.1 Air Masses

Key Concepts

- An air mass is an immense body of air that is characterized by similar temperatures and amounts of moisture at any given altitude.

- As an air mass moves, its characteristics can change and so does the weather in the area over which the air mass moves.

- Air masses are classified according to their source region, the place where they form.

- Much of the weather in North America is influenced by continental polar (cP) and maritime tropical (mT) air masses.

- Polar (P) or tropical (T) indicates the temperature of an air mass. Continental (c) or maritime (m) indicates whether the air mass is dry or humid.

Vocabulary
air mass, *p. 559*

20.2 Fronts

Key Concepts

- When two air masses meet, they form a front, which is a boundary that separates two contrasting air masses.

- A warm front forms when warm air moves into an area formerly covered by cooler air.

- A cold front forms when cold, dense air moves into a region occupied by warmer air.

- A stationary front forms when the surface position between two air masses does not move.

- An occluded front forms when a cold front overtakes a warm front, producing a complex weather pattern.

- A middle-latitude cyclone is a large center of low pressure that generally travels from west to east and causes stormy weather.

Vocabulary
front, *p. 564;* warm front, *p. 565;* cold front, *p. 566;* stationary front, *p. 566;* occluded front, *p. 567*

20.3 Severe Storms

Key Concepts

- A thunderstorm generates thunder and lightning and frequently produces gusty winds, heavy rain, and hail. Thunderstorms form when warm, humid air rises in an unstable environment.

- Tornadoes are violent windstorms that take the form of a rotating column of air called a vortex, which extends downward from a cumulonimbus cloud. Most tornadoes are associated with severe thunderstorms.

- Hurricanes are whirling tropical cyclones with high winds that sometimes develop over the ocean when water temperatures are warm enough to provide the necessary heat and moisture to fuel the storms.

Vocabulary
thunderstorm, *p. 571;* tornado, *p. 573;* hurricane, *p. 575;* eye wall, *p. 576;* eye, *p. 576;* storm surge, *p. 577*

Thinking Visually

Concept Map Use what you know about fronts and air masses to complete this concept map.

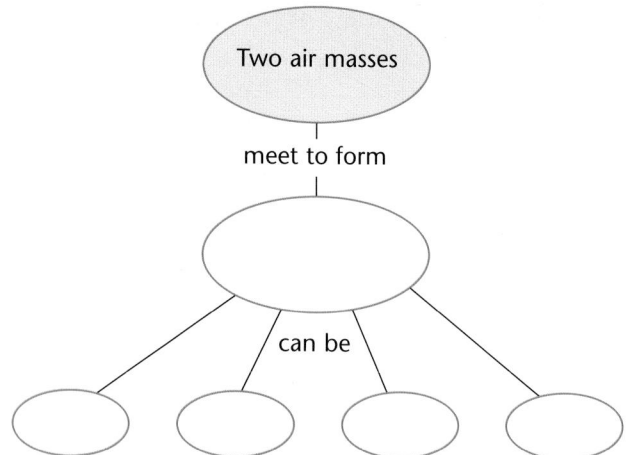

Reviewing Content

Choose the letter that best answers the question or completes the statement.

1. If an area is experiencing consecutive days of constant weather, this weather is called
   a. air-mass weather.
   b. warm-front weather.
   c. cold-front weather.
   d. occluded-front weather.

2. An air mass that forms over the Gulf of Mexico is a(n)
   a. cP air mass.   b. mP air mass.
   c. cT air mass.   d. mT air mass.

3. Air masses that have the greatest influence on weather in the midwestern United States are
   a. mT and cT air masses.
   b. cP and mT air masses.
   c. mP and cP air masses.
   d. cT and cP air masses.

4. Lake-effect snow is associated with a(n)
   a. mP air mass.   b. mT air mass.
   c. cP air mass.   d. cT air mass.

5. "Rain long foretold, long last; short notice, soon past." The first five words of this weather proverb refer to a(n)
   a. warm front.   b. cold front.
   c. anticyclone.   d. tornado.

6. Which front often produces hours of moderate-to-light precipitation over a large area?
   a. polar   b. maritime
   c. cold   d. warm

7. A thunderstorm is most intense during its
   a. cumulus stage.   b. wave stage.
   c. mature stage.   d. dissipating stage.

8. When a hurricane reaches land, its intensity decreases as the result of
   a. increase in pressure and temperature.
   b. lack of cold, dry air to fuel the storm.
   c. successive updrafts into the eye wall.
   d. friction and the lack of warm, moist air.

9. The eye of a hurricane
   a. has the greatest wind speeds.
   b. is warmer than the rest of the storm.
   c. experiences high pressures.
   d. is responsible for heavy precipitation.

Understanding Concepts

10. What kinds of changes occur as an air mass moves over an area?

11. Describe the effects of cP and mT air masses on much of the weather in the United States.

12. Describe weather associated with a warm front.

13. What kind of weather is associated with a cold front while it is over an area and once it passes?

14. What is a stationary front?

15. Sequence the steps that lead to the formation of an occluded front.

16. Describe the stages involved in the development of a middle-latitude cyclone.

17. How are cyclones and anticyclones related?

18. Describe the formation of a thunderstorm.

19. What is a mesocyclone and how does it form?

20. Describe the different parts of a hurricane.

Use this map to answer Questions 21–24.

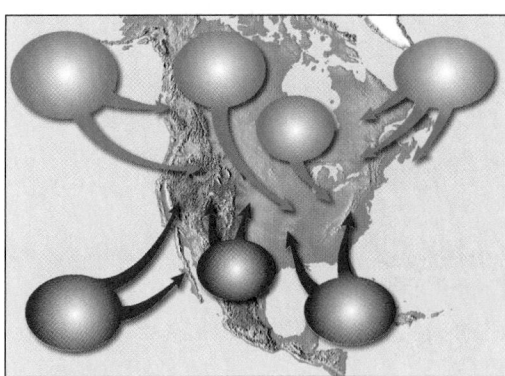

21. Name the three red air masses and identify the source region of each.

22. Identify the cold air masses, starting with the air mass farthest west and moving eastward.

23. Which air masses would supply the largest amount of precipitation to the area east of the Rocky Mountains?

24. Which of the air masses has the greatest influence on weather along the northwest coast?

Critical Thinking

25. **Comparing and Contrasting** Compare and contrast polar air masses with tropical air masses.

26. **Synthesizing** What type of air mass is responsible for most of the warm fronts east of the Rocky Mountains?

27. **Inferring** What kinds of weather conditions would you expect in regions north of a middle-latitude cyclone during winter?

28. **Comparing and Contrasting** Compare and contrast tornadoes and hurricanes.

29. **Identifying Cause and Effect** Great damage and significant loss of life can take place a day or more after a hurricane has moved ashore and weakened. Explain why this might happen.

Map Skills

Use the map to answer Questions 30–34.

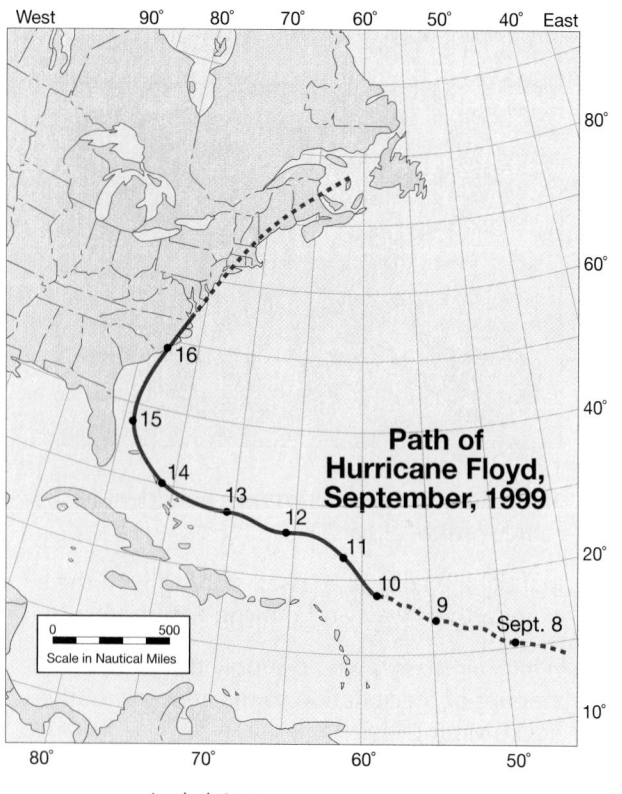

Path of Hurricane Floyd, September, 1999

0 — 500 Scale in Nautical Miles

- - - - - - - - - - tropical storm
———————— hurricane

30. **Reading Maps** Over which ocean did Hurricane Floyd develop and move?

31. **Interpreting Graphs** On which days was Floyd a tropical storm?

32. **Describing** Describe the path of Hurricane Floyd from September 10 through September 16.

33. **Inferring** When was Hurricane Floyd most intense? Explain.

34. **Reading Maps** When and where did Hurricane Floyd move onto land?

Concepts in Action

35. **Synthesizing** Describe weather conditions that you would observe if the center of a middle-latitude cyclone passed north of you.

36. **Applying Concepts** What kinds of negative effects might a hurricane have on coastal ecosystems?

37. **Writing in Science** Use what you know about weather patterns to write a paragraph to explain which parts of the Earth system interact to produce the high snowfall in the Great Lakes region of North America.

Performance-Based Assessment

Applying Concepts Find out about precautions people should take during any of the three types of severe storms discussed in this chapter. Summarize your findings in three separate posters.

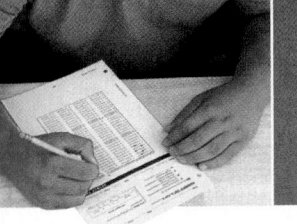

Standardized Test Prep

Use the maps below and what you know about thunderstorms and tornadoes to answer the questions on this page.

Choose the letter that best answers the question or completes the statement.

1. What part of Texas experiences the greatest average number of days with thunderstorms per year?
   (A) the southernmost tip
   (B) the southwestern portion of the state
   (C) the northern panhandle
   (D) the southeastern corner

2. The part of Texas that experiences the greatest average number of tornadoes per 26,000 km^2 is the area colored
   (A) tan.
   (B) green.
   (C) yellow.
   (D) orange.

3. How many tornadoes on average are experienced in the area referred to in Question 2?
   (A) 1.0–2.0
   (B) 2.0–3.0
   (C) 5.0–7.0
   (D) 7.0–9.0

Answer the following question in complete sentences.

4. Does there appear to be a relationship between the number of days with thunderstorms and the average number of tornadoes in Texas? Explain.

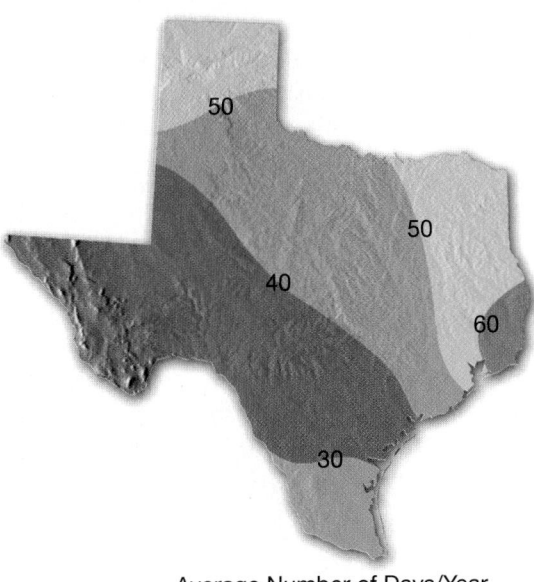

Average Number of Days/Year
with Thunderstorms

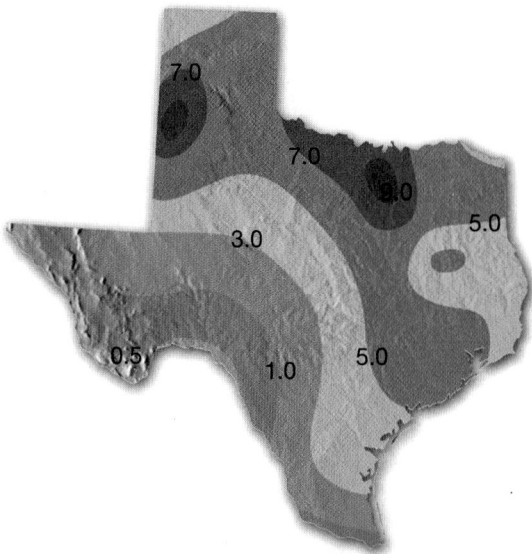

Average Annual Tornadoes
per 26,000 km^2

CONCEPTS in Action

Quick Lab
Observing How Land and Water Absorb and Release Energy

Exploration Lab
Human Impact on Climate and Weather

How the Earth Works
Coniferous Forests

 GEODe EARTH SCIENCE Heating the Atmosphere
↳ The Greenhouse Effect

DISCOVERY CHANNEL SCHOOL **Video Field Trip**

Polar Weather

Take a field trip to the North and South Poles with Discovery Channel and learn about the coldest places on Earth. Answer the following questions after watching the video.

1. Why is Antarctica, which holds 80 percent of the world's ice, technically called a desert?

2. What would happen to the ocean if the ice shelves around Antarctica melted?

 **Go Online PHSchool.com**

For: Chapter 21 Resources
Visit: PHSchool.com
Web Code: cjk-9999

Climate determines the types of vegetation ▶ that grow in an area. This forest in Denali Park, Alaska, includes a mix of coniferous forest and tundra vegetation.

Chapter Preview

Inquiry Activity

Global Warming: Fact or Fiction?

Global warming is perhaps one of the most hotly debated environmental issues. Is the world getting warmer? Do we need to worry about it? What are the economic and political issues behind the debate? In this activity, you will gather the evidence to decide for yourself.

Procedure

1. Gather information on the topic using the Internet. Focus your search to answer questions 1 through 4 under Think About It.

2. Now evaluate opposing points of view on this topic from credible sources. Search the Internet to find three articles that present the view that the damaging consequences of global warming are real. Find three articles that suggest that concerns about global warming are overstated.

3. Print each article and analyze the information you've collected by completing items 5 and 6. If your analysis shows that you don't have enough information, search for some additional articles.

4. Formulate your own opinion on the global warming issue based on your research. Complete items 7 and 8.

Think About It

1. What is the greenhouse effect?

2. List three greenhouse gases.

3. List three facts about global warming.

4. List three uncertainties about global warming.

5. Use a marker to highlight the facts in each article that are supported by data.

6. Use a marker of another color to highlight the claims in each article that are not well supported.

7. What did you decide? Is global warming a real threat, or are there more important environmental issues to resolve?

8. Write a letter in which you attempt to persuade your state senator to agree with your position. Support your stance with facts based on your research.

21.1 Factors That Affect Climate

Reading Focus

Key Concepts

- How does latitude affect climate?
- How does elevation affect climate?
- What effect does a mountain range have on climate?
- How do large bodies of water affect climate?
- What effect do global winds have on climate?
- How does vegetation affect climate?

Vocabulary

- ◆ tropical zone
- ◆ temperate zone
- ◆ polar zone

Reading Strategy

Summarizing Information Copy the table. As you read, summarize the effect(s) each factor has on climate.

Factor	Effect(s) on Climate
1. Latitude	a. _____?_____
2. Elevation	b. _____?_____
3. Topography	c. _____?_____
4. Water bodies	d. _____?_____
5. Global wind	e. _____?_____
6. Vegetation	f. _____?_____

Figure 1 Maroon Bells Area, Colorado All of Earth's spheres interact to affect climate.
Identifying *In the photograph, identify at least two components of each of the spheres shown.*

Recall from Chapter 17 that climate includes not only the average weather conditions of an area, but also any variations from those norms. In this section, you will learn that climate involves more than just the atmosphere. Powered by the sun, the climate system is a complex exchange of energy and moisture among Earth's different spheres, all of which are shown in Figure 1.

Factors That Affect Climate

The varied nature of Earth's surface and the many interactions that occur among Earth's spheres give every location a distinctive climate. You will now find out how latitude, elevation, topography, large bodies of water, global winds, and vegetation affect the two most important elements of climate—temperature and precipitation.

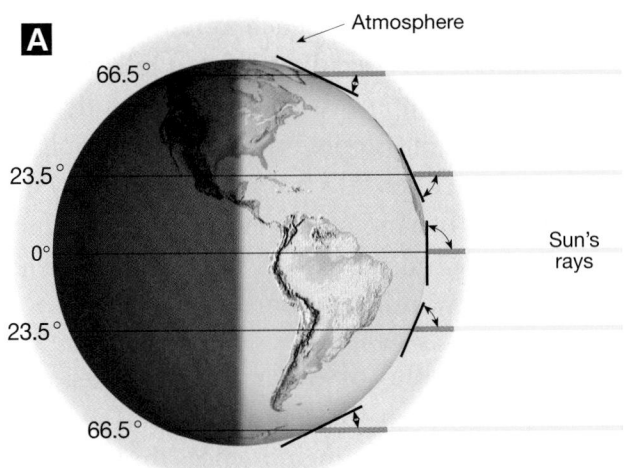

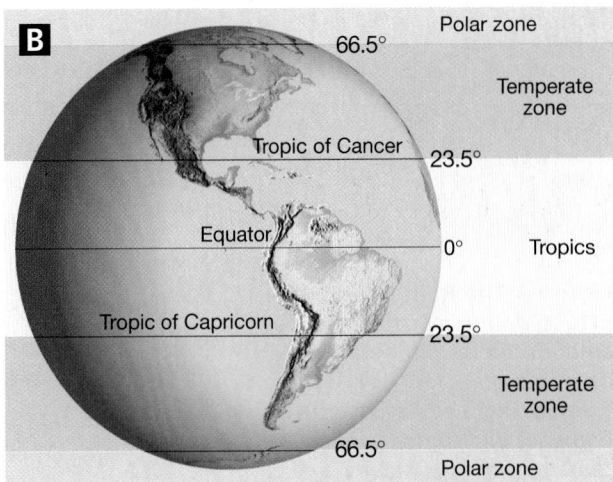

Latitude Latitude is the distance north or south of the equator. As latitude increases, the intensity of solar energy decreases. Can you explain why? Study Figures 2A and 2B. Notice that near the equator, the sun's energy strikes the planet at nearly right angles. Therefore, in this region, between about 23.5° north (Tropic of Cancer) and 23.5° south (Tropic of Capricorn) of the equator, the sun's rays are most intense. This region is called the tropics, or the **tropical zones.** Temperatures in the tropical zones are generally warm year-round. In the **temperate zones,** which are between about 23.5° and 66.5° north and south of the equator, the sun's energy strikes Earth at a smaller angle than near the equator. This causes solar energy to be spread out over a larger area. In addition, the length of daylight in the summer is much greater than in the winter. As a result, temperate zones have hot summers and rather cold winters. In the **polar zones,** which are between 66.5° north and south latitudes and the poles, the energy strikes at an even smaller angle, causing the light and heat to spread out over an even larger area. Therefore, the polar regions experience very cold temperatures, even in the summer.

Elevation Elevation, or height above sea level, is another factor that affects the climate of an area. Recall from Chapter 17 that air temperature decreases with elevation by an average of about 6.5°C Celsius every 1000 meters. The higher the elevation is, the colder the climate. The elevation of an area also determines the amount of precipitation it receives. Examine the graph in Figure 3 to see how the climates of two cities at roughly the same latitude are affected by their height above sea level.

 **Reading Checkpoint** *How does the intensity of solar radiation vary at different parts of Earth?*

Figure 2 Earth's Major Climate Zones A Solar energy striking Earth's surface near the poles is less intense than radiation striking near the equator. **B** Earth can be divided into three zones based on these differences in incoming solar radiation.

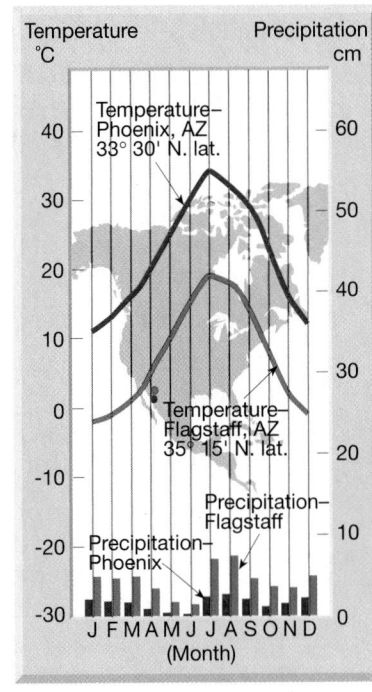

Figure 3 Climate Data for Two Cities This climate graph shows data for two cities in Arizona. Phoenix has an elevation of 338 m. Flagstaff has an elevation of 2134 m.
Interpreting Graphs *How does elevation affect annual temperatures and precipitation?*

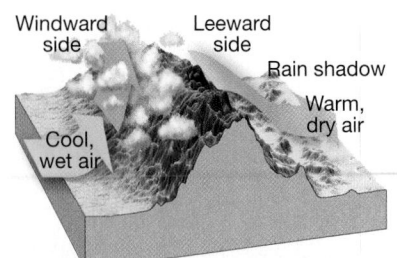

Windward side   Leeward side

Rain shadow

Warm, dry air

Cool, wet air

Figure 4 The Rain Shadow Effect Mountains influence the amount of precipitation that falls over an area.
Comparing and Contrasting *Compare and contrast the climates on either side of a mountain.*

Topography 🌀Topographic features such as mountains play an important role in the amount of precipitation that falls over an area. As shown in Figure 4, humid air on the windward side of a mountain moves up the mountain's slopes and eventually cools to form clouds. Heavy precipitation often falls from these clouds. By the time air reaches the leeward side of a mountain, much of the moisture is lost. This dry area is called a rain shadow. Rain shadows can extend for hundreds of kilometers downwind of a mountain range.

Water Bodies 🌀Large bodies of water such as lakes and oceans have an important effect on the temperature of an area because the temperature of the water body influences the temperature of the air above it. Places downwind of a large body of water generally have cooler summers and milder winters than places at the same latitude that are farther inland. In the Quick Lab below, you can observe how a body of water can influence climate.

Quick Lab

Observing How Land and Water Absorb and Release Energy

Materials

2 small, identical containers; 2 laboratory thermometers; water; dry sand; masking tape; watch or clock; book; paper towels or rags for spills

Procedure

1. On a separate sheet of paper, make a copy of the data table shown.
2. Fill one container three-quarters full of dry sand.
3. Fill the other container three-quarters full of water.
4. Place the containers in a sunny area on a flat surface such as a tabletop or a lab bench.
5. Place the bulb of one of the thermometers into the sand. Prop up the thermometer with a book. Tape the thermometer in place so that only the bulb is covered with sand.

6. Repeat Step 5 with the water.
7. Record the initial temperature of each substance in your data table.
8. Record the temperature of each thermometer every 5 minutes for about 20 minutes.
9. Remove the containers from the sunny area.
10. Record the temperature of each thermometer for another 20 minutes.

Analyze and Conclude

1. **Comparing and Contrasting** Which substance heated faster? Which substance cooled faster?
2. **Drawing Conclusions** How does a large body of water affect the temperature of nearby areas?

Heat Absorption and Retention of Water and Sand								
	Time	Temp H$_2$O	Temp Sand			Time	Temp H$_2$O	Temp Sand
Sunny Area	0				Shady Area	0		
	5					5		
	10					10		
	15					15		
	20					20		

Atmospheric Circulation

🔵Global winds are another factor that influences climate because they distribute heat and moisture around Earth. Recall from Chapter 19 that winds constantly move warm air toward the poles and cool air toward the equator. The low-pressure zones at the equator and in the subpolar regions lead to the formation of clouds that drop precipitation as rain or snow.

Vegetation You probably already know that the types of plants that grow in a region depend on climate, as shown in Figures 5A and 5B. But did you know that vegetation affects climate? 🔵**Vegetation can affect both temperature and the precipitation patterns in an area.** Vegetation influences how much of the sun's energy is absorbed and how quickly this energy is released. This affects temperature. During a process called transpiration, plants release water vapor from their leaves into the air. So, transpiration influences precipitation. Studies also indicate that some vegetation releases particles that act as cloud seeds. This increase in particles promotes the formation of clouds, which also influences regional precipitation patterns.

Figure 5 Arizona Vegetation
A Cacti and scrub are common types of vegetation in the hot, dry climate of Phoenix, Arizona.
B The vegetation in the highlands of Flagstaff, Arizona, is much different.
Formulating Hypotheses
Which of these areas would receive more precipitation? Why?

Section 21.1 Assessment

Reviewing Concepts

1. 🔵 How does latitude affect climate?
2. 🔵 How does elevation affect climate?
3. 🔵 How does a mountain range affect climate?
4. 🔵 How do large bodies of water affect climate?
5. 🔵 What effect do global winds have on climate?
6. 🔵 Describe different ways in which vegetation affects climate.

Critical Thinking

7. **Comparing and Contrasting** Compare and contrast tropical zones, temperate zones, and polar zones in terms of location and the intensity of solar radiation that each receives.

8. **Explaining** Explain why deserts are common on the leeward sides of mountain ranges.
9. **Applying Concepts** Look again at Figures 3 and 5. What two factors contribute to the average annual temperature in both areas?

Writing in Science

Explanatory Paragraph Write a paragraph to explain how three of the factors discussed in this section affect the climate of your area.

21.2 World Climates

Reading Focus

Key Concepts

- What is the Köppen climate classification system?
- What are humid tropical climates?
- Contrast the different types of humid mid-latitude climates.
- What are the characteristics of dry climates?
- What are the characteristics of polar climates?
- How do highland climates compare with nearby lowlands?

Vocabulary

- Köppen climate classification system
- wet tropical climate
- tropical wet and dry climate
- humid subtropical climate
- marine west coast climate
- dry-summer subtropical climate
- subarctic climate

Reading Strategy

Outlining Copy and continue the outline for each climate type discussed in this section. Include temperature and precipitation information for each climate type, as well as at least one location with that climate type.

```
I.  World Climates
    A.  Humid tropical
        1. Wet tropics
        2. _____?_____
    B.  Humid mid-latitude
        1. _____?_____
        2. _____?_____
    C.  Dry
        1. _____?_____
        2. _____?_____
```

Figure 6 An ice cap climate is a polar climate in which the average monthly temperature is always below freezing.

If you were to travel around the world, you would find an incredible variety of climates. So many, in fact, that it might be hard to believe they could all occur on the same planet! Despite the diversity, climates can be classified according to average temperatures and amount of precipitation. In this section, you will learn about the Köppen climate classification system, which is commonly used to group climates.

The Köppen Climate Classification System

Many classification systems have been used to group climates. Perhaps the best-known and most commonly used system is the Köppen climate classification system. **The Köppen climate classification system uses mean monthly and annual values of temperature and precipitation to classify climates.** This system is often used because it classifies the world into climatic regions in a realistic way.

The Köppen system has five principal groups: humid tropical climates, dry climates, humid mid-latitude climates, polar climates, and highland climates. An example of a polar climate is shown in Figure 6. Note that all of these groups, except climates classified as dry, are defined on the basis of temperature. Dry climates are classified according to the amount of precipitation that falls over an area. Each of the five major groups is further subdivided. See Figure 9 on page 594.

Figure 7 Rain Forest in Malaysia The vegetation in the tropical rain forest is the most luxuriant found anywhere on Earth.

Humid Tropical Climates

Humid tropical climates are climates without winters. Every month in such a climate has a mean temperature above 18°C. The amount of precipitation can exceed 200 cm per year. There are two types of humid tropical climates: wet tropical climates and tropical wet and dry climates.

Wet Tropical The tropical rain forest shown in Figure 7 is typical of a **wet tropical climate.** Wet tropical climates have high temperatures and much annual precipitation. Why? Recall what you've learned about how latitude affects climate. The intensity of the sun's rays in the tropics is consistently high. Because the sun is directly overhead much of the time, changes in the length of daylight throughout the year are slight. The winds that blow over the tropics cause the warm, humid, unstable air to rise, cool, condense, and fall as precipitation. Look at Figure 9 on pages 594 and 595. Notice that regions with humid tropical climates form a belt on either side of the equator.

Tropical Wet and Dry

Refer again to Figure 9. Bordering the wet tropics are climates classified as tropical wet and dry climates. **Tropical wet and dry climates** have temperatures and total precipitation similar to those in the wet tropics, but experience distinct periods of low precipitation. Savannas, which are tropical grasslands with drought-resistant trees, are typical of tropical wet and dry climates. A savanna in Africa is shown in Figure 8.

Figure 8 African Savanna Drought-resistant trees and tall grasses are typical vegetation of a savanna.

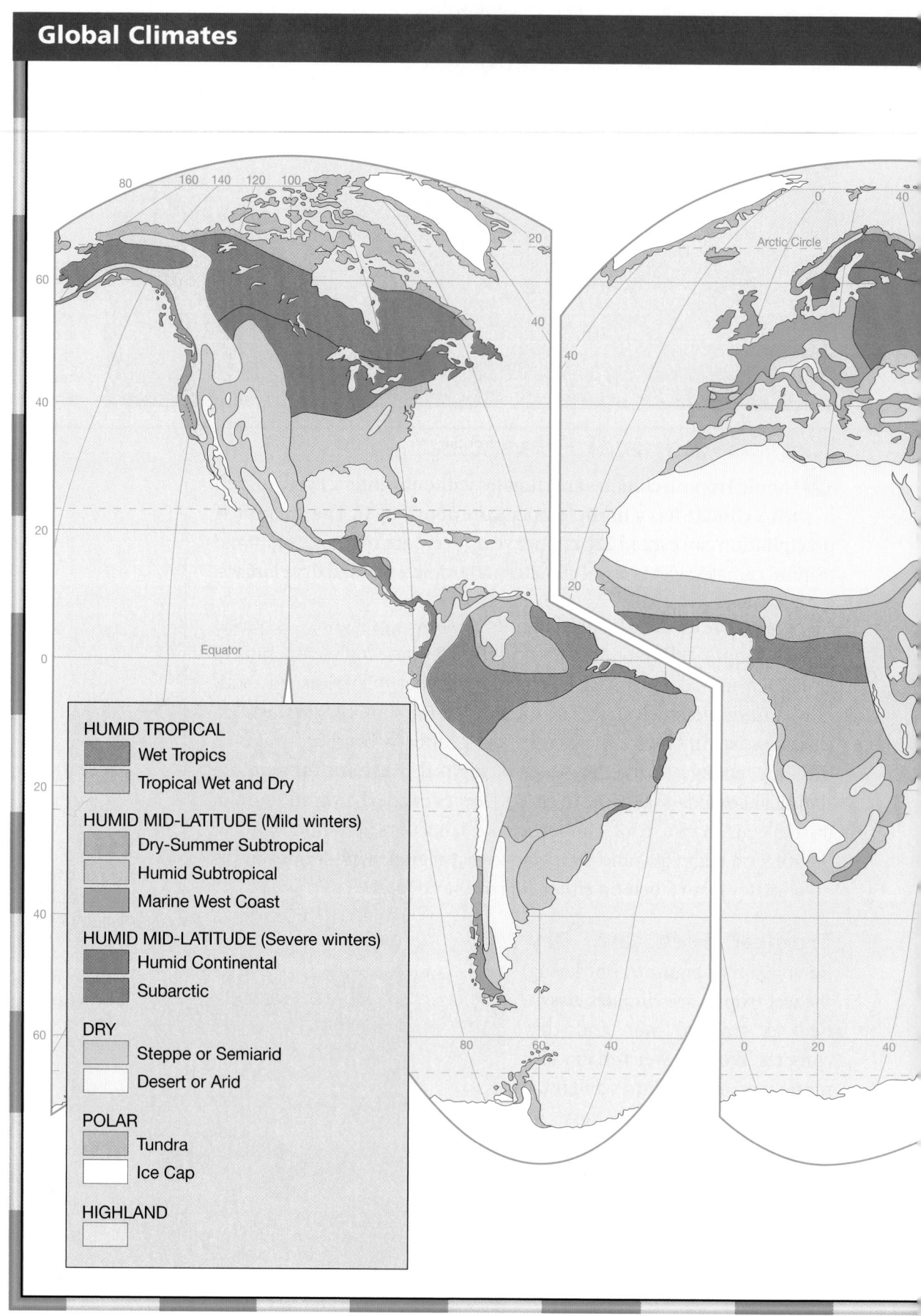

HUMID TROPICAL
- Wet Tropics
- Tropical Wet and Dry

HUMID MID-LATITUDE (Mild winters)
- Dry-Summer Subtropical
- Humid Subtropical
- Marine West Coast

HUMID MID-LATITUDE (Severe winters)
- Humid Continental
- Subarctic

DRY
- Steppe or Semiarid
- Desert or Arid

POLAR
- Tundra
- Ice Cap

HIGHLAND

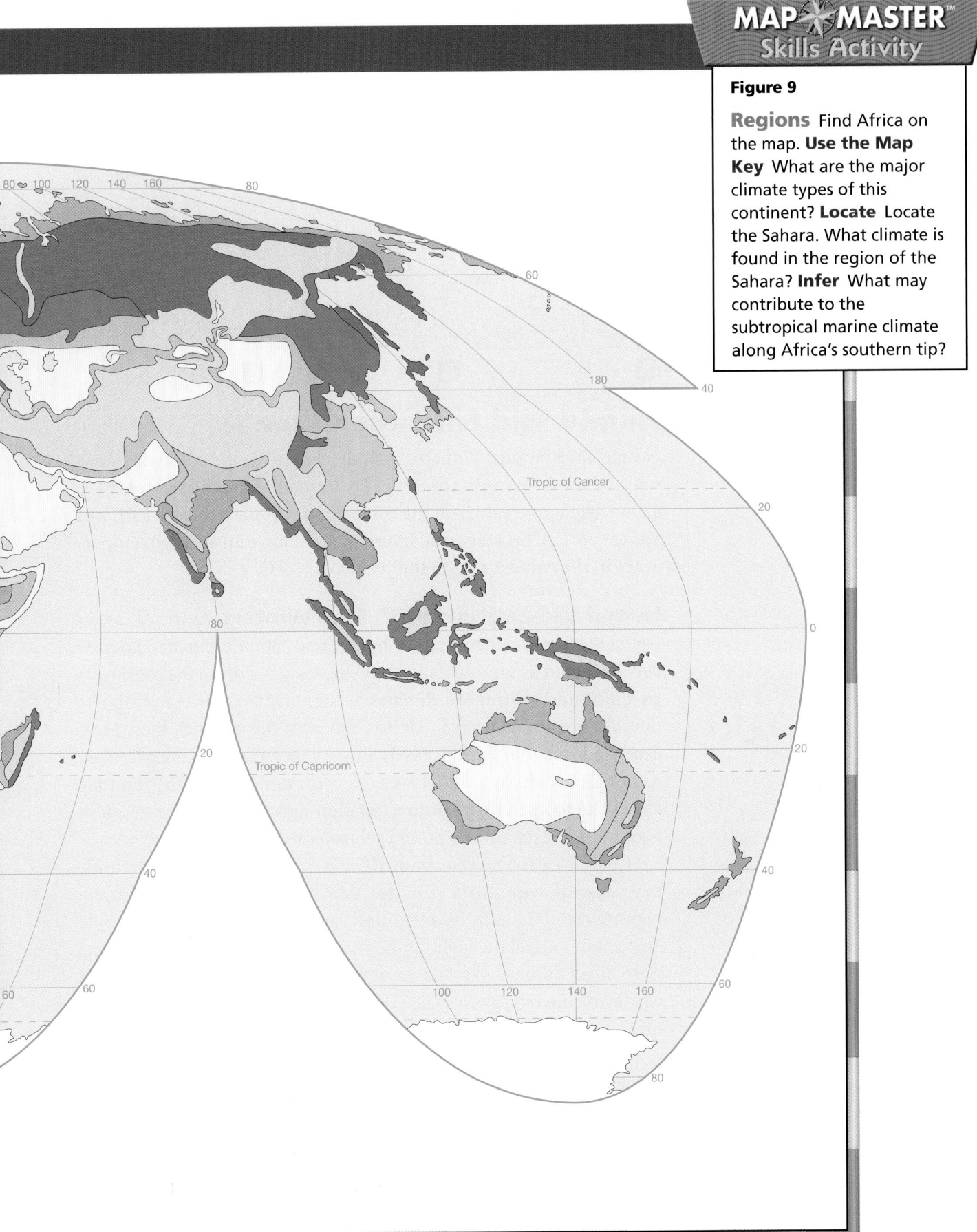

Figure 9

Regions Find Africa on the map. **Use the Map Key** What are the major climate types of this continent? **Locate** Locate the Sahara. What climate is found in the region of the Sahara? **Infer** What may contribute to the subtropical marine climate along Africa's southern tip?

80 100 120 140 160

80

60

180

40

Tropic of Cancer

20

80

0

20

Tropic of Capricorn

20

40

40

60

60

100 120 140 160

60

80

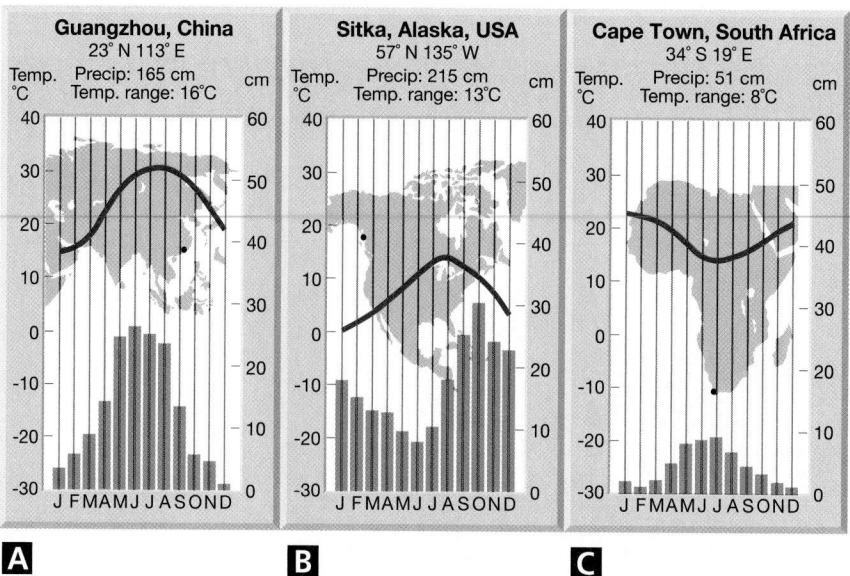

Figure 10 Each of these graphs shows typical climate data of the mid-latitude climates with mild winters. Graph **A** shows a humid subtropical climate. Graph **B** shows a marine west coast climate. Graph **C** shows a dry-summer subtropical climate.

Humid Mid-Latitude Climates

Humid mid-latitude climates include climates with mild winters as well as those with severe winters. **Climates with mild winters have an average temperature in the coldest month that is below 18°C but above −3°C. Climates with severe winters have an average temperature in the coldest month that is below −3°C.**

Humid Mid-Latitude With Mild Winters As you can see in Figure 9, there are three types of humid mid-latitude climates. Located between about 25° and 40° latitude on the eastern sides of the continents are the **humid subtropical climates.** Notice that the subtropical climate dominates the southeastern United States. In the summer, these areas experience hot, sultry weather as daytime temperatures are generally high. Although winters are mild, frosts are common in the higher-latitude areas. The temperature and precipitation data shown in the graph in Figure 10A are typical of a humid subtropical climate.

Coastal areas between about 40° and 65° north and south latitude have **marine west coast climates.** Maritime air masses over these regions result in mild winters and cool summers with an ample amount of rainfall throughout the year. In North America, the marine west coast climate extends as a narrow belt from northernmost California into southern Alaska. The data in Figure 10B are typical of marine west coast climates.

As you can see in Figure 9, regions with **dry-summer subtropical climates** are located between about 30° and 45° latitude. These climatic regions are unique because they are the only humid climate that has a strong winter rainfall maximum, as shown in Figure 10C. In the United States, dry-summer subtropical climate is found only in California. It is sometimes referred to as a mediterranean climate.

 *Describe the conditions typical of a humid subtropical climate.*

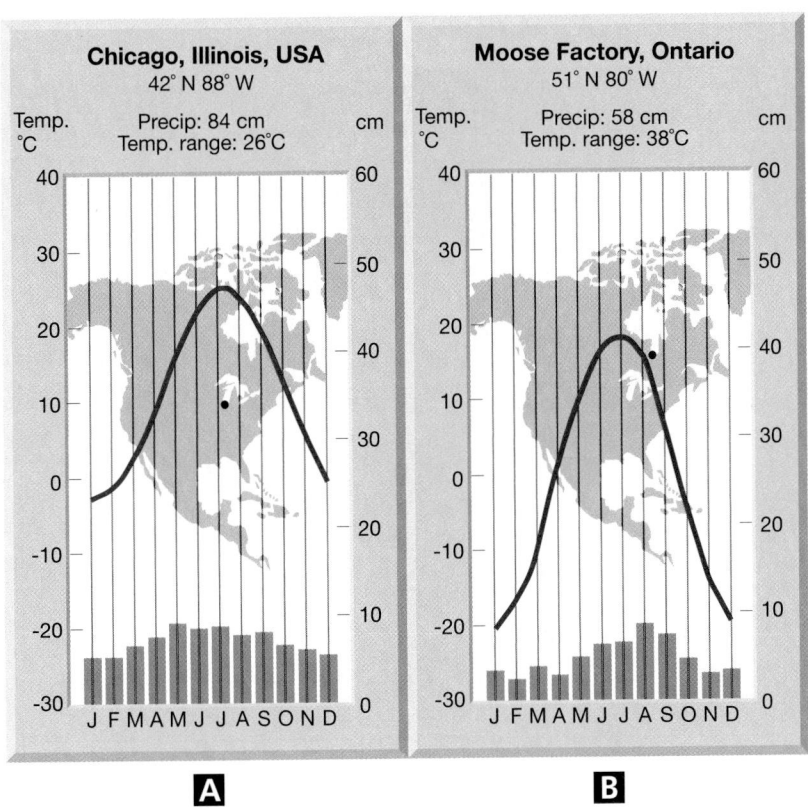

Chicago, Illinois, USA
42° N 88° W

Temp.
°C

Precip: 84 cm
Temp. range: 26°C

cm

Moose Factory, Ontario
51° N 80° W

Temp.
°C

Precip: 58 cm
Temp. range: 38°C

cm

Figure 11 Graph **A** displays data typical of a humid continental climate. The trends shown in graph **B** are typical of a subarctic climate.
Interpreting Graphs *What are the typical temperatures and amounts of precipitation for Chicago, Illinois, in May and June?*

Humid Mid-Latitude With Severe Winters There are two types of humid mid-latitude climates with severe winters: the humid continental climates and the subarctic climates. Continental landmasses strongly influence both of these climates. As a result, such climates are absent in the Southern Hemisphere. There, oceans dominate the middle-latitude zone. Locate the regions having a humid continental climate, which are shown in blue, on Figure 9. Note that areas with such climates lie between approximately 40° and 50° north latitude. As you can see in Figure 11A the winters are severe, while the summers are typically quite warm. Note, too, that precipitation is generally greater in summer than in winter.

North of the humid continental climate and south of the tundra is an extensive **subarctic climate** region. From Figure 9, you can see that this climate zone covers a broad expanse. Such climates stretch from western Alaska to Newfoundland in North America, and from Norway to the Pacific coast of Russia in Eurasia. Winters in these regions are long and bitterly cold. By contrast, summers in the subarctic are remarkably warm but very short. The extremely cold winters and relatively warm summers combine to produce the highest annual temperature ranges on Earth.

Compare and contrast two types of humid mid-latitude climates with severe winters.

Extent of Dry Climate Zones

[World map showing dry climate zones with labels: Great Basin, Sonoran, Turkestan, Gobi, Sahara, Arabian, Iranian, Great Indian, Atacama, Namib, Kalahari, Patagonian, Great Sandy, Simpson. Latitude lines marked: Tropic of Cancer, Equator, Tropic of Capricorn. Legend: Desert (arid), Steppe (semiarid). Scale bars: 0–3000 Miles, 0–4000 Kilometers]

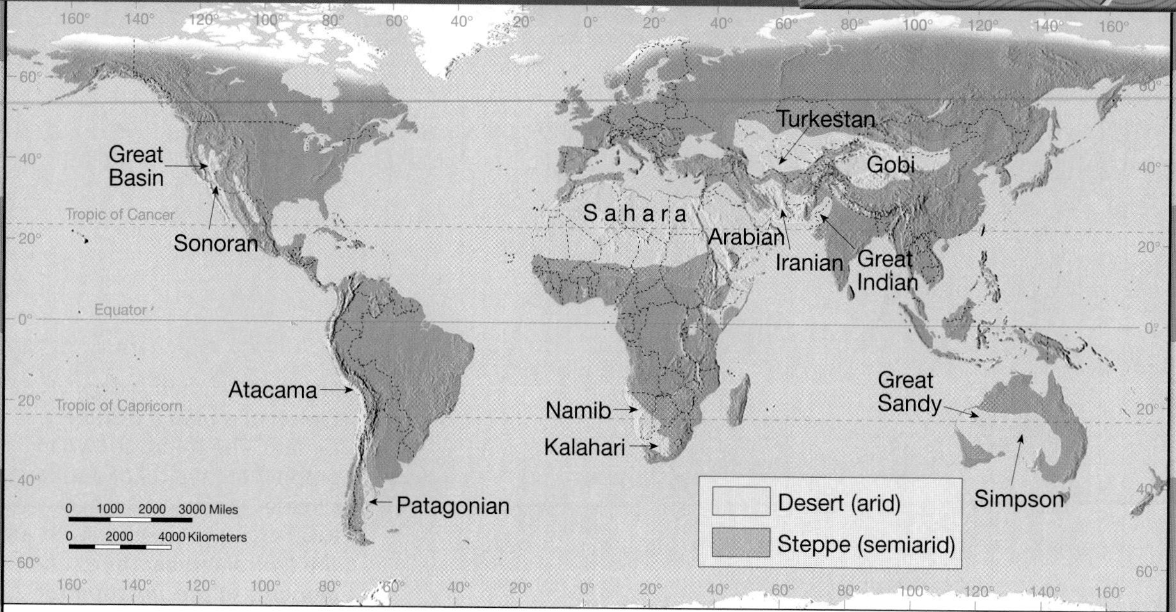

Figure 12

Location Locate each of the places listed.
Identify Identify the desert(s) in each place or region.
1. Chile
2. southwestern United States
3. central Australia
4. northwestern India
5. southern Africa

Describe About how much of Australia has a desert climate?

Q *Are deserts always hot?*

A Deserts can certainly be hot places. The record high temperature for the United States, 57°C, was set at Death Valley, California. However, deserts also experience very cold temperatures. The average daily minimum in January in Phoenix, Arizona, is 1.7°C, a temperature just barely above freezing. At Ulan Bator in Mongolia's Gobi Desert, the average high temperature in January is only −19°C!

Dry Climates

A dry climate is one in which the yearly precipitation is not as great as the potential loss of water by evaporation. In other words, dryness is not only related to annual rainfall, but is also a function of evaporation. Evaporation, in turn, is closely dependent upon temperature. There are two types of dry climates: arid or desert and semi-arid or steppe, as shown in Figure 12. These two climate types are classified as BW and BS, respectively, in the Köppen classification system. Arid and semi-arid climates have many features in common. In fact, the difference between them is slight. The steppe is a marginal and more humid variant of the desert. The steppe represents a transition zone that surrounds the desert and separates it from humid climates.

Dry climates exist as the result of the global distribution of air pressure and winds. In regions near the tropics of Cancer and Capricorn, air is subsiding. When air sinks, it is compressed and warmed. Such conditions are opposite of those needed for clouds to form precipitation. As a result, regions with dry climates experience mostly clear, sunny skies and dry climates. Other dry areas including the Great Basin in North America and the Gobi Desert of Eurasia occur where prevailing winds meet mountain barriers. These arid regions are called rain shadow deserts.

Polar Climates

Polar climates are those in which the mean temperature of the warmest month is below 10°C. Winters in these regions are periods of perpetual night, or nearly so, making temperatures at most polar locations extremely cold. During the summer months, temperatures remain cool despite the long days. Very little precipitation falls in polar regions. Evaporation, too, in these areas is limited.

There are two types of polar climates. The tundra climate, like that shown in Figure 13, is a treeless region found almost exclusively in the Northern Hemisphere. The ice cap climate does not have a single monthly mean above 0°C. Little vegetation grows and the landscape in these regions is covered by permanent ice and snow. Ice cap climates occur in scattered high mountain areas and in Greenland and Antarctica.

Figure 13 Tundra North of Nome, Alaska Tundra plant life includes mostly mosses, shrubs, and flowering herbs.

Highland Climates

The climate types discussed so far are very similar from place to place and extend over large areas. Some climates, however, are localized, which means that they are much different from climates in surrounding areas. One such climate is a highland climate. Conditions of highland climates often vary from one place to another. For example, south-facing slopes are warmer than north-facing slopes, and air on the windward sides of mountains is wetter than air on the leeward sides. **In general, highland climates are cooler and wetter than nearby areas at lower elevations.** Locate the highland climate regions on Figure 9. What do they all have in common?

Go Online

SciLINKS NSTA

For: Links on climates of the world
Visit: www.SciLinks.org
Web Code: cjn-6212

Section 21.2 Assessment

Reviewing Concepts

1. What is the Köppen climate classification system?
2. Describe the characteristics of humid tropical climates.
3. What are some characteristics of humid mid-latitude climates?
4. What defines a dry climate?
5. What are the characteristics of polar climates?
6. How do highland climates compare with nearby lowlands?

Critical Thinking

7. **Identifying** Use Figure 9 to identify the climate type of your city. Describe some characteristics of your city's climate type.
8. **Formulating Conclusions** Can tundra climates exist at low latitudes? Explain.

Writing in Science

Explanatory Paragraph Write a paragraph in which you explain why Antarctica can be classified as a desert.

21.3 Climate Changes

Reading Focus

Key Concepts

- Describe natural processes that can cause changes in climate.
- What is the greenhouse effect?
- What is global warming?
- What are some of the consequences of global warming?

Vocabulary

- greenhouse effect
- global warming

Reading Strategy

Identifying Cause and Effect Copy the table. Identify the causes and effects of climate change presented in this section.

Climate Changes	
Causes	**Effects**
a. ___?___	b. ___?___
c. ___?___	d. ___?___
e. ___?___	f. ___?___

Like most conditions on Earth, climate is always changing. Some of these changes are short-term. Others occur over long periods of geologic time. Some climate changes are the result of natural processes, such as the volcanic eruption shown in Figure 14. Others are related to human activities. In this section, you will learn about some of the ways in which climate changes.

Natural Processes That Change Climate

Many different natural processes can cause a climate to change. Some of the climate-changing processes that you will learn about include volcanic eruptions as well as changes in ocean circulation, solar activity, and Earth motions.

Figure 14 Eruption of Mount Pinatubo

Volcanic Eruptions As you can see in Figure 14, volcanic eruptions can emit large volumes of ash and dust into Earth's atmosphere. What you can't see in the photograph is that volcanic eruptions also send minute particles containing sulfur, into the air. If the volume of these very fine particles called aerosols, is great enough, it can cause short-term changes in Earth's surface temperature. Can you hypothesize why? **The presence of aerosols (volcanic ash, dust, and sulfur-based aerosols) in the air increases the amount of solar radiation that is reflected back into space. This causes Earth's lower atmosphere to cool.**

Ocean Circulation Recall from Chapter 19 that El Niño is a change in ocean circulation that causes parts of the eastern tropical Pacific Ocean to become warmer than usual. ⬤ **These changes in ocean circulation also can result in short-term climate fluctuations.** For example, some areas that are normally arid receive large amounts of rain during El Niño. Refer to Figure 15. Also, some regions that receive abundant precipitation may experience dry periods when ocean circulation patterns change.

Solar Activity The most studied hypotheses for the causes of climate change are based on changes in the output of solar energy. When the sun is most active, it contains dark blemishes called sunspots. The formation of sunspots appears to correspond with warm periods in Europe and North America. Although variations in solar output may cause short-term climatic change, no evidence for long-term variations due to solar activity exist.

Earth Motions A number of Earth motions are thought to cause changes in climate. Most of these changes are long-term changes. Tectonic plate movements, for example, cause the crust and upper mantle to move slowly over Earth's surface. These movements cause ocean basins to open and close. Plate movements also cause changes in the positions of landmasses. ⬤ **These geographic changes in Earth's land and water bodies cause changes in climate.**

⬤ **Changes in the shape of Earth's orbit and the tilt of Earth on its axis are other Earth motions that affect global climates.** Earth's orbit, or path around the sun, is always elliptical. But over a 100,000-year period, the path becomes more and then less elliptical. This change in shape brings Earth closer to and then farther from the sun. This affects global climates. Like its orbit, the tilt of Earth on its axis changes about 2 degrees over a 41,000-year period. Because the angle of tilt varies, the severity of the seasons also changes. The smaller the tilt, the smaller the temperature difference between summer and winter.

Figure 15 Effect of El Niño In 1998, bad weather conditions and flooding in Alabama were attributed to El Niño.

Reading Checkpoint *Identify four natural processes that can result in climate changes.*

Human Impact on Climate Changes

Natural processes have certainly contributed to many climatic changes throughout Earth's 4.6-billion year history. These processes will also be responsible for some of the future shifts in Earth's climates. Besides these processes of nature, human activities have contributed and will contribute to global climatic change.

The Greenhouse Effect 🔊 **The greenhouse effect is a natural warming of both Earth's lower atmosphere and Earth's surface.** The major gases involved in the greenhouse effect are water vapor and carbon dioxide. These greenhouse gases, as they are often called, are transparent to incoming solar radiation and therefore much of this energy reaches Earth's surface. Most of this energy is then reradiated skyward. The greenhouse gases are good absorbers of Earth's radiation, which accounts for the warm temperatures of the lower atmosphere.

The greenhouse effect is very important because it makes life as we know it possible on Earth. Without this effect, Earth would be much too cold to support any kind of complex life forms. However, an increase in the greenhouse effect could also prove devastating to Earth's billions of organisms.

Studies indicate that human activities for the past 200 or so years have had a huge impact on the greenhouse effect. As you can see in Figure 16, carbon dioxide levels in the air have risen at a rapid pace since about 1850. Much of this greenhouse gas has been added by the burning of fossil fuels such as coal, petroleum, and natural gas. The clearing of forests also contributes to an increase in carbon dioxide because this gas is released when vegetation is burned or when it decays.

Figure 16 The rapid increase in carbon dioxide concentration since 1850 has closely followed the increase in carbon dioxide emissions from burning fossil fuels. **Inferring** *What do you think initiated this increase in carbon dioxide levels?*

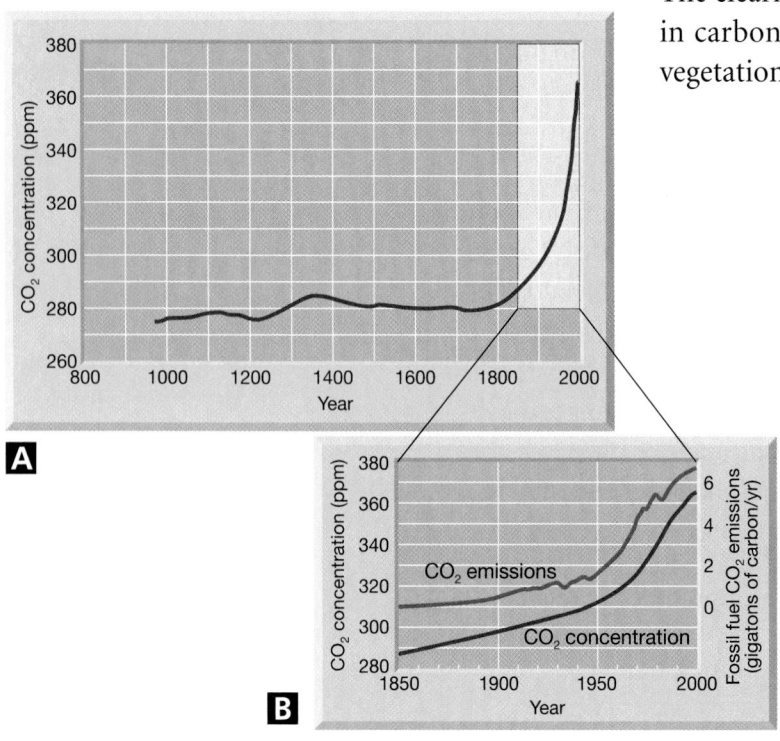

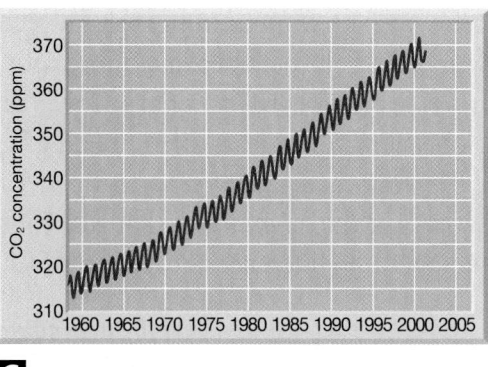

Global Warming 🌐 **As a result of increases in carbon dioxide levels, as well as other greenhouse gases, global temperatures have increased. This increase is called global warming.** Refer to Figure 17. Note that during the twentieth century, Earth's average surface temperatures increased about 0.6°C. Scientists predict that by the year 2100, temperatures will increase by 1.4°C to 5.8°C. How will these temperature increases affect Earth?

Warmer surface temperatures increase evaporation rates. This, in turn, increases the amount of water vapor in the atmosphere. Water vapor is an even more powerful absorber of radiation emitted by Earth than is carbon dioxide. Therefore, more water vapor in the air will magnify the effect of carbon dioxide and other gases.

Temperature increases will also cause sea ice to melt. Ice reflects more incoming solar radiation than liquid water does. The melting of the ice will cause a substantial increase in the solar energy absorbed at the surface. This, in turn, will magnify the temperature increase created by higher levels of greenhouse gases. The melting of sea ice and ice sheets will also cause a global rise in sea level. This will lead to shoreline erosion and coastal flooding.

Scientists also expect that weather patterns will change as a result of the projected global warming. More intense heat waves and droughts in some regions and fewer such events in other places are also predicted. What other consequences of global warming do you think might occur?

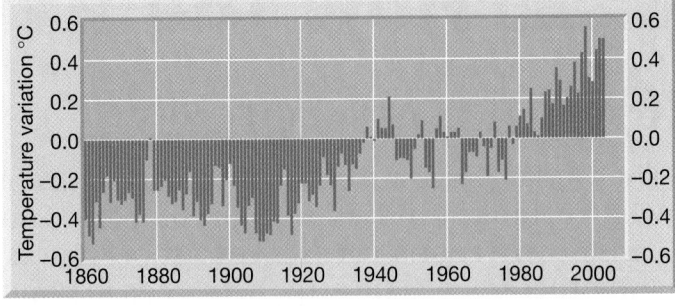

Figure 17 Increases in the levels of greenhouse gases have caused changes in Earth's average surface temperatures.
Interpreting Graphs *What year was the warmest to date?*

Go **O**nline
SCi LINKS
NSTA

For: Links on the carbon cycle/global warming
Visit: www.SciLinks.org
Web Code: cjn-6213

Section 21.3 Assessment

Reviewing Concepts

1. 🌐 Describe four natural processes that can cause climate change.
2. 🌐 What is the greenhouse effect?
3. 🌐 What is global warming?
4. 🌐 What are some of the possible effects of global warming?

Critical Thinking

5. **Formulating Hypotheses** Which would have a longer effect on climate changes—volcanic ash and dust or the same volume of sulfur-based aerosols? Why?

6. **Formulating Conclusions** How do you think cloud cover might change as the result of global warming?
7. **Synthesizing** How might global warming affect Earth's inhabitants, including humans?

Writing in Science

Persuasive Paragraphs Write at least two paragraphs to persuade your friends and family to reduce their consumption of fossil fuels. Be sure to explain why the usage of such energy sources should be reduced.

 **How the Earth Works**

Coniferous Forests

The world's largest forests extend across the far north, where winters can last for eight months. These dense **coniferous forests** consist of spruces, pines, and other trees that carry their seeds in cones. They are particularly suited for coping with cold conditions. Animals in northern forests find plentiful food during the long days of summer, but the season is brief and cold weather soon returns. To survive the harsh winter, many animals migrate south, while others hibernate.

Distribution of northern coniferous forests

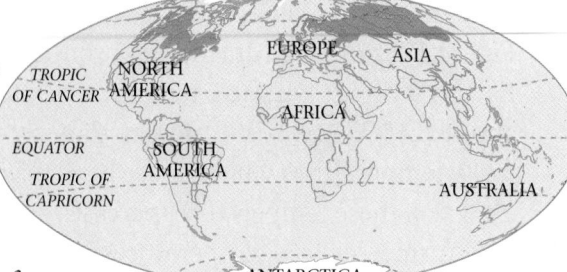

FORESTS AND LAKES
Coniferous forests often grow on land once covered by ice age glaciers. These glaciers scoured the ground, scraping away soil and creating rounded hills and hollows. When the glaciers melted, the hills became covered with trees and the hollows turned into lakes.

CONIFER LEAVES
Most conifers have small evergreen leaves that are tough enough to withstand the coldest winters. A narrow shape helps the leaves to cope with strong winds.

White spruce

Waterlogged soil beneath trees is acidic and infertile.

Bobcat

PREDATORS
Mammals are relatively scarce in northern forests, so the **predators** that feed upon other animals sometimes have to cover vast distances to find food. Bobcats may roam many miles searching for small prey. Wolves hunt in packs for deer and other large mammals.

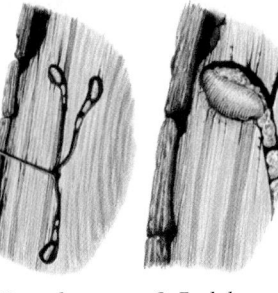
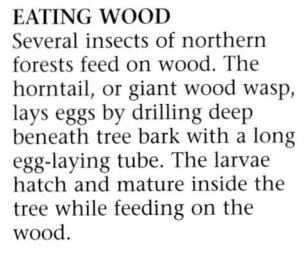

1. A horntail lays eggs deep in a tree trunk.

2. Young larvae bore away from the drill-hole.

3. Each larva matures inside a chamber near the bark of the tree.

EATING WOOD

Several insects of northern forests feed on wood. The horntail, or giant wood wasp, lays eggs by drilling deep beneath tree bark with a long egg-laying tube. The larvae hatch and mature inside the tree while feeding on the wood.

Red crossbill

SEED EATERS

Some birds rely on conifer seeds for food. Crossbill finches have unique bills that are crossed at the tips. This helps them remove seeds from cones. Clark's nutcracker, a member of the crow family, hides 20,000 or more seeds each fall. It is able to remember the locations of many of these seeds for up to nine months.

Spruce cone

Cold lake water contains few nutrients but is often rich in oxygen.

Caribou

ADAPTED FOR TRAVEL

To help them walk across thick layers of snow without sinking, caribou and elk have hooves with broadly splayed toes that help to distribute their weight. Lynx and snowshoe hares have similar adaptations.

Caribou hooves act as snowshoes.

COPING WITH COLD

To avoid extreme winter temperatures, bears, woodchucks, and other mammals hibernate. During the fall, they build up a store of fat in their bodies that will last until spring. They then go into **hibernation,** which slows their bodily functions to a minimum.

Woodchuck

ASSESSMENT

1. **Key Terms** Define **(a)** coniferous forest, **(b)** predator, **(c)** hibernation.

2. **Climates** Describe the climatic conditions that are generally found in northern coniferous forests.

3. **Ecosystems** How do trees serve as a food source for birds and insects?

4. **Ecosystems** How are mammals of northern coniferous forests well suited for survival in their natural environment?

5. **Critical Thinking Developing a Hypothesis** Deforestation has not reduced northern coniferous forests to the same degree that it has reduced mid-latitude deciduous forests. Why do you think that northern coniferous forests have fared better than deciduous forests to the south?

Human Impact on Climate and Weather

Scientists are now closely monitoring how daily human activity is changing microclimates. There is concern that changing microclimates can have an effect on global climates. In this investigation, you will explore some of the ways that human activities are changing the atmosphere.

Problem
How do we know that human activity is changing Earth's climates?

Materials
- paper
- pen or pencil

Skills
Calculating, Measuring, Using Tables, Analyzing Data

Procedure

1. Table 1 lists many of the types, sources, and amounts of primary pollutants. Use this table to answer items 1, 2, 3, and 4 under Analyze and Conclude.

2. Look at Figure A. The pollutants listed are linked to a wide variety of negative health effects such as eye irritation, heart damage, and lung damage. The pollutants shown are also linked to reduced visibility, reduced crop yields, and damage to ecosystems. Study the figure and answer items 5, 6, and 7.

3. Look at Figure B. Scientists have noted the increasing levels of carbon dioxide in the atmosphere. Research continues to determine whether these increasing levels are affecting global climates. Use Figure B to answer item 8.

4. Look at Table 2. This table presents data on the effects of large cities on their surrounding microclimates. Temperatures in cities can be higher than the surrounding countryside. Meteorologists call this effect "the urban heat island". Study the data in the table and answer items 9, 10, and 11.

Analyze and Conclude

1. **Interpreting Data** What is the leading source (by weight) of primary pollutants? How many metric tons of this pollutant are added to the atmosphere each year?

2. **Interpreting Data** Which of the following is the most abundant primary pollutant?
   a. carbon monoxide
   b. sulfur oxides

3. **Calculating** Your answer for item 2 is what percentage of all primary pollutants?
   a. 25%   b. 50%   c. 75%

4. **Calculating** What is the approximate total weight (in million metric tons) of all primary pollutants added to the atmosphere?

Table 1 Estimated Nationwide Emissions (millions of metric tons/year)						
Source	Carbon Monoxide	Partic-ulates	Sulfur Oxides	Volatile Organics	Nitrogen Oxides	Total
Transportation	43.5	1.6	1.0	5.1	7.3	58.5
Stationary Source Fuel Combustion	4.7	1.9	16.6	0.7	10.6	34.5
Industrial Processes	4.7	2.6	3.2	7.9	0.6	19.0
Solid Waste Disposal	2.1	0.3	0.0	0.7	0.1	3.2
Miscellaneous	7.2	1.2	0.0	2.8	0.2	11.4
Total	62.2	7.6	20.8	17.2	18.8	126.6

Source: U.S. Environmental Protection Agency

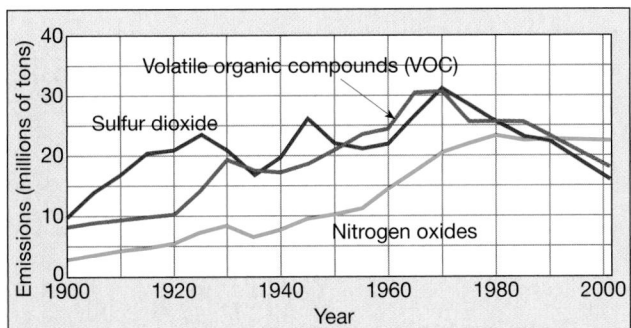

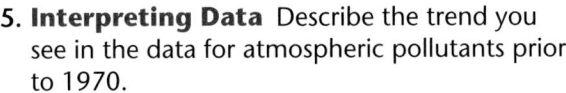

Figure A

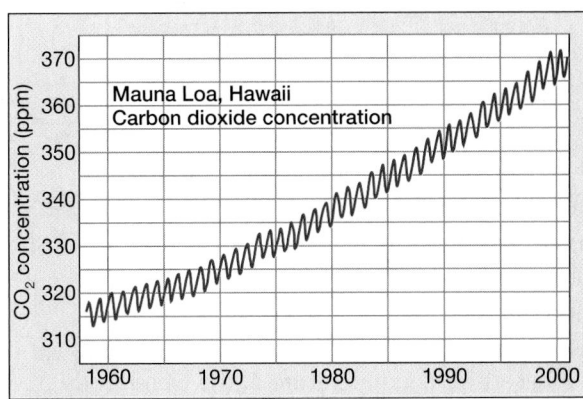

Figure B

5. **Interpreting Data** Describe the trend you see in the data for atmospheric pollutants prior to 1970.

6. **Interpreting Data** Describe the trend you see in the data for atmospheric pollutants since 1970.

7. **Inferring** Suggest a reason for the changing trend.

8. **Calculating** What has been the approximate percentage increase in atmospheric carbon dioxide near Mauna Loa since 1958?

9. **Interpreting Data** Compared to rural areas, which factors are increased by urbanization? Which factors are decreased?

10. **Interpreting Data** Of all of the factors shown, which shows the greatest increase due to urbanization?

11. **Predicting** Suggest a possible reason for each of the following effects on the weather that is influenced by a city.
    a. increased frequency of thunderstorms
    b. lower wind speed
    c. increased precipitation

Go Further Use the internet to search for climate data for your region. What trends do you see in the data since 1970? Suggest a hypothesis that could be used to test your conclusions.

Table 2 Average Climatic Changes Produced by Cities	
Element	**Comparison with Rural Areas**
Particulate matter	10 times more
Temperature	
Annual mean	0.5–1.5°C higher
Winter	1–2°C higher
Solar radiation	15–30% less
Ultraviolet, winter	30% less
Ultraviolet, summer	5% less
Precipitation	5–15% more
Thunderstorm frequency	16% more
Winter	5% more
Summer	29% more
Relative humidity	6% lower
Winter	2% lower
Summer	8% lower
Cloudiness (frequency)	5–10% more
Fog (frequency)	60% more
Winter	100% more
Summer	30% more
Wind speed	25% lower
Calms	5–20% more

Source: After Landsberg, Changnon, and others.

21.1 Factors That Affect Climate

🌐 Key Concepts

- As latitude increases, the intensity of solar energy decreases.
- The higher the elevation is, the colder the climate.
- Mountains play an important role in the amount of precipitation that falls over an area.
- Large bodies of water such as lakes and oceans have an important effect on the temperature of an area because the temperature of the water body influences the temperature of the air above it.
- Global winds affect climate because they distribute heat and moisture around Earth.
- Vegetation can affect both temperature and the precipitation patterns in an area.

Vocabulary

tropical zone, *p. 589;* temperate zone, *p. 589;* polar zone, *p. 589*

21.2 World Climates

🌐 Key Concepts

- The Köppen climate classification system uses mean values of temperature and precipitation to classify climates.
- Humid tropical climates have no winters.
- Humid mid-latitude climates with mild winters have an average temperature in the coldest month that is below 18°C but above −3°C. Humid mid-latitude climates with severe winters have an average temperature in the coldest month that is below −3°C.
- A dry climate is one in which the yearly precipitation is not as great as the potential loss of water by evaporation.
- Polar climates have a mean temperature in the warmest month that is below 10°C.
- Highland climates are generally cooler and wetter than nearby areas at lower elevations.

Vocabulary

Köppen climate classification system, *p. 592;* wet tropical climate, *p. 593;* tropical wet and dry climate, *p. 593;* humid subtropical climate, *p. 596;* marine west coast climate, *p. 596;* dry-summer subtropical climate, *p. 596;* subarctic climate, *p. 597*

21.3 Climate Changes

🌐 Key Concepts

- Aerosols, volcanic ash, dust, and sulfur-based aerosols in the air can cause a short-term cooling of the lower atmosphere.
- Changes in ocean circulation can result in short-term climate fluctuations.
- Changes in the shape of Earth's orbit and the tilt of Earth's axis affect global climates.
- The greenhouse effect is a natural warming of Earth's lower atmosphere and Earth's surface.
- As a result of increases in carbon dioxide levels, as well as other greenhouse gases, global temperatures have increased to cause global warming.
- Global warming causes changes in sea level.

Vocabulary

greenhouse effect, *p. 602;* global warming, *p. 603*

Thinking Visually

Identifying Causes and Effects Copy the table below onto a sheet of paper. Use the information in the chapter to complete the table.

Some Factors That Influence Climate	
Causes	**Effects**
1. Increase in latitude	1. _____?_____
2. _____?_____	2. Highland climate
3. Increase in greenhouse gases	3. _____?_____
4. _____?_____	4. More coastal erosion
5. Large volcanic eruption	5. _____?_____
6. Nearby lake	6. _____?_____

Reviewing Content

Choose the letter that best answers the question or completes the statement.

1. Which of the following is true?
   a. Climates at high latitudes are very warm.
   b. A nearby lake causes a climate to be colder.
   c. Vegetation can increase the amount of precipitation that falls over an area.
   d. Places at lower elevations generally have lower temperatures.

2. Humid tropical climates always experience
   a. severe winters.   b. dry summers.
   c. low humidity.   d. warm temperatures.

3. In a dry climate, yearly precipitation is
   a. less than the rate of evaporation.
   b. greater than the rate of evaporation.
   c. greater in a desert than a steppe.
   d. less than that in a polar climate.

4. The greenhouse effect is best described as
   a. an increase in Earth's surface temperature.
   b. a natural warming effect of the atmosphere.
   c. a result of global warming.
   d. any short-term change in climate.

5. Recent global warming appears to be the result of
   a. changes in global wind patterns.
   b. a decrease in the greenhouse effect.
   c. increases in greenhouse gases in the air.
   d. changes in Earth's revolution around the sun.

6. Melting ice caps can result in which of the following?
   a. a rise in sea level
   b. a fall in sea level
   c. colder temperatures
   d. less precipitation

7. An increase in ocean temperatures can cause
   a. melting of sea ice.
   b. most forms of ocean life to flourish.
   c. a decrease in sea level.
   d. global wind patterns to stabilize.

Understanding Concepts

Use this map to answer Questions 8–10.

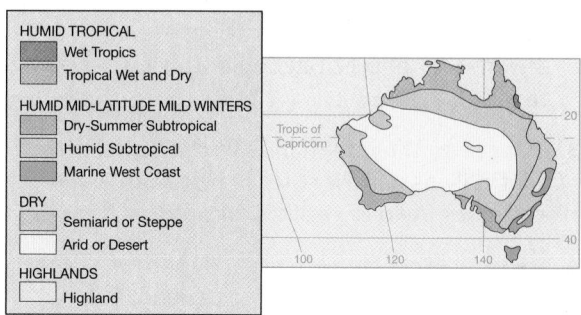

HUMID TROPICAL
Wet Tropics
Tropical Wet and Dry
HUMID MID-LATITUDE MILD WINTERS
Dry-Summer Subtropical
Humid Subtropical
Marine West Coast
DRY
Semiarid or Steppe
Arid or Desert
HIGHLANDS
Highland

8. Describe the dominant climate in Australia.

9. Identify the type of climate found on the other parts of the continent.

10. What causes much of the east-southeastern part of the country to experience warm, humid, and marine west coast climates?

11. What powers Earth's climate system, and which of Earth's spheres are involved in this system?

12. Name the three major climate zones, and explain why their overall temperatures differ.

13. Why can two places at the same latitude have different climates?

14. What climate data are needed in order to classify a climate using the Köppen climate classification system?

15. Describe the characteristics of a wet tropical climate.

16. Describe the characteristics of a humid continental climate, and give one example of a place with such a climate.

17. Explain the greenhouse effect caused by Earth's atmosphere.

18. How have humans contributed to the increase in the levels of carbon dioxide in the atmosphere?

19. What is global warming?

20. How might global warming affect global precipitation?

Critical Thinking

21. **Synthesizing** Can a region at low latitudes have snow? Explain.

22. **Applying Concepts** How does elevation affect the amount of precipitation that falls over an area?

23. **Inferring** Why do marine west coast climates exist only as narrow strips in North America, yet are widespread in western Europe?

24. **Formulating Hypotheses** Hypothesize why rain shadow deserts rarely experience fog.

Using Graphs

Use the graph below to answer Questions 25–29.

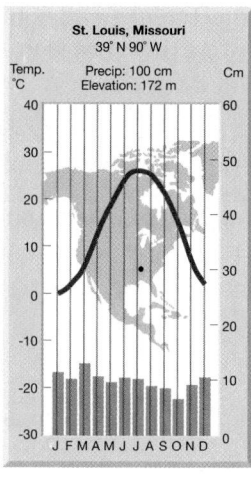

St. Louis, Missouri
39° N 90° W
Temp. °C
Precip: 100 cm
Elevation: 172 m
Cm

25. **Reading Graphs** What is the highest average annual temperature, and during which month does it occur?

26. **Reading Graphs** What is the lowest annual temperature, and during which month does it occur?

27. **Calculating** What is the average annual temperature range for St. Louis?

28. **Inferring** What is the wettest season of the year in St. Louis?

29. **Classifying** Classify the climate of St. Louis using the Köppen climate classification system.

Concepts in Action

30. **Synthesizing** Cities are referred to as urban heat islands. Use what you know about factors that affect climate to explain this statement.

31. **Applying Concepts** What do you think can be done to reduce the steady increase in global carbon dioxide levels?

32. **Writing in Science** Suppose you're a writer for the school newspaper. You are doing a story on how global warming might affect your area. Write an article that explains at least three effects that an increase in Earth's surface temperature might have on the climate of your area.

Performance-Based Assessment

Applying Concepts Make flyers with catchy slogans to suggest ways to reduce your community's use of fossil fuels. Get permission to post the flyers in grocery stores, community halls, shopping malls, and other common areas.

Standardized Test Prep

Test-Taking Tip

Using More Than One Visual
Sometimes an answer to a test question requires that you use or interpret more than one visual. When this occurs, carefully study the visuals before you read the questions pertaining to them. Look for similarities and differences between the visuals. Refer to the visuals again as you read each of the questions associated with the visuals. Use the graphs to answer the questions on this page.

Choose the letter that best answers the question or completes the statement.

1. Earth's temperatures were similar to the temperatures on our planet today
   (A) about 150,000 years ago.
   (B) about 135,000 years ago.
   (C) about 50,000 years ago.
   (D) about 25,000 years ago.

2. When do you think Earth was covered with more ice than is on our planet today?
   (A) between 150,000 and 140,000 years ago
   (B) between 140,000 and 120,000 years ago
   (C) between 135,000 and 20,000 years ago
   (D) between 20,000 and 10,000 years ago

3. Which part of the temperature graph shows the global warming trend discussed in the chapter?
   (A) the time from about 170,000 to 140,000 years ago
   (B) the time from about 120,000 to 100,000 years ago
   (C) the time from about 70,000 to 60,000 years ago
   (D) the time from about 100 years ago to the present

4. When during the past 160,000 years were carbon dioxide concentrations the highest?
   (A) about 150,000 years ago
   (B) about 120,000 years ago
   (C) about 40,000 years ago
   (D) about 1000 years ago

5. What were the carbon dioxide levels in the atmosphere during Earth's coldest period in the past 160,000 years?
   (A) between about 190 and 200 ppm
   (B) between about 220 and 240 ppm
   (C) between about 240 and 260 ppm
   (D) between about 260 and 280 ppm

Write one or two complete sentences to answer each of the following questions.

6. Describe the trends shown on the graphs.

7. Based on what you know about global warming and the data shown in these graphs, do you think the current global warming trends are natural changes or are they only the result of human activities? Support your answer with reasons.

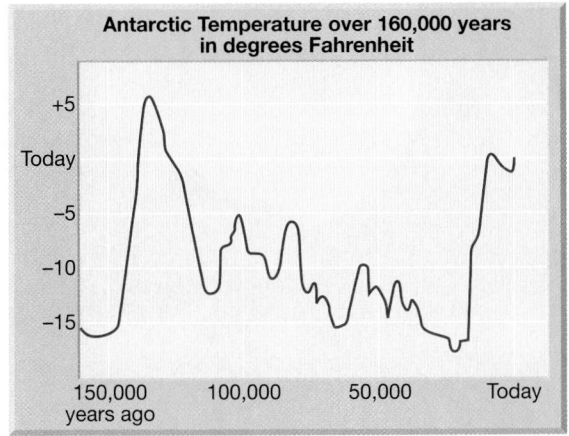

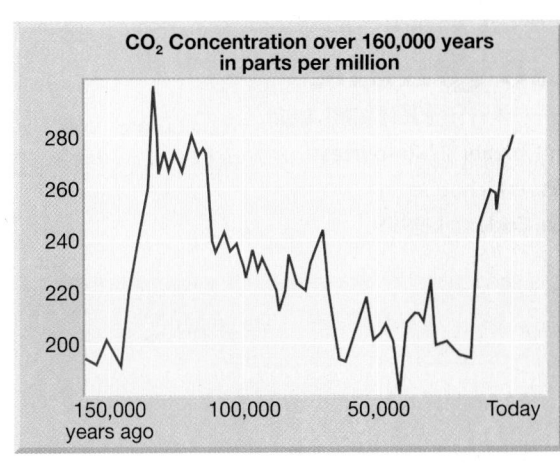

CONCEPTS
in Action

Exploration Lab
Modeling Synodic and Sidereal Months

Understanding Earth
Foucault's Experiment

 **GEODe** Astronomy
↳ Earth's Moon

 **Video Field Trip**

*Introduction to Space
Exploration*

Take a historical field trip with the Discovery
Channel and find out about the history of space
exploration. Answer the following questions
after watching the video.

1. What was Galileo's major astronomical
invention, and what theory did it enable
him to confirm?

2. How was Pluto discovered?

 Go Online
PHSchool.com

For: Chapter 22 Resources
Visit: PHSchool.com
Web Code: cjk-9999

**This photograph shows the moon ▶
over Mount Humphreys, in California's
eastern Sierras.**

Chapter Preview

How Do Impact Craters Form?

Procedure

1. Fill a large, plastic container with sand to a depth of about 3 cm. Flatten the surface of the sand with a wooden ruler.

2. One at a time, drop each of the different-sized balls from heights of 0.5 m, 1 m, and 2 m into the container. Make sure to smooth the surface of the sand between each drop.

3. Measure the diameter and height of the crater produced each time. Record your measurements in a data table.

Think About It

1. **Making Graphs** Identify your dependent and independent variables. Then plot your data on a line graph.

2. **Controlling Variables** Which of the variables is directly related to the velocity of the falling objects?

3. **Drawing Conclusions** Examine your data closely. What can you conclude about the general relationships between crater size and the size, mass, and velocity of the object that produced the crater?

22.1 Early Astronomy

Reading Focus

Key Concepts

- How does the geocentric model of the solar system differ from the heliocentric model?

- What were the accomplishments of early astronomers?

Vocabulary

- astronomy
- geocentric
- heliocentric
- retrograde motion
- ellipse
- astronomical unit (AU)

Reading Strategy

Comparing and Contrasting Copy the table below. As you read about the geocentric and heliocentric models of the solar system, fill in the table.

	Location of Earth	Location of Sun	Supporters of Model
Geocentric Model	center of universe	a. __?__	b. __?__
Heliocentric Model	c. __?__	d. __?__	e. __?__

Earth is one of nine planets and many smaller bodies that orbit the sun. The sun is part of a much larger family of perhaps 100 billion stars that make up our galaxy, the Milky Way. There are billions of galaxies in the universe. A few hundred years ago scientists thought that Earth was the center of the universe. In this chapter, you will explore some events that changed the view of Earth's place in space. You will also examine Earth's moon.

Figure 1 Early astronomers often used instruments called astrolabes to track the positions of the sun and stars.

Ancient Greeks

Astronomy is the science that studies the universe. Astronomy deals with the properties of objects in space and the laws under which the universe operates. The "Golden Age" of early astronomy (600 B.C.–A.D. 150) was centered in Greece. The early Greeks used philosophical arguments to explain natural events. However, they also relied on observations. The Greeks used instruments such as the one in Figure 1. The Greeks developed the basics of geometry and trigonometry. Using these branches of mathematics, they measured the sizes and distances of the sun and the moon.

The Greeks made many astronomical discoveries. The famous Greek philosopher Aristotle (384–322 B.C.) concluded that Earth is round because it always casts a curved shadow on the moon when it passes between the sun and the moon. Aristotle's belief that Earth is round was largely abandoned in the Middle Ages.

The first successful attempt to establish the size of Earth is credited to Eratosthenes (276–194 B.C.). As shown in Figure 2, Eratosthenes observed the angles of the noonday sun in two Egyptian cities that were roughly north and south of each other—Syene (presently Aswan) and Alexandria. Finding that the angles differed by 7 degrees, or 1/50 of a complete circle, he concluded that the circumference of Earth must be 50 times the distance between these two cities. The cities were 5000 stadia apart, giving him a measurement of 250,000 stadia. Many historians believe the stadia was 157.6 meters. This would make Eratosthenes' calculation of Earth's circumference—39,400 kilometers—a measurement very close to the modern circumference of 40,075 kilometers.

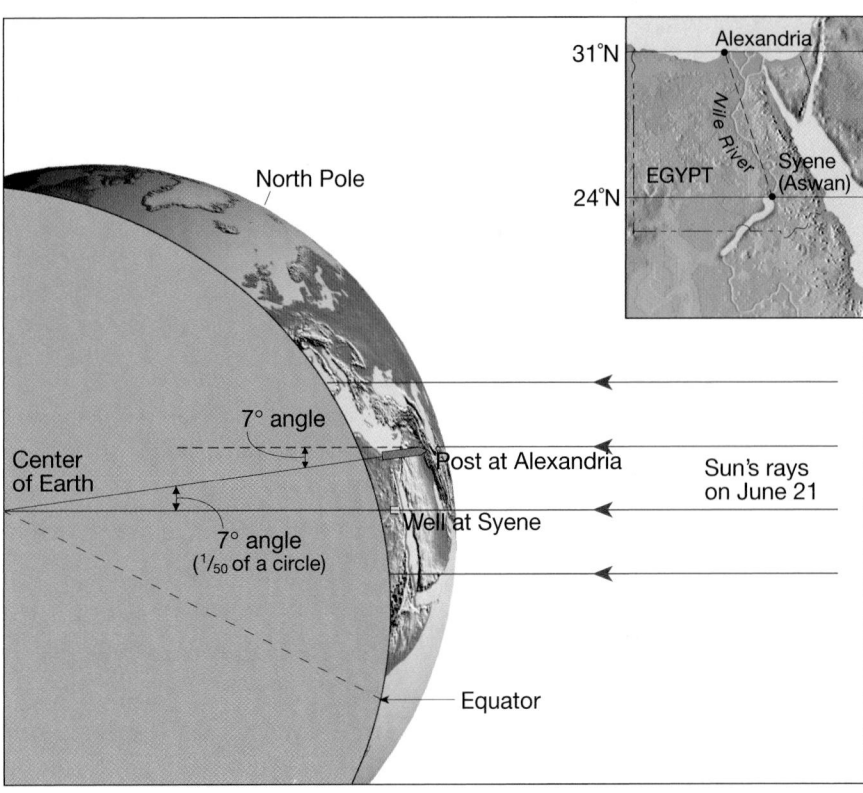

Figure 2 This diagram shows the orientation of the sun's rays at Syene (Aswan) and Alexandria in Egypt on June 21 when Eratosthenes calculated Earth's circumference.

Probably the greatest of the early Greek astronomers was Hipparchus (second century B.C.), best known for his star catalog. Hipparchus determined the location of almost 850 stars, which he divided into six groups according to their brightness. He measured the length of the year to within minutes of the modern year and developed a method for predicting the times of lunar eclipses to within a few hours.

Geocentric Model The Greeks believed in the **geocentric** view. They thought that Earth was a sphere that stayed motionless at the center of the universe. ☉**In the geocentric model, the moon, sun, and the known planets—Mercury, Venus, Mars, and Jupiter—orbit Earth.** Beyond the planets was a transparent, hollow sphere on which the stars traveled daily around Earth. This was called the celestial sphere. To the Greeks, all of the heavenly bodies, except seven, appeared to remain in the same relative position to one another. These seven wanderers included the sun, the moon, Mercury, Venus, Mars, Jupiter, and Saturn. Each was thought to have a circular orbit around Earth. The Greeks were able to explain the apparent movements of all celestial bodies in space by using this model. This model, however, was not correct. Figure 3A on page 616 illustrates the geocentric model.

For: Links on early astronomers
Visit: www.SciLinks.org
Web Code: cjn-7221

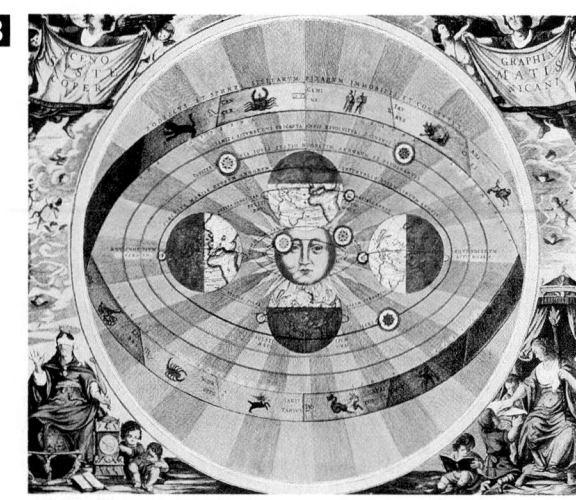

Figure 3 A Geocentric Model of the Universe
B Heliocentric Model of the Universe

Heliocentric Model Aristarchus (312–230 B.C.) was the first Greek to believe in a sun-centered, or **heliocentric,** universe. ⬭**In the heliocentric model, Earth and the other planets orbit the sun.** Aristarchus used geometry to calculate the relative distances from Earth to the sun and from Earth to the moon. He later used these distances to calculate the size of the sun and the moon. But Aristarchus came up with measurements that were much too small. However, he did learn that the sun was many times more distant than the moon and many times larger than Earth. Though there was evidence to support the heliocentric model, as shown in Figure 3B, the Earth-centered view, shown in Figure 3A, dominated Western thought for nearly 2000 years.

Ptolemaic System Much of our knowledge of Greek astronomy comes from Claudius Ptolemy. In a 13-volume work published in A.D. 141, Ptolemy presented a model of the universe that was called the Ptolemaic system. It accounted for the movements of the planets. The precision with which his model was able to predict the motion of the planets allowed it to go unchallenged for nearly 13 centuries.

Just like the Greeks, Ptolemy's model had the planets moving in circular orbits around a motionless Earth. However, the motion of the planets against the background of stars seemed odd. Each planet, if watched night after night, moves slightly eastward among the stars. Periodically, each planet appears to stop, reverse direction for a time, and then resume an eastward motion. The apparent westward drift is called **retrograde motion** and is diagrammed in Figure 4 on page 617. This rather odd apparent motion results from the combination of the motion of Earth and the planet's own motion around the sun, as shown in Figure 4.

It is difficult to accurately represent retrograde motion by using the Earth-centered model. Even though Ptolemy used the wrong model, he was able to account for the planets' motions.

 *What is retrograde motion?*

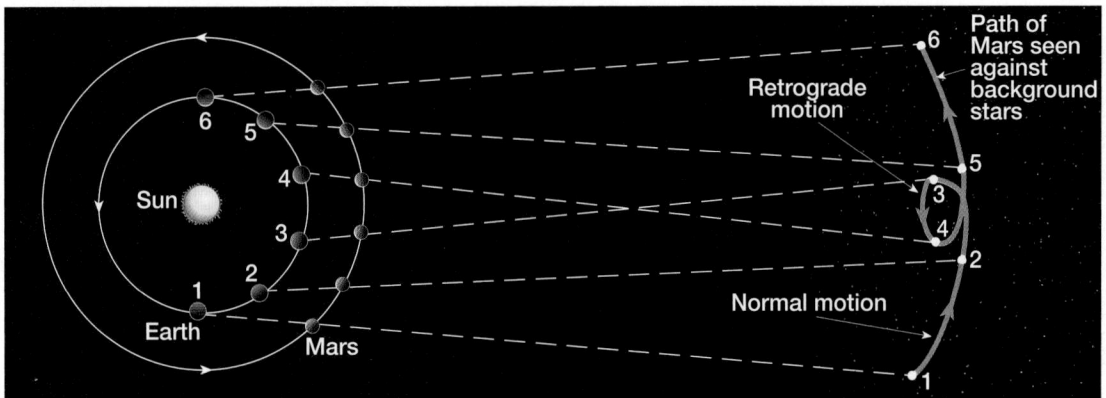

Retrograde motion

Path of Mars seen against background stars

Normal motion

The Birth of Modern Astronomy

The development of modern astronomy involved a break from previous philosophical and religious views. Scientists began to discover a universe governed by natural laws. We will examine the work of five noted scientists: Nicolaus Copernicus, Tycho Brahe, Johannes Kepler, Galileo Galilei, and Sir Isaac Newton.

Nicolaus Copernicus For almost 13 centuries after the time of Ptolemy, very few astronomical advances were made in Europe. The first great astronomer to emerge after the Middle Ages was Nicolaus Copernicus (1473–1543) from Poland. Copernicus became convinced that Earth is a planet, just like the other five planets that were known. The daily motions of the heavens, he reasoned, could be better explained by a rotating Earth.

🔑 **Copernicus concluded that Earth is a planet. He proposed a model of the solar system with the sun at the center.** This was a major break from the ancient idea that a motionless Earth lies at the center. Copernicus used circles, which were considered to be the perfect geometric shape, to represent the orbits of the planets. However, the planets seemed to stray from their predicted positions.

Tycho Brahe Tycho Brahe (1546–1601) was born of Danish nobility three years after the death of Copernicus. Brahe became interested in astronomy while viewing a solar eclipse that had been predicted by astronomers. He persuaded King Frederick II to build an observatory near Copenhagen. The telescope had not yet been invented. At the observatory, Brahe designed and built instruments, such as the angle-measuring device shown in Figure 5. He used these instruments for 20 years to measure the locations of the heavenly bodies. 🌐 **Brahe's observations, especially of Mars, were far more precise than any made previously.** In the last year of his life, Brahe found an able assistant, Johannes Kepler. Kepler kept most of Brahe's observations and put them to exceptional use.

Figure 4 Retrograde Motion When viewed from Earth, Mars moves eastward among the stars each day. Then periodically it appears to stop and reverse direction. This apparent movement, called retrograde motion, occurs because Earth has a faster orbital speed than Mars and overtakes it.

Figure 5 Tycho Brahe in His Observatory Brahe (central figure) is painted on the wall within the arc of a sighting instrument called a quadrant.

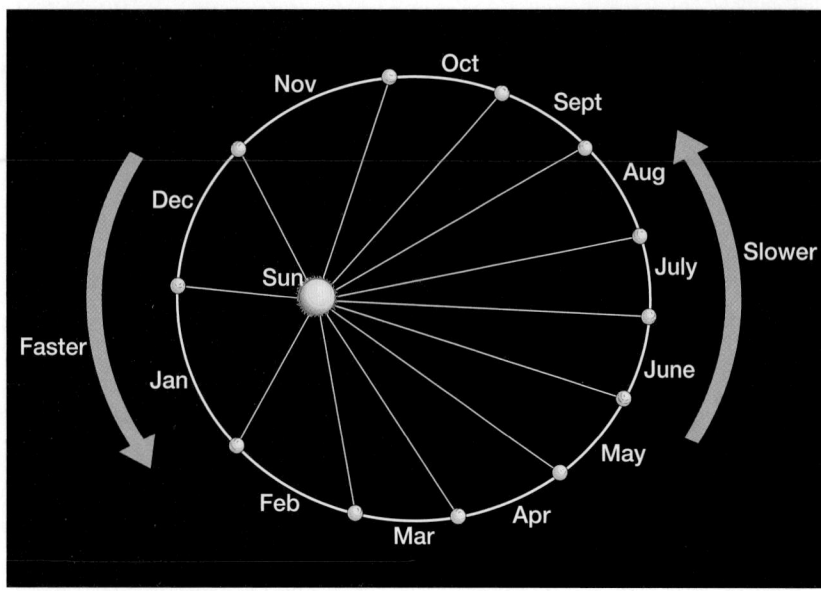

Figure 6 Planet Revolution
A line connecting a planet to the sun would move in such a manner that equal areas are swept out in equal times. Thus, planets revolve slower when they are farther from the sun and faster when they are closer.

Johannes Kepler Copernicus ushered out the old astronomy, and Johannes Kepler (1571–1630) ushered in the new. Kepler had a good mathematical mind and a strong faith in the accuracy of Brahe's work. 🔵**Kepler discovered three laws of planetary motion.** The first two laws resulted from his inability to fit Brahe's observations of Mars to a circular orbit. Kepler discovered that the orbit of Mars around the sun is not a perfect circle. Instead, it is an oval-shaped path called an **ellipse.** About the same time, he realized that the speed of Mars in its orbit changes in a predictable way. As Mars approaches the sun, it speeds up. As it moves away from the sun, it slows down.

After decades of work, Kepler summarized three laws of planetary motion:

1. The path of each planet around the sun is an ellipse, with the sun at one focus. The other focus is symmetrically located at the opposite end of the ellipse.

2. Each planet revolves so that an imaginary line connecting it to the sun sweeps over equal areas in equal time intervals, as shown in Figure 6. If a planet is to sweep equal areas in the same amount of time, it must travel more rapidly when it is nearer the sun and more slowly when it is farther from the sun.

3. The square of the length of time it takes a planet to orbit the sun (orbital period) is proportional to the cube of its mean distance to the sun.

In its simplest form, the orbital period of revolution is measured in Earth years. The planet's distance to the sun is expressed in astronomical units. The **astronomical unit (AU)** is the average distance between Earth and the sun. It is about 150 million kilometers.

Using these units, Kepler's third law states that the planet's orbital period squared is equal to its mean solar distance cubed ($T^2 = d^3$). Therefore, the solar distances of the planets can be calculated when their periods of revolution are known. For example, Mars has a period of 1.88 years, which squared equals 3.54. The cube root of 3.54 is 1.52, and that is the distance to Mars in astronomical units shown in Table 1.

Table 1 Period of Revolution and Solar Distances of Planets		
Planet	Solar Distance (d) (AU)*	Period (T) (Earth years)
Mercury	0.39	0.24
Venus	0.72	0.62
Earth	1.00	1.00
Mars	1.52	1.88
Jupiter	5.20	11.86
Saturn	9.54	29.46
Uranus	19.18	84.01
Neptune	30.06	164.80
Pluto	39.44	247.70

*AU = astronomical unit.

Galileo Galilei Galileo Galilei (1564–1642) was the greatest Italian scientist of the Renaissance. 👁 **Galileo's most important contributions were his descriptions of the behavior of moving objects.** All astronomical discoveries before his time were made without the aid of a telescope. In 1609, Galileo heard that a Dutch lens maker had devised a system of lenses that magnified objects. Apparently without ever seeing a telescope, Galileo constructed his own. It magnified distant objects to three times the size seen by the unaided eye.

Using the telescope, Galileo was able to view the universe in a new way. He made many important discoveries that supported Copernicus's view of the universe, such as the following:

1. *The discovery of four satellites, or moons, orbiting Jupiter.* This proved that the old idea of Earth being the only center of motion in the universe was wrong. Here, plainly visible, was another center of motion—Jupiter. People who opposed the sun-centered system said that the moon would be left behind if Earth really revolved around the sun. Galileo's discovery disproved this argument.

2. *The discovery that the planets are circular disks, not just points of light, as was previously thought.* This showed that the planets must be Earth-like.

3. *The discovery that Venus has phases just like the moon.* So Venus orbits its source of light—the sun. Galileo saw that Venus appears smallest when it is in full phase and therefore farthest from Earth, as shown in Figure 7.

4. *The discovery that the moon's surface was not smooth.* Galileo saw mountains, craters, and plains. He thought the plains might be bodies of water. This idea was also believed by others, as we can tell from the names given to these features (Sea of Tranquility, Sea of Storms, and so forth).

5. *The discovery that the sun had sunspots, or dark regions.* Galileo tracked the movement of these spots and estimated the rotational period of the sun as just under a month.

The Solar System Model Evolves

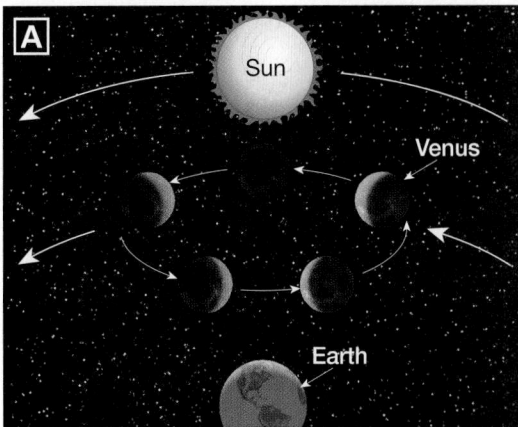

In the Ptolemaic system, the orbit of Venus lies between the sun and Earth.

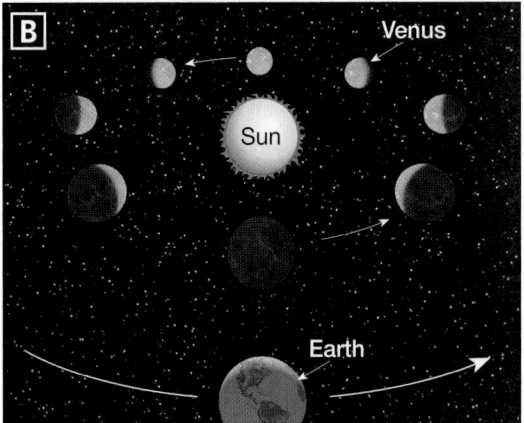

In the Copernican system, Venus orbits the sun and all its phases are visible from Earth.

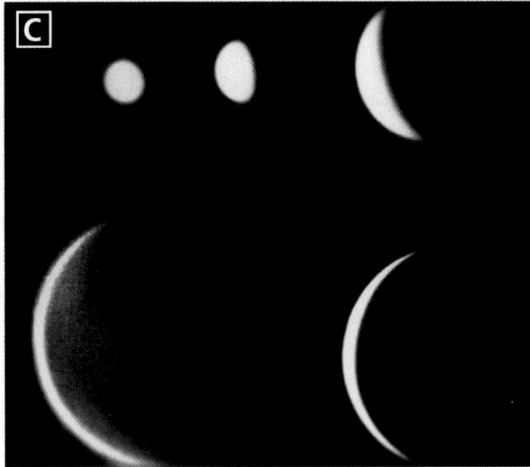

As Galileo observed, Venus goes through phases similar to the moon.

Figure 7
Relating Cause and Effect *In the geocentric model, which phase of Venus would be visible from Earth?*

Figure 8 Sir Isaac Newton

Sir Isaac Newton Sir Isaac Newton (1642–1727) was born in the year of Galileo's death. See Figure 8. Many scientists had attempted to explain the forces involved in planetary motion. Kepler believed that some force pushed the planets along in their orbits. Galileo correctly reasoned that no force is required to keep an object in motion. And he proposed that a moving object will continue to move at a constant speed and in a straight line. This concept is called inertia.

The problem, then, was not to explain the force that keeps the planets moving but rather to determine the force that keeps them from going in a straight line out into space. At the age of 23, Newton described a force that extends from Earth into space and holds the moon in orbit around Earth. **Although others had theorized the existence of such a force, Newton was the first to formulate and test the law of universal gravitation.**

Universal Gravitation According to Newton, every body in the universe attracts every other body with a force that is directly proportional to their masses and inversely proportional to the square of the distance between their centers of mass.

The gravitational force decreases with distance, so that two objects 3 kilometers apart have 3^2, or 9, times less gravitational attraction than if the same objects were 1 kilometer apart.

The law of universal gravitation also states that the greater the mass of the object, the greater is its gravitational force. For example, the mass of the moon creates a gravitational force strong enough to cause ocean tides on Earth. But the tiny mass of a satellite has no measurable effect on Earth. The mass of an object is a measure of the total amount of matter it contains. But more often mass is measured by finding how much an object resists any effort to change its state of motion.

Often we confuse the concept of mass with weight. Weight is the force of gravity acting upon an object. Weight is properly expressed in newtons (N). Therefore, weight varies when gravitational forces change. See Figure 9.

Figure 9 Weight is the force of gravity acting on an object. **A** An astronaut with a mass of 88 kg weighs 863 N on Earth. **B** An astronaut with a mass of 88 kg weighs 141 N on the moon. **Calculating** *If the same astronaut stood on Mars where the acceleration due to gravity is about 3.7 m/s², how much would the astronaut weigh?*

A **Astronaut on Earth**
Mass = 88.0 kg; Weight = 863 N

B **Astronaut on Moon**
Mass = 88.0 kg; Weight = 141 N

Newton proved that the force of gravity, combined with the tendency of a planet to remain in straight-line motion, results in the elliptical orbits that Kepler discovered. Earth, for example, moves forward in its orbit about 30 kilometers each second. During the same second, the force of gravity pulls it toward the sun about 0.5 centimeter. Newton concluded that it is the combination of Earth's forward motion and its "falling" motion that defines its orbit. As Figure 10 shows, if gravity were somehow eliminated, Earth would move in a straight line out into space. If Earth's forward motion suddenly stopped, gravity would pull it directly toward the sun.

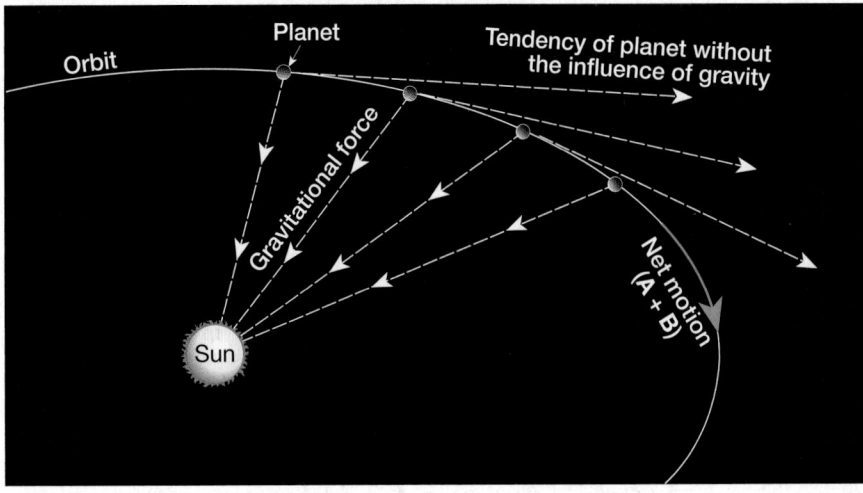

Figure 10 Without the influence of gravity, planets would move in a straight line out into space.

Newton used the law of universal gravitation to redefine Kepler's third law, which states the relationship between the orbital periods of the planets and their solar distances. When restated, Kepler's third law takes into account the masses of the bodies involved and provides a method for determining the mass of a body when the orbit of one of its satellites is known.

Section 22.1 Assessment

Reviewing Concepts

1. Compare and contrast the geocentric and heliocentric models of the universe.

2. What produces the retrograde motion of Mars?

3. What geometric arrangements did Ptolemy use to explain retrograde motion?

4. What major change did Copernicus make in the Ptolemaic system? Why was this change significant?

Critical Thinking

5. **Applying Concepts** What role did the telescope play in Galileo's contributions to science?

6. **Summarizing** In your own words, summarize Kepler's three laws of planetary motion.

Math **Practice**

7. Use Kepler's third law to show that the distance of a planet whose period is 5 years is 2.9 AU from the sun. Do the same for a planet with a period of 10 years at 4.6 AU from the sun, and a planet with a period of 10 days at 0.09 AU from the sun.

Key Concepts

- In what ways does Earth move?
- What causes the phases of the moon?
- Why are eclipses relatively rare events?

Vocabulary

- rotation
- revolution
- precession
- perihelion
- aphelion
- perigee
- apogee
- phases of the moon
- solar eclipse
- lunar eclipse

Reading Strategy

Monitoring Your Understanding Copy the flowchart below. As you read, complete it to show how eclipses occur.

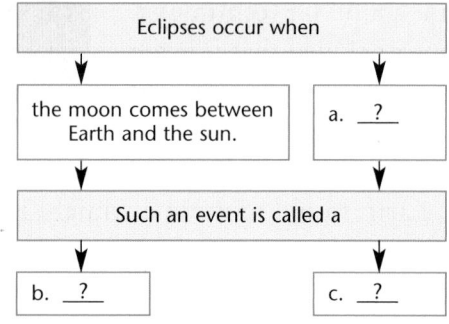

If you gaze away from the city lights on a clear night, it will seem that the stars produce a spherical shell surrounding Earth. This impression seems so real that it is easy to understand why many early Greeks regarded the stars as being fixed to a solid, celestial sphere. People have always been fascinated by the changing positions of the sun and moon in the sky. Prehistoric people, for example, built observatories. The structure known as Stonehenge, shown in Figure 11, was probably an attempt at better solar predictions. At the beginning of summer in the Northern Hemisphere (the summer solstice on June 21 or 22), the rising sun comes up directly above the heel stone of Stonehenge. Besides keeping this calendar, Stonehenge may also have provided a method of determining eclipses. In this section, you'll learn more about the movements of bodies in space that cause events such as eclipses.

Figure 11 On the summer solstice, the sun can be observed rising above the heel stone of Stonehenge, an ancient observatory in England.

Motions of Earth

The two main motions of Earth are rotation and revolution. **Rotation** is the turning, or spinning, of a body on its axis. **Revolution** is the motion of a body, such as a planet or moon, along a path around some point in space. For example, Earth revolves around the sun, and the moon revolves around Earth. Earth also has another very slow motion known as **precession,** which is the slight movement, over a period of 26,000 years, of Earth's axis.

Rotation The main results of Earth's rotation are day and night. Earth's rotation has become a standard method of measuring time because it is so dependable and easy to use. Each rotation equals about 24 hours. You may be surprised to learn that we can measure Earth's rotation in two ways, making two kinds of days. Most familiar is the mean solar day, the time interval from one noon to the next, which averages about 24 hours. Noon is when the sun has reached its zenith, or highest point in the sky.

The sidereal day, on the other hand, is the time it takes for Earth to make one complete rotation (360 degrees) with respect to a star other than our sun. The sidereal day is measured by the time required for a star to reappear at the identical position in the sky where it was observed the day before. The sidereal day has a period of 23 hours, 56 minutes, and 4 seconds (measured in solar time), which is almost 4 minutes shorter than the mean solar day. This difference results because the direction to distant stars barely changes because of Earth's slow revolution along its orbit. The direction to the sun, on the other hand, changes by almost 1 degree each day. This difference is shown in Figure 12.

Why do we use the mean solar day instead of the sidereal day as a measurement of our day? In sidereal time, "noon" occurs four minutes earlier each day. Therefore, after six months, "noon" occurs at "midnight." Astronomers use sidereal time because the stars appear in the same position in the sky every 24 sidereal hours. Usually, an observatory will begin its sidereal day when the position of the spring equinox is directly overhead.

Figure 12 Sidereal Day It takes Earth 23 hours and 56 minutes to make one rotation with respect to the stars (sidereal day). However, after Earth has completed one sidereal day, point Y has not yet returned to the "noon position" with respect to the sun. Earth has to rotate another 4 minutes to complete the solar day.

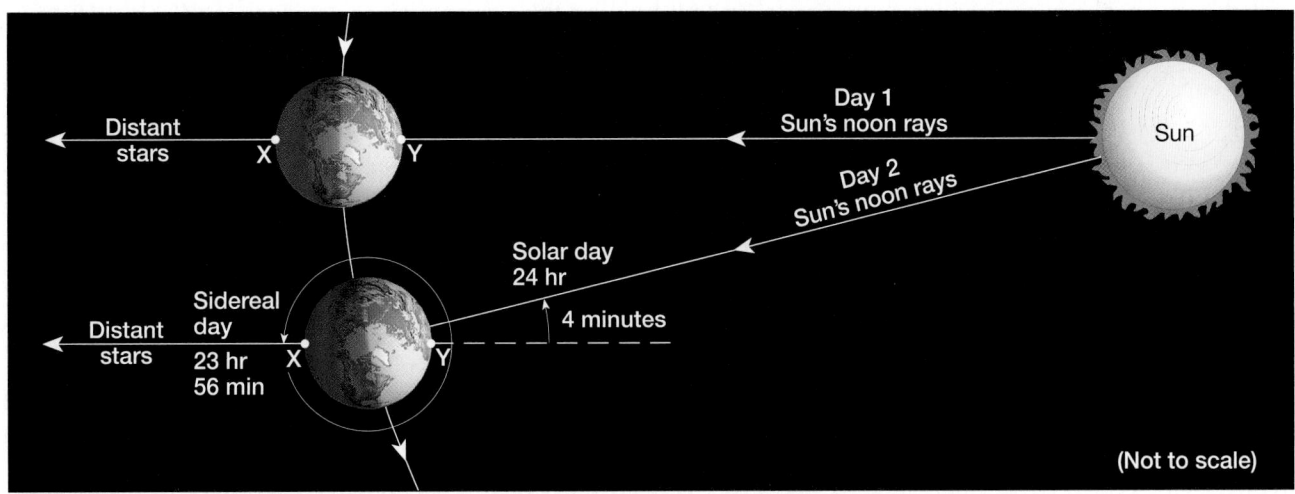

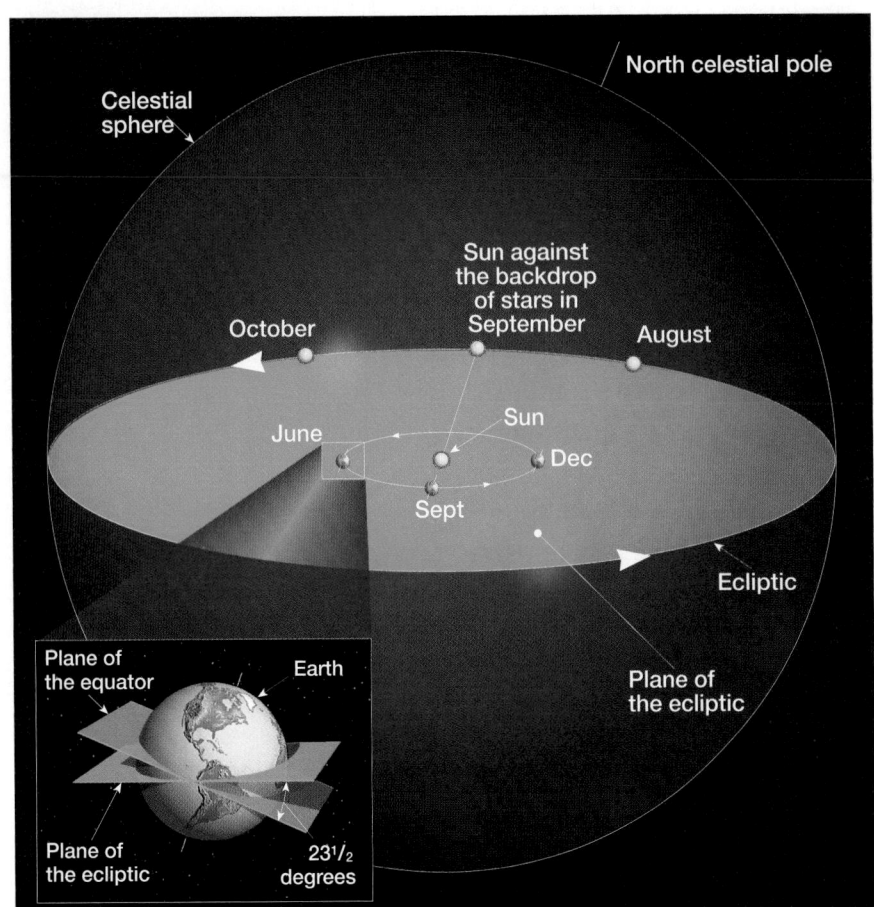

Revolution Earth revolves around the sun in an elliptical orbit at an average speed of 107,000 kilometers per hour. Its average distance from the sun is 150 million kilometers. But because its orbit is an ellipse, Earth's distance from the sun varies. At **perihelion,** Earth is closet to the sun—about 147 million kilometers away. Perihelion occurs about January 3 each year. At **aphelion,** Earth is farthest from the sun—about 152 million kilometers away. Aphelion occurs about July 4. So Earth is farthest from the sun in July and closest to the sun in January.

Because of Earth's annual movement around the sun, each day the sun appears to be displaced among the constellations at a distance equal to about twice its width, or 1 degree. The apparent annual path of the sun against the backdrop of the celestial sphere is called the ecliptic, as shown in Figure 13. Generally, the planets and the moon travel in nearly the same plane as Earth. So their paths on the celestial sphere lie near the ecliptic.

Figure 13 The Ecliptic Earth's orbital motion causes the apparent position of the sun to shift about 1 degree each day on the celestial sphere.

Earth's Axis and Seasons The imaginary plane that connects Earth's orbit with the celestial sphere is called the plane of the ecliptic. From the reference plane, Earth's axis of rotation is tilted about 23.5 degrees. Because of Earth's tilt, the apparent path of the sun and the celestial equator intersect each other at an angle of 23.5 degrees. This angle is very important to Earth's inhabitants. Because of the inclination of Earth's axis to the plane of the ecliptic, Earth has its yearly cycle of seasons.

When the apparent position of the sun is plotted on the celestial sphere over a period of a year's time, its path intersects the celestial equator at two points. From a Northern Hemisphere point of view, these intersections are called the spring equinox (March 20 or 21) and autumn equinox (September 22 or 23). On June 21 or 22, the date of the summer solstice, the sun appears 23.5 degrees north of the celestial equator. Six months later, on December 21–22, the date of the winter solstice, the sun appears 23.5 degrees south of the celestial equator.

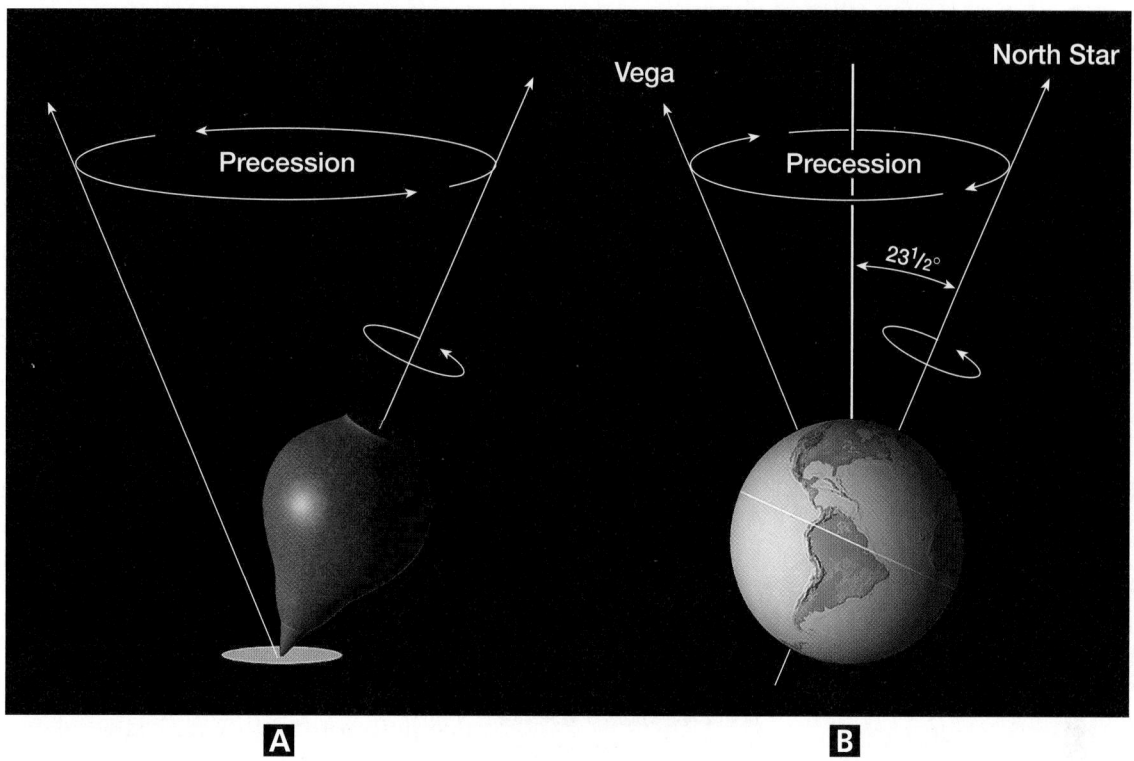

A **B**

Precession

A third and very slow movement of Earth is called precession. Earth's axis maintains approximately the same angle of tilt. But the direction in which the axis points continually changes. As a result, the axis traces a circle on the sky. This movement is very similar to the wobble of a spinning top, as shown in Figure 14A. At the present time, the axis points toward the bright star Polaris. In the year 14,000, it will point toward the bright star Vega, which will then become the North Star, as shown in Figure 14B. The period of precession is 26,000 years. By the year 28,000, Polaris will once again be the North Star.

Precession has only a minor effect on the seasons, because the angle of tilt changes only slightly. It does, however, cause the positions of the seasons (equinox and solstice) to move slightly each year among the stars.

Earth-Sun Motion

In addition to its own movements, Earth accompanies the sun as the entire solar system speeds in the direction of the bright star Vega at 20 kilometers per second. Also, the sun, like other nearby stars, revolves around the galaxy. This trip takes 230 million years to traverse at speeds approaching 250 kilometers per second. The galaxies themselves are also in motion. Earth is presently approaching one of its nearest galactic neighbors, the Great Galaxy in Andromeda. The motions of Earth are many and complex, and its speed in space is very great.

 **What is precession?**

Figure 14 Precession
A Precession is similar to a spinning top. It causes the North Pole to point at different parts of the sky during a 26,000-year cycle.
B Today, the North Pole points to Polaris.
Interpreting Illustrations *What star will the North Pole point to in 13,000 years?*

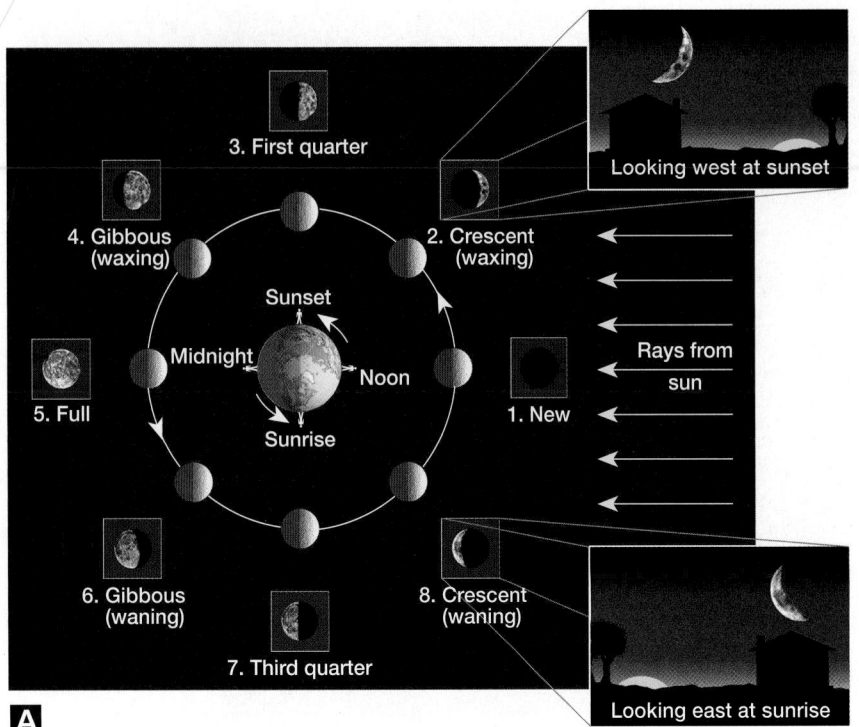

3. First quarter

Looking west at sunset

4. Gibbous (waxing)

Sunset

2. Crescent (waxing)

Midnight

Noon

Rays from sun

5. Full

Sunrise

1. New

6. Gibbous (waning)

8. Crescent (waning)

7. Third quarter

Looking east at sunrise

A

Motions of the Earth-Moon System

Earth has one natural satellite, the moon. In addition to accompanying Earth in its annual trip around the sun, our moon orbits Earth within a period of about one month. When viewed from above the North Pole, the direction of this motion is counterclockwise. Because the moon's orbit is elliptical, its distance to Earth varies by about 6 percent, averaging 384,401 kilometers. At a point known as **perigee,** the moon is closest to Earth. At a point known as **apogee,** the moon is farthest from Earth.

The motions of the Earth-moon system constantly change the relative positions of the sun, Earth, and moon. This results in changes in the appearance of the moon, as you'll read about next.

Phases of the Moon The first astronomical event to be understood was the regular cycle of the phases of the moon. On a monthly basis, we observe the **phases of the moon** as a change in the amount of the moon that appears lit. Look at the new moon shown in Figure 15A. About two days after the new moon, a thin sliver (crescent phase) appears low in the western sky just after sunset. During the following week, the lighted portion of the moon visible from Earth increases (waxing) to a half circle (first-quarter phase) and can be seen from about noon to midnight. In another week, the complete disk (full-moon phase) can be seen rising in the east as the sun is sinking in the west. During the next two weeks, the percentage of the moon that can be seen steadily declines (waning), until the moon disappears altogether (new-moon phase). The cycle soon begins again with the reappearance of the crescent moon.

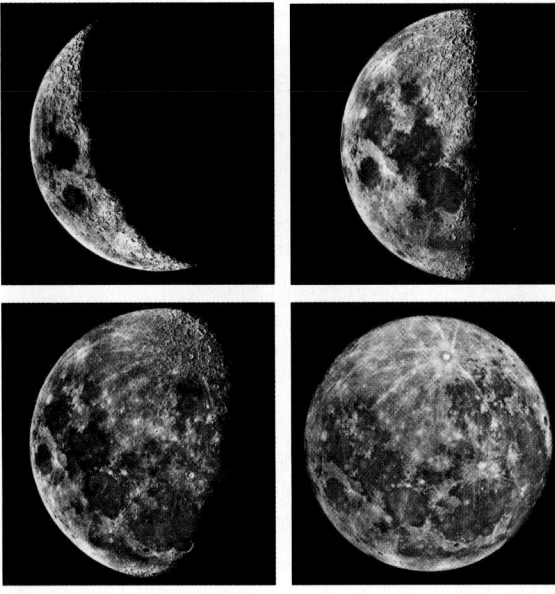

B

Figure 15 Phases of the Moon
A The outer figures show the phases as seen from Earth.
B Compare these photographs with the diagram.

Lunar phases are a result of the motion of the moon and the sunlight that is reflected from its surface. See Figure 15B. Half of the moon is illuminated at all times. But to an observer on Earth, the percentage of the bright side that is visible depends on the location of the moon with respect to the sun and Earth. When the moon lies between the sun and Earth, none of its bright side faces Earth.

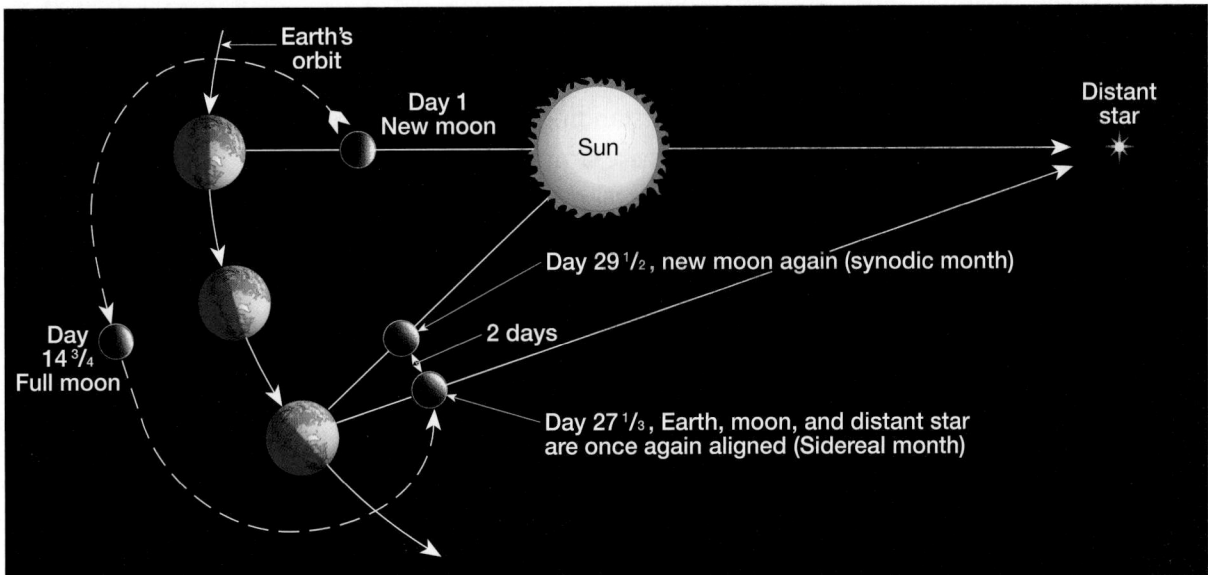

Labels within the figure:
Earth's orbit
Day 1 New moon
Sun
Distant star
Day 29 1/2, new moon again (synodic month)
2 days
Day 14 3/4 Full moon
Day 27 1/3, Earth, moon, and distant star are once again aligned (Sidereal month)

When the moon lies on the side of Earth opposite the sun, all of its lighted side faces Earth. So we see the full moon. At all positions between the new moon and the full moon, a part of the moon's lit side is visible from Earth.

Lunar Motions The cycle of the moon through its phases requires 29 1/2 days, a time span called the synodic month. This cycle was the basis for the first Roman calendar. However, this is the apparent period of the moon's revolution around Earth and not the true period, which takes only 27 1/3 days and is known as the sidereal month. The reason for the difference of nearly two days each cycle is shown in Figure 16. Note that as the moon orbits Earth, the Earth-moon system also moves in an orbit around the sun. Even after the moon has made a complete revolution around Earth, it has not yet reached its starting position, which was directly between the sun and Earth (new-moon phase). The additional motion to reach the starting point takes another two days.

An interesting fact about the motions of the moon is that the moon's period of rotation about its axis and its revolution around Earth are the same. They are both 27 1/3 days. Because of this, the same side of the moon always faces Earth. All of the crewed Apollo missions took place on the side of the moon facing Earth. Only orbiting satellites and astronauts have seen the "back" side of the moon.

Because the moon rotates on its axis only once every 27 1/3 days, any location on its surface experiences periods of daylight and darkness lasting about two weeks. This, along with the absence of an atmosphere, accounts for the high surface temperature of 127°C on the day side of the moon and the low surface temperature of −173°C on its night side.

Reading Checkpoint *Why does the same side of the moon always face Earth?*

Figure 16 Lunar Motion As the moon orbits Earth, the Earth-moon system also moves in orbit around the sun. Thus, even after the moon makes one revolution around Earth, it has not yet reached its starting point in relation to the stars.

Q *Why do we sometimes see the moon in daytime?*

A During phases of the lunar cycle other than the full moon, the moon and sun are not directly opposite each other. This makes it possible to see the moon during daylight hours.

Eclipses

Along with understanding the moon's phases, the early Greeks also realized that eclipses are simply shadow effects. When the moon moves in a line directly between Earth and the sun, it casts a dark shadow on Earth. This produces a **solar eclipse.** This situation occurs during new-moon phases. The moon is eclipsed when it moves within Earth's shadow, producing a **lunar eclipse.** This situation occurs during full-moon phases. Figure 17 illustrates solar and lunar eclipses.

Why doesn't a solar eclipse occur with every new moon and a lunar eclipse with every full moon? They would if the orbit of the moon lay exactly along the plane of Earth's orbit. However, the moon's orbit is inclined about 5 degrees to the plane that contains Earth and the sun. During most new-moon phases, the shadow of the moon misses Earth (passes above or below). During most full-moon phases, the shadow of Earth misses the moon. **During a new-moon or full-moon phase, the moon's orbit must cross the plane of the ecliptic for an eclipse to take place.** Because these conditions are normally met only twice a year, the usual number of eclipses is four. These occur as a set of one solar and one lunar eclipse, followed six months later with another set. Occasionally, the alignment can result in additional eclipses. However, the total number of eclipses in one year isn't more than seven.

Figure 17 A Observers in the umbra see a total solar eclipse. Those in the penumbra see a partial eclipse. The path of the solar eclipse moves eastward across the globe. The figure shows a total solar eclipse.
B During a total lunar eclipse, the moon's orbit carries it into Earth's umbra. During a partial eclipse, only a portion of the moon enters the umbra.

Solar and Lunar Eclipse

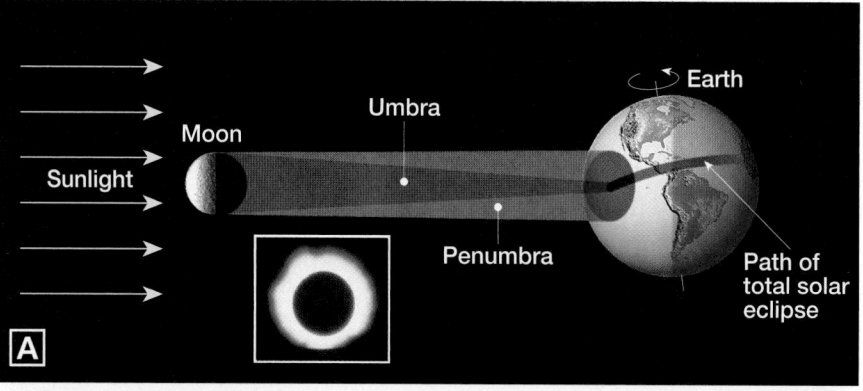

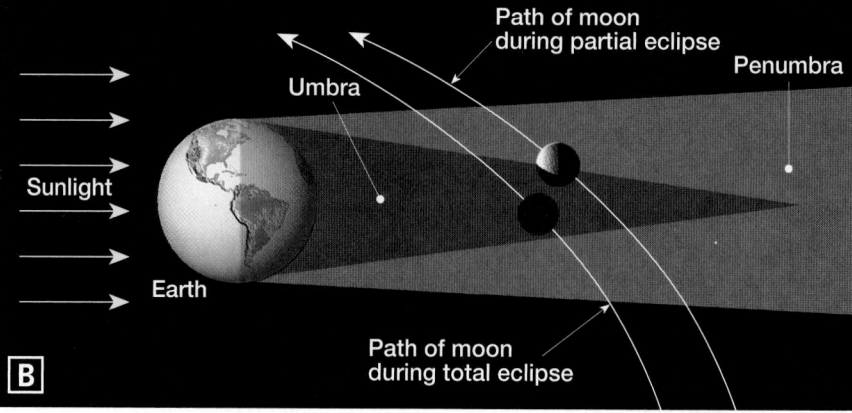

During a total lunar eclipse, Earth's circular shadow can be seen moving slowly across the disk of the full moon. When totally eclipsed, the moon is completely within Earth's shadow, but it is still visible as a coppery disk. This happens because Earth's atmosphere bends and transmits some long-wavelength light (red) into its shadow. A total eclipse of the moon can last up to four hours and is visible to anyone on the side of Earth facing the moon.

During a total solar eclipse, the moon casts a circular shadow that is never wider than 275 kilometers, about the size of South Carolina. Anyone observing in this region will see the moon slowly block the sun from view and the sky darken. When the eclipse is almost complete, the temperature sharply drops a few degrees. The solar disk is completely blocked for seven minutes at the most. This happens because the moon's shadow is so small. Then one edge reappears.

When the eclipse is complete, the dark moon is seen covering the complete solar disk. Only the sun's brilliant white outer atmosphere is visible. Total solar eclipses are visible only to people in the dark part of the moon's shadow known as the umbra. A partial eclipse is seen by those in the light portion of the shadow, known as the penumbra.

Partial solar eclipses are more common in the polar regions. In this zone, the penumbra covers the dark umbra of the moon's shadow, just missing Earth. A total solar eclipse is a rare event at any location. The next one that will be visible from the United States will take place on August 21, 2017.

Section 22.2. Assessment

Reviewing Concepts

1. In what ways does Earth move?
2. What phenomena result from Earth's rotation and revolution?
3. What causes the phases of the moon?
4. How does the crescent phase that precedes the new moon differ from the crescent phase that follows the new moon?
5. Why don't eclipses occur during every full-moon or new-moon phase?
6. Describe the locations of the sun, moon, and Earth during a solar eclipse and during a lunar eclipse.

Critical Thinking

7. **Predicting** Currently, Earth is closest to the sun in January (perihelion) and farthest from the sun in July (aphelion). However, 13,000 years from now, precession will cause perihelion to occur in July and aphelion to occur in January. Assuming no other changes, how might this affect average summer temperatures for your location? What about average winter temperatures?

Writing in Science

Firsthand Account Imagine you are an assistant for one of the ancient astronomers. You are present when the astronomer makes an important discovery. Write a firsthand account describing the discovery and its impact on science.

22.3 Earth's Moon

Reading Focus

Key Concepts

- What processes create surface features on the moon?
- How did the moon form?

Vocabulary

- ◆ crater
- ◆ ray
- ◆ mare
- ◆ rille
- ◆ lunar regolith

Reading Strategy

Sequencing Copy Copy the flowchart below. As you read, fill in the stages leading to the formation of the moon.

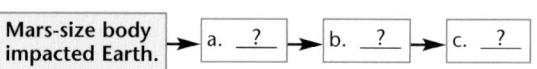

Figure 18 This is what the moon's surface looks like from Earth when viewed through a telescope.

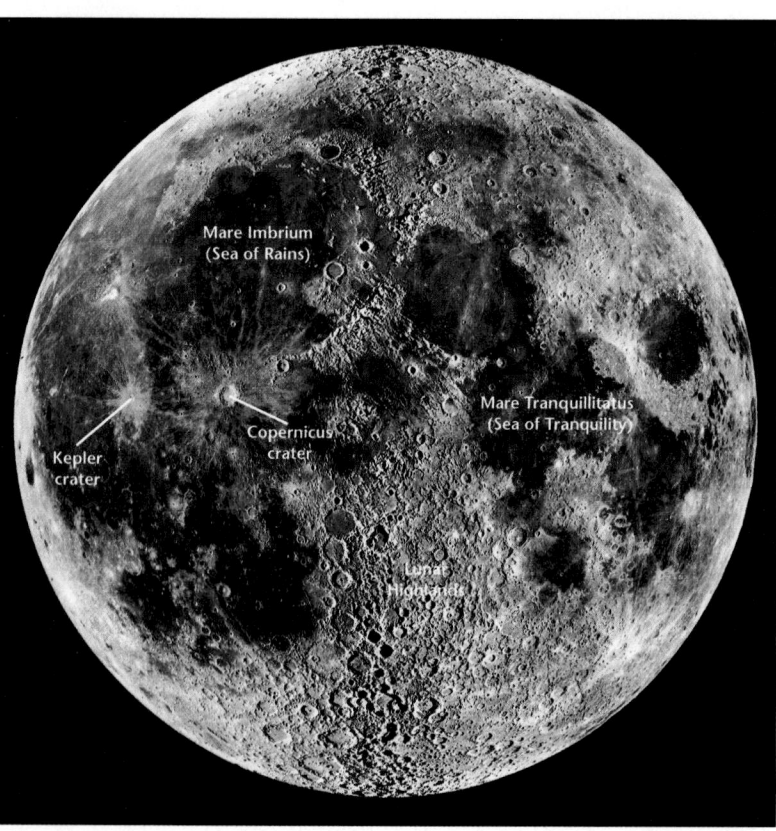

Earth now has hundreds of satellites. Only one natural satellite, the moon, accompanies us on our annual journey around the sun. Other planets have moons. But our planet-satellite system is unusual in the solar system, because Earth's moon is unusually large compared to its parent planet. The diameter of the moon is 3475 kilometers, about one-fourth of Earth's 12,756 kilometers.

Much of what we know about the moon, shown in Figure 18, comes from data gathered by the *Apollo* moon missions. Six *Apollo* spacecraft landed on the moon between 1969 and 1972. Uncrewed spacecraft such as the *Lunar Prospector* have also explored the moon's surface. From calculation of the moon's mass, we know that its density is 3.3 times that of water. This density is comparable to that of mantle rocks on Earth. But it is considerably less than Earth's average density, which is 5.5 times that of water. Geologists have suggested that this difference can be accounted for if the moon's iron core is small. The gravitational attraction at the lunar surface is one-sixth of that experienced on Earth's surface. (A 150-pound person on Earth weighs only 25 pounds on the moon). This difference allows an astronaut to carry a heavy life-support system easily. An astronaut on the moon could jump six times higher than on Earth.

The Lunar Surface

When Galileo first pointed his telescope toward the moon, he saw two different types of landscape—dark lowlands and bright highlands. Because the dark regions resembled seas on Earth, they were later named maria, which comes from the Latin word for *sea.* Today we know that the moon has no atmosphere or water. Therefore, the moon doesn't have the weathering and erosion that continually change Earth's surface. Also, tectonic forces aren't active on the moon, therefore volcanic eruptions no longer occur. However, because the moon is unprotected by an atmosphere, a different kind of erosion occurs. Tiny particles from space continually bombard its surface and gradually smooth out the landscape. Moon rocks become slightly rounded on top after a long time at the lunar surface. Even so, it is unlikely that the moon has changed very much in the last 3 billion years, except for a few craters.

Craters The most obvious features of the lunar surface are **craters,** which are round depressions in the surface of the moon. There are many craters on the moon. The moon even has craters within craters! The larger craters are about 250 kilometers in diameter, about the width of Indiana. **Most craters were produced by the impact of rapidly moving debris.**

By contrast, Earth has only about a dozen easily recognized impact craters. Friction with Earth's atmosphere burns up small debris before it reaches the ground. Evidence for most of the craters that formed in Earth's history has been destroyed by erosion or tectonic processes.

The formation of an impact crater is modeled in Figure 19. Upon impact, the colliding object compresses the material it strikes. This process is similar to the splash that occurs when a rock is dropped into water. A central peak forms after the impact.

Most of the ejected material lands near the crater, building a rim around it. The heat generated by the impact is enough to melt rock. Astronauts have brought back samples of glass and rock formed when fragments and dust were welded together by the impact.

Formation of a Crater

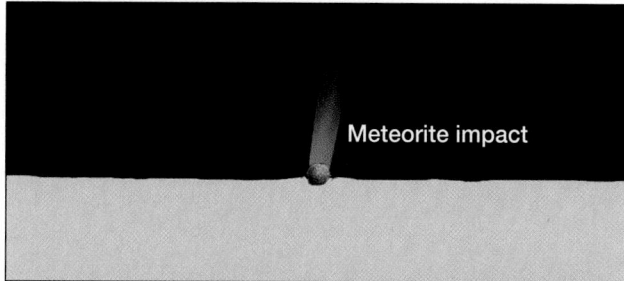

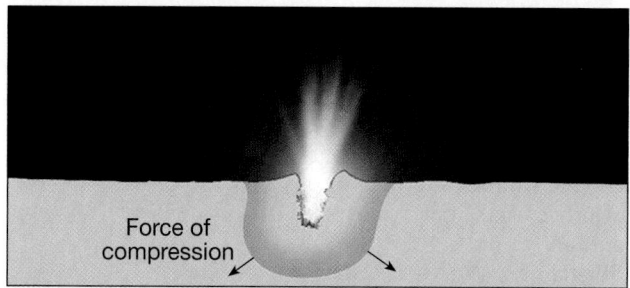

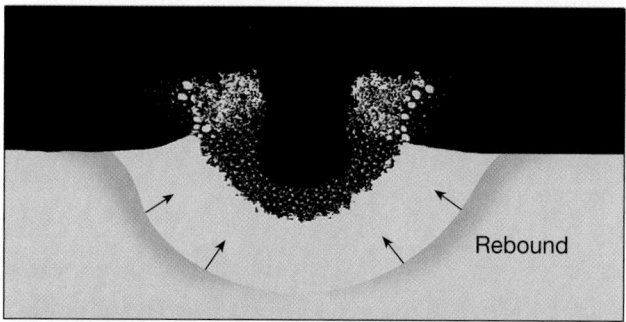

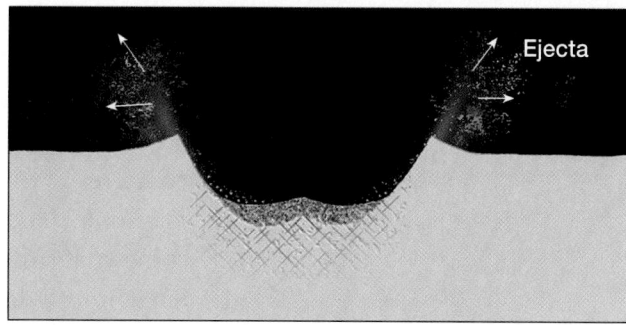

Figure 19 The energy of the rapidly moving meteoroid is transformed into heat energy. Rock compresses, then quickly rebounds. The rebounding rock causes debris to be ejected from the crater.

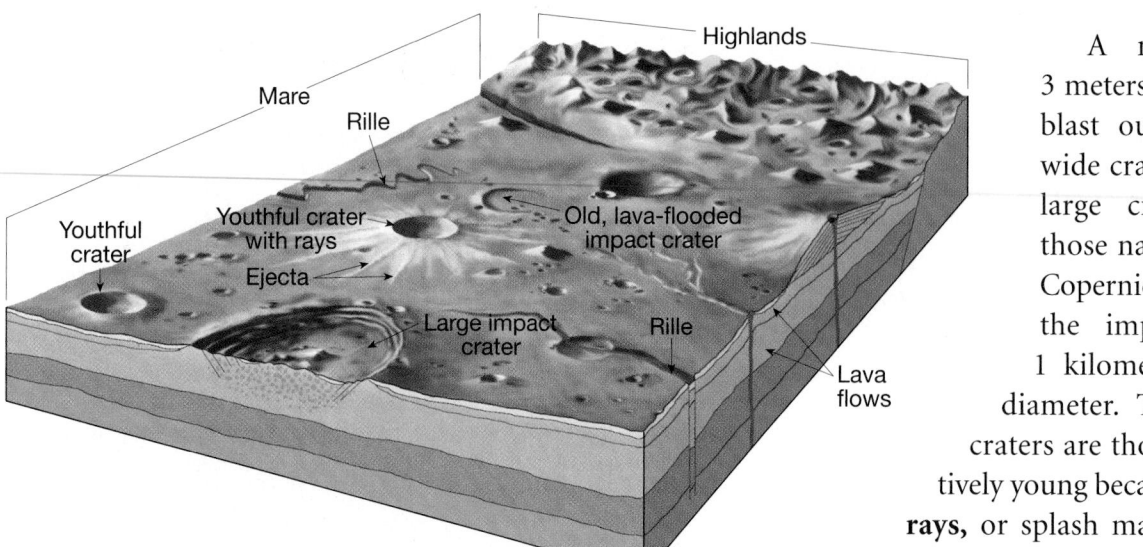

Mare

Rille

Youthful crater

Youthful crater with rays

Ejecta

Highlands

Old, lava-flooded impact crater

Large impact crater

Rille

Lava flows

Figure 20 Major topographic features on the moon's surface include craters, maria, and highlands.
Identifying *Where are rilles located?*

A meteoroid only 3 meters in diameter can blast out a 150-meter-wide crater. A few of the large craters, such as those named Kepler and Copernicus, formed from the impact of bodies 1 kilometer or more in diameter. These two large craters are thought to be relatively young because of the bright **rays,** or splash marks that radiate outward for hundreds of kilometers.

Highlands Most of the lunar surface is made up of densely pitted, light-colored areas known as highlands. In fact, highlands cover the surface of the far side of the moon. The same side of the moon always faces Earth. Within the highland regions are mountain ranges. The highest lunar peaks reach elevations of almost 8 kilometers. This is only 1 kilometer lower than Mount Everest. Figure 20 shows highlands and other features of the moon.

Maria The dark, relatively smooth area on the moon's surface is called a **mare** (plural: maria). **Maria, ancient beds of basaltic lava, originated when asteroids punctured the lunar surface, letting magma bleed out.** Apparently the craters were flooded with layer upon layer of very fluid basaltic lava somewhat resembling the Columbia Plateau in the northwestern United States. The lava flows are often over 30 meters thick. The total thickness of the material that fills the maria could reach thousands of meters.

Long channels called **rilles** are associated with maria. Rilles look somewhat similar to valleys or trenches. Rilles may be the remnants of ancient lava flows.

Regolith All lunar terrains are mantled with a layer of gray debris derived from a few billion years of bombardment from meteorites. This soil-like layer, called **lunar regolith,** is composed of igneous rocks, glass beads, and fine lunar dust. In the maria that have been explored by *Apollo* astronauts, the lunar regolith is just over 3 meters thick.

Reading Checkpoint

What is lunar regolith?

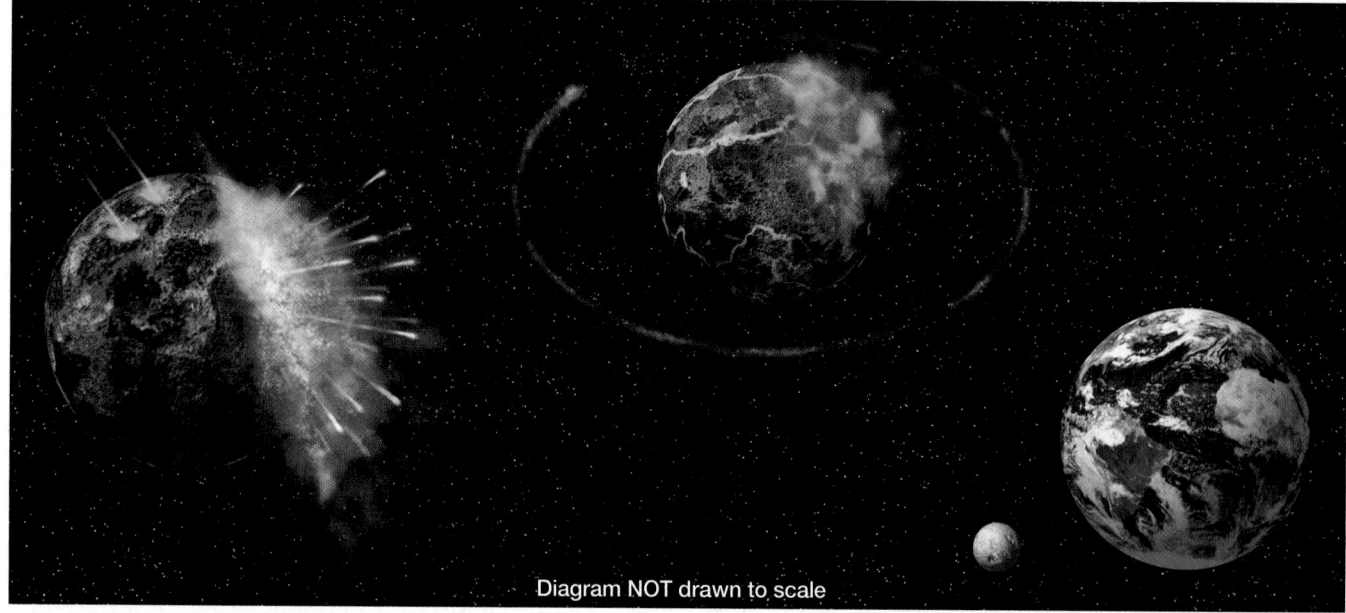

Diagram NOT drawn to scale

Lunar History

The moon is our nearest planetary neighbor. Although astronauts have walked on its surface, much is still unknown about its origin. **The most widely accepted model for the origin of the moon is that when the solar system was forming, a body the size of Mars impacted Earth.** The impact, shown in Figure 21, would have liquefied Earth's surface and ejected huge quantities of crustal and mantle rock from an infant Earth. A portion of this ejected debris would have entered an orbit around Earth where it combined to form the moon.

The giant-impact hypothesis is consistent with other facts known about the moon. The ejected material would have been mostly iron-poor mantle and crustal rocks. These would account for the lack of a sizable iron core on the moon. The ejected material would have remained in orbit long enough to have lost the water that the moon lacks. Despite this supporting evidence, some questions remain unanswered.

Geologists have worked out the basic details of the moon's later history. One of their methods is to observe variations in crater density (the number of craters per unit area). The greater the crater density, the older the surface must be. From such evidence, scientists concluded that the moon evolved in three phases—the original crust (highlands), maria basins, and rayed craters.

During its early history, the moon was continually impacted as it swept up debris. This continuous attack, combined with radioactive decay, generated enough heat to melt the moon's outer shell and possibly the interior as well. Remnants of this original crust occupy the densely cratered highlands. These highlands have been estimated to be as much as 4.5 billion years old, about the same age as Earth.

Figure 21 The moon may have formed when a large object collided with Earth. The resulting debris was ejected into space. The debris began orbiting around Earth and eventually united to form the moon.

Figure 22 Rayed craters such as Copernicus were the last major features to form on the moon.

One important event in the moon's evolution was the formation of maria basins. Radiometric dating of the maria basalts puts their age between 3.2 billion and 3.8 billion years, about a billion years younger than the initial crust. In places, the lava flows overlap the highlands, which also explains the younger age of the maria deposits.

The last prominent features to form were the rayed craters. Material ejected from these young depressions is clearly seen covering the surface of the maria and many older rayless craters. Even a relatively young crater like Copernicus, shown in Figure 22, must be millions of years old. If it had formed on Earth, erosional forces would have erased it long ago. If photographs of the moon taken several hundreds of millions of years ago were available, they would show that the moon has changed little. The moon is an inactive body wandering through space and time.

Section 22.3 Assessment

Reviewing Concepts

1. ⬤ How do craters form?
2. ⬤ How did maria originate?
3. ⬤ What are the stages that formed the moon?

Critical Thinking

4. **Identifying** On Earth, the four major spheres (atmosphere, hydrosphere, solid Earth, and biosphere) interact as a system. Which of these spheres are absent, or nearly absent, on the moon? Based on your answer, identify at least five processes that operate on Earth but not on the moon.

5. **Inferring** Why are craters more common on the moon than on Earth, even though the moon is a much smaller target?

Connecting ⊂ Concepts

Scientific Evidence Write a paragraph explaining what evidence scientists use to reconstruct the history of the moon.

Foucault's Experiment

Earth rotates on its axis once each day to produce periods of daylight and darkness. However, day and night and the apparent motions of the stars can be accounted for equally well by a sun and celestial sphere that revolve around a stationary Earth.

Copernicus realized that a rotating Earth greatly simplified the existing model of the universe. He was unable, however, to prove that Earth rotates. The first real proof was presented 300 years after his death by the French physicist Jean Foucault.

The Swinging Pendulum

In 1851, Foucault used a free-swinging pendulum to demonstrate that Earth does, in fact, turn on its axis. To picture Foucault's experiment, imagine a large pendulum swinging over the North Pole, as shown in the illustration on this page. Keep in mind that once a pendulum is put into motion, it continues swinging in the same plane unless acted upon by some outside force. Assume that a sharp point is attached to the bottom of this pendulum, marking the snow as it swings. If we were to observe the marks made by the point, we would see that the pendulum is slowly but continually changing position. At the end of 24 hours, the pendulum would have returned to its starting position.

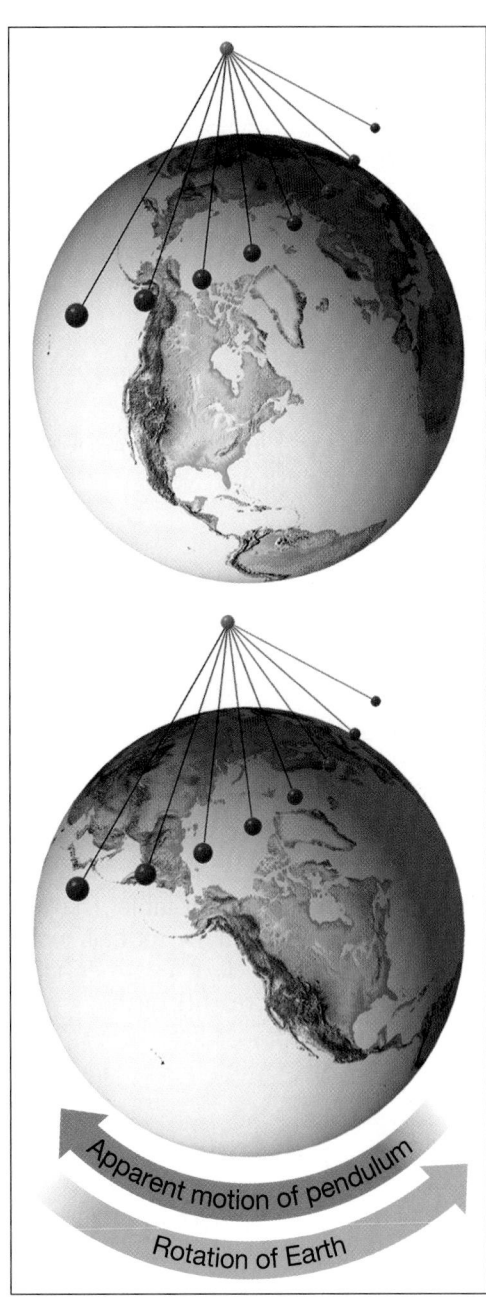

Apparent motion of pendulum

Rotation of Earth

Evidence of Earth's Rotation

No outside force acted on the pendulum to change its position. So what we observed must have been Earth rotating beneath the pendulum. Foucault conducted a similar experiment when he suspended a long pendulum from the dome of the Pantheon in Paris. Today, Foucault pendulums can be found in some museums to re-create this famous scientific experiment.

Modeling Synodic and Sidereal Months

The time interval required for the moon to complete a full cycle of phases is 29.5 days, or one synodic month. The true period of the moon's revolution around Earth, however, takes only 27.3 days and is known as the sidereal month. In this lab, you will model the differences between synodic and sidereal months.

Problem
How do synodic and sidereal months differ?

Materials
- pencil
- paper
- lamp
- basketball
- softball

Skills
Observing, Using Models, Analyzing Data, Drawing Conclusions

Procedure

1. Copy the diagram on the next page on a piece of paper. In Month 1, indicate the dark half of the moon on each of the eight lunar positions by shading the appropriate area with a pencil.

2. On the diagram of Month 1, label the position of the new moon. Do the same for the other lunar phases.

3. Repeat Steps 1 and 2 for the diagram of Month 2.

4. Place the lamp on a desk or table. The lamp represents the sun. Hold the softball, which represents the moon. Have a partner hold the basketball, which represents Earth.

5. Stand so that the "moon" is in the position of the new-moon phase in Month 1, relative to "Earth" and the "sun." Revolve the moon around Earth while at the same time moving both Earth and the moon to Month 2. Stop at the same numbered position at which you began. Use the diagrams to guide your movements.

Analyze and Conclude

1. **Using Models** After one complete revolution beginning at the new-moon phase in Month 1, in what position is the moon located in Month 2?

2. **Interpreting Data** Based on your answer to the previous question, does this position occur before or after the moon has completed one full cycle of phases?

3. **Identifying** In Month 2, what position represents the new-moon phase? When the moon reaches this position, will it have completed a synodic or sidereal month?

4. **Summarizing** In your own words, explain the difference between a sidereal and synodic month.

Go Further With your partner's help, use the lamp, softball, and basketball to model the positions of the sun, Earth, and moon during a lunar eclipse and a solar eclipse. On your diagram, label the position of the moon during each eclipse.

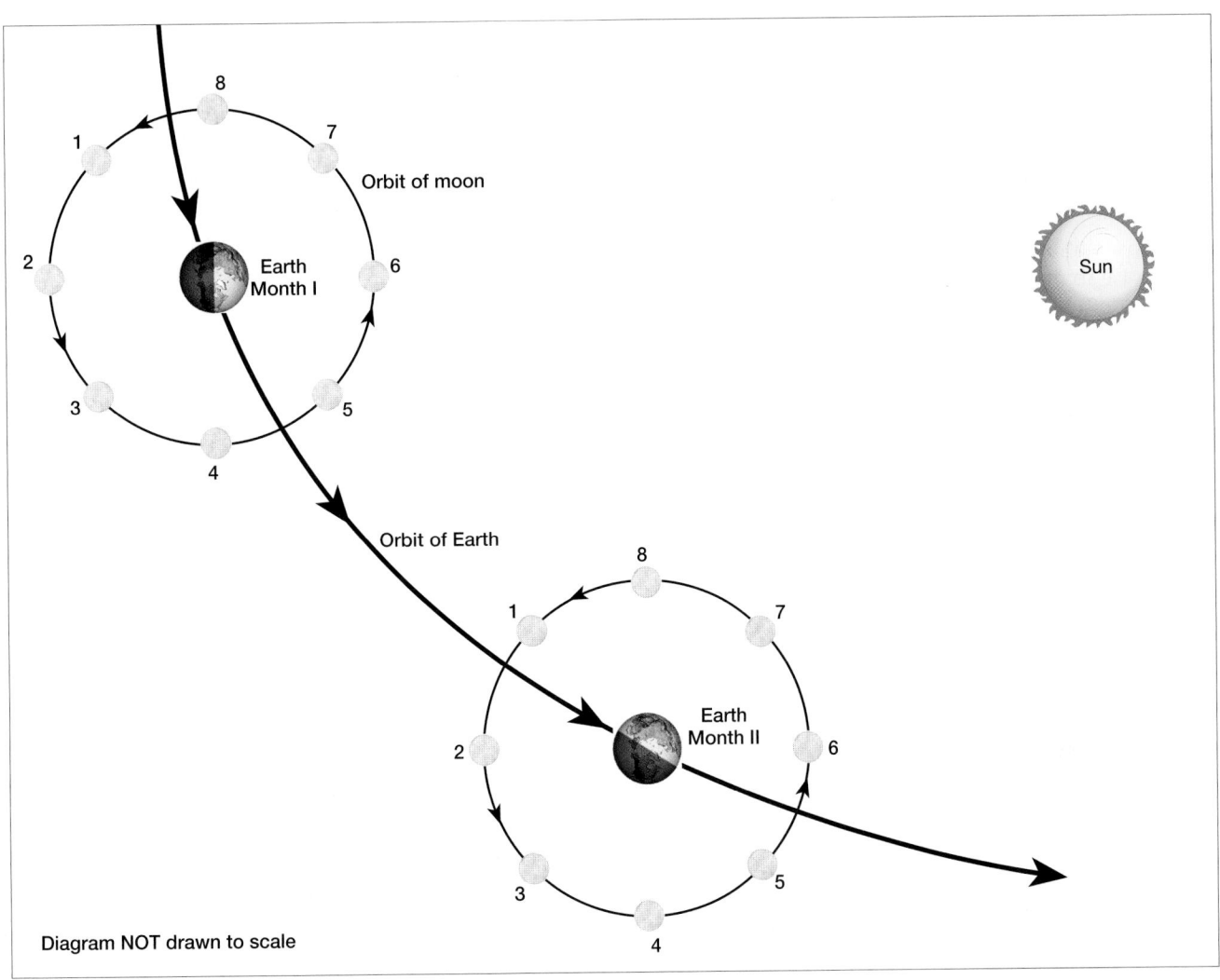

Orbit of moon

Earth
Month I

Sun

Orbit of Earth

Earth
Month II

Diagram NOT drawn to scale

22.1 Early Astronomy

Key Concepts

- In the geocentric model, the moon, sun, and the known planets—Mercury, Venus, Mars, and Jupiter—orbit Earth.
- In the heliocentric model, Earth and the other planets orbit the sun.
- Copernicus placed the sun at the center of the solar system, with the planets orbiting around it.
- Brahe's observations, especially of Mars, were far more precise than any made previously.
- Using Brahe's precise observations, Kepler discovered three laws of planetary motion.
- Galileo described the behavior of moving objects.
- Newton was the first to formulate and test the law of universal gravitation.

Vocabulary

astronomy, p. 614; geocentric, p. 615; heliocentric, p. 616; retrograde motion, p. 616; ellipse, p. 618; astronomical unit (AU), p. 618

22.2 The Earth-Moon-Sun System

Key Concepts

- The two main motions of Earth are rotation and revolution.
- Lunar phases are a result of the motion of the moon and the sunlight that is reflected from its surface.
- An eclipse can only occur during a new moon or full moon when the moon's orbit crosses the plane of the ecliptic.

Vocabulary

rotation, p. 622; revolution, p. 622; precession, p. 622; perihelion, p. 624; aphelion, p. 624; perigee, p. 626; apogee, p. 626; phases of the moon, p. 626; solar eclipse, p. 628; lunar eclipse, p. 628

22.3 Earth's Moon

Key Concepts

- Most craters were produced by the impact of rapidly moving debris.
- Mare, an ancient bed of basaltic lava, originated when asteroids punctured the lunar surface, letting the magma bleed out.
- The most widely accepted model for the origin of the moon is that when solar system was forming, a body the size of Mars impacted Earth.

Vocabulary

crater, p. 631; ray, p. 632; mare, p. 632; rille, p. 632; lunar regolith, p. 632

Thinking Visually

Use the information from the chapter to complete the concept map below.

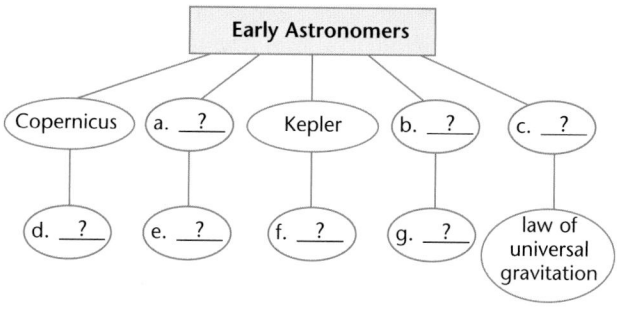

Reviewing Content

Choose the letter that best answers the question or completes the statement.

1. Which Greek first proposed that the sun was the center of the universe?
   a. Aristotle
   b. Aristarchus
   c. Anaxogoras
   d. Hipparchus

2. One astronomical unit averages about
   a. 93 million kilometers.
   b. 150 million kilometers.
   c. 210 million kilometers.
   d. 300 million kilometers.

3. During which month is Earth farthest from the sun?
   a. January
   b. April
   c. July
   d. October

4. In the year 14,000, Earth's axis will point toward
   a. Polaris.
   b. Vega.
   c. the sun.
   d. the moon.

5. When is the moon nearest to Earth during its orbit?
   a. at apogee
   b. at perihelion
   c. during an eclipse
   d. at perigee

6. What type of eclipse occurs when the moon casts its shadow on Earth?
   a. lunar
   b. sidereal
   c. solar
   d. synodic

7. During the period that the moon's phases are changing from new to full, the moon is
   a. waning.
   b. approaching Earth.
   c. waxing.
   d. receding from Earth.

8. The large, dark regions on the moon are called
   a. highlands.
   b. craters.
   c. mountains.
   d. maria.

9. Rilles are associated with which of the following lunar features?
   a. craters
   b. maria
   c. rays
   d. highlands

10. The oldest lunar features are
    a. highlands.
    b. rayed craters.
    c. rilles.
    d. maria.

Understanding Concepts

11. List three accomplishments of Hipparchus.

12. Describe how Eratosthenes measured the size of Earth.

13. What was Tycho Brahe's contribution to science?

14. Use Kepler's third law ($T^2 = d^3$) to determine the period of a planet whose solar distance is 10 AU.

15. What is an astronomical unit?

16. Newton learned that the orbits of planets are the results of what two forces?

17. Explain the difference between the mean solar day and the sidereal day.

18. What is the approximate length of the cycle of the phases of the moon?

19. What phase of the moon occurs approximately one week after the new moon?

20. How many eclipses normally occur each year?

21. How long can a total eclipse of the moon last? A total eclipse of the sun?

22. Describe three features found on the moon's surface.

23. Briefly outline the history of the moon.

Critical Thinking

24. Drawing Conclusions Does Earth move faster in its orbit near perihelion (January) or near aphelion (July)? Based on your answer, is the solar day longest in January or July?

25. Predicting The moon rotates very slowly on its axis. Predict how this affects the lunar surface temperature.

26. Applying Concepts Solar eclipses are slightly more common than lunar eclipses. Why then is it more likely that your region of the country will experience a lunar eclipse?

27. Making Generalizations In what ways do the interactions between Earth and its moon influence the Earth-moon system? If Earth did not have a moon, would the atmosphere, hydrosphere, solid Earth, and biosphere be any different? Explain.

Analyzing Data

Use the photograph below to answer Questions 28–30.

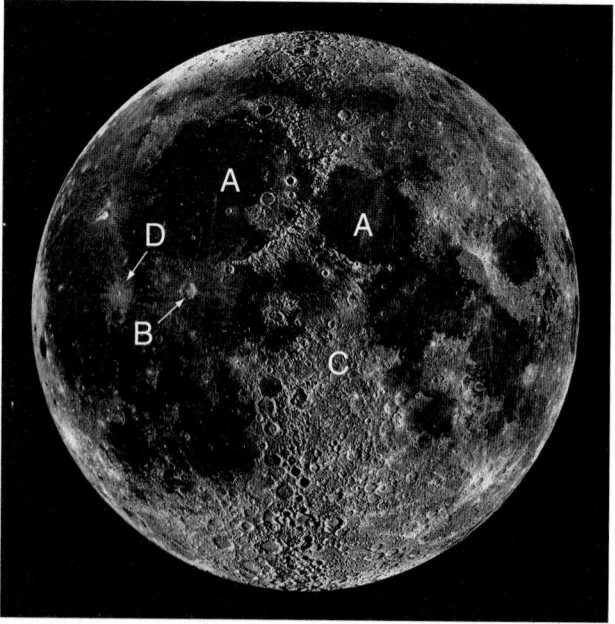

28. Interpreting Data What feature exists at point A? How did this feature likely form?

29. Identifying Which point represents a ray? Which point represents highlands?

30. Inferring What is the oldest feature in the photograph? How do you know?

Concepts in Action

31. Relating Cause and Effect How does the fact that Venus appears full when it is smallest support Copernicus's view rather than the Ptolemaic system?

32. Explaining Explain how Galileo's discovery of a rotating sun supported the heliocentric model.

33. Identifying What is the result of the moon's period of rotation and revolution being the same?

34. Applying Concepts How is crater density used in the relative dating of features on the moon?

Performance-Based Assessment

Observing Record at least four observations of the moon over the next two weeks. Sketch the moon at each observation. Use shading to show the phase you see. Note the date and time of each observation. Afterwards, write a paragraph describing how the size and shape of the lit portion of the moon changed over the length of your observations.

Standardized Test Prep

Eliminating Unreasonable Answers
When you answer a multiple-choice question, you can often eliminate at least one answer because it is clearly incorrect. If you eliminate one or more choices, you increase your odds of choosing the correct answer. In the question below, you can immediately eliminate choice A because the moon does not have rivers on its surface. Clearly, choices B and D cannot both be true because they relate to the same phenomenon. You can eliminate both of these choices because volcanic activity is not currently occurring on the moon. The remaining choice, C, must be the correct answer.

The most important forces currently modifying the moon's surface are

(A) rivers.
(B) lava flows.
(C) tiny particles from space.
(D) volcanoes.

1. The Ptolemy system proposed that
   (A) Earth revolved around the sun.
   (B) the sun was the center of the universe.
   (C) Earth was a wanderer.
   (D) Earth was the center of the universe.

2. What is the shape of a planet's orbit?
   (A) circular
   (B) irregular
   (C) elliptical
   (D) constantly changing

3. Explain why the planets appear to have retrograde motion.

4. List and describe four motions that Earth continuously experiences.

5. Compare and contrast an umbra and a penumbra.

Use the diagram below to answer Questions 6 and 7.

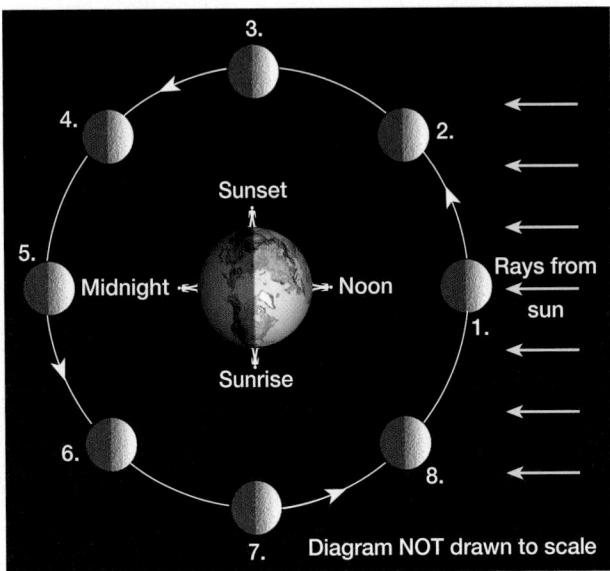

Diagram NOT drawn to scale

6. Select the number that illustrates the moon's position in its orbit for each of the following phases: full, third quarter, waxing crescent, new, waning.

7. What number represents the position of the moon during a lunar eclipse? A solar eclipse?

Touring Our Solar System

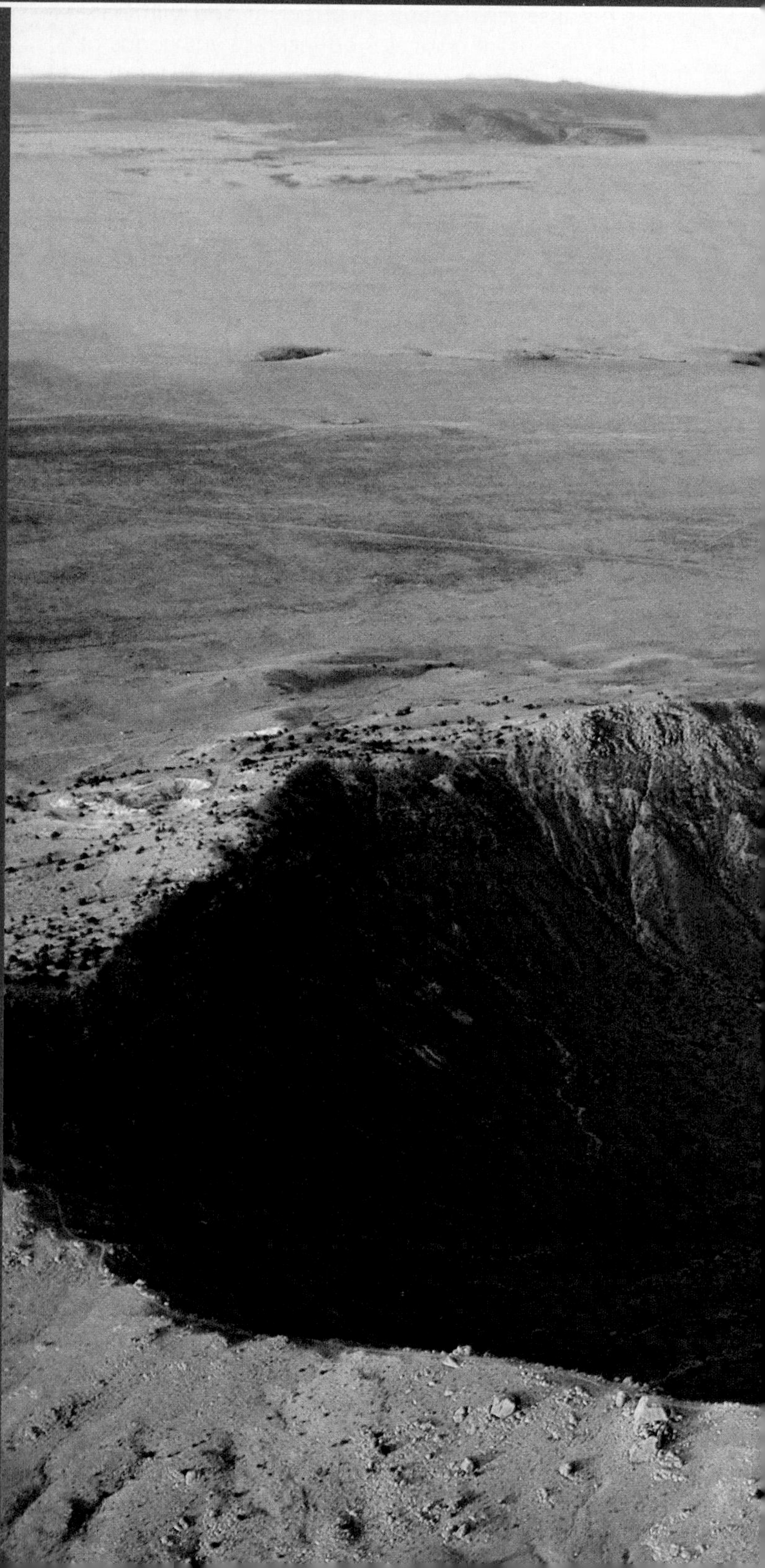

CONCEPTS
— in Action —

Exploration Lab
Modeling the Solar System

Earth as A System
Is Earth on a Collision Course?

 **GEODe** Astronomy
↳ The Planets: An Overview
Calculating Your Age and
Weight on Other Planets
Earth's Moon
A Brief Tour of the Planets

DISCOVERY **Video Field Trip**
CHANNEL
SCHOOL
Heavenly Bodies

Take a field trip through our solar system with
Discovery Channel and learn about some of our
neighboring planets.

1. Name one reason scientists think it is
   possible that life has existed on Mars.

2. Why are scientists certain that no life can exist
   on Saturn, Jupiter, Neptune, and Uranus?

Go Online
PHSchool.com

For: Chapter 23 Resources
Visit: PHSchool.com
Web Code: cjk-9999

**Meteor Crater, near Winslow, Arizona, is ▶
about 1.2 kilometers across and 170 meters
deep. The solar system is cluttered with
meteoroids and other objects that can strike
Earth with explosive force.**

Chapter Preview

Inquiry Activity

What Is the Shape of a Planetary Orbit?

Procedure

1. Place a piece of cardboard about 20 cm square on a flat surface. Place two push pins into the cardboard about 3 cm apart.

2. Tie the ends of a piece of string together. Loop the string around the pushpins.

3. Using a pencil to keep the string taut, trace around the pins.

4. Repeat steps 1 through 3, varying the distance between the two pins.

Think About It

1. **Observing** What type of shape did you draw?

2. **Observing** What happened when the pins were moved farther apart?

3. **Comparing** How do your drawings compare with the shapes you see in Figure 1 on the next page?

23.1 The Solar System

Reading Focus

Key Concepts
- How do terrestrial planets differ from Jovian planets?
- How did the solar system form?

Vocabulary
- terrestrial planet
- Jovian planet
- nebula
- planetesimal

Reading Strategy
Relating Text and Diagrams As you read, refer to Figure 3 to complete the flowchart on the formation of the solar system.

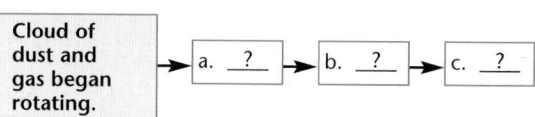

T he sun is the hub of a huge rotating system of nine planets, their satellites, and numerous smaller bodies. An estimated 99.85 percent of the mass of our solar system is contained within the sun. The planets collectively make up most of the remaining 0.15 percent. As Figure 1 shows, the planets, traveling outward from the sun, are Mercury, Venus, Earth, Mars, Jupiter, Saturn, Uranus, Neptune, and Pluto.

Guided by the sun's gravitational force, each planet moves in an elliptical orbit, and all travel in the same direction. The nearest planet to the sun—Mercury—has the fastest orbital motion at 48 kilometers per second, and it has the shortest period of revolution. By contrast, the most distant planet, Pluto, has an orbital speed of 5 kilometers per second, and it requires 248 Earth-years to complete one revolution.

Imagine a planet's orbit drawn on a flat sheet of paper. The paper represents the planet's orbital plane. The orbital planes of seven planets lie within 3 degrees of the plane of the sun's equator. The other two, Mercury and Pluto, are inclined 7 and 17 degrees, respectively.

Figure 1 Orbits of the Planets
The positions of the planets are shown to scale along the bottom of the diagram.

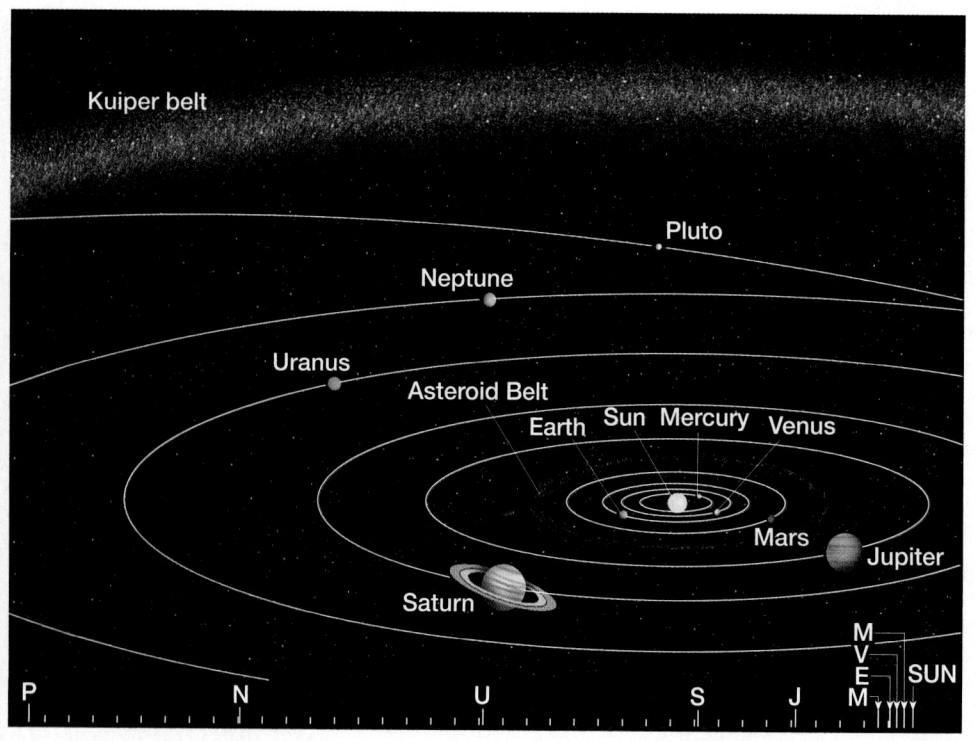

The Planets: An Overview

Careful examination of Table 1 shows that the planets fall quite nicely into two groups. The **terrestrial planets**—Mercury, Venus, Earth, and Mars—are relatively small and rocky. (*Terrestrial* = Earth-like.)The **Jovian planets**—Jupiter, Saturn, Uranus, and Neptune—are huge gas giants. (*Jovian* = Jupiter-like.) Small, cold Pluto does not fit neatly into either category.

   Size is the most obvious difference between the terrestrial and the Jovian planets. The diameter of the largest terrestrial planet, Earth, is only one-quarter the diameter of the smallest Jovian planet, Neptune. Also, Earth's mass is only 1/17 as great as Neptune's. Hence, the Jovian planets are often called giants. Because of their distant locations from the sun, the four Jovian planets and Pluto are also called the outer planets. The terrestrial planets are closer to the sun and are called the inner planets. As we shall see, there appears to be a correlation between the positions of these planets and their sizes.

   Density, chemical makeup, and rate of rotation are other ways in which the two groups of planets differ. The densities of the terrestrial planets average about five times the density of water. The Jovian planets, however, have densities that average only 1.5 times the density of water. One of the outer planets, Saturn, has a density only 0.7 times that of water, which means that Saturn would float if placed in a large enough water tank. The different chemical compositions of the planets are largely responsible for these density differences.

 **Reading Checkpoint**   *Compare the densities of terrestrial planets and Jovian planets.*

Table 1 Planetary Data									
Planet	Average Distance from Sun		Period of Revolution	Orbital Velocity km/s	Period of Rotation	Diameter (km)	Relative Mass (Earth = 1)	Average Density (g/cm³)	Number of Known Satellites*
	AU	Millions of km							
Mercury	0.39	58	88^d	47.5	59^d	4878	0.06	5.4	0
Venus	0.72	108	225^d	35.0	244^d	12,104	0.82	5.2	0
Earth	1.00	150	365.25^d	29.8	23^h 56^m 04^s	12,756	1.00	5.5	1
Mars	1.52	228	687^d	24.1	24^h 37^m 23^s	6794	0.11	3.9	2
Jupiter	5.20	778	12^{yr}	13.1	9^h 50^m	143,884	317.87	1.3	63
Saturn	9.54	1427	29.5^{yr}	9.6	10^h 14^m	120,536	95.14	0.7	31
Uranus	19.18	2870	84^{yr}	6.8	17^h 14^m	51,118	14.56	1.2	25
Neptune	30.06	4497	165^{yr}	5.3	16^h 03^m	50,530	17.21	1.7	13
Pluto	39.44	5900	248^{yr}	4.7	6.4^d	approx. 2300	0.002	1.8	1

*Includes all satellites discovered as of March 2004.

Mercury

Venus

Earth

Mars

Sun

Jupiter

Saturn

Uranus

Neptune

Pluto

Figure 2 The planets are drawn to scale.
Interpreting Diagrams *How do the sizes of the terrestrial planets compare with the sizes of the Jovian planets?*

The Interiors of the Planets

The planets are shown to scale in Figure 2. The substances that make up the planets are divided into three groups: gases, rocks, and ices. The classification of these substances is based on their melting points.

1. The gases—hydrogen and helium—are those with melting points near absolute zero ($-273°C$ or 0 kelvin).

2. The rocks are mainly silicate minerals and metallic iron, which have melting points above 700°C.

3. The ices include ammonia (NH_3), methane (CH_4), carbon dioxide (CO_2), and water (H_2O). They have intermediate melting points. For example, H_2O has a melting point of 0°C.

The terrestrial planets are dense, consisting mostly of rocky and metallic substances, and only minor amounts of gases and ices. The Jovian planets, on the other hand, contain large amounts of gases (hydrogen and helium) and ices (mostly water, ammonia, and methane). This accounts for their low densities. The outer planets also contain substantial amounts of rocky and metallic materials, which are concentrated in their cores.

The Atmospheres of the Planets

The Jovian planets have very thick atmospheres of hydrogen, helium, methane, and ammonia. By contrast, the terrestrial planets, including Earth, have meager atmospheres at best. A planet's ability to retain an atmosphere depends on its mass and temperature, which accounts for the difference between Jovian and terrestrial planets.

Simply stated, a gas molecule can escape from a planet if it reaches a speed known as the escape velocity. For Earth, this velocity is 11 kilometers per second. Any material, including a rocket, must reach this speed before it can escape Earth's gravity and go into space.

A comparatively warm body with a small surface gravity, such as our moon, cannot hold even heavy gases, like carbon dioxide and radon. Thus, the moon lacks an atmosphere. The more massive terrestrial planets of Earth, Venus, and Mars retain some heavy gases. Still, their atmospheres make up only a very small portion of their total mass.

In contrast, the Jovian planets have much greater surface gravities. This gives them escape velocities of 21 to 60 kilometers per second—much higher than the terrestrial planets. Consequently, it is more difficult for gases to escape from their gravitational pulls. Also, because the molecular motion of a gas depends upon temperature, at the low temperatures of the Jovian planets even the lightest gases are unlikely to acquire the speed needed to escape.

Formation of the Solar System

Between existing stars is "the vacuum of space." However, it is far from being a pure vacuum because it is populated with clouds of dust and gases. A cloud of dust and gas in space is called a **nebula** (*nebula* = cloud; plural: *nebulae*). A nebula, shown in Figure 3A, often consists of 92 percent hydrogen, 7 percent helium, and less than 1 percent of the remaining heavier elements. For some reason not yet fully understood, these thin gaseous clouds begin to rotate slowly and contract gravitationally. As the clouds contract, they spin faster. For an analogy, think of ice skaters—their speed increases as they bring their arms near their bodies.

Nebular Theory Scientific studies of nebulae have led to a theory concerning the origin of our solar system. ⬤ **According to the nebular theory, the sun and planets formed from a rotating disk of dust and gases.** As the speed of rotation increased, the center of the disk began to flatten out, as shown in Figure 3B. Matter became more concentrated in this center, where the sun eventually formed.

Figure 3 Formation of the Universe A According to the nebular theory, the solar system formed from a rotating cloud of dust and gas. **B** The sun formed at the center of the rotating disk. **C** Planetesimals collided, eventually gaining enough mass to be planets.

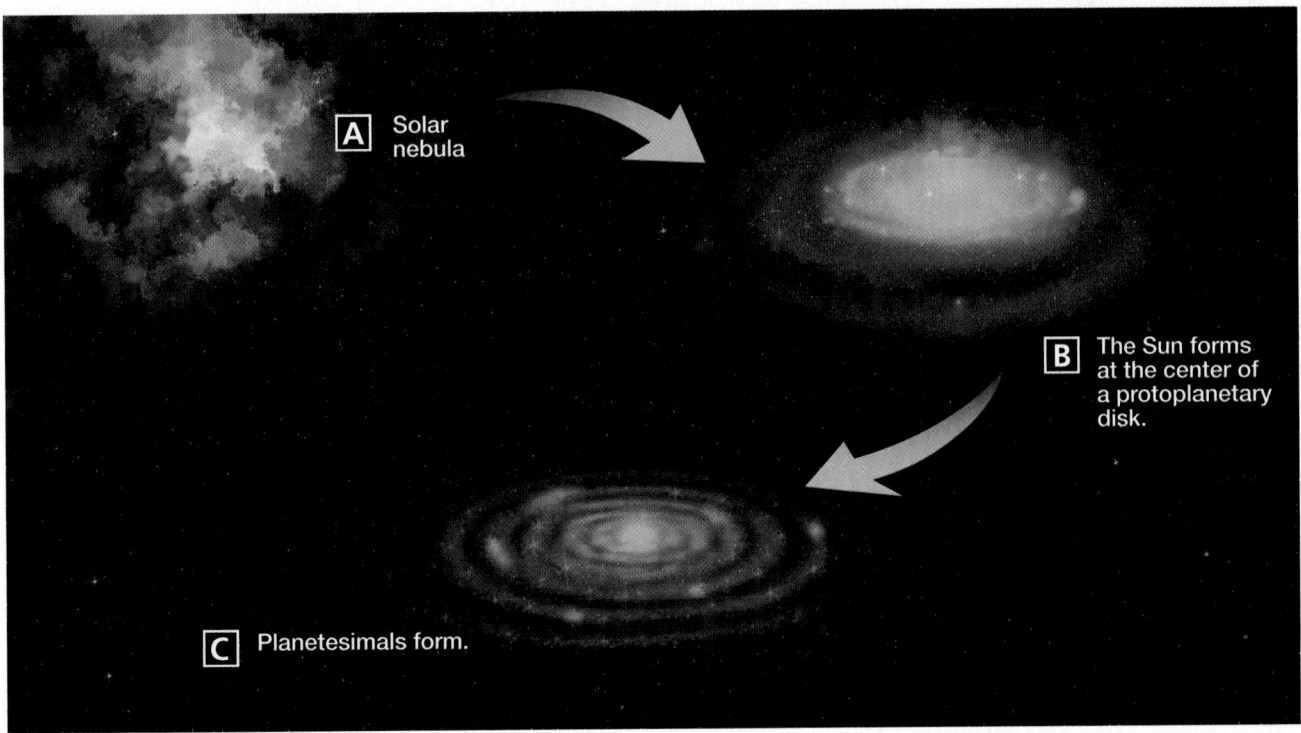

A Solar nebula

B The Sun forms at the center of a protoplanetary disk.

C Planetesimals form.

Planetesimals The growth of planets began as solid bits of matter began to collide and clump together through a process known as accretion. The colliding matter formed small, irregularly shaped bodies called **planetesimals.** As the collisions continued, the planetesimals grew larger, as shown in Figure 3C on page 647. They acquired enough mass to exert a gravitational pull on surrounding objects. In this way, they added still more mass and grew into true planets.

In the inner solar system, close to the sun, temperatures were so high that only metals and silicate minerals could form solid grains. It was too hot for ices of water, carbon dioxide, and methane to form. As shown in Figure 4, the inner planets grew mainly from substances with high melting points.

In the frigid outer reaches of the solar system, on the other hand, it was cold enough for ices of water and other substances to form. Consequently, the Jovian planets grew not only from accumulations of solid bits of material but also from large quantities of ices. Eventually, the Jovian planets became large enough to gravitationally capture even the lightest gases, such as hydrogen and helium. This enabled them to grow into giants.

Figure 4 The terrestrial planets formed mainly from silicate minerals and metallic iron that have high melting points. The Jovian planets formed from large quantities of gases and ices.

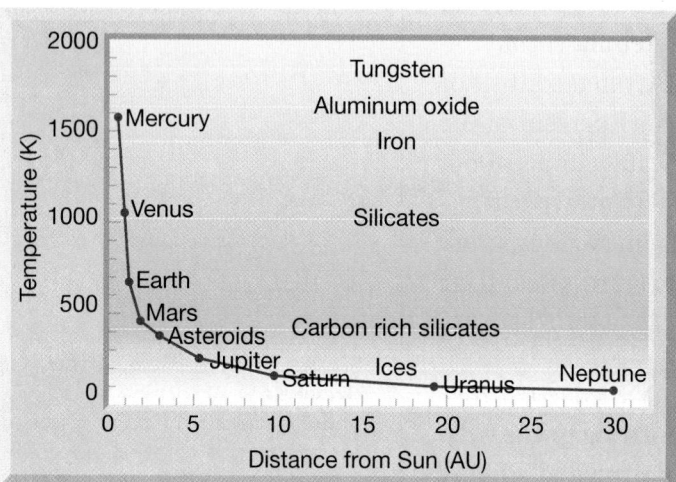

Section 23.1 Assessment

Reviewing Concepts

1. Which planets are classified as terrestrial? Which planets are classified as Jovian?

2. Sequence the nine planets in order, beginning with the planet closest to the sun.

3. 🔵 How do the terrestrial planets differ from the Jovian planets?

4. What is a nebula?

5. 🔵 How did distance from the sun affect the size and composition of the planets?

Critical Thinking

6. 🔵 **Summarizing** Summarize the nebular theory of the formation of the solar system.

7. **Inferring** Among the planets in our solar system, Earth is unique because water exists in all three states—solid, liquid, and gas—on its surface. How would Earth's water cycle be different if its orbit was outside the orbit of Mars?

Math Practice

8. Jupiter is 6.3×10^8 (630 million kilometers) from Earth. Calculate how long it would take to reach Jupiter if you traveled at
   1) 100 km/h (freeway speed);
   2) 1,000 km/h (jetliner speed);
   3) 40,000 km/h (rocket speed); and
   4) 3.0×10^8 km/s (speed of light).

23.2 The Terrestrial Planets

Reading Focus

Key Concepts

- What are the distinguishing characteristics of each terrestrial planet?

Reading Strategy

Using Prior Knowledge Copy the web diagram below. Before you read, add properties that you already know about Mars. Then add details about each property as you read. Make a similar web diagram for the other terrestrial planets.

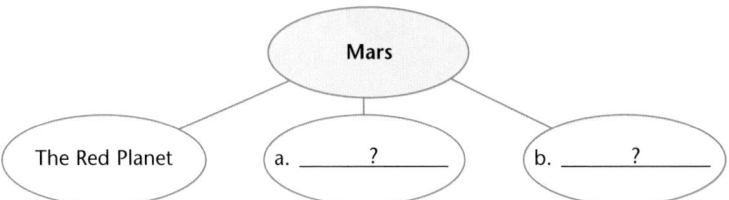

Mars

The Red Planet

a. _____?_____

b. _____?_____

In January 2004, the space rover, *Spirit,* bounced onto the rock-littered surface of Mars, known as the Red Planet. Shown in Figure 5, *Spirit* and its companion rover, *Opportunity,* were on the Red Planet to study minerals and geological processes, both past and present. They also searched for signs of the liquid water—such as eroded rocks or dry stream channels on Mars's surface. For the next few months, the rovers sent back to Earth numerous images and chemical analysis of Mars's surface. Much of what we learn about the planets has been gathered by rovers, such as *Spirit,* or space probes that travel to the far reaches of the solar system, such as *Voyager.* In this section, we'll explore three terrestrial planets—Mercury, Venus, and Mars—and see how they compare with the fourth terrestrial planet, Earth.

Mercury: The Innermost Planet

Mercury, the innermost and second smallest planet, is hardly larger than Earth's moon and is smaller than three other moons in the solar system. Like our own moon, it absorbs most of the sunlight that strikes it and reflects only 6 percent of sunlight back into space. This low percentage of reflection is characteristic of terrestrial bodies that have no atmosphere. Earth, on the other hand, reflects about 30 percent of the light that strikes it. Most of this reflection is from clouds.

Figure 5 *Spirit* roved the surface of Mars and gathered data about the Red Planet's geologic past and present.

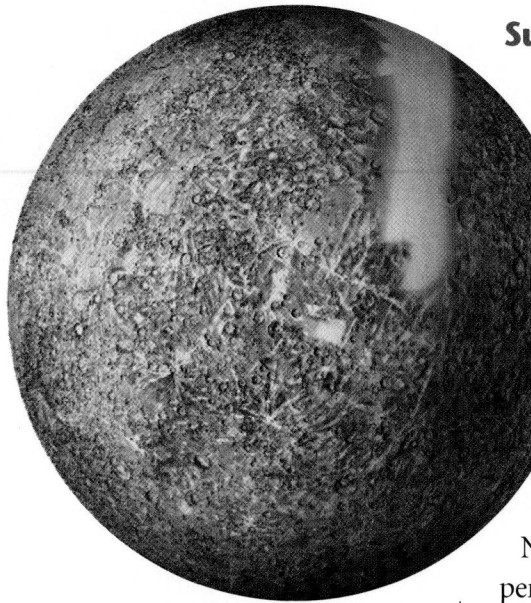

Figure 6 Mercury's surface looks somewhat similar to the far side of Earth's moon.

Surface Features Mercury has cratered highlands, much like the moon, and some smooth terrains that resemble maria. Unlike the moon, however, Mercury is a very dense planet, which implies that it contains a large iron core for its size. Also, Mercury has very long scarps (deep slopes) that cut across the plains and craters alike. These scarps may have resulted from crustal changes as the planet cooled and shrank.

Surface Temperature Mercury, shown in Figure 6, revolves around the sun quickly, but it rotates slowly. One full day-night cycle on Earth takes 24 hours. On Mercury, one rotation requires 59 Earth-days. Thus, a night on Mercury lasts for about three months and is followed by three months of daylight. Nighttime temperatures drop as low as −173°C, and noontime temperatures exceed 427°C—hot enough to melt lead. ◖**Mercury has the greatest temperature extremes of any planet.** The odds of life as we know it existing on Mercury are almost nonexistent.

 Reading Checkpoint) *How does Mercury's period of rotation compare with Earth's?*

Venus: The Veiled Planet

Venus, second only to the moon in brilliance in the night sky, is named for the goddess of love and beauty. It orbits the sun in a nearly perfect circle once every 255 Earth-days. Venus is similar to Earth in size, density, mass, and location in the solar system. Thus, it has been referred to as "Earth's twin." Because of these similarities, it is hoped that a detailed study of Venus will provide geologists with a better understanding of Earth's history.

Figure 7 Venus This global view of the surface of Venus is computer generated from two years of Magellan Project radar mapping. The twisting bright features that cross the planet are highly fractured mountains and canyons of the eastern Aphrodite highland.

Surface Features Venus is covered in thick clouds that visible light cannot penetrate. Nevertheless, radar mapping by the uncrewed *Magellan* spacecraft and by instruments on Earth have revealed a varied topography with features somewhat between those of Earth and Mars, as shown in Figure 7. To map Venus, radar pulses are sent toward the planet's surface, and the heights of plateaus and mountains are measured by timing the return of the radar echo. ◖**These data have confirmed that basaltic volcanism and tectonic activity shape Venus's surface. Based on the low density of impact craters, these forces must have been very active during the recent geologic past.**

About 80 percent of Venus's surface consists of plains covered by volcanic flows. Some lava channels extend hundreds of kilometers—one is 6800 kilometers long. Scientists have identified thousands of volcanic structures. Most are small shield volcanoes, although more than 1500 volcanoes greater than 20 kilometers across have been mapped. Figure 8 shows two of these volcanoes—one is Sapas Mons, 400 kilometers across and 1.5 kilometers high. Flows from this volcano mostly erupted from its flanks rather than its summit, in the manner of Hawaiian shield volcanoes.

Only 8 percent of Venus's surface consists of highlands that may be similar to continental areas on Earth. Tectonic activity on Venus seems to be driven by upwelling and downwelling of material in the planet's interior.

Figure 8 Sapas Mons and Maat Mons In this computer-generated image from Venus, Maat Mons, a large volcano, is near the horizon. Sapas Mons is the bright feature in the foreground.
Comparing and Contrasting *What features on Venus are similar to those on Earth? What features are different?*

Surface Temperature Before the advent of spacecraft, Venus was considered to be a possible habitat for living things. However, evidence from space probes indicates otherwise. The surface temperature of Venus reaches 475°C, and its atmosphere is 97 percent carbon dioxide. Only small amounts of water vapor and nitrogen have been detected. Venus's atmosphere contains a cloud layer about 25 kilometers thick. The atmospheric pressure is 90 times that at Earth's surface. This hostile environment makes it unlikely that life as we know it exists on Venus.

 **Reading Checkpoint** *Describe the composition of Venus's atmosphere.*

Mars: The Red Planet

Mars has evoked greater interest than any other planet. When one imagines intelligent life on other worlds, little green Martians may come to mind. Mars is easy to observe, which may explain why so many people are fascinated by it. The surfaces of all other planets within telescopic range are hidden by clouds—except for Mercury, whose nearness to the sun makes viewing it difficult. Mars is known as the Red Planet because it appears as a reddish ball when viewed through a telescope. Mars also has some dark regions that change intensity during the Martian year. The most prominent telescopic features of Mars are its brilliant white polar caps.

Figure 9 Many parts of Mars's landscape resemble desert areas on Earth.

The Martian Atmosphere

The Martian atmosphere has only 1 percent the density of Earth's. It is made up primarily of carbon dioxide with tiny amounts of water vapor. Data from Mars probes confirm that the polar caps of Mars are made of water ice, covered by a thin layer of frozen carbon dioxide. As winter nears in either hemisphere, temperatures drop to −125°C, and additional carbon dioxide is deposited.

🔑 **Although the atmosphere of Mars is very thin, extensive dust storms occur and may cause the color changes observed from Earth. Hurricane-force winds up to 270 kilometers per hour can persist for weeks.** As shown in Figure 9, images from *Spirit* reveal a Martian landscape remarkably similar to a rocky desert on Earth, with abundant sand dunes and impact craters partially filled with dust.

Surface Features *Mariner 9*, the first spacecraft to orbit another planet, reached Mars in 1971 amid a raging dust storm. When the dust cleared, images of Mars' northern hemisphere revealed numerous large volcanoes. The biggest, Olympus Mons, is the size of Ohio and is 23 kilometers high—over two and a half times higher than Mount Everest. This gigantic volcano and others resemble Hawaiian shield volcanoes on Earth.

Most Martian surface features are old by Earth standards. The highly cratered southern hemisphere is probably 3.5 billion to 4.5 billion years old. Even the relatively "fresh" volcanic features of the northern hemisphere may be older than 1 billion years.

Another surprising find made by *Mariner 9* was the existence of several canyons that are much larger than Earth's Grand Canyon. The largest, Valles Marineris, is shown in Figure 10. It is thought to have formed by slippage of material along huge faults in the crustal layer. In this respect, it would be comparable to the rift valleys of Africa.

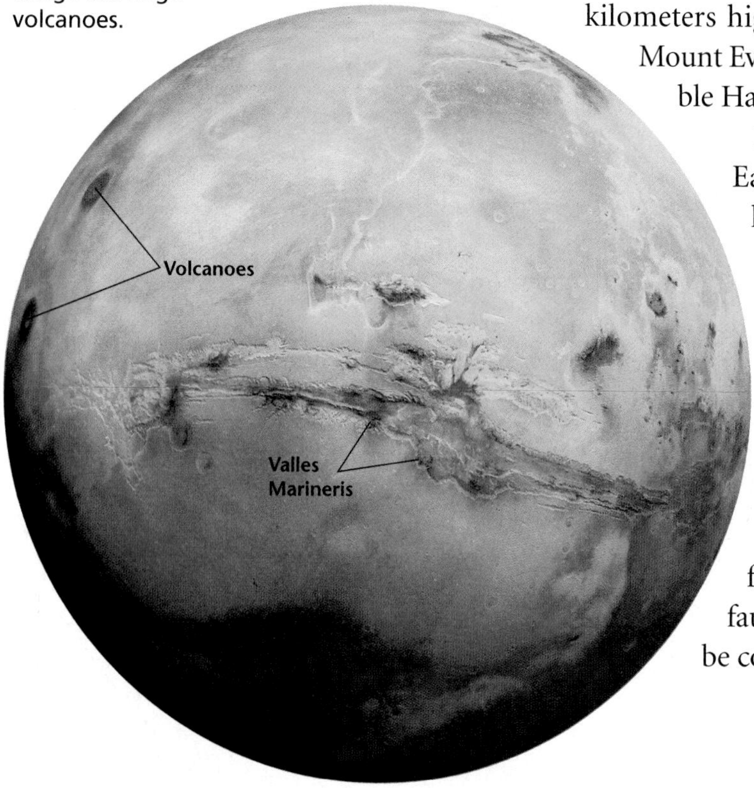

Figure 10 Valles Marineris Mars's Valles Marineris canyon system is more than 5000 kilometers long and up to 8 kilometers deep. The dark spots on the left edge of the image are huge volcanoes.

Volcanoes

Valles Marineris

Water on Mars Some areas of Mars exhibit drainage patterns similar to those created by streams on Earth. The rover *Opportunity,* for example, found evidence of evaporite minerals and geologic formations associated with liquid water, as shown in Figure 11. In addition, *Viking* images have revealed ancient islands in what is now a dry streambed. When these streamlike channels were first discovered, some observers speculated that a thick water-laden atmosphere capable of generating torrential downpours once existed on Mars. If so, what happened to this water? The present Martian atmosphere contains only traces of water.

Images from the *Mars Global Surveyor* indicate that groundwater has recently migrated to the surface. These spring-like seeps have created gullies where they emerge from valley and crater walls. Some of the escaping water may have initially frozen due to the average Martian temperatures that range between −70°C and −100°C. Eventually, however, it seeped out as a slurry of sediment, ice, and liquid that formed the gullies.

Many scientists do not accept the theory that Mars once had an active water cycle similar to Earth's. Rather, they believe that most of the large stream-like valleys were created by the collapse of surface material caused by the slow melting of subsurface ice. Data from *Opportunity,* however, indicate that some areas were "drenched" in water. It will take scientists many months, if not years, to analyze the data gathered by the latest Mars mission. Because water is an essential ingredient for life, scientists and nonscientists alike are enthusiastic about exploring this phenomenon.

Figure 11 The composition and markings of some Martian rocks indicate that liquid water was once present on Mars's surface. The marking shown in the center of the rock, however, was created by a NASA rover during chemical analysis.

Section 23.2 Assessment

Reviewing Concepts

1. Which inner planet is smallest?
2. How does Venus compare with Earth?
3. Identify one distinguishing characteristic of each inner planet.
4. What surface features does Mars have that are also common on Earth?

Critical Thinking

5. **Making Judgments** Besides Earth, which inner planet may have been most able to support life? Explain your answer.
6. **Relating Cause and Effect** Why are surface temperatures so high on Venus?

Writing in Science

Editorial A space mission to the moon or Mars often costs millions of dollars. Yet, it is hoped that space exploration can give us valuable knowledge about the solar system. Consider the pros and cons of space exploration. Then write an editorial stating whether or not you believe the costs are worth the potential benefits.

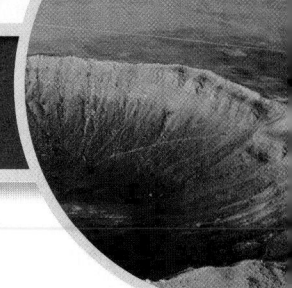

23.3 The Outer Planets

Reading Focus

Key Concepts

- What characteristics distinguish each outer planet?

Reading Strategy

Summarizing Make a table like the one on the right that includes a row for each outer planet. Write a brief summary of the characteristics of each planet.

Outer Planets	Characteristics
Jupiter	largest; most mass, Great Red Spot
a. ____?____	b. ____?____
c. ____?____	d. ____?____

Figure 12 This artist's rendition shows *Cassini* approaching Saturn.

$\mathbf{I}$n 2004, the space probe *Cassini,* launched seven years earlier, finally reached the planet Saturn. The mission of *Cassini,* shown in Figure 12, is to explore Saturn's stunning ring system and its moons, including the unique moon Titan. During its four-year tour, *Cassini* is expected to orbit the ringed giant 74 times and make nearly four dozen flybys of Titan. The *Hugyens* probe, carried into space by the *Cassini* orbiter, will descend to Titan's surface for further studies. In this section, we'll take a clue from *Cassini* and explore the outer planets—Jupiter, Saturn, Neptune, Uranus, and Pluto.

Jupiter: Giant Among Planets

Jupiter is only 1/800 as massive as the sun. Still, it is the largest planet by far. **Jupiter has a mass that is 2 1/2 times greater than the mass of all the other planets and moons combined.** In fact, had Jupiter been about 10 times larger, it would have evolved into a small star. Jupiter rotates more rapidly than any other planet, completing one rotation in slightly less than 10 Earth-hours. The effect of this fast spin is to make its equatorial region bulge and its poles flatten slightly.

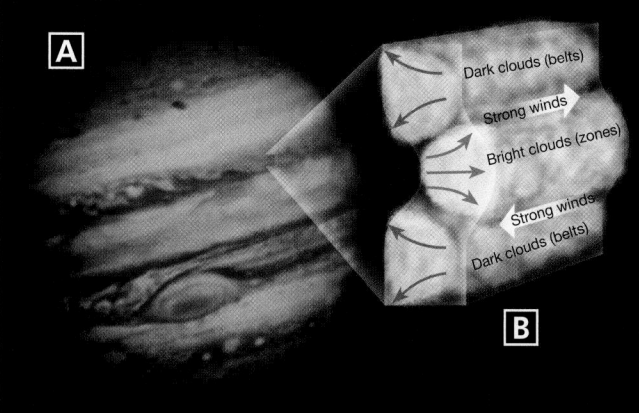

Figure 13 A When photographed by *Voyager 2,* the Great Red Spot was the size of two Earth-size circles placed side by side. **B** The light clouds are regions where gases are sinking and cooling. The convection currents and the rapid rotation of the planet generate high-speed winds.

When viewed through a telescope or binoculars, Jupiter appears to be covered with alternating bands of multicolored clouds that run parallel to its equator. The most striking feature is the Great Red Spot in the southern hemisphere, shown in Figure 13A. The Great Red Spot was first discovered more than three centuries ago. However, when *Pioneer 11* moved within 42,000 kilometers of Jupiter's cloud tops, images from the orbiter indicated that the Great Red Spot is a cyclonic storm.

Structure of Jupiter Jupiter's hydrogen-helium atmosphere also contains small amounts of methane, ammonia, water, and sulfur compounds. The wind systems, shown in Figure 13B, generate the light- and dark-colored bands that encircle this giant. Unlike the winds on Earth, which are driven by solar energy, Jupiter itself gives off nearly twice as much heat as it receives from the sun. Thus, the interior heat from Jupiter produces huge convection currents in the atmosphere.

Atmospheric pressure at the top of the clouds is equal to sea-level pressure on Earth. Because of Jupiter's immense gravity, the pressure increases rapidly toward its surface. At 1000 kilometers below the clouds, the pressure is great enough to compress hydrogen gas into a liquid. Consequently, Jupiter is thought to be a gigantic ocean of liquid hydrogen. Less than halfway into Jupiter's interior, extreme pressures cause the liquid hydrogen to turn into liquid metallic hydrogen. Jupiter is also believed to have a rocky and metallic central core.

Jupiter's Moons Jupiter's satellite system, consisting of 28 moons discovered so far, resembles a miniature solar system. The four largest moons were discovered by Galileo. They travel in nearly circular orbits around the planet. To the surprise of almost everyone images from *Voyagers 1* and *2* in 1979 revealed that each of the four Galilean satellites is a unique geological world. The moons are shown in Figure 14. The innermost of the Galilean moons, Io, is one of three known volcanically active bodies in our solar system. The other volcanically active bodies are Earth—and Neptune's moon Triton. The heat source for volcanic activity on Io is thought to be tidal energy generated by a relentless "tug of war" between Jupiter and the other Galilean moons. The gravitational power of Jupiter and nearby moons pulls and pushes on Io's tidal bulge as its orbit takes it alternately closer to and farther from Jupiter. This gravitational flexing of Io is transformed into heat energy and results in Io's volcanic eruptions.

Go Online
SciLINKS NSTA

For: Links on the outer planets
Visit: www.SciLinks.org
Web Code: cjn-7233

Figure 14 Jupiter's Moons
A Io is the innermost moon and is one of only three volcanically active bodies in the solar system. **B** Europa—the smallest of the Galilean moons—has an icy surface that is crossed by many linear features. **C** Ganymede is the largest Jovian moon, and it contains cratered areas, smooth regions, and areas covered by numerous parallel grooves. **D** Callisto—the outermost of the Galilean moons—is densely cratered, much like Earth's moon.

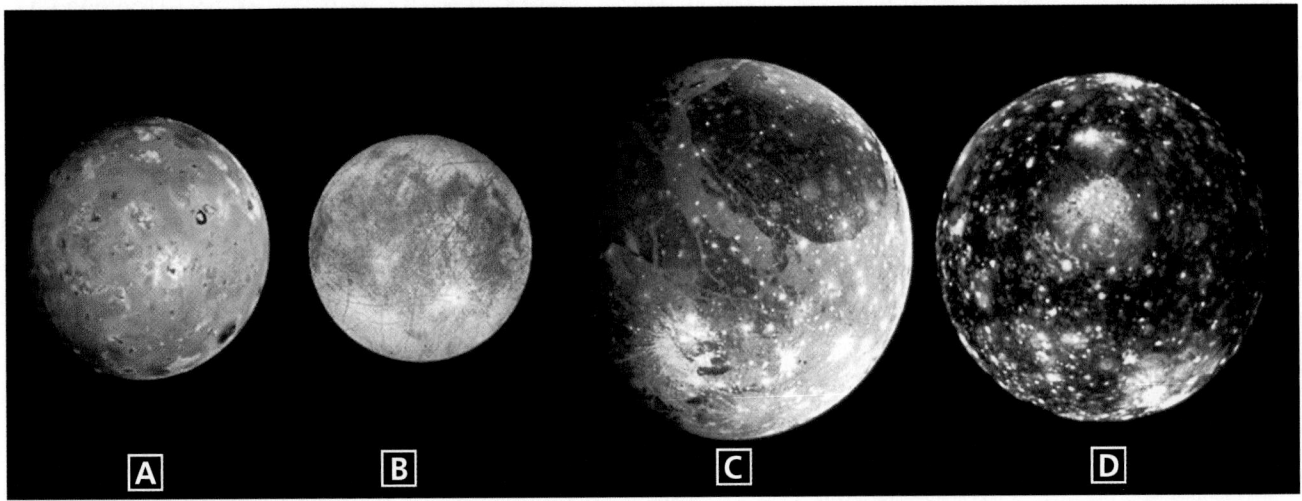

Jupiter's Rings Jupiter's ring system was one of the most unexpected discoveries made by *Voyager 1*. By analyzing how these rings scatter light, researchers concluded that the rings are composed of fine, dark particles, similar in size to smoke particles. The faint nature of the rings also indicates that these minute fragments are widely dispersed. The particles are thought to be fragments blasted by meteorite impacts from the surfaces of Metis and Adrastea, two small moons of Jupiter.

 **Reading Checkpoint** *Which Galilean moon is volcanically active?*

Saturn: The Elegant Planet

Requiring 29.46 Earth-years to make one revolution, Saturn is almost twice as far from the sun as Jupiter. However, its atmosphere, composition, and internal structure are thought to be remarkably similar to Jupiter's. **The most prominent feature of Saturn is its system of rings, shown in Figure 15.** In 1610, Galileo used a primitive telescope and first saw the structures that were later found to be the rings. They appeared as two small bodies adjacent to the planet. Their ring nature was explained 50 years later by the Dutch astronomer Christian Huygens.

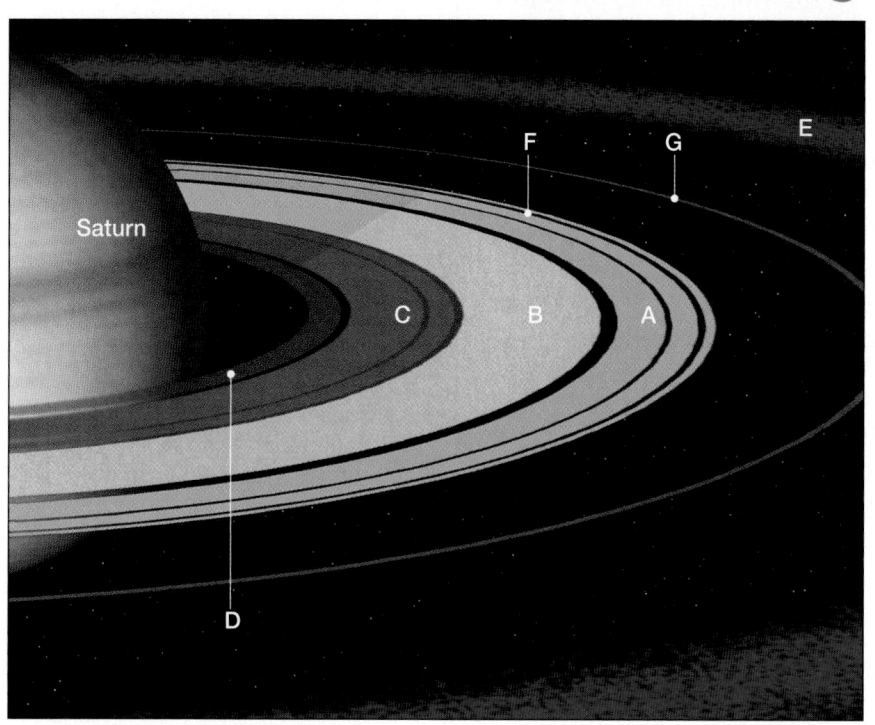

Figure 15 Saturn's Rings Saturn's rings fall into two categories based on particle density. The main rings (A and B) are densely packed. In contrast, the outer rings are composed of widely dispersed particles.

Features of Saturn In 1980 and 1981, flyby missions of the nuclear-powered *Voyagers 1* and *2* spacecraft came within 100,000 kilometers of Saturn. More information was gained in a few days than had been acquired since Galileo first viewed this elegant planet.

1. Saturn's atmosphere is very active, with winds roaring at up to 1500 kilometers per hour.
2. Large cyclonic "storms" similar to Jupiter's Great Red Spot, although smaller, occur in Saturn's atmosphere.
3. Eleven additional moons were discovered.
4. The rings of Saturn were found to be more complex than expected.

More recently, observations from ground-based telescopes, the Hubble Space Telescope, and *Cassini* have added to our knowledge of Saturn's ring and moon system. When the positions of Earth and Saturn allowed the rings to be viewed edge-on—thereby reducing the glare from the main rings—Saturn's faintest rings and satellites became visible.

Saturn's Rings Until the discovery that Jupiter, Uranus, and Neptune also have ring systems, this phenomenon was thought to be unique to Saturn. Although the four known ring systems differ in detail, they share many attributes. They all consist of multiple concentric rings separated by gaps of various widths. In addition, each ring is composed of individual particles—"moonlets" of ice and rock—that circle the planet while regularly impacting one another.

Most rings fall into one of two categories based on particle density. Saturn's main rings, designated A and B in Figure 15, and the bright rings of Uranus are tightly packed and contain "moonlets" that range in size from a few centimeters to several meters. These particles are thought to collide frequently as they orbit the parent planet. Despite the fact that Saturn's dense rings stretch across several hundred kilometers, they are very thin, perhaps less than 100 meters from top to bottom.

At the other extreme, the faintest rings, such as Jupiter's ring system and Saturn's outermost rings, are composed of very fine particles that are widely dispersed. Saturn's outermost rings are designated E in Figure 15. In addition to having very low particle densities, these rings tend to be thicker than Saturn's bright rings.

Saturn's Moons Saturn's satellite system consists of 31 moons, some of which are shown in Figure 16. Titan is the largest moon and is bigger than Mercury. It is the second-largest moon in the solar system. Titan and Neptune's Triton are the only moons in the solar system known to have substantial atmospheres. Because of its dense gaseous cover, the atmospheric pressure at Titan's surface is about 1.5 times that at Earth's surface. Another moon, Phoebe, exhibits retrograde motion. It, like other moons with retrograde orbits, is most likely a captured asteroid or large planetesimal left over from the formation of the planets.

 *How many moons of Saturn have been discovered thus far?*

Figure 16 Saturn's Moons This image of Saturn shows several of its moons.

Uranus: The Sideways Planet

A unique feature of Uranus is that it rotates "on its side."  **Instead of being generally perpendicular to the plane of its orbit like the other planets, Uranus's axis of rotation lies nearly parallel with the plane of its orbit.** Its rotational motion, therefore, has the appearance of rolling, rather than the top-like spinning of the other planets. Uranus's spin may have been altered by a giant impact.

A surprise discovery in 1977 revealed that Uranus has a ring system. This find occurred as Uranus passed in front of a distant star and blocked its view. Observers saw the star "wink" briefly both before and after Uranus passed by. Later studies indicate that Uranus has at least nine distinct ring belts.

Spectacular views from *Voyager 2*, such as seen in Figure 17, show the varied terrains of the five largest moons of Uranus. Some have long, deep canyons and linear scars, whereas others possess large, smooth areas on otherwise crater-riddled surfaces. Miranda, the innermost of the five largest moons, has a greater variety of landforms than any body yet examined in the solar system.

Figure 17 This image of Titania, one of Uranus's moons, was taken by *Voyager 2* from a distance of 1 million kilometers.

✓ Reading Checkpoint *What is unique about Uranus's axis of rotation?*

Neptune: The Windy Planet

As shown in Figure 18, Neptune has a dynamic atmosphere, much like those of Jupiter and Saturn. **Winds exceeding 1000 kilometers per hour encircle Neptune, making it one of the windiest places in the solar system.** It also has an Earth-size blemish called the Great Dark Spot that is reminiscent of Jupiter's Great Red Spot. The Great Dark Spot is assumed to be a large rotating storm. About five years after the Great Dark Spot was discovered, it vanished, only to be replaced by another dark spot in the planet's northern hemisphere.

Perhaps most surprising are the white, cirrus-like clouds that occupy a layer about 50 kilometers above the main cloud deck. The clouds are most likely frozen methane. Neptune has 13 known moons. *Voyager* images revealed that the bluish planet also has a ring system.

Triton, Neptune's largest moon, is nearly the size of Earth's moon. Triton is the only large moon in the solar system that exhibits retrograde motion. This motion indicates that Triton formed independently of Neptune and was gravitationally captured.

Triton also has the lowest surface temperature yet measured on any body in the solar system at −200°C. Its atmosphere is mostly nitrogen with a little methane. Despite low surface temperatures, Triton displays volcanic-like activity.

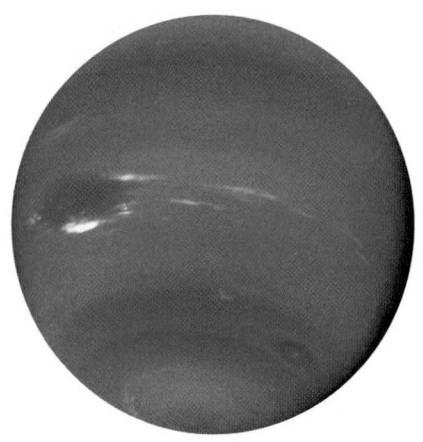

Figure 18 The Great Dark Spot of Neptune is visible in the center of the left of the image. Bright cirrus-like clouds that travel at high speeds around the planet are also visible.
Identifying *What is the Great Dark Spot?*

Pluto: Planet X

Pluto lies on the fringe of the solar system, almost 40 times farther from the sun than Earth. It is 10,000 times too dim to be visible to the unaided eye. Because of its great distance and slow orbital speed, it takes Pluto 248 Earth-years to orbit the sun. Since its discovery in 1930, it has completed about one-fourth of a revolution. **Pluto's orbit is highly eccentric, causing it to occasionally travel inside the orbit of Neptune, where it resided from 1979 through February 1999.**

In 1978 the moon Charon was discovered orbiting Pluto. Because of its close proximity to the planet, the best ground-based images of Charon show it only as an elongated bulge. In 1990 the Hubble Space Telescope produced a clearer image of the two icy worlds, shown in Figure 19. Charon orbits Pluto once every 6.4 Earth-days at a distance 20 times closer to Pluto than our moon is to Earth.

Current data indicate that Pluto has a diameter of approximately 2300 kilometers, making it the smallest planet in the solar system. Charon is about 1300 kilometers across, exceptionally large in proportion to its parent.

The average temperature of Pluto is estimated at −210°C, which is cold enough to solidify most gases that might be present. Thus, Pluto might best be described as a dirty iceball of frozen gases with lesser amounts of rocky substances.

A growing number of astronomers assert that Pluto's small size and location within a swarm of similar icy objects means that it should be reclassified as a minor planet. Other astronomers insist that demoting Pluto to a minor planet would dishonor astronomical history and confuse the public.

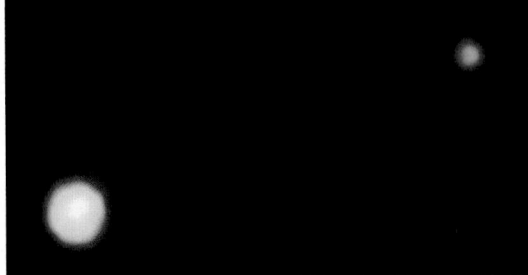

Figure 19 This Hubble image shows Pluto and its moon Charon.

Section 23.3 Assessment

Reviewing Concepts

1. What is the largest planet? What is the smallest?
2. What is Jupiter's Great Red Spot?
3. Identify one distinguishing characteristic of each outer planet.
4. How are Saturn's moon, Titan, and Neptune's Triton similar?
5. In what way is Io similar to Earth? What other body shows this similarity?

Critical Thinking

6. **Relating Cause and Effect** What may have caused Uranus's unique axis of rotation?
7. **Making Judgments** Should Pluto be reclassified as a minor planet? Explain your answer.

Connecting Concepts

Convection Currents Write a brief paragraph comparing and contrasting atmospheric convection currents on Jupiter and Earth.

23.4 Minor Members of the Solar System

Reading Focus

Key Concepts

- Where are most asteroids located?
- What is the structure of a comet?
- What is the origin of most meteoroids?

Vocabulary

- ◆ asteroid
- ◆ comet
- ◆ coma
- ◆ meteoroid
- ◆ meteor
- ◆ meteorite

Reading Strategy

Building Vocabulary Copy the table below. Then as you read the section, write a definition for each vocabulary term in your own words.

Vocabulary	Definition
asteroid	a. ____?____
b. ____?____	c. ____?____
d. ____?____	e. ____?____

Figure 20 This artist's rendition shows *NEAR Shoemaker* touching down on the asteroid Eros.

In February 2001 an American spacecraft, *NEAR Shoemaker,* finished its mission in spectacular fashion—it became the first visitor to an asteroid. This historic accomplishment was not part of *NEAR Shoemaker's* original goal, which was to orbit the asteroid, taking images and gathering data about these objects in space. With this mission accomplished, however, NASA engineers wanted to see if they could actually land a spacecraft on an asteroid. The data they would gather would be priceless. As an added benefit, NASA would gain valuable experience that might help in the future to deflect an asteroid on a collision course with Earth.

Although it was not designed for landing, *NEAR Shoemaker*—shown in Figure 20—successfully touched down on the asteroid, Eros. It generated information that has planetary geologists both intrigued and perplexed. The spacecraft drifted toward the surface of Eros at the rate of 6 kilometers per hour. The images obtained revealed a barren, rocky surface composed of particles ranging in size from fine dust to boulders up to 8 meters across. Researchers unexpectedly discovered that fine debris is concentrated in the low areas that form flat deposits resembling ponds. Surrounding the low areas, the landscape is marked by an abundance of large boulders.

Seismic shaking is one of several hypotheses being considered as an explanation for the boulder-laden topography. This shaking would move the boulders upward. The larger materials rise to the top while the smaller materials settle to the bottom, which is similar to what happens when a can of mixed nuts is shaken.

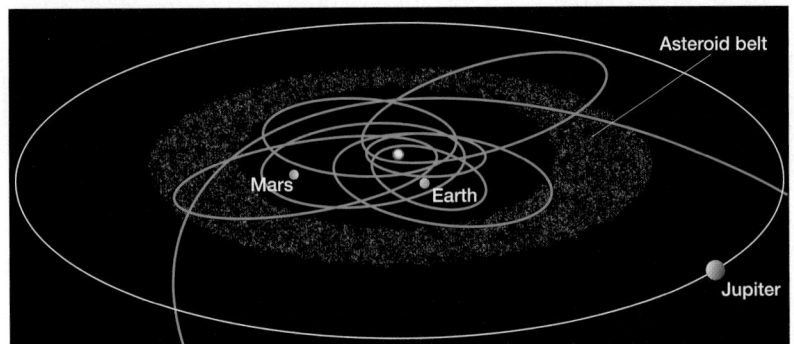

Figure 21 The orbits of most asteroids lie between Mars and Jupiter. Also shown are the orbits of a few near-Earth asteroids. Perhaps a thousand or more asteroids pass close to Earth. Luckily, only a few dozen are thought to be larger than 1 kilometer in diameter.

Asteroids: Microplanets

What exactly is an asteroid? **Asteroids** are small rocky bodies that have been likened to "flying mountains." The largest, Ceres, is about 1000 kilometers in diameter, but most are only about 1 kilometer across. The smallest asteroids are assumed to be no larger than grains of sand. **Most asteroids lie between the orbits of Mars and Jupiter. They have orbital periods of three to six years.** Some asteroids have very eccentric orbits and travel very near the sun, and a few larger ones regularly pass close to Earth and the moon as shown by the diagram in Figure 21. Many of the most recent impact craters on the moon and Earth were probably caused by collisions with asteroids. Inevitably, future Earth–asteroid collisions will occur, as discussed in this chapter's feature on page 665.

Many asteroids have irregular shapes, as shown in Figure 22. Because of this, planetary geologists first speculated that they might be fragments of a broken planet that once orbited between Mars and Jupiter. However, the total mass of the asteroids is estimated to be only 1/1000 that of Earth, which itself is not a large planet. What happened to the remainder of the original planet? Others have hypothesized that several larger bodies once coexisted in close proximity, and their collisions produced numerous smaller ones. The existence of several families of asteroids has been used to support this explanation. However, no conclusive evidence has been found for either hypothesis.

Figure 22 Asteroid 951, also called Gaspra, is probably the fragment of a larger body that was torn apart by a collision.

 **Reading Checkpoint** *What is an asteroid?*

Comets

Comets are among the most interesting and unpredictable bodies in the solar system. **Comets** are pieces of rocky and metallic materials held together by frozen gases, such as water, ammonia, methane, carbon dioxide, and carbon monoxide. Many comets travel in very elongated orbits that carry them far beyond Pluto. These comets take hundreds of thousands of years to complete a single orbit around the sun. However, a few have orbital periods of less than 200 years and make regular encounters with the inner solar system.

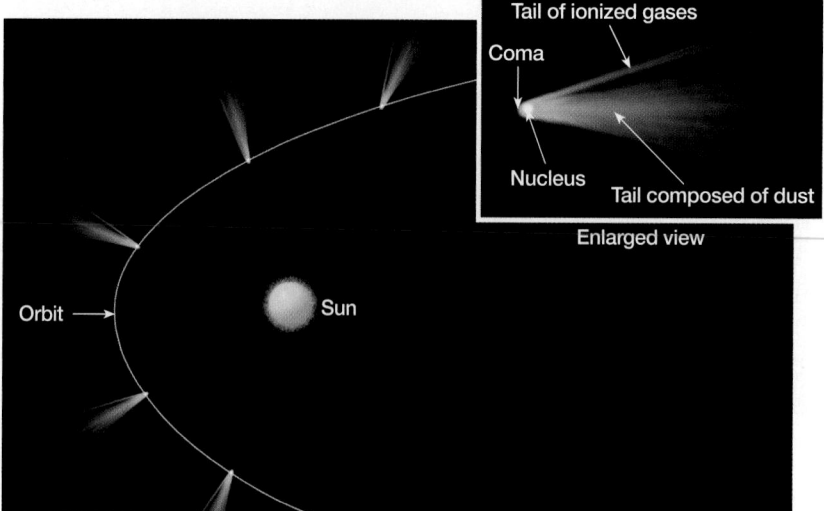

Figure 23 A comet's tail always points away from the sun.

Tail of ionized gases

Coma

Nucleus

Tail composed of dust

Enlarged view

Orbit

Sun

Coma When first observed, a comet appears very small. But as it approaches the sun, solar energy begins to vaporize the frozen gases. This produces a glowing head called the **coma,** shown in Figure 23. **A small glowing nucleus with a diameter of only a few kilometers can sometimes be detected within a coma. As comets approach the sun, some, but not all, develop a tail that extends for millions of kilometers.**

The fact that the tail of a comet points away from the sun in a slightly curved manner led early astronomers to propose that the sun has a repulsive force that pushes the particles of the coma away, thus forming the tail. Today, two solar forces are known to contribute to this formation. One, radiation pressure, pushes dust particles away from the coma. The second, known as solar wind, is responsible for moving the ionized gases, particularly carbon monoxide. You'll learn more about solar wind in the next chapter. Sometimes a single tail composed of both dust and ionized gases is produced, but often two tails are observed.

As a comet moves away from the sun, the gases forming the coma recondense, the tail disappears, and the comet returns to cold storage. Material that was blown from the coma to form the tail is lost from the comet forever. Therefore it is believed that most comets cannot survive more than a few hundred close orbits of the sun. Once all the gases are expelled, the remaining material—a swarm of tiny metallic and stony particles—continues the orbit without a coma or a tail.

Kuiper Belt Comets apparently originate in two regions of the outer solar system. Those with short orbital periods are thought to orbit beyond Neptune in a region called the Kuiper belt. Like the asteroids in the inner solar system, most Kuiper belt comets move in nearly circular orbits that lie roughly in the same plane as the planets. A chance collision between two Kuiper belt comets, or the gravitational influence of one of the Jovian planets, may occasionally alter the orbit of a comet enough to send it to the inner solar system, and into our view.

 Reading Checkpoint   *In which direction does the tail of a comet point?*

Oort Cloud Unlike Kuiper belt comets, comets with long orbital periods aren't confined to the plane of the solar system. These comets appear to be distributed in all directions from the sun, forming a spherical shell around the solar system called the Oort cloud. See Figure 24. Millions of comets are believed to orbit the sun at distances greater than 100,000 times the Earth-sun distance. The gravitational effect of another object in space is thought to send an occasional Oort cloud comet into a highly eccentric orbit that carries it toward the sun. However, only a tiny portion of the Oort cloud comets pass into the inner solar system.

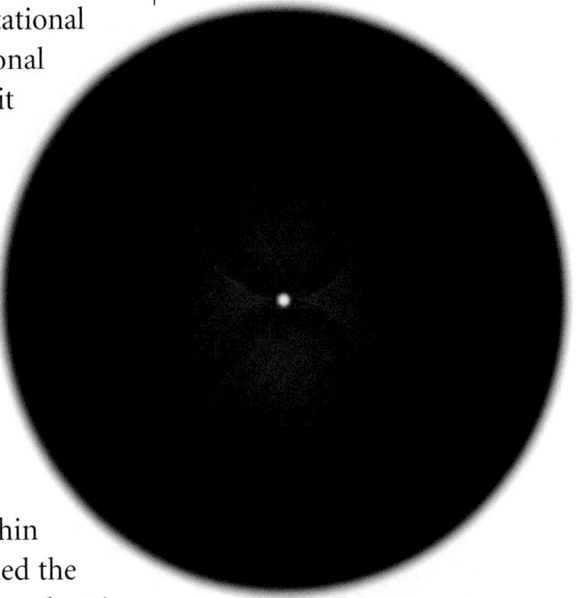

Halley's Comet The most famous short-period comet is Halley's comet. Its orbital period averages 76 years, and every one of its 29 appearances since 240 B.C. has been recorded by Chinese astronomers. When seen in 1910, Halley's comet had developed a tail nearly 1.6 million kilometers long and was visible during the daylight hours.

In 1986, the European probe *Giotto* approached to within 600 kilometers of the nucleus of Halley's comet and obtained the first images of this elusive structure. We now know that the nucleus is potato-shaped, 16 kilometers by 8 kilometers. The surface is irregular and full of craterlike pits. Gases and dust that vaporize from the nucleus to form the coma and tail appear to gush from its surface as bright jets or streams. Only about 10 percent of the comet's total surface was emitting these jets at the time of the rendezvous. The remaining surface area of the comet appeared to be covered with a dark layer that may consist of organic material.

Meteoroids

Nearly everyone has seen a "shooting star." This streak of light occurs when a meteoroid enters Earth's atmosphere. A **meteoroid** is a small solid particle that travels through space. **Most meteoroids originate from any one of the following three sources: (1) interplanetary debris that was not gravitationally swept up by the planets during the formation of the solar system, (2) material from the asteroid belt, or (3) the solid remains of comets that once traveled near Earth's orbit.** A few meteoroids are believed to be fragments of the moon, or possibly Mars, that were ejected when an asteroid impacted these bodies.

Some meteoroids are as large as asteroids. Most, however, are the size of sand grains. Consequently, they vaporize before reaching Earth's surface. Those that do enter Earth's atmosphere and burn up are called **meteors.** The light that we see is caused by friction between the particle and the air, which produces heat.

Figure 24 The Oort cloud is a sphere of comets surrounding the sun and planets.

Table 2 Major Meteor Showers		
Shower	Approximate Dates	Associated Comet
Quadrantids	Jan. 4–6	
Lyrids	Apr. 20–23	Comet 1861 I
Eta Aquarids	May 3–5	Halley's comet
Delta Aquarids	July 30	
Perseids	Aug. 12	Comet 1862 III
Draconids	Oct. 7–10	Comet Giacobini-Zinner
Orionids	Oct. 20	Halley's comet
Taurids	Nov. 3–13	Comet Encke
Andromedids	Nov. 14	Comet Biela
Leonids	Nov. 18	Comet 1866 I
Geminids	Dec. 4–16	

Figure 25 This meteorite, made up of mostly iron, was found in the desert sands.

Occasionally, meteor sightings can reach 60 or more per hour. These displays, called meteor showers, result when Earth encounters a swarm of meteoroids traveling in the same direction and at nearly the same speed as Earth. As shown in Table 2, the close association of these swarms to the orbits of some comets strongly suggests that they are material lost by these comets. The notable Perseid meteor shower occurs each year around August 12 and is believed to be the remains of the Comet 1862 III.

Reading Checkpoint   *What is a meteor shower?*

A meteoroid that actually reaches Earth's surface is called a **meteorite.** A few very large meteorites have blasted out craters on Earth's surface, similar to those on the moon. The most famous is Meteor Crater in Arizona. (See pages 642–643.) This huge cavity is about 1.2 kilometers across, 170 meters deep, and has an upturned rim that rises 50 meters above the surrounding countryside. Over 30 tons of iron fragments have been found in the immediate area, but attempts to locate the main body have been unsuccessful. Based on erosion, the impact likely occurred within the last 20,000 years.

Prior to moon rocks brought back by astronauts, meteorites such as the one in Figure 25 were the only extraterrestrial materials that could be directly examined. Meteorite dating indicates that our solar system's age exceeds 4.5 billion years. This "old age" has been confirmed by data from lunar samples.

Section 23.4 Assessment

Reviewing Concepts

1. Where are most asteroids located?
2. Describe the structure of a comet.
3. Where do short-period comets come from? What about long-period comets?
4. Meteoroids originate from what three sources?

Critical Thinking

5. **Comparing and Contrasting** Compare and contrast a meteoroid, meteor, and meteorite.
6. **Predicting** What do you think would happen if Earth passed through the tail of a comet?

Math Practice

7. It has been estimated that Halley's comet has a mass of 1×10^{11} tons. This comet is estimated to lose 1×10^8 tons of material each time its orbit brings it close to the sun. With an orbital period of 76 years, what is the maximum remaining life span of Halley's comet?

earth as a SYSTEM

Is Earth on a Collision Course?

The solar system is cluttered with meteoroids, asteroids, active comets, and extinct comets. These fragments travel at great speeds and can strike Earth with the explosive force of a powerful nuclear weapon.

Ancient Collisions

During the last few decades, it has become increasingly clear that comets and asteroids have collided with Earth far more frequently than was previously known. The evidence for these collisions is giant impact structures. See Figure 26. More than 100 impact structures have been identified as shown on the map in Figure 27. Most are so old that they no longer resemble impact craters. However, evidence of their intense impact remains. One notable exception is a very fresh-looking crater near Winslow, Arizona, known as Meteor Crater.

Evidence is mounting that about 65 million years ago a large asteroid about 10 kilometers in diameter collided with Earth. This impact may have caused the extinction of the dinosaurs, as well as nearly 50 percent of all plant and animal species.

Close Calls

More recently, a spectacular explosion has been linked to the collision of our planet with a comet or asteroid. In 1908, in a remote region of Siberia, a "fireball" that appeared more brilliant than the sun exploded with a violent force. The shock waves rattled windows and triggered reverberations heard up to 1000 kilometers away. The "Tunguska event," as it is called, scorched, de-limbed, and flattened trees up to 30 kilometers from the epicenter. However, expeditions to the area did not find any evidence of an impact crater or metallic fragments. It is believed that the explosion—which equaled at least a 10-megaton nuclear bomb—occurred a few kilometers above the surface. It was most likely the end of a comet or perhaps a stony asteroid. The reason it exploded prior to impact remains unclear.

A reminder of the dangers of living with these small but deadly objects from space came in 1989 when an asteroid—nearly 1 kilometer across—shot past Earth. The asteroid came close to Earth, passing it by only twice the distance to the moon. It traveled at a speed of 70,000 kilometers per hour, and it could have made an impact crater 10 kilometers in diameter and perhaps 2 kilometers deep.

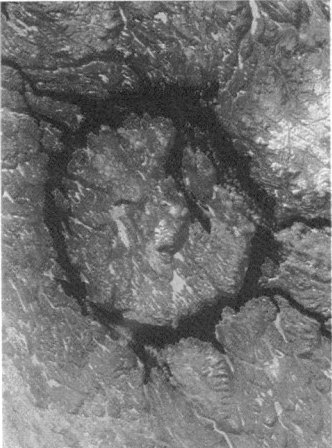

Figure 26 Manicouagan, Quebec, is a 200-million-year-old eroded impact structure. The lake outlines the crater remnant.

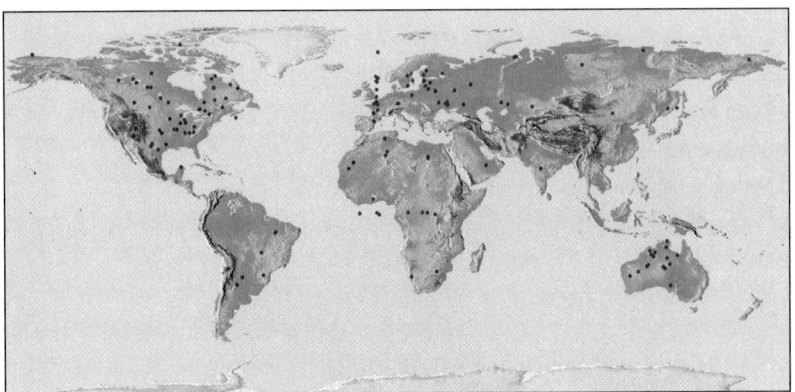

Figure 27 World Map of Major Impact Structures

Modeling the Solar System

An examination of any scale model of the solar system reveals that the distances from the sun and the spacing between the planets appear to follow a regular pattern. The best way to examine this pattern is to build an actual scale model of the solar system.

Problem How can you model distances among the planets and their distances from the sun?

Materials
- meter stick
- colored pencils
- calculator
- 6-meter length of adding machine paper

Skills Calculating, Using Models

Procedure

Note: Figure A on page 667 may help you model the solar system.

1. Place the 6-meter length of adding machine paper on the floor.

2. Draw an "X" about 10 centimeters from one end of the adding machine paper. Label this mark "sun."

Table 3			
Planet	Distance from Sun		Diameter (km)
	AU	Millions of km	
Mercury	0.39	58	4878
Venus	0.72	108	12,104
Earth	1.00	150	12,756
Mars	1.52	228	6794
Jupiter	5.20	778	143,884
Saturn	9.54	1427	120,536
Uranus	19.18	2870	51,118
Neptune	30.06	4497	50,530
Pluto	39.44	5900	2300

3. Table 3 shows the mean distances of the planets from the sun, as well as their diameters. Use the table and the following scale to calculate the proper scale distance of each planet from the sun:

   1 millimeter = 1 million kilometers

   1 centimeter = 10 million kilometers

   1 meter = 1000 million kilometers

4. After calculating the scale distances, draw a small circle for each planet at its proper scale distance from the sun. Use a different-colored pencil for the inner and outer planets. Write the name of each planet next to its position.

Analyze and Conclude

1. **Using Models** Where is Earth located on your model? Where are the rest of the planets located?

2. **Observing** What pattern of spacing do you observe? Summarize the pattern for both the inner and outer planets.

3. **Interpreting Data** Which planet or planets vary most from the general pattern of spacing?

Go Further Determine how to expand your model to include the scale sizes of the planets. Refer to the table for the diameters of each planet (Table 3). Develop a scale, and then calculate the proper scale size of the planets. Draw the planets to scale on your model.

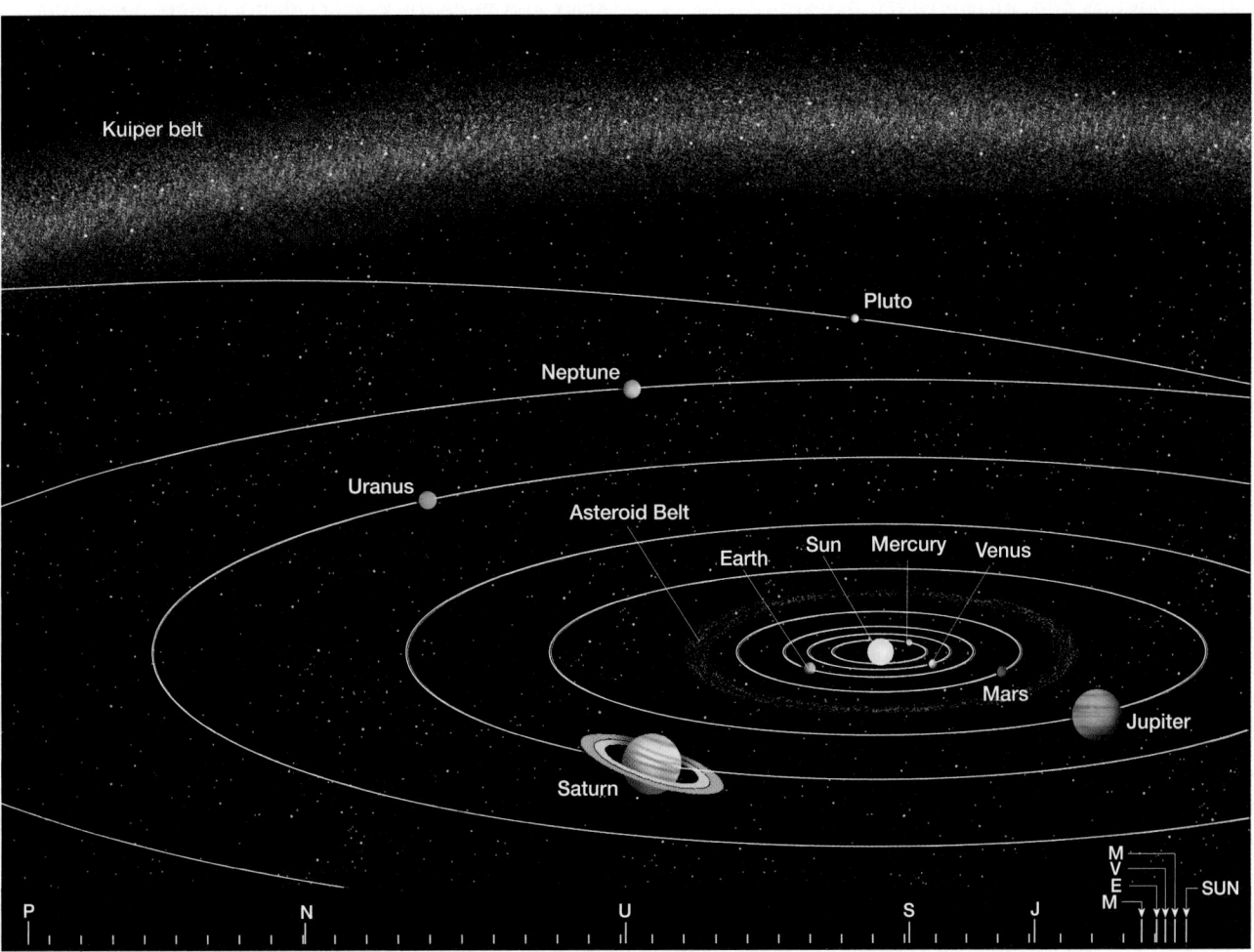

Figure A

23.1 The Solar System

Key Concepts

- Size is the most obvious difference between the terrestrial and the Jovian planets.
- Density, chemical makeup, and rate of rotation are other ways in which the two groups of planets differ.
- According to the nebular theory, the sun and planets formed from a rotating disk of dust and gases.

Vocabulary

terrestrial planet, *p. 645;* Jovian planet, *p. 645;* nebula, *p. 647;* planetesimal, *p. 648*

23.2 The Terrestrial Planets

Key Concepts

- Mercury has the greatest temperature extremes of any planet.
- The surface temperature of Venus reaches 475°C, and its atmosphere is 97 percent carbon dioxide.
- Some areas of Mars exhibit drainage patterns similar to those created by streams on Earth.

23.3 The Outer Planets

Key Concepts

- Jupiter has a mass that is 2 1/2 times greater than the mass of all the other planets and moons combined.
- The most prominent feature of Saturn is its system of rings.
- Instead of being generally perpendicular to the plane of its orbit like the other planets, Uranus's axis of rotation lies nearly parallel with the plane of its orbit.
- Winds exceeding 1000 kilometers per hour encircle Neptune, making it one of the windiest places in the solar system.
- Pluto's orbit is highly eccentric, causing it to occasionally travel inside the orbit of Neptune, where it resided from 1979 through February 1999.

23.4 Minor Members of the Solar System

Key Concepts

- Most asteroids lie between the orbits of Mars and Jupiter. They have orbital periods of three to six years.
- A small glowing nucleus with a diameter of only a few kilometers can sometimes be detected within a coma. As comets approach the sun, some, but not all, develop a tail that extends for millions of kilometers.
- Most meteoroids originate from any one of the following three sources: (1) interplanetary debris that was not gravitationally swept up by the planets during the formation of the solar system, (2) material from the asteroid belt, or (3) the solid remains of comets that once traveled near Earth's orbit.

Vocabulary

asteroid, *p. 661;* comet, *p. 661;* coma, *p. 662;* meteoroid, *p. 663;* meteor, *p. 663;* meteorite, *p. 664*

Thinking Visually

Copy and complete the table below comparing and contrasting the inner and outer planets. Include information about each planet's diameter, distance from the sun, composition, and number of moons.

Inner and Outer Planets		
Inner Planets		
	Diameter	**Distance from Sun**
Mercury	4878 km	0.39 AU
a. ___?___		
b. ___?___		
c. ___?___		
Outer Planets		
	Diameter	**Distance from Sun**
Jupiter	143,884 km	5.3 AU
d. ___?___		
e. ___?___		
f. ___?___		
g. ___?___		

Reviewing Content

Choose the letter that best answers the question or completes the statement.

1. Which of these planets is not a terrestrial planet?
   - **a.** Earth
   - **b.** Mercury
   - **c.** Venus
   - **d.** Uranus

2. What theory describes the formation of the solar system from a huge cloud of dust and gases?
   - **a.** protoplanet theory
   - **b.** nebular theory
   - **c.** planetesimal theory
   - **d.** solar theory

3. Which of the following is NOT a characteristic of Jovian planets?
   - **a.** large size
   - **b.** composed mostly of gases and ice
   - **c.** lack of moons
   - **d.** located beyond the orbit of Mars

4. Which planet was explored by the rovers *Spirit* and *Opportunity?*
   - **a.** Mercury
   - **b.** Pluto
   - **c.** Mars
   - **d.** Venus

5. Which two planets are most alike?
   - **a.** Jupiter and Pluto
   - **b.** Earth and Mercury
   - **c.** Mars and Uranus
   - **d.** Uranus and Saturn

6. Which of the following is NOT true of Jupiter?
   - **a.** It is more massive than all the other planets and moons combined.
   - **b.** It has huge rotating storms.
   - **c.** It has a thin ring system.
   - **d.** It has a solid surface.

7. Which moon is known to have active volcanism?
   - **a.** Io
   - **b.** Phobos
   - **c.** Europa
   - **d.** Titan

8. What bodies in the solar system orbit between Mars and Jupiter?
   - **a.** comets
   - **b.** stars
   - **c.** asteroids
   - **d.** meteorites

9. A comet's tail always points
   - **a.** away from the sun.
   - **b.** toward the sun.
   - **c.** up.
   - **d.** down.

10. Meteoroids that strike Earth are called
    - **a.** asteroids.
    - **b.** comets.
    - **c.** meteors.
    - **d.** meteorites.

Understanding Concepts

11. What objects are found in the solar system?

12. What substances make up most of the solar system? Classify them as gas, rock, or ice.

13. Describe general characteristics and location of the terrestrial planets.

14. What is Olympus Mons? Where is it found?

15. Why has Mars been the planet most studied by telescopes?

16. Why is life unlikely to exist on Venus?

17. Which planets have ring systems?

18. What three bodies in the solar system exhibit volcanic activity?

19. What are moonlets?

20. How are Uranus and Neptune similar?

21. Why isn't Pluto classified as either a terrestrial planet or a Jovian planet?

22. How big is the largest asteroid?

23. Which minor members of the solar system are thought to have formed beyond the orbit of Pluto?

24. What is the bright glowing head of a comet called?

25. What evidence indicates that our solar system is about 4.5 billion years old?

Critical Thinking

26. Analyzing Data What evidence supports the theory that liquid water may have existed on Mars? What evidence refutes the possibility of a wet Martian climate?

27. Drawing Conclusions Mercury is closer to the sun than Venus. Venus, however, is hotter. Why?

28. Inferring What can you infer about a moon that exhibits retrograde motion?

29. Making Generalizations Why is it more difficult for gases to escape from the Jovian planets than from the terrestrial planets?

30. Applying Concepts Why would it be difficult to verify that an impact may have altered Uranus's axis of rotation?

Analyzing Data

Use the table in the right column to answer Questions 31–34.

31. Identifying Which two planets have similar atmospheric compositions?

32. Interpreting Data What makes these two planets' atmospheres very different?

33. Inferring What gas is present in Earth's atmosphere, but nearly absent in the atmospheres of Venus and Mars? What do you think explains its presence on Earth? (*Hint:* What does Earth have that Venus and Mars both lack?)

34. Analyzing Data Based on the data in the table, how would you describe the effect of increasing atmospheric pressure on surface temperature?

Concepts in Action

35. Relating Cause and Effect Weight is a function of the gravitational attraction of an object on your mass. On which planet would you weigh the least? Explain your answer.

36. Calculating Refer to Table 1 on page 645. Using the table, determine how old you are in Jupiter-years.

37. Identifying Which features on Earth offer clear evidence that comets and asteroids have struck its surface?

Performance-Based Assessment

Using Models Use a fan, a Styrofoam ball, several pushpins, and several pieces of ribbon to create a model of a comet. Explain what each part of the model represents. Work with a partner to demonstrate the orbit of your model. Make sure that the "tail" points in the proper direction.

Comparison of the Atmospheres and Surface Temperatures of Mercury, Venus, Earth, Mars

Planet or Body	Gases (% by volume)			Surface Temperature (range)	Surface Atmospheric Pressure (bars)
	N_2	O_2	CO_2		
Mercury	0	trace	0	−173° to 427°C	10^{-15}
Venus	3.5	< 0.01	96.5	475°C (small range)	92
Earth	78.01	20.95	0.03	−40° to 75°C	1.014
Mars	2.7	1.3	95.32	−120° to 25°C	0.008

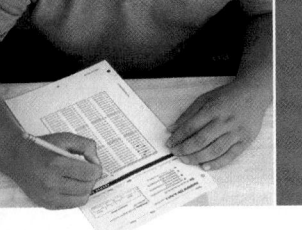

Standardized Test Prep

1. Which is NOT the most obvious difference between the terrestrial and Jovian planets?
   (A) mass
   (B) color
   (C) density
   (D) chemical makeup

2. Which planet does NOT have a density that is greater than water?
   (A) Mercury
   (B) Pluto
   (C) Venus
   (D) Saturn

3. Why was Mercury unable to retain an atmosphere during its formation?
   (A) Mercury has a high surface temperature and has a low mass.
   (B) Mercury is the largest planet.
   (C) Mercury is the farthest planet from the sun.
   (D) Mercury revolves slowly.

4. What causes the bright streak in the sky known as a meteor?

Use the photograph below to answer Questions 5 and 6.

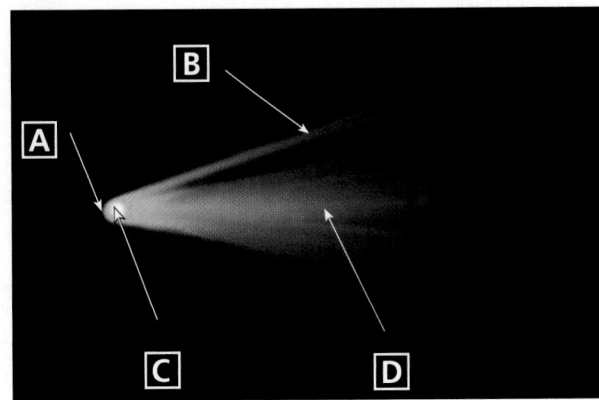

5. What features do labels B and D represent? What forces produce these features?

6. What are features A and C? How do they differ?

24 Studying the Sun

CONCEPTS
in Action

Exploration Lab
Tracking Sunspots

Earth as a System
Solar Activity and Climatic Change

Video Field Trip
Fireball

Take a solar field trip with Discovery Channel and learn about the inner core and the outer surface of our sun. Answer the following questions after watching the video.

1. How did scientists discover the activity of the sun's core?

2. How do auroras occur?

Go Online
PHSchool.com

For: Chapter 24 Resources
Visit: PHSchool.com
Web Code: cjk-9999

This photograph shows Kitt Peak National ▶ Observatory near Tucson, Arizona.

Chapter Preview

Inquiry > Activity

How Does the Position of the Setting Sun Change?

Procedure

1. Several minutes before sunset, estimate where the sun will set on the western horizon. Draw prominent features, such as buildings and trees, to the north and south of the sun's setting position.

2. As the sun sets, draw its position relative to the fixed features on the horizon. **CAUTION** *Never look directly at the sun; eye damage may result.*

3. Note the date and time of your observation.

4. Return to the same position several days later. Repeat the activity and record the results. Wait several more days then do the activity one more time.

Think About It

1. **Observing** How did the sun's position at sunset change over the course of your observations?

2. **Predicting** Based on your observations, predict where the sun might set in several weeks time. Sketch the sun on your drawing relative to the fixed features on the horizon.

24.1 The Study of Light

Reading Focus

Key Concepts

- What types of radiation make up the electromagnetic spectrum?
- What can scientists learn about a star by studying its spectrum?
- How can astronomers determine whether a star is moving toward or away from Earth?

Vocabulary

- electromagnetic spectrum
- photon
- spectroscopy
- continuous spectrum
- absorption spectrum
- emission spectrum
- Doppler effect

Reading Strategy

Predicting Copy the table. Before you read, predict the meaning of the term *electromagnetic spectrum*. After you read, revise your definition if it was incorrect.

Vocabulary Term	Before You Read	After You Read
electromagnetic spectrum	a. ____?____	b. ____?____

Astronomers are in the business of gathering and studying light. Almost everything that is known about the universe beyond Earth comes by analyzing light from distant sources. Consequently, an understanding of the nature of light is basic to modern astronomy. This chapter deals with the study of light and the tools used by astronomers to gather light in order to probe the universe. In addition, we will examine the nearest source of light, our sun. By understanding how the sun works, astronomers can better grasp the nature of more distant objects in space.

Electromagnetic Radiation

The vast majority of our information about the universe is obtained from the study of the light emitted from stars and other bodies in space. Although visible light is most familiar to us, it makes up only a small part of the different types of energy known as electromagnetic radiation. **Electromagnetic radiation includes gamma rays, X-rays, ultraviolet light, visible light, infrared radiation, microwaves, and radio waves.** The arrangement of these waves according to their wavelengths and frequencies is called the **electromagnetic spectrum.** Figure 1 shows the electromagnetic spectrum. All energy, regardless of wavelength, travels through the vacuum of space at the speed of light, or 300,000 kilometers per second. Over a 24-hour day, this equals a staggering 26 billion kilometers.

Figure 1 Electromagnetic Spectrum The electromagnetic spectrum classifies radiation according to wavelength and frequency.
Interpreting Diagrams *Which type of radiation has the shortest wavelength?*

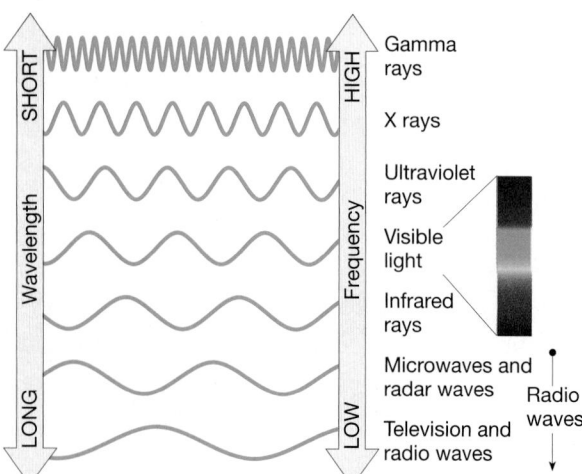

Nature of Light Experiments have shown that light can be described in two ways. In some instances light behaves like waves, and in others like particles. In the wave sense, light can be thought of as swells in the ocean. This motion is characterized by a property known as wavelength, which is the distance from one wave crest to the next. Wavelengths vary from several kilometers for radio waves to less than a billionth of a centimeter for gamma rays, as shown in Figure 1. Most of these waves are either too long or too short for our eyes to see.

The narrow band of electromagnetic radiation we can see is sometimes called visible light. However, visible light consists of a range of waves with various wavelengths. This fact is easily demonstrated with a prism, as shown in Figure 2. As visible light passes through a prism, the color with the shortest wavelength, violet, is bent more than blue, which is bent more than green, and so forth. Thus, visible light can be separated into its component colors in the order of their wavelengths, producing the familiar rainbow of colors.

Table 1 Colors and Corresponding Wavelengths	
Color	Wavelength (nanometers*)
Violet	380–440
Blue	440–500
Green	500–560
Yellow	560–590
Orange	590–640
Red	640–750

*One nanometer is 10^{-9} meter.

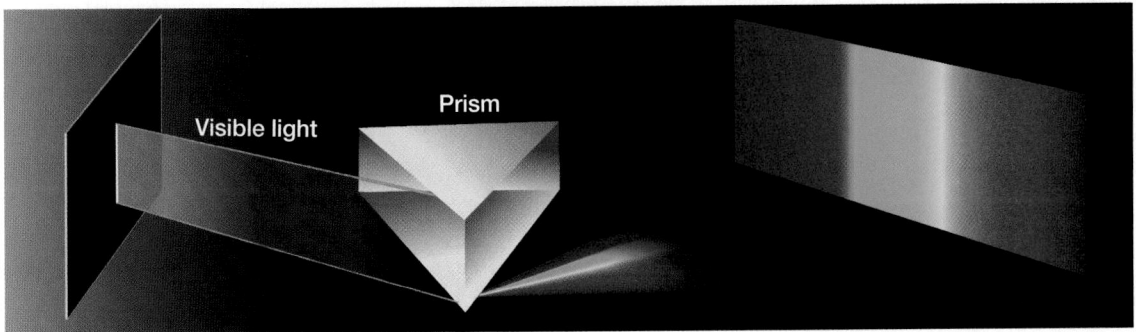

Visible light   Prism

Photons Wave theory, however, cannot explain some effects of light. In some cases, light acts like a stream of particles called **photons.** Photons can be thought of as extremely small bullets fired from a machine gun. They can push on matter. The force they exert is called radiation pressure. Photons from the sun are responsible for pushing material away from a comet to produce its tail. Each photon has a specific amount of energy, which is related to its wavelength in a simple way: Shorter wavelengths have more energetic photons. Thus, blue light has more energetic photons than does red light.

Which theory of light—the wave theory or the particle theory—is correct? Both, because each will predict the behavior of light for certain phenomena. As George Abell, a well-known astronomer, stated about all scientific laws, "The mistake is only to apply them to situations that are outside their range of validity."

 *What are photons?*

Figure 2 Spectrum A spectrum is produced when sunlight or visible light is passed through a prism, which bends each wavelength at different angles.

For: Links on the electromagnetic spectrum
Visit: www.SciLinks.org
Web Code: cjn-7441

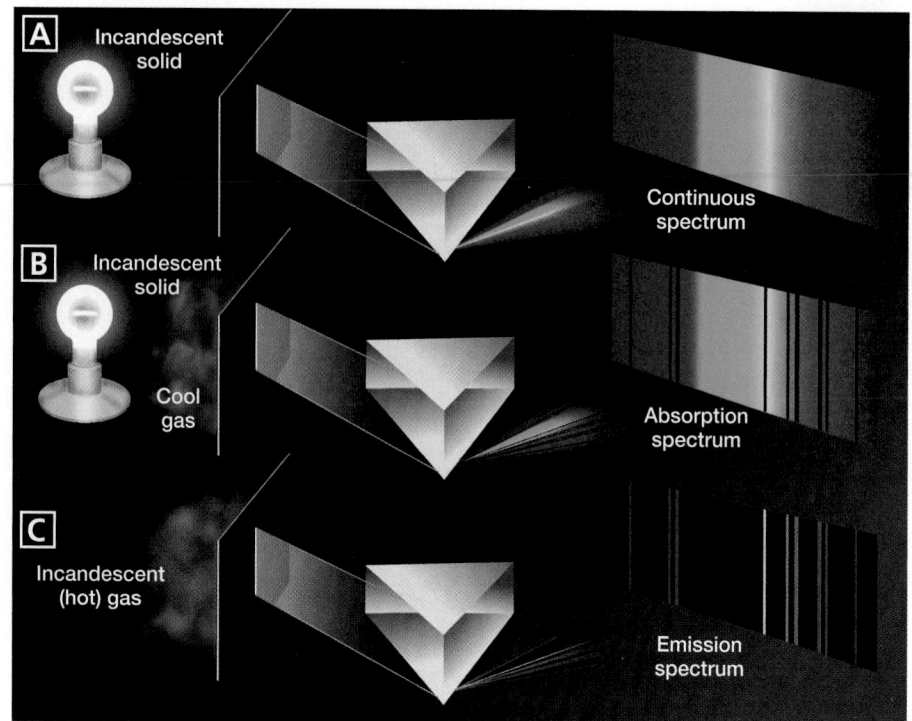

Figure 3 Formation of Spectra
A A continuous spectrum consists of a band of uninterrupted color. **B** An absorption spectrum contains dark lines. **C** An emission spectrum contains bright lines.

Spectroscopy

When Sir Isaac Newton used a prism to disperse visible light into its component colors, he unknowingly introduced the field of spectroscopy. **Spectroscopy** is the study of the properties of light that depend on wavelength. The rainbow of colors Newton produced included all wavelengths of light. It was later learned that two other types of spectra exist. Each is generated under somewhat different conditions.

Continuous Spectrum

A **continuous spectrum** is produced by an incandescent solid, liquid, or gas under high pressure. (*Incandescent* means "to emit light when hot.") The spectrum consists of an uninterrupted band of color, as shown in Figure 3A. One example would be light generated by a common light bulb. This is the type of spectrum Newton produced.

Absorption Spectrum

An **absorption spectrum** is produced when visible light is passed through a relatively cool gas under low pressure. The gas absorbs selected wavelengths of light. So the spectrum appears continuous, but with a series of dark lines running through it, as shown in Figure 3B.

Emission Spectrum

An **emission spectrum** is produced by a hot gas under low pressure. It is a series of bright lines of particular wavelengths, depending on the gas that produces them. As shown in Figure 3C, these bright lines appear in the exact location as the dark lines that are produced by the same gas in an absorption spectrum.

The spectra of most stars are of the dark-line, or absorption, type. The importance of these spectra is that each element or compound in its gaseous form produces a unique set of spectral lines. When the spectrum of a star is studied, the spectral lines act as "fingerprints." These lines identify the elements present and thus the star's chemical composition. The spectrum of the sun contains thousands of dark lines. More than 60 elements have been identified by matching these lines with those of elements known on Earth.

 *What is spectroscopy?*

676 *Chapter 24*

The Doppler Effect

When an ambulance approaches, the siren seems to have a higher-than-normal pitch. When it is moving away, the pitch sounds lower than normal. This effect, which occurs for both sound and light waves, is called the Doppler effect. The **Doppler effect** refers to the perceived change in wavelength of a wave that is emitted from a source that is moving away or toward an object. It takes time for the wave to be emitted. If the source is moving away from you, the beginning of the wave is emitted nearer to you than the end. From the listener's perspective the wave appears to be stretched, as shown in the model for Figure 4. The opposite is true for a wave moving toward you.

The light from a source that is moving away from an observer appears redder than it actually is because its waves are lengthened. This effect is only noticeable to the human eye at velocities approaching the speed of light. Objects moving toward an object have their light waves shifted toward the blue, or shorter wavelength. In addition, the amount of shift is related to the rate of movement. Thus, if a source of red light moved toward you, it could actually appear blue. The same effect would be produced if you moved and the light source was stationary.

In astronomy, the Doppler effect is used to determine whether a star or other body in space is moving away from or toward Earth. Larger Doppler shifts indicate higher speeds; smaller Doppler shifts indicate slower speeds. Doppler shifts are generally measured from the dark lines in the spectra of stars by comparing them with a standard spectrum produced in the laboratory.

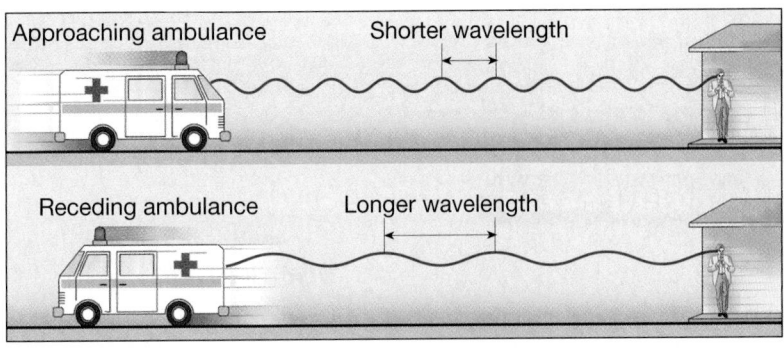

Figure 4 The Doppler Effect
The wavelength of the sound of an approaching ambulance is compressed as it approaches an observer. For a receding ambulance, the wavelength is stretched out and the observer notes a lower-pitched sound. When this effect is applied to light, a shorter wavelength is noted for an approaching object and is seen as blue light. A longer wavelength is noted for a receding object, which is seen as red light.

Section 24.1 Assessment

Reviewing Concepts

1. What types of radiation make up the electromagnetic spectrum?

2. Compare and contrast the three different types of spectra.

3. How do scientists determine the elements present in a star?

4. How can scientists determine whether a star is moving toward or away from Earth?

Critical Thinking

5. **Sequencing** Sequence the components of visible light according to wavelength, beginning with the shortest wavelength.

6. **Applying Concepts** Based on what you know about visible light, how do rainbows form in Earth's atmosphere?

Writing in Science

List of Questions Make a list of questions that you would like to ask a scientist about the nature of light. Your questions should cover both the wave theory and the particle theory of light.

24.2 Tools for Studying Space

Reading Focus

Key Concepts

- How does a refracting telescope produce an image?
- Why are most large telescopes reflecting telescopes?
- How does a radio telescope gather data?
- What advantages do space telescopes have over Earth-based telescopes?

Vocabulary

- refracting telescope
- chromatic aberration
- reflecting telescope
- radio telescope

Reading Strategy

Comparing and Contrasting Copy the Venn diagram. As you read, complete it to show the differences between refracting and reflecting telescopes.

Refracting Telescopes   Reflecting Telescopes

a. _?_   light-gathering, resolving, and magnifying power   b. _?_

Now that we've examined the nature of light, let's turn our attention to the tools astronomers use to intercept and study the energy emitted by distant objects in the universe. Because the basic principles of detecting radiation were originally developed through visual observations, the astronomical tools we'll explore first will be optical telescopes. An example is shown in Figure 5. The 10-meter Keck Telescope, located on Mauna Kea in Hawaii, uses a mosaic of 36 six-sided, 1.8-meter mirrors. The mirrors are carefully positioned by a computer to give the optical effect of a 10-meter mirror. The Keck Telescope is a type of optical telescope. To create an image that is a great distance away, a telescope must collect as much light as possible. Optical telescopes contain mirrors, lenses, or both to accomplish this task.

Figure 5 Keck Telescope
This optical telescope is located at the summit of Hawaii's Mauna Kea volcano.

Refracting Telescopes

Galileo is considered to be the first person to have used telescopes for astronomical observations. Having learned about the newly invented instrument, Galileo built one of his own that was capable of magnifying objects 30 times. Because this early instrument, as well as its modern counterparts, used a lens to bend or refract light, it is known as a **refracting telescope.**

Focus The most important lens in a refracting telescope, the objective lens, produces an image by bending light from a distant object so that the light converges at an area called the focus (*focus =* central point). For an object such as a star, the image appears as a point of light. For nearby objects it appears as an inverted replica of the original.

You can easily demonstrate the latter case by holding a lens in one hand and, with the other hand, placing a white card behind the lens. Now vary the distance between them until an image appears on the card. The distance between the focus (where the image appears) and the lens is called the focal length of the lens.

Astronomers usually study an image from a telescope by first photographing the image. However, if a telescope is used to examine an image directly, a second lens, called an eyepiece, is required. The eyepiece magnifies the image produced by the objective lens. In this respect, it is similar to a magnifying glass. The objective lens produces a very small, bright image of an object, and the eyepiece enlarges the image so that details can be seen. Figure 6 shows the parts of a refracting telescope.

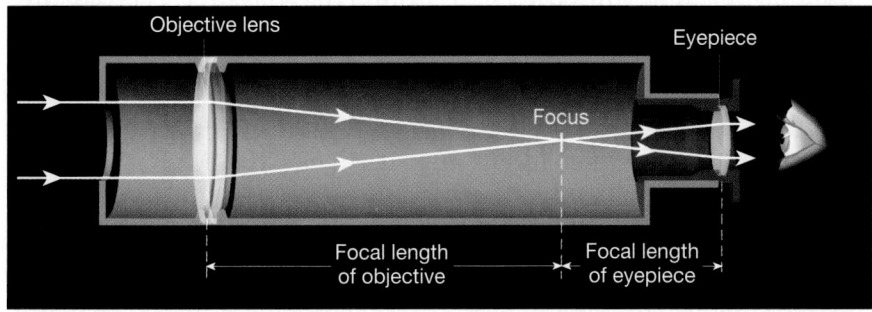

Figure 6 Simple Refracting Telescope A refracting telescope uses a lens to bend light.

Chromatic Aberration Although used extensively in the nineteenth century, refracting telescopes suffer a major optical defect. As light passes through any lens, the shorter wavelengths of light are bent more than the longer wavelengths. Consequently, when a refracting telescope is in focus for red light, blue and violet light are out of focus. The troublesome effect, known as **chromatic** (*chroma =* color) **aberration** (*aberrare =* to go astray), weakens the image and produces a halo of color around it. When blue light is in focus, a reddish halo appears. When red light is in focus, a bluish halo appears. Although this effect cannot be eliminated completely, it is reduced by using a second lens made of a different type of glass.

 *What is chromatic aberration?*

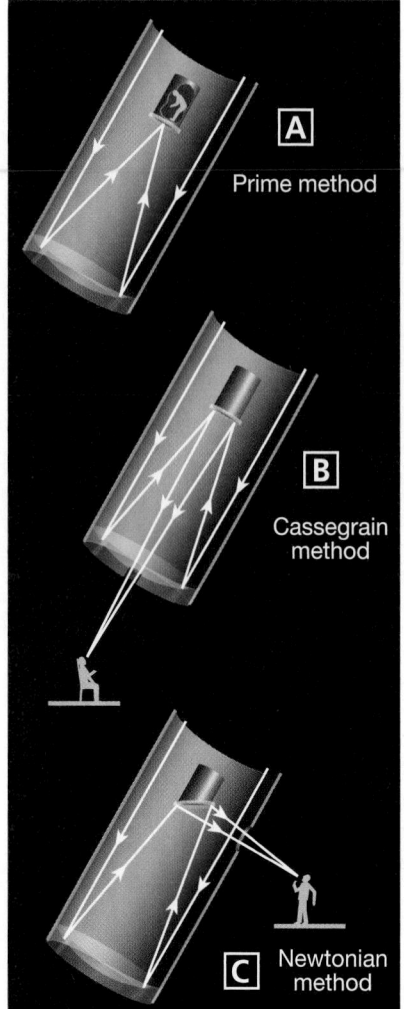

Figure 7 Viewing Methods with Reflecting Telescopes
A The prime method is only used with very large telescopes.
B The Cassegrain method is most commonly used. Note that a small hole in the center of the mirror allows light to pass through.
C This figure shows the Newtonian method.

For: Links on telescopes
Visit: www.SciLinks.org
Web Code: cjn-7242

Reflecting Telescopes

Newton was bothered by chromatic aberration so he built telescopes that reflected light from a shiny surface—a mirror. Because reflected light is not dispersed into its component colors, the chromatic aberration is avoided. **Reflecting telescopes** use a concave mirror that focuses the light in front of a mirror, rather than behind it, like a lens. The mirror is generally made of glass that is finely ground and coated with a highly reflective material, usually an aluminum compound.

Because the focus of a reflecting telescope is in front of the mirror, an observer must be able to view the image without blocking too much incoming light. Figure 7A shows a viewing cage for the observer within the telescope. Figures 7B and 7C show that the observer can remain indoors. Most large telescopes employ more than one type.

Advantages of Reflecting Telescopes As you might guess, it's a huge task to produce a large piece of high-quality, bubble-free glass for refracting telescopes. **Most large optical telescopes are reflectors. Light does not pass through a mirror so the glass for a reflecting telescope does not have to be of optical quality.** In addition, a lens can be supported only around the edge, so it sags. Mirrors, on the other hand, can be supported fully from behind. One disadvantage of reflecting telescopes is that the secondary mirror blocks some light entering the telescope. Thus, a reflecting telescope with a 10-inch opening will not collect as much light as a 10-inch refractor.

Properties of Optical Telescopes Both refracting and reflecting telescopes have three properties that aid astronomers in their work: 1) light-gathering power, 2) resolving power, and 3) magnifying power. Light-gathering power refers to the telescope's ability to intercept more light from distant objects, thereby producing brighter images. Telescopes with large lenses or mirrors "see" farther into space than do those with small ones.

Another advantage of telescopes with large objectives is their greater resolving power, which allows for sharper images and finer detail. For example, with the naked eye, the Milky Way appears as a vague band of light in the night sky. But even a small telescope is capable of resolving, or separating it into, individual stars. Lastly, telescopes have magnifying power, which is the ability to make an object larger. Magnification is calculated by dividing the focal length of the objective by the focal length of the eyepiece. Thus, the magnification of a telescope can be changed by simply changing the eyepiece.

 *What is light-gathering power?*

A

B

Detecting Invisible Radiation

As you learned earlier, sunlight is made up of more than just the radiation that is visible to our eyes. Gamma rays, X-rays, ultraviolet radiation, infrared radiation, and radio waves are also produced by stars. Photographic film that is sensitive to ultraviolet and infrared radiation has been developed. This extends the limits of our vision. However, most of this radiation cannot penetrate our atmosphere, so balloons, rockets, and satellites must transport cameras "above" the atmosphere to record it.

A narrow band of radio waves is able to penetrate the atmosphere. Measurement of this radiation is important because we can map the galactic distribution of hydrogen. Hydrogen is the main material from which stars are made.

Radio Telescopes The detection of radio waves is accomplished by big dishes called **radio telescopes,** shown in Figure 8A. In principle, the dish of one of these telescopes operates in the same manner as the mirror of an optical telescope. **A radio telescope focuses the incoming radio waves on an antenna, which absorbs and transmits these waves to an amplifier, just like a radio antenna.**

Because radio waves are about 100,000 times longer than visible radiation, the surface of the dish doesn't need to be as smooth as a mirror. Except for the shortest radio waves, a wire mesh is a good reflector. However, because radio signals from celestial sources are very weak, large dishes are necessary to intercept an adequate signal.

Radio telescopes have poor resolution, making it difficult to pinpoint the radio source. Pairs or groups of telescopes reduce this problem. When several radio telescopes are wired together, as shown in Figure 8B, the resulting network is called a radio interferometer.

Figure 8 A The 43-meter Radio Telescope at Green Bank, West Virginia The dish acts like the mirror of a reflecting telescope, focusing radio waves onto the antenna. **B The Very Large Array Near Socorro, New Mexico** Twenty-seven identical antennas operate together to form this radio network. **Identifying** *What is a network of radio telescopes called?*

Q *Why do astronomers build observatories on mountaintops?*

A Observatories are most often located on mountaintops because sites above the densest part of the atmosphere provide better conditions for "seeing."

Advantages of Radio Telescopes Radio telescopes have some advantages over optical telescopes. They are much less affected by turbulence in the atmosphere, clouds, and the weather. No protective dome is required, which reduces the cost of construction. "Viewing" is possible 24 hours a day. More important, radio telescopes can "see" through interstellar dust clouds that obscure visible wavelengths. Radio signals from distant points in the universe pass unhindered through the dust, giving us an unobstructed view. Furthermore, radio telescopes can detect clouds of gases too cool to emit visible light. These cold gas clouds are important because they are the sites of star formation.

Radio telescopes are, however, hindered by human-made radio interference. While optical telescopes are placed on remote mountaintops to reduce interference from city lights, radio telescopes are often hidden in valleys to block human-made radio interference.

Radio telescopes have revealed such spectacular events as the collision of two galaxies. They led to the important discovery of quasars and pulsars.

 **Reading Checkpoint** *Why can radio telescopes be used 24 hours a day?*

Space Telescopes

Have you ever seen a blurring effect caused by the movement of air on a hot summer day? That blurring effect also distorts the images produced by most telescopes on Earth. On a night when the stars twinkle, viewing is difficult because the air is moving rapidly. This causes the image to move about and blur.

Observatories are most often located on mountaintops. This is because sites above the densest part of the atmosphere provide better conditions for "seeing." At high elevations, there is less air to scatter and dim the incoming light. Also, there is less water vapor to absorb infrared radiation. Further, the thin air on mountaintops causes less distortion of the images being observed.

There is one other way to get around the distorting effects of Earth's atmosphere—send telescopes into space. **Space telescopes orbit above Earth's atmosphere and thus produce clearer images than Earth-based telescopes.**

Hubble Space Telescope The first space telescope, built by NASA, was the Hubble Space Telescope, shown in Figure 9. Hubble was put into orbit around Earth in April 1990. This 2.4-meter space telescope has 10 billion times more light-gathering power than the human eye. Hubble has given us many spectacular images. For example, the

Figure 9 Hubble Space Telescope Hubble was deployed into Earth orbit by the space shuttle *Discovery*.

Hubble Space Telescope has provided images that clearly resolve the
separation between Pluto and its
moon, Charon. It has also provided
data about planets that orbit other
stars, the birth of stars, black holes,
the age of the universe, and the
expansion of the universe.

Other Space Telescopes

Other types of radiation are also
affected by Earth's atmosphere. To
study X-rays, NASA uses the
Chandra X-Ray Observatory. This
space telescope was launched in
1999. One of its main missions is to
gather data about black holes—
objects whose gravity is so strong
that visible light cannot escape them. Another space telescope, the
Compton Gamma-Ray Observatory, was used to study both visible
light and gamma rays. In 2011, NASA plans to launch the James Webb
Space Telescope to study infrared radiation. As Figure 10 shows, images
obtained by different telescopes offer different information about the
same object in space—in this case, the Milky Way galaxy. By studying
all the images together, astronomers obtain a more thorough understanding of the galaxy.

**Figure 10 Images of the Milky
Way Galaxy** These images were
taken by different types of
telescopes, including visible light,
X-ray, gamma ray, and infrared.

Section 24.2 Assessment

Reviewing Concepts

1. How does a refracting telescope work?
2. How does a reflecting telescope differ from a refracting telescope?
3. Why are most large telescopes reflecting telescopes?
4. How do radio telescopes gather data?
5. Why do space telescopes obtain clearer images than Earth-based telescopes?

Critical Thinking

6. **Calculating** If a telescope has an objective with a focal length of 50 centimeters and an eyepiece with a focal length of 25 millimeter, what will be the magnification?

7. **Applying Concepts** Using the numbers from the previous question, would an eye-piece with a greater focal length increase or decrease magnification? Explain.

Connecting Concepts

Electromagnetic Radiation Recall the different types of electromagnetic radiation. Based on what you've learned in this section, would you recommend sending a telescope into space to study radio waves? Why or why not?

24.3 The Sun

The sun is one of the 100 billion stars that make up the Milky Way galaxy. Although the sun is of no significance to the universe as a whole, it is Earth's primary source of energy. Everything—from the fossil fuels we burn in our automobiles to the food that we eat—is ultimately derived from solar energy. The sun is also important to astronomers, since it is the only star whose surface we can study. Even with the largest telescopes, other stars appear only as points of light. Because of the sun's brightness and its damaging radiation, it is not safe to observe it directly. However, a telescope can project its image on a piece of cardboard held behind the telescope's eyepiece. In this manner, the sun can be studied safely. This basic method is used in several telescopes around the world, which keep a constant watch of the sun. One of the finest is at the Kitt Peak National Observatory in southern Arizona, shown in Figure 11. It consists of an enclosure with moving mirrors that directs sunlight to an underground mirror. From the mirror, an image of the sun is projected to an observing room, where it is studied.

Compared to other stars, the sun is an "average star." However, on the scale of our solar system, it is truly gigantic. Its diameter is equal to 109 Earth diameters, or 1.35 million kilometers. Its volume is 1.25 million times as great as Earth's. Its mass is 332,000 times the mass of Earth and its density is only one quarter that of solid Earth.

Figure 11 The McMath-Pierce Solar Telescope at Kitt Peak Near Tucson, Arizona Movable mirrors at the top follow the sun, reflecting its light down the sloping tunnel.

Structure of the Sun

Because the sun is made of gas, no sharp boundaries exist between its various layers. ⊙ **Keeping this in mind, we can divide the sun into four parts: the solar interior; the visible surface, or photosphere; and two atmospheric layers, the chromosphere and corona.** These parts are shown in Figure 12. The sun's interior makes up all but a tiny fraction of the solar mass. Unlike the outer three layers, the solar interior cannot be directly observed. Let's discuss the visible layers first.

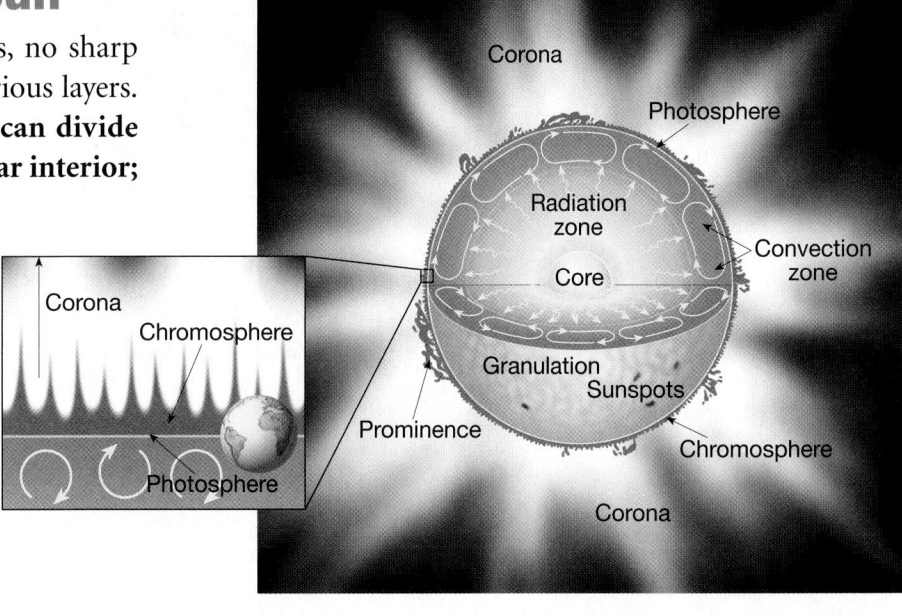

Photosphere The **photosphere** (*photos* = light, *sphere* = a ball) radiates most of the sunlight we see and can be thought of as the visible "surface" of the sun. The photosphere consists of a layer of gas less than 500 kilometers thick. It is neither smooth nor uniformly bright, as the ancients had imagined.

When viewed through a telescope, the photosphere's grainy texture is apparent. This is the result of numerous relatively small, bright markings called granules, which are surrounded by narrow, dark regions, as shown in Figure 13. Granules are typically the size of Texas, and they owe their brightness to hotter gases that are rising from below. As this gas spreads, cooling causes it to darken and sink back into the interior. Each granule survives only 10 to 20 minutes. The combined motion of new granules replacing old ones gives the photosphere the appearance of boiling. This up-and-down movement of gas is called convection. Besides producing the grainy appearance of the photosphere, convection is believed to be responsible for the transfer of energy in the uppermost part of the sun's interior.

The composition of the photosphere is revealed by the dark lines of its absorption spectrum. Studies reveal that 90 percent of the sun's surface atoms are hydrogen, almost 10 percent are helium, and only minor amounts of the other detectable elements are present. Other stars also have high proportions of these two lightest elements, a fact we shall discuss later.

Figure 12 Structure of the Sun The sun can be divided into four parts: the solar interior, the photosphere, the chromosphere, and the corona.

Figure 13 Granules Granules are the yellowish-orange patches on the photosphere. **Describing** *Describe the movement of gases in the convection zone.*

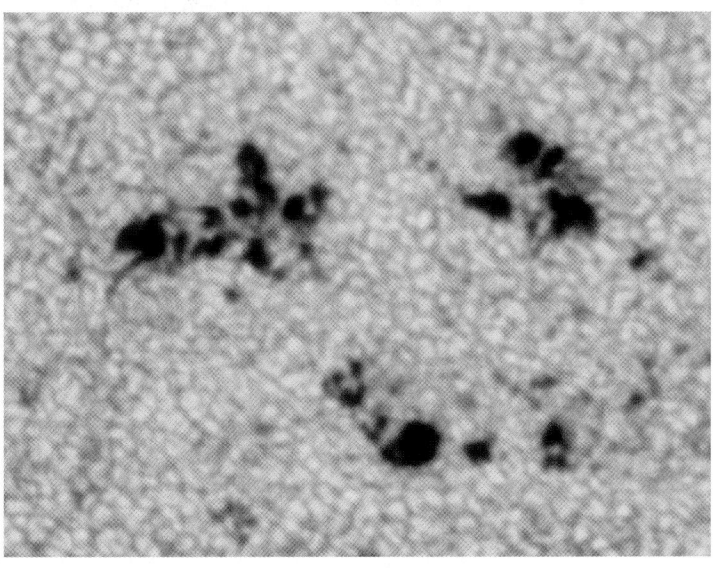

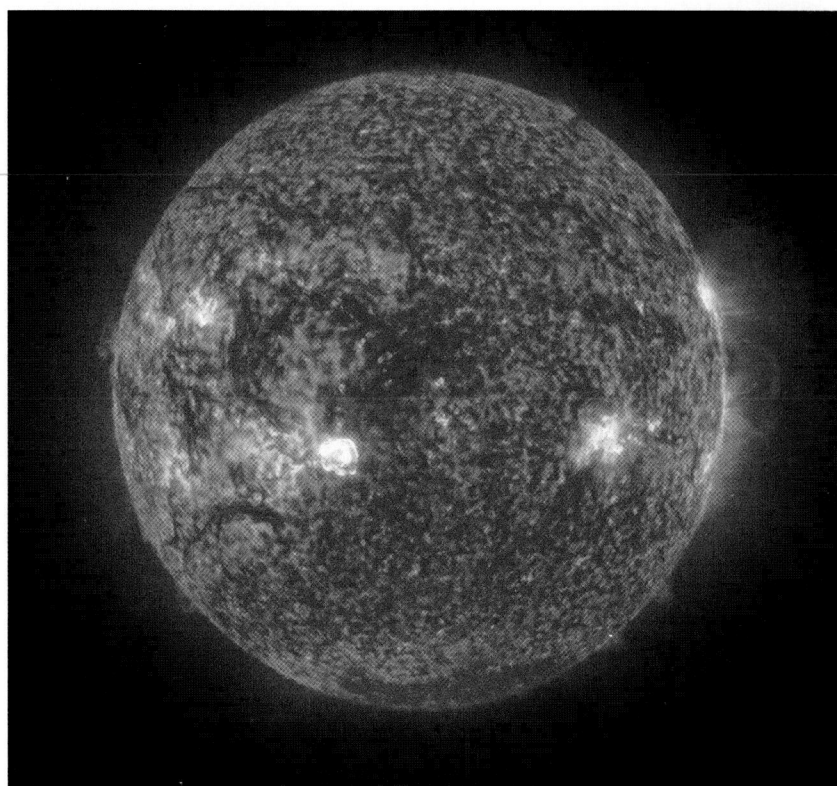

Figure 14 Chromosphere The chromosphere is a thin layer of hot gases that appears as a red rim around the sun.

Chromosphere Just above the photosphere lies the **chromosphere,** a relatively thin layer of hot gases a few thousand kilometers thick. The chromosphere is observable for a few moments during a total solar eclipse or by using a special instrument that blocks out the light from the photosphere. Under such conditions, it appears as a thin red rim around the sun. Because the chromosphere consists of hot, incandescent gases under low pressure, it produces an emission spectrum that is nearly the reverse of the absorption spectrum of the photosphere. One of the bright lines of hydrogen contributes a good portion of its total light and accounts for this sphere's red color.

Corona The outermost portion of the solar atmosphere, the **corona** (*corona* = crown) is very weak and, as with the chromosphere, is visible only when the brilliant photosphere is covered. This envelope of ionized gases normally extends a million kilometers from the sun and produces a glow about half as bright as the full moon.

At the outer fringe of the corona, the ionized gases have speeds great enough to escape the gravitational pull of the sun. The streams of protons and electrons that boil from the corona constitute the **solar wind.** This wind travels outward through the solar system at speeds up to 800 kilometers per second and eventually is lost to space. During its journey, the solar wind interacts with the bodies of the solar system, continually bombarding lunar rocks and altering their appearance. Although Earth's magnetic field prevents the solar winds from reaching our surface, these winds do affect our atmosphere, as we'll discuss later.

Studies of the energy emitted from the photosphere indicate that its temperature averages about 6000 K. Upward from the photosphere, the temperature unexpectedly increases, exceeding 1 million K at the top of the corona. Although the corona temperature is much higher than that of the photosphere, it radiates much less energy because of its very low density.

 *What is the solar wind?*

The Active Sun

The most conspicuous features on the surface of the sun are the dark regions. They were occasionally observed before the advent of the telescope, but were generally regarded as objects located somewhere between the sun and Earth. In 1610, Galileo concluded that these regions were part of the solar surface. From their motion, he deduced that the sun rotates on its axis about once a month. Later observations indicated that not all parts of the sun rotate at the same speed. The sun's equator rotates once in 25 days, while a location 70 degrees from the solar equator, whether north or south, requires 33 days for one rotation. Imagine if Earth rotated in a similar manner! The sun's nonuniform rotation is evidence of its gaseous nature.

Sunspots What are those dark areas Galileo observed? The dark regions on the surface of the photosphere are called **sunspots.** As Figure 15 shows, an individual spot contains a black center rimmed by a lighter region. **Sunspots appear dark because of their temperature, which is about 1500 K less than that of the surrounding solar surface.** If these dark spots could be observed away from the sun, they would appear many times brighter than the full moon.

During the early nineteenth century, it was believed that a tiny planet named Vulcan orbited between Mercury and the sun. In the search for Vulcan an accurate record of sunspot occurrences was kept. Although the planet was never found, the sunspot data revealed that the number of sunspots observable varies in an 11-year cycle.

First, the number of sunspots increases to a maximum, with perhaps a hundred or more visible at a given time. Then their numbers gradually decline to a minimum, when only a few or even none are visible.

Figure 15 Sunspots A Sunspots often appear as groups of dark areas on the sun. **B** A close-up of an individual sunspot shows a black center surrounded by a lighter region.

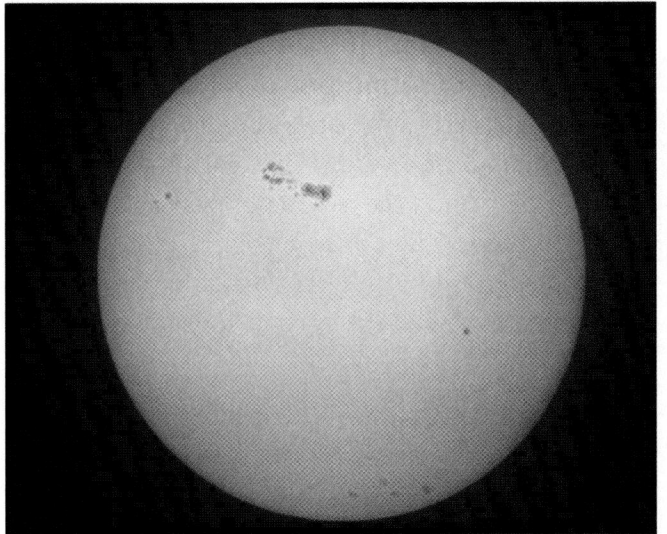

A

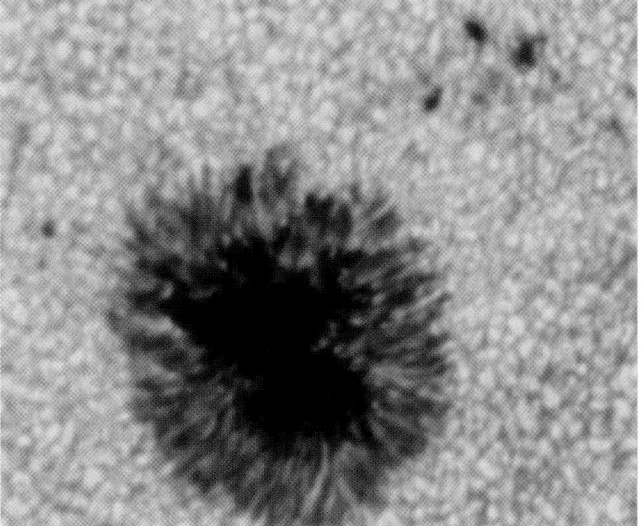

B

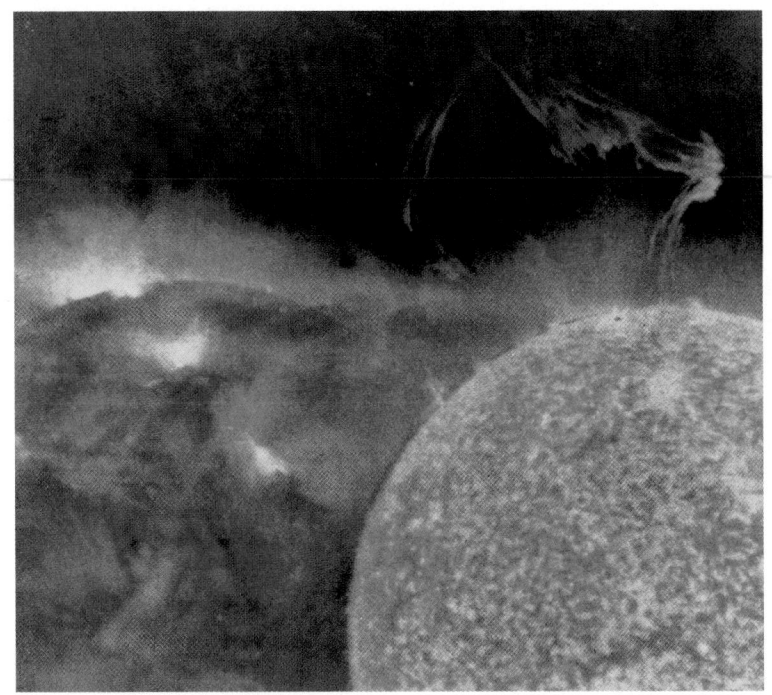

Figure 16 Solar Prominence
Solar prominences are huge, arched structures, best observed when they are on the edge of the sun.

Figure 17 Aurora Borealis or Northern Lights in Alaska
The same phenomenon occurs toward the south pole, where it is called the aurora australis or southern lights.

Prominences Among the more spectacular features of the active sun are prominences (*prominere* = to jut out). **Prominences** are huge cloudlike structures consisting of chromospheric gases. They often appear as great arches that extend well into the corona. Many prominences have the appearance of a fine tapestry and seem to hang motionless for days at a time. Others rise almost explosively away from the sun. These eruptive prominences reach speeds up to 1000 kilometers per second and may leave the sun entirely. **Prominences are ionized gases trapped by magnetic fields that extend from regions of intense solar activity.** Refer to Figure 16.

Solar Flares The most explosive events associated with sunspots are solar flares. **Solar flares** are brief outbursts that normally last about an hour and appear as a sudden brightening of the region above a sunspot cluster. **During their existence, solar flares release enormous amounts of energy, much of it in the form of ultraviolet, radio, and X-ray radiation.** At the same time, fast-moving atomic particles are ejected, causing the solar wind to intensify. Although a major flare could conceivably endanger the crew of a space flight, they are relatively rare. About a day after a large outburst, the ejected particles reach Earth, where they can affect long-distance radio communications.

The most spectacular effects of solar flares, however, are the **auroras,** also called the northern and southern lights. Following a strong solar flare, Earth's upper atmosphere near its magnetic poles is set aglow for several nights. The auroras appear in a wide variety of forms, one of which is shown in Figure 17. Sometimes the display looks like colorful ribbons moving with the breeze. At other times, the auroras appear as a series of luminous arcs or as a foglike glow. Auroral displays, like other solar activities, vary in intensity with the 11-year sunspot cycle.

 *What are solar flares?*

The Solar Interior

The interior of the sun cannot be observed directly. For that reason, all we know about it is based on information acquired from the energy it radiates and from theoretical studies. The source of the sun's energy was not discovered until the late 1930s.

Nuclear Fusion Deep in its interior, the sun produces energy by a process known as **nuclear fusion.** This nuclear reaction converts four hydrogen nuclei into the nucleus of a helium atom. Tremendous energy is released. ◖**During nuclear fusion, energy is released because some matter is actually converted to energy, as shown in Figure 18.** How does this process work? Consider that four hydrogen atoms have a combined atomic mass of 4.032 atomic mass units (4 × 1.008) whereas the atomic mass of helium is 4.003 atomic mass units, or 0.029 less than the combined mass of the hydrogen. The tiny missing mass is emitted as energy according to Einstein's equation:

$$E = mc^2$$

E equals energy, *m* equals mass, and *c* equals the speed of light. Because the speed of light is very great (300,000 km/s), the amount of energy released from even a small amount of mass is enormous.

The conversion of just one pinhead's worth of hydrogen to helium generates more energy than burning thousands of tons of coal. Most of this energy is in the form of high-energy photons that work their way toward the solar surface. The photons are absorbed and reemitted many times until they reach a layer just below the photosphere. Here, convection currents help transport this energy to the solar surface, where it radiates through the transparent chromosphere and corona.

Only a small percentage of the hydrogen in the nuclear reaction is actually converted to energy. Nevertheless, the sun is consuming an estimated 600 million tons of hydrogen each second; about 4 million tons are converted to energy. As hydrogen is consumed, the product of this reaction—helium—forms the solar core, which continually grows in size.

 **Reading Checkpoint** *What happens during the process of nuclear fusion?*

Go Online

SciLINKS NSTA

For: Links on nuclear fusion in the sun
Visit: www.SciLinks.org
Web Code: cjn-7243

Figure 18 Nuclear Fusion During nuclear fusion, four hydrogen nuclei combine to form one helium nucleus. Some matter is converted to energy.

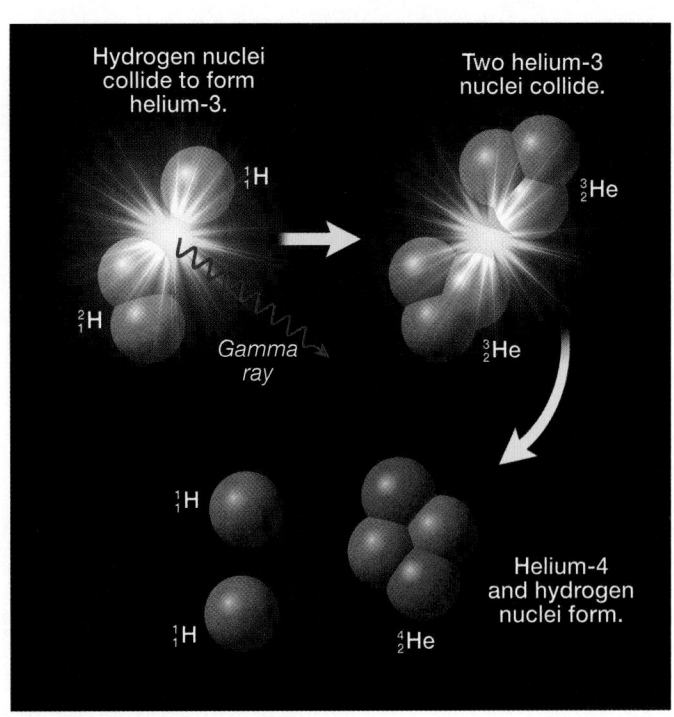

Figure 19 The sun is the source of more than 99 percent of all energy on Earth.

Just how long can the sun produce energy at its present rate before all of its hydrogen fuel is consumed? Even at the enormous rate of consumption, the sun, shown in Figure 19, has enough fuel to last easily another 100 billion years. However, evidence from other stars indicates that the sun will grow dramatically and engulf Earth long before all of its hydrogen is gone. It is thought that a star the size of the sun can exist in its present stable state for 10 billion years. As the sun is already 4.5 billion years old, it is "middle-aged."

To initiate nuclear fusion, the sun's internal temperature must have reached several million degrees. But what was the source of this heat? The solar system is believed to have formed from an enormous compressed cloud of dust and gases—mostly hydrogen. When gases are compressed, their temperature increases. All of the bodies in the solar system were compressed. However, the sun was the only one, because of its size, that became hot enough to trigger nuclear fusion. Astronomers currently estimate its internal temperature at 15 million K.

The planet Jupiter is basically a hydrogen-rich gas ball; if it were about 10 times more massive, it too might have become a star. The idea of one star orbiting another may seem odd, but recent evidence indicates that about 50 percent of the stars in the universe probably occur in pairs or multiples!

Section 24.3 Assessment

Reviewing Concepts

1. What is the structure of the sun?
2. Which layer of the sun can be thought of as its surface?
3. Describe some characteristics of features on the sun.
4. Are the same number of sunspots always present on the sun? Explain.
5. How does the sun produce energy?
6. How much longer will the sun likely exist in its present state?

Critical Thinking

7. **Relating Cause and Effect** Why do sunspots appear dark?
8. **Applying Concepts** What is the effect on Earth's atmosphere of a strong solar flare?

Math Practice

9. Of the 6×10^8 tons of hydrogen the sun consumes each second, about 4×10^8 tons are converted to energy. What percentage of the total energy consumed per second is converted to energy?

Solar Activity and Climatic Change

Some people believe that changes in solar activity relate to climatic change. The effect of such changes would seem direct and easily understood: Increases in solar output would cause the atmosphere to warm, and reductions would result in cooling. This notion is appealing because it can be used to explain climatic changes of any length or intensity.

Still, there is at least one major drawback: No major long-term variations in the total intensity of solar radiation have yet been measured. Such measurements were not even possible until satellite technology became available. Now that it is possible, we will need many years of records before we begin to sense how variable the sun really is.

Sunspot Cycles

Several theories for climatic change based on a variable sun relate to sunspot cycles. The most recognizable features on the surface of the sun are the dark regions called sunspots. See Figure 20. The number of sunspots seems to increase and decrease over a cycle of about 11 years. The graph in Figure 21 below shows the annual number of sunspots, beginning in the early 1700s. However, this pattern is not always regular.

There have been long periods when sunspots have been absent or nearly absent. These events correspond closely with cold periods in Europe and North America. In contrast, periods of high sunspot activity have been associated with warmer times in these regions.

Conflicting Evidence

Because of these data, some scientists have suggested that changes in solar activity are an important cause of climatic change. But other scientists seriously question this notion. Their hesitation stems in part from investigations using different climatic records from around the world that failed to find a significant relationship between solar activity and climate. Even more troubling is that there is no way to test the relationship.

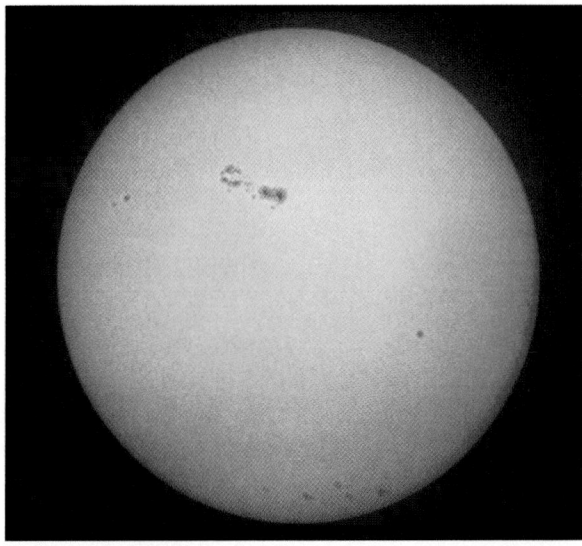

Figure 20 Dark regions on the surface of the sun are called sunspots.

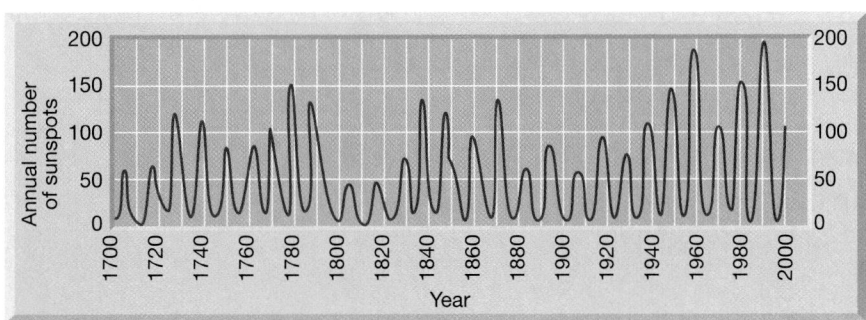

Figure 21 Mean Annual Sunspot Numbers

Tracking Sunspots

Sunspots begin as small areas about 1600 kilometers in diameter. Most last for only a few hours. However, some grow into dark regions many times larger than Earth and last for a month or more. In this lab you will count the number of sunspots over the course of several days.

Problem
How can you use a telescope to safely view and count the number of sunspots on the sun's surface?

Materials
- telescope
- small cardboard box
- large cardboard box
- piece of white paper
- metric ruler
- pencil
- tape

Skills
Observing, Interpreting Data, Making and Using Graphs

Procedure

1. Position a telescope on a tripod outside in a sunny spot away from trees and other obstacles. The eyepiece should face away from the sun. ⚠**CAUTION** *Never look at the sun directly. Do not view the sun through the telescope. These actions could cause eye damage.*

2. Place the large cardboard box on the ground about 15 centimeters in front of the telescope's eyepiece.

3. Use the pencil to punch a hole in one side of the small cardboard box. Tape a sheet of white paper inside the opposite end of the box, as shown in the illustration on this page.

4. Place the small box on top of the large box so that its front is open for viewing. The hole in the small box should face the eyepiece of the telescope. Adjust the telescope so that the eyepiece, the hole, and the white paper are aligned.

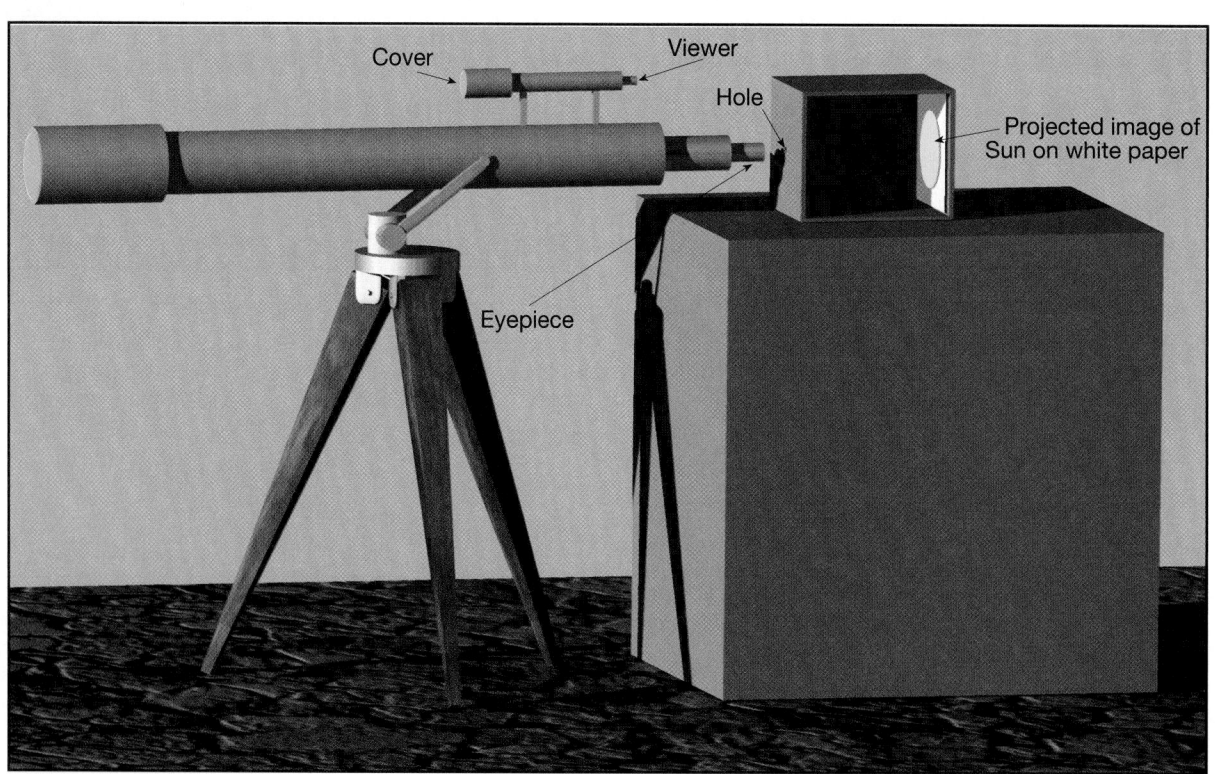

Cover   Viewer   Hole   Projected image of Sun on white paper   Eyepiece

5. Adjust the small box until you see an image of the sun projected onto the paper. You may adjust the telescope to obtain a clearer image, but do not look through the viewer to accomplish this. You may also vary the distance between the box and the telescope to obtain better images.

6. Record the number of sunspots that you observe in a data table similar to the one below. Trace the outlines of sunspots on the paper. Shade in the sunspots and use the ruler to measure their size.

7. As weather permits, make several more viewings of sunspots over the course of the next few days. During each viewing, repeat steps 1–6. Be sure to note the movement of the sunspots.

Analyze and Conclude

1. **Making Graphs** How many sunspots did you observe? Make a line graph of your data using your data table.

2. **Observing** How did the number of sunspots vary over the course of your observations?

3. **Interpreting Data** Why did the sunspots move?

Go Further The diameter of the sun is approximately 1.35 million kilometers. Use this number to develop a scale to estimate the sizes of the sunspots.

Sample Data Table		
Day	Number of Sunspots	Movement?
1		
2		
3		
4		
5		

24.1 The Study of Light

Key Concepts

- Electromagnetic radiation includes gamma rays, X-rays, ultraviolet light, visible light, infrared radiation, microwaves, and radio waves.

- When the spectrum of a star is studied, the spectral lines act as "fingerprints." These lines identify the elements present and thus the star's chemical composition.

- In astronomy, the Doppler effect is used to determine whether a star or other body in space is moving away from or toward Earth.

Vocabulary

electromagnetic spectrum, *p. 674;* photon, *p. 675;* spectroscopy, *p. 676;* continuous spectrum, *p. 676;* absorption spectrum, *p. 676;* emission spectrum, *p. 676;* Doppler effect, *p. 677*

24.2 Tools for Studying Space

Key Concepts

- In a refracting telescope, the objective lens produces an image by bending light from a distant object in such a way that the light converges at an area called the focus.

- Most large optical telescopes are reflectors. Light does not pass through a mirror so the glass for a reflecting telescope does not have to be of optical quality. This means chromatic aberration is not a problem.

- A radio telescope focuses the incoming radio waves on an antenna, which absorbs and transmits these waves to an amplifier, just like any radio antenna.

- Space telescopes orbit above Earth's atmosphere and thus produce clearer images than Earth-based telescopes.

Vocabulary

refracting telescope, *p. 678;* chromatic aberration, *p. 679;* reflecting telescope, *p. 680;* radio telescope, *p. 681*

24.3 The Sun

Key Concepts

- The sun can be divided into four parts: the solar interior; the visible surface, or photosphere; and two atmospheric layers, the chromosphere and corona.

- Sunspots appear dark because of their temperature, which is about 1500 K less than that of the surrounding solar surface.

- Prominences are ionized gases trapped by magnetic fields that extend from regions of intense solar activity.

- Solar flares release enormous amounts of energy, much of it in the form of ultraviolet, radio, and X-ray radiation.

- During nuclear fusion, energy is released because some matter is converted to energy.

Vocabulary

photosphere, *p. 685;* chromosphere, *p. 686;* corona, *p. 686;* solar wind, *p. 686;* sunspot, *p. 687;* prominence, *p. 688;* solar flare, *p. 688;* aurora, *p. 688;* nuclear fusion, *p. 689*

Thinking Visually

Concept Map Use information from the chapter to complete the concept map below.

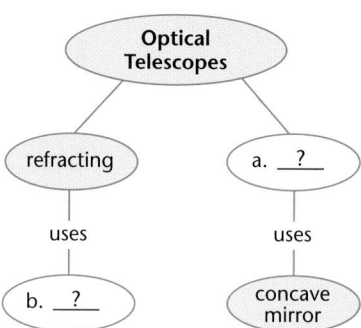

Reviewing Content

Choose the letter that best answers the question or completes the statement.

1. Which type of radiation has the shortest wavelength?
   a. gamma rays   b. X-rays
   c. visible light   d. radio waves

2. The energy of a photon is related to its
   a. size.   b. mass.
   c. density.   d. wavelength.

3. As light passes through a prism, which color will bend the most?
   a. red   b. violet
   c. yellow   d. blue

4. Which type of telescope uses a concave mirror?
   a. refracting   b. reflecting
   c. ultraviolet   d. infrared

5. Which of the following is not a property of optical telescopes?
   a. resolving power
   b. magnifying power
   c. reflecting power
   d. light-gathering power

6. When several radio telescopes are wired together, the resulting network is called a radio
   a. receiver.
   b. interferometer.
   c. tuner.
   d. antenna.

7. The numerous, relatively small bright markings on the sun's photosphere are called
   a. auroras.   b. sunspots.
   c. granules.   d. prominences.

8. The thin, red rim seen around the sun during a total solar eclipse is the
   a. chromosphere.   b. corona.
   c. solar wind.   d. photosphere.

9. Which features of the sun look like huge cloudlike arches?
   a. solar flares   b. sunspots
   c. auroras   d. prominences

10. What is the source of the sun's energy?
    a. magnetism
    b. nuclear fission
    c. nuclear fusion
    d. radiation pressure

Understanding Concepts

11. What two factors determine how radiation is arranged on the electromagnetic spectrum?

12. Which color has the longest wavelength? The shortest?

13. Compare and contrast the wave theory and the particle theory of light.

14. Describe a continuous spectrum. Give an example of a natural phenomenon that exhibits a continuous spectrum.

15. Which type of spectrum do most stars have?

16. What optical defect is associated with refracting telescopes?

17. What three properties do optical telescopes have that aid astronomers?

18. What are some advantages of radio telescopes over optical telescopes?

19. List three space telescopes and describe the type of radiation studied by each.

20. Compare the diameter of the sun to that of Earth.

21. What is solar wind?

22. What "fuel" does the sun consume?

23. What happens to the matter that is consumed in nuclear fusion?

Critical Thinking

24. Summarizing Briefly summarize the relationship between Doppler shift and the speed of a moving object.

25. Inferring Why would the moon make a good site for an observatory?

26. Relating Cause and Effect The photosphere has a boiling appearance. Why?

27. Drawing Conclusions The solar wind can be thought of as evidence for which theory of light? Explain your answer.

Analyzing Data

Use the graph to answer Questions 28–31.

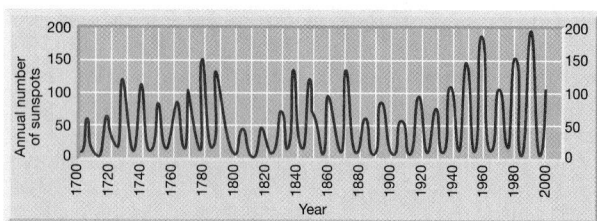

28. Identifying Which years had the lowest number of sunspots? The highest?

29. Interpreting Data Describe any patterns in the data.

30. Predicting When will the next period of maximum sunspot activity occur?

31. Analyzing Data Based on the data alone, is it possible to predict how many sunspots will occur during the next peak? Why or why not?

Concepts in Action

32. Inferring What can you infer about a star that exhibits a red shift in its spectra?

33. Explaining Why do astronomers seek to design telescopes with larger and larger objectives?

34. Relating Cause and Effect What could you infer about solar activity if you spotted an aurora that lasted several nights?

Performance-Based Assessment

Oral Presentation The sun is Earth's main source of energy. Work in a group to develop a presentation describing what might happen if the sun's energy increased by 10 percent. Discuss the effects on global temperatures, ocean shorelines, and polar caps. Be sure to consider changes in the amount of surface vegetation, and the impact of these changes on levels of atmospheric carbon dioxide.

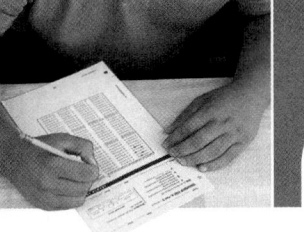

Standardized Test Prep

Test-Taking Tip

Scientific Drawings

Some test questions may include a drawing of a scientific instrument, such as a telescope, or an object studied by scientists, such as the sun. It is important that you carefully study the information presented in the question, as well as the picture provided. Keep these tips in mind when answering a question with drawings of objects or scientific instruments.

- Identify the item shown so you can determine what information the drawing can provide.

- Think of similar drawings or questions you have seen. These may help you determine information available from the drawing.

- The illustrations may not be drawn to scale. You must read and interpret the scales carefully.

- Carefully read the question. You may not need all the information. You may need more information than is presented in the drawing.

Practice using these tips in Questions 5 and 6.

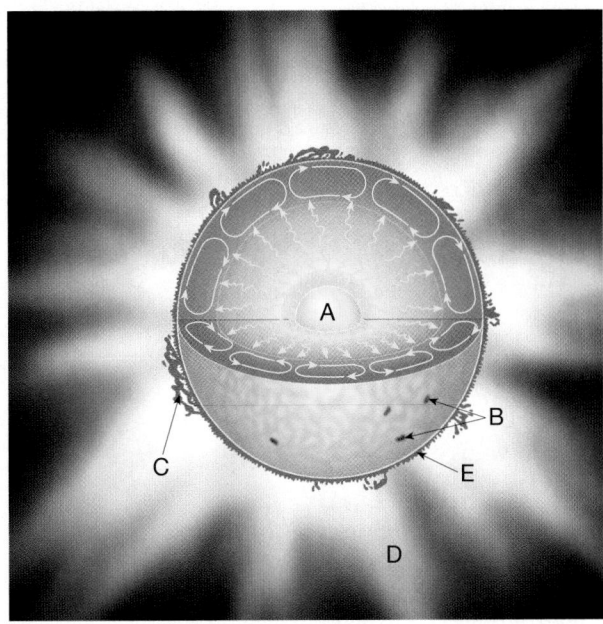

Use the diagram above to answer Questions 5 and 6.

5. What is the innermost layer of the sun called? What is the outermost layer?

6. What letters represent features found on the sun? Identify each feature.

Choose the letter that best answers the question or completes the statement.

1. Which of the following is NOT considered a form of electromagnetic radiation?
   (A) radio waves
   (B) gravity
   (C) gamma rays
   (D) visible light

2. The sun produces energy by converting
   (A) oxygen nuclei to carbon dioxide.
   (B) oxygen nuclei to nitrogen nuclei.
   (C) hydrogen nuclei to helium nuclei.
   (D) helium nuclei to hydrogen nuclei.

Answer the following questions in complete sentences.

3. What happens to the temperature of a gas when it is compressed?

4. Describe the composition of the sun's surface and compare it with that of other stars.

Beyond Our Solar System

CONCEPTS
— in Action —

Exploration Lab
Observing Stars

Understanding Earth
Astrology—Forerunner of Astronomy

Video Field Trip

Stars: Life and Death

Take a field trip through outer space with Discovery Channel and find out how stars are born, and why they die. Answer the following questions after watching the video.

1. What happens when a star runs out of hydrogen fuel?

2. Describe what will happen to the sun when it dies.

Go Online
PHSchool.com

For: Chapter 25 Resources
Visit: PHSchool.com
Web Code: cjk-9999

Stars embedded in clouds of dust and gases ▶ produce colorful nebulae.

Chapter Preview

Inquiry Activity

How Do Astronomers Measure Distances to Nearby Stars?

Procedure

1. Close your left eye. With your index finger in a vertical position, use your right eye to line up your finger with a distant object, such as a tree.

2. Without moving your finger, view the object with your left eye opened and your right eye closed.

Think About It

1. **Observing** What happened to the position of your finger when you observed it with your left eye?

2. **Predicting** What might happen if you repeated the activity, holding your finger farther from your eyes? Test your prediction.

25.1 Properties of Stars

Reading Focus

Key Concepts

- What can we learn by studying star properties?
- How does distance affect parallax?
- What factors determine a star's apparent magnitude?
- What relationship is shown on a Hertzsprung-Russell diagram?

Vocabulary

- constellation
- binary star
- light-year
- apparent magnitude
- absolute magnitude
- main-sequence star
- red giant
- supergiant
- Cepheid variable
- nova
- nebulae

Reading Strategy

Previewing Copy the table below. Before you read, write two questions about the Hertzsprung-Russell diagram on page 704. As you read, write answers to your questions.

Questions about the Hertzsprung-Russell Diagram	
Question	Answer
a. _____ ?	b. _____ ?
c. _____ ?	d. _____ ?

T he star Proxima Centauri is about 100 million times farther away from Earth than the moon. Yet, besides the sun, it is the closest star to Earth. The universe is incomprehensibly large. What is the nature of this vast universe? Do stars move, or do they remain in one place? Does the universe extend infinitely in all directions, or does it have boundaries? This chapter will answer these questions by examining the universe and the most numerous objects in the night sky—the stars.

As early as 5000 years ago, people became fascinated with the star-studded skies and began to name the patterns they saw. These patterns of stars, called **constellations,** were named in honor of mythological characters or great heroes, such as Orion, shown in Figure 1.

Although the stars that make up a constellation all appear to be the same distance from Earth, some are many times farther away than others. So, the stars in a particular constellation are not associated with one another in any physical way.

Today 88 constellations are recognized. They are used to divide the sky into units, just as state boundaries divide the United States. Every star in the sky is in, but is not necessarily part of, one of these constellations. Therefore, constellations can be used as a "map" of the night sky.

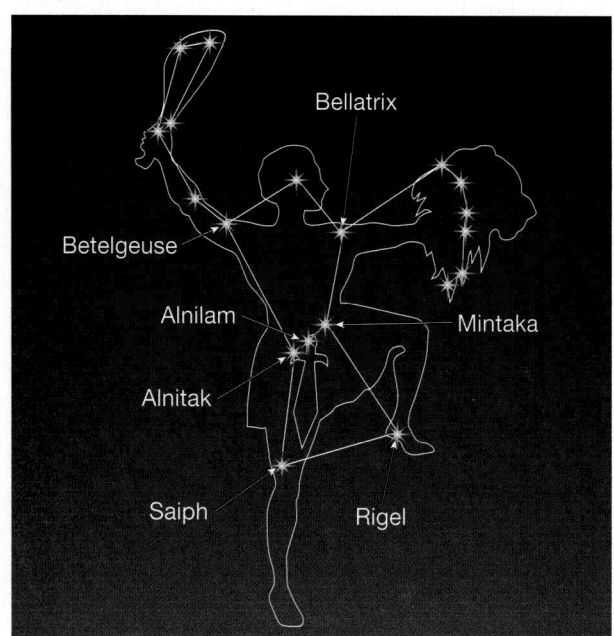

Figure 1 Orion The constellation Orion was named for a hunter.

Bellatrix

Betelgeuse

Alnilam

Mintaka

Alnitak

Saiph

Rigel

Characteristics of Stars

A great deal is known about the universe beyond our solar system. This knowledge hinges on the fact that stars, and even gases in the "empty" space between stars, radiate energy in all directions into space. The key to understanding the universe is to collect this radiation and unravel the secrets it holds. Astronomers have devised many ways to do just that. We will begin by examining some properties of stars, such as color, temperature, and mass.

Figure 2 Stars of Orion This time-lapse photograph shows stars as streaks across the night sky as Earth rotates. The streaks clearly show different star colors.

Star Color and Temperature Study the stars in Figure 2 and note their color. ● **Color is a clue to a star's temperature.** Very hot stars with surface temperatures above 30,000 K emit most of their energy in the form of short-wavelength light and therefore appear blue. Red stars are much cooler, and most of their energy is emitted as longer-wavelength red light. Stars with temperatures between 5000 and 6000 K appear yellow, like the sun.

Binary Stars and Stellar Mass In the early nineteenth century, astronomers discovered that many stars orbit each other. These pairs of stars, pulled toward each other by gravity, are called **binary stars.** More than 50 percent of the stars in the universe may occur in pairs or multiples.

● **Binary stars are used to determine the star property most difficult to calculate—its mass.** The mass of a body can be calculated if it is attached by gravity to a partner. This is the case for any binary star system. As shown in Figure 3, binary stars orbit each other around a common point called the center of mass. For stars of equal mass, the center of mass lies exactly halfway between them. If one star is more massive than its partner, their common center will be closer to the more massive one. If the sizes of their orbits are known, the stars' masses can be determined.

 **Reading Checkpoint** *What is a binary star system?*

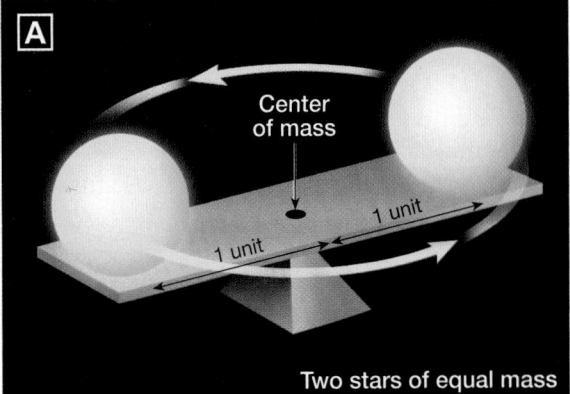

Two stars of equal mass

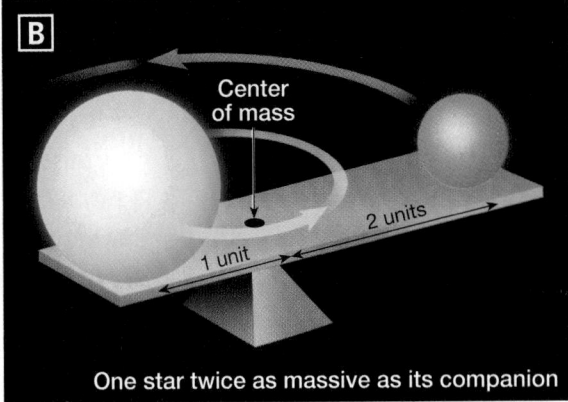

One star twice as massive as its companion

Figure 3 Common Center of Mass
A For stars of equal mass, the center of mass lies in the middle. **B** A star twice as massive as its partner is twice as close to the center of mass. It therefore has a smaller orbit than its less massive partner.

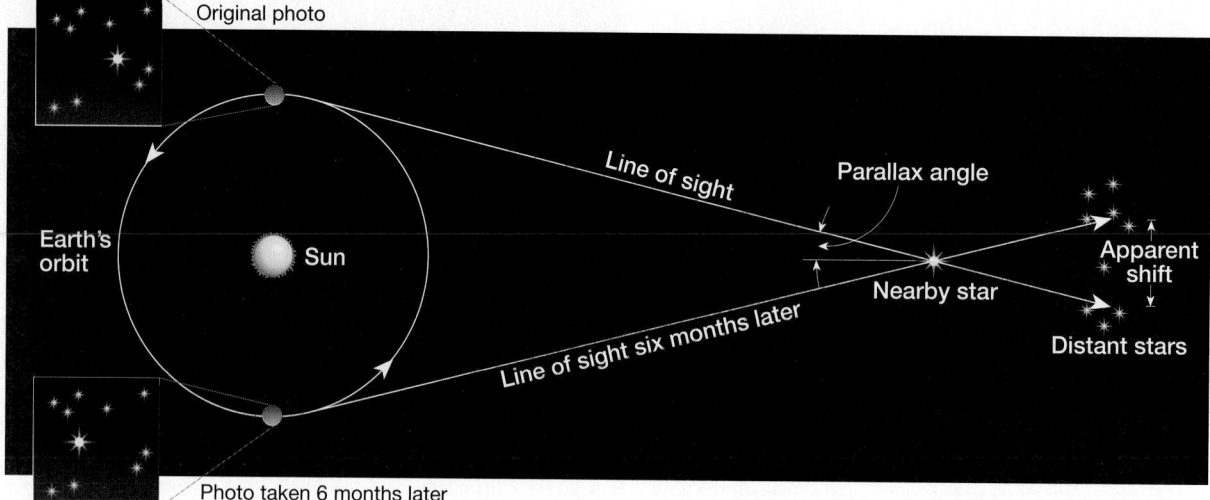

Original photo

Line of sight

Parallax angle

Earth's orbit

Sun

Apparent shift

Line of sight six months later

Nearby star

Distant stars

Photo taken 6 months later

Figure 4 Parallax The parallax angle shown here is exaggerated to illustrate the principle. Because the distances to even the nearest stars are huge, astronomers work with very small angles.
Relating Cause and Effect *What caused the star to appear to shift?*

Measuring Distances to Stars

Although measuring the distance to a star is very difficult, astronomers have developed some methods of determining stellar distances.

Parallax The most basic way to measure star distance is parallax. Parallax is the slight shifting in the apparent position of a nearby star due to the orbital motion of Earth. Parallax is determined by photographing a nearby star against the background of distant stars. Then, six months later, when Earth has moved halfway around its orbit, a second photograph is taken. When these photographs are compared, the position of the nearby star appears to have shifted with respect to the background stars. Figure 4 shows this shift and the resulting parallax angle.

The nearest stars have the largest parallax angles, while those of distant stars are too small to measure. In fact, all parallax angles are very small. The parallax angle to the nearest star (besides the sun), Proxima Centauri, is less than 1 second of arc, which equals 1/3600 of a degree. To put this in perspective, fully extend your arm and raise your little finger. Your finger is roughly 1 degree wide. Now imagine tracking a movement that is only 1/3600 as wide as your finger.

In principle, the method used to measure stellar distances may seem simple. But in practice, measurements are greatly complicated because of the tiny angles involved and because the sun, as well as the star being measured, also move through space. Even with today's technology, parallax angles for only a few thousand of the nearest stars are known with certainty.

Light-Year Distances to stars are so large that units such as kilometers or astronomical units are often too hard to use. A better unit to express stellar distance is the **light-year,** which is the distance light travels in one year—about 9.5×10^{12} or 9.5 trillion kilometers. Proxima Centauri is about 4.3 light-years away from the sun.

Reading Checkpoint

What is a light-year?

Stellar Brightness

The measure of a star's brightness is its magnitude. The stars in the night sky have an assortment of sizes, temperatures, and distances, so their brightnesses vary widely.

Apparent Magnitude Some stars may appear dimmer than others only because they are farther away. A star's brightness as it appears from Earth is called its **apparent magnitude.** Three factors control the apparent brightness of a star as seen from Earth: how big it is, how hot it is, and how far away it is.

Astronomers use numbers to rank apparent magnitude. The larger the number is, the dimmer the star. Just as we can compare the brightness of a 50-watt bulb to that of a 100-watt bulb, we can compare the brightness of stars having different magnitudes. A first-magnitude star is about 100 times brighter than a sixth-magnitude star. Therefore, two stars that differ by 5 magnitudes have a ratio in brightness of 100 to 1. It follows, then, that the brightness ratio of two stars differing by only one magnitude is about 2.5. A star of the first magnitude is about 2.5 times brighter than a star of the second magnitude.

 **Reading Checkpoint** *What is apparent magnitude?*

Absolute Magnitude Astronomers are also interested in how bright a star actually is, or its **absolute magnitude.** Two stars of the same absolute magnitude usually do not have the same apparent magnitude because one may be much farther from us than the other. The one that is farther away will appear dimmer. To compare their absolute brightness, astronomers determine what magnitude the stars would have if they were at a standard distance of about 32.6 light-years. For example, the sun, which has an apparent magnitude of −26.7, would, if located at a distance of 32.6 light-years, have an absolute magnitude of about 5. Stars with absolute magnitude values lower than 5 are actually brighter than the sun. Because of their distance, however, they appear much dimmer. Table 1 lists the absolute and apparent magnitudes of some stars as well as their distances from Earth.

Table 1 Distance, Apparent Magnitude, and Absolute Magnitude of Some Stars

Name	Distance (light-years)	Apparent Magnitude*	Absolute Magnitude*
Sun	NA	−26.7	5.0
Alpha Centauri	4.27	0.0	4.4
Sirius	8.70	−1.4	1.5
Arcturus	36	−0.1	−0.3
Betelgeuse	520	0.8	−5.5
Deneb	1600	1.3	−6.9

*The more negative, the brighter; the more positive, the dimmer.

 **Reading Checkpoint** *What is absolute magnitude?*

Hertzsprung-Russell Diagram

Early in the twentieth century, Einar Hertzsprung and Henry Russell independently developed a graph used to study stars. It is now called a Hertzsprung-Russell diagram (H-R diagram). 🔑A Hertzsprung-Russell diagram shows the relationship between the absolute magnitude and temperature of stars. By studying H-R diagrams, we learn a great deal about the sizes, colors, and temperatures of stars.

In the H-R diagram shown in Figure 5, notice that the stars are not uniformly distributed. About 90 percent are **main-sequence stars** that fall along a band that runs from the upper-left corner to the lower-right corner of the diagram. As you can see, the hottest main-sequence stars are the brightest, and the coolest main-sequence stars are the dimmest.

The brightness of the main-sequence stars is also related to their mass. The hottest blue stars are about 50 times more massive than the sun, while the coolest red stars are only 1/10 as massive. Therefore, on the H-R diagram, the main-sequence stars appear in decreasing order, from hotter, more massive blue stars to cooler, less massive red stars.

Above and to the right of the main sequence in the H-R diagram lies a group of very bright stars called **red giants.** The size of these giants can be estimated by comparing them with stars of known size that have the same surface temperature. Objects with equal surface temperatures radiate the same amount of energy per unit area. Therefore, any difference in the brightness of two stars having the same surface temperature is due to their relative sizes. Some stars are so large that they are called **supergiants.** Betelgeuse, a bright red supergiant in the constellation Orion, has a radius about 800 times that of the sun.

Stars in the lower-central part of the H-R diagram are much fainter than main-sequence stars of the same temperature. Some probably are no bigger than Earth. This group is called white dwarfs, although not all are white.

Figure 5 Hertzsprung-Russell Diagram In this idealized chart, stars are plotted according to temperature and absolute magnitude.

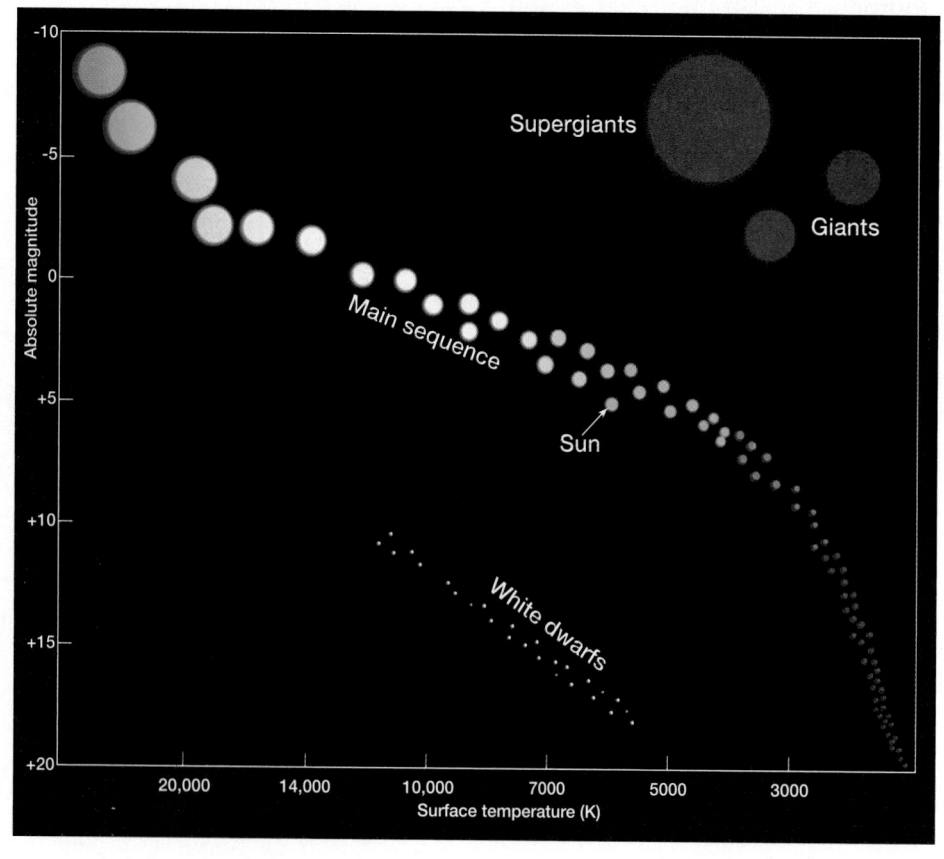

Soon after the first H-R diagrams were developed, astronomers realized their importance in interpreting stellar evolution. Just as with living things, a star is born, ages, and dies. After considering some variable stars and the nature of interstellar matter, we'll return to the topic of stellar evolution.

Variable Stars Stars may fluctuate in brightness. Some stars, called **Cepheid variables,** get brighter and fainter in a regular pattern. The interval between two successive occurrences of maximum brightness is called a light period. In general, the longer the light period of a Cepheid, the greater its absolute magnitude is. Once the absolute magnitude is known, it can be compared to the apparent magnitude of the Cepheid. Measuring Cepheid variable periods is an important means of determining distances within our universe.

A different type of variable is associated with a **nova,** or sudden brightening of a star. During a nova eruption, the outer layer of the star is ejected at high speed. A nova, shown in Figure 6, generally reaches maximum brightness in a few days, remains bright for only a few weeks, then slowly returns in a year or so to its original brightness. Only a small amount of its mass is lost during the flare-up. Some stars have experienced more than one such event. In fact, the process probably occurs repeatedly.

Scientists think that novas occur in binary systems consisting of an expanding red giant and a nearby hot white dwarf. Hydrogen-rich gas from the oversized giant is transferred by gravity to the white dwarf. Eventually, the added gas causes the dwarf to ignite explosively. Such a reaction rapidly heats and expands the outer layer of the hot dwarf to produce a nova. In a relatively short time, the white dwarf returns to its prenova state, where it remains inactive until the next buildup occurs.

Figure 6 Nova These photographs, taken two months apart, show the decrease in brightness that follows a nova flare-up.

Figure 7 Dark Nebula The Horsehead Nebula is found in the constellation Orion.

Interstellar Matter Between existing stars is "the vacuum of space." However, it is not a pure vacuum, for there are clouds of dust and gases known as **nebulae.** If this interstellar matter is close to a very hot star, it will glow and is called a bright nebula. The two main types of bright nebulae are emission nebulae and reflection nebulae.

Emission nebulae consist largely of hydrogen. They absorb ultraviolet radiation emitted by a nearby hot star. Because these gases are under very low pressure, they emit this energy as visible light. This conversion of ultraviolet light to visible light is known as fluorescence. You can see this effect in fluorescent lights. Reflection nebulae, as the name implies, merely reflect the light of nearby stars. Reflection nebulae are thought to be composed of dense clouds of large particles called interstellar dust.

Some nebulae are not close enough to a bright star to be lit up. They are called dark nebulae. Dark nebulae, such as the one shown in Figure 7, can easily be seen as starless regions when viewing the Milky Way.

Although nebulae appear very dense, they actually consist of thinly scattered matter. Because of their enormous size, however, their total mass may be many times that of the sun. Astronomers study nebulae because stars and planets form from this interstellar matter.

Section 25.1 Assessment

Reviewing Concepts

1. What can astronomers learn by studying a star's color?
2. Binary stars can be used to establish what property of stars?
3. How does distance affect parallax?
4. What factors determine a star's apparent magnitude?
5. The H-R diagram shows the relationship between what two factors?

Critical Thinking

6. **Problem Solving** How many times brighter is a star with a magnitude of 7 than a star with a magnitude of 12?

7. **Inferring** Scientists think that only a small amount of a star's mass is lost during a nova. Based on what you have learned about novas, infer what evidence scientists use to support this theory.

Writing in Science

Web Site Make an educational Web site about the H-R diagram for younger students. Use Figure 5 as a guide. Include a color key and other elements to help clarify concepts such as star temperature, the Kelvin scale, and absolute magnitude.

25.2 Stellar Evolution

Reading Focus

Key Concepts

- What stage marks the birth of a star?
- Why do all stars eventually die?
- What stages make up the sun's life cycle?

Vocabulary

- protostar
- supernova
- white dwarf
- neutron star
- pulsar
- black hole

Reading Strategy

Sequencing Copy the flowchart below. As you read, complete it to show how the sun evolves. Expand the chart to show the evolution of low-mass and high-mass stars.

Evolution of Sun → a. ___?___ → b. ___?___

Determining how stars are born, age, and then die was difficult because the life of a star can span billions of years. However, by studying stars of different ages, astronomers have been able to piece together the evolution of a star. Imagine that an alien from outer space lands on Earth. This alien wants to study the stages of human life. By examining a large number of humans, the alien observes the birth of babies, the activities of children and adults, and the death of elderly people. From this information, the alien then attempts to put the stages of human development into proper sequence. Based on the number of humans in each stage of development, the alien would conclude that humans spend more of their lives as adults than as children. In a similar way, astronomers have pieced together the story of stars.

Star Birth

The birthplaces of stars are dark, cool interstellar clouds, such as the one in Figure 8. These nebulae are made up of dust and gases. In the Milky Way, nebulae consist of 92 percent hydrogen, 7 percent helium, and less than 1 percent of the remaining heavier elements. For some reason not yet fully understood, some nebulae become dense enough to begin to contract. A shock wave from an explosion of a nearby star may trigger the contraction. Once the process begins, gravity squeezes particles in the nebula, pulling every particle toward the center. As the nebula shrinks, gravitational energy is converted into heat energy.

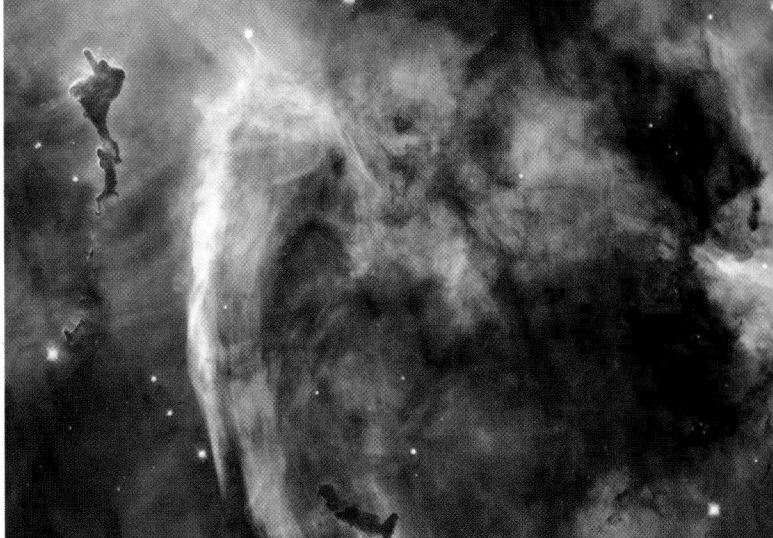

Figure 8 Nebula Dark, cool clouds full of interstellar matter are the birthplace of stars.

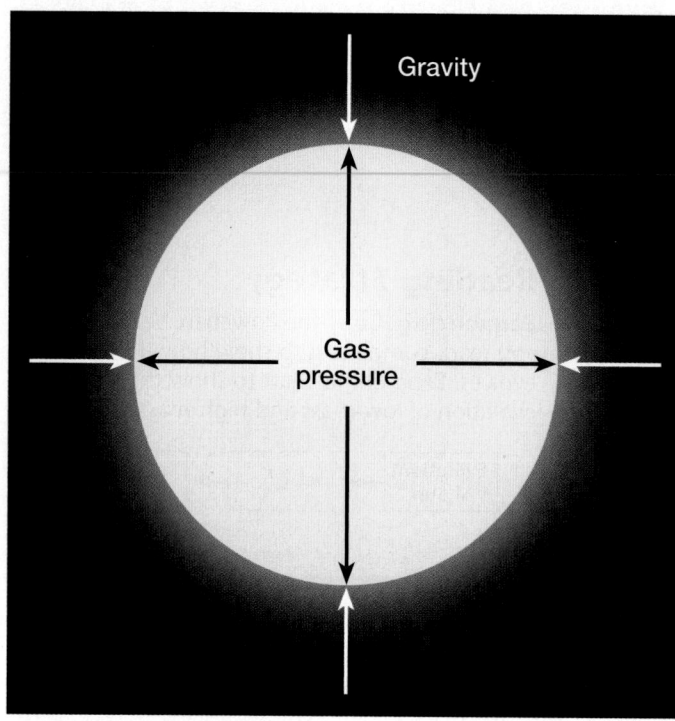

Gravity

Gas pressure

Figure 9 Balanced Forces A main-sequence star is balanced between gravity, which is trying to squeeze it, and gas pressure, which is trying to expand it.

Protostar Stage The initial contraction spans a million years or so. As time passes, the temperature of this gaseous body slowly rises until it is hot enough to radiate energy from its surface in the form of long-wavelength red light. This large red object is called a protostar. A **protostar** is a developing star not yet hot enough to engage in nuclear fusion.

During the protostar stage, gravitational contraction continues—slowly at first, then much more rapidly. This collapse causes the core of the protostar to heat much more intensely than the outer layer. ⬤ **When the core of a protostar has reached about 10 million K, pressure within is so great that nuclear fusion of hydrogen begins, and a star is born.**

Heat from hydrogen fusion causes the gases to increase their motion. This in turn causes an increase in the outward gas pressure. At some point, this outward pressure exactly balances the inward force of gravity, as shown in Figure 9. When this balance is reached, the star becomes a stable main-sequence star. Stated another way, a stable main-sequence star is balanced between two forces: gravity, which is trying to squeeze it into a smaller sphere, and gas pressure, which is trying to expand it.

Main-Sequence Stage From this point in the evolution of a main-sequence star until its death, the internal gas pressure struggles to offset the unyielding force of gravity. Typically, hydrogen fusion continues for a few billion years and provides the outward pressure required to support the star from gravitational collapse.

Different stars age at different rates. Hot, massive blue stars radiate energy at such an enormous rate that they deplete their hydrogen fuel in only a few million years. By contrast, the least massive main-sequence stars may remain stable for hundreds of billions of years. A yellow star, such as the sun, remains a main-sequence star for about 10 billion years.

An average star spends 90 percent of its life as a hydrogen-burning, main-sequence star. Once the hydrogen fuel in the star's core is depleted, it evolves rapidly and dies. However, with the exception of the least-massive red stars, a star can delay its death by fusing heavier elements and becoming a giant.

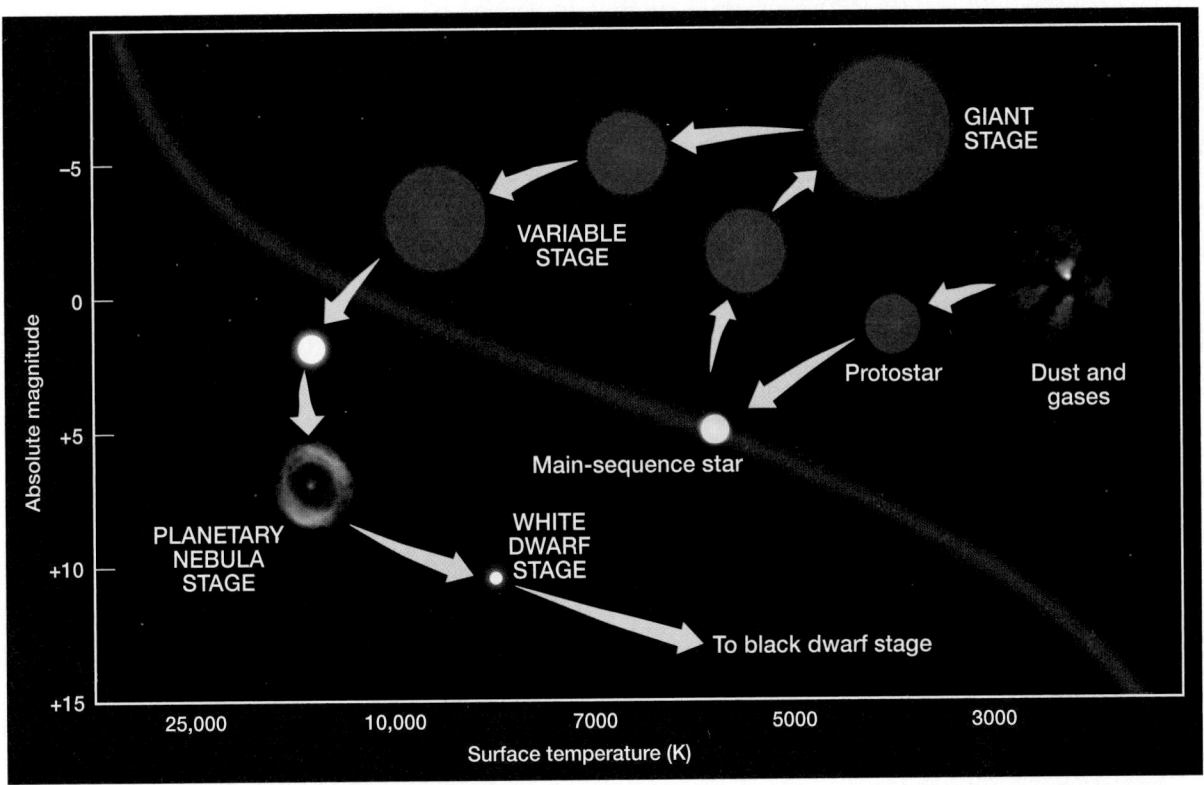

Absolute magnitude scale (vertical): −5, 0, +5, +10, +15
Surface temperature (K) scale (horizontal): 25,000, 10,000, 7000, 5000, 3000

GIANT STAGE

VARIABLE STAGE

Protostar

Dust and gases

PLANETARY NEBULA STAGE

WHITE DWARF STAGE

Main-sequence star

To black dwarf stage

Red-Giant Stage The red-giant stage occurs because the zone of hydrogen fusion continually moves outward, leaving behind a helium core. Eventually, all the hydrogen in the star's core is consumed. While hydrogen fusion is still progressing in the star's outer shell, no fusion is taking place in the core. Without a source of energy, the core no longer has enough pressure to support itself against the inward force of gravity. As a result, the core begins to contract.

As the core contracts, it grows hotter by converting gravitational energy into heat energy. Some of this energy is radiated outward, increasing hydrogen fusion in the star's outer shell. This energy in turn heats and expands the star's outer layer. The result is a giant body hundreds to thousands of times its main-sequence size, as shown in Figure 10.

As the star expands, its surface cools, which explains the star's reddish appearance. During expansion, the core continues to collapse and heat until it reaches 100 million K. At this temperature, it is hot enough to convert helium to carbon. So, a red giant consumes both hydrogen and helium to produce energy.

Eventually, all the usable nuclear fuel in these giants will be consumed. The sun, for example, will spend less than a billion years as a giant. More massive stars will pass through this stage even more rapidly. The force of gravity will again control the star's destiny as it squeezes the star into the smallest, most dense piece of matter possible.

 **Reading Checkpoint** *Why do red giants have a reddish appearance?*

Figure 10 Life Cycle of a Sunlike Star A medium-mass star, similar to the sun, will evolve along the path shown here. **Interpreting Diagrams** *What is the first stage in the formation of the star? What is the last stage?*

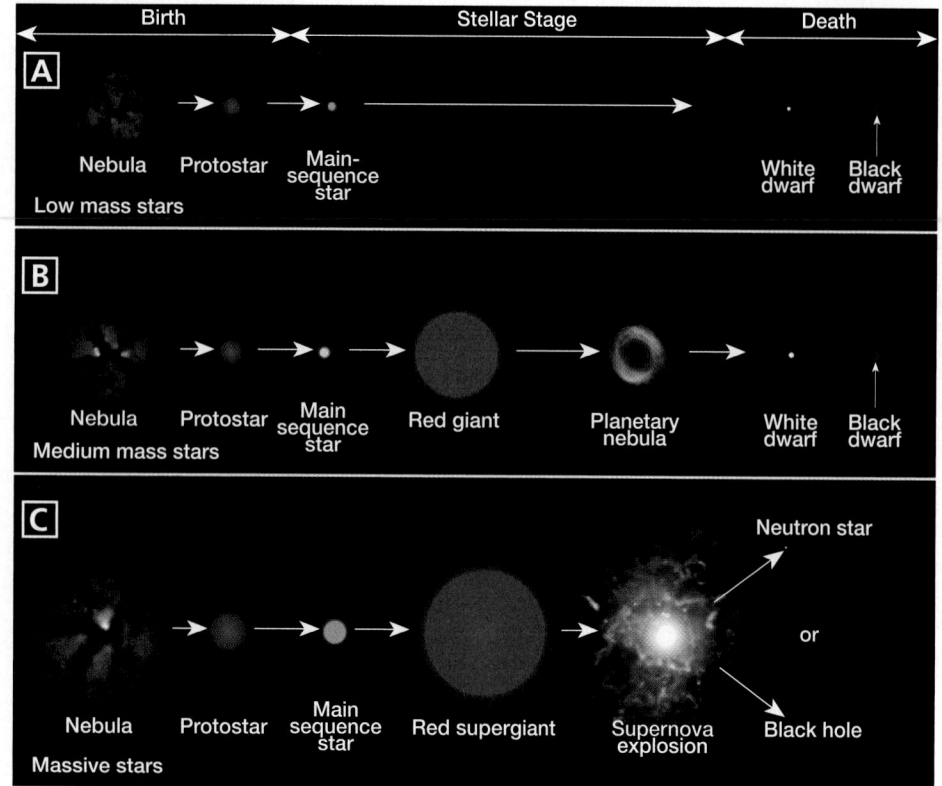

| Birth | Stellar Stage | Death |

A

Nebula　Protostar　Main-sequence star　　　　White dwarf　Black dwarf

Low mass stars

B

Nebula　Protostar　Main sequence star　Red giant　Planetary nebula　White dwarf　Black dwarf

Medium mass stars

C

Neutron star

Nebula　Protostar　Main sequence star　Red supergiant　Supernova explosion　or　Black hole

Massive stars

Figure 11 Stellar Evolution
A A low-mass star uses fuel at a low rate and has a long life span.
B Like a low-mass star, a medium-mass star ends as a black dwarf.
C Massive stars end in huge explosions, then become either neutron stars or black holes.

Burnout and Death

Most of the events of stellar evolution discussed so far are well documented. What happens next is based more on theory. **We do know that all stars, regardless of their size, eventually run out of fuel and collapse due to gravity.** With this in mind, let's consider the final stages of stars of different masses.

Death of Low-Mass Stars

As shown in Figure 11A, stars less than one half the mass of the sun consume their fuel at a fairly slow rate. Consequently, these small, cool red stars may remain on the main sequence for up to 100 billion years. Because the interior of a low-mass star never reaches high enough temperatures and pressures to fuse helium, its only energy source is hydrogen. So, low-mass stars never evolve into red giants. Instead, they remain as stable main-sequence stars until they consume their hydrogen fuel and collapse into a white dwarf, which you will learn more about later.

Death of Medium-Mass Stars

As shown in Figure 11B, stars with masses similar to the sun evolve in essentially the same way. During their giant phase, sunlike stars fuse hydrogen and helium fuel at a fast rate. Once this fuel is exhausted, these stars also collapse into white dwarfs.

During their collapse from red giants to white dwarfs, medium-mass stars are thought to cast off their bloated outer layer, creating an expanding round cloud of gas. The remaining hot, central white dwarf heats the gas cloud, causing it to glow. These often beautiful, gleaming spherical clouds are called planetary nebulae. An example of a planetary nebula is shown in Figure 12.

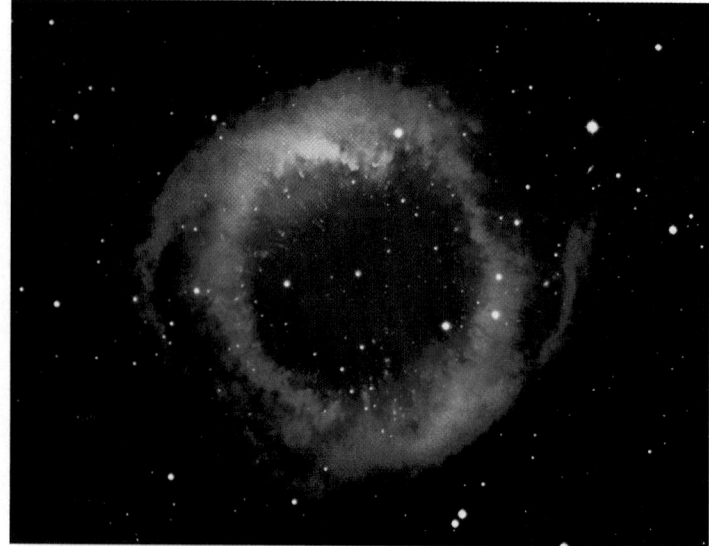

Figure 12 Planetary Nebula
During its collapse from a red giant to a white dwarf, a medium-mass star ejects its outer layer, forming a round cloud of gas.

Death of Massive Stars

In contrast to sunlike stars, which die gracefully, stars with masses three times that of the sun have relatively short life spans, as shown in Figure 11C. These stars end their lives in a brilliant explosion called a **supernova.** During a supernova, a star becomes millions of times brighter than its prenova stage. If one of the nearest stars to Earth produced such an outburst, it would be brighter than the sun. Supernovae are rare. None have been observed in our galaxy since the invention of the telescope, although Tycho Brahe and Galileo each recorded one about 30 years apart. An even larger supernova was recorded in 1054 by the Chinese. Today, the remnant of this great outburst is the Crab Nebula, shown in Figure 13.

A supernova event is thought to be triggered when a massive star consumes most of its nuclear fuel. Without a heat engine to generate the gas pressure required to balance its immense gravitational field, the star collapses. This implosion, or bursting inward, is huge, resulting in a shock wave that moves out from the star's interior. This energetic shock wave destroys the star and blasts the outer shell into space, generating the supernova event.

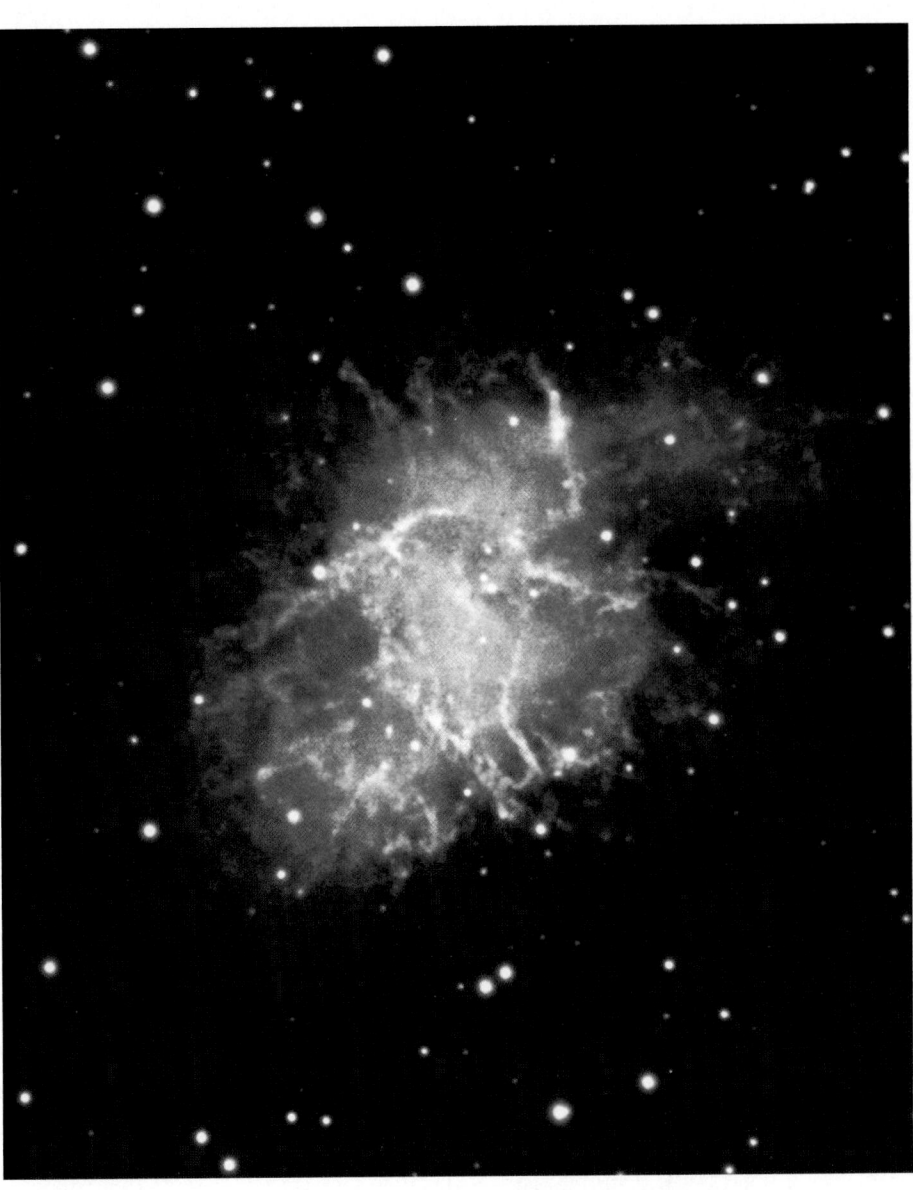

Figure 13 Crab Nebula
This nebula, found in the constellation Taurus, is the remains of a supernova that took place in 1054.

H-R Diagrams and Stellar Evolution Hertzsprung-Russell diagrams have been helpful in formulating and testing models of stellar evolution. They are also useful for illustrating the changes that take place in an individual star during its life span. Refer back to Figure 10, which shows the evolution of a star about the size of the sun. Keep in mind that the star does not physically move along this path. Its position on the H-R diagram represents the color and absolute magnitude of the star at various stages in its evolution.

 Reading Checkpoint *What is a supernova?*

Stellar Remnants

Eventually, all stars consume their nuclear fuel and collapse into one of three documented states—white dwarf, neutron star, or black hole. Although different in some ways, these small, compact objects are all composed of incomprehensibly dense material and all have extreme surface gravity.

White Dwarfs **White dwarfs** are the remains of low-mass and medium-mass stars. They are extremely small stars with densities greater than any known material on Earth. Although some white dwarfs are no larger than Earth, the mass of such a dwarf can equal 1.4 times that of the sun. So, their densities may be a million times greater than water. A spoonful of such matter would weigh several tons. Densities this great are possible only when electrons are displaced inward from their regular orbits, around an atom's nucleus, allowing the atoms to take up less than the "normal" amount of space. Material in this state is called degenerate matter.

In degenerate matter, the atoms have been squeezed together so tightly that the electrons are displaced much nearer to the nucleus. Degenerate matter uses electrical repulsion instead of molecular motion to support itself from total collapse. Although atomic particles in degenerate matter are much closer together than in normal Earth matter, they still are not packed as tightly as possible. Stars made of matter that has an even greater density are thought to exist.

As a star contracts into a white dwarf, its surface becomes very hot, sometimes exceeding 25,000 K. Even so, without a source of energy, it can only become cooler and dimmer. Although none have been observed, the last stage of a white dwarf must be a small, cold body called a black dwarf. Table 2 summarizes the evolution of stars of various masses. **As you can see, the sun begins as a nebula, spends much of its life as a main-sequence star, becomes a red giant, planetary nebula, white dwarf, and finally, black dwarf.**

Table 2 Summary of Evolution for Stars of Various Masses				
Initial Mass of Interstellar Cloud (Sun = 1)	Main-Sequence Stage	Giant Phase	Evolution After Giant Phase	Final Stage
1–3	Yellow	Yes	Planetary nebula	White dwarf
6	White	Yes	Supernova	Neutron star
20	Blue	Yes (Supergiant)	Supernova	Black hole

Neutron Stars After studying white dwarfs, scientists made what might at first appear to be a surprising conclusion. The smallest white dwarfs are the most massive, and the largest are the least massive. The explanation for this is that a more massive star, because of its greater gravitational force, is able to squeeze itself into a smaller, more densely packed object than can a less massive star. So, the smaller white dwarfs were produced from the collapse of larger, more massive stars than were the larger white dwarfs.

This conclusion led to the prediction that stars smaller and more massive than white dwarfs must exist. These objects, called **neutron stars,** are thought to be the remnants of supernova events. In a white dwarf, the electrons are pushed close to the nucleus, while in a neutron star, the electrons are forced to combine with protons to produce neutrons. If Earth were to collapse to the density of a neutron star, it would have a diameter equal to the length of a football field. A pea-size sample of this matter would weigh 100 million tons. This is approximately the density of an atomic nucleus. Neutron stars can be thought of as large atomic nuclei.

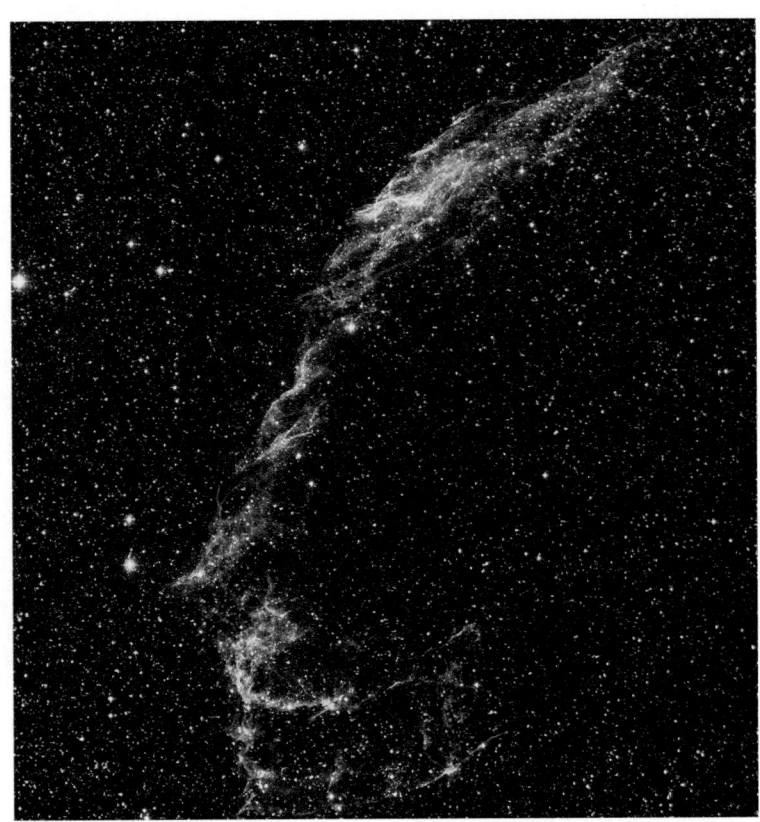

Figure 14 Veil Nebula Located in the constellation Cygnus, this nebula is the remnant of an ancient supernova.

Supernovae During a supernova, the outer layer of the star is ejected, while the core collapses into a very hot neutron star about 20 kilometers in diameter. Although neutron stars have high surface temperatures, their small size would greatly limit their brightness. Finding one with a telescope would be extremely difficult.

However, astronomers think that a neutron star would have a very strong magnetic field. Further, as a star collapses, it will rotate faster, for the same reason ice skaters rotate faster as they pull in their arms. Radio waves generated by these rotating stars would be concentrated into two narrow zones that would align with the star's magnetic poles. Consequently, these stars would resemble a rapidly rotating beacon emitting strong radio waves. If Earth happened to be in the path of these beacons, the star would appear to blink on and off, or pulsate, as the waves swept past.

In the early 1970s, a source that radiates short bursts or pulses of radio energy, called a **pulsar**, was discovered in the Crab Nebula. Studies of this radio source revealed it to be a small spinning star centered in the nebula. The pulsar found in the Crab Nebula is undoubtedly the remains of the supernova of 1054.

Black Holes Are neutron stars made of the most dense materials possible? No. During a supernova event, remnants of stars three times more massive than the sun apparently collapse into objects even smaller and denser than neutron stars. Even though these objects, called **black holes,** are very hot, their gravity is so strong that not even light can escape their surface. So they disappear from sight. Anything that moves too near a black hole would be swept in by its gravity and lost forever.

How can astronomers find an object whose gravitational field prevents the escape of all matter and energy? One strategy is to find evidence of matter being rapidly swept into a region of apparent nothingness. Scientists think that as matter is pulled into a black hole, it should become very hot and emit a flood of X-rays before being pulled in. Because isolated black holes would not have a source of matter to swallow up, astronomers first looked at binary-star systems.

A likely candidate for a black hole is Cygnus X-1, a strong X-ray source in the constellation Cygnus. In this case, the X-ray source can be observed orbiting a supergiant companion with a period of 5.6 days. It appears that gases are pulled from this companion and spiral into the disk-shaped structure around the black hole, as shown in Figure 15.

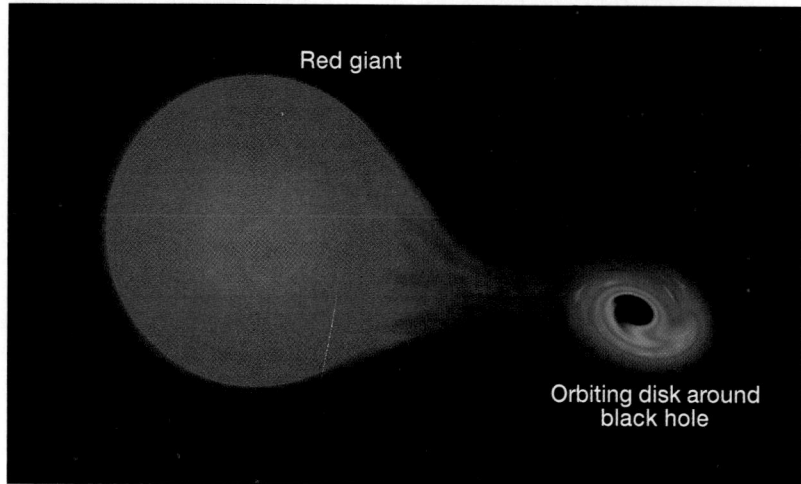

Red giant

Orbiting disk around black hole

Figure 15 Black Hole Gases from the red giant spiral into the black hole.

Go Online
SCi LINKS. NSTA

For: Links on black holes
Visit: www.SciLinks.org
Web Code: cjn-7252

Section 25.2 Assessment

Reviewing Concepts

1. What is a protostar?
2. At what point is a star born?
3. What causes a star to die?
4. Describe the life cycle of the sun.

Critical Thinking

5. **Inferring** Why are less massive stars thought to age more slowly than more massive stars, even though less massive stars have much less "fuel"?

6. **Relating Cause and Effect** Why is interstellar matter important to stellar evolution?

Connecting Concepts

Supernova If a supernova explosion were to occur near our solar system, what might be some possible consequences of the intense X-ray radiation that would reach Earth?

25.3 The Universe

Reading Focus

Key Concepts

- What is the size and structure of the Milky Way Galaxy?

- In what ways do galaxies differ from one another?

- What evidence indicates that the universe is expanding?

- According to the big bang theory, how did the universe begin?

Vocabulary

- galaxy
- galaxy cluster
- Hubble's law
- big bang theory

Reading Strategy

Outlining As you read, make an outline of the most important ideas in this section.

I. The Universe
    A. Milky Way Galaxy
        1. _____?_____
        2. _____?_____
    B. _____?_____
        1. Spiral Galaxy
        2. Elliptical Galaxy
        3. _____?_____

On a clear and moonless night away from city lights, you can see a truly marvelous sight—our own Milky Way Galaxy, as shown in Figure 16. **Galaxies** are groups of stars, dust, and gases held together by gravity. There may be more than 100 billion stars in the Milky Way Galaxy alone. Our galaxy looks milky because the solar system is located within a flat disk —the galactic disk. We view it from the inside and see stars in every direction.

The Milky Way Galaxy

When astronomers began to survey the stars located along the plane of the Milky Way, it appeared that equal numbers lay in every direction. Could Earth actually be at the center of the galaxy? Scientists came up with a better explanation. Imagine that the trees in an enormous forest represent the stars in the galaxy. After hiking into this forest, you look around. You see an equal number of trees in every direction. Are you in the center of the forest? Not necessarily. Anywhere in the forest will seem to be the center, except at the very edge.

For: Links on galaxies
Visit: www.SciLinks.org
Web Code: cjn-7253

Figure 16 Milky Way Galaxy
Notice the dark band caused by interstellar dark nebulae.

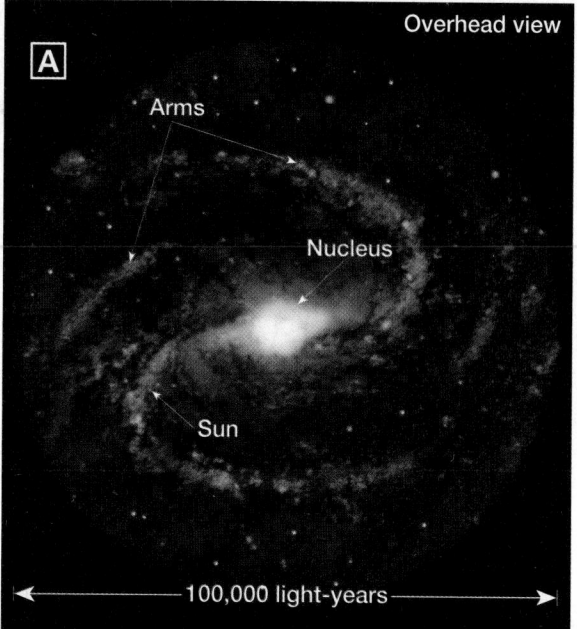

Overhead view

A

Arms

Nucleus

Sun

◄————— 100,000 light-years —————►

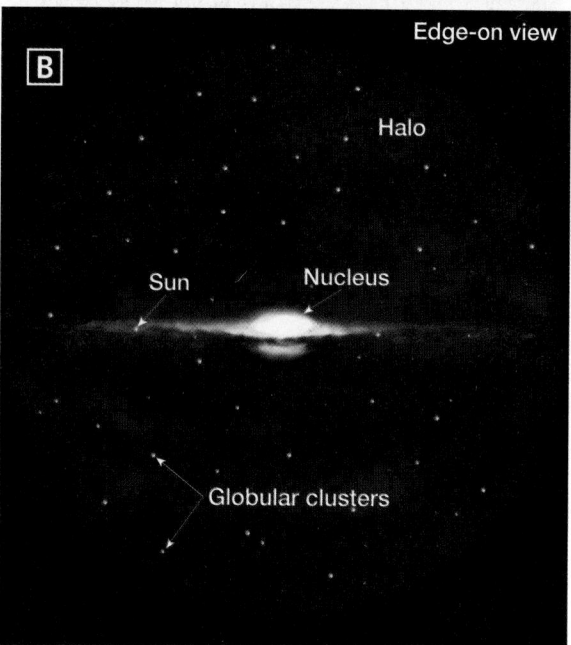

Edge-on view

B

Halo

Sun   Nucleus

Globular clusters

Figure 17 Structure of the Milky Way A The spiral arms are clearly visible in the overhead view of our galaxy. **B** Our solar system is located about 30,000 light-years from the galactic nucleus.

Size of the Milky Way It's hard to study the Milky Way Galaxy with optical telescopes because large quantities of interstellar matter block our vision. With the aid of radio telescopes, scientists have determined the structure of our galaxy. ◯**The Milky Way is a large spiral galaxy whose disk is about 100,000 light-years wide and about 10,000 light-years thick at the nucleus, as shown in Figure 17A.** As viewed from Earth, the center of the galaxy lies beyond the constellation Sagittarius. Figure 17B shows an edge-on view of the Milky Way.

How big is the Milky Way Galaxy?

Structure of the Milky Way Radio telescopes reveal that the Milky Way has at least three distinct spiral arms, with some signs of splintering. The sun is positioned in one of these arms about two thirds of the way from the center, or galactic nucleus, at a distance of about 30,000 light-years. The stars in the arms of the Milky Way rotate around the galactic nucleus. The most outward arms move the slowest, and the ends of the arms appear to trail. Our solar system orbits the galactic nucleus about every 200 million years.

Surrounding the galactic disk is a nearly round halo made of thin gas and numerous clusters of stars. These star clusters do not participate in the rotating motion of the arms but have their own orbits that carry them through the disk. Although some clusters are very dense, they pass among the stars of the arms with plenty of room to spare.

Where is our solar system located within the Milky Way Galaxy?

Types of Galaxies

In the mid-1700s, German philosopher Immanuel Kant proposed that the fuzzy patches of light scattered among the stars were actually distant galaxies like the Milky Way. Today we know that the universe includes hundreds of billions of galaxies, each containing hundreds of billions of stars. From these hundreds of billions of galaxies, scientists have identified several basic types.

Spiral Galaxies As shown in Figure 18A, spiral galaxies are usually disk-shaped, with a somewhat greater concentration of stars near their centers. There are numerous variations, though. Viewed broadside, the arms are often seen extending from the central nucleus and sweeping gracefully away. The outermost stars of these arms rotate most slowly, giving the galaxy the appearance of a pinwheel.

One type of spiral galaxy, however, has its stars arranged in the shape of a bar, which rotates as a rigid system. Attached to each end of these bars are curved spiral arms. These have become known as barred spiral galaxies, as shown in Figure 18B. Recent evidence indicates that the Milky Way may be a barred spiral galaxy. Spiral galaxies are generally quite large. About 10 percent of all galaxies are thought to be barred spirals, and another 20 percent are regular spiral galaxies.

Elliptical Galaxies About 60 percent of galaxies are classified as elliptical galaxies. Elliptical galaxies range in shape from round to oval. Although most are small, the very largest known galaxies—200,000 light-years in diameter—are elliptical. This type of galaxy, shown in Figure 19, does not have spiral arms.

Irregular Galaxies Only 10 percent of the known galaxies have irregular shapes and are classified as irregular galaxies. The best-known irregular galaxies, the Large and Small Magellanic Clouds, are easily visible with the unaided eye. These galaxies were named after the explorer Ferdinand Magellan, who observed them when he sailed around Earth in 1520. They are our nearest galactic neighbors—only 150,000 light-years away. An irregular galaxy is shown in Figure 20.

In addition to shape and size, one of the major differences among different types of galaxies is the age of their stars. Irregular galaxies are composed mostly of young stars, while elliptical galaxies contain old stars. The Milky Way and other spiral galaxies have both young and old stars, with the youngest located in the arms.

Figure 18 Spiral Galaxies
A A spiral galaxy looks somewhat like a pinwheel. **B** A barred spiral galaxy has a bar through its center, with arms extending outward from the bar.

Figure 19 Elliptical Galaxy Most galaxies are classified as elliptical with shapes ranging from round to oval.

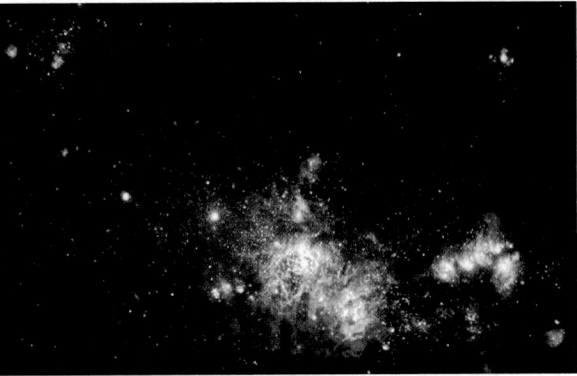

Figure 20 Irregular Galaxy Irregular galaxies have irregular shapes.
Describing *What type of stars would you find in an irregular galaxy?*

Figure 21 Galaxy Cluster This cluster of galaxies is located about 1 million light-years from Earth.

Galaxy Clusters Once astronomers discovered that stars were found in groups, they wondered whether galaxies also were grouped or just randomly distributed throughout the universe. They found that, like stars, galaxies are grouped in **clusters.** One such cluster is shown in Figure 21. Some clusters may contain thousands of galaxies. Our own cluster, called the Local Group, contains at least 28 galaxies. Of these, three are spirals, 11 are irregulars, and 14 are ellipticals. Galaxy clusters also make up huge groups called superclusters. Studies indicate that superclusters may be the largest entities in the universe.

 *Describe the shape of elliptical galaxies.*

The Expanding Universe

Recall the Doppler effect that you read about in Chapter 24. Remember that when a source is moving away, its light appears redder than it actually is, because its waves appear lengthened. Objects approaching have their light waves shifted toward the blue or shorter wavelengths. Therefore, the Doppler effect reveals whether a star or other body in space is moving away from Earth or toward Earth. The amount of shift allows us to calculate the rate at which the relative movement is occurring. Large Doppler shifts indicate higher speeds; smaller Doppler shifts indicate lower speeds.

Red Shifts One of the most important discoveries of modern astronomy was made in 1929 by Edwin Hubble. Observations completed several years earlier revealed that most galaxies have Doppler shifts toward the red end of the spectrum. The red shift occurs because the light waves are "stretched," which shows that Earth and the source are moving away from each other. Hubble set out to explain this red shift phenomenon.

Hubble realized that dimmer galaxies were probably farther away than were brighter galaxies. He tried to determine whether a relationship existed between the distances to galaxies and their red shifts. Hubble used estimated distances based on relative brightness and Doppler red shifts to discover that galaxies that exhibit the greatest red shifts are the most distant.

 *What relationship did Hubble discover between red shifts and the distances of galaxies from Earth?*

Hubble's Law A consequence of the universal red shift is that it predicts that most galaxies—except for a few nearby—are moving away from us. Recall that the amount of Doppler red shift depends on the speed at which the object is moving away. Greater red shifts indicate faster speeds. Because more distant galaxies have greater red shifts, Hubble concluded that they must be retreating from us at greater speeds. This idea is currently termed **Hubble's law.** It states that galaxies are retreating from us at a speed that is proportional to their distance.

Hubble was surprised at this discovery because it implied that the most distant galaxies are moving away from us many times faster than those nearby. What does this mean? ⟸ **The red shifts of distant galaxies indicate that the universe is expanding.**

To help visualize the nature of this expanding universe, imagine a loaf of raisin bread dough that has been set out to rise for a few hours. As shown in Figure 22 , as the dough doubles in size, so does the distance between all of the raisins. However, the raisins that were originally farther apart traveled a greater distance in the same time span than those located closer together. We therefore conclude that in an expanding universe, as in the raisin bread dough analogy, those objects located farther apart move away from each other more rapidly.

Another feature of the expanding universe can be demonstrated. No matter which raisin you select, it will move away from all the other raisins. Likewise, no matter where one is located in the universe, every other galaxy—again, except those in the same cluster—will be moving away. Hubble had indeed advanced our understanding of the universe. The Hubble Space Telescope is named in his honor.

 **Reading Checkpoint** *What is Hubble's law?*

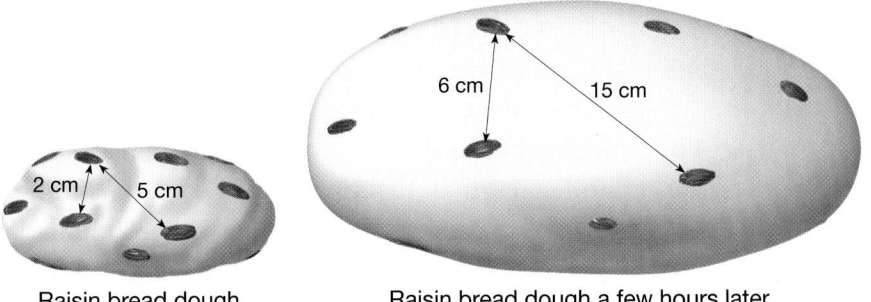

6 cm   15 cm

2 cm   5 cm

Raisin bread dough before it rises.

A

Raisin bread dough a few hours later.

B

Figure 22 Raisin Dough Analogy As the dough rises, raisins that were farther apart travel a greater distance in the same time as those that were closer together. Like galaxies in an expanding universe, the distant raisins move away from one another more rapidly than those that are near one another.

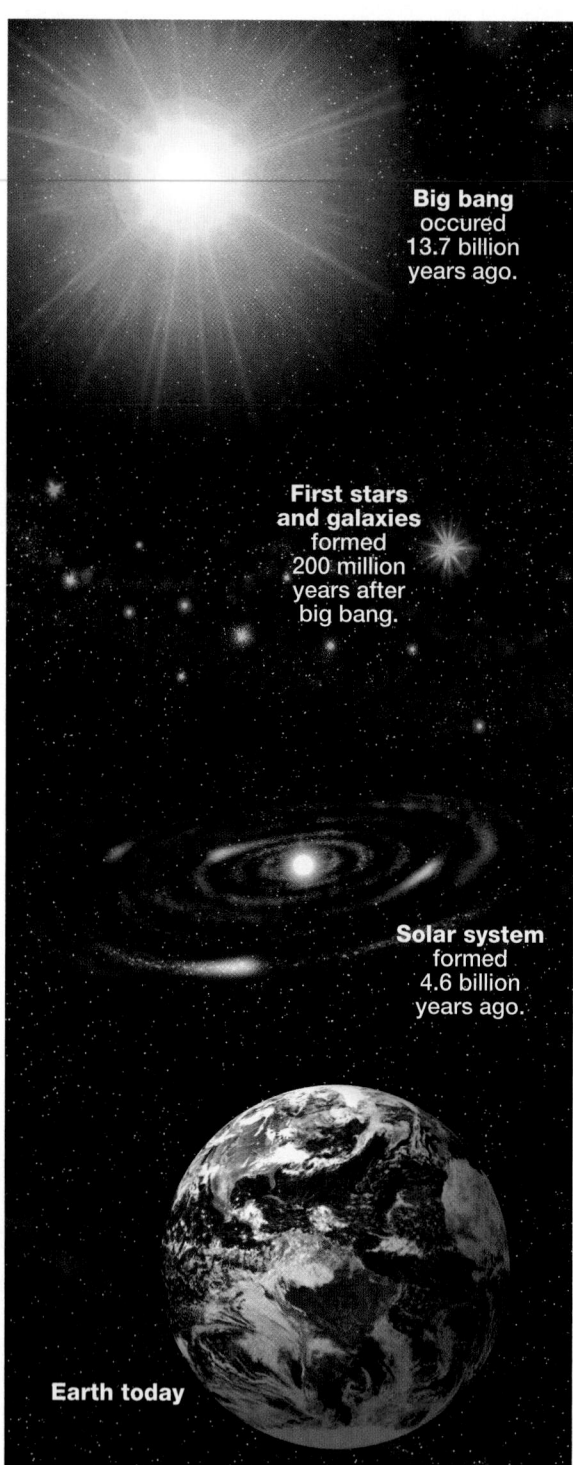

Figure 23 The Big Bang
According to the big bang theory, the universe began 13.7 billion years ago. Two hundred million years later, the first stars and galaxies began to form.

Labels in figure:
Big bang occured 13.7 billion years ago.

First stars and galaxies formed 200 million years after big bang.

Solar system formed 4.6 billion years ago.

Earth today

The Big Bang

Did the universe have a beginning? Will it have an end? Scientists are trying to answer these questions.

Any theory about the origin of the universe must account for the fact that all distant galaxies are moving away from us. Because all galaxies appear to be moving away from Earth, is our planet in the center of the universe? Probably not, because if we are not even in the center of our own solar system, and our solar system is not even in the center of the galaxy, it seems unlikely that we could be in the center of the universe.

A more probable explanation exists. Imagine a balloon with paper-punch dots glued to its surface. When the balloon is inflated, each dot spreads apart from every other dot. Similarly, if the universe is expanding, every galaxy would be moving away from every other galaxy.

This concept of an expanding universe led to the widely accepted big bang theory. According to the **big bang theory,** the universe began as a violent explosion from which the universe continues to expand, evolve, and cool. **The big bang theory states that at one time, the entire universe was confined to a dense, hot, supermassive ball. Then, about 13.7 billion years ago, a violent explosion occurred, hurling this material in all directions.** The big bang, as shown in Figure 23, marks the beginning of the universe. All matter and space were created at that instant. After several hundred thousand years, the universe became cool enough for atoms to form. Gases in the universe continued to cool and condense. They eventually formed the stars that make up the galaxies we now observe moving away from us.

Supporting Evidence Through decades of experimentation and observation, scientists have gathered substantial evidence that supports the big bang theory. For example, the red shift of galaxies that you read about earlier indicates that the universe is still expanding. Scientists discovered a type of energy called cosmic background radiation. This energy was detected as faint radio signals coming from every direction in space. Scientists think that this radiation was produced during the big bang.

What evidence supports the big bang?

The Big Crunch? If the universe began with a big bang, how will it end? One view is that the universe will last forever. In this scenario, the stars will slowly burn out, being replaced by invisible degenerate matter and black holes that will travel outward through an endless, dark, cold universe. The other possibility is that the outward flight of the galaxies will slow and eventually stop. Gravitational contraction would follow, causing the galaxies to collide and combine into the high-energy, high-density mass from which the universe began. This fiery death of the universe, the big bang operating in reverse, has been called the "big crunch."

Whether or not the universe will expand forever or eventually collapse upon itself depends on its average density. If the average density of the universe is more than its critical density—about one atom for every cubic meter—the gravitational field is enough to stop the outward expansion and cause the universe to contract. On the other hand, if the density of the universe is less than the critical value, it will expand forever. Current estimates of the density of the universe place it below the critical density, which predicts an ever-expanding, or open, universe. Additional support for an open universe comes from studies that indicate the universe is expanding faster now than in the past. The view currently favored by most scientists is an expanding universe with no ending point.

It should be noted, however, that the methods used to determine the ultimate fate of the universe have substantial uncertainties. It is possible that previously undetected matter exists in great quantities in the universe. If this is so, the galaxies could, in fact, collapse in the "big crunch."

Section 25.3 Assessment

Reviewing Concepts

1. What is a galaxy?
2. 🔵 Describe the size and structure of the Milky Way Galaxy.
3. 🔵 How do galaxies differ?
4. 🔵 What evidence indicates that the universe is expanding?
5. 🔵 What is the big bang theory?

Critical Thinking

6. **Comparing and Contrasting** Compare and contrast the three types of galaxies.
7. **Inferring** If the universe is an open universe, what can you infer about its average density?

Writing in Science

Descriptive Paragraph Scientists are continuously searching the Milky Way Galaxy for other stars that may have planets. What types of stars would most likely have a planet or planets suitable for life as we know it? Write a paragraph describing these stars.

Astrology—Forerunner of Astronomy

Many people confuse astrology and astronomy to the point of believing these terms to be synonymous. Nothing can be further from the truth. Astronomy is a scientific investigation of the universe to discover the properties of celestial objects and the laws under which the universe operates. Astrology, on the other hand, is based on ancient superstitions that a person's actions and personality are based on the positions of the planets and stars now, and at the person's birth. Scientists do not accept astrology, regarding it as a pseudoscience ("false science"). Most people who read horoscopes do so only as a pastime and do not let them influence their daily living.

Figure 24 The Constellations of the Zodiac Earth is shown in its autumn (September) position in orbit, from which the sun is seen against the background of the constellation Virgo.

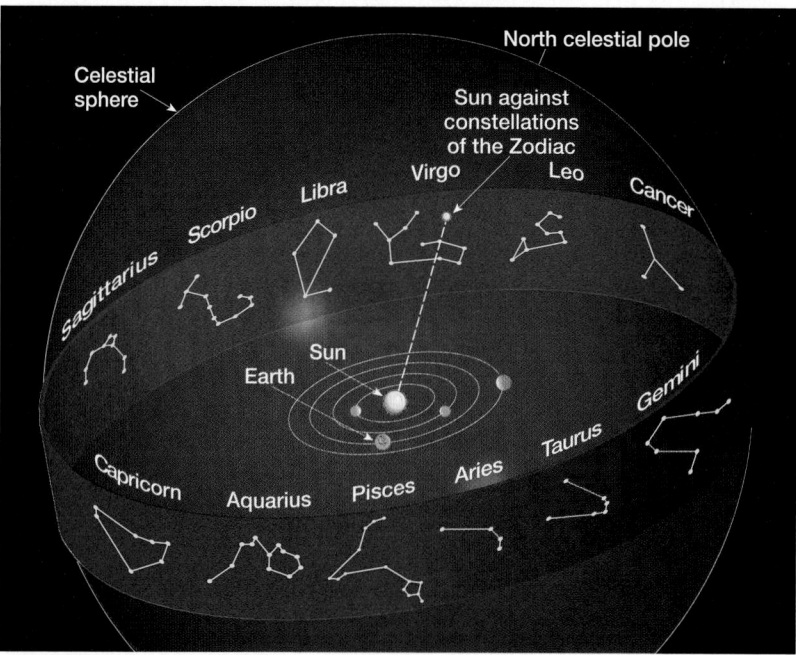

Astrology began more than 3000 years ago when the positions of the planets were plotted as they regularly migrated against the background of the "fixed" stars. Because the solar system is "flat," like a whirling Frisbee, the planets orbit the sun along nearly the same plane. Therefore, the planets, sun, and moon all appear to move along a band around the sky known as the zodiac. Because Earth's moon cycles through its phases about 12 times each year, the Babylonians divided the zodiac into 12 constellations, as shown in Figure 24. Thus, each successive full moon can be seen against the backdrop of the next constellation.

When the zodiac was first established, the vernal equinox (first day of spring) occurred when the sun was viewed against the constellation Aries. However, during each succeeding vernal equinox, the position of the sun shifts very slightly against the background of stars. Now, over 2000 years later, the vernal equinox occurs when the sun is in Pisces. In several years, the vernal equinox will occur when the sun appears against Aquarius.

Although astrology is not a science and has no basis in fact, it did contribute to the science of astronomy. The positions of the moon, sun, and planets at the time of a person's birth (sign of the zodiac) were considered to have great influence on that person's life. Even the great astronomer Kepler was required to make horoscopes part of his duties. To make horoscopes for the future, astrologers tried to predict the future positions of the celestial bodies. Thus, some of the improvements in astronomical instruments were made because of the desire for more accurate predictions of events such as eclipses, which were considered highly significant in a person's life.

Observing Stars

Throughout history, people have been recording the nightly movement of stars that results from Earth's rotation, as well as the seasonal changes in the constellations as Earth revolves around the sun. Early astronomers offered many explanations for the changes before the true nature of the motions was understood in the seventeenth century. In this lab, you'll observe and identify stars.

Problem
How can you use star charts to identify constellations and track star movements?

Materials
- star charts (in the Appendix)
- penlight
- notebook

Skills
Observing, Summarizing, Interpreting Data

Procedure
1. On a clear, moonless night far from street lights, go outside and observe the stars.

2. In a data table like the one below, make a list of the different colors of stars that you see.

3. Select one star that is overhead or nearly so. Observe and record its movement over a period of one hour. Also note the direction of its movement (eastward, westward).

4. Select a star chart suitable for your location and season. Locate several constellations. Sketch and label the constellations in your notebook.

5. Locate the North Star (Polaris) in the night sky. Observe the motion of stars that surround the North Star.

6. Repeat your observations several weeks later at the exact location.

Analyze and Conclude
1. **Observing** How many different colors of stars did you observe? How do these colors relate to star temperature?

2. **Interpreting Data** In which direction did the star that you observed appear to move? How is this movement related to the direction of Earth's rotation?

3. **Summarizing** Write a brief summary of the motion of the stars that surround the North Star. Be sure to include any changes you observed during your second viewing.

Go Further Find the Big Dipper, which is part of the constellation Ursa Minor. A binary star system makes up the stars of the Big Dipper. Locate the star pair and sketch them in their proper location in the Big Dipper.

Data Table				
Date	Star Colors	Star Movement	Constellations	Motions of Stars Around North Star

25.1 Properties of Stars

⬤ Key Concepts

- Color is a clue to a star's temperature.
- Binary stars can be used to determine stellar mass.
- The nearest stars have the largest parallax angles, while those of distant stars are too small to measure.
- Three factors control the apparent brightness of a star as seen from Earth: how big it is, how hot it is, and how far away it is.
- A Hertzsprung-Russell diagram shows the relationship between the absolute magnitude and temperature of stars.

Vocabulary

constellation, *p. 700;* binary star, *p. 701;* light-year, *p. 702;* apparent magnitude, *p. 703;* absolute magnitude, *p. 703;* main-sequence star, *p. 704;* red giant, *p. 704;* supergiant, *p. 704;* Cepheid variable, *p. 705;* nova, *p. 705;* nebulae, *p. 706*

25.2 Stellar Evolution

⬤ Key Concepts

- When the core of a protostar has reached at least 10 million K, pressure within is so great that nuclear fusion of hydrogen begins, and a star is born.
- All stars, regardless of their size, eventually run out of fuel and collapse due to gravity.
- Stars like the sun begin as a nebula, spend much of their lives as main-sequence stars, become red giants, planetary nebulae, white dwarfs, and finally, black dwarfs.

Vocabulary

protostar, *p. 708;* supernova, *p. 711;* white dwarf, *p. 712;* neutron star, *p. 713;* pulsar, *p. 713;* black hole, *p. 714*

25.3 The Universe

⬤ Key Concepts

- The Milky Way is a large spiral galaxy whose disk is about 100,000 light-years wide and about 10,000 light-years thick at the nucleus.
- In addition to shape and size, one of the major differences among different types of galaxies is the age of their stars.
- The red shifts of distant galaxies indicate that the universe is expanding.
- The big bang theory states that at one time, the entire universe was confined to a dense, hot, supermassive ball. Then, about 13.7 billion years ago, a violent explosion occurred, hurling this material in all directions.

Vocabulary

galaxy, *p. 715;* galaxy cluster, *p. 718;* Hubble's law, *p. 719;* big bang theory, *p. 720*

Thinking Visually

Concept Map Use information from the chapter to complete the concept map below.

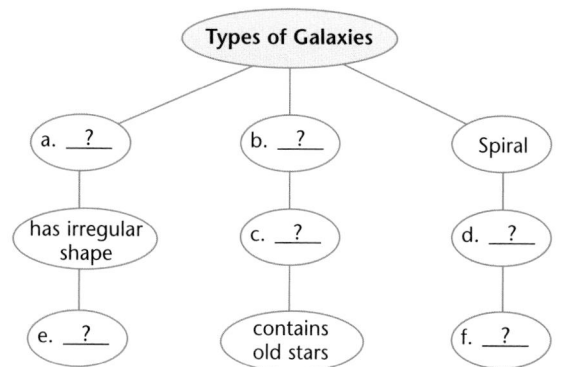

Reviewing Content

Choose the letter that best answers the question or completes the statement.

1. Distances to stars are usually expressed in units called
   - **a.** miles.
   - **b.** kilometers.
   - **c.** light-years.
   - **d.** astronomical units.

2. The measure of a star's brightness is called its
   - **a.** parallax.
   - **b.** color index.
   - **c.** visual binary.
   - **d.** magnitude.

3. Distances to nearby stars can be determined from
   - **a.** fluorescence.
   - **b.** stellar parallax.
   - **c.** stellar mass.
   - **d.** emission nebulae.

4. Which color stars have the highest surface temperature?
   - **a.** red
   - **b.** orange
   - **c.** yellow
   - **d.** blue

5. Which type of star is the sun?
   - **a.** black hole
   - **b.** black dwarf
   - **c.** main sequence
   - **d.** red giant

6. What happens to a sun-like star after it has used up all the fuel in its core?
   - **a.** supernova
   - **b.** neutron star
   - **c.** red giant
   - **d.** nebula

7. Which object has such a strong surface gravity that light cannot escape it?
   - **a.** black hole
   - **b.** black dwarf
   - **c.** red giant
   - **d.** white dwarf

8. Stars that are composed of matter in which electrons have combined with protons are called
   - **a.** black holes.
   - **b.** neutron stars.
   - **c.** red giants.
   - **d.** white dwarfs.

9. Hubble's law states that galaxies are retreating from Earth at a speed that is proportional to their
   - **a.** distance.
   - **b.** volume.
   - **c.** mass.
   - **d.** temperature.

10. What theory states that the universe began in a violent explosion?
    - **a.** the big crunch
    - **b.** the Doppler effect
    - **c.** Hubble's law
    - **d.** the big bang

Understanding Concepts

11. Which property of a star can be determined by its color?

12. About how many stars are estimated to occur in pairs or multiples?

13. What is parallax?

14. Compare and contrast apparent magnitude and absolute magnitude.

15. What color is the most massive type of main-sequence star? The least massive?

16. At what temperature does nuclear fusion begin?

17. A stable main-sequence star is balanced between which two forces?

18. What element is the main fuel for main-sequence stars? For red giants?

19. What type of stars end their lives as supernovae?

20. What is a pulsar?

21. How long does it take our solar system to orbit the Milky Way Galaxy?

22. More distant galaxies have greater red shifts. What does this indicate about the universe?

23. What is cosmic background radiation?

Critical Thinking

24. Explaining Why are radio telescopes instead of optical telescopes used to determine the structure of the Milky Way Galaxy?

25. Drawing Conclusions Imagine that you are a scientist studying the birth of stars in a spiral galaxy. Which part of the galaxy would you study? Explain your answer.

Analyzing Data

Use the diagram below to answer Questions 28–30.

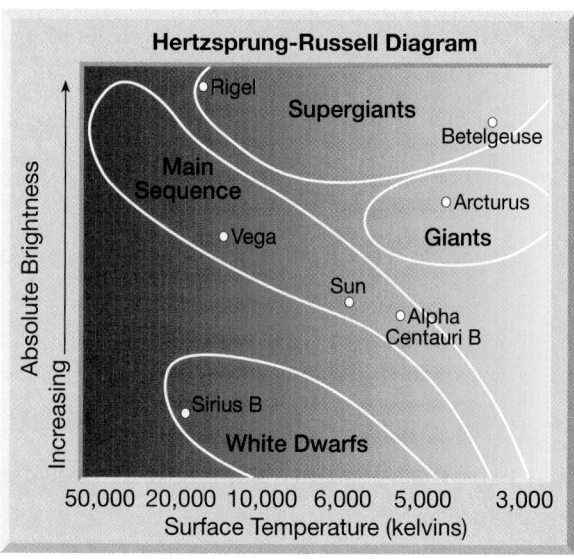

Hertzsprung-Russell Diagram

26. Interpreting Graphs What is the brightest star in the diagram? The hottest?

27. Analyzing Data How does the absolute brightness of white dwarfs compare with that of supergiants?

28. Summarizing What is the relationship between absolute brightness and temperature for a main-sequence star?

Concepts in Action

29. Explaining How can a binary star system be used to determine a star's mass?

30. Inferring Would you use parallax to determine the distance to a faraway star? Why or why not?

31. Calculating The closest star to the sun, Proxima Centauri, is 4.3 light-years away. How many kilometers from the sun is Proxima Centauri?

Performance-Based Assessment

Using Models Use materials provided by your teacher to construct a scale model of the Milky Way Galaxy. Before you begin, be sure to develop a workable scale for your model.

Standardized Test Prep

Test-Taking Tip

Sequencing a Series of Events

When a test question requires you to sequence a series of events, first try to predict the correct sequence before looking at the answer choices. Then compare your sequence to those listed. Be sure to pay attention to qualifiers in the question, such as *first, earliest, increasing,* or *decreasing,* as these may help you eliminate choices.

Which sequence of events describes the big bang theory? Begin with the earliest event.

(A) Explosion; atoms form; stars form; all matter concentrated at a single point.
(B) All matter concentrated at a single point; explosion; atoms form; stars form.
(C) Explosion; stars form; all matter concentrated at a single point; atoms form.
(D) Stars form; atoms form; all matter concentrated at a single point; explosion.

(Answer: B)

Choose the letter that best answers the question or completes the statement.

1. What can you estimate about a Cepheid variable if you know its absolute magnitude and apparent magnitude?
   (A) mass
   (B) distance
   (C) temperature
   (D) volume

2. Based on the red shifts of distant galaxies, astronomers conclude that
   (A) Earth is in the center of the universe.
   (B) the universe is contracting.
   (C) the universe is expanding.
   (D) new galaxies are continually being added to the universe.

Answer the following questions in complete sentences.

3. What types of stars are thought to be the remnants of supernova explosions?

4. How do the lives of the most massive stars end? What are the two possible products of this event?

Use the illustration below to answer Questions 5 and 6.

5. Sequence the steps in the evolution of a medium-mass star, such as the sun.

6. At which stage in its evolution is the star the hottest? The brightest?

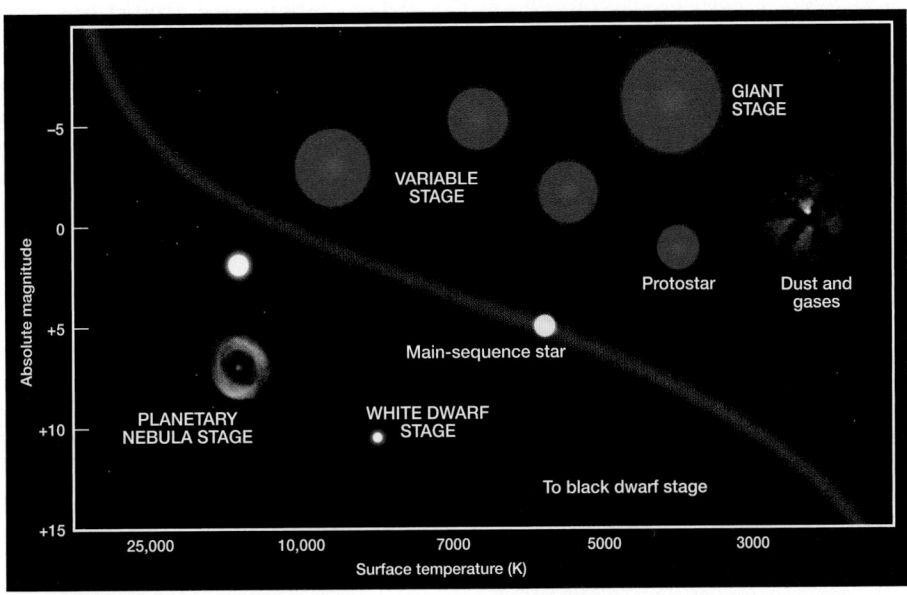

Science Skills

Basic Process Skills

During a science course, you often carry out some short lab activities as well as more detailed experiments. Here are some skills that you will use as you work.

Observing

In every science activity, you make a variety of observations. **Observing** is using one or more of the five senses to gather information. Many observations involve the senses of sight, hearing, touch, and smell.

Sometimes you will use tools that increase the power of your senses or make observations more precise. For example, hand lenses enable you to see things in greater detail. Tools may help you eliminate personal opinions or preferences.

In science it is customary to record your observations at the time they are made, usually by writing or drawing in a notebook. You may occasionally make records by using computers, cameras, videotapes, and other tools. As a rule, scientists keep complete accounts of their observations, often using tables to help organize their observations in a regular way.

Inferring

In science as in everyday life, observations are usually followed by inferences. **Inferring** is interpreting an observation or statement based on prior knowledge. For example, you can make several observations using the strobe photograph below. You can observe that the

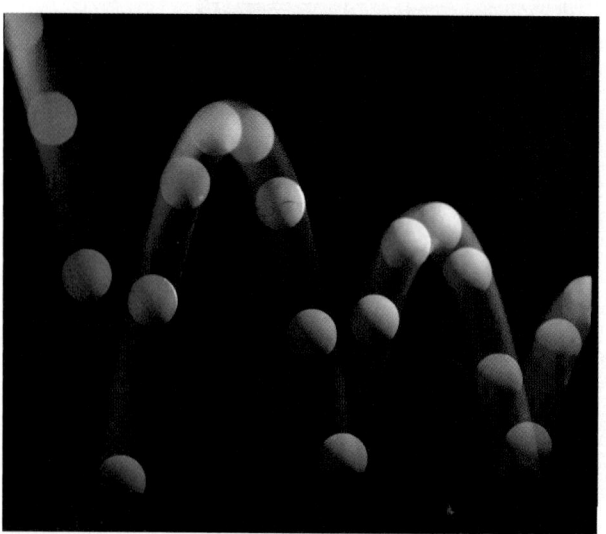

ball is moving. Based on the motion of the ball, you might infer that the ball was thrown downward at an angle by an experimenter. In making that inference, you would use your knowledge about the motion of projectiles. Someone who knew more about projectile motion might infer that the ball loses energy with each bounce. That is why the height decreases with each bounce.

Notice that an inference is an act of reasoning, not a fact. That means an inference may be logical but not true. It is often necessary to gather further information before you can be confident that an inference is correct. For scientists, that information may come from further observations or from research into the work done by others.

Comparing Observations and Inferences	
Sample Observation	**Sample Inference**
The ball moves less and less vertical distance in the time between each flash of the strobe light.	Gravity is slowing down the ball's upward motion.
The ball moves the same distance to the right in the time between each flash of the strobe light.	Air resistance is so small that it does not slow down the ball's horizontal motion.

Predicting

People often make predictions, but their statements about the future could be either guesses or inferences. In science, a **prediction** is an inference about a future event based on evidence, experience, or knowledge. For example, you can say, *On the first day next month, it will be sunny all day.* If your statement is based on evidence of weather patterns in the area, then the prediction is scientific. If the statement was made without considering any evidence, it's just a guess.

Predictions play a major role in science because they offer scientists a way to test ideas. If scientists understand an event or the properties of a particular object, they should be able to make accurate predictions about that event or object. Some predictions can be tested simply by making observations. For others, carefully designed experiments are needed.

Measuring

Measurements are important in science because they provide specific information and help observers avoid bias. **Measuring** is comparing an object or process to a standard. Scientists use a common set of standards, called the International System of Units, abbreviated as SI (for its French name, *Système International d'Unités*).

What distance does the ball travel in each time interval in the strobe photograph? You can make measurements on the photograph to make more precise statements about the ball's motion.

Calculating

Once scientists have made measurements, calculations are a very important part of analyzing data. How fast is a ball moving? You could directly measure the speed of a ball using probeware such as a motion sensor. But you can also calculate the speed using distance and time measurements. **Calculating** is a process in which a person uses mathematical operations to manipulate numbers and symbols.

Classifying

Classifying is grouping items according to some organizing idea or system. Classifying occurs in every branch of science but it's especially important in chemistry because there are so many different ways that elements can combine to form compounds.

Sometimes you place objects into groups using an established system. Other times you create a system by observing a variety of objects and identifying their properties. For example, you could group household cleaners into those that are abrasive and those that are not. Or you could categorize cleaners as toxic or nontoxic. Ammonia is toxic, whereas vinegar is not.

Using Tables and Graphs

Scientists represent and organize data in tables and graphs as part of experiments and other activities. Organizing data in tables and graphs makes it easier to see patterns in data. Scientists analyze and interpret data tables and graphs to determine the relationship of one variable to another and to make predictions based on the data.

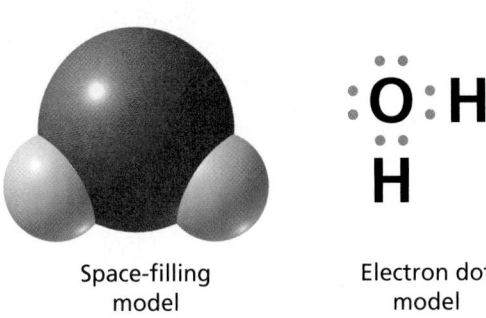

Space-filling model   Electron dot model

Using Models

Some cities refuse to approve new tall buildings if they would cast shadows on existing parks. As architects plan buildings in such locations, they use models to show where a proposed building's shadow will fall at any time of day at any season of the year. A **model** is a mental or physical representation of an object, process, or event. In science, models are usually made to help people understand natural objects and the processes that affect these objects.

Models can be varied. Mental models, such as mathematical equations, can represent some kinds of ideas or processes. For example, the equation for the surface area of a sphere can model the surface of Earth, enabling scientists to determine its size. Models can be two-dimensional (flat) or three-dimensional (having depth). In chemistry, for example, there are several ways to model the arrangement of atoms in a molecule. Two models for a water molecule are shown above. The electron dot model is two-dimensional. It has the advantage of clearly showing how electrons are shared among atoms in the molecule. The space-filling model cannot show the number of electrons inside the atoms or between atoms, but it does show the arrangement of atoms in space.

Experimental Methods

A science experiment is a procedure designed so that there is only one logical explanation for the results. Some types of experiments are fairly simple to design. Others may require ingenious problem solving.

Posing Questions

As a gardener harvested corn in her vegetable garden, she noticed that on one side of the garden the plants produced very few ears of corn. The gardener wondered, *Why didn't the plants on one side of the garden produce as much corn?*

An experiment may begin when someone like the gardener asks a specific question or wants to solve a particular problem. Sometimes the original question leads directly to an experiment, but often researchers need to restate the problem before they can design an appropriate experiment. The gardener's question about the corn, for example, is too broad to be tested by an experiment, since there are so many possible different answers. To narrow the topic, the gardener might think about several related questions: *Were the seeds the same on both sides of the garden? Was the sunlight the same? Is there something different about the soil?*

Formulating Hypotheses

In science, a question about an event is answered by developing a possible explanation called a **hypothesis**. The hypothesis may be developed after long thought and research or come to a scientist "in a flash." To be useful, a hypothesis must lead to predictions that can be tested.

In this case, the gardener decided to focus on the quality of the soil on each side of her garden. She did some tests and discovered that the soil had a lower pH on the side where the plants did not produce well. That led her to propose this hypothesis: *If the pH of the soil is too low, the plants will produce less corn.* The next step is to make a prediction based on the hypothesis, for example, *If the pH of the soil is increased using lime, the plants will yield more corn.* Notice that the prediction suggests the basic idea for an experiment.

Designing Experiments

A carefully designed experiment can test a prediction in a reliable way, ruling out other possible explanations. As scientists plan their experimental procedures, they pay particular attention to the variables that must be controlled and the procedures that must be defined.

The gardener decided to study three groups of plants:
Group 1—20 plants on the side of the garden with a low pH;
Group 2—20 plants on the side of the garden with a low pH, but with lime added; and
Group 3—20 plants on the side of the garden with a high pH.

Controlling Variables

As researchers design an experiment, they identify the **variables**, factors that can change. Some common variables include mass, volume, time, temperature, light, and the presence or absence of specific materials. An experiment involves three categories of variables. The factor that scientists purposely change is called the **manipulated variable**. The factor that may change because of the manipulated variable and that scientists want to observe is called the **responding variable**. And the factors that scientists purposely keep the same are called the **controlled variables**. Controlling variables helps make researchers confident that the observed changes in the responding variable are due to changes in the manipulated variable.

For the gardener, the manipulated variable is the pH of the soil. The responding variable is the number of ears of corn produced by the plants. Among the variables that must be controlled are the amount of sunlight received each day, the time of year when seeds are planted, and the amount of water the plants receive.

Forming Operational Definitions

In an experiment, it is often necessary to define one or more variables explicitly so that any researcher could measure or control the variable in exactly the same way. An **operational definition** describes how a particular variable is to be measured or how a term is to be defined. In this context, the term *operational* means "describing what to do."

The gardener, for example, has to decide exactly how much lime to add to the soil. Can lime be added after the seeds are planted or only before planting? At what pH should no more lime be added to the soil? In this case, the gardener decided to add lime only before planting, and to add enough lime to make the pH equal in Groups 2 and 3.

Analyzing Data

The observations and measurements that are made in an experiment are called **data**. Scientists customarily record data in an orderly way. When an experiment is done, the researcher analyzes the data for trends or patterns, often by doing calculations or making graphs, to determine whether the results support the hypothesis.

For example, the gardener regularly measured and recorded data such as the soil moisture, daily sunlight, and pH of the soil. She found that the soil pH in Groups 2 and 3 started the same, but after two months the soil pH for Group 3 was a little higher than the soil pH for Group 2.

After harvesting the corn, the gardener recorded the numbers of ears of corn produced by each plant. She totaled the number of ears for each group. Her results were the following.

Group 1: 67 ears of corn
Group 2: 102 ears of corn
Group 3: 126 ears of corn

The overall trend was clear: The gardener's prediction was correct.

Drawing Conclusions

Based on whether the results confirm or refute the hypothesis, researchers make a final statement that summarizes the experiment. That final statement is called the **conclusion**. For example, the gardener's conclusion was, *Adding lime to soil with a low pH will improve the production of corn plants.*

Communicating Results

When an experiment has been completed, one or more events may follow. Researchers may repeat the experiment to verify the results. They may publish the experiment so that others can evaluate and replicate their procedures. They may compare their conclusion with the discoveries made by other scientists. And they may raise new questions that lead to new experiments. For example, *Why does the pH level decrease over time when soil is treated with lime?*

Evaluating and Revising

Scientists must be flexible about the conclusions drawn from an experiment. Further research may help confirm the results of the experiment or make it necessary to revise the initial conclusions. For example, a new experiment may show that lime can be effective only when certain microbes are present in the soil. Scientists continuously evaluate and revise experiments based on the findings in new research.

Science Skills

Science Safety

Laboratory work can be exciting, but it can be dangerous if you don't follow safety rules. Ask your teacher to explain any rules you don't understand. Always pay attention to safety symbols and **CAUTION** statements.

General Safety Rules and First Aid

1. Read all directions for an experiment several times. Follow the directions exactly as they are written. If you are in doubt, ask your teacher for assistance.
2. Never perform unauthorized or unsupervised labs, or handle equipment without specific permission.
3. When you design an experiment, do not start until your teacher has approved your plan.
4. If a lab includes physical activity, use caution to avoid injuring yourself or others. Tell your teacher if there is a reason that you should not participate.
5. Never eat, drink, or bring food into the laboratory.
6. Report all accidents to your teacher immediately.
7. Learn the correct ways to deal with a burn, a cut, and acid splashed in your eyes or on your skin.
8. Be aware of the location of the first-aid kit. Your teacher should administer any required first aid.
9. Report any fire to your teacher immediately. Find out the location of the fire extinguisher, the fire alarm, and the phone where emergency numbers are listed.

Dress Code

10. Always wear safety goggles to protect your eyes when working in the lab. Avoid wearing contact lenses. If you must wear contact lenses, ask your teacher what precautions you should take.
11. Wear a laboratory apron to protect your skin and clothing from harmful chemicals or hot materials.
12. Wear disposable plastic gloves to protect yourself from contact with chemicals that can be harmful. Keep your hands away from your face. Dispose of gloves according to your teacher's instructions.
13. Tie back long hair and loose clothing. Remove any jewelry that could contact chemicals or flames.

Heating and Fire Safety

14. Hot plates, hot water, and hot glassware can cause burns. Never touch hot objects with your bare hands. Use an oven mitt or other hand protection.
15. Use a clamp or tongs to hold hot objects. Test an object by first holding the back of your hand near it. If you feel heat on the back of your hand, the object may be too hot to handle.
16. Tie back long hair and loose clothing, and put on safety goggles before using a burner. Follow instructions from your teacher for lighting and extinguishing burners. If the flame leaps out of a burner as you are lighting it, turn the gas off. Never leave a flame unattended or reach across a flame. Make sure your work area is not cluttered with materials.
17. If flammable materials are present, make sure there are no flames, sparks, or exposed sources of heat.
18. Never heat a chemical without your teacher's permission. Chemicals that are harmless when cool can be dangerous when heated. When heating a test tube, point the opening away from you and others in case the contents splash or boil out of the test tube.
19. Never heat a closed container. Expanding hot gases may cause the container to explode.

Using Electricity Safely

20. To avoid an electric shock, never use electrical equipment near water, or when the equipment or your hands are wet. Use ground fault circuit interrupter (GFCI) outlets if you or your equipment may come into contact with moisture.
21. Use only sockets that accept a three-prong plug. Never use two-prong extension cords or adapters. When removing an electrical plug from a socket or extension cord, grasp the plug, not the cord.
22. Disconnect equipment that is not in use. Be sure cords are untangled and cannot trip anyone.
23. Do not use damaged electrical equipment. Look for dangerous conditions such as bare wires or frayed cords. Report damaged equipment immediately.

Using Glassware Safely

24. Handle fragile glassware, such as thermometers, test tubes, and beakers, with care. Do not touch broken glass. Notify your teacher if glassware breaks. Never use chipped or cracked glassware.
25. Never force glass tubing into a stopper. Your teacher will demonstrate the proper methods.
26. Never heat glassware that is not thoroughly dry. Use a wire screen to protect glassware from flames.
27. Hot glassware may not appear hot. Never pick up glassware without first checking to see if it is hot.
28. Never eat or drink from laboratory glassware.

Using Chemicals Safely

29. Do not let any corrosive or poisonous chemicals get on your skin or clothing, or in your eyes. When working with poisonous or irritating vapors, work in a well-ventilated area and wash your hands thoroughly after completing the activity.

30. Never test for an odor unless instructed by your teacher. Avoid inhaling a vapor directly. Use a wafting motion to direct vapor toward your nose.

31. Never mix chemicals "for the fun of it." You might produce a dangerous, possibly explosive substance.

32. Never touch, taste, or smell a chemical that you do not know for certain to be harmless.

33. Use only those chemicals listed in an investigation. Keep the lids on the containers when chemicals are not being used. To avoid contamination, never return chemicals to their original containers.

34. Take extreme care not to spill any chemicals. If a spill occurs, immediately ask your teacher about the proper cleanup procedure. Dispose of all chemicals as instructed by your teacher.

35. Be careful when working with acids or bases. Pour these chemicals over the sink, not over your workbench. If an acid or base gets on your skin or clothing, rinse it off with plenty of cold water. Immediately notify your teacher about an acid or base spill.

36. When diluting an acid, pour the acid into water. Never pour water into the acid.

Using Sharp Instruments

37. Use sharp instruments only as directed. Scissors, scalpels, pins, and knives are sharp and can cut or puncture your skin. Always direct sharp edges and points away from yourself and others.

38. Notify your teacher immediately if you cut yourself when in the laboratory.

End-of-Experiment Rules

39. All chemicals and any other materials used in the laboratory must be disposed of safely. Follow your teacher's instructions.

40. Clean up your work area and return all equipment to its proper place. Thoroughly clean glassware before putting it away.

41. Wash your hands thoroughly with soap, or detergent, and warm water. Lather both sides of your hands and between your fingers. Rinse well.

42. Check that all burners are off and the gas supply for the burners is turned off.

Safety Symbols

 General Safety Awareness
Follow all safety instructions.

 Physical Safety
Use caution in physical activities.

 Safety Goggles
Always wear goggles in the laboratory.

 Lab Apron
Always wear a lab apron in the laboratory.

 Plastic Gloves
Protect your hands from unsafe chemicals.

 Heating
Be careful using sources of heat.

 Heat-Resistant Gloves
Do not touch hot objects with bare hands.

 Flames
Work carefully around open flames.

 No Flames
Flammable materials may be present.

 Electric Shock
Take precautions to avoid electric shock.

 Fragile Glassware
Handle glassware carefully.

 Corrosive Chemical
Work carefully with corrosive chemicals.

 Poison
Avoid contact with poisonous chemicals.

 Fumes
Avoid inhaling dangerous vapors.

 Sharp Object
Use caution with sharp or pointed tools.

 Disposal
Follow instructions for disposal.

 Hand Washing
Wash your hands before leaving the lab.

Reading and Study Skills

At the beginning of each section, you will find a reading strategy to help you study. Each strategy uses a graphic organizer to help you stay organized. The following strategies and graphic organizers are used throughout the text.

Reading Strategies

Using Prior Knowledge

This strategy helps you think about your own experience before you read a section. Research has shown that you learn new material better if you can relate it to something you already know.

Previewing

Previewing a lesson can give you a sense of how the textbook is organized and what lies ahead. One technique is to look at the section topics (in green and blue type). You also can preview by reading captions. Sometimes previewing helps you simply because you find out a topic isn't as hard as you thought it might be.

Predicting

You can preview a section and then make a prediction. For example, you might predict the meaning of an important concept. Then, as you read, check to see if your prediction was correct. Often you find out that you knew more about a topic than you realized.

Building Vocabulary

Start building new vocabulary by previewing a section and listing boldface terms you don't recognize. Then look for each term as you read. Writing a sentence with a term, and defining a term in your own words are two techniques that will help you remember definitions.

Identifying the Main Idea

The key symbols next to boldface sentences identify the main ideas in a section. You can use topic sentences to find the main idea in a paragraph. Often, a topic sentence is the first or second sentence in a paragraph.

Identifying Cause and Effect

Cause-and-effect relationships are very important in science. A flowchart will help you identify cause-and-effect relationships as you read about a process.

Comparing and Contrasting

Comparing and contrasting can help you understand how concepts are related. Comparing is identifying both similarities and differences, while contrasting focuses on the differences. Compare-and-contrast tables and Venn diagrams work best with this strategy.

Sequencing

When you sequence events, it helps you to visualize the steps in a process and to remember the order in which they occur. Sequences often involve cause-and-effect relationships. Use flowcharts for linear sequences and cycle diagrams for repeating sequences.

Relating Text and Figures

You can use diagrams and photographs to focus on the essential concepts in a section. Then find text that extends the information in the figures. You can also reinforce concepts by comparing different figures.

Summarizing

Summarizing requires you to identify key ideas and state them briefly in your own words. You will remember the content of an entire section better even if you summarize only a portion of the section.

Outlining

You can quickly organize an outline by writing down the green and blue headings in a section. Then add phrases or sentences from the boldface sentences to expand the outline with the most important concepts.

Monitoring Your Understanding

You can evaluate your progress with graphic organizers such as a Know-Write-Learn (KWL) table. To make a KWL table, construct a table with three columns, labeled K, W, and L. Before you read, write what you already know in the first column (K). In the middle column, write what you want to learn (W). After you read, write what you learned (L).

Graphic Organizers

Concept Maps and Web Diagrams

A **concept map** is a diagram that contains concept words in ovals and connects the ovals with linking words. Often the most general concept is placed at the top of the map. The content of the other ovals becomes more specific as you move away from the main concept. Linking words are written on a line between two ovals.

A **web diagram** is a type of concept map that shows how several ideas relate to one central idea. Each subtopic may also link to subtopics, creating the visual effect of a spider web. Linking words are usually not included.

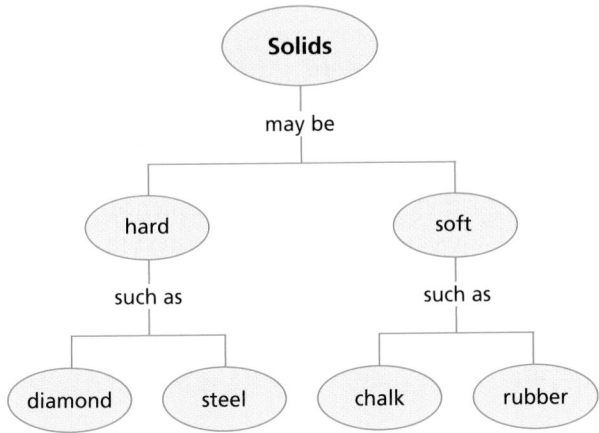

Compare-and-Contrast Tables

A **compare-and-contrast table** is a way of showing the similarities and differences between two or more objects or processes. The table provides an organized framework for making comparisons based on specific characteristics.

The items to be compared are usually column headings across the top of the table. Characteristics for comparison are listed in the first column. You complete the table by filling in information for each item.

Compare-and-Contrast Table		
Contents	Book	CD-ROM
Paper pages	Yes	No
Photographs	Yes	Yes
Videos	No	Yes

Venn Diagrams

A **Venn diagram** consists of two or more ovals that overlap. Each oval represents a particular object or idea. Unique characteristics are shown in the part of each oval that does not overlap. Shared characteristics are shown in the area of overlap.

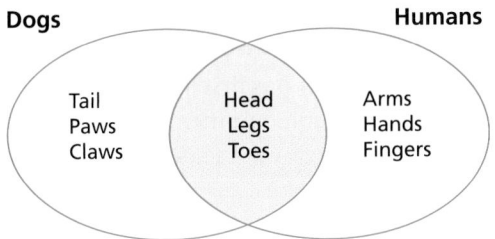

Flowcharts

A **flowchart** is used to represent the order in which a set of events occurs. Each step in the sequence is described in a box. Each box is linked to the next box with an arrow. The flowchart shows a sequence from beginning to end.

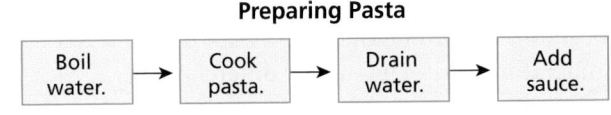

Cycle Diagrams

A **cycle diagram** shows boxes representing a cyclical sequence of events. As in a flowchart, boxes are linked with arrows, but the sequence does not have a beginning or end. The boxes are usually arranged in a clockwise circle.

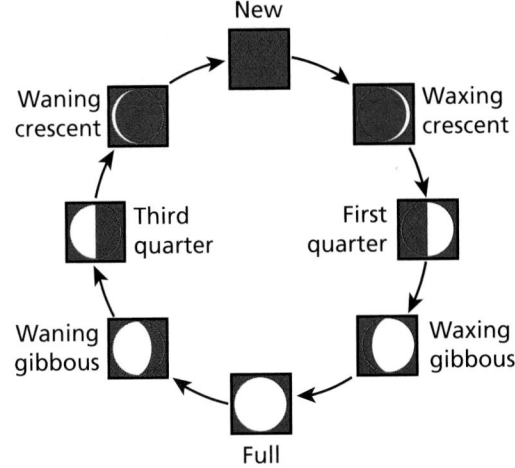

Throughout your study of science, you will often need to solve math problems. This appendix is designed to help you quickly review the basic math skills you will use most often.

Fractions

Adding and Subtracting Fractions

To add or subtract fractions that have the same denominator, add or subtract the numerators, and then write the sum or difference over the denominator. Express the answer in lowest terms.

Examples

$$\frac{3}{10} + \frac{1}{10} = \frac{3+1}{10} = \frac{4}{10} = \frac{2}{5}$$

$$\frac{5}{7} - \frac{2}{7} = \frac{5-2}{7} = \frac{3}{7}$$

To add or subtract fractions with different denominators, find the least common denominator. Write an equivalent fraction for each fraction using the least common denominator. Then add or subtract the numerators. Write the sum or difference over the least common denominator and express the answer in lowest terms.

Examples

$$\frac{1}{3} + \frac{3}{5} = \frac{5}{15} + \frac{9}{15} = \frac{5+9}{15} = \frac{14}{15}$$

$$\frac{7}{8} - \frac{1}{4} = \frac{7}{8} - \frac{2}{8} = \frac{7-2}{8} = \frac{5}{8}$$

Multiplying Fractions

When multiplying two fractions, multiply the numerators to find the product's numerator. Then multiply the denominators to find the product's denominator. It helps to divide any numerator or denominator by the greatest common factor before multiplying. Express the answer in lowest terms.

Examples

$$\frac{3}{5} \times \frac{2}{7} = \frac{3 \times 2}{5 \times 7} = \frac{6}{35}$$

$$\frac{4}{14} \times \frac{6}{9} = \frac{2 \times 2}{7 \times 2} \times \frac{2 \times 3}{3 \times 3} = \frac{2 \times 2}{7 \times 3} = \frac{4}{21}$$

Dividing Fractions

To divide one fraction by another, invert and multiply. Express the answer in lowest terms.

Examples

$$\frac{2}{5} \div \frac{3}{4} = \frac{2}{5} \times \frac{4}{3} = \frac{2 \times 4}{5 \times 3} = \frac{8}{15}$$

$$\frac{9}{16} \div \frac{5}{8} = \frac{9}{16} \times \frac{8}{5} = \frac{9 \times 1}{2 \times 5} = \frac{9}{10}$$

Ratios and Proportions

A ratio compares two numbers or quantities. A ratio is often written as a fraction expressed in lowest terms. A ratio also may be written with a colon.

Examples

The ratio of 3 to 4 is written as 3 to 4, $\frac{3}{4}$, or 3 : 4.

The ratio of 10 to 5 is written as $\frac{10}{5} = \frac{2}{1}$, or 2 : 1.

A proportion is a mathematical sentence that states that two ratios are equivalent. To write a proportion, place an equal sign between the two equivalent ratios.

Examples

The ratio of 6 to 9 is the same as the ratio of 8 to 12.

$$\frac{6}{9} = \frac{8}{12}$$

The ratio of 2 to 4 is the same as the ratio of 7 to 14.

$$\frac{2}{4} = \frac{7}{14}$$

You can set up a proportion to determine an unknown quantity. Use x to represent the unknown. To find the value of x, cross multiply and then divide both sides of the equation by the number that comes before x.

Example

Two out of five students have blue notebooks. If this same ratio exists in a class of twenty students, how many students in the class have blue notebooks?

$$\frac{2}{5} = \frac{x}{20} \qquad \leftarrow \textbf{Cross multiply.}$$

$$2 \times 20 = 5x \qquad \leftarrow \textbf{Divide.}$$

$$8 = x$$

Percents and Decimals

To convert a percent to a decimal value, write the number without the percent sign and move the decimal point two places to the left. Add a zero before the decimal point.

Examples

$$38\% = 0.38$$
$$13.92\% = 0.1392$$

You can convert a decimal value to a percent value by moving the decimal point two places to the right and adding the percent sign.

Examples

$$0.46 = 46\%$$
$$0.8215 = 82.15\%$$

Exponents

A base is a number that is used as a factor. An exponent is a number that tells how many times the base is to be used as a factor.

Example

$$2^5 = 2 \times 2 \times 2 \times 2 \times 2 = 32$$

A power is any number that can be expressed as a product in which all of the factors are the same. Any number raised to the zero power is 1. Any number raised to the first power is that number. The only exception is the number 0, which is zero regardless of the power it is raised to.

Exponents	
Powers of 2	**Powers of 10**
$2^2 = 4$	$10^2 = 100$
$2^1 = 2$	$10^1 = 10$
$2^0 = 1$	$10^0 = 1$
$2^{-1} = \frac{1}{2}$	$10^{-1} = \frac{1}{10}$
$2^{-2} = \frac{1}{4}$	$10^{-2} = \frac{1}{100}$

Multiplying Exponents

To multiply exponential expressions with the same base, add the exponents. The general expression for exponents with the same base is $x^a \times x^b = x^{a+b}$.

Example

$$3^2 \times 3^4 = (3 \times 3) \times (3 \times 3 \times 3 \times 3) = 3^6 = 729$$

To raise a power to a power, keep the base and multiply the exponents. The general expression is $(x^a)^b = x^{ab}$.

Example

$$(3^2)^3 = (3^2) \times (3^2) \times (3^2) = 3^6 = 729$$

To raise a product to a power, raise each factor to the power. The general expression is $(xy)^n = x^n y^n$.

Example

$$(3 \times 9)^2 = 3^2 \times 9^2 = 9 \times 81 = 729$$

Dividing Exponents

To divide exponential expressions with the same base, keep the base and subtract the exponents. The general expression is:

$$\frac{x^a}{x^b} = x^{a-b}$$

Example

$$\frac{5^6}{5^4} = 5^{6-4} = 5^2 = 25$$

When the exponent of the denominator is greater than the exponent of the numerator, the exponent of the result is negative. A negative exponent follows the general expression:

$$x^{-n} = \frac{1}{x^n}$$

Example

$$2^3 \div 2^5 = 2^{3-5} = 2^{-2} = \frac{1}{2^2} = \frac{1}{4}$$

Scientific Notation

Scientific notation is used to express very large numbers or very small numbers. To convert a large number to scientific notation, move the decimal point to the left until it is located to the right of the first nonzero number. The number of places that you move the decimal point becomes the positive exponent of 10.

Example

$18{,}930{,}000 = 1.893 \times 10^7$

To write a number less than 1 in scientific notation, move the decimal point to the right of the first nonzero number. Use the number of places you moved the decimal point as the negative exponent of 10.

Example

$0.0027 = \dfrac{2.7}{10 \times 10 \times 10} = 2.7 \times 10^{-3}$

Adding and Subtracting

To add or subtract numbers in scientific notation, the exponents must be the same. If they are different, rewrite one of the numbers to make the exponents the same. Then write the answer so that only one number is to the left of the decimal point.

Example

$3.20 \times 10^3 + 5.1 \times 10^2$

$$= 32.0 \times 10^2 + 5.1 \times 10^2$$
$$= 37.1 \times 10^2$$
$$= 3.71 \times 10^3$$

Multiplying and Dividing

To multiply or divide numbers in scientific notation, the exponents are added or subtracted.

Examples

$$(1.2 \times 10^3) \times (3.4 \times 10^4) = (4.1 \times 10^{3+4})$$
$$= 4.1 \times 10^7$$

$$(5.0 \times 10^9) \div (2.5 \times 10^6) = (2.0 \times 10^{9-6})$$
$$= 2.0 \times 10^3$$

Significant Figures

When measurements are combined in calculations, the uncertainty of each measurement must be correctly reflected in the final result. The digits that are accurate in the answer are called significant figures. When the result of a calculation has more significant figures than needed, the result must be rounded off. If the first digit after the last significant digit is less than 5, round down. If the first digit after the last significant digit is 5 or more, round up.

Examples

1577 rounded to three significant figures is 1580.
1574 rounded to three significant figures is 1570.
2.458462 rounded to three significant figures is 2.46.
2.458462 rounded to four significant figures is 2.458.

Adding and Subtracting

In addition and subtraction, the number of significant figures in the answer depends on the number with the largest uncertainty.

Example

$$\begin{array}{r} 25.34 \text{ g} \\ 152 \text{ g} \\ +\quad 4.009 \text{ g} \\ \hline 181 \text{ g} \end{array}$$

The measurement with the largest uncertainty is 152 g and it is measured to the nearest gram. Therefore, the answer is given to the nearest gram.

Multiplying and Dividing

In multiplication and division, the measurement with the smallest number of significant figures determines the number of significant figures in the answer.

Example

$$\text{Density} = \dfrac{\text{Mass}}{\text{Volume}}$$
$$= \dfrac{20.79 \text{ g}}{5.5 \text{ mL}}$$
$$= 3.8 \text{ g/mL}$$

Because 5.5 mL has only two significant figures, the answer must be rounded to two significant figures.

Formulas and Equations

An equation is a mathematical sentence that contains one or more variables and one or more mathematical operators (such as $+$, $-$, $\div$, $\times$, and $=$). An equation expresses a relationship between two or more quantities.

A formula is a special kind of equation. A formula such as $V = l \times w \times h$ states the relationship between unknown quantities represented by the variables V, l, w, and h. The formula means that volume (of a rectangular solid) equals length times width times height. Some formulas have numbers that do not vary, such as the formula for the perimeter of a square: $P = 4s$. In this formula, the number 4 is a constant.

To solve for a quantity in an equation or formula, substitute known values for the variables. Be sure to include units.

Example

An airplane travels in a straight line at a speed of 600 km/h. How far does it fly in 3.5 hours?

Write the formula that relates speed, distance, and time.

$$\text{Speed} = \frac{\text{Distance}}{\text{Time}}$$

$$v = \frac{d}{t}$$

To solve for distance, multiply both sides of the equation by t.

$$v = \frac{d}{t}$$
$$v \times t = \frac{d}{t} \times t$$
$$v \times t = d$$

Substitute in the known values.

$$600 \text{ km/h} \times 3.5 \text{ h} = d$$
$$d = 2100 \text{ km}$$

Conversion Factors

Many problems involve converting measurements from one unit to another. You can convert units by using an equation that shows how units are related. For example, 1 in. = 2.54 cm relates inches and centimeters.

To write a conversion factor, divide both sides of the equation by 1 in.

$$\frac{1 \text{ in.}}{1 \text{ in.}} = \frac{2.54 \text{ cm}}{1 \text{ in.}}$$

$$1 = 2.54 \text{ cm/in.}$$

Because the conversion factor is equal to 1, you can multiply one side of an equation by it and preserve equality. You can make a second conversion factor by dividing both sides of the equation by 2.54 cm.

$$\frac{1 \text{ in.}}{2.54 \text{ cm}} = \frac{2.54 \text{ cm}}{2.54 \text{ cm}} = 1$$

One conversion factor converts inches to centimeters and the other converts centimeters to inches. Choose the conversion factor that cancels out the unit that you have a measurement for.

Example

Convert 25 inches to centimeters. Use d to represent the unknown number of centimeters.

$$d = 25 \text{ in.} \times \frac{2.54 \text{ cm}}{1 \text{ in.}}$$
$$= 64 \text{ cm}$$

Some conversions are more complicated and require multiple steps.

Example

Convert 23°F to a Celsius temperature.

The conversion formula is
$$°F = \left(\frac{9}{5} \times °C\right) + 32°F$$

Substitute in 23°F:

$$23°F = \left(\frac{9}{5} \times °C\right) + 32°F$$

$$23°F - 32°F = \frac{9}{5} \times °C$$

$$-9°F = \frac{9}{5} \times °C$$

$$-9°F \times \frac{5}{9} = -5°C$$

Math Skills

Skills Handbook

Data Tables

Data tables help to organize data and make it easier to see patterns in data. If you plan data tables before doing an experiment, they will help you record observations in an orderly fashion.

The data table below shows United States immigration data for the year 2001. Always include units of measurement so people can understand the data.

Immigration to the United States, 2001	
Place of Origin	Number of Legal Immigrants
Africa	53,948
Asia	349,776
Europe	175,371
North America	407,888
South America	68,888

Bar Graphs

To make a bar graph, begin by placing category labels along the bottom axis. Add an overall label for the axis *Place of Origin*. Decide on a scale for the vertical axis. An appropriate scale for the data in the table is 0 to 500,000. Label the vertical axis *Number of People*. For each continent, draw a bar whose height corresponds to the number of immigrants. You will need to round off the values. For example, the bar for Africa should correspond to 54,000 people. Add a graph title to make it clear what the graph shows.

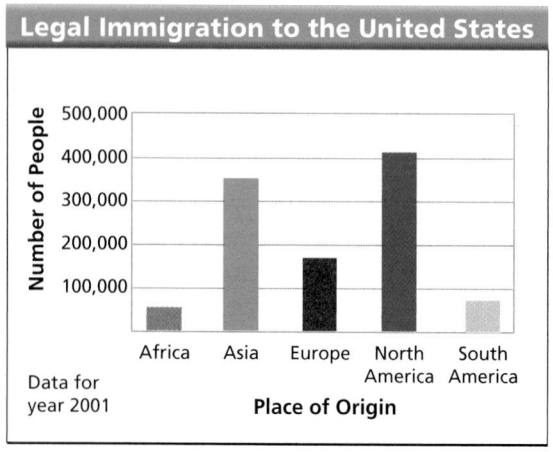

Circle Graphs

Use the total number to calculate percentages. For example, the percentage of immigrants from Africa in 2001 was 53,948 ÷ 1,061,984 = 0.051 ≈ 5%. Multiply each percent by 360° to find the central angle of each wedge. For Africa, the central angle is 18°. Use a protractor to draw each central angle. Color and label the wedges and finish your graph with a title.

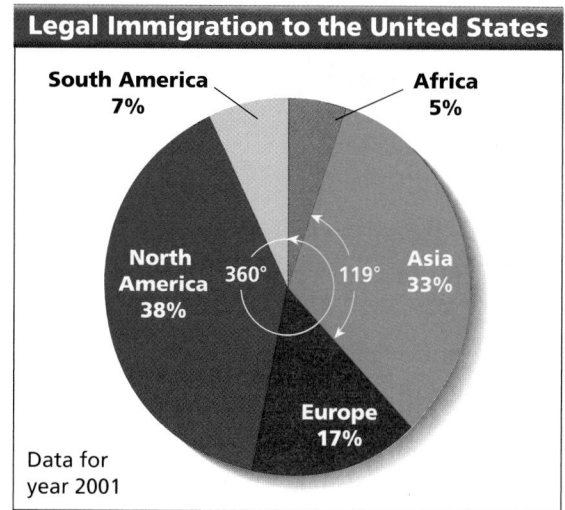

Line Graphs

The slope of a straight-line graph equals the "rise over the run." The rise is the change in the y values and the run is the change in the x values. Using points A and B on the graph below gives

$$\text{Slope} = \frac{\text{Rise}}{\text{Run}} = \frac{5-3}{9-3} = \frac{2}{6} = 0.33$$

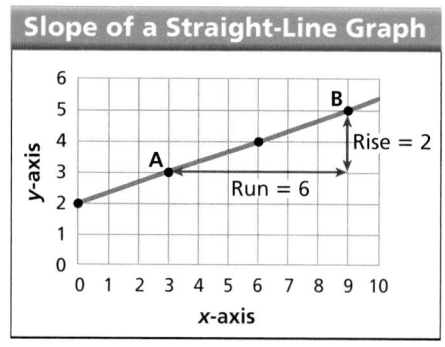

Appendix A SI Units

SI *(Système International d'Unités)* is a revised version of the metric system, which was originally developed in France in 1791. SI units of measurement are used by scientists throughout the world. The system is based on multiples of ten. Each unit is ten times larger or ten times smaller than the next unit. The most commonly used SI units are given below.

You can use conversion factors to convert between SI and non-SI units. Try the following conversions. How tall are you in meters? What is your weight in newtons? What is your normal body temperature in degrees Celsius?

Commonly Used Metric Units

Length	The distance from one point to another
meter (m)	A meter is slightly longer than a yard.
	1 meter = 1000 millimeters (mm)
	1 meter = 100 centimeters (cm)
	1000 meters = 1 kilometer (km)

Volume	The amount of space an object takes up
liter (L)	A liter is slightly more than a quart.
	1 liter = 1000 milliliters (mL)

Mass	The amount of matter in an object
gram (g)	A gram has a mass equal to about one paper clip.
	1000 grams = 1 kilogram (kg)

Temperature	The measure of hotness or coldness
degrees Celsius (°C)	0°C = freezing point of water at sea level
	100°C = boiling point of water at sea level

Metric–Customary Equivalents

2.54 centimeters (cm) = 1 inch (in.)
1 meter (m) = 39.37 inches (in.)
1 kilometer (km) = 0.62 miles (mi)
1 liter (L) = 1.06 quarts (qt)
250 milliliters (mL) = 1 cup (c)
9.8 newtons (N) = 2.2 pounds (lb)
$°C = 5/9 \times (°F - 32)$

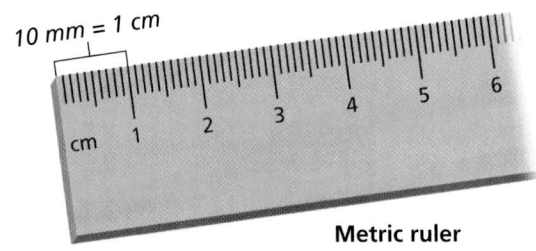

10 mm = 1 cm

Metric ruler

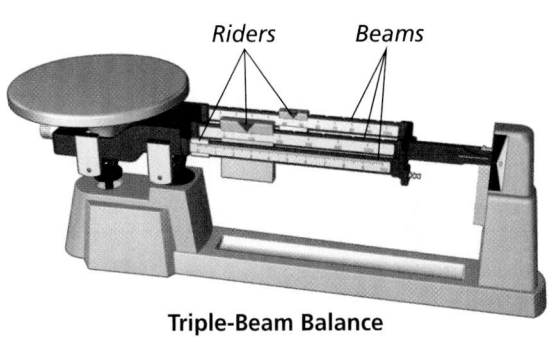

Riders   Beams

Triple-Beam Balance

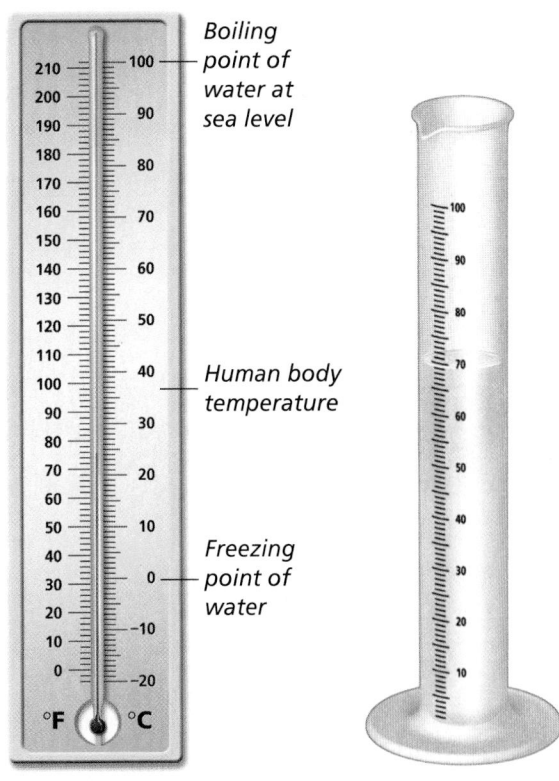

Boiling point of water at sea level

Human body temperature

Freezing point of water

Thermometer

Graduated cylinder

Appendices

The laboratory balance is an important tool in scientific investigations. You can use a balance to determine the masses of materials that you study or experiment with in the laboratory.

Different kinds of balances are used in the laboratory. One kind of balance is the triple-beam balance. The balance that you may use in your science class is probably similar to the balance illustrated. To use the balance properly, you should learn the name, location, and function of each part of the balance you are using.

The Triple-Beam Balance

The triple-beam balance is a single-pan balance with three beams The back, or 100-gram, beam is divided into ten units of 10 grams. The middle, or 500-gram, beam is divided into five units of 100 grams. The front, or 10-gram, beam is divided into ten major units, each of which is 1 gram. Each 1-gram unit is further divided into units of 0.1 gram. What is the largest mass you could measure with a triple-beam balance?

The following procedure can be used to find the mass of an object with a triple-beam balance.

1. When no object is on the pan, and the riders are at zero, make sure the pointer is at zero. If it is not, use the adjustment screw to zero the balance.
2. Place the object on the pan.
3. Move the rider on the middle beam notch by notch until the horizontal pointer drops below zero. Move the rider back one notch.
4. Move the rider on the back beam notch by notch until the pointer again drops below zero. Move the rider back one notch.
5. Slowly slide the rider along the front beam until the pointer stops at zero. The mass of the object is the sum of the readings on the three beams.

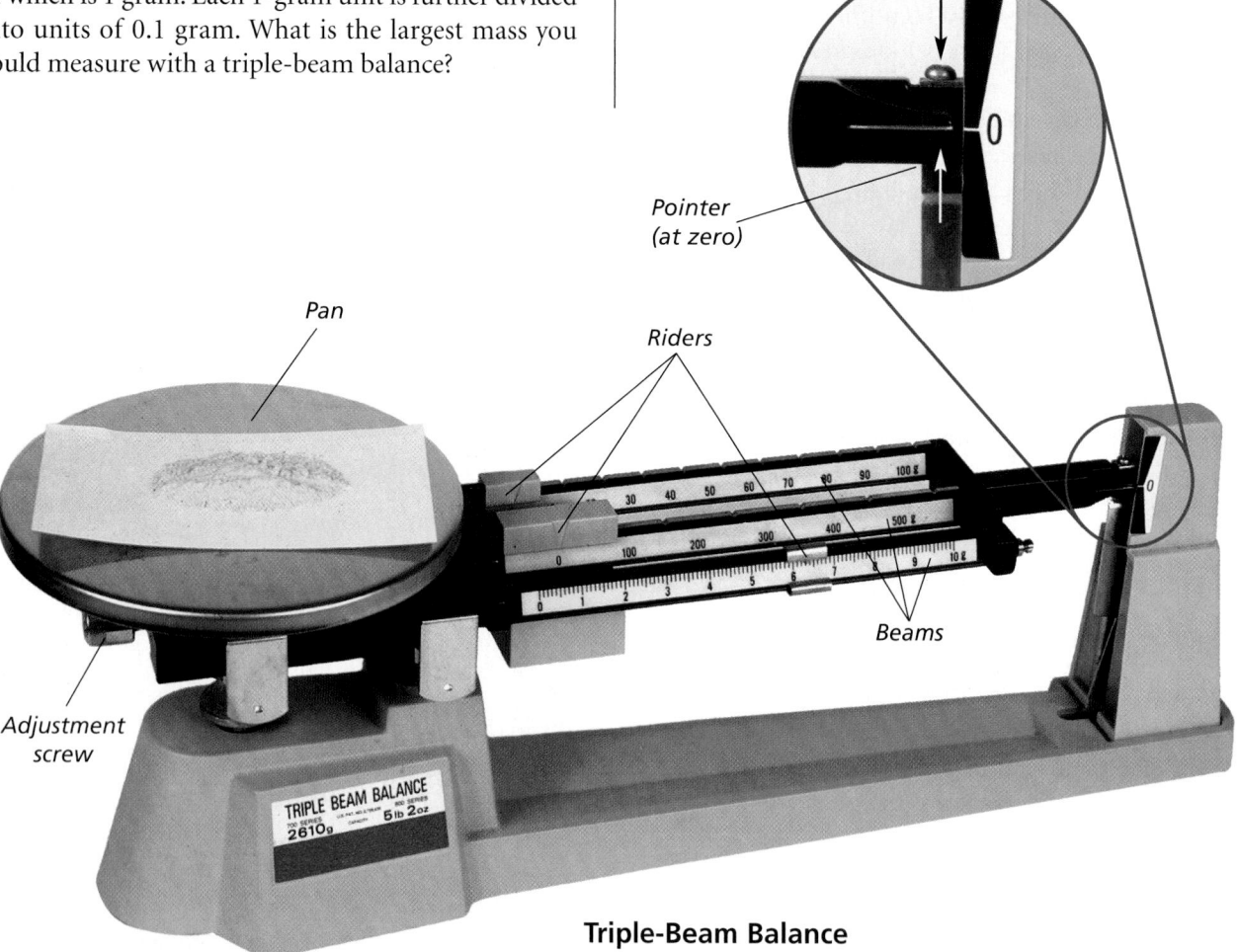

Pointer
(at zero)

Pan

Riders

Adjustment
screw

Beams

Triple-Beam Balance

Appendices

Element	Symbol	Atomic Number	Atomic Mass†	Element	Symbol	Atomic Number	Atomic Mass†
Actinium	Ac	89	(277)	Neodymium	Nd	60	144.24
Aluminum	Al	13	26.982	Neon	Ne	10	20.179
Americium	Am	95	(243)	Neptunium	Np	93	(237)
Antimony	Sb	51	121.75	Nickel	Ni	28	58.71
Argon	Ar	18	39.948	Niobium	Nb	41	92.906
Arsenic	As	33	74.922	Nitrogen	N	7	14.007
Astatine	At	85	(210)	Nobelium	No	102	(259)
Barium	Ba	56	137.33	Osmium	Os	76	190.2
Berkelium	Bk	97	(247)	Oxygen	O	8	15.999
Beryllium	Be	4	9.0122	Palladium	Pd	46	106.4
Bismuth	Bi	83	208.98	Phosphorus	P	15	30.974
Bohrium	Bh	107	(264)	Platinum	Pt	78	195.09
Boron	B	5	10.81	Plutonium	Pu	94	(244)
Bromine	Br	35	79.904	Polonium	Po	84	(209)
Cadmium	Cd	48	112.41	Potassium	K	19	39.098
Calcium	Ca	20	40.08	Praseodymium	Pr	59	140.91
Californium	Cf	98	(251)	Promethium	Pm	61	(145)
Carbon	C	6	12.011	Protactinium	Pa	91	231.04
Cerium	Ce	58	140.12	Radium	Ra	88	(226)
Cesium	Cs	55	132.91	Radon	Rn	86	(222)
Chlorine	Cl	17	35.453	Rhenium	Re	75	186.21
Chromium	Cr	24	51.996	Rhodium	Rh	45	102.91
Cobalt	Co	27	58.933	Rubidium	Rb	37	85.468
Copper	Cu	29	63.546	Ruthenium	Ru	44	101.07
Curium	Cm	96	(247)	Rutherfordium	Rf	104	(261)
Dubnium	Db	105	(262)	Samarium	Sm	62	150.4
Dysprosium	Dy	66	162.50	Scandium	Sc	21	44.956
Einsteinium	Es	99	(252)	Seaborgium	Sg	106	(263)
Erbium	Er	68	167.26	Selenium	Se	34	78.96
Europium	Eu	63	151.96	Silicon	Si	14	28.086
Fermium	Fm	100	(257)	Silver	Ag	47	107.87
Fluorine	F	9	18.998	Sodium	Na	11	22.990
Francium	Fr	87	(223)	Strontium	Sr	38	87.62
Gadolinium	Gd	64	157.25	Sulfur	S	16	32.06
Gallium	Ga	31	69.72	Tantalum	Ta	73	180.95
Germanium	Ge	32	72.59	Technetium	Tc	43	(98)
Gold	Au	79	196.97	Tellurium	Te	52	127.60
Hafnium	Hf	72	178.49	Terbium	Tb	65	158.93
Hassium	Hs	108	(265)	Thallium	Tl	81	204.37
Helium	He	2	4.0026	Thorium	Th	90	232.04
Holmium	Ho	67	164.93	Thulium	Tm	69	168.93
Hydrogen	H	1	1.0079	Tin	Sn	50	118.69
Indium	In	49	114.82	Titanium	Ti	22	47.90
Iodine	I	53	126.90	Tungsten	W	74	183.85
Iridium	Ir	77	192.22	Ununbium	Uub*	112	(277)
Iron	Fe	26	55.847	Ununnilium	Uun*	110	(269)
Krypton	Kr	36	83.80	Ununquadium	Uuq*	114	—
Lanthanum	La	57	138.91	Unununium	Uuu*	111	(272)
Lawrencium	Lr	103	(262)	Uranium	U	92	238.03
Lead	Pb	82	207.2	Vanadium	V	23	50.941
Lithium	Li	3	6.941	Xenon	Xe	54	131.30
Lutetium	Lu	71	174.97	Ytterbium	Yb	70	173.04
Magnesium	Mg	12	24.305	Yttrium	Y	39	88.906
Manganese	Mn	25	54.938	Zinc	Zn	30	65.38
Meitnerium	Mt	109	(268)	Zirconium	Zr	40	91.22
Mendelevium	Md	101	(258)				
Mercury	Hg	80	200.59				
Molybdenum	Mo	42	95.94				

† Number in parentheses gives the mass number of the most stable isotope.

* Name not officially assigned

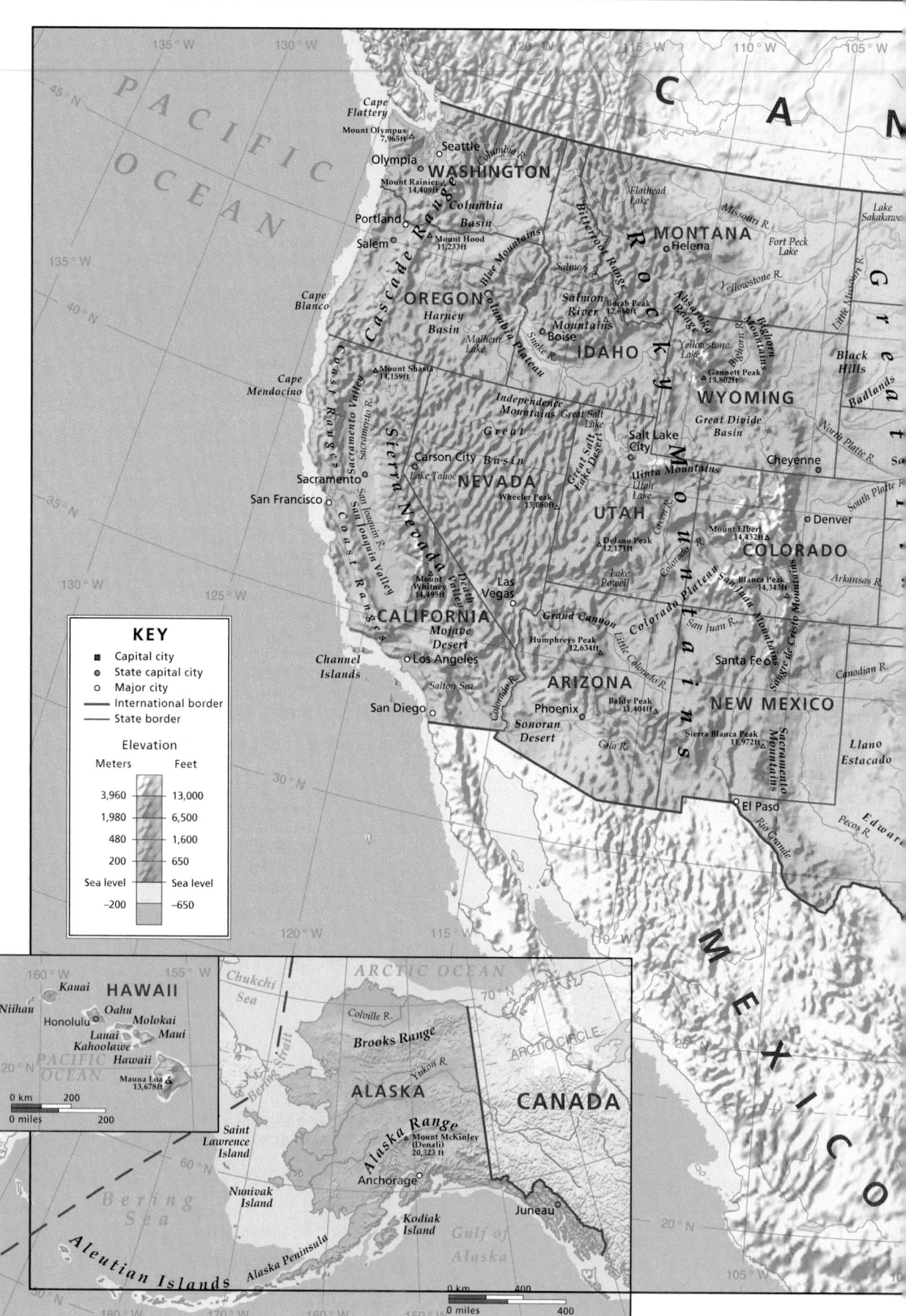

KEY

■ Capital city
● State capital city
○ Major city
— International border
— State border

Elevation

Meters	Feet
3,960	13,000
1,980	6,500
480	1,600
200	650
Sea level	Sea level
−200	−650

Appendices

This weather map shows data collected from many weather stations.
Below the map is an explanation of what the symbols mean.

Weather Map

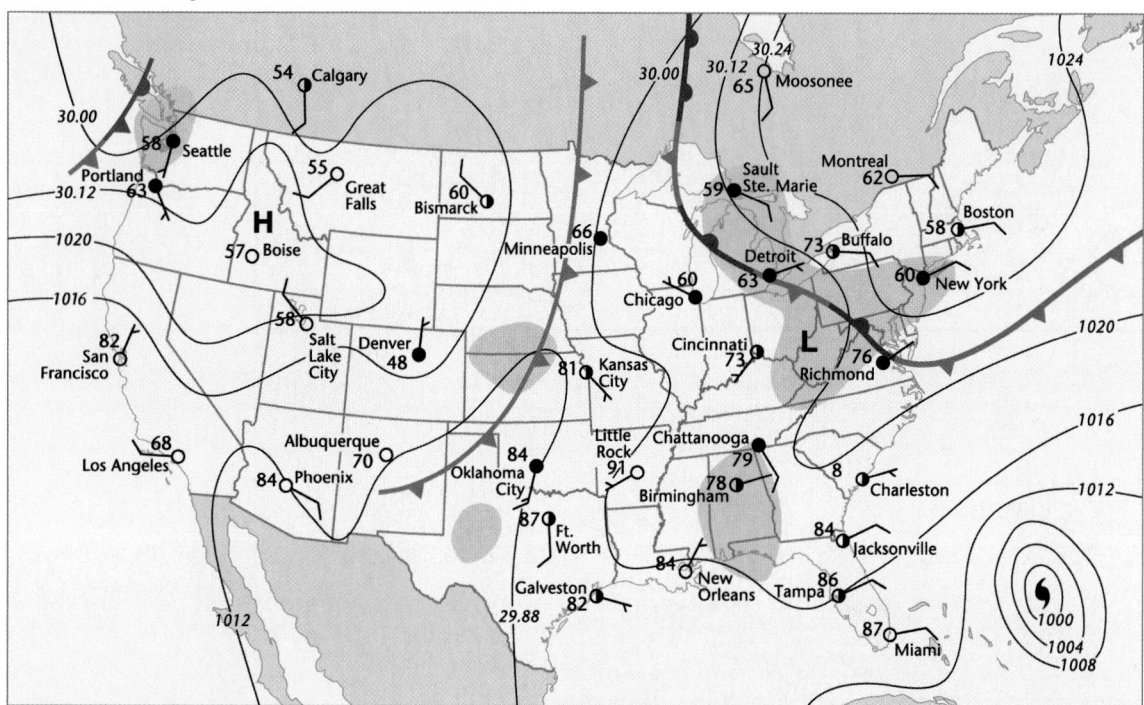

Explanation of Fronts

Cold Front
Boundary between a cold air mass and a warm air mass. Brings brief storms and cooler weather.

Warm Front
Boundary between a warm air mass and a cold air mass. Usually accompanied by precipitation.

Stationary Front
Boundary between warm and cold air masses when no movement occurs. Long periods of precipitation.

Occluded Front
Boundary on which a warm front has been overtaken by a cold front. Brings precipitation.

Weather	Symbol
Drizzle	,
Fog	≡
Hail	△
Haze	∞
Rain	●
Shower	▽
Sleet	⍍
Smoke	⌇
Snow	✳
Thunderstorm	↳
Hurricane	◗

Wind Speed (mph)	Symbol
1–2	
3–8	
9–14	
15–20	
21–25	
26–31	
32–37	
38–43	
44–49	
50–54	
55–60	
61–66	
67–71	
72–77	

Cloud Cover (%)	Symbol
0	○
10	◐
20–30	◔
40	◑
50	◑
60	◕
70–80	◕
90	◑
100	●

How Symbols Are Used on a Weather Map

Amount of cloud cover (100%)

Atmospheric pressure (millibars)

Temperature (°F)

38 ● 1018

Wind direction (from the southwest)

Wind speed (21–25 mph)

To find the relative humidity, measure the wet-bulb and dry-bulb temperatures with a sling psychrometer. Find the dry-bulb reading in the left column and the difference between readings at the top of the table. The number where these readings intersect is the relative humidity in percent.

Relative Humidity (percent)														
Dry-Bulb Reading (°C)	Difference Between Wet-Bulb and Dry-Bulb Readings (°C)													
	1	2	3	4	5	6	7	8	9	10	11	12	13	14
5	86	72	58	45	33	20	7							
6	86	73	60	48	35	24	11							
7	87	74	62	50	38	26	15							
8	87	75	63	51	40	29	19	8						
9	88	76	64	53	42	32	22	12						
10	88	77	66	55	44	34	24	15	6					
11	89	78	67	56	46	36	27	18	9					
12	89	78	68	58	48	39	29	21	12					
13	89	79	69	59	50	41	32	23	15	7				
14	90	79	70	60	51	42	34	26	18	10				
15	90	80	71	61	53	44	36	27	20	13	6			
16	90	81	71	63	54	46	38	30	23	15	8			
17	90	81	72	64	55	47	40	32	25	18	11			
18	91	82	73	65	57	49	41	34	27	20	14	7		
19	91	82	74	65	58	50	43	36	29	22	16	10		
20	91	83	74	66	59	51	44	37	31	24	18	12	6	
21	91	83	75	67	60	53	46	39	32	26	20	14	9	
22	92	83	76	68	61	54	47	40	34	28	22	17	11	6
23	92	84	76	69	62	55	48	42	36	30	24	19	13	8
24	92	84	77	69	62	56	49	43	37	31	26	20	15	10
25	92	84	77	70	63	57	50	44	39	33	28	22	17	12
26	92	85	78	71	64	58	51	46	40	34	29	24	19	14
27	92	85	78	71	65	58	52	47	41	36	31	26	21	16
28	93	85	78	72	65	59	53	48	42	37	32	27	22	18
29	93	86	79	72	66	60	54	49	43	38	33	28	24	19
30	93	86	79	73	67	61	55	50	44	39	35	30	25	21

Autumn Sky

To use this chart, hold it up in front of you and turn it so the direction you are facing is at the bottom of the chart. The chart works best at 35° N latitude, but it can be used at other latitudes. It works best at the following dates and times: September 1 at 10:00 P.M., October 1 at 8 P.M., and November 1 at 6 P.M.

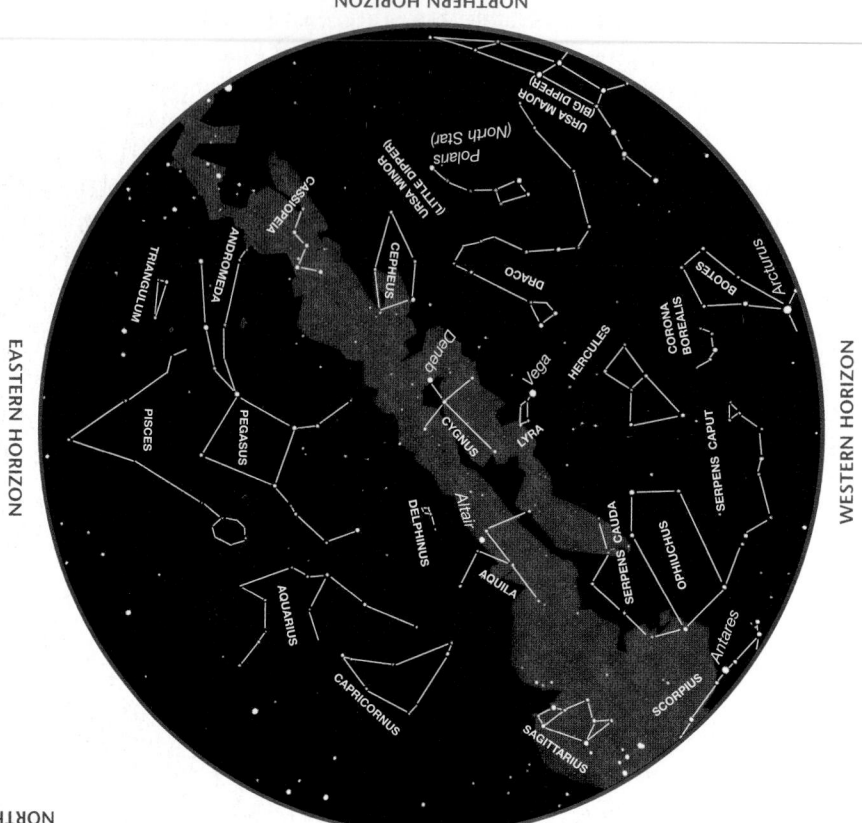

Winter Sky

To use this chart, hold it up in front of you and turn it so the direction you are facing is at the bottom of the chart. The chart works best at 35° N latitude, but it can be used at other latitudes. It works best at the following dates and times: December 1 at 10:00 P.M., January 1 at 8 P.M., and February 1 at 6 P.M.

Spring Sky

To use this chart, hold it up in front of you and turn it so the direction you are facing is at the bottom of the chart. The chart works best at 35° N latitude, but it can be used at other latitudes. It works best at the following dates and times: March 1 at 10:00 P.M. and April 1 at 8 P.M.

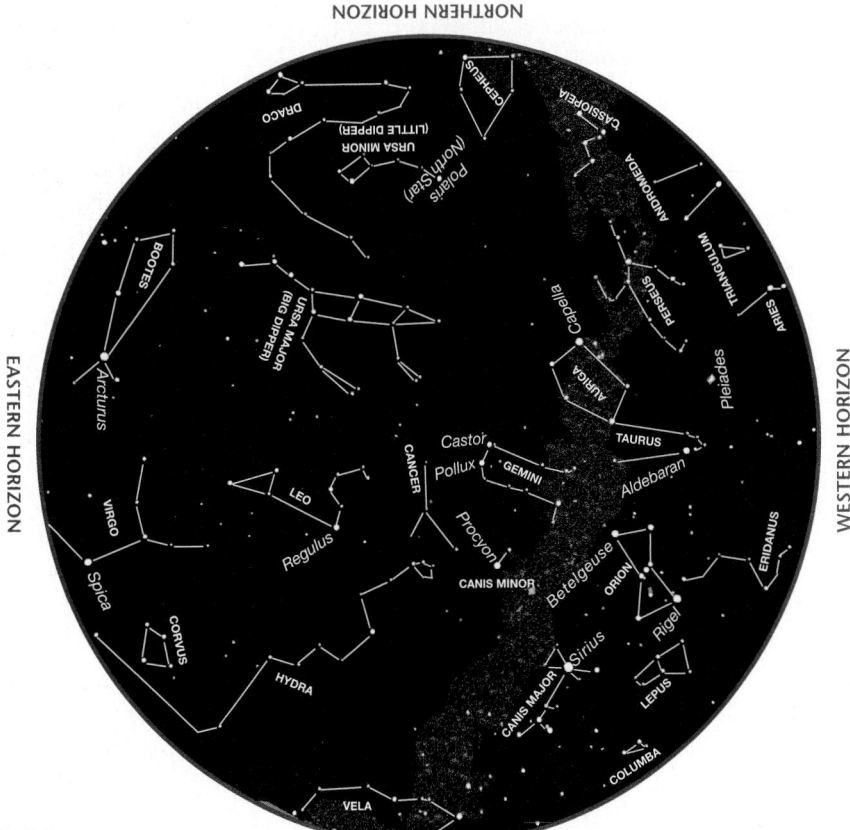

Summer Sky

To use this chart, hold it up in front of you and turn it so the direction you are facing is at the bottom of the chart. The chart works best at 35° N latitude, but it can be used at other latitudes. It works best at the following dates and times: May 15 at 11:00 P.M. and June 15 at 9 P.M.

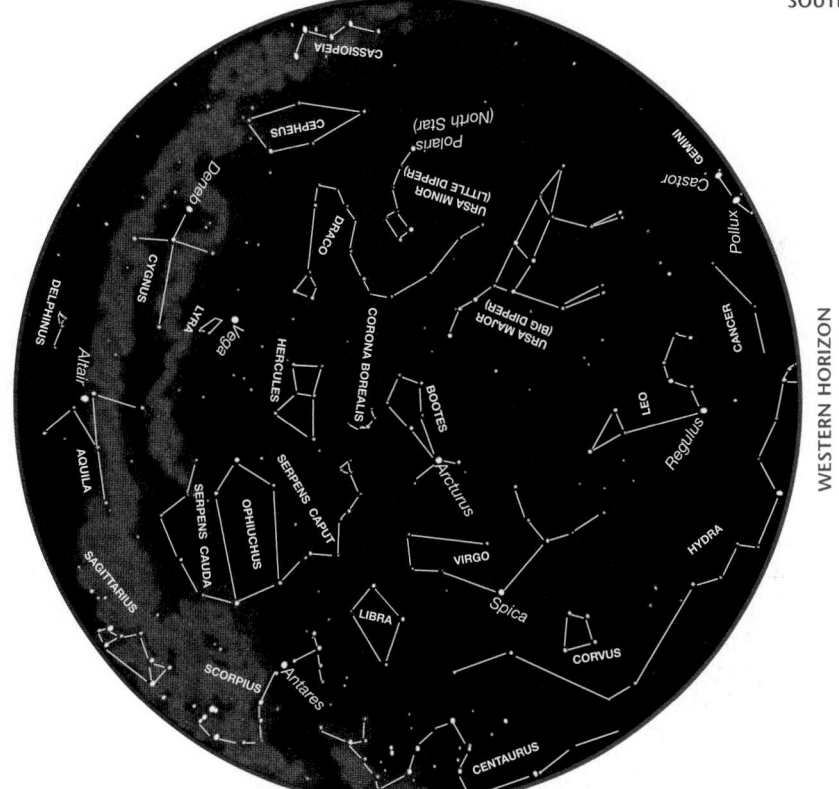

Dew-point temperature (°C)

Dry bulb (°C)	1	2	3	4	5	6	7	8	9	10	11	12	13	14	15	16	17	18	19	20	21	22
−20	−33																					
−18	−28																					
−16	−24																					
−14	−21	−36																				
−12	−18	−28																				
−10	−14	−22																				
−8	−12	−18	−29																			
−6	−10	−14	−22																			
−4	−7	−12	−17	−29																		
−2	−5	−8	−13	−20																		
0	−3	−6	−9	−15	−24																	
2	−1	−3	−6	−11	−17																	
4	1	−1	−4	−7	−11	−19																
6	4	1	−1	−4	−7	−13	−21															
8	6	3	1	2	−5	−9	−14															
10	8	6	4	1	−2	−5	−9	−14	−18													
12	10	8	6	4	1	−2	−5	−9	−16													
14	12	11	9	6	4	1	−2	−5	−10	−17												
16	14	13	11	9	7	4	1	−1	−6	−10	−17											
18	16	15	13	11	9	7	4	2	−2	5	10	−19										
20	19	17	15	14	12	10	7	4	2	−2	−5	−10	−19									
22	21	19	17	16	74	12	10	8	5	3	−1	−5	−10	−19								
24	23	21	20	18	16	14	12	10	8	6	2	−1	−5	−10	−18							
26	25	23	22	20	18	17	15	13	11	9	6	3	0	−4	−9	−18						
28	27	25	24	22	27	19	17	16	14	11	9	7	4	1	−3	−9	16					
30	29	27	26	24	23	21	19	18	16	14	12	70	8	5	1	−2	−8	−15				
32	31	29	28	27	25	24	22	21	19	17	15	13	11	8	5	2	−2	−7	−14			
34	33	31	30	29	27	26	24	23	21	20	18	16	14	12	9	6	3	−1	−5	−12	−29	
36	35	33	32	31	29	28	27	25	24	22	20	19	17	15	13	10	7	4	0	−4	−10	
38	37	35	34	33	32	30	29	28	26	25	23	21	19	17	15	13	11	8	5	1	−3	9
40	39	37	36	35	34	32	31	30	28	27	25	24	22	20	18	16	14	12	9	6	2	−2

(Dry-Bulb Temperature Minus Wet-Bulb Temperature = Depression of the Wet Bulb)

Dry-Bulb (Air) Temperature

Dew-Point Values

The map on the next page shows the generalized pattern of global soil orders according to the *Comprehensive Soil Classification System* (CSCS). It should be examined in conjunction with the table below, which briefly describes each of the soil orders depicted on the map. To avoid subjective decisions as to classification (a problem that plagued earlier systems), the CSCS defined its classes strictly in terms of soil characterisitics. That is, it is based on features that can be observed or inferred.

The CSCS uses a hierarchy of six categories, or levels. The system recognizes 10 major global *orders* that can be further subdivided into *suborders, great groups, subgroups, families,* and *series.* Note, however, that on the scale of a world map, only the largest units (soil orders) can be shown and then only in an extremely generalized way. Although the distribution pattern of major soil orders is more complex than can be shown, the major distinguishing regional properties of world soils are depicted.

World Soil Orders.

Entisols	Youngest soils on the Earth. Just beginning to develop in response to the weathering phenomena in the environment. Do not display natural horizons. Found in all climates. They weather slowly over thousands of years; consequently, volcanic ash deposits or sand deposits form the basis for entisols.
Vertisols	Soils containing large amounts of clay, which shrink upon drying and swell with the addition of water. Found in subhumid to arid climates, provided that adequate supplies of water are available to saturate the soil after periods of drought. Soil expansion and contraction exert stresses on human structures.
Inceptisols	Young soils that reveal developmental characteristics (horizons) in response to climate and vegetation. Exist from the Arctic to the tropics on young land surfaces. Common in alpine areas, on river floodplains, in stables and dune areas, and in areas once glaciated.
Aridsols	Soils that develop in dry places, such as the desert, where water—precipitation and groundwater—is insufficient to remove soluble minerals. Frequently irrigated for intensive agricultural production, although salt accumulation poses a problem.
Mollisols	Dark, soft soils that have developed under grass vegetation, generally found in prairie areas. Soil fertility is excellent because potential evaporation generally exceeds precipitation. Also found in hardwood forests with significant earthworm activity. Climatic range is boreal or alpine to tropical. Dry seasons are normal.
Spodosols	Soils found only in humid regions on sandy material. Range from the boreal coniferous forests into tropical forests. Beneath the dark upper horizon of weathered organic material lies a light-colored horizon of leached material, the distinctive property of this soil.
Alfisols	Mineral soils that form under boreal forests or broadleaf deciduous forests, rich in iron and aluminum. Clay particles accumulate in a subsurface layer in response to leaching in moist environments. Fertile, productive soils, because they are neither too wet nor too dry.
Ultisols	Soils that represent the products of long periods of weathering. Water percolating through the soil concentrates clay particles in the lower horizons (argillic horizons). Restricted to humid climates in the temperate regions and the tropics where the growing season is long. Abundant water and a long frost-free period contribute to extensive leaching, hence poorer soil quality.
Oxisols	Soils that occur on old land surfaces unless parent materials were strongly weathered before they were deposited. Generally found in the tropics and subtropical regions. Rich in iron and aluminum oxides, oxisols are heavily leached; hence are poor soils for agricultural activity. Few, if any, exist in the United States.
Histosols	Organic soils with little or no climatic implications. Can be found in any climate where organic debris can accumulate to form a bog soil. Dark, partially decomposed organic material commonly referred to as *peat.*

Source: Robert E. Norris et al., *Geography: An Introductory Perspective*, Columbus, Ohio: Merrill, 1982.

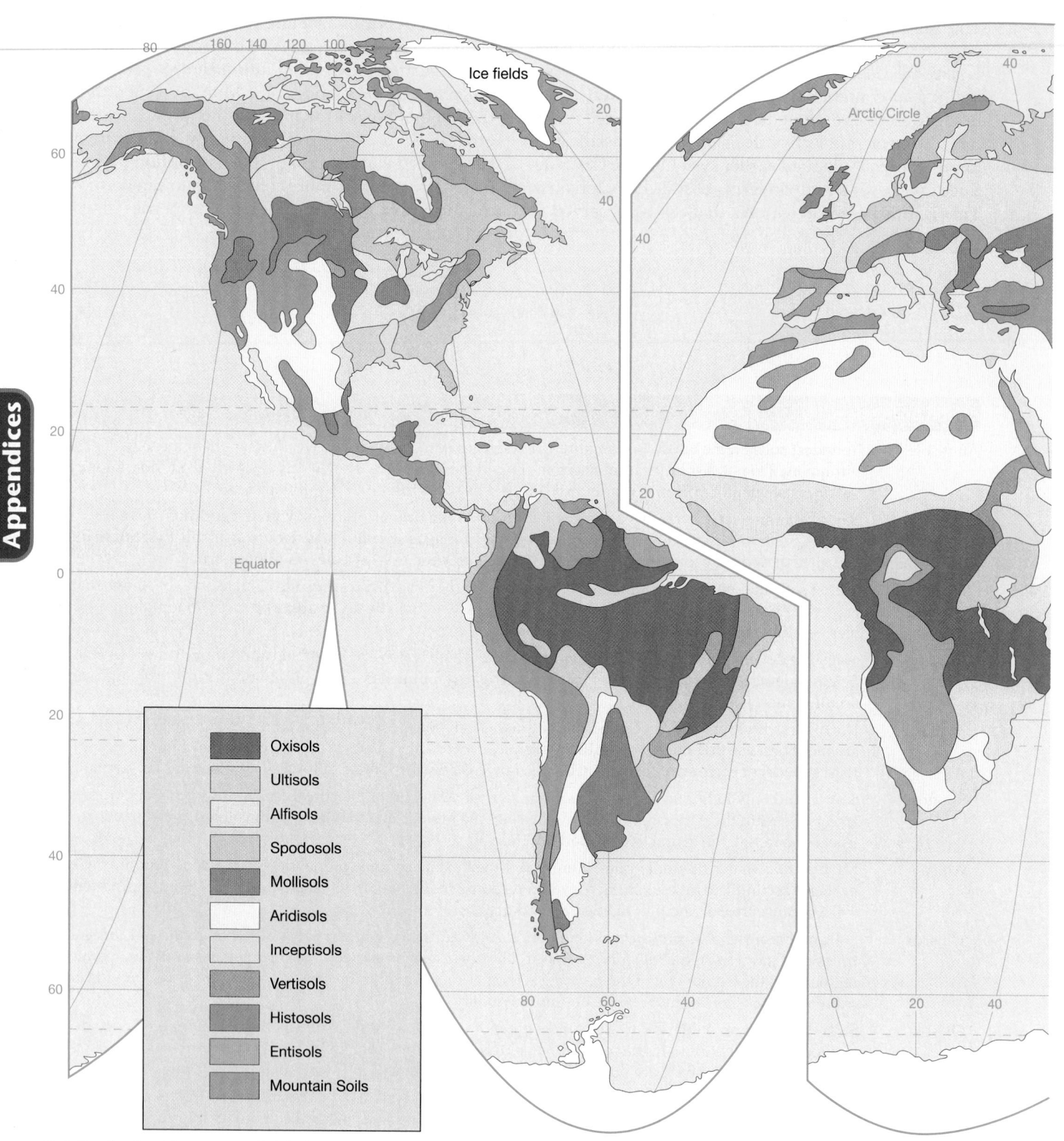

Soil distribution. The pattern of global soil orders is remarkably similar to the pattern of major climates. Soil classification is from the *Comprehensive Soil Classification System*.

Legend:
- Oxisols
- Ultisols
- Alfisols
- Spodosols
- Mollisols
- Aridisols
- Inceptisols
- Vertisols
- Histosols
- Entisols
- Mountain Soils

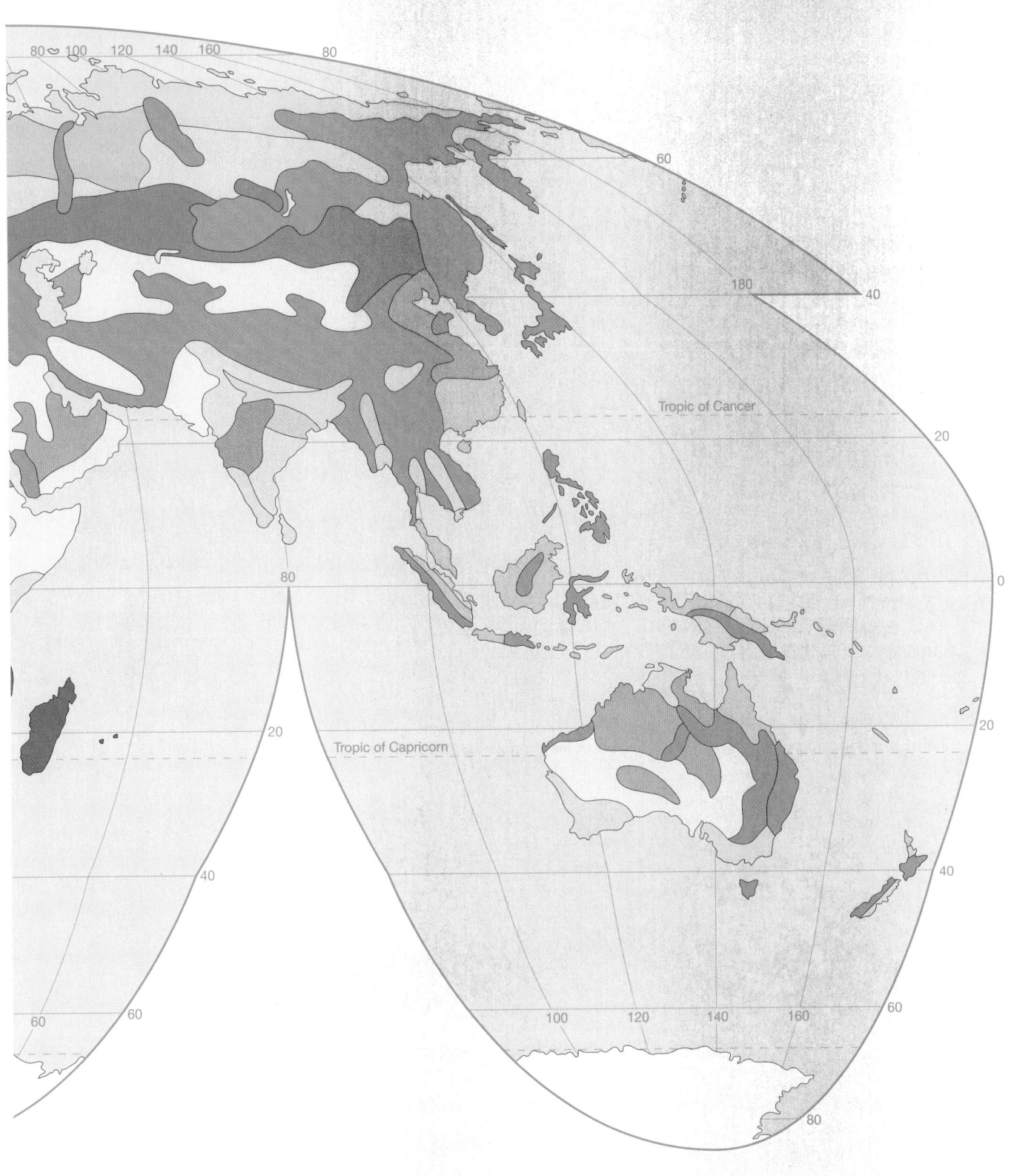

Tropic of Cancer

Tropic of Capricorn

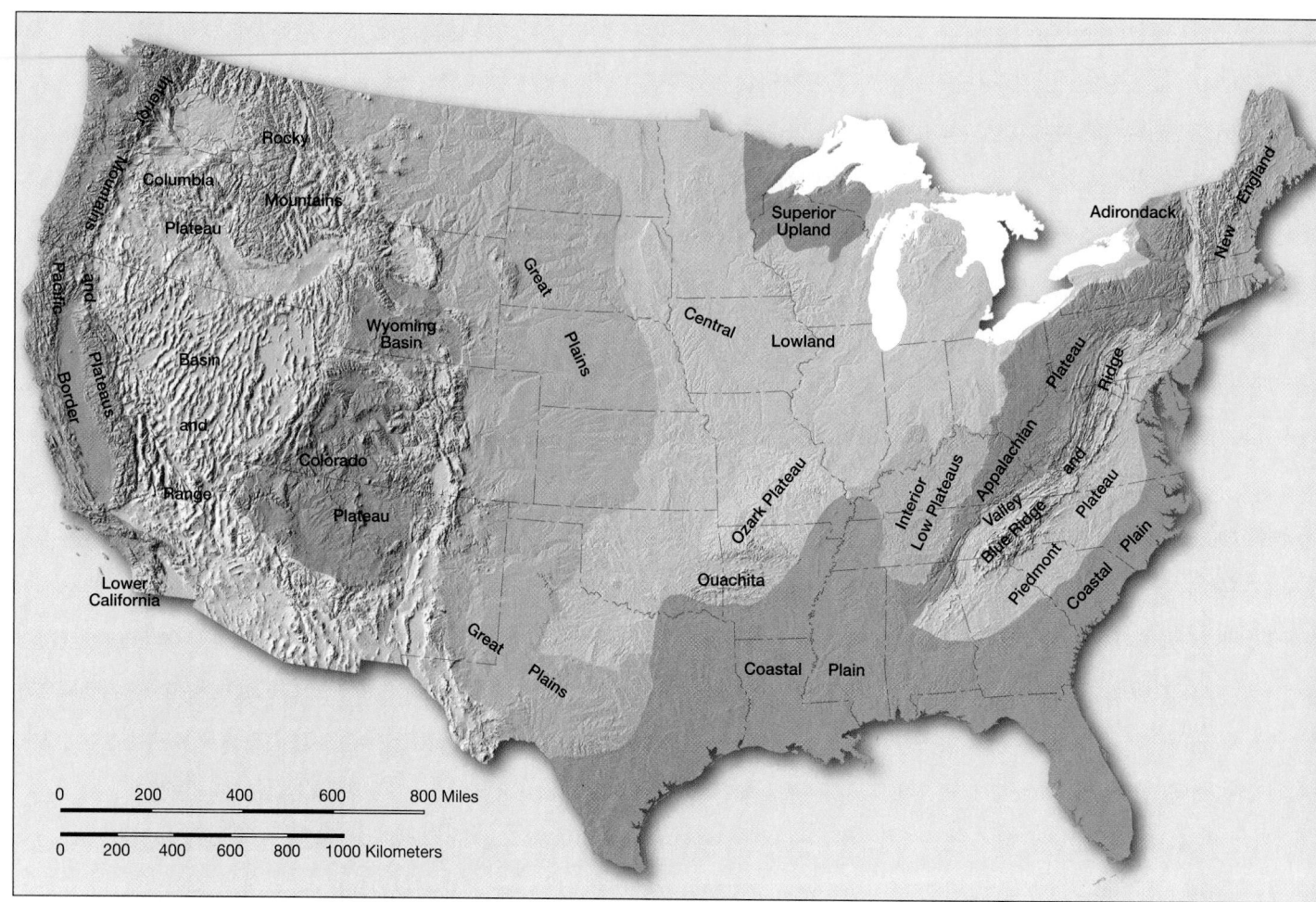

Outline map showing major physiographic provinces of the contiguous United States.

Landforms of the Contiguous United States

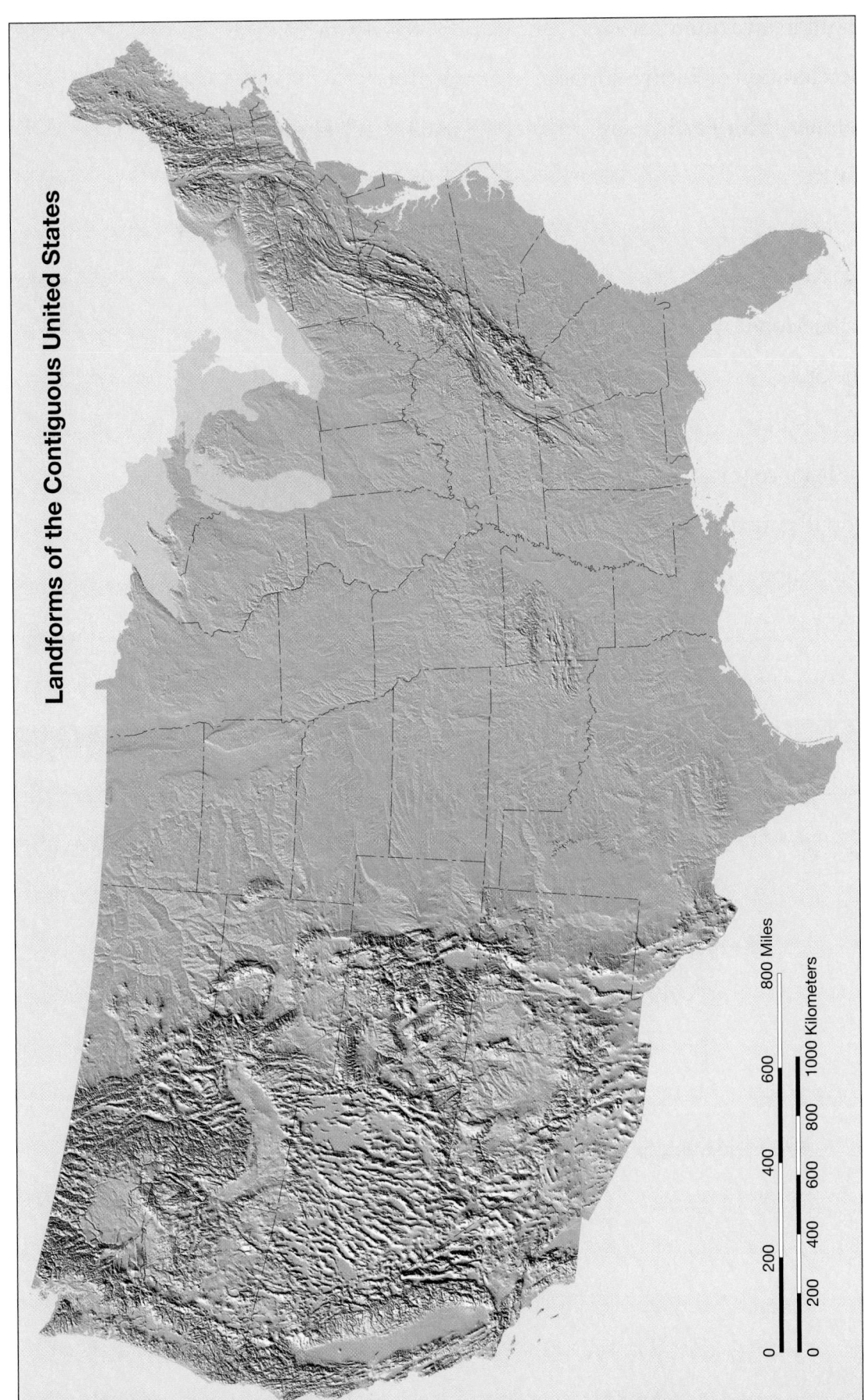

Digital shaded relief landform map of the United States. (Data provided by the U.S. Geological Survey)

Speed of light in a vacuum	3.00×10^8 m/s
Free fall acceleration of Earth's surface	9.81 m/s^2
Moment of inertia for Earth	8.03×10^{31} kg$\bullet$m^2
Mass of Earth	5.98×10^{24} kg
Radius of Earth	6.37×10^6 m
Mass of the Moon	7.35×10^{22} kg
Radius of the Moon	1.74×10^6 m
Mass of the Sun	1.99×10^{30} kg
Radius of the Sun	6.96×10^5 km
Earth-Sun distance (mean)	1.496×10^8 km
Earth-Moon distance (mean)	3.84×10^5 km
Earth's gravitational constant	6.67×10^{11} N$\bullet$m^2/kg^2

Some SI Derived Units

Quantity	Unit name	Abbreviation
Force	newton	N
Energy and work	joule	J
Power	watt	W
Pressure	pascal	Pa

A

absolute magnitude the apparent brightness of a star if it were viewed from a distance of 32.6 light-years; used to compare the true brightness of stars (p. 703)

absolute magnitude/magnitud absoluta luminosidad aparente de una estrella si se observara a una distancia de 32.6 años luz; usada para comparar la luminosidad real de las estrellas (pág. 703)

absorption spectrum a continuous spectrum produced when white light is passed through a cool gas under low pressure; The gas absorbs selected wavelengths of light, and the spectrum looks like it has dark lines superimposed. (p. 676)

absorption spectrum/espectro de absorción espectro continuo producido cuando pasa luz blanca a través de un gas frío a presión baja; el gas absorbe determinadas longitudes de onda de luz y el espectro pareciera tener líneas oscuras superpuestas (pág. 676)

abyssal plain very level area of the deep-ocean floor, usually lying at the foot of the continental rise (p. 404)

abyssal plain/planicie abisal área muy nivelada del fondo oceánico profundo, que se encuentra por lo general en la base del pie continental (pág. 404)

abyssal zone a subdivision of the benthic zone characterized by extremely high pressures, low temperatures, low oxygen, few nutrients, and no sunlight (p. 431)

abyssal zone/zona abisal subdivisión de la zona bentónica caracterizada por tener presiones extremadamente altas, bajas temperaturas, poco oxígeno, pocas sustancias nutrientes y ausencia de luz solar (pág. 431)

accretion process that occurs when crustal fragments collide with and stay connected to a continental plate (p. 321)

accretion/acreción proceso que ocurre cuando los fragmentos corticales chocan con una placa continental y permanecen conectados a ella (pág. 321)

accretionary wedge a large wedge-shaped mass of sediment that accumulates in subduction zones; Here sediment is scraped from the subducting oceanic plate and accreted to the overriding crustal block. (p. 319)

accretionary wedge/prisma acrecionario masa grande de sedimento en forma de prisma que se acumula en las zonas de subducción; el sedimento es raspado de la placa oceánica de subducción y acrecentado al bloque cortical preponderante (pág. 319)

aftershock a small earthquake that follows the main earthquake (p. 221)

aftershock/réplica terremoto pequeño que sigue al terremoto mayor (pág. 221)

air mass a large body of air that is characterized by similar temperatures and amounts of moisture at any given altitude (p. 559)

air mass/masa de aire cuerpo grande de aire que se caracteriza por tener temperatura y humedad similares a cualquier altitud dada (pág. 559)

air pressure the force exerted by the weight of a column of air above a given point (p. 532)

air pressure/ presión de aire fuerza ejercida por el peso de una columna de aire sobre un punto dado (pág. 532)

albedo the fraction of total radiation that is reflected back by a surface (p. 492)

albedo/albedo fracción de la radiación total que es reflejada por una superficie (pág. 492)

alluvial fan a fan-shaped deposit of sediment formed when a stream's slope is abruptly reduced (p. 201)

alluvial fan/abanico alluvial depósito de sedimentos en forma de abanico, formado cuando la vertiente de una corriente de agua se reduce abruptamente (pág. 201)

andesitic composition the composition of igneous rocks lying between felsic and mafic (p. 73)

andesitic composition/composición andesítica composición de rocas ígneas que se encuentra entre las rocas félsicas y máficas (pág. 73)

anemometer an instrument used to determine wind speed (p. 545)

anemometer/anemómetro instrumento usado para determinar la velocidad del viento (pág. 545)

Glossary

angiosperm flowering plant that produces seeds within a fruit (p. 383)

angiosperm/angiosperma planta que da flores y produce semillas dentro de una fruta (pág. 383)

anticline a fold in sedimentary strata resembling an arch (p. 310)

anticline/anticlinal pliegue en el estrato sedimentario que parece un arco (pág. 310)

anticyclone a high-pressure center characterized by a clockwise flow of air in the Northern Hemisphere (p. 538)

anticyclon/anticiclón centro de alta presión en el hemisferio norte que se caracteriza por una masa de aire que se mueve en dirección de las agujas del reloj (pág. 538)

aphelion the place in the orbit of a planet where the planet is farthest from the sun (p. 624)

aphelion/afelio punto en la órbita de un planeta en el que éste se encuentra más alejado del Sol (pág. 624)

apogee the point where the moon is farthest from Earth (p. 626)

apogee/apogeo punto donde la Luna se encuentra más alejada de la Tierra (pág. 626)

apparent magnitude the brightness of a star when viewed from Earth (p. 703)

apparent magnitude/magnitud aparente luminosidad de una estrella vista desde la Tierra (pág. 703)

aquifer rock or soil through which groundwater moves easily (p. 171)

aquifer/acuífero roca o tierra a través de la cual el agua subterránea se mueve fácilmente (pág. 171)

artesian well a well in which the water naturally rises above the level of the water table (p. 173)

artesian well/pozo artesiano pozo en el cual el agua sube naturalmente por encima del nivel freático (pág. 173)

asteroid a small, rocky body, which can range in size from a few hundred kilometers to less than a kilometer; The asteroids' orbits lie mainly between those of Mars and Jupiter. (p. 661)

asteroid/asteroide cuerpo rocoso y pequeño, cuyo tamaño puede variar entre cientos de kilómetros a menos de un kilómetro; las órbitas de los asteroides se encuentran principalmente entre las órbitas de Marte y Júpiter (pág. 661)

asthenosphere a weak plastic layer of the mantle situated below the lithosphere; The rock within this zone is easily deformed. (p. 235)

asthenosphere/astenosfera capa plástica y débil del manto situada debajo de la litosfera; la roca en esta zona se deforma fácilmente (pág. 235)

astronomical unit (AU) average distance from Earth to the sun; 1.5×10^8, or 150 million kilometers (p. 618)

astronomical unit (AU)/unidad astronómica (UA) distancia promedio de la Tierra al Sol; 1.5×10^8, ó 150 millones de kilómetros (pág. 618)

astronomy the scientific study of the universe; It includes the observation and interpretation of celestial bodies and phenomena. (p. 3)

astronomy/astronomía estudio científico del universo; incluye la observación y la interpretación de cuerpos y fenómenos celestes (pág. 3)

atmosphere the gaseous portion of a planet; the planet's envelope of air; one of the traditional subdivisions of Earth's physical environment (p. 7)

atmosphere/atmósfera porción gaseosa de un planeta; envoltura de aire del planeta; una de las subdivisiones tradicionales del medio ambiente físico de la Tierra (pág. 7)

atomic number the number of protons in the nucleus of an atom (p. 35)

atomic number/número atómico número de protones en el núcleo de un átomo (pág. 35)

aurora a bright display of ever-changing light caused by solar radiation interacting with the upper atmosphere in the region of the poles (p. 688)

aurora/aurora polar luz brillante en constante movimiento causada por la radiación solar que interactúa con la parte superior de la atmósfera en la región de los polos (pág. 688)

autumnal equinox the equinox that occurs on September 22 or 23 in the Northern Hemisphere and on March 21 or 22 in the Southern Hemisphere (p. 482)

autummal equinox/equinoccio de otoño equinoccio que ocurre el 22 ó 23 de septiembre en el hemisferio norte y el 21 ó 22 de marzo en el hemisferio sur (pág. 482)

B

barometer an instrument that measures atmospheric pressure (p. 533)

barometer/barómetro instrumento que mide la presión atmosférica (pág. 533)

barrier island a low, elongated ridge of sand that parallels the coast (p. 466)

barrier island/isla barrera lomo de arena bajo y alargado que se encuentra paralelo a la costa (pág. 466)

basaltic composition a compositional group of igneous rocks indicating that the rock contains substantial dark silicate minerals and calcium-rich plagioclase feldspar (p. 73)

basaltic composition/composición basáltica grupo composicional de rocas ígneas que indica que la roca contiene cantidades sustanciales de minerales de silicato oscuros y feldespato de plagioclasa rico en calcio (pág. 73)

batholith a large mass of igneous rock that formed when magma intruded at depth, became crystallized, and subsequently was exposed by erosion; Batholiths have a surface exposure greater than 100 square kilometers. (p. 290)

batholith/batolito masa grande de roca ígnea que se forma cuando el magma penetra en la profundidad, se cristaliza y luego queda expuesta debido a la erosión; los batolitos tienen una superficie expuesta mayor a los 100 kilómetros cuadrados (pág. 290)

bathymetry the measurement of ocean depths and the charting of the shape or topography of the ocean floor (p. 396)

bathymetry/batimetría medición de las profundidades marinas y trazado de la forma o topografía del fondo marino (pág. 396)

beach the accumulation of sediment found along the shore of a lake or an ocean (p. 461)

beach/playa acumulación de sedimento que se encuentra a lo largo de la costa de un lago u océano (pág. 461)

bed load sediment that is carried by a stream along the bottom of its channel (p. 165)

bed load/carga del lecho sedimento arrastrado por una corriente de agua a lo largo del fondo de su canal (pág. 165)

benthic zone 0the marine-life zone that includes any sea-bottom surface regardless of its distance from shore (p. 431)

benthic zone/zona béntica zona de vida marina que incluye cualquier superficie del fondo del mar sin importar su distancia de la costa (pág. 431)

benthos the forms of marine life that live on or in the ocean bottom; includes marine algae, sea stars, and crabs (p. 429)

benthos/bentos organismos marinos que viven en el fondo marino; incluyen algas marinas, estrellas de mar y cangrejos (pág. 429)

Bergeron process a theory that relates the formation of precipitation to supercooled clouds, freezing nuclei, and the different saturation levels of ice and liquid water (p. 521)

Bergeron process/proceso de Bergeron teoría que relaciona la formación de precipitación con nubes sobreenfriadas, núcleos congelados y los diferentes niveles de saturación del agua helada y el agua líquida (pág. 521)

big bang theory the theory that proposes that the universe originated as a single mass, which subsequently exploded (p. 720)

big bang theory/teoría del Big Bang teoría que propone que el universo se originó como una masa única, la cual estalló posteriormente (pág. 720)

binary star one of two stars revolving around a common center of mass under their mutual gravitational attraction (p. 701)

binary star/estrella binaria una de dos estrellas que giran alrededor de un centro de masa común atraídas por su fuerza gravitacional mutua (pág. 701)

biogenous sediment seafloor sediment of biological origin, such as shells and skeletons of marine life (p. 408)

biogenous sediment/sedimento biogénico sedimento del fondo marino de origen biológico, como conchas y esqueletos de organismos marinos (pág. 408)

biosphere all life on Earth; the parts of the solid Earth, hydrosphere, and atmosphere in which living organisms can be found (p. 7)

biosphere/biosfera toda la vida en la Tierra; partes de la Tierra sólida, la hidrosfera y la atmósfera en las que se encuentran los organismos vivos (pág. 7)

black hole a massive star that has collapsed to such a small volume that its gravity prevents the escape of everything, including light (p. 714)

black hole/agujero negro estrella masiva que se ha reducido a un volumen tan pequeño que su fuerza de gravedad no permite que nada se escape, incluyendo la luz (pág. 714)

C

calcareous ooze thick, common biogenous sediment produced by dissolving calcium carbonate shells (p. 408)

calcareous ooze/fango calcáreo sedimento biógeno común y grueso, producido por la disolución de conchas de carbonato de calcio (pág. 408)

caldera a large depression typically caused by collapse or ejection of the summit area of a volcano (p. 287)

caldera/caldera depresión grande causada típicamente por el colapso o la expulsión de la cima de un volcán (pág. 287)

capacity the total amount of sediment a stream is able to transport (p. 165)

capacity/capacidad cantidad total de sedimento que puede transportar una corriente de agua (pág. 165)

cavern a naturally formed underground chamber or series of chambers most commonly produced by solution activity in limestone (p. 176)

cavern/caverna cámara subterráneas o serie de cámaras subterráneas formadas naturalmente y producidas comúnmente por actividad de solución sobre piedra caliza (pág. 176)

cementation solidification of sediments by the deposition of dissolved minerals in the tiny spaces between the sedimentary particles (p. 76)

cementation/cementación solidificación de sedimentos por el depósito de minerales disueltos en los espacios diminutos entre las partículas sedimentarias (pág. 76)

Cepheid variable a star whose brightness varies periodically because it expands and contracts; a type of pulsating star (p. 705)

Cepheid variable/variable Cefeida estrella cuya luminosidad varía periódicamente porque se expande y se contrae; tipo de estrella púlsar (pág. 705)

chemical bond a force that holds together atoms that form a compound (p. 38)

chemical bond/enlace químico fuerza que une los átomos que forman un compuesto (pág. 38)

chemical sedimentary rock sedimentary rock consisting of material that was precipitated from water by either inorganic or organic means (p. 77)

chemical sedimentary rock/roca sedimentaria química roca sedimentaria formada de material precipitado del agua por medios inorgánicos u orgánicos (pág. 77)

chemical weathering the processes by which the internal structure of a mineral is altered by the removal and/or addition of elements (p. 129)

chemical weathering/meteorización química proceso mediante el cual la estructura interna de un mineral es alterada por la extracción y/o la suma de elementos (pág. 129)

chemosynthesis the process by which certain microorganisms use chemical energy to produce food (p. 433)

chemosynthesis/quimiosíntesis proceso por el cual ciertos microorganismos usan energía química para producir alimento (pág. 433)

chromatic aberration the property of a lens whereby light of different colors is focused at different places (p. 679)

chromatic aberration/aberración cromática propiedad de una lente en la cual se enfoca luz de diferentes colores en distintos lugares (pág. 679)

chromosphere the first layer of the solar atmosphere found directly above the photosphere (p. 686)

chromosphere/cromosfera primera capa de la atmósfera solar que se encuentra directamente por encima de la fotosfera (pág. 686)

cinder cone a small volcano built primarily of pyroclastic material ejected from a single vent (p. 284)

cinder cone/cono de escoria volcán pequeño formado principalmente de material piroclástico expulsado por una sola abertura (pág. 284)

cirque an amphitheater-shaped basin at the head of a glaciated valley produced by frost wedging and plucking (p. 193)

cirque/circo cuenca en forma de anfiteatro en la cabecera de un valle glaciar producida por la erosión de hielo (pág. 193)

cirrus one of three basic cloud forms; also one of the three high cloud types; They are thin, delicate ice-crystal clouds often appearing as veil-like patches or thin, wispy fibers. (p. 517)

cirrus/cirro una de las tres formaciones básicas de las nubes; también uno de los tres tipos de nubes altas; son nubes cristalinas delicadas que parecen retazos de velo o fibras tenues y finas (pág. 517)

clastic sedimentary rock a sedimentary rock made of broken fragments of preexisting rock (p. 77)

clastic sedimentary rock/roca sedimentaria clástica roca sedimentaria hecha de fragmentos rotos de roca preexistente (pág. 77)

cleavage the tendency of a mineral to break along planes of weak bonding (p. 52)

cleavage/clivaje tendencia de un mineral a fracturarse a lo largo de planos de enlace débiles (pág. 52)

cold front a front along which a cold air mass thrusts beneath a warmer air mass (p. 566)

cold front/frente frío frente en el que una masa de aire frío avanza bajo una masa de aire caliente (pág. 566)

collision-coalescence process a theory of raindrop formation in warm clouds (above 0°C) in which large cloud droplets collide and join together with smaller droplets to form a raindrop; Opposite electrical charges may bind the cloud droplets together. (p. 521)

collision-coalescence process/proceso de coalescencia y colisión teoría sobre la formación de gotas de agua en nubes cálidas (por encima de los 0 °C), en la cual las gotas grandes de agua en una nube chocan y se unen con gotitas más pequeñas para formar una gota de mayor tamaño; las corrientes eléctricas opuestas pueden unir las gotitas (pág. 521)

coma the fuzzy, gaseous component of a comet's head (p. 662)

coma/coma componente gaseoso y difuso que rodea el núcleo de un cometa (pág. 662)

comet a small body made of rocky and metallic pieces held together by frozen gases; Comets generally revolve about the sun in an elongated orbit. (p. 661)

comet/cometa cuerpo pequeño formado por materiales rocosos y metálicos unidos por medio de gases congelados; los cometas generalmente giran alrededor del Sol en una órbita alargada (pág. 661)

compaction process by which sediments are squeezed together by the weight of overlying materials driving out water (p. 76)

compaction/compactación proceso por el cual los sedimentos se unen y expulsan agua debido al peso de los materiales que los cubren (pág. 76)

composite cone a volcano composed of both lava flows and pyroclastic material (p. 285)

composite cone/estratovolcán volcán compuesto de flujos de lava y material piroclástico (pág. 285)

compost partly decomposed organic material that is used as fertilizer (p. 115)

compost/compost material orgánico parcialmente descompuesto que se usa como fertilizante (pág. 115)

compound a substance formed by the chemical combination of two or more elements in definite proportions and usually having properties different from those of its constituent elements (p. 37)

compound/compuesto sustancia formada por la combinación química de dos o más elementos en proporciones definidas y que tiene usualmente propiedades diferentes a las de los elementos que la componen (pág. 37)

condensation the change of state from a gas to a liquid (p. 506)

condensation/condensación cambio de estado de un gas a un líquido (pág. 506)

condensation nuclei tiny bits of particulate matter that serve as surfaces on which water vapor condenses (p. 516)

condensation nuclei/núcleos de condensación partículas muy pequeñas de materia que sirven como superficies para que se condense el vapor (pág. 516)

conduction the transfer of heat through matter by molecular activity; Energy is transferred through collisions from one molecule to another. (p. 483)

conduction/conducción transferencia de calor a través de la materia por actividad molecular; la energía se transfiere a través de choques de una molécula contra otra (pág. 483)

conservation the careful use of resources (p. 113)

conservation/conservación uso cuidadoso de los recursos (pág. 113)

constellation an apparent group of stars originally named for mythical characters; The sky is presently divided into 88 constellations. (p. 700)

constellation/constelación grupo aparente de estrellas nombrado originalmente a partir de personajes míticos; el cielo se encuentra en la actualidad dividido en 88 constelaciones (pág. 700)

contact metamorphism changes in rock caused by the heat from a nearby magma body (p. 81)

contact metamorphism/metamorfismo de contacto cambios en una roca causados por el calor de una masa de magma cercano (pág. 81)

continental drift a hypothesis that originally proposed that the continents had once been joined to form a single supercontinent; The supercontinent broke into pieces, which drifted into their present-day positions. (p. 248)

continental drift/deriva continental hipótesis que propuso originalmente que los continentes estuvieron unidos formando un solo supercontinente; el supercontinente se quebró en pedazos, los cuales se desplazaron hasta sus posiciones actuales (pág. 248)

continental glacier a very large, thick mass of glacial ice that covers a large region and flows outward in all directions from one or more accumulation centers; also called a continental ice sheet (p. 189)

continental glacier/glaciar continental masa muy grande y gruesa de hielo glacial que cubre una región grande y fluye hacia afuera en todas direcciones desde uno o más centros de acumulación; también se le llama capa de hielo continental (pág. 189)

continental margin that portion of the seafloor adjacent to the continents; It may include the continental shelf, continental slope, and continental rise. (p. 402)

continental margin/margen continental porción del suelo marino adyacente a los continentes; puede incluir la plataforma continental, el talud continental y el pie continental (pág. 402)

continental rise the gently sloping surface at the base of the continental slope (p. 403)

continental rise/pie continental superficie que se encuentra levemente en declive en la base del talud continental (pág. 403)

continental shelf the gently sloping submerged portion of the continental margin, extending from the shoreline to the continental slope (p. 402)

continental shelf/plataforma continental porción sumergida y levemente en declive del margen continental, que se extiende desde la costa hasta el talud continental (pág. 402)

continental slope the steep gradient that leads to the deep-ocean floor and marks the seaward edge of the continental shelf (p. 403)

continental slope/talud continental pendiente empinada que conduce al suelo marino profundo y marca el límite de la plataforma continental que da al mar (pág. 403)

continental volcanic arc mountains formed in part by volcanic activity caused by the subduction of oceanic lithosphere beneath a continent (p. 261)

continental volcanic arc/arco volcánico continental montañas formadas en parte por actividad volcánica causada por la subducción de la litosfera volcánica debajo de un continente (pág. 261)

continuous spectrum an uninterrupted band of light emitted by an incandescent solid, liquid, or gas under pressure (p. 676)

continuos spectrum/espectro continuo banda de luz continua emitida por un sólido, un líquido o un gas incandescente bajo presión (pág. 676)

contour interval on a topographic map, tells the distance in elevation between adjacent contour lines (p. 14)

contour interval/intervalo entre curvas de nivel en un mapa topográfico, indica la diferencia de altitud entre dos curvas de nivel adyacentes (pág. 14)

contour line line on a topographic map that indicates an elevation; Every point along a contour line has the same elevation. (p. 14)

contour line/curva de nivel línea en un mapa topográfico que indica una altitud; todos los puntos a lo largo de una curva de nivel tienen la misma altitud (pág. 14)

convection the transfer of heat by the movement of a mass or substance; It can take place only in fluids. (p. 484)

convection/convección transferencia de calor por el movimiento de una masa o sustancia; puede ocurrir sólo en líquidos (pág. 484)

convective flow the motion of matter resulting from changes in temperature; The convective flow of material in the mantle is due to Earth's unequal heating and causes the tectonic plates to move. (p. 269)

convective flow/flujo convectivo movimiento de materia resultante de cambios en la temperatura; el flujo convectivo de material en el manto se debe al calentamiento desigual de la tierra y hace que las placas tectónicas se muevan (pág. 269)

convergent boundary a boundary in which two plates move together (p. 255)

convergent boundary/límite convergente límite en el cual dos placas se muevan juntas (pág. 255)

core the innermost layer of Earth, located beneath the mantle; The core is divided into an outer core and an inner core. (p. 8)

core/núcleo capa más interna de la tierra, ubicada debajo del manto; el núcleo está dividido en un núcleo exterior y un núcleo interior (pág. 8)

Coriolis effect the apparent deflective force of Earth's rotation on all free-moving objects, including the atmosphere and oceans; Deflection is to the right in the Northern Hemisphere and to the left in the Southern Hemisphere. (p. 449)

Coriolis effect/efecto de Coriolis aparente fuerza desviadora que la rotación de la Tierra ejerce sobre todos los objetos que están en movimiento libre, incluyendo la atmósfera y los océanos; el desvío es hacia la derecha en el hemisferio norte y hacia la izquierda en el hemisferio sur (pág. 449)

corona the outer weak layer of the solar atmosphere (p. 686)

corona/corona solar débil capa exterior de la atmósfera solar (pág. 686)

correlation establishing the equivalence of rocks of similar age in different areas (p. 342)

correlation/correlación establecimiento de la equivalencia de rocas de edades similares en diferentes áreas (pág. 342)

covalent bond a bond that forms when atoms share electrons (p. 39)

covalent bond/enlace covalente enlace que se forma cuando los átomos comparten electrones (pág. 39)

crater the depression at the summit of a volcano or that which is produced by a meteorite impact (p. 283)

crater/cráter depresión en la cumbre de un volcán o la que se produce por el impacto de un meteorito (pág. 283)

creep the slow downhill movement of soil and regolith (p. 147)

creep/reptación movimiento lento cuesta abajo de tierra y regolitos (pág. 147)

crevasse a deep crack in the brittle surface of a glacier (p. 190)

crevasse/hendidura grieta profunda en la superficie frágil de un glaciar (pág. 190)

cross-cutting relationships, principle of a principle of relative dating; A rock or fault is younger than any rock or fault through which it cuts. (p. 341)

cross-cutting relationships, principle of/relaciones de corte transversal, principio de principio de datación relativa; una roca o falla es más joven que cualquier roca o falla que atraviesa (pág. 341)

crust the thin, rocky outer layer of Earth (p. 8)

crust/corteza capa exterior fina y rocosa de la tierra (pág. 8)

crystal form the external appearance of a mineral as determined by its internal arrangement of atoms (p. 49)

crystal form/forma cristalina apariencia externa de un mineral determinada según la distribución interna de los átomos (pág. 49)

cumulus one of three basic cloud forms; also the name given to one of the clouds of vertical development; They are billowy individual cloud masses that often have flat bases. (p. 517)

cumulus/cúmulo una de las tres formas básicas de las nubes; nombre dado también a una de las nubes de desarrollo vertical; son masas de nubes individuales ondulantes que tienen a menudo bases planas (pág. 517)

cyclone a low-pressure center characterized by a counterclockwise flow of air in the Northern Hemisphere (p. 538)

cyclone/ciclón centro de baja presión en el hemisferio norte caracterizado por una corriente de aire que corre en sentido contrario a las manecillas del reloj (pág. 538)

D

decompression melting melting due to a drop in confining pressure that occurs as rock rises (p. 292)

decompression melting/fusión por descompresión fusión debida a una disminución de la presión restrictiva que ocurre a medida que una roca va subiendo (pág. 292)

deflation the lifting and removal of loose material by wind (p. 203)

deflation/deflación levantamiento y remoción de material suelto por el viento (pág. 203)

deformation general term for the processes of folding, faulting, shearing, compression, or extension of rocks as the result of various natural forces (p. 308)

deformation/deformación término general para los procesos de plegamiento, formación de fallas, partición, comprensión o extensión en rocas, como resultado de diferentes fuerzas naturales (pág. 308)

delta an accumulation of sediment formed where a stream enters a lake or an ocean (p. 166)

delta/delta acumulación de sedimento que se forma donde una corriente de agua entra a un lago u océano (pág. 166)

density mass per unit volume of a substance, usually expressed as grams per cubic centimeter (p. 53)

density/densidad masa por unidad de volumen de una sustancia, expresada por lo general en gramos por centímetro cúbico (pág. 53)

density current current of ocean water that results from density differences among water masses (p. 451)

density current/corriente de densidad corriente de agua oceánica que resulta de las diferencias de densidad entre las masas de agua (pág. 451)

deposition the process by which an agent of erosion loses energy and drops the sediment it is carrying; also the process by which water vapor is changed directly to a solid without passing through the liquid state (p. 76, p. 506)

desposition/deposición proceso por el cual un agente de erosión pierde energía y deja caer el sedimento que arrastra; también es el proceso por el cual el vapor de agua pasa al estado sólido sin pasar por el estado líquido (pág. 76, pág. 506)

desert pavement a layer of coarse pebbles and gravel created when wind removed the finer material (p. 204)

desert pavement/pavimento desértico capa de guijarros gruesos y grava que se forma cuando el viento remueve el material más fino (pág. 204)

dew point the temperature to which air has to be cooled in order to reach saturation (p. 508)

dew point/punto de condensación temperatura a la cual se tiene que enfriar el aire para que alcance la saturación (pág. 508)

dike a tabular-shaped intrusive igneous feature that occurs when magma is injected into fractures in the surrounding rock, cutting across preexisting rock layers (p. 290)

dike/dique masa intrusiva de magma solidificado de forma tabular que se forma cuando el magma es inyectado en las fracturas de la roca circundante, penetrando transversalmente las capas de rocas preexistentes (pág. 290)

dinosaur land-dwelling reptile of the Mesozoic era (p. 377)

dinosaur/dinosaurio reptil de tierra de la era Mesozoica (pág. 377)

discharge the quantity of water in a stream that passes a given point in a period of time (p. 161)

discharge/caudal cantidad de agua en una corriente que pasa por un punto determinado en un período (pág. 161)

divergent boundary a region where the rigid plates are moving apart, typified by the oceanic ridges (p. 255)

divergent boundary/límite divergente zona donde las placas tectónicas se separan, tipificada por las dorsales oceánicas (pág. 255)

divide an imaginary line that separates the drainage of two streams; often found along a ridge (p. 169)

divide/divisoria de aguas línea imaginaria que separa el drenaje de dos corrientes de agua; frecuentemente se encuentra a lo largo de una elevación (pág. 169)

Doppler effect the apparent change in frequency of electromagnetic or sound waves caused by the relative motions of the source and the observer (p. 677)

Doppler effect/efecto Doppler variación aparente en la frecuencia de una onda sonora o electromagnética debido al movimiento relativo entre la fuente de la onda y el observador (pág. 677)

drainage basin the land area that contributes water to a stream (p. 169)

drainage basin/cuenca de avenamiento área de tierra que aporta agua a un arroyo (pág. 169)

drumlin a streamlined asymmetrical hill composed of glacial till; The steep side of the hill faces the direction from which the ice advanced. (p. 196)

drumlin/drumlin colina asimétrica compuesta de tilita glacial; el lado empinado de la colina mira hacia la dirección desde la cual avanzó el hielo (pág. 196)

dry adiabatic rate the rate of adiabatic cooling or warming in unsaturated air; The rate of temperature change is 1°C per 100 meters. (p. 511)

dry adiabatic rate/tasa adiabática seca tasa de enfriamiento o calentamiento adiabático en el aire no saturado; la tasa de cambio en la temperatura es de 1 °C por cada 100 metros (pág. 511)

dry-summer subtropical climate a climate located on the west sides of continents between 30° and 45° latitude; It is the only humid climate with a strong winter precipitation maximum. (p. 596)

dry-summer subtropical climate/clima subtropical de veranos secos clima que se encuentra en el occidente de los continentes entre los 30° y 45° de latitud; es el único clima húmedo que tiene una precipitación máxima elevada en invierno (pág. 596)

dune a hill or ridge of wind-deposited sand (p. 204)

dune/duna colina o elevación formada por arena depositada por el viento (pág. 204)

E

earthflow slow-moving downslope movement of water-saturated, clay-rich sediment, most characteristic of humid regions (p. 146)

earthflow/deslizamiento de tierra movimiento lento y descendente de sedimento saturado con agua, rico en arcilla, muy característico de las regiones húmedas (pág. 146)

earthquake the vibration of Earth produced by the rapid release of energy (p. 218)

earthquake/terremoto vibración de la Tierra producida por una liberación rápida de energía (pág. 218)

Earth science the name for all the sciences that collectively seek to understand Earth; It includes geology, oceanography, meteorology, and astronomy. (p. 2)

Earth science/ciencias de la Tierra nombre dado a todas las ciencias que colectivamente estudian la Tierra; incluye la geología, la oceanografía, la meteorología y la astronomía (pág. 2)

elastic rebound hypothesis the explanation stating that when rocks are deformed, they break, releasing the stored energy that results in the vibrations of an earthquake (p. 220)

elastic rebound hypothesis/teoría del rebote elástico explicación que dice que al deformarse las rocas, éstas se rompen, liberando energía que causa las vibraciones de un terremoto (pág. 220)

electromagnetic spectrum the arrangement of electromagnetic radiation according to wavelength (p. 674)

electromagnetic spectrum/espectro electromagnético orden de la radiación electromagnética según la longitud de onda (pág. 674)

element a substance that cannot be broken down into simpler substances by ordinary chemical or physical means (p. 34)

element/elemento sustancia que no puede ser descompuesta en sustancias más sencillas a través de métodos químicos o físicos comunes (pág. 34)

ellipse an oval (p. 618)

ellipse/elipse óvalo (pág. 618)

El Niño the name given to the periodic warming of the ocean that occurs in the central and eastern Pacific; A major El Niño episode can cause extreme weather in many parts of the world. (p. 546)

El Niño/El Niño nombre dado al calentamiento periódico que ocurre en las regiones central y oriental del océano Pacífico; un episodio intenso de El Niño puede causar fenómenos climáticos extremos en muchas partes del mundo (pág. 546)

emission spectrum a series of bright lines of particular wavelengths produced by a hot gas under low pressure (p. 676)

emission spectrum/espectro de emisión serie de luces brillantes con longitudes de onda específicas, producidas por un gas caliente sometido a bajas presiones (pág. 676)

energy level one of several distinct regions around the nucleus of an atom where electrons are located (p. 35)

energy level/nivel de energía una de varias regiones específicas que rodea el núcleo de un átomo y en donde se ubican los electrones (pág. 35)

eon the largest time unit on the geologic time scale, next in order of magnitude above era (p. 353)

eon/eón unidad de mayor intervalo en la escala geocronológica, mayor que una era (pág. 353)

epicenter the location on Earth's surface directly above the focus, or origin, of an earthquake (p. 219)

epicenter/epicentro punto en la superficie de la Tierra que está justo sobre el foco, u origen, de un terremoto (pág. 219)

epoch a unit of the geologic time scale that is a subdivision of a period (p. 353)

epoch/época unidad de la escala geocronológica, que es una subdivisión de un período (pág. 353)

era a major division on the geologic time scale; Eras are divided into shorter units called periods. (p. 353)

era/era una de las grandes divisiones de la escala geocronológica; las eras se dividen en unidades más pequeñas llamadas períodos (pág. 353)

erosion the incorporation and transportation of material by a mobile agent, such as water, wind, or ice (p. 76)

erosion/erosión incorporación y transporte de un material por un agente móvil, como el agua, el viento o el hielo (pág. 76)

esker sinuous ridge composed largely of sand and gravel deposited by a stream flowing in a tunnel beneath a glacier near its terminus (p. 197)

esker/esker elevación alargada y sinuosa, compuesta por arena y grava que han sido depositadas por un arroyo que fluye por el túnel de un glaciar, cerca de su punta. (pág. 197)

evaporation the process of converting a liquid to a gas (p. 505)

evaporation/evaporación proceso mediante el cual un líquido se convierte en gas (pág. 505)

exfoliation type of weathering caused by reducing pressure on a rock surface, allowing slabs of outer rock to break off in layers (p. 128)

exfoliation/exfoliación tipo de meteorización causada por la disminución de la presión en una superficie rocosa, lo que permite que los estratos externos de la roca se desprendan en láminas (pág. 128)

extrusive igneous rock igneous rock that has formed on Earth's surface (p. 71)

extrusive igneous rock/roca ígnea extrusiva roca ígnea que ha sido formada en la superficie de la Tierra (pág. 71)

eye a zone of scattered clouds and calm averaging about 20 kilometers in diameter at the center of a hurricane (p. 576)

eye/ojo zona de calma, con pocas nubes, que en promedio mide 20 kilómetros de diámetro y que se encuentra en el centro de un huracán (pág. 576)

eye wall the doughnut-shaped area of intense cumulonimbus development and very strong winds that surrounds the eye of a hurricane (p. 576)

eye wall/pared del ojo zona en forma de rosquilla con gran intensidad de cumulonimbos y fuertes vientos, que rodea el ojo de un huracán (pág. 576)

F

fault a fracture in Earth along which movement has occurred (p. 219)

fault/falla fractura en la Tierra en la cual ha habido movimiento (pág. 219)

fault-block mountain a mountain formed when large blocks of crust are tilted, uplifted, or dropped between large normal faults (p. 315)

fault block mountain/montaña de bloque de falla montaña formada cuando los bloques grandes de corteza terrestre se inclinan, se elevan o caen entre fallas grandes (pág. 315)

fetch the distance that the wind has traveled across open water (p. 456)

fetch/alcance del viento distancia que ha recorrido el viento sobre aguas abiertas (pág. 456)

firn coarse grains of ice resulting from recrystallization of compressed snow (p. 189)

firn/neviza granos gruesos de hielo formados cuando la nieve comprimida se vuelve a cristalizar (pág. 189)

flood occurs when the discharge of a stream becomes so great that it exceeds the carrying capacity of its channel and overflows its banks (p. 168)

flood/inundación ocurre cuando el caudal de una corriente de agua es tan grande que sobrepasa la capacidad de su canal y se desborda por sus riberas (pág. 168)

floodplain the flat, low-lying portion of a stream valley subject to periodic flooding (p. 167)

floodplain/planicie aluvial parte plana y baja del valle de un arroyo que está expuesta a inundaciones periódicas (pág. 167)

focus the point within Earth where an earthquake originates (p. 218)

focus/foco punto dentro de la Tierra en el cual se origina un terremoto (pág. 218)

folded mountain a mountain created primarily by compressional stresses, which create folds in the rock layers (p. 314)

folded mountain/montaña de pligues montaña que ha sido creada principalmente por esfuerzos de compresión, los caules causan pliegues en los estratos de roca (pág. 314)

foliated metamorphic rock a metamorphic rock with a texture that gives the rock a layered appearance (p. 83)

foliated metamorphic rock/roca metamórfica esquistosa roca metamórfica que tiene una textura que le da una apariencia de capas (pág. 83)

food chain a succession of organisms through which food energy is transferred, starting with primary producers (p. 437)

food chain/cadena alimentaria serie de organismos a través de los cuales se transfiere la energía de los alimentos y que empieza por los productores primarios (pág. 437)

food web a group of interrelated food chains (p. 437)

food web/red alimentaria grupo de cadenas alimentarias interrelacionadas (pág. 437)

foreshock a small earthquake that often precedes a major earthquake (p. 221)

foreshock/sismo premonitor pequeño terremoto que generalmente precede a un terremoto mayor (pág. 221)

fossil the remains or traces of an organism preserved from the geologic past (p. 343)

fossil/fósil remanentes o vestigios de un organismo que ha sido preservado del pasado geológico (pág. 343)

fossil fuel general term for any hydrocarbon that may be used as a fuel, including coal, oil, and natural gas (p. 95)

fossil fuel/combustible fósil término general usado para describir los hidrocarburos que se utilizan como combustible, entre los cuales están el carbón mineral, el petróleo y el gas natural (pág. 95)

fracture any break or rupture in rock along which no appreciable movement has taken place (p. 53)

fracture/fractura discontinuidad en una roca en la cual no se manifiesta que haya ocurrido movimiento alguno (pág. 53)

front the boundary between two adjoining air masses having contrasting characteristics (p. 512)

front/frente límite entre dos masas de aire adyacentes que tienen características que contrastan (pág. 512)

frost wedging the mechanical breakup of rock caused by the expansion of freezing water in cracks and crevices (p. 127)

frost wedging/gelifracción fragmentación mecánica de una roca, causada por la expansión tras la congelación del agua en sus grietas y poros (pág. 127)

G

galaxy a group of stars, dust, and gases held together by gravity (p. 715)

galaxy/galaxia grupo de estrellas, polvo y gas unidos por la gravedad (pág. 715)

galaxy cluster a system of galaxies containing from several to thousands of member galaxies (p. 718)

galaxy cluster/cúmulo de galaxias sistema que puede contener hasta miles de galaxias (pág. 718)

gas hydrate a gas, such as methane, trapped in a lattice-like structure of water molecules (p. 411)

gas hydrate/hidrato de gas un gas, por ejemplo el metano, que queda atrapado en una red de moléculas de agua (pág. 411)

geocentric describes the concept of an Earth-centered universe (p. 615)

geocentric/geocéntrico describe un universo cuyo centro es la Tierra (pág. 615)

geologic time scale the division of Earth history into blocks of time—eons, eras, periods, and epochs; The time scale was created using relative dating principles. (p. 353)

geologic time scale/escala geocronológica división de la historia de la Tierra en bloques de tiempo: eones, eras, períodos y épocas; la escala cronológica fue creada usando los principios de datación relativa (pág. 353)

geology the science that examines Earth, its form and composition, and the changes it has undergone and is undergoing (p. 2)

geology/geología ciencia que estudia la Tierra, su forma, su composición y los cambios que ha tenido y que continúa teniendo (pág. 2)

geosphere layer of Earth under both the atmosphere and the oceans; It is composed of the core, the mantle, and the crust. (p. 7)

geosphere/geosfera estrato de la Tierra que se encuentra bajo la atmósfera y los océanos; está compuesta por el núcleo, el manto y la corteza (pág. 7)

geothermal energy energy that can be extracted from Earth's internal heat, for example, natural steam used for power generation (p. 105)

geothermal energy/energía geotérmica energía que puede extraerse del calor interno de la Tierra; por ejemplo, el vapor natural que se usa para generar electricidad (pág. 105)

geothermal gradient the gradual increase in temperature with depth in the crust; The average is 30°C per kilometer in the upper crust. (p. 291)

geothermal gradient/gradiente geotérmico aumento gradual de la temperatura a medida que se penetra en la corteza; la media es 30 °C por kilómetro en la corteza superior (pág. 291)

geyser a hot spring or fountain that ejects water at various intervals (p. 172)

geyser/géiser manantial o fuente de agua caliente que expele agua a intervalos (pág. 172)

glacial erratic an ice-transported boulder that was not derived from bedrock near its present site (p. 194)

glacial erratic/bloque errático roca transportada por el hielo y que no se originó del lecho rocoso donde se encuentra (pág. 194)

glacier a thick mass of ice originating on land

from the compaction and recrystallization of snow that shows evidence of past or present flow (p. 188)

glacier/glaciar masa gruesa de hielo que se origina en la superficie terrestre por compactación y recristalización de la nieve, mostrando evidencias de flujo en el pasado o en la actualidad (pág. 188)

global warming the increase in average temperatures of Earth and the atmosphere due in part to increased carbon dioxide levels (p. 110)

global warming/calentamiento global aumento de la temperatura media de la Tierra y de la atmósfera causado en parte por el aumento en los niveles de dióxido de carbono (pág. 110)

Gondwana late Paleozoic continent that formed the southern portion of Pangaea, consisting of all or parts of present-day South America, Africa, Australia, India, and Antarctica (p. 370)

Gondwana/Gondwana continente de finales del paleozoico, que formaba la porción austral de Pangea y que abarcaba lo que hoy en día son América del Sur, África, Australia, India y la Antártida (pág. 370)

graben a valley formed by the downward displacement of a fault-bounded block (p. 315)

graben/fosa tectónica valle formado por el desplazamiento descendente de un bloque rodeado de fallas (pág. 315)

gradient the slope of a stream over a certain distance (p. 161)

gradient/gradiente pendiente de un arroyo a lo largo de una distancia determinada (pág. 161)

granitic composition a compositional group of igneous rocks that indicate a rock is composed almost entirely of light-colored silicates, mainly quartz and feldspar (p. 73)

granitic composition/composición de granito grupo estructural de rocas ígneas que indica que una roca está compuesta casi enteramente de silicatos de color claro, principalmente cuarzo y feldespato (pág. 73)

greenhouse effect the heating of Earth's surface and atmosphere from solar radiation being absorbed and emitted by the atmosphere, mainly by water vapor and carbon dioxide (p. 487)

greenhouse effect/efecto invernadero calentamiento de la superficie y la atmósfera de la Tierra debido a la absorción y emisión de radiación solar por la atmósfera, principalmente por el vapor de agua y el dióxido de carbono (pág. 487)

groundwater water underground in the zone of saturation (p. 171)

groundwater/agua subterránea agua que se encuentra bajo la tierra, en las zonas de saturación (pág. 171)

gymnosperm seed-bearing plant that bears its seeds on the surfaces of cones (p. 379)

gymnosperm/gimnosperma planta cuyas semillas se encuentran en las superficies de los conos (pág. 379)

gyre the large circular surface current pattern found in each ocean (p. 449)

gyre/giro patrón de corriente circular grande que se encuentra en todos los océanos (pág. 449)

H

half-life the time required for one half of the atoms of a radioactive substance to decay (p. 348)

half-life/vida media tiempo requerido para que se desintegre la mitad de los átomos de una sustancia radiactiva (pág. 348)

hardness the resistance a mineral offers to scratching (p. 52)

hardness/dureza resistencia que ofrece un mineral a ser rayado (pág. 52)

heliocentric describes the view that the sun is at the center of the solar system (p. 616)

heliocentric/heliocéntrico describe la idea de que el Sol es el centro del sistema solar (pág. 616)

heat thermal energy transferred from one object to another (p. 483)

heat/calor energía térmica que se transfiere de un objeto a otro (pág. 483)

Hertzsprung-Russell diagram *See* H-R diagram

Hertzsprung-Russell diagram/diagrama Hertzprung-Russell *ver* diagrama HR

horst an elongated, uplifted block of crust bounded by faults (p. 315)

horst/pilar tectónico bloque de corteza alargado que ha sido empujado hacia arriba y se encuentra rodeado de fallas (pág. 315)

hot spot a concentration of heat in the mantle capable of producing magma, which rises to Earth's surface; The Pacific plate moves over a hot spot, producing the Hawaiian Islands. (p. 268)

hot spot/punto caliente concentración de calor en el manto capaz de producir magma, la cual sube a la superficie terrestre; la placa tectónica del Pacífico se mueve sobre un punto caliente que formó las islas hawaianas (pág. 268)

H-R diagram a plot of stars according to their absolute magnitudes and temperatures (p. 704)

H-R diagram/diagrama HR diagrama de estrellas basado en las temperaturas y magnitudes absolutas de las mismas (pág. 704)

Hubble's law a law that states that the galaxies are retreating from the Milky Way at a speed that is proportional to their distance (p. 719)

Hubble's law/ley de Hubble ley que establece que las galaxias se alejan de la vía láctea a una velocidad proporcional a sus distancias (pág. 719)

humidity a general term referring to water vapor in the air but not to liquid droplets of fog, cloud, or rain (p. 506)

humidity/humedad término general que se refiere al vapor de agua en el aire, excluyendo las gotas líquidas de niebla, nubes o lluvia (pág. 506)

humid subtropical climate a climate generally located on the eastern side of a continent and characterized by hot, sultry summers and cool winters (p. 596)

humid subtropical climate/clima subtropical húmedo clima que generalmente se encuentra en la parte oriental de un continente y que se caracteriza por tener veranos calientes y sofocantes, e inviernos templados (pág. 596)

hurricane a tropical cyclonic storm having winds in excess of 119 kilometers per hour (p. 575)

hurricane/huracán tormenta tropical ciclónica con vientos cuyas velocidades exceden los 119 kilómetros por hora (pág. 575)

hydroelectric power the power generated by

falling water (p. 105)

hydroelectric power/energía hidroeléctrica energía generada por el agua en movimiento (pág. 105)

hydrogenous sediment seafloor sediment consisting of minerals that crystallize from seawater; An important example is manganese nodules. (p. 409)

hydrogenous sediment/sedimento hidrogenado sedimento del fondo oceánico, formado por minerales que se han cristalizado a partir del agua marina; un ejemplo importante son los nódulos de manganeso (pág. 409)

hydrosphere the water portion of Earth; one of the traditional subdivisions of Earth's physical environment (p. 7)

hydrosphere/hidrosfera parte acuática de la Tierra; una de las divisiones tradicionales del medio ambiente físico de la Tierra (pág. 7)

hydrothermal solution the hot, watery solution that escapes from a mass of magma during the later stages of crystallization; Such solutions may alter the surrounding rock. (p. 83)

hydrothermal solution/solución hidrotérmica solución acuosa y caliente que sale del magma durante las últimas fases de la cristalización; estas soluciones pueden alterar las rocas que las rodean (pág. 83)

hygrometer an instrument designed to measure relative humidity (p. 508)

hygrometer/higrómetro instrumento diseñado para medir la humedad relativa (pág. 508)

hypothesis a tentative explanation that is tested to determine if it is valid (p. 23)

hypothesis/hipótesis explicación tentativa cuya validez es sometida a prueba (pág. 23)

I

ice age a period of time when much of Earth's land is covered by glaciers (p. 88)

ice age/era glacial período en el que gran parte de la Tierra estaba cubierta por glaciares (pág. 88)

igneous rock a rock formed by the crystallization of molten magma (p. 66)

igneous rock/roca ígnea roca formada por la cristalización de magma líquido (pág. 66)

index fossil a fossil that is associated with a particular span of geologic time (p. 346)

index fossil/fósil índice fósil asociado a un período específico en la escala geocronológica (pág. 346)

infiltration the movement of surface water into rock or soil through cracks and pore spaces (p. 159)

infiltration/infiltración movimiento del agua desde la superficie hacia las rocas o la tierra a través de grietas y aperturas porosas (pág. 159)

inner core the solid innermost layer of Earth, about 1220 kilometers in radius (p. 235)

inner core/núcleo interno estrato sólido más profundo de la Tierra; tiene un radio de 1220 kilómetros (pág. 235)

intertidal zone the area where land and sea meet and overlap; the zone between high and low tides (p. 431)

intertidal zone/zona intermareal área donde se encuentran y se solapan la tierra y el mar; zona entre la marea alta y la marea baja (pág. 431)

intraplate volcanism igneous activity that occurs within a tectonic plate away from plate boundaries (p. 295)

intraplate volcanism/vulcanismo de placa actividad ígnea que ocurre en una placa tectónica lejos de sus límites (pág. 295)

intrusive igneous rock igneous rock that formed below Earth's surface (p. 71)

intrusive igneous rock/roca ígnea intrusiva roca ígnea formada bajo la superficie de la Tierra (pág. 71)

ion an atom or a molecule that possesses an electrical charge (p. 37)

ion/ion átomo o molécula que tiene una carga eléctrica (pág. 37)

ionic bond a bond that forms between negative and positive ions (p. 38)

ionic bond/enlace iónico enlace que se forma entre iones negativos e iones positivos (pág. 38)

isostasy the concept that Earth's crust is floating in gravitational balance upon the material of the mantle (p. 323)

isostasy/isostasia concepto que explica que la corteza terrestre está flotando sobre el material

del manto gracias a un equilibrio gravitacional (pág. 323)

isostatic adjustment process of establishing a new level of gravitational equilibrium (p. 323)

isostatic adjustment/ajuste isostático proceso en el cual se establece un nuevo nivel de equilibrio gravitacional (pág. 323)

isotherm a line connecting points of equal temperature (p. 492)

isotherm/isoterma línea que conecta puntos que tienen temperaturas idénticas (pág. 492)

isotope an atom with the same number of protons but different numbers of neutrons for a given element; An isotope's mass number is different from that of the given element. (p. 36)

isotope/isótopo para cualquier elemento, es un átomo con igual número de protones pero distinto número de neutrones; el número de masa de un isótopo es distinto al de ese elemento (pág. 36)

J

jet stream swift (120–240 kilometers per hour), high-altitude winds (p. 536)

jet stream/corriente de chorro vientos de alta velocidad (120–240 kilómetros por hora) que se encuentran a grandes altitudes (pág. 536)

Jovian planet the Jupiter-like planets: Jupiter, Saturn, Uranus, and Neptune; These planets have relatively low densities and are huge gas giants. (p. 645)

Jovian planet/planeta joviano cualquier planeta de la familia de Júpiter: Júpiter, Saturno, Urano y Neptuno; estos planetas tienen densidades relativamente bajas y están compuestos principalmente de gas (pág. 645)

K

karst topography an area that has a land surface or topography with numerous depressions called sinkholes (p. 178)

karst topography/relieve kárstico zona cuya superficie o topografía presenta numerosas depresiones llamadas dolinas (pág. 178)

kettle depression created when a block of ice

became lodged in glacial deposits and subsequently melted (p. 196)

kettle/marmita depresión creada cuando se derrite un bloque de hielo que se había alojado en un depósito glacial (pág. 196)

Köppen climate classification system a system for classifying climates that is based on mean monthly and annual values of temperature and precipitation (p. 592)

Köppen climate classification system/sistema de clasificación de climas de Köppen sistema para clasificar los climas en base a los valores promedio de las temperaturas y de las precipitaciones mensuales y anuales (pág. 592)

L

laccolith a massive igneous body intruded between preexisting strata (p. 290)

laccolith/lacolito cuerpo ígneo gigantesco que ha penetrado entre dos estratos preexistentes (pág. 290)

latent heat the energy absorbed or released during a change in state (p. 505)

latent heat/calor latente energía absorbida o desprendida durante un cambio de estado físico (pág. 505)

laterite a red, highly leached soil type found in the tropics that is rich in oxides of iron and aluminum (p. 139)

laterite/laterita suelo rojizo y altamente lixiviado de las regiones tropicales, rico en óxidos de hierro y aluminio (pág. 139)

latitude the distance north or south of the equator, measured in degrees (p. 11)

latitude/latitud distancia al norte o al sur del ecuador, que se mide en grados (pág. 11)

Laurasia the continental mass that formed the northern portion of Pangaea, consisting of present-day North America and Eurasia (p. 372)

Laurasia/Laurasia masa continental que se formó en la parte norte de Pangaea, y que abarcaba lo que hoy en día son América del Norte y Eurasia (pág. 372)

lava magma that reaches Earth's surface (p. 67)

lava/lava magma que ha llegado a la superficie de la Tierra (pág. 67)

light-year the distance light travels in a year, about 9.5 trillion kilometers (p. 702)

light-year/año luz distancia recorrida por la luz en un año o aproximadamente 9.5 billones de kilómetros (pág. 702)

liquefaction a phenomenon, sometimes associated with earthquakes, in which soils and other unconsolidated materials saturated with water are turned into a liquid that is not able to support buildings (p. 230)

liquefaction/licuefacción fenómeno, a veces asociado con los terremotos, en el cual la tierra, junto con otros materiales no consolidados saturados con agua, se convierten en un líquido que no es capaz de sostener los edificios (pág. 230)

lithosphere the rigid outer layer of Earth, including the crust and upper mantle (p. 234)

lithosphere/litosfera capa externa y rígida de la Tierra, que incluye la corteza y el manto superior (pág. 234)

loess deposits of windblown silt, lacking visible layers, generally light yellow, and capable of maintaining a nearly vertical cliff (p. 204)

loess/loes depósitos de limo transportado por el viento, generalmente amarillos y sin estratos visibles, y que son capaces de crear precipicios casi verticales (pág. 204)

longitude the distance east or west of the prime meridian, measure in degrees (p. 11)

longitude/longitud distancia hacia el este o el oeste del Primer meridiano; se mide en grados (pág. 11)

longshore current a near-shore current that flows parallel to the shore (p. 463)

longshore current/corriente litoral corriente que está cerca de la costa y que fluye paralela a la misma (pág. 463)

lunar eclipse an eclipse of the moon; A lunar eclipse occurs when the moon passes through Earth's shadow. (p. 628)

lunar eclipse/eclipse lunar eclipse de la Luna; ocurre cuando la Luna pasa a través de la sombra de la Tierra (pág. 628)

lunar regolith a thin, gray layer on the surface of

the moon, consisting of loosely compacted, fragmented material believed to have been formed by repeated impacts of meteorites (p. 632)

lunar regolith/regolito lunar capa gris y delgada sobre la superficie lunar compuesta de material fragmentado y ligeramente compactado, el cual se cree que fue formado por los impactos repetidos de meteoritos (pág. 632)

luster the appearance or quality of light reflected from the surface of a mineral (p. 49)

luster/brillo apariencia o calidad de la luz que es reflejada por la superficie de un mineral (pág. 49)

M

magma a body of molten rock found at depth, including any dissolved gases and crystals (p. 67)

magma/magma roca fundida que se encuentra en las profundidades de la Tierra; puede contener gas y cristales disueltos (pág. 67)

main-sequence star a star that falls into the main sequence category on the H-R diagram; This category contains the majority of stars and runs diagonally from the upper left to the lower right on the H-R diagram. (p. 704)

main-sequence star/estrella de secuencia principal estrella que pertenece a la categoría de Secuencia Principal en el diagrama HR; esta categoría contiene la mayoría de las estrellas y pasa diagonalmente de la esquina superior izquierda a la esquina inferior derecha en el diagrama HR (pág. 704)

mammal animal that bears live young and maintains a steady body temperature (p. 383)

mammal/mamífero animal que da a luz y es capaz de regular su temperatura corporal (pág. 383)

manganese nodule rounded lump of hydrogenous sediment scattered on the ocean floor, consisting mainly of manganese and iron and usually containing small amounts of copper, nickel, and cobalt (p. 412)

manganese nodule/nódulo de manganeso masa redonda de sedimento hidrogenado que se encuentra esparcida por el fondo oceánico; está formado principalmente por manganeso y hierro, y generalmente tiene pequeñas cantidades de cobre, níquel y cobalto (pág. 412)

mantle the 2890-kilometer-thick layer of Earth located below the crust (p. 8)

mantle/manto estrato de la Tierra que se encuentra justo por debajo de la corteza; tiene 2890 kilómetros de profundidad (pág. 8)

mantle plume a mass of hotter-than-normal mantle material that ascends toward the surface, where it may lead to igneous activity (p. 269)

mantle plume/pluma eruptiva masa de material del manto caliente que sube hacia la superficie, donde puede desencadenar una actividad ígnea (pág. 269)

mare (*plural* maria) the Latin name for the smooth areas of the moon formerly thought to be seas (p. 632)

mare/mare (plural: maria) nombre en Latín para las zonas lisas de la Luna que antiguamente se pensaba eran mares (pág. 632)

marine west coast climate a climate found on windward coasts from latitudes 40° to 65° and dominated by maritime air masses; Winters are mild, and summers are cool. (p. 596)

marine west coast climate/clima marítimo de la costa oeste clima de las costas expuestas al viento que se encuentran entre las latitudes 40° y 65°; en este clima predominan los aires marinos, los inviernos son templados y los veranos son frescos (pág. 596)

mass movement the downslope movement of rock, regolith, and soil under the direct influence of gravity (p. 143)

mass movement/movimiento de masas movimiento descendente de rocas, regolito y tierra por influencia directa de la gravedad (pág. 143)

mass number the number of neutrons and protons in the nucleus of an atom (p. 36)

mass number/número de masa número de neutrones y protones en el núcleo de un átomo (pág. 36)

meander a looplike bend in the course of a stream (p. 163)

meander/meandro sinuosidad en el recorrido de un arroyo (pág. 163)

mechanical weathering the physical disintegration of rock, resulting in smaller fragments (p. 126)

mechanical weathering/meteorización mecánica desintegración física de las rocas que produce fragmentos más pequeños (pág. 126)

mesosphere the layer of the atmosphere immediately above the stratosphere and characterized by decreasing temperatures with height (p. 480)

mesosphere/mesosfera estrato de la atmósfera que se encuentra inmediatamente por encima de la estratosfera y está caracterizada por el descenso de la temperatura con el aumento de la altura (pág. 480)

metallic bond a bond that forms when electrons are shared by metal ions (p. 39)

metallic bond/enlace metálico enlace que se forma cuando los iones metálicos comparten electrones (pág. 39)

metamorphic rock rock formed by the alteration of preexisting rock deep within Earth (but still in the solid state) by heat, pressure, and/or chemically active fluids (p. 66)

metamorphic rock/roca metamórfica roca formada por la alteración de una roca preexistente en las profundidades de la Tierra (pero todavía en estado sólido) debido al calor, la presión o líquidos químicamente activos (pág. 66)

metamorphism the changes in mineral composition and texture of a rock subjected to high temperature and pressure within Earth (p. 80)

metamorphism/metamorfismo cambios en la composición mineral y la textura de una roca sometida a temperaturas y presiones elevadas dentro de la Tierra (pág. 80)

meteor the luminous phenomenon observed when a meteoroid enters Earth's atmosphere and burns up, popularly called a shooting star (p. 663)

meteor/meteoro fenómeno luminoso que se observa cuando un meteoroide entra a la atmósfera de la Tierra y se desintegra, conocido popularmente como estrella fugaz (pág. 663)

meteorite any portion of a meteoroid that reaches Earth's surface (p. 664)

meteorite/meteorito cualquier fragmento de un meteoroide que llega a la superficie terrestre (pág. 664)

meteoroid a small, solid particle that travels through space (p. 663)

meteoroid/meteoroide partícula sólida y pequeña que viaja a través del espacio (pág. 663)

meteorology the scientific study of the atmosphere and atmospheric phenomena; the study of weather and climate (p. 3)

meteorology/meteorología estudio científico de la atmósfera y los fenómenos que ocurren en ella; estudio del estado del tiempo y el clima (pág. 3)

mid-ocean ridge *See* oceanic ridge

mid-ocean ridge/dorsal mesooceánica *ver* dorsal oceánica

mineral a naturally occurring, inorganic crystalline material with a unique chemical composition (p. 43)

mineral/mineral material cristalino inorgánico que ocurre de manera natural y que tiene una composición química única (pág. 43)

mixed zone an area of the ocean surface with uniform temperatures created by the mixing of water by waves, currents, and tides (p. 426)

mixed zone/zona mixta área de la superficie del océano que tiene una temperatura uniforme mantenida por la mezcla de aguas por el viento, las corrientes y las mareas (pág. 426)

Moho the Mohorovičić discontinuity, which is shortened to Moho; It is the boundary separating the crust from the mantle, discernible by an increase in the velocity of seismic waves. (p. 236)

Moho/Moho la discontinuidad de Mohorovičić, abreviada Moho; es el límite que separa la corteza del manto y que se distingue por un aumento en la velocidad de las ondas sísmicas (pág. 236)

Mohs scale a series of 10 minerals used as a standard in determining hardness (p. 52)

Mohs scale/escala de Mohs serie de 10 minerales usados como guía para determinar la dureza (pág. 52)

moment magnitude a more precise measure of earthquake magnitude than the Richter scale, which is derived from the amount of displacement that occurs along a fault zone and estimates the energy released by an earthquake (p. 227)

moment magnitude/magnitud de momento medida más exacta para la magnitud de un terremoto que la escala de Richter, que se deriva del desplazamiento que ocurre a lo largo de una zona de falla y estima la energía que libera un terremoto (pág. 227)

monocline a large steplike fold in otherwise horizontal sedimentary strata (p. 310)

monocline/pliegue monoclinal pliegue grande en forma de escalón en un estrato horizontal de sedimento (pág. 310)

monsoon seasonal reversal of wind direction associated with large continents, especially Asia; In winter, the wind blows from land to sea. In summer, the wind blows from sea to land. (p. 542)

monsoon/monzón cambio estacional en la dirección del viento asociado con los grandes continentes, particularmente Asia; en invierno, el viento sopla de la tierra al mar y en verano, sopla del mar a la tierra (pág. 542)

moraine a ridge of unsorted sediment left by a glacier (p. 194)

moraine/morrena loma de sedimento mixto depositado por un glaciar (pág. 194)

mudflow quickly moving downhill flow of soil and rock fragments containing a large amount of water (p. 146)

mudflow/corriente de barro movimiento descendente y rápido de tierra y fragmentos de roca que contienen gran cantidad de agua (pág. 146)

N

natural levee an elevated landform that parallels a stream and acts to confine its waters, except during floodstage (p. 167)

natural levee/terraplén natural formación de tierra elevada paralela a un arroyo y que sirve para contener sus aguas, excepto durante una etapa de inundación (pág. 167)

neap tide lowest tidal range, occurring near the times of the first-quarter and third-quarter phases of the moon (p. 459)

neap tide/marea muerta menor rango entre mareas, que ocurre aproximadamente cuando la Luna está en cuarto creciente y en cuarto menguante (pág. 459)

nebula a cloud of gas and/or dust in space (p. 647)

nebula/nébula nube de gas y/o polvo en el espacio (pág. 647)

nekton organisms that can move independently of ocean currents by swimming or other means of propulsion; includes most adult fish and squid, marine mammals, and marine reptiles (p. 429)

nekton/necton grupo de organismos que pueden moverse independientemente de las corrientes del océano, nadando o mediante otros medios de propulsión; incluye la mayoría de los peces y calamares adultos, y los mamíferos y reptiles marinos (pág. 429)

neritic zone the marine-life zone that extends from the low-tide line out to the shelf break (p. 431)

neritic zone/zona nerítica zona con vida marítima que se extiende desde la línea de marea baja hasta el talud continental (pág. 431)

neutron star a star of extremely high density composed entirely of neutrons (p. 713)

neutron star/estrella de neutrones estrella de gran densidad, compuesta enteramente de neutrones (pág. 713)

nonfoliated metamorphic rock metamorphic rock that does not exhibit a banded or layered appearance (p. 83)

nonfoliated metamorphic rock/roca metamórfica no esquistosa roca metamórfica que no tiene una apariencia estratificada (pág. 83)

nonpoint source pollution water pollution that does not have a specific point of origin (p. 109)

nonpoint source pollution/contaminación no localizada contaminación del agua que no tiene un origen determinado (pág. 109)

nonrenewable resource resource that takes millions of years to form (p. 94)

nonrenewable resource/recurso no renovable recurso que toma millones de años en formarse (pág. 94)

normal fault a fault in which the rock above the fault plane has moved down relative to the rock below (p. 311)

normal fault/falla normal falla en la que la roca que está por encima del plano de la falla se desplaza hacia abajo, en relación a la roca que está por debajo (pág. 311)

normal polarity a magnetic field that is the same as that which exists at present (p. 266)

normal polarity/polaridad normal campo magnético igual al que existe en el presente (pág. 266)

nova a star that explosively increases in brightness (p. 705)

nova/nova estrella cuyo brillo aumenta repentinamente (pág. 705)

nuclear fusion the way in which the sun produces energy; Nuclear fusion occurs when less massive nuclei combine into more massive nuclei, releasing tremendous amounts of energy. (p. 689)

nuclear fusion/fusión nuclear proceso mediante el cual el Sol genera energía; la fusión nuclear ocurre cuando los núcleos menos masivos se unen para formar núcleos más masivos y desprenden enormes cantidades de energía en el proceso (pág. 689)

O

occluded front a front formed when a cold front overtakes a warm front; It marks the beginning of the end of a middle-latitude cyclone. (p. 567)

occluded front/frente ocluido frente que se forma cuando un frente frío alcanza a un frente cálido; indica el principio del fin de un ciclón de las latitudes medias (pág. 567)

ocean basin floor area of the deep-ocean floor between the continental margin and the oceanic ridge (p. 404)

ocean basin floor/cuenca del fondo oceánico zona del fondo de los océanos profundos, ubicada entre el margen continental y la elevación oceánica (pág. 404)

ocean current mass of ocean water that flows from one place to another (p. 448)

ocean current/corriente oceánica masa de agua oceánica que fluye de un lugar a otro (pág. 448)

oceanic ridge a continuous elevated zone on the floor of all the major ocean basins and varying in width from 1000 to 4000 kilometers; The rifts at the crests of ridges represent divergent plate boundaries. (p. 258)

oceanic ridge/dorsal oceánica zona de elevación continua en el fondo de todas las cuencas de los océanos, cuya anchura varía entre 1000 y 4000 kilómetros; las grietas en las cimas de las elevaciones representan límites divergentes de las placas tectónicas (pág. 258)

oceanic zone the marine-life zone beyond the continental shelf (p. 431)

oceanic zone/zona oceánica zona con vida marina que se encuentra más allá de la plataforma continental (pág. 431)

oceanography the scientific study of the oceans and oceanic phenomena (p. 3)

oceanography/oceanografía estudio científico de los océanos y sus fenómenos (pág. 3)

ore a material from which a useful mineral or minerals can be mined at a profit (p. 98)

ore/mena material a partir del cual se pueden explotar minerales útiles para obtener un beneficio económico (pág. 98)

original horizontality, principle of a principle of relative dating; Layers of sediments are generally deposited in a horizontal or nearly horizontal position. (p. 340)

original horizontality, principle of/horizontalidad original, principio de la principio de la datación relativa; los estratos de sedimentos generalmente son depositadas en posición horizontal o casi horizontal (pág. 340)

orogenesis the processes that collectively result in the formation of mountains (p. 314)

orogenesis/orogénesis aquellos procesos que en colectivo resultan en la formación de las montañas (pág. 314)

orographic lifting mountains acting as barriers to the flow of air, forcing the air to ascend; The air cools adiabatically, and clouds and precipitation may result. (p. 512)

orographic lifting/elevación orográfica montaña o montañas que forman una barrera para el flujo del aire, empujando el aire hacia arriba; el aire se enfría de manera adiabática, lo cual causa la formación de nubes y precipitación (pág. 512)

outer core a layer beneath the mantle about 2260 kilometers thick; The outer core contains liquid iron and generates Earth's magnetic field. (p. 235)

outer core/núcleo exterior estrato que se encuentra por debajo del manto, con un grosor de aproximadamente 2260 kilómetros; el núcleo exterior contiene hierro líquido y genera el campo magnético de la Tierra (pág. 235)

outwash plain a relatively flat, gently sloping plain consisting of materials deposited by meltwater streams in front of the margin of an ice sheet (p. 196)

outwash plain/llanura aluvial llanura relativamente plana y con leves inclinaciones formada por materiales depositados por los arroyos de aguanieve al borde de un helero (pág. 196)

ozone a molecule of oxygen containing three oxygen atoms (p. 478)

ozone/ozono molécula de oxígeno que contiene tres átomos de oxígeno (pág. 478)

P

P wave earthquake wave that pushes and pulls rocks in the direction of the wave; also known as a compression wave (p. 223)

P wave/onda P onda sísmica que empuja y atrae las rocas; también se llama onda de compresión (pág. 223)

paleomagnetism the natural remnant magnetism in rock bodies; the permanent magnetization acquired by rock that can be used to determine the location of the magnetic poles at the time it became magnetized (p. 265)

paleomagnetism/paleomagnetismo restos de magnetismo natural en cuerpos rocosos; magnetización permanente que adquieren las rocas, que se puede usar para determinar la localización de los polos magnéticos en el momento en que se magnetizaron (pág. 265)

Pangaea the proposed supercontinent that 200 million years ago began to break apart and form the present landmasses (p. 248)

Pangaea/Pangea supercontinente que hace 200 millones de años comenzó a fragmentarse y a formar las masas de tierra actuales (pág. 248)

pedalfer soil of humid regions characterized by the accumulation of iron oxides and aluminum-rich clays in the B horizon (p. 139)

pedalfer/pedalfer suelo de las regiones húmedas que se caracteriza por la acumulación de óxidos de hierro y de arcillas ricas en aluminio en el horizonte B (pág. 139)

pedocal soil associated with drier regions and characterized by an accumulation of calcium carbonate in the upper horizons (p. 139)

pedocal/pedocal suelo asociado con las regiones más secas y que se caracteriza por una acumulación de carbonato de calcio en los horizontes superiores (pág. 139)

pelagic zone open ocean of any depth; Animals in this zone swim or float freely. (p. 431)

pelagic zone/zona pelágica océano abierto de cualquier profundidad; los animales de esta zona nadan o flotan libremente (pág. 431)

perigee the point at which the moon is closest to Earth (p. 626)

perigee/perigeo el punto en el que la Luna está más cerca de la Tierra (pág. 626)

perihelion the point in the orbit of a planet where it is closest to the sun (p. 624)

perihelion/perihelio el punto en la órbita de un planeta en el que éste está más cerca del Sol (pág. 624)

period a basic unit of the geologic time scale that is a subdivision of an era; Periods may be divided into smaller units called epochs. (p. 353)

period/período unidad básica de la escala geocronológica que es una subdivisión de una era; los períodos pueden dividirse en unidades más pequeñas llamadas épocas (pág. 353)

permeability a measure of a material's ability to transmit fluids (p. 171)

permeability/permeabilidad la capacidad de un material para transmitir fluidos (pág. 171)

phases of the moon the progression of changes in the moon's appearance during the month (p. 626)

phases of the moon/fases de la Luna la progresión de los cambios de la apariencia de la Luna a lo largo del mes (pág. 626)

photic zone the upper part of the ocean into which sunlight penetrates (p. 430)

photic zone/zona fótica parte superior del océano en la que penetra la luz solar (pág. 430)

photon a small packet of light energy (p. 675)

photon/fotón partícula de energía luminosa (pág. 675)

photosphere the region of the sun that radiates energy to space; visible surface of the sun (p. 685)

photosphere/fotosfera región del Sol que irradia energía al espacio; la superficie visible del Sol (pág. 685)

photosynthesis the process by which plants, algae, and certain prokaryotes use light energy to convert water and carbon dioxide into energy-rich glucose molecules (p. 433)

photosynthesis/fotosíntesis proceso mediante el cual plantas, algas y ciertos procariotas usan la energía luminosa para convertir agua y dióxido de carbono en moléculas de glucosa ricas en energía (pág. 433)

phytoplankton algal plankton, which are the most important community of primary producers in the ocean (p. 429)

phytoplankton/fitoplancton plancton algal, que es la comunidad más importante de productores primarios del océano (pág. 429)

planetesimal small, irregularly shaped body formed by colliding matter (p. 648)

planetesimal/planetésimo cuerpo pequeño, de forma irregular, formado por materia en colisión (pág. 648)

plankton passively drifting or weakly swimming organisms that cannot move independently of ocean currents; includes microscopic algae, protozoa, jellyfish, and larval forms of many animals (p. 428)

plankton/plancton organismos que flotan pasivamente o nadan débilmente, que no se pueden mover independientemente de corrientes oceánicas; incluyen algas microscópicas, protozoos, medusas y formas larvales de muchos animales (pág. 428)

plate one of numerous rigid sections of the lithosphere that moves as a unit over the material of the asthenosphere (p. 254)

plate/placa una de las numerosas secciones rígidas de la litosfera que se mueve como unidad sobre la materia de la astenosfera (pág. 254)

plate tectonics the theory that proposes that Earth's outer shell consists of individual plates that interact in various ways and thereby produce earthquakes, volcanoes, mountains, and the crust itself (p. 254)

plate tectonics/tectónica de placas teoría que propone que la capa exterior de la Tierra se compone de placas individuales que interactúan de varias maneras y producen como resultado terremotos, volcanes, montañas y la corteza en sí (pág. 254)

playa lake a flat area on the floor of an undrained desert basin (playa) that fills and becomes a lake after heavy rain (p. 201)

playa lake/salar superficie plana en el suelo de una cuenca desértica sin drenaje que se llena y se convierte en un lago tras lluvias fuertes (pág. 201)

pluton an intrusive igneous structure that results from the cooling and hardening of magma beneath the surface of Earth (p. 289)

pluton/plutón estructura intrusiva ígnea que resulta del enfriamiento y endurecimiento del magma bajo la superficie de la Tierra (pág. 289)

point source pollution water pollution that comes from a known and specific location (p. 108)

point source pollution/contaminación de fuentes localizadas contaminación acuática que procede de una fuente conocida y específica (pág. 108)

polar easterlies in the global pattern of prevailing winds, winds that blow from the polar high toward the subpolar low; These winds, however, should not be thought of as persistent winds, such as the trade winds. (p. 541)

polar easterlies/vientos polares del este en el patrón global de vientos dominantes, los vientos que soplan desde la zona polar de alta presión a la zona subpolar de baja presión; sin embargo, estos vientos no deben considerarse como vientos persistentes, como por ejemplo los vientos alisios (pág. 541)

polar front the stormy frontal zone separating cold air masses of polar origin from warm air masses of tropical origin (p. 541)

polar front/frente polar la zona frontal tormentosa que separa masas de aire frío de origen polar de masas de aire cálido de origen tropical (pág. 541)

polar zone the region between 66.5° north and south latitudes and the poles; The sun's rays strike at a very small angle in the polar zone. (p. 589)

polar zone/zona polar la región entre los 66.5° de latitud y los polos; los rayos del Sol llegan a la zona polar en un ángulo muy pequeño (pág. 589)

porosity the volume of open spaces in rock or soil (p. 171)

porosity/porosidad el volumen de espacios abiertos en una roca o suelo (pág. 171)

porphyritic texture an igneous texture consisting of large crystals embedded in a matrix of much smaller crystals (p. 72)

porphyritic texture/textura porfirítica textura ígnea formada por grandes cristales incrustados en una matriz de cristales mucho más pequeños (pág. 72)

precession a slow motion of Earth's axis that traces out a cone over a period of 26,000 years (p. 622)

precession/precesión movimiento lento del eje de la Tierra que traza un cono a lo largo de un período de 26,000 años (pág. 622)

precipitation any form of water that falls from a cloud (p. 504)

precipitation/precipitación cualquier forma de agua que cae de una nube (pág. 504)

pressure gradient the amount of pressure change occurring over a given distance (p. 534)

pressure gradient/gradiente de presión medida del cambio de presión que ocurre a lo largo de una distancia dada (pág. 534)

prevailing wind a wind that consistently blows from one direction more than from another (p. 545)

prevailing wind/viento dominante un viento que

sopla constantemente de una dirección más que de otra (pág. 545)

primary productivity the production of organic matter from inorganic substances through photosynthesis or chemosynthesis (p. 433)

primary productivity/productividad primaria la producción de materia orgánica a partir de sustancias inorgánicas a través de la fotosíntesis o quimiosíntesis (pág. 433)

prominence a concentration of gases above the solar surface that appears as a bright archlike structure (p. 688)

prominence/prominencia concentración de gases sobre la superficie solar que aparece como una estructura brillante en forma de arco (pág. 688)

protostar a collapsing cloud of gas and dust destined to become a star; a developing star not yet hot enough to engage in nuclear fusion (p. 708)

protostar/protoestrella nube de gas y polvo en colapso destinada a convertirse en una estrella; una estrella en desarrollo que todavía no está lo suficientemente caliente para iniciar la fusión nuclear (pág. 708)

pulsar a variable radio source of small size that emits radio pulses in very regular periods (p. 713)

pulsar/púlsar fuente de radio variable de tamaño pequeño que emite pulsaciones de radio en períodos muy regulares (pág. 713)

pycnocline a layer of water in which there is a rapid change of density with depth (p. 426)

pycnocline/picnoclina capa de agua en la que se produce un rápido cambio de densidad con la profundidad (pág. 426)

pyroclastic material the volcanic rock ejected during an eruption, including ash, bombs, and blocks (p. 283)

pyroclastic material/material piroclástico roca volcánica expulsada durante una erupción, incluyendo cenizas, bombas y bloques (pág. 283)

R

radiation the transfer of energy (heat) through space by electromagnetic waves (p. 485)

radiation/radiación transferencia de energía (calor) a través del espacio mediante ondas electromagnéticas (pág. 485)

radioactivity the spontaneous decay of certain unstable atomic nuclei (p. 347)

radioactivity/radiactividad desintegración espontánea de ciertos núcleos atómicos inestables (pág. 347)

radiocarbon (carbon-14) dating method for determining age by comparing the amount of carbon-14 to the amount of carbon-12 in a sample (p. 349)

radiocarbon (carbon-14) dating/datación por radiocarbono (carbono-14) método para determinar la edad mediante la comparación de la cantidad de carbono-14 con la cantidad de carbono-12 en una muestra (pág. 349)

radiometric dating the procedure of calculating the absolute ages of rocks and minerals that contain radioactive isotopes (p. 348)

radiometric dating/datación radiométrica procedimiento para calcular las edades absolutas de rocas y minerales que contienen isótopos radiactivos (pág. 348)

radio telescope a telescope designed to make observations in radio wavelengths (p. 681)

radio telescope/radiotelescopio telescopio diseñado para hacer observaciones en longitud de ondas de radio (pág. 681)

ray any of a system of bright elongated streaks, sometimes associated with a crater on the moon (p. 632)

ray/rayo cualquiera de los sistemas de haces alargados luminosos, a veces asociados con un cráter en la Luna (pág. 632)

recycling the collecting and processing of used items so they can be made into new products (p. 116)

recycling/reciclaje recolección y procesamiento de objetos usados para que puedan convertirse en nuevos productos (pág. 116)

red giant a large, cool star of high luminosity; a star occupying the upper-right portion of the H-R diagram (p. 704)

red giant/gigante roja estrella grande, fría, de gran luminosidad; estrella que ocupa la parte superior

derecha del diagrama HR (pág. 704)

reflecting telescope a telescope that concentrates light from distant objects by using a concave mirror (p. 680)

reflecting telescope/telescopio reflector telescopio que concentra la luz de objetos distantes usando un espejo cóncavo (pág. 680)

reflection the process whereby light bounces back from an object at the same angle at which it encounters a surface and with the same intensity (p. 486)

reflection/reflexión proceso por el cual la luz rebota de un objeto en el mismo ángulo en el que llega a su superficie y con la misma intensidad (pág. 486)

refracting telescope a telescope that uses a lens to bend and concentrate the light from distant objects (p. 678)

refracting telescope/telescopio refractor telescopio que usa una lente para doblar y concentrar la luz de objetos distantes (pág. 678)

refraction *See* wave refraction.

refraction/refracción *ver* onda de refracción

regional metamorphism metamorphism associated with large-scale mountain-building processes (p. 81)

regional metamorphism/metamorfismo regional metamorfismo asociado con procesos de formación de montañas a gran escala (pág. 81)

regolith the layer of rock and mineral fragments that nearly everywhere covers Earth's surface (p. 133)

regolith/regolito manto de fragmentos de rocas y minerales que cubre casi toda la superficie de la Tierra (pág. 133)

rejuvenation a change in the base level of a stream, often caused by regional uplift (p. 163)

rejuvenation/rejuvenecimiento cambio en el nivel bajo de un arroyo, a menudo causado por levantamiento regional (pág. 163)

relative dating process by which rocks are placed in their proper sequence or order; Only the chronological order of events is determined, not the absolute age in years. (p. 339)

relative dating/datación relativa proceso por el que las rocas se colocan en su propia secuencia u orden; sólo se determina el orden cronológico de los sucesos, no la edad absoluta en años (pág. 339)

relative humidity the ratio of the air's water-vapor content to its water-vapor capacity (p. 506)

relative humidity/humedad relativa la proporción del contenido de vapor de agua en el aire y su capacidad de vapor de agua (pág. 506)

renewable resource a resource that is virtually inexhaustible or that can be replenished over relatively short time spans (p. 94)

renewable resource/recurso renovable recurso que virtualmente no se puede agotar o que se puede renovar en un lapso relativamente corto (pág. 94)

retrograde motion the apparent westward motion of the planets with respect to the stars (p. 616)

retrograde motion/movimiento retrógrado el aparente movimiento hacia el oeste de los planetas con respecto a las estrellas (pág. 616)

reverse fault a fault in which the material above the fault plane moves up in relation to the material below (p. 312)

reverse fault/falla inversa falla en la que el material sobre el plano de la falla se desliza hacia arriba en relación con el material de abajo (pág. 312)

reverse polarity a magnetic field opposite to that which exists at present (p. 266)

reverse polarity/polaridad inversa campo magnético opuesto al que existe en el momento (pág. 266)

revolution the motion of one body about another, as Earth about the sun (p. 622)

revolution/revolución o traslación movimiento de un cuerpo alrededor de otro, como el de la Tierra alrededor del Sol (pág. 622)

ridge-push a mechanism that may contribute to plate motion; It involves the oceanic lithosphere sliding down the oceanic ridge under the pull of gravity. (p.269)

ridge-push/empuje de dorsal mecanismo que puede contribuir al movimiento de placas; implica que la litosfera oceánica se desliza hacia abajo por la dorsal oceánica bajo la atracción de la gravedad (pág. 269)

rift valley deep faulted structure found along the axes of divergent plate boundaries; Rift valleys can develop on the seafloor or on land. (p. 258)

rift valley/valle de rift estructura de fallas profundas que se encuentra a lo largo de los ejes de los límites de placas divergentes; los valles de rift pueden formarse en el suelo marino o en la tierra (pág. 258)

rille long channel associated with lunar maria; A rille looks similar to a valley or a trench. (p. 632)

rille/rille canal alargado asociado con los maria lunares; un rille es parecido a un valle o una fosa (pág. 632)

rock a consolidated mixture of minerals (p. 66)

rock/roca mezcla de minerales consolidados (pág. 66)

rock cycle a model that illustrates the origin of the three basic rock types and the interrelatedness of Earth materials and processes (p. 67)

rock cycle/ciclo de la roca modelo que ilustra el origen de los tres tipos básicos de rocas y la interrelación de materiales y procesos de la Tierra (pág. 67)

rockfall occurs when rocks or rock fragments fall freely through the air; common on steep slopes (p. 145)

rockfall/desprendimiento de rocas ocurre cuando rocas o fragmentos de roca caen libremente por el aire; son comunes en pendientes pronunciadas (pág. 145)

rockslide occurs when a mass of rock slides rapidly downslope along planes of weakness (p. 145)

rockslide/deslizamiento de rocas ocurre cuando una masa de rocas se desliza rápidamente pendiente a lo largo de taludes inestables (pág. 145)

rotation the spinning of a body, such as Earth, about its axis (p. 622)

rotation/rotación el giro de un cuerpo, como la Tierra, alrededor de su eje (pág. 622)

runoff water that flows over the land surface rather than seeping into the ground (p. 109)

runoff/escorrentía agua que fluye sobre la superficie del suelo, en lugar de filtrarse en ella (pág. 109)

S wave a seismic wave that shakes particles perpendicular to the direction the wave is traveling (p. 223)

S wave/onda S onda sísmica que sacude partículas perpendiculares a la dirección en que viaja la onda (pág. 223)

salinity the proportion of dissolved salts to pure water, usually expressed in parts per thousand (‰) (p. 422)

salinity/salinidad la proporción de sales disueltas en agua pura, generalmente expresada en partes por miles (‰) (pág. 422)

saturated the state of air that contains the maximum quantity of water vapor that it can hold at any given temperature and pressure (p. 506)

saturated/saturado el estado del aire que contiene la máxima cantidad de vapor de agua que puede retener a una temperatura y presión determinadas (pág. 506)

scattering the redirecting (in all directions) of light by small particles and gas molecules in the atmosphere; The result is more light rays with weaker intensity. (p. 486)

scattering/dispersión la redirección (en todas direcciones) de luz por pequeñas partículas y moléculas de gas en la atmósfera; el resultado es más rayos de luz con menos intensidad (pág. 486)

seafloor spreading the process by which plate tectonics produces new oceanic lithosphere at ocean ridges (p. 259)

seafloor spreading/expansión de los suelos oceánicos proceso por el cual la tectónica de placas produce una nueva litosfera oceánica en las dorsales oceánicas (pág. 259)

seamount an isolated volcanic peak that rises at least 1000 meters above the deep-ocean floor (p. 404)

seamount/monte marino pico volcánico aislado que se eleva al menos 1000 metros sobre el suelo oceánico (pág. 404)

sediment loose particles created by the weathering and erosion of rock, by chemical precipitation from solution in water, or from the secretions of organisms and transported by water, wind, or glaciers (p. 68)

sediment/sedimento partículas sueltas formadas por la meteorización y la erosión de una roca, por la precipitación química de una solución en agua o por las secreciones de organismos, y transportadas por el agua, el viento o los glaciares (pág. 68)

sedimentary rock rock formed from the weathered products of preexisting rocks that have been transported, deposited, compacted, and cemented (p. 66)

sedimentary rock/roca sedimentaria roca formada a partir de productos erosionados de rocas anteriores que han sido transportados, depositados, endurecidos y cimentados (pág. 66)

seismic gap an area along a fault where there has not been any earthquake activity for a long period of time (p. 232)

seismic gap/brecha sísmica área a lo largo de una falla donde no ha habido actividad sísmica durante un largo período (pág. 232)

seismogram the record made by a seismograph (p. 222)

seismogram/sismograma registro hecho por un sismógrafo (pág. 222)

seismograph an instrument that records earthquake waves (p. 222)

seismograph/sismógrafo instrumento que registra ondas sísmicas (pág. 222)

shield A large, relatively flat expanse of ancient metamorphic rock within the stable continental interior (p. 365)

shield/escudo extensión grande y relativamente plana de roca metamórfica antigua dentro del interior continental estable (pág. 365)

shield volcano a broad, gently sloping volcano built from fluid basaltic lavas (p. 284)

shield volcano/volcán en escudo volcán ancho, de laderas poco inclinadas, formado por el fluido de lavas basálticas (pág. 284)

silicate any one of numerous minerals that have the oxygen and silicon tetrahedron as their basic structure (p. 45)

silicate/silicato cualquiera de los numerosos

minerales que tienen como su estructura básica el tetraedro de oxígeno y silicio (pág. 45)

siliceous ooze biogenous sediment composed of the silica-based shells of single-celled animals and algae (p. 408)

siliceous ooze/fango silíceo sedimento biógeno compuesto de esqueletos de sílice de animales unicelulares y algas (pág. 408)

silicon-oxygen tetrahedron a structure composed of four oxygen atoms surrounding a silicon atom, which constitutes the basic building block of silicate minerals (p. 45)

silicon-oxygen tetrahedron/tetraedro de oxígeno y silicio estructura compuesta de cuatro átomos de oxígeno que rodean un átomo de silicio, que constituye la pieza clave para formar los silicatos (pág. 45)

sill a tabular igneous body formed when magma is injected along sedimentary bedding surfaces (p. 298)

sill/sill cuerpo tabular ígneo que se forma cuando el magma es inyectado a lo largo de superficies de lechos sedimentarios (pág. 298)

sinkhole a depression produced in a region where soluble rock has been removed by groundwater (p. 178)

sinkhole/dolina depresión que se produce en una región cuando el agua subterránea disuelve la roca soluble (pág. 178)

slab-pull a mechanism that contributes to plate motion in which cool, dense oceanic crust sinks into the mantle and "pulls" the trailing lithosphere along (p. 269)

slab-pull/subducción de placa mecanismo que contribuye al movimiento de placas en el cual la corteza oceánica, densa y fría se hunde en el manto, arrastrando consigo la listosfera (pág. 269)

slump the downward slipping of a mass of rock or unconsolidated material moving as a unit along a curved surface (p. 146)

slump/desprendimienro el movimiento hacia abajo de una masa de rocas o material no consolidado que se mueve como unidad a lo largo de una superficie curva (pág. 146)

snowline lowest elevation in a particular area that remains covered in snow all year (p. 188)

snowline/línea de nieve elevación más baja en un área concreta que queda cubierta por la nieve todo el año (pág. 188)

soil a combination of mineral and organic matter, water, and air; that portion of the regolith that supports plant growth (p. 133)

soil/suelo combinación de materia mineral y orgánica, agua y aire; parte del regolito que permite el crecimiento de plantas (pág. 138)

soil horizon a layer of soil that has identifiable characteristics produced by chemical weathering and other soil-forming processes (p. 138)

soil horizon/horizonte capa del suelo que tiene unas características identificables producidas por alteraciones químicas y otros procesos de formación del suelo (p. 138)

soil profile a vertical section through a soil showing its succession of horizons and the underlying parent material (p. 138)

soil profile/perfil del suelo sección vertical de un suelo que muestra la sucesión de horizontes y los materiales litológicos subyacentes (pág. 138)

solar eclipse an eclipse of the sun; A solar eclipse occurs when the moon moves in a line directly between Earth and the sun, casting a shadow on Earth. (p. 628)

solar eclipse/eclipse solar eclipse del Sol; un eclipse solar ocurre cuando la Luna se mueve en línea directa entre la Tierra y el Sol, formando una sombra sobre la Tierra (pág. 268)

solar flare a sudden and tremendous eruption in the solar chromosphere (p. 688)

solar flare/destello solar gran erupción de energía repentina en la cromosfera solar (pág. 688)

solar wind streams of protons and electrons ejected at high speed from the solar corona (p. 686)

solar wind/viento solar ráfagas de protones y electrones lanzadas a alta velocidad desde la corona solar (pág. 686)

sonar An electronic depth-sounding mechanism; Sonar is an acronym for sound navigation and ranging. Sonar calculates ocean depth by recording the time it takes for an energy pulse to reach the ocean floor and return. (p. 398)

sonar/sonar mecanismo electrónico de sonido de profundidad; *sonar* es un acrónimo en inglés para *Sound Navigation and Ranging* (navegación y rango de sonido); un sonar calcula la profundidad del océano al registrar el tiempo que tarda una pulsación de energía en llegar al suelo oceánico y volver (pág. 398)

spectroscopy the study of the properties of light that depend on wavelength (p. 676)

spectroscopy/espectroscopia estudio de las propiedades de la luz que depende de la longitud de onda (pág. 676)

spring a flow of groundwater that emerges naturally at the ground surface (p. 171)

spring/manantial fuente de agua subterránea que emerge de forma natural en la superficie de la tierra (pág. 171)

spring equinox the equinox that occurs on March 21 or 22 in the Northern Hemisphere (p. 482)

spring equinox/equinoccio de primavera el equinoccio que tiene lugar el 21 ó 22 de marzo en el hemisferio norte (pág. 482)

spring tide highest tidal range that occurs due to the alignment of Earth, the moon, and the sun (p. 459)

spring tide/marea viva rango de marea más alto que ocurre debido a la alineación de la Tierra, la Luna y el Sol (pág. 459)

stalactite an icicle-like structure that hangs from the ceiling of a cavern (p. 177)

stalactite/estalactita estructura en forma de carámbano que cuelga del techo de una caverna (pág. 177)

stalagmite a columnlike form that grows upward from the floor of a cavern (p. 177)

stalagmite/estalagmita estructura en forma de columna que crece hacia arriba desde el suelo de una caverna (pág. 177)

stationary front a situation in which the surface position of a front does not move; The flow on either side of such a boundary is nearly parallel to the position of the front. (p. 566)

stationary front/frente estacionario situación en la que la posición de la superficie de un frente no se mueve; el movimiento a cada lado de ese límite es casi paralelo a la posición del frente (pág. 566)

storm surge the abnormal rise of the sea along a shore as a result of strong winds (p. 577)

storm surge/marea de tempestad la subida anormal del mar a lo largo de la costa como resultado de fuertes vientos (p. 577)

strain the change in shape or volume of a body of rock as a result of stress (p. 308)

strain/deformación el cambio en la forma o el volumen de un cuerpo rocoso como resultado del esfuerzo (pág. 308)

stratosphere the layer of the atmosphere immediately above the troposphere, characterized by increasing temperatures with height, due to the concentration of ozone (p. 480)

stratosphere/estratosfera la capa de la atmósfera inmediatamente por encima de la troposfera, que se caracteriza por el aumento de la temperatura con la altura, debido a la concentración de ozono (pág. 480)

stratus one of three basic cloud forms; They are sheets or layers that cover much or all of the sky. (p. 518)

stratus/estrato una de las tres formas básicas de las nubes; son como sábanas o capas que cubren todo o casi todo el cielo (pág. 518)

streak the color of a mineral in powdered form (p. 51)

streak/raya el color de un mineral en forma pulverizada (pág. 51)

stream channel the course that the water in a stream follows (p. 161)

stream channel/cauce el curso que sigue el agua de una corriente (pág. 161)

stress the force per unit area acting on a solid (p. 308)

stress/esfuerzo la fuerza por unidad de área que actúa sobre un sólido (pág. 308)

strike-slip fault a fault along which the movement is horizontal and parallel to the trend of the fault (p. 313)

strike-slip fault/falla de desgarre falla a lo largo de la cual el movimiento es horizontal y paralelo a la tendencia de la falla (pág. 313)

stromatolite structure produced by algae trapping

sediment and forming layered mounds of calcium carbonate (p. 368)

stromatolite/estromatolito estructura producida por algas atrapadas en sedimento que forma pilas estratificadas de carbonato de calcio (pág. 368)

subarctic climate A climate found north of the humid continental climate and south of the polar climate; characterized by bitterly cold winters and short cool summers; Places within this climatic realm experience the highest annual temperature ranges on Earth. (p. 597)

subartic climate/clima subártico clima que prevalece al norte del clima húmedo continental y al sur del clima polar; se caracteriza por inviernos fríos rigurosos y veranos frescos y cortos; los lugares que se hallan en este ambiente tienen el rango de temperaturas más elevado de la Tierra (pág. 597)

subduction zone a destructive plate margin where oceanic crust is being pushed down into the mantle beneath a second plate (p. 261)

subduction zone/zona de subducción margen de placa destructivo donde la corteza oceánica es empujada hacia abajo, al manto, bajo una segunda placa (pág. 261)

sublimation the conversion of a solid directly to a gas without passing through the liquid state (p. 506)

sublimation/sublimación conversión de un sólido directamente a gas sin pasar por estado líquido (pág. 506)

submarine canyon a seaward extension of a valley that was cut on the continental shelf during a time when sea level was lower; a canyon carved into the outer continental shelf, slope, and rise by turbidity currents (p. 403)

submarine canyon/cañón submarino extensión de un valle hacia el mar que se cortó en la plataforma continental durante una era en la que el nivel del mar era más bajo; un cañón cavado en la parte exterior de la plataforma continental, el talud continental y el pie continental por corrientes de turbidez (pág. 403)

submersible a small underwater craft used for deep-sea research (p. 400)

submersible/sumergible nave submarina pequeña que se usa en la investigación oceánica (pág. 400)

summer solstice the solstice that occurs on June 21 or 22 in the Northern Hemisphere and on December 21 or 22 in the Southern Hemisphere (p. 482)

summer solstice/solsticio de verano solsticio que tiene lugar el 21 ó 22 de junio en el hemisferio norte y el 21 ó 22 de diciembre en el hemisferio sur (pág. 482)

sunspot a dark spot on the sun, which is cool by contrast to the surrounding photosphere (p. 687)

sunspot/mancha solar área oscura del Sol que está más fría que la fotosfera que la rodea (pág. 687)

supercooled water the condition of water droplets that remain in the liquid state at temperatures well below 0°C (p. 521)

supercooled water/agua subenfriada condición en que las gotas de agua permanecen en estado líquido a temperaturas inferiores a 0 °C (pág. 521)

supergiant a very large, very bright red giant star (p. 704)

supergiant/supergigante estrella roja muy grande y muy brillante (pág. 704)

supernova an exploding star that increases in brightness many thousands of times (p. 711)

supernova/supernova estrella en explosión que aumenta su brillo muchos miles de veces (pág. 711)

superposition, law of a law that states that in any undeformed sequence of sedimentary rocks, each bed is older than the layers above and younger than the layers below. (p. 340)

superposition, law of/ley de superposición ley que enuncia que en cualquier secuencia no deformada de rocas sedimentarias, cada capa es más antigua que los estratos de arriba y más joven que los estratos de abajo (pág. 340)

supersaturated air the condition of air that is more highly concentrated than is normally possible under given temperature and pressure conditions; When describing humidity, it refers to a relative humidity that is greater than 100 percent. (p. 521)

supersaturated air/aire sobresaturado condición del aire con un nivel de concentración mucho más alto de lo que es normalmente posible bajo ciertas condiciones de temperatura y presión; al describir la humedad, se refiere a una humedad relativa que es mayor que el 100 por ciento (pág. 521)

surface current movement of water that flows horizontally in the upper part of the ocean's surface (p. 448)

surface current/corriente superficial movimiento de agua que fluye horizontalmente en la parte superior de la superficie oceánica (pág. 448)

surface wave a seismic wave that travels along the surface of Earth (p. 223)

surface wave/onda superficial onda sísmica que viaja a lo largo de la superficie de la Tierra (pág. 223)

syncline a linear downfold in sedimentary strata; the opposite of anticline (p. 310)

syncline/sinclinal pliegue lineal en el estrato sedimentario; lo opuesto de anticlinal (pág. 310)

system any size group of interacting parts that form a complex whole (p. 18)

system/sistema grupo de cualquier tamaño de partes relacionadas que forman un conjunto complejo (pág. 18)

T

talus an accumulation of rock debris at the base of a cliff (p. 127)

talus/talud acumulación de restos de roca al pie de un acantilado (pág. 127)

temperate zone region located between 23.5° and 66.5° north and south of the equator; The sun's rays strike Earth at a smaller angle in the temperate zone than near the equator. (p. 589)

temperate zone/zona templada región situada entre 23.5° y 66.5° norte y sur del ecuador; los rayos de Sol llegan a la Tierra formando un ángulo más pequeño en la zona templada que en el ecuador. (pág. 589)

temperature a measure of the average kinetic energy of individual atoms or molecules in a substance (p. 483)

temperature/temperatura medición de la energía cinética promedio de los átomos o moléculas individuales en una sustancia (pág. 483)

temperature inversion a layer of limited depth in the atmosphere of limited depth where the temperature increases rather than decreases with height (p. 514)

temperature inversion/inversión de temperatura capa de poca densidad en la atmósfera de poca densidad donde la temperatura aumenta con la altura en vez de descender (pág. 514)

terrane a crustal block bounded by faults, whose geologic history is distinct from the histories of adjoining crustal blocks (p. 322)

terrane/terreno formación de rocas de la corteza rodeada de fallas, cuya historia geológica es distinta a la historias de las formaciones de rocas lindantes (pág. 322)

terrestrial planet any of the Earth-like planets, including Mercury, Venus, Mars, and Earth (p. 645)

terrestrial planet/planeta terrestre cualquiera de los planetas similares a la Tierra, como Mercurio, Venus, Marte y Tierra (pág. 645)

terrigenous sediment seafloor sediment derived from eroded rocks on land (p. 408)

terrigenous sediment/sedimento terrígeno sedimento en el fondo oceánico que se deriva de la erosión de rocas en la tierra (pág. 408)

theory a well-tested and widely accepted view that explains certain observable facts (p. 24)

theory/teoría perspectiva comprobada y generalmente aceptada que explica ciertos hechos observables (pág. 24)

thermocline a layer of water in which there is a rapid change in temperature with depth (p. 424)

thermocline/termoclina capa de agua en la cual se observa un rápido cambio de temperatura con la profundidad (pág. 424)

thermosphere the region of the atmosphere immediately above the mesosphere and characterized by increasing temperatures due to absorption of very short-wave solar energy by oxygen (p. 480)

thermosphere/termosfera capa de la atmósfera inmediatamente superior a la mesosfera y que se caracteriza por un aumento de temperatura causado por la absorción de energía solar de ondas muy cortas por el oxígeno (pág. 480)

thrust fault a reverse fault with a dip less than 45°, normally about 10–15° (p. 312)

thrust fault/falla de empuje falla inversa con una depresión de menos de 45°, normalmente entre 10°y 15° (pág. 312)

thunderstorm a storm produced by a cumulonimbus cloud and always accompanied by lightning and thunder; It is of relatively short duration and usually accompanied by strong wind gusts, heavy rain, and sometimes hail. (p. 571)

thunderstorm/tormenta eléctrica tormenta causada por una nube cumulonimbo y siempre acompañada de relámpagos y truenos; es de duración relativamente corta y va generalmente acompañada de fuertes ráfagas de viento, precipitaciones y a veces granizo (pág. 571)

tidal range the difference in height between successive high and low tides (p. 459)

tidal range/rango de marea diferencia en altura entre sucesivas mareas altas y bajas (pág. 459)

tide daily change in the elevation of the ocean surface (p. 458)

tide/marea cambios diarios en el ascenso de la superficie oceánica (pág. 458)

till sediment of different sizes deposited directly by a glacier (p. 194)

till/tillita sedimentos de diferentes tamaños depositados directamente por un glaciar (pág. 194)

topographic map a map that represents Earth's surface in three dimensions; It shows elevation, distance, directions, and slope angles. (p. 14)

topographic map/mapa topográfico mapa que representa la superficie de la Tierra en tres dimensiones; muestra elevación, distancia, direcciones y ángulos de inclinación (pág. 14)

tornado a small, very intense cyclonic storm with exceedingly high winds, most often produced along cold fronts in conjunction with severe thunderstorms (p. 573)

tornado/tornado pequeña tormenta ciclónica pero sumamente intensa, con vientos de gran velocidad, que a menudo ocurre a lo largo de

frentes fríos acompañados de poderosas tormentas eléctricas (pág. 573)

trade winds two belts of winds that blow almost constantly from easterly directions and are located on the north and south sides of the subtropical highs (p. 541)

trade winds/vientos alisios dos cinturones de viento que soplan casi constantemente desde la dirección del este y que se encuentran al norte y al sur de los centros de las altas presiones subtropicales (pág. 541)

transform fault boundary a boundary in which two plates slide past each other without creating or destroying lithosphere (p. 255)

transform fault boundary/límite de falla de transformación límite en el que dos placas se deslizan a lo largo de la falla sin generar o destruir litosfera (pág. 255)

travertine a form of limestone that is deposited by hot springs or as a cave deposit (p. 177)

travertine/travertino tipo de piedra caliza que es depositada por fuentes termales o que forma parte del depósito de cuevas (pág. 177)

trench a surface feature in the seafloor produced by the descending plate during subduction (p. 261)

trench/fosa depresión en el fondo oceánico causada por la placa descediente durante la subducción (pág. 261)

tributary a stream that empties itself into another stream (p. 162)

tributary/afluente corriente de agua que desemboca en otra corriente (pág. 162)

trophic level a nourishment level in a food chain; Plant and algae producers constitute the lowest level, followed by herbivores and a series of carnivores at progressively higher levels. (p. 436)

trophic level/nivel trófico nivel de alimentación en la cadena alimenticia; los productores como las plantas y las algas forman parte del nivel más bajo, seguidos de herbívoros y una serie de carnívoros en los niveles superiores progresivos (pág. 436)

tropical wet and dry climate a climate that is transitional between the wet tropics and the subtropical steppes (p. 593)

tropical wet and dry climate/clima tropical seco y húmedo clima de transición entre los húmedos trópicos y las estepas subtropicales (pág. 593)

tropical zone region between 23.5° north (the tropic of Cancer) and 23.5° south (the tropic of Capricorn) of the equator; The sun's rays are most intense and the temperatures are always warm. (p. 589)

tropical zone/zona tropical región entre 23.5° norte (trópico de Cáncer) y 23.5° sur (trópico de Capricornio) del ecuador; los rayos solares son de mayor intensidad y la temperatura es siempre cálida (pág. 589)

troposphere the lowermost layer of the atmosphere; It is generally characterized by a decrease in temperature with height. (p. 480)

troposphere/troposfera capa más inferior de la atmósfera; generalmente se caracteriza por un decrecimiento de la temperatura con la altura (pág. 480)

tsunami the Japanese word for a seismic sea wave (p. 230)

tsunami/tsunami palabra japonesa con la que se denomina a una ola sísmica marina (pág. 230)

turbidity current a downslope movement of dense, sediment-laden water created when sand and mud on the continental shelf and slope are dislodged and thrown into suspension (p. 403)

turbidity current/corriente de turbidez movimiento descendente de una densa masa de agua cargada de sedimentos que ocurre cuando la arena y el barro de la plataforma y el talud continental se desplazan y quedan en suspensión (pág. 403)

U

ultramafic igneous rock composed mainly of iron and magnesium-rich minerals (p. 73)

ultramafic/ultramáfica roca ígnea compuesta principalmente de hierro y minerales ricos en magnesio (pág. 73)

unconformity a surface that represents a break in the rock record, caused by erosion or lack of deposition (p. 341)

unconformity/discordancia superficie que representa una interrupción en la evolución de la roca, causada por erosión o por falta de deposición (pág. 341)

uniformitarianism the concept that processes that have shaped Earth in the past are essentially the same as those operating today (p. 337)

uniformitarianism/uniformismo principio que dice que los procesos que dieron forma a la Tierra en el pasado geológico son esencialmente los mismos que ocurren en la actualidad (pág. 337)

uplifted mountain a circular or an elongated structure formed by uplifting of the underlying basement rock (p. 316)

uplifted mountain/montaña formada por elevación estructura circular o elongada formada por el levantamiento de rocas subyacentes del basamento (pág. 316)

upwelling the rising of cold water from deeper layers to replace warmer surface water that has been moved away (p. 450)

upwelling/afloramiento movimiento ascendente de aguas frías desde las profundidades del mar para reemplazar las aguas más calidas de la superficie que han sido desplazadas (pág. 450)

V

valley glacier a glacier confined to a mountain valley, which in most instances had previously been a stream valley; also known as an alpine glacier (p. 189)

valley glacier/glaciar de valle glaciar localizado en un valle de montaña, que en varias etapas anteriores había sido un valle fluvial; también conocido como glaciar alpino (pág. 189)

vent an opening in the surface of Earth through which molten rock and gases are released (p. 281)

vent/chimenea abertura en la superficie de la Tierra a través de la cual salen roca derretida y gases (pág. 281)

ventifact a cobble or pebble polished and shaped by the sandblasting effect of wind (p. 204)

ventifact/ventifacto canto o guijarro pulido y esculpido por el efecto abrasivo del viento (pág. 204)

viscosity a measure of a fluid's resistance to flow (p. 281)

viscosity/viscosidad una medida que indica la resistencia de un líquido al fluir (pág. 281)

volcanic island arc a chain of volcanic islands generally located a few hundred kilometers from a trench where subduction of one oceanic slab beneath another is occurring (p. 262)

volcanic island arc/arco de islas volcánicas una cadena de islas volcánicas generalmente ubicada a unos cientos de kilómetros de una fosa donde está ocurriendo la subducción de una placa océanica debajo de otra (pág. 262)

volcano a mountain formed of lava and/or pyroclastic material (p. 283)

volcano/volcán montaña formada de lava y/o material piroclástico (pág. 283)

W

warm front a front along which a warm air mass overrides a retreating mass of cooler air (p. 565)

warm front/frente cálido zona frontal de una masa de aire cálido que avanza para reemplazar una masa de aire frío que retrocede (pág. 656)

water cycle the constant movement of water among the oceans, the atmosphere, geosphere, and the biosphere (p. 158)

water cycle/ciclo del agua movimiento constante del agua en los océanos, la atmósfera, la geosfera y la biosfera (pág. 283)

water table the upper level of the saturated zone of groundwater (p. 171)

water table/nivel freático nivel superior de la zona de saturación de las aguas subterráneas (pág. 171)

wave height the vertical distance between the trough and crest of a wave (p. 456)

wave height/altura de la ola distancia vertical entre el valle y la cresta de una ola (pág. 456)

wavelength the horizontal distance separating successive crests or troughs (p. 456)

wavelength/longitud de la ola distancia horizontal que separa crestas o valles sucesivos (pág. 456)

wave period the time interval between the passage of successive crests at a stationary point (p. 456)

wave period/período de la ola el intervalo entre el paso de crestas sucesivas por un mismo punto (pág. 462)

wave refraction the process by which the portion of a wave in shallow water slows, causing the wave to bend and tend to align itself with the underwater contours (p. 462)

wave refraction/refracción de la ola proceso en que la porción de una ola en aguas poco profundas disminuye su velocidad, lo cual causa que la ola se rompa y tienda a alinearse con las curvas de la superficie submarina (pág. 462)

weathering the disintegration and decomposition of rock at or near Earth's surface (p. 68)

weathering/meteorización la desintegración y descomposición de una roca en o cerca de la superficie de la Tierra (pág. 68)

well an opening bored into the zone of saturation (p. 173)

well/pozo abertura excavada dentro de la zona de saturación (pág. 173)

westerlies the dominant west-to-east motion of the atmosphere that characterizes the regions on the poleward side of the subtropical highs (p. 541)

westerlies/vientos del oeste el movimiento dominante de oeste a este de la atmósfera que caracteriza las regiones en el lado polar de las zonas de alta presión subtropicales (pág. 541)

wet adiabatic rate the rate of adiabatic temperature change in saturated air; The rate of temperature change is variable, but it is always less than the dry adiabatic rate. (p. 511)

wet adiabatic rate/tasa adiabática húmeda la tasa del cambio de temperatura adiabática en el aire saturado; la tasa de cambio de temperatura es variable, pero siempre es menor que la tasa adiabática seca (pág. 511)

wet tropical climate a climate with high temperatures and high annual precipitation (p. 593)

wet tropical climate/clima tropical húmedo clima de altas temperaturas y alta precipitación anual (pág. 593)

white dwarf a star that has exhausted most or all of its nuclear fuel and has collapsed to a very small size, believed to be near its final stage of evolution (p. 712)

white dwarf/enana blanca estrella que ha agotado todo o casi todo su combustible nuclear y que se desvanece hasta alcanzar un tamaño pequeño, que se considera el estado final de su evolución (pág. 712)

winter solstice the solstice that occurs on December 21 or 22 in the Northern Hemisphere and on June 21 or 22 in the Southern Hemisphere (p. 482)

winter solstice/solsticio de invierno el solsticio que tiene lugar el 21 ó 22 de diciembre en el hemisferio norte, y el 21 ó 22 de junio en el hemisferio sur (pág. 482)

Z

zone of saturation zone where all open spaces in sediment and rock are completely filled with water (p. 171)

zone of saturation/zona de saturación zona donde todos los espacios abiertos en el sedimento y la roca están completamente llenos de agua (pág. 171)

zooplankton animal plankton (p. 429)

zooplankton/zooplancton plancton animal (pág. 429)

Index

brittle failure, 309
bromine (Br), 423
Bronowski, Jacob, 24
Bryce Canyon National Park (Utah), 64, 132
building design, 229
building materials, 101
    buoyancy, 484
burrows, 344
Bushveld Complex, 98

Calaveras fault, 325
calcareous ooze, 408
calcite ($CaCO_3$), 48, 52, 53, 54, 85
calcium (Ca), 38, 42, 46, 71, 175
calcium bicarbonate, 176
calcium carbonates, 131, 368, 409
calcium fluoride, 42
calcium sulfate, 409
calculating, 729
calderas, 287
California, 598
California Current, 449, 450, 520
calories, 505
calving, 191
Cambrian period, 354, 367, 369, 370, 371
Cambridge (Massachusetts), earthquake in, 333
Canadian Rockies, 145, 253
Canadian Shield, 366
canyon, 209
Canyonlands National Park (Utah), 75
Cape Cod, 188, 195
carbon (C), 38, 49
    fossil fuels and, 85
carbon-12, 38
carbon-13, 38
carbon-14, 38
    dating with, 349
carbonates, 45, 48
carbon cycle, 85, 110
carbon dioxide, 110, 487, 602
    in atmosphere, 42, 85, 477
    in chemical weathering, 129
    in planets, 646
carbonic acid, 85, 129, 176
carbonization, 344
carbon monoxide, 110, 662
Caribbean Sea, 395
Carlsbad Caverns (New Mexico), 176
carnivores, 381
Cascade Range, 285, 316
Cassini (orbiter), 654, 656
cast fossils, 344
catalyst, 478
caverns, 176–177
celestial sphere, 615
cementation, 76
Cenozoic era, 354, 382–384
center of mass, 701
cephalopods, 371
cepheid variables, 705
Ceres, 661
chalk, 78
Challenger Deep, 404
HMS Challenger, 397
Chandra X-ray Observatory, 683
Charleston (South Carolina), earthquake in, 333
Charon, 659, 682

chemical bonds, 40, 42–43
chemicals, safe use of, 733
chemical sedimentary rocks, 77–78
chemical weathering, 76, 85, 129–131, 136, 139, 199, 423
    effect of temperature on, 150–151
chemosynthesis, 433
Chernobyl, 104
chert, 72, 77, 368
Chicxulub crater, 385
chitin, 371
chlorine (Cl), 39, 41, 49, 423
chlorite, 81
chlorofluorocarbons (CFCs), 111
C horizons, 138
chromatic aberration, 679, 680
chromite, 98
chromium (Cr), mining of, 366
chromosphere, 686
cinder cones, 284–285, 287
circle graphs, 740
circular orbital motion, 456–457
circum-Pacific belt, 226
cirques, 193
cirrocumulus clouds, 518
cirrostratus clouds, 518, 565
cirrus clouds, 517, 518, 565
classifying, 729
clastic sedimentary rocks, 77
clay minerals, 48
Clean Air Act (1970), 114–115
Clean Water Act (CWA), 114
clear-cutting, 112, 115
cleavage, 52–53
climates, 188, 476, 588–603
    in continental drift theory, 251–252
    factors that affect, 588–590
    human impact on changes in, 602–603
    natural processes that change, 600–601
    ocean currents and, 450
    in soil formation, 136, 139
    sunspot cycles in changes in, 691
    weathering and, 132
    world, 592–599
climate system, 20
closed system, 19, 349
cloud cover, 492
clouds, 494
    altocumulus, 518–519
    altostratus, 519, 565
    cirrocumulus, 518
    cirrostratus, 518, 565
    cirrus, 517, 518, 565
    cumulonimbus, 520, 522, 571, 573, 574
    cumulus, 517, 520
    nimbostratus, 519, 565
    stratocumulus, 519
    stratus, 518, 519
coal, 21, 66, 94, 95–96
coalescence, 521
coastal upwelling, 450
cobalt (Co), 413
Coeur D'Alene (Idaho), 99
cold currents, 450
cold fronts, 566, 569
Colorado Plateau, 310, 342
Colorado River, 202
Columbia Plateau, 204, 288, 295, 632
columnar rocks, 298

coma, 662
comets, 661–663
compaction, 76
compare-and-contrast tables, 735
composite cones, 285–286
compost, 115
compounds, 39
    covalent, 42
    ionic, 42
    properties of, 41
Comprehensive Environmental Response, Compensation, and Liability Act (CERCLA) (1980), 116
compressional stress, 309, 312, 314
compression waves, 223
Compton Gamma-Ray Observatory, 683
Comstock Lode, 99
concept map, 735
conclusions, drawing, 731
condensation, 504, 506, 516
condensation nuclei, 516
conduction, 483–484
cone of depression, 173
conglomerate, 76, 77
conic projection maps, 13
coniferous forests, 604–605
conifers, 379
conservation, 113
constellations, 700
constructive forces, 8–9
constructive plate margins, 258
contact metamorphism, 81, 84
contamination, groundwater, 174–175
continental accretion, 321–323
continental air masses, 560
continental drift, 248–253, 254, 265
continental glaciers, 189
continental ice sheets, 189
continental lithosphere, 262
continental margins, 401, 402–403
continental polar air mass, 560, 561
continental rifts, 260
continental rise, 403
continental shelf, 402
continental slope, 403
continental tropical air masses, 560, 563
continental volcanic arc, 261, 294
continent-continent convergence, 320
continents, influence of, on global winds, 542
continuous spectrum, 676
contour interval, 14
contour lines, 14, 15
contour plowing, 115, 142
contraction, 147
control group, 731
controlled variables, 730
convection, 484
    thermal, 270
    whole-mantle, 270
convective flow, 269
convergence, 513, 515
    horizontal, 538
    surface, 539
convergent boundaries, 255, 261–263, 293–294
    mountain building at, 317
conversion factors, 739
cooling, fogs caused by, 520

Index

Index

Index

Ulan Bator, 598
ultramafic, 73
ultraviolet (UV) radiation, 110, 111, 478, 674, 681
unaltered remains, 343–344
unconformities, 341–342
underground mining, 128
underground water, 170–171
uniformitarianism, 337, 338
universal gravitation, 620–621
universe, 715–721
    Earth's place in, 10
    expanding, 718–719
unloading, 128, 131
unstable air, 514
uplift, 260, 327
uplifted mountains, 316
upwelling, 450–451
Ural Mountains, 263, 320, 372
uranium (U), 94
    mining of, 366
uranium-238, 347
Uranus, 644, 645, 658
U-shaped valleys, 192, 193
Ussher, James, 337

Valentine (Texas), earthquake in, 333
Valles Marineris, 652
valley breeze, 544
valley glaciers, 189
variables, controlling, 730
Vega, 625
vegetation
    effect of, on climate, 591
    removal of, in mass movements, 145
Venn diagrams, 735
vent, 281
ventifacts, 204
Venus, 619, 644, 645, 650–651
    atmosphere of, 646
    in geocenter model, 615
    surface features of, 650–651
Very Long Baseline Interferometry (VLBI), 17
Viking, 653
viscosity, 281
visible light, 485, 674, 675, 676
volcanic eruptions, 66, 67, 126, 280–281
    effect on climate, 600
    factors affecting, 281
volcanic gases, 495
volcanic island arcs, 262, 294
volcanic material, 282
volcanic mountains, 316
volcanic neck, 287, 290
volcanic pipes, 287
volcanic rocks, 66
volcanism, 8
    intraplate, 295
    zones of, 296

volcanoes, 2, 254, 298
    anatomy of, 283–284
    effects of, 298–299
    major, 294
    types of, 283–288
vortex, 573
Voyager 1, 655, 656
Voyager 2, 655, 656, 658
V-shaped valley, 192
Vulcan, 687

Walsh, Don, 404
warm fronts, 565, 569
washes, 200–201
water, 42
    changes of state, 504–506
    in chemical weathering, 129–130
    hard, 175
    heating, 496–497
    in mass movements, 144
    in origin of magma, 292
    in planets, 646
    role of, in deserts, 200–202
    in soil erosion, 140–141
water bodies, effect of, on climate, 590
water cycle, 158–159
water density, effect of temperature on, 440–441
water pollution, 114
    freshwater, 108
    prevention of, 114
    types of, 109
water table, 171, 173, 177
water vapor, 110, 477, 487, 504, 602
wave-cut cliffs, 464
wave-cut platform, 464
wave height, 456
wave impact, 461–462
wavelength, 456, 675
wave motion, 456–457
wave period, 456
wave refraction, 462
waves, 455–457
weather, 476, 481, 558–563
    airflow aloft and, 569–570
    air masses in, 558–563
    air pressure and, 538–539
    forecasting, 539
    fronts in, 564–567
    hurricanes in, 575–577
    middle-latitude cyclones and, 567–569
    in North America, 561–563
    thunderstorms in, 571–572
    tornadoes in, 573–575
weathering, 8, 68, 69, 76, 78, 126–132, 164, 199
    chemical, 76, 85, 129–131, 136, 139, 199, 423
    differential, 132
    mechanical, 126–128, 199
    rate of, 131–132, 136
    spheroidal, 130–131

weather map, 746
weather satellites, 17
web diagram, 735
Wegener, Alfred, 248, 249, 251, 252, 253, 254
weight, 620
wells, 173
westerlies, 541, 543, 545
Western Deep Levels mine (South Africa), 81
West Wind Drift, 449
wet adiabatic rate, 511
wet-bulb thermometer, 508
whitecaps, 456
white dwarfs, 705, 710, 712
white light, 485
White Sands National Monument, 205
whole-mantle convection, 270
wind, 578
    direction of, 545
    effect of friction on, 536
    in erosion, 141, 203–204
    factors affecting, 534–536
    global, 540–542
    local, 543–544
    measurement of, 545
    observing patterns in, 550–551
    speed of, 545
windbreaks, 142
wind deposits, 204–205
wind energy, 104
wind flags, 534
wind power, 115
wind vanes, 545
winter monsoon, 542
winter solstice, 482, 624
Wizard Island, 287
world climates, 592–599
Wrangell-St. Elias National Park (Alaska), 191
wulfenite, 32

X-rays, 674, 681

Yellow River, 204
Yellowstone National Park, 172, 295
Yellowstone River, 167
Yosemite National Park, 68, 193
Yosemite Valley, 188
Yukon Territory, 193

zinc (Zn), 111
    in mid-ocean ridges, 405
zone
    of accumulation, 190
    of aeration, 171
    of fracture, 190
    of saturation, 171, 177
    of wastage, 190
zooplankton, 429, 432, 436

Acknowledgments

Editorial development, design, and production
Navta Associates, Inc.

Pages 148–149, **Soil** Taken from *Dictionary of the Earth,* published by Dorling Kindersley Limited. © Dorling Kindersley Limited, 1994, pp. 130–132; *Ecology* published by Dorling Kindersley Limited. © Dorling Kindersley Limited, 2000, pp. 22–23; *Earth,* published by Dorling Kindersley Limited. © Dorling Kindersley Limited, 2000, pp. 52–53. Pages 208–209, **Erosion** Taken from *Earth,* published by Dorling Kindersley Limited. © Dorling Kindersley Limited, 2000, pp. 54–55; *Dictionary of the Earth,* published by Dorling Kindersley Limited. © Dorling Kindersley Limited, 1994, pp. 112–113, 123. Pages 238–239, **Effects of Earthquakes** Taken from *Volcano & Earthquake,* published by Dorling Kindersley Limited. © Dorling Kindersley Limited, 2000, pp.46–47, 56–57. Pages 298–299, **Effects of Volcanoes** Taken from *Volcano & Earthquake,* published by Dorling Kindersley Limited. © Dorling Kindersley Limited, 2000, pp. 14–15, 22, 34–35, 39, 40–41. Pages 438–439, **Ocean Life** Taken from *Nature Encyclopedia,* published by Dorling Kindersley Limited. © Dorling Kindersley Limited, 1998, pp. 68–69, 72–73, 188. Pages 494–495, **Earth's Atmosphere** Taken from *Earth,* published by Dorling Kindersley Limited. © Dorling Kindersley Limited, 2000, pp. 10–11. Pages 578–579, **Winds and Storms** Taken from *Weather,* published by Dorling Kindersley Limited. © Dorling Kindersley Limited, 2000, pp. 38–39, 44–45. Pages 604–605, **Coniferous Forests** Taken from *Nature Encyclopedia,* published by Dorling Kindersley Limited. © Dorling Kindersley Limited, 1998, pp. 78–79.

Illustration
All illustrations by Dennis Tasa

Cover design Jan Calek/Navta Associates, Inc.

Cover photo Carr Clifton Photography

Photo research Navta Associates, Inc.

Front matter
Page iv, Art Wolfe, Inc.; **vi tl,** GeoScience Resources/American Geological Institute (AGI); **vi ml, vi bl,** Edward J. Tarbuck; **vi r,** Dennis Tasa; **vii,** Carl Purcell/Photo Researchers, Inc.; **viii,** Tom & Susan Bean, Inc./DRK Photo; **ix t,** Greg Vaughn Photography; **ix b,** Ira Block/National Geographic Image Collection; **x,** Gary Bell/Seapics.com/Innerspace Visions; **xi,** Kent Wood/Science Source/Photo Researchers, Inc.; **xiii,** Royal Observatory, Edinburgh/AATB/Science Photo Library/Photo Researchers, Inc.; **xv t,** Bettmann/Corbis; **xv m,** Ted Spiegel/Black Star; **xv b,** Science Photo Library; **xviii tl,** Reuters/Corbis; **xviii tr,** David Parker/ Science Photo Library/Photo Researchers, Inc.; **xviii b,** David Frazier/Photo Researchers, Inc.; **xix tl,** Owen Franken/Stock Boston; **xix tm,** Bill & Sally Fletcher/Tom Stack & Associates, Inc.; **xix tr,** Bojan Breceli/Corbis; **xix galaxy,** Pat Lanza-Field/Bruce Coleman, Inc.; **xix scientist,** James King-Holmes/Science Photo Library/Photo Researchers, Inc.

Chapter 1
Pages **x–1, 2 t,** Art Wolfe, Inc.; **2 b,** James L. Amos/Corbis; **3,** Randy M. Ury/ Corbis; **6, 7 t,** Art Wolfe, Inc.; **7 bl,** NASA; **7 br,** NASA/Science Source/Photo Researchers, Inc.; **11,** Art Wolfe, Inc.; **16,** NASA; **18,** Art Wolfe, Inc.; **19,** Jack Dykinga Photography; **20,** Roger Wood/Corbis; **22 t,** Mike Yamashita/Woodfin Camp & Associates; **22 b,** Reuters/STR/Getty Images; **23, 25 t,** Art Wolfe, Inc.; **25 b,** NASA.

Chapter 2
Pages **32–33, 34,** Jeffrey A. Scovil; **41,** Tom Pantages; **42 both,** Dennis Tasa; **43,** Corbis; **44 t,** Jeffrey A. Scovil; **44 bl,** Mark Schneider/Visuals Unlimited; **44 br,** Corbis; **45 t,** GeoScience Resources/American Geological Institute (AGI); **45 mt, 45 mb,** Edward J. Tarbuck; **45 b,** GeoScience Resources/American Geological Institute (AGI); **46 tl,** Tom & Susan Bean, Inc.; **46 tr,** GeoScience Resources/American Geological Institute (AGI); **46 b,** Dennis Tasa; **47,** Breck P. Kent; **49 both,** GeoScience Resources/American Geological Institute (AGI); **50 t,** Jeffrey A. Scovil; **50 b,** Fred Ward/Black Star; **51 tl, 51 tr,** Edward J. Tarbuck; **51 m,** G. Tompkinson/Photo Researchers, Inc.; **51 b,** Herve Berthoule/Photo Researchers, Inc.; **53 t,** Chip Clark; **53 b,** Edward J. Tarbuck; **54,** Paul Silverman/ Fundamental Photographs; **56 t,** Jeffrey A. Scovil; **56 bl,** Science Photo Library; **56 br,** Dorling Kindersley; **57 t,** Jeffrey A. Scovil; **57 bl,** Ken Lucas/Visuals Unlimited; **57 br,** Stone/Getty Images; **58, 60,** Dennis Tasa.

Chapter 3
Pages **64–65,** Carr Clifton Photography; **66 tl, 66 bl,** GeoScience Resources; **66 r,** Carr Clifton Photography; **68,** Jeff Gnass/Corbis; **69,** Edward J. Tarbuck;

70 t, Carr Clifton Photography; **70 b,** G. Brad Lewis/Getty Images; **71 both, 72,** Edward J. Tarbuck; **73,** Hubert Stadler/Corbis; **75 t,** Carr Clifton Photography; **75 b,** Jeff Gnass Photography; **76 both, 77 both, 78 t,** Edward J. Tarbuck; **78 bl,** Stephen Trimble; **78 br,** Gary Yeowell/Getty Images; **80 t,** Carr Clifton Photography; **80 b,** Michael Collier; **81,** Andrew Ward/Getty Images; **82,** Phil Dombrowski; **83 t,** Edward J. Tarbuck; **83 b,** Breck P. Kent; **85,** Carr Clifton Photography; **86, 87 all, 91 all,** Edward J. Tarbuck.

Chapter 4
Pages **92–93, 94 t,** Bettmann/Corbis; **94 b,** Kim Heacox/DRK Photo; **99,** James E. Patterson; **100,** Seaver Center for Western History Research/Natural History Museum of Los Angeles County; **102 t,** Bettmann/Corbis; **102 b,** Thomas Braise/Corbis; **103 t,** Martin Bond/Science Photo Library/Photo Researchers, Inc.; **103 b,** Comstock Images; **104,** John Mead/Science Photo Library/Photo Researchers, Inc.; **105,** Michael Collier; **106,** Pacific Gas & Electric Company; **108 t,** Bettmann/Corbis; **108 b,** Stocktrek/Corbis; **109,** Janis Burger/Bruce Coleman, Inc.; **110,** Stefan Zaklin/Getty Images; **111,** R. Ian Lloyd/Masterfile; **113 t,** Bettmann/Corbis; **113 b,** Steve Starr/Corbis; **114,** SuperStock, Inc.; **116,** Phil Degginger/Bruce Coleman, Inc.; **117 t,** Bettmann/Corbis; **117 b,** Michael Collier.

Chapter 5
Pages **124–125, 126 t,** David Muench/Muench Photography, Inc.; **126 b,** Tom & Susan Bean, Inc.; **127,** Photo Researchers, Inc.; **128,** Breck P. Kent; **129 t,** Tom & Susan Bean, Inc./DRK Photo; **129 bl,** Stephen J. Krasemann/DRK Photo; **129 bm, 129 br,** Edward J. Tarbuck; **130,** Doug Plummer/Photo Researchers, Inc.; **131 l,** Edward J. Tarbuck; **131 r,** Martin Schmidt, Jr.; **132,** Art Wolfe, Inc.; **133,** David Muench/Muench Photography, Inc.; **137 l,** Corbis; **137 r,** Dan Richter/ Visuals Unlimited; **138,** Dick Roberts/Visuals Unlimited; **139,** R. Ian Lloyd/Corbis; **140 t,** Wayne Lawler/Photo Researchers, Inc.; **140 b,** U.S. Department of Agriculture; **141,** Carl Purcell/Photo Researchers, Inc.; **143 t,** David Muench/ Muench Photography, Inc.; **143 b,** ChromoSohm/Sohm/Corbis; **144,** Noel Quidu/ Getty Images; **145,** Stephen Trimble; **146 t,** Chuck Place Photography; **146 b,** Edward J. Tarbuck; **147,** Science VU/Visuals Unlimited; **148–149,** Dorling Kindersley.

Chapter 6
Pages **156–157, 158,** Carr Clifton Photography; **163 both,** Michael Collier; **164,** Carr Clifton Photography; **165,** Mark Lyons/Getty Images; **167,** Art Wolfe, Inc.; **168,** Space Imaging; **171,** Carr Clifton Photography; **172,** Ken Hamblin; **175,** U.S. Geological Survey, Denver; **176 t,** Roy Morsch/Corbis; **176 b,** F. Rossotto/Corbis; **177,** Harris Photographic/Tom Stack & Associates, Inc.; **178,** Tom & Susan Bean, Inc.; **179,** St. Petersburg Times/Getty Images; **180,** Carr Clifton Photography.

Chapter 7
Pages **186–187, 188 t,** Tom & Susan Bean, Inc.; **188 b,** Carr Clifton Photography; **190,** Galen Rowell/Mountain Light Photography, Inc.; **191,** Tom & Susan Bean, Inc.; **192,** Carr Clifton Photography; **194 t,** Martin G. Miller; **194 b,** Edward J. Tarbuck; **195, 199 t,** Tom & Susan Bean, Inc.; **199 b,** David Muench/ Muench Photography, Inc.; **200 both,** Edward J. Tarbuck; **201,** Michael Collier; **203 t,** Tom & Susan Bean, Inc.; **203 b,** State Historical Society of North Dakota; **204 t,** David Muench/Muench Photography, Inc.; **204 b,** James E. Patterson; **205 l,** Michael Collier; **205 r,** Muench Photography, Inc.; **208–209,** Dorling Kindersley.

Chapter 8
Pages **216–217, 218 t,** Yann Arthus-Bertrand "Earth From Above"/Altitude/Peter Arnold, Inc.; **218 b,** David Weintraub/Photo Researchers, Inc.; **219,** Edward J. Tarbuck; **222, 229 t,** Yann Arthus-Bertrand "Earth From Above"/Altitude/Peter Arnold, Inc.; **229 b,** National Oceanic and Atmospheric Administration/Seattle; **231,** James L. Beck; **232,** U.S. Geological Survey, Denver; **233,** Yann Arthus-Bertrand "Earth From Above"/Altitude/Peter Arnold, Inc.; **238–239,** Dorling Kindersley.

Chapter 9
Pages **246–247, 248,** WorldSat International Inc., 2001. www.worldsat.ca. All Rights Reserved.; **253,** Carr Clifton Photography; **254, 258,** WorldSat International Inc., 2001. www.worldsat.ca. All Rights Reserved.; **260,** M. Timothy O'Keefe/Bruce Coleman, Inc.; **265, 269, 271,** WorldSat International Inc., 2001. www.worldsat.ca. All Rights Reserved.

Chapter 10
Pages **278–279, 280 t,** Art Wolfe, Inc.; **280 all,** U.S. Geological Survey, Denver; **282 l,** Doug Perrine/DRK Photo; **282 r,** J.D. Griggs/U.S. Geological Survey,

Denver; **284,** Greg Vaughn Photography; **285,** Michael Collier; **286,** David Muench/Muench Photography, Inc.; **287,** Greg Vaughn/Tom Stack & Associates, Inc.; **288 l,** Tom & Susan Bean, Inc./DRK Photo; **288 r,** John S. Shelton; **289 t,** Art Wolfe, Inc.; **289 b,** Edward J. Tarbuck; **291,** Art Wolfe, Inc.; **292,** Greg Vaughn Photography; **293 t,** Art Wolfe, Inc.; **293 b,** David Weintraub/Photo Researchers, Inc.; **295,** Arthur Roy/National Audubon Society/Photo Researchers, Inc.; **298–299,** Dorling Kindersley.

Chapter 11
Pages **306–307, 308 both,** Art Wolfe, Inc.; **311 both,** Tom & Susan Bean, Inc./DRK Photo; **313,** Michael Collier; **314 t,** Art Wolfe, Inc.; **314 b,** Peter French/DRK Photo; **315,** Michael Collier; **317 t,** Art Wolfe, Inc.; **317 b,** David Muench/Muench Photography, Inc.; **325, 332,** Art Wolfe, Inc.; **333 t,** Art Wolfe, Inc.; **333 b,** U.S. Geological Survey, Denver.

Chapter 12
Pages **334–335, 336 t,** Carr Clifton Photography; **336 m, 336 b,** U.S. Geological Survey, Denver; **338 t,** Edward J. Tarbuck; **338 b,** Michael Fogden/DRK Photo; **341 all,** Edward J. Tarbuck; **343 t,** Carr Clifton Photography; **343 b,** Reuters/Corbis; **344 tl,** Florissant Fossil Beds National Monument; **344 tr,** Edward J. Tarbuck; **344 ml,** Breck P. Kent; **344 mr,** Edward J. Tarbuck; **344 bl,** Muench Photography, Inc.; **344 br,** Edward J. Tarbuck; **347,** Carr Clifton Photography; **350,** Reuters/Corbis; **351 t,** Carr Clifton Photography; **351 b,** Stephen J. Krasemann/DRK Photo; **352,** Carr Clifton Photography.

Chapter 13
Pages **362–363, 364 t,** David Muench/Muench Photography, Inc.; **364 b,** Ira Block/National Geographic Image Collection; **368,** Sinclair Stammers/Science Photo Library/Photo Researchers, Inc.; **369,** David Muench/Muench Photography, Inc.; **371 t,** The Field Museum, Neg #GEO 80820C, Chicago.; **371 b,** GeoScience Resources/American Geological Institute (AGI); **375,** The Field Museum, Neg #GEO85637C, Chicago. Photographer: John Weinstein.; **377,** David Muench/Muench Photography, Inc.; **379,** Carr Clifton/Minden Pictures; **381,** Project Exploration P.A.S.T.; **382,** David Muench/Muench Photography, Inc.; **383,** Courtesy of the George C. Page Museum; **385,** David Muench/Muench Photography, Inc.; **389,** Sinclair Stammers/Science Photo Library/Photo Researchers, Inc.

Chapter 14
Pages **392–393, 394, 401,** Mark Muench/Muench Photography, Inc.; **406,** Douglas Peebles Photography; **406, 407,** Mark Muench/Muench Photography, Inc.; **409,** Deep Sea Drilling Project, Scripps Institution of Oceanography; **410 t,** Mark Muench/Muench Photography, Inc.; **410 b,** Gregory Ochocki/Photo Researchers, Inc.; **411 both,** GEOMAR Research Center; **412,** Lawrence Sullivan/Lamont Doherty Earth Observatory/Columbia University; **413,** William E. Townsend, Jr./Photo Researchers, Inc.

Chapter 15
Pages **420–421, 422,** Gary Bell/Seapics.com/Innerspace Visions; **423 tl,** Tom & Susan Bean, Inc.; **423 tr,** Wolfgang Kaehler Photography; **423 bl,** NASA; **423 br,** Paul Steel/Corbis; **428 t,** Gary Bell/Seapics.com/Innerspace Visions; **428 m, 428 b,** Norman T. Nicoll; **429 t,** Tom McHugh/Photo Researchers, Inc.; **429 m,** Larry Lisky/DRK Photo; **429 bl,** David Hall/Photo Researchers, Inc.; **429 br,** Fred Bavendam/Peter Arnold, Inc.; **432 t,** Dudley Foster/Woods Hole Oceanographic Institution; **432 b,** Al Giddings Images, Inc.; **433,** Gary Bell/Seapics.com/Innerspace Visions; **438–439,** Dorling Kindersley; **440,** Edward J. Tarbuck.

Chapter 16
Pages **446–447, 448 t,** Carr Clifton Photography; **448 b,** Marc Muench/Muench Photography, Inc.; **450,** O. Brown, R. Evans, and M. Carle, University of Miami Rosenstiel School of Marine and Atmospheric Science, Miami, Florida; **451,** Provided by the SeaWiFS Project, NASA/Goddard Space Flight Center and ORBIMAGE; **452,** Wayne Lynch/DRK Photo; **454, 455 t,** Carr Clifton Photography; **455 b,** Rafael Macia/Photo Researchers, Inc.; **461 t,** Carr Clifton Photography; **461 b,** Fletcher & Baylis/Photo Researchers, Inc.; **464 t,** Mark A. Johnson/Corbis; **464 b,** U.S. Department of Agriculture; **466,** Sandy Stockwell/London Aerial Photo Library/Bettmann/Corbis; **467 both,** U.S. Army Corps of Engineers, Headquarters; **468 both,** Nova Scotia Department of Tourism and Culture.

Chapter 17
Pages **474–475, 476 t,** Stone/Getty Images; **476 b,** Mike Groll/Getty Images; **479,** Carr Clifton/Minden Pictures; **482,** Brian Stablyk/Getty Images; **483,** Stone/Getty Images; **485,** Carr Clifton Photography; **488 t,** Stone/Getty Images; **488 b,** Bobbe Z. Christopherson; **494–495,** Dorling Kindersley; **496,** Edward J. Tarbuck.

Chapter 18
Pages **502–503, 504 t,** Gary Gray/DRK Photo; **504 b,** Mary Fulton/Getty Images; **508 t,** Wolfgang Kaehler Photography; **508 b,** Edward J. Tarbuck; **510 t,** Gary Gray/DRK Photo; **510 b,** Edward J. Tarbuck; **514,** Barbara Cushman Rowell/Mountain Light Photography, Inc.; **515,** Dick Canby/DRK Photo; **517 t,** Gary Gray/DRK Photo; **517 b,** Edward J. Tarbuck; **520,** Jim Brown/Corbis; **522,** Visual Communications/National Center for Atmospheric Research/University Corporation for Atmospheric Research/National Science Foundation; **523 t,** Gary Gray/DRK Photo; **523 b,** Ted Spiegel/Black Star.

Chapter 19
Pages **530–531, 532 t,** The Image Bank/Getty Images; **532 b,** National Geographic Image Collection/Getty Images; **537 t,** The Image Bank/Getty Images; **537 b,** Mark E. Gibson/DRK Photo; **543,** The Image Bank/Getty Images; **545,** Belfort Instrument Company; **549 t,** The Image Bank/Getty Images; **549 b,** Courtesy of NASA Goddard Space Flight Center.

Chapter 20
Pages **556–557, 558 t,** Kent Wood/Science Source/Photo Researchers, Inc.; **558 b,** John Sokich/National Oceanic and Atmospheric Administration/Seattle; **561,** AP/Wide World Photos; **562,** Tony Arruza/Corbis; **563,** Layne Kennedy/Corbis; **564 t,** Kent Wood/Science Source/Photo Researchers, Inc.; **564 b,** Kenneth Garrett/National Geographic Image Collection; **568,** John Jensenius/National Weather Service; **571 t,** Kent Wood/Science Source/Photo Researchers, Inc.; **571 b,** T.A. Wiewandt/DRK Photo; **574,** Warren Faidley/Weatherstock; **575,** AP/Wide World Photos; **578–579,** Dorling Kindersley.

Chapter 21
Pages **586–587, 588 t,** Yva Momatiuk & John Eastcott/Photo Researchers, Inc.; **588 b,** Pete Saloutos/Corbis; **591 l,** Charlie Ott Photography/Photo Researchers, Inc.; **591 r,** Larry Ulrich/DRK Photo; **592 t,** Yva Momatiuk & John Eastcott/Photo Researchers, Inc.; **592 b,** David Keaton/Corbis; **593 t,** Art Wolfe/Photo Researchers, Inc.; **593 b,** Stan Osolinski/Dembinsky Photo Associates; **599,** Fred Bruemmer/DRK Photo; **600 t,** Yva Momatiuk & John Eastcott/Photo Researchers, Inc.; **600 b,** Getty Images; **601,** Michey Welsh/Montgomery Advisor/Corbis Sygma; **604–605,** Dorling Kindersley.

Chapter 22
Pages **612–613, 614 t,** Galen Rowell/Mountain Light Photography, Inc.; **614 b,** David Lees/Corbis; **616 l,** Stapleton Collection/Corbis; **616 r,** Bettmann/Corbis; **617, 619,** With permission of the Royal Ontario Museum ©ROM.; **620 t,** Yerkes Observatory Photograph/University of Chicago; **620 bl,** AP/Wide World Photos; **620 br,** NASA; **622 t,** Galen Rowell/Mountain Light Photography, Inc.; **622 b,** Robin Scagell/Science Photo Library/Photo Researchers, Inc.; **626 all,** UC Regents/Lick Observatory; **628,** From Foundations of Astronomy, 3rd Edition, p. 54, by Michael Seeds. ©1992. Reprinted with permission of Brooks/Cole Publishing, a division of Thomson Learning.; **630 t,** Galen Rowell/Mountain Light Photography, Inc.; **630 b,** UC Regents/Lick Observatory; **634,** NASA; **635 t,** Galen Rowell/Mountain Light Photography, Inc.; **635 b,** Museum of Science and Industry; **640,** UC Regents/Lick Observatory.

Chapter 23
Pages **642–643, 644, 649 t,** Michael Collier; **649 b, 650 t,** NASA; **650 b,** NASA/Jet Propulsion Laboratory; **651,** David P. Anderson, SMU/NASA/Science Photo Library/Photo Researchers, Inc.; **652 t,** NASA; **652 b,** U.S. Geological Survey, Denver; **653,** NASA; **654,** Michael Collier; **655, 657, 658 both, 659,** NASA; **660,** Michael Collier; **661,** NASA; **664,** Jon Mandaville/Aramco World Magazine; **665 t,** Michael Collier; **665 b,** U.S. Geological Survey, Denver.

Chapter 24
Pages **672–673, 674, 678 t,** David Parker/Science Photo Library/Photo Researchers, Inc.; **678 b,** Roger Ressmeyer/Bettmann/Corbis; **681 l,** National Astronomy and Ionosphere Center's Arecibo Observatory, operated by Cornell University under contract with the National Science Foundation. Photo courtesy of David Parker, 1997/Science Photo Library; **681 r,** National Radio Astronomy Observatory; **682, 683,** NASA; **684 t,** David Parker/Science Photo Library/Photo Researchers, Inc.; **684 b,** Kent Wood/Photo Researchers, Inc.; **685,** National Optical Astronomy Observatories; **686,** NASA; **687 l,** Celestron International; **687 r,** National Optical Astronomy Observatories; **688 t,** Photri/Corbis; **688 b,** Michio Hoshino/Minden Pictures; **690,** Thomas Dimock/Corbis; **691 t,** David Parker/Science Photo Library/Photo Researchers, Inc.; **691 b,** Celestron International.

Chapter 25
Pages **698–699, 700,** Royal Observatory, Edinburgh/AATB/Science Photo Library/Photo Researchers, Inc.; **701,** National Optical Astronomy Observatories;

705 both, UC Regents/Lick Observatory; **706,** Anglo-Australian Observatory/ Royal Observatory, Edinburgh. Photograph from UK Schmidt plates by David Malin.; **707 t,** Royal Observatory, Edinburgh/AATB/Science Photo Library/Photo Researchers, Inc.; **707 b,** NASA; **710,** Anglo-Australian Observatory. Photography by David Malin.; **711,** UC Regents/Lick Observatory; **713,** California Inst. of Technology/Palomar/Hale Observatory; **715 t,** Royal Observatory, Edinburgh/ AATB/Science Photo Library/Photo Researchers, Inc.; **715 b,** Dr. Axel Mellinger; **717 t,** Anglo-Australian Observatory. Photography by David Malin.; **717 m,** Palomar Observatories/California Institute of Technology (Caltech); **717 bl,** ESO Education & Public Relations; **717 br, 718,** NASA; **722,** Royal Observatory, Edinburgh/AATB/Science Photo Library/Photo Researchers, Inc.

Skills and Reference Handbook
Page 728, Richard Megna/Fundamental Photographs; **729,** Russ Lappa; **730,** Jerry Howard; **731,** David Young-Wolff/PhotoEdit, Inc.; **742,** Russ Lappa.

Periodic Table of the Elements

Legend:

Nonmetals	Metals	Metalloids	
C	Li	B	Solid
Br	Hg		Liquid
H			Gas
	Tc		Not found in nature

1
1A

1
H
Hydrogen
1.0079

2
2A

3	4
Li	**Be**
Lithium	Beryllium
6.941	9.0122

11	12
Na	**Mg**
Sodium	Magnesium
22.990	24.305

		3 3B	**4** 4B	**5** 5B	**6** 6B	**7** 7B	**8** 8B	**9**
19	20	21	22	23	24	25	26	27
K	**Ca**	**Sc**	**Ti**	**V**	**Cr**	**Mn**	**Fe**	**Co**
Potassium	Calcium	Scandium	Titanium	Vanadium	Chromium	Manganese	Iron	Cobalt
39.098	40.08	44.956	47.90	50.941	51.996	54.938	55.847	58.933
37	38	39	40	41	42	43	44	45
Rb	**Sr**	**Y**	**Zr**	**Nb**	**Mo**	**Tc**	**Ru**	**Rh**
Rubidium	Strontium	Yttrium	Zirconium	Niobium	Molybdenum	Technetium	Ruthenium	Rhodium
85.468	87.62	88.906	91.22	92.906	95.94	(98)	101.07	102.91
55	56	71	72	73	74	75	76	77
Cs	**Ba**	**Lu**	**Hf**	**Ta**	**W**	**Re**	**Os**	**Ir**
Cesium	Barium	Lutetium	Hafnium	Tantalum	Tungsten	Rhenium	Osmium	Iridium
132.91	137.33	174.97	178.49	180.95	183.85	186.21	190.2	192.22
87	88	103	104	105	106	107	108	109
Fr	**Ra**	**Lr**	**Rf**	**Db**	**Sg**	**Bh**	**Hs**	**Mt**
Francium	Radium	Lawrencium	Rutherfordium	Dubnium	Seaborgium	Bohrium	Hassium	Meitnerium
(223)	(226)	(262)	(261)	(262)	(263)	(264)	(265)	(268)

Lanthanide Series

57	58	59	60	61	62
La	**Ce**	**Pr**	**Nd**	**Pm**	**Sm**
Lanthanum	Cerium	Praseodymium	Neodymium	Promethium	Samarium
138.91	140.12	140.91	144.24	(145)	150.4

Actinide Series

89	90	91	92	93	94
Ac	**Th**	**Pa**	**U**	**Np**	**Pu**
Actinium	Thorium	Protactinium	Uranium	Neptunium	Plutonium
(227)	232.04	231.04	238.03	(237)	(244)

Science *of* **EARTH** **SYSTEMS**

Second Edition

Science *of* EARTH SYSTEMS

Second Edition

STEPHEN D. BUTZ

THOMSON
DELMAR LEARNING™

Australia Brazil Canada Mexico Singapore Spain United Kingdom United States

THOMSON

DELMAR LEARNING

Science of Earth Systems, *Second Edition*
Stephen D. Butz

Vice President, Career Education Strategic Business Unit:
Dawn Gerrain

Director of Learning Solutions:
John Fedor

Managing Editor:
Robert L. Serenka, Jr.

Acquisitions Editor:
David Rosenbaum

Product Manager:
Christina Gifford

Editorial Assistant:
Scott Royael

Director of Production:
Wendy A. Troeger

Production Manager:
Mark Bernard

Senior Content Project Manager:
Kathryn B. Kucharek

Technology Project Manager:
Sandy Charette

Director of Marketing:
Wendy Mapstone

Channel Manager:
Gerard McAvey

Cover Images:
Getty Images Inc.

Cover Design:
Suzanne Nelson

For permission to use material from this text or product, submit a request online at http://www.thomsonrights.com
Any additional questions about permissions can be submitted by email to thomsonrights@thomson.com

Library of Congress Cataloging-in-Publication Data.

Butz, Stephen D.
Science of earth systems / Stephen D. Butz— 2nd ed.
p. cm.
Includes index.
ISBN 1-4180-4122-X
1. Earth sciences—Textbooks. I. Title.
QE28.B967 2007

550–dc22

2006038076

NOTICE TO THE READER

Preface

For much of the twentieth century, science has been divided into unique, highly specialized disciplines that have attempted to unlock the workings of nature. Until recently, each of these branches of science have remained virtually isolated from one another. Not only has this scientific isolation existed at the higher academic levels, but it is also standard practice in much of the secondary school science curriculum. Today, because of the changes that are being made by humankind on the Earth, scientists in these separate academic disciplines are finding it necessary to collaborate with one another on a unprecedented scale. It has now become necessary for them to share their research to try to understand the Earth's complex systems, and how those systems are being affected by human activity. This new area of collaborative research is called Earth system science, which is a combination of all the scientific disciplines into one body of knowledge. *Science of Earth Systems*, 2nd edition, is a textbook designed to introduce this new scientific discipline to secondary school students. This textbook brings together in one volume, the interactions that occur in the living and nonliving world. Whether students are studying the Earth sciences, agriculture, or environmental science, this text provides an understanding of the physical and biological processes that exist on our planet. *Science of Earth Systems* was written to meet the National Science Education Standards developed by the National Academy of Sciences for the Earth and space sciences, and can be easily aligned with Earth science-related standards and curriculum taught throughout the United States. This text provides an overview of all of the principle physical, chemical, and biological systems that occur on the Earth, and how they are being altered by human activity. Major topics include the role of science and technology in society, matter, energy, astronomy, geology, meteorology, oceanography, biology, environmental science, and much more. *Science of Earth Systems* introduces students to the processes that occur on our Earth by dividing the planet into five unique spheres, the exosphere, lithosphere, atmosphere, hydrosphere, and biosphere. Together these five spheres cover all the principal interactions between the Earth's physical and biological properties that make our planet unique. Any educator who needs to teach secondary students about the basic functions of the Earth and how those functions interact with the living world will find this textbook extremely useful. *Science of Earth Systems* begins with an introduction to the foundations of science and technology and an overview of the basic concepts of matter and energy. The textbook then presents the five individual spheres that together make up all of the Earth's systems.

Each unit in the textbook begins with a list of topics to be covered, and is divided into individual chapters that cover each specific subject to be learned. All of the chapters in this textbook begin with clear educational **objectives** to be learned by the student in the reading, and a list of important **terms to know.**

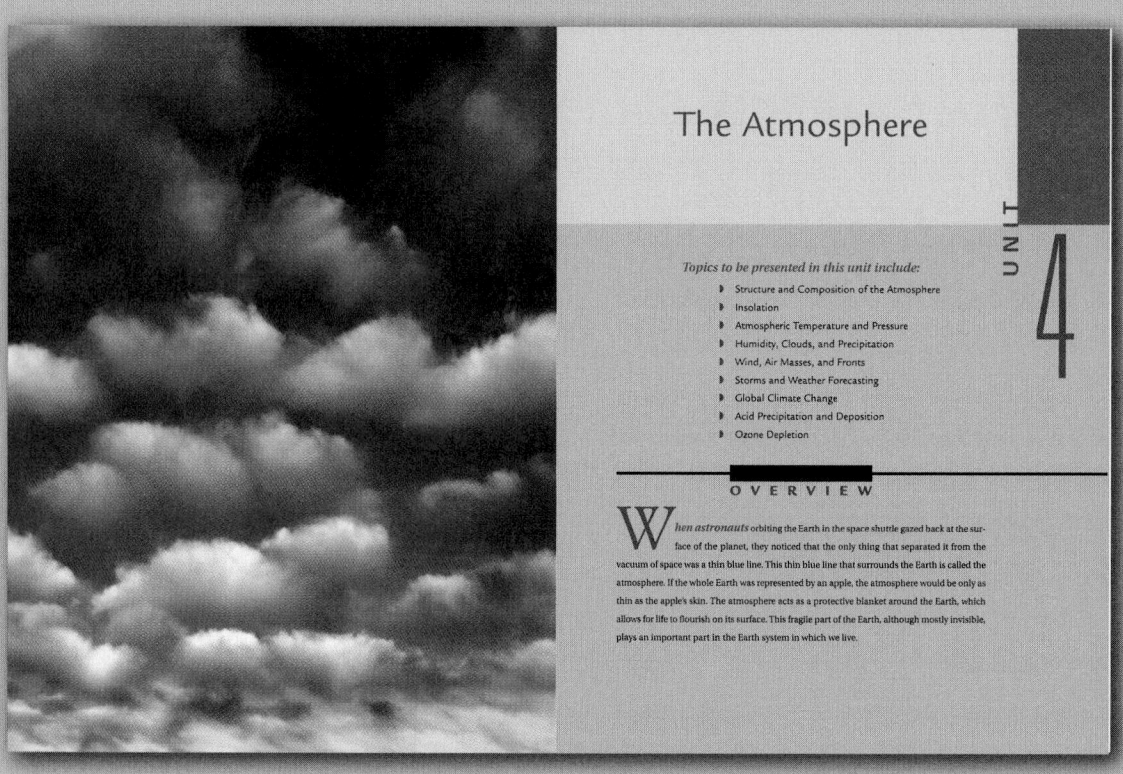

The Atmosphere

Topics to be presented in this unit include:

▶ Structure and Composition of the Atmosphere
▶ Insolation
▶ Atmospheric Temperature and Pressure
▶ Humidity, Clouds, and Precipitation
▶ Wind, Air Masses, and Fronts
▶ Storms and Weather Forecasting
▶ Global Climate Change
▶ Acid Precipitation and Deposition
▶ Ozone Depletion

UNIT 4

OVERVIEW

When astronauts orbiting the Earth in the space shuttle gazed back at the surface of the planet, they noticed that the only thing that separated it from the vacuum of space was a thin blue line. This thin blue line that surrounds the Earth is called the atmosphere. If the whole Earth was represented by an apple, the atmosphere would be only as thin as the apple's skin. The atmosphere acts as a protective blanket around the Earth, which allows for life to flourish on its surface. This fragile part of the Earth, although mostly invisible, plays an important part in the Earth system in which we live.

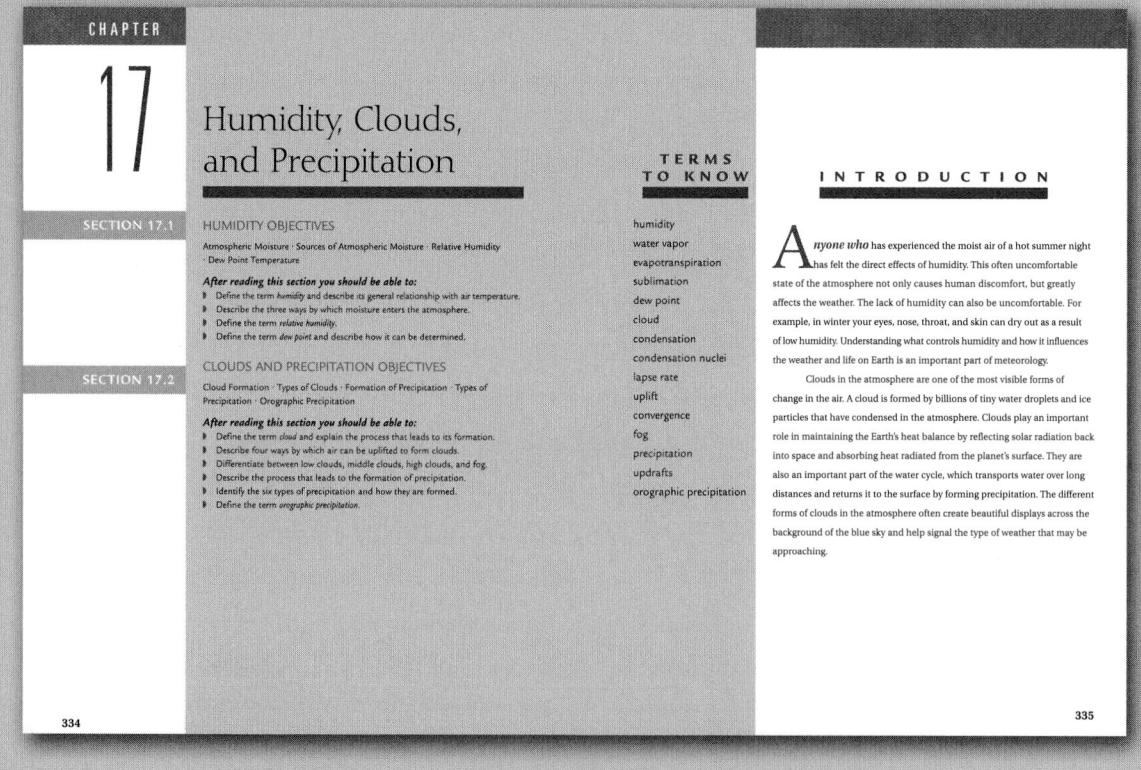

CHAPTER 17

Humidity, Clouds, and Precipitation

SECTION 17.1

HUMIDITY OBJECTIVES

Atmospheric Moisture · Sources of Atmospheric Moisture · Relative Humidity · Dew Point Temperature

After reading this section you should be able to:
▶ Define the term *humidity* and describe its general relationship with air temperature.
▶ Describe the three ways by which moisture enters the atmosphere.
▶ Define the term *relative humidity.*
▶ Define the term *dew point* and describe how it can be determined.

CLOUDS AND PRECIPITATION OBJECTIVES

Cloud Formation · Types of Clouds · Formation of Precipitation · Types of Precipitation · Orographic Precipitation

SECTION 17.2

After reading this section you should be able to:
▶ Define the term *cloud* and explain the process that leads to its formation.
▶ Describe four ways by which air can be uplifted to form clouds.
▶ Differentiate between low clouds, middle clouds, high clouds, and fog.
▶ Describe the process that leads to the formation of precipitation.
▶ Identify the six types of precipitation and how they are formed.
▶ Define the term *orographic precipitation.*

TERMS TO KNOW

humidity
water vapor
evapotranspiration
sublimation
dew point
cloud
condensation
condensation nuclei
lapse rate
uplift
convergence
fog
precipitation
updrafts
orographic precipitation

INTRODUCTION

Anyone who has experienced the moist air of a hot summer night has felt the direct effects of humidity. This often uncomfortable state of the atmosphere not only causes human discomfort, but greatly affects the weather. The lack of humidity can also be uncomfortable. For example, in winter your eyes, nose, throat, and skin can dry out as a result of low humidity. Understanding what controls humidity and how it influences the weather and life on Earth is an important part of meteorology.

Clouds in the atmosphere are one of the most visible forms of change in the air. A cloud is formed by billions of tiny water droplets and ice particles that have condensed in the atmosphere. Clouds play an important role in maintaining the Earth's heat balance by reflecting solar radiation back into space and absorbing heat radiated from the planet's surface. They are also an important part of the water cycle, which transports water over long distances and returns it to the surface by forming precipitation. The different forms of clouds in the atmosphere often create beautiful displays across the background of the blue sky and help signal the type of weather that may be approaching.

E ach chapter contains **key vocabulary words** highlighted in bold, **Career Connections**, and many colorful **pictures** and **diagrams** that help illustrate the concepts presented.

---

476 UNIT 5 The Hydrosphere

Transpiration and evaporation from plants

Precipitation

Evaporation from land and water

Runoff to rivers and streams

Runoff

Soil moisture

Ground infiltration and percolation

Groundwater (zone of saturation)

Water table

FIGURE 24–5 The pathways that water can take when it comes into contact with the soil include runoff, infiltration, and evapotranspiration.

EVAPOTRANSPIRATION

The fourth pathway that precipitation can take once it arrives at the surface is absorption by plants. Plants take water up through their root systems and distribute it throughout their bodies. Some of this water eventually reaches the leaves, where it evaporates back into the atmosphere. The process of water entering the root system of a plant, moving through the plant body, and then evaporating off the leaf surface is called evapotranspiration, also known simply as transpiration (Figure 24–5). Evapotranspiration can often play an important role in determining local climate by adding water vapor to the atmosphere. Large forests can add millions of gallons of water into the atmosphere by the process of evapotranspiration. One birch tree alone can add approximately 70 gal (265 l) of water, and one mature corn plant contributes more than 1 gal (3.8 l) of water each day to the atmosphere by evapotranspiration.

INFILTRATION AND GROUNDWATER

The final pathway that precipitation can take once it strikes the land surface is called infiltration. Infiltration is the movement of water into soil or rock. The rate of infiltration of water into the ground

CHAPTER 24 The Hydrologic Cycle | 477

depends on a few factors. The size of the pore spaces within the ground greatly affects the rate at which water infiltrates. Generally, the larger the size of the pores, the greater the rate of infiltration. Also, the amount of water within the pore spaces affects the rate of infiltration. The more water contained in the pore spaces within the ground, the slower the rate of infiltration. Pore spaces that are completely saturated with water will prevent any water from infiltrating into the soil, causing it to run off instead. The arrangement of particles in a soil also affects the rate of infiltration. Particles of mixed size tend to pack tightly together and reduce the amount of pores in the ground. This then reduces the infiltration rate. Sorted particles of similar size increase the pore spaces and therefore increase the infiltration rate.

Once the water infiltrates the ground, it is called groundwater. Groundwater holds approximately 0.6 percent of Earth's total water, which is a greater volume than all the world's lakes and rivers combined. Groundwater is an important source of freshwater for drinking and irrigation. Most groundwater eventually returns to the surface as flowing springs or is pumped out by mechanical wells. Approximately 50 percent of all Americans get their water from wells supplied by groundwater.

No matter which pathway precipitation takes when it reaches the land surface, eventually all water on Earth returns to the oceans, and the hydrologic cycle begins again. This might take days, years, or thousands of years depending on the specific pathway the water is traveling. The processes that help to move water around the planet involve the use of a great amount of energy. Mostly it is the power of the Sun that drives the hydrologic cycle, along with the force of gravity.

CAREER CONNECTIONS
Water Resource Engineer

A water resource engineer works in the planning, design, construction, and operation of all aspects of water use. This includes the management of all engineering projects that use water resources. Water resource engineers design systems for specific water resource projects such as flood control, dam construction, sewer systems, municipal water supplies, irrigation, and water transportation. These engineers work both in the field and in the laboratory, where they conduct surveys, perform tests, design projects, oversee construction, and monitor systems. They require knowledge of engineering, hydrology, and construction. Water resource engineers can find employment in private industry or with state and local governments.

---

658 UNIT 6 The Biosphere

A Section of a Dicot Leaf

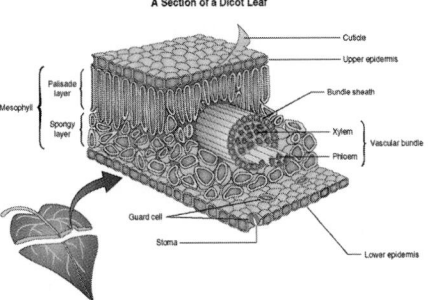

Cuticle
Upper epidermis
Mesophyll — Palisade layer, Spongy layer
Bundle sheath
Xylem
Phloem — Vascular bundle
Guard cell
Stoma
Lower epidermis

FIGURE 35–6 Cross section of the leaf of a vascular plant showing the tiny tubes that transport water and nutrients throughout the body of the plant.

CHAPTER 35 Classification of the Living World | 659

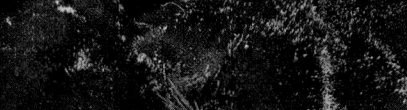

FIGURE 35–9 A close-up view of a moss, a nonvascular plant, producing spores. (*Courtesy of PhotoDisc.*)

cover that protects the seed. These include cone-bearing trees, also known as conifers (Figure 35–7). Common conifers include pine and spruce trees.

Angiosperms, which means "enclosed seed," are also called flowering plants. These green plants reproduce by producing seeds with a protective shell. Angiosperms are also known as flowering plants because these organisms produce flowers that bear the seeds (Figure 35–8). Flowering plants must be pollinated before they can form a seed. Insects and wind are important for the pollination of flowering plants.

Once a flower is pollinated, it produces a fruit. A fruit is a fleshy organ that protects seeds and helps them to be transported. Many plant fruits are eaten by animals and are then dispersed. Humans use many fruits for their nutrition. Technically, a fruit is anything that contains a seed. Therefore common vegetables such as cucumbers, squash, and tomatoes are truly fruits. Seedless vascular plants include ferns, which reproduce by producing spores. Spores are tiny cells that float on the wind and eventually land on the ground, where they grow into a mature plant.

Nonvascular green plants include mosses and liverworts (Figure 35–9). These organisms form matlike green carpets along the soil. Mosses also use spores for reproduction.

The plant kingdom forms the base for primary productivity in all terrestrial ecosystems. Many organisms rely on plants for food and shelter. Human beings cultivate specific plants for use as food and for industry. Trees are an important source of wood for construction and

for fiber used in making paper. Other green plants are used for making cloth, such as cotton, and flax, which is used to make linen. Green plants are also an important source of chemicals for use in medicine. It is estimated that green plants make up 90 percent of all the living material on land, making them an important part of the biosphere.

THE KINGDOM ANIMALIA

The kingdom Animalia includes all multicellular organisms that gain their nutrition by ingestion. Ingestion means to take in parts of or a whole organism. The animal kingdom is divided into two broad categories called invertebrates and vertebrates (Figure 35–10).

INVERTEBRATE ANIMALS

Invertebrates are animals that have no backbone or spine. Approximately 95 percent of all animals are classified as invertebrates. Invertebrates are further divided into specific phyla based on similar characteristics. The phylum Porifera includes organisms such as sponges. Sponges are marine animals that filter water through porelike openings in their bodies. Sponges were once harvested from the ocean by sponge divers.

FIGURE 35–7 Pine cones protect the seeds of a gymnosperm such as a pine tree. (*Courtesy of PhotoDisc.*)

FIGURE 35–8 Angiosperms, also known as flowering plants, growing over a rolling hillside. (*Courtesy of PhotoDisc.*)

In addition, each chapter contains **current research topics** and **internet sites**. Each chapter also highlights the lives and achievements of various **Earth System Scientists** throughout history.

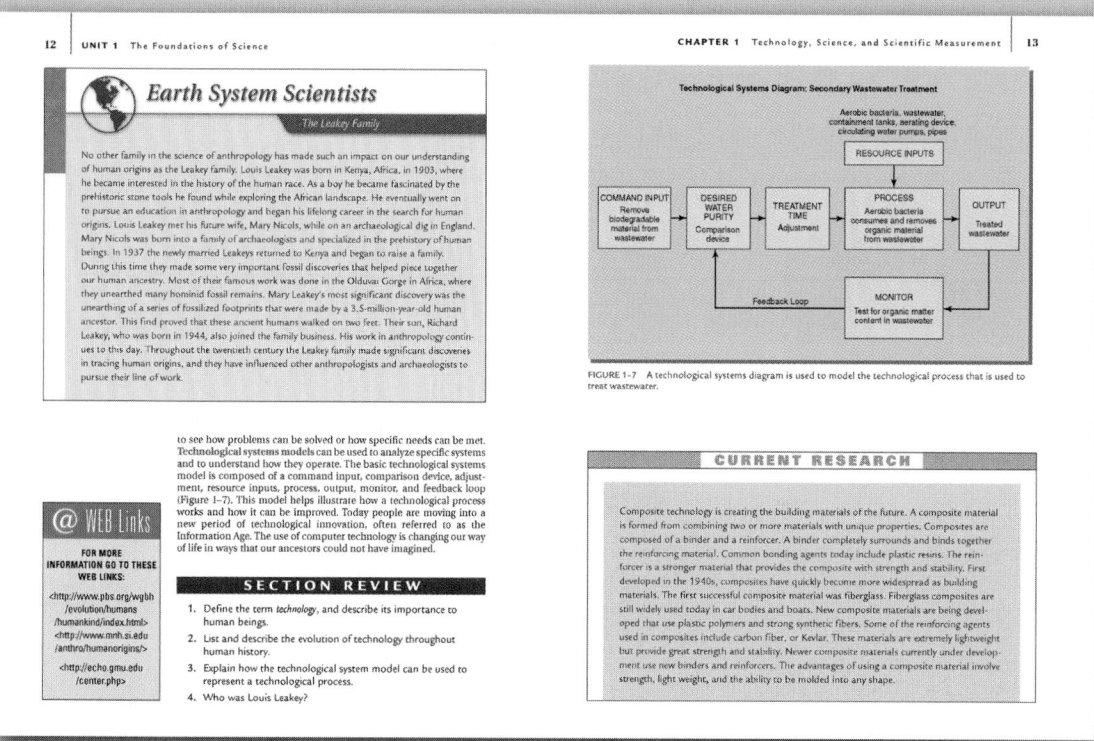

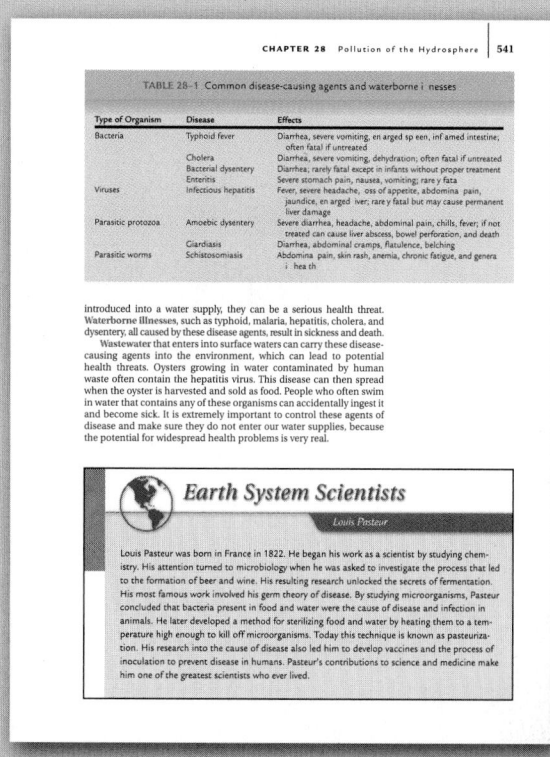

The end of each chapter is followed by a series of **review questions.** These questions include short answer, **Earth Math,** multiple choice, matching, and critical thinking. A **Chapter Summary** also highlights the topics that have been presented.

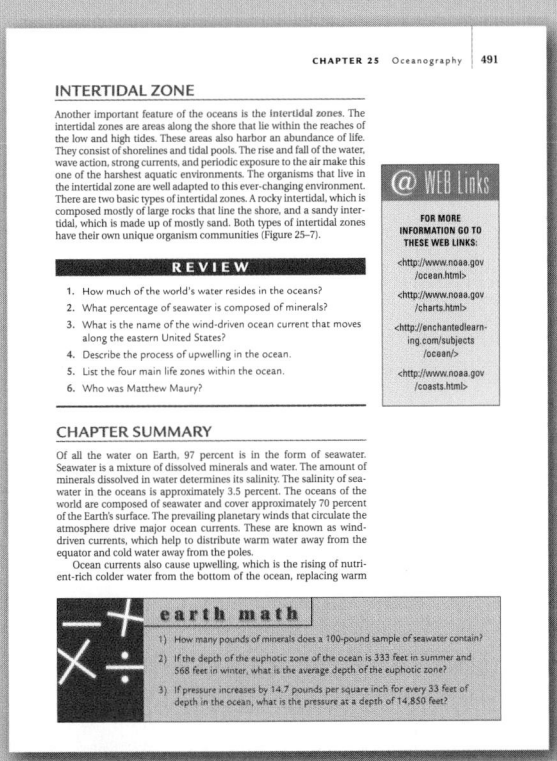

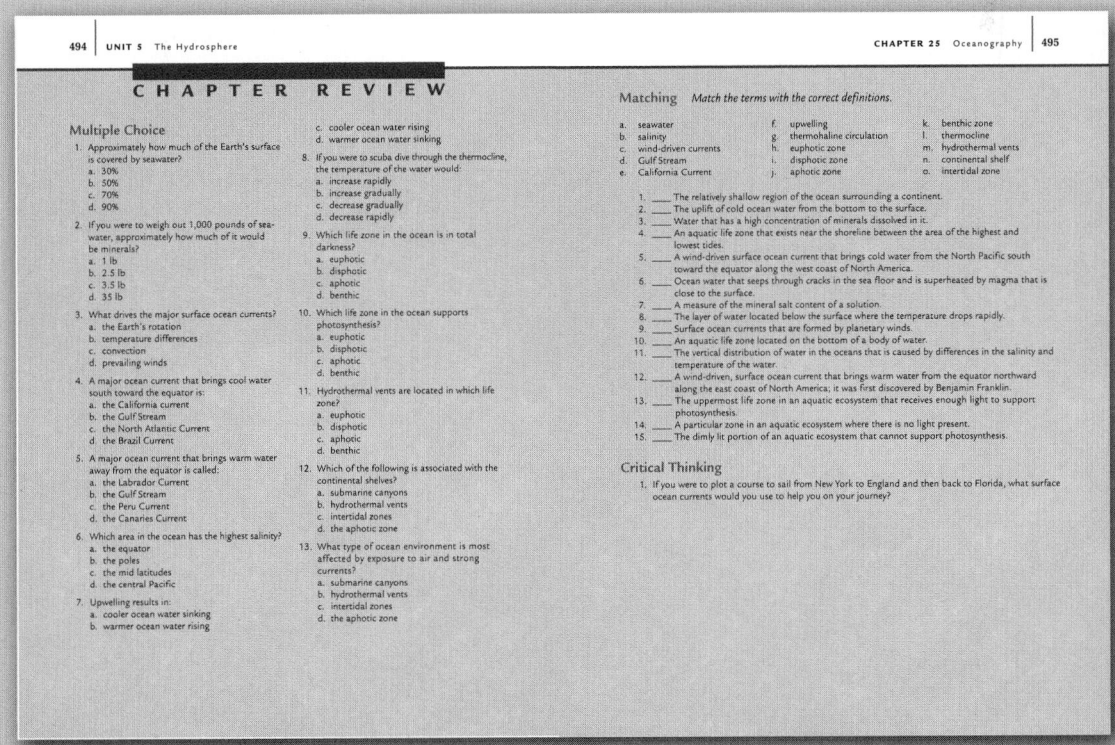

Also available with this textbook is a comprehensive **Instructor's Guide** and **Classmaster CD-ROM** that contains lesson planning suggestions, PowerPoint slides, and a test bank. *Science of Earth Systems* also offers a companion **Laboratory Manual** that includes 55 laboratory experiments and activities that help reinforce the material learned in each chapter and a corresponding **Lab Manual Instructor's Guide.** The laboratory manual and lab manual instructor's guide are available in either a print form or via CD-ROM. The **Lab Manual CD-ROM** affords the instructors the license to unlimited use to all of the lab material provided and the ability to provide copies to all their students, resulting in a cost savings. In addition, a **Classroom Interactivity CD-ROM** is available, which allows the instructor to create a dynamic learning environment through the use of four different software applications, each resembling a popular game show format. Overall, *Science of Earth Systems* is a textbook with ancillary materials that offers the complete instructional materials needed for introducing secondary students to the physical systems of the Earth and the interactions that exist between its living and nonliving components.

Contents

Common units of measurement used in science

Length
Metric
1 kilometer (km) = 1,000 meters (m)
1 meter (m) = 100 centimeters (cm)
1 meter (m) = 1,000 millimeters (mm)
1 centimeter (cm) = 0.01 meter (m)
1 millimeter (mm) = 0.001 meter (m)

English
1 foot (ft) = 12 inches (in)
1 yard (yd) = 3 feet (ft)
1 mile (mi) = 5,280 feet (ft)
1 nautical mile = 1.15 miles

Metric-English
1 kilometer (km) = 0.621 mile (mi)
1 meter (m) = 39.4 inches (in)
1 inch (in) = 2.54 centimeters (cm)
1 foot (ft) = 0.305 meter (m)
1 yard (yd) = 0.914 meter (m)
1 nautical mile = 1.85 kilometers (km)

Area
Metric
1 square kilometer (km^2) = 1,000,000 square meters (m^2)
1 square meter (m^2) = 1,000,000 square
    millimeters (mm^2)
1 hectare (ha) = 10,000 square meters (m^2)
1 hectare (ha) = 0.01 square kilometer (km^2)

English
1 square foot (ft^2) = 144 square inches (in^2)
1 square yard (yd^2) = 9 square feet (ft^2)
1 square mile (mi^2) = 27,880,000 square feet (ft^2)
1 acre (ac) = 43,560 square feet (ft^2)

Metric-English
1 hectare (ha) = 2.471 acres (ac)
1 square kilometer (km^2) = 0.386 square mile (mi^2)
1 square meter (m^2) = 1.196 square yards (yd^2)
1 square meter (m^2) = 10.76 square feet (ft^2)
1 square centimeter (cm^2) = 0.155 square inch (in^2)

Volume
Metric
1 cubic kilometer (km^3) = 1,000,000,000 cubic
    meters (m^3)
1 cubic meter (m$_3$) = 1,000,000 cubic centimeters (cm^3)
1 liter (L) = 1,000 milliliters (mL) = 1,000 cubic
    centimeters (cm^3)
1 milliliter (mL) = 0.001 liter (L)
1 milliliter (mL) = 1 cubic centimeter (cm^3)

English
1 gallon (gal) = 4 quarts (qt)
1 quart (qt) = 2 pints (pt)

Metric-English
1 liter (L) = 0.265 gallon (gal)
1 liter (L) = 1.06 quarts (qt)
1 liter (L) = 0.0353 cubic foot (ft^3)
1 cubic meter (m^3) = 35.3 cubic feet (ft^3)
1 cubic meter (m^3) = 1.30 cubic yard (yd^3)
1 cubic kilometer (km^3) = 0.24 cubic mile (mi^3)
1 barrel (bbl) = 159 liters (L)
1 barrel (bbl) = 42 U.S. gallons (gal)

Mass
Metric
1 kilogram (kg) = 1,000 grams (g)
1 gram (g) = 1,000 milligrams (mg)
1 gram (g) = 1,000,000 micrograms (μg)
1 milligram (mg) = 0.001 gram (g)
1 metric ton (mt) = 1,000 kilograms (kg)

English
1 ton (t) = 2,000 pounds (lb)
1 pound (lb) = 16 ounces (oz)

Metric-English
1 metric ton (mt) = 2,200 pounds (lb) = 1.1 tons (t)
1 kilogram (kg) = 2.20 pounds (lb)
1 pound (lb) = 454 grams (g)
1 gram (g) = 0.035 ounce (oz)

Energy and Power
Metric
1 kilojoule (kJ) = 1,000 joules (J)
1 kilocalorie (kcal) = 1,000 calories (cal)
1 calorie (cal) = 4,184 joules (J)

Metric-English
1 kilojoule (kJ) = 0.949 British thermal unit (Btu)
1 kilojoule (kJ) = 0.000278 kilowatt-hour (kW-h)
1 kilocalorie (kcal) = 3.97 British thermal units (Btu)
1 kilocalorie (kcal) = 0.00116 kilowatt-hour (kW-h)
1 kilowatt-hour (kW-h) = 860 kilocalories (kcal)
1 kilowatt-hour (kW-h) = 3,400 British thermal units (Btu)
1 quad (Q) = 1,050,000,000,000,000 kilojoules (kJ)
1 quad (Q) = 2,930,000,000,000 kilowatt-hours (kW-h)

Fahrenheit (°F) to Celsius (°C): $°C = \dfrac{°F - 32.0}{1.80}$

Celsius (°C) to Fahrenheit (°F): °F 5 (°C × 1.80) + 32.0

The Foundations of Science

UNIT 1

Topics to be presented in this unit include:

- ▶ The Foundations of Technology
- ▶ The Foundations of Science
- ▶ Scientific Observation and Measurement
- ▶ The Properties of Matter
- ▶ The Properties of Energy

OVERVIEW

From the beginnings of humankind, ancient people were at one with their world. Their understanding of the processes of nature were vital for their own survival. It was only a natural development for early humans to want to learn about the world in which they lived. Other creatures who shared the Earth with early humans used their own special adaptations to survive. Humans, on the other hand, used the power of thought to help them survive in the often harsh conditions that exist in nature. From these early beginnings, humans were learning about the environment in which they lived, and experimenting with new ways to improve their situation. This was certainly the beginning of what we know today as science and technology. Gathering information about the natural world, and then putting that knowledge to use in a practical form, has been a human trait for tens of thousands of years. This has resulted in a lasting relationship between science and technology, which continues to advance the human condition.

1 Technology, Science, and Scientific Measurement

TECHNOLOGY OBJECTIVES

Human Origins · Stone Age Technology · The Agricultural Revolution · Bronze Age and Iron Age Technology · The Industrial Revolution · Technological Systems

After reading this section you should be able to:
▶ Define the term *technology*, and describe its importance to human beings.
▶ Identify the progressive evolutionary developments of human technology.
▶ Explain the systems approach to understanding how technologies solve problems.
▶ Identify the different parts of a technological systems model.

THE FOUNDATIONS OF SCIENCE OBJECTIVES

The Birth of Science · The Scientific Method · Scientific Experiments · Science, Technology, and Engineering

After reading this section you should be able to:
▶ Define the term *science*.
▶ Explain the three main processes that together make up the scientific method.
▶ Discuss the importance of performing experiments in the process of scientific investigation.
▶ Explain the differences between science and engineering.

SCIENTIFIC MEASUREMENT OBJECTIVES

Observation and Measurement · Units of Measurement · Density · Scientific Notation · Percent Error

After reading this section you should be able to:
▶ Define the term *observation*.
▶ Explain why scientists use scientific instruments.
▶ Identify the fundamental units of measurement.
▶ Differentiate between the standard and metric systems of measurement.
▶ Define the term *density*, and explain how it affects a substance's physical properties.
▶ Explain why scientists use scientific notation.
▶ Explain why calculating percent error is an important part of scientific measurement.

INTRODUCTION

Try to imagine a world without science and technology. What would it be like, and more important, would you want to live in that world? For most of us the answer would certainly be no, for science and technology affect every aspect of our lives. The use of tools, materials, and technological processes are as important to human beings as wings are to a bird or claws are to a bear. These animals rely on these adaptations for their own survival, as humans rely on science and technology for our own survival. The link between human beings and technology is inseparable because technology is an important extension of the human mind that allows us to do things and live like no other organism on the Earth. Equally important to humans is our search for knowledge and understanding of the world in which we live. This forms the base of what we call science, which has changed our understanding of the Earth and its place in the universe. But what exactly are science and technology and how have they changed our lives?

1.1 Technology

HUMAN ORIGINS

Humans possess the ability to extend their own capabilities by using tools. Since ancient times, people have devised ways to make specialized devices to improve their situation. This was the beginning of technology. The appearance of a new type of primate occurred on the African continent approximately 4 million years ago. This new species belonged to a family of what anthropologists called the hominid. Although this creature would hardly have looked like a modern-day human being, it possessed two very unique adaptations. The first was the ability to walk upright on two legs. The second was the ability to make stone tools. Walking upright is called bipedalism, which literally means "two feet." Probably the most significant aspect of the ability to stand and walk upright is that it allows for the arms and hands to be used in other ways. The first hominid to possess this skill is called Homo habilis ("clever human") by anthropologists. It lived about 2 million years ago. These are the first known human ancestors to create customized tools. Over the next 4 million years, the hominid family began to disperse and form new species, which eventually led to the development of modern humans (Homo sapiens) (Figure 1–1).

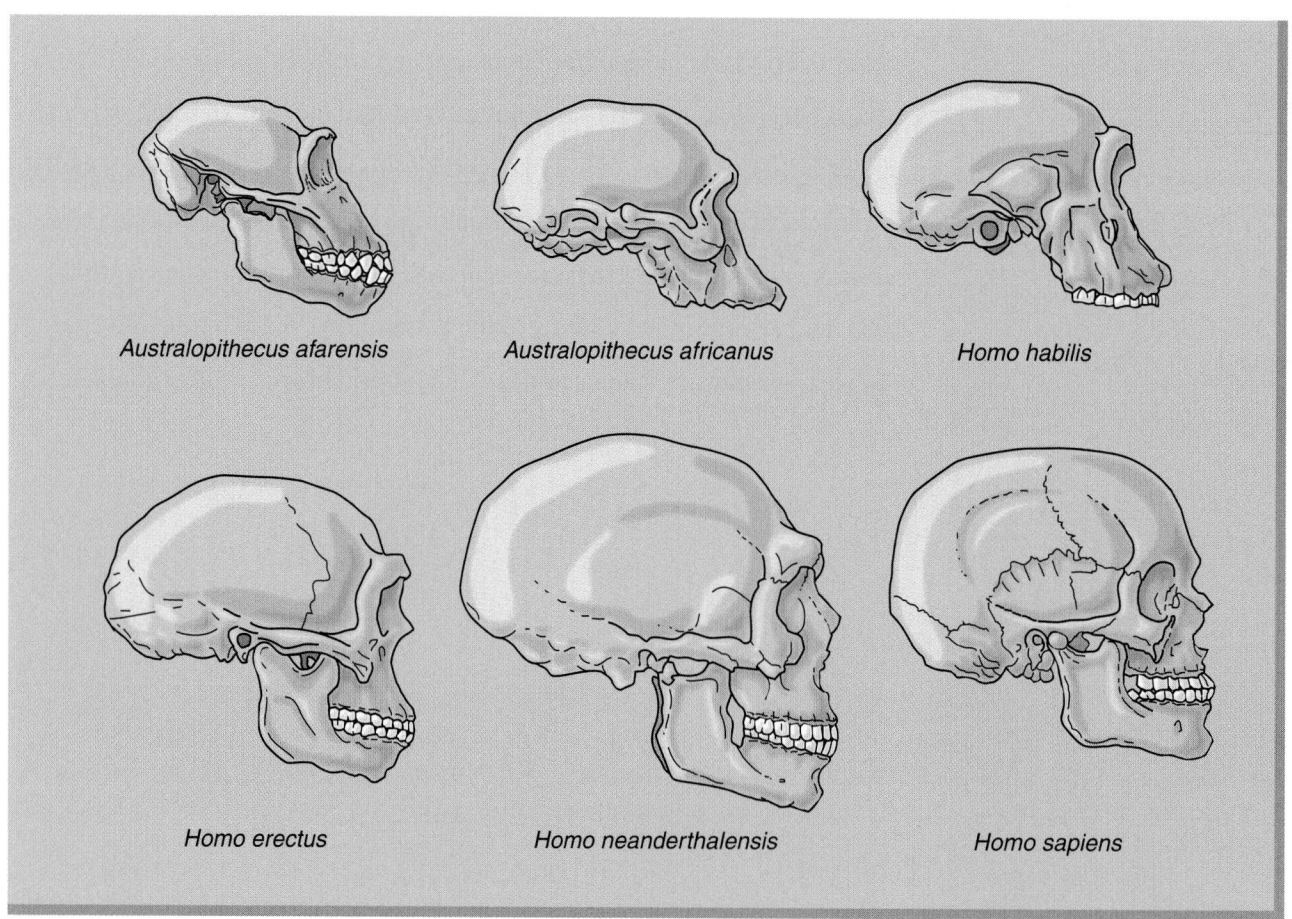

Australopithecus afarensis   *Australopithecus africanus*   *Homo habilis*

Homo erectus   *Homo neanderthalensis*   *Homo sapiens*

FIGURE 1–1   Comparison of hominid skull fossils traces the evolutionary development of human beings.

RECENT BREAKTHROUGH

The fossilized remains of a hominid, known as the Flores Man, were recently discovered in a cave on the remote island of Flores in Indonesia. Skeletal remains of this small hominid reveal that it stood at only 3 ft when fully grown, and might have lived about 13,000 years ago. Because of its small size, this small human-like creature has gained the nickname "Hobbit," from The Lord of the Rings novels. Stone tools and bones found at the site reveal that Flores Man made tools and hunted pygmy elephants, giant rodents, and Komodo Dragons that inhabited the island. After careful examination by anthropologists, this new species has been classified as Homo floresienses, and it is considered to be a smaller form of Homo erectus, which became extinct between 50,000 and 400,000 years ago. This new discovery suggests that this smaller form of Homo erectus survived until much more recently. More research is ongoing to determine how this species lived and might have interacted with modern humans, providing a new understanding of how our human ancestors coexisted.

Our early ancestors' ability to use their hands provided them with the opportunity to explore new ways in which to put them to use. Eventually this unique feature lead to the development of what we call technology. Modern humans, or Homo sapiens, ("intelligent human") are not the only hominid to have used tools. There is sufficient archeological evidence to suggest that many of our hominid ancestors also used primitive tools. The oldest tools discovered so far are approximately 2 million years old. These consist of crude stone implements called "choppers." Examples of these early stone tools are shown in Figure 1–2. Today, even modern chimpanzees and other animals like sea otters use primitive tools like these.

STONE AGE TECHNOLOGY

The use of tools by our early ancestors began what we call **technology**. Technology ("the science of skill") is defined as all the ways that human beings extend their capabilities to meet their wants and needs and to solve problems. Our early hominid ancestors used stone tool technology to extend their capabilities for more than 2 million years. The period of time that covers the use of stone tools is often called the Stone Age. The Stone Age is divided into two periods; the first is called the Paleolithic ("old stone") period. During the Paleolithic period, hominids used crude stones mainly for chopping and for breaking open animal bones to expose the nutritious marrow. Stone tools were also used for carving wood and for digging up plant roots. The later period of the Stone Age is called the Neolithic ("new stone"). During this period our ancestors began to manipulate stones to form customized sharp cutting tools for use in farming the land.

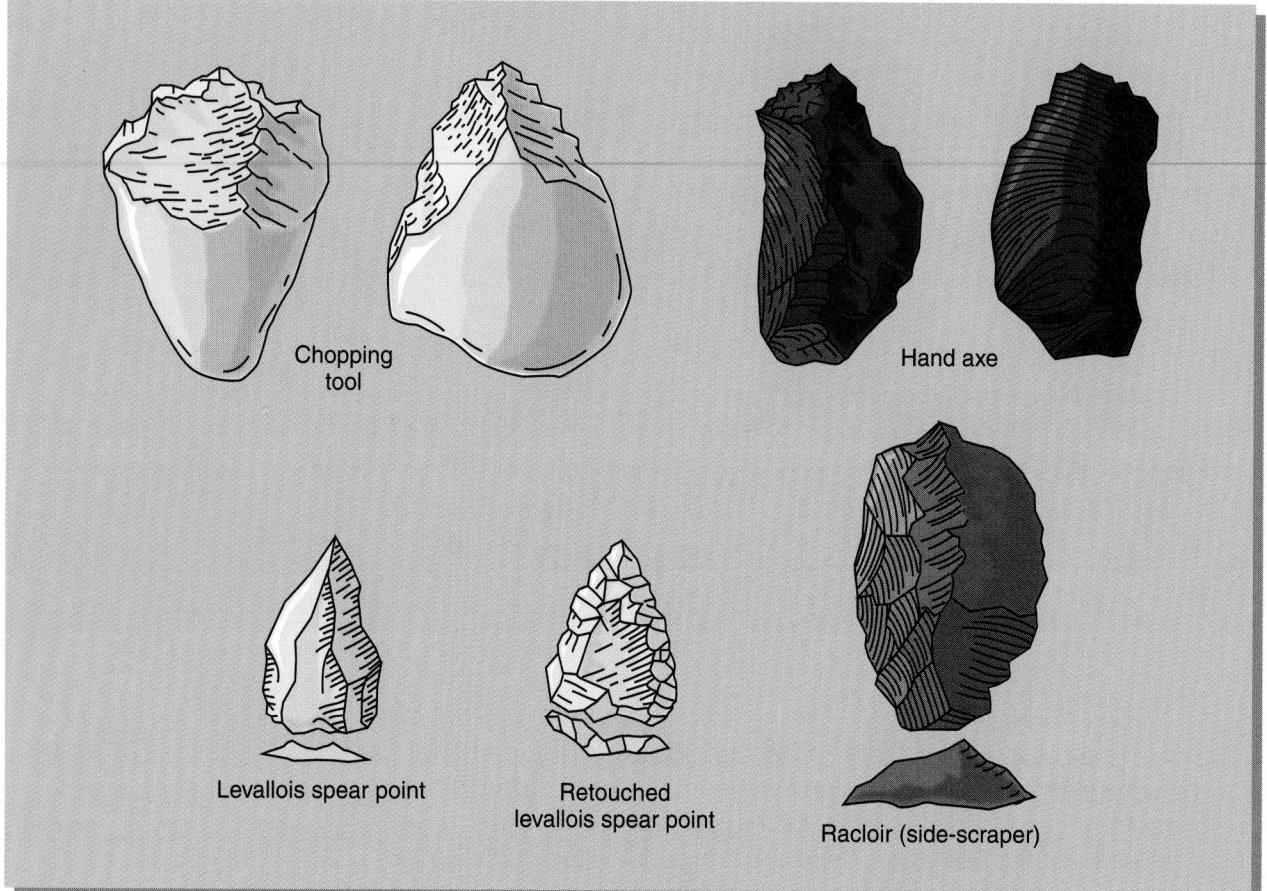

FIGURE 1–2   Examples of stone tools used by early humans for chopping and cutting.

THE AGRICULTURAL REVOLUTION

The appearance of modern humans approximately 100,000 years ago led to major advancements in technology. Modern humans began to craft very specialized tools in the form of spears and knives. About 35,000 years ago, people began creating pieces of art and primitive musical instruments. Over time, technology improved and became a part of everyday life. After fire and the wheel, one of the greatest (if not the most important) advancements in human technology was human domestication of plants and animals. This is called the Agricultural Revolution, which began approximately 10,000 years ago in southwest Asia (Figure 1–3).

During the Agricultural Revolution, humans created many customized tools made from stone, wood, and animal bones for growing and harvesting food crops. Until then, people hunted and scavenged off the land to meet their food needs. Agriculture created a whole new, better way of life for humans. No longer did they need to move around the land in search of food; now they could settle in one area and grow their own food. One of the tools that helped tremendously in this endeavor was the wooden plow, which humans built approximately 7,000 years ago (Figure 1–4). This development allowed humans to farm larger areas of land and grow more food.

FIGURE 1–3 The shift by early humans from a hunter-gather society to harvesting crops they have grown marked the beginning of the Agricultural Revolution more than 10,000 years ago. (*Courtesy of Getty Image Inc.*)

CAREER CONNECTIONS
Anthropology

Scientists who study human beings, their culture, and their origins are called anthropologists. Anthropology is divided into four major fields: Physical anthropology, cultural anthropology, archaeology, and linguistics. Physical anthropologists, also called biological anthropologists, study the unique biological adaptations of humans and also the origin of the human species. Cultural anthropologists study the social behavior and specific cultures of humans throughout the world both in the past and today. Archaeologists study the history of humans by searching for the remains of ancient cultures. Linguists study the origins and development of human language. Careers in anthropology usually require a four-year college degree and can lead to jobs in academic fields, corporations, nonprofit organizations, and state and federal governments.

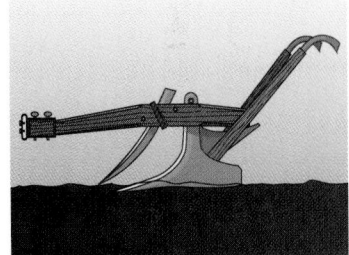

FIGURE 1–4 The moldboard plow enabled humans to efficiently prepare the land for the growth of crops.

BRONZE AGE AND IRON AGE TECHNOLOGY

FIGURE 1–5 Smelting iron ore at high temperatures creates molten metal, which can then be molded into tools. (*Courtesy of PhotoDisc.*)

As the human population grew, so did the number of technological advancements. One of these was the use of naturally occurring metal ore deposits such as copper and tin to create new, stronger tools. This began more than 5,000 years ago and marked the beginning of the Bronze Age. Bronze is an alloy, or mixture, of copper and tin. Humans learned that different metals could be mixed together to form strong new tools. Eventually they found that iron was better than bronze for making tools. Iron was much stronger than bronze and quickly improved human tool-making abilities (Figure 1–5). This led to what is called the Iron Age.

THE INDUSTRIAL REVOLUTION

As time passed, human beings began to manipulate their world with many different tools and processes that improved the quality of life. Never before had the Earth seen such resourcefulness as in the human species. Human beings began to build cities, conquer the oceans, and construct complicated machinery. The culmination of human ingenuity began a new era called the Technological Revolution (or the Industrial Revolution), which started in the late 1800s (Figure 1–6).

Technology Timeline	
Paleolithic Period	• First use of stone tools by Homo habilis~2.5 million years ago • Emergence of modern humans (Homo sapiens)~100,000 years ago
Neolithic Period	• Use of stone, wood, and animal bone tools • Emergence of art and musical instruments~35,000 years ago • Beginning of agricultural revolution~10,000 years ago • First known use of wooden plow in southwest Asia~7000 years ago • First known use of the wheel~5500 years ago
Bronze Age	• Emergence of copper and bronze in tool making~5000 years ago • Beginning of textile production in Mesopotamia~5000 years ago
Iron Age	• Smelting of iron in Africa~3000 years ago • Use of iron in Europe and China~2000 years ago • Construction of the Roman aqueducts~300 B.C.
Industrial Age	• Invention of the steam engine–1720 A.D. • Invention of the steamboat–1807 A.D. • First airplane flight–1903 A.D. • First moon landing–1969 A.D.
Information Age (the present)	

FIGURE 1–6 The technology timeline is divided into different historical periods based on advances in technology.

Human beings now possessed the ability to build machines and use industrial processes to perform work that would have been unthinkable only 100 years earlier.

The technology of stone tools has long been surpassed; however, it is important to realize that new technologies are usually the result of manipulating or combining older technological processes. Today complicated machines and tools perform the same tasks that were once performed by primitive stone tools. Many profound technological advancements have occurred over the course of human history, including the harnessing and manipulation of fire, the development of spears and the bow and arrow, the invention of the agricultural plow, use of the wheel, the development of shipbuilding, the invention of the steam engine and the railroad, the development of the internal combustion engine, the invention of the light bulb, the development of the telephone, and the development of modern computers (Table 1–1). The list could go on, but the point is quite clear: Technology has been used in countless ways to perform countless tasks to improve the human condition.

TECHNOLOGICAL SYSTEMS

Human problems and needs are now being addressed and resolved by complex technological systems that began with simple ideas and tools. A technological system is a system through which a process combines resources to provide a desired output. These systems are then studied

TABLE 1–1 Important technological inventions throughout history

Woven cloth, 5000 B.C.	Typewriter, 1867 A.D.
Wheeled vehicles, 3500 B.C.	Bicycle, 1867 A.D.
Ox-drawn plow, 2500 B.C.	Four-stroke engine, 1876 A.D.
Maps, 510 B.C.	Telephones, 1876 A.D.
Lever, 250 B.C.	Light bulb, 1879 A.D.
Paper, 100 A.D.	Gasoline automobile, 1885 A.D.
Gunpowder, 850 A.D.	Radio, 1901 A.D.
Eyeglasses, 1249 A.D.	Airplane, 1903 A.D.
Mechanical clock, 1360 A.D.	SONAR, 1917 A.D.
Printing press, 1454 A.D.	Refrigerator, 1918 A.D.
Screwdriver, 1550 A.D.	Jet engine, 1936 A.D.
Graphite pencil, 1565 A.D.	Photocopier, 1938 A.D.
Thermometer, 1592 A.D.	Atomic bomb, 1945 A.D.
Telescope, 1608 A.D.	Transistor, 1948 A.D.
Barometer, 1643 A.D.	Satellite, 1957 A.D.
Microscope, 1673 A.D.	Argon laser, 1960 A.D.
Steam engine, 1712 A.D.	Manned spaceflight, 1961 A.D.
Hot air ballon, 1782 A.D.	Word processor, 1965 A.D.
Steam locomotive, 1804 A.D.	Videotape cassette, 1970 A.D.
Photography, 1822 A.D.	Computer floppy disk, 1970 A.D.
Electric motor, 1831 A.D.	Laser printer, 1980 A.D.
Steam shovel, 1836 A.D.	CD-ROM, 1984 A.D.
Telegraph, 1844 A.D.	Gene-altered bacteria, 1987 A.D.
Sewing machine, 1846 A.D.	

Earth System Scientists

The Leakey Family

No other family in the science of anthropology has made such an impact on our understanding of human origins as the Leakey family. Louis Leakey was born in Kenya, Africa, in 1903, where he became interested in the history of the human race. As a boy he became fascinated by the prehistoric stone tools he found while exploring the African landscape. He eventually went on to pursue an education in anthropology and began his lifelong career in the search for human origins. Louis Leakey met his future wife, Mary Nicols, while on an archaeological dig in England. Mary Nicols was born into a family of archaeologists and specialized in the prehistory of human beings. In 1937 the newly married Leakeys returned to Kenya and began to raise a family. During this time they made some very important fossil discoveries that helped piece together our human ancestry. Most of their famous work was done in the Olduvai Gorge in Africa, where they unearthed many hominid fossil remains. Mary Leakey's most significant discovery was the unearthing of a series of fossilized footprints that were made by a 3.5-million-year-old human ancestor. This find proved that these ancient humans walked on two feet. Their son, Richard Leakey, who was born in 1944, also joined the family business. His work in anthropology continues to this day. Throughout the twentieth century the Leakey family made significant discoveries in tracing human origins, and they have influenced other anthropologists and archaeologists to pursue their line of work.

FOR MORE INFORMATION GO TO THESE WEB LINKS:

<http://www.pbs.org/wgbh /evolution/humans /humankind/index.html>

<http://www.mnh.si.edu /anthro/humanorigins/>

<http://echo.gmu.edu /center.php>

to see how problems can be solved or how specific needs can be met. **Technological systems models** can be used to analyze specific systems and to understand how they operate. The basic technological systems model is composed of a command input, comparison device, adjustment, resource inputs, process, output, monitor, and feedback loop (Figure 1–7). This model helps illustrate how a technological process works and how it can be improved. Today people are moving into a new period of technological innovation, often referred to as the Information Age. The use of computer technology is changing our way of life in ways that our ancestors could not have imagined.

SECTION REVIEW

1. Define the term *technology*, and describe its importance to human beings.

2. List and describe the evolution of technology throughout human history.

3. Explain how the technological system model can be used to represent a technological process.

4. Who was Louis Leakey?

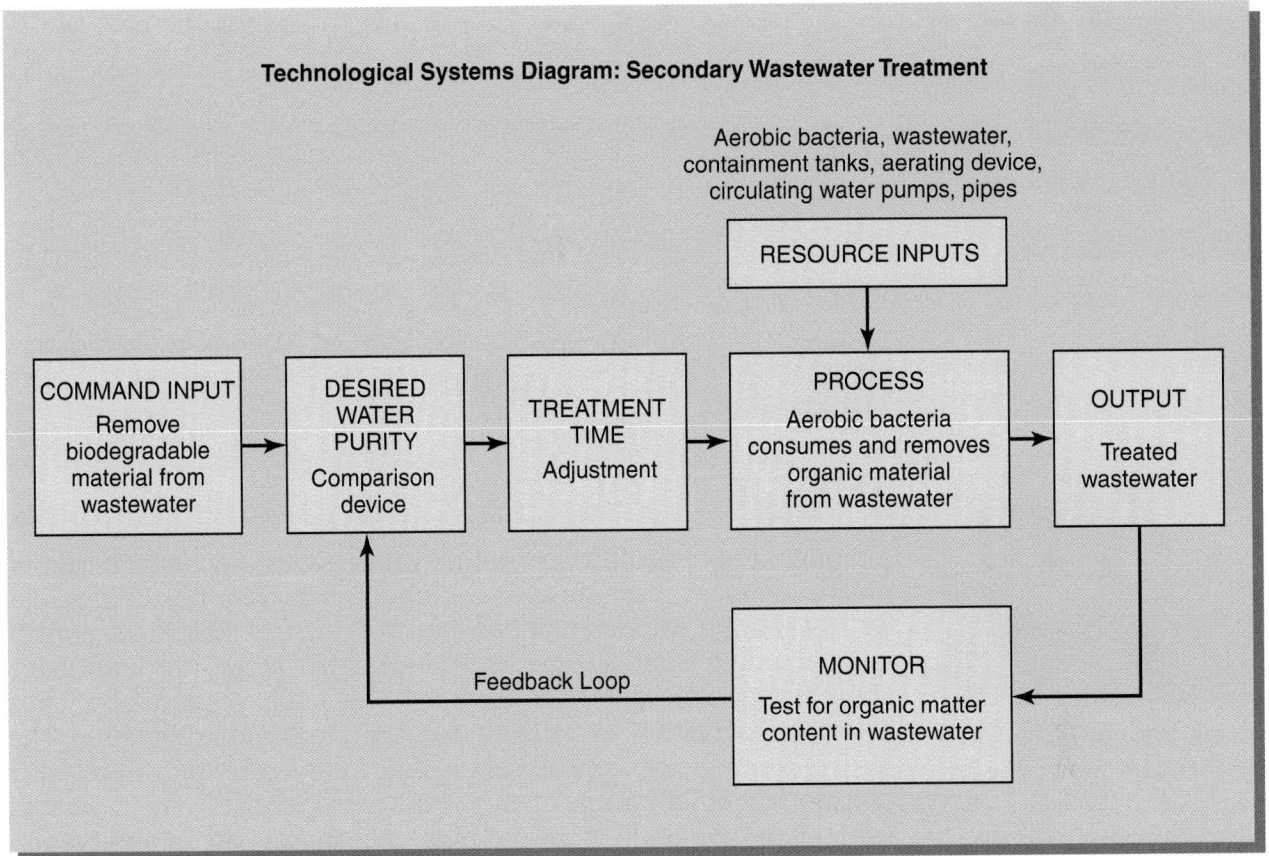

Technological Systems Diagram: Secondary Wastewater Treatment

FIGURE 1–7   A technological systems diagram is used to model the technological process that is used to treat wastewater.

CURRENT RESEARCH

Composite technology is creating the building materials of the future. A composite material is formed from combining two or more materials with unique properties. Composites are composed of a binder and a reinforcer. A binder completely surrounds and binds together the reinforcing material. Common bonding agents today include plastic resins. The reinforcer is a stronger material that provides the composite with strength and stability. First developed in the 1940s, composites have quickly become more widespread as building materials. The first successful composite material was fiberglass. Fiberglass composites are still widely used today in car bodies and boats. New composite materials are being developed that use plastic polymers and strong synthetic fibers. Some of the reinforcing agents used in composites include carbon fiber, or Kevlar. These materials are extremely lightweight but provide great strength and stability. Newer composite materials currently under development use new binders and reinforcers. The advantages of using a composite material involve strength, light weight, and the ability to be molded into any shape.

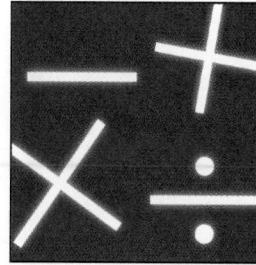

e a r t h   m a t h

1) If the Paleolithic period began 2.5 million years ago and ended approximately 100,000 years ago, how many years did the Paleolithic period last?

2) If the Information Age began in 1990, how long did the Industrial Age last?

1.2 The Foundations of Science

THE BIRTH OF SCIENCE

FIGURE 1–8   Stonehenge in England is believed to be an ancient astronomical calendar used to track the movement of the heavens that was built more than 2000 years ago. (*Courtesy of PhotoDisc.*)

Although it is difficult to determine when humans actually began to practice science, it can be assumed from our ancient beginnings that we have always wondered at how our world works. This is the core of understanding what science is. **Science** is the search for knowledge about how the natural world operates. The actual practice of science involves observation, investigation, description, and explanation. The birth of formal science most likely had its roots in the study of celestial objects (Figure 1–8). Some of the world's first scientists were fascinated with the motion of the stars and planets in space. Careful observation and measurement of astronomical phenomena led to the birth of astronomy and to the birth of modern science. Many of the world's best-known scientists were and are astronomers. Famous names such as Aristotle, Newton, Kepler, Galileo, Copernicus, Einstein, Hubble, Hawking, and Sagan are all famous astronomers who helped revolutionize science. Today science continues to improve our world and increase our understanding of how it works. To do this, scientists often use a formal method of inquiry to attempt to unlock the secrets of nature; this is called the scientific method.

THE SCIENTIFIC METHOD

The **scientific method** of inquiry is based on three main concepts: observation, experimentation, and the development of theories or natural laws (Table 1–2). The first step in the scientific method is the actual observation and recording of facts. Much of the work of a scientist involves **observation** and the collection of data. This helps scientists gain as much information as they can about the natural phenomena they are studying, and then to record that information in an organized way. Observation also involves conducting experiments. **Experiments** are controlled observations that help answer questions about what scientists are trying to discover (Figure 1–9). The next step in the scientific method is the formulation of a **theory** that might explain how or why the natural phenomenon that is being studied is occurring. This is also called a **hypothesis**, which is an explanation that is supported by a set of facts. The final step in the scientific process is the formulation of a natural law that explains the phenomenon that is being studied.

TABLE 1–2 The scientific method is a formal procedure that scientists use to answer questions

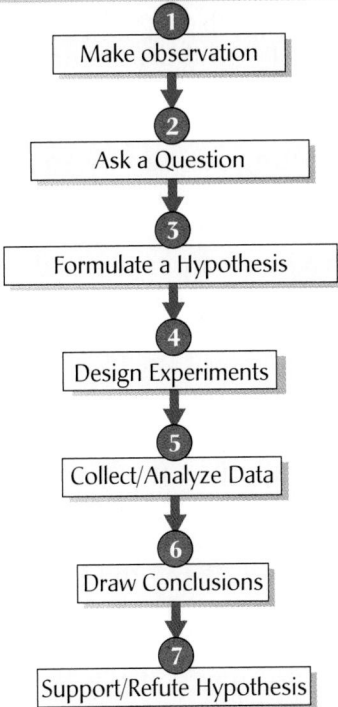

1. Make observation
2. Ask a Question
3. Formulate a Hypothesis
4. Design Experiments
5. Collect/Analyze Data
6. Draw Conclusions
7. Support/Refute Hypothesis

FIGURE 1–9 Scientists commonly conduct experiments to prove or disprove their theories. (*Courtesy of USDA/ARS #K1968-13.*)

The formulation of a natural or a physical law helps explain how certain aspects of the natural world operate and, more important, how they can be used to make predictions. Scientists often use observations they have made in the past to make inferences about what might occur in the future. An **inference** is a prediction or conclusion that is made about a future event based on previous scientific observations. The scientific method is a formal and organized procedure that scientists around the world use to make accurate investigations of the natural world.

Earth System Scientists

Thales of Miletus

Thales was born in ancient Greece in approximately 620 BCE (Before Common Era). He is considered by many historians to be the founder of scientific inquiry. His main achievements centered around the notion that natural events were the work of observable properties and processes, not the work of the gods. His achievements involved geography, engineering, mathematics, science, and politics. He is best known for his development of the scientific method and for his practical search for knowledge. He also did extensive work in astronomy and the prediction of eclipses. Thales' study of philosophy and science influenced many Greek philosophers, including Aristotle, Plato, Socrates, Pythagoras, and Diogenes.

SCIENTIFIC EXPERIMENTS

One of the most important aspects of the scientific method is experimentation. An experiment allows scientists to prove or disprove a hypothesis. Experiments are also an important way for students of science to learn about the natural world and gain knowledge by actually practicing science. Conducting experiments also follows an organized pattern, which includes stating the purpose of the experiment, creating a hypothesis, writing out step-by-step procedures, collecting and analyzing data, and formulating a conclusion. All experiments begin by stating the purpose for performing the experiment. The purpose explains exactly what you are trying to determine in your experiment. For example, if you wanted to know at what temperature water boiled, you could determine it by performing a simple experiment. Your purpose is simple: to discover the exact temperature at which water boils.

The next step in experimentation is formulating a hypothesis that might explain your experiment. A hypothesis is an explanation of how or why the phenomenon you are studying is occurring. A hypothesis is usually based on any previous knowledge you have about what you are studying. Using the boiling water example, you might already have an idea at what temperature water boils, so your hypothesis would state this. Or if you have no idea about the boiling temperature of water, you may state in your hypothesis that you believe water always boils at the same temperature, which you are trying to discover.

Writing out the procedures that you took to perform your experiment is another important aspect of experimentation. This allows other scientists or students to understand how the experiment is to be conducted. The procedure is also important because it allows for your experiment to be re-created by other scientists. A procedure is just a step-by-step explanation of what you did to conduct your experiment. It also may include special safety concerns and specific materials or instruments required to conduct your experiment. For example, if you are trying to determine the temperature of boiling water, you must take special precautions to prevent yourself from being scalded by the water.

Collecting and recording data from your experiment is the next step in experimentation. Data collection is a precise way of making accurate observations during your experiment. Often experiments are conducted more than once to collect more than one set of data, which allows for more accuracy. For this portion of your experiment, you may choose to record the temperature of the water every 30 seconds until it boils, and then repeat the experiment to gain a more accurate result. You must also consider what units of measurement you will use to record your data. In most scientific experiments the metric system is used, and temperature is often recorded in degrees Celsius. Calculating the results of your experiment involves analyzing and organizing the data you have collected. Creating a graph or chart to analyze your data often is an effective way to organize your results. A graph is a way to visually display numbers and data that you have collected during an experiment. Graphs are an important tool in the scientific method because they can reveal trends that are occurring in your data.

The final portion of an experiment is stating a conclusion. The conclusion of your experiment should summarize the results of your experiment, which will either support or disprove your hypothesis. If your experiment revealed that the boiling point of water was 100° Celsius, then this should be stated in your conclusion. Carefully conducting an experiment in an organized way ensures that scientific discovery can be well documented and re-created.

SCIENCE, TECHNOLOGY, AND ENGINEERING

There has always been an important link between science and technology. The general goal of science has been to try to understand how the natural world works. The goal of technology is to take the knowledge gained by scientific inquiry and apply it in a practical way. Today many of the technologies that our society uses are the direct result of scientific inquiry and research. These include technologies such as the airplane, the telephone, radio, computers, satellites, the light bulb, lasers, and countless more inventions. People who use scientific principles and apply them in a practical way are called engineers. Today engineers use math and science in a variety of ways to improve our way of life. Structural engineers, also called civil engineers, design buildings, bridges, tunnels, roads, airports, water supplies, and sewers that we depend on every day. Electrical engineers design all the electrical devices we use, including computers, communication equipment, entertainment devices, electrical power creation and distribution, appliances, and lighting. Chemical engineers create chemical substances that are used by both science and industry. Agricultural engineers help design new and efficient ways of producing food. One of the fastest growing fields of engineering today involves the use of biotechnology, also called bioengineering. Biotechnology is the use of living organisms to produce a usable product, or to accomplish a specific task. Science and technology will play an important role in the future of the human race as more knowledge is gained about the world in which we live and, more important, how this knowledge can be used to improve the human condition.

SECTION REVIEW

1. What are the three main processes that together make up the scientific method?

2. Describe the series of steps involved in conducting an experiment.

3. What is the difference between a scientist and an engineer?

4. Who was Thales?

WEB Links

FOR MORE INFORMATION GO TO THESE WEB LINK:

<http://echo.gmu.edu/center.php>

CAREER CONNECTIONS
Engineers

Engineers are professional problem solvers who apply math and science to improve the human condition. There are many different types of engineers who work on many new and unique ways to benefit society. Engineers need a four-year college degree in one of the four major branches of engineering: electrical, chemical, mechanical, or civil engineering. Electrical engineers develop and work with all kinds of electronic equipment. Chemical engineers use chemistry to produce new or existing chemicals. Mechanical engineers design, research, create, test, and produce all types of mechanical devices. This includes simple tools or complex machines such as airplanes and automobiles. Civil engineers design and supervise the building of bridges, railroads, tunnels, roads, water supplies, sewers, and airports. Once out of college, engineers can make an excellent salary by working for industry, business, the military, government, education, or research. Another related occupation is engineering technician, a technician who works in the practical applications of engineering. This includes jobs in all the engineering fields but requires a less formal education. Some of the many engineering fields include the following:

automotive

aerospace (aero or astronautical)

agricultural

architectural

bioengineering (biomedical, biomechanical, biochemical)

ceramic

computer

environmental

fire protection

geological

geothermal

heating, ventilating, air-conditioning, and refrigeration industrial

manufacturing

materials

metallurgy and materials

mineral and mining

naval

nuclear

ocean

optical

petroleum

plant

plastics robotics and automated systems

safety

software

transportation

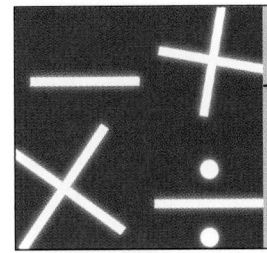

earth math

1) In 1543 CE, Nicolaus Copernicus hypothesized that the Earth and other planets revolve around the Sun. How old is this fundamental theory of astronomy?

1.3 Scientific Measurement

OBSERVATION AND MEASUREMENT

Much of a scientist's job involves making observations of the natural world. An observation can be as simple as using one of the five human senses. These are sight, touch, taste, smelling, and hearing. Today scientists extend their own senses by using scientific instruments. Instruments are devices that are designed to extend the human senses and make accurate measurements of the natural world. Scientific instruments can be as simple as a scale or meter stick or as complex as a satellite or radio telescope (Figure 1–10). Measurement is an important part of science, for it allows observations to be made more precisely.

Accurate measurements are also important for identifying unique physical or chemical properties of the Earth. Today scientists use four fundamental measurements to help observe the natural world: length, mass,

FIGURE 1–10 Scientific instruments, such as a balance, rulers, satellites, telescopes, and compasses, are used to extend the human senses. (*Courtesy of PhotoDisc.*)

time, and energy. **Length** measures the distance between two fixed points. **Mass** is a measure of the amount of matter in an object. On Earth the mass of an object is measured by determining its **weight**. Although weight can be used to measure mass, mass and weight are not always equal, because weight is just a measure of the pull of gravity on an object's mass. Therefore an object's weight can be different on the Moon than on the Earth; however, its mass remains constant. **Time** is forward movement, or specific interval between two events. **Energy** is measured as the electric charge of matter, which can be either positive or negative. Energy is also a measure of the movement of matter, called its kinetic energy. Common energy measurements include the heat or temperature of a substance.

UNITS OF MEASUREMENT

All scientific measurements consist of a numerical quantity and a specific unit. A unit is a specific measurement that has a fixed value. One of the oldest length units of measurement still in use today is the foot. The Romans first introduced the foot as a unit of length that divided the distance from a person's heel to the tip of the big toe into 12 equal parts. They also introduced the mile as a measure of length that equaled 1,000 paces. A pace was the distance a person could travel in two walking steps. Another ancient unit of measuring length is the yard, which was the distance between the tip of a person's nose and the thumb when the arm was fully extended. Today in the United States we recognize two systems of measurement. One is called the standard system of measurement, which includes units like the inch, foot, mile, pound, ounce, and yard. In the 1780s the French government developed a new system of measurement called the international system, also known as the metric system. Today the entire scientific community around the world uses the metric system for observation and measurement (Table 1–3). The metric system is based on the fundamental unit of length called the meter. The meter is further divided into divisions of 100 called centimeters. Another fundamental unit of mass in the metric system is called the gram. The gram is equal to the mass of 1 cubic centimeter of liquid water.

Many measurable quantities of the natural world include two or more fundamental quantities. These are called derived units; for example, the volume of a substance is measured by determining its length, width, and height. Common units of volume in science include the cubic centimeter and milliliter. Another derived unit often used in observation is speed or acceleration. Speed is a measure of a specific distance traveled in a specific amount of time. Common speed or acceleration units of measurement include kilometers per hour and miles per hour.

DENSITY

Density is an important derived unit of measurement that is used in science to determine the specific amount of mass per unit volume a substance has. Therefore density measures the amount of atoms and molecules that occupy a specific space. Density is determined by the following formula: density = mass/volume. The density of an object is important because it affects many of the physical properties of a substance (Figure 1–12). There is an important relationship between density

TABLE 1–3 Common units of measurement used in science

Length
Metric
1 kilometer (km) = 1,000 meters (m)
1 meter (m) = 100 centimeters (cm)
1 meter (m) = 1,000 millimeters (mm)
1 centimeter (cm) = 0.01 meter (m)
1 millimeter (mm) = 0.001 meter (m)

English
1 foot (ft) = 12 inches (in)
1 yard (yd) = 3 feet (ft)
1 mile (mi) = 5,280 feet (ft)
1 nautical mile = 1.15 miles

Metric-English
1 kilometer (km) = 0.621 mile (mi)
1 meter (m) = 39.4 inches (in)
1 inch (in) = 2.54 centimeters (cm)
1 foot (ft) = 0.305 meter (m)
1 yard (yd) = 0.914 meter (m)
1 nautical mile = 1.85 kilometers (km)

Area
Metric
1 square kilometer (km^2) = 1,000,000 square meters (m^2)
1 square meter (m^2) = 1,000,000 square millimeters (mm^2)
1 hectare (ha) = 10,000 square meters (m^2)
1 hectare (ha) = 0.01 square kilometer (km^2)

English
1 square foot (ft^2) = 144 square inches (in^2)
1 square yard (yd^2) = 9 square feet (ft^2)
1 square mile (mi^2) = 27,880,000 square feet (ft^2)
1 acre (ac) = 43,560 square feet (ft^2)

Metric-English
1 hectare (ha) = 2.471 acres (ac)
1 square kilometer (km^2) = 0.386 square mile (mi^2)
1 square meter (m^2) = 1.196 square yards (yd^2)
1 square meter (m^2) = 10.76 square feet (ft^2)
1 square centimeter (cm^2) = 0.155 square inch (in^2)

Volume
Metric
1 cubic kilometer (km^3) = 1,000,000,000 cubic meters (m^3)
1 cubic meter (m$_3$) = 1,000,000 cubic centimeters (cm^3)
1 liter (L) = 1,000 milliliters (mL) = 1,000 cubic centimeters (cm^3)
1 milliliter (mL) = 0.001 liter (L)
1 milliliter (mL) = 1 cubic centimeter (cm^3)

English
1 gallon (gal) = 4 quarts (qt)
1 quart (qt) = 2 pints (pt)

Metric-English
1 liter (L) = 0.265 gallon (gal)
1 liter (L) = 1.06 quarts (qt)
1 liter (L) = 0.0353 cubic foot (ft^3)
1 cubic meter (m^3) = 35.3 cubic feet (ft^3)
1 cubic meter (m^3) = 1.30 cubic yard (yd^3)
1 cubic kilometer (km^3) = 0.24 cubic mile (mi^3)
1 barrel (bbl) = 159 liters (L)
1 barrel (bbl) = 42 U.S. gallons (gal)

Mass
Metric
1 kilogram (kg) = 1,000 grams (g)
1 gram (g) = 1,000 milligrams (mg)
1 gram (g) = 1,000,000 micrograms (μg)
1 milligram (mg) = 0.001 gram (g)
1 metric ton (mt) = 1,000 kilograms (kg)

English
1 ton (t) = 2,000 pounds (lb)
1 pound (lb) = 16 ounces (oz)

Metric-English
1 metric ton (mt) = 2,200 pounds (lb) = 1.1 tons (t)
1 kilogram (kg) = 2.20 pounds (lb)
1 pound (lb) = 454 grams (g)
1 gram (g) = 0.035 ounce (oz)

Energy and Power
Metric
1 kilojoule (kJ) = 1,000 joules (J)
1 kilocalorie (kcal) = 1,000 calories (cal)
1 calorie (cal) = 4,184 joules (J)

Metric-English
1 kilojoule (kJ) = 0.949 British thermal unit (Btu)
1 kilojoule (kJ) = 0.000278 kilowatt-hour (kW-h)
1 kilocalorie (kcal) = 3.97 British thermal units (Btu)
1 kilocalorie (kcal) = 0.00116 kilowatt-hour (kW-h)
1 kilowatt-hour (kW-h) = 860 kilocalories (kcal)
1 kilowatt-hour (kW-h) = 3,400 British thermal units (Btu)
1 quad (Q) = 1,050,000,000,000,000 kilojoules (kJ)
1 quad (Q) = 2,930,000,000,000 kilowatt-hours (kW-h)

Fahrenheit (°F) to Celsius (°C): $°C = \dfrac{(°F - 32.0)}{1.80}$

Celsius (°C) to Fahrenheit (°F): °F 5 (°C × 1.80) + 32.0

Earth System Scientists

The Invention of Numbers

The invention of numbers that we use every day has played an important part in the development of human civilization. Almost all ancient societies, such as the Babylonians, Egyptians, Mayans, Hindus, and Arabs, developed methods of counting. The base 10 system, which we still use today, is based on the digits 1, 2, 3, 4, 5, 6, 7, 8, and 9. This most likely developed as a result of humans' having 10 fingers to count with. The writing of these numbers was first used in India during the third century BCE. They are known as the Brahmi numbers. This system of numbers was adapted by other civilizations and eventually became known as the Hindu-Arabic numeral system (Figure 1–11). This system, which we still use today, is more than 2,000 years old!

A similar system is the Roman numeral system, which uses hash marks to represent numbers from 1 to 9. The concept of the zero in number systems and mathematics came much later. The first recorded rules using a zero in mathematical expressions are found in a book called *The Opening of the Universe*, written in 630 CE by the Indian mathematician Brahmagupta. The significance of the zero in math and counting continues to this day. Even with our sophisticated computer technology, the concept of the zero, when applied to recording the year, created a worldwide scare and cost billions of dollars to fix. People around the world nervously waited to see how computers would be affected by the year 2000!

1	2	3	4	5	6	7	8	9
—	=	☰	+	h	౭	౧	౮	౨

FIGURE 1–11 An early numbering system developed, which forms the base of our modern numbers.

CAREER CONNECTIONS

Surveyors and Surveying Technicians

Surveyors and their technicians operate instruments that are used to measure and map all parts of our world. Surveying involves many aspects of the modern world, including the accurate measurement of land for the sale of property. Surveyors also help measure and lay out plans for the construction of roads, airports, bridges, and all other construction sites. Accurate surveys also help generate many different maps of our world. Surveying work involves a lot of time outdoors, where accurate measurements are made using precise instruments. Surveyors usually must pass state tests to become certified and a four-year college degree is often required. Surveying technicians can learn their trade on the job or in a two-year college program. Many vocational schools also offer surveying instruction.

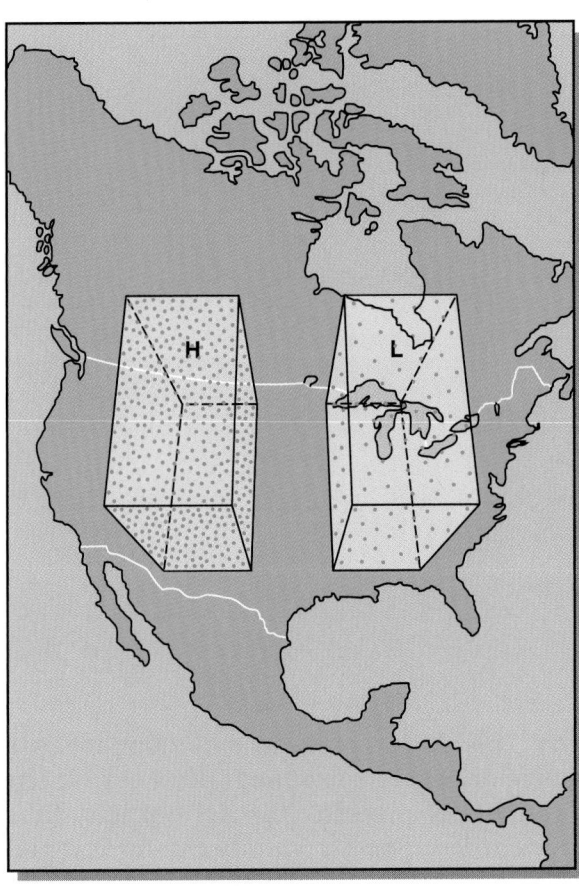

FIGURE 1–12 Two parcels of air with the same volume and different masses have different densities.

and the three states of matter. For all objects, excluding water, the solid form is the most dense, liquid being less dense, and the gaseous form being the least dense form of matter. Objects that are less dense tend to float on more dense objects. Observe the results when you mix oil and water. The less dense oil floats on top of the more dense water. The temperature of an object also has a relationship to density. Generally, as you increase the temperature of a substance, its density decreases; therefore hot objects tend to be less dense than cooler objects. Pressure also has an effect on the density of a substance. When you increase the pressure on a substance, its density increases. Water is a unique substance that has unusual properties associated with density. The most dense form of water is its liquid form, at 4° Celsius (39.2° F). The reason that the liquid form of water is more dense than the solid form has to do with the crystal structure of ice. When liquid water freezes to form ice, the water molecules link together in an organized crystal pattern. This crystal pattern has a larger volume per unit mass than the liquid form of water, which causes ice to be less dense. The density of ice is 0.91 grams per cubic centimeter, and the density of liquid water is 1.0 grams per cubic centimeter. The lower density of ice compared with liquid water causes ice to float. In all other substances on Earth, the solid form of matter is always denser than the liquid form, which causes it to sink (Table 1–4).

SCIENTIFIC NOTATION

Scientific measurements are often recorded in a form called scientific notation, or exponential notation. This allows extremely large or very small numbers to be written much more easily. Scientific notation is

TABLE 1–4 Densities of common substances

Solid	Density (g/cm³, 20°C)	Liquid	Density (g/cm³, 20°C)	Gas	Density (g/L, 0°C)
Gold	19.3	Water	1.00	Air	1.29
Lead	11.3	Gasoline	0.67	Oxygen	1.43
Copper	8.92	Milk	1.03	Hydrogen	0.090
Iron	7.86	Sea water	1.03	Helium	0.178
Aluminum	2.70	Blood	1.06	Carbon dioxide	1.96
Salt	2.16	Mercury	13.6		
Paper	0.70	Olive oil	0.92		
Balsa	0.20	Alcohol	0.79		
Redwood	0.44	Vinegar	1.01		
Rubber	1.1	Ether	0.70		
Ice	0.92	Carbon tetrachloride	1.59		

written in the following way: $N \times 10^e$. N represents a number between 1 and 10, and e is the positive or negative exponent power of 10. The exponent represents the number of places to the right or left of the decimal point. If the exponent is a positive number, then it represents the number of decimal places to the right of the number N. This represents very large numbers that are greater than 1. For example, 4.5×10^6 is the scientific notation form of the number 4,500,000. If the exponent is a negative number, it represents the number of decimal places to the left of N. This is a very small number that is less than 1. For example, 2×10^{-3} is the scientific notation form of 0.002.

PERCENT ERROR

Another important aspect of scientific measurement is the concept of percent deviation, also known as percent error. The percent deviation is a measure of how accurate a measurement is to that of an accepted value. This helps scientists gauge how good their measurements are when they make an observation. Human error or faulty scientific instruments are a constant variable that can create inaccurate measurements. Calculating percent deviation involves the use of the following formula: percent deviation = ((the difference between the accepted value and the measured value/the accepted value) × 100). For example, if you determine the mass of a mineral sample to be 35 gm, and the accepted mass is actually 40 grams, then your percent error calculation is determined by the following calculation: ((40 gm – 35 gm)/ 40 gm) × 100 = 12.5 percent. No measurement in the science classroom is completely accurate; therefore calculating the percent error helps reveal how good your measurement is. Common devices used for measuring, such as the speedometer of your car, have percent errors of approximately 3 percent. This means that the speed of your car is actually 3 percent more or less than the actual speed. An accurate measurement usually has a percent error of less than 3 percent.

SECTION REVIEW

1. Describe how a scientific observation is made.
2. What are the four fundamental units of measurement?
3. What system of measurement do scientists use?
4. What is a derived unit? Give two examples of derived units.
5. Define density.
6. What are three examples of how the density of an object can be affected?
7. What is the densest form of water?
8. Approximately how old is our modern system of numbers, and who was the first to use them?

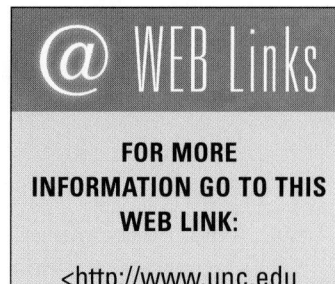

@ WEB Links

FOR MORE INFORMATION GO TO THIS WEB LINK:

<http://www.unc.edu/~rowlett/units/>

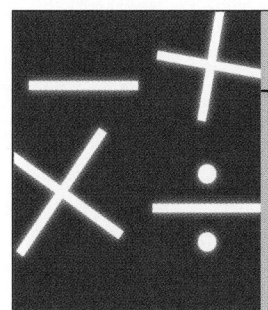

earth math

1) Write the following numbers in their long form: 1.2×10^9 and 6×10^{-5}

2) Write the following numbers in scientific notation: 91,000,000 and 0.00003

3) Determine the percent deviation of a measurement of 12 centimeters, when the accepted value is 11.5 centimeters.

CHAPTER SUMMARY

Throughout history, human beings have used technology to improve their lives by applying their knowledge to solve problems or perform tasks. This has resulted in a wealth of materials, tools, and processes that affect all aspects of our lives. Humans have often increased their knowledge of the world by careful investigation, which led to the development of what we know today as science. Science advances human knowledge by a systematic process called the scientific method. This formal process consists of observation, experimentation, and the development of theories. Observation often involves the use of scientific instruments that extend the use of the human senses and help scientists collect accurate data. Performing experiments is probably the most important part of the scientific method because it allows scientists to test their theories and learn more about the world. There will always be an important relationship between science and technology because many technologies are often developed as a result of a scientific investigation. Practicing science often involves the recording of precise measurements. The fundamental units of measurement include length, mass, weight, time, and energy. Two systems of measurement are commonly used in the United States for accurate measurement. These are the standard system and metric system. Often two or more fundamental units of measurement are combined to form what is called a derived unit, such as density. Density is a measure of the amount of mass per unit volume of a substance, which is an important physical characteristic of many substances on the Earth. Other important aspects of scientific measurement include percent error calculation, which reveals the accuracy of a measurement, and scientific notation, which is used to record very large or very small measurements in an abbreviated form.

CHAPTER REVIEW

Multiple Choice

1. How old are the oldest stone tools discovered that represent early human technology?
   a. 10,000 years
   b. 100,000 years
   c. 500,000 years
   d. 2,000,000 years

2. The period that began when humans first started to grow their own food is called:
   a. the Stone Age
   b. the Agricultural Revolution
   c. the Industrial Revolution
   d. the Information Age

3. The application of scientific knowledge for a practical purpose is called:
   a. science
   b. a technological systems model
   c. technology
   d. an instrument

4. The search for knowledge about how the natural world operates is called:
   a. science
   b. a technological systems model
   c. technology
   d. an instrument

5. The scientific method consists of:
   a. proof, facts, and experiments
   b. purpose, procedure, and conclusion
   c. input, process, and output
   d. observation, hypothesis, and natural law

6. The part of an experiment that relates the step-by-step directions of what was d is called the:
   a. purpose
   b. hypothesis
   c. procedure
   d. conclusion

7. To make an observation, a person must use:
   a. experiments
   b. the senses
   c. mathematical calculations
   d. proportions

8. An interpretation based on previous observations is:
   a. an inference
   b. a fact
   c. a classification
   d. a measurement

9. Which unit of measurement defines the amount of matter an object contains?
   a. weight
   b. volume
   c. mass
   d. density

10. Which term best describes the amount of space a substance occupies?
    a. density
    b. volume
    c. mass
    d. weight

11. In which state of matter do most materials on the Earth have their greatest density?
    a. gas
    b. liquid
    c. solid
    d. plasma

12. Compared with the density of liquid water, the density of ice is:
    a. always less
    b. always greater
    c. always the same
    d. sometimes less and sometimes more

13. What is the density of a rock with a mass of 35 grams and a volume of 7.0 cubic centimeters?
    a. 42 g/cm^3
    b. 28 g/cm^3
    c. 0.2 g/cm^3
    d. 5.0 g/cm^3

14. How many centimeters are there in 1 m?
    a. 1
    b. 10
    c. 100
    d. 1,000

15. The mass of a rock is measured to be 51 gm, but its actual mass is 60 gm. What is the percent error of the rock's mass?
    a. 7%
    b. 9%
    c. 15%
    d. 18%

16. The circumference of the Earth is approximately 4.0×104 km. This value is equal to:
    a. 400 km
    b. 4,000 km
    c. 40,000 km
    d. 400,000 km

17. The distance from the Earth to the Sun is approximately 93,000,000 mi. This value is equal to:
    a. 9.3×10^7 mi
    b. 9.3×10^6 mi
    c. 93×10^7 mi
    d. 93×10^6 mi

Matching   *Match the terms with the correct definitions.*

a. technology
b. technological systems model
c. science
d. scientific method
e. observation

f. experiment
g. theory
h. hypothesis
i. inference
j. length

k. mass
l. weight
m. time
n. energy
o. density

1. _____ A statement or statements used to describe a phenomenon.
2. _____ The application of human knowledge to solve problems or perform tasks.
3. _____ An explanation based on a set of facts that can be tested.
4. _____ A model used to illustrate the steps in a technological process.
5. _____ A conclusion based on a set of observed facts.
6. _____ The practice of observing, identifying, describing, and explaining natural phenomena.
7. _____ A fundamental form of measurement that measures horizontal distance.
8. _____ The specific set of procedures that scientists use to gain knowledge.
9. _____ A fundamental unit of measurement that measures the amount of matter a substance contains.
10. _____ The direct perception of something by use of one of the five human senses.
11. _____ The force that results from the gravitational attraction of the Earth on an object, which is dependent on its mass (commonly known as how heavy something is).
12. _____ A controlled test to prove or disprove a hypothesis.
13. _____ A fundamental unit of measurement that records the specific interval that separates events.
14. _____ The mass per unit volume of a substance, usually expressed in grams per cubic centimeter.
15. _____ The ability to cause change, or perform work.

Critical Thinking

1. Briefly discuss some positive and negative effects of science and technology on humans and the Earth.

2

Matter and Energy

THE PROPERTIES OF MATTER OBJECTIVES

Atoms · The Elements · States of Matter · Compounds and Molecules

After reading this section you should be able to:

▶ Define the term *matter*.
▶ Describe the three particles that make up an atom.
▶ Identify the four states of matter.
▶ Explain what a phase change is.
▶ Describe the difference between an element and a compound.

ENERGY OBJECTIVES

Energy · The Law of the Conservation of Energy · Electromagnetic Radiation · Energy Transfer · Heat and Temperature

After reading this section you should be able to:

▶ Define the term *energy*.
▶ Discuss the difference between potential energy and kinetic energy.
▶ Identify the eight different forms of energy.
▶ Describe the relationship between wavelength and energy on the electromagnetic spectrum.
▶ Identify the five ways in which electromagnetic energy can interact with the environment.
▶ Differentiate between heat and temperature.
▶ Explain the three fundamental ways in which energy is transferred on the Earth.
▶ Define the term *latent heat*.

TERMS TO KNOW

INTRODUCTION

What do you, cars, buildings, trees, flowers, your family pet, computers, and television all have in common? They are all made up of a complex interaction of matter and energy. All things in the universe as we know it are made up of matter and energy. These two fundamental items enable all the wonders of our world to exist. We rely on their interactions every day to feed us, keep us safe, provide us with knowledge, and entertain us. Understanding the basic concepts of matter and energy provides us with the ability to unlock the secrets of the world around us.

2.1   The Properties of Matter

ATOMS

All substances that exist on the Earth consist of matter. **Matter** is something that occupies space and has mass. The amount of space that matter occupies is known as its volume. The mass of the matter is a measure of the number of atoms that compose it. All matter is made up of fundamental particles called atoms. Atoms are extremely small particles that possess unique physical and chemical properties. The Greek philosopher Democritus first proposed the concept of an atom more than 2,000 years ago. Democritus believed that all things were composed of tiny particles that could not be further divided. He called these particles *atomos*, which in Greek means "indivisible," or unable to divide. All atoms are composed of three subatomic particles: protons, electrons, and neutrons. Protons and neutrons form an atom's nucleus, around which electrons revolve. Because the atom is so small and cannot be seen with the human eye, many different models have been developed to represent how the atom might look (Figure 2–1). In 1913 physicist Niels Bohr proposed the Bohr model of the atom. His model showed the atomic nucleus being orbited by its electrons at specific levels. The Bohr model has become the most popular model of the

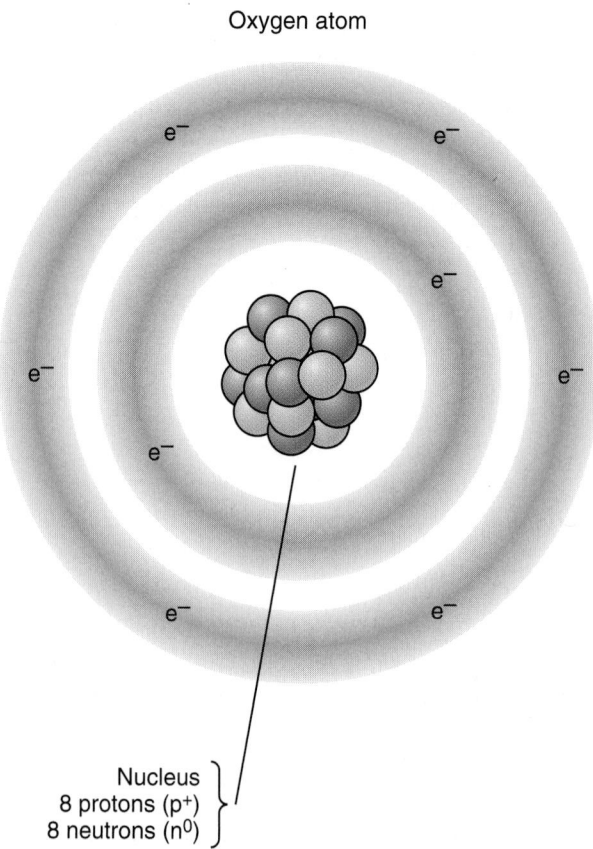

Oxygen atom

Nucleus
8 protons (p^+)
8 neutrons (n^0)

FIGURE 2–1   A model of an atom of oxygen, which shows the nucleus surrounded by an electron cloud.

atom; however, today it is believed that the atomic nucleus is surrounded by an electron "cloud," which is composed of electrons that possess different energy levels. This electron cloud model is a variation of the original Bohr model.

THE ELEMENTS

The subatomic particles that together form the atom provide matter with its unique properties. Protons are subatomic particles that have a positive electric charge, whereas the electron possesses a negative electric charge. The third subatomic particle, the neutron, has no electric charge. Recent research has demonstrated that these subatomic particles are made up of even smaller basic particles called quarks, which form protons and neutrons when combined. Together the mass of the particular number of protons and neutrons in an atom's nucleus creates its atomic mass. Although the atomic mass is an important physical characteristic of an atom, atoms are classified by their atomic number. The atomic number is the number of protons in an atom's nucleus. The atomic number of an atom helps to classify the different atoms that exist, which are also known as **elements**. Together there are 109 different atoms or elements that have been identified based on their atomic number. Each element possesses its own unique chemical and physical properties. The element hydrogen has an atomic number of 1, which means that it has one proton. The 109 elements are arranged in an organized chart called the periodic table of elements, shown in Figure 2–2.

Elements usually have the same number of electrons and protons. For example, the element hydrogen, with an atomic number of 1, has one proton and one electron. Sometimes elements lose electrons, creating an imbalance in their electric charge. These atoms are called ions (Table 2–1). Ions with a positive electric charge are called cations. Ions with a negative electric charge are called anions. Common table salt (sodium chloride) is made up of the anion sodium (Na^+) and the cation chloride (Cl^-; Figure 2–3). A variety of a specific element can exist when the number of neutrons differs in the nucleus of the same element; this is called an isotope. Many elements have different isotopes. Isotopes usually have the same chemical properties as atoms, but they possess a different atomic mass.

STATES OF MATTER

All matter in the universe exists in four distinct states that possess unique physical properties. These are known as the four states of matter: solids, liquids, gases, and plasma. The solid form of matter is the state in which atoms are most tightly packed together and are most restricted in their movement. Many solids are composed of atoms organized into a crystal pattern, which is an orderly, reoccurring arrangement of atoms (Figure 2–4). Atoms in a solid state possess the least amount of atomic movement (Figure 2–5). Because of the energy that is contained within an atom, they are always in constant motion. Atoms in a solid state of matter have movement that is limited to

Periodic Table of Elements

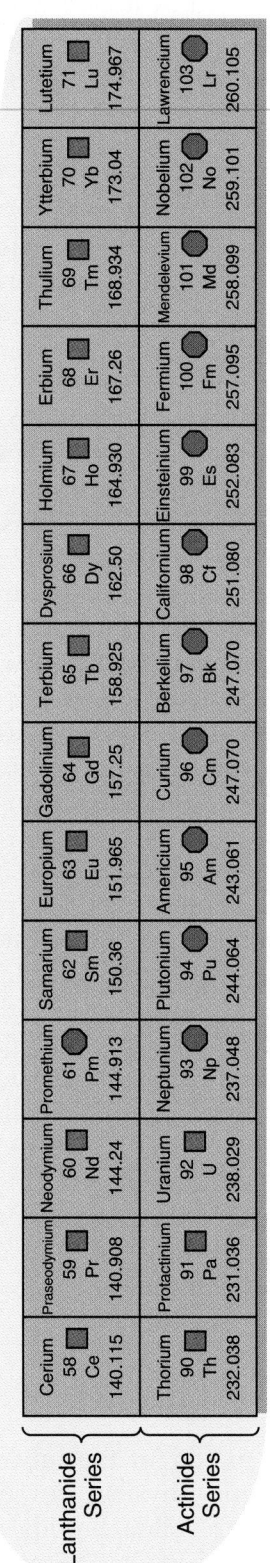

FIGURE 2–2 The periodic table of the elements.

*Names not officially assigned. Discovery of elements 114, 116, and 118 recently reported. Further information not yet available.

TABLE 2–1   Common ions and their electric charges

Cations

1+	2+	3+
Ammonium (NH_4^+)	Calcium (Ca^{2+})	Aluminum (Al^{3+})
Copper(I) (Cu^+)	Copper(II) (Cu^{2+})	Iron(III) (Fe^{3+})
Potassium (K^+)	Iron(II) (Fe^{2+})	
Silver (Ag^+)	Lead(II) (Pb^{2+})	
Sodium (Na^+)	Magnesium (Mg^{2+})	
	Mercury(I) (Hg_2^{2+})	
	Nickel (Ni^{2+})	
	Zinc (Zn^{2+})	

Anions

1–	2–	3–
Chloride (Cl^-)	Carbonate (CO_3^{2-})	Phosphate (PO_4^{3-})
Cyanide (CN^-)	Oxide (O^{2-})	
Fluoride (F^-)	Peroxide (O_2^{2-})	
Hydrogen carbonate or bicarbonate (HCO_3^-)	Sulfate (SO_4^{2-})	
Hydrogen sulfide (HS^-)	Sulfide (S^{2-})	
Hydroxide (OH^-)		
Nitrate (NO_3^-)		

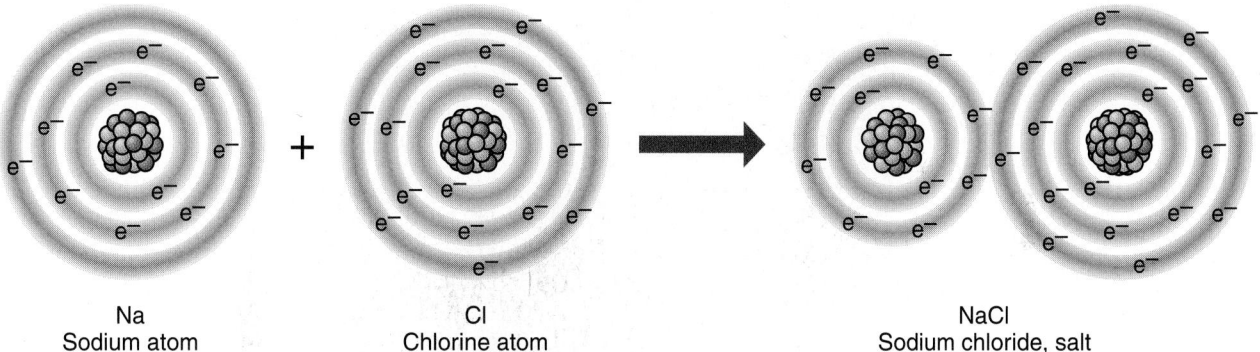

Na	Cl	NaCl
Sodium atom	Chlorine atom	Sodium chloride, salt

FIGURE 2–3   The sodium ion and chloride ion combine to form the compound known as table salt.

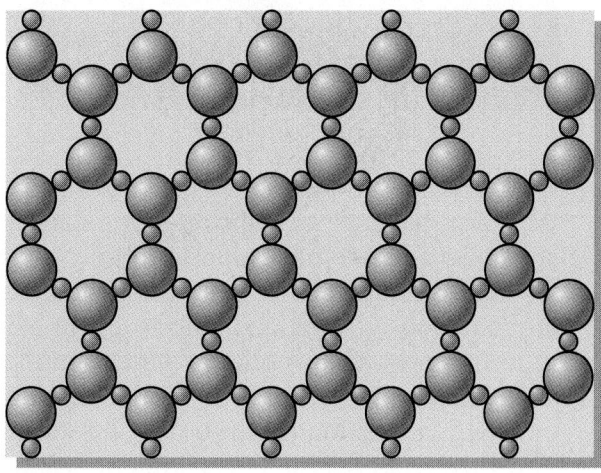

FIGURE 2–4   The orderly arrangement of molecules forming a crystal structure in a solid.

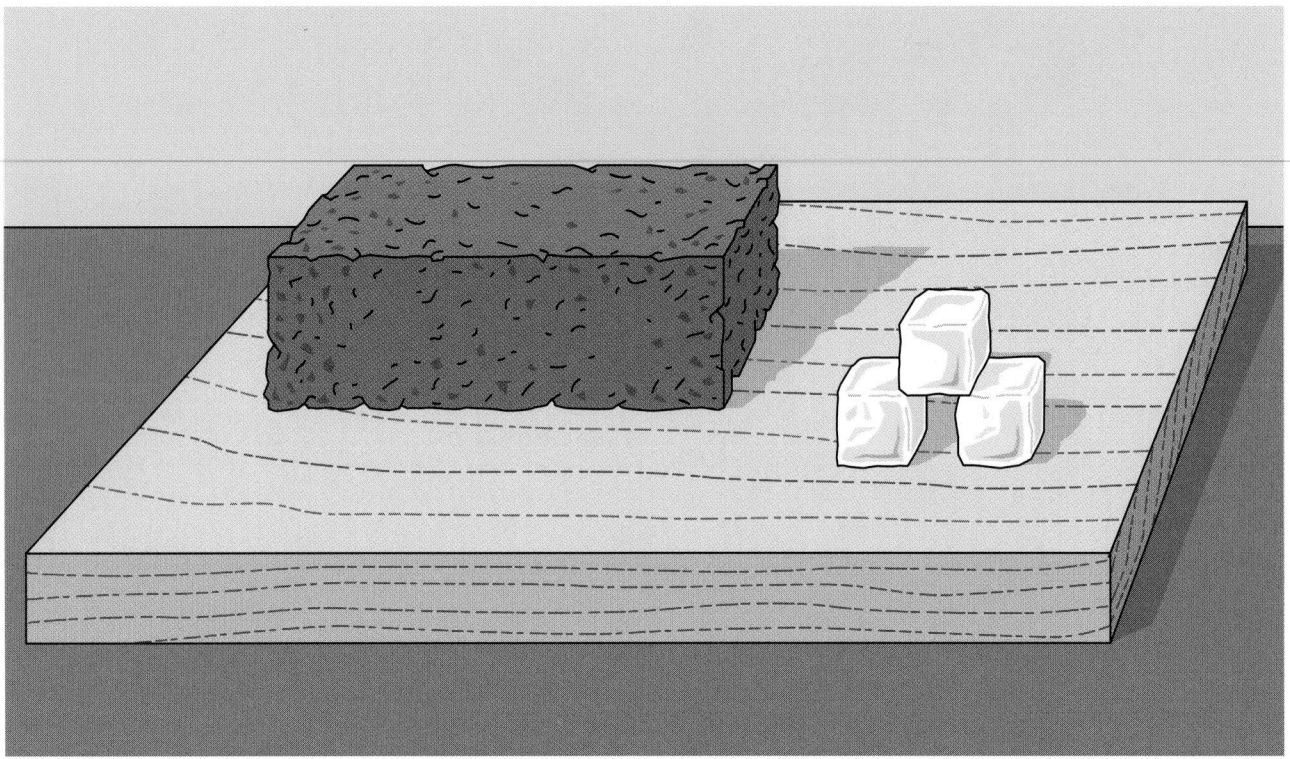

FIGURE 2–5 Examples of substances in the solid phase of matter.

FIGURE 2–6 Matter in the liquid state is fluid, which can be poured, and takes on the shape of its container. (*Courtesy of PhotoDisc.*)

vibration because of their relative fixed position. Matter in the solid state also tends to have a definite shape.

The next state of matter is liquid. Liquids are composed of atoms that are more loosely arranged. The atoms in a liquid have more freedom of movement, which gives liquid a more fluid property that has no definite shape (Figure 2–6). Atoms in a liquid tend to be arranged in long chains or clumps, rather than in the orderly crystal patterns in a solid (Figure 2–7). The movement of atoms in a liquid is also less restrictive than in a solid. When a solid turns into a liquid, it is referred to as a change in state, or phase change. Phase changes usually depend on a certain temperature

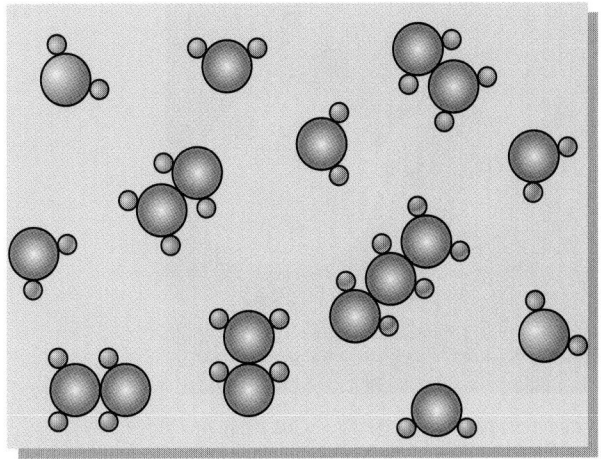

FIGURE 2–7 The chainlike configuration of molecules in a liquid.

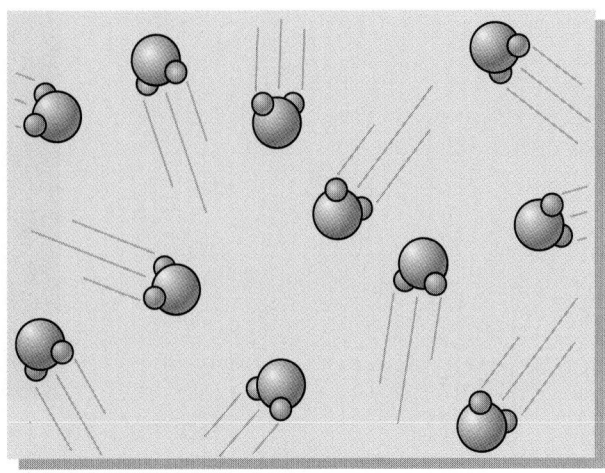

FIGURE 2–8 The rapidly moving molecules of a gas.

FIGURE 2–9 Steam rising from a volcano is the gaseous form of water. (*Courtesy of PhotoDisc.*)

and pressure to which the matter is exposed. The temperature at which a solid changes into a liquid at a specific pressure is called its melting point. When a liquid changes into a solid it is called freezing.

The gaseous state of matter provides atoms with the highest degree of movement. Atoms in a gas move at high rates and undergo constant collisions with other atoms (Figure 2–8). The high degree of movement that the atoms experience in a gaseous form causes them to have no defined shape. When a gas is enclosed in a solid container, the number of collisions that the freely moving molecules have with the walls of the container is known as pressure. The higher the number of collisions, the greater the pressure of the gas. When a liquid changes phase into a gas, it is called **vaporization** (Figure 2–9). The specific temperature required to change a liquid into a gas is known as its **boiling point.** The change from a gas to a liquid is called **condensation.** On some occasions a solid can change directly into a gas; this is called **sublimation.**

The fourth state of matter is called plasma, which is not as common as the other three. Plasma forms when the atoms that compose a gas become exposed to such high energy that they begin to ionize, or lose their electrons (Figure 2–10). The electrons are stripped away from the atoms, creating a high-energy fluid gas mixture composed of ions and electrons. Stars are composed of plasma.

FIGURE 2–10   The Sun is composed of plasma. (*Courtesy of PhotoDisc.*)

TABLE 2-2 Common compounds and the elements they are composed of

Common Name	Formula	Chemical Substance
Aspirin	$CH_3CO_2C_6H_4COOH$	Acetylsalicylic acid
Beet and cane sugars	$C_{12}H_{22}O_{11}$	Sucrose
Bleaching powder	$CaOCl_2$	Calcium oxychloride
Charcoal	$Ca_3(PO_4)_2 + C$	Calcium phosphate plus carbon
Clay	$H_2Al_2(SiO_4)_2 \cdot H_2O$	Hydrated ferric oxide
Common glass	$CaSiO_3 + Na_2SiO_3$	Calcium and other silicates
Diamond, graphite, fullerene (C_{60})	C	Carbon
Dry ice	CO_2	Frozen carbon dioxide
Fool's gold, pyrite	FeS_2	Iron disulfide
Grain alcohol	C_2H_3OH	Ethyl alcohol
Laughing gas	N_2O	Nitrous oxide
Limestone	$CaCO_3$	Calcium carbonate
Moth balls	$C_{10}H_8$	Naphthalene
Natural gas	CH_4^-	Impure methane
Nitroglycerin	$C_3H_5(NO_3)_3$	Glyceryl trinitrate
Quartz, agate, flint, chert	SiO_2	Silicon dioxide
Ruby, sapphire	Al_2O_3	Aluminum oxide
Rust	$(Fe_2O_3)_3 \cdot H_2O$	Hydrated ferric oxide
Soap lye	$NaOH$	Sodium hydroxide
Table and rock salts	$NaCl$	Sodium chloride

COMPOUNDS AND MOLECULES

Although the basic building blocks of matter are the 109 different atoms that make up the Earth's elements, combinations of these atoms really form the physical aspects of the Earth. Combinations of atoms that are chemically joined are called compounds (Table 2–2). A compound is a substance composed of two or more elements chemically combined in specific proportions. Compounds are also known as molecules. The Earth is composed of more than 10 million different compounds that together form unique substances. One of the most important molecules on Earth is the water molecule. Water is a compound that is composed of two atoms of hydrogen with one atom of

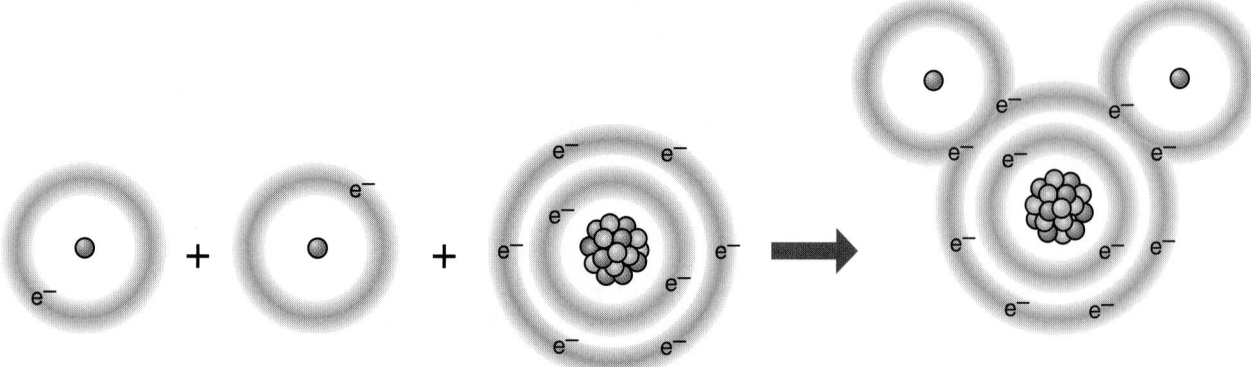

FIGURE 2-11   The formation of a water molecule by combining two atoms of hydrogen with one atom of oxygen.

oxygen (Figure 2–11). When two or more compounds are mixed together and still maintain their unique physical and chemical properties, it is called a mixture. Air is a mixture of many gases, including nitrogen, oxygen, and carbon dioxide. When two substances are mixed to form a uniform substance, it is called a solution. Seawater is a solution of salt and other minerals in water.

CAREER CONNECTIONS
Chemists

Chemistry is one of the most important scientific careers in the modern world. This vast career path involves the study of materials and compounds and how they interact with one another. Chemists analyze existing chemical compounds and perform experiments to discover new chemicals and materials. Chemists also often work with other scientists and engineers when conducting research. Branches of chemistry include analytical chemistry, organic chemistry, physical chemistry, and biochemistry. Analytical chemists identify the composition, structure, and properties of chemical substances. Organic chemists study the chemistry of living things, especially carbon-containing compounds, along with the synthesis of new drugs and commercial materials. Physical chemists study the properties of atoms and molecules and how they interact with one another, and biochemists study the chemistry of the human body and other living organisms. Chemistry courses in high school provide a good opportunity to experience what a career in chemistry might include. There are many jobs available for chemists once they gain a four-year college degree. A related occupation is the chemistry technician, who works with chemists, helping them to perform their daily tasks. This type of work requires a less formal education.

Earth System Scientists

John Dalton

John Dalton was born in England in 1766. He started his scientific career as a meteorologist, which began a lifelong dedication to weather observation in the area surrounding Manchester, England. One of his first scientific achievements was proposing that precipitation was formed by a change in atmospheric temperature, not by a change in air pressure. He also proposed the theory of the partial pressure of gases that today is known as Dalton's law of partial pressure. Later in his life he switched his scientific focus from meteorology and the study of the atmosphere to chemistry. In 1803 he developed his famous atomic theory, which stated that all matter was composed of small indivisible particles called atoms. He furthered hypothesized that atoms of a given element possess unique characteristics and weight and that three types of atoms exist: elements, compounds, and complex molecules. He published this theory in his book *New Systems of Chemical Philosophy* in 1808. Because of this theory, he is regarded by many to be the father of modern chemistry.

@ WEB Links

FOR MORE INFORMATION GO TO THIS WEB LINK:

<http://www.stcms.si.edu/pom/pom_student.htm>

SECTION REVIEW

1. What is matter?
2. Describe the three subatomic particles that make up the atom.
3. What is the difference between the atomic mass and atomic number of an atom?
4. What are isotopes and ions?
5. Describe the four states of matter.
6. What is a phase change?
7. What is an element, and how many have been identified on Earth?
8. Describe the difference between an atom and a compound.
9. Who was John Dalton?

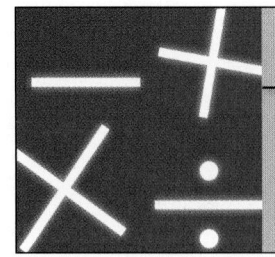

earth math

1) Determine the total atomic mass of a molecule of water using the following information: Hydrogen has an atomic mass of 1.0079, and oxygen has an atomic mass of 15.9994.

2.2 Energy

The relationship between matter and energy in the universe is the fundamental cause for the existence of the living and nonliving world. To fully understand the properties of matter, a full understanding of the properties of energy is equally important. In his world-famous equation $E = mc^2$, Albert Einstein revealed that energy and mass have a mutual relationship. But what exactly is energy, and how is it related to mass?

ENERGY

Energy is defined as the ability to do work or cause change. Matter that is exposed to energy is said to be in motion. Energy is classified in two basic forms: kinetic energy and potential energy. Kinetic energy is the energy of motion. When mass is in motion it is experiencing kinetic energy. The movement of the Earth around the Sun is kinetic energy. The movement of an athlete on a playing field is kinetic energy. The other type of energy is potential energy. Potential energy is stored energy. The gasoline in the tank of your car is a type of potential energy. It has the potential of powering your motor for a specific period. After riding a ski lift to the top of a mountain, you have a form of potential energy. The gravitational pull of the Earth will cause your body to move downhill on your snowboard (Figure 2–12). The sandwich in your

FIGURE 2–12 The snowboarder at the top of a mountain is an example of potential energy, whereas the snowboarder rapidly moving down the mountain illustrates kinetic energy.

lunch bag is also potential energy in the form of stored chemical energy—it will power your body for part of the school day.

THE LAW OF THE CONSERVATION OF ENERGY

Another important aspect of understanding energy is the law of the conservation of energy. This fundamental scientific law states that energy cannot be created or destroyed, but only changes form. This law means that energy can constantly change from one form to another, with no real gain or loss. The different forms in which energy can exist include mechanical, gravitational, radiant, thermal, electrical, magnetic, nuclear, and chemical. The light bulb that illuminates your classroom is an example of the law of the conservation of energy. The electricity that powers the light might have been generated by burning coal, which is a form of potential chemical energy. The burning coal produced heat energy that created steam, which turned a turbine generator by mechanical energy. The generator converted the mechanical energy into electrical energy that traveled to the light bulb through a network of wires. The light bulb converted the electrical energy into both radiant energy (light) and thermal energy (heat). So in the end no energy was really lost; it just changed forms.

ELECTROMAGNETIC RADIATION

Einstein's energy equivalency of mass equation ($E = mc^2$) means that all mass possesses energy. This type of energy is known as **electromagnetic radiation** (Figure 2–13). Electromagnetic radiation is the kinetic energy of movement or vibration given off by individual atoms or subatomic particles. All matter gives off electromagnetic radiation. Electromagnetic radiation travels in the form of a wave. Higher-energy

Type of Radiation	Relative wavelength	Actual wavelength (meters)	Energy carried per wave or photon
Gamma rays		10^{-13}	Increasing
X rays		10^{-9}	
Ultraviolet waves		10^{-7}	
Visible light waves		5×10^{-7}	
Infared waves		10^{-6}	
Microwaves		10^{-3}	
Television waves		1	
Radio waves	Wavelength	100	

FIGURE 2–13 A chart showing the different types of radiation that make up the electromagnetic spectrum, their wavelengths, and energy levels.

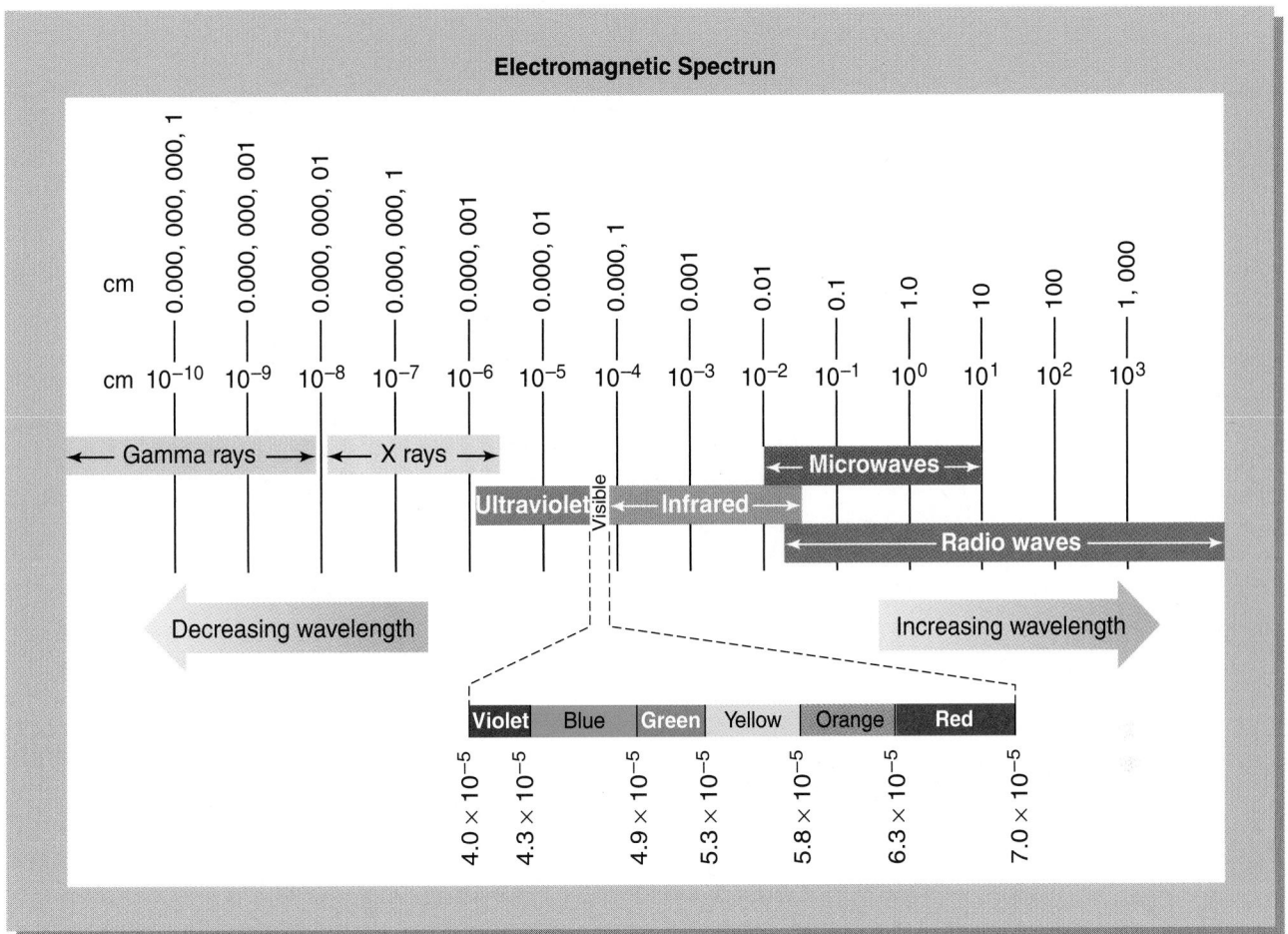

FIGURE 2–14   The electromagnetic spectrum.

electromagnetic radiation has smaller wavelengths than lower-energy electromagnetic waves. The **electromagnetic spectrum** indicates the energy and wavelength of the different forms of electromagnetic energy (Figure 2–14). The highest-energy electromagnetic waves are called gamma rays, which have a wavelength of approximately 1 billionth of a centimeter. The lowest-energy electromagnetic waves are radio waves, which have wavelengths that are as large as 10 km (6 mi). Visible light is also a form of electromagnetic radiation, which our eyes use to see. All electromagnetic waves travel at the speed of light, which is 186,000 miles per second (300,000 km/sec.).

The way in which electromagnetic radiation interacts with the environment plays an important role in many Earth processes. There are four basic ways that electromagnetic energy can interact with matter (Figure 2–15). Refraction causes electromagnetic waves to change direction or bend when they interact with matter. When a stick is placed halfway in water, it appears to be bent because of light being refracted by the water. Reflection is the bouncing of electromagnetic waves off a substance, like an image reflecting off a mirror. Scattering occurs when electromagnetic waves are refracted or reflected when they pass through a material. Some sunlight entering the atmosphere is scattered, which causes the sky to appear blue. Electromagnetic radiation can also be absorbed when matter takes in energy. The blacktop of a parking lot absorbs a great amount of solar energy, which

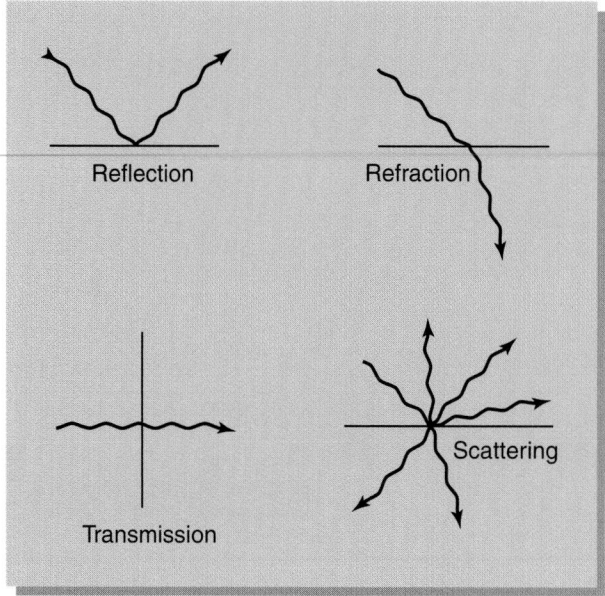

FIGURE 2–15 Four ways in which electromagnetic energy interacts with matter.

makes it very hot in summer. Substances that are good at absorbing electromagnetic radiation also tend to be good at emitting electromagnetic radiation. Usually, materials that absorb high-energy, smaller-wavelength electromagnetic radiation reradiate it at longer, lower-energy wavelengths. The final way in which electromagnetic radiation interacts with matter is called transmission. Transmission is when electromagnetic radiation passes through matter without interacting with it, like light passing through a window.

Earth System Scientists

Max Planck

Max Planck was born in 1858 in Germany. Most of his life was devoted to the study of theoretical physics. He began his work by researching thermodynamics and the nature of electromagnetic radiation. His early contributions to physics dealt with the relationship of electromagnetic radiation to wavelengths and energy. He derived the Planck constant, which is used to determine the energy associated with a particular frequency of the electromagnetic spectrum. This breakthrough revealed that the shorter the wavelength of electromagnetic energy, the higher the energy level. His most famous contribution to physics came in 1900 with his development of quantum theory. This groundbreaking theory explained how heat, light, and other forms of energy come in the form of individual bundles, which he called quanta. His theories revolutionized modern physics. In his later life he helped apply his knowledge to support Einstein's famous theory of relativity.

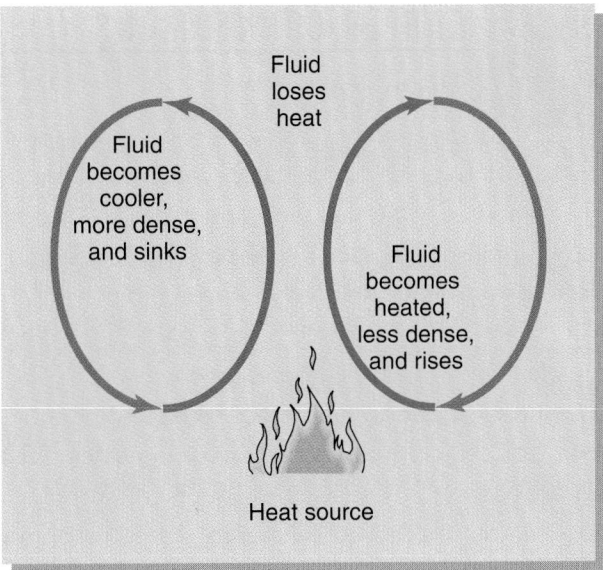

FIGURE 2–16 The formation of a convection cell in a fluid as result of differences in temperature and density.

ENERGY TRANSFER

All electromagnetic energy on Earth comes from the Sun. The Sun emits electromagnetic energy in all wavelengths. However, the Earth's surface receives most of the Sun's electromagnetic energy in the visible light range, with smaller amounts in the ultraviolet and infrared wavelengths. The interaction of energy and matter in, on, and around Earth is an important part of many Earth systems. The transfer of energy through the Earth takes place by three fundamental processes. **Conduction** is the transfer of kinetic energy by the direct contact of atoms and molecules. When you place a metal skillet on a fire, the heat of the fire is conducted through the metal and up the handle. Conduction is an important way that heat is transferred from the solid Earth to the atmosphere. Another way that heat is transferred throughout the Earth is **radiation**. Radiation is the movement of energy in empty space by electromagnetic waves. Feeling the heat of the Sun on your face on a hot summer day is sensing energy in the form of radiation. Radiation from the Sun is the main source of energy on Earth. The last method of energy transfer on Earth is **convection**. Convection is the circular movement of heat in a freely moving substance (gas or liquid), which is caused by differences in temperature and density (Figure 2–16). This form of energy transfer causes hot air to rise up toward the ceiling of your house and cooler air to sink toward the floor. Convection of heat in the Earth's mantle and atmosphere is an important way that heat is distributed around the Earth.

HEAT AND TEMPERATURE

Energy is measured on the Earth in the form of both heat and temperature. **Temperature** is the average kinetic energy of the molecules and atoms of a substance. Remember that all atoms are in motion; this motion can be in the form of vibrations, such as in a solid, or moving

CAREER CONNECTIONS

Physicists

Physicists work to discover the basic principles of matter and energy and how they interact with one another. Their research leads to improved materials, better power generation, new electronics, and knowledge about the universe in which we live. There are many different branches of physics, including nuclear physics, elementary particle physics, molecular physics, acoustics, astrophysics, optics, biophysics, and fluid physics. Nuclear physicists study the processes that occur in nuclear reactions. Elementary particle physicists study the basic particles that compose matter and how they interact. Molecular physicists study the behavior of molecules and atoms. Acoustical physics includes the study of sound. Astrophysicists study the structure and movement of all objects in the universe. Optical physicists study the properties of light energy. Biophysicists research the physics associated with the human body and other living organisms, and fluid physics studies the properties of fluids. Physics requires a good knowledge of mathematics and requires at least a four-year college degree. High school physics courses provide a good introduction to the type of work that physicists do.

over long distances and colliding rapidly, such as what occurs in gases. The greater the amount of motion of the atoms in a substance, the higher the temperature.

Temperature on Earth is measured using three different scales (Figure 2–17). Degrees Fahrenheit and Celsius measure the various temperatures associated with the physical properties of the water molecule. The freezing point of water is 32° F (0° C). This is the temperature at which liquid water becomes a solid. Water vaporizes at 212° F (100° C). This is the temperature at which liquid water becomes water vapor, or the gaseous form of water. The third temperature scale is Kelvin, which measures the average kinetic energy of atoms or molecules. Zero Kelvin is the theoretical temperature at which all particle motion stops, causing the particles to emit no electromagnetic radiation. This temperature has never been reached on Earth. Zero Kelvin equals –459.67° F and –273.16° C.

Heat is a measure of the flow of kinetic energy from one material to another, or the total amount of kinetic energy in a system. All heat flows from substances with high kinetic energy, or a source, to substances with low kinetic energy, called a sink. Therefore the energy flow in a system moves from a source to a sink. We sense this change in kinetic energy as heat. Heat is measured by using the calorie, which is a unit that denotes the amount of energy it takes to raise the temperature

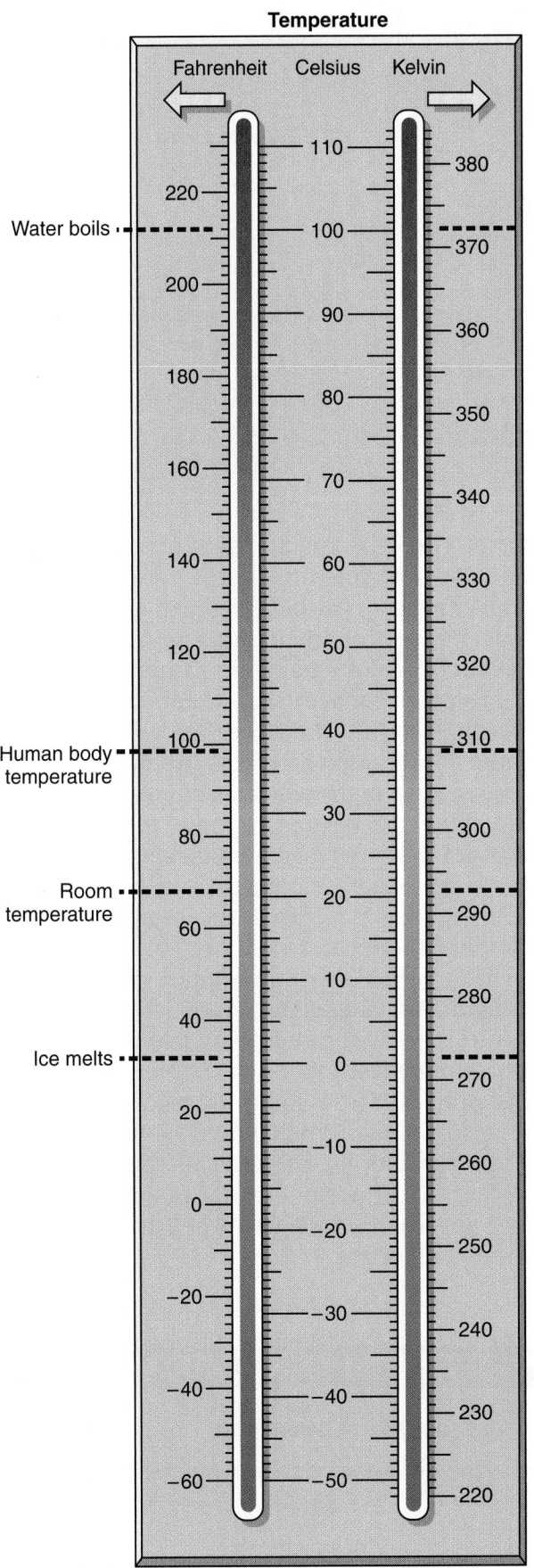

FIGURE 2–17 A comparison of the three scales used to measure temperature.

TABLE 2–3 The specific heat of common materials

Material		Specific Heat (calories/gram · C°)
Water	solid	0.5
	liquid	1.0
	gas	0.5
Dry air		0.24
Basalt		0.20
Granite		0.19
Iron		0.11
Copper		0.09
Lead		0.03

of 1 gm of water 1° C. The specific heat of a substance is a measure of how much heat is required to raise 1 gm of the substance to 1° C (Table 2–3). Specific heat is also called heat capacity. Liquid water has the highest specific heat of any natural substance on Earth. The specific heat of water is 1 calorie per gram. Other common substances on Earth have a lower heat capacity than water. The average heat capacity of rocks on Earth is about 0.2 calories per gram. Therefore water can hold much more heat energy than rock. This is why rocks heat and cool faster than water. The high heat capacity of water is an important property that helps the oceans regulate the climate of the Earth. Another important aspect of heat and its relationship to matter is that when matter changes state, heat energy is either absorbed or released. The potential energy that is released when a gas condenses into a liquid is called the **latent heat of condensation**. This means that heat is given off to the environment when a substance changes from a gas to a liquid. When 1 gram of water vapor condenses into liquid, 840 calories are released into the environment. The latent heat of freezing liquid water releases less energy into the environment, only 80 calories. When a solid changes phase into a liquid, or a liquid into a gas, energy is absorbed by a substance. When liquid water vaporizes into water vapor, it absorbs 840 calories. This is called the latent heat of vaporization. Latent heat is an important source of energy in the atmosphere, which is either absorbed or released when water vapor condenses or when liquid water vaporizes.

SECTION REVIEW

1. What is the definition of energy?
2. Describe the difference between kinetic energy and potential energy.
3. What is electromagnetic energy?
4. What is the relationship between wavelength and energy on the electromagnetic spectrum?

5. What is the source of all electromagnetic energy on Earth?

6. Which wavelengths of electromagnetic energy does the Earth's surface receive the most of?

7. List the five ways that electromagnetic energy can interact with the environment.

8. What is the difference between heat and temperature?

9. What are three ways by which heat can be transferred on Earth?

10. What is the specific heat of a substance?

11. Define the term *latent heat*.

12. Who was Max Planck?

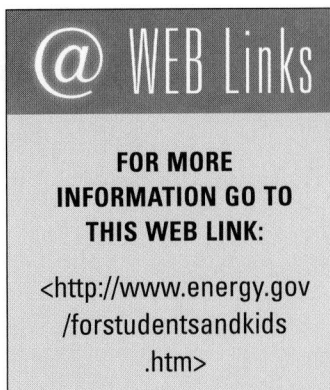

FOR MORE INFORMATION GO TO THIS WEB LINK:

<http://www.energy.gov/forstudentsandkids.htm>

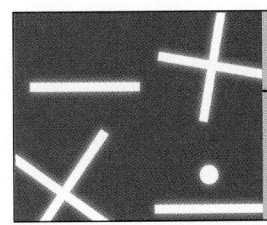

earth math

1) How many calories are released into the atmosphere when 3 grams of water vapor condenses to form a cloud?

CHAPTER SUMMARY

The universe is made up of two fundamental things: matter and energy. Matter is anything that occupies space and has mass. Matter is made up of individual particles called atoms. Atoms are composed of the subatomic particles called protons, neutrons, and electrons. Differing amounts of these subatomic particles make up unique atoms called elements. There are 109 different elements that have been identified on the Earth. Elements can be chemically combined to form complex substances called compounds. Energy is the ability to do work or cause change. There are two general types of energy: kinetic and potential. Kinetic energy is the energy of movement, and potential energy is stored energy. The law of the conservation of energy states that energy cannot be created or destroyed; it just changes forms. The different forms of energy include radiant energy, thermal energy, electrical energy, chemical energy, mechanical energy, nuclear energy, and magnetic energy. Electromagnetic energy, also called radiation, is a type of energy that travels in the form of a wave. The different types of electromagnetic energy are indicated by the electromagnetic spectrum, which classifies electromagnetic energy according to its wavelength. In general, short-wave radiation is higher in energy than long-wave radiation. The Sun emits all wavelengths of electromagnetic energy, but the surface of the Earth receives mostly the visible light form. Energy can be transferred in the environment by the processes of conduction, convection, or radiation. All these processes play an important role in the movement of energy through the Earth's systems. Energy is often measured in the form of heat or temperature. The temperature of a substance is a measure of the average kinetic energy of its atoms, which is commonly expressed as degrees Fahrenheit or Celsius.

CHAPTER REVIEW

Multiple Choice

1. Something that occupies space and has mass is called:
   a. energy
   b. weight
   c. matter
   d. volume

2. A particle that is composed of a nucleus surrounded by an electron is called:
   a. a proton
   b. an atom
   c. a neutron
   d. molecule

3. The state of matter that allows atoms to move freely is known as a:
   a. solid
   b. liquid
   c. gas
   d. plasma

4. Vaporization describes the phase change from a:
   a. solid to liquid
   b. liquid to gas
   c. gas to liquid
   d. liquid to solid

5. Condensation describes the phase change from a:
   a. solid to liquid
   b. liquid to gas
   c. gas to liquid
   d. liquid to solid

6. The process by which a solid changes phase into gas is called:
   a. boiling
   b. freezing
   c. melting
   d. sublimation

7. Two or more elements that are chemically combined create a:
   a. compound
   b. ion
   c. isotope
   d. atom

8. The energy that is associated with movement is called:
   a. radiant energy
   b. kinetic energy
   c. potential energy
   d. electromagnetic energy

9. The stored energy in gasoline, or in a sandwich, is classified as:
   a. radiant energy
   b. kinetic energy
   c. potential energy
   d. electromagnetic energy

10. High-energy electromagnetic radiation has:
    a. short wavelengths
    b. tall waves
    c. long wavelengths
    d. no waves

11. Hot air rising and cool air sinking in a room is an example of:
    a. conduction
    b. radiation
    c. convection
    d. reflection

12. Burning your hand on the handle of a pot on a stove is an example of heat transfer by:
    a. conduction
    b. radiation
    c. convection
    d. reflection

13. Which type of energy transfer travels in the form of a wave?
    a. conduction
    b. radiation
    c. convection
    d. reflection

14. The average kinetic energy of the atoms in a substance is known as:
    a. refraction
    b. heat
    c. latent heat
    d. temperature

15. Which type of energy is absorbed or released when a substance changes phase?
    a. heat
    b. latent heat
    c. temperature
    d. radiation

Matching   *Match the terms with the correct definitions.*

a. matter
b. elements
c. vaporization
d. boiling point
e. condensation

f. sublimation
g. energy
h. electromagnetic radiation
i. electromagnetic spectrum
j. conduction

k. radiation
l. convection
m. heat
n. temperature
o. latent heat

1. _____ The phase change from a solid to a gas.
2. _____ Something that occupies space and has mass.
3. _____ The ability to cause change or to perform work.
4. _____ The 109 identified atoms that have a definite number of protons, neutrons, and electrons.
5. _____ A type of energy that travels in the form of a wave and needs no medium for transfer.
6. _____ The phase change that occurs when a liquid changes into a gas.
7. _____ The range of specific wavelengths and frequencies that identify the specific forms of electromagnetic energy.
8. _____ The specific temperature at which a substance begins to change its phase from a liquid to a gas.
9. _____ The transfer of heat energy by direct molecular contact.
10. _____ The change in phase from a gas to a liquid.
11. _____ Waves or particles that are emitted from a substance.
12. _____ Heat energy that is either absorbed or released during a phase change.
13. _____ The transfer of heat energy in a fluid as a result of a change in density associated with a change in temperature.
14. _____ The average amount of kinetic energy of the atoms and molecules in a substance.
15. _____ The measurable or perceived effect of energy that is transferred between two objects that have different temperatures.

Critical Thinking

1. Construct a flow chart that depicts all the energy transfers that occur from the Sun to the milk in your cereal.
2. Construct a list of all the elements you can identify that are found in common substances around your home or in school.

The Exosphere

UNIT

2

OVERVIEW

The exosphere is the area that is located outside of Earth's atmosphere, also known as outer space. Understanding the Earth's place in the exosphere and the specific regions of outer space is important to understanding the systems of the Earth. Many processes that occur on the Earth every day are the direct result of the processes that occur in the exosphere. Even in ancient times, thousands of years before humans left the Earth and began to explore space, people were fascinated with the world outside our own. The length of the day, the changing seasons, tides, and time are all influenced by the exosphere. This has in turn influenced every living thing on the Earth. Unlocking the secrets of outer space has helped us learn more about our unique planet and how it functions.

The Earth as a Planet

THE PLANET EARTH OBJECTIVES

The Earth's Composition · The Earth's Shape · The Size of the Earth · The Earth's Rotation · The Earth's Tilted Axis · The Earth's Coordinate System: Latitude and Longitude · Topographical Maps

After reading this chapter you should be able to:

▌ Identify the four basic parts of the Earth's interior.

▌ Describe the true shape of the Earth, and explain three observations to prove its shape.

▌ Explain the characteristics of Earth's rotation and how it affects the planet.

▌ Describe an observation that can be used to prove the Earth is rotating.

▌ Describe the time period to complete one complete rotation of the Earth.

▌ Describe the position of the Earth's axis relative to the Sun during the equinoxes, summer solstice, and winter solstice.

▌ Explain how lines of latitude and longitude are used to locate an object on the Earth's surface.

▌ Describe how you can locate your latitude in the Northern Hemisphere.

▌ Explain what information you need to determine your longitude location on the Earth.

▌ Describe the type of information that can be found on a topographic map.

▌ Define the terms contour line and contour interval.

EARTH MOTIONS OBJECTIVES

Apparent Motion of Celestial Objects · Early Models of the Universe · Orbital Motion

After reading this chapter you should be able to:

▌ Discuss the differences between the Geocentric and Heliocentric views of the universe.

▌ Explain the concept of the apparent motion of celestial objects.

▌ Identify the contributions to astronomy made by Copernicus, Kepler, Galileo, and Newton.

▌ Describe the actual orbital paths of the planets around the Sun.

▌ Label all the parts of an ellipse.

▌ Explain the eccentricity of an ellipse, and how it affects the orbit of a planet.

▌ Describe how to calculate the eccentricity of an ellipse.

▌ Define the terms aphelion and perihelion.

- ▶ Describe how the velocity of a planet is related to its distance from the Sun.
- ▶ Explain the time period that is related to the Earth's revolution
- ▶ Identify the times of year when the Earth is at aphelion and perihelion.

TOOLS OF ASTRONOMY OBJECTIVES

Locating Celestial Objects · Telescopes · Space Exploration

After reading this chapter you should be able to:

- ▶ Describe how azimuth and altitude are used to locate celestial objects.
- ▶ Define the terms right ascension and declination, and explain how they are used to locate celestial objects.
- ▶ Identify three different types of telescopes used by astronomers.
- ▶ Define the term spectroscope and explain how astronomers use spectroscopes to study celestial objects.
- ▶ Discuss some of the milestones of spaceflight.
- ▶ Describe some of the challenges facing long range manned spaceflight.
- ▶ Explain the concept of technology transfer, and provide three examples from the space program.

INTRODUCTION

It is hard to imagine that we are all standing on a huge ball that is spinning like a top at more than 1,000 miles per hour (1,609 kilometers per hour) near the equator while also being propelled through space at speeds of approximately 66,000 miles per hour (106,217 kilometers per hour). The Earth's place in the solar system and its interactions with the Sun affect many of the Earth's systems. The length of the day, changing seasons of the year, and rise and fall of the tides are all examples of these complex interactions. It has taken human beings hundreds of years of careful observations to fully understand our planet's place in the solar system. As a result, human knowledge now rises out of the atmosphere and into the universe, revealing much about the planet we call home.

3.1 The Planet Earth

THE EARTH'S COMPOSITION

The Earth is a **terrestrial planet**. A planet is any large body that orbits around a star. The term *terrestrial* means that it is composed mainly of rock and metal. Because the Earth is composed of rock, it has a relatively high density, approximately 5.5 grams per cubic centimeter. The interior of the Earth is made up of a dense combination of molten iron and nickel, which is surrounded by a plastic-like, less dense rock called the mantle (Figure 3–1). The movements of the liquid interior of the Earth generate a strong magnetic field that surrounds the planet. This causes the Earth to act much like a large magnet, with the poles of the magnet located near the poles of the Earth. This magnetic field stretches out through the atmosphere and acts as a protective barrier to deadly, high-energy solar radiation. This portion of the Earth is called the magnetosphere (Figure 3–2). The Earth's magnetic field allows us to use compasses to locate direction on the planet. A small magnetic needle that is allowed to spin freely aligns itself with the Earth's magnetic field and points to the magnetic North Pole. The outer portion of the Earth, also called the crust, is made up of two basic types

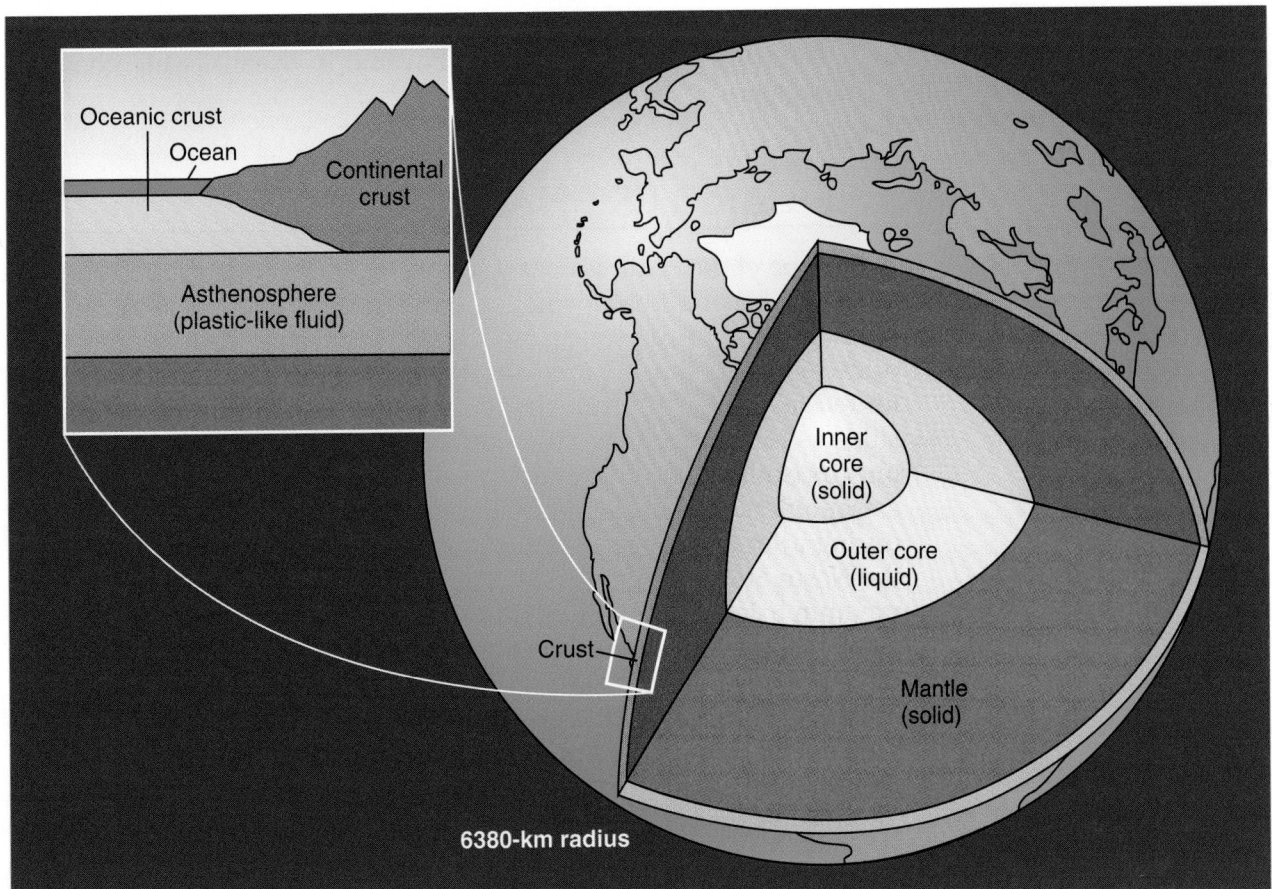

FIGURE 3–1 This cross section of the Earth reveals its internal structure, which is made up of the inner and outer core, mantle, and crust.

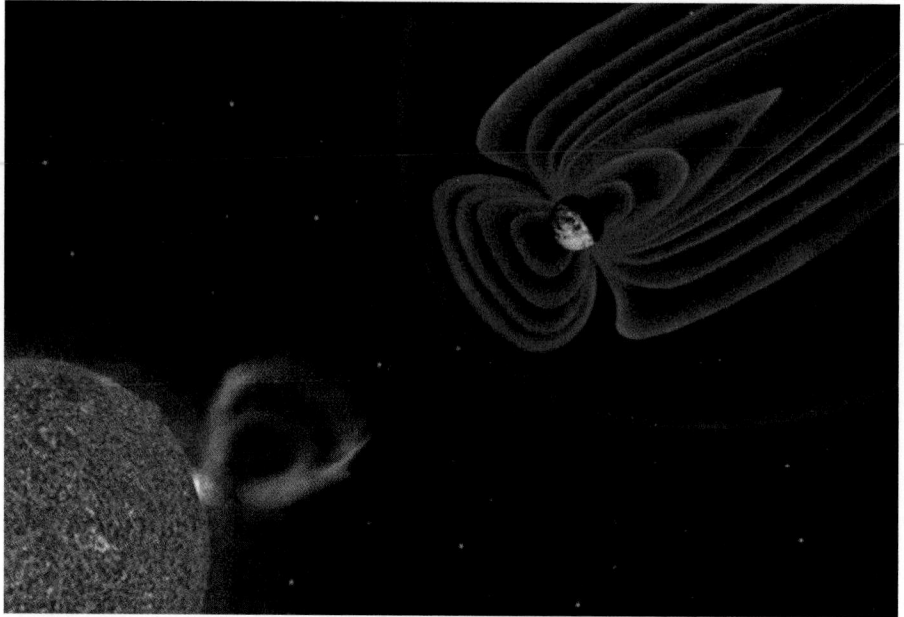

FIGURE 3–2 The Earth's magnetosphere acts as an invisible shield, protecting the planet from high level radiation. (*Courtesy of NASA.*)

of solid rock: granites and basalts. Granite rocks make up most of the Earth's continents, and basalts compose most of the ocean floor. Although the Earth is classified as a terrestrial planet, it also is surrounded by a thin envelope of gas called the atmosphere. Approximately 70 percent of the planet is covered in oceans, which have an average depth of 2 mi (3.2 km).

THE EARTH'S SHAPE

The shape of the Earth is nearly spherical, which means it resembles a round ball. Long before satellites or spacecraft were able to photograph the Earth from space and reveal its spherical form, humans theorized about its shape. Three observations made hundreds of years ago hinted at the Earth's true shape. The first was the disappearance of ships as they moved over the horizon. This simple observation could only be explained by the ships' traveling over a curved surface. Ancient astronomers also observed a curved shadow move across the moon during a lunar eclipse. Another observation included the altitude of the North Star in the night sky. The North Star, also called Polaris, is a medium bright star that lies almost directly over the North Pole. Early astronomers noticed that the altitude of Polaris—that is, the height of the star above the horizon—changed as they moved farther south or north. As an observer traveled north, toward the North Pole, the altitude of Polaris increased until it was exactly 90 degrees above the horizon directly at the North Pole. Then, as an observer traveled south toward the equator, the altitude of Polaris decreased. Eventually, as the observer moves past the equator and into the Southern Hemisphere, the North Star dips below the horizon and can no longer be seen. The only explanation for this apparent change in altitude is the Earth's shape being round. The actual shape of the Earth, however, is not perfectly round, but is referred to as an oblate spheroid. The term *oblate* means that it is slightly flattened. The slight flattening of the Earth near the equator is caused by its rapid rotation. Because the Earth is slightly oblate, its diameter is slightly larger around the equator than around the poles. The equatorial diameter of the Earth is approximately 7928 mi (12,759 km), whereas the diameter of the Earth between the North and South Poles is 7,900 mi (12,714 km). As a result of this slight bulging at the equator, if you were to fly around the world at the equator, you would have to travel 24,900 mi (40,073 km). This is 43 mi (69 km) more than if you flew around the Earth starting at the North Pole. Because of this relatively small bulge at the equator, it can be assumed that the Earth is nearly a perfect sphere when viewed from space.

THE SIZE OF THE EARTH

The total surface area of the Earth is approximately 197 million square miles (510 million square kilometers), of which more than 70 percent is covered by ocean. This is why the planet Earth appears blue when seen from space. Long before precise instruments were able to measure the size of the Earth, the Greek scientist Eratosthenes, who lived more than 2,000 years ago, accurately measured the circumference of the Earth. He observed that the Sun shone directly down at the bottom of a well in the city of Syene, Egypt. He then measured the length of a shadow cast by an obelisk at the same time in the city of Alexandria. Finally, Eratosthenes used his knowledge of geometry and the distance between Syene and Alexandria to calculate the circumference of the Earth. His calculations revealed the circumference of Earth to be approximately 25,054 mi (40,321 km), which is only 175 mi (282 km) off from the Earth's actual average circumference.

Earth System Scientists

Eratosthenes

Eratosthenes was a Greek scientist and philosopher who lived during the third century BCE. He also served as the librarian in the greatest library of the ancient world, in Alexandria, Egypt. Eratosthenes accomplished many things during his 80-year life. He was the first person to accurately measure the circumference of the Earth, and he calculated the distance of the Sun from the Earth. He studied the importance of prime numbers in mathematics. Eratosthenes created star charts that cataloged more than 500 stars, and he developed a calendar that included leap years. He created accurate maps and charts of the Nile River and was the first to suggest that heavy rains in the mountains and lakes above the river were the cause of floods downriver. He also wrote an epic poem titled *Hermes*, which explains the fundamentals of the science of astronomy at the time.

THE EARTH'S ROTATION

The Earth, like all planets that orbit the Sun, rotates on its axis. The **axis** of the Earth is an imaginary line through the center of the Earth that connects the North and South Poles. Early observations of the movement of stars, planets, and the Sun around the Earth caused ancient astronomers to believe that either the heavens were spinning around the Earth or the Earth was spinning on its axis. It was not until 1851 that the French scientist Jean Foucault proved that the Earth was spinning by performing an original experiment. He suspended a pendulum from the ceiling and let it swing back and forth across the room. The pendulum would continue to swing in the same direction if the Earth were not spinning. Much to the onlookers' amazement, the pendulum slowly changed direction as Foucault had predicted. The pendulum altered its course because the Earth was rotating underneath it. Today copies of Foucault's pendulum swing to and fro in many science museums across the world. The changing direction of the pendulums knock over objects to prove the Earth is indeed spinning on its axis.

The speed at which the Earth is rotating depends on how far north or south of the equator you are. The greatest velocity is at the equator, and the least is located near the North and South Poles. This is because the Earth is spherical. For example, if a line of roller skaters were skating around in a circle, the skater on the outside of the circle would have to skate the fastest to keep up with the other skaters in the line. The skater near the center of the circle, closest to the axis of rotation, would skate the slowest. The equator is the farthest point on the Earth from the axis of rotation, and therefore acts like the skater on the outside of the circle moving at the greatest speed. The North and South Poles are closest to the axis of rotation and act like the skaters near the center of the circle moving the slowest. If you are standing on the equator, the Earth's rotational speed is approximately 1,037 miles per hour (1,669 km/hr). At this speed the Earth makes one full **rotation**, or one rotational period, on its axis every 23 hours, 56 minutes, and 4.1 seconds. We round off this period to 24 hours, or 1 day. The rotation of the Earth causes half the world to be exposed to sunlight while the other half is bathed in darkness. This is why we experience day and night on Earth. This change in sunlight exposure causes the Earth to receive unequal heating, which helps define the Earth's weather and climate regions.

THE EARTH'S TILTED AXIS

The axis of the Earth is tilted approximately 23.5 degrees toward the plane of the ecliptic. The plane of the ecliptic is an imaginary plane in which the Earth orbits the Sun. The Earth's celestial equator is an imaginary line drawn from the Earth's equator out into space. The tilt of the Earth's axis causes parts of the Earth to receive more sunlight than other parts of the Earth during the year. This causes the Earth's four seasons. When the Earth's North Pole is pointing towards the Sun, the Northern Hemisphere experiences the summer season, during which the day length increases. The longest days in the middle latitudes of the Northern Hemisphere during the summer are between 14 and 15 hours long. The longest day falls around June 21, which is called the summer solstice. The North Pole experiences 24 hours of light for a period of six months during the summer season. When the Sun's path passes through the celestial equator, the planet experiences the fall and spring seasons. On these days the Sun is directly overhead at the equator. These are also known as the equinoxes, which means that the length of day and night are equal, or twelve hours in length. The autumnal equinox (fall) occurs around September 23, and the vernal equinox (spring) occurs around March 21. When the North Pole is tilted away from the Sun, the winter season has arrived. During this time of year, the middle latitudes in the Northern Hemisphere experience short days that are approximately 9 to 10 hours long. The shortest day is called the winter solstice, which occurs around December 21. The cycle of seasons repeats itself every year, which is the time it takes for the Earth to make one complete revolution around the Sun.

THE EARTH'S COORDINATE SYSTEM: LATITUDE AND LONGITUDE

A coordinate system is a method of locating an exact location on a two-dimensional surface. Although the Earth's surface is not truly two-dimensional, a coordinate system that uses intersecting horizontal and vertical lines is used to mark locations on the Earth. The Earth's coordinate system uses an imaginary horizontal line that divides the Earth in half, called the **equator**. This divides the planet into two hemispheres. The region north of the equator all the way to the North Pole is called the Northern Hemisphere. The region south of the equator all the way to the South Pole is called the Southern Hemisphere. Each hemisphere is further divided by horizontal lines that mark the location north or south of the equator. These parallel lines are called lines of **latitude** and are marked in degrees. The equator represents 0 degrees latitude, the North Pole is 90 degrees north latitude, and the South Pole represents 90 degrees south latitude. Each degree of latitude is further divided into 60 minutes, and 1 minute of latitude equals 60 seconds. This enables you to precisely measure your location on Earth either north or south of the equator (Figure 3–3). You can determine

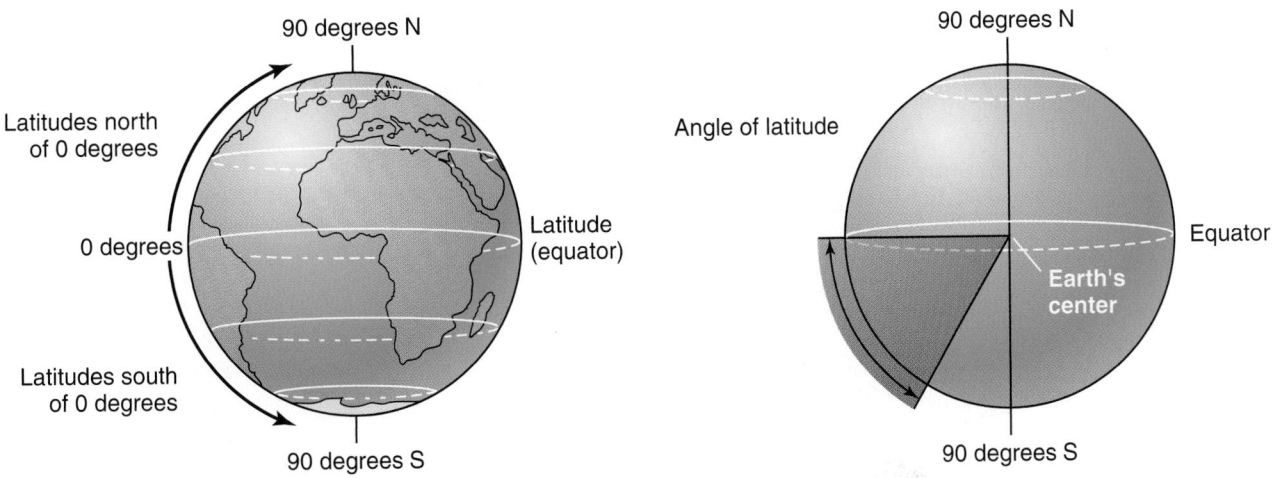

FIGURE 3–3   Lines of latitude on the Earth mark positions north and south of the equator.

your latitude in the Northern Hemisphere by using the North Star, also called Polaris. The North Star is a bright star that is located directly above the Earth's axis at the North Pole. At the North Pole, Polaris is exactly 90 degrees above the horizon. As you begin to move south toward the equator, the altitude of Polaris in the nighttime sky begins to decrease. Therefore the angle at which the North Star is above the horizon equals your latitude location. For example, if you measured the altitude of the North Star above the horizon to be 45 degrees, your latitude location is 45 degrees north of the equator. Because the North Star is above the North Pole, it can be used to determine your latitude only north of the equator. Once you reach the equator, the North Star is no longer visible because it dips below the horizon. In the Southern Hemisphere, you can use the brightest star located in the constellation called the Southern Cross to estimate your latitude. The Southern Cross is located almost directly over the South Pole and acts like the Northern Hemisphere's Polaris.

Lines of latitude are useful only for determining an exact location either north or south of the equator. Another set of lines that run perpendicular to latitude lines are needed to mark a precise location on Earth. These lines are called lines of **longitude**, which are vertical lines that run from the North Pole to the South Pole. Lines of longitude also use degrees, minutes, and seconds as units of measurement. Unlike lines of latitude, which use the exact halfway point between the North and South Poles to represent 0 degrees, there is no natural halfway point that divides the Earth in half vertically. Therefore English astronomers used the location of the national observatory at Greenwich, England, to represent 0 degrees longitude. This imaginary line is called the prime meridian, or the Greenwich meridian. From this starting point, lines of longitude, also called meridians, mark a location on the Earth either west or east of the prime meridian (Figure 3–4).

There are 180 degrees of longitude west of the prime meridian, and 180 degrees east of the prime meridian. The 180th meridian is also called the International Date Line. To determine a location in longitude, you must know the time difference between your location and the time at the prime meridian, also called Greenwich Mean Time (GMT). This is because the Earth is spinning on its axis from west to east. Every 15 degrees of longitude represents 1 hour of time; therefore the time

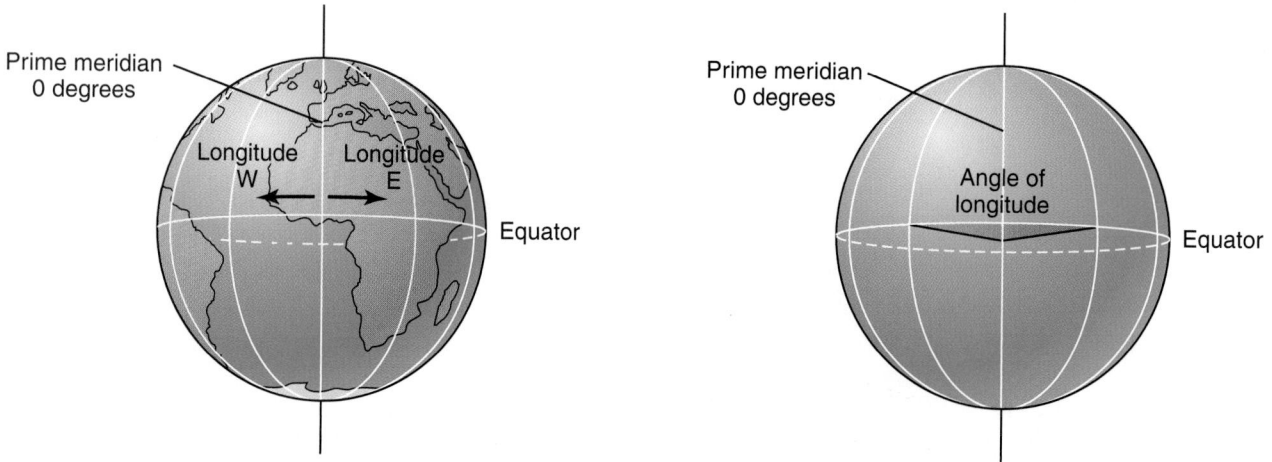

FIGURE 3–4 Lines of longitude on the Earth mark positions east and west of the prime meridian.

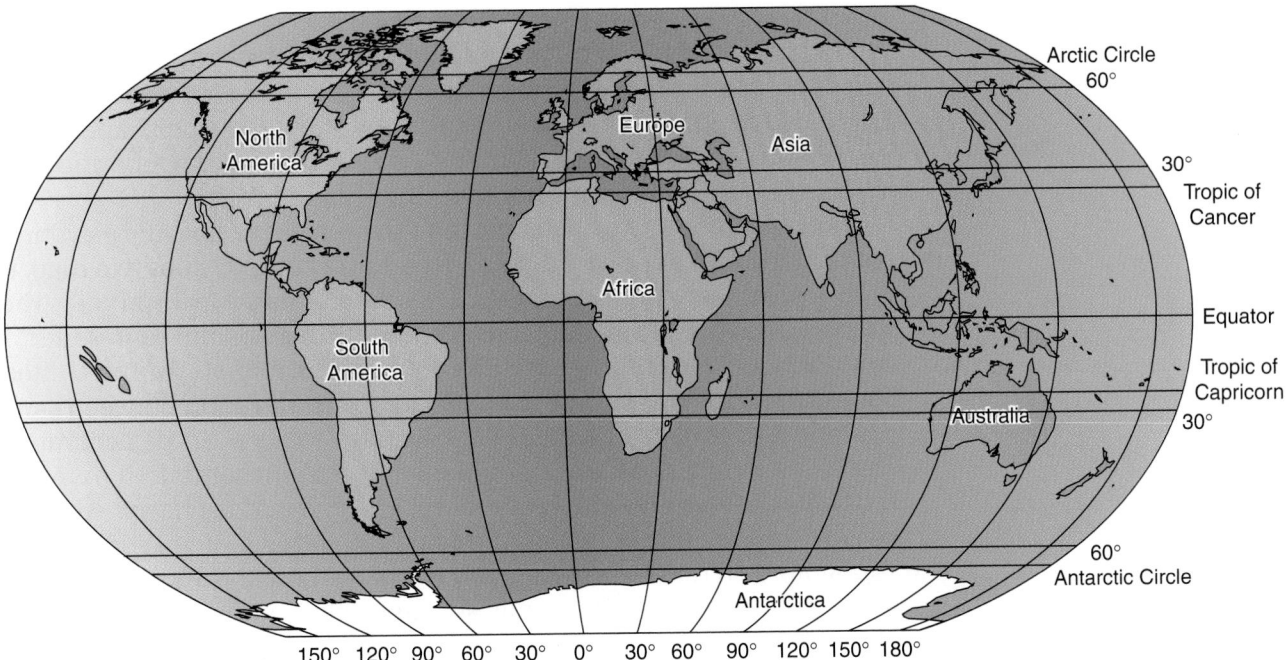

FIGURE 3–5 World map showing the latitude longitude coordinate system.

difference between your location and the time at the prime meridian can be used to determine your longitude. For example, if your time is 3 hours ahead of Greenwich Mean Time, then your longitude is 45 degrees east of the prime meridian. Because longitude requires an accurate knowledge of time, it wasn't possible to calculate longitude at sea until an accurate portable clock that could be used on board a ship was invented. This was achieved in 1728 by English clock maker John Harrison. By using the latitude and longitude coordinate system, it is possible to exactly locate any point on the Earth (Figure 3–5).

CAREER CONNECTIONS

Cartographer

Cartographers use accurate measurements of the Earth to produce precision maps of its surface. They gather many different types of information to make accurate maps. Geographers collect data on specific latitude and longitude locations of specific places on the Earth. They also collect geographical data and political information about a specific region. Cartographers use information about population, transportation routes, and local vegetation to create high-quality maps. Today, many cartographers use computers to help them create maps. Cartographers must be good at performing precision work, with attention to detail. Almost all cartography-related careers require a four-year college education.

TOPOGRAPHICAL MAPS

Maps that are used to represent the three-dimensional surface of the Earth are called topographical maps; they show the true shape of the Earth's surface. Topographical maps represent changes in elevation on the Earth's surface by using contour lines (Figure 3–6).

Contour lines are drawn on a map to represent a specific elevation of the land surface above sea level. By adding contour lines to a map, it is possible to see the true shape of the land. A **contour interval** is the specific division in height above sea level that each line represents. A common contour interval used on topographical maps in the United States is 20 feet. This means that the change in elevation between each contour line equals 20 feet. Mountains and valleys can be accurately represented on a two-dimensional map by adding contour lines. All of the United States and much of the world's land surface have been surveyed, and accurate topographical maps have been produced. Topographical maps show detailed features of the Earth's surface such as the locations of rivers, roads, swamps, lakes, ponds, railroads, and other interesting features (Figure 3–7). These maps are useful to a variety of people and are easily available.

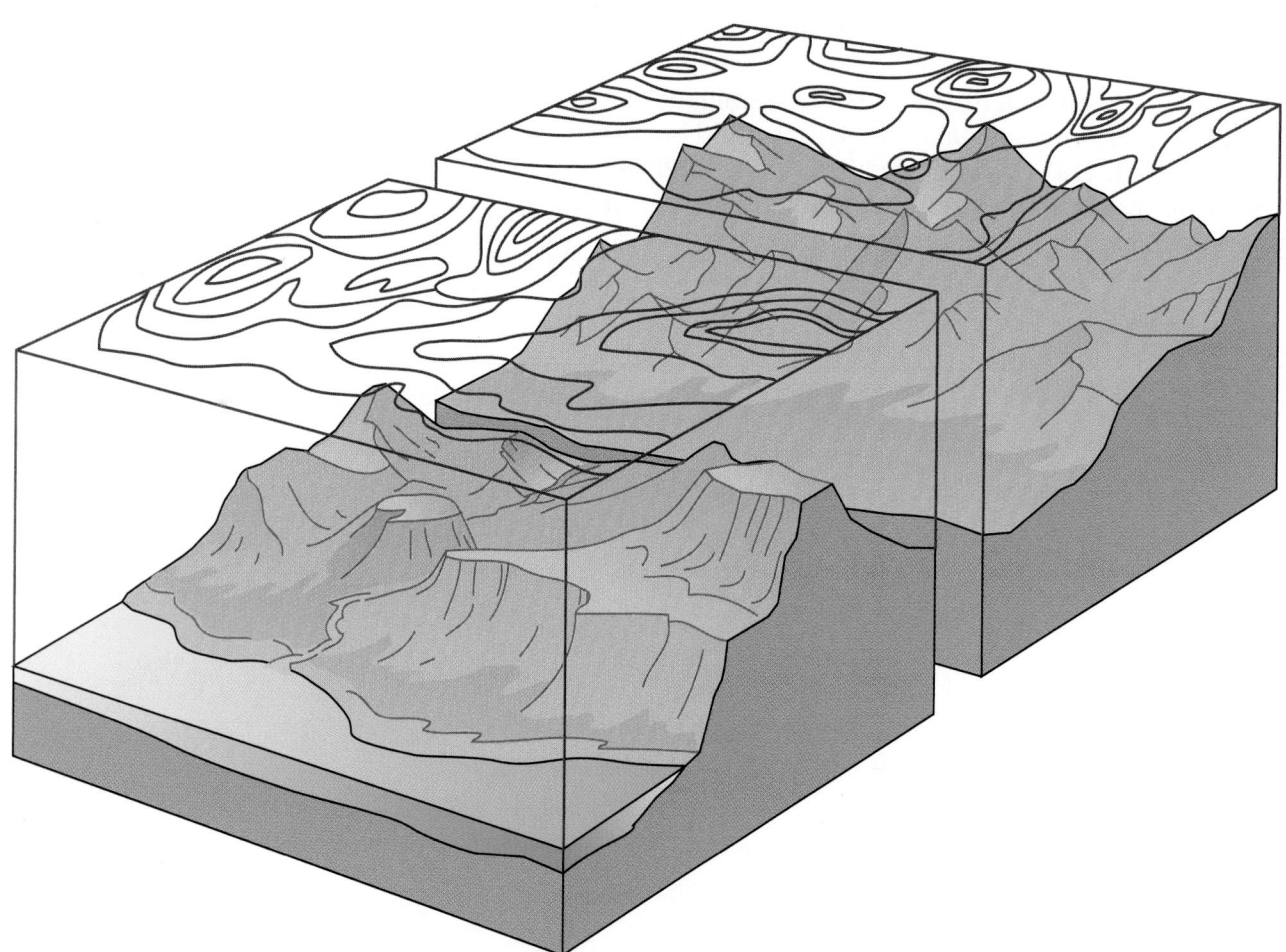

FIGURE 3–6 Contour lines are used to represent changes in elevation on a topographical map.

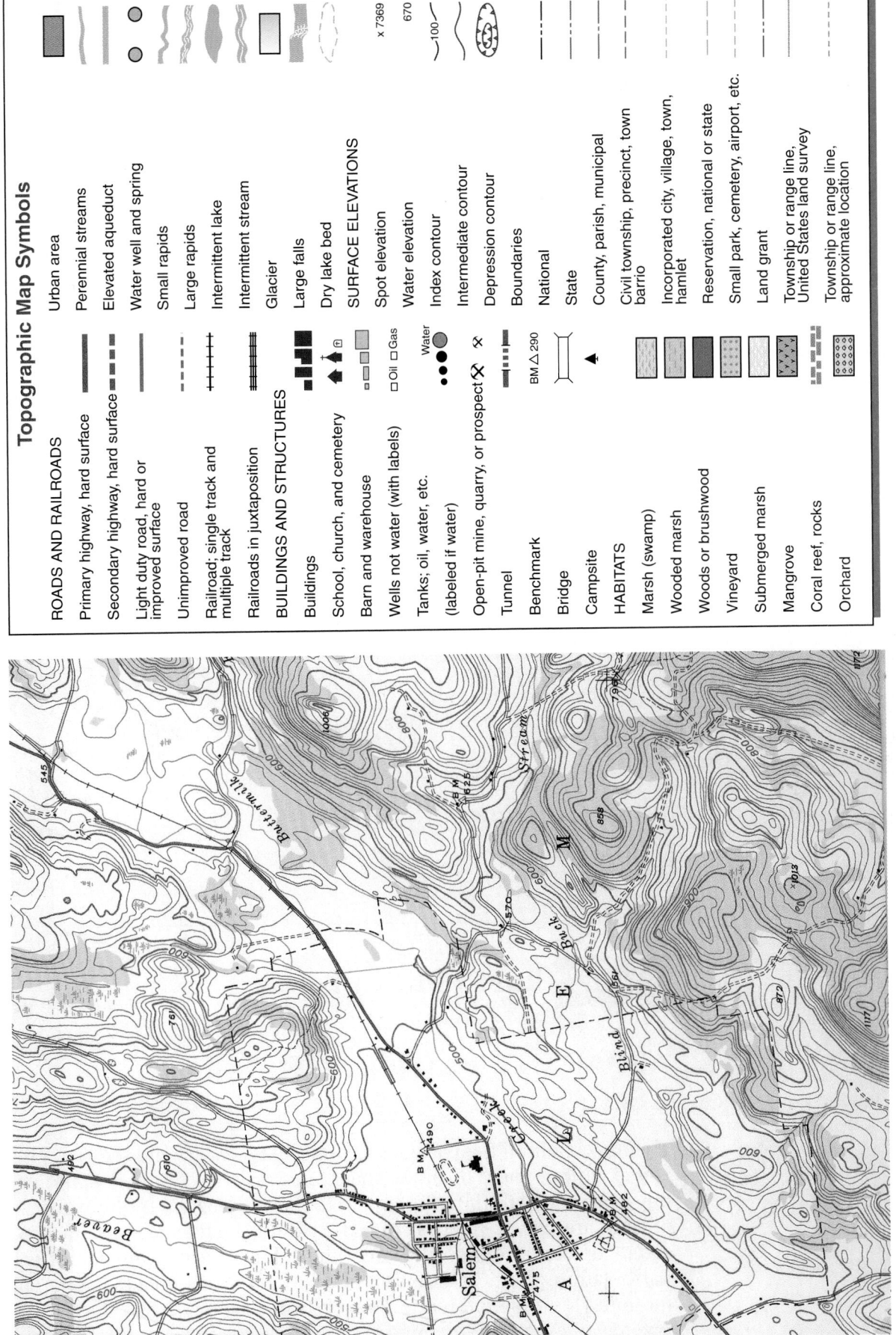

FIGURE 3–7   Topographical maps contain detailed information about the Earth's surface. (*Map courtesy of USGS.*)

SECTION REVIEW

1. What is a terrestrial planet?

2. What is the true shape of the Earth, and what are three pieces of evidence that prove its shape?

3. What is the exact time period for one rotation of the Earth?

4. Describe the positions of the Northern Hemisphere, with respect to the Earth's tilted axis and the four seasons of the year.

5. What is the significance of the following dates, December 21, March 21, June 22, and September 23?

6. What do lines of latitude measure on the Earth?

7. How can you determine your latitude in the Northern Hemisphere?

8. What do lines of longitude measure on the Earth?

9. What information do you need to determine your longitude?

10. What are topographic maps?

11. What are contour lines?

12. Who was Eratosthenes?

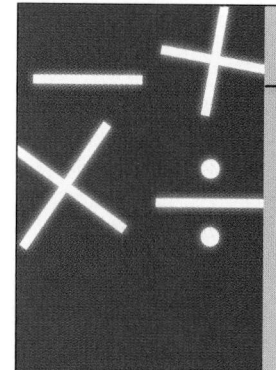

earth math

1) Determine the equatorial radius if the Earth's equatorial diameter is 7,928 miles.

2) What is your approximate longitude if it is noon at the Prime Meridian, and 5:00 PM at your location?

3) What is your approximate longitude if it is midnight at your location, and 6:00 AM at the Prime Meridian?

3.2 Earth Motions

APPARENT MOTION OF CELESTIAL OBJECTS

The movement of the Earth, both on its axis and around the Sun, creates a unique view of outer space. Because the Earth is spinning, objects in the nighttime sky appear to move in regular motions. These objects are called celestial objects, which include planets, moons, stars, comets, asteroids and any other object located outside of the Earth's atmosphere. The motion of celestial objects is called apparent motion. This apparent motion travels from east to west across the sky. The speed at which apparent motion travels is measured in degrees, with the sky representing 180 degrees from horizon to horizon. The apparent motion of celestial objects is approximately 15 degrees of sky per hour. Celestial objects appear to move at this rate because it takes 24 hours for the Earth to make one rotation. If you divide the 360 degrees that makes a complete circle around the Earth, by the 24 hours it takes to make one complete rotation, you come up with 15 degrees of movement per hour. Celestial objects are not really moving around the planet; the spinning of the Earth makes them appear to move this way. This is why it is called apparent motion.

EARLY MODELS OF THE UNIVERSE

As a result of the apparent motion of celestial objects, for thousands of years humans had the view that the planets and stars revolved around the Earth. Even observing the nighttime sky today reveals why people thought this way for so long. Claudius Ptolemy, the great Roman mathematician, geographer, and astronomer, who lived in Alexandria, Egypt, almost 2,000 years ago, was the first scientist to formalize this idea. In the Ptolemaic system, or **geocentric** view of the universe, Ptolemy described the planets and stars as revolving around the Earth in concentric crystalline spheres. This model of the universe also held the notion that all celestial objects moved around the Earth in perfect circular orbits (Figure 3–8).

The Geocentric model was accepted for over one thousand years until a Polish astronomer changed the way humans looked at the heavens.

FIGURE 3–8 An early drawing of a model of the geocentric view of the universe. (*Courtesy of NASA.*)

Nicolaus Copernicus observed the motions of stars and planets for decades, and realized that there were problems with the long-established geocentric model. Copernicus finally published his theory, now known as the Copernican **heliocentric** system, in 1543. This view put the Sun at the center of the solar system, with the planets, including the Earth, revolving around it. Copernicus' theory created much controversy, and lacked sufficient proof to verify it. Galileo Galilei, born in Italy in 1564, took up Copernicus' idea when he used improved telescopes of his own design to help support the heliocentric model through careful scientific observation. Galileo first observed the Earth's moon with his new telescopes, revealing that its surface was much like the Earth, consisting of mountains, valleys and craters. Then the brilliant scientist began to observe the planet Jupiter with his telescope. His observations not only discovered four of its moons, but more important that they were revolving around Jupiter like a miniature model of the heliocentric solar system. Next, Galileo began to observe the planet Venus. He correctly observed that the phases of Venus could only be explained by it revolving around the Sun, providing the proof he needed to verify the heliocentric model of Copernicus. Unfortunately, Galileo faced much opposition to his scientific ponderings, and was forced to live under house arrest for the rest of his life by powerful church officials who strongly supported the geocentric model. Incredibly, before his trouble with the church, Galileo also had observed the surface of the Sun with his telescopes. Although it made him nearly blind, Galileo's observation of the Sun discovered its unique sunspots. After carefully plotting the location of these dark patches on the Sun, Galileo further revealed that the Sun was most likely rotating on its axis, like the Earth. While Galileo struggled to prove the heliocentric model, another breakthrough for modern astronomy was made in 1609 from the work of the German astronomer, Johannes Kepler. Kepler was a student and assistant of the meticulous Danish astronomer Tycho Brahe, who had compiled the most accurate observations of celestial objects. Kepler used Brahe's work to reveal the true nature of the orbits of the planets. Up until Kepler, it was believed that the orbits of celestial objects were circular. Kepler recognized that the only way to accurately explain the positions of the planets was to describe their orbits as being elliptical. He then proposed what is now known as Kepler's laws of planetary motion. His first law states that the planets all revolve around the Sun in elliptical orbits. His second law explains that as the planets revolve around the Sun, their velocity changes in relationship to their distance from the Sun. Kepler's third law explains that the period of time it takes for a planet to orbit the Sun is related to the size of its elliptical path. Slowly the work of these astronomers were unlocking the mysteries of the solar system. Finally in 1687, the English astronomer and mathematician Isaac Newton published his three laws of gravitation. These helped explain how Kepler's laws worked, therefore revealing the physics behind orbital motion. The history of the development of the heliocentric model and the astronomical observations and mathematics used to prove it reveal the true process of scientific discovery. It shows how the advancement of human knowledge progresses through time as scientists build upon the theories of others, therefore furthering our understanding of the workings of nature.

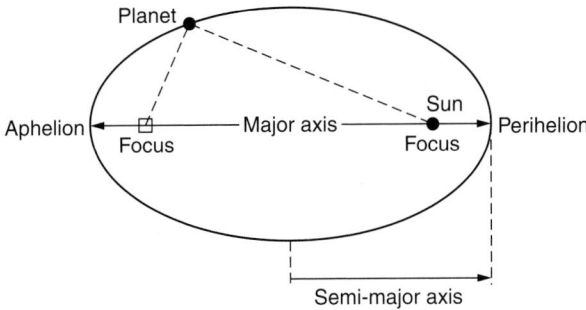

FIGURE 3–9   The parts of an ellipse.

ORBITAL MOTION

The motions of all celestial objects are based on the concept of an **ellipse**. In astronomy, the ellipse can be generally described as the oval-like path of a celestial object. The path of the ellipse, known as the orbit, is defined by two points, individually known as a focus, and together called foci. The Sun acts as one of the focus points for the elliptical path of objects orbiting the Sun. The other focus point is an imaginary position in space. A line connecting one side of the orbit, through the two foci points to the opposite side of the orbit, is known as the major axis (Figure 3–9). The oval nature of elliptical paths can be mathematically described as their eccentricity. The **eccentricity** of an orbit reveals how far from a perfect circle the elliptical path is.

An ellipse with an eccentricity of 0 represents a perfect circle. An ellipse with an eccentricity of 1 is regarded as a flat line; therefore the closer the eccentricity is to 1, the more eccentric or oval shaped the orbital path is. The time it takes for a planet to make one complete orbit around the Sun is called one **revolution**.

The eccentricity of an ellipse can be calculated by dividing the distance between the foci, by the length of the major axis. Table 3–1 reveals the eccentricities for all the planets in the solar system. Pluto's orbit is the most eccentric, or the farthest from being a perfect circle, meaning it is more oval shaped. Venus has the least eccentric orbit, which is the closest to being a perfect circle. Kepler's laws reveal the precise movement of the planets in their elliptical orbits. Because the Sun acts as one of the focus positions for the orbital paths of the planets, there are times in the orbit that planets are closer to the Sun, and other times when they are farther from the Sun.

For the Earth, the position in its orbit when it is closest to the Sun is called the **perihelion**. This occurs around the first of January, when the Earth is approximately 91,349,000 mi (147,011,965 km) from the Sun. The **aphelion** is the position when the Earth is farthest from the Sun in its orbit. This happens during the first week in July, when the Earth is approximately 94,454,000 mi (152,008,978 km) from the Sun (Figure 3–10). Observations of the Sun during these times support this concept as the Sun's apparent diameter at perihelion is larger because we are closer to the Sun. The apparent diameter of an object is its diameter measured from a specific distance. At aphelion, the Sun's apparent diameter becomes smaller because the Earth is farthest from the Sun in its orbit. Although the distance from the Earth to the Sun changes as a result of its elliptical orbit, this does not affect the Earth's

TABLE 3–1 Eccentricity of orbits for the planets of the solar system

Object	SUN	MERCURY	VENUS	EARTH	MARS	CERES	JUPITER	SATURN	URANUS	NEPTUNE	PLUTO	ERIS
Eccentricity of Orbit	—	0.206	0.007	0.017	0.093	0.080	0.048	0.056	0.047	0.009	0.250	0.442

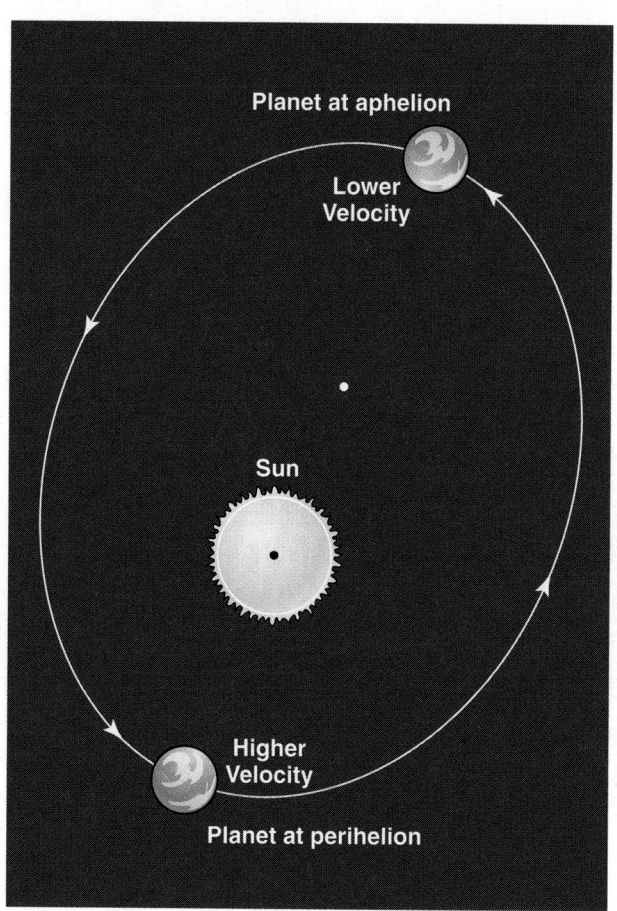

FIGURE 3–10 An exaggerated view of the Earth's elliptical orbit around the Sun, showing its aphelion and perihelion locations.

climate. The Earth's tilted axis has a much greater effect on seasonal change and temperature than the aphelion or perihelion.

Kepler's second law describes how the velocity of a planet changes in its orbital path relative to it distance from the Sun. Although Kepler came up with the idea, he couldn't explain how it occurred. Newton's laws of gravity solved that problem. Newton's work on gravity described that the gravitational attraction between two objects decreases as they get further apart, and increases when they are closer together. This notion helped explain the changing velocity of a planet relative to its distance from the Sun. When the Earth is at perihelion its velocity increases in its orbit. This is the result of the increased gravitational attraction of the Sun. The opposite effect occurs at aphelion when the Earth's velocity decreases. This is because it is farther from the Sun's gravitational influence. Studying the elliptical path of the

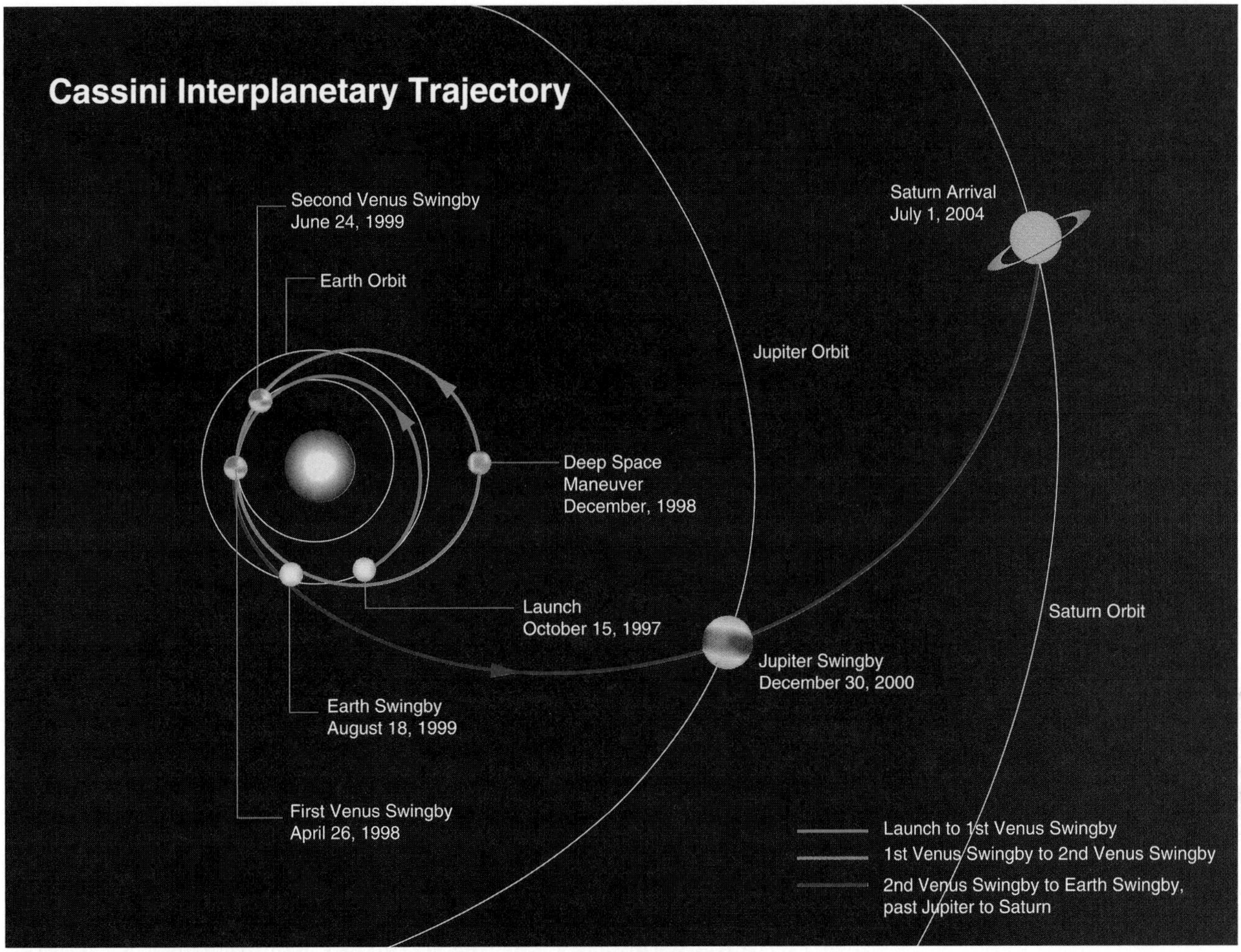

Cassini Interplanetary Trajectory

Second Venus Swingby
June 24, 1999

Earth Orbit

Deep Space
Maneuver
December, 1998

Launch
October 15, 1997

Earth Swingby
August 18, 1999

First Venus Swingby
April 26, 1998

Saturn Arrival
July 1, 2004

Jupiter Orbit

Saturn Orbit

Jupiter Swingby
December 30, 2000

Launch to 1st Venus Swingby
1st Venus Swingby to 2nd Venus Swingby
2nd Venus Swingby to Earth Swingby,
past Jupiter to Saturn

FIGURE 3–11   The gravity assist technique for propelling spacecraft.

Earth has revealed that our planet is traveling at an average speed of about 66,000 miles per hour (106,217 kilometer per hour)! Even at this incredible velocity, it still takes 365.25 days to make one complete revolution around the Sun. Knowledge of the elliptical orbits of planets and how they are governed by gravity has become a useful tool for exploring outer space. Astronomers have put this knowledge to practical use with what is called **gravity assist**. This is used to propel spacecraft far out into the solar system. Also known as the "slingshot" effect, the direction and velocity of many interplanetary spacecraft are controlled by applying an understanding of elliptical orbits and gravitational acceleration (Figure 3–11).

SECTION REVIEW

1. What is apparent motion, and what is its rate?
2. Describe the geocentric and heliocentric views of the universe.
3. What contributions to astronomy did Copernicus, Kepler, Galileo, and Newton make?
4. Explain what an ellipse is and describe its major parts.

@ WEB Links

FOR MORE INFORMATION GO TO THIS WEB LINK:

<http://obs.nineplanets.org/psc/theman.html>

<http://en.wikipedia.org/wiki/Copernicus>

<http://kepler.nasa.gov/johannes/>

<http://galileo.rice.edu/>

5. What is the eccentricity of an ellipse?

7. Define the terms aphelion and perihelion.

8. Describe how a planet's distance from the Sun affects its velocity.

9. What is the time period used to describe one revolution of the Earth, and how many days does it take?

10. What is gravity assist?

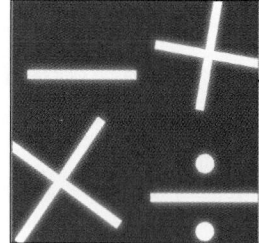

earth math

1) What is the eccentricity of an ellipse that has a distance between foci of 1, and a distance along the major axis of 4? Which planet in the solar system also has this same eccentricity?

3.3 Tools of Astronomy

LOCATING CELESTIAL OBJECTS

Astronomers have used various coordinate systems, known as celestial coordinates, to help them map the locations of celestial objects, and also track their movements. One of these systems is called the horizontal coordinate system. This uses coordinates called azimuth and altitude to mark precise locations in the sky. The azimuth is the location of an object around the horizon, which is divided into the 360 degrees of a circle. Due north on the horizon marks an azimuth of 0 degrees, with east representing 90 degrees, south 180 degrees, and west 270 degrees of azimuth. The altitude coordinate marks the angle of a celestial object above the horizon, which represents an angle between 0 and 90 degrees. The horizon represents 0 degrees of altitude with the **zenith** representing 90 degrees above the horizon. By using the azimuth and the altitude, an observer on the Earth can mark the location of a celestial object (Figure 3–12).

Another system more widely used by astronomers is called the equatorial coordinate system. This system is based on the Earth's latitude/longitude coordinate system, which is extended out into space into what is called the celestial sphere. In this system declination and right ascension are used to mark specific locations in space. Declination extends lines of latitude out into space, with objects located directly over the equator representing 0 degrees of declination, also known as the celestial equator. The North Pole represents +90 degrees, and the South Pole –90 degrees of declination. Right ascension is similar to extending lines of longitude out into space, and is measured in hours, minutes, and seconds, based on the Earth's 24-hour rotational period. The Prime Meridian, however, does not represent 0 hours 0 minutes and 0 seconds of right ascension. This point is called the vernal equinox point, which is located where the plane of the ecliptic meets the celestial equator (Figure 3–13).

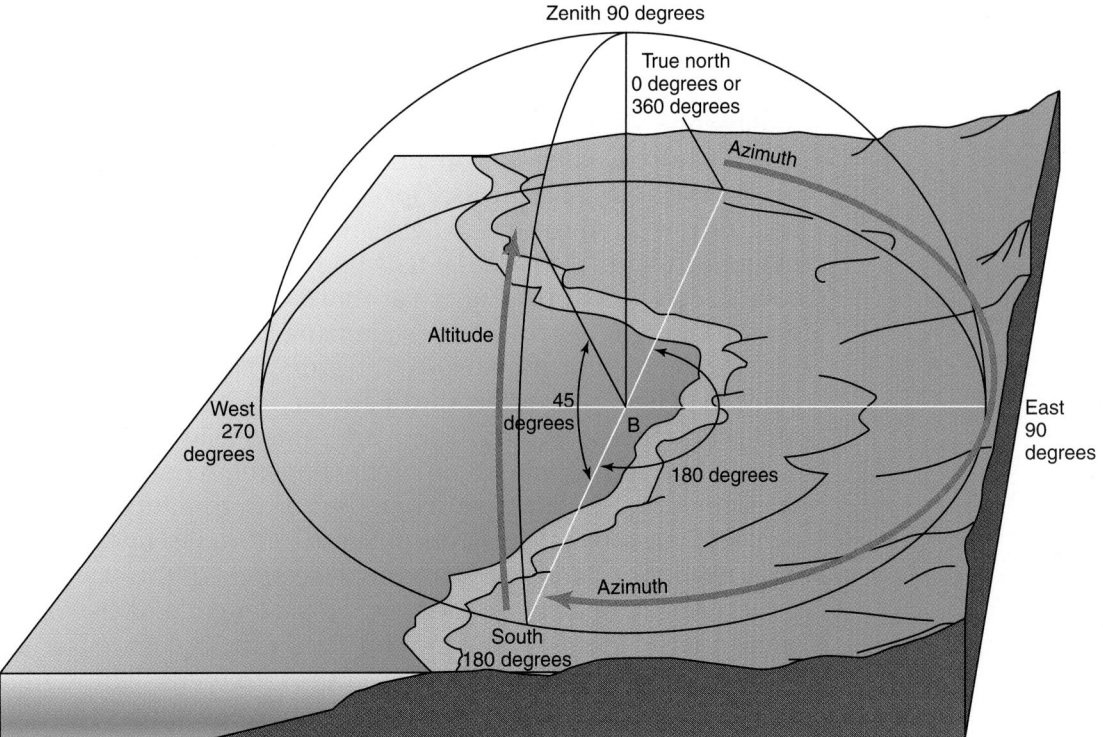

FIGURE 3–12 The location of the zenith and the horizon on the Earth and the use of altitude and azimuth to locate celestial objects.

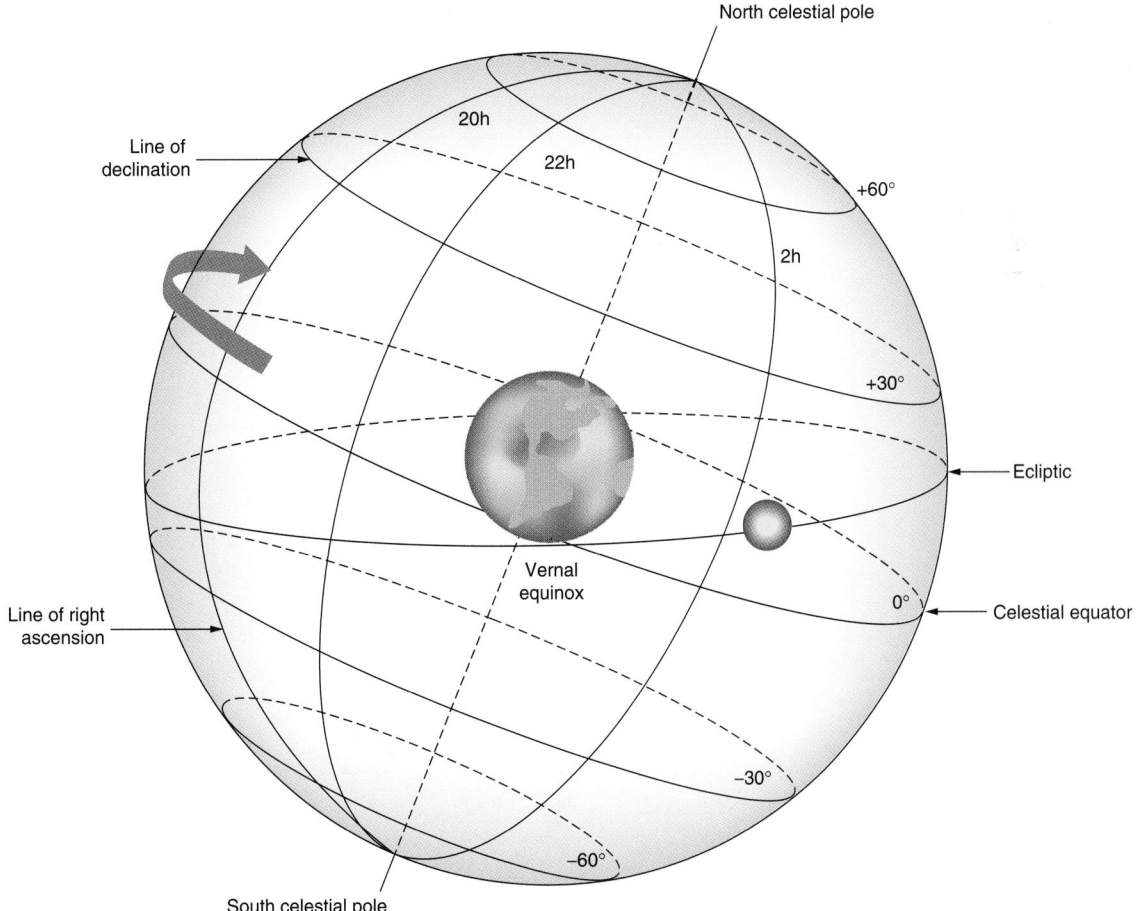

FIGURE 3–13 The equatorial coordinate system and the celestial sphere uses declination and right ascension to mark locations of celestial objects.

TELESCOPES

Probably the most widely used tool of astronomers is the **telescope**. A telescope is a scientific instrument used to observe objects that are very far away. Galileo was the first person we know of to use this device to observe celestial objects. **Optical telescopes** use both glass lenses and mirrors to magnify the light given off by an object. The power of magnification of a telescope tells how much larger an object appears compared to its normal size. Far more important than magnification power, though, is a telescope's aperture. The aperture of a telescope is the diameter of its lenses or mirrors. This greatly influences the amount of light that enters the telescope, and also the resolution of the image you are observing. There are three basic types of optical telescopes: refracting telescopes, reflecting telescopes, and compound telescopes. A refracting telescope uses a combination of concave and convex lenses to magnify an image. These telescopes provide clear, high-resolution images of very small sections of the sky. They tend to be very long as a result of their large focal length and also usually have small apertures due to the limited size of their glass lenses. A reflecting telescope uses a large concave mirror to focus light to magnify an image. These telescopes can have very large apertures providing a wide view of the sky with excellent clarity and brightness (Figure 3–14).

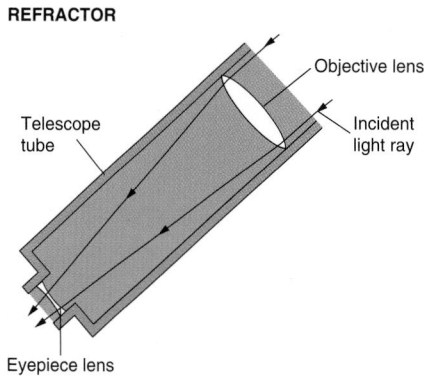

REFRACTOR

Objective lens

Telescope tube

Incident light ray

Eyepiece lens

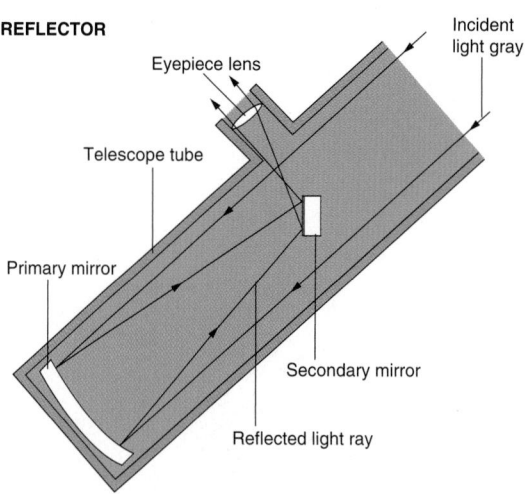

REFLECTOR

Incident light gray

Eyepiece lens

Telescope tube

Primary mirror

Secondary mirror

Reflected light ray

FIGURE 3–14 The two basic types of optical telescopes commonly used in astronomy.

The compound telescope uses a combination of both lenses and mirrors to provide an excellent high-resolution magnification of the sky. These telescopes are also more compact in size, making them easy to use. Many large-scale optical telescopes used by astronomers around the world are multiple-mirror telescopes like the Keck telescope in Hawaii. These telescopes use an array of mirrors to magnify the image. The Hale reflecting telescope on Mount Palomar in California was once the world's largest optical telescope, using a mirror over 16 ft (26 km) in diameter! One of the newest optical telescope projects is The Very Large Telescope Project in Chile, South America. This observatory combines an array of four large reflecting telescopes working together to provide high resolution images. One of the limits of ground based optical telescopes is the distortion and interference caused by the Earth's atmosphere. To alleviate this problem, NASA has designed and launched new space based telescopes like the famous Hubble Space Telescope. This large reflecting telescope orbits the Earth at about 375 mi (604 km) above the surface of our planet, far out of the atmosphere. The location of the Hubble telescope above the atmosphere, along with its large reflecting mirror, provides some of the highest resolution images of space ever seen by astronomers (Figure 3–15).

Photography and computer technology also have added to the capabilities of optical telescopes. Now cameras and computers are used to detect faint celestial objects that the human eye couldn't. Special sensors are used to pick up different wavelengths of electromagnetic radiation other than visible light, providing a new way of using optical telescopes to learn more about space. NASA's Spitzer Space Telescope uses its reflecting mirrors to sense infrared radiation that is normally blocked by the atmosphere. Launched in 2003, the Spitzer telescope does not orbit around the Earth itself, but orbits the Sun, just lagging behind the Earth in its orbit. This keeps it far from

FIGURE 3–15 The Hubble Space telescope has provided some of the best images ever taken of space. (*Courtesy of NASA.*)

the interference of Earth's own infrared radiation. Many optical telescopes are also fitted with spectroscopes. **Spectroscopes** are scientific instruments that are used to analyze the visible light portion of the electromagnetic spectrum. Working like a prism, which separates light into its individual colors, spectroscopes allow astronomers to view the unique spectrum of celestial objects. A continuous spectrum shows all of the colors of visible light, however the interaction of visible light with matter causes specific wavelengths of light to be absorbed. The wavelengths of light that are absorbed leave gaps in the spectrum. This is known as an absorption or **dark line spectrum**. Every element and compound has its own unique dark line signature, which can be used like a fingerprint to identify specific substances. A similar process also occurs when objects give off radiation. This is called an emission, or **bright line spectrum**, where bright lines of specific wavelengths appear within the spectrum. Again, astronomers can use these unique spectral lines to identify the substances present in celestial objects. The use of spectroscopes with optical telescopes is called spectral analysis. It has provided an incredible amount of information for astronomers about the composition of objects like stars, moons, planets, and many other celestial objects (Figure 3–16).

Radio telescopes are another type of telescope used by astronomers. These instruments pick up longer wave electromagnetic radiation in the form of microwaves and radio waves. The main component of a radio telescope is the antenna, which is usually disk shaped. A modern television satellite dish is an example of a small-scale radio telescope antenna. Radio telescopes sense radiation from far out into the universe and send it to computers to be analyzed. The Arecibo radio telescope in Puerto Rico is the world's largest single dish radio telescope. This telescope, in operation since 1963, uses a 1,000 ft (1,609 km) diameter dish. It has made many significant contributions to astronomy, including the detection of the first planets discovered outside of the solar system (Figure 3–17).

Often a network of radio telescopes is used to improve their resolution. The combination of radio signals received by a network of radio telescopes is called **interferometry**. This allows smaller telescopes to be combined to create one large telescope with a much greater resolution. The Very Large Array in New Mexico is an example of this.

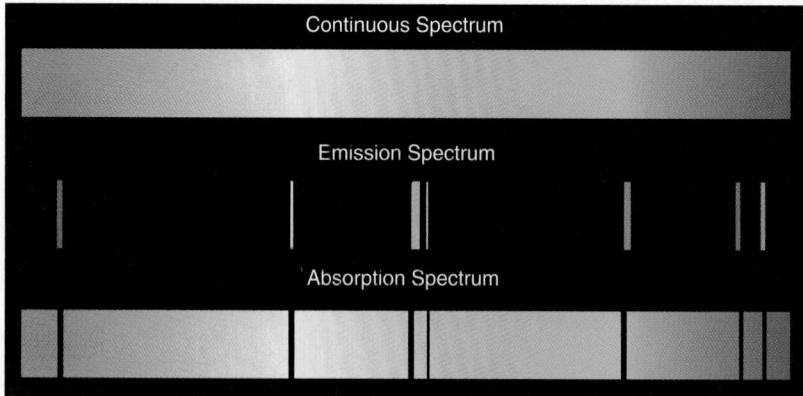

FIGURE 3–16 Spectral analysis used with optical telescopes can reveal the composition of celestial objects.

FIGURE 3–17 The Arecibo radio telescope, located in Puerto Rico, is the largest single radio telescope in the world. (*Courtesy of NASA.*)

This radio telescope network consists of 27 separate antenna dishes. Another even larger example of interferometry is The Very Long Baseline Array. This combined network of radio telescopes combines signals all the way from Hawaii through North America, and into the Caribbean. This creates an equivalent radio telescope dish that is larger than North America!

SPACE EXPLORATION

Although researchers will continue to develop and build larger and more powerful telescopes, there are limits that ground based, or even space telescopes have for the study of celestial objects. Ultimately, astronomers want to get a close-up view or even visit objects in the universe. Space exploration is the physical investigation of celestial objects outside of the Earth's atmosphere. Space exploration is undertaken in two fundamental ways. The first employs the use of robotic spacecraft or satellites to visit objects in the solar system. The other is human spaceflight, which utilizes spacecraft to transport humans into space for the purpose of exploration. One of the most difficult aspects of both methods of space exploration is the problem of getting off the Earth itself. So far the best way to do this is to use rocketry. Rockets use solid and liquid fuels, which are burned rapidly to create great amounts of thrust that rapidly accelerates the vehicle. The first great advances in modern rocketry were made by Robert Goddard, who is now known as the father of modern rocketry. Goddard designed and built the first successful rockets, and laid the foundation for the science and engineering of rocketry that we still use today. The first use of a rocket to propel a human made object into space was by the Russians, who launched the Sputnik satellite

FIGURE 3-18 Neil Armstrong was the first human to set foot on the Moon during the Apollo 11 mission in 1969. (*Courtesy of NASA.*)

in 1957. The Americans followed one year later with the launch of Explorer I, a satellite used to study the Van Allen Radiation Belt that surrounds the Earth. These amazing technological advancements began what is now known as the space race between The United States and Russia. Many missions followed that launched both manned and unmanned spacecraft and satellites into space to learn more about the Earth and solar system. The culmination of the space race occurred on July 20, 1969, when the American Apollo 11 mission landed Neil Armstrong and Edwin "Buzz" Aldrin on the Moon (Figure 3-18).

Earth System Law

The Outer Space Treaty

In January of 1967 the United States, Britain, and Russia signed the *Treaty on Principles Governing the Activities of States in the Exploration and Use of Outer Space, Including the Moon and Other Celestial Bodies* agreement. This treaty is commonly known as the Outer Space Treaty, which governs the peaceful use of outer space. This agreement prevents the deployment of nuclear or any other weapons of mass destruction on the Moon, orbiting space vehicles, or celestial bodies. The agreement also prevents the testing of weapons, or the establishment of military installations in space, on the Moon, or other celestial bodies. To date this treaty has been signed by more than 90 nations.

FIGURE 3–19 The Mars Explorer mission rover, Spirit has collected an incredible amount of data from the Martian surface. (*Courtesy of NASA.*)

For the next three decades famous unmanned spacecraft like the Mariner, Pioneer, Voyager, Viking, Magellan, Galileo, and Cassini-Huygens missions successfully surveyed nearly the entire solar system. The Pathfinder and Mars Exploration Rover missions even deployed remotely operated vehicles that traveled across the Martian surface. They analyzed rocks, soil, and characteristics of the atmosphere, and sent back incredibly detailed pictures of the Martian surface (Figure 3–19).

NASA's human spaceflight program has continued since the Apollo missions, with the creation of Skylab, the Space Shuttle fleet, and the International Space Station. Today, NASA is planning more manned missions to space including a return trip to the Moon and a visit to the planet Mars. Although the complexities of human space-flight for near Earth missions are demanding, the vast distances between celestial objects like Mars, which is many times farther from the Earth than the Moon, make space travel far more challenging. Engineers must design a spacecraft that can propel and sustain a crew of astronauts for long periods of time. Unlike a trip to the Moon, which takes only a few days, a trip to Mars using present propulsion technology will take over a year! And that is just to get there! Then the astronauts must return to Earth, making the whole mission almost three years to complete. Problems of providing energy, food, and living quarters that will protect the crew from the harsh environment of space for such long periods of time is indeed a daunting challenge. The development of new technologies to propel spacecraft are currently under way, and will certainly play an important role in the future of space exploration. The quest to explore space has always resulted in the development of new technologies, which have improved the quality of life on Earth. Cordless power tools, smoke detectors, light emitting diodes (LED), protective helmets, robotics, global positioning systems, wireless communication, night vision cameras, heart monitors, and scratch-resistant lenses are just a few of the examples of technologies that are the result of space exploration. This is known as **technology transfer**, or spin-off technology, which is sometimes used as way to justify the high costs associated with space exploration. Whether it be to learn more about the Earth, the solar system and the universe, or just the nature of humans to explore and colonize new worlds, the exploration of Space by both manned and robotic spacecraft will no doubt continue into the future.

@ WEB Links

FOR MORE INFORMATION GO TO THIS WEB LINK:

<http://amazing-space
.stsci.edu/resources
/explorations/groundup/>

<http://hubble.nasa
.gov/index.php>

<http://www.spitzer.caltech
.edu/spitzer/index.shtml>

<http://www.naic
.edu/index.htm>

<http://www.vlba.nrao.edu/>

<http://www.nrao.edu/>

<http://www.jpl.nasa
.gov/missions/>

<http://history.msfc.nasa
.gov/index.html>

<http://spaceflight.nasa
.gov/home/index.html>

<http://www.seasky.org
/spacexp/sky5d.html>

SECTION REVIEW

1. Describe how the horizontal coordinate system is used to locate celestial objects.

2. Describe how the equatorial coordinate system is used to locate celestial objects.

3. What are the different types of telescopes used by astronomers?

4. What is the main advantage for using space-based telescopes?

5. Describe the process of spectral analysis?

6. What is interferometry?

7. Describe some of the milestones of both manned and unmanned space exploration.

8. Describe some of the challenges facing long-distance manned spaceflight.

9. What is technology transfer, and describe two reasons it is an important part of space exploration.

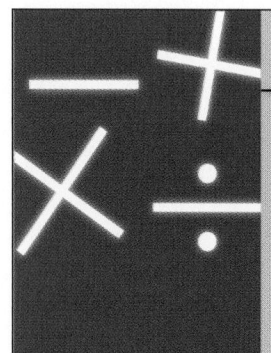

earth math

1) Two minutes after the launch of a space shuttle, the thrust of its primary rockets accelerates the vehicle to approximately 0.9 miles per second. How fast is the space shuttle going in miles per hour?

2) Eight minutes after the launch of the space shuttle, the vehicle reaches its orbit and is now traveling at 5.0 miles per second. How fast is the space shuttle traveling in miles per hour?

CHAPTER SUMMARY

The Earth is a terrestrial planet that is composed mostly of a thin outer layer of rock which surrounds a hot, molten mantle and dense iron core. Approximately 70 percent of the surface of the Earth is covered in water, and is surrounded by an atmosphere. The Earth's shape is considered an oblate spheroid, because it is slightly bulged at the equator. Evidence to support the Earth's nearly spherical shape include photographs from space, the Earth's curved shadow on the Moon during a lunar eclipse, and the changing altitude of Polaris as you move southward from the North pole toward the Equator. Precise locations are identified on the Earth using the latitude and longitude coordinate system. Lines of latitude run parallel across the Earth's surface, and mark locations north or south of the equator. Lines of longitude run from North pole to the South pole and mark locations east and west of the prime meridian. The use of topographic maps enables the three dimensional surface of the Earth to be displayed on a two-dimensional map. Contour lines are used to mark areas of equal elevation on a topographic map, which reveals the shape of the land. Topographical maps contain detailed information about the Earth's surface. The Earth is spinning on its axis, which is called rotation, at approximately 1,000 miles per hour near the equator. The time it takes for our planet to make one complete rotation is approximately 24 hours. This is commonly known as a day. The Earth's axis of rotation is tilted 23.5 degrees. This tilt causes the different seasons of the year. In addition to the spinning of the Earth on its axis, it is also traveling around the Sun. This is known as a revolution. One complete revolution of the Earth around the Sun takes approximately 365 days, also known as a year. The path of the Earth moving around the Sun is called an orbit. The Earth's orbit is elliptical. An ellipse is the oval-like path of a celestial object. The point in the Earth's orbit when it is closest to the Sun is known as the perihelion. The point in its orbit when it is farthest from the Sun is called the aphelion. Astronomers like Kepler and Newton helped describe the elliptical orbits of celestial objects. For many thousands of years the geocentric model of the universe was widely accepted. This puts the Earth at the center of the universe, with the planets and stars revolving around it. Great astronomers like Copernicus and Galileo helped advance the heliocentric model. This puts the Sun at the center of the solar system with the planets revolving around it. Observations of celestial objects from the Earth's surface reveal they are moving in an arc across the sky. This movement is called apparent motion, because it is actually caused by the Earth's rotation. This causes stars, planets, and the Sun to appear as if they are moving, when it is really the Earth that is moving relative to them. Astronomers use celestial coordinate systems to mark the precise locations of celestial objects. The horizontal coordinate system uses the altitude and azimuth of an object to mark its location. The equatorial coordinate system uses the declination and right ascension to mark the location of a celestial object. Astronomers use a wide array of technologies to learn more about celestial objects and space. These include optical telescopes, radio telescopes, space based telescopes, and both manned and unmanned spacecraft.

CHAPTER REVIEW

Multiple Choice

1. The true shape of the Earth is best described as a:
   a. perfect sphere
   b. perfect ellipse
   c. slightly oblate sphere
   d. highly eccentric ellipse

2. At sea level, which location is closest to the Earth?
   a. 45 degrees south latitude
   b. the equator
   c. 23 degrees north latitude
   d. the North pole

3. The best evidence that the Earth has a spherical shape is provided by:
   a. the spherical shape of the Sun
   b. the change in time of sunrise and sunset through the year
   c. photographs from space
   d. viewing the stars at night

4. The spinning of an object on its axis is called:
   a. revolution
   b. rotation
   c. an ellipse
   d. an orbit

5. The tilted axis of the Earth points the Northern Hemisphere toward the Sun at which time?
   a. the autumnal equinox
   b. the winter solstice
   c. the vernal equinox
   d. the summer solstice

6. The movement of the Earth around the Sun is known as:
   a. a revolution
   b. a rotation
   c. an ellipse
   d. an axis

7. The orbit of the Earth around the Sun is best described as:
   a. a perfect circle
   b. slightly elliptical
   c. oblate
   d. extremely elliptical

8. The point in the Earth's orbit when it is closest to the sun is known as the:
   a. aphelion
   b. axis
   c. perihelion
   d. apparent motion

9. During which season of the year is the Earth farthest from the Sun?
   a. spring
   b. summer
   c. fall
   d. winter

10. A star viewed at night appears to move at a rate of:
    a. 15 degrees per hour
    b. 30 degrees per hour
    c. 360 degrees per hour
    d. does not move at all

11. At which latitude is Polaris directly overhead?
    a. 0 degrees
    b. 23.5 degrees north
    c. 90 degrees south
    d. 90 degrees north

12. What is your latitude location if you have determined the altitude of Polaris to be 37 degrees above the horizon?
    a. 37 degrees south
    b. 53 degrees north
    c. 37 degrees north
    d. 90 degrees north

13. As a ship crosses the prime meridian and the altitude of Polaris is sighted as 45 degrees above the horizon, what is the ship's location?
    a. 45 degrees south latitude, 0 degrees longitude
    b. 45 degrees north latitude, 0 degrees longitude
    c. 0 degrees latitude, 45 degrees west longitude
    d. 0 degrees latitude, 45 degrees east longitude

14. What is your longitude location if your local time is 11:00 A.M. and the time at the prime meridian is 12:00 P.M.?
    a. 0 degrees longitude
    b. 15 degrees east longitude
    c. 15 degrees west longitude
    d. 30 degrees west longitude

15. Contour lines showing elevations in feet above sea level on a topographical map are labeled in the following order: 20, 40, 60, 80, 100. What is the contour interval used on this map?
    a. 20 feet
    b. 10 feet
    c. 80 feet
    d. 1 foot

16. Blue lines on a contour map indicate:
    a. The location of streams
    b. Contour lines
    c. The locations of trees
    d. Town lines

Matching *Match the terms with the correct definitions.*

a. exosphere
b. axis
c. rotation
d. revolution
e. ellipse

f. perihelion
g. aphelion
h. zenith
i. equator
j. latitude

k. longitude
l. contour lines
m. contour interval

1. _____ The zone outside the Earth's atmosphere that is commonly known as outer space.
2. _____ A straight line on which an object rotates.
3. _____ The point in the sky that is directly above the observer, or 90 degrees above the horizon.
4. _____ The circular movement of a body around a central point called an axis.
5. _____ The imaginary line, also known as 0 degrees latitude, that divides the Earth into the northern and southern hemispheres.
6. _____ The movement of an object in an orbit around another object.
7. _____ Parallel lines that run east and west across the Earth's surface that measure location north or south of the equator.
8. _____ The flattened circular path of the orbits of most celestial objects around two foci, one of which is the Sun.
9. _____ Coordinate lines used on the Earth's surface that run north and south from pole to pole and measure a location east or west of the prime meridian.
10. _____ The point in a planet's orbit around the Sun when it is closest to the Sun.
11. _____ Lines that mark areas of equal elevation on a topographical map.
12. _____ The point in the orbit of a planet when it is farthest from the Sun.
13. _____ The specific change in elevation associated with each contour line on a topographical map.

Critical Thinking

1. Describe the possible effects on the Earth if the Earth were tilted 30 degrees on its axis.

4

The Moon: Earth's Closest Neighbor

OBJECTIVES

The Moon's Formation · The Composition of the Moon · The Moon's Surface · The Moon's Orbit · The Phases of the Moon · Eclipses · Tides

After reading this chapter you should be able to:

▶ Identify the approximate age of the Moon.

▶ Describe how the Moon is believed to have formed and explain some evidence used to support these theories.

▶ Explain the composition of the Moon.

▶ Identify the various features found on the Moon's surface.

▶ Define the term *lunar month*.

▶ Identify the eight phases of the Moon and how they appear as viewed from the Earth's surface.

▶ Describe the positions of the Moon in its orbit around the Earth for each phase of the Moon.

▶ Define the term *eclipse*.

▶ Explain the difference between a lunar eclipse and a solar eclipse.

▶ Describe how tides are formed on the Earth.

▶ Explain the difference between neap and spring tides.

INTRODUCTION

On July 20, 1969, human beings realized an age-old dream of landing on the Moon. The flight of Apollo 11 breached the previously uncrossable gap of space and placed the first human being on another object in our solar system other than Earth. Not only was this a great feat of modern technology, but it also revealed much about the composition of the Moon and the origins of the solar system. The Moon has fascinated human beings since our early beginnings. It is a source of wonder and inspiration for all who gaze at it. The Moon also influences the natural rhythms of life on Earth. Our calendar is set by the phases of the Moon, along with the functions of the human body. The influence of the Moon's gravity affects the oceans by creating tides and causes periodic eclipses of the Sun. Understanding the origin and composition of the Moon and role that the Moon plays in the Earth's system has helped us understand much about our own planet.

THE MOON'S FORMATION

Rock samples brought back from the Moon reveal that our closest neighbor in space is approximately 4.5 billion years old. This is just as old as the Earth, which suggests that the Earth and the Moon formed at about the same time. The origin of the Moon is still being debated. One theory proposes that the Moon formed elsewhere in the solar system and was captured by the Earth's gravity as it passed close to our planet. Another theory suggests that debris orbiting the Earth that was left over from the formation of the planet eventually came together to form the Moon. The latest theory of how the Moon formed is gaining the most popularity. This theory states that a large object, perhaps as large as the planet Mars, struck the Earth and sent a large amount of the Earth's crust into space (Figure 4–1). This material eventually cooled and formed the Moon. Because of the age of the Moon, this event probably occurred early in the Earth's formation.

Evidence to support this theory comes from rock samples recovered from the Moon. They reveal that the Moon is mainly composed of **silicate** minerals and is **deficient** in iron. The lack of iron on the Moon, as compared with Earth, suggests that it was formed from the outer crust of the Earth, which contains much less iron than is located in its core. The average density of the Moon is approximately 3.3 grams per cubic centimeter, which is much less than Earth's density of 5.5 grams per cubic centimeter.

THE COMPOSITION OF THE MOON

The rocks that were brought back from the Moon are very similar to **volcanic rocks** produced on the Earth. The volcanic eruptions that formed these rocks on the Moon occurred early in the Moon's history, between 4 and 2.5 billion years ago. These ancient eruptions created large plains of **basalt** lava that are called **mares**. The term *mare* comes from the Latin word for "sea," which is what early astronomers thought these flat regions on the Moon's surface to be. Since the formation of the mares, the Moon has had no known volcanic eruptions. The most

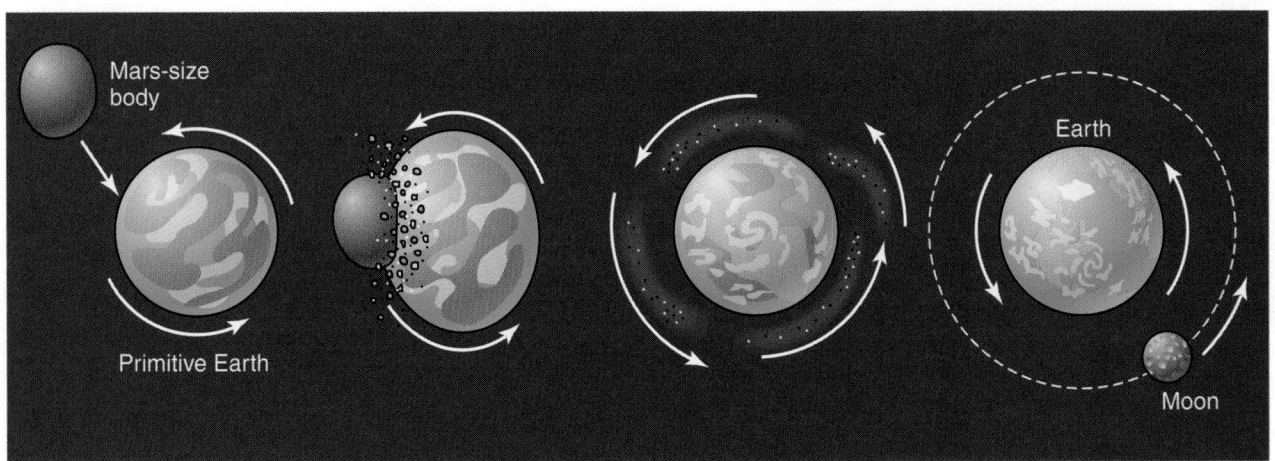

FIGURE 4–1   The theory of the Moon's formation by the impact of a Mars-sized object colliding with the Earth is known as the impact theory.

FIGURE 4–2 The surface of the Moon is covered in dark, flat regions called mares, and by large impact craters. (*Courtesy of PhotoDisc.*)

recognizable feature of the Moon's surface are its **impact craters** (Figure 4–2). Impact craters are the bowl-like remains of celestial objects such as asteroids that collided with the Moon. Dating of the craters has revealed that the majority of the Moon's craters were formed more than 4 billion years ago and that the number of impacts of celestial bodies with the Moon surface has declined ever since. Scientists believe that the early Earth was also bombarded by celestial objects at the same time as the Moon; however, the Earth's craters have been long lost as a result of weathering and erosion.

THE MOON'S SURFACE

Astronauts who landed on the Moon discovered that the surface is covered with a fine volcanic dust, which was formed by the impact craters. The Moon's surface has no atmosphere, and its gravity is 17 percent of Earth's gravity. The average surface temperature of the moon varies greatly during the day. At noon the temperature on the Moon can reach almost 200° F (93° C), and during the lunar night the temperature plummets to lower than −250° F (−157° C)! Until recently it was believed that the Moon had no water, but explorations of the Moon's polar regions suggest that there might be some frozen water on the Moon. The Moon's diameter is approximately 2,160 mi (3,475 km), which is roughly 27 percent of the Earth's diameter. The Moon is approximately 238,866 mi (384,418 km) from the Earth and completes one orbit around the Earth in 27 days and 7 hours. The period of the Moon's revolution around the Earth and the Moon's rotation on its own axis are the same; therefore the same side of the Moon always faces the Earth.

Earth System Scientists

Galileo Galilei

Galileo was born in Pisa, Italy, in 1564. He began his life in the pursuit of science by studying mathematics. In 1583 he discovered the properties of pendulums. Later he experimented with the physics of motion and demonstrated how two objects of two different masses fall at the same rate. This famous experiment was reportedly enacted at the famous leaning tower of Pisa. In 1970 Galileo's famous experiment was demonstrated on the Moon, when an astronaut dropped a feather and a hammer, which fell at the same rate toward the Moon's surface. In 1593 Galileo began to study the properties of water and invented the thermometer. Galileo next turned his attentions to working with telescopes and used them to make the first accurate observations of the Moon surface. He also discovered the moons of Jupiter using the telescopes that he himself designed, including the Galilean refracting telescope. In 1632 Galileo published a book titled *Dialogue Concerning the Two Chief World Systems*. This book supported his belief that the Earth and other planets orbited around the Sun. This was known as the heliocentric theory, which was first proposed by Nicolaus Copernicus. This controversial theory was in conflict with the geocentric theory, which proposed that all planets and the Sun revolve around the Earth. The geocentric theory was supported by the church in Rome, which in 1633 charged Galileo with heresy. He was then placed under house arrest for the rest of his life. Galileo's life work helped form the foundation for modern physics and astronomy.

CAREER CONNECTIONS
Lunar Geologist

A lunar geologist is a highly specialized geologist and astronomer who studies the geology of the Moon. Lunar geologists have analyzed the Moon rocks that were collected and brought back to the Earth during the Apollo missions. These scientists have unlocked the composition of the Moon and have pieced together its geological history. Today lunar geologists continue to study the Moon as a possible site for the future mining of mineral resources. Many space scientists believe that the Moon someday might be mined for minerals that can be used on Earth or for long-range space flight. Lunar geologists require a college education in both geology and space science and can be employed by NASA, academic institutions, or private industry.

THE MOON'S ORBIT

As the Moon orbits around the Earth, one side of it is always illuminated by the Sun. This causes the different Moon phases as viewed from the Earth's surface. Different phases of the Moon occur at different points in its revolution around the Earth. The cycle of **Moon phases**, also called the **lunar month**, is approximately 29 days and 12 hours long. This is slightly longer than the time it takes the Moon to complete one orbit around the Earth, which takes approximately 27 days 7 hours. The reason for the difference in time between the Moon's orbital period and the lunar month is caused by the orbit of the Earth around the Sun. By the time the Moon has completed one full orbit, the Earth also has moved relative to the Sun. This causes the time period between two New Moons to be 29.5 days. The orbit of the Moon, as with all celestial objects, is elliptical. This causes it to be closest to the Earth at one point in its orbit. This point is called the **perigee**. At the point of perigee the Moon is about 221,473 mi (356,426 km) from the Earth. The point in its orbit when the Moon is farthest from the Earth is called the **apogee**. This puts the Moon about 252,722 mi (406,717 km) from the Earth. The time of month when the Moon is at apogee and perigee varies over the course of a year.

THE PHASES OF THE MOON

The lunar month begins when the dark side of the Moon is facing Earth (Figure 4–3). This is called the New Moon, and because no sunlight is striking the Moon's surface, it appears as a dark disk in the sky. An eclipse of the Sun does not occur during every New Moon phase because the orbit of the Moon is tilted approximately 5 degrees from the plane of the ecliptic. The next phase of the Moon is called the Waxing Crescent phase; this phase occurs approximately 3 days after the New Moon. The Moon's surface is lit in a crescent shape and has completed one-eighth of its orbit around the Earth. The first Quarter Moon phase occurs approximately 7 days into the lunar cycle, when the Moon's surface as viewed from the Earth is half lit by sunlight. This is also called a Half Moon. The Waxing Gibbous phase occurs when three-quarters of the Moon's surface, as viewed from the Earth, is lit by sunlight. This occurs approximately 10 days into the lunar cycle. A Full Moon occurs when the side of the Moon facing the Earth is totally bathed in sunlight. This phase occurs about 14 days into the lunar cycle and marks the approximate halfway point of the Moon's orbit around the Earth. The next phase of the Moon is called the Waning Gibbous phase, which marks the point when three-quarters of the Moon's surface is lit by the Sun, as viewed from the Earth. This occurs approximately 17 days into the lunar cycle. The third Quarter Moon phase takes place when the Moon has completed 75 percent of its orbit around the Earth. The Moon's surface facing the Earth is once again half bathed in sunlight, causing another Half Moon. This phase occurs approximately 20 days into the lunar cycle. The Waning Crescent phase is marked by one-quarter of the moon's surface, as viewed from the Earth, being lit by the Sun. This occurs approximately 23 days into the lunar cycle. Finally, one lunar month is complete with the arrival of

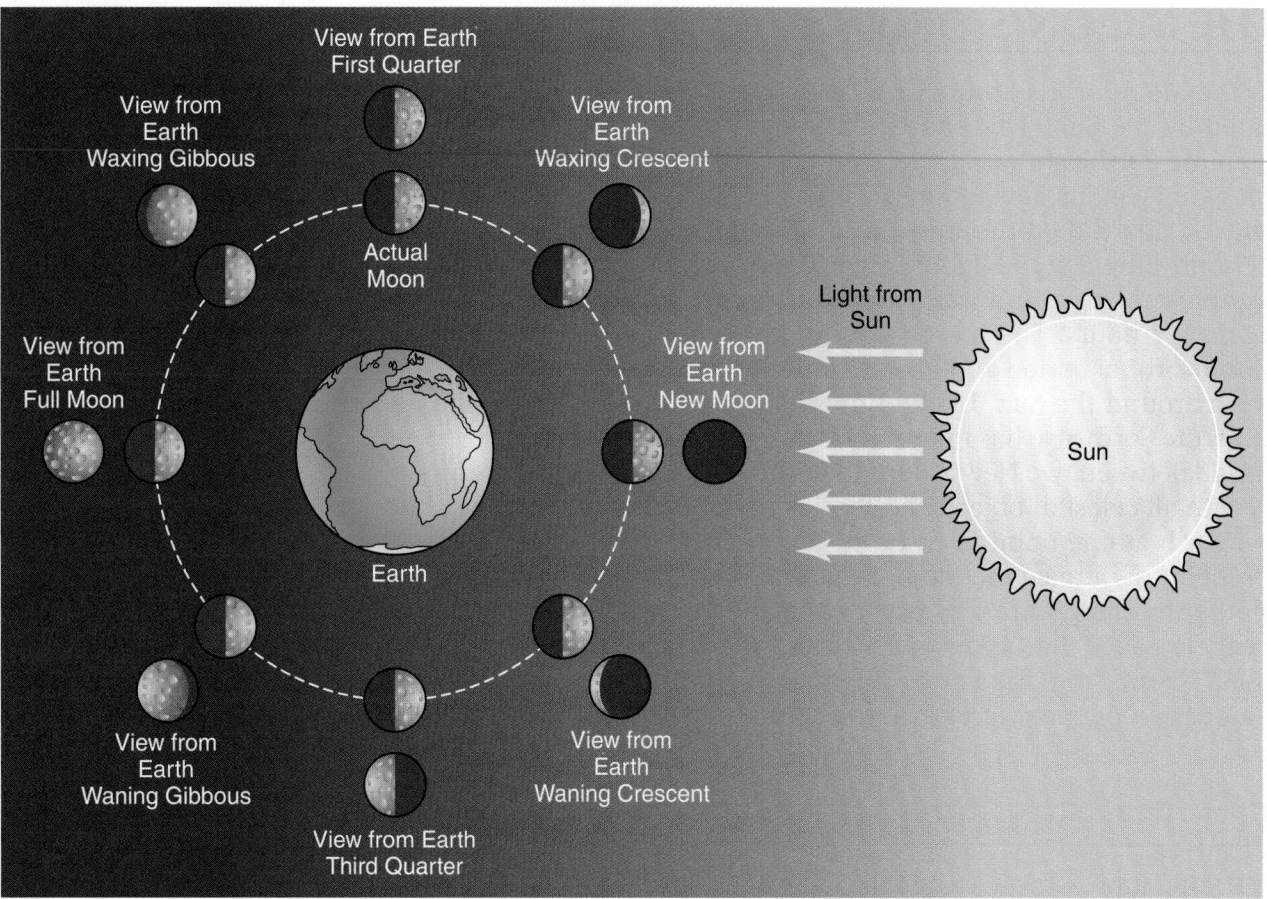

FIGURE 4-3 The eight different phases of the Moon as viewed from the Earth, and their locations in the Moon's orbit around the Earth.

another New Moon. This occurs when the Moon has made one full lunar cycle, a full 29.5 days later.

ECLIPSES

Another important result of the Moon's orbit around the Earth is the occurrence of eclipses. An **eclipse** occurs when either the Moon or the Earth is shadowed from the Sun by the other. The shadow of one celestial object that completely passes over another object is called the **umbra**. A partial shadow that occurs during an eclipse is called the **penumbra**. A **lunar eclipse** occurs when the Moon is shadowed from the Sun by the Earth (Figure 4-4). This type of eclipse can only occur during the Full Moon phase and can either be a partial eclipse or a total eclipse. A **solar eclipse** occurs when the Moon passes in front of the Sun. This is the result of the Sun and Moon being the same apparent size in the sky. Even though the Moon is much smaller than the Sun, it is much closer to the Earth than the Sun, which causes these celestial objects to appear to be the same size in the sky. A total solar eclipse causes the daytime sky to darken for a short time and allows for the unique view of the solar corona. The corona is the extremely hot outer atmosphere of the Sun. Both lunar and solar eclipses occur on Earth at various times during the year and are visible at different locations.

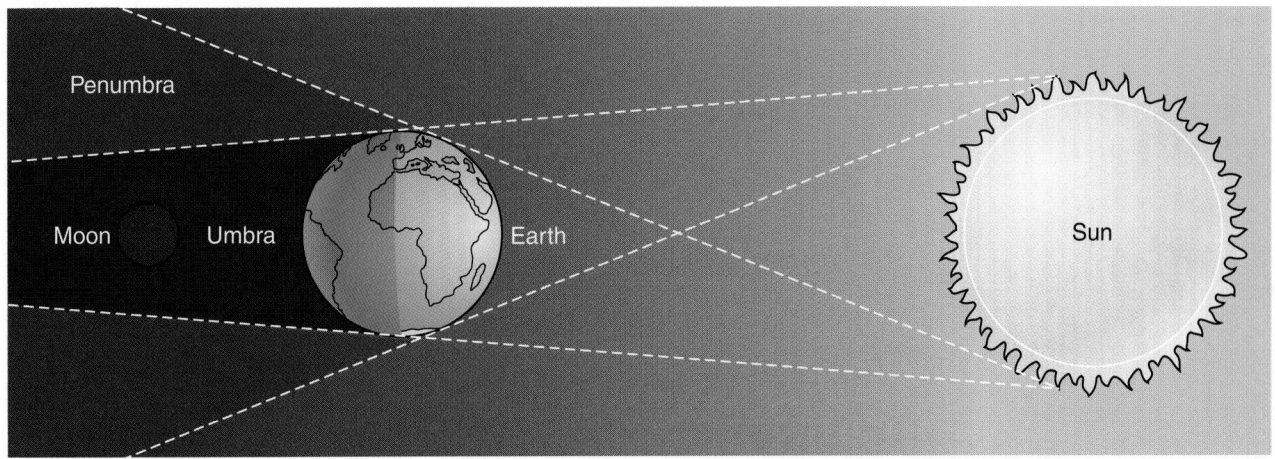

FIGURE 4–4   A lunar eclipse occurs when the Earth's shadow covers the Moon.

Even though the Sun can be partially or totally blocked during a solar eclipse, it is still extremely dangerous to look directly at the Sun during any eclipse event.

TIDES

The influence of gravity between the Earth, Sun, and the Moon creates a noticeable effect on the Earth's oceans, called tides. Tides are bulges that are created on the Earth's surface by the gravitational attraction of the Moon and Sun. These bulges create a rise in sea level near the coastlines. Because the Moon is closer to the Earth than the Sun, it has a greater influence on the formation of tides than the Sun. As the Moon moves around the Earth, the tidal bulge of ocean water follows it along, creating distinct times when high and low tides occur. The local geography of the coastlines of land masses also influences tides. This causes some places on Earth to experience one low and one high tide each day. These are called diurnal tides, which are common in the Caribbean. Semi diurnal tides occur when there are two high tides and two low tides each day. This is also the result of the local geography, which occurs along much of the coast of the Northeastern United States. During the times of the year when the Sun and the Moon are on the same side, or on the opposite sides of the Earth, **spring tides** are created. A spring tide creates the highest and lowest tides of the year. The difference between the height of the high tide and the height of the low tide is called the tidal range. When the Sun and Moon are at right angles to one another relative to the Earth, a **neap tide** occurs (Figure 4–5). The gravitational attraction of the Sun and Moon cancel out each other, and create the lowest tidal range of the year. The place on the Earth that experiences the greatest tidal range is the Bay of Fundy, in Nova Scotia. The tidal range there is more than 47 feet each day! Tides have a great influence on the shipping industry and the currents associated with waterways. Many tidal currents can be extremely strong, and very dangerous to swimmers or boaters.

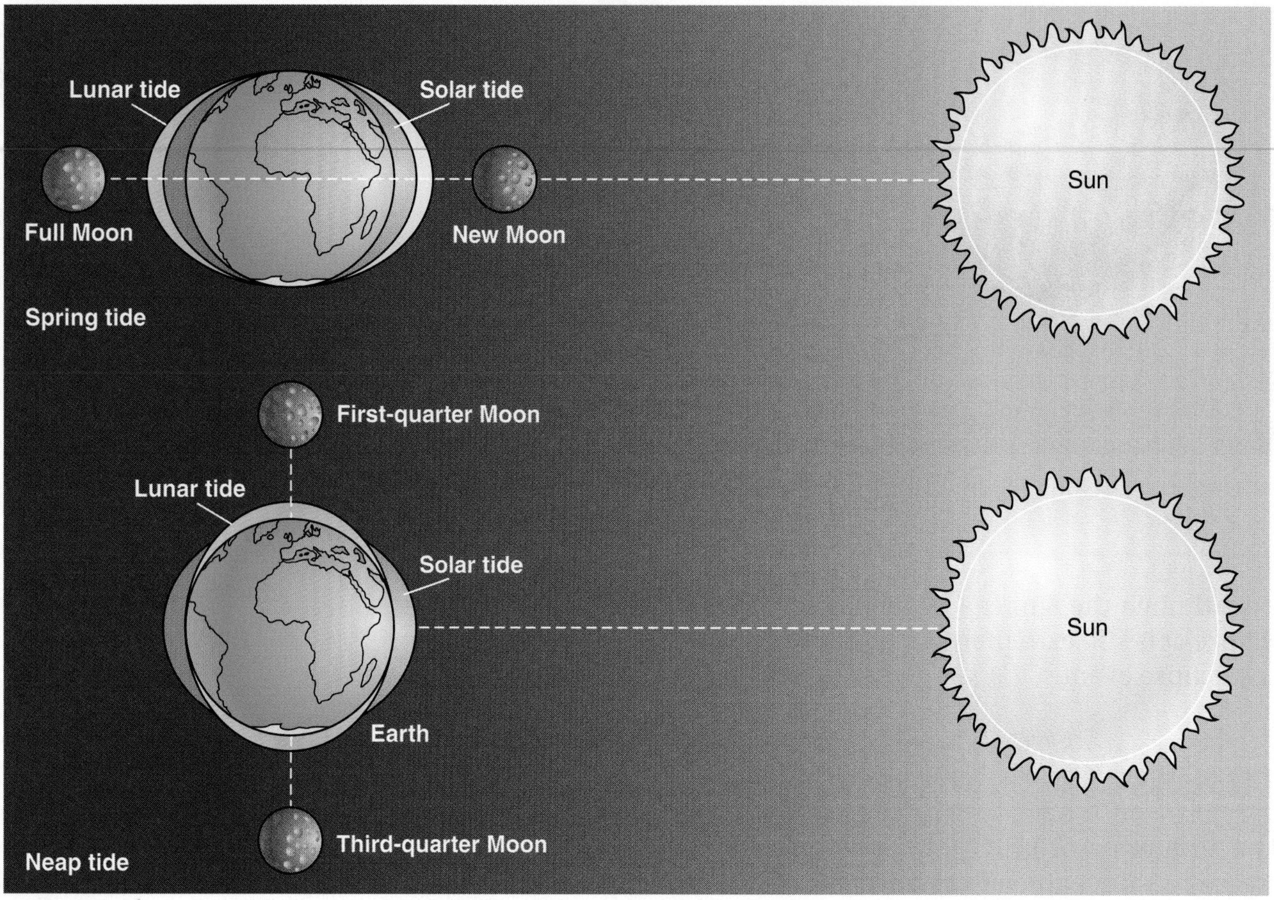

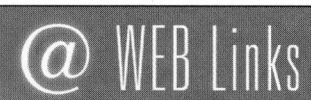

FIGURE 4–5 The effects of the Sun and Moon on the formation of spring and neap tides on the Earth.

REVIEW

1. How old is the Moon, and how do scientists believe it may have formed?
2. What are the mares on the Moon's surface?
3. What is the period of one orbit of the Moon around the Earth?
4. Why does the same side of the Moon face the Earth all the time?
5. What is a lunar month?
6. What are the eight main phases of the Moon?
7. What is a lunar eclipse?
8. Describe a solar eclipse.
9. How are tides formed on the Earth?
10. Explain the difference between neap and spring tides, and when they occur:
11. Who was Galileo?

@ WEB Links

FOR MORE INFORMATION GO TO THIS WEB LINK:

<http://www.nineplanets.org/luna.html>

<http://www.solarviews.com/eng/moon.htm>

<http://solarsystem.jpl.nasa.gov/planets/profile.cfm?Object=Moon>

<http://tidesonline.nos.noaa.gov>

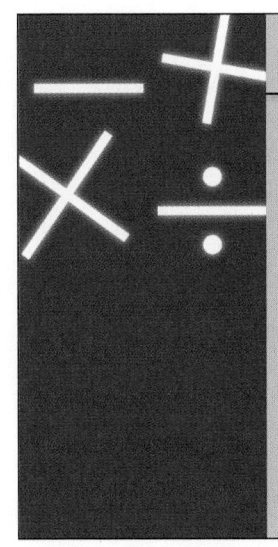

earth math

1) If the Moon's perigee (closest distance from the Earth) is approximately 222,756 miles and the Moon's apogee (farthest distance from the Earth) is approximately 254,866 miles, what is the average distance from the Earth to the Moon?

2) If the Sun's diameter is approximately 400 times the diameter of the Moon and the Moon's diameter is approximately 2160 miles, what is the approximate diameter of the Sun?

3) If the Moon travels 13 degrees of arc in space, as viewed from Earth as it orbits the planet each day, how many days does it take to travel 360 degrees of arc?

CHAPTER SUMMARY

The Moon is a celestial object that is approximately one-quarter the size of the Earth. It is believed to have formed 4.5 billion years ago at the same time that the Earth was forming. Several theories explain the formation of the Moon. The most popular of these states that the Moon formed when an object roughly the size of Mars collided with the Earth. The resulting debris thrown up into space formed the Moon. The Moon's surface is made up of two distinct features: mares and impact craters. Mares are large, dark, flat areas on the Moon's surface formed by volcanic eruptions that occurred between 2.5 and 4.5 million years ago. Impact craters are large bowl-like impressions on the Moon's surface caused by asteroid and meteorite impacts. The surface of the Moon is also covered in a fine volcanic ash, which was revealed when NASA's Apollo missions sent humans to explore its surface. The rocks on the Moon are similar to volcanic rocks found on the Earth and are rich in silicates. It is now believed that frozen water might exist in the craters of the Moon near its polar regions. The Moon makes one complete orbit around the Earth in approximately 29 days, which is called a lunar month. The same side of the Moon always faces toward the Earth. Different phases of the Moon are seen from the Earth depending on what point the Moon is at during its orbit. Moon phases are described by the amount of sunlight illuminating its surface as viewed from the Earth. Periodically the Moon passes in front of the Sun, which blocks the Sun from the Earth. This is called a solar eclipse. When the Earth passes between the Sun and the Moon and the Earth's shadow blocks the light illuminating the Moon, a lunar eclipse occurs. The Sun and Moon's gravitational attraction have an effect on the Earth's oceans, which we call tides. Tides are formed when the gravity of the Sun and Moon form large bulges in the ocean. This causes changes in the level of ocean water called high and low tides.

CHAPTER REVIEW

Multiple Choice

1. The composition of the Moon most closely resembles:
   a. the Earth's core
   b. the Earth's mantle
   c. the Earth's crust
   d. the planet Mars
2. The craters on the Moon's surface were formed by:
   a. an impact with the Earth
   b. meteorites and asteroid impacts
   c. volcanic eruptions
   d. basaltic rocks
3. The age of the Moon is approximately:
   a. 4.5 billion years
   b. 2.5 billion years
   c. 15 billion years
   d. unknown
4. The periods of the Moon's rotation and revolution are equal. This results in:
   a. lunar eclipses
   b. the eight phases of the Moon
   c. neap tides
   d. the same side of the Moon facing the Earth
5. Which motion causes the Moon to show phases as viewed from the Earth:
   a. the rotation of the Moon on its axis
   b. the revolution of the Moon around the Earth
   c. the rotation of the Sun on its axis
   d. the revolution of the Sun around the Moon
6. As viewed from the Earth, the Moon's phases have shown which type of changes over the past fifty years:
   a. noncyclic and predictable
   b. noncyclic and unpredictable
   c. cyclic and predictable
   d. cyclic and unpredictable

7. Which phase of the Moon occurs halfway in the orbit of the Moon around the Earth?
   a. New Moon
   b. Waxing Gibbous
   c. Full Moon
   d. Waning Gibbous
8. The New Moon phase occurs when the Moon is positioned between the Earth and Sun, but these positions do not always cause an eclipse of the Sun because:
   a. the Moon's orbit is tilted relative to the Earth's orbit
   b. the New Moon phase is visible only at night
   c. the night side of the Moon faces the Earth
   d. the apparent diameter of the Moon is greatest during these phases
9. When the Moon is completely covered within the Earth's umbra, which occurs?
   a. a lunar eclipse
   b. a solar eclipse
   c. an annular eclipse
   d. no eclipse
10. When the Moon passes in front of the Sun, which occurs?
    a. a lunar eclipse
    b. a solar eclipse
    c. an annular eclipse
    d. no eclipse
11. The high tides that occur at both the New Moon and Full Moon phases are called:
    a. flood tides
    b. neap tides
    c. spring tides
    d. ebb tides

Matching   *Match the terms with the correct definitions.*

a. silicate
b. deficient
c. volcanic rocks
d. basalt
e. mares

f. impact craters
g. Moon phases
h. lunar month
i. eclipse
j. umbra

k. penumbra
l. lunar eclipse
m. solar eclipse

1. ____ The series of different appearances of the Moon as observed from Earth, which results from the varying amount of light that illuminates the Moon at specific points in its orbit.
2. ____ A chemical compound that is composed of atoms of silicon and oxygen.
3. ____ The time it takes for the Moon to make one complete orbit around the Earth, which is approximately 29 days.
4. ____ Lacking something essential to life.
5. ____ The cutting off of all or part of the light of one celestial body by another.
6. ____ A common fine-grained volcanic rock that is dark in color, mafic, and dense.
7. ____ The area in shadow during an eclipse, which is totally blocked from the light.
8. ____ A Latin word for "seas" that is used to describe the flat, dark, plain-like areas that cover the surface of the Moon.
9. ____ The lighter area located next to the umbra, or darkened shadow, that occurs during an eclipse.
10. ____ Large bowl-like depressions that are left on the surface of a celestial object as the result of an impact by another celestial object, usually an asteroid or comet.
11. ____ The total or partial blocking of the Sun as viewed from the Earth when the Moon passes in front of it.
12. ____ Igneous rocks that form from cooled lava produced by a volcano.
13. ____ The total or partial blocking of sunlight striking the Moon's surface by the Earth as it moves directly in between the Moon and Sun.

Critical Thinking

1. One scientist once believed that the Moon should be destroyed, so that it no longer orbits our planet. How would the Earth be affected if the Moon did not exist?

5

The Life of Stars

LIFE CYCLE OF STARS OBJECTIVES

Star Formation and Life Cycle · Classification of Stars · Dwarf Stars · Giant and Supergiant Stars · Neutron Stars · Black Holes

After reading this chapter you should be able to:

▶ Define the term *star*.

▶ Identify the four ways by which stars are classified.

▶ Explain the basic stages of a star's life cycle.

▶ Describe the characteristics of dwarf, giant, and supergiant stars.

▶ Explain the concept of a black hole.

THE SUN OBJECTIVES

Formation of the Sun · Composition of the Sun · The Sun's Life Cycle

After reading this chapter you should be able to:

▶ Identify the approximate age of the Sun.

▶ Describe the composition of the Sun and its unique layers.

▶ Define the terms *solar cycle* and *solar wind* and explain how they affect the Earth.

INTRODUCTION

On a clear night, besides the Moon, the stars are by far the most visible of celestial objects. The grand display of twinkling starlight has captured the imagination of most all who have ever gazed up at the heavens. Ancient humans looked to the stars and grouped them into recognizable objects, like people or animals, called the constellations. Constellations are still used today to help locate specific stars. Stars also served as the first guides for navigation around the world. Studying the stars, learning how they form, and understanding their unique life cycles enables us to further understand our place in the universe. The closest star to the Earth, and the most important to life, is the Sun. All the energy that sustains life on our planet is derived from the Sun. The rising and setting of the Sun mark the beginning and ending of our day, and our calendars and watches are all set to its rhythms. Almost all ancient peoples worshiped the life-giving properties of the Sun in their own unique ways. The Sun provides the mechanism for the movement of matter and energy for many of the Earth's systems. Human beings have created many myths and legends to explain what the Sun is, but it wasn't until the beginning of the nineteenth century that we began to fully understand this bright object that is so important to our lives.

5.1 Life Cycle of Stars

STAR FORMATION AND LIFE CYCLE

By far the most visible objects in the nighttime sky are stars. These pinpoints of light surround the Earth in incredible numbers. A **star** is defined as a large, hot, glowing ball of gas that is powered by **nuclear fusion**. On the clearest of nights, far from the interference of artificial lights, there are approximately 9,000 stars visible to the naked eye. With the advent of telescopes, astronomers now estimate the number of stars in the Milky Way at approximately 200 billion! Even more amazing about stars is the distance they are from the Earth. The closest star to us, other than the Sun, is called Proxima Centauri. This star is more than 24 trillion mi (39 trillion km) away! Because stars are so far from the Earth, astronomers use the unit known as the light year to measure the distance between them. One light year is the distance that light can travel in one year, moving at a velocity of 186,000 miles per second (300,000 km/sec). This is roughly equivalent to about 5.8 trillion mi (9.3 trillion km). This puts Proxima Centauri about 4.2 light years away from us. Most stars we see at night are much farther from the Earth than Proxima Centauri. For example, the North Star, Polaris, is approximately 430 light years from Earth. Observing stars at night, even without a telescope, reveals that not all stars appear alike; in fact, they differ greatly in their size, color, and brightness. These characteristics are usually related to the stage of life the star is and its mass. It is believed that stars begin their lives as a large cloud of dust and gas, called a **stellar nebula** (Figure 5–1). Eventually the gravitational attraction of the atoms that compose the cloud cause it to begin to collapse. As the cloud collapses it begins to heat up and increase in its density and pressure. This stage in the life of a star is known as the proto star stage. Eventually, the cloud heats to extreme temperatures, and the pressure and gravity of the star are great enough to start a fusion reaction. The fusion reaction is caused by atoms of hydrogen joining together to form atoms of helium. The result is the release of an incredible amount of energy that causes a star to shine. This begins the stage in the life of a star known as the **main sequence** stage, when the star begins to give off radiation. Main sequence stars are in the middle stage of a star's life cycle, and are actively undergoing nuclear fusion. Astronomers believe that many of the stars in the Milky Way galaxy are main sequence stars, including our own Sun. Eventually, after a star has used up all of its hydrogen, the nuclear reactions that have kept it burning begin to slow down. This causes the star to begin to expand and cool, and eventually the star burns itself out.

FIGURE 5–1 This image shows the Orion Nebula against a background of stars. (*Courtesy of PhotoDisc.*)

CLASSIFICATION OF STARS

Stars are classified by their size, temperature, color, and brightness. This classification is usually based on a star's, mass, age, or stage of life. Two astronomers, Ejnar Hertzsprung and Henry Russell, developed a key that is used to classify stars. This is called the Hertzsprung-Russell diagram, or HR Diagram. The HR diagram is used to classify stars by

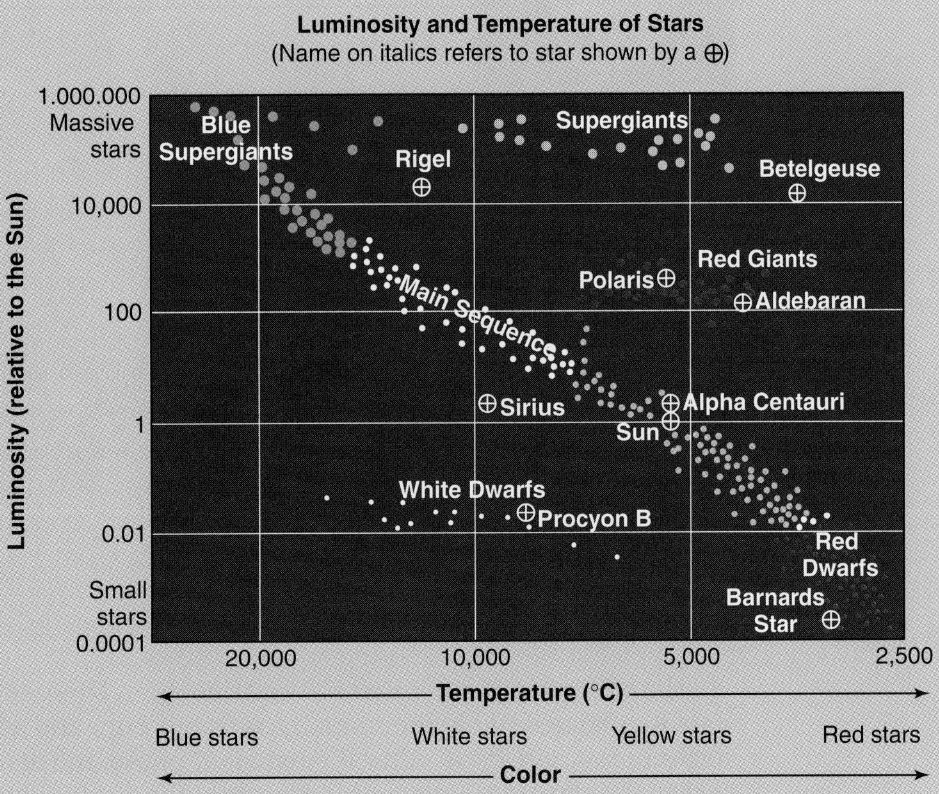

Luminosity and Temperature of Stars
(Name on italics refers to star shown by a ⊕)

[HR diagram showing Luminosity (relative to the Sun) on the vertical axis from 0.0001 to 1,000,000 and Temperature (°C) on the horizontal axis from 20,000 to 2,500. Regions labeled: Blue Supergiants, Rigel, Supergiants, Betelgeuse, Main Sequence, Polaris, Red Giants, Aldebaran, Sirius, Alpha Centauri, Sun, White Dwarfs, Procyon B, Red Dwarfs, Barnards Star. Bottom labels: Blue stars, White stars, Yellow stars, Red stars — Color]

- Vertical axis: Luminosity (relative to the Sun): 1.000.000 Massive stars, 10,000, 100, 1, 0.01, Small stars 0.0001
- Horizontal axis: Temperature (°C): 20,000, 10,000, 5,000, 2,500
- Color: Blue stars, White stars, Yellow stars, Red stars

FIGURE 5–2   The HR diagram is used to classify stars by their color, temperature, luminosity, and size.

their color, temperature, and **luminosity** (Figure 5-2). The luminosity of a star measures how bright a star is, or how much radiation it gives off relative to that of our Sun. The Sun has a luminosity of 1. The dimmest stars can have a luminosity of only 0.0001, and the brightest stars can have a luminosity of up to 1,000,000. These extremely bright stars are one million times brighter than our Sun. The color of a star, also known as its **spectral class**, can range from blue to white, yellow and red. A star's color is influenced by its temperature. The temperature of a star can be classified in either Kelvins or degrees Celsius. The coolest stars have temperatures around 2,500° C and appear red. The hottest stars can have temperatures over 20,000° C and are blue.

DWARF STARS

The coolest stars with the lowest luminosity on the HR Diagram are called **red dwarf** stars. These low mass stars have temperatures between 2,500 and 3,000 degrees Celsius. The color of these stars is red, due to their relatively low temperatures (Figure 5–3). An example of a red dwarf star is Proxima Centauri, the closest star to the Earth. **Brown dwarfs** are cool stars that have masses well below that of the Sun, and are at the end of their life cycle. After the red giant phase, these stars cool rapidly to the point where they are so dim that they barely give off enough radiation to be detected. New infrared telescopes are now being used to detect brown dwarf stars, adding more to our knowledge of star life cycles.

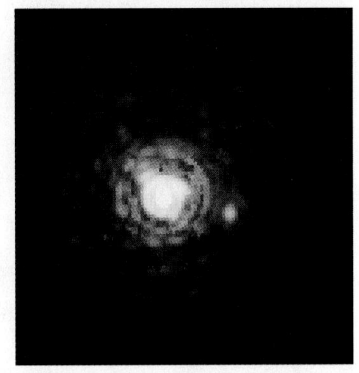

FIGURE 5–3   The small red dwarf star on the right, Gliese 623b, is 60,000 times dimmer and 10 times smaller than the Sun. The larger red dwarf star at center is its companion, Gliese 623a. (*Courtesy of C. Barbieri [University of Padua], NASA, ESA.*)

CAREER CONNECTIONS
Astronomer

Astronomers are specialized physicists who observe and study the universe, galaxies, stars, planets, moons, and other celestial objects. They are also interested in using their knowledge for practical applications such as space flight, communication, and navigation. Many astronomers also work to develop new instruments that can be used to study objects in space. These include specialized optical and radio telescopes, remote-operated spacecraft, and satellites. Astronomers often conduct research for universities or with NASA. Some astronomers are employed by private industry or museums. To be an astronomer you must be interested in physics, mathematics, computers, and celestial phenomena. All astronomers must have a college education.

The **white dwarf** is another star classification. These stars form from stars that have roughly the same mass as our Sun, and are in the final stages of their life cycle. After the red giant phase, the dense white-hot core of the star continues to shine brightly, forming a white dwarf. The high temperature of the white dwarf is the result of left-over heat that the core of the star is still radiating into space (Figure 5–4). Although classified as white dwarfs, these stars can vary in color, being light blue, true white, or even pale yellow. White dwarfs have temperatures that

FIGURE 5–4 This image of the Red Spider Nebula shows the formation of a white dwarf at the center of the cloud of gas that has just been blown off the star's surface. (*Courtesy of Garrelt Mellema [Leiden University] et al., HST, ESA, NASA.*)

range from 6,000 to 16,000 degrees Celsius, with an average luminosity of 0.01. These stars appear so dim as a result of their small size. The star Procyon B is an example of a white dwarf that is approximately 11.3 light years from the Earth, in the constellation Canis Minor.

GIANT AND SUPERGIANT STARS

Very large stars that are in the later stages of their lives are called **red giants**. These stars form as the aging star begins to expand as it uses up its hydrogen fuel. This causes the star to enlarge in size and shine more brightly. These massive stars have a luminosity that is more than 100 times that of our Sun, as a result of their extreme size. Red giants also have relatively moderate temperatures, between 4,000 and 7,500 degrees Celsius. An example of a red giant star is Aldebaran, in the constellation Taurus. This red giant is approximately 68 light years from Earth. Another red giant is Polaris, also called the North Star. This is probably the best-known star on Earth. It is located over the North Pole. Polaris is part of the Ursa Minor (Little Dipper) constellation. Both the red giants Aldebaran and Polaris have a luminosity that is approximately 100 times that of our Sun.

Supergiant stars are the largest of all stars. These stars can either be red supergiants or **blue supergiants**. These extremely massive objects are also the brightest of all stars with luminosities ranging between 10,000 and 1,000,000 times brighter than our Sun. An example of a red supergiant star is Betelgeuse, which has a temperature of approximately 3,000 degrees Celsius. The massive red supergiant is more than 1,000 times larger than the Sun. If Betelgeuse were located at the center of the solar system, its diameter would stretch out to the orbit of Jupiter! Betelgeuse is in the constellation of Orion, approximately 650 light years from the Earth (Figure 5–5). An example of a blue supergiant is Rigel, an extremely hot star with a temperature higher than 10,000 degrees Celsius. Rigel is also in the constellation of Orion, approximately 815 light years from Earth (Figure 5–6).

FIGURE 5–5   The red supergiant star Betelgeuse, which is 1000 times larger than the Sun but has a much lower temperature. (*Courtesy of A. Dupree [CFA], R. Gilliland [STScI], NASA.*)

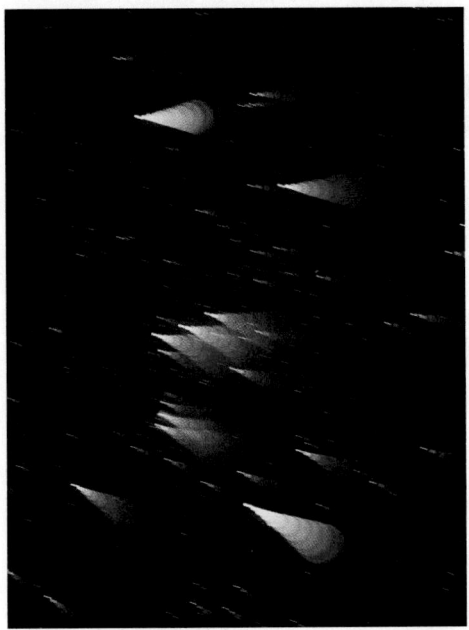

FIGURE 5–6   Stars in the constellation of Orion are photographed using a technique that reveals their unique colors. At the lower right is the blue supergiant Rigel. (© *David Malin.*)

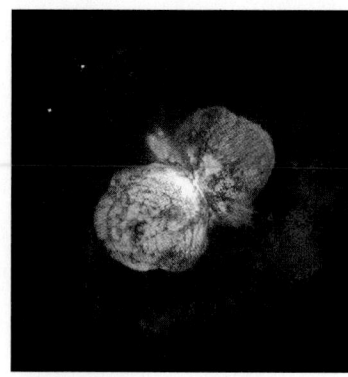

FIGURE 5–7 Gas and dust billows outward as a result of a supernova explosion of the star Eta Carinae, which exploded violently approximately 150 years ago. (*Courtesy of Jon Morse [University of Colorado] and NASA.*)

NEUTRON STARS

Most all stars end their lives as white dwarf stars; however, stars that are more massive than the Sun can result in the formation of very unique objects. A **neutron star** forms when a massive star has burned up all its fuel and suddenly collapses under its own gravity. The result is one of the most violent occurrences in the universe, a super nova (Figure 5–7). A super nova occurs when a dying star violently blows itself apart as it becomes unstable. Although rare, super nova explosions are so bright that they can even be observed in the daytime sky. A super nova explosion was recorded by ancient astronomers more than 1,000 years ago. Today the remains of this super nova form the Crab Nebula in the constellation Taurus. The result of a super nova event is the formation of an extremely dense neutron star. The density of a neutron star is so great that a tablespoon's worth of the star would have the equivalent mass of the entire Earth itself! Some neutron stars develop very powerful magnetic fields that emit radio waves at regular intervals as they spin on their axes. These neutron stars are known as **pulsars**. Acting much like a lighthouse, the rapidly rotating pulsar emits radio waves out into space. Because the star is rapidly spinning, the radio waves it sends out are observed from the Earth at regular intervals.

BLACK HOLES

Although most stars end their lives as brown dwarfs, white dwarfs, and neutron stars, some extremely massive stars can form an object known as a **black hole**. A black hole forms when a massive star ends its life in a violent super nova. The resulting neutron star is so extremely dense that its gravitational pull is strong enough to prevent light from escaping off its surface. This creates an object known as a black hole. These objects are known as black holes because they cannot be seen, and

Earth System Scientists

Stephen Hawking

Astronomer Stephen Hawking was born in England in 1942. His early work in physics and mathematics involved the concepts of space and time. While in graduate school, Hawking was diagnosed with a degenerative disease that eventually left him in a wheelchair and unable to speak. However, this disability did not prevent him from achieving his goal of becoming a respected mathematician and astrophysicist. In 1970 Hawking began to research the most bizarre of celestial phenomena, black holes. His work centered on the interaction of matter and energy within and around a black hole. In 1988 he published his famous book, *A Brief History of Time*, which explained the theories of space, time, relativity, and black holes to the general public. Today he still continues his work and holds the highly esteemed position of Lucasian Professor of Mathematics at Cambridge University in England, a position once held by Sir Isaac Newton.

their intense gravitational attraction is so great that they pull matter into them. Although they cannot be directly observed, black holes can be detected. The extreme gravitational attraction of a black hole causes matter surrounding it to heat up greatly as it is drawn in at the speed of light. This produces jets of x-rays that can be detected from the Earth. NASA's Chandra X-Ray Observatory is a satellite that is used to detect x-rays in space. So far the Chandra observatory has been used to discover and study many black holes. A black hole may exist in the constellation of Cygnus, and possibly at the center of the Milky Way galaxy. One of the farthest stars ever detected, Deneb, is also located in the constellation of Cygnus. This supergiant star is located approximately 1,600 light years from the Earth.

SECTION REVIEW

1. What is a star?
2. How are stars classified?
3. Describe how a star forms.
4. Describe the characteristics of the three types of dwarf stars.
5. What are the characteristics of the giant and supergiant stars?
6. What is a neutron star?
7. What is a pulsar?
8. What is a black hole?
9. Who is Stephen Hawking?

@ WEB Links

FOR MORE INFORMATION GO TO THESE WEB LINKS:

<http://aspire.cosmic-ray.org/labs/star_life/starlife_main.html>

<http://cse.ssl.berkeley.edu/bmendez/ay10/2000/cycle/cycle.html>

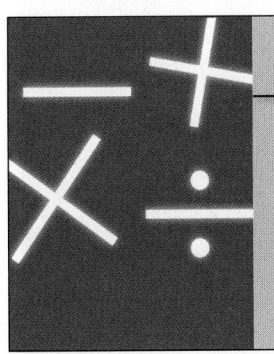

earth math

1) If one light year is equal to approximately 5.8 trillion mi, how many miles from Earth is the star Rigel?

2) Another way to measure the distance to a star is by using the unit called the parsec. One parsec is equal to approximately 3.26 light years. Knowing this, determine how many parsecs Proxima Centauri is from the Earth.

5.2 The Sun

FORMATION OF THE SUN

The Sun is a main sequence star of medium size that radiates energy into space at all wavelengths of the electromagnetic spectrum. It lies at the center of the solar system, approximately 93 million mi (150 million km) from the Earth. At this distance the energy from the Sun takes approximately 8 minutes to reach the Earth. The Sun is believed to have

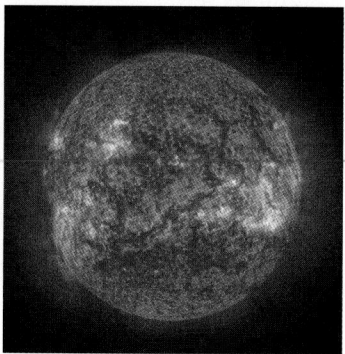

FIGURE 5–8 This image of the Sun, taken by NASA's Solar and Heliospheric Observatory (SOHO) satellite, reveals its surface. (*Courtesy of NASA.*)

formed from a swirling cloud of dust and gas called the Solar Nebula approximately 4.5 to 4.7 billion years ago (Figure 5–8). This nebula eventually collapsed under its own gravity, and the process of nuclear fusion began, which caused the Sun to shine.

COMPOSITION OF THE SUN

The Sun's mass is composed of approximately 74 percent hydrogen, 24 percent helium, and trace amounts of other elements, such as carbon, oxygen, silicon, and iron. The Sun is made up of four principal layers that surround a central core (Figure 5–9). The core of the Sun is where the thermonuclear reactions occur that power the Sun. There hydrogen atoms are fused together to create helium and extreme amounts of energy. The pressure inside the Sun's core is approximately 7 trillion pounds per square inch (0.5 trillion kilogram per square centimeter). This is an incredible force considering that the pressure at the Earth's surface is only 14.7 pounds per square inch (1 kilogram per square centimeter)! The temperature in the Sun's core is approximately 27 million° Fahrenheit (15 million° C). The layer that surrounds the Sun's core is called the convective zone. The convective zone is where the heat and light energy created in the Sun's core are transferred outward by convection currents.

The next layer of the Sun is called the photosphere. This is the visible surface of the Sun, which is composed of hot gases that act like a

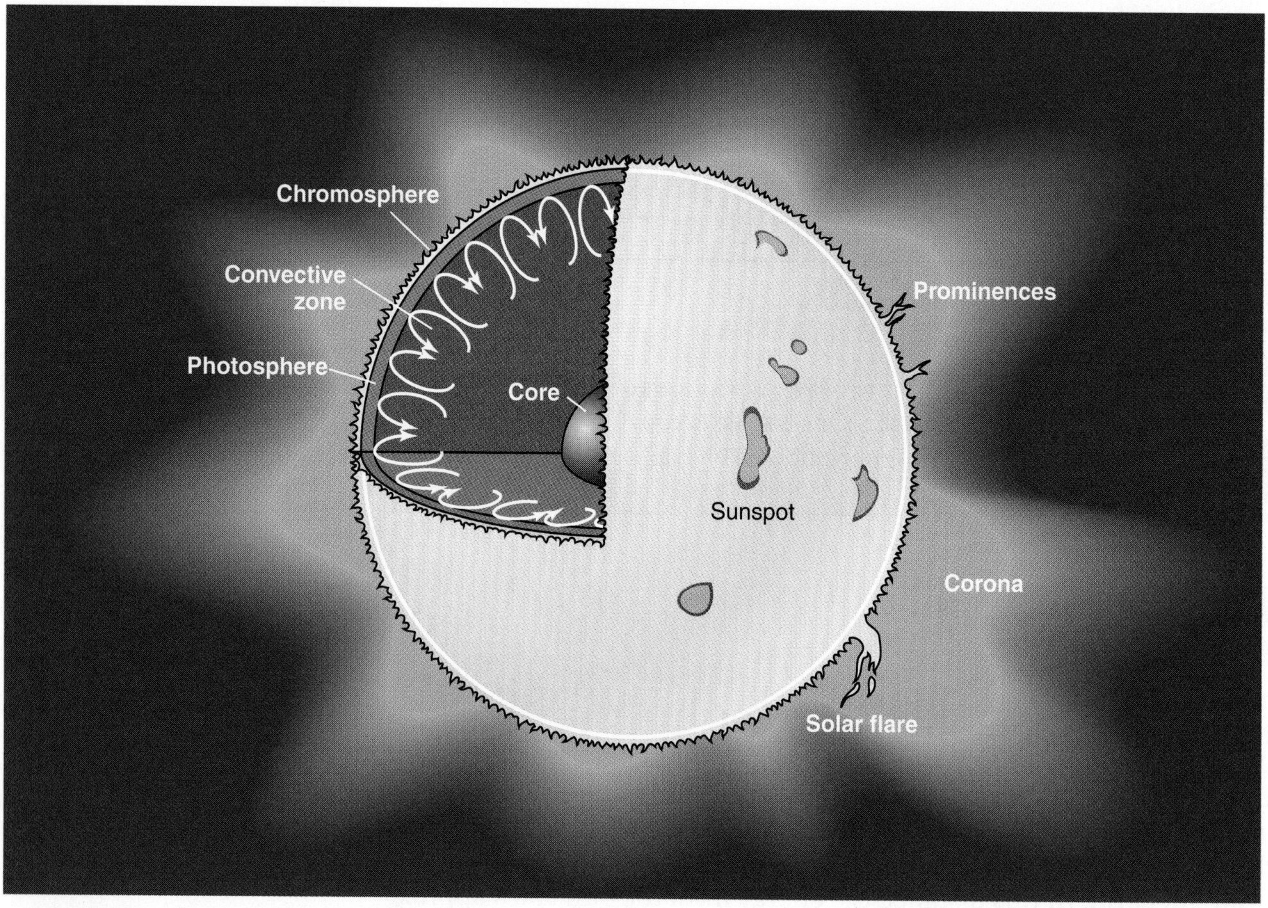

FIGURE 5–9 The different parts and layers of the Sun.

cloud surrounding the inner core and convection zone. The photosphere has a diameter of approximately 864,000 mi (1,390,473 km), which is approximately 109 times larger than the Earth. The photosphere is the region where hot gases rise and cooler gases descend back toward the Sun's center. These regions are known as granules, which are approximately 620 mi (998 km) across. These granules give the photosphere a rough surface (Figure 5–10).

The average temperature of the photosphere is approximately 9,700° F (5,371° C). Darker regions of cooler gas appear on the surface of the photosphere; these are called **sunspots** (Figure 5–11). Sunspot regions are about 3,000° Fahrenheit (1,649 ° C) cooler than the rest of the photosphere. Sunspots are also related to the occurrence of **solar flares**, which are hot regions of gas that leap off the Sun, sending out bursts of solar energy (Figure 5–12).

The number of sunspots on the Sun's surface changes from year to year, creating what is called a solar cycle. A solar cycle, or sunspot cycle, is the time from a period of high sunspot activity to a time when there are very few sunspots. The time of high sunspot activity is called the maxima, and the time of low sunspot activity is called the minima. One complete solar cycle, which is the time it takes to go from maxima to maxima, is 11.1 years. Scientists have related sunspot activity to periodic climate changes on the Earth. For example, periodic droughts that affect the Midwestern United States often occur on the same solar cycle as sunspot activity. Scientists are also concerned with the occurrence of solar flares because these violent eruptions on the Sun can cause disruptions to satellite communications and electrical power distribution on Earth. These are caused by solar flares emitting large bursts of radiation that eventually strike the Earth's atmosphere.

The layer of the Sun above the photosphere is called the chromosphere. This invisible layer of hot gas is approximately 2,000 mi thick and has temperatures ranging from 7,000 to 90,000° Fahrenheit (3,871

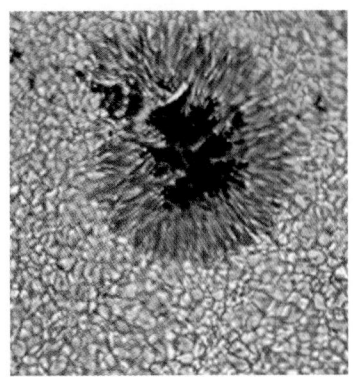

FIGURE 5–10 Close-up view of a sunspot surrounded by granules on the Sun's surface. (*Courtesy of T. Rimmele, M. Hannal/NOAO/AURA/NSF.*)

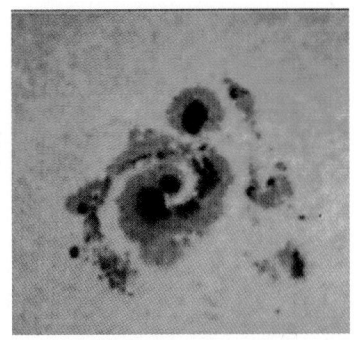

FIGURE 5–11 Image of a group of dark sunspots on the surface of the Sun. (*Courtesy of NOAO/AUEA/NSF.*)

Earth System Scientists

Hans Bethe

Hans Bethe was born in 1906 in Germany. He earned his doctorate in physics in 1928 at the University of Munich and became a professor of physics. He fled Germany in 1933, when Hitler gained power, and moved to England. His major contribution to science was unraveling the mechanics behind the energy production in stars. He was the first to propose that stars gain their energy from a fusion reaction that combines two atoms of hydrogen to form one atom of helium, along with a great amount of energy. He also became the chief of theoretical physics at the Los Alamos laboratory in New Mexico during World War II. This work was part of the Manhattan Project, which developed the first atomic bombs. In 1975 he moved to the United States and became a professor of physics at Cornell University. His work on the energy of stars eventually won him the Nobel Prize for Physics in 1976. For much of his life he was also involved in ensuring that scientists maintain a social responsibility for their work.

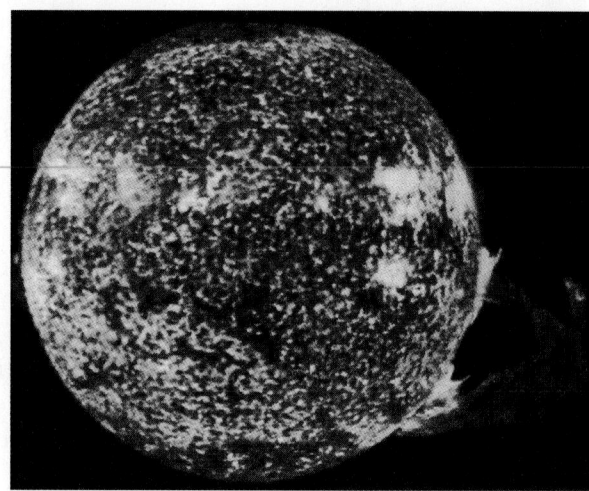

FIGURE 5-12 A large solar flare leaps off the surface of the Sun (lower right). (*Courtesy of NASA.*)

FIGURE 5-13 The aurora borealis, also called the northern lights, lights up the sky in the Northern Hemisphere as a result of the solar wind interacting with the magnetosphere and atmosphere. (*Courtesy of PhotoDisc.*)

to 49,982° C). The chromosphere merges with the final layer of the Sun, called the corona. The corona is visible only during a solar eclipse and reaches approximately 1 million mi (1.6 million km) into space. The corona can have temperatures greater than 3 million degrees F (1.7 million° C). The corona produces the **solar wind**, which is a stream of charged particles that move outward from the Sun at approximately 18,000 miles per hour (28,968 kilometers per hour.). The Earth is shielded from this stream of particles by its magnetic field; however, at the North and South Poles, the solar wind collides with the atmosphere and lights up the nighttime sky with brilliant colors. This is known as the northern lights, or the aurora borealis, in the Northern Hemisphere and the australis borealis in the Southern Hemisphere (Figure 5–13). Solar flares that leap off the surface of the Sun can also cause a temporary increase in the intensity of the solar wind.

CAREER CONNECTIONS
Solar Astronomer

A solar astronomer studies all aspects of our Sun. The Sun is the closest star to the Earth and has an important relationship with life on Earth. Solar astronomers study the Sun to better understand how it works and, more important, how it affects life on Earth. This specialized aspect of astronomy is also known as "space weather." Space weather is the change in space as a result of changes that occur with the Sun. Solar astronomers study these changes that occur within the Sun and how they affect our technology and life on the planet. Predicting periodic solar flares and other solar storms is one of the important jobs of a solar astronomer. Solar storms can interrupt power distribution and communication on Earth, so it is the job of the solar astronomer to study these events and determine how they may affect the Earth. Solar astronomers use several specialized telescopes, spacecraft, and other scientific instruments to study the Sun. Solar astronomers can work in the academic fields, for the government, or for private industries such as power companies.

CURRENT RESEARCH

Scientists working for the National Aeronautics and Space Administration (NASA) who have been studying the Sun have discovered a unique feature never before seen on our nearest star. Recent images taken of the Sun's surface have revealed explosions that create earthquakelike ripples on the Sun's surface. The explosions on the Sun's surface that cause these ripples are being called sunquakes. The power of these sunquakes would measure 11.1 on the Richter scale if they occurred on Earth. The explosions that cause sunquakes are connected to the Sun's increased activity. Activity on the Sun is marked by increases in the occurrence of solar storms that cause sunspots and solar flares. An increase in the number of solar storms that cause these sunquakes occurs during the Sun's solar maximum on an average of every 11 years. Scientists are interested in these solar storms because of the effect that they might have on the Earth. Much of the current research that is discovering new information about the nature of the Sun is being done with observations taken through NASA's Solar and Heliospheric Observatory, or SOHO satellite. This satellite is designed to observe the Sun continually and orbits around the Sun approximately 930,000 mi (1,496,690 km) away from the Earth.

FIGURE 5–14 The Sun's mass will increase drastically when it becomes a red giant in approximately 5 billion years, which will incinerate many of the planets of the solar system. (*Courtesy of James Gitlin/STScI AVL.*)

THE SUN'S LIFE CYCLE

The Sun, like any star, must go through the stages of a star's life cycle. Because the Sun is believed to be approximately 4.5 to 4.7 billion years old, it is estimated that it will take another 5 to 6 billion years to use up all of its fuel. When this happens the Sun will begin to enter the red giant phase of its life (Figure 5–14). When the sun becomes a red giant, it will be approximately 100 times larger than it is now. This will cause the hydrosphere on Earth to boil away and the atmosphere to be blown off, which will end life on Earth as we know it.

The outer planets, such as Saturn and Jupiter, will also have their atmospheres blown off during this phase of the Sun's life. Eventually the Sun will expel its outer layers of hot gas and develop into a white dwarf. The Sun during this time will be about the size of the Earth but will have an extreme density of more than 1,000 grams per cubic centimeter. Although this scenario means certain doom to our solar system, we should not worry, for this will not begin to occur for approximately 5 billion more years!

@ WEB Links

FOR MORE INFORMATION GO TO THIS WEB LINK:

< http://sohowww .nascom.nasa.gov/>

SECTION REVIEW

1. Approximately how old is the Sun?
2. What is the Sun made of?
3. Describe the different layers that together make up the Sun.
4. What is a solar cycle, and why is it important to the Earth?
5. What is the solar wind, and how does it affect the Earth?
6. Who is Hans Bethe?

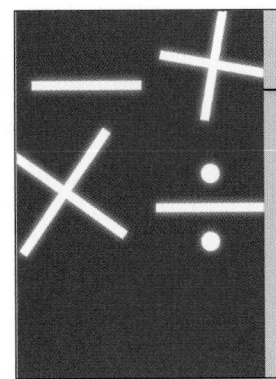

earth math

1) If the diameter of the Earth is approximately 7,918 miles and the Sun is 109 times the diameter of the Earth, what is the approximate diameter of the Sun?

2) Using the diameter you calculated from question 1, if the chromosphere of the Sun is 2000 miles thick, what percentage of the total size of the Sun does this layer occupy?

CHAPTER SUMMARY

Stars are luminous balls of gas that are powered by nuclear fusion. Billions of stars exist in the universe. Stars are classified by their particular color, temperature, size, and luminosity. This is often displayed on the HR diagram. All stars begin their lives in the form of a stellar nebula, which is a large cloud of collapsing dust and gas. Eventually the nebula collapses to the point where nuclear fusion begins to occur, causing the star to shine. This is called the main sequence stage of a star's life cycle. Eventually a star uses up all its fuel and begins to expand and cool. During this stage of a star's life, it is called a red giant. The red giant is a very large star that has a red appearance and is cooler than a main sequence star. The outer layer of gas of a red giant eventually is blown off into space, leaving a small, extremely hot, dense object called a white dwarf. The white dwarf then cools to form a neutron star, and the life cycle is complete. Many neutron stars emit radio waves at regular intervals and are known as pulsars. Some massive stars can also explode violently during their red giant phase, causing what is called a supernova. Another type of object, called a black hole, can form from a massive star. A black hole is created from the remnants of a star; it has a gravitational attraction so great that it prevents light from leaving its surface.

The closest star to the planet Earth is the Sun. The Sun is a medium-aged, main sequence star. Like all stars, the Sun is powered by the process of nuclear fusion. The Sun's central core is surrounded by four unique layers: the convective zone, photosphere, chromosphere, and corona. The photosphere is the visible surface of the Sun that we see from Earth. The surface of the photosphere has darker, cooler regions called sunspots. The number of sunspots on the photosphere changes periodically in what is called a solar cycle. The point in the solar cycle when there is a high number of sunspots is called the solar maxima. The point when there are very few sunspots is known as the solar minima. The average period between solar maxima and minima is 11 years. Increased solar activity also coincides with an increasing number of solar flares. A solar flare is a large eruption of hot gas off the surface of the Sun. Solar flares and increased sunspot activity can affect the Earth in several ways. The sun emits a stream of particles into space known as the solar wind. The interaction of the solar wind with the Earth's magnetic field creates the phenomenon known as the northern lights. The Sun is estimated to be approximately 5 billion years old, which is in the middle of its life cycle. Scientists believe the Sun will enter its red giant phase in approximately 5 billion years.

CHAPTER REVIEW

Multiple Choice

1. Which process causes a star to shine?
   a. nuclear fission
   b. nuclear fusion
   c. radioactive decay
   d. sunspots

2. Which is the correct sequence of events in a star's life cycle?
   a. white dwarf, red giant, main sequence, nebula
   b. red giant, nebula, white dwarf, main sequence
   c. nebula, main sequence, red giant, white dwarf
   d. main sequence, white dwarf, red giant, nebula

3. Which star classification causes a star's unique color?
   a. luminosity
   b. brightness
   c. size
   d. temperature

4. During which of the following stages of a star's life is it hottest?
   a. proto star
   b. red giant
   c. red dwarf
   d. white dwarf

5. Which of the following is the hottest type of star?
   a. blue supergiant
   b. white dwarf
   c. red giants
   d. red dwarf

6. Which type of star acts like a "lighthouse" that periodically emits radio waves into space?
   a. black hole
   b. neutron star
   c. pulsar
   d. supernova

7. Which of the following stars is closest to the Earth?
   a. Rigel
   b. Polaris
   c. Betelgeuse
   d. Alpha Centauri

8. What stage of a star's life is the Sun in now?
   a. proto star
   b. main sequence
   c. red giant
   d. white dwarf

9. What is the approximate age of the Sun?
   a. 2.5 billion years old
   b. 5 million years old
   c. 5 billion years old
   d. 10 billion years old

10. Which layer of the Sun is visible only during a solar eclipse?
    a. convective layer
    b. photosphere
    c. chromosphere
    d. corona

11. On which layer of the Sun do sunspots occur?
    a. convective layer
    b. photosphere
    c. chromosphere
    d. corona

12. Approximately how long is a solar cycle?
    a. 11 years
    b. 22 years
    c. 5 billion years
    d. 10 billion years

13. Climate change, power interruption, communication problems, and the northern lights are all associated with:
    a. granules
    b. solar flares
    c. nuclear fusion
    d. supernovas

14. The Sun is approximately how many times bigger than the Earth?
    a. 10 times
    b. 20 times
    c. 50 times
    d. 100 times

15. Scientists estimate the Sun will enter the red giant phase in approximately:
    a. 11 years
    b. 11 billion years
    c. 5 billion years
    d. never

Matching   *Match the terms with the correct definitions.*

a. star
b. nuclear fusion
c. stellar nebula
d. luminosity
e. spectral class

f. red dwarf stars
g. white dwarf
h. red giant
i. blue supergiant
j. neutron star

k. pulsars
l. black hole
m. sunspots
n. solar flares
o. solar wind

1. _____ A classification of a star that is dimmer than the Sun, white, small, and extremely hot.
2. _____ A large, shining, spherical celestial object that is held together by its own gravity and is undergoing nuclear fusion.
3. _____ A classification for a dim star that is small, red, and relatively cool.
4. _____ A nuclear reaction that is caused by combining, or fusing, two elements, which results in the creation of a great amount of energy.
5. _____ A classification used to describe a star's unique spectrum.
6. _____ The stream of particles and electromagnetic radiation that is emitted by the Sun and travels out into space in all directions.
7. _____ A classification for a star that is very bright, large, red, and relatively cool.
8. _____ Large flamelike emissions of hot plasma and radiation that leap off the surface of the Sun.
9. _____ A classification of massive stars that are blue, bright, and extremely hot.
10. _____ Dark spots that appear on the surface of the Sun, which are believed to be cooler areas on its surface.
11. _____ A classification for a star that is extremely dense and mostly composed of neutrons.
12. _____ A theoretical celestial object with a strong gravitational attraction that prevents light from escaping its surface.
13. _____ A type of neutron star that regularly emits periodic radio signals.
14. _____ A large mass of collapsing gas and dust that forms stars and planets.
15. _____ A measure of the rate at which stars radiate electromagnetic energy into space.

Critical Thinking

1. Explain what you think humans will need to do on Earth to survive when the Sun begins to enter the red giant phase.

The Solar System and Its Place in the Universe

THE SOLAR SYSTEM OBJECTIVES

The Formation of the Solar System · The Terrestrial Planets · The Gas Giants · Dwarf Planets · Small Solar System Bodies · Asteroids · Meteoroids · Comets

After reading this section you should be able to:

▶ Identify all the celestial objects that together make up the solar system.
▶ Differentiate between a terrestrial planet and a gas giant.
▶ Identify the eight planets and three dwarf planets in the solar system and some of their unique features.
▶ Define the terms *trans-neptunian object* and *small solar system body*.
▶ Define the term *asteroid* and identify the location of the asteroid belt within the solar system.
▶ Differentiate among meteoroid, meteor, and meteorite.
▶ Define the terms *comet* and *Oort cloud*.

THE EARTH'S PLACE IN THE UNIVERSE OBJECTIVES

Galaxies · Quasars · Life in the Universe · Cosmology

After reading this section you should be able to:

▶ Define the term galaxy, and identify the three different types of galaxies.
▶ Identify the approximate location of the solar system within the Milky Way galaxy.
▶ Define the term *quasar*.
▶ Define the term *universe*.
▶ Explain the Big Bang theory.
▶ Identify the approximate age of the universe.
▶ Explain the Doppler Effect.
▶ Describe the concept of red shift as applied to galaxies.
▶ Explain what cosmic background radiation is.
▶ Describe two observations used to support the Big Bang theory.
▶ Explain the three theories that predict the future of the universe.

INTRODUCTION

When you are gazing up at the sky on a clear night, you are sharing a view that has been seen by countless people for thousands of years. Technology may have changed our world, but the one thing that has remained the same is the view of the heavens. This creates a unique connection between all people who are living and have lived on the Earth. Because the universe is so vast and contains billions of star systems, it is possible that we are not the only ones who are trying to unlock its secrets. The awesome display of the celestial sphere has inspired generations of humans to ponder their place in the universe. Over time our explanations of the heavens have changed, revealing much about the vastness of space and all the wonders it contains. Each time a scientific discovery is made that reveals new information about the universe, further questions are raised and the universe becomes more fascinating to us.

6.1 The Solar System

THE FORMATION OF THE SOLAR SYSTEM

The solar system is a group of celestial objects that exist in a region centered by our Sun. The celestial objects that make up the solar system include planets, dwarf planets, moons, small solar system bodies, and the Sun. Our solar system is believed to have been formed from a swirling cloud of dust and gas called the Solar Nebula about 4.5 to 4.7 billion years ago (Figure 6–1). Eventually the inner portions of this nebula created the Sun, and the outer portions formed the **planets**; their **moons**, also called satellites; and other interplanetary material found in our solar system. The largest objects in the solar system, excluding the Sun, are known as planets. The solar system has eight major planets and three dwarf planets that have been positively identified so far. A planet is a large body composed of rock and gas that orbits a star, and has a nearly spherical shape from its own gravity. In our solar system we divide the planets into three main groups, the inner **terrestrial planets**, the outer gaseous planets known as **gas giants**, and the **dwarf planets**.

Earth System Scientists

Nicolaus Copernicus

Nicolaus Copernicus was born in Poland in 1473. During his life, he devoted much of his time to the science of astronomy. Using mostly the observations of other astronomers of his time, he developed his own theory about the Earth's place in the universe. Since 200 CE, scholars and the Roman Catholic Church believed that the Earth was the center of the universe, around which all other celestial objects revolved. This was known as the geocentric model of the universe, which was developed by a philosopher named Ptolemy. Copernicus's theory proposed that the Earth was not the center of the solar system or the universe. His observations suggested that the Earth, along with the other planets, revolved around the Sun, which also moved around the universe. He also proposed that the Earth's axis was tilted at approximately 23.5 degrees, which accounted for the apparent motion of celestial objects. Copernicus went on to explain that the Earth's atmosphere rotated with the Earth. His theory is known as the heliocentric theory. It was first published in 1513 as an anonymous text. Copernicus also calculated the distance of the planets from the Earth using the astronomical unit, which is the distance of the Earth from the Sun. Because of the controversial nature of his theories, which went against the views of the church in Rome, Copernicus did not publish his full work on heliocentric theory until he was on his deathbed in 1543. Ironically, he dedicated his controversial book, *De Revolutionibus*, to Pope Paul III. Copernicus's groundbreaking book, which formed the foundations of modern astronomy, was on the Catholic Church's forbidden book list until 1835.

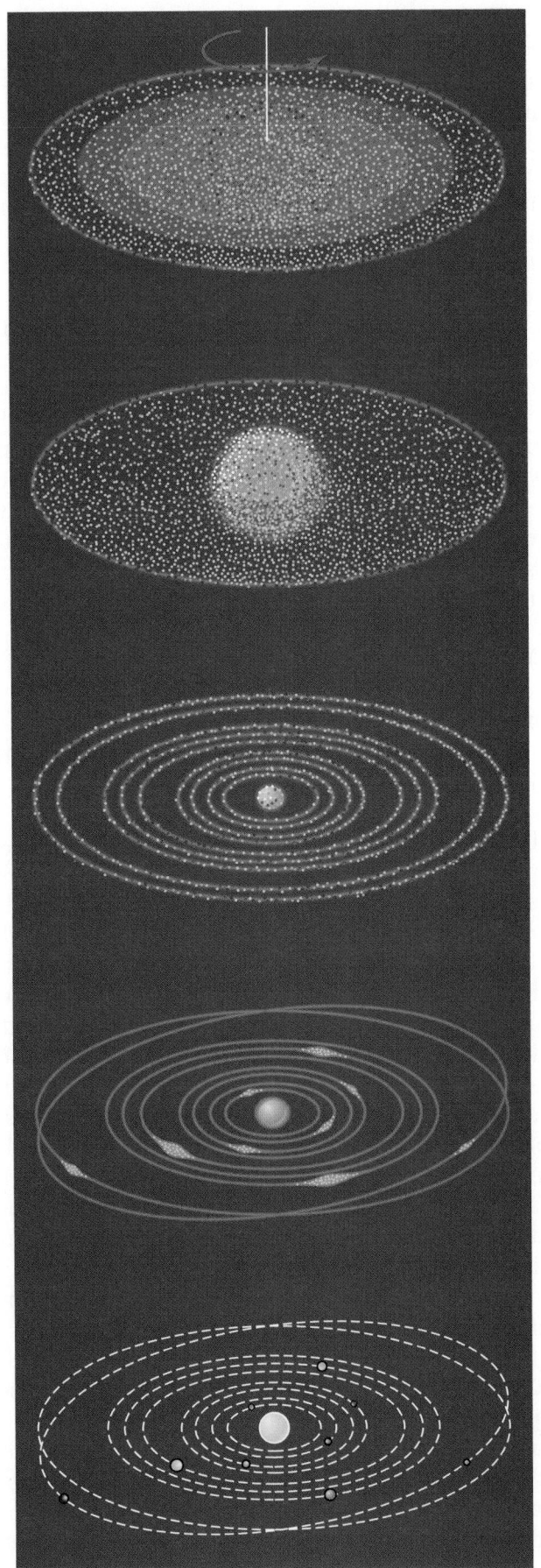

FIGURE 6–1 The formation of the solar system from the Solar Nebula.

THE TERRESTRIAL PLANETS

The inner terrestrial planets are relatively close to the Sun and are mainly composed of rock. These include Mercury, Venus, Earth, and Mars. The outer gaseous planets, also called the gas giants, lie further out in space from the Sun and are composed mainly of gases, although some might have rocky cores. The gaseous planets include Jupiter, Saturn, Uranus, and Neptune. The distance that is used to measure how far a planet is from the Sun is called the astronomical unit, or AU. One astronomical unit is equal to the distance of the Earth from the Sun, which is approximately 93 million mi (150 million km).

Mercury is the planet that is closest to the Sun, at a distance of 0.387 AU, or approximately 36 million mi (58 million km). Mercury is about one-third the size of Earth and has no atmosphere. This tiny planet is also the fastest of all planets, moving at approximately 29 miles per second around the Sun. Because Mercury has no atmosphere, it experiences wide temperature variations between day and night. At night the surface of Mercury can be as cold as –300° F (–184° C), and during the day the surface heats up to more than 700° F (371° C). This is the greatest temperature fluctuation of any planet in the solar system. The surface of Mercury is covered with impact craters much like our own Moon (Figure 6–2). Mercury has a slow rotation rate of almost 59 days and takes more than 87 days to orbit around the Sun.

The planet Venus is located 0.723 AU from the Sun, or approximately 67 million mi (108 million km). Venus is roughly the same size as the Earth and has an atmosphere that mainly consists of carbon dioxide gas and sulfuric acid clouds (Figure 6–3). Venus's clouds also reflect sunlight from the planet, which makes it the brightest planet in the sky. Venus is usually visible shortly after sunset, resembling a very bright star. The surface of Venus is shrouded by thick clouds of sulfuric acid that are most likely the result of volcanic eruptions. These clouds exist high above the planet's surface, where temperatures are approximately 70° F (21° C). This moderate temperature allows liquid water to mix with sulfur compounds and form sulfuric acid. Far down below these clouds, however, the average surface temperature of Venus is approximately 800° F (427° C), with a surface pressure 90 times that on Earth. The extreme surface temperatures on Venus are believed to be the result of a runaway greenhouse effect. This is caused by the great amount of carbon dioxide in the planet's atmosphere, which traps heat on the surface. It takes more than 224 days for Venus to orbit around the Sun and 243 days to make one rotation on its axis. Venus's rotation on its axis is opposite to that of Earth's rotation. This is called retrograde motion, and it causes the Sun to rise in the west and set in the east on Venus!

Earth is the third planet from the Sun, at a distance of 1 AU, or 93 million mi (150 million km). Earth is the only planet in the solar system that has liquid water and supports life. The Earth takes 365 days to orbit the Sun and 24 hours to make one full rotation on its axis. Our home planet also is orbited by one moon. The atmosphere on Earth is composed mainly of nitrogen and oxygen gas.

Mars is the fourth planet from the Sun and is the last of the four terrestrial planets. Mars is roughly half the size of the Earth and is located 1.52 AU from the Sun, or 141.5 million mi (228 million km) (Figure 6–4).

FIGURE 6–2 An image of the cratered surface of the planet Mercury. (*Courtesy of NASA/NSSDC.*)

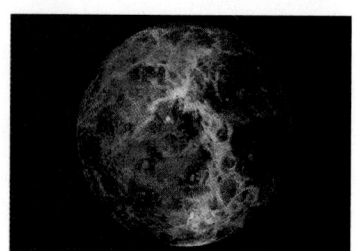

FIGURE 6–3 An image of the planet Venus, which is roughly the same size as Earth. (*Courtesy of PhotoDisc.*)

FIGURE 6–4 An image of the planet Mars. (*Courtesy of PhotoDisc.*)

Mars has a very thin atmosphere that is composed mainly of carbon dioxide gas. This causes wide temperature fluctuations on the surface of Mars. During the Martian day, the surface temperature can be more than –27° F (–33° C), and at night the temperature can plummet to less than –117° F (–83° C). Although the Martian atmosphere is thin, it can develop winds at speeds exceeding 62 miles per hour. Winds can create dust storms that cover large parts of the planet. The Martian atmosphere can also contain clouds. Martian clouds are composed of frozen water or dry ice (frozen carbon dioxide).

The surface of Mars has large canyons and channels that look much as if they were formed from flowing liquid water. Because of this evidence, scientists believe that at some time in Mars's past, the surface might have contained liquid water. Since that time, the Martian climate has been much too cold to contain liquid water. Some researchers believe that the evidence of once-flowing water on the Martian surface suggests that it also once contained life. Mars Exploration Rovers Spirit and Opportunity have also detected evidence that liquid water might have existed on Mars. Salt crystals found in sediment on the surface, cross bedding of sandstone rocks, along with the presence of hematite, a mineral commonly formed in water, suggest that liquid water once existed on Mars.

Others believe that there might still be living organisms on Mars. Scientists have discovered unique forms of bacteria that live in the ice and rock of Antarctica and in the extreme temperatures of hot springs on the Earth. This points to the possibility of some type of hardy life form that could also exist on Mars. Future missions to the planet will search for possible fossil evidence of extinct Martian life, and of existing life forms. A meteor found in Antarctica recently is believed to be a piece of Mars that was blasted into space by an asteroid impact with the Martian surface. This meteor has been studied, and microscopic features that look very similar to fossilized bacteria on Earth were found in the meteor. Some scientists believe that this might be the first sign of a life form on a planet other than Earth. Mars is also home to the solar system's largest volcano, called Olympus Mons (Figure 6–5). This volcano is more than 78,000 ft high (24 km) and 310 mi (499 km) wide.

Mars also contains two polar ice caps. These are not composed of water, however, but of frozen carbon dioxide. Mars orbits the Sun in about 686 days and takes 1 day to make a complete rotation on its axis. Mars also is orbited by two moons, Phobos and Demos. Neither of the Martian moons possesses an atmosphere.

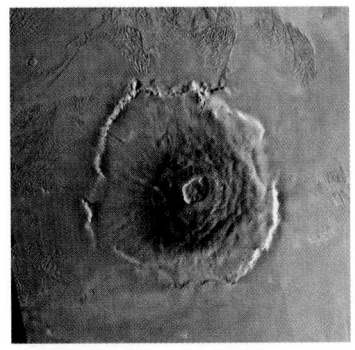

FIGURE 6–5 An image of the Olympus Mons on Mars, which is the largest known volcano in the solar system at more than 78,000 ft high and 310 mi wide. (*Courtesy of NASA/NSSDC.*)

THE GAS GIANTS

The first of the four gaseous planets, Jupiter, is located 5.2 AU from the Earth, or 483 million mi (777 million km). Jupiter is the largest planet in the solar system, with a mass that is only one-thousandth that of the Sun's mass (Figure 6–6). Jupiter's diameter is 88,730 mi (142,797 km), and it takes a little more than 11 years to orbit the Sun. Unlike the inner terrestrial planets, Jupiter is composed mainly of hydrogen, helium, ammonia, and methane gas.

Jupiter's cloudy surface is a variety of colors, including brown, red, orange, and white. These clouds, mostly composed of ammonia, form

FIGURE 6–6 An image of the planet Jupiter, the largest of the gas giants. (*Courtesy of PhotoDisc.*)

CAREER CONNECTIONS
Planetary Scientist

Planetary scientists study the origin, evolution, and environments of planets in both the solar system and around other stars. To do this, planetary scientists must have a wide-ranging knowledge of meteorology, geology, biology, chemistry, and physics. They must then apply this knowledge to the study of planets beyond Earth. Because it is not easy to send scientists to other planets, planetary scientists must use long-range observations to infer what a planet's environment is like. This requires the use of many scientific instruments to gather data to learn more about planets. Remote sensing spacecraft, telescopes, and powerful computers aid planetary scientists in their attempts to learn more about planets. Although early astronomers made discoveries about the properties of planets in the solar system, the work of planetary scientists over the past 20 to 30 years has given us detailed knowledge of other worlds. These specialized astronomers are also interested in discovering how humans might live someday on other planets, and if any life exists other than on Earth. Planetary scientists require a college education and usually conduct research in academic fields or with NASA.

FIGURE 6–7 An image of Ganymede, one of Jupiter's moons, which is the most heavily cratered object in the solar system. (*Courtesy of NASA/NSSDC.*)

turbulent swirls around the planet in unique bands. These bands often result in large storms that can be seen on the planet. The most famous of Jupiter's storms is the great red spot. This storm resembles a hurricane on Earth but is large enough to hold two Earths. The great red spot is a storm that has been raging on Jupiter for more than 300 years. Below the thick atmosphere of Jupiter is believed to be layers of liquid hydrogen. There may also be a slushy liquid core located deep within the planet. Jupiter is also surrounded by three ring systems. Jupiter's rings are not as visible as Saturn's rings because they are made up of tiny dark particles. These particles are most likely the debris that was kicked up into space when asteroids collided with Jupiter's moons.

Jupiter is surrounded by at least 39 moons. The first moons of Jupiter were discovered in the year 1610 A.D. by Galileo using his newly invented telescope. These include Io, Europa, Ganymede, and Callisto. The remainder of Jupiter's moons are designated by numbers, such as J6, J7, and so on. Ganymede is the largest moon in the solar system, with a diameter of approximately 3,274 mi (Figure 6–7). This is about the size of the planet Mercury. This moon is composed of rock and water ice. Ganymede's surface also contains the most impact craters of any object in the solar system.

The moon Callisto is also composed of water ice and rock but appears very different from Ganymede (Figure 6–8). Its surface has been shaped by large outflows of water from its interior. This has created lines of frozen water that radiate outward from the impact craters.

The two inner moons of Jupiter include Io and Europa. Io is the closest moon to Jupiter and is also one of the solar system's most active moons. The surface of Io is covered with active volcanoes and has a thin atmosphere composed of sulfur dioxide. At one time Io was observed to have eight volcanic eruptions occurring at once (Figure 6–9). Io's volcanoes spew out molten rock, which spreads out onto the planet's surface, and gaseous sulfur compounds that are blasted more than 190 mi (306 km) into the atmosphere. These sulfur compounds then condense in the cold atmosphere into solid particles that float down to the surface like snow. This sulfur "snow" covers the surface of the planet with a fine dust of white and orange sulfur compounds. The extreme volcanic activity that occurs on Io is believed to be caused by tidal forces that squeeze the moon and generate internal heat that powers the volcanoes. This is much like the heat that is generated when you twist a piece of metal wire. The surface temperature of Io is approximately –225° F (–143° C), although some volcanic regions can have temperatures as high as 70° F (21° C). In these regions, large pools of liquid sulfur are believed to exist.

Jupiter's second closest moon to its surface is Europa. This moon is unique in that its surface is completely covered with frozen water. Some scientists believe that below this frozen water there might exist liquid water. Evidence of this lies on the surface of Europa, which is covered with large cracks. Some of these cracks resemble the cracked ice fields off the coast of Antarctica on Earth. Future missions planned by the National Aeronautic and Space Administration (NASA) will try to locate a possible liquid ocean beneath the ice of Europa (Figure 6–10). If liquid

FIGURE 6–8 An image of Callisto, one of Jupiter's moons, which has a surface covered in rock and water ice. (*Courtesy of NASA/NSSDC.*)

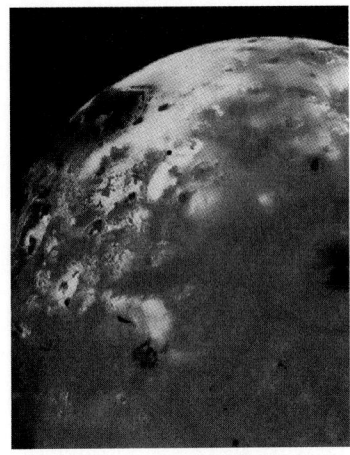

FIGURE 6–9 An image of the colorful surface of Io, one of Jupiter's moons, which is covered in many active volcanoes that spew out sulfur compounds. (*Courtesy of NASA/NSSDC.*)

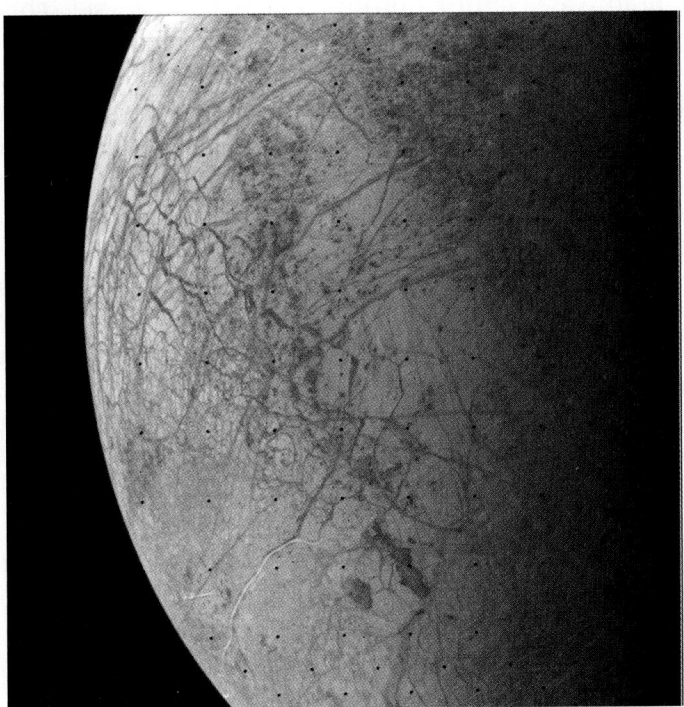

FIGURE 6–10 An image of the cracked ice on the surface of Europa, one of Jupiter's moons, which is believed to contain a liquid ocean beneath the ice. (*Courtesy of NASA/NSSDC.*)

FIGURE 6–11 An image of the planet Saturn, showing its distinctive rings. (*Courtesy of PhotoDisc.*)

FIGURE 6–12 An image of the planet Uranus. (*Courtesy of NASA/NSSDC.*)

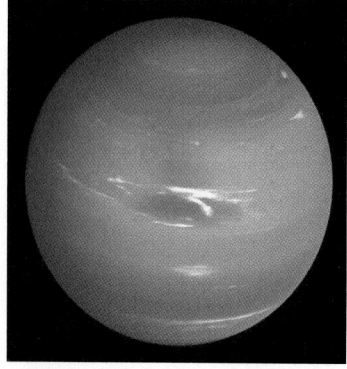

FIGURE 6–13 An image of the planet Neptune, which appears blue as a result of the high percentage of methane in its atmosphere. (*Courtesy of PhotoDisc.*)

water does exist on Europa, it might be one of the most likely places in the solar system, besides the Earth, to support life in some form.

The second gaseous planet in the solar system is Saturn. Saturn is probably the most visually stunning of all the planets because of its colorful rings. Saturn is located 9.6 AU from the Sun, or 886.2 million mi (1,426 km). Saturn is also composed mainly of hydrogen and helium gas, with clouds made of ammonia and methane. These clouds are not as spectacular as Jupiter's clouds. They form regular bands around the planet. The bands move in alternating east-west directions at speeds of more than 1,000 miles per hour. The most striking attribute of the planet Saturn is its unique rings (Figure 6–11). The planet is orbited by seven main ring systems, which are composed of billions of ice particles. These particles range in size from tiny grains of sand to giant boulders. This debris reflects different wavelengths of light, which give each ring its unique color. If we could enter the ring systems of Saturn, it would appear as if we were in a great blizzard. Saturn also is orbited by at least 22 moons. The largest of Saturn's moons, Titan, is the only moon in the solar system that contains a substantial atmosphere. Titan is larger than the planets Mercury and Pluto and has an atmosphere that is composed mainly of nitrogen gas. Researchers believe that Titan might have an atmosphere that is similar to that of the primitive Earth. Below Titan's thick atmosphere, the surface temperature is –289° Fahrenheit (–183° C). At this temperature there may be large lakes composed of hydrocarbons like ethane and methane covering portions of the surface. In 2005 the Cassini spacecraft launched the Huygens probe down through Titan's atmosphere, which sent back incredible images showing what might be hydrocarbon rivers flowing into a methane sea. The Cassini mission also flew by another moon of Saturn, named Enceladus in 2006. It revealed a surface covered in water ice with periodic eruptions of liquid water jetting out into space like a geyser. This exciting discovery suggests that Enceladus, like Jupiter's Europa, might also contain liquid water just beneath its icy surface.

Uranus is the seventh planet from the sun, located 19.2 AU, or 1.783 billion mi (2.869 billion km), from the center of the solar system (Figure 6–12). Uranus is also a gaseous planet that is about four times larger than the Earth. It takes 84 years for Uranus to orbit the Sun and more than 17 hours to make one full rotation. Uranus is unique among the planets in that its axis of rotation is tilted 90 degrees, so it appears to be spinning on its side as compared with the rotation of the other planets. The planet is composed mostly of ammonia and methane, with an atmosphere of hydrogen and helium. The methane and ammonia give Uranus its blue-green color. Uranus also is surrounded by a ring system and at least 18 moons.

Neptune is the eighth planet in the solar system, located 30.1 AU, or 2.794 billion mi (4.497 billion km), from the Sun. Neptune is also a gaseous planet composed of hydrogen, helium, and methane. The methane gives Neptune its blue color (Figure 6–13). Neptune orbits the Sun in approximately 168 years and makes one complete rotation on its axis every 19 hours. Neptune also has a small ring system and eight moons. One of Neptune's moons, Triton, is the coldest object in space so far recorded. The surface temperature of this moon is –390° F (–234° C)! Astronomers believe that this moon will eventually collide with Neptune in about 10 million to 100 million years.

DWARF PLANETS

Pluto had long been regarded as the solar system's ninth and final planet; however, with the discovery of a potential tenth planet in July of 2005, astronomers were faced with a new challenge on how best to scientifically define what a planet is. For more than 100 years, astronomers have loosely defined a planet as a large body that orbits around a central star. Now the International Astronomical Union (IAU) has redefined what constitutes a planet. The IAU is a worldwide organization of astronomers who support and promote the science of astronomy and oversee the classification and naming of celestial objects. In August of 2006, the IAU created new criteria defining a planet as a non-luminous object that orbits around a star, has sufficient gravity to form a spherical shape, and whose orbit has cleared its path of other celestial objects. As a result of this updated version of what defines a planet, Pluto is no longer considered a planet because its orbit crosses that of the planet Neptune. As a result of Pluto's new status, the IAU has created a new class of planets called dwarf planets. A **dwarf planet** is defined as a non-luminous object that orbits around a star, has sufficient gravity to form a spherical shape, and whose orbit has not cleared its path of other celestial objects. Currently three objects in the solar system are now considered dwarf planets: Ceres, Pluto, and Eris, which until September 2006 was known as 2003 UB-313.

Ceres, a dwarf planet located closest to the Sun, was once regarded as the largest asteroid lying in the asteroid belt between the orbits of Mars and Jupiter. Italian astronomer Giuseppe Piazzi discovered Ceres in 1801, and first classified it as a planet. However one year later it was reclassified as an asteroid. Ceres is approximately 580 mi in diameter and is located 2.9 AU, or approximately 277 million mi (446 million km) from the Sun. Little is known about its surface characteristics although scientists will learn more about this dwarf planet when NASA's unmanned Dawn probe arrives there in 2015 (Figure 6–14).

Pluto, the second dwarf planet, is located in the outer fringes of the solar system at 39.4 AU, or 3.666 billion mi (5.9 billion km) from the Sun. Pluto is very small, with a diameter of only 1,430 mi (2,301 km). Unlike Ceres, Pluto is a gaseous dwarf planet composed of frozen methane, nitrogen, and carbon monoxide. It takes Pluto more than 247 years to orbit the Sun, and it completes one rotation on its axis in 6 days. Pluto has one moon, Charon, which is half its size (Figure 6–15). This cold moon is believed to be composed mostly of frozen water.

In July of 2005, American astronomers announced the discovery of a third dwarf planet located in the outer reaches of the solar system, in the region known as the Kuiper Belt. This dwarf planet was given the temporary name of 2003 UB-313 until it was officially named as Eris by the IAU in September of 2006. This celestial object is larger than the dwarf planet Pluto and also falls under the category of being a Trans-Neptunian Object. **Trans-Neptunian Objects** are objects that orbit the Sun at a greater distance than the orbit of the planet Neptune. Eris orbits the Earth approximately 97 AU, or roughly 9 billion mi (14.5 billion km) from the Sun, and also has it own moon called Dysnomia. This dwarf planet is about 1,500 mi (2,414 km) in diameter, has an extremely eccentric orbit, and takes about 560 years to complete one revolution around the Sun. It was discovered by astronomers Mike

FIGURE 6–14 An image of the dwarf planet Ceres taken by the Hubble Space Telescope. (*Courtesy of NASA.*)

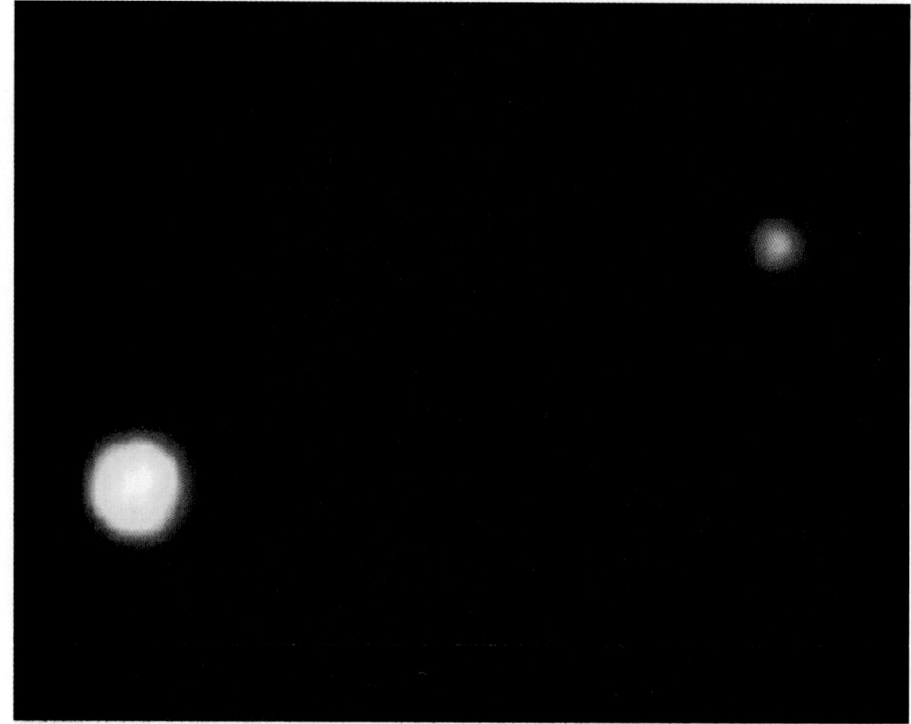

FIGURE 6–15 An image of the dwarf planet Pluto and its moon, Charon. (*Courtesy of NASA/NSSDC.*)

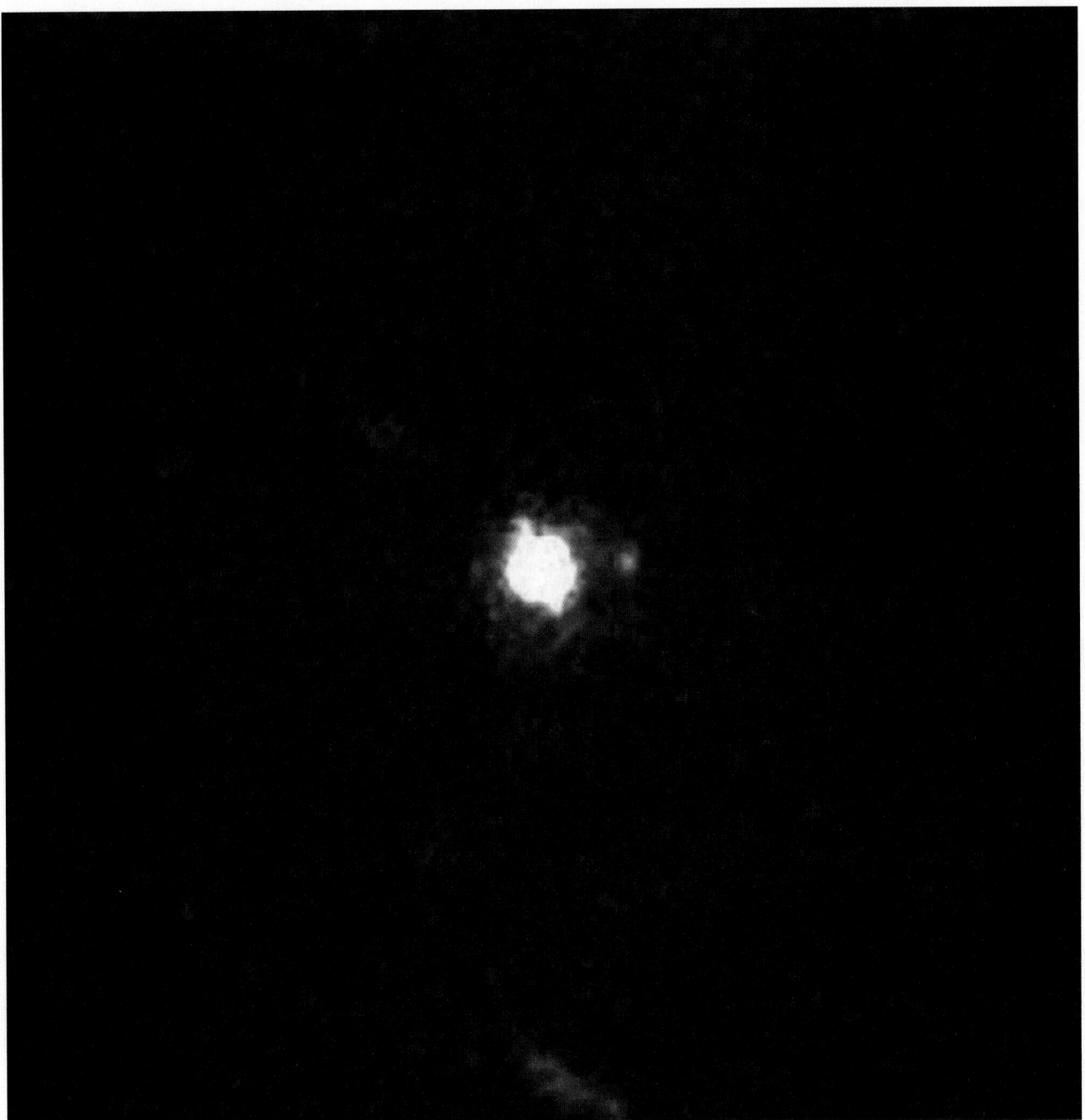

FIGURE 6-16 An image of the dwarf planet Eris and its moon Dysnomina, taken by the Keck Observatory. (*Courtesy of M.E. Brown, W.M. Keck Observatory.*)

Brown, Chad Trujillo, and David Rabinowitz using the Mount Palomar Observatory in California (Figure 6–16). Table 6–1 summarizes information about all the planets in our solar system.

SMALL SOLAR SYSTEM BODIES

A **small solar system body** is a category of celestial objects orbiting the Sun that are not classified as planets, dwarf planets, or moons. This includes objects known as asteroids, meteors, comets, and some transneptunian objects.

TABLE 6–1 Solar system data table

Object	Mean Distance from Sun (millions of km)	Period of Revolution	Period of Rotation	Eccentricity of Orbit	Equatorial Diameter (km)	Mass (Earth = 1)	Density (g/cm^3)	Number of Moons
Sun	—	—	27 days	—	1,392,000	333,000.00	1.4	—
Mercury	57.9	88 days	59 days	0.206	4,880	0.553	5.4	0
Venus	108.2	224.7 days	243 days	0.007	12,104	0.815	5.2	0
Earth	149.6	365.26 days	23 hr 56 min 4 sec	0.017	12,756	1.00	5.5	1
Mars	227.9	687 days	24 hr 37 min 23 sec	0.093	6,787	0.1074	3.9	2
Ceres (dwarf planet)	413.9	4.6 years	9 hr 5 min	0.080	933	0.00035	2.1	1
Jupiter	778.3	11.86 years	9 hr 50 min 30 sec	0.048	142,800	317.896	1.3	61
Saturn	1,427	29.46 years	10 hr 14 min	0.056	120,000	95.185	0.7	30
Uranus	2,869	84.0 years	17 hr 14 min	0.047	51,800	14.537	1.2	21
Neptune	4,496	164.8 years	16 hr	0.009	49,500	17.151	1.7	8
Pluto (dwarf planet)	5,900	247.7 years	6 days 9 hr	0.250	2,300	0.0025	2.0	1
Eris (dwarf planet)	10,127.8	556.7 years	8 hr	0.442	2,500	?	?	1
Earth's Moon	149.6 (0.386 from Earth)	27.3 days	27 days 8 hr	0.055	3,476	0.0123	3.3	—

ASTEROIDS

Lying between Mars and Jupiter is a region of our solar system known as the **asteroid belt**. This area is filled with a debris field of rocky **asteroids** that also orbit the Sun between a distance of 2.2 and 3.3 AU from the center of the solar system. Asteroids are the rocky remains of the solar system's formation (Figure 6–17). There may be thousands of asteroids in the asteroid belt that range in size from a small car to more than 600 miles (966 km) in diameter. Some of the largest asteroids in this region include Vesta, Pallas, and Hygeia.

Not all asteroids lie within the asteroid belt. Some are located inside the orbit of the Earth around the Sun; these are called Aten asteroids. One of the largest asteroids ever discovered, Chiron, orbits

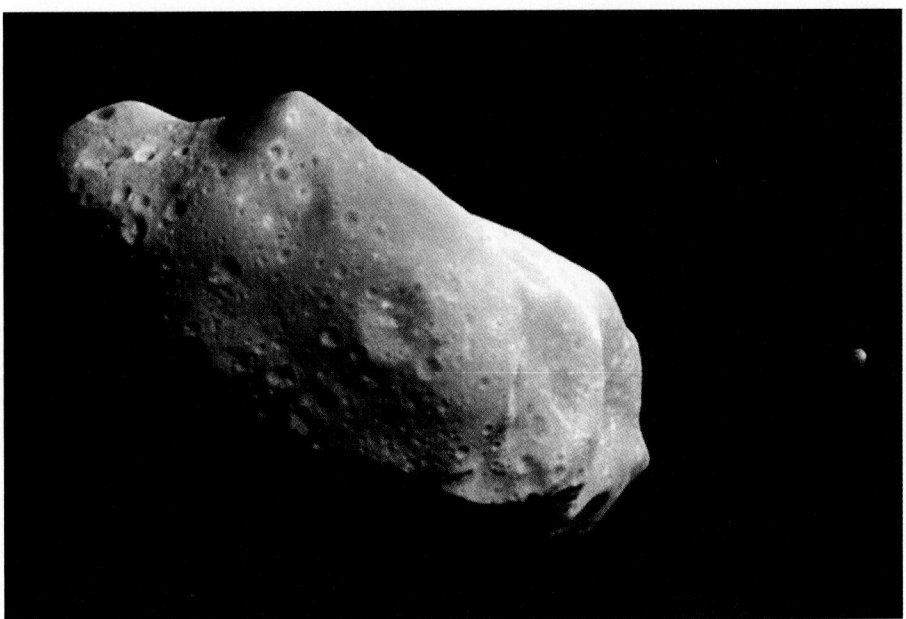

FIGURE 6-17 An image of the cratered surface of an asteroid. (*Courtesy of NASA/NSSDC.*)

the Sun near the planet Jupiter. This large asteroid is estimated to be more than 248 mi (399 km) in diameter. Some asteroids are classified by their ability to cross the Earth's orbit. These are a concern to astronomers because they have the potential to strike the Earth's surface. This class of asteroids is known as Apollo asteroids. Researchers estimate that there are between 300 and 700 of this type of asteroid. Most Apollo asteroids are no larger than 3,000 ft (914 m) in diameter. In 1989 Asteroid 1989 FC passed within 430,000 mi (692,017 km) of the Earth, which is the closest an asteroid has come to the Earth so far. Astronomers estimate that an asteroid strikes the Earth once every 2,000 years. The last recorded strike by a celestial object occurred in 1908 over Northern Siberia in Asia. This event, known as the Tunguska blast, happened in an extremely remote region of Russia. The object exploded above the Earth's surface and leveled thousands of acres of trees. This explosion did not leave an impact crater behind and might have been a comet instead of an asteroid.

METEOROIDS

Smaller chunks of rock that are located in the solar system are called **meteoroids, meteors,** and **meteorites.** Meteoroids are fast-moving chunks of rock that travel through space at high velocities. These rocks are the remains of the early solar system, comets, and fragments of our own Moon and nearby planets. These objects range in size from tiny grains of sand to large boulders. When a meteoroid's orbit crosses that of Earth, it may burn up in the atmosphere, creating a meteor, also known as a shooting star (Figure 6–18). It is estimated that more than 1,000 tons of meteoroid material rains down on the Earth every day! Meteors that make it all the way to the Earth's surface are called meteorites. Meteorites are grouped into three categories based on their composition.

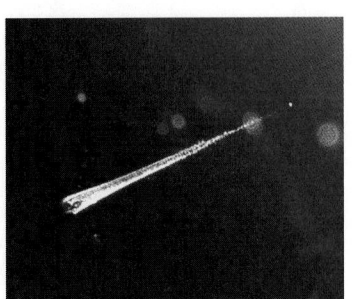

FIGURE 6-18 An image of a meteor burning up as it enters the Earth's atmosphere. (*Courtesy of ESA, NASA.*)

Stony meteorites are composed of silicate rock material. Iron meteorites are composed of an iron-nickel alloy and are very dense. Stony-iron meteorites are composed of a mixture of silicate rock and iron.

During certain times of the year, many meteors enter the Earth's atmosphere at once. These events are called **meteor showers**. Many meteor showers are associated with the debris left behind by a comet as it orbits around the Sun. The Perseid meteor shower occurs around the middle of August every year, when the Earth's orbit passes through the debris of comet 1862 III. During the height of this periodic meteor shower, on average a meteor enters the atmosphere once every minute. The largest iron meteorite found on the Earth fell in Southwest Africa and weighed more than 119,000 lb (53,977 kg). The largest stony meteorite fell in Kansas in the United States and weighed approximately 2,200 lb (998 kg). Many meteorites are found on the ice fields of Antarctica, where they are easily visible.

In 1984 a team of meteorite hunters found a stony meteorite that probably came from the planet Mars. After careful analysis, this meteorite, called ALH 840001, was determined to have been a piece of the Martian surface that was launched into space by an asteroid impact with the planet approximately 16 million years ago. This Martian rock then entered the Earth's atmosphere and landed on Antarctica as a meteorite approximately 13,000 years ago. Most fascinating about this meteorite is what was found inside it. Scientists have found what they believe are the fossil remains of bacteria inside of the meteorite. If this is the case, it would be the first known example of life existing elsewhere in the solar system.

COMETS

Comets are celestial objects that are composed of rock and ice that orbit the Sun. Once referred to as dirty snowballs, these objects are unique in their appearance among the heavens. A comet consists of three parts: nucleus, coma, and tail (Figure 6–19). A comet's nucleus is the rock and ice portion of the comet, which can range in size from half a mile to 6 mi (9.7 km) in diameter. The nucleus of a comet is composed of rock and icy chunks of water, methane, carbon dioxide, and ammonia. The coma surrounds the nucleus and is composed of the dust and gas that was once held within the nucleus. The coma can be

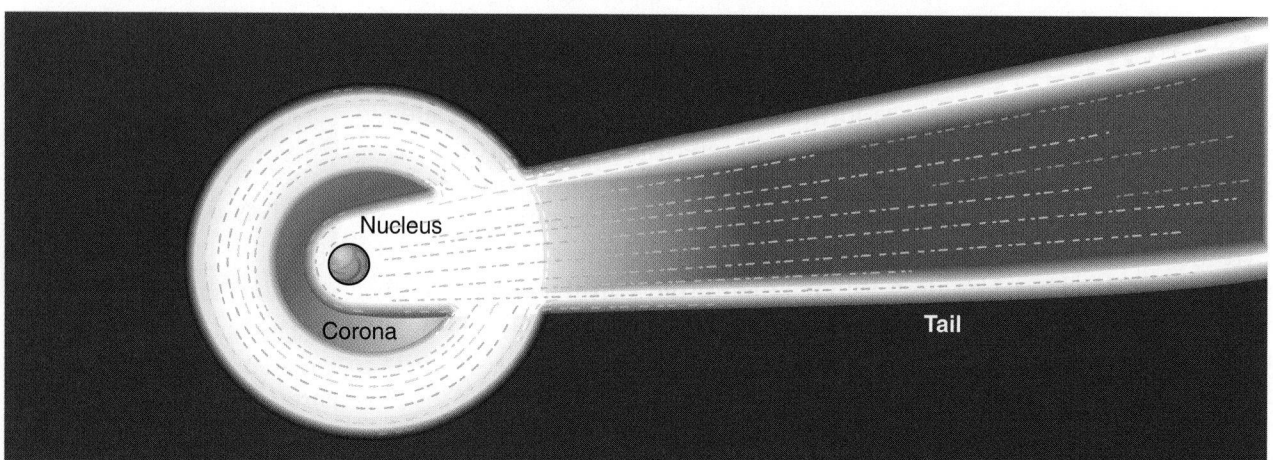

FIGURE 6–19   The parts of a comet.

extremely large, sometimes reaching the size of the planet Jupiter. Behind the comet lies the comet's tail. This is a stream of ionized gas blown away from the coma by the solar wind. The tail always points away from the Sun, as the solar wind interacts with the gas and dust of the comet. Comets are believed to be another remnant of the solar system's formation. Most comets come from a region at the edge of the solar system called the **Oort cloud**. The Oort cloud is located about 100,000 AU from the Sun and might contain as many as 1 trillion comets. Comets probably leave the Oort cloud as a result of the gravity from nearby stars and galaxies disturbing their orbits. Another source region for comets in the solar system could be just outside Pluto's orbit. This area, known as the Kuiper belt, might contain billions of comets.

There are two main types of comets, which are classified based on their period of revolution around the Sun. Long-period comets take an extremely long time to orbit the Sun, such as 30 million years. Short-period comets orbit the sun in periods less than 200 years. The famous Halley's comet takes 76 years to make one complete orbit around the Sun. This comet was last seen in 1986 and will be visible again on Earth in the year 2061. Some short-period comets move at much faster orbits around the Sun. Many of these comets take only 3 to 14 years to complete one orbit. In July 1994 the comet Shoemaker-Levy 9 collided with Jupiter, creating an incredible opportunity to see the effects of a comet impact with the massive planet.

CURRENT RESEARCH

Extrasolar Planets

As science and technology increase our ability to observe celestial objects, astronomers are now looking beyond our own solar system for planets similar to the Earth that also might support life. Up until recent times the only objects discovered outside of the solar system were stars and galaxies. Although there was no proof, scientists believed that the existence of other planets that orbit stars similar to our Sun was very likely. The development of new, more powerful scientific instruments has now enabled astronomers to verify the existence of extrasolar planets. The first extrasolar planet discovered orbiting around a star like the Sun was made by two Swiss astronomers in 1995. Since then scientists have discovered more than 190 extrasolar planets. Because of the great distances that exist between stars, most of these planets are believed to be massive gas giants like Saturn and Jupiter. Smaller terrestrial planets like the Earth are much harder to locate and observe over these vast distances. This soon might change with the creation of NASA's Planet Quest initiative. Planet Quest will be made up of a series of missions and the deployment of technology over the next 15 years, which scientists will use to try and discover Earth-like extrasolar planets. New, more powerful instruments like the Keck and Large Binocular Interferometers, along with the Kepler and Spitzer Space telescopes, and the Terrestrial Planet Finder observatories will allow astronomers to locate, observe, and study extrasolar planets. This important research will hopefully reveal the answer to one of the most pressing questions in astronomy: Is there life elsewhere in the universe?

WEB Links

FOR MORE INFORMATION GO TO THESE WEB LINKS:

<http://www.nineplanets.org/>

<http://pds.jpl.nasa.gov/planets/>

<http://www.nationalgeographic.com/solarsystem/>

<http://www.gps.caltech.edu/~mbrown/planetlila/>

<http://planetquest.jpl.nasa.gov/index.cfm>

SECTION REVIEW

1. What is the solar system, and how long ago did it form?
2. What are terrestrial planets, and how many are there in the solar system?
3. List all the terrestrial planets.
4. What are the gaseous planets, and how many are there in the solar system?
5. List all the gaseous planets.
6. What are dwarf planets, and how many are there in the solar system?
7. List all the dwarf planets.
8. Which two moons in the solar system are scientists eager to study, and why?
9. What is an asteroid, and where do most of them originate?
10. What is the difference between a meteoroid, a meteor, and a meteorite?
11. What are the three types of meteorites?
12. What is a comet, and where do they originate?
13. Who was Copernicus?

earth math

1) How many miles away is the Oort cloud located from the Sun?

2) If Jupiter has a diameter that is approximately 11.21 times greater than the Earth and the Earth's diameter is approximately 7,926 miles, determine the approximate diameter of Jupiter.

6.2 The Earth's Place in the Universe

GALAXIES

When peering up at the nighttime sky with the unaided eye, it appears that it is filled with thousands of stars. However, not all these objects look like the pinpoints of light that are characteristic of stars. When viewed through a telescope, much of what we thought were stars actually appear as bright fuzzy objects. These are known as galaxies. A **galaxy** is a grouping of millions or billions of individual stars that are located millions of light years from the Earth (Figure 6–20). French astronomer Charles Messier was the first scientist to begin to catalog these amazing objects that he called Messier objects. In 1758 he discovered the first of these, known as M1 or Messier 1, also called the Crab Nebula.

FIGURE 6–20 An image showing a cluster of galaxies in the constellation of Hydra. (© *Anglo-Australian Observatory. Photograph by David Malin.*)

Earth System Scientists

Edwin Hubble

Edwin Hubble was an American astronomer who was born in 1889. He began his career as an astronomer by attending the University of Chicago. After serving in the United States Army during World War I, he became the astronomer for the Mount Wilson Observatory in Pasadena, California, where he spent the rest of his career. There he began to research stellar nebulae and other objects outside our own galaxy. His work led to the classification of galaxies, the study of their speed, and their particular direction of movement. This led him to develop Hubble's law, which stated that the more distant a galaxy, the greater its speed. Hubble also developed the Hubble constant, which was the ratio of a galaxy's speed to its distance. His work led to the understanding that all objects in the universe are moving away from a central point. Using Hubble's observations, astronomers can now estimate the approximate age of the universe. Hubble died in 1953. He will forever be linked to the advancement of our knowledge of the universe and to the famous space telescope that today bears his name.

When viewed with very powerful telescopes, galaxies are revealed to be some of the most beautiful objects in space.

There are three main types of galaxies: spirals, elliptical, and irregular. A spiral galaxy appears much like a rotating pinwheel. At the center of a spiral galaxy is the nucleus, which is surrounded by many spiral arms. The nucleus of a spiral galaxy appears like a large bulge of

FIGURE 6–21   An image of the M51 spiral galaxy. (*Courtesy of T.A. Rector and Monica Ramirez/NOAO/AURA/NSF.*)

light, also called a halo, that is composed of millions of stars. Large groups of stars that surround the halo make up a globular cluster. The outlying spiral arms are also composed of stars that all rotate around the central nucleus (Figure 6–21).

The solar system is located in a spiral galaxy called the **Milky Way**. The solar system's location in the Milky Way galaxy is in one of the spiral arms, about halfway from the galactic center. The solar system revolves around the center of the Milky Way galaxy at approximately 136 miles per second (219 kilometers per second). The Milky Way galaxy is approximately 100,000 light years in diameter, and contains billions of individual stars. Many of these stars are similar to our Sun. All of the stars that fill the nighttime sky are in the Milky Way galaxy (Figure 6–22).

Many astronomers believe there is a black hole at the center of our galaxy. The Milky Way is part of group of galaxies that is known as the Local Group. The Local Group contains approximately 27 galaxies, including another spiral galaxy called M31 or the Andromeda galaxy, which is the closest galaxy to the Earth. This galaxy is located approximately 2 million light years from the Earth.

Elliptical galaxies are galaxies that have a nucleus and a halo of stars but no spiral arms. These galaxies can range in size from 300,000 light years or more in diameter, to only a few thousand light years across. The smaller elliptical galaxies are known as dwarf elliptical. Astronomers believe that elliptical galaxies are the most common type of galaxy found in the universe (Figure 6–23).

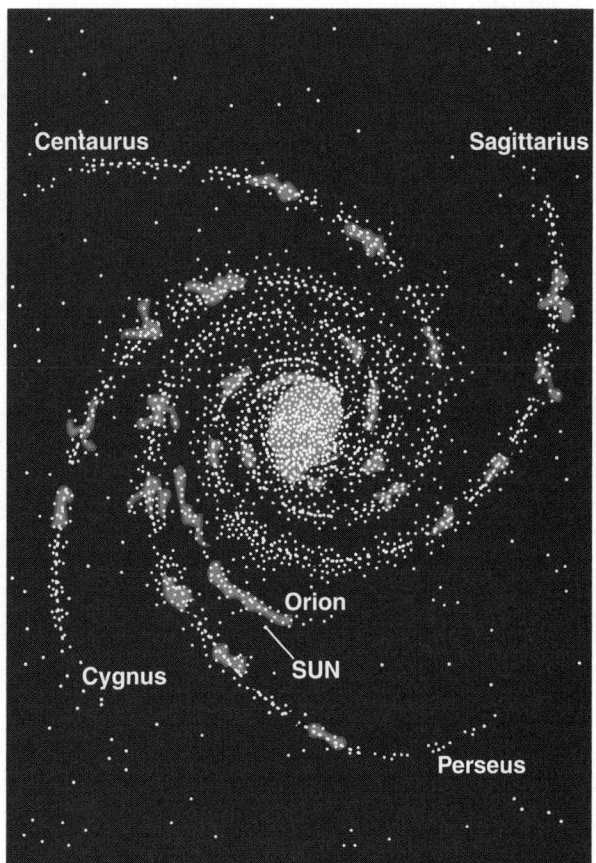

FIGURE 6-22 The location of the solar system within the Milky Way galaxy, near the center of one of its spiral arms.

FIGURE 6-23 An image of the elliptical galaxy M87. (*Courtesy of NOAO/AURA/NSF.*)

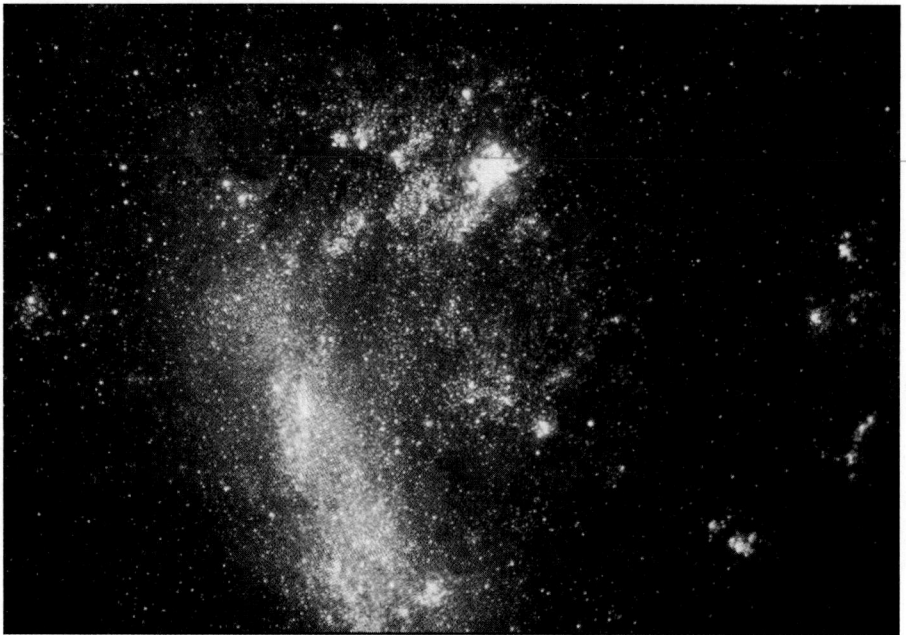

FIGURE 6–24 An image of an irregular galaxy called the Large Magellanic Cloud. (*Courtesy of NOAO/AURA/NSF.*)

The third type of galaxy is called the irregular galaxy. These galaxies have no well-defined shape. An example of an irregular galaxy is the Large Magellanic Cloud, which is the closest galaxy to the solar system. The Large Magellanic Cloud is approximately 175,000 light years away from Earth (Figure 6–24). Galaxies are believed to be well distributed throughout the universe. Astronomers estimate that there might be a billion galaxies in the universe, with each galaxy made up of over one billion stars!

QUASARS

Besides galaxies, another structure is found out on the edges of the universe. These objects are called **quasars**. Quasars are faint clouds of light that are racing away from the center of the universe at incredible speeds. These objects are the farthest objects ever discovered. Quasars get their name from the term *quasi stellar radio sources* because many of them were discovered to emit radio waves. Some quasars are moving away from the Earth at incredible speeds of almost 90 percent of the speed of light! These are indeed the fastest objects yet discovered in the universe. Quasars also emit incredible amounts of energy, which is more than 100 times the amount of energy released by the entire Milky Way galaxy. Astronomers believe that quasars may get their energy from extremely large black holes located at their centers. To create the energy emitted from a quasar, these black holes would have to be one billion times larger than our own sun!

LIFE IN THE UNIVERSE

The brilliant objects that make up the universe, the stars, galaxies, and quasars are amazing, to say the least. Although these objects have been studied, there still are many questions about the nature of the universe.

Earth System Scientists

Carl Sagan

Carl Sagan was an American astronomer who devoted his life to the study of astronomy and to sharing his love and knowledge of the universe with the general public. Sagan began his career in astronomy by obtaining his doctorate from the University of Chicago in 1960. In 1968 he took up the position of Director of Planetary Studies and eventually became the David Duncan Professor of Astronomy and Space Science at Cornell University. His early work involved research of the planet Venus, which revealed its hostile surface temperatures and physical features. His work also showed that Venus was experiencing a runaway greenhouse effect, which caused its high surface temperatures, and also resulted from increased levels of carbon dioxide gas in its atmosphere. Sagan also co-founded the Planetary Society, which has become the largest space interest group in the world. In 1980 he produced and starred in the famous television series *Cosmos*, which helped present the science of astronomy to the general public. His work also included the search for the origins of life on Earth and the possibility of life elsewhere in the universe. This began the science of exobiology. In the 1970s he helped to design a series of plaques and records that were attached to the Pioneer 10 and Voyager spacecraft. They contained a message from Earth to possible extraterrestrial beings. During his life he published eight books, one of which won the Pulitzer Prize. Sagan died in 1996, leaving behind a legacy of a life devoted to the search for understanding the universe and humanity's place within it.

Probably the most pressing of these questions asks if there are other planets in the universe like our own Earth. Recent discoveries have revealed that some stars in our own galaxies are being orbited by planets. This discovery suggests that all stars might indeed have their own planetary systems. If this is true, could some of these planets support life? The size and scale of the universe suggests that there could be millions of planets like our own Earth. If so, then it would be possible that some of these planets do harbor life. As one astronomer stated, "If the Earth were the only place in the universe to support life, what a great waste of space!" The distances between stars, however, are so great that we might never be able to visit or even communicate with planets outside of our own solar system. The distance between the stars in the Milky Way is so vast that even the speed of light seems slow. For example, if there was intelligent life on a planet orbiting the closest star to the Earth, Proxima Centauri, it would take 4.2 years to send them a message. Their reply would then take another 4.2 years. In total, the time it would take for us just to say, "Hello, we are here!" And for them to reply "So are we!" would take more than eight years! And this is for a star that is close to the Earth. Many stars are much farther away. Even with these vast distances, researchers are searching the universe for radio signals or laser pulses that might indicate intelligent life on other planets. This field of research is known as the SETI program, or Search for Extraterrestrial Intelligence.

COSMOLOGY

The universe is defined as the total amount of volume in which all energy and matter exist. The study of how the universe formed, how big it is, its shape, how it has changed over time, and what will happen to it in the future is called cosmology. The science of cosmology relies upon the assumption that the physical laws that govern basic processes in the solar system like gravity, electromagnetic radiation, and matter are the same throughout the universe. This allows scientists to infer what is occurring at different locations throughout the universe, what happened in the past, and what the future might hold. The foundation of modern cosmology is the theory known as the Big Bang. This widely accepted theory explains that the universe formed between 10 and 13 billion years ago from one colossal explosion. This single event is where all of the matter and energy that make up the universe today is believed to have come from. Scientists have made many important observations to support this theory. In 1929, the American astronomer Edwin Hubble used spectral analysis to observe the emission spectrum of light coming from distant galaxies. Hubble's discoveries would change human understanding of the universe. He saw that the unique spectral lines for common elements like hydrogen were not located in the correct positions that they should occupy within a bright line spectrum. Recall from Chapter 3 that each substance has its own unique spectral signature, which can be used to identify it. Hubble was puzzled by these inconsistencies until he realized what was causing the spectral lines of galaxies to be shifted—the Doppler Effect. The Doppler Effect is named for Christian Doppler, an Austrian scientist who in 1842 published a theory regarding the changing wavelengths of light or sound as a result of their motion relative to an observer. A simple example of the Doppler Effect is the change in pitch of sound coming from a siren on a fire truck that rapidly passes by an observer. As the fire truck quickly approaches the observer, sound waves emitted from the siren are compressed slightly by the truck's forward motion. This crowding up of sound waves coming from the siren reduces their wavelength, which causes the pitch of the siren to rise. As the fire truck passes by, and is now traveling away from the observer, the sound waves emitted from the siren are stretched somewhat by the quickly receding truck. The wavelengths of sound are now slightly elongated, which therefore causes the pitch of the siren to lower. This same principle can be observed for any moving vehicle that is emitting sound as it passes by an observer at high velocity (Figure 6–25).

Hubble used the Doppler Effect to explain the shift he observed in the wavelengths of light coming from distance galaxies. His observations discovered that the light of most all galaxies was shifted toward the red end of the visible spectrum. This is known as a red shift. A red shift occurs when the motion of a celestial object moving away from an observer causes the wavelengths of light in a bright line spectrum to be increased slightly. This motion causes their spectral lines to shift toward the red end of the visible light spectrum, as the wavelength is increased (Figure 6–26).

Recall from Chapter 2 that the wavelength of visible light increases as you move from the blue end towards the red end of the visible light portion of the electromagnetic spectrum. Once Hubble

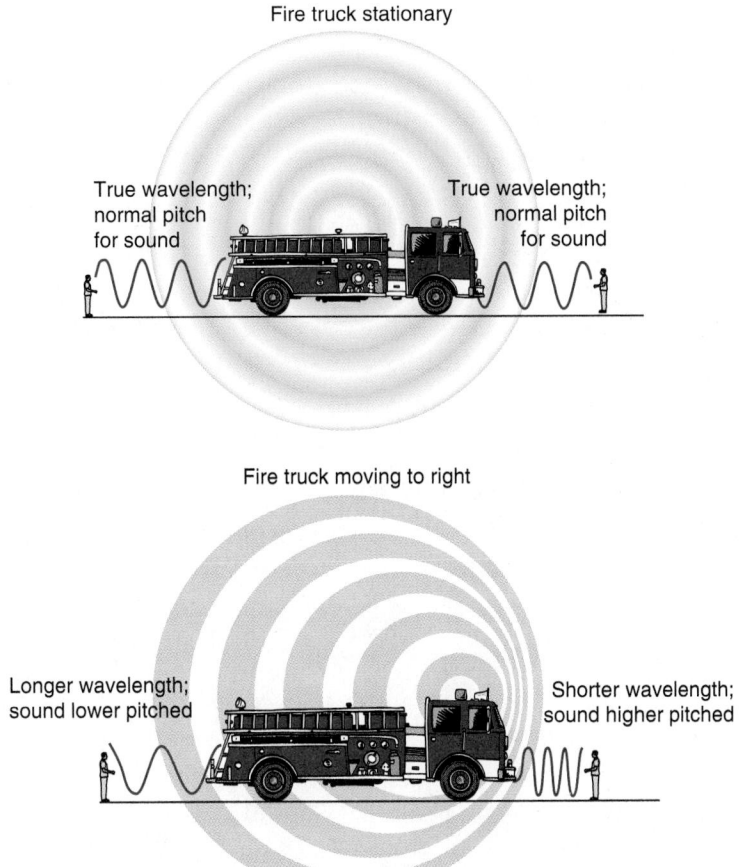

FIGURE 6–25   An example of the Doppler Effect as applied to sound.

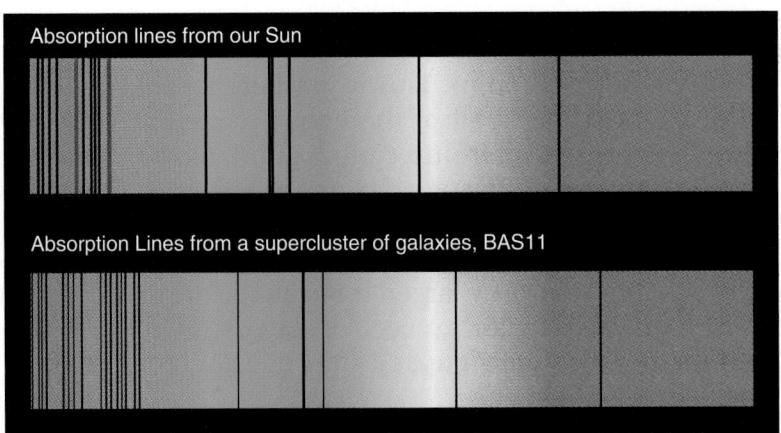

FIGURE 6–26   The shift in the spectral lines of the light emitted from a galaxy that is moving away from the Earth is known as a red shift.

realized what his observations meant, he continued to perform spectral analysis on more galaxies. His continued observations brought him to only one conclusion, that the universe must be expanding. Hubble's work laid the foundation for the Big Bang theory. It revealed that if the universe is currently expanding, then at one time in the past, all the galaxies, and therefore all matter and energy, must have

FIGURE 6–27   An image of Orion A, a giant molecular cloud. (*Courtesy of T.A. Rector, B. Wolpa, G. Jacoby, AURA, NOAO, NSF.*)

come from one central point. This event became known as the Big Bang. This event released all of the known energy in the universe, which began to spread out from a central point. As the energy created from the Big Bang began to spread wider, it began to cool and create clumps of matter. This was in the form of elements such as hydrogen and helium. Eventually as energy and matter continued to spread apart and the universe grew larger, it began to form random clumps of dust and gas called giant molecular clouds (Figure 6–27). These clouds of matter eventually created stars and the galaxies that comprise them.

Hubble's work also allowed scientists to calculate how long ago the Big Bang occurred, and therefore how old the universe is. Observations of the distances of galaxies from one another and the velocity at which they are moving can be used to determine how long it took for them to get to their present positions. Using this information, along with other observations, scientists believe the universe is approximately 10–14 billion years old. Another observation used to support the Big Bang has to do with the violent explosion that occurred at the birth of the universe. The extremely hot temperatures that must have existed at the time of the Big Bang left behind traces of its existence known as Cosmic Background Radiation. The intense heat that was generated at the

FIGURE 6–28 A map of the Cosmic Background Radiation created by the Big Bang. (*Courtesy of Wilkinson Microwave Anistrophy Probe (WMAP) NASA.*)

time of the big bang sent electromagnetic radiation out into space. In 1965, Arno Penzias and Robert Wilson first detected this radiation using a microwave receiver. Their discovery was awarded the Nobel Prize for physics and became more proof to support the Big Bang theory. More recently, NASA has used the Wilkinson Microwave Anisotropy Probe to make accurate maps of the Cosmic Background Radiation (Figure 6–28). Knowing today that the universe is expanding, scientists are turning their attention to what will happen to the universe in the future. Currently there are three possibilities for the fate of the universe. This first is called the closed universe model. This model predicts that the gravitational attraction of all matter in the universe will cause its expansion to slow down, eventually stop, and then to cause it to collapse in on itself. This will lead to what is called the Big Crunch. The closed universe model predicts that the universe will continue to expand and contract indefinitely, therefore continually creating and destroying itself. Another theory of the universe is called the open model. This predicts that the expansion of the universe will continue, causing galaxies to continue to move farther and farther away form one another. The third idea is called the flat universe model. This predicts that the universal expansion will slowly decline over vast period of time to almost a steady state.

SECTION REVIEW

1. How old is the universe estimated to be, and what event began the universe as we know it?

2. What is a galaxy, and what are the three types of galaxies?

3. What is the name of the galaxy in which the solar system is located, and what type of galaxy is it?

4. What is the approximate size of our galaxy?

5. How many galaxies are believed to exist in the universe?

6. Which galaxy is closest to our own galaxy, and how far away is it?

7. What is a quasar?

8. Who were Edwin Hubble and Carl Sagan?

CAREER CONNECTIONS

Exobiologist

An exobiologist studies the possibilities of life existing somewhere else in the universe other than on Earth. Exobiology closely resembles traditional biology but applies its knowledge of life processes to other planets, moons, or in space. Today an exobiologist studies how life might exist on other worlds and what types of life might be found there. A branch of exobiology also studies how living organisms from Earth survive in the microgravity of space. Many exobiologists are interested in studying life on Earth that can withstand extreme environments. Organisms like bacteria found living in hot springs and deep in the ice and rock of Antarctica are of special interest to exobiologists. If these organisms can survive in these harsh environments on Earth, then similar organisms might exist elsewhere in our solar system. Someday in the near future exobiologists might travel to Mars or to Jupiter's moon Europa to search for life. Exobiologists require a college education in biology and planetary science and can find work in the academic fields or with NASA.

@ WEB Links

FOR MORE INFORMATION GO TO THESE WEB LINKS:

<http://csep10.phys.utk.edu/astr162/lect/index.html>

<http://csep10.phys.utk.edu/astr161/lect/index.html>

earth math

1) If the fastest quasar is moving at 90 percent of the speed of light and the speed of light is 186,000 miles per second, determine how fast this quasar is moving away from the center of the universe.

2) Using the speed you determined for the fastest quasar in question 1, how long would it take for a quasar to travel from the Earth to the Sun? The distance from the Earth to the Sun is approximately 93 million miles.

CHAPTER SUMMARY

The solar system is a group of celestial objects that all orbit around a central star called the Sun. A celestial object includes any object that is outside the Earth's atmosphere. The celestial objects that together make up the solar system include planets, moons, asteroids, comets, and meteoroids. There are eight planets in the solar system, which are divided into two categories, the terrestrial planets and the gas giants. Terrestrial planets are composed mainly of rock, and orbit closest to the Sun. These include Mercury, Venus, Earth, and Mars. The gas giants are large planets composed mainly of gases. These planets orbit farther from the Sun and include Jupiter, Saturn, Uranus, and Neptune. Each planet has its own unique physical features; Earth is the only known planet in the solar system that supports life. Many planets are orbited by a moon or moons. Dwarf planets are smaller celestial objects that orbit the Sun. They currently include Ceres, Pluto, and Eris. Small solar system bodies include Trans-neptunian objects, asteroids, meteors, and comets.

Asteroids are large chunks of rock that orbit the Sun. Many asteroids are believed to originate in the asteroid belt, which is located between the orbits of Mars and Jupiter. Meteoroids are smaller chunks of rock that travel through space at high speeds and occasionally enter the Earth's atmosphere. These are commonly known as shooting stars. Comets also exist in the solar system; they are composed of frozen compounds that surround a rocky core. As a comet orbits around the Sun, the solar wind vaporizes its frozen compounds and sends them trailing off into space, forming their characteristic tail.

The solar system is part of a large group of stars that together form the Milky Way galaxy. A galaxy is an extremely large cluster of stars. Millions of galaxies exist in the universe. The universe is believed to have begun approximately 10 to 13 billion years ago with an event called the big bang. All the stars and galaxies in the universe appear to be traveling away from one central point as a result of the big bang. The most distant objects ever detected in space are bright, high-energy quasars. These celestial objects are believed to be traveling near the speed of light.

CHAPTER REVIEW

Multiple Choice

1. Which of the following is not part of the solar system?
   a. the Sun
   b. the Milky Way
   c. the Moon
   d. comets

2. The planets that orbit closest to the Sun are also known as:
   a. gas giants
   b. elliptical
   c. irregular
   d. terrestrial

3. The planets that are the largest and orbit farthest from the Sun are also known as:
   a. gas giants
   b. elliptical
   c. irregular
   d. terrestrial

4. Which of the following planets is one third the size of the Earth and has no atmosphere?
   a. Jupiter
   b. Mars
   c. Venus
   d. Mercury

5. Which of the following planets is approximately the same size of the Earth and has an atmosphere containing mostly carbon dioxide?
   a. Jupiter
   b. Mars
   c. Venus
   d. Mercury

6. Which of the following planets is believed to have once contained flowing liquid water?
   a. Jupiter
   b. Mars
   c. Venus
   d. Mercury

7. Which of the following planets contains a giant hurricane the size of three Earths?
   a. Neptune
   b. Pluto
   c. Jupiter
   d. Saturn

8. Which of the following planets contains a highly visible ring system?
   a. Uranus
   b. Pluto
   c. Jupiter
   d. Saturn

9. Which of the following planets has an axis of rotation that is tilted 90 degrees?
   a. Uranus
   b. Pluto
   c. Jupiter
   d. Saturn

10. Which of the following is located between the orbits of Mars and Jupiter?
    a. Oort cloud
    b. Halley's comet
    c. asteroid belt
    d. Perseid showers

11. What celestial object is also called a "dirty snowball"?
    a. asteroid
    b. comet
    c. meteoroid
    d. gas giant

12. Approximately how long ago do astronomers believe the Big Bang occurred?
    a. 20 billion years ago
    b. 10 billion years ago
    c. 5 billion years ago
    d. 4.5 billion years ago

13. What type of galaxy is the Milky Way?
    a. irregular
    b. spiral
    c. elliptical
    d. circular

14. The solar system is located in what part of the Milky Way galaxy?
    a. near the center
    b. in the middle of one of its arms
    c. between two arms
    d. on the outside edge

15. What are the fastest-moving celestial objects discovered so far in the universe?
    a. quasars
    b. galaxies
    c. meteoroids
    d. pulsars

Matching   *Match the terms with the correct definitions.*

a. planet
b. terrestrial planet
c. gas giant
d. meteor
e. moon

f. asteroid belt
g. asteroid
h. meteoroids
i. meteorites
j. meteor shower

k. comet
l. Oort cloud
m. galaxy
n. Milky Way
o. quasars

1. _____ A very high energy celestial object believed to be a type of galaxy, which is rapidly moving away from the center of the universe.
2. _____ An object that is orbiting the Sun, is smaller than a planet, and has no atmosphere.
3. _____ Small chunks of rock, no larger than a few feet in diameter, that travel through space.
4. _____ The name for the galaxy of stars in which the solar system is located.
5. _____ A meteor that does not burn up in the atmosphere and strikes the Earth's surface.
6. _____ A large grouping of stars.
7. _____ An event that describes a group of meteors entering into and burning up in the Earth's atmosphere.
8. _____ A hypothetical area that is located approximately 100,000 AU from the orbit of Pluto, where comets are believed to originate.
9. _____ A mixture of frozen compounds and rock that orbits the Sun; its distinct tail, composed of vaporized gas and dust, always points away from the Sun.
10. _____ A region in the solar system located between the orbits of Mars and Jupiter, where there are a high number of asteroids.
11. _____ A large celestial object that orbits around a star.
12. _____ The name for any large celestial body that orbits around a planet.
13. _____ A planet that is mostly composed of rock.
14. _____ A small chunk of rock, no larger than a few feet in diameter, that is traveling through space and enters the Earth's atmosphere, commonly known as a shooting star.
15. _____ A classification of planets that are extremely large and are composed mainly of gases.

Critical Thinking

1. Most all astronomers believe that life may exist elsewhere in the universe. Why do you think they have come to this conclusion?

The Lithosphere

UNIT

3

OVERVIEW

When we study the lithosphere, we are attempting to unlock the secrets of the ground beneath our feet, the mountains that tower over our heads, and the strange world that exists at the bottom of the oceans. Human beings have had a long relationship with the solid Earth. Millions of years ago, our primitive ancestors made the first tools from stone. They found shelter in natural caves, where they also created some of the first known art forms. Today a close relationship still exists with the solid Earth. We mine it to extract building materials and precious stones. We drill into it to search for fossil fuels. We also excavate the solid Earth to search for information about its history and the history of the human race. But what exactly is the solid Earth? Why are there so many different kinds of rocks, and how did they form? Humans have been asking these questions for hundreds if not thousands of years. Even today, geologists are still attempting to unravel the mysteries that lie both deep within the Earth and on its surface. The Earth's lithosphere is complex and dynamic and has a profound effect on how the whole Earth system operates.

Minerals, Rocks, and Mineral Resources

MINERALS OBJECTIVES

Mineral Properties · Mineral Composition · Rocks and Minerals

After reading this section you should be able to:

▶ Define the term *mineral* and describe the physical and chemical properties that are commonly used to identify them.
▶ Describe what generally gives a mineral its unique physical characteristics.
▶ Explain the basic structure of a silicate.

ROCKS OBJECTIVES

Igneous Rocks · Sedimentary Rocks · Metamorphic Rocks · The Rock Cycle

After reading this section you should be able to:

▶ Identify the three main types of rocks found on Earth.
▶ Describe four characteristics used to identify igneous rocks.
▶ Differentiate between extrusive and intrusive rocks.
▶ Differentiate between mafic rocks and felsic rocks.
▶ Describe the processes that lead to the formation of sedimentary rocks.
▶ Describe three characteristics used to identify sedimentary rocks.
▶ Explain the processes that lead to the formation of metamorphic rocks.
▶ Describe three characteristics used to identify metamorphic rocks.
▶ Explain the rock cycle.

MINERAL RESOURCES OBJECTIVES

Mineral Resources · Mineral Ores · Mineral Deposits · Mining Techniques

After reading this section you should be able to:

▶ Define the term *mineral resource* and differentiate between metallic and nonmetallic mineral resources.
▶ Identify the four different processes that form mineral deposits.
▶ Describe three ways in which mineral resources can be removed from the Earth's crust.

INTRODUCTION

The rocks that compose the Earth's crust and cover its landscape hold the secrets of our planet's history. Many geologists regard rocks as history books that tell the tale of the Earth's past environments and geological events. The stories that rocks hold reveal the creation and destruction of mountains and oceans, along with the occurrence of violent events such as volcanic eruptions and asteroid impacts. Learning to read the story that rocks tell involves simple observations of their physical characteristics, which can reveal much about their formation. This can then be used to piece together geological events of the past. The minerals that compose the Earth's rocks have been a fascination of humans for thousands of years. The precious metals and gemstones that are found in rocks are some of the most valued items on Earth. Understanding how these minerals form and what they are composed of provides more insight into the processes that occur within the lithosphere. The technological society in which we live is constructed from the minerals extracted from the lithosphere. Almost everything we use in our everyday lives contains minerals that were mined from the Earth's crust. Building materials, jewelry, automobiles, and most technological machines or devices contain minerals or precious metals taken from the ground. The dependence of human society on the wealth that lies deep within the Earth cannot be overstated; the access to mineral resources provides us the world we live in today.

7.1 Minerals

MINERAL PROPERTIES

The Earth's crust is composed of **minerals**. Minerals are naturally occurring, crystalline, inorganic substances that have unique physical and chemical properties. The definition of a mineral is complex and therefore should be further explored to fully understand what a mineral is. The term *naturally occurring* refers to the process by which a material is formed naturally on the Earth. Minerals are not created by humans; they exist naturally in the Earth. Minerals are also **crystalline**. This means that they are made up from atoms and molecules that are arranged in definite patterns. The term *inorganic* means nonliving, or not formed from a living thing. All minerals are inorganic. Rocks such as amber, for example, are not formed from minerals because amber is the hardened sap from a tree that grew millions of years ago.

Minerals are identified by a series of specific physical and chemical properties that make them unique. The color of a mineral can be used to identify it because some minerals possess unique colors (Figure 7–1). Sulfur is a bright yellow mineral that can be easily identified by its color. Color alone, however, is not sufficient to identify all minerals. This is because many minerals share the same color, such as pyroxine and olivine. These two minerals are both green, making it difficult to identify them by color alone. Other minerals, such as quartz, can come in a range of colors. Rosy quartz is pink, smoky quartz is gray, and some quartz is clear, lacking any color at all.

The *luster* of a mineral is the way that its surface reflects light. Luster is also an identifying characteristic for minerals. Some minerals possess a metallic luster that resembles polished metal. Magnetite has a metallic luster, as does galena (Figure 7–2). Other minerals can be classified as having a glassy luster. The minerals halite and quartz are examples of these because they both appear like transparent glass. Other luster categories include dull, pearly, greasy, and earthy.

The streak of a mineral is the small powder trail that is left behind when a mineral is rubbed against a rough surface (Figure 7–3). Often a

FIGURE 7–1   The various colors of the mineral calcite. (*Courtesy of The Rockdoctor.*)

FIGURE 7–2 The mineral magnetite showing its metallic luster (*Courtesy of Coolrox.com.*)

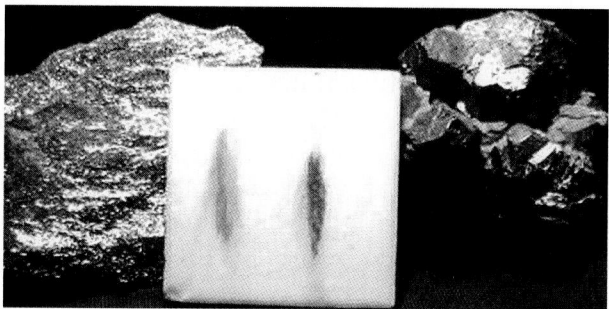

FIGURE 7–3 The characteristic streaks for the minerals hematite and galena. (*Courtesy of The Rockdoctor.*)

white plate made from porcelain, called a streak plate, is used to determine a mineral's streak. Many minerals produce a streak that is different from their overall color. The mineral fluorite, for example, has a light blue-green color, but it produces a white streak when rubbed against a porcelain plate. Some minerals are so hard that they do not produce a streak.

Hardness is the ability of a mineral to resist being scratched; it is often used to identify particular minerals. The Mohs scale of mineral hardness can be used to determine a mineral's hardness (Table 7–1). This measures mineral hardness on a scale from 1 to 10. A mineral hardness of 1 represents an extremely soft mineral, such as talc. Talc can easily be scratched by a fingernail. A harder mineral such as quartz has a hardness of 7 on the scale. It can be used to scratch glass. The hardest of all minerals is represented by a 10 on the hardness scale. A diamond, with a hardness of 10, cannot be scratched by any other mineral.

Cleavage is the tendency for minerals to break apart along specific surfaces or planes. A mineral's crystalline structure determines

TABLE 7–1 Mohs scale of mineral hardness

Mineral	Hardness	Relative Hardness
Graphite	1	Can be scratched by fingernail
Talc	1	
Gypsum	2	
Calcite	3	Can be scratched by copper penny
Flourite	4	Can be scratched by steel
Apatite	5	
Orthoclase	6	Can scratch glass
Quartz	7	
Topaz	8	Can be scratched by quartz
Corundum	9	Can be scratched by topaz
Diamond	10	Hardest of all minerals

how a mineral forms cleavage (Figure 7–4). Minerals such as mica produce cleavage in only one direction. This results in mica's breaking apart into thin sheets. Other minerals show different types of cleavage. Halite, the mineral that forms rock salt, cleaves in three directions or planes. This causes it to always break apart into cubes or rectangles. Calcite is a common mineral that always breaks apart along cleavage planes at 75-degree angles. Minerals that do not have particular cleavage patterns and break apart randomly are called fractured.

Specific gravity is a measure of a mineral's relative density. The density of a mineral is recorded in grams per cubic centimeter. The least dense minerals, such as calcite and talc, have a specific gravity of approximately 3. Hematite and magnetite are more dense and possess a specific gravity of approximately 5. The densest of all minerals is

Earth System Scientists

Friedrich Mohs

Friedrich Mohs was born in Germany in 1773 and was educated at the Freiberg Mining Academy. He spent his life teaching and studying the unique properties of minerals. He continued to teach mining science in Vienna until his death in 1839. Mohs developed a mineral classification system similar to the ones developed for use in biology. To help classify minerals, he created the Mohs scale of hardness, which identifies unique minerals by their ability to be scratched by certain materials. His scale is still widely used today to identify specific minerals.

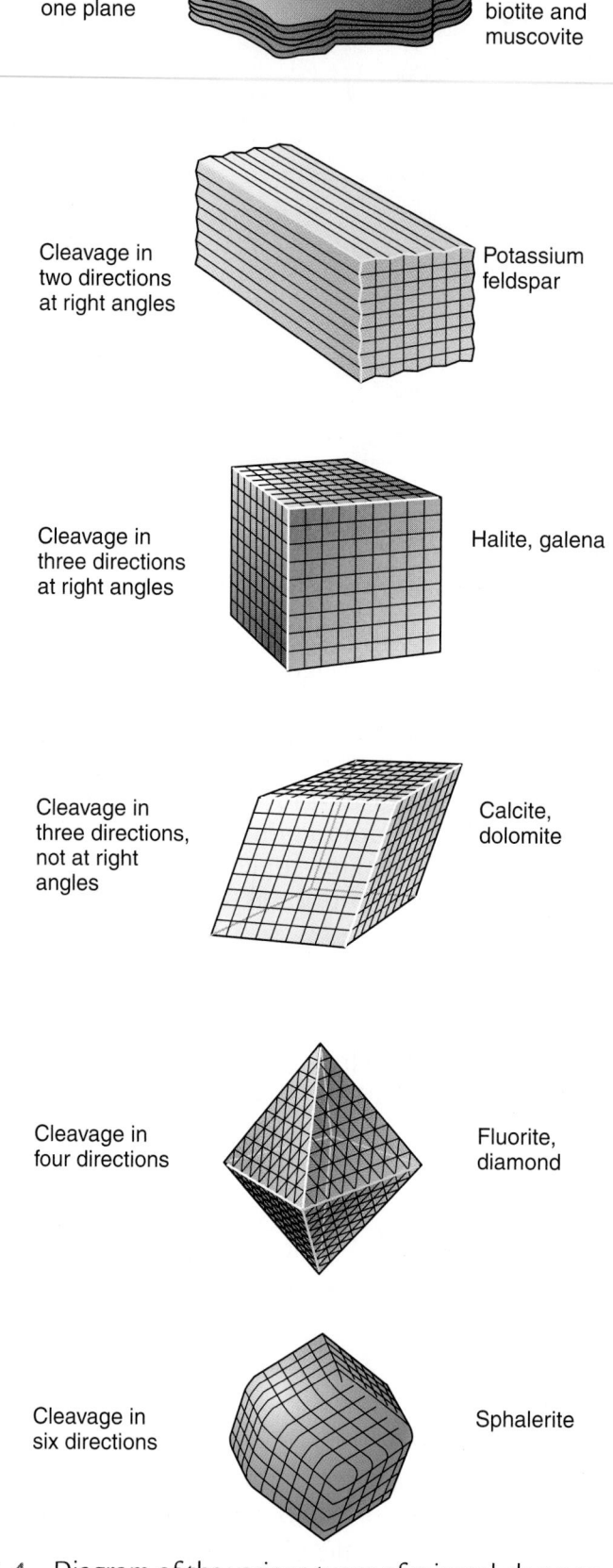

Cleavage in one plane — Micas – biotite and muscovite

Cleavage in two directions at right angles — Potassium feldspar

Cleavage in three directions at right angles — Halite, galena

Cleavage in three directions, not at right angles — Calcite, dolomite

Cleavage in four directions — Fluorite, diamond

Cleavage in six directions — Sphalerite

FIGURE 7–4 Diagram of the various types of mineral cleavage.

A mineralogist works to identify and classify all crystalline minerals. This includes the study of the elements that make up individual minerals and their structural arrangement. Mineralogists also determine the unique properties of individual minerals and the conditions by which they form in the Earth. This knowledge is then applied to the practical use of particular minerals. The work of a mineralogist involves the use of precise instruments to help identify specific minerals. These include powerful electron microscopes, x-ray diffraction machines, spectrometers, and computers. Many mining companies employ mineralogists to help identify regions where particular minerals might be found and how to process them. Other private industries employ mineralogists for use in industrial processes and commercial applications in which minerals are used. A career in mineralogy requires a college education.

gold, which, in its pure form, has a specific gravity of 19.3. This means that gold is more than 19 times heavier than talc.

Some minerals can be identified by using specific chemical tests. Minerals that contain calcite, which is composed of calcium carbonate, can be identified by dropping a small amount of hydrochloric acid onto them. The acid breaks apart the calcium carbonate molecule to form carbon dioxide gas. This causes the surface of the mineral to fizz. Geologists often use the acid test to determine if a rock contains calcium carbonate.

Minerals can possess special properties that are also used to identify them (Table 7–2). Some minerals are magnetic, such as magnetite, and can be easily identified by their magnetic properties. Other minerals are luminescent, meaning that they glow when exposed to ultraviolet light. Fluorite is a luminescent mineral. Other minerals, such as quartz, are piezoelectric, which means that they produce a weak electric current when exposed to increased pressure. A unique flame color produced when a mineral is exposed to fire is also a special property that can be used for identification.

MINERAL COMPOSITION

Different minerals are composed of specific elements that together give them their unique properties. Even though many unique minerals exist, most are made up of only two elements, silicon and oxygen. Silicon and oxygen are by far the most abundant elements in the Earth's crust by mass. Molecules that are formed from atoms of oxygen and silicon are also called silicates. Oxygen atoms make up more than 46 percent of the

TABLE 7–2 Characteristic properties of common minerals

Properties of Common Minerals

LUSTER	HARDNESS	CLEAVAGE	FRACTURE	COMMON COLORS	DISTINGUISHING CHARACTERISTICS	USE(S)	MINERAL NAME	COMPOSITION*
Nonmetallic luster	1	★		White to green	Greasy feel	Talcum powder, soapstone	Talc	$Mg_3Si_4O_{10}(OH)_2$
	2		★	Yellow to amber	Easily melted, may smell	Vulcanize rubber, sulfuric acid	Sulfur	S
	2	★		White to pink or gray	Easily scratched by fingernail	Plaster of Paris and drywall	Gypsum (Selenite)	$CaSO_4 \cdot 2H_2O$
	2–2.5	★		Colorless to yellow	Flexible in thin sheets	Electrical insulator	Muscovite Mica	$KAl_3Si_3O_{10}(OH_2)$
	2.5	★		Colorless to white	Cubic cleavage, salty taste	Food additive, melts ice	Halite	$NaCl$
	2.5–3	★		Black to dark brown	Flexible in thin sheets	Electrical insulator	Biotite Mica	$K(Mg,Fe)_3$ $AlSi_3O_{10}(OH)_2$
	3	★		Colorless or variable	Bubbles with acid	Cement, polarizing prisms	Calcite	$CaCO_3$
	3.5	★		Colorless or variable	Bubbles with acid when powdered	Source of magnesium	Dolomite	$CaMg(CO_3)_2$
	4	★		Colorless or variable	Cleaves in 4 directions	Hydrofluoric acid	Flourite	CaF_2
	5–6	★		Black to dark green	Cleaves in 2 directions at 90°	Mineral collections	Pyroxene (commonly Augite)	$(Ca,Na)(Mg,Fe,Al)$ $(Si,Al)_2O_6$
	5–5	★		Black to dark green	Cleaves at 56° and 124°	Mineral collections	Amphiboles (commonly Hornblende)	$Ca,Na(Mg,Fe)4(Al,Fe,Ti)3$ $Si_6O_{22}(O,OH)_2$
	6	★		White to pink	Cleaves in 2 directions at 90°	Ceramics and glass	Potassium Feldspar (Orthoclase)	$KAlSi_3O_8$
	6	★		White to gray	Cleaves in 2 directions, striations visible	Ceramics and glass	Potassium Feldspar (Na-Ca Feldspar)	$(Na,Ca)AlSi_3O_8$
	6.5		★	Green to gray or brown	Commonly light green and granular	Furnace bricks and jewelry	Olivine	$(Fe,Mg)_2SiO_4$
	7		★	Colorless or variable	Glassy luster, may form hexagonal crystals	Glass, jewelry, and electronics	Quartz	SiO_4
	7		★	Dark red to green	Glassy luster, often seen as red grains in NYS metamorphic rocks	Jewelry and abrasives	Garnet (commonly Almandine)	$Fe_3Al_2Si_3O_{12}$
Either	1–6.5		★	Metallic silver or earthy red	Red-brown streak	Ore or iron	Hematite	Fe_2O_3
Metallic luster	1–2	★		Silver to gray	Black streak, greasy feel	Pencil lead, lubricants	Graphite	C
	2.5	★		Metallic silver	Very dense (7.6 g/cm3), gray-black streak	Ore of lead	Galena	PbS
	5.5–6.5		★	Black to silver	Attracted by magnet black streak	Ore of iron	Magnetite	Fe_3O_4
	6.5		★	Brassy yellow	Green-black streak, cubic crystals	Ore of sulfur	Pyrite	FeS_2

Al = aluminum	Cl = chlorine	H = hydrogen	Na = sodium	S = sulfur
C = carbon	F = fluorine	K = potassium	O = oxygen	Si = silicon
Ca = calcium	Fe = iron	Mg = magnesium	Pb = lead	Ti = titanium

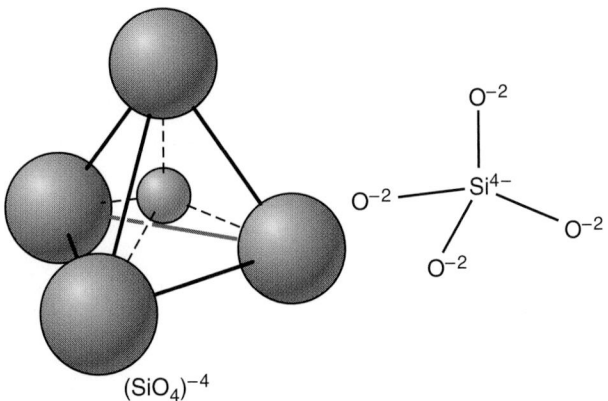

FIGURE 7–5   The structure of a silicate tetrahedron.

Earth's crust by mass. Silicon composes more than 28 percent of the Earth's crust by mass. The other important elements that compose most minerals are aluminum, iron, calcium, sodium, magnesium, and potassium.

Because silicon and oxygen account for most minerals, it is important to understand how they combine to form a mineral's unique structure. The joining of four oxygen atoms with one atom of silicon results in the formation of a silicon-oxygen tetrahedron (Figure 7–5). A tetrahedron is a four-sided object that resembles a three-dimensional triangle. The four corners of the tetrahedron are composed of oxygen atoms, which surround a central silicon atom. The silicon-oxygen tetrahedron is an important structure that gives many minerals their unique properties. The way that these tetrahedrons are arranged within a mineral creates its unique crystalline structure. Quartz is a common mineral that is composed of only silicon and oxygen atoms.

ROCKS AND MINERALS

Almost all rocks are composed of minerals. Exceptions to this include coal and amber, which are rocks formed from the remains of once-living organisms. Rocks that are formed from only one specific mineral are called **monomineralic rocks.** Rock salt is a monomineralic rock because it contains only the mineral halite. Another monomineralic rock is limestone; it contains only the mineral calcite. Rocks that are formed from more than one mineral are called **polymineralic rocks.** Most rocks that form the Earth's crust are polymineralic. Approximately 2,000 minerals have been identified in the Earth's crust, with only about 20 to 30 making up most of the rocks on Earth. The minerals that form the rocks in the Earth's crust are called the rock-forming minerals (Table 7–3). They include feldspar, quartz, talc, calcite, olivine, magnetite, pyrite, and mica.

@ WEB Links

FOR MORE INFORMATION GO TO THESE WEB LINKS:

<http://csmres.jmu.edu/geollab/Fichter/Minerals/index.html>

<http://www.mindat.org/>

<http://webmineral.com/>

<http://www.fi.edu/tfi/units/rocks/rocks.html>

<http://volcano.und.edu/vwdocs/vwlessons/lessons/Slideshow/Slideindex.html>

SECTION REVIEW

1. What is the definition of a mineral?

2. List the chemical and physical properties that are used to identify minerals.

TABLE 7–3 Common rock-forming minerals

Mineral	Abundance in Crust, %	Rock in Which Found
Plagioclase*	39	Igneous rocks mostly
Quartz	12	Detrital sedimentary rocks, granites
Orthoclase	12	Granites, detrital sedimentary rocks
Pyroxenes	11	Dark-colored igneous rocks
Micas	5	All rock types as accessory minerals
Amphiboles	5	Granites and other igneous rocks
Clay minerals	5	Shales, slates, decomposed granites
Olivine	3	Iron-rich igneous rocks, basalt
Others	11	Rock salt, gypsum, limestone, etc.

*Feldspar group of minerals

3. Draw a model of the silicon-oxygen tetrahedron.
4. Provide two examples of a monomineralic rock.
5. List five rock-forming minerals.
6. Who was Friedrich Mohs?

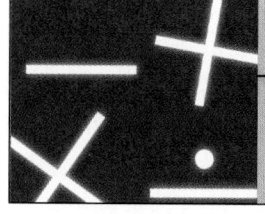

earth math

1) Determine the density for a mineral sample that has a mass of 104 grams and a volume of 20 cubic centimeters.

7.2 Rocks

Rocks are the naturally formed, solid material that makes up the Earth's crust. Most rocks are made up of one or more minerals, which are called the rock-forming minerals. Rocks on Earth are classified on the basis of their origin and formation. The three main categories of rocks on Earth are igneous, sedimentary, and metamorphic.

IGNEOUS ROCKS

Igneous rocks are rocks that have formed from the cooling and solidification of molten rock. Molten rock, called magma, comes from the Earth's upper mantle. When magma reaches the Earth's surface and

FIGURE 7–6   Extrusive rock forming from cooling lava at the Earth's surface. (*Courtesy of PhotoDisc.*)

comes into contact with air or water, it is called lava. When molten rock cools, it becomes a solid by forming crystals. The cooling and solidification of molten rock is also called **crystallization**. This process also occurs when liquid water reaches its freezing point. At 32° Fahrenheit (0° C), liquid water freezes and forms a network of crystals, which becomes ice. When magma cools to form igneous rock beneath the Earth's surface, these rocks are classified as intrusive. This is because the magma has intruded into the Earth's crust. The opposite of **intrusive rock** is **extrusive rock**, which forms when lava cools on the Earth's surface (Figure 7–6).

Igneous rocks are identified by their texture, color, density, and mineral composition. The texture of a rock is influenced by the size, shape, and arrangement of a rock's crystals. The texture of an igneous rock is defined by the time it took for the rock to cool and solidify. Rocks that cool slowly form very large crystals. These igneous rocks are usually formed from intrusive molten rock that has slowly cooled deep in the Earth's crust. Granite is an intrusive igneous rock that forms from slow cooling (Figure 7–7). The larger crystals that make up granite can be seen easily with the naked eye.

Rocks that are cooled quickly form very small crystals or even no crystals at all. These rocks are extrusive and are the result of volcanic activity (Figure 7–8). Basalt is a common extrusive rock, formed from volcanoes, that contains small crystals. Some extrusive rocks that are formed beneath the ocean cool so quickly that they develop a glassy texture. Obsidian, also called volcanic glass, is formed when lava cools rapidly. Some extrusive rock cools so quickly that air gets trapped inside, giving the rock a porous texture, which is referred to as vesicular. Pumice is a fine-grained extrusive rock with a porous texture that resembles a sponge.

The color of an igneous rock can also help classify it. Color is usually referred to as being either light or dark. Lighter-colored igneous rocks tend to contain feldspar and silicate minerals, which are not very dense. These include rocks such as granite and pumice. Darker-colored igneous rocks are rich in iron and magnesium and are much more dense. Basalt and gabbro are examples of darker-colored igneous rocks. The composition of minerals in igneous rock can also help identify them. Igneous rocks containing high percentages of

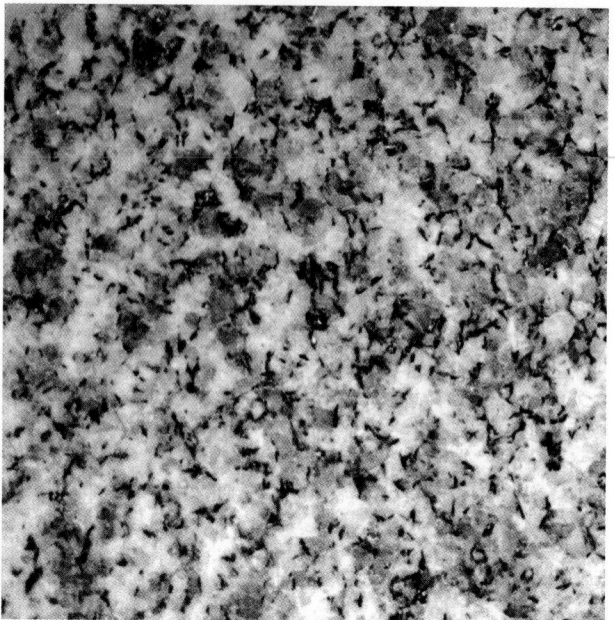

FIGURE 7–7   Coarse-textured granite formed from the slow cooling of intrusive magma below the Earth's surface. (*Photo by Pamela Gore, Georgia Perimeter College.*)

quartz and potassium feldspar minerals are classified as **felsic rocks**. These are rocks that are lighter in color and lower in density. The term *felsic* is derived from the words *feldspar* and *silicate*. Igneous rocks that contain high percentages of pyroxine, olivine, and plagioclase minerals are called **mafic rocks**. The term *mafic* is derived from the symbols for the chemical elements magnesium (Mg) and iron (Fe). These igneous rocks are darker in color and have a high density. Igneous rocks can be

FIGURE 7–8   The fine texture of rhyolite formed from the rapid cooling of extrusive lava. (*Photo by Pamela Gore, Georgia Perimeter College.*)

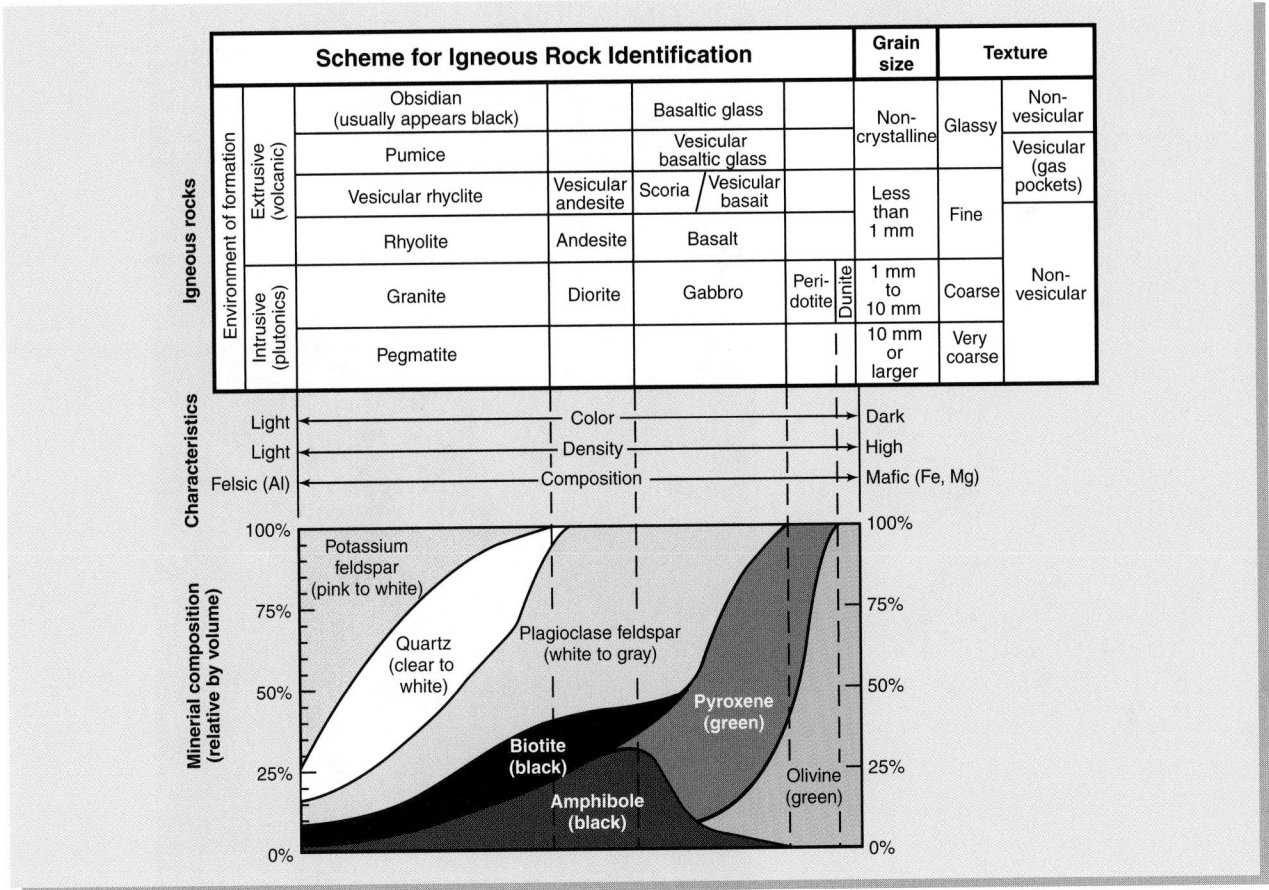

FIGURE 7–9 The scheme for igneous rock identification.

easily identified by using the scheme for igneous rock identification shown in Figure 7–9.

SEDIMENTARY ROCKS

Sedimentary rocks are formed from the accumulation of sediments, which are tiny rock particles that were weathered from, or broken off from, preexisting rock or organic material. These tiny rock particles are chemically or physically removed from their parent rock and then transported by wind, water, or glacial action to form sedimentary rock. The sediments that form these rocks are often classified by their unique texture. The texture of a sedimentary rock can be clastic and crystalline. The term *clastic* refers to the rock's being composed of individual rock fragments that have been bonded together. *Crystalline* texture refers to the rock's being composed of crystals. Another texture type, called *bioclastic*, refers to the rock's being formed from the remains of living organisms. Many sedimentary rocks form at the bottom of large bodies of water where large amounts of sediments have settled. Sedimentary rocks also usually contain horizontally arranged parallel layers called strata (Figure 7–10). These mark the different layers of accumulated sediments that formed the rock. Because sedimentary rocks are formed from accumulating sediment, they also

FIGURE 7–10   Horizontal layers, or strata, of sandstone, which is characteristic of sedimentary rock formations. (*Courtesy of PhotoDisc.*)

may contain fossils. Fossils are the hardened impressions of once-living organisms that died long ago and were buried in the sediments that eventually turned into rock. Sedimentary rocks are the only type of rocks that contain fossils. The process by which accumulating sediment turns into a solid mass, or sedimentary rock, is called **lithification**. There are four main processes that cause accumulated sediments to undergo lithification.

Cementation is the lithification of sediments by binding them together with a substance such as iron oxide, silicates, or calcium carbonate. These substances act as cement to tightly bond the sediments together to form a solid mass (Figure 7–11). Iron oxide, commonly called rust, is an excellent binding agent. For example, old automobile engines can become seized when their parts are allowed to rust. This is the same process that binds together sediment. Concrete uses the same binding action to form a solid mass that is used in construction. Cement is a mixture of iron, silica, and limestone (calcium carbonate) that binds together crushed stone. Common sedimentary rocks that are formed by the process of cementation are sandstone and conglomerate.

Compression and compaction is another way that sediments can become lithified to form sedimentary rock. As fine sediment settles to the bottom of a large lake or ocean, it begins to collect and is slowly

FIGURE 7–11   Large sediment particles that are cemented together to form conglomerate. (*Photo by Pamela Gore, Georgia Perimeter College.*)

compressed together. As newer sediments collect on top of older sediments, they increase the overlying weight and pressure, also known as overburden. Eventually the weight and pressure from the accumulating overburden becomes so great that the underlying sediments become compacted together to form a solid mass. Many sedimentary rocks form at the bottom of the ocean, where the extreme weight of the overlying water helps compress and compact the sediment particles together. Shale is a sedimentary rock that is formed from the compression and compaction of clay and silt-sized sediment. Approximately 70 percent of all the sedimentary rocks on Earth are shale.

Chemical processes such as precipitation and evaporation can also form sedimentary rocks. Minerals such as calcite can become dissolved in water to form a solution of calcium carbonate and water. Eventually the calcium carbonate can precipitate out of solution to form small mineral particles of calcite. The term **precipitation**, when used in geology, means the separation of solid particles out of a solution. These minerals can precipitate and build up over time to form solid rock masses. This process occurs underground when slightly acidic groundwater dissolves the calcite. If the groundwater penetrates into underground caverns and caves, the calcite precipitates out of solution and forms sedimentary rocks such as stalagmites and stalactites, which are also known as chemical limestone.

Another method of chemically forming sedimentary rocks involves evaporation. Seawater contains high amounts of dissolved sodium and chloride ions. If the seawater becomes trapped in some way and is exposed to warm temperatures for a long time, eventually all the water will evaporate. The sodium chloride that is left behind binds together to form halite. Together the halite makes up rock salt, also called an evaporate sedimentary rock, because it was formed as a result of evaporation. Large rock salt deposits can be found deep in the Earth's crust in the middle of continents far from the ocean. These deposits can be more than 10 feet thick in some places. This suggests that at one time the area was covered by a shallow sea that must have evaporated as a result of change in the environment. Sedimentary rocks that are formed from chemical action all tend to be monomineralic in composition. Rock salt contains only the mineral halite, and chemical limestone is composed of the mineral calcite.

The last method of sedimentary rock formation involves some type of living organism. In the ocean many microscopic organisms such as phytoplankton and zooplankton spend their lives floating freely through the water. Eventually these organisms die and settle at the bottom of the ocean. Over time a great amount of these once-living organisms can accumulate on the sea floor and become compacted into a solid mass. Many of the tiny organisms that collect on the sea floor build tiny shells composed of calcium. When these organisms collect on the sea floor and are lithified by compression and compaction, they form a solid mass called fossil limestone.

Another biological method of sedimentary rock formation involves the remains of ancient plants that once thrived around swamps. These plants died and fell to the bottom of the swamp, where they collected over time. Eventually the swamp dried up and became buried under accumulating sediments. The plant remains trapped deep in the Earth were then compressed and compacted together to form what is called bituminous coal, a biologically derived sedimentary rock. Although it appears to be black, and looks nothing like a plant, it is made from the fossilized remains of plants. Coal is one of the few rocks on the Earth that is not made up of minerals. It is made up of hydrocarbon, which is a compound formed mainly from atoms of carbon and hydrogen by living things. Because of the differences in the formation of sedimentary rocks, geologists divide them into two distinct categories (Figure 7–12). The first are the inorganic, land-derived sedimentary rocks. This category includes all sedimentary rocks that are formed from the weathering of preexisting rock. Examples of inorganic, land-derived sedimentary rocks include siltstone, conglomerate, shale, and sandstone. The other category of sedimentary rock is chemically or organically formed sedimentary rock. These are rocks that are formed from some type of chemical process such as precipitation or evaporation or are the remains of once-living organisms. Examples of these type of sedimentary rocks include chemical limestone, rock salt, gypsum, fossil limestone, and bituminous coal.

METAMORPHIC ROCKS

Metamorphic rocks form when preexisting rocks undergo a change as a result of exposure to intense heat and pressure. The rocks from which metamorphic rocks form are also known as parent rocks. Often these rocks are either sedimentary or igneous rocks. The formation of metamorphic rocks requires a great amount of heat and pressure; therefore metamorphic rocks are often associated with mountains. The forces that cause mountains to rise up from the Earth's surface are great enough to produce metamorphic rocks. The formation of metamorphic rocks usually involves the recrystallization of the minerals inside the parent rock. Recrystallization is the new arrangement of the atoms and molecules in the rock that gives it new properties.

Scheme for Sedimentary Rock Identification

CHEMICALLY AND/OR ORGANICALLY FORMED SEDIMENTARY ROCKS					
Texture	**Grain Size**	**Composition**	**Comments**	**Rock Name**	**Map & Symbol**
CRYSTALLINE	Coarse to fine	Calcite	Crystals from chemical precipitates and evaporites	Chemical limestone	
	Varied	Halite		Rock salt	
	Varied	Gypsum		Rock gypsum	
	Varied	Dolomite		Dolostone	
BIOCLASTIC	Microscoptic to coarse	Calcite	Cemented shell fragments or precipitates of biologic origin	Limestone	
	Varied	Carbon	Plant remains	Coal	

INORGANIC LAND-DERIVED SEDIMENTARY ROCKS					
Texture	**Grain Size**	**Composition**	**Comments**	**Rock Name**	**Map & Symbol**
CLASTIC (fragmental)	Pebbles, cobbles, and/or boulders embedded in sand, silt, and/or clay	Mostly quartz, feldspar, and clay minerals; may contain fragments of other rocks and minerals	Rounded fragments	Conglomerate	
			Angular fragments	Breccia	
	Sand (0.2 to 0.006 cm)		Fine to coarse	Sandstone	
	Silt (0.006 to 0.0004 cm)		Very fine grain	Siltstone	
	Clay (less than 0.0004 cm)		Compact: may split easily	Shale	

FIGURE 7–12 The scheme for sedimentary rock identification.

Earth System Scientists

William Smith

William Smith was born in England in 1769. His primary occupation for most of his life was builder of canals. Although he had no formal education, Smith became interested in the geology of England. In 1799 he began to record the detailed arrangement of rock strata all across England. His research lead to the creation of some of the first detailed geological maps. In 1815 he published a map titled *A Delineation of the Strata of England and Wales*, which showed in detail and scale the unique rock formations of his native country. Later he published geological charts, maps, and descriptions that identified the unique fossil species that were found within particular rock formations in England. Smith's work formed the foundation for the creation of accurate geological maps that eventually were made for all parts of the world. Much of his life's work was unappreciated because of his lack of education and his work as a canal builder. It was not until 8 years before his death in 1839 that he was recognized for his achievements by the Geological Society of London.

FIGURE 7–13   Foliation of minerals in a gneiss. (*Photo by Pamela Gore, Georgia Perimeter College.*)

Recrystallization does not require the rock to melt. The only rocks that form from melted rock are igneous rocks. The recrystallization that occurs to form metamorphic rocks is the result of intense heat and pressure, not melting. Metamorphic rocks also become **foliated** when they are exposed to heat and pressure. Foliation is the formation of distinct layers in the rock. The more intense the heat and pressure that the rock is exposed to, the thicker the bands of foliation; however, not all metamorphic rocks become foliated (Figure 7–13).

Metamorphic rocks often show a distorted structure, such as folding or curving (Figure 7–14). This is the result of the intense heat and

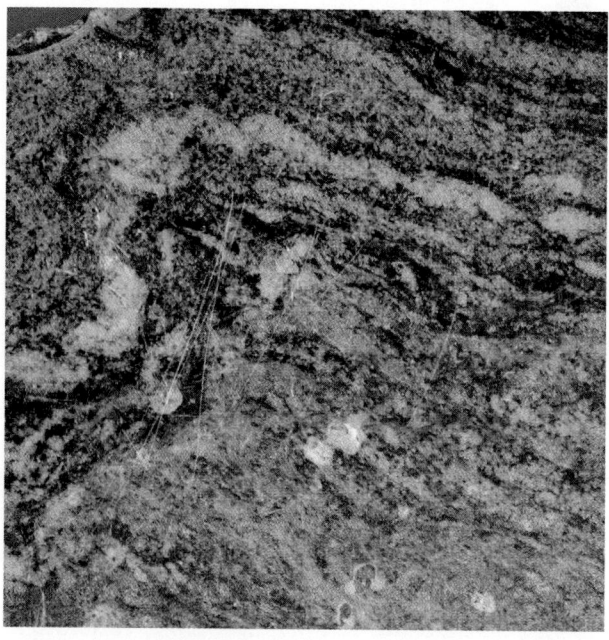

FIGURE 7–14   The distorted structure of a metamorphic rock. (*Photo by Pamela Gore, Georgia Perimeter College.*)

Scheme for Metamorphic Rock Identification

Texture		Grain Size	Composition	Type of Metamorphism	Comments	Rock Name	Map & Symbol
FOLIATED	MINERAL ALIGNMENT	Fine	MICA	Regional	Low-grade metamorphism of shale	Slate	
FOLIATED	MINERAL ALIGNMENT	Fine to medium	MICA, QUARTZ, FELDSPAR, AMPHIBOLE, GARNET	(Heat and pressure increase with depth) ↓	Foliation surfaces shiny from microscopic mica crystals	Phyllite	
FOLIATED	MINERAL ALIGNMENT	Fine to medium	MICA, QUARTZ, FELDSPAR, AMPHIBOLE, GARNET, PYROXENE	(Heat and pressure increase with depth) ↓	Platy mica crystals visible from metamorphism of clay or feldspar	Schist	
FOLIATED	BAND-ING	Medium to coarse	MICA, QUARTZ, FELDSPAR, AMPHIBOLE, GARNET, PYROXENE	(Heat and pressure increase with depth) ↓	High-grade metamorphism; some mica changed to feldspar; segregated by mineral type into bands	Gneiss	
CRYSTALLINE		Fine	Variable	Contact (Heat)	Various rocks changed by heat from nearby magna/lava	Hornfels	
CRYSTALLINE		Fine to coarse	Quartz	Regional or Contact	Metamorphism of quartz sandstone	Quartzite	
CRYSTALLINE		Fine to coarse	Calcite and/or dolomite	Regional or Contact	Metamorphism of limestone or dolostone	Marble	
CRYSTALLINE		Coarse	Various minerals in particles and matrix	Regional or Contact	Pebbles may be distorted or stretched	Meta-conglomerate	

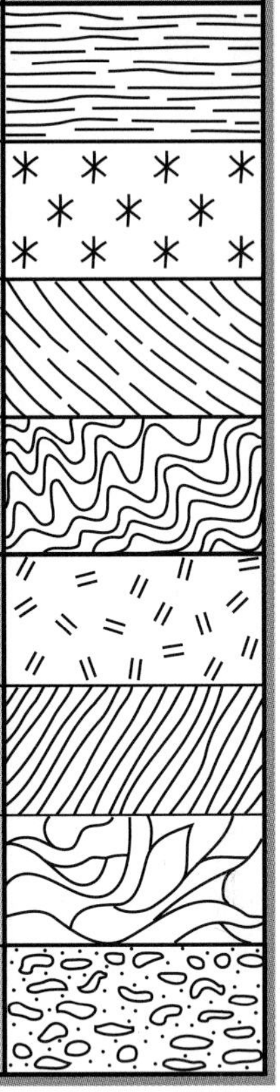

FIGURE 7–15 The scheme for metamorphic rock identification

pressure to which the rock was exposed at one time. Metamorphic rocks also have a higher density than their parent rocks. The increased density is due to the extreme pressure they have experienced.

Metamorphic rocks are often located within an existing mass of either igneous or sedimentary rock. This is caused by the process of contact metamorphism, which occurs when magma intrudes into an existing rock layer and the heat of contact between the magma and the rock layer causes a metamorphic rock to form. An example of this is the intrusion of magma into an existing layer of limestone. The magma eventually cools to form an igneous rock, such as granite, within the limestone. The area of limestone that was exposed to the heat of contact with the magma may metamorphose to form marble. Marble is a metamorphic rock whose parent rock was limestone.

Metamorphic rocks are classified mainly by their mineral composition, foliation, and texture (Figure 7–15). Common metamorphic rocks include slate, which forms from shale; quartzite, whose parent rock is sandstone; gneiss, which forms from basalt; and anthracite coal, which forms from bituminous coal.

THE ROCK CYCLE

Because of the dynamic nature of the Earth's crust, geologists have constructed a model that represents the cycling of rock material on Earth. This model is called the rock cycle, which is represented by a series of

CAREER CONNECTIONS

Petrologist

A petrologist studies the formation, composition, distribution, and classification of rocks. This includes a thorough knowledge of the conditions that lead to the formation of igneous, metamorphic, and sedimentary rocks. Identifying particular rock types and their unique properties is another important part of the work done by a petrologist. Many petrologists work for the mining or materials industry, in which they help locate specific rock types required for commercial or industrial uses. Other research performed by a petrologist includes the dating of rocks. Determining how long ago a rock formed, and therefore how old it is, is an important part of putting together the geological time scale of the Earth's history. This aspect of petrology is called geochronology. A career in petrology requires a college education and time spent in both the outdoors, where rock samples are collected, and in the lab, where they can be analyzed and tested.

interconnecting processes that lead to the formation of all three main rock types (Figure 7–16). The rock cycle is based on a cyclic pattern because there is no real starting point for rock formation. However, billions of years ago when the Earth was forming, all rocks began as igneous rock. Today many different processes are occurring on and in the Earth's crust to form or re-form rock. These processes are illustrated in the rock cycle. They include important terms such as *uplift, weathering and erosion, burial, heat, pressure, melting, compaction,*

Earth System Scientists

Abraham Werner

Abraham Werner was a German geologist, born in 1749. After receiving his education at the Freiberg Mining School, he went on to become a world-renowned geology instructor. His research involved the explanation of how the different rocks were formed on the Earth. He developed an early version of the rock cycle that explained the processes that lead to the formation of rocks he called primary, sedimentary, recent, and volcanic. Werner's theory proposed that most rocks on Earth were formed from water as the principal agent. At that time, other scientists disagreed with Werner and believed that rocks were formed from cooling molten rock. Today both these processes are considered responsible for rock formation on Earth.

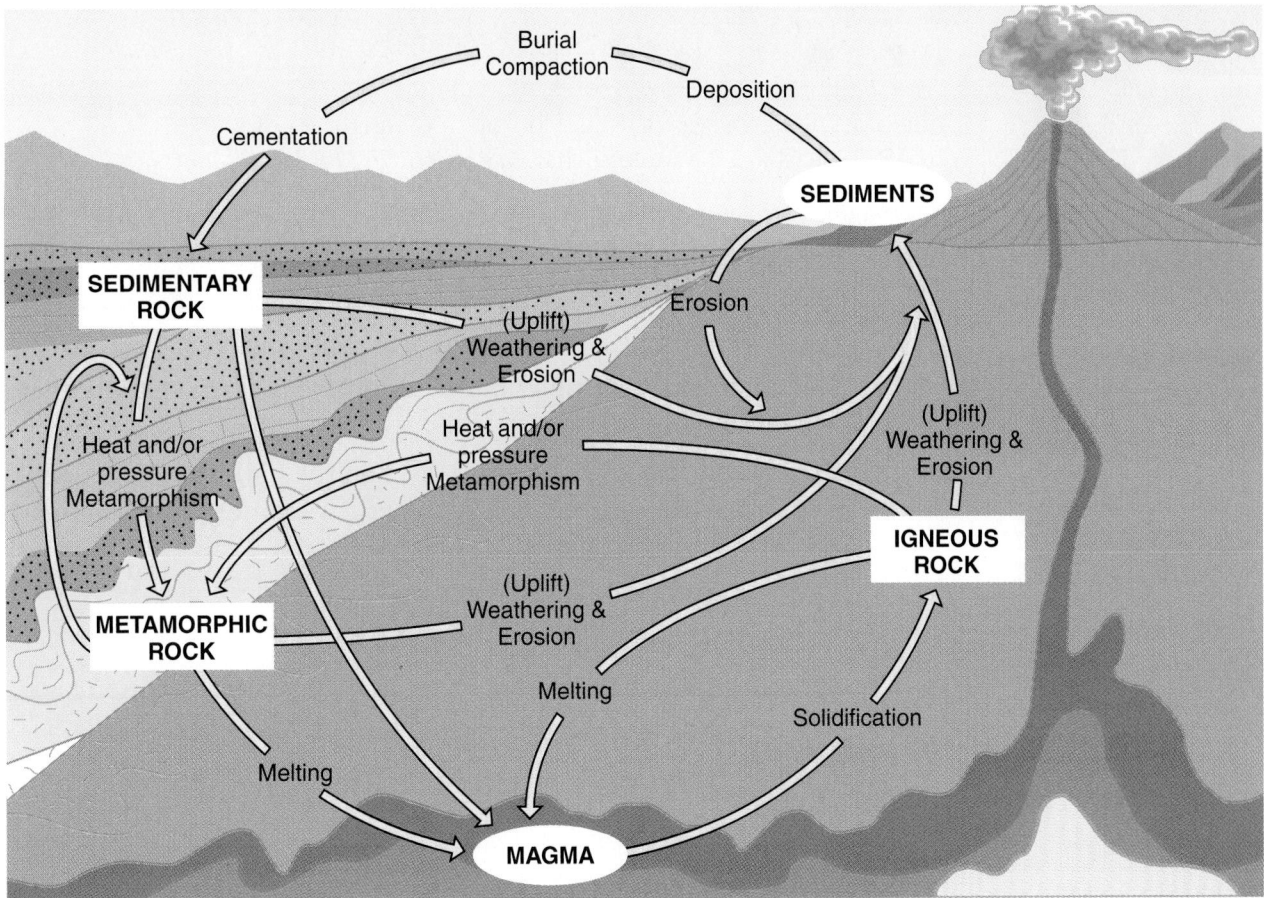

FIGURE 7–16 The rock cycle illustrates the processes that form rocks on the Earth.

sedimentation, and *solidification.* All these terms refer to the specific processes that lead to rock formation and are important in understanding how rocks form on Earth.

SECTION REVIEW

1. Describe the difference between intrusive and extrusive igneous rocks.

2. How does the rate of cooling affect the size of crystals in igneous rocks?

3. What is the difference between mafic and felsic igneous rocks?

4. What are the four methods of lithification that form sedimentary rocks?

5. What are three examples of inorganic, land-derived sedimentary rocks?

6. What are three examples of chemically or organically formed sedimentary rocks?

7. What causes sedimentary or igneous rocks to metamorphose?

8. List three characteristics of metamorphic rocks.

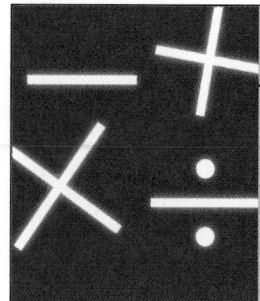

earth math

1) If lava at the Earth's surface cooled from a temperature of 450° Celsius to 35° Celsius in 30 minutes, what was its cooling rate per minute?

2) If a magma intrusion cooled from a temperature of 700° Celsius to 90° Celsius in 2 days, what was its cooling rate per minute?

@ WEB Links

FOR MORE INFORMATION GO TO THESE WEB LINKS:

<http://csmres.jmu.edu/geollab/Fichter/IgnRx/IgHome.html>

< http://csmres.jmu.edu/geollab/Fichter/SedRx/index.html>

<http://csmres.jmu.edu/geollab/Fichter/MetaRx/index.html>

<http://seis.natsci.csulb.edu/basicgeo/IGNEOUS_TOUR.html>

<http://seis.natsci.csulb.edu/bperry/Sedimentary%20Rocks%20Tour/introduction_to_sedimentary_rocks.htm>

<http://seis.natsci.csulb.edu/bperry/metarock/INTRODUCTION.htm>

<http://www.minsocam.org/MSA/K12/rkcycle/rkcycleindex.html>

<http://www.windows.ucar.edu/cgi-bin/tour_def/earth/geology/rocks_intro.html>

9. What are four examples of metamorphic rocks? What are their parent rocks?

10. Using the rock cycle diagram, explain the path that a sedimentary rock can take when it becomes a metamorphic rock, then a sedimentary rock once again.

11. Who was William Smith?

12. What did Abraham Werner develop?

7.3 Mineral Resources

MINERAL RESOURCES

A **mineral resource** is any mineral, compound, or pure element that exists naturally in the Earth's crust and is used by humans in some way. Mineral resources are classified in two broad categories: metallic mineral resources and nonmetallic mineral resources (Table 7–4). Metallic mineral resources are the abundant metal elements that exist in the Earth in large quantities. These include iron, aluminum, magnesium, titanium, and manganese. Other metallic mineral resources that are not so abundant in the Earth's crust are called scarce metals; these include gold, silver, copper, zinc, lead, tin, and nickel. Nonmetallic mineral resources include construction materials such as gravel, sand, clay, sandstone, shale, and limestone. Limestone is a major component of cement. Other nonmetallic mineral resources include phosphates, sodium chloride, and sulfur. Phosphate mined from the Earth is used for agricultural fertilizers, and sodium chloride is also known as common salt. Some nonmetallic mineral resources are used for abrasives such as garnet, which is used for sandpaper, or for ceramics such as clay, pumice, and quartz.

MINERAL ORES

Minerals are often found in the Earth in a form called ore. Mineral ores are natural rocks that contain the desired mineral to be extracted. Mineral ores are often found in specific rock formations called mineral deposits. A mineral deposit usually contains rocks with a high percentage of the desired mineral resource. A mineral ore deposit that contains a relatively high concentration of the desired mineral resource is considered a high-concentration deposit. For example, a high

TABLE 7–4 Classification of mineral resources

Metallic Mineral Resources	Nonmetallic Mineral Resources
Abundant Metals Iron, aluminum, manganese, magnesium, titanium	**Minerals for Industrial and Agricultural Use** Phosphates, nitrates, carbonates, sodium chloride, fluorite, sulfur, borax
Scarce Metals Copper, lead, zinc, tin, gold, silver, platinum-group metals, molybdenum, uranium, mercury, tungsten, bismuth, chromium, nickel, cobalt, columbium	**Construction Materials** Sand, gravel, clay, gypsum, building stone, shale and limestone (for cement) **Ceramics and Abrasives** Feldspar, quartz, clay, corundum, garnet, pumice, diamond

SOURCE: James R. Craig, David L. Vaughan, and Brian J. Skinner, *Resources of the Earth* (Englewood Cliffs, N.J.: Prentice Hall, 1988).

concentration of aluminum ore, also called bauxite, contains about 35 percent aluminum. The remaining 65 percent is unusable rock. A high-concentration deposit of iron ore can contain almost 70 percent iron. Some high-concentration ores, such as copper, contain only 3 percent to 4 percent copper. A low-concentration deposit contains lower percentages of the desired mineral resource. A low-concentration deposit of iron contains only 20 percent iron.

Earth System Scientists

John Wesley Powell

John Wesley Powell was born in 1834 in Illinois. He became interested in the study of natural history at a young age, especially with gathering specimens while exploring the outdoors. In 1850 he became the head of the Illinois Society of Natural History, where he continued his study of the Illinois landscapes. Powell's interest centered around the study of geology. After serving as a Union officer during the American Civil War, in which he lost his arm, he conducted a boating expedition down the Colorado River through the Grand Canyon. The results of his journey were published in his book titled *The Exploration of the Colorado River* in 1875. Shortly after his famous trip, Powell was appointed as the head of the U.S. Geological Survey. He continued his work in geomorphology by conducting a survey of the natural resources in Colorado, Utah, and Arizona. The results of his expeditions opened up many parts of the American Southwest, which had previously been unexplored and unmapped. His research also helped reveal the geological processes that led to the formations of much of the Southwest. In addition, Powell studied the processes of erosion, mountain formation, and volcanoes. Later in his life he began to work on plans to create dams and irrigation canals to supply water to the desert regions of the American Southwest.

MINERAL DEPOSITS

Mineral deposits originate from four different processes. Igneous mineral deposits occur as a result of the formation of igneous rocks that contain mineral resources. These mineral deposits form by volcanic activity, intrusive magma, near hydrothermal vents. Examples of igneous mineral deposits include copper, diamonds, lead, and zinc. Sedimentary mineral deposits form by sedimentary processes such as precipitation and evaporation associated with the ocean. Typical sedimentary mineral resources include rock salt, manganese, and iron. Weathered deposits of mineral resources also occur as a result of the leaching of minerals from soil. The aluminum ore bauxite is an example of a weathered mineral deposit.

MINING TECHNIQUES

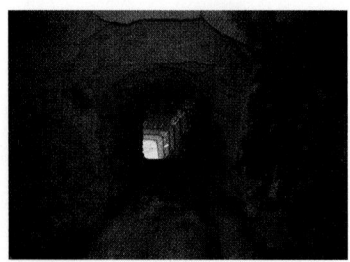

FIGURE 7–17 The shaft of a deep underground mine. (*Courtesy of Corbis.*)

Because mineral resources often exist deep within the Earth's crust, techniques have been developed to remove them and make them available for use. The removal of mineral resources from the lithosphere is called mining. Mining practices fall under two broad categories, underground mining and surface mining. Underground mining involves the digging of mine shafts directly into the Earth's crust (Figure 7–17). This is an extremely dangerous undertaking because the potential for collapse of the mine shaft is very real. Mine shafts are dug using a variety of methods that include rock drills and explosives. Once the ore deposit is drilled or blasted free, it must be transported out of the mine shaft. This involves a complex arrangement of elevators and railroad tracks that transport the heavy ore back to the surface. The deepest mine that has ever been excavated is in South Africa. It burrows 2.3 mi (3.7 km) into the Earth. Many ore deposits that lie deep within the Earth's crust can be accessed only by underground mines. One of the problems associated with underground mining involves the release of toxic heavy metals into the environment. Many deep underground mines become filled with groundwater, which must be pumped to the surface to keep the mine shafts from filling with water. Some of this water is naturally acidic and can dissolve toxic heavy metals exposed in the mine. When the water is discharged at the surface, it can pollute nearby surface waters.

Surface mining is the practice of removing mineral ore deposits from near the Earth's surface. There are many different types of surface mining operations. Open pit mining involves the removal of massive amounts of ore by some of the world's largest machines (Figure 7–18). The bucket excavators that extract ore in open pit mines can remove more than 100 tons in one single scoop (Figure 7–19). The Bingham Canyon open

FIGURE 7–18   Open pit mines remove massive amounts of ore from the Earth's crust. (*Courtesy of PhotoDisc.*)

FIGURE 7–19   An open pit coal mining operation. (*Courtesy of Corbis.*)

pit copper mine in Utah is the world's largest mine (Figure 7–20). It has created a hole in the Earth almost 3,000 ft (914 m) deep and has produced more than 3 billion tons of copper ore. Open pit mines cause extreme damage to the landscape as a result of massive erosion and runoff of water carrying toxic metals and sediments.

Another type of surface mining operation is strip mining. This involves the excavation of shallow strips along the Earth's surface. This

FIGURE 7–20   The Bingham Canyon copper mine, located in Utah, is the world's largest open pit mine. (*Courtesy of EyeWire.*)

Earth System Law

Mining Law

In August of 1977 the United States Congress enacted the *Surface Mining Control and Reclamation Act*. This legislation provides protection of land and water resources from the destructive processes of surface coal mining. This important law also requires that land from which coal has been mined shall be returned to a state where environmental quality and public health are not in danger of damage. In 1991 an international agreement was also enacted that protects Antarctica from mining operations. Forty-five countries signed the *Protocol on Environmental Protection to the Antarctic Treaty*. This international agreement, also known as the Madrid Protocol, prevents the mining of the Antarctic continent for the next 50 years. This treaty also designates Antarctica as a natural reserve devoted to peaceful scientific research and protects its natural resources from environmental degradation.

is less disruptive to the environment because the mine is backfilled immediately after the ore is removed. Many strip mines are also replanted with vegetation to stabilize the landscape and prevent erosion. Hydraulic mining also removes ore from the surface. This is done by blasting high-pressure water at the rock containing the ore deposit. This method of mining is also damaging to the environment because the water used causes massive erosion and flooding to the surrounding landscape. Gold is mined in this way today in many parts of the world.

The last type of surface mining method is called dredging. Dredging is done when mineral ore deposits lie beneath a body of water. A large dredging bucket is used to remove the ore, which creates sediment plumes that can disrupt the aquatic environment. Today many mining practices are being improved to help lessen the impact that they have on the environment.

SECTION REVIEW

1. Define the term *mineral resource* and explain the two categories of mineral resources.

2. What are some examples of metallic mineral resources?

3. What are two examples of nonmetallic mineral resources?

4. What are the four ways that mineral ore deposits form on the Earth?

5. Describe three ways that mineral resources are mined from the Earth's crust.

6. Who was John Wesley Powell?

FOR MORE INFORMATION GO TO THIS WEB LINK:

<http://minerals.usgs.gov/>

earth math

1) If 3 billion tons of copper ore has been mined from the Bingham Canyon mine in Utah and the ore contains an average of 6 percent copper, how much copper has the mine produced?

CHAPTER SUMMARY

Minerals are the naturally occurring, inorganic, crystalline substances formed in the Earth's crust that have unique physical and chemical properties. Individual minerals are identified by their unique properties, which include color, luster, hardness, streak, and cleavage. Many minerals that make up the rocks in the Earth's crust are composed of oxygen and silicon. These elements combine to form the chemical compound known as a silicate. Silicates possess a unique structure that is formed from four atoms of oxygen surrounding one atom of silicon. This structure is known as a silicate tetrahedron. The internal arrangement of atoms in a mineral provides it with its unique physical and chemical properties. Although hundreds of different minerals exist in the Earth's crust, only a few make up most of the rocks in the crust. These are called the common rock-forming minerals, which include feldspar, quartz, talc, calcite, olivine, magnetite, pyrite, and mica. Rocks are formed from one or many types of minerals.

There are three types of rocks that form on the Earth: igneous, sedimentary, and metamorphic. Igneous rocks are formed from the crystallization of cooling lava or magma. These types of rocks are classified by their relative color, texture, composition, and density. Common igneous rocks include granite, gabbro, and basalt. Sedimentary rocks are formed from the lithification of accumulating sediments. The sediments are bonded together by different processes to form one solid mass of rock. These processes include cementation, compression, compaction, precipitation, or evaporation. Sedimentary rocks are the only type of rocks that contain fossils. They are commonly classified by their texture, grain size, and composition. Common sedimentary rocks include sandstone, shale, and limestone. The third type of rock that is found on the Earth is metamorphic rock. Metamorphic rock is formed from preexisting rock that has been exposed to extreme heat and pressure. This causes the minerals in the rock to recrystallize, forming a new type of rock. Metamorphic rocks can be foliated, which means that the minerals that they contain align themselves into unique layers. Other metamorphic rocks can be folded, bent, or distorted in some way. Common metamorphic rocks include slate, gneiss, and marble.

The processes that form rocks on the Earth are often displayed in a model called the rock cycle. This model shows the various pathways and processes by which rocks form and re-form on the Earth.

Many rocks in the Earth's crust contain valuable mineral resources. A mineral resource is a mineral that is useful to society. There are two basic types of mineral resources: metallic and nonmetallic. Metallic resources include iron, zinc, aluminum, gold, and silver. Nonmetallic resources are mostly used as building materials, such as gravel, limestone, slate, and granite. A concentration of a mineral resource in the Earth is called a mineral deposit. The raw form of the mineral that is extracted from the Earth is called mineral ore. Various techniques are used to extract, or mine, mineral resources from the ground. These can often be large-scale above-ground or below-ground operations, which can cause damage to the environment.

CHAPTER REVIEW

Multiple Choice

1. The physical properties of minerals are largely caused by:
   a. volume
   b. melting point
   c. organic composition
   d. internal arrangement of atoms

2. A student rubs a mineral sample on a porcelain plate. The student is trying to determine a mineral's:
   a. density
   b. luster
   c. hardness
   d. streak

3. A student scratches the mineral with a fingernail. The student is trying to determine a mineral's:
   a. density
   b. luster
   c. hardness
   d. streak

4. Which mineral is mostly made from silicate?
   a. quartz
   b. magnetite
   c. mica
   d. calcite

5. Which mineral fizzes when exposed to acid?
   a. quartz
   b. magnetite
   c. mica
   d. calcite

6. Which physical property is classified as metallic, glassy, earthy, or dull?
   a. density
   b. luster
   c. hardness
   d. streak

7. Which two processes result in the formation of igneous rocks?
   a. evaporation
   b. recrystallization
   c. crystallization
   d. cementation

8. Which property is common to mafic rocks?
   a. high density
   b. intrusive formation
   c. quartz composed
   d. light color

9. Which igneous rock cools most rapidly?
   a. granite
   b. gabbro
   c. basalt
   d. marble

10. Which of the following is a coarse-grained, intrusive, light-colored, low-density igneous rock?
    a. granite
    b. gabbro
    c. basalt
    d. marble

11. Which process most likely formed sandstone?
    a. evaporation
    b. recrystallization
    c. crystallization
    d. cementation

12. Which rock is most likely organic in origin?
    a. limestone
    b. sandstone
    c. basalt
    d. conglomerate

13. Which rock is most likely to contain fossils?
    a. basalt
    b. granite
    c. shale
    d. marble

14. Which rock has a clastic texture?
    a. rock salt
    b. gypsum
    c. marble
    d. sandstone

15. Metamorphic rocks result from the:
    a. erosion of rocks
    b. recrystallization of rocks
    c. crystallization of magma
    d. cementation of sediments

16. The metamorphism of preexisting rock most likely results in the rock's becoming:
    a. melted
    b. more dense
    c. fossilized
    d. eroded

17. The alignment of minerals forming bands in a rock caused by recrystallization is called:
    a. folding
    b. clastic
    c. foliation
    d. cementation

18. Heat and pressure of a rock mass caused by an igneous intrusion is also known as:
    a. vertical sorting
    b. foliation
    c. contact metamorphism
    d. chemical evaporation

19. Which of the following is considered a nonmetallic mineral resource?
    a. gold
    b. limestone
    c. zinc
    d. copper

20. Which of the following mineral resources is classified as a sedimentary deposit?
    a. iron
    b. rock salt
    c. aluminum
    d. copper

Matching *Match the terms with the correct definitions.*

a. mineral
b. crystalline
c. monomineralic rocks
d. polymineralic rocks
e. igneous rocks

f. crystallization
g. intrusive rock
h. extrusive rock
i. felsic rocks
j. mafic rocks

k. sedimentary rocks
l. lithification
m. metamorphic rocks
n. foliated
o. mineral resource

1. _____ A type of igneous rock that is formed at the Earth's surface from the solidification of lava.
2. _____ The valuable minerals that are located in specific locations in the Earth's crust that can be mined.
3. _____ A classification of igneous rocks that are light colored, low density, and contain silicates and aluminum.
4. _____ A naturally occurring, inorganic, crystalline substance that has specific physical properties.
5. _____ The layered or wavy structure that forms in some metamorphic rocks.
6. _____ A substance or structure that is made up of crystals.
7. _____ A class of rocks that are formed when igneous or sedimentary rocks are changed into a new rock by exposure to intense heat and pressure.
8. _____ A specific type of rock that is made from only one mineral, such as rock salt or limestone.
9. _____ The process of converting sediments into one solid mass of rock.
10. _____ A type of rock formed on the Earth from solidifying magma or lava.
11. _____ Rocks that are composed of two or more different minerals.
12. _____ A type of rock that is formed from rock particles that are compacted or cemented together into one solid mass.
13. _____ A specific class of igneous rocks that are generally dark, dense, and contain iron and magnesium.
14. _____ Igneous rock that is formed from magma seeping into an existing rock mass.
15. _____ Rock changing phase from a liquid to a solid, also called solidification.

Critical Thinking

1. List the items in or around your home or at school that contain minerals, rocks, or mineral resources. Explain how your life would be changed if they did not exist.

The Earth's Interior

OBJECTIVES

The Earth's Core · The Mantle · The Earth's Crust · The Model of Earth's Interior

After reading this chapter you should be able to:

▶ Describe the composition of the Earth's inner and outer cores.

▶ Identify the main features of the Earth's mantle.

▶ Define the term *lithosphere*.

▶ Differentiate between oceanic and continental crust.

▶ Define the term *asthenosphere*.

▶ Explain how geologists were able to construct a model of the Earth's interior.

INTRODUCTION

The nineteenth-century novel *A Journey to the Center of the Earth,* written by Jules Verne, tells of an incredible scientific journey that went deep into the Earth. The story follows an expedition that discovered a fascinating underground world where strange seas and bizarre creatures existed. This classic work of fiction drew on the human fascination with what lies below the surface of the Earth. Many religions describe the underground world as a hot, hellish place where demons and monsters reside. Ancient peoples held funeral ceremonies deep in natural caves and caverns, which were believed to be the entrance to the underground world. This led to the term *underworld,* which soon became synonymous with death and the afterlife. Some early scientists actually believed they could dig through the Earth from one side to the other. They even developed plans for special drilling vehicles designed to take up the task. The Earth's interior has been part of myth and wonder throughout the ages. The ground beneath our feet provides stability for us to walk on, build on, and drive on. The solid rock that lies below the surface is extremely hard and dense, as compared with most other substances on the Earth. But is the Earth totally composed of solid rock? Certainly the first time human beings gazed at the hot, molten rock spewing out from a volcano, they must have wondered what really lies below the surface. The advancement of science and technology in the twentieth century has finally given us a realistic view of what lies below us and has opened the door to further understanding of the Earth's systems.

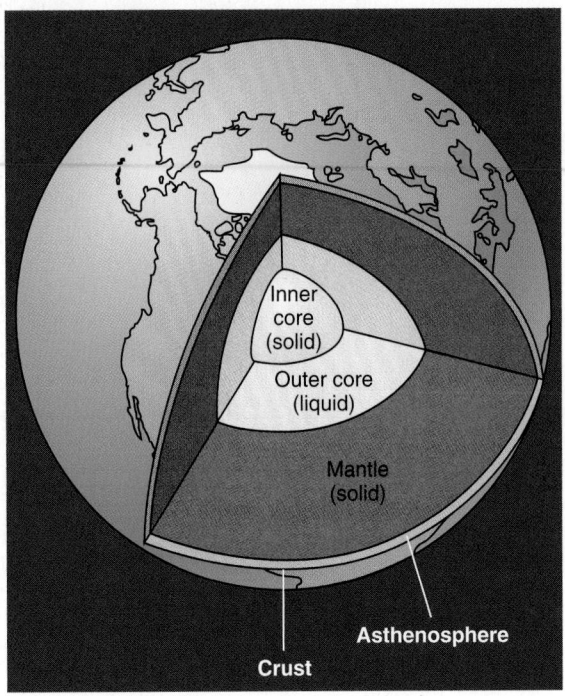

FIGURE 8–1 The Earth's interior, which consists of the solid inner core, liquid outer core, mantle, and crust.

THE EARTH'S CORE

The **lithosphere** is the solid outer crust of the Earth, which is made up of solid rock and the hot plasticlike upper **mantle**. If we could take the Earth and cut it in half, we would discover that it is made up of three major parts or layers (Figure 8–1). **Earth's core** is the very center of the Earth; it is divided into two parts, an outer liquid portion and an inner solid portion. The composition of both parts of the core are believed to be iron and nickel. You would have to travel more than 1,800 mi (2,897 km) to reach the Earth's outer core and another 1,300 mi (2,092 km) to reach the solid core. Geologists have used information gathered from the composition of meteorites to theorize that the Earth's core is made up of iron and nickel. These very dense elements are believed to have settled toward the center of the Earth during its formation. The Earth's core is extremely hot, reaching temperatures of more than 8,000° F (4,427° C). The movement of seismic waves through the Earth, generated by earthquakes, have revealed that the Earth's core is divided into a solid inner portion and a liquid outer portion. This is due to the different way in which these waves interact with liquids and solids. Geologists have used techniques like this to study the Earth's interior, because it is extremely hot and under high pressure, making it impossible to observe directly.

THE MANTLE

The next layer of the Earth's interior is called the mantle. The mantle makes up most of the Earth's total volume and is mostly composed of a hot solid material consisting of the elements silicon, oxygen, iron, aluminum, and magnesium. The mantle is an approximately 1,800-mi (2,897 km)-thick region that is also exposed to extremely high pressures.

It is believed that heat from the Earth's hot core moves upward through the mantle, forming large **convection cells**. much like in air or water. The extreme heat that is generated deep within the core and mantle comes from **radioactive decay, friction**, and **residual heat** left over from the Earth's formation. The upper part of the mantle is made up of a plasticlike material called the asthenosphere, which flows like thick syrup. It is estimated that the Earth's heat increases approximately 1° F for every 50 ft in depth (0.5° C every 15 m).

THE EARTH'S CRUST

The outer part of the Earth is composed of solid rock called the **crust**. The Earth's crust varies in its thickness from more than 40 miles (64 km) underneath high mountains to only 3 mi (4.8 km) underlying some parts of the ocean. The crust is relatively thin compared with the other parts that make up the Earth's interior. The Earth's crust varies in its density depending on its location around the planet. The crust that lies under the world's oceans, also called **oceanic crust**, has an average density of 3 grams per cubic centimeter. The crust that makes up the world's continents, also known as the **continental crust**, has an average density of 2.7 grams per cubic centimeter and is composed mainly of granitic rock. The oceanic crust is slightly denser than continental crust because it forms under the intense pressure of the deep ocean and is composed mainly of basalt rock. The solid crust of the Earth floats on top of the plasticlike upper mantle, much like a cracker floating on hot soup. Only seven elements make up nearly 99 percent of the Earth's crust. Oxygen and silicon are the most abundant elements, composing approximately 72 percent of the rocks in the crust. The remaining elements that make up most of the Earth's crust include aluminum, iron, calcium, magnesium, and sodium. Together, the lower part of the crust and the upper mantle form a unique layer called the **asthenosphere**. The **asthenosphere** is the plasticlike layer of rock on which the solid crust "floats" (Figure 8–2).

CAREER CONNECTIONS

Geophysicist

A geophysicist uses a knowledge of physics to study the Earth's interior, along with its gravitational and magnetic fields. These scientists are trying to unlock the secrets of the mechanisms that exist deep within the Earth and how they affect life at the surface and our planet's magnetic field. Geophysicists study the heat that is generated deep within the Earth and how it is distributed around the globe. This work is an important aspect of understanding plate tectonics. Geophysicists are also interested in the stress that builds up in the Earth's plates, which eventually leads to earthquakes. These scientists use a wide array of computers and sensing instruments to study the Earth's interior.

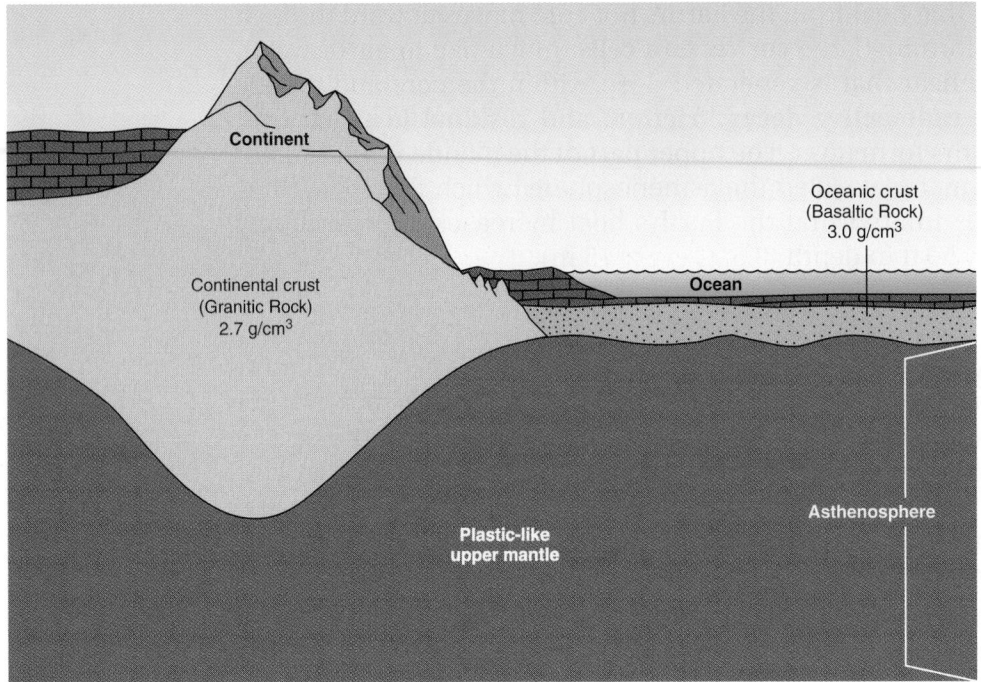

FIGURE 8-2 The Earth's lithosphere, showing the oceaning and continental crust floating on the plastic-like upper mantle called the athenosphere.

THE MODEL OF EARTH'S INTERIOR

Amazingly, geologists have developed a model of the Earth's interior by studying the way that seismic waves, which are produced by earthquakes, travel through the Earth. They have also studied the composition of the interior of meteorites to help them better understand the Earth's interior. The deepest that humans have penetrated into the Earth by drilling is only

Earth System Scientists

James Hutton

James Hutton was born in Edinburgh, Scotland, in 1726. After receiving his doctorate in medicine in 1749, he spent the next 20 years farming the land and traveling extensively in his native Scotland. His travels and his growing interest in geology gave him unique insight into the geological history of the Earth. He was the first scientist to propose that the Earth was continually undergoing a slow process of erosion and creation of new landforms. His greatest contribution to modern geology included the theory of uniformitarianism, which stated that the same geological processes that are occurring on Earth today have been occurring throughout its history. This fundamental geological concept forms the base of modern geology. He also proposed that the erosion of the continents led to the formation of sedimentary rocks on the floor of the ocean. These rocks were then thrust up to form new mountain chains by the internal heat of the Earth. He also pointed out the difference between igneous rock formation and sedimentary rock formation. His theories were published in his book titled *Theory of the Earth*.

9 mi (14.5 km), and the deepest mine has only reached a little more than 2 mi (3.2 km) deep. Therefore the model of the Earth's interior is constructed by inference, because we are unable to actually observe what exists deep below the surface. An **inference** is a conclusion based on gathered evidence. Geologists can only make inferences about the Earth's interior because it is impossible for humans to travel there. Many theories in geology are based on inference because the scale of the Earth is so large and much of the lithosphere cannot be studied by direct observation, such as the oceans or the atmosphere.

REVIEW

1. What is the composition of the Earth's inner and outer core?
2. Approximately how thick is the mantle region of the Earth's interior?
3. Describe the effect on temperature and pressure of increasing depth into the Earth's interior.
4. What elements make up 99 percent of the Earth's crust?
5. How do geologists know what the Earth's interior is like?
6. Who was James Hutton?

FOR MORE INFORMATION GO TO THIS WEB LINK:

<http://www.seismo.unr. edu/ftp/pub/louie/class/ 100/interior.html>

CHAPTER SUMMARY

The Earth is divided into three distinct layers: the core, mantle, and lithosphere. The Earth's core is divided into two parts, the liquid outer core and the solid inner core. Both are believed to be composed of iron and nickel. The mantle is the next layer, which is located between the core and the lithosphere. The mantle makes up most of the total volume of the Earth and is extremely hot and dense. The extreme heat of the inner portions of the Earth is derived mainly from radioactive decay, friction, and residual heat left over from when the planet formed. The outer layer of the Earth is called the lithosphere. The lithosphere is further subdivided into the solid outer layer of rock called the crust and the hot, plasticlike upper mantle called the asthenosphere. There are two basic types of crust: oceanic and continental. Oceanic crust forms below the oceans, is composed of basalt rock, and is denser than continental crust. Continental crust makes up the continents, is composed of granite rock, and is less dense than oceanic crust. Both types of crust float on the hot, plasticlike asthenosphere. Because humans cannot actually explore the Earth's interior, they have constructed a model of what they believe to exist below the surface by analyzing the way seismic waves travel through the Earth.

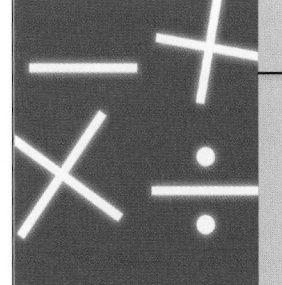

earth math

1) If the radius of the Earth is approximately 4,000 miles, determine the percentage that each portion of the Earth's interior occupies (crust, mantle, outer core, inner core).
   Assume that the average thickness of the crust is 20 miles and the average thickness of the mantle is 1,800 miles.

CHAPTER REVIEW

Multiple Choice

1. The inner core of the Earth is believed to contain:
   a. liquid iron
   b. solid iron
   c. liquid iron and nickel
   d. solid iron and nickel

2. Which objects have geologists studied to learn about the composition of the Earth's core?
   a. comets
   b. asteroids
   c. planets
   d. meteorites

3. Which of the following portions of the Earth's interior make up most of the total volume of the planet?
   a. crust
   b. mantle
   c. outer core
   d. inner core

4. As compared with oceanic crust, continental crust is:
   a. less dense and composed of granite
   b. more dense and composed of granite
   c. less dense and composed of basalt
   d. more dense and composed of basalt

5. As compared with continental crust, oceanic crust is:
   a. less dense and composed of granite
   b. more dense and composed of granite
   c. less dense and composed of basalt
   d. more dense and composed of basalt

6. The thin outer crust of rock is also called the:
   a. asthenosphere
   b. mantle
   c. continents
   d. lithosphere

7. The hot, plasticlike layer of rock on which the Earth's crust floats is known as the:
   a. asthenosphere
   b. mantle
   c. continents
   d. lithosphere

8. Geologists have constructed a model of the Earth's interior by:
   a. direct observation
   b. inference
   c. guessing
   d. tunneling

9. Which of the following is used to reveal the composition of the Earth's interior?
   a. satellite images
   b. seismic waves
   c. maps
   d. drills

10. Which elements compose most of the Earth's crust?
    a. hydrogen and oxygen
    b. aluminum and magnesium
    c. silicon and oxygen
    d. iron and nickel

Matching *Match the terms with the correct definitions.*

a. lithosphere
b. Earth's core
c. mantle
d. convection cells

e. radioactive decay
f. friction
g. residual heat
h. crust

i. oceanic crust
j. continental crust
k. asthenosphere
l. inference

1. _____ The extremely hot and dense center of the Earth that is believed to be composed of iron and nickel.
2. _____ An area of flowing, plasticlike molten rock located directly below the Earth's crust.
3. _____ The solid outer layer of the Earth that is composed of rock.
4. _____ A conclusion based on a set of observed facts.
5. _____ The solid outer layer of the Earth that is composed of rock and soil.

INTRODUCTION

The theory of plate tectonics is one of the most exciting scientific discoveries of our time. Rarely in science is there the development of one explanation for the cause of many phenomena. This is known as a unifying theory. Plate tectonics explains some of the best-known natural phenomena on the Earth, including earthquakes, volcanoes, continental drift, deep ocean trenches, mid-ocean ridges, mountains, and deformed rocks, to name a few. Today, plate tectonics is widely accepted, but it wasn't that long ago when a group of scientists were laughed at by their peers when they declared that the continents floated along the surface of the Earth like boats in a pond. The story of plate tectonics is also interesting because its development reveals the way that science progresses and how theories develop. It is a perfect illustration of the scientific method at work and the advancement of human knowledge, all of which is the result of the development of new ideas based on careful observation, experimentation, and use of technology.

THE DYNAMIC CRUST

One of the most fundamental concepts in geology, which also provides evidence to support the theory of plate tectonics, is the notion that the Earth's crust is constantly in motion. At first this may seem like an outlandish idea, for how could the solid rock that composes the landscape move? All it takes is a trip to the mountains or a drive down the highway where the road cuts through rock formations to reveal that the Earth's crust is moving. Sometimes the rocks exposed near a road cut appear to have been tilted or folded by some great amount of force. Evidence that the Earth is dynamic, or constantly in motion, can be found all around the globe.

EVIDENCE OF CRUSTAL MOVEMENT

The appearance of deformed rock layers suggests that the Earth's crust is moving in some way. To understand how deformed rocks lead to the notion that the Earth's crust is in a state of motion, you must understand the concept of original horizontality. Original horizontality is a fundamental principle in geology that assumes that most all rock forms in horizontal layers on the Earth's surface. These horizontal layers are called **strata** (Figure 9–1).

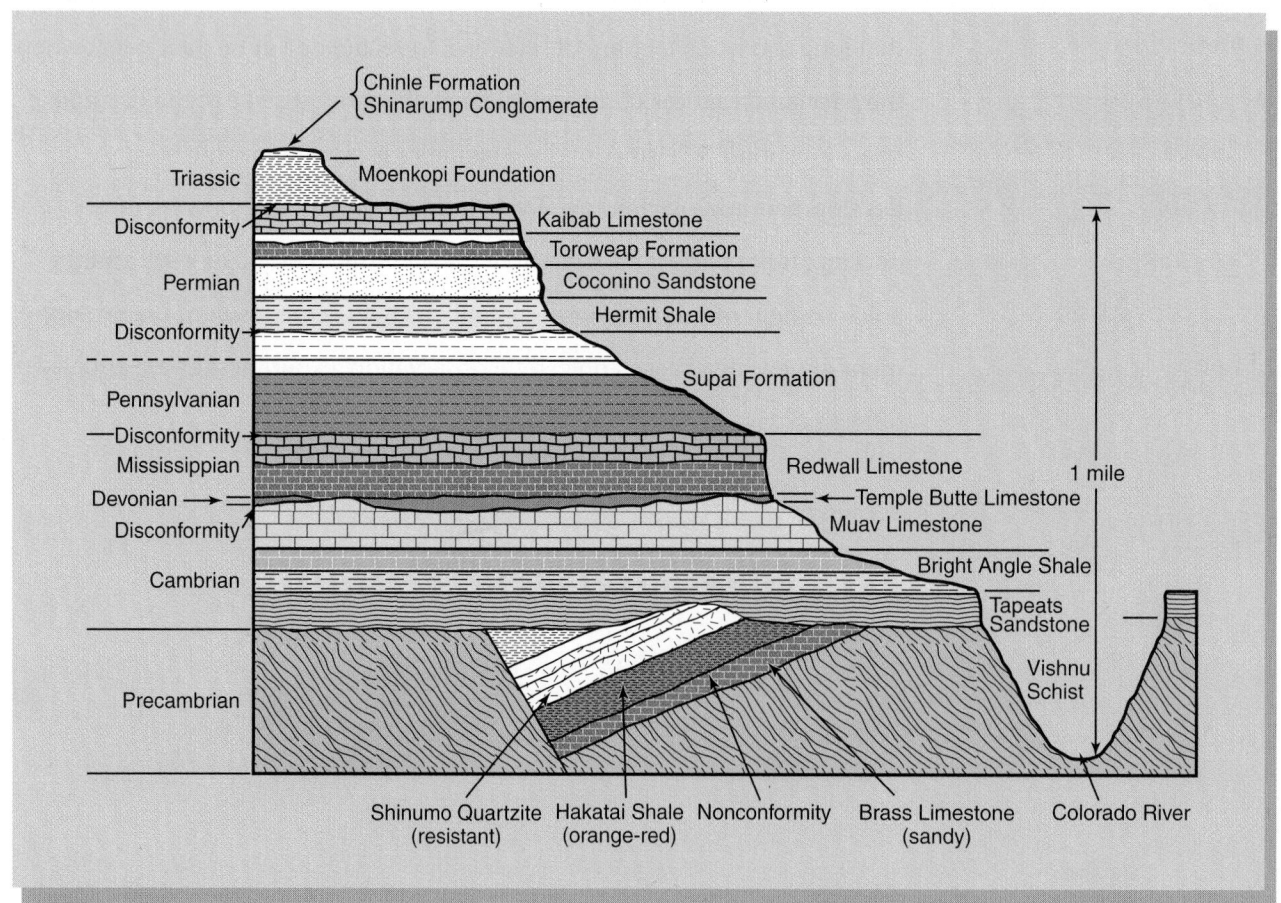

FIGURE 9–1 Diagram of the rock strata that make up the Grand Canyon.

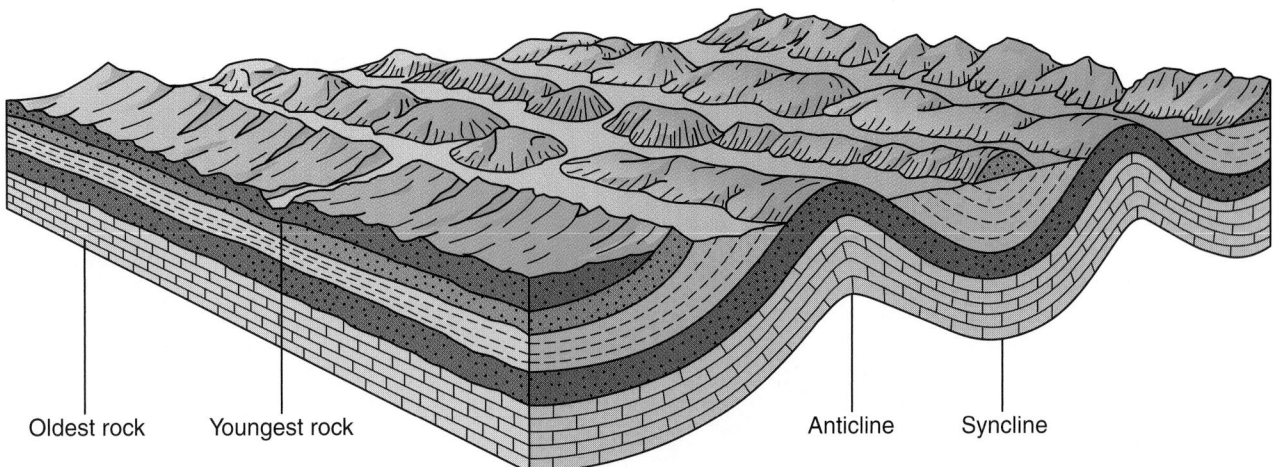

FIGURE 9–2 Deformed rock strata showing an anticline and syncline.

Just like the layers of cake, strata reveal the original orientation of the rock when it formed. There are three categories of deformed rock. Folded deformed rock occurs when **lateral forces** on the Earth's crust push together and fold strata either upward or downward. Folded rock strata creating an archlike formation is called an **anticline**. Folded rock strata forming a bowl-like depression is called a **syncline** (Figure 9–2). The second type of deformed rock is called tilted rock. This occurs when rock strata tilt upward or downward at an angle as a result of crustal movement (Figure 9–3). The third type of deformed rock is

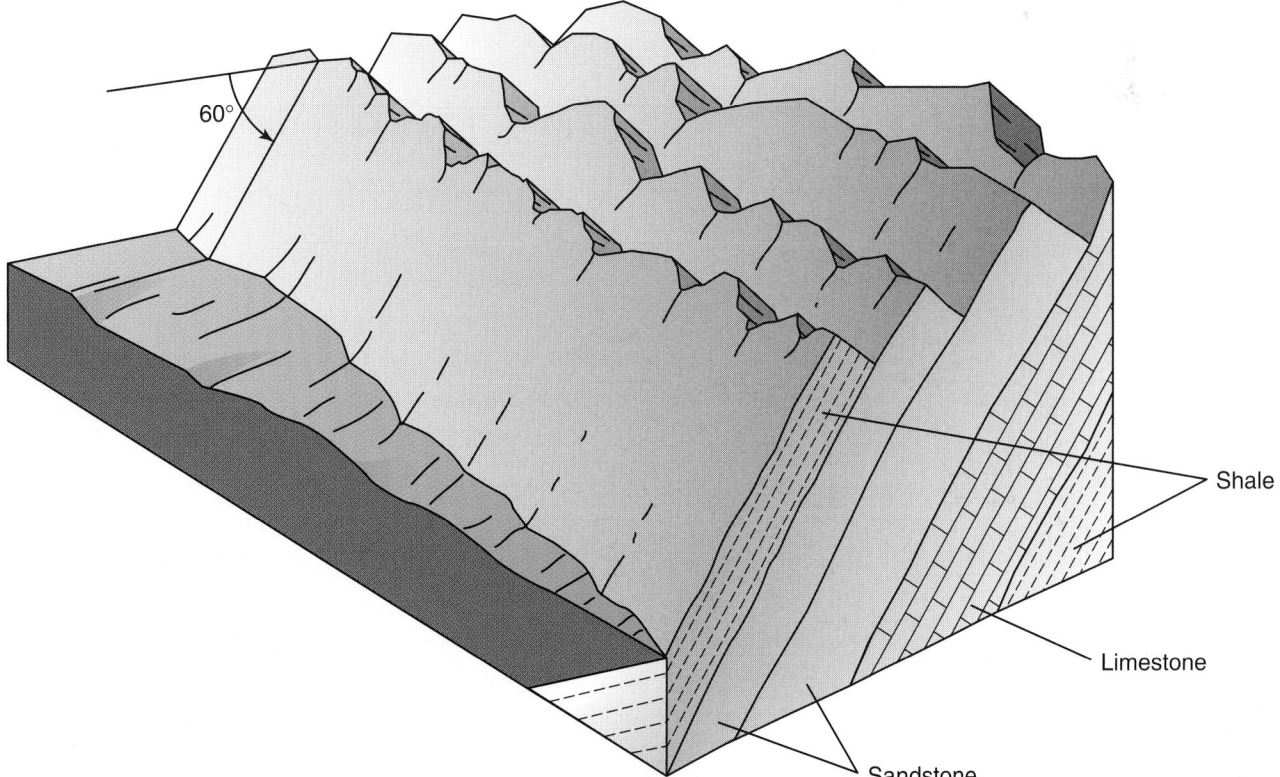

FIGURE 9–3 Rock strata that have been tilted 60 degrees to the horizon.

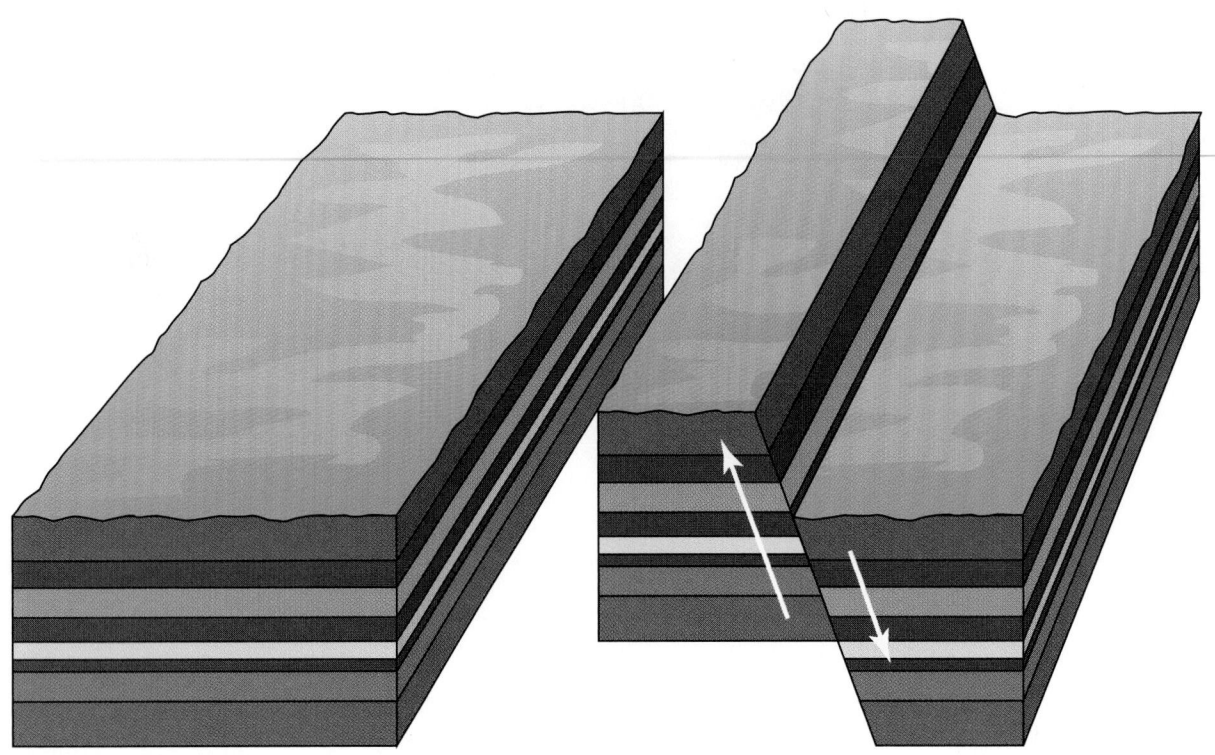

A   B

FIGURE 9–4   The development of a fault that displaces rock strata.

called faulted rock. This occurs when a large crack occurs in the rock, also called a **fault**, and the strata move upward or downward along the fault line (Figure 9–4).

The location of fossils in sedimentary rocks can also reveal that the Earth's crust is indeed dynamic. The fossils of marine organisms found

CAREER CONNECTIONS
Structural Geologist

A structural geologist studies the processes that deform the Earth's crust. This includes researching the mechanisms that lead to faulting, fracturing, and folding of rock; tectonic stress; crust deformation; and mountain building. Structural geologists travel the world to study rock formations to piece together the processes that have shaped our planet. They also use sophisticated computers and sensors to study the Earth's crust and the forces that continue to alter it. A career in structural geology begins with a 4-year degree in geology. Many structural geologists are employed by the oil industry because of the relationship between oil and deformed rock formations. Other career opportunities include academic research and employment with a government agency.

high in the mountains suggest that the rocks that contain the fossils were moved there by some geological force. All marine organisms live their lives in the ocean, far from the tops of mountains. Many marine fossils are found high in the Himalayan mountains, which are thousands of feet above sea level and hundreds of miles from the ocean. Also, some shallow water marine fossils, like coral, are found deep at the bottom of the ocean. These phenomena are known as displaced fossils, which suggests that the Earth's crust and the rocks it contains are moving in some way (Figure 9–5).

Benchmarks are specific elevation markers that geologists have placed all over the world. They usually consist of a bronze disk on top of a cement pillar and are marked on topographical maps. Benchmarks are used to mark the exact latitude and longitude coordinates and elevation of a specific point on the Earth's surface. Measurements taken over time at these benchmarks reveal that their positions are changing. This also provides evidence that the surface of the Earth is moving.

A **geosyncline** is a large, shallow ocean basin where sediments are accumulating near the edges of continents. The thickness of some of the sediment layers has been measured, revealing that the sediment layer is deeper than the water that it is in. This suggests that the accumulating sediments must be pushing down on the crust beneath the ocean, creating a large depression. This depression is called a geosyncline (Figure 9–6). The weight of the sediments in a geosyncline also causes the nearby continent to rise upward in elevation as it becomes lighter from the lost sediments. Geosynclines can also form as a result of the accumulation of calcite forming in the oceans. The buildup of limestone sediments in tropical waters can also push down on the crust, causing these depressions. The concept of the lighter, less dense continents floating higher on the Earth's mantle and the more dense ocean basins sinking into the mantle is called **isostasy**. Isostasy is the theory that states that the Earth's crust is always in a state of equilibrium. This means that as weight is added to one part of the Earth's crust, it will cause it to become heavier and sink into the mantle. The part of the crust that is losing weight becomes lighter and floats higher on the mantle, causing it to rise, much like when a lighter person rises up on

FIGURE 9–5 The discovery of displaced marine fossils located high above sea level suggests that the Earth's crust has been moved. (*Courtesy of Coolrox.com.*)

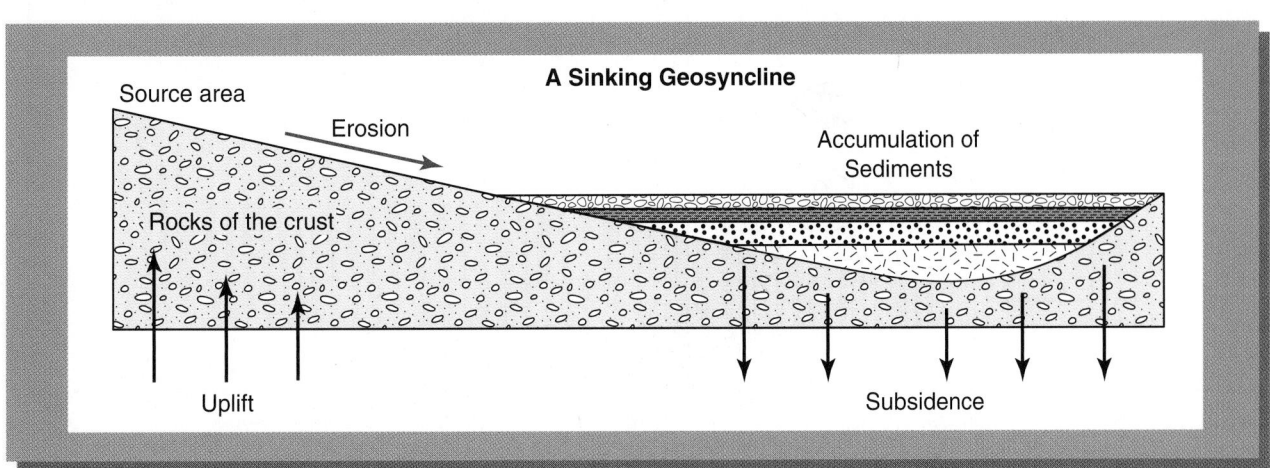

FIGURE 9–6 The formation of a geosyncline.

the mattress of a bed when a heavier person sits down on the mattress. Isostasy and the occurrence of geosynclines indicate that the Earth's crust is indeed dynamic.

CONTINENTAL DRIFT

From the time when the first maps were being drawn showing the accurate shapes of the world's continents, scientists have wondered at the jigsaw puzzle–like shapes of the land. One cannot help but notice the way that the South American and African continents appear to fit together (Figure 9–7). Geologists began to wonder if this was a coincidence or if at some time during the Earth's past they were once joined as one landmass. The first theories of how the Earth formed were developed around the idea that the planet was once composed of liquid rock. Once this rock began to cool, the outer surface of the Earth began to wrinkle and shrink. This was the explanation that described the formation of mountains and valleys, that the Earth's crust was only capable of vertical movement. It meant that the Earth's surface could only move upward to form mountains or downward to form ocean basins.

When scientists studied fossils located on the western coast of Africa and the Eastern coast of South America, they found many of them to be of the same species of organism. To explain this phenomenon, scientists theorized that ancient land bridges once connected the two continents but had long ago disappeared. It wasn't

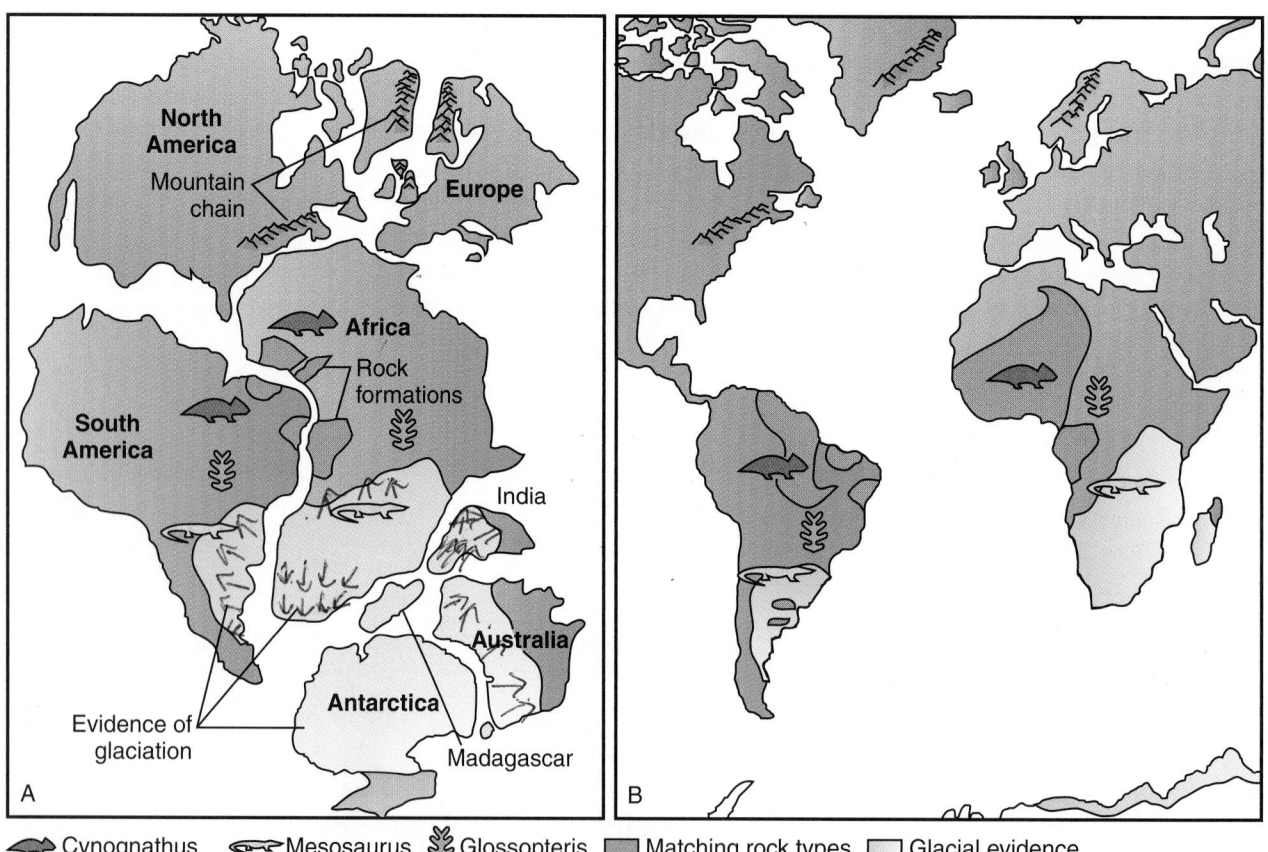

🐊 Cynognathus   🦎 Mesosaurus   🌿 Glossopteris   ⬛ Matching rock types   ⬜ Glacial evidence

FIGURE 9–7 The fossil and rock formation correlations used to support the theory of continental drift.

until 1912 that a meteorologist by the name of Alfred Wegner proposed a new theory that explained the jigsaw puzzle–like appearance of the continents and the similarities of fossils found there. He called it the theory of continental drift, which explained that the continents had once been joined together and have slowly drifted apart by some unknown mechanism. He supported his theory by continuing to compare fossil samples on either side of the continents, which revealed that many of them were of the same species. He also compared rock types on the different continents and showed that they were similar in their composition. The last piece of supporting evidence for his theory was the similarities that existed in the way glaciers left scars in rocks on the separate continents. He showed that the direction of the glacial movement lined up perfectly if the separate continents were rejoined (Figure 9–7). Wegner's fellow scientists at the time rejected his theory for two reasons. Their first argument was that Wegner was a meteorologist, not a geologist, and could not know about the Earth's continents. Secondly, Wegner failed to provide a mechanism for how the massive continents were able to drift across the Earth's surface. Today geologists have gathered enough evidence from around the world to prove continental drift and have pieced together a timeline of how the continents have moved relative to one another in the past. At one time all the continents were joined together to form one supercontinent called Pangaea. Pangaea formed about 290 million years ago.

Earth System Scientists

Alfred Wegner

Alfred Wegner was born in Germany in 1880 and began his career in science as a meteorologist. While traveling and studying the various climates of the world, he began to notice that the shapes of the continents, along with their regional geology, were very similar. He observed how some of the continents appeared to be large pieces of a jigsaw puzzle. This led him to begin formulating his theory of continental drift, which proposed that the continents were joined at some time in the Earth's past and had somehow drifted apart. To support this theory he traveled the world comparing fossils and rock formations in areas around Brazil and West Africa. He published his theory in his 1929 book, titled *The Origins of Continents and Oceans*. His theory was widely rejected by geologists at the time because Wegner was a meteorologist, not a geologist. They also rejected his theory because of the lack of an explanation of the mechanisms that had caused the continents to drift. Through much of his life, Wegner also continued to pursue meteorology, especially in the polar regions of the world. He died at the age of 50 during an expedition in Greenland. It took more than 30 years after Wegner's death for his theory of continental drift, now known as plate tectonics, to become validated by the scientific community.

SEA FLOOR SPREADING

During the period after World War II, detailed maps that were being constructed of the ocean floor revealed large underwater mountain ranges called **mid-ocean ridges**. One of these underwater mountain chains runs down the center of the Atlantic Ocean and is known as the Mid-Atlantic Ridge. During the 1950s and 1960s, scientists who studied the mid-ocean ridges began to put together theories on how new crust was being formed at the center of these ridges and was moving outward from the ridge center. This was called sea floor spreading, and it helped to explain how the continents might drift apart (Figure 9–8).

Further evidence to support sea floor spreading was gathered by studying how the crust on either side of the mid-ocean ridges contained alternating bands of magnetic crystals. Scientists had known that the Earth's magnetic field has periodically flipped at different times in the past. This meant that the locations of the **magnetic north** and south would periodically change from time to time. When liquid rock containing iron cools, the resulting iron crystals that form align themselves toward magnetic north. Maps made of the magnetic orientation of rocks on either side of the ridge appeared like a mirror image. After studying these maps, scientists then concluded that new crust was being formed at the mid-ocean ridge, which was then being pushed outward and away on both sides from the ridge center by the formation of newer rock (Figure 9–9).

Scientists also dated the rock samples around the mid-ocean ridges, which showed that the farther the rock was located from the

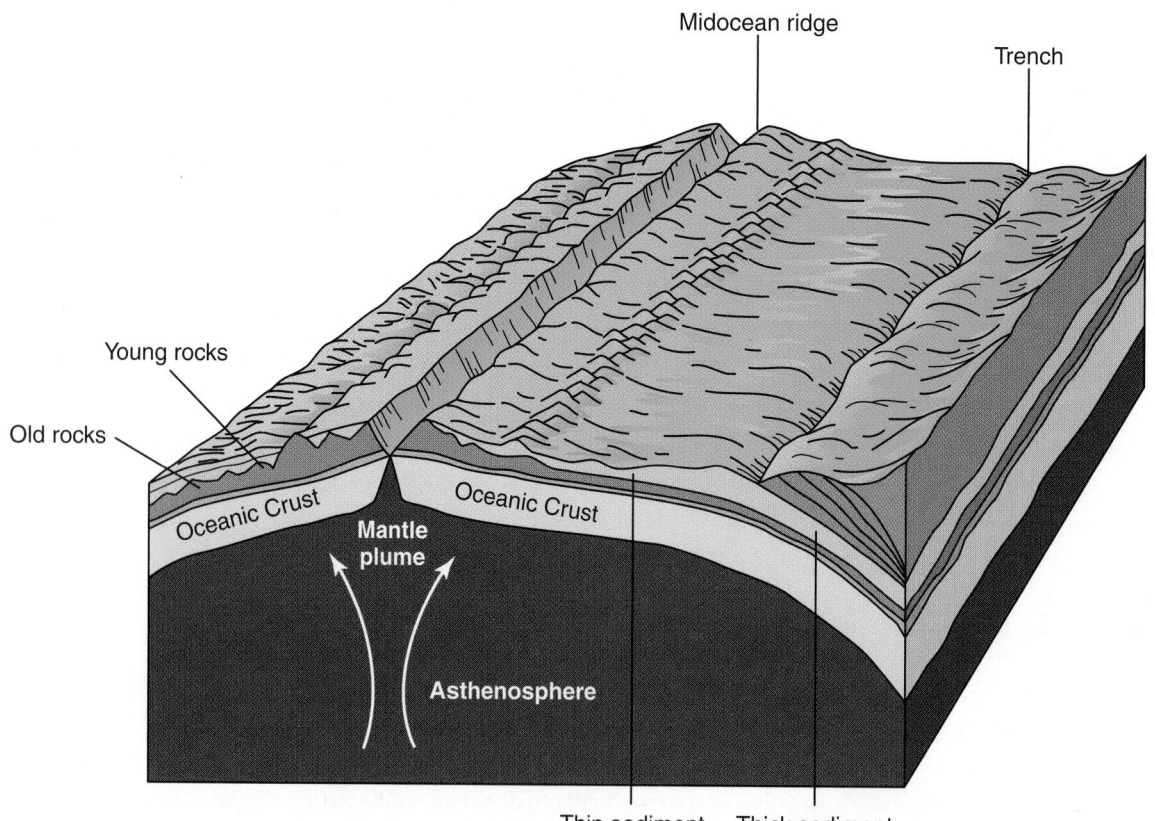

FIGURE 9–8 A cross section of a mid-ocean ridge showing the formation of new ocean crust at the ridge center, causing the sea floor to spread apart.

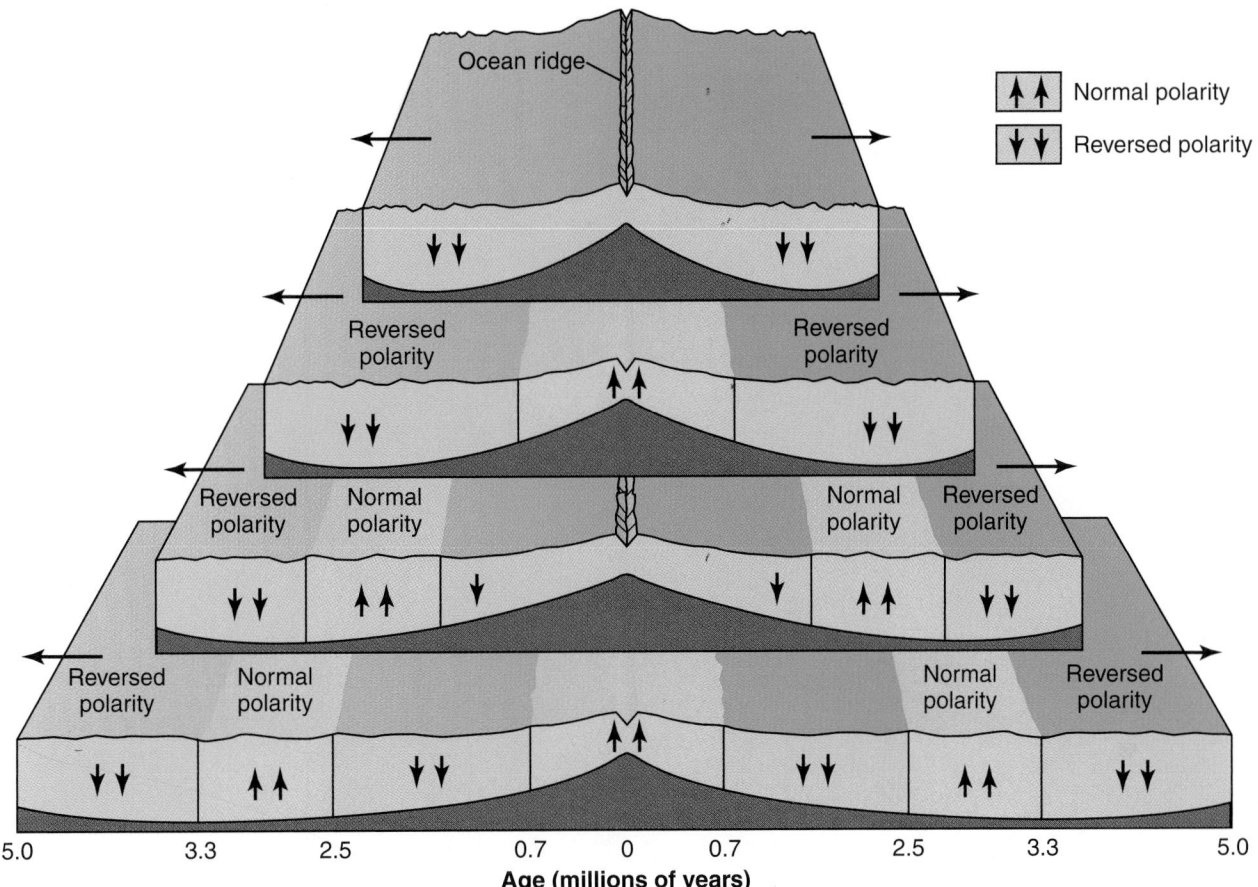

FIGURE 9–9   A map of the magnetic reversals associated with the Mid-Atlantic Ridge, which supports the concept of sea floor spreading.

ridge center, the older it was. Further analysis of heat around the mid-ocean ridges revealed that the ocean crust became cooler as you moved away from the ridge center. This pointed to the possibility that large convection cells in the underlying mantle may be the force causing the Earth's crust to move around on the Earth's surface. These discoveries were providing Wegner's continental drift theory with the mechanism needed to explain what caused the continents to move.

TECTONIC PLATES

As the theory of continental drift progressed, scientists were beginning to put together the idea that the Earth's surface is composed of a series of large, moving plates. This new theory, called plate tectonics, was built on the foundations of Alfred Wegner's theory of continental drift. Plate tectonics describes the Earth's surface as being divided into distinct plates that move relative to one another. These solid plates float on the semiliquid upper mantle, making the Earth's surface resemble a broken eggshell. It was also observed that edges of the tectonic plates, known as **plate boundaries**, are areas where volcanoes are located and also where frequent earthquakes occur. These areas, known as zones of earthquakes and volcanoes, mark the locations of plate boundaries. The movement of plates and the buildup of tectonic stress along plate boundaries cause earthquakes (Figure 9–10). There have been 14 major

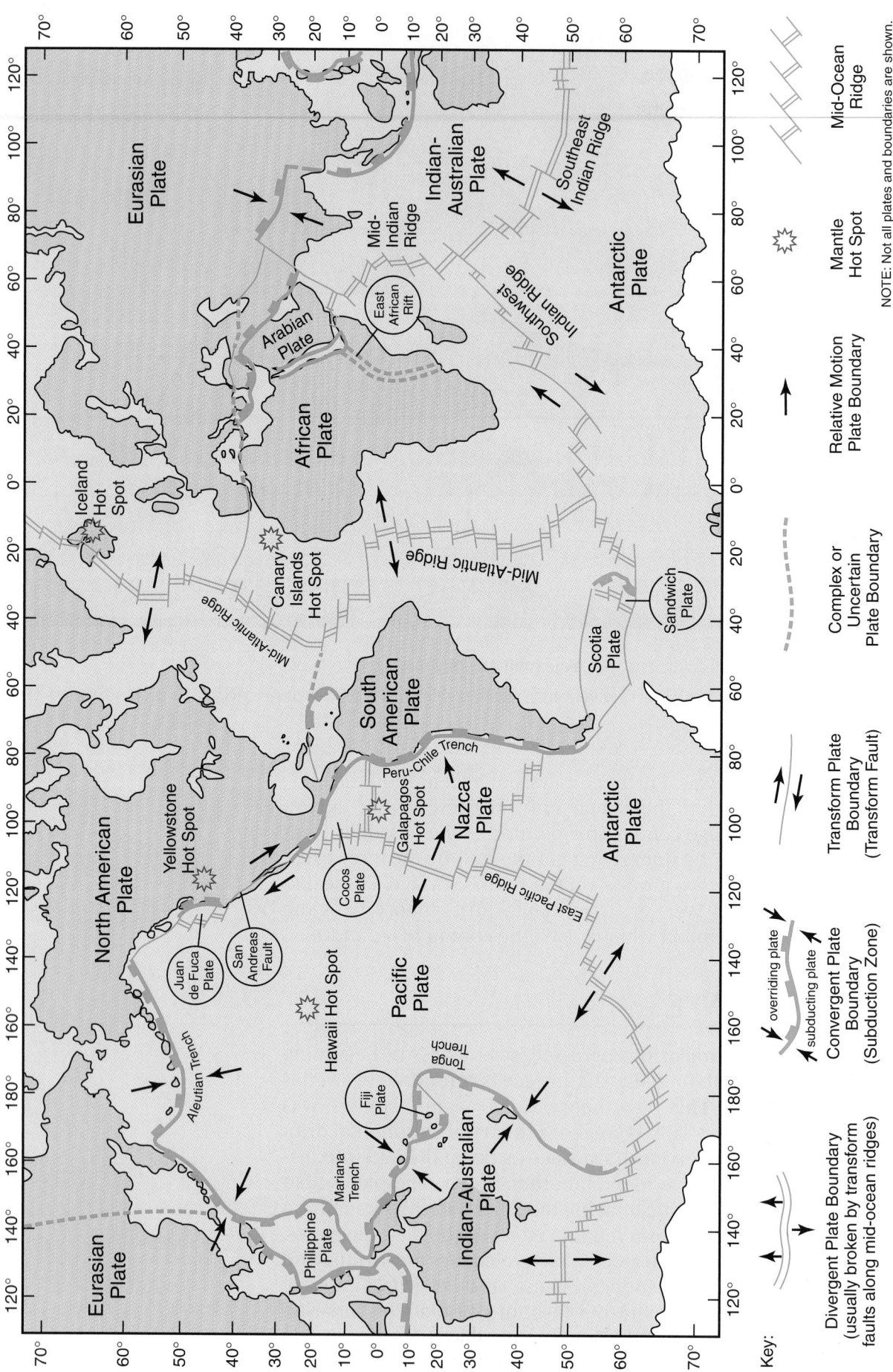

FIGURE 9–10 A map of the tectonic plates showing their relative movement and the different plate boundaries.

Earth System Scientists

Harry Hess

Harry Hess was born in New York in 1906. After attending Yale and Princeton, where he studied electrical engineering and geology, Hess began his research in geophysics and oceanography. In 1931 he began his lifelong study of the ocean floor. He conducted his research by taking soundings and samples of the bottom of the ocean from all parts of the world. His research led him to observe that certain parts of the ocean floor were younger than other portions. He eventually developed his theory of sea floor spreading in 1962. This groundbreaking theory proposed that new portions of the ocean floor were being formed at the mid-ocean ridges from rising currents of molten mantle. The new rock formed at the ridges and was then pushed outward as new rock rose up from the Earth's mantle and cooled, much like a conveyor belt. Hess's theory of sea floor spreading gave the struggling theory of continental drift the mechanism it needed to be proven. He then further hypothesized that the crust would be pushed along until it collided or ran under other tectonic plates. Harry Hess's work revolutionized the theory of plate tectonics and our knowledge of the Earth's systems.

plates identified on the Earth that together form the solid outer crust. All the plates float on the underlying asthenosphere and move relative to one another. Tectonic plates move at varying rates, with some moving at only 0.5 in (1.3 cm) per year and others moving more rapidly, up to 4 in (10 cm) per year.

PLATE BOUNDARIES

The point where two tectonic plates meet is called a plate boundary. There are three main types of plate boundaries on the Earth (Figure 9–11). The first type is called a divergent plate boundary. This is the boundary where two plates are moving away from one another. These are usually areas where new crust is formed from magma. Magma is hot, liquid rock that flows beneath the Earth's surface. Divergent plate boundaries are usually associated with mid-ocean ridges, like the Mid-Atlantic Ridge that runs down the middle of the Atlantic Ocean. Divergent plate boundaries on land form **rift valleys**, like the great African Rift Valley located near the eastern side of the African continent.

Areas where two plates come together and collide into one another are called convergent plate boundaries (Figure 9–12). Two things can occur when plates converge. First, if the two plates are both composed of less dense continental crust, they will collide, buckle, and rise upward in elevation to form mountains. This is what is occurring today as India continues to collide into Asia to form the Himalayan mountains. The Himalayas are continuing to rise in elevation as a result of the collision of these two plates. The Appalachian mountain range, located along the east coast of North America, formed when the African

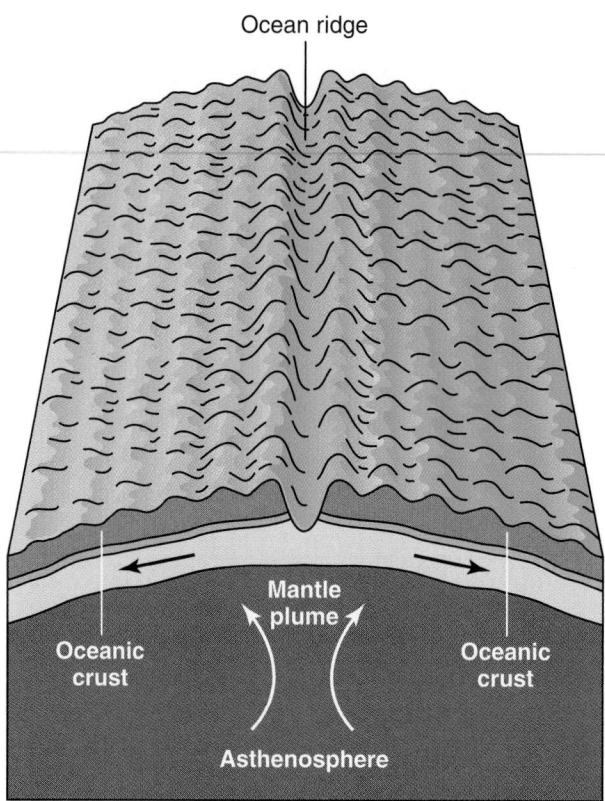

Ocean ridge

Mantle plume

Oceanic crust

Oceanic crust

Asthenosphere

FIGURE 9–11 A mid-ocean ridge is an example of a divergent plate boundary.

continent collided with North America approximately 290 million years ago. This important geological event also formed the supercontinent called Pangaea.

The other result of two plates converging is when an oceanic plate collides with a continental plate. The oceanic crust is more dense than the continental crust, which causes the oceanic plate to slide under the continental plate. When this occurs, it is called **subduction** and it results in the solid crust of the oceanic plate descending downward into the mantle, where it melts. The area where subduction occurs is called a subduction zone. Subduction zones form some of the deepest ocean trenches in the world. The Marianas trench, at the bottom of the Pacific Ocean near Japan, is the deepest point in the ocean at more than 7 mi (11 km) deep. Another feature associated with convergent boundaries is a **volcanic arc** system. A volcanic arc is a series of volcanoes that form near subduction zones. They form as a result of the sinking crust of an oceanic plate, which melts under great heat and pressure as it slides beneath the plate it is converging with. The sinking crust brings with it a great amount of sea water, which rises back toward the Earth's surface as a mixture of magma and steam in a network of faults and volcanic vents. It eventually reaches the Earth's surface to form a chain of active volcanoes. A subduction zone like this exists along the western edge of South America where it meets the Pacific Ocean. This convergent boundary formed the volcanic chain of mountains that runs along the coast of South America known as the Andes Mountains.

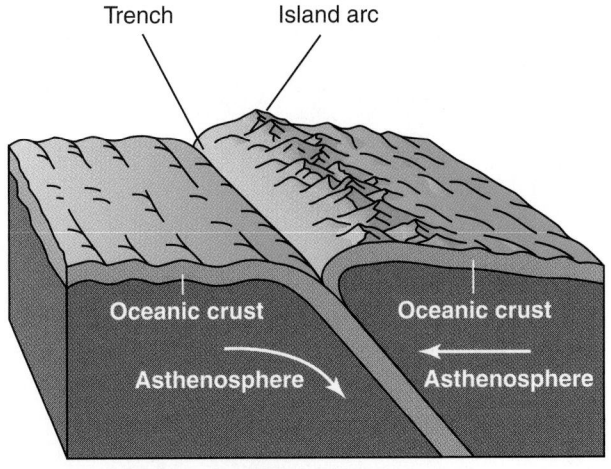

Oceanic-Oceanic

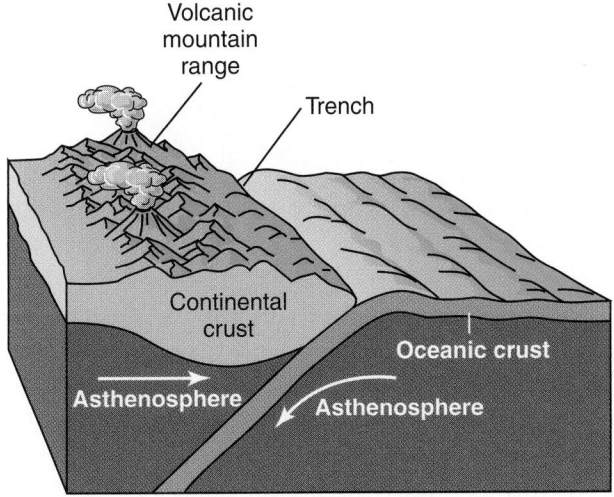

Oceanic-Continental

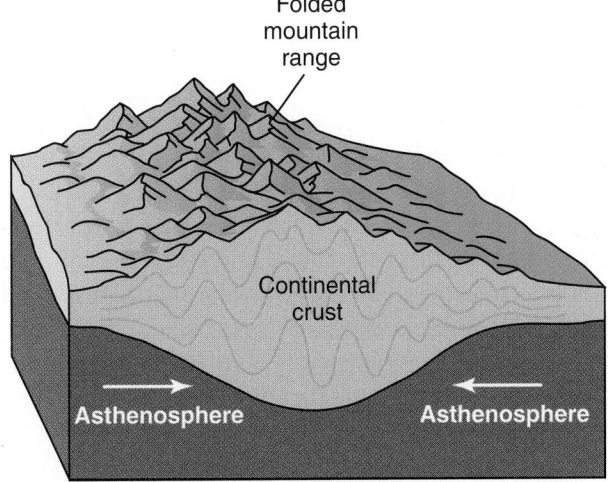

Continental-Continental

FIGURE 9–12 Three different types of convergent plate boundaries.

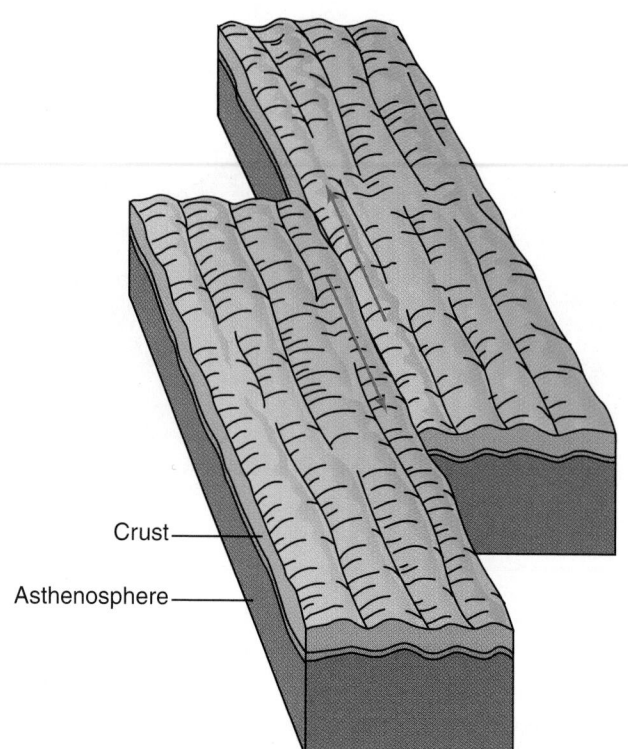

Crust

Asthenosphere

FIGURE 9–13 An example of a transform fault plate boundary.

The third type of plate boundary occurs when two tectonic plates slide along one another. This is called a transform fault plate boundary (Figure 9–13). Also known as a lateral fault, these areas can build up a great amount of tension between the two plates as a result of friction. Eventually the plates slip past one another and cause earthquakes. The famous San Andreas fault in California is an example of a transform fault plate boundary.

MANTLE CONVECTION

Mantle convection is the driving force that causes the tectonic plates to move around the Earth's surface. Convection is the way that the Earth's extremely hot interior dissipates heat toward the surface. Hot plumes of mantle rise upward toward the crust from deep within the asthenosphere, forming large convection cells. The specific area where hot magma rises up from the Earth's interior and breaks through the crust is called a **hot spot**. Hot spots are areas where magma breaks through the Earth's surface, forming lava that solidifies to form new crust. Mid-ocean ridges are located over hot spots, as are some volcanic island chains. The Hawaiian Islands in the middle of the Pacific Ocean were formed as the Pacific plate moved over a hot spot (Figure 9–14). The result is a chain of active volcanic islands, with the oldest islands being the least active. As the Pacific plate moves over the hot spot, the older islands, which formed earlier, slowly move away from the hot spot and begin to cool. Mantle convection and hot spots act like giant conveyor belts on which the tectonic plates move. Once the mantle

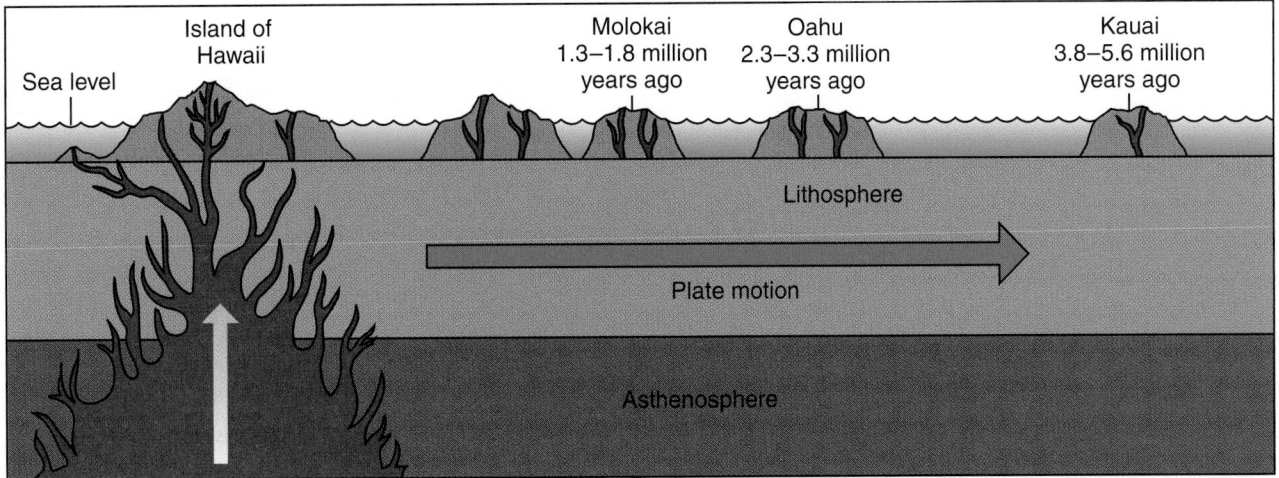

FIGURE 9–14 The formation of the Hawaiian Islands as the Pacific plate moves over a hot spot.

dissipates its heat to the crust, the cooler mantle sinks downward back into the Earth and the whole convection cycle begins again. The result of mantle convection and plate tectonics is an active crust that is constantly changing as new rock is produced and older rock is returned to the mantle.

REVIEW

1. What are the three types of deformed rock formations?

2. List four things that might suggest that the Earth's crust is dynamic.

3. What are three pieces of evidence that Wegner used to prove his theory of continental drift?

4. What are the three tectonic plate boundaries?

5. Explain how sea floor spreading is related to the theory of plate tectonics.

6. What is the mechanism by which the tectonic plates are forced to move?

7. Who were Alfred Wegner and Harry Hess?

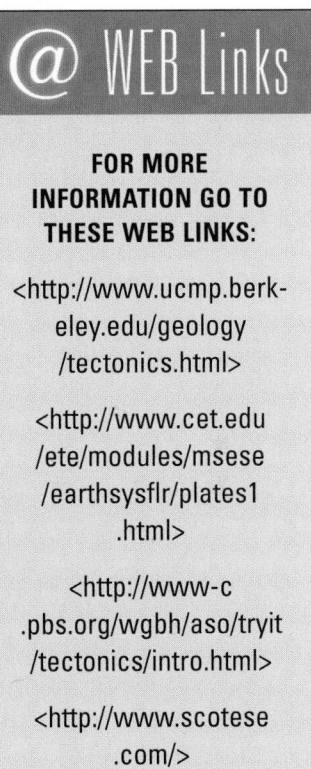

@ WEB Links

FOR MORE INFORMATION GO TO THESE WEB LINKS:

<http://www.ucmp.berk-eley.edu/geology/tectonics.html>

<http://www.cet.edu/ete/modules/msese/earthsysflr/plates1.html>

<http://www-c.pbs.org/wgbh/aso/tryit/tectonics/intro.html>

<http://www.scotese.com/>

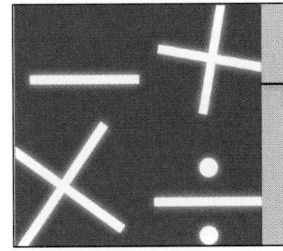

earth math

1) If a rock sample is located 50 miles to the east of the Mid-Atlantic Ridge and moves at approximately 1 inch per year, how many years ago did the rock form?

CHAPTER SUMMARY

Plate tectonics is a unifying theory that explains the occurrence of earthquakes, volcanoes, deformed rocks, mountains, continental drift, deep ocean trenches, and mid-ocean ridges. Simple observations of the rock formations on the Earth reveal that they have been moved and deformed by geological forces. This implies that the Earth's crust is dynamic, or in a state of motion. The geological principle of original horizontality is used to support the dynamic nature of the Earth's crust. Original horizontality states that all sedimentary rock layers were laid down horizontally on the Earth's surface. Evidence to support the notion that the crust is dynamic includes displaced fossils, tilted or folded rock formations, moving benchmarks, the presence of geosynclines, and continental drift.

The continental drift theory was first proposed by Alfred Wegner in 1912. It stated that the continents were joined together at one time in the past and have now drifted apart. Wegner used the jigsaw puzzle–like appearance of the coasts of Africa and South America, along with similar fossils and rock formations found on both continents, to prove that they were once joined. The lack of a mechanism to explain how the massive continents were moved made Wegner's theory unacceptable to many geologists at the time. Shortly after World War II, scientists began to make detailed maps of the sea floor. These maps revealed the existence of the Mid-Atlantic Ridge, which is a long chain of mountains that runs directly down the center of the Atlantic Ocean. Further investigation of this ridge system revealed that the age of the rocks increases as you move away from the ridge center. Studies were also made of the magnetic orientation of the rocks on either side of the ridge. This revealed a mirrorlike pattern of magnetic reversals on both sides of the ridge. Monitoring heat flow along the ridge has revealed that as you move away from the ridge center, the crust cools. All this evidence suggests that new crust is being formed at the center of the mid-ocean ridges, which is causing the sea floor to spread apart. This is the mechanism that can explain the continental drift theory.

The theory of plate tectonics states that the Earth's crust is divided into distinct plates that move relative to one another on the Earth's surface. Areas where plates interact form what are called plate boundaries. These areas are also zones where frequent earthquakes and volcanoes occur. The movement of the plates and buildup of tectonic stress cause earthquakes. There are three different types of plate boundaries: divergent, convergent, and transform. Divergent boundaries occur where two plates are moving apart, like at the mid-ocean ridges. Convergent boundaries occur where two plates come together. This results in the formation of mountain ranges and volcanic island arcs. When one plate slides underneath another plate, it is called subduction. Transform fault plate boundaries occur where two plates slide alongside one another, such as at the famous San Andreas fault in California. The mechanism that moves tectonic plates is caused by convection currents in the Earth's mantle. These form as the heat from the Earth's core is dissipated outward toward the crust. Mantle convection acts like large conveyor belts on which the tectonic plates move. Hot spots occur in the Earth's crust where mantle plumes break through the surface, forming volcanoes and mid-ocean ridges.

CHAPTER REVIEW

Multiple Choice

1. An observer discovers shallow-water marine fossils at an elevation of 15,000 feet above sea level. What is the best explanation for this observation?
   a. the level of the ocean was once 15,000 feet higher
   b. violent earthquakes caused the crust to collapse
   c. marine organisms evolved into land organisms
   d. the crust was lifted up by some force

2. A sandstone layer is found tilted 75 degrees from the horizon. What most likely caused this tilt?
   a. the sediments that formed the sandstone were laid down at a 75-degree angle
   b. the sandstone layer has changed positions because of crustal movement
   c. the sandstone has recrystallized in that orientation.
   d. all sandstone is deposited by the wind

3. Which is the best evidence of crustal movement?
   a. molten rock in the Earth's outer core
   b. tilted sedimentary rock layers
   c. sediment found on top of bedrock
   d. marine fossils found below sea level

4. A sequence of thickly bedded rock containing shallow marine fossils was most likely formed by:
   a. an ocean trench
   b. a meandering stream
   c. a geosyncline
   d. a glacial lake

5. The term isostasy refers to a:
   a. line of equal air pressure
   b. series of anticlines
   c. deflection of the winds by the Earth's rotation
   d. condition of balance between segments of the Earth's crust

6. Which statement best supports the theory that all the continents were once a single landmass?
   a. rocks of the ocean ridges are older than the surrounding sea floor
   b. rock and fossil correlations can be made where the continents appear to fit together
   c. marine fossils can be found at high elevations on all continents
   d. great thicknesses of shallow water sediments are found in the middle of continents

7. Which is the best evidence supporting the concept of sea floor spreading?
   a. earthquakes occur at great depth beneath the sea floor
   b. sandstones and limestones can be found in both North America and Africa
   c. volcanoes appear at random within the ocean crust
   d. rock along the mid-ocean ridges are younger than those farther from the ridge

8. Which best describes a major characteristic of earthquakes and volcanoes?
   a. they are centered at the poles
   b. they are located at the same geographical areas
   c. they are related to the formation of glaciers
   d. they are restricted to the Southern Hemisphere

9. Approximately how many tectonic plates make up the Earth's crust?
   a. 5
   b. 9
   c. 14
   d. 20

10. The area where two tectonic plates come together is known as a:
    a. convergent boundary
    b. divergent boundary
    c. transform boundary
    d. hot spot

11. The area where two tectonic plates move apart from each other is called a:
    a. convergent boundary
    b. divergent boundary
    c. transform boundary
    d. hot spot

12. The area where two tectonic plates slide along one another is known as a:
    a. convergent boundary
    b. divergent boundary
    c. transform boundary
    d. hot spot

13. Evidence of subduction occurs between the:
    a. African and South American plates
    b. Australian and Antarctic plates
    c. Pacific and Antarctic plates
    d. Nazca and South American plates

14. Heat detected below the mid-ocean ridges that gradually decreases as you move away from the ridge center is evidence that:
    a. subduction is occurring
    b. new crust is formed at the ridge center
    c. the Earth's magnetic poles are reversed
    d. earthquakes occur there

15. What is the mechanism that drives plate tectonics?
    a. the Earth's rotation
    b. sea floor spreading
    c. hot spots
    d. mantle convection

Matching   *Match the terms with the correct definitions.*

a. strata
b. lateral forces
c. anticline
d. syncline
e. fault

f. geosynclines
g. isostasy
h. mid-ocean ridge
i. magnetic north
j. plate boundaries

k. rift valley
l. subduction
m. volcanic arc
n. mantle convection
o. hot spot

1. _____ The direction on the Earth where a magnetic needle points north.
2. _____ Horizontal layers of sedimentary rocks.
3. _____ A type of divergent tectonic plate boundary located on the ocean floor where new crust is formed that pushes on the two plates, causing them to spread apart.
4. _____ Forces that push in on something from both sides.
5. _____ Large convection cells that are believed to exist in the Earth's upper mantle.
6. _____ A type of fold in rock strata that forms an archlike shape.
7. _____ A chain of volcanic islands that forms near a convergent plate boundary located below the ocean.
8. _____ A bowl-like fold or depression in rock strata.
9. _____ The movement of one tectonic plate underneath another at a convergent plate boundary.
10. _____ A large break or crack in a rock mass formed by tectonic stress that results in the displacement of rock strata.
11. _____ A valley that forms along a divergent plate boundary, where two tectonic plates are spreading apart.
12. _____ A bowl-like depression in the Earth's crust formed from the deposition of large amounts of sediments.
13. _____ Specific areas on the Earth's crust where two or more tectonic plates interact with one another.
14. _____ The theory that explains how the Earth's crust is in balance, causing the continents to float at different levels on the asthenosphere below.
15. _____ A term used to describe a specific point located near the middle of a tectonic plate that experiences volcanic activity.

Critical Thinking

1. If Africa and North America continue to move apart, what geological events will most likely occur and where?

10

Earthquakes and Volcanoes

EARTHQUAKES OBJECTIVES

Causes of Earthquakes · Seismic Waves · Epicenter Location · Earthquake Measurement

After reading this section you should be able to:
- Define the term *earthquake* and explain how earthquakes are caused.
- Define the term *seismic wave* and identify the characteristics associated with P-waves and S-waves.
- Differentiate between the focus and epicenter of an earthquake.
- Describe the process by which an earthquake's epicenter can be located.
- Differentiate between the Richter and Mercalli scales used to measure earthquakes.

VOLCANOES OBJECTIVES

Formation of a Volcano · Quiet Eruption Volcanoes · Explosive Eruption Volcanoes · Volcano Hazards

After reading this section you should be able to:
- Define the terms *volcano*, *lava*, and *eruption*.
- Differentiate between quiet eruptions and violent eruptions.
- Identify the six different types of volcanoes found on Earth.
- Describe the specific hazards that are associated with volcanoes.

INTRODUCTION

In 79 A.D. a violent volcanic eruption of Mount Vesuvius buried the Roman cities of Pompeii and Herculaneum. Almost 2,000 years later, archaeologists working in Italy continue to excavate these ancient cities and are learning more about the culture of ancient Roman society. Geologists, too, are interested in cities like Pompeii and Herculaneum because they reveal the violent nature of volcanic eruptions and how they can affect human civilization. These cities illustrate the long-standing relationship that humans have had with natural disasters such as earthquakes and volcanoes. This relationship continues today; millions of people live in areas that might be affected by these natural disasters. Understanding what causes these often violent events, and the potential damage to human life and property that they can cause, is the best way to minimize their threat. As a result of intensive research, geologists and engineers are now enabling human society to coexist with the dynamic nature of the Earth, which causes volcanoes and earthquakes (Figure 10–1). Although we might never be able to control these massive events, it is becoming increasingly possible to warn people when they might occur and also to create methods to prevent the loss of life and destruction they have caused too often in the past.

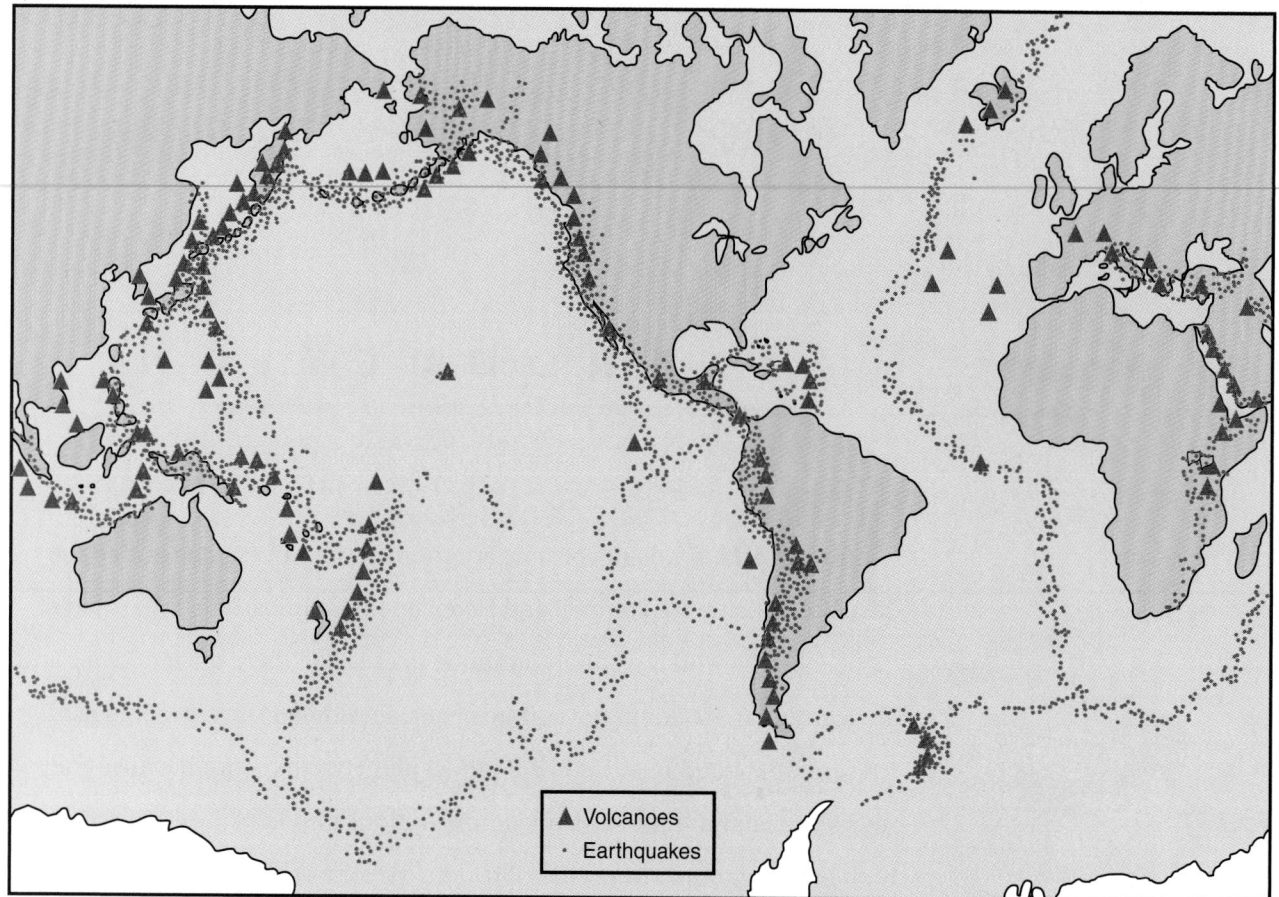

FIGURE 10–1   A map showing the locations of earthquakes and volcanoes on the Earth reveals a definite pattern, which geologists have linked to interactions occurring between tectonic plates.

10.1 Earthquakes

CAUSES OF EARTHQUAKES

One of the most destructive forces on Earth is the **earthquake**. An earthquake is caused by a natural rapid shaking of the ground, which is the result of displaced rocks (Figure 10–2). Displaced rocks are rocks that have been moved by tectonic forces. These forces cause strain to build up in the rigid rocks that form the Earth's crust. Eventually the rocks can no longer take the strain, and they break, much like bending a wooden ruler. If you gently apply force to both ends of the ruler, at first it will bend; however, if you increase the force at the ends of the ruler, the strain becomes too great and the ruler breaks. When this occurs in rock, it causes energy to dissipate outward from where the rock mass has fractured. The energy travels through the Earth in **seismic waves**. When seismic waves reach the Earth's surface, they move the ground and cause earthquakes. Some earthquakes occur on the ocean floor and can cause undersea landslides or displacement of the sea floor, which can form tidal waves, also known as tsunamis.

FIGURE 10-2 The massive displacement of the Earth's surface, caused by an earthquake. (*Photograph by Edwin L. Harp/ U.S. Geological Survey.*)

SEISMIC WAVES

The seismic waves produced by earthquakes can be detected using a **seismograph** (Figure 10–3). A seismograph uses a series of springs and weights to detect the waves produced when earthquakes occur. Earthquakes produce three distinct types of seismic wave. The first type of wave produced by an earthquake is called a compressional primary wave, also known as a **P-wave**. These waves travel through the

Earth System Scientists

Robert Mallet

Robert Mallet was born in Dublin, Ireland, in 1810. Shortly after attending college, he worked, along with his father, as a structural engineer. Together they helped design and build many large structures in Ireland, such as churches, railroads, and bridges. Mallet was also interested in the dynamics of earthquakes. He was one of the first scientists to conduct experiments to determine the speed and direction of movement of shock waves through rock and sand generated by blasts of dynamite. He also wrote the first research papers explaining the properties of earthquakes. In 1850 he moved to London, England, where he continued to practice as a consulting engineer while also writing scientific articles about the nature and location of earthquakes around the world.

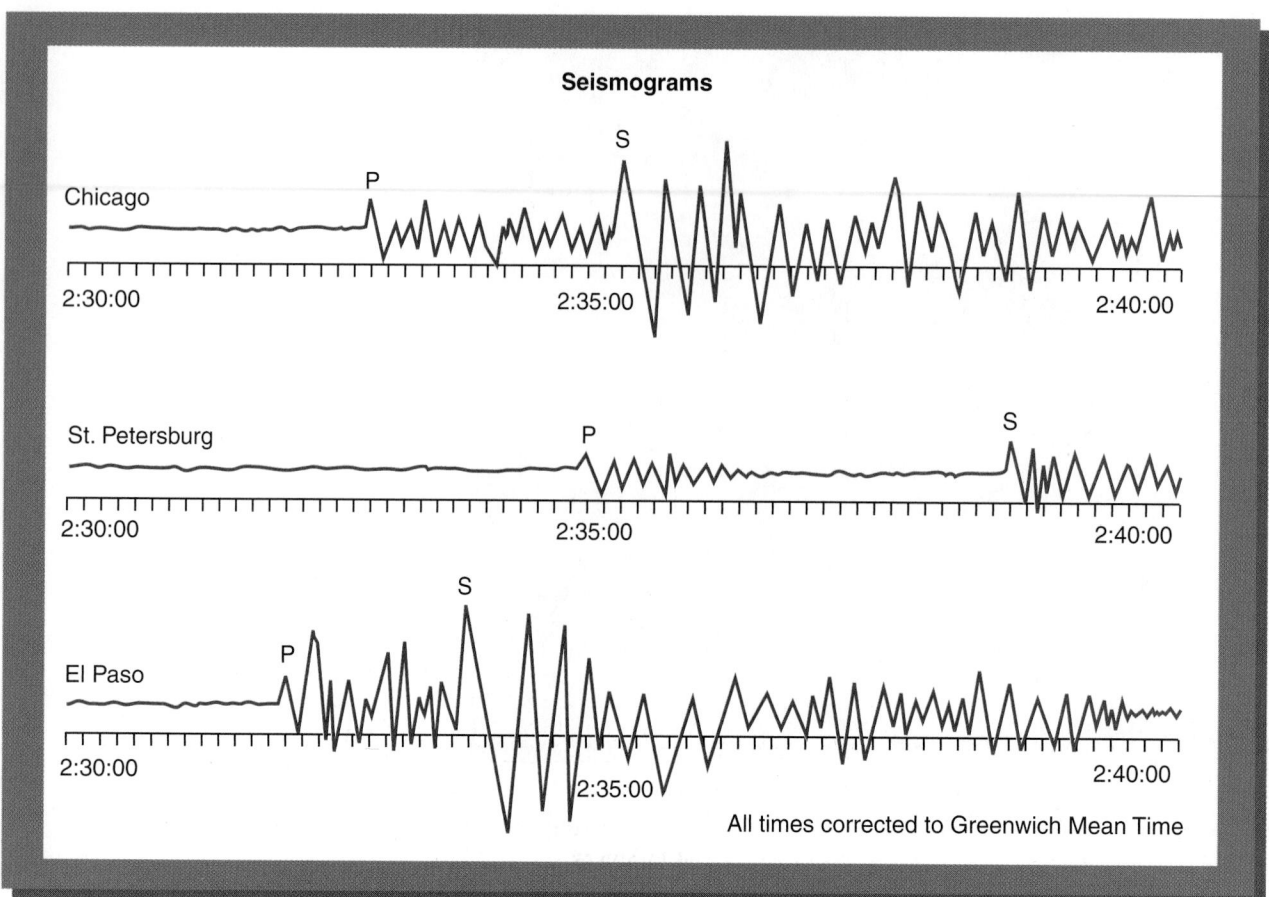

FIGURE 10–3   Seismographs record the arrival of seismic waves generated by an earthquake.

Earth by compressing and expanding the material through which they pass. P-waves move like sound waves and vibrate the particles of rock in which they travel. They can therefore travel through solids, liquids, and gases. P-waves are the fastest type of seismic wave. The second type of seismic wave is the secondary wave, or **S-wave**. S-waves travel through the ground perpendicular to their forward motion, which is in an up-and-down pattern much like the waves that move through water. S-waves move much more slowly than P-waves and can only travel through solid material, not liquids or gases. The third type of seismic wave is a **surface wave**. Surface waves are produced by a complex interaction of P- and S-waves reaching the Earth's surface. The result is a rolling motion of the ground as the surface waves move along the surface of the Earth. Surface waves are the most destructive of all seismic waves. The source of seismic waves is the area in the Earth where rock has broken apart violently; this is called the **focus**. The area on the Earth's surface located directly above the focus is known as the earthquake's **epicenter**.

EPICENTER LOCATION

It is possible to discover the exact location of an earthquake's epicenter by recording the arrival of P- and S-waves on a seismograph. Because P-waves travel faster than S-waves, it is possible to use the

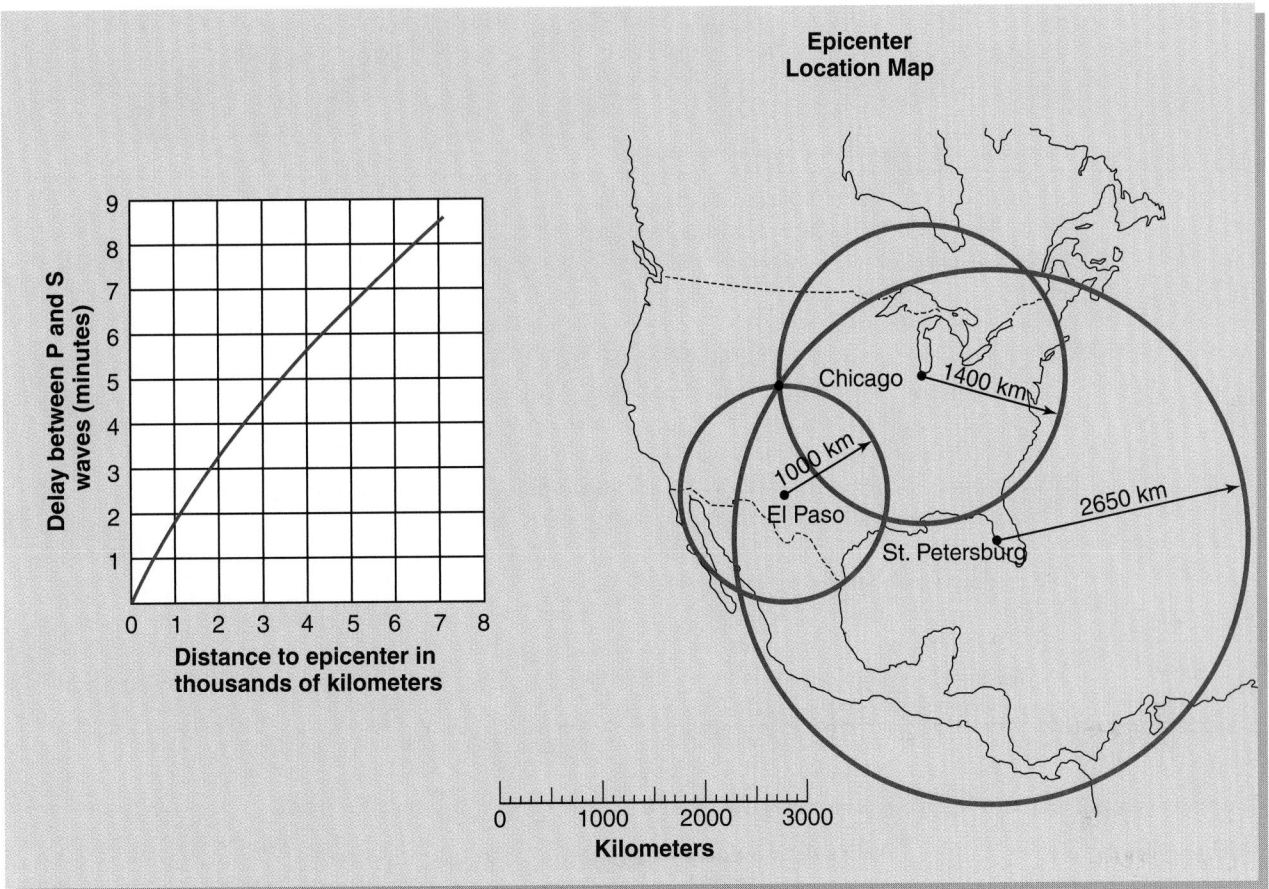

FIGURE 10–4 P- and S-wave arrival times at different seismograph stations can be used to locate the epicenter of an earthquake.

difference in their arrival times to a seismograph station to locate the distance to the epicenter (Figure 10–4). This is easy if you know the speeds at which both P- and S-waves travel through the Earth. This information can be used to develop a chart that uses the difference in arrival times of P- and S-waves and distance to the epicenter. Because this chart reveals only distance and not direction, data from at least three different seismograph stations are required to pinpoint the epicenter accurately.

EARTHQUAKE MEASUREMENT

The strength of earthquakes is measured using two different types of scales (Table 10–1). The Richter scale measures the equivalent energy produced by an earthquake on a scale from 0 to 9. The Richter scale is a logarithmic scale, which means that for every increase in number, the earthquake gains a tenfold increase in magnitude. For example, an earthquake with a Richter magnitude of 5 has the equivalent energy of a medium-sized atomic bomb. Another method of measuring earthquakes is the modified Mercalli scale. This scale categorizes earthquakes on a scale from I to XII and measures the amount of destruction the earthquake can cause to society. For example, a level II earthquake

TABLE 10–1 The Richter and modified Mercalli scales used to measure earthquakes

Level	Characteristic Effects in Populated Areas
I	Generally not felt; detectable by seismographs
II	Felt by few people; objects may swing if suspended
III	Felt by few people, mostly indoors; vibrations like a passing truck
IV	Felt by many people indoors but few outdoors; windows, dishes, and doors rattle
V	Felt by nearly everyone; sleepers awaken; small, unstable objects may fall and break; doors move
VI	Felt by everyone; some heavy furniture moves; people walk unsteadily; windows and dishes break; books fall from shelf; bushes and trees visibly shake
VII	Difficult to stand; moderate to heavy damage to poorly constructed buildings; plaster, loose bricks, titles, and stones fall; small landslides along slopes; water becomes turbid
VIII	Difficult to steer cars; damage to good unbraced masonry; chimneys, monuments, towers, and elevated tanks fall; tree branches break; steep slopes crack
IX	Extensive building damage; good masonry damaged seriously; foundations crack; serious damage to reservoirs; underground pipes break
X	Most masonry, frame structures, and foundations destroyed; numerous large landslides; water thrown on banks of rivers and lakes; railroad tracks bend slightly
XI	Few masonry buildings stand; railroad tracks bend severely; many bridges destroyed; underground pipelines completely inoperative
XII	Nearly total destruction; large rock masses displaced; objects thrown into the air

Comparison of Richter Magnitude and Energy Released

Richter Magnitude	Approximate Energy Released (Amount of TNT)	Earthquake Effects
1	170 grams	
2	6 kilograms	Usually not felt, but detected by seismographs
3	179 kilograms	
4	5 metric tons	Often felt, minor damage
5	179 metric tons	Slight damage to buildings
6	5,643 metric tons	
7	179,100 metric tons	Major earthquake, serious damage
8	5,643,000 metric tons	

is felt by few people, and suspended objects may swing. A level X earthquake would level most masonry buildings and bend railroad tracks.

FOR MORE INFORMATION GO TO THESE WEB LINKS:

<http://earthquake.usgs.gov/>

<http://www.geo.mtu.edu/UPSeis/index.html>

SECTION REVIEW

1. Describe what happens in the Earth to cause earthquakes.

2. What are the three types of seismic waves generated by earthquakes? Describe their general characteristics.

3. What is the equivalent energy of a magnitude 8 earthquake?

4. Who was Robert Mallet?

CAREER CONNECTIONS
Seismologist

Seismologists study the occurrence of earthquakes and the properties of the Earth's interior. The science of seismology uses shock waves to reveal the composition of the Earth's interior. By setting off controlled explosions, seismologists use sensors and other scientific instruments to study the movement of the shock waves through different parts of the Earth. This important research has revealed many underground features, such as faults. Seismologists also use these techniques to help locate oil and mineral resources. Studying earthquakes is another important aspect of seismology. Using seismographs, seismologists monitor and track earthquakes all over the world. Their research also involves earthquake prediction, which might someday prevent the loss of life associated with these natural disasters.

CURRENT RESEARCH

Current research

Satellite technology is now being applied to the monitoring of earthquakes. Researchers at the National Aeronautic and Space Administration's Jet Propulsion Laboratory have been using satellite images taken by the European Space Agency's Remote Sensing-2 satellite to map the precise movements of tectonic plates after an earthquake. The satellite photographs an image of a region on the Earth's surface from an angle to reveal the three-dimensional changes that have occurred as a result of an earthquake. Using images photographed before and after an earthquake occurs, researchers then combine data to produce a map that shows precise plate movements along fault lines. The data gained from these satellite images can then be applied to predicting future earthquakes. Often earthquake movement is unknown in remote regions that have not been studied at ground level. The satellite images provide researchers with data from all along the fault lines. By determining how much a plate has moved along a fault line, scientists can increase their ability to locate areas that might experience earthquakes in the near future.

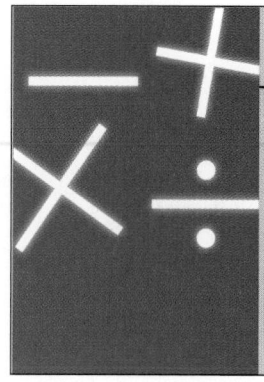

10.2 Volcanoes

FORMATION OF A VOLCANO

A **volcano** marks a point on the Earth's surface where hot molten rock, or **lava**, flows from beneath the crust. The location of volcanoes is often associated with convergent tectonic plate boundaries, where the solid crust of a subducting tectonic plate begins to descend back into the Earth's mantle and melt. The sinking plate brings with it a large amount of seawater that mixes with the molten rock to make steam that expands in the rock, making it less dense. This causes the molten rock to rise upward toward the Earth's surface, where it forms large chambers called **magma chambers**. Magma chambers feed a small network of **lava vents** that lead to the Earth's surface (Figure 10–5).

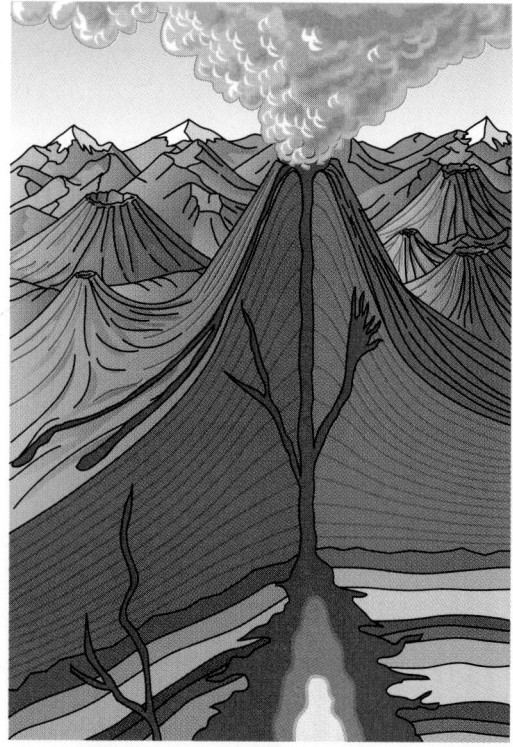

FIGURE 10–5 A cross section of a volcano showing the magma chambers and volcanic vents, which feed lava up to the surface.

This is where the lava that forms volcanoes originates. Volcanoes can also form near divergent plate boundaries such as the Mid-Atlantic Ridge, or over hot spots such as the Hawaiian Islands.

QUIET ERUPTION VOLCANOES

Volcanoes are often classified by the types of **eruption** they produce. An eruption is the release of lava, ash, steam, and gases from deep within the Earth. Quiet eruptions occur from volcanoes called shield cones. Shield cones are formed when lava gently flows up from a central vent. A vent is a pipelike crack in the Earth's crust through which lava flows. The lava cools at the surface and solidifies, forming a series of layers that resemble a shield lying on the ground. The volcanoes that formed the Hawaiian islands are classified as shield cones (Figure 10–6). Many volcanic islands in the ocean were formed from shield cones that slowly built up from layers of cooling lava, which eventually rose above sea level.

Another type of quiet eruption volcano is called a fissure eruption. A fissure is a long crack in the Earth's crust from which lava flows (Figure 10–7). These types of eruptions can produce large amounts of lava that cool to form huge sheets, or plateaus. The Deccan lava flows in India are probably the world's largest lava flow produced from a fissure. This massive lava flow occurred approximately 65 million years ago and has been linked by some researchers with the extinction of the dinosaurs. A fissure eruption of this size could have spewed millions of tons of toxic gas and ash that could have altered the environment on a scale that might have lead to a mass extinction. Another large-scale fissure eruption formed the Columbia River plateau, which covers parts of Washington, Oregon, and Idaho in the United States. Both these lava flows cover thousands of square miles and are hundreds of feet thick. Fissure eruptions also frequently occur on the island of Iceland, which lies over the Mid-Atlantic Ridge.

FIGURE 10–6   The Mauna Loa shield cone volcano, located on the island of Hawaii. (*Courtesy of PhotoDisc.*)

FIGURE 10–7   Lava pours from a fissure, creating a lava flow. (*Courtesy of PhotoDisc.*)

EXPLOSIVE ERUPTION VOLCANOES

The other classification of volcanoes is the explosive eruption. These are much more violent than quiet eruptions and pose the greatest threat to human life and property. One type of volcano that produces explosive exceptions is called a composite cone. Composite cone volcanoes are large, mountainlike structures that have formed from layers of lava and pyroclastic material (Figure 10–8). The term *pyroclastic* means "fire broken" and refers to rocks that were blasted apart as a result of an explosive eruption. Composite cones usually surround one central vent and are located on the continents near subduction zones associated with convergent plate boundaries. The hot magma that rises up in the central vent of a composite cone does not flow as easily as lava produced from fissures or shield cones. Therefore great amounts of pressure build up behind the "sticky" lava, until a great explosion occurs. The result is one of the most destructive occurrences on Earth. Some eruptions from composite cone volcanoes can be so destructive that the entire mountain can be blown apart. Examples of composite cone volcanoes include Mount Rainier in Washington State and the famous Mount Vesuvius in Italy (Figure 10–9).

When a composite cone is completely destroyed by an eruption, it leaves behind a large crater that sinks down into the magma chamber that once fed the volcano. This type of structure is called a **caldera**, or volcanic crater. When calderas eventually cool down, they can be filled

FIGURE 10–8   Mount St. Helens in Washington State is an example of a composite cone volcano. (*Courtesy of PhotoDisc.*)

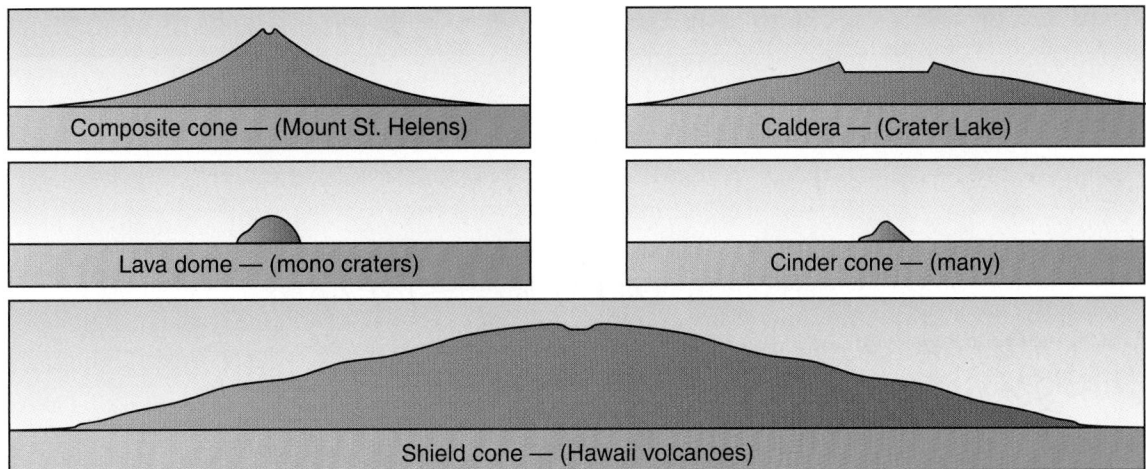

FIGURE 10-9 The size and shapes of different types of volcanoes.

with water to form large lakes. Crater Lake in Oregon is a large caldera (Figure 10–10). Many calderas can still produce explosive eruptions, although they appear to be inactive. One of the world's largest calderas exists in Yellowstone National Park. The hot magma below the surface of the caldera heats groundwater and produces the active geysers, mud pots, and hot springs that attract millions of tourists to the park each year. Geologists believe that the Yellowstone caldera might be a super-volcano that erupts catastrophically every half million years or so (see Current Research).

Another type of volcano that produces explosive eruptions is called a lava dome. Lava domes are smaller mounds of hardened lava that cover a lava vent. These structures can grow slowly as new lava forms underneath the dome and pushes outward. Lava domes are often

FIGURE 10–10 The caldera that formed Crater Lake in Oregon. (*Courtesy of PhotoDisc.*)

CAREER CONNECTIONS

Volcanologist

A volcanologist studies all aspects of volcanoes. This often dangerous profession puts scientists in the path of one of nature's deadliest forces. The study of volcanoes includes researching the forces that lead to volcano formation and the characteristics of molten rock that form lava. Volcanologists are also interested in studying volcanic eruptions and their deadly consequences. Currently, volcanologists are researching ways to better predict the eruptions associated with volcanoes to prevent loss of life. Some volcanologists also study mineral resources that are associated with volcanic rocks. Careers in volcanology require a college degree in geology and the willingness to work in sometimes dangerous environments.

CURRENT RESEARCH

Current research

Researchers from England believe that supervolcanoes can cause drastic changes in the global climate. Unlike common eruptions from volcanic mountains, supervolcanoes erupt from calderas. Calderas are craterlike volcanoes that lie over large magma chambers. Over thousands of years, pressure builds up under these calderas, and eventually they explode with great force. The explosions that are caused from a caldera equal that of an asteroid or comet impact on the Earth, which is thousands of times more violent than common eruptions. The result can be a drastic change in global climate, caused by the gas and dust kicked up high into the atmosphere. Surprisingly, the research team points to the Yellowstone caldera in the United States as the next likely supervolcano to erupt. Professor Bill McGuire believes the Yellowstone caldera is due to explode in the year 2076. This is based on a periodic eruption rate of 600,000 years. The last time Yellowstone erupted was 640,000 years ago. A supervolcano in Italy, which is much smaller than the one in Yellowstone, is also expected to erupt sometime in the future. McGuire points out that ice core data have shown that the explosions of supervolcanoes in the Earth's past have lowered global temperatures during spring and summer by up to 20° F (11° C). In comparison, large-scale mountain volcanoes affect the global temperature by only 3° Fahrenheit (1.7° C).

FIGURE 10–11 A lava dome developing in the crater of Mount St. Helens. (*Photograph by Lyn Topinka/U.S. Geological Survey.*)

found in the center of the craters of cinder cones. Often the lava vents that feed the lava dome become plugged. This results in a buildup of great pressure that eventually can cause an explosive eruption. After the famous Mount St. Helens volcanic eruption that occurred in Washington State in 1980, a small lava dome formed at the center of its crater (Figure 10–11).

The last type of volcano that can cause an explosive eruption is the cinder cone. A cinder cone is a small mound composed of lava, ash, and other pyroclastic material. This type of volcano is found in many places around the Earth. They are also the smallest type of volcano. Cinder cones usually form when lava breaks through the surface of the Earth for the first time. The resulting eruption can spew lava high into the air. Often the lava that is thrown into the air hardens before it hits the ground and forms what is called a volcanic bomb. Once the eruption that has formed the cinder cone stops, it usually remains inactive permanently.

VOLCANIC HAZARDS

One of the most dangerous results of an erupting volcano is **pyroclastic flow**. Unlike lava, which moves at a fairly slow pace, pyroclastic flows can move at speeds of more than 100 miles per hour (161 kilometer per hour). These rapidly moving flows contain extremely hot gases, water, ash, and debris that rush down the side of an erupting volcano, destroying

TABLE 10–2 Some of the world's most active volcanoes

Volcano Name	Location
Africa and the Indian Ocean	
Lengai Ol Doinyo	Tanzania
Nyamuragira	Zaire
Piton de la Foumaise	Zaire
Antarctica	
Mount Erebus	Ross Island
Big Ben	Heard Island
Deception Island	South Shetland Island
Asia	
Aso	Japan
Krakatau (Anak Krakatau)	Indonesia
Mayon	Philippines
Sakura-jima	Japan
Sheveluch	Russia
Central America and the Caribbean	
Arenal	Costa Rica
Pacaya	Guatemala
Santiaguito (Santa Maria) Dome	Guatemala
Rincon de la Vieja	Costa Rica
Poas	Costa Rica
North America	
Mount St. Helens	Washington State
Mauna Loa Kilauea	Hawaii

everything in its path. The famous Roman cities of Pompeii and Herculaneum were destroyed by the immense pyroclastic flow created when Mount Vesuvius erupted in 79 CE. Fine ash produced from volcanic eruptions, called volcanic ash, can be sent high into the atmosphere, where it can be transported over long distances. The result is the buildup of ash on the ground miles away from the erupting volcano. This ash collects like gray snow on the ground and can fill the air, making it difficult to breathe. Airplanes that fly through these ash clouds can experience engine failure and crash. Ash sent into the atmosphere from the Mount St. Helens eruption in 1980 traveled all the way to New York (Table 10–2).

The 1991 Mount Pinatubo eruption in the Philippines created so much ash that it fell thousands of miles away (Figure 10–12). So much ash entered the Earth's atmosphere from this eruption that it is believed to have altered the climate of the entire planet. The ash buildup can become so heavy that the roofs of buildings can collapse. Heavy rains caused by the huge amount of steam sent into the atmosphere during an eruption can mix with the ash fall and cause dangerous mudflows. These rapidly moving flows of wet volcanic ash can completely destroy whole towns. The Roman city of Herculaneum

FIGURE 10–12   The massive eruption of the Mount Pinatubo volcano in the Philippine Islands during July 1991. (*Courtesy of PhotoDisc.*)

was covered by mudflows that were more than 60 ft (18.3 m) deep after the eruption of Mount Vesuvius in 79 CE. The Mount Pinatubo eruption in 1991 created mudflows that were more than 650 ft deep (198 m).

Another product of volcanic eruptions can be the release of large amounts of toxic gas. Gases like sulfur dioxide can mix with steam to form sulfuric acid, which can rain down on the surrounding area. Volcanoes can also emit carbon dioxide. This colorless, odorless gas can flow down the sides of volcanoes and suffocate all the living things in its path. Debris flows, also known as **lahars**, are generated when melting snow that has collected on volcanoes with high elevations suddenly melts during an eruption (Figure 10–13). Lahars can move rapidly down the side of the volcano, taking with them trees, rock, mud, and water. The result is a deadly wall of rapidly moving debris that can easily destroy anything in its path. A lahar formed from the Nevado Del Ruiz volcano in Colombia was more than 120 ft (37 m) high and traveled more than 30 mi (48 km) away from the volcano. This lahar completely destroyed the town of Armero, killing more than 20,000 people.

FIGURE 10–13   An immense lahar created by the 1982 eruption of Mount St. Helens. (*Photograph by U.S. Geological Survey.*)

@ WEB Links

FOR MORE INFORMATION GO TO THESE WEB LINKS:

<http://wwwhvo.wr.usgs.gov/>

<http://volcano.und.edu/>

<http://vulcan.wr.usgs.gov/>

<http://www.volcanolive.com/>

<http://www.geo.mtu.edu/volcanoes/>

<http://vulcan.wr.usgs.gov/Volcanoes/Yellowstone/description_yellowstone.html>

SECTION REVIEW

1. What are the types of volcanoes associated with quiet eruptions?
2. What are the types of volcanoes associated with explosive eruptions?
3. Describe the direct effects that volcanoes can have on the surrounding area.
4. Who was Eduard Suess?

Earth System Scientists

Eduard Suess

Eduard Suess was born in London in 1831 and became a professor of geology at the University of Prague. He studied many aspects of geology, including paleontology, economic geology, and structural geology. In 1909 he published a book that presented many of his geologic theories, titled *The Face of the Earth*. Some of the research that Suess presented in his book included the history of the world's oceans, the nature of crustal movement, the structure of mountain chains around the globe, and the unique structural geology of the continents. He also proposed that there once was a large supercontinent on the Earth, which he called Gondwanaland. This marked the beginnings of the concept of continental drift, which was later developed by Alfred Wegner. Suess's other research included work on seismology and the fossils of the Danube River Basin.

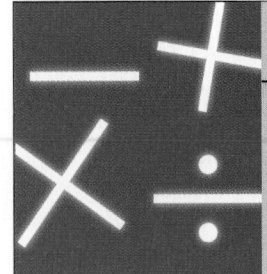

earth math

1) A huge fissure volcano poured lava onto the land surface in southeastern Washington State more than a million years ago. The lava covered an area of 30,000 square miles, with an average depth of 5,000 ft. How many cubic feet of lava were produced by this eruption?

CHAPTER SUMMARY

An earthquake is the violent shaking of the ground caused by the energy released from fractured rock below the Earth's surface. The energy of an earthquake travels in the form of waves through the Earth's interior, called seismic waves. Three types of seismic waves cause earthquakes. P-waves are the fastest traveling seismic waves and can move through solids, liquids, and gases. S-waves move more slowly than P-waves and can only travel through solids. The third type of seismic wave is called a surface wave. Surface waves form at the Earth's surface by an interaction of P- and S-waves and are the most damaging of all seismic waves. The point in the Earth's interior where a rock mass is fractured, causing an earthquake, is called the focus. The area on the Earth's surface that is directly over the focus is called the epicenter. Earthquakes are often located near tectonic plate boundaries, where the Earth's crust is under constant strain. The epicenters of earthquakes can be located by using a seismograph, a scientific instrument that detects seismic waves. Because P- and S-waves travel at different rates through the Earth, the difference in their arrival time, recorded on a seismograph, can be used to calculate how far away the earthquake occurred. Using data from at least three different seismographs pinpoints the earthquake's epicenter location. Two scales are used to measure the intensity of earthquakes, the Richter scale and the modified Mercalli scale. The Richter scale measures the energy equivalency of an earthquake. The modified Mercalli scale measures the potential damage to structures caused by an earthquake.

Volcanoes occur where hot, molten rock called lava erupts at the Earth's surface. Volcanoes are often associated with convergent tectonic plate boundaries where one oceanic plate is subducting beneath another plate. This causes seawater to mix with the upper mantle, forming a less dense magma, which rises toward the surface, forming a volcano. Volcanoes are classified by the type of eruptions they produce. Quiet eruptions occur when lava slowly flows from the ground, forming fissure volcanoes and shield cone volcanoes. Violent eruptions occur when gases, ash, rock, and lava are violently released from a volcano. These are associated with composite cones, calderas, lava domes, and cinder cones. Violent eruptions usually produce pyroclastic material, which is a mixture of hot gas, ash, lava, and rock. Two types of hazards are often associated with violent erupting volcanoes: lahars and mudflows. A lahar is a rapidly moving mixture of lava, gas, water, and ash that flows down the side of a volcano at speeds of more than 100 miles per hour. Mudflows are formed by melting snow on high-altitude volcanoes, which mixes with rock, ash, and other debris that races down the side of a volcano.

CHAPTER REVIEW

Multiple Choice

1. The sudden break of a rock mass beneath the Earth's surface causes:
   a. isostasy
   b. an earthquake
   c. erosion
   d. mantle convection

2. The locations of earthquakes are usually associated with:
   a. the center of continents
   b. the centers of landscape regions
   c. plate boundaries
   d. zones of erosion

3. The place in the Earth's crust where a rock mass has moved, causing an earthquake, is called the:
   a. epicenter
   b. zenith
   c. core
   d. focus

4. The point on the Earth's surface above where an earthquake originates is called the:
   a. epicenter
   b. zenith
   c. core
   d. focus

5. When the sea floor moves as a result of an earthquake, what can occur?
   a. seismic waves
   b. volcanoes
   c. a tsunami
   d. a focus

6. Which statement is true regarding the speed of P- and S-waves?
   a. S-waves travel faster than P-waves
   b. P-waves travel faster than S-waves
   c. They both travel at the same speed
   d. Their speed cannot be determined

7. Which statement is true regarding P-waves?
   a. They travel through solids, liquids, and gases
   b. They can only travel through solids
   c. They travel more slowly than S-waves
   d. They are the most damaging of all seismic waves

8. Which statement is true regarding S-waves?
   a. They travel through solids, liquids, and gases
   b. They can only travel through solids
   c. They travel more slowly than P-waves
   d. They are the most damaging of all seismic waves

9. Which statement is true regarding surface waves?
   a. They travel through solids, liquids, and gases
   b. They can only travel through solids
   c. They travel more slowly than S-waves
   d. They are the most damaging of all seismic waves

10. A seismograph station recorded the difference in arrival times between P- and S-waves to be 4 minutes. Using the P- and S-wave travel time diagram, how far away is the epicenter from this station?
    a. 1,000 km
    b. 1,900 km
    c. 2,600 km
    d. 5,200 km

11. Many volcanoes occur in specific regions associated with:
    a. subduction zones
    b. mountain ranges
    c. islands
    d. transform plate boundaries

12. Magma rises to the Earth's surface forming lava and volcanoes as a result of:
    a. earthquakes
    b. sliding rock along faults
    c. tsunamis
    d. mantle mixing with seawater

13. Shield cones and fissure eruptions cause:
    a. violent eruptions
    b. lahars
    c. quiet eruptions
    d. mudflows

14. Composite cones, lava domes, calderas, and cinder cones all cause:
    a. violent eruptions
    b. lava fields
    c. quiet eruptions
    d. plateaus

15. A rapidly moving mass of hot gas, ash, lava, and rock material is called a:
    a. mudflow
    b. pyroclastic flow
    c. lava flow
    d. lahar

16. A large mass of melted snow and debris that runs down the side of an erupting volcano is known as a:
    a. mudflow
    b. pyroclastic flow
    c. lava flow
    d. lahar

Matching   *Match the terms with the correct definitions.*

a. earthquake
b. seismic waves
c. seismograph
d. P-wave
e. S-wave

f. surface wave
g. focus
h. epicenter
i. volcano
j. lava

k. magma chambers
l. eruption
m. caldera
n. pyroclastic flow
o. lahars

1. _____ The point on the Earth's surface directly above the focus of an earthquake.
2. _____ A rapid flow of mud and debris formed from the rapid melting of snow and ice associated with a volcanic eruption.
3. _____ The violent, rapid shaking of the Earth caused by a rupture in the crust.
4. _____ An opening in the Earth's crust through which gas, dust, lava, and other pyroclastic materials flow to the surface.
5. _____ The extremely hot gas, ash, and volcanic material that is ejected from a volcano during an eruption and rapidly moves downhill.
6. _____ Energy released by an earthquake that travels through the Earth in the form of waves.
7. _____ The point in the Earth's crust where a rock mass is broken or moved, causing an earthquake.
8. _____ A large crater (more than 1 mile in diameter) caused by a violent volcanic eruption.
9. _____ A seismic wave formed from the interaction of other seismic waves at the Earth's surface caused by an earthquake, which causes the ground to move in a wavelike rolling motion.
10. _____ A scientific instrument that is used to detect seismic waves generated by earthquakes.
11. _____ The sudden release of lava or pyroclastic material from a volcano.
12. _____ A seismic wave generated at the focus of an earthquake that travels in the form of a wave and can only pass through solids.
13. _____ Tubes, tunnels, or large cavities in the Earth's crust through which magma travels or collects.
14. _____ A seismic wave produced at the focus of an earthquake that is the fastest of all seismic waves and can travel through all states of matter.
15. _____ Hot, molten volcanic rock that flows freely on the Earth's surface.

Critical Thinking

1. Describe the reasons why you would or would not choose to live near a tectonic plate boundary.

CHAPTER 11

Weathering, Erosion, Deposition, and Landform Development

SECTION 11.1

WEATHERING, EROSION, AND DEPOSITION OBJECTIVES

Physical and Chemical Weathering · The Process of Erosion · Agents of Erosion · The Process of Deposition

After reading this section you should be able to:

▶ Define the term *physical weathering* and provide three examples of this type of weathering.
▶ Define the term *chemical weathering* and provide three examples of this type of weathering.
▶ Describe the factors that affect the rate of weathering.
▶ Define the terms *sediment* and *erosion*.
▶ Describe three agents of erosion.
▶ Identify the factors that lead to mass wasting.
▶ Explain the relationship between transported sediment size and velocity of water.
▶ Describe how a sediment's size, shape, and density affect its settling rate.
▶ Differentiate between horizontal sorting and graded bedding.
▶ Explain how glaciers erode and deposit sediments.

SECTION 11.2

LANDFORMS OBJECTIVES

Landform Types · Factors that Effect Landforms · Stream Drainage Patterns · Geologic Provinces

After reading this section you should be able to:

▶ Describe the three general types of landforms and their basic characteristics.
▶ Explain four factors that affect the development of landforms.
▶ Describe the three basic stream drainage patterns.
▶ Identify the 10 basic geologic provinces of the United States.

INTRODUCTION

One of the most dynamic systems on the Earth is the breakdown and movement of rock material on its surface. This three-part system consists of the weathering, erosion, and deposition of rocks and sediments. It involves larger rocks being reduced into smaller rock particles, transporting them over long distances, and then placing them in a new location. When children scoop up a shovel full of sand to make a sand castle at the beach, they are touching rock particles that have made a long journey from the mountains to the sea. The breakdown and movement of rock on the Earth is an important part of the rock cycle, which constantly recycles this material on the planet. Weathering, erosion, and deposition also affect many aspects of our modern society. Agriculture depends on the deposition of sediments to renew the fertility of the soil. Farmers are also concerned about erosion because they want to keep their soil in place. Our buildings, homes, and transportation systems are constantly being affected by these processes, which costs millions of dollars each year to combat. Learning about the powerful forces that drive weathering, erosion, and deposition is vital to a complete understanding of the Earth's systems, and how these forces shape the landscape.

11.1 Weathering, Erosion, and Deposition

PHYSICAL AND CHEMICAL WEATHERING

The weathering of rock at the Earth's surface is an important part of understanding the dynamic nature of the Earth's lithosphere system. Weathering is simply the breakdown of rocks into smaller rock particles known as sediment. The formation of sediment is an important part of the rock cycle and also important to life on Earth. Weathering on Earth is divided into two categories: physical weathering and chemical weathering. **Physical weathering**, also called mechanical weathering, is the process by which rock is broken down into smaller particles by a physical process, with no chemical changes occurring (Figure 11–1). An example of physical weathering includes freezing and thawing, also known as frost action. When water freezes it expands, and can apply a great amount of pressure on any surrounding rock. The pressure can actually break the rock apart into smaller pieces. Rocks exposed to climates that experience freezing and thawing can be weathered rapidly. Another example of physical weathering is heating and cooling. When rocks are heated, they expand as their

FIGURE 11–1   A combination of heating and cooling and frost action has physically weathered this rock outcrop, creating a pile of smaller rocks at its base, called talus. (*Courtesy of the National Park Service.*)

molecules move farther apart. Then, when they cool rapidly, they contract as their molecules pack more tightly together. The action of expansion and contraction can break rocks apart and weather them over time. Physical weathering by expansion and contraction usually occurs in climates that experience severe temperature changes in a short time, such as in deserts. During the daylight hours in a desert climate, the temperature can rise rapidly, causing the rocks to heat up quickly. Then at night the temperature drops quickly, causing the rocks to cool rapidly. This causes the rocks to expand and contract continually day after day, which eventually breaks them apart.

Abrasion is another means of physical weathering; this is the rubbing together of rock particles. Much as sandpaper breaks down wood, sediments in either water or wind can weather rock (Figure 11–2). The action of living organisms can also break down rock. The roots of trees can grow into the cracks of rocks and pry them apart. Burrowing organisms such as ants or rodents can break rocks apart over time. Some minerals in rock can absorb water, causing the rock to swell and expand. Eventually when it dries out, the outer layer of rock can peel away. This is called exfoliation, or the peeling away of layers of rock, which is an example of physical weathering. Finally, another physical weathering process that breaks rock down into particles or sediments is called pressure unloading. Pressure unloading occurs when rocks that have been

FIGURE 11–2 The unique shape of this rock formation is the result of the physical weathering process of abrasion by wind. (*Courtesy of PhotoDisc.*)

buried deep in the ground and have been subject to extreme pressure are exposed at the surface. The release of the pressure causes the rocks to expand and break apart. This process affected many rocks that were covered by thick glaciers. The weight of the overlying ice compressed the rock. When the glaciers melted and retreated, the weight was removed, causing the rock to expand and crack. This physical weathering process is still occurring in parts of the northeastern United States.

Chemical weathering occurs when rock breaks down into smaller particles as a result of a chemical process. **Oxidation** is a chemical weathering process that occurs when minerals in the rock react with atmospheric oxygen. Oxidation changes the physical properties of the rock, causing it to break down. The formation of iron oxide, commonly known as rust, occurs when iron-containing rocks combine with oxygen in the air to form iron oxide. This causes the rock to crumble and break apart. If you have ever observed the effect that rust has on automobiles, you can appreciate the power that chemical weathering has on solid objects. Another form of chemical weathering is called **carbonation**. This occurs when carbon dioxide mixes with water to form carbonic acid. Carbonic acid can then break down rock into smaller particles. This type of weathering can occur at the Earth's surface when atmospheric moisture mixes with carbon dioxide in the air to form carbonic acid. This weak acid then rains down on exposed rocks and chemically weathers them. Limestone rocks are chemically weathered by this process. Carbonation can also occur underground when groundwater containing carbon dioxide slowly dissolves surrounding rocks. This eventually leads to the formation of large underground caverns and caves. Many caves and caverns on the Earth are formed when rock formations containing limestone are slowly dissolved by groundwater (Figure 11–3). As a result of atmospheric pollution, stronger acids are also now present in the atmosphere. Pollutants like nitrogen oxides and sulfur oxides created from burning fossil fuels form nitric and sulfuric acids in clouds that falls to the Earth's surface as acid precipitation. These strong acids have greatly increased the rate of chemical weathering in many regions of the world.

The last form of chemical weathering is called hydration. Hydration is the absorption of water by certain minerals in rock. Some minerals, such as feldspar, hornblende, and biotite, break down as a result of hydrolysis, or the splitting of water. Other minerals, such as halite and calcite, can also be dissolved by water.

The rate of weathering, or how long it takes for rock to be weathered, depends on a few specific factors. The climate in which the rock is located greatly affects the rate of weathering. Generally rock that is exposed to warm, **humid** climates weathers at a higher rate. A climate is classified as humid if it receives a good amount of precipitation each year. The size of the rock particle that is being weathered is also an important factor in determining how long it takes a rock to weather. Smaller rock particles expose more surface area per unit volume than larger particles and therefore weather at a higher rate. The mineral composition of the particular rock that is being weathered is also an important factor for weathering rates. Some minerals are more resistant to weathering than others. For example, quartz and orthoclase minerals are very weather resistant. Olivine and pyroxene minerals weather very easily. Probably the most important factor that determines weathering

FIGURE 11–3 Spectacular caverns and caves like this one were formed by the chemical weathering of limestone by groundwater. (*Courtesy of PhotoDisc.*)

rates is time. The more time that a rock is exposed to the forces of weathering, the more it will break down into smaller particles.

Once a rock has been weathered, it usually ends up in one of two forms: sediments or soil. Sediments are the rock particles or fragments that are produced by the weathering of rock. Sediments are classified by their size; the smallest rock particles are clay, silt, and sand, and the larger fragments are pebbles, cobbles, and boulders. Soil is the other result of weathered rock, which is actually a mixture of mineral particles with organic material, air, and water. Soil formation and the classification of soils will be discussed in depth in Chapter 12.

THE PROCESS OF EROSION

Erosion is another important process that affects the lithosphere system. Erosion is the process of transporting sediments from their place of origin and depositing them elsewhere. The principal force that transports sediments is gravity. The force of gravity along with some type of transporting material is called a transporting agent. Water is by far the most significant agent of erosion. It is responsible for moving millions of tons of sediments around the world every year.

CAREER CONNECTIONS
Geomorphologist

A geomorphologist studies the geological processes that lead to the formation of unique landscapes on the Earth. This includes researching conditions that lead to the formation of mountains, valleys, plains, and canyons. They examine the effects of climate and geological processes in specific regions around the world. Geomorphologists study the short-term and long-term effects of erosion and deposition in specific regions. They also examine how human beings are altering landscapes. This information is then used to prevent environmental damage and for land use planning. Geomorphologists require a college education with an emphasis on developing skills in map making, geology, surveying, computers, and environmental science. They can find employment with state and federal government agencies and in academic fields.

There are four main ways by which water erodes sediments on Earth. Raindrop and runoff erosion are caused when liquid precipitation, rain, hits the Earth's surface and dislodges, or moves, sediment from its location. Heavy rains can cause a great amount of sediment to be dislodged. Precipitation that does not infiltrate the ground collects on the surface and can flow down slopes, carrying with it dislodged sediments. This is called **runoff**. It accounts for millions of tons of eroded sediments each year. Exposed farm fields and construction sites are extremely susceptible to erosion by raindrop impact and runoff. Once sediments enter into water, they become transported by **stream erosion**. Stream erosion transports sediments either by dissolving the sediments into solution, carrying the smaller sediments in **suspension**, or by the force of the moving water bouncing and rolling the sediments downstream. The transportation of sediments by stream erosion greatly depends on the velocity of the flowing water. The greater the velocity of the water, the greater the size of the sediment that is transported (Figure 11–4). Sediments that have been transported by moving water eventually become rounded by the abrasion that occurs as the particles bounce and roll downstream.

Another method of water transport of sediment involves the ocean. The coastal interface between the ocean and the land is an area that experiences massive erosion by water. The power of waves and ocean currents can both erode and transport rock particles over long distances. A sandy beach along the shoreline is constantly changing its shape as sediment, in the form of sand, is transported by the power of the ocean.

When frozen water accumulates on land in great quantities over a long period, glaciers can form. Glaciers are large masses of ice that can move along the surface of the Earth. Glaciers are like great bulldozers that plow through rock and move it to new locations. Glaciers are also called

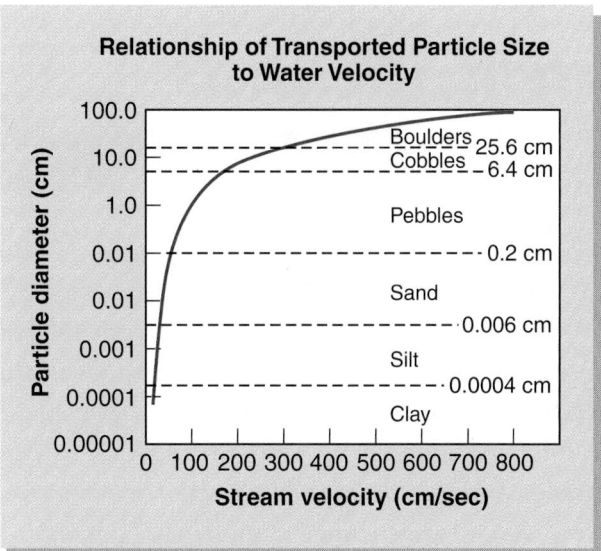

FIGURE 11-4 The relationship between sediment particle size and the velocity of the water needed to transport it.

"dirty snowballs" because there is a great amount of rock and sediment trapped in the ice. When glaciers melt and retreat, the rock particles that were trapped in the ice are deposited to form glacial sediments. The glacial sediments that were deposited to form New York's Long Island were transported all the way from Canada by glacial action (Figure 11–5).

FIGURE 11-5 A glacial moraine composed of unsorted, angular sediments. (*Courtesy of Duncan Heron.*)

Earth System Scientists

William Morris Davis

William Morris Davis was born in Philadelphia in 1850. He gained his college education at Harvard University, where he later taught meteorology, geology, and geomorphology. At the start of his career, he conducted many geographical surveys around the world. His major achievements in science included the study of the formation of landforms and landscapes. Because of this, he is regarded as the father of geomorphology. In 1889 he developed theories to explain the regular cycle of erosion and deposition. Davis developed a theory to explain the life cycle of rivers. This included a detailed explanation of the formation of steep river valleys, which signify young rivers, and the wide, flat meanders and floodplains of a mature river.

AGENTS OF EROSION

Water is definitely the dominant agent of erosion on Earth, but not the only one. The action of air moving across the Earth's surface, or wind, can also transport sediments over long distances. Wind erosion often occurs in dry climates where sediments are dried out and exposed to the power of wind, which moves them. Some wind-deposited sediments found in the midwestern United States are more than 100 feet (30 m) thick and have been built up over thousands of years. Wind erosion can also greatly affect agriculture if farm fields are left exposed to the atmosphere. In the 1930s a series of droughts and windstorms caused disastrous wind erosion in the midwest. This was called the dust bowl, and it resulted in a mass migration of farmers from the region because of the extreme effects of wind erosion. The constantly shifting sand dunes in the world's deserts illustrate the movement of sediments by the force of wind.

The last agent of erosion is called **mass wasting**. Mass wasting is the downhill movement of sediments by the force of gravity. As sediments are formed on slopes, they are exposed to the tug of gravity, which moves them downward. As the slope increases, the potential for the downward movement of sediments also increases. This is because the frictional forces that hold sediments in place on a slope lessen as slope increases; therefore, land with a steeper slope also has a greater erosion rate. Rapid mass wasting occurs when sediments on a slope are forced to move down slope suddenly (Figure 11–6). These type of events are called rock slides, mud slides, or avalanches.

Rapid mass wasting usually occurs when water accumulates on the slope, which greatly reduces the friction and increases the weight of the sediments. This causes the sediments to suddenly slide downhill. The opposite of rapid mass wasting is called creep. Creep occurs as sediments slowly move downhill over a long period. Evidence of creep can be seen in the leaning of fence posts pointing downhill as a result of the sediments that they are laid in slowly moving downward (Figure 11–7). Trees can also lean downhill as a result of creep.

FIGURE 11–6 The result of the rapid mass wasting of a hillside. (*Photograph by U.S. Geological Survey.*)

CURRENT RESEARCH

An atmospheric scientist from the University of Miami is studying the effects of the long-distance transport of dust from Africa on the citizens of Florida. Professor Joseph Prospero's research has revealed that dust kicked up from storms in West Africa rises up into the atmosphere to an elevation of 15,000 to 20,000 ft (4,572 to 6,096 m) above sea level. This dust is then carried across the Atlantic Ocean by planetary-scale easterly winds, where it eventually settles on the state of Florida. Prospero is concerned about the level at which the dust enters the air over Florida. The levels of dust in the air in Florida, also known as particulate matter, are above the limits set by the Environmental Protection Agency for atmospheric pollutants. Prospero believes that the haze that is visible in many parts of Florida is often mistaken for human pollution. His research suggests that the haze is the result of the African dust particles. When this dust enters into the lungs, it can react with sensitive lung tissue. Prospero's research reveals the amazing long-distance wind erosion that affects two continents and bridges the Atlantic Ocean.

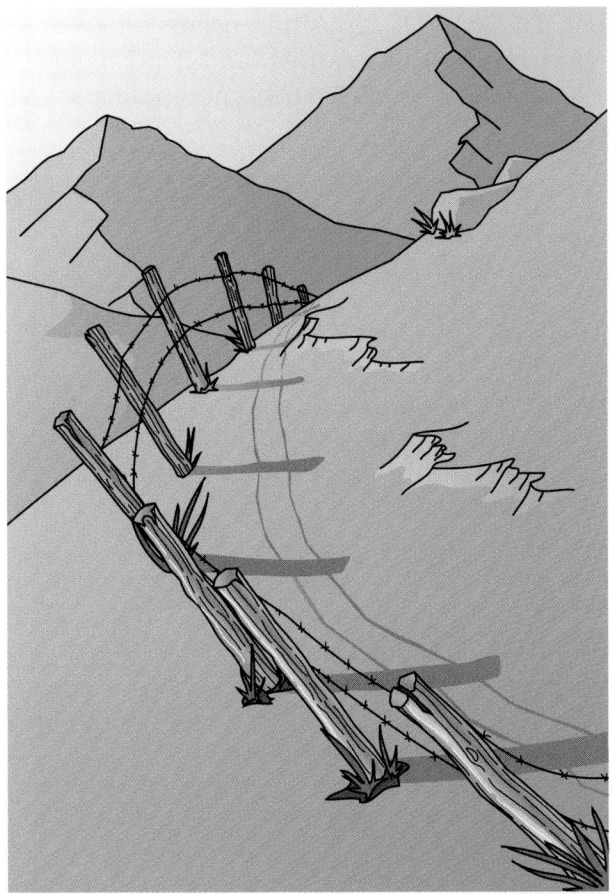

FIGURE 11–7 A line of fence posts points downhill, revealing evidence of creep on a hillside.

THE PROCESS OF DEPOSITION

Once sediments have been transported by some type of agent, they are released and then settle in a new location. This is called **deposition**. Deposition of sediments is usually caused when the velocity of the transporting agent, usually wind or water, decreases. The decrease in velocity causes the rock particles to settle out of suspension, forming a sediment deposit. Factors that also affect the deposition of sediments include particles' size, shape, and density. Smaller particles tend to settle at a slower rate than larger particles. The more spherical a sediment particle is, the faster its rate of settling; and flatter particles tend to settle at slower rates. In addition, the greater the density of a particle, the greater its settling rate. Taken together, these factors result in unique sediment deposits.

When the velocity of the transporting agent of sediments of mixed sizes is reduced quickly, they are deposited in a pattern called **graded bedding**. Graded bedding is a sediment deposit in which the size of the sediment increases with depth (Figure 11–8). This pattern results when the larger particles settle out first, and the smallest last. Graded bedding of sediments is often found near the area where streams enter into a large, deep lake.

Another type of sediment deposit is called **horizontal sorting** (Figure 11–9). This occurs as a result of the transporting agent's velocity decreasing at a slow rate over a long distance. Horizontal sorting results in a deposit in which larger particles settle first, and then the smaller particles settle farther out in the direction of the movement of the transporting agent. This type of deposition occurs where rivers empty into the ocean. Horizontal sorting causes sand deposits to settle nearer the shore and silt and clay deposits to form out in deeper water.

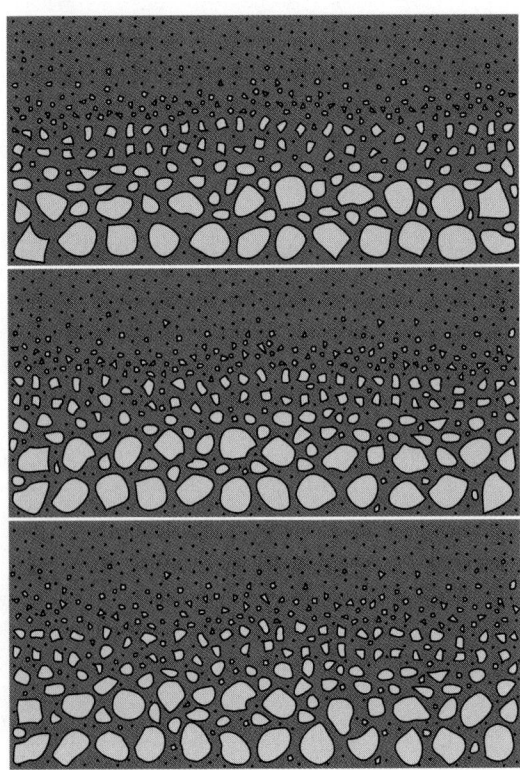

FIGURE 11–8 A series of vertically sorted sediment deposits known as graded bedding.

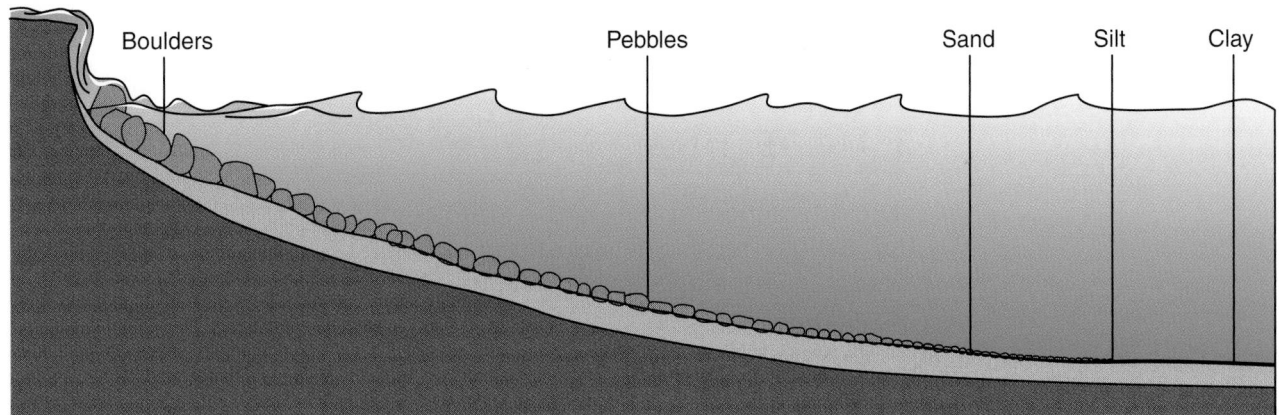

FIGURE 11-9 The horizontal sorting of sediments deposited by flowing water.

Another unique type of deposition is related to glaciers. When glaciers begin to melt, the sediments that they are carrying are left behind in large deposits called **moraines**. Moraines form large, unsorted sediment deposits also known as **glacial till**. In this type of deposition, sediment particles are randomly deposited. You can often differentiate between glacial deposits and deposits associated with moving liquid water by the shape and sorting of the sediment particles. Unlike sediments transported by liquid water, which become rounded because of abrasion, glacial sediments remain jagged and angular. This is because the particles are frozen in glacial ice and are not as heavily abraded. Also, glacial deposits are usually unsorted because the particles do not settle at different rates as a result of melting, unlike the sorted sediments associated with liquid water deposits. Almost all naturally occurring gravel pits are the remains of sediments that were deposited by either glaciers or moving water thousands of years ago. They often reveal much about what the environment was like when the sediments were deposited.

SECTION REVIEW

1. Define physical weathering and provide four examples.
2. Define chemical weathering and provide two examples.
3. What are some of the factors that affect the rate of weathering?
4. Describe two specific agents of erosion.
5. Describe three ways by which sediments can be deposited.
6. Who was William Morris Davis?

 **WEB Links**

FOR MORE INFORMATION GO TO THIS WEB LINK:

<http://www.gpc.edu/~pgore/geology/geo101/weather.htm>

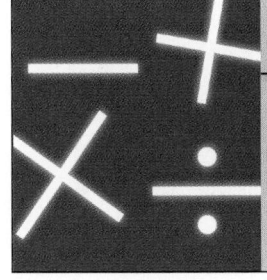

earth math

1) Calculate the density of the following sediment particles, and then determine which one will settle out of water first: Sample A weighs 50 grams, and its area is determined to be 15 cubic centimeters. Sample B weighs 60 grams, and its area is determined to be 20 cubic centimeters.

11.2 Landforms

LANDFORM TYPES

The interaction of the Earth's atmosphere and hydrosphere with the lithosphere forms specific surface topography known as a **landform**, also known as a landscape. The study of landforms and how they develop is known as geomorphology. Landforms fall under three general categories that are based on the elevation of the land, its slope, and soil and bedrock characteristics. The first type is called a mountain landform. **Mountains** or uplands, are high elevation areas that are found far above sea level. These regions tend to have very steep slopes, and are composed mostly of exposed bedrock. The rocks in mountain regions are usually composed of sedimentary and metamorphic rocks which are tilted, folded, and faulted as a result of the tectonic forces that formed the mountains. Streams and rivers within these regions move at high velocities as they flow over the steep sloping terrain, forming rapids and waterfalls. The soils in mountain regions also tend to be thin as a result of increased runoff. The next type of basic landform is called the plateau. **Plateaus** are medium to high elevation flat areas with a lesser slope. The term plateau is a derivation of the French word "plat" meaning "flat." Much of the bedrock that underlies a plateau consists of stratified sedimentary rocks, although there are some plateaus that were formed by massive outpourings of lava. These include the Columbian plateau that makes up parts of Washington, Oregon, and Idaho, and the Deccan plateau in India. The soils of a plateau are thicker than in the mountains, and bedrock is less exposed, except in canyons were running water has cut down deep into the rock. This is known as a dissected plateau. The third type of landform is known a plain. **Plains**, or lowlands, are low elevation, flat areas with very gentle slopes. These landscapes have well-developed deep soils and very little exposed bedrock (Figure 11–10).

FIGURE 11–10   Basic landforms.

FIGURE 11–11 The effect of climate on landform characteristics.

FACTORS THAT AFFECT LANDFORMS

There are many factors that affect the development of a particular landform region. Probably the most important of these is the interaction between leveling and uplift forces. Leveling forces include weathering and erosion, which cause a decrease in the elevation of a landscape, eventually bringing it down to sea level. Uplift forces cause an increase in the elevation of a landform as a result of tectonic activity such as convergence along plate boundaries, earthquakes, and volcanic eruptions. The slope and elevation of a landform is determined by the dominant force, whether it be leveling or uplift. If the leveling force is greater than uplift, a landform will decrease both its slope and elevation over time. If uplift forces are greater than leveling, then the elevation and slope of a landform will increase. Other factors that affect the development of landforms include the type of bedrock present and the amount of time it has been exposed to the atmosphere. Some types of bedrock are more resistant to weathering than others, which can greatly influence the development of landforms. Climate also has a role in creating unique landscapes. Generally, humid climates tend to weather and erode at a greater rate than arid climates. Also colder climates that support glacial activity can greatly affect the topography of an area. Over time these different climate types have created unique regional landforms (Figure 11–11).

STREAM DRAINAGE PATTERNS

A watershed, also called a drainage basin, is defined as the total area of a region that is drained by specific bodies of water including streams, rivers, and wetlands. Landform regions may be part of only one watershed, or may contain multiple watersheds. The unique topography of a landform greatly influences the way in which water will run off its surface. This is known as a stream drainage pattern,

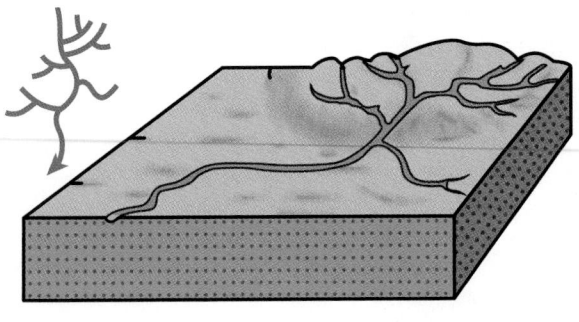

Dendritic

Radial

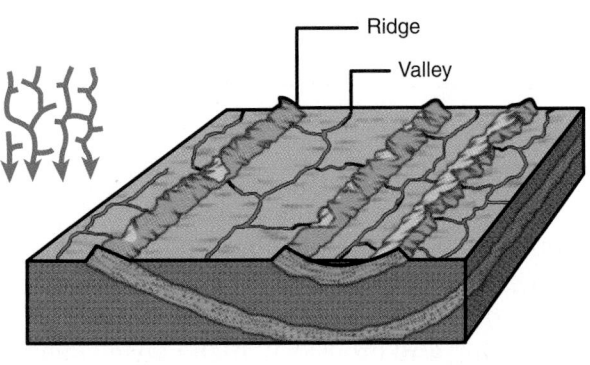

Trellis

FIGURE 11-12 Three different stream drainage patterns.

the specific way in which water is collected and drained from a land-form. These patterns can reveal much about the underlying geology of the region. A dendritic pattern usually occurs over landforms with a gradual slope, made up of easily eroded rocks and sediment. The trellis drainage pattern is associated with the rigid bedrock structure of a mountain landform. In this type of drainage the topography forces the streams and rivers to run in well-defined channels that are often parallel to the mountains. Radial drainage occurs around coni-cal landscapes with a central elevation point like a volcano, which drains water off in all directions (Figure 11–12).

GEOLOGIC PROVINCES

A geologic province is a well-defined landform area that occupies large regions on the Earth. The contiguous United States is made of ten geo-logic provinces. The east coast of the United States is composed of the Atlantic Plain and the Appalachian Uplands. The Atlantic Plain is a wide flat landscape region that stretches from Massachusetts south through Florida and westward into Texas. The Appalachian Uplands province is the remains of the ancient Appalachian Mountains that formed about 290 million years ago with the creation of the super-continent, Pangaea. This landscape region stretches from Maine all the way south into Georgia and Alabama. The weathering and erosion of the rocks of the Appalachian Mountains helped form the Atlantic Plain. Together these two provinces make up about 25 percent of the United States. The interior portions of the United States are composed of the Ouachita-Ozark Highlands, the Interior Plains, and the Laurentian Uplands. The Ouachita-Ozark Highlands comprise parts of Arkansas, Missouri, and Oklahoma. This province contains the folded and deformed rocks of the Ozark Mountains, which are very similar in rock structure to that of the southern portion of the Appalachian chain. The Interior Plains, also known the Great Plains, make up roughly 33 percent of the United States. This gently sloping landscape contains America's most productive farmland. The Laurentian Uplands are in Wisconsin, Minnesota, and the northern parts of Michigan. The metamorphic rocks here were formed 2.5 billion years ago. They make up the ancient core of the North American continent. The end of the last ice age, approximately 10,000 years ago, has greatly shaped this landscape region by covering it with glacial sediments. The western portion of the United States begins with the Rocky Mountain province. This relatively young mountain range was formed between 40 and 70 million years ago, and contains the highest elevations and steepest slopes of all the provinces in the United States. The Rockies stretch from Canada all the way down into Mexico. West of the Rockies are three Plateau provinces together known as the Intermontane Plateaus. This region contains the Columbian Plateau, which makes up parts of Washington, Oregon, and Idaho, the Basin and Range province of the American Southwest, and the Colorado Plateau. Formed approximately 17 million years ago by a massive lava outflow, the Columbian Plateau is one of the world's largest deposits of basaltic lava. The Basin and Range comprises the high deserts and canyon lands of Nevada, New Mexico, Arizona, and Utah, along with parts of Southern California. Some of the most beautiful landscapes in the United States make up the Colorado Plateau. This geologic province contains the Colorado River and the Grand Canyon. Colorful stratified layers of sedimentary rocks make up this picturesque landform region. Over the past few million years the power of running water has cut through the rocks in this area, creating a dissected plateau with a network of deep canyons. The Pacific Province is the western most region of the United States It comprises California, Oregon, and Washington. This is the most tectonically active landscape region as a result of the interactions between the Pacific Plate, Juan de Fuca Plate, and the North American Plate. The famous San Andreas Fault runs through the southern part of the region. To the north is located the volcanic mountain chain known as the Cascades (Figure 11–13).

SECTION REVIEW

1. What are the three general types of landforms, and their basic characteristics?
2. Describe three factors that affect the development of landforms:
3. What are the three basic stream drainage patterns?
4. Name the 10 basic geologic provinces of the United States.

@ WEB Links

FOR MORE INFORMATION GO TO THESE WEB LINKS:

<http://wrgis.wr.usgs.gov/parks/province/index.html>

<http://fermi.jhuapl.edu/states/states.html>

<http://www2.cerritos.edu/earth-science/tutor/landform_identification.htm>

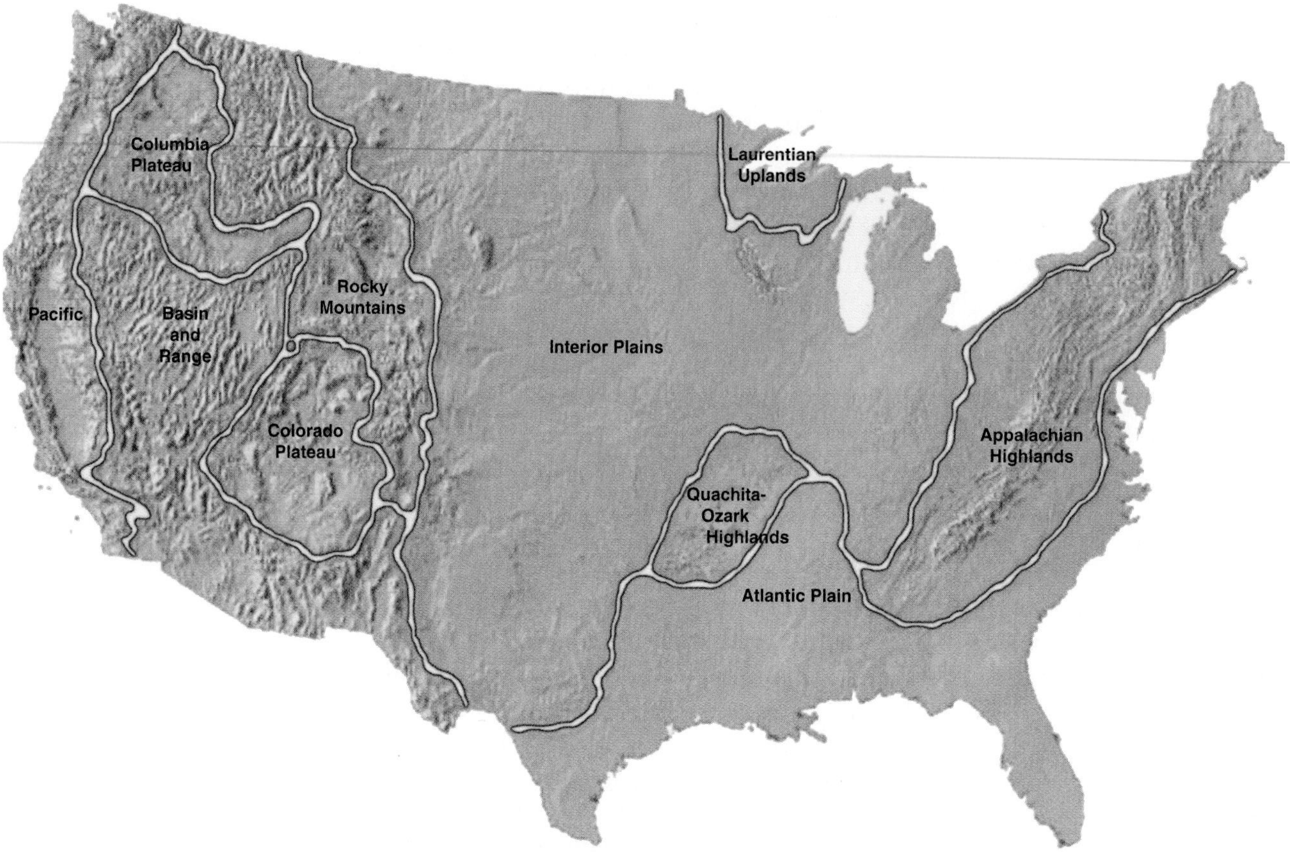

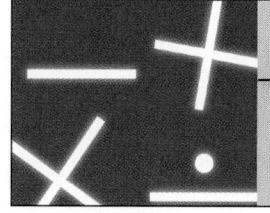

FIGURE 11–13 The ten major geologic provinces of the contiguous United States.

CHAPTER SUMMARY

The breakdown and movement of rock material on the Earth involves three fundamental processes. These are weathering, erosion, and deposition. Weathering is the breakdown of large rocks into smaller rock particles. There are two types of weathering processes on the Earth: physical weathering and chemical weathering. Physical weathering involves the breakdown of rock by a physical process. Examples of physical weathering include freezing and thawing, heating and cooling, abrasion, and root action. Chemical weathering is the breakdown of rock as a result of a chemical change. Examples of chemical weathering include hydration, carbonation, and oxidation.

The product of weathering is called sediment. Sediment is classified by its size, smaller particles being clay, silt, and sand. Larger sediments include pebbles, cobbles, and boulders. Once sediments are created, they are eventually transported to a new location. This process

earth math

1) Determine the gradient in feet per mile for a lowland plain that decreases its elevation by 200 ft over a distance of 4 mi.

is known as erosion. The specific way that sediments are transported is called an agent of erosion. The three principal agents of erosion are water, wind, and glaciers. The movement of sediment by water depends on two factors: the velocity of the water and the size of the sediment. Generally, the higher the velocity of the water, the larger the size of sediment that can be transported.

The erosion of large amounts of sediment and soil from land into a body of water is known as runoff. The rapid movement of sediment down a hillside is called mass wasting. Rapid mass wasting occurs very quickly and is known as a rockslide, mudslide, or avalanche. Slow mass wasting is called creep, which occurs over a long period. Once sediments are eroded, they eventually settle in a new location. This is called deposition. Deposition usually occurs when the transporting agent slows its velocity, causing the sediment particles to settle. The rate at which particles settle depends on the particles' size, shape, and density.

There are two main types of sediment deposits: graded bedding and horizontal sorting. Most sediment deposits are associated with liquid water, but glacial ice can also result in deposition. Glaciers scrape along rocks and gather sediments as they advance across the landscape. The sediments then become mixed in with the ice and carried along with the glacier. Eventually, when the glacial ice that contains the sediments melts, the sediments are deposited in large piles called moraines. Glacial deposits are usually composed of unsorted, angular sediments also known as glacial till. The specific surface topography of the Earth's surface is known as a landform. Landforms are divided into three basic categories based mainly on elevation, slope, and bedrock structure. The three basic landforms are mountains, plateaus and plains. Other factors that affect the formation of landscapes include climate, time, and the interaction between leveling and uplift forces. The specific way in which water drains off a landform is called a stream drainage pattern. Three basic types of stream drainage patterns include dendritic, radial, and trellis. Landforms that cover a wide geographic region are known as geologic provinces. The United States is composed of ten geologic provinces, which are known as the Atlantic Plain, Appalachian Highlands, Ouachita-Ozark Highlands, Interior Plains, Laurentian Uplands, Rocky Mountains, Columbian Plateau, Basin and Range, and the Pacific.

CHAPTER REVIEW

Multiple Choice

1. Which is the best example of physical weathering?
   a. the cracking of a rock mass by the freezing and thawing of water
   b. the transportation of sediment in a stream
   c. the reaction of limestone with acids in rainwater
   d. the formation of a sandbar along the side of a stream

2. Which property of water makes frost action a common form of physical weathering?
   a. Water dissolves many Earth materials.
   b. Water expands when it freezes.
   c. Water cools the surrounding area when it evaporates.
   d. Water loses heat when it freezes.

3. The main cause of chemical weathering on the Earth is:
   a. rock abrasion
   b. heating and cooling of a rock
   c. reactions of rock material with air and water
   d. contraction of water when it freezes

4. Which type of climate causes the fastest chemical weathering?
   a. cool and dry
   b. cold and humid
   c. hot and dry
   d. hot and humid

5. On Earth the dominant agent of erosion is:
   a. wave action
   b. moving ice
   c. running water
   d. moving air

6. As the velocity of the water increases, the size of the sediment particle transported:
   a. decreases
   b. stays the same
   c. increases
   d. varies

7. Which of the following causes an increase in runoff?
   a. an increase in slope
   b. a decrease in rainfall
   c. an increase in biological activity
   d. a decrease in air temperature

8. A flowing body of water transports sediments by rolling and bouncing, in solution, and by:
   a. sublimation
   b. transpiration
   c. suspension
   d. evaporation

9. Generally, if the particle size of sediments increases from clay to sand, the settling time:
   a. decreases
   b. increases
   c. remains the same
   d. varies

10. As the velocity of a stream decreases, there will most likely be an increase in:
    a. erosion by the stream
    b. deposition by the stream
    c. the size of particles transported by the stream
    d. the amount of material transported by solution in the stream

11. A sediment deposit that contains larger particles on the bottom and increasingly smaller particles toward the top is known as:
    a. graded bedding
    b. glacial till
    c. moraine
    d. horizontal sorting

12. A sediment deposit that is formed as moving water slowly decreases its velocity over a long distance is called:
    a. graded bedding
    b. glacial till
    c. moraine
    d. horizontal sorting

13. A hill consisting of angular sediments that are unsorted was most likely deposited by:
    a. wind
    b. a glacier
    c. a river
    d. a landslide

14. A gravel pit containing rounded sediments that are horizontally sorted was most likely deposited by:
    a. wind
    b. a glacier
    c. a river
    d. a landslide

15. Which sediment particle takes the least amount of time to settle: Particle A, a flat, low-density particle; or Particle B, a spherical, high-density particle?
    a. Particle A
    b. Particle B
    c. They would both settle at the same rate
    d. They would both float

16. Which rock would weather at a faster rate?
    a. a very large rock
    b. a very tiny rock
    c. a rock located in a dry climate
    d. a rock frozen in glacial ice

17. Which landform has a medium elevation with a gradual slope?
    a. mountain
    b. plateau
    c. plain
    d. basin

18. The type of stream drainage pattern associated with a volcano would be:
    a. dendritic
    b. trellis
    c. radial
    d. conical

Matching   *Match the terms with the correct definitions.*

a. physical weathering
b. chemical weathering
c. oxidation
d. carbonation
e. humid

f. erosion
g. runoff
h. stream erosion
i. suspension
j. mass wasting

k. deposition
l. graded bedding
m. horizontal sorting
n. moraines
o. glacial till

1. _____ The breakdown of rocks into smaller rock particles by a chemical process.
2. _____ Large amounts of unsorted glacial sediments that are deposited by a melting glacier.
3. _____ The process of breaking down rocks into smaller rock particles by a physical process in which no chemical changes take place.
4. _____ An accumulation of glacial sediments.
5. _____ The process of adding oxygen to a chemical compound.
6. _____ A specific type of sediment deposition, occurring in still water, which results in larger particles settling first, then progressively smaller particles settling on top of the larger ones.
7. _____ The addition of carbon dioxide gas to something.
8. _____ A specific form of deposition of sediments that results from the reduction of the velocity of water at the mouth of a river that enters into a body of water. This causes larger particles to settle closest to the mouth and decrease in size as you move farther into the still water.
9. _____ A term used to describe a region that has high atmospheric moisture.
10. _____ To put or place something down.
11. _____ The movement of rock particles or soil by wind, water, and the force of gravity.
12. _____ The rapid, down-slope movement of large masses of rock and soil.
13. _____ The rapid loss of soil, sediments, or other substances as a result of being washed away by rain or melting snow.
14. _____ Free-moving, solid particles that are hanging in a liquid.
15. _____ The movement of rock, soil, or sediments in a flowing body of water.

Critical Thinking

1. A gravel pit was discovered that contained horizontally sorted, rounded sediment particles at its base, covered by angular, unsorted sediments. Describe the series of events and changes in the environment that would result in this geological formation.

12

Soils

OBJECTIVES

Soil Minerals · Soil Organic Material · Soil Water and Air · Soil Organisms · Soil Structure · Parent Material · Soil Horizons · Soil Classification

After reading this chapter you should be able to:

▶ Define the term *soil*.

▶ Describe the composition of a typical soil.

▶ Explain how minerals are gained by or lost from soil.

▶ Define the term *humus* and explain why it is an important part of healthy soil.

▶ Differentiate between fertile soil and infertile soil.

▶ Describe the three main states of soil moisture.

▶ Identify the organisms that are important for the formation of healthy soil.

▶ Define the term *loam*.

▶ Define the term *parent material* and describe the four different types of parent material.

▶ Describe the five different soil horizons.

▶ Identify one soil order and describe its unique characteristics.

TERMS TO KNOW

soil

leaching

organic material

humus

soil moisture

tilling

nitrogen-fixing bacteria

loam

parent material

alluvial soils

loess

soil profile

soil horizon

top soil

subsoil

INTRODUCTION

Probably the most important aspect of the lithosphere, with regard to sustaining life on Earth, is the existence and formation of soil. The green plants that grow in soil and depend on it to sustain their lives convert the sun's energy into stored chemical energy that other animals require to live. Without soils, life on land would not exist in its present form. Soils have also helped shape civilization as we know it. This natural resource is of great importance to human beings. All the great societies that have flourished on the planet owe their success to fertile soils. Without a stable and plentiful food base grown in soil, advancement in civilization surely could not take place. This relationship continues today, as more people are added to the planet who depend on soils to sustain their food supply.

SOIL MINERALS

Soil is a complex arrangement of minerals and organic material mixed with air, water, and microorganisms. Approximately 45 percent of a typical soil is made up of minerals. This an important aspect of soil because plants require minerals for healthy growth. The minerals that make up the soil's inorganic material are classified by their size. From smallest to largest, they include clay, silt, sand, and gravel. Soils receive their minerals from the weathering of rock, decomposing organic material, and fertilizer created by human beings. Plants require 16 essential elements for healthy growth, making the mineral content of the soil extremely important for crops.

Soils lose minerals and gain them (Figure 12–1). The loss of the essential elements for plant growth can make a soil infertile, or unable to support the healthy growth of crops. Soil minerals are lost by erosion, or the removal of minerals by an agent of erosion. Soil minerals can also be lost by **leaching**. Leaching is the downward movement of minerals that are dissolved in water. Leaching moves essential minerals deep down into the soil where they cannot be accessed by plants. Minerals are also removed from soil by plant uptake. Over time plants remove essential minerals to build their bodies, which can create deficiencies in a soil. This is why farmers periodically spread fertilizers on their fields.

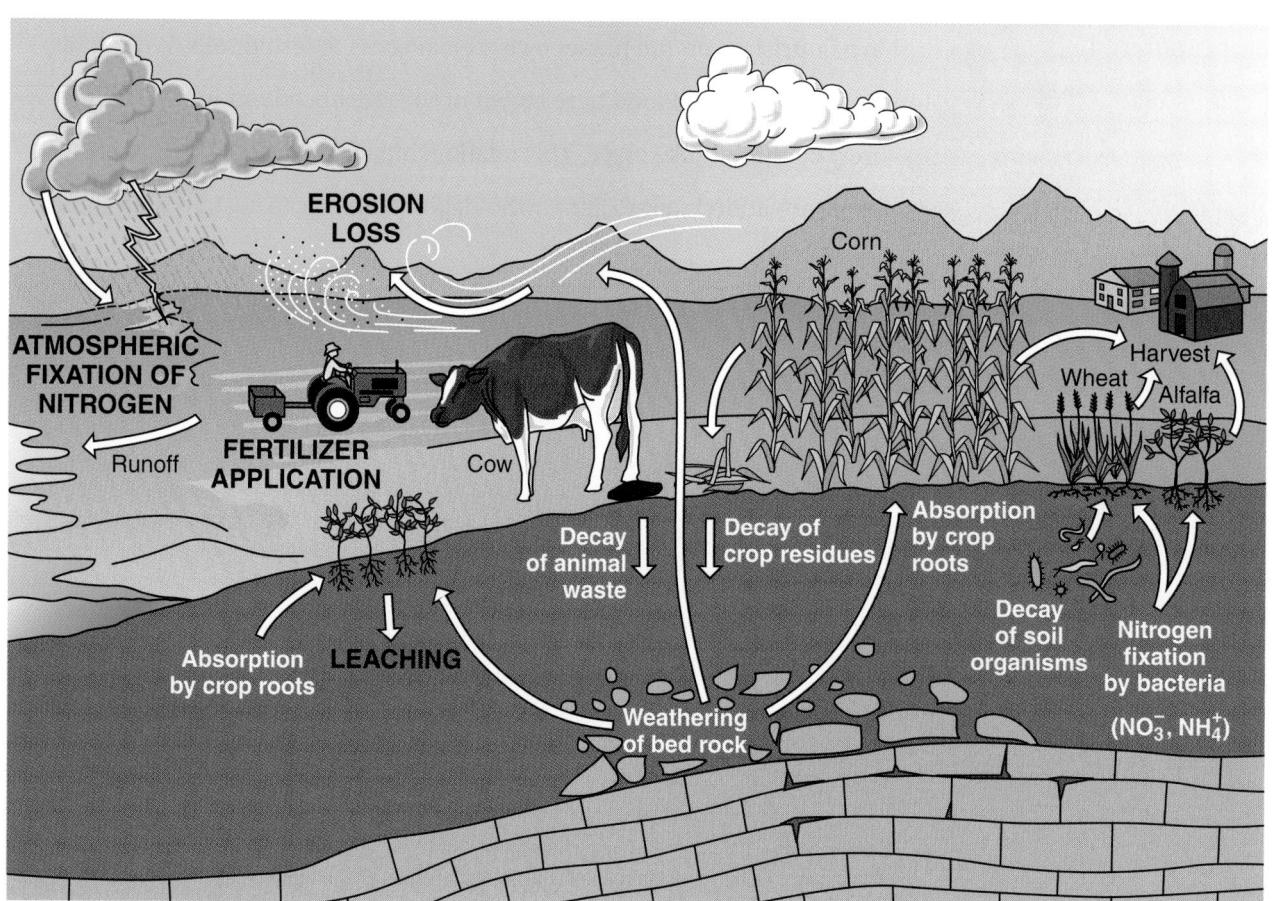

FIGURE 12–1 Soils can gain and lose essential minerals in a variety of ways.

SOIL ORGANIC MATERIAL

The **organic material** in a soil composes approximately 5 percent of its total bulk. The organic matter in a soil is made from the decayed remains of living organisms. This dark organic material is also called **humus**; it is made up of decomposed leaves, roots, twigs, insects, animals, worms, and so on. Any living thing that dies, falls to the Earth's surface, and decays can form humus. Humus is also the result of composting. When composted grass, leaves, or vegetable matter turns into a dark material, it has formed into humus. Although humus only makes up 5 percent of soil, it is extremely important because it acts like glue to hold the mineral particles together in a soil. This enables soils to resist erosion. The humus in a soil also helps form pore spaces. These little pockets that form in the soil hold water and air. A soil with a good amount of humus becomes spongy and provides a good home for the many beneficial bacteria that also live in the soil. It is important to add organic material to a soil to maintain its fertility. Farmers periodically spread animal manure or grow grass and other crops that they plow under into their fields. Both these practices help maintain organic material in the soil.

SOIL WATER AND AIR

The amount of water that is held in a soil's pore spaces is called **soil moisture** (Figure 12–2). Soil moisture is important for plant growth, but it also helps to bind together all the soil particles. Soil with good

Water Content of the Soil

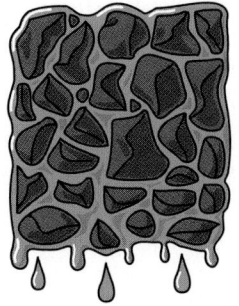

Saturation

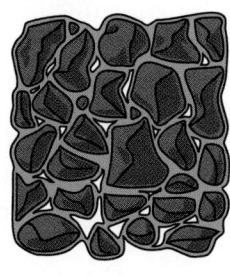

Field capacity

Thin film of moisture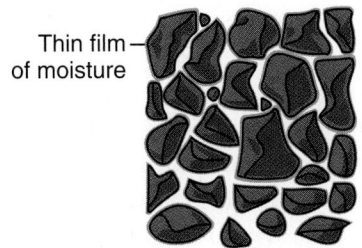

Wilting point

FIGURE 12–2 The three states of moisture in a soil's pore spaces are saturation, field capacity, and the wilting point.

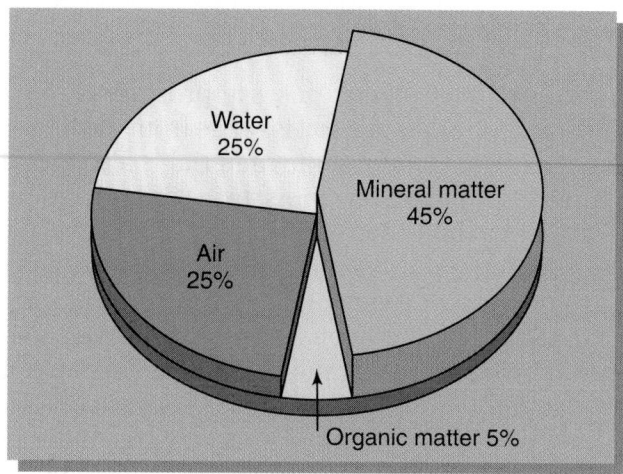

FIGURE 12–3 The composition of a typical soil that is good for crop growth.

moisture levels resists erosion better than drier soil. Soil can also contain too much moisture and become saturated. Saturation of a soil occurs when the soil's pore spaces are completely filled with water. The optimum amount of moisture in a soil is called field capacity. It occurs when the soil's pore spaces contain 50 percent water and 50 percent air. When a soil loses almost all its moisture, it is at its wilting point. This type of soil moisture is called the wilting point because the water levels in the soil are so low that plants begin to dry out and wilt. If this goes on for an extended period, the plants will eventually die.

A fertile soil also needs to contain air. The air in soil is similar to the air in the atmosphere because it contains the same amounts of nitrogen and oxygen and slightly higher amounts of carbon dioxide (Figure 12–3). Oxygen is especially important for a productive soil, because the cells that make up a plant's root system require oxygen for healthy growth. Air in a soil is located in the pores, along with the water. Turning over the soil and mixing it, also called **tilling**, is how air is introduced into a soil. It is important to ensure that soils used for growing plants are well aerated by occasionally tilling them.

SOIL ORGANISMS

Living organisms are also an important part of a soil. The organism that is most associated with soil is probably the earthworm. Earthworms help mix and aerate soils but are not the only organisms in soil. Bacteria are important soil organisms that help add nitrogen to the soil. Nitrogen is an essential element for plant growth. It is not derived from soil minerals. **Nitrogen-fixing bacteria** that reside in soil convert atmospheric nitrogen into plant-available forms such as nitrates. Other organisms, such as fungi and insects, help improve the structure of a soil and also add organic material. Rodents that burrow into soil also help mix a soil by digging deep into the ground. Another important living organism that helps form soil is lichen. Lichen are actually two organisms that live symbiotically. This means that they

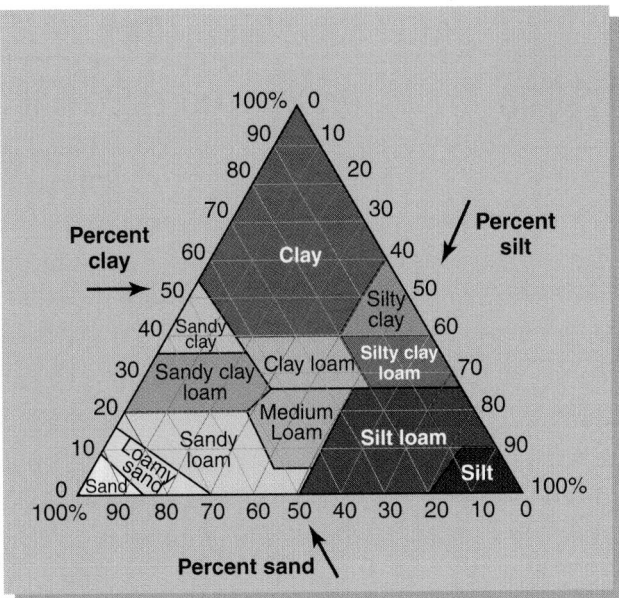

FIGURE 12–4 The soil textural triangle is used to classify a soil based on its mineral composition.

help each other survive. Lichen are composed of algae and fungi. The algae produce food from sunlight through the process of photosynthesis. The algae share the food with the fungi, which in turn secrete a weak acid that helps break down the material on which the lichen is growing. The minerals that are released by the action of the weak acid are then used by the algae as nutrients. The symbiotic relationship of lichen helps to create soil over time by slowly breaking down rock to form soil minerals.

SOIL STRUCTURE

The *structure* of a soil refers to the arrangement of the mineral particles and organic material in a specific soil (Figure 12–4). A well-structured soil tends to be spongy, with a high amount of humus and a mixture of mineral particle sizes. The mixture of mineral sizes can reveal a lot about how a soil will grow crops. A well-structured soil for crop growth is classified as **loam**. Loam contains nearly equal portions of sand, silt, and clay. Soil that contains a higher percentage of sand is called sandy loam. Sandy loams tend to have excessive drainage and cannot maintain good soil moisture. The opposite of this is a soil that has a high percentage of clay. This reduces the amount of pore spaces in the soil and prevents water from infiltrating it. Most poor-structured soils are classified as dense. They do not support good crop growth and are highly erodible.

PARENT MATERIAL

The **parent material** of a soil is the rock from which the soil minerals were derived. Rocks exposed to weathering break down to form mineral particles in a soil. The type of parent material that formed a

CAREER CONNECTIONS

Soil Conservation Technician

A soil conservation technician provides technical assistance to anyone who is concerned with the appropriate use of soil. The soil conservation technician works with farmers, foresters, landowners, state and local governments, and builders. The main goals of people in this occupation are to prevent the loss of fertile soil, the pollution of local waterways, and the destruction of natural resources. Soil conservationists must have knowledge in soil science, erosion control, agricultural engineering, hydrology, and chemistry. They apply their knowledge to develop land use plans to get the most productivity from the land without creating environmental damage. Most soil conservation technicians work with the soil and water conservation services that exist throughout the country. College programs in natural resource conservation provide an excellent foundation for a career in soil conservation.

particular soil greatly influences the fertility of that soil. For example, if the parent material for a particular soil is granite or sandstone, which are high in silicates, then the resulting soil tends to be nutrient deficient. Other types of parent rock, such as limestone, siltstone, and shale, are high in calcium and other essential elements that help form fertile soils.

There are two main types of parent material: residual and transported. Residual soils are formed from parent rock that is located directly below them. These soils tend to be younger, thin, and not yet fully developed. Transported parent material falls into three main categories, depending on how the parent rock material was transported. Glacial transport soils are soils formed from the parent material created by glaciers. Glacial till is the sedimentary remains of glaciers. It is composed of sediment in a variety of sizes. This makes glacial soils very rocky but also extremely fertile, because they contain an assortment of ground-up minerals. Water-transported soils are formed from the deposition of sediments transported by liquid water. These are also called **alluvial soils**. The periodic flooding that occurs near rivers deposits deep layers of sediments that help form rich, fine-grained, fertile soils. These soils tend to be excellent for crop growth. The third type of transported parent material is a wind-transported soil, also known as a **loess**. Soils formed from loess occur in areas where the wind has deposited thick layers of sediments. The American Midwest has excellent, fine-grained, loess-formed soil that is some of the most productive agricultural soil in the world.

Earth System Scientists

Edmund Ruffin

Edmund Ruffin, born in Virginia in 1794, became the United States' first soil researcher. After years of farming, Ruffin began to realize that techniques needed to be developed to revitalize the soil. A mostly self-educated man, Ruffin began to experiment with different techniques to return fertility to the soil and to understand the chemistry of the soil. He studied the effects of poor plowing and drainage on the soil and devised ways to increase the productivity of the soil. He used mixtures of clay, sand, and crushed seashells to return soil nutrients. In 1832 he published *An Essay on Calcareous Manures*, which presented techniques for improving the fertility of the soil. Ruffin also toured the southern United States giving lectures about the science of soil management. When the U.S. Civil War broke out, Ruffin became an outspoken Confederate and was one of the volunteers to fire the first cannon shots at Fort Sumter, which began the war in 1861.

SOIL HORIZONS

A **soil profile** is a cross-sectional view of a soil that helps classify it by identifying its unique horizons (Figure 12–5). A **soil horizon** is a unified layer in the soil that has similar physical and chemical features. Soils are usually divided into five horizons. The O-horizon, also called the organic layer, is the layer of decaying organic material that forms at the top of a soil. The leaf litter that collects on the forest floor is an example of an O-horizon. This is an important horizon that helps to add organic matter to a soil and also helps increase soil moisture by preventing excess evaporation. The next horizon in a soil is the A-horizon, or **top soil**. This is the darker soil that is rich in minerals, air, and water; it is the zone in which most plant root systems grow and forms the base for all productive agriculture in the world. The B-horizon lies below the A-horizon and is known as the **subsoil**. This horizon is usually a light tan or reddish brown colored layer that is low in organic material and very dense. The subsoil may be high in iron content as a result of the leaching of minerals that occurs from the A-horizon to the B-horizon. The next layer in a typical soil is the C-horizon, or unconsolidated parent material. *Unconsolidated* means "broken up," which describes the fractured rock of the soil's parent material. The final layer in a soil profile is the D-horizon, also called the bedrock. This is the solid mass of rock on which a soil rests. The bedrock is either an igneous, metamorphic, or sedimentary rock mass. It is important to note that not all soil types have all soil horizons. Some soils lack an O-horizon because of the lack of available organic material, such as a desert soil. Other soils might not have A-horizons or C-horizons because of the unique geography, climate, and living organisms in the area where the soils are formed. The type of soil

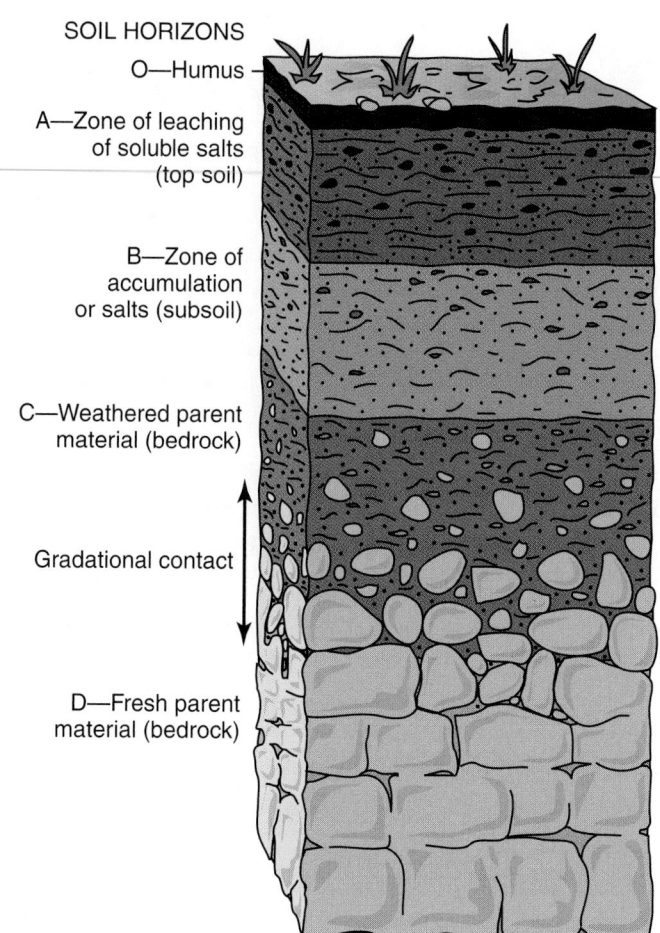

SOIL HORIZONS
O—Humus
A—Zone of leaching of soluble salts (top soil)
B—Zone of accumulation or salts (subsoil)
C—Weathered parent material (bedrock)
Gradational contact
D—Fresh parent material (bedrock)

FIGURE 12–5 A soil profile reveals the different horizons that make up a soil.

profile and its unique horizon arrangement help soil scientists classify the soils of the world.

SOIL CLASSIFICATION

Soils around the world is classified into groups called orders. There are a total of 10 soil orders identified on the Earth. Alfisols are a soil order that describes soils that form in the deciduous forest of the northeastern United States (Figure 12–6). These soils have extensive O-horizons, dark rich A-horizons that support excellent plant growth, and C-horizons that are formed from glacial deposits.

Mollisols make up a soil order containing soils that form under the grasslands in the midwestern United States (Figure 12–7). These soils have no O-horizon, an extremely deep and rich A-horizon, and a C-horizon that is composed from loess, alluvial, or glacial till.

The Oxisol soil order describes the type of soil that forms in the tropical rainforest regions (Figure 12–8). This soil has a thin O-horizon, barely any A-horizon, and a B-horizon that is dense and high in iron. When the vegetation of tropical rainforests is cleared away, the B-horizon is exposed to heavy rains and the hot tropical sun, which bakes it into a hard, bricklike material. This type of soil is not good for crop growth. Many thousands of acres of tropical rainforests are cleared each year

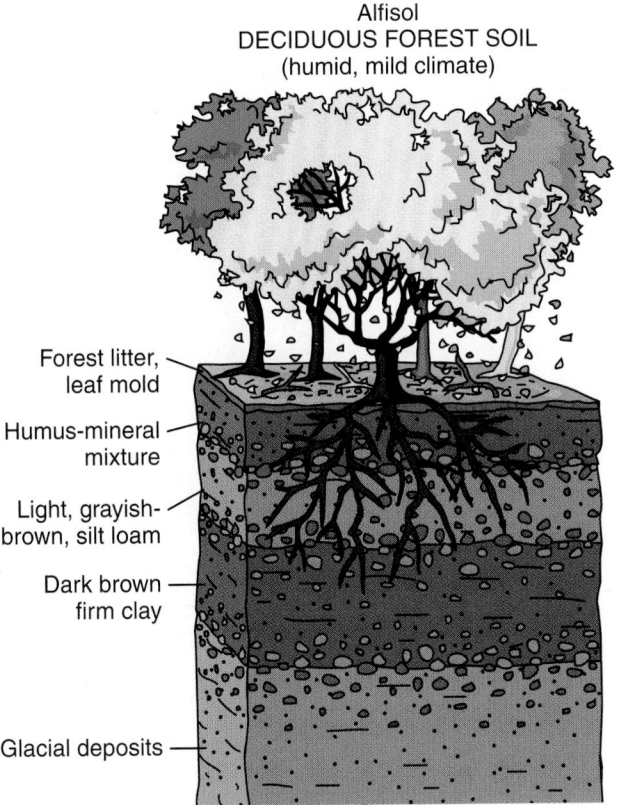

FIGURE 12–6   The profile of an Alfisol soil order associated with the deciduous forests of the northeastern United States reveals its unique horizon characteristics.

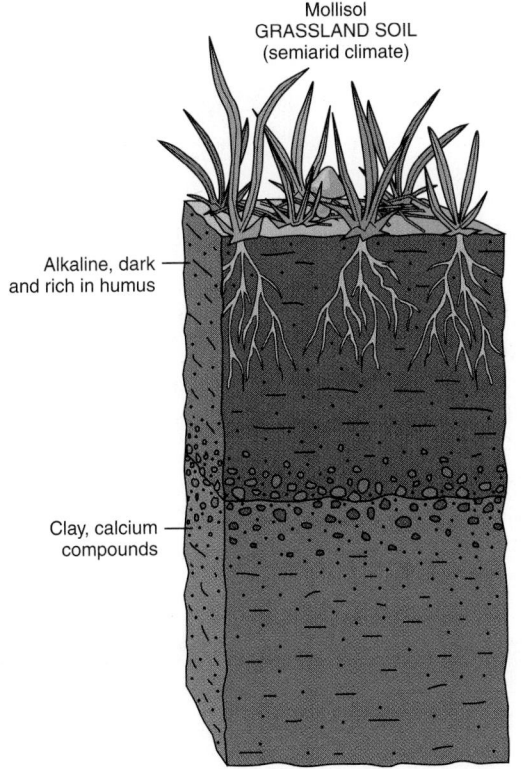

FIGURE 12–7   The profile of a Mollisol soil order associated with the grasslands of the midwestern United States reveals its unique horizon characteristics.

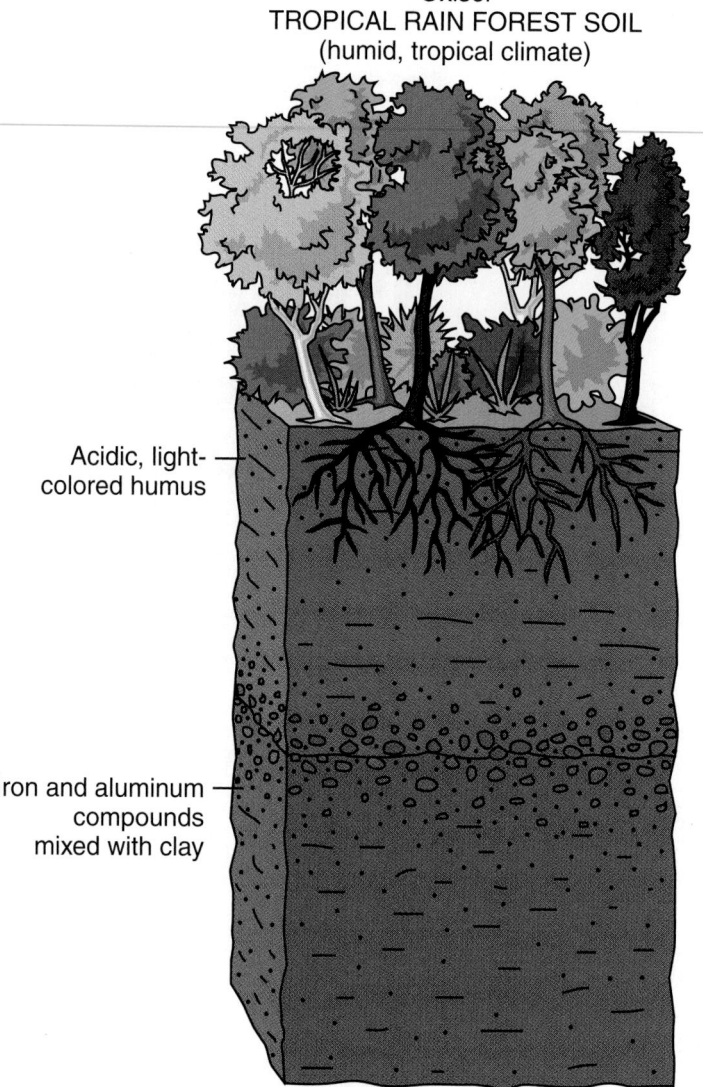

Oxisol
TROPICAL RAIN FOREST SOIL
(humid, tropical climate)

Acidic, light-colored humus

Iron and aluminum compounds mixed with clay

FIGURE 12–8 The profile of an Oxisol soil order associated with tropical rainforests reveals its unique horizon characteristics.

for agriculture, and unfortunately Oxisol soils do not support long-term crop growth.

The world's soil is an important natural resource on which our food supply relies (Figure 12–9). The formation of just 1 inch (2.5 cm) of soil might take a thousand years, making it important to practice sound soil conservation techniques that will protect and sustain this fragile part of the lithosphere.

@ WEB Links

FOR MORE INFORMATION GO TO THESE WEB LINKS:

<http://www.soils.org /smithsonian/index.html>

<http://soils.usda.gov/>

<http://www .fieldmuseum.org/under-groundadventure/>

<http://www.usda.gov /wps/portal/usdahome>

REVIEW

1. What is the composition of a typical soil?

2. What is humus, and why is it important to soil?

3. What are three processes by which soil loses mineral nutrients?

FIGURE 12–9 A map of North America showing the location of the continent's main soil orders.

4. What is the optimum amount of air and water content in a soil's pore spaces?

5. What are the three types of transported parent material that forms soil?

6. List the five soil horizons and describe their unique features.

7. Who was Edmund Ruffin?

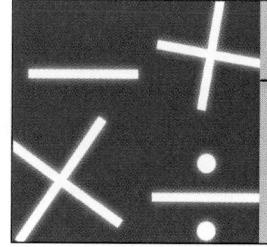

earth math

1) If it takes approximately 1,000 years for 1 inch of top soil to develop in a particular part of the world, how deep is the soil after the glacier retreated 12,500 years ago?

CHAPTER SUMMARY

Soil is an important natural resource on which many organisms, including humans, depend for their survival. A soil is a mixture of minerals, organic material, air, and water in specific proportions. Minerals make up approximately 45 percent of a typical soil. Plants that grow in soil use these minerals for healthy growth. Minerals in a soil are classified by their size, from the smallest to the largest, which include clay, silt, sand, and gravel. A soil gains minerals from decaying organic material, weathering of rocks, and fertilizer. Soils lose minerals by plant uptake, leaching, and runoff. Organic material composes about 5 percent of a typical soil. Organic material in a soil is often in the form of humus. Humus is the dark, moist, completely decayed remains of organic matter. It holds together the mineral particles of a soil, which helps a soil resist erosion. Humus also forms pore spaces in a soil, which are tiny spaces that contain water and air. The amount of water in the pore spaces of a soil is called soil moisture, which composes approximately 25 percent of a typical soil. There are three types of soil moisture: saturation, wilting point, and field capacity. Field capacity occurs when 50 percent of the pores in a soil are filled with air and 50 percent are filled with water. This is the optimum amount of moisture needed for healthy crop growth. The remaining 25 percent of a typical soil is composed of air, which is also required by plants for healthy growth. The composition of air in a soil is similar to the air in the atmosphere.

Many organisms reside in the soil. Earthworms burrow through soil, helping to turn it over and aerate it. Bacteria also live in the soil, some of which add nitrogen to the soil, which is needed by plants. The structure of a soil is the arrangement and composition of its minerals. Loam is a type of soil structure that is good for crop growth and is composed of nearly equal parts of sand, silt, and clay. The rocks that supply the minerals in a soil are known as parent material. There are four different types of parent material: alluvial, loess, glacial, and residual. Soils are classified by their unique profile, which is a cross-sectional view of a soil. Soil profiles reveal the unique layers of soil, called horizons. These horizons all have their own unique physical and chemical characteristics. The five soil horizons are the O-horizon, A-horizon, B-horizon, C-horizon, and D-horizon. Specific soils are classified into unique soil orders that are based on the characteristics of a soil's horizons.

CHAPTER REVIEW

Multiple Choice

1. A typical soil contains approximately what percentage of minerals?
   a. 5 percentage
   b. 10 percentage
   c. 25 percentage
   d. 45 percentage

2. The smallest mineral particle in a soil is called:
   a. clay
   b. silt
   c. sand
   d. gravel

3. A source of minerals in a soil is:
   a. leaching
   b. runoff
   c. plant uptake
   d. organic material

4. Organic material makes up approximately what percentage of a typical soil?
   a. 5 percentage
   b. 10 percentage
   c. 25 percentage
   d. 45 percentage

5. The dark, moist, decayed organic material that holds the mineral particles together in a soil is called:
   a. top soil
   b. subsoil
   c. humus
   d. parent material

6. When a soil's pore spaces contain 50% water and 50% air it is known as:
   a. saturation
   b. the wilting point
   c. full
   d. field capacity

7. Air and water compose approximately what percentage of a typical soil?
   a. 25 percentage air, 25 percentage water
   b. 50 percentage air, 50 percentage water
   c. 45 percentage air, 5 percentage water
   d. 5 percentage air, 45 percentage water

8. Which type of organism fixes nitrogen in the soil?
   a. earthworms
   b. lichen
   c. bacteria
   d. fungus

9. Which of the following parent material is transported by wind?
   a. loess
   b. alluvial
   c. glacial
   d. residual

10. When liquid water deposits parent material that forms soil it is known as:
    a. loess
    b. alluvial
    c. glacial
    d. residual

11. Which soil horizon is commonly called top soil?
    a. O-horizon
    b. A-horizon
    c. B-horizon
    d. C-horizon

12. Which soil horizon is known as the subsoil?
    a. O-horizon
    b. A-horizon
    c. B-horizon
    d. C-horizon

13. Which soil horizon is mostly composed of decaying organic material?
    a. O-horizon
    b. A-horizon
    c. B-horizon
    d. C-horizon

14. This type of soil order is commonly associated with the fertile grassland soils of the American Midwest:
    a. Alfisol
    b. Mollisol
    c. Oxisol
    d. Aridosol

15. The tropical rainforests that are being cleared for agriculture in South America grow in which type of soil?
    a. Alfisol
    b. Mollisol
    c. Oxisol
    d. Aridosol

Matching   *Match the terms with the correct definitions.*

a. soil
b. leaching
c. organic material
d. humus
e. soil moisture

f. tilling
g. nitrogen-fixing bacteria
h. loam
i. parent material
j. alluvial soils

k. loess
l. soil profile
m. soil horizon
n. top soil
o. subsoil

1. _____ The movement of chemicals that are dissolved in water from a higher layer of soil downward into a lower level of soil or groundwater.
2. _____ The layer of soil, also known as the B-horizon, that lies directly below the top soil.
3. _____ A mixture of minerals, organic material, air, and water that forms at the surface of the Earth.
4. _____ The uppermost layer of soil that contains a high amount of organic material, also called the A-horizon.
5. _____ A term used to describe a soil that contains specific portions of sand, silt, and clay.
6. _____ A well-defined layer of soil that has specific characteristics.
7. _____ A specific type of bacteria that converts atmospheric nitrogen (N_2) to plant-usable forms of nitrogen such as nitrate (NO_3^-)
8. _____ The term used to describe the specific rocks from which soil minerals are derived.
9. _____ A term used to describe material that is derived from a living thing.
10. _____ Rich, fertile soil formed by the deposition of minerals by liquid water.
11. _____ The completely decomposed remains of organic debris that is an important part of a soil.
12. _____ The cross-sectional view of a particular soil that shows all the soil's horizons.
13. _____ The amount of water that is present in a soil.
14. _____ A type of soil found in the American Midwest that is formed from wind-transported parent material.
15. _____ The process of turning over, or plowing, the soil.

Critical Thinking

1. As the world's population grows, our dependence on soil used to grow crops increases. What specific practices do you think can ensure that our soils will continue to produce healthy crops in the future?

13

The Earth's Geologic History

TERMS TO KNOW

geologic time scale

relative dating

principle of uniformity

principle of superposition

principle of cross-cutting
 relationships

unconformity

original preservation

mineralization

index fossils

half-life

radiometric dating

eon

stromatolites

Precambrian

eras

mass extinctions

Pangaea

epochs

evolution

gene

trait

heredity

transitional species

INTRODUCTION

Scientists believe that the Earth is approximately 4.6 billion years old. Discovering the events that occurred and the type of organisms that lived during this long period is like unraveling a great mystery. Scientists must act like detectives and gather clues using many different techniques of investigation and observation to help them reveal the mysteries of the Earth's past. These techniques have helped develop theories of how our planet formed and how it has changed over time, what life forms it has supported, and how those life forms have evolved during its long past.

13.1 Geologic Dating Techniques

GEOLOGIC PRINCIPLES

Scientists have pieced together the history of the Earth using the **geologic time scale**, which divides the Earth's history into distinct relative time periods. Geologic time and the techniques of **relative dating** are based on important geologic principles. The first is the **principle of uniformity**, which states that the processes occurring today on the Earth are the same processes that have occurred throughout the planet's history. This means that the conditions that lead to the formation of rocks today are the same as in the past. This important scientific concept was first proposed by Scottish farmer James Hutton in the late eighteenth century. Using this concept, geologists began to piece together other important geologic concepts such as the **principle of superposition**, which states that in undisturbed rock layers, the older rocks lie below younger rocks. Therefore it is possible to create a time scale that shows the formation of rocks relative to one another, where old rocks are on the bottom and younger rocks are on top. In addition, sedimentary rock layers can be identified and traced from one location on the Earth to another. This helps correlate geologic history over wide geographical areas.

Other important clues that help create relative dates include the identification of unique volcanic ash layers in rock layers. These layers act like time markers in rock strata that can also be traced over wide areas. Another relative dating technique used by geologists is known as the **principle of cross-cutting relationships**. Geologic features such as igneous intrusions, which occur when hot molten rock flows into cracks and crevices of older rock layers and solidifies, can reveal much about the dates of rock. The intrusion, also known as a cross-cut, is younger than the rock layers that it is in, which helps determine the relative date of its formation. Rock features such as faults, another type of cross-cut, and volcanic rocks can also help piece together the Earth's history. Faults are younger than the rock formations in which they are found, and volcanic rock usually flows through and over older rock. The presence of an unconformity in a rock sequence can also establish relative dates of rock formations. An **unconformity** is a buried erosional surface. Unconformities form when rocks are uplifted, eroded away, and reburied. This process takes an extremely long time and represents a significant gap in the geologic record. Together all these relative dating techniques help establish the series of events that have occurred in a rock formation (Figure 13–1).

FOSSILS

The discovery of the fossil remains of living organisms add more information to the geologic time scale. For an organism to be fossilized, it usually has to die and be buried quickly to prevent it from being decomposed. Fossil evidence can reveal much about what the environment was like when these organisms lived. For example, the remains of a marine organism found in the mountains today suggest that the environment has changed dramatically. This gives us clues as to what the world was like when these organisms were alive (Figure 13–2).

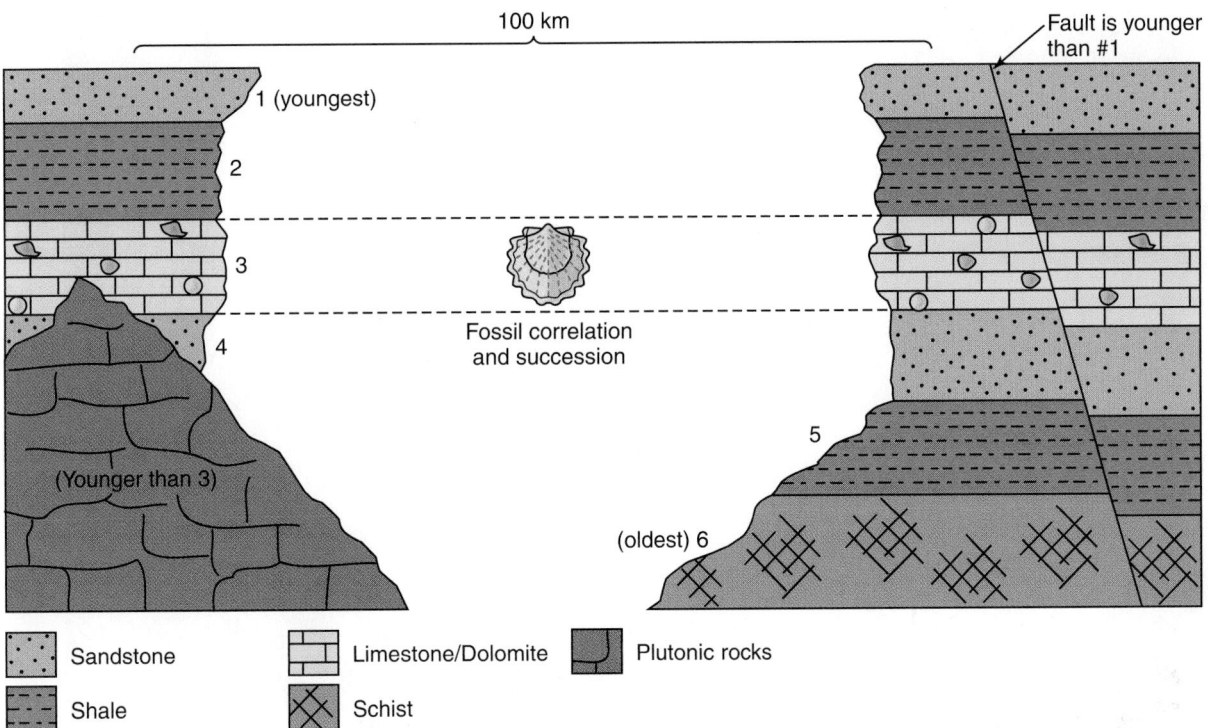

FIGURE 13–1 This geologic cross section shows how superposition, faults, igneous intrusions, index fossils, and rock correlations are used to relatively date rock formations.

FIGURE 13–2 Fossils of marine organisms found in rocks located high above sea level suggest that the environment was much different during the time these organisms were alive. (*Courtesy of PhotoDisc.*)

FIGURE 13-3   A mineralized dinosaur bone fossil. (*Courtesy of Alamy Images.*)

There are three basic ways in which organisms can be preserved as fossils. One way is called original preservation. **Original preservation** involves the process of preserving the actual body of the organism. This can occur by freezing, or as a result of the rapid drying out of an organism known as mummification. Tree sap that traps organisms and then solidifies into a rock-like substance known as amber can also preserve the whole body.

Other forms of original preservation include the remains of organisms preserved in acidic bog water or in tar pits. The second method of fossilization is called **mineralization**. Mineralization is a process that slowly replaces the atoms that make up the tissue of a dead organism with minerals like quartz or calcite. Over time the hard parts of an organism, such as bone and shells, become an exact rock-like copy of the original. Many dinosaurs have been preserved in this manner (Figure 13-3). The third method of fossilization is in the form of a fossil impression. Organisms that die in water can leave an impression of their bodies in soft sediments. Over time these impressions become buried in sediments and eventually lithify. Many marine organisms have left fossil impressions behind, and terrestrial organisms have left footprints that are known as trackways.

Fossils that lived for a relatively short time on the Earth, but are found all over the globe, can be used to establish relative dates of rock formations. These fossils are known as **index fossils**. If an index fossil is identified as living during a specific time period, then whenever the same species is found in a new rock formation that can help establish

TABLE 13–1 The half-lives and daughter elements of radioactive isotopes commonly used for radiometric dating

Radioactive Isotope	Approximate Half-Life	Decay Product
Rubidium 87	50 billion years	Strontium 87
Potassium 40	1.3 billion years	Argon 40
Uranium 238	4.5 billion years	Lead 206
Uranium 235	700 million years	Lead 207
Carbon 14	5730 years	Nitrogen 14

its relative age. Using all of these methods, geologists began to create a geologic history of the Earth, along with assumptions of what life was like during these periods.

RADIOMETRIC DATING

In 1895 the French physicist Antoine Henri Becquerel discovered that uranium atoms undergo radioactive decay. His discovery revealed that uranium breaks down over time to form a new element, lead. The original element is called the parent element, and the product of its decay is known as the daughter element. Uranium is the parent element, and lead is the resulting daughter element. Becquerel also discovered that radioactive decay occurs at a specific rate, called the **half-life**. The half-life of an element is the time it takes for half of a number of parent elements to decay into their daughter elements (Table 13–1). For example, if you start with 2 gm of uranium 238, 1 gm will remain after one half-life has elapsed. This technique is called **radiometric dating**. It allows geologists to estimate how old rocks were when they formed. By calculating the ratio of parent elements to daughter elements and using the half-life of the known element, it is possible to date rocks accurately and determine the absolute age of a rock. For example, the half-life of uranium 238 is 4.5 billion years. This means that it will take 4.5 billion years for half, or 50 percent, of the uranium in the rock to break down into lead. Therefore, if you found a rock that contained 50 percent lead and 50 percent uranium, you could estimate that it formed 4.5 billion years ago because half the element has decayed. The element uranium is good for dating only extremely old rocks, but other elements that have shorter half-lives can be used to date younger rocks. These elements include potassium 40, which has a half-life of 1.3 billion years; uranium 235, with a half-life of 700 million years; and carbon 14, with a half-life of 5,730 years. Because all living things contain carbon, the isotope carbon 14 can be used to radiometrically date the remains of living things (Figure 13–4).

Current exploration of objects in the solar system has also helped piece together the Earth's history. When astronauts brought back rock samples from the Moon, scientists were able to accurately date the rocks' age. The age of many meteorites has also been determined. The dating of rocks by radioactive decay, the existence of fossil evidence, and the well-established principles of geology combine to

FIGURE 13–4 The process by which Carbon 14 enters living organisms. Determining the ratio of Carbon 14 to its daughter element, Nitrogen 14, can reveal how long ago the organism died.

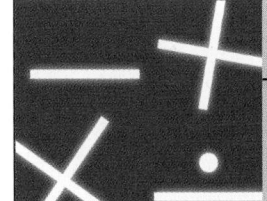

earth math

1) How long ago did a mastodon die if you determine that the Carbon 14 in one of its teeth has gone through three half-lives?

create the fascinating story of our planet's history. Our knowledge of this history is constantly being expanded as more scientific discoveries are made about the geology of Earth.

SECTION REVIEW

1. What is the principle of uniformity?
2. Describe the principle of superposition.
3. What is the half-life of an element?
4. What is radiometric dating?
5. What are the four principal elements used for radiometric dating?
6. Describe the three methods of fossilization:

FOR MORE INFORMATION GO TO THIS WEB LINK:

<http://www.c14dating.com/>

13.2   Geologic Time

THE GEOLOGIC TIME SCALE

The geologic time scale is used to represent the history of the Earth (Figure 13–5). The largest period represented in the geologic time scale is the **eon**. Three eons make up the Earth's history: the Archean, Proterozoic, and Phanerozoic eons.

Earth System Scientists

Arthur Holmes

Arthur Holmes was a geologist who in 1913 first proposed a geologic time scale that described the history of the Earth. Using the new science of radioactive dating, he theorized that the Earth was approximately 4.5 billion years old. He also helped date the different eras that together make up the geologic time scale. Later in his career he hypothesized that the mechanism behind plate tectonics might be large-scale convection cells in the Earth's mantle. This hypothesis was given without any research to back it up, however, and was not truly proven until 30 years later. Arthur Holmes continued his work in geology until his death in 1965.

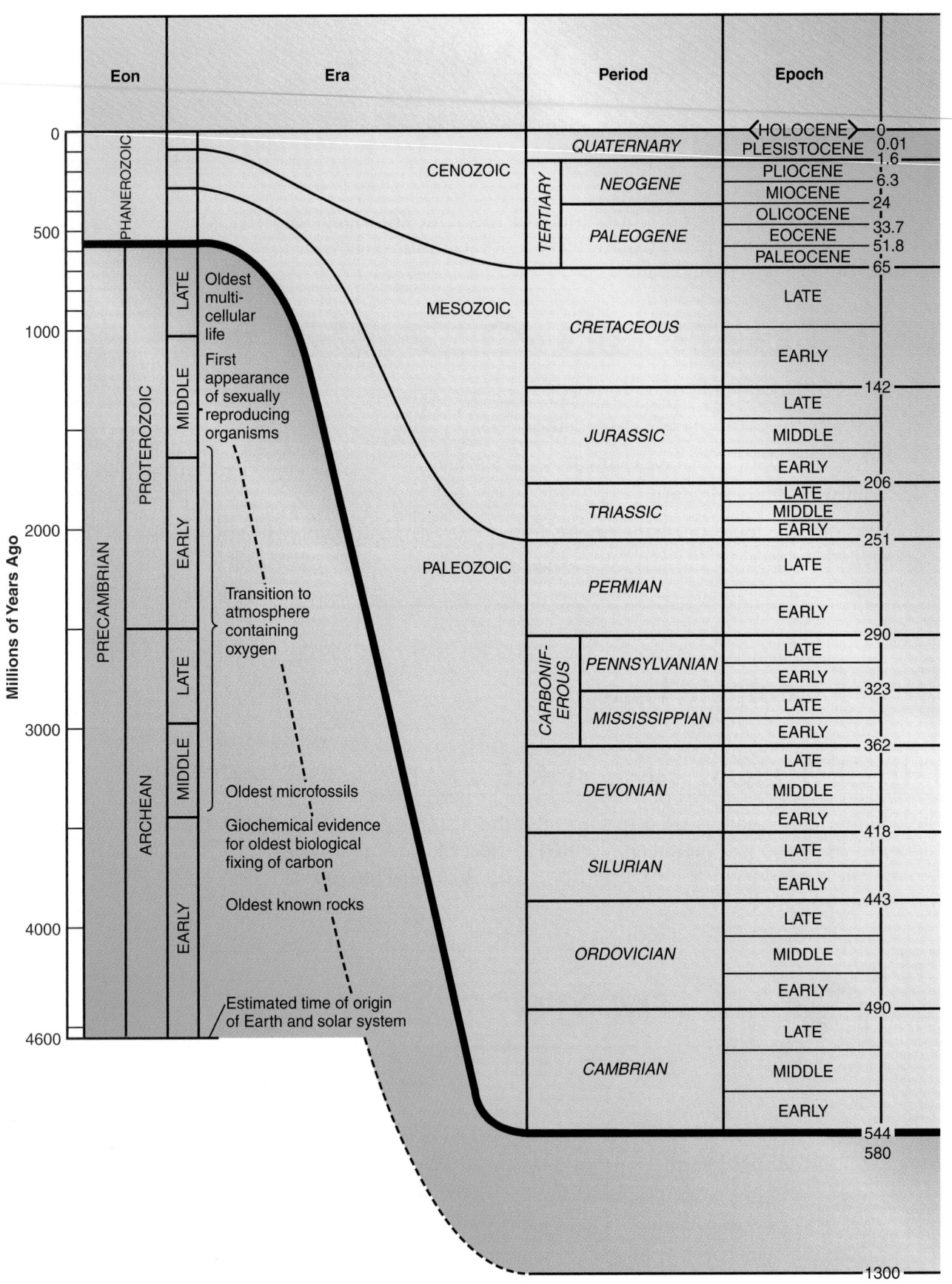

FIGURE 13–5 The geologic time scale.

Life on Earth	Inferred Position of Earth's Land Masses
Millions of years ago	

Humans, mastodonts, mammoths

Large carnivores
Abundant grazing mammals
Earliest grasses
Large running mammals
Many modern groups of mammals

Extinction of dinosaurs and amminoids

Earliest placental mammals
Climax of dinosaurs and amminoids

Earliest flowering plants
Decline of brachiopods
Diverse bony fishes

Earliest birds
Abundant dinosaurs and amminoids

Modern coral groups appear
Earliest dinosaurs and mammals with abundant
   cycads and conifers
Extinction of many kinds of marine animals,
   including trilobites
First mammal-like reptiles

Earliest reptiles
Extensive coal-forming forests

Abundant sharks and amphibians
Large and numerous scale trees and arid ferns

Earliest amphibians, ammonoids, sharks
Extinction of armored fish, other fish
   abundant

Earliest insects
Earliest land plants and animals
Peak development of Euryptecids

Invertebrates dominant
   – mollusks become abundant
Diverse coral and echinoderms

Graptolites abundant

Earliest fish
Algal reefs
Burgess shale fauna
Earliest chordates, diverse trilobites
Earliest trilobites
Earliest marine animals with shells

Edicaran fauna

Soft-bodied organisms

Stromatolites

TERTIARY — 59 million years ago

CRETACEOUS — 119 million years ago

TRIASSIC — 232 million years ago

DEVONIAN/MISSISSIPPIAN — 352 million years ago

ORDOVICIAN — 458 million years ago

FIGURE 13–5, Cont'd The geologic time scale.

THE ARCHEAN EON

The Archean eon began approximately 4.5 billion years ago, when scientists believe the Earth formed (Figure 13–6). The beginning of the Archean eon was a violent time in the Earth's history. The planet was exposed to constant bombardment by meteorites and asteroids, as evidenced by the surface of the Moon. During this time, the Earth was extremely hot, and much of the surface was covered in molten rock. As the Earth began to cool, it expelled gases from its interior, which is called outgassing. These gases were mainly carbon dioxide, water vapor, and hydrogen. The lighter element hydrogen was released into space, leaving carbon dioxide and water vapor to make up the Earth's early atmosphere.

Eventually the Earth cooled to the point that the surface began to solidify and form the Earth's crust. This marked the time when rocks first formed on Earth. The oldest rocks found on the planet today are located in parts of Canada, Greenland, and Australia, and are between 4- and 3.8-billion-year-old metamorphic and sedimentary rocks. They reveal that the Earth's crust might have formed more than 4 billion years ago. During the formation of the Earth's crust, the water vapor that was being expelled from the Earth's interior was condensing in the atmosphere and raining down on the Earth's surface. This began the creation of today's oceans. The first billion years of Earth's history resulted in the formation of the Earth's crust and oceans. Eventually, as the planet's environment became more stable, the first life forms appeared.

The Earth was unique compared with other planets in the solar system because it contained a great amount of liquid water. It was in the oceans that the first organisms flourished. The oldest fossils discovered on Earth are the remains of **stromatolites** that were found in Australia (Figure 13–7). Stromatolites are colonies of single-celled cyanobacteria that form large, slimy mats in warm, shallow saltwater. These ancient bacteria, also called blue-green algae, use photosynthesis as an energy source. These single-celled creatures secrete a sticky, glue-like material that traps sand grains. These grains help form the rocklike structures called stromatolites, which are approximately 3.5 billion years old.

Amazingly, there are stromatolites still living today in the warm, shallow waters off Australia (Figure 13–8). These are the oldest living organisms on the Earth. For the next billion years, stromatolites and most likely bacteria were the principal life forms on the Earth. The photosynthetic action of the stromatolites produced oxygen as a by-product; this oxygen began to fill the early atmosphere. Recent discoveries of communities of organisms living at the bottom of the ocean near volcanic vents suggest that life also might have existed on the early Earth in a similar deep-water environment.

THE PROTEROZOIC EON

The end of the Archean eon came approximately 2.5 billion years ago, and the Proterozoic eon began. Geologic evidence suggests that during this eon crustal plate movements began, which led to the formation of

FIGURE 13–6 The early Earth as it may have appeared during the Archean eon.

FIGURE 13-7 Stromatolite fossils, which are approximately 3.5 billion years old, are some of the oldest living things discovered on the Earth. (*Courtesy of Joseph Deuel/Petrified Sea Gardens.*)

FIGURE 13-8 Today stromatolites still thrive in the shallow waters off the coast of Australia. (*Courtesy of Eva Boogaard/Lochman Transparencies.*)

the first mountain ranges. Stromatolites were also widespread during the Proterozoic eon. The microscopic fossil remains of bacteria and other single-celled organisms were found in rocks near Lake Superior. They are approximately 1.9 billion years old. Some of these bacteria are similar to species that are alive today. These organisms used respiration to gain energy, which suggests that the atmosphere contained a level of oxygen similar to that found in today's atmosphere. Later in the Proterozoic eon, multicelled creatures began to flourish in the Earth's oceans for the first time. The fossil remains of algae and soft-bodied aquatic creatures have been found to be 570 to 900 million years old.

There is also geologic evidence to suggest that the first glaciers began to appear during this time. Remains of glacial deposits formed when ice that contained rocks, also called glacial till, melted and was deposited at the bottom of either a glacial lake or coastal ocean. Rocks formed from glacial till are known as tillites. During the late Proterozoic eon, approximately 700 million years ago, tillite glacial deposits were found on many continents, suggesting that much of the land was covered by glaciers.

The period before 570 million years ago, which includes the Archean and Proterozoic eons, is also known as the **Precambrian** time. By the end of Precambrian time, much of the North American continent was formed. One of the oldest Precambrian rock formations in the world is called the Canadian Shield, which today makes up parts of eastern Canada, Greenland, and the Adirondack Mountains of New York. This ancient land mass is approximately 2 billion years old. The end of the Proterozoic eon occurred approximately 570 billion years ago, and the eon in which we live today, the Phanerozoic eon, began.

THE PALEOZOIC ERA

The Phanerozoic eon is subdivided into three different periods called **eras.** This division is based on the occurrence of **mass extinctions** of organisms. Each era is then further subdivided into specific periods. The Paleozoic, or "early life," era consists of six specific periods based on the principal life forms that were alive at that time. The early Paleozoic era consists of the Cambrian period and the Ordovician period (Figure 13–9).

The Cambrian period began 570 million years ago and lasted for about 65 million years. The beginning of this important point in the history and development of life on Earth is also referred to as the Cambrian explosion. This is because it marks the appearance of many diverse forms of life for the first time in the fossil record. Many of the continents on the planet during this time were flooded by shallow inland seas. The Cambrian period is also when many shelled marine creatures such as trilobites first emerged. The Ordovician period began approximately 505 million years ago with the emergence of a variety of marine life forms, including crinoids, corals, snails, starfish, and segmented worms. There is some fossil evidence to suggest that during the late Ordovician period plants might have begun to inhabit land.

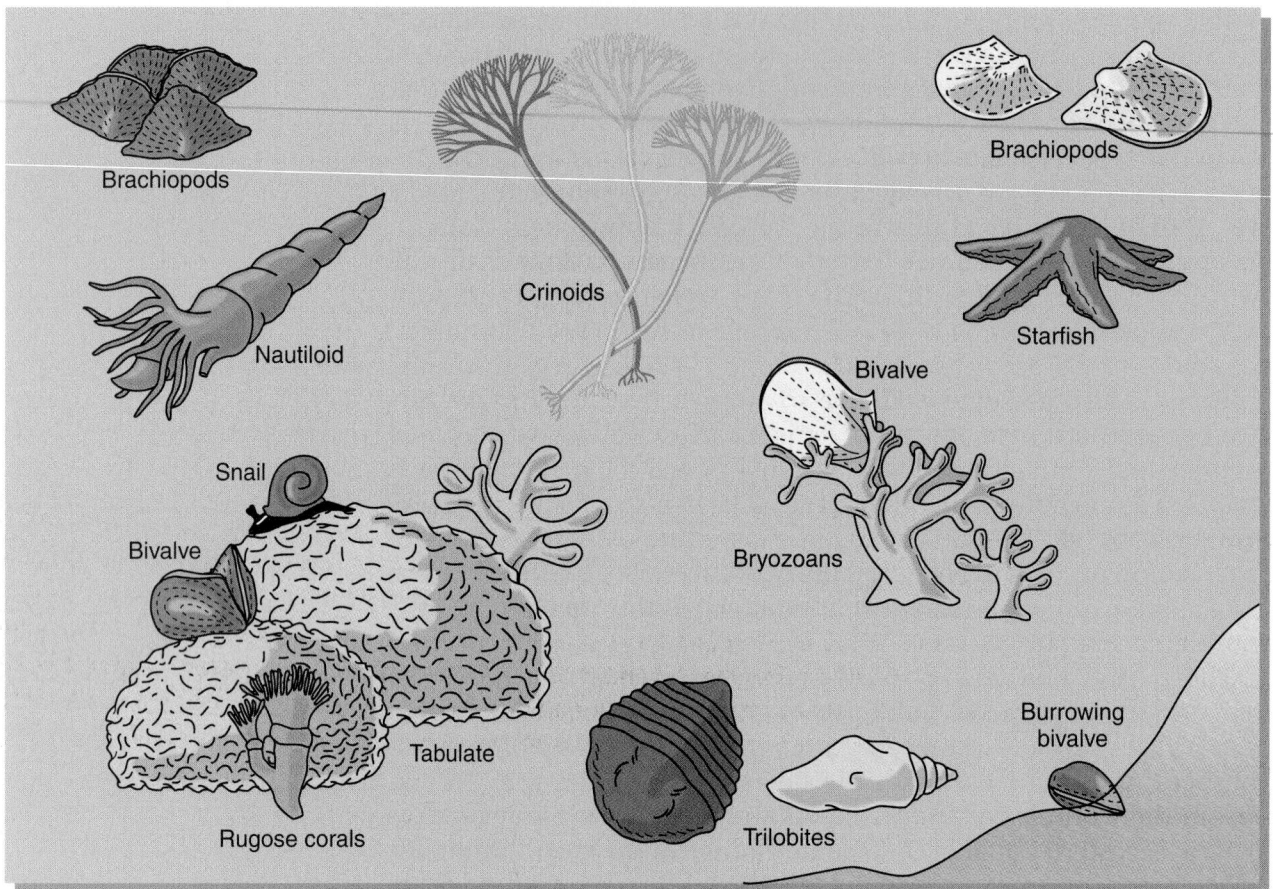

FIGURE 13-9 An example of marine organisms that lived during the Cambrian and Ordovician periods between 544 and 443 million years ago.

Much of the globe was covered in water as in the Cambrian period, providing the perfect shallow sea habitats that are preserved in Ordovician sediments; these sediments contain some of the best-preserved fossils on the planet.

Some regions of the planet might have been covered in glaciers during the later part of the Ordovician period. The Taconic Mountains were formed on the eastern part of North America when the continent collided with a string of volcanic islands in the proto-Atlantic Ocean, called the Iapetus Ocean. The end of the Ordovician period was marked by the mass extinction of the trilobite species.

The middle Paleozoic era, which began 438 million years ago, is divided into two periods: the Silurian and the Devonian. During the Silurian period, complex coral reefs began to form and swimming organisms such as the eurypterid emerged (Figure 13–10). This sea creature, which resembled a large aquatic scorpion, swam along the bottom of shallow water in search of prey.

The first true land plants also emerged during the Silurian period. These semiaquatic plants resembled today's marsh vegetation but were much simpler in their design. During this time, much of North America was flooded by a large inland sea. During the late Silurian period, this sea began to evaporate and shrink, leaving behind large salt deposits that are still being mined today.

FIGURE 13-10 Eurypterid fossils from the Silurian period, between 443 and 418 million years ago. (*Photo by Pamela Gore, Courtesy of the Denver Museum of Nature and Science.*)

The Devonian period began about 408 million years ago with the emergence of jawed fish. These were the first fish that had scales and fins like today's modern freshwater and marine fish species. Some of the jawed fish that lived during the late Devonian period grew to more than 30 feet (9 meters) in length. Other strange fish also flourished during this time, including the armored fish (Figure 13–11). These heavily protected fish were covered in unique armor; some even had armor that covered parts of their eyes!

FIGURE 13-11 The fossilized remains of a placoderm, a type of armored fish that became extinct in the middle of the Devonian period approximately 400 million years ago. (*Photo by Pamela Gore, Georgia Perimeter College.*)

The armored fish became extinct during the end of the Devonian period. During the late Devonian period the first trees began to appear on Earth, leading to the development of the first forests. The once barren landscape of Earth was now populated by many different plants, which contributed to the development of fertile soils. The first animals to inhabit the land began to emerge during the late Devonian period. These animals were amphibians that periodically crawled out from the water to search for food on land. Many of these creatures were primitive lungfish, which had strong, footlike fins that might have helped them move about on land. The end of the Devonian period was marked by the mass extinction of many tropical marine species. This extinction is believed to have been caused by the cooling of the planet because apparently only tropical species were affected. Geologic evidence from the late Devonian also supports that global cooling occurred during this time because there appear to have been glaciers covering many land areas.

The middle Paleozoic era ended approximately 363 million years ago and the rise of large coal swamps began. This is known as the Carboniferous period because a great amount of hydrocarbons were produced and buried deep in the ground. Hydrocarbons are molecules that contain hydrogen and carbon, and eventually they were transformed into coal. Coal swamps were large areas of the Earth that were partially flooded with freshwater (Figure 13–12). Large trees, ferns, and other plants grew in abundance in and around these swamps.

FIGURE 13–12 A Carboniferous period coal swamp that existed between 323 and 290 million years ago.

CAREER CONNECTIONS
Paleontologist

Paleontologists are specialized geologists who study the rock formations of the world in search of the fossilized remains of once living organisms. These scientists explore many parts of the globe to uncover knowledge about the Earth's living history. Paleontologists painstakingly uncover the remains of ancient plants and animals to piece together our planet's past (Figure 13–13). The most well-known paleontologists search for dinosaurs and are attempting to reveal the lives of these amazing creatures. Much of the paleontologist's career is spent in the laboratory analyzing and restoring fossil remains extracted from the Earth. All paleontologists are highly specialized and must have a solid understanding of geology. It is also important for paleontologists to have knowledge of biology so they can apply it to the ancient creatures that they are studying. Paleontologists require at least a 4-year college degree and often work within the academic fields. Many paleontologists become college professors or museum curators and travel to exotic places all over the world. There are also career opportunities for laboratory technicians who work with paleontologists. These jobs require less education but can be extremely rewarding because they are often involved in the restoration and preparation of fossil remains.

FIGURE 13–13 A paleontologist exposes a fossilized jaw bone as part of his laboratory work. (*Courtesy of PhotoDisc.*)

When these plants died, they fell into the swamps and became buried in sediments. Over time the remains of this decaying swamp vegetation were transformed by the heat and pressure of the Earth into coal.

During the Carboniferous period, large winged insects also began to appear. These creatures resembled today's houseflies and dragonflies. The ancestor of the modern cockroach first appeared during the Carboniferous period. Although the first amphibians appeared during the late Devonian period, the Carboniferous period marked the true rise of land-dwelling amphibians, which ranged from mouse sized to more than 20 feet (6 meters) in length. Many of the shallow seas of the world during this time contained a variety of crinoids (Figure 13–14).

Crinoids are fernlike creatures that attach themselves to the sea floor with long stems and filter out tiny microorganisms with their fan-like arms. These widespread organisms covered the bottom of the ocean, forming underwater meadows. Ancestors of modern sharks also lived in the oceans during this time. The end of the Carboniferous period, about 290 million years ago, marked the appearance of two important organisms: the conifers and the reptiles. Conifers are cone-bearing trees often called evergreens. The ancestors of today's pine,

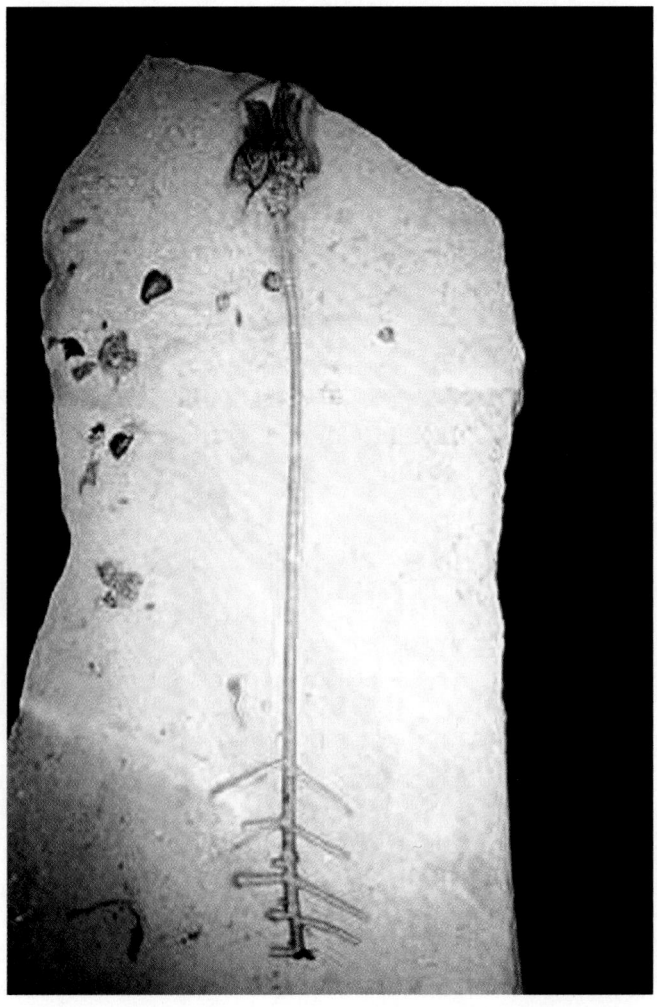

FIGURE 13–14   Crinoid fossils from the Mississippian period, between 362 and 232 million years ago. (*Courtesy of Coolrox.com.*)

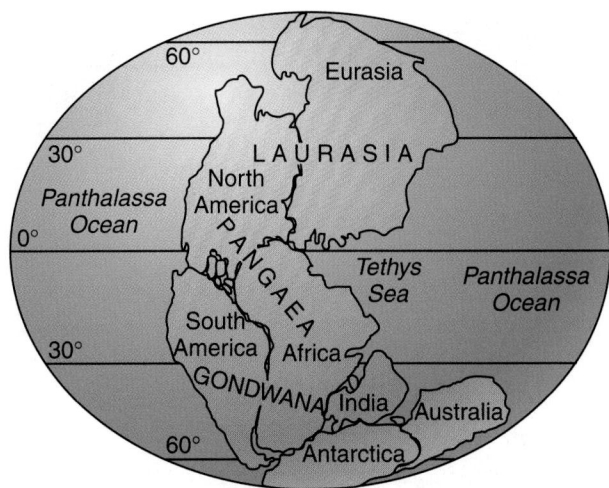

FIGURE 13–15 The supercontinent of Pangaea as it appeared 250 million years ago.

spruce, and fir trees began to appear at the start of the Permian period 290 million years ago. The formation of the Appalachian Mountain chain in eastern North America, known as the Appalachian orogeny, began at this time. It occurred as a result of the ancient African continent colliding with North America, which helped form the supercontinent called **Pangaea** (Figure 13–15).

The first reptiles appeared during this time. Reptiles were the first creatures known to lay eggs that could survive on dry land. Many of these early reptiles resembled today's lizards and alligators; however, some had large fins on their backs. Much of the climate during the later part of the Permian period was very hot and dry. The end of the Permian was marked by a mass extinction of both aquatic and land-based organisms. This was probably the greatest mass extinction of species in the Earth's history. The cause of the extinction is not well understood, but it is believed that a drop in sea level along with global cooling might have been contributing factors. The end of the Permian period came about 245 million years ago. This also marked the end of the Paleozoic era.

THE MESOZOIC ERA

The Mesozoic era, which began approximately 245 million years ago, is known as the age of the dinosaurs. The beginning of the Mesozoic era, called the Triassic period, marked the rise of many new species of both aquatic and land-based organisms. The rise of large fish and swimming reptiles occurred during this period, along with many clams and other bivalve mollusks. The appearance of modern corals occurred during this time. On land the dominant plants were ferns; the first mammals also appeared. These mammals were small rodents similar to mice and rats.

The supercontinent called Pangaea began to break apart during the Triassic period. This began the formation of the Atlantic Ocean, which formed as North America began to move apart from Africa, South America, and Eurasia. The first turtles and flying reptiles appeared during the Jurassic period. The pterosaur, or flying lizard, grew to approximately 2 feet (0.6 meters) in length. The rise of the first true

FIGURE 13–16 Dinosaurs that roamed Earth during the Jurassic period, between 206 and 142 million years ago.

dinosaurs came about 208 million years ago, at the start of the Jurassic period (Figure 13–16).

During the Jurassic period, the sauropods appeared; these were immense land-dwelling dinosaurs that grew to more than 90 ft (27 m) in length. Other smaller dinosaurs, such as the stegosaurus, which had large armored plates and a spiked tail, also lived during this period. Many marine reptiles flourished, including the plesiosaur, which had a long neck and four large fins and grew to more than 40 ft (12 m) in length. Much of the land was covered by forests that contained fernlike trees called cycads, along with many cone-bearing trees and the ancestors of modern broad-leafed trees such as the ginkgo. The end of the Jurassic period came approximately 146 million years ago with the appearance of the first birdlike organisms, called archaeopteryx. The archaeopteryx was the first winged reptile-like creature to be covered in feathers.

Much of North America was covered by a large inland sea during the Jurassic period, which today is represented by sedimentary rock known as the Morrison Formation. Many excellent dinosaur fossils have been preserved in these rocks.

The Cretaceous period began approximately 146 million years ago with the continued domination of the dinosaurs. During this time flowering plants and broad-leafed trees began to dominate the land. The first crabs and snails began to emerge during the Cretaceous period, along with much of the marine plankton that we see today. Many well-known dinosaurs, such as the tyrannosaurus, the triceratops, and the duck-billed dinosaur, flourished at this time. Other smaller creatures, such as snakes, salamanders, frogs, and turtles, lived alongside the great dinosaurs of the Cretaceous period.

The breakup of Pangaea occurred throughout the Cretaceous period, creating the continents that exist today. The climate of the time was very hot and humid, which might have been the result of global warming caused by extensive volcanic activity. The end of the Cretaceous period was marked by the most famous extinction in all the Earth's history, the extinction of the dinosaurs. The Cretaceous extinction, which occurred approximately 65 million years ago, is the subject of great debate. Some scientists believe that the extinction of the dinosaurs was caused by the spread of disease, whereas others believe that a change in climate was the cause.

The most fascinating theory to explain the extinction of the dinosaurs came from Luis Alvarez, a scientist studying a unique layer of ash that was deposited around the world during the time of the great extinction. The ash layer contained an element called iridium, which is found in high levels in comets and asteroids. Alvarez hypothesized that a large asteroid or comet might have struck the Earth 65 million years ago, causing massive damage and climate change. He believed that the climate change led to the extinction of the dinosaurs. Recently the remains of a large crater were discovered in the Gulf of Mexico, near Central America. This crater has been dated to approximately 65 million years ago and might have been created by an asteroid impact that led to the extinction of the dinosaurs (Figure 13–17).

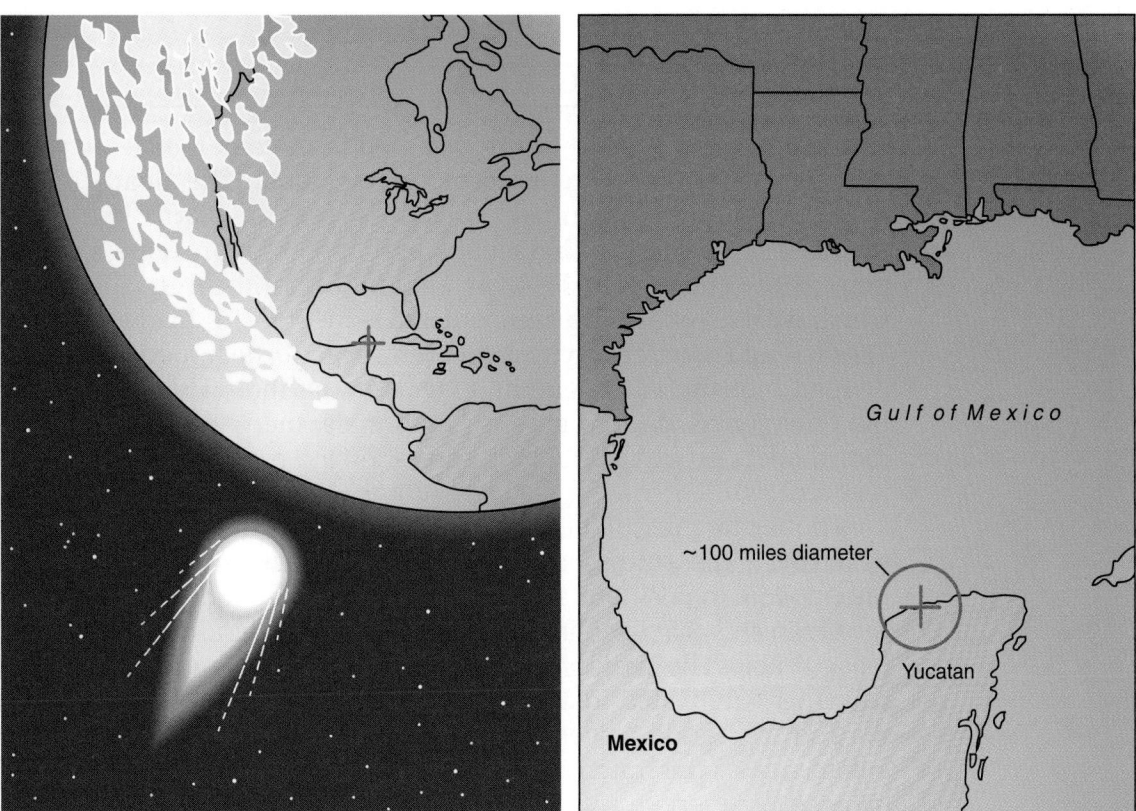

FIGURE 13–17 The asteroid impact theory suggests the extinction of the dinosaurs was caused by a 6-mile-wide asteroid that impacted the Earth near the present-day Yucatan Peninsula. The discovery of the 100-mile-wide Chicxulub crater in the Gulf of Mexico is believed to have been caused by this asteroid impact 65 million years ago.

Earth System Scientists

Luis Alvarez

Luis Alvarez began his career as a physicist who studied light, radar, and the nucleus of the atom. During World War II, he worked on the Manhattan Project, the top secret development of the atomic bomb at Los Alamos. While there he developed a detonating trigger for the first atomic bombs. He also flew on the Enola Gay, the B-29 bomber that dropped the first atomic bomb on Japan. In 1968 he received the Nobel Prize for his work in high-energy physics. Alvarez served as a member of the Warren Commission, which was a panel of scientists and government officials assigned to investigate the assassination of President John F. Kennedy.

Luis Alvarez gained most of his fame late in his life, when he teamed up with his son, Walter, a geologist. In 1980 Luis and Walter Alvarez theorized that the dinosaurs had become extinct as a result of an asteroid impact. Their theory was based on a thin layer of volcanic ash that appeared at about the same time the dinosaurs became extinct. This ash layer contained traces of a rare element, iridium, which is found in asteroids and comets. The Alvarez team gathered evidence from around the world to support their theory, which is still being debated. Luis Alvarez died in 1988.

THE CENOZOIC ERA

The extinction of the dinosaurs resulted in the emergence of mammals as the dominant life form on the land. The death of the dinosaurs allowed mammals to flourish on the Earth like never before. The end of the Cretaceous period 65 million years ago also marked the end of the Mesozoic era and began the Cenozoic era in which we live today. The Cenozoic era is further subdivided into the Tertiary and Quaternary periods, and the Tertiary period can be divided into the Paleogene and Neogene periods. This time began the emergence of large modern mammals, many of which survive today, such as whales, tigers, lions, horses, monkeys, and wolves (Figure 13–18).

The Tertiary period began the appearance of grasses on the Earth, which led to the widespread development of grazing animals. The continents were in positions similar to where they are today, and many of the organisms that lived in the oceans and on the land would be easily recognizable. The Tertiary period lasted for about 63 million years and is further subdivided into distinct periods called **epochs**. The end of the Tertiary period came approximately 2 million years ago with the emergence of the hominids, which marked the beginning of human beings.

The emergence of our human ancestors approximately 2 million years ago brings us to the present period, the Quaternary. This period has included large-scale glaciation of much of the North American

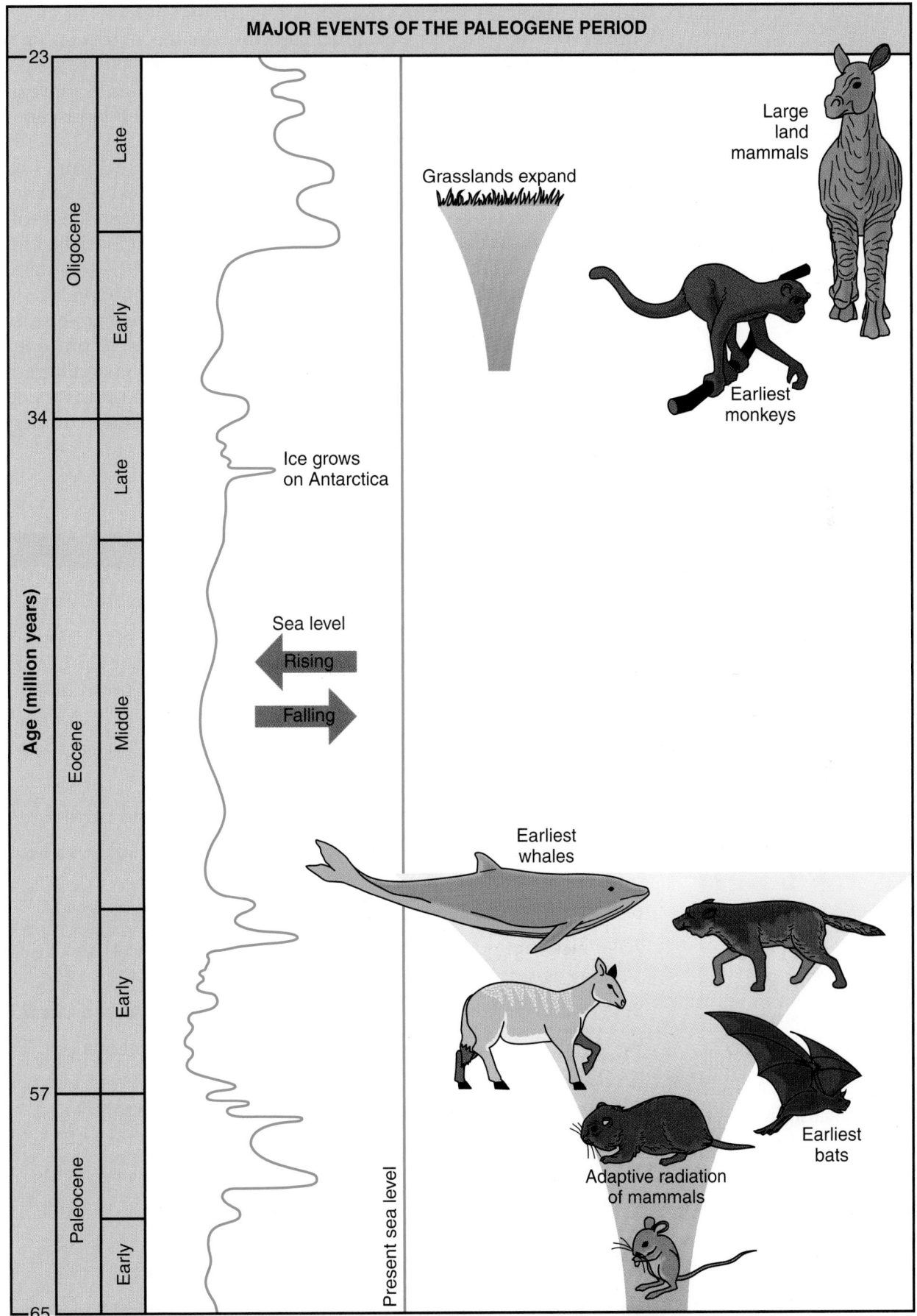

FIGURE 13–18 Animals that first appeared during the Tertiary period, 65 million years ago.

continent. It was during this cold time on Earth that humans began to flourish. The oldest fossil evidence for the existence of our own species, Homo sapiens, is dated to approximately 100,000 years ago. The glaciers in North America did not begin to melt until approximately 11,000 years ago. This glacial melting created the landscapes that we live in today throughout much of the world.

The geologic time scale is an important aspect of the Earth's history; it reveals the gradual changes that have occurred on our planet over time. Piecing together the history of the planet has been the result of exhausting research by countless numbers of scientists and researchers regarding rock formations and the fossils they contain. Although many pieces of Earth's fascinating history were not preserved and have been lost forever, it is still possible to tell a reasonable story of the Earth's past. There is one thing that the geologic record does show, however; it is the gradual advancement of life in many different forms over time, from its earliest beginnings to its most advanced forms. Understanding the Earth's geologic history is indeed understanding ourselves.

SECTION REVIEW

1. Briefly describe some of the events that took place on Earth during the Archean eon.

2. Briefly describe some of the events that took place on Earth during the Proterozoic eon, also known as Precambrian time.

3. When did the Cambrian period begin, and what were some of the organisms alive during that time?

4. What were some of the highlights of the Ordovician period?

5. How long ago did the Devonian period begin? Describe some of the organisms that lived during that time.

6. What was the significance of the Carboniferous period?

7. Which mountains formed during the Permian period, and how long ago did they begin to form?

8. What organisms flourished on Earth during the Mesozoic era?

9. What event is believed to have ended the Cretaceous period?

10. During what geologic period did our human ancestors first appear, and how long ago did this occur?

11. How old is the first fossil evidence of our own species, Homo sapiens?

12. Explain who Arthur Holmes was.

13. What were Luis Alvarez's contributions to science?

 **@ WEB Links**

FOR MORE INFORMATION GO TO THESE WEB LINKS:

<http://www.palaeos.com/Timescale/default.htm>

<http://www.cotf.edu/ete/modules/msese/earthsysflr/geotime.html>

<http://www.ucmp.berkeley.edu/help/timeform.html>

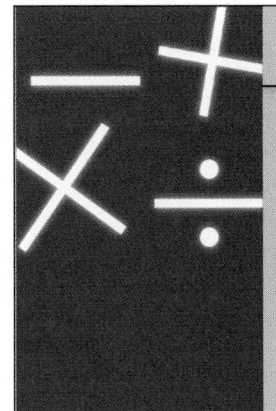

earth math

1) Determine approximately how many years the dinosaurs lived on the Earth.

2) What percentage of the Earth's total geologic history (4.5 billion years) did the Archean eon occupy?

3) What percentage of the Cenozoic era (65 million years) have humans occupied?

4) How much longer did the dinosaurs exist on the Earth compared with humans?

13.3 Evolution and Geologic History

THE THEORY OF EVOLUTION

In 1859 the British naturalist Charles Darwin published *On the Origin of Species*. This now famous book proposed a new theory on the process of how new species develop, which Darwin called natural selection. This became the foundation of the theory of evolution. **Evolution** describes how natural changes in the genes of organisms lead to the development of new traits, and therefore new species. **Genes** are the genetic instructions coded in an organism's DNA that usually form proteins. These proteins are then used to express unique traits of an organism. A **trait** is an inherited feature of an organism derived from its genes, like eye color, how tall you are, or whether you'll be covered in hair, fur, scales, or feathers. Darwin theorized that some changes in traits may provide an organism with an advantage in its ability to survive in its environment over other organisms that do not possess the trait. These traits are then passed on to its offspring, causing them to spread. Eventually, the change in traits of an organism leads to the creation of a new species (Figure 13–19). Thus evolution can be explained as the change in the traits of a population over long periods of time as a result of changes in **heredity**. Heredity is the transfer of the unique characteristics of an organism from a parent to its offspring. This is why many children resemble their parents in certain ways. Although Darwin proposed the theory of evolution, he could not explain how the modified traits of organisms were passed on to their offspring. This mechanism was revealed over the next hundred years by a variety of scientists studying heredity, which culminated in 1953 with the discovery of the structure of the DNA molecule. Today evolution is universally accepted by scientists as the best explanation for the diversity and structure of life, and has become the foundation for the study of biology. Ever since Darwin first proposed the idea, the theory of evolution has been controversial. Even today, this fundamental aspect of science is often characterized as just a mere theory; however, in science theories are not taken lightly and are developed as a result of intense scientific investigation. A scientific theory represents a high level of understanding that is used to describe an observable aspect of nature which has been

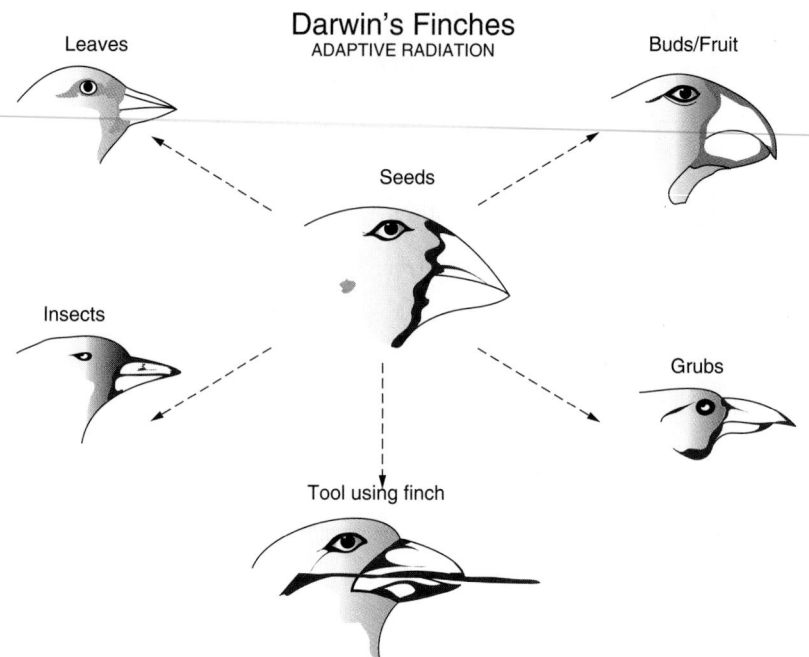

FIGURE 13-19 The unique beaks of Darwin's Finches, a group consisting of 14 different species of birds native to the Galapagos Islands, illustrates natural selection.

verified through many experiments and observations. Fundamental theories such as evolution, plate tectonics, and the heliocentric model of the solar system are as close to being factual as possible in science. These theories have been developed by careful observation and experimentation, and are widely accepted within the scientific community. Biologists have observed evolution at work over short periods of time in the form of the selective breeding of plants and animals used for agriculture, the development of resistance to antibiotics of certain bacteria, and the resistance to pesticides by insects. This is known as microevolution. It results from the changes in the traits of organisms within a species and usually does not result in the formation of a new species. This has also been observed in the study of fruit flies. Macroevolution is a longer-term, larger-scale change in the traits of an organism that leads to the development of a complete new species. Macroevolution has been observed by studying the fossil record, and by comparing, classifying, and studying the distribution of living things on Earth.

EVOLUTION AND THE FOSSIL RECORD

Geologists and paleontologists who study the Earth's geologic history have added greatly to our understanding of evolution. Studying the fossil record has exposed many evolutionary processes, showing how life has developed throughout the Earth's history. The discovery of many **transitional species** by paleontologists has revealed how certain species have evolved through time. A transitional species is an organism that displays primitive traits that lead to the development of a later species. The study of comparative anatomy, which compares the body structures of organisms, has been a very useful tool in the discovery of transitional species. The similarities that exist between many organisms

Earth System Scientists

Charles Darwin

Charles Darwin was born in Britain in 1809. At age 22, he signed on board the *H.M.S. Beagle* as a naturalist. The mission of the *Beagle* was to explore the west coast of South America and the islands of the south Pacific Ocean. Over the next 5 years, Darwin collected and recorded the natural history of many parts of the south Pacific, including the Galapagos Islands. Darwin became famous as a result of his journey. Over the next few years he compiled his records from his expedition and published a book about his discoveries. What Darwin saw on his expedition changed his life forever. His observations led him to develop his theory of natural selection, which proposed that species undergo a change in their form as a result of adaptations to their environment. This theory began the modern concept of evolution. Darwin published his theory in 1859 in his book *On the Origin of Species by Means of Natural Selection or the Preservation of Favoured Races in the Struggle of Life*. This controversial book forever changed the viewpoint on how life evolved on the Earth. In 1871 Darwin applied his theory of natural selection and evolution to human beings. He proposed that humans also underwent changes in their form over the years and that our early ancestors would be classified as primates. This sent shock waves through the religious and scientific worlds, but today this theory has become a fundamental aspect of biology.

alive today suggests that these organisms most likely came from common ancestors. A Tetrapod is a general term that describes all creatures that have four legs with toes at the ends. This includes many different species from mammals to amphibians, reptiles, even some forms of fish. Looking at the bone structures of all tetrapods reveals their similarities and suggests that they must all be related in some way (Figure 13–20). The science of comparative anatomy has helped track the evolution of body structure that has led to development of many species both alive and extinct. Famous fossils like those of A rchaeopteryx reveal the evolutionary transition of reptiles into birds. Many fossils of transitional species have been discovered that reveal the evolutionary development of organisms including sharks, fish, horses, birds, amphibians, mammals, and even humans (Figure 13–21). The geologic timescale not only reveals the history of life on the Earth, but also provides more evidence to support the theory of evolution, giving us a detailed view of how life has developed and changed over time.

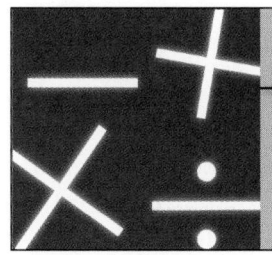

earth math

1) If the first human fossils appear in the fossil record approximately 100,000 years ago, what percentage of the Earth's total 4.5 billion history have we occupied?

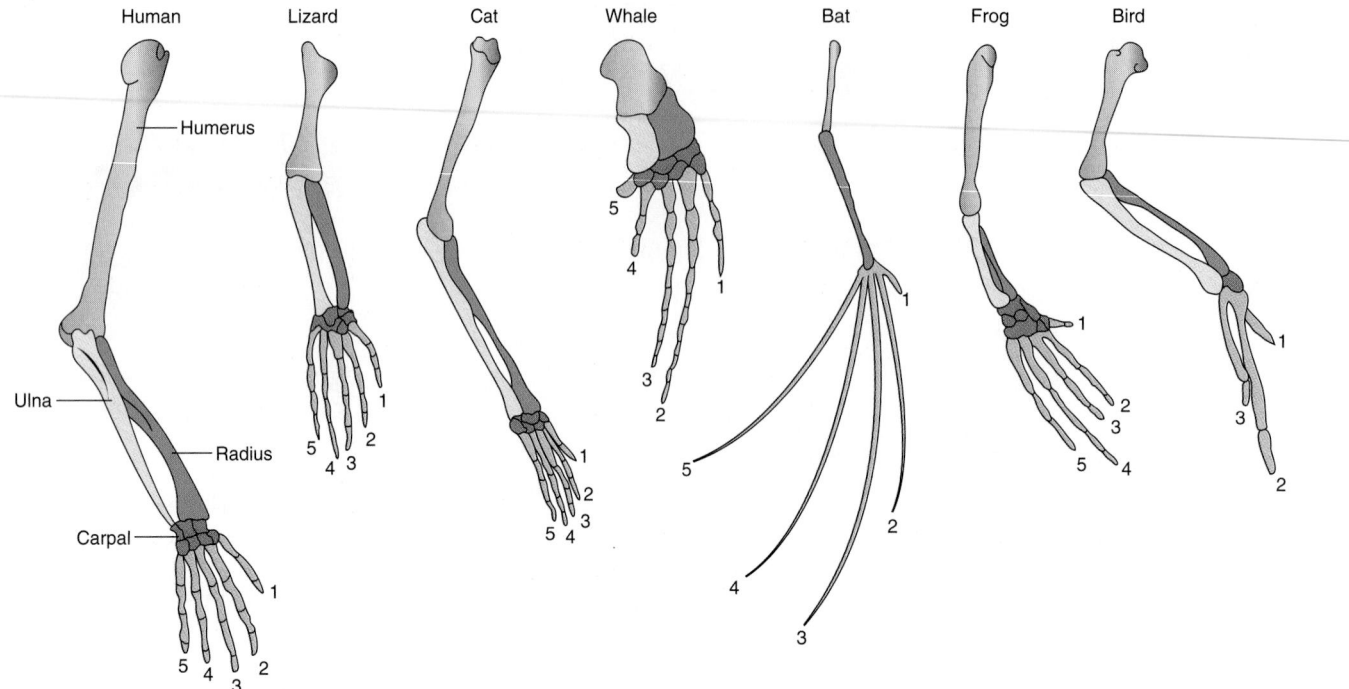

FIGURE 13–20 A comparison of tetrapod limbs showing their similar bone structures, suggesting a link to a common ancestor.

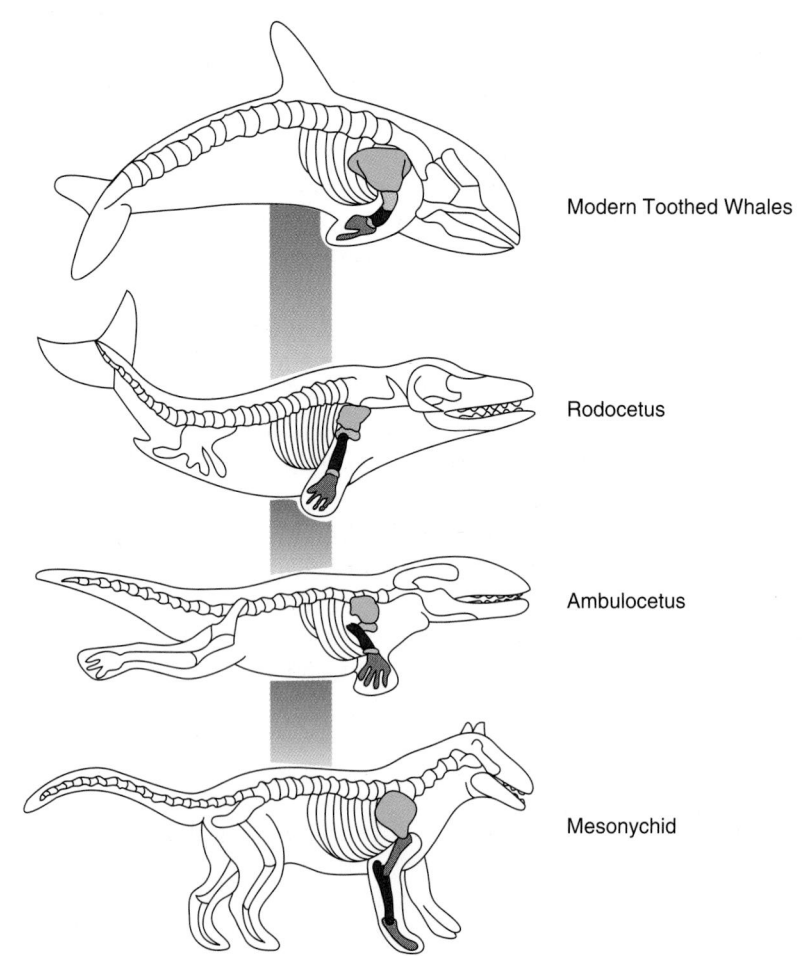

FIGURE 13–21 The transitional forms of mammals based on fossil evidence that shows the evolution of modern toothed whales.

SECTION REVIEW

1. Describe the theory of evolution:

2. How does the fossil record help to support the theory of evolution?

3. Who was Charles Darwin?

CHAPTER SUMMARY

The history of the Earth stretches back over 4.5 billion years. This long span of time is divided into unique sections that together make up the geologic time scale. The geologic time scale divides the Earth's history into distinct periods based on specific geologic events and the appearance or disappearance of unique life forms. Geologists use the geologic principles of uniformity and superposition to relatively date the age of rock formations. Other relative dating techniques involve the use of unique volcanic ash layers in rocks, igneous intrusions, faults, and index fossils. Radioactive isotopes can also be used by geologists to determine the absolute age of a rock by using the known half-life of an element. This technique is known as radiometric dating. Elements that are commonly used for radiometric dating include uranium 238, potassium 40, and carbon 14.

Both relative and absolute dating techniques have been used to construct the geologic time scale, which is divided into three large spans of time called eons. The Archean eon began approximately 4.5 billion years ago with the formation of the Earth, and it ended 2.5 billion years ago. The Proterozoic eon began 2.5 billion years ago and ended approximately 544 million years ago. Together these two eons are also known as Precambrian time, which means "before life." This is because most of the life forms on the Earth appear in the fossil record beginning 544 million years ago. The current eon, known as the Phanerozoic, began 544 million years ago and continues today. This span of time is further subdivided into geologic eras, periods, and epochs based on the first appearance of a species of organisms in the fossil record and when they disappeared.

Geologic time is often marked by mass extinctions, which occur when a large number of the species alive on the Earth die suddenly. Mass extinctions have occurred many times during the Earth's past, including the one 65 million years ago that marked the extinction of the dinosaurs. As more evidence is revealed about the Earth's history, new pieces of information will be added to the geologic time scale that will provide more detail about the Earth's past. The theory of evolution describes how natural changes in the genes of organisms lead to the development of new traits, and therefore new species over time. The fossil record supports evolution by revealing the changes that have occurred over time in the development of new species on Earth.

@ WEB Links

FOR MORE INFORMATION GO TO THESE WEB LINKS:

<http://evolution.berkeley.edu/>

<http://www.pbs.org/wgbh/evolution/>

<http://www.agiweb.org/news/evolution/foreword.html>

<http://www.becominghuman.org/>

CHAPTER REVIEW

Multiple Choice

1. Which geologic principle states that the same geologic processes occurring today have occurred throughout the Earth's history?
   a. superposition
   b. uniformity
   c. catastrophism
   d. radiometric

2. Unless a series of rock layers are overturned, the layers at the bottom are:
   a. the same age as the ones at the top
   b. the youngest rocks
   c. the oldest rocks
   d. the result of an intrusion

3. What is the relative age of a fault that cuts across many rock layers?
   a. the fault is the same age as the bottom layer it cuts across
   b. the fault is the same age as the top layer it cuts across
   c. the fault is older than all the rock layers it cuts across
   d. the fault is younger than all the layers it cuts across

4. An igneous intrusion is 50 million years old. What is the most probable age of the rock surrounding the intrusion?
   a. 10 million years
   b. 25 million years
   c. 40 million years
   d. 60 million years

5. Which of the following elements is used for radiometric dating?
   a. cobalt 60
   b. plutonium 244
   c. potassium 40
   d. silicon 28

6. If a rock sample contains half the original amount of potassium 40, approximately how old is the rock?
   a. 2.6 billion years
   b. 4.5 billion years
   c. 1.3 billion years
   d. 0.7 billion years

7. The geologic time unit known as the era is based on the occurrence of:
   a. life
   b. asteroids
   c. mass extinctions
   d. rock formations

8. The geologic time scale has been subdivided into time units called periods based on:
   a. fossil evidence
   b. rock thickness
   c. rock types
   d. radiometric dating

9. During which geologic period did the first forms of life appear?
   a. Archean
   b. Proterozoic
   c. Phanerozoic
   d. Paleozoic

10. Which geologic period marked the first appearance of trilobites on Earth?
    a. Cretaceous
    b. Cambrian
    c. Ordovician
    d. Tertiary

11. How many years ago did the Permian period begin?
    a. 544 million
    b. 142 million
    c. 490 million
    d. 290 million

12. The end of what geologic period marked the extinction of the dinosaurs?
    a. Carboniferous
    b. Cretaceous
    c. Devonian
    d. Jurassic

13. Approximately how long ago did the supercontinent Pangaea begin to break apart?
    a. 251 million years
    b. 490 million years
    c. 119 million years
    d. 65 million years

14. During what geologic period did the Appalachian Mountains begin to form?
    a. Cambrian
    b. Silurian
    c. Permian
    d. Quaternary

15. Approximately how long ago did the glaciers that
    covered much of North America begin to melt?
    a. 11,000 years
    b. 100,000 years
    c. 1 million years
    d. 4 million years

Matching   *Match the terms with the correct definitions.*

a. geologic time scale
b. principle of uniformity
c. principle of superposition
d. index fossils
e. half-life

f. radiometric dating
g. eon
h. stromatolites
i. Precambrian
j. era

k. mass extinction
l. Pangaea
m. epoch
n. evolution

1. _____ The largest division of geologic time, measured in billions or hundreds of millions of years.
2. _____ The scale of time that divides the Earth's history into distinct periods based on geologic events and the appearance or disappearance of specific life forms.
3. _____ A large unit of geologic time when not much life flourished on the Earth; it started with the formation of the planet and ended approximately 544 million years ago.
4. _____ A natural law used in geology that states that the geologic processes that are currently shaping the Earth have been occurring throughout the Earth's history.
5. _____ Large moundlike layers of sediments that form when cyanobacteria traps sand in warm, shallow ocean water.
6. _____ A natural law used in geology that states that in undisturbed rock layers the oldest layers are located at the bottom and the youngest are at the top.
7. _____ A specific type of fossil organism that lived for a short time over a wide geographical area; it is used to identify specific rock formations and the period when they were formed.
8. _____ A method of dating objects using the known decay rate of certain radio isotopes.
9. _____ The smallest division of geologic time that is measured in millions or thousands of years.
10. _____ The time it takes for half of a mass of a radioactive isotope to decay into its daughter element.
11. _____ The name of a supercontinent that existed more than 250 million years ago, when all the present-day continents were joined together into one great landmass.
12. _____ The widespread disappearance of a great number of species on Earth in a short time.
13. _____ The second largest division of geologic time; it is measured in hundreds of millions or millions of years and marks the mass extinction of species on Earth.
14. _____ The theory that describes how natural changes in the genes of organisms lead to the development of new traits, and therefore new species over time.

Critical Thinking

1. The geologic record reveals that many extinctions have occurred on the Earth, and the planet's environment has constantly undergone change. What do these two things tell you about the nature of life on Earth?

The Atmosphere

OVERVIEW

When astronauts orbiting the Earth in the space shuttle gazed back at the surface of the planet, they noticed that the only thing that separated it from the vacuum of space was a thin blue line. This thin blue line that surrounds the Earth is called the atmosphere. If the whole Earth was represented by an apple, the atmosphere would be only as thin as the apple's skin. The atmosphere acts as a protective blanket around the Earth, which allows for life to flourish on its surface. This fragile part of the Earth, although mostly invisible, plays an important part in the Earth system in which we live.

Structure and Composition of the Atmosphere

OBJECTIVES

Atmospheric Composition · Atmospheric Structure

After reading this chapter you should be able to:

▶ Define the terms *atmosphere* and *air*.
▶ Identify the main gases that make up the atmosphere.
▶ Identify the five layers of the atmosphere.
▶ Define the term *isothermal layer*.
▶ Explain where the ozone layer is located in the atmosphere and what function it performs.
▶ Describe the characteristics of the ionosphere.

INTRODUCTION

The air in which we live is an invisible sea of molecules that surrounds us and sustains life. We sense this invisible sea every time the wind blows or we look up at clouds moving through the bright blue sky. Not only does air sustain life on Earth, it plays an important role in distributing heat and water around the planet. Air also acts as a barrier that surrounds the Earth and protects its surface from the harsh environment of space. Probably the most well-known aspect of the air in which we live is how it forms weather. All these things point to the importance of understanding the Earth's atmosphere and its role in the Earth's systems.

FIGURE 14–1 The atmosphere of the Earth as viewed from space appears to be a thin blue line. (*Courtesy of PhotoDisc.*)

ATMOSPHERIC COMPOSITION

The **atmosphere** is defined as the thin envelope of gas that surrounds the Earth (Figure 14–1). From the Earth's surface, the gases that surround the planet stretch approximately 375 miles (604 km) above sea level. Past this point lies the near vacuum of space.

The atmosphere is composed of gases that together are commonly known as **air**. These gases are divided into two main groups: permanent and variable (Table 14–1). **Permanent gases** are gases that maintain a constant level in the atmosphere. These include nitrogen,

TABLE 14–1 The permanent and variable gases that make up the Earth's atmosphere, and their composition

Permanent Gases			Variable Gases			
Gas	Symbol	Percent (by Volume) Dry Air	Gas (and Particles)	Symbol	Percent (by Volume)	Parts per Million (ppm)*
Nitrogen	N_2	78.08	Water vapor	H_2O	0 to 4	
Oxygen	O_2	20.95	Carbon dioxide	CO_2	0.035	355
Argon	Ar	0.93	Methane	CH_4	0.00017	1.7
Neon	Ne	0.0018	Nitrous oxide	N_2O	0.00003	0.3
Helium	He	0.0005	Ozone	O_3	0.000004	0.04
Hydrogen	H_2	0.00006	Particles (dust, soot, etc.)		0.000001	0.01
Xenon	Xe	0.000009	Chlorofluorocarbons (CFCs)		0.00000001	0.0001

*For CO_2, 355 parts per million means that out of every million air molecules, 355 are CO_2 molecules.

oxygen, argon, neon, helium, hydrogen, and xenon. Nitrogen gas is a diatomic molecule, meaning that it contains two atoms of nitrogen. It composes approximately 78 percent of the Earth's atmosphere. Oxygen gas in the atmosphere is also a diatomic molecule, made from two atoms of oxygen. Oxygen composes approximately 21 percent of the Earth's atmosphere and is vital to life on Earth.

Geological evidence suggests that more than 2 billion years ago the atmosphere was much different than today, containing no oxygen. The photosynthetic action of aquatic plants and algae eventually filled the atmosphere with oxygen to its present levels. Before this, much of the Earth's early atmosphere was composed primarily of water vapor and carbon dioxide. Eventually much of the carbon dioxide was absorbed by the oceans and by rocks. The water vapor in the Earth's early atmosphere condensed and rained down to the surface to collect and form the oceans and fresh surface water that cover the planet today. The remaining permanent gases that make up today's atmosphere are found at much smaller levels than nitrogen or oxygen. These are known as trace gases.

The **variable gases** that make up the Earth's atmosphere include water vapor, carbon dioxide, methane, ozone, nitrous oxide, and chlorofluorocarbons (CFCs). **Water vapor** is the gaseous form of water in the atmosphere, which varies in its composition around the globe. In humid tropical climates near the Earth's equator, water vapor content can be as high as 4 percent in the atmosphere. In the drier polar regions, water vapor is as low as 0.5 percent. Water vapor content in the atmosphere changes daily and is an important aspect of the local weather.

Carbon dioxide is another variable gas in the atmosphere, composing a small portion of the air with levels of 0.035 percent; however, as a result of industrial processes, levels of this gas are slowly increasing. Even though carbon dioxide composes a small portion of the total atmosphere, it plays an important role in trapping the Earth's heat. Because of this, it is known as a greenhouse gas; it traps heat much like the glass of a greenhouse. Methane, another variable gas in the atmosphere, is produced as a by-product of anaerobic decomposition, which is the breakdown of organic material without oxygen. The main sources of methane in the Earth's atmosphere are from decomposing bacteria in livestock and rice paddies. The remaining variable gases that compose air are found in extremely small amounts but can play equally important roles in the atmosphere. Chlorofluorocarbons (CFCs) are human-created gases that now exist in the stratosphere, where they are destroying the ozone layer.

Both permanent and variable gases have one thing in common: They are invisible. This is especially apparent on a clear night, when you can see the stars shining in space. Why then does the sky appear blue during the day? The blue appearance of the sky during the day is caused by the scattering of blue visible light by gas molecules and particles in the atmosphere. At sunrise and sunset, the sky often appears red or orange in color. This is also caused by the scattering of light by the atmosphere. The sky appears red or orange because the light has to travel through more of the atmosphere, therefore scattering more blue wavelengths of light and allowing only colors such as red or orange to pass through.

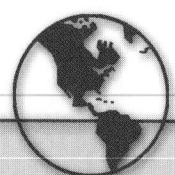

Earth System Scientists

Aristotle was born in Macedonia in 384 B.C. during the rise of ancient Greece. He studied under the great philosopher Plato and eventually became one of the greatest thinkers of the ancient world. He was the tutor of the future king of Greece, later known as Alexander the Great. In 335 B.C. he established his own school in Athens, where he taught philosophy, natural history, mathematics, and astronomy. He also helped establish the great library of Alexandria in Egypt. Aristotle's book *Meteorologica* was the first to describe the processes that lead to the formation of clouds, precipitation, wind, lightning, and other phenomena associated with weather. This book is where the term *meteorology* was derived. It was widely accepted as scientific fact for almost 2,000 years.

ATMOSPHERIC STRUCTURE

The atmosphere is divided into five distinct layers based on their unique characteristics. The **troposphere** is the layer that lies closest to the Earth's surface. It is approximately 7 mi (11 km) thick. All weather on Earth takes place in the troposphere, which also contains more than 90 percent of the atmosphere's gases. All the clouds that float through the skies form in the troposphere. The troposphere also contains all the oxygen we need to breathe. As you ascend into the troposphere, the temperature of the surrounding air decreases (Figure 14–2). The pressure of the air also decreases with height in the troposphere. This is apparent when you climb high mountains or visit areas that are located at higher elevations. Because these places are higher in the troposphere, the air is thinner, making it harder for you to breathe. You can also sense the change in pressure with height in the troposphere when your ears pop as you rise in elevation. This is caused by the air located in your inner ear equalizing with the air pressure outside your ear.

You also might notice a decline in temperature as you climb a high mountain. In some places on Earth it can be a sunny and warm day at the base of a mountain. When you climb the mountain and move higher in the troposphere, eventually it can be cold enough to form snow. The average decline in temperature in the troposphere is approximately 3.5° F for every 1,000 ft (2° C every 305 m) in elevation. At the top of the troposphere, temperatures can be as low as –80° F (–62° C). Eventually, as you rise toward the top of the troposphere, the air temperature begins to level off. The transitional layer that lies at the top of the troposphere is called the tropopause. In the tropopause, temperature remains stable as you increase in height. This is also called an **isothermal layer**, which is a layer that maintains the same temperature as you increase in altitude. The tropopause is approximately 6 mi (9.7 km) thick, and eventually the air temperature begins

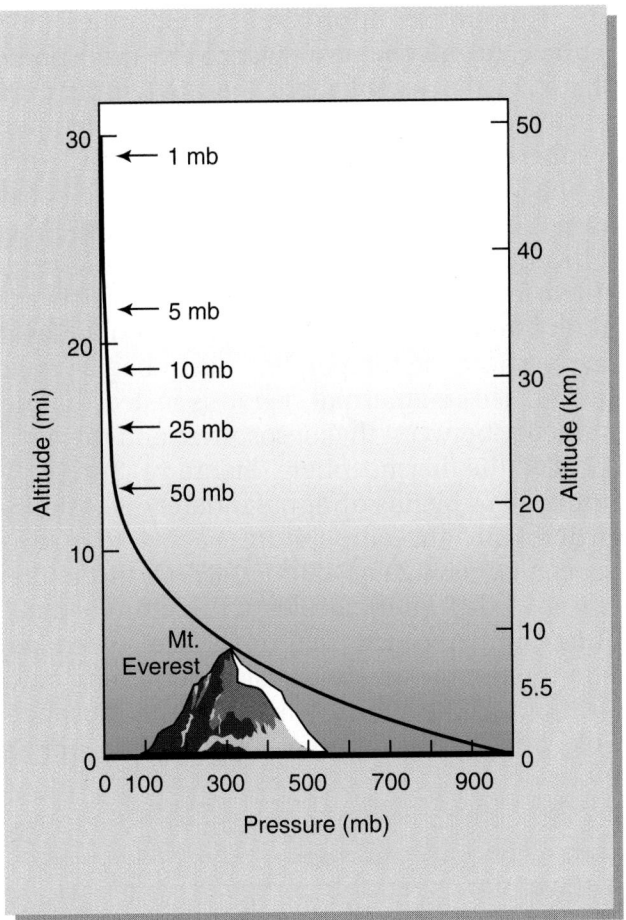

FIGURE 14–2 Air pressure decreases with height in the troposphere.

to rise again. This marks the entry into the next layer of the atmosphere, called the stratosphere.

The base of the **stratosphere** is located approximately 7 to 10 mi (11 to 16 km) above the Earth's surface. It rises to a height of approximately 30 miles (48 km) above the Earth. The stratosphere is the area of the atmosphere where temperature rises as you increase in height. When the air temperature increases with altitude in the atmosphere, it is known as a **temperature inversion**. Although the temperature increases with height, it is still very cold in the stratosphere. The highest temperature in the stratosphere is about 25° F (–3.9° C). Approximately 99.9 percent of all the gases that together form the Earth's atmosphere lie below the stratosphere.

One of the most important aspects of the stratosphere is the region called the **ozone layer**. Ozone is an unstable molecule composed of three atoms of oxygen that helps block deadly **ultraviolet radiation** coming from the sun. The ozone layer is the main reason that the stratosphere experiences a temperature inversion. Heat energy is released into the air in the stratosphere when ultraviolet radiation strikes the ozone layer. The ozone layer lies approximately 15 mi (24 km) above the Earth's surface. The air temperature at the top of the stratosphere eventually begins to level off, forming another isothermal transition layer called the stratopause.

Above the stratopause, approximately 35 miles (56 km) above the Earth's surface, begins the next layer of the atmosphere, known as the mesosphere. In the mesosphere the air temperature begins to decrease again as you increase in height. The lowest temperature in the Earth's atmosphere, approximately –130° F (–90° C), occurs in the mesosphere. This portion of the Earth's atmosphere rises to approximately 55 mi (88 km) above the Earth. The air in the mesosphere is extremely thin and has very low pressure. The mesosphere is also exposed to high levels of ultraviolet radiation, which would burn a person's skin if it were exposed. Another transitional layer lies above the mesosphere, where the temperature again begins to level off with increasing height. This isothermal region is called the mesopause. It marks the boundary between the mesosphere and the next layer of the atmosphere, called the thermosphere (Figure 14–3).

The thermosphere begins at approximately 60 mi (97 km) above the Earth, where the air temperature begins to rise once again. Temperatures can be as high as 120° F (–62° C) in the thermosphere; however, there are so few air molecules at this altitude that the temperature cannot be compared with that of surface air temperatures. The temperature in the thermosphere is just a measure of how fast the air molecules are moving. The air is so thin in the thermosphere that an air molecule will collide with another air molecule only after it has

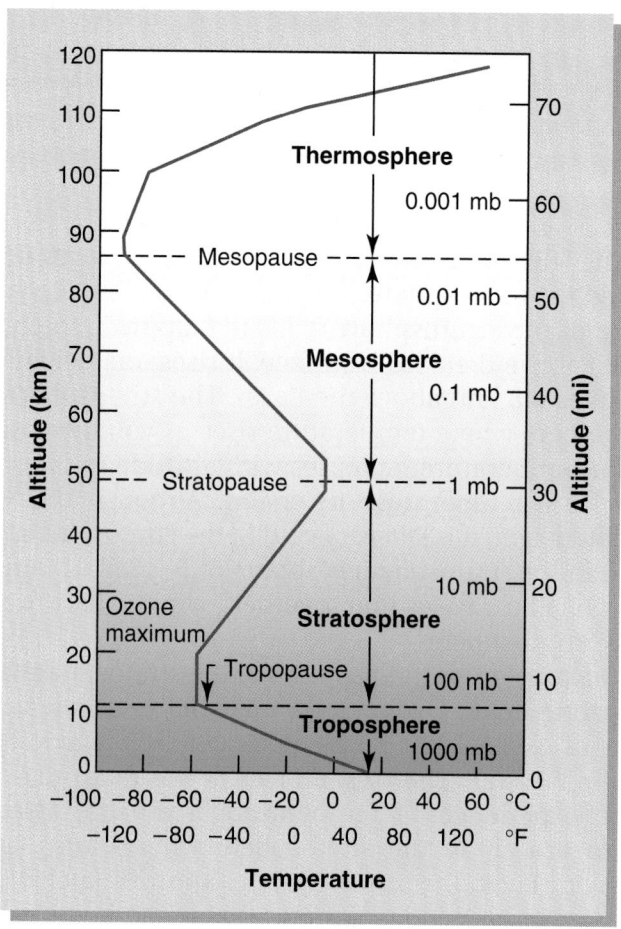

FIGURE 14–3   The layers of the atmosphere and their characteristic temperatures, pressures, and altitudes.

traveled an approximate distance of more than 3 mi (4.8 km). In comparison, an air molecule traveling in the troposphere will strike another air molecule after it has traveled only one millionth of an inch!

The top of the thermosphere is approximately 312 mi (502 km) above the Earth's surface, where the final layer of the atmosphere, the exosphere, begins. The exosphere is the region where air molecules escape the gravitational pull of Earth and travel off into space. This marks the top of the Earth's atmosphere and is where the cold near-vacuum of space begins.

Another important aspect of the Earth's atmosphere is a region called the ionosphere, which is an area in the atmosphere that contains a high concentration of **ions**. An ion is an atom or molecule that has an electric charge. The ions that make up the ionosphere are formed by incoming **solar radiation** that strikes the air in the atmosphere. The solar radiation strips away electrons from atoms in the atmosphere and forms ions. Because the formation of ions requires sunlight, the size of the ionosphere tends to be larger during the daytime and smaller at night. During the day, the ionosphere can form at approximately 37 mi (59 km) above the Earth's surface, near the top of the stratosphere. At night the ionosphere shrinks and begins at a higher altitude of about 75 mi (120 km) above the Earth, in the thermosphere. On average the ionosphere is approximately 200 mi (321 km) thick.

The ionosphere plays an important role in radio communication on Earth. AM radio waves emitted from stations on the Earth's surface are reflected back when they strike the ionosphere. During the day, the sun prompts the ionosphere to thicken, causing the bottom layer to form closer to the Earth's surface. This causes the radio waves to bounce back toward the surface more quickly, forcing them to travel shorter distances. At night, when the ionosphere thins, its bottom layer rises higher in the atmosphere and radio waves take longer to bounce back. This causes them to travel extremely long distances at night. As a result of this, radio stations increase their transmission power in the daytime and decrease it at night to compensate for the changing effects of the ionosphere on the distance a radio wave travels (Figure 14–4). At night it is possible to pick up radio stations on your AM radio from far around the Earth.

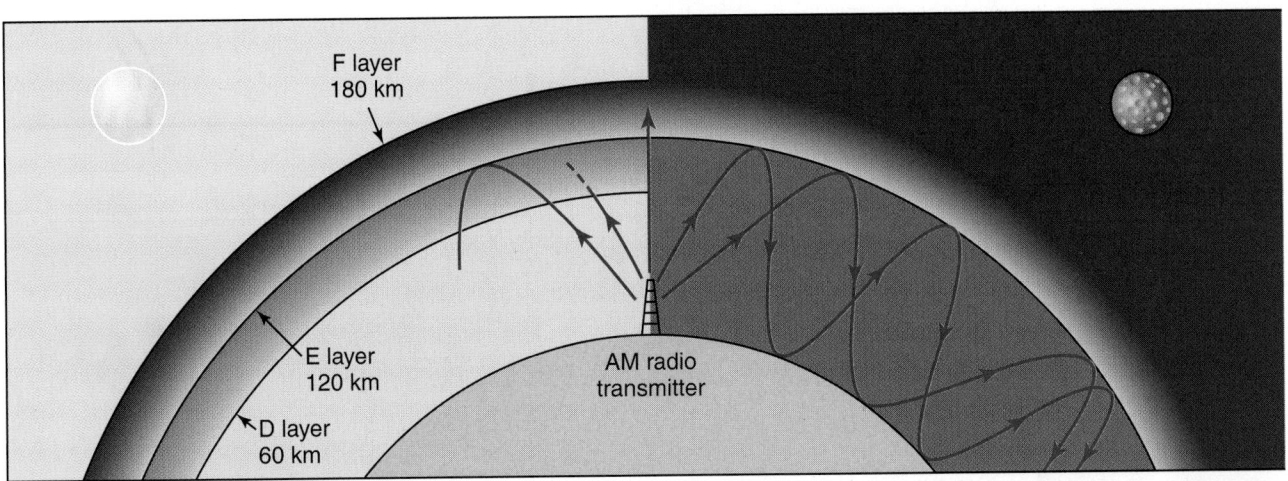

FIGURE 14–4 The effect of the changing size of the ionosphere on radio communications during the day and night.

CAREER CONNECTIONS
Physical Meteorologist

A physical meteorologist studies the physical and chemical properties of the atmosphere. This includes the transfer of heat and light energy through the atmosphere, the characteristics of its gases, and the formation of clouds, precipitation, and storms. Physical meteorologists conduct research to further understand the natural processes that occur in the atmosphere and how they affect life on Earth. Their work involves the use of sophisticated scientific instruments such as satellites, weather balloons, radar, and aircraft, along with the use of computers to collect and analyze atmospheric data. Physical meteorologists can find employment at colleges and universities or at government agencies such as the National Aeronautic and Space Administration (NASA) or the National Oceanic and Atmospheric Administration. A college degree in meteorology or atmospheric science is required for this occupation.

@ WEB Links

FOR MORE INFORMATION GO TO THESE WEB LINKS:

<http://csep10.phys.utk.edu/astr161/lect/earth/atmosphere.html>

<http://science.hq.nasa.gov/earth-sun/science/atmosphere.html>

<http://www.pbs.org/wgbh/nova/balloon/science/atmosphere.html>

REVIEW

1. What is the atmosphere?
2. Describe what a permanent atmospheric gas is and list all the Earth's permanent gases.
3. Describe what a variable gas is and list all the Earth's variable gases.
4. Name the unique layers of the atmosphere.
5. Which layers of the atmosphere experience temperature inversions?
6. Which layers of the atmosphere are isothermal?
7. Describe the ionosphere and explain how it affects radio waves.
8. Who was Aristotle?

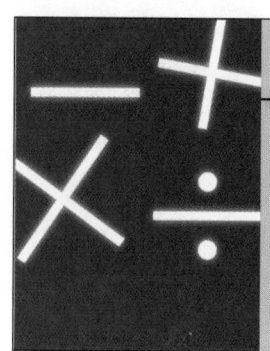

earth math

1) Using the information provided in the chapter, determine the thickness of both the thermosphere and the mesosphere.

2) If the temperature in the troposphere declines 3.5° F for every 1,000 ft in elevation, what would the approximate temperature be at the top of Mount Everest (29,022 ft) if the temperature is 70° F at sea level?

CHAPTER SUMMARY

The atmosphere is the thin envelope of gases that surrounds the Earth. The atmosphere is commonly known as air, which is composed of 78 percent nitrogen, 21 percent oxygen, and other trace gases. The gases in the atmosphere are classified as permanent or variable. Permanent gases remain at fixed levels in the atmosphere and include nitrogen, oxygen, argon, neon, helium, hydrogen, and xenon. Variable gases change in their composition and include water vapor, carbon dioxide, methane, ozone, nitrous oxide, and chlorofluorocarbons (CFCs).

The atmosphere is divided into five layers based on their own unique characteristics. The troposphere is the layer of the atmosphere that lies closest to the Earth. This is the part of the atmosphere in which we all live and where all weather takes place. As you rise in the troposphere, both temperature and pressure decrease with height. Above the troposphere lies another layer of the atmosphere called the stratosphere. The stratosphere contains a layer of ozone gas called the ozone layer. The ozone layer acts as a shield that protects the Earth's surface from deadly ultraviolet radiation. The other layers of the atmosphere include the mesosphere and the thermosphere. Transitional layers located between all the layers of the atmosphere are called isothermal layers. These are parts of the atmosphere where temperature remains the same with an increase in height. Another part of the atmosphere is the ionosphere. It is located within the stratosphere and the thermosphere and is composed of ions created by incoming solar radiation.

CHAPTER REVIEW

Multiple Choice

1. The atmosphere stretches into space approximately how far above the Earth's surface?
   a. 10 mi
   b. 75 mi
   c. 100 mi
   d. 375 mi

2. Which gas makes up most of the Earth's atmosphere?
   a. nitrogen
   b. oxygen
   c. carbon dioxide
   d. water vapor

3. Approximately 21 percent of the Earth's atmosphere is composed of:
   a. nitrogen
   b. oxygen
   c. carbon dioxide
   d. water vapor

4. Which of the following gases varies in its atmospheric composition?
   a. argon
   b. nitrogen
   c. water vapor
   d. oxygen

5. What layer in the atmosphere contains 90 percent of all the gases on Earth?
   a. thermosphere
   b. mesosphere
   c. stratosphere
   d. troposphere

6. The ozone exists in which layer of the atmosphere?
   a. thermosphere
   b. mesosphere
   c. stratosphere
   d. troposphere

7. As you rise up in the troposphere, temperature and pressure:
   a. increase
   b. decrease
   c. remain the same
   d. fluctuate

8. An area in the atmosphere where temperature remains the same as you increase in height is known as:
   a. the exosphere
   b. an isothermal layer
   c. the ionosphere
   d. an inversion

9. Which layer of the atmosphere has the coldest temperature?
   a. thermosphere
   b. mesosphere
   c. stratosphere
   d. troposphere

10. The ionosphere grows to its greatest thickness during which time?
    a. at night
    b. during a full Moon
    c. during the day
    d. at sunrise

Matching   *Match the terms with the correct definitions.*

a. atmosphere
b. air
c. permanent gases
d. variable gases
e. water vapor

f. troposphere
g. isothermal layer
h. stratosphere
i. temperature inversion
j. ozone layer

k. ultraviolet radiation
l. ions
m. solar radiation

1. _____ The process by which a warm layer of air overlies a cold layer of air.
2. _____ The electromagnetic radiation emitted from the Sun.
3. _____ The outer layer of gas that surrounds a planet.
4. _____ An atom or group of atoms that have an electric charge as a result of gaining or losing electrons.

5. ____ The gases that together make up Earth's atmosphere, including nitrogen, oxygen, argon, water vapor, carbon dioxide, and other trace elements.
6. ____ A layer in the Earth's atmosphere containing the ozone, where temperature increases with an increase in altitude.
7. ____ Gases that exist in fixed amounts in the Earth's atmosphere.
8. ____ A specific high-energy form of electromagnetic radiation emitted from the Sun that can be harmful to living things.
9. ____ Gases in the Earth's atmosphere that change in their composition.
10. ____ The specific area in the stratosphere, located at an altitude between 10 and 20 miles, that contains a high concentration of ozone gas.
11. ____ The gaseous form of water.
12. ____ The lowest layer of the Earth's atmosphere; it lies closest to the surface and is where all weather takes place and the temperature decreases with an increase in altitude.
13. ____ A layer in the atmosphere where temperature remains the same as altitude increases.

Critical Thinking

1. Describe some of the ways that humans use the atmosphere and the air it contains.

15

Insolation

OBJECTIVES

The Sun's Radiation · Insolation and the Atmosphere · Insolation and the Earth's Surface · Angle of Insolation · Duration of Insolation · Heating the Atmosphere

After reading this chapter you should be able to:

▶ Define the term *insolation*.

▶ Differentiate between long-wave and short-wave radiation emitted from the Sun.

▶ Identify all the pathways insolation can take when it strikes the Earth's atmosphere.

▶ Explain what happens to insolation when it strikes the Earth's surface.

▶ Describe how water and land differ in their ability to absorb and release heat.

▶ Explain the relationship between the intensity of insolation and the angle at which it strikes the Earth's surface.

▶ Describe the relationship between the intensity and angle of insolation and latitude location on the Earth's surface.

▶ Explain what causes the duration of insolation striking the Earth's surface to change throughout the year.

▶ Identify four ways by which the atmosphere is heated.

TERMS TO KNOW

insolation

short-wave radiation

long-wave radiation

albedo

heat capacity

reradiate

angle of insolation

duration

terrestrial radiation

latent heat of
condensation

INTRODUCTION

The warm sun on your face, a hot car seat, and a scalding parking lot beneath your feet on a sunny summer day all illustrate ways in which the Sun's energy can interact with our planet. Even though the Sun is 93 million mi (149 million km) away, the radiation it emits is so strong that it greatly affects many aspects of the Earth. Almost all the energy on our planet is derived from the Sun, which drives many processes on the Earth's surface. Knowing how solar energy interacts with the atmosphere, hydrosphere, and lithosphere is fundamental to a clear understanding of the Earth's systems.

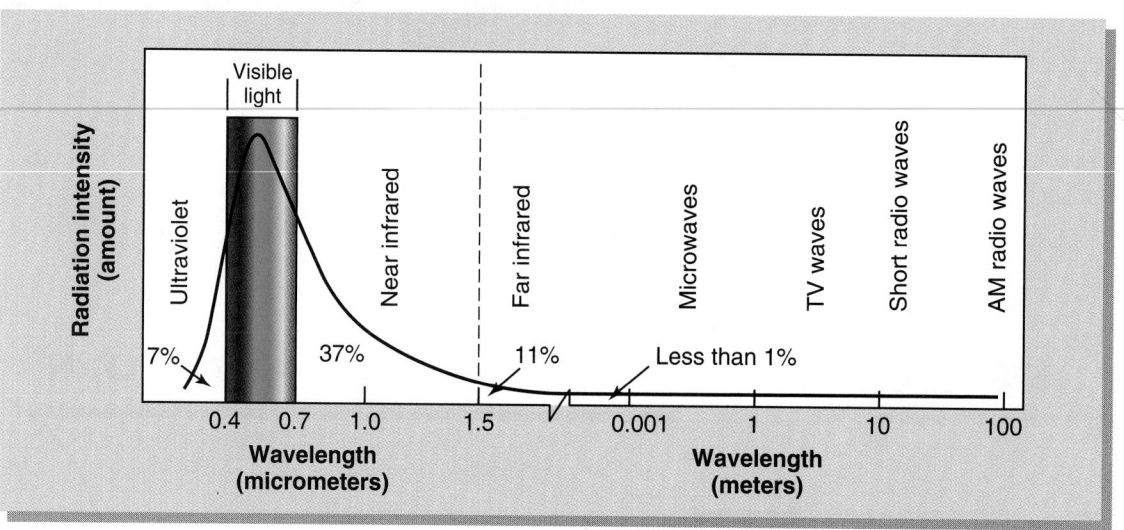

FIGURE 15–1   A portion of the amount and type of electromagnetic energy emitted by the Sun.

THE SUN'S RADIATION

Insolation is the incoming radiation from the Sun that is received by the Earth's atmosphere and surface. Insolation is the driving force that moves the atmosphere and creates weather on Earth. The Sun emits radiation in all wavelengths of the electromagnetic spectrum (Figure 15–1). Most of the Sun's radiation received by the Earth is in the form of **short-wave radiation**. This high-energy radiation makes up approximately 88 percent of the radiation that is received on Earth. Short-wave radiation emitted by the Sun includes ultraviolet, visible light, and near-infrared radiation. The remaining 12 percent of the radiation received on Earth from the Sun is low-energy **long-wave radiation**. This includes far-infrared and microwave radiation.

INSOLATION AND THE ATMOSPHERE

Short-wave and long-wave radiation can take many different paths after they come into contact with the Earth's atmosphere (Figure 15–2). When the Sun's radiation strikes the atmosphere, much of it can be directly absorbed by the gases present in the air. This is what causes the thermosphere and the stratosphere to experience an increase in temperature with height, known as a temperature inversion. Some gases, such as stratospheric ozone, absorb a large amount of incoming ultraviolet short-wave radiation. On average, 19 percent of the insolation received on Earth is absorbed by the atmosphere. Some of the solar radiation that strikes the Earth's atmosphere is scattered or reflected back into space. The scattering of short-wavelength visible light by gas molecules and particles in the atmosphere gives the sky its blue appearance during the day. Clouds present in the atmosphere also can reflect radiation back into space.

Approximately 26 percent of the insolation received by the Earth's atmosphere is scattered or reflected back into space by clouds.

The insolation that is not absorbed, scattered, or reflected back into space by the atmosphere strikes the land surface or the oceans. When short-wave radiation strikes the surface of the Earth, some of it

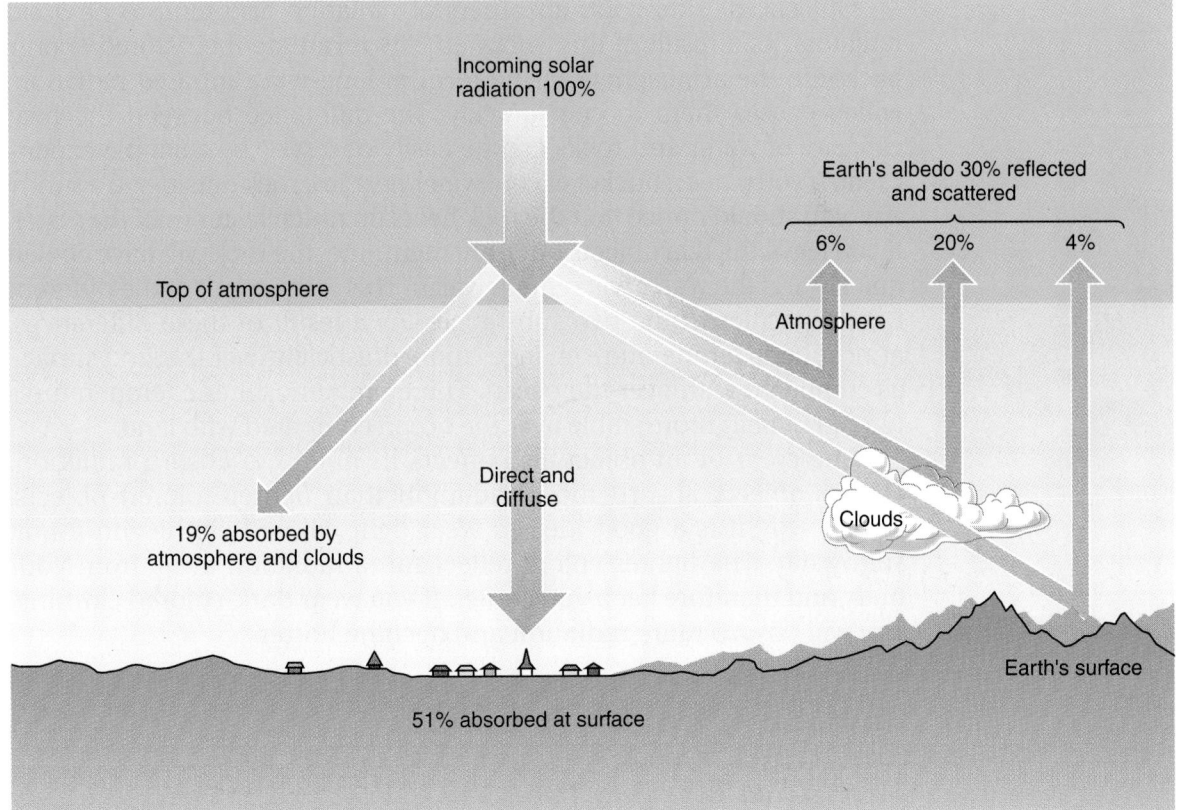

FIGURE 15–2 The general pathways that insolation takes when it strikes the Earth's atmosphere.

is immediately reflected back into space. This often occurs on snow-covered landscapes or on glaciers. White objects such as snow reflect 95 percent of the radiation received from the sun. Calm water can reflect up to 10 percent of the solar radiation received. Overall, land or water on the Earth reflects back approximately 4 percent of the Sun's incoming radiation. Combining this with the 26 percent that is reflected or scattered by the atmosphere means that a total of 30 percent of the insolation received on Earth is returned to space.

The ability of an object in space to reflect radiation is also called its **albedo**. The albedo measures the reflectivity of objects in space. The Earth's albedo is therefore approximately 30 percent; that is, 30 percent of the radiation it receives is reflected back into space. Thus, approximately 51 percent of the Earth's incoming solar radiation is absorbed at the surface by the world's oceans or land masses.

INSOLATION AND THE EARTH'S SURFACE

The land surface absorbs and releases heat from the Sun at a much higher rate than water because the rocks that make up the land surface have a lower **heat capacity** than water. Heat capacity is the ability of a substance to absorb or release heat and therefore alter its temperature. Water has a higher heat capacity than rock, which causes it to absorb a great amount of heat without a sudden change in temperature. This means that insolation absorbed by the ocean is stored for a longer time and released back into the atmosphere at a much slower rate. Rocks possess a lower heat capacity than water, which causes them to rapidly absorb heat.

Objects that are good absorbers of radiation also tend to be good radiators. As a result of this, rocks quickly **reradiate** their stored energy back into the atmosphere in the form of long-wave infrared radiation, which causes them to cool quickly. The difference between the heat capacity of water and rocks can be easily observed by a simple experiment. If you place a bucket of cool water next to a rock outside on a sunny day, you should notice that the rock heats up much faster than the water. If you leave the two objects out until nighttime, the rock will have cooled quickly and the water will remain warm. This is the result of the different heat capacities of the two substances. As a result of these differences, atmospheric temperature changes more drastically over the land surface as compared with over the ocean. Therefore atmospheric temperatures tend to remain more stable over the ocean compared with land.

The color of an object also affects its ability to absorb radiation. Darker objects absorb more radiation than lighter-colored objects. This is why it is a good idea to wear light-colored clothes on a hot, sunny day. The lighter colors reflect more radiation away from your body and therefore keep you cooler. If you wear dark-colored clothing, you will absorb more radiation and become hotter.

ANGLE OF INSOLATION

The amount of solar radiation that strikes the surface of the Earth greatly depends on the angle at which the radiation is received on the surface. The angle at which the sun's radiation strikes the Earth is called the **angle of insolation** (Figure 15–3).

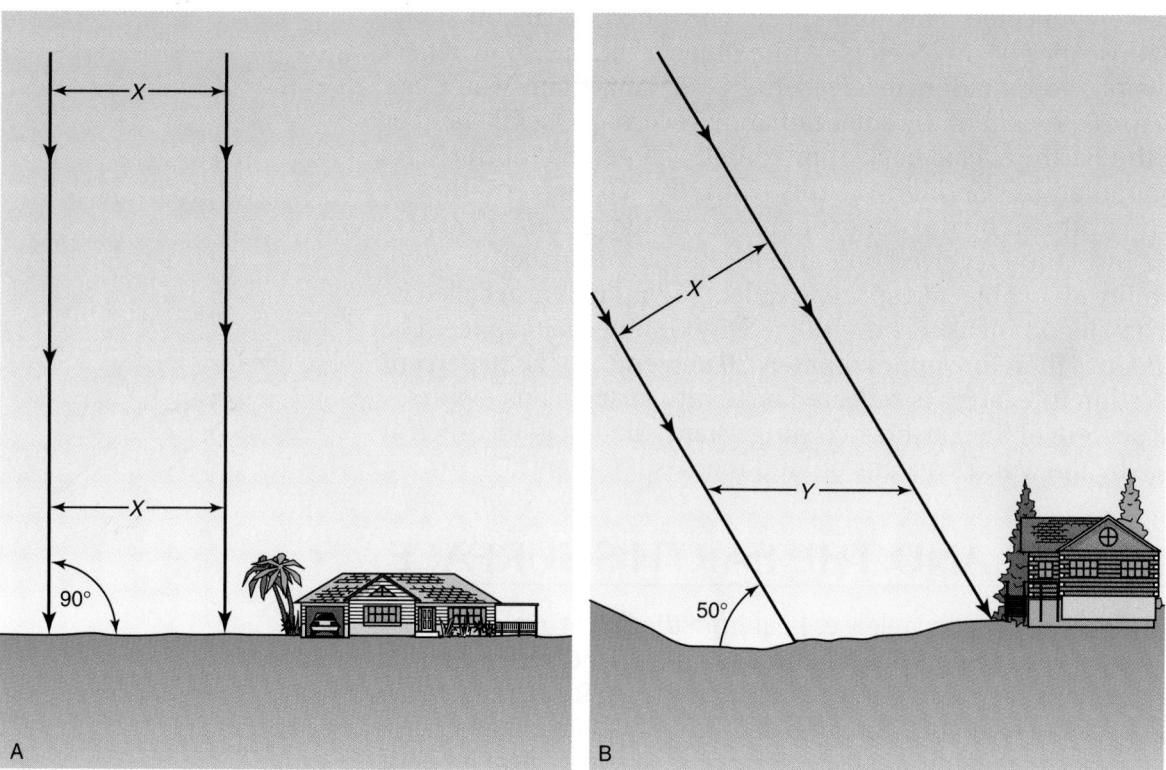

FIGURE 15–3 The intensity of insolation that strikes the Earth's surface is related to the angle at which it is received. The maximum insolation angle of 90° degrees has more intensity per unit area than an insolation angle of 50° degrees.

The angle of insolation depends on two factors: (1) the latitude at which the Sun is striking the Earth's surface and (2) the season of the year. Because the Earth's axis of rotation is tilted 23.5 degrees to the plane of the Sun, the angle at which the Sun's radiation strikes the Earth varies around the globe during the different seasons of the year (Table 15–1). For example, as the Northern Hemisphere begins to tilt away from the Sun when winter arrives, the angle of insolation striking the higher northern latitudes decreases. This causes the Northern Hemisphere to receive lower angles of insolation during winter, when it is tilted away from the Sun. During summer in the Northern Hemisphere, the angle of insolation is increased because the Earth is tilted toward the Sun. Therefore it receives a greater amount of insolation per unit area.

The nearly spherical shape of the Earth also affects the angle at which the Sun's energy strikes the Earth. This is because the curving surface of the Earth causes insolation to strike the higher latitudes at a lower angle. Generally the lower the angle of insolation, the lower the amount of solar energy received at the surface and therefore the lower the surface temperature. Areas located in the higher latitudes have a lower angle of insolation than areas closer to the equator. This results in a general decrease in surface temperature at latitudes farther

TABLE 15–1 Changing angle of insolation throughout the year for specific latitudes on Earth

Latitude	Summer Solstice June 21 — Angle of Insolation at Noon	Equinoxes March 21 September 23 — Angle of Insolation at Noon	Winter Solstice December 21 — Angle of Insolation at Noon
90° N	$23\frac{1}{2}°$	0°	—
80° N	$33\frac{1}{2}°$	10°	—
70° N	$43\frac{1}{2}°$	20°	—
60° N	$53\frac{1}{2}°$	30°	$6\frac{1}{2}°$
50° N	$63\frac{1}{2}°$	40°	$16\frac{1}{2}°$
40° N	$73\frac{1}{2}°$	50°	$26\frac{1}{2}°$
30° N	$83\frac{1}{2}°$	60°	$36\frac{1}{2}°$
20° N	$86\frac{1}{2}°$	70°	$46\frac{1}{2}°$
10° N	$76\frac{1}{2}°$	80°	$56\frac{1}{2}°$
0°	$66\frac{1}{2}°$	90°	$66\frac{1}{2}°$
10° S	$56\frac{1}{2}°$	80°	$76\frac{1}{2}°$
20° S	$46\frac{1}{2}°$	70°	$86\frac{1}{2}°$
30° S	$36\frac{1}{2}°$	60°	$83\frac{1}{2}°$
40° S	$26\frac{1}{2}°$	50°	$73\frac{1}{2}°$
50° S	$16\frac{1}{2}°$	40°	$63\frac{1}{2}°$
60° S	$6\frac{1}{2}°$	30°	$53\frac{1}{2}°$
70° S	—	20°	$43\frac{1}{2}°$
80° S	—	10°	$33\frac{1}{2}°$
90° S	—	0°	$23\frac{1}{2}°$

north or south of the equator. Near the equator the Sun strikes the Earth at nearly a 90°-degree angle all year. This concentrates a greater amount of solar radiation over a smaller area and creates high surface temperatures. Near the poles the angle of insolation is much lower, which results in cooler surface temperatures. The changing seasons on Earth reveal how the changing angle of insolation can affect the temperature throughout the year. In the United States during winter the angle of insolation is at its lowest; therefore the surface receives less insolation and experiences colder temperatures. During the summer, however, the Sun's angle of insolation is much greater, which concentrates more solar energy at the surface, therefore raising the temperature.

DURATION OF INSOLATION

Another factor that affects the amount of insolation received at the Earth's surface involves the **duration** that the surface is exposed to the Sun. Areas on the Earth in the higher latitudes receive differing amounts of sunlight throughout the year. Generally in the United States the Sun shines for a longer period in summer than it does in winter. This is the result of the Earth's tilted axis of rotation, which causes greater amounts of insolation to be received by the Northern Hemisphere during summer and lesser amounts during winter. The difference in heating that results from the effect of the Sun's changing angle of insolation and duration throughout the year creates an unequal distribution of heat in the atmosphere (Figure 15–4).

Length of Time from Sunrise to Sunset for Various Latitudes on Different Dates

Northern Hemisphere (read down)				
Latitude	March 20	June 21	Sep. 22	Dec. 21
0°	12 hr	12.0 hr	12 hr	12.0 hr
10°	12 hr	12.6 hr	12 hr	11.4 hr
20°	12 hr	13.2 hr	12 hr	10.8 hr
30°	12 hr	13.9 hr	12 hr	10.1 hr
40°	12 hr	14.9 hr	12 hr	9.1 hr
50°	12 hr	16.3 hr	12 hr	7.7 hr
60°	12 hr	18.4 hr	12 hr	5.6 hr
70°	12 hr	2 mo	12 hr	0 hr
80°	12 hr	4 mo	12 hr	0 hr
90°	12 hr	6 mo	12 hr	0 hr
Latitude	Sept. 22	Dec. 21	March 20	June 21
Southern Hemisphere (read up)				

FIGURE 15–4 The change in the duration of insolation for different latitudes during the different seasons of the year.

HEATING THE ATMOSPHERE

The Earth's atmosphere is heated by four processes. The first process by which the atmosphere is heated is from the direct absorption of radiation from the sun. As we have seen, gases in the atmosphere absorb both long-wave and short-wave radiation. The absorption of radiation by molecules in the atmosphere is then transferred into heat energy.

The second process by which the atmosphere is heated is from the reradiation of long-wave radiation from the Earth's surface. High-energy, short-wavelength radiation that strikes the Earth's surface is absorbed by the land surface. The land then reradiates long-wave, low-energy infrared radiation back into the atmosphere. This type of radiation is also called **terrestrial radiation**. Gases in the atmosphere absorb this infrared radiation and are heated.

The third way by which the atmosphere is heated is called conduction. Conduction is the transfer of heat by direct molecular contact. Not all the heat energy stored in the rocks at the Earth's surface is reradiated back into the atmosphere. Some of this energy is transferred by conduction through the direct contact of the hot rocks with the gas molecules in the atmosphere.

The fourth process that heats the atmosphere is called **latent heat of condensation**. This occurs when water vapor, which is the gaseous form of water, condenses to form liquid water. This change in phase results in the release of heat into the surrounding environment. When water vapor condenses, it gives off latent heat to the surrounding atmosphere. The absorption or release of heat energy when a change in phase occurs is known as latent heat. The heat energy that is released into the atmosphere when water condenses is gained by water molecules when they change phase from a liquid to a gas, known as evaporation. This change in phase removes heat from the surrounding

Earth System Scientists

Edmund Halley

Edmund Halley was born in England in 1656. He studied astronomy at Oxford University, which began a lifelong interest in celestial objects. From 1676 to 1678, using a telescope, he created the first chart of stars in the Southern Hemisphere. Later he became friends with the famous Sir Isaac Newton, whom he greatly admired. Halley traveled throughout Europe, often meeting many of the famous astronomers of the time. He also served as captain aboard a British Navy ship. During this time he formulated theories on the creation of the trade winds, atmospheric pressure, and insolation. He was the first to propose that the unequal heating of the planet caused the formation of the trade winds. He also researched the change in air pressure that is associated with elevation. His work studying climate helped reveal the distribution of heat and air around the globe. Halley is most remembered for his work with comets. He used mathematics to predict the orbital period of comets, especially the one that bears his name, Halley's comet.

environment, causing a cooling effect. This is what happens to your body when you sweat. The sweat on your skin evaporates and draws heat away from your body. This heat is then stored in water vapor as it rises into the atmosphere. Eventually, when the water vapor condenses, the heat it contained is released to the surrounding environment as latent heat. Large clouds in the atmosphere that are formed by the condensation of water vapor give off large amounts of latent heat to the air. This helps form massive storm systems. In this way the heat from your body that causes you to sweat is transferred into the atmosphere and helps form a cloud!

REVIEW

1. Define the term *insolation*.
2. Name the two main forms of radiation emitted from the Sun and provide one example of each form that strikes the Earth.
3. Approximately how much of the radiation received by the Earth is reflected back into space?
4. Approximately how much of the radiation received by the Earth is directly absorbed by the atmosphere?
5. What is the angle of insolation, and why does it vary around the globe?
6. List the four ways by which the atmosphere is heated.
7. Who was Edmund Halley?

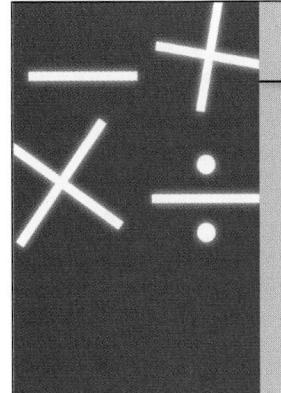

earth math

1) Wien's law (wavelength in micrometers = 2,897 micrometers/the surface temperature of an object in degrees Kelvin) describes the calculation that converts the temperature of an object in degrees Kelvin into the peak wavelength of radiation it emits in micrometers. Using Wien's law, at what peak wavelength does the Sun emit its radiation if its surface temperature is 6,000 degrees Kelvin?

2) Using Wien's law, determine the peak wavelength of radiation in micrometers that the Earth's surface emits with an average temperature of 300 degrees Kelvin.

CHAPTER SUMMARY

Insolation is the amount of incoming solar radiation received by the Earth. The Sun emits radiation in all wavelengths of the electromagnetic spectrum. Most insolation striking the Earth is high-energy, short-wave radiation in the ultraviolet and visible light range and low-energy, long-wave radiation in the infrared and microwave range. Insolation can interact with the atmosphere in several ways. Approximately 19 percent of the insolation that strikes the Earth is absorbed by the atmosphere, and 26 percent is reflected back into space by clouds or scattered throughout the atmosphere. The remaining 55 percent strikes the Earth's surface. Approximately 4 percent of this insolation is reflected back into space by snow, ice, or calm water. The remaining 51 percent of the insolation is then absorbed by objects on land or by water. Once this high-energy short-wave radiation is absorbed at the surface, it eventually gets reradiated back into the atmosphere in a lower-energy, long-wave infrared form.

The angle at which insolation strikes the Earth's surface greatly affects the intensity of the radiation received. Generally the greater the angle of insolation, the greater the intensity of radiation received at the surface. Because the Earth is spherical, its curved surface receives different angles of insolation, which causes some parts of the planet to receive more intense insolation than others. This results in a decrease in the angle of insolation at higher latitudes; that is, it causes areas on the Earth that are located at the higher latitudes to receive insolation at a lower intensity. Areas near the equator receive insolation at the highest angle and therefore receive the most intense insolation on the planet.

The duration of insolation is also important; this refers to how long the Sun is shining on one spot on the Earth. Because the Earth's axis of rotation is tilted 23.5 degrees, different parts of the planet receive varying amounts of sunlight during different seasons of the year. When winter arrives in the Northern Hemisphere, the duration of insolation is very short. Six months later, during summer, the duration of insolation is greatest. Both latitude and season of the year greatly affect insolation, which in turn influences weather and climate on the Earth. This is due to an increase in surface temperatures as a result of the increasing angle or duration of insolation. Insolation heats the atmosphere in four principal ways. These include the direct absorption of short-wave radiation from the Sun; absorption of long-wave radiation reradiated from the Earth's surface; conduction; and latent heat of condensation.

CHAPTER REVIEW

Multiple Choice

1. Electromagnetic energy that reaches the Earth from the Sun is called:
   a. insolation
   b. conduction
   c. specific heat
   d. terrestrial radiation

2. Approximately how much insolation is reflected back into space?
   a. 19%
   b. 30%
   c. 51%
   d. 75%

3. Which type of electromagnetic energy radiated from the Sun does the Earth's surface receive most?
   a. infrared
   b. ultraviolet
   c. gamma rays
   d. visible light

4. Approximately what percentage of insolation is absorbed by the Earth's surface?
   a. 19%
   b. 30%
   c. 51%
   d. 75%

5. Rocks heat and cool quicker than water because they:
   a. are harder
   b. have a higher heat capacity
   c. have a lower heat capacity
   d. are less dense

6. Which substance would absorb the greatest amount of radiation in the shortest amount of time?
   a. a white rock
   b. a black rock
   c. a cup of water
   d. a glacier

7. During which time of the year is the angle of insolation greatest at 45 degrees north latitude?
   a. winter
   b. spring
   c. summer
   d. fall

8. Generally as latitude increases, the angle of insolation:
   a. decreases
   b. increases
   c. stays the same
   d. varies

9. As its angle decreases, the intensity of insolation:
   a. remains the same
   b. decreases
   c. varies
   d. increases

10. As latitude decreases, the angle of insolation:
    a. remains the same
    b. decreases
    c. varies
    d. increases

11. During what time of the year is the duration of insolation longest in the Northern Hemisphere?
    a. winter
    b. spring
    c. summer
    d. fall

12. Which latitude would generally receive the greatest amount of insolation?
    a. 90 degrees
    b. 45 degrees
    c. 23.5 degrees
    d. 0 degrees

13. As the angle of insolation decreases, the surface temperature generally:
    a. remains the same
    b. decreases
    c. varies
    d. increases

14. Long-wave radiation emitted from the Earth's surface is also called:
    a. insolation
    b. conduction
    c. specific heat
    d. terrestrial radiation

15. Which method of heating the Earth's atmosphere involves a phase change?
    a. conduction
    b. latent heat
    c. radiation
    d. absorption

16. Which method of heating the atmosphere involves direct molecular contact?
    a. conduction
    b. latent heat
    c. radiation
    d. absorption

Matching *Match the terms with the correct definitions.*

a. insolation
b. short-wave radiation
c. long-wave radiation
d. albedo

e. heat capacity
f. reradiate
g. angle of insolation
h. duration

i. terrestrial radiation
j. latent heat of condensation

1. _____ The process by which an object takes in electromagnetic radiation and re-emits it into the atmosphere.
2. _____ Heat energy that is released into the atmosphere by the condensation of water vapor.
3. _____ The ability of a substance to absorb, contain, and release heat energy.
4. _____ The specific angle at which incoming solar radiation strikes the Earth's surface.
5. _____ The amount of incoming solar radiation on the Earth.
6. _____ The length of time that it takes for an event to occur.
7. _____ A high-energy, short-wavelength form of electromagnetic energy.
8. _____ Long-wavelength infrared radiation that is reradiated into the Earth's atmosphere from the land surface.
9. _____ A low-energy form of electromagnetic radiation such as infrared or radio waves.
10. _____ The reflective ability of an object or surface.

Critical Thinking

1. Some astronomers have proposed that the ice caps on Mars that contain both frozen water and carbon dioxide should be spray-painted black. Why do you think they believe this is a good idea?

16 Atmospheric Temperature and Pressure

ATMOSPHERIC TEMPERATURE OBJECTIVES

Temperature in the Atmosphere · Distribution of Heat on Earth · Radiative Cooling · The Greenhouse Effect

After reading this section you should be able to:

▌ Define the term *temperature* and differentiate between the molecular motions associated with cool temperatures and warm temperatures.

▌ Identify the freezing and boiling points of water in degrees Fahrenheit and Celsius.

▌ Describe three factors that cause heat to be unequally distributed on the Earth.

▌ Explain the way that heat is distributed in a convection cell.

▌ Describe the process of radiative cooling.

▌ Explain the greenhouse effect and identify three greenhouse gases.

ATMOSPHERIC PRESSURE OBJECTIVES

Pressure in the Atmosphere · Measuring Atmospheric Pressure · High and Low Atmospheric Pressure · Atmospheric Pressure and Moisture

After reading this section you should be able to:

▌ Define the term *atmospheric pressure*.

▌ Identify the two units commonly used to measure atmospheric pressure.

▌ Describe the processes that form low and high atmospheric pressure on the Earth.

▌ Explain how atmospheric moisture affects air pressure.

TERMS TO KNOW

temperature

thermometer

freezing point

boiling point

heat gradient

convection cell

radiative cooling

greenhouse effect

greenhouse gases

atmospheric pressure

barometer

adiabatic cooling

atmospheric moisture

INTRODUCTION

The *narrow* temperature range that exists on Earth enables our planet to support water in all three states of matter. This is unique among all the planets of the solar system, and it allows life to flourish on the Earth. The changes in temperature and pressure that occur on Earth are important indicators of changing weather. Today, because of our understanding of the relationship between temperature and pressure in the atmosphere, it is possible to provide better short-term and long-term forecasts. As a result, human society is able to better adapt to our planet's dynamic environment.

16.1 Atmospheric Temperature

TEMPERATURE IN THE ATMOSPHERE

The temperature on the Earth is greatly dependent on the atmosphere. **Temperature** is a measure of the average speed of atoms or molecules. The greater the speed of the molecules or atoms in a substance, the higher the temperature. When you go outside on a warm summer day, you are actually sensing the effects of rapidly moving atoms and molecules in the air. On a cold winter day, the movement of the molecules is much slower and you experience a lower temperature. The movement of the molecules is also known as kinetic energy, or the energy of movement. Generally, the greater the kinetic energy, the higher the temperature. You sense heat as a result of the kinetic energy of the surrounding air. The faster the movement of the molecules, the higher the kinetic energy and therefore the greater the amount of heat generated.

Temperature is measured using an instrument called a **thermometer**. Today many electronic thermometers are used to measure the kinetic energy of a substance; however, the first widespread thermometers were made of glass and mercury. Mercury is a metal that is in its liquid form at temperatures above –35° F (–37° C). In the original thermometers the mercury was kept in a small tube, and it expanded or contracted when it was exposed to different temperatures. The tube could then be calibrated using a scale, and temperatures could be recorded. In the United States, temperature is commonly recorded using the Fahrenheit scale, which was introduced in 1714 by the German scientist Gabriel Fahrenheit. This temperature scale is based on the **freezing point** of water being 32 degrees and the **boiling point** of water being 212 degrees. In 1742 a Swedish astronomer by the name of Anders Celsius derived a new type of temperature scale based on 0° marking the freezing point of water and 100° marking the boiling point of water. Today almost every country in the world uses the Celsius scale, although the United States still clings to the Fahrenheit scale. During the nineteenth century in England, Lord Kelvin created another temperature scale, which was based on the actual kinetic energy of the atoms or molecules. The Kelvin scale begins at absolute zero, which is the theoretical temperature at which all molecules stop moving. Using the Kelvin scale, the freezing point of water occurs at 273 Kelvins and the boiling point of water is 373 Kelvins (Figure 16–1).

DISTRIBUTION OF HEAT ON EARTH

As we saw in Chapter 15, the Earth is unequally heated by differences in insolation received at the surface. This is mainly the result of the Earth's tilted axis and nearly spherical shape. The length of time that the Earth's surface is exposed to solar radiation also changes throughout the year, depending on the season. Another factor that affects the unequal distribution of solar radiation on the Earth is the rotation of the Earth itself. Half the Earth receives sunlight while the other half is bathed in darkness. All these factors lead to the unequal distribution of

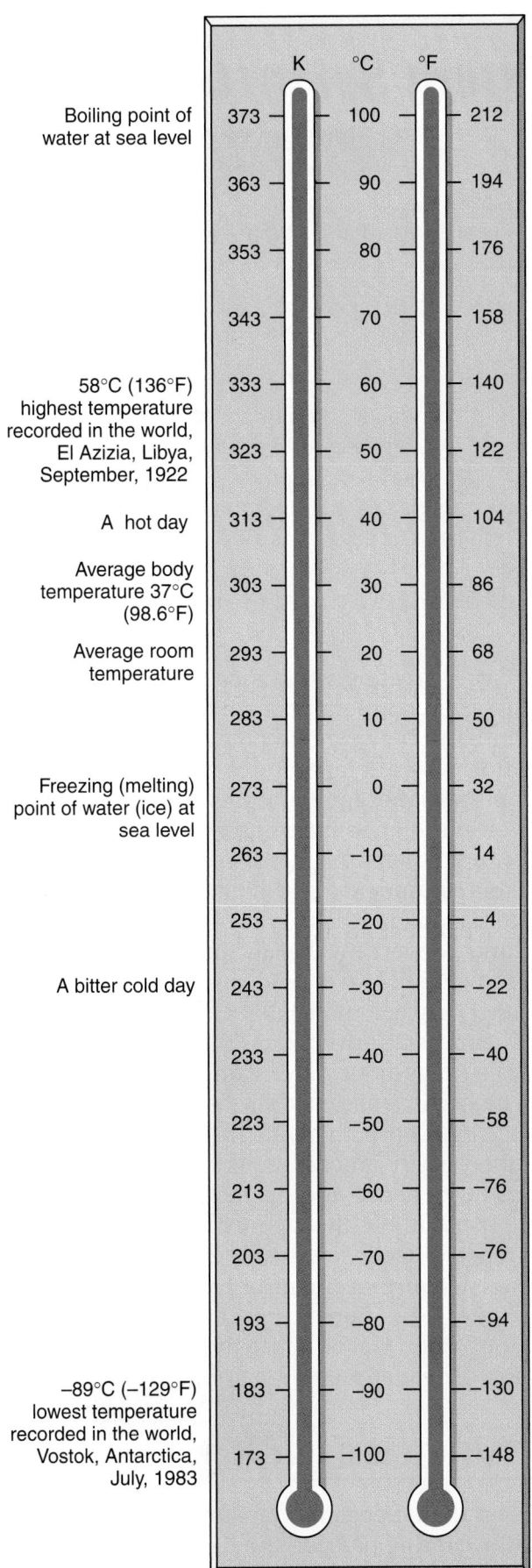

FIGURE 16-1 A comparison of the three principal temperature scales.

Earth System Scientists

Daniel Gabriel Fahrenheit

Daniel Gabriel Fahrenheit was born in Poland in 1686 but lived most of his life in Amsterdam. He became interested in the building of precise scientific instruments. He traveled Europe for many years, learning from other instrument makers, and eventually returned to Amsterdam to produce his own instruments. He invented the first mercury glass thermometer in 1714. He then used his thermometer to create a precise scale for the accurate measurement of temperature. His scale marked the freezing point of water at 32 degrees, the heat of the body at approximately 90 degrees, and the boiling point of water at 212 degrees. Today his name still identifies the name of the scale he devised almost 300 years ago. The creation of an accurate thermometer was a great advancement for science because it allowed for the study of the effects of temperature on the physical properties of many substances.

heat on the Earth, creating what is called a **heat gradient**, which is simply the change in temperature over a specific distance. A heat gradient exists on Earth between the poles, where temperatures are low, and the equator, where temperatures are high. A heat gradient also exists between the higher temperatures at the Earth's surface and the cooler temperatures high in the troposphere.

Temperature gradients on Earth result in the flow of heat from areas of high temperature to areas of low temperature. The flow of heat in a temperature gradient leads to the distribution of heat by radiation, conduction, and convection. Recall that radiation is the transfer of heat by electromagnetic waves, and conduction is the transfer of heat by direct contact between molecules. Convection, however, is a much more dynamic process. Convection is the transfer of heat by the movement of a fluid such as air or water. Convection begins when a portion of the fluid is heated in some way. The heat causes the molecules of the fluid to become less dense; therefore the fluid begins to rise. The rising heated fluid then begins to cool as its heat is dissipated. The cooling fluid becomes more dense and begins to sink downward again. The sinking fluid pushes under the warmer fluid and causes it to rise, and the process repeats itself. The result is a **convection cell**, which is formed by the circular movement of hot rising fluid and descending cooler fluid (Figure 16–2). Convection can occur in the Earth's air, water, and mantle. Convection that occurs in the troposphere is responsible for the distribution of heat around the Earth.

RADIATIVE COOLING

Another process that affects the transfer of heat in the atmosphere is called **radiative cooling**. During the daytime, insolation received by the Earth's surface is absorbed, causing the temperature of the surface to rise. As insolation continues throughout the day, the surface is

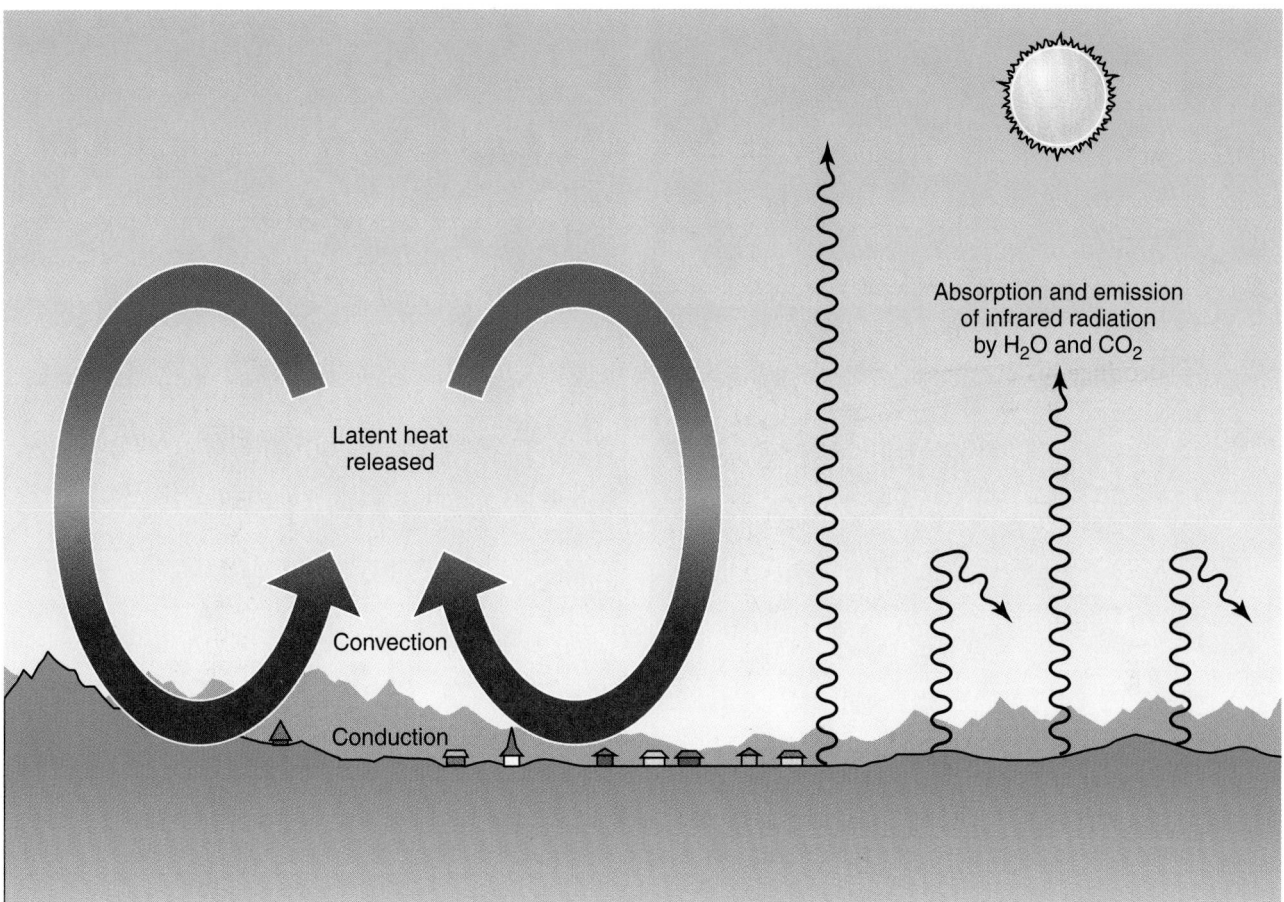

FIGURE 16–2 The formation of convection cells in the atmosphere helps distribute heat around the planet.

continually heated; the heat is then either conducted or radiated back into the atmosphere. This process continually heats the atmosphere during the day. As a result, the warmest temperatures during the day tend to occur around 3:00 P.M. At night, even though insolation stops, the Earth's surface continues to heat the atmosphere by radiating and conducting its stored heat. Eventually the surface cools and the heating of the atmosphere stops. The atmosphere then begins to cool as it radiates its heat back into space. Radiative cooling can result in the rapid decline of the temperature in the atmosphere. Extreme radiative cooling occurs on cloudless nights (Figure 16–3). Thus the coldest temperatures occur at night during winter. Cloudy nights can trap some of the heat that is being radiated back into space by acting as a blanket that slows down the cooling of the atmosphere. Therefore cloudy nights are usually much warmer in winter than cloudless nights.

THE GREENHOUSE EFFECT

High-energy, short-wave radiation penetrates the atmosphere to heat the Earth's surface. The surface then reradiates this energy back into the atmosphere in a low-energy, long-wave form, called infrared radiation.

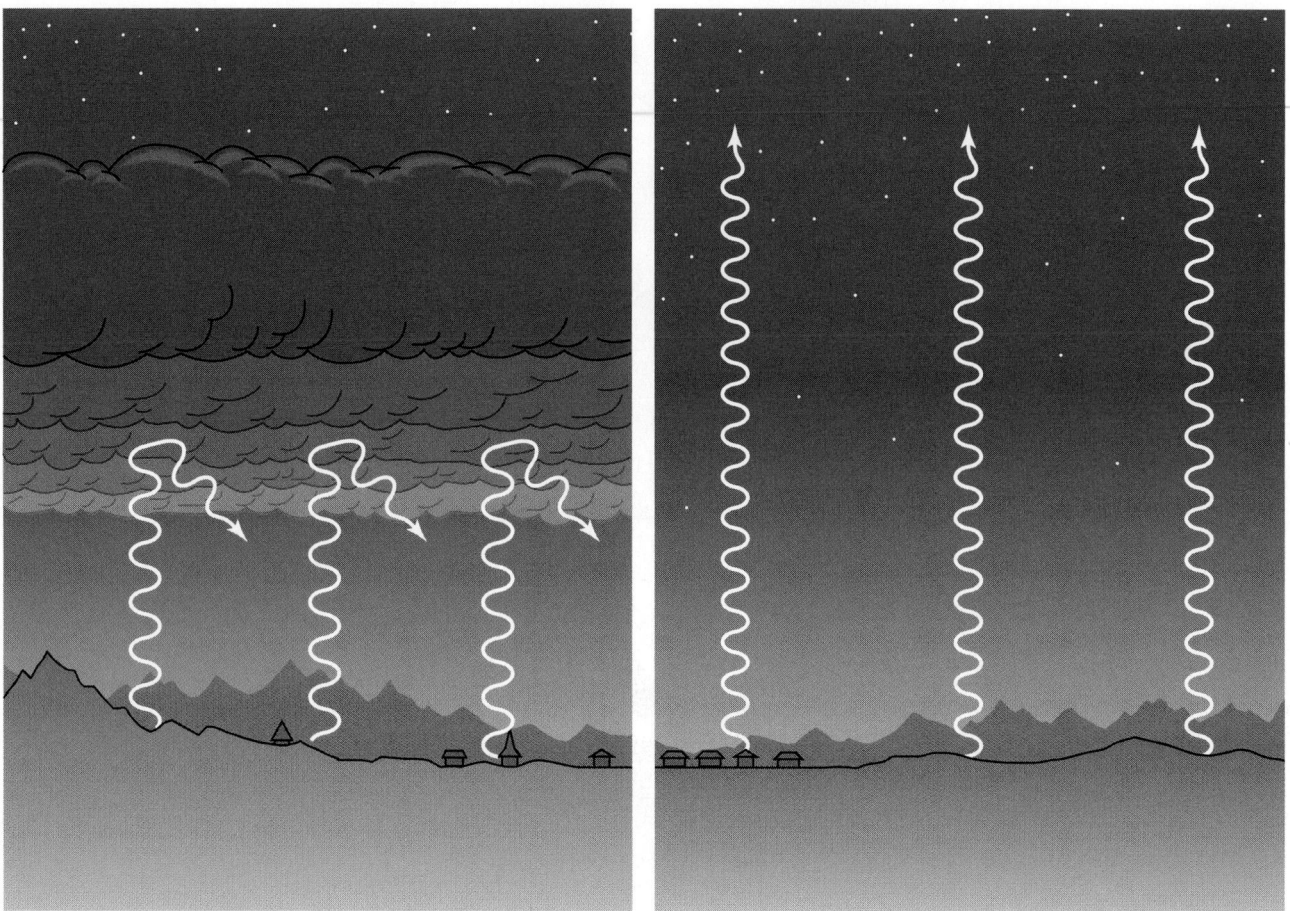

FIGURE 16–3 Radiative cooling of the atmosphere occurs rapidly on a clear night as heat is lost to space. Cloudy nights help trap heat in the atmosphere and keep it relatively warm.

The infrared radiation can then be absorbed by some of the gases in the atmosphere, which causes its temperature to rise. This process that heats our planet is often referred to as the **greenhouse effect**, because a similar process also occurs in a greenhouse (Figure 16–4). The short-wave infrared radiation that the Sun emits travels through the clear glass of a greenhouse and is absorbed by the solid floor and walls inside. These solid materials then reradiate long-wave (infrared) radiation back into the air of the greenhouse, which is trapped by the glass. This trapping of the long-wave infrared radiation can cause the air temperature inside the greenhouse to rise rapidly. The same process can also occur in a car. Short-wave radiation penetrates the windows of a car and is absorbed by the seats and dashboard. The seats and dashboard then reradiate long-wave radiation into the car and it is trapped by the glass, causing the air temperature inside the car to rise rapidly.

Gases in the atmosphere act like the glass in a greenhouse and absorb the long-wave radiation, thereby heating the planet. These types of gases are also known as **greenhouse gases**. Greenhouse gases in the Earth's atmosphere include water vapor, carbon dioxide, and methane. The concentrations of some of these gases are increasing in the atmosphere, which might be causing the temperature of the atmosphere to rise over time.

CAREER CONNECTIONS
Atmospheric Scientist

An atmospheric scientist conducts specific research dealing with the unique aspects of the Earth's atmosphere. This includes the physical and chemical properties of the gases that surround the planet. Some atmospheric scientists also research the atmospheric characteristics of other planets within the solar system. Today much of the work of an atmospheric scientist involves the study of human-created pollutants on Earth. The effects of atmospheric pollution have begun to interrupt the natural balance of the Earth's ecosystems. Atmospheric scientists are researching the ways these pollutants are interacting with the atmosphere and how they are altering its chemistry. Major topics such as global warming and ozone destruction are an important part of the work of atmospheric scientists, who are searching for ways to lessen the impact of human beings on the atmosphere. Jobs in the atmospheric sciences can be found in government agencies, such as the National Oceanic and Atmospheric Administration (NOAA) or the National Aeronautics and Space Administration (NASA), and in academic research. Atmospheric scientists must have at least a 4-year college degree.

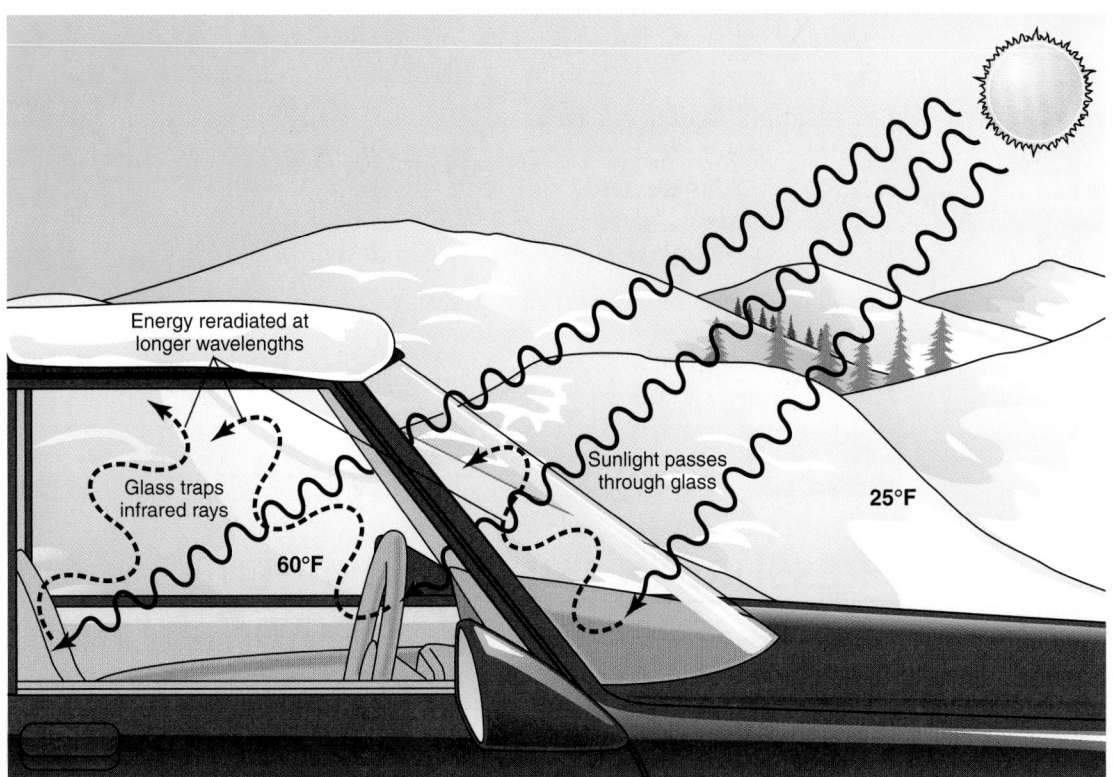

FIGURE 16–4 The greenhouse effect helps heat the Earth in the same way that it heats the inside of a car.

FOR MORE INFORMATION GO TO THIS WEB LINK:

<http://www.epa.gov
/globalwarming/kids
/greenhouse.html>

<http://earthguide.ucsd
.edu/earthguide
/diagrams/greenhouse/>

SECTION REVIEW

1. Define the term *temperature*.

2. What are the three scales used to measure temperature?

3. Describe the two types of temperature gradients that occur on Earth.

4. Briefly explain the process by which convection distributes heat.

5. What is radiative cooling?

6. Describe the greenhouse effect.

7. Who was Daniel Gabriel Fahrenheit?

earth math

1) During the month of January the average temperature at the North Pole is −50° F and the average temperature at the equator is 80° F, with a distance of 6,250 mi between them. Determine the temperature gradient in the Northern Hemisphere using the following formula: gradient = change in temperature/change in distance.

2) A temperature reading of −52° Fahrenheit is recorded at a height of 19 mi above sea level in the stratosphere, and at sea level the temperature is recorded at 52° F. Using the gradient calculation from Question 1, determine the temperature gradient from the stratosphere to the Earth's surface.

3) Temperature values often need to be converted from one unit to another. Use the following formulas to convert 68° F to Celsius and Kelvin and 37° C to Fahrenheit and Kelvin:

$$F = 9/5 \times C + 32 \quad C = 5/9 \times (F-32) \quad K = 5/9 \times F + 255.36$$

16.2 Atmospheric Pressure

PRESSURE IN THE ATMOSPHERE

Atmospheric pressure is simply the weight of all the air molecules pressing down at a specific level somewhere on Earth (Figure 16–5). Even though the air in the atmosphere appears invisible, it is made up of atoms and molecules that have mass. The mass of the air presses down on the Earth, and we call this atmospheric pressure, or air pressure.

Generally as you get closer to the surface of the Earth, the air pressure increases. This is because there are more air molecules above you

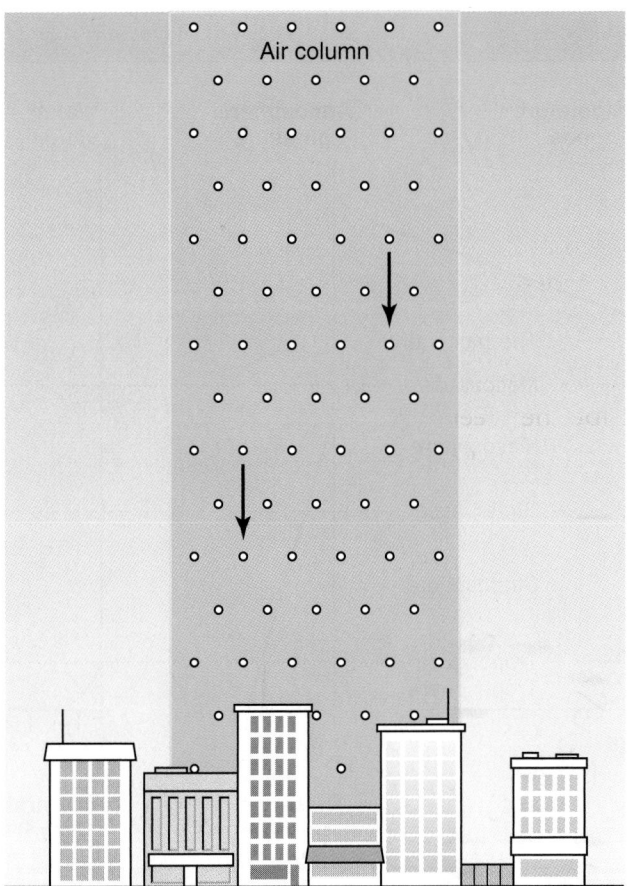

FIGURE 16-5 Air pressure on the Earth is a measure of the weight of a column of air pressing down on a specific point on the surface.

when you are closer to the Earth's surface. At sea level the weight of the air above you presses on your body with a force of 14.7 pounds per square inch (1 kilogram per square meter). You do not sense this weight because you have been surrounded by it all your life, but it is there. As you move farther away from the Earth's surface, the air pressure begins to decrease (Figure 16–6). This is because there are fewer air molecules over your head as you rise in the atmosphere and therefore less weight pressing on you. Air pressure is extremely low when you reach the upper part of the stratosphere.

MEASURING ATMOSPHERIC PRESSURE

Air pressure on Earth is measured by using a **barometer**, which is an instrument that measures the weight of the air at a specific point on the Earth. Air pressure is also known as barometric pressure. Barometric pressure is measured using two types of units: inches of mercury and millibars. Inches of mercury is the oldest unit used to measure barometric pressure (Figure 16–7). It was derived by the use of a barometer that contained mercury to record the changes in air pressure. As the air pressure increased, it pressed down on a dish that held a pool of mercury inside a glass tube. The increased air pressure caused the mercury to rise in the tube, and the change in air pressure was

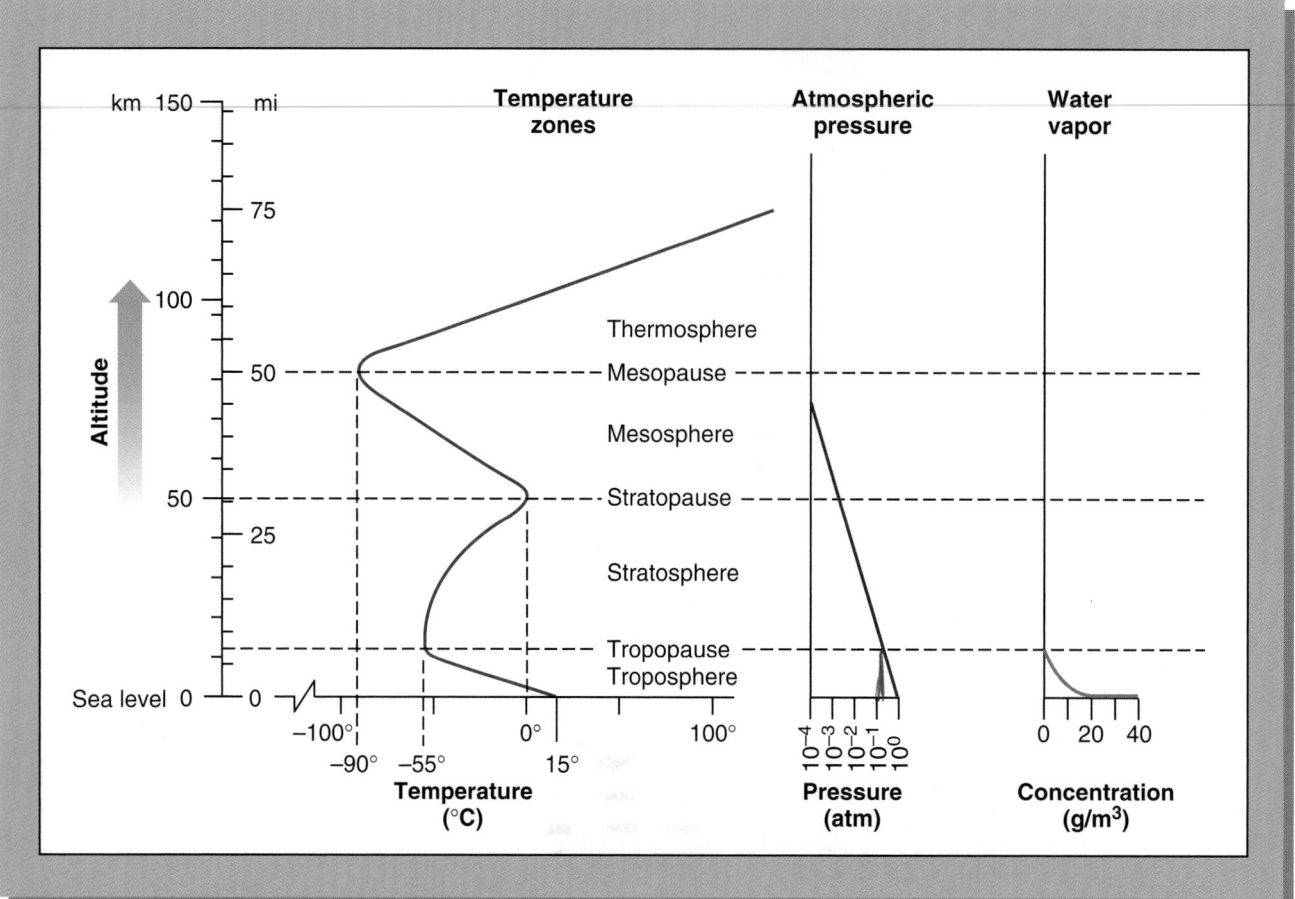

FIGURE 16–6   Air temperature, pressure, and water vapor decrease with an increase in height in the atmosphere.

recorded as the inches of mercury that the liquid metal occupied in the tube. The mercury barometer was invented in 1643 by an Italian scientist named Evangelista Torricelli.

The average air pressure at sea level, also known as 1 standard atmosphere, is 29.92 inches of mercury (1013.2 millibars). Today there are many different types of barometers that record atmospheric pressure without the need for mercury. The most common unit of measurement to record air pressure is the millibar. This is the form of barometric pressure used in meteorology and weather forecasting.

HIGH AND LOW ATMOSPHERIC PRESSURE

Atmospheric pressure on Earth is often influenced by the air temperature. Warm air that is heated near the Earth's surface begins to rise in the atmosphere because warm air is less dense than cooler air. The lifting of warm air that is less dense than the surrounding air and that weighs less creates an area of low pressure at the surface. Low pressure at the surface is usually associated with warmer, lighter, less dense air. When the warm air rises into the atmosphere, it begins to expand and cool. This is called **adiabatic cooling**, which is the cooling of air as a result of expansion (Figure 16–8).

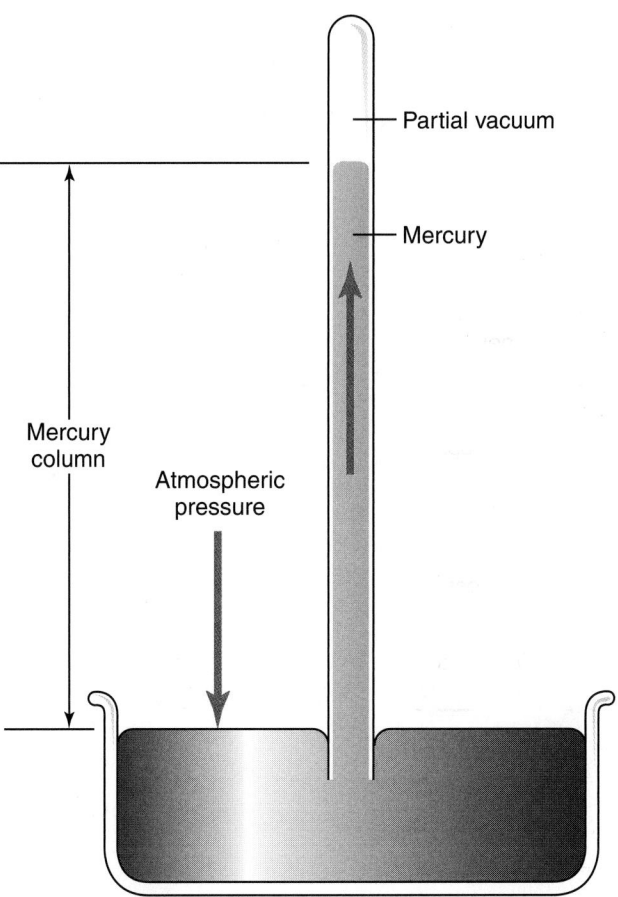

- Partial vacuum
- Mercury
- Mercury column
- Atmospheric pressure

FIGURE 16–7 A mercury barometer measures the air pressure as a result of the weight of the air pushing down on a pool of mercury, causing it to rise or lower in the tube. This type of barometer was invented by Evangelista Torricelli in 1643.

Earth System Scientists

Evangelista Torricelli

Evangelista Torricelli was born in Italy in 1608. He studied mathematics in Rome and eventually became the personal secretary to Galileo. After Galileo's death, he became a professor of mathematics in Florence, Italy. Torricelli began to work on the concept that the air that made up the atmosphere must have weight. In 1643 he invented a device to measure the weight of the air. He took a long glass tube that was closed on one end and filled it with mercury. He then inverted the tube into a pool of mercury and measured the height of the column of liquid metal. He theorized that the weight of the air was pushing on the pool of mercury, causing it to rise into the tube. This device eventually became known as the mercury barometer. Torricelli also noticed that the height of the column often changed from day to day. This observation led to the belief that air pressure also changed daily.

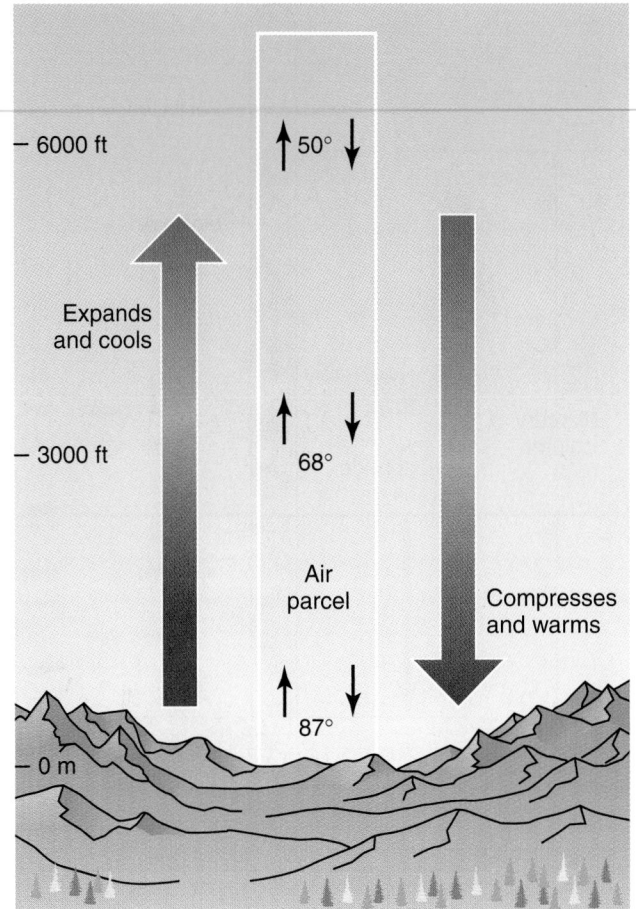

FIGURE 16–8 As air rises into the atmosphere, its pressure decreases, causing it to expand and cool. This is known as adiabatic cooling.

When the rising warm air begins to cool, the cooler air becomes more dense and begins to sink back toward the Earth's surface. The area on the Earth's surface where cool, dense air sinks downward experiences high atmospheric pressure. Therefore warm air is generally associated with low pressure and cooler air associated with high pressure (Figure 16–9). Meteorologists identify areas of low and high pressure on weather maps because they can be used to help forecast the weather. Areas of low pressure on a weather map are marked with a red capital L. Areas of high pressure on weather maps are marked with a blue capital H. Generally, low pressure indicates poor weather and high pressure indicates good weather.

ATMOSPHERIC PRESSURE AND MOISTURE

Air pressure is also influenced by the amount of water vapor present in the air, also known as **atmospheric moisture**. Generally, the more moisture in the air, the less dense it is. The water molecule weighs much less than the molecules of nitrogen and oxygen that compose most of the atmosphere. When the air has a higher moisture

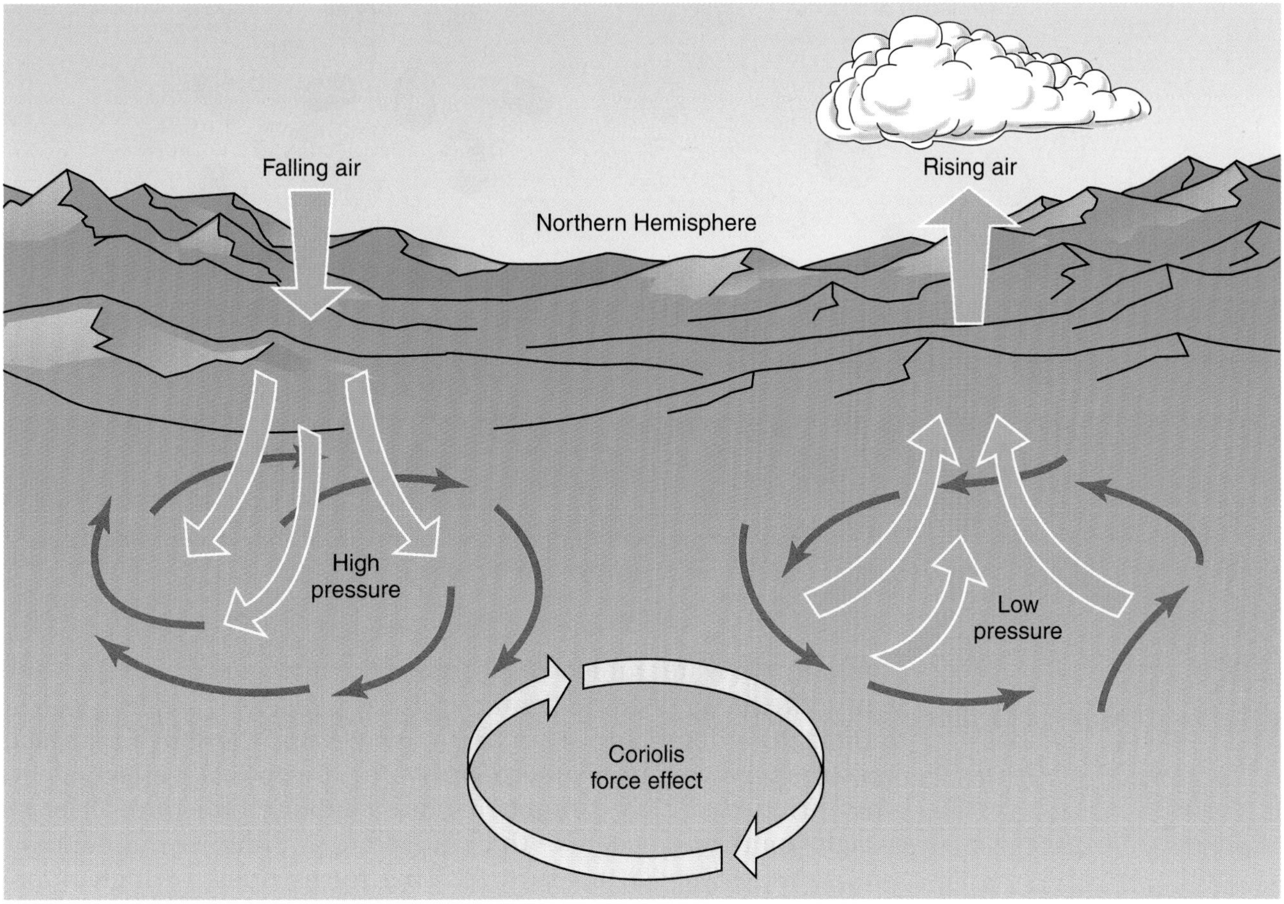

Falling air

Rising air

Northern Hemisphere

High pressure

Low pressure

Coriolis force effect

FIGURE 16–9 The creation of high or low pressure at the Earth's surface as a result of warm air rising or cooler air sinking.

CAREER CONNECTIONS
Biometeorologist

A biometeorologist studies the interactions between atmospheric phenomena and living things. This unique branch of atmospheric science attempts to understand the ways in which weather can influence organisms on Earth. Changes in atmospheric pressure and moisture can cause discomfort for many people in the form of aches and pains in their joints or by inducing headaches. Some animals are also very sensitive to changes in the atmosphere. A biometeorologist is interested in researching these phenomena to try to reverse their effects or to use them to better forecast the weather. Biometeorologists require a college education in both meteorology and biology. They often work in academic research.

Moist air   **Dry air**

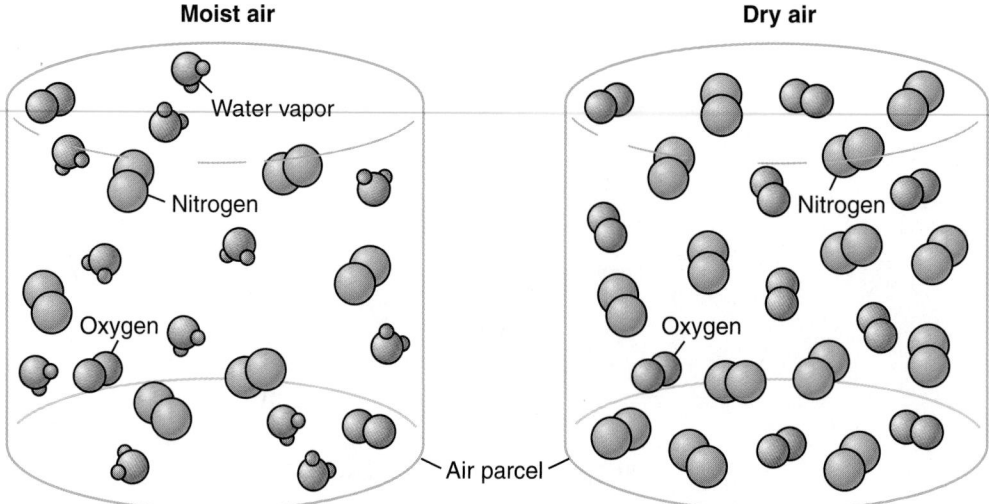

FIGURE 16–10   Moist air is lighter and lower in pressure than dry air as a result of the water molecules weighing less and displacing the heavier molecules of nitrogen and oxygen.

content, the water molecules displace the nitrogen and oxygen and cause the air to become lighter and less dense (Figure 16–10). The lighter, less dense moist air rises away from the Earth's surface, resulting in lower atmospheric pressure. The opposite effect occurs with drier air, which contains less atmospheric moisture. Drier air weighs more and is denser than moist air, and therefore it tends to sink toward the Earth's surface. This forms areas of high atmospheric pressure.

FOR MORE INFORMATION GO TO THIS WEB LINK:

<http://kids.earth.nasa
.gov/archive/air
_pressure/>

SECTION REVIEW

1. Define the term atmospheric pressure.
2. How is atmospheric pressure measured?
3. Describe the characteristics of low-pressure air.
4. Describe the characteristics of high-pressure air.
5. What type of general weather conditions are associated with low pressure and with high pressure?
6. Who was Torricelli?

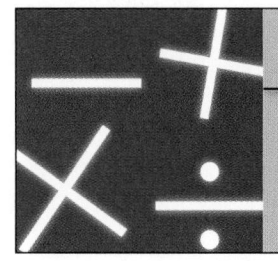

earth math

1) Barometric pressure is measured in both millibars and inches of mercury. If 1 inch of mercury equals 33.865 millibars, how many millibars equal 29.92 inches of mercury?

CHAPTER SUMMARY

The surface temperatures on the Earth depend on the atmosphere. Temperature is a measure of the average kinetic energy of a substance. Molecules of air that are moving relatively slowly have a cooler temperature. Rapidly moving molecules of air are higher in temperature. The specific temperature of a substance is measured using a thermometer. This scientific instrument records the temperature in degrees Fahrenheit, degrees Celsius, or Kelvins. The Earth's tilted axis, rotation, and spherical shape cause it to be unequally heated by the Sun. This results in specific heat gradients on the planet, which create unique climate and weather. A heat gradient is the specific change in temperature over a specific distance.

Heat is distributed throughout the atmosphere in three ways: radiation, conduction, and convection. The unequal heating of the Earth helps to form large-scale convection cells, which distribute heat around the planet. Heat can also be lost from the atmosphere, which cools the planet. This is known as radiative cooling. On a clear night the atmosphere can radiate its heat into space, causing rapid cooling. The coldest nights on the Earth usually occur on clear nights as a result of radiative cooling.

Heat is trapped on the Earth by a mechanism known as the greenhouse effect. The atmosphere acts like the glass in a greenhouse, which traps the long-wave infrared radiation that is reradiated into the atmosphere from the land surface. Atmospheric gases that trap this heat are known as greenhouse gases. These include water vapor, carbon dioxide, and methane.

Air pressure on the Earth is caused by the weight of the molecules of air pressing down on the surface. This is also known as barometric pressure. Generally the weight of the air at the Earth's surface is approximately 14.7 pounds per square inch (1 kilogram per square meter). The pressure in the atmosphere decreases with an increase in height, because there are fewer air molecules as you move away from the surface. The pressure of the atmosphere is measured with a scientific instrument called a barometer. Atmospheric pressure is usually recorded in either inches of mercury or millibars.

The temperature of the air influences air pressure on the Earth. Warm air tends to be less dense and therefore rises away from the surface. This helps form an area of low pressure at the surface. Cooler air is denser and sinks toward the surface. This helps form an area of high pressure at the surface. Changes in air pressure are good indicators of changes in the weather. Low air pressure is usually associated with poor weather and high pressure with fair weather. The amount of water in the air, also known as atmospheric moisture, can influence the air pressure. Moist air tends to be lower in air pressure than drier air.

CHAPTER REVIEW

Multiple Choice

1. As the temperature of the atmosphere increases, the average kinetic energy of the air molecules:
   a. decreases
   b. stays the same
   c. increases
   d. varies

2. At what temperature does water freeze in degrees Celsius?
   a. 0 degrees
   b. 32 degrees
   c. 100 degrees
   d. 212 degrees

3. What is the equivalent temperature in degrees Fahrenheit of 21° Celsius?
   a. −4 degrees
   b. 65 degrees
   c. 70 degrees
   d. 37 degrees

4. A weather balloon is released into the atmosphere. What changes will it record as it increases its altitude?
   a. increasing air temperature and pressure
   b. increasing air temperature and decreasing pressure
   c. decreasing air temperature and pressure
   d. decreasing air temperature and increasing pressure

5. The Earth's tilted axis, rotation, and curved surface all cause:
   a. tides on the Earth
   b. wind on the Earth
   c. convection cells on the Earth
   d. unequal heating of the Earth

6. Which type of radiation is trapped by greenhouse gases?
   a. short wave
   b. ultraviolet
   c. long wave
   d. visible light

7. Which of the following is not a greenhouse gas?
   a. water vapor
   b. oxygen

   c. methane
   d. carbon dioxide

8. The process by which the atmosphere cools on a clear night is called:
   a. conduction cooling
   b. convection cooling
   c. adiabatic cooling
   d. radiative cooling

9. The process of air expanding as it rises is called:
   a. conduction cooling
   b. convection cooling
   c. adiabatic cooling
   d. radiative cooling

10. As the temperature of the air increases, its density:
    a. decreases
    b. stays the same
    c. increases
    d. varies

11. An air pressure of 29.65 inches of mercury is equivalent to:
    a. 984.0 millibars
    b. 999.0 millibars
    c. 1001.0 millibars
    d. 1004.0 millibars

12. Which type of atmospheric pressure results from warm, rising air?
    a. low pressure
    b. adiabatic pressure
    c. high pressure
    d. radiative pressure

13. When air loses moisture, air pressure generally:
    a. increases
    b. remains the same
    c. decreases
    d. fluctuates rapidly

14. Which types of weather conditions are usually associated with low-pressure systems:
    a. fair weather
    b. high pressure and clear skies
    c. poor weather
    d. cool temperatures

Matching   *Match the terms with the correct definitions.*

a. temperature
b. thermometer
c. freezing point
d. boiling point
e. heat gradient

f. convection cell
g. radiative cooling
h. greenhouse effect
i. greenhouse gases
j. atmospheric pressure

k. barometer
l. adiabatic cooling
m. atmospheric moisture

1. _____ A scientific instrument used to measure temperature.
2. _____ The amount of water vapor present in the air.
3. _____ The specific temperature at which a substance begins to change its phase from a liquid to a gas, also known as the boiling point.
4. _____ The average amount of kinetic energy of the atoms and molecules in a substance, which is commonly expressed as the degree of hot or cold measured by a thermometer.
5. _____ The process by which rising air is cooled by expansion.
6. _____ The specific temperature at which a liquid changes phase into a solid.
7. _____ A term used to describe short-wave radiation passing through the atmosphere and being absorbed by the Earth's surface, which then reradiates the energy in a long-wave form that is trapped by gases in the atmosphere and heats the planet.
8. _____ An instrument used to measure atmospheric pressure, also called barometric pressure.
9. _____ The change in heat energy over a specific distance.
10. _____ The weight of a column of air at a specific point in the atmosphere, usually measured in millibars or inches of mercury.
11. _____ The circular movement of a fluid caused by a change in temperature and density associated with the transfer of heat.
12. _____ The cooling of an object as a result of its emitting electromagnetic radiation into the atmosphere or into space.
13. _____ Specific gases in the atmosphere that trap long-wave radiation, such as water vapor, methane, and carbon dioxide.

Critical Thinking

1. Explain why hot air balloons are launched early in the morning and not during the middle of the day during fall in the Northern Hemisphere.

Humidity, Clouds, and Precipitation

HUMIDITY OBJECTIVES

Atmospheric Moisture · Sources of Atmospheric Moisture · Relative Humidity · Dew Point Temperature

After reading this section you should be able to:

▶ Define the term *humidity* and describe its general relationship with air temperature.
▶ Describe the three ways by which moisture enters the atmosphere.
▶ Define the term *relative humidity*.
▶ Define the term *dew point* and describe how it can be determined.

CLOUDS AND PRECIPITATION OBJECTIVES

Cloud Formation · Types of Clouds · Formation of Precipitation · Types of Precipitation · Orographic Precipitation

After reading this section you should be able to:

▶ Define the term *cloud* and explain the process that leads to its formation.
▶ Describe four ways by which air can be uplifted to form clouds.
▶ Differentiate between low clouds, middle clouds, high clouds, and fog.
▶ Describe the process that leads to the formation of precipitation.
▶ Identify the six types of precipitation and how they are formed.
▶ Define the term *orographic precipitation*.

INTRODUCTION

Anyone who has experienced the moist air of a hot summer night has felt the direct effects of humidity. This often uncomfortable state of the atmosphere not only causes human discomfort, but greatly affects the weather. The lack of humidity can also be uncomfortable. For example, in winter your eyes, nose, throat, and skin can dry out as a result of low humidity. Understanding what controls humidity and how it influences the weather and life on Earth is an important part of meteorology.

Clouds in the atmosphere are one of the most visible forms of change in the air. A cloud is formed by billions of tiny water droplets and ice particles that have condensed in the atmosphere. Clouds play an important role in maintaining the Earth's heat balance by reflecting solar radiation back into space and absorbing heat radiated from the planet's surface. They are also an important part of the water cycle, which transports water over long distances and returns it to the surface by forming precipitation. The different forms of clouds in the atmosphere often create beautiful displays across the background of the blue sky and help signal the type of weather that may be approaching.

17.1 Humidity

ATMOSPHERIC MOISTURE

Humidity is a measure of how much water vapor is present in the atmosphere. **Water vapor** is the invisible gaseous form of water, also called atmospheric moisture. When water enters the air as vapor, it coexists with the other gases that make up the Earth's atmosphere. In tropical regions near the ocean, the atmospheric moisture content can be as high as 4 percent. This means that if you took a sample of air, 4 percent of it would be composed of water vapor. The ability of water vapor to exist in the atmosphere can depend on the temperature of the air. Generally an increase in air temperature increases the ability of water vapor to exist in the atmosphere, meaning that warmer air has a higher atmospheric moisture level than colder air. This is apparent during different times of the year.

In the colder months of winter, the air has a low atmospheric moisture level and is considered dry. This causes air in winter to dry out the mucous membranes in your eyes and throat. People develop colds during winter because they lose the protective barrier that mucus provides. Many people use humidifiers in their homes during the colder months to increase the atmospheric moisture content of the air they breathe. Cooler air with low atmospheric moisture creates the clear, dry weather that is associated with high atmospheric pressure.

In contrast, warmer air has much higher atmospheric moisture content and is considered humid. During warm, humid summer days, you can almost feel the moisture in the air. The visibility of the air is also greatly reduced as a result of the high amount of water vapor present in the atmosphere. The water vapor scatters light in the atmosphere, making it difficult to see over long distances. Because warm air

Earth System Scientists

Henry Cavendish

Henry Cavendish, born in France in 1731, spent most of his life in England. As the son of rich parents, Cavendish was free to pursue his interest in mathematics and physics. In 1776 he published his first scientific paper, which reported his discovery of the element hydrogen. He also studied many other properties of gases and proved that water was not an element but a compound of hydrogen and oxygen. In 1783 Cavendish discovered that the composition of the atmosphere was the same all over the globe. He went on to describe the actual composition of the atmosphere as approximately 79 percent nitrogen, 21 percent oxygen, and trace amounts of other gases. Cavendish also experimented with electricity and gravity and derived the gravitational constant. Much of Cavendish's work went unpublished and was not discovered until more than 100 years after his death.

is often associated with air that has high atmospheric moisture content, it also tends to be lower in barometric pressure.

SOURCES OF ATMOSPHERIC MOISTURE

Water vapor in the atmosphere is an important part of the hydrological cycle, and there are three main ways by which water can enter into the air. The main source of atmospheric moisture is evaporation. Evaporation is the process by which liquid changes into a gas. Much of the water that enters the atmosphere as water vapor is evaporated from the surface of the ocean (Figure 17–1).

This is because approximately 70 percent of the Earth's surface is covered by the oceans. Insolation strikes the ocean and heats the water molecules at its surface, which then causes the water to evaporate into the atmosphere. Another way that water enters the atmosphere is by **evapotranspiration** (Figure 17–2). Evapotranspiration is the movement of water from the soil into a plant's root system and up through the body of a plant; it then evaporates off the surface of the leaves.

Evapotranspiration is an often overlooked source of atmospheric moisture that contributes large amounts of water vapor to the air. Approximately 8,800 gallons per day of water is transpired by 2.5 acres of corn plants. Extensive evapotranspiration over large forested areas

FIGURE 17–1 One of the main sources of atmospheric moisture is the evaporation of water from the ocean surface. (*Courtesy of PhotoDisc.*)

FIGURE 17–2 Evapotranspiration transports water from the soil, through a plant, and into the atmosphere where it evaporates off the leaf surface.

FIGURE 17–3 The dramatic effects of the sublimation of a field of snow on a sunny day. (*Courtesy of PhotoDisc.*)

helps regulate the local climate. When the forest is removed by logging or for agriculture, a rapid reduction in atmospheric moisture takes place as a result of the loss of evapotranspiration. This can cause a shift in climate that often results in drier weather.

The third way in which water enters the atmosphere is by **sublimation**. Sublimation is the process of ice changing directly into water vapor; it occurs in areas that experience snowfall. When snow is exposed to bright sunlight, it absorbs the radiant energy and begins to sublimate (Figure 17–3). Large amounts of snow can sublimate on a cold, clear day, greatly reducing the depth of the snow.

RELATIVE HUMIDITY

The most common way to measure the amount of water vapor in the atmosphere is to determine the relative humidity. Relative humidity is the ratio of the amount of water vapor in the air compared with its saturation point at a specific temperature and pressure. Saturation is the total amount of water a specific parcel of air can hold. When air becomes saturated, it can no longer hold any more water vapor, much like a sponge that has absorbed all the water it can hold. Relative humidity is expressed in the form of a percentage. A relative humidity of 80 percent means that the air contains 80 percent of the total amount of water vapor it can hold at that specific temperature. When the relative humidity reaches 100 percent, water must then condense in the air and form precipitation.

DEW POINT TEMPERATURE

Another term that is related to atmospheric moisture and relative humidity is the **dew point**. The dew point is the temperature to which the air must be cooled for saturation to occur (Figure 17–4). For example, if the dew point is 65° F, when the air temperature reaches 65° F, the air becomes saturated. Both the dew point and the relative humidity can be calculated by using an instrument called a psychrometer.

A psychrometer consists of two thermometers. One thermometer records the dry bulb temperature, which is equal to the current air temperature. The other thermometer records the wet bulb temperature. It is called the wet bulb temperature because the end of the thermometer is covered with a damp cloth, which records the cooling temperature of the evaporation of the water from the cloth into the air. When water evaporates, it removes heat energy from the surrounding

FIGURE 17–4 A psychrometer determines the wet bulb and dry bulb temperatures, which are used to establish the relative humidity and dew point temperature of the air. (*Courtesy of NOAA.*)

TABLE 17–1 The chart used to determine dew point temperature

Dry Bulb Temperature (°C)	Difference Between Wet Bulb and Dry Bulb Temperatures (C°)															
	0	1	2	3	4	5	6	7	8	9	10	11	12	13	14	15
−20	−20	−33														
−18	−18	−28														
−16	−16	−24														
−14	−14	−21	−36													
−12	−12	−18	−28													
−10	−10	−14	−22													
−8	−8	−12	−18	−29												
−6	−6	−10	−14	−22												
−4	−4	−7	−12	−17	−29											
−2	−2	−5	−8	−12	−20											
0	0	−3	−6	−9	−15	−24										
2	2	−1	−3	−6	−11	−17										
4	4	1	−1	−4	−7	−11	−19									
6	6	4	1	−1	−4	−7	−13	−21								
8	8	6	3	1	−2	−5	−9	−14								
10	10	8	6	4	1	−2	−5	−9	−14	−28						
12	12	10	8	6	4	1	−2	−5	−9	−16						
14	14	12	11	9	6	4	1	−2	−5	−10	−17					
16	16	14	13	11	9	7	4	1	−1	−6	−10	−17				
18	18	16	15	13	11	9	7	4	2	−2	−5	−10	−19			
20	20	19	17	15	14	12	10	7	4	2	−2	−5	−10	−19		
22	22	21	19	17	16	14	12	10	8	5	3	−1	−5	−10	−19	
24	24	23	21	20	18	16	14	12	10	8	6	2	21	−5	−10	−18
26	26	25	23	22	20	18	17	15	13	11	9	6	3	0	−4	−9
28	28	27	25	24	22	21	19	17	16	14	11	9	7	4	1	−3
30	30	29	27	26	24	23	21	19	18	16	14	12	10	8	5	1

air, causing it to cool; therefore evaporation is a cooling process. Generally, the drier the air, the lower the wet bulb temperature. This is because more water is evaporating from the cloth, therefore causing more evaporative cooling. Air containing more water vapor causes the wet bulb temperature to be higher because less evaporative cooling occurs. The difference between the dry bulb and wet bulb temperatures is called the dew point depression. The dew point depression can then be used to calculate the dew point temperature and the relative humidity. Generally the greater the dew point depression, the drier the air. When the dew point depression becomes smaller, it signifies that the air contains more water vapor. This is often used as an indicator to predict cloud formation and the formation of precipitation. By using the difference between the wet bulb and dry bulb temperatures and a dew point or relative humidity table, you can easily determine the dew point temperature and relative humidity of the surrounding air (Tables 17–1 and 17–2).

SECTION REVIEW

1. Define the term *humidity*.

2. What is the highest percentage of water vapor in the Earth's atmosphere?

TABLE 17–2 The chart used to determine relative humidity

Dry bulb Temperature (°C)	Difference Between Wet Bulb and Dry Bulb Temperatures (C°)															
	0	1	2	3	4	5	6	7	8	9	10	11	12	13	14	15
−20	100	28														
−18	100	40														
−16	100	48														
−14	100	55	11													
−12	100	61	23													
−10	100	66	33													
−8	100	71	41	13												
−6	100	73	48	20												
−4	100	77	54	32	11											
−2	100	79	58	37	20	1										
0	100	81	63	45	28	11										
2	100	83	67	51	36	20	6									
4	100	85	70	56	42	27	14									
6	100	86	72	59	46	35	22	10								
8	100	87	74	62	51	39	28	17	6							
10	100	88	76	65	54	43	33	24	13	4						
12	100	88	78	67	57	48	38	28	19	10	2					
14	100	89	79	69	70	50	41	33	25	16	81					
16	100	90	80	71	62	54	45	37	29	21	14	7	1			
18	100	91	81	72	64	56	48	40	33	26	19	12	6			
20	100	91	82	74	66	58	51	44	36	30	23	17	11	5		
22	100	92	83	75	68	60	53	46	40	33	27	21	15	10	4	
24	100	92	84	76	69	62	55	49	42	36	30	25	20	14	9	4
26	100	92	85	77	70	64	57	51	45	39	34	28	23	18	13	9
28	100	93	86	8	71	65	59	53	47	42	36	31	26	21	17	12
30	100	93	86	79	72	66	61	55	49	44	39	34	29	25	20	16

3. What type of humidity is associated with low air pressure and with high pressure?

4. Describe the three ways by which water enters the atmosphere.

5. What is relative humidity?

6. Describe how the dew point depression can be used to determine the amount of moisture in the air?

7. Who was Henry Cavendish?

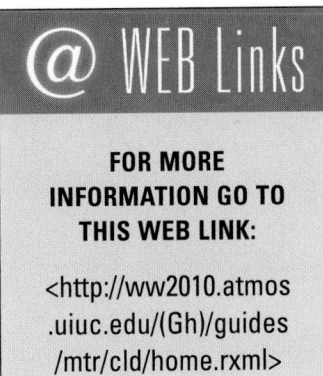

@ WEB Links

FOR MORE INFORMATION GO TO THIS WEB LINK:

<http://ww2010.atmos.uiuc.edu/(Gh)/guides/mtr/cld/home.rxml>

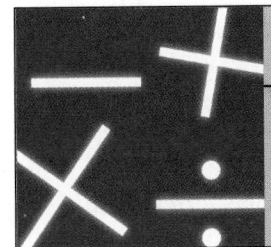

earth math

1) Which parcel of air contains more water vapor: Parcel A with a dry bulb temperature of 73° F and a wet bulb temperature of 57° F, or Parcel B with a dry bulb temperature of 79° F and a wet bulb temperature of 58° F?

CAREER CONNECTIONS

Paleoclimatologist

A paleoclimatologist studies the climate history of the Earth. This includes piecing together the ancient composition of gases in the atmosphere, along with estimating regional temperatures, wind direction, humidity, and precipitation patterns. The work of a paleoclimatologist involves the study of the fossil record, landscapes, and rock formations to search for clues to past climates. These scientists also explore glaciers to learn about past glaciations and ice ages. Paleoclimatologists travel the world in search of evidence that may be used to infer what the Earth's climate was like throughout its history. This research involves the study of ice cores, tree rings, coral reefs, and ocean sediments, which all help reveal the Earth's past climates. A paleoclimatologist needs a college education in many different scientific disciplines, including paleontology, meteorology, geology, biology, and chemistry. These scientists are often employed by the petroleum and mineral industries, where they help reveal places on the Earth that once had climates that might have led to oil formation or specific mineral deposits. Paleoclimatologists also conduct academic research and can work for government agencies.

17.2 Clouds and Precipitation

CLOUD FORMATION

A **cloud** is a large mass of condensing water droplets and ice crystals that forms in the atmosphere when the air is cooled to its dew point. Remember that the dew point is the temperature of the air at which it becomes saturated. Once air becomes saturated, the water vapor it contains begins to condense. **Condensation** is the process of water vapor changing into a liquid. When water vapor condenses in the atmosphere, it forms tiny droplets of water or ice on small solid particles that float through the air. These microscopic particles are composed of sea salt, ash, dust, and other substances and are called **condensation nuclei**. The small water droplets or ice crystals that form on the condensation nuclei together make up a cloud. The process that cools air to its dew point begins when a parcel of air rises up into the atmosphere. The rising air begins to expand and then cools. This expansion and cooling of rising air is called adiabatic cooling. The rate at which air cools adiabatically in the atmosphere is called the **lapse rate** (Figure 17–5). The rate at which a moist parcel of air cools

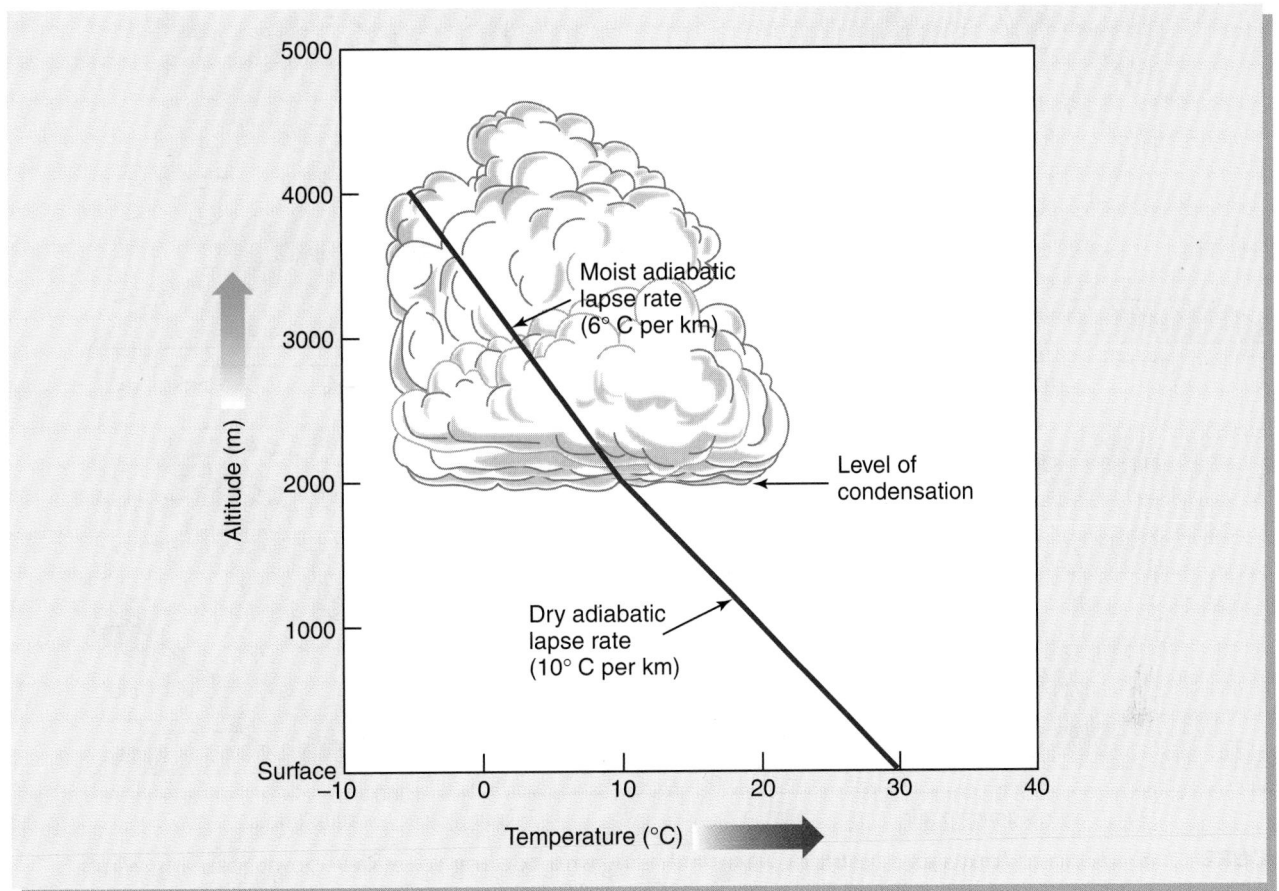

FIGURE 17-5   The lapse rate measures the decline in temperature with an increase in altitude of a parcel of air. The lapse rate can be used to determine at what height clouds are likely to form.

as it rises and expands is known as the moist adiabatic lapse rate, which is approximately 3.3° F for every 1,000 ft of elevation (1.9° C every 305 m). The moist adiabatic lapse rate helps determine the altitude at which a cloud forms. For example, a parcel of air at the surface with a temperature of 70° F and a dew point of 60 degrees forms a cloud when it is raised to a height of approximately 3,000 ft.

Clouds form when air is forced to rise and cool; therefore it is important to understand the processes that cause air to rise (Figure 17–6). Rising air is also known as **uplift**. The warming of air from the heat radiated by the Earth's surface is one way that air is forced to rise in the atmosphere. Warm air becomes less dense than the air around it and therefore begins to rise. This same process is used to raise hot air balloons into the air. The balloon traps air that is heated by a flame, which raises the temperature of the air inside the balloon. This causes the air to become less dense than the cooler air outside the balloon and forces it to rise upward. In the atmosphere, hot rising air can form massive clouds that produce strong thunderstorms.

Another way that air is forced to rise in the atmosphere to form clouds is by topography. Air that encounters a mountain is forced to rise as the elevation of the land increases (Figure 17–7). This type of lifting process is also called orographic lifting. Orographic lifting often causes the tops of mountains to be hidden in the clouds.

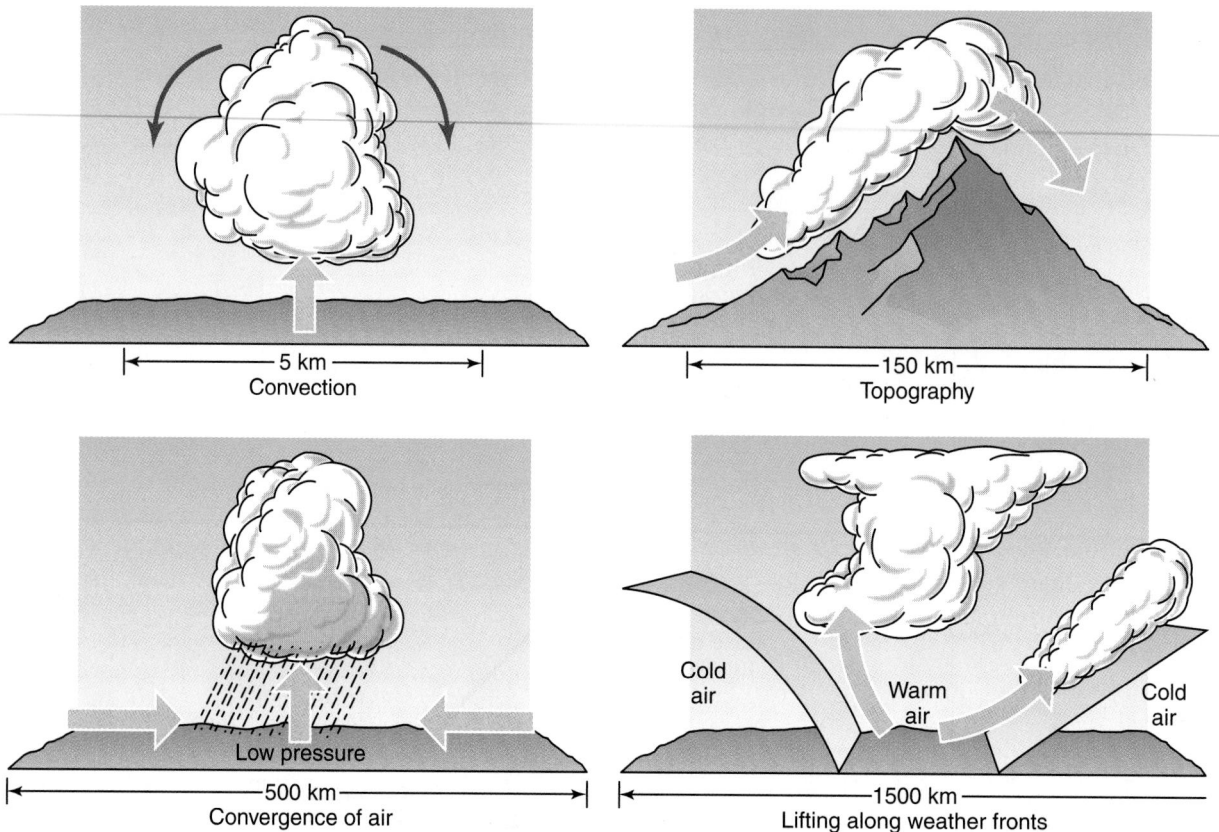

FIGURE 17–6 A cloud forms as a result of warm air rising and cooling to its dew point, causing water vapor to condense in the atmosphere; this occurs by four different processes.

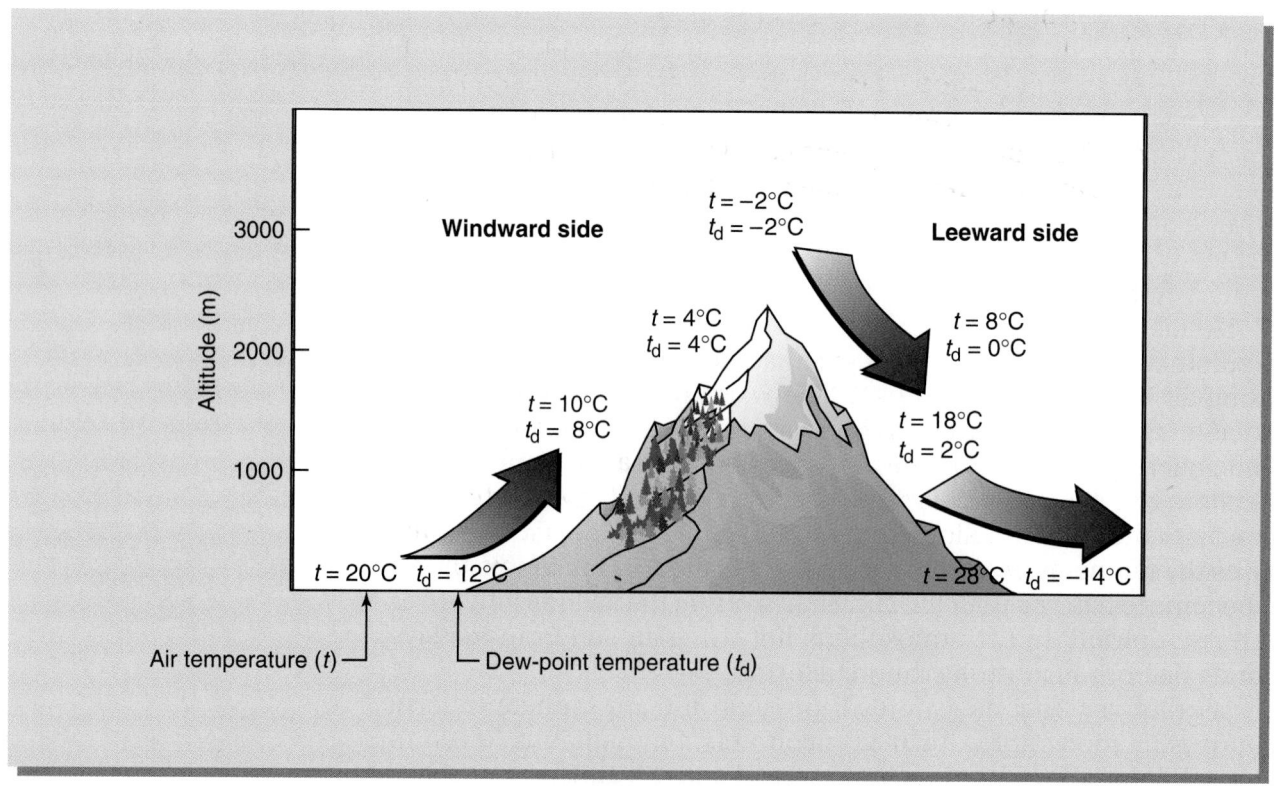

FIGURE 17–7 When an air mass encounters a mountain, it is forced to rise and cool. This process is known as orographic lifting and leads to the formation of clouds on the windward side of a mountain.

Earth System Scientists

John Tyndall

John Tyndall, born in 1820, was an Irish physicist. Tyndall became a teacher of mathematics and eventually a professor of physics. In 1869 he discovered that when light passes through certain substances it can be scattered. This led to his conclusion that sunlight passing through the atmosphere was scattered with invisible particles, causing the sky to appear blue. Tyndall also worked on the interaction of specific gases with radiant energy. He proposed that gases in the atmosphere, such as water vapor and carbon dioxide, are capable of absorbing heat energy. This work led to the discovery of how the Earth's atmosphere is heated. Tyndall also experimented with the notion that the air held microscopic bacteria that could spoil food. He then derived ways of sterilization by using heat.

Another type of lifting mechanism that causes air to rise, cool to its dew point, and then form clouds, is the **convergence** of surface winds. Areas on the Earth's surface where winds converge, or come together, can force air upward into the atmosphere. Wind often converges along the shoreline of a large body of water, when fast-moving wind traveling over the relatively smooth water comes into contact with the rough surface of the land. The friction from the rough land surface causes the wind velocity to slow, resulting in a pileup of air, or a convergence zone. This then can force air upward into the atmosphere.

The last way that uplift causes air to rise and cool is by the action of a cold air mass moving underneath a warm air mass. Because cold air is denser than warm air, it can wedge itself underneath warmer air and force it to rise. It occurs as cold fronts collide with a warm air mass in front of them. This often results in the formation of clouds.

TYPES OF CLOUDS

The condensation of water vapor into liquid droplets or ice in the atmosphere forms many unique types of clouds, which are classified both by general appearance and height of formation (Figure 17–8). Clouds that form at levels just above the surface and to a height of 6,500 ft (1.9 km) are called low clouds. These clouds form when the temperature of the atmosphere is above 23° F (–5° C). Because of this they are often composed of tiny liquid water droplets. Low clouds include cumulus clouds, which appear like large cotton balls and are often separated by clear blue sky. Cumulus clouds form on clear days when convection begins to force warm air upward, causing the water vapor in the air to condense. As the day progresses, cumulus clouds grow bigger. Eventually, large cumulus clouds may produce light rain or snow showers. When the sun goes down and the atmosphere cools, cumulus clouds begin to dissipate as the water droplets they contain vaporize. Stratus, another type of low cloud, consists of one gray, uniform

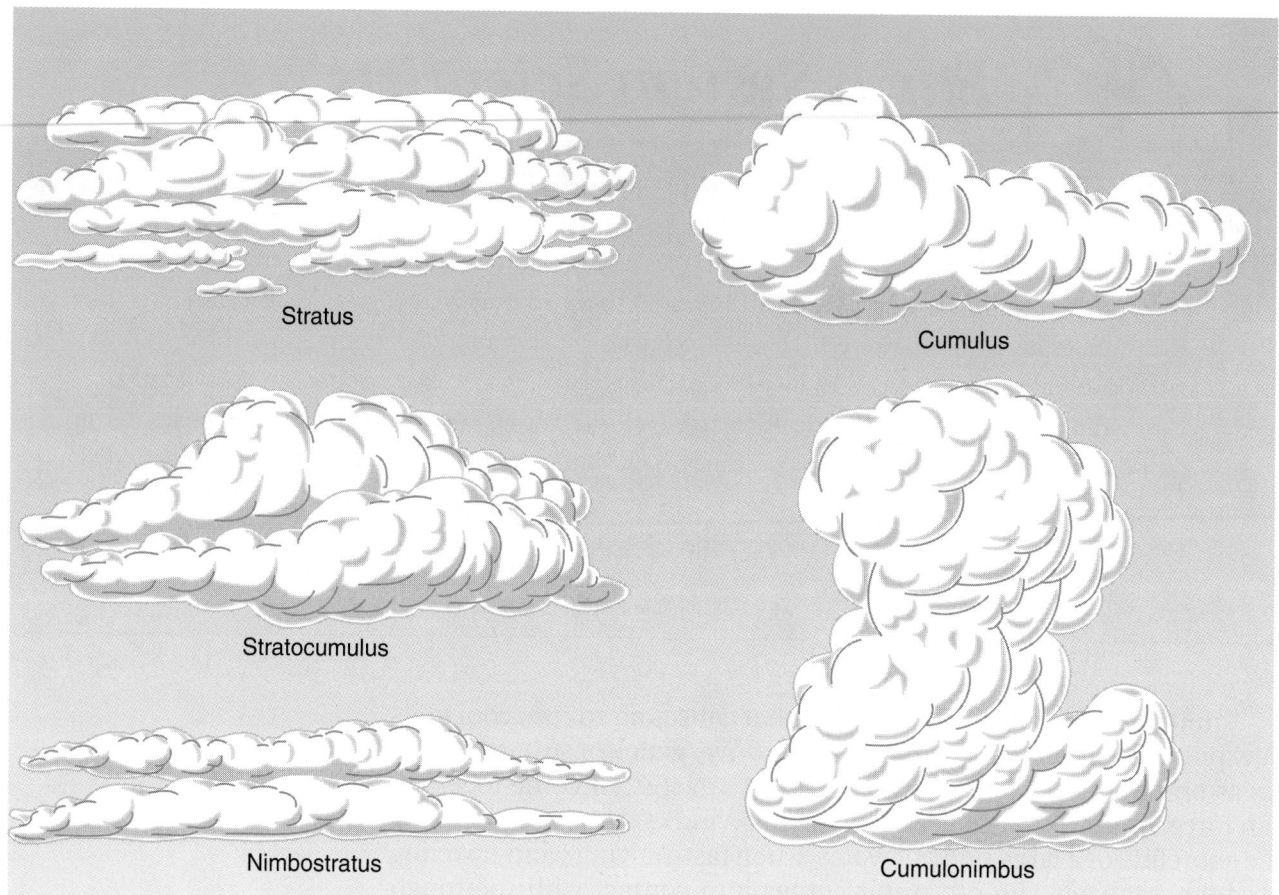

FIGURE 17–8   The different types of low clouds that form at elevations between 1500 and 6500 feet above the ground.

layer that covers the entire sky. Nimbostratus is a low cloud that is thicker than a stratus cloud and much darker; they produce light precipitation for extended periods. Cumulonimbus clouds begin as small cumulus clouds and evolve into large clouds with high vertical development. These clouds form thunderstorms and heavy precipitation. Some cumulonimbus clouds can develop vertical heights of more than 23,000 ft.

The next major cloud type is the middle clouds. Middle clouds form at elevations between 6,600 ft (2 km) and 23,000 ft (7 km) where temperatures fall between 32° F (0° C) and –13° F (–25° C). Middle clouds are composed of a mixture of supercooled water droplets and ice crystals. Common forms of middle clouds include the altostratus and altocumulus clouds (Figure 17–9). Altostratus clouds are composed of one uniform layer that appears white or gray. Altocumulus clouds are thick, white, puffy clouds that form long bands in the sky. Altostratus and altocumulus clouds rarely produce precipitation that reaches the ground (it usually evaporates before it reaches the surface).

The highest clouds to form in the atmosphere, also known as high clouds, are called cirrus clouds. These highest of clouds form at heights above 23,000 ft (7 km). Cirrus clouds are composed of ice crystals. They appear like thin wisps that float through the sky (Figure 17–10). Cirrostratus and cirrocumulus clouds form thin veils high in the atmosphere through which the sun can easily penetrate.

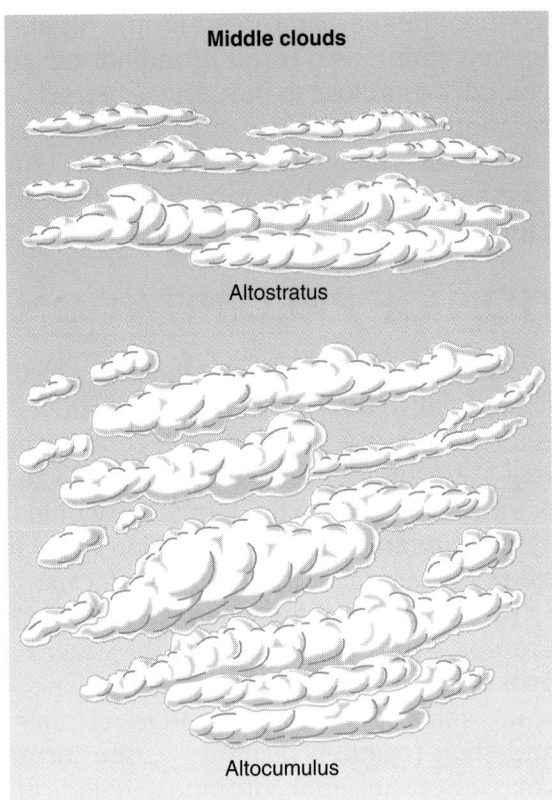

FIGURE 17–9 Altostratus and altocumulus are types of middle clouds that form between 6,600 and 23,000 ft above the ground.

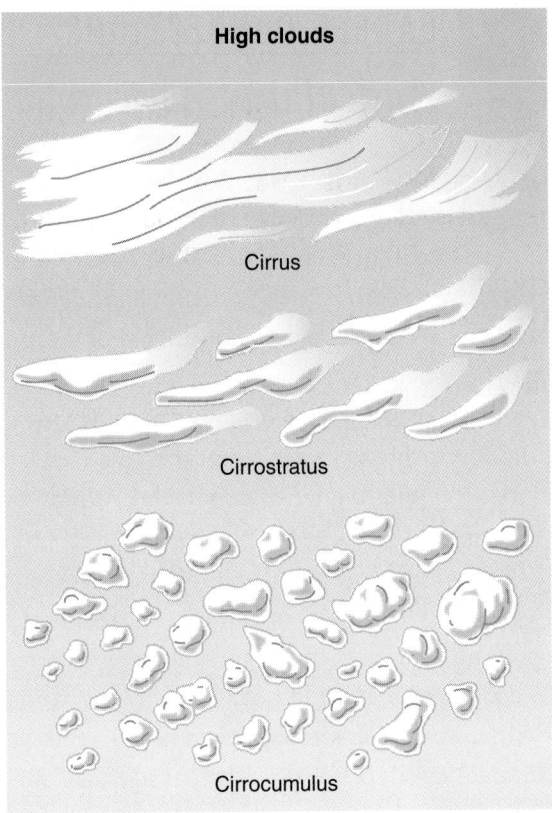

FIGURE 17–10 Cirrus clouds are classified as high clouds, forming at heights between 23,000 and 40,000 ft above the ground.

Sometimes, when the temperature of humid air above the ground is lowered to its dew point, as a result of radiational cooling, a cloud forms. When a cloud forms close to the surface of the Earth, it is known as **fog**. The formation of fog usually occurs in the morning or at night when the ground is cool enough so that it lowers the temperature of air above it to its dew point. Fog then rapidly dissipates when sunlight begins to heat the ground once again.

FORMATION OF PRECIPITATION

Precipitation is the process by which water vapor in the atmosphere condenses and falls back to the Earth's surface (Figure 17–11). Although this process seems simple, it actually is quite complex and is the result of many different atmospheric processes. The tiny water droplets and ice crystals that form clouds are so light that they would float high up in the atmosphere indefinitely if not for the action of updrafts. **Updrafts** are winds that flow upward from the Earth's surface as a result of convection. The formation of cumulus clouds is usually associated with updrafts. As cumulus clouds begin to build, the water droplets and ice crystals that form from condensation begin to get knocked around by updrafts. This causes the water droplets and ice crystals to collide into one another and stick together, resulting in the formation of larger water droplets and ice crystals that continue to collide and grow in size. Eventually the growing water droplets or ice crystals become too heavy, and the updrafts can no longer keep them suspended in the cloud. They then fall toward the Earth's surface as precipitation.

CAREER CONNECTIONS

Agricultural Meteorologist

Agricultural meteorologists are highly specialized atmospheric scientists who apply a knowledge of weather to the field of agriculture. These researchers study weather patterns and how they affect crop growth. Atmospheric phenomena such as droughts, floods, and storms cause millions of dollars of crop damage each year. These occurrences might be prevented, or at least the damage they cause reduced, with a better understanding of the interaction of weather with agricultural crops. Research in this field includes the possibilities of controlling rainfall by seeding clouds, along with the study of the adverse affects of atmospheric pollution on crop growth. Agricultural meteorologists are also interested in long-term climate changes that might affect agricultural regions throughout the world. These scientists require a college education in both meteorology and agricultural science. Agricultural meteorologists can work in private industry, in academic research, or for government agencies such as the U. S. Department of Agriculture or the National Weather Service.

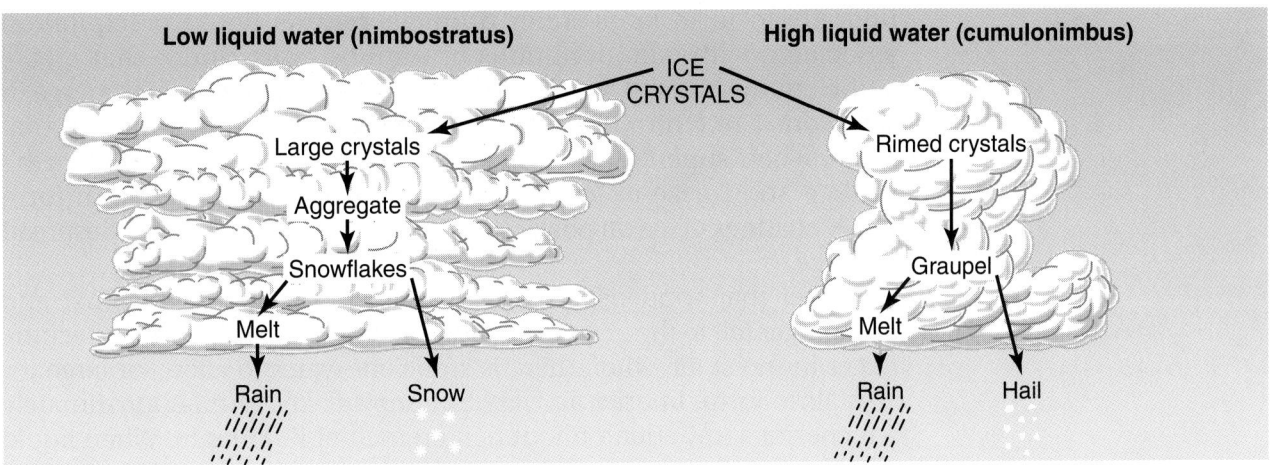

FIGURE 17–11 Precipitation forms in clouds when ice crystals and tiny water droplets clump together to the point that they are heavy enough to fall to the Earth's surface.

TYPES OF PRECIPITATION

Once the water droplets or ice crystals begin to get heavy enough to become precipitation, they can fall to Earth in many different forms (Figure 17–12). Drizzle is precipitation that consists of very tiny water droplets no bigger than 0.5 mm in diameter. Drizzle develops in stratus clouds, which do not have sufficient convection and

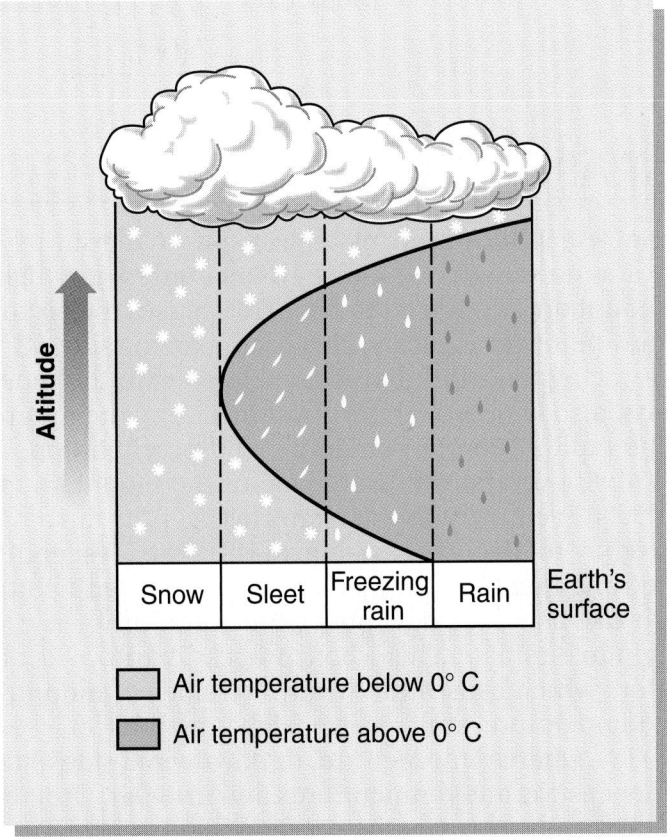

FIGURE 17–12 Different types of precipitation can form as a result of the air temperature above the surface.

updrafts to form large water droplets. Rain is liquid precipitation associated with cumulonimbus or nimbostratus clouds that create sufficient updrafts to form fairly large water droplets, which range in size from 1 to 6 mm in diameter. Freezing rain is precipitation that forms when supercooled droplets of liquid water fall to the Earth's surface and freeze on contact. This type of precipitation can form heavy coatings of ice on power lines and tree limbs, causing widespread damage.

Water that condenses as only ice crystals that stick together and grow larger fall to the ground as snowflakes. Snowflakes usually become larger in moist air, when there is sufficient water to allow for large ice crystals to form. In drier air, very fine snow flakes form. Approximately 4 inches of snow equals about half an inch of liquid rain. When liquid rain droplets freeze before they reach the Earth's surface, they form ice pellets. These pellets, which appear to be white, bounce off the ground on impact.

The last type of precipitation to form in clouds is called hail. Hail is associated with clouds that have strong updrafts, such as cumulonimbus clouds, which also form thunderstorms. Ice pellets form high in the clouds and are kept suspended by strong updrafts. They periodically melt and then refreeze to form concentric rings much like an onion. The stronger the updraft, the larger the size of the hail that can form. Hail is commonly no larger than one half inch in diameter when it finally falls to the ground, but if the updrafts within the cloud are extremely powerful, large hailstones can form. Hailstones are very large hail that can be as big as golf balls. The largest hailstones ever observed to fall to the Earth were equal in size to a small grapefruit.

@ WEB Links

FOR MORE INFORMATION GO TO THESE WEB LINKS:

<http://vortex .plymouth.edu /cloudboutique/>>

<http://ww2010.atmos .uiuc.edu/(Gh)/guides /mtr/cld/home.rxml>

<http://www .cloudman.com/>

<http://ww2010.atmos .uiuc.edu/(Gh)/guides/mtr /cld/prcp/home.rxml>

OROGRAPHIC PRECIPITATION

Orographic precipitation forms as a result of the lifting of an air mass over a mountain. When moist air encounters the higher elevation of a mountain, it is forced to rise. This causes the air to cool and reach its dew point very quickly. This occurs on the side of the mountain that is facing the wind that is associated with the movement of the air mass, also known as the windward side of the mountain. The result is the rapid formation of clouds and precipitation. As the air continues to rise up the windward side of the mountain, more precipitation falls. Eventually, as the air moves over the top of the mountain, it begins to decrease in elevation. The descending air is compressed and therefore warms. This causes the temperature of the air mass to rise above its dew point. Precipitation then ceases, and clouds begin to dissipate. This whole process is known as orographic precipitation, which causes the windward sides of mountains to be cooler in temperature and receive high amounts of precipitation (Figure 17–13), whereas the leeward, or downwind, side of the mountain experiences warmer temperatures and drier air. Orographic precipitation controls the weather and climate of many different geographic areas around the world that are either on the windward or leeward sides of mountain ranges.

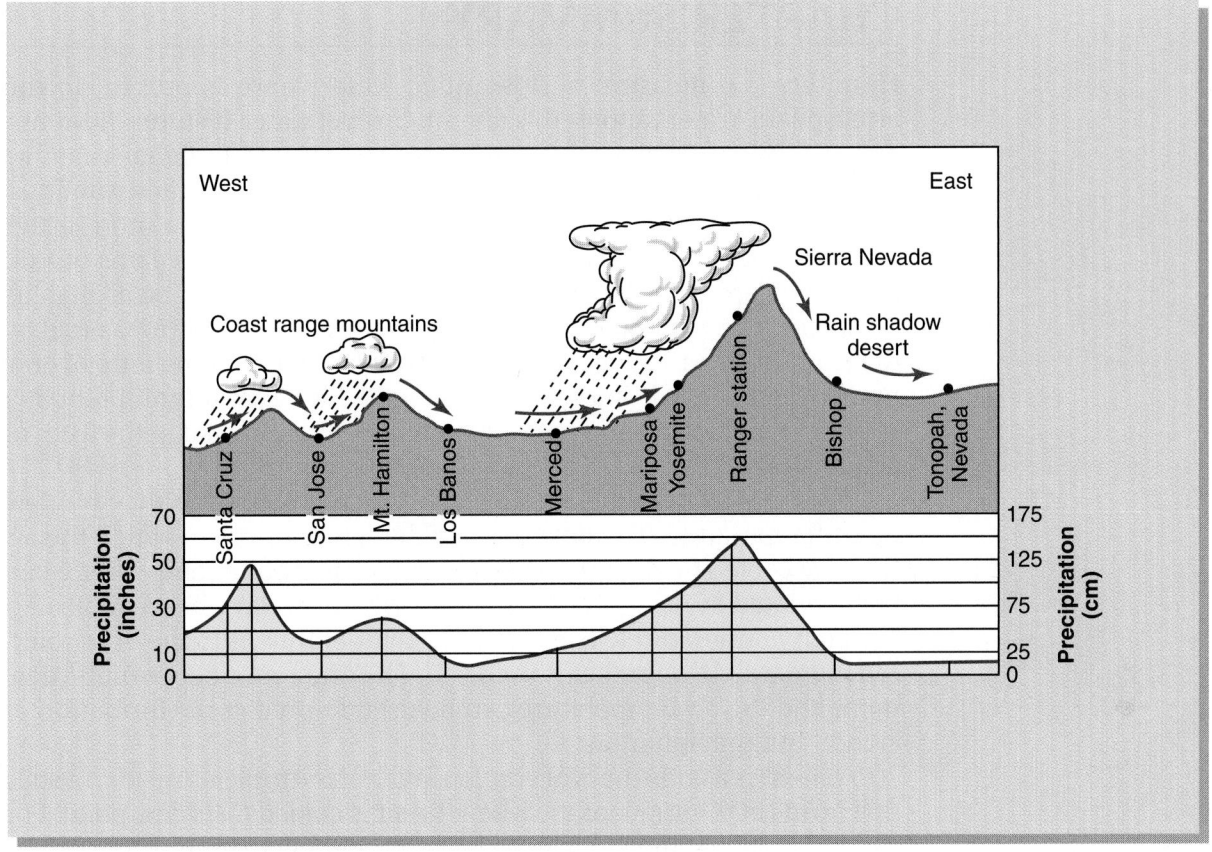

FIGURE 17–13 Orographic precipitation affects the amount of precipitation received by the windward and leeward sides of mountains.

SECTION REVIEW

1. Describe the process by which clouds form.
2. Explain the moist adiabatic lapse rate.
3. What are three things that cause air to rise in the atmosphere?
4. Explain the three basic types of clouds and the heights where they form.
5. Describe how precipitation forms in clouds.
6. What are the six forms of precipitation?
7. What is orographic precipitation?
8. Who was John Tyndall?

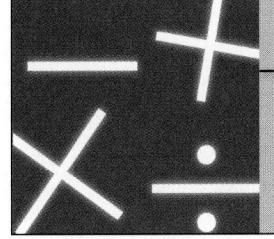

earth math

1) Using the approximate moist adiabatic lapse rate of 3.3° F for every 1,000 ft in elevation, determine the height at which a cloud forms in a parcel of air at sea level that has a temperature of 52° F and a dew point of 32° F.

CHAPTER SUMMARY

Humidity is a measure of how much water vapor is present in the atmosphere. Water vapor is the gaseous form of water. It enters the atmosphere in three principal ways: evaporation of water from the oceans or from surface freshwater, evapotranspiration by plants, and sublimation of snow and ice. Generally the warmer the air, the more water vapor it can hold. This causes warm air to be more humid than cold air. Near the tropics, the water vapor content of the air can be as high as 4 percent. The amount of water vapor in the air is usually measured by determining the relative humidity. Relative humidity is the ratio of how much water vapor is in the air compared with its saturation point at a specific temperature and pressure. It is usually expressed in the form of a percentage.

The relative humidity of the atmosphere is related to the air's dew point temperature. The dew point is the temperature to which the air must be cooled for saturation to occur. The dew point temperature can be calculated by using a psychrometer, which records the wet bulb and dry bulb temperatures. The closer the temperature is to the dew point, the more water vapor that is in the air. The difference between the dew point and the air temperature can be used to predict the formation of clouds and precipitation.

A cloud is a large mass of condensing water droplets and ice crystals that forms in the atmosphere when the air is cooled to its dew point. For a cloud to form, moist air from the surface must rise into the atmosphere, where it cools to its dew point temperature and causes water vapor to condense. There are four ways by which air can be forced to rise to form clouds. Warm air at the surface becomes less dense than the surrounding air and rises. Topography with high elevations can also cause air to rise, therefore causing it to cool. The convergence of wind at the surface of the Earth can force air upward, and the movement of a cold air mass into a warm air mass can cause air to rise. This occurs when the cold air wedges itself underneath the warm air, forcing it upward. A cloud that forms at the Earth's surface is called fog.

Once clouds form in the atmosphere, they can produce precipitation. Precipitation forms when the tiny water droplets and ice crystals in clouds clump together and fall back to the Earth's surface. There are six different forms of precipitation: drizzle, rain, freezing rain, snow, ice pellets, and hail. Orographic precipitation occurs when moist air comes into contact with a mountain. The mountain forces the air to rise, cool, and condense. This causes the formation of clouds and precipitation on the windward side of the mountain. Once the air moves over the mountain, it descends, compresses, and heats. This causes the clouds and precipitation to dissipate on the leeward side of the mountain.

CHAPTER REVIEW

Multiple Choice

1. Most moisture enters the atmosphere by the processes of:
   a. convection and conduction
   b. condensation and radiation
   c. reflection and absorption
   d. evapotranspiration and evaporation

2. Which area on the Earth is most likely to have an atmospheric moisture content of 4%?
   a. the poles
   b. 45 degrees north and south
   c. the tropics
   d. nowhere

3. As compared with warm air, cold air:
   a. is lower in pressure
   b. is drier
   c. is less dense
   d. holds more water

4. The movement of water from the soil up through a plant and off its leaf surface is called:
   a. condensation
   b. evapotranspiration
   c. evaporation
   d. sublimation

5. Snow changing phase into water vapor occurs by the process of:
   a. condensation
   b. evapotranspiration
   c. evaporation
   d. cublimation

6. The change in phase from water vapor to liquid water is called:
   a. condensation
   b. evapotranspiration
   c. evaporation
   d. sublimation

7. Which temperature and dew point indicate the lowest humidity?
   a. temperature 17° C, dew point 12° Celsius
   b. temperature 13° C, dew point 12° Celsius
   c. temperature 17° C, dew point 11° Celsius
   d. temperature 21° C, dew point 7° Celsius

8. What is the approximate relative humidity if the dry bulb temperature is 12° Celsius and the wet bulb temperature is 7° Celsius?
   a. 28%
   b. 35%
   c. 48%
   d. 65%

9. What is the dew point of the air if the wet bulb temperature is 10° Celsius and the dry bulb is 14° Celsius?
   a. −25° C
   b. 6° C
   c. 3° C
   d. 4° C

10. For clouds to form, which of the following must occur?
    a. Cool air must sink and warm.
    b. Cool air must rise and warm.
    c. Warm air must rise and cool.
    d. Warm air must sink and cool.

11. The formation of clouds requires air to be:
    a. saturated and have condensation nuclei
    b. saturated and have no condensation nuclei
    c. unsaturated and have condensation nuclei
    d. unsaturated and have no condensation nuclei

12. Why is it possible for no rain to be falling from a cloud?
    a. There are no condensation nuclei in the cloud.
    b. The cloud is water vapor.
    c. The dew point has not yet reached the cloud.
    d. The water droplets are too small to fall.

13. If the air temperature is 10° Celsius, which dew point results in the highest probability of precipitation?
    a. 8° C
    b. 6° C
    c. 0° C
    d. −4° C

14. Which of the following is a form of liquid precipitation that is less than 0.5 mm in diameter?
    a. rain
    b. drizzle
    c. fog
    d. sleet

15. Compared with the windward side of a
    mountain, the leeward side is:
    a. cooler and drier
    b. warmer and drier
    c. moist and cool
    d. moist and warm

Matching *Match the terms with the correct definitions.*

a. humidity
b. water vapor
c. evapotranspiration
d. sublimation
e. dew point

f. cloud
g. condensation
h. condensation nuclei
i. lapse rate
j. uplift

k. convergence
l. fog
m. precipitation
n. updrafts
o. orographic precipitation

1. _____ The term to describe the phase change from a solid to a gas.
2. _____ A common term that refers to the amount of water vapor content in the air.
3. _____ A type of precipitation that occurs as a result of orographic lifting, which causes moist air to cool and condense when it is forced to rise up the windward side of a mountain.
4. _____ The temperature to which the air needs to be cooled to become saturated with water at a specific atmospheric pressure.
5. _____ Strong, vertical winds that move upward through a cloud.
6. _____ The gaseous form of water.
7. _____ Liquid or solid water formed in clouds that falls to the surface of the Earth.
8. _____ A large mass of condensing water droplets and ice crystals in the atmosphere.
9. _____ The important pathway by which water moves from the soil, through the body of a plant, and evaporates off the leaf surface back into the atmosphere.
10. _____ Microscopic particles floating in the atmosphere on which water condenses to form clouds.
11. _____ A cloud that forms near or at the Earth's surface and is composed of tiny water droplets.
12. _____ The change in phase from a gas to a liquid.
13. _____ The process of coming together.
14. _____ The rate at which temperature or moisture decreases with height.
15. _____ The process of lifting something up.

Critical Thinking

1. Explain why pilots should try to avoid flying through developing cumulonimbus clouds.
2. Why do you think your skin feels hotter on a day that has 99 percent relative humidity, compared with a day that has 50 percent relative humidity?

Wind, Air Masses, and Fronts

SECTION 18.1

WIND OBJECTIVES

Pressure Gradient · Planetary Winds · Pressure Systems · Mesoscale Winds · Local Winds · The Jet Stream · Wind Measurement

After reading this section you should be able to:

▶ Define the term *wind*.

▶ Determine the pressure gradient between two points on the Earth's surface.

▶ Describe the formation of planetary winds on the Earth.

▶ Identify the locations of the low- and high-pressure centers on the Earth that are associated with prevailing winds.

▶ Describe the Coriolis effect and how it affects winds on the Earth.

▶ Identify the specific wind circulation around high- and low-pressure centers in the Northern Hemisphere.

▶ Explain the conditions that lead to the formation of land and sea breezes.

▶ Define the term *jet stream*.

SECTION 18.2

AIR MASSES AND FRONTS OBJECTIVES

Air Mass Formation · Source Regions and Classification of Air Masses · Fronts · Mid-latitude Cyclones

After reading this section you should be able to:

▶ Define the term *air mass*.

▶ Identify the different regions that form unique air masses.

▶ Describe the characteristic temperature, moisture, and pressure associated with the five different air mass types.

▶ Identify the four different types of fronts and their characteristic changes in temperature, pressure, and precipitation.

▶ Describe the development of a mid-latitude cyclone.

INTRODUCTION

For thousands of years, human civilizations have harnessed the wind to move ships and power machines. The prevailing winds that blow across the oceans opened up new lands for both trade and colonization and forever changed our relationship with the sea. Humans have long respected the winds on the planet, for they not only provide easily accessible power, but they also can be some of the most damaging aspects of the environment. Events such as hurricanes, tornadoes, and thunderstorms can generate winds with deadly force. Even our modern technology cannot prevent the potential destruction that strong winds can cause. Wind is also an important aspect of the Earth's climate. It is the natural way by which our planet distributes energy and heat throughout the atmosphere. Most everyone on Earth can appreciate the cooling effects of a gentle breeze on a hot summer day or the power of the wind to raise a kite into the sky. The movement of air across the Earth is an important part of weather. This is especially noticeable when a hot, humid summer day suddenly cools off as a result of a cold front passing through the area. The passing of fronts is often the cause for change in weather, but what actually is a front, and what causes air to have unique characteristics of temperature and moisture? All these phenomena are part of the complex interaction of the atmosphere, oceans, and land surface that creates weather and climate on the Earth.

18.1 Wind

PRESSURE GRADIENT

The only time we can really feel the atmosphere around us is when the wind blows. **Wind** on Earth is the horizontal movement of air across the Earth's surface. Wind is also known as a pressure gradient force, because it is caused by a difference in air pressure. A **pressure gradient** is a change in air pressure over a specific distance (Figure 18–1). Air on Earth always moves from areas of high atmospheric pressure to areas of low atmospheric pressure. This movement of air from high pressure to low pressure is called wind.

Wind is a **vector force**, which means that it has both a direction and a velocity. The direction that wind moves is always recorded from where it originates. A wind that is blowing from the northwest is actually traveling from the northwest toward the southeast. Because wind is caused by changes in air pressure, atmospheric pressure centers on the Earth can reveal a lot about the force and direction of wind. Rapid changes in air pressure over short distances result in a strong pressure gradient, which causes strong winds. The more slowly the pressure changes over a distance, the weaker the pressure gradient, which therefore creates weaker winds. Winds on the Earth are divided into three main categories: planetary winds, mesoscale winds, and local winds.

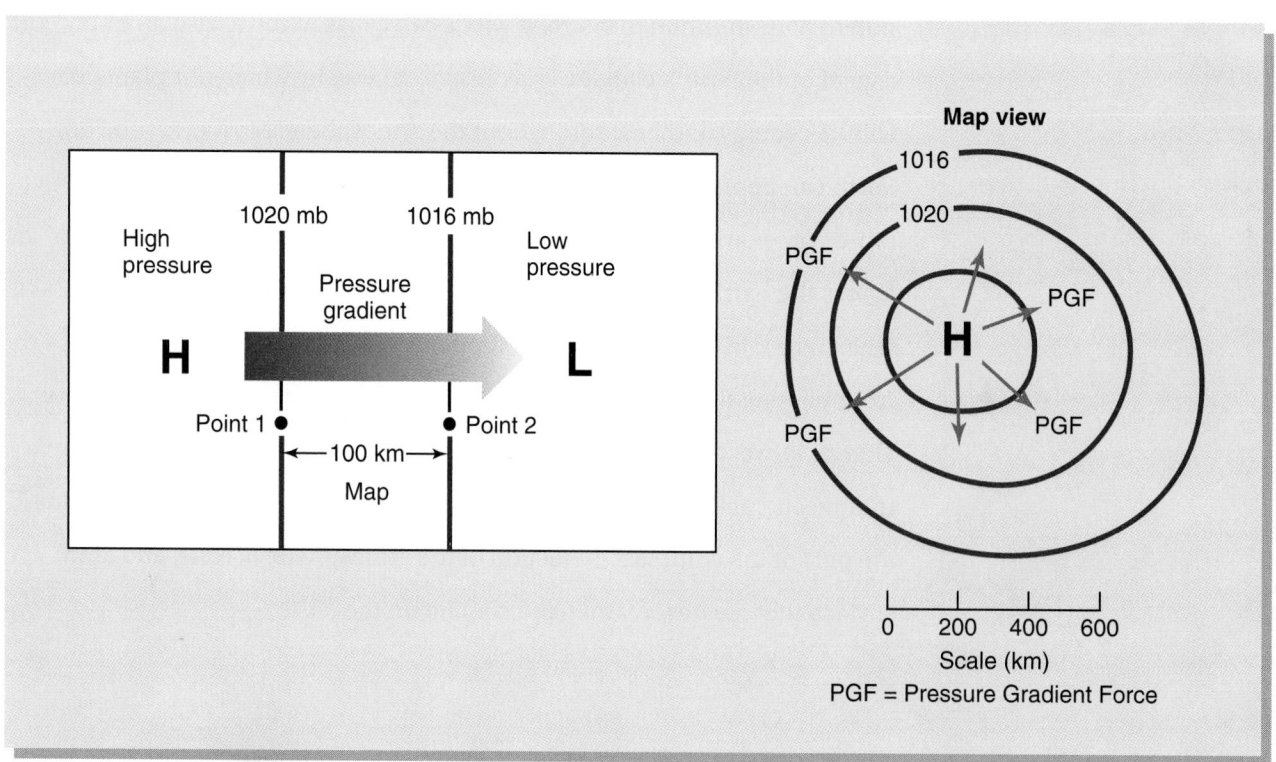

FIGURE 18–1   The formation of winds by the flow of air from areas of high pressure toward areas of low pressure over a specific distance on the Earth, also called the pressure gradient.

PLANETARY WINDS

Planetary winds are the large-scale wind patterns that flow across the Earth as a result of the unequal distribution of insolation received by the Earth's surface. Common planetary winds, also called prevailing winds, include the trade winds, which blow from the northeast between 30 degrees north latitude and the equator (Figure 18–2). The westerlies are also prevailing planetary winds; they blow from the southwest across the Earth's surface between 30 degrees and 60 degrees north latitude. Many explorers who sailed the ocean in ships took advantage of these prevailing winds, which steered them to their destinations.

Planetary winds are caused by large pressure differences that occur near the Earth's surface as a result of the unequal distribution of heat on Earth. At the equator, the Sun strikes the Earth at nearly a 90-degree angle all throughout the year, which causes rapid heating of the surface near the tropics. This results in the formation of warm air at the surface, which begins to rise in the atmosphere as a result of its lower density. The area of warm, rising air is also known as an area of convergence because air molecules are converging, or coming together, at the surface to replace the air that is rising into the atmosphere. This warm, rising air causes areas of low pressure to form near the equator. As this air continues to rise into the atmosphere, it begins to cool as it

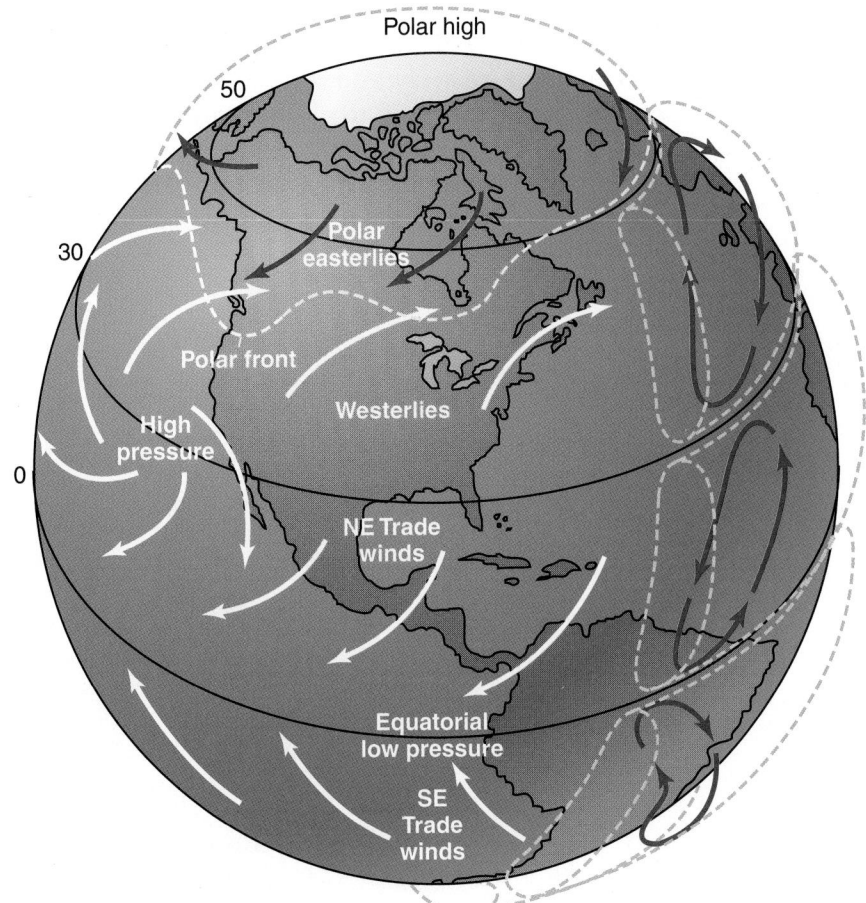

FIGURE 18–2 Planetary winds on the Earth's surface, also known as prevailing winds.

expands. The cooling air then becomes denser and begins to sink back toward the surface of the Earth. This cool, dense, sinking air returns to the surface at about 30 degrees north and south latitude. As the cooler air sinks, it begins to form areas of high pressure at the surface. These areas are called areas of divergence, because the cool, dense air is pushing downward and causing the air at the surface to spread apart, or diverge.

The result of the warm air rising and cooler air sinking is the formation of a large-scale atmospheric convection cell, also called a **Hadley cell**, after the English meteorologist who first theorized the process. Because the Hadley cell results in low pressure at the equator and high pressure at 30 degrees north and south of the equator, large-scale winds develop that blow from the areas of high pressure to the areas of low pressure (Figure 18–3). These are planetary winds. The low-pressure area near the equator is also called the intertropical convergence zone (ITCZ), and the areas of high pressure that form near 30 degrees north and south of the equator are known as the subtropical highs. Farther north and south of these pressure areas, at approximately 60 degrees north and south latitude, another low pressure system forms, called the subpolar lows. The cooler air located at the poles forms areas of high pressure, known as the polar highs. This causes air to flow from the polar highs to the subpolar lows, creating planetary winds between the higher latitudes.

If you were to add all the major pressure centers to a map of the Earth and draw the direction of air flow from areas of high pressure to areas of low pressure, you would find that the planetary winds blow directly from the north or from the south. This, however, does not explain the occurrence of the easterly and westerly prevailing planetary winds that actually occur on the Earth. The prevailing winds do not blow directly from the north or from the south because of the Earth's rotation. The Earth is spinning on its axis at a speed of approximately 1,000 miles per hour (1,609 kilometers per hour) near the equator,

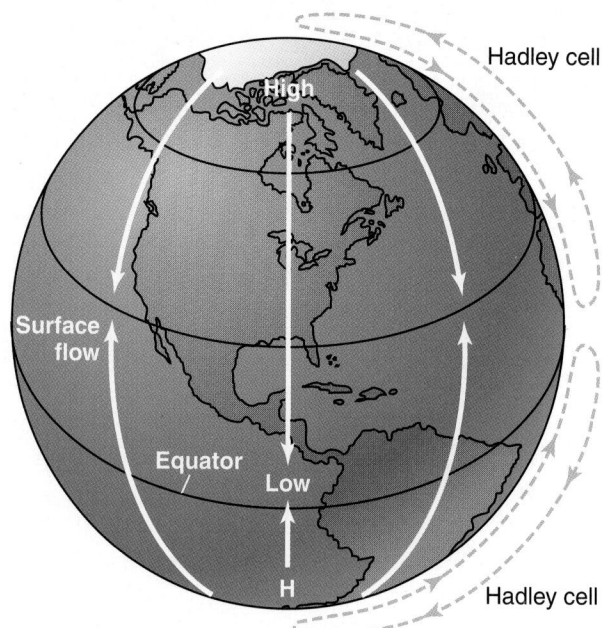

FIGURE 18–3 The formation of large-scale convection currents, called Hadley cells, creates distinct areas of low and high pressure at the Earth's surface. This results in the formation of planetary winds.

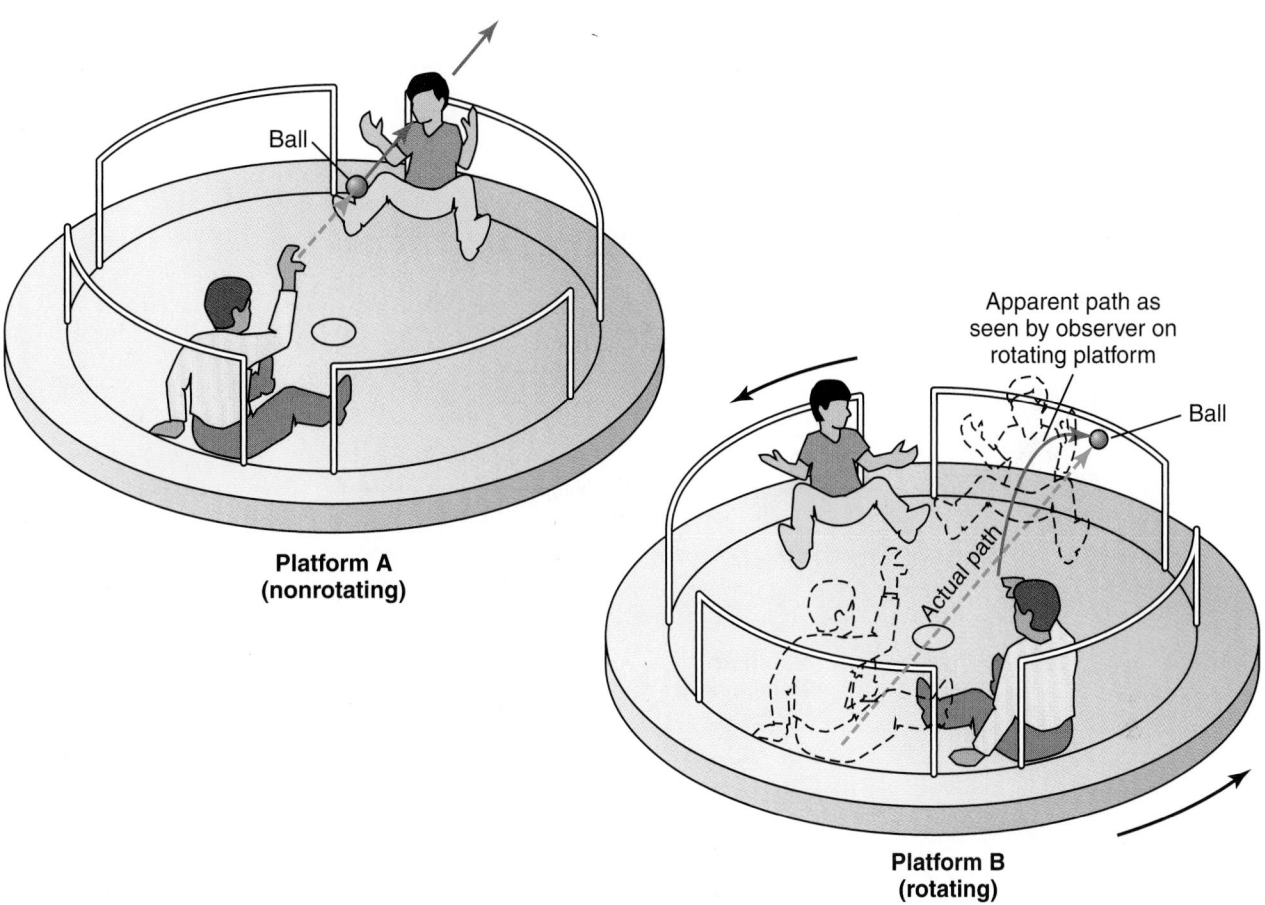

FIGURE 18–4 An example of what causes the Coriolis effect can be seen by two children playing catch on a merry-go-round. As the ball is thrown from the center, it appears to curve to the right of motion as the child on the outside moves away from it.

which causes winds on the Earth's surface to experience the **Coriolis effect**. The Coriolis effect causes free-floating objects on the Earth, such as air molecules, water, or things in the atmosphere, to move to the right or left as they travel on the Earth. This is actually caused by the movement of the Earth underneath the free-floating objects. The Coriolis effect can be illustrated by two children playing on a merry-go-round (Figure 18–4). Picture one child standing outside the merry-go-round and the other child standing at its center. If the child at the center of the merry-go-round tried to throw a ball straight toward the child spinning around on the outside, the ball would never reach the friend, because she would have moved away before it gets to her. If you observed this from above the merry-go-round looking down, it would appear that the ball was being deflected to the right or left, depending on which way the merry-go-round was spinning as it was thrown from the center.

This is exactly what causes the Coriolis effect on the Earth. Because the Earth is spinning on its axis, its surface moves under objects in the atmosphere, which causes them to be deflected to the right or left of travel. The first evidence of the Coriolis effect was noticed by French artillery officers when they were practicing firing their cannons at targets located long distances away. No matter how well they aimed their cannons, the artillery shells always landed to the right of the target, even when they adjusted for the wind. After careful investigation, the effect was finally explained by French physicist Gustave-Gaspard Coriolis in

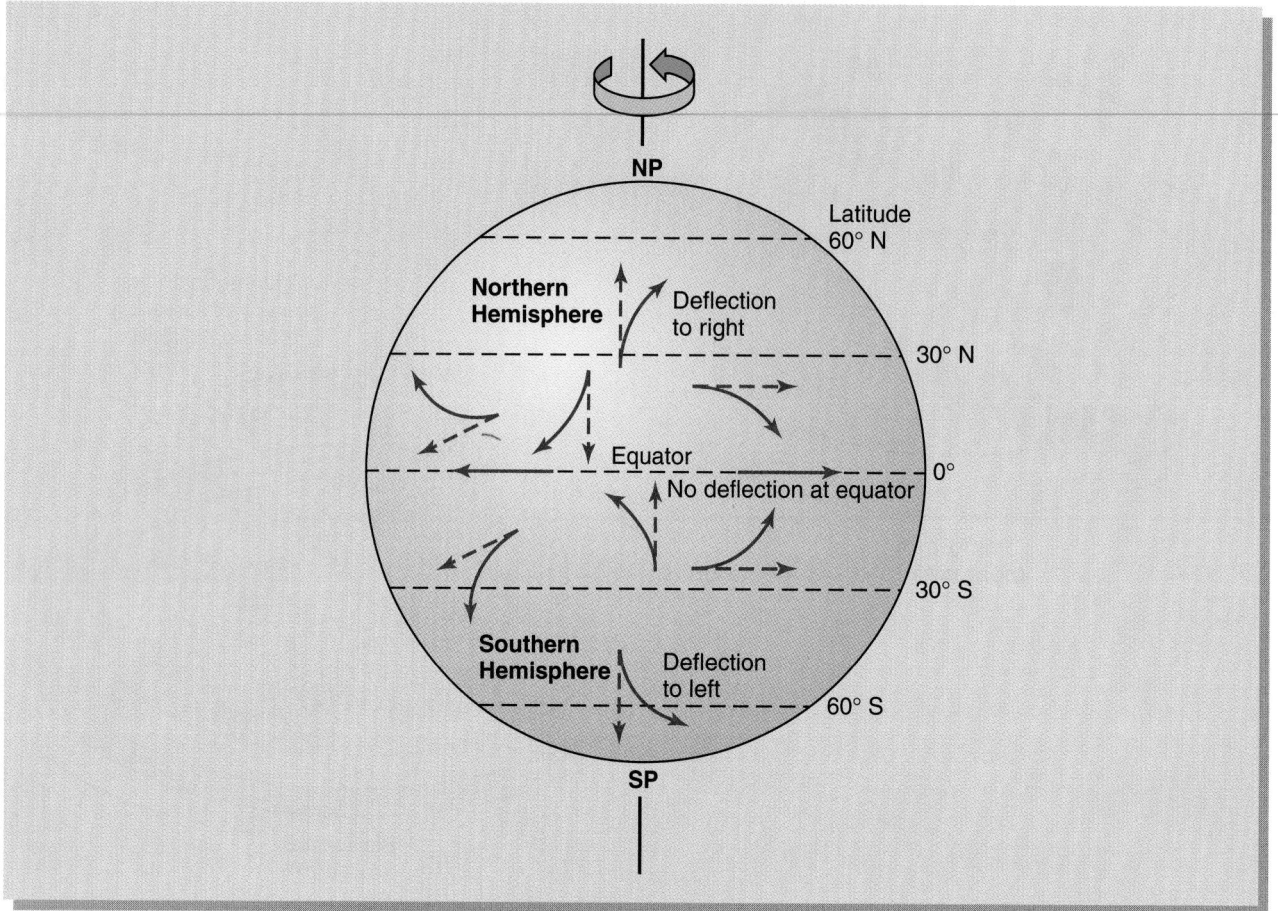

FIGURE 18–5 The Coriolis effect causes winds to be deflected to the right of travel in the Northern Hemisphere and to the left of travel in the Southern Hemisphere as a result of the Earth's rotation.

1835: The Earth was actually rotating underneath the long-range artillery shells, causing them to miss their target every time. The Coriolis effect also affects wind on the Earth and results in the path of the wind being deflected to the right of travel in the Northern Hemisphere and to the left of travel in the Southern Hemisphere (Figure 18–5). If you then adjust your map of planetary winds by curving them to the right of travel in the Northern Hemisphere and to the left of travel in the Southern Hemisphere, you can see the correct direction of the Earth's prevailing winds.

PRESSURE SYSTEMS

A pressure system is a mass of air with a well-defined **pressure center**. A pressure center is an area of relatively low pressure or high pressure within an air mass. Air masses that possess cold, dry, dense air tend to contain a high atmospheric pressure center. Because wind moves from areas of high atmospheric pressure to areas of low atmospheric pressure, pressure centers are also associated with specific wind patterns. Wind associated with a high-pressure system travels outward from the high-pressure center in a clockwise pattern in the Northern Hemisphere (Figure 18–6). This is also known as an anticyclone. The reason that the wind spirals outward in a clockwise direction around a high-pressure center has to do with the Coriolis effect that is caused by

Earth System Scientists

George Hadley

George Hadley, born in England in 1685, was a meteorologist who took the ideas of Edmund Halley and applied them to his theory of atmospheric circulation. In 1735 Hadley proposed that the trade winds were formed when hot, rising air near the equator moved north and south and eventually cooled and sank back toward the Earth's surface. His theory explained how areas of high and low atmospheric pressure formed at the surface, leading to the formation of planetary winds. Hadley also theorized that the rotation of the Earth on its axis caused these planetary winds to be deflected to the right of travel in the Northern Hemisphere and to the left of travel in the Southern Hemisphere. These large-scale convection cells that Hadley discovered are known as Hadley cells.

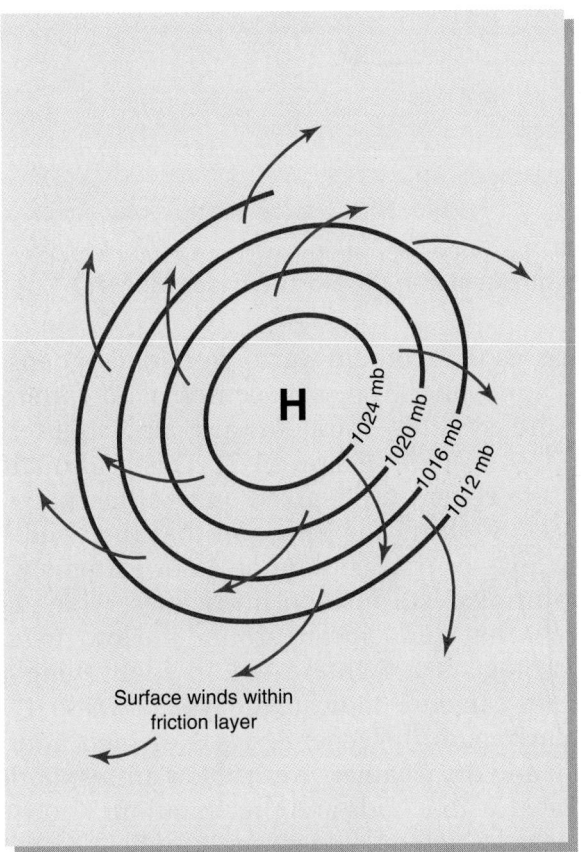

FIGURE 18-6 Winds spiral outward in a clockwise direction around a high-pressure center in the Northern Hemisphere.

the Earth's rotation. Recall that winds are deflected to the right of travel in the Northern Hemisphere. The air that is moving outward from the high-pressure center is deflected to the right, causing a clockwise rotation. High-pressure centers are noted on a weather map by a blue capital *H* and can indicate the direction that the wind is blowing.

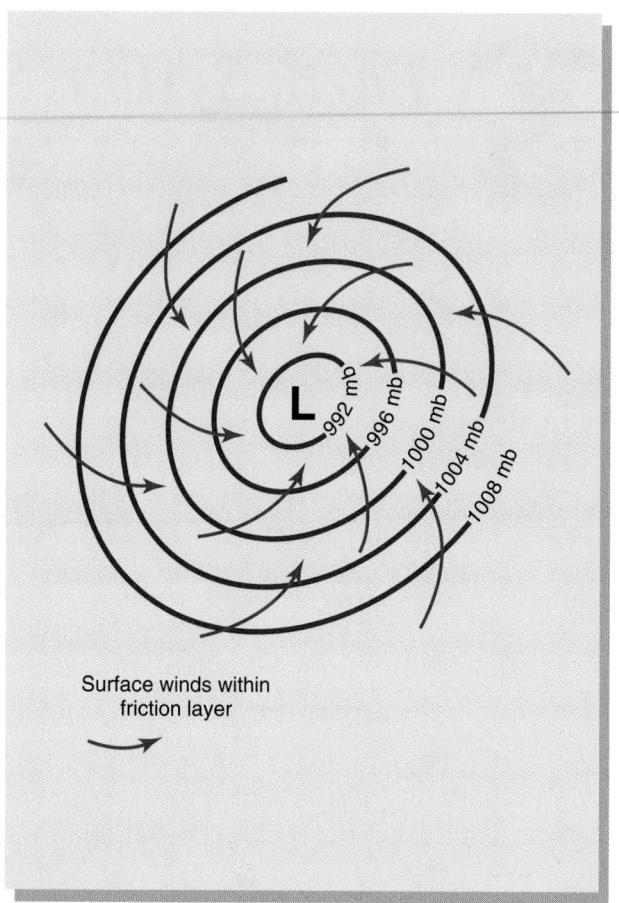

Surface winds within
friction layer

FIGURE 18-7 Winds spiral inward in a counterclockwise direction around a low-pressure center in the Northern Hemisphere.

Air masses that contain warm, humid, less dense air tend to contain a low atmospheric pressure center. Wind patterns associated with low-pressure systems spiral inward and counterclockwise in the Northern Hemisphere (Figure 18–7). This is also known as a cyclone. Low-pressure centers are marked on weather maps by a red capital *L* and can also indicate the direction that the wind is moving. Warm, humid air masses that contain areas of extremely low pressure can form into tropical storms and hurricanes, which can generate high wind speeds that spiral inward around the low-pressure center.

Meteorologists are interested in identifying pressure centers because they can often indicate the type of weather that might form in a particular region. In general, areas of high atmospheric pressure bring clear and dry weather. Areas of low atmospheric pressure tend to be associated with clouds and precipitation. Knowing how air moves around areas of high or low pressure can help meteorologists forecast the wind direction.

MESOSCALE WINDS

Mesoscale winds, also known as regional winds, develop as a result of smaller-scale interactions of changing pressure near the Earth's surface. A good example of the formation of mesoscale winds is the land and sea breeze. On a hot day, insolation received by the land surface

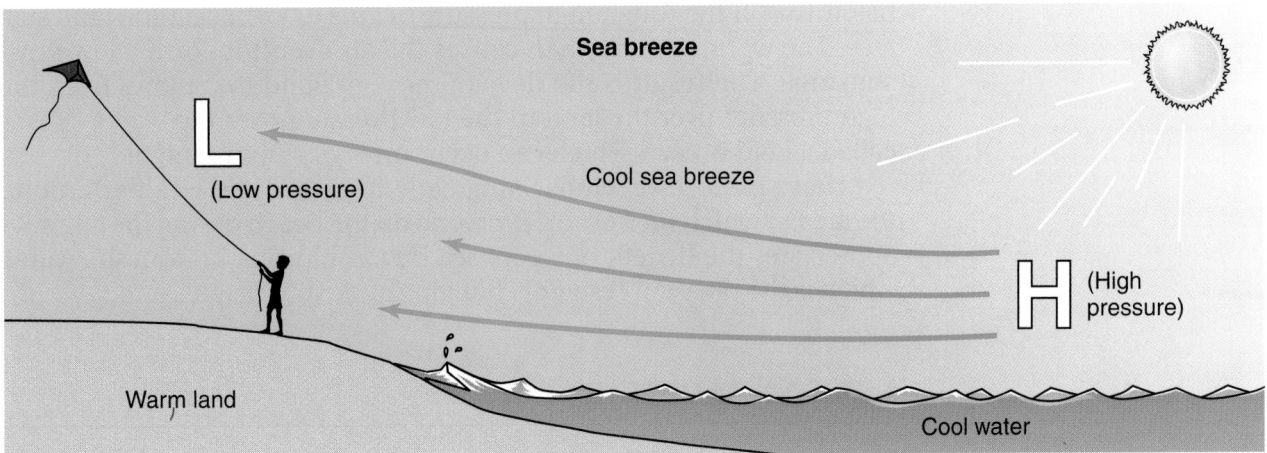

FIGURE 18–8 A sea breeze develops as a result of low pressure forming over the rapidly heating land surface during the day and high pressure forming over the cooler water.

located next to a large body of water heats rapidly. This causes hot air to form near the surface; the hot air begins to rise as it becomes less dense. The rising hot air creates an area of low barometric pressure near the surface, as air molecules are heated and move upward into the atmosphere. Next to land, cooler air is forming over the water, which is not heating as rapidly as the land surface. This is a result of the water's high heat capacity. This cooler, denser air begins to form an area of high pressure over the water. The result of the formation of high pressure over the cool water and low pressure over the warm land is wind that travels from the high pressure toward low pressure. This is also called a sea breeze, which blows cool air toward the coast on a hot day. The formation of a sea breeze can occur on a hot, sunny day wherever land lies next to a large body of water (Figure 18–8).

Eventually, as the sun goes down, the land surface begins to cool quickly and cool air begins to form over the land surface (Figure 18–9). The temperature of the water stays relatively the same when the sun is down and results in warmer air forming over its surface as compared with the land. After the temperature of the land cools to a temperature

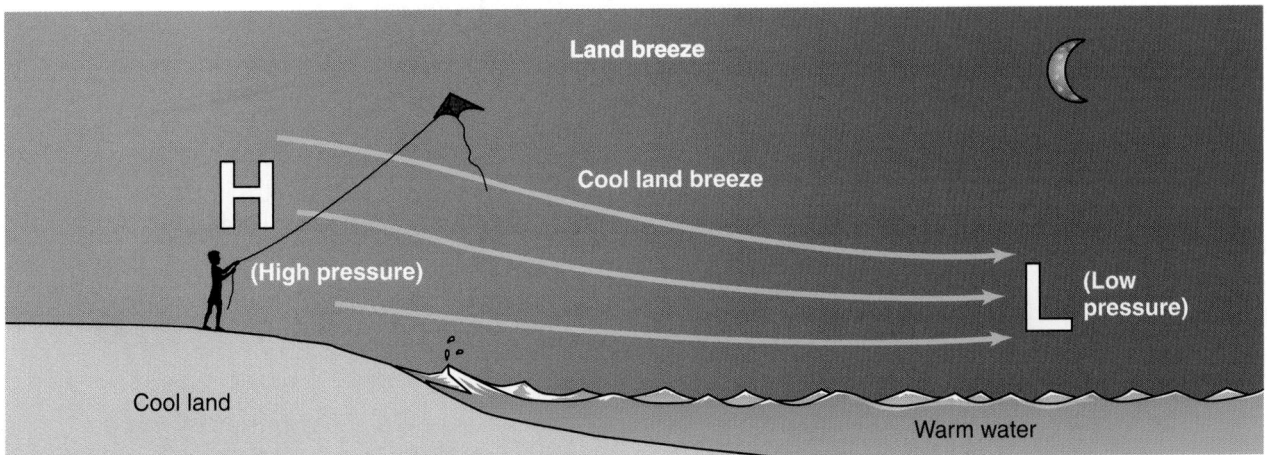

FIGURE 18–9 A land breeze develops as a result of high pressure forming over the cooler land surface at night and low pressure forming over the warmer water.

below that of the water, high pressure begins to form over the land surface. The warmer water then causes the air over it to form a low pressure area. The result is the development of wind that blows from the high pressure over the land to the low pressure over the water. This is called a land breeze, which can occur on cool summer nights.

These mesoscale winds can greatly influence the weather around the area in which they occur. Everyone on the beach during the summer appreciates the benefit of a cool sea breeze blowing in from the water, which is the pleasant result of changing atmospheric pressure.

LOCAL WINDS

Local winds are created by local geographic features. When air rides up and over a mountain range and picks up colder temperatures, it then descends into a warmer valley, creating a cool mountain breeze. The opposite effect can occur when warmer air developing in a low valley rises up the slopes of the surrounding cooler mountains, creating a warm valley breeze. Similar effects can also occur when cold air moving over a high plain spills down into adjacent lower regions, creating a cold katabatic wind. *Katabatic* means "to fall." Local katabatic winds generated in Greenland can rush down off the ice fields at speeds of more than 100 miles per hour (161 kilometers per hour).

CAREER CONNECTIONS
Operational Meteorologist

Operational meteorologists gather information about the pressure, wind direction and speed, temperature, and humidity of specific points on the Earth. They then use this information to make short-term and long-term forecasts about regional weather. Operational meteorologists apply the principles of atmospheric science to predict weather conditions. By using sophisticated computer models, radar, satellite images, and ground-based observations, these scientists provide detailed predictions about the state of the atmosphere in a particular place on Earth. Many aspects of daily life depend on the work of operational meteorologists, especially in the transportation industry. Forecasting potentially dangerous events such as tornadoes, hurricanes, blizzards, and flooding helps to prevent the loss of life and property and is one of the most important aspects of this type of career. Operational meteorologists require a college degree and can find work in the armed forces, transportation industry, and academic research or in government agencies such as the National Weather Service.

Another type of local wind is the famous Santa Ana winds of California. This wind forms over the hot desert and picks up speed as it moves through dry canyons and valleys. Eventually it reaches the populated areas of Los Angeles as a hot, harsh, dry wind. Local topography or buildings can also create local winds. Chicago is called the Windy City because cold winds blowing across the great lakes slam into the buildings of the city and swiftly move through the streets, creating strong cold wind gusts. Whirlwinds or dust devils, another example of a local wind, are spiraling winds that form in certain areas as moving air circles around rapidly, bringing with it dust and debris. These local wind gusts usually dissipate as quickly as they form. The famous nor'easters that blow in from the Atlantic Ocean along the northeastern coast of the United States are composed of high winds that blow in from the North Atlantic. These large-scale local winds can cause damaging winter storms in New England.

THE JET STREAM

Winds on Earth do not only occur near the surface; some winds form high up in the atmosphere at the level of the tropopause. Areas high in the tropopause, where cool air begins to descend back toward the surface, form belts of high winds called the **jet stream** (Figure 18–10). Jet streams are bands of high-speed winds located high in the atmosphere. The rapid decline in pressure associated with the descending air of a Hadley cell can generate winds of more than 100 miles per hour (161 km/hr.). Jet streams are located 6 to 9 mi (9 and 14 km) up in the atmosphere over the subtropical and polar highs. These fast-moving streams of air are approximately 200 mi (322 km) wide and less than a

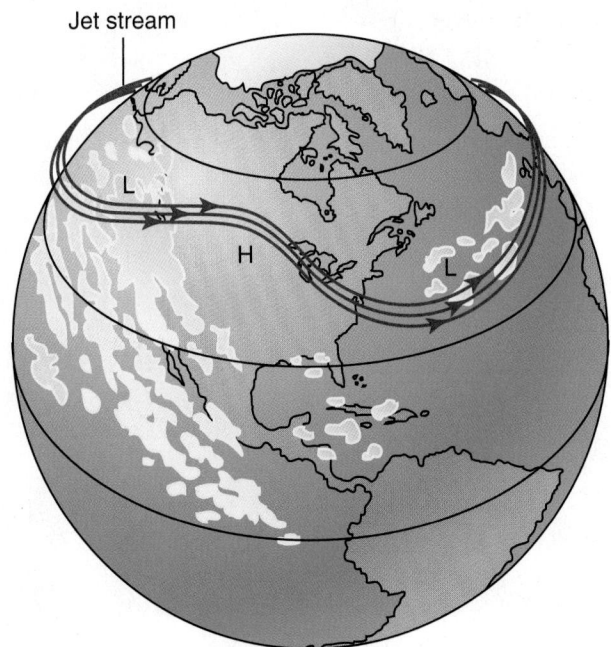

FIGURE 18–10   Rapidly moving winds high in the tropopause form the polar front jet stream.

mile thick. Over the United States the polar jet stream travels from west to east and helps move air masses and their associated weather in a westward to eastward direction. The subtropical jet stream, which is located over the lower latitudes, plays an important role in moving warm tropical air, and many hurricanes, along the east coast of the United States.

WIND MEASUREMENT

The movement of wind across the Earth's surface is measured in both its direction and speed. The wind direction is recorded in degrees from which direction the wind is blowing. Wind blowing directly from the north is recorded as 0 degrees, and wind blowing directly from the south has a direction of 180 degrees. The direction of the wind is recorded by a wind vane. This instrument consists of a long metal arrow that swings freely on a vertical pole. The wind vane is then calibrated to the directions of the compass (Figure 18–11). Another way to measure wind direction is by using a wind sock, a cloth tube through which the wind blows and points in the direction the wind is blowing.

FIGURE 18–11   A weather vane is one of the oldest weather instruments; it is used to record wind direction. (*Courtesy of PhotoDisc.*)

TABLE 18-1 The Beaufort wind scale measures wind by its effects on the environment

Beaufort Number	Description	Wind Speed			Observations
		ml/hr	knots	km/hr	
0	Calm	0–1	0–1	0–2	Smoke rises vertically
1	Light air	1–3	1–3	2–6	Direction of wind shown by drifting smoke, but not by wind vanes
2	Slight breeze	4–7	4–6	7–11	Wind felt on face; leaves rustle; wind vanes moved by wind; flags stir
3	Gentle breeze	8–12	7–10	12–19	Leaves and small twigs move; wind will extend light flag
4	Moderate breeze	13–18	11–16	20–29	Wind raises dust and loose paper; small branches move; flags flap
5	Fresh breeze	19–24	17–21	30–39	Small trees with leaves begin to sway; flags ripple
6	Strong breeze	25–31	22–27	40–50	Large tree branches in motion; whistling heard in power lines; umbrellas used with difficulty
7	High wind	32–38	28–33	51–61	Whole trees in motion; inconvenience felt walking against wind; flags extend
8	Gale	39–46	34–40	62–74	Wind breaks twigs off trees; walking is difficult
9	Strong gale	47–54	41–47	75–87	Slight structural damage occurs (signs and antennas blown down)
10	Whole gale	55–63	48–55	88–101	Trees uprooted; considerable damage occurs
11	Storm	64–74	56–64	102–119	Winds produce widespread damage
12	Hurricane	≥75	≥65	≥120	Winds produce extensive damage

The velocity of the wind is a measure of how fast the air is moving across the Earth's surface. Wind speed is usually measured in knots. One knot is equivalent to 1.15 miles per hour (1.85 kilometers per hour). Wind velocity, or the speed of the wind, is measured by an instrument called an anemometer, which is composed of three metal cups that are allowed to swing freely around a vertical pole. The speed with which the cups spin around the pole, caused by the force of the wind, is calibrated to record the wind speed. An aerovane is a modern device that uses a propeller mounted on a weather vane to record both the wind speed and direction.

The relative wind speed can also be recorded by using the Beaufort scale of wind force (Table 18–1). This uses common observations on a scale from 0 to 12 to estimate the speed of the wind. For example, a Beaufort wind scale score of 2 is considered a light breeze that can be felt on your face and may rustle leaves on the ground. In contrast, a Beaufort wind scale score of 9 is a strong gale force wind that can produce slight structural damage and cause waves to crest and roll over.

@ WEB Links

FOR MORE INFORMATION GO TO THIS WEB LINK:

<http://ww2010.atmos .uiuc.edu/(Gh)/guides /mtr/fw/home.rxml>

SECTION REVIEW

1. What is the definition of *wind*?
2. Describe the process that forms planetary scale winds.
3. Describe the process that causes sea breezes to form.
4. What are three examples of local winds?
5. What are jet streams, and where are they located?
6. Who was George Hadley?

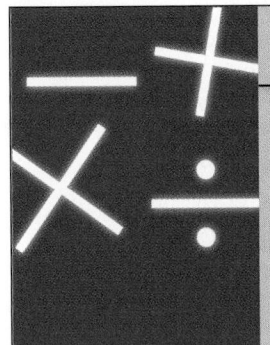

earth math

1) Using the following information, determine the pressure gradient that helps form the planetary winds: the pressure at the equator (ITCZ) is 1008 millibars, and the pressure at 30 degrees north latitude (subtropical high) is 1020 millibars. The distance between the two pressure zones is approximately 3000 mi. Remember: Gradient = change in value/change in distance.

18.2 Air Masses and Fronts

AIR MASS FORMATION

An **air mass** is a large body of moving air in the troposphere that has similar characteristics of temperature, pressure, and moisture. Air masses derive their characteristics from source regions, which are geographical areas that give an air mass its unique qualities. Generally, if an air mass forms in an area located in the higher latitudes, it has a cooler air temperature. Conversely, air masses that form near the equator possess warmer temperatures. The atmospheric moisture of an air mass also is related to its source region. Air masses that form over the ocean have higher atmospheric moisture content and are considered moist. Air masses that form over the continents tend to be lower in atmospheric moisture content and are considered dry.

SOURCE REGIONS AND CLASSIFICATION OF AIR MASSES

The source region from which an air mass originates can reveal a lot about the weather it may create. Air masses are classified in five categories. Four of those categories are shown in Table 18–2. The first is a continental polar air mass, which develops over a land mass near the poles. This particular air mass contains cool, dry air. Continental polar air masses that affect the United States often originate over northern

TABLE 18–2 Classification of air masses and their unique characteristics

Source Region	Polar (P)	Tropical (T)
Land continental (c)	cP cold, dry, stable	cT hot, dry, stable air aloft; unstable surface air
Water maritime (m)	mP cool, moist, unstable	mT warm, moist; usually unstable

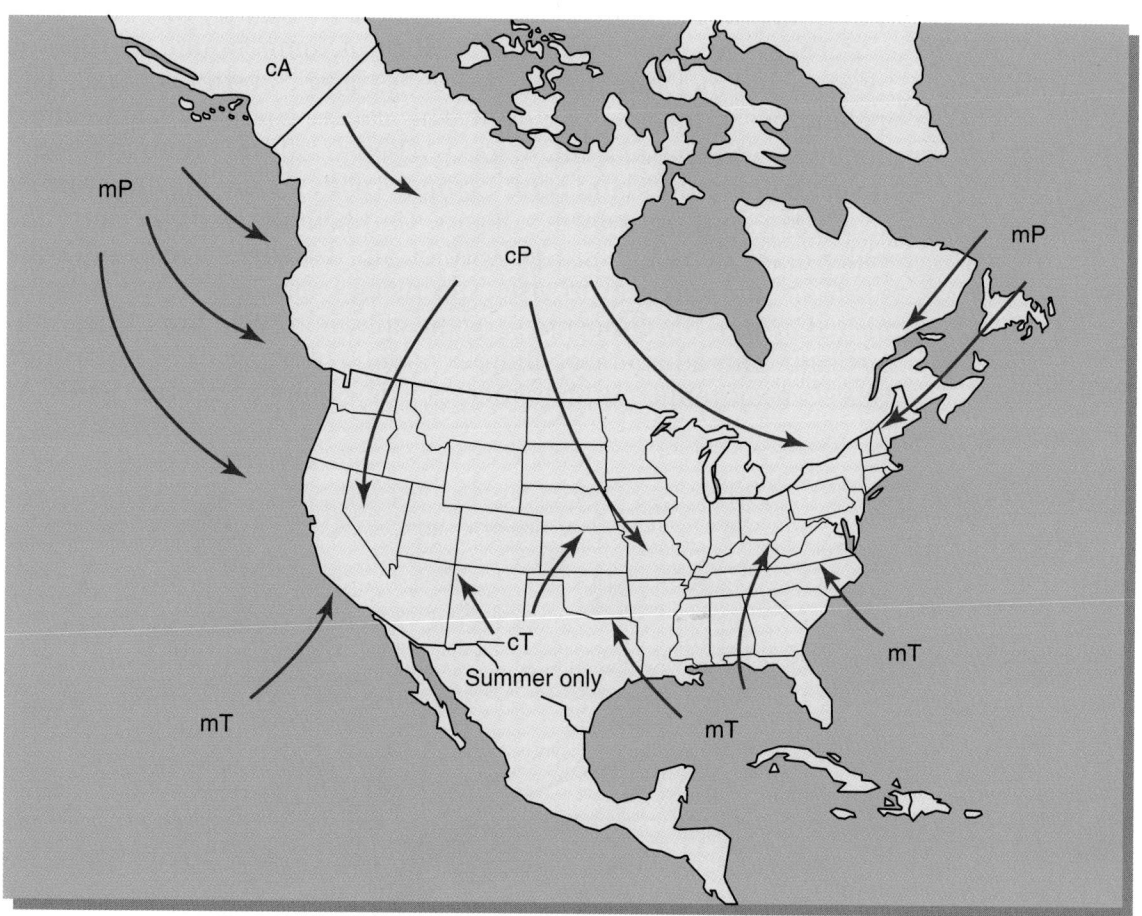

FIGURE 18–12 Air mass source regions that affect North America, and their general paths of movement.

Canada (Figure 18–12). A maritime polar air mass originates near the poles over the ocean. This type of air mass contains cool, moist air and is often associated with cold winter rains. Source areas for maritime polar air masses include the North Atlantic and North Pacific oceans. Continental tropical air masses develop over a land mass near the equator and contain warm, dry air; those that affect North America form over Mexico and Texas. Maritime tropical air masses form over the ocean near the equator and contain warm, humid air; they are often associated with the development of hurricanes. Source regions for these air masses include the South Atlantic Ocean and the Gulf of

Mexico. The arctic air mass, which contains extremely cold and dry air, forms north of 60 degrees north latitude on the ice fields of Siberia, Greenland, and the Arctic Ocean. Arctic air masses can bring extremely cold and dry weather to the United States during winter, known as the arctic express.

FRONTS

The Earth's surface is covered with many different types of air masses moving relative to one another. Not all air masses move at the same speed; some are moving faster than others. When one air mass comes into contact with another air mass, the area where they meet is known as a **front**. The different characteristics of temperature, barometric pressure, and moisture that each air mass have come into contact with one another in the area of a front. This causes characteristic weather, unique to each type of front, to form. When an advancing air mass with cooler temperatures comes into contact with a slow-moving warmer air mass, a **cold front** forms (Figure 18–13, Table 18–3). Because the colder air is denser than the warmer air, it wedges itself under the warm air and forces it to rise. The rising warm air, which is being pushed up into the atmosphere by the advancing cold front, cools adiabatically. This adiabatic cooling, or cooling of rising air by expansion, causes the air temperature to meet the dew point and form clouds. As

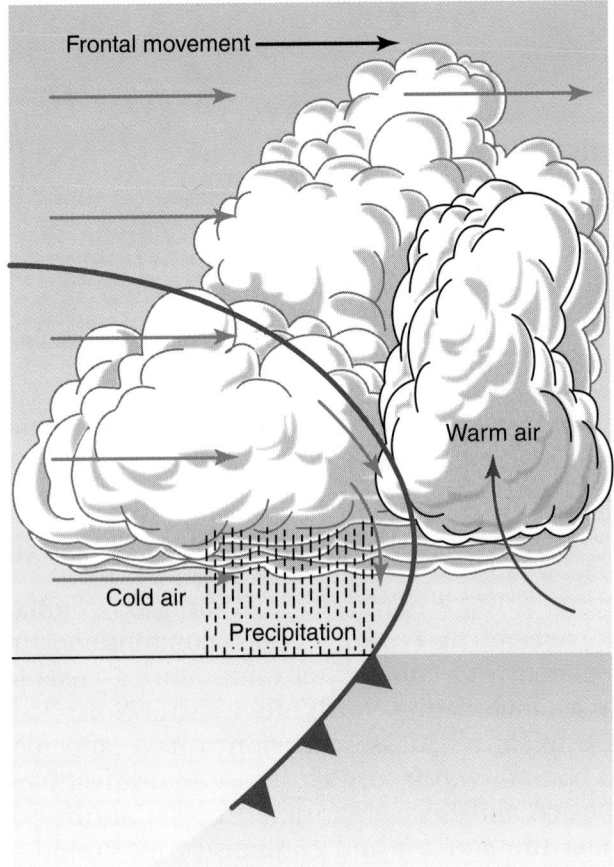

FIGURE 18–13 The unique cross section of a cold front.

TABLE 18–3 Characteristic weather conditions associated with a cold front

Weather Element	Before Passing	While Passing	After Passing
Winds	South-southwest	Gusty, shifting	West-northwest
Temperature	Warm	Sudden drop	Steadily dropping
Pressure	Falling steadily	Minimum, then sharp rise	Rising steadily
Clouds	Increasing Ci, Cs, then either Tcu or Cb	Tcu or Cb*	Often Cu
Precipitation	Short period of showers	Heavy showers of rain or snow, sometimes with hail, thunder, and lightning	Decreasing intensity of showers, then clearing
Visibility	Fair to poor in haze	Poor, followed by improving	Good except in showers
Dew point	High; remains steady	Sharp drop	Lowering

*Tcu stands for towering cumulus, such as cumulus congestus; Cb stands for cumulonimbus; Ci stands for cirrus; Cs stands for cirrostratus; and Cu stands for cumulus.

a result of the rapid rising air, caused by the wedging action of cold air, cumulonimbus clouds quickly form, creating heavy precipitation and thunderstorms. Therefore cold fronts are often associated with weather that forms cumulus clouds with strong vertical development, producing heavy rains for a short period.

Fast-moving cold fronts produce a band of intense thunderstorms called a squall line. Slower moving cold fronts cause the warm air ahead to rise slowly, which produces brief showers. A shift in the wind direction is also associated with the passage of a cold front. As the cold front passes, the wind direction shifts from the southwest and begins to blow from the northwest. A change in atmospheric pressure also occurs when a cold front moves through a region. The cooler, denser air has a higher atmospheric air pressure than the warm air it is replacing; therefore a rise in pressure often occurs after a cold front passes through a region. Cold fronts are represented on weather maps by a blue line with triangles pointing in the direction that the front is moving.

When a warm air mass comes into contact with a slower moving cold air mass, it is called a **warm front** (Figure 18–14). Warm air that makes up a warm front is less dense than the cooler air of a cold air mass, which causes the warm air to slowly override the cold air beneath it. This causes the formation of high clouds first, then mid-level clouds, and finally low clouds. The advancing warm front is preceded by a gradually thickening layer of clouds that produce light precipitation for extended periods. This type of light rain is good for agriculture because it allows the precipitation to infiltrate the soil. If a warm front is producing precipitation in the form of snow, it can lead to heavy accumulations. As the warm air overrides the cold air around a warm front, fog may also form along the thin boundary that separates the warm air from the cold air just above the Earth's surface. This is called a prefrontal fog.

The shift in wind that is associated with the passage of a warm front changes from the southeast to the southwest (Table 18–4). The less dense warm air that is replacing the cooler, denser air also brings a

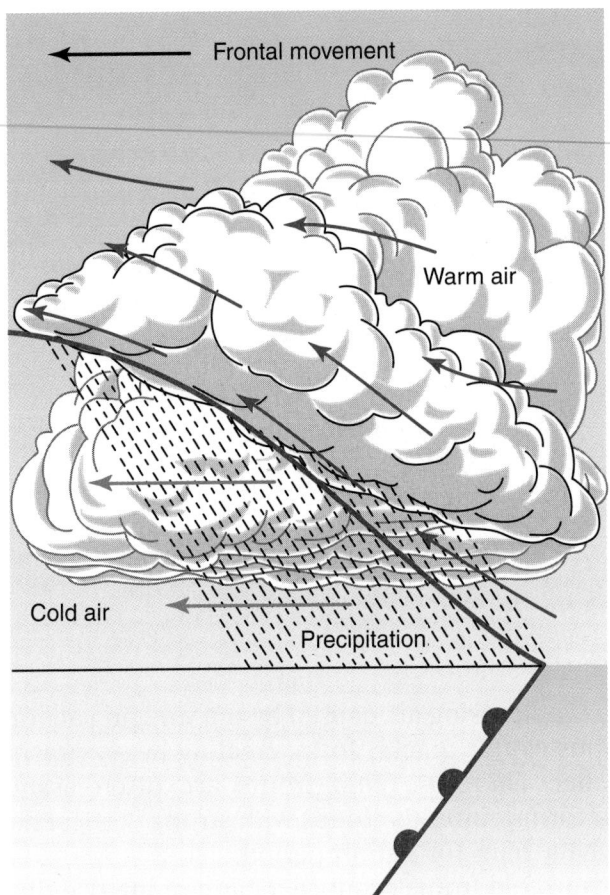

Frontal movement

Warm air

Cold air

Precipitation

FIGURE 18–14 The unique cross section of a warm front.

TABLE 18–4 Characteristic weather conditions associated with a warm front

Weather Element	Before Passing	While Passing	After Passing
Winds	South-southeast	Variable	South-southwest
Temperature	Cool, cold, slow warming	Steady rise	Warmer, then steady
Pressure	Usually falling	Leveling off	Slight rise, followed by fall
Clouds	In this order: Ci, Cs, As, Ns, St, and fog; occasionally Cb in summer	Stratus-type	Clearing with scattered Sc; occasionally Cb in summer
Precipitation	Light-to-moderate rain, snow, sleet, or drizzle	Drizzle or none	Usually none; sometimes light rain or showers
Visibility	Poor	Poor, but improving	Fair in haze
Dew point	Steady rise	Steady	Rise, then steady

Ci, cirrus; *Cs*, cirrostratus; *As*, altostratus; *Ns*, nimbostratus; *St*, Stratus; *Cb*, cumulonimbus.

change in barometric pressure. The pressure usually drops after a warm front passes through an area. Warm fronts are represented on weather maps by a red line with half circles pointing in the direction the front is traveling.

Another type of front that forms between two different air masses is an **occluded front** (Figure 18–15). An occluded front forms when a

Earth System Scientists

Svante Arrhenius

Svante Arrhenius was born in Sweden in 1869. Most of his life's work was devoted to the study of chemistry. His research involved the study of the electrical conductivity of solutions. He received the Nobel Prize for chemistry in 1903 as a result of this pursuit. Arrhenius's contribution to atmospheric science came from what he called a hobby. In 1895 he presented a scientific paper titled "On the Influence of Carbonic Acid in the Air Upon the Temperature on the Ground." This groundbreaking hypothesis revealed the effects of carbon dioxide gas and water vapor on the surface temperature of the Earth. In his paper, Arrhenius unlocked the mechanisms of the greenhouse effect. He also hypothesized that changes in the composition of carbon dioxide in the atmosphere might have led to ice ages in the past.

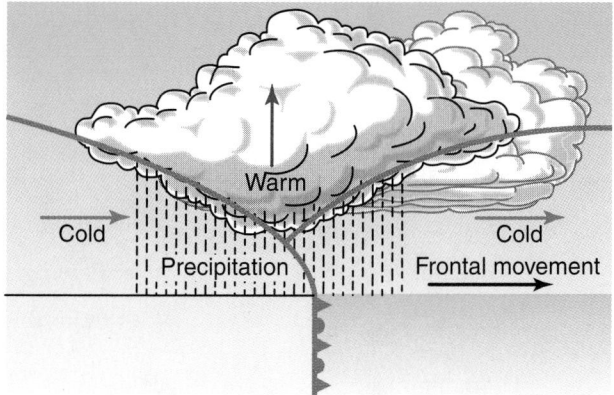

FIGURE 18–15 The unique cross section of an occluded front.

rapidly moving cold front moves under a slow-moving warm front and causes it to uplift. The rapid movement of the cold air completely raises the entire warm air mass off the surface.

This results in widespread precipitation, which can be intense or sustained, depending on the lifting action of the cold air (Table 18–5). Wind shifts associated with the passage of an occluded front are usually from the southeast to the northwest, which is almost a 180-degree shift in winds. An occluded front is represented by a purple line with both triangles and half circles pointing in the direction of travel of the front.

Not all air masses run into one another to form cold, warm, or occluded fronts; sometimes air masses slide past one another. The type of front that forms when cold air and warm air sit next to each other is called a **stationary front** (Figure 18–16). This type of front usually creates clear weather with no appreciable cloud development. This is because the cold air stays on one side of the front and the warm air stays on the other, with no interactions occurring. Eventually one of the air masses begins to overtake the other, and the stationary front becomes either a cold front or a warm front. Stationary fronts are

CAREER CONNECTIONS
Weather Observer

A weather observer is a trained individual who makes hourly observations about the present state of the atmosphere. Surface weather observations form the base for all types of meteorology, by providing current atmospheric conditions at many points around the world. These technicians record hourly temperature, humidity, cloud cover, precipitation, winds, pressure, and visibility at their weather stations. These data are then collected and used to create synoptic weather maps. These maps are then analyzed, and weather forecasts are made. Weather observers work in weather stations located in airports and colleges, on board ships, and in other special locations around the globe. Many weather observers gain their training while serving in the military, or they can gain experience in college by majoring in meteorology.

TABLE 18–5 Characteristic weather conditions associated with an occluded front

Weather Element	Before Passing	While Passing	After Passing
Winds	Southeast-south	Variable	West to northwest
Temperature			
Cold type	Cold, cool	Dropping	Colder
Warm type	Cold	Rising	Milder
Pressure	Usually falling	Low point	Usually rising
Clouds	In this order: Ci, Cs, As, Ns	Ns, sometimes Tcu and Cb	Ns, As, or scattered Cu
Precipitation	Light, moderate, or heavy precipitation	Light, moderate, or heavy continuous precipitation or showers	Light-to-moderate precipitation followed by general clearing
Visibility	Poor in precipitation	Poor in precipitation	Improving
Dew point	Steady	Usually slight drop, especially if cold/occluded	Slight drop, although may rise a bit if warm/occluded

Ci, cirrus; *Cs*, cirrostratus; *As*, altostratus; *Ns*, nimbostratus; *Cb*, cumulonimbus.

represented on weather maps by a blue and red line with blue triangles pointing toward the cold air mass and red half circles pointed at the warm air mass.

Air masses usually move across the surface of the Earth with a relative velocity and direction. The speed and direction of air masses and their associated fronts can be tracked by meteorologists, helping them forecast the weather. In the United States, air masses and fronts generally move from west to east across the continent.

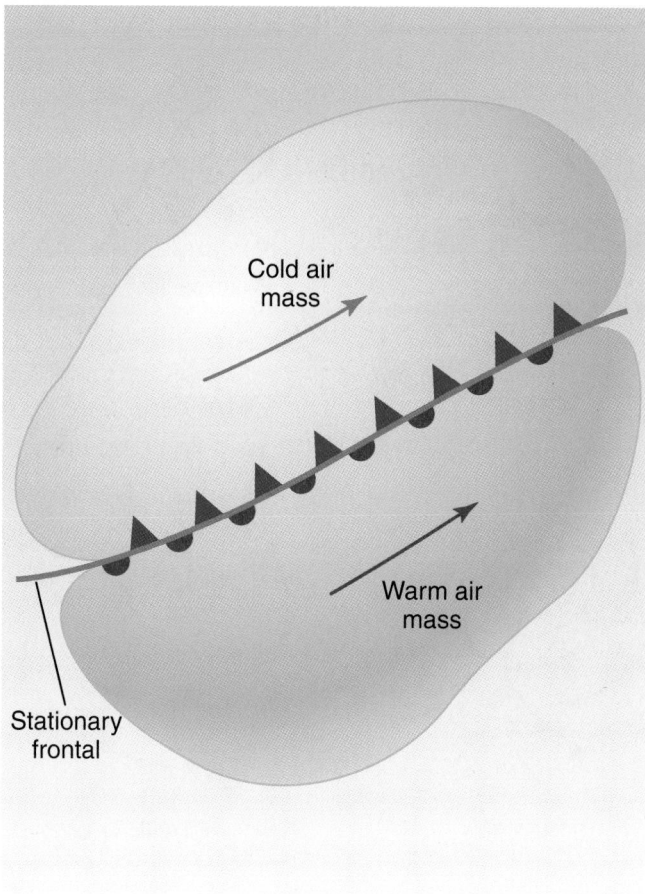

FIGURE 18-16 A stationary front forms when a cold air mass moves alongside a warm air mass.

MID-LATITUDE CYCLONES

The formation of fronts along the boundaries of air masses constantly undergoes change as the temperature, humidity, and pressure of the colliding air masses also change. The type of changes associated with interacting fronts help form a unique storm system called the mid-latitude cyclone. A mid-latitude cyclone forms in the Northern Hemisphere around a low-pressure system. A **cyclone** is a counterclockwise, inward rotation of air around a low-pressure center. Mid-latitude cyclones form when an advancing cold air mass moves up behind a slower moving warm air mass. Both frontal systems are centered around the spiraling low-pressure center. The clouds and precipitation associated with the two frontal boundaries cause a wide band of precipitation that precedes the fronts (Figure 18-17).

Eventually, as the low-pressure system intensifies, the precipitation begins to spiral inward toward the pressure center, forming a unique cloud formation called a comma cloud. The comma cloud gets its name from the shape of the clouds that result from the cold and warm fronts spiraling around the center of low pressure. As the air masses move across the land surface, the cold front begins to overtake the

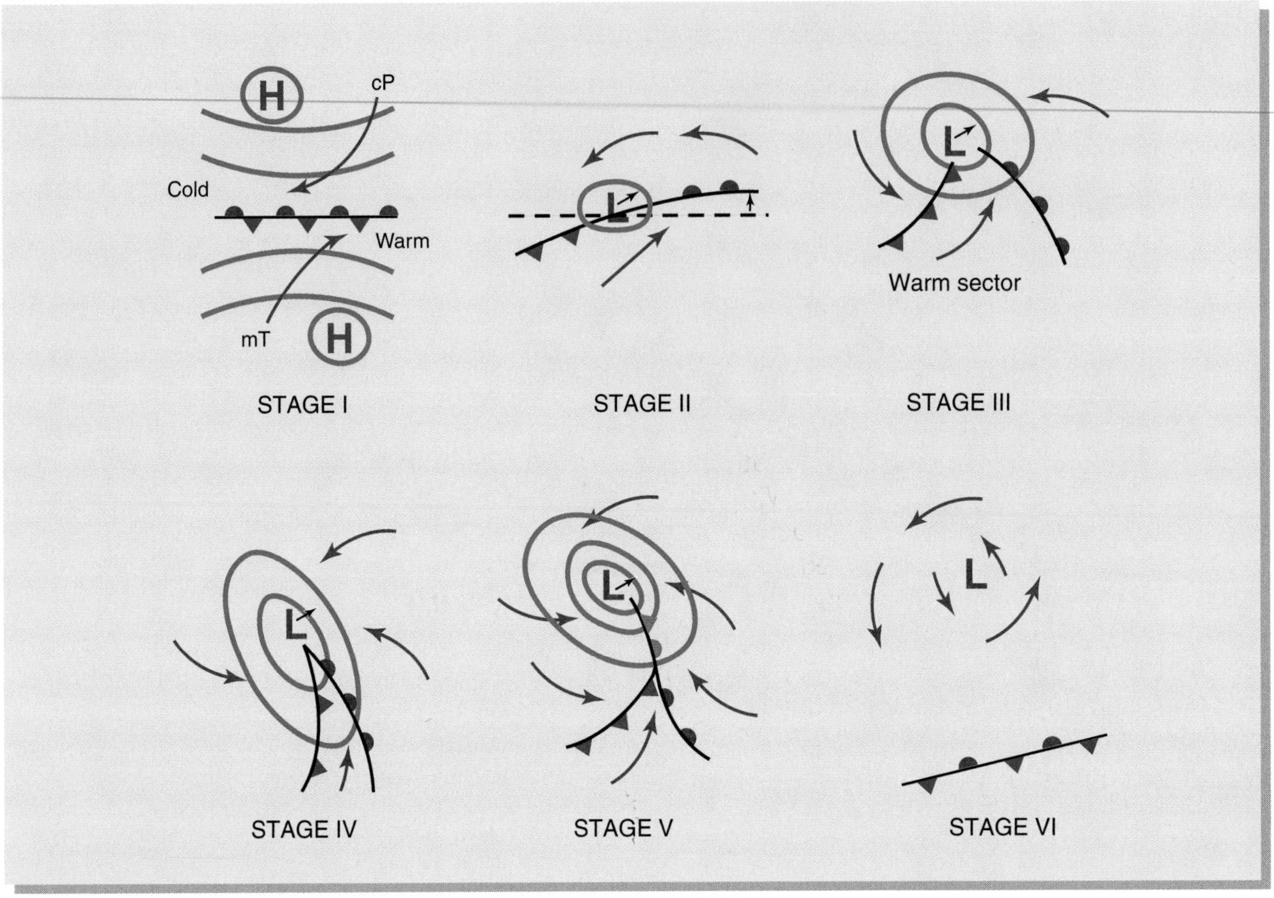

STAGE I

STAGE II

STAGE III

Warm sector

STAGE IV

STAGE V

STAGE VI

FIGURE 18–17 The different stages of development of a mid-latitude cyclone.

warm air mass and forms an occluded front. The pressure system then begins to weaken, and the cyclone breaks apart as it moves out over the Atlantic Ocean. Many of the strong storms that affect the northeastern United States, creating heavy precipitation, are caused by the formation of mid-latitude cyclones.

SECTION REVIEW

1. Define the term *air mass.*
2. What are the five source regions for air masses?
3. Define the term *front.*
4. What is a cold front? Describe some of its characteristics.
5. What is a warm front? Describe some of its characteristics.
6. What is an occluded front? Describe some of its characteristics.
7. What is a stationary front? Describe some of its characteristics.
8. Draw a rough sketch of a mid-latitude cyclone, using the correct fronts.
9. Who was Svante Arrhenius?

@ WEB Links

FOR MORE INFORMATION GO TO THIS WEB LINK:

<http://ww2010.atmos .uiuc.edu/(Gh)/guides /mtr/af/home.rxml>

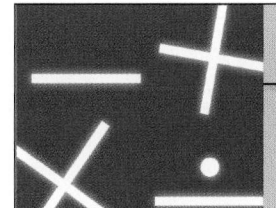

earth math

1) If a cold front is located in Chicago at noon and arrives in Cleveland (363 mi away) at 11:00 P.M., approximately how fast is the front moving?

CHAPTER SUMMARY

Wind is the horizontal movement of air across the Earth's surface. It is caused by differences in atmospheric pressure as air moves from areas of high pressure to areas of low pressure. The speed of the wind is affected by the pressure gradient. Pressure gradient is the change in pressure that occurs over a specific distance. The greater the pressure gradient, the greater the wind speed over an area. Wind is known as a vector force because it has both direction and velocity. Large-scale winds that move air through the atmosphere are called planetary winds. Planetary winds form as a result of the unequal heating of the Earth. Warm, rising air at the equator forms areas of low atmospheric pressure. The air eventually cools and sinks back toward the surface at approximately 30 degrees north and south latitude, forming areas of high atmospheric pressure. Air then flows from the high pressure toward the low pressure, creating planetary winds. This also occurs at the higher latitudes when air flows from the polar highs toward the subpolar lows.

Wind on Earth is affected by the Coriolis effect, which is caused by the Earth's rotation. This results in winds being deflected to the right of travel in the Northern Hemisphere and to the left of travel in the Southern Hemisphere. The Coriolis effect also influences wind that is associated with pressure centers on the Earth. It causes winds to spiral inward and counterclockwise around low pressure and outward and clockwise around high pressure in the Northern Hemisphere.

Mesoscale winds can form as a result of local pressure differences. A sea breeze occurs when air flows from the higher pressure forming over cooler water toward low pressure forming over the rapidly heated land surface. At night the opposite, called a land breeze, occurs. This forms when air flows from high pressure over the cooler land toward low pressure over the warmer water. Other smaller scale winds that can form at the Earth's surface include mountain and valley breezes, along with cold katabatic winds.

An air mass is a large mass of air that has uniform temperature, pressure, and moisture. Air masses are characterized by where they form, known as air mass source regions. These regions produce five basic types of air masses: continental tropical, continental polar, maritime tropical, maritime polar, and arctic. When two air masses come into contact with one another, they form a front.

Fronts are areas where unique weather develops as a result of the collision of two different air masses. There are four types of fronts: cold, warm, occluded, and stationary. All fronts have their own characteristic change in temperature, pressure, wind direction, cloud type, and precipitation. In North America a unique type of weather pattern forms as a result of the interaction between cold and warm air masses. This is known as a mid-latitude cyclone. A cyclone is a low-pressure system. The mid-latitude cyclone goes through unique stages of development that bring stormy weather to the United States.

CHAPTER REVIEW

Multiple Choice

1. Winds blow from regions of:
   a. high air temperature to regions of low air temperature
   b. high air pressure to regions of low air pressure
   c. high precipitation to regions of low precipitation
   d. convergence to regions of divergence

2. The primary cause of winds on the Earth's surface is the:
   a. unequal heating of the Earth's atmosphere
   b. uniform density of the atmosphere
   c. friction between the atmosphere and lithosphere
   d. rotation of the Earth

3. The wind speed between two nearby locations is affected most directly by the differences in the:
   a. latitude between the two locations
   b. longitude between the two locations
   c. air pressure between the two locations
   d. Coriolis effect between the two locations

4. The Coriolis effect is caused by the:
   a. movement of the Earth in relation to the Milky Way
   b. movement of the Earth in relation to the Moon
   c. revolution of the Earth around the Sun
   d. the rotation of the Earth on its axis

5. In the Northern Hemisphere the wind blowing from the north is deflected toward which direction as a result of the Coriolis effect?
   a. northwest
   b. northeast
   c. southwest
   d. southeast

6. What are the planetary winds that form between 30 degrees north latitude and the equator?
   a. the ITCZ winds
   b. the westerlies
   c. the trade winds
   d. the katabatic winds

7. In the Northern Hemisphere, winds move around a low-pressure system:
   a. spiraling outward and clockwise
   b. spiraling inward and clockwise
   c. spiraling outward and counterclockwise
   d. spiraling inward and counterclockwise

8. Which type of wind results from high pressure forming over the ocean and low pressure forming over the land?
   a. a land breeze
   b. a sea breeze
   c. a cyclone
   d. a katabatic wind

9. In the Northern Hemisphere a high-pressure center is also known as:
   a. a cyclone
   b. an anti-cyclone
   c. a whirlwind
   d. a mid-latitude cyclone

10. What type of air mass forms over central Canada?
    a. continental tropical
    b. continental polar
    c. maritime tropical
    d. maritime polar

11. What type of air mass forms over the South Atlantic Ocean?
    a. continental tropical
    b. continental polar
    c. maritime tropical
    d. maritime polar

12. When a warm air mass overtakes a cold air mass, what type of front forms?
    a. a cold front
    b. an occluded front
    c. a warm front
    d. a stationary front

13. When a cold air mass completely lifts a warm air mass off the surface, it forms:
    a. a cold front
    b. an occluded front
    c. a warm front
    d. a stationary front

14. Generally fronts move across the United States from:
    a. north to south
    b. south to north
    c. east to west
    d. west to east

15. Heavy, short-duration rain and lowering then rising air pressure signal the passing of:
    a. a cold front
    b. an occluded front
    c. a warm front
    d. a stationary front

Matching   *Match the terms with the correct definitions.*

a. wind
b. pressure gradient
c. vector force
d. planetary winds
e. Hadley cell

f. Coriolis effect
g. pressure center
h. jet stream
i. air mass
j. front

k. cold front
l. warm front
m. occluded front
n. stationary front
o. cyclone

1. _____ A front that develops between two air masses that are not moving.
2. _____ A large body of air that has similar temperature and moisture characteristics.
3. _____ The horizontal movement of air across the Earth's surface, from areas of high atmospheric pressure to areas of low atmospheric pressure.
4. _____ An area where two different air masses come together.
5. _____ A term for winds that spiral inward and around a low-pressure center.
6. _____ The change in atmospheric pressure that occurs over a specific distance.
7. _____ The zone where a cold air mass overtakes and replaces a warm air mass.
8. _____ A force that has both speed and direction.
9. _____ A frontal boundary that usually occurs when a rapidly moving cold air mass overtakes a warm air mass by wedging underneath it and lifting upward, creating very unstable weather.
10. _____ Large-scale winds that circulate air around the Earth, such as the trade winds or the westerlies.
11. _____ A front that develops when a warm air mass replaces a cold air mass.
12. _____ A region of high-velocity winds that exist high up in the atmosphere.
13. _____ The large-scale convection cell that forms low pressure at the equator and high pressure at 30 degrees north and south of the equator, producing planetary winds.
14. _____ A region on the Earth's surface around which air circulates, where the atmospheric pressure is relatively low or high compared with the surrounding air.
15. _____ The deflection of free-floating objects to the right of travel in the Northern Hemisphere and to the left of travel in the Southern Hemisphere as a result of the Earth's rotation.

Critical Thinking

1. Describe the rotation of the winds around the low-pressure center of a hurricane that forms in the Southern Hemisphere and slowly moves over the equator into the Northern Hemisphere.

19

Storms and Weather Forecasting

STORMS OBJECTIVES

Thunderstorms · Tornadoes · Hurricanes

After reading this section you should be able to:

▶ Describe specific aspects of all three stages of thunderstorm development.

▶ Identify the dangerous weather that accompanies a thunderstorm.

▶ Define the term *tornado* and describe how tornadoes form.

▶ Explain how the Fujita scale is used to classify a tornado.

▶ Describe the conditions that lead to the formation of a hurricane.

▶ Differentiate between a tropical disturbance, tropical storm, and a hurricane.

▶ Define the term *storm surge* and explain how it forms.

▶ Explain how the Saffir-Simpson scale is used to classify hurricanes.

WEATHER FORECASTING OBJECTIVES

Weather Data Collection · Synoptic Weather Maps · Weather Forecasts · Weather Radar and Satellites

After reading this section you should be able to:

▶ Describe the three processes involved in making weather forecasts.

▶ Identify the specific weather data that are commonly observed and collected at weather stations around the world.

▶ Decode the information recorded in a station model.

▶ Define the terms *isotherm* and *isobar*.

▶ Describe the information displayed on weather forecast maps, and differentiate between long-term and short-term weather forecasts.

▶ Describe how radar is used to forecast the weather.

▶ Describe some simple observations of the environment that may be used to forecast the weather.

TERMS TO KNOW

thunderstorm

lightning

tornado

hurricane

cyclone

tropical disturbance

tropical depression

tropical storm

storm surge

typhoons

station model

isotherms

isobars

radar

infrared satellite images

INTRODUCTION

The most deadly aspect of the atmosphere is the formation of strong storms at the Earth's surface. The advances in meteorology over the past 50 years have been centered around understanding how and when storms form. Deadly storms such as thunderstorms, hurricanes, and tornadoes can cause severe damage to populated areas and lead to the loss of life. Hurricane Andrew struck southern Florida in 1992, causing more than 30 billion dollars in damage and taking the lives of 25 people. Predicting these dangerous storms involves the constant observation of changing weather conditions by meteorologists around the country. These observations are then used to make maps and computer models of the atmosphere, which are used to forecast the weather. Today's society is highly dependent on weather forecasts for many aspects of modern life.

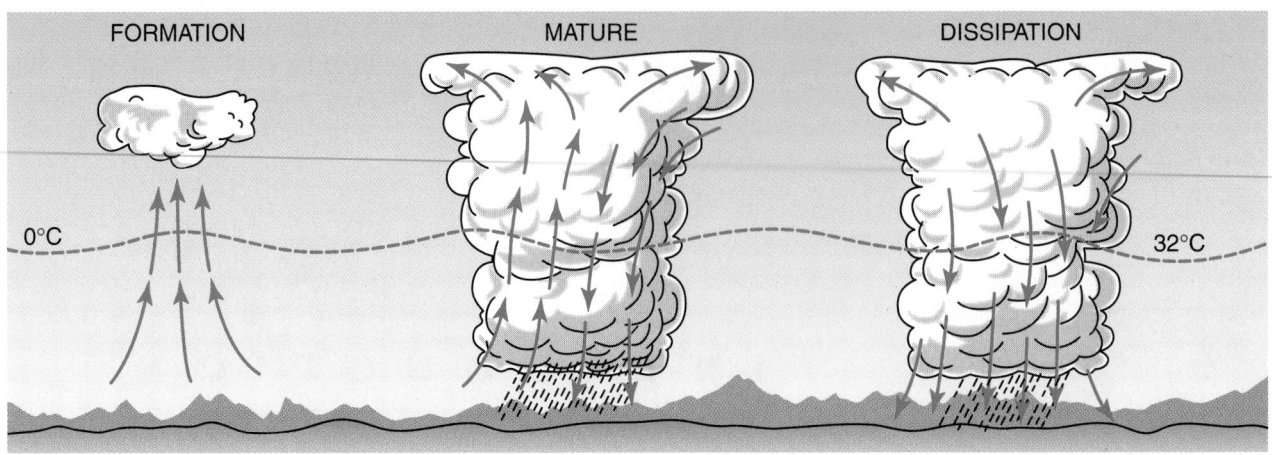

FIGURE 19-1   The three main stages in the life cycle of a thunderstorm.

19.1 Storms

THUNDERSTORMS

Probably the most widespread type of storm to affect the United States is the **thunderstorm**. Thunderstorms form as a result of intense convection associated with the heating of the Earth's surface during spring, summer, and fall. Thunderstorms go through a typical life cycle that is divided into three stages of development (Figure 19–1). The beginning stages of a thunderstorm involve the formation of a cumulus cloud. The rapid heating of the land during a hot day causes warm air to form at the surface. The warm air begins to rise because it is less dense than the surrounding air. Eventually the rising air begins to cool, causing water vapor to condense and form a cloud. As the ground continues to be heated, the cloud grows bigger and small-scale convection cells form. The rising air from the surface creates an area of low pressure beneath the cloud, which draws in air from the surrounding area. This begins to form winds at the surface. During the beginning stages of growth, cumulus clouds can experience rapid vertical development of more than 26,000 ft (8 km) in only 15 minutes; eventually its base can cover a distance of more than 6 mi (10 km). As the cloud grows, the convection intensifies, creating strong winds at the surface of the cloud as air rushes in to replace the warm air that is rising into the cloud. The rapidly rising air also creates strong updrafts within the cloud. These updrafts cause the water droplets and ice crystals that make up the cloud to clump together, forming precipitation. When the top of the cloud reaches a height of more than 7 mi (11 km), it begins to produce heavy precipitation and is known as a cumulonimbus cloud. The thunderstorm is now entering in the mature stage of formation.

During the mature phase, strong updrafts and downdrafts of wind continue to intensify in the cloud. Downdrafts are formed by cooler air sinking toward the Earth's surface. The updrafts and downdrafts cause the separation of lighter ice crystals near the top of the cloud and heavier hail at the lower part of the cloud. The ice crystals become positively

FIGURE 19–2 The formation of lightning within a thunderstorm as a result of opposite electrical charges forming within the cloud.

charged with static electricity, and the hail becomes negatively charged. A large electrical potential is formed between the two different particles in the cloud. This potential is eventually released in the form of **lightning** (Figure 19–2).

Lightning is an electrical discharge of more than 100 million volts that heats the surrounding air to about 45,000° Fahrenheit (25,000° C) (Figure 19–3). This causes the cool air in the cloud to rapidly expand

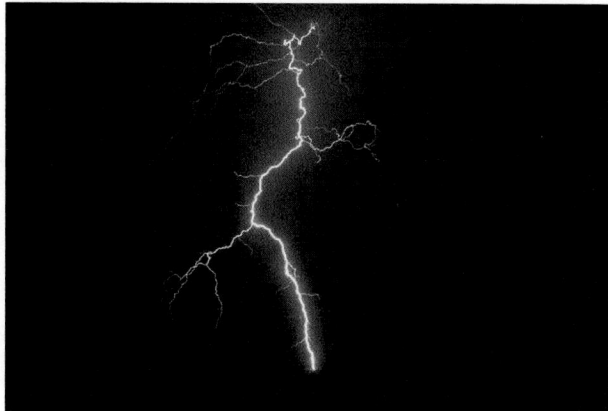

FIGURE 19–3 When lightning strikes, it can generate more than 100 million volts of electricity and heat the surrounding air to more than 45,000° F. (*Courtesy of PhotoDisc.*)

and create a loud noise known as thunder. The lightning that is produced during a thunderstorm is classified by where it travels. Lightning can travel many different ways, including cloud to cloud, cloud to ground, and cloud to air. All forms of lightning can be potentially dangerous. Lightning can start fires, destroy electrical equipment, and kill or injure people. One of the most dangerous things a person can do during a thunderstorm is to talk on the telephone. Lightning can strike telephone lines, travel into homes, and electrocute a person using a phone that has a cord. Cordless phones and cell phones are safe to use during thunderstorms. It also dangerous to stand beneath trees during a thunderstorm, because lightning is often attracted to the tops of tall objects such as trees. The safest place to be during a thunderstorm is indoors.

Another deadly aspect of thunderstorms can be the strong, damaging winds they can generate. Many lives are lost and property damaged by the strong winds that thunderstorms can bring to an area. Often thunderstorms travel so quickly there is little warning and little time for people to seek shelter. Lives are lost each summer in campgrounds where thunderstorms cause trees to blow over onto tents and campers who are seeking shelter from the quickly arriving storm. Heavy rains produced by thunderstorms can also cause flash flooding. The downpours that accompany thunderstorms quickly dump large amounts of water on the surface of the Earth, causing rapid flooding of low-lying areas. Eventually the strong convection that formed the thunderstorm begins to diminish, and the storm enters the dissipating stage. This results in a decline in winds and rain as the cloud begins to dissipate and the skies clear.

Earth System Scientists

Wilhelm Bjerknes

Wilhelm Bjerknes was born in Norway in 1862. Today many meteorologists regard him as the father of weather forecasting and modern meteorology. Bjerknes's early work in physics and electricity had him working with Heinrich Hertz in Germany. Their research on the flow of electrical currents helped lead to the development of the radio. Upon his return to Norway, Bjerknes turned his attention to the study of atmospheric and oceanic circulation. In 1905 he presented his theory of weather prediction, which proposed that the weather could be predicted by applying mathematical models to the present state of the atmosphere. This led to the development of modern forecasting techniques. Bjerknes was one of the first meteorologists to set up a network of weather observation points to collect data about the state of the atmosphere at a particular time over a wide geographic region. Later in his life, while working with his son Jakob, he also discovered the phenomena known as air masses and fronts and helped create a model that explains the stages of the formation of a mid-latitude cyclone.

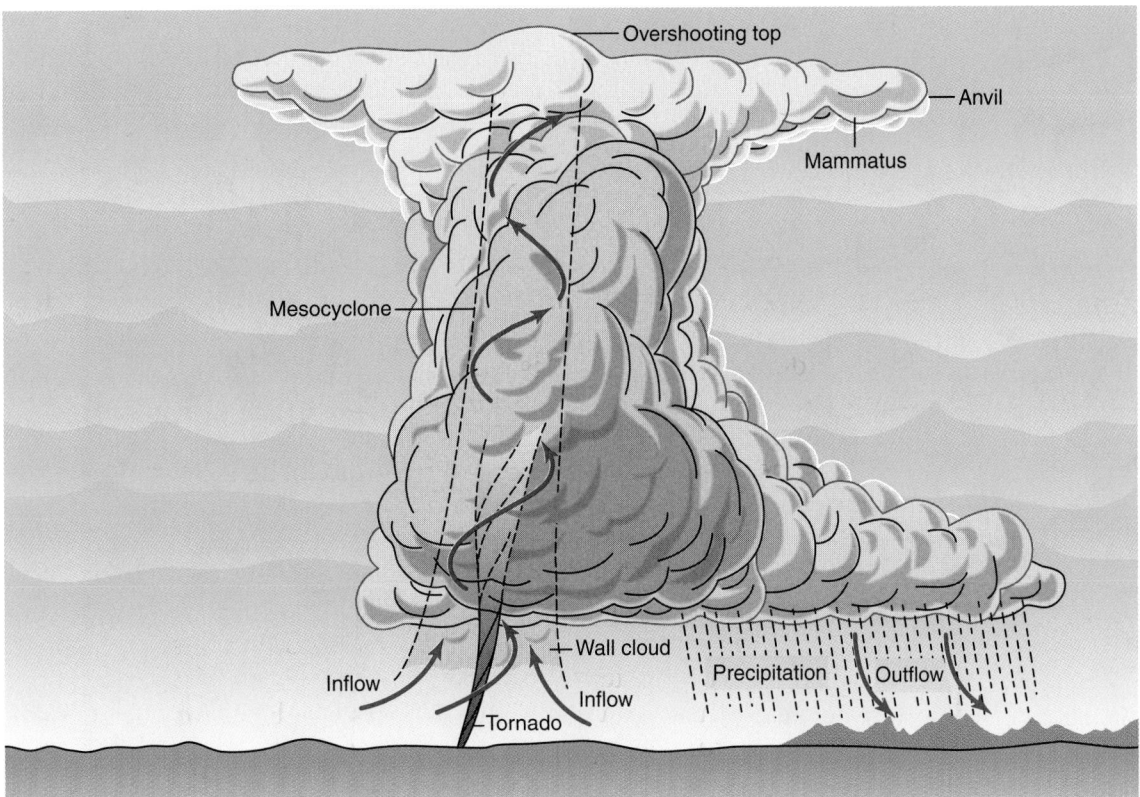

FIGURE 19–4 The formation of a tornado at the base of a thunderstorm results from strong updrafts.

TORNADOES

A **tornado** is a rapidly spiraling column of air that comes into contact with the ground; it is one of the most deadly and unpredictable forms of weather on the Earth. Tornadoes form at the base of thunderstorms when an extremely steep pressure gradient develops as a result of strong convection (Figure 19–4). Tornadoes produce visible columns of swirling air called funnel clouds, which are composed of rapidly moving dust and debris that are being picked up from the ground by the extremely powerful winds.

Tornadoes can produce wind speeds of up to 300 miles per hour (483 kilometers per hour) (Figure 19–5). Although extremely violent and deadly, tornadoes usually last only a few minutes; however, some tornadoes have lasted up to 2 hours. Every year in the United States approximately 800 tornadoes are formed. Most tornadoes develop during the warmest part of the day, between 10:00 A.M. and 6:00 P.M., and occur between the months of March and July. Tornadoes have been reported in every state in the United States, but most occur in the south central part of the country, known as Tornado Alley (Figure 19–6).

Professor T. Theodore Fujita of the University of Chicago created what is called the Fujita scale of tornado intensity. This scale rates tornadoes by their wind speed on a scale from F0 to F5 (Table 19–1). A tornado classified as F0 on the Fujita scale produces winds of up to 73 miles per hour (117 kilometers per hour). An F5 tornado can sustain winds between 261 to 318 miles per hour (420 to 512 kilometers per hour). When tornadoes move over water, they produce what is known

FIGURE 19–5 A tornado is one of the most powerful natural forces on the Earth. (*Courtesy of NOAA.*)

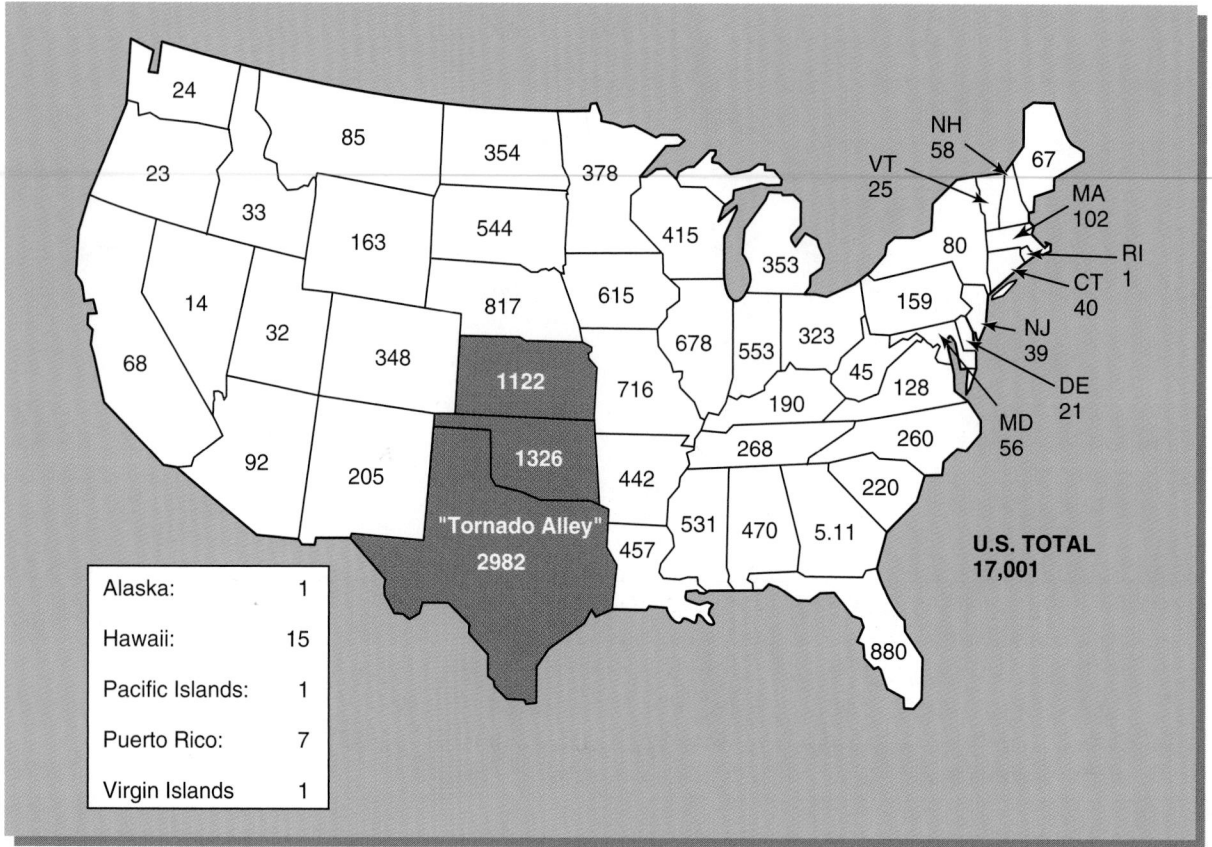

FIGURE 19-6 Tornado occurrences during a 25-year period for each state. Notice the high number of tornadoes in the Midwest, known as Tornado Alley.

CURRENT RESEARCH

A joint study between scientists at the National Aeronautic and Space Administration (NASA) and the University of Georgia has revealed the effects of urban heat islands on thunderstorm formation. An urban heat island is an area where natural forests and vegetation have been replaced by buildings and blacktop roads. The roads and buildings absorb a greater amount of heat energy than vegetation, causing an increase in the surface temperature of the area. The study centers around the metropolis of Atlanta, Georgia, where more than 350,000 acres of land has been replaced by urban sprawl since 1973. The heat island effect caused by the urbanization of Atlanta has raised the surface temperatures there by as much as 10 degrees. This excess heat has several adverse effects on the region. Because of the higher temperatures, people must use more electricity to cool their homes with air conditioners. The researchers also revealed that Atlanta is creating its own thunderstorms. The excess heat causes air to rise rapidly, developing into violent storms. Other urban areas around the world are also believed to be experiencing the heat island effect. The team of scientists suggest that the effect could be reduced if the roofs of buildings were painted white, if lighter colored construction materials were used, and if more trees were planted.

TABLE 19–1 The Fujita scale classifies the intensity of tornadoes

Scale	Category	Mi/Hr	Knots	Expected Damage
F0	Weak	40–72	35–62	Light: tree branches broken, sign boards damaged
F1		73–112	63–97	Moderate: trees snapped, windows broken
F2	Strong	113–157	98–136	Considerable: large trees uprooted, weak structures destroyed
F3		158–206	137–179	Severe: trees leveled, cars overturned, walls removed from buildings
F4	Violent	207–260	180–226	Devastating: frame houses destroyed
F5		261–318	227–276	Incredible: structures the size of autos moved more than 100 meters, steel-reinforced structures highly damaged

as a waterspout. This occurs as water is drawn up into the spiraling winds that make up the tornado. Both waterspouts and tornadoes can move across the landscape with speeds from 30 to 75 miles per hour (48 to 121 kilometers per hour). Because of the unpredictable nature of tornado formation and their rapid movement, they are the most difficult storms to predict, allowing only a few minutes of warning to those who might be affected by the tornado.

HURRICANES

A **hurricane** is a violent storm that is associated with a large low-pressure system, also called a **cyclone**. Cyclones rotate counterclockwise around a center of low pressure in the Northern Hemisphere, with winds spiraling inward at high speeds (Figure 19–7). Hurricanes begin to form over the Atlantic Ocean near the equator as a center of low pressure. As the pressure center moves over the ocean toward the United States, it picks up energy and moisture from the warm surface water. At this point the low-pressure system is called a **tropical disturbance**. The wind speeds associated with a tropical disturbance are less than 20 miles per hour (32 kilometers per hour).

FIGURE 19–7   A satellite image shows the characteristic cyclonic movement of clouds around the eye of a hurricane. (*Courtesy of NOAA.*)

CAREER CONNECTIONS

Synoptic Meteorologist

A synoptic meteorologist helps to create new methods of studying and forecasting the weather. This involves the use of new technologies such as satellites, Doppler radar, and complex computer models. Synoptic meteorologists must have a solid background in weather forecasting and the principles of atmospheric science. They then use this knowledge to discover new and more effective methods of weather prediction. Synoptic meteorology is searching for ways to better understand the chaotic nature of weather, which might make it easier to predict. This research is especially important when it is applied to forecasting potentially dangerous storms. An interest in technology and computers is required for this profession because technical advances have greatly improved the forecasting abilities of synoptic meteorologists. Persons in this occupation can find employment in private industry and academic research or with government agencies. It also requires at least a 4-year college degree in meteorology.

As the disturbance moves over the warm ocean, it gathers more heat and moisture and begins to intensify. At this point the storm is known as a **tropical depression**, with wind speeds between 21 and 39 miles per hour (34 to 63 kilometers per hour). As the storm moves across the ocean, its clouds begin to thicken and rotate around the center of low pressure. Wind speeds then increase to between 40 and 70 miles per hour (64 to 116 kilometers per hour) and the system is known as a **tropical storm**. When the sustained winds of the cyclone reach more than 74 miles per hour (119 kilometers per hour), the tropical storm becomes a hurricane. The characteristic spiraling clouds of a hurricane swirl around the center of low pressure, which is also called the eye, and the storm strengthens. Winds generated by a strong hurricane can be in excess of 250 miles per hour (402 kilometers per hour).

The rotation of the winds and clouds in a hurricane is the same for any low-pressure system in the Northern Hemisphere: They move inward and counterclockwise. Because of this counterclockwise rotation, the strong winds build up high waves on the northwestern edge of the hurricane as it moves westward toward the coast. This pileup of water ahead of the hurricane is called a **storm surge**, which can raise tides along the coast by up to 16 ft (5 m). Waves generated by the strong winds can also top 10 ft (3 m). When the hurricane strikes land, the storm surge it creates often causes disastrous flooding. Approximately 90 percent of all deaths associated with hurricanes are caused by flooding as a result of the storm surge.

Because hurricanes form in the Atlantic Ocean and move toward the coast, it is possible to predict the speed and direction that the

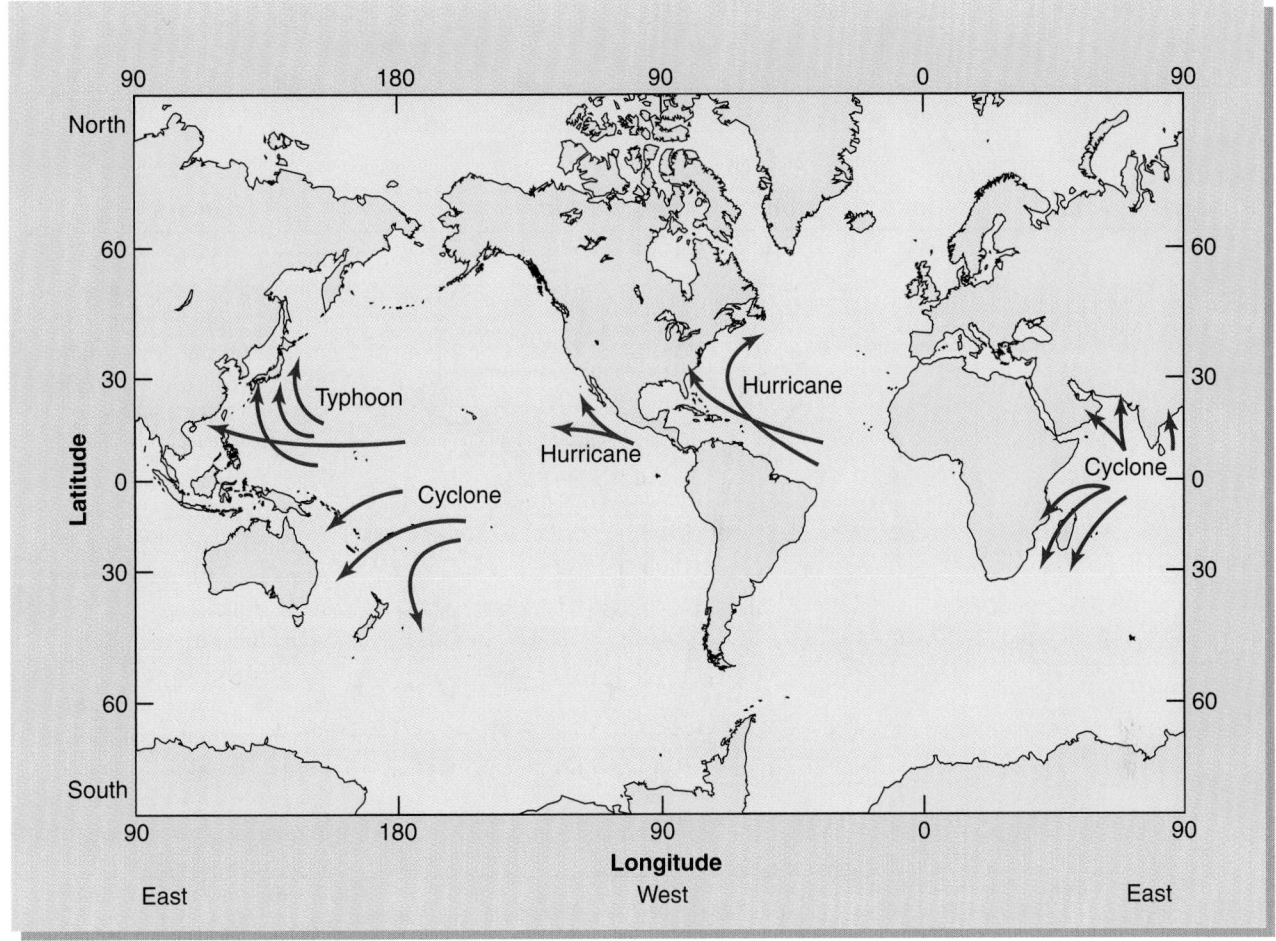

FIGURE 19–8 The average paths of movement for hurricanes around the world.

hurricane will move (Figure 19–8). Hurricanes typically travel between 6 and 12 miles per hour (10 and 19 kilometers per hour). This information is extremely important to the people who live along the coast, who can then be warned and have time to evacuate the area. Once a hurricane strikes land, it usually begins to weaken as its energy and moisture supply is cut off. Besides strong winds and storm surges, hurricanes can also cause inland areas to flood as a result of heavy rains. Rainfall amounts associated with hurricanes can reach 10 to 20 in (25 to 50 cm) in 24 hours. Hurricanes can also generate tornadoes from any of the thunderstorm systems associated with the mass of clouds that surround the eye.

The intensity of hurricanes is often measured using the Saffir-Simpson scale, which measures the pressure, wind speed, and storm surge of hurricanes on a scale from 1 to 5 (Table 19–2). Hurricanes usually occur during specific times of the year in the United States. This is called the hurricane season, which begins in June and ends in late November. When a tropical depression that may develop into a hurricane forms in the Atlantic, it is given a name. The naming of hurricanes is done alphabetically and alternates between male and female names each year. Strong low-pressure centers that form hurricanes can also form in the Pacific Ocean, where, they are referred to as **typhoons**; therefore typhoons strike Hawaii, and hurricanes strike the East Coast.

TABLE 19–2 The Saffir-Simpson scale used to classify hurricanes

Scale Number (Category)	Central Pressure		Winds		Storm Surge		Damage
	mb	in.	mi/hr	knots	ft	m	
1	≥980	≥28.94	74–95	64–82	4–5	~1.5	Damage mainly to trees, shrubbery, and unanchored mobile homes
2	965–979	28.50–28.91	96–110	83–95	6–8	~2.0–2.5	Some trees blow down; major damage to exposed mobile homes; some damage to roofs of buildings
3	945–964	27.91–28.47	111–130	96–113	9–12	~2.5–4.0	Foliage removed from trees; large trees blown down; mobile homes destroyed; some structural damage to small buildings
4	920–944	27.17–27.88	131–155	114–135	13–18	~4.0–5.5	All signs blow down; extensive damage to roofs, windows, and doors; complete destruction of mobile homes; flooding inland as far as 6 mi; (10 km) major damage to lower floors of structures near shore
5	<920	<27.17	>155	>135	>18	>5.5	Severe damage to windows and doors; extensive damage to roofs of homes and industrial buildings; small buildings overturned and blown away; major damage to lower floors of all structures less than 915 ft (4.5 m) above sea level within 500 m of shore

The worst hurricane to hit the United States in the past 100 years struck the coast of Texas in September 1900. This occurred before hurricanes were named and produced winds in excess of 130 miles per hour (209 kilometers per hour). The storm surge created at the northwestern edge of the hurricane rose tides more than 18 ft, killing more than 6,000 people.

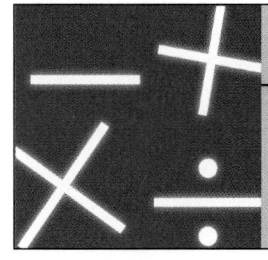

earth math

1) A westward-moving tropical storm, located 200 miles off the East Coast, becomes a hurricane at 1:00 A.M. and is moving at approximately 12 miles per hour. At approximately what time will it strike the coast?

SECTION REVIEW

1. Describe the process of thunderstorm formation.
2. What are the hazards associated with thunderstorms?
3. What are tornadoes, and where can they occur in the United States?
4. Describe the process that leads to the formation of a hurricane.
5. What are the hazards associated with hurricanes?
6. Who was Wilhelm Bjerknes?

@ WEB Links

FOR MORE INFORMATION GO TO THESE WEB LINKS:

<http://ww2010.atmos.uiuc.edu/(Gh)/guides/mtr/svr/home.rxml>

<http://www.spc.noaa.gov/>

<http://www.noaa.gov/tornadoes.html>

<http://hurricanes.noaa.gov/>

19.2 Weather Forecasting

WEATHER DATA COLLECTION

The knowledge of all the processes that occur in the atmosphere is put to use by meteorologists who try to forecast the weather. Forecasting weather involves three main processes. The first is the gathering of current weather information. Second, this information is recorded on charts and maps or entered into computer models. Last, the charts, maps, and computer models are analyzed and the weather is predicted, or forecasted. The first step in the forecasting process involves the gathering of current weather data from around the region. In the United States, there are almost 1,000 weather stations around the country that gather weather data (Figure 19–9).

These stations are mostly run by the National Weather Service, airports, the military, and private citizens. Many ships at sea and automated buoys in the ocean also record weather data. Information about the current state of the weather is usually recorded every hour, using Greenwich Mean Time. The weather data that are recorded each hour by these weather stations includes the surface air temperature, dew point, barometric pressure, precipitation, cloud cover, visibility, and wind speed and direction. Some weather stations use weather balloons to record data about weather conditions high in the atmosphere. These balloons carry radio transmitters that send back weather data at specific altitudes, including air temperature, dew point, wind direction and speed, and barometric pressure.

SYNOPTIC WEATHER MAPS

All the weather data gathered by each weather station are then plotted on weather maps every 3 hours. The data are displayed on these maps using the **station model**, which shows the current weather data for each station in a coded form (Figure 19–10). Meteorologists then use the information plotted on the maps to construct detailed weather maps.

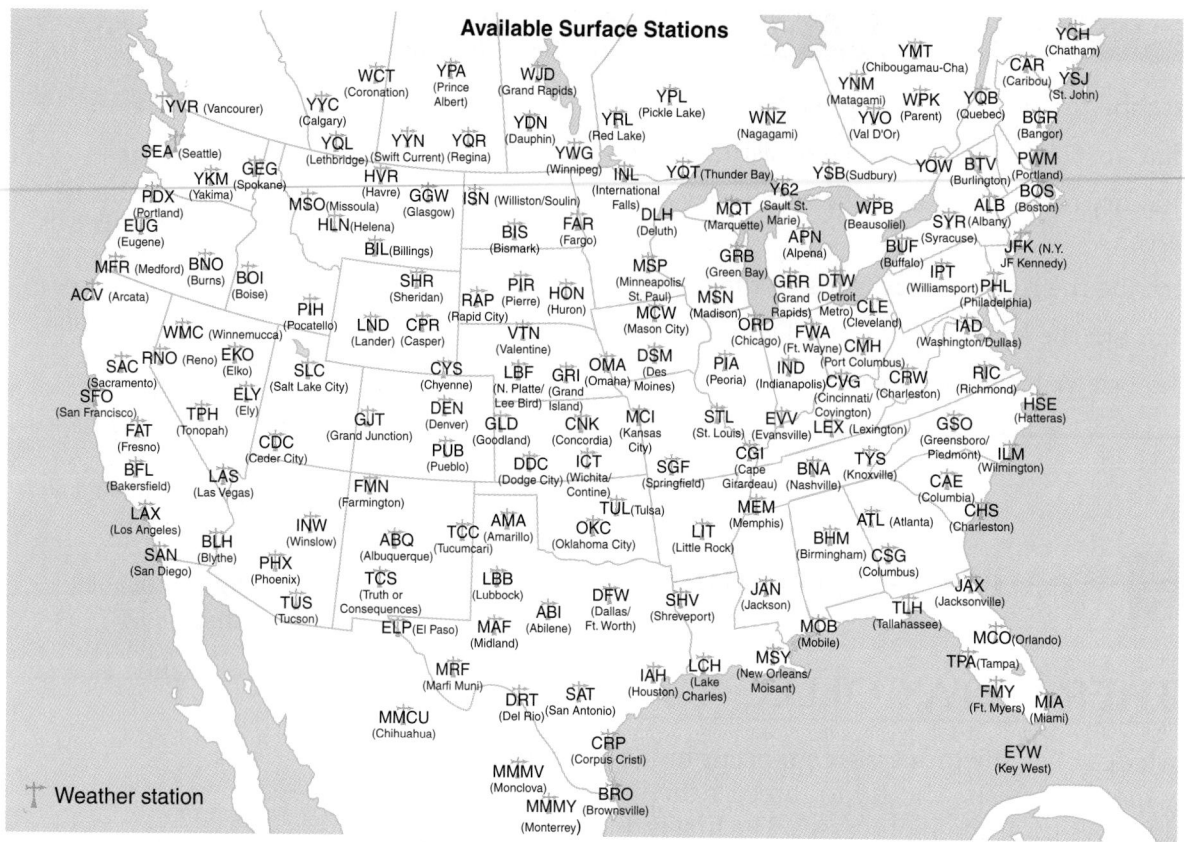

FIGURE 19–9 The network of weather stations around the United States that records hourly weather observations.

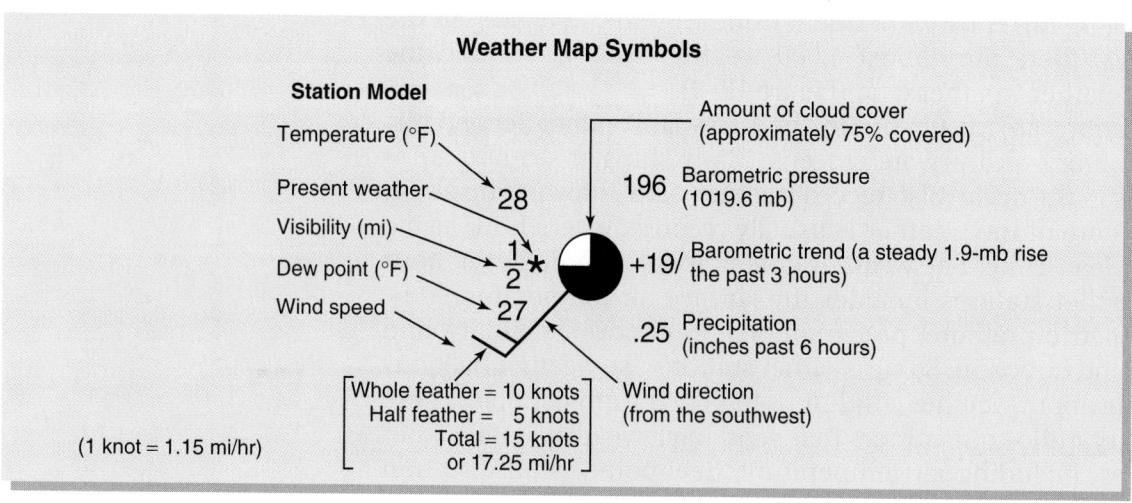

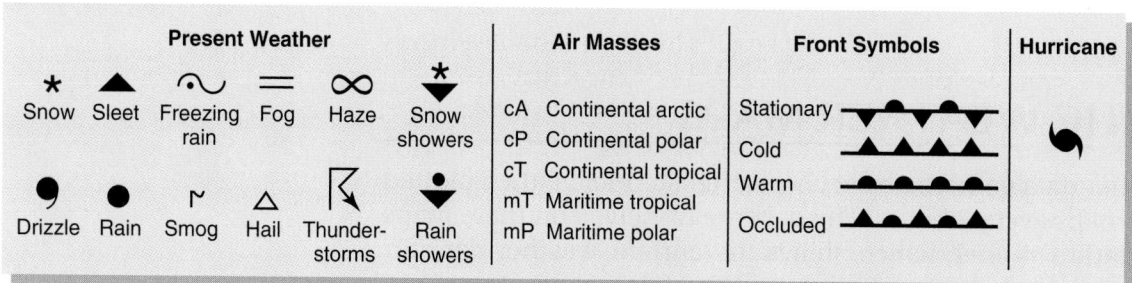

FIGURE 19–10 The weather station model is used on weather maps to encode weather observations.

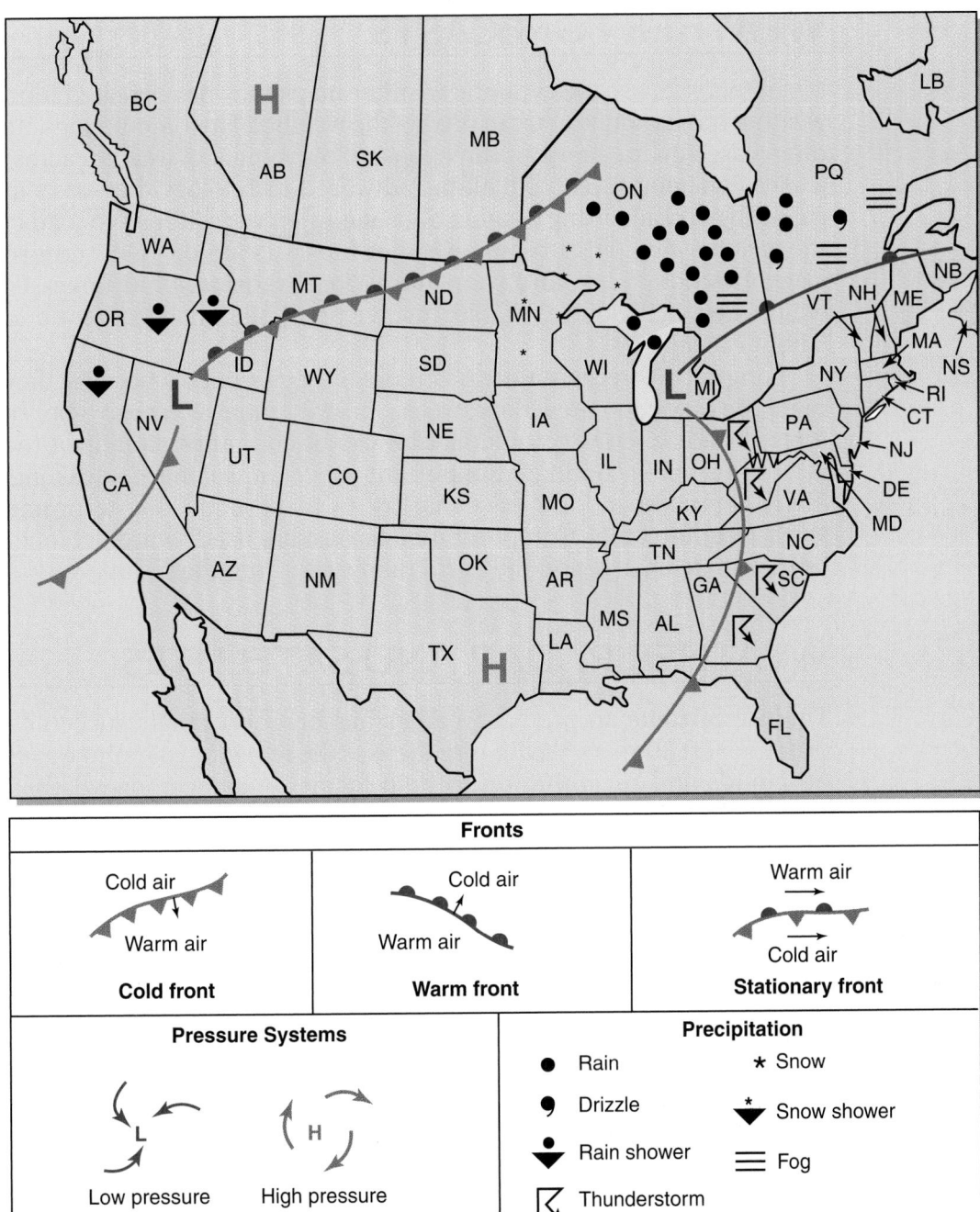

FIGURE 19–11   A typical surface weather map showing the locations of pressure centers, fronts, and precipitation.

Surface weather maps usually show the locations of high- and low-pressure systems, temperatures, fronts, and precipitation (Figure 19–11). Often surface temperature maps are created using **isotherms**, which are lines that connect equal values of temperature along the surface. Pressure maps can also be created by using **isobars**, which are lines that connect values of equal pressure. Both temperature and pressure maps can also be generated for different levels in the atmosphere; these are called upper air maps. Today computers are used to create many weather maps that depict current weather every three hours.

WEATHER FORECASTS

Meteorologists use the synoptic weather maps they have created from weather observations to try to predict the weather. Their predictions are often based on the previous direction and movement of weather across a specific region. Even with all the advanced technology that exists in gathering and analyzing weather data, it is often very difficult to predict the weather exactly. Currently weather forecasts are divided into two categories: long term and short term. Short-term weather forecasts, which are usually quite reliable, involve predicting the weather up to 6 hours ahead.

Long-term forecasts are much more difficult to make because they might be made for a few days, weeks, or even months. These types of forecasts are often very general. The use of computer models of the atmosphere is becoming an important aspect of weather forecasting. Many computer models exist that try to make both long-term and short-term forecasts. Computer models also are used to predict long-term climate changes on the Earth many years into the future.

WEATHER RADAR AND SATELLITES

The use of **radar** to predict weather has been extremely successful over the past 20 years. Weather radar uses the reflection of radio waves off clouds and precipitation to help locate areas of poor weather.

Earth System Scientists

Benjamin Franklin

Benjamin Franklin was born in Boston, Massachusetts, in 1706. Franklin was to become one of the most famous men of his time, highly respected in both America and Europe. Franklin was a self-educated man who had an interest in many things well beyond his role in the American Revolution. He spent much of the first part of his life as a printer and writer. Later he became famous as an inventor, politician, and scientist, most notably for his experiments to prove that lightning was a form of electricity. Franklin also made important advances for the understanding of weather, climate, and the oceans. Franklin was the first person to reveal that weather systems and storms moved from west to east across North America. He published long-term weather forecasts in his widely read *Poor Richard's Almanac.* Franklin also became interested in the warm water current off the east coast of North America, known as the Gulf Stream. In 1775 he took measurements of the water temperature of the Gulf Stream and produced the first chart that showed its location and movement. He went on to further propose that the Gulf Stream originated near the Gulf of Mexico and was driven northward along the coast by the trade winds. Franklin theorized about the effects of deforestation, hypothesizing that cleared farmlands might have an effect on local climate. In 1784 he became interested in the possible effects of volcanic eruptions on regional climate patterns. He proposed that ash and dust produced from a volcano would block incoming solar radiation and therefore cool the planet.

CURRENT RESEARCH

Researchers at NASA's Goddard Space Science Center are using a supercomputer to predict short-term climate changes and to improve long-term weather forecasts. By entering data on surface temperature and moisture conditions and applying mathematical models, the super-computer then crunches numbers to predict regional rainfall patterns. The climate research team uses the Cray T3E supercomputer, which makes billions of calculations per second. The models that the team develop use data from the atmosphere, hydrosphere, and land surface. So far their predictions have been surprisingly accurate. One day the team hopes their research will lead to a better understanding of weather and might help predict short-term climate events such as droughts or floods.

CAREER CONNECTIONS
Weather Reporter

A career in reporting weather on television or radio is one of the most well-known occupations in the field of meteorology. No news report on television or radio is complete without a weather forecast. There are also specialty television stations that deal with only weather-related topics. A weather reporter requires a solid background in meteorology and communications and can find employment all over the country. Another fast-growing opportunity in this field is forecasting the weather for one of the many Internet-related weather services. There are many World Wide Web sites that provide up-to-date weather forecasts 24 hours a day. These companies require meteorologists to make forecasts, create weather maps, and to keep their Web pages current. Opportunities in all these fields are expected to increase in the future.

The United States is nearly covered by regional radar stations that can give an accurate view of the current precipitation patterns across the country. These up-to-date radar images are easily accessible today on the Internet. They can help determine when and where precipitation will occur. New radar systems can also differentiate between different forms of precipitation, making it easier for meteorologists to predict where snow or freezing rain might form. The use of weather satellites is also an important advancement in technology that can aid in the forecasting of weather. **Infrared satellite images** can identify cloud formations and height across the country during both day and night.

Weather prediction does not always require sophisticated technology and a network of weather stations. Some simple local observations can also be used to predict the weather. Because low air pressure is often associated with poor weather, a drop in barometric pressure can signal the coming of poor weather and an increase in barometric pressure can indicate good weather. The type of clouds that are present in the sky can also indicate the coming weather. Cumulus clouds with strong vertical development could indicate oncoming thunderstorms. Higher stratocumulus clouds moving into the region might signal an approaching warm front bringing extended precipitation to the region. Clearing night skies during winter can also signal an extreme drop in temperature.

@ WEB Links

FOR MORE INFORMATION GO TO THESE WEB LINKS:

<http://ww2010.atmos
.uiuc.edu/(Gh)/guides
/maps/home.rxml>

<http://ww2010.atmos
.uiuc.edu/(Gh)/guides
/mtr/fcst/home.rxml>

<http://www.nws
.noaa.gov/>

SECTION REVIEW

1. What are the three main processes used to forecast the weather?

2. What weather information is commonly recorded by weather stations?

3. What are the common weather maps that depict the current state of the weather?

4. Describe how radar and satellites are used to forecast the weather.

5. What are some common changes that occur in the local conditions that can be used to forecast the weather?

6. Draw a station model for the following weather observation: temperature 24° F, dew point 20° F, 50 percent cloud cover, winds from the southwest at 25 knots, atmospheric pressure 1011.1 millibars.

7. Who was Benjamin Franklin?

CHAPTER SUMMARY

Storms in the atmosphere can form dangerous conditions, leading to the damage of property and loss of life. There are three main types of potentially dangerous storms on the Earth: thunderstorms, tornadoes, and hurricanes. Thunderstorms form when the Earth's surface is heated, causing warm air to rise rapidly. This causes the formation of a small-scale convection cell that leads to the creation of a cumulonimbus cloud. Eventually the cloud grows large enough to create heavy precipitation and generate strong winds. The vertical winds inside a thunderstorm are called updrafts and downdrafts. These winds cause

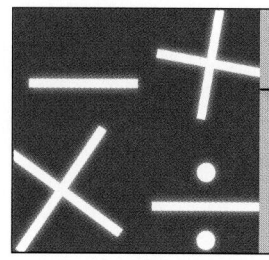

earth math

1) The following atmospheric pressure readings in millibars were recorded at a weather station over the past 12 hours: 1005, 1006, 1012, 1014, 1017, and 1024. What was the rate of change in pressure over this time?

the separation of lighter ice crystals near the top of the cloud and heavier hail near the cloud base. The two different forms of precipitation build up opposite electrical charges within the cloud, eventually forming lightning. Lightning can strike from cloud to cloud, cloud to air, or cloud to ground. When the convection that formed the thunderstorm ceases, the cloud begins to dissipate and the thunderstorm is over. The most damaging aspects of a thunderstorm involve heavy winds and rain, along with lightning.

Some very strong thunderstorms cause wind to rush in toward the base at such high velocities that they can form a tornado. A tornado is a rapidly spiraling column of air that comes into contact with the ground. Tornadoes can generate wind at speeds more than 300 miles per hour (483 kilometers per hour), making them one of the most deadly forces on Earth. Tornadoes usually only last for a few minutes and are very difficult to predict.

Hurricanes are another type of storm system that can generate strong winds and heavy rain. These are the largest storms that form on Earth. They can affect hundreds of square miles. Hurricanes form from developing low-pressure systems over warm ocean water near the tropics. They gain energy and moisture as they move across the ocean, leading to the formation of a massive cyclone around which clouds rotate. The winds of a hurricane spiral around the central eye of a hurricane in a counterclockwise motion in the Northern Hemisphere. This causes water to build up on the northwestern edge of the hurricane, forming a storm surge. This wall of water can raise tides by up to 16 feet (5 meters), causing massive flooding when the hurricane strikes land. Eventually, if the hurricane moves over land, it loses its source of energy and begins to dissipate. Hurricane season in the eastern United States is usually from June to November.

Meteorologists try to predict storms by studying weather observations taken from weather stations all around the country, recording the surface air temperature, dew point, barometric pressure, precipitation, cloud cover, visibility, and wind speed and direction at specific locations. They then enter these data into computers and plot them on weather maps, which are then analyzed to make forecasts about the weather. Data on surface weather maps are in a form called the station model, which encodes surface weather information for each specific weather station. Meteorologists also use radar and satellite images to make predictions about the weather. Some simple observations made of the surrounding environment can also be used to forecast the weather. These include observing changes in atmospheric pressure, approaching clouds, and sky conditions.

CHAPTER REVIEW

Multiple Choice

1. In the United States, during which month are thunderstorms most likely to occur?
   a. January
   b. March
   c. August
   d. November

2. Which conditions are favorable for the formation of thunderstorms?
   a. cool, sinking air
   b. an approaching warm front
   c. an approaching stationary front
   d. hot, rising air

3. The strong vertical winds inside a thunderstorm are called:
   a. updrafts
   b. a tornado
   c. prevailing winds
   d. cyclones

4. The separation of hail at the base of the cloud and tiny ice crystals near the top of the cloud results in:
   a. updrafts
   b. downdrafts
   c. lightning
   d. tornadoes

5. The most difficult type of weather event to predict a few hours in advance of its development is a:
   a. thunderstorm
   b. tornado
   c. hurricane
   d. cyclone

6. Which storm usually lasts the shortest time?
   a. a thunderstorm
   b. a tornado
   c. a hurricane
   d. a cyclone

7. What conditions are favorable for the formation of a hurricane?
   a. cool, moist air
   b. a continental tropical air mass
   c. warm ocean water
   d. rapidly heating land

8. The circulation of clouds and wind around the eye of a hurricane in the Northern Hemisphere is best described as:
   a. counterclockwise and inward
   b. counterclockwise and outward
   c. clockwise and inward
   d. clockwise and outward

9. Another term for the low-pressure system that forms a hurricane is:
   a. anticyclone
   b. typhoon disturbance
   c. maritime polar air mass
   d. cyclone

10. A tornado that can cause severe damage with 200-mile-per-hour winds has a Fujita intensity of:
    a. F1
    b. F2
    c. F3
    d. F4

11. Hurricanes that form in the Atlantic Ocean near the equator travel in what general direction?
    a. west
    b. southwest
    c. northeast
    d. southeast

12. During which month is a hurricane most likely to form near the equator in the Atlantic ocean?
    a. January
    b. March
    c. September
    d. April

13. A hurricane with an atmospheric pressure reading in the eye of 28.00 inches of mercury is classified on the Saffir-Simpson scale as what type?
    a. 1
    b. 2
    c. 3
    d. 4

14. Lines that connect equal temperatures on a weather map are called:
    a. isobars
    b. isotachs
    c. isotherms
    d. contour lines

15. Lines that connect equal pressure on a weather map are called:
    a. isobars
    b. isotachs
    c. isotherms
    d. contour lines

16. The atmospheric pressure on a station model is recorded as 164. This is equal to:
    a. 164 inches of mercury
    b. 916.4 millibars
    c. 1016.4 millibars
    d. 1016.4 inches of mercury

17. Decreasing atmospheric pressure usually indicates what type of approaching weather?
    a. fair weather
    b. partly cloudy weather
    c. poor weather
    d. cold weather

Matching   *Match the terms with the correct definitions.*

a. thunderstorm
b. lightning
c. tornado
d. hurricane
e. cyclone

f. tropical disturbance
g. tropical storm
h. storm surge
i. tropical depression
j. typhoon

k. station model
l. isotherms
m. isobar
n. radar
o. infrared satellite images

1. _____ A rapidly rotating, funnel-shaped column of air located at the base of a cumulonimbus cloud, resulting in deadly high-velocity winds.
2. _____ Isolines that are used to connect points of equal temperature on a weather map.
3. _____ A large-scale tropical cyclone with winds in excess of 74 miles per hour.
4. _____ An organized group of thunderstorms associated with a strong low-pressure system with cyclonic winds between 40 and 70 miles per hour.
5. _____ A low atmospheric pressure system that forms in the tropics over the ocean, consisting of group of thunderstorms and cyclonic winds between 20 and 40 miles per hour.
6. _____ An organized group of thunderstorms with cyclonic winds less than 20 miles per hour.
7. _____ A hurricane that forms and is located over the western Pacific ocean.
8. _____ Satellite imagery created by sensing the infrared energy given off by a substance, which allows images to be recorded at night without the presence of light.
9. _____ A coded symbol used on weather maps to display specific atmospheric variables.
10. _____ A small-scale storm caused by the formation of a cumulonimbus cloud, producing strong winds, heavy rain or hail, lightning, and thunder.
11. _____ A term for winds that spiral inward and around a low-pressure center.
12. _____ A term that stands for "radio detecting and ranging," which describes a device that bounces radio waves off an object to track its location, speed, and movement.
13. _____ The rise in water level that is caused by the strong winds associated with an approaching hurricane.
14. _____ A naturally occurring electrical discharge in the atmosphere usually associated with thunderstorms.
15. _____ An isoline that connects points of equal atmospheric pressure on a weather map.

Critical Thinking

1. If predictions are correct about the Earth's increasing surface temperatures, explain three ways you think this will affect the weather in the United States.
2. What observations of the local weather might be used to predict the formation of a tornado?

20

Global Climate Change

OBJECTIVES

Revealing the Earth's Past Climate · Ice Ages and Glaciations · The Milankovitch Cycle · Hot House Climates · Goldilocks Syndrome · Humans and Global Climate Change

After reading this chapter you should be able to:

▶ Define the term *climate*.

▶ Identify six ways that paleoclimatologists can infer what the Earth's past climate was like.

▶ Differentiate between a hot house climate and an ice age.

▶ Describe the effects that an ice age has on the planet.

▶ Explain the three aspects of the Milankovitch cycle and how they relate to global climate.

▶ Describe the effects that a hot house climate has on the Earth.

▶ Explain what scientists believe caused the Earth's temperature to increase in the past.

▶ Describe the Goldilocks syndrome.

▶ Explain the evidence used to suggest that humans are causing an increase in global temperatures.

▶ Describe the possible effects of increasing global temperatures on the Earth.

TERMS TO KNOW

climate

hot house climate

ice age

paleoclimatology

tree ring

pollen

ice cores

precession

eccentricity

Goldilocks syndrome

fossil fuels

rice paddies

chlorofluorocarbons

nitrous oxide

INTRODUCTION

The long-term weather conditions that occur in specific regions are known as the climate. Climate is usually classified by the average temperature and precipitation that an area receives annually. Very cold climates are known as polar, warmer climates as tropical, and areas with moderate temperatures are usually classified as mid-latitude climates. An area that receives an ample amount of precipitation throughout the year is known as a humid climate, whereas an area with a lack of water is classified as arid. Together these terms are used to identify the different types of climates that exist on the planet. The climate of the Earth is the direct result of the state of the atmosphere and its relationship to the Earth's surface. Research has revealed that the Earth's climate has gone through many changes in its long history. Many think that these changes are part of the natural cycle of interactions that occur in our planet's atmosphere, hydrosphere, and lithosphere. Changes in these aspects of the Earth's systems may be the result of variations in atmospheric gases, ocean currents, insolation, and tectonic plate movements. The concept of global climate change is not new. In fact, scientists have determined that the Earth has experienced changes in global climate many times in its 4.5-billion-year history.

REVEALING THE EARTH'S PAST CLIMATE

Geologists refer to the Earth's climate in two general terms: **hot house climate** and **ice age**. A hot house climate occurs when the average surface temperature of the Earth is much warmer than it is today. An ice age occurs when the average surface temperature of the planet drops well below that of today, resulting in many portions of the Earth becoming covered with ice and snow. Researchers can reveal what the average surface temperature of the Earth was like before humans used instruments to record global temperatures and other climate data. This branch of science is called **paleoclimatology**. Paleoclimatology uses several different methods to hypothesize about what the climate was like during different times in the Earth's past. One of these techniques involves careful study of the fossil record. By looking at fossil evidence, paleoclimatologists can determine what the climate was like when that particular organism flourished. For example, fossilized palm trees and ferns found in Alaska suggest that the climate was much different in that region when these organisms were alive (Figure 20–1).

Studying coral reefs can also reveal much about the past temperatures of the ocean. Coral reefs are large colonies of individual organisms called corals. When a coral dies, it is covered by new generations of corals, leading to the formation of a large reef. By drilling into a coral reef and extracting a core sample, scientists can study its chemical composition to learn about the conditions that existed in the oceans when the ancient corals were alive. Studying **tree ring** data is another means by which climate change can be revealed (Figure 20–2). Trees grow thick rings during wet, warm summers and thinner rings during drier seasons. By analyzing the thickness of a tree's rings, scientists can infer what the climate was like during the time that it was growing.

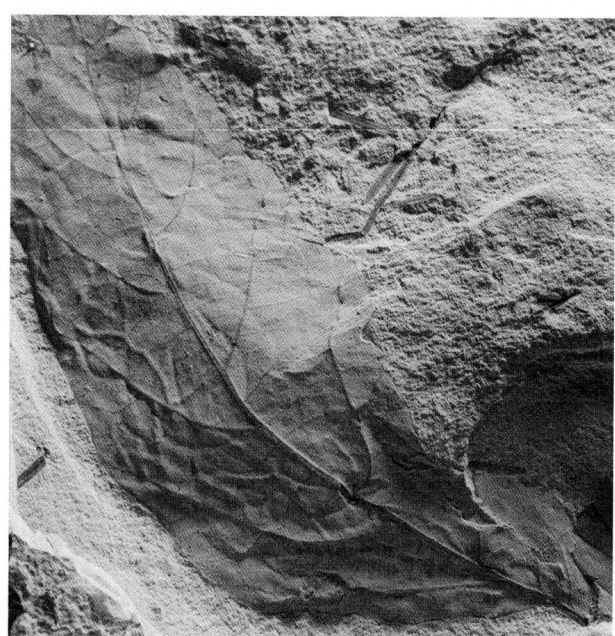

FIGURE 20–1 Fossils of warm climate tree leaves found in areas that are extremely cold today suggest that the climate was different when the trees were alive. (*Courtesy of PhotoDisc.*)

FIGURE 20–2   Tree rings can provide clues to the Earth's past climate by examining its growth rates in the past. (*Courtesy of PhotoDisc.*)

In addition, lake and ocean sediments can reveal a lot about the climate that existed when they were deposited in the water. This is because different types of sediments are associated with changes in the landscape. Analyzing fossilized **pollen** samples is another method by which scientists can reveal past climates. Certain species of plants grow only in specific climates. By identifying the pollen that existed in an area, scientists can piece together what plants grew there and therefore infer what the climate might have been like. **Ice cores** drilled into glaciers and ice sheets are another important way to determine past climate. When snow falls and compacts to form a glacier, it traps tiny air bubbles that represent the composition of the atmosphere during the time it snowed. Scientists can analyze these trapped air bubbles and determine what the global atmosphere and climate might have been like (Figure 20–3). Using all these methods has enabled scientists to piece together the climate history of the Earth with reasonable accuracy.

ICE AGES AND GLACIATIONS

Research has revealed that at several times in the past the Earth was much colder than it is today. This resulted in the widespread formation of ice sheets and glaciers on many of the continents. When this

FIGURE 20-3 Ice cores contain tiny bubbles of gas that represent the composition of the Earth's atmosphere during the past. They can be analyzed to reveal the Earth's past climates. (*Courtesy of PhotoDisc.*)

type of event lasts more than a million years, it is called an ice age. Over shorter periods, such as thousands of years, these events are known as glaciations. It is estimated that four major ice ages have occurred on the Earth. The earliest of these occurred about 800 to 600 million years ago in the late Proterozoic eon. Another major ice age took place during the late Ordovician and early Silurian periods between 430 to 460 million years ago. The late Carboniferous and early Permian periods also experienced an ice age between 250 to 350 million years ago. The last known ice age on Earth occurred approximately 4 million years ago, during the late Tertiary period. During this ice age, approximately 30 percent of the land surfaces on the Earth were covered in ice. The most extensive ice coverage of the continents during this time occurred approximately 20,000 years ago. Since then the glaciers have been retreating, leading to the formation of many of the landscapes that we recognize today. Evidence based on global temperature averages during the past 100,000 years suggests that the Earth is still in a cooler climate period. It is only in the past 1,000 years or so that the Earth's climate has begun to warm up (Figure 20-4).

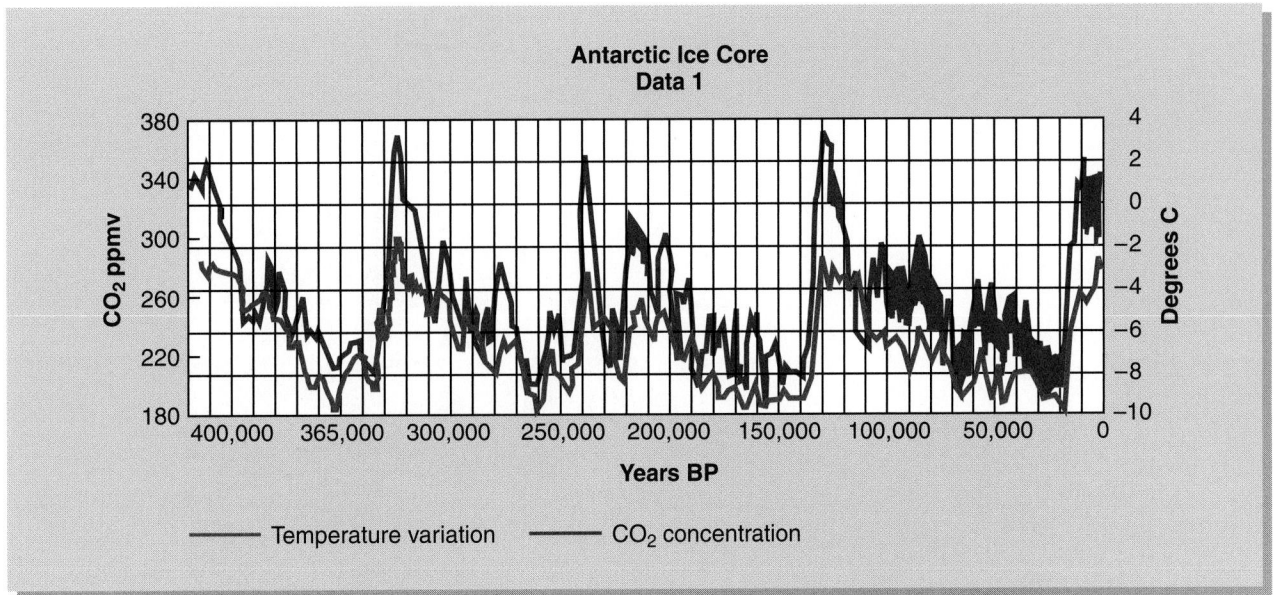

FIGURE 20–4 Ice core data show the relationship between carbon dioxide concentration in the Earth's atmosphere and global temperature. This record reveals the changes in the Earth's climate that have occurred for the past 420,000 years.

THE MILANKOVITCH CYCLE

One question scientists are trying to answer is what causes an ice age. Scientists agree that the interactions among the oceans, land, and atmosphere play an important role; however, changes in the Earth's position relative to the Sun also might influence the occurrence of ice ages. This hypothesis was first proposed by Milutin Milankovitch in the mid-nineteenth century. Milankovitch revealed that changes in the Earth's tilted axis, along with its orbit around the Sun, occur on a periodic scale. The Earth's axis does not remain at a constant tilt of 23.5 degrees. It actually fluctuates between a maximum tilt of 24.5 degrees and a minimum tilt of 22 degrees every 41,000 years. This causes changes in the insolation received at higher latitudes, which could lead to glaciations (Figure 20–5).

Milankovitch also determined that the Earth wobbles on its axis, which is known as **precession** (Figure 20–6). Precession can be easily demonstrated by observing a spinning top. As the top spins on its axis rapidly, it also slowly wobbles back and forth. This is precession. The Earth's rapid rotation on its axis also causes it to slowly wobble back and forth on a periodic scale. This change in the orientation of the Earth to the Sun is a result of precession. The time it takes for the Earth to wobble back and forth once is approximately 22,000 years.

The **eccentricity** of the Earth's orbit around the Sun is a measure of how close to a perfect circle the orbit is (Figure 20–7). The Earth's orbital eccentricity also changes on a periodic scale approximately every 100,000 years due to the gravitational interaction of other planets in the solar system. This results in a periodic change in the distance between the Earth and the Sun, which causes variations in the intensity of

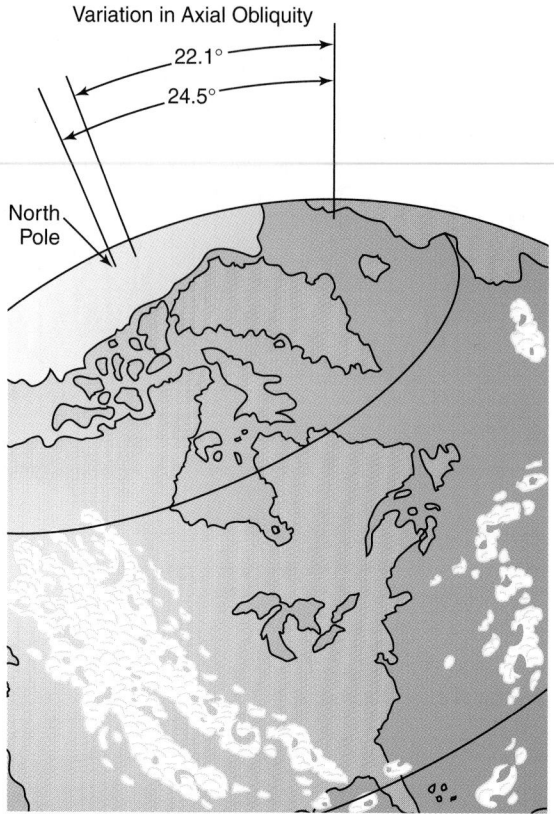

FIGURE 20-5 The periodic change that occurs in the Earth's tilt between 22 degrees and 24.5 degrees every 41,000 years is part of the Milankovitch cycle.

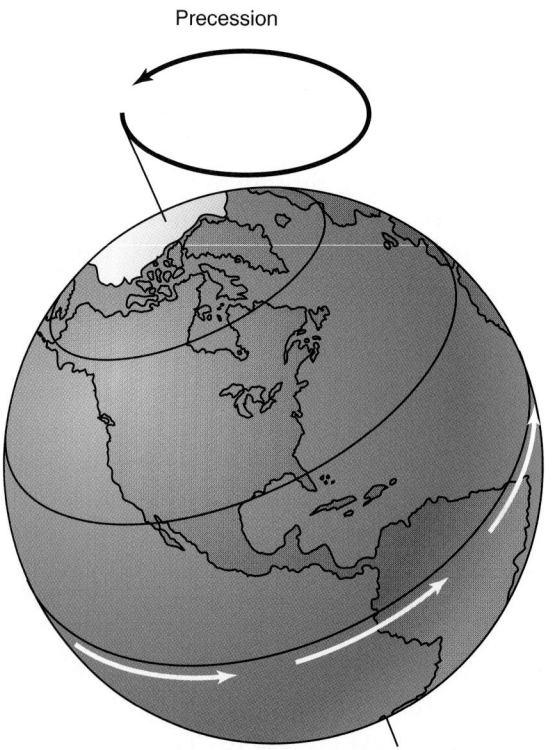

FIGURE 20-6 The wobble of the Earth as it spins on its axis, known as precession, occurs on a 22,000-year cycle. This is part of Milankovitch's theory of climate change.

Variation in Orbital Eccentricity

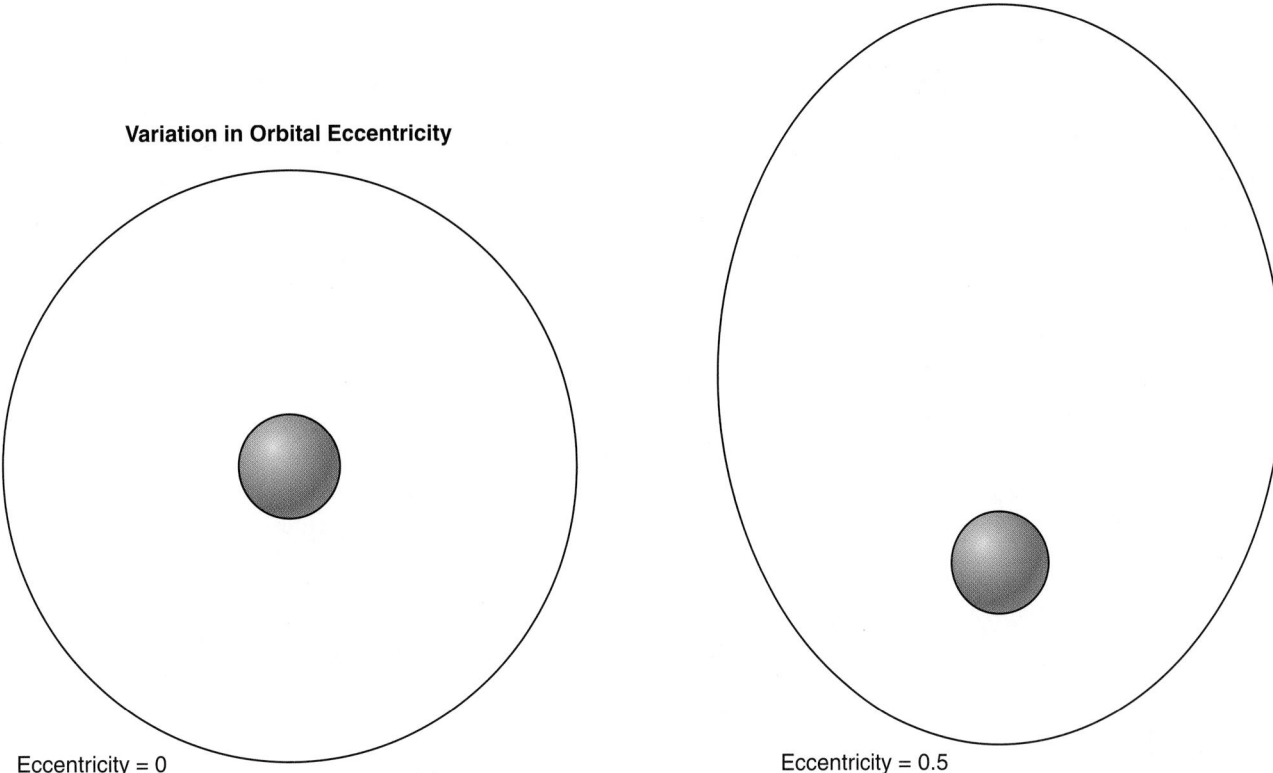

Eccentricity = 0   Eccentricity = 0.5

FIGURE 20-7 The changing eccentricity of Earth's orbit was also proposed by Milankovitch to influence the Earth's climate; these exaggerated views show how changes in eccentricity affect orbital paths.

insolation received by the Earth. Together these changes in the Earth's position relative to the Sun are called Milankovitch cycles (Figure 20–8). These cycles are believed to be part of the cause of ice ages and glaciations.

Other smaller scale changes on the Earth can also lead to global cooling. Large volcanic eruptions can spew millions of tons of dust and

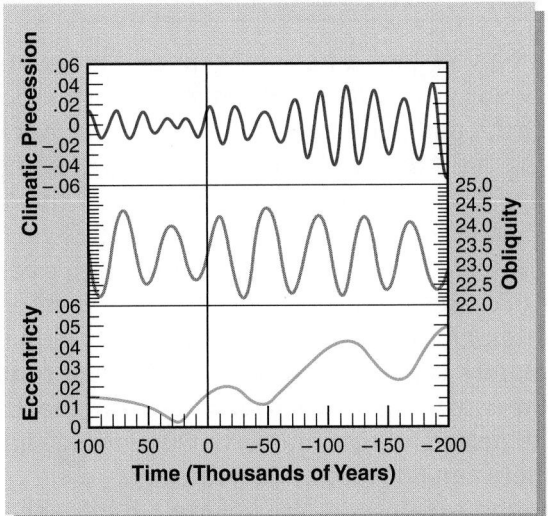

FIGURE 20-8 Milankovitch used the periodic changes in the Earth's tilted axis, precession, and orbital eccentricity, known as the Milankovitch cycle, to explain the changes in the Earth's climate for the past 200,000 years. Compare his data to the ice core data in Figure 20–4 and see if you can find a relationship between temperature and the Milankovitch cycles.

Earth System Scientists

Milutin Milankovitch

Milutin Milankovitch was born in Serbia in 1879. He was educated at the Vienna Institute of Technology and later became a professor of applied mathematics. Milankovitch is best known for his theory of how the Earth's motions may be related to climate change. Known as the Milankovitch theory, he proposed that the periodic change in the motions of the Earth around the Sun and the Earth's tilted axis lead to periodic changes in the insolation received by the Earth. He then applied a mathematical model to these cyclical changes and developed an insolation and average temperature record for the Earth dating back 600,000 years. Milankovitch applied this record to try to explain past ice ages. Unfortunately, Milankovitch's theory of climate change and the Earth's orbit was ignored by the scientific community for more than 50 years. In 1976 new research revealed that Milankovitch's model correlated with past temperatures derived from studying deep sea sediments. The Milankovitch theory has since been widely accepted as one of the major factors affecting the Earth's climate.

ash high into the atmosphere. This dust can act as a shield that blocks incoming solar radiation. The resulting reduction in solar energy received by the Earth's surface can cool the planet and alter the climate. Volcanoes can put large amounts of sulfur dioxide gas (SO_2) into the atmosphere. This gas helps reflect sunlight away from the planet, which can help cool the climate. These examples illustrate how the lithosphere and plate tectonics can also help alter global climate.

HOT HOUSE CLIMATES

The opposite of an ice age, a hot house period is when the Earth's climate is significantly warmer than today. This has occurred several times in the Earth's past. The most ancient of these hot house climates occurred during the mid-Cretaceous period approximately 90 to 120 million years ago. During this time, tropical plants and animals lived as far north as 55 degrees north latitude. Today this region is near the Arctic Circle, where only cold-hardy plants can exist. Another hot house period occurred approximately 125,000 years ago, during the Penultimate Interglacial period. During this time, global temperatures were approximately 4° to 6° F (2.6° to 3.6° C) warmer than today. Since then, two more warming periods occurred on the Earth: the mid-Holocene warm period approximately 6,000 years ago and the Medieval warm period between 600 and 1,100 years ago.

All these hot house episodes are believed to have been caused by an increase in carbon dioxide gas (CO_2) in the Earth's atmosphere. During all the warm periods, levels of carbon dioxide have been found to be 2 to 4 times greater than today. Carbon dioxide gas is a greenhouse gas that helps trap the Earth's heat. Scientists are still trying to determine what caused an increase in carbon dioxide concentration in the past. Volcanoes, along with the weathering of carbonate rocks, can put large amounts of carbon dioxide into the atmosphere. Changes in the populations of organisms that use carbon dioxide for photosynthesis or produce it by respiration can also affect global levels. The exact reason for the past increases in carbon dioxide might always remain a mystery.

GOLDILOCKS SYNDROME

The role that carbon dioxide gas plays in determining the surface temperature of our planet is often referred to as the greenhouse effect. The greenhouse effect occurs as a result of our atmosphere's ability to allow incoming short-wave radiation from the Sun to strike the Earth's surface. The gases in the atmosphere transmit short-wavelength visible light radiation. This radiation is absorbed by the Earth's surface and is then reradiated back into the atmosphere as long-wave infrared radiation. Greenhouse gases such as carbon dioxide absorb this energy, which regulates the temperature of the atmosphere and the Earth's surface (Figure 20–9).

The important link between carbon dioxide and surface temperatures does not exist only on Earth. Astronomers refer to the effect of carbon dioxide on a planet's surface temperature as the **Goldilocks syndrome** (Figure 20–10). "Goldilocks and the Three Bears" is the fable of a girl who tasted three different bowls of porridge. The first was too hot, the second was too cold, and the third was just right. This analogy is also used to describe the surface temperatures of the planets Venus, Mars, and Earth. Venus has a thick atmosphere that is 95 percent carbon dioxide, which causes the surface temperature to reach 800° Fahrenheit (427° C). This planet has too much carbon dioxide and is therefore too hot. Mars

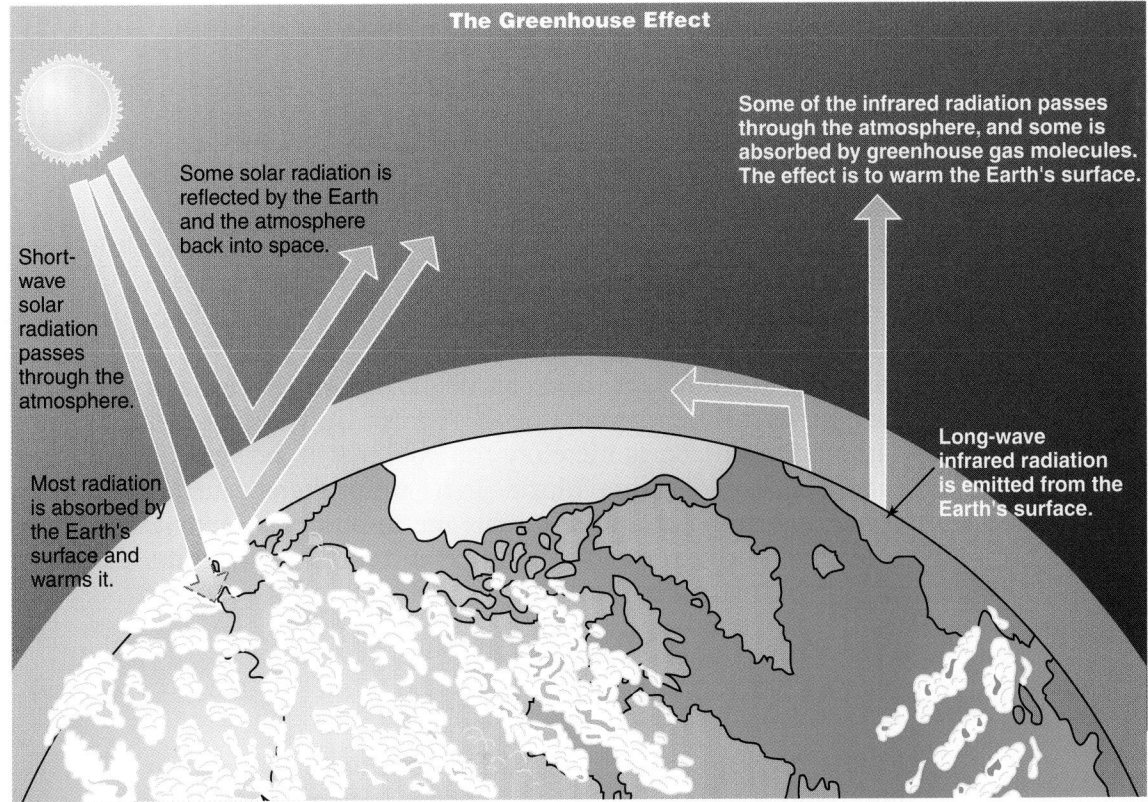

The Greenhouse Effect

Some of the infrared radiation passes through the atmosphere, and some is absorbed by greenhouse gas molecules. The effect is to warm the Earth's surface.

Some solar radiation is reflected by the Earth and the atmosphere back into space.

Short-wave solar radiation passes through the atmosphere.

Most radiation is absorbed by the Earth's surface and warms it.

Long-wave infrared radiation is emitted from the Earth's surface.

FIGURE 20–9 The greenhouse effect regulates the surface temperature on the Earth and depends on the amount of greenhouse gases, such as carbon dioxide, that are present in the atmosphere.

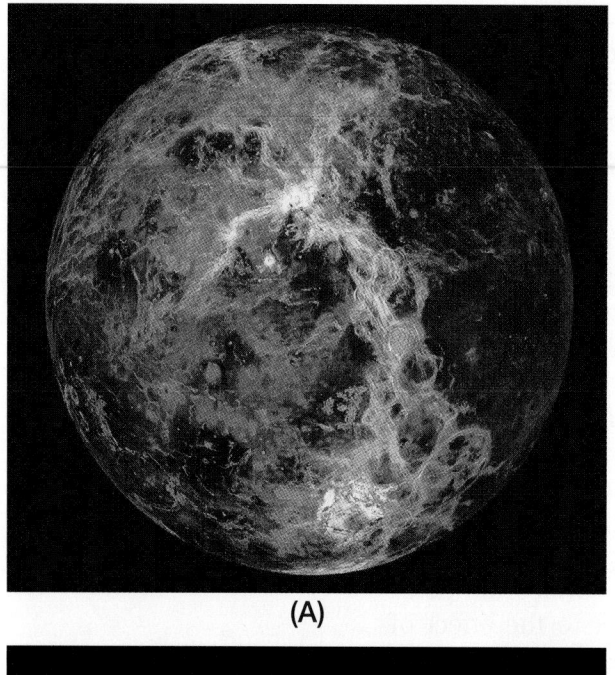

(A)

(B)

(C)

FIGURE 20–10 The Goldilocks syndrome illustrates how the surface temperatures of Venus (A), Earth (B), and Mars (C) are affected by carbon dioxide concentration in their atmospheres. (*Courtesy of PhotoDisc.*)

has a very thin atmosphere of carbon dioxide, which causes it to have an average surface temperature of –72° F (–58° C). This planet has too little carbon dioxide and is therefore too cold. Earth, however, maintains a careful balance of carbon dioxide in its atmosphere, which makes it just right. This simple example reveals the important link between atmospheric carbon dioxide concentration and surface temperature.

HUMANS AND GLOBAL CLIMATE CHANGE

During the past 1,000 years, global temperatures have been slowly increasing (Figure 20–11). The greatest increases in temperatures have occurred during the past 100 years and might be the result of human activity.

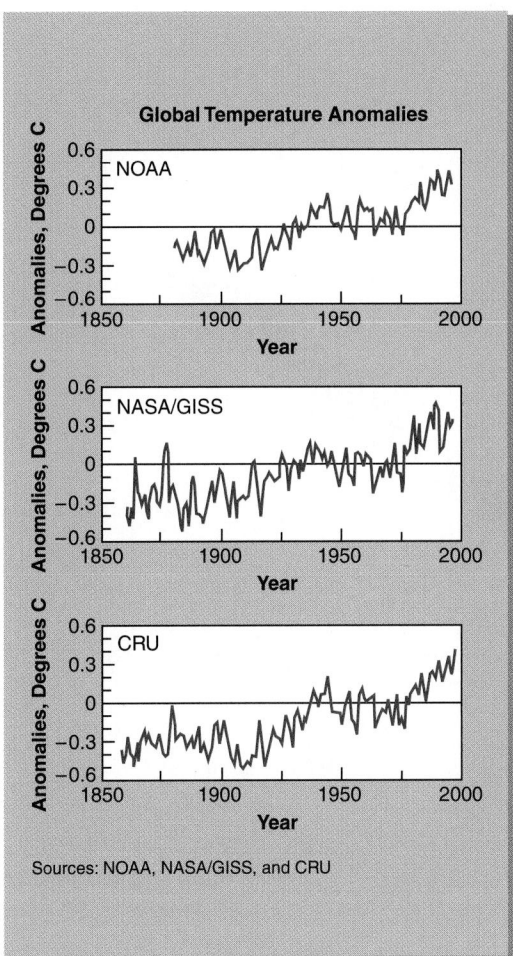

FIGURE 20-11 The average change in global temperature from three different sources going back to 1860 reveals that the Earth's average surface temperature is increasing.

The use of **fossil fuels** such as coal and oil has been causing an increase in atmospheric carbon dioxide levels since the end of the nineteenth century (Figure 20–12). Fossil fuels are hydrocarbon compounds, which, when burned, produce carbon dioxide gas. The increases in both industrial carbon dioxide production and atmospheric carbon dioxide concentration are most certainly linked (Figure 20–13).

Carbon dioxide is not the only greenhouse gas whose levels have been increasing in the Earth's atmosphere. The levels of methane gas (CH_4) have also increased in the past 100 years (Figure 20–14). On Earth, methane is produced mainly by livestock and **rice paddies**.

In addition, the levels of greenhouse gases such as **chlorofluorocarbons** (CFCs) and **nitrous oxide** (N_2O) are increasing. Evidence of rising global temperatures and increased concentrations of greenhouse gases suggests that human beings are indeed altering the climate of our planet. Increased temperatures around the globe may have worldwide effects. As the Earth begins to get warmer, seasonal storms such as thunderstorms, hurricanes, and tornadoes might become more powerful and occur more frequently. A shift in general climate types also might occur, resulting in widespread drought in some places and excess rainfall in others. A change in climate types could also impact regional vegetation.

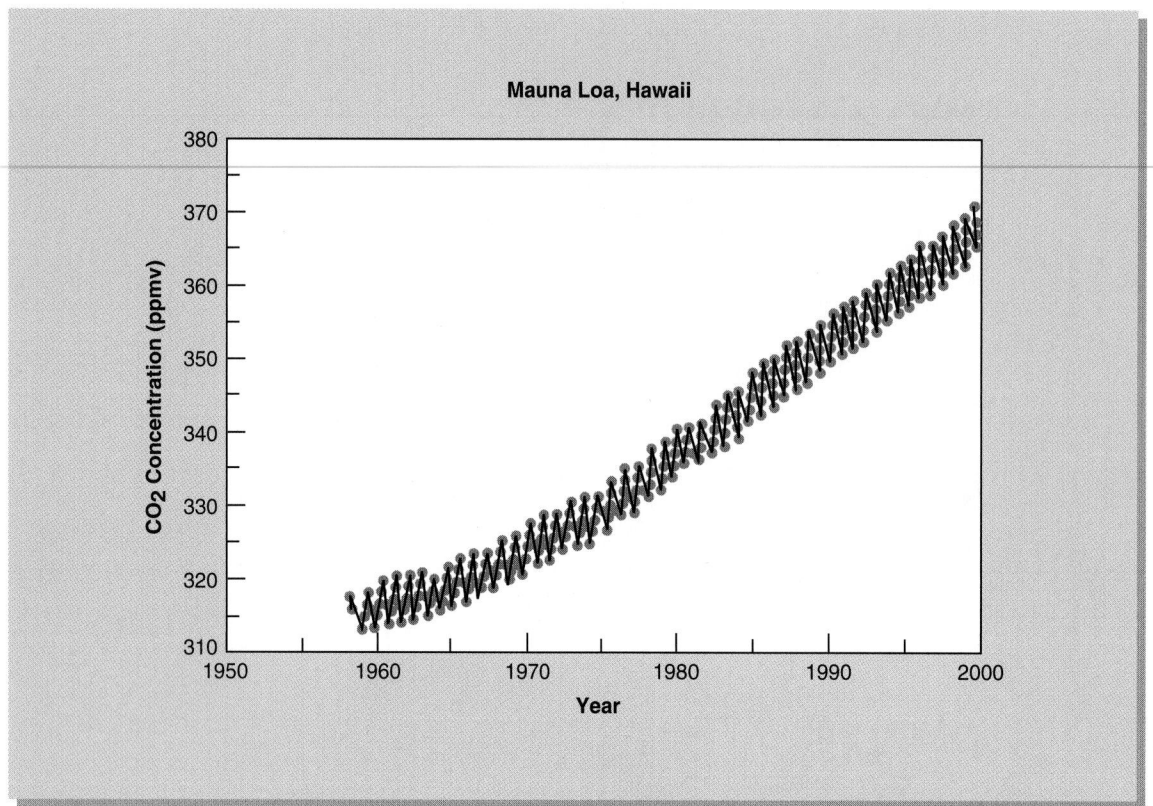

FIGURE 20-12 Atmospheric carbon dioxide levels have been steadily increasing since 1960, as this data show. The cyclical nature shown on the graph is the result of the periodic drop in carbon dioxide that occurs every spring when vegetation removes carbon dioxide from the atmosphere to grow new leaves.

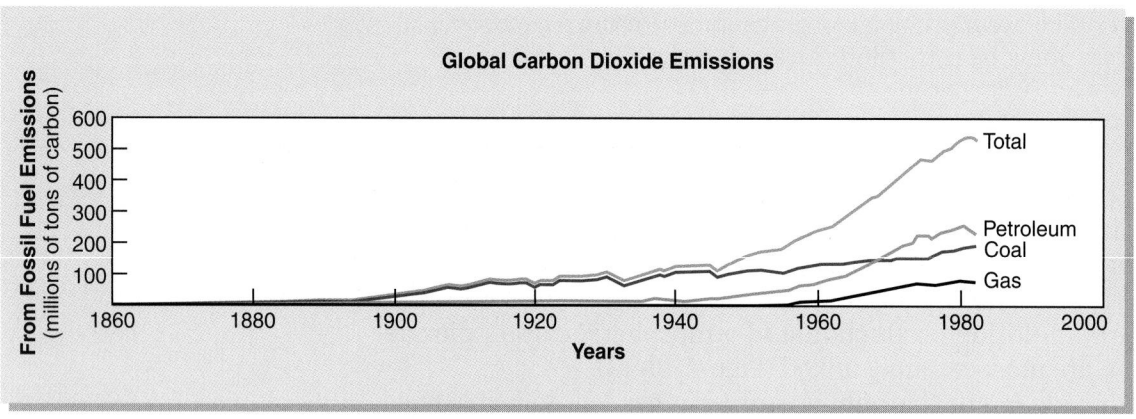

FIGURE 20-13 The rise in the production of carbon dioxide gas since 1860 as a result of the burning of fossil fuels.

Warmer varieties of plants would be able to grow in higher latitudes than today. A changing climate also could cause ice sheets and glaciers to melt, which would lead to a gradual rise in the sea level around the globe as the melting ice adds more water to the world's oceans.

Although the levels of carbon dioxide and other greenhouse gases are increasing, along with the average global temperature, researchers are not sure exactly when, if at all, the Earth's global climate will begin to change. Much more research needs to be conducted to fully understand the effects of global climate change. One thing is clear, however: Human practices and technology are interrupting the natural balance

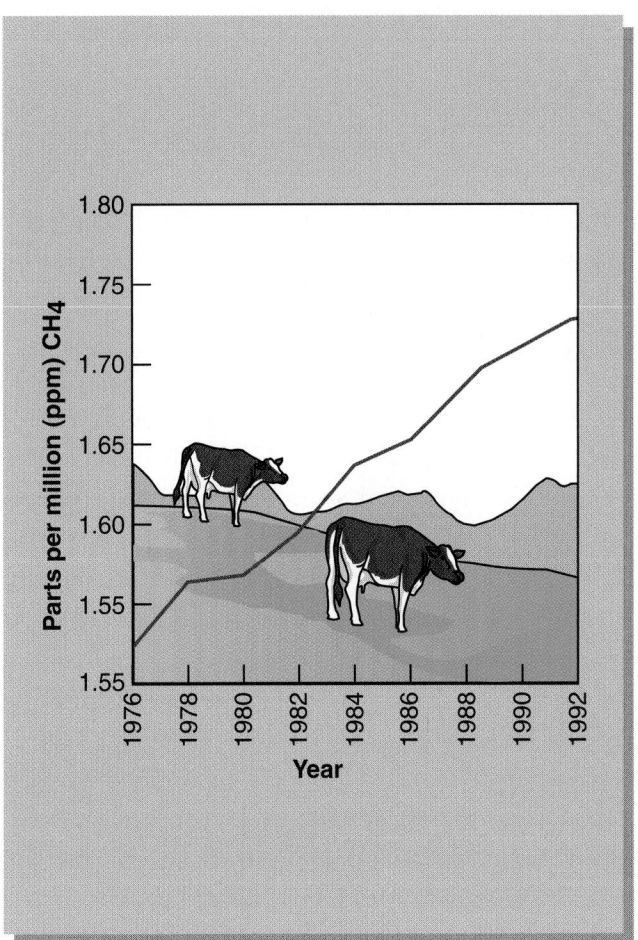

FIGURE 20–14 The atmospheric concentration of methane, a greenhouse gas, has steadily increased since 1976.

Earth System Law

The Kyoto Protocol

As part of the United Nations Framework Convention on Climate Change, the Kyoto Protocol is a binding agreement that is directed at reducing greenhouse gas emissions worldwide. The agreement was adopted on December 11, 1997 in Kyoto, Japan, and creates a 5.2 percent total reduction in the amount of greenhouse gases emitted by industrialized nations that signed the agreement. The time period for the reductions takes place between 2008 and 2012, and is based on levels of greenhouse gases produced in 1990. Industrialized nations bound by the protocol have specific target emission standards, and developing nations are excluded from emission controls. Currently 163 countries have ratified the protocol. The United States, which is the world's largest contributor of greenhouse gas emissions, signed the Kyoto Protocol in 1998, but withdrew its signature in 2001. The President and Congress felt that both developing and industrialized nations should reduce their emissions, and did not want to sign into an international agreement that might harm the economy.

CURRENT RESEARCH

Global Dimming

Scientists studying the atmosphere and the amount of sunlight reaching the Earth's surface have discovered that the Earth may now be experiencing a cooling effect known as global dimming. Research conducted by Dr. Gerald Stanhill of the Israeli Ministry of Agriculture has revealed that since the 1950s the Earth's surface has been receiving 22 percent less sunlight. Stanhill was astonished at his findings but was not alone. Scientists in Germany, Australia, and the United States were also coming to the same conclusion, that the Earth was being cooled by an average of 1.8° F (1.8° C) by a reduction of solar energy received at the surface. The cause of this cooling effect is believed to have two main sources, atmospheric pollution and air travel. Atmospheric pollution in the form of particulate matter, such as ash and soot, and gases such as sulfur dioxide, reflect solar energy back into space. High altitude flying jet airplanes create white trails of condensing water called contrails. These artificial, high altitude clouds crisscross the sky and also reflect sunlight back into space. Together contrails and atmospheric pollutants cause the Earth's surface to receive less sunlight, therefore cooling the planet. A dramatic effect of the impact that contrails have on the Earth's heat budget were observed in the days following the September 11th, 2001 attack in the United States. Atmospheric scientist Dr. David Travis of the University of Wisconsin had been studying the effects of contrails on weather when he had a unique opportunity to observe the atmosphere with no contrails. This was the result of airplanes being grounded for several days after the September 11th attack. Dr. Travis was amazed to find that without contrails reflecting sunlight back into space, the temperature range between night and day in the U. S. increased by an average of 2° F (1.2° C). Ironically, scientists also believe that a reduction in atmospheric pollutants may offset global dimming, therefore enhancing global warming, thus illustrating the complex ways in which humans are affecting global climate.

of the atmosphere at an unprecedented rate. This suggests that we should attempt to lessen our impact on the Earth's systems so we do not continue to interrupt the natural balance that has evolved among the atmosphere, lithosphere, and hydrosphere over billions of years.

REVIEW

1. What is paleoclimatology?
2. What methods do scientists use to determine the Earth's past climates?
3. What is the difference between an ice age and a glaciation?
4. How many ice ages have occurred during the Earth's past, and when did they occur?
5. What may cause global cooling of the planet?
6. What are hot house periods, and when have they occurred in the past?

CAREER CONNECTIONS

Geographic Information Systems Specialist

A geographic information systems specialist uses computers and geographic information system (GIS) software to analyze all types of geographic data. The job includes the creation, retrieval, and viewing of specific geographic information. GIS-created maps display layers of different information to reveal any trends or relationships that are occurring in unique geographic areas. This includes data on population, vegetation, water use, disease, droughts, floods, utilities, sewer systems, agriculture, and any other information being researched. GIS systems specialists must be able to use GIS software to sort data and to create colorful layered maps, and be able to operate digital cameras, scanners, plotters, and printers. They must also have knowledge of coordinate systems, latitude and longitude, cartography, topography, and map scales. A college degree with an emphasis on geography and computer programming is required for this type of career. Jobs within government agencies or in private industry are becoming more widespread as the use of GIS software increases around the world. Many free versions of GIS software are available for download via the Internet, which can be explored to see how this new technology is used and what type of work a GIS systems specialist performs.

@ WEB Links

FOR MORE INFORMATION GO TO THESE WEB LINKS:

<http://museum.state.il.us/exhibits/ice_ages/>

<http://www.noaa.gov/climate.html>

<http://www.cotf.edu/ete/modules/climate/GCmain.html>

<http://epa.gov/climatechange/index.html>

<http://www.noaa.gov/greenhouse.html>

<http://www.cotf.edu/ete/modules/carbon/earthfire.html>

<http://www.earth.nasa.gov/science/Science_ecosystems.html>

7. What may cause global warming?

8. Describe the Goldilocks syndrome.

9. How have humans contributed to possible global warming?

10. Who was Milutin Milankovitch?

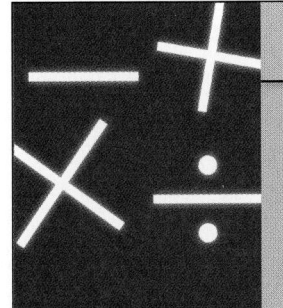

earth math

1) If the four major ice ages occurred approximately 700, 445, 300, and 4 million years ago, what is the average number of years between ice ages?

2) The concentration of carbon dioxide gas in the Earth's atmosphere was approximately 320 parts per million (ppm) in 1960 and 365 ppm in 2000. Determine the rate of change for carbon dioxide gas concentration for this period.

CHAPTER SUMMARY

The long-term weather on Earth is known as climate. Scientists believe that the Earth's climate has undergone drastic changes in the past. Scientists who study the Earth's past climate are known as paleoclimatologists. They use several techniques to infer what the past climate was like at different periods of geologic time. These techniques include examining fossils, tree rings, ice cores, sediment deposits, pollen, and coral reefs. The results of their investigations reveal several different times in the Earth's past when the climate was either much warmer than today or much colder. Ice ages occurred at different times in the past when temperatures were much colder than today. They resulted in much of the continents being covered with ice sheets or glaciers.

The Milankovitch cycle proposes that variations in the Earth's orbit and axis of rotation cause changes in the amount of insolation received by the Earth on a periodic basis. This is believed to cause ice ages. Hot house climates occur when the Earth's past temperature was much higher than it is today. This has also occurred at different times in the past. Scientists believe the main cause for the increase in temperature during hot house climates is an increase in carbon dioxide gas in the atmosphere. Carbon dioxide is a greenhouse gas that helps trap heat on the planet. The relationship between atmospheric carbon dioxide gas concentration and the surface temperature of the planet can be illustrated by observing our two neighboring planets. Venus has too much carbon dioxide in its atmosphere and therefore has a very high surface temperature. Mars has too little carbon dioxide in its atmosphere and has a very cold surface temperature. Recent evidence suggests that the Earth has been experiencing a gradual rise in surface temperatures over the past 100 years. This is thought to be the result of human activity. The increasing use of fossil fuels by industry and for transportation has led to a gradual increase in atmospheric carbon dioxide levels on Earth. Other greenhouse gases, such as methane and CFCs, have also been increasing in their atmospheric concentration. An increase in global temperatures may result in a change in global climate. This may lead to an increase in the intensity of storms, widespread drought, and rising sea levels.

CHAPTER REVIEW

Multiple Choice

1. Long-term patterns of temperature and moisture in a particular region are called:
   a. weather
   b. paleoclimatology
   c. climate
   d. meteorology

2. How can studying sediment deposits reveal past climates?
   a. Different landscapes form different sediments.
   b. Sediments only form in warm climates.
   c. Sediments trap gas bubbles that can be analyzed.
   d. Sediments only form in cold climates.

3. What effect do volcanic ash and sulfur dioxide have on climate?
   a. They both cool the climate.
   b. They both increase the surface temperature.
   c. They cause hot house climates and ice ages.
   d. They create a balance in global temperatures.

4. The wobbling of a spinning object on its axis is known as:
   a. eccentricity
   b. tilting
   c. precession
   d. rotation

5. What is the result of the Milankovitch cycle?
   a. varying orbital speed of the Earth
   b. varying insolation received by the Earth
   c. a change in the axis of the Sun
   d. the slowing down of the Earth

6. How long ago did the last ice age cover much of North America with glaciers?
   a. 5,000 years
   b. 10,000 years
   c. 20,000 years
   d. 100,000 years

7. What is believed to be responsible for the creation of hot house climates in the past?
   a. the Milankovitch cycle
   b. volcanic ash
   c. carbon dioxide gas
   d. CFCs

8. For the past 100 years, scientific evidence suggests that:
   a. Earth is about to enter another ice age
   b. Earth's average temperature is increasing
   c. Earth's average temperature is decreasing
   d. Earth's climate is stable

9. An increase in carbon dioxide in the atmosphere over the past 100 years is the result of:
   a. rice paddies
   b. melting glaciers
   c. volcanic eruptions
   d. burning of fossil fuels

10. Which of the following is not a greenhouse gas?
    a. carbon dioxide
    b. methane
    c. water vapor
    d. nitrogen gas

Matching   *Match the terms with the correct definitions.*

a. climate
b. hot house climate
c. ice age
d. paleoclimatology
e. tree ring

f. pollen
g. ice cores
h. precession
i. eccentricity
j. Goldilocks syndrome

k. fossil fuels
l. rice paddies
m. chlorofluorocarbons
n. nitrous oxide

1. _____ Long cylindrical sections of ice that are removed from glaciers by drilling and can be used to study the Earth's past climate.

2. _____ A chemical compound that is the form of a gas containing two atoms of nitrogen and one atom of oxygen (N_2O).

3. _____ The long-term weather patterns of a specific region on the Earth, usually defined by the area's annual temperature and precipitation values.

4. _____ The wobbling motion of the axis of a rapidly rotating body, such as the Earth, which causes the tilt of the axis to change periodically.

5. _____ Tiny, dustlike male reproductive cells produced by a flower.

6. _____ The mathematical expression of how far an ellipse is from a perfect circle, which can be determined by dividing the distance between the foci by the length of the major axis.

7. _____ A term used to describe a period in the Earth's history when the average surface temperature was much warmer than today.

8. _____ A class of human-created molecules commonly used as refrigerants and in electrical manufacturing and foam production that is responsible for ozone destruction and is also greenhouse gas.

9. _____ A specific period in the Earth's history when the average surface temperature was much lower than today, causing the widespread formation of glaciers.

10. _____ A illustration of the relationship among the atmospheric carbon dioxide concentrations on Venus, Earth, and Mars and their surface temperatures.

11. _____ A type of agricultural field used to grow rice; it is periodically flooded with water.

12. _____ The scientific discipline that studies the history of the Earth's climates.

13. _____ A term used to describe hydrocarbon fuels such as coal and oil, which were formed from the remains of once living organisms.

14. _____ The ringlike growth of new wood in the trunk of tree that marks the occurrence of one growing season.

Critical Thinking

1. The Milankovitch cycle involves the changing tilt of the Earth's axis between 24.5 and 22 degrees. Explain how the climate would be affected in the United States if the Earth's axis was tilted 21.5 degrees instead of its present 23.5 degrees.

21

Acid Precipitation and Deposition

OBJECTIVES

The pH of Precipitation · Formation of Precipitation · Anthropogenic Gases · Long Distance Transport of Acid-Causing Pollutants · Effects of Acid Deposition on Aquatic Ecosystems · Effects of Acid Precipitation on Terrestrial Ecosystems · Effects of Acid Deposition on Human Beings and Building Materials · Control of Acid Deposition

After reading this chapter you should be able to:

▶ Define the term *acid precipitation*.

▶ Explain why the pH of unpolluted rain is slightly acidic.

▶ Identify three natural sources that produce acid-forming compounds.

▶ Describe the process by which nitric acid and sulfuric acid are formed in the atmosphere.

▶ Identify the two main anthropogenic sources of sulfur dioxide and nitrogen oxide gases.

▶ Describe how acid precipitation is transported over long distances.

▶ Identify the main source area for sulfur dioxide gas, which creates acid precipitation that affects the northeastern United States.

▶ Explain two ways by which aquatic ecosystems are negatively affected by acid precipitation.

▶ Define the term *acid shock*.

▶ Explain two ways by which terrestrial ecosystems are negatively affected by acid precipitation.

▶ Identify five building materials that can be damaged by acid precipitation.

TERMS TO KNOW

acidic

pH

alkalinity

acid precipitation

sulfur dioxide

sulfuric acid

nitric acid

fossil fuels

hydrocarbon

combustion

anthropogenic

acid deposition

toxic heavy metals

acid shock

buffer

INTRODUCTION

One of the most shocking examples of how human activities can alter the chemistry of the atmosphere, resulting in widespread damage to the environment, is the formation of acid precipitation. Acid precipitation is a form of global pollution that is the direct result of human activities altering the Earth's systems. Following the pathways through the environment that pollutants take to form acid precipitation reveals the complex interaction that occurs among human activity, the atmosphere, the hydrosphere, and the biosphere.

THE pH OF PRECIPITATION

Under normal conditions, precipitation is naturally **acidic**. This is due to the effect of carbon dioxide gas in the atmosphere. Carbon dioxide dissolves in water high up in the atmosphere to form weak carbonic acid. Because of this, normal, unpolluted rain has a pH value between 5.2 and 5.6. The **pH** scale measures the acidity or **alkalinity** of a solution on a scale from 0 to 14. A pH of 7 is considered neutral. Any solution that is less than 7 is acidic, and any solution that is greater than 7 is considered basic or alkaline (Figure 21–1). **Acid precipitation** is formed when atmospheric pollutants create rain, snow, or fog with a pH level of 5 or less.

FORMATION OF ACID PRECIPITATION

Some natural events also create slightly acidic precipitation. Volcanic eruptions can emit **sulfur dioxide** gas into the atmosphere, which can also mix with atmospheric moisture. This combination forms **sulfuric acid**. Forest fires and lightning can naturally lower the pH of precipitation (Figure 21–2). These natural phenomena form nitrogen oxide compounds that can mix with moisture in the atmosphere to form **nitric acid**. Together, these natural forms of acid precipitation occur on such a small level that they pose no threat to the environment; however, human technology is altering this process.

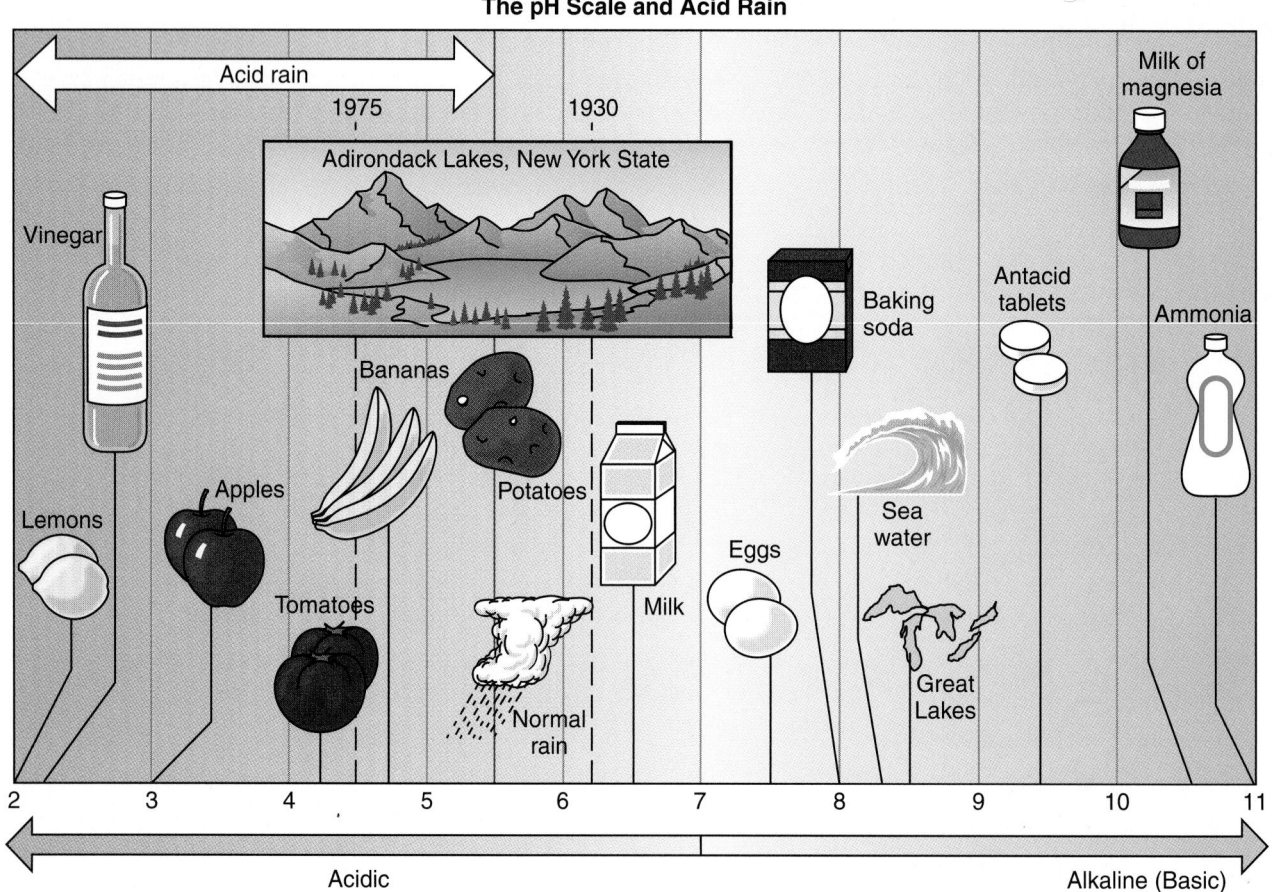

FIGURE 21-1   The pH scale and the acidity or alkalinity of some common substances.

FIGURE 21–2 Volcanic eruptions and forest fires are natural sources of acid-forming compounds in the atmosphere. (*Left image courtesy of PhotoDisc. Right image courtesy of Boise National Forest.*)

Earth System Scientists

Robert Angus Smith

Robert Angus Smith was born in Scotland in 1817. He was educated as a chemist and became interested in the pollution that was being created by the industrial revolution. Smith became one of the first scientists concerned about the negative effects of industry on the environment. He theorized that factory smoke and fumes could mix with precipitation and raise its acidity. In 1852 he presented his findings in a paper titled "On the Air and Rain of Manchester." Smith was the first scientist to call this phenomenon acid rain; it is now one of the most damaging forms of air pollution around the world. In 1872 Smith published *Air and Rain: The Beginnings of Chemical Climatology*, a book that presented his theories of how precipitation formed. Later in his life he also became interested in the effects of pollution on public health.

ANTHROPOGENIC GASES

The combustion of **fossil fuels** such as gasoline, coal, or natural gas is adding large amounts of nitrogen oxides (NO_x) and sulfur dioxide (SO_2) to the Earth's atmosphere. Most automobiles and trucks get their power by mixing a **hydrocarbon** fuel, such as gasoline, with oxygen in the air. This mixture is then ignited to create a controlled explosion that powers the vehicle. The burning of a substance is also known as **combustion**. Because 78 percent of the atmosphere is nitrogen gas, the combustion inside of an engine combines this nitrogen with atmospheric oxygen to form nitrogen oxide compounds. These nitrogen oxides, the by-product of combustion, end up in the Earth's atmosphere. In a different process, coal is also burned as a source of energy. Unlike gasoline, oil, or natural gas, coal contains sulfur. When this sulfur is heated as a result of combustion, it is joined with atmospheric oxygen to form sulfur dioxide gas. This gas also enters the Earth's atmosphere.

Both the nitrogen oxides and sulfur dioxide that are created as a result of technological combustion are known as **anthropogenic** gases. The term *anthropogenic* means "human created." Both these gases rise into the atmosphere and combine with atmospheric moisture to form nitric and sulfuric acids. These anthropogenic acids create acid precipitation (Figure 21–3).

Acid deposition is a different process than acid precipitation. Acid deposition occurs when dry nitrogen and sulfur compounds are deposited directly onto the Earth's surface. This causes a reaction with the surrounding environment that leads to the formation of strong acids. Acid deposition is also caused by anthropogenic gases.

LONG DISTANCE TRANSPORT OF ACID-CAUSING POLLUTANTS

Since 1987 more than 50 million tons of sulfur dioxide gas has been emitted into the atmosphere by utility companies burning coal in the United States, and more than 210 million tons of sulfur compounds fall to the Earth's surface every year. The combustion of coal is used to create steam that generates electrical power. The majority of the sulfur dioxide emissions in the United States originate in the Midwest. About 90 percent of all the acid precipitation and deposition that occurs on the Earth is derived from sulfur dioxide. Nitrogen oxide emissions into the atmosphere from the United States since 1987 equal about 250 million tons. It is estimated that more than 56 million tons of nitrogen compounds are deposited on the Earth's surface annually. The nitrogen compounds are derived from both transportation and industrial combustion of fossil fuels. The amount of these gases that have entered the atmosphere is altering the chemistry of precipitation.

Because of the prevailing winds that move weather across North America from west to east, the northeastern portions of the continent receive the greatest amount of acid precipitation (Figure 21–4). Nitrogen oxides and sulfur dioxide gas that are produced west of the Appalachian Mountains rise into the atmosphere and mix with atmospheric moisture to form acid precipitation. By the time weather systems reach the northeast, the pH of the precipitation is between 4.3 and 4.5. This is called

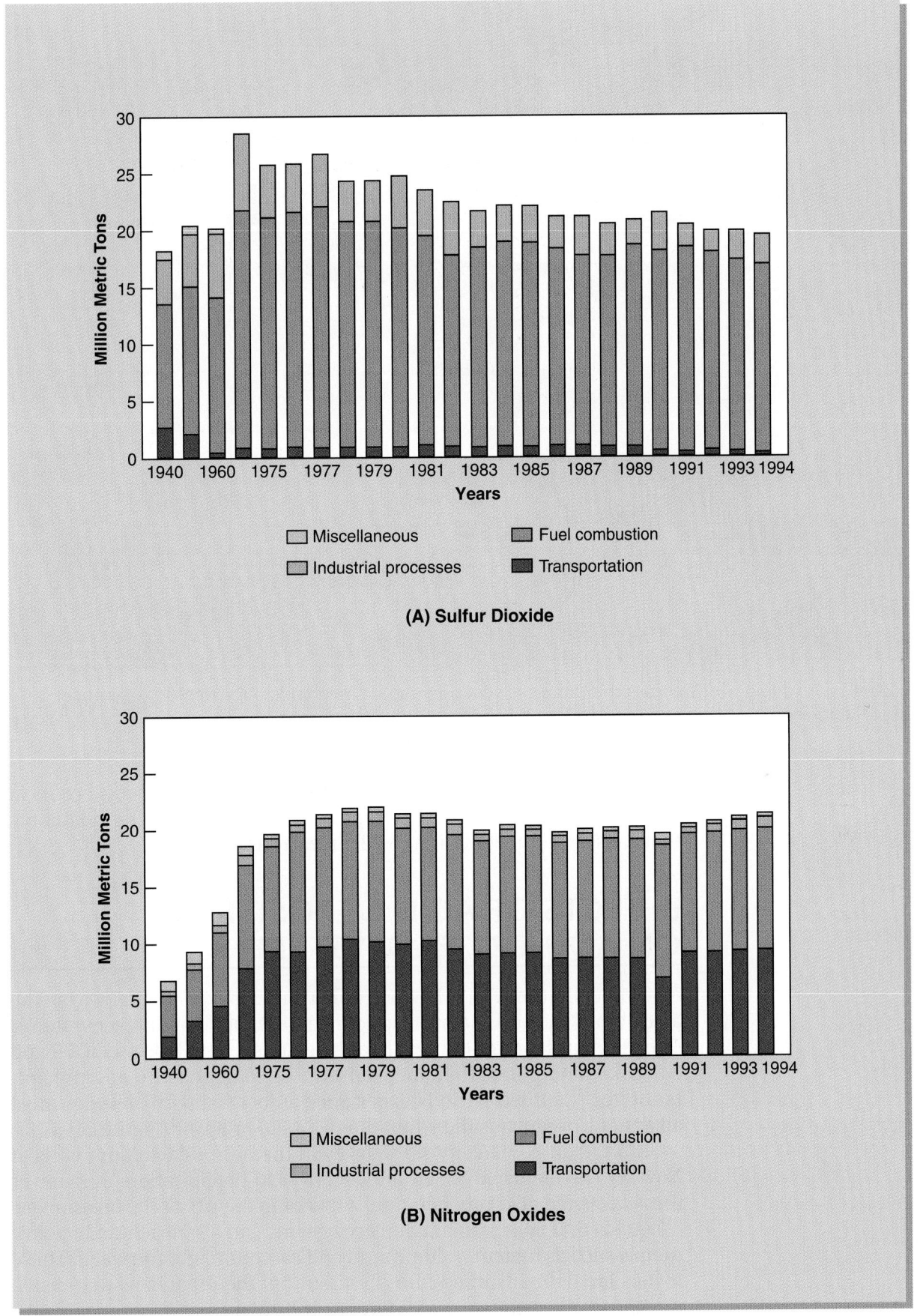

FIGURE 21-3 Anthropogenic sources and their annual emissions of sulfur dioxide and nitrogen oxides, which form acid precipitation.

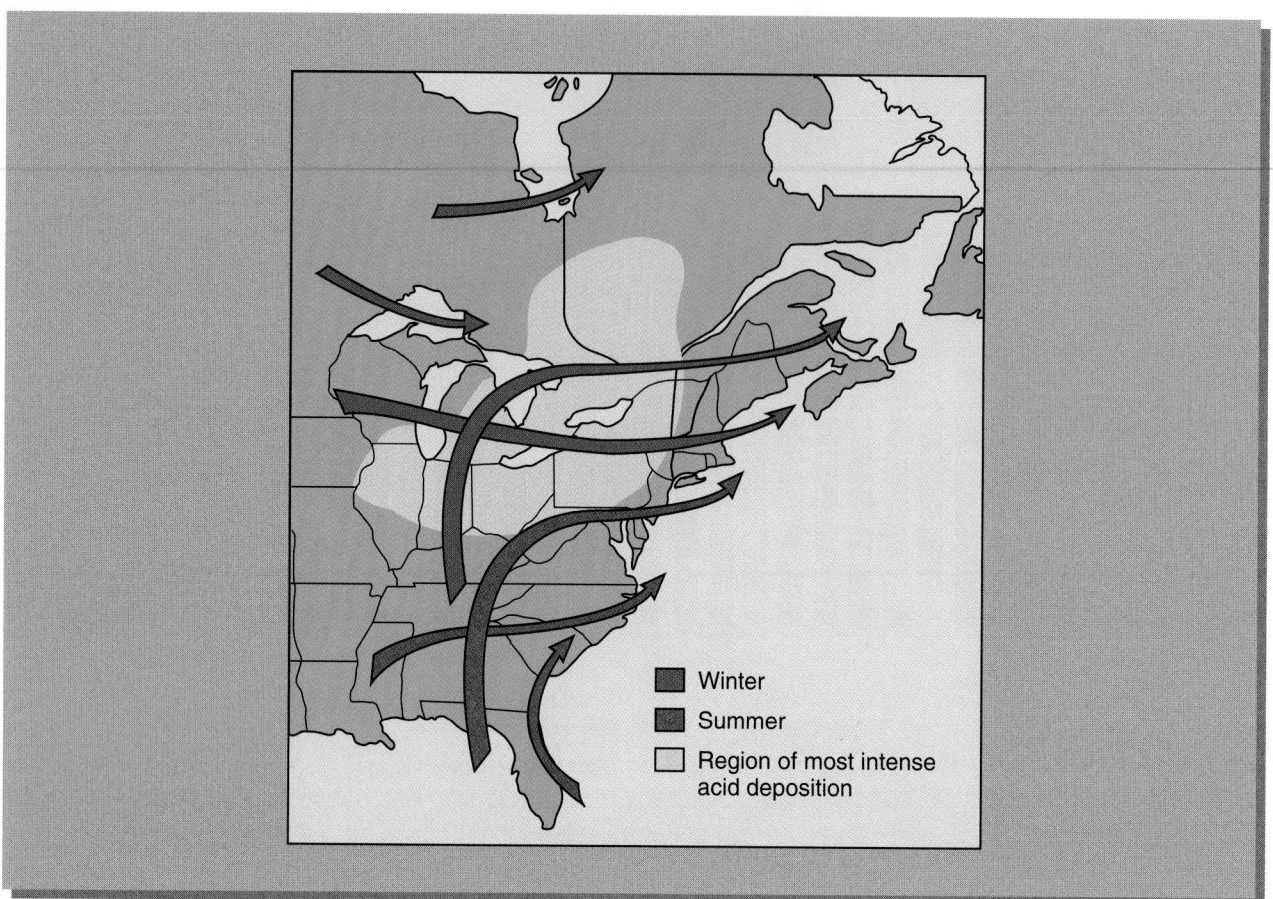

FIGURE 21–4 Prevailing winds across the United States provide the mechanism for the long-distance transport of acid-forming compounds in the atmosphere.

long-distance transport of acid precipitation. A similar process occurs in Europe, where the western European countries create the pollutants that cause acid precipitation to fall on eastern Europe.

EFFECTS OF ACID DEPOSITION ON AQUATIC ECOSYSTEMS

Acid precipitation can adversely affect the Earth in several ways. The acids that fall from the atmosphere can damage aquatic ecosystems. The pH values for unpolluted, healthy ecosystems fall between 6.0 and 8.0. Lakes and ponds that are exposed to acid deposition and precipitation for extended periods experience a decreasing pH level. Almost all aquatic organisms die when the pH is 4.0 or lower (Figure 21–5).

More than 70 percent of the lakes in the Adirondack Mountains of New York are being adversely affected by acid precipitation. In many of these lakes the acid precipitation is lowering the pH of the lakes below 4.0. Acids that collect in aquatic ecosystems can also leach **toxic heavy metals** such as mercury, aluminum, and cadmium into the water. These metals are then absorbed into the tissues of the organisms that reside there, causing adverse health effects. If humans eat these organisms, the toxic metals can build up in human tissue, causing health problems. One of the worst effects of acid deposition on aquatic ecosystems occurs during the winter. Over the winter, acidic snow accumulates; then during the

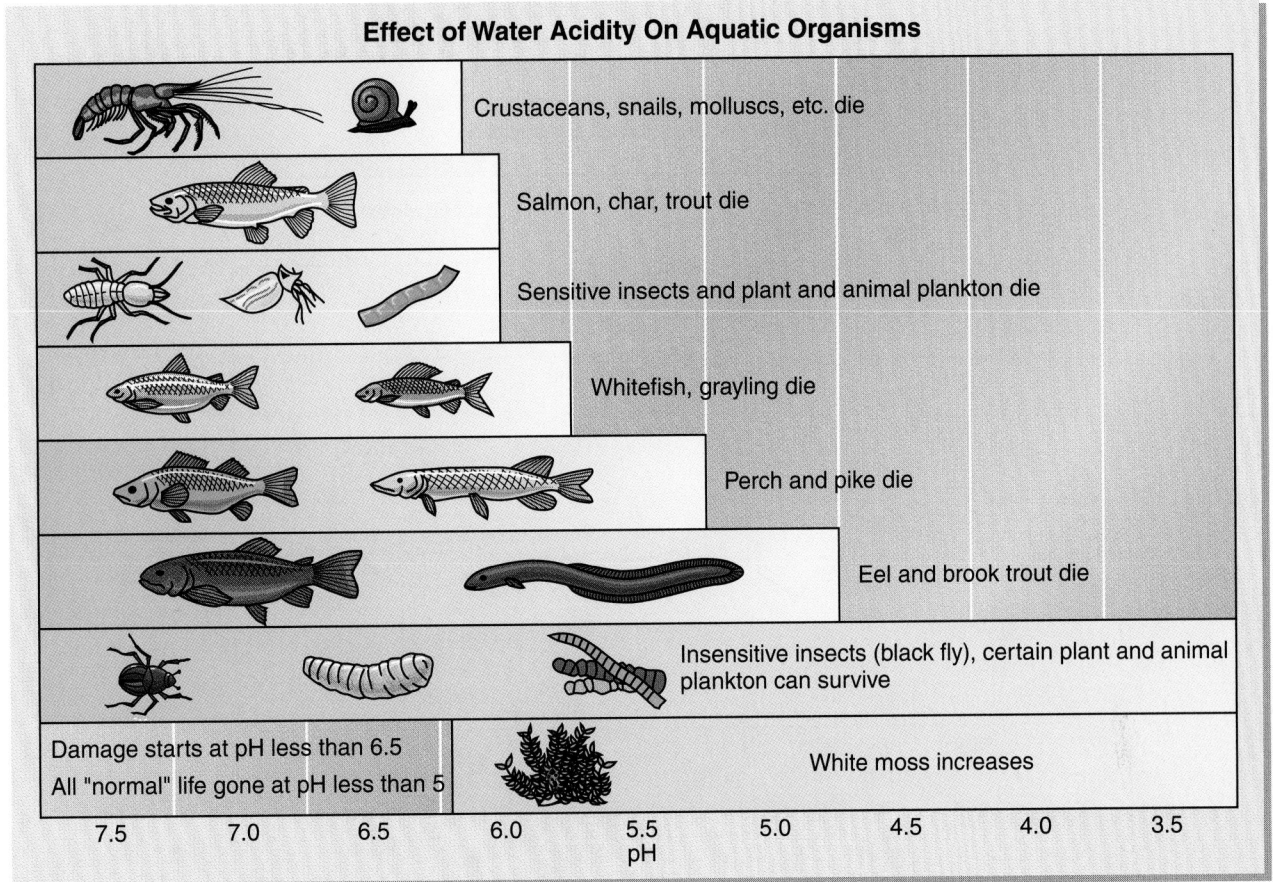

FIGURE 21-5 The effect of increased acidity on aquatic organisms.

spring thaw this snow releases a large amount of acidic water into nearby lakes and streams. This is called an **acid shock**, which is caused by acidic melt water rapidly entering aquatic ecosystems. The organisms that live there are then exposed to a rapid drop in the pH of the water, which causes adverse health effects. Most adult organisms can survive an acid shock, but younger organisms and eggs are usually killed off by this phenomenon. Some aquatic ecosystems are able to neutralize the effects of acid deposition. This is caused by natural limestone rock outcrops that act as a **buffer** to the acids (Figure 21–6).

EFFECTS OF ACID PRECIPITATION ON TERRESTRIAL ECOSYSTEMS

Acid deposition and precipitation can also have adverse effects on land-based environments, also known as terrestrial ecosystems. Many plants and trees experience stress from acids burning their leaves and stems. The acids break down the protective waxy layer on many plants, which exposes their leaves and stems to disease and causes them to lose water. Trees that are located at higher elevations and are constantly bathed in fog and mist are especially susceptible to acid damage. Acids can also leach important plant nutrients from the soil, including potassium, calcium, and magnesium. Other elements in soil can be released by the increased acidity, which causes plants to become damaged by their exposure. Aluminum is responsible for the

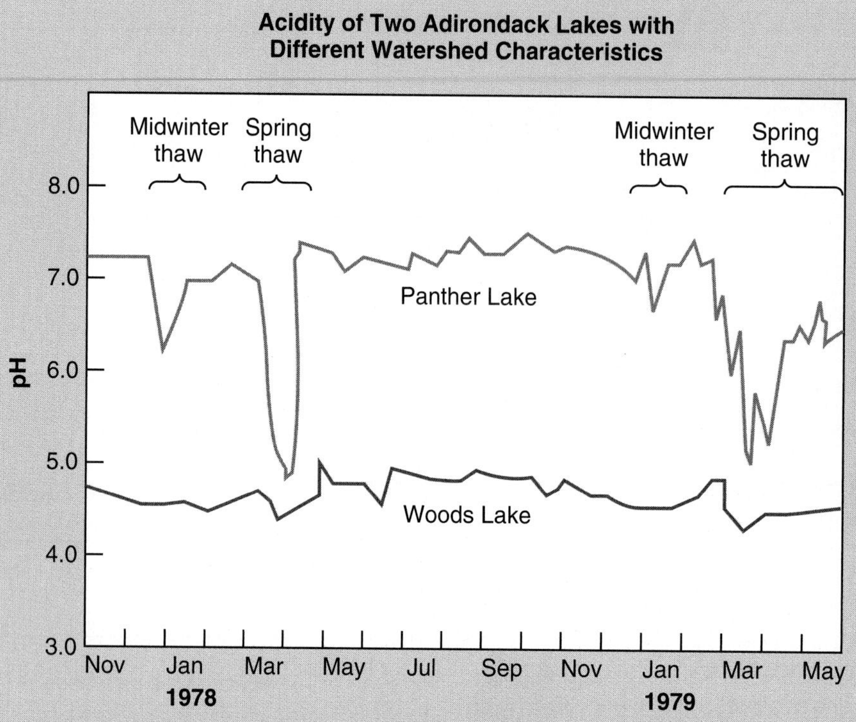

Acidity of Two Adirondack Lakes with Different Watershed Characteristics

FIGURE 21–6   The buffering capacity of rock outcrops can lessen the impact of acid shock during the spring thaw, as shown by the pH data for two different lakes in the Adirondack Mountains of New York.

CAREER CONNECTIONS

Air Quality Environmental Technician

An air quality environmental technician applies a knowledge of science, technology, and communication to the monitoring of acid precipitation and other air quality problems. This job includes the collection, labeling, and storing of both air and precipitation samples for use in the monitoring of acid precipitation. These environmental technicians also operate, calibrate, maintain, and repair monitoring equipment in the field; input data into computer databases; and help analyze samples in the laboratory. This profession requires a 2- or 4-year college degree in environmental science; people who meet this requirement can seek employment with state or local government agencies and in academic institutions.

FIGURE 21-7   The damage caused to trees in the mountains of New York State as a result of acid deposition. (*Courtesy of PhotoDisc.*)

die-off of many evergreen trees that are exposed to acid precipitation and deposition (Figure 21–7).

Acid precipitation that falls on soil can also kill off beneficial microorganisms, such as bacteria and fungi, that add to soil fertility. Extremely acidic soils can also inhibit the germination of plant seeds, directly affecting agricultural production.

EFFECTS OF ACID DEPOSITION ON HUMAN BEINGS AND BUILDING MATERIALS

Human beings can also be affected by acid precipitation and deposition. Humans who consume fish that live in acidic waters can be affected by the intake of toxic heavy metals. Also, because acid precipitation affects plants, it can affect food production and forest products, such as timber, pulp, and maple sugar. Trees and plants that are damaged by acid precipitation are not as productive. Humans can also develop respiratory illness and irritation of the eyes, nose, and throat when they are exposed to sulfur dioxide gas and other acid-forming compounds.

Living organisms are not the only things that are affected by acid precipitation. Structures and building materials can also be damaged. Concrete and stone can experience enhanced weathering as a result of exposure to acids. Bridges, buildings, and other concrete structures are slowly dissolved and weaken with exposure to acids. Other materials, such as stone and brick, are broken down over time. Many old gravestones made from stone are almost unreadable today as a result of acid precipitation damage (Figure 21–8). Many ancient stone statues around the world are also slowly wearing away as a result of acid damage.

Metals such as steel, iron, and copper are corroded by the acids that fall from the atmosphere. Paints, varnish, rubber, and ceramics are damaged by acid deposition. The costs associated with maintaining or replacing these structures or artifacts reach billions of dollars annually.

Another negative aspect of excess acids in the atmosphere is the reduction of visibility. Nitrogen oxides and sulfur oxides greatly reduce visibility. This is becoming quite a problem for many of the national parks. Millions of people travel to these parks to experience their amazing visual beauty; however, these pollutants are causing reduced visibility at many of these parks.

CONTROL OF ACID DEPOSITION

The federal and state governments are attempting to regulate the amount of nitrogen oxides and sulfur dioxide gas that are emitted into the atmosphere. Northeastern states are especially concerned about

FIGURE 21–8   Many gravestones in cemeteries across the Northeastern United States have been severely degraded by the accelerated chemical weathering caused by acid precipitation. (*Courtesy of PhotoDisc.*)

Earth System Law

The Clean Air Act and The Acid Rain Program

The Clean Air Act of 1990 is the amended version of The Clean Air Act that was originally created in 1970. This important American legislation sets limits on the emission of air pollutants, including carbon monoxide, nitrogen oxides, sulfur oxides, particulate matter, volatile organic compounds, ozone, and lead. The Acid Rain Program was also an important amendment to the Clean Air Act, which is designed to reduce the damage caused by the long-distance transport of acid-forming compounds. This law sets limits on the levels of sulfur oxides and nitrogen oxides emitted by electrical power plants in the United States. The goal of this program is to reduce sulfur oxide emissions by 10 tons and nitrogen oxide by 2 tons by the year 2010. The Acid Rain Program also allows for the market trading of pollution allowances. One allowance is equal to 1 ton of sulfur oxide or nitrogen oxide emissions. If a company has allowances left over at the end of the year they may sell it to another company that requires it. This market-based incentive for pollution control is also known as cap and trade. In the future, pollution trading might act as an important way to induce industry to meet pollution standards.

controlling these atmospheric pollutants. Forests in eastern New York and western Vermont are experiencing the worst damage by acid deposition (Figure 21–9). The interactions that occur among human technology, the atmosphere, and the biosphere are responsible for the damaging affects of acid precipitation. Now that the process by which this pollution is formed is fully understood, efforts must be made to stop it before the damage becomes too great.

REVIEW

1. What is the normal, unpolluted pH value of precipitation?
2. What causes unpolluted precipitation to be slightly acidic?
3. What is the definition of acid precipitation?
4. How does acid precipitation form?
5. What processes produce the gases that form acid precipitation?
6. How does acid precipitation affect aquatic ecosystems?
7. How does acid precipitation affect terrestrial ecosystems?
8. How can human beings be affected by acid precipitation?
9. Explain how building materials are damaged by acid precipitation.
10. Who was Robert Angus Smith?

@ WEB Links

FOR MORE INFORMATION GO TO THIS WEB LINK:

<http://www.epa.gov /airmarkets/acidrain/>

<http://www.epa.gov /acidrain/site_students /index.html>

<http://www .adkmuseum.org /acidrain/>

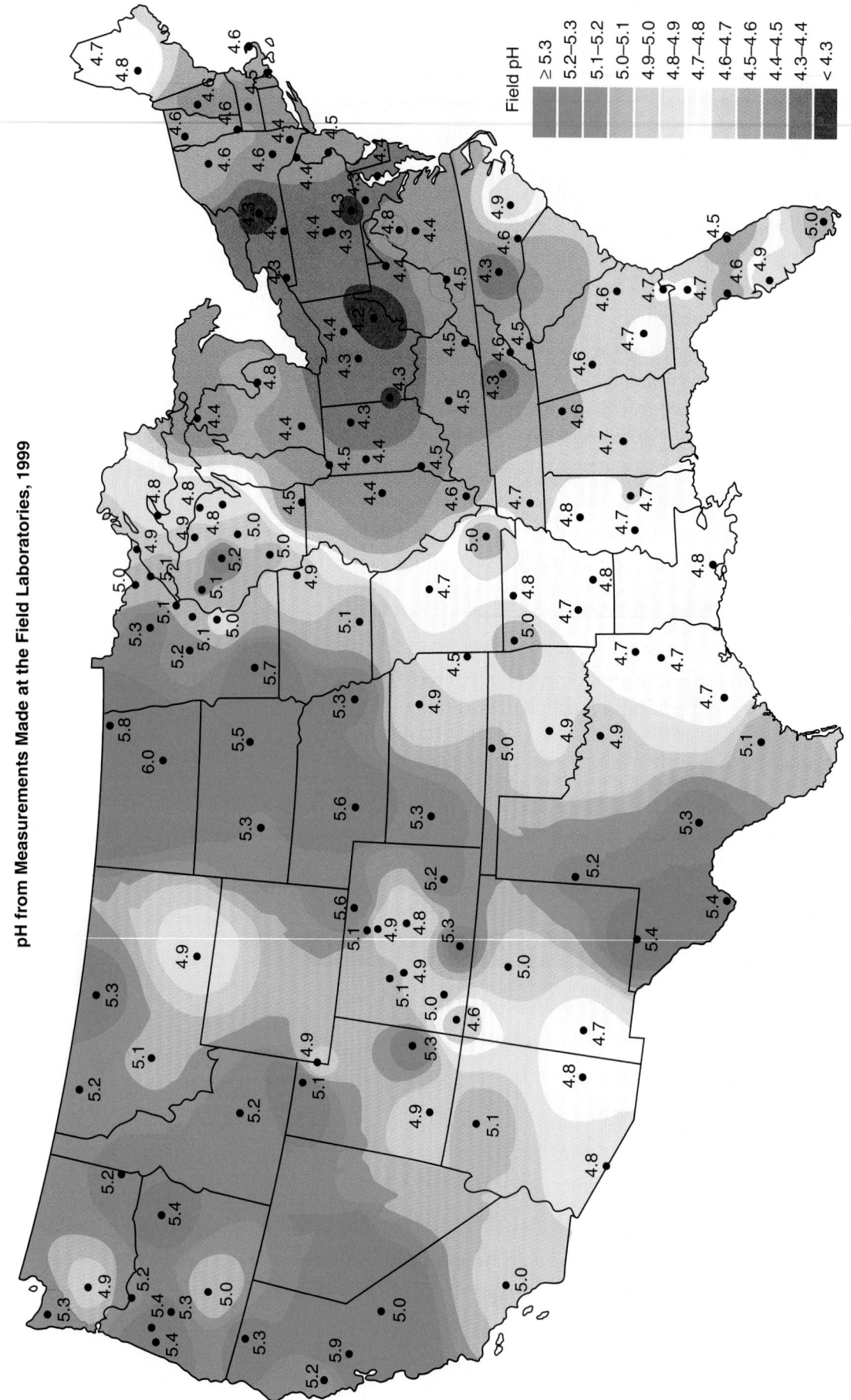

pH from Measurements Made at the Field Laboratories, 1999

FIGURE 21–9 A map of the United States showing the average pH levels for different regions.

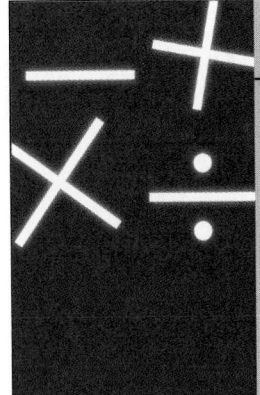

earth math

1) If 250 million tons of nitrogen oxides were put into the atmosphere between 1987 and 1997, approximately how many tons of nitrogen oxides enter the atmosphere each year?

2) By the year 2010 the Environmental Protection Agency plans to have utility companies reduce their nitrogen oxide emissions by 2 million tons each year. If their annual levels of nitrogen oxides are approximately 22 million tons, by what percentage will their emissions be reduced?

CHAPTER SUMMARY

Acid precipitation occurs when the pH of rain is lower than 5.0. The pH of a solution measures its acidity or alkalinity on a scale from 0 to 14, with 7 being neutral. A pH of less than 7 is considered an acid, and a pH greater than 7 is considered alkaline or basic. Unpolluted rain is naturally acidic, with a pH between 5.4 and 5.6, because it can mix with carbon dioxide in the atmosphere to form weak carbonic acid. Other natural events, such as volcanic eruptions and forest fires, also naturally lower the pH of rain. Acid precipitation forms when chemicals such as sulfur dioxide and nitrogen oxides mix with water in the atmosphere to form sulfuric and nitric acids. These then return to the surface in the form of rain or snow with a greatly reduced pH. Human activities such as the burning of fossil fuels create these anthropogenic gases.

The two major sources of anthropogenic gases are the burning of coal and the combustion of gasoline used for transportation. Acid precipitation can cause many adverse effects on the environment. When acid precipitation falls into aquatic ecosystems, the pH of the water can be reduced. This can cause stress or even death to the organisms that reside in the water. When the pH of an aquatic ecosystem drops below 4.0, nothing will survive. Many lakes in the northeastern United States have been adversely affected by acid precipitation.

Terrestrial ecosystems can also be harmed by acid precipitation. The leaves of trees and plants can be damaged by the acids, as can organisms residing in the soil, such as bacteria. Many buildings and structures built from materials such as concrete, stone, brick, and iron are damaged by exposure to acid precipitation. These building materials are rapidly degraded by the acids. The structures damaged by this pollution cost millions of dollars to repair or replace. Human health also is affected by exposure to acid precipitation. The eyes, nose, throat, and lungs can be irritated by exposure to the acids in the atmosphere.

Much of the acid precipitation that falls on the United States is formed by power companies in the Midwestern part of the country. These utility companies burn coal to produce electricity, which emits millions of tons of acid-forming gases into the atmosphere. These gases are then transported over long distances toward the East Coast by the prevailing winds, which move weather across the country. The long-distance transport of acid precipitation has caused eastern New York and western Vermont to experience the worst damage by acid rain. New regulations and cleaner forms of transportation are required to reduce this threat to our environment.

CHAPTER REVIEW

Multiple Choice

1. Which of the following atmospheric gases causes precipitation to be naturally acidic?
   a. nitrogen
   b. oxygen
   c. carbon dioxide
   d. argon

2. Lightning, forest fires, and vehicle exhaust all produce this gas, which combines with water in the atmosphere and lowers its pH:
   a. oxygen
   b. nitrogen oxides
   c. sulfur dioxide
   d. argon

3. The burning of coal and volcanic eruptions produce this gas, which combines with water in the atmosphere and lowers its pH:
   a. oxygen
   b. nitrogen oxides
   c. sulfur dioxide
   d. argon

4. These two acids are primarily responsible for the formation of acid precipitation:
   a. acetic and carbonic
   b. citric and carbonic
   c. vinegar and soda
   d. nitric and sulfuric

5. Most acid rain that falls on Vermont and New York originates in:
   a. New York City
   b. the Midwest
   c. California
   d. Canada

6. Most all aquatic organisms die when the pH of the water drops below:
   a. 6.0
   b. 5.0
   c. 4.0
   d. 3.0

7. In the northeastern United States the annual spring thaw can cause:
   a. acid rain
   b. acid shock
   c. acid melt
   d. algal bloom

8. Which type of aquatic organism is most affected by lowering the pH of water?
   a. young
   b. old
   c. carp
   d. bacteria

9. What percentage of lakes in the Adirondack Mountains of New York are affected by acid precipitation?
   a. 10%
   b. 25%
   c. 50%
   d. 70%

10. Which element can be leached from rock and soil into water by acid precipitation, harming organisms?
    a. nitrogen
    b. sulfur
    c. aluminum
    d. calcium

Matching   *Match the terms with the correct definitions.*

a. acid precipitation
b. pH
c. acidic
d. alkalinity
e. sulfur dioxide

f. sulfuric acid
g. nitric acid
h. fossil fuels
i. hydrocarbon
j. combustion

k. anthropogenic
l. acid deposition
m. toxic heavy metals
n. acid shock
o. buffer

1. _____ A gaseous chemical compound composed of one atom of sulfur and two atoms of oxygen (SO_2).
2. _____ The deposit of acidic substances on the Earth's surface.
3. _____ A term used to describe hydrocarbon fuels such as coal and oil, which were formed from the remains of once living organisms.
4. _____ A substance that is capable of stabilizing the acidity or alkalinity of a solution.
5. _____ Precipitation that contains high concentrations of sulfuric or nitric acids and has a pH of 5.0 or lower.
6. _____ Rapid introduction of acidic water into lakes and streams caused by melting snow.
7. _____ The unit of measurement used to measure the acidity or alkalinity of a solution.
8. _____ Naturally occurring, poisonous metal elements such as lead or mercury.
9. _____ A chemical reaction that results in light and heat, commonly called burning.
10. _____ A solution that possesses a pH lower than 7.0.
11. _____ A term that describes any substance that is created or introduced into the environment by human activity.
12. _____ A solution that has a pH greater than 7.0, also called a base.
13. _____ A type of chemical compound composed of hydrogen and carbon and commonly associated with fuels.
14. _____ A strong acid (H_2SO_4) that forms in the atmosphere when sulfur dioxide gas reacts with atmospheric moisture.
15. _____ A strong acid (HNO_3) that is formed in the atmosphere when rain mixes with nitrogen compounds to create acid precipitation.

Critical Thinking:

1. Some researchers believe that acid rain may actually be beneficial to agriculture. Why do you think they believe this true?

22

Ozone Depletion

OBJECTIVES

Ozone Gas · The Ozone Layer · Measuring Stratospheric Ozone · Effects of Ozone Depletion · The Ozone Hole · Reducing Ozone Depletion

After reading this chapter you should be able to:

▶ Describe how ozone gas forms in the atmosphere.

▶ Identify the location of the ozone layer within the atmosphere.

▶ Explain the process of how ozone gas prevents ultraviolet radiation from striking the Earth's surface.

▶ Identify the gases that are responsible for the destruction of the ozone layer.

▶ Describe the process by which ozone is being destroyed.

▶ Explain the negative effect that ozone depletion has on the Earth's surface.

▶ Define the term *ozone hole*.

▶ Describe two ways by which humans can be affected by the destruction of the ozone layer.

▶ Explain three things that you can do to protect yourself from the loss of ozone.

TERMS TO KNOW

ozone

stratosphere

ultraviolet radiation

ozone layer

regeneration

dynamic equilibrium

depletion

chlorofluorocarbon

Freon

immune systems

mutated

ozone hole

INTRODUCTION

The discovery of a decrease in atmospheric ozone is one of the most serious threats that our planet has faced since the last mass extinction 65 million years ago. The layer of ozone gas that surrounds the planet acts as a protective barrier that prevents ultraviolet radiation from striking the Earth's surface at deadly levels. Today the ozone layer is being depleted around the world as a result of human activity, which is directly threatening life on the surface of the Earth. Understanding how ozone forms, what part it plays in the Earth's systems, and how we can prevent its loss is one of the most important scientific topics of the twenty-first century.

OZONE GAS

Ozone is an unstable gas composed of three atoms of oxygen that naturally exists between 12 and 15 mi (19 to 24 km) up in the **stratosphere**. Ozone gas is formed when atmospheric oxygen, which is composed of two atoms of oxygen (O_2), is bombarded by incoming **ultraviolet radiation** from the Sun. This high-energy radiation breaks apart the two oxygen atoms, which recombine with other individual atoms of oxygen to form a molecule of ozone gas (O_3). As a result of this process, ozone gas has built up in the stratosphere over time to form what is called the ozone layer (Figure 22–1). The **ozone layer** is an important part of the Earth's atmosphere because it acts as a shield that protects the surface from deadly ultraviolet radiation emitted by the Sun.

THE OZONE LAYER

When an ozone molecule is struck by high-energy ultraviolet radiation, it breaks apart and converts the energy into heat (Figure 22–2). The release of this heat causes the temperatures to increase at higher altitudes in the stratosphere. This process prevents the high-energy ultraviolet radiation from reaching the surface of the Earth. The individual

FIGURE 22–1 The location of the ozone layer in the stratosphere, high up in the Earth's atmosphere. (*Courtesy of PhotoDisc.*)

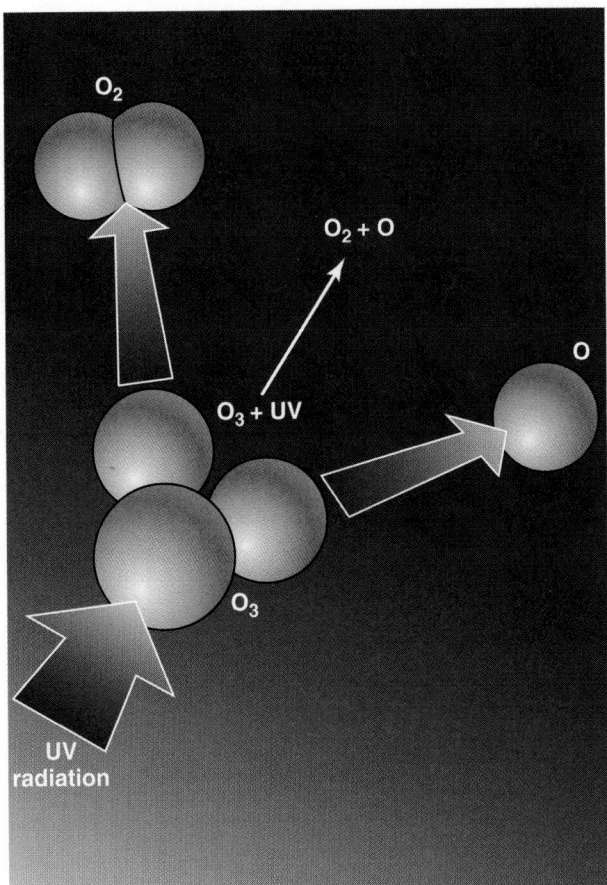

FIGURE 22–2   The destruction of a molecule of ozone as it absorbs ultraviolet radiation.

atoms of oxygen that are split apart by the ultraviolet radiation then recombine to form more ozone. The process of the destruction and **regeneration** of ozone molecules in the stratosphere has reached a state of **dynamic equilibrium**. This means that over time, the amount of ozone gas that is destroyed by ultraviolet radiation equals the amount that is reformed. This natural balance has existed in the atmosphere for billions of years.

Before the Earth's atmosphere contained oxygen, there was no ozone layer. This allowed deadly ultraviolet radiation to strike the Earth's surface, making it impossible for life to exist on land. Ultraviolet radiation does not penetrate deep into water, so during the first 2 billion years of Earth's history, life could exist only in the oceans. Eventually, as the atmosphere became filled with oxygen, the ozone layer began to form, enabling life to exist on land for the first time.

MEASURING STRATOSPHERIC OZONE

To study how much ozone exists in the stratosphere, scientists set up a series of ground-based instruments that determined the amount of ozone over specific spots on the Earth. This was done by measuring the amount of ultraviolet radiation that was reaching the surface at each particular location. The more radiation received at the surface, the less the amount of ozone gas present in the ozone layer above

CAREER CONNECTIONS
Aeronomer

An aeronomer is a specialized scientist who works to improve the ability to observe, understand, predict, and protect the quality of the atmosphere. The job of an aeronomer is to study the atmosphere in three distinct ways. These include theoretical research, field monitoring, and laboratory science. Theoretical research involves an improved knowledge of atmospheric movement and the transport of chemicals in the air. Field monitoring involves the measurement of the chemical and physical properties of the atmosphere around the world. Laboratory science investigates the chemical processes and reactions that occur within the atmosphere and how they are being altered by human activity. All three of the areas that make up the science of aeronomy work together to create an improved understanding of how the atmosphere operates and how it is being affected by human activity. Major research topics include the El Niño, southern oscillation, stratospheric ozone depletion, ozone in the troposphere, the effects of aircraft on the atmosphere, and global warming. Scientists in the field of aeronomy must have a college education in atmospheric science and are employed in academic research or with a government agency such as the National Oceanic and Atmospheric Administration or the National Aeronautics and Space Administration (NASA).

that location. The less the amount of radiation at the surface, the greater the amount of ozone gas. This research revealed that ozone levels change naturally with the seasons and with the global circulation of the atmosphere. These natural changes were minimal and showed no threat to the Earth's surface. However, in the 1970s it was noticed that ozone levels were beginning to decrease. This depletion was not understood at first, but as time went on, researchers realized that the ozone layer was indeed becoming thinner in some regions (Figure 22–3).

The **depletion** of the ozone layer was found to be the result of human-created gases that are interrupting the natural chemistry of the ozone layer in the stratosphere. During the early part of the twentieth century, scientists were experimenting with different gases that could be used for refrigeration. These gases needed to be able to remove heat from the air efficiently and enable it to cool to a low temperature. The first gas used for refrigeration was ammonia; however, this could be deadly to the surrounding environment if it leaked out. Chemists then synthesized a gas that could be used for refrigeration but was not

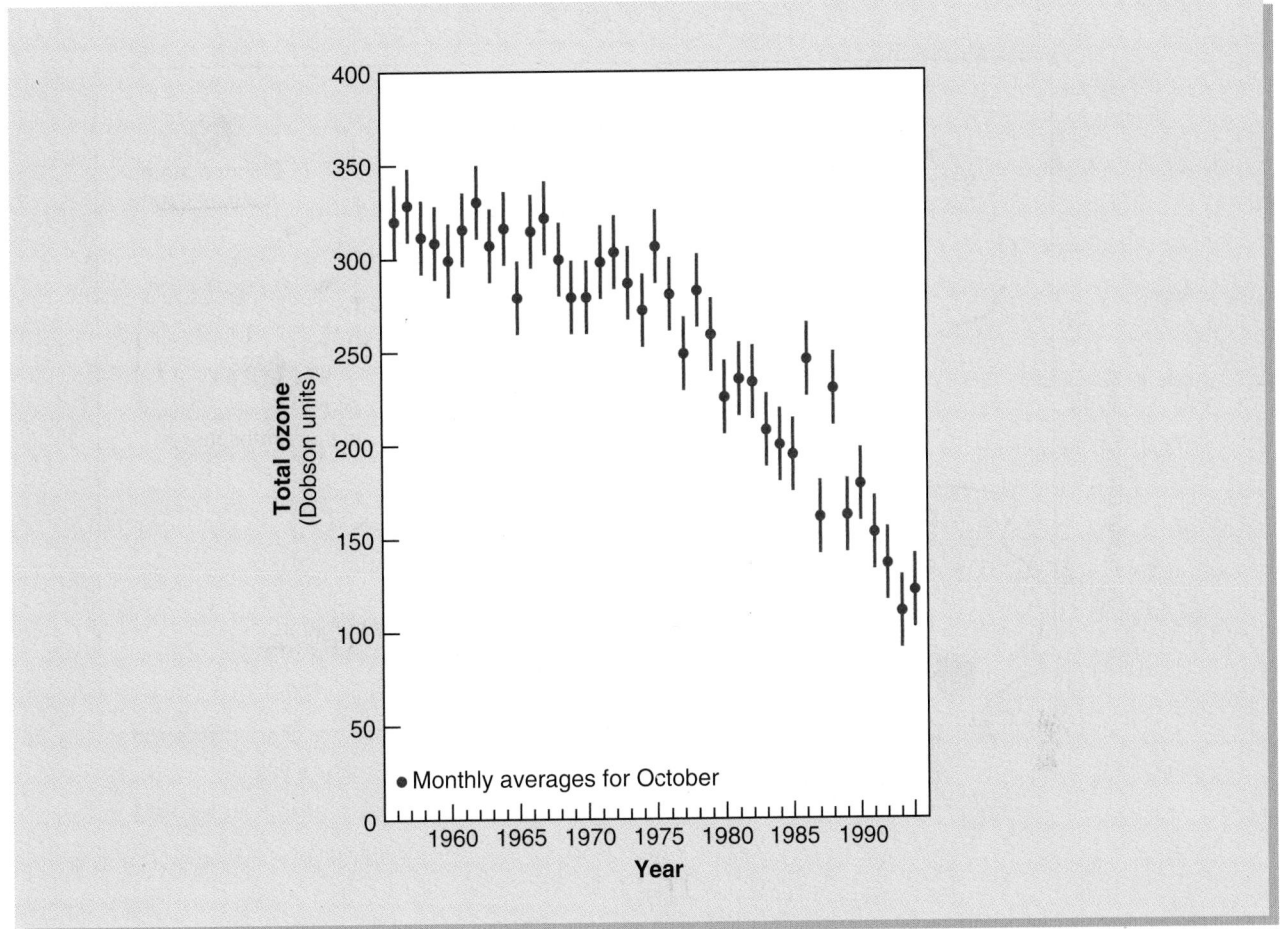

FIGURE 22-3 The decline in the level of ozone in the stratosphere between the years 1955 and 1995.

deadly if it leaked. This gas was called a **chlorofluorocarbon**, or CFC. One popular CFC gas used in refrigerators and air conditioners was **Freon**. CFCs were also used for industrial processes, as propellants in aerosol spray cans, in foam production, and for cleaning electrical parts. Over time it began to increase in concentration in the atmosphere. When CFCs are released into the atmosphere, it takes approximately 2 years for them to rise up to the level of the stratosphere. At low atmospheric levels, CFC gas does not react with other molecules and is harmless to life; however, as it rises up into the stratosphere, it undergoes chemical changes that lead to ozone destruction.

A CFC molecule is composed from atoms of fluorine, chlorine, and carbon. When a CFC molecule enters the stratosphere, it is exposed to high-level ultraviolet radiation (Figure 22–4). Like a molecule of ozone, high-energy radiation strikes the CFC molecule and breaks it apart. When this occurs, chlorine atoms are freed and begin to join with the oxygen atoms in the ozone layer. This creates chloride compounds that remove individual oxygen atoms from the stratosphere, causing a decrease in oxygen molecules that normally combine to create protective ozone gas. Therefore CFCs are primarily responsible for depleting the ozone layer. Other chemical compounds, such as bromide and halons, are also responsible for some ozone destruction.

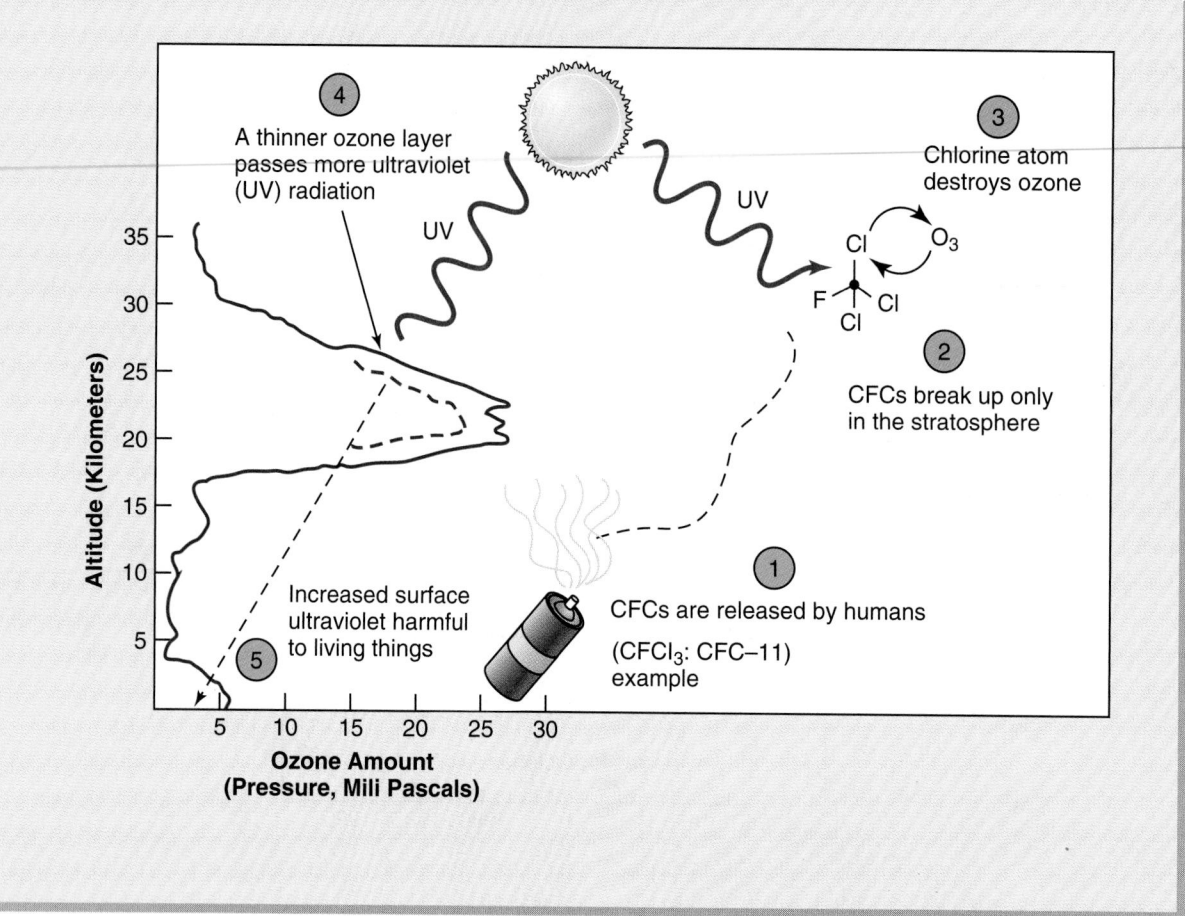

FIGURE 22–4 The pathway by which CFC gases travel through the atmosphere to destroy ozone in the stratosphere, thereby allowing more ultraviolet radiation to strike the Earth's surface.

 # Earth System Scientists

Gordon Dobson

Gordon Dobson was born in England in 1889. In 1920 he became a lecturer in meteorology at Oxford University. His research involved the properties of the stratosphere. In 1924 Dobson became interested in the levels of ozone gas within the stratosphere. He developed and built a device known as the Dobson ozone spectrometer, which he used to measure ozone levels around the world. In 1925 he discovered that ozone levels experienced seasonal changes around the globe. Later in his career he became interested in the effects of pollutants on the atmosphere. Dobson's work on ozone helped pave the way to an understanding of what role ozone gas plays in the Earth's systems. He also helped identify changes in the levels of ozone that led to an understanding of ozone depletion. The Dobson unit is still used today to measure the amount of ozone within the stratosphere.

EFFECTS OF OZONE DEPLETION

A reduction of ozone in the stratosphere results in a greater amount of ultraviolet radiation striking the Earth's surface. This can lead to potential damage to the world's ecosystems, as organisms become exposed to this high-energy radiation. Ultraviolet radiation can damage cells that are exposed to the atmosphere. The high-energy radiation strikes the cells much like a baseball striking a tower made of blocks. This results in damage to the structure of the cell. In human beings this can lead to skin cancer, degradation of the eyes, and weakened **immune systems**. Some researchers believe that many species of amphibians, such as frogs and salamanders, are especially susceptible to damage from depleted ozone. These organisms have sensitive skin, making them more likely to be damaged by ultraviolet radiation. Widespread incidence of **mutated** frogs might be the first signs of how a depleted ozone is affecting the biosphere.

THE OZONE HOLE

Today the National Aeronautics and Space Administration (NASA) and the National Oceanic and Atmospheric Administration (NOAA) use advanced satellites like the Ozone Mapping Instrument (OMI) and the Total Ozone Mapping Spectrometer (TOMS) to monitor ozone levels around the world. The continued monitoring of stratospheric ozone revealed an alarming decrease in ozone gas over Antarctica (Figure 22–5). For the past 20 years, data have revealed that ozone over the South Pole

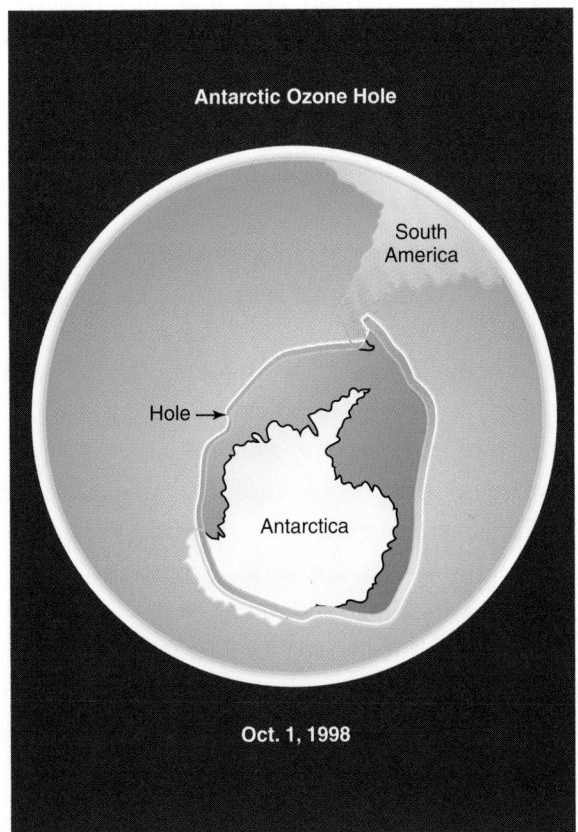

FIGURE 22–5 The location and size of the ozone hole over Antarctica.

has been depleted rapidly. The low concentration of ozone gas over Antarctica is known as the **ozone hole**. The formation of the ozone hole over Antarctica occurs during the Antarctic spring between September and November. Since the 1950s the seasonal ozone over Antarctica has been reduced by 60 percent.

A similar ozone loss also occurs over the North Pole during the Northern Hemisphere's spring season. These reductions have amounted to approximately a 20 percent to 25 percent loss of ozone. Other parts of the globe are also experiencing ozone loss. The mid-latitudes typically have experienced a reduction in ozone of approximately 4 percent to 6 percent. Areas between the equator and 20 degrees north and south latitude have experienced no loss of ozone.

Studies reveal that the loss of ozone is related to an increase in ultraviolet radiation reaching the surface. On average, a 10 percent reduction in ozone can lead to a 10 percent increase in ultraviolet radiation at the surface. A 30 percent loss of ozone can lead to a 50 percent increase in ultraviolet radiation striking the surface, and a 60 percent loss of ozone, such as in Antarctica, can result in an increase of ultraviolet radiation at the surface of almost 150 percent. Doctors have found that there is a direct relationship between increased exposure to ultraviolet light and skin cancer in humans. These statistics reveal the actual threat to the Earth's surface that ozone depletion can cause.

REDUCING OZONE DEPLETION

As scientists discovered that the chemistry of ozone destruction was being caused by chemicals such as CFCs, governments around the world began to control the use of these gases. In 1996 CFCs were completely

Earth System Law

The Montreal Protocol

On September 16, 1987, The Montreal Protocol on Substances that Deplete the Ozone Layer was adopted at a conference in Montreal, Canada, which was attended by more than 29 countries. This international agreement between industrial and developing nations sets reductions and phase-out timelines for stratospheric ozone-destroying compounds. Human-created gases such as chlorofluorocarbons (CFCs), halons, carbon tetrachloride, hydrochlorofluorocarbons (HCFCs), methyl chloroform, hydrobromofluorocarbons (HBFCs), and methyl bromide have all been targeted for elimination. The results of this international agreement have been recently observed by scientists monitoring the ozone layer. Researchers from NASA and the World Meteorological Organization have recorded a reduction in the concentration of ozone-destroying chemicals in the atmosphere, and a decline in the size of the Antarctic ozone hole over the past 10 years. The Montreal Protocol is now being hailed as a successful example of the importance of international agreements in reducing environmental degradation.

banned around the world; however, leftover CFCs that are still in the atmosphere continue to destroy ozone. Old refrigerators and air conditioners in wrecked cars located in landfills and junkyards will continue to leak CFCs into the atmosphere for many years. These chemicals will take between 50 and 100 years to be removed from the atmosphere by natural processes. It is hoped that the ozone layer will then begin to rebuild itself and return to its natural state. Until then, careful monitoring of ozone depletion will be necessary to provide information about how much ultraviolet radiation is reaching the Earth's surface.

Protecting exposed skin from the Sun can help lessen the effect of these potentially harmful forms of radiation (Figure 22–6). This includes the use of sunscreen, wearing hats and sunglasses, and reducing the time that your skin is exposed to the Sun. Scientists hope the biosphere will not be too adversely affected by this period of increased ultraviolet radiation. Ozone depletion provides yet another example of the effects of human technology on the Earth's systems. It also reveals that with careful scientific study and governmental cooperation, many environmental threats can be controlled.

FIGURE 22–6   Loss of stratospheric ozone results in an increase in harmful ultraviolet radiation reaching the Earth's surface. This has been linked to the increasing incidence of skin cancer in humans. (*Courtesy of PhotoDisc.*)

REVIEW

1. What is ozone gas, and where is it found naturally on the Earth?
2. What is the ozone layer, and why is it important?
3. What is causing the depletion of the ozone layer?
4. How is ozone gas destroyed?
5. How much of the ozone layer has been lost in different parts of the world?
6. What is the ozone hole?
7. What are some of the negative effects of increased ultraviolet radiation striking the Earth's surface?
8. Who was Gordon Dobson?

CHAPTER SUMMARY

Ozone is an unstable molecule that is composed of three atoms of oxygen (O_3). It exists naturally in the stratosphere, where it forms the ozone layer. The ozone layer acts as a protective barrier to deadly ultraviolet radiation. It prevents high levels of this radiation from striking the Earth's surface, which enables life to flourish here. In the late 1950s scientists detected reduced levels of ozone gas in the stratosphere. They discovered that human-created gases such as chlorofluorocarbons were responsible for the depletion of the ozone layer. These compounds were rising into the stratosphere and releasing atoms of chlorine, which combined with the oxygen there. As a result, the amount of free oxygen that normally formed ozone was becoming depleted. The reduction of ozone caused an increase in the amount of ultraviolet radiation striking the Earth's surface. A large amount of ozone was lost over Antarctica; this is known as the ozone hole.

The increase in ultraviolet radiation striking the Earth's surface as a result of ozone destruction can damage an organism's cells. The eyes and skin are especially susceptible to damage by increased exposure to this high-energy radiation. This can lead to the development of skin cancer in humans. The discovery that gases such as CFCs were responsible for ozone destruction led governments around the world to ban their use. Although they are no longer used, CFCs still exist in the atmosphere and will continue to deplete ozone in the stratosphere. Until they are removed by natural processes, it will be necessary to take precautions to protect your skin and eyes from increased levels of ultraviolet radiation.

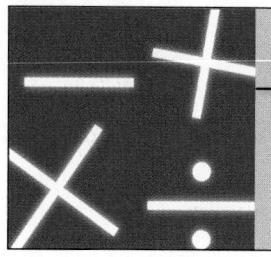

earth math

1) If the ozone concentration over Antarctica has decreased by 60 percent from 1960 to 2001, by what percentage did the ozone decrease over the South Pole each year?

C H A P T E R   R E V I E W

Multiple Choice

1. Ozone gas is formed from how many molecules of oxygen?
   a. one
   b. two
   c. three
   d. four

2. Ozone exists naturally in which part of the atmosphere?
   a. troposphere
   b. stratosphere
   c. mesosphere
   d. thermosphere

3. The ozone protects the Earth's surface from:
   a. insolation
   b. visible light radiation
   c. infrared radiation
   d. ultraviolet radiation

4. What happens to the oxygen molecules that compose ozone when it breaks apart?
   a. They recombine to form more ozone.
   b. They fly off into space.
   c. They turn into heat energy.
   d. They combine with water vapor.

5. As the amount of ozone gas in the ozone layer decreases, what occurs on the Earth?
   a. The stratosphere gets hotter.
   b. More ultraviolet light strikes the surface.
   c. Oxygen in the atmosphere decreases.
   d. The surface temperature increases.

6. What is responsible for the depletion of the ozone layer?
   a. climate change
   b. burning of fossil fuels
   c. CFCs
   d. acid precipitation

7. Approximately how much time does it take for ozone-destroying compounds to rise up to the ozone layer?
   a. 6 months
   b. 2 years
   c. 50 years
   d. 100 years

8. Which part of the Earth is not experiencing depletion in the ozone layer?
   a. the area between the equator and 20 degrees north and south latitude
   b. the mid-latitudes
   c. the North Pole
   d. the South Pole

9. Which part of the Earth is experiencing a reduction in the ozone layer between 4 percent and 6 percent?
   a. the area between the equator and 20 degrees north and south latitude
   b. the mid-latitudes
   c. the North Pole
   d. the South Pole

10. Where is the ozone hole located?
    a. the area between the equator and 20 degrees north and south latitude
    b. the mid-latitudes
    c. the North Pole
    d. the South Pole

11. A 30 percent reduction of ozone in the ozone layer can increase the level of ultraviolet radiation striking the Earth's surface by how much?
    a. 10%
    b. 30%
    c. 50%
    d. 150%

12. How does the depletion of the ozone layer affect humans?
    a. It is altering the climate.
    b. It is raising sea level.
    c. It is increasing the threat of skin cancer.
    d. It is polluting the air we breathe.

13. What is likely to occur if humans stop polluting the atmosphere with ozone-destroying compounds?
    a. The ozone layer will return to its normal levels.
    b. The ozone level will remain at its present levels.
    c. Ozone will continue to be destroyed.
    d. Scientists are not sure what will happen.

Matching *Match the terms with the correct definitions.*

a. ozone
b. stratosphere
c. ultraviolet radiation
d. ozone layer

e. regeneration
f. dynamic equilibrium
g. depletion
h. chlorofluorocarbon

i. freon
j. immune system
k. mutated
l. ozone hole

1. _____ The system in the body that is responsible for fighting off disease.
2. _____ The process of reconstructing something.
3. _____ A colorless, gaseous compound composed of three atoms of oxygen (O_3).
4. _____ A class of human-created molecules commonly used as refrigerants, in electrical manufacturing, and in foam production that is responsible for ozone destruction; it is also a greenhouse gas.
5. _____ The loss of something.
6. _____ A type of chlorofluorocarbon gas that was commonly used in air conditioners and refrigerators.
7. _____ An area over Antarctica that has a reduced level of ozone gas in the stratosphere.
8. _____ The specific area in the stratosphere, located at an altitude between 10 and 20 miles, that contains a high concentration of ozone gas.
9. _____ To be altered by a change in the structure of an organism's genes.
10. _____ A layer in the Earth's atmosphere where the ozone layer exists and temperature increases with an increase in altitude.
11. _____ A balance between two opposing processes that occur at the same rate in an energetic system such as a river or stream.
12. _____ A specific high-energy form of electromagnetic radiation emitted from the Sun that can be harmful to living things.

Critical Thinking

1. If astronomers are searching for life on other planets in the solar system, what should they look for that might indicate that life could exist there, and why?

The Hydrosphere

UNIT

5

OVERVIEW

In 1968 the mission of the Apollo 8 spacecraft was to allow human beings to orbit the Moon for the first time. Mission commander Jim Lovell knew he was making lunar history; the view of his home planet rising from the Moon's horizon forever changed the view human beings have of the Earth. Lovell stared through the small window of the Apollo 8 spacecraft and saw the Earth as a tiny blue marble hanging in the vast emptiness of black space. The pictures he took of the Earth during that mission more than 30 years ago still remind us today of how precious our planet is. The Earth appears to be a blue marble when viewed from outer space because most of its surface is covered in water, its most abundant resource.

23

Earth, The Water Planet

INTRODUCTION

The term *Earth* is derived from the Old English word eorthe, which means "ground" or "soil." We use a derivation of this term as the name for our planet, which is ironic because most of it is covered in water. The Earth is indeed a water planet. Water surrounds us in a multitude of ways. If you were to remove all the water from a plant, you would find that it would lose almost 90 percent of its weight. It would be almost the same for any living organism on Earth. Water falls from the sky, collects in puddles, and soaks the ground. The sky is filled with water, both visible as clouds and invisible as water vapor. Every day we depend on water to be where we want it to be, so we can use its special properties. The water molecule is unique among other molecules on the Earth. Water's unique properties allow life to flourish on our planet and shape the world in which we live.

23.1 The Blue Marble

THE EARTH'S OCEANS

Together, in all its forms, all water on Earth is known as the **hydrosphere**. More than 70 percent of the Earth's surface is covered in liquid water (Figure 23–1). All this water, which makes the planet appear blue from space, comprises the planet's three main oceans (Figure 23–2). The largest of Earth's oceans is the Pacific Ocean, which covers more than 64 million square miles (166 million square kilometers), or 35 percent of the Earth's surface, with an average depth of 14,045 ft (4,281 m). The next largest ocean is the Atlantic, which stretches for more than 33 million square mi (85 million square kilometers), or 21 percent of the Earth's surface, and has an average depth of 12,254 ft (3,735 m). The third largest of the Earth's oceans is the Indian Ocean. This covers more than 28 million square mi (73 million square kilometers), or 15 percent of the planet's surface, at an average depth of 12,704 ft (3,872 m). In total, all the oceans combined cover much of our planet with water that is more than 2 mi (3 km) deep! So it is not hard to imagine why water is Earth's most abundant resource.

FIGURE 23–1 The planet Earth as viewed from space appears like a blue marble because of the abundance of water that covers its surface. (*Courtesy of PhotoDisc.*)

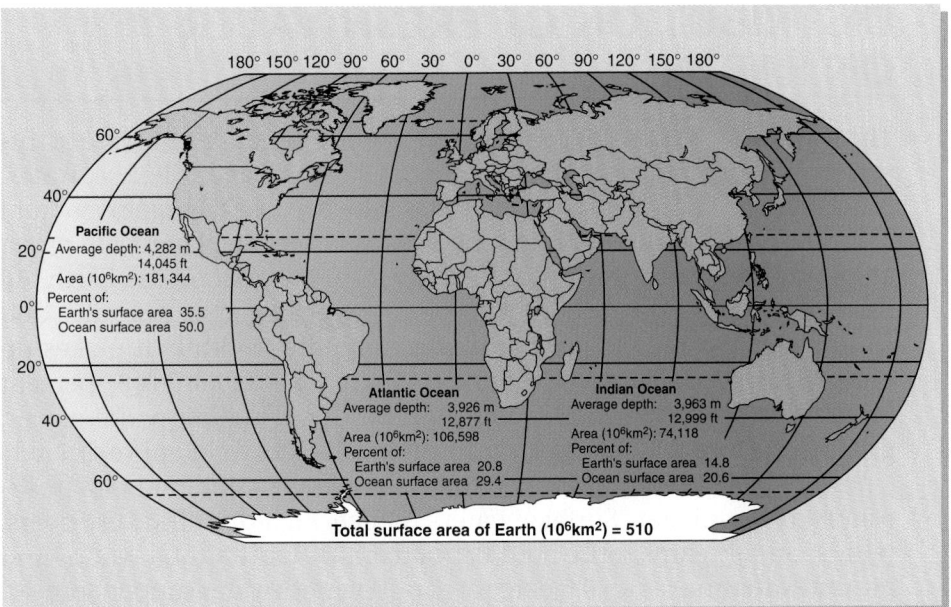

FIGURE 23–2 The average size and depth of the world's three principal oceans, which together cover approximately 70 percent of the Earth's surface.

Earth System Scientists

Jacques-Yves Cousteau

Jacques-Yves Cousteau was born in France in 1910 and began his lifelong attachment to the sea by joining the French Navy. During World War II, he began to experiment with a variety of diving techniques that would enable a person to remain underwater for extended lengths of time. After two failed attempts at trying out experimental diving equipment that nearly cost him his life, Cousteau finally achieved his dream in 1943. With Emile Gagnan, Cousteau invented the first self-contained underwater breathing apparatus, or SCUBA, which enabled him to breathe while underwater. In 1951 Cousteau set out on the first of many expeditions to explore the world's oceans. Using his now famous ship, the *Calypso*, he revealed the mysteries of the underwater world. His expeditions were filmed and eventually made into a series of popular television shows. No other person has provided the world with a better understanding of the oceans than Jacques Cousteau. As a result of his underwater expeditions, Cousteau turned his attentions to the health of the oceans and the influence of human pollutants on sea life. He created the Cousteau Foundation to both explore and protect the world's water resources and to educate the public about sustaining the life within them. Cousteau also experimented with the possibilities of living under the sea. He researched the long-term effects of living deep below the ocean in specially created submersible laboratories; this was known as the Conshelf program. In 1965 three of Cousteau's men lived at a depth of 330 feet below the surface for three weeks. Over the next three decades, Cousteau conducted countless expeditions, published books in more than 20 languages, and produced film documentaries about all aspects of the Earth's hydrosphere. Cousteau died in 1997. He will be forever remembered as an inventor, explorer, and environmentalist, and the man who introduced humanity to the wonders of the world's oceans.

DISTRIBUTION OF FRESHWATER ON EARTH

The world's oceans do not contain pure water, but rather a mixture of dissolved minerals and gases that together make up what is called **seawater**. Seawater, also known as saltwater, tastes salty because it contains sodium chloride, or table salt. Although the oceans cover the planet with a vast amount of seawater, this is not the only form of water on the Earth. All the water on Earth can be divided into two categories, seawater and **freshwater**. Freshwater is what humans require to drink. It makes up only 3 percent of all the water found on Earth. The remaining 97 percent is seawater. The Earth's freshwater supply is found in three major places: glaciers, surface water, and groundwater. **Glaciers** hold approximately 2 percent of all the world's water and are the largest storehouse of freshwater on the planet. Surface waters, which includes all lakes, rivers, ponds, and streams, only hold 0.4 percent of Earth's total water. And **groundwater** makes up 0.6 percent of our planet's water supply. Some of the Earth's water is present in the atmosphere in the form of water vapor, and all the organisms that live on the Earth contain water in their bodies. Even though most of our planet is covered in water, only a small amount of it is available as freshwater, which is required for growing food and drinking (Figure 23–3). This is why many people are so concerned about maintaining the quality of our freshwater supply. The blue marble of the Earth is indeed like Samuel Coleridge's *The Rime of the Ancient Mariner*: "Water, water everywhere, nor any drop to drink."

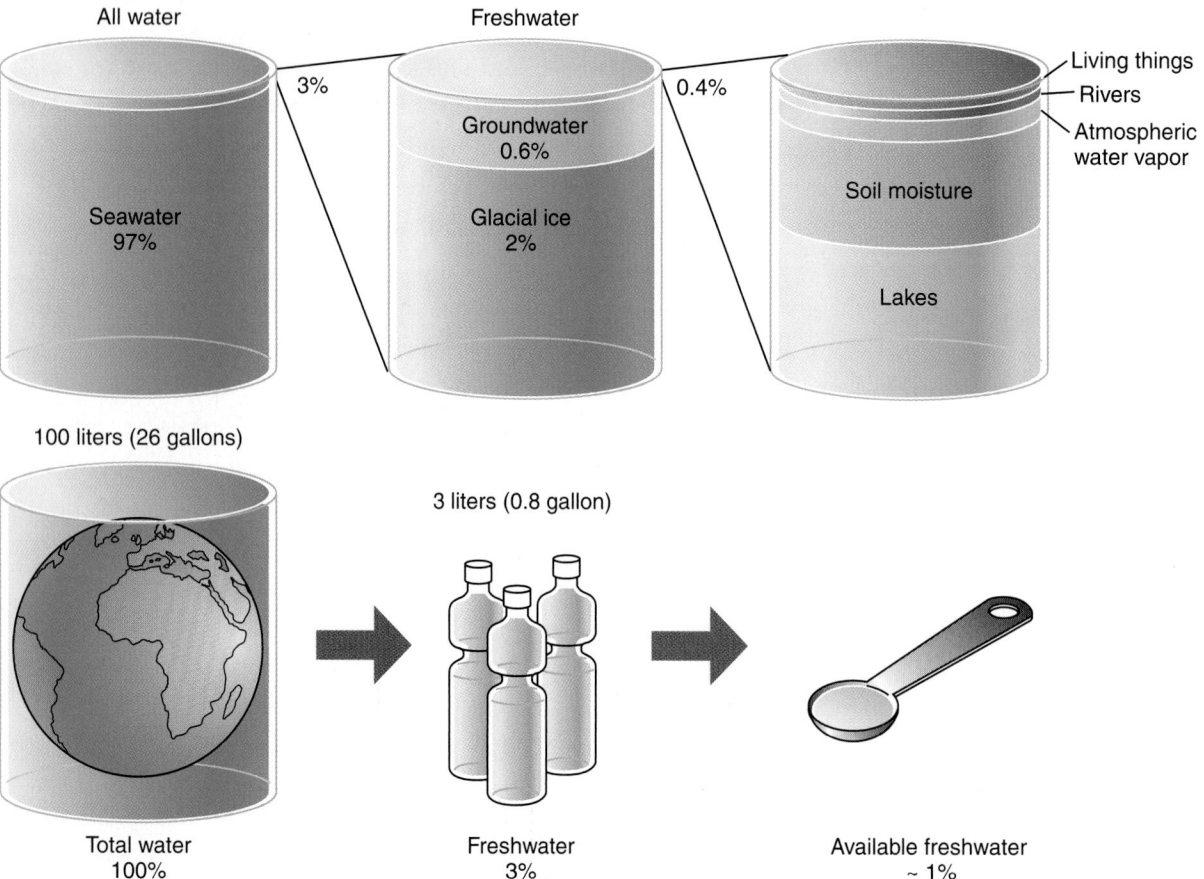

FIGURE 23–3   The distribution of water on the Earth.

CAREER CONNECTIONS
Chemical Oceanographer

Chemical oceanographers study the chemistry of water within the ocean. Their research involves the understanding of chemical processes that occur all throughout the world's oceans. This includes the chemistry of both ocean sediments and the open water. Today much of the work of a chemical oceanographer involves the study of the effects of pollutants in the ocean. Research on the effects of oil spills, garbage, human waste, and toxic chemicals on ocean water is becoming increasingly important. Chemical oceanographers must spend time at sea and in the laboratory to successfully perform their research. This occupation requires a college education in oceanography, chemistry, and hydrology. Chemical oceanographers can work in private industry, in the academic fields, or for a government agency.

FOR MORE INFORMATION GO TO THESE WEB SITES:

<http://www.ec.gc.ca /water/en/nature /e_nature.htm>

<http://interactive2 .usgs.gov/learningweb /students/homework _hydrology.asp>

<http://water.usgs.gov/>

SECTION REVIEW

1. How much of the Earth's surface is covered by water?
2. What is the average depth of the world's oceans?
3. How much of the Earth's water is freshwater?
4. Who was Jacques-Yves Cousteau?

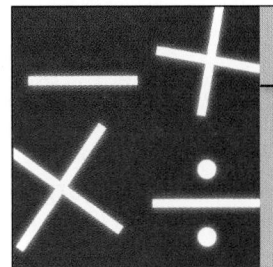

earth math

1) How many square miles do all three of the Earth's largest oceans cover?

2) Use the average depths of the Pacific, Atlantic, and Indian Oceans, in feet, to determine the average depth of the Earth's oceans in miles.

23.2 The Amazing Water Molecule

THE WATER MOLECULE

Not only is water the most abundant resource on Earth, it is also one of the most interesting molecules, possessing many unique features. The water molecule, or H_2O, consists of two hydrogen atoms attached to one oxygen atom. The arrangement of these atoms creates a unique

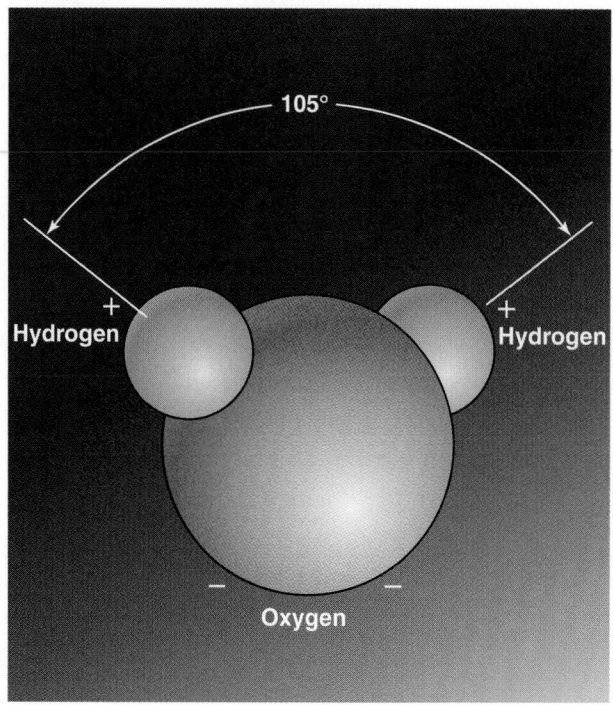

FIGURE 23–4 The characteristic shape of the water molecule gives it unique properties.

shape that resembles the head of the Mickey Mouse cartoon character. This unique shape also contributes to water's unique properties (Figure 23–4). The hydrogen atoms, or the "ears" of the water molecule, carry a positive electrical charge, whereas the oxygen atom, or "head" of the molecule, possesses a negative electrical charge. These opposite charges make water a **polar molecule**. A polar molecule is a molecule that has a positive charge on one end and a negative charge on the other end. Items such as batteries and magnets are also polar.

ADHESION AND COHESION

The result of water's polarity creates its first unique property, **cohesion**. Cohesion is the attraction of water molecules to one another (Figure 23–5). This occurs as a result of the attraction of the positively charged hydrogen molecules to a neighboring water molecule's negatively charged oxygen atom. This attraction occurs because opposite electrical charges are attracted to one another. Cohesion tends to clump water molecules together in chains, which is why drops of liquid clump together as they fall toward the ground, forming a characteristic raindrop shape.

Another unique property of the water molecule is **adhesion**. Adhesion is the attraction of water molecules to molecules of other substances (Figure 23–6). Adhesion is also caused by the polarity of the water molecule. It results in water clinging to certain surfaces. These surfaces are **hydrophilic**, meaning "water loving." Adhesion can be seen when you look at the surface of water inside a glass. You will notice that the water is higher near the edges of the glass. This is the result of the water molecules "climbing" up the glass because of adhesion. You can also observe adhesion after you empty a glass of water and hold it

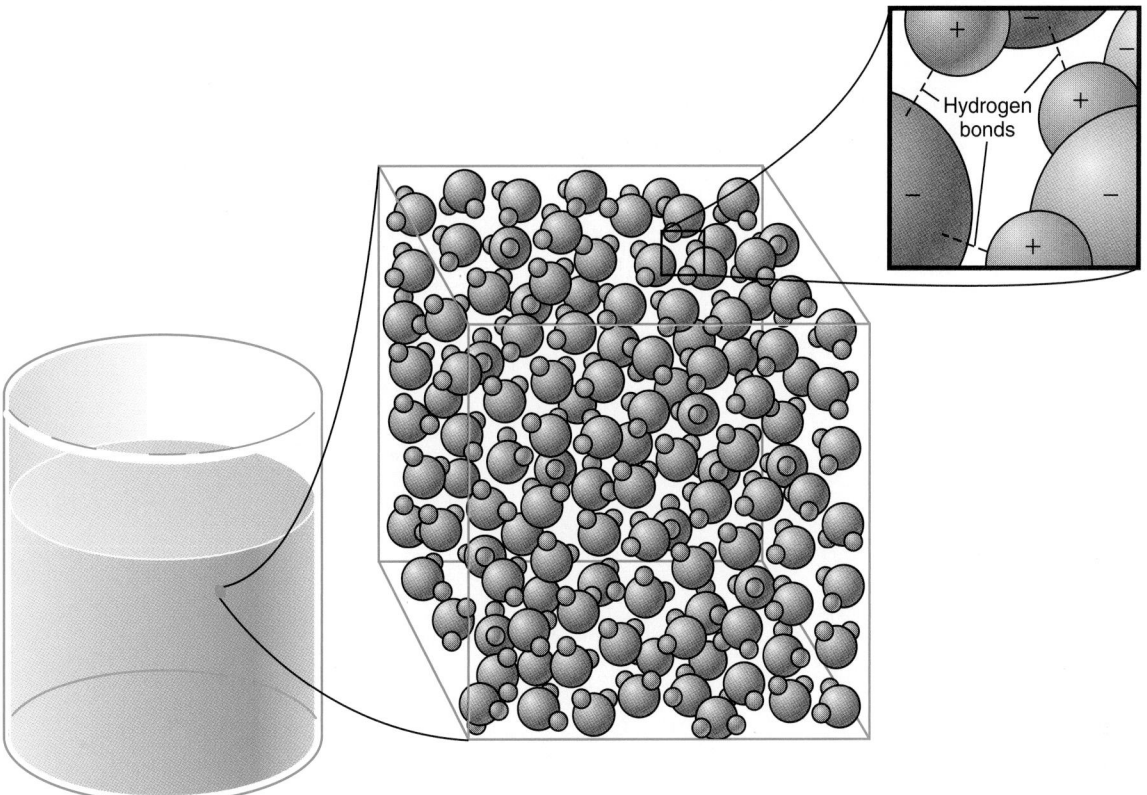

FIGURE 23-5 The attraction of water molecules to one another as a result of their polarity is called cohesion.

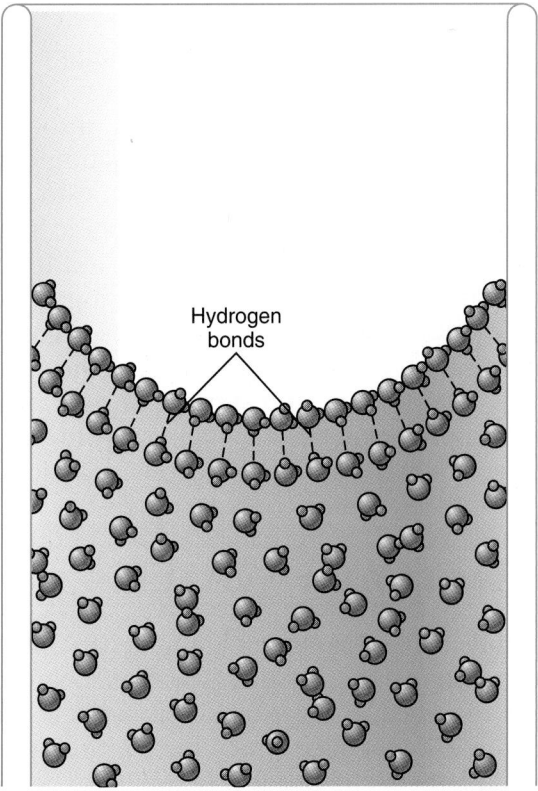

FIGURE 23-6 The attraction of water molecules to specific substances, such as glass, forming a meniscus is called adhesion.

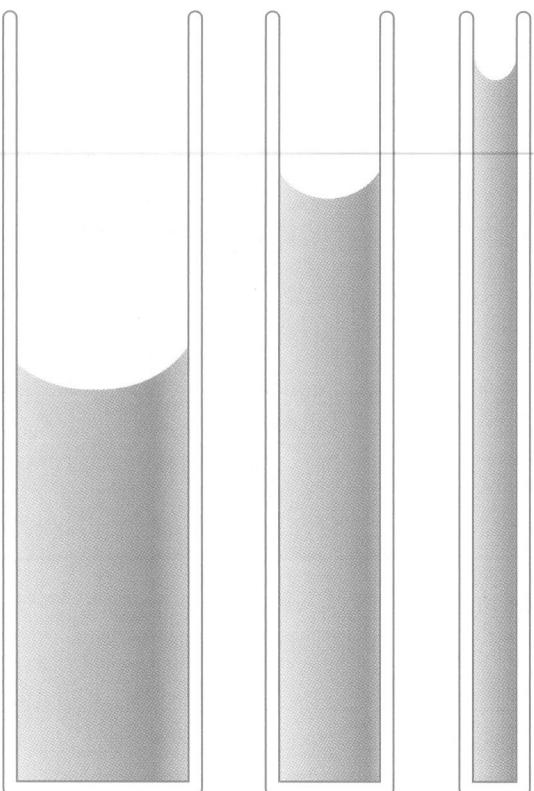

FIGURE 23-7 The ability of water to rise upward in tiny tubes or vessels as a result of adhesion and cohesion is known as capillary action.

upside down. Water droplets will still cling to the sides of the glass as a result of adhesion.

Together, adhesion and cohesion cause **capillary action**. Capillary action is the ability of water to move upward in small tubes or vessels (Figure 23–7). The smaller the diameter of the tube, the higher the water column rises. This is caused by the attraction of water to other substances (adhesion) and the attraction of water to itself (cohesion). The attraction of water molecules to a hydrophilic substance causes water to pull other water molecules along behind it in a long chain, which results in the whole water column rising upward. Capillary action is a fundamental life process that helps organisms distribute water throughout their bodies. You can observe the power of capillary action if you take a dry sponge and stand it upright in a small puddle of water. Without applying any force at all, water in the puddle will be drawn into the vessels of the sponge by capillary action.

HEAT CAPACITY OF WATER

The water molecule also possesses a high **heat capacity**. Heat capacity is the ability of a substance to store energy without changing its temperature. Water has a high heat capacity; in contrast, metal has a low heat capacity. For example, if you filled a metal pot with water and set it on a stove, what would happen when heat was applied? The metal pot would become hot very fast, while the water would remain cool for a much longer time. This is the result of heat capacity. The metal pot has a low heat capacity; therefore its temperature is easy to change when heat energy is applied to it. The result is that the metal quickly becomes hot. The water, however, takes a much longer time to become hot because of its high heat capacity. Water's high heat capacity makes it a valuable reservoir for storing heat on Earth. The world's oceans are vast storehouses of heat that has been absorbed from the sun and is important for global climate. Storms such as hurricanes and typhoons are one way that the oceans give off this stored heat. The strength of these tropical storms provides a good example of how much energy is actually stored in the world's oceans.

PROPERTIES OF ICE

Water has yet another unique feature: It is one of the only substances that expands when it freezes. Most substances on Earth contract, or reduce their size, when they become colder. Water, however, expands, or increases its size, when it freezes. For example, if you fill a plastic bottle with water and then place it in your freezer, what will happen? The water will freeze in the bottle, expand, and crack the plastic container. Water increases its volume by approximately 9 percent when it freezes. Other substances, such as steel bridges, usually contract, or become smaller, when they get colder. Engineers use large expansion joints when they construct large bridges because bridges shrink during cold weather and expand in hot weather. If bridge engineers did not install these expansion joints, the bridges would eventually pull themselves apart! Water's ability to expand when it freezes also makes it less dense (Figure 23–8). Most substances become more dense when they freeze, unlike water. Frozen water is less dense than liquid water, which

FIGURE 23–8   Ice is the solid form of water, which is less dense than liquid water, causing it to float. (*Courtesy of PhotoDisc.*)

allows ice to float. The ability of ice to float is important for aquatic life on Earth because it allows life to flourish beneath the ice in lakes and ponds during winter. If ice were more dense than liquid water, every winter the aquatic plants and animals that reside in ponds and lakes would be crushed by the sinking ice. Unlike most substances on Earth, which have their greatest density in the solid form, water's density is greatest when it is in liquid form at 39.2° F (4° Celsius).

Water is unique because it is one of the only substances found on Earth that exists in all three states of matter (Figure 23–9). Solid water forms **ice** and snow in colder parts of the planet. Liquid water fills the oceans and lakes and flows in rivers and streams. The gaseous form of water, called **water vapor**, exists in the atmosphere and creates weather and climate. The interactions between all of water's three states of matter help drive many of the processes that shape our Earth and enable life to exist on our planet.

WATER AS A SOLVENT

The last unique property of water is its ability to be a **solvent**. Water is sometimes referred to as the universal solvent because it can **dissolve** many substances. All water on the planet, even freshwater, contains dissolved minerals and gases. Fish and other aquatic organisms depend on dissolved gases in water, such as oxygen, to live. The ability of water to

FIGURE 23–9 Water exists in all three states of matter on Earth. (*Courtesy of PhotoDisc.*)

CAREER CONNECTIONS
Hydrologist

A hydrologist applies scientific knowledge to all aspects of water-related problems that affect society. This includes maintaining healthy surface waters and improving water quality. Hydrologists help with the management of municipal water supplies and all surface freshwater resources. These scientists monitor the water quality of reservoirs, rivers, and any type of surface water for human use or recreation. They are also concerned with irrigation of agricultural lands and the problems associated with flooding. Hydrologists monitor snow packs in the mountains, along with local precipitation, to determine the future availability of surface water. They are concerned with the chemical study of surface waters to maintain their ability to support healthy wildlife populations. Some surface water hydrologists also monitor water for pollutants and are charged with keeping water safe for recreational uses such as swimming, boating, and fishing. These scientists must have a college education in hydrology and environmental science and can find employment with state and local governments, and with private industry.

dissolve substances makes it extremely important for life on Earth. Plants depend on water to distribute dissolved nutrients and manufactured food throughout their bodies. Humans rely on the water in blood to circulate oxygen and food throughout the body, while also transporting waste materials away from cells. None of this would be possible without

Earth System Scientists

Sir John Ross

John Ross was born in England in 1777. He was best known as an arctic explorer who was in search of a northwest passage from the Atlantic Ocean to the Pacific Ocean. While at sea, Ross took many bottom measurements and began to develop some of the first accurate charts that revealed the depth of the ocean. He also took samples from the bottom of the ocean to learn about the types of organisms that lived there. In 1817 he recovered living organisms from the ocean floor at a depth of more than 1 mi (1.6 km). Previous to this discovery, scientists thought that no life could survive in the deep ocean. Later, while exploring the waters off Antarctica, Ross recovered bottom-dwelling organisms from depths of more than 4 mi (6.4 km). His research proved that life could exist in the deep, dark, cold, and high-pressure environment of the ocean floor.

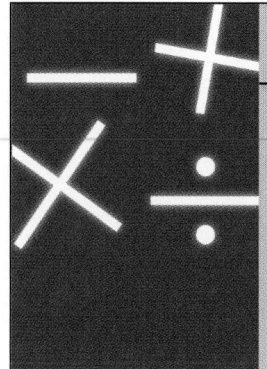

1) If the density of ice is 0.9170 grams per cubic centimeter and the density of liquid water at 20° C is 0.9982 grams per cubic centimeter, what is the difference in density between the liquid and solid forms of water in grams per cubic centimeter?

2) If liquid water becomes water vapor at a temperature of 212° F, what is the difference in temperature between water vapor and ice?

@ WEB Links

FOR MORE INFORMATION GO TO THESE WEB LINKS:

<http://interactive2 .usgs.gov/learningweb /students/homework _hydrology.asp>

<http://www.epa.gov /students/water.htm>

the ability of water to be an effective solvent. Not only is the water molecule one of the most abundant substances on Earth, it also possesses many unique qualities that make it indispensable to life on Earth.

SECTION REVIEW

1. Draw the shape and label the polarity of the water molecule.
2. Describe the difference between adhesion and cohesion.
3. What are the three states of matter for water?
4. Explain why ice floats.
5. Who was John Ross?

CHAPTER SUMMARY

The Earth is a water planet. More than 70 percent of the Earth's surface is covered in water, including three major oceans that have an average depth of more than 2 mi. Water on the Earth is divided into two main categories: seawater and freshwater. Seawater contains many dissolved minerals, including sodium chloride, and makes up 97 percent of all the water on the Earth. Freshwater composes the remaining 3 percent of all the world's water and is what we use to drink and for agriculture. Freshwater occurs in three different forms on the Earth: glaciers, groundwater, and surface water.

Water is a unique substance because it possesses many special properties. The water molecule, H_2O, is made up of two molecules of hydrogen and one molecule of oxygen. This results in the unique shape of the water molecule that also makes it a polar molecule, meaning that one side of the water molecule has a positive charge and the other has a negative charge. The polarity of the water molecule causes it to be attracted to other water molecules. This is known as cohesion. Polarity also causes water to be attracted to certain hydrophilic, or water-loving, substances. This is known as adhesion. Together adhesion and cohesion create capillary action. Capillary action is the ability of water molecules to rise upward in tiny tubes or vessels and is an important mechanism by which living things distribute water throughout their bodies.

Another unique property of the water molecule is its high heat capacity. Heat capacity is the ability of substances to absorb heat without changing their temperature. Water's high heat capacity allows it to store large amounts of heat. This enables the oceans to store great amounts of heat energy, helping to moderate the planet's climate. Water is also unique because it becomes less dense when it freezes to form ice. Almost all substances on the Earth become more dense when they are in their solid forms. Because ice is less dense than liquid water, it floats. The most dense form of water is the liquid form at 4° C.

Water exists on the Earth in all three states of matter, which is also unique. The interaction among ice, liquid water, and water vapor affects many processes on the Earth. Water is considered the universal solvent, because it can dissolve many substances. This property of water is essential to all living things on the planet.

CHAPTER REVIEW

Multiple Choice

1. What percentage of the Earth's surface is covered by water?
   a. 15%
   b. 21%
   c. 35%
   d. 70%

2. What percentage of the Earth's surface does the Pacific Ocean cover?
   a. 15%
   b. 21%
   c. 35%
   d. 70%

3. The average depth of the world's oceans is approximately:
   a. 100 feet
   b. 5,000 feet
   c. 13,000 feet
   d. 21,000 feet

4. Where is most of the world's freshwater located?
   a. glaciers
   b. lakes and ponds
   c. groundwater
   d. plants and animals

5. The water molecule is a polar molecule, which means that it:
   a. formed near the poles
   b. has an electrical charge
   c. sinks when frozen
   d. has a low heat capacity

6. The ability of water molecules to be attracted to one another is called:
   a. adhesion
   b. cohesion
   c. polarity
   d. capillary action

7. Water rising into a sponge is an example of:
   a. adhesion
   b. cohesion
   c. polarity
   d. capillary action

8. Water sticking to the sides of a glass is an example of:
   a. adhesion
   b. cohesion
   c. polarity
   d. capillary action

9. Water's high heat capacity enables it to:
   a. boil rapidly
   b. quickly change temperature
   c. store heat
   d. form water vapor

10. Water's density is greatest when:
    a. it is frozen solid, at 0° Celsius
    b. it is liquid, at 4° Celsius
    c. it is packed inside a glacier
    d. it is in the form of hail

11. When it freezes, water's volume increases by approximately:
    a. 1%
    b. 3%
    c. 9%
    d. 50%

Matching   *Match the terms with the correct definitions.*

a. hydrosphere
b. seawater
c. freshwater
d. glacier
e. groundwater

f. polar molecule
g. cohesion
h. adhesion
i. hydrophilic
j. capillary action

k. heat capacity
l. ice
m. water vapor
n. solvent
o. dissolve

1. _____ A term that describes a substance that attracts water molecules.
2. _____ The gaseous form of water.
3. _____ All the water on the Earth.
4. _____ To enter into a solution.
5. _____ Water that has a high concentration of minerals dissolved in it, also known as saltwater.
6. _____ A substance that is capable of dissolving another substance.
7. _____ The attraction of water molecules to one another.
8. _____ The solid form of water, which is less dense than liquid water, causing it to float.
9. _____ Water on or below the Earth's surface that contains a small amount of dissolved mineral salts and is good for drinking.
10. _____ The attraction of water molecules to a hydrophilic substance.
11. _____ A long-lasting, large mass of snow and ice that forms over land from the accumulation and compaction of snow that creeps down slope.
12. _____ A molecule that has a weak positive and negative electrical charge.
13. _____ The movement of water molecules upward in tiny tubes as a result of adhesion and cohesion.
14. _____ Naturally occurring freshwater that flows or is stored underground in rock or sediments.
15. _____ The ability of a substance to absorb, contain, and release heat energy.

Critical Thinking

1. If water were truly a universal solvent, how would this affect life on Earth?

The Hydrologic Cycle

OBJECTIVES

Evaporation · Water Vapor and Condensation · Precipitation and Surface Water · Runoff · Evapotranspiration · Infiltration and Groundwater

After reading this chapter you should be able to:

▶ Define the term *hydrologic cycle*.

▶ Describe the process by which water enters the atmosphere.

▶ Explain what happens to water vapor when it is in the atmosphere.

▶ Describe the five pathways that water can take when it falls back to the surface.

▶ Define the term *evapotranspiration*.

▶ Identify the factors that affect the rate at which water infiltrates the ground.

▶ Identify the sources of energy that drive the hydrologic cycle.

INTRODUCTION

One of the most important aspects of understanding the role that the hydrosphere plays on Earth is examining the function of the **hydrologic cycle**. The hydrologic cycle is the circular movement of water between the oceans, atmosphere, and land surface. The term *hydrologic* means "the study of water"; therefore, the hydrologic cycle is the study of how water moves through the environment and the role it plays in the Earth's systems.

EVAPORATION

The term *cycle* refers to the circular movement of something, so there really is no starting point for the hydrologic cycle on the Earth; however, because the world's oceans contain 97 percent of all the world's water, this is a good theoretical starting point for the hydrologic cycle (Figure 24–1). Radiant energy from the Sun strikes the surface of the oceans and begins to heat the liquid water molecules. Eventually there is enough heat energy absorbed by the water molecules to cause them to evaporate off the ocean surface. **Evaporation** is the phase change from a liquid to a gas. The gaseous form of water is known as **water vapor**. Millions of gallons of water evaporates from the surface of the oceans each day around the world. This is by far the largest contributor of water into the Earth's atmosphere.

WATER VAPOR AND CONDENSATION

Once water from the ocean evaporates into water vapor, it then becomes an important part of the atmosphere (Figure 24–2). Water vapor makes up anywhere from 0 to 4 percent of the atmosphere, depending on the location and time of the year. The warmer areas

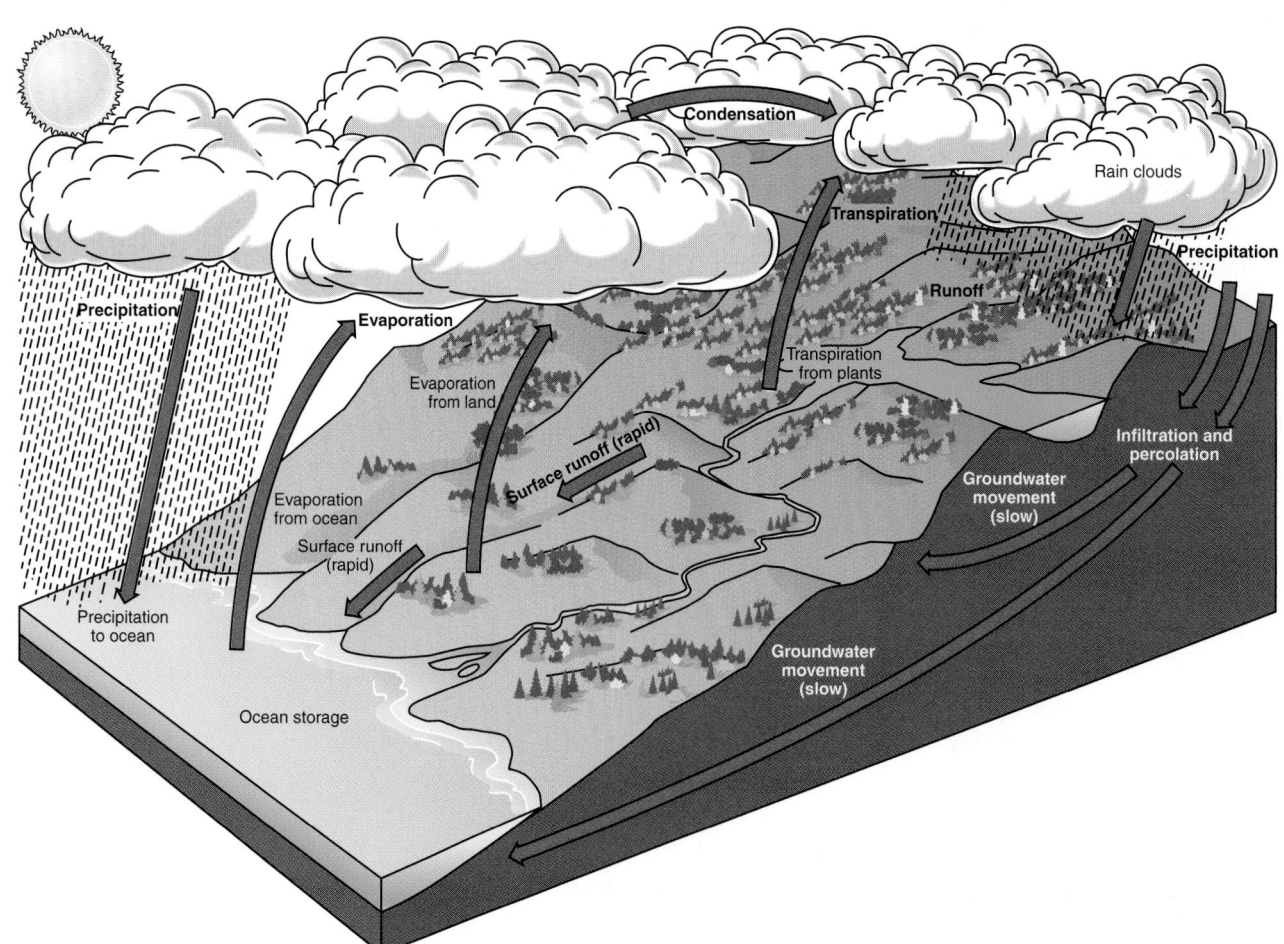

FIGURE 24–1   The hydrologic cycle is a model of the movement of water through the environment.

FIGURE 24-2 The evaporation of water from the ocean, forming water vapor that eventually condenses in the atmosphere to create clouds. This process transports water from the oceans to the land surface. (*Courtesy of PhotoDisc.*)

closer to the equator typically have the greatest amount of water vapor in the atmosphere. Areas close to the poles of the Earth have the least amount of water vapor in the atmosphere. This is the result of warmer air having the ability to absorb more water than cooler air. Although water vapor in the atmosphere composes only 0.001 percent of the Earth's total water supply, it is an important pathway by which water moves from the oceans to the land surface. All the surface freshwater on the planet, which is located in glaciers, rivers, lakes, and groundwater, was once atmospheric water vapor. This illustrates the important link that the atmosphere provides between the water in the oceans and the water on land. Once water vapor enters the atmosphere, it rises and begins to cool. This is because moist air is less dense than dry air. The cooling action of the upper portions of the atmosphere causes water vapor in the rising air to condense.

The average time water spends in the Earth's atmosphere is 10 days, because eventually air will cool enough and cause the water vapor to condense. **Condensation** is the phase change from a gas to a liquid. Eventually enough water vapor condenses in the atmosphere and begins to collect as clouds. As the clouds begin to grow, so does the liquid water contained within them. The clouds are driven over the land by atmospheric winds, and soon liquid water begins to fall toward the land surface. This is known as **precipitation**.

PRECIPITATION AND SURFACE WATER

Precipitation can be either in the form of a liquid (rain) or a solid (snow). Once the precipitation arrives on the land surface, it can take one of five pathways (Figure 24-3). The first path it can possibly take is to collect on the surface in lakes or ponds. These freshwater storage areas can be extremely large. Lake Superior in North America covers more than 31,000 square miles (80,290 square kilometers) and has an

FIGURE 24–3   Precipitation returns water back to the Earth's surface. (*Courtesy of PhotoDisc.*)

Earth System Scientists

Robert Horton

Robert Horton was born in Michigan in 1875. After receiving a college education, he began working with his uncle, a civil engineer who had worked on the Erie Canal. Their work together involved the measurement of stream flow in rivers and creeks in New York State. In 1900 Horton became the New York district engineer for the U.S. Geological Survey. His research of stream flow helped him to develop theories on the interaction of precipitation with the ground. He proposed that water can take one of four pathways when it reaches the Earth's surface. Horton discovered that precipitation could either run off, infiltrate the ground, transpire through plants, or evaporate. This important discovery helped form a better understanding of the hydrologic cycle. Horton's research in hydrology revealed that stream flow during the drier months was attributed to groundwater discharge. He also helped establish flood stages for major flowing waterways in New York State to help prevent flood damage and the loss of life.

average depth of 3,264 ft (995 m). **Surface water** can also be very shallow, such as a pond, which can cover only 1,000 square feet (93 square meter). The surface water of lakes and ponds can also evaporate and return the water to the atmosphere once again to repeat the cycle.

The second pathway that water can take when it falls to the Earth is to collect as snow and ice to form glaciers. In this way freshwater can be stored on the Earth's surface for thousands of years. Approximately 2 percent of all water on the Earth is locked in the ice that composes the world's glaciers. Eventually, when the leading edge of a glacier meets the sea, the ice melts and the water once again returns to the oceans.

RUNOFF

The next pathway that precipitation can take when it reaches the land surface is called **runoff**. Rain or melting snow is driven by the force of gravity to collect in streams and rivers that eventually find their way back to the ocean (Figure 24–4). This is another way that the hydrologic cycle can complete itself. The largest of the world's rivers is the Nile River in Africa, which is more than 4,100 mi (6,598 km) long. All the minerals that are dissolved in the water of the oceans were transported there by the world's river systems.

FIGURE 24–4   Precipitation that does not collect in surface water or infiltrate into the ground can run off the surface into streams and rivers. (*Courtesy of PhotoDisc.*)

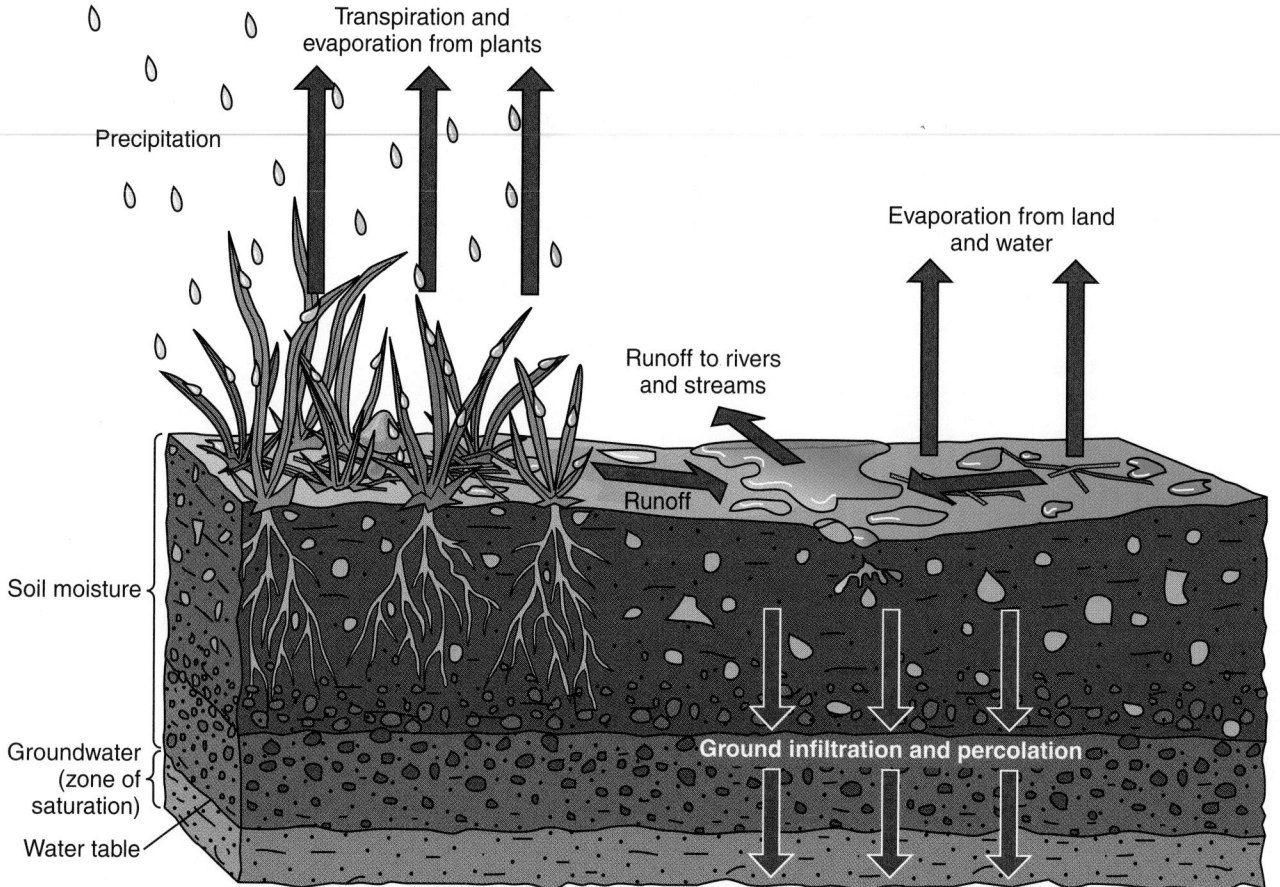

Transpiration and
evaporation from plants

Precipitation

Evaporation from land
and water

Runoff to rivers
and streams

Runoff

Soil moisture

Ground infiltration and percolation

Groundwater
(zone of
saturation)

Water table

FIGURE 24–5   The pathways that water can take when it comes into contact with the soil include runoff, infiltration, and evapotranspiration.

EVAPOTRANSPIRATION

The fourth pathway that precipitation can take once it arrives at the surface is **absorption** by plants. Plants take water up through their root systems and distribute it throughout their bodies. Some of this water eventually reaches the leaves, where it evaporates back into the atmosphere. The process of water entering the root system of a plant, moving through the plant body, and then evaporating off the leaf surface is called **evapotranspiration**, also known simply as transpiration (Figure 24–5). Evapotranspiration can often play an important role in determining local climate by adding water vapor to the atmosphere. Large forests can add millions of gallons of water into the atmosphere by the process of evapotranspiration. One birch tree alone can add approximately 70 gal (265 l) of water, and one mature corn plant contributes more than 1 gal (3.8 l) of water each day to the atmosphere by evapotranspiration.

INFILTRATION AND GROUNDWATER

The final pathway that precipitation can take once it strikes the land surface is called **infiltration**. Infiltration is the movement of water into soil or rock. The rate of infiltration of water into the ground depends on a few factors. The size of the pore spaces within the ground greatly affects the rate at which water infiltrates. Generally, the larger the size of the pores, the greater the rate of infiltration. Also, the amount of water within the pore spaces affects the rate of infiltration. The more water contained in the pore spaces within the ground, the slower the rate of infiltration. Pore spaces that are completely saturated with water will prevent any water from infiltrating into the soil, causing it to run off instead. The arrangement of particles in a soil also affects the rate of infiltration. Particles of mixed size tend to pack tightly together and reduce the amount of pores in the ground. This then reduces the infiltration rate. Sorted particles of similar size increase the pore spaces and therefore increase the infiltration rate.

Once the water infiltrates the ground, it is called **groundwater**. Groundwater holds approximately 0.6 percent of Earth's total water, which is a greater volume than all the world's lakes and rivers combined. Groundwater is an important source of freshwater for drinking and **irrigation**. Most groundwater eventually returns to the surface as **flowing springs** or is pumped out by mechanical wells. Approximately 50 percent of all Americans get their water from wells supplied by groundwater.

No matter which pathway precipitation takes when it reaches the land surface, eventually all water on Earth returns to the oceans, and the hydrologic cycle begins again. This might take days, years, or thousands of years depending on the specific pathway the water is traveling. The processes that help to move water around the planet involve the use of a great amount of energy. Mostly it is the power of the Sun that drives the hydrologic cycle, along with the force of gravity.

CAREER CONNECTIONS

Water Resource Engineer

A water resource engineer works in the planning, design, construction, and operation of all aspects of water use. This includes the management of all engineering projects that use water resources. Water resource engineers design systems for specific water resource projects such as flood control, dam construction, sewer systems, municipal water supplies, irrigation, and water transportation. These engineers work both in the field and in the laboratory, where they conduct surveys, perform tests, design projects, oversee construction, and monitor systems. They require knowledge of engineering, hydrology, and construction. Water resource engineers can find employment in private industry or with state and local governments.

REVIEW

1. How much of the Earth's water is located in the oceans?
2. Define the term *evaporation* and explain its importance to the hydrologic cycle.
3. Describe the five pathways water can take when it reaches the land surface.
4. Who was Robert Horton?

CHAPTER SUMMARY

The hydrologic cycle is the circular movement of water through the environment. The theoretical starting point for the hydrologic cycle is in the oceans. Solar energy heats the ocean surface and causes the water to evaporate. The water enters the atmosphere in the gaseous state called water vapor. Eventually the water vapor in the atmosphere rises, cools, and condenses. This forms clouds, which then move through the atmosphere and form precipitation. Precipitation returns water to the Earth's surface in the form of rain or snow.

Once water strikes the land surface, it can take five possible pathways. These include collecting as surface water in lakes or ponds or as the snow and ice in glaciers. Precipitation can also run off the land surface, forming streams and rivers that flow toward the oceans. Some precipitation can infiltrate into the rock and soil, forming groundwater. The rate at which water infiltrates the ground is affected by the size of the pore spaces within the ground and by the amount of water that is already there. Once water enters the ground, it can be stored there for long periods or can be taken up into the root systems of plants. The movement of water through the roots of plants and up through the plant body, eventually evaporating off the leaf surface back into the atmosphere, is called evapotranspiration. All these pathways eventually return water either to the ocean or to the atmosphere, which starts the cycle over again. The driving force of the hydrologic cycle is energy from the Sun, along with gravity.

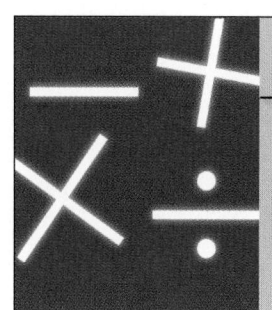

earth math

1) If one plant transpires 80 ml of water per day, how many liters of water does the plant transpire in a week?

2) If it takes a water molecule 88 minutes to travel 1 mi down the Nile River, how many days will it take water to travel the entire length of the river?

CHAPTER REVIEW

Multiple Choice

1. The movement of water from the oceans to the atmosphere is by the process of:
   a. evaporation
   b. condensation
   c. precipitation
   d. evapotranspiration

2. Generally, the amount of water vapor in the atmosphere is greatest near the:
   a. North Pole
   b. mid-latitudes
   c. equator
   d. South Pole

3. The process by which water forms clouds in the atmosphere is called:
   a. evaporation
   b. condensation
   c. precipitation
   d. evapotranspiration

4. Ponds, lakes, and glaciers are all examples of:
   a. groundwater
   b. precipitation
   c. stored surface water
   d. runoff

5. Which of the following increases the amount of runoff?
   a. small pore spaces in an unsaturated soil
   b. small pore spaces in a saturated soil
   c. large pore spaces in an unsaturated soil
   d. large pore spaces in a saturated soil

6. Which type of soil particles have the greatest infiltration rate?
   a. mixed saturated particles
   b. mixed unsaturated particles
   c. sorted saturated particles
   d. sorted unsaturated particles

7. Plants move water from the ground by the process of:
   a. infiltration
   b. condensation
   c. precipitation
   d. evapotranspiration

8. Approximately how long does water vapor remain in the atmosphere?
   a. 1 day
   b. 10 days
   c. 1 month
   d. 1 year

9. What is the driving force for much of the hydrologic cycle?
   a. adhesion and cohesion
   b. the Sun
   c. capillary action
   d. prevailing winds

Matching   Match the terms with the correct definitions.

a. hydrologic cycle
b. evaporation
c. water vapor
d. condensation
e. precipitation

f. surface water
g. runoff
h. absorbed
i. evapotranspiration
j. infiltration

k. groundwater
l. irrigation
m. flowing spring

1. _____ The phase change when a liquid changes into a gas.
2. _____ The rapid loss of soil, sediments, or other substances as a result of being washed away by rain or melting snow.
3. _____ The circular pathway of water molecules as they move through the environment, also called the water cycle.
4. _____ An area where groundwater is discharged at the surface and flows freely.
5. _____ The gaseous form of water.

6. _____ An artificial means of supplying water to plants.
7. _____ To take in or soak up matter or energy.
8. _____ Naturally occurring freshwater that flows or is stored underground in rock or sediments.
9. _____ The change in phase from a gas to a liquid.
10. _____ The important pathway by which water moves from the soil, through the body of a plant, and evaporates off the leaf surface back into the atmosphere.
11. _____ Liquid or solid water formed in clouds that falls to the surface of the Earth.
12. _____ The process of infiltrating, or entering into something.
13. _____ Water that is located on the surface of the Earth.

Critical Thinking

1. Explain how cutting down a forest might affect the hydrologic cycle.

25

Oceanography

OBJECTIVES

Seawater · Ocean Currents · Deep Ocean Circulation · Life Zones in the Ocean
· Continental Shelves · Intertidal Zone

After reading this chapter you should be able to:

▶ Describe the approximate salinity of the ocean.
▶ Identify some of minerals that compose seawater.
▶ Describe the mechanism that drives surface ocean currents.
▶ Identify at least four major surface ocean currents.
▶ Explain the process of thermohaline circulation.
▶ Define the terms *upwelling* and *thermocline*.
▶ Identify the four main life zones within the ocean.
▶ Describe some of the characteristics of the continental shelves.
▶ Define the term *intertidal zone*.

INTRODUCTION

Of all water on Earth, 97 percent resides in the oceans, which cover more than 70 percent of the planet. These vast storehouses of water have an average depth of more than 2 mi (3.2 km) and remain largely unexplored. Some oceanographers argue that we know more about other planets in our solar system than we do about our own oceans. It is believed that life on Earth began in the ocean. This vast resource has also helped to sustain life for more than 3 billion years with its abundant resources. Our dependence on the ocean continues to this day. The oceans of the world also store incredible amounts of heat energy, which help to regulate global climate. Understanding the physical and chemical properties of the ocean is important to understanding its role in the Earth's complex systems and how it influences life on Earth.

TABLE 25–1 The major components of seawater

Constituent	Percent of Substances by Mass
Oxygen	85.4
Hydrogen	10.7
Chlorine	1.85
Sodium	1.03
Magnesium	0.127
Sulfur	0.087
Calcium	0.040
Potassium	0.038
Bromine	0.0065
Carbon	0.0027
Nitrogen	0.0016
Strontium	0.00079
Boron	0.00043
Silicon	0.00028
Fluorine	0.00013

SEAWATER

The water that resides in the oceans is called **seawater**. Seawater is a mixture of water and more than 70 other chemical elements. The measure of the amount of chemical elements in seawater is called **salinity**. The salinity of the ocean is approximately 3.5 percent, which means that 3.5 percent of seawater is made up of dissolved minerals (Table 25–1). For example, if a little more than 100 gal (379 l) of seawater evaporates, approximately 30 lb (13.6 kg) of mineral salts is left behind. The principal mineral salts in seawater are sodium, chloride, sulfur, and magnesium. The salinity of the ocean remains fairly constant all around the globe, although near the polar regions it is slightly higher. This is the result of the freezing of water that forms the ice caps, which helps increase the concentration of mineral salts dissolved in the ocean around the poles.

OCEAN CURRENTS

Another important feature of Earth's oceans involves the circulation of seawater around the planet. The circulation of water throughout the oceans is known as currents, which are divided into two main types (Figure 25–1). The first type of ocean current is called a **wind-driven current**. Wind-driven currents move the upper parts of the ocean horizontally by wind action that strikes the ocean surface. The planetary-scale prevailing winds that circulate the atmosphere create these currents. Major wind-driven currents begin near the equator and then move along the edge of the continents, bringing warm equatorial water northward or southward toward the poles. Other wind-driven currents transport cold water from the poles back toward the equator,

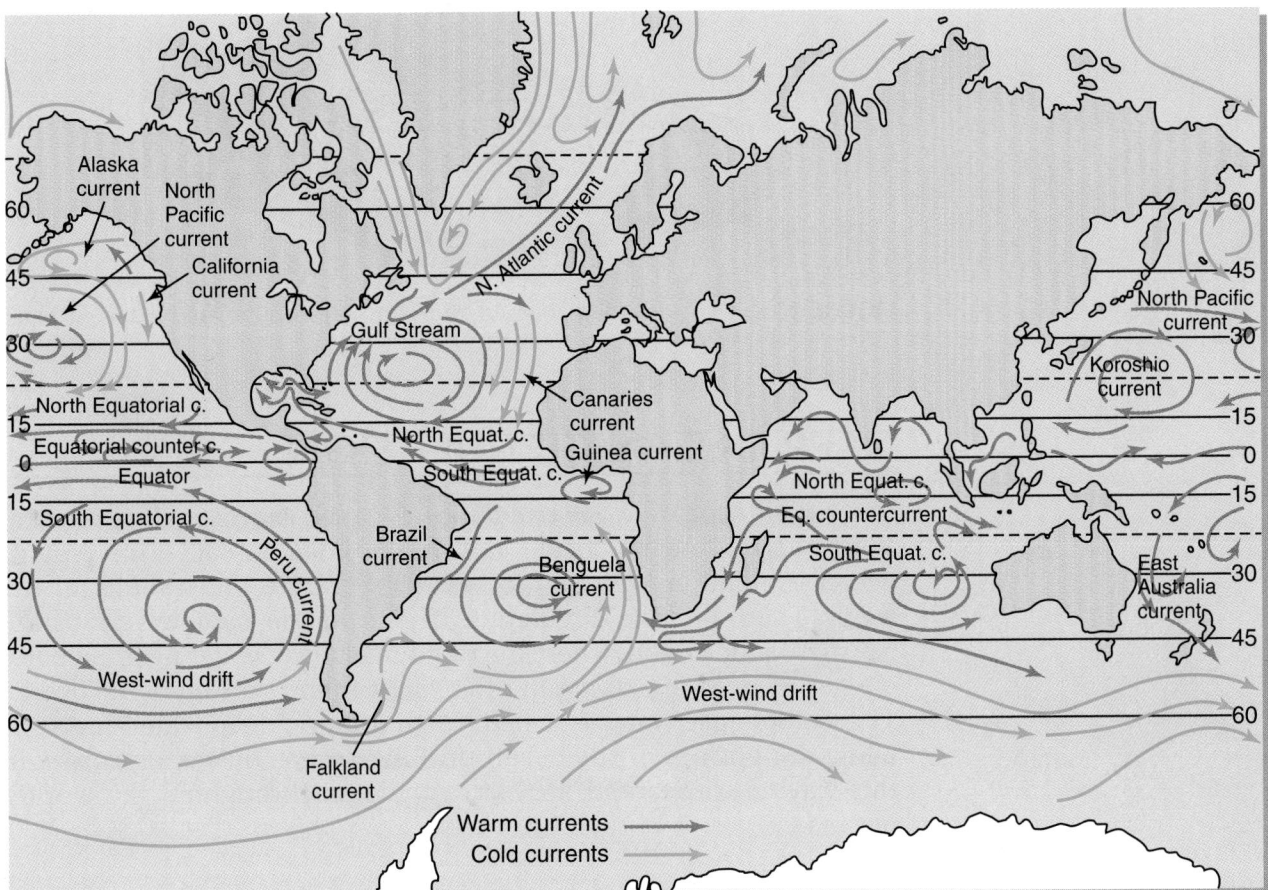

FIGURE 25-1 The world's major surface ocean currents.

where it is heated once again. Wind-driven currents help transport heat energy from the Earth's equatorial regions and bring it to the colder high latitudes. The **Gulf Stream** is a major wind-driven current that moves warm water from the Caribbean Sea up along the east coast of the United States, where it eventually reaches Greenland.

The warm waters that the Gulf Stream current moves northward help moderate the climate of England. Although the British Isles are located at high colder latitudes, its climate is mild because of the influence of the Gulf Stream. Other wind-driven currents, such as the **California Current**, move colder arctic waters southward. The California Current brings cold water down the western coast of North America, which can also influence local climate.

Another important aspect of wind-driven ocean currents involves the vertical distribution of heat throughout the ocean. This is called **upwelling**. Upwelling occurs when winds move warm surface waters away from the equator or the coasts of continents (Figure 25–2). The cooler deep water moves upward and then replaces the warm surface waters. Major upwelling zones occur along the western coast of South America and along the equator in the Pacific Ocean. Upwelling also helps bring cold, nutrient-rich water up to the surface, where it is used by aquatic organisms. Changes in the upwelling zones near the equator, off the western coast of South America, are linked to changes in global climate patterns.

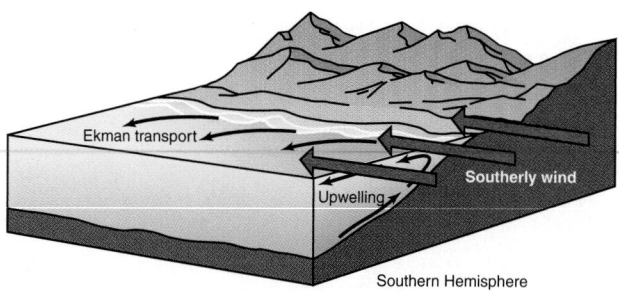

FIGURE 25–2 The upwelling of cold, nutrient-rich water from the deep ocean.

DEEP OCEAN CIRCULATION

The second type of ocean circulation is called **thermohaline circulation.** *Thermo* means "heat," and *haline* means "sal." This type of ocean circulation is driven by the temperature and salinity of the water. Thermohaline circulation begins in the cold waters of the North Atlantic Ocean, where the rapid freezing of water near the poles creates cold, saline-rich water that sinks to the bottom of the ocean. This cold, dense water is called North Atlantic deep water. It creeps along the bottom of the ocean until it reaches upwelling zones. In this way, nutrients and heat are circulated throughout the world's oceans.

Earth System Scientists

Matthew Maury

Matthew Maury was born in 1803 in Virginia and joined the Navy as a young midshipman. His love for the sea was rivaled only by his love of knowledge. Early in his naval career, Maury was aboard the first U.S. ship to circumnavigate the globe, in 1830. During his life he wrote many scientific papers that dealt with navigation and the physical aspects of the oceans. In 1839 his leg was badly broken in a stagecoach accident, which ended his career at sea. He became the superintendent of the U.S. Naval Observatory in 1844. While there he began to analyze the data that were contained in the thousands of ships' logs stored at the observatory. Maury recognized that these logs held valuable information about winds, currents, and weather conditions at many points in the ocean. Over the next 10 years, Maury created the first detailed navigation charts of the world's oceans. By using the information contained in the ships' logs, Maury charted ocean currents, prevailing winds, and other important information that could be used by ship captains. In 1855 he published *The Physical Geography of the Sea*, which became the first book to present the science of oceanography. Maury was also responsible for developing standardized methods for recording weather and nautical information gathered at sea. Because of his lifelong work, Maury is often regarded as the father of modern oceanography.

CAREER CONNECTIONS

Physical Oceanographer

A physical oceanographer studies all the physical aspects of the world's oceans. This includes ocean temperatures, currents, salinity, wave formation, density, and tidal forces. These marine scientists are interested in revealing the interactions that occur in the oceans. They collect data about the ocean by using remote sensing satellites, sonar, radar, and a wide array of different sensors. They also collect water samples from different parts of the world and at different depths from within the ocean. Physical oceanographers are interested in the relationship among the ocean, the atmosphere, and global climate. Specialized physical oceanographers study the topography and composition of the ocean floor. These scientists create accurate maps of the ocean floor. Some physical oceanographers search for mineral resources or oil that might be located in ocean sediments. Careers in this field require at least a 4-year college degree. Work can be found within academic research, government agencies, or private industry.

LIFE ZONES IN THE OCEAN

Because the ocean is so deep, scientists also study vertical layers, or zones, that affect marine life (Figure 25–3). The top zone, or layer, of the ocean, is called the **euphotic zone**. This is where enough sunlight reaches into the ocean to support photosynthesis. The euphotic zone usually extends no deeper than 600 feet (183 meters), although that varies depending on the regional clarity of ocean water. The next layer of the ocean is called the **disphotic zone**. The disphotic zone receives a small amount of light but not enough to support photosynthesis. The depth of this zone reaches to approximately 3,000 feet (914 meters). Below the disphotic zone lies the largest layer of the ocean, called the **aphotic zone**. This zone receives no light at all. It supports many strange species of aquatic organisms that live in total darkness. The bottom of the ocean is called the **benthic zone**, which is subject to extreme pressure and near freezing water. This zone is mostly composed of a thick mudlike sediments, which form as the bodies of tiny dead aquatic organisms sink to the ocean bottom. The fecal pellets of aquatic organisms also collect on the ocean bottom, helping form the benthic environment. Some of the loose sediments that cover the ocean floor can be more than 1 mile (1.6 km) thick.

Another important feature of the ocean is called the **thermocline**. The thermocline is the area where warm, nutrient-poor surface water mixes with cold, nutrient-rich bottom water. This is an area of extreme temperature change (Figure 25–4). The depth of the thermocline varies depending on the time of year and latitude. In tropical ocean waters

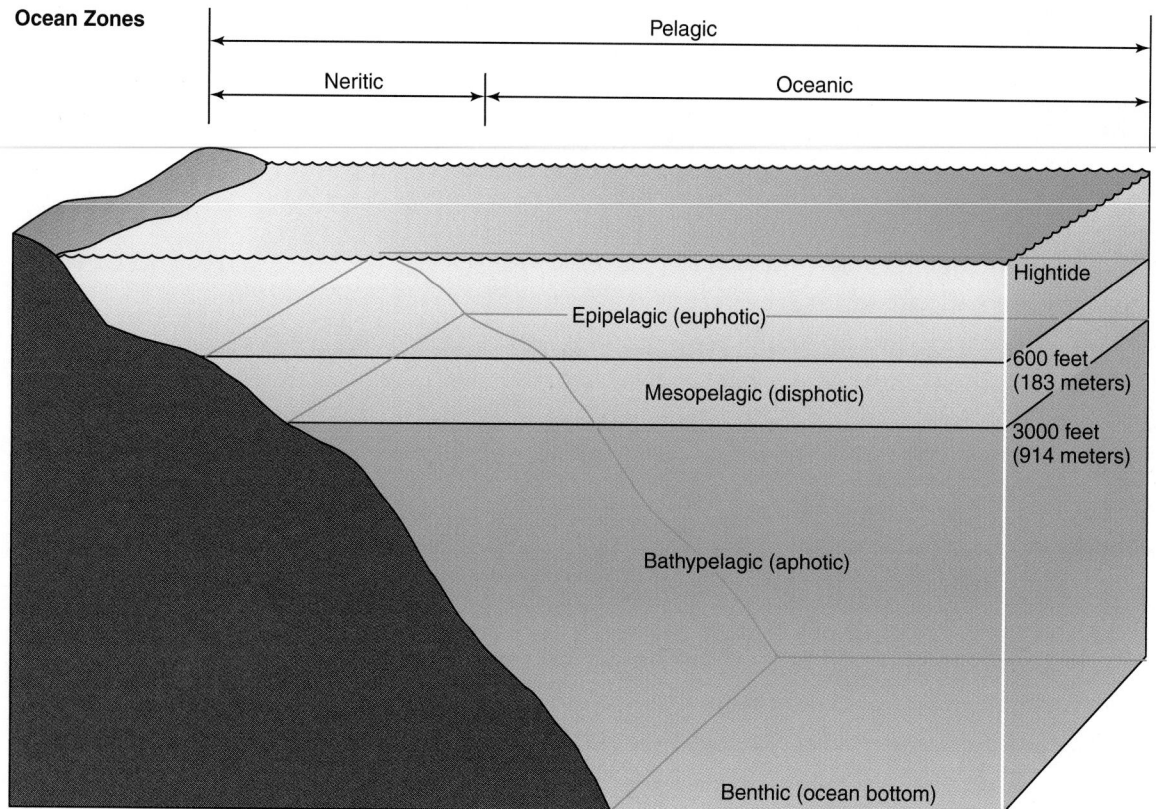

FIGURE 25–3 The aquatic life zones within the ocean.

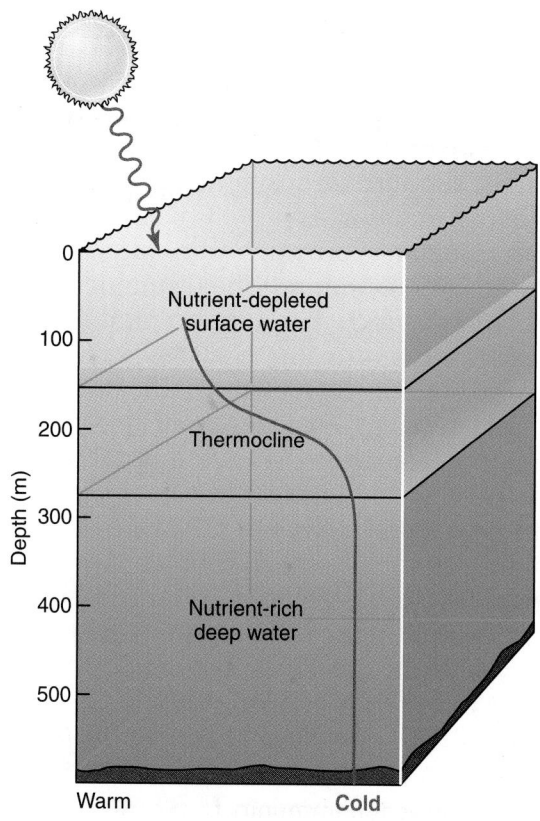

FIGURE 25–4 The location of the thermocline, which is the depth at which the temperature of the water declines rapidly.

CURRENT RESEARCH

Researchers from Japan and Australia believe that fertilizing the Pacific Ocean off the coast of South America might help curb global warming. Australian oceanographer Ian Jones and a Japanese engineering firm are proposing that nitrogen fertilizer pumped into the ocean off the coast of Chile would help boost the plankton population residing in its coastal waters. Plankton removes carbon dioxide from the atmosphere as it builds its body, which could result in a reduction in global atmospheric carbon dioxide levels as the plankton population grows. The so-called ocean enrichment plan is reported to be less expensive and easier to carry out than planting trees or using industrial scrubbers to remove carbon dioxide. Skeptics of the plan are not sure what the effect would be if nitrogen were added to the ocean, therefore increasing the plankton population.

near the equator, the thermocline can be located more than 600 feet (183 meters) from the surface. In the higher latitudes of temperate climates, the thermocline can be found only 50 feet (15 meters) from the surface. Many aquatic organisms live within the thermocline, seeking the nutrients that it provides. These organisms also migrate with the thermocline as its depth fluctuates throughout the year.

Although much of the benthic zone in the world's oceans is located almost 3 miles below the surface, it still is home to many varieties of living organisms. Recently oceanographers have been studying a unique feature of the deep ocean benthic zone called **hydrothermal vents**. Hydrothermal vents are areas where volcanic activity emits rich minerals and extreme heat into the cold bottom waters of some parts of the oceans (Figure 25–5). The pressure around these benthic zone vents can be 300 times that of the Earth's surface, and temperatures can be as high as 750° Fahrenheit (390° C). The vents, however, support a variety of organisms, such as tube worms, clams, crabs, and bacteria, that thrive in these deep, harsh conditions.

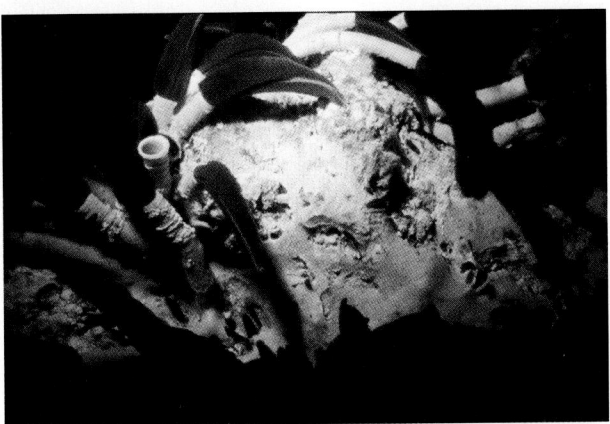

FIGURE 25–5 A hydrothermal vent community that survives in the intense heat and crushing pressure of the ocean floor, near a volcanic vent. (*Courtesy of NOAA.*)

CONTINENTAL SHELVES

Most organisms that reside in the world's oceans survive in the relatively shallow waters of the continental shelves. A **continental shelf** is a shallow, sloping area located around the margins of continents. The average depth of a continental shelf is approximately 400 ft (122 m). Most of the continental shelves around the world lie within the euphotic zone, which supports a variety of aquatic life. Approximately 90 percent of all the fish and shellfish harvested from the oceans comes from the continental shelves. On average, the world's continental shelves stretch out from the land about 45 mi (72 km); however, some continental shelves can be as wide as 900 mi (1,448 km). Along the edges of the continental shelves, where the depth of the ocean increases rapidly, there exist large, deep canyons called submarine canyons (Figure 25–6). Some of these canyons can have depths of more than 12,000 ft (366 m). Many submarine canyons are associated with the world's large rivers. Scientists believe that submarine canyons form from turbidity currents that result from flowing sediments caused by undersea earthquakes. Today these canyons are still being shaped by the sediments and currents that large river systems bring into the oceans. The Hudson Canyon is a large submarine canyon that extends out from the Hudson River; it has a depth of 3,600 ft (1,097 m) and is more than 5 mi (8 km) wide.

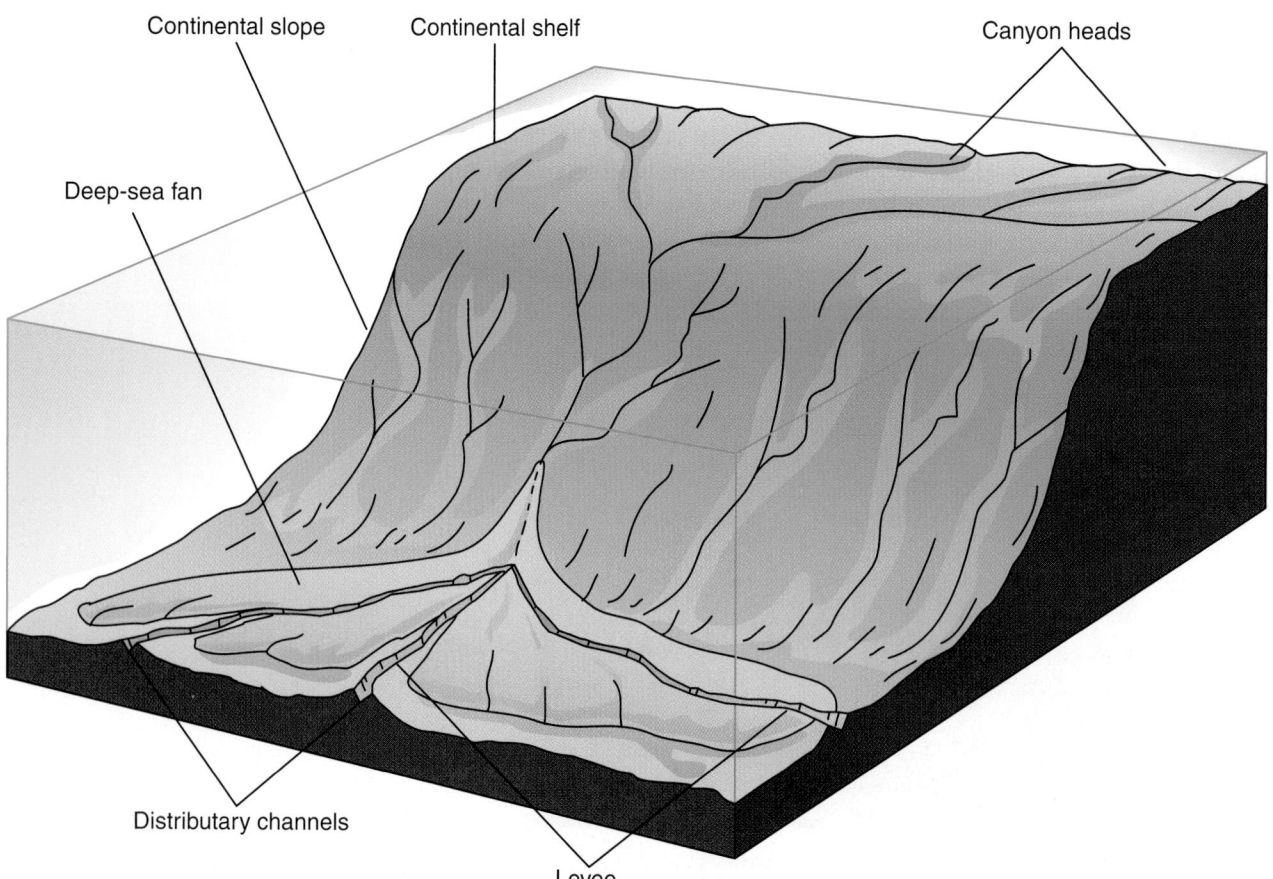

FIGURE 25–6 The location of a submarine canyon near the edge of a continental shelf.

INTERTIDAL ZONE

Another important feature of the oceans is the **intertidal zones**. The intertidal zones are areas along the shore that lie within the reaches of the low and high tides. These areas also harbor an abundance of life. They consist of shorelines and tidal pools. The rise and fall of the water, wave action, strong currents, and periodic exposure to the air make this one of the harshest aquatic environments. The organisms that live in the intertidal zone are well adapted to this ever-changing environment. There are two basic types of intertidal zones. A rocky intertidal, which is composed mostly of large rocks that line the shore, and a sandy intertidal, which is made up of mostly sand. Both types of intertidal zones have their own unique organism communities (Figure 25–7).

@ WEB Links

FOR MORE INFORMATION GO TO THESE WEB LINKS:

<http://www.noaa.gov/ocean.html>

<http://www.noaa.gov/charts.html>

<http://enchantedlearning.com/subjects/ocean/>

<http://www.noaa.gov/coasts.html>

REVIEW

1. How much of the world's water resides in the oceans?
2. What percentage of seawater is composed of minerals?
3. What is the name of the wind-driven ocean current that moves along the eastern United States?
4. Describe the process of upwelling in the ocean.
5. List the four main life zones within the ocean.
6. Who was Matthew Maury?

CHAPTER SUMMARY

Of all the water on Earth, 97 percent is in the form of seawater. Seawater is a mixture of dissolved minerals and water. The amount of minerals dissolved in water determines its salinity. The salinity of seawater in the oceans is approximately 3.5 percent. The oceans of the world are composed of seawater and cover approximately 70 percent of the Earth's surface. The prevailing planetary winds that circulate the atmosphere drive major ocean currents. These are known as wind-driven currents, which help to distribute warm water away from the equator and cold water away from the poles.

Ocean currents also cause upwelling, which is the rising of nutrient-rich colder water from the bottom of the ocean, replacing warm

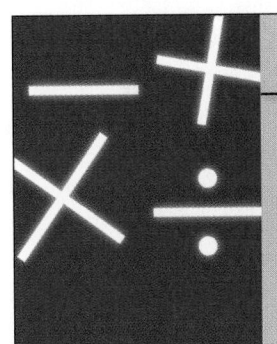

earth math

1) How many pounds of minerals does a 100-pound sample of seawater contain?

2) If the depth of the euphotic zone of the ocean is 333 feet in summer and 568 feet in winter, what is the average depth of the euphotic zone?

3) If pressure increases by 14.7 pounds per square inch for every 33 feet of depth in the ocean, what is the pressure at a depth of 14,850 feet?

FIGURE 25–7   The community of organisms that reside in the harsh conditions of the rocky intertidal zone.

surface waters that are moved away by prevailing winds. This is known as the vertical mixing of the ocean. Another type of ocean circulation, called thermohaline circulation, moves cold, saline-rich water from the poles down along the bottom of the ocean toward the equator.

The thermocline is the layer of the ocean where the temperature drops rapidly with depth. This is where cold, nutrient-rich water mixes with warmer surface water. The ocean is divided into four distinct vertical layers called life zones. The uppermost layer of the ocean is called the euphotic zone. This is where enough light penetrates into the water to support photosynthesis. Below this layer is the disphotic zone, where a small amount of light reaches but cannot support photosynthesis. Most of the ocean exists in the aphotic zone, which is the deep zone where no light reaches. The bottom of the ocean is called the benthic zone. In some places this can be more than 5 mi (8 km) deep; the pressure is extremely high, and the water is near freezing. Although the benthic zone is a harsh environment, it supports a variety of aquatic life.

Some communities of organisms reside on the bottom of the ocean near volcanic vents. These nutrient-rich areas are known as hydrothermal vent communities, where the temperature of the water can be more than 200° F (93° C). Although the water is extremely hot, specially adapted organisms thrive there. The relatively shallow regions of the ocean that surround the continents are called the continental shelves. These areas are usually no deeper than 400 feet (122 meters). They support a great amount of aquatic life. Near the edges of the continental shelves are natural deep canyons called submarine canyons, which are extensions of large river systems that drain into the oceans. The area closest to the shore line is called the intertidal zone. This area exists between the lowest and highest tides, where wave action, strong currents, and periodic exposure to air make it difficult to survive.

CHAPTER REVIEW

Multiple Choice

1. Approximately how much of the Earth's surface is covered by seawater?
   a. 30%
   b. 50%
   c. 70%
   d. 90%

2. If you were to weigh out 1,000 pounds of seawater, approximately how much of it would be minerals?
   a. 1 lb
   b. 2.5 lb
   c. 3.5 lb
   d. 35 lb

3. What drives the major surface ocean currents?
   a. the Earth's rotation
   b. temperature differences
   c. convection
   d. prevailing winds

4. A major ocean current that brings cool water south toward the equator is:
   a. the California current
   b. the Gulf Stream
   c. the North Atlantic Current
   d. the Brazil Current

5. A major ocean current that brings warm water away from the equator is called:
   a. the Labrador Current
   b. the Gulf Stream
   c. the Peru Current
   d. the Canaries Current

6. Which area in the ocean has the highest salinity?
   a. the equator
   b. the poles
   c. the mid latitudes
   d. the central Pacific

7. Upwelling results in:
   a. cooler ocean water sinking
   b. warmer ocean water rising
   c. cooler ocean water rising
   d. warmer ocean water sinking

8. If you were to scuba dive through the thermocline, the temperature of the water would:
   a. increase rapidly
   b. increase gradually
   c. decrease gradually
   d. decrease rapidly

9. Which life zone in the ocean is in total darkness?
   a. euphotic
   b. disphotic
   c. aphotic
   d. benthic

10. Which life zone in the ocean supports photosynthesis?
    a. euphotic
    b. disphotic
    c. aphotic
    d. benthic

11. Hydrothermal vents are located in which life zone?
    a. euphotic
    b. disphotic
    c. aphotic
    d. benthic

12. Which of the following is associated with the continental shelves?
    a. submarine canyons
    b. hydrothermal vents
    c. intertidal zones
    d. the aphotic zone

13. What type of ocean environment is most affected by exposure to air and strong currents?
    a. submarine canyons
    b. hydrothermal vents
    c. intertidal zones
    d. the aphotic zone

Matching   *Match the terms with the correct definitions.*

a. seawater
b. salinity
c. wind-driven currents
d. Gulf Stream
e. California Current

f. upwelling
g. thermohaline circulation
h. euphotic zone
i. disphotic zone
j. aphotic zone

k. benthic zone
l. thermocline
m. hydrothermal vents
n. continental shelf
o. intertidal zone

1. _____ The relatively shallow region of the ocean surrounding a continent.
2. _____ The uplift of cold ocean water from the bottom to the surface.
3. _____ Water that has a high concentration of minerals dissolved in it.
4. _____ An aquatic life zone that exists near the shoreline between the area of the highest and lowest tides.
5. _____ A wind-driven surface ocean current that brings cold water from the North Pacific south toward the equator along the west coast of North America.
6. _____ Ocean water that seeps through cracks in the sea floor and is superheated by magma that is close to the surface.
7. _____ A measure of the mineral salt content of a solution.
8. _____ The layer of water located below the surface where the temperature drops rapidly.
9. _____ Surface ocean currents that are formed by planetary winds.
10. _____ An aquatic life zone located on the bottom of a body of water.
11. _____ The vertical distribution of water in the oceans that is caused by differences in the salinity and temperature of the water.
12. _____ A wind-driven, surface ocean current that brings warm water from the equator northward along the east coast of North America; it was first discovered by Benjamin Franklin.
13. _____ The uppermost life zone in an aquatic ecosystem that receives enough light to support photosynthesis.
14. _____ A particular zone in an aquatic ecosystem where there is no light present.
15. _____ The dimly lit portion of an aquatic ecosystem that cannot support photosynthesis.

Critical Thinking

1. If you were to plot a course to sail from New York to England and then back to Florida, what surface ocean currents would you use to help you on your journey?

26

Fresh Surface Water and Groundwater

SECTION 26.1

FRESH SURFACE WATER OBJECTIVES

Lakes · Lake Productivity · Life Zones in Lakes · Watersheds and Rivers · Stream Features · Floodplains · Stages of River Development

After reading this section you should be able to:

▶ Explain the unique characteristics of the three lake classifications based on their productivity.

▶ Identify the four aquatic life zones that exist in lakes.

▶ Define the term *watershed*.

▶ Describe the relationship between the slope and velocity of a river.

▶ Define the term *meandering* and describe the four primary stream features.

▶ Define the terms *dynamic equilibrium* and *discharge rate*.

▶ Describe the three stages of the development of a river.

SECTION 26.2

GROUNDWATER OBJECTIVES

Groundwater Recharge and the Water Table · Groundwater Flow · Aquifers and Groundwater Discharge · Groundwater Pollution

After reading this section you should be able to:

▶ Explain the process by which groundwater is recharged and define the term *water table*.

▶ Describe what causes groundwater to flow and what controls the rate at which it flows.

▶ Differentiate between an aquifer and a confined aquifer.

▶ Identify three sources of groundwater pollution.

INTRODUCTION

The distribution and movement of freshwater, both above and below the ground, is an important part of the Earth's systems. All the freshwater on Earth that is not locked up in glaciers makes up less than 1 percent of the water on the planet. This small percentage, however, plays a crucial role in the hydrological cycle, shaping the Earth's surface and supporting life. Today it is rare, if not impossible, to actually drink from any surface water supply because they have all been polluted to some degree by human activity. Almost every lake, stream, pond, and river in the United States could potentially make you sick if you drank from it without treating the water. The only water supply that humans can safely drink from without any type of filtration is groundwater. The world's groundwater supply is more than 90 times greater than all the world's fresh surface water supplies combined. Every day in the United States more than 78.5 billion gal (297 billion l) of freshwater are pumped from the ground to be used for drinking or irrigation. This water supplies more than 40 percent of our nation's drinking water. This important water resource is often overlooked because it is out of sight. It has been abused by both pollution and overuse. Understanding the dynamics of surface freshwater and groundwater—how we can improve their quality and sustain their use—is vital to the future of our planet.

26.1 Fresh Surface Water

LAKES

The Earth's fresh surface water is either flowing or standing. The standing freshwater on the surface of the Earth is commonly known as lakes, ponds, and swamps. Lakes can be extremely large and deep, such as Lake Baikal in Russia, which covers more than 12,000 square miles (31,080 km^2) and is more than 5,000 feet (1,524 meters) deep. The largest of the Great Lakes in North America, Lake Superior, covers more than 22,000 square miles (56,980 km^2), with an average depth of 1,300 feet (396 meters) (Figure 26–1). Ponds, on the other hand, can be extremely small and shallow, and are located all over the Earth's surface. Both lakes and ponds form when flowing surface waters become trapped and begin to accumulate. Lake and pond formation is a result of the local topography, glacial action, volcanoes, landslides, earthquakes, meteorites, and shifting river patterns. Some of the world's deepest lakes were formed by retreating glaciers. These large masses of ice carved deep into the Earth's crust. Later, when the glaciers melted, the deep canyons they left behind became deep glacial lakes.

LAKE PRODUCTIVITY

Lakes are often classified by their age and productivity (Figure 26–2). Productivity is the amount of solar energy that is converted to plant material by the process of photosynthesis. Young, crystal clear lakes

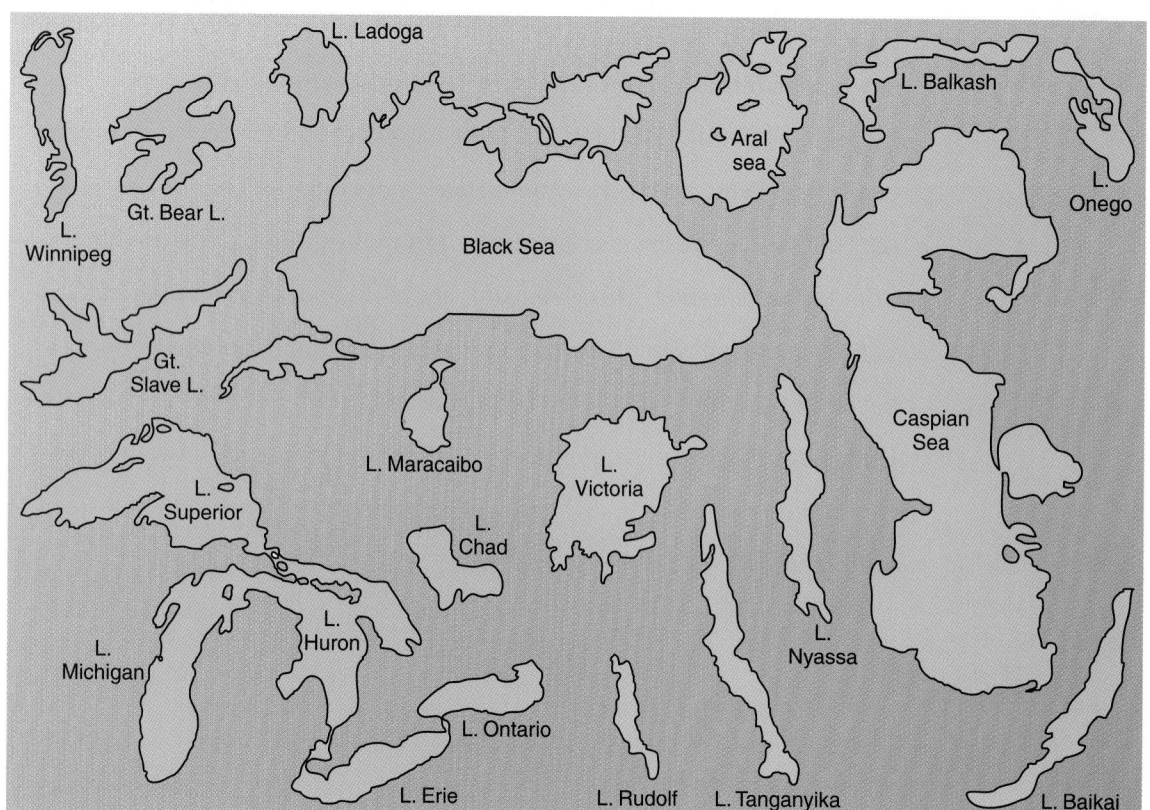

FIGURE 26–1 A comparison of the relative sizes of the major lakes of the world.

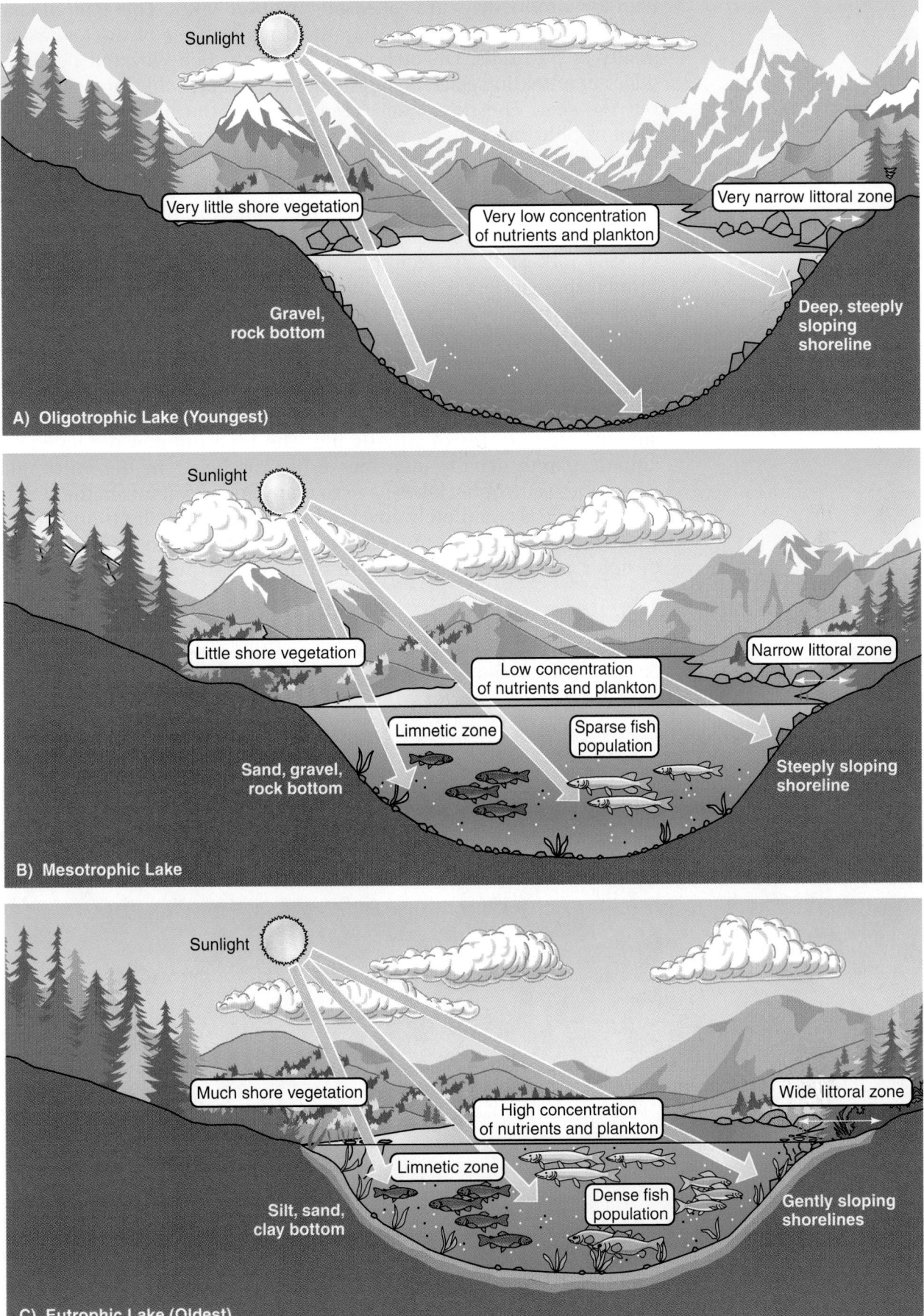

FIGURE 26–2   The unique characteristics of the three classifications of lakes.

Qualitative description
Quant Nutrients
Quantity/type of life

with low productivity are called **oligotrophic lakes**. This type of lake has limited amounts of aquatic organisms because of the low availability of nutrients. Oligotrophic lakes are usually located near the edges of retreating glaciers and therefore contain cold water throughout the year. The next lake classification is the **mesotrophic lake**. Mesotrophic lakes have medium productivity resulting from the increased availability of nutrients. The water is clear and usually cool, supporting an abundance of fish and other aquatic organisms. Many of the larger, clear lakes in the United States are mesotrophic lakes; these are used for water supplies and for recreation. The Finger Lakes in New York State are examples of mesotrophic lakes. These lakes formed after glaciers retreated back into Canada approximately 10,000 years ago. They are extremely deep and clear and support large populations of aquatic organisms.

The third classification for lakes is called eutrophic. **Eutrophic lakes** have an abundance of nutrients and high productivity (Figure 26–3). These lakes are usually very shallow with cloudy warm water, and support many forms of aquatic life. The high number of algae and aquatic plants usually identifies a lake as being in the eutrophic stage. Some eutrophic lakes have so many aquatic plants in them that their surface is completely covered in green mats of plants and algae. Lakes undergo a succession of development beginning with the oligotrophic stage. Over time, runoff from the surrounding area brings

FIGURE 26–3   Large populations of aquatic plants and algae in a eutrophic lake as a result of the high amount of nutrients. (*Courtesy of PhotoDisc.*)

Earth System Scientists

Alexander Agassiz was born in Switzerland in 1835 and eventually settled in the United States. After graduating from Harvard University in 1855, he took over the operation of a large copper mine. By 1875 Agassiz was a millionaire, and he turned his attention to the study of the world's oceans. He backed many scientific expeditions to research the oceans. In 1871 the British government launched an expedition that was designed to study the physical and biological aspects of the ocean. The ship, H. M. S. *Challenger,* sailed around the globe collecting important information about the oceans. Agassiz became involved with this epic voyage. He helped to classify and organize much of the samples that were collected during the 4-year expedition. He also helped to finance many scientific studies conducted by researchers in the United States and aided in the acceptance of oceanography as a true science. Agassiz's talent as a scientist was in the design and construction of marine sampling devices and the ability to classify marine organisms.

nutrients into the lake. Eventually the lake reaches a point at which it becomes mesotrophic. The time it takes to reach the mesotrophic stage is usually recorded in thousands of years. As a lake's nutrients continue to accumulate and it becomes filled with sediments, it eventually becomes eutrophic. This can take tens of thousand of years to occur, except if the lake is very shallow. Eventually all lakes become shallow swamps. Sediments washed into lakes from the surrounding land eventually fill up all lakes. Because of pollution, many mesotrophic lakes are becoming eutrophic lakes in a very short period. Lakes that were once clear are now being overgrown with aquatic plants and algae because of the increased productivity caused by the introduction of fertilizers and sewage leaking into the water as a result of human activity.

LIFE ZONES IN LAKES

Like the oceans, lakes also possess unique vertical layers called aquatic life zones (Figure 26–4). The shallow area that surrounds a lake is the littoral zone, which supports many aquatic plants and animals. This zone is the most productive in the lake; it exists where sunlight can reach the lake bottom. The open waters of the lake, where light can penetrate and photosynthesis can occur, is called the limnetic zone. The depth of the limnetic zone can vary greatly depending on the lake. The clear waters of mesotrophic lakes can have deep limnetic zones reaching 100 feet (30 meters) or more. Cloudy eutrophic lakes can have a very shallow limnetic zone, where sunlight can only penetrate a few feet into the water. Very deep lakes may also possess a profundal zone that sunlight cannot reach. In this zone the water is cold and is in perpetual darkness. Not all lakes have a profundal zone.

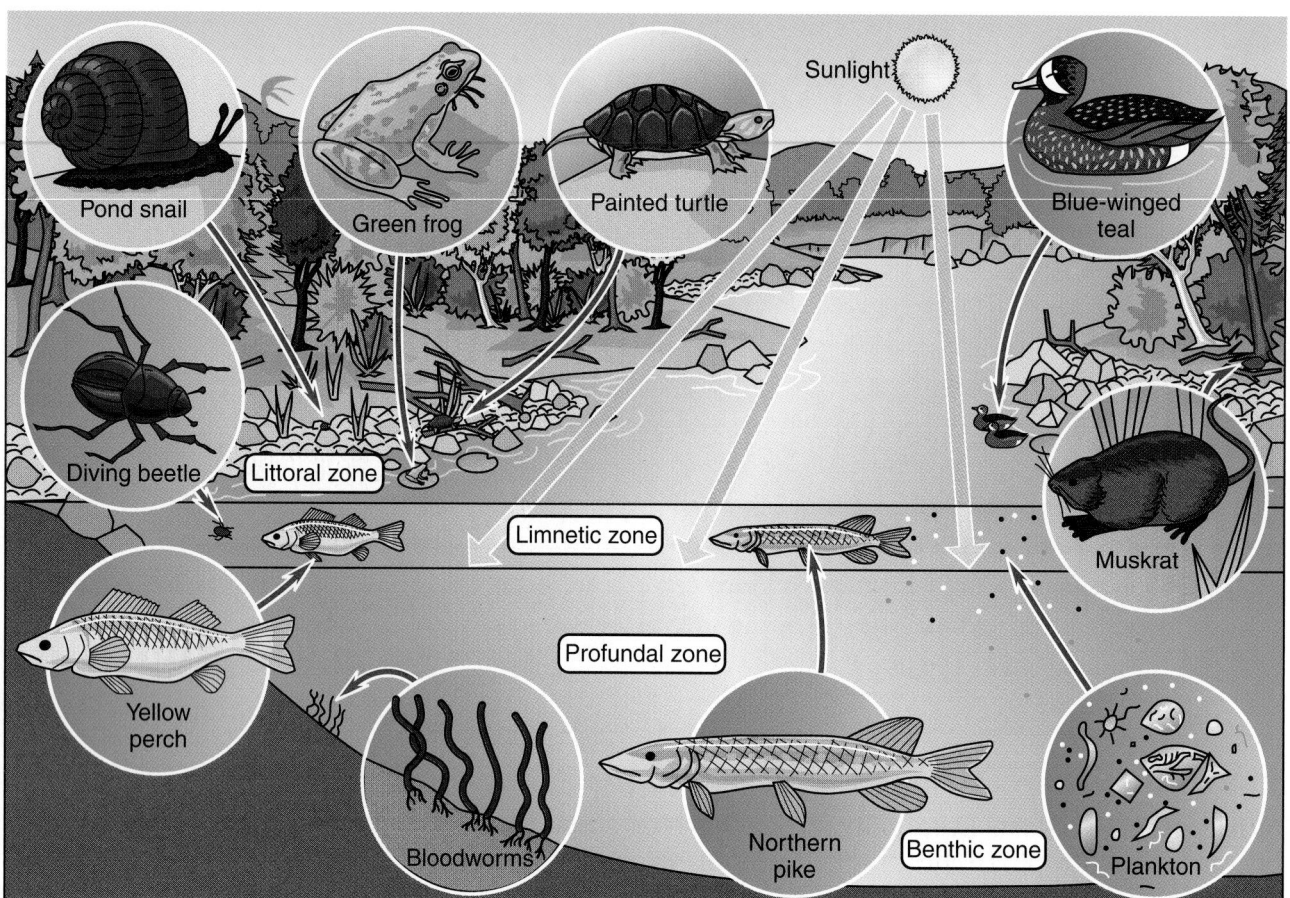

FIGURE 26-4 The aquatic life zones that exist in lakes.

The bottom of the lake is called the benthic zone. The benthic zone can be home to many aquatic organisms, depending on the depth of the lake. Some glacial lakes have depths in excess of 600 ft (183 m). Many benthic zones of large lakes around the world have been virtually unexplored and may contain many unique forms of aquatic life. Lakes also possess a thermocline like the ocean. This is an area where cold deep water meets the warmer surface waters. Sometimes in early summer you can feel the thermocline when you jump into a lake, as your body plunges into the colder water below the surface. The thermocline is an important mixing zone where nutrients and oxygen are transferred from surface water to the deeper parts of the lake.

WATERSHEDS AND RIVERS

The other classification of fresh surface water on Earth is known as flowing water. Flowing water is also known as rivers and streams. As precipitation falls onto the land surface, any water that does not infiltrate into the ground begins to flow toward lower elevations as a result of gravity. Eventually the flowing water, also called runoff, gathers in small creeks and streams. These streams begin to converge into larger flowing bodies of water called rivers, which are in constant motion flowing toward the sea. The total land area from which these flowing waters collect precipitation is called a drainage basin or **watershed**

CAREER CONNECTIONS

Limnologist

Limnologists study the biological, chemical, geologic, and physical characteristics of inland freshwater systems. This includes all aspects of lakes, ponds, rivers, streams, and wetlands. Their research involves the circulation of water in a specific region, light transmission through water, bottom sediments, water temperature, seasonal changes, and the interaction of aquatic organisms with the physical aspects of freshwater systems. Limnologists also study the events that lead to the formation and evolution of inland bodies of freshwater. Current research also surrounds the effects of human society on freshwater systems, especially water use and pollution. Many of these aquatic scientists conduct research in the academic fields, but they can also find employment with state and local government agencies.

(Figure 26–5). Drainage basins can cover thousands of square miles for large river systems or a few square miles for small creeks. Small creeks and streams that contribute water to larger river systems are called tributaries. Most major river systems have thousands of smaller tributaries that feed water into them.

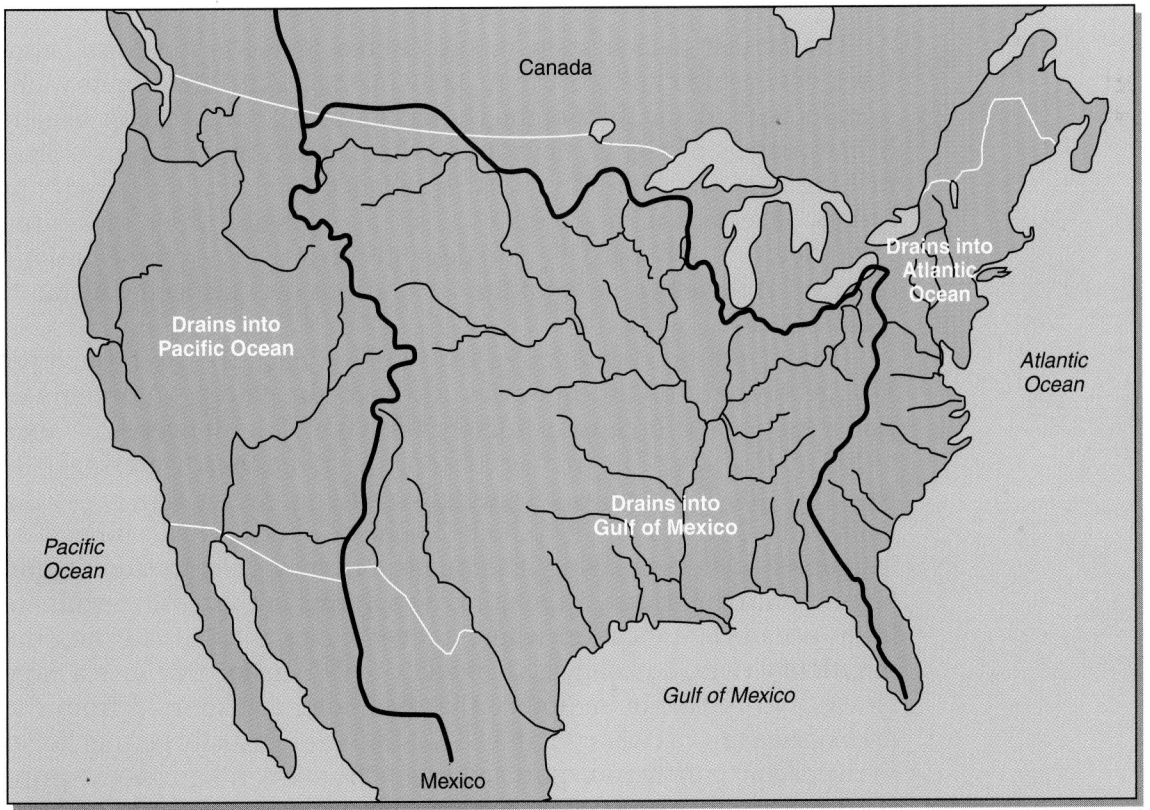

FIGURE 26–5 The drainage areas for the major river systems of the United States.

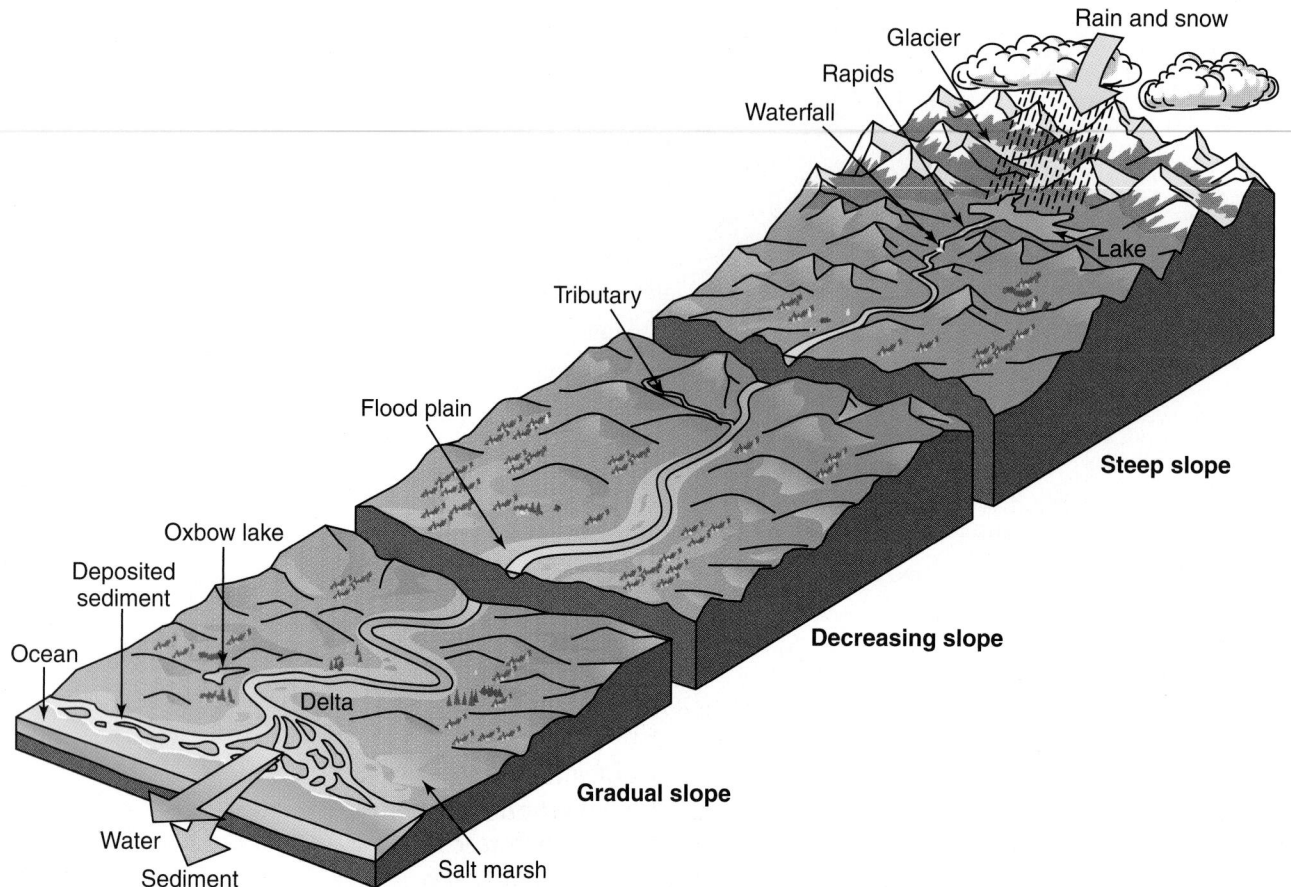

FIGURE 26-6 The slope of a river system gradually decreases from its source to its mouth.

The largest river system in the United States is the Mississippi River, which stretches more than 3,000 mi (4,828 km) and drains water from more than one third of the United States. All river systems usually begin in areas of higher elevations, where creeks and streams collect melting snow or rain. This area is called the headwaters of a river system. Rivers are all powered by the force of gravity, which moves the water at a specific rate. This rate depends on a river's slope. The slope of a river is the elevation that the water drops over a specific distance (Figure 26-6).

Usually the headwaters of a river system have the greatest slope. The headwaters of the Arkansas River, in the Rocky Mountains of North America, drop approximately 4,000 ft (1,219 m) over a distance of 100 mi (161 km). The increased slope of a river's headwaters usually results in the formation of waterfalls and whitewater rapids. As the river lowers in elevation, its velocity begins to decrease. This is because its slope is also decreasing. Eventually the river runs its course and empties into the ocean. All major river systems in the world terminate in an ocean. The location where a river meets the sea is called the mouth of a river. It usually is marked by a wide delta. A delta is a large fan-shaped region of sediment that has been transported from the drainage basins of rivers (Figure 26-7). Deltas are usually getting larger as rivers continually transport sediments from inland areas. The principal action of river systems is to move water and sediment from the inland regions of land masses and transport them to the sea.

FIGURE 26–7 An area of deposition where sediment is being deposited by flowing water. (*Courtesy of USDA/NRCS.*)

STREAM FEATURES

Because river systems drop from areas of higher elevation to areas of lower elevation, they contain an abundance of energy. The power of flowing water has been used as a source of energy for hundreds of years. Many types of mills and factories were built next to rivers and streams to harness their immense power. The energy that river systems contain creates many unique stream features. Stream features are formed as a result of a river trying to dissipate its excess energy. The primary way a river system dissipates energy is by **meandering**. Meandering is the series of S-shaped curves that make up a body of flowing water (Figure 26–8). Rivers rarely flow in a straight line, but tend to form a snakelike pattern. This meandering results in a continual pattern of erosion and deposition along the total length of a river.

Areas of erosion, or removal of rocks and soil along a river, are called cut banks. Cut banks are formed where the river cuts into the soil and rock along the bank and removes it. This area forms along the outside curve of a river. This is because the velocity of the water is greatest along the outside curve of a meander. This area of erosion also forms another

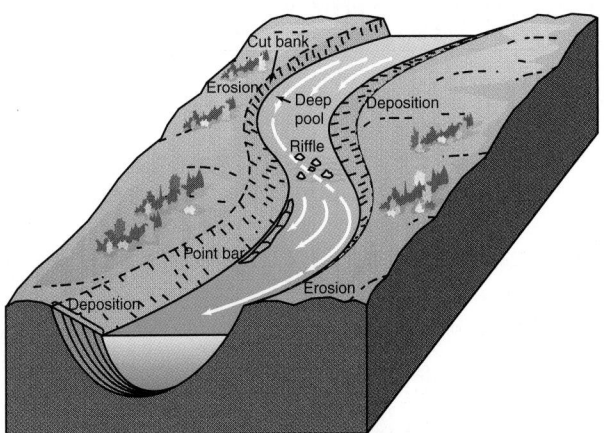

FIGURE 26–8 The meandering of a stream results in the formation of deep pools, cut banks, point bars, and riffles as a result of the erosion and deposition of sediments by the flowing water.

unique stream feature called a deep pool. A deep pool is also formed on the outside curve of a meander where the river bottom is being eroded. Trout fishermen usually know the locations of these deep pools because this is where many fish like to reside on hot summer days. The force of the flowing water in the river moves the eroded material from the cut bank and deep pool downstream and deposits it as a point bar. A point bar is a shallow area of deposition located on the inside curve of a river. This is an area of deposition because the inside curve of a meander is where the velocity of the flowing water is at its least.

After the water moves through a meander, the river channel begins to straighten out. This part of a river is called a riffle. A riffle is a relatively straight shallow portion of a river located between meanders. Riffles are also areas of deposition where the material eroded from upstream is deposited. Riffles are shallow regions usually marked by whitewater and rapids. The riffle then enters into another meander and the whole process repeats itself. This series of erosions and depositions, which is caused by meandering, continues until the river reaches its mouth. The meandering process continually erodes and deposits rock and sediments all along a river and eventually transports the mountains to the sea.

A flowing river is in a state of **dynamic equilibrium**, because the erosion of material by the water is equal to the amount of material that it deposits. The amount of water that flows past a specific point in a river is called its **discharge rate**. Discharge rates are recorded in both cubic centimeters per second and gallons per second and are important indicators used for flood prediction (Figure 26–9).

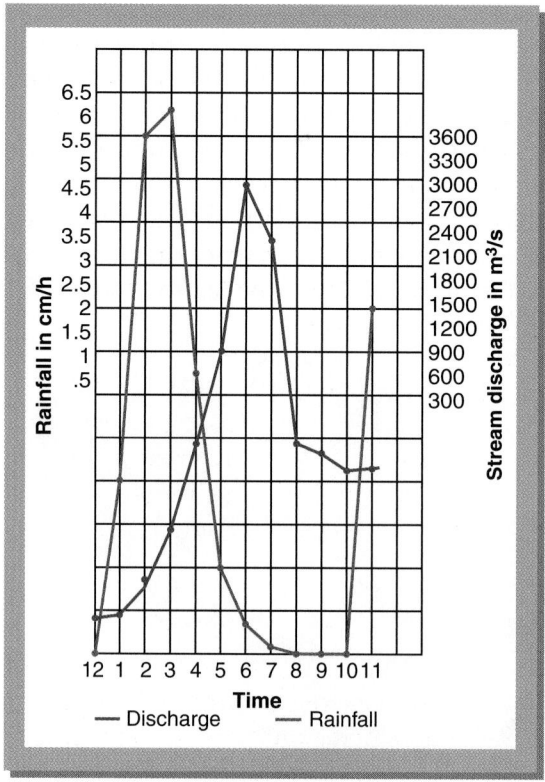

FIGURE 26–9 The relationship between rainfall and the discharge rate of a river shows the time delay between the time of maximum rainfall and the time of maximum discharge.

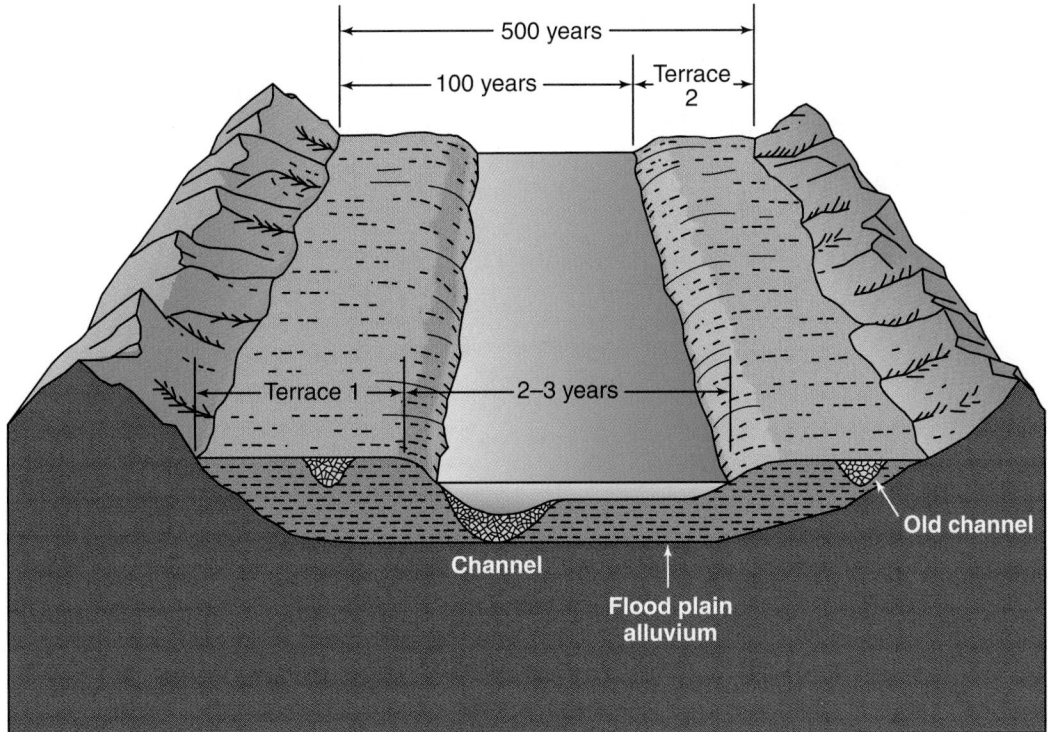

FIGURE 26–10 The cross section of a floodplain showing the location of the channel and terraces.

FLOODPLAINS

Another important feature of a river system is called the floodplain. A **floodplain** is a gently sloping area that surrounds the **channel** of a river. The channel is the portion of the river that contains flowing water. Floodplains are formed by sediments that were deposited by a past flood event. Over time the sediments build up wide, flat areas alongside the river channel. Floodplains often contain a series of small steps that lead to the current river channel. These steps are called terraces. They mark areas where the channel of the river was located during a past flood (Figure 26–10). Floodplains are usually wetland areas that contain low-growing vegetation. This is due to the periodic flooding that can occur along river systems. Because floodplains are naturally flat areas near flowing water, towns and farms often have been established near them. The periodic flooding that formed the floodplains can destroy lives and property located in these areas. It is important to identify floodplain areas to prevent the loss of life that occurs as a result of excess rainfall or snow melt.

STAGES OF RIVER DEVELOPMENT

All rivers have a similar series of developmental stages that are based mainly on their slope and velocity, along with the surrounding topography (Figure 26–11). The upper stage or source area of a river was once referred to as the youthful stage. This section of a river flows over a steep slope and has a high water velocity. The upper stage of a river is mainly an area of erosion, which has a stream channel that is confined

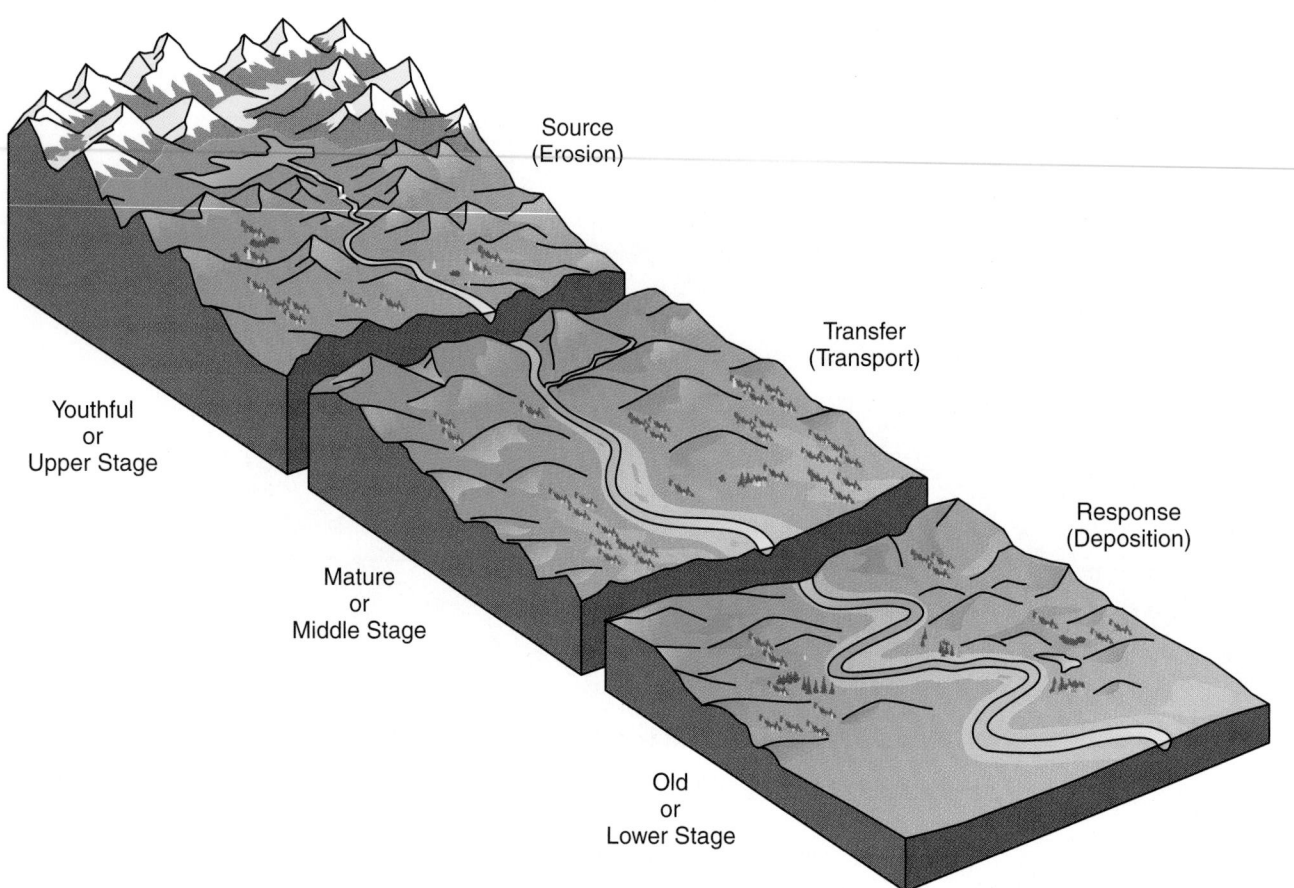

Source
(Erosion)

Transfer
(Transport)

Response
(Deposition)

Youthful
or
Upper Stage

Mature
or
Middle Stage

Old
or
Lower Stage

FIGURE 26-11   The three stages in the development of a river.

by the surrounding landscape. The rapidly moving water cuts through rock and sediment, forming deep canyons. The upper stage also has many rapids and waterfalls that form as a result of the steep gradient, and has a fairly straight stream channel. The rapidly moving headwaters of the Colorado River that cut through the mountains to form steep canyons are an example of an upper stage or source river.

Eventually, as the river cuts down into the landscape, its slope decreases, causing the velocity of the river to begin to slow. The river is now in the middle or transfer stage of development where the erosion and deposition of sediments are in dynamic equilibrium. Dynamic equilibrium is a balance between two opposing processes that occur at the same rate. The transfer stage was once known as the old age stage of a river, which is identified by the formation of a wide floodplain. This stage of a river also begins to form more developed meanders as it cuts into the floodplain. The middle stage of a river moves through a wide river valley lined with gently sloping hills. The Hudson River, which flows through the rolling hills of the Hudson Valley in New York State, is an example of a river in the middle or transfer stage.

The lower or response stage of river development, once known as the old age stage, occurs when the slope of the river is greatly reduced, causing it to flow slowly. Large meanders form in the flat surrounding floodplain. Some of these meanders get cut off from the main channel of the river as it changes its course, forming oxbow lakes. Oxbow lakes formed from the Mississippi River in parts of Louisiana are called bayous. During the lower stage of development, deposition is occurring at a higher rate than erosion. The lower Mississippi River is a good example of a river in the lower stage.

SECTION REVIEW

1. List the three age classifications of lakes.
2. Describe the four zones found within a lake.
3. What causes rivers to flow?
4. Define the term *watershed*.
5. Describe the process of meandering.
6. What is a floodplain?
7. Briefly describe the three stages of river development, and their unique characteristics.
8. Who was Alexander Agassiz?

@ WEB Links

FOR MORE INFORMATION GO TO THESE WEB LINKS:

<http://www.epa.gov/highschool/water.htm>

<http://www.mbgnet.net/fresh/index.htm>

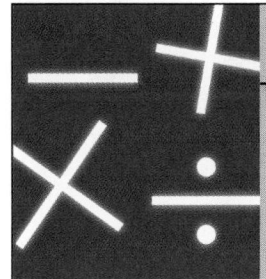

earth math

1) The discharge rate of a river is determined by multiplying the average velocity of the water by its cross-sectional area. If a section of river is 75 ft wide with an average depth of 5 ft and the water is flowing at 0.7 ft per second, what is the discharge rate for this river?

26.2 Groundwater

GROUNDWATER RECHARGE AND THE WATER TABLE

Water that is stored in pores and crevices located in rock and soil is called groundwater. All groundwater enters, or infiltrates, the ground as precipitation or as seepage. Infiltration occurs when precipitation falls to the ground and soaks into the soil. Seepage occurs as surface waters slowly leak into the ground. Areas of infiltration are also called recharge areas, because this is where groundwater supplies are recharged. As water infiltrates into the soil, the force of gravity drives it downward, where it begins to collect and saturate the soil. This area is called the zone of saturation. It is where the pores in soil or rock underground are completely filled with water (Figure 26–12). The zone of saturation varies in its depth depending on the local climate. In some areas that receive high amounts of rainfall, the zone of saturation can be located only 8 to 10 ft below the surface. Other dry areas might

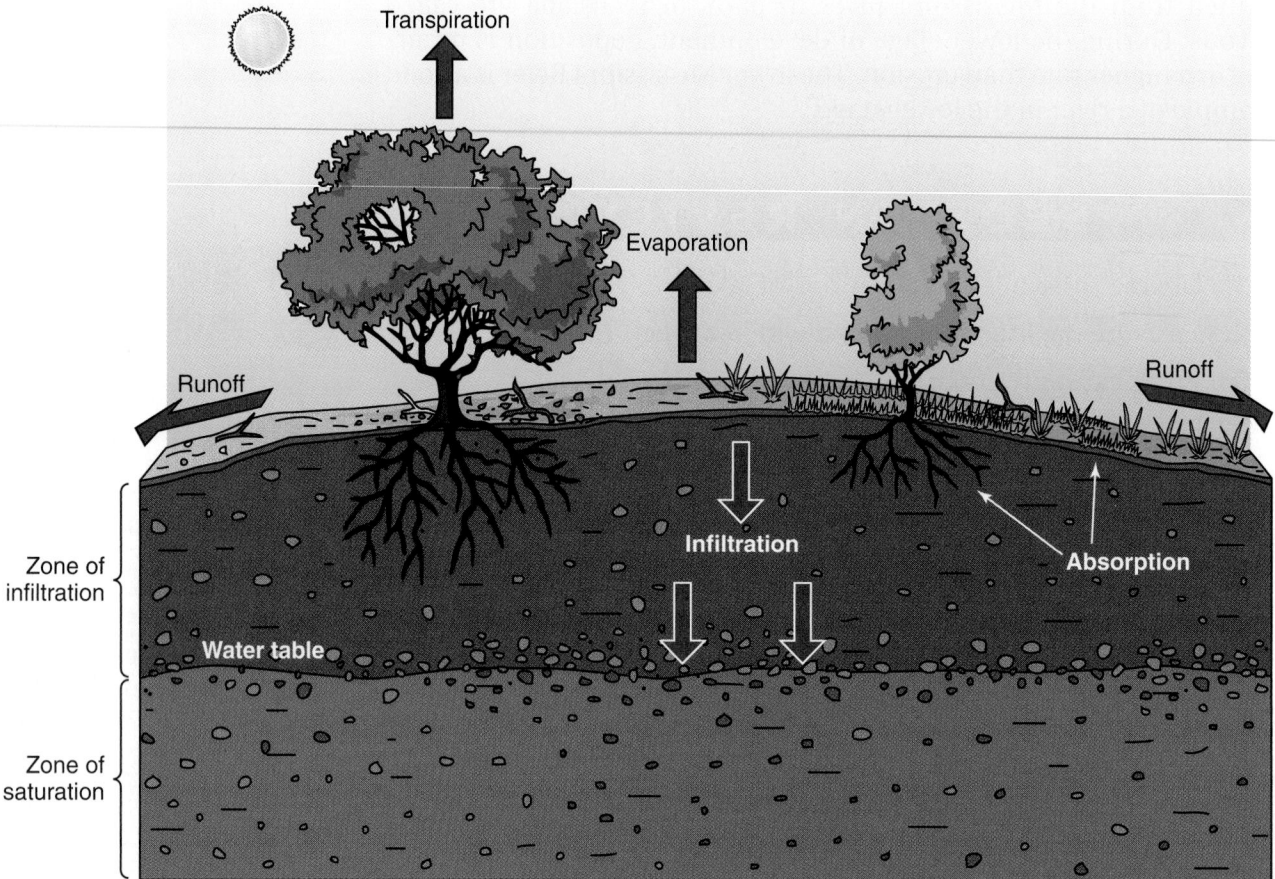

FIGURE 26–12 Groundwater that completely saturates the pores in rock and soil forms the zone of saturation. The top of the zone of saturation is known as the water table.

have very deep zones of saturation. The top portion of the zone of saturation is called the **water table**. The water table can also vary in its depth seasonally. During rainy seasons the water table can move up toward the surface as infiltration is increased. Then during the drier months the water table might descend deeper as the infiltration rates decline.

GROUNDWATER FLOW

All groundwater, like flowing surface water, is in a constant state of movement, called groundwater flow. The flow of groundwater moves by the force of gravity; therefore it travels from areas of high elevation to areas of low elevation. Eventually all groundwater exits the ground and returns to the surface. The area where groundwater reaches the surface is called the area of discharge (Figure 26–13). Common areas of discharge are flowing springs, where cool fresh groundwater flows out of the ground. During times of the year when there are low amounts of rainfall, the groundwater that is discharged from flowing springs continues to feed water into streams and rivers. This is what keeps these bodies of water flowing throughout the year. The time and distance that it takes for groundwater to travel from an area of recharge to an area of discharge can vary greatly and depends on the soil or rock in which

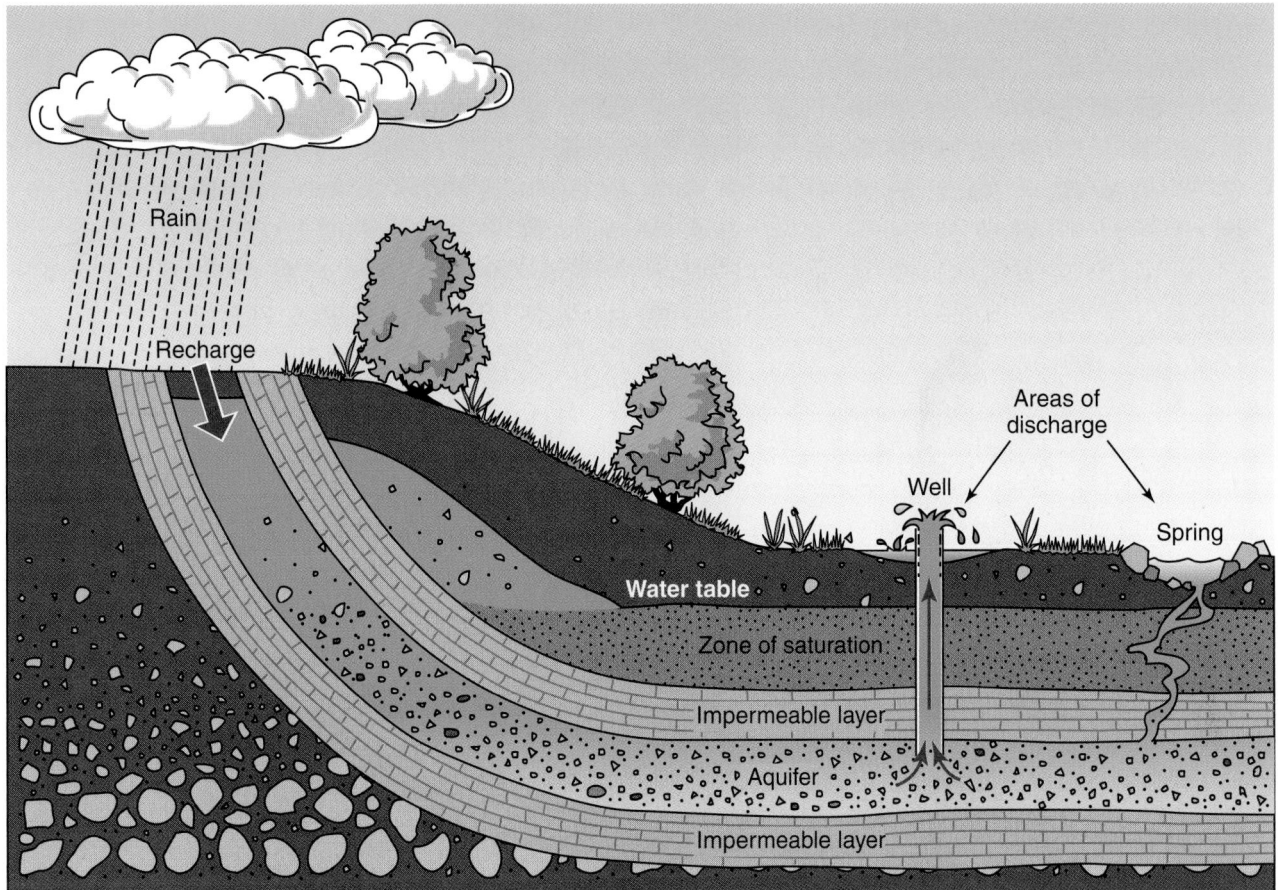

FIGURE 26-13 Groundwater flows from areas of recharge to areas of discharge.

it is flowing. Groundwater located in large porous rock formations can flow at a very high rate. If the groundwater is located in small, tightly packed pores of rock and soil, it flows at a much slower rate.

AQUIFERS AND GROUNDWATER DISCHARGE

Another important aspect of groundwater is called the **aquifer**. Aquifers are areas of porous rock that store large amounts of groundwater. One of the largest aquifers in the United States, the Oglalla aquifer, underlies more than 174,000 square miles (450,658 square kilometers) of Texas, New Mexico, Oklahoma, Kansas, Colorado, Nebraska, Wyoming, and South Dakota (Figure 26-14). This aquifer holds approximately the same amount of water as Lake Huron. The average thickness of the zone of saturation that makes up the Oglalla aquifer is approximately 200 ft (61 m). Most of the water that is stored in this huge aquifer infiltrated the ground as glaciers began to melt approximately 10,000 years ago.

Some aquifers are located between two layers of water-impermeable rock. **Impermeable** means that water cannot infiltrate the rocks. The trapped water between the two rock layers is called a **confined aquifer** (Figure 26-15). Wells drilled into confined aquifers are called flowing or **artesian wells**, because the trapped water becomes pressurized and flows forcefully from underground.

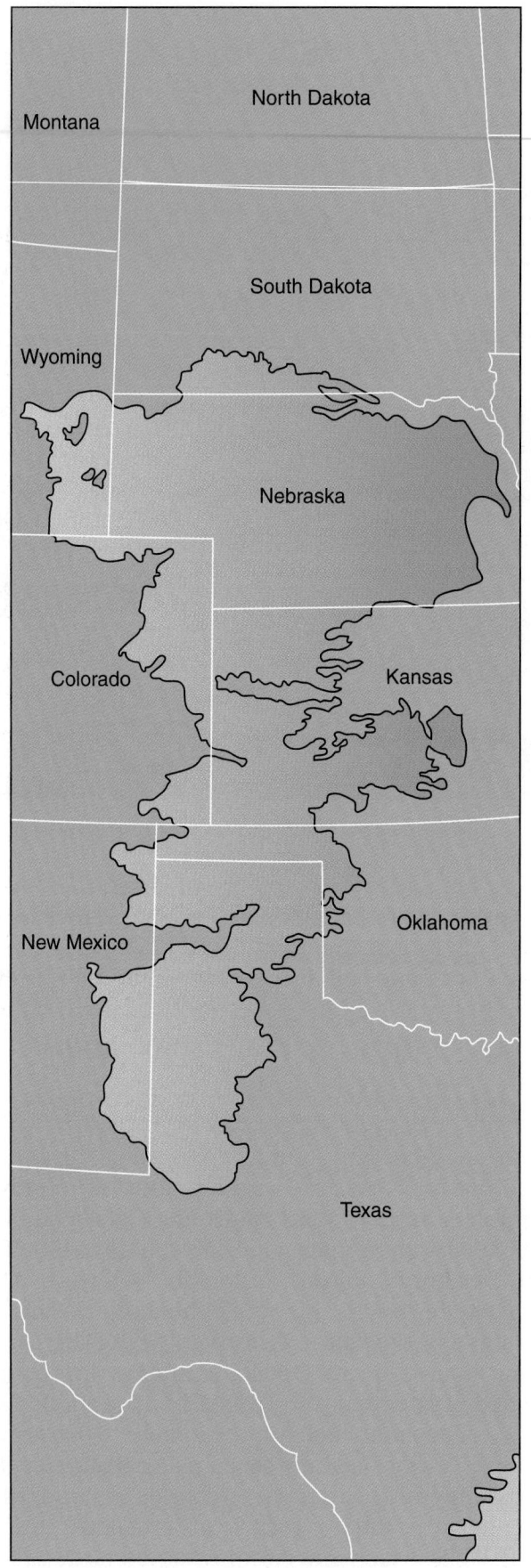

FIGURE 26–14 The Oglalla aquifer stores millions of gallons of water in the ground under large parts of the Midwest.

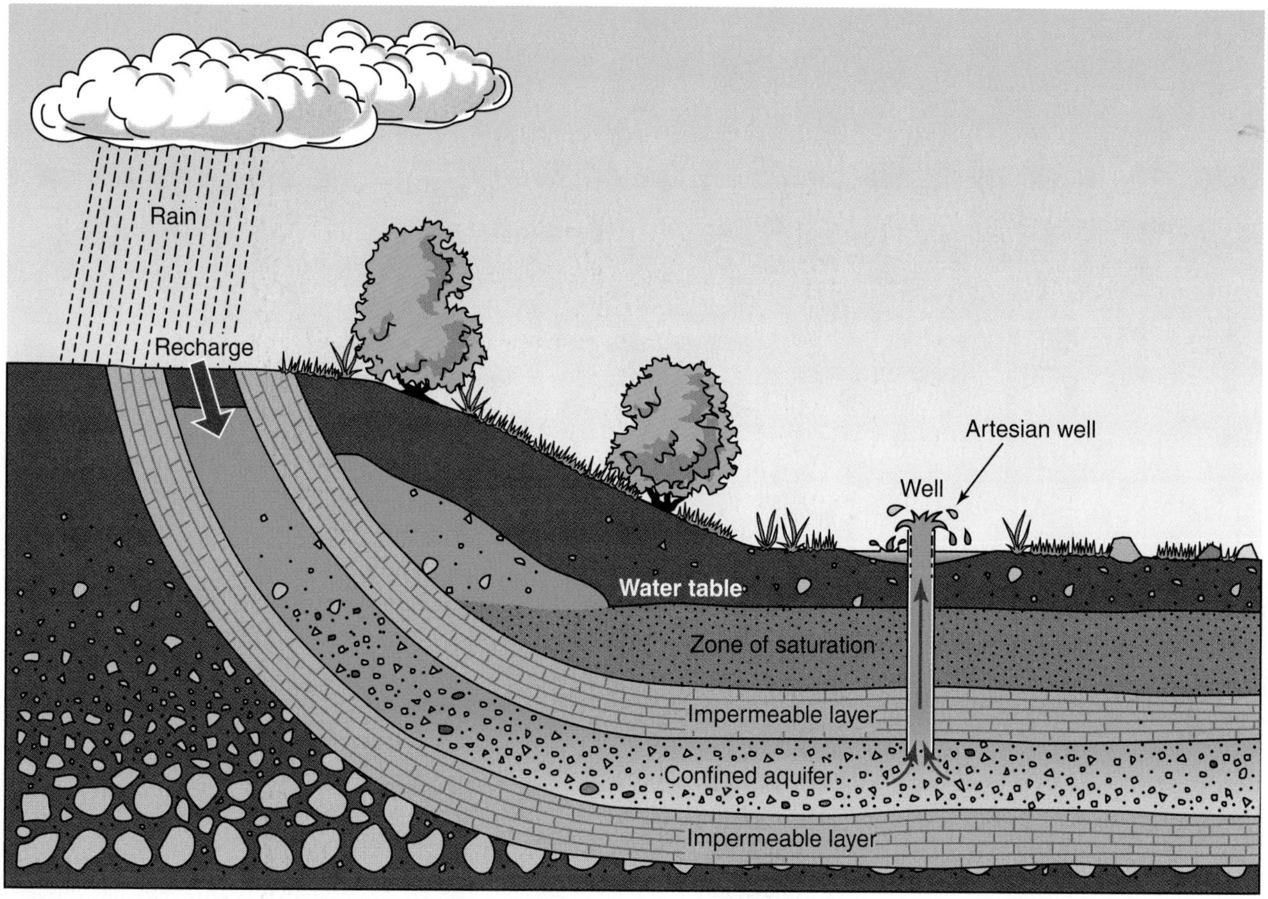

FIGURE 26–15 The location of a confined aquifer between two layers of impermeable rock.

Earth System Scientists

Rachel Carson

Rachel Carson was born in Philadelphia in 1907. She received her education in zoology and worked at the Woods Hole Oceanographic Institute as a teacher and researcher. She also became the head biologist for the U.S. Fish and Wildlife Service, where she wrote fisheries information for the government. Eventually she became a published writer of books that presented the biology of the sea. In 1962 her world-famous book *Silent Spring* was published. In this groundbreaking publication, Carson presented the ill effects of pesticides on the food chain. She wrote of the evils of DDT, a widely used pesticide that was moving through groundwater and surface waters and eventually entering the bodies of living organisms. Her study on the effects of pesticides on the environment led to the birth of the environmental movement in the United States. Because of Carson's research, the world was introduced to the dangers of chemicals being spread throughout the environment and the problems associated with industrialization and water resources.

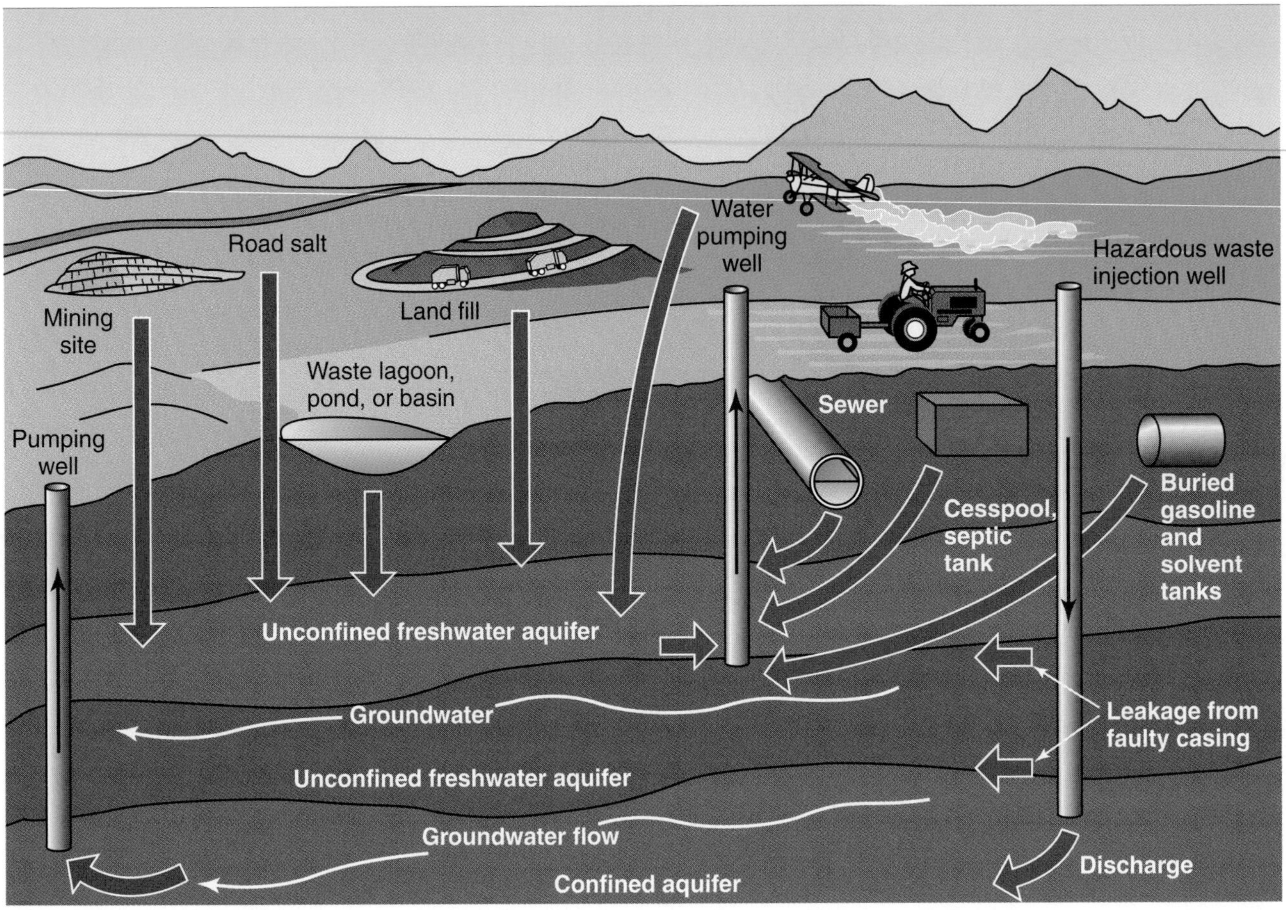

The diagram shows labels:

Mining site

Road salt

Land fill

Water pumping well

Hazardous waste injection well

Pumping well

Waste lagoon, pond, or basin

Sewer

Cesspool, septic tank

Buried gasoline and solvent tanks

Unconfined freshwater aquifer

Groundwater

Leakage from faulty casing

Unconfined freshwater aquifer

Groundwater flow

Confined aquifer

Discharge

FIGURE 26–16 The main sources of groundwater pollution.

GROUNDWATER POLLUTION

Unfortunately, many groundwater supplies can be easily contaminated or polluted. When water infiltrates the ground, it can carry with it many dissolved pollutants, such as chemicals, fertilizers, and heavy metals. Landfills, leaking underground chemical storage tanks, manure piles, and leaking septic systems are all sources of groundwater pollutants (Figure 26–16). Groundwater pollution can often be the most difficult form of water pollution to detect and clean up. This is because groundwater is not visible, which makes it difficult to locate the source and determine the extent of the groundwater pollution. The best way to protect the quality of groundwater is to prevent pollutants from entering the ground.

@ WEB Links

FOR MORE INFORMATION GO TO THIS WEB LINK:

<http://www.epa.gov /highschool/water.htm>

SECTION REVIEW

1. What percentage of the United States' drinking water supply comes from groundwater?

2. Define the term *infiltration*.

3. What are the two areas called where groundwater enters and then leaves the ground?

CAREER CONNECTIONS

Hydrogeologist

A hydrogeologist, also called a groundwater hydrologist, studies and monitors the world's groundwater resources. This includes the tracking of how much groundwater is stored in a particular region. These scientists determine the amount of groundwater that is available for use and the rate at which it is being used or replenished. They also help to locate underground water sources and determine where to drill wells. These researchers study the way that groundwater flows underground, from areas of recharge to areas of discharge. Hydrogeologists also research the pollution of groundwater resources. This aspect of their field involves tracking polluted groundwater, locating the source of pollution, and cleaning contaminated groundwater. Hydrogeologists study ways in which the pollution of groundwater can also be prevented. A career in this field requires a college degree with an emphasis on geology and hydrology. Hydrogeologists can find work in private industry or for state and local governments.

4. Where is the water table located?
5. Define the term *confined aquifer*.
6. Who was Rachel Carson?

CHAPTER SUMMARY

The world's freshwater supply that is not locked up in glacial ice makes up approximately 1 percent of all the water on the planet. This water exists on the Earth in lakes and rivers and as groundwater. Lakes are large inland bodies of water that are often classified by their level of

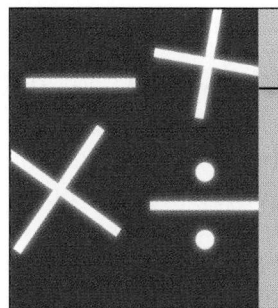

earth math

1) How many gallons of water are pumped from the ground for drinking water and irrigation in the United States each week?

2) If 1 cubic foot of water equals approximately 7 gal of water, how many gallons of water does an aquifer hold if it has an area of 12.5 million cubic feet?

productivity. An oligotrophic lake is a cold and deep lake with crystal clear water that has very low productivity as a result of the lack of available nutrients. These lakes support a small amount of aquatic organisms and are often formed by melting glaciers. Mesotrophic lakes are cool, deep lakes with clear water and medium productivity. These lakes support a healthy population of both aquatic plants and animals as a result of the increased amount of nutrients in the water. Eutrophic lakes are shallow, warm-water lakes that are very cloudy and have a muddy bottom. These lakes support a high number of aquatic plants and algae as a result of the increased amount of nutrients in the water.

Lakes also have unique aquatic life zones similar to those in the ocean. The area near the shore, where light can penetrate all the way to the lake bottom, is called the littoral zone. The limnetic zone is located out in the deeper water of the lake, from the surface to the depth where photosynthesis can occur. Some deep lakes have profundal zones where no light reaches, making it perpetually dark. The bottom of the lake is called the benthic zone. The depth of the lake at which a rapid drop in the water temperature occurs is called the thermocline.

Flowing bodies of water on the Earth's surface are called streams and rivers. They flow over the surface of the land by the power of gravity from areas of high elevation to areas of lower elevation. The total land area that a river system drains is called a watershed. All flowing bodies of water have characteristic S-shaped curves called meanders. These form as a result of the flowing water trying to dissipate its energy. The meandering of a flowing body of water creates unique stream features. These include areas of erosion called cut banks and deep pools, which form on the outside curve of a meander. The point bar is a stream feature that forms on the inside curve of a meander where sediment is deposited. A riffle is the relatively straight, shallow area of deposition downstream from a meander.

A flowing body of water such as a stream or river is in a state of dynamic equilibrium, which means that its rate of erosion is equal to its rate of deposition. The amount of water that is flowing past a particular point in a river or stream is called its discharge rate.

All rivers go through a series of stages that together make up the life cycle of a river. The youthful stage is marked by the river's steep slope, which causes the velocity of the water to increase. This forms rapids and waterfalls and creates deep, narrow canyons through which the water flows. The mature stage of a river occurs when the slope is reduced and the river begins to form meanders that cut into its flat floodplain. Mature rivers also flow through wide river valleys. The old age stage of a river is marked by a very gradual slope, which causes the river to flow slowly. Large meanders develop as the river cuts through the wide floodplain. Some of these meanders get cut off from the main channel, forming oxbow lakes.

Water that seeps into the ground from surface water or from the infiltration of precipitation is called groundwater. Groundwater exists in the pore spaces of soil and rock. The top of the area where all the pore spaces are filled with water is called the water table. This important freshwater resource flows from areas of high elevation to areas of low elevation. The rate at which groundwater flows depends on the size and distribution of pore spaces within rock and soil.

A large amount of groundwater stored in rocks and soil is called an aquifer. Aquifers that are trapped between two layers of impermeable rock are known as confined aquifers. All groundwater eventually flows out of the ground from an area of discharge. These are commonly known as flowing springs. Groundwater supplies approximately 40 percent of drinking water in the United States; it can be polluted by leaking fuel tanks, fertilizers, sewage, and toxic chemicals.

CHAPTER REVIEW

Multiple Choice

1. Which of the following is a characteristic of a eutrophic lake?
   a. clear water and cold water
   b. little aquatic life
   c. low productivity
   d. high amounts of nutrients

2. A clear lake with medium productivity that supports a variety of aquatic life is called:
   a. oligotrophic
   b. mesotrophic
   c. eutrophic
   d. autotrophic

3. Which aquatic life zone exists in deep water where photosynthesis can occur?
   a. limnetic zone
   b. littoral zone
   c. profundal zone
   d. benthic zone

4. What aquatic life zone supports plants growing on the bottom of the lake?
   a. limnetic zone
   b. littoral zone
   c. profundal zone
   d. aphotic zone

5. Approximately one third of the United States is part of the Mississippi River's:
   a. watershed
   b. discharge area
   c. recharge area
   d. aquifer

6. An area of deposition located on the inside curve of a river's meander is called a:
   a. deep pool
   b. cut bank
   c. point bar
   d. riffle

7. This area of erosion located on the bottom of the outside curve of a meander is where a fisherman would most likely find trout on a hot day:
   a. deep pool
   b. cut bank
   c. point bar
   d. riffle

8. Rapidly moving water that cuts a deep, narrow canyon in the surrounding rock is in what stage of river development?
   a. youth
   b. maturity
   c. old age
   d. rejuvenation

9. The Hudson River in New York is an example of what type of river?
   a. youthful
   b. mature
   c. old age
   d. rejuvenated

10. When the amount of erosion equals the amount of deposition in river, it is:
    a. youthful
    b. in dynamic equilibrium
    c. mature
    d. meandering

11. What decreases in depth during wet seasons and increases its depth during dry seasons?
    a. soil pores
    b. the water table
    c. artesian wells
    d. flowing springs

12. Groundwater flows more rapidly when:
    a. pore spaces are large and the rock is permeable
    b. pore spaces are small and the rock is permeable
    c. pore spaces are large and the rock is impermeable
    d. pore spaces are small and the rock is impermeable

13. A large amount of water stored in the ground below impermeable rock is known as:
    a. soil pores
    b. the water table
    c. a confined aquifer
    d. flowing springs

14. Approximately what percentage of Americans get their drinking water from groundwater?
    a. 10 percent
    b. 20 percent
    c. 30 percent
    d. 40 percent

Matching   *Match the terms with the correct definitions.*

a. oligotrophic lake
b. mesotrophic lake
c. eutrophic lake
d. watershed
e. meandering

f. dynamic equilibrium
g. discharge rate
h. floodplain
i. channel
j. water table

k. aquifer
l. impermeable
m. confined aquifer
n. artesian wells

1. _____ The flat area of a river valley, located along both sides of a river channel, that is formed from the deposition of sediments during periodic floods.
2. _____ The total land area that is drained by a particular river system.
3. _____ A free-flowing well that discharges water from the ground that is recharged from a higher elevation.
4. _____ A classification of lake that has been recently formed from glacial melt waters; it has very clear, cold water and is very low in nutrients or aquatic life.
5. _____ The top of the zone of saturation.
6. _____ The portion of a moving body of water where water is currently flowing.
7. _____ Groundwater that is located below an impermeable rock layer.
8. _____ The classification for a middle-aged lake that is relatively clear, deep, and low in available nutrients.
9. _____ A term meaning *unable to pass through,* such as certain rocks that do not allow water to pass through them.
10. _____ A classification for a lake that is relatively cloudy, warm, and shallow and has an abundance of nutrients that support a large population of aquatic plants and animals.
11. _____ Large amounts of water stored in porous or fragmented rock underground.
12. _____ The reoccurring S-shaped curves of a river or stream.
13. _____ A balance between two opposing processes that occur at the same rate in an energetic system, such as a river or stream.
14. _____ The amount of water passing by a particular point in a flowing body of water.

Critical Thinking

1. If toxic chemicals were mixed in with river sediments, what do you think would happen to them over time?

27

Glaciers

OBJECTIVES

Anatomy of a Glacier · Glacial Movement and Moraines · Types of Glaciers
· Glaciers and Global Climate

After reading this chapter you should be able to:

▶ Define the term *glacier*.
▶ Differentiate among the zones of accumulation, flowage, and ablation
  on a glacier.
▶ Explain the process that causes a glacier to flow.
▶ Describe the location and formation of terminal, medial, and lateral moraines.
▶ Identify the five different types of glaciers and their unique characteristics.
▶ Describe the processes that lead to glacial advance and glacial retreat.
▶ Explain the relationship among global climate, glaciers, and sea level.
▶ Identify how much sea level has risen over the past 100 years and how much
  it is expected to rise in the future.

TERMS TO KNOW

glaciers

zone of accumulation

glacial front

zone of flowage

glacial till

moraines

terminal moraines

zone of ablation

lateral moraines

medial moraines

icebergs

glacial advance

glacial retreat

INTRODUCTION

The largest storehouse of freshwater on Earth is located in the world's glaciers. Approximately one tenth of all the land surfaces on the Earth are covered in glaciers, and as recently as 11,000 years ago, more than 30 percent of the land surface was located under glacial ice. The entire continent of Antarctica is covered entirely by ice. The average thickness of the glacial ice there is approximately 7,000 ft (2,134 m), with the thickest ice being more than 14,000 ft (4,267 m). Recent investigations of the glaciers that exist around the world suggest that they are all shrinking. Scientists fear that the melting of the world's glaciers might indicate a change in the global climate.

The amount of water that the world's glaciers hold is more than two times as much as all the world's groundwater and surface freshwater supplies combined. Scientists are not sure of what the effect would be on the environment if all this water were to melt. During the height of the last ice age approximately 18,000 years ago, global sea level was almost 400 ft (122 m) lower than it is today. This reveals the important relationship between glaciers and sea level. Understanding the processes that form glaciers and how they interact with the environment is an important aspect of Earth systems science.

ANATOMY OF A GLACIER

Glaciers are large masses of ice formed by the compaction of snow over long periods. Glaciers form in the higher latitudes, where temperatures remain below freezing for much of the year and where more snow accumulates than melts. Eventually the snow builds up and becomes compressed by the accumulating weight of the snow that continues to collect on top of the glacier. The compressed snow begins to crystallize into glacial ice. As the ice begins to build up, crystallizing ice begins to change from the white color of snow to the bluish tint of glacial ice. The area where snow falls to form the glacier is called the **zone of accumulation**. This area is often located in higher elevations, where the temperature remains below freezing throughout the year, allowing snow to continually accumulate. When the ice reaches a thickness of more than 100 feet, the pressure from the zone of accumulation begins to force the ice below to flow outward. This causes glaciers to advance, or move away from the zone of accumulation. The flow of a glacier can be demonstrated by observing a piece of Play-Doh. If you took a ball of Play-Doh, laid it down on a table, and pressed your hand down on top of it, it would begin to spread apart all along its sides. This is the same way that a glacier flows. The weight from the zone of accumulation presses downward and causes the glacial ice to spread outward.

The advancing edge of glacier is called the **glacial front** (Figure 27–1). The lower portion of a glacier is the portion that undergoes the most movement or flow. This **zone of flowage** varies in its rate of movement by a few inches or up to 25 ft (7.6 m) per day. Some areas of the Antarctic have zones of flowage that are rapidly transporting glacial ice toward the sea. Studies of these glaciers have revealed that a layer of pressurized liquid was located below the glacier, which causes the ice

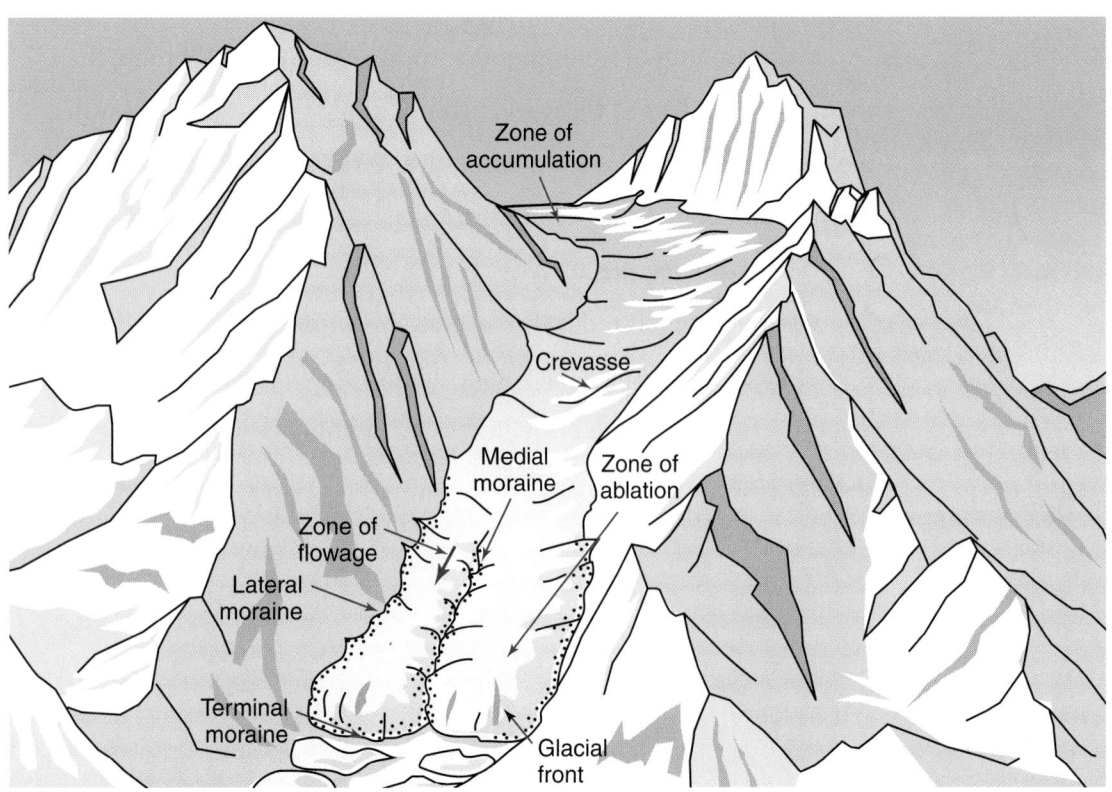

FIGURE 27–1 The main features of a glacier.

to flow rapidly over the surface. These portions of Antarctica move like rivers of ice across the frozen landscape.

GLACIAL MOVEMENT AND MORAINES

As glaciers flow outward from their zone of accumulation, they usually move toward areas of lower elevation. Much like flowing rivers, glaciers tend to push their way through mountain valleys and eventually reach the oceans. As glaciers move through these valleys, their immense weight and forward movement grind up rocks and soil much like a large bulldozer. These rocks and debris become mixed up within the glacial ice and are transported along within the glacier. When the glacier begins to melt away, large mounds of unsorted glacial sediments are left behind which are called **glacial till**. Specific formations of glacial till that are transported and deposited by a glacier are also known as **moraines**.

Terminal moraines are formed when the leading edge of the glacier begins to melt and retreat. This deposits large mounds of glacial sediments on the land surface that marked the position of the glacial front. The leading edge of a glacier is also known as the **zone of ablation**. Ablation is the loss of ice from the glacial front. This can occur on land or in water. **Lateral moraines** are formed along the sides of glaciers as they scrape the edges of mountain valleys. These result in long, dark lines of sediment that form along the sides of glaciers as they remove rock from the valley walls (Figure 27–2). **Medial moraines** are formed in

FIGURE 27–2 Lateral moraines form along the sides of a glacier as it scrapes the valley walls, and terminal moraines are deposited along the glacial front. (*Courtesy of PhotoDisc.*)

CAREER CONNECTIONS

Glaciologist

A glaciologist studies the physical aspects of snow and ice. This includes research involving ice sheets, glaciers, and ice fields all over the world. These scientists monitor the changes that occur within glaciers, especially if they are advancing or retreating. Glaciologists also map glaciers to determine their size and elevation and study how glaciers move and flow. Their research is especially important in monitoring the effects of global climate change. Glaciologists must work in the often harsh, cold environments where glaciers are found. Much of their work involves collecting data on, around, and within a glacier. They take core samples of ice from glaciers to study their age and composition. A glaciologist requires a college background in geology and often works in research for colleges or government agencies.

the center of glaciers where two separate valley glaciers join together to form one large glacier. Glacial moraines result in unique patterns in glacial ice that can often be used to identify its pattern of movement. In many parts of the United States, the remains of these moraines identify areas where glaciers once existed. Today many of these moraines are used as a source for gravel in construction. Glacial moraines can be distinguished because they consist of angular, unsorted sediments.

Some glaciers move large boulders in their ice that can be deposited when they melt. These large boulders are called glacial erratics, because they often exist in random locations. When rocks become trapped in glacial ice near the bottom of the glacier, they move and scrape over rock. When the glacier melts, it leaves behind characteristic scrapes on bedrock that can be used to identify the direction and movement of glaciers in the past. These marks still exist today in many rocks exposed at the Earth's surface, which reveal the movement of glacial ice during the last ice age.

TYPES OF GLACIERS

Glaciers can be divided into different categories, usually classified by their location and size. The largest glaciers, called continental glaciers, cover entire continents; they are also known as ice sheets. The two continental glaciers on Earth are located in Antarctica and Greenland. The Antarctic continental glacier covers more land area than the United States and Central America combined, at an average thickness of more than 7,000 ft (2,134 m) (Figure 27–3). The thickest portion of the Antarctic ice sheet is more than 2.5 mi (4 km)!

The next classification of a glacier is called an ice field (Figure 27–4). Ice fields are large areas of connecting glaciers where only the tops of mountains extend from the surface of the ice. Ice fields are located in high-latitude mountain regions, such as the Juneau ice field in Alaska.

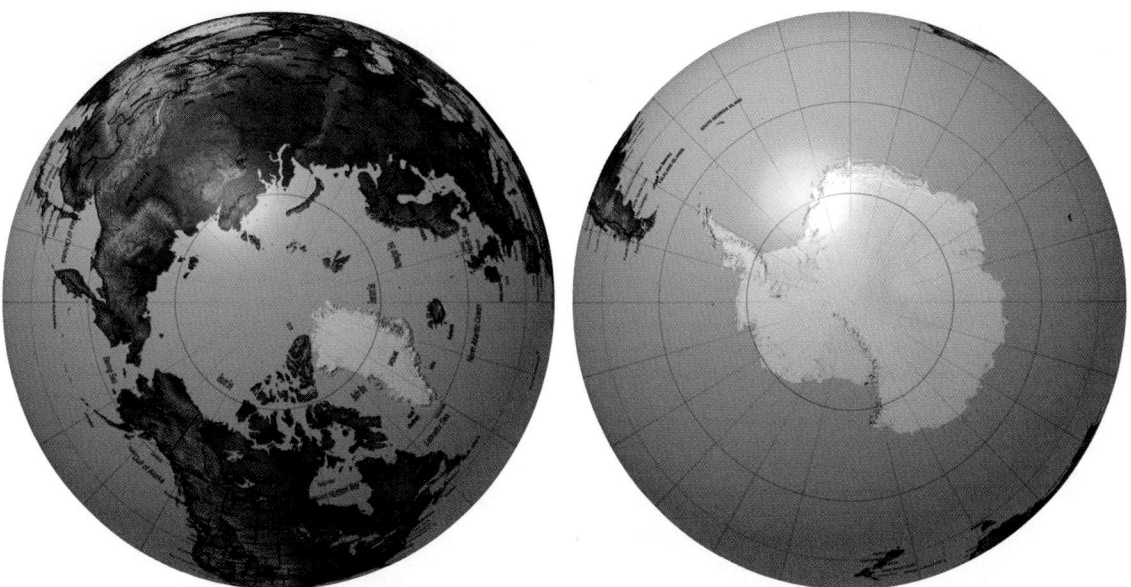

FIGURE 27-3 Ice sheets cover both Greenland and Antartica. (*Courtesy of EyeWire.*)

FIGURE 27-4 Many of the world's ice fields and glaciers terminate in the ocean. (*Courtesy of PhotoDisc.*)

Ice caps are large glaciers that form over the top of a mountain peak and flow outward down the slopes of the mountain. Many ice caps exist in Iceland and usually appear as large, smooth domes. Valley glaciers form in mountain valleys as ice caps flow down into lower elevations (Figure 27–5). These are also called alpine glaciers. They resemble rivers of ice flowing toward the sea. The last type of glacier is the piedmont glacier, which is formed from many valley glaciers joining together in a large, gently sloping plain. Piedmont glaciers can be found along the coast in Alaska.

FIGURE 27–5 A glacier flows from its zone of accumulation in the mountains of Alaska. (*Courtesy of PhotoDisc.*)

The glacial front can occur in one of two locations: the land or the ocean. When the glacial front occurs in the ocean, large chunks of glacial ice break off the glacial front and float away as **icebergs**. The breaking off of large chunks of glacial ice to form icebergs is called calving. When the glacial front occurs on land, the melting glacial ice forms huge glacial lakes that flow into cold subglacial rivers. Some lakes formed from melting glaciers have characteristic bowl-like shapes that result from the deposition of glacial sediments around a large melting chunk of ice. These are called kettle lakes.

Glaciers can be also be classified according to their state of movement. A glacier is in a state of advance when the rate of melting of the glacial front is exceeded by the forward movement of the ice. **Glacial advance** occurs when accumulation of ice is greater than the ablation at the glacial front. Many glaciers in Greenland and Antarctica are in a constant state of advance. A glacier can be in a stationary state when the rate of melting at the glacial front equals the rate of advancement, or accumulation equals ablation. **Glacial retreat** occurs when melting at the front is faster than the forward advancement. This is the result of ablation occurring at a higher rate than accumulation. Glaciers that

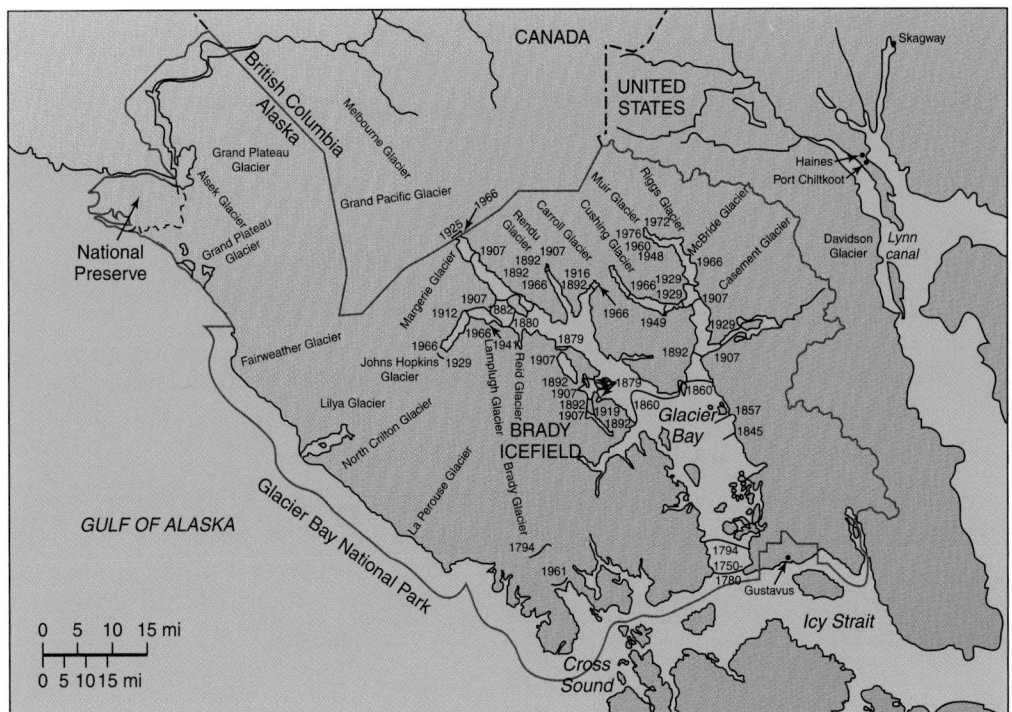

FIGURE 27–6 The specific years and locations of the glacial fronts of the retreating glaciers in Glacier Bay National Park, Alaska.

feed into Glacier Bay, Alaska, have been in a rapid state of retreat over the past few hundred years (Figure 27–6). It is estimated that these glaciers have retreated more than 60 mi (97 km) during this period; some researchers believe this has been caused by increasing global temperatures.

Earth System Scientists

Jean-Louis Agassiz

Jean-Louis Agassiz, the father of Alexander Agassiz (see Chapter 26), was born in Switzerland in 1807. He was educated in both comparative anatomy and paleontology, although his fame would later come from his interest in glacial geology. Early in his career, Agassiz helped classify more than 1,700 fossil fish species collected from around the world. His most famous work, however, involved the study of glaciers. In 1836 he proposed that glaciers were in a constant state of motion. He examined rocks that appeared to have been scarred by glacial movement and theorized that glaciers in Europe were once more widespread. This led him to develop the concept of the ice age. In 1840 he published *Studies on Glaciers,* which presented his theories on how much of Europe was once covered by ice and his theory of ice ages. He further proposed that these ice ages might have caused mass extinctions of living organisms. In 1847 he moved to the United States, where he became a professor at Harvard University. While there, he concluded that North America had also experienced ice ages in the past.

CURRENT RESEARCH

Research conducted by Lonnie Thompson, a professor of geology at Ohio State University, is revealing the disappearance of ice caps from Africa and South America. Thompson's research on Mount Kilimanjaro, in Africa, has shown a reduction in the ice caps by up to 82 percent since 1912. His research has also shown a reduction of ice caps in the Andes Mountains in South America. If the present melting rate continues, the ice caps are expected to totally disappear in the next 10 to 15 years. Similar research has also shown a reduction of ice caps in both China and Tibet. Thompson compares the loss of these ice caps to the "canary in the coal mine" syndrome. Canaries were once used to detect deadly gases in coal mines; if the canary died, it signaled to miners the presence of the odorless gases. Thompson theorizes that the disappearance of ice caps from Africa and South America might be a signal of the changes that are occurring in the global climate.

GLACIERS AND GLOBAL CLIMATE

Recent research by scientists around the world suggests that many glaciers are retreating. This means that the water that they hold is melting and being added to the oceans. If all the water trapped in the world's glaciers melted into the ocean, it is estimated that sea level would rise more than 100 ft (31 m). Scientists have revealed that sea level has risen approximately 4 in (10 cm) over the past 100 years. They predict that at the present rate of increase, the level of the oceans could rise by 12 in (31 cm) in the next 70 years. Most researchers believe this increase in sea level is the result of the melting of the world's glaciers. They do not agree, however, on what is causing the glaciers to melt. Some believe it is the result of global warming caused by human activity. Others suggest that it is the continued warming of the planet that led to the end of the last ice age 11,000 years ago. Whatever the cause, the effect that melting glacial ice will have on modern society could threaten many of the world's major cities. Most of the world's major cities and more than 50 percent of the planet's population live near a coast. The predicted rise in sea level as a result of melting glaciers would be a disaster for these population centers. Many major coastal cities are located only a few feet above sea level; therefore, this change could be catastrophic.

Although glaciers make up a cold, harsh environment on Earth, their role in the cycling and storage of water makes them an important aspect of the hydrosphere. Glaciers in the past have also helped transform much of the world's landscape and have contributed to the formation of many fertile soils that support agriculture. More important, today glaciers might be indicators of a changing global climate.

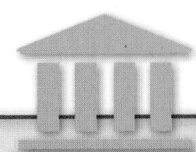

Earth System Law

The Antarctic Treaty

The vast Antarctic continent is the last pristine environment of the Earth, officially recognized as such by the creation of the Antarctic Treaty on December 1, 1959. The 12 nations that forged this treaty, including the United States, took an important step in preserving this unique place on the Earth. Subsequent amendments to the treaty made in 1964 (Agreed Measures for the Conservation of Antarctic Fauna and Flora), 1972 (Convention for the Conservation of Antarctic Seals), 1980 (Convention for the Conservation of Antarctic Marine Living Resources), 1988 (Convention on the Regulation of Antarctic Mineral Resource Activities), and 1991 (Protocol for the Environmental Protection of the Antarctic Treaty) were added to further preserve Antarctica. The treaty applies to all areas south of 60 degrees south latitude, and prevents the use of the region for military installations or weapons testing, nuclear testing or disposal, and the mining of natural resources. The treaty also protects the Antarctic environment, its native plants and animals and its historic sites, manages tourism, and encourages scientific cooperation. Today the Antarctic Treaty is supported by 45 nations.

REVIEW

1. Explain how glaciers form.
2. What are the three type of moraines associated with glaciers?
3. List the five types of glaciers that occur on Earth.
4. Explain the difference between a glacial advance and a glacial retreat.
5. Who was Jean-Louis Agassiz?

@ WEB Links

FOR MORE INFORMATION GO TO THESE WEB LINKS:

<http://www.glacier.rice.edu/>

<http://nsidc.org/glaciers/>

<http://ak.water.usgs.gov/glaciology>

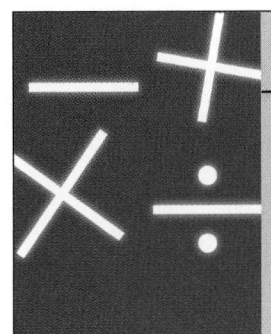

earth math

1) If a glacier is moving at a rate of 9 ft per day, how many days will it take to travel 1 mi?

2) How many gallons of water does a 1-square-foot, 7130-foot-long core section of the Antarctic ice sheet contain if 1 cubic foot of water equals approximately 7 gal of water?

CHAPTER SUMMARY

Glaciers are large masses of ice that form by the accumulation of snow over long periods. The glaciers around the world contain approximately 2 percent of all the planet's freshwater supply. Glacial ice flows outward from the zone of accumulation. This is where snow accumulates and presses down on the glacier, causing it to flow outward. The area of the glacier where the ice is flowing is called the zone of flowage. The zone of flowage eventually reaches the zone of ablation, where the ice is lost from a glacier by melting. As glaciers flow, they scrape along rock to form a mixture of ice and sediment called glacial till. These sediments form unique glacial deposits called moraines.

Moraines that form along the sides of glaciers are known as lateral moraines. Terminal moraines form at the front of a glacier where sediments are deposited by the melting ice. Medial moraines form along the center of a glacier as a result of two valley glaciers joining together.

Glaciers are classified by their size and location on the Earth. Continental glaciers, also known as ice sheets, cover complete continents, such as in Antarctica. Ice fields are large glaciers that cover wide areas, leaving only the tops of mountains exposed. Ice caps are dome-like glaciers that cover the top of a mountain and flow downward into surrounding valleys. Valley glaciers exist where ice flows down through mountain valleys. The last type of glacier, the piedmont, forms on flat plains where valley glaciers come together.

Glaciers that are growing are in a state known as glacial advance. This occurs when the accumulation of snow exceeds the ablation of ice, causing the glacial front to advance. Glacial retreat occurs when ablation occurs at a higher rate than accumulation, causing the glacial front to retreat. Scientists have linked the retreat of many of the world's glaciers to a change in global climate. As glaciers melt, they add water into the oceans, which causes a change in sea level. As a result of this, the level of the oceans has risen by 4 in (10 cm) over the past 100 years and is expected to continue to rise as a result of glacial melting.

CHAPTER REVIEW

Multiple Choice

1. Glaciers during the last ice age lowered sea level by approximately how much?
   a. 4 in
   b. 12 in
   c. 100 ft
   d. 400 ft

2. The area of a glacier where snow collects and compacts to form glacial ice is called the:
   a. zone of accumulation
   b. zone of flowage
   c. zone of ablation
   d. zone of formation

3. In which area of a glacier would you most likely find icebergs?
   a. zone of accumulation
   b. zone of flowage
   c. zone of ablation
   d. zone of formation

4. Which part of a glacier is most likely to form a lateral moraine?
   a. zone of accumulation
   b. zone of flowage
   c. zone of ablation
   d. zone of formation

5. A pile of unsorted glacial sediment deposited by the glacial front is known as:
   a. lateral moraine
   b. terminal moraine
   c. medial moraine
   d. glacial erratic

6. What is the result when ablation occurs at a higher rate than accumulation?
   a. glacial advance
   b. glacial flow
   c. glacial retreat
   d. glacial equilibrium

7. The entire continent of Antarctica is covered by which type of glacier?
   a. ice sheet
   b. ice field
   c. ice cap
   d. ice dome

8. The type of glacier that covers much of Iceland is called:
   a. ice sheet
   b. ice field
   c. ice cap
   d. ice dome

9. When a glacier's rate of accumulation is higher than its rate of ablation, what occurs?
   a. glacial advance
   b. glacial flow
   c. glacial retreat
   d. glacial equilibrium

10. Approximately how much is sea level expected to rise in the next 70 years as glaciers continue to retreat?
    a. 4 in
    b. 12 in
    c. 100 ft
    d. 400 ft

Matching   *Match the terms with the correct definitions.*

a. glacier
b. zone of accumulation
c. glacial front
d. zone of flowage
e. glacial till

f. moraines
g. terminal moraines
h. zone of ablation
i. lateral moraines
j. medial moraines

l. icebergs
m. glacial advance
n. glacial retreat

1. _____ The face of a glacier where the ice breaks off and melts.
2. _____ Large chunks of glacial ice that break off the leading edge of a glacier and float into the sea.
3. _____ Unsorted glacial sediments that are located at the front or deposited near the front of a glacier.
4. _____ Glacial sediments that are located near the middle of a glacier.

5. _____ A large, long-lasting mass of snow and ice that forms over land from the accumulation and compaction of snow that creeps down slope.
6. _____ The zone of a glacier where ice is breaking off and melting.
7. _____ The forward movement of a glacier caused when snow accumulation is greater than melting.
8. _____ Glacial sediments that form along the sides of a glacier as it scrapes along rock.
9. _____ The area on a glacier where snowfall is building up, forming new glacial ice.
10. _____ The shrinking of a glacier caused when melting exceeds snow accumulation.
11. _____ Unsorted glacial sediments.
12. _____ The area on a glacier where glacial ice is currently flowing.
13. _____ An accumulation of glacial sediments.

Critical Thinking

1. Describe the effects on society and the environment if glaciers began to increase in size instead of shrinking.

Pollution of the Hydrosphere

OBJECTIVES

Sediment Pollution · Nutrition Pollution and Eutrophication · Toxic Organic Compounds · Toxic Inorganic Compounds · Disease-Causing Agents · Thermal Pollution

After reading this chapter you should be able to:

▶ Define the term *sediment pollution* and describe two of its sources.

▶ Explain the negative effects of sediment pollution.

▶ Describe what causes an algal bloom and how this affects an aquatic ecosystem.

▶ Identify three sources of toxic organic water pollutants.

▶ Describe three toxic inorganic water pollutants and their sources.

▶ Define the terms *disease-causing agent* and *waterborne illness*.

▶ Describe two waterborne illnesses and their sources.

▶ Differentiate between the two different types of thermal pollution and describe their negative effects on aquatic ecosystems.

pollution

sediment pollution

nutrient pollution

eutrophication

algal bloom

aerobic bacteria

polychlorinated biphenyls

landfills

disease-causing agents

waterborne illnesses

wastewater

thermal pollution

dissolved oxygen

INTRODUCTION

Pollution of the hydrosphere is one of the most life-threatening impacts that human beings have had on the Earth. Because of water's abundance and usefulness, it has been contaminated in a multitude of ways by a variety of human practices. The importance of water to living things cannot be overstated because every organism alive on the planet requires clean water to survive. The availability of clean freshwater is especially important because it makes up such a small portion of the Earth's total water supply. Freshwater resources on the planet are unequally distributed around the globe, making it an even more precious resource. Today on our planet the freshwater that is used for drinking, agriculture, and industry often contains some form of pollutant. As the human population continues to grow, more and more people will depend on the small amount of freshwater that is available on the Earth. Understanding how water becomes polluted, preventing further pollution of this important resource, and conserving it for sustained use are vital to the future of our planet.

SEDIMENT POLLUTION

The number one form of water pollution on the Earth is sediment pollution. **Sediment pollution** of water occurs when eroding soil particles are washed into water by the process of runoff (Figure 28–1). Runoff occurs when soil is exposed to precipitation that washes it into nearby lakes or streams. The main sources of sediment pollution are exposed agricultural fields, clear-cut logging operations, and construction sites. These practices clear land of the vegetation that naturally protects the soil from erosion. When the vegetation is removed, the soil is exposed and can be easily washed away. The sediment that is washed into nearby streams or lakes clouds the water and reduces the amount of sunlight that can penetrate the water. This then reduces the amount of photosynthesis that can occur in the water, which reduces the amount of food available to the aquatic organisms that live there. Introduction of sediments into water can also clog the gills of fish and other aquatic organisms. This reduces their ability to absorb oxygen from the water. Some fish species, such as trout, require clear water to live because they use their vision to hunt for insects. When the water becomes cloudy, they are unable to find food. Increased sediment in water can also negatively affect the spawning of fish, lowering their ability to reproduce. Sediment washed into water slowly builds up on the bottom of lakes and streams, making the water shallow over time. This can cause an eventual overflow of water to the surrounding land. Many rivers and

FIGURE 28–1 Clear-cut logging can contribute large amounts of sediments into surrounding bodies of water. (*Courtesy of PhotoDisc.*)

lakes that are used for transportation by the shipping industry must be continually dredged to remove the accumulating sediments each year. It is estimated that more than 75 billion tons of sediments are washed into the water annually. Much of this sediment was once productive soil that supported plant growth but has now been lost to the water.

NUTRIENT POLLUTION AND EUTROPHICATION

Another form of water contamination is called nutrient pollution. **Nutrient pollution** is caused by the increase of water soluble chemicals such as nitrates and phosphates in water (Figure 28–2). These chemicals act as nutrient fertilizers to aquatic plants and algae. The increasing amount of nutrients in a body of water is called **eutrophication**. The plants that live in water that are exposed to these nutrients begin to grow in abundance, which creates an imbalance in the aquatic ecosystem. This imbalance is known as an **algal bloom**, which is the rapid increase in the population of algae and aquatic plants caused by the increasing amount of fertilizer in the water.

Algal blooms also cause an increase in dying algae, which sink to the bottom of the body of water being affected. The decaying algae is then decomposed by **aerobic bacteria**. These bacteria require oxygen to live. The mass of dead algae causes a rise in the population

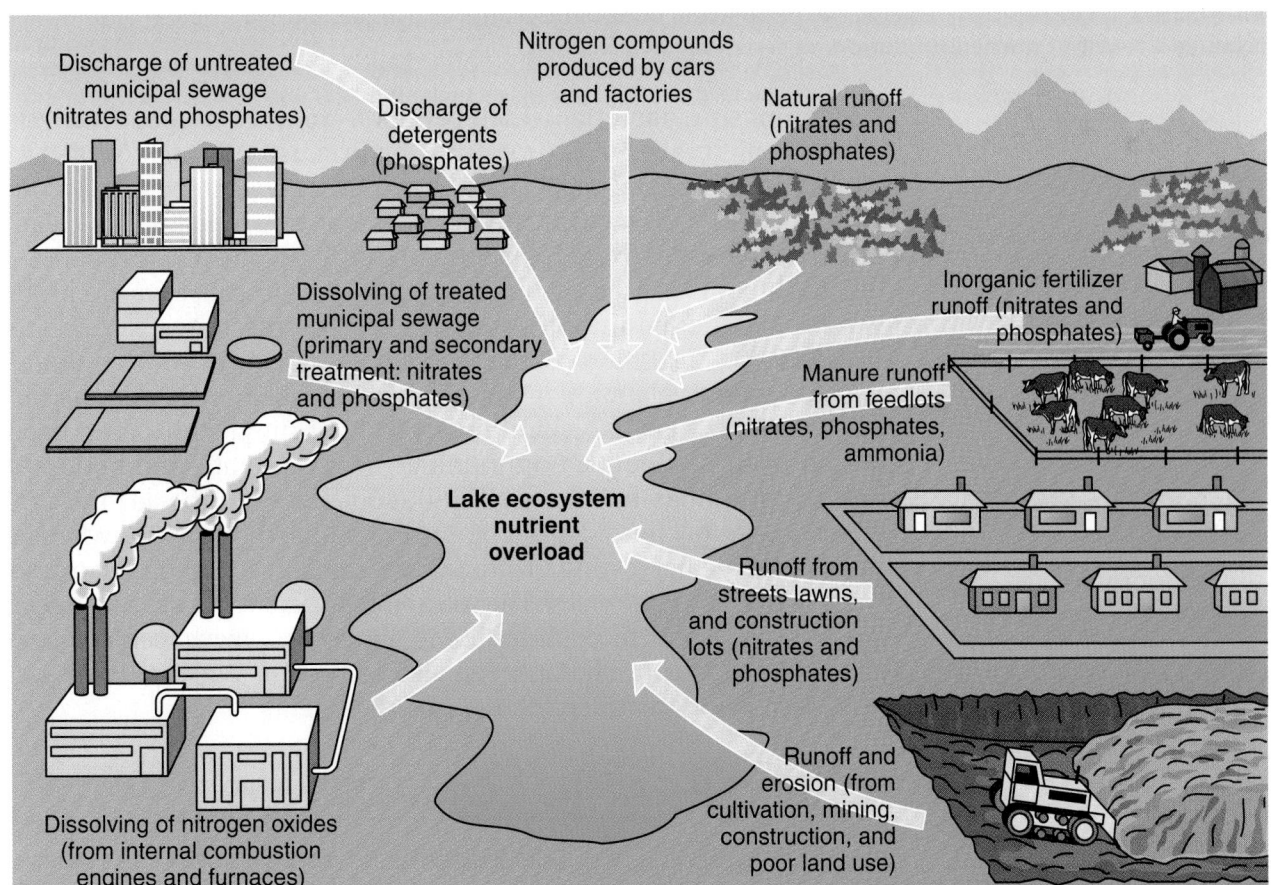

FIGURE 28–2 The major sources of nutrient pollutants in water.

FIGURE 28–3 The rapid increase in the population of aquatic plants and algae, known as algal bloom, occurs as a result of nutrient pollution. (*Courtesy of PhotoDisc.*)

of decomposing bacteria, which begins to remove oxygen from the water at a high rate. Sometimes the bacteria use so much oxygen to break down the dead algae that eventually the water contains no oxygen at all. At this point the body of water is classified as dead, because there is no oxygen for other aquatic organisms to breathe.

Algal blooms caused by nutrient pollution can cause severe problems for aquatic life in both standing and flowing water ecosystems (Figure 28–3). Algal blooms can also choke the water with an abundance of aquatic plants that can clog water intake pipes and disrupt boating traffic. Many lakes and ponds in the United States have been affected by algal blooms. Communities near these affected bodies of water try to combat the increased amount of plants and algae in several ways. Some apply herbicides to control the growth of plants, whereas others use large harvesting machines that cut and scoop up the excess aquatic plants from the water. The source of nutrients that can cause algal blooms originates with plant fertilizers applied on lawns, gardens, and farm fields. Nutrient pollutants can also come from leaking septic systems, wastewater treatment plants, and detergents.

TOXIC ORGANIC COMPOUNDS

One of the most widely publicized forms of water pollution around the world are oil spills. This type of contamination is called toxic organic compound water pollution. The term organic refers to any molecule that

FIGURE 28–4   The pollution of water by toxic organic compounds such as oil can cause widespread contamination of the environment. (*Courtesy of PhotoDisc.*)

contains carbon. Toxic organic compounds include oil, gasoline, solvents, and pesticides, which, when mixed with water, can be deadly to many different organisms (Figure 28–4). Toxic organic compounds enter the water in many different ways. Oil spills from leaking tanker ships are the most widely known because of their immense size, but smaller spills of chemicals can be just as harmful. The Environmental Protection Agency estimates that more than 1 million underground fuel storage tanks are leaking into groundwater in the United States, resulting in widespread contamination of drinking water. These types of spills are difficult to trace because they often come from old abandoned fuel tanks. Because most of this pollution occurs underground, it is often hard to determine how much groundwater has been polluted and where it is traveling. Another source of toxic organic compounds is pesticides that are applied to plants to protect them from insects, weeds, and disease. If not applied at the correct time, pesticides can be washed into water by precipitation and runoff, where they can contaminate the water.

TOXIC INORGANIC COMPOUNDS

Toxic inorganic chemicals are another class of water pollutants. These include synthetic industrial chemicals and heavy metals such as lead, mercury, and arsenic. The presence of these chemicals in water can cause long-term health problems and even death. Many of these deadly chemicals have been introduced into water by poor waste

FIGURE 28–5 Contamination of water by industrial processes has decreased water quality all over the world. (*Courtesy of PhotoDisc.*)

disposal practices. Toxic chemicals stored in leaking metal drums enter both groundwater and surface water, causing widespread contamination. Unlike toxic organic chemicals, which usually break down in the environment after a few days or weeks, inorganic compounds and heavy metals can remain deadly for many years. The use of **polychlorinated biphenyls**, or PCBs, to manufacture electrical components led to one of the worst forms of toxic inorganic water pollution. PCBs were washed into the Hudson River in New York State for many years (Figure 28–5). As a result, traces of PCBs are found in the tissue of many birds and fish that live in or along the Hudson River. Long stretches of the Hudson River are contaminated by PCBs, which resulted in a ban on fishing in the area for many years. Today the river's sediments still contain high concentrations of PCBs, which are to be removed by an advanced dredging operation. Other sources of toxic inorganic chemicals include leaking **landfills** and old abandoned industrial sites.

DISEASE-CAUSING AGENTS

The introduction of **disease-causing agents** into water supplies is a very serious water pollutant (Table 28–1). Viruses, bacteria, amoeba, protozoa, and parasitic worms are all agents of disease that can enter water supplies and affect human health. Most of these disease-causing agents enter water through human or animal waste. *Escherichia coli*, or *E. coli*, bacteria are present in the waste of all animals; however, when they are

TABLE 28-1 Common disease-causing agents and waterborne illnesses

Type of Organism	Disease	Effects
Bacteria	Typhoid fever	Diarrhea, severe vomiting, enlarged spleen, inflamed intestine; often fatal if untreated
	Cholera	Diarrhea, severe vomiting, dehydration; often fatal if untreated
	Bacterial dysentery	Diarrhea; rarely fatal except in infants without proper treatment
	Enteritis	Severe stomach pain, nausea, vomiting; rarely fatal
Viruses	Infectious hepatitis	Fever, severe headache, loss of appetite, abdominal pain, jaundice, enlarged liver; rarely fatal but may cause permanent liver damage
Parasitic protozoa	Amoebic dysentery	Severe diarrhea, headache, abdominal pain, chills, fever; if not treated can cause liver abscess, bowel perforation, and death
	Giardiasis	Diarrhea, abdominal cramps, flatulence, belching
Parasitic worms	Schistosomiasis	Abdominal pain, skin rash, anemia, chronic fatigue, and general ill health

introduced into a water supply, they can be a serious health threat. **Waterborne illnesses**, such as typhoid, malaria, hepatitis, cholera, and dysentery, all caused by these disease agents, result in sickness and death.

Wastewater that enters into surface waters can carry these disease-causing agents into the environment, which can lead to potential health threats. Oysters growing in water contaminated by human waste often contain the hepatitis virus. This disease can then spread when the oyster is harvested and sold as food. People who often swim in water that contains any of these organisms can accidentally ingest it and become sick. It is extremely important to control these agents of disease and make sure they do not enter our water supplies, because the potential for widespread health problems is very real.

Earth System Scientists

Louis Pasteur

Louis Pasteur was born in France in 1822. He began his work as a scientist by studying chemistry. His attention turned to microbiology when he was asked to investigate the process that led to the formation of beer and wine. His resulting research unlocked the secrets of fermentation. His most famous work involved his germ theory of disease. By studying microorganisms, Pasteur concluded that bacteria present in food and water were the cause of disease and infection in animals. He later developed a method for sterilizing food and water by heating them to a temperature high enough to kill off microorganisms. Today this technique is known as pasteurization. His research into the cause of disease also led him to develop vaccines and the process of inoculation to prevent disease in humans. Pasteur's contributions to science and medicine make him one of the greatest scientists who ever lived.

CAREER CONNECTIONS
Wastewater Treatment Operator

Wastewater treatment operators are responsible for the removal of harmful pollutants from industrial and domestic wastewater. They do this by managing a network of pipes, pumps, valves, tanks, filters, and chemical processes to cleanse wastewater. Their job also involves the periodic testing of water as it passes through the treatment process to maintain quality control. They must have a knowledge of the systems that together make up the wastewater treatment plant and should be able to perform routine maintenance or repairs when necessary. Wastewater treatment operators are usually employed by cities or towns that have wastewater treatment plants. Many of these jobs require a high school diploma and technicians receive on-the-job training. There are also 2-year college degree programs available in wastewater treatment technology. Large wastewater treatment facilities may employ several engineers, chemists, and technicians to operate these facilities. Because of the increasing importance of this type of service, job outlooks in this profession are expected to be excellent in the future.

THERMAL POLLUTION

The last method of water pollution involves the introduction of excess heat into water. This form of water contamination is called **thermal pollution**. Many factories and electrical power plants are built near water because they use this resource to cool many of their industrial processes. Colder water taken from the environment is heated in these factories and then released back into the environment at a higher temperature. This can cause a drastic change in the aquatic ecosystems that exist near these areas. The amount of oxygen that is dissolved in water greatly depends on the temperature of the water (Figure 28–6). Colder water holds more **dissolved oxygen** than warmer water, and as the water is heated, this oxygen is driven out into the atmosphere.

Aquatic species such as fish require high amounts of dissolved oxygen in water to survive. When water is heated by factories and power plants and then reintroduced into the environment, it can lead to the reduction of oxygen in the water. As a result, water environments around these factories will no longer be able to support certain aquatic organisms. Nuclear power plants can cause extreme changes in the water temperature surrounding the plants (Figure 28–7). The change in water temperature caused by nuclear power plants in Florida is causing a disruption in the migration of manatees. Manatees are large aquatic mammals that reside in coastal rivers and bays; they normally migrate to areas with warmer water during the winter. As a result of thermal pollution, manatees are staying in warmer waters near the nuclear power plants. This interrupts their normal migration, causing overpopulation and interbreeding of the manatees.

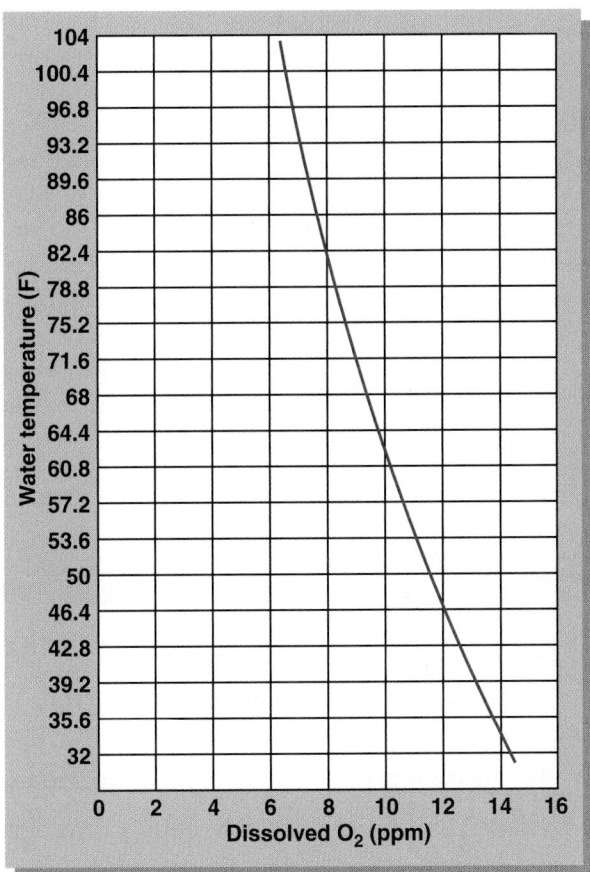

FIGURE 28-6 An increase in the temperature of the water caused by thermal pollution causes a decrease in the amount of dissolved oxygen available to aquatic organisms.

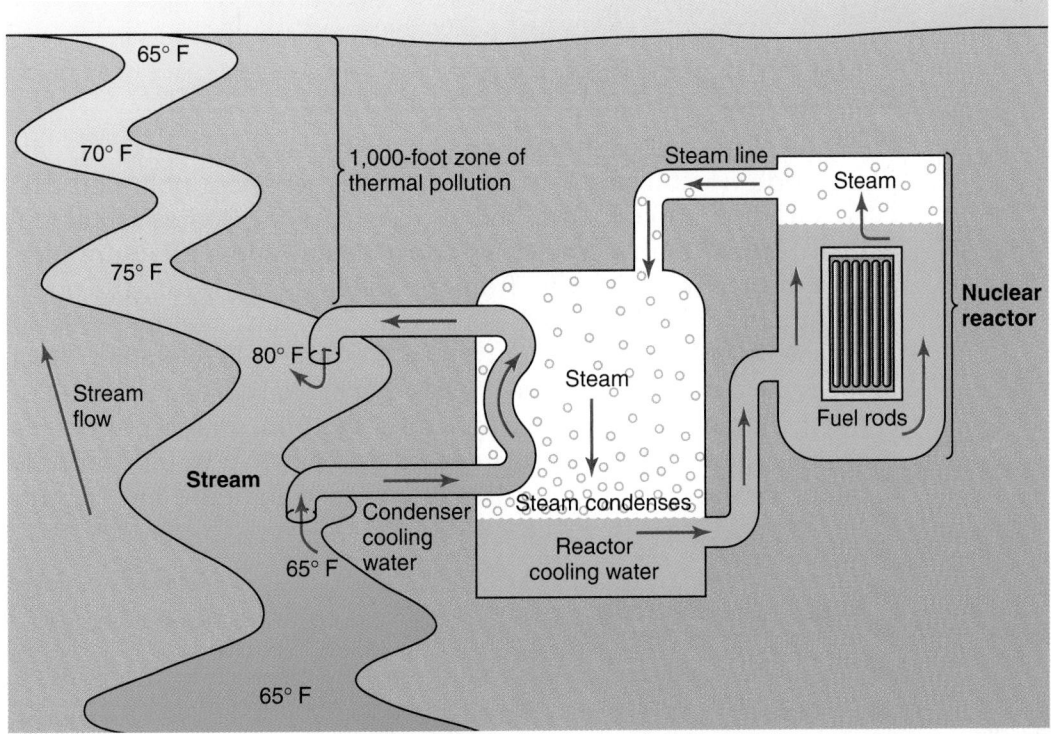

FIGURE 28-7 The effects of a nuclear power plant on the water temperature of a river illustrates the concept of thermal water pollution.

Another type of thermal pollution can be caused by the construction of large dams on rivers. This type of thermal pollution is the result of the lowering of water temperature rather than the heating of the water. Large dams create deep artificial reservoirs of water behind them. The deep water at the bottom of the reservoir becomes much colder than the normal temperature of the water in the river. When the cooler water from the base of the dam is released, it can lower the temperature of the river water by 10 degrees or more. The native fish species of the river cannot tolerate this temperature change and can no longer live there. This type of thermal water pollution is occurring in the Colorado River, where artificial reservoirs are responsible for greatly lowering the water temperatures downriver from these massive dams. Today many cold-water trout are being stocked in the river, where they would normally not be able to survive.

REVIEW

1. What are the two main sources of sediment pollution?
2. Describe the process of eutrophication and how it affects aquatic ecosystems.
3. What are three examples of toxic organic compounds?
4. What are three examples of toxic inorganic compounds?
5. How do disease-causing organisms contaminate water?
6. Explain how thermal pollution affects an aquatic ecosystem.
7. Who was Louis Pasteur?

@ WEB Links

FOR MORE INFORMATION GO TO THIS WEB LINK:

<http://www.epa.gov/students/water.htm>

CHAPTER SUMMARY

Pollution of the hydrosphere has resulted directly from human activity. The world's worst form of water pollution is sediment pollution. This occurs when sediment is washed into surrounding bodies of water by runoff. Human practices such as construction and agriculture often remove protective vegetation from the soil and expose it to the power of wind and rain, which washes rocks and soil into nearby bodies of water. Sediment pollution can cause the water to be clouded, which reduces the amount of photosynthesis that can take place there. It also can clog the gills of fish, reduce their ability to hunt for food, and interrupt their spawning. Sediments can fill up bodies of water over time, creating the need for periodic dredging to keep shipping lanes open.

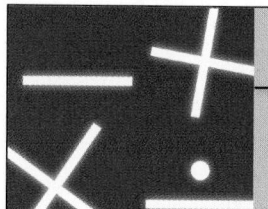

earth math

1) How many tons of sediment are washed into the world's oceans each month?

Another widespread form of water pollution is nutrient pollution. This occurs as a result of the introduction of nutrient fertilizers such as nitrates and phosphates into water. These excess fertilizers cause algal blooms, which can disrupt the balance of aquatic ecosystems. Nutrient pollution is also called eutrophication. It is caused by fertilizer runoff, leaking septic systems, wastewater, and detergents.

Toxic organic water pollution occurs when toxic organic chemicals such as fuels and pesticides leak into water. This form of pollutant can occur in both groundwater and surface water. Toxic inorganic water pollution is caused by the introduction of heavy metals such as mercury or lead into water, along with human-created compounds such as PCBs. These often can contaminate water supplies for long periods because they do not break down rapidly by natural processes. These chemicals can leak into water from old waste dumps, landfills, and industrial processes.

The introduction of disease-causing agents such as bacteria, parasitic worms, and viruses into water can pose a serious threat to the environment. Diseases associated with these organisms include dysentery, cholera, malaria, and hepatitis. Wastewater from human sewage is usually the source of these waterborne illnesses.

The last type of water pollutant is called thermal pollution. This occurs when the water temperature of a body of water is changed drastically as a result of human activity. Often, thermal pollution results in an increase in the temperature of the water, which leads to a decrease in the amount of dissolved oxygen available for aquatic organisms. This is caused by the water being heated when it is used for an industrial process or for generating electricity. Another form of thermal pollution is the result of the lowering of the temperature of the water, which is associated with the construction of large dams on rivers.

Earth System Law

Water Pollution Control

The U.S. Government has enacted several important laws designed to protect water resources. The Clean Water Act of 1972 was the first legislation to protect freshwater resources from pollution and destruction. This law has also been amended over the past 30 years. It establishes strict limits on the discharge of pollutants into water bodies, and aims to make all freshwater safe for fishing, swimming, and other recreational activities. The Clean Water Act has resulted in many significant improvements in the health of many surface water resources. The Safe Drinking Water Act was enacted originally in 1974, and was designed to protect the nation's drinking water supplies. This law was subsequently updated in 1986 and 1996 to add protection to groundwater resources. The Ocean Dumping Ban Act took effect in 1991 as part of the Marine Protection, Research, and Sanctuaries Act. It prevents the dumping of sewage sludge and industrial waste into the ocean. The Oil Pollution Act went into effect in 1990. It is designed to help prevent oil spills and improve the planning and response to the discharge of oil into the environment.

CHAPTER REVIEW

Multiple Choice

1. The most widespread form of water pollution is:
   a. nutrient pollution
   b. toxic inorganic compounds
   c. sediment pollution
   d. thermal pollution

2. The enrichment of fertilizers in aquatic ecosystems is called:
   a. nutrient pollution
   b. toxic inorganic compounds
   c. sediment pollution
   d. thermal pollution

3. Runoff from a construction site can result in:
   a. increased water temperature
   b. decreased photosynthesis by aquatic plants and algae
   c. decreased water temperature
   d. waterborne illnesses

4. Leaking septic systems located around lakes and ponds can cause:
   a. nutrient pollution
   b. toxic inorganic compounds
   c. sediment pollution
   d. thermal pollution

5. A rapid increase in the population of aquatic plants is known as:
   a. eutrophication
   b. an algal bloom
   c. thermal pollution
   d. a waterborne illness

6. Increasing amounts of nitrates and phosphate fertilizers in water cause:
   a. eutrophication
   b. an algal bloom
   c. thermal pollution
   d. a waterborne illness

7. As the temperature of the water increases, what happens to the level of dissolved oxygen within the water?
   a. it decreases
   b. it increases
   c. it remains the same
   d. it disappears

8. The main source of waterborne illness is:
   a. runoff
   b. oil spills
   c. leaking fuel tanks
   d. wastewater

9. Polychlorinated biphenyls (PCBs) are an example of:
   a. toxic organic compounds
   b. toxic inorganic compounds
   c. nutrient pollutants
   d. thermal pollutants

10. An increase or decrease in water temperature caused by human activity is known as:
    a. nutrient pollution
    b. toxic inorganic compounds
    c. sediment pollution
    d. thermal pollution

Matching   *Match the terms with the correct definitions.*

a. pollution
b. sediment pollution
c. nutrient pollution
d. eutrophication
e. algal bloom

f. aerobic bacteria
g. polychlorinated biphenyls
h. landfills
i. disease-causing agents
j. waterborne illnesses

k. wastewater
l. thermal pollution
m. dissolved oxygen

1. _____ A rapid increase in the population of algae caused by the introduction of nutrient fertilizers into an aquatic ecosystem.
2. _____ Specific organisms that cause or spread disease.
3. _____ The amount of oxygen gas that is dissolved in water.

4. ____ An undesirable change in the quality of the environment that negatively affects the health of organisms living there.
5. ____ Bacteria that require oxygen to live.
6. ____ A form of pollution associated with a change in temperature.
7. ____ A form of water pollution caused by the rapid introduction of sediments into an aquatic ecosystem as a result of runoff.
8. ____ A class of human-created chemical compounds used in the production of electrical parts.
9. ____ A form of water pollution caused by an increase in nutrients in an aquatic ecosystem, leading to a rapid increase in aquatic plants and algae.
10. ____ A type of disease or sickness caused by an organism that lives in water.
11. ____ A term used to describe a place where large amounts of garbage are deposited.
12. ____ Polluted water that is unfit for drinking or introduction into the environment because it has been used for some purpose and made unclean.
13. ____ The rapid introduction of nutrient fertilizers into an aquatic ecosystem, leading to an increase in aquatic plants and algae.

Critical Thinking

1. Some people believe that thermal pollution is not a true form of water pollution because it does not affect human beings. Explain why you agree or disagree with this point of view.

29

El Niño and the Southern Oscillation

OBJECTIVES

The South Equatorial Current and Upwelling · The Southern Oscillation · The Effects of an El Niño Event · La Niña Events · Monitoring the Pacific Ocean

After reading this chapter you should be able to:

▶ Describe the normal conditions that exist between the atmosphere and the ocean along the equator off the west coast of South America.

▶ Define the term *upwelling* and explain how it affects fish populations off the coast of South America.

▶ Explain the changes in the atmosphere and ocean that cause an El Niño event.

▶ Describe the relationship between atmospheric pressure and climate that is known as the southern oscillation.

▶ Identify three effects that an El Niño Southern Oscillation (ENSO) event has on the Earth's climate.

▶ Explain the changes in the atmosphere and ocean that cause a La Niña event.

INTRODUCTION

Humans beings have had a long relationship with the sea. The world's oceans have supplied us with a bountiful food supply for thousands of years. Today's ocean fishing industry is important not only for the food it supplies, but also because it supports the economy of many communities that depend on the sea for their livelihood. Fishermen's observations of the natural rhythms of the sea have helped scientists understand the nature of the ocean and its role in the Earth's systems. In 1972 a massive die-off of fish populations off the west coast of South America nearly destroyed the communities that have depended on these fish for their survival. Similar events have occurred in the same region since then, and they have become known as El Niño events. After decades of study, it has been revealed that the changes that periodically occur in the ocean not only affect fish populations but affect the world's climate. As a result, El Niño has become a household phrase; it illustrates the interactions that occur between the hydrosphere and atmosphere and how they affect life on our planet.

THE SOUTH EQUATORIAL CURRENT AND UPWELLING

The event known as El Niño is a **climate** phenomenon that is linked to changes in the temperature of ocean currents off the western coast of South America. The name El Niño, which is Spanish for "the child," originated from local fishermen who first noticed the warmer waters that appeared around Christmas time off the South American coast. During normal conditions, planetary scale winds that blow from east to west along the equator, also known as the **trade winds**, drive the westerly moving ocean current called the **South Equatorial Current**. This ocean current moves warm equatorial waters from the coast of South America toward the western Pacific Ocean (Figure 29–1). As this current moves warm water westward, cold water moves up the continental slope off South America from the deep ocean to replace it.

The upward movement of deep ocean water toward the surface is known as **upwelling**. This process brings nutrient-rich, cooler ocean water up to the ocean surface. This nutrient-rich cold water sustains the food chain in the ocean waters off the Pacific coast of South America. Local fisherman rely on this cold water to provide nutrients for the fish that they catch for food. During an El Niño event, the easterly trade winds slow down, which also slows down the south equatorial current. The result is warmer water lying off the South American coast, which reduces the upwelling of colder, nutrient-rich water. The reduction of nutrients causes a decline in the fish populations off the coast of South America, which affects the local fisherman (Figure 29–2).

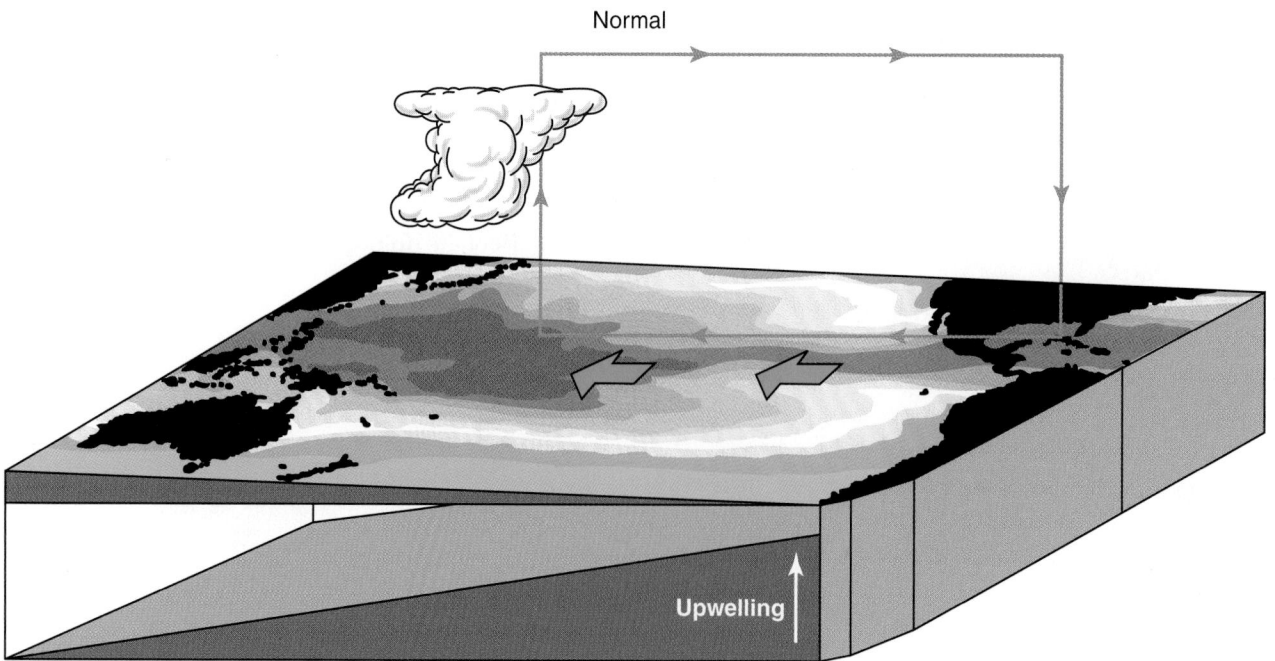

FIGURE 29–1 The normal circulation of surface ocean currents off the west coast of South America moves warm ocean water toward the west, where it is replaced by the upwelling of cold bottom water. This causes clouds and wet weather to form near the South Pacific.

El Niño

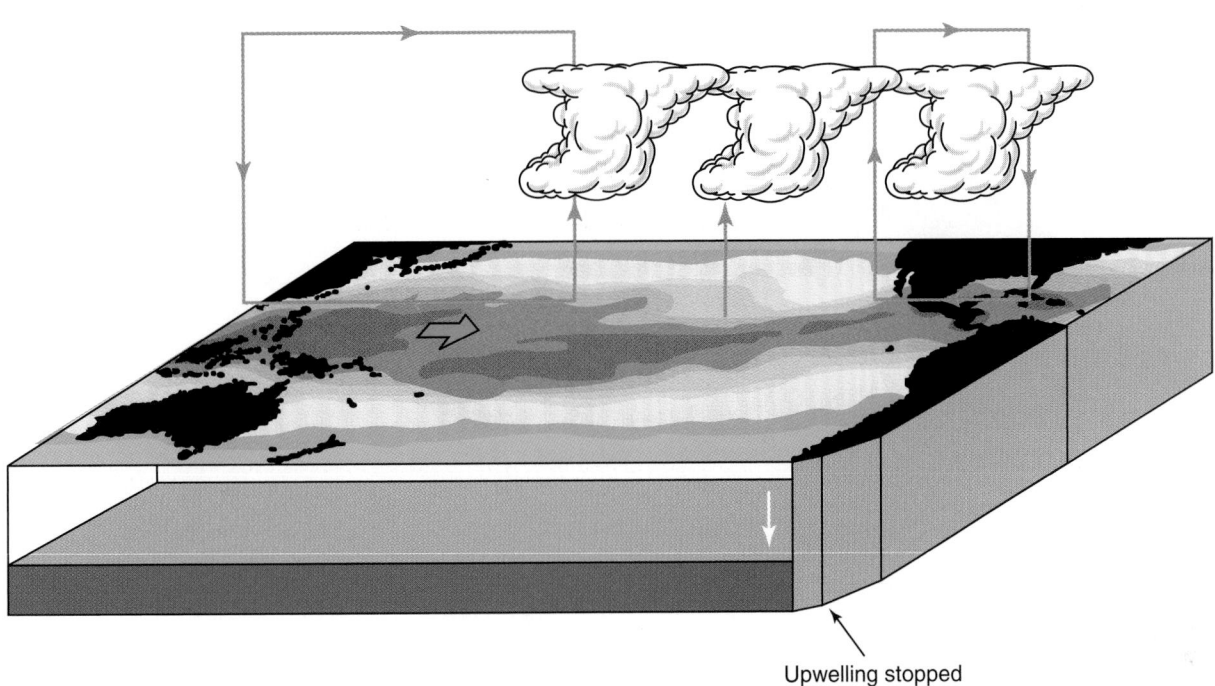

Upwelling stopped

FIGURE 29–2 The stalled circulation of surface ocean currents during an El Niño event along the equator causes warm water to spread eastward, preventing upwelling along the west coast of South America. This causes clouds and wet weather to form farther east than normal.

THE SOUTHERN OSCILLATION

The El Niño phenomenon is linked to another climate variation called the **southern oscillation**. During the 1920s, the British meteorologist Sir Gilbert Walker was studying the formations of monsoons off the coast of southeast Asia. Monsoons are strong seasonal winds that often bring heavy rains to this region (Figure 29–3). Walker determined that they were associated with the development of low and high surface air pressure over the Pacific Ocean. Under normal conditions, a strong low atmospheric pressure system develops over Indonesia, bringing wet weather to the southwestern Pacific Ocean. On the other side of the Pacific, a high atmospheric pressure system develops over the eastern south Pacific Ocean, bringing cool and dry weather to the region.

Walker also noticed that these pressure systems tend to move in relation to ocean currents. During normal years, strong easterly trade winds develop between these two pressure systems. This causes the strong southern equatorial current to move warm water toward southeast Asia, forming the seasonal monsoons. For reasons unknown, this pattern shifts, which results in increased atmospheric pressure over the western Pacific and decreased pressure over the eastern Pacific. This reduces the strength of the trade winds. The movement of these pressure systems occurs on a 2- to 7-year cycle, which Walker called the southern oscillation. Walker also hypothesized that this oscillation was responsible for the periodic droughts that occur in Australia, Africa, and India. Skeptics at the time of Walker's hypothesis laughed at the notion that weather could be influenced on a global scale.

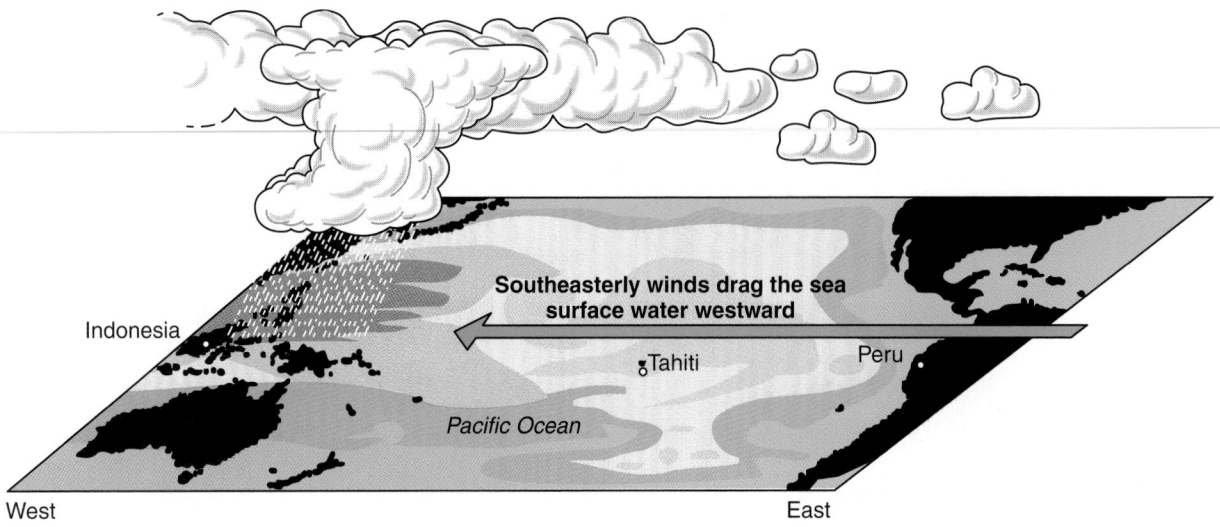

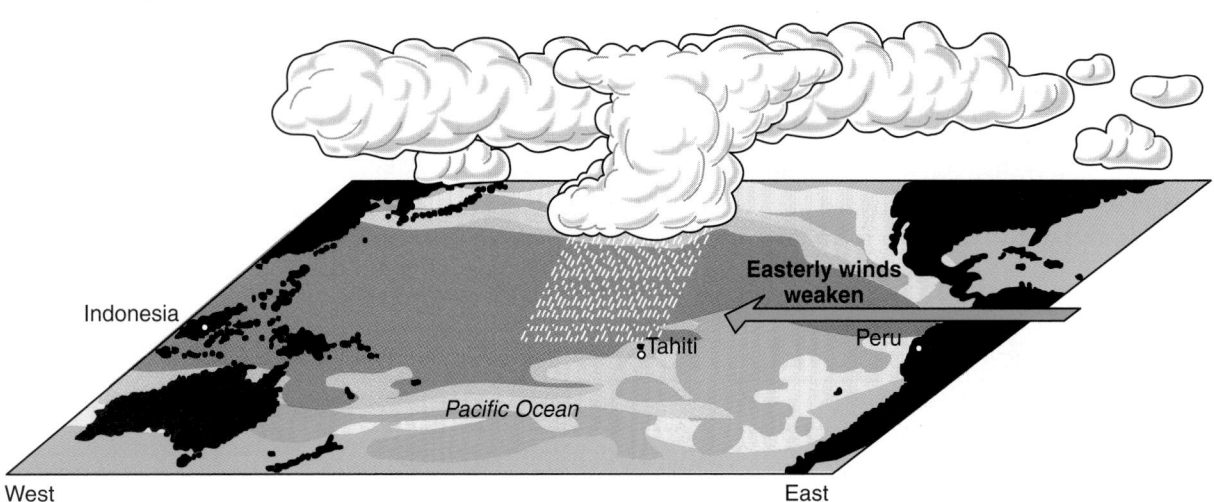

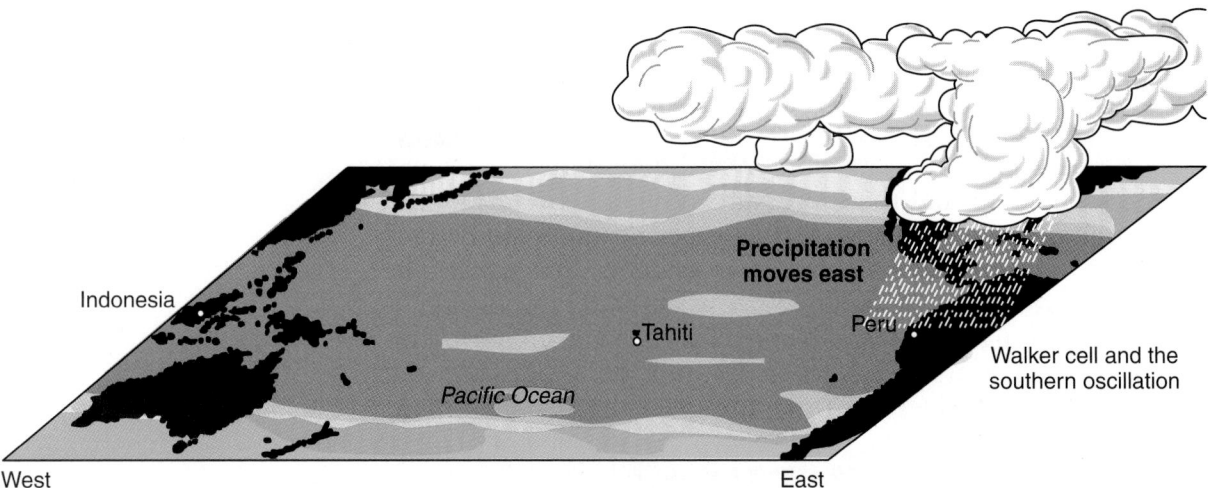

FIGURE 29–3 The movement of low-pressure systems and the precipitation they produce, which Gilbert Walker termed the southern oscillation. During normal years, the trade winds drive warm ocean water and low pressure westward. The reduction of the trade winds and the stalled movement of warm ocean water periodically causes the low pressure to form farther east. This phenomenon was later linked to the occurrence of an El Niño event.

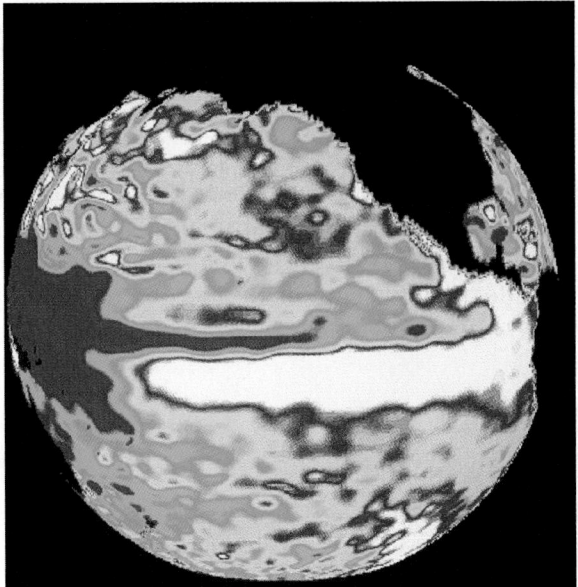

FIGURE 29-4   The abnormally high sea surface temperatures along the equator during an El Niño event. (*Courtesy of Corbis.*)

During the 1950s another meteorologist, Jacob Bjerknes, determined that the changes in the temperature of the ocean currents off the South American coast were related to Walker's southern oscillation (Figure 29–4). Bjerknes found that the warm water that normally flowed along the equator toward the western Pacific helped form the moist low-pressure systems over Indonesia. He further hypothesized that when these currents were reduced, the lows would form farther east than normal. The result was a change in global climate patterns. This was the first time that the El Niño event and the southern oscillation were linked together. The two phenomena have been linked ever since and are now known as the **El Niño Southern Oscillation,** or **ENSO.**

Earth System Scientists

Sir Gilbert Walker

Gilbert Walker was a British meteorologist who was the head of the Indian Meteorological Service. In 1904 the British government asked Walker to investigate the seasonal monsoons that affected the Indian subcontinent. They were concerned with the periodic droughts that occurred in the region. Walker began to sift through the meteorological records of the area and discovered a relationship between the droughts and a change in atmospheric pressure, which he termed the southern oscillation. Walker noticed that when there was high atmospheric pressure in the western Pacific Ocean, there was low atmospheric pressure in the eastern Pacific Ocean. Walker then charted a pattern of precipitation that was associated with this phenomenon, which is now called the Walker circulation. He also became the first scientist to propose that regional changes in weather can lead to changes in global climate. Later, scientists linked Walker's southern oscillation to the phenomenon known as El Niño.

THE EFFECTS OF AN EL NIÑO EVENT

The occurrence of an ENSO event can be traced back to the year 1567, when Peruvian fisherman were first known to experience the warm waters of an El Niño and the reduced fish populations that are associated with it. Since that time, it is believed that more than 25 ENSO events have occurred. Not all ENSO events are the same; they vary in their duration, water temperature, and effect on atmospheric pressure.

An ENSO event affects global climate by altering the moisture patterns that occur around the world (Figure 29–5). During normal conditions,

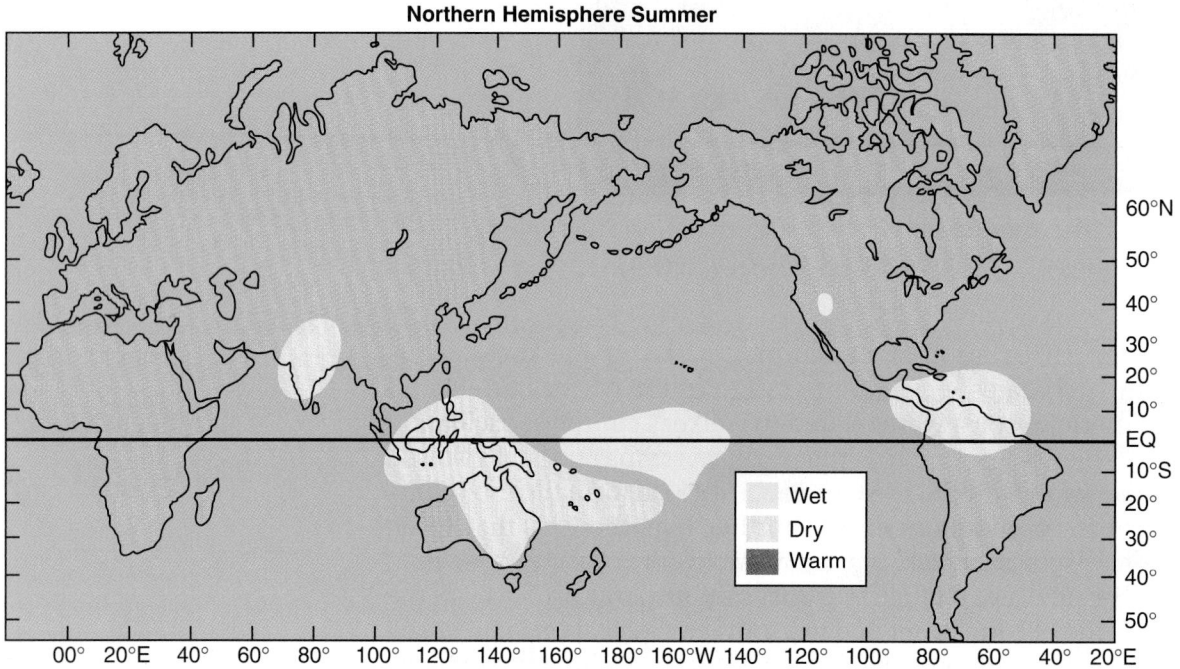

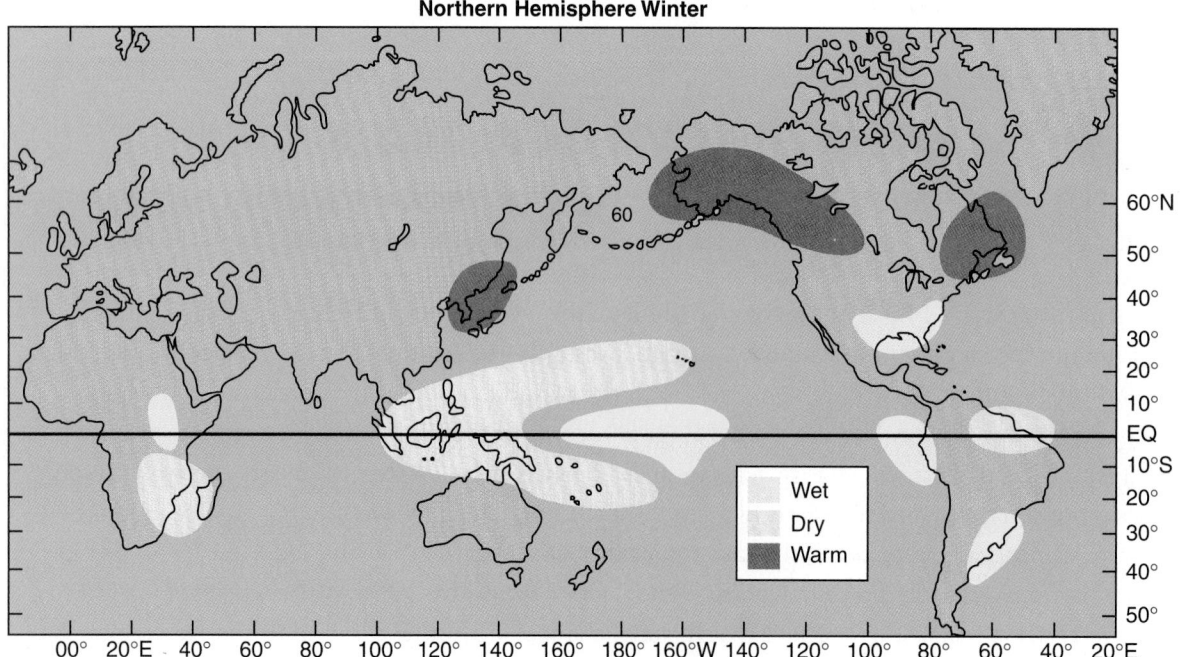

FIGURE 29–5   The effects on global climate during an El Niño event.

low-pressure systems develop over the southwestern Pacific Ocean and bring rains to the region. During an ENSO event, the low-pressure system moves eastward, bringing the moisture with it. This causes drought conditions in parts of Australia, the South Pacific, and India. This also causes wet conditions and more storms to form over western North America and Central America. In northeastern North America, warmer winters are created, and the southern United States experiences more rainfall.

One of the most recent and most severe ENSO events occurred from 1982 to 1983. It resulted in terrible drought conditions in parts of Australia, South Africa, and Indonesia. It caused grain crop production in Australia to be cut in half. The abnormally warm waters off the coast of South America during this ENSO event caused a massive die-off of fish and sea birds, the result of the loss of cold, nutrient-rich water that affected their food supply. The commercial fish catch for that year was reduced by 50 percent compared with the previous year's catch. This event also resulted in excessive storms along the California coast, which created floods and caused widespread shoreline damage. The last El Niño event occurred in 1998, the strongest ENSO event on record. It caused severe flooding in Chile and South America and heavy rainfall in parts of North America.

CAREER CONNECTIONS
Marine Engineer

Marine engineers are specialized engineers who design equipment for studying all aspects of the ocean. They also design structures that must withstand the rough conditions associated with the ocean and along coastlines. This includes breakwaters, jetties, oil drilling platforms, docks, piers, and other marine structures. Their knowledge must include an understanding of the effects of saltwater, currents, tides, waves, and marine organisms on structural materials. Marine engineers also design and help construct scientific equipment that is used to research the oceans. These devices include specialized buoys that collect scientific data, water and marine organism sampling devices, remotely operated vehicles, and small research submarines. These engineers often work with other scientists and specialists to best meet their needs for the design and construction of specific equipment. Marine engineers often accompany the equipment that they design out into the field to test it and to ensure that it is operating properly. They also go along on scientific expeditions to adjust and repair their equipment if necessary. Marine engineers must have a college education specializing in ocean engineering. They can work for the military, academic research, government agencies, or private industry.

Cold Episode Relationships December–February

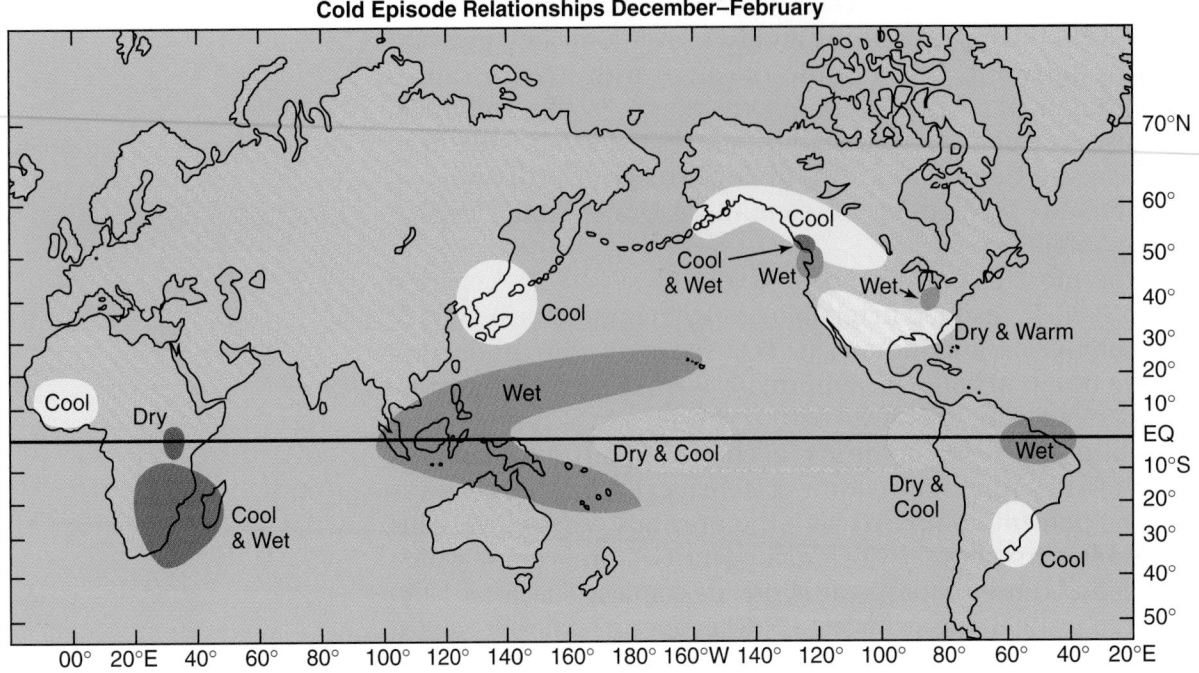

Cold Episode Relationships June–August

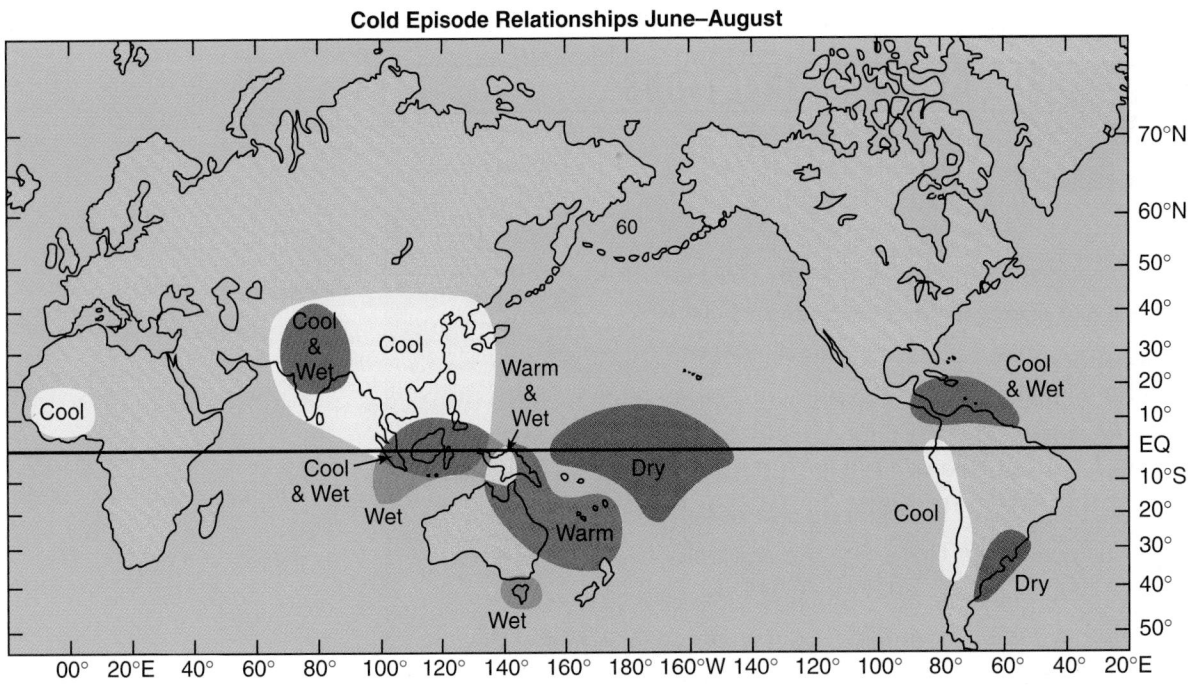

FIGURE 29–6 The effects on global climate during a La Niña event.

LA NIÑA EVENTS

The opposite of an ENSO event is known as **La Niña**. A La Niña event occurs when colder ocean currents spread farther east across the Pacific ocean.

A La Niña event causes a shift in atmospheric pressure and moisture, which has the opposite effects on climate as El Niño (Figure 29–6).

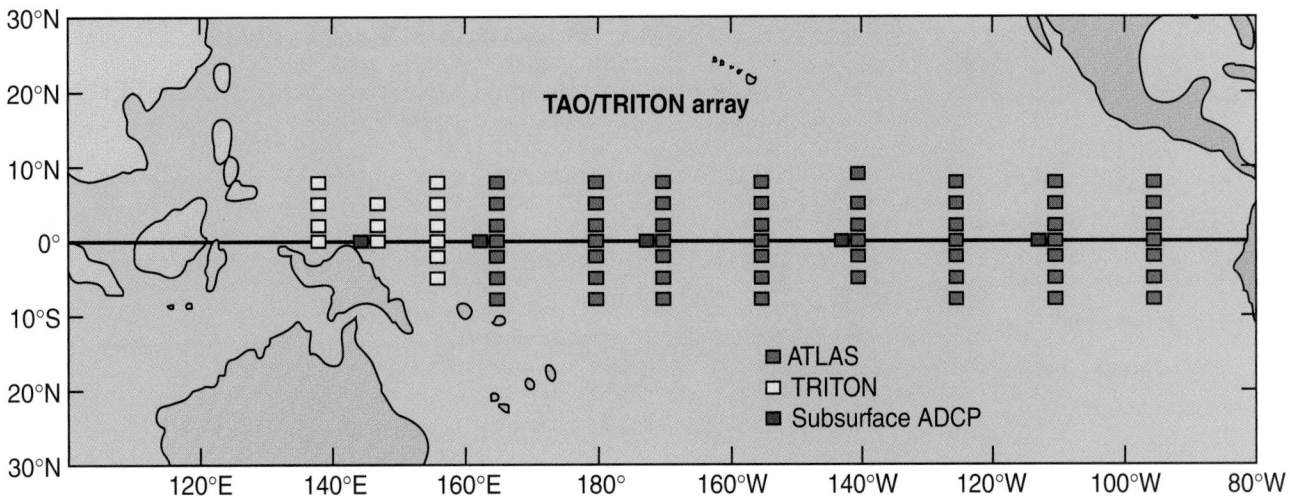

FIGURE 29-7   The location of the TAO array, which records data about the state of the atmosphere and the ocean along the equator. This information is then used to help predict El Niño and La Niña events.

In 1999 the last La Niña caused a heavy monsoon season in Indonesia and dry conditions in the southern United States. There appears to be no connection between El Niño and La Niña years; however, these events are still not fully understood.

MONITORING THE PACIFIC OCEAN

After the strong ENSO event of 1983 to 1984, the National Oceanic and Atmospheric Administration (NOAA) began the Equatorial Pacific Ocean Climate Studies program. The project was designed to study the effects of the El Niño southern oscillation and possibly predict when it might occur. This would greatly help forecast climate changes that are associated with these events. The highlight of this program was the development of the Tropical Atmosphere Ocean, or TAO, array (Figure 29–7). This consists of a network of 400 **buoys** that lie along the equator between 10 degrees north and 10 degrees south latitude in the Pacific Ocean. These buoys record air temperature, wind speed and direction, relative humidity, barometric pressure, and ocean temperature at depths to approximately 1,500 ft (457 m), and ocean current direction and speed. The buoys transmit their data via satellite to researchers working on the project. These data help scientists monitor the physical aspects of the atmosphere and ocean in that region and will be used to help forecast future ENSO events.

The ENSO and La Niña events are a perfect example of how the systems of the Earth interact to form unique patterns of global climate. The collaboration of meteorologists and oceanographers has made it possible to begin to understand this complex relationship that exists between the hydrosphere and the atmosphere.

FOR MORE INFORMATION GO TO THESE WEB LINKS:

<http://www.elnino .noaa.gov/>

<http://airsea-www .jpl.nasa.gov/ENSO /welcome.html>

<http://www.jpl.nasa .gov/earth/ocean_motion /el_nino_index.cfm>

<http://kids.earth.nasa .gov/archive/nino/>

REVIEW

1. Who were the first people to experience the effects of El Niño, and why?

2. What was the importance of Sir Gilbert Walker's work in the 1920s?

3. What did Jacob Bjerknes reveal in the 1950s about the southern oscillation?

4. Describe the conditions of the ocean and the atmosphere that lead to an ENSO event.

5. What effects does an ENSO event have on the Earth?

6. What is a La Niña event, and how does it affect the Earth?

7. What is the TAO array, and what does it monitor?

CHAPTER SUMMARY

An El Niño event is linked to changes in the surface ocean temperatures near the equator off the western coast of South America. The term *El Niño* is Spanish for "the child," which was the term used by Peruvian fisherman to describe the occurrence of warm ocean water that occurred periodically during Christmas time. During normal conditions, the trade winds move warm water from east to west along the equator. This produces the ocean current called the southern equatorial current. This movement causes cold, nutrient-rich ocean water to rise to the surface off the west coast of South America. This process is known as upwelling, which brings nutrients to fish and other marine organisms that live in this region.

An El Niño event occurs when the trade winds begin to slow down and cause the south equatorial current to also slow. This prevents the movement of warm ocean water off the coast of South America and reduces upwelling. The loss of nutrients as a result of reduced upwelling causes a decline in fish populations.

During the 1920s, British meteorologist Gilbert Walker began to study the periodic weather patterns that form seasonal monsoons in the South Pacific Ocean. He discovered that low atmospheric pressure was associated with warm water in the Pacific Ocean and high atmospheric pressure with cooler ocean water. He hypothesized that these

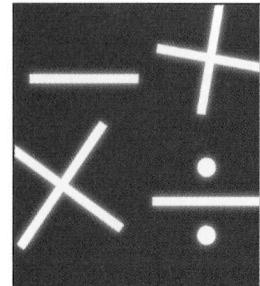

earth math

1) If ENSO events occurred in the years 1900, 1902, 1915, 1920, 1941, 1973, 1983, 1988, 1995, and 1998, what is the average period of their occurrence?

2) Using the period you determined in the previous question, when do you predict that the next ENSO event might occur?

pressure systems formed the seasonal monsoons and were linked to ocean currents along the equator. He called this phenomenon the southern oscillation. Later it was discovered that the southern oscillation was linked to the changes in ocean temperatures that caused El Niño events. The change in surface ocean water temperatures was then linked to changes in regional climate and became known as the El Niño Southern Oscillation, or ENSO. An ENSO event can cause widespread changes in climate conditions, resulting in droughts, floods, changes in precipitation patterns, and reduced fish populations. The opposite of an ENSO event is called a La Niña event. This occurs when cooler ocean currents extend farther west in the Pacific Ocean. This also affects worldwide climate patterns.

To better predict the occurrence of these events, scientists have deployed a series of buoys in the Pacific Ocean along the equator. These buoys record the physical aspects of both the atmosphere and ocean in this region to help researchers better understand these phenomena and better prepare the world for the resulting changes in climate they may cause.

CHAPTER REVIEW

Multiple Choice

1. Which planetary scale wind is associated with an El Niño event?
   a. the westerlies
   b. the trade winds
   c. the jet stream
   d. a sea breeze

2. What process moves cold ocean water toward the surface?
   a. the Coriolis effect
   b. monsoons
   c. upwelling
   d. tides

3. Which surface ocean current is associated with an El Niño event?
   a. the Gulf Stream
   b. the North Atlantic Current
   c. the Equatorial Countercurrent
   d. the South Equatorial Current

4. Warm ocean water in the Pacific Ocean is responsible for forming:
   a. high atmospheric pressure and dry weather
   b. low atmospheric pressure and wet weather
   c. upwelling
   d. La Niña

5. The periodic shifting of low- and high-pressure systems over the Pacific Ocean near the equator is called:
   a. La Niña
   b. the southern oscillation
   c. upwelling
   d. monsoons

6. An El Niño event is associated with:
   a. colder ocean water, low atmospheric pressure moving east, and increased upwelling
   b. warmer ocean water, high atmospheric pressure moving west, and decreased upwelling
   c. warmer ocean water, low atmospheric pressure moving west, and decreased upwelling
   d. colder ocean water, high atmospheric pressure moving east, and increased upwelling

7. An ENSO event causes what changes in global climate?
   a. drought in southeast Asia and Australia
   b. heavy rain in southeast Asia and Australia
   c. drought in North America
   d. drought in Central America

8. During non–El Niño years, what normal climate conditions exist?
   a. drought in southeast Asia and Australia
   b. heavy rain in southeast Asia and Australia
   c. drought in North America
   d. drought in Central America

9. A La Niña event is associated with:
   a. colder ocean water, low atmospheric pressure moving east, and increased upwelling
   b. warmer ocean water, high atmospheric pressure moving west, and decreased upwelling
   c. warmer ocean water, low atmospheric pressure moving west, and decreased upwelling
   d. colder ocean water, high atmospheric pressure moving east, and increased upwelling

10. During a La Niña event, what climate conditions exist?
    a. drought in Southeast Asia and Australia
    b. heavy rain in Southeast Asia and Australia
    c. heavy rain in North America
    d. increased hurricanes in Central America

Matching   *Match the terms with the correct definitions.*

a. climate
b. trade winds
c. South Equatorial Current

d. upwelling
e. southern oscillation
f. El Niño

g. La Niña
h. buoy

1. _____ The uplift of cold ocean water from the bottom to the surface.
2. _____ When sea surface temperatures along the equator off the western coast of South America are cooler than normal, resulting in widespread change in climate.
3. _____ A wind-driven, surface ocean current that moves water westward along the equator away from the west coast of South America.
4. _____ The long-term weather patterns of a specific region on the Earth, usually defined by the area's annual temperature and precipitation values.
5. _____ An increase in the sea surface temperature off the western coast of South America near the equator that leads to changes in climate around the world.
6. _____ The periodic change in the locations of low and high atmospheric pressure systems over the Pacific Ocean near the equator.
7. _____ Planetary scale winds in the Earth's atmosphere that form when areas of high atmospheric pressure, located near 30 degrees north and south of the equator, move air toward low pressure at the equator.
8. _____ A floating marker that is anchored to a specific spot in a body of water.

Critical Thinking

1. Describe two ways in which the Sun is related to an ENSO event.

30

Coral Bleaching

OBJECTIVES

Coral and Coral Reef Systems · The Bleaching of Corals · Occurrence of Coral Bleaching · Causes of Coral Bleaching

After reading this chapter you should be able to:

▶ Describe the environment in which coral reefs are located.
▶ Explain the symbiotic relationship between algae and coral.
▶ Describe the process by which coral reefs are formed.
▶ Define the term *coral bleaching*.
▶ Identify five possible causes of coral bleaching.

INTRODUCTION

Coral reefs are some of the most amazing and beautiful living structures on the Earth. Almost everyone has seen pictures or moving images of the variety of colors and diversity of the marine organisms that live there. Because of the incredible diversity of marine life that coral reefs support, they are often known as the rainforests of the sea. These beautiful natural treasures, however, are now being threatened around the world by a phenomenon known as coral bleaching. Studying the causes and effects of coral bleaching reveals the careful balance that exists between the living and nonliving aspects of the Earth and how human activity might be harming these delicate structures.

CORAL AND CORAL REEF SYSTEMS

Coral reefs are located in shallow, warm ocean waters and are composed of colonies of small organisms known as **corals**. Corals are marine organisms that build protective shells from calcium carbonate and attach themselves to one another with a gluelike substance. They filter feed on tiny plankton and debris that float freely through the water. Corals maintain a **symbiotic relationship** with single-celled **algae** that reside in the protective shell of the coral. This algae help provide the coral with nutrients, while the coral provides carbon dioxide and a home for the algae. Over time, millions of these organisms form huge underwater structures called coral reefs (Figure 30–1).

THE BLEACHING OF CORALS

In recent years a phenomenon known as **coral bleaching** has been occurring at high rates in reefs around the world. Coral bleaching is the whitening of corals caused by the death of the algae that reside inside. These algae give coral their unique colors, and when they die, the coral appears white, or bleached. The death of the algae within the coral can eventually lead to the death of the coral itself (Figure 30–2). If the environmental stress that causes the death of the algae ends, it might be possible for the coral to recover. However, the longer the coral survives without the symbiotic algae, the greater the chance that it will not be able to recover.

FIGURE 30–1 Coral reefs, the rainforests of the sea, are one of nature's most beautiful structures and are home to a variety of colorful marine life. (*Courtesy of PhotoDisc.*)

FIGURE 30-2 This set of photographs, taken from the same vantage point 10 years apart, illustrates the rapid degradation of coral reefs that has occurred throughout the Florida Keys and Caribbean Sea. Carysfort Reef, the largest and most luxuriant reef in the Keys, has lost more than 92 percent of it living coral cover from pollution, disease, and physical damage. Ocean warming, which can cause bleaching, adds additional stress to already threatened reefs. (*Photos © P. Dustan.*)

OCCURRENCE OF CORAL BLEACHING

Scientists have been interested in coral bleaching because it is becoming more common around the world and may be caused by environmental stress (Figure 30–3). Since 1980 the occurrence of coral bleaching has dramatically increased, causing concern for the fate of coral reef systems around the world. More than 57 percent of coral deaths that occurred between 1979 and 1990 were attributed to coral bleaching. This is a substantial increase compared with a 4 percent coral death rate from bleaching during the previous 100 years.

CAUSES OF CORAL BLEACHING

Scientists have identified several factors that can cause coral bleaching. Changes in the temperature of the water in which the corals reside can cause the death of algae. A sudden drop in temperature by 5 degrees or 10 degrees for a period of 10 days or more can cause the death of the algae. A sudden increase in water temperature by 2 degrees to 4 degrees for a period of months can also cause the die-off. Two factors could be leading to the temperature fluctuations in the oceans that are affecting the coral. The **El Niño Southern Oscillation**, which affects water temperatures near the equatorial Pacific Ocean, might affect some regional

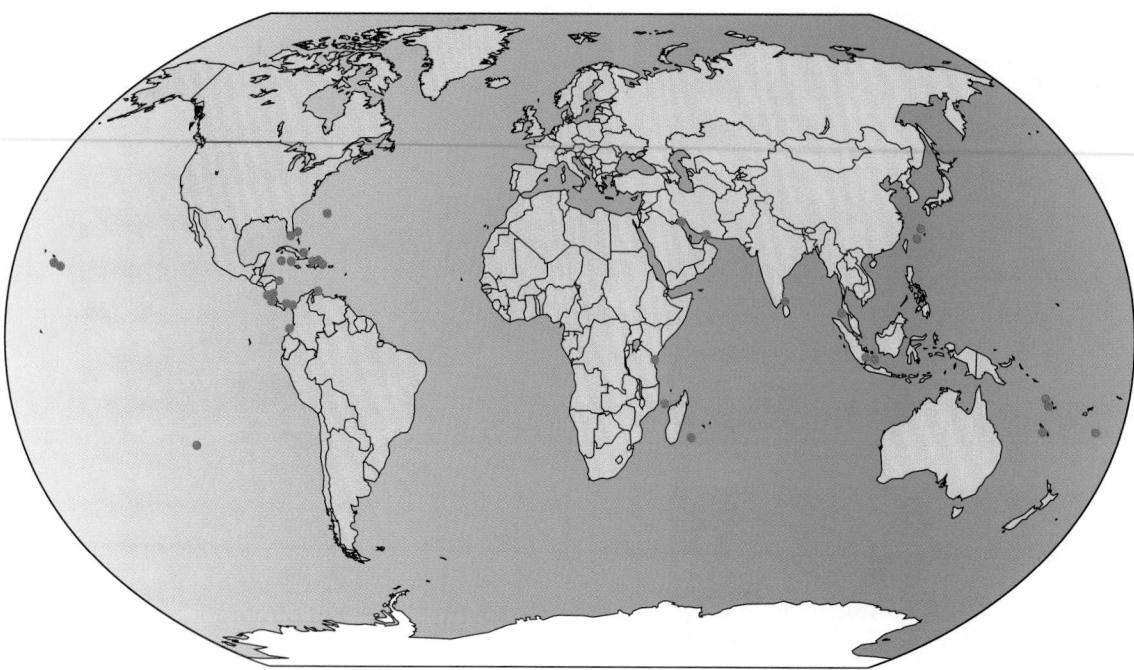

FIGURE 30–3 Areas around the world that are affected by coral bleaching.

coral reefs. Increasing global temperatures could be leading to an increase of ocean temperatures in some regions. Satellite analysis of global sea surface temperatures shows that some regions of the world are experiencing a rise in temperature (Figure 30–4).

Increased exposure to ultraviolet radiation in shallow-water corals is believed to cause coral bleaching. The algae cannot survive the deadly

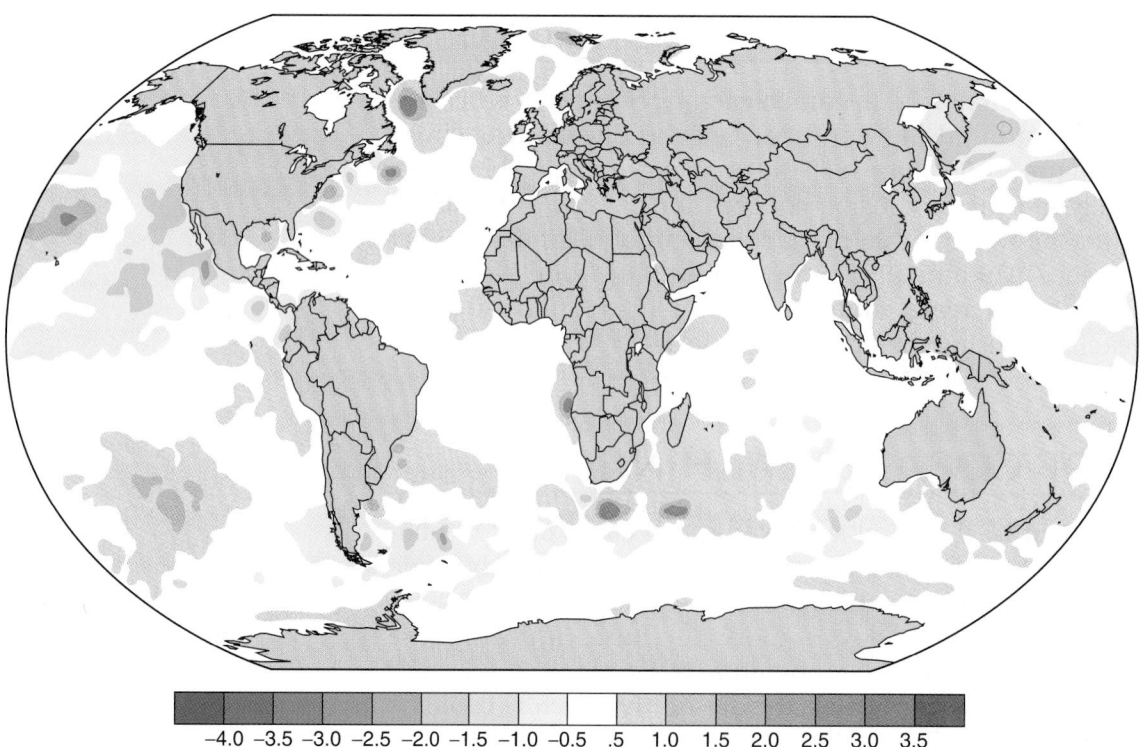

–4.0 –3.5 –3.0 –2.5 –2.0 –1.5 –1.0 –0.5 .5 1.0 1.5 2.0 2.5 3.0 3.5

FIGURE 30–4 Change in sea surface temperatures around the world is one of the causes of coral bleaching.

Earth System Scientists

Dr. Sylvia Earle

Sylvia Earle was born in New Jersey in 1935 and received her education in marine biology. She has spent most of her life exploring the world's oceans. She was one of the first women scientists to use scuba gear to study life below the surface. Since 1961 Earle has written more than 100 publications about life in the sea. In 1970 she participated in the Hydrolab project, which was an underwater laboratory experiment sponsored by the U.S. government. She spent 2 weeks living underwater and helped pave the way for the National Aeronautics and Space Administration's Skylab space station. Earle used the Hydrolab to study coral reefs off the coast of Florida. In 1979 she made the world's deepest untethered dive while strapped to the front of a submarine that took her to a depth of 1,250 ft (381 m). She then walked around on the bottom of the ocean in a special dive suit and planted an American flag. In 1981 Earle cofounded Deep Ocean Engineering, a company that designs and builds underwater research equipment. She also became the first woman to serve as the chief scientist for the National Oceanographic and Atmospheric Administration (NOAA). Today Earle continues her study of the marine environment and her efforts to prevent its destruction.

effects of ultraviolet radiation on their sensitive tissue. The increase in ultraviolet radiation may be the result of ozone depletion in the stratosphere. Increased sediments entering the ocean as a result of erosion, runoff, and heavy rains might be leading to the death of corals near the shoreline. The sediments cloud the water and prevent sunlight from reaching the algae within the corals. This reduces their ability to use photosynthesis to produce food. Also, toxic chemicals such as **herbicides**, oils, and other organic compounds that are washed into the ocean can cause coral bleaching. These compounds can kill off the algae and harm the coral. The input of **wastewater** from human sewage or animal manure can also negatively affect corals. Wastewater often contains **infectious agents** such as bacteria and viruses that affect the reef system.

The many environmental stresses that lead to coral bleaching could be the result of human activity and the disruption of the natural cycles within Earth's system. Not all the possible causes may be prevented by human action, but some human practices could be changed, which would lessen the impact of coral bleaching on the world's reef systems.

REVIEW

1. What is coral?
2. Why are coral reefs important, and where are they found?
3. What is coral bleaching?
4. What may cause coral bleaching?
5. Who is Dr. Sylvia Earle?

FOR MORE INFORMATION GO TO THIS WEB LINK:

<http://www.coralreef .noaa.gov/>

CAREER CONNECTIONS
Coral Reef Scientist

A coral reef scientist studies all aspects of a coral reef ecosystem. This includes an understanding of the life cycle and other biological properties of corals, of coral habitats and their distribution around the world, and of the interactions of other marine organisms with coral reefs and the reefs' relationship to other marine ecosystems. Today much of the work of a coral reef scientist involves the conservation of coral reef systems and the understanding of how human activity is affecting these important marine resources. Coral reef scientists must be certified scuba divers because much of their work involves the underwater observation of coral reefs and the collection of both living and nonliving samples from the reef system. A love for working on and in the ocean, a willingness to travel to exotic locations, and a college education in marine biology and oceanography are musts for this type of occupation. Career opportunities are available in academic research or with government agencies.

CURRENT RESEARCH

Research conducted by the National Center for Atmospheric Research has revealed that increased levels of carbon dioxide in the Earth's atmosphere might be causing the deaths of coral reefs. A report prepared by John Klepas has shown that in the laboratory, increased levels of carbon dioxide have caused the decline of coral. Carbon dioxide gas in the atmosphere is absorbed into the oceans, where it disrupts the natural chemistry of the water. The team of researchers has shown that the higher levels of carbon dioxide in the ocean interrupt the uptake of calcium carbonate that corals use to build their protective shells. This research has revealed the first possible negative effects of increasing levels of carbon dioxide on a marine ecosystem. The scientists hope that their research will help reduce the global emissions of carbon dioxide and save the world's fragile coral reefs.

earth math

1) A typical brain coral grows about 0.14 inches per year. If it is 36 in. tall today, approximately how old is this coral?

2) Coral reefs off the island of Jamaica rise 40 ft off the ocean floor. They took approximately 5,000 years to form. Using this information, approximately how much does this reef grow in inches each year?

CHAPTER SUMMARY

Coral reefs support a great degree of diversity within the ocean and are among nature's most beautiful structures. Coral reefs are composed of colonies of tiny marine organisms called corals. These creatures filter out plankton and organic debris from the water as a source of food. They also build protective shells out of calcium carbonate, which builds up over time to form large structures called coral reefs. Corals have a symbiotic relationship with algae that reside within the body of the coral. The algae produce food for the coral, while the coral provides carbon dioxide for the algae. Coral reefs are located in warm, shallow ocean water.

A phenomenon known as coral bleaching is killing off many corals around the world. Coral bleaching is caused by the death of the symbiotic algae that live within the coral. This causes the corals to appear white, or bleached. More than 50 percent of the deaths of corals around the world since 1980 are the result of coral bleaching. Coral bleaching is caused by many different environmental stresses, including changes in water temperature, increased amounts of sediments in the ocean, runoff of pesticides, toxic chemicals spilled in the ocean, and animal waste. Most of these causes are the result of human activity, which can be controlled to prevent further damage to the world's coral reef systems.

CHAPTER REVIEW

Multiple Choice

1. Coral reefs are located in what type of environment?
   a. deep, cold saltwater
   b. deep, cold freshwater
   c. shallow, warm saltwater
   d. shallow, warm freshwater

2. Which organism has a symbiotic relationship with coral?
   a. zooplankton
   b. tiny fish
   c. humans
   d. algae

3. Coral reefs are mostly composed of:
   a. calcium carbonate
   b. algae
   c. carbon dioxide
   d. sand

4. The white appearance of bleached coral is the result of:
   a. excess chlorine in the water
   b. excess carbon dioxide in the water
   c. the death of the symbiotic algae
   d. the death of the coral

5. Approximately what percentage of coral deaths since 1980 were caused by coral bleaching?
   a. 10 percent
   b. 27 percent
   c. 57 percent
   d. 100 percent

6. Which of the following does not cause coral bleaching?
   a. increased salinity
   b. change in water temperature
   c. sediment pollution
   d. ultraviolet radiation

Matching   *Match the terms with the correct definitions.*

a. coral reefs
b. corals
c. symbiotic

d. algae
e. coral bleaching
f. El Niño Southern Oscillation

g. herbicides
h. wastewater
i. infectious agents

1. _____ Single-celled or multicelled aquatic organisms that derive their energy from photosynthesis.
2. _____ A group of chemicals that are used to kill or control the growth of undesired plants.
3. _____ Large underwater structures located in warm, shallow saltwater that are built by colonies of coral and are composed primarily of calcium carbonate and sand.
4. _____ A relationship between two different species of organisms in which one or both organisms benefit from the action of the other.
5. _____ Polluted water that is unfit for drinking or introduction into the environment because it has been used for some purpose, and made unclean.
6. _____ The whitening of living coral as a result of the die-off of the coral's symbiotic algae, possibly leading to the death of the coral itself.
7. _____ An increase in the sea surface temperature off the western coast of South America near the Equator, which leads to changes in climate around the world.
8. _____ Any substance or organism that transmits disease.
9. _____ A group of benthic aquatic organisms that live in warm, shallow saltwater and may build shells from calcium carbonate.

Critical Thinking

1. Describe the specific human activities that have led to coral bleaching by increased runoff, increased global temperatures, and increased ultraviolet radiation reaching the Earth's surface.

The Biosphere

Topics to be presented in this unit include:

▌ Ecological Systems

▌ World Biomes and Marine Ecosystems

▌ The Flow of Energy and Matter Through Ecosystems

▌ Biological Succession

▌ Classification of the Living World

▌ Threats to Biodiversity

O V E R V I E W

T*he interactions* that occur between the living and nonliving world are an important part of the Earth system as a whole. The biosphere is a term used to describe all of the living components of the Earth's ecosystems. Many of the physical aspects of our planet have been shaped by living organisms. The gases that compose the atmosphere are the result of biological activity. The soils that support all the world's plants are a mixture of both living and nonliving components. And the effects of the human race on the Earth are altering the planet at unprecedented rates. It is with this in mind that the biosphere becomes another important part of the Earth's systems.

Ecological Systems

OBJECTIVES

Ecology · Habitats · Populations · Communities · Ecosystems

After reading this chapter you should be able to:

▶ Define the terms *ecology, biotic,* and *abiotic.*

▶ Identify the four aspects that make an organism's habitat.

▶ Define the terms *population* and *species* and provide two examples of a population.

▶ Differentiate between specialist and generalist populations.

▶ Define the term *community* and describe three examples of symbiotic relationships.

▶ Define the term *ecosystem* and identify four abiotic factors that exist within ecosystems.

▶ Describe the ecosphere.

TERMS TO KNOW

ecology

biotic

abiotic

habitat

population

species

community

symbiotic relationship

mutualism

lichen

commensalisms

parasitism

ecosystem

ecosphere

INTRODUCTION

The study of living things and the way that they interact with the physical environment is called **ecology**. The word ecology is derived from the ancient Greek words *oikos,* meaning "house" or "place to live," and *logic,* meaning "to learn." Indeed, ecology is the study of where organisms live. Learning about how living organisms interact with the environment is important for determining what role they play in the Earth's systems and how best to maintain them for future generations.

ECOLOGY

Two words that are important to the study of ecology are *biotic* and *abiotic*. The term **biotic** refers to any living organism, including plants, animals, bacteria, and fungi. **Abiotic** refers to the nonliving factors of the environment that interact with the biotic world. These include air, water, rocks, minerals, temperature, altitude, light, and soil. Scientists who study ecology are called ecologists. Ecologists study the interaction of the biotic and abiotic world in different levels of relationships on the Earth.

HABITATS

The smallest level of relationship that ecologists study is an organism's **habitat**. *Habitat* refers to an organism's specific food, water, shelter, and space requirements. All organisms require these four fundamental things to survive (Figure 31–1). Food requirements for living organisms can vary greatly in the natural world; however, they all form the basis for how an organism derives energy. Some organisms, such as green plants, gain their energy from sunlight. Other organisms must consume other living things to gain energy.

Another important habitat requirement is a source of water. All living things on the Earth require water to survive. Some organisms

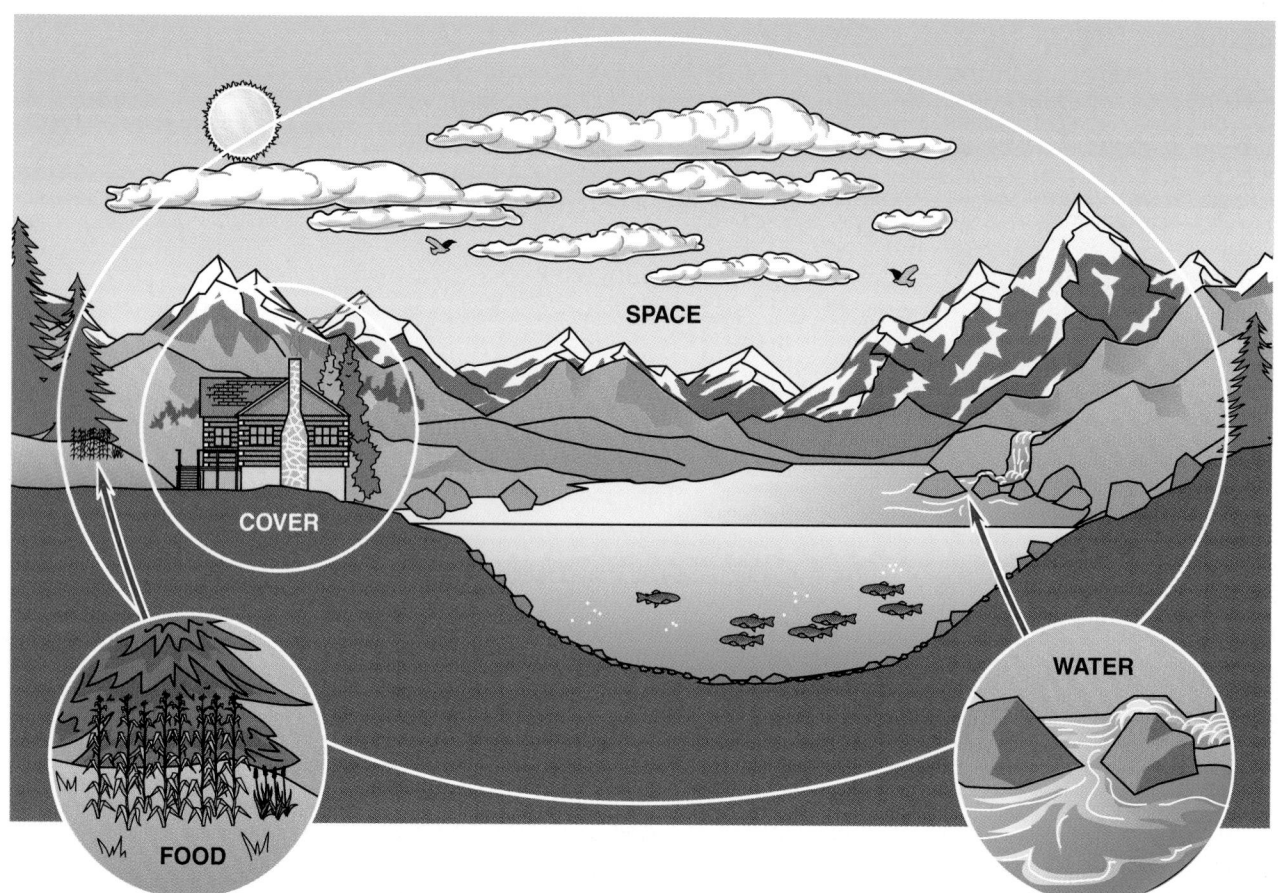

FIGURE 31–1   The four elements that together make up an organism's habitat.

CAREER CONNECTIONS

Ecologist

An ecologist studies the ecological issues associated with a wide range of environments. These scientists use this knowledge to solve problems with supplying food and shelter and with improving the health of human beings. Their job also includes monitoring and managing natural resources to sustain ecosystems and wildlife populations. Ecologists help to design sustainable land use plans and help develop environmental impact statements. Much of their work today involves using their knowledge to solve many environmental problems around the world, especially those associated with habitat destruction. These scientists often work in the outdoors gathering data about specific interactions that occur within ecosystems. The field of ecology requires a 4-year college degree. Ecologists can find employment in research or with government agencies.

spend their entire lives in water; these are called aquatic organisms. Organisms that live on the land, called terrestrial organisms, must absorb water from the environment.

The third habitat requirement for all living things is shelter. Shelter is the particular way that an organism protects itself from the environment. This can include protective body parts, such as shells, or the ability to find or build a shelter.

The final habitat requirement for all living things is space. All living things require space in which to live their lives. Some organisms, such as bacteria and algae, have extremely small space requirements. Other organisms, such as bears and migratory birds, require large amounts of space to live. The arctic tern is a bird that migrates from the North Pole arctic regions all the way to Antarctica every year. This is the largest space requirement for a living thing on the Earth.

POPULATIONS

The next level of relationship that ecologists study is the **population**. A population is a group of the same organisms living in a specific area (Figure 31–2). Groups of the same organism are also known as a **species**. A species is a group of organisms that resemble one another genetically and can reproduce with one another. Groups of the same species that live in a particular area are known collectively as a population. Populations can occupy an extremely small space, such as a population of bacteria on a particle of soil, or can be as large as all the human beings who live in the United States.

Many ecologists study specific populations to learn about the way that they interact with the environment. Some populations require

FIGURE 31–2   A population of organisms consists of a group of the same species residing in a particular area.

special habitat requirements that make them very specialized. If there is an interruption or change in their habitat, these specialist populations can be threatened. Populations that include wolves, elephants, tigers, and many others are being threatened as a result of the loss of their habitats. Other populations, called generalists, can survive in a wide range of habitats. Examples of these types of populations include human beings, squirrels, mice, rats, and many insects. Generalists can tolerate extreme change in their habitats and can easily adapt to their altered surroundings.

COMMUNITIES

The third level of relationship that ecologists study is the **community**. A community is the interaction of different populations that reside in a particular area (Figure 31–3). Communities are composed of many different species of organisms that share similar habitats. Communities can exist in a very small area, such as the organisms found in one drop of pond water. Communities can also occupy extremely large areas, such as entire forests, lakes, or geographical regions. Often the removal of one species or population from a community can have a negative impact on the other members of the community.

Many populations that together form unique communities depend on one another for survival. The relationships that exist between populations in a community can sometimes be called symbiotic. A **symbiotic relationship** occurs when one or more organisms benefit from the actions of another organism (Figure 31–4). Another type of relationship that occurs in communities is **mutualism**, which is the interaction of two species that both benefit from actions of one another. An example of mutualism is the **lichen** community. A lichen is actually a community of two organisms, an alga and a fungus, that reside together on the surface of rocks and trees. The alga produces food from sunlight, in the form of sugar and starches, through the process of photosynthesis. The fungus consumes some of this food and in return secretes weak acids that help break down the organic material and minerals from the surfaces on which the lichen reside. This is an important source of nutrients for the alga.

FIGURE 31–3 A community consists of all the living things in a specific region.

FIGURE 31–4 Examples of the symbiotic relationships include mutualism between the algae and fungus of a lichen on rock (left) and parasitism between a tick (right) and a dog. (*Left image courtesy of PhotoDisc.*)

Another type of symbiotic relationship is called **commensalism**. This is a relationship between two organisms in which one organism benefits from another organism without any expense to its host. An example of commensalism is the relationship between the remora fish and its shark hosts. The remora harmlessly attaches itself to the body of a shark and benefits from the leftovers of the shark's meals.

A third type of symbiotic relationship between species is **parasitism**. This occurs when one organism harms a host organism by taking its nutrition from it. An example of this is a tick on a dog. The tick attaches itself to the dog and feeds on the dog's blood.

ECOSYSTEMS

The next level of relationship that ecologists study is called the **ecosystem**. *Ecosystem* is the short word for ecological system. An ecosystem is the interaction of a community of organisms with the abiotic factors in a specific area. Some examples of abiotic factors include the amount of sunlight a region receives and the amount of moisture in an area. The temperature of the environment where the organism resides is also an important abiotic factor, along with the surrounding landscape.

The particular size of an ecosystem varies, depending on the region an ecologist is studying. Generally ecosystems cover large geographical areas such as entire forests or even parts of entire continents. The largest ecosystem that scientists study is called the **ecosphere**. This is the relationship between the biotic and abiotic components of the entire planet, which includes every living and nonliving thing on the Earth, and how they interact. Two broad categories of ecosystems on the planet include aquatic ecosystems and terrestrial ecosystems. Aquatic ecosystems exist in water, and terrestrial ecosystems are found on land (Figures 31–5 and 31–6).

FIGURE 31–5 A terrestrial ecosystem consists of all the biotic and abiotic factors in a specific location on land.

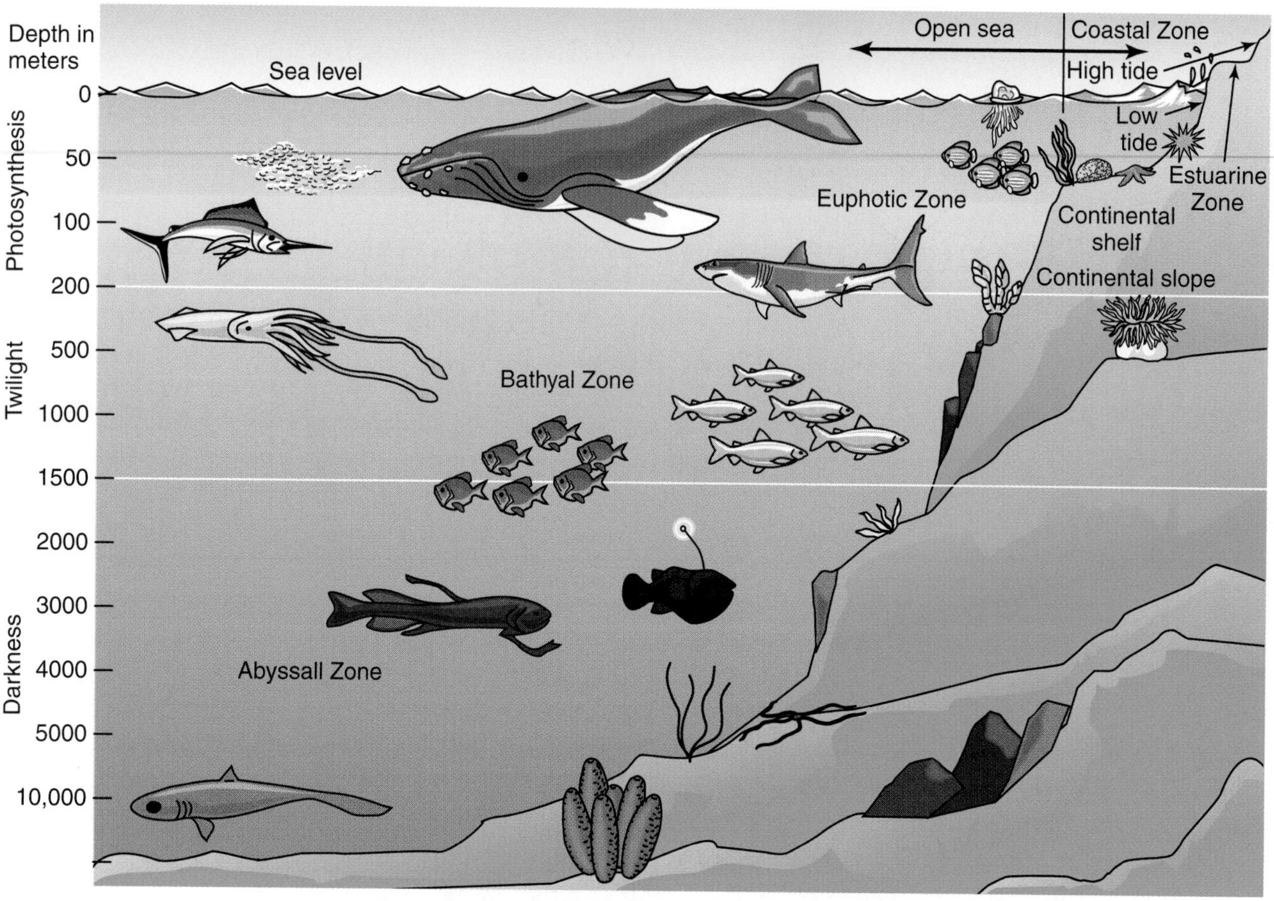

FIGURE 31–6 An aquatic ecosystem consists of all the biotic and abiotic factors in a specific location within a water environment.

@ **WEB Links**

FOR MORE INFORMATION GO TO THIS WEB LINK:

<http://www.ucmp .berkeley.edu/glossary /gloss5/biome/>

REVIEW

1. Define the term *ecology*.
2. What are the four aspects of an organism's habitat?
3. What is a population of organisms?
4. Define the term *community*.
5. What are three examples of symbiotic relationships?
6. What is an ecosystem?

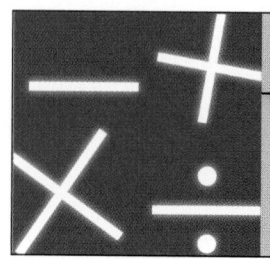

earth math

1) Some ecologists believe there are 5 million different species of organisms on the Earth; still others believe there are 30 million species on the planet. What is the average estimated number of living species on the Earth?

CHAPTER REVIEW

Ecology is the study of the interactions between organisms and the environment in which they live. An ecologist is a specialized scientist who studies organisms and their environment. This includes a detailed knowledge of the biotic and abiotic factors in an organism's environment. The term *biotic* means "living"; *abiotic* means "nonliving." Ecologists study the relationship of organisms with their environment on four main levels. The first level of study is called the habitat. A habitat is the specific water, food, shelter, and space requirements for an organism. Every living thing requires these four fundamental items to survive. The next level of relationship studied in ecology is the population. A population is a group of the same species of organism that live in the same area. A species is a group of organisms that are genetically the same and can breed with one another. For example, all the brook trout that live in the Battenkill River in New York make up a population. Populations can be extremely small, such as bacteria in the soil, or very large, such as the human population.

The next level of ecology is called the community. A community is a group of different populations that live in the same geographical area and interact with one another. Communities can extend over a wide area, such as an entire forest, or exist in a very small space, such as a drop of pond water. The interactions between organisms in a community are important for the survival of many different species. Often if one species is removed from a community, it can harm the remaining populations.

Symbiotic relationships, in which two organisms benefit from one another, can exist within a community. Some specific types of symbiotic relationships include commensalism, mutualism, and parasitism.

The highest level of ecological relationship is called the ecosystem. An ecosystem is the interaction between a community and the abiotic factors in the environment. This relationship includes the interactions between all the living and nonliving things in a specific area. Examples of abiotic factors in an ecosystem include the amount of sunlight, temperature, moisture, and nutrient elements. There are two general types of ecosystems recognized on the Earth: aquatic and terrestrial. Aquatic ecosystems exist in water, and terrestrial ecosystems are found on land. The largest ecosystem studied on the Earth is called the ecosphere. The ecosphere is the interaction between all the biotic and abiotic factors on the entire planet.

CHAPTER REVIEW

Multiple Choice

1. An example of an abiotic element is:
   a. lichen
   b. sunlight
   c. trees
   d. bacteria

2. Which of the following is not part of an organism's habitat?
   a. air
   b. space
   c. cover
   d. water

3. An example of a biotic element in an organism's habitat is:
   a. minerals
   b. sunlight
   c. plants
   d. water

4. Organisms that can breed with one another are known as:
   a. generalists
   b. species
   c. communities
   d. specialists

5. All the brook trout in a river are an example of:
   a. a habitat
   b. a population
   c. a community
   d. an ecosystem

6. Human beings are an example of:
   a. a generalist population
   b. a specialist population

   c. a community
   d. abiotic factors in an ecosystem

7. The interaction between the alga and fungus of a lichen is an example of:
   a. commensalism
   b. parasitism
   c. abiosis
   d. mutualism

8. A tick attached to the skin of a dog is an example of:
   a. commensalism
   b. parasitism
   c. abiosis
   d. mutualism

9. The interaction between the living and nonliving aspects of a particular area is called:
   a. a habitat
   b. a population
   c. a community
   d. an ecosystem

10. All the trees in a particular forest are an example of:
    a. a habitat
    b. a population
    c. a community
    d. an ecosystem

11. Which is the highest level of relationship studied by ecologists?
    a. habitat
    b. population
    c. community
    d. ecosystem

Matching   *Match the terms with the correct definitions.*

a. ecology
b. biotic
c. abiotic
d. habitat
e. population

f. species
g. community
h. symbiotic relationship
i. mutualism
j. lichen

k. commensalism
l. parasitism
m. ecosystem
n. ecosphere

1. _____ A relationship between two different species of organisms in which one or both organisms benefit from the action of the other.

2. _____ The interaction between the biotic and abiotic factors in a specific area.

3. _____ All the species of organisms that reside in a particular area.
4. _____ The scientific discipline that studies how organisms interact with their environment.
5. _____ The specific food, water, cover, and space requirements for a particular organism.
6. _____ A taxonomical classification used to describe a fundamental group of organisms that can interbreed.
7. _____ A symbiotic relationship between two organisms in which the host organism is harmed by a parasite.
8. _____ A term that describes all the life zones that exist on Earth and is made up of the atmosphere, hydrosphere, lithosphere, and biosphere.
9. _____ A type of symbiotic relationship in which both organisms benefit from each other.
10. _____ A symbiotic organism consisting of an alga and fungus that lives on rocks and trees.
11. _____ A nonliving organism.
12. _____ A living organism.
13. _____ A specific type of symbiotic relationship in which one organism benefits from a host, and the host is neither helped nor harmed.
14. _____ A group of one species of organism that resides in a particular area.

Critical Thinking

1. Explain why the biosphere is an important aspect of the Earth's systems.

32

World Biomes and Marine Ecosystems

WORLD BIOMES OBJECTIVES

Biomes · Tundra · Coniferous Forests · Temperate Forests · Grasslands · Savannas · Deserts · Tropical Rain Forests · Chaparral · Mountains

After reading this section you should be able to:

▶ Define the term *biome*.
▶ Identify the two main factors that create unique biomes on the Earth.
▶ Describe the unique features of the tundra biome.
▶ Differentiate between the coniferous forest and deciduous forest biomes.
▶ Describe the unique features of the grassland biome.
▶ Differentiate between the grassland and savanna biomes.
▶ Describe the unique features of the desert biome.
▶ Describe the unique features of the tropical rain forest biome.
▶ Describe the unique features of the chaparral and mountain biomes.

MARINE ECOSYSTEMS OBJECTIVES

Coastal Wetlands · The Neritic and Intertidal Zones · The Oceanic Zone · The Benthic Zone · Hydrothermal Vent Communities

After reading this section you should be able to:

▶ Identify the four types of coastal wetlands.
▶ Differentiate between the neritic zone and the oceanic zones.
▶ Describe the harsh conditions that exist in the intertidal zone.
▶ Differentiate between plankton and nekton.
▶ Describe the conditions that exist in a hydrothermal vent community.

INTRODUCTION

The large-scale interactions between the biotic and abiotic elements of specific regions are known as ecosystems. Much of the world that we live in has been shaped by the relationships that occur in the unique ecosystems that exist around the world. Often the nonliving aspects of a particular region determine what type of organisms reside in a specific ecosystem. Two types of ecosystems cover most of the world's surface: terrestrial ecosystems and aquatic ecosystems. Terrestrial ecosystems occur on the land surface, and aquatic ecosystems exist in water. The terrestrial ecosystems we live in today have been altered by human activity, which has interrupted the natural balance these systems have maintained for thousands of years. Understanding the natural interactions that occur in terrestrial ecosystems is vital to maintaining a healthy environment for humans and the organisms that share the ecosystems in which we live.

Although the oceans cover approximately 70 percent of the Earth's surface, we are just now beginning to unlock the secrets of the marine ecosystems that exist there. Recent research has revealed the complex interactions that occur within marine ecosystems and how they influence the entire planet. The existence of marine communities that thrive in the harsh environment of the deep ocean are revealing the ability of life to exist in many environments. Studying the interactions between the living and nonliving elements in the world's ecosystems is important for revealing the role that all living things play in the Earth's systems.

32.1 World Biomes

BIOMES

A **terrestrial** ecosystem is the land-based relationship between organisms and the nonliving components in a specific area. Terrestrial ecosystems are also called **biomes**. Biomes are large terrestrial ecosystems that cover wide geographical areas. Ecologists recognize nine major biomes around the world, which are classified by two main abiotic factors. These factors include the average yearly temperature and precipitation that each region receives.

TUNDRA

The **tundra** biome is one of the harshest environments on the planet; it is located in the higher latitudes. The tundra supports the northernmost limits of plant growth, with vegetation consisting of moss, lichen, hardy grasses, and small shrubs. Tundra biomes cover approximately 19 percent of the Earth's land surface and can be found in the higher latitudes in Northern Canada, Greenland, and Northern Asia. The average annual temperature for the tundra biome is 10° Fahrenheit (–12° C). The soil of the tundra is classified as **permafrost**, which means that it is frozen throughout the year (Figure 32–1).

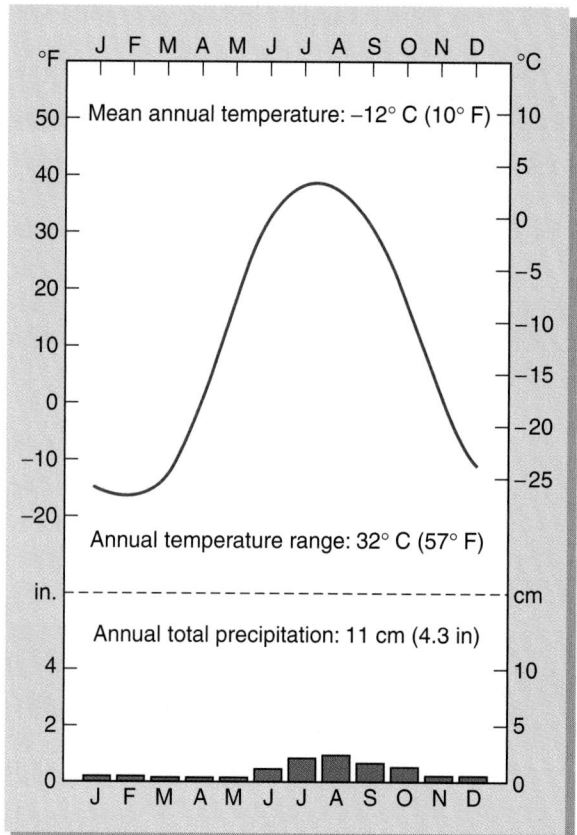

FIGURE 32–1 The monthly temperature and precipitation values over the course of a year for a tundra biome.

FIGURE 32-2 The low-growing, matlike vegetation of a tundra biome. (*Courtesy of EyeWire.*)

The top portion of the permafrost soil melts to form small pools of liquid water during the short summer months. This is the principal source of liquid water for the organisms that reside there. The tundra biome experiences long, cold winters with barely any sunlight, which creates temperatures well below freezing. When the short summers do arrive in the tundra regions, the average high temperatures are around 50° F (10° C). The tundra is also considered arid, with less than 10 in (25 cm) of precipitation each year on average (Figure 32-2). Large organisms that reside in the tundra biome include musk ox, caribou, arctic fox, polar bear, arctic hare, and human beings.

CONIFEROUS FORESTS

The next type of biome lies in the latitudes next to the tundra. It is called the coniferous forest biome. This biome, also known as the taiga or boreal forest, is located at the higher latitudes just below the tundra and covers approximately 11 percent of the Earth's land surface. Coniferous forest biomes experience long, cold winters and short, hot summers. As the name states, this biome is home to many cone-bearing tree species, including pine, spruce, and fir. The coniferous forest receives higher amounts of precipitation than the tundra, with averages around 20 in (51 cm) annually. Temperatures during the summer months can exceed 60° F (16° C) and then can drop below freezing for most of the winter (Figure 32-3).

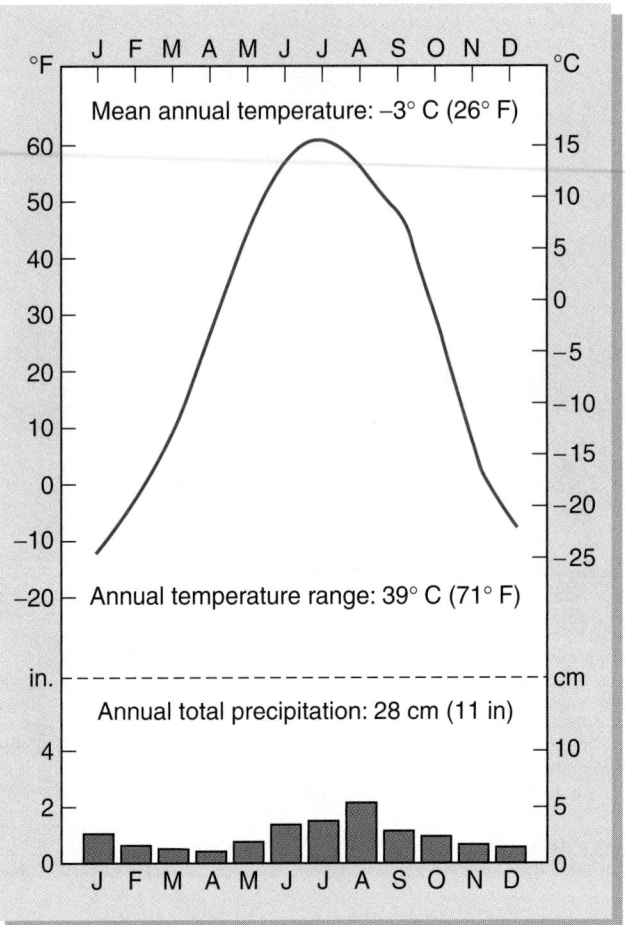

FIGURE 32–3 The monthly temperature and precipitation values over the course of a year for a coniferous forest biome.

Coniferous forests support a wide variety of animal species, including wolves, bears, squirrels, rabbits, hawks, deer, moose, and of course humans (Figure 32–4). Large parts of North America, including parts of the United States and Canada, contain coniferous forests. Much of Northern Europe and Asia also have coniferous forest biomes.

TEMPERATE FORESTS

The biome that lies adjacent to the coniferous forests, near the middle latitudes, is called the temperate forest biome. This type of climate is also known as a deciduous forest, because the primary form of vegetation growing there is the deciduous tree. A deciduous tree is a type of broad-leafed tree that drops its leaves every fall (Figure 32–5).

Common deciduous trees found in the temperate forests include maple, birch, ash, hickory, beech, and oak. The annual change in the color of the leaves in a temperate forest each autumn is one of nature's most beautiful displays. The temperate forest biome experiences long, hot summers and cold winters. This biome also receives a high amount of precipitation in both rain and snow. The average annual temperature of the temperate forest is 49° F (9° C), although through most of

FIGURE 32–4 Evergreen trees are the principal vegetation in the coniferous forest biome. (*Courtesy of PhotoDisc.*)

FIGURE 32–5 Deciduous trees lose their leaves each fall in the deciduous forest, also known as the temperate forest biome. (*Courtesy of PhotoDisc.*)

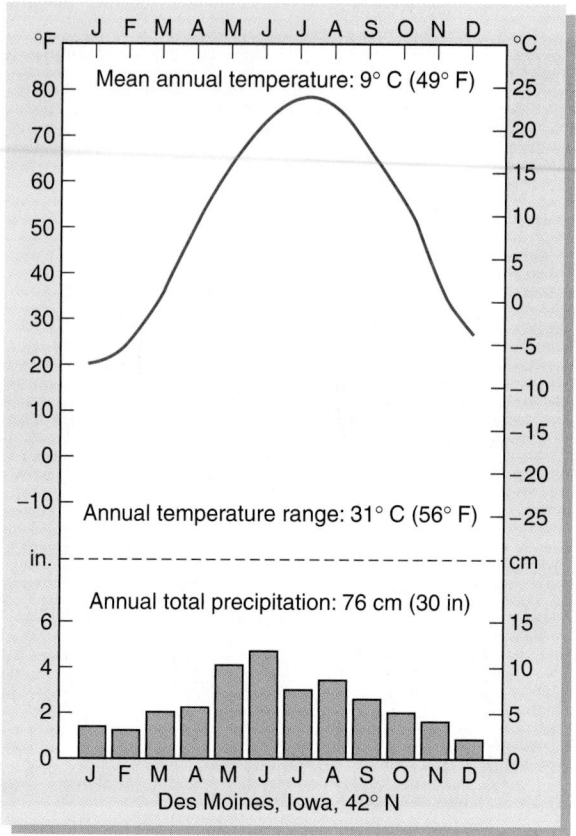

FIGURE 32–6 The monthly temperature and precipitation values over the course of a year for a deciduous forest biome.

the winter the temperature falls below freezing (Figure 32–6). Because of this, many parts of the temperate forests are snow covered during the winter months. During the summer months temperatures are usually above 70° F (21° C).

CAREER CONNECTIONS

Biogeographer

Biogeographers study the geographical distribution of living things on the Earth. Their work researches the way that regional geography and climate influence the types of plants and animals that live in particular region. Biogeographers also study the past relationships that have existed between the land and living things all through the Earth's history. This work involves the search for fossils and other clues to past climates. Biogeographers are also interested in plate tectonics and how the movement of land masses around the world has influenced the distribution of living things on Earth. Most of the work of a biogeographer is in academic research that requires knowledge of geography, biology, and geology.

Much of the eastern coast of the United States is a deciduous forest biome, as are major parts of Europe and China. Most of the temperate forests of the eastern United States have been cut down for use as lumber or cleared for farmland. Many of the current deciduous forests of the eastern United States are second-generation forests, which means they have grown back after they were originally cut down by Europeans when they settled North America. Less than 1 percent of all deciduous forests are old-growth forests that have not been altered by humans. The temperate forest biome also supports a variety of animals and birds.

GRASSLANDS

The next type of terrestrial ecosystem, or biome, is called the grassland. The grassland biome also is located near the middle latitudes but mostly is found near the interior of continents. Grasslands experience long, hot summers that are accompanied by periodic **droughts** (Figure 32–7). During these drought periods, wildfires may be started by lightning, which quickly burns the dried vegetation. These periodic wildfires prevent larger plants such as trees from growing. This limits the type of vegetation that grows in these regions to grasses and shrubs. The grassland

FIGURE 32–7 The wide-open plains of the grasslands of the American midwest experience periodic droughts. (*Courtesy of PhotoDisc.*)

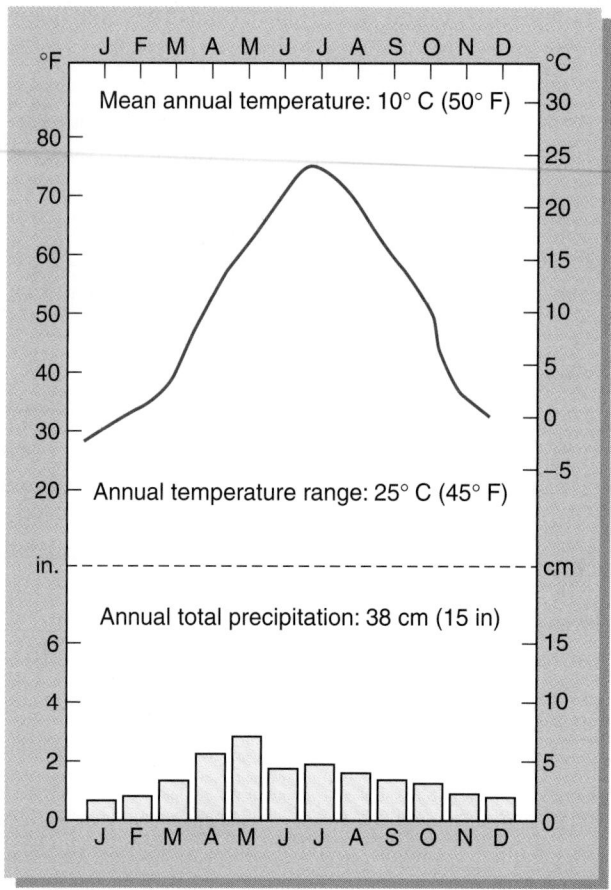

FIGURE 32-8 The monthly temperature and precipitation values over the course of a year for a grassland biome.

receives less than 15 in (38 cm) of rain each year, receiving as little as 1 in (2.5 cm) per month in summer (Figure 32–8).

Grassland biomes are located in the midwestern United States, parts of South America, Africa, and Asia. The grassland biome supports large herds of animals that graze on the wealth of grass found in the grasslands. This type of biome also supports much of the world's agriculture. The "bread basket" grassland in the midwestern United States is the most productive farmland in the world.

SAVANNAS

Another type of biome that also supports a large amount of grassy vegetation is called the savanna. Savannas are also known as tropical grasslands, because they are found near the equator. Savannas are also located in the interior of continents, but they differ from the grassland biome in that they experience a long rainy season. Average rainfall is approximately 40 in (102 cm), but less than 2 in (5 cm) falls over a 2-month period (Figure 32–9). This annual drought period reduces the vegetation to mostly tall grass, shrubs, and widely spread drought-resistant trees. Because the savanna is near the tropical regions of the world, the annual temperatures remain fairly constant, with an average of approximately 77° F (25° C) throughout the year.

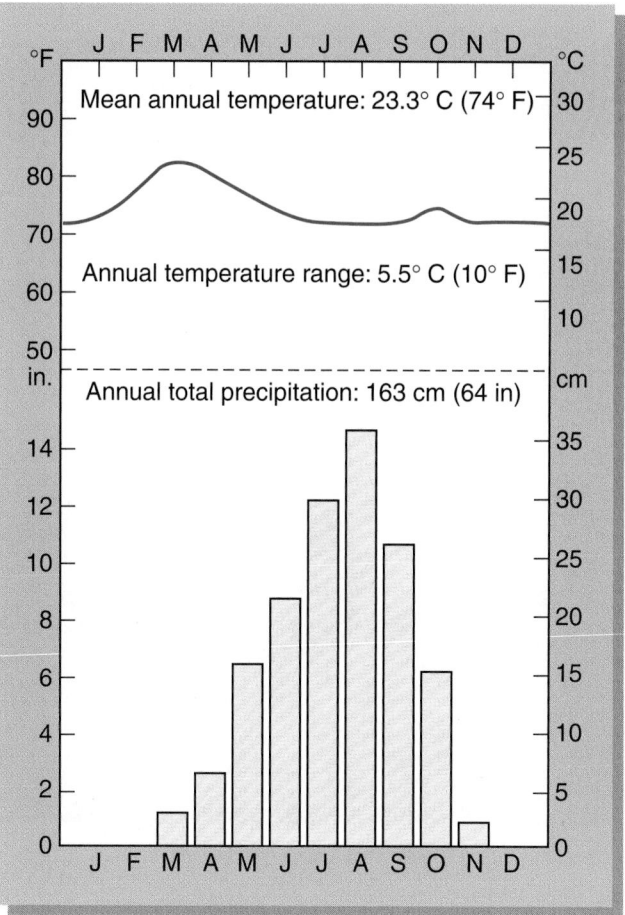

FIGURE 32-9 The monthly temperature and precipitation values over the course of a year for a savanna biome.

Earth System Scientists

Aldo Leopold

Aldo Leopold was born in Iowa in 1887. He became interested in the outdoors and gained an appreciation for wildlife at a young age. Leopold graduated from Yale University with a degree in forestry. After college he worked for the U.S. Forest Service and began to develop an understanding of the interaction of different organisms in a specific area. His observations and research led to the concept known in ecology as a community. In 1933 he published his book titled *Game Management,* which quickly became one of the most influential books on wildlife management. Leopold began the modern science of restoring wildlife populations by using a variety of management techniques. As a result of his work, he has become known as the father of wildlife ecology. His most famous book, *A Sand County Almanac,* is a collection of essays devoted to restoring our nation's landscapes. Leopold believed that the same type of science and technology that led to the destruction of wildlife habitat should be applied to its restoration.

FIGURE 32–10   The Serengeti Plains of Africa are an example of a savanna biome, also called a tropical grassland. (*Courtesy of PhotoDisc.*)

The famous Serengeti Plains of central Africa are a savanna that supports some of the world's most exotic animals (Figure 32–10). These include lions, giraffes, cheetahs, zebras, and elephants. Savannas also exist in South America and Southeast Asia.

DESERTS

The desert biome is one of the Earth's harshest environments because it receives very little rainfall throughout the year. Deserts are usually located near the interior of continents and are found at many different latitudes. The desert biome receives the least amount of precipitation of any biome on Earth. Annual rainfalls in most deserts of the world are less than 2 in (5 cm). This extremely dry climate is also known as an arid climate. Although most people believe that deserts are also hot, this is not always the case. Cold deserts also exist in the higher and middle latitudes. China's Gobi Desert is a cold desert where temperatures often fall below freezing. The entire continent of Antarctica is often classified as a polar desert, where temperatures are extremely cold throughout the year and very little precipitation is received.

Deserts can also be located at very high altitudes. The driest place on Earth is believed to be a cold desert located high in the Andes Mountains of South America. This desert is so dry that it has not rained there in nearly 100 years! The deserts of the United States are primarily located in the southwestern part of North America. These include the Sonoran and Mojave Deserts.

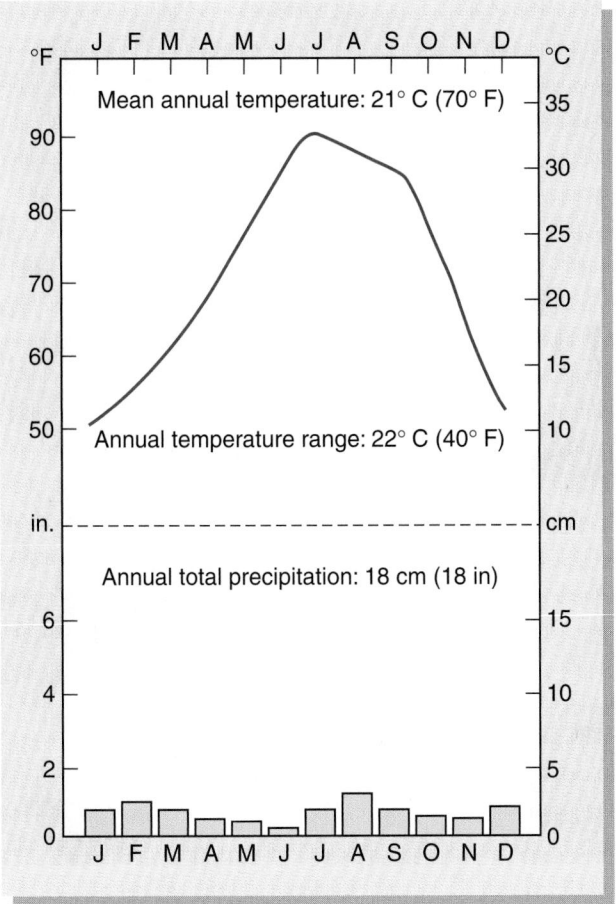

FIGURE 32–11 The monthly temperature and precipitation values over the course of a year for a hot desert biome.

Desert biomes cover approximately 30 percent of all the land surfaces on the Earth. The world's largest hot desert is the Sahara, which is located in North Africa (Figure 32–11). Some deserts experience very wide temperature fluctuations throughout the day. During the daytime, temperatures can be as high as 100° F (38° C), and at night the temperature can drop to almost 40° F (4° C). This is due to the general lack of clouds that can act as a protective blanket helping regulate heat on the Earth's surface. This extreme temperature change during a 24-hour period adds to the harsh environment of the desert biome.

Even though a desert is exposed to extremes in both temperature and lack of precipitation, it still supports a variety of living organisms. All of the plants and animals that reside in the deserts of the world have adapted to the extreme temperatures and lack of water (Figure 32–12). Desert plants such as cactus and animals such as the kangaroo rat can survive on very little water throughout the year.

TROPICAL RAIN FORESTS

The tropical rain forest biome is the most productive land-based ecosystem in the world and supports the greatest amount of **biological diversity**. Tropical rain forests are located near the equator in the **tropics**.

FIGURE 32-12 The rugged landscape of the deserts of the American southwest show the drought-resistant plants that survive in a desert biome. (*Courtesy of PhotoDisc.*)

This ecosystem receives high amounts of rainfall throughout the year and approximately 12 hours of sunlight every day. This results in rapid growth of plants that support a variety of animal species. The average amount of rainfall in the tropical rain forest biome is approximately 110 in (279 cm) annually. This biome also maintains a stable temperature throughout the year of approximately 77° F (25° C) (Figure 32-13).

The trees that make up the rain forest are called broad-leafed evergreens because they have large leaves and keep them throughout the year, unlike deciduous trees. Tropical rain forests cover approximately 2 percent of the Earth's land surface and are found in Central America, South America, Africa, and Southeast Asia. Although the tropical rain forests cover a small amount of the land on the planet, they are home to more than 70 percent of all the species on the Earth. This makes them a valuable biological resource that must be preserved (Figure 32-14).

CHAPARRAL

Another type of biome found on the Earth is called the chaparral. A chaparral is a warm coastal climate that experiences cool, rainy winters and hot, dry summers. The primary vegetation in a chaparral includes shrubs, grasses, and drought-resistant trees (Figure 32-15).

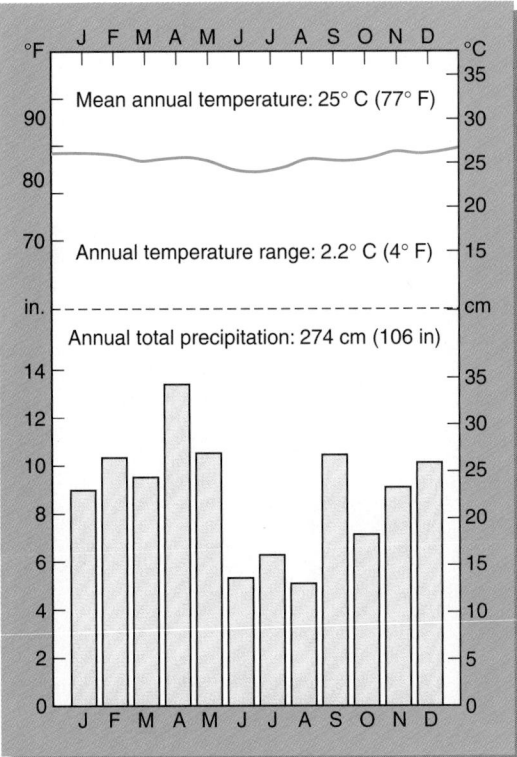

FIGURE 32–13 The monthly temperature and precipitation values over the course of a year for a tropical rain forest biome.

FIGURE 32–14 The lush vegetation of a tropical rain forest biome. This is the most productive biome on the Earth and supports a great amount of biological diversity. (*Courtesy of PhotoDisc.*)

FIGURE 32–15 The shrubs and small trees that grow in the chaparral biome. (*Courtesy of PhotoDisc.*)

Chaparral biomes can be found around the coast of the Mediterranean Sea and in southern California. Because the chaparral has a dry season, it also experiences periodic wildfires that can burn the dried vegetation. People who live in the chaparral biomes of California are susceptible to these wildfires, which can destroy life and property.

MOUNTAINS

The final biome type found on the Earth is called the mountain biome. A mountain biome is unique because it shares the same attributes as a coniferous forest biome and the tundra; however, the extremes in temperatures are caused by altitude, not latitude (Figure 32–16). Mountain biomes can be located anywhere on the planet where there are extremely high mountains. Mountain biomes contain coniferous trees at lower altitudes, which eventually give way to tundra vegetation if the altitude is high enough. Mount Washington in New Hampshire is one of the most extreme mountain biomes in North America. At the top of Mount Washington tundra vegetation exists where some of the world's coldest temperatures and strongest winds have been recorded. Mountain biomes can also be located near the equator, where mountain ranges reach high elevations (Figure 32–17).

FIGURE 32–16   A mountain biome exists at high elevations, where cooler temperatures create conditions similar to the coniferous forest and tundra biomes as a result of increasing altitude. (*Courtesy of PhotoDisc.*)

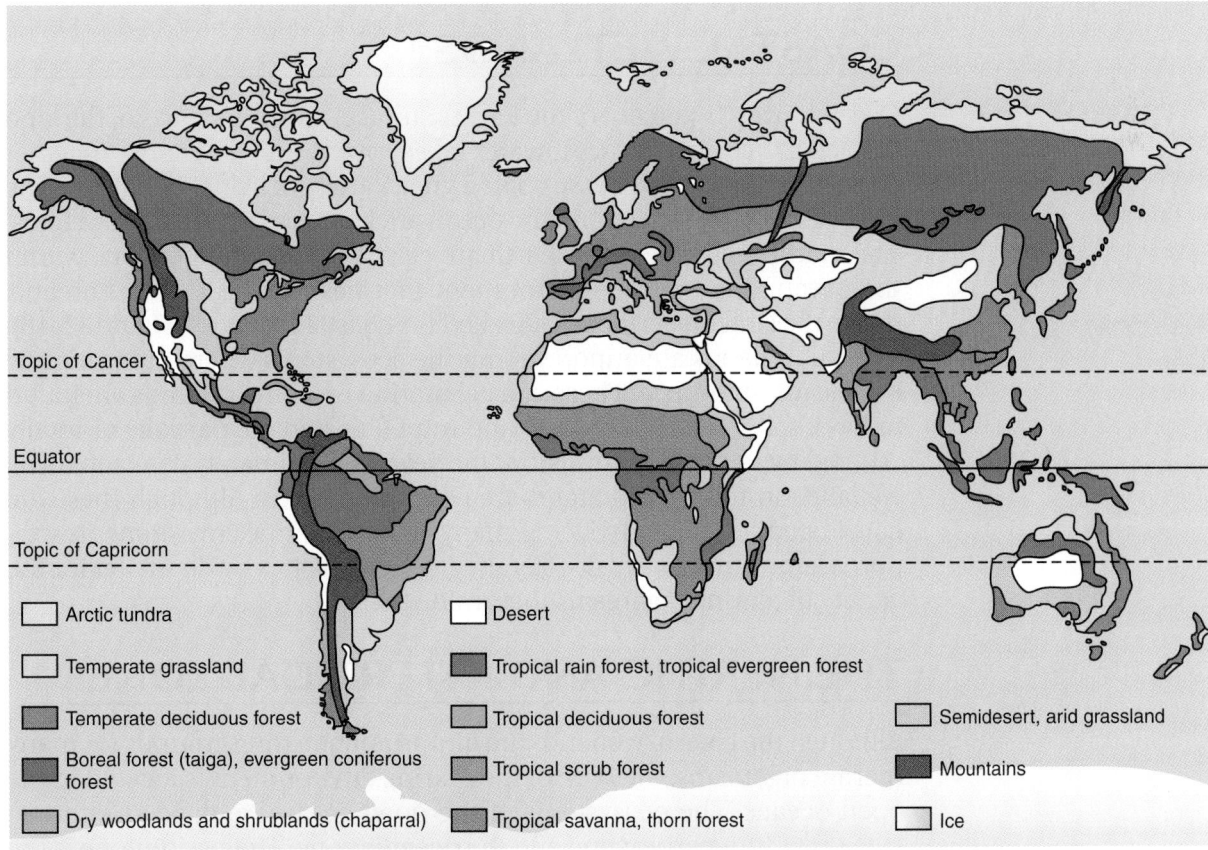

Topic of Cancer

Equator

Topic of Capricorn

☐ Arctic tundra

☐ Temperate grassland

☐ Temperate deciduous forest

☐ Boreal forest (taiga), evergreen coniferous forest

☐ Dry woodlands and shrublands (chaparral)

☐ Desert

☐ Tropical rain forest, tropical evergreen forest

☐ Tropical deciduous forest

☐ Tropical scrub forest

☐ Tropical savanna, thorn forest

☐ Semidesert, arid grassland

☐ Mountains

☐ Ice

FIGURE 32–17   A map showing the locations of major biomes around the world.

FOR MORE INFORMATION GO TO THESE WEB LINKS:

<http://www.blueplanet-
biomes.org/table_of
_contents.htm>

<http://www.mbgnet
.net/sets/index.htm>

SECTION REVIEW

1. What abiotic factors are used to classify the Earth's biomes?
2. Which two biomes experience harsh conditions throughout the year?
3. What type of trees make up most of the vegetation in a temperate forest biome?
4. Which biome supports the greatest amount of biological diversity on the Earth?
5. In which biome are most of the world's food crops grown?
6. Who was Aldo Leopold?

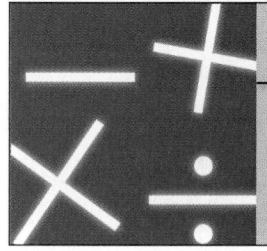

earth math

1) If the total surface area of all the land on Earth is approximately 60 million square miles, determine the approximate surface area of the following biomes: tropical rain forests (2 percent), tundra (11 percent), and deserts (30 percent).

32.2 Marine Ecosystems

COASTAL WETLANDS

Oceans cover 71 percent of the Earth's surface, and other parts of the land surface are covered by freshwater lakes, rivers, and wetlands. Together these **aquatic** ecosystems support a great variety of living organisms. The ecosystems that exist within the ocean are known as **marine** ecosystems. The marine ecosystems on Earth are classified by their locations within the ocean. The marine environment that lies closest to the shoreline, where the land meets the sea, is called the coastal wetlands (Figure 32–18). Coastal wetlands are important marine ecosystems where many marine organisms reproduce. These coastal marine breeding grounds are found in bays, salt marshes, lagoons, and mud flats and are partially or totally covered by salt water throughout the year. Approximately 3 percent of all wetlands in the United States are coastal wetlands. Although these are considered aquatic ecosystems, many of these marine environments support a large number of salt-tolerant grasses, which provide shelter for the variety of marine organisms that reside there.

THE NERITIC AND INTERTIDAL ZONES

Although the coastal wetlands are important breeding grounds for many marine organisms, the bulk of the marine environment is located in the open oceans. The ecosystems of the open ocean are divided into two categories: the neritic zone and the oceanic zone. The neritic zone is the ecosystem that lies along the coasts. It begins at the shoreline, which experiences high and low tides each day (Figure 32–19).

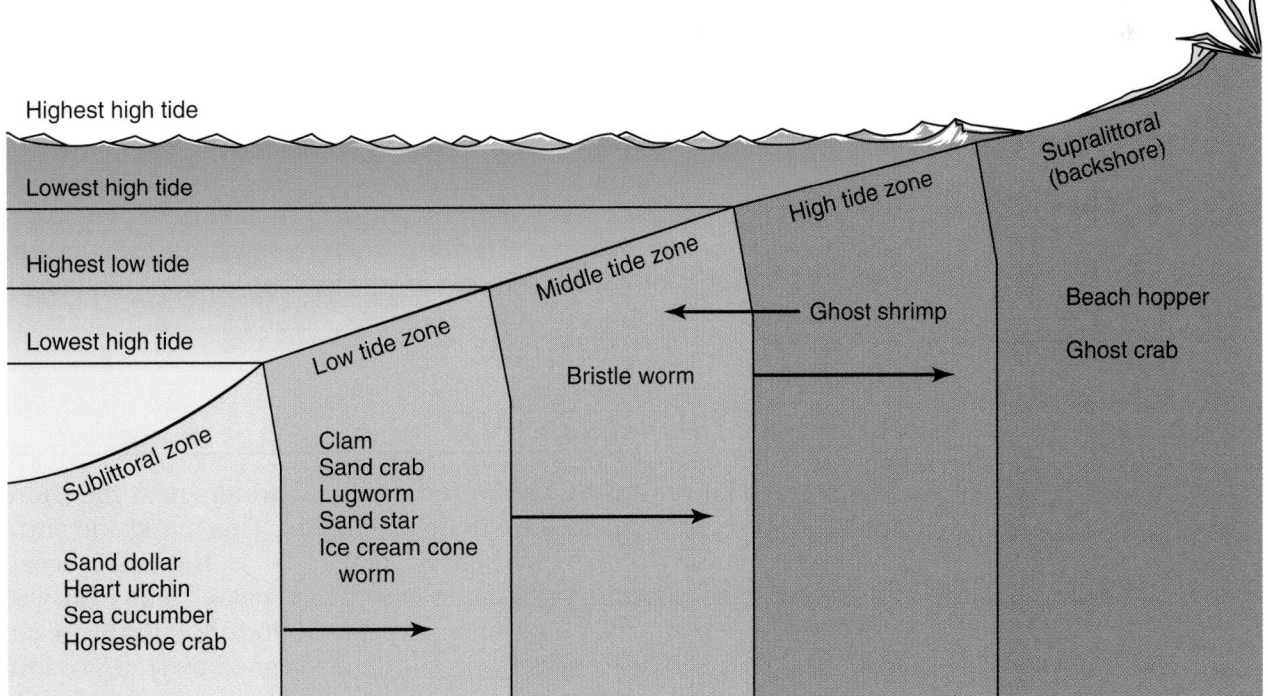

FIGURE 32-18 The coastal wetlands located along the coast of the Atlantic Ocean off of Maryland. (*Courtesy of PhotoDisc.*)

FIGURE 32-19 The different zones and the organisms that live along the shoreline in the intertidal ecosystem, which is located between the area of low and high tides.

FIGURE 32–20 Marine organisms that live in the neritic zone of the ocean.

The neritic zone is also called the **intertidal zone**; it is a marine ecosystem that is home to many well-known marine organisms such as mussels, hermit crabs, starfish, seaweeds, sea anemones, algae, and barnacles (Figure 32–20). This ecosystem is one of the harshest marine environments because the organisms that live there are exposed to dry periods when the tide is low and submerged conditions when the tide is high. This environment is also exposed to the constant impact of waves and tidal forces. Many of the organisms that reside in the inter-tidal ecosystem are extremely flexible, such as algae and grasses, or extremely hard, such as mussels and barnacles. These adaptations help them survive in this harsh environment.

THE OCEANIC ZONE

The neritic zone stretches out from the shallow waters near the shore into the ocean to a depth of about 600 ft (183 m). This marks the entry into the oceanic zone marine ecosystem. This is the open-ocean ecosystem that supports two main life forms, called plankton and nekton. Plankton are free-floating organisms that drift with the ocean currents. They include microscopic algae, also called **phytoplankton**, and single-celled animals called **zooplankton** (Figure 32–21). Larger plankton include the many species of jellyfish.

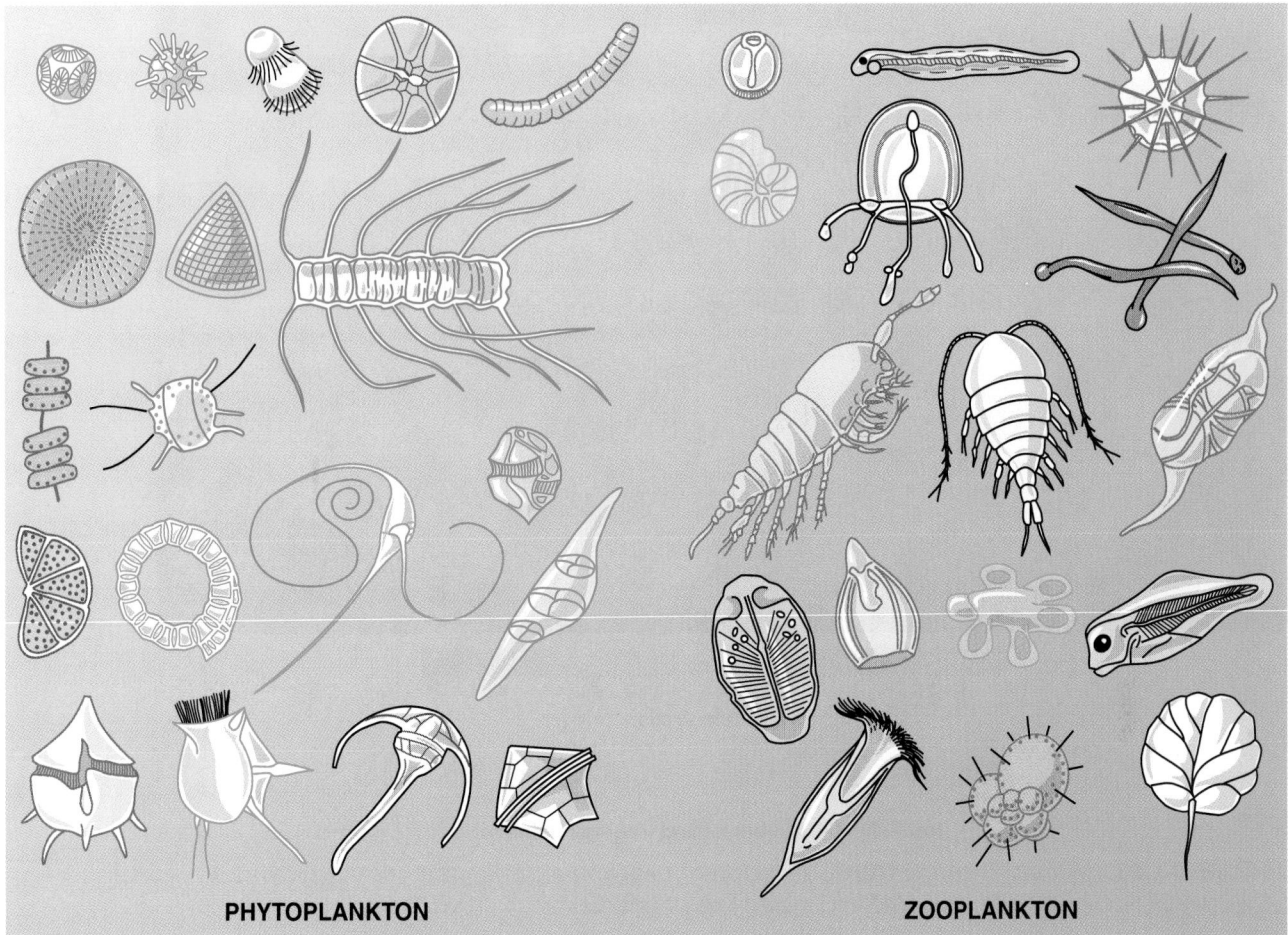

PHYTOPLANKTON   **ZOOPLANKTON**

FIGURE 32–21   Examples of zooplankton and phytoplankton that live in the oceanic zone.

Most plankton float freely throughout the ocean to a depth of about 1,000 ft (305 m). Although plankton can exist anywhere in the oceanic zone, the highest populations occur close to the continental shelves (Figure 32–22). This is due to the greater amount of nutrients available to the plankton there.

The other type of organism that resides in the oceanic zone is the nekton. Nekton are marine organisms that are capable of moving under their own power. These include all fish, squid, octopus, and marine mammals such as whales and dolphins (Figure 32–23). Nekton can live at all depths in the open ocean; some prefer to stay near the surface to feed and live out their lives, whereas others survive in the total darkness of the deep ocean. Some marine nekton will live part of their lives in the ocean and the remaining part in freshwater ecosystems on land. The Atlantic eel is a marine fish that is born in the oceanic zone and eventually migrates into freshwater rivers to live. These types of marine organisms are classified as catadromous, which means they are born in saltwater and live in freshwater. The Atlantic and Pacific salmon do the opposite; they are born in freshwater streams and rivers and migrate out into the open ocean, where they live out their adult lives. These are called anadromous fish.

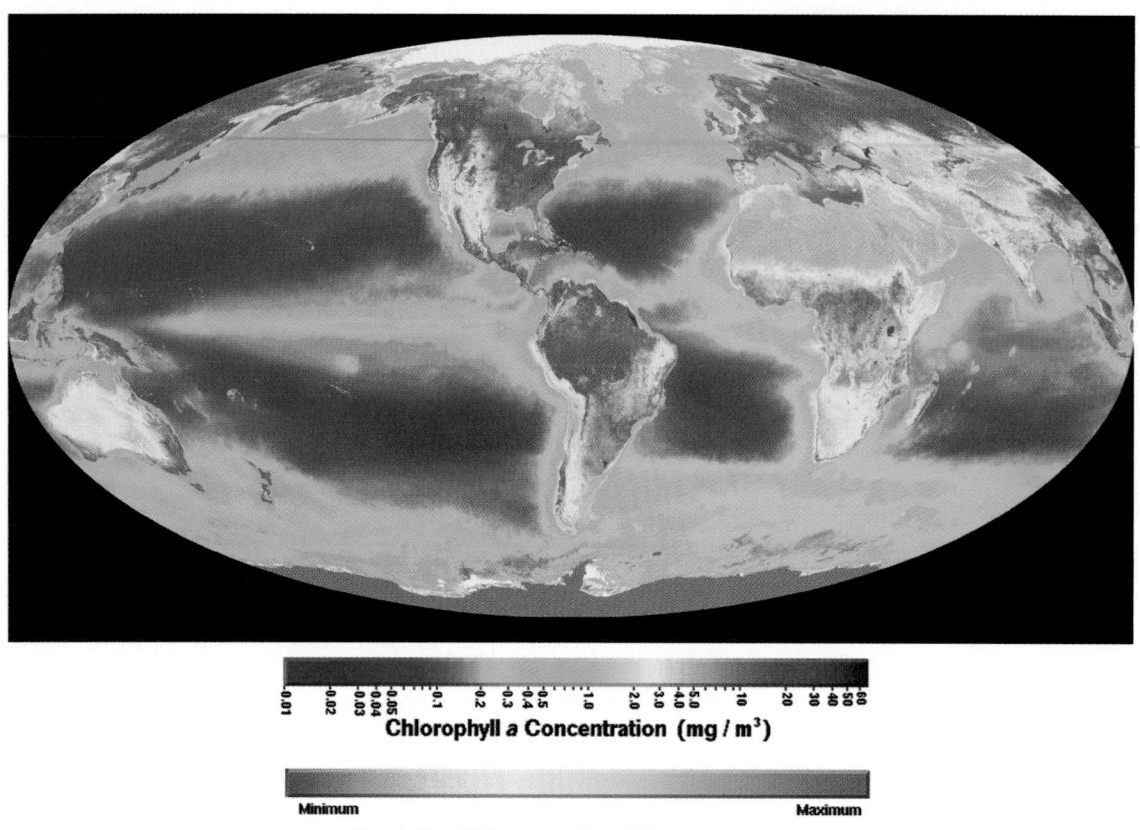

Chlorophyll *a* Concentration (mg / m³)

Minimum   Maximum

Normalized Difference Land Vegetation Index

FIGURE 32–22 A map showing the distribution of phytoplankton in the oceans around the world. (*Courtsey of the SeaWiFS Project, NASA/Goddard Space Flight Center, and ORBIMAGE.*)

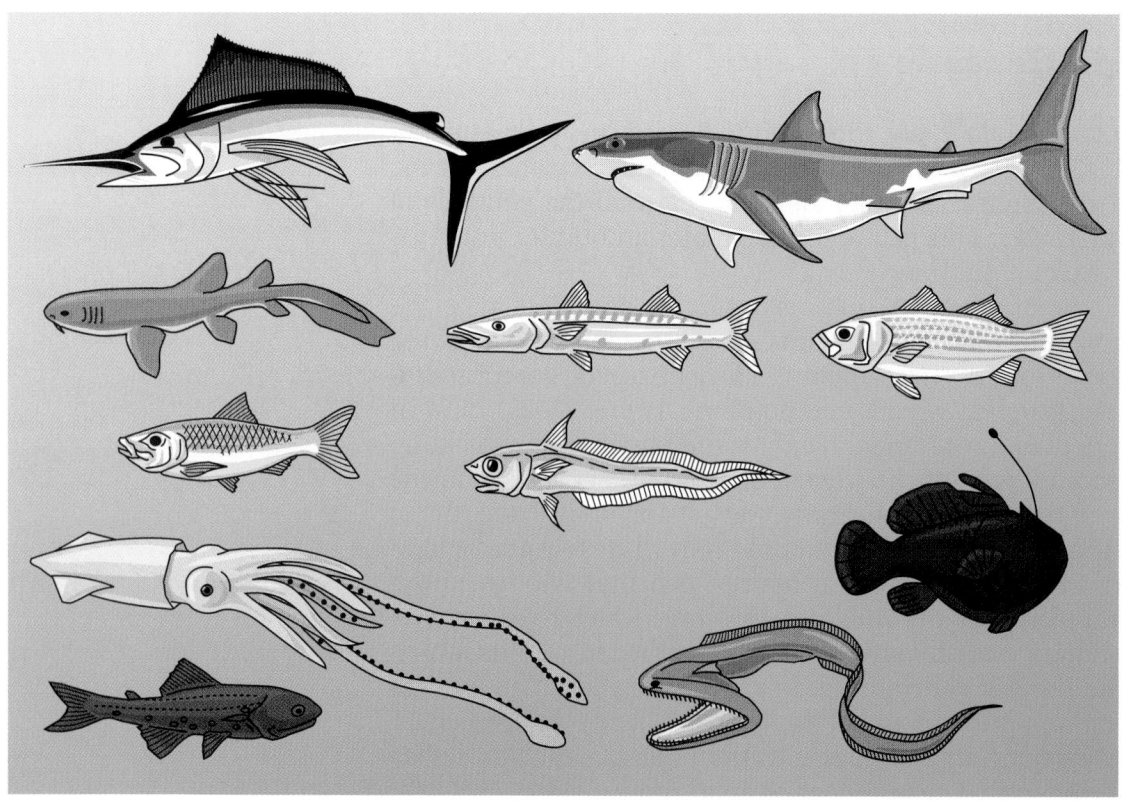

FIGURE 32–23 Examples of nekton that live in the oceanic zone.

Earth System Scientists

Victor Hensen

Victor Hensen was born in Germany in 1835. Trained in anatomy and physiology, Henson became interested in life in the oceans. In 1887 he coined the term plankton to describe the tiny organisms that float freely in the sea and form the base of the aquatic food chain. Hensen led many marine expeditions to survey the extent of plankton in the oceans. In 1889 he revealed that the cooler, nutrient-rich waters of the Arctic and Antarctic supported higher populations than the warm, nutrient-poor waters of the tropics.

THE BENTHIC ZONE

The benthic zone, another major marine ecosystem that exists in the world's oceans, includes all organisms that live at the bottom of the ocean. In some areas close to the shore and in shallow water, the benthic environment receives a great amount of sunlight. This creates highly productive marine communities known as coral reefs. Coral reefs are the largest living structures on the Earth. They are composed of tiny organisms called coral that secrete calcium carbonate to make a protective shell. Over time the colonies of coral grow and produce large structures composed of calcium carbonate and sand. When the older colonies die, new colonies grow on top of the remaining shells of the dead coral. This leads to the buildup of what is called the coral reef.

Coral maintain a symbiotic relationship with algae that together form the base of the coral reef ecosystem. The single-celled algae reside within the protective shell of the coral. The algae produce nutrients for the coral while the coral offers protection and carbon dioxide to the algae. Coral can exist only in shallow water that receives ample amounts of sunlight and that maintains a temperature above 64° F (18° C). Because of this, they are found in only the tropical regions (Figure 32–24). Coral reefs form one of the most beautiful underwater environments on the planet, which supports a wide array of life.

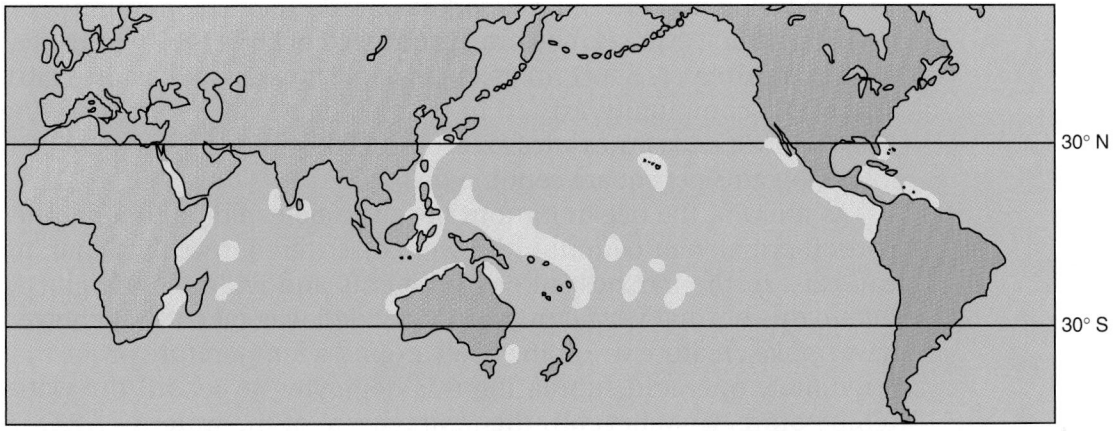

FIGURE 32–24 The locations of the world's major coral reef systems.

HYDROTHERMAL VENT COMMUNITIES

Another interesting community that forms a benthic marine ecosystem resides in the extremely deep and dark waters of the ocean. These are called deep sea hydrothermal vent communities. A **hydrothermal vent** is a chimneylike structure that spews out extremely hot water that is rich in minerals. The source of the water, which can reach temperatures of more than 600° F (316° C), is volcanic activity. Ocean water seeps into cracks in the Earth's crust and is then superheated by the Earth's hot interior. In 1977 the first hydrothermal vent community was discovered near the equator in the Pacific Ocean. Located at a depth of more than 8,000 ft (2,438 m), and in total darkness, this aquatic community was unlike anything ever seen before. It consisted of large tube worms that were approximately 3 ft (1 m) in length, large mussels, and white crabs. The whole community existed in total darkness, in water exceeding 200° F (93°C), and at pressures exceeding 5,000 pounds per square inch (352 kilograms per square centimeters).

As more of the ocean bottom began to be explored, many other hydrothermal vent communities were discovered, revealing that life can exist in the harshest of environments and without sunlight. At one hydrothermal vent community a video was taken that showed a wormlike creature wrapping itself around a temperature probe that a remotely operated submarine was deploying to record the water temperature. Unbelievably, the temperature of the water was 221° F (105° C)!

Earth System Law

Protecting the Ocean and Its Resources

Preserving marine ecosystems has been an important part of environmental legislation in the United States. The Ocean Dumping Act prevents the dumping of sewage and industrial waste into the ocean, and the Coastal Zone Management Act of 1972, protects, manages, and restores the nation's coastal zones. The Marine Mammal Protection Act prevents the harvest of Marine Mammals in U.S. waters and by U.S. citizens. This law also prevents the importation and sale of marine mammal products into the country. In 1972 the Fishery Conservation and Management Act was passed by Congress to establish a zone in the ocean surrounding the United States for the conservation and management of marine fisheries. The Endangered Species Act of 1973 is also applied to the protection of marine organisms that are in danger of becoming extinct due to human activity.

SECTION REVIEW

1. What are some of the ecosystems that are classified as coastal wetlands?

2. Describe two conditions that make the intertidal ecosystem extremely harsh.

3. How have organisms adapted to surviving in the intertidal ecosystem?

4. What are the two categories of organisms found in the oceanic zone? Give two examples for each.

5. Where is the benthic environment located within the ocean?

6. Under what conditions can coral reefs form?

7. Describe the relationship between algae and coral in a reef ecosystem.

8. What is a hydrothermal vent community, and under what conditions do they exist within the ocean?

9. Who was Victor Hensen?

@ WEB Links

FOR MORE INFORMATION GO TO THESE WEB LINKS:

<http://www.mbgnet.net/salt/index.htm>

<http://oceanexplorer.noaa.gov/>

<http://www.nmfs.noaa.gov/>

<http://www.pmel.noaa.gov/vents/>

<http://seawifs.gsfc.nasa.gov/OCEAN_PLANET/HTML/oceanography_recently_revealed1.html>

<http://www.botos.com/marine/vents01.html>

CHAPTER SUMMARY

The interaction between the living and nonliving elements of a specific region on the Earth is called an ecosystem. Two main types of ecosystems are studied on the planet: terrestrial ecosystems and aquatic ecosystems. Terrestrial ecosystems exist on the land, and aquatic ecosystems are found in the water. Terrestrial ecosystems are also called

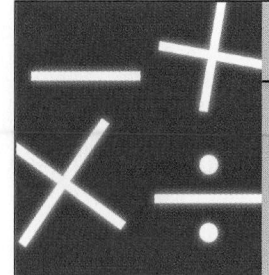

earth math

1) If a hydrothermal vent community exists at a depth of 10,890 feet below the ocean surface and pressure increases 14.7 pounds per square inch for every 33 feet of depth, what is the pressure in pounds per square inch where this community is located?

biomes. Ecologists recognize nine major biomes on the Earth, which are determined by the temperature and precipitation they experience each year. The tundra biome is located in the higher latitudes where the temperature remains below freezing for most of the year. The tundra exists on permafrost, which is soil that is frozen throughout the year.

Located below the tundra biome is the coniferous forest biome. This ecosystem experiences long, cold winters and short, hot summers. The principal vegetation growing there is the coniferous tree, also known as the evergreen tree. The deciduous forest biome, also called the temperate forest, is located near the middle latitudes and experiences cold winters and hot summers. The principal vegetation in the temperate forests are deciduous trees. These are trees that lose their leaves each fall.

Another type of biome is grassland. This ecosystem is located in the middle latitudes near the interior of continents. Grasslands experience periodic droughts during the year, which causes periodic wildfires to burn through the region. This allows grasses and shrubs to be the principal vegetation in this biome. Grasslands that grow near the equator are called savannas or tropical grasslands. These ecosystems receive greater amounts of precipitation and support grasses, shrubs, and drought-resistant trees.

The desert biome is one of the harshest ecosystems on the planet, receiving very little precipitation each year. These extremely dry environments can be hot or cold. The Sahara Desert in North Africa is the world's largest hot desert. Cold deserts, such as the Gobi Desert in China, experience temperatures that can fall below freezing at certain times during the year. Even though deserts are very harsh environments, they still support life.

The chaparral biome is a coastal ecosystem that experiences hot, dry summers and cool, rainy winters. These biomes exist around the Mediterranean Sea and along the coast of California. The last major biome is called the mountain biome. These ecosystems resemble coniferous forests and tundra biomes but exist in the higher altitudes of mountain ranges. Marine ecosystems exist within the world's oceans. The coastal wetlands are areas that lie close to the shore and are covered with saltwater for most of the year. These marine ecosystems include mudflats, salt marshes, bays, and lagoons, and are important breeding grounds for many marine organisms. The open ocean is divided into two distinct types of marine ecosystems called the neritic zone and the oceanic zone. The neritic zone extends from the shoreline out to a depth of approximately 600 ft (183 m). It includes the area known as the intertidal zone, which lies between the zones of high and low tides.

The organisms that live in this area must withstand a harsh environment exposed to the air, wave action, and tidal currents.

The oceanic zone includes all of the deep ocean. The organisms that live there are divided into two main categories, called plankton and nekton. Plankton are free-floating marine organisms such as algae or jellyfish. Nekton are capable of swimming, such as fish or whales.

The benthic zone is another type of marine ecosystem that exists on the ocean bottom. This can include the shallow water, where coral reefs exist, or the deep, dark ocean. Recently a unique benthic marine ecosystem was discovered that exists in total darkness near hydrothermal vents. These volcanic vents spew out superheated water that is rich in minerals and supports a community of marine organisms. The temperature of the water around hydrothermal vents can be more than 200° F (93° C). The organisms that thrive in this unique ecosystem illustrate the ability for life to exist in extreme environments.

CHAPTER REVIEW

Multiple Choice

1. Which biome exists in the higher latitudes in the zone of permafrost?
   a. tropical rain forest
   b. grassland
   c. coniferous forest
   d. tundra

2. Which biome is exposed to periodic wildfires during the summer?
   a. tropical rain forest
   b. grassland
   c. coniferous forest
   d. tundra

3. Trees that lose their leaves each fall are the principal vegetation in what biome?
   a. deciduous forest
   b. savanna
   c. chaparral
   d. desert

4. These type of biomes are also called tropical grasslands:
   a. deciduous forest
   b. savanna
   c. chaparral
   d. desert

5. The two most important abiotic factors that determine a biome are:
   a. altitude and latitude
   b. temperature and altitude
   c. temperature and precipitation
   d. precipitation and latitude

6. Which type of biome exists along the coast of California?
   a. deciduous forest
   b. savanna
   c. chaparral
   d. desert

7. The marine ecosystem that is periodically exposed to the air and wave action is called:
   a. the intertidal zone
   b. coastal wetland
   c. the oceanic zone
   d. the benthic zone

8. The marine ecosystem that exists from the shoreline to a depth of approximately 600 feet is called:
   a. the coastal wetland
   b. the neritic zone
   c. the oceanic zone
   d. the benthic zone

9. The free-floating organisms that live in the open ocean are known as:
   a. plankton
   b. nekton
   c. catadromous
   d. anadromous

10. Coral reefs and hydrothermal vent communities exist in which type of marine ecosystem?
    a. the coastal wetland
    b. the neritic zone
    c. the oceanic zone
    d. the benthic zone

Matching   *Match the terms with the correct definitions.*

a. terrestrial
b. biomes
c. tundra
d. permafrost
e. droughts

f. biological diversity
g. tropics
h. aquatic
i. marine
j. intertidal zone

k. phytoplankton
l. zooplankton
m. hydrothermal vent

1. _____ A term that refers to anything associated with the oceans.
2. _____ Tiny animals that float freely in water.
3. _____ Another term for a land-based ecosystem, also called a terrestrial ecosystem.
4. _____ A term that refers to land.

5. ____ A type of plankton that uses photosynthesis to gain energy.
6. ____ A term that refers to the area located near the equator.
7. ____ An extended period when little or no precipitation is received by a specific region.
8. ____ Ocean water that seeps through cracks in the sea floor and is superheated by magma that is close to the surface.
9. ____ An aquatic life zone that exists near the shoreline between the area of the highest and lowest tides.
10. ____ Permanently frozen soil.
11. ____ The variety of living species on Earth and their unique genes.
12. ____ A term that describes anything that lives in water.
13. ____ A biome that is found in the higher latitudes, where the temperature is below freezing for most of the year, and supports matlike vegetation.

Critical Thinking

1. Identify the biome in which you live, and describe some of the specific biotic and abiotic factors in your particular biome.

33 The Flow of Energy and Matter Through Ecosystems

ENERGY FLOW WITHIN LIVING SYSTEMS OBJECTIVES

Photosynthesis and Chemosynthesis · Autotrophs and Heterotrophs · Primary Production · Primary and Secondary Consumers · Food Chains and Webs · The Energy Pyramid

After reading this chapter you should be able to:

▶ Identify where most energy on the Earth comes from.
▶ Describe the photosynthesis and chemosynthesis chemical reactions.
▶ Differentiate between autotrophic and heterotrophic organisms.
▶ Describe the process of primary production.
▶ Explain the relationship among producers, primary consumers, secondary consumers, and decomposers in an ecosystem.
▶ Define the terms *herbivore*, *carnivore*, *omnivore*, and *detritivore*.
▶ Draw a diagram of a simple food chain.
▶ Describe the transfer of energy from one trophic level to another in a food pyramid.

BIOGEOCHEMICAL CYCLING OBJECTIVES

Biogeochemical Cycling · Carbon Cycling · Oxygen Cycling · Nitrogen Cycling · Phosphorus Cycling

After reading this chapter you should be able to:

▶ Define the term *biogeochemical cycling*.
▶ Identify the four main biogeochemical cycles on the Earth.
▶ Describe three examples of how carbon moves through the carbon cycle.
▶ Explain the relationship between photosynthesis and respiration in the oxygen cycle.
▶ Describe the pathway by which nitrogen moves from the atmosphere into plants.
▶ Identify the main sources of phosphorus for ecosystems on the Earth.

TERMS TO KNOW

autotrophs

chemosynthesis

heterotrophs

primary production

biomass

herbivores

carnivores

omnivores

detritivores

decomposers

food chain

biogeochemical cycling

respiration

reservoir

limiting factor

INTRODUCTION

The interactions that occur in the world's ecosystems involve the exchange and movement of energy and matter between the living and nonliving worlds. The source of all the energy used in most of the world's ecosystems is the Sun. The pathways through which solar energy moves once it strikes the planet link all living things together. Every living thing on the Earth depends on the flow of energy through ecosystems for survival. The movement of matter through ecosystems is equally important for life to flourish on the Earth. The chemical elements that make up the nonliving world are the building blocks for life. These important molecules and nutrients are continually recycled between the nonliving and living world. Understanding the interactions between matter, energy, and life on the planet reveals the importance of the biosphere as part of the Earth's systems and how life on the Earth has flourished for more than 3 billion years.

33.1 Energy Flow Within Living Systems

PHOTOSYNTHESIS AND CHEMOSYNTHESIS

All life on Earth requires energy to live, and the way that an organism gains energy is vital for its survival. An organism that can derive energy from sunlight or from chemical reactions is called an **autotroph**, which means "self-feeder." Autotrophs use two different processes to gain energy. The first is the process of photosynthesis. Photosynthesis is the chemical reaction by which organisms transform light energy from the sun into stored chemical energy (Figure 33–1). This is accomplished by creating sugars and starches. Photosynthesis is probably the most important chemical reaction on Earth. The photosynthesis reaction takes light energy from sunlight and combines it with carbon dioxide and water to form the sugar glucose, as well as oxygen as a by-product. The oxygen is then released into the atmosphere.

All the oxygen in the atmosphere is the result of photosynthesis. Glucose molecules produced by photosynthesis are then joined together to form long, chainlike molecules called starches. Green plants and phytoplankton are the two main types of organisms that utilize photosynthesis. **Chemosynthesis** is the other process by which autotrophs gain energy (Figure 33–2). Organisms that use chemosynthesis gain energy released from chemical reactions. Many organisms that use chemosynthesis derive their energy from sulfur-containing molecules. This is how bacteria that reside in deep sea hydrothermal vent communities gain their energy. These communities are unique on the Earth because they do not derive their energy from sunlight as most ecosystems do.

AUTOTROPHS AND HETEROTROPHS

Another method by which organisms gain their energy on Earth is the consumption of other organisms. Such a living thing is called a **heterotroph**, which means "other feeder." Heterotrophs use the chemical energy stored in the bodies of other organisms, such as plants and animals, to gain energy. Human beings are heterotrophs; they must consume food to gain energy.

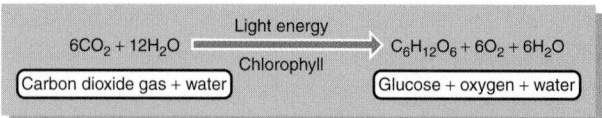

FIGURE 33–1   The photosynthesis reaction combines carbon dioxide and water in the presence of sunlight to form glucose sugar, water, and oxygen.

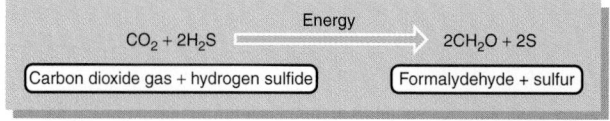

FIGURE 33–2   A chemosynthesis reaction that is used by bacteria near hydrothermal vents deep within the ocean utilizes hydrogen sulfide and carbon dioxide gas to gain energy while producing pure sulfur.

Earth System Scientists

Linus Pauling

Linus Pauling, born in Oregon in 1901, received an education in chemical engineering. Pauling's early work involved the understanding of chemical bonds. In 1939 he published this research in his book *The Nature of the Chemical Bond*, which opened the door to a better understanding of molecular structure. In 1954 his work earned him the Nobel Prize for chemistry. His later research involved the chemistry of living things and their molecular structure. His research helped reveal the structure of the DNA molecule, proteins, and human blood. Pauling also became a proponent of the benefits of vitamin C to the health of the human body. In 1963 Pauling gained another Nobel Prize, this time for his work in helping ban nuclear testing. He is the only person to receive two Nobel Prizes.

CAREER CONNECTIONS

Biophysicist

A biophysicist studies the properties of molecules within organisms. This includes an understanding of their structure and their unique physical and electrical properties. These scientists also study the chemical reactions that are vital to life on Earth, such as photosynthesis and respiration. A biophysicist uses sophisticated laboratory equipment to unlock the secrets of molecules and their interactions, which are important to life. Biophysicists perform experiments and analysis on specific chromosomes and DNA molecules to further understand heredity and genetics. The work of a biophysicist someday might lead to cures for disease and improved health. Biophysicists also are researching ways to safely degrade toxic chemicals and oils that have polluted the environment. Biophysicists must have a college education with an emphasis on chemistry and biology. They can work in academic research, in medicine, or in the environmental sciences.

PRIMARY PRODUCTION

Although it is important to understand how individual organisms gain their energy, it is the flow of energy through entire ecosystems that enables life to exist as it does on our planet. Autotrophic organisms such as plants and algae form the base for energy in all ecosystems. With the exception of the deep sea hydrothermal vent communities, all energy flow in both aquatic and terrestrial ecosystems begins with green plants and algae. These autotrophs convert radiant energy from

FIGURE 33–3 Example of green plants that are the producers for an ecosystem; they convert radiant energy from the Sun into stored chemical energy. (*Courtesy of PhotoDisc.*)

the Sun into stored chemical energy (Figure 33–3). This forms a vital link between the Sun and the rest of the organisms on Earth. Photosynthesizing autotrophs are also called producers because they produce the energy for the entire ecosystem. The amount of chemical energy that an autotroph converts from solar energy by the process of photosynthesis is called **primary production**. Primary production is measured by determining the amount of **biomass** a plant has. *Biomass* is a short term for biological mass, which is the total dry weight of an organism.

PRIMARY AND SECONDARY CONSUMERS

The heterotrophic organisms that consume the producers are called primary consumers. These include all organisms that eat plants or algae as a source of energy. Known as **herbivores**, or "plant eaters," primary consumers come in all shapes and sizes in a specific ecosystem. Many insects are primary consumers in ecosystems around the world. Fish and larger animals such as deer, moose, and cows are also primary consumers, or herbivores that only consume plants (Figure 33–4).

Organisms that consume the herbivores are known as secondary consumers. These organisms are sometimes called **carnivores**, or "meat eaters." Tigers, killer whales, and hawks are all secondary consumers.

FIGURE 33–4   Cattle are examples of primary consumers, also called herbivores, who eat the producers in an ecosystem. (*Courtesy of PhotoDisc.*)

Sometimes an organism can act as both a primary consumer and secondary consumer by eating both producers and herbivores. These organisms are known as **omnivores**, or "all eaters." Humans are omnivores, as are bears and dogs (Figure 33–5). Some ecosystems contain higher-level consumers who eat secondary consumers. These types of organisms are called tertiary consumers. The producers form the vital link between the Sun and the primary consumers in an ecosystem; however, there exists another important category of organisms that helps recycle nutrients in a community. These organisms are called **detritivores**, or **decomposers**, and eat dead organisms (Figure 33–6). Although considered gruesome, detritivores perform an invaluable service to the ecosystem by breaking down, or consuming, the remains of dead organisms. This allows valuable nutrients to be recycled in an ecosystem. If not for the detritivores, things would be quite messy here on Earth. Decomposers are like nature's garbage collectors. Common detritivores include vultures, many types of insects, fungi, and bacteria.

FOOD CHAINS AND WEBS

The specific way that energy flows through a community of organisms in a ecosystem is called a **food chain** (Figure 33–7). The food chain is a series of eating processes by which energy and nutrients flow from one organism to another. A food web is a complex interaction of food chains within a specific ecosystem.

FIGURE 33–5 A brown bear is an upper-level consumer in an ecosystem, also known as an omnivore, who eats both plants and animals. (*Courtesy of PhotoDisc.*)

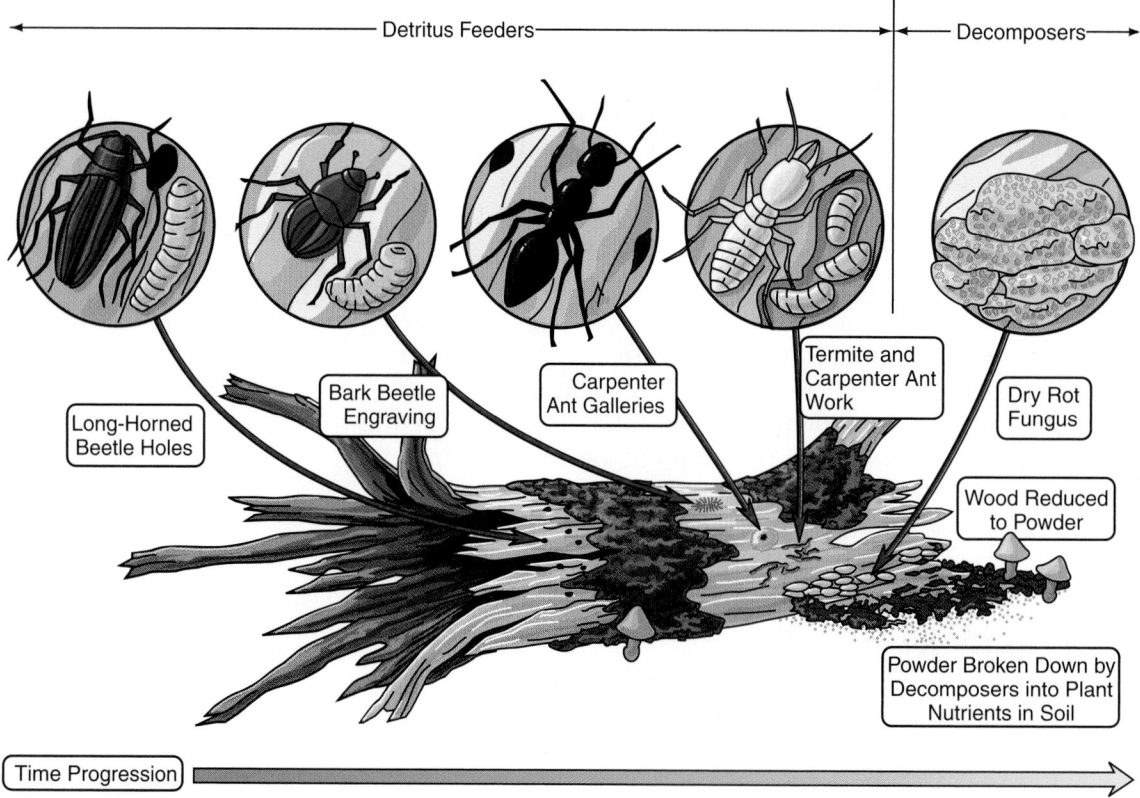

FIGURE 33–6 A variety of organisms act as decomposers, also known as detritivores, which consume dead organisms.

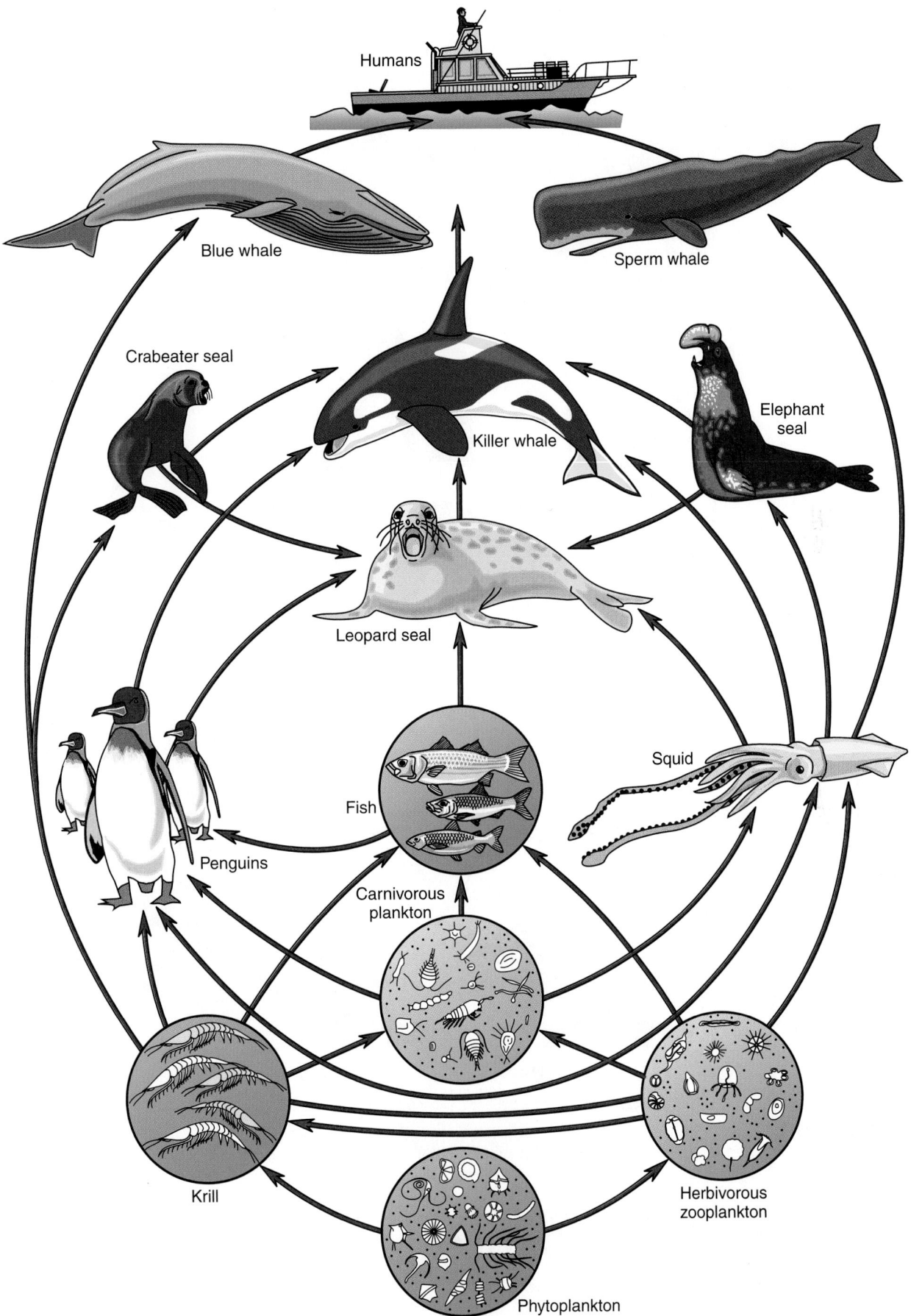

FIGURE 33–7 Interrelated food chains in the ocean form an aquatic food web.

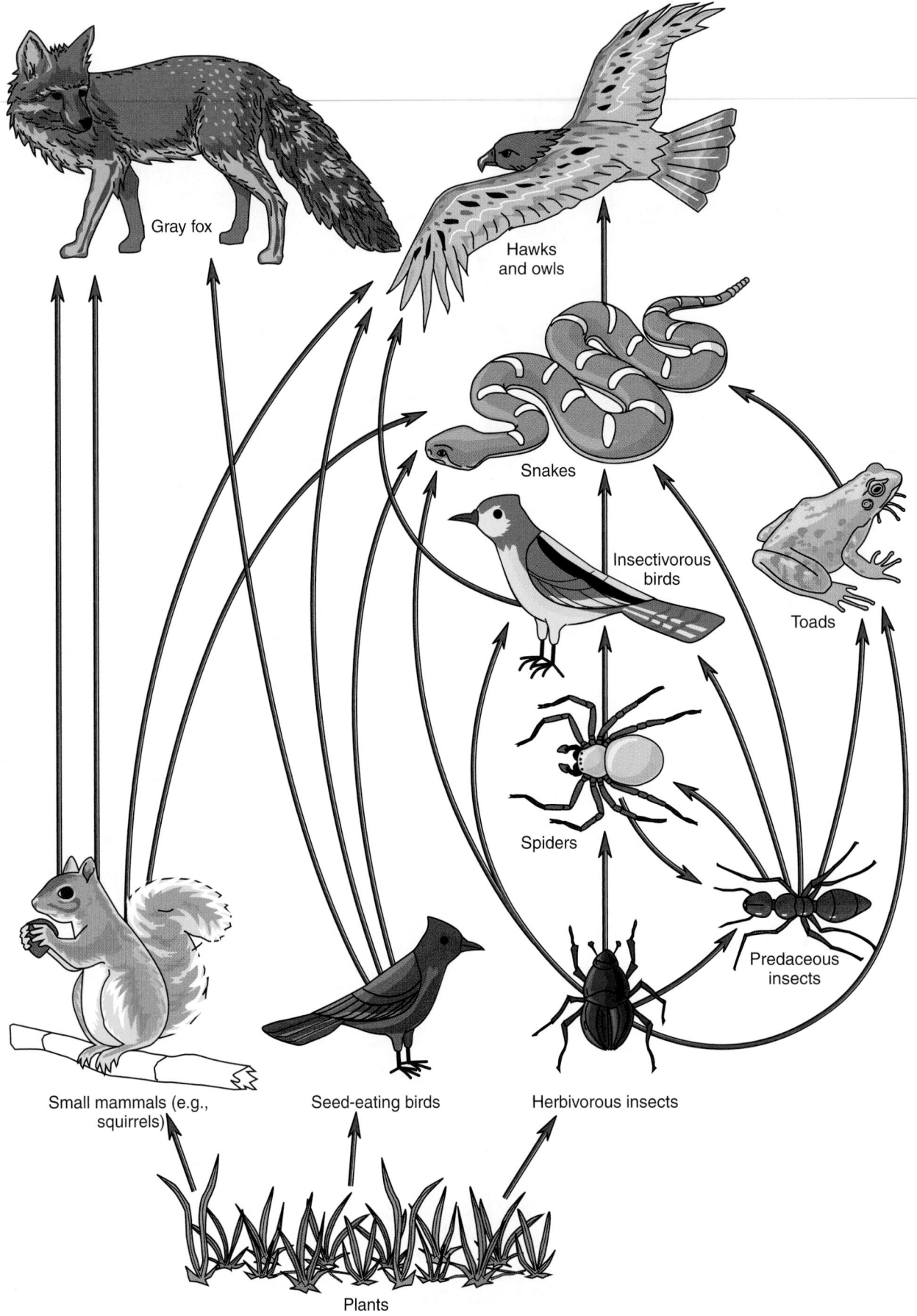

Gray fox

Hawks and owls

Snakes

Insectivorous birds

Toads

Spiders

Predaceous insects

Small mammals (e.g., squirrels)

Seed-eating birds

Herbivorous insects

Plants

FIGURE 33–8 An example of a terrestrial food web.

All ecosystems have their own unique food chains or webs that sustain all the living things in an ecosystem's community (Figure 33–8). All food chains or webs always contain their own unique producers, primary consumers, secondary consumers, and decomposers.

THE ENERGY PYRAMID

The movement of energy through an ecosystem can also be illustrated by the energy pyramid. The energy pyramid is a visual representation of the way energy moves through a food chain. Each step in the food chain, illustrated by the energy pyramid, is called a trophic, or feeding, level. The base of the pyramid is formed by the producers, who take in radiant energy from the Sun and transform it into chemical energy in the form of sugar and starches.

The next level in the energy pyramid is occupied by the primary consumers, who eat the producers. This is the second trophic level. When a primary consumer eats a producer, approximately 10 percent of the total energy contained by the producer is gained by the primary consumer. Almost 90 percent of the total chemical energy contained in the producer is given off as heat when the organism digests, uses, and stores the chemical energy derived from the first trophic level. This "loss" of energy is an important part of the movement of energy through a food chain (Figure 33–9). The energy is really not lost, but it is no longer available for

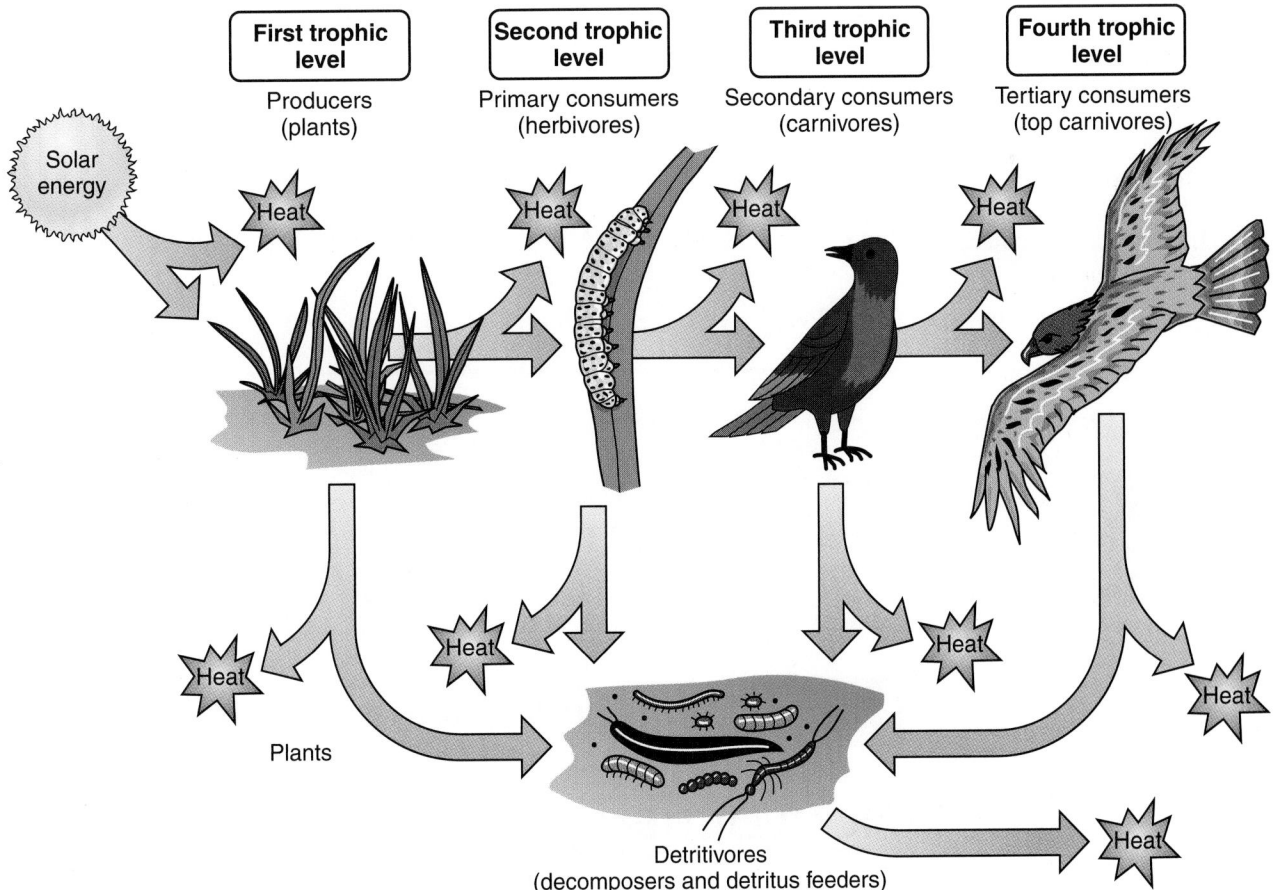

FIGURE 33–9 The movement of energy through a food chain reveals the loss of energy as heat to the atmosphere with each transfer between different trophic levels.

use by organisms in the food chain. Typically when an organism eats something, approximately 90 percent of the energy is given off to the atmosphere as heat.

Above the primary consumer in an energy pyramid is the third trophic level, which is occupied by the secondary consumer. Once again, when the secondary consumer eats the primary consumer, it only gains approximately 10 percent of the total chemical energy of the second trophic level.

The purpose of the energy pyramid is to show how energy moves through a food chain and, more important, how much of the energy in an ecosystem is lost to the atmosphere as heat. Each successive step of a trophic level in a food chain results in a large loss of energy. This is why upper-level consumers must eat large quantities of food to survive. The other important aspect of the energy pyramid is how it illustrates that the Sun forms the base for all energy in an ecosystem. It also shows how the producers act as the important link between the Sun and all other organisms on the Earth.

@ WEB Links

FOR MORE INFORMATION GO TO THESE WEB LINKS:

<http://www.flyingturtle.org/photosyn/photosynth.html>

<http://www.flyingturtle.org/me/pyramid.html>

<http://www.mesa.edu.au/friends/seashores/energy_pyramid.html>

SECTION REVIEW

1. Define the term *autotroph* and provide one example.

2. Describe the difference between chemosynthesis and photosynthesis.

3. Define the term *heterotroph* and provide one example.

4. Define the terms *producer*, *primary consumer*, and *secondary consumer* and explain how energy moves up through a food chain.

5. Provide an example for each of the following: herbivore, carnivore, omnivore, and detritivore.

6. Draw a simple food chain.

7. Approximately how much energy is lost between each trophic level in an energy pyramid?

8. Who was Linus Pauling?

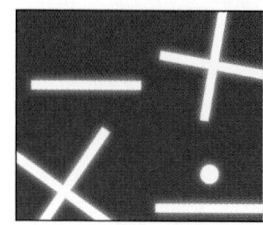

earth math

1) If the first trophic level in a food chain contains 5,000 units of energy, how many units of energy are transferred to the third trophic level?

33.2 Biogeochemical Cycling

BIOGEOCHEMICAL CYCLING

Energy is not the only thing that flows through ecosystems. Important nutrients that are vital to life move through communities and are constantly being recycled. The cycling of nutrients through an ecosystem

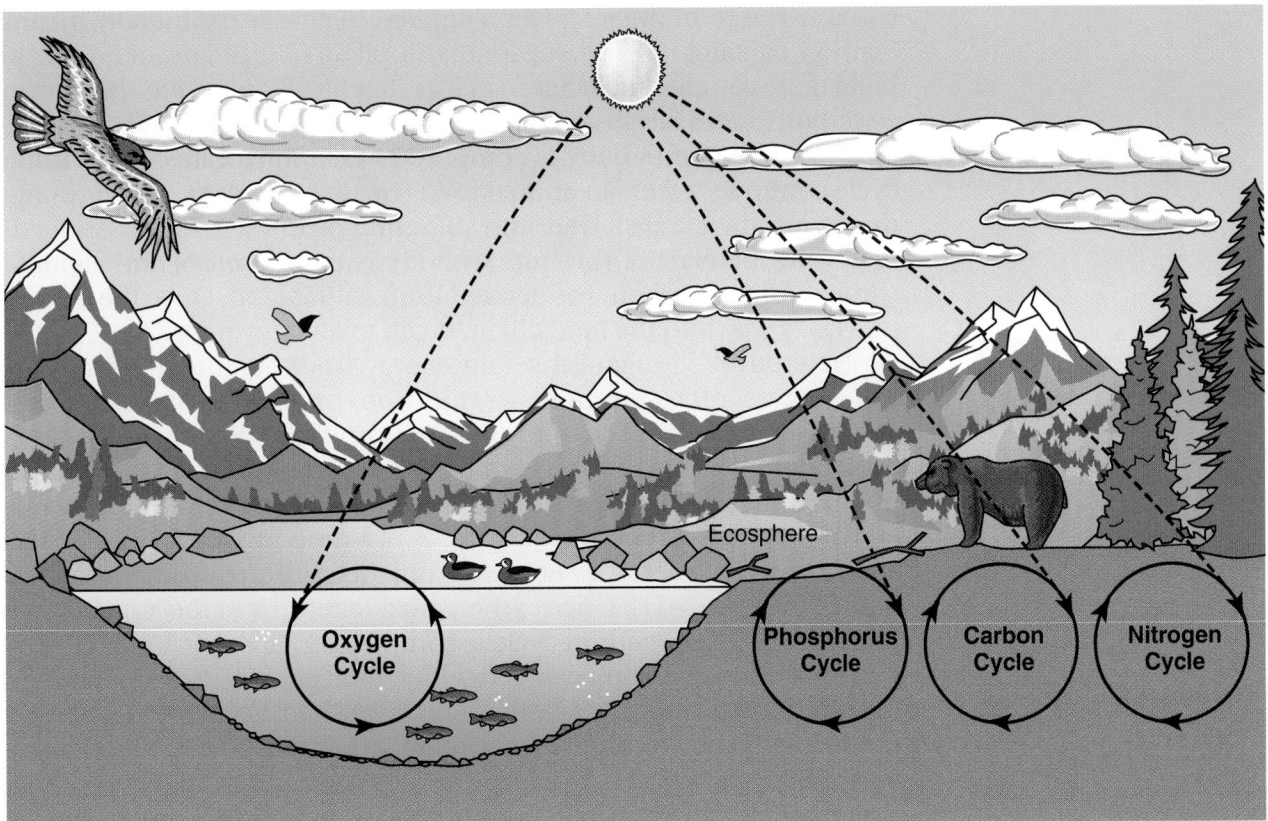

FIGURE 33–10   The four main biogeochemical cycles on the Earth.

is called **biogeochemical cycling**. Biogeochemical cycles move nutrients from the nonliving world into living organisms, and then back again. Without the recycling of nutrients on Earth, life could not exist in its present form. The Earth contains a fixed amount of elements that are required for life. Some of these elements are readily available to organisms, but others are in short supply. Over time, the availability of these important nutrients has reached a careful balance between the living and nonliving world. This makes the understanding of biogeochemical cycles an important part of the Earth's systems. There are four main biogeochemical cycles that play important roles in ecosystems (Figure 33–10).

CARBON CYCLING

The first biogeochemical cycle is called the carbon cycle. Carbon molecules form the base for all life, making the availability of carbon to living things essential. Because a cycle refers to the circular movement of elements from the abiotic world and into the biotic world, there is really no starting point; however, most carbon that finds its way into living organisms comes from the atmosphere. Carbon dioxide gas (CO_2) present in the Earth's atmosphere is used by green plants and algae for photosynthesis. Photosynthesis uses solar energy to take carbon dioxide from the atmosphere and combines it with water to form sugars. A common form of sugar that is a product of photosynthesis is glucose. Glucose is classified as an organic molecule, which means it contains carbon. The term organic, when applied to chemistry, literally means "carbon containing." The sugars that a plant creates are then used to build more complex molecules, such as starches. Starches are also known as carbohydrates because they contain carbon, hydrogen, and oxygen.

Most of a plant's body is composed of carbohydrates. The carbon cycle continues when an animal then consumes a plant. The carbohydrates are then transferred into the body of the herbivore. Approximately 19 percent of the human body is composed of the element carbon. All this carbon was derived from eating food. Once the carbon moves its way into the food chain, it can take many pathways.

Heterotrophic organisms gain energy from organic molecules by the process of respiration. **Respiration** breaks down sugars and starches in the presence of oxygen and produces carbon dioxide as a by-product. The respiration chemical reaction is the exact opposite of photosynthesis. It uses glucose, oxygen, and water to gain energy while also producing carbon dioxide gas. Every time human beings exhale air out of their lungs, they are removing this carbon dioxide from their bodies (Figure 33–11). Once carbon dioxide returns to the atmosphere, the pathway of the carbon cycle is complete.

Another path carbon can take in the food chain is to be eliminated from an organism in its waste. The waste then becomes part of the nonliving soil environment. Once there, the organic molecules that are in waste can be used by decomposers such as fungi or bacteria. Eventually this carbon is also returned to the atmosphere as carbon

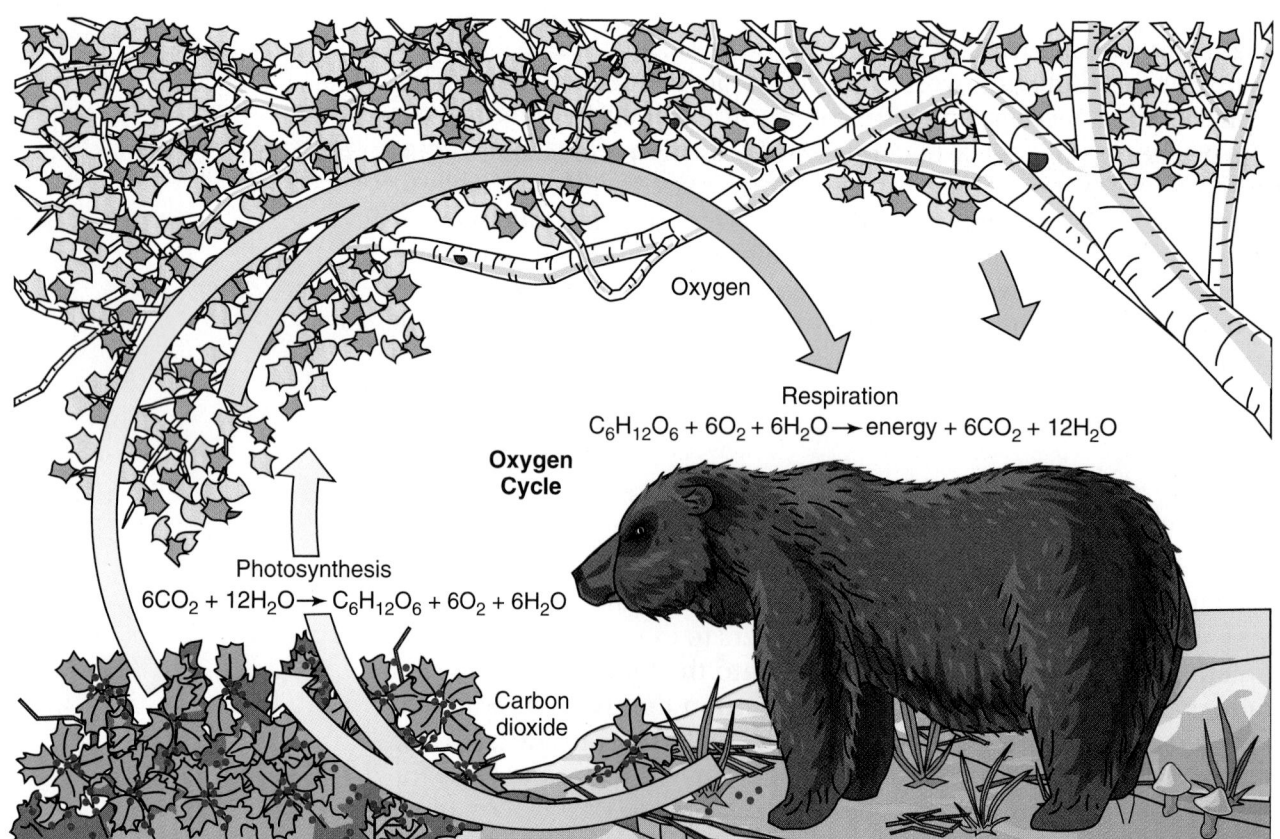

Oxygen

Respiration
$C_6H_{12}O_6 + 6O_2 + 6H_2O \rightarrow$ energy $+ 6CO_2 + 12H_2O$

Oxygen Cycle

Photosynthesis
$6CO_2 + 12H_2O \rightarrow C_6H_{12}O_6 + 6O_2 + 6H_2O$

Carbon dioxide

FIGURE 33–11   The exchange of carbon dioxide between the processes of photosynthesis and respiration sustains life on the Earth.

dioxide. When organic molecules decay, such as in a compost pile, carbon dioxide is produced as a by-product of respiration by decomposers and reenters the atmosphere.

Not all carbon dioxide in the atmosphere is used for photosynthesis; some of it finds its way into the bodies of organisms that reside in the oceans. These marine animals take carbon dioxide from the atmosphere and combine it with calcium to form hard limestone shells. Clams, mussels, and coral are all examples of marine animals that build protective shells from calcium carbonate, commonly called limestone (Figure 33–12). Over time these organisms die and their shells settle to the bottom of the world's oceans. This forms deep sediments of calcium carbonate that eventually form large layers of limestone rock. Limestone sediments store carbon in rocks for millions of years. This is also known as a **carbon reservoir**. A reservoir is anything that is used to store something. Over time, as a result of plate tectonics, the limestone may become exposed at the Earth's surface once again. Once there, it is weathered and the carbon finds its way back into the atmosphere in the form of carbon dioxide gas once again. Some limestone rock can be subducted underneath a tectonic plate, and the carbon it contains is blasted back into the atmosphere in a volcanic eruption. Volcanic eruptions can add millions of tons of carbon dioxide gas into the atmosphere in a short period.

An alternate path that carbon can take through an ecosystem occurs when the bodies of plants and animals are buried deep in the

FIGURE 33–12 Marine organisms that build shells from calcium carbonate are an important part of the carbon cycle. (*Courtesy of PhotoDisc.*)

Earth for millions of years. These carbon-containing organisms are then exposed to the great heat and pressure below the Earth's surface. This causes chemical changes that transform the long-dead organisms into what we call fossil fuels. Common fossil fuels include oil and coal. Oil is the remains of once living plankton that collected at the bottom of the ocean and became buried by sediments. Coal is the dead remains of plants that were buried in swamps millions of years ago.

All fossil fuels are also known as hydrocarbons, because they are mostly composed of hydrogen and carbon. When fossil fuels are removed from deep within the Earth by human activity and are then burned, the carbon that was locked in the Earth for millions of years is released back into the atmosphere as carbon dioxide gas. When something is burned it also called combustion. Fossil fuels act as a reservoir for carbon, which in the past 100 years has been used as an energy source and is causing an imbalance of carbon dioxide in the Earth's atmosphere. Many scientists believe this is leading to increased temperatures around the planet, which may be causing global warming.

Part of the carbon cycle also involves the creation of methane gas (CH_4). Methane is a hydrocarbon molecule that is produced by anaerobic bacteria. *Anaerobic* means without oxygen. Anaerobic bacteria can survive only without the presence of oxygen. They produce methane gas as a by-product of their feeding process. Many herbivores, such as cows, contain anaerobic bacteria in their digestive tracts. These bacteria help digest the tough grasses, while also producing methane. Another source of methane is the mud of rice paddies in Asia. Anaerobic bacteria that reside there release methane into the atmosphere. No matter which pathway carbon takes through the environment, the carbon cycle is an important aspect of many of the Earth's systems (Figure 33–13).

OXYGEN CYCLING

The movement of oxygen through ecosystems is an important biogeochemical cycle (Figure 33–14). Oxygen is another vital element for life on Earth. All heterotrophs on Earth require oxygen for respiration. Oxygen is the most abundant element in the Earth's crust, composing approximately 45 percent of the lithosphere. Oxygen is also the second most abundant gas in the atmosphere, with a concentration of approximately 21 percent. This important element also makes up about 63 percent of the human body. Some oxygen is combined with other elements such as silicon, iron, or aluminum to form many of the Earth's minerals and rocks. The water molecule, which is one of the most abundant molecules on Earth, is composed of one oxygen atom and two hydrogen atoms.

One of the most important interactions of the oxygen cycle occurs between the photosynthesis and respiration reactions. Photosynthesis takes in carbon dioxide gas, water, and sunlight to yield simple sugars, water, and oxygen. Respiration then uses the oxygen produced by plants and combines it with simple sugars and water to yield energy, water, and carbon dioxide. This relationship forms a vital link between plants and animals on Earth. At one time in the Earth's past, there was no oxygen in the atmosphere. It took the photosynthetic action of ancient

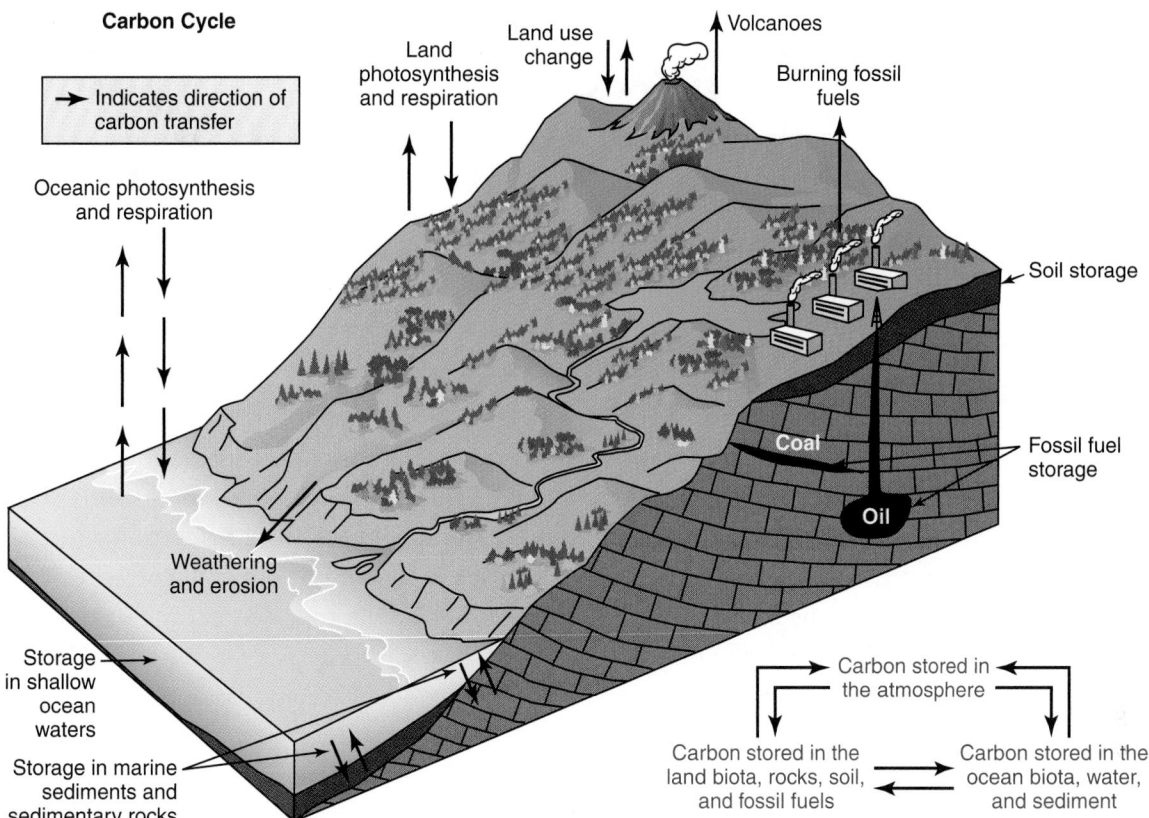

FIGURE 33–13 The storage and movement of carbon through the environment is known as the carbon cycle.

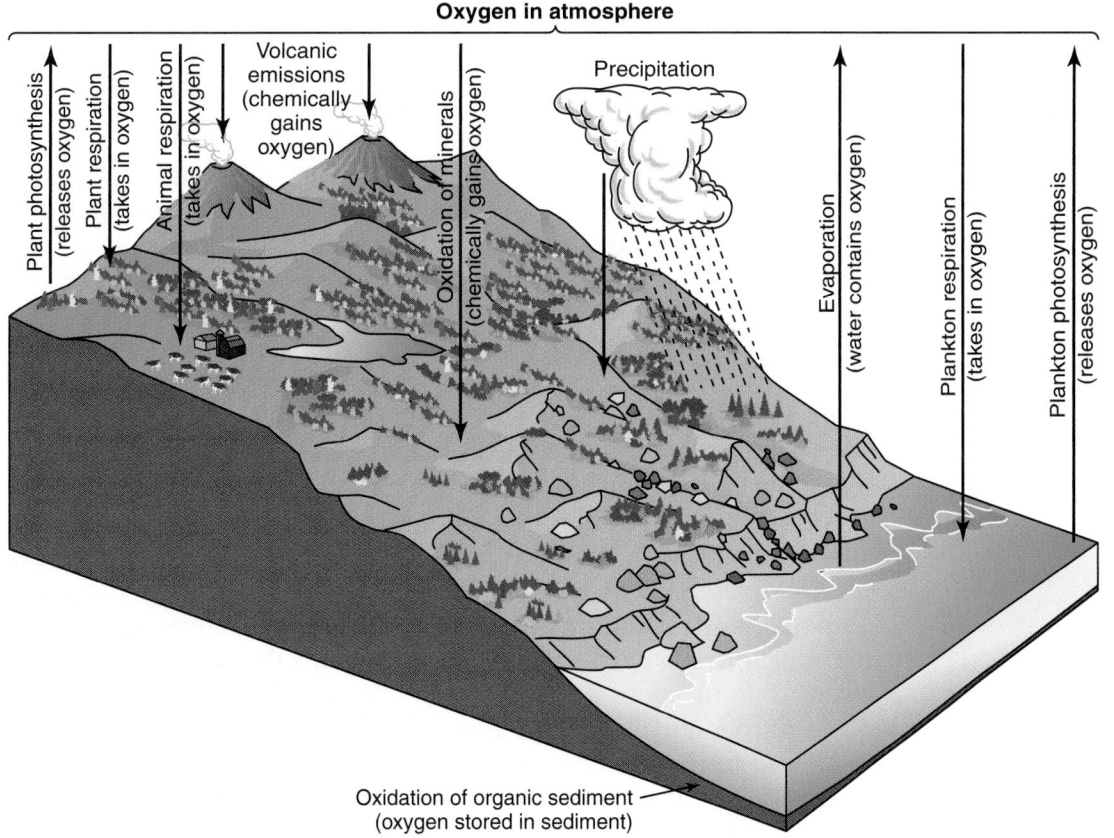

FIGURE 33–14 The oxygen cycle.

Earth System Scientists

Roger Revelle

Roger Revelle was born in Seattle, Washington, in 1901. He earned his college degree in geology and later studied oceanography. He received his doctorate for his study of the sediments of the Pacific Ocean. Revelle next became interested in studying the global carbon cycle, especially the role of the oceans in this important biogeochemical cycle. As a result of his research on the carbon cycle, he began to notice that global levels of carbon dioxide were rising steadily. His research him to write a groundbreaking scientific paper that proposed that the increasing levels of carbon dioxide gas were the result of burning fossil fuels. This broke open the concept of global warming and the effects of human technology on global climate. As a result of his research, Revelle's career turned to working with world governments and helping them accept the fact that global warming was indeed a worldwide problem. Revelle concluded that global warming would lead to a melting of the polar ice caps and therefore cause sea levels to rise. He also worked on the problems of deforestation and its effect on global carbon dioxide concentration. The latter part of his career involved the applications of science and technology to food production.

algae to fill the atmosphere with oxygen to its current level. Oxygen can also be dissolved in water, where it is used by marine organisms for respiration.

The ozone layer high in the stratosphere is made up of oxygen. Ozone gas is composed of three atoms of oxygen (O_3). It acts as a protective barrier that blocks harmful ultraviolet radiation from striking the Earth's surface. The cycling of oxygen from the biotic world into the abiotic world and back again is another important aspect of the biosphere.

NITROGEN CYCLING

The third biogeochemical cycle is called the nitrogen cycle. Nitrogen is an important element that is part of the DNA molecule, which is responsible for the replication of living cells. Nitrogen is also an important component of protein molecules. Approximately 5 percent of the human body is composed of nitrogen. The source of nitrogen for the world's ecosystems is the atmosphere. Earth's atmosphere is composed of 78 percent nitrogen. The nitrogen gas that fills the atmosphere is in a diatomic form (N_2). The term diatomic means that it is composed of two atoms of nitrogen.

The nitrogen cycle begins when microscopic bacteria located in the soil and in the root systems of specialized plants combine atmospheric nitrogen with other atoms to form nitrogen compounds. This process is called nitrification, and it produces nitrogen-containing molecules such as nitrates and ammonia. These nitrogen compounds can then be taken up by the root systems of plants to be used to make proteins. The plants that harbor these specialized bacteria in their root systems are called legumes (Figure 33–15). Small nodules on the roots of legumes contain the nitrifying bacteria that convert atmospheric nitrogen into plant-available nitrogen. These can then be used to form proteins and other compounds within plants. Common legumes include clover, beans, peanuts, and alfalfa. Legumes are often used in agriculture to add nitrogen to the soil, and they act as natural fertilizers.

Once plants take up the nitrogen that the bacteria produce, it is then available for other organisms in the food chain (Figure 33–16). All the proteins and other nitrogen-containing molecules in our bodies were once part of plants. Animals produce waste that contains nitrogen that is expelled from the body. This returns nitrogen compounds back into the environment, where they are decomposed by the detritivores. Some bacteria convert these nitrogen compounds back into diatomic nitrogen that reenters the atmosphere. These bacteria, called denitrifying bacteria, are also found in the soil. Some human activities, such as the burning of fossil fuels, cause atmospheric nitrogen to combine with oxygen to produce compounds called nitrogen oxides. These compounds can mix with water in the atmosphere to form nitric acid. This is the also known as acid precipitation, which has become one of the worst forms of air pollution.

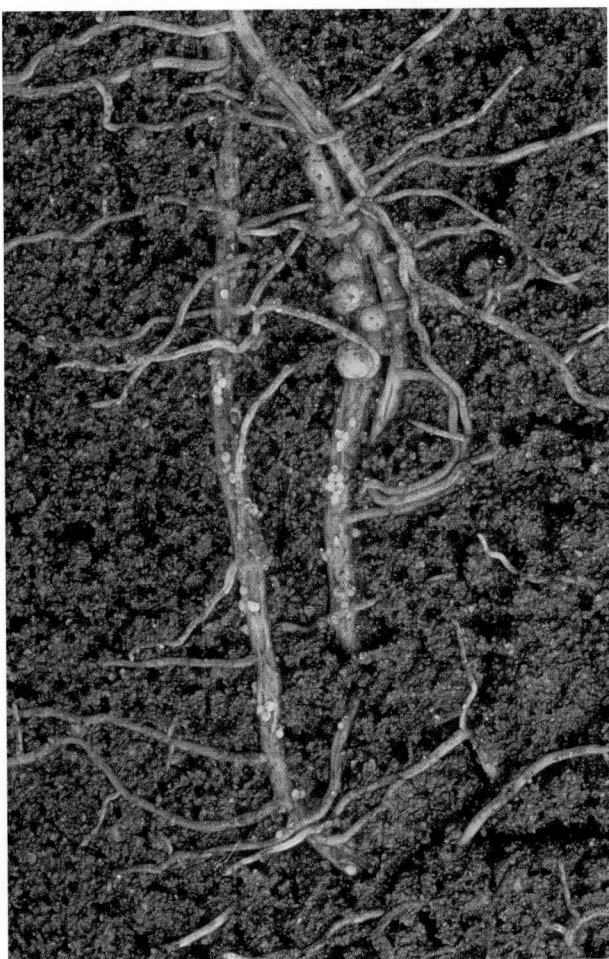

FIGURE 33–15 Legume nodules on the roots of a soybean plant contain bacteria that convert atmospheric nitrogen into nitrogen compounds that can be used by plants. (*Courtesy of USDA-ARS.*)

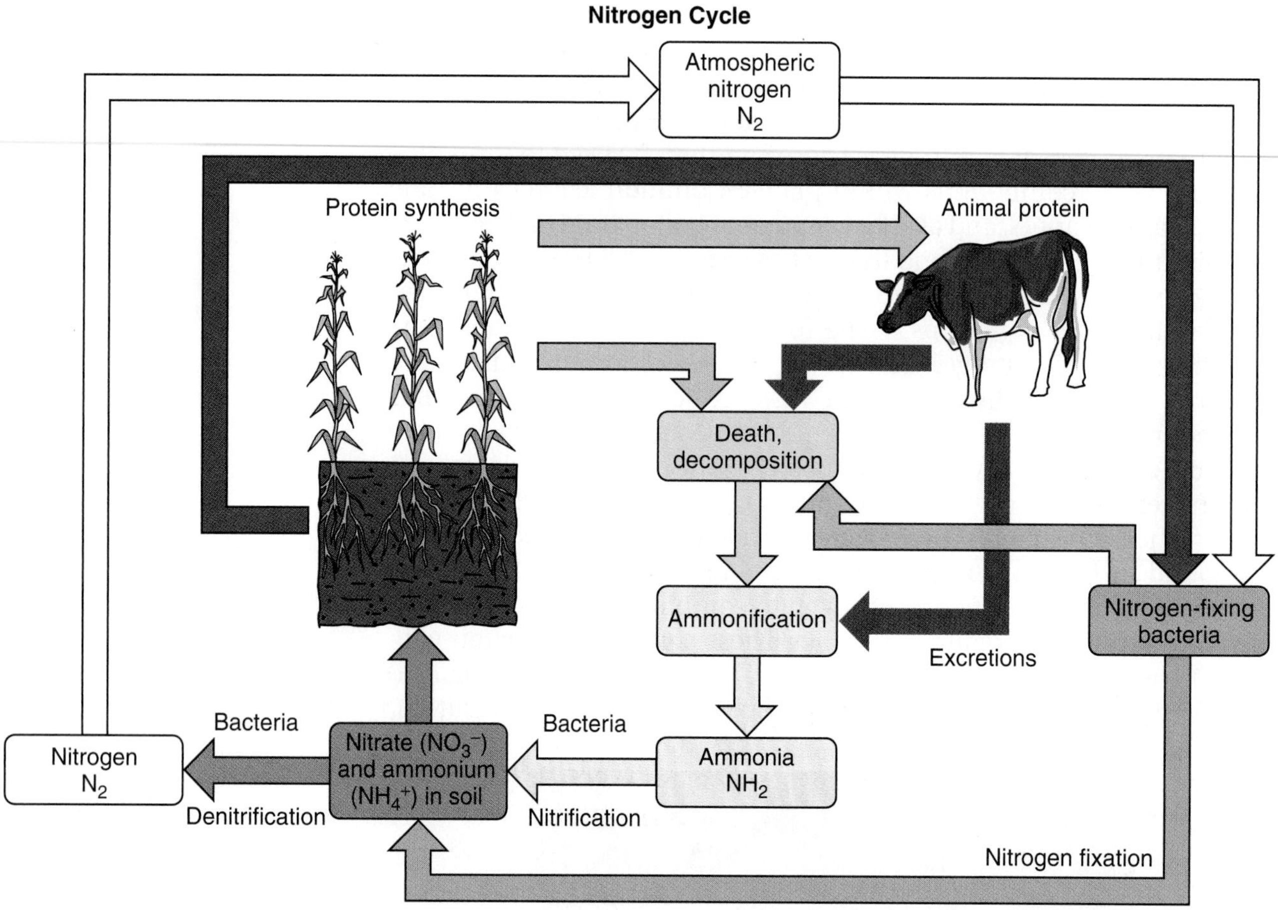

Nitrogen Cycle

FIGURE 33–16   The nitrogen cycle. (*Courtesy of USDA-ARS.*)

CAREER CONNECTIONS
Biochemist

Biochemists study the chemistry of all living organisms. Their work includes an understanding of the chemical processes that take place in the body that are responsible for growth, reproduction, metabolism, and heredity. Biochemists also help to understand the cause and spread of disease and illness in the human body. Current research in biochemistry involves the use of living organisms to perform specific tasks. This is called biotechnology, and it is one of the most exciting aspects of modern science. Biochemists are also searching for ways to produce new drugs or to improve food sources. These scientists work in three major areas: medicine, agriculture, and nutrition. The main goal of all biochemists is to further understand the complex chemistry of living organisms. Biochemists need a college education in both chemistry and biology. Career opportunities are available in private industry or in academic research.

PHOSPHORUS CYCLING

The final biogeochemical cycle is the phosphorus cycle (Figure 33–17). Phosphorus is an important nutrient that is needed by plants. It is also part of the DNA molecule. Individual cells use phosphorus-containing molecules as an energy source. Unlike the other biogeochemical cycles, the major source of phosphorus is not found in the atmosphere, but rather in rocks. Phosphate-containing rocks that become exposed at the Earth's surface become weathered and begin to break down. This is the main source of phosphorus for the ecosystems of the world. Plants take up the phosphorus minerals and use them for their body functions. Plants are then eaten by other organisms in a food chain, and the phosphorus is transferred. Animal waste contains a high amount of phosphorus and helps to recycle this important element back through the food chain. In many ecosystems, phosphorus is in short supply; it is therefore known as a **limiting factor**. A limiting factor is something that limits the productivity of an ecosystem. As a result of human activity, which includes waste disposal and the use of phosphorus-containing fertilizers, phosphorus is entering aquatic ecosystems in higher levels than normal. This causes a rapid growth of aquatic plants and algae, which use the phosphorus as an important nutrient. The result is called an algal bloom, which chokes waterways with the overgrowth of algae and other aquatic plants.

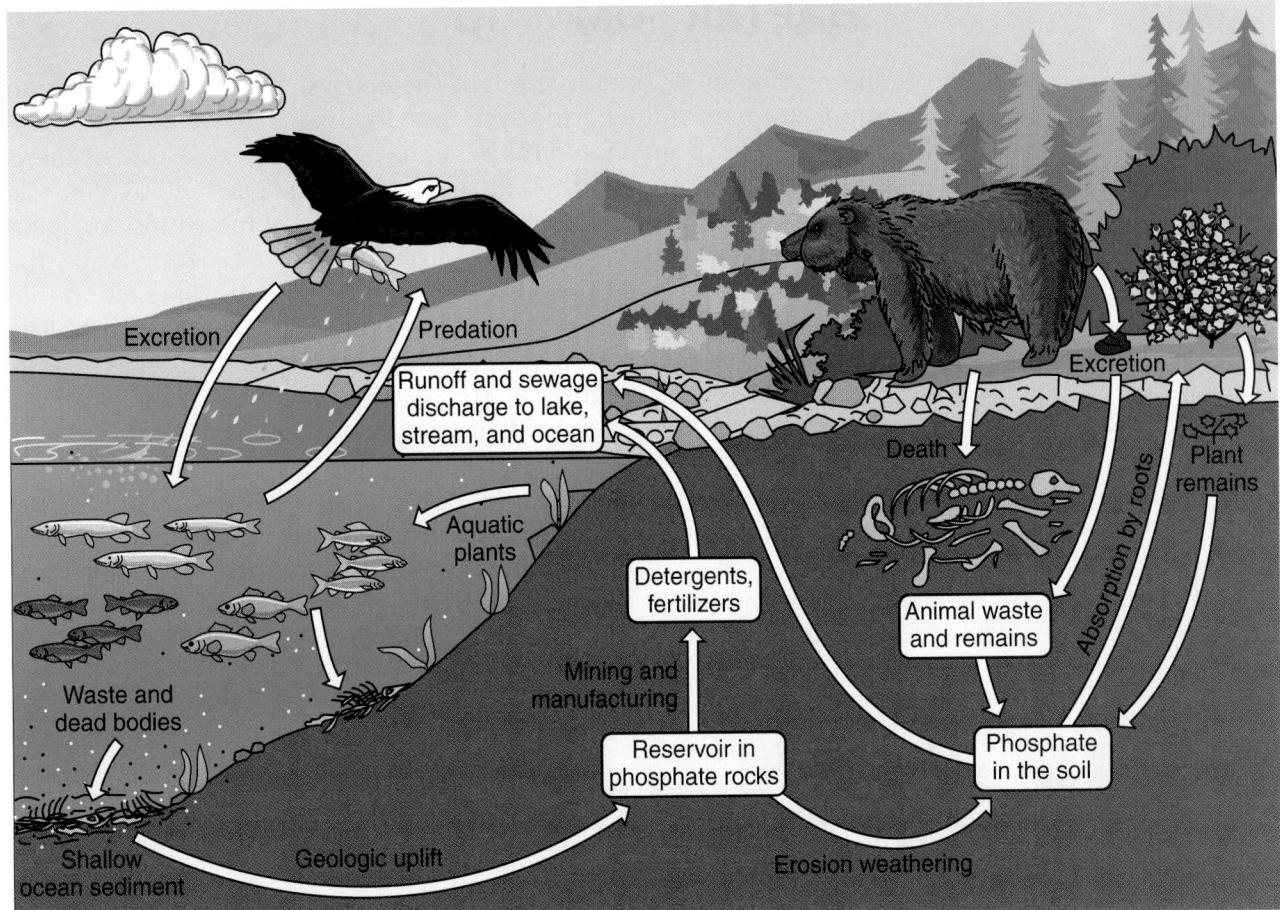

FIGURE 33–17 The phosphorus cycle.

FOR MORE INFORMATION GO TO THESE WEB LINKS:

<http://observe.arc
.nasa.gov/nasa/earth
/hydrocycle/hydro1
.html>

<http://library.thinkquest
.org/11226/>

<http://www.earth.nasa
.gov/science/Science
_ecosystems.html>

Although the carbon, oxygen, nitrogen, and phosphorus cycles make up the four main biogeochemical cycles on Earth, there are many other elements and nutrients that also travel through ecosystems. Without the recycling of nutrients through the food chains of the world, and their movement from the abiotic environment to the biotic environment, life could not exist on Earth as we know it. Following the pathways that particular elements take through an ecosystem illustrates the complexities that exist in the Earth's systems and reveals the careful balance that has evolved over time between living things and their nonliving environment.

SECTION REVIEW

1. Define the term *biogeochemical cycle*.
2. Draw a simple diagram of the carbon cycle.
3. Draw a simple diagram of the oxygen cycle.
4. Draw a simple diagram of the nitrogen cycle.
5. Draw a simple diagram of the phosphorus cycle.
6. Who was Roger Revelle?

CHAPTER SUMMARY

The movement of energy through the ecosystems of the world is an important part of the Earth's systems. Organisms derive energy in two principal ways, from photosynthesis and chemosynthesis. Photosynthesis uses solar energy and carbon dioxide to create sugars and oxygen as a by-product. All green plants and algae use photosynthesis to gain energy. Photosynthesis is the way by which most ecosystems on the Earth derive their energy. Chemosynthesis is a chemical reaction that gains energy from the breakdown of specific molecules. This is the way that deep sea hydrothermal vent communities derive their energy without access to sunlight.

Organisms that produce their own energy by these two processes are called autotrophs, or "self-feeders." Another way that organisms derive energy on the Earth is by consuming other organisms. These type of living things are called heterotrophs, or "other feeders." The amount of chemical energy that is created by autotrophs is called primary production. It is measured in the amount of biomass produced by an organism. Autotrophs are also known as producers in an ecosystem because they produce food.

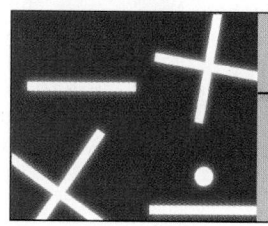

earth math

1) If approximately 19 percent of the human body is composed of carbon, how much carbon does an average adult human weighing 150 lb contain?

Organisms that consume the producers are called primary consumers. Because they consume plants, the primary consumers are also called herbivores. Other organisms that eat the primary consumers are called secondary consumers. These animals are known as carnivores because they eat meat. Organisms that consume both plants and animals, such as humans, are called omnivores. Some ecosystems have tertiary consumers who eat the secondary consumers; these are also known as upper level consumers. Another important aspect of an ecosystem is the decomposers. These organisms consume waste and dead organisms and are called detritivores.

The specific movement of energy through an ecosystem by a series of eating processes is called a food chain. Many interrelated food chains are known as food webs. An energy pyramid is used to illustrate the way that energy is used in a specific food chain. It is composed of a series of feeding levels called trophic levels. The movement of energy from one trophic level to another results in the loss of energy from a food chain as heat to the atmosphere. Energy pyramids also reveal the important link between the Sun and all living things within an ecosystem.

The recycling of matter within ecosystems is another important aspect of the Earth's systems. The Earth has a fixed amount of chemical elements that can be used by organisms. These elements form molecules, act as nutrients for organisms in ecosystems, and are continually recycled between the living and nonliving world. This is called biogeochemical cycling. There are four main biogeochemical cycles on the Earth: carbon cycle, oxygen cycle, nitrogen cycle, and phosphorus cycle. The way that these nutrients move through the environment and their constant reuse allow for life to flourish on the Earth.

CHAPTER REVIEW

Multiple Choice

1. Most energy on the Earth is derived from:
   a. ecosystems
   b. producers
   c. the Sun
   d. autotrophs

2. An organism that makes its own food is called:
   a. a secondary consumer
   b. an autotroph
   c. a heterotroph
   d. a decomposer

3. Bacteria in hydrothermal vent communities deep in the ocean use which process to gain energy?
   a. chemosynthesis
   b. primary production
   c. photosynthesis
   d. nitrification

4. Combining carbon dioxide with water and sunlight to produce glucose sugar is an example of:
   a. chemosynthesis
   b. respiration
   c. photosynthesis
   d. nitrification

5. The amount of biomass that an ecosystem produces is called:
   a. chemosynthesis
   b. primary production
   c. photosynthesis
   d. nitrification

6. An organism that consumes only plants is called:
   a. an omnivore
   b. a herbivore
   c. a carnivore
   d. a decomposer

7. The bacteria, fungi, and insects that eat waste and dead organisms are known as:
   a. omnivores
   b. herbivores
   c. carnivores
   d. decomposers

8. Approximately how much energy is given off to the atmosphere as heat between trophic levels in a food pyramid?
   a. 10%
   b. 30%
   c. 50%
   d. 90%

9. The movement of matter between the living and nonliving world is called:
   a. the food chain
   b. biogeochemical cycling
   c. the energy pyramid
   d. a food web

10. The source of most carbon in the carbon cycle is:
    a. the hydrosphere
    b. rocks in the Earth's crust
    c. the atmosphere
    d. fossil fuels

11. The process of gaining energy by breaking down sugars in the presence of oxygen is called:
    a. photosynthesis
    b. respiration
    c. chemosynthesis
    d. nitrification

12. Which geochemical cycle uses limestone rock and fossil fuels as a reservoir?
    a. the carbon cycle
    b. the nitrogen cycle
    c. the oxygen cycle
    d. the phosphorus cycle

13. The main source of phosphorus for the phosphorus cycle is:
    a. the hydrosphere
    b. rocks in the Earth's crust
    c. the atmosphere
    d. fossil fuels

14. The process by which bacteria convert atmospheric nitrogen into plant-available forms is called:
    a. photosynthesis
    b. respiration
    c. chemosynthesis
    d. nitrification

15. Which biogeochemical cycle is linked to global warming?
    a. the carbon cycle
    b. the nitrogen cycle
    c. the oxygen cycle
    d. the phosphorus cycle

16. The limiting factor in most ecosystems is associated with which biogeochemical cycle?
    a. the carbon cycle
    b. the nitrogen cycle
    c. the oxygen cycle
    d. the phosphorus cycle

17. Which of the following plants is not a legume that helps fix nitrogen in the soil?
    a. grass
    b. clover
    c. alfalfa
    d. peanuts

Matching   *Match the terms with the correct definitions.*

a. autotrophs
b. chemosynthesis
c. heterotrophs
d. primary production
e. biomass

f. herbivores
g. carnivores
h. omnivores
i. detritivores
j. decomposers

k. food chain
l. biogeochemical cycling
m. respiration
n. reservoir
o. limiting factor

1. ____ A classification of organisms that must consume other organisms to gain energy, such as humans.
2. ____ A classification of organisms that eat both plants and animals.
3. ____ A type of organism that produces its own food by photosynthesis, such as a plant or algae, or by chemosynthesis, such as certain bacteria.
4. ____ A specific nutrient that is lacking in an ecosystem and limits the growth of organisms.
5. ____ A method of deriving energy from the breakdown or formation of organic compounds.
6. ____ The model pathway that energy and matter take through an ecosystem by a series of eating processes.
7. ____ A storage place for something.
8. ____ A type of animal that only eats plants.
9. ____ An organism that breaks down and decays dead organisms or waste.
10. ____ The chemical process by which carbohydrates are broken down in the presence of oxygen to derive energy and produce carbon dioxide.
11. ____ Meat-eating organisms.
12. ____ The process by which plants use photosynthesis to convert solar energy into chemical energy that is stored in plant material.
13. ____ A type of organism that consumes dead and decayed organisms or waste.
14. ____ The natural recycling of elements between the nonliving world and the living world.
15. ____ The total dry weight of an organism.

Critical Thinking

1. Explain the differences and similarities between a naturally occurring food web and a human-created agricultural food chain.
2. In your opinion is human activity a natural or artificial process? Explain your answer.

34

Biological Succession

OBJECTIVES

Primary Succession · Primary Succession and Pioneer Communities · Secondary Succession

After reading this chapter you should be able to:

▶ Define the term *biological succession*.

▶ Differentiate between primary and secondary succession.

▶ Define the term *pioneer community*.

▶ Identify areas on the Earth where primary succession occurs.

▶ Provide an example of primary succession.

▶ Provide an example of secondary succession.

INTRODUCTION

The interactions between a community of organisms and the environment in which they live is a **dynamic** system. Over time, ecosystems experience gradual changes in both their abiotic and biotic factors. The constant change that ecosystems experience is barely perceptible to human beings, but on a geologic time scale these changes are quite apparent. The geologic forces of weathering, erosion, and plate tectonics, along with the dynamic nature of life, cause gradual changes to occur in all aspects of the Earth's systems. These natural changes are continually reshaping the landscape and providing the regeneration necessary to sustain life all over the planet.

BIOLOGICAL SUCCESSION

One of the key scientific principles that helps explain the changes ecosystems go through over time is called **biological succession**. Biological succession is the gradual replacement of one community of organisms by another in a slow, orderly, and predictable manner. Scientists have observed the process of biological succession in many parts of the world and now understand it as a natural force of change on the Earth. Biological succession is divided into two categories: primary succession and secondary succession.

PRIMARY SUCCESSION AND PIONEER COMMUNITIES

Primary succession occurs when living organisms first begin to inhabit a part of the Earth. As time goes by, communities of organisms begin to flourish and are slowly replaced by other communities of organisms. An example of primary succession can be seen in the wake of a retreating glacier (Figure 34–1). The land that was once covered by a thick ice sheet becomes exposed to the elements when the ice melts away as the glacier retreats. Over time, the barren rocks that were

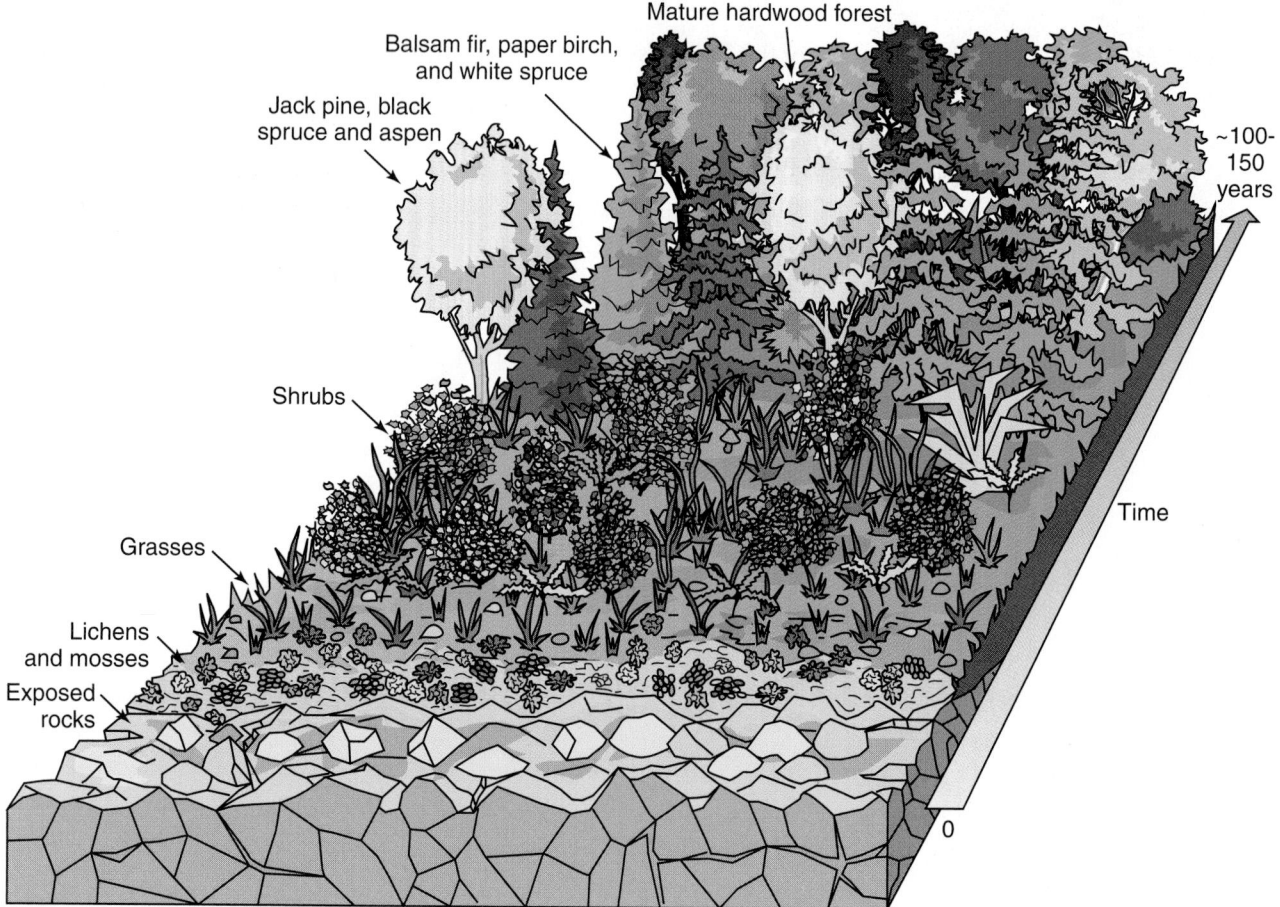

FIGURE 34–1 An example of the stages of primary succession on bare rock exposed by a retreating glacier.

exposed by the melting glacier are colonized by a **pioneer community**. A pioneer community consists of a rapidly growing group of organisms that can reside in a place where no life presently exists. Examples of pioneer communities include microorganisms such as bacteria, mosses, and lichen.

Lichen are actually composed of two organisms, algae and a fungus, that maintain a symbiotic relationship (Figure 34–2). The algae use the process of photosynthesis to create food for themselves and their companion fungus. In return, the fungus secretes a weak acid that breaks down rock into usable minerals that the algae require. When lichen establish themselves on barren rock, they slowly create an environment that becomes suitable for other organisms. Eventually, a thin soil layer forms over the rocks as the lichen colony breaks it down and mixes it with the decaying organic material of dead lichen. When the soil becomes thick enough, seeds and spores brought to the area by birds or on the wind can become established. Eventually the area can support hardy grasses, ferns, and small shrubs. This makes way for other organisms to inhabit the area, such as insects, rodents, birds, and migrating grazing animals. As more time passes, the community of organisms creates a rich environment that may begin to support trees. Over a period of a few thousand years, a mature forest ecosystem can become established where once there was no life at all. This is how the process of primary succession works.

FIGURE 34–2 Lichen growing on bare rocks are an example of a pioneer community that can live in harsh environments where no other life exists.

Earth System Scientists

Gifford Pinchot

Gifford Pinchot was born in Connecticut in 1865. He graduated from Yale University and then attended the French Forestry School. While in France, he learned about the selective cutting of trees and responsible forest management. Upon his return to the United States, Pinchot was made the head of the Division of Forestry, which would later become the U.S. Forest Service. His job involved the management of all of the U.S. forest land. Under Pinchot's leadership, the Forest Service began the process of managing forests as a valuable natural resource. He realized that forests were vital to the U.S. economy and that they should be managed scientifically. Pinchot created management schemes that would ensure the continued availability of forest resources and help to create millions of acres of national forest. His techniques prevented the overharvesting of trees and regulated the use of forest land. Pinchot, along with President Theodore Roosevelt, helped form the conservation movement of the early twentieth century. Later in his life Pinchot became a two-term governor of Pennsylvania.

Much of North America was once covered in thick ice sheets that were more than 1 mi (1.6 km) thick. Then as the glaciers retreated approximately 11,000 years ago, the process of primary succession transformed the landscape into what it looks like today. Although the abiotic environment plays an important role in primary succession, the action of the living organisms that form communities does much of the work. The interactions that occur between organisms and their environment are the driving force for change that causes succession.

Retreating glaciers are not the only force that can lead to primary succession. Shifting rivers or shorelines can expose sandbars out of the water, which quickly become inhabited by pioneer communities. Volcanic islands in the oceans are also creating new landforms that can be shaped by primary succession. A new island is being formed off the Hawaiian Island chain in the south Pacific. Some day this new island will break the ocean's surface and be transformed into a tropical paradise, much like its sister islands, by the process of primary succession.

SECONDARY SUCCESSION

The other type of biological succession that occurs on Earth is known as **secondary succession**. Secondary succession is the gradual replacement of one community of organisms by another in a slow, predictable manner in an area where life has already flourished (Figure 34–3). The common cause of secondary succession is usually some type of **catastrophic** event such as a volcanic eruption, forest fire, or flood. Human activities have also interrupted the landscape to the point at which secondary succession can occur.

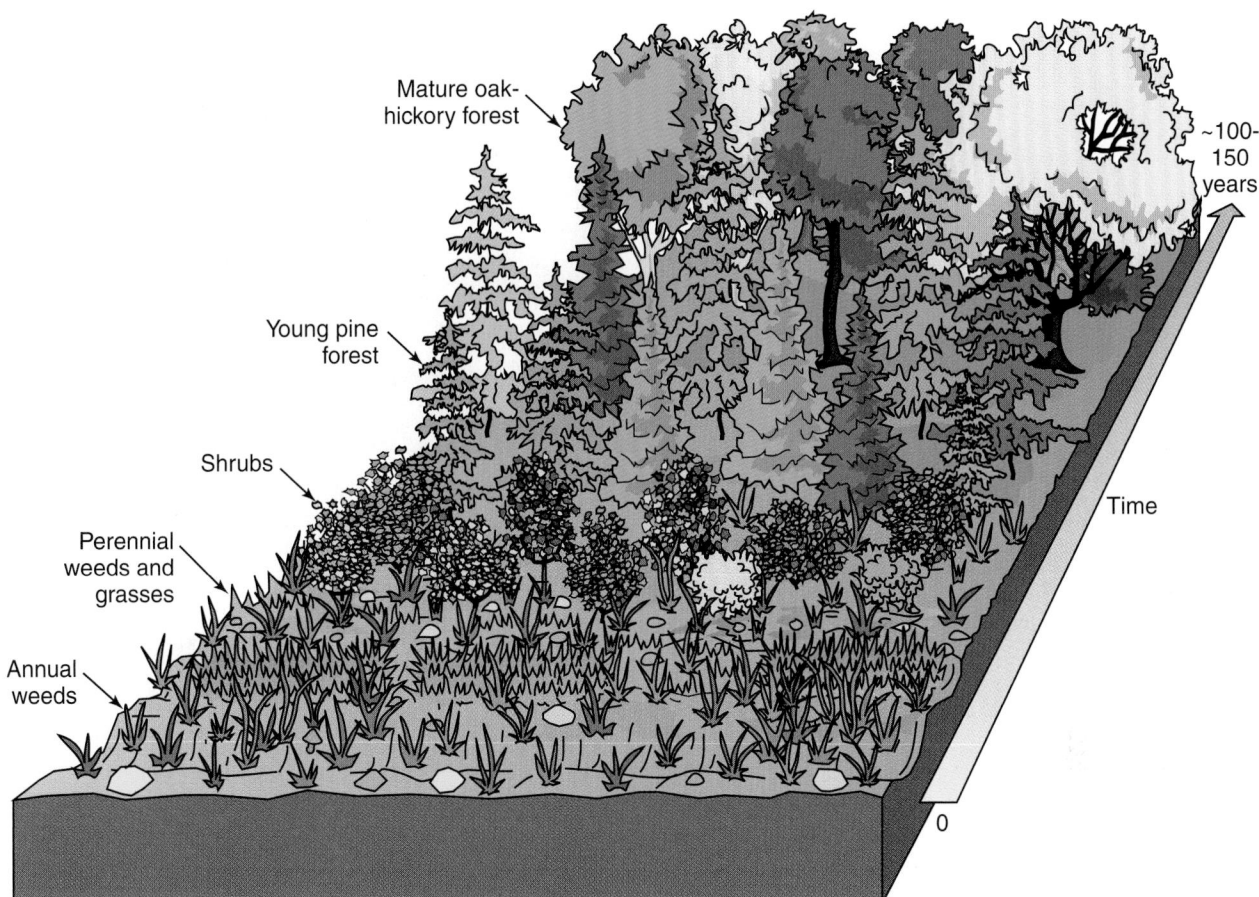

FIGURE 34-3   An example of the stages of secondary succession that occurred after a farm field was abandoned.

When a forest fire completely burns away a forest ecosystem and leaves behind nothing but burnt debris, secondary succession begins almost immediately. Seeds and spores carried on the wind **germinate** in the charred soil and begin to sprout. This leads to the establishment of grasses and ferns that quickly overtake the area. Eventually the grasses give way to sprouting trees, which shade out the grass. Small shrubs may also become established in the burnt remains of the forest. Soon the area that was once completely devastated harbors life again. As the trees grow taller, birds, insects, and mammals begin to inhabit the area. Approximately 70 to 100 years after the fire, the forest ecosystem completely reestablishes itself.

Secondary succession is an important way that the Earth heals itself after devastating events. It truly shows how strong the force of life is on our planet. Scientists received a firsthand look at the process of secondary succession after the catastrophic volcanic eruption of Mount St. Helens in Washington State. The eruption of Mount St. Helens in 1980 destroyed thousands of acres of forest land and killed millions of aquatic and terrestrial organisms (Figure 34–4). After the eruption, the landscape was completely void of life. The blast of the volcano incinerated everything in its path and created devastating mudflows that choked lakes and streams.

Not long after the disaster occurred, primary succession began. Seeds and insects blown in on the wind from surrounding areas began to

FIGURE 34-4 The catastrophic destruction caused by the eruption of Mount St. Helens in Washington State is an example of a disturbed landscape. (*Courtesy of P. Frenzen, USDA Forest Service.*)

FIGURE 34-5 The same disturbed landscape near Mount St. Helens shown in Figure 34-4. Here, 11 years after the volcanic eruption, the regeneration of the forest as a result of biological succession is evident. (*Courtesy of P. Frenzen, USDA Forest Service.*)

inhabit the region once again. As time went by, the once black and gray charred remains of the area were transformed into the lush green colors of plant life. Today the landscape around Mount St. Helens has developed into a healthy ecosystem once again as a result of the powers of secondary succession (Figure 34-5).

Many parts of the northeastern United States have also experienced secondary succession over the past 100 years. Shortly after the American Civil War, the western frontier was opened up to settlers, which created a mass migration of people to the Great Plains. Many of these settlers abandoned their farms in the north for the much flatter, more forgiving soil of the Midwest. Over time the abandoned farms of the northeast gave way to secondary succession. The fields that lay fallow eventually returned to the mixed hardwood deciduous forests that make up much of the landscape of New York and New England (Figure 34-6). As you walk through these forests today, you can still find the remains of old stone fences that once divided the farm fields. Most of the trees that inhabit these forests are the result of secondary succession.

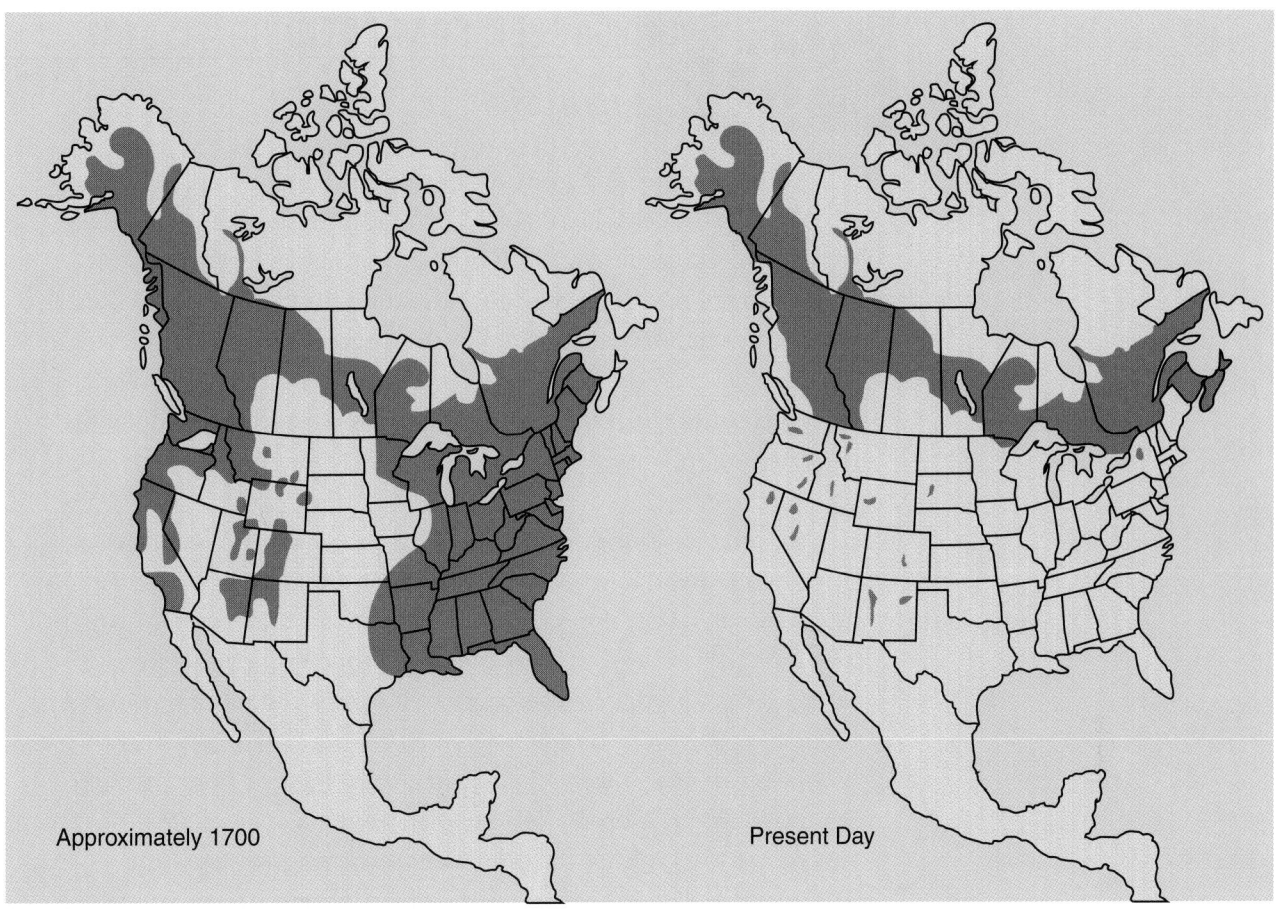

FIGURE 34-6 A map showing the comparison between the distribution of old growth forests of North America in 1700 and the present. This reveals that most of the forests that grow in the United States today are the products of secondary succession.

Biological succession is the way that the Earth allows life to reclaim **disturbed areas**. It is a force that is driven by living things, that paves the way for other life forms to flourish in an area where once they could not. Understanding the process of biological succession has become an important management tool for reclaiming many disturbed areas. Whether it be old abandoned lots sprouting new growth in the middle of large cities or the sounds of birds in the once silent valley near Mount St. Helens, biological succession gives life the ability to flourish in the harshest of environments and paves the way for future communities.

REVIEW

1. Define the term *primary succession*.
2. What is a pioneer community?
3. Provide an example of primary succession.
4. Define the term *secondary succession*.
5. Provide an example of secondary succession.
6. Who was Gifford Pinchot?

@ WEB Links

FOR MORE INFORMATION GO TO THIS WEB LINK:

<http://jimswan.com /111/succession /succession.htm>

CAREER CONNECTIONS
Forester

Foresters manage forests for both public and private land. They develop and carry out specific management techniques to sustain forest resources. Both private and public forest lands are managed for use in outdoor recreation, timber use, watersheds, wildlife habitat, and other forest resources such as maple sugar production. Forest management includes conducting forest inventories, creating maps, planting trees, studying wildlife, fire prevention, improving trails and roads, monitoring for disease and insects, and overseeing timber cutting. Foresters can work for private industry or for the state and federal government. Their work involves a love for the outdoors in all types of weather. There are managed forest lands in all parts of North America and throughout the world that employ foresters. Foresters need a college degree in forestry and natural resource management. Often forest technicians work with foresters to help carry out specific management techniques. Forest technicians can gain on-the-job experience with a professional forester or in a high school vocational conservation program. Many 2-year technical colleges offer instruction for careers as a forest technician.

CHAPTER SUMMARY

Biological succession is the gradual replacement of one community of organisms by another in a slow, predictable manner. It is the natural way that Earth continues to renew itself and allows for life to flourish in disturbed areas. There are two main types of biological succession: primary and secondary. Primary succession takes place in a location where no life has existed previously. This is often associated with retreating glaciers, volcanic eruptions, and shifting bodies of water. The first organisms to inhabit an area during primary succession are known as a pioneer community. These are often hardy, rapidly growing

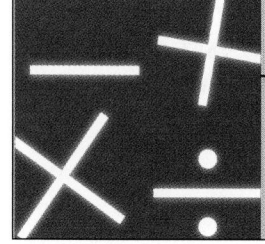

earth math

1) If approximately 20,000 hectares of forest were destroyed by the Mount St. Helens eruption, what were the approximate amount of acres destroyed (1 hectare = 2.47 acres)?

species that can survive in harsh conditions. Eventually the pioneer community alters the area to the point at which other species, such as grass, trees, and shrubs, can grow. Over time the area that was once void of life supports a healthy ecosystem.

The other type of succession, called secondary succession, occurs in an area where life already exists. These areas are usually disturbed in some way by a natural or human-induced event. Forest fires commonly destroy areas and allow secondary succession to take over. The area that was affected by the fire eventually supports rapidly growing grasses and small plants. Over time, small trees and shrubs take over the area, and eventually the forest returns to its former state. This process can occur in as little as 70 to 100 years. Many of the forests of the northeastern United States are the result of secondary succession, which took place when farm fields were abandoned after the Civil War. Understanding and using the processes of biological succession is often useful as a management technique to restore damaged areas.

CHAPTER REVIEW

Multiple Choice

1. The area inhabited by organisms shortly after a glacier has retreated is an example of:
   a. primary succession
   b. secondary succession
   c. pioneer communities
   d. forestry management

2. A rapidly growing, hardy population of organisms that colonize an area for the first time is known as:
   a. primary succession
   b. secondary succession
   c. a pioneer community
   d. forestry management

3. The regeneration of farm fields into a forest is called:
   a. primary succession
   b. secondary succession
   c. a pioneer community
   d. forestry management

4. Which of the following areas is not usually associated with primary succession?
   a. volcanoes in the ocean
   b. retreating glaciers
   c. a sand bar
   d. abandoned farm fields

5. Which organism would most likely begin the process of biological succession in a disturbed area?
   a. trees
   b. shrubs
   c. birds
   d. lichen

Matching   *Match the terms with the correct definitions.*

a. dynamic
b. biological succession
c. primary succession

d. pioneer community
e. lichen
f. secondary succession

g. catastrophic
h. germinate
i. disturbed areas

1. _____ The gradual replacement of one community of species by another in a slow, predictable manner.
2. _____ A symbiotic organism that consists of an algae and a fungus that live on rocks and trees.
3. _____ Energetic, always changing or moving.
4. _____ Ecosystems or parts of ecosystems that have been destroyed or disrupted.
5. _____ The introduction of a community of organisms into an area where life has not existed before.
6. _____ A great and sudden disaster.
7. _____ The process that a plant seed undergoes when it begins to grow.
8. _____ The slow, gradual, and predictable replacement of one community of organisms by another in a specific area where life has already existed.
9. _____ A group of organisms that populate an area on the Earth where no organisms have lived before.

Critical Thinking

1. Explain how you think the Earth would be affected if biological succession did not occur.
2. What role have humans played in the process of biological succession in your community?

35

Classification of the Living World

OBJECTIVES

Taxonomy · The Kingdom Monera · The Kingdom Protista · The Kingdom Fungi · The Kingdom Plantae · The Kingdom Animalia · Invertebrate Animals · Vertebrate Animals

After reading this chapter you should be able to:

▶ Describe the taxonomic system used to classify organisms on the Earth.

▶ Explain how organisms are divided into specific taxonomic groups.

▶ Identify the five main taxonomic kingdoms used to classify organisms on the Earth.

▶ Describe some of the characteristics of organisms within the kingdom Monera and provide an example of one of these organisms.

▶ Describe some of the characteristics of organisms within the kingdom Protista and provide an example of one of these organisms.

▶ Describe some of the characteristics of organisms within the kingdom Fungi and provide an example of one of these organisms.

▶ Differentiate between vascular and nonvascular plants that make up the kingdom Plantae and provide an example of each.

▶ Differentiate between invertebrate and vertebrate organisms within the kingdom Animalia.

▶ Identify three invertebrate organisms within the animal kingdom.

▶ Identify five vertebrate organisms within the animal kingdom.

INTRODUCTION

The biosphere on Earth is home to more than 5 million different species of living things. The different shapes, sizes, and life cycles of all the organisms alive today illustrate the great diversity of life on our planet. Studying the fossil record has revealed an amazing variety of organisms that once lived on the Earth. As humans explored more of the planet, different forms of life were continually being discovered. To better classify organisms that compose the biosphere, a universal classification system was required. By formally grouping together all living things, scientists have discovered that all the creatures on the Earth share related characteristics. This has led to the remarkable story of the evolution of life on our planet. Classifying organisms on the Earth is also important for identifying the role they play in ecosystems. Ecologists recognize that the greater the diversity of life in an ecosystem, the healthier it is. Appreciating the variety of life on the Earth and understanding the role each organism plays in the biosphere is an important aspect of the science of Earth's systems.

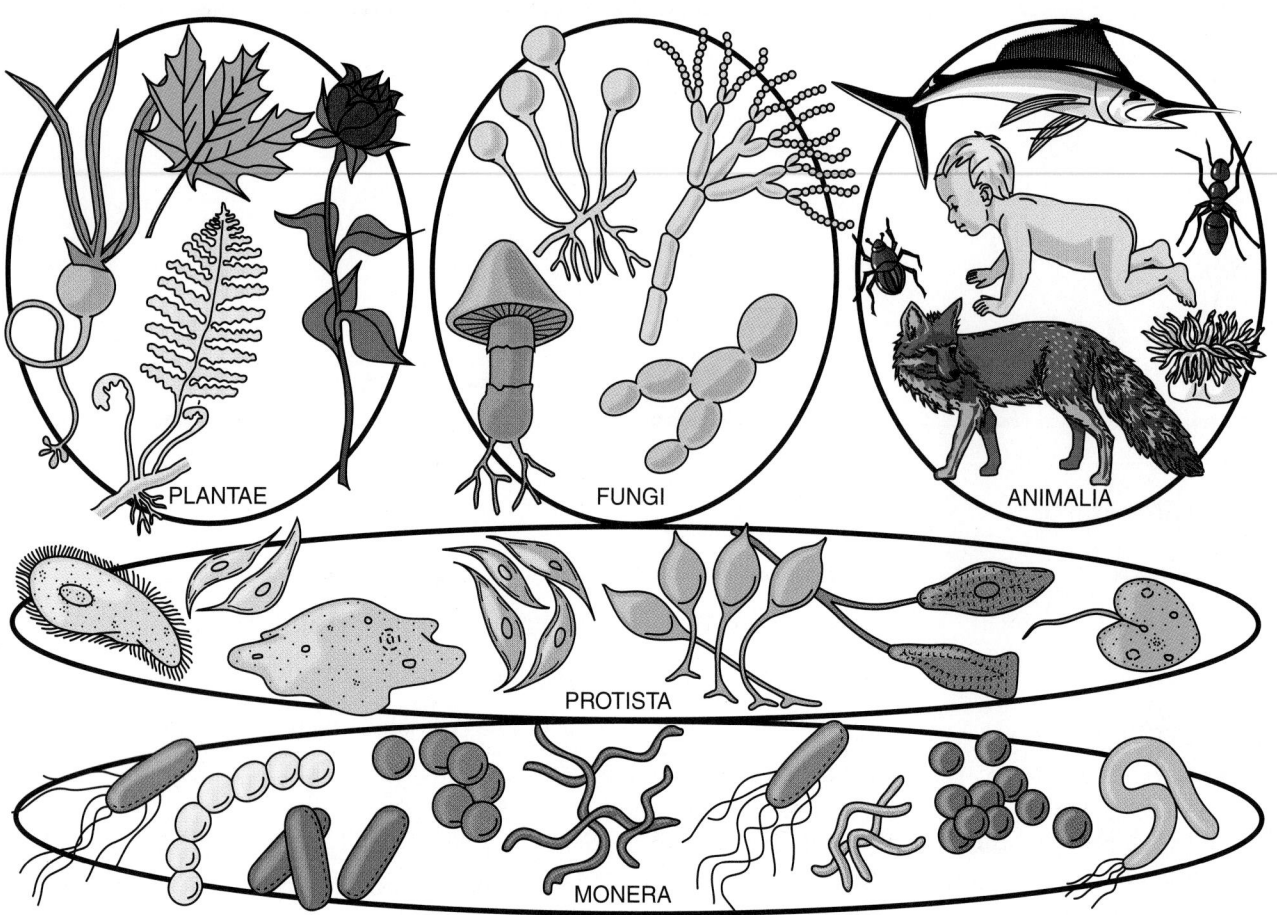

FIGURE 35–1 The five kingdoms used to classify organisms on the Earth.

TAXONOMY

Organisms on Earth are categorized into groups that possess similar **biological characteristics**. Today all the living things on the Earth are grouped into five broad categories also known as kingdoms. The classification of different organisms is called **taxonomy**. It was first formally conceived by Carolus Linnaeus in the eighteenth century. He created a system for classifying animals that is known as the binomial method. *Binomial* means "two names," and this system uses two Latin words that represent the genus and species of a unique organism.

The taxonomic system that Linnaeus created is based on seven levels of classification that groups together similar organisms. This taxonomic system includes classification within a kingdom, phylum, class, order, family, genus, and species. When Linnaeus created his taxonomic key, he had only two kingdoms: the plants and the animals. Today five kingdoms are used to classify organisms: Monera, Protista, Fungi, Plantae, and Animalia (Figure 35–1).

THE KINGDOM MONERA

The kingdom Monera includes all single-celled organisms, such as bacteria and blue-green algae, that do not have a cell nucleus. A nucleus is a membrane that surrounds a cell's DNA molecules. The organisms that

Earth System Scientists

Carolus Linnaeus

Carolus Linnaeus was born in Sweden in 1707. Linnaeus became interested in the study of plants at a young age. He then went on to study and eventually teach botany. In 1735 he published a method for the formal classification of plants based on the anatomy of their flowers. In 1753 he developed his binomial system of nomenclature, which identified plants by using a specific genus and species name. His system of classification became known as the binomial system, which he applied to animals in 1758. The system that Linnaeus devised to classify plants and animals is still in use today. During his life, Linnaeus also wrote many books on the classification of the natural world, botany, and his travels in Europe.

are classified as Monera lack a nucleus, which allows their DNA to freely move throughout the cell. Bacteria are one of the most abundant life forms on the Earth; they are found living virtually everywhere. The human skin alone is home to more than 500 million bacteria. Bacteria colonize deep in the soil and at the bottom of the ocean. Many bacteria act as important decomposers in the world's ecosystems and are responsible for the recycling of nutrients in a food chain. Bacteria are also an important part of the nitrogen cycle. They convert atmospheric nitrogen into forms that plants can use. Many bacteria live inside the intestines of animals and help break down food. Some bacteria, however, can be deadly. Many kinds of bacteria can cause infections and sickness in both plants and animals.

Blue-green algae, also known as cyanobacteria, are also part of the kingdom Monera. These single-celled organisms produce their own food by the process of photosynthesis, although they are biologically different from plants and algae. Cyanobacteria can live in some of the harshest environments found on the Earth. Cyanobacteria grow in hot springs that reach 170° F (77° C) and are also found alive in the ice of Antarctica (Figure 35–2).

Scientists believe that cyanobacteria are the oldest living things found alive today. Fossils of cyanobacteria colonies called stromatolites are the remains of the oldest living things that have ever been identified. Stromatolites are believed to have been the primary form of life on Earth more than 3.5 billion years ago. Today stromatolites can be found alive off the coast of Australia, making them the oldest living things on the planet. The cyanobacteria that lived more than 3 billion years ago may have been the source of oxygen in the atmosphere. Some researchers believe that cyanobacteria may one day be discovered on other planets or moons in our solar system. The planet Mars or Europa, one of Jupiter's moons, may be home to cyanobacteria. Scientists at the National Aeronautics and Space Administration (NASA) are designing remotely operated space vehicles to search these places for signs of life beyond the Earth.

FIGURE 35–2 Brightly colored mats of bacteria growing in scalding water around a hot spring are examples of organisms in the kingdom Monera. (*Courtesy of PhotoDisc.*)

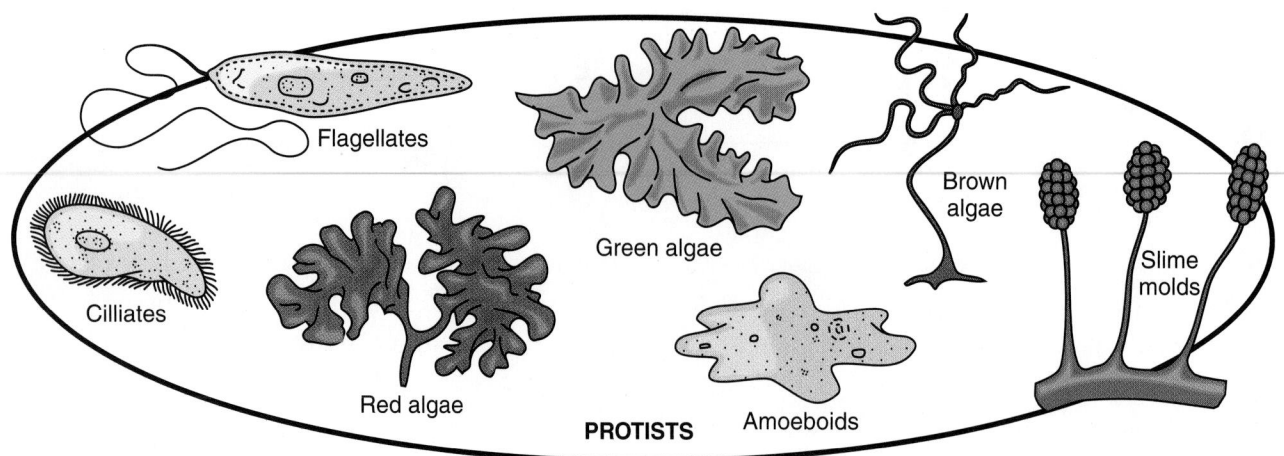

Flagellates

Brown algae

Green algae

Slime molds

Cilliates

Red algae

PROTISTS

Amoeboids

FIGURE 35-3 Examples of organisms in the kingdom Protista.

THE KINGDOM PROTISTA

The kingdom Protista includes all single-celled organisms that have a cell nucleus (Figure 35–3). These organisms can be both photosynthetic and heterotrophic. Most plankton that live in water are protists. Amoebae are also protists, which float through the water like small blobs and consume their food by completely surrounding it. Diatoms are also protists, which live in the world's oceans. These free-floating, single-celled organisms use photosynthesis to produce food from sunlight and construct protective shells made from silica.

Diatoms are an important part of the food chain in the open oceans. When diatoms die, their microscopic shells settle to the bottom of the ocean and collect over time to form sediments that are rich in silica. This is known as a **siliceous ooze**, which is found mainly near the equator and surrounding Antarctica. Both these locations support high populations of diatoms.

Another important protist is the single-celled algae, which form the base for many aquatic food chains around the world. These microscopic organisms convert sunlight into chemical energy stored in sugars and starches. They are also responsible for the production of atmospheric oxygen. Some biologists prefer to classify algae as part of the Plant kingdom because of their similar methods of photosynthesis; however, in this text they are considered protists.

Brown algae, commonly known as seaweed, include some of the most complex colonies of protists. Brown algae grow along the coast of the world's oceans and are used as a food by human beings. Other algae, such as red algae, also reside in the ocean and can produce **neurotoxins**. Neurotoxins are deadly poisons that affect the nervous systems of animals. Large populations of red algae, also called a red tide, can kill thousands of fish and be harmful to humans.

Protists also include the slime molds. These brightly colored, slimy colonies of protozoans grow in the damp debris on the forest floor. You can often find these protists when you look under a rotting log. Often mistaken for a fungus, slime molds actually move along the ground at extremely slow rates. Some protists can cause disease and sickness in animals. When these protists enter an organism's bloodstream, they can be deadly. Malaria is caused by a protozoan that is transferred into an organism's blood by a mosquito bite. The protozoan called Giardia is found in many freshwater lakes and streams in the United States and causes intestinal discomfort in humans. This is why it is wise to use some method of water purification when you are camping to kill protozoans that could be present in your drinking water.

THE KINGDOM FUNGI

Organisms in the Fungi kingdom include yeasts, mildew, molds, and mushrooms (Figure 35–4). Many organisms in the fungi kingdom are important decomposers in the world's ecosystems. Yeasts are single-celled fungi that consume sugars and starches as food and produce

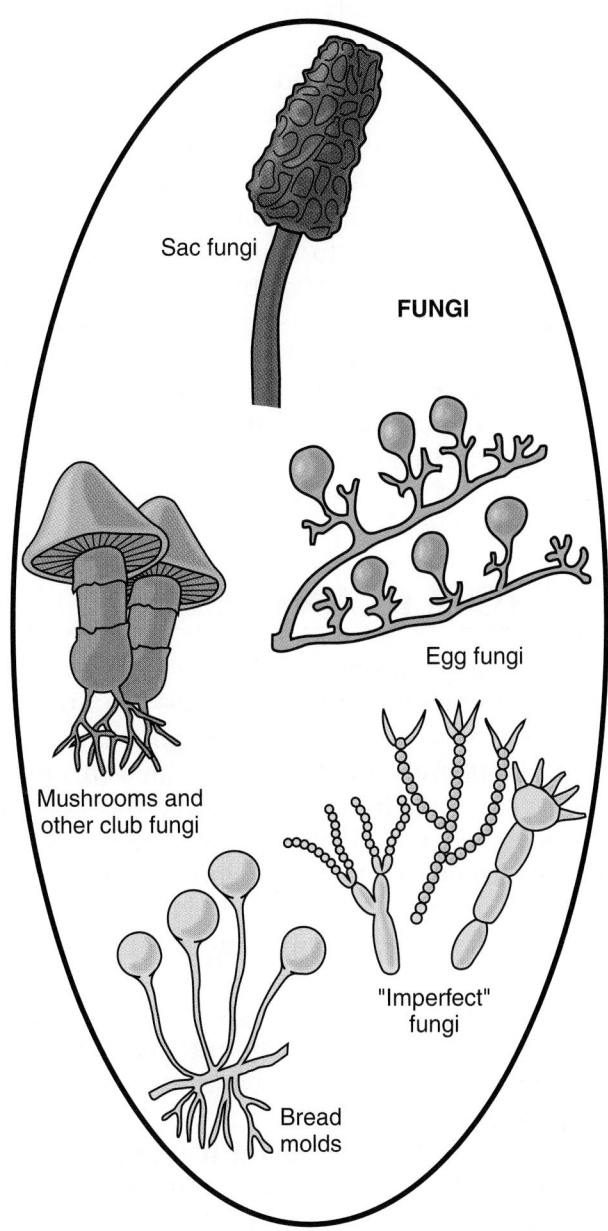

FIGURE 35–4 Examples of organisms in the kingdom Fungi include mushrooms and molds.

both carbon dioxide and alcohol as by-products. Humans use the power of yeasts for baking; cheese making; **fermentation** of beer, wine, and alcohol; and industrial processes. The use of a living organism to produce a usable product is called biotechnology. Yeasts are one of the most widely used organisms in biotechnology.

Other fungi include mildew, which are multicolored colonies of fungus that grow in damp areas. Almost everyone has encountered mildew trying to grow in a shower or in a damp corner of a basement. Mildew, like all fungi, reproduce by producing spores. Spores float on air and transport mildews all over the planet. Some people can become sick or have allergic reactions when they breathe in these spores.

Mushrooms and molds are also fungi. These organisms are decomposers that consume the decaying organic material of both plants and animals. Most mushrooms are poisonous to humans when they are eaten, but some, such as white button mushrooms, are a popular food.

Many fungi secrete weak acids from their cells that help break down the organic material on which they grow. This results in a solution of nutrients that the fungus uses for nutrition. Many fungi form mutualistic relationships with plants that they are growing near. These fungi are called **mycorrhizae**, which means "fungus roots." The fungus breaks down minerals in the soil by secreting weak acids. Plant roots then absorb the minerals for use in their bodies. In return, the plants supply organic material for the fungus to use as food. Scientists have determined that more than 90 percent of plants and trees have mycorrhizae.

Many fungi can be a problem in the storage of food. This is called spoilage, which is caused by molds that decompose food. Bread, fruits, and vegetables can be spoiled when molds begin to decompose them. We have all seen the effects of mold on food. When mold is found on food, the food is usually uneatable.

THE KINGDOM PLANTAE

The kingdom Plantae includes all multicelled organisms that are autotrophs, known as green plants (Figure 35–5). In the Plantae kingdom organisms make their own food through the process of photosynthesis. Most plants are also terrestrial, which means they live on land. Some plants do reside in water, but by far most organisms in the Plantae kingdom live on land. Seaweeds and algae are similar to green plants but are not part of the Plantae kingdom. Many green plants also have a rigid cell wall around their cells, which gives them strength and stability. Green plants are divided into two main categories: vascular and nonvascular.

Vascular means that the organism has a network of tiny tubes that transport water and nutrients throughout the body (Figure 35–6). Vascular green plants include trees. Trees are some of the largest and oldest living organisms on the Earth.

The bristlecone pine that grows in the mountains of California and Nevada has been dated at 4,600 years old. These trees are believed to live as long as 5,500 years. The tallest trees include the giant redwoods also found in California. These trees reach almost 400 ft (122 m) in height. Vascular green plants are classified into two broad categories:

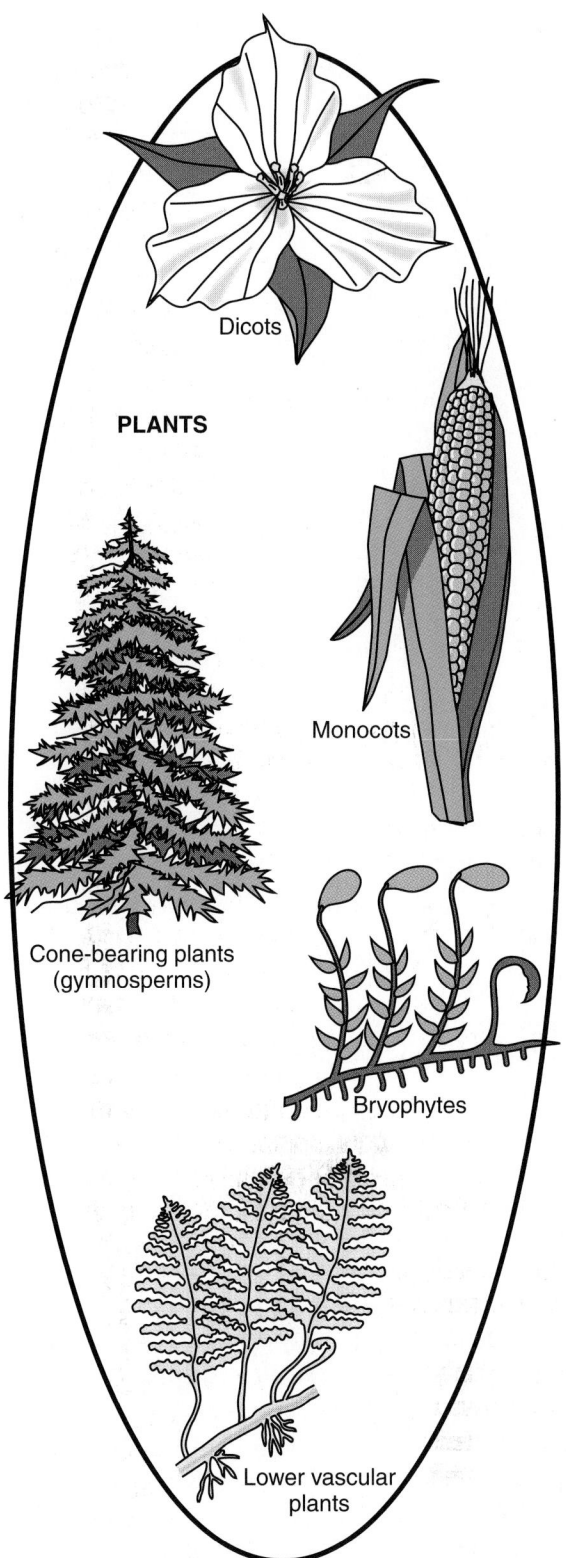

FIGURE 35–5 Examples of organisms in the kingdom Plantae.

seed plants and seedless plants. Seed plants are green plants that reproduce by producing seeds. These include categories of plants called angiosperms and gymnosperms.

Gymnosperms, which means "naked seed," are green plants that reproduce by producing seeds without seed coats. A seed coat is a hard

A Section of a Dicot Leaf

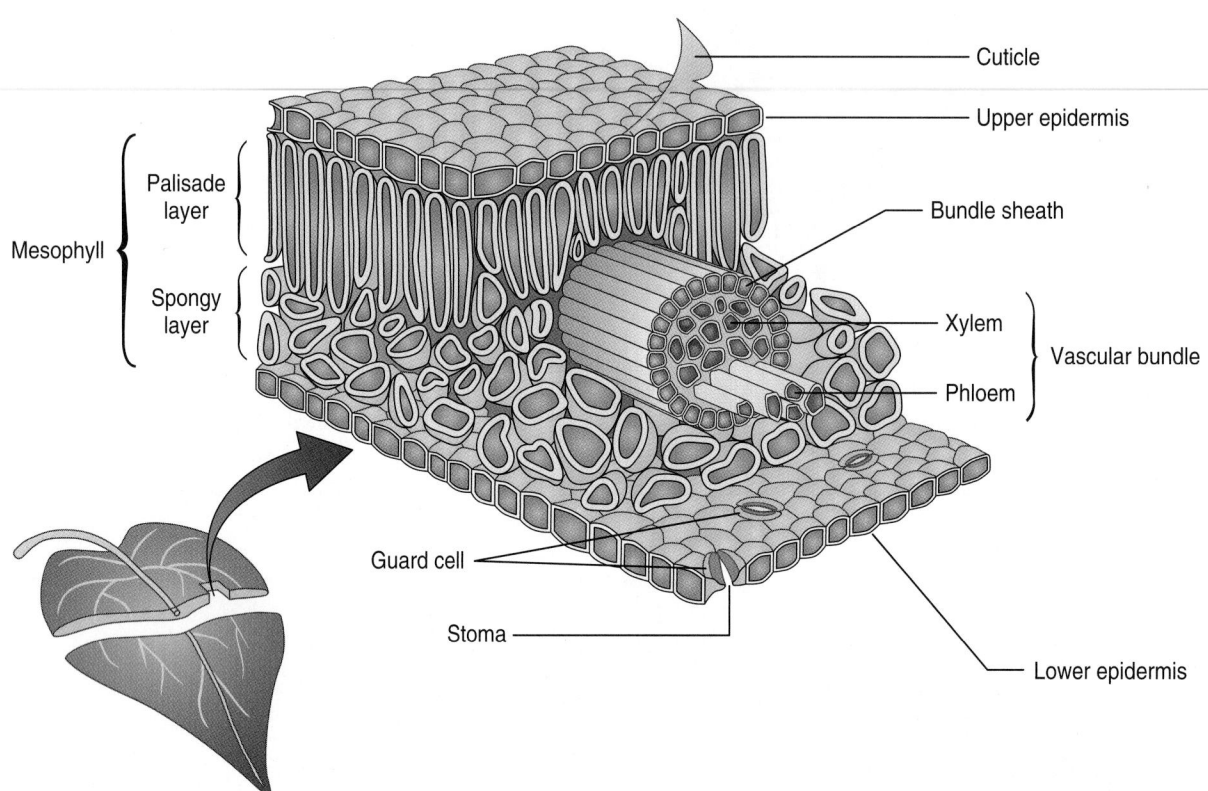

FIGURE 35–6   Cross section of the leaf of a vascular plant showing the tiny tubes that transport water and nutrients throughout the body of the plant.

FIGURE 35–7   Pine cones protect the seeds of a gymnosperm such as a pine tree. (*Courtesy of PhotoDisc.*)

cover that protects the seed. These include cone-bearing trees, also known as conifers (Figure 35–7). Common conifers include pine and spruce trees.

Angiosperms, which means "enclosed seed," are also called flowering plants. These green plants reproduce by producing seeds with a protective shell. Angiosperms are also known as flowering plants because these organisms produce flowers that bear the seeds (Figure 35–8). Flowering plants must be pollinated before they can form a seed. Insects and wind are important for the pollination of flowering plants.

Once a flower is pollinated, it produces a fruit. A fruit is a fleshy organ that protects seeds and helps them to be transported. Many plant fruits are eaten by animals and are then dispersed. Humans use many fruits for their nutrition. Technically, a fruit is anything that contains a seed. Therefore common vegetables such as cucumbers, squash, and tomatoes are truly fruits. Seedless vascular plants include ferns, which reproduce by producing **spores**. Spores are tiny cells that float on the wind and eventually land on the ground, where they grow into a mature plant.

Nonvascular green plants include mosses and liverworts (Figure 35–9). These organisms form matlike green carpets along the soil. Mosses also use spores for reproduction.

The plant kingdom forms the base for primary productivity in all terrestrial ecosystems. Many organisms rely on plants for food and shelter. Human beings cultivate specific plants for use as food and for industry. Trees are an important source of wood for construction and

FIGURE 35–9 A close-up view of a moss, a nonvascular plant, producing spores. (*Courtesy of PhotoDisc.*)

for fiber used in making paper. Other green plants are used for making cloth, such as cotton, and flax, which is used to make linen. Green plants are also an important source of chemicals for use in medicine. It is estimated that green plants make up 90 percent of all the living material on land, making them an important part of the biosphere.

THE KINGDOM ANIMALIA

The kingdom Animalia includes all multicellular organisms that gain their nutrition by ingestion. Ingestion means to take in parts of or a whole organism. The animal kingdom is divided into two broad categories called invertebrates and vertebrates (Figure 35–10).

INVERTEBRATE ANIMALS

Invertebrates are animals that have no backbone or spine. Approximately 95 percent of all animals are classified as invertebrates. Invertebrates are further divided into specific phyla based on similar characteristics. The phylum Porifera includes organisms such as sponges. Sponges are marine animals that filter water through porelike openings in their bodies. Sponges were once harvested from the ocean by sponge divers.

FIGURE 35–8 Angiosperms, also known as flowering plants, growing over a rolling hillside. (*Courtesy of PhotoDisc.*)

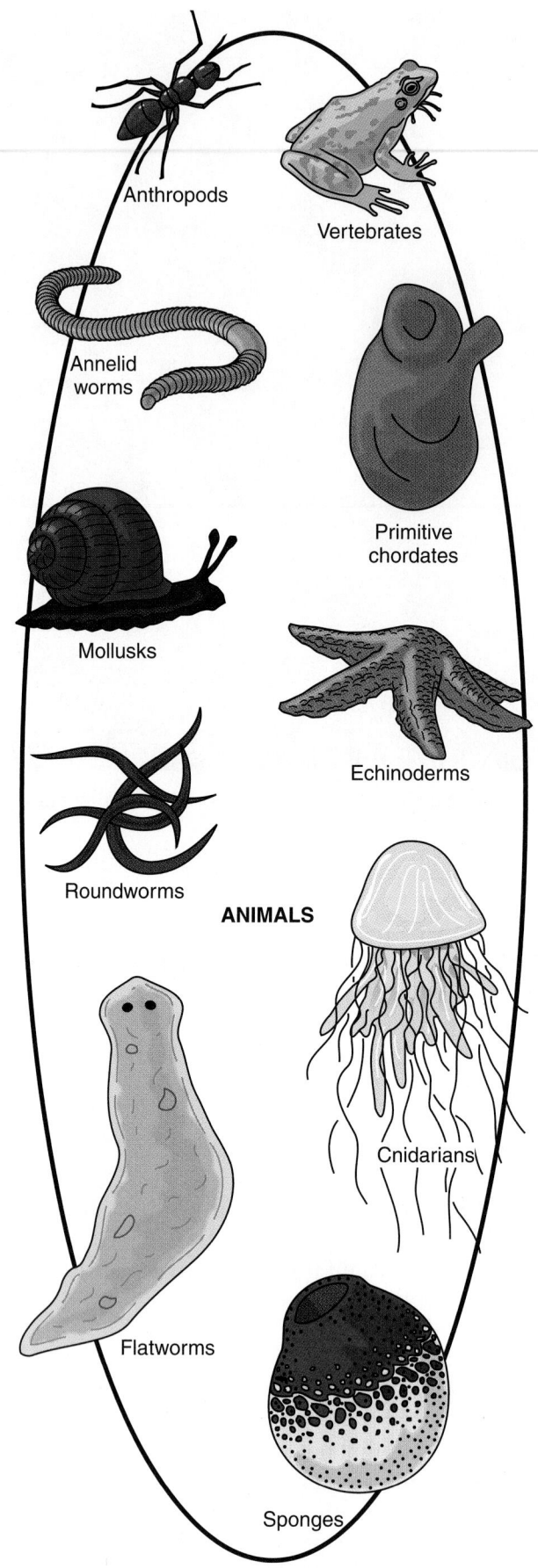

FIGURE 35-10 Examples of organisms within the kingdom Animalia.

FIGURE 35–11   A jellyfish freely floating through the water is an invertebrate animal in the phylum Cnidaria. (*Courtesy of NOAA.*)

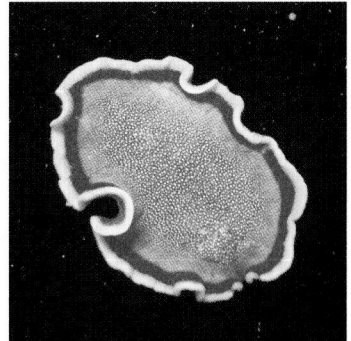

FIGURE 35–12   A flatworm grazing on a coral reef is an example of an animal in the phylum Platyhelminthes. (*Courtesy of NOAA.*)

Sponge divers were people who could hold their breath for a long time and swim under water to retrieve sponges. The bodies of dead sponges were useful in absorbing great amounts of spilled liquids. The fibrous body material was also useful for cleaning. Today most sponges we use in homes are synthetic.

The phylum Cnidaria includes marine organisms such as jellyfish, coral, and sea anemones. Animals in this phylum are similar in that they have a body that surrounds a large digestive sac. Jellyfish float through the water and are often washed up on the beach. Some jellyfish can cause a painful sting if you accidentally touch them while swimming (Figure 35–11). One of the largest cnidarians is called the Portuguese man-of-war, which floats on the surface of the ocean and has tentacles that can reach 50 feet in length.

The phylum Platyhelminthes includes flat, wormlike animals such as flukes, tapeworms, and flatworms (Figure 35–12). These tiny organisms are often parasites that attach themselves to the wall of the intestines of larger animals or burrow into the skin and travel in the bloodstream. Some flatworms that live in the ocean are not parasites, can grow fairly large, and are quite colorful. These organisms are often found living on coral reefs.

The phylum Nematoda includes microscopic worms such as roundworms and nematodes. Nematodes reside in the soil and can infect the root systems of plants, causing damage to food crops (Figure 35–13).

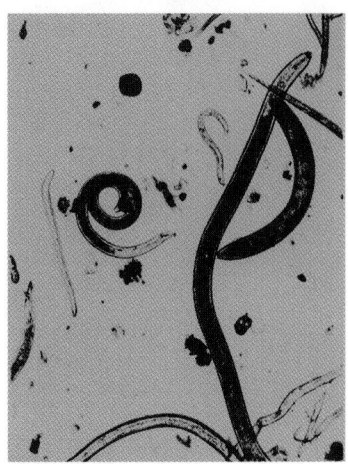

FIGURE 35–13   Microscopic nematodes reside in the soil and are part of the phylum Nematoda in the animal kingdom. (*Courtesy of Patricia Sanders and the Pennsylvania Turfgrass Council.*)

FIGURE 35–14   Organisms in the phylum Annelida include earthworms. (*Courtesy of PhotoDisc.*)

Roundworms can also infect humans either by being ingested or by burrowing into the skin. Trichinosis is a disease caused by eating meat that is infected by parasitic roundworms. It is usually associated with undercooked pork. The roundworm can multiply in the host organism and cause damage to organs throughout the body.

The phylum Annelida includes animals such as earthworms or sea worms, also known as segmented worms (Figure 35–14). Earthworms are an important part of the soil environment, where they break down organic material. Thousands of earthworms can be found in just one acre of soil, where they help turn over the soil and create channels through which air can pass into the ground. This helps aerate the soil and create pore spaces for water to infiltrate more easily into the soil. Earthworms are usually forced to the surface of the soil after a heavy rain. This occurs when the small channels through which they are burrowing become saturated with water. The worms must surface so they can have access to atmospheric oxygen. These annelids are also raised in captivity on worm farms where they are sold as fish bait.

The phylum Mollusca includes a variety of snails, squid, octopus, and **bivalves**. Bivalves are mollusks that have shells with two halves. These include scallops, clams, mussels, and oysters. Scallops flap their hinged shells like wings, which pushes them through the water, making them one of the few bivalves that actually swims. Mussels attach themselves to wood, rocks, and other submerged substances by secreting a strong gluelike substance.

All bivalves are filter feeders. They pump water into their shells and filter out tiny plankton and organic material that they use for food. Oysters sometimes filter out tiny pieces of sand that become trapped in their bodies. As a defense, the oyster coats the sand grain with a hard substance that eventually forms a pearl. Although most pearls are white, some oysters make colored pearls such as the rare black pearl.

The clam, another bivalve, can grow very large. The giant clam can grow to almost 3 ft (1 m) in length. The clam shell also contains growth rings similar to those found in trees. You can count these rings on the clam's shell to estimate its age.

The **zebra mussel**, a bivalve species, is a freshwater mollusk that lives in Europe (Figure 35–15). The tiny larvae of the zebra mussel were

FIGURE 35–15   The zebra mussel, a bivalve mollusk, is an exotic species that is overpopulating lakes in North America. (*Courtesy of PhotoDisc.*)

CAREER CONNECTIONS
Zoologist

A zoologist is a scientist who studies all types of living organisms and their life processes, behavior, diseases, and origins. These scientists research animals in many different settings, including their natural habitat, in captivity, and in the laboratory. They also study the bodies of dead animals to learn more about their anatomy. Zoologists are often specialized in studying particular types of organisms. A protozoologist studies single-celled organisms such as protozoans and bacteria. An entomologist works solely on insects. An ichthyologist studies all types of freshwater and marine fish. A herpetologist studies amphibians and reptiles. An ornithologist works with birds of all kinds, and a mammalogist studies mammals. All zoologists must have a college degree in biology and animal behavior, along with a special emphasis on a unique type of organism. Zoologists often work in research within an academic institution. Zoologists spend much of their time outdoors in the natural habitat, where their organisms live, and conduct observations and collect specimens. Employment opportunities are available in zoos, aquariums, and other animal-related parks and sanctuaries.

transported across the ocean in the ballast water of ships coming to the United States. Ballast water is pumped into a ship to add weight and stabilize it. The zebra mussel has spread quickly through freshwater lakes and is interrupting the balance of aquatic ecosystems in the United States. Because the zebra mussel has no natural predators in North America, its populations are increasing and the organism is taking over whole lakes. Organisms that populate ecosystems where they do not naturally grow are called exotic species.

The Cephalopods are a class of mollusks that include octopus and squid. These organisms have long arms called tentacles. Octopuses use these long tentacles to trap and hold their prey. These annelids also have a sharp beak, much like a bird, that is used to tear apart their food. Squid are also annelids and are the fastest swimming invertebrates in the world. Squids use jetlike propulsion that forces water quickly through their bodies, propelling them to speeds of more than 20 miles per hour (32 kilometers per hour). The largest squid species is called the giant squid. These cephalopods live deep in the ocean and can be more than 40 ft long. The giant squid also has the largest eyeball of any animal living on the planet. The eyeball of a giant squid is about the size of a volleyball. Many organisms in the annelid phylum are eaten by humans. Humans commonly ingest

FIGURE 35–16 A common garden snail is part of the Gastropod class of mollusks. (*Courtesy of PhotoDisc.*)

squid, clams, mussels, scallops, oysters, and occasionally even snails (Figure 35–16).

The phylum Arthropoda is one of the largest phyla on the planet, with more than 1 million species identified on Earth. Arthropods include the arachnids, which are land-dwelling arthropods such as scorpions, spiders, ticks, and mites (Figure 35–17). Crustaceans are another class of arthropods, which include aquatic organisms such as shrimp, crayfish, lobsters, and barnacles. Humans also dine on millions of pounds of crustaceans each year. Millipedes and centipedes also fall under the Arthropoda phylum, as do aquatic organisms such as sea stars, sea cucumbers, sea urchins, and starfish. Although they appear lifeless, starfish are fearsome predators that attack mollusks such as oysters and mussels.

The largest class of arthropods is the Insecta class. This includes all insects of the world, which by far outnumber any other class of organisms on the planet. More than 900,000 insect species have been identified on the Earth. Insects are some of the most adaptable organisms on the planet. They come in an amazing assortment of shapes and sizes. Insects play an important role in many ecosystems, especially as decomposers. They are also important for the pollination of flowering plants.

FIGURE 35–17 A spider is an arachnid within the Arthropod phylum. (*Courtesy of PhotoDisc.*)

Earth System Scientists

Georges Cuvier

Born in 1769, Georges Cuvier was a comparative anatomist who studied the similarities in all forms of animals and their unique physical characteristics. He continued the classification work begun by Carolus Linnaeus and helped to group organisms into unique categories called phyla. In 1812 his worked turned to the classification of the fossil remains of organisms. He was the first scientist to determine that fossil bones were the remains of once living organisms. Cuvier also theorized that catastrophic events at different times during the Earth's past had wiped out many species on the Earth, which caused new species to become more widespread. This was the first suggestion of the mass extinction, which is an important aspect of the geologic time scale. His work also involved the reconstruction of many fossil skeletons and the identification of extinct organisms. Because of this, he is often considered the father of paleontology.

VERTEBRATE ANIMALS

The other major category of organisms in the animal kingdom are called vertebrates. These are organisms that have a backbone. They fall under the phylum Chordata. The chordates include many different classes of animals that all have a notochord. A notochord is a flexible rod that lies between the spinal chord and an animal's gut. The Agnatha class includes jawless organisms such as lampreys. These parasites attach themselves to the sides of fish with hooklike devices located in their mouths. They then pierce the skin of their host with a sharp tongue and suck out the animal's blood. Lampreys begin life as microscopic larvae that float in the water. Many freshwater lakes in the eastern United States have been invaded by freshwater lamprey that were brought over in the ballast water of ships arriving from Europe. In their new environment, the lamprey have no natural predators and are quickly overpopulating lakes and killing many native species of fish (Figure 35–18).

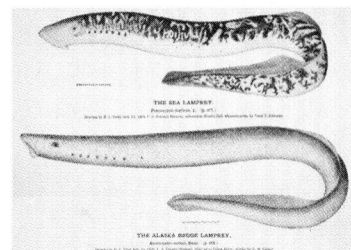

FIGURE 35–18   Lampreys are classified as a vertebrate in the Agnatha class. (*Courtesy of NOAA.*)

The class Chondrichthyes, also called the cartilaginous fish, include organisms that have skeletons made of cartilage. Cartilage is a soft, flexible, bonelike material. Sharks are probably the most well known of the cartilaginous fish (Figure 35–19). Approximately 370 different species of sharks live in the world's oceans. The largest shark is the whale shark, which grows to a length of more than 50 ft (15 m). The great white shark is also large, often growing more than 30 ft (9 m) long. Sharks can be deadly when they attack humans. Their razorlike teeth can be more than 2 in (5 cm) long. Approximately 100 people are attacked by sharks each year around the world. Scientists are interested in studying sharks because they can easily ward of diseases, especially cancer. Other cartilaginous fish include skates and rays, which "fly" through the water using winglike fins. The stingray has a sharp, swordlike tail that can pierce the skin, causing a stinging sensation. Manta rays can grow very large, with

FIGURE 35–19   The vertebrate class Chondrichthyes, also called the cartilaginous fish, include organisms such as sharks. (*Courtesy of Sea Images, Inc.*)

FIGURE 35–20 Both freshwater and saltwater fish are classified in the chordate class Osteichthyes, also called the bony fish. (*Courtesy of PhotoDisc.*)

wingspans of more than 25 ft (8 m). Although very large, these creatures are harmless to humans, because that they only eat plankton and small fish that they filter out of the water in their mouths.

The chordate class Osteichthyes, also called the bony fish, include all fish that have skeletons made of bone. This is the largest class of vertebrate animals. It includes more than 300,000 species. Because the ocean is difficult to explore, scientists believe there are even more species of bony fish that have not yet been identified. Bony fish come in many shapes and sizes and live in both freshwater and saltwater environments (Figure 35–20). All bony fish, however, have similar streamlined body shapes that are designed to propel them through the water. Almost all bony fish have a large fin near the tail, called a caudal fin, that pushes them forward through the water. Some fish use their powerful caudal fins to move at speeds near 60 miles per hour (97 kilometers per hour).

Bony fish are also an important food source for humans all around the world. The ocean fishing industry today is being regulated to prevent the overharvesting of fish. Once thriving fish populations in the Atlantic Ocean have been declining in recent years, making regulation necessary. Aquaculture, also called fish farming, is a method of raising fish species in captivity. Using aquaculture to provide fish for use as a food source is becoming more widespread in the United States. The three main bony fish that are raised on fish farms in the United States are catfish, trout, and salmon.

FIGURE 35–21   A common frog is an example of an amphibian. (*Courtesy of PhotoDisc.*)

The vertebrate class Amphibia includes all amphibians, such as frogs and salamanders (Figure 35–21). Amphibians are unique creatures that begin their lives in water; when they mature, they can survive on land. Amphibians are believed to be the first vertebrates on the Earth to have emerged from the water to live on dry land. Amphibians have moist skin that must not be allowed to dry out. Although many amphibians can survive on land, they usually stay near some type of water source to prevent their sensitive skin from drying out. Amphibians transport oxygen through their skin for use in respiration. The largest amphibian in the world is the giant salamander, which lives in freshwater streams in Japan. This amphibian can grow as long as 6 ft (1.8 m). Scientists are discovering that many amphibians are becoming deformed and their populations are declining. It is believed that pollution or increased ultraviolet radiation reaching the Earth's surface resulting from ozone depletion may be causing this phenomenon, although much research still remains to prove or disprove this theory.

The Reptilia class of vertebrates includes all reptiles, such as snakes, lizards, turtles, and alligators. Reptiles are cold-blooded invertebrates, meaning that their body temperatures depend on the temperature of the environment. This causes reptiles to live in warmer climates or to go into dormancy during cold seasons. Many reptiles warm their bodies by lying on hot rocks in the sunlight (Figure 35–22). The largest reptiles on the Earth today include the American alligator and Komodo dragon. Both these organisms are carnivores, or meat eaters. Turtles are unique

FIGURE 35–22 An iguana, a cold-blooded reptile, needs to warm its body in the Sun to raise its body temperature. (*Courtesy of EyeWire.*)

reptiles that protect themselves with hard shells. Some species of turtles can live extremely long lives, up to 100 years or more.

It was once thought that the long-extinct dinosaurs were reptiles, but recent debates have changed this viewpoint. Dinosaurs did have much in common with present-day reptiles. They both lay eggs to reproduce, and both have similar skin. The debate on whether dinosaurs were reptiles continues to this day. It is a common misconception that reptiles have slimy skin. All reptiles are covered with a dry, scaly skin that is rather soft and smooth to the touch. Some reptiles can be extremely deadly. Alligators have been known to attack humans and can be very dangerous. Poisonous snakes, such as rattlesnakes and cobras, can also kill a human being with their deadly venom.

The vertebrate class Aves includes all the birds in the world (Figure 35–23). Birds are unique organisms that possess many interesting features. Almost all birds have wings that enable them to fly. Birds have extremely light, hollow skeletons that makes them lightweight. This is an advantage that helps them to fly. Birds are warm-blooded creatures that regulate their own body temperatures. Birds come in many varieties and sizes; some are flightless. Ostriches, emus, and penguins are examples of birds that do not fly. Penguins are also unique birds because they hunt for their food beneath the ocean surface. They use their wings much like fins.

Birds have well-developed brains that allow them to live fairly complex lives. Many birds communicate with a variety of songs and are

FIGURE 35-23 Birds belong to the vertebrate class Aves. (*Courtesy of PhotoDisc.*)

able to mimic human speech. Birds also construct complex nests from which to raise their young. The smartest bird is believed to be the common crow, which has the ability to solve simple problems such as how to untie a knot to get to a food source.

Birds are also unique in that they can navigate over far distances. Many bird species migrate thousands of miles each year. The longest migration of any animal on Earth is performed by the arctic tern. The arctic tern spends its summer in the Arctic near the North Pole. Every year it travels all the way to Antarctica near the South Pole.

All birds have a unique covering on their bodies called feathers. Feathers are made from keratin, a protein that is found in fingernails. Feathers help to insulate a bird's body while also providing the extra surface area needed for flight. Another unique feature of birds is the **gizzard**. Birds do not have teeth with which to chew their food; instead they use a gizzard. The gizzard is a special saclike organ that crushes and grinds food before it reaches a bird's stomach. Birds must fill their gizzards with small stones, called grit, to help grind down their food. Eventually the grit within the gizzard becomes rounded and polished by abrasion.

Many scientists believe that dinosaurs are the ancestors of modern birds. Unlike reptiles, some dinosaurs were believed to be warm blooded like birds. The fossil remains of some dinosaurs have also been found with piles of polished gizzard stones, much like birds. The debate over what dinosaurs were related to, birds or reptiles, goes on to this day.

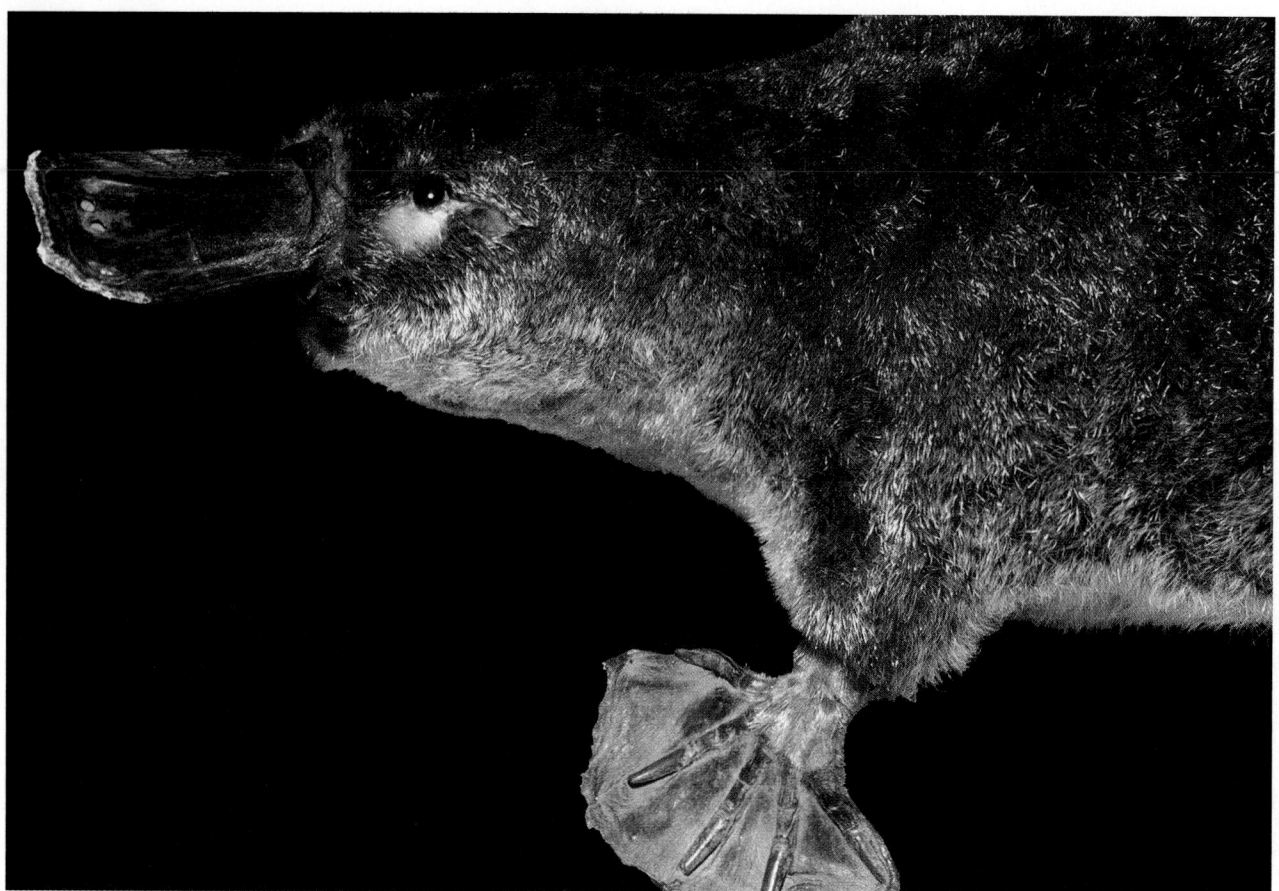

FIGURE 35–24 The platypus is an egg-laying mammal classified in the order Monotremata. (*Courtesy of Wernher Krutein/photovault.com.*)

The final class of vertebrate animals is Mammalia, also called the mammals. Mammals are animals that have bodies that are mostly covered in hair. They also nourish their offspring with milk produced from mammary glands. This is where the Mammalia class derives its name. Human beings are part of the mammal class, which totals approximately 4,000 different species. Mammals are further divided into specific orders that group together animals with similar characteristics. The order Monotremata include unique mammals such as the platypus and the spiny anteater. These organisms are unlike any other mammal because they lay eggs. The platypus has a bill, much like a duck, and resides near water (Figure 35–24). Both these strange mammals are found only on the island of New Guinea and in Australia.

Another order of mammals are the Marsupials. Marsupials carry their offspring in pouches on their bodies. They include the koala bear, opossum, and kangaroo (Figure 35–25). When these organisms are born, they crawl along their mother's fur and into her pouch. They stay in the pouch until they are completely developed. The continent of Australia has the largest number of marsupial species on the planet. The only other species of marsupial that lives in other parts of the world is the opossum.

The next order of mammals is the Artiodactyla. These include mammals that have an even number of toes or hooves on their legs. Organisms such as deer, moose, elk, cows, sheep, and goats are all

FIGURE 35–25 The koala bear is an example of a Marsupial mammal. (*Courtesy of PhotoDisc.*)

examples of Artiodactyla. All the organisms in this order are also herbivores, meaning that they eat only plants. Another similar order of mammals is the Perissodactyla. This order includes organisms that have an odd number of toes or hooves on their legs (Figure 35–26). Horses, rhinoceroses, zebras, and donkeys fall under this order of animals. These organisms are also herbivores.

The Carnivora order of mammals includes the meat eaters, or carnivores. This order of mammals is further subdivided into two infraorders. One of these has retractable claws. This means that the claw can move in and out of the animal's foot. This infraorder includes all cats, such as lions, cheetahs, and house cats, along with the mongoose and hyenas (Figure 35–27). The other infraorder of carnivore includes all animals that have nonretractable claws. These are claws that cannot move in and out of the animal's foot. This includes wolves, dogs, bears, raccoons, foxes, skunks, weasels, seals, otters, walruses, and sea lions. Many carnivores have well-developed brains and show a complex social structure. For example, wolves depend on the coordinated group actions of their pack for survival. Domestic dogs are also intelligent carnivores that can complete many complex tasks.

The next order of mammals is the Chiroptera, which includes bats. Bats are the only type of mammal adapted for flying. Bats are **nocturnal** animals, which means that they are active mainly at night. Bats use a type of sonar, which bounces sound waves off objects to detect them (Figure 35–28).

FIGURE 35–26 Examples of an even-toed deer (top) in the order Artiodactyla and an odd-toed zebra (bottom) in the order Perissodactyla. (*Photos courtesy of PhotoDisc.*)

FIGURE 35–27 A male lion is an example of a mammal with retractable claws in the Carnivora order. (*Courtesy of PhotoDisc.*)

FIGURE 35–28 Flying mammals in the Chiroptera class, such as bats, are nocturnal and use a type of sonar to help them hunt and fly at night. (*Courtesy of PhotoDisc.*)

FIGURE 35-29 Dolphins and whales are aquatic mammals that belong to the Cetacea order of animals. (*Courtesy of PhotoDisc.*)

Other mammals that use sonar include dolphins, which are in a different order of chordates. Whales, dolphins, and porpoises make up the Cetacea order of mammals (Figure 35–29). These aquatic mammals are unique in that they live their lives entirely in the water. Although they resemble fish, with their streamlined bodies and fins, the cetaceans all must breathe air to survive. These sea mammals all nourish their young with milk, unlike fish. Fossil evidence has revealed that the ancient ancestors of the dolphin were wolflike creatures who lived near the coastline on land. Another order of aquatic mammals are the Sirenia. These include the manatee and dugongs, also called sea cows. These marine mammals are herbivores that dine on aquatic vegetation. Many manatees that live in the warm waters around Florida have become endangered as a result of their slow movement. This causes them to be run over by motorboats. These gentle sea mammals are believed to be the source of the mermaid myth. Sailors who were at sea for long periods may have mistakenly seen these creatures as half human, half fish.

The Edentata order of mammals are organisms that have few or no teeth. These include mammals such as armadillos, sloths, and anteaters (Figure 35–30). The tree sloth is an extremely docile animal. *Docile* means slow and gentle. The tree sloth moves so slowly through the tree tops that moss often grows in the hair on its back.

The Rodentia order of mammals groups together all rodents. Rodents are mammals that have front teeth that are continually growing.

FIGURE 35-30 An armadillo is an animal with very little teeth that is grouped in the Edentata order of mammals. (*Courtesy of EyeWire.*)

FIGURE 35–31   Rodents, such as squirrels, are mammals that have constantly growing teeth, requiring them to continually chew on things. (*Courtesy of PhotoDisc.*)

This causes them to be active chewers, which reduces the size of their teeth. Rodents include rats, mice, gerbils, gophers, hamsters, squirrels, and beavers (Figure 35–31). Another similar class of mammals is the Lagomorpha order, which also has well-developed teeth. These include rabbits and hares. Animals in this order also have long legs, which helps them to move by jumping or hoping.

The Insectivora order of mammals include animals that eat only insects. Animals in this order are the moles, hedgehogs, and shrews.

The final order of mammals are the Primates. This order includes animals that have opposable thumbs, forward-facing eyes, and well-developed brains (Figure 35–32). An opposable thumb is one that can be used to grasp and manipulate objects. Animals in the Primate class include lemurs, monkeys, chimpanzees, gorillas, orangutans, and humans. All these mammals are highly intelligent and live in organized social groups. Human beings are in the genus *Homo* and the *species sapiens*. *Homo sapiens* is Latin for "intelligent humans."

The taxonomic classification of living things that make up the Earth's biosphere is a very important part of understanding the Earth's systems. Taxonomy helps to organize living things by their similar characteristics It also illustrates the amazing variety of organisms on the Earth and the roles that they fill within their ecosystems. But more important, taxonomy helps us to see how all living things on the Earth are related.

FIGURE 35–32   Primates are an order of mammals with highly developed brains that includes lemurs, monkeys, chimpanzees, gorillas, orangutans, and humans.

FOR MORE INFORMATION GO TO THIS WEB LINK:

<http://www.estrellam-ountain.edu/faculty /farabee/biobk /biobooktoc.html>

<http://mclibrary .nhmccd.edu /taxonomy/taxonomy .html>

REVIEW

1. What is taxonomy?

2. What is the binomial method of taxonomy?

3. Name the five kingdoms used to classify organisms on Earth.

4. What are stromatolites, in which kingdom do they belong, and why were they important?

5. What is a diatom and in which kingdom does it belong?

6. What are mycorrhizae and in which kingdom do they belong?

7. Describe the difference between vascular and nonvascular plants and provide one example for each.

8. List 10 organisms that are classified as invertebrates.

9. What are two examples of cartilaginous fish?

10. Give three examples of amphibians.

11. What are three examples of reptiles?

12. How do birds grind up food before it enters the stomach?

13. What are mammals?

14. To which phylum do humans belong?

15. What is the genus and species of a human being?

16. Who was Carolus Linnaeus?

17. Who was Georges Cuvier?

CHAPTER SUMMARY

The biosphere consists of all the living things on the Earth. These organisms have helped to shape the world in which we live and perform important roles in the ecosystems in which they reside. All the living things on Earth are classified into specific groups based on their similar biological characteristics. The classification of things is called taxonomy. Botanist Carolus Linnaeus devised a system for classifying the world's organisms during the eighteenth century. He invented the binomial system of classification that identifies an organisms by its unique genus and species names.

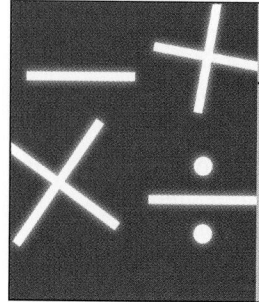

earth math

1) If there are 5 million species of organisms on the Earth and there are 4,000 mammal species, what percentage of species are mammals?

2) If there are 5 million species of organisms on the Earth and 18 percent are classified as insects, how many insect species are there on the planet?

Today organisms on the Earth are divided into five general categories called kingdoms: Monera, Protista, Fungi, Plantae, and Animalia. Organisms in the kingdom Monera include all single-celled organisms that have no cell nucleus. Examples of this type of organism are bacteria and blue-green algae; they are believed to be the first living things to inhabit the Earth. The kingdom Protista contains all the single-celled organisms that have a cell nucleus. Protists are free-floating organisms such as diatoms and algae, which play an important part in all aquatic ecosystems. The kingdom Fungi includes all the molds, yeasts, mildew, and mushrooms. These organisms act as decomposers in many of the world's ecosystems, helping to break down organic material.

The kingdom Plantae includes all the green plants. Plants are divided into two main categories: vascular and nonvascular. Vascular plants have a network of tiny tubes that transport water and nutrients throughout their bodies. Common vascular plants include trees, ferns, grass, and many of the plants we use for food. Nonvascular plants are matlike vegetation, including mosses and liverworts.

The kingdom Animalia consists of all the animals on the Earth that consume other organisms as food. The animal kingdom is subdivided into two main categories called vertebrates and invertebrates. Invertebrate animals have no backbone and include sponges, jellyfish, worms, mollusks, squid, crustaceans, spiders, and insects. The vertebrate animals all have a backbone and include organisms such as sharks, fish, amphibians, reptiles, birds, and mammals.

Human beings are classified in the genus and species *Homo sapiens*, within the class of mammals in the primate order. The taxonomic classification of living things that make up the Earth's biosphere is a very important part of understanding the Earth's systems. Taxonomy helps to organize living things by their similar characteristics It also illustrates the amazing variety of organisms on the Earth, the role that they fill within their ecosystems, and how all living things on the Earth are related.

CHAPTER REVIEW

Multiple Choice

1. Organisms on the Earth are classified according to:
   a. their size and shape
   b. their similar biological characteristics
   c. whether they live on land or in water
   d. their specific geographical location

2. The binomial classification of organisms identifies a specific living thing by its unique:
   a. kingdom
   b. adaptations
   c. genus and species
   d. phylum and order

3. The taxonomic classification of living things on the Earth is organized in which way?
   a. kingdom, phylum, class, order, family, genus, species
   b. kingdom, order, class, species, phylum, genus, family
   c. species, genus, family, order, class, phylum, kingdom
   d. phylum, order, species, genus, family, kingdom, class

4. Bacteria belong to which taxonomic kingdom?
   a. animalia
   b. protista
   c. monera
   d. fungi

5. The kingdom Protista includes which of the following organisms?
   a. cyanobacteria
   b. liverworts
   c. mildew
   d. algae

6. Which taxonomic kingdom includes the first forms of life believed to have existed on the Earth?
   a. animalia
   b. protista
   c. monera
   d. fungi

7. Flowering plants are classified under which category in the Plant kingdom?
   a. nonvascular
   b. angiosperm

   c. gymnosperm
   d. conifer

8. Which ta-xonomic kingdom composes approximately 90% of all living things on land within the biosphere?
   a. animalia
   b. protista
   c. monera
   d. plantae

9. Sponges, jellyfish, worms, squid, and insects are classified as which type of animals?
   a. vertebrates
   b. annelids
   c. invertebrates
   d. mammals

10. Which kingdom contains the class of organisms with the greatest number of species identified on the planet?
    a. animalia
    b. protista
    c. monera
    d. fungi

11. Sharks belong to which class of animals?
    a. bony fish
    b. cartilaginous fish
    c. cephalopods
    d. reptiles

12. The animals grouped in the vertebrate class Aves are commonly called:
    a. mammals
    b. amphibians
    c. birds
    d. reptiles

13. Which class of animals is believed to be the first to live on land?
    a. mammals
    b. amphibians
    c. birds
    d. reptiles

14. What mammal is classified as a marsupial?
    a. a bat
    b. an opossum
    c. a platypus
    d. a manatee

15. Humans are grouped in which order of mammals?
   a. primates
   b. carnivores
   c. *Homo sapiens*
   d. sirenia

Matching   *Match the terms with the correct definitions.*

a. biological characteristics
b. taxonomy
c. siliceous ooze
d. neurotoxins
e. fermentation

f. mycorrhizae
g. gymnosperm
h. angiosperm
i. spores
j. invertebrates

k. bivalves
l. zebra mussel
m. gizzard
n. nocturnal
o. Homo sapiens

1. _____ A type of symbiotic associated with the root systems of plants.
2. _____ The taxonomic classification of a specific type of plant that reproduces by flowers that produce seeds with a protective coat.
3. _____ A discipline of science that deals with the classification of organisms.
4. _____ The genus and species classification of human beings.
5. _____ An organism's unique physical or chemical features.
6. _____ Mudlike sediments composed of silicates that form on the ocean floor.
7. _____ The classification of a green plant that produces a seed without a seed coat in cone, such as a pine tree.
8. _____ A term used to describe an organism that is active during the night.
9. _____ A type of toxic chemical compound that affects the nervous system of animals.
10. _____ The reproductive cells of fungi.
11. _____ An anaerobic chemical process by which complex compounds, such as sugars and starches, are reduced into simple compounds, such as alcohol and carbon dioxide, by microorganisms.
12. _____ The organ in a bird's digestive tract that helps to break down food by grinding it between stones.
13. _____ A classification of aquatic organisms that have a hinged shell that can open and close.
14. _____ A species of mollusk, named for its black and white shell, that is not native to North America and is currently overpopulating many fresh bodies of water in the northeastern United States.
15. _____ A taxonomic term used to describe all organisms within the animal kingdom that have no backbone.

Critical Thinking

1. Explain why you think biologists use the taxonomic classification of organisms to help support the theory of evolution.

36

Threats to Biodiversity

OBJECTIVES

Biodiversity · Extinction · The Endangered Species Act · Wildlife Management

After reading this chapter you will be able to:

▶ Define the term *biodiversity*.

▶ Describe three reasons why it is important to preserve biodiversity on Earth.

▶ Define the term *wildlife resource*.

▶ Identify the differences between renewable and nonrenewable resources.

▶ Define the term *extinction*.

▶ Describe three practices that cause extinction.

▶ Explain the concept known as the tragedy of the commons.

▶ Define the term *invasive species*, and provide three examples of an invasive species.

▶ Briefly describe the Endangered Species Act.

▶ Explain the difference between a generalist and a specialist organism.

▶ Define the term *habitat*.

▶ Explain three methods used for wildlife management.

▶ Describe the difference between an ecotone and an ecological island.

▶ Explain three techniques used for fisheries management.

TERMS TO KNOW

biodiversity

biosphere

intrinsic value

instrumental value

natural resource

renewable resource

nonrenewable resource

wildlife resource

extinction

invasive species

endangered species

threatened species

wildlife management

habitat

generalist

specialist

ecological island

ecotone

INTRODUCTION

The variety of life that that has lived on the Earth in the past and lives here now is incredible, to say the least. From the simplest of bacteria to the much more complex organisms like mammals, each species occupies its own unique place in the web of life. Although natural catastrophes have certainly affected the survival of organisms on the Earth in the past, today humans are currently causing the destruction of species at alarming rates. This is known as extinction. Sometimes the loss of a species due to extinction has direct observable effects on the Earth. At other times the disappearance of an organism might go virtually unnoticed, only much later revealing the important role it has played in the healthy function of the biosphere. Learning what leads to extinction, and the ways that it can be prevented, are among the most important issues that face Earth systems scientists today.

BIODIVERSITY

Imagine having the task of identifying and counting every living thing on the Earth. This would include a census of everything that is alive today, including every microorganism, plant, fungus, animal, and insect that lives in the water, on land, and beneath the Earth's surface. Obviously this would be an impossible task for just one person. Scientists, however, have estimated the total number of species alive on the Earth. Although it is an extremely rough estimate, it is believed that the Earth is home to somewhere between 1.7 and 13.6 million different species (Figure 36–1). The richness and diversity of life on Earth is called **biodiversity**. Scientists are not only concerned with quantifying the biodiversity on the planet, but more important, identifying the unique attributes of species, and the roles they play within the biosphere.

The **biosphere** is a term used to describe all of the living components of the Earth's ecosystems. Some people argue that we should maintain the biodiversity of the planet because every living thing has a right to live on the Earth. This is known as the **intrinsic value** of species. Others maintain that we should preserve biodiversity because certain species might be a resource to humans. This is called the **instrumental value** of species, and it includes the use of living things for agriculture, medicine, science, and recreation. These types

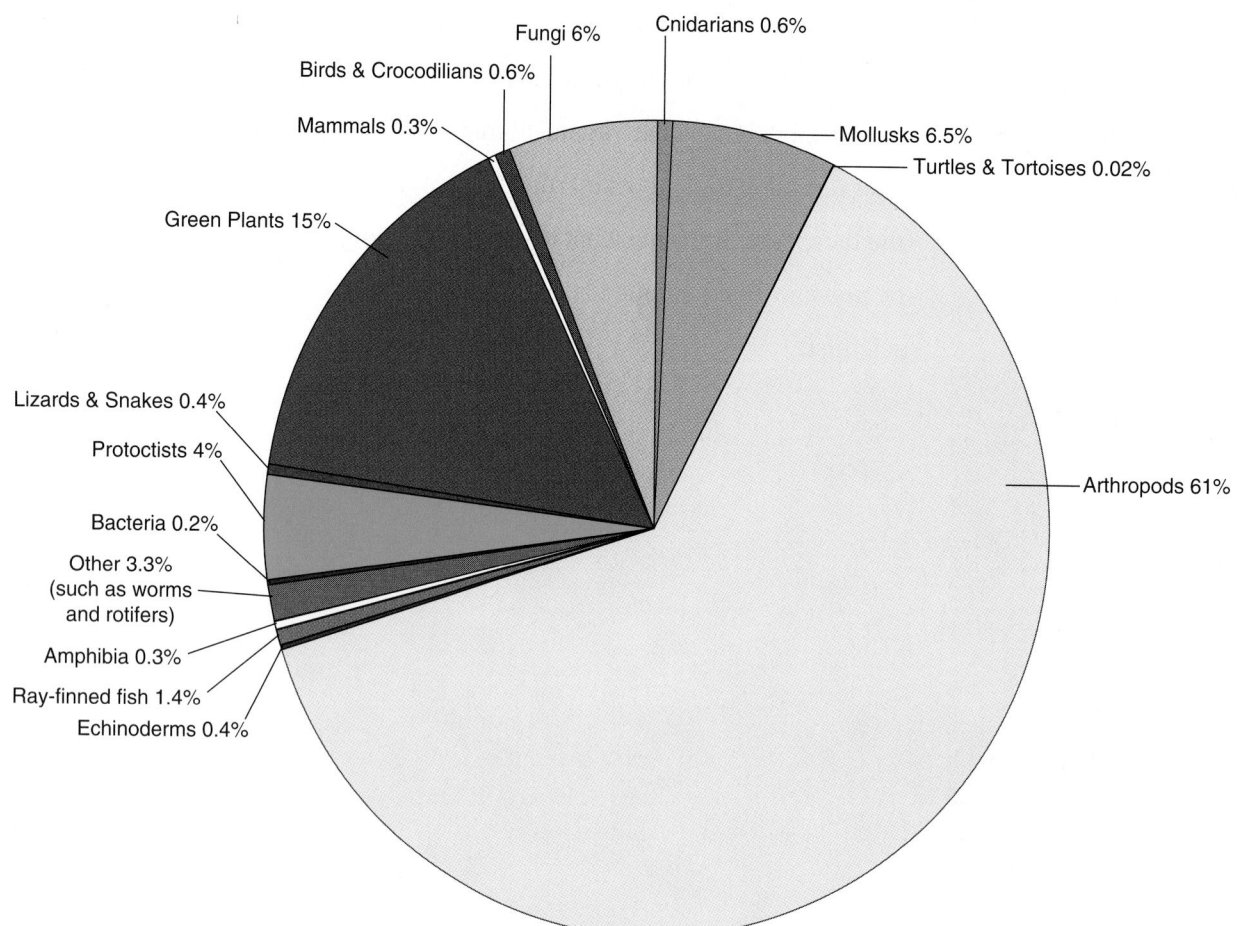

FIGURE 36–1 A chart showing the distribution of the Earth's biodiversity.

of species are known as wildlife resources. A **wildlife resource** is any free living organism, usually in the form of plants or animals, that has importance to humans. **Natural resources** are things found naturally on the Earth, both living and nonliving, that have a value to humans in some way. Natural resources usually fall under two categories, renewable resources and nonrenewable resources. A **renewable resource** is something that can be replaced in a reasonable amount of time. Examples of renewable resources include water, soil, air, and wildlife, along with the renewable energy resources like wind, solar, geothermal, and biomass in (Figure 36–2). A **nonrenewable resource** is something that cannot be replaced rapidly enough by natural processes, or that exists in fixed quantities on the Earth. Examples of

FIGURE 36–2 Examples of renewable resources like wind, solar energy, geothermal energy, and agricultural crops. (*Courtesy of Getty Images Inc.*)

FIGURE 36–2 Cont'd Examples of renewable resources like wind, solar energy, geothermal energy, and agricultural crops. (*Courtesy of Getty Images Inc.*)

FIGURE 36–3 Oil removed from the Earth's crust is an example of a nonrenewable resource. (*Courtesy of Getty Images Inc.*)

these kinds of resources include minerals and fossil fuels (Figure 36–3). The concern for conserving natural resources grows every year as human population continues to increase, resources are consumed in greater quantities, and the environment is degraded as a result of their use. The demand for resources by human society is one of the major threats to the Earth's biodiversity.

EXTINCTION

The complete loss of a species of organism from the Earth is called **extinction**. Once a species becomes extinct, it is gone from the planet forever. Studying the Earth's past history has revealed that extinction is a natural process. Amazingly, by studying the fossil record, paleontologists believe that over 99 percent of organisms that have ever lived on the planet have become extinct. Many of these organisms disappeared in what is known as mass extinctions. Scientists have identified five major mass extinction events in the Earth's past. The most famous of these is the Cretaceous/Tertiary extinction, which occurred 65 million years ago and wiped out the dinosaurs. Mass extinctions are believed to be caused by catastrophic natural disasters such as volcanic eruptions, asteroid impacts, the outbreak of disease, and rapid changes in climate. Today, many biologists believe that humans are causing the sixth mass extinction to occur on the Earth. Over the past 10,000 years, since the birth of civilization, humans have been responsible for the extinction of many species. Incredibly, scientists predict that current human activity could eradicate 50 percent of the Earth's species by the year 2100! Today many researchers estimate that we lose thousands of species each year. Most of these species are unidentified organisms lost in the destruction of tropical rainforests. Numerous compounds used in medicine and agriculture that have improved the quality of life have been derived from plants and animals. The potential loss of the benefits that these extinct organisms pose is reason enough to prevent their destruction. Human activity that causes extinction is the result of habitat destruction, commercial hunting, the introduction of invasive species, and environmental degradation. As human population increases, more land is needed for industry, housing, transportation, and agriculture. These are the main culprits of habitat destruction. The creation of dams, roadways, urban areas, mines, and agricultural fields has interrupted virtually every ecosystem on the planet. Some scientists estimate that 40 percent of the Sun's energy is now being used for agricultural practices alone. The loss of this energy by other species surely affects energy flow within ecosystems, therefore causing a decline in biodiversity. Commercial hunting is another leading cause of extinction that involves the practice of harvesting wildlife for its economic benefit. Commercial hunting was widely practiced in the past when large herds of animals roamed freely around the world. In the United States, the American bison was commercially hunted almost to extinction. In 1800 there were an estimated 60 million American bison roaming the west. In 1889 that number was reduced to just below 600 as a result of hunting (Figure 36–4).

The Passenger Pigeon was once one of the most numerous bird species in the United States. The size of their population during the 1800s

FIGURE 36–4 The American bison was nearly hunted to extinction in North America. (*Courtesy of Getty Images Inc.*)

FIGURE 36-5 The Passenger Pigeon, which was once one of the most numerous bird species in the United States, has became extinct as a result of human activity.

is estimated to be between 1 and 4 billion. Flocks of these birds were so large that it often took hours for them to cross the sky. The Passenger Pigeon became extinct around 1900 as a result of commercial hunting (Figure 36–5).

Today in Africa, elephants and rhinoceros are illegally hunted for the sale of their tusks and horns. The oceans are also open to commercial hunters. Many species of whales have become nearly extinct, along with the overharvest of fish such as the Atlantic Cod. This popular fish species has almost been wiped out over the past 200 years. In 1968, ecologist Garrett Hardin wrote an essay titled *The Tragedy of the Commons*. In this famous work, Hardin describes the destruction of shared resources as a result of their overuse. A shared resource is something that is not owned by anyone, like the ocean or public grazing lands. Hardin pointed out that because there is no ownership involved, the resources are exploited by their common use. Today, the tragedy of the commons is causing the loss of species and the decline of many ecosystems around the world.

The introduction of invasive species into an ecosystem can also lead to extinction. **Invasive species**, also known as exotic or alien species, are organisms that have been introduced into an area where they are not normally found. They are usually brought into a region by humans either purposely or by accident. Invasive species cause destruction to ecosystems because their populations can grow rapidly and spread as a result of the lack of natural enemies to keep their numbers in check. These organisms therefore compete with native species for resources. Invasive species in the form of plants, animals, fish, insects, and even fungi have caused the nearly complete destruction of many species in the United States. An Asian fungus that causes the disease known as chestnut blight is believed to have come into the United States on one tree that was brought to New York City from Asia. Fifty years later, this fungus has wiped out the American Chestnut tree from virtually every North America forest.

FIGURE 36-6   The zebra mussel is an example of an invasive species that is threatening the health of freshwater ecosystems in North America. (*Courtesy of U.S. Geological Survey.*)

The zebra mussel is another example of an invasive species that has been introduced into North America. This small freshwater mollusk is currently taking over many freshwater lakes and streams. Originating in Western Europe, the zebra mussel was transported to the United States in the ballast water of cargo ships. This small mussel increases its population so quickly that it rapidly covers the bottoms of boats, docks, water intake pipes, and other submerged structures. The rapid spread of this invasive creature is crowding out native species and disrupting many freshwater ecosystems (Figure 36–6).

The final contributing cause of extinction around the world is environmental degradation. Pollution of air, water, and soil is currently destroying or depleting the habitats of many species on the Earth. Industrial processes and the need for natural resources, along with the production of energy that supplies our modern world, are the main culprits of environmental destruction. Short-term damage to ecosystems, like oil spills and the use of pesticides, can cause an immediate loss of species. Longer-term damage such as climate change, acid precipitation, and ozone depletion can cause the gradual demise of organisms. Certainly the prevention and cleanup of environmental pollutants will result in the dramatic decline of the loss of species. Some species' only chance of survival today depends on keeping them alive in captivity. This is known as the zoo approach to species management. Although successful, this is not the best option, because organisms that are raised in captivity are susceptible to the loss of genetic diversity and the threat of inbreeding.

THE ENDANGERED SPECIES ACT

In 1973, the United States Government enacted the Endangered Species Act. This legislation was designed to protect endangered or threatened species. An **endangered species** is any living organism whose population has decreased to the point where it is in immediate danger of becoming extinct. A **threatened species** is any organism whose numbers are currently

Earth System Scientists

Edward O. Wilson

Born in 1929, Edward Wilson began his scientific career as an entomologist. An entomologist is a scientist who studies insects. His main research first focused on ant species. Wilson was one of the first scientists to identify the role of pheromones in insect communication. He dramatically displayed his findings by tracing out a line of pheromones extracted from the abdomen of an ant. He then demonstrated their significance when he displayed how a long line of ants diligently followed its trail. Wilson's focus on ants began to shift during the 1980s when he helped to found a new scientific discipline based on the social systems on non-human creatures, which he called sociobiology. Sociobiology looks at the effect of genetics on the role of behavior. Wilson first applied this to the study of social insects, such as ants and bees. Eventually his research was applied to humans, which created much controversy because of the notion that human behavior might be influenced by genetics. His focus began to shift again in the 1990s to the subject of biodiversity. In his famous book, *The Diversity of Life*, Wilson began to describe the incredible amount of diversity on the Earth, and more important, its present demise. Wilson called this the sixth extinction, and predicted that between 30 percent and 50 percent of species on the Earth might be extinct by the 21st century as a result of human activity. Currently E. O. Wilson is a professor at Harvard University.

declining, but can be easily saved if steps are taken to protect it. This important law prevents the loss of protected species as a result of their harvest or the destruction of their habitat. Currently the U. S. Department of the Interior and the Fish and Wildlife Service keeps a comprehensive list of 1,300 organisms that are endangered or threatened in the United States. Worldwide there are more than 1,800 identified endangered or threatened species. Since 1973, the Endangered Species Act has successfully saved many organisms that were on the verge of becoming extinct, such as the Peregrine Falcon, American Alligator, Gray Whale, and Brown Pelican. Another important piece of legislation is the Convention on International Trade in Endangered Species of Wild Fauna and Flora, also known as CITES. This agreement among 169 countries around the world took effect on July 1, 1975. CITES is designed to protect organisms that might be harmed as a result of trade between nations. There are approximately 5,000 animal and 28,000 plant species protected by this international agreement.

WILDLIFE MANAGEMENT

Along with the cleanup and reduction of environmental pollution, reducing the destruction of, improving, or maintaining habitats are important ways to prevent extinction. This is known as wildlife management. **Wildlife management** is the planned use, protection, and control of wildlife using sound ecological principles. The goal of wildlife management is to maintain a healthy population of a specific target species. One of the most important concepts in wildlife management is identifying the specific habitat of an organism. Every living thing on the Earth requires a habitat to live. A **habitat** is the specific food, water, cover, and space requirements that an organism needs. Habitats vary greatly for different species. For example, one drop of pond water can provide a healthy habitat for an aquatic microorganism. In contrast, hundreds of square miles of forestland makes up the habitat for one grizzly bear. Many organisms on the Earth make long distance movements known as migrations. These include many bird species, which require habitats spread over thousands of miles. Biologists sometimes classify organisms as being a generalist or specialist when it comes to habitat requirements. A **generalist** is a type of organism that can live in a variety of habitats, and is easily adaptable. Many organisms that have managed to live among human society, like some bird species, rodents, insects, and dogs, are good examples of generalists. A **specialist** requires very specific habitat requirements, which make it more susceptible to becoming endangered. Panda bears, for example, eat only specific types of bamboo found in the mountainous regions of China.

Techniques used in wildlife management include habitat improvement. This involves identifying and providing the specific habitat requirements for an organism. Habitat improvement is often achieved through the manipulation of vegetation in an area. Establishing wildlife refuges and wilderness areas are also useful for the protection of species. A wildlife refuge is an area that has been set aside for the protection of wildlife. These include large tracts of land that are protected from human activity. Sometimes a series of small stopover refuges are used to help migratory bird species move through an area. Wilderness areas are large areas of undisturbed and uninhabited land used for the protection of wildlife. The use of smaller areas of undisturbed ecosystems are sometimes referred to as ecological islands. An **ecological island** is a protected ecosystem, containing only native species, that is completely surrounded by disturbed land. Another wildlife management tool is controlled hunting. This is a method often used to keep the populations of certain species down, to prevent starvation and disease, and to allow other species to thrive. Maintaining ecotones is another effective method of wildlife management. An **ecotone** is an area where two different ecosystems come together, also known as the edge effect. Often these areas are very diverse, and support high populations of species (Figure 36-7). Managing wildlife also include fisheries management, which encourages the growth of populations of certain aquatic species. Regulating fishing seasons, putting limits on the size and number of species harvested, restocking, and the protection of breeding grounds are some of the techniques used to manage fisheries.

SECTION REVIEW

1. What is biodiversity?

2. What are three reasons why it is important to preserve biodiversity on Earth?

FIGURE 36–7 The area where a forest meets a field is known as an ecotone, a zone of high biodiversity where two ecosystems come together, also known as the edge effect. (*Courtesy of Getty Images Inc.*)

3. Define the term wildlife resource:

4. Describe the differences between renewable and nonrenewable resources:

5. What is extinction, and list three practices that cause extinction:

7. What is the tragedy of the commons?

8. Define the term invasive species, and provide two examples of an invasive species:

9. Briefly describe the Endangered Species Act:

10. What is a habitat?

12. Explain three methods used for wildlife management:

13. Describe the difference between an ecotone and an ecological island.

14. What are three techniques used for fisheries management?

@ WEB Links

FOR MORE INFORMATION GO TO THESE WEB LINKS:

<http://www.biodiversityhotspots.org/xp/Hotspots>

<http://www.fws.gov/endangered/>

<http://www.natureserve.org/>

<http://www.invasivespeciesinfo.gov/>

<http://www.invasive.org/>

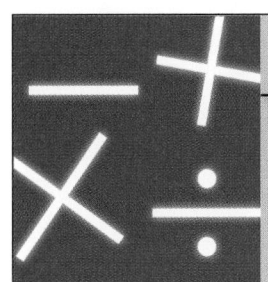

earth math

1) If the total number of species on the Earth is estimated at 13,620,000, and there are approximately 320,000 plant species and 8,000,000 insects, what percentage of all species on the planet are plants? What percentage are insects?

CHAPTER SUMMARY

Biodiversity is the richness and variety of living organisms on the Earth. Preserving biodiversity is important for the healthy function of the biosphere. A wildlife resource is any organism that has a value to human beings. A natural resource is a naturally occurring thing on the Earth, both living and non-living, that has value to humans in some way. Natural resources are classified as renewable and nonrenewable. A renewable resource is one that can be replenished in a reasonable amount of time. A nonrenewable resource comes in fixed quantities on the Earth or cannot be replaced in a reasonable amount of time. When a species is lost from the Earth forever it is known as extinction. It is estimated that 99 percent of all things that have ever lived on the Earth have become extinct. This has usually occurred in the form of natural disasters known as mass extinctions. Today human activity is causing the extinction of species on Earth at an alarming rate. Extinction is caused as a result of pollution, habitat destruction, commercial hunting, and by invasive species. The tragedy of the commons is a concept that describes the destruction of a shared resource as a result of its overuse. This is causing the loss of species and the decline of many ecosystems around the world. Invasive species are organisms that have been introduced into an area where they do not normally live. Their populations therefore grow unchecked and compete with native organisms for resources. The Endangered Species Act is a law that is designed to protect certain species from becoming extinct. Wildlife management is the planned use, protection, and control of wildlife using sound ecological principles. The main goal of wildlife management is to sustain the habitats of specific organisms. A habitat is the food, water, space, and cover requirements of a specific organism. An organism that has very specific habitat requirements is known as a specialist. An organism that can survive in a variety of habitats is called a generalist. Techniques used for management include manipulating the vegetation in an area, creating wildlife refuges and wilderness areas, and controlled hunting. An ecological island is a protected ecosystem, containing only native species, that is completely surrounded by disturbed land. Maintaining ecotones, which are areas where two ecosystems come together, is also another method of wildlife management. These locations tend to support a high amount of biodiversity. Fisheries management is another part of managing wildlife. It includes setting size limits, controlling the numbers of aquatic organism that can be harvested, establishing specific times for harvesting, restocking programs, and protecting breeding grounds.

CHAPTER REVIEW

Multiple Choice

1. The use of living things for agriculture, medicine, and recreation is an example of:
   a. intrinsic value
   b. biodiversity
   c. instrumental value
   d. tragedy of the commons

2. Which of the following is a renewable resource:
   a. oil
   b. coal
   c. uranium
   d. soil

3. Which of the following is a nonrenewable resource:
   a. minerals
   b. water
   c. trees
   d. wildlife

4. Extinction is caused by all of the following except:
   a. habitat destruction
   b. wildlife management
   c. commercial hunting
   d. pollution

5. Commercial hunting resulted in the extinction of which species:
   a. passenger pigeon
   b. American bison
   c. brown pelican
   d. American alligator

6. An organism's specific water, food, cover, and space requirements are known as its:
   a. ecotone
   b. ecological Island
   c. habitat
   d. species

7. An organism that can live in a variety of habitats is called:
   a. a specialist
   b. an invasive species
   c. extinct
   d. a generalist

8. An organism that can live only in a specific habitat is called:
   a. a specialist
   b. an invasive species
   c. extinct
   d. a generalist

9. Which of the following is an example of an invasive species:
   a. passenger pigeon
   b. zebra mussel
   c. American bison
   d. peregrine falcon

10. The area where two ecosystems meet is known as:
    a. an ecotone
    b. an Ecological Island
    c. a habitat
    d. the tragedy of the commons

Matching   *Match the terms with the correct definitions*

a. biodiversity
b. biosphere
c. intrinsic value
d. instrumental value
e. natural resource

f. renewable resource
g. nonrenewable resource
h. wildlife resource
i. extinction
j. invasive species

k. endangered species
l. habitat
m. ecological island
m. ecotone

1. _____ something that cannot be replaced rapidly enough by natural processes, or that exists in fixed quantities on the Earth.
2. _____ organisms that have been introduced into an area where they are not normally found.
3. _____ an area where two different ecosystems come together, known as the edge effect.
4. _____ The richness and diversity of life on Earth.

5. _____ Maintaining biodiversity of the planet because every living thing has a right to live on the Earth.
6. _____ All of the living components of the Earth's ecosystems.
7. _____ Something that can be replaced in a reasonable amount of time.
8. _____ A protected ecosystem, containing only native species, which is completely surrounded by disturbed land.
9. _____ Things found naturally on the Earth, both living and nonliving, that have a value to humans in some way.
10. _____ The specific food, water, cover, and space requirements that an organism needs to live.
11. _____ Any free living organism, usually plants or animals, that has importance to humans.
12. _____ preserving biodiversity because certain species might be a resource to humans.
13. _____ The complete loss of a species of organism from the Earth forever.
14. _____ Any living organism whose population has decreased to the point where it is in immediate danger of becoming extinct.

Critical Thinking

1. Which argument for preserving biodiversity do you think is most important: the intrinsic or instrumental? Explain.

Glossary

A

A-horizon Uppermost layer of a soil, commonly called topsoil.

abiotic Nonliving.

abiotic factors Nonliving factors in the environment, such as wind, temperature, humidity, or minerals.

abrasion Physical weathering of rocks by the action of particles rubbing against one another.

absorbed Taken in or soaked up matter or energy.

absorption The process of absorbing, or when a solid, liquid, or gas takes in matter or energy and holds it.

absorption spectrum A spectrum of light where specific wavelengths are absorbed leaving gaps in the form of dark lines within the spectrum, also known as a dark line spectrum.

accumulation To collect or build up a substance or substances.

acid deposition The deposit of acidic substances on the Earth's surface.

acid precipitation Precipitation that contains high concentrations of sulfuric or nitric acids and has a pH of 5.0 or lower.

acid shock Rapid introduction of acidic water into lakes and streams caused by melting snow.

acidic A solution with a pH lower than 7.0.

adaptations Adjusting to new conditions by the process of natural selection and evolution.

adhesion The attraction of water molecules to a hydrophilic substance.

adiabatic cooling The process by which rising air is cooled by expansion.

aerobic bacteria Bacteria that require oxygen to live.

aerovane A wind instrument that records both air speed and direction.

Agnatha The taxonomical classification of a jawless class of invertebrates that includes the lampreys.

Agricultural Revolution A historic period that included the development and improvement of agriculture that is believed to have begun approximately 10,000 years ago.

air The gases that together make up Earth's atmosphere; they include nitrogen, oxygen, argon, water vapor, carbon dioxide, and other trace elements.

air mass A large body of air that has similar temperature and moisture characteristics.

albedo The reflective ability of an object or surface.

alfisols A particular order of fertile soils that contain high amounts of aluminum and iron, with a well-developed topsoil; associated with deciduous forests.

algae Single-celled or multicelled aquatic organisms that derive their energy from photosynthesis.

algal bloom A rapid increase in the population of algae resulting from the introduction of nutrient fertilizers into an aquatic ecosystem.

alkalinity Having a pH greater than 7.0; also called a base.

alluvial soils Rich, fertile soils that are formed by the deposition of minerals by liquid water.

alpine glaciers Glaciers that are located within mountain ranges; also known as mountain glaciers.

altitude The particular elevation or height of something above sea level, or the angle of a celestial object above the horizon.

amber A yellow or brownish yellow petrified tree sap.

ammonia A colorless compound consisting of nitrogen and hydrogen (NH_3); used by plants as a source of nitrogen and commonly used as fertilizer.

amoebae A type of free-moving single-celled Protoctista.

Amphibia The taxonomical classification of a class of vertebrates, commonly called amphibians, that include frogs and salamanders.

anadromous A type of fish that reproduces in freshwater and lives its adult life in saltwater, such as salmon.

anaerobic bacteria A type of bacteria that live in an environment without oxygen.

anemometer An instrument that measures wind speed.

angiosperm The taxonomical classification of a specific type of plant that reproduces by flowers that produce seeds with a protective coat.

angle of insolation The specific angle at which incoming solar radiation strikes the Earth's surface.

Animalia A taxonomical classification of the kingdom of organisms that are commonly known as animals.

anions A negatively charged ion such as chloride (Cl^-) or nitrate (NO_3^-).

Annelida A taxonomical classification for the phylum that includes all segmented worms such as the earthworm.

anthropogenic A term that describes any substance that is created or introduced into the environment by human activity.

anthropologist A scientist who specializes in the study of the origin, development, and culture of human beings.

anticline A type of fold in rock strata that forms an arched shape.

aphelion The point in the orbit of a planet when it is farthest from the Sun.

aphotic zone A particular zone in an aquatic ecosystem where there is no light.

apogee The point in the orbit of the Moon or an artificial satellite when it is farthest from the Earth.

Apollo asteroids A classification of asteroids with orbits that cross the Earth's orbit.

Appalachian orogeny The geologic event that formed the Appalachian Mountains approximately 290 million years ago by the collision of Africa with North America.

apparent motion The perceived movement of celestial objects caused by the Earth's rotation as they arc across the sky.

aquatic A term that describes anything that lives in water.

aquatic organisms Living things whose habitat is water.

aquifer Large amounts of water stored in porous or fragmented rock under ground.

arachnids A taxonomical classification of arthropods that includes spiders and ticks.

archaeopteryx The fossilized remains of a 150-million-year-old birdlike reptile.

Archean eon A division of the geologic time scale marking the beginning of Earth's history from 4.6 to 2.5 billion years ago; also part of the Precambrian period.

archaeology A specialized division of anthropology that searches for and studies the remains of ancient human culture.

arctic air mass A large body of air that forms over the high latitudes and is usually very cold and dry.

armored fish A type of jawed fish that was covered with armor plates; it became extinct more than 362 million years ago.

artesian wells Free-flowing wells that discharge water from the ground and are recharged from a higher elevation.

Arthropoda A taxonomical classification for the phylum that includes insects, spiders, and crustaceans.

Artiodactyla A taxonomical classification for an order of mammals with even numbers of toes on each foot. These include sheep, deer, cattle, and pigs.

asteroid belt A region in the solar system located between the orbits of Mars and Jupiter where there are a high number of asteroids.

asteroid An object orbiting the Sun that is smaller than a planet and has no atmosphere.

asthenosphere An area of flowing plastic-like molten rock located directly below the Earth's crust to a depth of approximately 700 km.

astronomical unit A unit of measurement used to mark the distance of a planet from the Sun. One astronomical unit is equivalent to 93 million miles, which is also the approximate distance of the Earth from the Sun.

astronomy The scientific discipline that studies all aspects of outer space.

Aten asteroids Asteroids with orbits that lie between the Earth and the Sun.

atmosphere The outer layer of gas that surrounds a planet.

atmospheric moisture The amount of water vapor that is present in the air.

atmospheric pressure The weight of a column of air at a specific point in the atmosphere, usually measured in millibars or inches of mercury.

atomic mass The exact mass of the protons and neutrons in the nucleus of an atom, measured in atomic mass units.

atomic number The number of protons in the nucleus of an atom.

atoms The smallest particles, also called elements, that can be combined to form compounds. Atoms consists of a nucleus that is made up of subatomic particles known as protons and neutrons, which are orbited by electrons.

aurora australis The Southern Hemisphere's equivalent of the northern lights, or aurora borealis, which is caused by streams of particles interacting with the Earth's magnetic field.

autotrophs Organisms that produce their own food by photosynthesis, such as plants or algae, or by chemosynthesis, such as certain bacteria.

autumnal equinox The time of the year, on or around September 21, when the Earth's axis of rotation is aligned perpendicular to the plane of the Sun and the length of daylight (12 hours) equals the length of darkness (12 hours).

avalanche A large mass of snow, ice, or rock rapidly sliding downhill.

Aves A taxonomical classification of a class of vertebrates commonly called birds.

axis A straight line around which an object rotates.

axis of rotation An imaginary line drawn through an object, around which it seems to rotate.

azimuth The location of an object above the horizon, which is divided into the 360 degrees of a circle.

B

B-horizon The second layer of soil, also known as the subsoil, that lies below the topsoil or A-horizon.

backbone The common term for the hard skeleton, or vertebrae, that makes up an organism's spinal column.

bacteria Microscopic, single-celled organisms that do not have a cell nucleus and are part of the kingdom Monera.

barometer An instrument that is used to measure atmospheric pressure, also called barometric pressure.

barometric pressure The measure of the weight of a column of air at a particular location on a planet; also known as atmospheric pressure.

barren An area that is lifeless or lacking vegetation.

basalt A common fine-grained volcanic rock that is dark, mafic, and dense.

BCE The acronym for Before Contemporary Era, which denotes the period formerly referred to as B.C. or the time prior to the birth of Jesus Christ.

bedrock A large mass of unbroken or undisturbed rock usually buried deep within the ground.

benchmarks A series of human-created markers or monuments that designate the precise latitude, longitude, and elevation of a specific point on the Earth's surface.

benthic zone An aquatic life zone located on the bottom of a body of water.

Big Bang A popular theory of the origin of the universe, which is believed to have begun after a violent explosion that propelled matter and energy away from one central point.

binomial An ancient Greek term meaning "two names," which is commonly used for the classification of organisms.

biodiversity The richness and diversity of life on Earth.

biogeochemical cycling The natural recycling of elements between the nonliving world and the living world.

biological characteristics An organism's unique physical or chemical features.

biological diversity The variety of living species on Earth and their unique genes.

biological succession The gradual replacement of one community of species by another in a slow, predictable manner.

biomass A shortened term for biological mass, which is the total dry weight of an organism.

biomes Another term for a land-based ecosystem, also called a terrestrial ecosystem.

biosphere A term used to describe all of the living components of the Earth's ecosystems.

biotechnology The scientific discipline that studies the use or manipulation of living organisms to perform specific tasks.

biotic Living.

bipedalism A term used to describe an organism that walks on two feet.

bivalve mollusks A classification of aquatic organisms that have a hinged shell that can open and close.

bivalves *See* bivalve mollusks.

black hole A theoretical celestial object with a strong gravitational attraction that prevents light from escaping its surface.

blue supergiant A classification of massive stars that are blue, extremely hot, and bright.

blue-green algae An aquatic organism that is similar to bacteria but gains its energy from photosynthesis; *see* cyanobacteria.

boiling point The specific temperature at which a substance begins to change its phase from a liquid to a gas; also known as vaporization.

boreal forest Another term for the coniferous forest biome.

bright line spectrum A type of spectrum where bright lines of specific wavelengths of visible light appear within a spectrum that represent wavelengths of light emitted from a substance, also known as an emission spectrum.

broad-leafed trees A type of tree that photosynthesizes using large flat leaves.

Bronze Age A period beginning approximately 5,000 years ago and ending 3,000 years ago when bronze, a metal alloy composed of copper and tin, was widely used.

brown algae A brownish multicelled aquatic organism commonly called seaweed.

Brown dwarf Cool stars that have masses well below that of the Sun, and are at the end of their life cycle.

buffer A substance that is capable of stabilizing the acidity or alkalinity of a solution.

buoys Floating markers that are anchored to a specific spot in a body of water.

burial To cover something with soil or rock.

C

C-horizon The third layer of a soil, composed of unconsolidated rock or transported parent material.

calcium carbonate The chemical compound that makes up the mineral calcite, which forms limestone.

caldera A large crater (more than 1 mile in diameter) caused by a violent volcanic eruption.

California Current A wind-driven surface ocean current that brings cold water from the North Pacific south toward the equator along the coast of California.

Cambrian period A period of the geologic time scale marking the appearance of the earliest shelled marine organisms that began approximately 544 million years ago and ended 490 million years ago.

capillary action The movement of water molecules upward in tiny tubes as a result of adhesion and cohesion.

carbohydrates Chemical compounds that are made up of carbon, hydrogen, and oxygen, many of which are produced by the process of photosynthesis, such as sugar and starch.

carbon dioxide A chemical compound, usually in the form of a gas, that is made up of one atom of carbon and two atoms of oxygen (CO_2) and is the by-product of respiration and combustion.

carbonation The addition of carbon dioxide gas to something.

Carboniferous period A period in the geologic time scale beginning approximately 362 million years ago and ending 290 million years ago, when an abundance of coal-forming trees and ferns lived.

Carnivora A taxonomical classification for an order of mammals that includes carnivores, which have sharp canine teeth, such as bears and lions.

carnivores Meat-eating organisms.

catadromous A type of fish that reproduces in saltwater and lives its life in freshwater, such as the Atlantic eel.

catastrophic A great and sudden disaster.

cations Positively charged elements such as sodium (Na^+) or calcium (Ca_2^+).

CE The acronym for Contemporary Era, which denotes the period formerly referred to as A.D. or the time after the birth of Jesus Christ.

celestial A term that pertains to something outside the Earth's atmosphere.

Celestial equator An imaginary line drawn from the Earth's equator out into space.

celestial object An object that is located outside the Earth's atmosphere.

cement A substance that binds things together.

cementation The process of binding something together.

Cenozoic era A division of the geologic time scale that began 65 million years ago with the extinction of the dinosaurs and stretches to the present day.

centripetal force The force that keeps an object moving in a circular path.

Cephalopods A taxonomical classification for a class of mollusks, such as octopuses and squids.

Cetacea A taxonomical classification for an order of aquatic mammals, such as dolphins and whales.

CFCs *See* chlorofluorocarbons.

channel The portion of a moving body of water where water is currently flowing.

chaparral A type of biome that has hot dry summers and cool rainy winters.

chemical energy A form of energy that is stored in the chemical bonds between atoms and molecules.

chemical weathering The breakdown of rocks into smaller rock particles by a chemical process.

chemosynthesis A method of deriving energy from the breakdown or formation of organic compounds.

chlorofluorocarbons Human-created molecules, commonly used as refrigerants, in electrical manufacturing, and in foam production, that are responsible for ozone destruction; also a greenhouse gas.

Chondrichthyes A taxonomical classification for a class of chordates commonly known as cartilaginous fish, such as sharks.

Chordata A taxonomical classification for the phylum of animals that have a spinal chord.

chromosphere The specific layer of the Sun that is located above the photosphere.

cinder cone A small, straight-sided volcanic cone made up of pyroclastic material.

class A taxonomical classification for things that have at least one similar feature.

clay The smallest size classification of a rock particle that is between 0.00001 and 0.0004 centimeters in diameter.

cleavage The breaking of minerals along specific planes of weakness caused by the internal arrangement of their atoms.

climate The long-term weather patterns of a specific region on the Earth, usually defined by the area's annual temperature and precipitation values.

cloud A large mass of condensing water droplets and ice crystals in the atmosphere.

Cnidaria A taxonomical classification for the phylum of animals that includes jellyfish, corals, and sea anemones.

coal The rocklike fossilized remains of ancient plants, which is used as fuel.

coastal wetlands A type of wetland that is located near the coastline of a land mass.

cohesion The attraction of water molecules to one another.

cold front The zone where a cold air mass overtakes and replaces a warm air mass.

colonies A large grouping of a particular species of organism in a specific area.

color The specific appearance of an object that is caused by its ability to absorb or reflect visible light energy in specific wavelengths.

coma The gas and dust that are released from and surround the nucleus of a comet.

combustion A chemical reaction that results in light and heat, commonly called burning.

comet A mixture of frozen compounds and rock that orbits the Sun and which has a distinct tail composed of vaporized gas and dust that always points away from the Sun.

comet's nucleus The frozen compounds and rock that form the core of a comet.

comet's tail The vaporized gas and dust that trail away from the nucleus of a comet.

commensalism A specific type of symbiotic relationship in which one organism benefits from a host and the host is neither helped nor harmed.

community All the species of organisms that reside in a particular area.

compaction The reduction in volume of a substance as a result of extreme pressure or weight.

composite cone volcano A volcano that is composed of both solidified lava and pyroclastic material.

composting The breakdown of organic material by decomposing bacteria, insects, and fungi into humus.

compounds Substances that are formed from joining two or more elements in specific proportions.

compression To press something together into a smaller space.

compressional primary wave (P wave) A seismic wave produced at the focus of an earthquake that is the fastest of all seismic waves and can travel through all states of matter.

conclusion The final summation of the scientific method that states what has been learned.

condensation The change in phase from a gas to a liquid.

condensation nuclei Microscopic particles floating in the atmosphere on which water condenses to form clouds.

conduction The transfer of heat energy by direct molecular contact.

confined aquifer Groundwater that is located below an impermeable rock layer.

coniferous forest A specific type of biome that experiences long, cold winters and short, hot summers, where evergreen trees (conifers) are the main vegetation.

conifers A cone-bearing tree, also called an evergreen.

constellations Specific groupings of stars that resemble mythological figures, objects, or animals.

contact metamorphism Metamorphism of rock by the heat of contact associated with an igneous intrusion.

contaminated To pollute or make impure.

contiguous Connected or close together sharing a common boundary such as the 48 states of the United States. Hawaii and Alaska are not part of the contiguous United States.

continental crust The specific portion of the Earth's outer crust that is relatively thick, lower in density, and composed primarily of granitic rock that makes up the continents.

continental glaciers Large masses of accumulating snow and ice that cover an entire continent.

continental polar air mass A large mass of cold air that forms over land near the poles and has low moisture.

continental shelf The relatively shallow region of the ocean that surrounds a continent.

continental tropical air mass A large mass of warm air that forms over land near the equator and has low moisture.

contour interval The specific change in elevation associated with each contour line on a topographical map.

contour lines Isolines that mark areas of equal elevation on a topographical map.

contraction The reduction in the volume of a substance that is usually associated with lowering its temperature.

convection The transfer of heat energy in a fluid as a result of a change in density associated with a change in temperature.

convection cell The circular movement of a fluid caused by a change in temperature and density that is associated with the transfer of heat.

convection currents The specific pattern of movement of a fluid caused by convection.

convective zone An inner layer of the Sun where heat from the core is convected outward.

convergence The process of coming together.

convergent plate boundaries An area on the Earth's surface where two tectonic plates come together.

coordinate system A system of precise location using a grid pattern of intersecting lines.

coral bleaching The whitening of living coral as a result of the die-off of the coral's symbiotic algae, which can eventually lead to the death of the coral itself. It is believed to be caused by exposure to environmental stress.

coral reefs Large underwater structures located in warm, shallow saltwater that are built by colonies of coral; composed primarily of calcium carbonate and sand.

corals Benthic aquatic organisms that live in warm, shallow saltwater and can build shells from calcium carbonate.

Coriolis effect The deflection of free-floating objects to the right of travel in the Northern Hemisphere and to the left of travel in the Southern Hemisphere as a result of the Earth's rotation.

corona The outermost layer of the Sun, which stretches millions of miles out into space, where temperatures are in the millions of degrees.

creep The slow, almost imperceptible movement of soil and rock down a slope.

Cretaceous period A period of the geologic time scale that began approximately 142 million years ago and ended 65 million years ago and marks the height of the age of dinosaurs and the appearance of flowering plants.

crinoids Animals, commonly called sea lilies, that use branching arms to capture tiny floating prey in the water; can be free floating or attached to the bottom by a stalk.

cross-cutting relationship A natural law in geology that states that intrusions or faults are younger than the rocks they are in.

crust The solid outer layer of the Earth, composed of rock.

Crustaceans A taxonomical classification of arthropods that includes lobster, shrimp, and crabs.

crystalline A substance or structure that is made up of crystals.

crystallization Rock changing phase from a liquid to a solid; also called solidification.

crystal A term that describes the distinct recurring pattern of the atoms or molecules in a specific mineral that form a unique recognizable structure.

currents A specific pattern of movement within a fluid.

cut bank A specific physical feature of a flowing body of water caused by the erosion of material away from the outside curve of a meander, resulting in a steep dropoff.

cyanobacteria A photosynthetic, oxygen-producing single-celled organism; also known as blue-green algae.

cycads Ancient shrublike trees that are related to the conifers.

cyclic A periodic or recurring event.

cyclone A term for winds that spiral inward and around a low-pressure center.

D

D-horizon The fourth layer of soil; also known as the consolidated bedrock.

dark line spectrum A spectrum of light where specific wavelengths are absorbed leaving gaps in the form of dark lines within the spectrum, also known as an absorption spectrum.

data Specific information gathered for use or analysis.

daughter element The element that forms after the decay of a radioactive isotope.

deciduous forest A specific type of biome that is marked by long, hot summers and cold winters, where deciduous trees are the primary vegetation.

deciduous tree A type of tree that loses its leaves each autumn and goes into dormancy during winter.

declination The angular distance north or south of the celestial equator, used to mark the position of a celestial object in the equatorial coordinate system.

decomposers Organisms that break down and decay dead organisms or waste.

decomposing organic material The breakdown of the remains of a living thing.

deep pools A physical feature of a flowing body of water that results when the moving water erodes and deepens the stream bottom on the outside curve of a meander.

deficient Lacking something essential to life.

deformed rock layers Rock strata exposed to outside forces that have caused them to be tilted, folded, faulted, or overturned.

delta The formation that results at the mouth of a river where sediments carried by the river have been deposited.

denitrifying bacteria A specific type of bacteria that converts nitrogen compounds found in soil into atmospheric nitrogen.

density The mass per unit volume of a substance, usually expressed in grams per cubic centimeter.

depletion The loss of something.

deposition To put down or place something.

derived units The combination of two or more fundamental units of measurement, such as miles per hour.

desert A specific type of biome that receives little or no moisture throughout the year and generally lacks an abundance of vegetation.

destruction The act of tearing down or ruining something.

detritivores Organisms that consume dead and decayed organisms or waste; *see* decomposers.

Devonian period A period of the geologic time scale that began approximately 418 million years ago and ended 362 million years ago, marking the appearance of the first amphibians and the rise of fish.

dew point The temperature to which the air would need to be cooled to become saturated with water at a specific atmospheric pressure.

dew point depression The difference between the wet bulb and dry bulb temperatures; also called the wet bulb depression.

diatomic A term that refers to a molecule that consists of two atoms.

diatoms Microscopic algae that build a protective silicate shell.

dinosaurs A class of reptile and birdlike organisms that were dominant on the Earth for approximately 200 million years and became extinct 65 million years ago.

disassociate To pull apart or separate.

discharge To unload or empty.

discharge rate The amount of water passing by a particular point in a flowing body of water.

disease-causing agents Specific organisms that cause or spread disease.

dislodged To be removed or forced out.

disphotic zone The dimly lit portion of an aquatic ecosystem that cannot support photosynthesis.

displaced rocks Rocks that have been moved or transported to a new location.

dissolve To enter into a solution.

dissolved oxygen The amount of oxygen gas that is dissolved in water.

disturbed areas Ecosystems or parts of ecosystems on the Earth that have been destroyed or disrupted.

diurnal tides High and low tides that occur only once every day.

divergent plate boundary A point in the Earth's crust where two tectonic plates are moving away from one another.

diverging Moving apart or away from one another.

DNA The short form of deoxyribonucleic acid, which is the molecule that holds all of an organism's genes and is responsible for the replication of a cell.

domesticate To adapt for life with human beings.

downdrafts Strong vertical winds that blow downward from the base of a cloud.

drainage basin The total land area that contributes water to a river system, pond, or lake; also known as a watershed.

dredging A method of mining that involves the removal of sediments from the bottom of a body of water.

drizzle A form of precipitation that consists of tiny liquid water droplets.

droughts Extended periods when little or no precipitation is received by a specific region.

dry ice The solid form of carbon dioxide.

duration The length of time that it takes for an event to occur.

dust devils A term to describe very small cyclonic winds that kick up dust and whirl it across the landscape.

dwarf planet A non-luminous object that orbits around a star which has sufficient gravity to form a spherical shape, and whose orbit has not cleared its path of other celestial objects.

dynamic Energetic, always changing or moving.

dynamic equilibrium A balance between two opposing processes that occur at the same rate in an energetic system, such as a river or stream.

E

Earth's core The extremely hot and dense center of the Earth, which is believed to be composed of iron and nickel.

Earth's magnetic field The magnetic field that surrounds and protects the Earth from harmful radiation, which is believed to be generated by the Earth's core.

earthquake The violent, rapid shaking of the Earth caused by a rupture in the crust.

eccentricity The mathematical expression of how far an ellipse is from a perfect circle, which can be determined by dividing the distance between the foci by the length of the major axis.

eclipse The cutting off of all or part of the light of one celestial body by another.

ecliptic An imaginary plane in which the Earth orbits the Sun.

ecological island A protected ecosystem, containing only native species, which is completely surrounded by disturbed land.

ecology The scientific discipline that studies how organisms interact with their environment.

ecosphere A term that describes all the life zones that exist on Earth, which is made up of the atmosphere, hydrosphere, lithosphere, and biosphere.

ecosystem The interaction between the biotic and abiotic factors in a specific area.

ecotone An area where two different ecosystems come together, also known as the edge effect. Often these areas are very diverse, and support high populations of species.

Edentata A taxonomical classification for an order of mammals that have reduced or no teeth, such as anteaters and sloths.

El Niño *See* El Niño Southern Oscillation.

El Niño Southern Oscillation (ENSO) An increase in the sea surface temperature off the western coast of South America near the equator, which leads to changes in climate around the world.

electrical energy A form of energy that flows by exciting electrons in specific elements called conductors, which produces an electric current.

electrical potential An element or ion's electrical charge.

electromagnetic radiation A type of energy that travels in the form of a wave and needs no medium for transfer.

electromagnetic spectrum The range of specific wavelengths and frequencies that identify the specific forms of electromagnetic energy.

electrons Negatively charged subatomic particles that surround the nucleus of an atom.

elements The 109 identified atoms that have a definite number of protons, neutrons, and electrons.

ellipse The oval-like path of the orbit of a celestial object around two points known as foci, one of which is the Sun.

elliptical galaxy A type of galaxy whose stars form an elliptical shape.

emission spectrum A type of spectrum where bright lines of specific wavelengths of visible light appear within a spectrum that represent wavelengths of light emitted from a substance, also known as a bright line spectrum.

endangered species Any living organism whose population has decreased to the point where it is in immediate danger of becoming extinct.

energy The ability to cause change or perform work.

energy pyramid The mathematical model that describes the transfer of energy through a food chain, which illustrates the loss of energy at each trophic level.

engineer A skilled person who uses scientific principles to solve practical problems and design efficient systems.

eon The largest division of geologic time, which is measured in billions or hundreds of millions of years.

epicenter The point on the Earth's surface directly above the focus of an earthquake.

epoch The smallest division of geologic time, which is measured in millions or thousands of years.

equator The imaginary line, also known as zero degrees latitude, that divides the Earth in half into the Northern and Southern Hemispheres.

equatorial A term referring to a location near the equator.

equilibrium A state of balance.

era The second largest division of geologic time, which is measured in the hundreds of millions or millions of years and marks the mass extinction of species on Earth.

erosion The movement of rock particles or soil by wind, water, and the force of gravity.

eruption The sudden release of lava or pyroclastic material from a volcano.

euphotic zone The uppermost life zone in an aquatic ecosystem that receives enough light to support photosynthesis.

Eurasia The name for the large continent where Europe and Asia are located.

eurypterid An extinct marine organism that resembled a large scorpion; it flourished during the Permian and Devonian periods; also called the New York State fossil.

eutrophic lake A classification for a lake that is relatively cloudy, warm, and shallow and has an abundance of nutrients that support a large population of aquatic plants and animals.

eutrophication The rapid introduction of nutrient fertilizers into an aquatic ecosystem, which leads to an increase in aquatic plants and algae.

evaporation The phase change of a liquid changing into a gas.

evaporative cooling A cooling process caused by the evaporation of a liquid from a surface, which is the result of the evaporating liquid absorbing energy from the surrounding environment, therefore cooling it.

evapotranspiration The important pathway by which water moves from the soil, through the body of a plant, and evaporates off the leaf surface back into the atmosphere.

evidence A set of facts, proof, or demonstration used to support a theory.

evolution The theory that describes how natural changes in the genes of organisms lead to the development of new traits, and therefore new species, over time.

exfoliation The process by which layers of rock peel off the parent rock.

exosphere The zone outside of Earth's atmosphere that is commonly known as outer space.

expand To increase the volume of a substance.

expansion The process of increasing the volume of a substance.

expansion joints Flexible material constructed into bridges, buildings, and other large structures to allow for the building material to expand and contract when exposed to changes in temperature.

experiment A controlled test to prove or disprove a hypothesis.

explosive eruption The violent release of pyroclastic material from a volcano.

extinction The complete loss of a species of organism from the Earth.

extrusive rock A type of igneous rock that is formed at the Earth's surface from the solidification of lava.

F

family A taxonomical classification for a group of organisms that have similar characteristics.

fault A large break or crack in a rock mass formed by tectonic stress that results in the displacement of rock strata.

faulted rock Rock strata that contains a fault.

felsic rocks A classification of igneous rocks that are light colored and low density and contain silicates and aluminum.

fermentation An anaerobic chemical process by which complex compounds, such as sugars and starches, are reduced into simple compounds, such as alcohol and carbon dioxide, by microorganisms.

fertile soil A common term used to describe a soil that supports healthy crop growth.

fertilizers A term used to describe chemical compounds that are required by plants for healthy growth.

field capacity The moisture content of a soil when its pore spaces contain 50 percent air and 50 percent water, which is perfect for the growth of plants.

First Quarter Moon A phase of the Moon when it has completed the first quarter of its orbit around the Earth and half of its surface, as viewed from the Earth, is illuminated by the Sun; commonly called a Half Moon.

fissure eruption A specific type of volcanic eruption that occurs when lava flows out of a large crack in the Earth's surface.

floodplain The flat area of a river valley located along both sides of a river channel that is formed from the deposition of sediments during periodic floods.

flowering plants A classification of plants that reproduce by producing a flower that forms seeds with a protective coat.

flowing spring An area where groundwater is discharged at the surface and flows freely.

focus The point in the Earth's crust where a rock mass is broken or moved, causing an earthquake.

fog A cloud formed near or at the Earth's surface that is composed of tiny water droplets.

folded deformed rock Rock strata that has been folded by tectonic forces.

foliated The layered or wavy structure that forms in some metamorphic rocks.

food chain The model pathway that energy and matter take through an ecosystem by a series of eating processes.

food web Interrelated food chains that exist in an ecosystem.

fossil The remnant or trace of a once living organism preserved in sedimentary rock.

fossil fuels A term used to describe hydrocarbon fuels, such as coal and oil, that were formed from the remains of once living organisms.

fracture The process of breaking.

freezing The phase change of a liquid to a solid.

freezing point The specific temperature at which a liquid changes phase into a solid.

freezing rain A form of precipitation that occurs when rain freezes after it comes into contact with the Earth's surface.

Freon A type of chlorofluorocarbon gas that was commonly used in air conditioners and refrigerators.

fresh surface water Water on the Earth's surface that contains a small amount of dissolved mineral salts and is good for drinking.

freshwater Water on or below the Earth's surface that contains a small amount of dissolved mineral salts and is good for drinking.

friction The rubbing of one surface or object against another.

front An area where two different air masses come together.

Fujita scale of tornado intensity A scale that rates the power of a tornado based on its wind speed and potential damage.

Full Moon A phase of the Moon at which it has reached the halfway point of its orbit around the Earth, and its surface is completely illuminated by the Sun as viewed from Earth.

fundamental measurements Any basic form of measurement such as mass, length, or time.

Fungi A taxonomical classification for the kingdom of organisms commonly known as fungus.

funnel cloud A rapidly moving vortex of wind and debris, also called a tornado, that has not yet reached the ground and is formed at the base of a cloud.

fusion reaction A specific type of nuclear reaction that results when two atoms are joined together to produce a great amount of energy.

G

galaxy A large grouping of stars.

gas A state of matter that has a very low density, where molecules and atoms are allowed to move freely.

gas giants A classification of planets that are extremely large and are composed mainly of gases.

gaseous planets *See* gas giants.

generalist An organism that can live in a variety of habitats, and is easily adaptable.

genes The genetic instructions coded in an organism's DNA that usually form proteins. These proteins are then used to express unique traits of an organism.

genus A taxonomical classification of organisms that includes several species with very similar characteristics.

geocentric An early model of the universe which puts the Earth at the center of the solar system and universe.

geologic forces The main forces in geology that help form rocks and transform the landscape, which include gravity, erosion, and tectonic activity.

geologic province A well-defined landform area that occupies large regions on the Earth.

geologic time scale The scale of time that divides the Earth's history into distinct periods based on geologic events and the appearance or disappearance of specific life forms.

geosyncline A bowl-shaped depression in the Earth's crust formed from the deposition of large amounts of sediments.

germinate *See* germination.

germination The process that a plant seed undergoes when it begins to grow.

giant molecular cloud A large mass of gas and dust found in the universe.

Giardia A specific type of disease-causing microorganism that is associated with human waste and is found in fresh surface water.

ginkgo A type of broad-leafed deciduous tree that dates back to the time of the dinosaurs.

gizzard The organ in a bird's digestive tract that helps break down food by grinding it between stones.

glacial advance The forward movement of a glacier, caused when snow accumulation is greater than melting.

glacial deposits Unsorted sediments deposited by a melting glacier.

glacial front The face of a glacier where the ice breaks off and melts.

glacial lake A lake that is formed from glacial melt water.

glacial retreat The shrinking of a glacier caused when melting exceeds snow accumulation.

glacial sediments Unsorted, angular rock fragments deposited by a glacier.

glacial till An accumulation of glacial sediments.

glacial transport soils Soils that are formed from glacial sediments.

glacier A long-lasting, large mass of snow and ice that forms over land from the accumulation and compaction of snow that creeps downslope.

globular cluster A large grouping of stars that form portions of a galaxy.

glucose A common form of sugar that is produced by the process of photosynthesis.

Goldilocks syndrome A illustration of the relationship among the atmospheric carbon dioxide concentrations of Venus, Earth, and Mars and their surface temperatures that uses the Goldilocks fairy tale. Venus has too much carbon dioxide; therefore it is too hot. Mars has very little carbon dioxide and is too cold. The Earth is just right.

graded bedding A specific form of deposition of sediments that results from the reduction of the velocity of water at the mouth of a river that enters into a body of water. This causes larger particles to settle closest to the mouth and decrease in size as they move farther into the still water.

granite A type of intrusive, felsic igneous rock composed of coarse crystals that are primarily made up of quartz and feldspar minerals.

granule A small grain or particle.

graph A visual representation that shows the relationship between a specific set of numbers or data.

grassland A specific type of biome that experiences hot, dry summers and cold winters where grass is the main vegetation.

gravel A loose mixture of rock fragments.

gravity An attractive force between two bodies in the universe.

gravity assist A technique also known as the "slingshot" effect which is used to control the direction and velocity of many interplanetary spacecraft by applying an understanding of elliptical orbits and gravitational acceleration.

greenhouse effect A term that is used to describe short-wave radiation passing through the atmosphere and being absorbed by the Earth's surface, which then reradiates the energy in a long-wave form that is trapped by gases in the atmosphere and heats the planet. This process is the same method by which greenhouses are heated by the sun, whereby the glass of the greenhouse acts like the atmospheric gases.

greenhouse gases Specific gases in the atmosphere that trap long-wave radiation, such as water vapor, methane, and carbon dioxide.

Greenwich Mean Time The exact time of day on the Prime Meridian that is located in Greenwich, England, which is used to determine exact longitude locations on the Earth.

groundwater Naturally occurring freshwater that flows or is stored underground in rock or sediments.

groundwater flow The specific direction and movement of groundwater.

gulf stream A wind-driven, surface ocean current that brings warm water from the equator northward along the east coast of North America; first discovered by Benjamin Franklin.

gymnosperm The classification of a green plant that produces a seed without seed coat in a cone, such as a pine tree.

H

habitat The specific food, water, cover, and space requirements for a particular organism.

Hadley cell The large-scale convection cell that forms low pressure at the equator and high pressure at 30 degrees north and south of the equator, which produces the planetary scale winds; first proposed by George Hadley.

hail A ball-like type of precipitation that forms within a cumulonimbus cloud as a result of strong updrafts.

half-life The time it takes for half a mass of a radioactive isotope to decay into its daughter element.

halo Rings or arcs that encircle the Sun or Moon, caused by light passing through ice crystals in the atmosphere.

hardness A term used to describe a mineral's resistance to being scratched.

headwaters The point of origin of a river.

heat The measurable or perceived effect of energy that is transferred between two objects that have different temperatures.

heat capacity The ability of a substance to absorb, contain, and release heat energy.

heat gradient The change in heat energy over a specific distance.

heliocentric A model of the solar system that puts the Sun at its center with the Earth and other planets revolving around it.

hemisphere One half of a sphere.

herbicides A group of chemicals that are used to kill or control the growth of undesired plants.

herbivores Animals that eat only plants.

heredity The transfer of the unique characteristics of an organism from a parent to its offspring.

heterotrophs Organisms that must consume other organisms to gain energy, such as humans.

high atmospheric pressure system An air mass that has relatively high atmospheric pressure, is cool and dry, and produces winds that spiral outward and clockwise in the Northern Hemisphere.

high clouds A classification of clouds that generally form at altitudes above 20,000 ft.

high-concentration deposit A mineral ore deposit that has a high concentration of the desired element; also known as a high-grade deposit.

high-pressure center An area on the Earth's surface that has relatively high atmospheric pressure compared with the surrounding air, is generally cooler, and is dry. Air circulates around high pressure outward and clockwise in the Northern Hemisphere.

high tide The time or times of day when the surface of the ocean is raised to its highest point by the gravitational attraction of the Sun and Moon.

hominid A term used to identify all members of the human family.

Homo sapiens The genus and species classification of human beings.

horizon The horizontal plane on the Earth where the sky meets the land.

horizontal sorting A specific type of sediment deposition that occurs in still water, which results in larger particles settling first, then progressively smaller particles settling on top of the larger ones.

hot house climate A term used to describe a period in the Earth's history when the average surface temperature on Earth was much warmer than today.

hot spot A term used to describe a specific point located near the middle of a tectonic plate that experiences volcanic activity.

HR diagram The Hertzprung-Russell diagram, which classifies stars by their color, temperature, and luminosity.

humid A term used describe a region that has high atmospheric moisture.

humidity A common term that refers to the amount of water vapor in the air.

humus The completely decomposed remains of organic debris, which is an important part of a soil.

hurricane A large-scale tropical cyclone with winds in excess of 74 miles per hour.

hydration To add water to something.

hydraulic mining A method of mining minerals that uses high-pressure water.

hydrocarbon A chemical compound composed of hydrogen and carbon that is commonly associated with fuels.

hydrological cycle The circular pathway of water molecules as they move through the environment; also called the water cycle.

hydrophilic A term that describes a substance that attracts water molecules.

hydrosphere All the water on the Earth.

hydrothermal vents Ocean water that seeps through cracks in the sea floor and is superheated by magma close to the surface.

hypothesis An explanation based on a set of facts that can be tested.

I

ice The solid form of water that is less dense than liquid water, which causes it to float.

ice age A specific period in the Earth's history when the average surface temperature was much lower than today, causing the formation of widespread glaciers.

ice cap A platelike or dome-shaped mass of ice and snow that covers an entire mountain and spreads outward in all directions.

ice cores Long cylindrical sections of ice that are removed from glaciers by drilling and can be used to study the Earth's past climate.

ice field An extensive mass of ice that covers large areas of land, except high mountain peaks.

ice pellets A form of precipitation that consists of small frozen grains of ice.

ice sheet An extremely large and thick mass of glacial ice that covers an entire continent; also called a continental glacier.

icebergs Large chunks of glacial ice that break off the leading edge of a glacier and float away into the sea.

igneous intrusion Magma that seeps into an existing rock mass to form new igneous rock and may metamorphasize surrounding rock by the heat of contact.

igneous mineral deposits Specific mineral deposits that exist within igneous rock formations.

igneous rocks A type of rock on the Earth that forms from solidifying magma or lava.

immune system The system in the body that is responsible for fighting off disease.

impact craters Large bowl-like depressions that are left on the surface of a celestial object as the result of an impact by another celestial object, usually an asteroid or comet.

impermeable Unable to pass through, such as certain rocks that do not allow water to pass through them.

inches of mercury A unit of measurement used to record atmospheric pressure.

index fossils A specific type of fossil organism that lived for a short time over a wide geographical area, which is used to identify specific rock formations and the period when they formed.

infectious agents Any substance or organism that transmits disease.

inference A conclusion based on a set of observed facts.

infertile soil A common term for a soil that does not support healthy crop growth.

infiltrate To enter into something, such as water entering into the ground

infiltration The process of infiltrating, or entering into something.

infrared radiation A form of long-wavelength electromagnetic radiation.

infrared satellite images Satellite imagery that is created by sensing the infrared energy given off by a substance, which allows images to be recorded at night without the presence of light.

ingestion To eat.

Inorganic Not containing carbon; also referring to something that is not or was not alive.

Insecta A taxonomical classification for a class of arthropods commonly called insects.

Insectivora A taxonomical classification for an order of mammals that includes insect-eating moles and shrews.

insolation The amount of incoming solar radiation on the Earth.

instrumental value A school of thought that believes that humans should maintain biodiversity for the potential of using living things as resources for agriculture, medicine, science, and recreation.

interferometry The combination of radio signals received by a network of radio telescopes used to create one large telescope.

international date line A specific line of longitude located in the middle of the Pacific Ocean that is exactly 180 degrees east or west of the prime meridian.

intertidal zone An aquatic life zone that exists near the shoreline between the area of the highest and lowest tides.

intertropical convergence zone The zone surrounding the equator where warm rising air causes low pressure to form at the Earth's surface, resulting in the formation of planetary winds called the trade winds.

intrinsic value A school of thought which believes that humans should maintain the biodiversity of the planet because every living thing has a right to live on the Earth.

intrusive rock Igneous rock that is formed from magma seeping into an existing rock mass.

invasive species Organisms that have been introduced into an area where they are not normally found, also known as exotic or alien species.

invertebrates A taxonomical term used to describe all organisms within the animal kingdom that have no backbone.

ionosphere A layer of the Earth's atmosphere where there exists a large number of ions and free electrons.

ion An atom or group of atoms that have an electric charge as a result of gaining or losing electrons.

Iron Age A period in time when humans began to use iron to make tools, which began approximately 3,000 years ago.

iron meteorites A type of meteorite that is composed mostly of iron compounds.

irregular galaxy A type galaxy that has no definite shape.

irrigation An artificial means of supplying water to plants.

isobars Isolines that connect points of equal atmospheric pressure on a weather map.

isostasy The theory that explains how the Earth's crust is in balance, causing the continents to float at different levels on the asthenosphere below, much like different sized blocks of wood floating at different levels in water. The higher the continent above sea level, the lower it floats on the crust, and as material is eroded away from the continent, it tends to rise.

isothermal layer A layer in the atmosphere where temperature remains the same as the altitude increases.

isotherms Isolines that are used to connect points of equal temperature on a weather map.

isotopes Similar atoms that have the same number of protons but a different number of neutrons in the nucleus.

J

jawed fish A common name for the class Osteichthyes, also known as bony fish, which have jaws.

jet stream A region of high-velocity winds that exists high up in the atmosphere.

Jurassic period A period of the geologic time scale that began approximately 206 million years ago and ended 142 million years ago, marking the rise of the dinosaurs and the first appearance of birds.

K

katabatic wind A cold wind that blows down the side of a mountain.

kinetic energy The energy of motion or movement.

kingdom A broad, general category of living things.

Kuiper Belt An area located just outside of the orbit of the planet Pluto that may contain millions of comets.

L

La Niña The opposite effect of the El Niño Southern Oscillation, which occurs when the sea surface temperature along the equator off the western coast of South America is cooler than normal, resulting in widespread change in climate.

Lagomorpha A taxonomical classification for the order of mammals that has long back legs used for jumping, such as rabbits.

lahar A rapid flow of mud and debris formed from the rapid melting of snow and ice associated with a volcanic eruption.

lake A large inland body of water.

land breeze A coastal wind system that occurs when high pressure forms over cool land and low pressure forms over warmer water, causing air to flow from the land toward the water.

landfills A term used to describe a place where large amounts of garbage are deposited.

landform A specific feature of the Earth's surface that is based on elevation, slope, bedrock, and soil characteristics.

landscape *See* landform.

lapse rate The rate at which temperature or moisture decreases with height.

latent heat Heat energy that is either absorbed or released during a phase change.

latent heat of condensation Heat energy that is released into the atmosphere by the condensation of water vapor.

lateral fault A large rupture in a rock mass that runs horizontally; also known as a strike-slip fault.

lateral forces Forces that push in on something from both sides.

lateral moraines Glacial sediments that form along the sides of a glacier as it scrapes along rock.

latitude Parallel lines that run east and west across the Earth's surface, measuring location north or south of the equator.

lava Hot molten volcanic rock that flows freely on the Earth's surface.

lava dome A domelike structure of cooled lava that is located within a larger, active volcanic crater.

lava vents A system of pipes or tunnels that funnel lava outward along the sides of a volcano.

leaching The movement of chemicals that are dissolved in water, from a higher layer of soil downward into a lower level of soil or groundwater.

leeward The side of something opposite toward which the wind is blowing

legumes A specific type of plant that houses symbiotic bacteria in its root system, which puts nitrogen into the soil. Common legumes include clover, peas, and alfalfa.

length A measurement of horizontal distance.

lichen A symbiotic organism that consists of an alga and fungus that lives on rocks and trees.

light year A unit of measurement used in astronomy that records the distance that light travels in 1 year, based on the speed of light being 186,000 miles per second.

lightning A naturally occurring electrical discharge in the atmosphere usually associated with thunderstorms.

limestone A form of sedimentary rock composed of the mineral calcite (calcium carbonate).

limiting factor A specific nutrient that is lacking in an ecosystem and limits the growth of organisms.

limnetic zone The aquatic life zone that begins near the surface of a body of water and stretches down as far as light can penetrate and be used for photosynthesis.

liquid A state of matter between a solid and a gas where molecules are allowed to flow.

lithification The process of converting sediments into one solid mass of rock.

lithified Having undergone the process of lithification.

lithosphere The solid outer layer of the Earth, which is composed of rock and soil.

littoral zone The aquatic life zone of body of water that is located along the shore, where light can reach the bottom.

loam Soil that contains specific portions of sand, silt, and clay.

Local Group A term used in astronomy to describe the group of galaxies that are close to our own galaxy, called the Milky Way.

loess A type of soil found in the American Midwest that is formed from wind-transported parent material.

long-period comets Comets that take 200 or more years to complete one orbit around the Sun.

longitude Coordinate lines used on the Earth's surface that run north and south from pole to pole and measure a location east or west of the prime meridian.

long-wave radiation A low-energy form of electromagnetic radiation, such as infrared or radio waves.

low atmospheric pressure system An air mass that has relatively low atmospheric pressure, is warm and moist, and produces winds that spiral inward and counterclockwise in the Northern Hemisphere.

low clouds A classification of clouds with bases that form lower than 6,500 feet above the Earth's surface.

low-concentration deposit A mineral ore deposit that has a low concentration of the desired element, also known as a low-grade deposit.

low-pressure center An area on the Earth's surface that has relatively low atmospheric pressure compared with the surrounding air, is generally warmer, and is moist. Air circulates around low pressure inward and counterclockwise in the Northern Hemisphere.

low tide The time or times of day when the surface of the ocean is reduced to its lowest point by the gravitational attraction of the Sun and Moon.

luminescent The production of light without heat.

luminosity A measure of the rate at which stars radiate electromagnetic energy into space; commonly measured by comparing the luminosity of a star with that of the Sun's luminosity, which has a value of 1 Ls.

lunar eclipse The total or partial blocking of sunlight striking the Moon's surface by the Earth as it moves directly between the Moon and Sun.

lunar month The time it takes for the Moon to make one complete orbit around the Earth, which is approximately 29 days.

lungfish Specific fish species that have both lungs and gills, which allow them to breathe both underwater and on land.

luster A characteristic property of a mineral that describes how it reflects light from its surface; commonly classified as metallic or nonmetallic.

M

mafic rocks A specific class of igneous rocks that are generally dark and dense and contain iron and magnesium.

magma Hot molten rock located within the Earth's crust.

magma chambers Tubes, tunnels, or large cavities in the Earth's crust through which magma travels or collects.

magnetic energy A form of energy that is associated with magnetic fields.

magnetic north The direction on the Earth toward which a magnetic needle points, which is slightly different from the geographical North Pole, which is located directly on the Earth's axis of rotation.

magnetosphere The term used to describe the magnetic field that surrounds the Earth and stretches out into space.

main sequence A classification of a star that is in the middle part of its life cycle and is actively undergoing nuclear fusion.

Mammalia A taxonomical classification for a class of animals commonly known as mammals.

mammals Organisms that produce milk for their young from specialized glands called mammaries.

mantle The extremely hot, dense inner layer of the Earth that makes up most of the planet's total volume.

mantle convection Large convection cells that are believed to exist in the Earth's upper mantle.

mares A Latin word for "seas," used to describe the flat, dark plains that cover the surface of the Moon.

marine A term that refers to anything associated with the oceans.

maritime polar air mass A large mass of cold, moist air that forms over the oceans near the poles.

maritime tropical air mass A large mass of warm, moist air that forms over the ocean near the equator.

marrow The soft, nutritious material found at the center of a bone.

Marsupials An order of mammals that raise their young in pouches attached to their bodies.

mass A measurement of the amount of matter a substance contains.

mass extinction The widespread disappearance of a great number of species on Earth in a short period.

mass wasting The rapid, downslope movement of large masses of rock and soil.

matter Something that occupies space and has mass.

meandering The reoccurring S-shaped curves of a river or stream.

mechanical energy A form of energy that involves physical movement by a mechanism.

mechanism A system of parts that operate or interact like a machine.

medial moraines Glacial sediments that are located near the middle of a glacier.

melting The change in phase from a solid to a liquid.

membrane A thin, flexible layer of tissue.

mesopause A transitional layer in the Earth's atmosphere that lies between the mesosphere and thermosphere, where temperature does not change with an increase in height.

mesoscale winds Medium-scale winds that affect areas over distances between 1 and 900 miles.

mesosphere A layer of the Earth's atmosphere between 30 and 60 miles above the Earth's surface where temperature decreases with height.

mesotrophic lake The classification for a middle-aged lake that is relatively clear, deep, and low in available nutrients.

Mesozoic era A specific division of the geologic time scale that existed between 251 and 65 million years ago, which includes the rise and fall of dinosaur species.

metallic mineral resources Specific mined mineral resources that are composed of metal elements.

metamorphic rocks A class of rocks that are formed when igneous or sedimentary rocks are changed into a new rock by exposure to intense heat and pressure.

meteor A small chunk of rock, no larger than a few feet in diameter, that is traveling through space and enters the Earth's atmosphere; commonly known as a shooting star.

meteor shower An event that describes a group of meteors entering and burning up in the Earth's atmosphere.

meteorites A meteor that does not burn up in the atmosphere, and strikes the Earth's surface.

meteoroids Small chunks or rock, no larger than a few feet in diameter, that travel through space.

meteorologist A scientist who studies all aspects of the Earth's atmosphere and weather.

meteorology The scientific discipline that studies all aspects of the Earth's atmosphere and weather.

methane A colorless, odorless gas that is flammable and is composed of one carbon atom and four hydrogen atoms (CH_4).

metric system A specific system of measurement commonly used in science that uses the meter as a base for length, the kilogram as a base for mass, and the liter as a base for volume.

microscopic A term that describes something that is very small and cannot be seen with the naked eye.

mid-latitude cyclone A specific type of low-pressure weather system that develops over regions located in the middle latitudes.

mid-ocean ridges Divergent tectonic plate boundaries located on the ocean floor, where new crust is formed that pushes on the two plates, causing them to spread apart.

middle clouds Specific clouds that form between 6,500 and 23,00 feet above the Earth's surface.

mildew A common term used to describe a type of fungus that grows in dark, damp areas.

Milky Way The name for the galaxy of stars in which our solar system is located.

millibar A unit of measurement commonly used in meteorology to record atmospheric pressure.

mineral deposit A relatively high concentration of a specific mineral located within the Earth's crust.

mineral ore The raw, unprocessed rock form of a desired mineral resource found in the Earth's crust.

mineral resources The valuable minerals that are located in specific locations in the Earth's crust and can be mined.

mineral A naturally occurring, inorganic, crystalline substance that has specific physical properties.

mineralization A fossilization process that slowly replaces the atoms that make up the tissue of a dead organism with minerals like quartz or calcite. Over time the hard parts of an organism like bone and shells become an exact rock-like copy of the original.

mining The process or specific technique of removing mineral resources from the Earth's crust.

mixture A blend of different substances.

modified Mercalli scale A scale used to measure the intensity of an earthquake based on potential damage.

Moho The short term for the Mohorovicic discontinuity, which describes the zone within the Earth between the solid lithosphere and plastic-like upper mantle.

moist adiabatic lapse rate The rate of temperature decrease associated with an increase in height of moist air.

molds Fungus types that grow on organic material, such as food.

molecules An arrangement of atoms in specific proportions that are bound together and have specific physical and chemical properties.

mollisol A specific order of soil with a thick, rich A-horizon, or topsoil, that typically forms in grassland biomes, such as the American Midwest.

Mollusca A taxonomical classification for a phylum that includes all mollusks, such as snails, squid, clams, and octopuses.

molten rock Rock that is in the liquid state of matter that occurs at only extremely high temperatures.

Monera A taxonomical classification for the kingdom of single-celled organisms that include bacteria.

monomineralic rock A specific type of rock that is made up from only one mineral, such as rock salt or limestone.

Monotremata A taxonomical classification for the order of mammals that lay eggs, such as the platypus.

Moon The name for any large celestial body that orbits around a planet.

Moon phases The series of different appearances of the Moon as observed from Earth, which results from the varying amount of light that illuminates the Moon at specific points in its orbit.

moraines Large amounts of unsorted glacial sediments that are deposited by a melting glacier.

mountain High elevation landforms that are found far above sea level which tend to have very steep slopes, and are composed mostly of exposed bedrock. Also known as uplands or highlands.

mountain breeze A local wind system that occurs when air blows down the side of a mountain at night.

mouth The term used to describe the end point of a river where it empties into a lake or ocean.

mud slide The rapid downslope movement of soil that is saturated with water.

multicelled An organism that is composed of many cells.

mushrooms A type of fungus that reproduces by forming a large fruiting body.

mutated To be altered by a change in the structure of an organism's genes.

mutualism A type of symbiotic relationship in which both organisms benefit.

mutualistic A type of relationship by which both parties benefit.

mycorrhizae Symbiotic fungi that are associated with the root systems of plants.

N

natural law A well-accepted fact that describes a process or processes that occur in nature.

natural resource Things found naturally on the Earth, both living and nonliving, that have a value to humans in some way.

neap tides The least amount of tidal activity that occurs when the Moon is at its first and third quarter positions in its orbit.

nekton A term used to describe aquatic organisms that can move freely by swimming, such as fish.

Nematoda A taxonomical classification for a phylum of organisms commonly known as roundworms.

Neogene period A division of the geologic time scale that began approximately 24 million years ago and ended 1.6 million years ago, which marked the appearance of grasses and grazing animals on the Earth.

Neolithic A term that means "new stone age" and is a division of time that began more than 53,000 years ago and ended approximately 5,500 years ago; it was marked by the widespread use of stone tools by human beings.

neritic zone A life zone in an aquatic ecosystem that stretches from the shoreline out to water that is approximately 600 ft deep.

neurotoxins A type of toxic chemical compound that affects the nervous system of animals.

neutron star A star that is extremely dense and mostly composed of neutrons.

neutrons A subatomic particle with a neutral electrical charge that is found in the nucleus of an atom.

New Moon A particular phase of the Moon in which it appears totally darkened and that occurs when it is aligned between the Sun and Earth. The New Moon phase also marks the starting point of the orbit of the Moon around the Earth.

nitrate A chemical compound composed of one atom of nitrogen and three atoms of oxygen (NO_3^-); a common plant fertilizer.

nitric acid A strong acid (HNO_3) that is formed in the atmosphere when rain mixes with nitrogen compounds to create acid precipitation.

nitrification The process of converting atmospheric nitrogen (N_2) to nitrogen compounds such as nitrate (NO_3^-) that are usable by plants; called nitrogen fixation.

nitrifying bacteria A specific bacteria type that converts atmospheric nitrogen (N_2) to plant-usable forms of nitrogen, such as nitrate (NO_3^-).

nitrogen cycle The movement and recycling of nitrogen compounds through the environment.

nitrogen-fixing bacteria *See* nitrifying bacteria.

nitrogen oxides Compounds that are composed of nitrogen and oxygen (NO_x).

nitrous oxide A gas that contains two atoms of nitrogen and one atom of oxygen (N_2O).

nocturnal A term used to describe an organism that is active during the night.

nonmetallic mineral resources Mineral resources that are not considered metals, such as limestone, rock salt, gypsum, diamonds, and marble.

non renewable resource A natural resource that cannot be replaced rapidly enough by natural processes, or that exists in fixed quantities on the Earth.

nonvascular plants Plants that do not have an organized network of vascular bundles that delivers water and nutrients throughout the plant.

nor'easter A strong low-pressure storm system that affects the northeastern coast of North America, blowing in cold air and precipitation from the Northeast.

notochord A flexible rodlike structure that runs along the back of the embryos of all vertebrates.

nuclear fusion A nuclear reaction that is caused by combining, or fusing, two elements, which results in the creation of a great amount of energy.

nucleus The central core of an atom, which is composed of a specific number of protons and neutrons.

nutrient pollution A form of water pollution caused by an increase in nutrients in an aquatic ecosystem that leads to a rapid increase of aquatic plants and algae.

O

O-horizon The uppermost layer of a soil, which is composed of partially decayed organic material.

oblate A slightly flattened sphere.

observation The direct perception of something by use of one of the five human senses.

occluded front A frontal boundary that usually occurs when a rapidly moving cold air mass overtakes a warm air mass by wedging underneath it and lifting upward, creating very unstable weather.

ocean An extremely large body of saltwater that covers approximately 72 percent of the Earth's surface and divides the continents.

oceanic crust The portion of the Earth's crust that lies below the oceans; it is typically more dense than continental crust and is composed of basaltic rock.

oceanic zone A life zone in the open ocean that makes up the deep water environment that exists in water with a depth of 600 feet or greater.

oil A fossil fuel that is formed deep within the Earth's crust from the decayed remains of plankton that lived in the oceans millions of years ago.

oligotrophic lakes A classification of lake that has been recently formed from glacial melt waters, which has very clear, cold water and is very low in nutrients or aquatic life.

omnivores Organisms that eat both plants and animals, such as humans.

Oort cloud A hypothetical area that is located approximately 100,000 astronomical units from the orbit of the planet Pluto, where comets are believed to originate. It is named for the Dutch astronomer Jan Oort, who first proposed it.

open pit mining A method of mining that involves the extraction of minerals from the Earth by digging large open pits.

optical telescope A telescope that uses glass lenses and mirrors to magnify the light given off by an object.

orbit The elliptical path that a celestial object takes as it revolves around another celestial object.

order A taxonomical classification for a group of animals that have similar characteristics.

Ordovician period A division of the geologic time scale that existed between 490 and 443 million years ago, which marked the rise of corals and coral reefs in the ocean.

organic A term that is used to describe any compound that contains carbon; also refers to something that is associated with a living thing.

organic material Material that is derived from a living thing.

original horizontality A natural law used in geology that assumes that all sedimentary rock layers were laid down in horizontal layers when they originally were formed.

original preservation A fossilization process that preserves the actual body of the organism.

orographical lifting A process that occurs when a large mass of air is forced to rise upward along the windward side of a mountain.

orographical precipitation A type of precipitation that occurs as a result of orographic lifting, which causes moist air to cool and condense when it is forced to rise up the windward side of a mountain.

oscilloscope A type of instrument used to display electrical motion in the form of a wave.

Osteichthyes A taxonomical classification used to describe a class of vertebrates commonly known as bony fish.

outgassing The process of expelling gas from a substance.

overburden A large mass of rock, soil, or ice that lies on top of something.

oxidation The process of adding oxygen to a chemical compound.

oxisol A highly weathered soil found in tropical rainforest biomes that has a very thin A-horizon, or topsoil, and a deep B-horizon that contains a high concentration of iron oxide.

oxygen cycle The movement and recycling of oxygen through the environment.

ozone A colorless, gaseous compound composed of three atoms of oxygen (O_3).

ozone hole An area over Antarctica that has a reduced level of ozone gas in the stratosphere.

ozone layer The specific area in the stratosphere, located at an altitude between 10 and 20 mi, that contains a high concentration of ozone gas.

P

P wave *See* compressional primary wave.

paleoclimatology The scientific discipline that studies the history of the Earth's climates.

Paleogene period A division of the geologic time scale that occurred between 65 and 24 million years ago and began with the extinction of the dinosaurs.

Paleolithic A term used to describe a period of time that ended approximately 100,000 years ago; also called the Old Stone Age.

Paleozoic era A large division of the geologic time scale that occurred between 544 and 251 million years ago, which began with the appearance of a variety of aquatic organisms and ended with the first appearance of the dinosaurs.

Pangaea The name of a supercontinent that existed more than 250 million years ago, when all the present-day continents were joined together into one great landmass.

parallel A term to describe two objects that are located in the same plane and are equally distant from each other.

parasitism A symbiotic relationship between two organisms in which the host organism is harmed by a parasite.

parent element The specific element that is the starting point of the radioactive decay of a radioisotope.

parent material The term used to describe the specific rocks from which soil minerals come.

parent rocks The specific rocks from which the rock particles that make up sediments come.

partial eclipse A partial blocking of light caused by the movement of a celestial object in front of another celestial object.

pendulum A device that consists of a weight suspended from a fixed point, which is caused to swing back and forth under the influence of gravity.

penumbra The lighter area located next to the umbra, or darkened shadow, that occurs during an eclipse.

percent error A unit of measurement that mathematically describes the difference between a measured value and the accepted value (percentage error = difference between the measured value and the accepted value/ the accepted value (100); also known as percent deviation.

perigee The point in the orbit of the Moon or an artificial satellite when it is closest to the Earth.

perihelion The point in a planet's orbit around the Sun when it is closest to the Sun.

Perissodactyla A taxonomical classification used to describe a specific order of mammals that have hooves with an odd number of toes, such as horses, zebras, and rhinoceroses.

permafrost Permanently frozen soil.

permanent gases Gases that are in fixed amounts in the Earth's atmosphere.

Permian period A division of the geologic time scale that occurred between 251 and 290 million years ago; it was marked by the first appearance of mammal-like reptiles and the mass extinction of many marine species, including trilobites.

perpendicular Two objects or lines that are at a right angle to one another.

pH The unit of measurement used to measure the acidity or alkalinity of a solution.

Phanerozoic eon A large division of the geologic time scale that began 544 million years ago with the appearance of a variety of marine organisms and continues to this day.

phosphate A chemical compound composed of one atom of phosphorus and four atoms of oxygen (PO_4^{3-}); an important plant fertilizer.

phosphorus cycle The movement and recycling of phosphorus through the environment.

photosphere The outer, visible layer of the Sun.

photosynthesis A chemical reaction that certain organisms use for energy, combining water, carbon dioxide, and solar energy to form carbohydrates, oxygen, and water.

photosynthetic A term to describe an organism that uses photosynthesis to derive energy.

phylum A taxonomical classification for a group of organisms that share common traits.

psychrometer A weather instrument used to measure the dry and wet bulb temperatures, which determines the dew point and relative humidity of the atmosphere.

physical weathering The process of breaking down rocks into smaller rock particles by a physical process, where no chemical changes take place.

physicist A scientist who studies physics, which is the study of matter and energy and their interactions.

phytoplankton A type of plankton that utilizes photosynthesis to gain energy.

piedmont glacier A specific type of glacier that forms at the base of a mountain range where valley glaciers come together to form a large sheet of ice.

piezoelectric The generation of an electrical current by crystals that are subjected to mechanical stress.

pioneer community A group of organisms that populate an area on the Earth where no organisms have lived before.

plain Low elevation landforms that are flat with very gentle slopes. Also known as lowlands.

plane of the ecliptic An imaginary plane in which the Earth orbits the Sun.

planetary winds Large-scale winds that circulate air around the Earth, such as the trade winds or the westerlies.

planet A large celestial object that orbits around a star.

plankton Tiny, free-floating organisms that live in water.

plant uptake The process by which a plant absorbs water and nutrients into its root system.

Plantae The taxonomical classification for the kingdom of organisms that includes all plants.

plasma The fourth state of matter, which occurs when matter exists in the form of an ionized gas.

plate boundaries Specific areas on the Earth's crust where two or more tectonic plates interact with one another.

plate tectonics The theory that describes the Earth's crust as being divided into distinct plates that float on a semiliquid mantle and move relative to one another, which helps to explain the occurrence of earthquakes, volcanoes, mid-ocean ridges, mountain ranges, deep sea trenches, and deformed rock structures.

plateau Medium to high elevation landforms that are relatively flat with a medium slope.

Platyhelminthes A taxonomical classification for a phylum of organisms commonly known as flatworms.

plesiosaurs Aquatic, reptile-like dinosaurs that lived during the Cretaceous period, which grew to more than 40 feet in length and used paddle-like feet to propel themselves through the water.

point bar The point in a stream or river, located on the inside curve of a meander, where sediments are deposited.

polar jet stream An area of high-level winds located high in the atmosphere in the upper latitudes.

polar molecule A molecule that has a weak positive and negative electric charge.

polar regions The geographical areas that lie close to the poles of the planet.

Polaris A star that is located directly over the North Pole; also called the North Star.

pollen Tiny, dustlike male reproductive cells produced by a flower.

pollution An undesirable change in the quality of the environment that negatively affects the health of organisms living there.

polychlorinated biphenyls (PCBs) A class of human-created chemical compounds used in the production of electrical parts.

polymineralic rocks Rocks that are composed of two or more different minerals.

pond A very small inland body of water.

population A group of the same species of organisms living in the same area.

pore spaces Tiny vessels in soil or rock that hold air and water.

pores Tiny openings in a substance.

Porifera A taxonomical classification for a specific phylum of animals commonly known as sponges.

porous A substance that is composed of many pores, which allow liquids and gases to pass through.

potential energy The stored energy, or capacity for something to perform work or cause change.

Precambrian A large unit of geologic time when not much life flourished on the Earth, which started with the formation of the planet and ended approximately 544 million years ago.

precession The wobbling motion of the axis of a rapidly rotating body, such as the Earth, which causes the tilt of the axis to change periodically.

precipitate The process of a solid forming out of a solution.

precipitation Liquid or solid water formed in clouds that falls to the surface of the Earth.

prefrontal fog A layer of fog close to the ground that forms in front of an approaching air mass.

pressure Force applied over a surface, which is measured in force per unit area.

pressure center A region on the Earth's surface where the atmospheric pressure is relatively low or high as compared with the surrounding air, around which air circulates.

pressure gradient The change in atmospheric pressure that occurs over a specific distance.

pressure gradient force The rate of atmospheric pressure decrease over a specific area, which forces air to move, forming wind.

pressure unloading The release of pressure off a rock mass, caused when overlying rock or ice is removed.

prevailing winds Dominant, planetary scale winds that move air along the surface of the Earth, such as the trade winds or the westerlies.

primary consumers A feeding classification for any organism that consumes plants; also called herbivores.

primary production The process by which plants use photosynthesis to convert solar energy into chemical energy that is stored in plant material.

primary succession The introduction of a community of organisms into an area where life has not existed before.

primary wave *See* compressional primary wave.

primate A taxonomical classification for an order of animals that includes monkeys, apes, lemurs, and humans.

prime meridian An imaginary line drawn on the Earth's surface that connects the North Pole to the South Pole, which runs through Greenwich, England, and represents zero degrees longitude.

primitive An early or original state of development.

principle of cross-cutting relationships A natural law in geology that states that intrusions or faults are younger than the rocks they are in.

principle of superposition A natural law used in geology that states that in undisturbed rock layers, the oldest layers are located at the bottom and the youngest are at the top.

principle of uniformity A natural law, also known as uniformitarinism, used in geology that states that the geologic processes that are currently shaping the Earth have been occurring all throughout the Earth's history.

procedure The series of steps taken to perform an experiment.

producers A feeding classification for all organisms that use photosynthesis or chemosynthesis as means to derive energy and create food.

productivity A term used to describe how much biomass is created by plants in a specific area.

profundal zone An aquatic life zone located in deep open water where it is too dark for photosynthesis to occur.

protein A nitrogen-containing chemical compound that is important for the growth and repair of an organism's tissues.

Proterozoic eon A large division of the geologic time scale that began approximately 2.5 million years ago and ended 544 million years ago with the appearance of many aquatic life forms on the Earth.

Protista A taxonomical classification for the kingdom of organisms commonly called protists, which include plankton, algae, and diatoms.

proto star A stage in the life cycle of a star when a stellar nebula has collapsed and nuclear fusion is beginning to occur, forming an embryonic star.

protons Subatomic particles with a positive electrical charge found in the nucleus of an atom.

pterosaur A type of long-winged dinosaur that could fly.

pulsars A type of neutron star that regularly emits periodic radio signals.

purpose The reason an experiment is performed.

pyroclastic Fragmented material ejected from a volcano, which includes ash, cinders, and volcanic rock.

pyroclastic flow The extremely hot gas, ash, and volcanic material that is ejected from a volcano during an eruption and moves downhill rapidly.

Q

quarks The theoretical basic particles that make up all subatomic particles, such as protons and neutrons.

quasar A very high energy celestial object believed to be a type of galaxy that is rapidly moving away from the center of the universe.

Quaternary period A division of the geologic time scale that began 1.6 million years ago with the appearance of human beings and includes the present day.

quiet eruption A type of volcanic eruption that releases lava in a gentle outpouring associated with a shield cone or fissure eruption.

R

radar A term that stands for Radio Detecting and Ranging, which describes a device that uses radio waves to bounce off an object and track its location, speed, and movement.

radiant energy Energy in the form of visible light.

radiation Waves or particles that are emitted from a substance; *see* electromagnetic radiation.

radiative cooling The cooling of an object as a result of its emitting electromagnetic radiation into the atmosphere or into space.

radio telescope A type of telescope that senses longer wave electromagnetic radiation in the form of microwaves and radio waves.

radioactive decay The breakdown of one element by the release of subatomic particles, which forms a new element.

radiometric dating A method of dating objects using the known decay rate of certain radio isotopes.

rain The liquid form of precipitation.

recharge The process by which groundwater is replenished when surface water infiltrates into the ground.

recrystallization The rearrangement of crystals in a rock by exposure to extreme heat and pressure.

recycle To reuse something.

red algae A harmful form of marine algae that produces neurotoxins; commonly called the red tide.

red dwarf star A classification for a dim star that is small, red, and has a relatively cool temperature.

red giant A classification for a star that is very bright, large, red, and has a relatively cool temperature.

red supergiant A classification of a star that is extremely bright and large, red, and has a medium temperature.

reflection The act of electromagnetic energy bouncing off a surface.

refraction The act of electromagnetic energy being altered in its direction of travel when it passes through certain substances.

regeneration The process of reconstructing something.

relative dating Dating techniques in geology that estimate the age of rock layers and rock-formations to one another using geologic principles such as uniformity, superposition, cross-cutting, and unconformities.

relative humidity A unit of measurement that records the amount of moisture present in the air, usually expressed as a percentage.

renewable resource A natural resource that can be replaced in a reasonable amount of time.

replication The process of reproducing something.

reptiles A class of animals that reproduce by laying eggs and are cold blooded, such as lizards and snakes.

Reptilia A taxonomical classification for the class of animals commonly known as reptiles.

reradiate *See* reradiation.

reradiation The process by which an object takes in electromagnetic radiation and re-emits it into the atmosphere.

reservoir A storage place for something.

residual heat Heat left over from something.

residual parent material Parent rock on which a soil has formed that has not been transported.

respiration The chemical process by which carbohydrates are broken down in the presence of oxygen to derive energy and produce carbon dioxide.

retractable claws A type of claw that can be pushed into and pulled out of an animal's foot, such as a cat's claw.

retreat To move back.

retrograde To move backward or in an opposite direction.

revolution The movement of an object in an orbit around another object.

revolutionize To change drastically.

rice paddy A type of agricultural field that is used to grow rice, which is periodically flooded with water.

Richter scale A scale that measures the energy released by an earthquake.

riffle The particular point in a flowing body of water that is relatively straight and shallow, where sediments are deposited, forming turbulent water.

rift valley A valley that forms along a divergent plate boundary, where two tectonic plates are spreading apart.

right ascension A part of the equatorial coordinate system used to measure the east-west position of a celestial body.

ring system A well-defined area of debris composed of rock and ice that is orbiting a planet and appears to form a ring or series of rings around the planet.

river A large flowing body of water.

rock cycle A model of the processes that cause the formation, movement, and recycling of rock material on the Earth.

rock slide The rapid down-slope movement of rock.

rock The solid, crystalline substances that make up the Earth's crust, which are mostly composed of one or more minerals.

Rodentia A taxonomical classification for the order of mammals, commonly called rodents, that have continuously growing teeth, such as rats, mice, and squirrels.

rodents *See* Rodentia.

rotation The circular movement of a body around a central point called an axis.

runoff The rapid loss of soil, sediments, or other substances as a result of being washed away by rain or melting snow.

S

S wave (secondary wave) A seismic wave generated at the focus of an earthquake that travels in the form of a wave, is slower than a P wave, and can only pass through solids.

Saffir-Simpson scale A scale used to classify a hurricane by using its central pressure, wind speed, and damage.

salinity A measure of the mineral salt content of a solution.

sand A size classification for rock particles that are between 0.006 and 0.2 cm in diameter.

Santa Ana wind A warm, dry wind that blows off the high desert plateau of southern California.

saturated The point at which a substance can no longer absorb any more liquid.

sauropod A large type of long-necked, plant-eating dinosaur; commonly called the brontosaurus.

savanna A type of biome that experiences hot, dry summers and cool, rainy winters, where grass, shrubs, and small trees are the main type of vegetation. This biome is sometimes known as the tropical grassland.

scattering The random reflection and refraction of electromagnetic waves that occur when it comes into contact with certain substances

scavenge To feed on dead or decaying organic material.

science The practice of observing, identifying, describing, and explaining natural phenomena.

scientific instruments Devices that are used to extend the human senses.

scientific method The specific set of procedures that scientists use to gain knowledge.

scientific notation A method of writing very large or very small numbers that uses exponents.

sea breeze A coastal wind that develops during the day when air blows from high pressure forming over cool water toward low pressure developing over the warmer land.

sea floor spreading The process of forming new oceanic crust at a mid-ocean ridge, which causes two tectonic plates to move, or spread apart from one another.

seawater Water that has a high concentration of minerals dissolved in it; also known as saltwater.

secondary consumers A classification of organisms that consume herbivores; also known as carnivores.

secondary succession The slow, gradual, and predictable replacement of one community of organisms by another in a specific area where life has already existed.

secondary wave *See* S wave.

sediment pollution A form of water pollution that is caused by the rapid introduction of sediments into an aquatic ecosystem as a result of runoff.

sedimentary mineral deposits Mineral resources that were deposited in the form of sediments.

sedimentary rocks A type of rock formed from rock particles that are compacted or cemented together to form one solid mass.

sedimentation The process of depositing sediments.

sediments Small fragments or particles of rock.

seepage The process of a liquid passing slowly through small openings in a substance.

segmented worms A specific phylum of worms that includes earthworms and leeches.

seismic waves Energy released by an earthquake that travels through the Earth in the form of waves.

seismograph A scientific instrument that is used to detect seismic waves generated by earthquakes.

semi-diurnal tides Two high and two low tides occurring each day.

shield cones The largest type of volcano, which is composed of piles of lava that form a steep, sloping, cone-shaped mountain.

short-period comets Comets that take less than 200 years to complete one orbit around the Sun.

short-wave radiation A high-energy form of electromagnetic energy that has a short wavelength.

siliceous ooze Mudlike sediments composed of silicates that form on the ocean floor.

silicate A chemical compound that is composed of atoms of silicon and oxygen.

silt A size classification for rock particles that are between 0.0004 and 0.006 cm in diameter.

Silurian period A division of the geologic time scale that existed between 443 and 418 million years ago, during which the first land plants and animals appeared on the Earth.

single-celled organisms Organisms that are composed of only one cell, such as bacteria.

Sirenia A taxonomical classification for an order of aquatic mammals that eat plants, such as the manatee.

slime mold A type of protist that grows in the damp organic material located on the forest floor.

slope An inclined surface that is at a particular angle to the horizon.

small solar system body A category of celestial objects orbiting the Sun that are not classified as planets, dwarf planets, or moons. This includes objects known as asteroids, meteors, comets, and some trans-Neptunian objects.

snowflakes A solid form of precipitation that has unique crystal shapes.

soil A mixture of minerals, organic material, air, and water that forms at the surface of the Earth.

soil horizon A well-defined layer of soil that has specific characteristics.

soil minerals The rock particles that are found in a soil.

soil moisture The amount of water that is present in a soil.

soil orders Specific classifications of unique soils that are found on the Earth.

soil profile The cross-sectional view of a particular soil that shows all the soil's horizons.

solar cycle The time it takes the Sun to go from low sun spot activity to high sun spot activity and back again, which is approximately 11 years.

solar eclipse The total or partial blocking of the Sun as viewed from the Earth when the Moon passes in front of it.

solar flares Large flamelike emissions of hot plasma and radiation that leap off the surface of the Sun.

Solar Nebula The theoretical cloud of gas and dust that is believed to have formed the solar system.

solar radiation The electromagnetic radiation that is emitted from the Sun.

solar system The group of nine planets and other celestial bodies that orbit around a main sequence star called the Sun.

solar wind The stream of particles and electromagnetic radiation that is emitted from the Sun and travels out into space in all directions.

solid The state of matter in which atoms form a crystal structure and have the most restricted movement.

solidification The change in phase from a liquid to a solid; also called crystallization.

solution A mixture of two or more substances that have become dissolved.

solvent A substance that is capable of dissolving another substance.

south equatorial current A wind-driven, surface ocean current that moves water westward along the equator away from the west coast of South America.

southern oscillation The periodic change in the locations of low and high atmospheric pressure systems over the Pacific Ocean near the equator.

specialist An organism that requires very specific habitat requirements.

species A taxonomical classification used to describe a fundamental group of organisms that can interbreed.

specific gravity A unit of measurement used to describe the weight of a substance per unit volume.

specific heat A unit of measurement used to describe the ratio between the temperature change of a substance and its ability to absorb, hold, or release heat.

spectral class A classification used to describe a star's unique spectrum, luminosity, and color.

spectroscope A scientific instrument used to analyze the visible light portion of the electromagnetic spectrum.

spherical A three-dimensional ball-like shape.

spiral galaxy A type of galaxy in which the stars are arranged in a spiral shape.

spores The reproductive cells of fungi.

spring tides The time of maximum tides, which occurs during the time of a Full or New Moon.

squall line A rapidly moving line of thunderstorms that is located ahead of a cold front.

standard atmosphere A theoretical state of the atmosphere that assumes it has equal density, temperature, and a pressure of 29.92 in of mercury or 14.7 pounds per square inch.

standard system *See* metric system.

standing freshwater A still body of freshwater.

star A large, shining, spherical celestial object that is held together by its own gravity and is undergoing nuclear fusion.

starch A complex molecule that is made up of carbon, hydrogen, and oxygen and is produced by plants.

station model A coded symbol used on weather maps to display specific atmospheric variables.

stationary front A front that develops between two air masses that are not moving.

stegosaurus A type of dinosaur that had a series of large platelike scales running along its back and a tail that possessed four or five large spikes.

stellar nebula A large mass of collapsing gas and dust located in the universe that forms stars and planets.

stony meteorites A classification used to describe meteorites that are composed of silica.

stony-iron meteorites A classification used to describe meteorites that are composed of silica and iron.

storm surge The rise in water level that is caused by the strong winds associated with an approaching hurricane.

strata Horizontal layers of sedimentary rocks.

stratopause An isothermal layer in the atmosphere located between the stratosphere and the mesosphere.

stratosphere A layer in the Earth's atmosphere where the ozone layer exists and temperature increases with an increase in altitude.

streak The colored powder left behind after a mineral is rubbed against a surface.

stream erosion The movement of rock, soil, or sediments in a flowing body of water.

stream features The specific physical characteristics of a stream.

stream A small, flowing body of water.

strip mining A method of exposing and removing mineral resources from the ground that involves the digging up of rock and soil located above the mineral deposit.

stromatolites Large moundlike layers of sediments that form when cyanobacteria trap sand in warm, shallow ocean water.

subsoil The layer of soil, also known as the B-horizon, that lies directly below the topsoil.

subduction The movement of one tectonic plate underneath another at a convergent plate boundary.

subduction zone A narrow zone located at a convergent plate boundary where subduction is occurring, leading to the formation of deep ocean trenches, volcanoes, and earthquake activity.

sublimation The term that describes the phase change from a solid to a gas.

subtropical jet stream A narrow band of rapidly moving winds located in the upper atmosphere near the lower latitudes.

sulfur dioxide A gaseous chemical compound composed of one atom of sulfur and two atoms of oxygen (SO_2).

sulfuric acid A strong acid (H_2SO_4) that forms in the atmosphere when sulfur dioxide gas reacts with atmospheric moisture.

summer solstice The time of the year when the Earth's tilted axis points the Northern Hemisphere toward the Sun, which usually occurs around June 21.

Sun The name of a medium-aged, main sequence star that lies at the center of our solar system.

sunspots Dark spots that appear on the surface of the Sun that are believed to be cooler areas on its surface.

supernova The violent explosion that is caused by a dying star when it blows off its atmosphere.

supercooled droplets Tiny drops of water that have temperatures below 32° Fahrenheit and exist in clouds.

superposition A natural law used in geology that states that in undisturbed rock layers, the oldest layers are located at the bottom and the youngest are at the top.

surface mining A method of removing mineral resources from the Earth when they are located directly at the surface.

surface water Water that is located on the surface of the Earth.

surface wave A seismic wave formed from the interaction of other seismic waves at the Earth's surface caused by an earthquake, which causes the ground to move in a wavelike rolling pattern. This is the most destructive form of seismic wave; also known as a surface wave.

surface weather maps Maps that display weather conditions at the Earth's surface.

survey To determine the boundaries, elevations, distances, and other aspects of a specific portion of the Earth's surface.

suspension Free-moving, solid particles that are hanging in a liquid.

swamp A low region on land that is covered with shallow standing water.

symbiotic relationship A relationship between two different species of organisms in which one or both organisms benefit from the action of the other.

syncline A U-shaped fold or depression in rock strata.

T

taiga *See* coniferous forest.

taxonomy A discipline of science that deals with the classification of organisms.

Technological Revolution A period of time that marked the beginning of the widespread use of technological processes in industry, which began near the middle of the nineteenth century. This period is often associated with the use of coal as fuel; also known as the Industrial Revolution.

technological system The specific process or series of processes that are associated with a specific technology.

technological systems model A model used to illustrate the steps in a technological process.

technology The application of human knowledge to solve problems or perform tasks.

technology transfer The transfer and application of technology to improve the quality of life that was developed as a result of scientific investigation.

tectonic forces The geologic processes and forces that are associated with plate tectonics.

tectonic plate A large portion of the Earth's crust that floats on the plasticlike upper mantle.

telescope A scientific instrument used to observe objects that are very far away.

temperate forest A biome that exists in the middle latitudes, where the winters are very cold, the summers are hot, and the main type of vegetation is deciduous trees.

temperature The average amount of kinetic energy of the atoms and molecules in substance, which is commonly expressed as the degree of heat or cold measured by a thermometer.

temperature inversion The process by which a warm layer of air overlies a cold layer of air.

terminal moraines Unsorted glacial sediments that are located at the front or deposited near the front of a glacier.

terraces Steplike features located on a floodplain of a river or stream that mark the past location of the channel during a flood.

terrestrial A term that refers to land.

terrestrial ecosystems Ecosystems that are located on land.

terrestrial organisms Organisms that live on land.

terrestrial planet A planet that is composed mostly of rock.

terrestrial radiation Long-wavelength infrared radiation that is reradiated into the Earth's atmosphere from the land surface.

tertiary consumers A feeding classification used to describe carnivores that are at the top of a food chain.

Tertiary period A division of the geologic time scale that began approximately 65 million years ago with the extinction of the dinosaurs and ended 1.6 million years ago with the appearance of humans.

tetrahedron A four-sided geometric figure composed of four equilateral triangles.

texture The size and arrangements of crystals or sediments in a rock.

thawing The phase change that occurs when ice melts into liquid water.

theory A statement or statements used to describe a phenomenon.

thermal energy Energy associated with heat.

thermal pollution A form of pollution that is associated with a change in temperature.

thermocline The layer of water located below the surface where the temperature drops rapidly.

thermohaline circulation The vertical distribution of water in the oceans that is caused by differences in the salinity and temperature of the water.

thermometer A scientific instrument used to measure temperature.

thermosphere A layer in the Earth's upper atmosphere where temperature increases with an increase in altitude.

Third Quarter Moon A particular phase of the Moon when it has completed three quarters of its orbit around the Earth and appears like a Half Moon when viewed from Earth.

threatened species Any organism whose numbers are currently declining, but can be easily saved if steps are taken to protect it.

thunderstorm A small-scale storm that is caused by the formation of a cumulonimbus cloud, which produces strong winds, heavy rain or hail, lightning, and thunder.

tidal range The difference in height between the low and high tides.

tides The periodic rise and fall of the ocean surface that is caused by the gravitational attraction of the Sun and Moon.

tilling The process of turning over, or plowing, the soil.

tillites Sedimentary rocks made of sediments created by tilling.

tilted rock Disturbed rock strata that lies at an angle with the ground.

time A fundamental unit of measurement that records the specific interval that separates events.

topsoil The uppermost layer of soil that contains a high amount of organic material; also called the A-horizon.

topographic maps A two-dimensional map that displays the three-dimensional surface of the Earth by using contour lines that show the elevation and shape of the land surface

tornado A rapidly rotating, funnel-shaped column of air located at the base of a cumulonimbus cloud that results in deadly high-velocity winds.

total eclipse The total blocking of light by one celestial body passing in front of another.

toxic heavy metals Naturally occurring, poisonous metal elements such as lead or mercury.

toxic inorganic chemicals Human-created chemical compounds that are poisonous to living organisms.

toxic organic compound A naturally occurring poisonous chemical compound.

trade winds Planetary scale winds in the Earth's atmosphere that form when areas of high atmospheric pressure located near 30 degrees north and south of the equator move air toward low pressure at the equator. The trade winds blow from the northeast toward the southwest in the Northern Hemisphere.

trait An inherited feature of an organism derived from its genes.

trans-Neptunian object Objects that orbit the Sun at a greater distance than the orbit of the planet Neptune.

transform fault plate boundary A type of plate boundary where two tectonic plates slide along one another.

transitional species An organism that displays primitive traits that lead to the development of a later species.

transmission The movement of electromagnetic radiation through a substance, without a change in its wavelength.

transpiration The movement of water through a soil, into a plant's body, and then back into the atmosphere when it evaporates off the leaf surface.

transported parent material Rock material that forms a soil that has been transported by wind, water, or a glacier.

transporting agent The means by which a substance is moved.

tree ring The ringlike growth of new wood in the trunk of tree that marks the occurrence of one growing season.

Triassic period A division of the geologic time scale that occurred between 251 and 206 million years ago, which began after the mass extinction of trilobite species and the appearance of the first dinosaurs.

tributaries Smaller flowing bodies of water that drain into a larger river system.

triceratops A type of dinosaur that had three horns located on its massive shieldlike head.

trilobites A now extinct species of invertebrate aquatic animals that lived widely in the oceans of the Earth between 544 and 251 million years ago.

trophic level A term used to describe the feeding level classification of an organism in a food chain.

tropical A term that refers to something being located near the equator.

tropical depression A low atmospheric pressure system that forms in the tropics over the ocean, which consists of groups of thunderstorms and cyclonic winds between 20 and 40 miles per hour.

tropical disturbance An organized group of thunderstorms with cyclonic winds that are less than 20 miles per hour.

tropical rainforest a type of biome that exists near the equator and experiences high temperatures and rainfall throughout the year, which supports rainforest vegetation.

tropical storm An organized group of thunderstorms associated with a strong low pressure system with cyclonic winds between 40 and 70 miles per hour.

tropics The geographic areas that lie close to the equator.

tropopause An isothermal layer in the atmosphere located between the troposphere and the stratosphere.

troposphere The lowest layer of the Earth's atmosphere that lies closest to the surface, where all weather takes place and the temperature decreases with an increase in altitude.

tundra A biome that is found in the higher latitudes where the temperature is below freezing for most of the year, and supports matlike vegetation.

typhoon A hurricane that forms and is located over the western Pacific Ocean.

Tyrannosaurus A type of large meat-eating dinosaur that walked upright on two legs.

U

ultraviolet radiation A specific high-energy form of electromagnetic radiation emitted from the Sun that can be harmful to living things.

umbra The area in shadow during an eclipse that is totally blocked from the light.

unconformity A buried erosional surface that represents a significant gap of time in the geologic record.

unconsolidated parent material Parent rock that forms a soil that has been broken apart and is no longer one mass.

underground mining A method of removing mineral resources from the Earth's crust that involves the digging of long, deep mine shafts to access the minerals.

uniformity A natural law, also known as uniformitarinism, used in geology that states that the geologic processes that are currently shaping the Earth have been occurring all throughout the Earth's history.

unit A precise quantity that is used to describe a measurement.

universe The area in which all matter and energy exist.

updrafts Strong, vertical winds that move upward through a cloud.

uplift The process of lifting something upward.

upper air maps Weather maps that are used to display weather variables that exist in the upper atmosphere.

upwelling The uplift of cold ocean water from the bottom to the surface.

V

valley breeze A local wind that blows warm air up the sides of a mountain from the valley below.

valley glaciers Glaciers that are located in valleys between mountains.

vaporization The phase change that occurs when a liquid changes into a gas.

variable gases Gases in the Earth's atmosphere that change in their composition.

vascular plants A class of plants that have bundles of tiny tubes throughout their bodies that transport water and nutrients.

vector force A force that has both speed and direction.

velocity The speed at which something is moving.

vernal equinox The point in the Earth's orbit around the Sun, occurring on or around March 21, when the tilt of the Earth's axis is perpendicular to the plane of the Sun and the length of daylight (12 hours) equals the amount of darkness (12 hours).

vertebrates A classification of organisms that have backbones.

visibility The greatest distance an observer can see through the atmosphere or through water.

visible light radiation A form of electromagnetic radiation that includes all the visible colors.

volcanic arc A chain of volcanic islands that forms near a convergent plate boundary located below the ocean.

volcanic ash Tiny particles of pyroclastic material produced by a volcanic eruption.

volcanic bomb A chunk of lava that is ejected into the sky by a volcanic eruption, which hardens into an aerodynamic shape before it strikes the ground.

volcanic eruption The often sudden and violent release of gas, dust, lava, and other pyroclastic material from a volcano.

volcanic rocks Igneous rocks that form from cooled lava produced by a volcano.

volcanic vents Cracks and tubes that carry lava that run along the side or below a volcano.

volcano An opening in the Earth's crust through which gas, dust, lava, and other pyroclastic materials flow to the surface.

volume The amount of space occupied by something, or how large an object is.

W

waning crescent A phase of the Moon that occurs near the end of its orbital period around the Earth, during which only a crescent-shaped portion of the Moon is lit by the sun as viewed from Earth.

waning gibbous A phase of the Moon that occurs between the full and three quarter phases, during which three quarters of the Moon's surface is lit by the Sun as viewed from Earth.

warm front A front that develops when a warm air mass replaces a cold air mass.

wastewater Polluted water that is unfit for drinking or introduction into the environment because it has been used for some purpose and made unclean.

water molecule The chemical compound that is found in large quantities on the Earth which consists of two atoms of hydrogen and one atom of oxygen (H_2O).

water table The uppermost level of the soil where the pore spaces are completely saturated by groundwater.

water vapor The gaseous form of water.

waterborne illness A type of disease or sickness that is caused by an organism that lives in water.

watershed The total land area that is drained by a particular river system also known as a drainage basin.

waxing crescent A phase of the Moon that occurs near the beginning of its orbital period around the Earth, during which only a crescent-shaped

portion of the Moon is lit by the sun as viewed from Earth.

waxing gibbous A phase of the Moon that occurs between the first quarter and full Moon phases, during which three quarters of the Moon's surface is lit by the Sun as viewed from Earth.

weathered Something that has been exposed to the forces of weathering.

weathered mineral deposits Mineral resources that were formed as a result of the weathering of rocks.

weathering The physical or chemical processes by which large rocks are broken down into smaller rock particles.

weight The force that results from the gravitational attraction of the Earth on an object, which depends on its mass; commonly known as how heavy something is.

westerlies Planetary scale winds that occur in the middle latitudes, which move air from the southwest in the Northern Hemisphere and the northwest in the Southern Hemisphere.

wet bulb temperature The lowest temperature that can be obtained by the evaporation of water into the air, usually measured using a psychrometer.

wetland A terrestrial ecosystem that is covered by shallow water for most of the year.

whirlwinds Small rotating winds that create weak cyclones, which kick up dust and debris.

white dwarf A classification of a star that is dimmer than the Sun, white, small, and extremely hot.

wildlife management The planned use, protection, and control of wildlife using sound ecological principles.

wildlife resource Any free living organism, usually in the form of plants or animals, that has importance to humans.

wilting point A term used to describe the state of soil moisture when a soil's pore spaces only contain a thin film of water, which is unavailable for use by plants, causing them to wilt.

wind The horizontal movement of air across the Earth's surface, from areas of high atmospheric pressure to areas of low atmospheric pressure.

wind-driven currents Surface ocean currents that are formed by planetary winds.

wind erosion The movement of soil and sediments by the force of wind.

wind sock A large cloth tube that is used to indicate the direction of the wind

wind vane A metal device used to indicate the direction of the wind.

windward The side of something that is facing away from the direction of the wind.

winter solstice The time of the year when the Earth's tilted axis points the Northern Hemisphere away from the Sun, which usually occurs on or around December 21.

Y

yeast A single-celled fungus that converts sugar into carbon dioxide and alcohol by the process of fermentation.

Z

zebra mussel A species of mollusk, named for its black and white shell, that is not native to North America and is currently overpopulating many fresh bodies of water in the northeastern United States.

zenith The point in the sky that is directly above the observer, or 90 degrees above the horizon.

zone of ablation The front of a glacier where ice is breaking off and melting.

zone of accumulation The area on a glacier where snowfall is building up, forming new glacial ice.

zone of flowage The area on a glacier where glacial ice is currently flowing.

zone of saturation The area of a soil where all the pores in a soil are filled with water.

zooplankton Tiny animals that float freely in water.

Index